ArtScroll Mesorah Series®

Rabbi Nosson Scherman / Rabbi Meir Zlotowitz
General Editors

מחזור
בית יוסף

NUSACH ASHKENAZ — נוסח אשכנז

Published by

Mesorah Publications, ltd

The Complete ArtScroll machzor Succos

A new translation and anthologized commentary

composed by

Rabbi Avie Gold

in collaboration with

Rabbi Meir Zlotowitz

and Rabbi Nosson Scherman

Designed by

Rabbi Sheah Brander

FIRST EDITION
First Impression . . . September, 1987
SECOND EDITION
Revised and corrected
First Impression . . . August, 1988

Published and Distributed by
MESORAH PUBLICATIONS, Ltd.
Brooklyn, New York 11223

Distributed in Israel by
MESORAH MAFITZIM / J. GROSSMAN
Rechov Harav Uziel 117
Jerusalem, Israel

Distributed in Europe by
J. LEHMANN HEBREW BOOKSELLERS
20 Cambridge Terrace
Gateshead, Tyne and Wear
England NE8 1RP

THE ARTSCROLL MESORAH SERIES®
"MACHZOR BAIS YOSEF / THE COMPLETE ARTSCROLL MACHZOR"
Succos — Nusach Ashkenaz

1969 Coney Island Avenue / Brooklyn, N.Y. 11223 / (718) 339-1700

ISBN: 0-89906-683-6

Typography by CompuScribe at ArtScroll Studios, Ltd., Brooklyn, NY
Bound by **Sefercraft, Inc.**, Brooklyn, NY

This Machzor is dedicated to the memory of

Joseph Kushner ע״ה

ר׳ יוסף בן משה הלוי ע״ה

October 5, 1985 / ו׳ סכות תשמ״ו

Surviving the horrors of the Holocaust,
he came to a new land to build a glorious future.

Success never compromised his integrity;
nor did it cloud his vision of raising a loving, loyal family,
and building a community whose centerpiece would be
Torah, its values and its institutions.

In glowing memory, he remains the model of the Jew
whose character and prosperity,
the themes of Succos and Koheles,
are a means to help others.

Mrs. Rae Kushner

Linda & Murray Laulicht
Laurie & Bernard Hasten, Pamela, Shellie and Abigail

Lee & Murray Kushner
Ari, Jonathan, Marc and Melissa

Seryl & Charles Kushner
Dara Jared, Nicole and Joshua

Esther & William Schulder
Jessica, Jacob and Ruth

תנצב״ה

TABLE OF CONTENTS

שַׁבַּת חוֹל הַמּוֹעֵד — SABBATH OF CHOL HAMOED

SHEMINI ATZERES — שְׁמִינִי עֲצֶרֶת

SIMCHAS TORAH — שִׂמְחַת תּוֹרָה

◆§ Publisher's Preface

Succos, as our tefillos call it, is the "time of our joy," but it is also a time when there are many relatively unfamiliar additions to the order of prayer. Based on the kind reception given the ArtScroll Siddur and the ArtScroll Machzorim for Rosh Hashanah and Yom Kippur, we are hopeful that this Succos Machzor will help the public spend less time searching and seeking instructions for the services, and more time understanding them. Following is a brief description of the features of the Machzor:

◆§ **Contents** *The Machzor is as complete as possible. It includes such frequently omitted and almost never translated sections as Ushpizin, Mishnah Succah, Koheles/Ecclesiastes, Hoshanos, and piyutim; as well as commentaries to all of them and to the Torah readings. Everything is translated except for piyutim that are omitted by virtually all congregations, but those have been included in the back of the Machzor for the convenience of the congregations that require them. In addition there are full services for Chol HaMoed and Hoshana Rabbah, an expanded section on Simchas Torah with a commentary on the Hakafos, and an Overview providing a perspective on Succos and its deeper significance.*

◆§ **Translation** *The translation seeks to balance the lofty beauty of the heavily nuanced text and a readily understood English rendering. Where a choice had to be made, we generally preferred fidelity to the text over inaccurate simplicity, but occasionally, we had to stray from the literal translation in order to capture the essence of a phrase in an accessible English idiom. Especially in the piyutim, we had to go beyond a strictly literal translation, and sometimes rely on the commentary to clarify the meaning of the text.*

◆§ **Commentary** *The commentary has two goals; to explain the difficult passages and to involve the reader in the emotional, spiritual, and inspirational experience of prayer. We have avoided purely technical or grammatical comments. Unattributed comments are sometimes the author's own, but usually distill the general trend of several authorities of the Scriptural or Talmudic sources on which a phrase is based.*

◆§ **Laws and Instructions** *Clear instructions are provided throughout. More complex or lengthy halachos are discussed in the 'Laws' section at the end of the Machzor, which the reader will find to be a very helpful guide. In addition to halachos that relate specifically to Succos, the Laws section includes general halachos that are relevant to the regular prayer service. Throughout the Machzor, we refer to these laws by paragraph (§) number.*

◆§ **Layout and Typography** *While we have followed the pattern of the ArtScroll Siddur and Machzorim, which have been greatly praised for their ease of use and clarity of layout, this Machzor presents special challenges due to the fact that, on Succos, many omit part or all of the special piyutim. Consequently, we have provided separate repetitions of the chazzan's Shemoneh Esrei, one with piyutim and one without. This Machzor, with its clear instructions, copious subtitles, and precise page headings, was designed to* *make the service easy for everyone to follow. In addition, it incorporates the following popular features of the Siddur: The first and last phrases of the translation on each page parallel the first and last phrases of the Hebrew text; paragraphs begin with bold-type words to facilitate finding the individual tefillos; each paragraph in the translation is introduced with the parallel Hebrew world to ease cross-checking; portions said aloud by the chazzan are indicated by either the symbol ∴ or the word chazzan. An asterisk (*) after a word indicates that that word or phrase is treated in the commentary. Numbered footnotes give the Scriptural sources of countless verses that have been melded into the prayers. A footnote beginning 'Cf.' indicates that the Scriptural source is paraphrased.*

◆§ Hebrew Grammar *As a general rule in the Hebrew language, the accent is on the last syllable. Where the accent is on an earlier syllable, it is indicated with a messeg, a vertical line below the accented letter:* שִֽׁירוּ*. In the case of the Shema and the Song at the Sea, which are given with the cantillation [trop], the accent follows the trop. A* שְׁוָא נָע *[sh'va na] is indicated by a hyphen mark above the letter,* בָּרְכוּ*; except for a sh'va on the first letter of a word, which is always a sh'va na. In identifying a sh'va na, we have followed the rules of the Vilna Gaon and Rabbi Yaakov Emden.*

Acknowledgments

The ArtScroll Series has been privileged to benefit from the advice and support of the venerable leaders of our generation: MARAN HAGAON HARAV MOSHE FEINSTEIN, MARAN HAGAON HARAV YAAKOV KAMINETZKY, MARAN HAGAON HARAV SHNEUR KOTLER זצ״ל *and* להבחל״ח MARAN HAGAON HARAV MORDECHAI GIFTER שליט״א *among others.*

The profound influence of MARAN HAGAON HARAV GEDALIA SCHORR זצ״ל *pervades the Overviews. Quietly and self-effacingly, he put a lasting stamp on two generations of American Torah life.*

We are deeply grateful to HARAV DAVID FEINSTEIN, HARAV DAVID COHEN *and* HARAV HILLEL DAVID שליט״א *who have placed their encyclopedic scholarship at our disposal whenever needed.*

It is a source of great pride that so outstanding a Torah scholar as HARAV HERSH GOLDWURM שליט״א *has been associated with the ArtScroll Series virtually since its inception. In this Machzor Rabbi Goldwurm has contributed the 'Laws,' reviewed most of the instructions, and been available for research and guidance.*

Among those whose guidance was invaluable are such leaders of organizational and rabbinic life as RABBI MOSHE SHERER, RABBI PINCHAS STOLPER, RABBI BORUCH B. BORCHARDT, RABBI JOSHUA FISHMAN, RABBI FABIAN SCHONFELD, RABBI BENJAMIN WALFISH, RABBI EMANUEL HOLZER, RABBI YAAKOV MARCUS, MR. DAVID H. SCHWARTZ, RABBI SHLOMO LESIN, RABBI YISRAEL H. EIDELMAN, RABBI BURTON JAFFA, RABBI MICHOEL LEVI, *and* MR. YAAKOV KORNREICH.

A huge investment of time and resources was required to make this Machzor a reality. Only through the generous support of many people was it possible not only to produce the work, but to keep it within reach of the average family and congregation. Among those to whom we are grateful are:

The family of MR. JOSEPH KUSHNER ז״ל*, in whose memory it has been named Machzor* BEIS YOSEF. *He was a man of unusual warmth and generosity, who survived the Holocaust and went on to help rebuild what was lost, in his own family and in the host of institutions he supported, here and in Israel. He gained universal respect for his integrity, consistency, and the courage of his convictions. It is our privilege that this Machzor will help perpetuate a noble memory.*

MR. *and* MRS. ELI STERN *and* MR. *and* MRS. JOSEPH STERN *who dedicated the Nusach Sefard Rosh Hashanah Machzor* ZICHRON MOSHE *and the Nusach Sefard Yom Kippur Machzor* ZICHRON Z'EV. *People of unassuming gentility and gracious generosity, they benefit a host of Torah causes with vigor, imagination, and unselfish dedication;*

MRS. EMMA GLICK *of Wilmington Delaware and her sons* YITZCHOK (EDWARD) *and* NAFTALI (NORMAN), *who dedicated the Ashkenaz Rosh Hashanah Machzor* ZICHRON REUVEN *in memory of their late husband and father* REB REUVEN GLICK ז״ל;

MRS. LILLIE FEDER *and her children* NORMAN *and* MAUREEN *of Toronto, who dedicated the Ashkenaz Yom Kippur Machzor* ZICHRON YOSEF *in memory of their husband and father, Reb Yosef* ז״ל.

We are also grateful to the good and loyal friends who dedicated the various editions of the ArtScroll Siddur (in order of their publication): MR. *and* MRS. ZALMAN MARGULIES; MR. *and* MRS. JOSEPH BERLINER; MR. *and* MRS. AARON L. HEIMOWITZ; MRS. MALA WASSNER; MR. *and* MRS. HIRSH WOLF; *and* MR. *and* MRS. BEREL TENNENBAUM.

Many other people have provided the assistance needed to produce such Torah projects. In addition to those mentioned in previous editions of the Siddur and other ArtScroll works, we are grateful to MR. *and* MRS. LOUIS GLICK, *whose sponsorship of the ArtScroll Mishnah Series with the* YAD AVRAHAM *commentary is a jewel in the crown of Torah dissemination;* MR. *and* MRS. DAN SUKENIK *and* MR. *and* MRS. MOSHE SUKENIK, *who are living legends — for what they do and for the way they do it. May their work for Torah be a z'chus for the* נשמות *of their parents* ר׳ שלמה זאב ב״ר יחיאל ע״ה והאשה רודא בת ר׳ דניאל ע״ה.

The following people have been particularly helpful in making possible the publication of this Machzor: MEL *and* NAOMI BRODY לעילוי נשמות הרב דוד בונם ב״ר זאב ע״ה והאשה חוה בת הרב ישראל ע״ה; MR. *and* MRS. ABRAHAM FRUCHTHANDLER; MR. *and* MRS. ERWIN GRUNHUT; MR. *and* MRS. NACHMAN HERMAN; MR. CHAIM LEIBEL; RABBI *and* MRS. YEHUDAH LEVI; MR. *and* MRS. MORDECAI LIPSCHITZ לעילוי נשמות ר׳ גבריאל ב״ר ברוך ע״ה ור׳ רפאל יהודה אריה ב״ר מאיר ע״ה; MR. *and* MRS. SHLOMO PERL; MR. *and* MRS. ALBERT REICHMANN; MR. *and* MRS. SHMUEL RIEDER; MR. *and* MRS. NATHAN B. SILBERMAN; MR. *and* MRS. YAAKOV SINGER; MR. *and* MRS. LAURENCE A. TISCH; MR. *and* MRS. WILLY WIESNER; *and* MR. *and* MRS. HOWARD ZUCKERMAN.

RABBI AVIE GOLD, *Senior Editor, translated and commented on the piyutim and coordinated the editing and organization of the entire Machzor. His breadth and dedication are fixtures of the entire ArtScroll Series, and this Machzor is no exception. The balance of the Machzor was drawn from other works in the Series or was written by members of the ArtScroll staff especially for this work. With this Machzor, Reb Avie will earn the gratitude of the many thousands of people for whom the beauty of the Succos tefillos is now revealed.*

Only a fellow craftsman can perceive the excruciating hours that REB SHEAH BRANDER *expended in designing the Machzor for the mispallel's maximum ease. In this project he has outdone even his own standard of excellence. Moreover, his learned and incisive comments improved every aspect of this work.*

RABBI AVROHOM YOSAIF ROSENBERG *reviewed the vowelization and accenting of the piyutim, and* RABBI YEHEZKEL DANZIGER *and* GEDALIAH ZLOTOWITZ *reviewed and condensed the Mishnah commentary. We are grateful to them.*

MRS. ESTHER FEIERSTEIN, MRS. SIMIE KORN *and* MENUCHA MARCUS *typed the manuscript diligently and conscientiously.* RABBI YOSEF GESSER, MRS. FAYGIE WEINBAUM *and* MRS. TOVA FINKELMAN *carefully proofed the second edition.*

The entire ArtScroll staff has a share in our service to the community, each in his or her area of responsibility: SHMUEL BLITZ, *head of ArtScroll Jerusalem;* SHIMON GOLDING, *director of marketing;* SHEILA TENNENBAUM, *director of sales;* ELI KROEN, YOSEF TIMINSKY, MICHAEL ZIVITZ, MRS. JUDI DICK, LEA FREIER, MRS. ESTIE DICKER *and* SURIE ADLER. *We conclude with gratitude to Hashem Yisborach for His infinite blessings and for the opportunity to have been the quill that records His word. May He guide our work in the future for the benefit of His people.*

Elul 5748 *Rabbis Meir Zlotowitz / Nosson Scherman*
Brooklyn, NY

Overviews

◈ *An Overview / Succos and the Festival Cycle*

ANY DISCUSSION OF THE TORAH'S FESTIVALS must recognize that they are not merely commemorations of historic events. It would miss the point completely, for example, to say that we have a weekly Sabbath because people need a chance to relax and rejuvenate themselves, physically and mentally. That can be done just as easily on a Sunday or Wednesday. Rather, the Sabbath is our testimony that God created the universe in six days, that we can grow and elevate ourselves on the Sabbath, and that the holiness of the Sabbath nourishes the entire week. Just as kindhearted, ethical carpenters or accountants are different kinds of people than their unsympathetic, boorish counterparts — even though they all wear overalls or wield calculators — so, too, the person who absorbs holiness on the Sabbath is not the same as the one who devotes the day to gossip and gourmet food.

Spiritual Overtones

Similarly, the overtones of the individual Jewish festivals are primarily spiritual. Furthermore, the three Pilgrimage Festivals — Pesach, Shavuos, and Succos — form a cycle, in which one leads into the other. The cycle begins with Pesach, continues with Shavuos, and ends with Succos. Let us, therefore, try to understand Succos in the light of its role within the cycle.

Why is Succos the climax of the three Pilgrimage Festivals? What profound event is represented by Succos? Why do the Torah and our prayers emphasize that Succos is the Festival of Gladness? Finally, Succos appears to be part of another cycle as well, the Tishrei cycle of Rosh Hashanah, Ten Days of Repentance, Yom Kippur, and Succos — what is the connection between the festival of joy and the somber days of repentance, prayer, and fasting?

Significance of Seasons

EACH YEAR IS LIKE A NEW CREATION. We see this most clearly in the cycle of seasons. After the dreary respite of winter, "Creation" begins. In the spring, the fields come to life and the trees blossom. Birds chirp and children romp on the new grass. The earth has come to life again. Slowly, the crops grow until they are ready for harvest. The summer season of joy approaches as the first fruits mature and ripen under the benevolent smile of the sun. Finally, the earth's wealth is ready to be gathered from the fields and brought into homes, barns, and silos. It is autumn, and man is ready to enjoy the products of his sweat until the next season of rebirth and growth begins.

In the Torah's perspective, the "real" world is the spiritual one; the physical world is the way in which God translates His will into messages that human beings can understand. In everyday life, for example, we take it for granted that a person's actions are a reflection of his values. If someone secretly arranges to pay medical bills and send food packages to the indigent, it is fair to say that he is a person of great kindness and sensitivity. His deeds reflect his inner self. Similarly, the coming of spring is an indication that God smiles at man and offers him an opportunity to free himself from the shackles of his wintry discontent. It is time for man to aspire to freedom and a new beginning — just as Israel did centuries ago when it burst free from the physical and spiritual bondage of Egypt. Like an electronic printer translating impulses into a picture of a far-off event, "nature" translates God's gift of spiritual rejuvenation into the physical manifestations of springtime. What do the longer days and returning birds tell us? Surely not merely to plow, make vacation plans, and begin strolling in the park! We should recognize spring for what it *truly* is: a signal that the time is ripe for spiritual renewal.

Israel's national springtime came when the Exodus from Egypt took place. The Torah emphasizes and reemphasizes that it happened in חֹדֶשׁ הָאָבִיב, *the month of springtime*, reminding us that just as the earth comes to life, so must Israel rejuvenate its resolve every year, as it did in the first Nissan when it was elevated to nationhood.

The season of harvest coincides with Shavuos in *Eretz Yisrael*. Springtime works wonders on the fields, but it would all be a waste unless the crops are harvested. The crop of human freedom is more precious than any found on field or tree, but it too will do no good unless it is harvested. On Shavuos, God informed His foundling nation Israel of the purpose of its freedom — to make itself a *kingdom of priests and a holy nation* (*Exodus* 19:6). By accepting the Torah, Israel gave meaning to its existence. Otherwise, the crop of freedom would have become the rot of license and self-indulgence that has corrupted and destroyed so many civilizations.

For the farmer, the harvest season is not the end. The grain must dry in the sun and then be bundled, threshed, winnowed, gathered. The fruit must be processed and prepared for storage or market. Not until the end of this productive and exhausting season can the farmer rejoice and say that he has completed the cycle that spring began. Here, too, nature is but a reflection of the reality above. Man's freedom reaches its desired climax when his personal cycle of accomplishment is complete. Then he presents its end-product to God and says, "You gave me life and direction — this is what I have made of Your gifts." As Israel said in the Wilderness, "You gave us freedom; we dedicate it to Your Torah."

Clearly, the birth of the Jewish nation achieved heightened significance when the Torah was given on Shavuos, but how would God help Israel find the way to a successful ingathering of its spiritual crop? The message of Succos provides the answer.

Message of Succos

IN THE WILDERNESS God enveloped and sheltered Israel in His עֲנָנֵי הַכָּבוֹד, *Clouds of Glory*. The clouds were a sign that Israel had risen to the spiritual plateau that made it worthy of God's all-enveloping protection. Israel had completed the cycle. The promise of its springtime and the challenge of its harvest had been fulfilled as the nation was gathered into God's exalting, protecting, inspiring clouds. As the Torah says, *for in succah-booths did I settle the Children of Israel* (*Leviticus* 23:43).

As *Sfas Emes* and others point out, whenever an individual or nation scales a spiritual height, it becomes easier to regain it even after it has been lost. Like something that has been learned once and then forgotten, it is far easier to relearn it than to acquire new knowledge. Having once become worthy of God's protection and of being gathered into His spiritual bosom, as it were, Israel bequeathed to its posterity the potential to do so again. That means that *we* — all of us — can rise to the spiritual heights attained by our ancestors in the Wilderness. So the events of that year became a watershed and a model in Israel's history. What had happened then became the goal of every future year, every future historical cycle, because it *could* be done again.

Thus Succos concludes the cycle. In the world of nature, it represents the joy of successfully completing the agricultural cycle. In the world of the spirit, it represents the successful completion of the mission for which God created man and gave the Torah to Israel.

The commandment of *succah* tells Jews, צֵא מִדִּירַת קֶבַע וְשֵׁב בְּדִירַת עֲרַאי, *leave the permanent dwelling and settle in a temporary dwelling* (*Succah* 2a). In the context of the desert experience, even a *succah* offered little security. Makeshift walls and a thatched shade could not have provided true comfort in the vast, baked, sandy wilderness where there was neither food nor water, where snakes and scorpions were a constant danger (see *Deuteronomy* 8:15). Israel's comfortable survival for forty years in the wilderness was possible only because of God's constant mercy. Thus, when a Jew leaves his home in favor of his *succah*, he realizes that his own personal survival, like that of his forefathers, ultimately depends on God's protection. Even in modern times, the threats of human destructiveness and natural disaster make plain that man has no safer refuge than his fragile *succah*, and the Heavenly protection it represents.

R' Samson Raphael Hirsch (in his *Horeb*) finds this aspect of *succah* to be both sobering and encouraging. To the powerful and wealthy, the *succah* says, 'Do not rely on your fortune; it is transitory and can leave you more quickly than it came. Even your castle is no more secure than a *succah*. If you are safe, it is because God shelters you as He did your ancestors when they had but a booth to protect them against one of earth's harshest environments. Let the starry sky you see through your *s'chach* teach you to build your castle upon a firm foundation of faith in God and see the benevolent gaze of God even when you look at its sturdy, insulated roof. If you can do that, opulence will not blind you to the glow of God's beneficence.

To the poor and downtrodden, the *succah* says, 'Are you more helpless than millions of your ancestors in the Wilderness, without food, water, or permanent shelter? What sustained them? Who provided for them? Whose benevolent hand wiped their brow and soothed their worry? Look around you at your *succah's* frail walls and at the stars you see through its rustling roof. Let it remind you that Israel became a nation living in such "mansions." Those were the palaces of the *kingdom of priests and holy nation* (*Exodus* 19:6), the homes where they became a great and Godly nation, where they developed the faith that overcame fear, and the knowledge that God's word was their guarantor for tomorrow — every tomorrow.'

Memorials of the Past

OUR *SUCCAH* REFLECTS the phenomena experienced by Israel in the Wilderness. The people built booths, and so do we. But they were also privileged to enjoy an even greater protection, one that surpassed not only booths but fortresses: Israel was enveloped by God's Clouds of Glory. Heavenly clouds transport a people into a spiritual environment where they are impervious to the slings and barbs of earthly danger. In the desert, Israel was in a higher world where earthly dangers had no power. This is why the *Zohar* refers to the *succah* phenomenon as צִלָּא דִמְהֵימְנוּתָא, *the shelter of faith.*

In His compassion and mercy, God provided us with memorials to the miracles He performed for our forefathers. How can we, who have never seen Clouds of Glory achieve an attachment to the sublime experiences of our ancestors? There in the Wilderness, Israel was enveloped in Clouds of Glory; today we can wrap ourselves, as it were, in the *succah.* Out of our homes, stripped of our security, without the accoutrements that spell safety and convenience all year round, we sit completely enwrapped in our *succah*. In the twinkling stars that shimmer through the *s'chach,* we can see the One Above making us aware of His presence.

The man of faith integrates into his own experience the teachings and experiences of the Patriarchs, Moses and Aaron, the prophets, and all the teachers whose words still live *for* him and *within* him. When such a person sits in his *succah* he remembers that his ancestors sat in essentially similar booths. Like them, he has the benefit of Clouds of Glory, because he, too, is under the protection of צִלָּא דִמְהֵימְנוּתָא, *the shelter of faith.* This is why Succos is called "the festival of our joy" — who would not be joyous to know that God envelops and shelters him?

During the Russo-Japanese war in 1904-5, many young disciples of Ger were conscripted into the Russian army and sent to the Japanese front. The underfed, underclothed, undertrained young Torah scholars maintained a brisk correspondence — including the Talmudic novellae they composed at or near the front — with their *Rebbe*, Rabbi Yehudah Aryeh Leib Alter, known as the *Sfas Emes*, who grieved and allowed himself no rest as long as his disciples were in danger. Once they wrote him how those at the front made themselves a *succah* by digging a foxhole and covering it with branches. All through the night, they took turns scurrying to the *succah* with their rations so that they could fulfill the *mitzvah* of the festival.

The *Sfas Emes* wrote them back, 'Of people like you God says, "הַעִידֹתִי בָכֶם הַיּוֹם אֶת הַשָּׁמַיִם וְאֶת הָאָרֶץ, *I have adorned* [homiletically deriving הַעִידֹתִי from the word עֲדִי, *jewelry*] *heaven and earth with you today*" (*Deuteronomy* 4:26). You are the jewelry that beautifies heaven and earth!'

Didn't people of such faith see Clouds of Glory? Wasn't their Succos a festival of joy for themselves and their Maker Who adorned creation with them?

Completion

AS WE HAVE SEEN, the Three Pilgrimage Festivals form a progression: from the birth of the nation on Pesach, to the assumption of its mission on Shavuos, to the successful completion of its task on Succos. This ascending order of achievement is reflected in the Torah's description of the observance of the respective festivals. Nowhere is the term שִׂמְחָה, *gladness*, applied explicitly to Pesach (although Pesach is included in the *general* commandment to rejoice on the festivals). Only once does the Torah command Israel to rejoice on Shavuos (*Deuteronomy* 16:11) — but no less than three times is Israel enjoined to celebrate on Succos (*Leviticus* 23:40 and *Deuteronomy* 16:14,15). The implication is plain.

The greatest cause for celebration is the attainment of a goal. Succos symbolizes the successful completion and ingathering of Israel's *spiritual* harvest; that is surely ample reason for the Torah to stress three times, and for the Sages to incorporate into the prayers of the day, that Succos is זְמַן שִׂמְחָתֵנוּ, *the season of our gladness (Sfas Emes).*

The connection between the Days of Awe and Succos is based on more than their calendrical proximity. In various Midrashim, our Sages point out that Succos flows naturally from the cleansing and ennobling process of Rosh Hashanah and Yom Kippur. Only one who has cleansed himself through repentance is capable of being imbued with the message of faith and the joy of fulfillment represented by Succos.

In this sense, Succos belongs to both the Pilgrimage Festivals and the Days of Awe. If no one ever sinned, life would be a progression from Pesach to Shavuos to Succos, from birth to mission to fulfillment. But people *do* sin.

Nevertheless, all is not lost. The Sages teach that the universe would not have been created unless man were to have the ability to gain atonement — otherwise the world could not endure (*Nedarim* 39b). As man is about to fall, Rosh Hashanah and Yom Kippur and the Ten Days of Atonement arrive. He is accused. He repents. God judges — and forgives. Then the Jew emerges from his trial cleansed and vindicated — and walks to his *succah*, his awaiting Clouds of Glory. This is one reason why it is preferable to begin the construction of the *succah* immediately after Yom Kippur is over; the atonement of Yom Kippur makes possible the spiritual fulfillment of Succos.

Unity of the Four Species

THE ASPECT OF PEACE is related to the Four Species of Succos, the *esrog, lulav, hadassim,* and *aravos*. The Midrash likens the Four Species to various major organs of the human body, all of which can be used for good or for evil. The myrtle leaf [הֲדַס] is shaped like an eye and the *esrog* like a heart. As the Sages have taught, these two organs can unite in a partnership of sin: the eye sees and the heart lusts, with the result that the person's better instincts are inundated by the power of his temptations. The willow leaf is shaped like a mouth, the organ of speech, which is the tool of Torah, prayer, and encouragement, but which is so often used as a weapon that injures others and tears away at man's spiritual fiber. The straight, tall *lulav* resembles man's spinal column, the organ through which all the brain's impulses are conveyed to the rest of the body, for better or for worse. By combining these species in the performance of a *mitzvah*, we symbolize our repentance and desire to use all of our organs and faculties to serve God. The taking of the Four Species represents the resolve to unite our body and our emotional and intellectual drives for the good.

There is another organism in addition to the individual human body: the *national* organism of Israel with its many kinds of people. The Four Species symbolize them all. The *esrog* is a food containing both טַעַם וְרֵיחַ, *taste and pleasant aroma;* it symbolizes righteous people who possess both Torah and good deeds. The *lulav*, the branch of a date palm, is odorless, but it produces sweet, nourishing food; it symbolizes the scholar who possesses Torah knowlege but is deficient in good deeds. The fragrant, tasteless myrtle leaf represents common people who possess good deeds, but lack Torah scholarship. Finally, the odorless, tasteless willow leaf symbolizes someone who lacks both Torah and good deeds. God wishes the Jewish nation to unite into a *community* of Israel.

When all segments of Israel come together in the service of the common goal of national dedication to His will, then *everyone* belongs, from the august *esrog* to the lowly willow. And when every shade and manner of Jew joins with every other in pursuit of that good, then God accepts their common repentance.

The Closing Celebration

THERE IS SOMETHING UNIQUE about the Shemini Atzeres/Simchas Torah festival. Although it is attached to Succos chronologically and our prayers describe it, like Succos, as *the time of our gladness*, it has the status of a separate festival. Morever, unlike the three Pilgrimage Festivals, on Shemini Atzeres there is no commandment for Jews to appear at the Temple or to bring festive *Chagigah* offerings, as there is on the other three festivals (see *Rambam, Hil. Chagigah* 1:7).

As expounded by *HaRav Gedaliah Schorr*, there is a unique way in which Shemini Atzeres provides the Jew with the same spiritual sustenance as the other festivals. The Passover Haggadah quotes *Sifri* that וּבְמוֹרָא גָּדוֹל, *with great fear*, refers to God's revelation of His Presence [גִּלּוּי שְׁכִינָה], which brings fear of Heaven to those who perceive it. This same reverence was felt by people who came to the Temple, the resting place of God's Presence. In the absence of the Temple, we can attempt to reach that level of reverence through philosophical speculation and cultivation of sincere faith, but these can not truly approximate the feelings one had when he was face to face with revelation. That is a loss we feel keenly as we yearn for the faith and reverence of earlier times. One aspect of revelation was never lost, however.

According to *Sifri* on the last verse of the Torah, the phrase וּבְמוֹרָא גָּדוֹל, *with great fear*, refers to the teaching of the Torah, as well as to revelation. This is an astounding insight into the power of Torah study — it is equivalent to and just as awe-inspiring as revelation itself, as God's Presence in the Temple. Through its love and study of the Torah, the Jewish people can reach levels of reverence and closeness to God that are equal to those that were attained in the Temple. This is why the Sages teach that from the day the Temple was destroyed, all God has in His universe are the four cubits of the *Halachah*. This is the *miniature sanctuary* [מִקְדָּשׁ מְעַט] where God's holiness finds hospitality even in exile. Torah study — its halls and its scholars — are parallel to the Temple.

This is the uniqueness of Shemini Atzeres and Simchas Torah. We cannot appear at the Temple today; but even in Temple times there was no requirement to do so on Shemini Atzeres. Even then, this day was the celebration of Torah study, for as Kabbalistic literature teaches, Shemini Atzeres commemorates the merit of Moses, our teacher of Torah. Thus, it is the only festival that gives us as much today as it gave our ancestors in Temple days, because the Torah is with us today as much as it was with them. But it should be even more precious to us, because the Torah is all we have left.

Can there be a better reason for the joy of Simchas Torah? Succos with its commandments is over. On Succos we dwelled in the fragile yet indestructible "shelter of faith," the *succah*. We experienced the joy of unity — personal and national — by lovingly clutching our Four Species. On Shemini Atzeres we have no *succah* and no Four Species — but we have the Torah! Allegiance to it is our protection and in it we find unity. We all have a share in the Torah, whatever our level of scholarship. And even if we have no Torah knowledge, the Torah is still ours, because we can support its students and find fulfillment in their achievements.

So on Shemini Atzeres and Simchas Torah we reach the climax of Tishrei. From the yearning of repentance to the purity of atonement, we have gained the joy of Succos — and finally the ecstasy of Torah and revelation.

An Overview / The Hoshana Service

History Regained

ON SUCCOS, IN THE DAYS WHEN the Temple stood, Jews would go down to Motza, a valley below Jerusalem, and pick huge *aravah* branches, each eleven cubits long (approximately 17-22 feet). The branches would be placed upright on the יְסוֹד, *base*, of the Altar on all four sides. They would extend a cubit over the Altar with their tips hanging over its top. To the joyous sound of shofar blasts, Jews would enter the courtyard and encircle the Altar once on each of the first six days of Succos. On the seventh day, Hoshana Rabbah, they would encircle the Altar seven times. As they made their daily circuits, they would pray, אָנָּא ה׳ הוֹשִׁיעָה נָּא, אָנָּא ה׳ הַצְלִיחָה נָּא, *Please* HASHEM, *bring salvation now! Please,* HASHEM, *bring success now!* (*Psalms* 118:25). According to R' Yehudah, they would say אֲנִי וָהוֹ הוֹשִׁיעָה נָּא, *ANI VAHO* [i.e., two mystical Names of God] *bring salvation now!*

When the Second Temple was built, the *aravah* services were broadened. The prophets Chaggai, Zechariah, and Malachi, who were members of the Great Assembly, instituted the custom that on Hoshana Rabbah, Jews could take part in the *aravah* service wherever they were, even outside the Temple (*Succah* 44a-b, see *Rosh; Tosefos Yom Tov*).

After the Temple was destroyed, the entire practice of circuits and the *aravah* service came to an end — for a while.

But the people of Israel do not forget. Just as the spiritual genius of the people, thanks to its prophets, extended the *aravah* service throughout the land in happier times, so the collective soul of Israel would not remain stifled in the tragedy of exile. We do not know precisely when, but after the end of the Talmudic era, a new spirit arose: 'Let us make a זֵכֶר לְמִקְדָּשׁ, *a reminder of the Temple.*'

When the Temple was gone, the circuits of the Altar were no more. But in community after community, country after country, the custom was revived until no village or hamlet was without it. And so, today, wherever there are Jews, their synagogues feature a reminder of the Altar of old. It is the synagogue *bimah*, at which there stands a man holding a Torah scroll. Around that 'altar' a nation walks with *lulav* and *esrog* in hand, chanting its prayer for salvation.

Man, Speech and Deed

YESOD V'SHORESH HA'AVODAH WRITES that the *hakafah*-circuits of the *Hoshana* service have a profound influence on the Heavenly spheres, an influence that cannot be grasped by ordinary human intelligence. We can have some small idea of its significance if we understand that the cosmic effects of this *mitzvah* emanate from the nature of its performance. It combines three factors: Man, Speech, and Deed.

Man, Speech, and Deed. These concepts are symbolized by the individual Jew as he makes his way around the *bimah*, intoning his *Hoshana* prayers, and holding the Four Species as he does so. This combination of Man, Speech, and Deed forms the word אָדָם, *man* at his greatest.

The א represents אָדָם, *the human being;* ד represents דִיבּוּר, *the power of intelligent speech;* מ represents מַעֲשֶׂה, *deed*, the readiness to bring the abstract into reality. One who combines all three characteristics establishes himself as a total person, a Jew who dedicates himself, in mind and deed, to the goal represented by the *bimah*.

The 'deed' aspect of this complete man is represented by the Four Species, which, as noted above, symbolizes both the unity of all Jews and of all an individual's organs and faculties in the service of God.

Periods of Judgment

SUCCOS IN GENERAL and Hoshana Rabbah in particular are periods of judgment in two ways: one specific and the other general. During the Ten Days of Repentance between Rosh Hashanah and Yom Kippur, the overall decisions are made for humanity as a whole and for each individual in particular. At other times, God determines what will be done with regard to *particular* needs. On Pesach He judges man with regard to fruit crops, and on Succos with regard to water supply *(Rosh Hashanah* 16a; see ArtScroll Mishnah, *Rosh Hashanah* 1:2).

The decision regarding water is not rendered until the end of Succos; for this reason, certain specific *mitzvos* of Succos revolve around water: in the Temple, water libations [נִיסוּךְ הַמַּיִם] were offered at the altar; the *mitzvah* of the Four Species is performed with plants that depend on abundant water for their existence; and the willow, which assumes the spotlight on the climactic day of the water-judgment, Hoshana Rabbah, is identified by the Torah as a plant that grows alongside streams [*Leviticus* 23:40].

But Hoshana Rabbah's significance is broader than the universal need for water. The *Zohar* describes it as a judgment day akin to Yom Kippur itself, the day when the judgment of Yom Kippur is 'sealed' finally, and the 'parchments containing the decrees' are handed to 'angels' who deliver them. Consequently, Hoshana Rabbah assumes special importance as a day of prayer and repentance. Because the *aravah* service is unique to Hoshanah Rabbah, we must examine the *aravah* service in that light.

Commentators (cited by *Sefer HaToda'ah)* explain this process of 'angels, parchments and seals' that the *Zohar* associates with Hoshana Rabbah. We can better comprehend God's kingdom if we compare its procedure to that of human government.

When a merciful king passes judgment on his subjects, he seeks excuses for their behavior. Perhaps there were extenuating circumstances for their misdeeds. Even better, perhaps they feel a degree of remorse that guarantees a future better than the past. Examining the case before him, if the king finds grounds for vindication or mercy, he dismisses the indictment and declares the defendant innocent. If not — there is still hope. The offender may find witnesses who will come forward to defend him. There is always time to condemn and punish. Delay cannot hurt; a hasty decision may be irrevocable. So the king waits. Time goes by, and if grounds for mercy are found indeed, the relieved king hands down his decision for acquittal. But even if the evidence mounts against the defendant and the verdict must be guilty, there is still an option. The verdict will not take effect until it is inscribed, sealed and delivered — perhaps in the interval the defendant will repent or a defender will come forward. If not, the verdicts are handed to the officers of the court for delivery. Even then there is hope. If the messenger comes to the convict's home and finds him joyously engaged in the service of the king and devotedly carrying out his laws, he returns to his monarch and says, 'Surely, he *was* guilty, but now he is a changed man.' The king agrees and tears up the verdict.

The Heavenly kingdom is similar. On Rosh Hashanah all people are judged. The righteous are given a favorable judgment, those found wanting — but not totally evil — are given until Yom Kippur to repent. If they fail to do so, the verdict against them is written and sealed, but not yet delivered. That is not done until Hoshana Rabbah, a day when Jews assemble in prayer, dedication, and supplication. Then, when the joy of Succos reaches its climax not in dissolution but in devotion, God in His mercy may find ample reason to tear up the parchment bearing harsh sentences, as it were, and replace them with brighter tidings. This period of reprieve extends until the morning of Shemini Atzeres when Israel tarries for another period of rejoicing before God. The Four Species have been laid aside, the *aravah*-bundle has done its work, the *succah* is empty — but Israel remains with intense joy at having been privileged to serve God with love and awe. Then, even the guilty can mesh with the righteous and have their own spark of goodness break through the heavy overlays of sin.

Jericho and the Nations

EARLY IN ISRAEL'S HISTORY there was a time when its religious service was instrumental in bringing down the resistance of an enemy. The first Canaanite city faced by Joshua and Israel was Jericho, a fortress protected by impregnable walls backed by a powerful army (see *Joshua* 6). God told Joshua to have the army, led by seven *Kohanim* and the Ark, circle the city once a day for six days. On the seventh day, they were to circle Jericho seven times, then the *Kohanim* were to blow their *shofars*, and the mighty wall would collapse.

When the Temple stood, a total of seventy bullocks were offered as burnt-offerings on Succos (*Numbers* 29:12-34). These offerings were to protect the seventy nations of the world from suffering, to seek atonement for them, and to seek peace for all peoples (*Bamidbar Rabbah* 21). R' Yehoshua ben Levi exclaims, "If only the nations had known how the Temple benefited *them*, they would have surrounded it with legions to protect it!" But though the offerings helped the nations, they had another purpose as well. The seventy bullocks were offered in a diminishing order: thirteen the first day, twelve the second, and so on, until there were only seven on Hoshana Rabbah. This order symbolized our prayer that God diminish the power of the nations and individuals who flout His will. Thus, Succos represents their fall from dominance, and Hoshana Rabbah represents the climax of their downfall.

In the Temple, too, a procession circled the Altar once a day for the first six days of Succos, and seven times on Hoshana Rabbah. On that last day, Israel completed its decreasing order of seventy sacrifices that served to invoke God's protection on the nations, but also invoked the greatest benefit they could gain — that they be shorn of their illusory power and become subservient to the nation that represented God's will on earth. So the circuits of Hoshana Rabbah evoke Jericho, not merely in commemoration of an ancient event, but of the continuing goal of human history: that evil disappear and mankind recognize the purpose for which it was created.

First it was Jericho. Then it was all seventy nations. Now the embodiment of evil is primarily Edom, descendant of Esau and Amalek, initiator of the current, final exile that has plunged man into nearly twenty centuries of darkness.

Hoshana Rabbah

HOSHANA RABBAH BRINGS WITH IT the confluence of several factors of profound spiritual significance: the day when God applies the final seal to the judgment of Yom Kippur; the day when seventy offerings are completed and when seven circuits are made around the altar/*bimah;* the day that recalls the miracle at Jericho and portends the glorious day when far greater forces of evil than Jericho will suffer their downfall, leading to a triumph that will dwarf Joshua's.

When that day comes, it will bring the fulfillment of Isaiah's prophecy, יְשֻׂשׂוּם מִדְבָּר וְצִיָּה וְתָגֵל עֲרָבָה וְתִפְרַח כַּחֲבַצָּלֶת, *the arid desert will be joyous and* [עֲרָבָה] *the wilderness will exult and blossom like a rose* (*Isaiah* 35:1).

The word *aravah* means wilderness, it means willow, and it alludes to the *Aravos*, the highest of the spiritual realms (see *Psalms* 68:5, לָרֹכֵב בָּעֲרָבוֹת). The prophets and sages and the collective genius of the people of Israel chose the *aravah* branch for the particular *mitzvah* of this portentous day. The *aravah* proclaims God as Master of the *Aravos*, and its message will one day — finally — be heard universally. Then, the final redemption will come, and Zion, whose spiritual magnificence had been reduced to an unproductive wilderness, will blossom with a new birth of spiritual splendor.

As we saw above, the *aravah* symbolizes the human mouth and the simple folk who lack both learning and deeds. That the Sages chose Hoshana Rabbah as the day for these allusions, and the *aravah* as the symbol best suited to the day, is not coincidental.

Israel's Mouth

HOSHANA RABBAH IS A DAY of many prayers, and the *aravah* — resembling the mouth and lips, the organs of prayer — is the day's aptest symbol. Different nations have different characteristics. No less a personage than Isaac defined Jacob's essence as: הַקֹּל קוֹל יַעֲקֹב, *the voice is Jacob's voice* (*Genesis* 27:22).

Ideally, the mouth should be the tool that expounds, clarifies, and teaches the wisdom of God, but few people reach that pinnacle. Many can offer little Torah knowledge and few deeds. Often, even their faith seems doubtful. But in history's severest tests and worst times, the lips of ordinary Jews have given expression to the legacy of Jacob, even if they could say little more than הוֹשַׁעְנָא, *Please save!* They have sanctified God's Name with prayer and with *Shema Yisrael* on their lips.

On Hoshana Rabbah, therefore, when the opportunites for achieving God's help are so auspicious, the prophets and sages laid aside the *esrog* with its perfection, the *lulav* with its Torah, the myrtle with its good deeds, and picked up a bundle of *aravos.* Of course, the word *aravos* represents the very highest of the heavens — but how does one scale the heavens? Hoshana Rabbah offers its own unique way: Through prayer. Through being part of the Jewish people. Through recognizing that God longs for the repentance and prayer of *every* Jew, even the humblest *(Sfas Emes).*

The Midrash teaches that the three Pilgrimage Festivals commemorate the three Patriarchs. *Tur Orach Chaim* (417) explains the source for this statement: Pesach reminds us of Abraham who told Sarah to bake *matzos* for the three visiting angels *(Genesis* 18:6); Shavuos is for Isaac because the *shofar* blast at Sinai symbolizes the horn of the ram that replaced Isaac on the altar of the *Akeidah;* and Succos recalls Jacob who made סֻכּוֹת, *succah-tents,* for his flocks *(Genesis* 33:17, Overview to ArtScroll *Vayeitzei).*

It is noteworthy that Succos, the festival of Jacob, includes the Four Species and the *aravos* — the very *mitzvos* that stress the unity of the Jewish people. Of the three Patriarchs, Jacob was the only one whose family was perfect in its entirety, for — unlike the offspring of Abraham and Isaac — Jacob's children were righteous without exception and they all became the pillars of the nation. His children were very different, but each was essential to the integrity of the nation. The Four Species of Succos point up how every facet of Israel thrives best when it is united with all the others. And Hoshana Rabbah with its emphasis on the lowly *aravah* shows best of all how Israel needs its common folk just as it needs its finest.

The *aravah* people are an extension of Jacob whose identity lay in his 'voice.' When Israel is united in this manner, when it shows its appreciation of every offspring of Jacob, when it proves its understanding that its ultimate salvation is in the hands of God, when it stands at the climax of its judgment season with *aravah* in hand — then it is worthy of the gift of Moses, and to ascend to the realm of *Aravos.*

◈ *An Overview / Shemini Atzeres, Simchas Torah and Shavuos*

Just as Pesach and Shavuos are related, so too Succos and Shemini Atzeres are related. On Pesach, we went free; on Shavuos we received the Torah, which gave us the mission for which God had freed us. It is as if we received our body on

Pesach and our soul on Shavuos. Succos is a time to celebrate success and prosperity — and Shemini Atzeres/Simchas Torah shows us that the truest joy is defined by and devoted to the will of God, as expressed in the Torah. But why did it take seven weeks for the theme of Pesach to be interpreted while the theme of Succos was interpreted immediately?

Pesach was a time when Israel became filled with fear of God. The people saw every manner of miracle as He demonstrated His unlimited power. They saw Him alter the course of nature to effect His Will. They saw the unparalleled miracle of the Splitting of the Sea, when they were saved and their enemies destroyed. When they saw that miracle, the Torah tells us that, וַיִּירְאוּ הָעָם אֶת ה׳ וַיַּאֲמִינוּ בַּה׳ וּבְמֹשֶׁה עַבְדּוֹ, *the people feared* HASHEM *and they had faith in* HASHEM *and in Moses, His servant* (*Exodus* 14:31). As the verse indicates, their faith was born of fear — but fear can be a fleeting thing. That is why there had to be a delay before the Torah was given. The people were given seven weeks to ponder and examine themselves, so that they could make that fear and faith a permanent part of their being.

But Succos is unlike Pesach. We have emerged from the Days of Awe having repented and gained purity from sin. We have dwelled in the *succah*, demonstrating our trust that God provides greater protection than battlements and armies. We have experienced the days of joy that stem from awareness that God cares for us and provides our sustenance. Such feelings and experiences produce love for God. And in the long run, love and joy accomplish more than fear. So we move immediately to channel this love and joy into a celebration of Torah, a celebration which is simultaneously a covenant betweeen ourselves and God to remain loyal to Him and His teachings.

Everyone's Celebration

SIMCHAS TORAH IS NOT JUST FOR SCHOLARS. Every Jewish male, even young children, receives an *aliyah* to the Torah and the privilege of singing and dancing with it. Just as the Torah reading of the morning is repeated over and over until everyone has an *aliyah*, the *Hakafos* are extended until everyone has been able to express his love and joy at being able to hold the Torah, possess it, study it, observe it.

The celebration of the Torah is the only observance of Simchas Torah — because, ultimately, the Torah is our most cherished, most permanent possession. Today we have no Temple service, no *succah* and no Four Species, but we still have the Torah. In fact, as the poet says in the Yom Kippur service, אֵין לָנוּ שִׁיוּר רַק הַתּוֹרָה הַזֹּאת, *we have nothing left but this Torah!* Much has changed in Jewish history and much has been lost over the long, long exile, but the Torah is intact and it remains our soul. Sharing our celebration, so to speak, are the fathers of our nation, the seven *Ushpizin*/guests — Abraham, Isaac, Jacob, Moses, Aaron, Joseph, and David — who shared our *succah*. Therefore, many communities invoke their merit at the end of each respective *Hakafah*/circuit.

The Chassidic master R' Naftali of Ropshitz once said, "Only one time did someone get the better of me. He was an unlearned wagon driver who was rejoicing mightily on Simchas Torah. I said to him, 'Why are you so happy — you have not studied the Torah!' He replied, 'Rebbe, if my brother makes a celebration, shouldn't I rejoice with him? Don't I have a share in his happiness?'

"I said to him, 'You are right, my son. Please forgive me.' "

THE CLIMAX OF SUCCOS — which our prayers describe as זְמַן שִׂמְחָתֵנוּ, *our time of gladness* — is our heartfelt and ecstatic rejoicing with the Torah. In fact, as *Sfas Emes* comments, it is precisely because Succos and Shemini Atzeres represent an outpouring of joy that the Sages chose this festival for the annual completion and new beginning of the Torah-reading cycle, that we observe on Simchas Torah. [In Israel, Shemini Atzeres and Simchas Torah are observed on the same day.]

Hakafos

Why does the completion of the Torah call for a celebration? *Levush* finds an explanation in the early days of Solomon's kingship, when he became king as a lad of twelve. God came to him in a dream and asked him to request whatever he wished. Solomon replied that he wanted "an understanding heart with which to judge Your people, to discern between good and evil."

God was pleased with Solomon's request. He said,

> Because you requested this and you did not request long life for yourself and you did not request the life of your enemies — but you requested discernment to understand judgment: Behold I have fulfilled your words; behold I have given you a wise and discerning heart, so that there has never been your equal before you, nor will your equal arise after you. And I have even given you what you did not request, even wealth and even glory, so that no man will be your equal among kings all your days (I *Kings* 3:9-13).

When Solomon awoke, he went to the national altar in Giveon, brought offerings of gratitude and made a feast for all his subjects (ibid 3:15). Commenting on this incident, R' Yitzchak notes, מִכָּאן שֶׁעוֹשִׂין סְעֻדָּה לִגְמָרָהּ שֶׁל תּוֹרָה, *from here we derive that we should make a banquet upon completion of the Torah* (*Koheles Rabbah* 1:1 and *Shir Hashirim Rabbah* 1:1).

Solomon was taught an important principle in addition to the gift of wisdom. With a wise and discerning heart come all other human gifts, including wealth and glory, for knowledge of the Torah is the primary good. Solomon had hardly had a chance to use his newly granted wisdom, but the mere fact that he had it was sufficient cause for a celebration to which he would invite all Israel, because he had been granted the springboard to more knowledge of the Torah and the opportunity to use it in the service of God and Israel. On Simchas Torah, too, when we reflect that another cycle of Torah reading leads us into a new year of study and knowledge, we respond as Solomon did — with rejoicing and celebration.

Matteh Moshe (976) offers another Midrashic source. On Succos, Satan comes before God to condemn the Jewish people, saying, "They study the Torah, but will not complete it [i.e., they will be caught up in the festivities of Succos and will neglect the study of the Torah]." When we do indeed complete the reading of the Torah, God responds to Satan, "But they *have* completed it."

Satan answers, "Even though they have completed it, they will not begin it anew!" [i.e., if Israel does not begin its new cycle of Torah reading and study immediately, it signifies a lack of appreciation for the Torah's holiness.] As soon as Israel begins its new cycle of reading from *Bereishis*, God responds, "But they *have* begun it!" — and Satan retires in defeat. Because our devotion to the Torah provides God with grounds to defend us, this day is known as Simchas Torah.

מחזור
בית יוסף

ערוב תבשילין

When Succos falls on Thursday and Friday, an *eruv tavshilin* is made on Wednesday Erev Succos and again on Wednesday Hoshana Rabbah [see commentary]. The *eruv*-foods are held while the following blessing and declaration are recited.

בָּרוּךְ אַתָּה יהוה אֱלֹהֵינוּ מֶלֶךְ הָעוֹלָם, אֲשֶׁר קִדְּשָׁנוּ בְּמִצְוֹתָיו, וְצִוָּנוּ עַל מִצְוַת עֵרוּב.

בַּהֲדֵין עֵרוּבָא יְהֵא שָׁרֵא לָנָא לַאֲפוּיֵי וּלְבַשּׁוּלֵי וּלְאַטְמוּנֵי וּלְאַדְלוּקֵי שְׁרָגָא וּלְתַקָּנָא וּלְמֶעְבַּד כָּל צָרְכָּנָא, מִיּוֹמָא טָבָא לְשַׁבְּתָא [לָנָא וּלְכָל יִשְׂרָאֵל* הַדָּרִים בָּעִיר הַזֹּאת].

ערובי תחומין

The *eruv*-food is put in a safe place [see commentary] and the following blessing and declaration are recited. The appropriate bracketed phrases should be added.

בָּרוּךְ אַתָּה יהוה אֱלֹהֵינוּ מֶלֶךְ הָעוֹלָם, אֲשֶׁר קִדְּשָׁנוּ בְּמִצְוֹתָיו, וְצִוָּנוּ עַל מִצְוַת עֵרוּב.

בְּזֶה הָעֵרוּב יְהֵא מֻתָּר [לִי/לָנוּ] לֵילֵךְ מִמָּקוֹם זֶה אַלְפַּיִם אַמָּה לְכָל רוּחַ בְּ[שַׁבָּת וּבְ]יוֹם טוֹב זֶה.

ערובי חצרות

This *eruv* is required for the Sabbath, but not for a weekday Festival [see commentary]. The *eruv*-foods are held while the following blessing and declaration are recited. [If the *eruv* is made for the entire year, the bracketed passage is added.]

בָּרוּךְ אַתָּה יהוה אֱלֹהֵינוּ מֶלֶךְ הָעוֹלָם, אֲשֶׁר קִדְּשָׁנוּ בְּמִצְוֹתָיו, וְצִוָּנוּ עַל מִצְוַת עֵרוּב.

בַּהֲדֵין עֵרוּבָא יְהֵא שָׁרֵא לָנָא לְאַפּוּקֵי וּלְעַיּוּלֵי מִן הַבָּתִּים לֶחָצֵר, וּמִן הֶחָצֵר לְבָתִּים, וּמִבַּיִת לְבַיִת, וּמֵחָצֵר לְחָצֵר, וּמִגַּג לְגַג, כָּל מַאי דִּצְרִיךְ לָן, וּלְכָל יִשְׂרָאֵל הַדָּרִים בַּשְּׁכוּנָה זוּ [וּלְכָל מִי שֶׁיִּתּוֹסֵף בָּהּ, לְכָל שַׁבְּתוֹת הַשָּׁנָה, וּלְכָל יָמִים טוֹבִים].

עֵרוּב תַּבְשִׁילִין / ERUV TAVSHILIN

The Biblical prohibition against labor on the Festivals *(Exodus* 12:16) specifically excludes preparation of food. Still, it is forbidden to prepare food on a Festival for use on another day. When a Festival falls on Friday, however, it is permitted to prepare food needed for the Sabbath. But since this may lead people to think that they may even cook in preparation for a weekday, the Rabbis attached a condition to the preparation of Sabbath meals on a Festival — i.e., such preparations must be started before the Festival *(Pesachim* 46b). Thus, when Succos falls on Thursday and Friday, preparations for the Sabbath meal must begin on Wednesday. This enactment is called *eruv tavshilin,* literally, *mingling of cooked foods.* It consists of a *challah, matzah,* or loaf of bread, along with any other cooked food (such as fish, meat or an egg), set aside on the day before the Festival to be eaten on the Sabbath. The *eruv*-foods are held in the hand *(Orach Chaim* 527:2) and a blessing is recited. Since the person setting the *eruv* must understand its purpose, the accompanying declaration [beginning בַּהֲדֵין, *'Through this . . .'*] must be said in a language he understands.

וּלְכָל יִשְׂרָאֵל — *And for all Jews.* The bracketed phrase is recited only if the maker of the *eruv*

ERUV TAVSHILIN

When Succos falls on Thursday and Friday, an *eruv tavshilin* is made on Wednesday Erev Succos and again on Wednesday Hoshana Rabbah [see commentary]. The *eruv*-foods are held while the following blessing and declaration are recited.

בָּרוּךְ *Blessed are You, HASHEM, our God, King of the universe, Who has sanctified us with His commandments and has commanded us concerning the mitzvah of eruv.*

בַּהֲדֵין *Through this eruv may we be permitted to bake, cook, insulate, kindle flame, prepare, and do anything necessary on the Festival for the sake of the Sabbath [for ourselves and for all Jews* who live in this city].*

ERUVEI TECHUMIN

The *eruv*-food is put in a safe place [see commentary] and the following blessing and declaration are recited. The appropriate bracketed phrases should be added.

בָּרוּךְ *Blessed are You, HASHEM, our God, King of the universe, Who has sanctified us with His commandments and has commanded us concerning the mitzvah of eruv.*

בְּזֶה *Through this eruv may [I/we] be permitted to walk two thousand cubits in every direction from this place during this [Sabbath and] Festival.*

ERUVEI CHATZEIROS

This *eruv* is required for the Sabbath, but not for a weekday Festival [see commentary]. The *eruv*-foods are held while the following blessing and declaration are recited. [If the *eruv* is made for the entire year, the bracketed passage is added.]

בָּרוּךְ *Blessed are You, HASHEM, our God, King of the universe, Who has sanctified us with His commandments and has commanded us concerning the mitzvah of eruv.*

בַּהֲדֵין *Through this eruv may we be permitted to carry out or to carry in from the houses to the courtyard, and from the courtyard to the houses, from house to house, from courtyard to courtyard, and from roof to roof, all that we require, for ourselves and for all Jews who live in this area [and to all who will move into this area, for all the Sabbaths and Festivals of the year].*

---

wishes to include those who may not have made an *eruv* for themselves. If so, a second person (not the minor child of the maker) must act as agent for the townspeople and take possession of the *eruv*-foods on their behalf.

עֵרוּבֵי תְחוּמִין /MERGING OF BOUNDARIES

On the Sabbath and Festivals, one is forbidden to go more than 2,000 cubits from his halachically defined dwelling. This limit is called his תְּחוּם, *boundary*. Ordinarily, this 'dwelling' is the town in which one resides, but one has the option of establishing his dwelling elsewhere. By placing a sufficient amount of food for two Sabbath meals in a place as much as 2,000 cubits from his 'dwelling,' one establishes *that* place as his 'dwelling,' and his 2,000-cubit radius is reckoned from there. [For a full discussion of *eruvei chatzeiros* and *techumin*, see the Introduction to the ArtScroll Mishnah *Eruvin*.]

עֵרוּבֵי חֲצֵרוֹת / MERGING OF COURTYARDS

The Sages forbade carrying from the private domain of one person to that of another on the Sabbath. Similarly a courtyard, hall, or staircase shared by the residents of houses or apartments is regarded as a separate domain, and it is forbidden to carry from the private dwellings into the shared area. The Sages also provided a procedure to remove this prohibition against carrying. Known as *eruvei chatzeiros*, or the

❧ הדלקת הנרות ❧

On each *Yom Tov* night of Succos two blessings are recited. Preferably the lights should be kindled in the Succah, even if some will later be brought into the home (see *Laws* §12). When Succos coincides with the Sabbath, light the candles, then cover the eyes and recite the blessings. Uncover the eyes and gaze briefly at the candles. When Succos falls on a weekday, some follow the above procedure, while others recite the blessings before lighting the candles. When Succos coincides with the Sabbath, the words in brackets are added.

[It is forbidden to create a new flame — for example, by striking a match — on *Yom Tov*. Therefore, on the second night the candles must be lit from a flame that has been burning from before *Yom Tov*.]

בָּרוּךְ אַתָּה יהוה אֱלֹהֵינוּ מֶלֶךְ הָעוֹלָם, אֲשֶׁר קִדְּשָׁנוּ בְּמִצְוֹתָיו, וְצִוָּנוּ לְהַדְלִיק נֵר* שֶׁל [שַׁבָּת וְשֶׁל] יוֹם טוֹב.*

בָּרוּךְ אַתָּה יהוה אֱלֹהֵינוּ מֶלֶךְ הָעוֹלָם, שֶׁהֶחֱיָנוּ* וְקִיְּמָנוּ וְהִגִּיעָנוּ לַזְּמַן הַזֶּה.

It is customary to recite the following prayer after the kindling. The words in brackets are included as they apply.

יְהִי רָצוֹן* לְפָנֶיךָ, יהוה אֱלֹהַי וֵאלֹהֵי אֲבוֹתַי, שֶׁתְּחוֹנֵן אוֹתִי [וְאֶת אִישִׁי, וְאֶת בָּנַי, וְאֶת בְּנוֹתַי, וְאֶת אָבִי, וְאֶת אִמִּי] וְאֶת כָּל קְרוֹבַי; וְתִתֶּן לָנוּ וּלְכָל יִשְׂרָאֵל חַיִּים טוֹבִים וַאֲרוּכִים; וְתִזְכְּרֵנוּ בְּזִכְרוֹן טוֹבָה וּבְרָכָה; וְתִפְקְדֵנוּ בִּפְקֻדַּת יְשׁוּעָה וְרַחֲמִים; וּתְבָרְכֵנוּ בְּרָכוֹת גְּדוֹלוֹת; וְתַשְׁלִים בָּתֵּינוּ; וְתַשְׁכֵּן שְׁכִינָתְךָ בֵּינֵינוּ. וְזַכֵּנִי לְגַדֵּל בָּנִים וּבְנֵי בָנִים חֲכָמִים וּנְבוֹנִים, אוֹהֲבֵי יהוה, יִרְאֵי אֱלֹהִים, אַנְשֵׁי אֱמֶת, זֶרַע קֹדֶשׁ, בַּיהוה דְּבֵקִים, וּמְאִירִים אֶת הָעוֹלָם בַּתּוֹרָה וּבְמַעֲשִׂים טוֹבִים, וּבְכָל מְלֶאכֶת עֲבוֹדַת הַבּוֹרֵא. אָנָּא שְׁמַע אֶת תְּחִנָּתִי בָּעֵת הַזֹּאת, בִּזְכוּת שָׂרָה וְרִבְקָה וְרָחֵל וְלֵאָה אִמּוֹתֵינוּ, וְהָאֵר נֵרֵנוּ שֶׁלֹּא יִכְבֶּה לְעוֹלָם וָעֶד, וְהָאֵר פָּנֶיךָ וְנִוָּשֵׁעָה. אָמֵן.

'merging of courtyards,' this procedure considers all houses opening into the shared area as owned by a single consortium. This is done by collecting bread or *matzah* from each of the families and placing all the loaves in one of the dwelling units. [Even if only one person supplies the bread, it is still possible to make an *eruv*. In this case, a second person (not the minor child of the donor) must act as agent for all those involved and take possession of the bread on their behalf.] This symbolizes that all the contributors are legal residents of the unit where they have deposited their bread, and the entire area is regarded as a single dwelling. All the residents may carry in all its parts on the Sabbath, as long as the breads were intact and edible at the onset of the Sabbath. [The declaration as given here may not be used if the *eruv* area includes a public thoroughfare. Such an area requires complex additional procedures which should not be undertaken by a layman.]

The restrictions on carrying apply only to the Sabbath and not to the Festivals. Thus, *eruvei chatzeiros* is only necessary for *Yom Tov* that falls on the Sabbath but not for the other days of the Festival.

⊰ הַדְלָקַת הַנֵּרוֹת / KINDLING LIGHTS ⊱

Since women generally look after household matters, the *mitzvah* of kindling the lights has devolved upon the mistress of the house *(Rambam)*. Nevertheless, a man living alone is required to kindle the lights and recite the proper blessing. Similarly, if a woman is too ill to light, her husband should light the candles and recite the blessing *(Magen Avraham)*.

KINDLING LIGHTS

On each *Yom Tov* night of Succos two blessings are recited. Preferably the lights should be kindled in the Succah, even if some will later be brought into the home (see *Laws* §12). When Succos coincides with the Sabbath, light the candles, then cover the eyes and recite the blessings. Uncover the eyes and gaze briefly at the candles. When Succos falls on a weekday, some follow the above procedure, while others recite the blessings before lighting the candles. When Succos coincides with the Sabbath, the words in brackets are added.

[It is forbidden to create a new flame — for example, by striking a match — on *Yom Tov*. Therefore, on the second night the candles must be lit from a flame that has been burning from before *Yom Tov*.]

בָּרוּךְ *Blessed are You, HASHEM, our God, King of the universe, Who has sanctified us with His commandments, and has commanded us to kindle the light* of [the Sabbath and of] the Festival.**

בָּרוּךְ *Blessed are You, HASHEM, our God, King of the universe, Who has kept us alive,* sustained us, and brought us to this season.*

It is customary to recite the following prayer after the kindling. The words in brackets are included as they apply.

יְהִי רָצוֹן *May it be Your will,* HASHEM, my God and God of my forefathers, that You show favor to me [my husband, my sons, my daughters, my father, my mother] and all my relatives; and that You grant us and all Israel a good and long life; that You remember us with a beneficent memory and blessing; that You consider us with a consideration of salvation and compassion; that You bless us with great blessings; that You make our households complete; that You cause Your Presence to dwell among us. Privilege me to raise children and grandchildren who are wise and understanding, who love HASHEM and fear God, people of truth, holy offspring, attached to HASHEM, who illuminate the world with Torah and good deeds and with every labor in the service of the Creator. Please, hear my supplication at this time, in the merit of Sarah, Rebecca, Rachel, and Leah, our mothers, and cause our light to illuminate that it be not extinguished forever, and let Your countenance shine so that we are saved. Amen.*

There should be some light in every room where it will be needed—and indeed this is a halachic requirement—nevertheless, the blessing is recited upon the flames that are kindled in the dining room (*Mishnah Berurah*). The lights honor the Sabbath and Festival by brightening and dignifying the festive meal (*Rashi*).

נֵר — *The light.* Prevalent custom calls for at least two candles. According to *Eliyah Rabbah*, they symbolize man and wife. Nevertheless, since one can fulfill the *mitzvah* with a single candle [indeed, *Mishnah Berurah* advises one with extremely limited means to purchase one good candle rather than two inferior ones] the blessing is couched in the singular form, נֵר, *light*, and not נֵרוֹת, *lights*.

שֶׁל [שַׁבָּת וְשֶׁל] יוֹם טוֹב — *Of [the Sabbath and of] the Festival.* The Sabbath is mentioned first, following the Talmudic rule that a more frequently performed *mitzvah* takes precedence over a less frequent one.

שֶׁהֶחֱיָנוּ — *Who has kept us alive.* Some authorities rule that women should not recite the שֶׁהֶחֱיָנוּ blessing at this point, but instead should listen to the blessing during *Kiddush*, as does the rest of the family. However, it is a virtually universal custom that women do recite the blessing when kindling the lights.

יְהִי רָצוֹן — *May it be Your will.* It is customary to recite this prayer after the kindling. Because of the Talmudic declaration, 'One who is scrupulous in the kindling of lights will be blessed with children who are Torah scholars' (*Shabbos* 23b), the prayer stresses the supplication that the children of the home grow up learned and righteous.

מנחה לערב סוכות

אַשְׁרֵי יוֹשְׁבֵי בֵיתֶךָ, עוֹד יְהַלְּלְוּךָ סֶּלָה.[1] אַשְׁרֵי הָעָם שֶׁכָּכָה לוֹ, אַשְׁרֵי הָעָם שֶׁיהוה אֱלֹהָיו.[2]

תהלים קמה

תְּהִלָּה לְדָוִד,

אֲרוֹמִמְךָ* אֱלוֹהַי הַמֶּלֶךְ, וַאֲבָרְכָה שִׁמְךָ לְעוֹלָם וָעֶד.
בְּכָל יוֹם אֲבָרְכֶךָּ,* וַאֲהַלְלָה שִׁמְךָ לְעוֹלָם וָעֶד.
גָּדוֹל יהוה וּמְהֻלָּל מְאֹד, וְלִגְדֻלָּתוֹ אֵין חֵקֶר.*
דּוֹר לְדוֹר יְשַׁבַּח מַעֲשֶׂיךָ, וּגְבוּרֹתֶיךָ יַגִּידוּ.
הֲדַר כְּבוֹד הוֹדֶךָ, וְדִבְרֵי נִפְלְאֹתֶיךָ אָשִׂיחָה.
וֶעֱזוּז נוֹרְאוֹתֶיךָ יֹאמֵרוּ, וּגְדוּלָּתְךָ אֲסַפְּרֶנָּה.
זֵכֶר רַב טוּבְךָ יַבִּיעוּ, וְצִדְקָתְךָ יְרַנֵּנוּ.
חַנּוּן וְרַחוּם* יהוה, אֶרֶךְ אַפַּיִם וּגְדָל חָסֶד.
טוֹב יהוה לַכֹּל, וְרַחֲמָיו עַל כָּל מַעֲשָׂיו.
יוֹדְוּךָ יהוה כָּל מַעֲשֶׂיךָ, וַחֲסִידֶיךָ יְבָרְכוּכָה.
כְּבוֹד מַלְכוּתְךָ יֹאמֵרוּ, וּגְבוּרָתְךָ יְדַבֵּרוּ.
לְהוֹדִיעַ לִבְנֵי הָאָדָם גְּבוּרֹתָיו, וּכְבוֹד הֲדַר מַלְכוּתוֹ.
מַלְכוּתְךָ מַלְכוּת כָּל עֹלָמִים, וּמֶמְשַׁלְתְּךָ בְּכָל דּוֹר וָדֹר.

מִנְחָה לְעֶרֶב סוכות / MINCHAH FOR EREV SUCCOS

The Talmud tells us that *Minchah* corresponds to — and substitutes for — the *[tamid]* daily afternoon offering of the Temple service, and that this prayer was first introduced by the Patriarch Isaac (*Berachos* 26b). These two factors explain both the time and the mood of this prayer.

The daily afternoon *tamid* could be brought no earlier that half an hour after midday; consequently *Minchah* may be recited only from that time onward. It is preferable, however, not to begin *Minchah* earlier than three and a half hours after midday, because the *tamid* was customarily delayed until then (*Orach Chaim* 233:1). Another reason that *Minchah* is left for late afternoon is because that part of the day is a time of Divine mercy. It was then that God answered Elijah's prayer for vindication (*I Kings* 18:36) and that Isaac went out to the field to pray (*Genesis* 24:63).

Since Isaac originated the *Minchah* prayer, it is logical that we find in his life a clue to the prayer's significance. Unlike his father Abraham whose life was a story of uninterrupted success, ascension, and the gaining of universal respect, Isaac was envied and persecuted by the reigning kings and dominant peoples of Canaan, and ended his life in blindness, saddened by the conflicts that put an end to the domestic tranquility of his family. Thus, whereas Abraham's life is like the expectancy of a new day, Isaac's story is symbolized by the sun descending from its noontime zenith to the gloom and fear of night.

Abraham inaugurated the morning prayer, which is brightened by psalms of praise, the proclamation of God's Oneness and the blessings of the *Shema*, which acknowledge God as the Creator of light, wisdom, and salvation. In stark contrast, Isaac's *Minchah* prayer consists almost exclusively of the *Shemoneh Esrei* with its acknowledgment of our total dependence on God for all our personal and national needs.

אַשְׁרֵי / Ashrei

The Sages teach that one should pray in a state of joyous dedication to God's will. To accomplish this, they inserted *Ashrei* prior to *Shemoneh Esrei*, because *Ashrei* concludes with verses that express confidence in God's goodness and concern for His servants.

Psalm 145 begins with the verse תְּהִלָּה לְדָוִד;

MINCHAH FOR EREV SUCCOS

אַשְׁרֵי *Praiseworthy are those who dwell in Your house; may they always praise You, Selah!*[1] *Praiseworthy is the people for whom this is so, praiseworthy is the people whose God is* HASHEM.[2]

Psalm 145 *A psalm of praise by David:*

א *I will exalt You,* my God the King,*
and I will bless Your Name forever and ever.

ב *Every day I will bless You,**
and I will laud Your Name forever and ever.

ג HASHEM *is great and exceedingly lauded,*
*and His greatness is beyond investigation.**

ד *Each generation will praise Your deeds to the next*
and of Your mighty deeds they will tell;

ה *The splendrous glory of Your power*
and Your wondrous deeds I shall discuss.

ו *And of Your awesome power they will speak,*
and Your greatness I shall relate.

ז *A recollection of Your abundant goodness they will utter*
and of Your righteousness they will sing exultantly.

ח *Gracious and merciful* is* HASHEM,
slow to anger, and great in [bestowing] kindness.

ט HASHEM *is good to all; His mercies are on all His works.*

י *All Your works shall thank You,* HASHEM,
and Your devout ones will bless You.

כ *Of the glory of Your kingdom they will speak,*
and of Your power they will tell;

ל *To inform human beings of His mighty deeds,*
and the glorious splendor of His kingdom.

מ *Your kingdom is a kingdom spanning all eternities,*
and Your dominion is throughout every generation.

(1) *Psalms* 84:5. (2) 144:15.

---

the two preliminary verses, each beginning with the word אַשְׁרֵי, are affixed to תְּהִלָּה לְדָוִד for two reasons: (a) By expressing the idea that those who can dwell in God's house of prayer and service are praiseworthy, these verses set the stage for the succeeding psalm of praise, for we, the praiseworthy ones, are about to laud the God in Whose house we dwell; and (b) the word אַשְׁרֵי is found three times in these verses. This alludes to the Talmudic dictum that one who recites psalm 145 three times a day is assured of a share in the World to Come (*Berachos* 4b); thus, those who do so are indeed אַשְׁרֵי, *praiseworthy.*

תְּהִלָּה . . . אֲרוֹמִמְךָ — *A psalm . . . I will exalt You.* Beginning with the word אֲרוֹמִמְךָ, the initials of the respective verses follow the order of the *Aleph-Beis.* According to *Abudraham* the *Aleph-Beis* structure symbolizes that we praise God with every sound available to the organs of speech. *Midrash Tadshei* records that the Psalmists and Sages used the *Aleph-Beis* formula in chapters that they wanted people to follow more easily or memorize.

בְּכָל יוֹם אֲבָרְכֶךָּ — *Every day I will bless You.* True, no mortal can pretend to know God's essence, but each of us *is* equipped to appreciate life, health, sustenance, sunshine, rainfall, and so on. For them and their daily renewal, we give daily blessings *(Siach Yitzchak).*

וְלִגְדֻלָּתוֹ אֵין חֵקֶר — *And His greatness is beyond investigation.* Much though we may try, we can understand neither God's essence nor His ways through human analysis, for He is infinite. We *must* rely on the traditions that have come to us from earlier generations, as the next verse suggests *(Rama).*

חַנּוּן וְרַחוּם — *Gracious and merciful.* Because

סוֹמֵךְ יהוה* לְכָל הַנֹּפְלִים, וְזוֹקֵף לְכָל הַכְּפוּפִים.
עֵינֵי כֹל אֵלֶיךָ יְשַׂבֵּרוּ,* וְאַתָּה נוֹתֵן לָהֶם אֶת אָכְלָם בְּעִתּוֹ.

Concentrate intently while reciting the verse, פּוֹתֵחַ.

פּוֹתֵחַ* אֶת יָדֶךָ, וּמַשְׂבִּיעַ לְכָל חַי רָצוֹן.
צַדִּיק יהוה בְּכָל דְּרָכָיו, וְחָסִיד* בְּכָל מַעֲשָׂיו.
קָרוֹב יהוה לְכָל קֹרְאָיו, לְכֹל אֲשֶׁר יִקְרָאֻהוּ בֶאֱמֶת.
רְצוֹן יְרֵאָיו יַעֲשֶׂה, וְאֶת שַׁוְעָתָם יִשְׁמַע וְיוֹשִׁיעֵם.
שׁוֹמֵר יהוה אֶת כָּל אֹהֲבָיו, וְאֵת כָּל הָרְשָׁעִים יַשְׁמִיד.
❖ תְּהִלַּת יהוה יְדַבֶּר פִּי, וִיבָרֵךְ כָּל בָּשָׂר שֵׁם קָדְשׁוֹ לְעוֹלָם
וָעֶד. וַאֲנַחְנוּ נְבָרֵךְ* יָהּ, מֵעַתָּה וְעַד עוֹלָם, הַלְלוּיָהּ.*[1]

Chazzan recites חֲצִי קַדִּישׁ.

יִתְגַּדַּל וְיִתְקַדַּשׁ שְׁמֵהּ רַבָּא. (.Cong – אָמֵן.) בְּעָלְמָא דִּי בְרָא כִרְעוּתֵהּ. וְיַמְלִיךְ מַלְכוּתֵהּ, בְּחַיֵּיכוֹן וּבְיוֹמֵיכוֹן וּבְחַיֵּי דְכָל בֵּית יִשְׂרָאֵל, בַּעֲגָלָא וּבִזְמַן קָרִיב. וְאִמְרוּ: אָמֵן.

(.Cong – אָמֵן. יְהֵא שְׁמֵהּ רַבָּא מְבָרַךְ לְעָלַם וּלְעָלְמֵי עָלְמַיָּא.)

יְהֵא שְׁמֵהּ רַבָּא מְבָרַךְ לְעָלַם וּלְעָלְמֵי עָלְמַיָּא.

יִתְבָּרַךְ וְיִשְׁתַּבַּח וְיִתְפָּאַר וְיִתְרוֹמַם וְיִתְנַשֵּׂא וְיִתְהַדָּר וְיִתְעַלֶּה וְיִתְהַלָּל שְׁמֵהּ דְּקֻדְשָׁא בְּרִיךְ הוּא (.Cong – בְּרִיךְ הוּא) — לְעֵלָּא מִן כָּל בִּרְכָתָא וְשִׁירָתָא תֻּשְׁבְּחָתָא וְנֶחֱמָתָא, דַּאֲמִירָן בְּעָלְמָא. וְאִמְרוּ: אָמֵן. (.Cong – אָמֵן.)

God is *merciful,* He is אֶרֶךְ אַפַּיִם, *slow to anger,* so that punishment, although deserved, is delayed as long as possible to allow time for repentance. And because He is *gracious* He is גְּדָל חָסֶד, *great in bestowing kindness (Siach Yitzchak).*

סוֹמֵךְ ה׳ — *HASHEM supports.* No verse in *Ashrei* begins with a נ, because in the context of this verse that speaks of God supporting the fallen, the letter נ can be taken as an allusion to נְפִילָה, Israel's future *downfall,* ח״ו, and the Psalmist refused to use a letter that could suggest such tragedy. Nevertheless, knowing that downfalls would take place, the Psalmist comforted Israel by saying *God supports all the fallen ones.* This is an implied guarantee that even when a dreaded downfall happens, the people can look forward to His support *(Berachos* 4b). *Maharsha* comments that by omitting a direct mention of downfall, the Psalmist implies that even when Israel *does* suffer reverses, those reverses will never be complete. Rather, as the next verse declares, God will support the fallen.

עֵינֵי כֹל אֵלֶיךָ יְשַׂבֵּרוּ — *The eyes of all look to You with hope.* Even animals instinctively rely upon God for their sustenance [how much more so should man recognize the beneficence of his Maker!] *(Radak).*

פּוֹתֵחַ — *[You] open.* When reciting this verse, one must have in mind the translation of the words because this declaration of God's universal goodness is one of the two reasons the Sages required the thrice-daily recitation of this psalm. One who forgot to concentrate on the translation must recite the verse again *(Tur* and *Shulchan Aruch* 51:7). This verse should be recited with great joy at the knowledge that God cares for every creature *(Yesod V'Shoresh HaAvodah).*

צַדִּיק . . . וְחָסִיד — *Righteous . . . and magnanimous.* That God's ways are just and righteous means that He judges people only according to their deeds. Nevertheless, even when justice calls for grievous punishment He is *magnanimous* in softening the blow, for He is merciful *(Vilna Gaon).*

וַאֲנַחְנוּ נְבָרֵךְ — *We will bless.* After completing psalm 145 which holds an assurance of the World to Come, we append this verse in which we express the hope that we will bless God *forever* — that is, in both worlds *(Levush).*

הַלְלוּיָהּ — *Halleluyah.* This familiar word is a contraction of two words: הַלְלוּ יָהּ, *praise God.*

ס *HASHEM supports* all the fallen ones and straightens all the bent.*
ע *The eyes of all look to You with hope**
and You give them their food in its proper time;
פ *You open* Your hand,* Concentrate intently while reciting the verse, *'You open. . .'*
and satisfy the desire of every living thing.
צ *Righteous is HASHEM in all His ways*
and magnanimous in all His deeds.*
ק *HASHEM is close to all who call upon Him —*
to all who call upon Him sincerely.
ר *The will of those who fear Him He will do;*
and their cry He will hear, and save them.
ש *HASHEM protects all who love Him;*
but all the wicked He will destroy.
ת Chazzan– *May my mouth declare the praise of HASHEM*
and may all flesh bless His Holy Name forever and ever.
We will bless God from this time and forever, Halleluyah!**[1]

Chazzan recites Half-*Kaddish:*

יִתְגַּדַּל *May His great Name grow exalted and sanctified* (Cong.– *Amen.*) *in the world that He created as He willed. May He give reign to His kingship in your lifetimes and in your days, and in the lifetimes of the entire Family of Israel, swiftly and soon. Now respond: Amen.*

(Cong.– *Amen. May His great Name be blessed forever and ever.*)
May His great Name be blessed forever and ever.

Blessed, praised, glorified, exalted, extolled, mighty, upraised, and lauded be the Name of the Holy One, Blessed is He (Cong.– *Blessed is He*) *— beyond any blessing and song, praise and consolation that are uttered in the world. Now respond: Amen.* (Cong.– *Amen.*)

(1) *Psalms* 115:18.

The term הַלְלוּ denotes crying out in happy excitement, while the unique meaning implied by the Name יָהּ means 'the One Who is forever.' The Psalmist addresses everyone, saying: Use your energy to be *excited* over God and nothing else *(R' Avigdor Miller).*

שְׁמוֹנֶה עֶשְׂרֵה / SHEMONEH ESREI

The Talmud refers to *Shemoneh Esrei* simply as תְּפִלָּה, *The Prayer,* for it is only in *Shemoneh Esrei* that we formulate our needs and ask God to fulfill them. The three *Shemoneh Esrei* prayers of the day were instituted by the Patriarchs and they are in place of the daily Temple offerings *(Berachos* 26b).

The term *Shemoneh Esrei* means eighteen, and, indeed, the original *Shemoneh Esrei* consisted of eighteen blessings. The requirement that there be precisely eighteen is based on various Scriptural supports (*Megillah* 17b). The text of the individual blessings was composed by the Men of the Great Assembly at the beginning of the Second Temple period, and it was put into its final form under Rabban Gamliel II after the Destruction, over four centuries later (ibid.). A nineteenth blessing was added later (see commentary to וְלַמַּלְשִׁינִים, p. 16), but the name *Shemoneh Esrei* was left unchanged. The *Zohar* refers to the *Shemoneh Esrei* as the *Amidah* ['standing prayer'], and the two names are used interchangeably.

Shemoneh Esrei has three sections: (a) In the first three blessings, the supplicant pays homage to God, like a slave praising his master before he dares make a request; (b) the middle section of thirteen (originally, twelve) blessings contains the supplicant's requests; (c) in the last three blessings, he takes leave, expressing gratitude and confidence in his Master's graciousness *(Berachos* 34a).

Even the middle section is not merely a catalogue of selfish requests. In each blessing, we first acknowledge God's mastery, and only then make the request. Thus, each blessing is an affirmation of God's power *(Vilna Gaon).*

שמונה עשרה – עמידה

Take three steps backward, then three steps forward. Remain standing with feet together while reciting *Shemoneh Esrei*. Recite it with quiet devotion and without interruption, verbal or otherwise. Although it should not be audible to others, one must pray loudly enough to hear himself.

כִּי שֵׁם יהוה אֶקְרָא,* הָבוּ גֹדֶל לֵאלֹהֵינוּ.[1]
אֲדֹנָי שְׂפָתַי תִּפְתָּח,* וּפִי יַגִּיד תְּהִלָּתֶךָ.[2]

אבות

Bend the knees at בָּרוּךְ; bow at אַתָּה; straighten up at ה׳.

בָּרוּךְ אַתָּה* יהוה אֱלֹהֵינוּ וֵאלֹהֵי אֲבוֹתֵינוּ,* אֱלֹהֵי אַבְרָהָם, אֱלֹהֵי יִצְחָק, וֵאלֹהֵי יַעֲקֹב, הָאֵל הַגָּדוֹל הַגִּבּוֹר וְהַנּוֹרָא, אֵל עֶלְיוֹן,* גּוֹמֵל חֲסָדִים טוֹבִים וְקוֹנֵה הַכֹּל,* וְזוֹכֵר חַסְדֵי אָבוֹת, וּמֵבִיא גוֹאֵל* לִבְנֵי בְנֵיהֶם, לְמַעַן שְׁמוֹ בְּאַהֲבָה.

Bend the knees at בָּרוּךְ; bow at אַתָּה; straighten up at ה׳.

מֶלֶךְ עוֹזֵר וּמוֹשִׁיעַ וּמָגֵן.* בָּרוּךְ אַתָּה יהוה, מָגֵן אַבְרָהָם.*

גבורות

אַתָּה גִּבּוֹר לְעוֹלָם אֲדֹנָי, מְחַיֵּה מֵתִים* אַתָּה, רַב לְהוֹשִׁיעַ. מְכַלְכֵּל חַיִּים בְּחֶסֶד, מְחַיֵּה מֵתִים בְּרַחֲמִים רַבִּים, סוֹמֵךְ נוֹפְלִים, וְרוֹפֵא חוֹלִים, וּמַתִּיר אֲסוּרִים, וּמְקַיֵּם אֱמוּנָתוֹ לִישֵׁנֵי עָפָר. מִי כָמוֹךָ בַּעַל גְּבוּרוֹת, וּמִי דּוֹמֶה לָּךְ, מֶלֶךְ מֵמִית וּמְחַיֶּה וּמַצְמִיחַ יְשׁוּעָה.* וְנֶאֱמָן אַתָּה לְהַחֲיוֹת מֵתִים. בָּרוּךְ אַתָּה יהוה, מְחַיֵּה הַמֵּתִים.

☙ Introductory Phrases

כִּי שֵׁם ה׳ אֶקְרָא — *When I call out the Name of* HASHEM. Moses introduced his final prophecies and prayers for Israel's redemption with this verse [*Deuteronomy* 32:3]. In effect he said to Israel, 'When I call out God's Name in prayer, do not respond that He has forsaken us. God will keep His promises despite your shortcomings' (*Sforno*).

אֲדֹנָי שְׂפָתַי תִּפְתָּח — *My Lord, open my lips ... Ramban* notes that שְׂפָתַי, *my lips,* can also mean *my boundaries.* Thus we ask God to free us from our limitations so that we can praise Him properly.

☙ אָבוֹת / Patriarchs

The first blessing of *Shemoneh Esrei* is known as אָבוֹת, *Patriarchs,* because it recalls the greatness of our forefathers in whose merit God pledged to help Israel throughout history, even if we are unworthy.

בָּרוּךְ אַתָּה — *Blessed are You.* [Since God is perfect by definition, what benefit can man's blessing confer upon Him?]

— This is a declaration of fact: God *is* blessed in the sense that He is perfect and complete (*Sefer HaChinuch* 430).

— God is the *Source* of inexhaustible blessing, and He has created the world in order to do good to His creatures. Since this is His will, we pray for the Redemption, when man will be worthy of His utmost blessing (*Rashba; R' Bachya*).

אֱלֹהֵינוּ וֵאלֹהֵי אֲבוֹתֵינוּ — *Our God and the God of our forefathers.* First we call Him *our God* because we are obligated to serve Him and know Him to the limit of *our* capacity. But there is much about His ways that we cannot understand. In response to such doubts we proclaim that He is *the God of our forefathers,* and we have faith in the tradition they transmitted (*Dover Shalom*).

אֵל עֶלְיוֹן — *The supreme God.* The word עֶלְיוֹן, *supreme,* means that God is so exalted that He is far beyond the comprehension of even the holiest angels. We can understand Him only superficially, by studying His deeds, i.e., that He *bestows beneficial kindnesses* (*Siach Yitzchak*).

❧ SHEMONEH ESREI – AMIDAH ☙

Take three steps backward, then three steps forward. Remain standing with feet together while reciting *Shemoneh Esrei*. Recite it with quiet devotion and without interruption, verbal or otherwise. Although it should not be audible to others, one must pray loudly enough to hear himself.

When I call out the Name of HASHEM, ascribe greatness to our God.*[1]
My Lord, open my lips, that my mouth may declare Your praise.*[2]

PATRIARCHS

Bend the knees at *'Blessed'*; bow at *'You'*; straighten up at *'HASHEM.'*

בָּרוּךְ *Blessed are You,* HASHEM, our God and the God of our forefathers,* God of Abraham, God of Isaac, and God of Jacob; the great, mighty, and awesome God, the supreme God,* Who bestows beneficial kindnesses and creates everything,* Who recalls the kindnesses of the Patriarchs and brings a Redeemer* to their children's children, for His Name's sake, with love.*

Bend the knees at *'Blessed'*; bow at *'You'*; straighten up at *'HASHEM.'*

O King, Helper, Savior, and Shield. Blessed are You, HASHEM, Shield of Abraham.**

GOD'S MIGHT

אַתָּה *You are eternally mighty, my Lord, the Resuscitator of the dead* are You; abundantly able to save. He sustains the living with kindness, resuscitates the dead with abundant mercy, supports the fallen, heals the sick, releases the confined, and maintains His faith to those asleep in the dust. Who is like You, O Master of mighty deeds, and who is comparable to You, O King Who causes death and restores life and makes salvation sprout!* And You are faithful to resuscitate the dead. Blessed are You, HASHEM, Who resuscitates the dead.*

(1) *Deuteronomy* 32:3. (2) *Psalms* 51:17.

וְקוֹנֵה הַכֹּל — *And creates everything.* The translation is based on the consensus of commentators, both here and to *Genesis* 14:19. Some translate *the Owner of everything*. Either way, the sense of the phrase is that God is Master of all creation.

וּמֵבִיא גוֹאֵל — *And brings a Redeemer.* The phrase is in the present tense. Every event, no matter how terrible it may seem, is a step toward the ultimate redemption by the Messiah *(Siach Yitzchak)*.

עוֹזֵר וּמוֹשִׁיעַ וּמָגֵן — *Helper, Savior, and Shield.* God 'helps' [עוֹזֵר] those who try to help themselves; He 'saves' [מוֹשִׁיעַ] even without the victim's participation; and 'shields' [מָגֵן] to prevent danger from approaching *(Iyun Tefillah)*. In a different interpretation, *B'nai Yisas'char* comments that עוֹזֵר refers to the help that God gives without any prayer on the part of the victim, while מוֹשִׁיעַ refers to God's response to a prayer.

מָגֵן אַבְרָהָם — *Shield of Abraham.* God preserves the spark of Abraham within every Jew, no matter how far he may have strayed *(Chiddushei HaRim)*.

☙ גְּבוּרוֹת / God's Might

מְחַיֵּה מֵתִים — *The Resuscitator of the dead.* The concept that God restores life is found three times in this section, alluding to the three kinds of resuscitation: man's awakening every morning after deathlike slumber; the rain that has the life-sustaining quality of making vegetation grow; and the literal resuscitation of the dead, that will take place in the Messianic age *(Abudraham)*.

וּמַצְמִיחַ יְשׁוּעָה — *And makes salvation sprout.* Good deeds are like seeds that are planted and produce crops. People can earn resuscitation because of the good their children do or because of beneficial results of undertakings they initiated in their lifetimes *(Siach Yitzchak)*.

During the *chazzan's* repetition, *Kedushah* (below) is recited at this point.

קדושת השם

אַתָּה קָדוֹשׁ וְשִׁמְךָ קָדוֹשׁ,* וּקְדוֹשִׁים* בְּכָל יוֹם יְהַלְלוּךָ סֶּלָה. בָּרוּךְ אַתָּה יהוה, הָאֵל הַקָּדוֹשׁ.

בינה

אַתָּה חוֹנֵן לְאָדָם דַּעַת,* וּמְלַמֵּד לֶאֱנוֹשׁ בִּינָה. חָנֵּנוּ מֵאִתְּךָ דֵּעָה בִּינָה וְהַשְׂכֵּל. בָּרוּךְ אַתָּה יהוה, חוֹנֵן הַדָּעַת.

קדושה

When reciting *Kedushah,* one must stand with his feet together and avoid any interruptions. One should rise on his toes when saying the words קָדוֹשׁ, קָדוֹשׁ, קָדוֹשׁ; בָּרוּךְ (of בָּרוּךְ כְּבוֹד); and יִמְלֹךְ.

Cong. then *Chazzan* – **נְקַדֵּשׁ** אֶת שִׁמְךָ בָּעוֹלָם, כְּשֵׁם שֶׁמַּקְדִּישִׁים אוֹתוֹ בִּשְׁמֵי מָרוֹם, כַּכָּתוּב עַל יַד נְבִיאֶךָ, וְקָרָא זֶה אֶל זֶה וְאָמַר:

All – קָדוֹשׁ קָדוֹשׁ קָדוֹשׁ* יהוה צְבָאוֹת, מְלֹא כָל הָאָרֶץ כְּבוֹדוֹ.*[1]

Chazzan – לְעֻמָּתָם בָּרוּךְ יֹאמֵרוּ:*

All – בָּרוּךְ כְּבוֹד יהוה, מִמְּקוֹמוֹ.[2]

Chazzan – וּבְדִבְרֵי קָדְשְׁךָ כָּתוּב לֵאמֹר:

All – יִמְלֹךְ יהוה* לְעוֹלָם, אֱלֹהַיִךְ צִיּוֹן לְדֹר וָדֹר, הַלְלוּיָהּ.[3]

Chazzan only concludes – לְדוֹר וָדוֹר נַגִּיד גָּדְלֶךָ וּלְנֵצַח נְצָחִים קְדֻשָּׁתְךָ נַקְדִּישׁ, וְשִׁבְחֲךָ אֱלֹהֵינוּ מִפִּינוּ לֹא יָמוּשׁ לְעוֹלָם וָעֶד, כִּי אֵל מֶלֶךְ גָּדוֹל וְקָדוֹשׁ אָתָּה. בָּרוּךְ אַתָּה יהוה, הָאֵל הַקָּדוֹשׁ.

Chazzan continues . . . אַתָּה חוֹנֵן (above).

קְדֻשָּׁה / Kedushah

Kedushah, Sanctification, expresses the concept that God is exalted above and separated from the limitations of material existence. When a *minyan* (quorum of ten) is present, it becomes the representative of the nation and echoes the angels who sing God's praise by proclaiming His holiness and glory. We do this by reciting *Kedushah,* a prayer based on that of the angels themselves, and with feet together, in the manner of the angels *(Ezekiel* 1:7). When reciting the words קָדוֹשׁ, קָדוֹשׁ, קָדוֹשׁ; בָּרוּךְ (of בָּרוּךְ כְּבוֹד); and יִמְלֹךְ, we rise up on our toes to symbolize that we seek to break loose from the bonds of earth and unite our service with that of the angels.

Based on the teachings of *Arizal,* everyone recites the entire *Kedushah* (from נְקַדֵּשׁ until הַלְלוּיָהּ), even the parts labeled *'Chazzan.'* Many congregations, however, follow the custom recorded in *Shulchan Aruch* (ch. 125) that only the verses labeled 'Cong.' or 'All' are recited by everyone. Each congregation, of course, should maintain its own custom.

קָדוֹשׁ קָדוֹשׁ קָדוֹשׁ — *Holy, holy, holy.* God is *holy* with relation to the physical world, *holy* with relation to the spiritual world and *holy* with relation to the World to Come *(Targum Yonasan).*

מְלֹא כָל הָאָרֶץ כְּבוֹדוֹ — *The whole world is filled with His glory.* Man can bring God's holiness — awesome though it is — to earth, by fulfilling the Torah's commandments *(Zohar).*

לְעֻמָּתָם בָּרוּךְ יֹאמֵרוּ — *Those facing them say 'Blessed.'* They respond to קָדוֹשׁ, *Holy . . .,* with the verse . . . בָּרוּךְ כְּבוֹד, *Blessed is the glory,* which the congregation will now recite in full.

יִמְלֹךְ ה׳ — *HASHEM shall reign.* The Sages inserted this verse into *Kedushah* because they wanted all prayers to include an implied or

During the *chazzan's* repetition, *Kedushah* (below) is recited at this point.

HOLINESS OF GOD'S NAME

אַתָּה *You are holy and Your Name is holy,* and holy ones* praise You every day, forever. Blessed are You,* HASHEM, *the holy God.*

INSIGHT

אַתָּה *You graciously endow man with wisdom* and teach insight to a frail mortal. Endow us graciously from Yourself with wisdom, insight, and discernment. Blessed are You,* HASHEM, *gracious Giver of wisdom.*

KEDUSHAH

When reciting *Kedushah*, one must stand with his feet together and avoid any interruptions. One should rise on his toes when saying *Holy, holy, holy; Blessed is;* and *HASHEM shall reign.*

Cong. then *Chazzan* – **נְקַדֵּשׁ** *We shall sanctify Your Name in this world, just as they sanctify it in heaven above, as it is written by Your prophet, "And one [angel] will call another and say:*

All – *'Holy, holy, holy* is* HASHEM, *Master of Legions, the whole world is filled with His glory.' "*[1]*

Chazzan – *Those facing them say 'Blessed':**

All – *'Blessed is the glory of* HASHEM *from His place.'[2]*

Chazzan – *And in Your holy Writings the following is written:*

All – *'*HASHEM *shall reign* forever — your God, O Zion — from generation to generation, Halleluyah!'[3]*

Chazzan only concludes – *From generation to generation we shall relate Your greatness and for infinite eternities we shall proclaim Your holiness. Your praise, our God, shall not leave our mouth forever and ever, for You, O God, are a great and holy King. Blessed are You,* HASHEM, *the holy God.*

Chazzan continues אַתָּה חוֹנֵן, *You graciously endow . . .* (above).

(1) *Isaiah* 6:3. (2) *Ezekiel* 3:12. (3) *Psalms* 146:10.

---

direct plea for the rebuilding of Jerusalem [Zion] *(Abudraham).*

קְדוּשַּׁת הַשֵּׁם / Holiness of God's Name

See prefatory comment to *Kedushah.*

אַתָּה קָדוֹשׁ וְשִׁמְךָ קָדוֹשׁ — *You are holy and Your Name is holy.* The 'Name' of God refers to the manner in which we perceive His actions. The person who enjoys good health and prosperity perceives God as the 'Merciful One,' whereas the person who suffers pain and poverty sees Him as the God of Judgment.

וּקְדוֹשִׁים — *And holy ones.* The term may refer to the angels *(Iyun Tefillah)* or, as most commentators agree, to Israel *(Abudraham).* As *Ramban (Leviticus* 18:2) defines it, human holiness is measured by how well a person controls his permissible desires. Someone who seeks ways to indulge his lusts and passions without directly violating the law is described as a נָבָל בִּרְשׁוּת הַתּוֹרָה, *degenerate with the Torah's permission.*

בִּינָה / Insight

אַתָּה חוֹנֵן לְאָדָם דַּעַת — *You graciously endow man with wisdom.* [This blessing begins the middle section of the *Shemoneh Esrei,* in which man makes his requests of God. The first plea is for wisdom and understanding — because man's intelligence is his primary characteristic, the one that sets him apart from animals.] We ask for *wisdom* and for *insight,* so that we can draw proper conclusions and achieve intellectual *discernment (Vilna Gaon).*

Only wisdom that is in accord with God's will is our assurance that we will indeed act wisely *(Mei Marom).*

תשובה

הֲשִׁיבֵנוּ אָבִינוּ* לְתוֹרָתֶךָ, וְקָרְבֵנוּ מַלְכֵּנוּ לַעֲבוֹדָתֶךָ, וְהַחֲזִירֵנוּ* בִּתְשׁוּבָה שְׁלֵמָה לְפָנֶיךָ. בָּרוּךְ אַתָּה יהוה, הָרוֹצֶה בִּתְשׁוּבָה.

סליחה

Strike the left side of the chest with the right fist while reciting the words חָטָאנוּ and פָּשָׁעְנוּ.

סְלַח לָנוּ אָבִינוּ כִּי חָטָאנוּ, מְחַל לָנוּ מַלְכֵּנוּ* כִּי פָשָׁעְנוּ, כִּי מוֹחֵל וְסוֹלֵחַ אָתָּה. בָּרוּךְ אַתָּה יהוה, חַנּוּן הַמַּרְבֶּה לִסְלוֹחַ.

גאולה

רְאֵה בְעָנְיֵנוּ,* וְרִיבָה רִיבֵנוּ, וּגְאָלֵנוּ[1] מְהֵרָה לְמַעַן שְׁמֶךָ,* כִּי גוֹאֵל חָזָק אָתָּה. בָּרוּךְ אַתָּה יהוה, גּוֹאֵל יִשְׂרָאֵל.

רפואה

רְפָאֵנוּ יהוה וְנֵרָפֵא,* הוֹשִׁיעֵנוּ וְנִוָּשֵׁעָה, כִּי תְהִלָּתֵנוּ אָתָּה,[2] וְהַעֲלֵה רְפוּאָה שְׁלֵמָה לְכָל מַכּוֹתֵינוּ, °°כִּי אֵל מֶלֶךְ רוֹפֵא נֶאֱמָן וְרַחֲמָן אָתָּה. בָּרוּךְ אַתָּה יהוה, רוֹפֵא חוֹלֵי עַמּוֹ יִשְׂרָאֵל.

ברכת השנים

בָּרֵךְ עָלֵינוּ* יהוה אֱלֹהֵינוּ אֶת הַשָּׁנָה הַזֹּאת וְאֶת כָּל מִינֵי תְבוּאָתָהּ לְטוֹבָה, וְתֵן בְּרָכָה עַל פְּנֵי הָאֲדָמָה, וְשַׂבְּעֵנוּ מִטּוּבֶךָ, וּבָרֵךְ שְׁנָתֵנוּ כַּשָּׁנִים הַטּוֹבוֹת. בָּרוּךְ אַתָּה יהוה, מְבָרֵךְ הַשָּׁנִים.

°°At this point one may interject a prayer for one who is ill:

יְהִי רָצוֹן מִלְּפָנֶיךָ יהוה אֱלֹהַי וֵאלֹהֵי אֲבוֹתַי, שֶׁתִּשְׁלַח מְהֵרָה רְפוּאָה שְׁלֵמָה מִן הַשָּׁמַיִם, רְפוּאַת הַנֶּפֶשׁ וּרְפוּאַת הַגּוּף

for a male—לַחוֹלֶה (patient's name) בֶּן (mother's name) בְּתוֹךְ שְׁאָר חוֹלֵי יִשְׂרָאֵל.

for a female—לַחוֹלָה (patient's name) בַּת (mother's name) בְּתוֹךְ שְׁאָר חוֹלֵי יִשְׂרָאֵל.

Continue—כִּי אֵל . . .

תְּשׁוּבָה / Repentance

הֲשִׁיבֵנוּ אָבִינוּ — *Bring us back, our Father.* Only in this prayer for repentance, and in the next one, for forgiveness, do we refer to God as *our Father.* A father has the responsibility to teach his son the proper way to live — but even if a son has rebelled and become estranged, the father's compassion will assert itself if his son repents *(Etz Yosef).*

וְהַחֲזִירֵנוּ — *And influence us to return.* God never *compels* anyone to repent, but if a person makes a sincere beginning, God makes his way easier.

סְלִיחָה / Forgiveness

סְלַח לָנוּ אָבִינוּ . . . מְחַל לָנוּ מַלְכֵּנוּ — *Forgive us, our Father . . . pardon us, our King.* סְלִיחָה, *forgiveness,* means giving up the right to punish for a wrong, but מְחִילָה, *pardon,* means not even harboring resentment or ill will *(Abudraham).*

REPENTANCE

הֲשִׁיבֵנוּ *Bring us back, our Father,* to Your Torah, and bring us near, our King, to Your service, and influence us to return* in perfect repentance before You. Blessed are You, HASHEM, Who desires repentance.*

FORGIVENESS

Strike the left side of the chest with the right fist while reciting the words *'erred'* and *'sinned.'*

סְלַח *Forgive us, our Father, for we have erred; pardon us, our King,* for we have willfully sinned; for You pardon and forgive. Blessed are You, HASHEM, the gracious One Who pardons abundantly.*

REDEMPTION

רְאֵה *Behold our affliction,* take up our grievance, and redeem us[1] speedily for Your Name's sake,* for You are a powerful Redeemer. Blessed are You, HASHEM, Redeemer of Israel.*

HEALTH AND HEALING

רְפָאֵנוּ *Heal us, HASHEM — then we will be healed;* save us — then we will be saved, for You are our praise.[2] Bring complete recovery for all our ailments, °°for You are God, King, the faithful and compassionate Healer. Blessed are You, HASHEM, Who heals the sick of His people Israel.*

YEAR OF PROSPERITY

בָּרֵךְ *Bless on our behalf* — O HASHEM, our God — this year and all its kinds of crops for the best, and give a blessing on the face of the earth, and satisfy us from Your bounty, and bless our year like the best years. Blessed are You, HASHEM, Who blesses the years.*

°°At this point one may interject a prayer for one who is ill:

May it be Your will, HASHEM, my God, and the God of my forefathers, that You quickly send a complete recovery from heaven, spiritual healing and physical healing to the patient (name) *son/daughter of* (mother's name) *among the other patients of Israel.*

Continue: *For You are God . . .*

(1) Cf. *Psalms* 119:153-154. (2) Cf. *Jeremiah* 17:14.

גְּאוּלָה / Redemption

רְאֵה בְעָנְיֵנוּ — *Behold our affliction.* Though Israel suffers because of its own sins, our enemies have no right to claim that they are merely doing God's work, because they cause Israel to suffer much more than necessary. Similarly, many commentators explain that the Egyptians were punished for oppressing and enslaving the Jews, even though God had decreed slavery and suffering, because the Egyptians, in their wickedness, went far beyond God's decree *(Etz Yosef).*

לְמַעַן שְׁמֶךָ — *For Your Name's sake.* Israel's suffering is a reflection on our God, and, therefore, a desecration of His Name.

רְפוּאָה / Health and Healing

רְפָאֵנוּ ה׳ וְנֵרָפֵא — *Heal us, HASHEM — then we will be healed.* Sometimes human beings or angels are God's agents to heal illness, but in that case, the cure may be only partial or temporary. [Or the pain or other symptoms may be relieved, while the illness itself remains uncured *(Siach Yitzchak).*] But if God *Himself* undertakes to cure the patient, we are confident that it will not be a temporary nor a partial measure: *then we will be healed (Etz Yosef* from *Zohar).*

בִּרְכַּת הַשָּׁנִים / Year of Prosperity

בָּרֵךְ עָלֵינוּ — *Bless on our behalf.* We request a blessing on our general business activities and then go on to ask for abundant crops. Even in bad times some people prosper, and even in good times some farms and businesses fail. We ask not only for general prosperity, but that we be enabled to share in it *(R' S. R. Hirsch).*

קיבוץ גליות

תְּקַע בְּשׁוֹפָר גָּדוֹל* לְחֵרוּתֵנוּ, וְשָׂא נֵס לְקַבֵּץ גָּלֻיּוֹתֵינוּ, וְקַבְּצֵנוּ יַחַד מֵאַרְבַּע כַּנְפוֹת הָאָרֶץ.[1] בָּרוּךְ אַתָּה יהוה, מְקַבֵּץ נִדְחֵי עַמּוֹ יִשְׂרָאֵל.

דין

הָשִׁיבָה שׁוֹפְטֵינוּ כְּבָרִאשׁוֹנָה,* וְיוֹעֲצֵינוּ* כְּבַתְּחִלָּה,[2] וְהָסֵר מִמֶּנּוּ יָגוֹן וַאֲנָחָה,* וּמְלוֹךְ עָלֵינוּ אַתָּה יהוה לְבַדְּךָ בְּחֶסֶד וּבְרַחֲמִים, וְצַדְּקֵנוּ בַּמִּשְׁפָּט. בָּרוּךְ אַתָּה יהוה, מֶלֶךְ אוֹהֵב צְדָקָה וּמִשְׁפָּט.

ברכת המינים

וְלַמַּלְשִׁינִים* אַל תְּהִי תִקְוָה, וְכָל הָרִשְׁעָה כְּרֶגַע תֹּאבֵד, וְכָל אֹיְבֶיךָ* מְהֵרָה יִכָּרֵתוּ, וְהַזֵּדִים מְהֵרָה תְעַקֵּר וּתְשַׁבֵּר וּתְמַגֵּר וְתַכְנִיעַ בִּמְהֵרָה בְיָמֵינוּ. בָּרוּךְ אַתָּה יהוה, שׁוֹבֵר אֹיְבִים וּמַכְנִיעַ זֵדִים.

צדיקים

עַל הַצַּדִּיקִים וְעַל הַחֲסִידִים, וְעַל זִקְנֵי עַמְּךָ בֵּית יִשְׂרָאֵל, וְעַל פְּלֵיטַת סוֹפְרֵיהֶם,* וְעַל גֵּרֵי הַצֶּדֶק וְעָלֵינוּ, יֶהֱמוּ רַחֲמֶיךָ יהוה אֱלֹהֵינוּ, וְתֵן שָׂכָר טוֹב לְכָל הַבּוֹטְחִים בְּשִׁמְךָ בֶּאֱמֶת, וְשִׂים חֶלְקֵנוּ עִמָּהֶם לְעוֹלָם, וְלֹא נֵבוֹשׁ* כִּי בְךָ בָּטָחְנוּ. בָּרוּךְ אַתָּה יהוה, מִשְׁעָן וּמִבְטָח לַצַּדִּיקִים.

בנין ירושלים

וְלִירוּשָׁלַיִם* עִירְךָ בְּרַחֲמִים תָּשׁוּב, וְתִשְׁכּוֹן בְּתוֹכָהּ כַּאֲשֶׁר דִּבַּרְתָּ, וּבְנֵה אוֹתָהּ בְּקָרוֹב בְּיָמֵינוּ בִּנְיַן עוֹלָם,

---

◆§ קִבּוּץ גָּלֻיּוֹת / Ingathering of Exiles

תְּקַע בְּשׁוֹפָר גָּדוֹל — *Sound the great shofar.* There are three differences between this prayer for redemption and the earlier one of גְּאוּלָּה, *Redemption:* (a) The earlier blessing refers to God's *daily* help in all sorts of crises and suffering, while this one refers to the *future* Redemption from exile; (b) the earlier blessing refers only to *physical* salvation, while this one is a plea for *spiritual* deliverance; (c) this one specifies not only freedom from oppression, but the ingathering of all exiles to *Eretz Yisrael.*

◆§ דִּין / Restoration of Justice

הָשִׁיבָה שׁוֹפְטֵינוּ כְּבָרִאשׁוֹנָה — *Restore our judges as in earliest times.* When Elijah heralds Messiah's coming, he will first re-establish the Sanhedrin. A secondary theme of this prayer is the wish that God help all Jewish judges rule wisely and justly *(Yaaros D'vash).*

וְיוֹעֲצֵינוּ — *And our counselors,* i.e., the prophets who gave wise advice in both spiritual and temporal affairs *(Olas Tamid).*

יָגוֹן וַאֲנָחָה — *Sorrow and groan.* יָגוֹן, *sorrow,* results from actual want or pain, such as hunger or destruction. אֲנָחָה, *groan,* refers to inner turmoil, such as worry or fear *(Vilna Gaon).*

◆§ בִּרְכַּת הַמִּינִים / Against Heretics

וְלַמַּלְשִׁינִים — *And for slanderers.* Chronologically, this is the *nineteenth* blessing of *Shemoneh Esrei;* it was instituted in Yavneh, some time after the destruction of the Second Temple. The blessing was composed in response to the threats of such heretical Jewish sects as

INGATHERING OF EXILES

תְּקַע *Sound the great shofar* for our freedom, raise the banner to gather our exiles and gather us together from the four corners of the earth.*[1] *Blessed are You, HASHEM, Who gathers in the dispersed of His people Israel.*

RESTORATION OF JUSTICE

הָשִׁיבָה *Restore our judges as in earliest times* and our counselors* as at first;*[2] *remove from us sorrow and groan;* and reign over us — You, HASHEM, alone — with kindness and compassion, and justify us through judgment. Blessed are You, HASHEM, the King Who loves righteousness and judgment.*

AGAINST HERETICS

וְלַמַּלְשִׁינִים *And for slanderers* let there be no hope; and may all wickedness perish in an instant; and may all Your enemies* be cut down speedily. May You speedily uproot, smash, cast down, and humble the wanton sinners — speedily in our days. Blessed are You, HASHEM, Who breaks enemies and humbles wanton sinners.*

THE RIGHTEOUS

עַל הַצַּדִּיקִים *On the righteous, on the devout, on the elders of Your people the Family of Israel, on the remnant of their scholars,* on the righteous converts and on ourselves — may Your compassion be aroused, HASHEM, our God, and give goodly reward to all who sincerely believe in Your Name. Put our lot with them forever, and we will not feel ashamed,* for we trust in You. Blessed are You, HASHEM, Mainstay and Assurance of the righteous.*

REBUILDING JERUSALEM

וְלִירוּשָׁלַיִם *And to Jerusalem,* Your city, may You return in compassion, and may You rest within it, as You have spoken. May You rebuild it soon in our days as an eternal structure,*

(1) Cf. *Isaiah* 11:12. (2) Cf. 1:26.

---

the Sadducees, Boethusians, Essenes, and the early Christians. They tried to lead Jews astray through example and persuasion, and they used their political power to oppress observant Jews and to slander them to the anti-Semitic Roman government.

In this atmosphere, Rabban Gamliel felt the need for a prayer against the heretics and slanderers, and to incorporate it in the *Shemoneh Esrei* to make the populace aware of the danger.

Despite the disappearance from within Israel of the sects against whom it was directed, it is always relevant, because there are still non-believers and heretics who endanger the spiritual continuity of Israel *(Yaaros D'vash).*

אֹיְבֶיךָ — *Your enemies.* Any enemy of Israel is an enemy of God *(Tikun Tefillah).*

☙ צַדִּיקִים / The Righteous

פְּלֵיטַת סוֹפְרֵיהֶם — *The remnant of their scholars.* The term סוֹפְרִים, *scholars,* refers to those who transmit the Oral Torah from generation to generation *(Avodas Yisrael).* These four categories of people — righteous, devout, elders, scholars — are the leaders of the nation. Because the nation needs them, the Sages instituted a special prayer for their welfare *(R' Yehudah ben Yakar).*

וְלֹא נֵבוֹשׁ — *And we will not feel ashamed.* One who puts his faith in people feels shamed — because he has been shown to be helpless on his own. But he is not ashamed to have trusted in God, because no one can succeed without His help *(Dover Shalom).*

☙ בִּנְיַן יְרוּשָׁלַיִם / Rebuilding Jerusalem

וְלִירוּשָׁלַיִם — *And to Jerusalem.* After having sought God's blessing on Israel's leaders and righteous people, we seek His blessing for the Holy City. No blessing is complete until the seat

וְכִסֵּא דָוִד* מְהֵרָה לְתוֹכָהּ תָּכִין. בָּרוּךְ אַתָּה יהוה, בּוֹנֵה יְרוּשָׁלָיִם.

מלכות בית דוד

אֶת צֶמַח דָּוִד* עַבְדְּךָ מְהֵרָה תַצְמִיחַ, וְקַרְנוֹ תָּרוּם בִּישׁוּעָתֶךָ, כִּי לִישׁוּעָתְךָ קִוִּינוּ כָּל הַיּוֹם. בָּרוּךְ אַתָּה יהוה, מַצְמִיחַ קֶרֶן יְשׁוּעָה.

קבלת תפלה

שְׁמַע קוֹלֵנוּ יהוה אֱלֹהֵינוּ, חוּס וְרַחֵם* עָלֵינוּ, וְקַבֵּל בְּרַחֲמִים וּבְרָצוֹן אֶת תְּפִלָּתֵנוּ, כִּי אֵל שׁוֹמֵעַ תְּפִלּוֹת וְתַחֲנוּנִים* אָתָּה. וּמִלְּפָנֶיךָ מַלְכֵּנוּ רֵיקָם אַל תְּשִׁיבֵנוּ,°° כִּי אַתָּה שׁוֹמֵעַ תְּפִלַּת עַמְּךָ יִשְׂרָאֵל בְּרַחֲמִים. בָּרוּךְ אַתָּה יהוה, שׁוֹמֵעַ תְּפִלָּה.

עבודה

רְצֵה* יהוה אֱלֹהֵינוּ בְּעַמְּךָ יִשְׂרָאֵל וּבִתְפִלָּתָם, וְהָשֵׁב אֶת הָעֲבוֹדָה לִדְבִיר בֵּיתֶךָ. וְאִשֵּׁי יִשְׂרָאֵל* וּתְפִלָּתָם בְּאַהֲבָה

°°During the silent *Shemoneh Esrei* one may insert either or both of these personal prayers.

For forgiveness:

אָנָּא יהוה, חָטָאתִי עָוִיתִי וּפָשַׁעְתִּי לְפָנֶיךָ, מִיּוֹם הֱיוֹתִי עַל הָאֲדָמָה עַד הַיּוֹם הַזֶּה (וּבִפְרַט בַּחֵטְא ....). אָנָּא יהוה, עֲשֵׂה לְמַעַן שִׁמְךָ הַגָּדוֹל, וּתְכַפֶּר לִי עַל עֲוֹנַי וַחֲטָאַי וּפְשָׁעַי שֶׁחָטָאתִי וְשֶׁעָוִיתִי וְשֶׁפָּשַׁעְתִּי לְפָנֶיךָ, מִנְּעוּרַי עַד הַיּוֹם הַזֶּה. וּתְמַלֵּא כָּל הַשֵּׁמוֹת שֶׁפָּגַמְתִּי בְּשִׁמְךָ הַגָּדוֹל.

For livelihood:

אַתָּה הוּא יהוה הָאֱלֹהִים, הַזָּן וּמְפַרְנֵס וּמְכַלְכֵּל מִקַּרְנֵי רְאֵמִים עַד בֵּיצֵי כִנִּים. הַטְרִיפֵנִי לֶחֶם חֻקִּי, וְהַמְצֵא לִי וּלְכָל בְּנֵי בֵיתִי מְזוֹנוֹתַי קוֹדֶם שֶׁאֶצְטָרֵךְ לָהֶם, בְּנַחַת וְלֹא בְצַעַר, בְּהֶתֵּר וְלֹא בְאִסּוּר, בְּכָבוֹד וְלֹא בְבִזָּיוֹן, לְחַיִּים וּלְשָׁלוֹם, מִשֶּׁפַע בְּרָכָה וְהַצְלָחָה, וּמִשֶּׁפַע בְּרֵכָה עֶלְיוֹנָה, כְּדֵי שֶׁאוּכַל לַעֲשׂוֹת רְצוֹנֶךָ וְלַעֲסוֹק בְּתוֹרָתֶךָ וּלְקַיֵּם מִצְוֹתֶיךָ. וְאַל תַּצְרִיכֵנִי לִידֵי מַתְּנַת בָּשָׂר וָדָם. וִיקֻיַּם בִּי מִקְרָא שֶׁכָּתוּב: פּוֹתֵחַ אֶת יָדֶךָ, וּמַשְׂבִּיעַ לְכָל חַי רָצוֹן.[1] וְכָתוּב: הַשְׁלֵךְ עַל יהוה יְהָבְךָ וְהוּא יְכַלְכְּלֶךָ.[2]

Continue — כִּי אַתָּה . . .

---

of holiness, Jerusalem, is rebuilt in all its grandeur (*Iyun Tefillah*).

וְכִסֵּא דָוִד — *The throne of David.* Jerusalem cannot be considered rebuilt unless an heir of David sits on the throne (*R' Yitzchak Zev Soloveitchik*).

מַלְכוּת בֵּית דָּוִד / Davidic Reign

אֶת צֶמַח דָּוִד — *The offspring of . . . David.* Messiah's name will be צֶמַח, *Tzemach,* literally, the *sprouting* or *flourishing* of a plant (*Zechariah* 6:12). Thus, the normal process of redemption is like a plant's barely noticeable daily growth (*Iyun Tefillah*). David has been mentioned in the previous blessing as well. There, Jerusalem's rebirth depends on the Davidic heir. Here we learn that Israel's ultimate salvation is possible only through the Davidic Messiah.

קַבָּלַת תְּפִלָּה / Acceptance of Prayer

[In the middle section of *Shemoneh Esrei* we

and may You speedily establish the throne of David within it. Blessed are You,* HASHEM, *the Builder of Jerusalem.*

DAVIDIC REIGN

אֶת צֶמַח *The offspring of Your servant David* may You speedily cause to flourish, and enhance his pride through Your salvation, for we hope for Your salvation all day long. Blessed are You,* HASHEM, *Who causes the pride of salvation to flourish.*

ACCEPTANCE OF PRAYER

שְׁמַע קוֹלֵנוּ *Hear our voice,* HASHEM *our God, pity and be compassionate* to us, and accept — with compassion and favor — our prayer, for God Who hears prayers and supplications* are You. From before Yourself, our King, turn us not away empty-handed,°° for You hear the prayer of Your people Israel with compassion. Blessed are You,* HASHEM, *Who hears prayer.*

TEMPLE SERVICE

רְצֵה *Be favorable,** HASHEM, *our God, toward Your people Israel and their prayer and restore the service to the Holy of Holies of Your Temple. The fire-offerings of Israel* and their prayer*

°°During the silent *Shemoneh Esrei* one may insert either or both of these personal prayers.

For forgiveness:

אָנָּא *Please, O* HASHEM, *I have erred, been iniquitous, and willfully sinned before You, from the day I have existed on earth until this very day (and especially with the sin of ...). Please,* HASHEM, *act for the sake of Your Great Name and grant me atonement for my iniquities, my errors, and my willful sins through which I have erred, been iniquitous, and willfully sinned before You, from my youth until this day. And make whole all the Names that I have blemished in Your Great Name.*

For livelihood:

אַתָּה *It is You,* HASHEM *the God, Who nourishes, sustains, and supports, from the horns of re'eimim to the eggs of lice. Provide me with my allotment of bread; and bring forth for me and all members of my household, my food, before I have need for it; in contentment but not in pain, in a permissible but not a forbidden manner, in honor but not in disgrace, for life and for peace; from the flow of blessing and success and from the flow of the Heavenly spring, so that I be enabled to do Your will and engage in Your Torah and fulfill Your commandments. Make me not needful of people's largesse; and may there be fulfilled in me the verse that states, 'You open Your hand and satisfy the desire of every living thing'[1] and that states, 'Cast Your burden upon* HASHEM *and He will support you.'[2]*

Continue: *For You hear the prayer . . .*

(1) *Psalms* 145:16. (2) 55:23.

have asked God to grant our specific needs. We now close the section with a general plea that He take note of our call and grant our requests.]

חוּס וְרַחֵם — *Pity and be compassionate.* The term חוּס, *pity,* refers to an artisan's special regard for the product of his hands; while רַחֲמִים, *compassion,* describes the emotion aroused upon seeing someone who is pathetically helpless. O God — *pity* us because we are Your handiwork, and *be compassionate* because we are nothing without You! *(Vilna Gaon).*

תְּפִלּוֹת וְתַחֲנוּנִים — *Prayers and supplications.* תַּחֲנוּן is a request for מַתְּנַת חִנָּם, *an unearned gift (Rashi, Deut.* 3:23). The most righteous people use this expression because they are aware that no man can claim that God 'owes' him something. *Gur Aryeh* explains that the righteous use the term תַּחֲנוּן only when praying for themselves, but when praying for the community they use תְּפִלָּה, because Israel as a *community* deserves God's help.

עֲבוֹדָה / Temple Service

רְצֵה — *Be favorable.* This begins the final section of *Shemoneh Esrei.* Like a servant who is grateful for having had the opportunity to express himself before his master, we thank God

תְקַבֵּל בְּרָצוֹן, וּתְהִי לְרָצוֹן תָּמִיד עֲבוֹדַת יִשְׂרָאֵל עַמֶּךָ.

וְתֶחֱזֶינָה עֵינֵינוּ* בְּשׁוּבְךָ לְצִיּוֹן בְּרַחֲמִים. בָּרוּךְ אַתָּה יהוה, הַמַּחֲזִיר שְׁכִינָתוֹ לְצִיּוֹן.

הודאה

Bow at מודים; straighten up at 'ה. In his repetition the *chazzan* should recite the entire מודים aloud, while the congregation recites מודים דְּרַבָּנָן softly.

מוֹדִים אֲנַחְנוּ לָךְ, שָׁאַתָּה הוּא יהוה אֱלֹהֵינוּ וֵאלֹהֵי אֲבוֹתֵינוּ לְעוֹלָם וָעֶד. צוּר חַיֵּינוּ,* מָגֵן יִשְׁעֵנוּ אַתָּה הוּא לְדוֹר וָדוֹר. נוֹדֶה לְּךָ* וּנְסַפֵּר תְּהִלָּתֶךָ[1] עַל חַיֵּינוּ* הַמְּסוּרִים בְּיָדֶךָ, וְעַל נִשְׁמוֹתֵינוּ הַפְּקוּדוֹת לָךְ,* וְעַל נִסֶּיךָ שֶׁבְּכָל יוֹם עִמָּנוּ, וְעַל נִפְלְאוֹתֶיךָ* וְטוֹבוֹתֶיךָ שֶׁבְּכָל עֵת, עֶרֶב וָבֹקֶר וְצָהֳרָיִם. הַטּוֹב כִּי לֹא כָלוּ רַחֲמֶיךָ, וְהַמְּרַחֵם כִּי לֹא תַמּוּ חֲסָדֶיךָ,[2]* מֵעוֹלָם קִוִּינוּ לָךְ.

מודים דרבנן

מוֹדִים אֲנַחְנוּ לָךְ, שָׁאַתָּה הוּא יהוה אֱלֹהֵינוּ וֵאלֹהֵי אֲבוֹתֵינוּ, אֱלֹהֵי כָל בָּשָׂר, יוֹצְרֵנוּ, יוֹצֵר בְּרֵאשִׁית. בְּרָכוֹת וְהוֹדָאוֹת לְשִׁמְךָ הַגָּדוֹל וְהַקָּדוֹשׁ, עַל שֶׁהֶחֱיִיתָנוּ וְקִיַּמְתָּנוּ. כֵּן תְּחַיֵּנוּ וּתְקַיְּמֵנוּ, וְתֶאֱסוֹף גָּלֻיּוֹתֵינוּ לְחַצְרוֹת קָדְשֶׁךָ, לִשְׁמוֹר חֻקֶּיךָ וְלַעֲשׂוֹת רְצוֹנֶךָ, וּלְעָבְדְּךָ בְּלֵבָב שָׁלֵם, עַל שֶׁאֲנַחְנוּ מוֹדִים לָךְ. בָּרוּךְ אֵל הַהוֹדָאוֹת.

---

for hearing us out. As we conclude *Shemoneh Esrei,* which is our substitute for the Temple's sacrificial service, we ask that the *true* service be restored to the Temple *(Etz Yosef).*

וְאִשֵּׁי יִשְׂרָאֵל — *The fire-offerings of Israel.* Since the Temple is not standing this phrase is taken in an allegorical sense. It refers to: the souls and the deeds of the righteous, which are as pleasing as sacrifices; Jewish prayers that are like offerings; or the altar fires and sacrifices of Messianic times. Some repunctuate the blessing to read: . . . *and restore the service . . . and the fire-offerings of Israel. Their prayer accept with love . . .*

☙ **וְתֶחֱזֶינָה עֵינֵינוּ** — *May our eyes behold.* There is a principle that a person may not witness the downfall of his enemies unless he is personally worthy. As we find in the case of Lot's wife *(Genesis* 19:26), although God sent an angel to save her from the destruction of Sodom, she did not deserve to see the destruction of her neighbors. Similarly, one does not see the splendor of the miracles bringing about his salvation unless he is personally worthy. Therefore we pray that *we* may be worthy to witness the return to Zion with our own eyes *(Yaaros D'vash).*

☙ **הוֹדָאָה / Thanksgiving [Modim]**

צוּר חַיֵּינוּ — *Rock of our lives.* Our parents are the 'rocks' from whom our bodies are hewn, but from You we receive life itself *(Etz Yosef).*

נוֹדֶה לְּךָ — *We shall thank You.* Having described God's greatness and our relationship, we now specify what we thank Him for.

עַל חַיֵּינוּ — *For our lives.* Lest anyone think that he is master over his own life, we acknowledge that every breath and heartbeat is a direct result of God's mercy *(Olas Tamid).*

נִשְׁמוֹתֵינוּ הַפְּקוּדוֹת לָךְ — *Our souls that are entrusted to You.* The word נְשָׁמָה, *neshamah,* refers to the higher soul that gives man his holiness, as opposed to the lower soul that merely keeps him alive. During sleep, the animal soul remains in man; he remains alive and his body continues to function. But the *neshamah* leaves the body and ascends to higher spiritual

accept with love and favor, and may the service of Your people Israel always be favorable to You.

וְתֶחֱזֶינָה *May our eyes behold* Your return to Zion in compassion. Blessed are You,* HASHEM, *Who restores His Presence unto Zion.*

THANKSGIVING [MODIM]

Bow at *'We gratefully thank You'*; straighten up at *'HASHEM.'* In his repetition the *chazzan* should recite the entire *Modim* aloud, while the congregation recites *Modim of the Rabbis* softly.

מוֹדִים *We gratefully thank You, for it is You Who are* HASHEM, *our God and the God of our forefathers for all eternity; Rock of our lives,* Shield of our salvation are You from generation to generation. We shall thank You* and relate Your praise[1] — for our lives,* which are committed to Your power and for our souls that are entrusted to You;* for Your miracles that are with us every day; and for Your wonders* and favors in every season — evening, morning, and afternoon. The Beneficent One, for Your compassions were never exhausted, and the Compassionate One, for Your kindnesses* never ended[2] — always have we put our hope in You.*

MODIM OF THE RABBIS

מוֹדִים *We gratefully thank You, for it is You Who are* HASHEM, *our God and the God of our forefathers, the God of all flesh, our Molder, the Molder of the universe. Blessings and thanks are due Your great and holy Name for You have given us life and sustained us. So may You continue to give us life and sustain us and gather our exiles to the Courtyards of Your Sanctuary, to observe Your decrees, to do Your will and to serve You wholeheartedly. [We thank You] for inspiring us to thank You. Blessed is the God of thanksgivings.*

(1) Cf. *Psalms* 79:13. (2) Cf. *Lamentations* 3:22.

realms where it can conceivably receive Divine communications. Occasionally such messages become known to a person through dreams that may seem to be intuitive, but may be messages from on high, such as the prophetic dreams found in Scripture. During slumber, the *neshamah* leaves the body and is, so to speak, entrusted to God's safekeeping, to be returned to man in the morning *(Derech Hashem).*

נִסֶּיךָ ... נִפְלְאוֹתֶיךָ — *Your miracles ... Your wonders. Miracles* are the extraordinary events that everyone recognizes as the results of God's intervention. *Wonders* are the familiar things that we do not regard as miracles because we have grown accustomed to them, such as breathing, raining, and growing. We thank God for both *miracles* and *wonders,* because we know that He is their Creator *(Etz Yosef).*

הַטּוֹב ... רַחֲמֶיךָ ... חֲסָדֶיךָ — *The Beneficent One ... Your compassions ... Your kindnesses.* The three Hebrew terms טוֹב, רַחֲמִים and חֶסֶד all refer to God's attribute of Mercy. Specifically: טוֹב, *goodness* or *beneficence,* is the kind deed that was actually done; רַחֲמִים is the *compassion* with which God softens the decision called for by strict Justice. Thus, compassion will cause an offender to receive less than his deserved punishment; but he may well be punished to some degree; חֶסֶד is God's infinite store of *kindness.* It can either overcome completely the dictates of Justice, or it can provide the רַחֲמִים that mitigates Justice *(R' Munk).*

מוֹדִים דְּרַבָּנָן / Modim of the Rabbis

When the *chazzan* bows and recites *Modim* in the manner of a slave accepting the total authority of his master, the congregation must join him in accepting God's sovereignty. Therefore each member of the congregation must make his own declaration of submission

וְעַל כֻּלָּם יִתְבָּרַךְ וְיִתְרוֹמַם שִׁמְךָ מַלְכֵּנוּ תָּמִיד לְעוֹלָם וָעֶד.

Bend the knees at בָּרוּךְ; bow at אַתָּה; straighten up at 'ה.

וְכֹל הַחַיִּים* יוֹדוּךָ סֶּלָה, וִיהַלְּלוּ אֶת שִׁמְךָ בֶּאֱמֶת, הָאֵל יְשׁוּעָתֵנוּ וְעֶזְרָתֵנוּ סֶלָה. בָּרוּךְ אַתָּה יהוה, הַטּוֹב שִׁמְךָ וּלְךָ נָאֶה לְהוֹדוֹת.

שלום

שָׁלוֹם רָב עַל יִשְׂרָאֵל עַמְּךָ תָּשִׂים לְעוֹלָם, כִּי אַתָּה הוּא מֶלֶךְ אָדוֹן לְכָל הַשָּׁלוֹם. וְטוֹב בְּעֵינֶיךָ* לְבָרֵךְ אֶת עַמְּךָ יִשְׂרָאֵל בְּכָל עֵת וּבְכָל שָׁעָה בִּשְׁלוֹמֶךָ. בָּרוּךְ אַתָּה יהוה, הַמְּבָרֵךְ אֶת עַמּוֹ יִשְׂרָאֵל בַּשָּׁלוֹם.

יִהְיוּ לְרָצוֹן* אִמְרֵי פִי וְהֶגְיוֹן לִבִּי לְפָנֶיךָ, יהוה צוּרִי וְגֹאֲלִי.[1]

The *chazzan's* repetition of *Shemoneh Esrei* ends here. Individuals continue below. See commentary for permissible responses while reciting this final paragraph of *Shemoneh Esrei.*

אֱלֹהַי, נְצוֹר לְשׁוֹנִי מֵרָע,* וּשְׂפָתַי מִדַּבֵּר מִרְמָה,[2] וְלִמְקַלְלַי נַפְשִׁי תִדּוֹם, וְנַפְשִׁי כֶּעָפָר* לַכֹּל תִּהְיֶה. פְּתַח לִבִּי בְּתוֹרָתֶךָ,* וּבְמִצְוֹתֶיךָ תִּרְדּוֹף נַפְשִׁי. וְכֹל הַחוֹשְׁבִים עָלַי רָעָה, מְהֵרָה הָפֵר עֲצָתָם וְקַלְקֵל מַחֲשַׁבְתָּם. עֲשֵׂה לְמַעַן שְׁמֶךָ, עֲשֵׂה לְמַעַן יְמִינֶךָ, עֲשֵׂה לְמַעַן קְדֻשָּׁתֶךָ, עֲשֵׂה לְמַעַן תּוֹרָתֶךָ. לְמַעַן יֵחָלְצוּן יְדִידֶיךָ, הוֹשִׁיעָה יְמִינְךָ וַעֲנֵנִי.[3]

Some recite verses pertaining to their names at this point. See page 1301.

(*Abudraham*). The Talmud (*Sotah* 40a and *Yerushalmi* 1:8) cites the personal declarations used by a number of rabbis, and concludes that the proper custom is to recite them all. This collection of prayers was thus given the name *Modim of the Rabbis.*

וְכֹל הַחַיִּים — *Everything alive.* As long as there is life, people can express their thanks to God. This prayer refers specifically to the universal praise that will come with the restoration of the Divine service in the rebuilt Temple.

שָׁלוֹם / Peace

אָדוֹן לְכָל הַשָּׁלוֹם וְטוֹב בְּעֵינֶיךָ — *Master of all peace. May it be good in Your eyes.* For a blessing to come true, there must be two conditions: (a) the one from whom the blessing is sought must have the power to confer it, and (b) he must be willing to do so. Therefore, we declare that God is *Master of all peace* and we pray that *it be good in [His] eyes* to bestow it upon us (*Acharis Shalom*).

יִהְיוּ לְרָצוֹן — *May . . . find favor.* We conclude *Shemoneh Esrei* with this brief prayer that our prayers find favor before God. Kabbalistic literature attaches great sanctity to this verse and stresses that it be recited slowly and fervently.

Some authorities maintain that since יִהְיוּ לְרָצוֹן closes the *Shemoneh Esrei* prayer, it should be recited before אֱלֹהַי נְצוֹר, which is not an integral part of *Shemoneh Esrei* (see below). Others hold that since the Sages have appended אֱלֹהַי נְצוֹר, *Shemoneh Esrei* is not over until the end of אֱלֹהַי נְצוֹר, at which point יִהְיוּ לְרָצוֹן should be said. To accommodate both views, some authorities hold that יִהְיוּ לְרָצוֹן should be said both before and after אֱלֹהַי נְצוֹר.

אֱלֹהַי נְצוֹר / Concluding Prayers

Many of the Talmudic Sages composed individual supplications that they would recite at the conclusion of the prayer. Some of these supplications are cited in *Berachos* 16b-17a. The prayer now in universal use is based on that of Mar, son of Rabina (ibid. 18a).

While one is reciting אֱלֹהַי נְצוֹר, he may not respond to blessings and the like except for the exceptions given below. In the case of those exceptions, it is preferable to recite יִהְיוּ לְרָצוֹן

For all these, may Your Name be blessed and exalted, our King, continually forever and ever.

Bend the knees at *'Blessed'*; bow at *'You'*; straighten up at *'HASHEM.'*

Everything alive will gratefully acknowledge You, Selah! and praise Your Name sincerely, O God of our salvation and help, Selah! Blessed are You, HASHEM, Your Name is 'The Beneficent One' and to You it is fitting to give thanks.*

PEACE

שָׁלוֹם רָב *Establish abundant peace upon Your people Israel forever, for You are King, Master of all peace. May it be good in Your eyes* to bless Your people Israel at every time and every hour with Your peace. Blessed are You, HASHEM, Who blesses His people Israel with peace.*

May the expressions of my mouth and the thoughts of my heart find favor before You, HASHEM, my Rock and my Redeemer.*[1]

The *chazzan's* repetition of *Shemoneh Esrei* ends here. Individuals continue below.
See commentary for permissible responses while reciting this final paragraph of *Shemoneh Esrei.*

אֱלֹהַי *My God, guard my tongue from evil* and my lips from speaking deceitfully.*[2] *To those who curse me, let my soul be silent; and let my soul be like dust* to everyone. Open my heart to Your Torah,* then my soul will pursue Your commandments. As for all those who design evil against me, speedily nullify their counsel and disrupt their design. Act for Your Name's sake; act for Your right hand's sake; act for Your sanctity's sake; act for Your Torah's sake. That Your beloved ones may be given rest; let Your right hand save, and respond to me.*[3]

Some recite verses pertaining to their names at this point. See page 1301.

(1) *Psalms* 19:15. (2) Cf. *Psalms* 34:14. (3) 60:7; 108:7.

---

before responding, but if there is not enough time to do so, the responses should be said anyway. The responses are: *Borchu;* the *amens* after הָאֵל הַקָּדוֹשׁ and שׁוֹמֵעַ תְּפִלָּה; אָמֵן יְהֵא שְׁמֵהּ רַבָּא and the *amen* after דַּאֲמִירָן בְּעָלְמָא; in *Kedushah,* the two verses קָדוֹשׁ and בָּרוּךְ כְּבוֹד; and the three words מוֹדִים אֲנַחְנוּ לָךְ. [See *Orach Chaim* ch. 122.]

אֱלֹהַי נְצוֹר לְשׁוֹנִי מֵרָע — *My God, guard my tongue from evil.* We pray that God protect us from situations that would tempt us to speak ill of others *(Abudraham).*

The Midrash [*Vayikra Rabbah* 33:1] relates that Rabban Shimon ben Gamliel once sent his servant, Tavi, to buy 'good food.' Tavi, who was famous for his wisdom, brought back a tongue. Thereupon Rabban Shimon sent him to buy some 'bad food.' Again, he returned with a tongue. Rabban Shimon asked him to explain how the same food could be both good and bad. Tavi said, 'From a tongue can come good or bad. When a tongue speaks *good,* there is nothing better, but when a tongue speaks *ill,* there is nothing worse' *(Vayikra Rabbah* 33:1).

נַפְשִׁי תִדּוֹם ... כֶּעָפָר — *Let my soul be silent ... like dust.* We should ignore barbs and insults, because the less a person cares about his prestige, the less he will let selfishness interfere with his service of God and his efforts at self-improvement *(Ruach Chaim).*

פְּתַח לִבִּי בְּתוֹרָתֶךָ — *Open my heart to Your Torah.* Our goal is to serve God in a positive manner by studying Torah and fulfilling its commandments *(Abudraham).*

☙ Verses for People's Names

Kitzur Sh'lah teaches that it is a source of merit for people that before יִהְיוּ לְרָצוֹן they recite a Scriptural verse symbolizing their name. The verse should either contain the person's name or else begin and end with the first and last letters of his name. A list of such verses may be found on p. 1301.

יִהְיוּ לְרָצוֹן אִמְרֵי פִי וְהֶגְיוֹן לִבִּי לְפָנֶיךָ, יהוה צוּרִי וְגֹאֲלִי.[1]

Bow and take three steps back. Bow left and say ... עֹשֶׂה, bow right and say ... הוּא יַעֲשֶׂה; bow forward and say וְעַל כָּל ... אָמֵן.

עֹשֶׂה שָׁלוֹם בִּמְרוֹמָיו, הוּא יַעֲשֶׂה שָׁלוֹם עָלֵינוּ, וְעַל כָּל יִשְׂרָאֵל. וְאִמְרוּ: אָמֵן.

יְהִי רָצוֹן מִלְּפָנֶיךָ* יהוה אֱלֹהֵינוּ וֵאלֹהֵי אֲבוֹתֵינוּ, שֶׁיִּבָּנֶה בֵּית הַמִּקְדָּשׁ בִּמְהֵרָה בְיָמֵינוּ, וְתֵן חֶלְקֵנוּ בְּתוֹרָתֶךָ. וְשָׁם נַעֲבָדְךָ בְּיִרְאָה, כִּימֵי עוֹלָם וּכְשָׁנִים קַדְמוֹנִיּוֹת. וְעָרְבָה לַיהוה מִנְחַת יְהוּדָה וִירוּשָׁלָיִם, כִּימֵי עוֹלָם וּכְשָׁנִים קַדְמוֹנִיּוֹת.[2]

THE INDIVIDUAL'S RECITATION OF שְׁמוֹנֶה עֶשְׂרֵה ENDS HERE.

The individual remains standing in place until the *chazzan* reaches *Kedushah* — or at least until the *chazzan* begins his repetition — then he takes three steps forward. The *chazzan* himself, or one praying alone, should remain in place for a few moments before taking three steps forward.

קדיש שלם

The *chazzan* recites קַדִּישׁ שָׁלֵם.

יִתְגַּדַּל וְיִתְקַדַּשׁ שְׁמֵהּ רַבָּא. (.Cong – אָמֵן.) בְּעָלְמָא דִּי בְרָא כִרְעוּתֵהּ. וְיַמְלִיךְ מַלְכוּתֵהּ, בְּחַיֵּיכוֹן וּבְיוֹמֵיכוֹן וּבְחַיֵּי דְכָל בֵּית יִשְׂרָאֵל, בַּעֲגָלָא וּבִזְמַן קָרִיב. וְאִמְרוּ: אָמֵן.

(.Cong – אָמֵן. יְהֵא שְׁמֵהּ רַבָּא מְבָרַךְ לְעָלַם וּלְעָלְמֵי עָלְמַיָּא.)

יְהֵא שְׁמֵהּ רַבָּא מְבָרַךְ לְעָלַם וּלְעָלְמֵי עָלְמַיָּא.

יִתְבָּרַךְ וְיִשְׁתַּבַּח וְיִתְפָּאַר וְיִתְרוֹמַם וְיִתְנַשֵּׂא וְיִתְהַדָּר וְיִתְעַלֶּה וְיִתְהַלָּל שְׁמֵהּ דְּקֻדְשָׁא בְּרִיךְ הוּא (.Cong – בְּרִיךְ הוּא) — לְעֵלָּא מִן כָּל בִּרְכָתָא וְשִׁירָתָא תֻּשְׁבְּחָתָא וְנֶחֱמָתָא, דַּאֲמִירָן בְּעָלְמָא. וְאִמְרוּ: אָמֵן. (.Cong – אָמֵן.)

(.Cong – קַבֵּל בְּרַחֲמִים וּבְרָצוֹן אֶת תְּפִלָּתֵנוּ.)

תִּתְקַבֵּל צְלוֹתְהוֹן וּבָעוּתְהוֹן דְּכָל בֵּית יִשְׂרָאֵל קֳדָם אֲבוּהוֹן דִּי בִשְׁמַיָּא. וְאִמְרוּ: אָמֵן. (.Cong – אָמֵן.)

(.Cong – יְהִי שֵׁם יהוה מְבֹרָךְ, מֵעַתָּה וְעַד עוֹלָם.[3])

יְהֵא שְׁלָמָא רַבָּא מִן שְׁמַיָּא, וְחַיִּים עָלֵינוּ וְעַל כָּל יִשְׂרָאֵל. וְאִמְרוּ: אָמֵן. (.Cong – אָמֵן.)

(.Cong – עֶזְרִי מֵעִם יהוה, עֹשֵׂה שָׁמַיִם וָאָרֶץ.[4])

Take three steps back. Bow left and say ... עֹשֶׂה; bow right and say ... הוּא; bow forward and say וְעַל כָּל ... אָמֵן. Remain standing in place for a few moments, then take three steps forward.

עֹשֶׂה שָׁלוֹם בִּמְרוֹמָיו, הוּא יַעֲשֶׂה שָׁלוֹם עָלֵינוּ, וְעַל כָּל יִשְׂרָאֵל. וְאִמְרוּ: אָמֵן. (.Cong – אָמֵן.)

May the expressions of my mouth and the thoughts of my heart find favor before You, HASHEM, my Rock and my Redeemer.[1]

Bow and take three steps back. Bow left and say, *'He Who makes peace . . .'*; bow right and say, *'may He make peace . . .'*; bow forward and say, *'and upon all Israel . . . Amen.'*

He Who makes peace in His heights, may He make peace upon us, and upon all Israel. Now respond: Amen.

יְהִי רָצוֹן *May it be Your will,* HASHEM, our God and the God of our forefathers, that the Holy Temple be rebuilt, speedily in our days. Grant us our share in Your Torah, and may we serve You there with reverence, as in days of old and in former years. Then the offering of Judah and Jerusalem will be pleasing to HASHEM, as in days of old and in former years.*[2]

THE INDIVIDUAL'S RECITATION OF *SHEMONEH ESREI* ENDS HERE.

The individual remains standing in place until the *chazzan* reaches *Kedushah* — or at least until the *chazzan* begins his repetition — then he takes three steps forward. The *chazzan* himself, or one praying alone, should remain in place for a few moments before taking three steps forward.

FULL KADDISH

The *chazzan* recites the Full *Kaddish*.

יִתְגַּדַּל *May His great Name grow exalted and sanctified* (Cong.– *Amen.*) *in the world that He created as He willed. May He give reign to His kingship in your lifetimes and in your days, and in the lifetimes of the entire Family of Israel, swiftly and soon. Now respond: Amen.*

(Cong.– *Amen. May His great Name be blessed forever and ever.)*

May His great Name be blessed forever and ever.

Blessed, praised, glorified, exalted, extolled, mighty, upraised, and lauded be the Name of the Holy One, Blessed is He (Cong.– *Blessed is He*) *— beyond any blessing and song, praise and consolation that are uttered in the world. Now respond: Amen.* (Cong.– *Amen.*)

(Cong.– *Accept our prayers with mercy and favor.*)

May the prayers and supplications of the entire Family of Israel be accepted before their Father Who is in Heaven. Now respond: Amen. (Cong.– *Amen.*)

(Cong.– *Blessed be the Name of HASHEM, from this time and forever.*[3])

May there be abundant peace from Heaven, and life, upon us and upon all Israel. Now respond: Amen. (Cong.– *Amen.*)

(Cong.– *My help is from HASHEM, Maker of heaven and earth.*[4])

Take three steps back. Bow left and say, *'He Who makes peace . . .'*; bow right and say, *'may He . . .'*; bow forward and say, *'and upon all Israel . . .'* Remain standing in place for a few moments, then take three steps forward.

He Who makes peace in His heights, may He make peace upon us, and upon all Israel. Now respond: Amen. (Cong.– *Amen.*)

(1) *Psalms* 19:15. (2) *Malachi* 3:4. (3) *Psalms* 113:2. (4) 121:2.

✤ יְהִי רָצוֹן מִלְּפָנֶיךָ — *May it be Your will.* As noted above, the *Shemoneh Esrei*, as the primary prayer, takes the place of the Temple Service. Thus it is appropriate to conclude with this plea (from *Avos* 5:23) that God permit the rebuilding of the *Beis HaMikdash* so that we can perform the Temple Service in actuality. We ask further that God give us our share in the Torah, both because of the extreme importance of Torah study and because the study of the laws of the offerings takes the place of the offerings themselves.

Stand while reciting עָלֵינוּ.

עָלֵינוּ לְשַׁבֵּחַ לַאֲדוֹן הַכֹּל, לָתֵת גְּדֻלָּה לְיוֹצֵר בְּרֵאשִׁית, שֶׁלֹּא עָשָׂנוּ כְּגוֹיֵי הָאֲרָצוֹת, וְלֹא שָׂמָנוּ כְּמִשְׁפְּחוֹת הָאֲדָמָה. שֶׁלֹּא שָׂם חֶלְקֵנוּ כָּהֶם, וְגוֹרָלֵנוּ* כְּכָל הֲמוֹנָם. (שֶׁהֵם מִשְׁתַּחֲוִים* לְהֶבֶל וָרִיק, וּמִתְפַּלְּלִים אֶל אֵל לֹא יוֹשִׁיעַ.[1]) וַאֲנַחְנוּ כּוֹרְעִים וּמִשְׁתַּחֲוִים וּמוֹדִים, לִפְנֵי מֶלֶךְ מַלְכֵי הַמְּלָכִים הַקָּדוֹשׁ בָּרוּךְ הוּא. שֶׁהוּא נוֹטֶה שָׁמַיִם וְיֹסֵד אָרֶץ,[2] וּמוֹשַׁב יְקָרוֹ בַּשָּׁמַיִם מִמַּעַל, וּשְׁכִינַת עֻזּוֹ בְּגָבְהֵי מְרוֹמִים. הוּא אֱלֹהֵינוּ, אֵין עוֹד. אֱמֶת מַלְכֵּנוּ, אֶפֶס זוּלָתוֹ, כַּכָּתוּב בְּתוֹרָתוֹ: וְיָדַעְתָּ הַיּוֹם וַהֲשֵׁבֹתָ אֶל לְבָבֶךָ,* כִּי יהוה הוּא הָאֱלֹהִים בַּשָּׁמַיִם מִמַּעַל וְעַל הָאָרֶץ מִתָּחַת, אֵין עוֹד.[3]

Bow while reciting וַאֲנַחְנוּ כּוֹרְעִים וּמִשְׁתַּחֲוִים.

עַל כֵּן נְקַוֶּה לְּךָ* יהוה אֱלֹהֵינוּ לִרְאוֹת מְהֵרָה בְּתִפְאֶרֶת עֻזֶּךָ, לְהַעֲבִיר גִּלּוּלִים מִן הָאָרֶץ, וְהָאֱלִילִים כָּרוֹת יִכָּרֵתוּן, לְתַקֵּן עוֹלָם בְּמַלְכוּת שַׁדַּי. וְכָל בְּנֵי בָשָׂר יִקְרְאוּ בִשְׁמֶךָ, לְהַפְנוֹת אֵלֶיךָ כָּל רִשְׁעֵי אָרֶץ. יַכִּירוּ וְיֵדְעוּ כָּל יוֹשְׁבֵי תֵבֵל, כִּי לְךָ תִּכְרַע כָּל בֶּרֶךְ, תִּשָּׁבַע כָּל לָשׁוֹן.[4] לְפָנֶיךָ יהוה אֱלֹהֵינוּ יִכְרְעוּ וְיִפֹּלוּ, וְלִכְבוֹד שִׁמְךָ יְקָר יִתֵּנוּ. וִיקַבְּלוּ כֻלָּם אֶת עוֹל מַלְכוּתֶךָ, וְתִמְלֹךְ עֲלֵיהֶם מְהֵרָה לְעוֹלָם וָעֶד. כִּי הַמַּלְכוּת שֶׁלְּךָ הִיא וּלְעוֹלְמֵי עַד תִּמְלוֹךְ בְּכָבוֹד, כַּכָּתוּב בְּתוֹרָתֶךָ: יהוה יִמְלֹךְ

עָלֵינוּ / Aleinu

According to many early sources, among them *Rokeach, Kol Bo,* and a Gaonic responsum attributed to *Rabbi Hai Gaon,* this declaration of faith and dedication was composed by Joshua after he led Israel across the Jordan. During the Talmudic era it was part of the Rosh Hashanah *Mussaf* service. At some point during medieval times it began to find its way into the daily service.

Bach (Orach Chaim 133) explains that *Aleinu* was added to the daily prayers to implant faith in the Oneness of God's kingship, and the conviction that He will one day *remove detestable idolatry from the earth ...,* thus preventing Jews from being tempted to follow the beliefs and lifestyles of the nations among whom they dwell (see *Iyun Tefillah* and *Emek Brachah).*

As we can surmise from its authorship and its placement at the conclusion of every service, its significance is profound. Its first paragraph [עָלֵינוּ] proclaims the difference between Israel's concept of God and that of the other nations. The second paragraph [עַל כֵּן] expresses our confidence that all humanity will eventually recognize His sovereignty and declare its obedience to His commandments. It should be clear, however, that this does not imply a belief or even a hope that they will convert to Judaism. Rather, they will accept Him as *the only God* and obey the universal Noachide laws that are incumbent upon all nations *(R' Hirsch).*

חֶלְקֵנוּ ... וְגוֹרָלֵנוּ — *Our portion ... our lot.* God does not punish gentile nations until they have reached the full quota of sin, beyond which He no longer extends mercy. Then He brings retribution upon them, often wiping them out. Such powerful ancient empires as Egypt, Persia, Greece, Rome, and Carthage have disappeared or become inconsequential. God does not act this

Stand while reciting עָלֵינוּ, *'It is our duty . . .'*

עָלֵינוּ *It is our duty to praise the Master of all, to ascribe greatness to the Molder of primeval creation, for He has not made us like the nations of the lands and has not emplaced us like the families of the earth; for He has not assigned our portion like theirs nor our lot* like all their multitudes. (For they bow* to vanity and emptiness and pray to a god which helps not.[1]) But we bend our knees, bow, and acknowledge our thanks before the King Who reigns over kings, the Holy One, Blessed is He. He stretches out heaven and establishes earth's foundation,[2] the seat of His homage is in the heavens above and His powerful Presence is in the loftiest heights. He is our God and there is none other. True is our King, there is nothing beside Him, as it is written in His Torah: 'You are to know this day and take to your heart* that* HASHEM *is the only God — in heaven above and on the earth below — there is none other.'[3]*

Bow while reciting 'But we bend our knees.'

עַל כֵּן *Therefore we put our hope in You,** HASHEM, *our God, that we may soon see Your mighty splendor, to remove detestable idolatry from the earth, and false gods will be utterly cut off, to perfect the universe through the Almighty's sovereignty. Then all humanity will call upon Your Name, to turn all the earth's wicked toward You. All the world's inhabitants will recognize and know that to You every knee should bend, every tongue should swear.[4] Before You,* HASHEM, *our God, they will bend every knee and cast themselves down and to the glory of Your Name they will render homage, and they will all accept upon themselves the yoke of Your kingship that You may reign over them soon and eternally. For the kingdom is Yours and You will reign*

(1) *Isaiah* 45:20. (2) 51:13. (3) *Deuteronomy* 4:39. (4) Cf. *Isaiah* 45:23.

---

way with regard to Israel, however. The world survives whether or not there is a Roman Empire, but the world could not survive without Israel. Therefore, God punishes Israel piecemeal, so that it may never be destroyed *(Siach Yitzchak).*

שֶׁהֵם מִשְׁתַּחֲוִים . . . — *For they bow* . . . The inclusion of this verse follows the original version of *Aleinu*. In the year 1400, a baptized Jew, no doubt seeking to prove his loyalty to the Church, spread the slander that this passage was meant to slur Christianity. He 'proved' his contention by the coincidence that the numerical value of וָרִיק, *emptiness*, is 316, the same as יֵשׁוּ, the Hebrew name of their messiah. The charge was refuted time and again, particularly by Manasseh ben Israel, the seventeenth-century scholar, but repeated persecutions and Church insistence, backed by governmental enforcement, caused the line to be dropped from most Ashkenazic *siddurim*. While most congregations have not returned it to the *Aleinu* prayer, some prominent authorities, among them Rabbi Yehoshua Leib Diskin, insist that *Aleinu* be recited in its original form *(World of Prayer; Siach Yitzchak).*

וְיָדַעְתָּ הַיּוֹם וַהֲשֵׁבֹתָ אֶל לְבָבֶךָ — *You are to know this day and take to your heart.* The masters of *Mussar* explain that an abstract belief in God is not sufficient to make people observe the *mitzvos* as they should. After obtaining knowledge we must take it to heart; that is, develop an emotional commitment to act upon the knowledge.

עַל כֵּן נְקַוֶּה לְךָ — *Therefore we put our hope in You.* Having stated that God chose us from among all the nations to serve Him, we are entitled to hope that He will speedily reveal His greatness and rid the earth of spiritual abomination *(Abudraham).*

לְעֹלָם וָעֶד.[1] ❖ וְנֶאֱמַר: וְהָיָה יהוה לְמֶלֶךְ עַל כָּל הָאָרֶץ, בַּיּוֹם הַהוּא יִהְיֶה יהוה אֶחָד וּשְׁמוֹ אֶחָד.[2]

Some congregations recite the following after עָלֵינוּ:

אַל תִּירָא* מִפַּחַד פִּתְאֹם, וּמִשֹּׁאַת רְשָׁעִים כִּי תָבֹא.[3] עֻצוּ עֵצָה וְתֻפָר, דַּבְּרוּ דָבָר וְלֹא יָקוּם, כִּי עִמָּנוּ אֵל.[4] וְעַד זִקְנָה אֲנִי הוּא, וְעַד שֵׂיבָה אֲנִי אֶסְבֹּל, אֲנִי עָשִׂיתִי וַאֲנִי אֶשָּׂא, וַאֲנִי אֶסְבֹּל וַאֲמַלֵּט.[5]

קדיש יתום

Mourners recite קַדִּישׁ יָתוֹם, the Mourner's *Kaddish* (see *Laws* §81-83).

יִתְגַּדַּל וְיִתְקַדַּשׁ שְׁמֵהּ רַבָּא.* (Cong. – אָמֵן.*) בְּעָלְמָא דִּי בְרָא כִרְעוּתֵהּ.* וְיַמְלִיךְ מַלְכוּתֵהּ, בְּחַיֵּיכוֹן* וּבְיוֹמֵיכוֹן וּבְחַיֵּי דְכָל בֵּית יִשְׂרָאֵל, בַּעֲגָלָא וּבִזְמַן קָרִיב.* וְאִמְרוּ: אָמֵן.

(Cong. – אָמֵן. יְהֵא שְׁמֵהּ רַבָּא* מְבָרַךְ לְעָלַם וּלְעָלְמֵי עָלְמַיָּא.)

יְהֵא שְׁמֵהּ רַבָּא מְבָרַךְ לְעָלַם וּלְעָלְמֵי עָלְמַיָּא.

יִתְבָּרַךְ* וְיִשְׁתַּבַּח וְיִתְפָּאַר וְיִתְרוֹמַם וְיִתְנַשֵּׂא וְיִתְהַדָּר וְיִתְעַלֶּה וְיִתְהַלָּל שְׁמֵהּ דְּקֻדְשָׁא בְּרִיךְ הוּא (Cong. – בְּרִיךְ הוּא) — לְעֵלָּא מִן כָּל בִּרְכָתָא* וְשִׁירָתָא תֻּשְׁבְּחָתָא וְנֶחֱמָתָא, דַּאֲמִירָן בְּעָלְמָא. וְאִמְרוּ: אָמֵן. (Cong. – אָמֵן.)

יְהֵא שְׁלָמָא רַבָּא מִן שְׁמַיָּא, וְחַיִּים עָלֵינוּ וְעַל כָּל יִשְׂרָאֵל. וְאִמְרוּ: אָמֵן. (Cong. – אָמֵן.)

Take three steps back. Bow left and say . . . עֹשֶׂה; bow right and say . . . הוּא; bow forward and say וְעַל כָּל . . . אָמֵן. Remain standing in place for a few moments, then take three steps forward.

עֹשֶׂה שָׁלוֹם בִּמְרוֹמָיו, הוּא יַעֲשֶׂה שָׁלוֹם עָלֵינוּ, וְעַל כָּל יִשְׂרָאֵל. וְאִמְרוּ: אָמֵן. (Cong. – אָמֵן.)

⊲§ אַל תִּירָא — *Do not fear. Zichron Zion* cites the custom of reciting these three verses after *Aleinu.* They express confidence in God's protection and are regarded as auguries of deliverance: (a) Do not fear an evildoer's intention, no matter how dangerous it seems; (b) let the enemies of Israel conspire and plan — they will fail; (c) God remains the eternal protector of Israel, even though it has sinned.

⊲§ קַדִּישׁ יָתוֹם / The Mourner's Kaddish

For the eleven months following the death of a parent and on the *yahrzeit*, or anniversary of the death, a son is obligated to recite *Kaddish* as a source of merit for the soul of the departed. A discussion of the concept and basis underlying the recitation of the Mourner's *Kaddish* appears in the ArtScroll *Kaddish.*

יִתְגַּדַּל וְיִתְקַדַּשׁ שְׁמֵהּ רַבָּא — *May His great Name grow exalted and sanctified.* The ultimate sanctification of God's Name will come when Israel is redeemed; in this sense *Kaddish* is a plea for the final Redemption. It is also an expression of Israel's mission to bring recognition of His sovereignty to all people on earth. This mission is incumbent primarily upon the community as a whole, and *Kaddish* is therefore recited only in the presence of a *minyan* [a quorum of ten males over *bar mitzvah*] *(R' Munk).*

אָמֵן — *Amen.* The word אָמֵן, *Amen,* is the listener's acknowledgment that he believes in what the reader has just said. It is derived from the same root as אֱמוּנָה, *faithfulness (Tur, Orach Chaim* 124). Additionally, it stands for אֵל מֶלֶךְ נֶאֱמָן, *God, the trustworthy King (Shabbos* 119b).

בְּעָלְמָא דִּי בְרָא כִרְעוּתֵהּ — *In the world that He created as He willed.* God had His concept of a perfect world before He began creation. Then He began to create in accordance with His prior will *(Ran).* Or it refers to the *future.* Only then

for all eternity in glory as it is written in Your Torah: HASHEM shall reign for all eternity.[1] Chazzan– *And it is said: HASHEM will be King over all the world — on that day HASHEM will be One and His Name will be One.*[2]

Some congregations recite the following after *Aleinu:*

אַל תִּירָא *Do not fear* sudden terror, or the holocaust of the wicked when it comes.*[3] *Plan a conspiracy and it will be annulled; speak your piece and it shall not stand, for God is with us.*[4] *Even till your seniority, I remain unchanged; and even till your ripe old age, I shall endure. I created you and I shall bear you; I shall endure and rescue.*[5]

MOURNER'S KADDISH

Mourners recite the Mourner's *Kaddish* (see *Laws* §81-83).
[A transliteration of this *Kaddish* appears on page 1305.]

יִתְגַּדַּל *May His great Name grow exalted and sanctified** (Cong.– *Amen.**) *in the world that He created as He willed.* May He give reign to His kingship in your lifetimes* and in your days, and in the lifetimes of the entire Family of Israel, swiftly and soon.* Now respond: Amen.*

(Cong.– *Amen. May His great Name* be blessed forever and ever.*)
May His great Name be blessed forever and ever.

Blessed, praised, glorified, exalted, extolled, mighty, upraised, and lauded be the Name of the Holy One, Blessed is He* (Cong.– *Blessed is He*) — *beyond any blessing* and song, praise and consolation that are uttered in the world. Now respond: Amen.* (Cong.– *Amen.*)

May there be abundant peace from Heaven, and life, upon us and upon all Israel. Now respond: Amen. (Cong.– *Amen.*)

Take three steps back. Bow left and say, *'He Who makes peace . . .';* bow right and say, *'may He . . .';* bow forward and say, *'and upon all Israel . . .'*
Remain standing in place for a few moments, then take three steps forward.

He Who makes peace in His heights, may He make peace upon us, and upon all Israel. Now respond: Amen. (Cong.– *Amen.*)

(1) *Exodus* 15:18. (2) *Zechariah* 14:9. (3) *Proverbs* 3:25. (4) *Isaiah* 8:10. (5) 46:4.

---

will mankind function in accordance with God's original intention *(R' Yehudah ben Yakar).*

בְּחַיֵּיכוֹן — *In your lifetimes.* The one reciting the *Kaddish* expresses the hope that his fellow congregants may all live to witness the Redemption of Israel and the sanctification of God's Name *(Abudraham).*

בַּעֲגָלָא וּבִזְמַן קָרִיב — *Swiftly and soon.* May the travail preceding the Messianic epoch be over swiftly and not be drawn out; and may it begin very soon *(Aruch HaShulchan).*

יְהֵא שְׁמֵהּ רַבָּא — *May His great Name* . . . The Talmud stresses in several places that the response, יְהֵא שְׁמֵהּ רַבָּא, *May His great Name. . .,* has an enormous cosmic effect. Indeed, the *halachah* states that an opportunity to respond to *Kaddish* takes precedence over an opportunity to respond to any other prayer, even *Kedushah* and *Borchu*. Consequently, if *Kaddish* is about to be recited in one room and *Kedushah* in another, one should go to hear *Kaddish (Mishnah Berurah* 56:6).

The Talmud *(Shabbos* 19b) teaches that one must respond יְהֵא שְׁמֵהּ רַבָּא 'with all his power,' meaning his total concentration *(Rashi, Tosafos).* Though it is preferable to raise one's voice when saying it, one should not say it so loudly that he will invite ridicule *(R' Yonah).* And it must be enunciated clearly *(Maharal).*

יִתְבָּרַךְ — *Blessed.* This begins a series of praises that continue the central theme of *Kaddish:* namely that in time to come God's greatness will be acknowledged by all of mankind *(Emek Berachah).*

לְעֵלָּא מִן כָּל בִּרְכָתָא — *Beyond any blessing.* No words or ideas can praise God adequately.

WHEN SUCCOS FALLS ON A WEEKDAY, TURN TO *MAARIV*, PAGE 34.

קבלת שבת

When the first day of Succos coincides with the Sabbath, *Kabbalas Shabbos* [our acceptance upon ourselves of the holiness of the Sabbath] consists of Psalms 92 and 93.

תהלים צב

מִזְמוֹר שִׁיר לְיוֹם הַשַּׁבָּת.* טוֹב לְהֹדוֹת לַיהוה, וּלְזַמֵּר לְשִׁמְךָ עֶלְיוֹן. לְהַגִּיד בַּבֹּקֶר חַסְדֶּךָ, וֶאֱמוּנָתְךָ בַּלֵּילוֹת.* עֲלֵי עָשׂוֹר* וַעֲלֵי נָבֶל, עֲלֵי הִגָּיוֹן בְּכִנּוֹר. כִּי שִׂמַּחְתַּנִי יהוה בְּפָעֳלֶךָ, בְּמַעֲשֵׂי יָדֶיךָ אֲרַנֵּן. מַה גָּדְלוּ מַעֲשֶׂיךָ יהוה, מְאֹד עָמְקוּ מַחְשְׁבֹתֶיךָ.* אִישׁ בַּעַר לֹא יֵדָע, וּכְסִיל לֹא יָבִין אֶת זֹאת. בִּפְרֹחַ רְשָׁעִים* כְּמוֹ עֵשֶׂב, וַיָּצִיצוּ כָּל פֹּעֲלֵי אָוֶן, לְהִשָּׁמְדָם עֲדֵי עַד.* וְאַתָּה מָרוֹם לְעֹלָם יהוה. כִּי הִנֵּה אֹיְבֶיךָ יהוה, כִּי הִנֵּה אֹיְבֶיךָ יֹאבֵדוּ, יִתְפָּרְדוּ כָּל פֹּעֲלֵי אָוֶן. וַתָּרֶם כִּרְאֵים קַרְנִי,* בַּלֹּתִי בְּשֶׁמֶן רַעֲנָן.* וַתַּבֵּט עֵינִי בְּשׁוּרָי, בַּקָּמִים עָלַי מְרֵעִים, תִּשְׁמַעְנָה אָזְנָי. ❖ צַדִּיק כַּתָּמָר יִפְרָח, כְּאֶרֶז* בַּלְּבָנוֹן יִשְׂגֶּה. שְׁתוּלִים בְּבֵית יהוה,* בְּחַצְרוֹת אֱלֹהֵינוּ יַפְרִיחוּ. עוֹד יְנוּבוּן בְּשֵׂיבָה, דְּשֵׁנִים וְרַעֲנַנִּים יִהְיוּ. לְהַגִּיד כִּי יָשָׁר יהוה, צוּרִי וְלֹא עַוְלָתָה בּוֹ.

קַבָּלַת שַׁבָּת / KABBALAS SHABBOS

מִזְמוֹר שִׁיר לְיוֹם הַשַּׁבָּת / Psalm 92

The custom of reciting psalms ninety-two and ninety-three at the arrival of the Sabbath is ancient. In a responsa, *Rambam (Pe'er HaDor* 116) implies clearly that it predated him by many generations. With our recitation of this song of praise to the Sabbath, we accept its holiness upon ourselves together with all its positive and negative *mitzvos.*

מִזְמוֹר שִׁיר לְיוֹם הַשַּׁבָּת — *A psalm, a song for the Sabbath day.* Although this psalm is identified as belonging particularly to the theme of the Sabbath — indeed, it was the Levites' song for the Sabbath Temple service *(Rashi)* — the text contains not a single direct reference to the Sabbath. What is the connection? Many explanations are given. Among them are:

— The psalm refers not to the weekly Sabbath, but to the World to Come, when man will achieve the spiritual perfection we only glimpse during the Sabbath. The psalm is thus well suited to the Sabbath which is a semblance of that future spiritual perfection *(Rashi).*

— Praise of God is necessary, but difficult in the weekdays when people must struggle for a livelihood. On the Sabbath when Jews are free from the strictures of the week, they can turn their minds and hearts to the perception of God's ways and His praise — which are the topics of this psalm *(Radak).*

בַּבֹּקֶר . . . בַּלֵּילוֹת — *In the dawn . . . in the nights.* Dawn is an allusion to redemption, while night symbolizes exile. We express our faith that even when God made us suffer, that too was kindness, because He did it for our ultimate benefit. Thus we *relate* His *kindness,* whether it was as clear and pleasant as the bright *dawn* or whether it was as hard to accept as the dark *night.* During the harsh night of exile, we call it אֱמוּנָתְךָ, *Your faith,* because we have faith that God is good, even if we do not understand some of the things He does.

עֲלֵי עָשׂוֹר — *Upon ten-stringed instrument.* The Sages teach that the lyre of Messianic times will be ten-stringed, representing a beautiful enhancement of music, which is now limited to the octave of eight notes. Every period in life calls for its own unique expression of praise, just as each day has its own song of praise and each part of creation serves God in its own way. The

WHEN SUCCOS FALLS ON A WEEKDAY, TURN TO *MAARIV,* PAGE 34.

KABBALAS SHABBOS

When the first day of Succos coincides with the Sabbath, *Kabbalas Shabbos* [our acceptance upon ourselves of the holiness of the Sabbath] consists of Psalms 92 and 93.

Psalm 92

מִזְמוֹר שִׁיר *A psalm, a song for the Sabbath day.* It is good to thank* HASHEM *and to sing praise to Your Name, O Exalted One; to relate Your kindness in the dawn and Your faith in the nights.* Upon ten-stringed instrument* and lyre, with singing accompanied by a harp. For You have gladdened me,* HASHEM, *with Your deeds; at the works of Your Hands I sing glad song. How great are Your deeds,* HASHEM; *exceedingly profound are Your thoughts.* A boor cannot know, nor can a fool understand this: when the wicked bloom* like grass and all the doers of iniquity blossom — it is to destroy them till eternity.* But You remain exalted forever,* HASHEM. *For behold! — Your enemies,* HASHEM, *for behold! — Your enemies shall perish, dispersed shall be all doers of iniquity. As exalted as a re'eim's shall be my pride,* I will be saturated with ever-fresh oil.* My eyes have seen my vigilant foes; when those who would harm me rise up against me, my ears have heard their doom.* Chazzan– *A righteous man will flourish like a date palm, like a cedar* in the Lebanon he will grow tall. Planted in the house of* HASHEM,* *in the courtyards of our God they will flourish. They will still be fruitful in old age, vigorous and fresh they will be — to declare that* HASHEM *is just, my Rock in Whom there is no wrong.*

---

enhanced spirituality of Messianic times will demand a heightened form of song (*Sfas Emes;* see *Overview,* ArtScroll *Tehillim*).

מַעֲשֶׂיךָ ... מַחְשְׁבֹתֶיךָ — *Your deeds ... Your thoughts.* God's *deeds* are the tangible parts of Creation and the events we perceive with our senses. His *thoughts* are His purposes and goals; they are profound beyond human comprehension (*Sfas Emes*).

בִּפְרֹחַ רְשָׁעִים — *When the wicked bloom.* Most people can find no answer to the eternal human dilemma: Why do the wicked prosper? If only these inquisitors could look beyond what their senses tell them, they would realize that ...

לְהִשָּׁמְדָם עֲדֵי עַד — *To destroy them till eternity.* God gives temporal success and happiness to the wicked as reward for whatever good deeds they may have done. Having been recompensed, they will sink to destruction, while the righteous gain eternal reward (*Rashi*).

וַתָּרֶם כִּרְאֵים קַרְנִי — *As exalted as a re'eim's shall be my pride* [lit. *my horn*]. The once-downtrodden pride of the righteous will rise and be as exalted as the upraised horns of the haughty *re'eim* [a beast of uncertain identity, variously translated as unicorn, rhinoceros, buffalo, antelope, and others]. In any case, its use in Scripture indicates that it has a long and powerful horn.

בְּשֶׁמֶן רַעֲנָן — *With ever-fresh oil.* Oil is a common Scriptural simile for blessing, prosperity, and supremacy (*Rashi*).

כַּתָּמָר ... כְּאֶרֶז — *Like a date palm, like a cedar.* The *tzaddik* will be as fruitful as a date palm, and as sturdy in health as a cedar (*Rashi*).

שְׁתוּלִים בְּבֵית ה׳ — *Planted in the house of* HASHEM. The quality of a tree — described in the previous verse — is only half the formula for success; for maximum benefit it must be planted in luxuriant soil. The righteous will be firmly rooted in the spiritual riches of God's House. There they will blossom without limit (*Radak*).

תהלים צג

יהוה מָלָךְ גֵּאוּת לָבֵשׁ,* לָבֵשׁ יהוה עֹז הִתְאַזָּר, אַף תִּכּוֹן תֵּבֵל בַּל תִּמּוֹט. נָכוֹן כִּסְאֲךָ מֵאָז, מֵעוֹלָם אָתָּה. נָשְׂאוּ נְהָרוֹת, יהוה, נָשְׂאוּ נְהָרוֹת קוֹלָם,* יִשְׂאוּ נְהָרוֹת דָּכְיָם. ❖ מִקֹּלוֹת מַיִם רַבִּים* אַדִּירִים מִשְׁבְּרֵי יָם, אַדִּיר בַּמָּרוֹם יהוה. עֵדֹתֶיךָ* נֶאֶמְנוּ מְאֹד לְבֵיתְךָ נַאֲוָה קֹּדֶשׁ, יהוה, לְאֹרֶךְ יָמִים.*

קדיש יתום

Mourners recite קַדִּישׁ יָתוֹם, the Mourner's *Kaddish* (see *Laws* §81-83).

יִתְגַּדַּל וְיִתְקַדַּשׁ שְׁמֵהּ רַבָּא. (.Cong – אָמֵן.) בְּעָלְמָא דִּי בְרָא כִרְעוּתֵהּ. וְיַמְלִיךְ מַלְכוּתֵהּ, בְּחַיֵּיכוֹן וּבְיוֹמֵיכוֹן וּבְחַיֵּי דְכָל בֵּית יִשְׂרָאֵל, בַּעֲגָלָא וּבִזְמַן קָרִיב. וְאִמְרוּ: אָמֵן.

(.Cong – אָמֵן. יְהֵא שְׁמֵהּ רַבָּא מְבָרַךְ לְעָלַם וּלְעָלְמֵי עָלְמַיָּא.)

יְהֵא שְׁמֵהּ רַבָּא מְבָרַךְ לְעָלַם וּלְעָלְמֵי עָלְמַיָּא.

יִתְבָּרַךְ וְיִשְׁתַּבַּח וְיִתְפָּאַר וְיִתְרוֹמַם וְיִתְנַשֵּׂא וְיִתְהַדָּר וְיִתְעַלֶּה וְיִתְהַלָּל שְׁמֵהּ דְּקֻדְשָׁא בְּרִיךְ הוּא (.Cong – בְּרִיךְ הוּא) — לְעֵלָּא מִן כָּל בִּרְכָתָא וְשִׁירָתָא תֻּשְׁבְּחָתָא וְנֶחֱמָתָא, דַּאֲמִירָן בְּעָלְמָא. וְאִמְרוּ: אָמֵן. (.Cong – אָמֵן.)

יְהֵא שְׁלָמָא רַבָּא מִן שְׁמַיָּא, וְחַיִּים עָלֵינוּ וְעַל כָּל יִשְׂרָאֵל. וְאִמְרוּ: אָמֵן. (.Cong – אָמֵן.)

Take three steps back. Bow left and say . . . עֹשֶׂה; bow right and say . . . הוּא; bow forward and say וְעַל כָּל . . . אָמֵן. Remain standing in place for a few moments, then take three steps forward.

עֹשֶׂה שָׁלוֹם בִּמְרוֹמָיו, הוּא יַעֲשֶׂה שָׁלוֹם עָלֵינוּ, וְעַל כָּל יִשְׂרָאֵל. וְאִמְרוּ: אָמֵן. (.Cong – אָמֵן.)

ה׳ מָלָךְ / Psalm 93

This psalm is a direct continuation of the previous theme that God's greatness will be recognized by all in the Messianic era. Accordingly, the past-tense syntax of the psalm should be understood as uttered in retrospect. Because it describes God in His full grandeur and power as He was when He completed the six days of Creation, and because it describes Him as 'donning' grandeur and 'girding' Himself like one dressing in Sabbath finery, the psalm was designated as the Levite's 'Song of the Day' for Friday, when the footsteps of the Sabbath begin to be heard *(R' Yaakov Emden).*

An alternative interpretation of this psalm ascribes it to the beginning of Creation:

On the sixth day Adam was created. God blew a breath of life into his nostrils and invested him with a Divine soul. When Adam stood and scrutinized God's amazing creation, he realized how awesome and wonderful it was. As he sang God's praises, Adam truly looked Divine, because he was a reflection of God's image. The creatures of the earth were filled with awe, for they imagined that Adam was their creator. When they gathered to bow to him in submission, however, Adam was incredulous. 'Why do you bow to me?' he asked. 'Let us go together to pay homage to God, Who truly reigns. Let us robe the Creator in majesty.' Then Adam led all the creatures in this song, *HASHEM . . . reigned, He . . . donned grandeur (Pirkei deR' Eliezer* 11).

גֵּאוּת לָבֵשׁ — *He will have donned grandeur.* The concept of *grandeur* represents God's revelation as the dominant force before Whom yield the mightiest natural forces. In man, grandeur — or arrogance — is a contemptible trait, because man's power is limited at best. But to God, *grandeur* is becoming because all forces owe their existence to Him while He is dependent on nothing *(Midrash Shocher Tov).*

Iggeres HaRamban explains that the arrogant man is a rebel who defies the sovereignty of God. Such a person steals the royal vestments which belong to God alone, for, as our verse states, *HASHEM . . . reigned, He . . . donned grandeur.*

God 'dons' grandeur — it is similar to a person donning a garment; our comprehension of him is guided by the contours and quality of the

Psalm 93

יהוה מָלָךְ *HASHEM will have reigned, He will have donned grandeur;* He will have donned might and girded Himself; even firmed the world that it should not falter. Your throne was established from of old; eternal are You. Like rivers they raised, O HASHEM, like rivers they raised their voice;* like rivers they shall raise their destructiveness.* Chazzan– *More than the roars of many waters,* mightier than the waves of the sea — You are mighty on high, HASHEM. Your testimonies* are exceedingly trustworthy about Your House, the Sacred Dwelling — O HASHEM, may it be for long days.**

MOURNER'S KADDISH

Mourners recite the Mourner's *Kaddish* (see *Laws* §81-83).
[A transliteration of this *Kaddish* appears on page 1305.]

יִתְגַּדַּל *May His great Name grow exalted and sanctified* (Cong.– *Amen.*) *in the world that He created as He willed. May He give reign to His kingship in your lifetimes and in your days, and in the lifetimes of the entire Family of Israel, swiftly and soon. Now respond: Amen.*

(Cong.– *Amen. May His great Name be blessed forever and ever.*)

May His great Name be blessed forever and ever.

Blessed, praised, glorified, exalted, extolled, mighty, upraised, and lauded be the Name of the Holy One, Blessed is He (Cong.– *Blessed is He*) *— beyond any blessing and song, praise and consolation that are uttered in the world. Now respond: Amen.* (Cong. – *Amen.*)

May there be abundant peace from Heaven, and life, upon us and upon all Israel. Now respond: Amen. (Cong.– *Amen.*)

Take three steps back. Bow left and say, *'He Who makes peace . . .'*; bow right and say, *'may He . . .'*; bow forward and say, *'and upon all Israel . . .'* Remain standing in place for a few moments, then take three steps forward.

He Who makes peace in His heights, may He make peace upon us, and upon all Israel. Now respond: Amen. (Cong.– *Amen.*)

---

garment, but the garment is hardly his essence. No matter how much of God's greatness we think we understand, our puny intellect grasps but the minutest fraction of His infinite greatness. He does us the favor of allowing mankind this degree of perception so that we can aspire to the privilege of praising Him.

נָשְׂאוּ נְהָרוֹת קוֹלָם — *Like rivers they raised their voice.* The enemies of Israel will roar against Israel like raging rivers at flood stage *(Radak).*

The repetition of the phrase represents the destruction of the two Temples *(Etz Yosef).*

מִקֹּלוֹת מַיִם רַבִּים ... — *More than the roars of many waters* ... You, O God, are beyond the threatening roars of the hostile nations who wish to drown us. You are mightier than the powerful waves of the sea, i.e., the mighty forces of evil among those who wish to crush us.

עֵדֹתֶיךָ — *Your testimonies.* The assurances of Your prophets regarding the eventual rebuilding of the Temple *(Rashi).*

ה׳ לְאֹרֶךְ יָמִים — *O HASHEM, may it be for long days.* The psalm closes with a plea that when the *trustworthy* prophecies about the Third Temple are finally fulfilled, may it stand for *long days,* a Scriptural idiom meaning forever *(Radak).*

מַעֲרִיב / THE EVENING SERVICE

Like *Shacharis* and *Minchah* (see page 6), *Maariv* has its basis in the Temple service. In the Temple, no sacrifices were offered in the evening, but any sacrificial parts that had not been burned on the Altar during the day could be burned at night. Thus, although no sacrificial service was *required* during the night, the Altar was usually in use. This explains why *Maariv* began as a voluntary service; unlike *Shacharis* and *Minchah* that took the place of required offerings, *Maariv* corresponds to a service optional in the sense that it was unnecessary if all parts were burned during the day. During Talmudic times, Jewry universally adopted *Maariv* as an obligatory service, so it now has the status of *Shacharis* and *Minchah.* (It should be noted that the original optional status of

מעריב לסוכות

In some congregations the *chazzan* chants a melody during his recitation of בָּרְכוּ so that the congregation can then recite יִתְבָּרַךְ.

Chazzan bows at בָּרְכוּ and straightens up at ה׳.

בָּרְכוּ אֶת יהוה* הַמְּבֹרָךְ.

Congregation, followed by *chazzan*, responds, bowing at בָּרוּךְ and straightening up at ה׳.

בָּרוּךְ יהוה הַמְּבֹרָךְ* לְעוֹלָם וָעֶד.

יִתְבָּרַךְ[1] וְיִשְׁתַּבַּח וְיִתְפָּאַר וְיִתְרוֹמַם וְיִתְנַשֵּׂא שְׁמוֹ שֶׁל מֶלֶךְ מַלְכֵי הַמְּלָכִים, הַקָּדוֹשׁ בָּרוּךְ הוּא. שֶׁהוּא רִאשׁוֹן וְהוּא אַחֲרוֹן, וּמִבַּלְעָדָיו אֵין אֱלֹהִים.[2] סֹלּוּ, לָרֹכֵב בָּעֲרָבוֹת, בְּיָהּ שְׁמוֹ, וְעִלְזוּ לְפָנָיו.[3] וּשְׁמוֹ מְרוֹמָם עַל כָּל בְּרָכָה וּתְהִלָּה.[4] בָּרוּךְ שֵׁם כְּבוֹד מַלְכוּתוֹ לְעוֹלָם וָעֶד. יְהִי שֵׁם יהוה מְבֹרָךְ, מֵעַתָּה וְעַד עוֹלָם.[5]

ברכות קריאת שמע

בָּרוּךְ אַתָּה יהוה אֱלֹהֵינוּ מֶלֶךְ הָעוֹלָם, אֲשֶׁר בִּדְבָרוֹ* מַעֲרִיב עֲרָבִים, בְּחָכְמָה פּוֹתֵחַ שְׁעָרִים,* וּבִתְבוּנָה מְשַׁנֶּה עִתִּים,* וּמַחֲלִיף אֶת הַזְּמַנִּים, וּמְסַדֵּר אֶת הַכּוֹכָבִים בְּמִשְׁמְרוֹתֵיהֶם בָּרָקִיעַ כִּרְצוֹנוֹ. בּוֹרֵא יוֹם וָלָיְלָה, גּוֹלֵל אוֹר מִפְּנֵי חֹשֶׁךְ וְחֹשֶׁךְ מִפְּנֵי אוֹר. וּמַעֲבִיר יוֹם וּמֵבִיא לָיְלָה, וּמַבְדִּיל בֵּין יוֹם וּבֵין לָיְלָה, יהוה צְבָאוֹת* שְׁמוֹ. ❖ אֵל חַי וְקַיָּם, תָּמִיד יִמְלוֹךְ עָלֵינוּ, לְעוֹלָם וָעֶד.

Many congregations recite *piyutim* (liturgical poems) that are inserted at various points in the synagogue service, often in the middle of a paragraph. Those who do not recite *piyutim* should not assume their appearance to indicate a stop, but should continue until the next new paragraph as indicated by bold type for the first word.

Maariv applied only to *Shemoneh Esrei;* the *Shema* reading is Scripturally required.)

בָּרְכוּ / Borchu

בָּרְכוּ אֶת ה׳ — *Bless HASHEM.* בָּרְכוּ is recited only in the presence of a *minyan,* a quorum of ten adult males. The *chazzan* summons them to join in the forthcoming prayers known as בִּרְכוֹת קְרִיאַת שְׁמַע, *Blessings of the Shema.* As *Zohar* states: All sacred acts require summoning.

With relation to God, the term *bless* cannot mean adding to His powers. Rather it is our declaration that He is the *source* of all blessing *(Kad HaKemach).* It represents our dedication to fulfill His will by our obedience to His commandments. Thus, in a sense we *do* confer something upon Him, for it is in our power to accomplish His goals for man *(R' Hirsch).*

בָּרוּךְ ה׳ הַמְּבֹרָךְ — *Blessed is HASHEM, the blessed One.* With or without our acknowledgment, God is constantly 'blessed' by all aspects of Creation — from the celestial beings to the humblest pebble — for they function in accordance with His will *(Kad HaKemach).*

Having called upon the congregation to bless God, the *chazzan* must not let it appear as though he excludes himself from the obligation. Therefore, when the congregation has concluded its response, he repeats it *(Tur).*

בִּרְכוֹת קְרִיאַת שְׁמַע / Blessings of the Shema

The four nighttime Blessings of the *Shema* are similar in theme to the morning three (see page 216). The total of seven is based on the verse *(Psalms 119:164): Seven times a day I praise You (Berachos* 11a, *Rashi).* Of the evening blessings, the first describes God's control over nature, seasons, and the cycles of light. The second speaks of God's gift of the Torah, the very essence of Israel's survival. The third refers to the Exodus, but with emphasis on the future redemption. The fourth, described by the Talmud as an extension of the theme of redemption, stresses God's protection of His people from the terrors and dangers of night.

בָּרוּךְ אַתָּה . . . אֲשֶׁר בִּדְבָרוֹ — *Blessed are You . . . Who by His word.* The command of God created day just as it created night, for every moment has a purpose in God's plan. This recognition of God's everpresent will is especially important at night, which represents the period of fear, failure, and exile *(R' Hirsch).*

פּוֹתֵחַ שְׁעָרִים — *Opens gates.* A reference to the 'gates' which 'open' to release the light of the morning sun and 'close' upon it in the evening — as if the sun were brought out at dawn and

MAARIV FOR SUCCOS

In some congregations the *chazzan* chants a melody during his recitation of *Borchu* so that the congregation can then recite *'Blessed, praised . . .'*

Chazzan bows at *'Bless'* and straightens up at *'HASHEM.'*

Bless HASHEM,* the blessed One.

Congregation, followed by *chazzan,* responds, bowing at *'Blessed'* and straightening up at *'HASHEM.'*

Blessed is HASHEM, the blessed One,* for all eternity.

Blessed,[1] praised, glorified, exalted and upraised is the Name of the King Who rules over kings — the Holy One, Blessed is He. For He is the First and He is the Last and aside from Him there is no god.[2] Extol Him — Who rides the highest heavens — with His Name, YAH, and exult before Him.[3] His Name is exalted beyond every blessing and praise.[4] Blessed is the Name of His glorious kingdom for all eternity. Blessed be the Name of HASHEM from this time and forever.[5]

BLESSINGS OF THE SHEMA

בָּרוּךְ *Blessed are You, HASHEM, our God, King of the universe, Who by His word* brings on evenings, with wisdom opens gates,* with understanding alters periods,* changes the seasons, and orders the stars in their heavenly constellations as He wills. He creates day and night, removing light before darkness and darkness before light. He causes day to pass and brings night, and separates between day and night — HASHEM, Master of Legions,* is His Name.* Chazzan– *May the living and enduring God continuously reign over us, for all eternity.*

(1) See *Orach Chaim* 57:1 (2) Cf. *Isaiah* 44:6. (3) *Psalms* 68:5. (4) Cf. *Nechemiah* 9:5. (5) *Psalms* 113:2.

put to rest at dusk *(Iyun Tefillah).*

וּבִתְבוּנָה מְשַׁנֶּה עִתִּים — *With understanding alters periods.* With deep understanding of the needs of a particular time segment, God varies weather conditions from day to day and from hour to hour *(Siach Yitzchak).*

ה׳ צְבָאוֹת — *HASHEM, Master of Legions.* He takes the infinite number of forces and conditions that form the universe and harmonizes them to perform His will *(R' Hirsch).*

פִּיוּטִים / Piyutim

Piyutim (liturgical poems) are inserted at various points in the synagogue service on the Festivals and on certain Sabbaths during the year. These *piyutim* express the mood and theme of the day, and many of them have become highlights of the day's service.

The composers of these *piyutim* include some of the outstanding figures of ancient times. The first and greatest was R' Elazar HaKalir who, according to tradition, lived in the time of the Mishnah. [According to *Tosafos* (*Chagigah* 13a) and *Rosh* (*Berachos* 5:21), he is the second-century Tanna R' Elazar son of R' Shimon bar Yochai.] Most of the *piyutim* of the *Hoshana* service are ascribed to him (see p. 362). The other *paytanim* (composers of *piyutim*) were among the *Geonim* (7th-10th-century Torah authorities) and *Rishonim* (11th-15th-century authorities). Consequently, it should be clear that their compositions are not merely inspired poetry.

The *piyutim* for the first night of Succos contain (as indicated by the bold type) an acrostic of the *aleph-beis,* followed by the signature יוֹסֵף הַקָּטָן בַּר שְׁמוּאֵל, *Yosef the lesser, son of Shmuel.* Also known as *R' Yosef Tuv Elem,* he was spiritual leader of the Jewish communities in Limoges and Anjou, France,

Laws of Maariv (see also *Laws* §33-55 for the laws of *Shema*)

The ideal time for *Maariv* is after dark. However, one may recite *Maariv* earlier in which case he must repeat the three chapters of *Shema* after dark.

As a general rule, no אָמֵן, *Amen,* or other prayer response may be recited between *Borchu* and *Shemoneh Esrei,* but there are exceptions. The main exception is 'between chapters' [בֵּין הַפְּרָקִים] of the *Shema Blessings* — i.e., after each of the blessings, and between the three chapters of *Shema.* At those points, אָמֵן (but not בָּרוּךְ הוּא וּבָרוּךְ שְׁמוֹ) may be said in response to any blessing. Some responses, however, are so important that they are permitted at any point in the *Shema* blessings. They are: (a) In *Kaddish,* אָמֵן יְהֵא שְׁמֵהּ רַבָּא . . . עָלְמַיָּא and the אָמֵן after דַּאֲמִירָן בְּעָלְמָא; and (b) the response to בָּרְכוּ.

No interruptions whatever are permitted during the two verses of שְׁמַע and בָּרוּךְ שֵׁם.

FIRST NIGHT

אוֹחֲזֵי בְיָדָם אַרְבָּעָה מִינִים,
בָּאִים לְסַלְּדָךְ בְּעֻגָב וּבְמִנִּים,*
גְּמוּנֵי פָז* אוֹגְדִים וּמְזַמְּנִים,
דְּגָלֵימוֹ יָשִׂים
כְּכוֹכְבֵי שַׁחַק נִמְנִים.

SECOND NIGHT

יִשְׂמְחוּ בְחַגֵּיהֶם יְדִידִים וּנְעִימִים,
חֲסוּת בְּצֵל סֻכָּה[1] שִׁבְעַת יָמִים,
יִתְעַנְּגוּ בָהּ בְּמִינֵי מַטְעַמִּים,
אֲהוּבִים מִצְוֹתֶיהָ מְקַיְּמִים
לֵילוֹת וְיָמִים.*

בָּרוּךְ אַתָּה יהוה, הַמַּעֲרִיב עֲרָבִים. (Cong.– אָמֵן.)

אַהֲבַת עוֹלָם* בֵּית יִשְׂרָאֵל עַמְּךָ אָהָבְתָּ. תּוֹרָה וּמִצְוֹת, חֻקִּים וּמִשְׁפָּטִים, אוֹתָנוּ לִמַּדְתָּ. עַל כֵּן יהוה אֱלֹהֵינוּ, בְּשָׁכְבֵנוּ וּבְקוּמֵנוּ נָשִׂיחַ בְּחֻקֶּיךָ, וְנִשְׂמַח* בְּדִבְרֵי תוֹרָתֶךָ, וּבְמִצְוֹתֶיךָ לְעוֹלָם וָעֶד. ❖ כִּי הֵם חַיֵּינוּ, וְאֹרֶךְ יָמֵינוּ,* וּבָהֶם נֶהְגֶּה יוֹמָם וָלָיְלָה. וְאַהֲבָתְךָ, אַל תָּסִיר מִמֶּנּוּ לְעוֹלָמִים.

FIRST NIGHT

הוֹגֵי דָת מֵרֹאשׁ נְסוּכָה,*
וּבָאִים וְלָנִים שִׁבְעָה בַּסֻּכָּה,
זְכוּת הַמְצִיאֵם
וְגוֹנְנֵם מִמְּשֻׁכָּה,*
חֹק אֲהֵבָתָם
בְּלִי לְחָשְׁכָה.

SECOND NIGHT

בְּרֶנֶן וְהַלֵּל וְחֶדְוָה רַבָּה,
יְצַהֲלוּ כָּל שִׁבְעָה כַּדָּת הַכְּתוּבָה,
חֲגִיגוֹתֵיהֶם* וְשַׁלְמֵיהֶם
וּפָרֵיהֶם לְקָרְבָה,
קָרְבְּנוֹתֵיהֶם וְעוֹלוֹתֵיהֶם
יֵרָצוּ בְּאַהֲבָה.

בָּרוּךְ אַתָּה יהוה, אוֹהֵב עַמּוֹ יִשְׂרָאֵל. (Cong.– אָמֵן.)

---

early in the eleventh century. Of special importance among his many compositions is his *yotzer* for *Shabbos HaGadol* (the Sabbath before Pesach), a halachic-liturgical work quoted extensively by *Tosafos*.

The *piyutim* for the second night were composed by the otherwise unknown R' Yechiel ben Yitzchak of Zülpich, Germany (13th century?), whose name appears in the acrostic at least three times.

When the first night of Succos falls on the Sabbath, the *piyutim* are omitted on that night (*Orach Chaim* 275:2), and most congregations recite them on the second night. In such a case the *piyutim* usually recited on the second night are omitted entirely.

בְּעֻגָב וּבְמִנִּים — *With musical instruments.* This refers to the daily Temple services which were accompanied by a Levite choir and orchestra. More specifically this may allude to the *Simchas Beis HaSho'evah*, which was unique to Succos and at which musical instruments of every type were played (*Succah* 5:4, see p. 124).

גְּמוּנֵי פָז — *Bands of finest gold.* After binding their *haddasim* and *aravos* to their *lulavim*, the residents of Jerusalem would adorn the *lulavim* with golden bands (*Succah* 3:8, see p. 110).

לֵילוֹת וְיָמִים — *Night and day.* The *Succah* becomes their dwelling place for the duration of the Festival. They sleep in the *succah* at night and eat in it during the day.

אַהֲבַת עוֹלָם — [*With*] *an eternal love.* Like the blessing immediately before the morning *Shema*, this blessing is an ecstatic expression of gratitude to God for the gift of Torah. Only after acknowledging our dependence on, and love for, the Torah, can we go on to express our undivided loyalty and dedication to ה׳ אֶחָד, *HASHEM, the One and Only* God, Who gave us this most precious gift.

The blessing begins with an axiom of Judaism: God loves us. The fact that He chose to give us His Torah proves that it is the vehicle for our national fulfillment. Therefore we dedicate ourselves to study it — constantly, joyously, and devotedly (*Siach Yitzchak*).

וְנִשְׂמַח — *And we will rejoice.* Torah study must be seen not as a chore, but as a source of joy. A mourner is forbidden to study Torah except for tragic passages or relevant laws, because normal study would gladden him at a time when he is required to feel grief over his loss.

FIRST NIGHT	SECOND NIGHT
א *Those who hold the Four Species in hand,*	י *May the beloved and pleasant ones rejoice in their Festivals,*
ב *Come to exalt You with musical instruments,**	ח *Taking shelter in the shade of the succah[1] for seven days,*
ג *With bands of finest gold* they bind and prepare [their lulavim],*	י *May they find delight there with all manner of delicacies,*
ד *May their bannered tribes be countless as the stars of heaven.*	אל *The beloved ones, who fulfill the [succah's] mitzvos night and day.**

Blessed are You, HASHEM, *Who brings on evenings.* (Cong.– *Amen.*)

אַהֲבַת *With an eternal love* have You loved the House of Israel, Your nation. Torah and commandments, decrees and ordinances have You taught us. Therefore* HASHEM, *our God, upon our retiring and arising, we will discuss Your decrees and we will rejoice* with the words of Your Torah and with Your commandments for all eternity.* Chazzan– *For they are our life and the length of our days* and about them we will meditate day and night. May You not remove Your love from us forever.*

FIRST NIGHT	SECOND NIGHT
ה *Those who study the Torah which was chosen from the start,**	בר *With glad song, praise and abundant delight,*
ו *Come and spend seven nights in the succah,*	יצ *May they be jubilant all seven [days] as the Written Law [requires],*
ז *May You find them meritorious and protect them from pain,**	ח *To bring their chagigah-offerings,* peace-offerings and bulls,*
ח *Never to withhold the measure of their love.*	ק *May their offerings and olah-offerings be accepted with love.*

Blessed are You, HASHEM, *Who loves His nation Israel.* (Cong.– *Amen.*)

(1) Cf. *Isaiah* 4:6.

כִּי הֵם חַיֵּינוּ וְאֹרֶךְ יָמֵינוּ — *For they are our life and the length of our days.* The word life means different things to different people. The Torah teaches us that the only *true* life is one in the service of God, one that is dedicated to the study of Torah and the performance of *mitzvos.* When a person lives such a life on earth, he is assured that a natural consequence of his efforts is אֹרֶךְ יָמִים, *lengthy days,* of blessing and joy in the eternal World to Come *(Or HaChaim).*

דָּת מֵרֹאשׁ נְסוּכָה — *The Torah which was chosen from the start.* Wisdom and Understanding [i.e., the Torah *(Rashi)*] proclaim, 'HASHEM acquired me at the beginning of His way, before His works in times of yore. From the beginning of time was I chosen, from the start, even before there was an earth!' (*Proverbs* 8:22-23).

מִמְּשֻׂכָה — *From pain* (lit., *from a fence*). This is an allusion to מְשֻׂכַת חָדֶק, *a fence of thorns* (*Proverbs* 15:19). Thus, it refers to anything that causes pain the way a wall of thorns does.

... חֲגִיגוֹתֵיהֶם — *Their chagigah-offerings ...* The *paytan* lists the animal offerings brought during Succos:

Every Jewish male is commanded to appear at the *Beis HaMikdash* during the Pesach, Shavuos and Succos Festivals. Moreover, he must bring with him an animal as an elevation-offering (see *Deuteronomy* 16:16). The paytan refers to this sacrifice as עוֹלוֹתֵיהֶם, *their olah-offerings.*

Another commandment is that of תָּחֹג, *you shall celebrate* (*Exodus* 23:14), which, the Sages explain, requires the bringing of peace-offerings with which to celebrate the Festival. Hence, along with the *olah* each male must also bring a *chagigah,* referred to in our *piyut* as חֲגִיגוֹתֵיהֶם, *their chagigah-offering.*

A third offering is the שַׁלְמֵי שִׂמְחָה, *peace-offerings of joy.* The Jew is enjoined to be joyful when he appears before God during the Festivals. This joy is to be expressed by partaking of the meat of peace-offerings. Therefore, if the *chagigah*-offerings do not supply sufficient meat, then additional peace-offerings must be brought.

Accompanying every *olah-* and peace-offering is a *minchah* [flour-offering] (see p. 153). These are included here in the general term קָרְבְּנוֹתֵיהֶם, *their offerings.*

שמע

Immediately before its recitation concentrate on fulfilling the positive commandment of reciting the *Shema* twice daily. It is important to enunciate each word clearly and not to run words together. For this reason, vertical lines have been placed between two words that are prone to be slurred into one and are not separated by a comma or a hyphen. See *Laws* §40-52.

When praying without a *minyan,* begin with the following three-word formula:

אֵל מֶלֶךְ נֶאֱמָן.*

Recite the first verse aloud, with the right hand covering the eyes, and concentrate intently upon accepting God's absolute sovereignty.

שְׁמַע | יִשְׂרָאֵל,* יְהֹוָה | אֱלֹהֵינוּ, יְהֹוָה | אֶחָד:[1]

In an undertone — בָּרוּךְ שֵׁם* כְּבוֹד מַלְכוּתוֹ לְעוֹלָם וָעֶד.

While reciting the first paragraph (דברים ו:ה-ט), concentrate on accepting the commandment to love God.

וְאָהַבְתָּ* אֵת | יְהֹוָה | אֱלֹהֶיךָ, בְּכָל־לְבָבְךָ, וּבְכָל־נַפְשְׁךָ, וּבְכָל־מְאֹדֶךָ: וְהָיוּ הַדְּבָרִים הָאֵלֶּה, אֲשֶׁר | אָנֹכִי מְצַוְּךָ הַיּוֹם,* עַל־לְבָבֶךָ:* וְשִׁנַּנְתָּם לְבָנֶיךָ, וְדִבַּרְתָּ בָּם, בְּשִׁבְתְּךָ בְּבֵיתֶךָ, וּבְלֶכְתְּךָ בַדֶּרֶךְ, וּבְשָׁכְבְּךָ וּבְקוּמֶךָ: וּקְשַׁרְתָּם* לְאוֹת | עַל־יָדֶךָ, וְהָיוּ לְטֹטָפֹת בֵּין | עֵינֶיךָ: וּכְתַבְתָּם | עַל־מְזֻזוֹת בֵּיתֶךָ, וּבִשְׁעָרֶיךָ:

Finally, the communal *mussaf*-offerings of Succos differ from those of the other Festivals. Unique to Succos are the bulls of the *mussaf* (see p. 318), here called פָּרֵיהֶם, *their bulls.*

שְׁמַע ❧ / The Shema

The recitation of the three paragraphs of *Shema* is required by the Torah, and one must have in mind that he is about to fulfill this commandment. Although one should try to concentrate on the meaning of all three paragraphs, he must concentrate at least on the first (שְׁמַע, *Hear* . . .) and the second verses (בָּרוּךְ שֵׁם, *Blessed* . . .) because the recitation of *Shema* represents fulfillment of the paramount commandment of acceptance of God's absolute sovereignty [קַבָּלַת עוֹל מַלְכוּת שָׁמַיִם]. By declaring that God is One, Unique, and Indivisible, we subordinate every facet of our personalities, possessions — our very lives — to His will.

In the שְׁמַע we have included the cantillation symbols *(trop)* for the convenience of those who recite שְׁמַע in the manner it is read from the Torah. Nevertheless, to enable those unfamiliar with this notation to group the words properly, commas have been inserted.

אֵל מֶלֶךְ נֶאֱמָן ❧ — *God, trustworthy King.* The Sages teach that there are both 248 organs in the human body and 248 positive commandments. This parallel number symbolizes that the purpose of physical existence is to obey the precepts of the Torah. The total number of words in the three paragraphs of *Shema* is 245. The Sages wished to convey the above symbolism in the recitation of the *Shema,* so they added three words to it. If a *minyan* is present, the congregation listens to the *chazzan's* repetition aloud of the three words ה׳ אֱלֹהֵיכֶם אֱמֶת. If there is no *minyan,* the three words אֵל מֶלֶךְ נֶאֱמָן are recited before *Shema* is begun. The initials of these words spell אָמֵן [literally, *it is true*], thus testifying to our faith in the truths we are about to recite.

The three words of the verse mean: He is אֵל, *God,* the All-Powerful Source of all mercy; He is the מֶלֶךְ, *King,* Who rules, leads, and exercises supervision over all; and He is נֶאֱמָן, *trustworthy,* i.e., fair, apportioning no more suffering nor less good than one deserves *(Anaf Yosef).*

שְׁמַע יִשְׂרָאֵל ❧ — *Hear, O Israel.* Although the commentators find many layers of profound meaning in this seminal verse, there is a consensus among the halachic authorities that *Rashi's* explanation is the minimum that one should have in mind. It is the basis of our translation: At this point in history, HASHEM is only *our* God, for He is not acknowledged universally, but ultimately all will recognize Him as the *One and Only* God.

אֶחָד — *The One and Only.* The word אֶחָד has two connotations: (a) There is no God other than HASHEM *(Rashbam);* and, (b) though we perceive God in many roles — kind, angry, merciful, wise, judging, and so on — these different attitudes are not contradictory, even though human intelligence does not comprehend their harmony. *Harav Gedaliah Schorr* likened this concept to a ray of light seen through a prism. Though it is seen as a myriad of different colors, it is a single ray of light. So,

THE SHEMA

Immediately before its recitation concentrate on fulfilling the positive commandment of reciting the *Shema* twice daily. It is important to enunciate each word clearly and not to run words together. See *Laws* §40-52.

When praying without a *minyan,* begin with the following three-word formula:

*God, trustworthy King.**

Recite the first verse aloud, with the right hand covering the eyes, and concentrate intently upon accepting God's absolute sovereignty.

Hear, O Israel:* HASHEM is our God, HASHEM, the One and Only.*[1]

In an undertone— *Blessed is the Name* of His glorious kingdom for all eternity.*

While reciting the first paragraph (*Deuteronomy* 6:5-9), concentrate on accepting the commandment to love God.

וְאָהַבְתָּ *You shall love* HASHEM, your God, with all your heart, with all your soul and with all your resources. Let these matters that I command you today* be upon your heart.* Teach them thoroughly to your children and speak of them while you sit in your home, while you walk on the way, when you retire and when you arise. Bind them* as a sign upon your arm and let them be tefillin between your eyes. And write them on the doorposts of your house and upon your gates.*

(1) *Deuteronomy* 6:4.

too, God's many manifestations are truly one.

In saying the word אֶחָד, *the One and Only,* draw out the second syllable (חָ) a bit and emphasize the final consonant (ד). While drawing out the ח — a letter with the numerical value of eight — bear in mind that God is Master of the earth and the seven heavens. While clearly enunciating the final ד — which has the numerical value of four — bear in mind that God is Master in all four directions, meaning everywhere.

☙ The enlarged ע and ד

In Torah scrolls, the letters ע of שְׁמַע and ד of אֶחָד are written large. Together they form the word עֵד, *witness.* The enlarged letters allude to the thought that every Jew, by pronouncing the *Shema,* bears witness to HASHEM's unity and declares it to all the world *(Rokeach; Kol Bo; Abudraham).*

☙ בָּרוּךְ שֵׁם — *Blessed is the Name.* Having proclaimed God as our King, we are grateful for the privilege of serving the One Whose kingdom is eternal and unbounded *(Etz Yosef).*

The Sages give two reasons for saying this verse silently:

(a) At Jacob's deathbed his children affirmed their loyalty to God by proclaiming the verse *Shema* [the word 'Israel' in that context refers to Jacob]. Jacob responded with the words *'Blessed is the Name . . .'* The Sages taught: Should we say these words in our prayers because Jacob said them? Yes. But, on the other hand, Moses did not transmit them to us, for they are not found in the Torah. Therefore, let us say them silently *(Pesachim* 56a).

(b) Moses heard this beautiful prayer from the angels, and taught it to Israel. We dare not say it aloud, because we are sinful and therefore unworthy of using an angelic formula. On Yom Kippur, however, when Israel elevates itself to the sin-free level of angels, we may proclaim it loudly *(Devarim Rabbah* 2:36).

☙ וְאָהַבְתָּ — *You shall love.* One should learn to fulfill the commandments out of love, rather than fear — and certainly not out of habit. The Mishnah *(Berachos* 9:5) explains that one should serve God with all his emotions and desires *(with all your heart),* even to the point of giving up his life for God *(with all your soul),* and even at the cost of his wealth *(with all your resources).*

אֲשֶׁר אָנֹכִי מְצַוְּךָ הַיּוֹם — *That I command you today.* But have they all been commanded today? — This teaches that although the Torah was given thousands of years ago, we are not to regard the *mitzvos* as ancient rites followed out of loyalty and habit. Rather, we are to regard them with as much freshness and enthusiasm as if God had given them today.

עַל לְבָבֶךָ — *Upon your heart.* Always be conscious of the demands of God and His Torah. Then, you will convey them to your children and *speak of them,* i.e., study, concentrate, and review them wherever you are.

וּקְשַׁרְתָּם — *Bind them. Tefillin* on the arm, next to the heart, and on the head consecrate one's physical, emotional, and intellectual capacities to God's service *(Ramban).* The *mezuzah* on the doorpost consecrates one's home to Him.

While reciting the second paragraph (דברים יא:יג-כא), concentrate on accepting all the commandments and the concept of reward and punishment.

וְהָיָה,* אִם־שָׁמֹעַ תִּשְׁמְעוּ אֶל־מִצְוֹתַי, אֲשֶׁר | אָנֹכִי מְצַוֶּה |
אֶתְכֶם הַיּוֹם, לְאַהֲבָה אֶת־יהוה | אֱלֹהֵיכֶם וּלְעָבְדוֹ,
בְּכָל־לְבַבְכֶם, וּבְכָל־נַפְשְׁכֶם: וְנָתַתִּי מְטַר־אַרְצְכֶם בְּעִתּוֹ, יוֹרֶה
וּמַלְקוֹשׁ, וְאָסַפְתָּ דְגָנֶךָ וְתִירֹשְׁךָ וְיִצְהָרֶךָ: וְנָתַתִּי | עֵשֶׂב | בְּשָׂדְךָ
לִבְהֶמְתֶּךָ, וְאָכַלְתָּ וְשָׂבָעְתָּ: הִשָּׁמְרוּ* לָכֶם, פֶּן־יִפְתֶּה לְבַבְכֶם,
וְסַרְתֶּם וַעֲבַדְתֶּם | אֱלֹהִים | אֲחֵרִים, וְהִשְׁתַּחֲוִיתֶם לָהֶם:* וְחָרָה |
אַף־יהוה בָּכֶם, וְעָצַר | אֶת־הַשָּׁמַיִם, וְלֹא־יִהְיֶה מָטָר, וְהָאֲדָמָה לֹא
תִתֵּן אֶת־יְבוּלָהּ, וַאֲבַדְתֶּם* | מְהֵרָה מֵעַל הָאָרֶץ הַטֹּבָה | אֲשֶׁר |
יהוה נֹתֵן לָכֶם: וְשַׂמְתֶּם | אֶת־דְּבָרַי | אֵלֶּה, עַל־לְבַבְכֶם וְעַל־
נַפְשְׁכֶם, וּקְשַׁרְתֶּם | אֹתָם לְאוֹת | עַל־יֶדְכֶם, וְהָיוּ לְטוֹטָפֹת בֵּין |
עֵינֵיכֶם: וְלִמַּדְתֶּם | אֹתָם | אֶת־בְּנֵיכֶם, לְדַבֵּר בָּם, בְּשִׁבְתְּךָ* בְּבֵיתֶךָ,
וּבְלֶכְתְּךָ בַדֶּרֶךְ, וּבְשָׁכְבְּךָ וּבְקוּמֶךָ: וּכְתַבְתָּם | עַל־מְזוּזוֹת בֵּיתֶךָ,
וּבִשְׁעָרֶיךָ: לְמַעַן | יִרְבּוּ | יְמֵיכֶם* וִימֵי בְנֵיכֶם, עַל הָאֲדָמָה | אֲשֶׁר
נִשְׁבַּע | יהוה לַאֲבֹתֵיכֶם לָתֵת לָהֶם, כִּימֵי הַשָּׁמַיִם | עַל־הָאָרֶץ:*

במדבר טו:לז-מא

וַיֹּאמֶר | יהוה* | אֶל־מֹשֶׁה לֵּאמֹר: דַּבֵּר | אֶל־בְּנֵי | יִשְׂרָאֵל,
וְאָמַרְתָּ אֲלֵהֶם, וְעָשׂוּ לָהֶם צִיצִת, עַל־כַּנְפֵי בִגְדֵיהֶם
לְדֹרֹתָם, וְנָתְנוּ | עַל־צִיצִת הַכָּנָף, פְּתִיל תְּכֵלֶת:* וְהָיָה לָכֶם לְצִיצִת,
וּרְאִיתֶם | אֹתוֹ, וּזְכַרְתֶּם | אֶת־כָּל־מִצְוֹת | יהוה, וַעֲשִׂיתֶם | אֹתָם,
וְלֹא תָתוּרוּ* | אַחֲרֵי לְבַבְכֶם וְאַחֲרֵי | עֵינֵיכֶם, אֲשֶׁר־אַתֶּם זֹנִים |
אַחֲרֵיהֶם: לְמַעַן תִּזְכְּרוּ, וַעֲשִׂיתֶם | אֶת־כָּל־מִצְוֹתָי, וִהְיִיתֶם קְדֹשִׁים
לֵאלֹהֵיכֶם: אֲנִי יהוה | אֱלֹהֵיכֶם, אֲשֶׁר
הוֹצֵאתִי | אֶתְכֶם | מֵאֶרֶץ מִצְרַיִם, לִהְיוֹת
לָכֶם לֵאלֹהִים, אֲנִי | יהוה | אֱלֹהֵיכֶם: אֱמֶת —

Concentrate on fulfilling the commandment of remembering the Exodus from Egypt.

וְהָיָה — *And it will come to pass.* Unlike the first paragraph of *Shema,* this one specifies the duty to perform מִצְוֹתַי, *My commandments,* and teaches that when the nation is righteous, it will be rewarded with success and prosperity. When it sins, it must expect poverty and exile.

וְאָכַלְתָּ וְשָׂבָעְתָּ הִשָּׁמְרוּ — *And you will eat and be satisfied. Beware* ... Prosperity is often the greatest challenge to religious devotion. People who are rich in wealth but poor in sophistication often succumb to temptation *(Rashi).*

יִפְתֶּה ... וְהִשְׁתַּחֲוִיתֶם לָהֶם — *Be seduced ... and bow to them,* i.e., to strange gods. An imperceptible, seemingly innocent surrender to temptation can be the beginning of a course that will end in idolatry *(Rashi).*

וְלֹא יִהְיֶה מָטָר ... וַאֲבַדְתֶּם — *So there will be no rain ... and you will ... be banished.* First will come famine. If that does not bring repentance, exile will follow *(Vilna Gaon).*

וְלִמַּדְתֶּם ... בְּשִׁבְתְּךָ — *Teach them ... while you sit.* In giving the command to educate children in the Torah, the verse speaks in the plural (וְלִמַּדְתֶּם), while the other words in the verse (בְּשִׁבְתְּךָ and so on) are in the singular. This alludes to a communal responsibility to arrange

While reciting the second paragraph (*Deuteronomy* 11:13-21), concentrate on accepting all the commandments and the concept of reward and punishment.

וְהָיָה *And it will come to pass* that if you continually hearken to My commandments that I command you today, to love* HASHEM, *your God, and to serve Him, with all your heart and with all your soul — then I will provide rain for your land in its proper time, the early and late rains, that you may gather in your grain, your wine, and your oil. I will provide grass in your field for your cattle and you will eat and be satisfied. Beware* lest your heart be seduced and you turn astray and serve gods of others and bow to them.* Then the wrath of* HASHEM *will blaze against you. He will restrain the heaven so there will be no rain and the ground will not yield its produce. And you will swiftly be banished* from the goodly land which* HASHEM *gives you. Place these words of Mine upon your heart and upon your soul; bind them for a sign upon your arm and let them be tefillin between your eyes. Teach them to your children, to discuss them, while you sit* in your home, while you walk on the way, when you retire and when you arise. And write them on the doorposts of your house and upon your gates. In order to prolong your days* and the days of your children upon the ground that* HASHEM *has sworn to your ancestors to give them, like the days of the heaven on the earth.**

Numbers 15:37-41

וַיֹּאמֶר *And* HASHEM *said* to Moses saying: Speak to the Children of Israel and say to them that they are to make themselves tzitzis on the corners of their garments, throughout their generations. And they are to place upon the tzitzis of each corner a thread of techeiles.* And it shall constitute tzitzis for you, that you may see it and remember all the commandments of* HASHEM *and perform them; and not explore* after your heart and after your eyes after which you stray. So that you may remember and perform all My commandments; and be holy to your God. I am* HASHEM, *your God, Who has removed you from the land of Egypt to be a God to you; I am* HASHEM *your God — it is true —*

Concentrate on fulfilling the commandment of remembering the Exodus from Egypt.

---

for the Torah education of children *(Iyun Tefillah)*.

לְמַעַן יִרְבּוּ יְמֵיכֶם — *In order to prolong your days.* [Although many *siddurim* set this verse as a new paragraph, leading some to believe that there are *four* paragraphs in the *Shema*, the verse is part of the paragraph which begins וְהָיָה.]

כִּימֵי הַשָּׁמַיִם עַל הָאָרֶץ — *Like the days of the heaven on the earth. Eretz Yisrael* is the eternal heritage of the Jewish people, just as heaven will always remain above the earth. Alternatively, just as heaven always showers blessings upon the earth in the form of life-giving rain, so too Israel will be blessed in the land God has sworn to it.

⟫ וַיֹּאמֶר ה׳ — *And* HASHEM *said.* The third paragraph of *Shema* is recited to fulfill the commandment to recall the Exodus every day. By freeing Israel from Egypt, God laid claim to the nation's eternal allegiance. No Jew is free to absolve himself of that obligation *(Rashi)*.

פְּתִיל תְּכֵלֶת — *A thread of techeiles. Techeiles* is sky-blue wool dyed with the secretion of an amphibian called *chilazon*. For many centuries the identity of the animal has been unknown. Even in the absence of the *techeiles* thread, however, the commandment of *tzitzis* remains binding *(Menachos* 38a).

וְלֹא תָתוּרוּ — *And not explore.* First the eye sees, then the heart covets, then the body sins *(Rashi)*.

Although the word אֱמֶת belongs to the next paragraph, it is appended to the conclusion of the previous one, as explained in the commentary.

—*Chazzan* repeats **יהוה אֱלֹהֵיכֶם אֱמֶת.***

וֶאֱמוּנָה* כָּל זֹאת, וְקַיָּם עָלֵינוּ, כִּי הוּא יהוה אֱלֹהֵינוּ וְאֵין זוּלָתוֹ, וַאֲנַחְנוּ יִשְׂרָאֵל עַמּוֹ. הַפּוֹדֵנוּ מִיַּד מְלָכִים, מַלְכֵּנוּ הַגּוֹאֲלֵנוּ מִכַּף כָּל הֶעָרִיצִים. הָאֵל הַנִּפְרָע לָנוּ מִצָּרֵינוּ, וְהַמְשַׁלֵּם גְּמוּל לְכָל אֹיְבֵי נַפְשֵׁנוּ.* הָעֹשֶׂה גְדֹלוֹת עַד אֵין חֵקֶר,* וְנִפְלָאוֹת עַד אֵין מִסְפָּר.[1] הַשָּׂם נַפְשֵׁנוּ בַּחַיִּים,* וְלֹא נָתַן לַמּוֹט רַגְלֵנוּ.[2] הַמַּדְרִיכֵנוּ עַל בָּמוֹת אוֹיְבֵינוּ, וַיָּרֶם קַרְנֵנוּ עַל כָּל שׂוֹנְאֵינוּ. הָעֹשֶׂה לָּנוּ נִסִּים וּנְקָמָה בְּפַרְעֹה, אוֹתוֹת וּמוֹפְתִים בְּאַדְמַת בְּנֵי חָם.* הַמַּכֶּה בְעֶבְרָתוֹ כָּל בְּכוֹרֵי מִצְרָיִם, וַיּוֹצֵא אֶת עַמּוֹ יִשְׂרָאֵל מִתּוֹכָם לְחֵרוּת עוֹלָם. הַמַּעֲבִיר בָּנָיו בֵּין גִּזְרֵי יַם סוּף, אֶת רוֹדְפֵיהֶם וְאֶת שׂוֹנְאֵיהֶם בִּתְהוֹמוֹת טִבַּע. וְרָאוּ בָנָיו גְּבוּרָתוֹ, שִׁבְּחוּ וְהוֹדוּ לִשְׁמוֹ. ❖ וּמַלְכוּתוֹ בְּרָצוֹן קִבְּלוּ עֲלֵיהֶם. מֹשֶׁה וּבְנֵי יִשְׂרָאֵל לְךָ עָנוּ שִׁירָה,

FIRST NIGHT	SECOND NIGHT	
טוֹעֲנֵי נִטְעֵי צְמָחוֹת,	אַנְווּ בְּמִצְוֹת* וְאַדְּרוּ,	
יַשִּׂיגוּ שֹׂבַע שְׂמָחוֹת,*	תֵּשְׁבוּ כְּעֵין תְּדִוּרוּ,[3]	בְּחַג הַסֻּכּוֹת.
בְּחַג הַסֻּכּוֹת.	בָּרִאשׁוֹן תִּקְחוּ אַרְבַּעַת מִינִים,[4]	
כַּסֵּם בְּצֵל יְמִינֶךָ,	לְרַצּוֹת עַל מֵי עֲנָנִים,*	בְּחַג הַסֻּכּוֹת.

⊰ **אֱמֶת** — *True.* The law that one may not interrupt between the last words of the *Shema* and אֱמֶת is of ancient origin. The reason for it is so that we may declare, as did the prophet *[Jeremiah* 10:10]: וַה׳ אֱלֹהִים אֱמֶת, *HASHEM, God, is true (Berachos* 14a).

⊰ **אֱמֶת וֶאֱמוּנָה** — *True and faithful.* This paragraph continues our fulfillment of the obligation to recall the Exodus in the evening. The morning blessing of אֱמֶת וְיַצִּיב, *True and certain* (p. 238), concentrates on God's kindness in having redeemed us from Egypt, while אֱמֶת וֶאֱמוּנָה, *True and faithful,* recited at night, symbolizes exile and stresses our faith that God will redeem us from this exile just as He did at the time of the Exodus *(Berachos* 12a; *Rashi* and *Tosafos).*

Alternatively, the faithfulness of the nights refers to man's confidence that God will return his soul in the morning refreshed and rested after a night of sleep *(Talmidei R' Yonah; Tos., Berachos* 12a; *Rashi* in *Pardes).*

Chiddushei HaRim explains that אֱמֶת, *truth,* refers to something that we know to be true, either because our senses tell us so or because we have conclusive evidence. אֱמוּנָה, *faith,* refers to something that we *believe,* even though we have seen neither it nor proof that it happened. We know the Exodus to be *true,* because it was witnessed by millions of people, but the future redemption is not yet an accomplished fact. Nevertheless we have a perfect *faith* that God will bring it about, as He promised through the prophets. This is just as real for us as our *faith* in another phenomenon that has not yet taken place — that we will wake up from our sleep tomorrow morning.

מִצָּרֵינוּ ... אֹיְבֵי נַפְשֵׁנוּ — *From our foes ... enemies of our soul.* The term *foe* [צַר] refers to one who actually causes harm, while *enemy* [אוֹיֵב] is one who hates and who encourages harm, even though he has not done anything actively *(Malbim* to *Isaiah* 59:18). Later a third kind of enemy is mentioned: שׂוֹנֵא, *one who hates.* A שׂוֹנֵא does nothing against the object of his hate; he merely rejoices at his suffering and downfall *(Siach Yitzchak).*

The expression *enemies of our soul* implies enmity directed against Israel's spiritual essence. They do not desire the physical destruction of the Jewish people, but they cannot abide Israel's loyalty to the Torah *(Siach Yitzchak).*

גְּדֹלוֹת עַד אֵין חֵקֶר — *Great deeds that are beyond comprehension.* If our entire solar system were

Although the word אֱמֶת, *'true,'* belongs to the next paragraph, it is appended to the conclusion of the previous one, as explained in the commentary.

Chazzan repeats: **HASHEM, your God, is true.***

וֶאֱמוּנָה *And faithful* is all this, and it is firmly established for us that He is* HASHEM *our God, and there is none but Him, and we are Israel, His nation. He redeems us from the power of kings, our King Who delivers us from the hand of all the cruel tyrants. He is the God Who exacts vengeance for us from our foes and Who brings just retribution upon all enemies of our soul;* Who performs great deeds that are beyond comprehension,* and wonders beyond number.[1] Who set our soul in life* and did not allow our foot to falter.[2] Who led us upon the heights of our enemies and raised our pride above all who hate us; Who wrought for us miracles and vengeance upon Pharaoh; signs and wonders on the land of the offspring of Ham;* Who struck with His anger all the firstborn of Egypt and removed His nation Israel from their midst to eternal freedom; Who brought His children through the split parts of the Sea of Reeds while those who pursued them and hated them He caused to sink into the depths. When His children perceived His power, they lauded and gave grateful praise to His Name.* Chazzan– *And His Kingship they accepted upon themselves willingly. Moses and the Children of Israel raised their voices to You in song,*

FIRST NIGHT	SECOND NIGHT
ט *Those who carry the plantings of [the Four] Species,*	א *Beautify and glorify yourselves with mitzvos,* sit [in the succah] as you would dwell [in your home],[3] during the Festival of Succos.*
י *May they attain fullness of joy,* on the Festival of Succos.*	ב *On the first day, take the Four Species,[4] to find favor regarding the clouds' waters,* during the Festival of Succos.*
כ *Shelter them in the shade of Your right hand,*	

(1) *Job* 9:10. (2) *Psalms* 66:9. (3) Tractate *Succah* 26a. (4) Cf. *Leviticus* 23:40.

to disappear, the loss would not even be noticed in the vastness of space (*Malbim, Job* 9:10).

הַשָּׂם נַפְשֵׁנוּ בַּחַיִּים — *Who set our soul in life.* A reference to the night in Egypt when all non-Jewish firstborn died, but Jewish souls were preserved (*Abudraham*). This also implies God's protection from the murderous designs of our enemies in all generations (*Siach Yitzchak*).

בְּנֵי חָם — *The offspring of Ham.* Mitzrayim, forerunner of the Egyptian nation, was a son of Ham [*Genesis* 10:6].

שׂבַע שְׂמָחוֹת — *Fullness of joy.* This phrase comes from *Psalms* 16:11. Midrashically (*Vayikra Rabbah* 30:2), it is interpreted as if the word שׂבַע were vowelized שֶׁבַע, *seven,* and it alludes to the seven *mitzvos* of the Succos Festival: the Four Species; the *succah;* the *chagigah*-offering; and the *simchah*-offering (see p 37).

⊲§ אַנְווּ בְּמִצְוֹת — *Beautify ... yourselves with mitzvos.* The Sages interpret the verse וְאַנְוֵהוּ, *I will beautify Him* (*Exodus* 15:2): 'Beautify yourselves before Him with *mitzvos* — a beautiful *succah,* a beautiful *esrog*' (*Shabbos* 133b).

The first thirteen verses of this alphabetical *piyut* tell how Succos was celebrated during the Temple era. The remaining verses describe Succos as it is celebrated today, and the future rewards awaiting those who fulfill the *mitzvah* of the *succah.*

מֵי עֲנָנִים — *The clouds' waters.* Many of the prayers and rituals of Succos are based on the Mishnaic teaching: 'At four junctures of the year the world is judged ... and on the, Festival of Succos they are judged for the water [i.e., the rainfall] (*Rosh Hashanah* 1:2). Thus, the taking of the Four Species, all of which depend on water, is in part a symbolic prayer for abundant rainfall during the coming year.

FIRST NIGHT

לְמַעַן זְכוּת מַאֲמִינֶךָ,
נָתַץ מַסֵּכוֹת.*

מְחַנְּנִים בְּלֵב בָּשָׂר,*
נַהֲלֵם כְּיָחִיד נִתְבַּשַּׂר,
בַּעֲצֵי הַסְּבָכוֹת.[1]

סֻכָּה תִּהְיֶה לְצֵל,[2]
עֲבוּר תָּם הַמְּפַצֵּל,[3]
חָנָה בַּסֻּכּוֹת.[4]

פְּלִיטִים בְּצִלְּךָ
תַּסְתִּירֵם,
צְנִיף יֶשַׁע
תַּכְתִּירֵם,
מִנֶּשֶׁק לְסֻכּוֹת.

קָדוֹשׁ, בְּרִית תַּגְבִּיר,
רוּחַ טֻמְאָה תַּעֲבִיר,[5]
פְּרָעוֹת וּסְבָכוֹת.*

SECOND NIGHT

גַּם בַּשֵּׁנִי רֶמֶז לְנִסּוּךְ הַמַּיִם* לְעָרֵה,
תְּהוֹם אֶל תְּהוֹם קוֹרֵא,*[6] בְּחַג הַסֻּכּוֹת.
הֶרֶךְ יוֹם* רְבָעִי לְהַעֲלוֹת בְּשִׁירוֹת,
לְעַטֵּר שׁוּקֵי יְרוּשָׁלַיִם בַּפֵּרוֹת, בְּחַג הַסֻּכּוֹת.
הֲמוֹנִים עָלוּ לְצִיּוֹן בְּרִנָּה,
בְּחַג הָאָסִיף תְּקוּפַת הַשָּׁנָה,[7] בְּחַג הַסֻּכּוֹת.
וְשָׁם חוֹגְגִים בְּשִׂמְחָה רַבָּה,
שִׂמְחַת בֵּית הַשּׁוֹאֵבָה,* בְּחַג הַסֻּכּוֹת.
זְמִירוֹת וּנְגִינוֹת לְהַעֲלִיל,
בִּכְלֵי שִׁיר וּבֶחָלִיל, בְּחַג הַסֻּכּוֹת.
חָדִים כֻּלָּם בִּנְגִינָה,
עִם יְלָדִים פִּרְחֵי כְהֻנָּה, בְּחַג הַסֻּכּוֹת.
טוֹעֲנִים וּמְקַפְּצִים לְדִלֵּג,
וּבִידֵיהֶם כַּדֵּי שֶׁמֶן שֶׁל שְׁלֹשִׁים לֹג, בְּחַג הַסֻּכּוֹת.
יוֹדְעֵי דָת וְחַכְמֵי עֵדָה,
מַרְאִים לִפְנֵיהֶם קִדָּה, בְּחַג הַסֻּכּוֹת.
כֹּהֲנִים וּלְוִיִּם מְצַלְצְלִים וּמוֹדִים,
הַחֲסִידִים וְאַנְשֵׁי מַעֲשֶׂה מְרַקְּדִים, בְּחַג הַסֻּכּוֹת.
לָאֲנָשִׁים מִן הַנָּשִׁים לְהַפְרִישָׁם,
מְתַקְּנִים תִּקּוּן גָּדוֹל שָׁם, בְּחַג הַסֻּכּוֹת.

נָתַץ מַסֵּכוֹת – *Who smashed molten idols.* Terach, an idol manufacturer, asked his young son Abraham to mind the business. When his father had left, Abraham took a club and smashed all the idols except the largest one. Then he placed the club into that idol's hands.

Upon returning, Terach demanded, 'Who did this to my idols?'

Abraham explained, 'When I placed food before them, the idols began arguing, each claiming the right to the first portion. Finally, the largest of them settled the argument by smashing the others with his club.'

'What are you saying?' cried the incredulous Terach. 'Do they know what is happening?'

To which Abraham replied, 'Would that your ears would hear what your mouth said [i.e., why do you worship them if they do not know what is happening?]' (*Bereishis Rabbah* 38:13).

בְּלֵב בָּשָׂר – *With heart of flesh.* The prophet describes Israel's rejuvenation at the ingathering of the exiles: God says, *'I shall remove their heart of stone and shall give them a heart of flesh' (Ezekiel* 11:19). A *stone heart* is hard and unreceptive to admonition; a *heart of flesh* is pliant and submits readily to reproof *(Radak).*

Some *machzorim* read בְּלֵב וּבָשָׂר, *with heart and flesh.* The *heart* alludes to the intellectual and intuitive faculties, and the *flesh* to the physical powers (see *Psalms* 84:3).

פְּרָעוֹת וּסְבָכוֹת – *Protrusions and branchy canopies.* The Mishnah (*Nazir* 7:3) uses these terms to describe pieces protruding from a fence and tree branches forming a canopy over the ground. Under either of these may lie a *tumah*-contaminated object. The *paytan* uses *tumah*-contamination as a metaphor for the *Yetzer Hara,* or Evil Inclination, which lurks in hidden recesses — i.e., where it can find someone unaware — and tries to lure man into his snare and entice him to sin.

Alternatively, פְּרָעוֹת וּסְבָכוֹת means *the uncovered and the concealed,* and refers to overt and covert transgressions.

לְנִסּוּךְ הַמַּיִם — *The water libation.* Throughout the year, a wine libation accompanied the daily *tamid*-offering. Each day of Succos an additional libation of water was poured (see *Succah* 4:9, p. 120). Although this water libation is not mentioned specifically in the Torah, it is alluded to in the section (*Numbers* 29) describing the *Succos mussaf* sacrifices where three superfluous letters are inserted. In describing the *mussaf* of the second day (v. 19), the Torah uses the word וְנִסְכֵּיהֶם, *their libation* (rather than וְנִסְכָּהּ, *its libation* — the expression used for the other days). Thus, there is an extra מ. For the sixth day the Torah uses וּנְסָכֶיהָ, lit., *its libations* (v.

FIRST NIGHT	SECOND NIGHT
ל *In the merit of [Abraham] Your faithful one who smashed molten idols.**	ג *On the second day there is an allusion to the pouring of the water libation,* watery depth calls to watery depth,[6]* during the Festival of Succos.*
מ *Those who pray with heart of flesh,**	ד *Within a day's journey* bring up the fourth-year fruits with song, to adorn the streets of Jerusalem with fruit, during the Festival of Succos.*
נ *Lead them like [Isaac] the unique one who was informed [of his destiny], [when the ram was caught] in the trees of the thicket.*[1]	ה *The multitudes ascended to Zion with glad song, for the Festival of the Ingathering at the turn of the year,*[7] *during the Festival of Succos.*
ס *May the succah provide shelter,*[2]	ו *There they celebrated with great joy, the Festival of the Water Drawing,* during the Festival of Succos.*
ע *In the merit of [Jacob] the wholesome peeler of the sticks,*[3] *who dwelt in Succos.*[4]	ז *Hymns and songs to exalt, with musical instrument and flute, during the Festival of Succos.*
פ *Conceal the survivors [of the War of Gog and Magog] in Your shelter,*	ח *They all delight with song, together with the young Kohanim, during the Festival of Succos.*
צ *Crown them with a turban of salvation, to protect them from weaponry.*	ט *Carrying, leaping, skipping, in their hands thirty-login pitchers of oil, during the Festival of Succos.*
ק *O Holy One, strengthen the covenant,*	י *Knowers of the Law and scholars of the flock, appeared before them in prostration, during the Festival of Succos.*
ר *Make the spirit of contamination pass away,*[5] *[even from] protrusions and branchy canopies.**	כ *Kohanim and Levites would clash cymbals and offer thanks, men devout and of [good] deed would dance, during the Festival of Succos.*
	ל *To separate the men from the women, they would make a great improvement there, during the Festival of Succos.*

(1) See *Genesis* 19:13. (2) *Isaiah* 4:6. (3) See *Genesis* 30:37ff. (4) See 33:17.
(5) Cf. *Zechariah* 13:2. (6) *Psalms* 42:8. (7) *Exodus* 34:22.

31), providing an extra י. And in describing the seventh day (v. 33) the Torah uses the word כְּמִשְׁפָּטָם rather than the word כַּמִּשְׁפָּט which appears on all the other days — again, an extra ם. The three extra letters spell מַיִם, *water*, an allusion to the Succos water libation (*Taanis* 2b).

Thus, 'On the second day there is an allusion to the pouring of the water libation.'

תְּהוֹם אֶל תְּהוֹם קוֹרֵא — *Watery depth calls to watery depth.* The Talmud interprets this verse as an allusion to the water libations on Succos:

When the water libation is performed with the wine libation, watery depth [i.e., the heavenly waters] calls out to watery depth [i.e., the earthly waters], 'Let your waters spring forth, for I hear the voice of two friends [i.e., the water vessel and the wine vessel]'... The angel appointed over rainfall stands ... where the sea meets the heavens. To the heavenly depth he says, 'Let your waters drip,' and to the earthly depth he says, 'Let your waters spring forth ...' (*Taanis* 25b).

דֶּרֶךְ יוֹם — *A day's journey.* During the first three years after a tree has been planted or replanted, any fruit that it produces is called עָרְלָה, *orlah*, and is forbidden. Fruit grown during the tree's fourth year is called רְבָעִי, *revai*, and must either be (a) transported to Jerusalem to be eaten there, or (b) redeemed for coins which will be transported to Jerusalem and used to purchase foodstuffs there. At one point in history, the Rabbis decreed that any *revai* grapes that were less than one-day's journey from Jerusalem were not to be redeemed but were to be brought to Jerusalem (*Maaser Sheni* 5:2). R' Yochanan taught that this decree was promulgated in order to adorn the streets of Jerusalem with fruit (*Beitzah* 5a).

שִׂמְחַת בֵּית הַשּׁוֹאֵבָה — *The Festival of the (House of the) Water Drawing.* The next eight verses

FIRST NIGHT

שְׁבֹר זְרוֹעַ רֶשַׁע,[1]
שְׁלַח לְצֶדֶק יֶשַׁע,
אֹמֶץ וּסְמָכוֹת.[2]
תָּחֹן חוֹגְגֵי שִׁבְעָה,
תּוֹפְשֵׂי מְגָדִים
אַרְבָּעָה,
וְשַׁוְעָתָם סְכוֹת.
יִשְׁעִי, אֵל,
סְכוֹת שַׁוְעַת עַמֶּךָ,
וּרְעֵם וְעַנְּגֵם
בְּטוּב טַעְמֶךָ,
סַגִּיב, כְּדַשְׁתָּ צָרֵיהֶם[3]
בְּזַעְמֶךָ,
פְּאֵר וָזֶמֶר נָתְנוּ
לְהַנְעִימֶךָ,
בְּגִילָה, בְּרִנָּה,

SECOND NIGHT

מַרְבִּים הָיוּ בְּשִׂמְחָה וּבְצִלְצוּלִים,
מַה יָּפוּ פְעָמַיִךְ בַּנְּעָלִים,*[4] בְּחַג הַסֻּכּוֹת.
נוֹטְלִים לוּלָב שִׁבְעָה בְּהִלּוּלִים,
זֵכֶר לְמִקְדָּשׁ לַעֲשׂוֹת בִּגְבוּלִים, בְּחַג הַסֻּכּוֹת.
סֻכָּה לַעֲשׂוֹת בְּכָל מוֹשְׁבֹתֵיכֶם,
לְמַעַן יֵדְעוּ דֹרֹתֵיכֶם,[5] בְּחַג הַסֻּכּוֹת.
עֲדָנִים[6] לִהְיוֹת שֶׁבַע בְּצֵל רַעֲנַנִּים,
סִימָן לְשִׁבְעָה עֲנָנִים,* בְּחַג הַסֻּכּוֹת.
פַּחִים לְהָצֵן לֶהָבָה וְשָׁרָב,
וְסֻכָּה תִּהְיֶה לְצֵל יוֹמָם מֵחֹרֶב,*[7] בְּחַג הַסֻּכּוֹת.
צִלָּתָהּ לְהָגֵן מִלַּהַט וּלְסַכּוֹת,
כָּל הָאֶזְרָח בְּיִשְׂרָאֵל יֵשְׁבוּ בַּסֻּכֹּת,[8] בְּחַג הַסֻּכּוֹת.
קָמִים יְנַתְּקוּ מוֹסֵרוֹת*[9] לְיִרְאָתֶךָ,
וְשָׂמַחְתָּ אַתָּה וּבֵיתֶךָ,[10] בְּחַג הַסֻּכּוֹת.
רוֹזְנִים נוֹסְדוּ יַחַד[11] מֵרֹב אֲנָחָה,
וְכָל יִשְׂרָאֵל יָשִׂישׂוּ בְּהַלֵּל וּבְשִׂמְחָה, בְּחַג הַסֻּכּוֹת.
שֵׁם הַנִּכְבָּד שִׁבְעָה לְהָדֵר,
בְּלוּלָב וּבִפְרִי עֵץ הָדָר, בְּחַג הַסֻּכּוֹת.
תִּשְׁבָּחוֹת לוֹ לְמַלֵּל,
וְלִגְמֹר בּוֹ אֶת הַהַלֵּל, בְּחַג הַסֻּכּוֹת.
יְקַר חַסְדְּךָ יוֹצְרֵנוּ[12] בַּבֹּקֶר לְמַלְּלָם,
אֱמוּנָתְךָ לְסַפֵּר בַּלֵּילוֹת[13] מֵעֵין כֹּל נֶעְלָם,
חָזָק וְאַמִּיץ נְפָאֵר שִׁמְךָ לְעוֹלָם.[14]
בְּגִילָה, בְּרִנָּה,

בְּשִׂמְחָה רַבָּה וְאָמְרוּ כֻלָּם:

speak of these festivities which are described in tractate *Succah* (5:1-4, see pp. 122-124; 642).

מַה יָּפוּ פְעָמַיִךְ בַּנְּעָלִים — *O how lovely were your footsteps in sandals,* when your pilgrims walked to Jerusalem to celebrate the Festivals. With this line, the *paytan* ends his description of what was, and goes on to bewail the loss of the *Beis HaMikdash* and our inability to celebrate the *mitzvos* of Succos there.

לְשִׁבְעָה עֲנָנִים — *Of the seven clouds.* During their forty-year sojourn in the Wilderness, the Jews were protected by the עֲנְנֵי הַכָּבוֹד, *clouds of glory.* According to one opinion there were seven clouds: four on the four sides of their camp; one overhead to shade them from the desert sun; one beneath their feet to prevent scorpions and serpents from attacking them; and one that went before them, guiding them in their travels (*Mechilta* 13:32). The *paytan* interprets the seven-day period that we dwell in the *succah* as an allusion to those seven clouds.

פַּחִים לְהָצֵן . . . מֵחֹרֶב — *To cool . . . from hot winds.* Rabbi Levi taught that he who fulfills the *mitzvah* of *succah* in this world will be sheltered from the fires of the Day of Judgment (*Pesikta D'Rav Kahana* 29; see also commentary to *Ushpizin* p. 77).

קָמִים יְנַתְּקוּ מוֹסֵרוֹת — *Enemies will cut [themselves loose from] the binds.* The Talmud records that in the World to Come, God will castigate the gentiles for not accepting the Torah. They will reply, 'Offer us the Torah anew and we will obey it.'

To test them God will respond, 'I have an easy [i.e., inexpensive] *mitzvah* called *succah;* go and perform it.'

Immediately, every gentile will go and construct a *succah* on his roof [as was customary in ancient Israel]. But God will cause

FIRST NIGHT

ש *Break the arm of evil,*[1] *send to the righteous salvation, strength and support.*[2]

ת *Be gracious to those who celebrate the seven[-day festival] — those who hold the Four Species — and hearken to their cries.*

י *O my Salvation, O God, hearken to the cries of Your people;*

ו *Tend them and grant them delight in the goodness of Your reasoning.*

ס *O Supreme One, when You trampled their [Egyptian] oppressors*[3] *in Your fury,*

פ *They offered glory and song to praise You sweetly, with mirth, with glad song,*

SECOND NIGHT

מ *They would increase in joy and cymbal clashing: O how lovely were your footsteps in sandals,**[4] *during the Festival of Succos.*

נ *They take the lulav [all] seven [days] while reciting Hallel, to establish a remembrance of the Sanctuary in the provinces, during the Festival of Succos.*

ס *To erect a succah in all your dwelling places, so that your [future] generations may know,*[5] *during the Festival of Succos.*

ע *They delight*[6] *in being seven [days] in the shade of fresh branches, a symbol of the seven clouds,* during the Festival of Succos.*

פ *To cool coals, flame and heat, by day the succah shall be a shade from hot winds,**[7] *during the Festival of Succos.*

צ *Its shade to protect [them] from the sharpness and to cover them; every male in [the nation of] Israel shall dwell in succos,*[8] *during the Festival of Succos.*

ק *Enemies will cut [themselves loose from] the binds**[9] *of Your awesomeness, and you shall be joyous — you and your family,*[10] *during the Festival of Succos.*

ר *The lords take counsel together*[11] *against an abundance of woe, while all Israel will celebrate with praise and joy, during the Festival of Succos.*

ש *To glorify the honored Name for seven [days], with lulav and the fruit of the esrog tree, during the Festival of Succos.*

ת *To recite His praises to Him, and on it to complete the Hallel, during the Festival of Succos.*

יחי *Your precious kindness, our Creator,*[12] *each morning to recite,*

אל *Your faithfulness to retell each night,*[13] *You Who are hidden from every eye, O Strong and Firm One, we shall glorify Your Name forever.*[14] *with mirth, with glad song,*

with abundant gladness — and said unanimously:

(1) Cf. *Psalms* 10:15. (2) Some *machzorim* read: שְׁבֹר קָדְקֹד מֵאֱדָם, שַׁכֵּר חִצֶּיךָ מִדַּם אֻמּוֹת הַנְּסִיכוֹת – *Break the skull of Edom, may Your arrows become drunk with the blood of the dominating nations.* (3) Some *machzorim* read: שַׂגִּיא, כְּהִכְנַעְתָּ זֵדִים – *O exceedingly great One, when You humbled the wanton [Egyptians].* (4) *Song of Songs* 7:2. (5) *Leviticus* 23:43. (6) Some *machzorim* read עֲדוּיִים, *adorned,* i.e., wearing their festival finery; others read עִדּוֹנִים, *time periods,* i.e., a period of seven days. (7) *Isaiah* 4:6. (8) *Leviticus* 23:42. (9) *Psalms* 2:3. (10) *Deuteronomy* 14:26. (11) *Psalms* 2:2. (12) Some *machzorim* read . . . יְקַר חַסְדְּךָ בְּרִנָּה, *The preciousness of Your kindness in glad song,* and omit the word יוֹצְרֵנוּ, *Our Creator.* According to that reading, the author's name יְחִיאֵל does not appear in this verse. (13) Cf. *Psalms* 92:3. (14) Some *machzorim* add: כְּשׁוֹרְרוּ אֲהוּבִים וְאָמְרוּ כֻלָּם, *when the beloved ones sang and said unanimously.*

the sun to blaze upon them and each will kick over his *succah* [contemptuously, thus proving the insincerity of his commitment to *mitzvos*] (*Avodah Zarah* 3a).

מִי כָמֹכָה בָּאֵלִם יהוה, מִי כָּמֹכָה נֶאְדָּר בַּקֹּדֶשׁ, נוֹרָא תְהִלֹּת,* עֹשֵׂה פֶלֶא.[1] ❖ מַלְכוּתְךָ רָאוּ בָנֶיךָ* בּוֹקֵעַ יָם לִפְנֵי מֹשֶׁה,

FIRST NIGHT	SECOND NIGHT
הַלֵּל גּוֹמְרִים כָּל שְׁמוֹנָה, קוֹרְאֵי פָּרָשַׁת קָרְבָּנוֹת בִּזְמַנָּהּ, טְעֵם וְהוֹשִׁיבֵם בְּאֶרֶץ שְׁמֵנָה, נֶצַח צוּר יִשְׁעֵנוּ לְהֵאָמְנָה.	יְפִי עֲנָנֶיךָ סִכַּכְתָּ עַל גְּאוּלִים, חֻפַּת כְּבוֹדְךָ פָּרַשְׂתָּ עֲלֵיהֶם לִהְיוֹת סְלוּלִים, יִחֲדוּךָ וּפֵאֲרוּךָ כְּעוֹבְרֵי גַלִּים, אָז* לְשִׁמְךָ שִׁבְּחוּ בְּנֵי אֵלִים.

זֶה צוּר יִשְׁעֵנוּ פָּצוּ פֶה וְאָמְרוּ: Continue: ... ה׳ יִמְלֹךְ

זֶה אֵלִי[2] עָנוּ וְאָמְרוּ:

יהוה יִמְלֹךְ לְעֹלָם וָעֶד.[3] ❖ וְנֶאֱמַר: כִּי פָדָה יהוה אֶת יַעֲקֹב,* וּגְאָלוֹ מִיַּד חָזָק מִמֶּנּוּ.[4]

FIRST NIGHT	SECOND NIGHT
בְּהַדְרַת קֹדֶשׁ שׁוֹרְרוּ[5] בְּמִקְדָּשׁוֹ, רוֹחֲשִׁים שִׁיר וָשֶׁבַח לְחַדְּשׁוֹ, שָׁלוֹם תִּשְׁפֹּת לָהֶם[6] לְהַגְדִּישׁוֹ,[7] מֶלֶךְ צוּר יִשְׂרָאֵל וְקְדוֹשׁוֹ.	בְּנֵה סֻכָּתְךָ* וְהָקֵם הַנְּפוּלָה,[8] יְסוֹדוֹתֶיהָ לְשַׁתֵּת וְלִבְנוֹתָהּ עַל תִּלָּהּ,[9] צֹאנְךָ לִרְעוֹת עַל מִשְׁכְּנוֹתֶיךָ[10] לְהַנְחִילָהּ, חָפֵץ כְּמִקֶּדֶם זִבְחֵי צֶדֶק וְעוֹלָה.

[Some conclude the blessing as follows; others conclude with בָּרוּךְ ... גָּאַל יִשְׂרָאֵל.]

בָּרוּךְ אַתָּה יהוה, מֶלֶךְ צוּר יִשְׂרָאֵל וְגוֹאֲלוֹ. (.Cong. – אָמֵן)

בָּרוּךְ אַתָּה יהוה, גָּאַל יִשְׂרָאֵל.* (.Cong. – אָמֵן)

הַשְׁכִּיבֵנוּ* יהוה אֱלֹהֵינוּ לְשָׁלוֹם,* וְהַעֲמִידֵנוּ מַלְכֵּנוּ לְחַיִּים, וּפְרוֹשׂ עָלֵינוּ סֻכַּת שְׁלוֹמֶךָ, וְתַקְּנֵנוּ בְּעֵצָה טוֹבָה מִלְּפָנֶיךָ, וְהוֹשִׁיעֵנוּ לְמַעַן שְׁמֶךָ. וְהָגֵן בַּעֲדֵנוּ, וְהָסֵר מֵעָלֵינוּ אוֹיֵב,

---

נוֹרָא תְהִלֹּת — *Too awesome for praise.* We are too terrified to attempt a complete assessment of His greatness, because whatever we say is insufficient *(Rashi).* Alternatively, it is impossible for one to praise God adequately; the only way to laud Him is to recount His awe-inspiring deeds. Thus this phrase means: [God's] *awesomeness constitutes His praises (Ramban).*

מַלְכוּתְךָ רָאוּ בָנֶיךָ — *Your children beheld Your majesty.* The Sages taught: A maidservant saw more [of God's majesty] at the Sea than did even Ezekiel in his prophecies! *(Etz Yosef).*

אָז — *The 'Az Yashir' song.* After God split the Sea of Reeds allowing the Jewish people to cross it in safety, Moses led the people in the prophetic Song of the Sea (see p. 206) which begins אָז יָשִׁיר מֹשֶׁה, *Then Moses sang.*

כִּי פָדָה ה׳ אֶת יַעֲקֹב — *For HASHEM has redeemed Jacob.* Jacob faced more dangerous situations than either Abraham or Isaac *(Acharis Shalom).*

One should recite this blessing with intense joy, confident that God is our past and future Redeemer *(Yesod V'Shoresh HaAvodah).*

סֻכָּתְךָ — *Your Succah.* This refers to the *Beis HaMikdash.*

גָּאַל יִשְׂרָאֵל — *Who redeemed Israel.* Some *machzorim* follow the custom to substitute the phrase מֶלֶךְ צוּר יִשְׂרָאֵל וְגוֹאֲלוֹ, *King, Rock of*

מִי כָמֹכָה *Who is like You among the heavenly powers,* H*ASHEM! Who is like You, mighty in holiness, too awesome for praise,* doing wonders!*[1] Chazzan– *Your children beheld Your majesty,* as You split the sea before Moses,*

FIRST NIGHT	SECOND NIGHT
ה *Those who complete Hallel all eight [days],*	י *With Your beautiful clouds, You covered Your redeemed ones,*
ק *Who read the chapter of [each day's] offerings in its time,*	ח *You spread Your glorious canopy before them to clear the way,*
ט *Plant them and settle them in the land of abundance,*	י *They declared Your Oneness and glorified You as [befits] those who have crossed the waves,*
נ *Thus to verify the eternality of the Rock of our salvation.*	אל *The Patriarchs' offspring praised Your Name with the 'Az Yashir' song.**

'He is the Rock of our salvation!' they opened their mouths and said:

Continue: *'*H*ASHEM shall reign . . .'*

'This is my God!'[2] *they exclaimed, then they said:*

יהוה *'*H*ASHEM shall reign for all eternity!'*[3] Chazzan– *And it is further said: 'For* H*ASHEM has redeemed Jacob* and delivered him from a power mightier than he.'*[4]

FIRST NIGHT	SECOND NIGHT
ב *With the majesty of holiness they sang*[5] *in His Sanctuary,*	בן *Rebuild Your Succah* and erect the fallen one,*[8]
ר *They bestir themselves to inaugurate song and praise.*	י *Support its foundations to rebuild it on its hilltop,*[9]
ש *Prepare for them peace*[6] *in heaping measure,*[7]	צ *To graze Your flock beside Your Tabernacle,*[10] *to make it a heritage,*
מ *O King, Rock of Israel and its Holy One.*	ח *Accept as of old the righteous sacrifices and olah-offerings.*

[Some conclude the blessing as follows; others conclude with *'Blessed . . . Who redeemed Israel'.*]

Blessed are You, H*ASHEM, King, Rock of Israel and its Redeemer.*

Blessed are You, H*ASHEM, Who redeemed Israel.** (Cong.– *Amen.)*

הַשְׁכִּיבֵנוּ *Lay us down* to sleep,* H*ASHEM, our God, in peace,* raise us erect, our King, to life; and spread over us the shelter of Your peace. Set us aright with good counsel from before Your Presence, and save us for Your Name's sake. Shield us, remove from us foe,*

(1) *Exodus* 15:11. (2) 15:2. (3) 15:18. (4) *Jeremiah* 31:10. (5) Some *machzorim* read: מְחַנְּנִים*, they pray.* (6) Cf. *Isaiah* 26:12. (7) Some *machzorim* read: לְהַקְדִּישׁוֹ*, to sanctify them.* (8) Cf. *Amos* 9:11. (9) Cf. *Jeremiah* 30:18. (10) Cf. *Song of Songs* 1:8.

Israel and its Redeemer, whenever *piyutim* are recited. However, the halachic authorities disagree regarding the propriety of this change. *Mishnah Berurah* (66:33; 236:3) states that it is preferable that the conclusion not be altered.

הַשְׁכִּיבֵנוּ — *Lay us down.* This blessing is an extension of the theme of redemption. Whereas the earlier blessing spoke of Israel's redemption from Egypt [and alluded to the future redemption], this one describes God as our Savior from the dangers and afflictions associated with the terrors of the night, literally and figuratively.

הַשְׁכִּיבֵנוּ . . . לְשָׁלוֹם — *Lay us down to sleep . . . in peace.* The purpose of sleep is to allow the

דֶּבֶר, וְחֶרֶב, וְרָעָב, וְיָגוֹן, וְהָסֵר שָׂטָן מִלְּפָנֵינוּ וּמֵאַחֲרֵינוּ,* וּבְצֵל כְּנָפֶיךָ* תַּסְתִּירֵנוּ,[1] כִּי אֵל שׁוֹמְרֵנוּ וּמַצִּילֵנוּ אָתָּה, כִּי אֵל מֶלֶךְ חַנּוּן וְרַחוּם אָתָּה.[2] ❖ וּשְׁמוֹר צֵאתֵנוּ וּבוֹאֵנוּ, לְחַיִּים וּלְשָׁלוֹם מֵעַתָּה וְעַד עוֹלָם.[3] וּפְרוֹשׂ עָלֵינוּ* סֻכַּת שְׁלוֹמֶךָ.

FIRST NIGHT	SECOND NIGHT
וָתִיק, חַדֵּשׁ מְכוֹן אוּלָמֶךָ,	קוֹרֵא מִקְרָא קֹדֶשׁ וּמִשְׁמְּרוֹ,
אַמֵּץ אֲהוּבִים כּוֹנַנְתָּ בְּצִלְמֶךָ,	יְקַבֵּל לַיּוֹם הַבָּא שְׂכָרוֹ,*
לְבָרֵךְ וּלְקַדֵּשׁ שִׁמְךָ בְּעוֹלָמֶךָ,	גַּאֲוָה אֲפִיקֵי מָגִנִּים סְגוּרוֹ,[4]
תָּגֵן עָלֵינוּ בִּבְרִית שְׁלוֹמֶךָ.	דּוֹד לְמַלְּאוֹת לוֹ בְּשִׁכּוֹת עוֹרוֹ.[5]

בָּרוּךְ אַתָּה יהוה, הַפּוֹרֵשׂ סֻכַּת שָׁלוֹם עָלֵינוּ וְעַל כָּל עַמּוֹ יִשְׂרָאֵל וְעַל יְרוּשָׁלָיִם. (Cong. – אָמֵן.)

Congregation rises and remains standing until after *Shemoneh Esrei.*

On the Sabbath, the congregation, followed by the *chazzan,* recites:

וְשָׁמְרוּ* בְנֵי יִשְׂרָאֵל אֶת הַשַּׁבָּת, לַעֲשׂוֹת אֶת הַשַּׁבָּת* לְדֹרֹתָם בְּרִית עוֹלָם. בֵּינִי וּבֵין בְּנֵי יִשְׂרָאֵל* אוֹת הִיא לְעֹלָם, כִּי שֵׁשֶׁת יָמִים עָשָׂה יהוה אֶת הַשָּׁמַיִם וְאֶת הָאָרֶץ, וּבַיּוֹם הַשְּׁבִיעִי שָׁבַת וַיִּנָּפַשׁ.*[6]

Congregation, then *chazzan:*

וַיְדַבֵּר מֹשֶׁה* אֶת מֹעֲדֵי יהוה, אֶל בְּנֵי יִשְׂרָאֵל.[7]

The *chazzan* recites חֲצִי קַדִּישׁ.

יִתְגַּדַּל וְיִתְקַדַּשׁ שְׁמֵהּ רַבָּא. (Cong. – אָמֵן.) בְּעָלְמָא דִּי בְרָא כִרְעוּתֵהּ, וְיַמְלִיךְ מַלְכוּתֵהּ, בְּחַיֵּיכוֹן וּבְיוֹמֵיכוֹן וּבְחַיֵּי דְכָל בֵּית יִשְׂרָאֵל, בַּעֲגָלָא וּבִזְמַן קָרִיב. וְאִמְרוּ: אָמֵן.

(Cong. – אָמֵן. יְהֵא שְׁמֵהּ רַבָּא מְבָרַךְ לְעָלַם וּלְעָלְמֵי עָלְמַיָּא.)

---

body to rejuvenate itself, the better to serve God the next day *(R' Hirsch).*

מִלְּפָנֵינוּ וּמֵאַחֲרֵינוּ — *From before us and behind us.* Protect us from spiritual harm in the future *[before us]* and from the consequences of what has already occurred *[behind us]* *(R' Hirsch).*

וּבְצֵל כְּנָפֶיךָ — *And in the shadow of Your wings.* *Psalms* 91:4 likens God's protection to the wings of a mother bird sheltering her young.

וּפְרוֹשׂ עָלֵינוּ — *And spread over us.* This phrase was recited earlier in the paragraph, but it is repeated now because of its similarity to the closing of the blessing. There is a general rule that the conclusion of a blessing should be related to the content. Unlike the weekday הַשְׁכִּיבֵנוּ, which concludes with a request for Divine protection, the concluding blessing on the Sabbath and Festivals reflects the peace that comes with the holiness of the day *(Anaf Yosef).*

שְׂכָרוֹ — *His reward.* This refers to the *Succah* of Leviathan and the feast therein (see p. 1020) as the following verse attests.

❧ וְשָׁמְרוּ — *And . . . shall keep.* As noted above, there should be no interruption between the theme of redemption and *Shemoneh Esrei.* However, this Scriptural statement of Israel's Sabbath observance is related to the theme of redemption, because Israel will be redeemed from exile in the merit of Sabbath observance *(Abudraham).*

This chapter of Sabbath observance appears in the Torah immediately after the commandment to commence the construction of the Tabernacle. This teaches that even for the sake of building the Temple, one may not desecrate

plague, sword, famine, and woe; and remove spiritual impediment from before us and behind us, and in the shadow of Your wings* shelter us[1] — for God Who protects and rescues us are You; for God, the Gracious and Compassionate King, are You.[2]* Chazzan– *Safeguard our going and coming, for life and for peace from now to eternity.[3] And spread over us* the shelter of Your peace.*

FIRST NIGHT	SECOND NIGHT
ו *O All-worthy One, renew Your dwelling, Your Temple,*	ק *Whoever declares [Succos] a holy convocation and observes it,*
א *Strengthen the beloved [Israel] whom You have created in Your image,*	י *Will receive his reward, in Time to Come,**
ל *[Enable them] to bless and to sanctify Your Name in Your world, Protect us with the covenant of Your peace.*	ג *The haughty [Leviathan] wrapped in his shield-like scales,[4]*
	דל *The Beloved will fulfill his desires in the tents of its skin.[5]*

Blessed are You, HASHEM, Who spreads the shelter of peace upon us, upon all of His people Israel and upon Jerusalem. (Cong.– *Amen.*)

Congregation rises and remains standing until after *Shemoneh Esrei.*

On the Sabbath, the congregation, followed by the *chazzan,* recites:

וְשָׁמְרוּ *And the Children of Israel shall keep* the Sabbath, to make the Sabbath* an eternal covenant for their generations. Between Me and the Children of Israel* it is a sign forever that in six days HASHEM made heaven and earth, and on the seventh day He rested and was refreshed.*[6]*

Congregation, then *chazzan:*

And Moses declared* HASHEM's appointed festivals to the Children of Israel.[7]

The *chazzan* recites Half-*Kaddish.*

יִתְגַּדַּל *May His great Name grow exalted and sanctified* (Cong.– *Amen.*) *in the world that He created as He willed. May He give reign to His kingship in your lifetimes and in your days, and in the lifetimes of the entire Family of Israel, swiftly and soon. Now respond: Amen.*

(Cong.– *Amen. May His great Name be blessed forever and ever.*)

(1) Cf. *Psalms* 17:8. (2) Cf. *Nechemiah* 9:31. (3) Cf. *Psalms* 121:8. (4) Cf. *Job* 41:7. (5) Cf. 40:31. (6) *Exodus* 31:16-17. (7) *Leviticus* 23:44.

the Sabbath (*Rashi* to *Exodus* 31:13). [By logical extension, this concept refutes those who may tend to relax the observance of the Sabbath or other *mitzvos* for the sake of what they consider to be noble spiritual causes.]

לַעֲשׂוֹת אֶת הַשַּׁבָּת — *To make the Sabbath.* Each generation must *'make' the Sabbath,* by teaching its importance and holiness to those who are lax in sanctifying it because they fail to appreciate its importance (*Maor VaShemesh*).

בֵּינִי וּבֵין בְּנֵי יִשְׂרָאֵל — *Between Me and the Children of Israel.* Only Israel is commanded to observe the Sabbath, thereby bearing witness to God's creation of heaven and earth in six days. Consequently, the Sabbath is a *sign* of God's special relationship with Israel.

וַיִּנָּפַשׁ — *And was refreshed.* The translation follows *Rashi* who comments that this is an example of how God is described in human terms: God, of course, cannot become tired or refreshed, but a man would need a day of rest to refresh himself after six days of labor.

Other commentators, *Ramban* and *R' Yehudah HaChassid* among them, derive this word from נֶפֶשׁ, *soul.* They render וַיִּנָּפַשׁ, *and He gave them a soul,* i.e., the heaven and earth just mentioned *were given a soul,* as if to say that the creation of the Sabbath gave a new spiritual dimension to the universe.

◆§ וַיְדַבֵּר מֹשֶׁה – *And Moses declared.* This verse concludes a chapter that discusses the festivals. Thus, the verse alludes to all the specific laws

יְהֵא שְׁמֵהּ רַבָּא מְבָרַךְ לְעָלַם וּלְעָלְמֵי עָלְמַיָּא.

יִתְבָּרַךְ וְיִשְׁתַּבַּח וְיִתְפָּאַר וְיִתְרוֹמַם וְיִתְנַשֵּׂא וְיִתְהַדָּר וְיִתְעַלֶּה וְיִתְהַלָּל שְׁמֵהּ דְּקֻדְשָׁא בְּרִיךְ הוּא (.Cong– בְּרִיךְ הוּא) — לְעֵֽלָּא מִן כָּל בִּרְכָתָא וְשִׁירָתָא תֻּשְׁבְּחָתָא וְנֶחֱמָתָא, דַּאֲמִירָן בְּעָלְמָא. וְאִמְרוּ: אָמֵן. (.Cong– אָמֵן.)

❧ שמונה עשרה – עמידה ☙

Take three steps backward, then three steps forward. Remain standing with the feet together while reciting *Shemoneh Esrei*. Recite it with quiet devotion and without interruption, verbal or otherwise. Although its recitation should not be audible to others, one must pray loudly enough to hear himself.

אֲדֹנָי שְׂפָתַי תִּפְתָּח, וּפִי יַגִּיד תְּהִלָּתֶךָ.[1]

אבות

Bend the knees at בָּרוּךְ; bow at אַתָּה; straighten up at 'ה.

בָּרוּךְ אַתָּה יהוה אֱלֹהֵינוּ וֵאלֹהֵי אֲבוֹתֵינוּ, אֱלֹהֵי אַבְרָהָם, אֱלֹהֵי יִצְחָק, וֵאלֹהֵי יַעֲקֹב, הָאֵל הַגָּדוֹל הַגִּבּוֹר וְהַנּוֹרָא, אֵל עֶלְיוֹן, גּוֹמֵל חֲסָדִים טוֹבִים וְקוֹנֵה הַכֹּל, וְזוֹכֵר חַסְדֵי אָבוֹת, וּמֵבִיא גוֹאֵל לִבְנֵי בְנֵיהֶם, לְמַעַן שְׁמוֹ בְּאַהֲבָה.

Bend the knees at בָּרוּךְ; bow at אַתָּה; straighten up at 'ה.

מֶלֶךְ עוֹזֵר וּמוֹשִׁיעַ וּמָגֵן. בָּרוּךְ אַתָּה יהוה, מָגֵן אַבְרָהָם.

גבורות

אַתָּה גִּבּוֹר לְעוֹלָם אֲדֹנָי, מְחַיֵּה מֵתִים אַתָּה, רַב לְהוֹשִׁיעַ. מְכַלְכֵּל חַיִּים בְּחֶסֶד, מְחַיֵּה מֵתִים בְּרַחֲמִים רַבִּים, סוֹמֵךְ נוֹפְלִים, וְרוֹפֵא חוֹלִים, וּמַתִּיר אֲסוּרִים, וּמְקַיֵּם אֱמוּנָתוֹ לִישֵׁנֵי עָפָר. מִי כָמוֹךָ בַּעַל גְּבוּרוֹת, וּמִי דּוֹמֶה לָּךְ, מֶלֶךְ מֵמִית וּמְחַיֶּה וּמַצְמִיחַ יְשׁוּעָה. וְנֶאֱמָן אַתָּה לְהַחֲיוֹת מֵתִים. בָּרוּךְ אַתָּה יהוה, מְחַיֵּה הַמֵּתִים.

---

and teachings of each of the festivals.

❧ The Festival Shemoneh Esrei

The basic structure of the Festival *Shemoneh Esrei* is similar to that of the Sabbath in that it consists of seven blessings: the same three-blessing introduction and conclusion as those of every other *Shemoneh Esrei* all year round, and a single-blessing mid-section that contains the prayers of the day.

However, there are differences between the *Shemoneh Esrei* of the Sabbath and that of the festivals. Unlike the *Shemoneh Esrei* prayers of the Sabbath that concentrate primarily on the sanctity of the day, the Festival prayers stress Israel's status as God's Chosen People. The Sabbath derives its holiness from God Who rested on the seventh day of creation; its holiness predated Israel and is in no way dependent on the Jewish people. The Festivals, on the other hand, commemorate the history of Israel. Although the Sabbath, as the testimony to God the Creator, could exist without the Jewish people, there could be no Festivals unless there had been a nation that was freed from Egypt, given the Torah and sheltered in the

May His great Name be blessed forever and ever.

Blessed, praised, glorified, exalted, extolled, mighty, upraised, and lauded be the Name of the Holy One, Blessed is He (Cong.— *Blessed is He*) — *beyond any blessing and song, praise and consolation that are uttered in the world. Now respond: Amen.* (Cong.— *Amen.*)

SHEMONEH ESREI — AMIDAH

Take three steps backward, then three steps forward. Remain standing with the feet together while reciting *Shemoneh Esrei.* Recite it with quiet devotion and without interruption, verbal or otherwise. Although its recitation should not be audible to others, one must pray loudly enough to hear himself.

My Lord, open my lips, that my mouth may declare Your praise.[1]

PATRIARCHS

Bend the knees at *'Blessed'*; bow at *'You'*; straighten up at *'HASHEM.'*

בָּרוּךְ *Blessed are You, HASHEM, our God and the God of our forefathers, God of Abraham, God of Isaac, and God of Jacob; the great, mighty, and awesome God, the supreme God, Who bestows beneficial kindnesses and creates everything, Who recalls the kindnesses of the Patriarchs and brings a Redeemer to their children's children, for His Name's sake, with love.*

Bend the knees at *'Blessed'*; bow at *'You'*; straighten up at 'HASHEM.'

O King, Helper, Savior, and Shield. Blessed are You, HASHEM, Shield of Abraham.

GOD'S MIGHT

אַתָּה *You are eternally mighty, my Lord, the Resuscitator of the dead are You; abundantly able to save. He sustains the living with kindness, resuscitates the dead with abundant mercy, supports the fallen, heals the sick, releases the confined, and maintains His faith to those asleep in the dust. Who is like You, O Master of mighty deeds, and who is comparable to You, O King Who causes death and restores life and makes salvation sprout! And You are faithful to resuscitate the dead. Blessed are You, HASHEM, Who resuscitates the dead.*

(1) *Psalms* 51:17.

Wilderness. This emphasis is apparent from the very start of the middle section of the Festival *Shemoneh Esrei,* which declares that God has chosen Israel from among the nations, a concept that is absent from the Sabbath *Shemoneh Esrei.*

Furthermore, since the Festivals are dependent on the calendar and the sanctification of the months — which the Torah assigns to the Jewish people through their courts — the Festivals are creatures of the Jewish people, as it were.

Another feature unique to the Festivals is that joy is an integral part of their observance. Both of these features are reflected in the Festival *Shemoneh Esrei.*

There is yet another difference between the Festival and the Sabbath prayers. Each *Shemoneh Esrei* of the Sabbath refers to a different aspect of the day, and is therefore unique. These differences do not apply on Festivals with the result that all the *Shemoneh Esrei* services (with the exception of *Mussaf,* of course) are identical.

The commentary for the first section of *Shemoneh Esrei* may be found on page 10.

קדושת השם

אַתָּה קָדוֹשׁ וְשִׁמְךָ קָדוֹשׁ, וּקְדוֹשִׁים בְּכָל יוֹם יְהַלְלוּךָ סֶּלָה. בָּרוּךְ אַתָּה יהוה, הָאֵל הַקָּדוֹשׁ.

קדושת היום

אַתָּה בְחַרְתָּנוּ* מִכָּל הָעַמִּים, אָהַבְתָּ אוֹתָנוּ, וְרָצִיתָ בָּנוּ, וְרוֹמַמְתָּנוּ מִכָּל הַלְּשׁוֹנוֹת,* וְקִדַּשְׁתָּנוּ בְּמִצְוֹתֶיךָ,* וְקֵרַבְתָּנוּ מַלְכֵּנוּ לַעֲבוֹדָתֶךָ, וְשִׁמְךָ הַגָּדוֹל וְהַקָּדוֹשׁ עָלֵינוּ קָרָאתָ.*

On Saturday night add. [If forgotten, do not repeat *Shemoneh Esrei*. See *Laws* §91.]

וַתּוֹדִיעֵנוּ* יהוה אֱלֹהֵינוּ אֶת מִשְׁפְּטֵי צִדְקֶךָ, וַתְּלַמְּדֵנוּ לַעֲשׂוֹת (בָּהֶם) חֻקֵּי רְצוֹנֶךָ. וַתִּתֶּן לָנוּ יהוה אֱלֹהֵינוּ מִשְׁפָּטִים יְשָׁרִים* וְתוֹרוֹת אֱמֶת חֻקִּים וּמִצְוֹת טוֹבִים. וַתַּנְחִילֵנוּ זְמַנֵּי שָׂשׂוֹן וּמוֹעֲדֵי קֹדֶשׁ וְחַגֵּי נְדָבָה.* וַתּוֹרִישֵׁנוּ קְדֻשַּׁת שַׁבָּת וּכְבוֹד מוֹעֵד וַחֲגִיגַת הָרֶגֶל. וַתַּבְדֵּל* יהוה אֱלֹהֵינוּ בֵּין קֹדֶשׁ לְחוֹל, בֵּין אוֹר לְחֹשֶׁךְ, בֵּין יִשְׂרָאֵל לָעַמִּים, בֵּין יוֹם הַשְּׁבִיעִי לְשֵׁשֶׁת יְמֵי הַמַּעֲשֶׂה. בֵּין קְדֻשַּׁת שַׁבָּת לִקְדֻשַּׁת יוֹם טוֹב הִבְדַּלְתָּ, וְאֶת יוֹם הַשְּׁבִיעִי מִשֵּׁשֶׁת יְמֵי הַמַּעֲשֶׂה קִדַּשְׁתָּ, הִבְדַּלְתָּ וְקִדַּשְׁתָּ אֶת עַמְּךָ יִשְׂרָאֵל בִּקְדֻשָּׁתֶךָ.

אַתָּה בְחַרְתָּנוּ . . . — *You have chosen us. Anaf Yosef* gives this passage a different interpretation for each of the festivals. Regarding Succos the passage alludes to the Talmudic narrative (*Avodah Zarah* 3a,b) that the commandment of dwelling in a *succah* is an 'easy *mitzvah*,' which will be given to the nations as an opportunity to prove their willingness to accept the Torah. But they will reject it angrily at the first sign of discomfort. Thus, our acceptance and performance of this *mitzvah* is a symbol of our chosenness and of our acceptance of the entire Torah. For even when God is dissatisfied with our service, we accept His rejection as a call for a greater measure of devotion to Him.

מִכָּל הַלְּשׁוֹנוֹת — *Above all the tongues.* Human language can capture sublime thoughts and complex ideas, but Israel was granted the language of the Torah, which encompasses God's own wisdom and which is uniquely suited to expressing concepts of holiness.

וְקִדַּשְׁתָּנוּ בְּמִצְוֹתֶיךָ — *And You sanctified us with Your commandments.* Unlike the laws of human legislatures and monarchs, the laws of the Torah infuse holiness into those who observe them.

וְשִׁמְךָ . . . עָלֵינוּ קָרָאתָ — *And proclaimed Your . . . Name upon us.* We are proud and grateful that God wished to be known as the God of Israel.

The three expressions at the beginning of this paragraph — *chosen, loved,* and *found favor* — allude to the respective historical characteristics of the three pilgrimage Festivals, which will be named in וַתִּתֶּן לָנוּ, *And You gave us.* On Pesach, God chose us from among the Egyptians; on Shavuos, He showed His love for us by giving us His Torah; and on Succos, He showed us favor by forgiving the sin of the Golden Calf and bringing us under the Divine shelter which is symbolized by the *succah* booth *(Siach Yitzchak).*

These three terms are suited to their respective Festivals. The term "choose" implies that one selects one person or thing over others — not that it is perfect, but because it is the best of the lot, or because of its potential. Thus, Pesach

HOLINESS OF GOD'S NAME

אַתָּה *You are holy and Your Name is holy, and holy ones praise You every day, forever. Blessed are You, HASHEM, the holy God.*

SANCTIFICATION OF THE DAY

אַתָּה בְחַרְתָּנוּ *You have chosen us* from all the peoples; You loved us and found favor in us; You exalted us above all the tongues* and You sanctified us with Your commandments.* You drew us close, our King, to Your service and proclaimed Your great and Holy Name upon us.**

On Saturday night add. [If forgotten, do not repeat *Shemoneh Esrei.* See *Laws* §91.]

וַתּוֹדִיעֵנוּ *You made known to us,* HASHEM, our God, Your righteous ordinances, and You taught us to do the decrees of Your will. You gave us, HASHEM, our God, fair laws* and true teachings, good decrees and commandments. As a heritage You gave us seasons of joy, appointed festivals of holiness, and free-willed festive offerings.* You made us heir to the Sabbath holiness, the appointed festival glory, and festive offering of the pilgrimage. You distinguished,* O HASHEM, our God, between the sacred and secular, between light and darkness, between Israel and the peoples, between the seventh day and the six days of labor. Between the sanctity of the Sabbath and the sanctity of the holiday You have distinguished, and the seventh day, from among the six days of labor You have sanctified. You have distinguished and You have sanctified Your people Israel with Your holiness.*

---

marks the choice of an imperfect Israel that had enormous potential for good. One loves another because he is compatible emotionally or in deed. God showed His love on Shavuos by giving us the Torah. Favor is the highest of all levels, because it transcends logic. Even after Israel sinned with the Golden Calf, Israel found favor in God's eyes to such a degree that He forgave the sin on Yom Kippur and ushered in Succos, the most joyous of the Festivals (*Poras Yosef*).

⁂ **וַתּוֹדִיעֵנוּ** — *You made known to us.* This paragraph, which was composed by the Talmudic sages, Rav and Shmuel (*Berachos* 33b), takes the place of אַתָּה חוֹנַנְתָּנוּ, *You have graced us,* the insertion at the conclusion of the regular Sabbath that draws the distinction between the holy and the secular (see p. 622). Despite the great sanctity of the Festivals, they are less holy than the Sabbath; hence the requirement that *Havdalah* be recited here in *Shemoneh Esrei* and as part of the *Kiddush.*

וַתִּתֶּן לָנוּ ... מִשְׁפָּטִים יְשָׁרִים — *You gave us ... fair laws.* God gave us many commandments of various kinds — some that are comprehensible to the human mind, some that teach us to perceive our proper role in creation, some decrees that are above our comprehension, and commandments to regulate all facets of our behavior in a manner that will bring us closer to His service. The Sabbaths and Festivals are uniquely suited to inspire us with renewed sanctity to strive toward the fulfillment of the tasks God has set for us (*R' Hirsch*).

זְמַנֵּי שָׂשׂוֹן וּמוֹעֲדֵי קֹדֶשׁ וְחַגֵּי נְדָבָה — *Seasons of joy, appointed festivals of holiness, and free-willed festive offerings.* These three terms refer to three aspects of the Festivals. Firstly, they are seasons of joy as regards the agricultural cycle: Pesach comes in springtime; Shavuos ushers in the time of the first fruits; and Succos is the festive season of harvest. Secondly, they are appointed as Festivals because of their historical significance: Pesach commemorates the Exodus; Shavuos recalls the Revelation at Sinai; and Succos reminds us that God sheltered us in the Wilderness. Finally, these three terms recall the three kinds of offerings, expressing both devotion and joy, that were offered by the multitudes of Jews who came to Jerusalem for each of the three annual pilgrimage Festivals (*R' Hirsch*).

וַתַּבְדֵּל — *You distinguished.* The following list parallels the one found in the weekday *Shemoneh Esrei* recited at the conclusion of the Sabbath, except, of course, that this one includes the distinction betwen the Sabbath and Festival holiness.

On the Sabbath add the words in brackets. [If forgotten, see Laws §86-90.]

וַתִּתֶּן לָנוּ יהוה אֱלֹהֵינוּ בְּאַהֲבָה* [שַׁבָּתוֹת לִמְנוּחָה וּ]מוֹעֲדִים* לְשִׂמְחָה* חַגִּים* וּזְמַנִּים לְשָׂשׂוֹן, אֶת יוֹם [הַשַּׁבָּת הַזֶּה וְאֶת יוֹם] חַג הַסֻּכּוֹת הַזֶּה, זְמַן שִׂמְחָתֵנוּ* [בְּאַהֲבָה*], מִקְרָא קֹדֶשׁ,* זֵכֶר לִיצִיאַת מִצְרָיִם.*

אֱלֹהֵינוּ וֵאלֹהֵי אֲבוֹתֵינוּ, יַעֲלֶה, וְיָבֹא,* וְיַגִּיעַ, וְיֵרָאֶה, וְיֵרָצֶה, וְיִשָּׁמַע, וְיִפָּקֵד, וְיִזָּכֵר זִכְרוֹנֵנוּ וּפִקְדוֹנֵנוּ, וְזִכְרוֹן אֲבוֹתֵינוּ, וְזִכְרוֹן מָשִׁיחַ בֶּן דָּוִד עַבְדֶּךָ, וְזִכְרוֹן יְרוּשָׁלַיִם עִיר קָדְשֶׁךָ, וְזִכְרוֹן כָּל עַמְּךָ בֵּית יִשְׂרָאֵל לְפָנֶיךָ, לִפְלֵיטָה לְטוֹבָה לְחֵן וּלְחֶסֶד וּלְרַחֲמִים, לְחַיִּים וּלְשָׁלוֹם בְּיוֹם חַג הַסֻּכּוֹת הַזֶּה. זָכְרֵנוּ יהוה אֱלֹהֵינוּ בּוֹ לְטוֹבָה, וּפָקְדֵנוּ בוֹ לִבְרָכָה, וְהוֹשִׁיעֵנוּ בוֹ לְחַיִּים. וּבִדְבַר יְשׁוּעָה וְרַחֲמִים, חוּס וְחָנֵּנוּ וְרַחֵם עָלֵינוּ וְהוֹשִׁיעֵנוּ, כִּי אֵלֶיךָ עֵינֵינוּ, כִּי אֵל מֶלֶךְ חַנּוּן וְרַחוּם אָתָּה.[1]

On the Sabbath add the words in brackets. [If forgotten, see Laws §86-90.]

וְהַשִּׂיאֵנוּ* יהוה אֱלֹהֵינוּ אֶת בִּרְכַּת מוֹעֲדֶיךָ לְחַיִּים וּלְשָׁלוֹם, לְשִׂמְחָה וּלְשָׂשׂוֹן, כַּאֲשֶׁר רָצִיתָ* וְאָמַרְתָּ לְבָרְכֵנוּ. [אֱלֹהֵינוּ וֵאלֹהֵי אֲבוֹתֵינוּ רְצֵה בִמְנוּחָתֵנוּ] קַדְּשֵׁנוּ בְּמִצְוֹתֶיךָ וְתֵן חֶלְקֵנוּ בְּתוֹרָתֶךָ, שַׂבְּעֵנוּ מִטּוּבֶךָ וְשַׂמְּחֵנוּ בִּישׁוּעָתֶךָ, וְטַהֵר לִבֵּנוּ

וַתִּתֶּן לָנוּ . . . בְּאַהֲבָה — *And You gave us . . . with love.* Having chosen us, God gave us this special day. If the Festival falls on a Sabbath, that day, too, is mentioned here specifically. The difference in description between the Sabbath and the Festivals expresses a major difference between them. Although there is rest on the Festivals and gladness on the Sabbath, their primary features are, as we say here, Sabbath for *rest* and Festivals for *gladness.*

מוֹעֲדִים — *Appointed festivals.* This term for the Festivals has the connotation of meeting, i.e., God has designated times when Israel can greet His Presence.

מוֹעֲדִים לְשִׂמְחָה — *Appointed festivals for gladness.* The expression used here is *appointed festivals* **for** *gladness,* rather than **of** *gladness.* This tells us that *Yom Tov* is not only a day of rejoicing but a source from which to draw joy and inspiration for the rest of the year. In the same way, שַׁבָּתוֹת לִמְנוּחָה, *Sabbaths for rest,* teaches that the Sabbath furnishes us with the blessing of restfulness for the entire week *(Sfas Emes).*

חַגִּים — *Festivals.* The word חַג is sometimes used for the Festival day and sometimes to refer to the קָרְבַּן חֲגִיגָה, *festive offering,* that pilgrims brought in celebration of the day.

זְמַן שִׂמְחָתֵנוּ — *The time of our gladness.* During the solemn days of penitence just past, the Jew acquired spiritual strength and purification. On Succos, these sources of vigor and sanctity are released in a joyous display of confidence and trust in God which endows this festival with a unique character all its own. In the wilderness, too, it was on the tenth of Tishrei, the date of Yom Kippur, that Israel was forgiven for the sin of the Golden Calf and given the privilege of building the מִשְׁכָּן, *Tabernacle.* Then and now, Succos is *the season of our gladness,* when the Jewish people celebrate pardon and purity with a joy that reaches its peak with Simchas Torah (R' Elie Munk in *World of Prayer).*

בְּאַהֲבָה — *With love.* This extra expression of love, referring only to the Sabbath, denotes the particular affection with which Israel accepted the commandments of the Sabbath. Whereas the Festival observance represents our acknowledgment of God's kindness to our ancestors, the Sabbath shows our desire to honor Him as the Creator.

מִקְרָא קֹדֶשׁ — *A holy convocation.* On these days,

On the Sabbath add the words in brackets. [If forgotten, see *Laws* §86-90.]

וַתִּתֶּן לָנוּ *And You gave us, HASHEM, our God, with love* [Sabbaths for rest], appointed festivals* for gladness,* Festivals* and times for joy, [this day of Sabbath and] this day of the Festival of Succos, the time of our gladness* [with love*], a holy convocation,* a memorial of the Exodus from Egypt.**

אֱלֹהֵינוּ *Our God and God of our forefathers, may there rise, come,* reach, be noted, be favored, be heard, be considered, and be remembered — the remembrance and consideration of ourselves; the remembrance of our forefathers; the remembrance of Messiah, son of David, Your servant; the remembrance of Jerusalem, the City of Your Holiness; the remembrance of Your entire people the Family of Israel — before You for deliverance, for goodness, for grace, for kindness, and for compassion, for life, and for peace on this day of the Festival of Succos. Remember us on it, HASHEM, our God, for goodness, consider us on it for blessing, and help us on it for life. In the matter of salvation and compassion, pity, be gracious and compassionate with us and help us, for our eyes are turned to You, because You are God, the gracious and compassionate King.*[1]

On the Sabbath add the words in brackets. [If forgotten, see *Laws* §86-90.]

וְהַשִּׂיאֵנוּ *Bestow upon us,* O HASHEM, our God, the blessing of Your appointed festivals for life and for peace, for gladness and for joy, as You desired* and promised to bless us. [Our God and the God of our forefathers, may You be pleased with our rest.] Sanctify us withYour commandments and grant us our share in Your Torah; satisfy us from Your goodness and gladden us with Your salvation, and purify our heart*

(1) Cf. *Nechemiah* 9:31.

the nation is gathered to pursue holiness, and to sanctify the Festival through prayer and praise to God *(Ramban; Sforno)*.

זֵכֶר לִיצִיאַת מִצְרָיִם — *A memorial of the Exodus from Egypt*. There is a deep connection between all the Festivals and the Exodus. We are called upon constantly to renew our service of God. The key to doing so is our awareness that God revealed Himself at the Exodus, demonstrated His mastery over the universe, and made us His people. Our daily prayers stress our liberation from Egypt, and on Pesach we re-experience the initial self-revelation of God, and the creation of the Jewish people as a free nation. The freedom gained in Egypt is further unfolded on Shavuos, when we receive the Torah. It finds its final expression on Succos when we leave the temporal world, to take refuge in the *succah*, which symbolizes the sheltering wings of the *Shechinah*, the Divine Presence *(Maharal)*.

☙ אֱלֹהֵינוּ . . . יַעֲלֶה וְיָבֹא — *Our God . . . may there rise, come*. Our recollection of Israel's closeness to God brings home the poignant reality that we still lack the Temple. Therefore, we pray that He bring an end to the exile and reunite Israel, Jerusalem, and the Temple.

This prayer contains eight words [. . . יַעֲלֶה וְיִזָּכֵר] expressing the same general idea. *Rabbi S.R. Hirsch* interprets them: May our personal behavior and fortune *rise* [יַעֲלֶה] above ordinary human existence; and *come* [וְיָבֹא] before God to merit His interest; may nothing prevent them from *reaching* [וְיַגִּיעַ] God and gaining His acceptance; may they be *noted* [וְיֵרָאֶה] in the best possible light; may they be worthy of God's *favor* [וְיֵרָצֶה]; may God *hear* [וְיִשָּׁמַע] the impact these remembrances have on our lives; may God *consider* [וְיִפָּקֵד] our needs; and may He *remember* [וְיִזָּכֵר] us and our relationship to Him.

☙ וְהַשִּׂיאֵנוּ — *Bestow upon us*. In concluding the central portion of the *Shemoneh Esrei*, we ask God to give all the joyous blessings of the day and season.

כַּאֲשֶׁר רָצִיתָ — *As You desired*. God wishes to

לְעָבְדְּךָ בֶּאֱמֶת,* וְהַנְחִילֵנוּ יהוה אֱלֹהֵינוּ [בְּאַהֲבָה וּבְרָצוֹן*] בְּשִׂמְחָה וּבְשָׂשׂוֹן [שַׁבָּת וּ]מוֹעֲדֵי קָדְשֶׁךָ, וְיִשְׂמְחוּ בְךָ יִשְׂרָאֵל מְקַדְּשֵׁי שְׁמֶךָ. בָּרוּךְ אַתָּה יהוה, מְקַדֵּשׁ [הַשַּׁבָּת וְ]יִשְׂרָאֵל וְהַזְּמַנִּים.*

עבודה

רְצֵה יהוה אֱלֹהֵינוּ בְּעַמְּךָ יִשְׂרָאֵל וּבִתְפִלָּתָם, וְהָשֵׁב אֶת הָעֲבוֹדָה לִדְבִיר בֵּיתֶךָ. וְאִשֵּׁי יִשְׂרָאֵל וּתְפִלָּתָם בְּאַהֲבָה תְקַבֵּל בְּרָצוֹן, וּתְהִי לְרָצוֹן תָּמִיד עֲבוֹדַת יִשְׂרָאֵל עַמֶּךָ.

וְתֶחֱזֶינָה עֵינֵינוּ בְּשׁוּבְךָ לְצִיּוֹן בְּרַחֲמִים. בָּרוּךְ אַתָּה יהוה, הַמַּחֲזִיר שְׁכִינָתוֹ לְצִיּוֹן.

הודאה

Bow at מוֹדִים; straighten up at 'ה.

מוֹדִים אֲנַחְנוּ לָךְ, שָׁאַתָּה הוּא יהוה אֱלֹהֵינוּ וֵאלֹהֵי אֲבוֹתֵינוּ לְעוֹלָם וָעֶד. צוּר חַיֵּינוּ, מָגֵן יִשְׁעֵנוּ אַתָּה הוּא לְדוֹר וָדוֹר. נוֹדֶה לְּךָ וּנְסַפֵּר תְּהִלָּתֶךָ[1] עַל חַיֵּינוּ הַמְּסוּרִים בְּיָדֶךָ, וְעַל נִשְׁמוֹתֵינוּ הַפְּקוּדוֹת לָךְ, וְעַל נִסֶּיךָ שֶׁבְּכָל יוֹם עִמָּנוּ, וְעַל נִפְלְאוֹתֶיךָ וְטוֹבוֹתֶיךָ שֶׁבְּכָל עֵת, עֶרֶב וָבֹקֶר וְצָהֳרָיִם. הַטּוֹב כִּי לֹא כָלוּ רַחֲמֶיךָ, וְהַמְרַחֵם כִּי לֹא תַמּוּ חֲסָדֶיךָ,[2] מֵעוֹלָם קִוִּינוּ לָךְ.

וְעַל כֻּלָּם יִתְבָּרַךְ וְיִתְרוֹמַם שִׁמְךָ מַלְכֵּנוּ תָּמִיד לְעוֹלָם וָעֶד.

Bend the knees at בָּרוּךְ; bow at אַתָּה; straighten up at 'ה.

וְכֹל הַחַיִּים יוֹדוּךָ סֶּלָה, וִיהַלְלוּ אֶת שִׁמְךָ בֶּאֱמֶת, הָאֵל יְשׁוּעָתֵנוּ וְעֶזְרָתֵנוּ סֶלָה. בָּרוּךְ אַתָּה יהוה, הַטּוֹב שִׁמְךָ וּלְךָ נָאֶה לְהוֹדוֹת.

---

bless and help His people; it remains for us to be worthy of His blessings.

בֶּאֱמֶת — *Sincerely*. Human beings are all too prone to self-deception. Someone may *think* he is sincere in his service of God, while he is really acting out of habit or to impress others. 'God — purify us to serve You in *true* sincerity!' (*Yesod V'Shoresh HaAvodah*).

בְּאַהֲבָה וּבְרָצוֹן — *With love and with favor*. This term is uniquely associated with the Sabbath; it is not even recited on Festivals unless they fall on the Sabbath. As the eternal reminder that God is the Creator, the *mitzvah* of the Sabbath shows us that God wants us to remember Him and praise Him. Accordingly, the Sabbath expresses His love for us and ours for Him, because on it we become more conscious that He desires our homage (*R' Hirsch*); and He finds special *favor* in our Temple offerings (*Abudraham*).

מְקַדֵּשׁ יִשְׂרָאֵל וְהַזְּמַנִּים — *Who sanctifies Israel and the festive seasons*. The use of the word

to serve You sincerely. And grant us a heritage, O HASHEM, our God — [with love and with favor*] with gladness and with joy — [the Sabbath and] the appointed festivals of Your holiness, and may Israel, the sanctifiers of Your Name, rejoice in You. Blessed are You, HASHEM, Who sanctifies [the Sabbath,] Israel and the festive seasons.**

TEMPLE SERVICE

רְצֵה *Be favorable, HASHEM, our God, toward Your people Israel and their prayer and restore the service to the Holy of Holies of Your Temple. The fire-offerings of Israel and their prayer accept with love and favor, and may the service of Your people Israel always be favorable to You.*

וְתֶחֱזֶינָה *May our eyes behold Your return to Zion in compassion. Blessed are You, HASHEM, Who restores His Presence to Zion.*

THANKSGIVING [MODIM]

Bow at *'We gratefully thank You'*; straighten up at *'HASHEM.'*

מוֹדִים *We gratefully thank You, for it is You Who are HASHEM, our God and the God of our forefathers for all eternity; Rock of our lives, Shield of our salvation are You from generation to generation. We shall thank You and relate Your praise[1] — for our lives, which are committed to Your power and for our souls that are entrusted to You; for Your miracles that are with us every day; and for Your wonders and favors in every season — evening, morning, and afternoon. The Beneficent One, for Your compassions were never exhausted, and the Compassionate One, for Your kindnesses never ended[2] — always have we put our hope in You.*

For all these, may Your Name be blessed and exalted, our King, continually forever and ever.

Bend the knees at *'Blessed'*; bow at *'You'*; straighten up at *'HASHEM.'*

Everything alive will gratefully acknowledge You, Selah! and praise Your Name sincerely, O God of our salvation and help, Selah! Blessed are You, HASHEM, Your Name is 'The Beneficent One' and to You it is fitting to give thanks.

---

(1) Cf. *Psalms* 79:13. (2) Cf. *Lamentations* 3:22.

זְמַנִּים, *festive seasons,* rather than the Scriptural term מוֹעֲדִים, *appointed Festivals,* alludes to a special feature of the Jewish calendar. The Torah ordains that Pesach must fall in the springtime, thus the court must take the זְמַנִּים, *seasons,* into account in formulating the calendar *(R' Bachya).*

מְקַדֵּשׁ [הַשַּׁבָּת וְ]יִשְׂרָאֵל וְהַזְּמַנִּים — *Who sanctifies [the Sabbath,] Israel and the seasons.* The

שלום

שָׁלוֹם רָב* עַל יִשְׂרָאֵל עַמְּךָ תָּשִׂים לְעוֹלָם, כִּי אַתָּה הוּא מֶלֶךְ אָדוֹן לְכָל הַשָּׁלוֹם. וְטוֹב בְּעֵינֶיךָ לְבָרֵךְ אֶת עַמְּךָ יִשְׂרָאֵל, בְּכָל עֵת וּבְכָל שָׁעָה בִּשְׁלוֹמֶךָ. בָּרוּךְ אַתָּה יהוה, הַמְּבָרֵךְ אֶת עַמּוֹ יִשְׂרָאֵל בַּשָּׁלוֹם.

יִהְיוּ לְרָצוֹן אִמְרֵי פִי וְהֶגְיוֹן לִבִּי לְפָנֶיךָ, יהוה צוּרִי וְגֹאֲלִי.[1]

אֱלֹהַי, נְצוֹר לְשׁוֹנִי מֵרָע, וּשְׂפָתַי מִדַּבֵּר מִרְמָה,[2] וְלִמְקַלְלַי נַפְשִׁי תִדֹּם, וְנַפְשִׁי כֶּעָפָר לַכֹּל תִּהְיֶה. פְּתַח לִבִּי בְּתוֹרָתֶךָ, וּבְמִצְוֹתֶיךָ תִּרְדּוֹף נַפְשִׁי. וְכֹל הַחוֹשְׁבִים עָלַי רָעָה, מְהֵרָה הָפֵר עֲצָתָם וְקַלְקֵל מַחֲשַׁבְתָּם. עֲשֵׂה לְמַעַן שְׁמֶךָ, עֲשֵׂה לְמַעַן יְמִינֶךָ, עֲשֵׂה לְמַעַן קְדֻשָּׁתֶךָ, עֲשֵׂה לְמַעַן תּוֹרָתֶךָ. לְמַעַן יֵחָלְצוּן יְדִידֶיךָ, הוֹשִׁיעָה יְמִינְךָ וַעֲנֵנִי.[3] Some recite verses pertaining to their names here. See p. 1301.

יִהְיוּ לְרָצוֹן אִמְרֵי פִי וְהֶגְיוֹן לִבִּי לְפָנֶיךָ, יהוה צוּרִי וְגֹאֲלִי.[1]

Bow and take three steps back. Bow left and say ... עֹשֶׂה, bow right and say ... הוּא יַעֲשֶׂה; bow forward and say וְעַל כָּל ... אָמֵן.

עֹשֶׂה שָׁלוֹם בִּמְרוֹמָיו, הוּא יַעֲשֶׂה שָׁלוֹם עָלֵינוּ, וְעַל כָּל יִשְׂרָאֵל. וְאִמְרוּ: אָמֵן.

יְהִי רָצוֹן מִלְּפָנֶיךָ יהוה אֱלֹהֵינוּ וֵאלֹהֵי אֲבוֹתֵינוּ, שֶׁיִּבָּנֶה בֵּית הַמִּקְדָּשׁ בִּמְהֵרָה בְיָמֵינוּ, וְתֵן חֶלְקֵנוּ בְּתוֹרָתֶךָ. וְשָׁם נַעֲבָדְךָ בְּיִרְאָה, כִּימֵי עוֹלָם וּכְשָׁנִים קַדְמוֹנִיּוֹת. וְעָרְבָה לַיהוה מִנְחַת יְהוּדָה וִירוּשָׁלָיִם, כִּימֵי עוֹלָם וּכְשָׁנִים קַדְמוֹנִיּוֹת.[4]

SHEMONEH ESREI ENDS HERE.

Remain standing in place for at least a few moments before taking three steps forward.

ON FRIDAY NIGHT, THE SERVICE CONTINUES ON PAGE 62;
ON ALL OTHER NIGHTS, ON PAGE 64.

Kiddush recited on *Yom Tov* closes by blessing God Who *sanctifies the people of Israel and the seasons* — Israel is mentioned before the seasons. But if the *Yom Tov* coincides with a Sabbath, we mention the Sabbath before Israel: *God Who sanctifies the Sabbath and Israel and the seasons.* The seventh day of the week was sanctified at Creation, long before the Jewish nation was created. In the case of the Festivals, however, although the Torah ordains the date on which they are to be celebrated, this date actually depends on the Jewish people — represented by *Beis Din,* the Rabbinic Court — which the Torah assigns to regulate and fix the calendar. We can therefore make mention of the festive seasons only *after* first proclaiming the sanctity of the Jewish people itself *(Beitzah* 17a).

שָׁלוֹם רָב — *Abundant peace.* The last blessing of *Shemoneh Esrei* is a prayer for peace, because R' Shimon ben Chalafta said: The Holy One, Blessed is He, could find no container that

PEACE

שָׁלוֹם *Establish abundant peace* upon Your people Israel forever, for You are King, Master of all peace. May it be good in Your eyes to bless Your people Israel at every time and every hour with Your peace. Blessed are You, HASHEM, Who blesses His people Israel with peace.*

May the expressions of my mouth and the thoughts of my heart find favor before You, HASHEM, my Rock and my Redeemer.[1]

אֱלֹהַי *My God, guard my tongue from evil and my lips from speaking deceitfully.*[2] *To those who curse me, let my soul be silent; and let my soul be like dust to everyone. Open my heart to Your Torah, then my soul will pursue Your commandments. As for all those who design evil against me, speedily nullify their counsel and disrupt their design. Act for Your Name's sake; act for Your right hand's sake; act for Your sanctity's sake; act for Your Torah's sake. That Your beloved ones may be given rest; let Your right hand save, and respond to me.*[3]

Some recite verses pertaining to their names at this point. See page 1301.

May the expressions of my mouth and the thoughts of my heart find favor before You, HASHEM, my Rock and my Redeemer.[1] *He Who makes peace in His heights, may He make peace upon us, and upon all Israel. Now respond: Amen.*

Bow and take three steps back. Bow left and say, *'He Who makes peace . . .'*; bow right and say, *'may He make peace . . .'*; bow forward and say, *'and upon . . . Amen.'*

יְהִי רָצוֹן *May it be Your will, HASHEM, our God and the God of our forefathers, that the Holy Temple be rebuilt, speedily in our days. Grant us our share in Your Torah, and may we serve You there with reverence, as in days of old and in former years. Then the offering of Judah and Jerusalem will be pleasing to HASHEM, as in days of old and in former years.*[4]

SHEMONEH ESREI ENDS HERE.

Remain standing in place for at least a few moments before taking three steps forward.

ON FRIDAY NIGHT, THE SERVICE CONTINUES ON PAGE 62;
ON ALL OTHER NIGHTS, ON PAGE 64.

---

(1) *Psalms* 19:15. (2) Cf. 34:14. (3) 60:7; 108:7. (4) *Malachi* 3:4.

---

holds Israel's blessings as well as peace *(Uktzin* 3:12). Peace is the cement that holds the nation together. When reciting this prayer, one should have in mind the plea that all Jews feel affection for one another. Likewise he should pray that he be freed from the curse of anger, because there can be no peace where there is anger *(Yaaros D'vash)*. Furthermore, after the Morning and Afternoon Temple services, the *Kohanim* would bless the people with *Bircas Kohanim,* which concludes with a blessing for peace. This blessing in *Shemoneh Esrei* contains the word peace four times, alluding to a prayer for each of the Four Exiles *(Etz Yosef)*.

On Friday night, all present stand and recite וַיְכֻלּוּ aloud in unison. Conversation is forbidden until after the אָמֵן response to the blessing מְקַדֵּשׁ הַשַּׁבָּת (below).

וַיְכֻלּוּ* הַשָּׁמַיִם וְהָאָרֶץ וְכָל צְבָאָם. וַיְכַל אֱלֹהִים בַּיּוֹם הַשְּׁבִיעִי מְלַאכְתּוֹ אֲשֶׁר עָשָׂה, וַיִּשְׁבֹּת בַּיּוֹם הַשְּׁבִיעִי מִכָּל מְלַאכְתּוֹ אֲשֶׁר עָשָׂה. וַיְבָרֶךְ אֱלֹהִים אֶת יוֹם הַשְּׁבִיעִי, וַיְקַדֵּשׁ אֹתוֹ, כִּי בוֹ שָׁבַת מִכָּל מְלַאכְתּוֹ, אֲשֶׁר בָּרָא אֱלֹהִים לַעֲשׂוֹת.[1]

ברכה מעין שבע

Chazzan continues:

בָּרוּךְ אַתָּה יהוה אֱלֹהֵינוּ וֵאלֹהֵי אֲבוֹתֵינוּ, אֱלֹהֵי אַבְרָהָם, אֱלֹהֵי יִצְחָק, וֵאלֹהֵי יַעֲקֹב, הָאֵל הַגָּדוֹל הַגִּבּוֹר וְהַנּוֹרָא, אֵל עֶלְיוֹן, קוֹנֵה שָׁמַיִם וָאָרֶץ.

Congregation, then *chazzan:*

מָגֵן אָבוֹת בִּדְבָרוֹ, מְחַיֵּה מֵתִים בְּמַאֲמָרוֹ, הָאֵל הַקָּדוֹשׁ שֶׁאֵין כָּמוֹהוּ, הַמֵּנִיחַ לְעַמּוֹ בְּיוֹם שַׁבַּת קָדְשׁוֹ, כִּי בָם רָצָה לְהָנִיחַ לָהֶם. לְפָנָיו נַעֲבֹד בְּיִרְאָה וָפַחַד, וְנוֹדֶה לִשְׁמוֹ בְּכָל יוֹם תָּמִיד מֵעֵין הַבְּרָכוֹת. אֵל הַהוֹדָאוֹת, אֲדוֹן הַשָּׁלוֹם, מְקַדֵּשׁ הַשַּׁבָּת וּמְבָרֵךְ שְׁבִיעִי, וּמֵנִיחַ בִּקְדֻשָּׁה לְעַם מְדֻשְּׁנֵי עֹנֶג, זֵכֶר לְמַעֲשֵׂה בְרֵאשִׁית.

Chazzan continues:

אֱלֹהֵינוּ וֵאלֹהֵי אֲבוֹתֵינוּ רְצֵה בִמְנוּחָתֵנוּ. קַדְּשֵׁנוּ בְּמִצְוֹתֶיךָ, וְתֵן חֶלְקֵנוּ בְּתוֹרָתֶךָ. שַׂבְּעֵנוּ מִטּוּבֶךָ, וְשַׂמְּחֵנוּ בִּישׁוּעָתֶךָ, וְטַהֵר לִבֵּנוּ לְעָבְדְּךָ בֶּאֱמֶת. וְהַנְחִילֵנוּ יהוה אֱלֹהֵינוּ בְּאַהֲבָה וּבְרָצוֹן שַׁבַּת קָדְשֶׁךָ, וְיָנוּחוּ בָהּ יִשְׂרָאֵל מְקַדְּשֵׁי שְׁמֶךָ. בָּרוּךְ אַתָּה יהוה, מְקַדֵּשׁ הַשַּׁבָּת.* (Cong. — אָמֵן.)

וַיְכֻלּוּ — ... *were finished.* We stand and recite this paragraph aloud because it is a form of testimony that God created heaven and earth — and witnesses must give their testimony while standing and in a loud, clear voice *(Ibn Yarchi).*

Because of this paragraph's status as a testimony, it should preferably be said with the congregation, or at least in the company of one other person. However, it may be recited by an individual as well *(Orach Chaim* 268).

Tur (ibid.) notes that it is especially important not to speak during וַיְכֻלּוּ or during the recitation of the seven-faceted blessing.

בְּרָכָה מֵעֵין שֶׁבַע / The Seven-faceted Blessing

In Talmudic times, the synagogues were generally located outside town limits, in open fields. Since it was dangerous to walk home alone in the dark after *Maariv,* the Sages instituted an extra prayer for the congregation so that everyone would stay a little longer, in case someone was slow in finishing his own *Maariv (Shabbos* 24b). On weekdays, the prayer בָּרוּךְ ה׳ לְעוֹלָם, *Blessed is* HASHEM *forever,* alludes to the number of blessings in the weekday *Shemoneh Esrei.* On the eve of the Sabbath, this extra prayer was formulated as a synopsis of the

On Friday night, all present stand and recite וַיְכֻלּוּ, *'Thus the heavens . . .,'* aloud in unison. Conversation is forbidden until after the *'Amen'* response to the blessing, *'Who sanctifies the Sabbath'* (below).

וַיְכֻלּוּ *Thus the heavens and the earth were finished,* and all their legion. On the seventh day God completed His work which He had done, and He abstained on the seventh day from all His work which He had done. God blessed the seventh day and sanctified it, because on it He had abstained from all His work which God created to make.*[1]

THE SEVEN-FACETED BLESSING

Chazzan continues:

בָּרוּךְ *Blessed are You, HASHEM, our God and the God of our forefathers, God of Abraham, God of Isaac, and God of Jacob; the great, mighty, and awesome God, the supreme God, Creator of heaven and earth.*

Congregation, then *chazzan:*

מָגֵן *He Who was the shield of our forefathers with His word, Who resuscitates the dead with His utterance, the Holy God Who is unequalled, Who grants rest to His people on His holy Sabbath day, for He was pleased with them to grant them rest. Before Him we will serve with awe and dread and give thanks to His Name every day continually with appropriate blessings. God of grateful praise, Master of peace, Who sanctifies the Sabbath and blesses the seventh day, and gives rest with holiness to a people saturated with delight — in memory of the work of Creation.*

Chazzan continues:

אֱלֹהֵינוּ *Our God and the God of our forefathers, may You be pleased with our rest. Sanctify us with Your commandments and grant us our share in Your Torah; satisfy us from Your goodness and gladden us with Your salvation, and purify our heart to serve You sincerely. O HASHEM, our God, with love and favor grant us Your holy Sabbath as a heritage and may Israel, the sanctifiers of Your Name, rest on it. Blessed are You, HASHEM, Who sanctifies the Sabbath.** (Cong.– *Amen.)*

(1) *Genesis* 2:1-3.

---

seven blessings of the *Shemoneh Esrei.* It begins בָּרוּךְ אַתָּה ה׳, which is very similar to the beginning of *Shemoneh Esrei.* Then it continues with מָגֵן אָבוֹת, which has seven parts, as follows:

(1) מָגֵן אָבוֹת, *Shield of our forefathers* = the blessing of אָבוֹת, *forefathers;*

(2) מְחַיֵּה מֵתִים, *Who resuscitates the dead* = the blessing of resuscitation;

(3) הָאֵל הַקָּדוֹשׁ, *The Holy God* = the blessing of His holiness;

(4) הַמֵּנִיחַ לְעַמּוֹ, *Who grants rest to His people* = קְדוּשַּׁת הַיּוֹם, the intermediate blessing, which discusses the Sabbath;

(5) לְפָנָיו נַעֲבוֹד, *Before Him we serve* = רְצֵה, which appeals for acceptance of our service;

(6) וְנוֹדֶה לִשְׁמוֹ, *And give thanks to His Name* = the blessing of מוֹדִים, which thanks God for His many favors;

(7) אֲדוֹן הַשָּׁלוֹם, *Master of peace* = שָׁלוֹם רָב, the last blessing, which speaks of peace.

מְקַדֵּשׁ הַשַּׁבָּת – *Who sanctifies the Sabbath.* When a Festival falls on the Sabbath, this prayer is recited without any mention of the Festival, because the Sages did not compose a separate Seven-faceted Blessing for Festivals.

The *chazzan* recites קַדִּישׁ שָׁלֵם.

יִתְגַּדַּל וְיִתְקַדַּשׁ שְׁמֵהּ רַבָּא. (.Cong – אָמֵן.) בְּעָלְמָא דִּי בְרָא כִרְעוּתֵהּ. וְיַמְלִיךְ מַלְכוּתֵהּ, בְּחַיֵּיכוֹן וּבְיוֹמֵיכוֹן וּבְחַיֵּי דְכָל בֵּית יִשְׂרָאֵל, בַּעֲגָלָא וּבִזְמַן קָרִיב. וְאִמְרוּ: אָמֵן.

(.Cong – אָמֵן. יְהֵא שְׁמֵהּ רַבָּא מְבָרַךְ לְעָלַם וּלְעָלְמֵי עָלְמַיָּא.)

יְהֵא שְׁמֵהּ רַבָּא מְבָרַךְ לְעָלַם וּלְעָלְמֵי עָלְמַיָּא.

יִתְבָּרַךְ וְיִשְׁתַּבַּח וְיִתְפָּאַר וְיִתְרוֹמַם וְיִתְנַשֵּׂא וְיִתְהַדָּר וְיִתְעַלֶּה וְיִתְהַלָּל שְׁמֵהּ דְּקֻדְשָׁא בְּרִיךְ הוּא (.Cong – בְּרִיךְ הוּא) – לְעֵלָּא מִן כָּל בִּרְכָתָא וְשִׁירָתָא תֻּשְׁבְּחָתָא וְנֶחֱמָתָא, דַּאֲמִירָן בְּעָלְמָא. וְאִמְרוּ: אָמֵן. (.Cong – אָמֵן.)

(.Cong – קַבֵּל בְּרַחֲמִים וּבְרָצוֹן אֶת תְּפִלָּתֵנוּ.)

תִּתְקַבֵּל צְלוֹתְהוֹן וּבָעוּתְהוֹן דְּכָל בֵּית יִשְׂרָאֵל קֳדָם אֲבוּהוֹן דִּי בִשְׁמַיָּא. וְאִמְרוּ: אָמֵן. (.Cong – אָמֵן.)

(.Cong – יְהִי שֵׁם יהוה מְבֹרָךְ, מֵעַתָּה וְעַד עוֹלָם.[1])

יְהֵא שְׁלָמָא רַבָּא מִן שְׁמַיָּא, וְחַיִּים עָלֵינוּ וְעַל כָּל יִשְׂרָאֵל. וְאִמְרוּ: אָמֵן. (.Cong – אָמֵן.)

(.Cong – עֶזְרִי מֵעִם יהוה, עֹשֵׂה שָׁמַיִם וָאָרֶץ.[2])

Take three steps back. Bow left and say . . . עֹשֶׂה; bow right and say . . . הוּא; bow forward and say וְעַל כָּל . . . אָמֵן. Remain standing in place for a few moments, then take three steps forward.

עֹשֶׂה שָׁלוֹם בִּמְרוֹמָיו, הוּא יַעֲשֶׂה שָׁלוֹם עָלֵינוּ, וְעַל כָּל יִשְׂרָאֵל. וְאִמְרוּ: אָמֵן. (.Cong – אָמֵן.)

קידוש בבית הכנסת

In some congregations, the *chazzan* recites *Kiddush* [although he will repeat *Kiddush* at home]. *Chazzan's Kiddush* consists of the blessings over wine, the holiness of the day, and *Shehecheyanu*. On Saturday night, two *Havdalah* blessings are inserted.

סַבְרִי מָרָנָן וְרַבָּנָן וְרַבּוֹתַי:

בָּרוּךְ אַתָּה יהוה אֱלֹהֵינוּ מֶלֶךְ הָעוֹלָם, בּוֹרֵא פְּרִי הַגָּפֶן. (.Cong – אָמֵן.)

On Friday night, the words in brackets are included.

בָּרוּךְ אַתָּה יהוה אֱלֹהֵינוּ מֶלֶךְ הָעוֹלָם, אֲשֶׁר בָּחַר בָּנוּ מִכָּל עָם, וְרוֹמְמָנוּ מִכָּל לָשׁוֹן, וְקִדְּשָׁנוּ בְּמִצְוֹתָיו. וַתִּתֶּן לָנוּ יהוה אֱלֹהֵינוּ בְּאַהֲבָה [שַׁבָּתוֹת לִמְנוּחָה וּ]מוֹעֲדִים לְשִׂמְחָה חַגִּים וּזְמַנִּים לְשָׂשׂוֹן, אֶת יוֹם [הַשַּׁבָּת הַזֶּה וְאֶת יוֹם] חַג הַסֻּכּוֹת הַזֶּה, זְמַן שִׂמְחָתֵנוּ [בְּאַהֲבָה] מִקְרָא קֹדֶשׁ, זֵכֶר לִיצִיאַת מִצְרָיִם. כִּי בָנוּ בָחַרְתָּ וְאוֹתָנוּ קִדַּשְׁתָּ מִכָּל הָעַמִּים, [וְשַׁבָּת] וּמוֹעֲדֵי קָדְשֶׁךָ [בְּאַהֲבָה וּבְרָצוֹן] בְּשִׂמְחָה וּבְשָׂשׂוֹן הִנְחַלְתָּנוּ. בָּרוּךְ אַתָּה יהוה, מְקַדֵּשׁ [הַשַּׁבָּת וְ]יִשְׂרָאֵל וְהַזְּמַנִּים. (.Cong – אָמֵן.)

KIDDUSH CONTINUES ON NEXT PAGE.

The *chazzan* recites the Full *Kaddish*.

יִתְגַּדַּל *May His great Name grow exalted and sanctified* (Cong.– *Amen.*) *in the world that He created as He willed. May He give reign to His kingship in your lifetimes and in your days, and in the lifetimes of the entire Family of Israel, swiftly and soon. Now respond: Amen.*

(Cong.– *Amen. May His great Name be blessed forever and ever.*)

May His great Name be blessed forever and ever.

Blessed, praised, glorified, exalted, extolled, mighty, upraised, and lauded be the Name of the Holy One, Blessed is He (Cong.– *Blessed is He*) — *beyond any blessing and song, praise and consolation that are uttered in the world. Now respond: Amen.* (Cong.– *Amen.*)

(Cong.– *Accept our prayers with mercy and favor.*)

May the prayers and supplications of the entire Family of Israel be accepted before their Father Who is in Heaven. Now respond: Amen. (Cong.– *Amen.*)

(Cong.– *Blessed be the Name of* HASHEM, *from this time and forever.*[1])

May there be abundant peace from Heaven, and life, upon us and upon all Israel. Now respond: Amen. (Cong.– *Amen.*)

(Cong.– *My help is from* HASHEM, *Maker of heaven and earth.*[2])

Take three steps back. Bow left and say, *'He Who makes peace . . .'*; bow right and say, *'may He . . .'*; bow forward and say, *'and upon all Israel . . .'* Remain standing in place for a few moments, then take three steps forward.

He Who makes peace in His heights, may He make peace upon us, and upon all Israel. Now respond: Amen. (Cong.– *Amen.*)

KIDDUSH IN THE SYNAGOGUE

In some congregations, the *chazzan* recites *Kiddush* [although he will repeat *Kiddush* at home]. *Chazzan's Kiddush* consists of the blessings over wine,the holiness of the day, and *Shehecheyanu*. On Saturday night, two *Havdalah* blessings are inserted.

By your leave, my masters and teachers:

בָּרוּךְ *Blessed are You,* HASHEM, *our God, King of the universe, Who creates the fruit of the vine.* (Cong.– *Amen.*)

On Friday night, the words in brackets are included.

בָּרוּךְ *Blessed are You,* HASHEM, *our God, King of the universe, Who has chosen us from every people, exalted us above every tongue, and sanctified us with His commandments. And You gave us,* HASHEM, *our God, with love, [Sabbaths for rest], appointed festivals for gladness, festivals and times of joy, [this day of Sabbath and] Succos, the time of our gladness [with love], a holy convocation, a memorial of the Exodus from Egypt. For You have chosen us and You have sanctified us above all the peoples, [and the Sabbath] and Your holy festivals [in love and in favor] in gladness and in joy have You granted us as a heritage. Blessed are You,* HASHEM, *Who sanctifies [the Sabbath and] Israel and the seasons.*

(Cong.– *Amen.*)

KIDDUSH CONTINUES ON NEXT PAGE.

(1) *Psalms* 113:2. (2) 121:2.

◆§ Kiddush in the Synagogue

The custom of reciting *Kiddush* in the synagogue dates back to very early times. It was instituted for the benefit of homeless people or travelers who often ate and slept in the synagogue. They were thus able to discharge their obligation of *Kiddush* by listening to the *chazzan's* recitation. Although the need for this *Kiddush* ceased to exist as even people without homes would be invited home by other congregants, the custom is maintained by

On Saturday night, two candles with flames touching each other are held before the *chazzan*.

בָּרוּךְ אַתָּה יהוה אֱלֹהֵינוּ מֶלֶךְ הָעוֹלָם, בּוֹרֵא מְאוֹרֵי הָאֵשׁ.
(.Cong. – אָמֵן)

The fingers are held up to the flames to see their light reflected on the nails.

בָּרוּךְ אַתָּה יהוה אֱלֹהֵינוּ מֶלֶךְ הָעוֹלָם, הַמַּבְדִּיל בֵּין קֹדֶשׁ לְחוֹל, בֵּין אוֹר לְחֹשֶׁךְ, בֵּין יִשְׂרָאֵל לָעַמִּים, בֵּין יוֹם הַשְּׁבִיעִי לְשֵׁשֶׁת יְמֵי הַמַּעֲשֶׂה. בֵּין קְדֻשַּׁת שַׁבָּת לִקְדֻשַּׁת יוֹם טוֹב הִבְדַּלְתָּ, וְאֶת יוֹם הַשְּׁבִיעִי מִשֵּׁשֶׁת יְמֵי הַמַּעֲשֶׂה קִדַּשְׁתָּ, הִבְדַּלְתָּ וְקִדַּשְׁתָּ אֶת עַמְּךָ יִשְׂרָאֵל בִּקְדֻשָּׁתֶךָ. בָּרוּךְ אַתָּה יהוה, הַמַּבְדִּיל בֵּין קֹדֶשׁ לְקֹדֶשׁ.
(.Cong. – אָמֵן)

The following blessing is recited on both nights:

בָּרוּךְ אַתָּה יהוה אֱלֹהֵינוּ מֶלֶךְ הָעוֹלָם, שֶׁהֶחֱיָנוּ וְקִיְּמָנוּ וְהִגִּיעָנוּ לַזְּמַן הַזֶּה.
(.Cong. – אָמֵן)

A child who listened to the *Kiddush* and responded אָמֵן is given some of the wine. [If no child is present, the *chazzan* drinks the required amount; see commentary below.]

The congregation stands while reciting עָלֵינוּ.

עָלֵינוּ לְשַׁבֵּחַ לַאֲדוֹן הַכֹּל, לָתֵת גְּדֻלָּה לְיוֹצֵר בְּרֵאשִׁית, שֶׁלֹּא עָשָׂנוּ כְּגוֹיֵי הָאֲרָצוֹת, וְלֹא שָׂמָנוּ כְּמִשְׁפְּחוֹת הָאֲדָמָה. שֶׁלֹּא שָׂם חֶלְקֵנוּ כָּהֶם, וְגוֹרָלֵנוּ כְּכָל הֲמוֹנָם. (שֶׁהֵם מִשְׁתַּחֲוִים לְהֶבֶל וָרִיק, וּמִתְפַּלְּלִים אֶל אֵל לֹא יוֹשִׁיעַ.[1]) וַאֲנַחְנוּ כּוֹרְעִים וּמִשְׁתַּחֲוִים וּמוֹדִים, לִפְנֵי מֶלֶךְ מַלְכֵי הַמְּלָכִים הַקָּדוֹשׁ בָּרוּךְ הוּא. שֶׁהוּא נוֹטֶה שָׁמַיִם וְיֹסֵד אָרֶץ,[2] וּמוֹשַׁב יְקָרוֹ בַּשָּׁמַיִם מִמַּעַל, וּשְׁכִינַת עֻזּוֹ בְּגָבְהֵי מְרוֹמִים. הוּא אֱלֹהֵינוּ, אֵין עוֹד. אֱמֶת מַלְכֵּנוּ, אֶפֶס זוּלָתוֹ, כַּכָּתוּב בְּתוֹרָתוֹ: וְיָדַעְתָּ הַיּוֹם וַהֲשֵׁבֹתָ אֶל לְבָבֶךָ, כִּי יהוה הוּא הָאֱלֹהִים בַּשָּׁמַיִם מִמַּעַל וְעַל הָאָרֶץ מִתָּחַת, אֵין עוֹד.[3]

Bow while reciting וַאֲנַחְנוּ כּוֹרְעִים וּמִשְׁתַּחֲוִים.

עַל כֵּן נְקַוֶּה לְּךָ יהוה אֱלֹהֵינוּ לִרְאוֹת מְהֵרָה בְּתִפְאֶרֶת עֻזֶּךָ, לְהַעֲבִיר גִּלּוּלִים מִן הָאָרֶץ, וְהָאֱלִילִים כָּרוֹת יִכָּרֵתוּן, לְתַקֵּן עוֹלָם בְּמַלְכוּת שַׁדַּי. וְכָל בְּנֵי בָשָׂר יִקְרְאוּ בִשְׁמֶךָ, לְהַפְנוֹת אֵלֶיךָ כָּל רִשְׁעֵי אָרֶץ. יַכִּירוּ וְיֵדְעוּ כָּל יוֹשְׁבֵי תֵבֵל, כִּי לְךָ תִּכְרַע כָּל

---

virtually all Ashkenaz synagogues. Since the person reciting this *Kiddush* will be reciting *Kiddush* at home for the benefit of his family — and for himself, as well, since that is where he will have his *Yom Tov* meal — he should have in mind that he will not discharge his own

On Saturday night, two candles with flames touching each other are held before the *chazzan.*

בָּרוּךְ *Blessed are You, HASHEM, our God, King of the universe, Who creates the illumination of the fire.* (Cong. – *Amen.)*

The fingers are held up to the flames to see their light reflected on the nails.

בָּרוּךְ *Blessed are you, HASHEM, our God, King of the universe, Who distinguishes between the sacred and secular, between light and darkness, between Israel and the peoples, between the seventh day and the six days of labor. Between the sanctity of the Sabbath and the sanctity of the holidays You have distinguished; and the seventh day, from among the six days of labor, You have sanctified. You have distinguished and You have sanctified Your people Israel with Your holiness. Blessed are You, HASHEM, Who distinguishes between holiness and holiness.* (Cong. – *Amen.)*

The following blessing is recited on both nights:

בָּרוּךְ *Blessed are You, HASHEM, our God, King of the universe, Who has kept us alive, sustained us, and brought us to this season.* (Cong.– *Amen.)*

A child who listened to the *Kiddush* and responded *Amen* is given some of the wine. [If no child is present, the *chazzan* drinks the required amount; see commentary below.]

The congregation stands while reciting עָלֵינוּ, *'It is our duty . . .'*

עָלֵינוּ *It is our duty to praise the Master of all, to ascribe greatness to the Molder of primeval creation, for He has not made us like the nations of the lands, and has not emplaced us like the families of the earth; for He has not assigned our portion like theirs nor our lot like all their multitudes. (For they bow to vanity and emptiness and pray to a god which helps not.*[1]*) But we bend our knees, bow, and acknowledge our thanks before the King Who reigns over kings, the Holy One, Blessed is He. He stretches out heaven and establishes earth's foundation,*[2] *the seat of His homage is in the heavens above and His powerful Presence is in the loftiest heights. He is our God and there is none other. True is our King, there is nothing beside Him, as it is written in His Torah: 'You are to know this day and take to your heart that HASHEM is the only God — in heaven above and on the earth below — there is none other.'*[3]

Bow while reciting *'But we bend our knees.'*

עַל כֵּן *Therefore we put our hope in You, HASHEM our God, that we may soon see Your mighty splendor, to remove detestable idolatry from the earth, and false gods will be utterly cut off, to perfect the universe through the Almighty's sovereignty. Then all humanity will call upon Your Name, to turn all the earth's wicked toward You. All the world's inhabitants will recognize and know that to You every*

(1) *Isaiah* 45:20. (2) 51:13. (3) *Deuteronomy* 4:39.

obligation in the synagogue. Therefore, he should not drink from the wine, but instead give some to one or more young children who listened to the *Kiddush* and responded אָמֵן.

Some authorities hold that *Kiddush* should not be recited in the synagogue during Succos, for even the homeless (for whom this *Kiddush* is recited) must eat in the *succah* and recite

בָּרֶךְ, תִּשָּׁבַע כָּל לָשׁוֹן.[1] לְפָנֶיךָ יהוה אֱלֹהֵינוּ יִכְרְעוּ וְיִפֹּלוּ, וְלִכְבוֹד שִׁמְךָ יְקָר יִתֵּנוּ. וִיקַבְּלוּ כֻלָּם אֶת עוֹל מַלְכוּתֶךָ, וְתִמְלֹךְ עֲלֵיהֶם מְהֵרָה לְעוֹלָם וָעֶד. כִּי הַמַּלְכוּת שֶׁלְּךָ הִיא וּלְעוֹלְמֵי עַד תִּמְלוֹךְ בְּכָבוֹד, כַּכָּתוּב בְּתוֹרָתֶךָ: יהוה יִמְלֹךְ לְעֹלָם וָעֶד.[2] ❖ וְנֶאֱמַר: וְהָיָה יהוה לְמֶלֶךְ עַל כָּל הָאָרֶץ, בַּיּוֹם הַהוּא יִהְיֶה יהוה אֶחָד וּשְׁמוֹ אֶחָד.[3]

Some recite the following after עָלֵינוּ:

אַל תִּירָא מִפַּחַד פִּתְאֹם, וּמִשֹּׁאַת רְשָׁעִים כִּי תָבֹא.[4] עֻצוּ עֵצָה וְתֻפָר, דַּבְּרוּ דָבָר וְלֹא יָקוּם, כִּי עִמָּנוּ אֵל.[5] וְעַד זִקְנָה אֲנִי הוּא, וְעַד שֵׂיבָה אֲנִי אֶסְבֹּל, אֲנִי עָשִׂיתִי וַאֲנִי אֶשָּׂא, וַאֲנִי אֶסְבֹּל וַאֲמַלֵּט.[6]

קדיש יתום

Mourners recite קַדִּישׁ יָתוֹם (see *Laws* §81-83).

יִתְגַּדַּל וְיִתְקַדַּשׁ שְׁמֵהּ רַבָּא. (Cong. – אָמֵן.) בְּעָלְמָא דִּי בְרָא כִרְעוּתֵהּ. וְיַמְלִיךְ מַלְכוּתֵהּ, בְּחַיֵּיכוֹן וּבְיוֹמֵיכוֹן וּבְחַיֵּי דְכָל בֵּית יִשְׂרָאֵל, בַּעֲגָלָא וּבִזְמַן קָרִיב. וְאִמְרוּ: אָמֵן.

(Cong. – אָמֵן. יְהֵא שְׁמֵהּ רַבָּא מְבָרַךְ לְעָלַם וּלְעָלְמֵי עָלְמַיָּא.)

יְהֵא שְׁמֵהּ רַבָּא מְבָרַךְ לְעָלַם וּלְעָלְמֵי עָלְמַיָּא.

יִתְבָּרַךְ וְיִשְׁתַּבַּח וְיִתְפָּאַר וְיִתְרוֹמַם וְיִתְנַשֵּׂא וְיִתְהַדָּר וְיִתְעַלֶּה וְיִתְהַלָּל שְׁמֵהּ דְּקֻדְשָׁא בְּרִיךְ הוּא (Cong. – בְּרִיךְ הוּא) – לְעֵלָּא מִן כָּל בִּרְכָתָא וְשִׁירָתָא תֻּשְׁבְּחָתָא וְנֶחֱמָתָא, דַּאֲמִירָן בְּעָלְמָא. וְאִמְרוּ: אָמֵן. (Cong. – אָמֵן.)

יְהֵא שְׁלָמָא רַבָּא מִן שְׁמַיָּא, וְחַיִּים עָלֵינוּ וְעַל כָּל יִשְׂרָאֵל. וְאִמְרוּ: אָמֵן. (Cong. – אָמֵן.)

Take three steps back. Bow left and say . . . עֹשֶׂה; bow right and say . . . הוּא; bow forward and say וְעַל כָּל . . . אָמֵן. Remain standing in place for a few moments, then take three steps forward.

עֹשֶׂה שָׁלוֹם בִּמְרוֹמָיו, הוּא יַעֲשֶׂה שָׁלוֹם עָלֵינוּ, וְעַל כָּל יִשְׂרָאֵל. וְאִמְרוּ: אָמֵן. (Cong. – אָמֵן.)

תהלים כז

לְדָוִד, יהוה אוֹרִי* וְיִשְׁעִי, מִמִּי אִירָא, יהוה מָעוֹז חַיַּי, מִמִּי אֶפְחָד. בִּקְרֹב עָלַי מְרֵעִים לֶאֱכֹל אֶת בְּשָׂרִי, צָרַי וְאֹיְבַי לִי, הֵמָּה כָשְׁלוּ וְנָפָלוּ. אִם תַּחֲנֶה עָלַי מַחֲנֶה, לֹא יִירָא לִבִּי, אִם

Kiddush there. *Mateh Efraim* (625:40) and *Mishnah Berurah* (269:5) hold that the *Kiddush* should be recited. However, *Mateh Efraim* adds that a synagogue which does not have an established custom regarding this *Kiddush* should not recite it.

⊰ לְדָוִד ה׳ אוֹרִי / Psalm 27

ה׳ אוֹרִי — *HASHEM is my light.* It is customary to recite this psalm every morning and evening from Rosh Chodesh Elul until Shemini Atzeres. This custom is based on the Midrash that

knee should bend, every tongue should swear.[1] *Before You,* HASHEM, *our God, they will bend every knee and cast themselves down and to the glory of Your Name they will render homage, and they will all accept upon themselves the yoke of Your kingship that You may reign over them soon and eternally. For the kingdom is Yours and You will reign for all eternity in glory as it is written in Your Torah:* HASHEM *shall reign for all eternity.*[2] *And it is said:* HASHEM *will be King over all the world — on that day* HASHEM *will be One and His Name will be One.*[3]

Some recite the following after *Aleinu:*

אַל תִּירָא *Do not fear sudden terror, or the holocaust of the wicked when it comes.*[4] *Plan a conspiracy and it will be annulled; speak your piece and it shall not stand, for God is with us.*[5] *Even till your seniority, I remain unchanged; and even till your ripe old age, I shall endure. I created you and I shall bear you; I shall endure and rescue.*[6]

MOURNER'S KADDISH

Mourners recite the Mourner's *Kaddish* (see *Laws* §81-83).
[A transliteration of this *Kaddish* appears on page 1301.]

יִתְגַּדַּל *May His great Name grow exalted and sanctified* (Cong.– *Amen.*) *in the world that He created as He willed. May He give reign to His kingship in your lifetimes and in your days, and in the lifetimes of the entire Family of Israel, swiftly and soon. Now respond: Amen.*

(Cong.– *Amen. May His great Name be blessed forever and ever.*)

May His great Name be blessed forever and ever.

Blessed, praised, glorified, exalted, extolled, mighty, upraised, and lauded be the Name of the Holy One, Blessed is He (Cong.– *Blessed is He*) *— beyond any blessing and song, praise and consolation that are uttered in the world. Now respond: Amen.* (Cong.– *Amen.*)

May there be abundant peace from Heaven, and life, upon us and upon all Israel. Now respond: Amen. (Cong.– *Amen.*)

Take three steps back. Bow left and say, *'He Who makes peace . . .';* bow right and say, *'may He . . .';* bow forward and say, *'and upon all Israel . . .'* Remain standing in place for a few moments, then take three steps forward.

He Who makes peace in His heights, may He make peace upon us, and upon all Israel. Now respond: Amen. (Cong.– *Amen.*)

Psalm 27

לְדָוִד *Of David;* HASHEM *is my light* and my salvation, whom shall I fear?* HASHEM *is my life's strength, whom shall I dread? When evildoers approach me to devour my flesh, my tormentors and my foes against me — it is they who stumble and fall. Though an army would besiege me, my heart would not fear; though war*

(1) Cf. *Isaiah* 45:23. (2) *Exodus* 15:18. (3) *Zechariah* 14:9. (4) *Proverbs* 3:25. (5) *Isaiah* 8:10. (6) 46:4.

expounds: *HASHEM is my light,* on Rosh Hashanah; *and my salvation,* on Yom Kippur; *He will hide me in His shelter* (below), an allusion to Succos. The implication is that on Rosh Hashanah God helps us see the *light* and repent; on Yom Kippur He provides us *salvation* by forgiving our sins. Once we are forgiven, He shelters us from all foes and dangers, just as He sheltered our ancestors in the Wilderness.

תָּקוּם עָלַי מִלְחָמָה, בְּזֹאת אֲנִי בוֹטֵחַ.* אַחַת שָׁאַלְתִּי מֵאֵת יהוה,* אוֹתָהּ אֲבַקֵּשׁ, שִׁבְתִּי בְּבֵית יהוה כָּל יְמֵי חַיַּי, לַחֲזוֹת בְּנֹעַם יהוה, וּלְבַקֵּר בְּהֵיכָלוֹ. כִּי יִצְפְּנֵנִי בְּסֻכֹּה* בְּיוֹם רָעָה, יַסְתִּירֵנִי בְּסֵתֶר אָהֳלוֹ, בְּצוּר יְרוֹמְמֵנִי. וְעַתָּה יָרוּם רֹאשִׁי עַל אֹיְבַי סְבִיבוֹתַי, וְאֶזְבְּחָה בְאָהֳלוֹ זִבְחֵי תְרוּעָה, אָשִׁירָה וַאֲזַמְּרָה לַיהוה. שְׁמַע יהוה קוֹלִי אֶקְרָא,* וְחָנֵּנִי וַעֲנֵנִי. לְךָ אָמַר לִבִּי בַּקְּשׁוּ פָנָי,* אֶת פָּנֶיךָ יהוה אֲבַקֵּשׁ. אַל תַּסְתֵּר פָּנֶיךָ מִמֶּנִּי, אַל תַּט בְּאַף עַבְדֶּךָ, עֶזְרָתִי הָיִיתָ, אַל תִּטְּשֵׁנִי וְאַל תַּעַזְבֵנִי, אֱלֹהֵי יִשְׁעִי. כִּי אָבִי וְאִמִּי עֲזָבוּנִי,* וַיהוה יַאַסְפֵנִי. הוֹרֵנִי יהוה דַּרְכֶּךָ, וּנְחֵנִי בְּאֹרַח מִישׁוֹר, לְמַעַן שׁוֹרְרָי.* אַל תִּתְּנֵנִי בְּנֶפֶשׁ צָרָי, כִּי קָמוּ בִי עֵדֵי שֶׁקֶר, וִיפֵחַ חָמָס. ❖ לוּלֵא הֶאֱמַנְתִּי* לִרְאוֹת בְּטוּב יהוה בְּאֶרֶץ חַיִּים.* קַוֵּה אֶל יהוה,* חֲזַק וְיַאֲמֵץ לִבֶּךָ,* וְקַוֵּה אֶל יהוה.

Mourners recite קַדִּישׁ יָתוֹם, the Mourner's *Kaddish* (p. 68).

Many congregations recite either אֲדוֹן עוֹלָם or יִגְדַּל, or both, at this point.

אֲדוֹן עוֹלָם* אֲשֶׁר מָלַךְ, בְּטֶרֶם כָּל יְצִיר נִבְרָא.
לְעֵת נַעֲשָׂה בְחֶפְצוֹ כֹּל, אֲזַי מֶלֶךְ שְׁמוֹ נִקְרָא.
וְאַחֲרֵי כִּכְלוֹת הַכֹּל, לְבַדּוֹ יִמְלוֹךְ נוֹרָא.
וְהוּא הָיָה וְהוּא הֹוֶה, וְהוּא יִהְיֶה בְּתִפְאָרָה.
וְהוּא אֶחָד וְאֵין שֵׁנִי, לְהַמְשִׁיל לוֹ לְהַחְבִּירָה.

בְּזֹאת אֲנִי בוֹטֵחַ — *In this I trust.* I trust in the motto expressed in the opening verse, *HASHEM is my light and my salvation, whom shall I fear? (Rashi; Radak).*

According to *Ibn Ezra* and *Sforno,* the reason for this trust is expressed in the following verse: I trust in God because I have always requested only spiritual success, and nothing vain and worthless.

אַחַת שָׁאַלְתִּי מֵאֵת ה׳ — *One thing I asked of HASHEM.* Man's desires always change. Each moment breeds new whims and fresh requests, but I have had only one desire ... and what is more: אוֹתָהּ אֲבַקֵּשׁ, *that shall I* [continue to] *seek,* because this request embodies all of my desires: to serve God and understand His ways *(Malbim).*

בְּסֻכֹּה — *In His shelter.* Without vowel points the spelling of this word would lead us to pronounce it בְּסֻכָּה, *in a shelter;* but it is vowelized בְּסֻכּוֹ, *in His shelter.* David declares: 'Often, when I am in danger, *a shelter* seems to appear as if by chance. I am not misled. I know that God Himself has provided this salvation and that it is *His* shelter' *(R' A. Ch. Feuer).*

שְׁמַע ה׳ קוֹלִי אֶקְרָא — *HASHEM, hear my voice when I call.* Previously David had discussed his wars against human armies. In such battles, he is confident of Divine salvation. Now he turns his attention to the most difficult struggle of all, the struggle against the Evil Inclination *(Otzar Nechmad).*

לְךָ אָמַר לִבִּי בַּקְּשׁוּ פָנָי — *In Your behalf, my heart has said, 'Seek My Presence'* [lit. *My Face].* In expressing the desire to seek God's Presence, my own heart spoke as if it were God's emissary. It is He Who implants in the Jew's heart the noble aspiration that he wishes to dwell in the House of God all his life.

כִּי אָבִי וְאִמִּי עֲזָבוּנִי — *Though my father and mother have forsaken me.* After youth and adolescence, they sent me out on my own *(Sforno).*

לְמַעַן שׁוֹרְרָי — *Because of my watchful foes,* i.e.,

would arise against me, in this I trust. One thing I asked of* H*ASHEM*,* *that shall I seek: That I dwell in the House of* H*ASHEM* *all the days of my life; to behold the sweetness of* H*ASHEM* *and to contemplate in His Sanctuary. Indeed, He will hide me in His Shelter* on the day of evil; He will conceal me in the concealment of His Tent, He will lift me upon a rock. Now my head is raised above my enemies around me, and I will slaughter offerings in His Tent accompanied by joyous song; I will sing and make music to* H*ASHEM*. H*ASHEM*, *hear my voice when I call,* be gracious toward me and answer me. In Your behalf, my heart has said, 'Seek My Presence';* Your Presence,* H*ASHEM*, *do I seek. Conceal not Your Presence from me, repel not Your servant in anger. You have been my Helper, abandon me not, forsake me not, O God of my salvation. Though my father and mother have forsaken me,** H*ASHEM* *will gather me in. Teach me Your way,* H*ASHEM*, *and lead me on the path of integrity, because of my watchful foes.* Deliver me not to the wishes of my tormentors, for there have arisen against me false witnesses who breathe violence.* Chazzan– *Had I not trusted* that I would see the goodness of* H*ASHEM* *in the land of life!* Hope to* H*ASHEM*,* *strengthen yourself and He will give you courage;* and hope to* H*ASHEM*.

Mourners recite קַדִּישׁ יָתוֹם, the Mourner's *Kaddish* (p. 68).

Many congregations recite either אֲדוֹן עוֹלָם, *Master of the universe,* or יִגְדַּל, *Exalted be,* or both.

אֲדוֹן עוֹלָם *Master of the universe,* Who reigned*
before any form was created,
At the time when His will brought all into being —
then as 'King' was His Name proclaimed.
After all has ceased to be,
He, the Awesome One, will reign alone.
It is He Who was, He Who is,
and He Who shall remain, in splendor.
He is One — there is no second
to compare to Him, to declare as His equal.

---

in order to frustrate my enemies who enviously and maliciously seek out my flaws and scrutinize my ways [from שׁוּר, to stare] (*Radak*).

לוּלֵא הֶאֱמַנְתִּי — *Had I not trusted . . .!* The meaning of this exclamation is implied: If not for my faith, such false witnesses would have destroyed me long ago. I never stopped believing, so I ignored them and continued to serve God with devotion (*Rashi; Radak*).

בְּאֶרֶץ חַיִּים — *In the land of life.* A reference to the World to Come (*Berachos* 4a).

קַוֵּה אֶל ה׳ — *Hope to* H*ASHEM*. Because of my boundless faith in God I hope for His aid at all times and pay no heed to my enemies (*Radak*).

חֲזַק וְיַאֲמֵץ לִבֶּךָ — *Strengthen yourself and He will give you courage.* Just as someone trying to purify himself is given assistance (*Yoma* 38b), so too, someone trying to strengthen his faith is helped by God (*Alshich*).

Malbim observes that hoping for God's help is greatly different from hoping for the aid of man. Heartache and disillusionment are the lot of one who is dependent on people. Not so with God. Placing one's hope in Him is exhilarating, and brings renewed strength.

⊛ אֲדוֹן עוֹלָם — *Master of the universe.* This inspiring song of praise is attributed to R' Shlomo ibn Gabirol, one of the greatest early

בְּלִי רֵאשִׁית בְּלִי תַכְלִית, וְלוֹ הָעֹז וְהַמִּשְׂרָה.
וְהוּא אֵלִי וְחַי גֹּאֲלִי, וְצוּר חֶבְלִי בְּעֵת צָרָה.
וְהוּא נִסִּי וּמָנוֹס לִי, מְנָת כּוֹסִי בְּיוֹם אֶקְרָא.
בְּיָדוֹ אַפְקִיד רוּחִי, בְּעֵת אִישַׁן וְאָעִירָה.
וְעִם רוּחִי גְּוִיָּתִי, יהוה לִי וְלֹא אִירָא.

יִגְדַּל אֱלֹהִים חַי* וְיִשְׁתַּבַּח, נִמְצָא וְאֵין עֵת אֶל מְצִיאוּתוֹ.*
אֶחָד וְאֵין יָחִיד כְּיִחוּדוֹ, נֶעְלָם וְגַם אֵין סוֹף לְאַחְדוּתוֹ.
אֵין לוֹ דְּמוּת הַגּוּף וְאֵינוֹ גוּף,* לֹא נַעֲרוֹךְ אֵלָיו קְדֻשָּׁתוֹ.
קַדְמוֹן לְכָל דָּבָר אֲשֶׁר נִבְרָא, רִאשׁוֹן וְאֵין רֵאשִׁית לְרֵאשִׁיתוֹ.
הִנּוֹ אֲדוֹן עוֹלָם* לְכָל נוֹצָר, יוֹרֶה גְדֻלָּתוֹ וּמַלְכוּתוֹ.
שֶׁפַע נְבוּאָתוֹ* נְתָנוֹ, אֶל אַנְשֵׁי סְגֻלָּתוֹ וְתִפְאַרְתּוֹ.
לֹא קָם בְּיִשְׂרָאֵל כְּמֹשֶׁה* עוֹד, נָבִיא וּמַבִּיט אֶת תְּמוּנָתוֹ.
תּוֹרַת אֱמֶת* נָתַן לְעַמּוֹ אֵל, עַל יַד נְבִיאוֹ נֶאֱמַן בֵּיתוֹ.
לֹא יַחֲלִיף הָאֵל וְלֹא יָמִיר דָּתוֹ, לְעוֹלָמִים לְזוּלָתוֹ.
צוֹפֶה וְיוֹדֵעַ סְתָרֵינוּ, מַבִּיט לְסוֹף דָּבָר בְּקַדְמָתוֹ.
גּוֹמֵל לְאִישׁ חֶסֶד כְּמִפְעָלוֹ, נוֹתֵן לְרָשָׁע רָע כְּרִשְׁעָתוֹ.
יִשְׁלַח לְקֵץ הַיָּמִין מְשִׁיחֵנוּ, לִפְדּוֹת מְחַכֵּי קֵץ יְשׁוּעָתוֹ.
מֵתִים יְחַיֶּה אֵל בְּרֹב חַסְדּוֹ, בָּרוּךְ עֲדֵי עַד שֵׁם תְּהִלָּתוֹ.

---

paytanim [liturgical poets], who flourished in the eleventh century. The daily prayer service is inaugurated with the Name אָדוֹן to recall the merit of Abraham, the first one to address God with this title [*Genesis* 15:2] *(Etz Yosef)*, and the one who instituted the morning prayers [*Berachos* 26b] *(Vilna Gaon)*.

The song emphasizes that God is timeless, infinite and omnipotent. Mankind can offer Him only one thing: to proclaim Him as King, by doing His will and praising Him. Despite God's greatness, however, He involves Himself with man's personal needs in time of pain and distress. The prayer concludes on the inspiring note that, lofty though He is, *HASHEM is with me, I shall not fear.*

יִגְדַּל אֱלֹהִים חַי — *Exalted be the Living God.* This song of uncertain authorship summarizes the 'Thirteen Principles of Faith' expounded by *Rambam* [Maimonides] in his *Commentary to Mishnah, Sanhedrin,* ch. 10, and stated succinctly in the famous *Ani Maamin* prayer. They comprise the basic principles that every Jew is required to believe. In *Rambam's* view, to deny any of them constitutes heresy.

וְאֵין עֵת אֶל מְצִיאוּתוֹ — *Unbounded by time is His existence.* If God's existence were timebound, it would be no different in kind from that of any living, but not eternal, being. *Rambam* comments that the principle of God's timelessness, with neither beginning nor end, implies that He cannot be dependent in any way on any other being: the timebound is inherently inferior to the timeless. Nothing can exist without God, but He depends on no one and on nothing.

וְאֵינוֹ גוּף — *Nor is He corporeal.* God has no physicality, not even that of invisible, intangible angels.

הִנּוֹ אֲדוֹן עוֹלָם — *Behold! He is Master of the universe.* Because He is absolute Master, there is nothing else to which prayers may be directed.

שֶׁפַע נְבוּאָתוֹ — *His flow of prophecy.* Judaism depends on the principle that God, through His prophets, revealed His will to Israel.

כְּמֹשֶׁה — *Like Moses.* It is necessary to acknowledge that Moses' prophecy is unparalleled; otherwise another 'prophet' could conceiv-

Without beginning, without conclusion —
His is the power and dominion.
He is my God, my living Redeemer,
Rock of my pain in time of distress.
He is my banner, a refuge for me,
the portion in my cup on the day I call.
Into His hand I shall entrust my spirit
when I go to sleep — and I shall awaken!
With my spirit shall my body remain.
HASHEM is with me, I shall not fear.

יִגְדַּל *Exalted be the Living God* and praised,*
*He exists — unbounded by time is His existence.**
He is One — and there is no unity like His Oneness.
Inscrutable and infinite is His Oneness.
*He has no semblance of a body nor is He corporeal;**
nor has His holiness any comparison.
He preceded every being that was created —
the First, and nothing precedes His precedence.
Behold! He is Master of the universe to every creature,*
He demonstrates His greatness and His sovereignty.
*He granted His flow of prophecy**
to His treasured splendrous people.
In Israel none like Moses arose again —*
a prophet who perceived His vision clearly.
*God gave His people a Torah of truth,**
by means of His prophet, the most trusted of His household.
God will never amend nor exchange His law
for any other one, for all eternity.
He scrutinizes and knows our hiddenmost secrets;
He perceives a matter's outcome at its inception.
He recompenses man with kindness according to his deed;
He places evil on the wicked according to his wickedness.
By the End of Days He will send our Messiah,
to redeem those longing for His final salvation.
God will revive the dead in His abundant kindness —
Blessed forever is His praised Name.

---

ably challenge or amend it, thus challenging the authenticity of the Torah.

תּוֹרַת אֱמֶת — *A Torah of truth.* God gave Moses not only the Written Law, but the Oral Law as well. Neither can be complete without the other, and *Torah of truth* is a term that includes both.

אושפיזין

Upon entering the *succah* we invite the *Ushpizin*-guests [see commentary] to join us, and we offer prayers that our fulfillment of the *mitzvah* of *succah* be found worthy of Divine favor. Customs vary regarding these prayers. Some recite the full text, others omit various paragraphs. [The first paragraph is said only by those who follow the *Sefirah* order of the *Ushpizin*-guests (see below).]

עוּלוּ אוּשְׁפִּיזִין עִלָּאִין קַדִּישִׁין, עוּלוּ אֲבָהָן עִלָּאִין קַדִּישִׁין, לְמֵיתַב בְּצִלָּא דִמְהֵימְנוּתָא עִלָּאָה בְּצִלָּא דְקֻדְשָׁא בְּרִיךְ הוּא. לֵעוּל אַבְרָהָם רְחִימָא, וְעִמֵּיהּ יִצְחָק עֲקִידְתָּא, וְעִמֵּיהּ יַעֲקֹב שְׁלִמְתָּא, וְעִמֵּיהּ מֹשֶׁה רַעְיָא מְהֵימְנָא, וְעִמֵּיהּ אַהֲרֹן כַּהֲנָא קַדִּישָׁא, וְעִמֵּיהּ יוֹסֵף צַדִּיקָא, וְעִמֵּיהּ דָּוִד מַלְכָּא מְשִׁיחָא. בַּסֻּכּוֹת תֵּשְׁבוּ, תִּיבוּ אוּשְׁפִּיזִין עִלָּאִין תִּיבוּ, תִּיבוּ אוּשְׁפִּיזֵי מְהֵימְנוּתָא תִּיבוּ.

הֲרֵינִי מוּכָן וּמְזֻמָּן לְקַיֵּם מִצְוַת סֻכָּה כַּאֲשֶׁר צִוַּנִי הַבּוֹרֵא יִתְבָּרַךְ שְׁמוֹ: בַּסֻּכֹּת תֵּשְׁבוּ שִׁבְעַת יָמִים, כָּל הָאֶזְרָח בְּיִשְׂרָאֵל יֵשְׁבוּ בַּסֻּכֹּת. לְמַעַן יֵדְעוּ* דֹרֹתֵיכֶם, כִּי בַסֻּכּוֹת הוֹשַׁבְתִּי אֶת בְּנֵי יִשְׂרָאֵל, בְּהוֹצִיאִי אוֹתָם מֵאֶרֶץ מִצְרָיִם.[1]

תִּיבוּ תִּיבוּ אוּשְׁפִּיזִין עִילָּאִין, תִּיבוּ תִּיבוּ אוּשְׁפִּיזִין קַדִּישִׁין, תִּיבוּ תִּיבוּ אוּשְׁפִּיזִין דִּמְהֵימְנוּתָא, תִּיבוּ בְּצִלָּא דְקֻדְשָׁא בְּרִיךְ הוּא. זַכָּאָה חוּלְקָנָא, וְזַכָּאָה חוּלְקֵיהוֹן דְּיִשְׂרָאֵל, דִּכְתִיב: כִּי חֵלֶק יהוה עַמּוֹ, יַעֲקֹב חֶבֶל נַחֲלָתוֹ.*[2] לְשֵׁם יִחוּד* קֻדְשָׁא בְּרִיךְ הוּא וּשְׁכִינְתֵּהּ, לְיַחֲדָא שֵׁם י״ה בְּו״ה בְּיִחוּדָא שְׁלִים עַל יְדֵי הַהוּא טָמִיר וְנֶעְלָם, בְּשֵׁם כָּל יִשְׂרָאֵל.

וִיהִי נֹעַם אֲדֹנָי אֱלֹהֵינוּ עָלֵינוּ, וּמַעֲשֵׂה יָדֵינוּ כּוֹנְנָה עָלֵינוּ,* וּמַעֲשֵׂה יָדֵינוּ כּוֹנְנֵהוּ.[3]

אוּשְׁפִּיזִין/USHPIZIN

It is customary to invite and welcome seven exalted אוּשְׁפִּיזִין *[Ushpizin], guests*, to join us when we enter the *succah*. No ordinary guests, the *Ushpizin* are Abraham, Isaac, Jacob, Moses, Aaron, Joseph and David. Each day of Succos another of these guests leads the others into the *succah*.

This custom is based on a passage of *Zohar:* When a man sits in the *succah*, 'the shade of faithfulness' [צִלָּא דִמְהֵימְנוּתָא], the *Shechinah* spreads Its wings over him from above and ... Abraham, five other righteous ones, and King David make their dwelling with him ... Thus, a person should rejoice with shining countenance each and every day [of the festival] together with these guests who take lodging with him ... Upon entering the *succah*, Rav Hamnuna Sava would rejoice and, standing inside the doorway, say, 'Let us invite the guests and prepare the table.' Then he would remain on his feet and bless [them], saying '*In succos you shall dwell.* Be seated, exalted guests, be seated; be seated guests of faithfulness, be seated.' He would then raise his hands in joy and say, 'Worthy is our portion, worthy is the portion of Israel, as it is written (*Deuteronomy* 32:9): *For HASHEM's portion is His people.*' Then he would sit down (*Zohar, Emor* 103b).

However, the blessings to be gained by inviting the exalted *Ushpizin* to join us must be activated by our own conduct, by the acts of kindness and charity that we ourselves perform.

Indeed, the passage cited above goes on to say that the portions of food one would normally serve the honored *Ushpizin* should be distributed among the poor, preferably as guests in one's own *succah*. Moreover, "if one scrupulously serves and gladdens his guests, then God Himself rejoices with him. Abraham blesses the host, '*You shall be granted delight with HASHEM*' (*Isaiah* 58:14); Isaac proclaims, '*Mighty in the land will his offspring be*' (*Psalms* 112:2); Jacob says, '*Then shall your light burst forth just like the dawn*' (*Isaiah* 58:8); the other righteous ones [Moses, Aaron and Joseph] say, '*HASHEM will forever lead you, and He will satisfy you*' (ibid. 58:11); King David proclaims, '*Any weapons that are honed against you shall not succeed*' (ibid. 54:17) ... Praises to the portion of the person worthy of all this; praises to the portions

USHPIZIN

Upon entering the *succah* we invite the *Ushpizin*-guests [see commentary] to join us, and we offer prayers that our fulfillment of the *mitzvah* of *succah* be found worthy of Divine favor. Customs vary regarding these prayers. Some recite the full text, others omit various paragraphs. [The first paragraph is said only by those who follow the *Sefirah* order of the *Ushpizin*-guests (see below).]

עוּלוּ *Enter, exalted holy guests, enter, exalted holy Patriarchs, to be seated in the shade of exalted faithfulness in the shade of the Holy One, Blessed is He. Enter, Abraham the beloved one, Moses the faithful shepherd, Aaron the holy Kohen, Joseph the righteous one, and David the anointed king. In succos you shall dwell, be seated, exalted guests, be seated; be seated, guests of faithfulness, be seated.*

הֲרֵינִי *Behold, I am prepared and ready to perform the commandment of succah as the Creator, Blessed is His Name, commanded me: In succos shall you dwell for seven days; every citizen in Israel shall dwell in succos; in order that your generations may know* that I caused the Children of Israel to dwell in succos when I brought them forth from the land of Egypt.*[1]

Be seated, be seated, exalted guests; be seated, be seated, holy guests; be seated, be seated, guests of faithfulness; be seated in the shade of the Holy One, Blessed is He. Worthy is our portion, worthy is the portion of Israel, as it is written: For HASHEM*'s portion is His people, Jacob the lot of His heritage.**[2] *For the sake of the unification* of the Holy One, Blessed is He, and His Presence, to unify the Name Yud-Kei with Vav-Kei in perfect unity through Him Who is hidden and inscrutable — [I pray] in the name of all Israel.*

May the pleasantness of my Lord, our God, be upon us — may He establish our handiwork for us; our handiwork may He establish.*[3]

(1) *Leviticus* 23:42-43. (2) *Deuteronomy* 32:9. (3) *Psalms* 90:17.

---

of the righteous in this world and in the World to Come. About them it is written, '*Regarding your nation — all of them are righteous*' " (ibid. 60:21; *Zohar, Emor* 104a).

Customs regarding the invitation and the associated prayers differ. Some recite the full text presented above, others include some paragraphs and omit others. Additionally, some repeat the invitations and prayers before each meal, while others recite them only once each day. A third difference, regarding the order of the *Ushpizin*, is discussed below.

בַּסֻּכֹּת תֵּשְׁבוּ . . . לְמַעַן יֵדְעוּ — *In succos shall you dwell . . . in order that your generations may know . . .* The Torah specifies that the *mitzvah* of *succah* is to serve as a reminder '*that I caused the Children of Israel to dwell in succos when I brought them forth from the land of Egypt.*' Unlike the overwhelming majority of *mitzvos*, knowledge of this reason is necessary to the proper fulfillment of the *mitzvah* of *succah* — 'in order that your generations may know.' Two other *mitzvos* in which the reason for the *mitzvah* is an integral part of its fulfillment are *tzitzis* and *tefillin*. Due to this unusual relationship between performance and understanding, the author of the halachic code *Tur* — in addition to listing the halachic requirements — departs from his usual style of simply describing the form of the *mitzvah* and adds an interpretation of the verses along with the proper כַּוָּנוֹת, *intentions*, upon which one should concentrate while performing these three *mitzvos* (*Bach* 625). Thus, upon entering the *succah* we declare the reason for our doing so.

תִּיבוּ . . . נַחֲלָתוֹ — *Be seated . . . His heritage.* This passage is almost a direct quote from the words of Rav Hamnuna cited by *Zohar* [see above, prefatory note to *Ushpizin*].

לְשֵׁם יִחוּד — *For the sake of the unification.* This kabbalistic formulation, similar to that customarily recited before many *mitzvos*, is discussed on page 131.

וּמַעֲשֵׂה יָדֵינוּ כּוֹנְנָה עָלֵינוּ — *May He establish our handiwork for us* [lit. *upon us*]. In any material

יְהִי רָצוֹן מִלְּפָנֶיךָ, יהוה אֱלֹהַי וֵאלֹהֵי אֲבוֹתַי, שֶׁתַּשְׁרֶה שְׁכִינָתְךָ בֵּינֵינוּ, וְתִפְרוֹשׂ עָלֵינוּ סֻכַּת שְׁלוֹמֶךָ – בִּזְכוּת מִצְוַת סֻכָּה שֶׁאָנוּ מְקַיְּמִין* – לְיַחֲדָא שְׁמָא דְקֻדְשָׁא בְּרִיךְ הוּא וּשְׁכִינְתֵּהּ, בִּדְחִילוּ וּרְחִימוּ, לְיַחֲדָא שֵׁם י״ה בְּו״ה בְּיִחוּדָא שְׁלִים, בְּשֵׁם כָּל יִשְׂרָאֵל, וּלְהַקִּיף אוֹתָנוּ מִזִּיו כְּבוֹדְךָ הַקָּדוֹשׁ וְהַטָּהוֹר, נָטוּי עַל רָאשֵׁינוּ מִלְמַעְלָה כְּנֶשֶׁר יָעִיר קִנּוֹ;[1]* וּמִשָּׁם יֻשְׁפַּע שֶׁפַע הַחַיִּים לְעַבְדְּךָ (Hebrew name) בֶּן (mother's Hebrew name) אֲמָתֶךָ.* וּבִזְכוּת צֵאתִי מִבֵּיתִי הַחוּצָה – וְדֶרֶךְ מִצְוֹתֶיךָ אָרוּצָה[2] – יֵחָשֵׁב לִי בְּזֹאת כְּאִלּוּ הִרְחַקְתִּי נְדוֹד.[3] וְהֶרֶב כַּבְּסֵנִי מֵעֲוֹנִי, וּמֵחַטָּאתִי טַהֲרֵנִי.[4]* וּמֵאוּשְׁפִּיזִין עִילָּאִין, אוּשְׁפִּיזִין דִּמְהֵימְנוּתָא, תִּהְיֶינָה אָזְנֶיךָ קַשֻּׁבוֹת רַב בְּרָכוֹת. (וְלָרְעֵבִים גַּם צְמֵאִים תֵּן לַחְמָם וּמֵימָם הַנֶּאֱמָנִים.) וְתִתֵּן לִי זְכוּת לָשֶׁבֶת וְלַחֲסוֹת בְּסֵתֶר צֵל כְּנָפֶיךָ – בְּעֵת פְּטִירָתִי מִן הָעוֹלָם – וְלַחֲסוֹת מִזֶּרֶם וּמִמָּטָר,*[5] כִּי תַמְטִיר עַל רְשָׁעִים פַּחִים.[6] וּתְהֵא חֲשׁוּבָה מִצְוַת סֻכָּה זוּ שֶׁאֲנִי מְקַיֵּם כְּאִלּוּ קִיַּמְתִּיהָ בְּכָל פְּרָטֶיהָ וְדִקְדּוּקֶיהָ וּתְנָאֶיהָ וְכָל מִצְוֹת הַתְּלוּיִם בָּהּ. וְתֵיטִיב לָנוּ הַחֲתִימָה.* וּתְזַכֵּנוּ לֵישֵׁב יָמִים רַבִּים עַל הָאֲדָמָה, אַדְמַת קֹדֶשׁ, בַּעֲבוֹדָתְךָ וּבְיִרְאָתֶךָ. בָּרוּךְ יהוה לְעוֹלָם, אָמֵן וְאָמֵן.[7]

---

activity, a craftsman shapes his creation, but remains dependent on it, in a sense. For example, architects and builders can erect a structure, but it rests on the earth, not on them, and *they* must depend on *it* for shelter. In the spiritual world, the opposite is true. One's performance of a *mitzvah* has as much spiritual content as he puts into it. We pray now that our deeds be worthy of God's pleasure and that He 'establish' them *upon us,* i.e., on the basis of our own spiritual handiwork *(Malbim).*

וְתִפְרוֹשׂ עָלֵינוּ סֻכַּת שְׁלוֹמֶךָ – בִּזְכוּת מִצְוַת סֻכָּה שֶׁאָנוּ מְקַיְּמִין – *That You spread over us the succah of Your peace — in the merit of the mitzvah of succah that we are fulfilling.* In His dealings with mankind, God treats every person מִדָּה כְּנֶגֶד מִדָּה, *measure for measure (Sotah* 8b). This attribute may be understood in light of R' Yisrael *Baal Shem Tov's* explanation of the verse, ה׳ צִלְּךָ, *HASHEM is your shade*, i.e., shelter *(Psalms* 121:5). The words ה׳ צִלְּךָ may also be translated *HASHEM is your shadow.* When you jump, your shadow jumps; when you stand still, you shadow does too. And when you perform a *mitzvah,* then God — as your shadow — also performs that *mitzvah* (cited in *Kedushas Levi, Exodus* 15:1). Having performed the *mitzvah* of erecting and dwelling in the *succah,* we ask that God spread over us His *succah* of peace.

כְּנֶשֶׁר יָעִיר קִנּוֹ – *Like an eagle arousing its brood* [lit., *its nest*]. This phrase is taken from *Deuteronomy* 32:11. *Rashi* there explains that the eagle takes pity on its young. If, upon returning to its nest, the parent bird finds the eaglets asleep, it will first flit from branch to branch, beating its wings and shaking the foliage until the gentle sounds awaken the young ones so that they do not become startled when their parent enters the nest.

In like manner, we pray that God spread the aura of His honor over our heads — not in a way that will overwhelm us with the sudden manifestation of His full splendor and glory, but with a merciful gradual approach that enables us to bear His honor.

לְעַבְדְּךָ (. . .) בֶּן (. . .) אֲמָתֶךָ – *Your servant (...) son of (...) Your handmaid.* One who prays for a person's welfare — whether himself or someone else *(Sefer Chassidim* 237) — should mention the person's name and that of his mother *(Shabbos* 66b as explained by *Rashi).*

וּבִזְכוּת צֵאתִי מִבֵּיתִי ... כְּאִלּוּ הִרְחַקְתִּי נְדוֹד ... וּמֵחַטָּאתִי טַהֲרֵנִי – *And in the merit of my leaving my house . . . as if I have wandered afar . . . and from my sin purify me.* On Rosh Hashanah God sits in judgment over all of creation and on Yom Kippur the verdict is sealed. But perhaps Israel was not found worthy and was fated to exile! — In return for the Jewish 'exile' of leaving their homes and dwelling in the *succah,* God considers it as if they had been exiled all the way to Babylon *(Pesikta deRav Kahana* 29).

וְלַחֲסוֹת מִזֶּרֶם וּמִמָּטָר . . . – *To take refuge from the stream [of fire] and the [fiery] rain . . .* The prophet *(Isaiah* 4:6) describes the protective cloud which will be spread over the righteous in Messianic times: *It will be a succah . . . to give refuge . . . from the stream and the rain. Stream* refers to a stream of fire *(Daniel* 7:10) that will engulf the wicked (see *Jeremiah* 23:19). *Rain* refers to fiery coals that will rain upon them (see

יְהִי רָצוֹן *May it be Your will,* HASHEM, *my God and the God of my forefathers, that You cause Your Presence to reside among us; that You spread over us the succah of Your peace — in the merit of the mitzvah of succah that we are fulfilling* — to unify the Name of the Holy One, Blessed is He, and His Presence, in fear and love, to unify the Name Yud-Kei with Vav-Kei in perfect unity, in the name of all Israel; and to surround us with the aura of Your honor, holy and pure, spread over our heads from above like an eagle arousing its brood;*[1] and from there cause an abundant outpouring of life for Your servant* (Hebrew name) *son of* (mother's Hebrew name) *Your handmaid.* And in the merit of my leaving my house to go out — and I will enthusiastically pursue the path of Your commandments[2] — may this be reckoned for me as if I have wandered afar.[3] Cleanse me thoroughly from my iniquity, and from my sin purify me.*[4] From the exalted guests, the guests of faithfulness, may Your ears hear abundant blessings. (To the hungry and thirsty, may You give their food and their unfailing supply of water.) May You endow me with the privilege to dwell and take refuge in the sheltering protection of Your wings — at the time of my departure from the world — to take refuge from the stream [of fire] and the [fiery] rain,*[5] when You rain coals upon the wicked.[6] May this mitzvah of succah that I perform be reckoned as if I had fulfilled it in all its details, implications and specifications, as well as all the mitzvos dependent on it. May You seal [the Book of Life] for our benefit,* and allow us the opportunity to dwell many days upon the land, the Holy Land, in Your service and in Your reverence. Blessed is* HASHEM *forever, Amen and Amen.[7]*

(1) *Deuteronomy* 32:11. (2) Cf. *Psalms* 119:32. (3) Cf. 55:8. (4) 51:4. (5) Cf. *Isaiah* 4:6. (6) Cf. *Psalms* 11:6. (7) 89:53.

Psalms 11:6) in retribution for their evil (*Rashi*). In the merit of sitting in the *succah* today, may we, in time to come, be found worthy of dwelling under the protective cloud-*succah*.

וְתֵיטִיב לָנוּ הַחֲתִימָה – *May You seal [the Book of Life] for our benefit [*lit., *may You make beneficial for us the seal].* Succos in general and its seventh day, Hoshana Rabbah, in particular, are periods of judgment in two ways: one specific and the other general. During the ten Days of Awe overall decisions have been made for humanity as a whole and for each individual in particular. Later God determines what will be done with regard to *particular* needs. On Pesach He judges man with regard to the grain crops, on Shavuos with regard to fruit crops, and on Succos with regard to the water supply [the climactic day of the water judgment coming on Hoshana Rabbah] (ibid. 16a).

But Hoshana Rabbah has a significance broader than the universal need for water. *Zohar* (*Tzav* 31b) describes it as a judgment day akin to Yom Kippur itself. On this day the judgment of Yom Kippur is sealed finally, and 'the parchments containing the decrees are given to angels to deliver.' On Rosh Hashanah all people were judged. The righteous were given a favorable judgment, those found wanting — but not totally evil — were given until Yom Kippur to repent. If they failed to do so, the verdict against them was written and sealed, but is not delivered until Hoshana Rabbah, when Jews assemble in prayer, dedication and supplication. The joy of Succos reaches its climax not in dissolute behavior, but in devotion. Then, God in His mercy finds ample reason to tear up the parchment bearing harsh sentences, as it were, and replace them with brighter tidings.

Thus for as long as we sit in the *succah* we still pray to be sealed in the Book of Life for goodness.

◆§ The Order of the Ushpizin

Days	Sefirah-emanations	Ushpizin
1st	חֶסֶד, *Lovingkindness*	Abraham
2nd	גְּבוּרָה, *Power*	Isaac
3rd	תִּפְאֶרֶת, *Splendor*	Jacob
4th	נֶצַח, *Eternality*	Moses
5th	הוֹד, *Glory*	Aaron
6th	יְסוֹד, *Foundation*	Joseph
7th	מַלְכוּת, *Kingship*	David

רִבּוֹן כָּל הָעוֹלָמִים, יְהִי רָצוֹן מִלְּפָנֶיךָ שֶׁיְּהֵא חָשׁוּב לְפָנֶיךָ מִצְוַת יְשִׁיבַת סֻכָּה זוּ, כְּאִילוּ קִיַּמְתִּיהָ בְּכָל פְּרָטֶיהָ וְדִקְדּוּקֶיהָ וְתַרְיַ״ג מִצְוֹת הַתְּלוּיִם בָּהּ, וּכְאִילוּ כִּוַּנְתִּי בְּכָל הַכַּוָּנוֹת שֶׁכִּוְּנוּ בָהּ אַנְשֵׁי כְנֶסֶת הַגְּדוֹלָה.

There are two traditions regarding the order of the *Ushpizin* (see commentary).

SEFIRAH ORDER

Each day — אֲזַמֵּן לִסְעֻדָּתִי אֻשְׁפִּיזִין עִלָּאִין: אַבְרָהָם יִצְחָק יַעֲקֹב מֹשֶׁה אַהֲרֹן יוֹסֵף וְדָוִד.

On the first day — בְּמָטוּ מִנָּךְ אַבְרָהָם אֻשְׁפִּיזִי עִלָּאִי, דְּיֵתְבוּ עִמִּי וְעִמָּךְ כָּל אֻשְׁפִּיזֵי עִלָּאֵי, יִצְחָק יַעֲקֹב מֹשֶׁה אַהֲרֹן יוֹסֵף וְדָוִד.

On the second day — בְּמָטוּ מִנָּךְ יִצְחָק אֻשְׁפִּיזִי עִלָּאִי, דְּיֵתְבוּ עִמִּי וְעִמָּךְ כָּל אֻשְׁפִּיזֵי עִלָּאֵי, אַבְרָהָם יַעֲקֹב מֹשֶׁה אַהֲרֹן יוֹסֵף וְדָוִד.

On the third day — בְּמָטוּ מִנָּךְ יַעֲקֹב אֻשְׁפִּיזִי עִלָּאִי, דְּיֵתְבוּ עִמִּי וְעִמָּךְ כָּל אֻשְׁפִּיזֵי עִלָּאֵי, אַבְרָהָם יִצְחָק מֹשֶׁה אַהֲרֹן יוֹסֵף וְדָוִד.

On the fourth day — בְּמָטוּ מִנָּךְ מֹשֶׁה אֻשְׁפִּיזִי עִלָּאִי, דְּיֵתְבוּ עִמִּי וְעִמָּךְ כָּל אֻשְׁפִּיזֵי עִלָּאֵי, אַבְרָהָם יִצְחָק יַעֲקֹב אַהֲרֹן יוֹסֵף וְדָוִד.

On the fifth day — בְּמָטוּ מִנָּךְ אַהֲרֹן אֻשְׁפִּיזִי עִלָּאִי, דְּיֵתְבוּ עִמִּי וְעִמָּךְ כָּל אֻשְׁפִּיזֵי עִלָּאֵי, אַבְרָהָם יִצְחָק יַעֲקֹב מֹשֶׁה יוֹסֵף וְדָוִד.

On the sixth day — בְּמָטוּ מִנָּךְ יוֹסֵף אֻשְׁפִּיזִי עִלָּאִי, דְּיֵתְבוּ עִמִּי וְעִמָּךְ כָּל אֻשְׁפִּיזֵי עִלָּאֵי, אַבְרָהָם יִצְחָק יַעֲקֹב מֹשֶׁה אַהֲרֹן וְדָוִד.

On Hoshana Rabbah — בְּמָטוּ מִנָּךְ דָּוִד אֻשְׁפִּיזִי עִלָּאִי, דְּיֵתְבוּ עִמִּי וְעִמָּךְ כָּל אֻשְׁפִּיזֵי עִלָּאֵי, אַבְרָהָם יִצְחָק יַעֲקֹב מֹשֶׁה אַהֲרֹן וְיוֹסֵף.

CHRONOLOGICAL ORDER

Each day — אֲזַמֵּן לִסְעֻדָּתִי אֻשְׁפִּיזִין עִלָּאִין: אַבְרָהָם יִצְחָק יַעֲקֹב יוֹסֵף מֹשֶׁה אַהֲרֹן וְדָוִד.

On the first day — בְּמָטוּ מִנָּךְ אַבְרָהָם אֻשְׁפִּיזִי עִלָּאִי, דְּיֵתְבוּ עִמִּי וְעִמָּךְ כָּל אֻשְׁפִּיזֵי עִלָּאֵי, יִצְחָק יַעֲקֹב יוֹסֵף מֹשֶׁה אַהֲרֹן וְדָוִד.

On the second day — בְּמָטוּ מִנָּךְ יִצְחָק אֻשְׁפִּיזִי עִלָּאִי, דְּיֵתְבוּ עִמִּי וְעִמָּךְ כָּל אֻשְׁפִּיזֵי עִלָּאֵי, אַבְרָהָם יַעֲקֹב יוֹסֵף מֹשֶׁה אַהֲרֹן וְדָוִד.

On the third day — בְּמָטוּ מִנָּךְ יַעֲקֹב אֻשְׁפִּיזִי עִלָּאִי, דְּיֵתְבוּ עִמִּי וְעִמָּךְ כָּל אֻשְׁפִּיזֵי עִלָּאֵי, אַבְרָהָם יִצְחָק יוֹסֵף מֹשֶׁה אַהֲרֹן וְדָוִד.

On the fourth day — בְּמָטוּ מִנָּךְ יוֹסֵף אֻשְׁפִּיזִי עִלָּאִי, דְּיֵתְבוּ עִמִּי וְעִמָּךְ כָּל אֻשְׁפִּיזֵי עִלָּאֵי, אַבְרָהָם יִצְחָק יַעֲקֹב מֹשֶׁה אַהֲרֹן וְדָוִד.

On the fifth day — בְּמָטוּ מִנָּךְ מֹשֶׁה אֻשְׁפִּיזִי עִלָּאִי, דְּיֵתְבוּ עִמִּי וְעִמָּךְ כָּל אֻשְׁפִּיזֵי עִלָּאֵי, אַבְרָהָם יִצְחָק יַעֲקֹב יוֹסֵף אַהֲרֹן וְדָוִד.

On the sixth day — בְּמָטוּ מִנָּךְ אַהֲרֹן אֻשְׁפִּיזִי עִלָּאִי, דְּיֵתְבוּ עִמִּי וְעִמָּךְ כָּל אֻשְׁפִּיזֵי עִלָּאֵי, אַבְרָהָם יִצְחָק יַעֲקֹב יוֹסֵף מֹשֶׁה וְדָוִד.

On Hoshana Rabbah — בְּמָטוּ מִנָּךְ דָּוִד אֻשְׁפִּיזִי עִלָּאִי, דְּיֵתְבוּ עִמִּי וְעִמָּךְ כָּל אֻשְׁפִּיזֵי עִלָּאֵי, אַבְרָהָם יִצְחָק יַעֲקֹב יוֹסֵף מֹשֶׁה וְאַהֲרֹן.

In naming the *Ushpizin*-guests, the *Zohar* (cited above) lists, 'Abraham, five other righteous ones, and King David.' A second passage in *Zohar* adds Isaac and Jacob. Although the remaining three *Ushpizin* are not identified, they are universally recognized as Joseph, Moses and Aaron, and they are assigned the fourth, fifth and sixth days of Succos. But the order in which the days are assigned is a matter of controversy which has given rise to two distinct orderings. Most *machzorim* of *Nusach Ashkenaz* follow a chronological order according to when the respective *Ushpizin* lived, i.e., Joseph on the fourth day, Moses on the fifth, and

רִבּוֹן *Master of all the worlds, may it be Your will that this mitzvah of dwelling in the succah be reckoned before You as if I had fulfilled it in all its details and implications, as well as the six hundred thirteen mitzvos that are dependent upon it; and as if I had concentrated upon all the intentions which the Men of the Great Assembly concentrated upon regarding it.*

There are two traditions regarding the order of the *Ushpizin* (see commentary).

SEFIRAH ORDER

Each day: *I invite to my meal the exalted guests: Abraham, Isaac, Jacob, Moses, Aaron, Joseph and David.*

On the first day: *May it please you, Abraham, my exalted guest, that all the other exalted guests dwell here with me and with you — Isaac, Jacob, Moses, Aaron, Joseph and David.*

On the second day: *May it please you, Isaac, my exalted guest, that all the other exalted guests dwell here with me and with you — Abraham, Jacob, Moses, Aaron, Joseph and David.*

On the third day: *May it please you, Jacob, my exalted guest, that all the other exalted guests dwell here with me and with you — Abraham, Isaac, Moses, Aaron, Joseph and David.*

On the fourth day: *May it please you, Moses, my exalted guest, that all the other exalted guests dwell here with me and with you — Abraham, Isaac, Jacob, Aaron, Joseph and David.*

On the fifth day: *May it please you, Aaron, my exalted guest, that all the other exalted guests dwell here with me and with you — Abraham, Isaac, Jacob, Moses, Joseph, and David.*

On the sixth day: *May it please you, Joseph, my exalted guest, that all the other exalted guests dwell here with me and with you — Abraham, Isaac, Jacob, Moses, Aaron, and David.*

On Hoshana Rabbah: *May it please you, David, my exalted guest, that all the other exalted guests dwell here with me and with you — Abraham, Isaac, Jacob, Moses, Aaron and Joseph.*

CHRONOLOGICAL ORDER

Each day: *I invite to my meal the exalted guests: Abraham, Isaac, Jacob, Joseph, Moses, Aaron and David.*

On the first day: *May it please you, Abraham, my exalted guest, that all the other exalted guests dwell here with me and with you — Isaac, Jacob, Joseph, Moses, Aaron and David.*

On the second day: *May it please you, Isaac, my exalted guest, that all the other exalted guests dwell here with me and with you — Abraham, Jacob, Joseph, Moses, Aaron and David.*

On the third day: *May it please you, Jacob, my exalted guest, that all the other exalted guests dwell here with me and with you — Abraham, Isaac, Joseph, Moses, Aaron and David.*

On the fourth day: *May it please you, Joseph, my exalted guests, that all the other exalted guests dwell here with me and with you — Abraham, Isaac, Jacob, Moses, Aaron and David.*

On the fifth day: *May it please you, Moses, my exalted guest, that all the other exalted guests dwell here with me and with you — Abraham, Isaac, Jacob, Joseph, Aaron and David.*

On the sixth day: *May it please you, Aaron, my exalted guest, that all the other exalted guests dwell here with me and with you — Abraham, Isaac, Jacob, Joseph, Moses and David.*

On Hoshana Rabbah: *May it please you, David, my exalted guest, that all the other exalted guests dwell here with me and with you — Abraham, Isaac, Jacob, Joseph, Moses and Aaron.*

Aaron on the sixth. [Although Aaron was three years older than Moses, Moses takes precedence for he was the prophet and leader.] However, according to the kabbalistic tradition of R' Yitzchak Luria (known as *Arizal*), Joseph appears after Moses and Aaron even though he predated them by several generations.

Arizal's view is based on the kabbalistic concepts of *Sefiros*, generally translated *emanations*. This concept teaches that man can have

On Friday night, some recite the following before *Kiddush*.
Each of the first four stanzas is recited three times.

שָׁלוֹם עֲלֵיכֶם, מַלְאֲכֵי הַשָּׁרֵת, מַלְאֲכֵי עֶלְיוֹן, מִמֶּלֶךְ מַלְכֵי הַמְּלָכִים הַקָּדוֹשׁ בָּרוּךְ הוּא.

בּוֹאֲכֶם לְשָׁלוֹם, מַלְאֲכֵי הַשָּׁלוֹם, מַלְאֲכֵי עֶלְיוֹן, מִמֶּלֶךְ מַלְכֵי הַמְּלָכִים הַקָּדוֹשׁ בָּרוּךְ הוּא.

בָּרְכוּנִי לְשָׁלוֹם, מַלְאֲכֵי הַשָּׁלוֹם, מַלְאֲכֵי עֶלְיוֹן, מִמֶּלֶךְ מַלְכֵי הַמְּלָכִים הַקָּדוֹשׁ בָּרוּךְ הוּא.

צֵאתְכֶם לְשָׁלוֹם, מַלְאֲכֵי הַשָּׁלוֹם, מַלְאֲכֵי עֶלְיוֹן, מִמֶּלֶךְ מַלְכֵי הַמְּלָכִים הַקָּדוֹשׁ בָּרוּךְ הוּא.

כִּי מַלְאָכָיו יְצַוֶּה לָּךְ, לִשְׁמָרְךָ בְּכָל דְּרָכֶיךָ.[1]
יהוה יִשְׁמָר צֵאתְךָ וּבוֹאֶךָ, מֵעַתָּה וְעַד עוֹלָם.[2]

(משלי לא:י-לא)

אֵשֶׁת חַיִל מִי יִמְצָא, וְרָחֹק מִפְּנִינִים מִכְרָהּ.
בָּטַח בָּהּ לֵב בַּעְלָהּ, וְשָׁלָל לֹא יֶחְסָר.
גְּמָלַתְהוּ טוֹב וְלֹא רָע, כֹּל יְמֵי חַיֶּיהָ.
דָּרְשָׁה צֶמֶר וּפִשְׁתִּים, וַתַּעַשׂ בְּחֵפֶץ כַּפֶּיהָ.
הָיְתָה כָּאֳנִיּוֹת סוֹחֵר, מִמֶּרְחָק תָּבִיא לַחְמָהּ.
וַתָּקָם בְּעוֹד לַיְלָה, וַתִּתֵּן טֶרֶף לְבֵיתָהּ, וְחֹק לְנַעֲרֹתֶיהָ.
זָמְמָה שָׂדֶה וַתִּקָּחֵהוּ, מִפְּרִי כַפֶּיהָ נָטְעָה כָּרֶם.
חָגְרָה בְעוֹז מָתְנֶיהָ, וַתְּאַמֵּץ זְרוֹעֹתֶיהָ.
טָעֲמָה כִּי טוֹב סַחְרָהּ, לֹא יִכְבֶּה בַלַּיְלָה נֵרָהּ.
יָדֶיהָ שִׁלְּחָה בַכִּישׁוֹר, וְכַפֶּיהָ תָּמְכוּ פָלֶךְ.
כַּפָּהּ פָּרְשָׂה לֶעָנִי, וְיָדֶיהָ שִׁלְּחָה לָאֶבְיוֹן.
לֹא תִירָא לְבֵיתָהּ מִשָּׁלֶג, כִּי כָל בֵּיתָהּ לָבֻשׁ שָׁנִים.
מַרְבַדִּים עָשְׂתָה לָּהּ, שֵׁשׁ וְאַרְגָּמָן לְבוּשָׁהּ.
נוֹדָע בַּשְּׁעָרִים בַּעְלָהּ, בְּשִׁבְתּוֹ עִם זִקְנֵי אָרֶץ.
סָדִין עָשְׂתָה וַתִּמְכֹּר, וַחֲגוֹר נָתְנָה לַכְּנַעֲנִי.
עוֹז וְהָדָר לְבוּשָׁהּ, וַתִּשְׂחַק לְיוֹם אַחֲרוֹן.
פִּיהָ פָּתְחָה בְחָכְמָה, וְתוֹרַת חֶסֶד עַל לְשׁוֹנָהּ.
צוֹפִיָּה הֲלִיכוֹת בֵּיתָהּ, וְלֶחֶם עַצְלוּת לֹא תֹאכֵל.
קָמוּ בָנֶיהָ וַיְאַשְּׁרוּהָ, בַּעְלָהּ וַיְהַלְלָהּ.
רַבּוֹת בָּנוֹת עָשׂוּ חָיִל, וְאַתְּ עָלִית עַל כֻּלָּנָה.
שֶׁקֶר הַחֵן וְהֶבֶל הַיֹּפִי, אִשָּׁה יִרְאַת יהוה הִיא תִתְהַלָּל.
תְּנוּ לָהּ מִפְּרִי יָדֶיהָ, וִיהַלְלוּהָ בַשְּׁעָרִים מַעֲשֶׂיהָ.

---

no perception of God, for His true Being is beyond human intelligence. All we can know are His 'manifestations,' the various ways in which He seems to behave toward us, i.e., mercy, power, judgment, etc. Even these can come to us only through intermediaries, known as *Sefirah*-emanations, for we can never perceive God's essence. Each day of Succos is related to one of seven *Sefirah*-emanations, which in turn is represented by one of the seven *Ushpizin*-

On Friday night, some recite the following before *Kiddush*.
Each of the first four stanzas is recited three times.

שָׁלוֹם עֲלֵיכֶם *Peace upon you, O ministering angels, angels of the Exalted One — from the King Who reigns over kings, the Holy One, Blessed is He.*

בּוֹאֲכֶם לְשָׁלוֹם *May your coming be for peace, O angels of peace, angels of the Exalted One — from the King Who reigns over kings, the Holy One, Blessed is He.*

בָּרְכוּנִי לְשָׁלוֹם *Bless me for peace, O angels of peace, angels of the Exalted One — from the King Who reigns over kings, the Holy One, Blessed is He.*

צֵאתְכֶם לְשָׁלוֹם *May your departure be to peace, O angels of peace, angels of the Exalted One — from the King Who reigns over kings, the Holy One, Blessed is He.*

He will charge His angels for you, to protect you in all your ways.[1]
May HASHEM *protect your going and returning, from this time and forever.*[2]

(Proverbs 31:10-31)

אֵשֶׁת חַיִל *An accomplished woman, who can find? —*
Far beyond pearls is her value.
ב *Her husband's heart relies on her and he shall lack no fortune.*
ג *She repays his good, but never his harm, all the days of her life.*
ד *She seeks out wool and linen, and her hands work willingly.*
ה *She is like a merchant's ships, from afar she brings her sustenance.*
ו *She arises while it is yet nighttime,*
and gives food to her household and a ration to her maidens.
ז *She envisions a field and buys it,*
from the fruit of her handiwork she plants a vineyard.
ח *With strength she girds her loins, and invigorates her arms.*
ט *She discerns that her enterprise is good —*
so her lamp is not snuffed out by night.
י *Her hands she stretches out to the distaff, and her palms support the spindle.*
כ *She spreads out her palm to the poor, and extends her hands to the destitute.*
ל *She fears not snow for her household,*
for her entire household is clothed with scarlet wool.
מ *Luxurious bedspreads she made herself, linen and purple wool are her clothing.*
נ *Distinctive in the councils is her husband,*
when he sits with the elders of the land.
ס *She makes a cloak to sell, and delivers a belt to the peddler.*
ע *Strength and majesty are her raiment, she joyfully awaits the last day.*
פ *She opens her mouth with wisdom, and a lesson of kindness is on her tongue.*
צ *She anticipates the ways of her household,*
and partakes not of the bread of laziness.
ק *Her children arise and praise her, her husband, and he lauds her:*
ר *'Many daughters have amassed achievement, but you surpassed them all.'*
ש *False is grace and vain is beauty,*
a God-fearing woman — she should be praised.
ת *Give her the fruits of her hand*
and let her be praised in the gates by her very own deeds.

(1) *Psalms* 91:11. (2) 121:8.

guests (see chart above). Consequently, Moses and Aaron, who personify the fourth and fifth *Sefiros* of נֵצַח, *Eternality,* and הוד, *Glory,* are the *Ushpizin* on the fourth and fifth days. The righteous Joseph, who represents יְסוֹד, *Foundation* — צַדִּיק יְסוֹד עוֹלָם, *the righteous one is the foundation of the world* (*Proverbs* 10:25) — is the guest on the sixth day of the festival.

קידוש לליל ראשון ושני של סוכות

When the Festival falls on Friday night, begin here:

(Recite silently — וַיְהִי עֶרֶב* וַיְהִי בֹקֶר)

יוֹם הַשִּׁשִּׁי. וַיְכֻלּוּ* הַשָּׁמַיִם וְהָאָרֶץ* וְכָל צְבָאָם. וַיְכַל אֱלֹהִים בַּיּוֹם הַשְּׁבִיעִי מְלַאכְתּוֹ אֲשֶׁר עָשָׂה, וַיִּשְׁבֹּת בַּיּוֹם הַשְּׁבִיעִי מִכָּל מְלַאכְתּוֹ אֲשֶׁר עָשָׂה. וַיְבָרֶךְ אֱלֹהִים אֶת יוֹם הַשְּׁבִיעִי וַיְקַדֵּשׁ אֹתוֹ, כִּי בוֹ שָׁבַת מִכָּל מְלַאכְתּוֹ אֲשֶׁר בָּרָא אֱלֹהִים לַעֲשׂוֹת.[1]

On all nights other than Friday begin here (on Friday night include all words in brackets):

סַבְרִי מָרָנָן וְרַבָּנָן וְרַבּוֹתַי:

בָּרוּךְ אַתָּה יהוה אֱלֹהֵינוּ מֶלֶךְ הָעוֹלָם, בּוֹרֵא* פְּרִי הַגָּפֶן.

(All present respond — אָמֵן.)

בָּרוּךְ אַתָּה יהוה אֱלֹהֵינוּ מֶלֶךְ הָעוֹלָם, אֲשֶׁר בָּחַר בָּנוּ מִכָּל עָם,* וְרוֹמְמָנוּ מִכָּל לָשׁוֹן, וְקִדְּשָׁנוּ בְּמִצְוֹתָיו. וַתִּתֶּן לָנוּ יהוה אֱלֹהֵינוּ בְּאַהֲבָה [שַׁבָּתוֹת לִמְנוּחָה וּ]מוֹעֲדִים לְשִׂמְחָה חַגִּים וּזְמַנִּים לְשָׂשׂוֹן, אֶת יוֹם [הַשַּׁבָּת הַזֶּה וְאֶת יוֹם] חַג הַסֻּכּוֹת הַזֶּה, זְמַן שִׂמְחָתֵנוּ [בְּאַהֲבָה] מִקְרָא קֹדֶשׁ, זֵכֶר לִיצִיאַת מִצְרָיִם. כִּי בָנוּ בָחַרְתָּ וְאוֹתָנוּ קִדַּשְׁתָּ מִכָּל הָעַמִּים, [וְשַׁבָּת] וּמוֹעֲדֵי קָדְשֶׁךָ [בְּאַהֲבָה וּבְרָצוֹן] בְּשִׂמְחָה וּבְשָׂשׂוֹן הִנְחַלְתָּנוּ. בָּרוּךְ אַתָּה יהוה, מְקַדֵּשׁ [הַשַּׁבָּת וְ]יִשְׂרָאֵל וְהַזְּמַנִּים.

(All present respond — אָמֵן.)

ON SATURDAY NIGHT CONTINUE BELOW. ON ALL OTHER NIGHTS CONTINUE ON NEXT PAGE.

On Saturday night, add the following two *Havdalah** blessings. Two candles with flames touching each other should be held before the person reciting the *Havdalah*.
After the first blessing, hold the fingers up to the flames to see the reflected light.

[It is forbidden to create a new flame — for example, by striking a match — on *Yom Tov*. Therefore, the *Havdalah* candle must be lit from a flame that has been burning from before the Sabbath. It is likewise forbidden to extinguish the flame.]

בָּרוּךְ אַתָּה יהוה אֱלֹהֵינוּ מֶלֶךְ הָעוֹלָם, בּוֹרֵא מְאוֹרֵי הָאֵשׁ.

(All present respond — אָמֵן.)

Kiddush

Every Sabbath and *Yom Tov* is ushered in by *Kiddush*, a declaration of the day's sanctity. Even though we have already proclaimed the holiness of the day in our evening prayers, its proper celebration belongs in the home (tonight, of course, home is in the *succah*), where we usually pursue our weekday activities. As we begin our festive meal, therefore, we dedicate ourselves to the special message of the day.

וַיְהִי עֶרֶב — *And there was evening.* When *Yom Tov* falls on the Sabbath, we preface the *Kiddush* with the same verses that we recite every Friday night, and which describe the Sabbath of the week of creation, to remind us of the profound purpose of the Sabbath.

וַיְכֻלּוּ — *Were finished.* The Midrash interprets וַיְכֻלּוּ and וַיְכַל homiletically as *longing*, as we find כָּלְתָה נַפְשִׁי, *my soul longed* (*Psalms* 84:3). Heaven and earth, and God Himself, long for the coming of the Sabbath, because it infuses all of creation with holiness (*Tzror HaMor*).

וַיְכֻלּוּ הַשָּׁמַיִם וְהָאָרֶץ — *Thus the heavens and the*

KIDDUSH FOR THE FIRST AND SECOND NIGHTS OF SUCCOS

When the Festival falls on Friday night, begin here:
(Recite silently— *And there was evening* and there was morning)*

יוֹם הַשִּׁשִּׁי *The sixth day. Thus the heavens and the earth were finished,* and all their array. On the seventh day God completed His work which He had done, and He abstained on the seventh day from all His work which He had done. God blessed the seventh day and hallowed it, because on it He abstained from all His work which God created to make.*[1]

On all nights other than Friday begin here (on Friday night include all words in brackets):
By your leave, my masters, rabbis and teachers:

בָּרוּךְ *Blessed are You, HASHEM, our God, King of the universe, Who creates* the fruit of the vine.* (All present respond— *Amen.)*

בָּרוּךְ *Blessed are You, HASHEM, our God, King of the universe, Who has chosen us from every people,* exalted us above every tongue, and sanctified us with His commandments. And You gave us, HASHEM, our God, with love [Sabbaths for rest], appointed festivals for gladness, festivals and times for joy, [this day of Sabbath and] Succos, the time of our gladness [with love], a holy convocation, a memorial of the Exodus from Egypt. For You have chosen us and You have sanctified us above all the peoples, [and the Sabbath] and Your holy festivals [in love and in favor] in gladness and in joy have You granted us as a heritage. Blessed are You, HASHEM, Who sanctifies [the Sabbath and] Israel and the seasons.* (All present respond— *Amen.)*

ON SATURDAY NIGHT CONTINUE BELOW. ON ALL OTHER NIGHTS CONTINUE ON NEXT PAGE.

On Saturday night, add the following two *Havdalah** blessings. Two candles with flames touching each other should be held before the person reciting the *Havdalah.*
After the first blessing, hold the fingers up to the flames to see the reflected light.

[It is forbidden to create a new flame — for example, by striking a match — on *Yom Tov.* Therefore, the *Havdalah* candle must be lit from a flame that has been burning from before the Sabbath. It is likewise forbidden to extinguish the flame.]

בָּרוּךְ *Blessed are You, HASHEM, our God, King of the universe, Who creates the illumination of the fire.* (All present respond— *Amen.)*

(1) *Genesis* 1:31-2:3.

---

earth were finished. The verse uses the passive form *were finished* rather than the active *and HASHEM finished.* This implies that, despite the magnitude of the task, God expended only minimum effort in the creation of the universe *(Tzror HaMor).*

בָּרוּךְ אַתָּה ... בּוֹרֵא – *Blessed are You ... Who creates.* The blessing begins by addressing God directly in second person — אַתָּה, *You* — it then reverts to third person, בּוֹרֵא, *(He) Who creates.* This is also true of all blessings. They begin by addressing God in second person because prayer is so exalted that it enables mortal man to turn directly to God, so to speak. Then the blessings change to third person because the balance of the blessing speaks of His outward manifestations as He guides and controls the universe. Of that aspect of God, we have no direct understanding — only an imperfect perception of outward appearances *(Michtav MeEliyahu).*

... אֲשֶׁר בָּחַר בָּנוּ מִכָּל עָם – *Who has chosen us from every people ...* The wording of *Kiddush* is reminiscent of the Festival *Shemoneh Esrei* (see page 54).

Havdalah

If the second day of Succos falls on Sunday, we must mark the end of the Sabbath with הַבְדָּלָה, *Havdalah,* the ceremony by which we separate the Sabbath with its greater holiness

בָּרוּךְ אַתָּה יהוה אֱלֹהֵינוּ מֶלֶךְ הָעוֹלָם, הַמַּבְדִּיל בֵּין קֹדֶשׁ לְחוֹל, בֵּין אוֹר לְחֹשֶׁךְ, בֵּין יִשְׂרָאֵל לָעַמִּים, בֵּין יוֹם הַשְּׁבִיעִי לְשֵׁשֶׁת יְמֵי הַמַּעֲשֶׂה. בֵּין קְדֻשַּׁת שַׁבָּת לִקְדֻשַּׁת יוֹם טוֹב הִבְדַּלְתָּ, וְאֶת יוֹם הַשְּׁבִיעִי מִשֵּׁשֶׁת יְמֵי הַמַּעֲשֶׂה קִדַּשְׁתָּ, הִבְדַּלְתָּ וְקִדַּשְׁתָּ אֶת עַמְּךָ יִשְׂרָאֵל בִּקְדֻשָּׁתֶךָ. בָּרוּךְ אַתָּה יהוה, הַמַּבְדִּיל בֵּין קֹדֶשׁ לְקֹדֶשׁ.

(All present respond— אָמֵן.)

If, for whatever the reason, one does not recite *Kiddush* in a *succah,* the first of the following blessings is omitted. On the second night, some reverse the order of these two blessings.

בָּרוּךְ אַתָּה יהוה אֱלֹהֵינוּ מֶלֶךְ הָעוֹלָם, אֲשֶׁר קִדְּשָׁנוּ בְּמִצְוֹתָיו וְצִוָּנוּ לֵישֵׁב בַּסֻּכָּה.*

(All present respond— אָמֵן.)

בָּרוּךְ אַתָּה יהוה אֱלֹהֵינוּ מֶלֶךְ הָעוֹלָם, שֶׁהֶחֱיָנוּ* וְקִיְּמָנוּ וְהִגִּיעָנוּ לַזְּמַן הַזֶּה.

(All present respond— אָמֵן.)

ברכת המזון

תהלים קכו

שִׁיר הַמַּעֲלוֹת, בְּשׁוּב יהוה אֶת שִׁיבַת צִיּוֹן, הָיִינוּ כְּחֹלְמִים. אָז יִמָּלֵא שְׂחוֹק פִּינוּ וּלְשׁוֹנֵנוּ רִנָּה, אָז יֹאמְרוּ בַגּוֹיִם, הִגְדִּיל יהוה לַעֲשׂוֹת עִם אֵלֶּה. הִגְדִּיל יהוה לַעֲשׂוֹת עִמָּנוּ, הָיִינוּ שְׂמֵחִים. שׁוּבָה יהוה אֶת שְׁבִיתֵנוּ, כַּאֲפִיקִים בַּנֶּגֶב. הַזֹּרְעִים בְּדִמְעָה בְּרִנָּה יִקְצֹרוּ. הָלוֹךְ יֵלֵךְ וּבָכֹה נֹשֵׂא מֶשֶׁךְ הַזָּרַע, בֹּא יָבֹא בְרִנָּה, נֹשֵׂא אֲלֻמֹּתָיו.

תְּהִלַּת יהוה יְדַבֶּר פִּי, וִיבָרֵךְ כָּל בָּשָׂר שֵׁם קָדְשׁוֹ לְעוֹלָם וָעֶד.[1] וַאֲנַחְנוּ נְבָרֵךְ יָהּ, מֵעַתָּה וְעַד עוֹלָם, הַלְלוּיָהּ.[2] הוֹדוּ לַיהוה כִּי טוֹב, כִּי לְעוֹלָם חַסְדּוֹ.[3] מִי יְמַלֵּל גְּבוּרוֹת יהוה, יַשְׁמִיעַ כָּל תְּהִלָּתוֹ.[4]

---

from the rest of the week.

We are permitted certain activities on *Yom Tov,* such as baking or cooking, that are forbidden on the Sabbath; therefore it is necessary to declare the Sabbath as ended. For this purpose, we pronounce the blessing, *'Who creates the illumination of the fire,'* and also the blessing of *Havdalah,* which distinguishes between the greater holiness of Sabbath and the lesser holiness of *Yom Tov.* This latter blessing alludes to seven distinctions: the distinction between the sacred and the profane, between light and darkness, between Israel and the nations, between the Sabbath and weekdays, between the holiness of Sabbath and that of *Yom Tov* and *Chol HaMoed* (the Intermediate Days of the *Yom Tov),* and — within the Jewish people — between *Kohanim* and Levites, and between Levites and Israelites.

Succah Blessing

לֵישֵׁב בַּסֻּכָּה – *To dwell in the succah.* Blessings recited before the performance of a *mitzvah* take one of two forms. The more common form uses the word עַל, *upon* or *concerning,* to precede the name of the *mitzvah,* e.g., עַל אֲכִילַת מַצָּה, *concerning the eating of matzah.* The second form uses an infinitive clause, preceded by the prefix ל, e.g., לֵישֵׁב בַּסֻּכָּה, *to dwell in the succah.* Generally speaking, the former version is used when a short period is required for the performance of the *mitzvah,* e.g., the *mitzvah* of *matzah* is fulfilled as soon as the required amount is eaten. When the *mitzvah* consists of an activity performed over an extended time period, e.g., the *mitzvah* of *succah* lasts for seven full days, the infinitive form is used *(Mateh Moshe).*

בָּרוּךְ *Blessed are You, Hashem, our God, King of the universe, Who distinguishes between the sacred and secular, between light and darkness, between Israel and the peoples, between the seventh day and the six days of labor. Between sanctity of the Sabbaths and the sanctity of the holidays You have distinguished, and the seventh day, from among the six days of labor You have sanctified. You have distinguished and You have sanctified Your people Israel with Your holiness. Blessed are You, Hashem, Who distinguishes between holiness and holiness.*

(All present respond— *Amen.*)

If, for whatever the reason, one does not recite *Kiddush* in a *succah,* the first of the following blessings is omitted. On the second night, some reverse the order of these two blessings.

בָּרוּךְ *Blessed are You, Hashem, our God, King of the universe, Who has sanctified us with His commandments and has commanded us to dwell in the succah.** (All present respond— *Amen.*)

בָּרוּךְ *Blessed are You, Hashem, our God, King of the universe, Who has kept us alive,* sustained us, and brought us to this season.* (All present respond— *Amen.*)

GRACE AFTER MEALS

Psalm 126

שִׁיר הַמַּעֲלוֹת *A song of ascents. When Hashem will return the captivity of Zion, we will be like dreamers. Then our mouth will be filled with laughter and our tongue with glad song. Then they will declare among the nations, 'Hashem has done greatly with these.' Hashem has done greatly with us, we were gladdened. O Hashem — return our captivity like springs in the desert. Those who tearfully sow will reap in glad song. He who bears the measure of seeds walks along weeping, but will return in exultation, a bearer of his sheaves.*

תְּהִלַּת *May my mouth declare the praise of Hashem and may all flesh bless His Holy Name forever.*[1] *We will bless Hashem from this time and forever, Halleluyah!*[2] *Give thanks to God for He is good, His kindness endures forever.*[3] *Who can express the mighty acts of Hashem? Who can declare all His praise?*[4]

(1) *Psalms* 145:21. (2) 115:18. (3) 118:1 (4) 106:2.

Shehecheyanu

שֶׁהֶחֱיָנוּ – *Who has kept us alive.* This blessing is called בִּרְכַּת הַזְּמַן, *the blessing of the time,* or simply זְמַן, *time.* It is recited: on the festivals; over fruits of a new season, provided they ripen at recurring intervals and are not always available; upon *mitzvos* that are performed at seasonal interval such as *succah, lulav,* and others connected with the annual festivals; upon seeing a friend whom one has not seen for a significant interval; upon purchasing a new garment of significance; and upon benefiting from a significant event [see *Orach Chaim* 225].

This blessing is technically in the category of בִּרְכוֹת הוֹדָאָה, *blessings of thanksgiving.* It expresses our gratitude to God for having granted us the life and sustenance to celebrate another festive season.

בִּרְכַּת הַמָּזוֹן / GRACE AFTER MEALS

For commentary see the *ArtScroll Bircas HaMazon* or *The Complete ArtScroll Siddur.*

זימון

If three or more males, aged thirteen or older, participate in a meal, a leader is appointed to formally invite the others to join him in the recitation of *Bircas HaMazon*. This invitation is called *zimun*.

Leader – רַבּוֹתַי נְבָרֵךְ.

Others – יְהִי שֵׁם יהוה מְבֹרָךְ מֵעַתָּה וְעַד עוֹלָם.[1]

If ten men join in the *zimun* the words in parentheses are added.

Leader – יְהִי שֵׁם יהוה מְבֹרָךְ מֵעַתָּה וְעַד עוֹלָם.[1]

בִּרְשׁוּת מָרָנָן וְרַבָּנָן וְרַבּוֹתַי, נְבָרֵךְ (אֱלֹהֵינוּ) שֶׁאָכַלְנוּ מִשֶּׁלּוֹ.

Others° – בָּרוּךְ (אֱלֹהֵינוּ) שֶׁאָכַלְנוּ מִשֶּׁלּוֹ וּבְטוּבוֹ חָיִינוּ.

°Those who have not eaten respond:
בָּרוּךְ (אֱלֹהֵינוּ) וּמְבֹרָךְ שְׁמוֹ תָּמִיד לְעוֹלָם וָעֶד.

Leader – בָּרוּךְ (אֱלֹהֵינוּ) שֶׁאָכַלְנוּ מִשֶּׁלּוֹ וּבְטוּבוֹ חָיִינוּ.

בָּרוּךְ הוּא וּבָרוּךְ שְׁמוֹ.

The *zimun* leader should recite *Bircas HaMazon* (or, at least, the conclusion of each blessing) aloud thus allowing the others to respond *Amen* to his blessings. Otherwise it is forbidden to interrupt *Bircas HaMazon* for any response other than those permitted during the *Shema*.

ברכת הזן

בָּרוּךְ אַתָּה יהוה אֱלֹהֵינוּ מֶלֶךְ הָעוֹלָם, הַזָּן אֶת הָעוֹלָם כֻּלּוֹ, בְּטוּבוֹ, בְּחֵן בְּחֶסֶד וּבְרַחֲמִים, הוּא נֹתֵן לֶחֶם לְכָל בָּשָׂר, כִּי לְעוֹלָם חַסְדּוֹ.[2] וּבְטוּבוֹ הַגָּדוֹל, תָּמִיד לֹא חָסַר לָנוּ, וְאַל יֶחְסַר לָנוּ מָזוֹן לְעוֹלָם וָעֶד. בַּעֲבוּר שְׁמוֹ הַגָּדוֹל, כִּי הוּא אֵל זָן וּמְפַרְנֵס לַכֹּל, וּמֵטִיב לַכֹּל, וּמֵכִין מָזוֹן לְכָל בְּרִיּוֹתָיו אֲשֶׁר בָּרָא. ❖ בָּרוּךְ אַתָּה יהוה, הַזָּן אֶת הַכֹּל.

(Others – אָמֵן.)

ברכת הארץ

נוֹדֶה לְּךָ יהוה אֱלֹהֵינוּ, עַל שֶׁהִנְחַלְתָּ לַאֲבוֹתֵינוּ אֶרֶץ חֶמְדָּה טוֹבָה וּרְחָבָה. וְעַל שֶׁהוֹצֵאתָנוּ יהוה אֱלֹהֵינוּ מֵאֶרֶץ מִצְרַיִם, וּפְדִיתָנוּ מִבֵּית עֲבָדִים, וְעַל בְּרִיתְךָ שֶׁחָתַמְתָּ בִּבְשָׂרֵנוּ, וְעַל תּוֹרָתְךָ שֶׁלִּמַּדְתָּנוּ, וְעַל חֻקֶּיךָ שֶׁהוֹדַעְתָּנוּ, וְעַל חַיִּים חֵן וָחֶסֶד שֶׁחוֹנַנְתָּנוּ, וְעַל אֲכִילַת מָזוֹן שָׁאַתָּה זָן וּמְפַרְנֵס אוֹתָנוּ תָּמִיד, בְּכָל יוֹם וּבְכָל עֵת וּבְכָל שָׁעָה.

וְעַל הַכֹּל יהוה אֱלֹהֵינוּ אֲנַחְנוּ מוֹדִים לָךְ, וּמְבָרְכִים אוֹתָךְ, יִתְבָּרַךְ שִׁמְךָ בְּפִי כָּל חַי תָּמִיד לְעוֹלָם וָעֶד. כַּכָּתוּב, וְאָכַלְתָּ וְשָׂבָעְתָּ, וּבֵרַכְתָּ אֶת יהוה אֱלֹהֶיךָ, עַל הָאָרֶץ הַטֹּבָה אֲשֶׁר נָתַן לָךְ.[3] ❖ בָּרוּךְ אַתָּה יהוה, עַל הָאָרֶץ וְעַל הַמָּזוֹן.

(Others – אָמֵן.)

בנין ירושלים

רַחֵם יהוה אֱלֹהֵינוּ עַל יִשְׂרָאֵל עַמֶּךָ, וְעַל יְרוּשָׁלַיִם עִירֶךָ, וְעַל צִיּוֹן מִשְׁכַּן כְּבוֹדֶךָ, וְעַל מַלְכוּת בֵּית דָּוִד מְשִׁיחֶךָ, וְעַל הַבַּיִת הַגָּדוֹל וְהַקָּדוֹשׁ שֶׁנִּקְרָא שִׁמְךָ עָלָיו. אֱלֹהֵינוּ אָבִינוּ רְעֵנוּ זוּנֵנוּ פַּרְנְסֵנוּ

ZIMUN/INVITATION

If three or more males, aged thirteen or older, participate in a meal, a leader is appointed to formally invite the others to join him in the recitation of Grace after Meals. This invitation is called *zimun.*

Leader – *Gentlemen, let us bless.*

Others – *Blessed be the Name of* HASHEM *from this time and forever!*[1]

If ten men join in the *zimun* the words in brackets are added.

Leader – *Blessed be the Name of* HASHEM *from this time and forever!*[1]
With the permission of the distinguished people present,
let us bless [our God,] He of Whose we have eaten.

Others° – *Blessed is [our God,] He of Whose we have eaten and through Whose goodness we live.*

°Those who have not eaten respond: *Blessed is He [our God] and blessed is His Name continuously forever.*

Leader – *Blessed is [our God,] He of Whose we have eaten and through Whose goodness we live.*
Blessed is He and Blessed is His Name.

The *zimun* leader should recite Grace after Meals (or, at least, the conclusion of each blessing) aloud thus allowing the others to respond *Amen* to his blessings. Otherwise it is forbidden to interrupt Grace after Meals for any response other than those permitted during the *Shema.*

FIRST BLESSING: FOR THE NOURISHMENT

בָּרוּךְ *Blessed are You,* HASHEM, *our God, King of the universe, Who nourishes the entire world, in His goodness — with grace, with kindness, and with mercy. He gives nourishment to all flesh, for His kindness is eternal.*[2] *And through His great goodness, we have never lacked, and may we never lack, nourishment, for all eternity. For the sake of His great Name, because He is God Who nourishes and sustains all, and benefits all, and He prepares food for all of His creatures which He has created.* Leader – *Blessed are You,* HASHEM, *Who nourishes all.* (Others – *Amen.*)

SECOND BLESSING: FOR THE LAND

נוֹדֶה *We thank You,* HASHEM, *our God, because You have given to our forefathers as a heritage a desirable, good and spacious land; because You removed us,* HASHEM, *our God, from the land of Egypt and You redeemed us from the house of bondage; for Your covenant which You sealed in our flesh; for Your Torah which You taught us and for Your statutes which You made known to us; for life, grace, and lovingkindness which You granted us; and for the provision of food with which You nourish and sustain us constantly, in every day, in every season, and in every hour.*

וְעַל הַכֹּל *For all,* HASHEM, *our God, we thank You and bless You. May Your Name be blessed by the mouth of all the living, continuously for all eternity. As it is written: 'And you shall eat and you shall be satisfied and you shall bless* HASHEM, *your God, for the good land which He gave you.'*[3] Leader – *Blessed are You,* HASHEM, *for the land and for the nourishment.* (Others – *Amen.*)

THIRD BLESSING: FOR JERUSALEM

רַחֵם *Have mercy,* HASHEM, *our God, on Israel Your people; on Jerusalem, Your city, on Zion, the resting place of Your Glory; on the monarchy of the house of David, Your anointed; and on the great and holy House upon which Your Name is called. Our God, our Father — tend us, nourish us, sustain us,*

(1) *Psalms* 113:2. (2) 136:25. (3) *Deuteronomy* 8:10.

וְכַלְכְּלֵנוּ וְהַרְוִיחֵנוּ, וְהַרְוַח לָנוּ יהוה אֱלֹהֵינוּ מְהֵרָה מִכָּל צָרוֹתֵינוּ. וְנָא אַל תַּצְרִיכֵנוּ יהוה אֱלֹהֵינוּ, לֹא לִידֵי מַתְּנַת בָּשָׂר וָדָם, וְלֹא לִידֵי הַלְוָאָתָם, כִּי אִם לְיָדְךָ הַמְּלֵאָה הַפְּתוּחָה הַקְּדוֹשָׁה וְהָרְחָבָה, שֶׁלֹּא נֵבוֹשׁ וְלֹא נִכָּלֵם לְעוֹלָם וָעֶד.

On the Sabbath add the following. [If forgotten, see box below.]

רְצֵה וְהַחֲלִיצֵנוּ יהוה אֱלֹהֵינוּ בְּמִצְוֹתֶיךָ, וּבְמִצְוַת יוֹם הַשְּׁבִיעִי הַשַּׁבָּת הַגָּדוֹל וְהַקָּדוֹשׁ הַזֶּה, כִּי יוֹם זֶה גָּדוֹל וְקָדוֹשׁ הוּא לְפָנֶיךָ, לִשְׁבָּת בּוֹ וְלָנוּחַ בּוֹ בְּאַהֲבָה כְּמִצְוַת רְצוֹנֶךָ, וּבִרְצוֹנְךָ הָנִיחַ לָנוּ יהוה אֱלֹהֵינוּ, שֶׁלֹּא תְהֵא צָרָה וְיָגוֹן וַאֲנָחָה בְּיוֹם מְנוּחָתֵנוּ, וְהַרְאֵנוּ יהוה אֱלֹהֵינוּ בְּנֶחָמַת צִיּוֹן עִירֶךָ, וּבְבִנְיַן יְרוּשָׁלַיִם עִיר קָדְשֶׁךָ, כִּי אַתָּה הוּא בַּעַל הַיְשׁוּעוֹת וּבַעַל הַנֶּחָמוֹת.

אֱלֹהֵינוּ וֵאלֹהֵי אֲבוֹתֵינוּ, יַעֲלֶה, וְיָבֹא, וְיַגִּיעַ, וְיֵרָאֶה, וְיֵרָצֶה, וְיִשָּׁמַע, וְיִפָּקֵד, וְיִזָּכֵר זִכְרוֹנֵנוּ וּפִקְדוֹנֵנוּ, וְזִכְרוֹן אֲבוֹתֵינוּ, וְזִכְרוֹן מָשִׁיחַ בֶּן דָּוִד עַבְדֶּךָ, וְזִכְרוֹן יְרוּשָׁלַיִם עִיר קָדְשֶׁךָ, וְזִכְרוֹן כָּל עַמְּךָ בֵּית יִשְׂרָאֵל לְפָנֶיךָ, לִפְלֵיטָה לְטוֹבָה לְחֵן וּלְחֶסֶד וּלְרַחֲמִים, לְחַיִּים וּלְשָׁלוֹם בְּיוֹם

On Succos: חַג הַסֻּכּוֹת הַזֶּה.

On Shemini Atzeres and Simchas Torah: הַשְּׁמִינִי חַג הָעֲצֶרֶת הַזֶּה.

זָכְרֵנוּ יהוה אֱלֹהֵינוּ בּוֹ לְטוֹבָה, וּפָקְדֵנוּ בוֹ לִבְרָכָה, וְהוֹשִׁיעֵנוּ בוֹ לְחַיִּים. וּבִדְבַר יְשׁוּעָה וְרַחֲמִים, חוּס וְחָנֵּנוּ וְרַחֵם עָלֵינוּ וְהוֹשִׁיעֵנוּ, כִּי אֵלֶיךָ עֵינֵינוּ, כִּי אֵל חַנּוּן וְרַחוּם אָתָּה.[1]

❖ **וּבְנֵה** יְרוּשָׁלַיִם עִיר הַקֹּדֶשׁ בִּמְהֵרָה בְיָמֵינוּ. בָּרוּךְ אַתָּה יהוה, בּוֹנֵה (בְּרַחֲמָיו) יְרוּשָׁלָיִם. אָמֵן. (Others – אָמֵן.)

[When required, the compensatory blessing is recited here.]

◈ If One Omitted יַעֲלֶה וְיָבֹא or רְצֵה

If one omitted יַעֲלֶה וְיָבֹא on Succos (and/or רְצֵה on Succos that falls on the Sabbath):

(a) If he realizes his omission after having recited the word בּוֹנֵה, *Who rebuilds,* of the next paragraph, but has not yet begun the following blessing, he completes the blessing until אָמֵן, and then makes up for the omission by reciting the appropriate Compensatory Blessing (facing page).

(b) If he realizes his omission after reciting the words בָּרוּךְ אַתָּה ה׳, *Blessed are You, HASHEM,* but had not yet said the word בּוֹנֵה, *Who rebuilds,* he concludes with the phrase, לַמְּדֵנִי חֻקֶּיךָ, *teach me Your statutes;* then recites the omitted paragraph and continues from there. [This ruling is based on the fact that בָּרוּךְ אַתָּה ה׳ לַמְּדֵנִי חֻקֶּיךָ, *Blessed are You, HASHEM; teach me Your statutes,* is a verse in *Psalms* (119:12) and not a blessing. Only if one has recited the next blessing of *Bircas HaMazon* is it forbidden to go back to a previous blessing, but if one has merely inserted a verse from *Psalms,* he is still in the middle of the prayer and may go back to correct an omission.]

(c) If he realizes his omission after having recited the first six words of the fourth blessing, he may still switch immediately into the compensatory blessing since the words בָּרוּךְ אַתָּה . . . הָעוֹלָם are identical in both blessings.

(d) If he realizes his omission after having recited the word הָאֵל, *the Almighty,* of the fourth blessing, it is too late for the compensatory blessing to be recited. In that case, at the first two meals of *Shabbos* and *Yom Tov* (but not *Chol HaMoed*), *Bircas HaMazon* must be repeated in its entirety; at the third meal, nothing need be done.

support us, relieve us; HASHEM, our God, grant us speedy relief from all our troubles. Please, make us not needful — HASHEM, our God — of the gifts of human hands nor of their loans, but only of Your Hand that is full, open, holy, and generous, that we not feel inner shame nor be humiliated for ever and ever.

On the Sabbath add the following. [If forgotten, see box below.]

רְצֵה *May it please You, HASHEM, our God — give us rest through Your commandments and through the commandment of the seventh day, this great and holy Sabbath. For this day is great and holy before You to rest on it and be content on it in love, as ordained by Your will. May it be Your will, HASHEM, our God, that there be no distress, grief, or lament on this day of our contentment. And show us, HASHEM, our God, the consolation of Zion, Your city, and the rebuilding of Jerusalem, City of Your holiness, for You are the Master of salvations and Master of consolations.*

אֱלֹהֵינוּ *Our God and God of our forefathers, may there rise, come, reach, be noted, be favored, be heard, be considered, and be remembered — the remembrance and consideration of ourselves; the remembrance of our forefathers; the remembrance of Messiah, son of David, Your servant; the remembrance of Jerusalem, the City of Your Holiness; the remembrance of Your entire people the Family of Israel — before You for deliverance, for goodness, for grace, for kindness, and for compassion, for life, and for peace on this Day of the*

On Succos:	On Shemini Atzeres and Simchas Torah:
Succos Festival.	*Shemini Atzeres Festival.*

Remember us on it, HASHEM, our God, for goodness; consider us on it for blessing; and help us on it for life. In the matter of salvation and compassion, pity, be gracious and compassionate with us and help us, for our eyes are turned to You, because You are God, gracious and compassionate.[1]

❖ **וּבְנֵה** *Rebuild Jerusalem, the Holy City, soon in our days. Blessed are You, HASHEM, Who rebuilds Jerusalem (in His mercy). Amen.*

(Others— *Amen.*)

[When required, the compensatory blessing is recited here.]

(1) Cf. *Nechemiah* 9:31.

❧ Compensatory Blessings (see facing page)

If יַעֲלֶה וְיָבֹא was omitted on any day other than the Sabbath.

בָּרוּךְ אַתָּה יהוה אֱלֹהֵינוּ מֶלֶךְ הָעוֹלָם, אֲשֶׁר נָתַן יָמִים טוֹבִים לְעַמּוֹ יִשְׂרָאֵל לְשָׂשׂוֹן וּלְשִׂמְחָה, אֶת יוֹם [חַג הַסֻּכּוֹת/הַשְּׁמִינִי חַג הָעֲצֶרֶת] הַזֶּה. בָּרוּךְ אַתָּה יהוה, מְקַדֵּשׁ יִשְׂרָאֵל וְהַזְּמַנִּים.

Blessed are You, HASHEM, our God, King of the universe, Who gave festivals to His people Israel for happiness and gladness, this day of the [Succos/Shemini Atzeres] Festival. Blessed are You, HASHEM, Who sanctifies Israel and the seasons.

If both רְצֵה and יַעֲלֶה וְיָבֹא were omitted on Succos that falls on the Sabbath:

בָּרוּךְ אַתָּה יהוה אֱלֹהֵינוּ מֶלֶךְ הָעוֹלָם, אֲשֶׁר נָתַן שַׁבָּתוֹת לִמְנוּחָה לְעַמּוֹ יִשְׂרָאֵל בְּאַהֲבָה, לְאוֹת וְלִבְרִית, וְיָמִים טוֹבִים לְשָׂשׂוֹן וּלְשִׂמְחָה, אֶת יוֹם [חַג הַסֻּכּוֹת/הַשְּׁמִינִי חַג הָעֲצֶרֶת] הַזֶּה. בָּרוּךְ אַתָּה יהוה, מְקַדֵּשׁ הַשַּׁבָּת וְיִשְׂרָאֵל וְהַזְּמַנִּים.

Blessed are You, HASHEM, our God, King of the universe, Who gave Sabbaths for contentment to His people Israel with love as a sign and as a covenant, and festivals for happiness and gladness, this day of the [Succos/Shemini Atzeres] Festival. Blessed are You, HASHEM, Who sanctifies the Sabbath, Israel, and the seasons.

If יַעֲלֶה וְיָבֹא was recited, but רְצֵה was omitted on the Sabbath:

בָּרוּךְ אַתָּה יהוה אֱלֹהֵינוּ מֶלֶךְ הָעוֹלָם, אֲשֶׁר נָתַן שַׁבָּתוֹת לִמְנוּחָה לְעַמּוֹ יִשְׂרָאֵל בְּאַהֲבָה, לְאוֹת וְלִבְרִית. בָּרוּךְ אַתָּה יהוה, מְקַדֵּשׁ הַשַּׁבָּת.

Blessed are You, HASHEM, our God, King of the universe, Who gave Sabbaths for contentment to His people Israel with love, as a sign and as a covenant. Blessed are You, HASHEM, Who sanctifies the Sabbath.

הטוב והמטיב

בָּרוּךְ אַתָּה יהוה אֱלֹהֵינוּ מֶלֶךְ הָעוֹלָם, הָאֵל אָבִינוּ מַלְכֵּנוּ אַדִּירֵנוּ בּוֹרְאֵנוּ גּוֹאֲלֵנוּ יוֹצְרֵנוּ קְדוֹשֵׁנוּ קְדוֹשׁ יַעֲקֹב, רוֹעֵנוּ רוֹעֵה יִשְׂרָאֵל, הַמֶּלֶךְ הַטּוֹב וְהַמֵּטִיב לַכֹּל, שֶׁבְּכָל יוֹם וָיוֹם הוּא הֵטִיב, הוּא מֵטִיב, הוּא יֵיטִיב לָנוּ. הוּא גְמָלָנוּ הוּא גוֹמְלֵנוּ הוּא יִגְמְלֵנוּ לָעַד, לְחֵן וּלְחֶסֶד וּלְרַחֲמִים וּלְרֶוַח הַצָּלָה וְהַצְלָחָה, בְּרָכָה וִישׁוּעָה נֶחָמָה פַּרְנָסָה וְכַלְכָּלָה ❖ וְרַחֲמִים וְחַיִּים וְשָׁלוֹם וְכָל טוֹב, וּמִכָּל טוּב לְעוֹלָם אַל יְחַסְּרֵנוּ. (–Others אָמֵן.)

הָרַחֲמָן הוּא יִמְלוֹךְ עָלֵינוּ לְעוֹלָם וָעֶד. הָרַחֲמָן הוּא יִתְבָּרַךְ בַּשָּׁמַיִם וּבָאָרֶץ. הָרַחֲמָן הוּא יִשְׁתַּבַּח לְדוֹר דּוֹרִים, וְיִתְפָּאַר בָּנוּ לָעַד וּלְנֵצַח נְצָחִים, וְיִתְהַדַּר בָּנוּ לָעַד וּלְעוֹלְמֵי עוֹלָמִים. הָרַחֲמָן הוּא יְפַרְנְסֵנוּ בְּכָבוֹד. הָרַחֲמָן הוּא יִשְׁבּוֹר עֻלֵּנוּ מֵעַל צַוָּארֵנוּ, וְהוּא יוֹלִיכֵנוּ קוֹמְמִיּוּת לְאַרְצֵנוּ. הָרַחֲמָן הוּא יִשְׁלַח לָנוּ בְּרָכָה מְרֻבָּה בַּבַּיִת הַזֶּה, וְעַל שֻׁלְחָן זֶה שֶׁאָכַלְנוּ עָלָיו. הָרַחֲמָן הוּא יִשְׁלַח לָנוּ אֶת אֵלִיָּהוּ הַנָּבִיא זָכוּר לַטּוֹב, וִיבַשֶּׂר לָנוּ בְּשׂוֹרוֹת טוֹבוֹת יְשׁוּעוֹת וְנֶחָמוֹת.

The Talmud (*Berachos* 46a) gives a rather lengthy text of the blessing that a guest inserts here for the host. It is quoted with minor variations in *Shulchan Aruch* (*Orach Chaim* 201) and many authorities are at a loss to explain why the prescribed text has fallen into disuse in favor of the briefer version commonly used. The text found in *Shulchan Aruch* is:

יְהִי רָצוֹן שֶׁלֹּא יֵבוֹשׁ וְלֹא יִכָּלֵם בַּעַל הַבַּיִת הַזֶּה, לֹא בָעוֹלָם הַזֶּה וְלֹא בָעוֹלָם הַבָּא, וְיַצְלִיחַ בְּכָל נְכָסָיו, וְיִהְיוּ נְכָסָיו מוּצְלָחִים וּקְרוֹבִים לָעִיר, וְאַל יִשְׁלוֹט שָׂטָן בְּמַעֲשֵׂה יָדָיו, וְאַל יִזְדַּקֵּק לְפָנָיו שׁוּם דְּבַר חֵטְא וְהִרְהוּר עָוֹן, מֵעַתָּה וְעַד עוֹלָם.

Those eating at their own table recite (including the words in parentheses that apply):

הָרַחֲמָן הוּא יְבָרֵךְ אוֹתִי (וְאֶת אִשְׁתִּי / בַּעְלִי וְאֶת זַרְעִי) וְאֶת כָּל אֲשֶׁר לִי.

Guests recite the following (children at their parents' table include the words in parentheses):

הָרַחֲמָן הוּא יְבָרֵךְ אֶת (אָבִי מוֹרִי) בַּעַל הַבַּיִת הַזֶּה, וְאֶת (אִמִּי מוֹרָתִי) בַּעֲלַת הַבַּיִת הַזֶּה, אוֹתָם וְאֶת בֵּיתָם וְאֶת זַרְעָם וְאֶת כָּל אֲשֶׁר לָהֶם.

אוֹתָנוּ וְאֶת כָּל אֲשֶׁר לָנוּ, כְּמוֹ שֶׁנִּתְבָּרְכוּ אֲבוֹתֵינוּ אַבְרָהָם יִצְחָק וְיַעֲקֹב בַּכֹּל מִכֹּל כֹּל,[1] כֵּן יְבָרֵךְ אוֹתָנוּ כֻּלָּנוּ יַחַד בִּבְרָכָה שְׁלֵמָה, וְנֹאמַר, אָמֵן.

בַּמָּרוֹם יְלַמְּדוּ עֲלֵיהֶם וְעָלֵינוּ זְכוּת, שֶׁתְּהֵא לְמִשְׁמֶרֶת שָׁלוֹם. וְנִשָּׂא בְרָכָה מֵאֵת יהוה, וּצְדָקָה מֵאֱלֹהֵי יִשְׁעֵנוּ, וְנִמְצָא חֵן וְשֵׂכֶל טוֹב בְּעֵינֵי אֱלֹהִים וְאָדָם.[2]

On the Sabbath add:

הָרַחֲמָן הוּא יַנְחִילֵנוּ יוֹם שֶׁכֻּלּוֹ שַׁבָּת וּמְנוּחָה לְחַיֵּי הָעוֹלָמִים.

FOURTH BLESSING: GOD'S GOODNESS

בָּרוּךְ *Blessed are You, HASHEM, our God, King of the Universe, the Almighty, our Father, our King, our Sovereign, our Creator, our Redeemer, our Maker, our Holy One, Holy One of Jacob, our Shepherd, the Shepherd of Israel, the King Who is good and Who does good for all. For every single day He did good, He does good, and He will do good to us. He was bountiful with us, He is bountiful with us, and He will forever be bountiful with us — with grace and with kindness and with mercy, with relief, salvation, success, blessing, help, consolation, sustenance, support,* Leader– *mercy, life, peace, and all good; and of all good things may He never deprive us.* (Others– *Amen.)*

הָרַחֲמָן *The compassionate One! May He reign over us forever. The compassionate One! May He be blessed in heaven and on earth. The compassionate One! May He be praised throughout all generations, may He be glorified through us forever to the ultimate ends, and be honored through us forever and for all eternity. The compassionate One! May He sustain us in honor. The compassionate One! May He break the yoke of oppression from our necks and guide us erect to our Land. The compassionate One! May He send us abundant blessing to this house and upon this table at which we have eaten. The compassionate One! May He send us Elijah, the Prophet — he is remembered for good — to proclaim to us good tidings, salvations, and consolations.*

The Talmud (*Berachos* 46a) gives a rather lengthy text of the blessing that a guest inserts here for the host. It is quoted with minor variations in *Shulchan Aruch* (*Orach Chaim* 201) and many authorities are at a loss to explain why the prescribed text has fallen into disuse in favor of the briefer version commonly used. The text found in *Shulchan Aruch* is:

יְהִי רָצוֹן *May it be God's will that this host not be shamed nor humiliated in This World or in the World to Come. May he be successful in all his dealings. May his dealings be successful and conveniently close at hand. May no evil impediment reign over his handiwork, and may no semblance of sin or iniquitous thought attach itself to him from this time and forever.*

Those eating at their own table recite (including the words in parentheses that apply):

The compassionate One! May He bless me (my wife/husband and my children) and all that is mine.

Guests recite the following (children at their parents' table include the words in parentheses):

The compassionate One! May He bless (my father, my teacher) the master of this house, and (my mother, my teacher) lady of this house, them, their house, their family, and all that is theirs.

Ours and all that is ours — just as our forefathers Abraham, Isaac, and Jacob were blessed in everything, from everything, with everything.[1] *So may He bless us all together with a perfect blessing. And let us say: Amen!*

בַּמָּרוֹם *On high, may merit be pleaded upon them and upon us, for a safeguard of peace. May we receive a blessing from HASHEM and just kindness from the God of our salvation, and find favor and good understanding in the eyes of God and man.*[2]

On the Sabbath add:

The compassionate One! May He cause us to inherit the day which will be completely a Sabbath and rest day for eternal life.

(1) Cf. *Genesis* 24:1; 27:33; 33:11. (2) Cf. *Proverbs* 3:4.

הָרַחֲמָן הוּא יַנְחִילֵנוּ יוֹם שֶׁכֻּלּוֹ טוֹב.

The following paragraph is *not* recited on *Shemini Atzeres* and *Simchas Torah:*

הָרַחֲמָן הוּא יָקִים לָנוּ אֶת סֻכַּת דָּוִד הַנֹּפֶלֶת.[1]

הָרַחֲמָן הוּא יְזַכֵּנוּ לִימוֹת הַמָּשִׁיחַ וּלְחַיֵּי הָעוֹלָם הַבָּא. מִגְדּוֹל יְשׁוּעוֹת מַלְכּוֹ וְעֹשֶׂה חֶסֶד לִמְשִׁיחוֹ לְדָוִד וּלְזַרְעוֹ עַד עוֹלָם.[2] עֹשֶׂה שָׁלוֹם בִּמְרוֹמָיו, הוּא יַעֲשֶׂה שָׁלוֹם עָלֵינוּ וְעַל כָּל יִשְׂרָאֵל. וְאִמְרוּ, אָמֵן.

יְראוּ אֶת יהוה קְדֹשָׁיו, כִּי אֵין מַחְסוֹר לִירֵאָיו. כְּפִירִים רָשׁוּ וְרָעֵבוּ, וְדֹרְשֵׁי יהוה לֹא יַחְסְרוּ כָל טוֹב.[3] הוֹדוּ לַיהוה כִּי טוֹב, כִּי לְעוֹלָם חַסְדּוֹ.[4] פּוֹתֵחַ אֶת יָדֶךָ, וּמַשְׂבִּיעַ לְכָל חַי רָצוֹן.[5] בָּרוּךְ הַגֶּבֶר אֲשֶׁר יִבְטַח בַּיהוה, וְהָיָה יהוה מִבְטַחוֹ.[6] נַעַר הָיִיתִי גַּם זָקַנְתִּי, וְלֹא רָאִיתִי צַדִּיק נֶעֱזָב, וְזַרְעוֹ מְבַקֶּשׁ לָחֶם.[7] יהוה עֹז לְעַמּוֹ יִתֵּן, יהוה יְבָרֵךְ אֶת עַמּוֹ בַשָּׁלוֹם.[8]

מעין שלש

The following blessing is recited after partaking of (a) grain products (other than bread or matzah) made from wheat, barley, rye, oats, or spelt; (b) grape wine or grape juice; (c) grapes, figs, pomegranates, olives, or dates. (If foods from two or three of these groups were consumed, then the insertions for each group are connected with the conjunctive וְ, thus וְעַל. The order of insertion in such a case is grain, wine, fruit.)

בָּרוּךְ אַתָּה יהוה אֱלֹהֵינוּ מֶלֶךְ הָעוֹלָם,

After grain products:	After wine:	After fruits:
עַל הַמִּחְיָה	עַל הַגֶּפֶן	עַל הָעֵץ
וְעַל הַכַּלְכָּלָה,	וְעַל פְּרִי הַגֶּפֶן,	וְעַל פְּרִי הָעֵץ,

וְעַל תְּנוּבַת הַשָּׂדֶה, וְעַל אֶרֶץ חֶמְדָּה טוֹבָה וּרְחָבָה, שֶׁרָצִיתָ וְהִנְחַלְתָּ לַאֲבוֹתֵינוּ, לֶאֱכוֹל מִפִּרְיָהּ וְלִשְׂבּוֹעַ מִטּוּבָהּ. רַחֵם יהוה אֱלֹהֵינוּ עַל יִשְׂרָאֵל עַמֶּךָ, וְעַל יְרוּשָׁלַיִם עִירֶךָ, וְעַל צִיּוֹן מִשְׁכַּן כְּבוֹדֶךָ, וְעַל מִזְבְּחֶךָ וְעַל הֵיכָלֶךָ. וּבְנֵה יְרוּשָׁלַיִם עִיר הַקֹּדֶשׁ בִּמְהֵרָה בְיָמֵינוּ, וְהַעֲלֵנוּ לְתוֹכָהּ, וְשַׂמְּחֵנוּ בְּבִנְיָנָהּ, וְנֹאכַל מִפִּרְיָהּ, וְנִשְׂבַּע מִטּוּבָהּ, וּנְבָרֶכְךָ עָלֶיהָ בִּקְדֻשָּׁה וּבְטָהֳרָה. [On the Sabbath – וּרְצֵה וְהַחֲלִיצֵנוּ בְּיוֹם הַשַּׁבָּת הַזֶּה.] וְשַׂמְּחֵנוּ בְּיוֹם

On Succos:	On Shemini Atzeres/Simchas Torah:
חַג הַסֻּכּוֹת הַזֶּה.	בְּיוֹם הַשְּׁמִינִי חַג הָעֲצֶרֶת הַזֶּה.

כִּי אַתָּה יהוה טוֹב וּמֵטִיב לַכֹּל, וְנוֹדֶה לְּךָ עַל הָאָרֶץ

After grain products	After wine:	After fruit:
וְעַל הַמִּחְיָה.	וְעַל פְּרִי הַגָּפֶן.	וְעַל הַפֵּרוֹת.°
בָּרוּךְ אַתָּה יהוה, עַל הָאָרֶץ וְעַל הַמִּחְיָה.	בָּרוּךְ אַתָּה יהוה, עַל הָאָרֶץ וְעַל פְּרִי הַגָּפֶן.	בָּרוּךְ אַתָּה יהוה, עַל הָאָרֶץ וְעַל הַפֵּרוֹת.°

°If the fruit grew in *Eretz Yisrael,* substitute פֵּרוֹתֶיהָ for הַפֵּרוֹת.

After eating or drinking any food for which neither *Bircas HaMazon* nor the Three-Faceted Blessing applies, such as fruits other than the above, vegetables or beverages other than wine, recite:

בָּרוּךְ אַתָּה יהוה אֱלֹהֵינוּ מֶלֶךְ הָעוֹלָם, בּוֹרֵא נְפָשׁוֹת רַבּוֹת וְחֶסְרוֹנָן, עַל כָּל מַה שֶּׁבָּרָא(תָ) לְהַחֲיוֹת בָּהֶם נֶפֶשׁ כָּל חָי. בָּרוּךְ חֵי הָעוֹלָמִים.

הָרַחֲמָן *The compassionate One! May He cause us to inherit the day which is completely good.*

The following paragraph is *not* recited on *Shemini Atzeres* and *Simchas Torah:*

הָרַחֲמָן *The compassionate One! May He erect for us David's fallen booth.*[1]

הָרַחֲמָן *The compassionate One! May He make us worthy of the days of Messiah and the life of the World to Come. He Who is a tower of salvations to His king and does kindness for His anointed, to David and to his descendants forever.*[2] *He Who makes peace in His heights, may He make peace upon us and upon all Israel. Now respond: Amen!*

יְראוּ *Fear HASHEM, you — His holy ones — for there is no deprivation for His reverent ones. Young lions may want and hunger, but those who seek HASHEM will not lack any good.*[3] *Give thanks to God for He is good; His kindness endures forever.*[4] *You open Your hand and satisfy the desire of every living thing.*[5] *Blessed is the man who trusts in HASHEM, then HASHEM will be his security.*[6] *I was a youth and also have aged, and I have not seen a righteous man forsaken, with his children begging for bread.*[7] *HASHEM will give might to His people; HASHEM will bless His people with peace.*[8]

THE THREE-FACETED BLESSING

The following blessing is recited after partaking of (a) grain products (other than bread or matzah) made from wheat, barley, rye, oats or spelt; (b) grape wine or grape juice; (c) grapes, figs, pomegranates, olives, or dates. (If foods from two or three of these groups were consumed, then the insertions for each group are connected with the conjunctive ו, thus וְעַל. The order of insertion in such a case is grain, wine, fruit.)

בָּרוּךְ *Blessed are You, HASHEM, our God, King of the universe, for the*

After grain products:	After wine:	After fruits:
nourishment and the sustenance,	*vine and the fruit of the vine,*	*tree and the fruit of the tree,*

and for the produce of the field; for the desirable, good and spacious Land that You were pleased to give our forefathers as a heritage, to eat of its fruit and to be satisfied with its goodness. Have mercy, HASHEM, our God, on Israel, Your people; on Jerusalem, Your city; and on Zion, the resting place of Your glory; upon Your altar, and upon Your Temple. Rebuild Jerusalem, the city of holiness, speedily in our days. Bring us up into it and gladden us in its rebuilding and let us eat from its fruit and be satisfied with its goodness and bless You upon it in holiness and purity. [On the Sabbath— *And be pleased to let us rest on this Sabbath day.*] *And gladden us on this day of the [Succos/Shemini Atzeres] festival. For You, HASHEM, are good and do good to all and we thank You for the land and for the*

After grain products:	After wine:	After fruit:
nourishment.	*fruit of the vine.*	*fruit.*°

Blessed are You, HASHEM, for the land and for the

nourishment.	*fruit of the vine.*	*fruit.*°

°If the fruit grew in *Eretz Yisrael,* substitute *'its fruit.'*

After eating or drinking any food for which neither *Bircas HaMazon* nor the Three-Faceted Blessing applies, such as fruits other than the above, vegetables or beverages other than wine, recite:

בָּרוּךְ *Blessed are You, HASHEM, our God, King of the universe, Who creates numerous living things with their deficiencies; for all that You have created with which to maintain the life of every being. Blessed is He, the life of the worlds.*

---

(1) Cf. *Amos* 9:11. (2) *Psalms* 18:51. (3) 34:10-11. (4) 136:1 et al.
(5) 145:16. (6) *Jeremiah* 17:7. (7) *Psalms* 37:25. (8) 29:11.

משניות סוכה

It is customary to study the *mishnah* of Tractate Succah during Succos.

פרק ראשון

[א] סֻכָּה שֶׁהִיא גְבוֹהָה לְמַעְלָה מֵעֶשְׂרִים אַמָּה פְּסוּלָה. רַבִּי יְהוּדָה מַכְשִׁיר. וְשֶׁאֵינָהּ גְּבוֹהָה עֲשָׂרָה טְפָחִים, וְשֶׁאֵין לָהּ שְׁלֹשָׁה דְפָנוֹת, וְשֶׁחַמָּתָהּ מְרֻבָּה מִצִּלָּתָהּ, פְּסוּלָה. סֻכָּה יְשָׁנָה – בֵּית שַׁמַּאי פּוֹסְלִין, וּבֵית הִלֵּל מַכְשִׁירִין. וְאֵיזוֹ הִיא סֻכָּה יְשָׁנָה? כָּל־שֶׁעֲשָׂאָהּ קֹדֶם לֶחָג שְׁלֹשִׁים יוֹם. אֲבָל אִם עֲשָׂאָהּ לְשֵׁם חַג, אֲפִילוּ מִתְּחִלַּת הַשָּׁנָה, כְּשֵׁרָה.

[ב] הָעוֹשֶׂה סֻכָּתוֹ תַּחַת הָאִילָן, כְּאִלּוּ עֲשָׂאָהּ בְּתוֹךְ הַבַּיִת. סֻכָּה עַל־גַּבֵּי סֻכָּה הָעֶלְיוֹנָה כְּשֵׁרָה, וְהַתַּחְתּוֹנָה פְּסוּלָה. רַבִּי יְהוּדָה אוֹמֵר: אִם אֵין דִּיּוּרִין בָּעֶלְיוֹנָה, הַתַּחְתּוֹנָה כְּשֵׁרָה.

YAD AVRAHAM / יד אברהם

[A full treatment of these and all relevant mishnayos may be found in the ArtScroll Mishnah with the *Yad Avraham* commentary by Rabbi Yisroel P. Gornish, from which the following commentary has been adapted.]

☙ Tractate Succah

This tractate discusses the specific laws of the festival of Succos. [General laws of *Yom Tov*, such as those pertain to labor and food preparation, are detailed in tractate *Beitzah.*] It deals with three broad subject areas: the *succah* as a dwelling, the Four Species, and the Temple ritual and festivities.

CHAPTER ONE

A *succah* is the temporary dwelling which a Jew establishes as his domicile during the festival of Succos. It has two components: its סְכָךְ, *covering,* from which it takes its name (*Rashi* 2a), and its walls. Each of these has specific laws regarding composition, dimensions, and acceptable materials, as well as various other details.

Many of the *succah's* measurements are expressed in terms of cubits, handbreadths and so on. The codifiers disagree on the conversion of these measurements into meters and inches. The three most accepted views are the following:

	טפח – **Handbreadth**	אמה – **Cubit**
Chazon Ish	3.8 in. /9.6 cm.	22.7 in. /57.66 cm.
Igros Moshe	3.75 in. /9.1 cm.	22.5 in. /54.6 cm.
R' A. C. No'eh	3.2 in. /8 cm.	18.9 in. /48 cm.

1. סֻכָּה שֶׁהִיא גְבוֹהָה לְמַעְלָה מֵעֶשְׂרִים אַמָּה – *A succah that is more than twenty cubits high,* i.e., the *interior* height of the *succah.* The thickness of the *s'chach* is not included in this measurement.

פְּסוּלָה – *Is invalid.* This is because the word *succos* refers to buildings of a temporary nature, implying that one must settle in a דִירַת עֲרַאי, *temporary dwelling,* one for which flimsy walls suffice. Walls taller than twenty cubits must be built with a firmness which would make them permanent; walls of less than twenty cubits, however, can be built in a temporary manner (*Gem.* 2a).

If the *s'chach* is *exactly* twenty cubits above its floor, the *succah* is valid; the mishnah invalidates only a *succah* whose *s'chach* begins more than twenty cubits above the floor.

רַבִּי יְהוּדָה מַכְשִׁיר – *R' Yehudah validates it.* He holds that the *succah* must be able to serve as a permanent structure (*Gem.* 7b). The halachah, however, follows the first *Tanna* (*Orach Chaim* 613:1).

וְשֶׁאֵינָהּ גְּבוֹהָה עֲשָׂרָה טְפָחִים – *And [a succah] that is not ten handbreadths high.* The interior, from floor to *s'chach,* is less than ten handbreadths high. This is invalid because it is a דִירָה סְרוּחָה, *unpleasant dwelling,* since it is too confining for decent habitation (*Gem.* 4a). [The Torah requires that one 'dwell' in a *succah.*

MISHNAYOS SUCCAH

It is customary to study the *mishnah* of Tractate Succah during Succos.

CHAPTER ONE

[1] **סֻכָּה** *A succah that is more than twenty cubits high is invalid. R' Yehudah validates it. And [a succah] that is not ten handbreadths high, or [one] that does not have three walls, or [one] whose sun[ny area] is greater than its shade[d area], is invalid. An old succah — Beis Shammai invalidate it and Beis Hillel validate it. And what is [considered] an 'old' succah? Whatever one built thirty days prior to the Festival. But if one built it specifically for the Festival, even [if he put it up] at the beginning of the year, it is valid.*

[2] *If one builds his succah under a tree, it is as though he had built it inside the house. [If] a succah [is built] atop another succah the upper one is valid, and the lower one is invalid. R' Yehudah says: If there can be no tenancy in the upper one, [only] the lower one is valid.*

YAD AVRAHAM

The Rabbis understand this to mean תֵּשְׁבוּ כְּעֵין תָּדוּרוּ, *you are to dwell* (in the *succah) just as you would inhabit* (your home). By implication, the Sages derived that a *succah* must contain minimal living conditions, such as a height of ten handbreadths.

שְׁלֹשָׁה דְפָנוֹת – *Three walls.* A *succah* must have a minimum of three walls. Two of these walls must be at least seven handbreadths wide [the minimum width of a *succah*], in addition to being at least ten handbreadths high. The third wall, however, as defined in the oral tradition received by Moses at Sinai [הֲלָכָה לְמֹשֶׁה מִסִּינַי], need not always have seven handbreadths. See *Orach Chaim* 630:2,3 for details.

וְשֶׁחַמָּתָהּ מְרֻבָּה מִצִּלָּתָהּ – *Or [one] whose sun[ny area] is greater than its shade[ed area].* Since by definition, a *succah* must provide shade — *s'chach*=shelter — a *succah* that lets in more sunlight than it blocks out fails to perform its basic function.]

סֻכָּה יְשָׁנָה – *An old succah*, i.e., a *succah* erected more than thirty days before *Succos* whose *s'chach* was not put up expressly for the festival. Beis Shammai require that the *s'chach* be laid expressly for the *mitzvah*, while Beis Hillel holds there is no such requirement. The walls need not be constructed expressly for Succos *(Taz* 636:1). Although the halachah follows Beis Hillel, *Yerushalmi* teaches that it is preferable to make some minor change in the *s'chach* in honor of the Festival, such as lifting and replacing an area of *s'chach* measuring one square handbreadth (*Orach Chaim* 636:1).

כָּל שֶׁעֲשָׂאָהּ קֹדֶם לֶחָג שְׁלֹשִׁים יוֹם – *Whatever one built thirty days prior to the Festival.* [Throughout *Mishnayos* the Festival of Succos is referred to simply as חָג, *the Festival.*] The presumption is that a *succah* built before the festival season was made for the sake of shade, not the *mitzvah*. Within thirty days, when people have begun to study the laws of Succos, it is presumed to have been constructed expressly for this *mitzvah (Rav).*

2. תַּחַת הָאִילָן – *Under a tree,* i.e., the tree's branches and leaves are directly over the *s'chach* of the *succah*. While a tree is still rooted in the earth, its branches are not valid *s'chach* (mishnah 4).

כְּאִלּוּ עֲשָׂאָהּ בְּתוֹךְ הַבַּיִת – *It is as though he had built it inside the house.* A *succah* built under a roof is not valid because the Torah emphasizes that one must dwell in a [single] *succah*, not in a double-roofed one, such as a *succah* covered by a tree, a roof or the *s'chach* of another *succah (Gem.).* [Thus, the area covered by the branches and leaves is invalid.]

סֻכָּה עַל גַּבֵּי סֻכָּה – *[If] a succah [is built] atop another succah,* i.e., the *s'chach* of the lower *succah* serves as the floor of the upper *succah*.

וְהַתַּחְתּוֹנָה פְּסוּלָה – *and the lower one is invalid,* because it is under two 'roofs.' However, if the upper *succah* is less than ten handbreadths high, and thus not valid as a separate *succah*, (see m. 1), then the two *s'chachim* are regarded as a single thick one, and the lower *succah* is valid (*Orach Chaim* 628:1).

רַבִּי יְהוּדָה אוֹמֵר . . . – *R' Yehudah says . . .* that if the *s'chach* of the lower *succah* cannot support the weight of the upper *succah's* occupants, it has no standing as an independent dwelling. Consequently, its *s'chach* is not reckoned as a separate roof. In principle, even the anonymous *Tanna* agrees with this. The dispute is only where the *s'chach* of the lower *succah* is just strong enough to support the utensils of the upper one with difficulty. The first *Tanna* considers this enough to qualify the upper *succah* as fit for tenancy [since a *succah* need only be a temporary abode (see comm. to

[ג] פֵּרַס עָלֶיהָ סָדִין מִפְּנֵי הַחַמָּה, אוֹ תַחְתֶּיהָ מִפְּנֵי הַנְּשָׁר, אוֹ שֶׁפֵּרַס עַל־גַּבֵּי הַקִּינוֹף, פְּסוּלָה. אֲבָל, פּוֹרֵס הוּא עַל־גַּבֵּי נַקְלִיטֵי הַמִּטָּה.

[ד] הִדְלָה עָלֶיהָ אֶת־הַגֶּפֶן, וְאֶת־הַדְּלַעַת, וְאֶת־הַקִּסּוֹם, וְסִכֵּךְ עַל־גַּבָּהּ, פְּסוּלָה. וְאִם הָיָה סִכּוּךְ הַרְבֵּה מֵהֶן, אוֹ שֶׁקְּצָצָן, כְּשֵׁרָה. זֶה הַכְּלָל: כָּל־שֶׁהוּא מְקַבֵּל טֻמְאָה וְאֵין גִּדּוּלוֹ מִן־הָאָרֶץ, אֵין מְסַכְּכִים בּוֹ; וְכָל־דָּבָר שֶׁאֵינוֹ מְקַבֵּל טֻמְאָה וְגִדּוּלוֹ מִן־הָאָרֶץ, מְסַכְּכִין בּוֹ.

[ה] חֲבִילֵי קַשׁ וַחֲבִילֵי עֵצִים וַחֲבִילֵי זְרָדִין, אֵין מְסַכְּכִין בָּהֶן. וְכֻלָּן שֶׁהִתִּירָן כְּשֵׁרוֹת. וְכֻלָּן כְּשֵׁרוֹת לַדְּפָנוֹת.

[ו] מְסַכְּכִין בִּנְסָרִים; דִּבְרֵי רַבִּי יְהוּדָה. וְרַבִּי מֵאִיר אוֹסֵר. נָתַן עָלֶיהָ נֶסֶר שֶׁהוּא רָחָב אַרְבָּעָה טְפָחִים, כְּשֵׁרָה, וּבִלְבַד שֶׁלֹּא יִישַׁן תַּחְתָּיו.

יד אברהם

m. 1)]. Thus the lower *succah* is a *succah* beneath a *succah*. R' Yehudah, however, holds that a permanent structure is required (ibid.); and since the lower *s'chach* is too weak to qualify it as a 'permanent' floor, he rules the upper *succah* unfit for tenancy. Thus the lower *succah* is not a *succah* beneath a *succah (Rav)*.

3. One of the categories of materials not eligible to be used as *s'chach* are things which are susceptible to receiving *tumah* (see m. 4). This category includes finished utensils, garments, and sheets, the subject of our mishnah.

מִפְּנֵי הַחַמָּה — *Because of the sun.* Although the *succah* had sufficient *s'chach* to make it valid, a sheet was draped over it to block out sunlight. Since the purpose of the sheet is for protection, it is regarded as *s'chach* — but a sheet is invalid for *s'chach* because it can become *tamei (Rav)*.

מִפְּנֵי הַנְּשָׁר — *Because of the falling leaves*, i.e., to keep them from falling onto the table.

אוֹ שֶׁפֵּרַס עַל גַּבֵּי הַקִּינוֹף — *Or if one spread it over a four-poster bed*, to create a canopy for the bed. The canopy is not close to the *s'chach* so that it cannot be regarded as invalid *s'chach* as the previous cases. Nonetheless, since the canopy is horizontal, it is regarded as a separate roof intervening between the person and the *s'chach (Rav)*.

נַקְלִיטֵי הַמִּטָּה — *A two-poster bed* — one each at the head and foot of the bed, with a horizontal bar connecting the tops of the two posts. A sheet draped over this bar and sloping down on either side is not considered a tent, because the peak does not have a level width of at least one handbreadth, the minimum dimension qualifying as a 'roof.' [The slopes of the sheet are considered walls, not a roof.] Accordingly, the person in the bed is considered as dwelling solely under the *s'chach* of the *succah (Rav)*.

4. ... הִדְלָה עָלֶיהָ — *If one raised onto it* ... i.e., he drew any of these vines over the top of a *succah*. [Gourds and ivy also grow on vines and can easily be drawn over a large area.] They are, however, not valid as *s'chach*, since they are still attached to the ground [see m. 2] *(Rav)*.

וְסִכֵּךְ עַל גַּבָּהּ — *And covered it with [valid] s'chach.* As long as the vines constitute the majority of the *s'chach* it is invalid *(Rav)*.

וְאִם הָיָה סִכּוּךְ הַרְבֵּה — *But if the [valid] s'chach exceeded* the amount of vine, gourd, or ivy, the *succah* is valid based on the principle of בִּטּוּל בְּרוֹב, *nullification [of the legal qualities of the minority substance] in the majority*. However, one must mix the valid and invalid *s'chach* together so that the vines are not discernible *(Rav)*.

אוֹ שֶׁקְּצָצָן — *Or he detached them.* If the invalid *s'chach* exceeds the valid *s'chach*, the *succah* can be made valid by cutting the attached vines, so that they are no longer rooted in the ground. He must, however, lift each vine or branch and set it down again as part of the *s'chach*. By so doing he is, in effect, putting down new, valid *s'chach*. This is to avoid the legal pitfall of תַּעֲשֶׂה וְלֹא מִן הֶעָשׂוּי, *you must make [the s'chach], but it may not come into being indirectly (Gem.)*.

טֻמְאָה — *Tumah* is a legally defined state of ritual contamination which restricts the people or objects contaminated from contact with sanctified things or entry into the Temple. Our mishnah invalidates not only *s'chach* that has already become *tamei*, but any *s'chach* that *can* become *tamei*. Examples are finished utensils, clothing, food. [Raw materials, such as wood, can become *tamei* only if processed into finished utensils. Slats or bamboo, therefore, are commonly used as *s'chach*.]

וְאֵין גִּדּוּלוֹ מִן הָאָרֶץ — *Or does not grow from the ground.* This disqualifies hides even if they have

[3] *If one spread a sheet over [the s'chach] because of the sun, or beneath it because of the falling leaves, or if one spread it over a four-poster bed, it is invalid. However, one may spread it over a two-poster bed.*

[4] *If one raised onto it a grapevine, a gourd, or ivy, and covered it with s'chach, it is invalid. But if the s'chach exceeded them, or if he detached them, it is valid. This is the rule [regarding the validity of s'chach]: Whatever is susceptible to contamination or does not grow from the ground, we may not use for s'chach; but whatever is not susceptible to contamination and grows from the ground, we may use for s'chach.*

[5] *Bundles of straw, bundles of wood, or bundles of fresh cane may not be used for s'chach; but all of these are valid when they are untied. All of them are valid for the walls.*

[6] *We may cover the succah with boards; these are the words of R' Yehudah. But R' Meir forbids it. If one placed atop it a board that is four handbreadths wide, [the succah] is valid, except that one may not sleep under [the board].*

YAD AVRAHAM

not yet been fashioned into leather utensils or garments. Metal, earth or clay, although they *are* earth, do not grow from it (*Rama O. Ch.* 629:1).

5. ... חֲבִילֵי – *Bundles* ... are tied together to facilitate transport (*Rama* 629:15). When they are meant for kindling, they are left to dry so that they will burn better.

אֵין מְסַכְּכִין בָּהֶן – *May not be used for s'chach.* If a man places his bundle on top of the *succah* to dry out in the sun for use as fuel, and he then changes his mind and decides to leave his bundle on the *succah* as *s'chach*, it would not be valid because it would fall under the category of תַּעֲשֶׂה וְלֹא מִן הֶעָשׂוּי, *you must make [the s'chach], but it may not come into being indirectly* (see m. 4). Since his original intention had not been for shade, the *s'chach* was not 'made' by him. In order to preclude such a situation, the Sages banned the use of bundles even if they were originally set down as *s'chach* (*Rav*).

וְכֻלָּן שֶׁהִתִּירָן כְּשֵׁרוֹת – *But all of these are valid when they are untied* – if he originally set them in place as *s'chach*. Since the contents of the bundle are valid *s'chach* according to Torah law, it is sufficient to untie them and thereby remove the Rabbinical objection. But if he placed them on the *succah* in order to *dry* them, and then untied them for use as *s'chach*, they remain invalid until he lifts them and sets them back in place.

וְכֻלָּן – *All of them.* All the aforementioned classifications which are not valid as *s'chach:* (a) attached to the ground; (b) not growing from the soil; (c) susceptible to *tumah;* and (d) bundles (*Rav*).

כְּשֵׁרוֹת לַדְּפָנוֹת – *Are valid for the walls.* The word סֻכָּה *[succah]* implies the סְכָךְ *[s'chach], covering.* Thus all limitations on acceptable materials refer to the roof, not to the walls (*Rav*).

6. ... מְסַכְּכִין בִּנְסָרִים – *We may cover the succah with boards* ... Both R' Yehudah and R' Meir agree that a board four handbreadths wide or more is not valid. The Sages banned the use of such boards because they resemble the ceiling boards of a house, and one might see no difference between eating under the roofing of his house, and that of the *succah.* When boards are less than three handbreadths wide, both agree that they are valid, since they are regarded as no more than sticks. They disagree only regarding boards between three and four handbreadths wide. R' Meir considers their width to be significant, while R' Yehudah does not. The halachah follows R' Yehudah. However, it is our custom not to use boards even if they are less than four handbreadths wide (*Orach Chaim* 629:18), except in extenuating circumstances, because one might cover the *succah* in a way that would allow no rain to penetrate (*Mishnah Berurah*).

כְּשֵׁרָה – *It [the succah] is valid.* Even though a four-handbreadth board is not valid, that applies only to the area covered by the board itself, but it need not disqualify the rest of the *s'chach.* Thus, if the *succah* is large enough to retain the minimum area of seven handbreadths square even after the space from the board to the adjacent wall is subtracted from the total area of the *succah*, it is valid, except for the area directly beneath the board (*Orach Chaim* 632:1).

וּבִלְבַד שֶׁלֹּא יִישַׁן תַּחְתָּיו – *Except that one may not sleep* [or eat] *under [the board].*

[ז] תִּקְרָה שֶׁאֵין עָלֶיהָ מַעֲזִיבָה — רַבִּי יְהוּדָה אוֹמֵר: בֵּית שַׁמַּאי אוֹמְרִים, מְפַקְפֵּק וְנוֹטֵל אַחַת מִבֵּינְתַיִם; וּבֵית הִלֵּל אוֹמְרִים, מְפַקְפֵּק אוֹ נוֹטֵל אַחַת מִבֵּינְתַיִם. רַבִּי מֵאִיר אוֹמֵר: נוֹטֵל אַחַת מִבֵּינְתַיִם וְאֵין מְפַקְפֵּק.

[ח] הַמְקָרֶה סֻכָּתוֹ בַּשְּׁפוּדִין אוֹ בַּאֲרוּכוֹת הַמִּטָּה, אִם יֵשׁ־רֶוַח בֵּינֵיהֶן כְּמוֹתָן, כְּשֵׁרָה. הַחוֹטֵט בְּגָדִישׁ לַעֲשׂוֹת בּוֹ סֻכָּה, אֵינָהּ סֻכָּה.

[ט] הַמְשַׁלְשֵׁל דְּפָנוֹת מִלְמַעְלָה לְמַטָּה, אִם גָּבוֹהַּ מִן־הָאָרֶץ שְׁלֹשָׁה טְפָחִים, פְּסוּלָה; מִלְמַטָּה לְמַעְלָה, אִם גָּבוֹהַּ מִן־הָאָרֶץ עֲשָׂרָה טְפָחִים, כְּשֵׁרָה. רַבִּי יוֹסֵי אוֹמֵר: כְּשֵׁם שֶׁמִּלְמַטָּה לְמַעְלָה עֲשָׂרָה טְפָחִים, כָּךְ מִלְמַעְלָה לְמַטָּה עֲשָׂרָה טְפָחִים. הִרְחִיק אֶת־הַסִּכּוּךְ מִן הַדְּפָנוֹת שְׁלֹשָׁה טְפָחִים, פְּסוּלָה.

[י] בַּיִת שֶׁנִּפְחַת וְסִכֵּךְ עַל־גַּבָּיו, אִם יֵשׁ מִן־הַכֹּתֶל לַסִּכּוּךְ אַרְבַּע אַמּוֹת, פְּסוּלָה. וְכֵן חָצֵר שֶׁהִיא מֻקֶּפֶת אַכְסַדְרָה. סֻכָּה גְדוֹלָה שֶׁהִקִּיפוּהָ

יד אברהם

7. The mishnah now turns to the problem of how to convert an existing roof made of boards into valid *s'chach*. Some authorities (*Rambam, Ran,* and others) maintain that the planks under discussion in this mishnah are less than four handbreadths wide. As part of an actual roof, these boards would be disqualified as *s'chach* for the same reason used above to bar wider boards. A further reason for disqualification is that they were put down not for *s'chach,* but for roofing. Thus a later attempt to use them for *s'chach* would render them indirectly made *s'chach,* as in mishnah 4 [תַּעֲשֶׂה וְלֹא מִן הֶעָשׂוּי]. This mishnah discusses how to remove both of these disqualifications.

שֶׁאֵין עָלֶיהָ מַעֲזִיבָה — *That has no plaster on it.* The roofing boards have not yet been covered with plaster [or tar], substances ineligible for *s'chach (Rav).*

רַבִּי יְהוּדָה אוֹמֵר — *R' Yehudah says* that Beis Shammai and Beis Hillel disagree about which steps must be taken to turn the roof boards into *s'chach,* and he presents their dispute.

בֵּית שַׁמַּאי אוֹמְרִים — *Beis Shammai say.* As the *Gemara* (15a) understands this, Beis Shammai mean that even if one removed the nails (and lifted the boards), it is insufficient. Rather, he must replace every other board with valid *s'chach.* Having done so, he need not loosen the remaining boards. Though lifting the boards would correct the problem of indirectly made *s'chach,* it would not suffice to remove the disqualification based on the concern that someone might conclude that an ordinary roof was equally acceptable. Beis Shammai therefore require that every second plank be replaced with valid *s'chach.* This removes both disqualifications.

וּבֵית הִלֵּל אוֹמְרִים — *But Beis Hillel say* that either loosening or replacing is sufficient. Beis Hillel consider that merely *loosening* the planks removes them from the category of a 'roof,' since a permanent roof would surely have to be secured. Thus the loosened planks may be used for *s'chach* if they are less than four handbreadths wide.

רַבִּי מֵאִיר אוֹמֵר: נוֹטֵל אַחַת מִבֵּינְתַיִם וְאֵין מְפַקְפֵּק — *R' Meir says: He removes every other one but does not loosen [them].* This is identical to the position attributed by R' Yehudah to Beis Shammai. In R' Meir's opinion, this ruling was never disputed by Beis Hillel.

8. בַּשְּׁפוּדִין אוֹ בַּאֲרוּכוֹת הַמִּטָּה — *If one roofs his succah with spits or bed-boards.* Atop his *succah* someone laid out a framework of spits or bed-boards upon which he will pile *s'chach (Rashi).* Metal spits are invalid as *s'chach* because they do not grow from the ground, and bed-boards are disqualified because they are utensils *(Rav).*

אִם יֵשׁ רֶוַח בֵּינֵיהֶן כְּמוֹתָן — *If the space between them is equal to themselves.* The *s'chach*-covered space left between the spits or bed-boards is equal to the space covered by the spits or bed-boards themselves, with the result that at least half the *succah* is covered by valid *s'chach.*

הַחוֹטֵט בְּגָדִישׁ לַעֲשׂוֹת בּוֹ סֻכָּה — *If one hollowed out a haystack to make a succah inside it.* He removed the straw from within, until he had hollowed out a space large enough for a valid *succah (Rav).*

אֵינָהּ סֻכָּה — *It is not a succah.* Although the top layer of hay is an acceptable material for *s'chach,* the *succah* is not valid because the hay was not emplaced originally for the purpose of

[7] *A roof that has no plaster on it — R' Yehudah says: Beis Shammai say, one loosens them and removes every other board; but Beis Hillel say, he [either] loosens [them] or removes every other one. R' Meir says: He removes every other one but does not loosen [them].*

[8] *If one roofs his succah with spits or bed-boards, if the space between them is equal to themselves, it is valid. If one hollowed out a haystack to make a succah inside it, it is not a succah.*

[9] *If one suspends the walls from above downwards, if [they are] three handbreadths above the ground, it is invalid; from below upwards, if it reaches a height of ten handbreadths above the ground, it is valid. R' Yose says: Just as from below upwards ten handbreadths [suffice], so from above downwards ten handbreadths [suffice]. If one moved the s'chach three handbreadths away from the walls, it is invalid.*

[10] *A house that was breached and he placed s'chach over it, if there are four cubits from the wall to the s'chach, it is invalid. The same [applies to] a courtyard that is surrounded by a portico. A large succah that they ringed*

YAD AVRAHAM

shade; thus it is indirectly made *s'chach (Rav).*

9. הַמְשַׁלְשֵׁל דְּפָנוֹת מִלְמַעְלָה לְמַטָּה — *If one suspends the walls from above downwards.* He wove or plaited the *succah* walls working his way downwards from the *s'chach (Rav).*

אִם גְּבוֹהָ מִן הָאָרֶץ שְׁלֹשָׁה טְפָחִים — *If [they are] three handbreadths above the ground.* If the bottom of the wall is three or more handbreadths above the ground, it is invalid. Since the three-handbreadths gap is large enough to permit goats to crawl into the *succah,* it lacks the halachic status of a partition *(Rashi).*

מִלְּמַטָּה לְמַעְלָה — *From below upwards,* i.e., he builds the *succah* walls from the ground up.

גָּבוֹהַ מִן הָאָרֶץ עֲשָׂרָה טְפָחִים — *Ten handbreadths above the ground* is the minimum height for a partition in halachah (see m. 1). Thus, if the wall is directly below the *s'chach,* it is valid, even though there is a large gap from the top of the wall to the *s'chach.* We rely on the principle גּוּד אֲסִיק, *gud asik* (lit., *pull and bring up),* according to which the walls are seen as stretching upwards until the *s'chach.* This principle was transmitted orally to Moses on Sinai *(Gem.* 6b). If, however, the wall was not directly below the *s'chach,* but off to the side, the *succah* is valid only if the wall is within three handbreadths of the *s'chach (Orach Chaim* 630:9).

כָּךְ מִלְמַעְלָה לְמַטָּה עֲשָׂרָה טְפָחִים — *So from above downwards ten handbreadths [suffice].* Even though there may be a gap greater than three handbreadths from the ground to the bottom of the suspended wall, R' Yose considers it valid as long as the wall has the minimum height of ten handbreadths. The halachah, however, does not follows R' Yose *(Rav).*

הִרְחִיק אֶת הַסִּכּוּךְ מִן הַדְּפָנוֹת שְׁלֹשָׁה טְפָחִים — *If one moved the s'chach three handbreadths away from the walls.* This refers to a horizontal gap between the *s'chach* and the wall *(Rav).*

פְּסוּלָה — *It is invalid,* in a *succah* of three walls. A gap of three handbreadths, running between the *s'chach* and the wall along the entire length of the *succah,* separates the *s'chach* from the wall and thus disqualifies it as a *succah* wall. This leaves the *succah* with only two walls *(Orach Chaim* 632:2).

10. בַּיִת שֶׁנִּפְחַת — *A house that was breached,* i.e., the middle of a roof collapsed, leaving a large gap in the ceiling over which the owner placed *s'chach (Rav).*

פְּסוּלָה — *It is invalid.* A four-cubit distance between the *s'chach* and the wall is considered a separation; we do not consider the *s'chach* to have walls beneath it. But if the intact part of the ceiling between the *s'chach* and the walls is less than four cubits, the *succah* is valid. In line with the Sinaitic principle of דּוֹפֶן עֲקוּמָה, *bent wall,* we regard the intervening section of ceiling as part of the wall which bends over to meet the *s'chach.* But one may not eat or sleep under the ceiling part *(Rav; Orach Chaim* 632:1).

וְכֵן חָצֵר שֶׁהִיא מֻקֶּפֶת אַכְסַדְרָה — *The same [applies to] a courtyard that is surrounded by a portico,* i.e., a courtyard surrounded on three sides by houses which open into it. From each house, a roof projects toward the courtyard, shading some of it and leaving the rest exposed. If one were to lay *s'chach* over the exposed portion of the courtyard using the walls of the surrounding houses as the walls of the *succah,* the portico would separate the *s'chach* from the house walls. If the portico is four cubits, the *succah* is not valid; if less, then it is valid based on the principle of דּוֹפֶן עֲקוּמָה, *bent wall (Rashi; Rav).*

סֻכָּה גְדוֹלָה — *A large succah,* i.e., an area of at least seven handbreadths square of valid *s'chach*

בְּדָבָר שֶׁאֵין מְסַכְּכִים בּוֹ, אִם יֵשׁ־תַּחְתָּיו אַרְבַּע אַמּוֹת, פְּסוּלָה.

[יא] הָעוֹשֶׂה סֻכָּתוֹ כְּמִין צְרִיף, אוֹ שֶׁסְּמָכָהּ לַכֹּתֶל, רַבִּי אֱלִיעֶזֶר פּוֹסֵל, מִפְּנֵי שֶׁאֵין לָהּ גַּג; וַחֲכָמִים מַכְשִׁירִין. מַחֲצֶלֶת קָנִים גְּדוֹלָה, עֲשָׂאָהּ לִשְׁכִיבָה, מְקַבֶּלֶת טֻמְאָה וְאֵין מְסַכְּכִין בָּהּ; לְסִכּוּךְ, מְסַכְּכִין בָּהּ וְאֵינָהּ מְקַבֶּלֶת טֻמְאָה. רַבִּי אֱלִיעֶזֶר אוֹמֵר: אַחַת קְטַנָּה וְאַחַת גְּדוֹלָה, עֲשָׂאָהּ לִשְׁכִיבָה, מְקַבֶּלֶת טֻמְאָה וְאֵין מְסַכְּכִין בָּהּ; לְסִכּוּךְ, מְסַכְּכִין בָּהּ וְאֵינָהּ מְקַבֶּלֶת טֻמְאָה.

פרק שני

[א] **הַיָּשֵׁן** תַּחַת הַמִּטָּה בַּסֻּכָּה לֹא יָצָא יְדֵי חוֹבָתוֹ. אָמַר רַבִּי יְהוּדָה: נוֹהֲגִין הָיִינוּ, שֶׁהָיִינוּ יְשֵׁנִים תַּחַת הַמִּטָּה בִּפְנֵי הַזְּקֵנִים וְלֹא אָמְרוּ לָנוּ דָּבָר. אָמַר רַבִּי שִׁמְעוֹן: מַעֲשֶׂה בְטָבִי, עַבְדּוֹ שֶׁל רַבָּן גַּמְלִיאֵל, שֶׁהָיָה יָשֵׁן תַּחַת הַמִּטָּה. וְאָמַר לָהֶן רַבָּן גַּמְלִיאֵל לַזְּקֵנִים: ,,רְאִיתֶם טָבִי עַבְדִּי? שֶׁהוּא תַלְמִיד חָכָם וְיוֹדֵעַ שֶׁעֲבָדִים פְּטוּרִין מִן־הַסֻּכָּה — לְפִיכָךְ יָשֵׁן הוּא תַּחַת הַמִּטָּה.״ וּלְפִי דַרְכֵּנוּ לָמַדְנוּ שֶׁהַיָּשֵׁן תַּחַת הַמִּטָּה לֹא יָצָא יְדֵי חוֹבָתוֹ.

יד אברהם

was surrounded along its sides by non-valid *s'chach,* which lay between it and the walls *(Rav).*

אִם יֵשׁ תַּחְתָּיו אַרְבַּע אַמּוֹת — *If there were four cubits beneath it.* If the space covered by the invalid materials is four cubits.

פְּסוּלָה — *It is invalid,* because the walls are too far from the *s'chach* to be regarded as part of the *succah,* and the four-cubit expanse prevents us from considering the invalid materials part of a *bent wall.* An *empty* space of three handbreadths running through the length of the *succah* invalidates the *succah* regardless of whether it is in the middle or on the side (see m. 9).

11. הָעוֹשֶׂה סֻכָּתוֹ כְּמִין צְרִיף — *If one makes his succah like a conical hut.* A conical hut has no roof and the walls meet each other on top *(Rav).* In this respect the roof and the walls are one [the walls being made of valid *s'chach*] *(Rashi).*

אוֹ שֶׁסְּמָכָהּ לַכֹּתֶל — *Or he leaned it against the wall.* He built a lean-to — a single wall of valid *s'chach* leaning against the wall of a house with a seven-handbreadth square area beneath it *(Rav).*

רַבִּי אֱלִיעֶזֶר פּוֹסֵל, מִפְּנֵי שֶׁאֵין לָהּ גַּג — *R' Eliezer invalidates it, since it has no roof.* In both cases one cannot distinguish between roof and wall, and a *succah* must have a discernable roof at least one handbreadth wide (*Rav, Gem.* 19b). The halachah follows R' Eliezer *(Rav; Orach Chaim* 631:10).

עֲשָׂאָהּ לִשְׁכִיבָה, מְקַבֶּלֶת טֻמְאָה — *If made to lie upon, is susceptible to contamination.* Although such a mat is generally made for shade, if one designated it to recline upon it loses its acceptability because it then becomes a utensil and thus susceptible to *tumah* [see m. 4] *(Gem.* 20a).

לְסִיכּוּךְ, מְסַכְּכִין בָּהּ — *If for shade, we [may] use it for s'chach.* Even a small mat — which is generally made for reclining — is valid for *s'chach* if it was made expressly for *s'chach* *(Gem.).*

וְאֵינָהּ מְקַבֶּלֶת טֻמְאָה — *And it is not susceptible to contamination,* since he specifically intended it for shade, and not as a mat.

רַבִּי אֱלִיעֶזֶר אוֹמֵר — *R' Eliezer says:* The *Gemara* explains that R' Eliezer disagrees with the Sages and holds that even a large mat is generally made for reclining. Therefore, the words עֲשָׂאָהּ לִשְׁכִיבָה here imply that they are *usually* made for reclining *(Rav).*

לְסִכּוּךְ — *If for s'chach.* If he expressly designated it for *s'chach* [which is not its usual use], it never attains the status of a utensil. It is, therefore, not subject to *tumah* and is valid as *s'chach.* The halachah does not follow R' Eliezer *(Orach Chaim* 629:6).

CHAPTER TWO

Where the previous chapter discussed the laws governing the *succah* itself — its dimensions, the *s'chach,* and related matters — this chapter will discuss the act of performing the *mitzvah,* which requires one to sleep as well as to eat there. Indeed, the Torah states generally

with material that we may not use for s'chach, if there were four cubits beneath it, it is invalid.

[11] *If one makes his succah like a conical hut, or he leaned it against the wall, R' Eliezer invalidates it, since it has no roof; but the Sages declare it valid. A large reed mat, if made to lie upon, is susceptible to contamination and we may not use it for s'chach; if for shade, we may use it for s'chach and it is not susceptible to contamination. R' Eliezer says: Whether [the mat is] small or large, if he made it to lie upon, it is susceptible to contamination and we may not use it as s'chach; if for s'chach, we may use it for s'chach and it is not susceptible to contamination.*

CHAPTER TWO

[1] **הַיָּשֵׁן** *One who sleeps under the bed in the succah has not fulfilled his obligation [to sleep in a succah]. R' Yehudah said: We regularly slept under the bed in the presence of the Elders and they said nothing to us. R' Shimon said: There is a case of Tavi, Rabban Gamliel's slave, who used to sleep under the bed. Rabban Gamliel said to the Elders, 'Have you observed my slave Tavi? He is a scholar and knows that [gentile] slaves are exempt from [the obligation of] succah — that is why he sleeps under the bed.' And incidentally we deduced that one who sleeps under the bed does not fulfill his obligation [to sleep in a succah].*

YAD AVRAHAM

(*Lev.* 23:42): *In succos shall you dwell for seven days.* All activities and pastimes usually taking place in the home should be done in the *succah* so that it becomes one's temporary abode (see *Orach Chaim* 639:1). However, the mishnah singles out eating and sleeping as acts requiring a *succah,* because these activities are, as a rule, performed in the home.

In the temperate zones of Europe and North America, the *mitzvah* of sleeping in the *succah* has become regarded as a voluntary observance reserved for only the most devout. This apparent disregard of the law is itself based on a halachah — that of מִצְטַעֵר, *feeling distressed,* i.e., when climatic or other conditions are so severe that one feels a significant degree of discomfort in the *succah,* the *mitzvah* does not apply. The cool evening temperatures in temperate regions make sleeping outdoors a discomfort and consequently not obligatory.

1. הַיָּשֵׁן תַּחַת הַמִּטָּה — *One who sleeps under the bed.* The *Gemara* comments that the mishnah speaks of a bed where the area beneath is ten handbreadths high so that it is considered a 'tent' by itself. Thus, the bed acts as a barrier separating him from the *succah (Rav).* If the space beneath it was lower than ten handbreadths, it is considered to be part of the *succah* and one can discharge his obligation by sleeping there.

אָמַר רַבִּי יְהוּדָה: נוֹהֲגִין הָיִינוּ, שֶׁהָיִינוּ יְשֵׁנִים תַּחַת הַמִּטָּה בִּפְנֵי הַזְּקֵנִים — *R' Yehudah said: We regularly slept under the bed in the presence of the Elders.* R' Yehudah is consistent with his view (1:1) that a *succah* must be a permanent structure. Accordingly, a temporary shelter, such as the area underneath a movable bed, cannot nullify the permanent shelter of the *succah* proper *(Rav).* The halachah does not follow R' Yehudah (*Orach Chaim* 627:1).

שֶׁהוּא תַלְמִיד חָכָם וְיוֹדֵעַ שֶׁעֲבָדִים פְּטוּרִין מִן הַסֻּכָּה — *He is a scholar and knows that [gentile] slaves are exempt from [the obligation of] succah.* Non-Jews who have been purchased as slaves, must, within twelve months of their purchase, undergo circumcision, immerse in a *mikveh,* and accept voluntarily the *mitzvos* incumbent upon slaves owned by a Jew. Upon doing so, such slaves have the same obligations to observe *mitzvos* as Jewish women *(Chagigah* 4a). Since women are exempt from the *mitzvah* of *succah* because it has a fixed time (2:8), so are slaves *(Rav).*

לְפִיכָךְ יָשֵׁן הוּא תַּחַת הַמִּטָּה — *That is why he sleeps under the bed,* i.e., Tavi demonstrated his awareness of his exemption by sleeping unde the bed. If so, why was Tavi in the *succah* at all? Probably to serve his master, and at the same time to listen to the Torah discourses of the Sages. Presumably not wishing to take up space needed by those obligated to sleep in the *succah,* he slept under the bed (cf. *Yerushalmi* here cited by *Ran).*

וּלְפִי דַרְכֵּנוּ לָמַדְנוּ — *And · incidentally we deduced.* Although Rabban Gamliel mentioned Tavi's practice only in order to praise his slave, we learned a lesson *(Rav).* [Our practice is to derive lessons even from the casual conversation of scholars. It is axiomatic that a scholar does

[ב] הַסּוֹמֵךְ סֻכָּתוֹ בְּכַרְעֵי הַמִּטָּה, כְּשֵׁרָה. רַבִּי יְהוּדָה אוֹמֵר: אִם אֵינָהּ יְכוֹלָה לַעֲמוֹד בִּפְנֵי עַצְמָהּ, פְּסוּלָה. סֻכָּה הַמְדֻבְלֶלֶת, וְשֶׁצִּלָּתָהּ מְרֻבָּה מֵחַמָּתָהּ, כְּשֵׁרָה. הַמְעֻבָּה כְּמִין בַּיִת, אַף־עַל־פִּי שֶׁאֵין הַכּוֹכָבִים נִרְאִים מִתּוֹכָהּ, כְּשֵׁרָה.

[ג] הָעוֹשֶׂה סֻכָּתוֹ בְּרֹאשׁ הָעֲגָלָה אוֹ בְּרֹאשׁ הַסְּפִינָה כְּשֵׁרָה, וְעוֹלִין לָהּ בְּיוֹם טוֹב. בְּרֹאשׁ הָאִילָן אוֹ עַל־גַּבֵּי גָמָל כְּשֵׁרָה, וְאֵין עוֹלִין לָהּ בְּיוֹם טוֹב. שְׁתַּיִם בְּאִילָן וְאַחַת בִּידֵי אָדָם, אוֹ שְׁתַּיִם בִּידֵי אָדָם וְאַחַת בְּאִילָן, כְּשֵׁרָה, וְאֵין עוֹלִין לָהּ בְּיוֹם טוֹב. שָׁלֹשׁ בִּידֵי אָדָם וְאַחַת בְּאִילָן כְּשֵׁרָה, וְעוֹלִין לָהּ בְּיוֹם טוֹב. זֶה הַכְּלָל: כָּל־שֶׁנִּטַּל הָאִילָן וִיכוֹלָה לַעֲמוֹד בִּפְנֵי עַצְמָהּ, כְּשֵׁרָה, וְעוֹלִין לָהּ בְּיוֹם טוֹב.

[ד] הָעוֹשֶׂה סֻכָּתוֹ בֵּין הָאִילָנוֹת, וְהָאִילָנוֹת דְּפָנוֹת לָהּ, כְּשֵׁרָה. שְׁלוּחֵי מִצְוָה פְּטוּרִין מִן־הַסֻּכָּה. חוֹלִין וּמְשַׁמְּשֵׁיהֶן פְּטוּרִין מִן־הַסֻּכָּה. אוֹכְלִין וְשׁוֹתִין עֲרַאי חוּץ לַסֻּכָּה.

יד אברהם

not make statements unless they are well considered.]

2. הַסּוֹמֵךְ סֻכָּתוֹ בְּכַרְעֵי הַמִּטָּה — *If one supports his succah on the legs of a bed.* This refers to a bed with four boards around it, which extend above the mattress for at least ten more handbreadths. *S'chach* is placed on top of these four boards, which thus also serve as the walls of the *succah* (*Tur Orach Chaim* 630; *Bais Yosef* there).

כְּשֵׁרָה — *It is valid.* Even though when one moves the bed, he automatically moves the entire *succah* with it *(Tif. Yis.).*

רַבִּי יְהוּדָה אוֹמֵר — *R' Yehudah says* that is invalid. R' Yehudah is consistent with his view (1:1) that a *succah* must be a permanent structure; if it is movable it is invalid. The halachah does not follow R' Yehudah *(Rav).*

סֻכָּה הַמְדֻבְלֶלֶת — *A disarranged succah* [i.e. disarranged *s'chach].* Some of the *s'chach* points upward and some points downward, with the result that חַמָּתָהּ מְרֻבָּה מִצִּלָּתָהּ, *its sunny area is greater than its shaded area.* If the *s'chach* were lying evenly together, there would be more shaded area than sunny area. Since the spaces between the disarranged pieces are less than three handbreadths, we regard it as though it were all together and as such it is valid *(Rav; Orach Chaim* 631:5).

וְשֶׁצִּלָּתָהּ מְרֻבָּה מֵחַמָּתָהּ — *Or one whose shade[d area] is greater than its sun[lit] area.* There are many air spaces between the pieces of *s'chach,* each space being less than three handbreadths, but the total shaded area is greater than the sunny area [see m.1:1] *(Tif. Yis.; Orach Chaim* 631:4).

אַף עַל פִּי שֶׁאֵין הַכּוֹכָבִים נִרְאִים מִתּוֹכָהּ, כְּשֵׁרָה — *Even though the stars cannot be seen from inside it, it is valid.* However, it is preferable [לְכַתְּחִילָה] that the *s'chach* be laid on so that the stars are visible through it *(Orach Chaim* 631:3).

3. כְּשֵׁרָה — *It is valid.* Both *succos* meet the requirement of a temporary dwelling. A *succah* on a wagon is a livable abode even though it is mobile *(Rashi).*

So long as the *succah* is sturdy enough to stand up to normal *land* winds, it is a proper temporary dwelling, even if it could not withstand the impact of the turbulent winds that are more common at sea *(Gem.* 23a; *Orach Chaim* 629:2).

בְּרֹאשׁ הָאִילָן — *[If he makes a succah] in the top of a tree* by erecting partitions and covering them with *s'chach (Rashi* to 22b; *Rav).*

כְּשֵׁרָה, וְאֵין עוֹלִין לָהּ בְּיוֹם טוֹב — *It is valid, but we may not go up into it on the festival.* It meets the halachic requirements of a *succah* but runs afoul of the Rabbinic ban on the physical use of trees or live animals on festivals, instituted to prevent the breaking off of branches on *Yom Tov (Beitzah* 36b). [In the case of animals the fear is that he may break off a twig for use as a riding crop while riding the animal *(Rashi; Rav).*] Thus it may be used only during the Intermediate days of the festival *(Rashi, Rav).*

וְאַחַת בִּידֵי אָדָם — *And one [is] man-made.* A board is set into the ground to support the part of the floor that extends beyond the tree. The third wall of the *succah* is formed by that board, or something built on it, extending upward above the floor. The *s'chach* is laid across the top of all three walls *(Rashi; Rav).*

וְאֵין עוֹלִין לָהּ בְּיוֹם טוֹב — *But we may not go up into it on the festival.* In either case the tree is indispensable to the *succah;* without it,

[2] *If one supports his succah on the legs of a bed, it is valid. R' Yehudah says: If it cannot stand by itself, it is invalid. A disarranged succah, or one whose shade[d area] is greater than its sun[lit area], is valid. If [the succah] is thickly covered like a house, even though the stars cannot be seen from inside it, it is valid.*

[3] *If one makes his succah on top of a wagon or on the deck of a ship it is valid, and we may go up into it on the festival. [If he makes a succah] in the top of a tree or on the back of a camel it is valid, but we may not go up into it on the festival. [If] two [walls are] in a tree and one is man-made, or two [are] man-made and one [is] in a tree, it is valid, but we may not go up into it on the festival. [If] three [walls are] man-made and one [is] in a tree, it is valid, and we may go up into it on the festival. This is the general rule: Wherever the tree can be removed and [the succah] can stand by itself, it is valid, and we may go up into it on the festival.*

[4] *If one makes his succah between the trees, and the trees serve as its walls, it is valid. Those who are engaged in the performance of a mitzvah are exempt from the [mitzvah of] succah. Ill people and their attendants are exempt from the [mitzvah of] succah. We may eat and drink casually outside the succah.*

YAD AVRAHAM

the *succah* floor would collapse. Therefore, to dwell in the *succah* means to use the tree, an act that is forbidden on festivals. Consequently, it may be used only on Intermediate Days (*Rashi; Rav*).

שָׁלשׁ בִּידֵי אָדָם וְאַחַת בְּאִילָן כְּשֵׁרָה, וְעוֹלִין לָהּ בְּיוֹם טוֹב – *[If] three [walls are] man-made and one [is] in a tree, it is valid, and we may go up into it on the festival,* i.e., the *succah* is on the ground. Three of its walls are manmade and a tree is used as the fourth wall. Thus, even without the tree, enough remains to constitute a valid *succah* (see 1:1).

4. הָעוֹשֶׂה סֻכָּתוֹ בֵּין הָאִילָנוֹת, וְהָאִילָנוֹת דְּפָנוֹת לָהּ – *If one makes his succah between the trees, and the trees serve as its walls,* but the floor of the *succah* is on the ground (*Rashi*). [Otherwise, the mishnah would have added that he is not be permitted to 'go up into the *succah*' on Yom Tov.]

כְּשֵׁרָה – *It is valid.* We do not fear that he will make some direct use of the tree on the festival.

שְׁלוּחֵי מִצְוָה – *Those who are engaged in the performance [lit. agents] of a mitzvah.* For example: someone who is traveling to study Torah or to greet his rabbi, or is occupied with redeeming Jewish captives (*Rashi; Rav*).

פְּטוּרִין מִן הַסֻּכָּה – *Are exempt from the [mitzvah of] succah.* A person who is occupied with one *mitzvah* is exempt from another (הָעוֹסֵק בְּמִצְוָה פָּטוּר מִן הַמִּצְוָה). If performing the second *mitzvah* would require him to go out of his way. Consequently, people engaged in such a mission are obligated to sleep in a *succah* only if one is readily available. If it would be troublesome for them to build one or even look for one, they are exempt (*Rashi; Rama, Orach Chaim* 38:8).

פְּטוּרִין מִן הַסֻּכָּה – *Are exempt from the [mitzvah of] succah.* The sick person is exempt because Scripture states (*Lev.* 23:42): תֵּשְׁבוּ בַּסֻּכֹּת, *In succos you shall dwell.* This teaches תֵּשְׁבוּ כְּעֵין תָּדוּרוּ, *as you are accustomed to dwell all year long at home, so are you to dwell in a succah.* But under conditions of extreme discomfort such as illness, which would cause one to leave his normal dwelling to go to a more comfortable place, he is not required to live in a *succah* (*Rav* from *Gem.* 26a). The attendants are exempt because they are involved in the *mitvzah* of caring for the patient, and one who is involved in a *mitzvah* is exempt from another *mitzvah*. *Rama* (ibid.), however, cautions that on the first night of Succos, even those who suffer discomfort must eat at least כַּזַּיִת, *an olive's volume* of bread in the *succah*.

אוֹכְלִין וְשׁוֹתִין עֲרַאי חוּץ לַסֻּכָּה – *We may eat and drink casually outside the succah.* The *Shulchan Aruch* (*Orach Chaim* 639:2) follows the view that up to and including an egg's volume of bread is still considered a snack. More than this is considered a 'meal,' which must be eaten in the *succah.* The laws of the types and quantities of foods and drink that must be eaten in a *succah*, and the instances when the blessing לֵישֵׁב בַּסֻּכָּה, *to dwell in the succah,* must be recited, are discussed there at length.

[ה] מַעֲשֶׂה וְהֵבִיאוּ לוֹ לְרַבָּן יוֹחָנָן בֶּן־זַכַּאי לִטְעוֹם אֶת־הַתַּבְשִׁיל, וּלְרַבָּן גַּמְלִיאֵל שְׁתֵּי כוֹתָבוֹת וּדְלִי שֶׁל מַיִם, וְאָמְרוּ: „הַעֲלוּם לַסֻּכָּה." וּכְשֶׁנָּתְנוּ לוֹ לְרַבִּי צָדוֹק אֹכֶל פָּחוֹת מִכַּבֵּיצָה, נְטָלוֹ בְמַפָּה וַאֲכָלוֹ חוּץ לַסֻּכָּה, וְלֹא בֵרֵךְ אַחֲרָיו.

[ו] רַבִּי אֱלִיעֶזֶר אוֹמֵר: אַרְבַּע עֶשְׂרֵה סְעוּדוֹת חַיָּב אָדָם לֶאֱכוֹל בַּסֻּכָּה, אַחַת בַּיּוֹם וְאַחַת בַּלַּיְלָה. וַחֲכָמִים אוֹמְרִים: אֵין לַדָּבָר קִצְבָה, חוּץ מִלֵּילֵי יוֹם טוֹב רִאשׁוֹן שֶׁל חַג בִּלְבָד. וְעוֹד אָמַר רַבִּי אֱלִיעֶזֶר: מִי שֶׁלֹּא אָכַל לֵילֵי יוֹם טוֹב הָרִאשׁוֹן יַשְׁלִים בְּלֵילֵי יוֹם טוֹב הָאַחֲרוֹן. וַחֲכָמִים אוֹמְרִים: אֵין לַדָּבָר תַּשְׁלוּמִין. עַל־זֶה נֶאֱמַר: „מְעֻוָּת לֹא־יוּכַל לִתְקֹן, וְחֶסְרוֹן לֹא־יוּכַל לְהִמָּנוֹת."

[ז] מִי שֶׁהָיָה רֹאשׁוֹ וְרֻבּוֹ בַסֻּכָּה וְשֻׁלְחָנוֹ בְתוֹךְ הַבַּיִת — בֵּית שַׁמַּאי פּוֹסְלִין, וּבֵית הִלֵּל מַכְשִׁירִין. אָמְרוּ לָהֶן בֵּית הִלֵּל לְבֵית שַׁמַּאי: „לֹא כָךְ הָיָה מַעֲשֶׂה, שֶׁהָלְכוּ זִקְנֵי בֵית שַׁמַּאי וְזִקְנֵי בֵית הִלֵּל לְבַקֵּר אֶת־רַבִּי יוֹחָנָן בֶּן־הַחוֹרָנִי, וּמְצָאוּהוּ שֶׁהָיָה יוֹשֵׁב רֹאשׁוֹ וְרֻבּוֹ בַסֻּכָּה וְשֻׁלְחָנוֹ בְתוֹךְ הַבַּיִת, וְלֹא אָמְרוּ לוֹ דָבָר?" אָמְרוּ לָהֶן בֵּית שַׁמַּאי: „מִשָּׁם רְאָיָה? אַף הֵם אָמְרוּ לוֹ: ,אִם כֵּן הָיִיתָ נוֹהֵג, לֹא קִיַּמְתָּ מִצְוַת סֻכָּה מִיָּמֶיךָ'."

יד אברהם

5. וְאָמְרוּ: הַעֲלוּם לַסֻּכָּה — *And they* [i.e., both Rabban Yochanan and Rabban Gamliel] *said, 'Bring them up to the succah.'* This contradicts the previous mishnah which states that a snack may be eaten outside the *succah*. The *Gemara* (26a) resolves the contradiction by saying that they wished to be strict with themselves, and our mishnah teaches that a person is not regarded as haughty if he chooses to eat even fruit and water only in the *succah*. Though water in any amount may be drunk outside the *succah, Rambam,* quoted in *Orach Chaim* (639:2), states: Whoever wishes to be strict with himself and not drink even water outside the *succah* is praiseworthy.

נְטָלוֹ בְמַפָּה — *He took it with a cloth.* [This food required washing of the hands before eating, i.e., it was either bread or 'something which is dipped in liquid' (דָּבָר שֶׁטִּיבּוּלוֹ בְּמַשְׁקֶה) which required washing of the hands (at least in Talmudic times; see *Orach Chaim* 158:4).] R' Tzaddok holds that food smaller than the volume of an egg does not require washing. Had he been required to wash his hands, wrapping the food in a cloth to avoid touching it while eating would have been no substitute for washing; it is permitted only as an emergency measure when no water is to be found for a considerable distance *(Orach Chaim* 163:1). Though R' Tzaddok held that washing was not required, he held the food in a cloth for reasons of cleanliness *(Rashi)*.

וַאֲכָלוֹ חוּץ לַסֻּכָּה — *And ate it outside the succah,* thus demonstrating that one who is not strict with himself on this point is not to be considered careless in performing *mitzvos (Ran)*.

וְלֹא בֵרֵךְ אַחֲרָיו — *And did not recite the benediction after it.* R' Tzaddok held the view of R' Yehudah *(Berachos* 7:2) that one is obligated to recite *Bircas HaMazon* only after a meal of at least an egg's volume of bread. [The halachah, however, follows R' Meir who rules that eating an olive's volume of bread obligates one in *Bircas HaMazon (Orach Chaim* 184:6).]

6. רַבִּי אֱלִיעֶזֶר אוֹמֵר: אַרְבַּע עֶשְׂרֵה סְעוּדוֹת חַיָּב אָדָם לֶאֱכוֹל בַּסֻּכָּה — *R' Eliezer says: A man is obligated to eat fourteen meals in the succah.* Just as one eats a meal in the morning and a meal in the evening in his own house, he is to do the same in the *succah (Gem.* 27a).

וַחֲכָמִים אוֹמְרִים: אֵין לַדָּבָר קִצְבָה — *But the Sages say: This matter has no fixed obligation.* The Sages also agree with R' Eliezer that one should dwell in the *succah* just as he dwells at home. However, just as one is not *required* to eat at home twice a day, so it is in the *succah (Rav)*.

חוּץ מִלֵּילֵי יוֹם טוֹב רִאשׁוֹן שֶׁל חַג בִּלְבָד — *Except for the night of the first Yom Tov of the Festival only,* i.e., the first night of Succos. The *mitzvah* of dwelling in a *succah (Lev.* 23:24) applies to all seven days of Succos, but on the first night of

[5] *Once they brought Rabban Yochanan ben Zakkai some cooked food to taste, and to Rabban Gamliel [they brought] two dates and a pail of water, and they said, 'Bring them up to the succah.' But when they gave R' Tzaddok food smaller than the volume of an egg, he took it with a cloth and ate it outside the succah, and did not recite the benediction after it.*

[6] *R' Eliezer says: A man is obligated to eat fourteen meals in the succah, one each day and one each night. But the Sages say: This matter has no fixed obligation, except for the night of the first Yom Tov of the Festival only. R' Eliezer further stated: Whoever did not eat [in the succah] on the night of the first Yom Tov must compensate for it on the night of the last Yom Tov. But the Sages say: This matter has no compensation. About this matter it is said [Ecclesiastes 1:15]: A twisted thing cannot be made straight, and what is not there cannot be numbered.*

[7] *A person who had his head and most of his body inside the succah and his table inside the house — Beis Shammai invalidate [the succah], and Beis Hillel validate it. Said Beis Hillel to Beis Shammai, 'Did it not happen that the elders of Beis Shammai and the elders of Beis Hillel went to visit R' Yochanan son of the Choranite, and found him sitting with his head and most of his body inside the succah and his table within the house, and they said nothing to him?' Beis Shammai replied to them, 'Is that [your] proof? Actually they said to him, "If this is how you have [always] conducted yourself, [then] you have never in your life fulfilled the mitzvah of succah." '*

YAD AVRAHAM

Succos, a meal *must* be eaten in the *succah* מִדְאוֹרַיְתָא, *by Torah law.*

וְעוֹד אָמַר רַבִּי אֱלִיעֶזֶר – *R' Eliezer further stated* that that one who failed to eat a meal in the *succah* on the first night should add food to his regular *Shemini Atzeres* meal to compensate for the missed meal. [However, the *Shemini Atzeres* meal is not to be eaten in the *succah,* for the *mitzvah* of *succah* no longer applies, as will be discussed below *(Rashi; Rav).*] The *Gemara* explains that R' Eliezer changed his view about the requirement of fourteen meals and concurred with the Sages that there is no set number of required meals. But he compares eating in the *succah* to sacrifices. If one failed to bring the required sacrifices on the first day of *Yom Tov,* he may compensate by bringing them on the last day (*Gemara,* following *Rashi).*

וַחֲכָמִים אוֹמְרִים – *But the Sages say* that if one missed the obligatory meal on the first night there is no way to make it up.

7. מִי שֶׁהָיָה רֹאשׁוֹ וְרֻבּוֹ בַּסֻּכָּה – *A person who had his head and most of his body inside the succah.* In Talmudic times it was customary to eat lying on a couch, rather than sitting erect, and low tables were placed next to each couch. In our mishnah's case the table was not inside the *succah,* for reasons that will be discussed below.

בֵּית שַׁמַּאי פּוֹסְלִין, וּבֵית הִלֵּל מַכְשִׁירִין – *Beis Shammai invalidate [the succah] and Beis Hillel validate it.* Beis Shammai and Beis Hillel disagree in two cases. The first is when the *succah* is large enough to contain the person, his table, and even more people, but he chose to recline near the *succah* entrance and keep his table in the house. Beis Shammai forbid this for fear that 'he may follow his table into the house.' But Beis Hillel permitted this.

The second dispute is where the *succah* is so small that it can contain no more than his head and the greater part of his body [but not even a one-handbreadth table]; Beis Shammai invalidate that *succah* and Beis Hillel validate it. Here, too, the reason is that he may follow his table *(Rambam; Rav).* The *Gemara* notes that in this case the halachah follows Beis Shammai rather than Beis Hillel. *Seder* of *R' Amram* notes that this is one of only six disputes between the two schools where the halachah follows Beis Shammai *(Tosafos* 3a).

אִם כֵּן הָיִיתָ נוֹהֵג, לֹא קִיַּמְתָּ מִצְוַת סֻכָּה מִיָּמֶיךָ – *"If this is how you have [always] conducted yourself [then] you have never in your life fulfilled the mitzvah of succah." '* Beis Shammai admonished R' Yochanan that since he kept the table outside the *succah,* he had never fulfilled the *mitzah* properly in accordance with the regulation of the Sages, although he had satisfied the Torah requirement *(Ritva).*

[ח] נָשִׁים, וַעֲבָדִים, וּקְטַנִּים פְּטוּרִים מִן־הַסֻּכָּה. קָטָן שֶׁאֵינוֹ צָרִיךְ לְאִמּוֹ חַיָּב בַּסֻּכָּה. מַעֲשֶׂה וְיָלְדָה כַלָּתוֹ שֶׁל שַׁמַּאי הַזָּקֵן וּפִחֵת אֶת־הַמַּעֲזִיבָה וְסִכֵּךְ עַל־גַּבֵּי הַמִּטָּה בִּשְׁבִיל הַקָּטָן.

[ט] כָּל־שִׁבְעַת הַיָּמִים אָדָם עוֹשֶׂה סֻכָּתוֹ קֶבַע וּבֵיתוֹ עֲרַאי. יָרְדוּ גְשָׁמִים, מֵאֵימָתַי מֻתָּר לְפַנּוֹת? מִשֶּׁתִּסְרַח הַמִּקְפָּה. מָשְׁלוּ מָשָׁל: לְמָה הַדָּבָר דּוֹמֶה? לְעֶבֶד שֶׁבָּא לִמְזוֹג כּוֹס לְרַבּוֹ, וְשָׁפַךְ לוֹ קִיתוֹן עַל־פָּנָיו.

פרק שלישי

[א] **לוּלָב** הַגָּזוּל וְהַיָּבֵשׁ פָּסוּל. שֶׁל אֲשֵׁרָה וְשֶׁל עִיר הַנִּדַּחַת פָּסוּל. נִקְטַם רֹאשׁוֹ, נִפְרְצוּ עָלָיו, פָּסוּל. נִפְרְדוּ עָלָיו, כָּשֵׁר. רַבִּי

יד אברהם

8. נָשִׁים, וַעֲבָדִים — *Women, slaves,* i.e., non-Jewish slaves.

פְּטוּרִים מִן הַסֻּכָּה — *Are exempt from the [mitzvah of] succah.* Although we derive some laws of Succos from Pesach, in which women and slaves are obligated [in exception to the general rule exempting them from time — specific time-related *mitzvos*], this does not obligate them to eat in the *succah* (*Gem.* 28a).

קָטָן שֶׁאֵינוֹ צָרִיךְ לְאִמּוֹ — *A minor who does not need his mother.* The *Gemara* (28b) explains that this refers to a child who is not so dependent on her that he must *continually* call her. Rather, he calls once and then remains silent *(Rashi).*

חַיָּב בַּסֻּכָּה — *Is obligated [to dwell] in the succah.* His obligation is the Rabbinical one of חִנּוּךְ, *training,* in the performance of *mitzvos.* Circumstances determine the age of training for each particular *mitzvah (Tosafos).*

וְסִכֵּךְ עַל גַּבֵּי הַמִּטָּה בִּשְׁבִיל הַקָּטָן — *And placed s'chach above the bed for the child.* Shammai the Elder, disagreeing with the first Tanna, imposes training even upon children who still need their mothers. The Sages, on the other hand, maintain that since the mother is exempt from the *mitzvah* and the child needs the mother, there is no obligation to train him *(Ran).*

9. כָּל שִׁבְעַת הַיָּמִים אָדָם עוֹשֶׂה סֻכָּתוֹ קֶבַע — *All the seven days a man must make his succah [his] permanent [abode].* If he has beautiful vessels, he should bring them into the *succah;* if he has beautiful divans, he should bring them into the *succah;* he should eat, drink and spend his leisure time in the *succah.* He should also study Torah in the *succah,* but if it is difficult for him to concentrate in the *succah,* he may study outside the *succah (Gem.* 28b; *Orach Chaim* 639:4).

וּבֵיתוֹ עֲרַאי — *And his house [his] temporary [abode].* He should use his house only for functional matters (e.g., cooking), whereas the *succah* should serve as his abode *(Rambam).*

מֵאֵימָתַי מֻתָּר לְפַנּוֹת? מִשֶּׁתִּסְרַח הַמִּקְפָּה — *When is it permissible to leave? When the porridge becomes spoiled.* מִקְפָּה is any cooked food which is neither very loose nor very thick *(Rashi, Rav).* The porridge need not be in the *succah;* one need only estimate the amount of time needed for it to spoil if it were in the *succah.*

מָשְׁלוּ מָשָׁל: לְמָה הַדָּבָר דּוֹמֶה — *They* [the Sages] *illustrated this with a parable: To what is this comparable?* [i.e., being forced out of the *succah* by rain].

וְשָׁפַךְ לוֹ קִיתוֹן עַל פָּנָיו — *And he poured the jug at his face,* as if to say that the slave is not serving him properly, and his services are no longer needed. By causing it to rain, the Almighty is telling us that He is dissatisfied with our service and so He asks us to leave *(Rashi, Rav).*

CHAPTER THREE

◆§ The Four Species

As the *Gemara* states, אַרְבָּעָה מִינִים שֶׁבַּלּוּלָב מְעַכְּבִים זֶה אֶת זֶה, *the four species connected with the lulav are dependent upon one another;* i.e., the *mitzvah* cannot be performed in the absence of any one of them. The *mitzvah,* as ordained by the Torah, is actually two fold: on the first day of Succos, the obligation of taking the species applies everywhere; for the rest of the *Yom Tov,* the *mitzvah* applies only in the Temple. After the destruction of the Second Temple, Rabban Yochanan Ben Zakkai instituted the performance of the *mitzvah* throughout Succos everywhere (except for the Sabbath) in commemoration of the Temple ritual (m. 12).

1. לוּלָב הַגָּזוּל — *A stolen lulav.* The Four Species must be the property of the one using them; a stolen *lulav,* therefore, is invalid. This is derived from the word (*Lev.* 24:20) לָכֶם [lit., *for yourself*], which is expounded to mean מִשֶּׁלָּכֶם, *from*

[8] *Women, slaves, and minors are exempt from the succah. A minor who does not need his mother is obligated [to dwell] in the succah. It once happened that the daughter-in-law of Shammai the Elder gave birth and he removed the plaster [roof] and placed s'chach above the bed for the child.*

[9] *All the seven days a man must make his succah [his] permanent [abode] and his house [his] temporary [abode]. If it rained, when is it permissible to leave? When the porridge becomes spoiled. They [the Sages] illustrated this with a parable: To what is this comparable? To a slave who came to pour a cup for his master, and he poured the jug at his face.*

CHAPTER THREE

[1] **לוּלָב** *A stolen lulav or a dry one is invalid. [One] from an asherah or from a city that was led astray is invalid. If its top was broken off, [or] its leaves severed, it is invalid. If its leaves spread apart, it is valid.*

YAD AVRAHAM

your own property. For the same reason, even a borrowed *lulav* would be invalid. Another reason is the Talmudic dictum that מִצְוָה הַבָּאָה בַּעֲבֵרָה, *a mitzvah made possible by a transgression,* is unacceptable (*Gem.* 30a). It is this principle that distinguishes a stolen *lulav* from a borrowed one. Accordingly, though a borrowed *lulav* is unacceptable only on the first day, for its user does not own it, a stolen one is invalid for the entire Succos festival.

וְהַיָּבֵשׁ – *Or a dry one.* Either the majority of its leaves or its spine has dried out (*Orach Chaim* 645:5). The reason that a dry *lulav* is rendered invalid is because of the requirement that the Four Species possess הָדָר, *beauty [Lev.* 24:40] (*Tos.*).

The actual degree of dryness that invalidates the *lulav* is the subject of dispute. *Tosafos* and *Rosh* explain that *dry* means so brittle that one can crumble it with his nail. *Ravad* (quoted by *Rosh*) maintains that practical experience contradicts this definition, since a *lulav* may last many years without reaching that state. In the context of *lulav,* therefore, *Ravad* defines dryness as a total lack of greenness, where the *lulav* remains white because all its moisture is gone. The *Shulchan Aruch* (*Orach Chaim* 645:5) follows *Ravad's* view. *Rama* states that where *lulavim* were not available it was customary to rely on the more lenient view of *Tosafos* and *Rosh.*

שֶׁל אֲשֵׁרָה – *[One] from an asherah,* i.e., a tree worshiped by idolaters.

וְשֶׁל עִיר הַנִּדַּחַת – *Or from a city that was led astray.* The law of this city is outlined in *Deuteronomy* 13:13-19. In brief, if the majority of residents in a Jewish city are persuaded by local residents to worship idols, the city and all its contents must be burned (*Rambam, Hilchos Avodah Zarah* 4:2).

פָּסוּל – *Is invalid.* This invalidation is due to the failure to meet the שִׁיעוּר, [the halachically prescribed] size of the *lulav.* In the view of halachah, once an object is condemned to be burned — as are the *asherah* and the *city led astray* — it is considered as it if had already been burned and reduced to ashes. Thus it lacks the physical dimensions required for the *mitzvah.*

◆§ The Lulav

Invalidation of the *lulav* involves its three basic physical features: שִׁדְרָה, *spine;* עָלִים, *leaves;* and תְּיוֹמֶת, *twin-leaf.*

The *spine* is the thick green core which serves as the *lulav's* center. The leaves grow out of the spine and constitute the bulk of the *lulav.* According to most commentators, the *twin-leaf* refers to the uppermost double-leaf growing from the top of the *lulav* and forming its tip (*Tosafos; Rosh; Rama, Orach Chaim* 645:3). According to *Rambam* (*Lulav* 8:4) and *Shulchan Aruch* (*ibid.*), each of the *lulav's* leaves are referred to as a *twin-leaf,* for each is composed of two connected leaves.

There is a difference of opinion among the *Rishonim,* as to which leaves the mishnah refers to as ראשו, *its top:*

— *Rosh* maintains that the 'top' of the *lulav* means the top of the *majority* of its upper leaves.

— *Ran* and *Maggid Mishnah* (8:3) hold that the top of the *lulav* is the tip of the middle leaf (תְּיוֹמֶת) only, which, if broken off, is sufficient reason to invalidate the *lulav.*

— *Shulchan Aruch* (*Orach Chaim* 645:6) follows the view of *Rosh,* but *Rama* (*ibid.*) adds that we should be strict and follow the views of *Ran* and *Maggid Mishnah.*

נִפְרְצוּ עָלָיו – *[Or] its leaves severed.* The *Gemara* (32a) compares the leaves of this *lulav* to the leaves of a broom. According to *Rashi,* the *lulav's* leaves are completely severed from its spine and are tied to it like an old-fashioned broom (*Rav*). *Rif* and *Rambam* (8:3) understand that the leaves are partially torn from the spine but are still dangling from it, thus resembling the leaves that are used in fashioning a broom. *Shulcan Aruch* (*Orach Chaim* 645:2) follows the

יְהוּדָה אוֹמֵר: יֵאגְדֶנּוּ מִלְמַעְלָה. צִנֵּי הַר הַבַּרְזֶל כְּשֵׁרוֹת. לוּלָב שֶׁיֶּשׁ־בּוֹ שְׁלֹשָׁה טְפָחִים, כְּדֵי לְנַעֲנֵעַ בּוֹ, כָּשֵׁר.

[ב] הֲדַס הַגָּזוּל וְהַיָּבֵשׁ פָּסוּל. שֶׁל אֲשֵׁרָה וְשֶׁל עִיר הַנִּדַּחַת פָּסוּל. נִקְטַם רֹאשׁוֹ, נִפְרְצוּ עָלָיו, אוֹ שֶׁהָיוּ עֲנָבָיו מְרֻבּוֹת מֵעָלָיו, פָּסוּל. וְאִם מִעֲטָן כָּשֵׁר, וְאֵין מְמַעֲטִין בְּיוֹם טוֹב.

[ג] עֲרָבָה גְזוּלָה וִיבֵשָׁה פְּסוּלָה. שֶׁל אֲשֵׁרָה וְשֶׁל עִיר הַנִּדַּחַת פְּסוּלָה. נִקְטַם רֹאשָׁהּ, נִפְרְצוּ עָלֶיהָ, וְהַצַּפְצָפָה, פְּסוּלָה; כְּמוּשָׁה, וְשֶׁנָּשְׁרוּ מִקְצָת עָלֶיהָ, וְשֶׁל בַּעַל, כְּשֵׁרָה.

[ד] רַבִּי יִשְׁמָעֵאל אוֹמֵר: שְׁלֹשָׁה הֲדַסִּים, וּשְׁתֵּי עֲרָבוֹת, לוּלָב אֶחָד, וְאֶתְרוֹג אֶחָד; אֲפִילוּ שְׁנַיִם קְטוּמִים וְאֶחָד אֵינוֹ קָטוּם. רַבִּי טַרְפוֹן אוֹמֵר: אֲפִלּוּ שְׁלָשְׁתָּן קְטוּמִים. רַבִּי עֲקִיבָא אוֹמֵר: כְּשֵׁם שֶׁלּוּלָב אֶחָד וְאֶתְרוֹג אֶחָד, כָּךְ הֲדַס אֶחָד וַעֲרָבָה אַחַת.

[ה] אֶתְרוֹג הַגָּזוּל וְהַיָּבֵשׁ פָּסוּל. שֶׁל אֲשֵׁרָה וְשֶׁל עִיר הַנִּדַּחַת פָּסוּל. שֶׁל עָרְלָה פָּסוּל. שֶׁל תְּרוּמָה טְמֵאָה פָּסוּל. שֶׁל תְּרוּמָה טְהוֹרָה לֹא יִטֹּל,

---

יד אברהם

view of *Rif* and *Rambam.*

פָּסוּל – *It is invalid.* In both cases it is invalid due to a lack of הָדָר, *beauty.*

נִפְרְדוּ עָלָיו – *If its leaves spread apart,* i.e., they are fully attached to the spine but are spread apart on top like the branches of a tree *(Rashi, Rav).*

צִנֵּי הַר הַבַּרְזֶל – *The thorn palms of the Iron Mountain.* The spines of these palm branches are very sparsely covered with short leaves. In some such branches, the top of the lower leaf does not reach even as far as the beginning of the one above it *(Rashi; Rav).* They are valid only if the top of one leaf reaches the base of the next one *(Gem.* 32a; *Orach Chaim* 645:4).

כְּדֵי לְנַעֲנֵעַ בּוֹ – *[Long] enough to wave.* The *lulav* must be three handbreadths long — the length of the *hadas* and *aravah* — plus another handbreadth for waving (see m. 9). Thus, in total, the *lulav* must be at least *four* handbreadths long, while the *hadas* and *aravah* need be only three.

☙ The Hadas

2. From the Scriptural description (*Lev.* 23:40) of the *hadas* as עֲנַף עֵץ־עָבֹת, *twig of a plaited tree (Rambam, Lulav* 7:2), we derive the requirement that the *hadas* be covered with leaves in a fashion that resembles a plait or braid. The *Gemara* (32b) stipulates that the leaves of the *hadas* should grow in clusters of at least three — either from central points on the twig, or from three points on one level.

וְהַיָּבֵשׁ – *or a dry one.* [See comm. to previous mishnah, s.v. והיבש).] *Ravad* maintains that the myrtle is dried out only when it turns white. At this stage, the moisture is gone and cannot be restored. *Shulchan Aruch* (648:7) concurs.

נִקְטַם ראשו – *If its top was broken off.* In the case of the *hadas,* the commentators are in almost total agreement that the top of the *stem* is meant. However, the halachah follows R' Tarfon in mishnah 4, who disagrees *(Rav).*

נִפְרְצוּ עָלָיו – *[Or] its leaves were severed,* i.e., if a *hadas* lost most of its leaves.

או שֶׁהָיוּ עֲנָבָיו מְרֻבּוֹת מֵעָלָיו, פָּסוּל – *or its berries outnumbered its leaves, it is invalid. Hadas* twigs sometimes produce a small berry-like fruit. As long as the berries are green like the leaves, they are acceptable, but if the berries are black or red, and they outnumber the leaves, they create a spotted appearance that is inconsistent with the requirement of beauty, invalidating the *hadas (Rav).*

וְאִם מִעֲטָן – *If he decreased them,* i.e., he plucked off enough berries before *Yom Tov* so that they no longer outnumbered the leaves.

וְאֵין מְמַעֲטִין בְּיוֹם טוב – *But we may not decrease them on Yom Tov.* Since the removal is to validate the twig it is considered 'repairing,' and is prohibited on the Sabbath and *Yom Tov (Gemara* 33b).

☙ The Aravah

3. נִפְרְצוּ עָלֶיהָ – *[Or] its leaves were severed.* The majority of its leaves fell off, as in the case of the *hadas* (see comm. to mishnah 2).

R' Yehudah says: He should tie them together at the top. The thorn palms of the Iron Mountain are valid. A lulav that is three handbreadths long, [long] enough to wave, is valid.

[2] *A stolen myrtle twig or a dry one is invalid. [One] from an asherah or a city that was led astray is invalid. If its top was broken off, [or] its leaves were severed, or its berries outnumbered its leaves, it is invalid. If he decreased them it is valid, but we may not decrease them on Yom Tov.*

[3] *A stolen willow twig or a dry one is invalid. [One] from an asherah or from a city that was led astray is invalid. If its top was broken off, [or] its leaves were severed, or [it is] a tzaftzafah, it is invalid. [One whose leaves are] wilted, or part of its leaves have fallen off, or [one] from a field, is valid.*

[4] *R' Yishmael says: Three myrtle twigs, two willow twigs, one lulav, and one esrog [are required]; even if two are broken off and one is not broken off. R' Tarfon says: Even if all three are broken off. R' Akiva says: Just as there is one lulav and one esrog, so [there is] one myrtle twig and one willow twig.*

[5] *A stolen esrog or a dry one is invalid. [One] from an asherah or from a city that was led astray is invalid. [One] of orlah is invalid. [One] of contaminated terumah is invalid. [If it is] of pure terumah he should not use it,*

YAD AVRAHAM

וְהַצַּפְצָפָה – *Or [it is] a tzaftzafah.* This is a mountain plant that resembles the *aravah,* but is a different species. Its stem is white rather than reddish and its leaves are rounded with serrated edges, unlike the elongated, smooth leaves of the *aravah (Gem.; Rambam, Lulav* 7:4).

כְּמוּשָׁה – *[One whose leaves are] wilted,* i.e., no longer fresh, but not dried out.

וְשֶׁנָּשְׁרוּ מִקְצָת עָלֶיהָ – *Or part of its leaves have fallen off,* but only a minority of them.

וְשֶׁל בַּעַל – *Or [one] from a field.* It grew in a rain-watered field, and not near a brook *(Rav).* The *Gemara* explains that the phrase עַרְבֵי נַחַל, *willows of the stream,* does not exclude willows that grew elsewhere.

4. רַבִּי יִשְׁמָעֵאל אוֹמֵר: שְׁלֹשָׁה הֲדַסִּים, וּשְׁתֵּי עֲרָבוֹת, לוּלָב אֶחָד, וְאֶתְרוֹג אֶחָד – *R' Yishmael says: Three myrtle twigs, two willow twigs, one lulav, and one esrog [are required].* The *Gemara* (34b) explains that he derives these numbers from the wording of the verse *(Lev.* 23:40).

אֲפִילוּ שְׁנַיִם קְטוּמִים וְאֶחָד אֵינוֹ קָטוּם – *Even if two [hadas twigs] are broken off and one is not broken off.*

רַבִּי טַרְפוֹן אוֹמֵר: אֲפִלּוּ שְׁלָשְׁתָּן קְטוּמִים – *R' Tarfon says: Even if all three are broken off.* R' Tarfon, in opposition to mishnah 2, validates a broken *hadas* because he does not require הָדָר, *beauty,* for the *hadas* or *aravah (Rashi; Rav). Rambam,* however, explains that since the leaves cover the twig all the way to the top, the missing tip is not noticeable, and does not lack in beauty. *Shulchan Aruch (Orach Chaim* 646:1,10), following the opinion of *Rif, Rambam,* and *Rosh,* validates a *hadas* whose top is clipped off. *Rama,* however, rules that wherever possible, one should not use such a *hadas.*

רַבִּי עֲקִיבָא אוֹמֵר – *R' Akiva says* that just one each of the species is necessary to fulfill the *mitzvah.*

◆§ The Esrog

5. Since the *esrog* is the only one of the Four Species that is edible, laws relating to food will apply to it. Some of these laws are among the subjects of our mishnah.

וְהַיָּבֵשׁ – *Or a dry one. Ravad* defines the degree of dryness which invalidates an *esrog* as the complete lack of moisture *(Tur* 648).

שֶׁל עָרְלָה – *[One] of orlah.* For the first three years after a tree's planting, the fruit is forbidden for consumption and no benefit may be derived from it *(Leviticus* 19:23). Such fruit is called *'orlah'* (restricted), and it must be burned.

שֶׁל תְּרוּמָה טְמֵאָה פָּסוּל – *[One] of contaminated terumah is invalid.* If *terumah,* the tithe given to a *Kohen,* becomes *tamei* [contaminated], it must be burned. Thus, such an *esrog,* as well as the *orlah-esrog,* is not considered his property because they are forbidden to him.

שֶׁל תְּרוּמָה טְהוֹרָה לֹא יִטֹּל – *[If it is] of pure terumah he should not use it.* Although an uncontaminated *terumah-esrog* is valid according to the halachah, the Sages decreed that its use should be avoided in order to avoid the possibility that it might become contaminated.

וְאִם נָטַל, כָּשֵׁר. שֶׁל דְּמַאי, בֵּית שַׁמַּאי פּוֹסְלִין, וּבֵית הִלֵּל מַכְשִׁירִין. שֶׁל מַעֲשֵׂר שֵׁנִי בִּירוּשָׁלַיִם, לֹא יִטֹּל, וְאִם נָטַל, כָּשֵׁר.

[ו] עָלְתָה חֲזָזִית עַל־רֻבּוֹ, נִטְּלָה פִּטְמָתוֹ, נִקְלַף, נִסְדַּק, נִקַּב וְחָסֵר כָּל־שֶׁהוּא, פָּסוּל. עָלְתָה חֲזָזִית עַל־מִעוּטוֹ, נִטַּל עֻקְצוֹ, נִקַּב וְלֹא חָסַר כָּל־שֶׁהוּא, כָּשֵׁר. אֶתְרוֹג הַכּוּשִׁי פָּסוּל. וְהַיָּרֹק כְּכַרְתִי, רַבִּי מֵאִיר מַכְשִׁיר, וְרַבִּי יְהוּדָה פּוֹסֵל.

[ז] שִׁעוּר אֶתְרוֹג הַקָּטָן — רַבִּי מֵאִיר אוֹמֵר: כָּאֱגוֹז. רַבִּי יְהוּדָה אוֹמֵר: כַּבֵּיצָה. וּבַגָּדוֹל — כְּדֵי שֶׁיֹּאחֵז שְׁנַיִם בְּיָדוֹ אַחַת; דִּבְרֵי רַבִּי יְהוּדָה. רַבִּי יוֹסֵי אוֹמֵר: אֲפִילוּ אֶחָד בִּשְׁתֵּי יָדָיו.

[ח] אֵין אוֹגְדִין אֶת־הַלּוּלָב אֶלָּא בְמִינוֹ; דִּבְרֵי רַבִּי יְהוּדָה. רַבִּי מֵאִיר אוֹמֵר: אֲפִילוּ בִמְשִׁיחָה. אָמַר רַבִּי מֵאִיר: מַעֲשֶׂה בְּאַנְשֵׁי יְרוּשָׁלַיִם שֶׁהָיוּ אוֹגְדִין אֶת־לוּלְבֵיהֶן בְּגִימוֹנִיּוֹת שֶׁל זָהָב. אָמְרוּ לוֹ: בְּמִינוֹ הָיוּ אוֹגְדִין אוֹתוֹ מִלְּמַטָּה.

[ט] וְהֵיכָן הָיוּ מְנַעְנְעִין? בְּ,,הוֹדוּ לַה',״ תְּחִלָּה וָסוֹף, וּבְ,,אָנָּא ה',

---

יד אברהם

שֶׁל דְּמַאי — *[If it is] of demai.* In the times of Yochanan, the High Priest, it was found that many unlearned people were careful to separate *terumah*, but were lax in separating *maaser*. As a result the Sages decreed that one who buys produce from an עַם הָאָרֶץ, *unlearned person,* must separate *maaser* from it even if assured by the seller that he had already done so. This produce is called *demai*.

בֵּית שַׁמַּאי פּוֹסְלִין — *Beis Shammai invalidate it.* Since the *demai-esrog* may not be eaten until it is tithed, it lacks the necessary requirement of לָכֶם, *yours (Rashi; Rav).*

וּבֵית הִלֵּל מַכְשִׁירִין — *And Beis Hillel validate it.* Beis Hillel regard an *esrog* of *demai* as *'yours'* because the Sages permitted it to the poor for consumption without re-tithing. Beis Shammai, however, forbid *demai* even to the poor *(Ran).*

שֶׁל מַעֲשֵׂר שֵׁנִי בִּירוּשָׁלַיִם — *[If it is] of ma'aser sheni in Jerusalem.* In addition to מַעֲשֵׂר רִאשׁוֹן, *the first tithe,* which must be given to the Levite, the Torah requires the owner to separate מַעֲשֵׂר שֵׁנִי, *the second tithe,* which belongs to the owner but can be eaten only in Jerusalem. Unlike the Levite's tithe, *maaser sheni* is holy, and thus, like *terumah*, may not be contaminated *(Lev.* 27:30). Therefore, the Sages preferred that an esrog of *maaser sheni*, like one of *terumah*, not be used.

וְאִם נָטַל, כָּשֵׁר — *But if he used it, it is valid.* However, outside Jerusalem, where *maaser sheni* fruits may not be eaten, an *esrog* of *maaser sheni* would not be valid *(Rashi; Rav).*

6. עַל רֻבּוֹ — *On most of it.* Only if the boil cover the greater portion of the *esrog* is it considered invalid. An *esrog* with such a growth lacks beauty *(Rosh; Mishnah Berurah* 648:37). The *Gemara* (35b) adds that even a small boil can invalidate the *esrog* if it is on its חוֹטֶם, *nose,* i.e., the part that narrows towards its peak. This part of the *esrog* is more important because any blemish there is immediately visible *(Rashi).*

נִטְּלָה פִּטְמָתוֹ — *[Or] its pitam was removed,* i.e., the short stem that protrudes from the nose of the *esrog*. The tip of this stem is called the שׁוֹשַׁנְתָּא, *bud.* An *esrog* whose top stem, *pitam,* has been removed is invalid because it is חָסֵר, *deficient. Esrogim*, however, that grow without a *pitam* obviously are not deficient *(Mishnah Berurah* 648:32).

נִקְלַף — *[Or] it was peeled.* The *esrog* in our mishnah is missing its thin outer peel, leaving its body intact and not altering its color *(Ran).* It is invalid because it lacks beauty.

נִסְדַּק — *[Or] it was split.* Although no part of the *esrog* is missing, the fact that it is split invalidates it as it if were deficient *(Orach Chaim* 648:5).

נִקַּב וְחָסֵר כָּל שֶׁהוּא — *[Or] it was punctured and is missing a slight portion.* The *esrog* was both punctured *and* made partially deficient *(Rashi; Ravad).* According to *Rambam*, however, a puncture and a deficiency are two separate invalidations.

נִטַּל עֻקְצוֹ — *[Or] its stem was removed,* i.e., the stem at the base of the *esrog*, by which it was attached to the tree.

כָּשֵׁר — *It is valid.* In none of these latter cases

but if he used it, it is valid. [If it is] of demai, Beis Shammai invalidate it, and Beis Hillel validate it. [If it is of] ma'aser sheni in Jerusalem, he should not use it, but if he used it, it is valid.

[6] *If a scab-like boil grew on most of it, [or] its pitam was removed, [or] it was peeled, [or] it was split, [or] it was punctured and is missing a slight portion, it is invalid. If a boil covered a minority of it, [or] its stem was removed, [or] it was punctured and nothing was missing, it is valid. An Ethiopian esrog is invalid. If one is green as a leek, R' Meir validates it but R' Yehudah invalidates it.*

[7] *The minimum size of an esrog — R' Meir says: Like a nut. R' Yehudah says: Like an egg. And the maximum — so that he can hold two [esrogim] in one hand; these are the words of R' Yehudah. R' Yose says: Even one [that must be held] in both hands.*

[8] *We do not bind the lulav except with its own kind; these are the words of R' Yehudah. R' Meir says: Even with cord. R' Meir said: It happened that the men of Jerusalem would bind their lulavim with gold wire. The Sages said to him [in rebuttal]: They would bind it with its own kind underneath.*

[9] *At which point [in the Hallel service] did they wave [the lulav]? At 'Give thanks to* HASHEM,' *at the beginning and end, and at 'Please* HASHEM,

---

YAD AVRAHAM

is there sufficient lack of beauty to invalidate the *esrog.* Nor do these deficiencies disqualify it as not being intact.

אֶתְרוֹג הַכּוּשִׁי פָּסוּל — *An Ethiopian* (i.e., *dark*) *esrog is invalid.* Dark *esrogim* are invalid only in areas like *Eretz Yisrael* where *esrogim* do not grow that color. In Ethiopia or nearby, where a dark color is natural, they are valid.

וְהַיָּרֹק כְּכַרְתִי — *If one is green as a leek,* which resembles grass (*Rosh*).

רַבִּי מֵאִיר מַכְשִׁיר וְרַבִּי יְהוּדָה פּוֹסֵל — *R' Meir validates it but R' Yehudah invalidates it. Rosh* quotes *Tosafos* that a green *esrog* that will turn yellow eventually is valid, because the fact that it will turn yellow is sufficient indication of its ripeness. This is also the view of *Orach Chaim* 648:21.

7. רַבִּי יְהוּדָה אוֹמֵר: כַּבֵּיצָה — *R' Yehudah says: Like an egg.* The halachah follows R' Yehudah that an *esrog* smaller than an egg is not valid (*Orach Chaim* 648:22).

כְּדֵי שֶׁיֹּאחֵז שְׁנַיִם בְּיָדוֹ אַחַת — *So that he can hold two [esrogim] in one hand.* Sometimes people inadvertently take the *esrog* and *lulav* in the wrong hands and are forced to transfer them. If an *esrog* is oversized, it may fall and become invalid. If it is small enough for two to fit into one hand, we do not fear its falling (*Gem.* 31b). The halachah, however, follows R' Yose (*Orach Chaim* 648:22; 651:12).

8. אֶלָּא בְמִינוֹ — *Except with its own kind.* The *mitzvah* calls for the *lulav* to be bound together with the *hadasim* and *aravos.* Any part of the palm tree is considered material of its own kind — even strips of the bark or the vine-like material growing around the trunk (*Gem.* 36b). According to R' Yehudah, the binding is considered an essential part of the *mitzvah;* consequently, the use of a different material would be tantamount to adding a fifth species to the four specified by the Torah (*Gem.* 31b; *Rashi*).

רַבִּי מֵאִיר אוֹמֵר — *R' Meir says* that one may take the four species without tying them together. Accordingly, the binding material, because it is unessential, is not part of the *mitzvah,* so its material cannot be considered a forbidden addition to the *mitzvah.*

אָמְרוּ לוֹ: בְּמִינוֹ הָיוּ אוֹגְדִין אוֹתוֹ מִלְּמַטָּה — *The Sages* [lit., they] *said to him [in rebuttal]: They would bind it with its own kind underneath.* The noble Jews of Jerusalem first tied together the *lulav* and the other species with material of its own kind, and *over* that they placed gold bands to glorify the *mitzvah,* so the gold bands served only as adornment and were not an essential part of the *mitzvah* (*Rashi Rav*). Nevertheless, the halachah follows R' Meir (*Orach Chaim* 651:1).

9. וְהֵיכָן הָיוּ מְנַעְנְעִין — *At which point [in the Hallel service] did they wave [the lulav]?* The Rabbis instituted the procedure of נַעֲנוּעִים, which involves moving and shaking the *lulav* in all four directions, as well as upward and downward.

בְּ,,הוֹדוּ לַה׳,, תְּחִלָּה וָסוֹף — *At 'Give thanks to* HASHEM,' *at the beginning and end.* Psalm 118 begins and ends with the verse הוֹדוּ לַה׳ כִּי טוֹב

הוֹשִׁיעָה נָּא״; דִּבְרֵי בֵית הִלֵּל. וּבֵית שַׁמַּאי אוֹמְרִים: אַף בְּ,,אָנָּא ה׳, הַצְלִיחָה נָּא.״ אָמַר רַבִּי עֲקִיבָא: צוֹפֶה הָיִיתִי בְרַבָּן גַּמְלִיאֵל וְרַבִּי יְהוֹשֻׁעַ, שֶׁכָּל־הָעָם הָיוּ מְנַעַנְעִין אֶת־לוּלְבֵיהֶן, וְהֵן לֹא נִעְנְעוּ אֶלָּא בְ,,אָנָּא ה׳, הוֹשִׁיעָה נָּא.״ מִי שֶׁבָּא בַדֶּרֶךְ וְלֹא הָיָה בְיָדוֹ לוּלָב לִטּוֹל, לִכְשֶׁיִּכָּנֵס לְבֵיתוֹ יִטֹּל עַל־שֻׁלְחָנוֹ. לֹא נָטַל שַׁחֲרִית יִטֹּל בֵּין הָעַרְבַּיִם, שֶׁכָּל־הַיּוֹם כָּשֵׁר לַלּוּלָב.

[י] מִי שֶׁהָיָה עֶבֶד, אוֹ אִשָּׁה, אוֹ קָטָן מַקְרִין אוֹתוֹ, עוֹנֶה אַחֲרֵיהֶן מַה שֶּׁהֵן אוֹמְרִין — וּתְהִי לוֹ מְאֵרָה! אִם הָיָה גָדוֹל מַקְרֵא אוֹתוֹ, עוֹנֶה אַחֲרָיו: ,,הַלְלוּיָהּ.״

[יא] מָקוֹם שֶׁנָּהֲגוּ לִכְפֹּל, יִכְפֹּל; לִפְשֹׁט, יִפְשֹׁט; לְבָרֵךְ אַחֲרָיו, יְבָרֵךְ אַחֲרָיו — הַכֹּל כְּמִנְהַג הַמְּדִינָה. הַלּוֹקֵחַ לוּלָב מֵחֲבֵרוֹ בַּשְּׁבִיעִית, נוֹתֵן לוֹ אֶתְרוֹג בְּמַתָּנָה, לְפִי שֶׁאֵין רַשַּׁאי לְלָקְחוֹ בַּשְּׁבִיעִית.

יד אברהם

כִּי לְעוֹלָם חַסְדּוֹ, *Give thanks to HASHEM, for He is good, for His loving-kindness is eternal.* The waving of the *lulav* corresponds to the beginning and the end of the chapter *(Rashi)*.

אָמַר רַבִּי עֲקִיבָא — *Said R' Akiva.* He testified that Rabban Gamliel and R' Yehoshua, who were disciples of Beis Hillel, waved only during אָנָּא ה׳, and not during הודו לה׳. Thus, R' Akiva disagrees with the mishnah's version of Beis Hillel. The halachah, however, follows the *Tanna Kamma's* version of Beis Hillel, not R' Akiva's.

לִכְשֶׁיִּכָּנֵס לְבֵיתוֹ יִטֹּל עַל שֻׁלְחָנוֹ — *When he comes* [lit., *enters] home he should take it at his table.* If he began his meal in violation of the Rabbinic prohibition of eating before taking the *lulav*, he should interrupt his meal to perform the *mitzvah.*

שֶׁכָּל הַיּוֹם כָּשֵׁר לַלּוּלָב — *For the entire day is valid for the lulav.* The *mitzvah* is valid only during the day, but not at night. Nevertheless, it is always preferable to perform a *mitzvah* as early as possible.

10. In the times of the Mishnah, there were periods when not everyone was educated enough to read the *Hallel*. In order to insure that everyone fulfilled his obligation, the *chazzan* would recite the *Hallel* and the congregation merely listened, in much the same way that the Reading of the Torah and the *Megillah* are performed today *(Rashi)*. This is effective based on the principle of שׁוֹמֵעַ כְּעוֹנֶה, *listening is equivalent to answering,* by which one can fulfill such obligations as *Megillah* or *Kiddush* by listening to someone read for him. A prerequisite for this principle is that the reader be obligated to perform the reading just as is the listener. Since *Hallel* is a time-related *mitzvah*, it is not obligatory for women or for non-Jewish slaves. Accordingly, they cannot discharge males of their obligations.

עוֹנֶה אַחֲרֵיהֶן מַה שֶּׁהֵן אוֹמְרִין — *He must repeat after them whatever they say.* By repeating each phrase after them, he reads the *Hallel* himself *(Rashi; Rav).*

וּתְהִי לוֹ מְאֵרָה — *And let it be a curse upon him!* If he was compelled to resort to this form of *Hallel* reading because of his ignorance, let him be cursed for being so unlearned *(Rav).*

עוֹנֶה אַחֲרָיו: ,,הַלְלוּיָהּ״ — *He must respond after him, 'Halleluyah.'* The *chazzan* would recite the entire first verse of *Hallel* and the congregation would respond הַלְלוּיָהּ, *give praise to God,* and so on throughout the entire *Hallel.* However even if he does not respond with *Halleluyah,* he fulfills his obligation, for it is the listening to the *chazzan* that is essential to the *mitzvah,* not the response *(Gem.* 38b).

11. מָקוֹם שֶׁנָּהֲגוּ לִכְפֹּל — *In a place where they are accustomed to repeat.* The custom to repeat many verses in the *Hallel* prayer stems from *Psalm* 118 — a major part of the *Hallel* — many of whose verses have a repetitive character. For example, the chapter begins with four verses that end with the phrase כִּי לְעוֹלָם חַסְדּוֹ, *for His loving-kindness is eternal;* and the first of those verses ... הודו לה׳, *Give thanks to HASHEM,* is repeated in its entirety at the end of the chapter. According to *Rav,* the custom was to repeat the verses in chapter 118 that do not in themselves have a repetitive content, beginning with *v.* 21 אוֹדְךָ כִּי עֲנִיתָנִי, *I thank You, HASHEM, for You have answered me.* The custom of the locality

bring salvation now'; these are the words of Beis Hillel. Beis Shammai say: Also at 'Please HASHEM, bring success now.' Said R' Akiva: As I was watching Rabban Gamliel and R' Yehoshua, all the people were waving their lulavim, but they did not wave except during 'Please HASHEM, bring salvation now.' One who arrived from a journey where he did not have a lulav at hand to use, when he comes home he should take it at his table. If he did not take it in the morning he should take it in the afternoon, for the entire day is valid for the lulav.

[10] *If a [non-Jewish] slave, or a woman, or a minor recited [Hallel] for someone, he must repeat after them whatever they say — and let it be a curse upon him! If an adult was reciting for him, he must respond after him, 'Halleluyah.'*

[11] *In a place where they are accustomed to repeat, he repeats; [where the custom is] to recite as is, he recites as is; [where the custom is] to recite a blessing after it, he recites a blessing after it — everything [must be done] in accord with the local custom. If one purchases a lulav from his friend during Shemittah, he must give him the esrog as a gift, because it is forbidden to purchase it during Shemittah.*

YAD AVRAHAM

becomes an obligatory part of the performance of the *mitzvah* and must be followed.

לְבָרֵךְ אַחֲרָיו, יְבָרֵךְ אַחֲרָיו – *[Where the custom is] to recite a blessing after it, he recites a blessing after it.* Many places had the custom, in common use today, of concluding the Hallel with a blessing that begins with יְהַלְלוּךָ, *They shall praise You (Meiri).*

הַכֹּל כְּמִנְהַג הַמְּדִינָה – *Everything [must be done] in accord with the local custom* [lit., *the custom of the country]. Rama (Orach Chaim* 690:17) rules that we may not nullify any customs or amend them, for they were established with good reason.

◆§ Shemittah – Sabbatical Year

One may not purchase *Shemittah* produce from a person who is suspected of not using the money in compliance with the laws of *Shemittah*, specifically, for purchasing food by a certain deadline. If, however, the price does not exceed the cost of three meals, one may pay him for he will use the funds immediately *(Rambam, Shemittah* 8:10, 12).

There is a distinction between fruit and vegetables concerning the reckoning of the *Shemittah* year: fruits that reached the stage of חֲנָטָה, *budding,* before Rosh Hashanah of the seventh year have the status of sixth-year produce and are not subject to *Shemittah* restrictions even if they were picked during *Shemittah.* Vegetables, however, that were picked during *Shemittah* — even if they were grown in the sixth year — are considered *Shemittah* products. There is a question, however, whether an *esrog* has the halachic status of a fruit or whether it is an exception to the law of fruit and follows the law of vegetables (ibid. 4:12; see *Kesef Mishnah).*

הַלּוֹקֵחַ לוּלָב מֵחֲבֵרוֹ בַּשְּׁבִיעִית – *If one purchases a lulav from his friend during Shemittah* [lit., *during the seventh].* Although the mishnah speaks of purchasing a *lulav,* the problem of *Shemittah* produce in this context applies only to the *esrog* that presumably was purchased with the *lulav.* The prohibition of *Shemittah* does not apply to the *lulav* for it has the status of a tree product, whose growth is calculated according to its חֲנָטָה, *budding.* Since a *lulav* used on Succos of *Shemittah* was obviously past its budding stage by Rosh Hashanah, it is considered as a product of the sixth year *(Gem.* 39a; *Rashi).* The seller here is an unlearned person [*am haaretz*] to whom one may not give money for *Shemittah* products for fear he will not use them in accordance with the halachah.

נוֹתֵן לוֹ אֶתְרוֹג בְּמַתָּנָה. – *He must give him the esrog as a gift.* Since the price of the *esrog* usually exceeds the equivalent of three meals, one may not give the *am haaretz* money for the purchase, for fear he will hoard it past the time of בִּיעוּר, *removal,* when it is forbidden to keep it *(Rashi);* or he will spend it on products or services that one is forbidden to purchase with money of *Shemittah (Gem.* 39a; *Tos.).* The *Gemara* (39a) adds that if the *am haaretz* refuses to give the *esrog* as a gift, then he may raise the price of the *lulav* to cover the cost of the *esrog* so that it is considered as if the money is only in exchange for the *lulav* and thus not subject to the restrictions of *Shemittah.* This procedure is called הַבְלָעָה, *inclusion* [of the *esrog* for the price of the *lulav*].

[יב] בָּרִאשׁוֹנָה הָיָה לוּלָב נִטָּל בַּמִּקְדָּשׁ שִׁבְעָה, וּבַמְּדִינָה יוֹם אֶחָד. מִשֶּׁחָרַב בֵּית הַמִּקְדָּשׁ, הִתְקִין רַבָּן יוֹחָנָן בֶּן־זַכַּאי שֶׁיְּהֵא לוּלָב נִטָּל בַּמְּדִינָה שִׁבְעָה זֵכֶר לַמִּקְדָּשׁ; וְשֶׁיְּהֵא יוֹם הָנֵף כֻּלּוֹ אָסוּר.

[יג] יוֹם טוֹב הָרִאשׁוֹן שֶׁל חַג שֶׁחָל לִהְיוֹת בַּשַּׁבָּת, כָּל־הָעָם מוֹלִיכִין אֶת־לוּלְבֵיהֶן לְבֵית הַכְּנֶסֶת. לַמָּחֳרָת מַשְׁכִּימִין וּבָאִין. כָּל אֶחָד וְאֶחָד מַכִּיר אֶת־שֶׁלּוֹ וְנוֹטְלוֹ, מִפְּנֵי שֶׁאָמְרוּ חֲכָמִים: אֵין אָדָם יוֹצֵא יְדֵי חוֹבָתוֹ בְּיוֹם טוֹב הָרִאשׁוֹן שֶׁל חַג בְּלוּלָבוֹ שֶׁל חֲבֵרוֹ; וּשְׁאָר יְמוֹת הֶחָג, אָדָם יוֹצֵא יְדֵי חוֹבָתוֹ בְּלוּלָבוֹ שֶׁל חֲבֵרוֹ.

[יד] רַבִּי יוֹסֵי אוֹמֵר: יוֹם טוֹב הָרִאשׁוֹן שֶׁל חַג שֶׁחָל לִהְיוֹת בַּשַּׁבָּת, וְשָׁכַח וְהוֹצִיא אֶת־הַלּוּלָב לִרְשׁוּת הָרַבִּים, פָּטוּר — מִפְּנֵי שֶׁהוֹצִיאוֹ בִּרְשׁוּת.

[טו] מְקַבֶּלֶת אִשָּׁה מִיַּד בְּנָהּ וּמִיַּד בַּעְלָהּ וּמַחֲזִירַתּוֹ לַמַּיִם בַּשַּׁבָּת. רַבִּי יְהוּדָה אוֹמֵר: בַּשַּׁבָּת מַחֲזִירִין, בְּיוֹם טוֹב מוֹסִיפִין, וּבַמּוֹעֵד מַחֲלִיפִין. קָטָן הַיּוֹדֵעַ לְנַעְנֵעַ חַיָּב בַּלּוּלָב.

יד אברהם

12. בָּרִאשׁוֹנָה — *Originally.* [In the years when the Temple stood.]

הָיָה לוּלָב נִטָּל בַּמִּקְדָּשׁ — *The lulav was taken in the Temple seven [days].* The *mitzvah* of *lulav* was performed all seven days of Succos in the Temple. This Scriptural obligation, based on the verse (*Lev.* 23:40) which is the source of the *mitzvah* of *lulav,* stems from the words: וּשְׂמַחְתֶּם לִפְנֵי ה׳ אֱלֹהֵיכֶם שִׁבְעַת יָמִים, *And you shall rejoice before HASHEM your God for seven days.*

וּבַמְּדִינָה — *And in the provinces.* This includes all areas outside the Temple. Even Jerusalem is considered part of 'the provinces' in this context *(Rashi* 41a; *Rav; Ran).* But in the view of the *Rambam (Shofar* 2:8) and *Aruch,* the entire city of Jerusalem is included in the category of the Temple, while everywhere outside of Jerusalem is referred to as the provinces.

יוֹם אֶחָד — *[It was taken] one day.* This is stated in the first segment of the same verse (ibid.): וּלְקַחְתֶּם לָכֶם בַּיּוֹם הָרִאשׁוֹן, *and you shall take for yourselves on the first day.*

זֵכֶר לַמִּקְדָּשׁ — *In remembrance of the Temple.* The *Gemara* (41a) explains that the concept of performing *mitzvos* in remembrance of the Temple was first expressed by Jeremiah *(Jer.* 30:17): צִיּוֹן הִיא דֹּרֵשׁ אֵין לָהּ, *she is Zion; she has no one inquiring about her.* The way to show concern for Zion, the Sages determined, was to perform *mitzvos* in remembrance of the Temple.

וְשֶׁיְּהֵא יוֹם הָנֵף כֻּלּוֹ אָסוּר — *And that the entire Day of Waving be forbidden.* The Day of Waving refers to the Omer offering which was brought in the Temple on the sixteenth of Nissan. When the Temple stood, no new grain crop was permitted to be eaten until after the Omer service was complete. Following the destruction, Rabban Yochanan decreed that new crops not be eaten until the sixteenth of Nissan was over (see *Rosh Hashanah* 4:3).

13. יוֹם טוֹב הָרִאשׁוֹן שֶׁל חַג שֶׁחָל לִהְיוֹת בַּשַּׁבָּת — *On the first day of the Festival that fell on the Sabbath.* As explained in *Rosh Hashanah* (4:1), the Rabbis chose to nullify the *mitzvah* on the Sabbath, for fear that a person might inadvertently carry his *lulav* in the street to a learned person that he may teach him how to perform the *mitzvah,* thus violating the prohibition of carrying in a public domain. When the first day of Succos occurred on a Sabbath, however, the Rabbis placed no restrictions on the *mitzvah* of *lulav,* for on the first day the *mitzvah* is מִדְּאוֹרַיְיתָא, *of Scriptural origin.* [The *Gemara* (43a) adds, however, that since the destruction of the Temple, the *lulav* is never taken on the Sabbath, even on the first day.]

כָּל הָעָם מוֹלִיכִין אֶת לוּלְבֵיהֶן לְבֵית הַכְּנֶסֶת — *All the people would bring their lulavim to the synagogue.* They would do this on Friday before the commencement of the Sabbath, because carrying the Four Species in a public domain (or from a private domain to a public domain) does not override the Sabbath *(Rashi).*

[12] *Originally the lulav was taken in the Temple seven [days], and in the provinces [it was taken] one day. After the Temple was destroyed, Rabban Yochanan ben Zakkai instituted that the lulav be taken in the provinces seven [days] in remembrance of the Temple; and that the entire Day of Waving be forbidden.*

[13] *On the first day of the Festival that fell on the Sabbath, all the people would bring their lulavim to the synagogue. On the morrow they would awaken early and come. Everyone would recognize his own [lulav] and take it, for the Sages said: A man cannot fulfill his obligation on the first day of Succos with a lulav belonging to his friend; but on the other days of Succos a man can fulfill his obligation with a lulav belonging to his friend.*

[14] *R' Yose says: If the first day of Succos fell on the Sabbath, and one forgot and carried the lulav out into the public domain, he is exempt — for he carried it out with permission.*

[15] *A woman may accept [a lulav] from her son or from her husband and return it to the water on the Sabbath. R' Yehudah says: On the Sabbath we return [it], on the Festival we add [water], and during [the Intermediate Days of] the Festival we change [the water]. A minor who knows how to wave is obligated to take the lulav.*

YAD AVRAHAM

אֵין אָדָם יוֹצֵא יְדֵי חוֹבָתוֹ בְּיוֹם טוֹב הָרִאשׁוֹן שֶׁל חַג — *A man cannot fulfill his obligation on the first day of Succos*, the day on which the taking of the *lulav* is דְּאוֹרַיְתָא, *a Scriptural obligation*, with a *lulav* belonging to someone else, as explained above, 3:1.

14. וְשָׁכַח — *And one forgot.* Involved in the detail of this *mitzvah* he forgot that the day was also the Sabbath *(Rashi).*

וְהוֹצִיא אֶת הַלּוּלָב לִרְשׁוּת הָרַבִּים — *And carried the lulav out into the public domain.* Thereby unintentionally performing the forbidden labor of transporting an object from a private domain to the public domain.

פָּטוּר — *He is exempt.* Ordinarily when one violates the Sabbath unintentionally, he is obligated to bring a sin-offering (*Shabbos* 7:1). But in this case R' Yose holds that his involvement in the present *mitzvah* frees him from the need for expiation. Thus the performance of the *mitzvah* 'permitted' the unintentional transgression *(Rashi). Rambam (Shegagos* 2:10) rules according to R' Yose. The *Gemara* (42a) adds that R' Yose exempts one from a sin-offering only if his action was done in the course of fulfilling the *mitzvah*, not after the *mitzvah* was already fulfilled.

15. מְקַבֶּלֶת אִשָּׁה מִיַּד בְּנָהּ וּמִיַּד בַּעְלָהּ — *A woman may accept [a lulav] from her son or from her husband.* This mishnah addresses the question of *muktzeh* [lit., *set aside*], the category of objects that, for various reasons, were forbidden by the Rabbis to be moved. Although a woman is exempt from the *mitzvah* of *lulav*, the *lulav* is not *muktzeh* and a woman may take the *lulav* from her husband or son and return it to its place in the water. *Rashi* explains that since men are obligated to perform the *mitzvah*, it is not *muktzeh* for anyone; as long as something is useful to some people it is not *muktzeh* to others either.

וּמַחֲזִירַתּוֹ לַמַּיִם בְּשַׁבָּת — *And return it to the water on the Sabbath,* i.e., to the same water from which it was removed, in order to keep it from withering *(Rashi; Rav).* Nowadays, since the *lulav* is not taken on the Sabbath, it is *muktzeh* and may not even be handled on the Sabbath. Consequently, if the *lulav* was inadvertently removed from the water on the Sabbath, it is forbidden to replace it *(Orach Chaim* 658:2).

בְּיוֹם טוֹב מוֹסִיפִין — *On the Festival one may add* water to the vase where the *lulav* is kept, but may not replace the old water with fresh water. This is considered undue exertion, which is prohibited on *Yom Tov (Rashi; Rav).*

קָטָן הַיּוֹדֵעַ לְנַעְנֵעַ — *A minor who knows how to wave.* He knows how the *lulav* should be raised and lowered, and waved back and forth.

חַיָּב בַּלּוּלָב — *Is obligated to take the lulav,* i.e., at this point in his son's development, a father is obligated to train his son in the performance of *mitzvos (Rashi; Rav).*

פרק רביעי

[א] **לולב** וַעֲרָבָה שִׁשָּׁה וְשִׁבְעָה. הַהַלֵּל וְהַשִּׂמְחָה שְׁמוֹנָה. סֻכָּה וְנִסּוּךְ הַמַּיִם שִׁבְעָה. וְהֶחָלִיל חֲמִשָּׁה וְשִׁשָּׁה.

[ב] לוּלָב שִׁבְעָה כֵּיצַד? יוֹם טוֹב הָרִאשׁוֹן שֶׁל חַג שֶׁחָל לִהְיוֹת בַּשַּׁבָּת, לוּלָב שִׁבְעָה; וּשְׁאָר כָּל־הַיָּמִים, שִׁשָּׁה.

[ג] עֲרָבָה שִׁבְעָה כֵּיצַד? יוֹם שְׁבִיעִי שֶׁל עֲרָבָה שֶׁחָל לִהְיוֹת בַּשַּׁבָּת, עֲרָבָה שִׁבְעָה; וּשְׁאָר כָּל־הַיָּמִים, שִׁשָּׁה.

[ד] מִצְוַת לוּלָב כֵּיצַד? יוֹם טוֹב הָרִאשׁוֹן שֶׁל חַג שֶׁחָל לִהְיוֹת בַּשַּׁבָּת, מוֹלִיכִין אֶת־לוּלְבֵיהֶן לְהַר הַבַּיִת, וְהַחַזָּנִין מְקַבְּלִין מֵהֶן וְסוֹדְרִין אוֹתָן עַל־גַּב הָאִצְטַבָּא—וְהַזְּקֵנִים מַנִּיחִין אֶת־שֶׁלָּהֶן בְּלִשְׁכָּה—וּמְלַמְּדִים אוֹתָם לוֹמַר: ,,כָּל־מִי שֶׁמַּגִּיעַ לוּלָבִי בְיָדוֹ, הֲרֵי הוּא לוֹ בְמַתָּנָה.״ לְמָחָר מַשְׁכִּימִין וּבָאִין. וְהַחַזָּנִין זוֹרְקִין אוֹתָם לִפְנֵיהֶם וְהֵן מְחַטְּפִין, וּמַכִּין אִישׁ

יד אברהם

CHAPTER FOUR

The first mishnah introduces this chapter and the first four *mishnayos* of chapter 5. Each law mentioned here is reviewed in a subsequent mishnah and elaborated upon.

1. וַעֲרָבָה — *And the willow branch.* This refers to the ceremony of ringing the Altar with willow branches and then marching around it as described in mishnah 5 below (*Rav; Rashi* to 42b).

שִׁשָּׁה וְשִׁבְעָה — *[Are performed] six or seven [days].* Since Succos is seven days long (*Lev.* 23:39), one of the days must always be a Sabbath. Our mishnah teaches that in some years the commandments of *lulav* and *aravah* are performed even on the Sabbath and are thus fulfilled for seven days. In other years, though, neither is performed on the Sabbath, and is thus performed on only six days. *Mishnayos* 2 and 3 explain these variations in detail (*Rashi; Rav*).

הַהַלֵּל — *The [recitation of] Hallel.* On the seven days of Succos and *Shemini Atzeres*, the entire *Hallel* (*Psalms* 113-118) is recited [see mishnah 8], in contrast to Pesach when the entire *Hallel* is recited only on the first day (and on the first two days outside of *Eretz Yisrael*). The *Talmud* (*Arachin* 10a,b) explains that this distinction is based on the difference between their respective *mussaf* offerings (*Numbers* 28:19-25; 29:13-34). During Pesach, the *Mussaf* offering is the same every day, while on Succos each day's is different. *Rashi* and *Tosafos* (*Taanis* 28b) explain that this changing number of offerings demonstrates that Succos should be considered a set of seven one-day festivals, each of which requires its own recitation of *Hallel*, whereas all seven days of Pesach should be regarded as a single festival spread out over a seven-day period, for which a single *Hallel* at the beginning of the festival is sufficient.

וְהַשִּׂמְחָה — *And the [mitzvah of] rejoicing.* This refers to the eating of the *shlomim* [peace-offerings] (or of other sacrifices; see *Chagigah* 8a and *Rambam, Hil. Chagigah* 2:9) on each day of the festival (see m. 8).

Rambam (*Yom Tov* 6:17-18), however, in codifying our mishnah lists various forms of 'rejoicing' without mentioning sacrificial meat: children are given candies, women are given clothing and jewelry, and men are served meat and wine.

שְׁמוֹנָה — *[Are performed] eight [days].* These *mitzvos* are observed on the seven days of Succos and on Shemini Atzeres.

סֻכָּה — *The [mitzvos of] succah,* i.e., the commandment to dwell in the *succah.*

וְנִסּוּךְ הַמַּיִם — *And the water libation.* In a ceremony performed only during Succos, water was poured on the Altar as explained below in m. 8 and 9.

וְהֶחָלִיל — *And the flute [is played].* Musical instruments were played to accompany the jubilation that preceded the ceremony of water-drawing, as described in 5:2-4 (*Rashi; Rav*).

2. יוֹם טוֹב הָרִאשׁוֹן שֶׁל חַג שֶׁחָל לִהְיוֹת בַּשַּׁבָּת, לוּלָב שִׁבְעָה — *If the first day of the Festival falls on the Sabbath, the lulav [is taken] seven [days].* In the Temple era, if the first day fell on the Sabbath, the Four Species were taken — even in the provinces, where the Torah ordained the *mitzvah* for only one day (see above 3:13; *Gem.*).

וּשְׁאָר כָּל הַיָּמִים, שִׁשָּׁה — *But [if it falls] on any of the other days, [it is taken] six [days].* If the first day of the Festival fell on a weekday, one of the

CHAPTER FOUR

[1] **לוּלָב** *The [mitzvos of] lulav and the willow branch [are performed] six or seven [days]. The [recitation of] Hallel and the [mitzvah of] rejoicing [are performed] eight [days]. The [mitzvos of] succah and the water libation [are performed] seven [days]. And the flute [is played] five or six [days].*

[2] *How is [the mitzvah of] lulav [performed] seven [days]? If the first day of the Festival falls on the Sabbath, the lulav [is taken] seven [days]; but [if it falls] on any of the other days, [it is taken] six [days].*

[3] *How is [the mitzvah of the] willow branch [performed] seven [days]? If the seventh day of [the] willow [ceremony] falls on the Sabbath, the willow [ceremony] is seven [days]; but [if it falls] on any of the other days, [the ceremony is performed] six [days].*

[4] *How is the mitzvah of lulav [performed]? If the first day of Succos falls on the Sabbath, they bring their lulavim to the Temple Mount, and the attendants receive [the lulavim] from them and arrange them upon the bench — but the elderly place theirs in a chamber — and they teach them to say, 'My lulav is presented as a gift to whomever it may come.' On the morrow they arise early and come. The attendants throw [the lulavim] before them and they would snatch them, striking one another. When*

YAD AVRAHAM

Intermediate Days would fall on the Sabbath, and the *lulav* would not be taken. Thus it would be taken only six days *(Rashi; Rav)*.

Because the *mitzvah* on the first day applies in both the Temple and the provinces [and is therefore to be considered of greater importance *(Meiri)*], the Sages did not wish to hinder the performance of this *mitzvah*. Nowadays, the *lulav* is not taken on the Sabbath even on the first day of the Festival *(Orach Chaim* 658:2).

3. יוֹם שְׁבִיעִי שֶׁל עֲרָבָה שֶׁחָל לִהְיוֹת בַּשַּׁבָּת, עֲרָבָה שִׁבְעָה — *If the seventh day of [the] willow [ceremony] fell on the Sabbath, the willow [ceremony] is seven [days].* The *mitzvah* of circling the altar with the willow-branch is not performed on the Sabbath unless it is the seventh day of Succos, Hoshana Rabbah.

Why is this *mitzvah*, which involves no labor, prohibited on the Sabbath at all? The *Gemara* (43b) replies that if the *mitzvah* of *aravah* were permitted on the Sabbath while the taking of the *lulav* were not, unknowing people would come to the erroneous conclusion that the *mitzvah* of *lulav* was not done on the Sabbath because it was less important than the *mitzvah* of *aravah*. The Sages did not wish the *mitzvah* of *lulav* to be held in such low regard. Nowadays, since the advent of a fixed calendar the question is academic because the seventh day of Succos (21 Tishrei) can never fall on the Sabbath.

4. מוֹלִיכִין אֶת לוּלְבֵיהֶן לְהַר הַבַּיִת — *They bring their lulavim to the Temple Mount.* The populace bring their *lulavim* to the Temple Mount on the afternoon before the Sabbath *(Rashi* to 42b; *Rav)*, since it is forbidden to carry them four cubits in the public domain or from a private domain to the public domain on the Sabbath. [The *lulav* could be carried on the Temple Mount which was considered רְשׁוּת הַיָּחִיד, *a private domain* — even though it was open to the public — because it was surrounded by a wall (see *Middos* 1:3).]

וְהַחַזָּנִין מְקַבְּלִין מֵהֶן וְסוֹדְרִין אוֹתָן עַל גַּב הָאִצְטְבָא — *And the attendants receive [the lulavim] from them and arrange them* [i.e., the *lulavim*] *upon the bench.* Two long benches were built on the Temple Mount, one higher and closer to the Temple than the other. These benches were covered by pillared canopies so that people could rest in the shade. The masses of *lulavim* were placed on the benches so that the roofs would shade them from the sun *(Rashi* 45a).

וְהַזְּקֵנִים — *But the elderly.* They were provided with a special room to prevent injury the next day when everyone was jostling for his *lulav* *(Rashi; Rav)*.

וּמְלַמְּדִים אוֹתָם לוֹמַר — *And they teach them to say.* The *beis din* taught the entire populace to make this declaration, because one cannot fulfill the *mitzvah* of *lulav* on the first day with a *lulav* that belongs to someone else (3:13), whether borrowed or stolen (see 3:1). As a result of this statement, every *lulav* became the property of whoever had it *(Rashi; Rav)*.

וְהֵן מְחַטְּפִין, וּמַכִּין אִישׁ אֶת חֲבֵרוֹ — *And they would snatch them* [i.e., *the lulavim*], *striking one another.* [In their eagerness to retrieve their *lulavim*.]

אֶת־חֲבֵרוֹ. וּכְשֶׁרָאוּ בֵּית דִּין שֶׁבָּאוּ לִידֵי סַכָּנָה, הִתְקִינוּ שֶׁיְּהֵא כָּל־אֶחָד וְאֶחָד נוֹטֵל בְּבֵיתוֹ.

[ה] מִצְוַת עֲרָבָה כֵּיצַד? מָקוֹם הָיָה לְמַטָּה מִירוּשָׁלַיִם וְנִקְרָא מוֹצָא. יוֹרְדִין לְשָׁם, וּמְלַקְּטִין מִשָּׁם מֻרְבִּיּוֹת שֶׁל עֲרָבָה, וּבָאִין וְזוֹקְפִין אוֹתָן בְּצִדֵּי הַמִּזְבֵּחַ, וְרָאשֵׁיהֶן כְּפוּפִין עַל־גַּבֵּי הַמִּזְבֵּחַ. תָּקְעוּ, וְהֵרִיעוּ, וְתָקְעוּ. בְּכָל־יוֹם מַקִּיפִין אֶת־הַמִּזְבֵּחַ פַּעַם אַחַת וְאוֹמְרִים: „אָנָּא ה׳ הוֹשִׁיעָה נָּא, אָנָּא ה׳ הַצְלִיחָה נָא!" רַבִּי יְהוּדָה אוֹמֵר: „אֲנִי וָהוֹ, הוֹשִׁיעָה נָּא!" וְאוֹתוֹ הַיּוֹם מַקִּיפִין אֶת־הַמִּזְבֵּחַ שִׁבְעָה פְעָמִים. בִּשְׁעַת פְּטִירָתָן מָה הֵן אוֹמְרִים? „יֹפִי לְךָ, מִזְבֵּחַ! יֹפִי לְךָ, מִזְבֵּחַ!" רַבִּי אֱלִיעֶזֶר אוֹמֵר: „לְיָהּ וּלְךָ, מִזְבֵּחַ לְיָהּ וּלְךָ, מִזְבֵּחַ"

[ו] כְּמַעֲשֵׂהוּ בְּחֹל, כָּךְ מַעֲשֵׂהוּ בְּשַׁבָּת, אֶלָּא שֶׁהָיוּ מְלַקְּטִין אוֹתָן מֵעֶרֶב שַׁבָּת וּמַנִּיחִים אוֹתָן בְּגִיגִיּוֹת שֶׁל זָהָב כְּדֵי שֶׁלֹּא יִכְמֹשׁוּ. רַבִּי יוֹחָנָן בֶּן בְּרוֹקָה אוֹמֵר: חֲרִיּוֹת שֶׁל דֶּקֶל הָיוּ מְבִיאִין וְחוֹבְטִין אוֹתָן בַּקַּרְקַע בְּצִדֵּי הַמִּזְבֵּחַ. וְאוֹתוֹ הַיּוֹם נִקְרָא יוֹם חִבּוּט חֲרִיּוֹת.

[ז] מִיָּד הַתִּינוֹקוֹת שׁוֹמְטִין אֶת־לוּלְבֵיהֶן וְאוֹכְלִין אֶתְרוֹגֵיהֶן.

יד אברהם

הִתְקִינוּ שֶׁיְּהֵא כָּל אֶחָד וְאֶחָד נוֹטֵל בְּבֵיתוֹ — *they ordained that everyone should take [his lulav] at home* [lit., *in his house]*. One should perform the *mitzvah* at home, rather than bring his *lulav* to the Temple Mount on Friday.

5. מִצְוַת עֲרָבָה כֵּיצַד? — *How was the mitzvah of the willow [performed]?* I.e., how was the special *aravah* ceremony performed in the Temple? Although not stated explicitly in the Torah, this precept has the status of a Scriptural commandment, because it was transmitted to Moses at Sinai.

מוֹצָא — *Motza.* Willows grew there *(Rav).*

יוֹרְדִין לְשָׁם — *They descended there.* The emissaries of *beis din* would go to Motza to bring the willows. This procedure survives in the custom that the synagogue attendant (שַׁמָּשׁ) brings willows for the congregants for Hoshana Rabbah *(Ran).*

וּבָאִין וְזוֹקְפִין אוֹתָן — *And came and stood them up.* Some say they held the willow while they walked around the Altar, and the branches were set up after a circuit had been made around the Altar *(Tosafos).* Others say that first the willows were set up next to the Altar and then the circuit was made *(Tos. Yom Tov).*

בְּצִדֵּי הַמִּזְבֵּחַ — *Against the sides of the Altar.* They were placed on the base of the Altar, leaning against its sides *(Gem.* 45a).

וְרָאשֵׁיהֶן כְּפוּפִין עַל גַּבֵּי הַמִּזְבֵּחַ — *With their tops drooping over the top of the Altar.* The *Gemara* (45a) explains that in order for the willows to reach that far and droop down one cubit they had to be eleven cubits tall and be standing on the base of the Altar.

תָּקְעוּ, וְהֵרִיעוּ, וְתָקְעוּ — *They blew [on a trumpet] a tekiah, a teruah, and a tekiah. Rambam (Klei HaMikdash* 7:21) states that the trumpet was blown during the procession of bringing the willow branches and while arranging them around the Altar. The blowing created an atmosphere of joy and happiness *(Tosafos).*

בְּכָל יוֹם מַקִּיפִין אֶת הַמִּזְבֵּחַ פַּעַם אַחַת — *Each day they would circle the Altar one time.* Only the *Kohanim* would walk around the Altar, not the general public, because in order to circuit the Altar one had to pass between the אוּלָם, *antechamber of the Temple,* and the Altar, and only *Kohanim* were allowed to enter this part of the Temple (see *Keilim* 1:8,9).

רַבִּי יְהוּדָה אוֹמֵר: „אֲנִי וָהוֹ, הוֹשִׁיעָה נָּא" — *R' Yehudah says: [They would say] 'ANI VAHO, bring salvation now!'* Instead of saying אָנָּא ה׳, *Please* HASHEM, the *Kohanim* said the words אֲנִי וָהוֹ, *ANI VAHO.* The numerical value of both phrases is identical — 78 [which is three times the numerical value of HASHEM]. Furthermore, ANI and VAHO are two of the seventy-two Divine Names which are secreted in three verses in *Exodus* (14:19-21).

וְאוֹתוֹ הַיּוֹם — *But on that day,* i.e., the seventh day of Succos, Hoshana Rabbah.

מַקִּיפִין אֶת הַמִּזְבֵּחַ שִׁבְעָה פְּעָמִים — *They circled*

the beis din saw that they were endangered, they ordained that everyone should take [his lulav] at home.

[5] *How was the mitzvah of the willow [performed]? There was a place below Jerusalem called Motza. They descended there, gathered from there large willow branches, and came and stood them up against the sides of the altar, with their tops drooping over the top of the altar. They blew [on a trumpet] a tekiah, a teruah, and a tekiah. Each day they would circle the altar one time and say, 'Please* HASHEM *bring salvation now, please* HASHEM *bring success now!'* R' *Yehudah says: [They would say] 'Ani Vaho, bring salvation now!' But on that day they circled the altar seven times. When they left what did they say? 'Beauty is yours, O altar! Beauty is yours, O altar!'* R' *Eliezer says: [They said,] 'To Yah and to you, O altar! To Yah and to you, O altar!'*

[6] *Just as it was performed on the weekdays, so it was performed on the Sabbath, except they gathered them on the eve of the Sabbath and placed them in golden vessels so that they should not wilt.* R' *Yochanan ben Berokah says: They brought date-palm branches and beat them on the ground at the sides of the altar. That day was called the day of the beating of the [date-palm] branches.*

[7] *Immediately the children loosened their lulavim and ate their esrogim.*

YAD AVRAHAM

the Altar seven times. Yerushalmi (4:3) states that this is in commemoration of the conquest of Jericho. Each day the Jewish People walked around the city one time, and on the seventh day they walked around it seven times.

בִּשְׁעַת פְּטִירָתָן – *When they left.* When they finished the circuits and left the Altar.

רַבִּי אֱלִיעֶזֶר אוֹמֵר: ,,לְיָהּ וְלָךְ, מִזְבֵּחַ! לְיָהּ וְלָךְ מִזְבֵּחַ!" – *R' Eliezer says: [They said,] 'To* YAH *and to you, O Altar! To* YAH *and to you, O Altar,'* i.e., we believe in HASHEM and do not deny that He is our God, and we praise the Altar, which is so dear to God since it serves to atone for us *(Rashi).*

6. כָּךְ מַעֲשֵׂהוּ בְשַׁבָּת – *So it was performed on the Sabbath.* The ceremony is conducted in excatly the same manner when the seventh day falls on the Sabbath.

וּמַנִּיחִים אוֹתָן בְּגִיגִיּוֹת שֶׁל זָהָב כְּדֵי שֶׁלֹּא יִכְמשׁוּ – *And placed them in golden vessels so that they should not wilt.* These vessels were filled with water to prevent the leaves from withering *(Rav).*

רַבִּי יוֹחָנָן בֶּן בְּרוֹקָה אוֹמֵר: חֲרָיוֹת שֶׁל דֶּקֶל הָיוּ מְבִיאִין – *R' Yochanan ben Berokah says: They brought date-palm branches.* Not willow branches, as is the view of the first *Tanna.*

וְחוֹבְטִין אוֹתָן – *And beat them, i.e., the date-palm branches.* [It would seem that according to the first Tanna the same was done with the willow branches.]

וְאוֹתוֹ הַיּוֹם נִקְרָא יוֹם חִבּוּט חֲרָיוֹת – *That day was called the day of the beating of the [date-palm] branches. Rashi, Tosafos* and *Rav* maintain that R' Yochanan ben Berokah disagrees with the first *Tanna* regarding weekdays as well as the Sabbath. Accordingly, each day of the Festival was called "the day of the beating of the palm branches."

7. מִיָּד – *Immediately,* i.e., as soon as the *mitzvos* of the *lulav* and the willow branch had been performed [on the seventh day] *(Rosh).*

הַתִּינוֹקוֹת שׁוֹמְטִין אֶת לוּלְבֵיהֶן – *The children loosened their lulavim.* They untied the festive bindings of the *lulav (Meiri).*

וְאוֹכְלִין אֶתְרוֹגֵיהֶן – *And ate their esrogim.* Even though the *esrog* may not be used for any purpose but the *mitzvah* of the Four Species, beause it was set aside for *mitzvah* use for the whole seven-day period, nevertheless, the children ignored this law *(Rambam). Rashi* (46b) suggests that the *esrogim* of children, unlike those of adults, were not set aside for a מִצְוָה גְמוּרָה, complete *mitzvah.* [Presumably, since children take the Four Species only because of their parents' obligation to train them, their *esrogim* are not considered to be totally dedicated for the purpose of a *mitzvah.]* Therefore, the children were allowed to eat theirs on the seventh day, but the adults did not eat theirs.

[ח] הַהַלֵּל וְהַשִּׂמְחָה שְׁמוֹנָה כֵּיצַד? מְלַמֵּד שֶׁחַיָּב אָדָם בַּהַלֵּל, וּבַשִּׂמְחָה, וּבִכְבוֹד יוֹם טוֹב הָאַחֲרוֹן שֶׁל חַג, כִּשְׁאָר כָּל־יְמוֹת הֶחָג. סֻכָּה שִׁבְעָה כֵּיצַד? גָּמַר מִלֶּאֱכוֹל, לֹא יַתִּיר סֻכָּתוֹ, אֲבָל מוֹרִיד אֶת־הַכֵּלִים מִן־הַמִּנְחָה וּלְמַעְלָה, מִפְּנֵי כְבוֹד יוֹם טוֹב הָאַחֲרוֹן שֶׁל חַג.

[ט] נִסּוּךְ הַמַּיִם כֵּיצַד? צְלוֹחִית שֶׁל זָהָב מַחֲזֶקֶת שְׁלֹשֶׁת לֻגִּים, הָיָה מְמַלֵּא מִן־הַשִּׁלּוֹחַ. הִגִּיעוּ לְשַׁעַר הַמַּיִם תָּקְעוּ, וְהֵרִיעוּ, וְתָקְעוּ. עָלָה בַכֶּבֶשׁ וּפָנָה לִשְׂמֹאלוֹ. שְׁנֵי סְפָלִים שֶׁל כֶּסֶף הָיוּ שָׁם. רַבִּי יְהוּדָה אוֹמֵר: שֶׁל סִיד הָיוּ, אֶלָּא שֶׁהָיוּ מֻשְׁחָרִין פְּנֵיהֶם מִפְּנֵי הַיַּיִן. וּמְנֻקָּבִין כְּמִין שְׁנֵי חֳטָמִין דַּקִּין, אֶחָד מְעֻבֶּה וְאֶחָד דַּק, כְּדֵי שֶׁיְּהוּ שְׁנֵיהֶם כָּלִין בְּבַת אַחַת. מַעֲרָבִי שֶׁל מַיִם; מִזְרָחִי שֶׁל יַיִן. עֵרָה שֶׁל מַיִם לְתוֹךְ שֶׁל יַיִן, וְשֶׁל יַיִן לְתוֹךְ שֶׁל מַיִם, יָצָא. רַבִּי יְהוּדָה אוֹמֵר: בַּלֹּג הָיָה מְנַסֵּךְ כָּל־שְׁמוֹנָה. וְלַמְנַסֵּךְ אוֹמְרִים לוֹ: „הַגְבַּהּ יָדֶךָ!" שֶׁפַּעַם אַחַת נִסֵּךְ אֶחָד עַל־גַּבֵּי רַגְלָיו, וּרְגָמוּהוּ כָל־הָעָם בְּאֶתְרוֹגֵיהֶן.

יד אברהם

8. וּבַשִּׂמְחָה — *(And) in the [mitzvah of] rejoicing.* 'Rejoicing' here means eating the meat of the *shlomim*, peace-offerings (*Rashi* to 48a).

וּבִכְבוֹד יוֹם טוֹב הָאַחֲרוֹן שֶׁל חַג — *And in [the] honor of the last Festival day of Succos.* Succos proper is only seven days, but Shemini Atzeres is considered the last day of the Festival *season*, even though it is not part of Succos. Thus the eighth day for *Hallel* and rejoicing is Shemini Atzeres.

כִּשְׁאָר כָּל יְמוֹת הֶחָג — *Like all the other days of Succos.* The *Gemara* (48a) derives the obligation of rejoicing on Shemini Atzeres from *Deut.* (16:15): וְהָיִיתָ אַךְ שָׂמֵחַ, *and you shall be only joyful.* This verse teaches that the *mitzvah* of rejoicing applies to the night of Shemini Atzeres as a continuation of the first seven days of Succos.

גָּמַר מִלֶּאֱכוֹל — *When one has finished eating.* On the seventh day of Succos, Hoshana Rabbah *(Rashi).*

לֹא יַתִּיר סֻכָּתוֹ — *He may not take apart* [lit., *undo] his succah.* Because the *mitzvah* of *succah* is still in force the entire day *(Rav).*

Rashi emphasizes that there is always the possibility that he will eat another meal that day — and it will have to be eaten in the *succah.*

מִן הַמִּנְחָה וּלְמַעְלָה — *From Minchah time and later,* i.e., from two and a half hours before the end of the day *(Ritva).* One may not take his utensils back into the home until the time stated by the mishnah *(Rashi; Rav).*

9. נִסּוּךְ הַמַּיִם כֵּיצַד — *How is the water libation done?* This special libation was performed only during the seven days of Succos. All other libations in the Temple were of wine poured on the Altar, but during the seven days of Succos water was poured simultaneously with the wine libation as part of the daily burnt offering in the morning.

This water libation was commanded to Moses orally on Sinai [הֲלָכָה לְמֹשֶׁה מִסִּינַי] *(Gemara* 44a), and has the force of Scriptural law. However, R' Yehudah ben Besaira noted that the Torah alluded to the superfluous word מַיִם, *water,* in the section (*Numb.* 29) describing the *mussaf* sacrifices of Succos. In referring to the libations of Succos, the Torah generally uses the word וְנִסְכָּהּ. However, verse 19 uses the word וְנִסְכֵּיהֶם; thus, there is an extra ם. The Torah uses וּנְסָכֶיהָ in verse 31, providing an extra י. And in verse 33, the Torah uses the word כְּמִשְׁפָּטָם rather than the word כַּמִּשְׁפָּט which appears on all the other days. Thus, again, an extra ם. The three extra letters spell מַיִם, *water,* an allusion to the Succos water-libation *(Taanis* 2b).

צְלוֹחִית שֶׁל זָהָב מַחֲזֶקֶת שְׁלֹשֶׁת לֻגִּים הָיָה מְמַלֵּא — *He filled a golden flagon holding three lugim. Numbers* 15:8 describes this libation as רְבִיעִית הַהִין, *a quarter of a hin.* A *hin* is twelve *lugim;* thus three *lugim* mentioned in our mishnah are one quarter of a *hin.* Depending on the various opinions regarding the size of a *log,* it is at least approximately 30.6 fluid ounces; according to others it is much more.

מִן הַשִּׁלּוֹחַ — *From the Shiloach,* a fresh-water spring near the Temple Mount *(Rashi; Rav).*

הִגִּיעוּ לְשַׁעַר הַמַּיִם — *When they reached the Water Gate.* The Water Gate was one of the southern gates of the Temple Courtyard. It was

[8] *How are [the recitation of] the Hallel and the [mitzvah of] rejoicing [done for] eight [days]? This teaches that a man is obligated in [the recitation of] the Hallel, in the [mitzvah of] rejoicing, and in [the] honor of the last Festival day of Succos, like all the other days of Succos. How is [the mitzvah of] succah [observed for] seven [days]? When one has finished eating, he may not take apart his succah, but he may take down his utensils from Minchah time and later, in honor of the last day of Succos.*

[9] *How is the water libation done? He filled a golden flagon holding three lugim, from the Shiloach. When they reached the Water Gate they sounded a tekiah, a teruah, and a tekiah. He went up the ramp and turned to his left. There were two silver bowls there. R' Yehudah says: They were of plaster, but their surfaces were darkened from wine. Each had a hole like a thin nostril, one wider and the other narrower, so that both would drain out at the same time. The western one was for water; the eastern one was for wine. If he poured [the flagon] of water into [the bowl] for wine, or [the flagon] of wine into [the bowl] for water, he fulfilled the obligation. R' Yehudah says: He would pour with one log all eight [days]. To the pourer they would say, 'Raise your hand!' For once someone poured it over his feet, and all the people pelted him with their esrogim.*

YAD AVRAHAM

given this name because the flagon for the water libation was brought into the Courtyard through it *(Rashi; Rav).*

בַּכֶּבֶשׁ – *The ramp.* The *Kohen* chosen to carry the flagon went up the ramp to the Altar in the Temple Courtyard *(Rashi; Rav).*

שְׁנֵי סְפָלִים שֶׁל כֶּסֶף הָיוּ שָׁם – *There were two silver bowls there,* [on the southwestern corner] permanently cemented to the Altar (*Tosafos* 48a s.v. שְׁנֵי), one for wine and the other for water *(Tif. Yis.).*

וּמְנֻקָּבִין כְּמִין שְׁנֵי חֹטָמִין דַּקִּין – *Each had a hole like a thin nostril.* Beneath each bowl was a thin projection through which the liquid flowed. The *Kohen* would pour the wine and the water simultaneously into their respective bowls. The liquids would then flow through the projections onto the top of the Altar, and then through a hole in the top of the Altar, down into a deep cavity beneath the Altar called the *shissin* (*Rashi* 48b; *Rav; Tif. Yis.).*

כְּדֵי שֶׁיְּהוּ שְׁנֵיהֶם כָּלִין בְּבַת אַחַת – *So that both would drain out at the same time.* Since water flows more freely than wine, the hole of the wine bowl was made wider and that of the water bowl narrower, so that both bowls would empty at the same time *(Rashi; Rav).*

יָצָא – *He fulfilled the obligation.* Although this is not the proper manner of fulfilling the *mitzvah,* as long as both libations were made, the *mitzvah* is considered fulfilled.

רַבִּי יְהוּדָה אוֹמֵר: בַּלֹּג הָיָה מְנַסֵּךְ כָּל שְׁמוֹנָה – *R' Yehudah says: He would pour with one log all eight [days].* R' Yehudah argues with the first *Tanna* on two points: He maintains that the amount of water used in the water libation was one *log,* while the first *Tanna* holds three *lugim.* In addition, R' Yehudah says the water-libation ceremony was performed all eight days — seven of Succos and one of Shemini Atzeres, but the first *Tanna* holds that it was performed only during the seven days of Succos *(Rashi; Rav).*

The halachah does not follow R' Yehudah *(Rav).*

וְלַמְנַסֵּךְ אוֹמְרִים לוֹ: ,,הַגְבַּהּ יָדְךָ!" – *To the pourer they would say, 'Raise your hand!'* They would ask the *Kohen* who performed the water-libation to keep his hands high as he poured so that all could see that he was pouring it into the bowl. During the Second Temple era there arose a heretical sect called the Sadducees who rejected any law not stated explicitly in the Torah. This sect found adherents among Jerusalem's upper class, even among the *kohanim.* Since the water libation is an oral tradition transmitted to Moses and is not explicit in the Torah, the Sadducean *Kohanim* denied its validity and refused to perform it properly *(Rashi; Rav).*

שֶׁפַּעַם אַחַת נִסֵּךְ אֶחָד עַל גַּבֵּי רַגְלָיו – *For once someone poured it over his feet.* The *Kohen* performing the rite that time was a Sadducee and, instead of pouring the water into the proper bowl, he poured it over his feet *(Rashi; Rav).*

[י] כְּמַעֲשֵׂהוּ בְחֹל, כָּךְ מַעֲשֵׂהוּ בַשַּׁבָּת, אֶלָּא שֶׁהָיָה מְמַלֵּא מֵעֶרֶב שַׁבָּת חָבִית שֶׁל זָהָב שֶׁאֵינָהּ מְקֻדֶּשֶׁת מִן־הַשִּׁלוֹחַ, וּמַנִּיחָהּ בַּלִּשְׁכָּה. נִשְׁפְּכָה אוֹ נִתְגַּלְּתָה, הָיָה מְמַלֵּא מִן־הַכִּיּוֹר, שֶׁהַיַּיִן וְהַמַּיִם הַמְגֻלִּין פְּסוּלִים לְגַבֵּי הַמִּזְבֵּחַ.

פרק חמישי

[א] **הֶחָלִיל** חֲמִשָּׁה וְשִׁשָּׁה, זֶהוּ הֶחָלִיל שֶׁל בֵּית הַשּׁוֹאֵבָה, שֶׁאֵינוֹ דוֹחֶה לֹא אֶת־הַשַּׁבָּת וְלֹא אֶת־יוֹם טוֹב. אָמְרוּ: „כָּל־מִי שֶׁלֹּא רָאָה שִׂמְחַת בֵּית הַשּׁוֹאֵבָה לֹא רָאָה שִׂמְחָה מִיָּמָיו.״

[ב] בְּמוֹצָאֵי יוֹם טוֹב הָרִאשׁוֹן שֶׁל חַג יָרְדוּ לְעֶזְרַת נָשִׁים, וּמְתַקְּנִין שָׁם תִּקּוּן גָּדוֹל. וּמְנוֹרוֹת שֶׁל זָהָב הָיוּ שָׁם וְאַרְבָּעָה סְפָלִים שֶׁל זָהָב בְּרָאשֵׁיהֶן, וְאַרְבָּעָה סֻלָּמוֹת לְכָל אֶחָד וְאֶחָד, וְאַרְבָּעָה יְלָדִים מִפִּרְחֵי כְהֻנָּה וּבִידֵיהֶם כַּדִּים שֶׁל שֶׁמֶן שֶׁל מֵאָה וְעֶשְׂרִים לֹג, שֶׁהֵן מַטִּילִין לְכָל סֵפֶל וָסֵפֶל.

[ג] מִבְּלָאֵי מִכְנְסֵי כֹהֲנִים וּמֵהֶמְיָנֵיהֶן מֵהֶן הָיוּ מַפְקִיעִין וּבָהֶן הָיוּ מַדְלִיקִין. וְלֹא הָיָה חָצֵר בִּירוּשָׁלַיִם שֶׁאֵינָהּ מְאִירָה מֵאוֹר בֵּית הַשּׁוֹאֵבָה.

יד אברהם

10. אֶלָּא שֶׁהָיָה מְמַלֵּא מֵעֶרֶב שַׁבָּת חָבִית שֶׁל זָהָב שֶׁאֵינָהּ מְקֻדֶּשֶׁת — *Except that he would fill an unconsecrated golden barrel on the eve of the Sabbath.* To draw water on the Sabbath from the Shiloach would have required carrying it from a public domain into the Temple era, a private domain. Such carrying is forbidden on the Sabbath.

Why was a consecrated vessel not used to store the water until the following morning? A consecrated vessel sanctifies what is put into it, but sanctified matter becomes invalid by being left overnight. Since they drew the water on Friday for use the next morning, they stored the vessel in an unconsecrated golden barrel so that it could remain overnight (*Gem.* 50a; *Rav; Rashi*).

נִשְׁפְּכָה אוֹ נִתְגַּלְּתָה, הָיָה מְמַלֵּא מִן הַכִּיּוֹר — *If they were spilled or uncovered, he would refill it from the laver.* The laver, situated in the Temple Court, was a consecrated vessel that held water. Even though the laver was a consecrated vessel, a special device was invented by a *Kohel Gadol* named Ben-Katin to keep its water from being disqualified by remaining overnight (*Yoma* 3:10). He devised a wheel which lowered the entire laver into a well. There the water of the well and the water of the laver merged and became one, so that the water in the laver was considered part of the well rather than separate water stored in the laver. Since the laver water was not disqualified, it could be used for the libation (*Rashi* 48b; *Rav*).

שֶׁהַיַּיִן וְהַמַּיִם הַמְגֻלִּין פְּסוּלִים לְגַבֵּי הַמִּזְבֵּחַ — *For uncovered wine and water are unfit for the Altar.* But the laver was a *covered* vessel, and its water was therefore fit for the Altar. Wine and water left uncovered, for the amount of time it would take a snake to emerge from a nearby hole and drink, may not be drunk for fear that a snake may have drunk from them and left some of its venom behind (*Terumos* 8:4 and *Rav* ibid.). They are then surely unfit for Temple service.

CHAPTER FIVE

1. וְזֶהוּ הֶחָלִיל שֶׁל בֵּית הַשּׁוֹאֵבָה — *This is the flute of Beis HaSho'evah* [lit., *the place of Water Drawing*]. The water drawing is described in 4:9. The festivities that preceded the water drawing are discussed below (mishnayos 2-4). Many other instruments besides the flute were played during the festivities. However, since the flute was the main instrument and its sound was heard above that of the other instruments, it was singled out (*Rav; Rambam, Comm.*).

שֶׁאֵינוֹ דוֹחֶה לֹא אֶת הַשַּׁבָּת וְלֹא אֶת יוֹם טוֹב — *Which overrides neither Sabbath nor Festival.* If the first day of Succos fell on the Sabbath, the flute would be played each of the remaining six days. If the first day of Succos fell on a weekday, one of the intermediate days would be a Sabbath and the flute would only be played for five days (*Rashi* 50a; *Rav*).

[10] *Just as it is performed on a weekday, so it is performed on the Sabbath, except that he would fill an unconsecrated golden barrel on the eve of the Sabbath from the Shiloach, and place it in a chamber. If they were spilled or uncovered, he would refill it from the laver, for uncovered wine and water are unfit for the Altar.*

CHAPTER FIVE

[1] **הֶחָלִיל** *The flute [is played] five or six [days], this is the flute of Beis HaSho'evah, which overrides neither Sabbath nor Festival. They said, 'Whoever did not see the rejoicing of Beis HaSho'evah never saw rejoicing in his lifetime.'*

[2] *At the conclusion of the first Festival day of Succos they descended to the Women's Courtyard, where they made a great improvement. There were golden candelabra there with four golden bowls atop them, four ladders for each [candelabrum], and four youths from [among] the young Kohanim each holding a thirty-log pitcher of oil — for a total of one hundred and twenty log — which he poured into one of the bowls.*

[3] *From the worn-out trousers of the Kohanim and their belts they made wicks and they would kindle them. There was not a courtyard in Jerusalem that was not illuminated by the light of the Beis HaSho'evah.*

YAD AVRAHAM

כָּל מִי שֶׁלֹּא רָאָה שִׂמְחַת בֵּית הַשּׁוֹאֵבָה לֹא רָאָה שִׂמְחָה מִיָּמָיו. — *Whoever did not see the rejoicing of the Beis HaSho'evah never saw rejoicing in his lifetime.*

Rashi (50a) points out that these extraordinarily joyous festivities fulfilled the verse in *Isaiah* (12:3): וּשְׁאַבְתֶּם מַיִם בְּשָׂשׂוֹן — *And you shall draw water joyously.*

2. יָרְדוּ לְעֶזְרַת נָשִׁים — *They descended to the Women's Courtyard.* The *Kohanim* and Levites would descend from the Temple Courtyard to the Women's Courtyard which was situated lower down on the slope of the Temple Mount (*Rashi* 51a).

Adjoining the Courtyard (עֲזָרָה) surrounding the Temple was the עֶזְרַת נָשִׁים, *Women's Courtyard.* This court, occupying an area of 135x135 cubits, was situated on the east side of the Temple Courtyard. Its width (135 cubits) corresponded to the width of the Temple Courtyard, and the wall surrounding the Temple Courtyard separated it from the Women's Courtyard. Since the Temple stood on a mountain, the Temple Courtyard was higher than the Women's Courtyard. One had to ascend fifteen steps to go from one to the other (*Middos* 2:5).

וּמְתַקְּנִין שָׁם תִּקּוּן גָּדוֹל — *Where they made a great improvement. Rashi* explains that projecting brackets were built into the walls all around the Courtyard. Each year they would arrange planks of wood on the brackets [with a railing (*Tif. Yis.*)] to create a balcony from which the women could view the festivities without mingling with the men, thereby preventing frivolity. It was this great improvement that was made every year. *Rambam (Comm.)* comments that the balcony was built to keep the men from looking at the women.

The *mechitzah* or dividing wall separating the men and the women in synagogues is based on the separate courtyards for men and women in the Temple. The galleries of the large synagogues derive from the great improvement enacted in the Temple.

וּמְנוֹרוֹת שֶׁל זָהָב הָיוּ שָׁם — *There were golden candelabra there.* [In the Women's Courtyard stood candelabra that were used only for the water-drawing festivities.]

וְאַרְבָּעָה סְפָלִים שֶׁל זָהָב בְּרָאשֵׁיהֶן — *With four golden bowls atop them.* Into these bowls were placed very thick wicks (*Tif. Yis.*).

וְאַרְבָּעָה סֻלָּמוֹת לְכָל אֶחָד וְאֶחָד — *Four ladders for each [candelabrum].* The ladders were needed because the candelabra were fifty cubits high (*Gemara* 52b).

וְאַרְבָּעָה יְלָדִים מִפִּרְחֵי כְהֻנָּה — *And four youths from [among] the young kohanim.* Each youth was assigned a ladder which he climbed to light a wick in one bowl. Consequently, four youths were assigned for each candelabrum.

3. מִבְּלָאֵי מִכְנְסֵי כֹהֲנִים וּמֵהֶמְיָנֵיהֶן — *From the worn-out trousers of the Kohanim and their belts.* Both these garments were purchased from communal funds and were worn by the *Kohanim* when they performed the Temple service (*Rashi* 51a; see *Yoma* 7:5).

וְלֹא הָיָה חָצֵר בִּירוּשָׁלַיִם שֶׁאֵינָהּ מְאִירָה מֵאוֹר בֵּית הַשּׁוֹאֵבָה — *There was not a courtyard in Jerusalem that was not illuminated by the light of the Beis HaSho'evah.* Since the fifty-cubit-

[ד] חֲסִידִים וְאַנְשֵׁי מַעֲשֶׂה הָיוּ מְרַקְּדִים לִפְנֵיהֶם בַּאֲבוּקוֹת שֶׁל אוֹר שֶׁבִּידֵיהֶן וְאוֹמְרִים לִפְנֵיהֶן דִּבְרֵי שִׁירוֹת וְתִשְׁבָּחוֹת; וְהַלְוִיִּם בְּכִנּוֹרוֹת, וּבִנְבָלִים, וּבִמְצִלְתַּיִם, וּבַחֲצוֹצְרוֹת, וּבִכְלֵי שִׁיר בְּלֹא מִסְפָּר עַל־חֲמֵשׁ עֶשְׂרֵה מַעֲלוֹת הַיּוֹרְדוֹת מֵעֶזְרַת יִשְׂרָאֵל לְעֶזְרַת נָשִׁים – כְּנֶגֶד חֲמִשָּׁה עָשָׂר שִׁיר הַמַּעֲלוֹת שֶׁבַּתְּהִלִּים. שֶׁעֲלֵיהֶן לְוִיִּם עוֹמְדִין בִּכְלֵי שִׁיר וְאוֹמְרִים שִׁירָה. וְעָמְדוּ שְׁנֵי כֹהֲנִים בְּשַׁעַר הָעֶלְיוֹן שֶׁיּוֹרֵד מֵעֶזְרַת יִשְׂרָאֵל לְעֶזְרַת נָשִׁים, וּשְׁתֵּי חֲצוֹצְרוֹת בִּידֵיהֶן. קָרָא הַגֶּבֶר, תָּקְעוּ, וְהֵרִיעוּ, וְתָקְעוּ. הִגִּיעוּ לְמַעֲלָה עֲשִׂירִית, תָּקְעוּ, וְהֵרִיעוּ, וְתָקְעוּ. הִגִּיעוּ לָעֲזָרָה, תָּקְעוּ, וְהֵרִיעוּ, וְתָקְעוּ. הָיוּ תוֹקְעִין וְהוֹלְכִין עַד שֶׁמַּגִּיעִין לְשַׁעַר הַיּוֹצֵא מִזְרָח. הִגִּיעוּ לְשַׁעַר הַיּוֹצֵא מִמִּזְרָח, הָפְכוּ פְּנֵיהֶן לַמַּעֲרָב וְאָמְרוּ: „אֲבוֹתֵינוּ שֶׁהָיוּ בַּמָּקוֹם הַזֶּה אֲחוֹרֵיהֶם אֶל־הֵיכַל וּפְנֵיהֶם קֵדְמָה, וְהֵמָּה מִשְׁתַּחֲוִים קֵדְמָה לַשָּׁמֶשׁ. וְאָנוּ – לְיָהּ עֵינֵינוּ.״ רַבִּי יְהוּדָה אוֹמֵר: הָיוּ שׁוֹנִין וְאוֹמְרִין „אָנוּ לְיָהּ, וּלְיָהּ עֵינֵינוּ.״

[ה] אֵין פּוֹחֲתִין מֵעֶשְׂרִים וְאַחַת תְּקִיעוֹת בַּמִּקְדָּשׁ, וְאֵין מוֹסִיפִין עַל־אַרְבָּעִים וּשְׁמוֹנֶה. בְּכָל־יוֹם הָיוּ שָׁם עֶשְׂרִים וְאַחַת תְּקִיעוֹת בַּמִּקְדָּשׁ: שָׁלֹשׁ לִפְתִיחַת שְׁעָרִים; וְתֵשַׁע לְתָמִיד שֶׁל שַׁחַר; וְתֵשַׁע לְתָמִיד שֶׁל בֵּין הָעַרְבַּיִם. וּבַמּוּסָפִין הָיוּ מוֹסִיפִין עוֹד תֵּשַׁע וּבְעֶרֶב שַׁבָּת הָיוּ מוֹסִיפִין עוֹד שֵׁשׁ: שָׁלֹשׁ לְהַבְטִיל הָעָם מִמְּלָאכָה; וְשָׁלֹשׁ לְהַבְדִּיל

יד אברהם

high candelabra rose up above the eastern wall of the Temple, and the Temple Mount was higher than the rest of Jerusalem, the light shone out over the whole city (*Rashi* 51a; *Rav*).

4. וְאַנְשֵׁי מַעֲשֶׂה — *And men of [good] deeds,* who occupy themselves in communal matters, such as the collection of charity, raising orphans, helping poor brides and so on.

הָיוּ מְרַקְּדִים לִפְנֵיהֶם — *Would dance before them.* The outstanding scholars of Israel, the heads of the yeshivos, the Sanhedrin, and the pious men and men of good deeds, would dance and clap and sing and act joyously in the Temple during the days of Succos. The general populace, both men and women, would come to watch and listen (*Rambam Lulav* 8:4).

בַּאֲבוּקוֹת שֶׁל אוֹר שֶׁבִּידֵיהֶן — *With the flaming torches [that were] in their hands.* They would throw them up in the air and then catch them. Some were expert enough to juggle four torches and some could juggle eight (*Rashi* 51b; *Rav*).

וְאוֹמְרִים לִפְנֵיהֶן דִּבְרֵי שִׁירוֹת וְתִשְׁבָּחוֹת — *And would utter before them words of songs and praises.* Those elders who had led fully righteous lives would praise God by saying, 'Happy is our youth that has not shamed our old age' — i.e., we did not transgress in our youth and, as such, are not ashamed in our old age.

Penitents would say, 'Happy is our old age which has atoned for our youth.'

All of them would say together, 'Happy is he who did not sin, but if he has sinned let him repent and He will forgive him.'

עַל חֲמֵשׁ עֶשְׂרֵה מַעֲלוֹת — *[Stood] on the fifteen steps.* The Levites stood on these steps while they played their instruments during the *Beis HaSho'evah* festivities. Throughout the rest of the year when they sang and played for the daily sacrifices, they stood on a דּוּכָן, *platform,* near the Altar (*Rashi* 51b; *Rav*).

The steps ran across the width of the Courtyard. Each step ran across the width of the Courtyard. Each step was half a cubit deep and half a cubit high (*Rashi* 51b; *Middos* 2:3).

כְּנֶגֶד חֲמִשָּׁה עָשָׂר שִׁיר הַמַּעֲלוֹת שֶׁבַּתְּהִלִּים — *Corresponding to the fifteen Songs of Ascent in Psalms.* The fifteen steps corresponded to the fifteen Songs of Ascent (*Psalms* 120-134), each of which begins with the words שִׁיר הַמַּעֲלוֹת, *A Song of Ascents,* or *Steps.*

קָרָא הַגֶּבֶר — *[When] the crier called out. Gevini,* the Temple Crier (*Shekalim* 5:1), called out every morning at daybreak (or at some time prior to it), 'Arise *Kohanim* to perform your service; *Levites* to your platform; and Israelites to your stations' (*Yoma* 20b).

תָּקְעוּ, וְהֵרִיעוּ, וְתָקְעוּ — *They sounded a tekiah, a teruah, and a tekiah.* The two *Kohanim* sounded a *tekiah,* a *teruah,* and a *tekiah* [on

[4] *Devout men and men of [good] deeds would dance before them with the flaming torches [that were] in their hands and would utter before them words of songs and praises; and the Levites with harps, lyres, cymbals, trumpets, and countless musical instruments [stood] on the fifteen steps that descend from the Courtyard of the Israelites to the Women's Courtyard — corresponding to the fifteen Songs of Ascent in Psalms. Upon them the Levites would stand with musical instruments and chant songs. Two Kohanim stood at the Upper Gate that descends from the Courtyard of the Israelites to the Women's Courtyard, with two trumpets in their hands. [When] the crier called out, they sounded a tekiah, a teruah, and a tekiah. [When] they reached the tenth step, they sounded a tekiah, a teruah, and a tekiah. When they reached the Courtyard, they sounded a tekiah, a teruah, and a tekiah. They would continue sounding tekiah until they reached the gate leading out [to the] east. When they reached the gate leading out to the east, they turned to the west and said, 'Our forefathers who were in this place [had] their backs toward the Sanctuary and their faces toward the east, and they bowed eastward toward the sun. But as for us — our eyes are toward* Yah.' *R' Yehudah says: They repeated and said, 'We are for* Yah *and toward* Yah *are our eyes.'*

[5] *They make no fewer than twenty-one trumpet blasts in the Temple, and no more than forty-eight. Every day there were twenty-one trumpet blasts in the Temple: three for the opening of the gates; nine for the morning tamid offering; and nine for the afternoon tamid offering. With the mussaf offerings they added another nine. And on the eve of the Sabbath they added another six: three to stop the people from work; and three to distinguish*

YAD AVRAHAM

their trumpets] as a signal to proceed toward the Shiloach spring to draw the water for the libation (*Rashi* 51b; *Rav*).

עַד שֶׁמַּגִּיעִין לְשַׁעַר הַיּוֹצֵא מִזְרָח – *Until they reached the gate leading out [to the] east.* The gate led from the Women's Courtyard to the eastern slope of the Temple Mount. This gate faced the Upper Gate mentioned above. Their route of descent was from west to east. When they entered the Temple, they ascended from east to west (*Rashi* 51b).

הָפְכוּ פְּנֵיהֶן לְמַעֲרָב – *They turned to the west,* i.e., the entire group [which was about to exit] turned toward the Temple Courtyard and the more sanctified portions of the Temple (*Rashi* 51b; *Rav*).

וְאָמְרוּ: אֲבוֹתֵינוּ שֶׁהָיוּ בַּמָּקוֹם הַזֶּה – *And said, 'Our forefathers who were in this place.'* Some of the Jews at the end of the First Temple era were sun worshipers (see *Ezekiel* 8:16) and would deliberately turn their backs to the Temple in an obscene gesture of derision (see *Yoma* 77a) while bowing down eastward toward the rising sun (*Rashi* 51b).

וְאָנוּ לְיָהּ עֵינֵינוּ – *But as for us — our eyes are toward YAH.* In the First Temple period the sin of idol worship was prevalent, but in the Second Temple period this temptation was removed. [So they could truly state 'our eyes are toward God'] (*Yoma* 9b).

5. אֵין פּוֹחֲתִין מֵעֶשְׂרִים וְאַחַת תְּקִיעוֹת בַּמִּקְדָּשׁ – *They make no fewer than twenty-one trumpet blasts in the Temple.* Every sounding of the *trumpet* was a set of three blasts — a *tekiah,* a *teruah* and another *tekiah.* On any given day in the Temple, a minimum of twenty-one blasts was sounded in the Temple, and on specific occasions there were as many as forty-eight. The mishnah proceeds to explain.

וְתֵשַׁע לְתָמִיד שֶׁל שַׁחַר – *Nine for the morning tamid-offering.* Each morning when they poured the wine libation as part of the morning *tamid*-offering (see p. 152), the Levites would chant the Song of the Day. This daily psalm was divided into three parts. Before each part, the *Kohanim* sounded a *tekiah-teruah-tekiah* on their trumpets and the people bowed, for a total of nine blasts (*Tamid* 7:3; *Rashi* 53b; *Rav*).

הָיוּ מוֹסִיפִין עוֹד תֵּשַׁע – *They added another nine.* Consequently, on a day when there was a *mussaf* offering, the sum total of blasts was thirty: the daily twenty-one plus the additional nine.

The *Gemara* (55a) concludes that even when there is more than one additional offering (e.g., when a festival falls on the Sabbath — one for the festival and one for the Sabbath), they blew only nine blasts for all of them.

עוֹד שֵׁשׁ – *Another six.* Thus on most Fridays there would be twenty-seven blasts: the daily

בֵּין קֹדֶשׁ לְחֹל. עֶרֶב שַׁבָּת שֶׁבְּתוֹךְ הֶחָג, הָיוּ שָׁם אַרְבָּעִים וּשְׁמוֹנֶה: שָׁלֹשׁ לִפְתִיחַת שְׁעָרִים; שָׁלֹשׁ לְשַׁעַר הָעֶלְיוֹן; וְשָׁלֹשׁ לְשַׁעַר הַתַּחְתּוֹן; וְשָׁלֹשׁ לְמִלּוּי הַמַּיִם; וְשָׁלֹשׁ עַל־גַּבֵּי מִזְבֵּחַ; תֵּשַׁע לְתָמִיד שֶׁל שַׁחַר; וְתֵשַׁע לְתָמִיד שֶׁל בֵּין הָעַרְבַּיִם; וְתֵשַׁע לַמּוּסָפִין; שָׁלֹשׁ לְהַבְטִיל אֶת־הָעָם מִן־הַמְּלָאכָה; וְשָׁלֹשׁ לְהַבְדִּיל בֵּין קֹדֶשׁ לְחֹל.

[ו] יוֹם טוֹב הָרִאשׁוֹן שֶׁל חַג הָיוּ שָׁם שְׁלֹשָׁה עָשָׂר פָּרִים, וְאֵילִים שְׁנַיִם, וְשָׂעִיר אֶחָד; נִשְׁתַּיְּרוּ שָׁם אַרְבָּעָה עָשָׂר כְּבָשִׂים לִשְׁמוֹנֶה מִשְׁמָרוֹת. בַּיּוֹם הָרִאשׁוֹן שִׁשָּׁה מַקְרִיבִין שְׁנַיִם שְׁנַיִם, וְהַשְּׁאָר אֶחָד אֶחָד. בַּשֵּׁנִי חֲמִשָּׁה מַקְרִיבִין שְׁנַיִם שְׁנַיִם, וְהַשְּׁאָר אֶחָד. בַּשְּׁלִישִׁי אַרְבָּעָה מַקְרִיבִין שְׁנַיִם שְׁנַיִם, וְהַשְּׁאָר אֶחָד אֶחָד. בָּרְבִיעִי שְׁלֹשָׁה מַקְרִיבִין שְׁנַיִם שְׁנַיִם, וְהַשְּׁאָר אֶחָד אֶחָד. בַּחֲמִישִׁי שְׁנַיִם מַקְרִיבִין שְׁנַיִם שְׁנַיִם, וְהַשְּׁאָר אֶחָד אֶחָד. בַּשִּׁשִּׁי אֶחָד מַקְרִיב שְׁנַיִם, וְהַשְּׁאָר, אֶחָד אֶחָד. בַּשְּׁבִיעִי כֻּלָּן שָׁוִין. בַּשְּׁמִינִי חָזְרוּ לְפַיִס כְּבָרְגָלִים. אָמְרוּ: „מִי שֶׁהִקְרִיב פָּרִים הַיּוֹם לֹא יַקְרִיב לְמָחָר;" אֶלָּא חוֹזְרִין חֲלִילָה.

[ז] בִּשְׁלֹשָׁה פְרָקִים בַּשָּׁנָה הָיוּ כָל־מִשְׁמָרוֹת שָׁווֹת בְּאֵמוּרֵי הָרְגָלִים וּבְחִלּוּק לֶחֶם הַפָּנִים. בָּעֲצֶרֶת אוֹמְרִים לוֹ: „הֵילָךְ מַצָּה; הֵילָךְ

יד אברהם

twenty-one plus the additional six. When a *mussaf* offering was brought on a Friday, e.g., on Rosh Chodesh, the total was thirty-six.

שָׁלֹשׁ לְהַבְטִיל הָעָם מִמְּלָאכָה – *Three to stop the people from work.* The first *tekiah* signaled the stoppage of all work in the fields; the second blast, a *teruah*, was a signal for all the shops to close and lock up; the third blast, a second *tekiah*, was the signal to remove all the boiling pots from the fire, to store the hot food in the oven, to seal the oven, and to light the Sabbath candles *(Shabbos* 35b).

וְשָׁלֹשׁ לְהַבְדִּיל בֵּין קֹדֶשׁ לְחֹל – *And three to distinguish between the sacred and the secular.* After pausing long enough to roast a small fish or to attach an unbaked bread to the side of an over, they sounded a second set of *tekiah-teruah-tekiah.* This set signaled the arrival of the holy Sabbath. All work was forbidden from that moment on *(Shabbos* 35b).

וְשָׁלֹשׁ לְשַׁעַר הַתַּחְתּוֹן – *Three for the Lower Gate.* [This was the gate which led out from the Women's Courtyard to the eastern slope of the Temple Mount.] The mishnah states that the blasts were made as soon as the procession reached the floor of the Courtyard, which was before they arrived at the Lower Gate. However, they prolonged the blasts until they reached the gate of the Women's Courtyard, which was known as the Lower Gate. Because this series of blasts was stretched out until the *Kohanim* arrived at the gate, the blasts are identified with the Lower Gate *(Rashi* 53b; *Rav).*

The *Gemara* (54a) notes that the *Tanna* of this mishnah disagrees with the *Tanna* of mishnah 4 and therefore omits the three blasts which the latter said were sounded on the tenth step; the *Tanna* of that mishnah disagrees with the *Tanna* of this mishnah and therefore omits the three blasts which the latter said (below) were sounded at the Altar.

וְשָׁלֹשׁ לְמִלּוּי הַמַּיִם – *Three at the filling of the water.* After filling the gold flask with water they returned to the Temple and entered the Courtyard through the Water Gate as described in 4:9. It was at this gate that they sounded three blasts *(Rashi* 53b; *Rav)*

וְשָׁלֹשׁ עַל־גַּבֵּי מִזְבֵּחַ – *Three on top of the Altar.* This took place when the willow branches were set up against the side of the Altar as described in 4:5 *(Rashi; Rav).*

6. Samuel and David divided the *Kohanim* into twenty-four watches, each of which would be in charge of the Temple service for one week after which another watch would take its place. This continued until each of the twenty-four had a turn and then the rotation would begin again *(Rambam, K'lei HaMikdash* 4:3).

On the three pilgrimage festivals of Pesach, Shavuos, and Succos, however, all the watches shared in the service of the festival *mussaf* offering *(Deut.* 18:7-8 with *Rashi;* mishnah 7; *Rambam, ibid.* 4). However, the regular daily service, as well as sacrifices offered by individuals, belonged to the *Kohanim* in whose watch the festival fell. Our mishnah explains how the

between the sacred and the secular. On the eve of the Sabbath during Succos, there were forty-eight: three for the opening of the gates; three for the Upper Gate; three for the Lower Gate; three at the filling of the water; three on top of the altar; nine for the daily morning burnt offering; nine for the daily afternoon burnt offering; and nine for the mussaf offerings; three to stop the people from work; and three to distinguish between the sacred and the secular.

[6] *On the first festival day of Succos there were thirteen bulls, two rams, and one he-goat; there remained fourteen sheep in their first year for eight watches. On the first day six [of the watches] offered up two each, and the rest [offered] one each. On the second [day] five offered up two each, and the rest one each. On the third [day] four offered up two each, and the rest one each. On the fourth [day] three offered up two each, and the rest one each. On the fifth [day] two offered up two each, and the rest one each. On the sixth [day] one offered up two, and the rest, one each. On the seventh [day] all were equal. On the eighth [day] they reverted to [casting] lots as on the [other] festivals. [The Sages] said, 'Whoever offered up bulls today should not offer them tomorrow;' but they took turns in rotation.*

[7] *During three periods of the year all [twenty-four] watches were equal in the prescribed offerings of the Festival and in the division of the Panim Bread. On Shavuos they would say to him, 'Here is matzah for you; here*

YAD AVRAHAM

mussaf offerings were divided among the watches on Succos.

יום טוב הָרִאשׁוֹן שֶׁל חַג הָיוּ שָׁם שְׁלֹשָׁה עָשָׂר פָּרִים, וְאֵילִים שְׁנַיִם, וְשָׂעִיר אֶחָד — *On the first festival day of Succos there were thirteen bulls, two rams, and one he-goat.* The entire *mussaf* offering specified for the first day of Succos (*Numbers* 29:12-16) is: *And on the fifteenth day of the seventh month ... you shall offer [as] a burnt offering ... thirteen bulls, two rams, fourteen first-year sheep and one he-goat for a sin offering.* Our mishnah lists sixteen of them, which were offered by sixteen different watches, leaving fourteen first-year sheep not accounted for (*Rashi* 55b; *Rav*).

בַּיּוֹם הָרִאשׁוֹן — *On the first day.* [The eight watches divided the fourteen lambs as follows:]

בַּשֵּׁנִי — *On the second [day].* Scripture (*Num.* 29:13-32) requires one bull less on each successive day of Succos: twelve for the second day, eleven for the third day, and so on, together with the constant two rams and single he-goat. Thus on the second day there was a total of fifteen animals requiring fifteen watches. That left nine watches to offer the fourteen lambs (*Rashi* 55b; *Rav*).

כֻּלָּן שָׁוִין — *All were equal.* Since each of the remaining fourteen watches offered one lamb, every one of the twenty-four watches offered only one animal that day (*Rashi; Rav*).

חָזְרוּ לְפַיִס — *They reverted to [casting] lots.* For Shemini Atzeres the Torah (*Numbers* 29:25-38) requires one bull, one ram, one he-goat, and seven lambs to be offered. Since there were only ten offerings that day, all twenty-four watches participated in the lots to determine which ones would bring the ten offerings (*Rashi* 55b; *Rav*).

R' Elazar said: To what do those seventy bulls offered during the seven days of Succos correspond? To the seventy nations (*Gem.* 55b). These offerings were brought on behalf of the seventy nations to atone for their sins so that they would merit proper rainfall throughout the year [cf. *Zechariah* 14:17-18]. For it is on Succos that the world is judged on the year's water supply (*Rashi*).

To what does the single bull offered on Shemini Atzeres correspond? To the unique nation [Israel]. This may be compared to a mortal king who said to his servants, 'Prepare for me a great banquet.' But on the next day he said to his favorite, 'Prepare for me a simple feast, so that I may derive pleasure from you. [I can have pleasure and satisfaction only from you (Israel) and not from them]' (*Rashi, ibid.*).

7. וּבְחִלּוּק לֶחֶם הַפָּנִים — *And in the division of the Panim Bread.* Every Sabbath, twelve fresh breads, the *Panim* Breads, were arranged on the Table in the Sanctuary (*Lev.* 24:5-9), and the previous week's breads were removed and divided between the incoming and the outgoing watches, for it was on the Sabbath that the watches would relieve each other (mishnah 8). The mishnah informs us here that on a festival Sabbath the *Panim* Bread was divided equally among all twenty-four watches.

בָּעֲצֶרֶת — *On Shavuos.* When Shavuos falls on the Sabbath (*Rashi; Rav*), all watches shared not only the *Panim Bread,* but also the שְׁתֵּי

חָמֵץ!״ מִשְׁמָר שֶׁזְּמַנּוֹ קָבוּעַ — הוּא מַקְרִיב תְּמִידִין, נְדָרִים, וּנְדָבוֹת, וּשְׁאָר קָרְבְּנוֹת צִבּוּר, וּמַקְרִיב אֶת־הַכֹּל. יוֹם טוֹב הַסָּמוּךְ לַשַּׁבָּת, בֵּין מִלְּפָנֶיהָ בֵּין לְאַחֲרֶיהָ, הָיוּ כָל־הַמִּשְׁמָרוֹת שָׁווֹת בְּחִלּוּק לֶחֶם הַפָּנִים.

[ח] חָל לִהְיוֹת יוֹם אֶחָד לְהַפְסִיק בֵּינְתַיִם, מִשְׁמָר שֶׁזְּמַנּוֹ קָבוּעַ הָיָה נוֹטֵל עֶשֶׂר חַלּוֹת, וְהַמִּתְעַכֵּב נוֹטֵל שְׁתַּיִם. וּבִשְׁאָר יְמוֹת הַשָּׁנָה, הַנִּכְנָס נוֹטֵל שֵׁשׁ וְהַיּוֹצֵא נוֹטֵל שֵׁשׁ. רַבִּי יְהוּדָה אוֹמֵר: הַנִּכְנָס נוֹטֵל שֶׁבַע וְהַיּוֹצֵא נוֹטֵל חָמֵשׁ. הַנִּכְנָסִין חוֹלְקִין בַּצָּפוֹן וְהַיּוֹצְאִין בַּדָּרוֹם. בִּלְגָּה לְעוֹלָם חוֹלֶקֶת בַּדָּרוֹם, וְטַבַּעְתָּהּ קְבוּעָה, וְחַלּוֹנָהּ סְתוּמָה.

יד אברהם

הַלֶּחֶם, *Two Loaves,* that were brought as a special offering from the חָדָשׁ, *new wheat* that grew after Pesach (*Lev.* 23:16; *Menachos* 9:1). While the *Panim* Bread was *matzah* [unleavened], the Two Loaves were *chametz* [leavened bread] (*Lev.* 23:17; *Menachos* 5:1). Thus, on a Shavuos-Sabbath, the service included both *chametz* and *matzah (Rambam, Comm.).*

אוֹמְרִים לוֹ – *They would say to him.* Those who distributed portions from these two kinds of breads would say when they gave a *Kohen* his portions of the *Panim* Bread and the Two Loaves *(Rashi; Rav).*

מִשְׁמָר שֶׁזְּמַנּוֹ קָבוּעַ – *The watch whose time [of service] was fixed.* The watch whose turn it was to serve in the Temple on the week of the festival brings all the offerings listed below that were not brought specifically because of the festival *(Rashi; Rav)*

נְדָרִים וּנְדָבוֹת – *Vow offerings, freewill offerings.* Various personal offerings were pledged during the year and brought to the Temple in fulfillment of the pledges during the festival. The watches whose turns were not fixed for this week did not share in these offerings, for they were entitled to share only in offerings that were directly connected with the festival *(Rashi* 55b; *Rav).*

A נֶדֶר, *vow offering,* is an obligation undertaken when a man vows to bring an offering without designating a specific animal. A נְדָבָה, *freewill offering,* is an obligation when a person designates a specific animal and states, 'This one is an offering,' without, however, explicitly obligating *himself* to bring an offering. Accordingly, in the case of the vow offering if the eventually chosen animal dies or is stolen, it must be replaced, because the obligation to bring an offering is a personal one and remains incumbent upon him. In the case of a freewill offering, however, if the animal dies or is stolen, its owner is exempt from offering a different one, because his sole obligation was to offer the specifically designated animal *(Kinnim* 1:1).

וּשְׁאָר קָרְבְּנוֹת צִבּוּר – *The remaining public offerings.* This term includes the bull brought by each tribe in the rare instance when a majority of the entire Jewish People sinned following an erroneous ruling of the *Beis Din* which permitted a transgression whose deliberate violation would result in *kares* [spiritual excision]. If the *Beis Din* erred in permitting idol worship, then a he-goat must accompany the bull (*Gem.* 56a; *Rambam, Shegagos* 12:1; *Rashi* 56a; *Rav).*

יוֹם טוֹב הַסָּמוּךְ לַשַּׁבָּת בֵּין מִלְּפָנֶיהָ – *If a festival fell near a Sabbath, either before it.* For example, if a festival fell on Friday so that all the *Kohanim* who were not part of the regular watch could not leave for home until after the Sabbath *(Gem.* 56a and *Rashi; Rav).*

בֵּין לְאַחֲרֶיהָ – *Or after it.* If a festival fell on Sunday, all the *Kohanim* coming to serve during the festival had to arrive before the Sabbath *(Gem.* 56 and *Rashi; Rav).*

8. חָל לִהְיוֹת יוֹם אֶחָד לְהַפְסִיק בֵּינְתַיִם – *If one day intervened between them.* If the festival was to begin on Monday, many *Kohanim* would arrive on Friday instead of Sunday, and if the festival ended Thursday, many *Kohanim* would remain for the Sabbath rather than leave for home on Friday *(Rashi* 56a; *Rav).*

וְהַמִּתְעַכֵּב – *And the one that stayed behind.* Those were the *Kohanim* who came to the Temple on Friday and remained over the Sabbath, even though they could have come on Sunday, or the *Kohanim* who could have gone home on Friday but decided to stay over the Sabbath *(Rashi; Rav).*

וּבִשְׁאָר יְמוֹת הַשָּׁנָה – *But during the rest of the*

is chametz for you!' The watch whose time [of service] was fixed — [only] it offers the daily burnt offerings, vow offerings, freewill offerings, the remaining public offerings, and [this watch] offers everything. If a festival fell near a Sabbath, either before it or after it, all the watches shared equally in the division of the Panim Bread.

[8] *If one day intervened between them, the watch whose time was fixed took ten loaves, and the one that stayed behind took two. But during the rest of the year, the incoming [watch] took six [loaves] and the outgoing [watch] took six. R' Yehudah says: The incoming [watch] took seven and the outgoing [watch] took five. The incoming [watch] divided [the bread] in the north and the outgoing [watch] in the south. [The watch of] Bilgah always divided [the bread] in the south, its ring was permanently affixed, and its window was sealed.*

YAD AVRAHAM

year, i.e., on Sabbaths that were not festival days.

רַבִּי יְהוּדָה אוֹמֵר: הַנִּכְנָס נוֹטֵל שֶׁבַע — *R' Yehudah says: The incoming [watch] took seven.* The incoming watch is entitled to seven of the breads. The *Gemara* (56b) explains that it receives an extra loaf because that evening it will close the Temple gates which had been opened that morning by the outgoing watch.

Rashi (56b s.v. בשכר) implies that those who opened the gates in the morning should have had the duty of completing their task by closing them at night. Since the incoming watch closed them, its seems as though it were doing the work of the outgoing watch. Therefore the outgoing watch must yield one of its loaves in payment of this service.

הַנִּכְנָסִין חוֹלְקִין בַּצָּפוֹן — *The incoming [watch] divided [the bread] in the north.* They divided their loaves among themselves ... in the section of the Courtyard north of the Altar (see *Yoma* 36a).

בִּלְגָּה — *[The watch of] Bilgah.* Because of the following incident that brought the watch of Bilgah into disrepute, the Sages punished it in the three ways discussed in the mishnah below: A woman named Miriam from the family of Bilgah became an apostate and married a Greek officer. When the Greeks entered the Sanctuary during the time of Mattisyahu the son of Yochanan, she stamped with her sandal upon the Altar crying out, 'Lukos, Lukos, [wolf, wolf,] how long will you consume Israel's money and yet not stand by them in the time of oppression!'

[*Maharsha* explains Miriam's outburst as an allusion to the daily offerings. Wolves are known to eat sheep, and the Altar 'ate' the two sheep of the *tamid*-offering every day.]

When the Sages heard of this they punished Bilgah.

Others say that the reason for the penalties was the fact that Bilgah's watch was once tardy in coming and so Yeshevav, one of its fellow watches, replaced it.

The *Gemara* (56b) notes that according to the view that the whole watch was tardy, it is understandable that the whole watch was penalized. But according to the view that only one of its daughters left the fold, why was the whole watch penalized?

Abaye explained: "The child's statement in the marketplace is either of his father or of his mother. Moreover, 'Woe to the wicked and woe to his neighbor.' Thus, Miriam would not have degraded the Altar unless she had heard her family speak that way."

לְעוֹלָם חוֹלֶקֶת בַּדָּרוֹם — *Always divided [the bread] in the south.* Even when it was the incoming watch, Bilgah was required to divide its share in the southern part of the Courtyard; consequently, Bilgah always seemed to be leaving the Temple *(Rabbeinu Chananel)*. This was the first fine imposed upon the Bilgah watch.

וְטַבַּעְתָּהּ קְבוּעָה — *Its ring was permanently affixed.* Twenty-four rings were affixed to the floor of the Temple Courtyard where the slaughtering was done. The rings were stapled to the floor at one point, and were raised so that the animal's head could be inserted in them and locked in place during the slaughterings. The ring assigned to Bilgah, however, was permanently stapled to the floor at two points so that it could not be raised. This forced Bilgah to use the ring of another watch and thus suffer embarrassment.

וְחַלּוֹנָהּ סְתוּמָה — *And its [Bilgah's] window was sealed.* The אוּלָם, *antechamber,* of the Temple was thirty cubits wider than the Temple proper, and there were rooms at its northern and southern extremities. These were called בֵּית הַחֲלִיפוֹת, *the knife room(s).* Each of the watches had a window through which it would deposit its knives in the room. Bilgah's window was permanently sealed *(Rav; Rashi;* see *Meiri)*.

השכמת הבוקר

A Jew should wake up with gratitude to God for having restored his faculties and with a lionlike resolve to serve his Creator. Before getting off the bed or commencing any other conversation or activity, he declares his gratitude:

מוֹדֶה אֲנִי לְפָנֶיךָ,* מֶלֶךְ חַי וְקַיָּם, שֶׁהֶחֱזַרְתָּ בִּי נִשְׁמָתִי בְּחֶמְלָה — רַבָּה אֱמוּנָתֶךָ.

Wash the hands according to the ritual procedure: pick up the vessel of water with the right hand, pass it to the left, and pour water over the right. Then with the right hand pour over the left. Follow this procedure until water has been poured over each hand three times. Then, recite:

רֵאשִׁית חָכְמָה יִרְאַת יהוה, שֵׂכֶל טוֹב לְכָל עֹשֵׂיהֶם, תְּהִלָּתוֹ עֹמֶדֶת לָעַד.[1] בָּרוּךְ שֵׁם כְּבוֹד מַלְכוּתוֹ לְעוֹלָם וָעֶד.

לבישת ציצית

Hold the *tallis kattan* in readiness to put on, inspect the *tzitzis* (see commentary) and recite the following blessing. Then don the *tallis kattan* and kiss the *tzitzis*. One who wears a *tallis* for *Shacharis* does not recite this blessing (see commentary).

בָּרוּךְ אַתָּה יהוה אֱלֹהֵינוּ מֶלֶךְ הָעוֹלָם, אֲשֶׁר קִדְּשָׁנוּ בְּמִצְוֹתָיו, וְצִוָּנוּ עַל מִצְוַת צִיצִת.

יְהִי רָצוֹן מִלְּפָנֶיךָ, יהוה אֱלֹהַי וֵאלֹהֵי אֲבוֹתַי, שֶׁתְּהֵא חֲשׁוּבָה מִצְוַת צִיצִת לְפָנֶיךָ, כְּאִלּוּ קִיַּמְתִּיהָ בְּכָל פְּרָטֶיהָ וְדִקְדּוּקֶיהָ וְכַוָּנוֹתֶיהָ, וְתַרְיַ״ג מִצְוֹת הַתְּלוּיִם בָּהּ. אָמֵן סֶלָה.

עטיפת טלית

Before donning the *tallis,* inspect the *tzitzis* (see commentary) while reciting these verses:

בָּרְכִי נַפְשִׁי* אֶת יהוה, יהוה אֱלֹהַי גָּדַלְתָּ מְּאֹד, הוֹד וְהָדָר לָבָשְׁתָּ. עֹטֶה אוֹר כַּשַּׂלְמָה, נוֹטֶה שָׁמַיִם כַּיְרִיעָה.[2]

Many recite the following declaration of intent before donning the *tallis:*

לְשֵׁם יִחוּד* קֻדְשָׁא בְּרִיךְ הוּא וּשְׁכִינְתֵּהּ, בִּדְחִילוּ וּרְחִימוּ לְיַחֵד שֵׁם י״ה בְּו״ה בְּיִחוּדָא שְׁלִים, בְּשֵׁם כָּל יִשְׂרָאֵל.

השְׁכָּמַת הַבּוֹקֶר / UPON ARISING

מוֹדֶה אֲנִי לְפָנֶיךָ — *I gratefully thank You.* A Jew opens his eyes and thanks God for restoring his faculties to him in the morning. Then, he acknowledges that God did so in the expectation that he will serve Him, and that He is abundantly faithful to reward those who do.

לְבִישַׁת צִיצִית / DONNING THE TZITZIS

Since *tzitzis* need not be worn at night, the commandment of *tzitzis [Numbers* 15:38] is classified as a time-related *mitzvah*, and as such, is not required of women. It may be fulfilled in two ways: the *tallis kattan* (lit., small garment), worn all day, usually under the shirt; and the large *tallis,* worn during the morning prayers. Among Sephardic and German Jews, the large *tallis* is worn even by young boys, but in most Ashkenazic congregations it is worn only by one who is or has been married. Although, strictly speaking, one should recite the appropriate blessing over each garment, the custom is that one who wears a *tallis* at *Shacharis* does not recite a blessing over the *tallis kattan*. Instead, before donning the large *tallis,* he has in mind that its blessing apply to both garments.

Before donning his *tallis* or *tallis kattan,* one

❧ UPON ARISING ☙

A Jew should wake up with gratitude to God for having restored his faculties and with a lionlike resolve to serve his Creator. Before getting off the bed or commencing any other conversation or activity, he declares his gratitude:

מוֹדֶה אֲנִי *I gratefully thank You,* O living and eternal King, for You have returned my soul within me with compassion — abundant is Your faithfulness!*

Wash the hands according to the ritual procedure: pick up the vessel of water with the right hand, pass it to the left, and pour water over the right. Then with the right hand pour over the left. Follow this procedure until water has been poured over each hand three times. Then, recite:

רֵאשִׁית חָכְמָה *The beginning of wisdom is the fear of HASHEM — good understanding to all their practitioners; His praise endures forever.*[1] *Blessed is the Name of His glorious kingdom for all eternity.*

❧ DONNING THE TZITZIS ☙

Hold the *tallis kattan* in readiness to put on, inspect the *tzitzis* (see commentary) and recite the following blessing. Then don the *tallis kattan* and kiss the *tzitzis.* One who wears a *tallis* for *Shacharis* does not recite this blessing (see commentary).

בָּרוּךְ *Blessed are You, HASHEM, our God, King of the universe, Who has sanctified us with His commandments, and has commanded us regarding the commandment of tzitzis.*

יְהִי רָצוֹן *May it be Your will, HASHEM, my God and the God of my forefathers, that the commandment of tzitzis be as worthy before You as if I had fulfilled it in all its details, implications, and intentions, as well as the six hundred thirteen commandments that are dependent upon it. Amen, Selah!*

❧ DONNING THE TALLIS ☙

Before donning the *tallis,* inspect the *tzitzis* (see commentary) while reciting these verses:

בָּרְכִי נַפְשִׁי *Bless HASHEM, O my soul;* HASHEM, my God, You are very great; You have donned majesty and splendor; cloaked in light as with a garment, stretching out the heavens like a curtain.*[2]

Many recite the following declaration of intent before donning the *tallis:*

לְשֵׁם יִחוּד *For the sake of the unification* of the Holy One, Blessed is He, and His Presence, in fear and love to unify the Name* — yud-kei with vav-kei — in perfect unity, in the name of all Israel.*

(1) *Psalms* 111:10. (2) 104:1-2.

---

must examine the fringes carefully, especially at the point where the strings are looped through the holes in the corners of the garment, for if one of the strings is torn there, the *tzitzis* are invalid and the garment may not be worn.

❧ עֲטִיפַת טַלִּית / DONNING THE TALLIS ☙

❧ **בָּרְכִי נַפְשִׁי** — *Bless . . . O my soul.* Because the *tallis* symbolizes the splendor of God's commandments, we liken our wearing of it to wrapping ourselves in God's glory and brilliance.

❧ **לְשֵׁם יִחוּד** — *For the sake of the unification.* This preliminary formulation serves two purposes: a statement of intent that the act about to be performed fulfills the Torah's commandment; and a prayer that the spiritual qualities of the commandment be realized. Some omit the sentence beginning לְשֵׁם יִחוּד and start from הֲרֵינִי. Others omit the entire prayer, but all agree that one should have intent to fulfill the *mitzvah.*

לְיַחֵד שֵׁם . . . — *To unify the Name . . .* The first half of the Divine Name, formed of the letters *yud* and *hei,* symbolizes the Attribute of Judgment, while the second half, formed of the

הֲרֵינִי מִתְעַטֵּף גּוּפִי בְּצִיצִת, כֵּן תִּתְעַטֵּף נִשְׁמָתִי וּרְמַ״ח אֵבָרַי וּשְׁסָ״ה גִידַי* בְּאוֹר הַצִּיצִת הָעוֹלֶה תַרְיַ״ג. וּכְשֵׁם שֶׁאֲנִי מִתְכַּסֶּה בְּטַלִּית בָּעוֹלָם הַזֶּה, כַּךְ אֶזְכֶּה לַחֲלוּקָא דְרַבָּנָן וּלְטַלִּית נָאָה לָעוֹלָם הַבָּא בְּגַן עֵדֶן. וְעַל יְדֵי מִצְוַת צִיצִת תִּנָּצֵל נַפְשִׁי וְרוּחִי וְנִשְׁמָתִי וּתְפִלָּתִי מִן הַחִיצוֹנִים. וְהַטַּלִּית יִפְרוֹשׂ כְּנָפָיו עֲלֵיהֶם וְיַצִּילֵם כְּנֶשֶׁר יָעִיר קִנּוֹ, עַל גּוֹזָלָיו יְרַחֵף.[1] וּתְהֵא חֲשׁוּבָה מִצְוַת צִיצִת לִפְנֵי הַקָּדוֹשׁ בָּרוּךְ הוּא כְּאִלּוּ קִיַּמְתִּיהָ בְּכָל פְּרָטֶיהָ וְדִקְדּוּקֶיהָ וְכַוָּנוֹתֶיהָ וְתַרְיַ״ג מִצְוֹת הַתְּלוּיִם בָּהּ. אָמֵן סֶלָה.

Unfold the *tallis*, hold it in readiness to wrap around yourself, and recite the following blessing:

בָּרוּךְ אַתָּה יהוה אֱלֹהֵינוּ מֶלֶךְ הָעוֹלָם, אֲשֶׁר קִדְּשָׁנוּ בְּמִצְוֹתָיו, וְצִוָּנוּ לְהִתְעַטֵּף בַּצִּיצִת.

Wrap the *tallis* around your head and body, then recite:

מַה יָּקָר חַסְדְּךָ אֱלֹהִים, וּבְנֵי אָדָם בְּצֵל כְּנָפֶיךָ יֶחֱסָיוּן. יִרְוְיֻן מִדֶּשֶׁן בֵּיתֶךָ, וְנַחַל עֲדָנֶיךָ תַשְׁקֵם. כִּי עִמְּךָ מְקוֹר חַיִּים, בְּאוֹרְךָ נִרְאֶה אוֹר. מְשֹׁךְ חַסְדְּךָ לְיֹדְעֶיךָ, וְצִדְקָתְךָ לְיִשְׁרֵי לֵב.[2]

Recite the following collection of verses upon entering the synagogue:

מַה טֹּבוּ אֹהָלֶיךָ* יַעֲקֹב, מִשְׁכְּנֹתֶיךָ יִשְׂרָאֵל.[3] וַאֲנִי בְּרֹב חַסְדְּךָ אָבוֹא בֵיתֶךָ, אֶשְׁתַּחֲוֶה אֶל הֵיכַל קָדְשְׁךָ בְּיִרְאָתֶךָ.[4] יהוה אָהַבְתִּי מְעוֹן בֵּיתֶךָ, וּמְקוֹם מִשְׁכַּן כְּבוֹדֶךָ.[5] וַאֲנִי אֶשְׁתַּחֲוֶה וְאֶכְרָעָה, אֶבְרְכָה לִפְנֵי יהוה עֹשִׂי.[6] וַאֲנִי, תְפִלָּתִי לְךָ יהוה, עֵת רָצוֹן, אֱלֹהִים בְּרָב חַסְדֶּךָ, עֲנֵנִי בֶּאֱמֶת יִשְׁעֶךָ.[7]

Tefillin on Chol HaMoed

There are three different customs (all halachically valid) regarding the wearing of tefillin on Chol HaMoed:

a) *Tefillin* are worn but the blessings usually recited upon donning them are omitted (*Taz* to *O.C.* 31:2).

b) *Tefillin* are worn and the blessings recited, but silently *(Rama)*.

c) *Tefillin* should not be worn (*Orach Chaim* 31:2 and *Vilna Gaon)*.

Mishnah Berurah advises that before putting on the *tefillin* one should stipulate mentally the following: 'If I am obligated to wear *tefillin* today, then I am donning them in fulfillment of my obligation; but if I am not obligated to wear *tefillin* today, then I do not intend to fulfill any *mitzvah* by donning them;' and that the blessing not be recited.

It is not proper for a congregation to follow contradictory customs. Thus, if one whose custom is not to wear *tefillin* during Chol HaMoed prays with a *tefillin*-wearing *minyan,* he should don *tefillin* without a blessing. Conversely, if one whose custom is to wear *tefillin* prays with a non-*tefillin*-wearing *minyan,* he should not wear his *tefillin* while praying but may don them at home before going to the synagogue (*M.B.)*.

Those who wear *tefillin* customarily remove them before *Hallel*.

הֲרֵינִי *I am ready to wrap my body in tzitzis, so may my soul, my two hundred forty-eight organs and my three hundred sixty-five sinews* be wrapped in the illumination of tzitzis which has the numerical value of six hundred thirteen. Just as I cover myself with a tallis in This World, so may I merit the rabbinical garb and a beautiful cloak in the World to Come in the Garden of Eden. Through the commandment of tzitzis may my life-force, spirit, soul, and prayer be rescued from the external forces. May the tallis spread its wings over them and rescue them like an eagle rousing his nest, fluttering over his eaglets.[1] May the commandment of tzitzis be worthy before the Holy One, Blessed is He, as if I had fulfilled it in all its details, implications, and intentions, as well as the six hundred thirteen commandments that are dependent upon it. Amen, Selah!*

Unfold the *tallis*, hold it in readiness to wrap around yourself, and recite the following blessing:

בָּרוּךְ *Blessed are You, HASHEM, our God, King of the universe, Who has sanctified us with His commandments and has commanded us to wrap ourselves in tzitzis.*

Wrap the *tallis* around your head and body, then recite:

מַה יָּקָר *How precious is Your kindness, O God! The sons of man take refuge in the shadows of Your wings. May they be sated from the abundance of Your house; and may You give them to drink from the stream of Your delights. For with You is the source of life — by Your light we shall see light. Extend Your kindness to those who know You, and Your charity to the upright of heart.*[2]

Recite the following collection of verses upon entering the synagogue:

מַה טֹּבוּ *How goodly are your tents,* O Jacob, your dwelling places, O Israel.*[3] *As for me, through Your abundant kindness I will enter Your House; I will prostrate myself toward Your Holy Sanctuary in awe of You.*[4] *O HASHEM, I love the House where You dwell, and the place where Your glory resides.*[5] *I shall prostrate myself and bow, I shall kneel before HASHEM my Maker.*[6] *As for me, may my prayer to You, HASHEM, be at an opportune time; O God, in Your abundant kindness, answer me with the truth of Your salvation.*[7]

(1) *Deuteronomy* 32:11. (2) *Psalms* 36:8-11. (3) *Numbers* 24:5.
(4) *Psalms* 5:8. (5) 26:8. (6) Cf. 95:6. (7) 69:14.

letters *vav* and *hei*, symbolizes the Attribute of Mercy. The blend of both attributes leads to His desired goal for Creation. Since these letters form the sacred Four-Letter Name that is not to be uttered as it is spelled, and since many authorities maintain that this prohibition extends even to uttering the four letters of the Name, the commonly used pronunciation of these letters in the לְשֵׁם יִחוּד prayer is *yud-kei b'vav kei.*

רְמַ״ח אֵבָרַי וּשְׁסָ״ה גִידַי — *My two hundred forty-eight organs and my three hundred sixty-five sinews.* The Sages' computation of the important organs, two hundred forty-eight, is equal to the number of positive commandments, while the three hundred sixty-five sinews equal the number of negative commandments. This symbolizes the principle that man was created to perform God's will. The total number of sinews and organs in man, and the total of Divine commandments, are each six hundred thirteen.

☙ מה טבו אֹהָלֶיךָ — *How goodly are your tents.* The Sages interpret this praise of Israel as a reference to its 'tents of learning and prayer.' In a deeper sense, the Jewish home achieves its highest level when it incorporates the values of the synagogue and study hall. This collection of verses expresses love and reverence for the synagogue that, in the absence of the Holy Temple, is *the place where God's glory resides* among Israel.

אֲדוֹן עוֹלָם* אֲשֶׁר מָלַךְ, בְּטֶרֶם כָּל יְצִיר נִבְרָא.
לְעֵת נַעֲשָׂה בְחֶפְצוֹ כֹּל, אֲזַי מֶלֶךְ שְׁמוֹ נִקְרָא.
וְאַחֲרֵי כִּכְלוֹת הַכֹּל, לְבַדּוֹ יִמְלוֹךְ נוֹרָא.
וְהוּא הָיָה וְהוּא הֹוֶה, וְהוּא יִהְיֶה בְּתִפְאָרָה.
וְהוּא אֶחָד וְאֵין שֵׁנִי, לְהַמְשִׁיל לוֹ לְהַחְבִּירָה.
בְּלִי רֵאשִׁית בְּלִי תַכְלִית, וְלוֹ הָעֹז וְהַמִּשְׂרָה.
וְהוּא אֵלִי וְחַי גֹּאֲלִי, וְצוּר חֶבְלִי בְּעֵת צָרָה.
וְהוּא נִסִּי וּמָנוֹס לִי, מְנָת כּוֹסִי בְּיוֹם אֶקְרָא.
בְּיָדוֹ אַפְקִיד רוּחִי, בְּעֵת אִישַׁן וְאָעִירָה.
וְעִם רוּחִי גְּוִיָּתִי, יהוה לִי וְלֹא אִירָא.

יִגְדַּל אֱלֹהִים חַי* וְיִשְׁתַּבַּח, נִמְצָא וְאֵין עֵת אֶל מְצִיאוּתוֹ.
אֶחָד וְאֵין יָחִיד כְּיִחוּדוֹ, נֶעְלָם וְגַם אֵין סוֹף לְאַחְדוּתוֹ.
אֵין לוֹ דְּמוּת הַגּוּף וְאֵינוֹ גוּף, לֹא נַעֲרוֹךְ אֵלָיו קְדֻשָּׁתוֹ.
קַדְמוֹן לְכָל דָּבָר אֲשֶׁר נִבְרָא, רִאשׁוֹן וְאֵין רֵאשִׁית לְרֵאשִׁיתוֹ.
הִנּוֹ אֲדוֹן עוֹלָם לְכָל נוֹצָר, יוֹרֶה גְדֻלָּתוֹ וּמַלְכוּתוֹ.
שֶׁפַע נְבוּאָתוֹ נְתָנוֹ, אֶל אַנְשֵׁי סְגֻלָּתוֹ וְתִפְאַרְתּוֹ.
לֹא קָם בְּיִשְׂרָאֵל כְּמֹשֶׁה עוֹד, נָבִיא וּמַבִּיט אֶת תְּמוּנָתוֹ.
תּוֹרַת אֱמֶת נָתַן לְעַמּוֹ אֵל, עַל יַד נְבִיאוֹ נֶאֱמַן בֵּיתוֹ.
לֹא יַחֲלִיף הָאֵל וְלֹא יָמִיר דָּתוֹ, לְעוֹלָמִים לְזוּלָתוֹ.
צוֹפֶה וְיוֹדֵעַ סְתָרֵינוּ, מַבִּיט לְסוֹף דָּבָר בְּקַדְמָתוֹ.
גּוֹמֵל לְאִישׁ חֶסֶד כְּמִפְעָלוֹ, נוֹתֵן לְרָשָׁע רָע כְּרִשְׁעָתוֹ.
יִשְׁלַח לְקֵץ הַיָּמִין מְשִׁיחֵנוּ, לִפְדּוֹת מְחַכֵּי קֵץ יְשׁוּעָתוֹ.
מֵתִים יְחַיֶּה אֵל בְּרֹב חַסְדּוֹ, בָּרוּךְ עֲדֵי עַד שֵׁם תְּהִלָּתוֹ.

⌘ **אֲדוֹן עוֹלָם** — *Master of the universe.* This inspiring song of praise is attributed to R' Shlomo ibn Gabirol, one of the greatest early *paytanim* [liturgical poets], who flourished in the eleventh century. The daily prayer service is inaugurated with the Name אָדוֹן to recall the merit of Abraham, the first one to address God with this title [*Genesis* 15:2] *(Etz Yosef)*, and the one who instituted the morning prayers [*Berachos* 26b] *(Vilna Gaon)*.

The song emphasizes that God is timeless, infinite and omnipotent. Mankind can offer Him only one thing: to proclaim Him as King, by doing His will and praising Him. Despite God's greatness, however, He involves Himself with man's personal needs in time of pain and distress. The prayer concludes on the inspiring note that, lofty though He is, *HASHEM is with me, I shall not fear.*

⌘ **יִגְדַּל אֱלֹהִים חַי** — *Exalted be the Living God.* This song of uncertain authorship summarizes the 'Thirteen Principles of Faith' expounded by *Rambam* and stated succinctly in the famous *Ani Maamin* prayer. See commentary on page 72.

אֲדוֹן עוֹלָם *Master of the universe,* Who reigned*
before any form was created,
At the time when His will brought all into being —
then as 'King' was His Name proclaimed.
After all has ceased to be,
He, the Awesome One, will reign alone.
It is He Who was, He Who is,
and He Who shall remain, in splendor.
He is One — there is no second
to compare to Him, to declare as His equal.
Without beginning, without conclusion —
His is the power and dominion.
He is my God, my living Redeemer,
Rock of my pain in time of distress.
He is my banner, a refuge for me,
the portion in my cup on the day I call.
Into His hand I shall entrust my spirit
when I go to sleep — and I shall awaken!
With my spirit shall my body remain.
HASHEM is with me, I shall not fear.

יִגְדַּל *Exalted be the Living God* and praised,*
He exists — unbounded by time is His existence.
He is One — and there is no unity like His Oneness.
Inscrutable and infinite is His Oneness.
He has no semblance of a body nor is He corporeal;
nor has His holiness any comparison.
He preceded every being that was created —
the First, and nothing precedes His precedence.
Behold! He is Master of the universe to every creature,
He demonstrates His greatness and His sovereignty.
He granted His flow of prophecy
to His treasured splendrous people.
In Israel none like Moses arose again —
a prophet who perceived His vision clearly.
God gave His people a Torah of truth,
by means of His prophet, the most trusted of His household.
God will never amend nor exchange His law
for any other one, for all eternity.
He scrutinizes and knows our hiddenmost secrets;
He perceives a matter's outcome at its inception.
He recompenses man with kindness according to his deed;
He places evil on the wicked according to his wickedness.
By the End of Days He will send our Messiah,
to redeem those longing for His final salvation.
God will revive the dead in His abundant kindness —
Blessed forever is His praised Name.

ברכות השחר

Although many hold that the blessing עַל נְטִילַת יָדָיִם should be recited immediately after the ritual washing of the hands upon arising, others customarily recite it at this point. Similarly, some recite אֲשֶׁר יָצַר immediately after relieving themselves in the morning, while others recite it here.

בָּרוּךְ אַתָּה יהוה אֱלֹהֵינוּ מֶלֶךְ הָעוֹלָם, אֲשֶׁר קִדְּשָׁנוּ בְּמִצְוֹתָיו, וְצִוָּנוּ עַל נְטִילַת יָדָיִם.*

בָּרוּךְ אַתָּה יהוה אֱלֹהֵינוּ מֶלֶךְ הָעוֹלָם, אֲשֶׁר יָצַר אֶת הָאָדָם בְּחָכְמָה,* וּבָרָא בוֹ נְקָבִים נְקָבִים, חֲלוּלִים* חֲלוּלִים. גָּלוּי וְיָדוּעַ לִפְנֵי כִסֵּא כְבוֹדֶךָ, שֶׁאִם יִפָּתֵחַ אֶחָד מֵהֶם, אוֹ יִסָּתֵם אֶחָד מֵהֶם, אִי אֶפְשַׁר לְהִתְקַיֵּם וְלַעֲמוֹד לְפָנֶיךָ. בָּרוּךְ אַתָּה יהוה, רוֹפֵא כָל בָּשָׂר וּמַפְלִיא לַעֲשׂוֹת.*

At this point, some recite אֱלֹהַי נְשָׁמָה, (p. 138).

ברכות התורה

It is forbidden to study or recite Torah passages before reciting the following blessings. Since the commandment to study Torah is in effect all day long, these blessings need not be repeated if one studies at various times of the day. Although many *siddurim* begin a new paragraph at וְהַעֲרֶב נָא, according to the vast majority of commentators the first blessing does not end until לְעַמּוֹ יִשְׂרָאֵל.

בָּרוּךְ אַתָּה יהוה אֱלֹהֵינוּ מֶלֶךְ הָעוֹלָם, אֲשֶׁר קִדְּשָׁנוּ בְּמִצְוֹתָיו, וְצִוָּנוּ לַעֲסוֹק בְּדִבְרֵי תוֹרָה. וְהַעֲרֶב נָא יהוה אֱלֹהֵינוּ אֶת דִּבְרֵי תוֹרָתְךָ בְּפִינוּ וּבְפִי עַמְּךָ בֵּית יִשְׂרָאֵל. וְנִהְיֶה אֲנַחְנוּ וְצֶאֱצָאֵינוּ וְצֶאֱצָאֵי עַמְּךָ בֵּית יִשְׂרָאֵל, כֻּלָּנוּ יוֹדְעֵי שְׁמֶךָ וְלוֹמְדֵי תוֹרָתֶךָ לִשְׁמָהּ.* בָּרוּךְ אַתָּה יהוה, הַמְּלַמֵּד תּוֹרָה לְעַמּוֹ יִשְׂרָאֵל.

בָּרוּךְ אַתָּה יהוה אֱלֹהֵינוּ מֶלֶךְ הָעוֹלָם, אֲשֶׁר בָּחַר בָּנוּ מִכָּל הָעַמִּים וְנָתַן לָנוּ אֶת תּוֹרָתוֹ. בָּרוּךְ אַתָּה יהוה, נוֹתֵן הַתּוֹרָה.

במדבר ו:כד-כו

יְבָרֶכְךָ יהוה וְיִשְׁמְרֶךָ. יָאֵר יהוה פָּנָיו אֵלֶיךָ וִיחֻנֶּךָּ. יִשָּׂא יהוה פָּנָיו אֵלֶיךָ, וְיָשֵׂם לְךָ שָׁלוֹם.

בִּרְכוֹת הַשַּׁחַר / MORNING BLESSINGS

עַל נְטִילַת יָדָיִם — *Regarding washing the hands.* In the case of blessings, the general rule is that they should be recited in conjunction with the acts to which they apply. Nevertheless, some postpone the blessings עַל נְטִילַת יָדָיִם for washing the hands and אֲשֶׁר יָצַר for relieving oneself so that they will be recited as part of *Shacharis* (see *Mishnah Berurah* 4:4 and 6:9).

אֲשֶׁר יָצַר אֶת הָאָדָם בְּחָכְמָה — *Who fashioned man with wisdom.* This phrase has two meanings: (a) When God created man, He gave him the gift of wisdom; and (b) God used wisdom when He created man, as is demonstrated in the precise balance of his organs and functions.

נְקָבִים, חֲלוּלִים — *Openings and . . . cavities.* The mouth, nostrils, and other orifices are the *openings* that lead in and out of the body. The *cavities* are the inner hollows that contain such organs as the lungs, heart, stomach, and brain.

וּמַפְלִיא לַעֲשׂוֹת — *And acts wondrously.* The delicate balance of the organs is a wonder of wonders *(Beis Yosef);* alternatively, it is

MORNING BLESSINGS

Although many hold that the blessing עַל נְטִילַת יָדָיִם, '. . .*regarding washing the hands,*' should be recited immediately after the ritual washing of the hands upon arising, others customarily recite it at this point. Similarly, some recite אֲשֶׁר יָצַר, '*Who fashioned* . . .,' immediately after relieving themselves in the morning, while others recite it here.

בָּרוּךְ *Blessed are You, HASHEM, our God, King of the universe, Who has sanctified us with His commandments and has commanded us regarding washing the hands.**

בָּרוּךְ *Blessed are You, HASHEM, our God, King of the universe, Who fashioned man with wisdom* and created within him many openings and many cavities.* It is obvious and known before Your Throne of Glory that if but one of them were to be ruptured or but one of them were to be blocked it would be impossible to survive and to stand before You. Blessed are You, HASHEM, Who heals all flesh and acts wondrously.**

At this point, some recite אֱלֹהַי נְשָׁמָה, '*My God, the soul* . . .' (p. 138).

BLESSINGS OF THE TORAH

It is forbidden to study or recite Torah passages before reciting the following blessings. Since the commandment to study Torah is in effect all day long, these blessings need not be repeated if one studies at various times of the day. Although many *siddurim* begin a new paragraph at וְהַעֲרֶב נָא, '*Please, HASHEM,*' according to the vast majority of commentators the first blessing does not end until לְעַמּוֹ יִשְׂרָאֵל, '. . . *His people Israel.*'

בָּרוּךְ *Blessed are You, HASHEM, our God, King of the universe, Who has sanctified us with His commandments and has commanded us to engross ourselves in the words of Torah. Please, HASHEM, our God, sweeten the words of Your Torah in our mouth and in the mouth of Your people, the family of Israel. May we and our offspring and the offspring of Your people, the House of Israel — all of us — know Your Name and study Your Torah for its own sake.* Blessed are You, HASHEM, Who teaches Torah to His people Israel.*

בָּרוּךְ *Blessed are You, HASHEM, our God, King of the universe, Who selected us from all the peoples and gave us His Torah. Blessed are You, HASHEM, Giver of the Torah.*

Numbers 6:24-26

יְבָרֶכְךָ *May HASHEM bless you and safeguard you. May HASHEM illuminate His countenance for you and be gracious to you. May HASHEM turn His countenance to you and establish peace for you.*

---

wondrous that the spiritual soul fuses with the physical body to create a human being (*Rama*).

בִּרְכוֹת הַתּוֹרָה / Blessings of the Torah

As stated explicitly in the Talmudic selection[אֵלּוּ דְבָרִים] at the conclusion of these blessings, the study of Torah is the paramount commandment. Without it, man cannot know God's will; with it, he can penetrate the wisdom of the Creator Himself. Each part of the blessings expresses a different idea. The first, אֲשֶׁר קִדְּשָׁנוּ, *Who has sanctified us,* applies to the commandments; the second, וְהַעֲרֶב נָא, *Please . . . sweeten,* is a prayer; the third, אֲשֶׁר בָּחַר בָּנוּ, *Who selected us,* is an expression of thanks for the gift of the Torah.

לִשְׁמָהּ — *For its own sake.* May we study Torah for no other reason than to know it and become imbued with its wisdom.

Selections from the Written and Oral Torah

Whenever a blessing is recited for a *mitzvah,* the *mitzvah* must be performed immediately. Having recited the blessings for the study of Torah, we immediately recite selections from

משנה, פאה א:א

אֵלּוּ דְבָרִים שֶׁאֵין לָהֶם שִׁעוּר:* הַפֵּאָה וְהַבִּכּוּרִים וְהָרַאְיוֹן* וּגְמִילוּת חֲסָדִים וְתַלְמוּד תּוֹרָה.

שבת קכז.

אֵלּוּ דְבָרִים שֶׁאָדָם אוֹכֵל פֵּרוֹתֵיהֶם בָּעוֹלָם הַזֶּה וְהַקֶּרֶן קַיֶּמֶת לוֹ* לָעוֹלָם הַבָּא. וְאֵלּוּ הֵן: כִּבּוּד אָב וָאֵם, וּגְמִילוּת חֲסָדִים, וְהַשְׁכָּמַת בֵּית הַמִּדְרָשׁ שַׁחֲרִית וְעַרְבִית, וְהַכְנָסַת אוֹרְחִים, וּבִקּוּר חוֹלִים, וְהַכְנָסַת כַּלָּה, וּלְוָיַת הַמֵּת, וְעִיּוּן תְּפִלָּה, וַהֲבָאַת שָׁלוֹם בֵּין אָדָם לַחֲבֵרוֹ – וְתַלְמוּד תּוֹרָה כְּנֶגֶד כֻּלָּם.

אֱלֹהַי, נְשָׁמָה* שֶׁנָּתַתָּ בִּי טְהוֹרָה הִיא. אַתָּה בְרָאתָהּ אַתָּה יְצַרְתָּהּ, אַתָּה נְפַחְתָּהּ בִּי, וְאַתָּה מְשַׁמְּרָהּ בְּקִרְבִּי, וְאַתָּה עָתִיד לִטְּלָהּ מִמֶּנִּי, וּלְהַחֲזִירָהּ בִּי לֶעָתִיד לָבֹא. כָּל זְמַן שֶׁהַנְּשָׁמָה בְקִרְבִּי, מוֹדֶה אֲנִי לְפָנֶיךָ, יהוה אֱלֹהַי וֵאלֹהֵי אֲבוֹתַי, רִבּוֹן כָּל הַמַּעֲשִׂים, אֲדוֹן כָּל הַנְּשָׁמוֹת. בָּרוּךְ אַתָּה יהוה, הַמַּחֲזִיר נְשָׁמוֹת לִפְגָרִים מֵתִים.

The *chazzan* recites the following blessings aloud, and the congregation responds אָמֵן to each blessing. Nevertheless, each person must recite these blessings for himself. Some people recite the blessings aloud for one another so that each one can have the merit of responding אָמֵן many times (see commentary).

בָּרוּךְ אַתָּה יהוה אֱלֹהֵינוּ מֶלֶךְ הָעוֹלָם, אֲשֶׁר נָתַן לַשֶּׂכְוִי בִינָה*[1] לְהַבְחִין בֵּין יוֹם וּבֵין לָיְלָה.

בָּרוּךְ אַתָּה יהוה אֱלֹהֵינוּ מֶלֶךְ הָעוֹלָם, שֶׁלֹּא עָשַׂנִי גּוֹי.*

בָּרוּךְ אַתָּה יהוה אֱלֹהֵינוּ מֶלֶךְ הָעוֹלָם, שֶׁלֹּא עָשַׂנִי עָבֶד.*

Men say:

בָּרוּךְ אַתָּה יהוה אֱלֹהֵינוּ מֶלֶךְ הָעוֹלָם, שֶׁלֹּא עָשַׂנִי אִשָּׁה.*

Women say:

בָּרוּךְ אַתָּה יהוה אֱלֹהֵינוּ מֶלֶךְ הָעוֹלָם, שֶׁעָשַׂנִי כִּרְצוֹנוֹ.

---

both the Written and Oral Torah. First we recite the Scriptural verses of the Priestly Blessings (for commentary, see p. 355), then a Talmudic selection from the *Mishnah* [אֵלּוּ דְבָרִים שֶׁאֵין] *(Peah* 1:1) and *Gemara* [אֵלּוּ דְבָרִים שֶׁאָדָם] *(Shabbos* 127a). The Talmudic selection discusses the reward for various commandments and concludes with the declaration that Torah study is equivalent to them all, an appropriate addendum to the Blessings of the Torah.

§ **אֵלּוּ דְבָרִים שֶׁאֵין לָהֶם שִׁעוּר** — *These are the precepts that have no prescribed measure.* The Torah does not prescribe how much is involved in the performance of the following commandments *(Rav).*

וְהָרַאְיוֹן — *The pilgrimage.* Though the Torah ordains that a Jew visit the Temple on each of the three festivals (Pesach, Shavuos, and Succos), one may visit as often as he wishes. Alternatively, there is no set amount for the value of the elevation-offering [עוֹלַת רְאִיָּה] that one must bring at such times.

וְהַקֶּרֶן קַיֶּמֶת לוֹ — *But whose principal remains intact for him.* Though one is rewarded for these *mitzvos* in This World, his reward in the World to Come is not diminished.

Mishnah, *Peah* 1:1

אֵלּוּ דְבָרִים *These are the precepts that have no prescribed measure:* the corner of a field [which must be left for the poor], the first-fruit offering, the pilgrimage,* acts of kindness, and Torah study.*

Talmud, *Shabbos* 127a

אֵלּוּ דְבָרִים *These are the precepts whose fruits a person enjoys in This World but whose principal remains intact for him* in the World to Come. They are: the honor due to father and mother, acts of kindness, early attendance at the house of study morning and evening, hospitality to guests, visiting the sick, providing for a bride, escorting the dead, absorption in prayer, bringing peace between man and his fellow — and the study of Torah is equivalent to them all.*

אֱלֹהַי *My God, the soul* You placed within me is pure. You created it, You fashioned it, You breathed it into me, You safeguard it within me, and eventually You will take it from me, and restore it to me in Time to Come. As long as the soul is within me, I gratefully thank You, HASHEM, my God and the God of my forefathers, Master of all works, Lord of all souls. Blessed are You, HASHEM, Who restores souls to dead bodies.*

The *chazzan* recites the following blessings aloud, and the congregation responds *'Amen'* to each blessing. Nevertheless, each person must recite these blessings for himself. Some people recite the blessings aloud for one another so that each one can have the merit of responding *Amen* many times (see commentary).

בָּרוּךְ *Blessed are You, HASHEM, our God, King of the universe, Who gave the heart understanding*[1] to distinguish between day and night.*

*Blessed are You, HASHEM, our God, King of the universe, for not having made me a gentile.**

*Blessed are You, HASHEM, our God, King of the universe, for not having made me a slave.**

Men say:	Women say:
*Blessed are You, HASHEM, our God, King of the universe, for not having made me a woman.**	*Blessed are You, HASHEM, our God, King of the universe, for having made me according to His will.*

(1) Cf. *Job* 38:36.

⚜ אֱלֹהַי, נְשָׁמָה — *My God, the soul* ... This prayerful blessing is an expression of gratitude to God for restoring our vitality in the morning with a soul of pure, celestial origin, and for maintaining us in life and health.

⚜ בָּרוּךְ ... אֲשֶׁר נָתַן לַשֶּׂכְוִי בִינָה — *Blessed ... Who gave the heart understanding.* The word שֶׂכְוִי means both *heart* and *rooster.* In the context of this blessing, both meanings are implied: the rooster crows, but man's heart reacts and understands how to deal with new situations *(Rosh).*

שֶׁלֹּא עָשַׂנִי גּוֹי ... עָבֶד ... אִשָּׁה — *For not having made me a gentile ... a slave ... a woman.* The Torah assigns missions to respective groups of people. Within Israel, for example, the Davidic family, *Kohanim,* and Levites are set apart by virtue of their particular callings, in addition to their shared mission as Jews. All such missions carry extra responsibilities and call for the performance of the *mitzvos* associated with them. We thank God, therefore, for the challenge of improving His universe in accordance with

בָּרוּךְ אַתָּה יהוה אֱלֹהֵינוּ מֶלֶךְ הָעוֹלָם, פּוֹקֵחַ עִוְרִים.[1]
בָּרוּךְ אַתָּה יהוה אֱלֹהֵינוּ מֶלֶךְ הָעוֹלָם, מַלְבִּישׁ עֲרֻמִּים.
בָּרוּךְ אַתָּה יהוה אֱלֹהֵינוּ מֶלֶךְ הָעוֹלָם, מַתִּיר אֲסוּרִים.[2]
בָּרוּךְ אַתָּה יהוה אֱלֹהֵינוּ מֶלֶךְ הָעוֹלָם, זוֹקֵף כְּפוּפִים.[1]
בָּרוּךְ אַתָּה יהוה אֱלֹהֵינוּ מֶלֶךְ הָעוֹלָם, רוֹקַע הָאָרֶץ עַל הַמָּיִם.*[3]
בָּרוּךְ אַתָּה יהוה אֱלֹהֵינוּ מֶלֶךְ הָעוֹלָם, שֶׁעָשָׂה לִי כָּל צָרְכִּי.
בָּרוּךְ אַתָּה יהוה אֱלֹהֵינוּ מֶלֶךְ הָעוֹלָם, הַמֵּכִין מִצְעֲדֵי גָבֶר.[4]
בָּרוּךְ אַתָּה יהוה אֱלֹהֵינוּ מֶלֶךְ הָעוֹלָם, אוֹזֵר יִשְׂרָאֵל בִּגְבוּרָה.
בָּרוּךְ אַתָּה יהוה אֱלֹהֵינוּ מֶלֶךְ הָעוֹלָם, עוֹטֵר יִשְׂרָאֵל בְּתִפְאָרָה.
בָּרוּךְ אַתָּה יהוה אֱלֹהֵינוּ מֶלֶךְ הָעוֹלָם, הַנּוֹתֵן לַיָּעֵף כֹּחַ.[5]

Although many *siddurim* begin a new paragraph at וִיהִי רָצוֹן, the following is one long blessing that ends at לְעַמּוֹ יִשְׂרָאֵל.

בָּרוּךְ אַתָּה יהוה אֱלֹהֵינוּ מֶלֶךְ הָעוֹלָם, הַמַּעֲבִיר שֵׁנָה מֵעֵינָי וּתְנוּמָה מֵעַפְעַפָּי. וִיהִי רָצוֹן* מִלְּפָנֶיךָ, יהוה אֱלֹהֵינוּ וֵאלֹהֵי אֲבוֹתֵינוּ,* שֶׁתַּרְגִּילֵנוּ בְּתוֹרָתֶךָ וְדַבְּקֵנוּ בְּמִצְוֹתֶיךָ, וְאַל תְּבִיאֵנוּ לֹא לִידֵי חֵטְא, וְלֹא לִידֵי עֲבֵרָה וְעָוֹן, וְלֹא לִידֵי נִסָּיוֹן, וְלֹא לִידֵי בִזָּיוֹן, וְאַל תַּשְׁלֶט בָּנוּ יֵצֶר הָרָע. וְהַרְחִיקֵנוּ מֵאָדָם רָע וּמֵחָבֵר רָע. וְדַבְּקֵנוּ בְּיֵצֶר הַטּוֹב וּבְמַעֲשִׂים טוֹבִים, וְכוֹף אֶת יִצְרֵנוּ לְהִשְׁתַּעְבֶּד לָךְ. וּתְנֵנוּ הַיּוֹם וּבְכָל יוֹם לְחֵן וּלְחֶסֶד וּלְרַחֲמִים בְּעֵינֶיךָ, וּבְעֵינֵי כָל רוֹאֵינוּ, וְתִגְמְלֵנוּ חֲסָדִים טוֹבִים. בָּרוּךְ אַתָּה יהוה, גּוֹמֵל חֲסָדִים טוֹבִים לְעַמּוֹ יִשְׂרָאֵל.

His will. Male, free Jews have responsibilities and duties not shared by others. For this, they express gratitude that, unlike women, they were *not* freed from the obligation to perform the time-related commandments. This follows the Talmudic dictum that an obligatory performance of a *mitzvah* is superior to a voluntary one, because it is human nature to resist obligations [גָּדוֹל הַמְּצֻוֶּה וְעוֹשֶׂה מִמִּי שֶׁאֵינוֹ מְצֻוֶּה וְעוֹשֶׂה]. Women, on the other hand, both historically and because of their nature, are the guardians of tradition, the molders of character, children, and family. Furthermore, women have often been the protectors of Judaism when the impetuosity and aggressiveness of the male nature led the men astray. The classic precedent was in the Wilderness when men — not women — worshiped the Golden Calf. Thus, though women were not given the privilege of the challenge assigned to men, they are created closer to God's ideal of satisfaction. They express their gratitude in the blessing שֶׁעָשַׂנִי כִּרְצוֹנוֹ, *for having made me according to His will (R' Munk).*

רוֹקַע הָאָרֶץ עַל הַמָּיִם — *Who spreads out the earth upon the water.* By nature, water spreads and floods everything in its path, while earth tends to sink beneath the surface of the water. God formed the earth so that it remains always in place *(Radak).*

וִיהִי רָצוֹן — *And may it be Your will.* When a person starts off well, his chances for future success are enhanced immeasurably. Having thanked God for giving us new life, health, and vigor at the start of a new day, we pray that He provide us the conditions to serve Him and that He remove impediments to His service *(Siach Yitzchak).*

וֵאלֹהֵי אֲבוֹתֵינוּ — *And the God of our forefathers.* As is common in prayers, we call upon God as *the God of our forefathers,* because we wish to identify with the merit of our righteous forebears *(Etz Yosef).*

The above series of fifteen blessings is based on *Berachos* 60b, where the Sages teach that as one experiences the phenomena of the new day,

Blessed are You, HASHEM, our God, King of the universe, Who gives sight to the blind.[1]

Blessed are You, HASHEM, our God, King of the universe, Who clothes the naked.

Blessed are You, HASHEM, our God, King of the universe, Who releases the bound.[2]

Blessed are You, HASHEM, our God, King of the universe, Who straightens the bent.[1]

*Blessed are You, HASHEM, our God, King of the universe, Who spreads out the earth upon the waters.**[3]

Blessed are You, HASHEM, our God, King of the universe, Who has provided me my every need.

Blessed are You, HASHEM, our God, King of the universe, Who firms man's footsteps.[4]

Blessed are You, HASHEM, our God, King of the universe, Who girds Israel with strength.

Blessed are You, HASHEM, our God, King of the universe, Who crowns Israel with splendor.

Blessed are You, HASHEM, our God, King of the universe, Who gives strength to the weary.[5]

Although many *siddurim* begin a new paragraph at וִיהִי רָצוֹן, *'And may it be Your will,'* the following is one long blessing that ends at לְעַמּוֹ יִשְׂרָאֵל, *'. . . His people Israel.'*

בָּרוּךְ *Blessed are You, HASHEM, our God, King of the universe, Who removes sleep from my eyes and slumber from my eyelids. And may it be Your will,* HASHEM, our God, and the God of our forefathers,* that You accustom us to [study] Your Torah and attach us to Your commandments. Do not bring us into the power of error, nor into the power of transgression and sin, nor into the power of challenge, nor into the power of scorn. Let not the Evil Inclination dominate us. Distance us from an evil person and an evil companion. Attach us to the Good Inclination and to good deeds and compel our Evil Inclination to be subservient to You. Grant us today and every day grace, kindness, and mercy in Your eyes and in the eyes of all who see us, and bestow beneficent kindnesses upon us. Blessed are You, HASHEM, Who bestows beneficent kindnesses upon His people Israel.*

(1) *Psalms* 146:8. (2) v. 7. (3) Cf. 136:6. (4) Cf. 37:23. (5) *Isaiah* 40:29.

---

he should bless God for providing them. For example, one thanks God for giving man the crucial ability to make distinctions in life, such as that between day and night; when he rubs his eyes and sees; when he gets dressed, and so on. Some of these phenomena are not so obvious from the text of the blessing. Among them are: sitting up and stretching *[releases the bound]*; getting out of bed *[straightens the bent]*; standing on the floor *[spreads out the earth . . .]*; donning shoes which symbolizes man's ability to go on his way comfortably *[provided me my every need]*; setting out on one's destination *[firms . . . footsteps]*; fastening one's clothing *[girds Israel . . .]*; putting on a hat, which symbolizes the Jew's reminder that Someone is above him *[crowns Israel . . .]*; feeling the passing of nighttime exhaustion *[gives strength . . .* and *removes sleep . . .]*.

Arizal teaches that each day a righteous person should endeavor to respond to a minimum of ninety blessings, four times *Kedushah* (i.e., the verse קָדוֹשׁ קָדוֹשׁ קָדוֹשׁ, *Holy, Holy, Holy . . .*), ten times *Kaddish*, and to recite no less than one hundred blessings. These figures are alluded to by the letters of the word

יְהִי רָצוֹן* מִלְּפָנֶיךָ, יהוה אֱלֹהַי וֵאלֹהֵי אֲבוֹתַי, שֶׁתַּצִּילֵנִי הַיּוֹם וּבְכָל יוֹם מֵעַזֵּי פָנִים וּמֵעַזּוּת פָּנִים, מֵאָדָם רָע, וּמֵחָבֵר רָע, וּמִשָּׁכֵן רָע, וּמִפֶּגַע רָע, וּמִשָּׂטָן הַמַּשְׁחִית, מִדִּין קָשֶׁה וּמִבַּעַל דִּין קָשֶׁה, בֵּין שֶׁהוּא בֶן בְּרִית,* וּבֵין שֶׁאֵינוֹ בֶן בְּרִית.

עקדה

Some omit the following paragraph on the Sabbath and Yom Tov.

אֱלֹהֵינוּ* וֵאלֹהֵי אֲבוֹתֵינוּ, זָכְרֵנוּ בְּזִכָּרוֹן טוֹב לְפָנֶיךָ, וּפָקְדֵנוּ בִּפְקֻדַּת יְשׁוּעָה וְרַחֲמִים מִשְּׁמֵי שְׁמֵי קֶדֶם. וּזְכָר לָנוּ יהוה אֱלֹהֵינוּ אַהֲבַת הַקַּדְמוֹנִים אַבְרָהָם יִצְחָק וְיִשְׂרָאֵל עֲבָדֶיךָ, אֶת הַבְּרִית וְאֶת הַחֶסֶד וְאֶת הַשְּׁבוּעָה שֶׁנִּשְׁבַּעְתָּ לְאַבְרָהָם אָבִינוּ בְּהַר הַמּוֹרִיָּה, וְאֶת הָעֲקֵדָה שֶׁעָקַד אֶת יִצְחָק בְּנוֹ עַל גַּבֵּי הַמִּזְבֵּחַ, כַּכָּתוּב בְּתוֹרָתֶךָ:

בראשית כב:א-יט

וַיְהִי אַחַר הַדְּבָרִים הָאֵלֶּה, וְהָאֱלֹהִים נִסָּה אֶת אַבְרָהָם, וַיֹּאמֶר אֵלָיו, אַבְרָהָם. וַיֹּאמֶר, הִנֵּנִי. וַיֹּאמֶר, קַח נָא אֶת בִּנְךָ, אֶת יְחִידְךָ, אֲשֶׁר אָהַבְתָּ, אֶת יִצְחָק, וְלֶךְ לְךָ אֶל אֶרֶץ הַמֹּרִיָּה, וְהַעֲלֵהוּ שָׁם לְעֹלָה עַל אַחַד הֶהָרִים אֲשֶׁר אֹמַר אֵלֶיךָ. וַיַּשְׁכֵּם אַבְרָהָם בַּבֹּקֶר,* וַיַּחֲבֹשׁ אֶת חֲמֹרוֹ, וַיִּקַּח אֶת שְׁנֵי נְעָרָיו* אִתּוֹ, וְאֵת יִצְחָק בְּנוֹ, וַיְבַקַּע עֲצֵי עֹלָה, וַיָּקָם וַיֵּלֶךְ אֶל הַמָּקוֹם אֲשֶׁר אָמַר לוֹ הָאֱלֹהִים. בַּיּוֹם הַשְּׁלִישִׁי, וַיִּשָּׂא אַבְרָהָם אֶת עֵינָיו, וַיַּרְא אֶת הַמָּקוֹם מֵרָחֹק. וַיֹּאמֶר אַבְרָהָם אֶל נְעָרָיו, שְׁבוּ לָכֶם פֹּה עִם הַחֲמוֹר, וַאֲנִי וְהַנַּעַר נֵלְכָה עַד כֹּה, וְנִשְׁתַּחֲוֶה וְנָשׁוּבָה* אֲלֵיכֶם. וַיִּקַּח אַבְרָהָם אֶת עֲצֵי הָעֹלָה, וַיָּשֶׂם עַל יִצְחָק בְּנוֹ, וַיִּקַּח בְּיָדוֹ אֶת הָאֵשׁ וְאֶת הַמַּאֲכֶלֶת, וַיֵּלְכוּ שְׁנֵיהֶם יַחְדָּו. וַיֹּאמֶר יִצְחָק אֶל אַבְרָהָם אָבִיו, וַיֹּאמֶר, אָבִי. וַיֹּאמֶר, הִנֶּנִּי בְנִי. וַיֹּאמֶר, הִנֵּה הָאֵשׁ

צַדִּיק, *righteous one,* which have the numerical equivalents of 90, 4, 10, and 100 respectively. To assure ninety *Amen* responses, some people recite these fifteen blessings aloud for one another.

יְהִי רָצוֹן — *May it be Your will.* This personal prayer was recited by Rabbi Yehudah HaNassi every day after *Shacharis (Berachos* 16b). It is a prayer for protection in day-to-day dealings with one's fellow men. During the recitation, one may add his personal requests for God's help during the day *(Tur).*

בֶּן בְּרִית — *A member of the covenant,* i.e., Abraham's covenant of circumcision, the emblem of Israel's bond with God.

עֲקֵדָה / THE AKEIDAH

The *Akeidah* is the story of the most difficult challenge to Abraham's faith in God. He was commanded to sacrifice Isaac, his beloved son and sole heir, to God. Father and son jointly demonstrated their total devotion, upon which God ordered Abraham to release Isaac. The Kabbalistic masters, from *Zohar* to *Arizal,* have stressed the great importance of the daily recitation of the *Akeidah.* In response to their writings, the *Akeidah* has been incorporated into the great majority of *siddurim,* although it is not recited in all congregations. In some congregations, it is recited individually rather than as part of the public morning service. The *Zohar* records that this recitation of Abraham and Isaac's readiness to put love of God ahead of life itself is a source of heavenly mercy whenever Jewish lives are threatened. *Avodas HaKodesh* comments that the *Akeidah* should inspire us

יְהִי רָצוֹן *May it be Your will,* HASHEM, my God, and the God of my forefathers, that You rescue me today and every day from brazen men and from brazenness, from an evil man, an evil companion, an evil neighbor, an evil mishap, the destructive spiritual impediment, a harsh trial and a harsh opponent, whether he is a member of the covenant* or whether he is not a member of the covenant.*

THE AKEIDAH

Some omit the following paragraph on the Sabbath and Yom Tov.

אֱלֹהֵינוּ *Our God* and the God of our forefathers, remember us with a favorable memory before You, and recall us with a recollection of salvation and mercy from the primeval loftiest heavens. Remember on our behalf — O HASHEM, our God — the love of the Patriarchs, Abraham, Isaac and Israel, Your servants; the covenant, the kindness, and the oath that You swore to our father Abraham at Mount Moriah, and the Akeidah, when he bound his son Isaac atop the altar, as it is written in Your Torah:*

Genesis 22:1-19

וַיְהִי *And it happened after these things that God tested Abraham and said to him, 'Abraham.'*

And he replied, 'Here I am.'

And He said, 'Please take your son, your only one, whom you love — Isaac — and get yourself to the Land of Moriah; bring him up there as an offering, upon one of the mountains which I shall indicate to you.'

So Abraham awoke early in the morning and he saddled his donkey; he took his two young men* with him, and Isaac, his son. He split the wood for the offering, and rose and went toward the place which God had indicated to him.*

On the third day, Abraham looked up, and perceived the place from afar. And Abraham said to his young men, 'Stay here by yourselves with the donkey, while I and the lad will go yonder; we will prostrate ourselves and we will return to you.'*

And Abraham took the wood for the offering, and placed it on Isaac, his son. He took in his hand the fire and the knife, and the two of them went together. Then Isaac spoke to Abraham his father and said, 'Father — '

And he said, 'Here I am, my son.'

---

toward greater love of God, by following the example of Abraham and Isaac. *Arizal* teaches that the recitation brings atonement to someone who repents sincerely, for he identifies himself with the two Patriarchs who placed loyalty to God above all other considerations.

⊛ אֱלֹהֵינוּ — *Our God.* This preliminary supplication is one of the highlights of the Rosh Hashanah *Mussaf.*

וַיַּשְׁכֵּם אַבְרָהָם בַּבֹּקֶר — *So Abraham awoke early in the morning.* He began early, with alacrity, to do God's will, even though he had been commanded to slaughter his beloved Isaac. From this verse the Sages derive that one should perform his religious obligations (e.g., circumcision) as early in the day as possible (*Pesachim* 4a).

שְׁנֵי נְעָרָיו — *His two young men.* Ishmael, his older son, and Eliezer, his trusted servant.

וְנִשְׁתַּחֲוֶה וְנָשׁוּבָה — *We will prostrate ourselves and we will return.* An unintended prophecy came from Abraham's lips. Instead of saying 'I will return,' — without Isaac — he said 'we,' for

וְהָעֵצִים, וְאַיֵּה הַשֶּׂה לְעֹלָה. וַיֹּאמֶר אַבְרָהָם, אֱלֹהִים יִרְאֶה לּוֹ הַשֶּׂה* לְעֹלָה, בְּנִי, וַיֵּלְכוּ שְׁנֵיהֶם יַחְדָּו. וַיָּבֹאוּ אֶל הַמָּקוֹם אֲשֶׁר אָמַר לוֹ הָאֱלֹהִים, וַיִּבֶן שָׁם אַבְרָהָם אֶת הַמִּזְבֵּחַ, וַיַּעֲרֹךְ אֶת הָעֵצִים, וַיַּעֲקֹד אֶת יִצְחָק בְּנוֹ, וַיָּשֶׂם אֹתוֹ עַל הַמִּזְבֵּחַ מִמַּעַל לָעֵצִים. וַיִּשְׁלַח אַבְרָהָם אֶת יָדוֹ, וַיִּקַּח אֶת הַמַּאֲכֶלֶת לִשְׁחֹט אֶת בְּנוֹ. וַיִּקְרָא אֵלָיו מַלְאַךְ יהוה מִן הַשָּׁמַיִם, וַיֹּאמֶר, אַבְרָהָם, אַבְרָהָם. וַיֹּאמֶר, הִנֵּנִי. וַיֹּאמֶר, אַל תִּשְׁלַח יָדְךָ אֶל הַנַּעַר, וְאַל תַּעַשׂ לוֹ מְאוּמָה, כִּי עַתָּה יָדַעְתִּי כִּי יְרֵא אֱלֹהִים אַתָּה, וְלֹא חָשַׂכְתָּ אֶת בִּנְךָ אֶת יְחִידְךָ מִמֶּנִּי. וַיִּשָּׂא אַבְרָהָם אֶת עֵינָיו וַיַּרְא, וְהִנֵּה אַיִל, אַחַר, נֶאֱחַז בַּסְּבַךְ בְּקַרְנָיו, וַיֵּלֶךְ אַבְרָהָם וַיִּקַּח אֶת הָאַיִל, וַיַּעֲלֵהוּ לְעֹלָה תַּחַת בְּנוֹ. וַיִּקְרָא אַבְרָהָם שֵׁם הַמָּקוֹם הַהוּא יהוה יִרְאֶה,* אֲשֶׁר יֵאָמֵר הַיּוֹם, בְּהַר יהוה יֵרָאֶה. וַיִּקְרָא מַלְאַךְ יהוה אֶל אַבְרָהָם, שֵׁנִית מִן הַשָּׁמָיִם. וַיֹּאמֶר, בִּי נִשְׁבַּעְתִּי נְאֻם יהוה, כִּי יַעַן אֲשֶׁר עָשִׂיתָ אֶת הַדָּבָר הַזֶּה, וְלֹא חָשַׂכְתָּ אֶת בִּנְךָ אֶת יְחִידֶךָ. כִּי בָרֵךְ אֲבָרֶכְךָ, וְהַרְבָּה אַרְבֶּה אֶת זַרְעֲךָ כְּכוֹכְבֵי הַשָּׁמַיִם, וְכַחוֹל אֲשֶׁר עַל שְׂפַת הַיָּם, וְיִרַשׁ זַרְעֲךָ אֵת שַׁעַר אֹיְבָיו. וְהִתְבָּרְכוּ בְזַרְעֲךָ כֹּל גּוֹיֵי הָאָרֶץ, עֵקֶב אֲשֶׁר שָׁמַעְתָּ בְּקֹלִי. וַיָּשָׁב אַבְרָהָם אֶל נְעָרָיו, וַיָּקֻמוּ וַיֵּלְכוּ יַחְדָּו אֶל בְּאֵר שָׁבַע, וַיֵּשֶׁב אַבְרָהָם בִּבְאֵר שָׁבַע.

Some omit the following paragraph on the Sabbath and Yom Tov.

רִבּוֹנוֹ שֶׁל עוֹלָם, יְהִי רָצוֹן מִלְּפָנֶיךָ, יהוה אֱלֹהֵינוּ וֵאלֹהֵי אֲבוֹתֵינוּ, שֶׁתִּזְכָּר לָנוּ בְּרִית אֲבוֹתֵינוּ. כְּמוֹ שֶׁכָּבַשׁ אַבְרָהָם אָבִינוּ אֶת רַחֲמָיו מִבֶּן יְחִידוֹ, וְרָצָה לִשְׁחוֹט אוֹתוֹ כְּדֵי לַעֲשׂוֹת רְצוֹנֶךָ, כֵּן יִכְבְּשׁוּ רַחֲמֶיךָ אֶת כַּעַסְךָ מֵעָלֵינוּ, וְיִגֹּלּוּ רַחֲמֶיךָ עַל מִדּוֹתֶיךָ, וְתִכָּנֵס אִתָּנוּ לִפְנִים מִשּׁוּרַת דִּינֶךָ, וְתִתְנַהֵג עִמָּנוּ, יהוה אֱלֹהֵינוּ, בְּמִדַּת הַחֶסֶד וּבְמִדַּת הָרַחֲמִים. וּבְטוּבְךָ הַגָּדוֹל, יָשׁוּב חֲרוֹן אַפְּךָ מֵעַמְּךָ וּמֵעִירְךָ וּמֵאַרְצְךָ וּמִנַּחֲלָתֶךָ. וְקַיֶּם לָנוּ, יהוה אֱלֹהֵינוּ, אֶת הַדָּבָר שֶׁהִבְטַחְתָּנוּ עַל יְדֵי מֹשֶׁה עַבְדֶּךָ, כָּאָמוּר: וְזָכַרְתִּי אֶת בְּרִיתִי יַעֲקוֹב, וְאַף אֶת בְּרִיתִי יִצְחָק, וְאַף אֶת בְּרִיתִי אַבְרָהָם אֶזְכֹּר, וְהָאָרֶץ אֶזְכֹּר.[1]

---

such, indeed, was God's intention.

אֱלֹהִים יִרְאֶה לּוֹ הַשֶּׂה — *God will seek out for Himself the lamb.* The Midrash teaches that Isaac understood from this reply that he would be the sacrificial 'lamb.' Nevertheless, though Isaac was in the prime of life at the age of 37 and Abraham was a century his senior, *the two of them went together*, united in their dedication.

ה׳ יִרְאֶה — *HASHEM Yireh*, literally, *HASHEM will see*, i.e., God will see the mountain where the *Akeidah* took place as the appropriate site for His Temple. Indeed, the *Akeidah* took place on the future Temple Mount *(Onkelos)*. Alternatively, God will eternally 'see' the *Akeidah* as a source of merit for the offspring of Abraham and Isaac *(R' Bachya)*.

And he said, 'Here are the fire and the wood, but where is the lamb for the offering?'

And Abraham said, 'God will seek out for Himself the lamb for the offering, my son.' And the two of them went together.*

They arrived at the place which God indicated to him. Abraham built the altar there, and arranged the wood; he bound Isaac, his son, and he placed him on the altar atop the wood. Abraham stretched out his hand, and took the knife to slaughter his son.

And an angel of HASHEM called to him from heaven, and said, 'Abraham! Abraham!'

And he said, 'Here I am.'

And he [the angel quoting HASHEM] said, 'Do not stretch out your hand against the lad nor do anything to him, for now I know that you are a God-fearing man, since you have not withheld your son, your only one, from Me.'

And Abraham looked up and saw — behold a ram! — after it had been caught in the thicket by its horns. So Abraham went and took the ram and brought it as an offering instead of his son. And Abraham named that site 'HASHEM Yireh,' as it is said this day: On the mountain HASHEM is seen.*

The angel of HASHEM called to Abraham, a second time from heaven, and said, " 'By Myself I swear,' declared HASHEM, 'that since you have done this thing, and have not withheld your son, your only one, I shall surely bless you and greatly increase your offspring like the stars of the heavens and like the sand on the seashore; and your offspring shall inherit the gate of its enemy; and all the nations of the earth shall bless themselves by your offspring, because you have listened to My voice.' "

Abraham returned to his young men, and they rose and went together to Beer Sheba, and Abraham stayed at Beer Sheba.

Some omit the following paragraph on the Sabbath and Yom Tov.

רִבּוֹנוֹ שֶׁל עוֹלָם *Master of the universe! May it be Your will, HASHEM, our God, and the God of our forefathers, that You remember for our sake the covenant of our forefathers. Just as Abraham our forefather suppressed his mercy for his only son and wished to slaughter him in order to do Your will, so may Your mercy suppress Your anger from upon us and may Your mercy overwhelm Your attributes. May You overstep with us the line of Your law and deal with us — O HASHEM, our God — with the attribute of kindness and the attribute of mercy. In Your great goodness may You turn aside Your burning wrath from Your people, Your city, Your land, and Your heritage. Fulfill for us, HASHEM, our God, the word You pledged through Moses, Your servant, as it is said: 'I shall remember My covenant with Jacob; also My covenant with Isaac, and also My covenant with Abraham shall I remember; and the land shall I remember.'*[1]

(1) *Leviticus* 26:42.

לְעוֹלָם* יְהֵא אָדָם יְרֵא שָׁמַיִם בְּסֵתֶר וּבַגָּלוּי,* וּמוֹדֶה עַל הָאֱמֶת,* וְדוֹבֵר אֱמֶת בִּלְבָבוֹ,* וְיַשְׁכֵּם וְיֹאמַר:

רִבּוֹן כָּל הָעוֹלָמִים,* לֹא עַל צִדְקוֹתֵינוּ אֲנַחְנוּ מַפִּילִים תַּחֲנוּנֵינוּ לְפָנֶיךָ, כִּי עַל רַחֲמֶיךָ הָרַבִּים. מָה אֲנַחְנוּ, מֶה חַיֵּינוּ, מֶה חַסְדֵּנוּ, מַה צִּדְקוֹתֵינוּ, מַה יְּשׁוּעָתֵנוּ, מַה כֹּחֵנוּ, מַה גְּבוּרָתֵנוּ. מַה נֹּאמַר לְפָנֶיךָ, יהוה אֱלֹהֵינוּ וֵאלֹהֵי אֲבוֹתֵינוּ, הֲלֹא כָּל הַגִּבּוֹרִים כְּאַיִן לְפָנֶיךָ, וְאַנְשֵׁי הַשֵּׁם כְּלֹא הָיוּ, וַחֲכָמִים כִּבְלִי מַדָּע, וּנְבוֹנִים כִּבְלִי הַשְׂכֵּל. כִּי רוֹב מַעֲשֵׂיהֶם תֹּהוּ, וִימֵי חַיֵּיהֶם הֶבֶל לְפָנֶיךָ, וּמוֹתַר הָאָדָם מִן הַבְּהֵמָה אָיִן, כִּי הַכֹּל הָבֶל.[1]

אֲבָל אֲנַחְנוּ* עַמְּךָ, בְּנֵי בְרִיתֶךָ, בְּנֵי אַבְרָהָם אֹהַבְךָ שֶׁנִּשְׁבַּעְתָּ לּוֹ בְּהַר הַמּוֹרִיָּה, זֶרַע יִצְחָק יְחִידוֹ שֶׁנֶּעֱקַד עַל גַּב הַמִּזְבֵּחַ, עֲדַת יַעֲקֹב בִּנְךָ בְּכוֹרֶךָ, שֶׁמֵּאַהֲבָתְךָ שֶׁאָהַבְתָּ אוֹתוֹ וּמִשִּׂמְחָתְךָ שֶׁשָּׂמַחְתָּ בּוֹ, קָרָאתָ אֶת שְׁמוֹ יִשְׂרָאֵל וִישֻׁרוּן.*

לְפִיכָךְ אֲנַחְנוּ חַיָּבִים לְהוֹדוֹת לְךָ, וּלְשַׁבֵּחֲךָ, וּלְפָאֶרְךָ, וּלְבָרֵךְ וּלְקַדֵּשׁ וְלָתֵת שֶׁבַח וְהוֹדָיָה לִשְׁמֶךָ. אַשְׁרֵינוּ,* מַה טּוֹב חֶלְקֵנוּ, וּמַה נָּעִים גּוֹרָלֵנוּ, וּמַה יָּפָה יְרֻשָּׁתֵנוּ. ❖ אַשְׁרֵינוּ, שֶׁאֲנַחְנוּ מַשְׁכִּימִים וּמַעֲרִיבִים, עֶרֶב וָבֹקֶר וְאוֹמְרִים פַּעֲמַיִם בְּכָל יוֹם:

שְׁמַע יִשְׂרָאֵל,* יהוה אֱלֹהֵינוּ, יהוה אֶחָד.[2]

In an undertone— בָּרוּךְ שֵׁם כְּבוֹד מַלְכוּתוֹ לְעוֹלָם וָעֶד.

לְעוֹלָם ⁂ — *Always.* The section beginning with לְעוֹלָם and extending until קָרְבָּנוֹת/*Offerings*, is in its totality a profound and succinct summation of basic Jewish faith and loyalty to God. What is more, it is a ringing declaration of joyous pride in our Jewishness, a pride that overcomes all persecutions and that moves us to pray for the time when all will recognize the truth of the Torah's message, and we will proudly proclaim the message that the anti-Semites of the world attempt to still.

Furthermore, the declarations contained in this section represent the manner in which a Jew should conduct himself *always,* not merely on ceremonial occasions.

יְרֵא שָׁמַיִם בְּסֵתֶר וּבַגָּלוּי — *God-fearing privately and publicly.* Some people behave piously when in the view of others, but not when their behavior goes unseen. Others are God-fearing in private but are ashamed to do so in public for fear of being labeled as non-conformists. But the Jew must strive to be consistently God-fearing, whatever his surroundings.

וּמוֹדֶה עַל הָאֱמֶת — *[Let him] acknowledge the truth.* One who seeks the truth is not ashamed to concede his errors. But if he cares more about his reputation than the truth, he will stubbornly persist in falsehood and sin.

וְדוֹבֵר אֱמֶת בִּלְבָבוֹ — *[Let him] speak the truth within his heart.* The Sages cite Rav Safra as the prototype of inner honesty (*Chullin* 94b and *Rashi* to *Makkos* 24a). Once, while he was praying and therefore not permitted to speak, Rav Safra was offered a satisfactory price for something he wished to sell. The buyer did not realize why Rav Safra did not respond, so he kept raising his bid. When Rav Safra finished his prayers, he insisted on accepting no more than the first offer, because in his heart he had intended to sell for that price.

רִבּוֹן כָּל הָעוֹלָמִים — *Master of all worlds!* We now begin leading up to *Shema,* the affirmation of the Oneness of God and acknowledgment of His absolute mastery. We declare that, given the inherent powerlessness and inadequacy of man,

לְעוֹלָם *Always* let a person be God-fearing privately and publicly,* acknowledge the truth,* speak the truth within his heart,* and arise early and proclaim:*

Master of all worlds! Not in the merit of our righteousness do we cast our supplications before You, but in the merit of Your abundant mercy. What are we? What is our life? What is our kindness? What is our righteousness? What is our salvation? What is our strength? What is our might? What can we say before You, HASHEM, our God, and the God of our forefathers — are not all the heroes like nothing before You, the famous as if they had never existed, the wise as if devoid of wisdom and the perceptive as if devoid of intelligence? For most of their deeds are desolate and the days of their lives are empty before You. The pre-eminence of man over beast is non-existent for all is vain.*[1]

But we are Your people, members of Your covenant, children of Abraham, Your beloved, to whom You took an oath at Mount Moriah; the offspring of Isaac, his only son, who was bound atop the altar; the community of Jacob, Your firstborn son, whom — because of the love with which You adored him and the joy with which You delighted in him — You named Israel and Jeshurun.**

לְפִיכָךְ *Therefore, we are obliged to thank You, praise You, glorify You, bless, sanctify, and offer praise and thanks to Your Name. We are fortunate* — how good is our portion, how pleasant our lot, and how beautiful our heritage!* Chazzan— *We are fortunate for we come early and stay late, evening and morning, and proclaim twice each day:*

Hear, O Israel:* HASHEM is our God, HASHEM, the One and Only.[2]

In an undertone— *Blessed is the Name of His glorious kingdom for all eternity.*

(1) *Ecclesiastes* 3:19. (2) *Deuteronomy* 6:4.

Israel is enormously privileged in having been selected as God's Chosen People. Therefore, we dedicate ourselves to proclaim His Oneness through the *Shema.* After the blessing that follows the *Shema* we pray for Israel's salvation so that we may be able to sanctify His Name without hindrance. This prayer was composed by the Talmudic sage Rabbi Yochanan (*Yoma* 87b) for use in the Yom Kippur *vidui* (confession) service.

אֲבָל אֲנַחְנוּ — *But we are.* In contrast to the above-described futility of man, we Jews are privileged to carry on the legacy and mission of our forefathers. Abraham is described as God's beloved, which, our Sages explain, means that he sought always to make God beloved in the eyes of his fellow human beings. God made an oath to him at Mount Moriah where the *Akeidah* took place and where Isaac demonstrated his own devotion to God. Jacob is called God's firstborn because the Jewish nation, which bears his name, was given that title by God Himself (*Exodus* 4:22) and to ratify the fact that God considered Jacob, not Esau, to be the legitimate firstborn.

יִשְׂרָאֵל וִישֻׁרוּן — *Israel and Jeshurun.* These two names describe Jacob's stature. יִשְׂרָאֵל (from שְׂרָרָה, *mastery)* means that Jacob *triumphed* over an angel (see *Genesis* 35:10) and יְשֻׁרוּן (from יָשָׁר, *upright, fair)* refers to *dedication to justice* in accordance with God's will.

אַשְׁרֵינוּ — *We are fortunate.* Although, as noted in *Tikkun Tefillah,* this section of the service was compiled during a period of intense persecution, we do not feel downtrodden. To the contrary, we are fortunate to be God's Chosen People and proud to proclaim His Oneness.

שְׁמַע יִשְׂרָאֵל — *Hear, O Israel.* During the

Some congregations complete the first chapter of the *Shema* (following paragraph) at this point, although most omit it. However if you fear that you will not recite the full *Shema* later in *Shacharis* before the prescribed time has elapsed, recite all three chapters of *Shema* (p. 236-238) here.

דברים ו:ה-ט

וְאָהַבְתָּ אֵת יהוה אֱלֹהֶיךָ, בְּכָל לְבָבְךָ, וּבְכָל נַפְשְׁךָ, וּבְכָל מְאֹדֶךָ. וְהָיוּ הַדְּבָרִים הָאֵלֶּה, אֲשֶׁר אָנֹכִי מְצַוְּךָ הַיּוֹם, עַל לְבָבֶךָ. וְשִׁנַּנְתָּם לְבָנֶיךָ, וְדִבַּרְתָּ בָּם, בְּשִׁבְתְּךָ בְּבֵיתֶךָ, וּבְלֶכְתְּךָ בַדֶּרֶךְ, וּבְשָׁכְבְּךָ וּבְקוּמֶךָ. וּקְשַׁרְתָּם לְאוֹת עַל יָדֶךָ, וְהָיוּ לְטֹטָפֹת בֵּין עֵינֶיךָ. וּכְתַבְתָּם עַל מְזֻזוֹת בֵּיתֶךָ וּבִשְׁעָרֶיךָ.

אַתָּה הוּא* עַד שֶׁלֹּא נִבְרָא הָעוֹלָם, אַתָּה הוּא מִשֶּׁנִּבְרָא הָעוֹלָם, אַתָּה הוּא בָּעוֹלָם הַזֶּה, וְאַתָּה הוּא לָעוֹלָם הַבָּא. ❖ קַדֵּשׁ אֶת שִׁמְךָ עַל מַקְדִּישֵׁי שְׁמֶךָ,* וְקַדֵּשׁ אֶת שִׁמְךָ בְּעוֹלָמֶךָ. וּבִישׁוּעָתְךָ תָּרִים וְתַגְבִּיהַּ קַרְנֵנוּ. בָּרוּךְ אַתָּה יהוה, מְקַדֵּשׁ אֶת שִׁמְךָ בָּרַבִּים.* (.Cong. – אָמֵן)

אַתָּה הוּא יהוה אֱלֹהֵינוּ, בַּשָּׁמַיִם וּבָאָרֶץ וּבִשְׁמֵי הַשָּׁמַיִם הָעֶלְיוֹנִים. אֱמֶת, אַתָּה הוּא רִאשׁוֹן, וְאַתָּה הוּא אַחֲרוֹן,* וּמִבַּלְעָדֶיךָ אֵין אֱלֹהִים.[1] קַבֵּץ קֹוֶיךָ מֵאַרְבַּע כַּנְפוֹת הָאָרֶץ. יַכִּירוּ וְיֵדְעוּ כָּל בָּאֵי עוֹלָם כִּי אַתָּה הוּא הָאֱלֹהִים לְבַדְּךָ לְכֹל מַמְלְכוֹת הָאָרֶץ. אַתָּה עָשִׂיתָ אֶת הַשָּׁמַיִם וְאֶת הָאָרֶץ,[2] אֶת הַיָּם, וְאֶת כָּל אֲשֶׁר בָּם. וּמִי בְּכָל מַעֲשֵׂה יָדֶיךָ בָּעֶלְיוֹנִים אוֹ בַתַּחְתּוֹנִים שֶׁיֹּאמַר לְךָ, מַה תַּעֲשֶׂה. אָבִינוּ שֶׁבַּשָּׁמַיִם, עֲשֵׂה עִמָּנוּ חֶסֶד בַּעֲבוּר שִׁמְךָ הַגָּדוֹל שֶׁנִּקְרָא עָלֵינוּ, וְקַיֶּם לָנוּ יהוה אֱלֹהֵינוּ מַה שֶּׁכָּתוּב: בָּעֵת הַהִיא אָבִיא אֶתְכֶם, וּבָעֵת קַבְּצִי אֶתְכֶם, כִּי אֶתֵּן אֶתְכֶם לְשֵׁם וְלִתְהִלָּה בְּכֹל עַמֵּי הָאָרֶץ, בְּשׁוּבִי אֶת שְׁבוּתֵיכֶם לְעֵינֵיכֶם, אָמַר יהוה.[3]

---

middle of the fifth century the Persian king, Yezdegerd II, forbade the Jews to observe the Sabbath and to recite the *Shema*. His purpose was to eradicate belief in Hashem as the Creator (which is symbolized by the Sabbath) and in His Oneness, as it is proclaimed in the *Shema*. To insure that the *Shema* would not be read in defiance of his decree, the king stationed guards in the synagogue for the first quarter of the day, when the *Shema* must be read. To counteract his design, the Sages instituted two recitations of the first verse of *Shema:* the one here, which was to be recited at home, and another one as part of *Kedushah* of *Mussaf* (see p. 340). Although these services contain only the first verse of the *Shema*, this is sufficient to fulfill the *Shema* obligation in cases of extreme emergency (*Berachos* 13b). Even when Yezdegerd was killed in response to the prayers of the Sages and his decree was lifted, the two *Shema* recitations remained part of the regular ritual, and the one that had been recited at home was moved to this part of the synagogue service.

אַתָּה הוּא — *It was You.* The first four phrases of this prayer express the idea that God is eternal and unchanging, unaffected by time or place.

Some congregations complete the first chapter of the *Shema* (following paragraph) at this point, although most omit it. However if you fear that you will not recite the full *Shema* later in *Shacharis* before the prescribed time has elapsed, recite all three chapters of *Shema* (p. 236-238) here.

Deuteronomy 6:5-9

וְאָהַבְתָּ *You shall love* HASHEM, *your God, with all your heart, with all your soul and with all your resources. Let these matters, which I command you today, be upon your heart. Teach them thoroughly to your children and speak of them while you sit in your home, while you walk on the way, when you retire and when you arise. Bind them as a sign upon your arm and let them be tefillin between your eyes. And write them on the doorposts of your house and upon your gates.*

אַתָּה *It was You* before the world was created, it is You since the world was created, it is You in This World, and it is You in the World to Come.* Chazzan– *Sanctify Your Name through those who sanctify Your Name,* and sanctify Your Name in Your universe. Through Your salvation may You exalt and raise our pride. Blessed are You,* HASHEM, *Who sanctifies Your Name among the multitudes.**

(Cong.– *Amen.)*

אַתָּה *It is You Who are* HASHEM, *our God, in heaven and on earth and in the loftiest heavens. True — You are the First and You are the Last,* and other than You there is no God.*[1] *Gather in those who yearn for You, from the four corners of the earth. Let all who walk the earth recognize and know that You alone are the God over all the kingdoms of the earth. You have made the heavens, the earth,*[2] *the sea, and all that is in them. Who among all Your handiwork, those above and those below, can say to You, 'What are You doing?' Our Father in Heaven, do kindness with us for the sake of Your great Name that has been proclaimed upon us. Fulfill for us,* HASHEM, *our God, what is written: 'At that time I will bring you and at that time I will gather you in, for I will set you up for renown and praise among all the peoples of the earth, when I bring back your captivity, before your own eyes,' said* HASHEM.[3]

(1) Cf. *Isaiah* 44:6. (2) *II Kings* 19:15. (3) *Zephaniah* 3:20.

קַדֵּשׁ אֶת שִׁמְךָ עַל מַקְדִּישֵׁי שְׁמֶךָ — *Sanctify Your Name through those who sanctify Your Name.* When originally composed, this referred to the Jewish martyrs who had sanctified the Name through unyielding loyalty. In later times, it came to refer also to those who cling to the commandments despite hardship and temptation.

מְקַדֵּשׁ אֶת שִׁמְךָ בָּרַבִּים — *Who sanctifies Your Name* [some versions read שְׁמוֹ, *His Name] among the multitudes.* May the time come when no Jew need ever fear to express his Jewishness openly.

רִאשׁוֹן ... אַחֲרוֹן — *The First ... the Last.* We mean only to say that God pre-existed everything and will survive everything — not that He had a beginning or will have an end, for God is infinite and timeless.

❧ קרבנות ❧

הכיור

שמות ל:יז-כא

וַיְדַבֵּר יהוה אֶל מֹשֶׁה לֵּאמֹר. וְעָשִׂיתָ כִּיּוֹר נְחֹשֶׁת, וְכַנּוֹ נְחֹשֶׁת,
לְרָחְצָה, וְנָתַתָּ אֹתוֹ בֵּין אֹהֶל מוֹעֵד וּבֵין הַמִּזְבֵּחַ, וְנָתַתָּ
שָׁמָּה מָיִם. וְרָחֲצוּ אַהֲרֹן וּבָנָיו מִמֶּנּוּ, אֶת יְדֵיהֶם וְאֶת רַגְלֵיהֶם.
בְּבֹאָם אֶל אֹהֶל מוֹעֵד יִרְחֲצוּ מַיִם וְלֹא יָמֻתוּ,* אוֹ בְגִשְׁתָּם אֶל
הַמִּזְבֵּחַ לְשָׁרֵת לְהַקְטִיר אִשֶּׁה לַיהוה. וְרָחֲצוּ יְדֵיהֶם וְרַגְלֵיהֶם
וְלֹא יָמֻתוּ, וְהָיְתָה לָהֶם חָק עוֹלָם, לוֹ וּלְזַרְעוֹ לְדֹרֹתָם.

תרומת הדשן

ויקרא ו:א-ו

וַיְדַבֵּר יהוה אֶל מֹשֶׁה לֵּאמֹר. צַו אֶת אַהֲרֹן וְאֶת בָּנָיו לֵאמֹר,
זֹאת תּוֹרַת הָעֹלָה, הִוא הָעֹלָה עַל מוֹקְדָה עַל הַמִּזְבֵּחַ
כָּל הַלַּיְלָה* עַד הַבֹּקֶר, וְאֵשׁ הַמִּזְבֵּחַ תּוּקַד בּוֹ. וְלָבַשׁ הַכֹּהֵן
מִדּוֹ בַד,* וּמִכְנְסֵי בַד יִלְבַּשׁ עַל בְּשָׂרוֹ, וְהֵרִים אֶת הַדֶּשֶׁן* אֲשֶׁר
תֹּאכַל הָאֵשׁ אֶת הָעֹלָה עַל הַמִּזְבֵּחַ, וְשָׂמוֹ אֵצֶל הַמִּזְבֵּחַ. וּפָשַׁט
אֶת בְּגָדָיו,* וְלָבַשׁ בְּגָדִים אֲחֵרִים, וְהוֹצִיא אֶת הַדֶּשֶׁן אֶל מִחוּץ
לַמַּחֲנֶה, אֶל מָקוֹם טָהוֹר. וְהָאֵשׁ עַל הַמִּזְבֵּחַ תּוּקַד בּוֹ, לֹא

❧ קָרְבָּנוֹת / OFFERINGS ❧

From the beginning of its existence as a nation, Israel *saw* — whether or not it understood why or how — that the sacrificial service brought it a closeness to God and the manifestation of His Presence. The offerings represented the Jew's submission to God of his self and his resources.

Abraham asked God how Israel would achieve forgiveness when the Temple would lie in ruins and they could no longer offer sacrifices.

God replied, 'When Israel recites the Scriptural order of the offerings, I will consider it as if they had brought the sacrifices and I will forgive their sins' (*Megillah* 31a; *Taanis* 27b).

Rav Yitzchak said: The Torah writes זֹאת תּוֹרַת הַחַטָּאת, *this is the Torah* [i.e., teaching] *of the sin-offering (Leviticus* 6:18), to imply that whoever involves himself in the study of the sin-offering is regarded as if he had actually brought a sin-offering (*Menachos* 110a).

In the inspiring words of *R' Hirsch* (*Horeb* 624): 'The Temple has fallen, the Altar has disappeared, the harps of the singers are heard no more, but their spirit has become the heritage of Israel; it still infuses the word which alone survives as an expression of the inward Divine service.'

The section dealing with the קָרְבָּנוֹת, *offerings,* logically follows the previous prayer, אַתָּה הוּא, which longs for Israel's redemption. Given the fact that the offerings require the existence of the Holy Temple as the spiritual center of the nation, we pray that God gather us in from our dispersion. Then, our message will become a truly universal one, for God will have set us up *'for renown and praise among all the peoples of the earth.'*

The offerings whose laws are about to be recited are all communal ones; the Sages chose them because they illustrate our wish that Israel become united as a single nation in God's service.

❧ הַכִּיּוֹר / The Laver

Before the *Kohanim* could begin the Temple service, they had to take sanctified water and pour it over their hands and feet. This water was drawn from the כִּיּוֹר, *laver*, a large copper basin in the Temple Courtyard. In preparation for our 'verbal sacrificial service,' therefore, we 'wash' ourselves with water from the laver, as it were.

וְלֹא יָמֻתוּ — *So that they not die.* The offense of performing the service without washing does *not* incur a court-imposed death penalty, but the violator makes himself liable to a Heavenly

OFFERINGS

THE LAVER

Exodus 30:17-21

וַיְדַבֵּר *HASHEM spoke to Moses, saying: Make a laver of copper, and its base of copper, for washing; and place it between the Tent of Appointment and the Altar and put water there. Aaron and his sons are to wash their hands and feet from it. When they arrive at the Tent of Appointment they are to wash with water so that they not die,* or when they approach the Altar to serve, to burn a fire-offering to HASHEM. They are to wash their hands and feet so that they not die; and this shall be an eternal decree for them — for him and for his offspring — throughout their generations.*

THE TAKING OF ASHES

Leviticus 6:1-6

וַיְדַבֵּר *HASHEM spoke to Moses saying: Instruct Aaron and his sons saying: This is the teaching of the elevation-offering, it is the elevation-offering that stays on the pyre on the Altar all night* until morning, and the fire of the Altar should be kept burning on it. The Kohen should don his linen garment,* and he is to don linen breeches upon his flesh; he is to pick up the ashes* of what the fire consumed of the elevation-offering upon the Altar and place it next to the Altar. Then he should remove his garments* and don other garments; then he should remove the ashes to the outside of the camp to a pure place. The fire on the Altar shall be kept burning on it, it may not be*

---

punishment for his display of contempt.

תְּרוּמַת הַדֶּשֶׁן / The Taking of Ashes

These verses are recited here because they concern the first service of the day: to remove a small portion of the ashes from the previous day's offerings. It was done first thing in the morning, before the *tamid*, daily continual offering, was brought. In addition, the passage contains three references to fire on the Altar: (a) עַל מוֹקְדָה, *on the pyre;* (b) וְאֵשׁ הַמִּזְבֵּחַ, *the fire of the Altar;* (c) וְהָאֵשׁ עַל הַמִּזְבֵּחַ, *the fire on the Altar*. This teaches that three fires were kept burning on the Altar *(Yoma* 45a). They were: מַעֲרָכָה גְדוֹלָה, *the large pyre,* upon which the offerings were burned; מַעֲרָכָה שְׁנִיָּה שֶׁל קְטֹרֶת, *the second pyre for the incense,* from which burning coals were taken and brought into the Sanctuary for the morning and afternoon incense service; and מַעֲרָכָה לְקִיּוּם הָאֵשׁ, *the pyre for perpetuation of the flame,* which was kept burning at all times in case either of the other fires became extinguished.

הִוא הָעֹלָה ... כָּל הַלַּיְלָה — *It is the elevation-offering ... all night.* Although it was preferable to burn a day's offerings during the day, it was permitted to place them on the fires all night, provided the service of the blood was completed during the day.

מִדּוֹ בַד — *His linen garment.* The *Kohen* must wear his full priestly raiment; like all Temple services, this one may not be performed if the *Kohen* is lacking even one of the prescribed garments (described in *Exodus* 28).

וְהֵרִים אֶת הַדֶּשֶׁן — *He is to pick up the ashes.* He is to take glowing ashes from the burnt flesh of offerings, not from wood ashes. The portion taken for this service need be no larger than a handful and it is placed on the floor of the Courtyard, to the east of the ramp leading up to the Altar (the ramp is on the south side of the Altar). This removal of ashes is a required part of the daily morning service, whether or not the Altar had to be cleaned of excess ashes.

וּפָשַׁט אֶת בְּגָדָיו — *Then he should remove his garments.* Unlike the previous verse that discusses a daily *mitzvah,* this verse discusses the cleaning of the Altar, which was done whenever the accumulation of ashes atop the Altar interfered with the service, but was not done daily. The ashes were removed and taken to a designated place outside of Jerusalem; in the Wilderness, they were taken to a place outside of the Israelite camp. In speaking of 'removal' of the priestly garments the verse advises that the *Kohen* should wear less expensive or well-worn priestly garments when performing this service because the ashes would

תִּכְבֶּה, וּבִעֵר עָלֶיהָ הַכֹּהֵן עֵצִים בַּבֹּקֶר בַּבֹּקֶר,* וְעָרַךְ עָלֶיהָ הָעֹלָה, וְהִקְטִיר עָלֶיהָ חֶלְבֵי הַשְּׁלָמִים.* אֵשׁ תָּמִיד תּוּקַד עַל הַמִּזְבֵּחַ, לֹא תִכְבֶּה.

קרבן התמיד

Some authorities hold that the following (until קְטֹרֶת) should be recited standing.
Some omit the following paragraph on the Sabbath and *Yom Tov.*

יְהִי רָצוֹן מִלְּפָנֶיךָ,* יהוה אֱלֹהֵינוּ וֵאלֹהֵי אֲבוֹתֵינוּ, שֶׁתְּרַחֵם עָלֵינוּ וְתִמְחַל לָנוּ עַל כָּל חַטֹּאתֵינוּ, וּתְכַפֶּר לָנוּ אֶת כָּל עֲוֹנוֹתֵינוּ, וְתִסְלַח לְכָל פְּשָׁעֵינוּ, וְתִבְנֶה בֵּית הַמִּקְדָּשׁ בִּמְהֵרָה בְיָמֵינוּ, וְנַקְרִיב לְפָנֶיךָ קָרְבַּן הַתָּמִיד שֶׁיְּכַפֵּר בַּעֲדֵנוּ, כְּמוֹ שֶׁכָּתַבְתָּ עָלֵינוּ בְּתוֹרָתֶךָ עַל יְדֵי מֹשֶׁה עַבְדֶּךָ, מִפִּי כְבוֹדֶךָ, כָּאָמוּר:

במדבר כח:א־ח

וַיְדַבֵּר יהוה אֶל מֹשֶׁה לֵּאמֹר. צַו אֶת בְּנֵי יִשְׂרָאֵל וְאָמַרְתָּ אֲלֵהֶם, אֶת קָרְבָּנִי לַחְמִי* לְאִשַּׁי, רֵיחַ נִיחֹחִי, תִּשְׁמְרוּ לְהַקְרִיב לִי בְּמוֹעֲדוֹ. וְאָמַרְתָּ לָהֶם, זֶה הָאִשֶּׁה אֲשֶׁר תַּקְרִיבוּ לַיהוה, כְּבָשִׂים בְּנֵי שָׁנָה תְמִימִם, שְׁנַיִם לַיּוֹם, עֹלָה תָמִיד. אֶת הַכֶּבֶשׂ אֶחָד תַּעֲשֶׂה בַבֹּקֶר, וְאֵת הַכֶּבֶשׂ הַשֵּׁנִי תַּעֲשֶׂה בֵּין הָעַרְבָּיִם. וַעֲשִׂירִית הָאֵיפָה סֹלֶת לְמִנְחָה,* בְּלוּלָה בְּשֶׁמֶן כָּתִית רְבִיעִת הַהִין. עֹלַת תָּמִיד, הָעֲשֻׂיָה בְּהַר סִינַי, לְרֵיחַ נִיחֹחַ, אִשֶּׁה לַיהוה. וְנִסְכּוֹ רְבִיעִת הַהִין לַכֶּבֶשׂ הָאֶחָד, בַּקֹּדֶשׁ הַסֵּךְ נֶסֶךְ שֵׁכָר לַיהוה. וְאֵת הַכֶּבֶשׂ הַשֵּׁנִי תַּעֲשֶׂה בֵּין הָעַרְבָּיִם, כְּמִנְחַת הַבֹּקֶר וּכְנִסְכּוֹ תַּעֲשֶׂה, אִשֵּׁה רֵיחַ נִיחֹחַ לַיהוה.

וְשָׁחַט אֹתוֹ עַל יֶרֶךְ הַמִּזְבֵּחַ צָפֹנָה לִפְנֵי יהוה, וְזָרְקוּ בְּנֵי אַהֲרֹן הַכֹּהֲנִים אֶת דָּמוֹ עַל הַמִּזְבֵּחַ סָבִיב.*[1]

---

tend to soil his clothing: 'The outfit one wears while cooking his master's meal, one should not wear while filling his master's goblet' (*Yoma* 23a).

עֵצִים בַּבֹּקֶר בַּבֹּקֶר — *Wood ... every morning.* Wood must be placed on the Altar fire every morning.

הָעֹלָה ... הַשְּׁלָמִים — *The elevation-offering ... the peace-offerings.* The morning continual elevation-offering had to go on the Altar before any other offerings; similarly, the last offering of the day was the afternoon continual offering.

הַתָּמִיד / The Tamid (Continual) Offering

יְהִי רָצוֹן מִלְּפָנֶיךָ — *May it be Your will.* We are about to begin 'offering' our communal sacrifices, as it were. Before doing so, we recite a brief prayer that God end the exile and make it possible for us to offer the true offerings, not just the recitations that take their place.

וַיְדַבֵּר ה׳ . . . קָרְבָּנִי לַחְמִי — *HASHEM spoke . . . My offering, My food.* The offering referred to here is the עֹלַת תָּמִיד, *continual elevation-offering* or *tamid.* The offering is called תָּמִיד, *continual,* because it is brought regularly, day in and day out; it is a communal offering purchased with the annual half-*shekel* contributions, collected especially for this purpose. The offering is called *food* in the figurative sense, referring to the parts that are burned on the Altar. The *satisfying odor* does not refer to the odor *per se,* for just as God does not require our 'food,' He does not benefit from the aroma of burning flesh. Rather, the aroma of the burning offering is pleasing to God because it represents the culmination of our performance

extinguished, and the Kohen shall burn wood upon it every morning. He is to prepare the elevation-offering upon it and burn upon it the fats of the peace-offerings.* A permanent fire should remain burning on the Altar; it may not be extinguished.*

THE TAMID OFFERING

Some authorities hold that the following (until קְטֹרֶת /Incense) should be recited standing. Some omit the following paragraph on the Sabbath and *Yom Tov.*

יְהִי רָצוֹן *May it be Your will,* HASHEM, our God, and the God of our forefathers, that You have mercy on us and pardon us for all our errors, atone for us all our iniquities, forgive all our willful sins; and that You rebuild the Holy Temple speedily, in our days, so that we may offer to You the continual offering that it may atone for us, as You have prescribed for us in Your Torah through Moses, Your servant, from Your glorious mouth, as it is said:*

Numbers 28:1-8

וַיְדַבֵּר *HASHEM spoke to Moses, saying: Command the Children of Israel and tell them: My offering, My food* for My fires, My satisfying aroma, you are to be scrupulous to offer Me in its appointed time. And you are to tell them: 'This is the fire-offering that you are to bring to HASHEM: [male] first-year lambs, unblemished, two a day, as a continual elevation-offering. One lamb-service you are to perform in the morning and the second lamb-service you are to perform in the afternoon; with a tenth-ephah of fine flour as a meal-offering,* mixed with a quarter-hin of crushed olive oil. It is the continual elevation-offering that was done at Mount Sinai, for a satisfying aroma, a fire-offering to HASHEM. And its libation is a quarter-hin for each lamb, to be poured on the Holy [Altar], a fermented libation to HASHEM. And the second lamb-service you are to perform in the afternoon, like the meal-offering of the morning and its libation are you to make, a fire-offering for a satisfying aroma to HASHEM.'*

He is to slaughter it on the north side of the Altar before HASHEM, and Aaron's sons the Kohanim are to dash its blood upon the Altar, all around.[1]*

(1) *Leviticus* 1:11.

---

of His will. In the words of the Sages, God is pleased, שֶׁאָמַרְתִּי וְנַעֲשָׂה רְצוֹנִי, *for I have spoken, and My will has been done.*

סֹלֶת לְמִנְחָה — *Fine flour as a meal-offering.* Every elevation- and peace-offering, whether communal or private, is accompanied by a meal-offering, which is burned completely on the Altar, and a libation of wine, which is poured onto the Altar. The wine is called נְסָכִים and the meal-offering, which consists of fine flour mixed with olive oil, is called מִנְחַת נְסָכִים. The amount of flour, oil and wine depends on the species of the animal. For sheep — the animal used for the *tamid* — the amounts are a tenth-*ephah* (approximately 4½ lbs.) of flour, and a quarter-*hin* (approx. 30 fl. oz.) each of oil and wine. The amounts needed for other species may be found on page 344.

סָבִיב — *All around.* Immediately after slaughter, the blood of the *tamid* was caught by a *Kohen* in a sacred utensil and dashed on the northeast and southwest corners of the Altar. This is called 'all around' because blood thrown at a corner would spread out to the two adjacent

Some omit the following paragraph on the Sabbath and *Yom Tov.*

יְהִי רָצוֹן מִלְּפָנֶיךָ, יהוה אֱלֹהֵינוּ וֵאלֹהֵי אֲבוֹתֵינוּ, שֶׁתְּהֵא אֲמִירָה זוּ חֲשׁוּבָה וּמְקֻבֶּלֶת וּמְרֻצָּה לְפָנֶיךָ כְּאִלּוּ הִקְרַבְנוּ קָרְבַּן הַתָּמִיד בְּמוֹעֲדוֹ וּבִמְקוֹמוֹ וּכְהִלְכָתוֹ.

קטרת

אַתָּה הוּא יהוה אֱלֹהֵינוּ שֶׁהִקְטִירוּ אֲבוֹתֵינוּ לְפָנֶיךָ אֶת קְטֹרֶת הַסַּמִּים בִּזְמַן שֶׁבֵּית הַמִּקְדָּשׁ קַיָּם, כַּאֲשֶׁר צִוִּיתָ אוֹתָם עַל יְדֵי מֹשֶׁה נְבִיאֶךָ, כַּכָּתוּב בְּתוֹרָתֶךָ:

שמות ל:לד-לו, ז-ח

וַיֹּאמֶר יהוה אֶל מֹשֶׁה, קַח לְךָ סַמִּים, נָטָף וּשְׁחֵלֶת וְחֶלְבְּנָה, סַמִּים וּלְבֹנָה זַכָּה, בַּד בְּבַד יִהְיֶה.* וְעָשִׂיתָ אֹתָהּ קְטֹרֶת, רֹקַח, מַעֲשֵׂה רוֹקֵחַ, מְמֻלָּח, טָהוֹר, קֹדֶשׁ. וְשָׁחַקְתָּ* מִמֶּנָּה הָדֵק, וְנָתַתָּה מִמֶּנָּה* לִפְנֵי הָעֵדֻת בְּאֹהֶל מוֹעֵד אֲשֶׁר אִוָּעֵד לְךָ שָׁמָּה, קֹדֶשׁ קָדָשִׁים תִּהְיֶה לָכֶם.

וְנֶאֱמַר: וְהִקְטִיר עָלָיו אַהֲרֹן קְטֹרֶת סַמִּים, בַּבֹּקֶר בַּבֹּקֶר, בְּהֵיטִיבוֹ אֶת הַנֵּרֹת* יַקְטִירֶנָּה. וּבְהַעֲלֹת אַהֲרֹן אֶת הַנֵּרֹת בֵּין הָעַרְבַּיִם, יַקְטִירֶנָּה, קְטֹרֶת תָּמִיד לִפְנֵי יהוה לְדֹרֹתֵיכֶם.

כריתות ו., ירושלמי יומא ד:ה

תָּנוּ רַבָּנָן, פִּטּוּם הַקְּטֹרֶת כֵּיצַד.* שְׁלֹשׁ מֵאוֹת וְשִׁשִּׁים וּשְׁמוֹנָה מָנִים* הָיוּ בָהּ. שְׁלֹשׁ מֵאוֹת וְשִׁשִּׁים וַחֲמִשָּׁה כְּמִנְיַן יְמוֹת הַחַמָּה — מָנֶה לְכָל יוֹם, פְּרַס בְּשַׁחֲרִית וּפְרַס בֵּין הָעַרְבָּיִם; וּשְׁלֹשָׁה מָנִים יְתֵרִים,* שֶׁמֵּהֶם מַכְנִיס כֹּהֵן גָּדוֹל מְלֹא חָפְנָיו בְּיוֹם הַכִּפֻּרִים. וּמַחֲזִירָם לְמַכְתֶּשֶׁת בְּעֶרֶב יוֹם הַכִּפֻּרִים, וְשׁוֹחֲקָן יָפֶה יָפֶה כְּדֵי שֶׁתְּהֵא דַקָּה מִן הַדַּקָּה. וְאַחַד עָשָׂר סַמָּנִים*

---

sides, so there would be some blood on each of the Altar's four sides.

קְטֹרֶת / INCENSE

Incense, blended according to a strictly prescribed formula, was burned in the Temple on the Golden Altar, morning and evening. The Golden Altar was located inside the Temple building. It was much smaller than the Altar used for offerings, which was covered with copper plates and was located in the Courtyard. *Arizal* writes that the careful recitation of this section helps bring one to repentance. *R' Hirsch* comments that the incense symbolized Israel's duty to make all its actions pleasing to God.

According to *Zohar*, the chapter and laws of קְטֹרֶת should be recited here 'in order to remove impurity from the world prior to the prayers [i.e., the complete *Shacharis* service] that take the place of offerings.' In response to the *Zohar's* dictum, it has become customary to include קְטֹרֶת in this part of the service. *Rama* notes that it is important to pronounce each of the ingredients and measurements carefully and clearly, because the recitation takes the place of the actual mixture which, as we shall see below, had to be exact (*Orach Chaim* 132:2).

בַּד בְּבַד יִהְיֶה — *They are all to be of equal weight.* The four spices given by name are of equal weight. The other seven, however, were different from these four, as will be seen from the Talmudic passage that follows.

וְשָׁחַקְתָּ — *You are to grind.* The incense must

Some omit the following paragraph on the Sabbath and *Yom Tov*.

יְהִי רָצוֹן *May it be Your will,* HASHEM, *our God and the God of our forefathers, that this recital be worthy and acceptable, and favorable before You as if we had offered the continual offering in its set time, in its place, and according to its requirement.*

INCENSE

אַתָּה *It is You,* HASHEM, *our God, before Whom our forefathers burned the incense-spices in the time when the Holy Temple stood, as You commanded them through Moses Your prophet, as is written in Your Torah:*

Exodus 30:34-36, 7-8

וַיֹּאמֶר HASHEM *said to Moses: Take yourself spices — stacte, onycha, and galbanum — spices and pure frankincense; they are all to be of equal weight.* You are to make it into incense, a spice-compound, the handiwork of an expert spice-compounder, thoroughly mixed, pure and holy. You are to grind* some of it finely and place some of it* before the Testimony in the Tent of Appointment, where I shall designate a time to meet you; it shall be a holy of holies for you.*

It is also written: Aaron shall burn upon it the incense-spices every morning; when he cleans the lamps he is to burn it. And when Aaron ignites the lamps in the afternoon, he is to burn it, as continual incense before* HASHEM *throughout your generations.*

Talmud, *Kereisos* 6a, *Yerushalmi Yoma* 4:5

תָּנוּ רַבָּנָן *The Rabbis taught: How is the incense mixture formulated?* Three hundred sixty-eight maneh* were in it: three hundred sixty-five corresponding to the days of the solar year — a maneh for each day, half in the morning and half in the afternoon; and three extra maneh,* from which the Kohen Gadol would bring both his handfuls [into the Holy of Holies] on Yom Kippur. He would return them to the mortar on the day before Yom Kippur, and grind them very thoroughly so that it would be exceptionally fine. Eleven kinds of spices**

---

be pulverized into a fine powder.

מִמֶּנָּה . . . מִמֶּנָּה — *Some of it . . . some of it.* The repetition alludes to the special Yom Kippur incense service, when the incense is reground and the *Kohen Gadol* [High Priest] takes it into the Holy of Holies, the only time of the year when a human being enters that most sacred place. On all other days, incense is burned twice a day in the Sanctuary.

בְּהֵיטִיבוֹ אֶת הַנֵּרֹת — *When he cleans the lamps.* The *Kohen* cleans the lamps of the Menorah every morning, after which the incense is burned.

☙ תָּנוּ רַבָּנָן פִּטּוּם הַקְּטֹרֶת כֵּיצַד — *The Rabbis taught: How is the incense mixture formulated?* This passage explains how the incense mixture was prepared and it gives the names and amounts that are not specified in Scriptures.

מָנִים — *Maneh.* A *maneh* is equal to approximately twenty ounces.

וּשְׁלֹשָׁה מָנִים יְתֵרִים — *And three extra maneh.* In addition to the regular incense service on Yom Kippur, there was a special service that was performed in the Holy of Holies. Three *maneh* were taken before Yom Kippur and ground again to make them extra fine. From that incense, the *Kohen Gadol* filled both hands, which he used for the special Yom Kippur service.

☙ וְאַחַד עָשָׂר סַמָּנִים — *Eleven kinds of spices.* Eleven different spices were used in the incense mixture, but only four of them — stacte, onycha, galbanum, and frankincense — are named in the Scriptural verse, above. The identity of the other spices is part of the Oral Law. That there are a total of eleven spices is derived from this verse in the following manner:

הָיוּ בָהּ, וְאֵלּוּ הֵן: (א) הַצֳּרִי, (ב) וְהַצִּפֹּרֶן, (ג) הַחֶלְבְּנָה, (ד) וְהַלְּבוֹנָה, מִשְׁקַל שִׁבְעִים שִׁבְעִים מָנֶה; (ה) מוֹר, (ו) וּקְצִיעָה, (ז) שִׁבֹּלֶת נֵרְדְּ, (ח) וְכַרְכֹּם, מִשְׁקַל שִׁשָּׁה עָשָׂר שִׁשָּׁה עָשָׂר מָנֶה; (ט) הַקֹּשְׁטְ שְׁנֵים עָשָׂר, (י) וְקִלּוּפָה שְׁלֹשָׁה, (יא) וְקִנָּמוֹן תִּשְׁעָה. בֹּרִית כַּרְשִׁינָה תִּשְׁעָה קַבִּין, יֵין קַפְרִיסִין סְאִין* תְּלָתָא וְקַבִּין תְּלָתָא, וְאִם אֵין לוֹ יֵין קַפְרִיסִין, מֵבִיא חֲמַר חִוַּרְיָן עַתִּיק, מֶלַח סְדוֹמִית רֹבַע הַקָּב; מַעֲלֶה עָשָׁן* כָּל שֶׁהוּא. רַבִּי נָתָן הַבַּבְלִי אוֹמֵר: אַף כִּפַּת הַיַּרְדֵּן כָּל שֶׁהוּא. וְאִם נָתַן בָּהּ דְּבַשׁ, פְּסָלָהּ. וְאִם חִסַּר* אַחַת מִכָּל סַמָּנֶיהָ, חַיָּב מִיתָה.

רַבָּן שִׁמְעוֹן בֶּן גַּמְלִיאֵל אוֹמֵר: הַצֳּרִי אֵינוֹ אֶלָּא שְׂרָף הַנּוֹטֵף מֵעֲצֵי הַקְּטָף. בֹּרִית כַּרְשִׁינָה לָמָּה הִיא בָאָה, כְּדֵי לְיַפּוֹת בָּהּ אֶת הַצִּפֹּרֶן, כְּדֵי שֶׁתְּהֵא נָאָה. יֵין קַפְרִיסִין לָמָּה הוּא בָא, כְּדֵי לִשְׁרוֹת בּוֹ אֶת הַצִּפֹּרֶן, כְּדֵי שֶׁתְּהֵא עַזָּה. וַהֲלֹא מֵי רַגְלַיִם יָפִין לָהּ, אֶלָּא שֶׁאֵין מַכְנִיסִין מֵי רַגְלַיִם בַּמִּקְדָּשׁ מִפְּנֵי הַכָּבוֹד.

תַּנְיָא, רַבִּי נָתָן אוֹמֵר: כְּשֶׁהוּא שׁוֹחֵק, אוֹמֵר הָדֵק הֵיטֵב, הֵיטֵב הָדֵק, מִפְּנֵי שֶׁהַקּוֹל יָפֶה לַבְּשָׂמִים. פִּטְּמָהּ לַחֲצָאִין,* כְּשֵׁרָה; לִשְׁלִישׁ וְלִרְבִיעַ, לֹא שָׁמָעְנוּ. אָמַר רַבִּי יְהוּדָה: זֶה הַכְּלָל – אִם כְּמִדָּתָהּ, כְּשֵׁרָה לַחֲצָאִין; וְאִם חִסַּר אַחַת מִכָּל סַמָּנֶיהָ, חַיָּב מִיתָה.

תַּנְיָא, בַּר קַפָּרָא אוֹמֵר: אַחַת לְשִׁשִּׁים אוֹ לְשִׁבְעִים שָׁנָה* הָיְתָה בָאָה שֶׁל שִׁירַיִם לַחֲצָאִין. וְעוֹד תָּנֵי בַּר קַפָּרָא: אִלּוּ הָיָה נוֹתֵן בָּהּ קוֹרְטוֹב שֶׁל דְּבַשׁ,* אֵין אָדָם יָכוֹל לַעֲמֹד מִפְּנֵי רֵיחָהּ. וְלָמָּה אֵין מְעָרְבִין בָּהּ דְּבַשׁ, מִפְּנֵי שֶׁהַתּוֹרָה אָמְרָה: כִּי כָל שְׂאֹר וְכָל דְּבַשׁ לֹא תַקְטִירוּ מִמֶּנּוּ אִשֶּׁה לַיהוה.[1]

סַמִּים, *spices,* is plural, yielding two kinds; then three spices are named, for a total of five; the word סַמִּים appears again implying the addition of another group of five (equivalent to the five given above). Finally *frankincense* is added, for a total of eleven.

It should be noted that the exact translations of the spices are not known with absolute certainty.

סְאִין . . . קַבִּין — *Kab . . . se'ah.* A *kab* contains a volume of approximately forty fluid ounces. A *se'ah* is equal to six *kab.*

מַעֲלֶה עָשָׁן — *A smoke-raising herb.* The addition of this herb, which is not identified by name, caused the smoke of the incense to ascend straight as a pillar.

וְאִם חִסַּר — *But if he left out,* i.e., if he used either more or less than the prescribed amount of any ingredient, he is liable to the heavenly death penalty *(Etz Yosef).* According to *Rashi (Kereisos* 6b), this liability applies only to the annual Yom Kippur service performed in the Holy of Holies, because the *Kohen Gadol* is considered to have made a בִּיאָה רֵיקָנִית, *an empty-handed coming,* since he did not have the proper mixture. *Rambam,* however, applies this

were in it, as follows: (1) stacte, (2) onycha, (3) galbanum, (4) frankincense — each weighing seventy maneh; (5) myrrh, (6) cassia, (7) spikenard, (8) saffron — each weighing sixteen maneh; (9) costus — twelve maneh; (10) aromatic bark — three; and (11) cinnamon — nine. [Additionally] Carshina lye, nine kab; Cyprus wine, three se'ah and three kab — if he has no Cyprus wine, he brings old white wine; Sodom salt, a quarter-kab; and a minute amount of a smoke-raising herb.* Rabbi Nassan the Babylonian says: Also a minute amount of Jordan amber. If he placed fruit-honey into it, he invalidated it. But if he left out* any of its spices, he is liable to the death penalty.*

רַבָּן שִׁמְעוֹן *Rabban Shimon ben Gamliel says: The stacte is simply the sap that drips from balsam trees. Why is Carshina lye used? To bleach the onycha, to make it pleasing. Why is Cyprus wine used? So that the onycha could be soaked in it, to make it pungent. Even though urine is more suitable for that, nevertheless they do not bring urine into the Temple out of respect.*

תַּנְיָא *It is taught, Rabbi Nassan says: As one would grind [the incense] another would say, 'Grind thoroughly, thoroughly grind,' because the sound is beneficial for the spices. If one mixed it in half-quantities,* it was fit for use, but as to a third or a quarter — we have not heard the law. Rabbi Yehudah said: This is the general rule — In its proper proportion, it is fit for use in half the full amount; but if he left out any one of its spices, he is liable to the death penalty.*

תַּנְיָא *It is taught, Bar Kappara says: Once every sixty or seventy years,* the accumulated leftovers reached half the yearly quantity. Bar Kappara taught further: Had one put a kortov of fruit-honey* into it, no person could have resisted its scent. Why did they not mix fruit-honey into it? — because the Torah says: 'For any leaven or any fruit-honey, you are not to burn from them a fire-offering to HASHEM.'*[1]

(1) *Leviticus* 2:11.

---

ruling to the whole year (*Hil. Klei HaMikdash* 2:8) because it is regarded as קְטֹרֶת זָרָה, *strange* [i.e., unauthorized] *incense.*

פִּטְּמָהּ לַחֲצָאִין — *If one mixed it in half-quantities.* Instead of mixing 368 *maneh* as was customarily done, someone mixed only 184 *maneh.* Since the manner of compounding was transmitted orally, the question arose whether it was forbidden to prepare spice-mixtures totaling *less* than the usual 368 *maneh.* Rabbi Nassan stated that he had learned that it *was* permitted to make mixtures containing exactly half the normal amount, but he did not know whether smaller mixtures, too, were permitted. To this Rabbi Yehudah replied that any amount, even a one-day supply, was acceptable, provided the ingredients were in the correct proportion.

אַחַת לְשִׁשִּׁים אוֹ לְשִׁבְעִים שָׁנָה — *Once every sixty or seventy years.* We learned earlier that three *maneh* were set aside from which the *Kohen Gadol* filled his hands on Yom Kippur. A quantity (depending on the size of the *Kohen Gadol's* hands) of this mixture was unused, and was set aside. Over many years, enough of this leftover incense had accumulated to provide 184 *maneh,* or a half-year supply of incense. When that happened, only half the normal mixture had to be made for the coming year.

קוֹרְטוֹב שֶׁל דְּבַשׁ — *A kortov of fruit-honey.* Honey or any other fruit juice or product would have made the scent irresistible, but the Torah

The next three verses, each beginning ה׳, are recited three times each.

יהוה צְבָאוֹת עִמָּנוּ,* מִשְׂגָּב לָנוּ אֱלֹהֵי יַעֲקֹב, סֶלָה.[1]
יהוה צְבָאוֹת, אַשְׁרֵי אָדָם בֹּטֵחַ בָּךְ.[2]
יהוה הוֹשִׁיעָה, הַמֶּלֶךְ יַעֲנֵנוּ בְיוֹם קָרְאֵנוּ.[3]

אַתָּה סֵתֶר לִי, מִצַּר תִּצְּרֵנִי, רָנֵּי פַלֵּט, תְּסוֹבְבֵנִי, סֶלָה.[4] וְעָרְבָה לַיהוה מִנְחַת יְהוּדָה וִירוּשָׁלָיִם, כִּימֵי עוֹלָם וּכְשָׁנִים קַדְמוֹנִיּוֹת.[5]

יומא לג.

אַבַּיֵי הֲוָה מְסַדֵּר* סֵדֶר הַמַּעֲרָכָה מִשְּׁמָא דִגְמָרָא וְאַלִּבָּא דְאַבָּא שָׁאוּל: מַעֲרָכָה גְדוֹלָה* קוֹדֶמֶת לְמַעֲרָכָה שְׁנִיָּה* שֶׁל קְטֹרֶת; וּמַעֲרָכָה שְׁנִיָּה שֶׁל קְטֹרֶת קוֹדֶמֶת לְסִדּוּר שְׁנֵי גִזְרֵי עֵצִים;* וְסִדּוּר שְׁנֵי גִזְרֵי עֵצִים קוֹדֵם לְדִשּׁוּן מִזְבֵּחַ הַפְּנִימִי; וְדִשּׁוּן מִזְבֵּחַ הַפְּנִימִי קוֹדֵם לַהֲטָבַת חָמֵשׁ נֵרוֹת;* וַהֲטָבַת חָמֵשׁ נֵרוֹת קוֹדֶמֶת לְדַם הַתָּמִיד; וְדַם הַתָּמִיד קוֹדֵם לַהֲטָבַת שְׁתֵּי נֵרוֹת; וַהֲטָבַת שְׁתֵּי נֵרוֹת קוֹדֶמֶת לִקְטֹרֶת; וּקְטֹרֶת קוֹדֶמֶת לְאֵבָרִים; וְאֵבָרִים לְמִנְחָה; וּמִנְחָה לַחֲבִתִּין;* וַחֲבִתִּין לִנְסָכִין; וּנְסָכִין לְמוּסָפִין;* וּמוּסָפִין לְבָזִיכִין;* וּבָזִיכִין קוֹדְמִין לְתָמִיד שֶׁל בֵּין הָעַרְבָּיִם, שֶׁנֶּאֱמַר: וְעָרַךְ עָלֶיהָ הָעֹלָה, וְהִקְטִיר עָלֶיהָ חֶלְבֵי הַשְּׁלָמִים.[6] עָלֶיהָ הַשְׁלֵם* כָּל הַקָּרְבָּנוֹת כֻּלָּם.

---

forbids the use of fruit products in the incense (*Rashi* to *Leviticus* 2:11; see *Mishnah L'Melech* to *Hil. Issurei Mizbe'ach* 5:1).

A *kortov* equals 1/256 of a *kab*. Here it is used to mean a minimal amount, a touch.

ה׳ צְבָאוֹת עִמָּנוּ — *HASHEM, Master of Legions, is with us. Yerushalmi Berachos* 5:1 cites Rabbi Yochanan who says of the first two verses, 'One should never let them depart from his mouth.' Therefore, they have been introduced into the daily prayers at several points. *Arizal* teaches that they should be repeated three times after each mention of קְטֹרֶת, *incense*, which is why they are inserted here.

The first verse proclaims the principle of הַשְׁגָּחָה פְּרָטִית, *individual Providence*, while the second declares the praise of one who trusts in God. *Iyun Tefillah* points to two events that show how הַשְׁגָּחָה פְּרָטִית and total trust in God played important roles in shaping Rabbi Yochanan's life and lifestyle:

Once, Rabbi Yochanan and his colleague Ilfa were so poverty stricken that they had no choice but to leave the study hall to seek their fortune. On the way, Rabbi Yochanan — but not Ilfa — heard one angel say to another that the two former students deserve to die because 'they forsake the eternal life and go to engage in a temporary life.' Since Ilfa did not hear the message, Rabbi Yochanan understood that it was directed not at Ilfa but at himself. He returned to the yeshivah and became the outstanding sage of his time (*Taanis* 21a). Thus, Rabbi Yochanan's life was changed by a particular incident of individual Providence.

As an elderly man, Rabbi Yochanan, who had become wealthy despite his Torah study, pointed out to Rabbi Chiya bar Abba many valuable properties that he had sold in order to enable him not to interrupt his Torah study. Rabbi Chiya wept at the thought that Rabbi Yochanan had left nothing for his own old age. Rabbi Yochanan replied, 'Chiya, my son, do you think so little of what I have done? I have sold a material thing, that was presented after six days, as it says (*Exodus* 20:11): *For in six days HASHEM made heaven and earth.* But the Torah was given after forty days [of God's instruction to Moses] as it says (ibid. 34:28): *And* [Moses] *was there with HASHEM for forty days.'* It was because of such commitment that Rabbi Yochanan was regarded by his generation as the very symbol of dedication to Torah study and faith that God would provide for his material

The next three verses, each beginning *'HASHEM,'* are recited three times each.

*HASHEM, Master of Legions, is with us,**
a stronghold for us is the God of Jacob, Selah![1]
HASHEM, Master of Legions,
praiseworthy is the person who trusts in You.[2]
HASHEM, save! May the King answer us on the day we call![3]

You are a shelter for me; from distress You preserve me; with glad song of rescue, You envelop me, Selah![4] *May the offering of Judah and Jerusalem be pleasing to HASHEM, as in days of old and in former years.*[5]

Talmud, *Yoma* 33a

אַבַּיֵי *Abaye listed** *the order of the Altar service based on the tradition and according to Abba Shaul: The arrangement of the large pyre** *precedes that of the secondary pyre** *for the incense-offering; the secondary pyre for the incense-offering precedes the placement of two logs;** *the placement of two logs precedes the removal of ashes from the Inner Altar; the removal of ashes from the Inner Altar precedes the cleaning of five lamps [of the Menorah];** *the cleaning of the five lamps precedes the [dashing of the] blood of the continual offering; the blood of the continual offering precedes the cleaning of the [other] two lamps; the cleaning of the two lamps precedes the incense; the incense precedes the [burning of the] limbs; the [burning of the] limbs [precedes] the meal-offering; the meal-offering [precedes] the pancakes;** *the pancakes [precede] the wine-libations; the wine-libations [precede] the mussaf-offering;** *the mussaf-offering [precedes] the bowls [of frankincense];** *the bowls [precede] the afternoon continual offering, for it is said: 'And he is to arrange the elevation-offering upon it and burn the fats of the peace-offerings upon it,'*[6] *— 'upon it' [the elevation-offering] you are to complete** *all the [day's] offerings.*

(1) *Psalms* 46:8. (2) 84:13. (3) 20:10. (4) 32:7. (5) *Malachi* 3:4. (6) *Leviticus* 6:5.

needs (*Shir HaShirim Rabbah* to 8:7). As a man of such faith, Rabbi Yochanan personifies the verse ... *praiseworthy is the person who trusts in You.*

אַבַּיֵי הֲוָה מְסַדֵּר — *Abaye listed.* To conclude the description of the daily service, we recite the full order of the morning service as transmitted by Abaye. Although he lived several generations after the Destruction, he taught the order, as it had been transmitted orally, in the name of Abba Shaul, a Mishnaic sage *(Tanna).*

מַעֲרָכָה גְדוֹלָה — *The large pyre* at the center of the Altar, upon which the offerings were burned.

מַעֲרָכָה שְׁנִיָּה — *The secondary pyre* near the southwest corner of the Altar, from which glowing coals were taken into the Sanctuary for the burning of the daily incense.

סִדּוּר שְׁנֵי גִזְרֵי עֵצִים — *The placement of two logs.* Two large sections of wood were placed on the large pyre every morning. More wood could be added during the day, as needed.

הַטָבַת חָמֵשׁ נֵרוֹת — *The cleaning of five lamps [of the Menorah].* The Temple Menorah had seven lamps. Scriptural exegesis teaches that the lamps, which had burned all night, are cleaned in two steps, first five and then two.

חֲבִתִּין — *The pancakes.* The *Kohen Gadol* was required to bring a meal-offering every day, half in the morning and half in the afternoon. It was baked in a low, flat pan called a מַחֲבַת, hence the name מִנְחַת חֲבִתִּין.

מוּסָפִין — *The mussaf-offering,* on the Sabbath, Festivals, and Rosh Chodesh.

בָּזִיכִין — *The bowls [of frankincense].* These two bowls were placed with the showbread every week. The bread was eaten by the *Kohanim* and the incense was burned on the Altar after the showbread was removed from the Table.

הַשְּׁלָמִים עָלֶיהָ הַשְׁלֵם — *Of the peace-offerings ... upon it you are to complete.* The Sages expound the word הַשְּׁלָמִים, *the peace-offerings.* It is

אָנָּא בְּכֹחַ* גְּדֻלַּת יְמִינְךָ תַּתִּיר צְרוּרָה.* אב״ג ית״ץ
קַבֵּל רִנַּת עַמְּךָ שַׂגְּבֵנוּ טַהֲרֵנוּ נוֹרָא. קר״ע שט״ן
נָא גִבּוֹר דּוֹרְשֵׁי יִחוּדְךָ* כְּבָבַת שָׁמְרֵם. נג״ד יכ״ש
בָּרְכֵם טַהֲרֵם רַחֲמֵם* צִדְקָתְךָ תָּמִיד גָּמְלֵם. בט״ר צת״ג
חֲסִין קָדוֹשׁ בְּרוֹב טוּבְךָ נַהֵל עֲדָתֶךָ. חק״ב טנ״ע
יָחִיד גֵּאֶה לְעַמְּךָ פְּנֵה זוֹכְרֵי קְדֻשָּׁתֶךָ. יג״ל פז״ק
שַׁוְעָתֵנוּ קַבֵּל וּשְׁמַע צַעֲקָתֵנוּ יוֹדֵעַ תַּעֲלֻמוֹת. שק״ו צי״ת
בָּרוּךְ שֵׁם כְּבוֹד מַלְכוּתוֹ לְעוֹלָם וָעֶד.

Some omit the following paragraph on the Sabbath and *Yom Tov*.

רִבּוֹן הָעוֹלָמִים,* אַתָּה צִוִּיתָנוּ לְהַקְרִיב קָרְבַּן הַתָּמִיד בְּמוֹעֲדוֹ, וְלִהְיוֹת כֹּהֲנִים בַּעֲבוֹדָתָם, וּלְוִיִּם בְּדוּכָנָם, וְיִשְׂרָאֵל בְּמַעֲמָדָם. וְעַתָּה בַּעֲוֹנוֹתֵינוּ חָרַב בֵּית הַמִּקְדָּשׁ וּבָטֵל הַתָּמִיד, וְאֵין לָנוּ לֹא כֹהֵן בַּעֲבוֹדָתוֹ, וְלֹא לֵוִי בְּדוּכָנוֹ, וְלֹא יִשְׂרָאֵל בְּמַעֲמָדוֹ.* וְאַתָּה אָמַרְתָּ: וּנְשַׁלְּמָה פָרִים שְׂפָתֵינוּ.[1] לָכֵן יְהִי רָצוֹן מִלְּפָנֶיךָ, יהוה אֱלֹהֵינוּ וֵאלֹהֵי אֲבוֹתֵינוּ, שֶׁיְּהֵא שִׂיחַ שִׂפְתוֹתֵינוּ חָשׁוּב וּמְקֻבָּל וּמְרֻצֶּה לְפָנֶיךָ, כְּאִלּוּ הִקְרַבְנוּ קָרְבַּן הַתָּמִיד בְּמוֹעֲדוֹ, וְעָמַדְנוּ עַל מַעֲמָדוֹ.

On the Sabbath add (במדבר כח:ט-י):

וּבְיוֹם הַשַּׁבָּת* שְׁנֵי כְבָשִׂים בְּנֵי שָׁנָה תְּמִימִם, וּשְׁנֵי עֶשְׂרֹנִים סֹלֶת מִנְחָה בְּלוּלָה בַשֶּׁמֶן, וְנִסְכּוֹ. עֹלַת שַׁבַּת בְּשַׁבַּתּוֹ, עַל עֹלַת הַתָּמִיד וְנִסְכָּהּ.

---

interpreted as if pronounced הַשְּׁלֵמִים, *the completions,* meaning that all the services of the day should be completed after the morning *tamid,* and before the afternoon *tamid.*

אָנָּא בְּכֹחַ — *We beg You! With the strength* . . . Tradition ascribes this mystic prayer to the *tanna* R' Nechuniah ben Hakanah. It contains forty-two words, the initials of which form the secret forty-two letter Name of God. Moreover, the six initials of each of its seven verses form Divine Names. The Kabbalists teach that it should be divided into phrases of two words each, but our translation follows the division indicated by a simple reading of the phrases.

תַּתִּיר צְרוּרָה — *Untie the bundled sins.* The accumulated sins of Israel are bound together like a barrier that prevents our prayers from ascending to the Heavenly Throne. We ask God to remove this impediment *(Iyun Tefillah).*

דּוֹרְשֵׁי יִחוּדְךָ — *Those who foster Your Oneness.* The acknowledgment of God's Oneness is paramount (see commentary to שְׁמַע יִשְׂרָאֵל, p. 38). As the nation that accepts this obligation upon itself, Israel pleads for God's protection *(Iyun Tefillah).*

רַחֲמֵם — *Show them pity.* According to some versions, this phrase reads רַחֲמֵי צִדְקָתְךָ, *the mercy of Your righteousness.*

רִבּוֹן הָעוֹלָמִים — *Master of the worlds.* We pray that our recitation of the morning service be accepted in place of the Temple service that we cannot perform. As we say later in this prayer, *'Let our lips compensate for the bulls,'* meaning that our recitation must take the place of the actual offerings.

לֹא כֹהֵן בַּעֲבוֹדָתוֹ, וְלֹא לֵוִי בְּדוּכָנוֹ, וְלֹא יִשְׂרָאֵל בְּמַעֲמָדוֹ — *Neither Kohen at his service, nor Levite on his platform, nor Israelite at his*

אָנָּא בְּכֹחַ *We beg You! With the strength* of Your right hand's greatness, untie the bundled sins.* Accept the prayer of Your nation; strengthen us, purify us, O Awesome One. Please, O Strong One — those who foster Your Oneness,* guard them like the pupil of an eye. Bless them, purify them, show them pity,* may Your righteousness always recompense them. Powerful Holy One, with Your abundant goodness guide Your congregation. One and only Exalted One, turn to Your nation, which proclaims Your holiness. Accept our entreaty and hear our cry, O Knower of mysteries.*

Blessed is the Name of His glorious Kingdom for all eternity.

Some omit the following paragraph on the Sabbath and *Yom Tov.*

רִבּוֹן הָעוֹלָמִים *Master of the worlds,* You commanded us to bring the continual offering at its set time, and that the Kohanim be at their assigned service, the Levites on their platform, and the Israelites at their station. But now, through our sins, the Holy Temple is destroyed, the continual offering is discontinued, and we have neither Kohen at his service, nor Levite on his platform, nor Israelite at his station.* But You said: 'Let our lips compensate for the bulls'*[1] *— therefore may it be Your will,* HASHEM, *our God and the God of our forefathers, that the prayer of our lips be worthy, acceptable and favorable before You, as if we had brought the continual offering at its set time and we had stood at its station.*

On the Sabbath add (*Numbers* 28:9-10):

וּבְיוֹם *And on the Sabbath day* [the mussaf-offering is]: two [male] first-year lambs, unblemished; two tenth-ephah of fine flour for a meal-offering, mixed with olive oil, and its wine-libation. The elevation-offering of the Sabbath must be on its particular Sabbath, in addition to the continual elevation-offering and its wine-libation.*

(1) *Hoshea* 14:3.

---

station. All three categories of Jews were represented in the daily communal service. The *Kohanim* performed the service, Levites stood on a platform to sing the Song of the Day (see p. 388), and the rest of the nation had delegates who recited special prayers and Scriptural passages.

וּבְיוֹם הַשַּׁבָּת – *And on the Sabbath day.* The verses of the Sabbath additional offerings are recited at this point because they will not be read from the Torah. It is never necessary to recite the verses of the Succos or other Festival offerings because they will be read as the *Maftir* of the day. Although the portion of Rosh Chodesh is read from the Torah on all new moons (with the exception of Rosh Hashanah), the Rosh Chodesh verses are recited here (again with the exception of Rosh Hashanah) for a different reason: since the *Maariv Shemoneh Esrei* is essentially unchanged from that of other days (with the minor exception of יַעֲלֶה וְיָבֹא), the verses of Rosh Chodesh at this point serve as a reminder of the day to the congregants (*Orach Chaim* 48:1).

אֵיזֶהוּ מְקוֹמָן / What is the Location?

The Talmud (*Kiddushin* 30a) teaches that one should study Scripture, *Mishnah* [i.e., the compilation of laws], and *Gemara* [i.e., the explanation of the laws] every day. In fulfillment of that injunction, the Sages instituted that appropriate passages from each of these three categories be included in this section of *Shacharis.* Since Scriptural passages regarding the Temple offerings are part of the service in any case, the Sages chose a chapter of the Mishnah on the same subject. Chapter 5 of *Zevachim,* which begins אֵיזֶהוּ מְקוֹמָן, *What is the location,* was chosen for three reasons: (a) It discusses all the sacrifices; (b) it is the only chapter in the Mishnah in which there is no halachic dispute; and (c) its text is of very ancient origin, possibly even from the days of Moses.

משנה, זבחים פרק ה

[א] **אֵיזֶהוּ** מְקוֹמָן* שֶׁל זְבָחִים. קָדְשֵׁי קָדָשִׁים* שְׁחִיטָתָן בַּצָּפוֹן.* פַּר וְשָׂעִיר שֶׁל יוֹם הַכִּפּוּרִים שְׁחִיטָתָן בַּצָּפוֹן, וְקִבּוּל דָּמָן בִּכְלִי שָׁרֵת* בַּצָּפוֹן. וְדָמָן טָעוּן הַזָּיָה עַל בֵּין הַבַּדִּים,* וְעַל הַפָּרֹכֶת,* וְעַל מִזְבַּח הַזָּהָב.* מַתָּנָה אַחַת מֵהֶן מְעַכֶּבֶת.* שְׁיָרֵי הַדָּם הָיָה שׁוֹפֵךְ עַל יְסוֹד מַעֲרָבִי שֶׁל מִזְבֵּחַ הַחִיצוֹן; אִם לֹא נָתַן, לֹא עִכֵּב.

[ב] **פָּרִים** הַנִּשְׂרָפִים* וּשְׂעִירִים הַנִּשְׂרָפִים* שְׁחִיטָתָן בַּצָּפוֹן, וְקִבּוּל דָּמָן בִּכְלִי שָׁרֵת בַּצָּפוֹן. וְדָמָן טָעוּן הַזָּיָה עַל הַפָּרֹכֶת וְעַל מִזְבַּח הַזָּהָב. מַתָּנָה אַחַת מֵהֶן מְעַכֶּבֶת. שְׁיָרֵי הַדָּם הָיָה שׁוֹפֵךְ עַל יְסוֹד מַעֲרָבִי שֶׁל מִזְבֵּחַ הַחִיצוֹן; אִם לֹא נָתַן, לֹא עִכֵּב. אֵלּוּ וָאֵלּוּ נִשְׂרָפִין בְּבֵית הַדָּשֶׁן.*

[ג] **חַטֹּאת** הַצִּבּוּר וְהַיָּחִיד* – אֵלּוּ הֵן חַטֹּאת הַצִּבּוּר, שְׂעִירֵי רָאשֵׁי חֳדָשִׁים וְשֶׁל מוֹעֲדוֹת – שְׁחִיטָתָן בַּצָּפוֹן, וְקִבּוּל דָּמָן בִּכְלִי שָׁרֵת בַּצָּפוֹן. וְדָמָן טָעוּן אַרְבַּע מַתָּנוֹת עַל אַרְבַּע קְרָנוֹת. כֵּיצַד, עָלָה בַכֶּבֶשׁ, וּפָנָה לַסּוֹבֵב* וּבָא לוֹ לְקֶרֶן

---

1. אֵיזֶהוּ מְקוֹמָן — *What is the location?* In discussing the various categories of animal offerings, this chapter focuses on the location in the Courtyard where they were slaughtered and the part of the Altar upon which their blood was placed.

קָדְשֵׁי קָדָשִׁים — *The most holy offerings.* Sin- [חַטָּאוֹת], guilt- [אֲשָׁמוֹת], elevation- [עוֹלוֹת], and communal peace- [זִבְחֵי שַׁלְמֵי צִבּוּר] offerings are called 'most holy offerings' because they have stricter laws than individual peace- [שְׁלָמִים] and thanksgiving- [תּוֹדָה] offerings [see below, 6-8], which are called 'offerings of lesser holiness' [קָדָשִׁים קַלִּים]. Among the stricter laws that typify the most holy offerings are that they must be eaten in, and may not be removed from, the Temple Courtyard; and that anyone who makes personal use of them, even before their blood is sprinkled [מוֹעֵל בְּהֶקְדֵּשׁ], must undergo a procedure of atonement. Offerings of lesser holiness, on the other hand, may be eaten and taken anywhere within the walls of Jerusalem, and one who makes personal use of them requires atonement only if he does so after the blood has been sprinkled.

בַּצָּפוֹן — *In the north,* i.e., in the Courtyard to the north of the Altar.

בִּכְלִי שָׁרֵת — *In a service-vessel.* Special vessels were set aside in the Sanctuary for the purpose of receiving blood from the animal's neck after slaughter.

עַל בֵּין הַבַּדִּים — *Between the poles [of the Holy Ark].* On Yom Kippur, the *Kohen Gadol* brought blood into the Holy of Holies and sprinkled part of it toward the Holy Ark, between the two poles of the Ark that extended from either side of it toward the Sanctuary.

וְעַל הַפָּרֹכֶת — *And toward the Curtain,* that separated the Holy of Holies from the Sanctuary. Toward this Curtain, too, the *Kohen Gadol* sprinkled blood.

מִזְבַּח הַזָּהָב — *The Golden Altar.* This Altar, also referred to as מִזְבַּח הַפְּנִימִי, *the Inner Altar,* was actually made of wood and was plated with gold.

מַתָּנָה אַחַת מֵהֶן מְעַכֶּבֶת — *Every one of these applications [of blood] is essential* [lit. *prevents*], i.e., atonement has not been achieved if even one of the above blood applications was omitted.

2. פָּרִים הַנִּשְׂרָפִים — *The bulls that are completely burned.* Certain parts (see *Leviticus* 4:8-12) of the animal are placed upon the Altar-pyre to be consumed by the fire. The remainder of the animal is burned outside of Jerusalem (see below).

With the exception of the Yom Kippur sacrifices, only two kinds of bull offerings are completely burned, no part of them being eaten by the *Kohanim.* They are (a) פַּר הֶעְלֵם דָּבָר שֶׁל

Mishnah, *Zevachim* Chapter 5

[1] **אֵיזֶהוּ** *What is the location* of the offerings? [Regarding] the most holy offerings,* their slaughter is in the north.* The slaughter of the bull and the he-goat of Yom Kippur is in the north and the reception of their blood in a service-vessel* is in the north. Their blood requires sprinkling between the poles [of the Holy Ark],* and toward the Curtain* [of the Holy of Holies] and upon the Golden Altar.* Every one of these applications [of blood] is essential.* The leftover blood he would pour onto the western base of the Outer Altar; but if he failed to apply it [the leftover blood on the base], he has not prevented [atonement].*

[2] **פָּרִים** *[Regarding] the bulls that are completely burned* and he-goats that are completely burned,* their slaughter is in the north, and the reception of their blood in a service-vessel is in the north. Their blood requires sprinkling toward the Curtain and upon the Golden Altar. Every one of these applications is essential. The leftover blood he would pour onto the western base of the Outer Altar; but if he failed to apply it [the leftover blood on the base] he has not prevented [atonement]. Both these and those [the Yom Kippur offerings] are burned in the place where the [Altar] ashes are deposited.**

[3] **חַטֹּאת** *[Regarding] sin-offerings of the community and of the individual* — the communal sin-offerings are the following: the he-goats of Rosh Chodesh and festivals — their slaughter [of all sin-offerings] is in the north and the reception of their blood in a service-vessel is in the north. Their blood requires four applications, [one] on [each of] the four corners [of the Altar]. How is it done? He [the Kohen] ascended the [Altar] ramp, turned to the surrounding ledge* and*

צִבּוּר, the bull brought if the *Sanhedrin* erred in a halachic ruling, and, as a result of following that ruling, most of the people violated a commandment for which, if the sin had been committed intentionally, the penalty would be כָּרֵת, *spiritual excision;* (b) פַּר כֹּהֵן מָשִׁיחַ, the bull brought by the *Kohen Gadol* if he made an erroneous halachic decision regarding the above type of sin and himself acted on this ruling.

שְׂעִירִים הַנִּשְׂרָפִים — *He-goats that are completely burned.* If the *Sanhedrin* (highest court) erroneously permitted an act that was a violation of the laws against idol worship, and a majority of the community followed their ruling, their atonement consists of a communal sin-offering — a he-goat that is completely burned.

נִשְׂרָפִין בְּבֵית הַדֶּשֶׁן — *Are burned in the place where the [Altar] ashes are deposited.* The excess ashes from the Altar were removed daily (or as needed) to a ritually clean place outside of Jerusalem. The offerings mentioned in this mishnah and also the offerings of Yom Kippur were burned in that place.

3. חַטֹּאת הַצִּבּוּר וְהַיָּחִיד — *Sin-offerings of the community and of the individual.* Before giving the laws of sin-offerings, the mishnah lists the kinds of communal sin-offerings that fall under this category. The listing is necessary, because the earlier mishnayos, too, have discussed communal sin-offerings, but they fell under the special category of offerings that were completely burned.

וּפָנָה לַסּוֹבֵב — *Turned to the surrounding ledge.* The Altar was ten cubits high. Six cubits above the ground, a one-cubit-wide ledge went completely around the Altar. The walls ascended another three cubits to the Altar top upon which the pyres (see p. 159) burned. In the square cubit located at each corner of the Altar top, the walls rose an additional cubit. These four protrusions were called קַרְנוֹת הַמִּזְבֵּחַ, *the 'corners' of the Altar,* and it was on these 'corners' that the blood of the sin-offerings was placed. In order to reach these ten-cubit-high 'corners,' the *Kohen* walked around the Altar on the surrounding ledge, with the utensil containing the blood. He stopped at each 'corner' of

דְּרוֹמִית מִזְרָחִית, מִזְרָחִית צְפוֹנִית, צְפוֹנִית מַעֲרָבִית, מַעֲרָבִית דְּרוֹמִית. שְׁיָרֵי הַדָּם הָיָה שׁוֹפֵךְ עַל יְסוֹד דְּרוֹמִי. וְנֶאֱכָלִין לִפְנִים מִן הַקְּלָעִים,* לְזִכְרֵי כְהֻנָּה, בְּכָל מַאֲכָל, לְיוֹם וָלַיְלָה, עַד חֲצוֹת.*

[ד] **הָעוֹלָה** קֹדֶשׁ קָדָשִׁים. שְׁחִיטָתָהּ בַּצָּפוֹן, וְקִבּוּל דָּמָהּ בִּכְלִי שָׁרֵת בַּצָּפוֹן. וְדָמָהּ טָעוּן שְׁתֵּי מַתָּנוֹת שֶׁהֵן אַרְבַּע;* וּטְעוּנָה הַפְשֵׁט* וְנִתּוּחַ,* וְכָלִיל לָאִשִּׁים.

[ה] **זִבְחֵי** שַׁלְמֵי צִבּוּר* וַאֲשָׁמוֹת,* אֵלּוּ הֵן אֲשָׁמוֹת: אֲשַׁם גְּזֵלוֹת,* אֲשַׁם מְעִילוֹת,* אֲשַׁם שִׁפְחָה חֲרוּפָה,* אֲשַׁם נָזִיר,* אֲשַׁם מְצוֹרָע,* אָשָׁם תָּלוּי.* שְׁחִיטָתָן בַּצָּפוֹן, וְקִבּוּל דָּמָן בִּכְלִי שָׁרֵת בַּצָּפוֹן, וְדָמָן טָעוּן שְׁתֵּי מַתָּנוֹת שֶׁהֵן אַרְבַּע. וְנֶאֱכָלִין לִפְנִים מִן הַקְּלָעִים לְזִכְרֵי כְהֻנָּה, בְּכָל מַאֲכָל, לְיוֹם וָלַיְלָה, עַד חֲצוֹת.

[ו] **הַתּוֹדָה*** וְאֵיל נָזִיר* קָדָשִׁים קַלִּים.* שְׁחִיטָתָן בְּכָל מָקוֹם בָּעֲזָרָה, וְדָמָן טָעוּן שְׁתֵּי מַתָּנוֹת שֶׁהֵן אַרְבַּע. וְנֶאֱכָלִין בְּכָל הָעִיר, לְכָל אָדָם, בְּכָל מַאֲכָל, לְיוֹם וָלַיְלָה, עַד חֲצוֹת. הַמּוּרָם מֵהֶם כַּיּוֹצֵא בָהֶם, אֶלָּא שֶׁהַמּוּרָם נֶאֱכָל לַכֹּהֲנִים, לִנְשֵׁיהֶם וְלִבְנֵיהֶם וּלְעַבְדֵיהֶם.

---

the Altar, dipped his right index finger into the utensil containing the blood, and deposited the blood upon the 'corner.' Then he would go on to the next 'corner.'

וְנֶאֱכָלִין לִפְנִים מִן הַקְּלָעִים — *They are eaten within the [Courtyard] curtains.* After the specified fats are removed to be burned on the Altar, the flesh of the sin-offerings is distributed to be eaten by male *Kohanim.* It is prepared and eaten only within the Temple Courtyard. The term 'curtains' is borrowed from the period in the Wilderness, when the Tabernacle Courtyard was enclosed not by walls, but by curtains.

עַד חֲצוֹת — *Until midnight.* A sin-offering could be eaten for the remainder of the day on which it was sacrificed and for the following evening. Under Scriptural law it could be eaten until dawn, but the Sages imposed a deadline of midnight to prevent mishaps.

4. שְׁתֵּי מַתָּנוֹת שֶׁהֵן אַרְבַּע — *Two applications that are equivalent to four.* As explained above in the chapter of the *tamid,* p. 153, blood was thrown from the service-vessel at two corners of the Altar walls: the northeast and southwest. The blood would spread out to the two adjacent walls. Thus, the two applications of blood would put blood on all four walls of the Altar.

הַפְשֵׁט — *Flaying.* The hide of all offerings of greater holiness (other than those discussed in mishnah 2) was given to the *Kohanim.*

וְנִתּוּחַ — *And dismemberment.* The elevation offering was cut up in a prescribed way; only then was it completely burned.

5. זִבְחֵי שַׁלְמֵי צִבּוּר — *Communal peace-offerings.* The only such offerings are the two sheep that are brought in addition to the Shavuos *mussaf*-offering [*Leviticus* 23:19]. The other communal offerings are either sin- or elevation-offerings.

אֲשָׁמוֹת — *Guilt-offerings.* There are six kinds of guilt-offerings, all of which are listed in this mishnah. They are:

(a) אֲשַׁם גְּזֵלוֹת — *. . . for thefts.* If someone owed money — whether a loan, a theft, an article held in safekeeping, or whatever — and intentionally swore falsely that he did not owe it, he is required to bring a guilt-offering as an atonement. See *Leviticus* 5:20-26.

(b) אֲשַׁם מְעִילוֹת — *. . . for misuse of sacred objects.* If someone unintentionally used objects belonging to the Sanctuary for his personal benefit he must atone by bringing a guilt-offering. See ibid. 5:14-16.

(c) אֲשַׁם שִׁפְחָה חֲרוּפָה — *. . . [for violating] a*

arrived at the southeast [corner], the northeast, the northwest, and the southwest. The leftover blood he would pour out on the southern base. They are eaten within the [Courtyard] curtains, by males of the priesthood, prepared in any manner, on the same day and that night until midnight.**

[4] **הָעוֹלָה** *The elevation-offering is among the most holy offerings. Its slaughter is in the north and the reception of its blood in a service-vessel is in the north. Its blood requires two applications that are equivalent to four.* It requires flaying* and dismemberment,* and it is entirely consumed by the fire.*

[5] **זִבְחֵי** *[Regarding] communal peace-offerings* and [personal] guilt-offerings* — the guilt-offerings are as follows: the guilt-offering for thefts,* the guilt-offering for misuse of sacred objects,* the guilt-offering [for violating] a betrothed maidservant,* the guilt-offering of a Nazirite,* the guilt-offering of a metzora,* and a guilt-offering in case of doubt* — their slaughter is in the north and the reception of their blood in a service-vessel is in the north. Their blood requires two applications that are equivalent to four. They are eaten within the [Courtyard] curtains, by males of the priesthood, prepared in any manner, on the same day and that night until midnight.*

[6] **הַתּוֹדָה** *The thanksgiving-offering* and the ram of a Nazirite* are offerings of lesser holiness.* Their slaughter is anywhere in the Courtyard, and their blood requires two applications that are equivalent to four. They are eaten throughout the City [of Jerusalem] by anyone, prepared in any manner, on the same day and that night until midnight. The [priestly] portion separated from them is treated like them, except that that portion may be eaten only by the Kohanim, their wives, children and slaves.*

---

betrothed maidservant. The woman involved was a non-Jewish slave who had been owned by two Jewish partners. One of the partners freed her, thus making her half-free and half-slave. But since a freed non-Jewish slave has the same status as a proselyte, this half-free maidservant is half Jewish and half non-Jewish and is forbidden to marry either a non-Jew or a Jew. She is, however, permitted to a Jewish indentured servant [עֶבֶד עִבְרִי], who is permitted to both a Jewish woman and a non-Jewish maidservant. If she became betrothed to a Jewish indentured servant and subsequently had relations with another man, the adulterer must bring a guilt-offering in atonement.

(d) אֲשַׁם נָזִיר — *... of a Nazirite,* who became טָמֵא, *ritually contaminated,* through contact with a corpse. See *Numbers* 6:9-12.

(e) אֲשַׁם מְצוֹרָע — *... of a metzora.* One afflicted by the leprous disease described in *Leviticus* (ch. 13) regains his complete ritual purity upon bringing a series of offerings after he is cured. The guilt-offering is brought on the eighth day after he is pronounced cured. See *Leviticus* 14:10-12.

(f) אָשָׁם תָּלוּי — *... in case of doubt.* This is the only guilt-offering not prescribed for a specific offense or phenomenon. It is required whenever there is a question of whether one has become liable to bring a חַטָּאת, *sin-offering.* As long as such a doubt exists, the possible transgressor can protect himself from punishment through a guilt-offering. However, if and when it becomes established that the offense was indeed committed, the person must bring his sin-offering. See *Leviticus* 5:17-19.

6. הַתּוֹדָה — *The thanksgiving-offering.* This offering is brought by someone who survives serious danger or illness. See ibid. 7:12.

אֵיל נָזִיר — *Ram of a Nazirite,* which is brought when a Nazirite completes the period of abstinence he has accepted upon himself. See *Numbers* 6:13-21.

קָדָשִׁים קַלִּים — *Offerings of lesser holiness.* Their greater leniency is obvious from a comparison of

[ז] **שְׁלָמִים*** קָדָשִׁים קַלִּים. שְׁחִיטָתָן בְּכָל מָקוֹם בָּעֲזָרָה, וְדָמָן טָעוּן שְׁתֵּי מַתָּנוֹת שֶׁהֵן אַרְבַּע. וְנֶאֱכָלִין בְּכָל הָעִיר, לְכָל אָדָם, בְּכָל מַאֲכָל, לִשְׁנֵי יָמִים וְלַיְלָה אֶחָד. הַמּוּרָם מֵהֶם כַּיּוֹצֵא בָהֶם, אֶלָּא שֶׁהַמּוּרָם נֶאֱכָל לַכֹּהֲנִים, לִנְשֵׁיהֶם וְלִבְנֵיהֶם וּלְעַבְדֵיהֶם.

[ח] **הַבְּכוֹר** וְהַמַּעֲשֵׂר וְהַפֶּסַח קָדָשִׁים קַלִּים. שְׁחִיטָתָן בְּכָל מָקוֹם בָּעֲזָרָה, וְדָמָן טָעוּן מַתָּנָה אֶחָת,* וּבִלְבָד שֶׁיִּתֵּן כְּנֶגֶד הַיְסוֹד. שִׁנָּה בַאֲכִילָתָן: הַבְּכוֹר נֶאֱכָל לַכֹּהֲנִים, וְהַמַּעֲשֵׂר לְכָל אָדָם. וְנֶאֱכָלִין בְּכָל הָעִיר, בְּכָל מַאֲכָל, לִשְׁנֵי יָמִים וְלַיְלָה אֶחָד. הַפֶּסַח אֵינוֹ נֶאֱכָל אֶלָּא בַלַּיְלָה, וְאֵינוֹ נֶאֱכָל אֶלָּא עַד חֲצוֹת, וְאֵינוֹ נֶאֱכָל אֶלָּא לִמְנוּיָו,* וְאֵינוֹ נֶאֱכָל אֶלָּא צָלִי.

ברייתא דר' ישמעאל – ספרא, פתיחה

רַבִּי יִשְׁמָעֵאל אוֹמֵר: בִּשְׁלֹש עֶשְׂרֵה מִדּוֹת הַתּוֹרָה נִדְרֶשֶׁת בָּהֵן. (א) מִקַּל וָחֹמֶר; (ב) וּמִגְּזֵרָה שָׁוָה; (ג) מִבִּנְיַן אָב מִכָּתוּב אֶחָד, וּמִבִּנְיַן אָב מִשְּׁנֵי כְתוּבִים; (ד) מִכְּלָל

---

the laws in this mishnah with those above.

7. שְׁלָמִים — *Peace-offerings.* The peace-offerings may be eaten for *two* days and the night between them, while thanksgiving-offerings (mishnah 6) are eaten for only *one* day and a night.

8. וְדָמָן טָעוּן מַתָּנָה אֶחָת — *Their blood requires a single application.* Unlike all the offerings mentioned above, the offerings mentioned in this mishnah do not require multiple applications of blood. The יְסוֹד, *base,* is a part of the Altar, one cubit high and one cubit wide, that juts out along the entire lengths of the west and north walls, but only one cubit along the south and east walls. The blood may be applied only to a part of the Altar wall that is directly above the base.

הַפֶּסַח ... לִמְנוּיָו — *The Pesach-offering ... by those registered for it.* Those who eat from a particular Pesach-offering must reserve their share in it before the slaughter. [See *Exodus* 12:4.] In the case of all other offerings, any qualified person may partake of the flesh.

❧ רַבִּי יִשְׁמָעֵאל / Rabbi Yishmael

As noted above, the Sages prefaced *Shacharis* with selections from Scripture, *Mishnah,* and *Gemara.* As used in the Talmud, *Mishnah* means a listing of laws and *Gemara* means the logic behind and the application of the laws. As a selection from *Gemara,* the Sages chose one that gives the thirteen methods used in Scriptural interpretation. This passage is a *baraisa* [literally, *outside*], meaning that it is one of the countless Talmudic teachings that was 'left out' of the *Mishnah* when that basic compendium of laws was formulated. Though not part of the *Mishnah,* the *baraisos* are authoritative and are cited by the *Gemara* constantly. Unlike most *baraisos* which are statements of law, this one is a basic introduction to an understanding of the derivation of the laws. It shows us how the very brief statements of the Torah can be 'mined' to reveal a host of principles and teachings. This is why such use of these thirteen rules is called דְּרַשׁ, which implies *investigation* and *seeking out;* we seek to elicit principles and laws from the sometimes cryptic words of the Torah.

This particular *baraisa* is the introduction to *Sifra,* a midrashic work that exhaustively interprets the Book of *Leviticus.* Since most of *Sifra* is of a halachic nature, it was natural that it be introduced with a listing of the principles of halachic interpretation. And since *Sifra* deals mainly with the Temple service, this *baraisa* is particularly apt for this section of *Shacharis.*

❧ The Oral Law

The Torah was composed by God according to the rules of logic and textual analysis contained in Rabbi Yishmael's *baraisa.* (These rules are also known as hermeneutic principles.) The oral tradition governs the way in which these rules are applied and we have no authority to use them in a manner that contradicts or is not sanctioned by the Oral Law. Thus, when

[7] **שְׁלָמִים** *The peace-offerings* are offerings of lesser holiness. Their slaughter is anywhere in the Courtyard, and their blood requires two applications that are equivalent to four. They are eaten throughout the City [of Jerusalem] by anyone, prepared in any manner, for two days and one night. The [priestly] portion separated from them is treated like them, except that that portion may be eaten only by the Kohanim, their wives, children and slaves.*

[8] **הַבְּכוֹר** *The firstborn and tithe of animals and the Pesach-offering are offerings of lesser holiness. Their slaughter is anywhere in the Courtyard, and their blood requires a single application,* provided he applies it above the base. They differ in their consumption: The firstborn is eaten by Kohanim, and the tithe by anyone. They are eaten throughout the City [of Jerusalem], prepared in any manner, for two days and one night. The Pesach-offering is eaten only at night and it may be eaten only until midnight; it may be eaten only by those registered for it;* and it may be eaten only if roasted.*

Introduction to *Sifra*

רַבִּי יִשְׁמָעֵאל *Rabbi Yishmael says: Through thirteen rules is the Torah elucidated: (1) Through a conclusion inferred from a lenient law to a strict one, and vice versa; (2) through tradition that similar words in different contexts are meant to clarify one another; (3) through a general principle derived from one verse, and a general principle derived from two verses; (4) through a general*

---

we speak of Rabbinic exegesis, or the way in which the Torah is expounded, we do not speak of the invention of new laws, but of the means by which the Oral Law was implied in the Torah itself. It should also be noted that the great majority of the laws were handed down for many centuries from teacher to student, and they were well known without a need to search for their Scriptural sources. Consequently, in the Talmud era when the Sages attempted to set forth the Scriptural derivation of such well-known laws as the use of an *esrog* or the law that an eye for an eye refers to monetary compensation, there were disputes concerning the exact Scriptural interpretations although the laws were familiar.

☙ The Thirteen Rules

The following is a brief explanation with illustrations of the Thirteen Rules by means of which the Torah is expounded:

(1) קַל וָחֹמֶר. Logic dictates that if a lenient case has a stringency, the same stringency applies to a stricter case. Another way of putting it is that laws can be derived from less obvious situations and applied to more obvious ones. For example, if it is forbidden to pluck an apple from a tree on Festivals (when food may be prepared by cooking and other means that may be prohibited on the Sabbath), surely plucking is forbidden on the Sabbath. Conversely, if it is permitted to slice vegetables on the Sabbath, it is surely permitted on Festivals.

(2) גְּזֵרָה שָׁוָה. In strictly limited cases, the Sinaitic tradition teaches that two independent laws or cases are meant to shed light upon one another. The indication that the two laws are complementary can be seen in two ways: (a) The same or similar words appear in both cases, e.g., the word בְּמוֹעֲדוֹ, *in its proper time* (*Numbers* 28:2), is understood to indicate that the daily offering must be brought even on the Sabbath. Similarly, the same word in the context of the Pesach-offering (*Numbers* 9:2) should be interpreted to mean that it is offered even if its appointed day, too, falls on the Sabbath (*Pesachim* 66a); (b) When two different topics are placed next to one another (this is also called הֶיקֵּשׁ, *comparison*), e.g., many laws regarding the technical processes of divorce and betrothal are derived from one another because Scripture (*Deuteronomy* 24:2) mentions divorce and betrothal in the same phrase by saying . . . וְיָצְאָה, וְהָיְתָה לְאִישׁ אַחֵר, *she shall depart* [through divorce] . . . *and become betrothed to another man.* This juxtaposition implies that the two changes of marital status are accomplished through similar legal processes (*Kiddushin* 5a).

(3) בִּנְיַן אָב . . . A general principle derived from one verse is applied to all cases that

וּפְרָט; (ה) וּמִפְּרָט וּכְלָל; (ו) כְּלָל וּפְרָט וּכְלָל, אִי אַתָּה דָן אֶלָּא כְּעֵין הַפְּרָט; (ז) מִכְּלָל שֶׁהוּא צָרִיךְ לִפְרָט, וּמִפְּרָט שֶׁהוּא צָרִיךְ לִכְלָל; (ח) כָּל דָּבָר שֶׁהָיָה בִּכְלָל וְיָצָא מִן הַכְּלָל לְלַמֵּד, לֹא לְלַמֵּד עַל עַצְמוֹ יָצָא, אֶלָּא לְלַמֵּד עַל הַכְּלָל כֻּלּוֹ יָצָא; (ט) כָּל דָּבָר שֶׁהָיָה בִּכְלָל וְיָצָא לִטְעוֹן טוֹעַן אֶחָד שֶׁהוּא כְעִנְיָנוֹ, יָצָא לְהָקֵל וְלֹא לְהַחֲמִיר; (י) כָּל דָּבָר שֶׁהָיָה בִּכְלָל וְיָצָא לִטְעוֹן טְעַן אַחֵר שֶׁלֹּא כְעִנְיָנוֹ, יָצָא לְהָקֵל וּלְהַחֲמִיר; (יא) כָּל דָּבָר שֶׁהָיָה בִּכְלָל וְיָצָא לִדּוֹן בַּדָּבָר הֶחָדָשׁ, אִי אַתָּה יָכוֹל לְהַחֲזִירוֹ לִכְלָלוֹ, עַד שֶׁיַּחֲזִירֶנּוּ הַכָּתוּב לִכְלָלוֹ בְּפֵרוּשׁ; (יב) דָּבָר הַלָּמֵד מֵעִנְיָנוֹ, וְדָבָר הַלָּמֵד מִסּוֹפוֹ; (יג) וְכֵן שְׁנֵי כְתוּבִים הַמַּכְחִישִׁים זֶה אֶת זֶה, עַד שֶׁיָּבוֹא הַכָּתוּב הַשְּׁלִישִׁי וְיַכְרִיעַ בֵּינֵיהֶם.

---

logically appear to be similar. This rule is also known as a מַה מָּצִינוּ, lit., *'what do we find?'* For example, since the Torah specifies that one may not marry even his maternal half sister, this בִּנְיַן אָב, *general principle,* dictates that the prohibition against marrying one's father's sister applies equally to his father's maternal half sister (*Yevamos* 54b). The same rule applies when two different verses shed light on one another. Similar situations may be derived from the combination of the two verses.

(4) כְּלָל וּפְרָט. When a generality is followed by a specific, the law is applied only to the specific. For example, in listing the animals from which sacrificial offerings may be brought, the Torah says: *From the [domestic] animals, from the cattle and sheep/goats (Leviticus* 1:2). This rule teaches that no animals but cattle and sheep/goats may be used. In such cases the generality [i.e., domestic animals] is mentioned only to teach that no part of the species is included in the law except for the specified items.

(5) פְּרָט וּכְלָל. This is the reverse of the above case. In describing the obligation to return lost objects, the Torah says that one should return: *His donkey . . . his garment . . . any lost object (Deuteronomy* 22:3). The concluding generality teaches that there are *no* exceptions to this rule.

(6) כְּלָל וּפְרָט וּכְלָל. . . The difference between this rule and כְּלָל וּפְרָט (rule 4) is that here the Scriptural phrase is concluded by a general statement. The two general statements imply that everything is included while the specific items in the middle imply that only they are meant. The apparent contradiction is resolved this way: Everything *is* included, provided it is essentially similar to the items specified. For example, in the verse imposing a fine on a thief, there are two general terms — *for any matter of dishonesty* and *for any lost item* — implying that the thief is liable no matter what he has taken. However, sandwiched between these general terms, a number of specific items are mentioned: *an ox . . . or a garment (Exodus* 22:8). This teaches that the fine applies to any movable object that has intrinsic value, but *not* to real estate, which is not movable, or to contracts, which testify to a debt, but have no intrinsic value *(Bava Metzia* 57b).

(7) . . . כְּלָל שֶׁהוּא צָרִיךְ לִפְרָט. This rule tells us that the principles of כְּלָל וּפְרָט and פְּרָט וּכְלָל (numbers 4 and 5 above) do not apply in cases where the introductory general statement or specification requires further clarification for its meaning to be clear. For example, the Torah commands that after slaughtering fowl or non-domesticated kosher animals, וְכִסָּהוּ בֶּעָפָר, *he is to cover [its blood] with dirt (Leviticus* 17:13). The generalization *to cover* requires clarification because it could be taken to mean that it can be poured into an enclosed pot or covered with wood or some other solid. Therefore, *with dirt* is needed to indicate that the covering must be a soft substance that can easily mix with the blood. Accordingly, it is not a 'specification' in the sense of principle 4, but a clarification *(Chullin* 88b).

(8) . . . כָּל דָּבָר שֶׁהָיָה בִּכְלָל וְיָצָא . . . לְלַמֵּד. This principle is best explained by an example. The Torah *(Leviticus* 7:19) forbids the eating of sacrificial meat by anyone who is טָמֵא, *ritually contaminated.* The very next verse singles out the שְׁלָמִים, *peace-offering,* and states that a contaminated person who eats of it is liable to כָּרֵת, *spiritual excision.* This principle teaches that the peace-offering is not an exception to the general rule; rather, that the punishment specified for the peace-offering applies to all offerings.

(9) . . . וְיָצָא לִטְעוֹן . . . כְעִנְיָנוֹ . . . Again, this principle requires an example. In imposing the death penalty on a murderer *(Leviticus* 24:21),

statement limited by a specification; (5) through a specification broadened by a general statement; (6) through a general statement followed by a specification followed, in turn, by another general statement — you may only infer whatever is similar to the specification; (7) when a general statement requires a specification or a specification requires a general statement to clarify its meaning; (8) anything that was included in a general statement, but was then singled out from the general statement in order to teach something, was not singled out to teach only about itself, but to apply its teaching to the entire generality; (9) anything that was included in a general statement, but was then singled out to discuss a provision similar to the general category, has been singled out to be more lenient rather than more severe; (10) anything that was included in a general statement, but was then singled out to discuss a provision not similar to the general category, has been singled out both to be more lenient and more severe; (11) anything that was included in a general statement, but was then singled out to be treated as a new case, cannot be returned to its general statement unless Scripture returns it explicitly to its general statement; (12) a matter elucidated from its context, or from the following passage; (13) similarly, two passages that contradict one another — until a third passage comes to reconcile them.

---

the Torah does not differentiate between premeditated and careless murders. Then the Torah describes a person who chops wood carelessly with the result that someone is killed by a flying piece of wood. Although this case would seem to require the death penalty discussed earlier, the Torah requires such a murderer to go into exile. This principle teaches that he has been singled out for *lenient* treatment, meaning that his exile is *instead* of the death penalty, not in *addition* to it.

(10) ... וְיָצָא לִטְעוֹן ... שֶׁלֹּא כְעִנְיָנוֹ ... After describing the laws regulating a Jewish indentured servant (עֶבֶד עִבְרִי) who goes free after six years of service (*Exodus* 21:1-6), the Torah turns to a Jewish indentured maidservant — who should have been included with her male counterpart. Instead, the Torah says of her that her avenues of going free are entirely unlike those of the male. This has lenient applications, for she may go free even before six years of service (upon the onset of puberty or the death of her master) and it also has a stringent application, for her master can betroth her against her will to himself or to his son (see *Exodus* 21:7-11).

(11) ... וְיָצָא לִדּוֹן ... A *Kohen's* entire family is permitted to eat *terumah* [the priestly tithe], but if his daughter marries a non-*Kohen*, she is no longer permitted to eat *terumah* (*Leviticus* 22:11,12). What if she is widowed or divorced and returns to her father's household? Since marriage had removed her from the permitted status of the rest of the family, she would not have been permitted to eat *terumah* again unless the Torah had specifically returned her to the family group (which it did, ibid. 22:13).

(12) דָּבָר הַלָּמֵד מֵעִנְיָנוֹ. In the Ten Commandments, the Torah commands, *'You shall not steal.'* The Sages derive from the context that the theft in question must be a capital offense since the injunction against stealing is preceded by the commandments not to kill and not to commit adultery with a married woman which are both capital offenses. The only theft for which someone can receive the death penalty is kidnaping a fellow Jew and treating him as a slave. Thus, *You shall not steal* refers to kidnaping.

דָּבָר הַלָּמֵד מִסּוֹפוֹ. Another form of contextual clarification is that which is found in *Leviticus* 14:34,35. First the Torah teaches that a house with a 'leprous' spot must be torn down. From the end of the passage — which describes the cleansing of the stone, wood and mortar of the house — we derive that this law applies only to houses made of stone, wood, and mortar.

(13) ... שְׁנֵי כְתוּבִים. Two verses may seem to be contradictory, until a third verse explains that each of the two has its own application. After being commanded to remove Isaac from the altar, Abraham asked God to explain two contradictory verses. First God said that Isaac would be the forefather of Israel (*Genesis* 21:12) and then He commanded that Abraham slaughter him (ibid. 22:2). God explained that the wording of the command was to *place Isaac on the altar*, but not to *slaughter* him on it (*Midrash* to *Genesis* 22:12). Thus, there is no contradiction.

יְהִי רָצוֹן מִלְּפָנֶיךָ, יהוה אֱלֹהֵינוּ וֵאלֹהֵי אֲבוֹתֵינוּ, שֶׁיִּבָּנֶה בֵּית הַמִּקְדָּשׁ* בִּמְהֵרָה בְיָמֵינוּ, וְתֵן חֶלְקֵנוּ בְּתוֹרָתֶךָ. וְשָׁם נַעֲבָדְךָ בְּיִרְאָה כִּימֵי עוֹלָם וּכְשָׁנִים קַדְמוֹנִיּוֹת.

קדיש דרבנן

Mourners recite קַדִּישׁ דְּרַבָּנָן. See *Laws* §84-85.

יִתְגַּדַּל וְיִתְקַדַּשׁ שְׁמֵהּ רַבָּא. (.Cong – אָמֵן.) בְּעָלְמָא דִּי בְרָא כִרְעוּתֵהּ. וְיַמְלִיךְ מַלְכוּתֵהּ, בְּחַיֵּיכוֹן וּבְיוֹמֵיכוֹן וּבְחַיֵּי דְכָל בֵּית יִשְׂרָאֵל, בַּעֲגָלָא וּבִזְמַן קָרִיב. וְאִמְרוּ: אָמֵן.

(.Cong – אָמֵן. יְהֵא שְׁמֵהּ רַבָּא מְבָרַךְ לְעָלַם וּלְעָלְמֵי עָלְמַיָּא.)

יְהֵא שְׁמֵהּ רַבָּא מְבָרַךְ לְעָלַם וּלְעָלְמֵי עָלְמַיָּא.

יִתְבָּרַךְ וְיִשְׁתַּבַּח וְיִתְפָּאַר וְיִתְרוֹמַם וְיִתְנַשֵּׂא וְיִתְהַדָּר וְיִתְעַלֶּה וְיִתְהַלָּל שְׁמֵהּ דְּקֻדְשָׁא בְּרִיךְ הוּא (.Cong – בְּרִיךְ הוּא) לְעֵלָּא מִן כָּל בִּרְכָתָא וְשִׁירָתָא תֻּשְׁבְּחָתָא וְנֶחֱמָתָא, דַּאֲמִירָן בְּעָלְמָא. וְאִמְרוּ: אָמֵן. (.Cong – אָמֵן.)

עַל יִשְׂרָאֵל וְעַל רַבָּנָן,* וְעַל תַּלְמִידֵיהוֹן וְעַל כָּל תַּלְמִידֵי תַלְמִידֵיהוֹן, וְעַל כָּל מָאן דְּעָסְקִין בְּאוֹרַיְתָא, דִּי בְאַתְרָא הָדֵין וְדִי בְכָל אֲתַר וַאֲתַר.* יְהֵא לְהוֹן וּלְכוֹן* שְׁלָמָא רַבָּא, חִנָּא וְחִסְדָּא וְרַחֲמִין,* וְחַיִּין אֲרִיכִין, וּמְזוֹנֵי רְוִיחֵי, וּפֻרְקָנָא מִן קֳדָם אֲבוּהוֹן דִּי בִשְׁמַיָּא* (וְאַרְעָא). וְאִמְרוּ: אָמֵן. (.Cong – אָמֵן.)

יְהֵא שְׁלָמָא רַבָּא מִן שְׁמַיָּא, וְחַיִּים (טוֹבִים) עָלֵינוּ וְעַל כָּל יִשְׂרָאֵל. וְאִמְרוּ: אָמֵן. (.Cong – אָמֵן.)

Take three steps back. Bow left and say . . . עֹשֶׂה; bow right and say . . . הוּא; bow forward and say וְעַל כָּל . . . אָמֵן. Remain standing in place for a few moments, then take three steps forward.

עֹשֶׂה שָׁלוֹם בִּמְרוֹמָיו, הוּא בְּרַחֲמָיו יַעֲשֶׂה שָׁלוֹם עָלֵינוּ, וְעַל כָּל יִשְׂרָאֵל. וְאִמְרוּ: אָמֵן. (.Cong – אָמֵן.)

⁂ יְהִי רָצוֹן . . . שֶׁיִּבָּנֶה בֵּית הַמִּקְדָּשׁ — *May it be Your will . . . that the Holy Temple be rebuilt.* Having substituted the laws of the offerings for the actual Temple service, we pray that we may soon be able to offer them in the rebuilt Temple.

⁂ קַדִּישׁ דְּרַבָּנָן / The Rabbis' Kaddish

'Whenever ten or more Israelites engage in the study of the Oral Law — for example, *Mishnah, Halachah,* and even *Midrash* or *Aggadah* — one of them recites the Rabbis' *Kaddish* [upon conclusion of the study]' *(Rambam, Nusach HaKaddish).* Although the implication from *Rambam* is that this *Kaddish* is recited primarily after the study of halachic portions of the Oral Law, many other authorities maintain that it is recited only after Midrashic material or Scriptural exegesis. *Magen Avraham,* therefore, rules that unless Scriptural verses have been expounded upon, as in the above section of *Shacharis,* a brief Aggadic passage should be taught after halachic study in order that this *Kaddish* may be recited according to all opinions. It has become customary in most communities for this *Kaddish* to be recited by mourners.

עַל יִשְׂרָאֵל וְעַל רַבָּנָן — *Upon Israel, (and) upon the teachers.* The distinctive feature of the Rabbis' *Kaddish* is the paragraph containing a prayer for the welfare of the rabbis, students, and the people who support their study. In the text of the prayer, Israel is named first, out of respect for the nation and because Moses, too, gave first mention to those who provide the necessary support for Torah study. In *Deuteronomy* 33:18, where Moses referred to the partnership of Zevulun, the supporter of scholars, and Issachar, the scholarly tribe, he blessed Zevulun first.

Any prayer for Torah scholars is indeed a

יְהִי רָצוֹן *May it be Your will,* HASHEM, *our God and the God of our forefathers, that the Holy Temple be rebuilt,* speedily in our days, and grant us our share in Your Torah, and may we serve You there with reverence as in days of old and in former years.*

THE RABBIS' KADDISH

Mourners recite the Rabbis' *Kaddish*. See *Laws* §84-85.
[A transliteration of this *Kaddish* appears on page 1304.]

יִתְגַּדַּל *May His great Name grow exalted and sanctified* (Cong.— *Amen.*) *in the world that He created as He willed. May He give reign to His kingship in your lifetimes and in your days, and in the lifetimes of the entire Family of Israel, swiftly and soon. Now respond: Amen.*

(Cong.— *Amen. May His great Name be blessed forever and ever.*)

May His great Name be blessed forever and ever.

Blessed, praised, glorified, exalted, extolled, mighty, upraised, and lauded be the Name of the Holy One, Blessed is He (Cong.— *Blessed is He*) — *beyond any blessing and song, praise and consolation that are uttered in the world. Now respond: Amen.* (Cong.— *Amen.*)

Upon Israel, upon the teachers, their disciples and all of their disciples and upon all those who engage in the study of Torah, who are here or anywhere else;* may they and you have* abundant peace, grace, kindness, and mercy,* long life, ample nourishment, and salvation from before their Father Who is in Heaven* (and on earth). Now respond: Amen.* (Cong. — *Amen.*)

May there be abundant peace from Heaven, and (good) life, upon us and upon all Israel. Now respond: Amen. (Cong.— *Amen.*)

Take three steps back. Bow left and say, *'He Who makes peace . . .'*; bow right and say, *'may He . . .'*; bow forward and say, *'and upon all Israel . . .'* Remain standing in place for a few moments, then take three steps forward.

He Who makes peace in His heights, may He, in His compassion, make peace upon us, and upon all Israel. Now respond: Amen. (Cong.— *Amen.*)

---

prayer for the entire nation, because Israel's welfare is directly dependent on Torah study *(R' Hirsch).*

This special prayer for members of the Torah community was appended only to the study of the Oral — but not the Written — Law, because that part of the Torah, in particular, was left for the Sages to teach, expound, and study. Historically, the transmission of the Oral Law depended on the teacher-student relationship and tradition, hence the prayer for their welfare.

See commentary to the beginning of *Kaddish* on pages 28-29. [A full commentary and Overview appear in the ArtScroll *Kaddish.*]

דִּי בְאַתְרָא הָדֵין וְדִי בְכָל אֲתַר וַאֲתַר — *Who are here or anywhere else.* The references to all the various places are meant to imply that every town and neighborhood, individually, benefits from those who study Torah within it.

יְהֵא לְהוֹן וּלְכוֹן — *May they and you have.* The blessing is extended not only to the Torah teachers and their students, but to all the people present in the congregation.

חִנָּא וְחִסְדָּא וְרַחֲמִין — *Grace, kindness, and mercy.* [These terms are often used synonymously, but when they are used together we must assume that they have distinct meanings. Some interpretations are as follows:]

— These characteristics refer to how God views us: The most deserving people are nourished through God's חִנָּא, *grace,* while at the other extreme, even the least worthy are recipients of רַחֲמִין, *mercy,* because He displays compassion to every living thing. Those in between are provided for through חִסְדָּא, *kindness (R' Hirsch).*

— Or, these are characteristics that *we* hope to have: חִנָּא, *grace,* is the quality that makes a person beloved by others; חִסְדָּא, *kindness,* refers to a generous, considerate human being who is kind to others, even the undeserving; רַחֲמִין, *mercy,* is the quality of compassion by which one withholds punishment even when a wrongdoer has earned it *(Siach Yitzchak).*

אֲבוּהוֹן דִּי בִשְׁמַיָּא — *Their Father Who is in Heaven.* Some *siddurim* add the word וְאַרְעָא, *and on earth,* an addition which, although rejected by some commentators, is used in many congregations.

ON CHOL HAMOED WEEKDAYS AND HOSHANA RABBAH CONTINUE ON PAGE 646.
ON ALL OTHER DAYS CONTINUE BELOW.

INTRODUCTORY PSALM TO PESUKEI D'ZIMRAH

תהלים ל

מִזְמוֹר שִׁיר חֲנֻכַּת הַבַּיִת* לְדָוִד. אֲרוֹמִמְךָ יהוה כִּי דִלִּיתָנִי, וְלֹא שִׂמַּחְתָּ אֹיְבַי לִי. יהוה אֱלֹהָי, שִׁוַּעְתִּי אֵלֶיךָ וַתִּרְפָּאֵנִי. יהוה הֶעֱלִיתָ מִן שְׁאוֹל נַפְשִׁי,* חִיִּיתַנִי מִיָּרְדִי בוֹר. זַמְּרוּ לַיהוה חֲסִידָיו, וְהוֹדוּ לְזֵכֶר קָדְשׁוֹ. כִּי רֶגַע בְּאַפּוֹ, חַיִּים בִּרְצוֹנוֹ, בָּעֶרֶב יָלִין בֶּכִי וְלַבֹּקֶר רִנָּה. וַאֲנִי אָמַרְתִּי בְשַׁלְוִי, בַּל אֶמּוֹט לְעוֹלָם. יהוה בִּרְצוֹנְךָ הֶעֱמַדְתָּה לְהַרְרִי עֹז, הִסְתַּרְתָּ פָנֶיךָ הָיִיתִי נִבְהָל. אֵלֶיךָ יהוה אֶקְרָא, וְאֶל אֲדֹנָי אֶתְחַנָּן. מַה בֶּצַע בְּדָמִי, בְּרִדְתִּי אֶל שָׁחַת, הֲיוֹדְךָ עָפָר, הֲיַגִּיד אֲמִתֶּךָ. שְׁמַע יהוה וְחָנֵּנִי, יהוה הֱיֵה עֹזֵר לִי. ❖ הָפַכְתָּ מִסְפְּדִי לְמָחוֹל לִי, פִּתַּחְתָּ שַׂקִּי, וַתְּאַזְּרֵנִי שִׂמְחָה. לְמַעַן יְזַמֶּרְךָ כָבוֹד וְלֹא יִדֹּם, יהוה אֱלֹהַי לְעוֹלָם אוֹדֶךָּ.

Mourners recite קַדִּישׁ יָתוֹם. See *Laws* §81-83.

יִתְגַּדַּל וְיִתְקַדַּשׁ שְׁמֵהּ רַבָּא. (.Cong – אָמֵן.) בְּעָלְמָא דִּי בְרָא כִרְעוּתֵהּ. וְיַמְלִיךְ מַלְכוּתֵהּ, בְּחַיֵּיכוֹן וּבְיוֹמֵיכוֹן וּבְחַיֵּי דְכָל בֵּית יִשְׂרָאֵל, בַּעֲגָלָא וּבִזְמַן קָרִיב. וְאִמְרוּ: אָמֵן.

(.Cong – אָמֵן. יְהֵא שְׁמֵהּ רַבָּא מְבָרַךְ לְעָלַם וּלְעָלְמֵי עָלְמַיָּא.)

יְהֵא שְׁמֵהּ רַבָּא מְבָרַךְ לְעָלַם וּלְעָלְמֵי עָלְמַיָּא.

יִתְבָּרַךְ וְיִשְׁתַּבַּח וְיִתְפָּאַר וְיִתְרוֹמַם וְיִתְנַשֵּׂא וְיִתְהַדָּר וְיִתְעַלֶּה וְיִתְהַלָּל שְׁמֵהּ דְּקֻדְשָׁא בְּרִיךְ הוּא (.Cong – בְּרִיךְ הוּא) – לְעֵלָּא מִן כָּל בִּרְכָתָא וְשִׁירָתָא תֻּשְׁבְּחָתָא וְנֶחֱמָתָא, דַּאֲמִירָן בְּעָלְמָא. וְאִמְרוּ: אָמֵן. (.Cong – אָמֵן.)

יְהֵא שְׁלָמָא רַבָּא מִן שְׁמַיָּא, וְחַיִּים עָלֵינוּ וְעַל כָּל יִשְׂרָאֵל. וְאִמְרוּ: אָמֵן. (.Cong – אָמֵן.)

Take three steps back. Bow left and say . . . עֹשֶׂה; bow right and say . . . הוּא; bow forward and say וְעַל כָּל . . . אָמֵן. Remain standing in place for a few moments, then take three steps forward.

עֹשֶׂה שָׁלוֹם בִּמְרוֹמָיו, הוּא יַעֲשֶׂה שָׁלוֹם עָלֵינוּ, וְעַל כָּל יִשְׂרָאֵל. וְאִמְרוּ: אָמֵן. (.Cong – אָמֵן.)

מִזְמוֹר שִׁיר / Psalm 30

This psalm is not part of *Pesukei D'zimrah* (see below) and it did not become customary to include it in the morning prayers until the seventeenth century. Apparently, it was decided to include it in *Shacharis* because it was sung to inaugurate the morning Temple service, and thus is an appropriate prelude to the prayers that take the place of that service *(Tikun Tefillah)*. It is also a fitting conclusion to the Scriptural and Talmudical passages regarding the offerings. Additionally, מִזְמוֹר שִׁיר is an appropriate introduction to the morning psalms of praise because of its emphasis in the faith that God rescues from even the most hopeless situations *(R' Munk)*.

חֲנֻכַּת הַבַּיִת – *The inauguration of the Temple.* How is this psalm, which deals only with David's illness, related to the dedication of the Temple? *Radak* explains that Solomon's eventual inauguration of the Temple represented

ON CHOL HAMOED WEEKDAYS AND HOSHANA RABBAH CONTINUE ON PAGE 646.
ON ALL OTHER DAYS CONTINUE BELOW.

INTRODUCTORY PSALM TO PESUKEI D'ZIMRAH

Psalm 30

מִזְמוֹר *A psalm — a song for the inauguration of the Temple*— by David. I will exalt You, HASHEM, for You have drawn me up and not let my foes rejoice over me. HASHEM, my God, I cried out to You and You healed me. HASHEM, You have raised my soul from the lower world,* You have preserved me from my descent to the Pit. Make music to HASHEM, His devout ones, and give thanks to His Holy Name. For His anger endures but a moment; life results from His favor. In the evening one lies down weeping, but with dawn — a cry of joy! I had said in my serenity, 'I will never falter.' But, HASHEM, all is through Your favor — You supported my greatness with might; should You but conceal Your face, I would be confounded. To You, HASHEM, I would call and to my Lord I would appeal. What gain is there in my death, when I descend to the Pit? Will the dust acknowledge You? Will it declare Your truth? Hear, HASHEM, and favor me; HASHEM, be my Helper!* Chazzan– *You have changed for me my lament into dancing; You undid my sackcloth and girded me with gladness. So that my soul might make music to You and not be stilled, HASHEM my God, forever will I thank You.*

Mourners recite the Mourners' *Kaddish*. See *Laws* §81-83.
[A transliteration of this *Kaddish* appears on page 1305.]

יִתְגַּדַּל *May His great Name grow exalted and sanctified* (Cong.– *Amen.*) *in the world that He created as He willed. May He give reign to His kingship in your lifetimes and in your days, and in the lifetimes of the entire Family of Israel, swiftly and soon. Now respond: Amen.*

(Cong.– *Amen. May His great Name be blessed forever and ever.*)

May His great Name be blessed forever and ever.

Blessed, praised, glorified, exalted, extolled, mighty, upraised, and lauded be the Name of the Holy One, Blessed is He (Cong.– *Blessed is He*) — *beyond any blessing and song, praise and consolation that are uttered in the world. Now respond: Amen.* (Cong.– *Amen.*)

May there be abundant peace from Heaven, and life, upon us and upon all Israel. Now respond: Amen. (Cong.– *Amen.*)

Take three steps back. Bow left and say, *'He Who makes peace . . .'*; bow right and say, *'may He . . .'*; bow forward and say, *'and upon all Israel . . .'* Remain standing in place for a few moments, then take three steps forward.

He Who makes peace in His heights, may He make peace upon us, and upon all Israel. Now respond: Amen. (Cong.– *Amen.*)

David's vindication against the taunts and charges of his enemies. His offspring could not have gained the privilege of building the Temple if David had been a sinner.

Another explanation is that the Temple's purpose is best achieved when each individual Jew recognizes God's presence and help in his personal life. Accordingly, by never losing his faith in God, and by finally being vindicated through God's deliverance, David is the perfect embodiment of the Temple's role in the life of the nation (*R' Hirsch*).

ה׳ הֶעֱלִיתָ מִן שְׁאוֹל נַפְשִׁי — *HASHEM, You have raised my soul from the lower world. R' Yerucham Levovitz* notes that David speaks as if he had already died and descended to the 'lower world,' where sinners are punished after death. From this we learn that one can suffer the anguish of purgatory even while alive! As the Talmud (*Nedarim* 22a) teaches: 'Whoever be-

פסוקי דזמרה ליום טוב ולשבת חול המועד

(Some recite this short Kabbalistic declaration of intent before beginning *Pesukei D'zimrah:)*

(הֲרֵינִי מְזַמֵּן אֶת פִּי לְהוֹדוֹת וּלְהַלֵּל וּלְשַׁבֵּחַ אֶת בּוֹרְאִי. לְשֵׁם יִחוּד קֻדְשָׁא בְּרִיךְ הוּא וּשְׁכִינְתֵּיהּ עַל יְדֵי הַהוּא טָמִיר וְנֶעְלָם, בְּשֵׁם כָּל יִשְׂרָאֵל.)

Pesukei D'zimrah begins with the recital of בָּרוּךְ שֶׁאָמַר. Stand while reciting בָּרוּךְ שֶׁאָמַר. During its recitation, hold the two front *tzitzis* of the *tallis* (or *tallis kattan)* in the right hand, and at its conclusion kiss the *tzitzis* and release them. Conversation is forbidden from this point until after *Shemoneh Esrei,* except for certain prayer responses (see box below).

בָּרוּךְ שֶׁאָמַר וְהָיָה הָעוֹלָם,* בָּרוּךְ הוּא. בָּרוּךְ עֹשֶׂה בְרֵאשִׁית, בָּרוּךְ אוֹמֵר וְעֹשֶׂה,* בָּרוּךְ גּוֹזֵר וּמְקַיֵּם, בָּרוּךְ מְרַחֵם עַל הָאָרֶץ,* בָּרוּךְ מְרַחֵם עַל הַבְּרִיּוֹת, בָּרוּךְ מְשַׁלֵּם שָׂכָר טוֹב לִירֵאָיו,* בָּרוּךְ חַי לָעַד וְקַיָּם לָנֶצַח,* בָּרוּךְ פּוֹדֶה וּמַצִּיל,* בָּרוּךְ שְׁמוֹ.* בָּרוּךְ אַתָּה יהוה אֱלֹהֵינוּ מֶלֶךְ הָעוֹלָם, הָאֵל הָאָב הָרַחֲמָן* הַמְהֻלָּל בְּפֶה עַמּוֹ,* מְשֻׁבָּח וּמְפֹאָר בִּלְשׁוֹן חֲסִידָיו

---

comes angry is subjected to all types of *Gehinnom.'* The flames of frustration, anguish, and melancholy are the equivalent of the fires of *Gehinnom.* Throughout the Book of *Psalms,* most references to 'falling into the lower world' refer to this type of emotional inferno.

פְּסוּקֵי דְזִמְרָה / PESUKEI D'ZIMRAH

The Sages taught that one should set forth the praises of God before making requests of Him *(Berachos* 32a). In this section of *Shacharis,* we concentrate on God's revelation in nature and history — on how His glory can be seen in creation and in the unfolding of events. Accordingly פְּסוּקֵי דְזִמְרָה means *Verses of Praise.* However, many commentators relate the word דְזִמְרָה to the verb תִּזְמֹר, *prune (Leviticus* 25:4). In this view, we now recite 'Verses of Pruning,' which are designed to 'cut away' the mental and spiritual hindrances to proper prayer. Thus, by focusing on God's glory all around us, we prepare ourselves for the *Shema* and *Shemoneh Esrei,* when we accept Him as our King and pray for the needs of the Jewish people.

Because it is a separate section of *Shacharis* with a purpose all its own, *Pesukei D'zimrah* is introduced with a blessing [בָּרוּךְ שֶׁאָמַר] and concluded with a blessing [יִשְׁתַּבַּח]. In this way, it is similar to *Hallel,* which is a complete unit and is therefore introduced by, and concluded with, a blessing.

בָּרוּךְ שֶׁאָמַר / Baruch She'amar

The commentators record an ancient tradition that this prayer was transcribed by the Men of the Great Assembly approximately 2400 years ago from a script that fell from heaven. The prayer contains 87 words, equal to the numerical value of פָּז, *finest gold.* This alludes to the verse *(Song of Songs* 5:11): רֹאשׁוֹ כֶּתֶם פָּז, *His opening words* [i.e., the introductory words of *Pesukei D'zimrah] were finest gold.*

In recognition of its lofty status, one must stand when reciting *Baruch She'amar.* Kabbalists teach that one should hold his two front *tzitzis* during *Baruch She'amar* and kiss them upon concluding the prayer. Mystically, this signifies that *Baruch She'amar* has an effect on 'the higher regions.'

Baruch She'amar begins with a series of phrases in which we bless seven aspects of God. *Rabbi David Hoffmann,* cited and explained in *World of Prayer,* asserts that these seven ideas are all implied by the Four-Letter Name, י-ה-ו-ה. That Name contains the letters of הָיָה הֹוֶה יִהְיֶה, *He was, He is, He will be.* It is the Name that symbolizes God's eternity, mastery of all conditions, and the fact that He brought everything into being and will carry out His will and word. The seven ideas expressed by this Name are:

(1) שֶׁאָמַר וְהָיָה הָעוֹלָם — *Who spoke and the world came into being.* God is the Creator Who brought all of creation into being and maintains it [עוֹשֶׂה בְרֵאשִׁית] with no more than His word.

(2) אוֹמֵר וְעֹשֶׂה — *Who speaks and does.* God brings His promise into being even when people no longer seem to deserve His generosity. Conversely, גּוֹזֵר וּמְקַיֵּם, He *decrees and fulfills;* when He warns of punishment, the sinner cannot escape unless he repents sincerely.

(3) מְרַחֵם עַל הָאָרֶץ — *Who has mercy on the earth.* The Four-Letter Name also refers to Him as the merciful God, Who has compassion on the *earth* and all its בְּרִיּוֹת, *creatures,* human or otherwise.

(4) מְשַׁלֵּם שָׂכָר טוֹב לִירֵאָיו — *Who gives goodly reward to those who fear Him.* His reward may not be dispensed in This World, but it will surely be dispensed in the World to Come. Whatever the case, no good deed goes unrewarded.

(5) חַי לָעַד וְקַיָּם לָנֶצַח — *Who lives forever*

PESUKEI D'ZIMRAH FOR YOM TOV AND SHABBOS CHOL HAMOED

(Some recite this short Kabbalistic declaration of intent before beginning *Pesukei D'zimrah:)*

(I now prepare my mouth to thank, laud, and praise my Creator. For the sake of the unification of the Holy One, Blessed is He, and His Presence, through Him Who is hidden and inscrutable — [I pray] in the name of all Israel.)

Pesukei D'zimrah begins with the recital of בָּרוּךְ שֶׁאָמַר, *Blessed is He Who spoke . . .* Stand while reciting בָּרוּךְ שֶׁאָמַר. During its recitation, hold the two front *tzitzis* of the *tallis* (or *tallis kattan)* in the right hand, and at its conclusion kiss the *tzitzis* and release them. Conversation is forbidden from this point until after *Shemoneh Esrei,* except for certain prayer responses (see box below).

בָּרוּךְ שֶׁאָמַר *Blessed is He Who spoke, and the world came into being* — blessed is He. Blessed is He Who maintains creation; blessed is He Who speaks and does;* blessed is He Who decrees and fulfills; blessed is He Who has mercy on the earth;* blessed is He Who has mercy on the creatures; blessed is He Who gives goodly reward to those who fear Him;* blessed is He Who lives forever and endures to eternity;* blessed is He Who redeems and rescues* — blessed is His Name!* Blessed are You,* HASHEM, *our God, King of the universe, the God, the merciful Father,* Who is lauded by the mouth of His people,* praised and glorified by the tongue of His devout ones*

---

and endures to eternity. Not only is God's existence infinite and eternal, He *endures forever,* in the sense that He continues to involve Himself in the affairs of the universe.

(6) פּוֹדֶה וּמַצִּיל — *Who redeems* people from moral decline *and rescues* them from physical danger. The classic example is the Redemption from Egypt, when God took a degraded, powerless rabble and made it a great nation.

(7) בָּרוּךְ שְׁמוֹ — *Blessed is His Name!* The Name by which we call God can in no way express His true essence. Nevertheless, in His kindness to man, He allows us to glimpse some of His properties and express them in a Name.

הָאֵל הָאָב הָרַחֲמָן — *The God, the merciful Father.* We bless God with awareness that He is both all-powerful [אֵל] and filled with mercy, like a father whose behavior is a constant expression of mercy, even when he must be harsh *(Siach Yitzchak).*

בְּפֶה עַמּוֹ — *By the mouth of His people.* The Kabbalists comment that בְּפֶה has the numerical value of 87, and alludes to the number of words

Permitted responses during Pesukei D'zimrah

From this point until after *Shemoneh Esrei* conversation is forbidden. During *Pesukei D'zimrah* [from בָּרוּךְ שֶׁאָמַר until יִשְׁתַּבַּח, p. 214] certain congregational and individual responses [e.g., בָּרוּךְ הוּא וּבָרוּךְ שְׁמוֹ] are omitted. The following responses, however, should be made: אָמֵן, *Amen,* after any blessing; *Kaddish; Borchu; Kedushah;* and the Rabbis' *Modim.* Additionally, one should join the congregation in reciting the first verse of the *Shema,* and may recite the אֲשֶׁר יָצַר blessing if he had to relieve himself during *Pesukei D'zimrah.*

If one is in the middle of *Pesukei D'zimrah* and the congregation has already reached the Torah reading, it is preferable that he not be called to the Torah. However, if (a) one is the only *Kohen* or Levite present, or (b) the *gabbai* inadvertently called him to the Torah, then he may recite the blessings and even read the portion softly along with the Torah reader.

If after beginning *Pesukei D'zimrah* one realizes that he has forgotten to recite the morning Blessings of the Torah (p. 136), he should pause to recite them and their accompanying verses. Likewise, if he fears that he will not reach the *Shema* before the prescribed time (see *Laws* §55), he should recite all three paragraphs of *Shema.*

In all cases of permitted responses it is preferable to respond between psalms, whenever possible. Thus, for example, if one realizes that the congregation is approaching *Kedushah,* he should not begin a new psalm, but should wait for the congregation to recite *Kedushah,* then continue his prayers.

The responses permitted above do not apply during the 'blessing' portions of בָּרוּךְ שֶׁאָמַר and יִשְׁתַּבַּח [i.e., from the words בָּרוּךְ אַתָּה ה׳, *Blessed are You,* HASHEM, until the blessing's conclusion] where no interruptions are permitted.

וַעֲבָדָיו,* וּבְשִׁירֵי דָוִד עַבְדֶּךָ. נְהַלֶּלְךָ יהוה אֱלֹהֵינוּ, בִּשְׁבָחוֹת וּבִזְמִרוֹת. נְגַדֶּלְךָ וּנְשַׁבֵּחֲךָ וּנְפָאֶרְךָ וְנַזְכִּיר שִׁמְךָ וְנַמְלִיכְךָ, מַלְכֵּנוּ אֱלֹהֵינוּ. ❖ יָחִיד, חֵי הָעוֹלָמִים, מֶלֶךְ מְשֻׁבָּח וּמְפֹאָר עֲדֵי עַד שְׁמוֹ הַגָּדוֹל. בָּרוּךְ אַתָּה יהוה, מֶלֶךְ מְהֻלָּל בַּתִּשְׁבָּחוֹת. (.Cong. – אָמֵן)

דברי הימים א טז:ח-לו

הוֹדוּ לַיהוה* קִרְאוּ בִשְׁמוֹ,* הוֹדִיעוּ בָעַמִּים עֲלִילֹתָיו. שִׁירוּ לוֹ, זַמְּרוּ לוֹ, שִׂיחוּ בְּכָל נִפְלְאֹתָיו. הִתְהַלְּלוּ בְּשֵׁם קָדְשׁוֹ, יִשְׂמַח לֵב מְבַקְשֵׁי יהוה. דִּרְשׁוּ יהוה וְעֻזּוֹ, בַּקְּשׁוּ פָנָיו תָּמִיד. זִכְרוּ נִפְלְאֹתָיו אֲשֶׁר עָשָׂה, מֹפְתָיו וּמִשְׁפְּטֵי פִיהוּ. זֶרַע יִשְׂרָאֵל עַבְדּוֹ, בְּנֵי יַעֲקֹב בְּחִירָיו. הוּא יהוה אֱלֹהֵינוּ, בְּכָל הָאָרֶץ מִשְׁפָּטָיו. זִכְרוּ לְעוֹלָם בְּרִיתוֹ, דָּבָר צִוָּה לְאֶלֶף דּוֹר.* אֲשֶׁר כָּרַת אֶת אַבְרָהָם, וּשְׁבוּעָתוֹ לְיִצְחָק. וַיַּעֲמִידֶהָ לְיַעֲקֹב לְחֹק, לְיִשְׂרָאֵל בְּרִית עוֹלָם. לֵאמֹר, לְךָ אֶתֵּן אֶרֶץ כְּנָעַן, חֶבֶל נַחֲלַתְכֶם. בִּהְיוֹתְכֶם מְתֵי מִסְפָּר, כִּמְעַט וְגָרִים בָּהּ. וַיִּתְהַלְּכוּ מִגּוֹי אֶל גּוֹי, וּמִמַּמְלָכָה אֶל עַם אַחֵר. לֹא הִנִּיחַ לְאִישׁ לְעָשְׁקָם, וַיּוֹכַח עֲלֵיהֶם מְלָכִים. אַל תִּגְּעוּ בִּמְשִׁיחָי, וּבִנְבִיאַי אַל תָּרֵעוּ. שִׁירוּ לַיהוה* כָּל הָאָרֶץ, בַּשְּׂרוּ מִיּוֹם אֶל יוֹם יְשׁוּעָתוֹ. סַפְּרוּ בַגּוֹיִם אֶת כְּבוֹדוֹ, בְּכָל הָעַמִּים נִפְלְאוֹתָיו. כִּי גָדוֹל יהוה וּמְהֻלָּל מְאֹד, וְנוֹרָא הוּא עַל כָּל אֱלֹהִים. ❖ כִּי כָּל אֱלֹהֵי הָעַמִּים אֱלִילִים, (pause) וַיהוה שָׁמַיִם עָשָׂה.*

---

in this prayer. *Magen Avraham* and *Mishnah Berurah* (51:1) favor the usage of this word. Nevertheless, some authorities feel that the word בְּפִי, which has the same meaning, is the preferred grammatical form.

חֲסִידָיו וַעֲבָדָיו — *His devout ones and His servants.* We would not dare to compose praises on our own, for we are totally inadequate to evaluate God. We praise Him with the words of the great and holy people of the past and with the psalms of David, which are the backbone of *Pesukei D'zimrah (Etz Yosef).*

הודו / Give Thanks

הודו לה׳ — *Give thanks to* HASHEM. The first twenty-nine verses of this lengthy prayer form a jubilant song that David taught Assaf and his colleagues. Assaf and his family were musicians and psalmists whose own compositions are included in the *Book of Psalms.* This song was intended by David to be sung when the Holy Ark was brought to Jerusalem.

According to *Seder Olam,* during the last forty-three years before Solomon inaugurated the Temple, the first fifteen of these verses were sung in the Tabernacle every day during the morning *tamid*-offering service, and the last fourteen were sung during the afternoon *tamid* service. With very minor changes, these verses are also found in *Psalms* 105:1-15, 96:2-13, and 106:47-48. [Incidentally, it is because these verses were recited during the sacrificial service that the *Nusach Sefard* ritual places הודו before *Pesukei D'zimrah.* Given the fact that these verses relate to the offerings, they should be recited immediately after the *Korbanos* section of *Shacharis. Nusach Ashkenaz,* however, does not make this change, because the verses are in *general* praise, and thus similar to the rest of *Pesukei D'zimrah.*]

In its entirety this song calls upon Israel to maintain its faith in God and its confidence that He will bring it salvation from exile and persecution. The first fifteen verses refer to the miracles of past salvations and how our Patriarchs had complete faith in God even though they had nothing to go by but His covenant and oath. The second group of fourteen verses begins שִׁירוּ לַה׳ כָּל הָאָרֶץ, *Sing to* HASHEM, *everyone on earth.* It refers to the song of gratitude that everyone will sing in Messianic times. Thus, this section parallels the

and His servants and through the psalms of David Your servant. We shall laud You, HASHEM, our God, with praises and songs. We shall exalt You, praise You, glorify You, mention Your Name and proclaim Your reign, our King, our God.* Chazzan– *O Unique One, Life-giver of the worlds, King Whose great Name is eternally praised and glorified. Blessed are You, HASHEM, the King Who is lauded with praises.*

(Cong.– *Amen.*)

I Chronicles 16:8-36

הודו *Give thanks to HASHEM,* declare His Name,* make His acts known among the peoples. Sing to Him, make music to Him, speak of all His wonders. Glory in His holy Name, be glad of heart, you who seek HASHEM. Search out HASHEM and His might, seek His Presence always. Remember His wonders that He wrought, His marvels and the judgments of His mouth. O seed of Israel, His servant, O children of Jacob, His chosen ones — He is HASHEM, our God, over all the earth are His judgments. Remember His covenant forever — the word He commanded for a thousand generations* — that He made with Abraham and His vow to Isaac. Then He established it for Jacob as a statute, for Israel as an everlasting covenant; saying, 'To you I shall give the Land of Canaan, the lot of your heritage.' When you were but few in number, hardly dwelling there, and they wandered from nation to nation, from one kingdom to another people. He let no man rob them, and He rebuked kings for their sake: 'Dare not touch My anointed ones, and to My prophets do no harm.' Sing to HASHEM,* everyone on earth, announce His salvation daily. Relate His glory among the nations, among all the peoples His wonders. That HASHEM is great and exceedingly lauded, and awesome is He above all heavenly powers.* Chazzan– *For all the gods of the peoples are nothings — but HASHEM made heaven!**

---

theme of the morning *Shema* blessings (p. 216) in which we emphasize the redemption of the past, while the second section parallels the evening *Shema* blessings (p. 34) in which we stress the redemption of the future.

The third section of this prayer continues with a collection of verses. It is discussed on the next page, s.v. רוֹמְמוּ.

קִרְאוּ בִשְׁמוֹ — *Declare His Name.* Whatever you accomplish, ascribe it to God's help, and let even the gentile nations know that God's guiding hand is everywhere *(Vilna Gaon).*

לְאֶלֶף דּוֹר — *For a thousand generations.* God's *word,* i.e., His covenant with Israel lasts for a *thousand generations,* a poetic expression meaning forever. He sealed His covenant with Abraham, designated Isaac as Abraham's successor, and then chose Jacob over Esau, thus making Israel His chosen people everlastingly *(Tzilosa D'Avraham).*

שִׁירוּ לַה׳ — *Sing to HASHEM.* As we find repeatedly in the Prophets, in Messianic times all nations will follow Israel's lead in recognizing and serving God. The fourteen verses beginning here allude to those days. However, David also referred to a salvation that occurred in his own lifetime. The Philistines had captured the Holy Ark and destroyed the Tabernacle at Shiloh. But the presence of the Ark in the Philistine cities brought plagues upon them. Recognizing the hand of God in their suffering, the Philistines returned the Ark with a gift of tribute to God. The same will happen in future times when Israel's oppressors will recognize God's mastery.

וַה׳ שָׁמַיִם עָשָׂה — *But HASHEM made heaven.* After having proclaimed that the gods of the nations are vain and useless *nothings,* David made this logical argument: the most prominent and seemingly powerful idols were the heavenly

הוֹד וְהָדָר לְפָנָיו, עֹז וְחֶדְוָה בִּמְקֹמוֹ. הָבוּ לַיהוה מִשְׁפְּחוֹת
עַמִּים, הָבוּ לַיהוה כָּבוֹד וָעֹז. הָבוּ לַיהוה כְּבוֹד שְׁמוֹ, שְׂאוּ מִנְחָה
וּבֹאוּ לְפָנָיו, הִשְׁתַּחֲווּ לַיהוה בְּהַדְרַת קֹדֶשׁ. חִילוּ מִלְּפָנָיו כָּל
הָאָרֶץ, אַף תִּכּוֹן תֵּבֵל בַּל תִּמּוֹט.* יִשְׂמְחוּ הַשָּׁמַיִם וְתָגֵל הָאָרֶץ,
וְיֹאמְרוּ בַגּוֹיִם, יהוה מָלָךְ. יִרְעַם הַיָּם וּמְלוֹאוֹ, יַעֲלֹץ הַשָּׂדֶה וְכָל
אֲשֶׁר בּוֹ. אָז יְרַנְּנוּ עֲצֵי הַיָּעַר, מִלִּפְנֵי יהוה, כִּי בָא לִשְׁפּוֹט אֶת
הָאָרֶץ. הוֹדוּ לַיהוה כִּי טוֹב, כִּי לְעוֹלָם חַסְדּוֹ. וְאִמְרוּ הוֹשִׁיעֵנוּ
אֱלֹהֵי יִשְׁעֵנוּ, וְקַבְּצֵנוּ וְהַצִּילֵנוּ מִן הַגּוֹיִם, לְהֹדוֹת לְשֵׁם קָדְשֶׁךָ,
לְהִשְׁתַּבֵּחַ בִּתְהִלָּתֶךָ. בָּרוּךְ יהוה אֱלֹהֵי יִשְׂרָאֵל מִן הָעוֹלָם וְעַד
הָעֹלָם, וַיֹּאמְרוּ כָל הָעָם, אָמֵן, וְהַלֵּל לַיהוה.

❖ רוֹמְמוּ יהוה אֱלֹהֵינוּ* וְהִשְׁתַּחֲווּ לַהֲדֹם רַגְלָיו, קָדוֹשׁ הוּא.[1]
רוֹמְמוּ יהוה אֱלֹהֵינוּ וְהִשְׁתַּחֲווּ לְהַר קָדְשׁוֹ, כִּי קָדוֹשׁ יהוה אֱלֹהֵינוּ.[2]

וְהוּא רַחוּם יְכַפֵּר עָוֹן וְלֹא יַשְׁחִית, וְהִרְבָּה לְהָשִׁיב אַפּוֹ, וְלֹא
יָעִיר כָּל חֲמָתוֹ.[3] אַתָּה יהוה, לֹא תִכְלָא רַחֲמֶיךָ מִמֶּנִּי, חַסְדְּךָ
וַאֲמִתְּךָ תָּמִיד יִצְּרוּנִי.[4] זְכֹר רַחֲמֶיךָ יהוה וַחֲסָדֶיךָ, כִּי מֵעוֹלָם
הֵמָּה.[5] תְּנוּ עֹז לֵאלֹהִים, עַל יִשְׂרָאֵל גַּאֲוָתוֹ, וְעֻזּוֹ בַּשְּׁחָקִים. נוֹרָא
אֱלֹהִים מִמִּקְדָּשֶׁיךָ, אֵל יִשְׂרָאֵל הוּא נֹתֵן עֹז וְתַעֲצֻמוֹת לָעָם, בָּרוּךְ
אֱלֹהִים.[6] אֵל נְקָמוֹת יהוה, אֵל נְקָמוֹת הוֹפִיעַ. הִנָּשֵׂא שֹׁפֵט הָאָרֶץ,
הָשֵׁב גְּמוּל עַל גֵּאִים.[7] לַיהוה הַיְשׁוּעָה, עַל עַמְּךָ בִרְכָתֶךָ סֶּלָה.[8]

❖ יהוה צְבָאוֹת עִמָּנוּ, מִשְׂגָּב לָנוּ אֱלֹהֵי יַעֲקֹב סֶלָה.[9] יהוה צְבָאוֹת,
אַשְׁרֵי אָדָם בֹּטֵחַ בָּךְ.[10] יהוה הוֹשִׁיעָה, הַמֶּלֶךְ יַעֲנֵנוּ בְיוֹם קָרְאֵנוּ.[11]

הוֹשִׁיעָה אֶת עַמֶּךָ, וּבָרֵךְ אֶת נַחֲלָתֶךָ, וּרְעֵם וְנַשְּׂאֵם עַד
הָעוֹלָם.[12] נַפְשֵׁנוּ חִכְּתָה לַיהוה, עֶזְרֵנוּ וּמָגִנֵּנוּ הוּא. כִּי בוֹ יִשְׂמַח
לִבֵּנוּ, כִּי בְשֵׁם קָדְשׁוֹ בָטָחְנוּ. יְהִי חַסְדְּךָ יהוה עָלֵינוּ, כַּאֲשֶׁר
יִחַלְנוּ לָךְ.[13] הַרְאֵנוּ יהוה חַסְדֶּךָ, וְיֶשְׁעֲךָ תִּתֶּן לָנוּ.[14] קוּמָה

---

bodies — but since *HASHEM made heaven,* how can anyone justify worshiping His creatures in preference to Him? *(Radak).*

It is important to pause between אֱלִילִים, *nothings* [i.e., the idols] and וַה׳, *but* [lit. *and]* HASHEM. If the two words are read together, it could be understood to mean ח״ו, *all of the gods . . . are nothings and* HASHEM, as if to say that He is like them.

תֵּבֵל בַּל תִּמּוֹט — *The world . . . it cannot falter.* Though the turbulent history of war and conflict often makes it seem as though man will destroy his planet, the climax of history will be the peace and fulfillment of Messianic times. The world cannot be totally destroyed for God has ordained that it will survive *(Radak).*

רוֹמְמוּ ה׳ אֱלֹהֵינוּ — *Exalt* HASHEM, *our God . . .* From this point until its end, the prayer contains a collection of verses from throughout *Psalms. Tzilosa D'Avraham* cites Rabbi Profiat Duran, a refugee from the Spanish massacres of 1391, that these verses collectively were known as פְּסוּקֵי דְרַחֲמֵי, *Verses of Mercy,* because they are effective in pleading for God's mercy. Accord-

Glory and majesty are before Him, might and delight are in His place. Render to HASHEM, *O families of the peoples, render to* HASHEM *honor and might. Render to* HASHEM *honor worthy of His Name, take an offering and come before Him, prostrate yourselves before* HASHEM *in His intensely holy place. Tremble before Him, everyone on earth, indeed, the world is fixed so that it cannot falter.* The heavens will be glad and the earth will rejoice and say among the nations, '*HASHEM *has reigned!' The sea and its fullness will roar, the field and everything in it will exult. Then the trees of the forest will sing with joy before* HASHEM, *for He will have arrived to judge the earth. Give thanks to* HASHEM, *for He is good, for His kindness endures forever. And say, 'Save us, O God of our salvation, gather us and rescue us from the nations, to thank Your Holy Name and to glory in Your praise!' Blessed is* HASHEM, *the God of Israel, from This World to the World to Come — and let the entire people say, 'Amen and praise to God!'*

Chazzan– *Exalt* HASHEM, *our God,* and bow at His footstool; He is holy!*[1] *Exalt* HASHEM, *our God, and bow at His holy mountain; for holy is* HASHEM, *our God.*[2]

He, the Merciful One, is forgiving of iniquity and does not destroy; frequently, He withdraws His anger, not arousing His entire rage.[3] *You,* HASHEM *— withhold not Your mercy from me; may Your kindness and Your truth always protect me.*[4] *Remember Your mercies,* HASHEM, *and Your kindnesses, for they are from the beginning of the world.*[5] *Render might to God, Whose majesty hovers over Israel and Whose might is in the clouds. You are awesome, O God, from Your sanctuaries, O God of Israel — it is He Who grants might and power to the people, blessed is God.*[6] *O God of vengeance,* HASHEM, *O God of vengeance, appear! Arise, O Judge of the earth, render recompense to the haughty.*[7] *Salvation is* HASHEM*'s, upon Your people is Your blessing, Selah.*[8] Chazzan– HASHEM, *Master of Legions, is with us, a stronghold for us is the God of Jacob, Selah.*[9] HASHEM, *Master of Legions, praiseworthy is the person who trusts in You.*[10] HASHEM, *save! May the King answer us on the day we call.*[11]

Save Your people and bless Your heritage, tend them and elevate them forever.[12] *Our soul longed for* HASHEM *— our help and our shield is He. For in Him will our hearts be glad, for in His Holy Name we trusted. May Your kindness,* HASHEM, *be upon us, just as we awaited You.*[13] *Show us Your kindness,* HASHEM, *and grant us Your salvation.*[14] *Arise —*

(1) *Psalms* 99:5. (2) 99:9. (3) 78:38. (4) 40:12. (5) 25:6. (6) 68:35-36. (7) 94:1-2. (8) 3:9. (9) 46:8. (10) 84:13. (11) 20:10. (12) 28:9. (13) 33:20-22. (14) 85:8.

ingly, they were adopted in the prayers for an end to exile and dispersion.

From *Etz Yosef, World of Prayer* and others, the following progression of thought emerges from these verses. Even if הֲדֹם רַגְלָיו, *His footstool,* i.e., the Temple, has been destroyed, God heeds our prayers at הַר קָדְשׁוֹ, *His holy mountain.* But the millions of Jews who cannot come to the Temple Mount need not fear that their prayers are in vain because God is always merciful and ready to withdraw His anger in the face of sincere prayer. Though Israel may have suffered grievously in the many places of its dispersion, God avenges it and helps those who

עֶזְרָתָה לָּנוּ, וּפְדֵנוּ לְמַעַן חַסְדֶּךָ.[1] אָנֹכִי יהוה אֱלֹהֶיךָ הַמַּעַלְךָ מֵאֶרֶץ מִצְרָיִם, הַרְחֶב פִּיךָ וַאֲמַלְאֵהוּ.[2] אַשְׁרֵי הָעָם שֶׁכָּכָה לּוֹ, אַשְׁרֵי הָעָם שֶׁיהוה אֱלֹהָיו.[3] ❖ וַאֲנִי בְּחַסְדְּךָ בָטַחְתִּי, יָגֵל לִבִּי בִּישׁוּעָתֶךָ, אָשִׁירָה לַיהוה, כִּי גָמַל עָלָי.[4]

תהלים יט

לַמְנַצֵּחַ מִזְמוֹר לְדָוִד. הַשָּׁמַיִם מְסַפְּרִים כְּבוֹד אֵל, וּמַעֲשֵׂה יָדָיו מַגִּיד הָרָקִיעַ.* יוֹם לְיוֹם יַבִּיעַ אֹמֶר,* וְלַיְלָה לְּלַיְלָה יְחַוֶּה דָּעַת. אֵין אֹמֶר וְאֵין דְּבָרִים,* בְּלִי נִשְׁמָע קוֹלָם. בְּכָל הָאָרֶץ יָצָא קַוָּם,* וּבִקְצֵה תֵבֵל מִלֵּיהֶם,* לַשֶּׁמֶשׁ שָׂם אֹהֶל* בָּהֶם. וְהוּא כְּחָתָן יֹצֵא מֵחֻפָּתוֹ, יָשִׂישׂ כְּגִבּוֹר לָרוּץ אֹרַח.* מִקְצֵה הַשָּׁמַיִם מוֹצָאוֹ, וּתְקוּפָתוֹ עַל קְצוֹתָם, וְאֵין נִסְתָּר מֵחַמָּתוֹ. תּוֹרַת יהוה תְּמִימָה, מְשִׁיבַת נָפֶשׁ, עֵדוּת יהוה נֶאֱמָנָה,* מַחְכִּימַת פֶּתִי. פִּקּוּדֵי יהוה יְשָׁרִים, מְשַׂמְּחֵי לֵב,* מִצְוַת יהוה בָּרָה, מְאִירַת עֵינָיִם. יִרְאַת יהוה טְהוֹרָה,* עוֹמֶדֶת לָעַד, מִשְׁפְּטֵי יהוה אֱמֶת, צָדְקוּ יַחְדָּו.* הַנֶּחֱמָדִים מִזָּהָב וּמִפַּז רָב, וּמְתוּקִים מִדְּבַשׁ וְנֹפֶת צוּפִים. גַּם עַבְדְּךָ נִזְהָר בָּהֶם, בְּשָׁמְרָם עֵקֶב רָב. שְׁגִיאוֹת מִי יָבִין,* מִנִּסְתָּרוֹת נַקֵּנִי. גַּם מִזֵּדִים חֲשֹׂךְ עַבְדֶּךָ, אַל יִמְשְׁלוּ בִי,* אָז אֵיתָם, וְנִקֵּיתִי מִפֶּשַׁע רָב. ❖ יִהְיוּ לְרָצוֹן אִמְרֵי פִי, וְהֶגְיוֹן לִבִּי* לְפָנֶיךָ, יהוה צוּרִי וְגֹאֲלִי.

---

call upon Him.

The term God's 'footstool' refers to the place on earth where He rests His glory, as we find in *Isaiah* 66:1: *So says HASHEM, 'The heaven is My throne and the earth is My footstool.'*

⁂ לַמְנַצֵּחַ / Psalm 19

This psalm describes how the wonders of creation are a testimony to the glory of God Who made them. Nature sings to God in the sense that each part of the universe acts as God wanted it to and in harmony with all other parts. Seen this way, the universe is like a symphony orchestra playing a continuous song of praise. But after lyrically recounting the wonders of creation, the Psalmist says that all of this is merely an example of the greatness of the Torah — the blueprint that enables man to understand and fulfill God's will.

הַשָּׁמַיִם . . . הָרָקִיעַ — *The heavens . . . the expanse of the sky.* The upper reaches where the planets and stars orbit are called שָׁמַיִם, *the heavens.* The רָקִיעַ, *expanse of the sky,* contains the atmosphere and evaporated moisture that forms clouds and becomes precipitation *(Malbim).*

יוֹם לְיוֹם יַבִּיעַ אֹמֶר — *Day following day brings expressions [of praise].* The daily renewed works of creation, such as the rising and setting of the sun, stir mankind to speak and express God's praises *(Rashi).*

אֵין אֹמֶר וְאֵין דְּבָרִים — *There is no speech and there are no words.* The heavens do not speak, yet the inner soul of man can discern their message clearly *(Radak).*

קַוָּם — *Their line.* The precision of the universe is likened metaphorically to a surveyor's tape stretched out to the ends of the earth. This means that the precision of the cosmos is evident all over the earth to any observer.

מִלֵּיהֶם — *Their words.* The performance of the heavenly bodies speaks of God's wisdom with greater eloquence than the spoken word *(Radak).*

אֹהֶל — *A tent.* The sky is likened to a tent with the sun affixed in its roof *(Ibn Ezra).*

יָשִׂישׂ כְּגִבּוֹר לָרוּץ אֹרַח — *Rejoicing like a warrior to run the course.* The warrior rejoices at the opportunity to go out to war, for he has confidence in his strength. So too, the sun is confident that it will run its course with no interference *(Metzudos).*

עֵדוּת ה׳ נֶאֱמָנָה — *The testimony of HASHEM is*

assist us, and redeem us by virtue of Your kindness.[1] *I am* HASHEM, *your God, Who raised you from the land of Egypt, open wide your mouth and I will fill it.*[2] *Praiseworthy is the people for whom this is so, praiseworthy is the people whose God is* HASHEM.[3] Chazzan– *As for me, I trust in Your kindness; my heart will rejoice in Your salvation. I will sing to* HASHEM, *for He dealt kindly with me.*[4]

Psalm 19

לַמְנַצֵּחַ *For the Conductor; a song of David. The heavens declare the glory of God, and the expanse of the sky* tells of His handiwork. Day following day brings expressions of praise,* and night following night bespeaks wisdom. There is no speech and there are no words;* their sound is unheard. Their line* goes forth throughout the earth, and their words* reach the farthest ends of the land; He has set up a tent* for the sun in their midst. And it is like a groom coming forth from his bridal chamber, rejoicing like a warrior to run the course.* The end of the heavens is its source, and its circuit is to their other end; nothing is hidden from its heat. The Torah of* HASHEM *is perfect, restoring the soul; the testimony of* HASHEM *is trustworthy,* making the simple one wise. The orders of* HASHEM *are upright, gladdening the heart;* the command of* HASHEM *is clear, enlightening the eyes. The fear of* HASHEM *is pure,* enduring forever; the judgments of* HASHEM *are true, altogether righteous.* They are more desirable than gold, than even much fine gold; sweeter than honey and drippings from the combs. Even Your servant is careful of them, for in observing them there is great reward. Yet, who can discern mistakes?* From unperceived faults cleanse me. Also from intentional sins, restrain Your servant; let them not rule me;* then I shall be perfect and cleansed of great transgression.* Chazzan– *May the expressions of my mouth and the thoughts of my heart* find favor before You,* HASHEM, *my Rock and my Redeemer.*

(1) *Psalms* 44:27. (2) 81:11. (3) 144:15. (4) 13:6.

trustworthy. The *mitzvos* of the Torah are called *testimony,* because they attest to the *faith* of the people who fulfill them *(Metzudos).*

מְשַׂמְּחֵי לֵב — *Gladdening the heart.* The wise man will rejoice when his intellect will dominate the passions of his body *(Radak).*

יִרְאַת ה׳ טְהוֹרָה — *The fear of* HASHEM *is pure.* This refers to the negative commandments. The person who is careful not to transgress them is pure, for he has not sullied himself with sin *(Ibn Ezra).*

צָדְקוּ יַחְדָּו — *Altogether righteous.* There is no contradiction between one law of the Torah and another, whereas in civil law one will very often find inconsistencies and conflicts between different statutes *(Ibn Ezra).*

שְׁגִיאוֹת מִי יָבִין — *Yet, who can discern mistakes?* Though I try to keep Your commands, who can be so careful that he never errs unintentionally? *(Rashi; Radak).* שְׁגִיאָה, *mistake,* denotes an error due to imperfect understanding and reasoning from which no man is immune and of which he is unaware. Only Divine assistance can protect a person from these inborn human flaws *(R' Hirsch).*

אַל יִמְשְׁלוּ בִי — *Let them not rule me.* Do not let my evil inclination overpower me. For, God helps those whose hearts yearn to do what is right and proper [cf. *Yoma* 38b].

וְהֶגְיוֹן לִבִּי — *And the thoughts of my heart.* Please do not limit Your attention to the requests which I express orally. Be aware of the many inner thoughts that I am incapable of expressing *(Radak).*

תהלים לד

לְדָוִד, בְּשַׁנּוֹתוֹ אֶת טַעְמוֹ לִפְנֵי אֲבִימֶלֶךְ, וַיְגָרְשֵׁהוּ וַיֵּלַךְ.
אֲבָרְכָה* אֶת יהוה בְּכָל עֵת, תָּמִיד תְּהִלָּתוֹ בְּפִי.
בַּיהוה תִּתְהַלֵּל נַפְשִׁי, יִשְׁמְעוּ עֲנָוִים וְיִשְׂמָחוּ.
גַּדְּלוּ לַיהוה אִתִּי,* וּנְרוֹמְמָה שְׁמוֹ יַחְדָּו.
דָּרַשְׁתִּי אֶת יהוה וְעָנָנִי, וּמִכָּל מְגוּרוֹתַי הִצִּילָנִי.
הִבִּיטוּ אֵלָיו וְנָהָרוּ,
וּפְנֵיהֶם אַל יֶחְפָּרוּ.
זֶה עָנִי* קָרָא וַיהוה שָׁמֵעַ,* וּמִכָּל צָרוֹתָיו הוֹשִׁיעוֹ.
חֹנֶה מַלְאַךְ יהוה סָבִיב לִירֵאָיו, וַיְחַלְּצֵם.
טַעֲמוּ וּרְאוּ* כִּי טוֹב יהוה, אַשְׁרֵי הַגֶּבֶר יֶחֱסֶה בּוֹ.
יְראוּ אֶת יהוה קְדֹשָׁיו,* כִּי אֵין מַחְסוֹר לִירֵאָיו.
כְּפִירִים רָשׁוּ* וְרָעֵבוּ, וְדֹרְשֵׁי יהוה לֹא יַחְסְרוּ כָל טוֹב.*
לְכוּ בָנִים* שִׁמְעוּ לִי, יִרְאַת יהוה אֲלַמֶּדְכֶם.
מִי הָאִישׁ הֶחָפֵץ חַיִּים,* אֹהֵב יָמִים לִרְאוֹת טוֹב.
נְצֹר לְשׁוֹנְךָ מֵרָע, וּשְׂפָתֶיךָ מִדַּבֵּר מִרְמָה.*
סוּר מֵרָע וַעֲשֵׂה טוֹב, בַּקֵּשׁ שָׁלוֹם וְרָדְפֵהוּ.
עֵינֵי יהוה אֶל צַדִּיקִים, וְאָזְנָיו אֶל שַׁוְעָתָם.
פְּנֵי יהוה בְּעֹשֵׂי רָע, לְהַכְרִית מֵאֶרֶץ זִכְרָם.

⧼ לְדָוִד בְּשַׁנּוֹתוֹ / Psalm 34

Everything in creation has its place. The previous psalm spoke of the loftiest physical and spiritual forces in creation and how they sing to God. Here we see how His greatness can be perceived even in the most painful depths. David once said to God, 'All that You created is beautiful, and wisdom is the most beautiful of all. However, I fail to understand or to appreciate the value of madness. What satisfaction can You derive from having created a lunatic who walks about ripping his clothing, is chased by little children and is mocked by all?'

God replied, 'David, you will some day need this madness which you now criticize. Furthermore, you will even pray that I give this madness to you.'

A short time later, David was forced to flee for his life from King Saul. Only among the Philistines, Israel's sworn enemies, did he find safety. But even there he was recognized as Israel's greatest warrior and threatened with death. He pretended to be insane and King Abimelech — disgusted by David's lunatic behavior — drove him out. [See *I Samuel* 21:11-16.] Instead of feeling despair, David composed this beautiful and profound hymn. Its verses begin according to the letters of the *Aleph-Beis,* to show that we are to praise God with our every faculty, and to acknowledge that whatever He created — from *aleph* to *tav* — is for the good.

אֲבָרְכָה — *I shall bless.* David's frightening experiences and his miraculous escape inspired him to understand that God's ways are merciful. Hence, he responds with a blessing *(Sforno).*

גַּדְּלוּ לַה׳ אִתִּי — *Declare the greatness of* HASHEM *with me.* Not content merely to have been saved, he wants his salvation to be a lesson to others. Let everyone declare God's greatness.

זֶה עָנִי — *This poor man.* In his humility, David looks upon himself as poor and undeserving *(Radak).*

וַה׳ שָׁמֵעַ — *And* HASHEM *hears.* He hears and responds even before the supplicant has completed his prayer *(R' Chaim Vital).*

טַעֲמוּ וּרְאוּ — *Contemplate and see. Contemplate* intellectually, by analyzing events, and *see,* by noticing God's deeds — and you will realize *that* HASHEM *is good (Radak).*

Psalm 34

לְדָוִד *Of David: When he disguised his sanity before Abimelech who drove him out and he left.*

א *I shall bless* HASHEM at all times,*
always shall His praise be in my mouth.
ב *In HASHEM does my soul glory,*
may humble ones hear and be glad.
ג *Declare the greatness of HASHEM with me,**
and let us exalt His Name together.
ד *I sought out HASHEM and He answered me,*
and from all my terror He delivered me.
ה *They look to Him and become radiant,*
ו *and their faces were not shamed.*
ז *This poor man* calls and HASHEM hears* —*
and from all his troubles He saved him.
ח *The angel of HASHEM encamps around His reverent ones*
and releases them.
ט *Contemplate and see* that HASHEM is good —*
praiseworthy is the man who takes refuge in Him.
י *Fear HASHEM, you — His holy ones* —*
for there is no deprivation for His reverent ones.
כ *Young lions may want* and hunger,*
*but those who seek HASHEM will not lack any good.**
ל *Go, O sons,* heed me,*
the fear of HASHEM will I teach you.
מ *Which man desires life,**
who loves days of seeing good?
נ *Guard your tongue from evil,*
*and your lips from speaking deceit.**
ס *Turn from evil and do good,*
seek peace and pursue it.
ע *The eyes of HASHEM are toward the righteous,*
and His ears to their cry.
פ *The face of HASHEM is against evildoers,*
to cut off their memory from earth.

קְדֹשָׁיו — *His holy ones.* Holy people are those who control their lusts, even the permitted ones *(Ramban).*

כְּפִירִים רָשׁוּ — *Young lions may want.* Strong, vigorous people — like lions in the prime of life — become helpless and destitute, but God will provide for those who trust in Him.

לֹא יַחְסְרוּ כָל טוֹב — *Will not lack any good.* They may not have all the luxuries enjoyed by their neighbors, but they feel no lack of anything because they are content with their lot *(Sh'lah).*

לְכוּ בָנִים — *Go, O sons.* In this sense, go is an exhortation to accomplish a goal *(Radak).*

מִי הָאִישׁ הֶחָפֵץ חַיִּים — *Which man desires life,* i.e., in the World to Come *(Sforno).* In another vein, however, the Psalmist urged people to better their lives in This World by avoiding gossip and slander. David was the victim of constant slander and his generation suffered defeats in battle because they were not careful in their speech [*Yerushalmi Peah* 1:1] *(R' A. Ch. Feuer).*

The *Baal Shem Tov* taught that every person is allotted a given number of words during his life. When he has used up his quota, he dies. Thus, by guarding his tongue, one assures himself of greater longevity.

מֵרָע . . . מִרְמָה — *From evil . . . deceit,* i.e., slander, false testimony, and cursing. *Deceit* refers to

צָעֲקוּ וַיהוה שָׁמֵעַ, וּמִכָּל צָרוֹתָם הִצִּילָם.
קָרוֹב יהוה לְנִשְׁבְּרֵי לֵב, וְאֶת דַּכְּאֵי רוּחַ יוֹשִׁיעַ.
רַבּוֹת רָעוֹת צַדִּיק,* וּמִכֻּלָּם יַצִּילֶנּוּ יהוה.
שֹׁמֵר כָּל עַצְמוֹתָיו, אַחַת מֵהֵנָּה לֹא נִשְׁבָּרָה.
תְּמוֹתֵת רָשָׁע רָעָה,* וְשֹׂנְאֵי צַדִּיק יֶאְשָׁמוּ.
❖ פּוֹדֶה יהוה נֶפֶשׁ עֲבָדָיו, וְלֹא יֶאְשְׁמוּ כָּל הַחֹסִים בּוֹ.

תהלים צ

תְּפִלָּה לְמֹשֶׁה אִישׁ הָאֱלֹהִים,* אֲדֹנָי מָעוֹן אַתָּה הָיִיתָ לָּנוּ בְּדֹר וָדֹר. בְּטֶרֶם הָרִים יֻלָּדוּ וַתְּחוֹלֵל אֶרֶץ וְתֵבֵל, וּמֵעוֹלָם עַד עוֹלָם אַתָּה אֵל. תָּשֵׁב אֱנוֹשׁ* עַד דַּכָּא, וַתֹּאמֶר שׁוּבוּ* בְנֵי אָדָם. כִּי אֶלֶף שָׁנִים בְּעֵינֶיךָ כְּיוֹם אֶתְמוֹל כִּי יַעֲבֹר, וְאַשְׁמוּרָה בַלָּיְלָה. זְרַמְתָּם, שֵׁנָה יִהְיוּ,* בַּבֹּקֶר כֶּחָצִיר יַחֲלֹף. בַּבֹּקֶר יָצִיץ וְחָלָף, לָעֶרֶב יְמוֹלֵל וְיָבֵשׁ. כִּי כָלִינוּ בְאַפֶּךָ, וּבַחֲמָתְךָ נִבְהָלְנוּ. שַׁתָּ עֲוֹנֹתֵינוּ לְנֶגְדֶּךָ,* עֲלֻמֵנוּ לִמְאוֹר פָּנֶיךָ. כִּי כָל יָמֵינוּ פָּנוּ* בְעֶבְרָתֶךָ, כִּלִּינוּ שָׁנֵינוּ כְמוֹ הֶגֶה. יְמֵי שְׁנוֹתֵינוּ בָהֶם* שִׁבְעִים שָׁנָה, וְאִם בִּגְבוּרֹת שְׁמוֹנִים* שָׁנָה, וְרָהְבָּם עָמָל וָאָוֶן, כִּי גָז חִישׁ וַנָּעֻפָה.* מִי יוֹדֵעַ עֹז אַפֶּךָ,* וּכְיִרְאָתְךָ עֶבְרָתֶךָ. לִמְנוֹת יָמֵינוּ* כֵּן הוֹדַע, וְנָבִא לְבַב חָכְמָה. שׁוּבָה יהוה עַד מָתָי,* וְהִנָּחֵם עַל עֲבָדֶיךָ. שַׂבְּעֵנוּ בַבֹּקֶר חַסְדֶּךָ, וּנְרַנְּנָה וְנִשְׂמְחָה בְּכָל יָמֵינוּ. שַׂמְּחֵנוּ כִּימוֹת עִנִּיתָנוּ,* שְׁנוֹת רָאִינוּ רָעָה. יֵרָאֶה אֶל עֲבָדֶיךָ פָעֳלֶךָ, וַהֲדָרְךָ

---

insincere friendship that masks evil designs *(Radak)*. It also includes exaggerated praise that lays the groundwork for discussing vices. 'He is a wonderful person, *but . . .*' *(Chazeh Zion)*.

רַבּוֹת רָעוֹת צַדִּיק — *Many are the mishaps of the righteous.* Greatness is a product of challenges, brave attempts, and many mistakes. No one becomes truly *righteous* without his share of *mishaps (Sfas Emes)*.

תְּמוֹתֵת רָשָׁע רָעָה — *The death blow of the wicked is evil.* Wicked people will be destroyed by the very evil they set in motion *(Radak; Rashi)*.

תְּפִלָּה לְמֹשֶׁה / Psalm 90

In composing *Psalms*, David drew upon the works of ten psalmists — including Moses — in addition to his own *(Bava Basra* 14b). According to *Radak*, David found an ancient scroll written by Moses. It contained eleven psalms (90-100), which David adapted for incorporation in the Book of *Psalms*. The Talmud *(Nedarim* 39b) teaches that repentance was a prerequisite to creation, for man is the centerpoint of the universe, and unless he can free himself of sin, he will neither fulfill his purpose nor survive. Therefore, this psalm is appended to those that recall the Sabbath, the day dedicated as the memorial of creation.

אִישׁ הָאֱלֹהִים — *The man of God.* Though Moses was a flesh-and-blood man, he elevated himself to the level of a Godly being *(Devarim Rabbah* 11:4).

תָּשֵׁב אֱנוֹשׁ — *You reduce* [lit., *return*] *man.* God crushes the pride of arrogant people *(Rashi)*.

וַתֹּאמֶר שׁוּבוּ — *And You say, 'Repent.'* By showing vulnerable man that he is powerless, God 'tells' him to *repent*.

זְרַמְתָּם שֵׁנָה יִהְיוּ — *You flood them away, they become sleeplike.* The Psalmist continues to describe man's transitory nature. His life is like a dream that vanishes without a trace *(Radak)*.

שַׁתָּ עֲוֹנֹתֵינוּ לְנֶגְדֶּךָ — *You have set our iniquities before Yourself.* Man may forget his sins, but God's memory is eternal *(Radak)*.

יָמֵינוּ פָּנוּ — *Our days passed by.* Because we

צ *They cried out and HASHEM heeds,*
and from all their troubles He rescues them.
ק *HASHEM is close to the brokenhearted;*
and those crushed in spirit, He saves.
ר *Many are the mishaps of the righteous,**
but from them all HASHEM rescues him.
ש *He guards all his bones,*
even one of them was not broken.
ת *The death blow of the wicked is evil,**
and the haters of the righteous will be condemned.
Chazzan– *HASHEM redeems the soul of His servants,*
and all those who take refuge in Him will not be condemned.

Psalm 90

תְּפִלָּה *A prayer by Moses, the man of God:* My Lord, an abode have You been for us in all generations; before the mountains were born and You had not yet fashioned the earth and the inhabited land, and from This World to the World to Come You are God. You reduce man* to pulp and You say, 'Repent,* O sons of man.' For a thousand years in Your eyes are but a bygone yesterday, and like a watch in the night. You flood them away, they become sleeplike,* by morning they are like grass that withers. In the morning it blossoms and is rejuvenated, by evening it is cut down and brittle. For we are consumed by Your fury; and we are confounded by Your wrath. You have set our iniquities before Yourself,* our immaturity before the light of Your countenance. For all our days passed by* because of Your anger, we consumed our years like a fleeting thought. The days of our years among them* are seventy years, and if with strength, eighty* years; their proudest success is but toil and pain, for it is cut off swiftly and we fly away.* Who knows the power of Your fury?* As You are feared, so is Your anger. According to the count of our days,* so may You teach us; then we shall acquire a heart of wisdom. Return, HASHEM, how long?* Relent concerning Your servants. Satisfy us in the morning with Your kindness, then we shall sing out and rejoice throughout our days. Gladden us according to the days You afflicted us,* the years when we saw evil. May Your works be visible to Your servants, and Your majesty*

---

incurred God's wrath, our days passed by unproductively *(Rashi).*

יְמֵי שְׁנוֹתֵינוּ בָהֶם — *The days of our years among them.* Our time on earth surrounded by the sins and immaturity mentioned above consists of seventy years, on average *(Rashi).*

שִׁבְעִים ... שְׁמוֹנִים — *Seventy ... eighty.* Although Moses, who composed this psalm, lived to one hundred twenty years, this verse speaks of average people *(Radak);* or it was inserted by David [who lived seventy years], since life spans were shorter in his time *(Tosafos).*

כִּי גָז חִישׁ וַנָּעֻפָה — *For it is cut off swiftly and we fly away.* Man's success is fleeting. When our souls fly away, life and accomplishment go with it.

מִי יוֹדֵעַ עֹז אַפֶּךָ — *Who knows the power of Your fury?* Once God's wrath is unleashed, who can guard against it? *(Radak).*

לִמְנוֹת יָמֵינוּ — *According to the count of our days.* Since our lives are so short, make the truth known to us so that we may comprehend it *(Sforno).*

שׁוּבָה ה׳ עַד מָתָי — *Return, HASHEM, how long?* Come back to us — how long will You abandon us? *(Radak).*

שַׂמְּחֵנוּ כִּימוֹת עִנִּיתָנוּ — *Gladden us according to*

עַל בְּנֵיהֶם. ❖ וִיהִי נֹעַם* אֲדֹנָי אֱלֹהֵינוּ עָלֵינוּ, וּמַעֲשֵׂה יָדֵינוּ כּוֹנְנָה עָלֵינוּ, וּמַעֲשֵׂה יָדֵינוּ* כּוֹנְנֵהוּ.

תהלים צא

יֹשֵׁב בְּסֵתֶר עֶלְיוֹן,* בְּצֵל שַׁדַּי יִתְלוֹנָן. אֹמַר לַיהוה מַחְסִי וּמְצוּדָתִי, אֱלֹהַי אֶבְטַח בּוֹ. כִּי הוּא יַצִּילְךָ מִפַּח יָקוּשׁ, מִדֶּבֶר הַוּוֹת. בְּאֶבְרָתוֹ יָסֶךְ לָךְ, וְתַחַת כְּנָפָיו תֶּחְסֶה, צִנָּה וְסֹחֵרָה אֲמִתּוֹ. לֹא תִירָא מִפַּחַד לָיְלָה,* מֵחֵץ יָעוּף יוֹמָם. מִדֶּבֶר בָּאֹפֶל יַהֲלֹךְ, מִקֶּטֶב יָשׁוּד צָהֳרָיִם. יִפֹּל מִצִּדְּךָ אֶלֶף, וּרְבָבָה מִימִינֶךָ,* אֵלֶיךָ לֹא יִגָּשׁ. רַק בְּעֵינֶיךָ תַבִּיט, וְשִׁלֻּמַת רְשָׁעִים תִּרְאֶה. כִּי אַתָּה יהוה מַחְסִי, עֶלְיוֹן שַׂמְתָּ מְעוֹנֶךָ. לֹא תְאֻנֶּה אֵלֶיךָ רָעָה, וְנֶגַע לֹא יִקְרַב בְּאָהֳלֶךָ.* כִּי מַלְאָכָיו יְצַוֶּה לָּךְ, לִשְׁמָרְךָ בְּכָל דְּרָכֶיךָ. עַל כַּפַּיִם יִשָּׂאוּנְךָ,* פֶּן תִּגֹּף בָּאֶבֶן רַגְלֶךָ. עַל שַׁחַל וָפֶתֶן* תִּדְרֹךְ, תִּרְמֹס כְּפִיר וְתַנִּין. כִּי בִי חָשַׁק* וַאֲפַלְּטֵהוּ, אֲשַׂגְּבֵהוּ כִּי יָדַע שְׁמִי. יִקְרָאֵנִי וְאֶעֱנֵהוּ, עִמּוֹ אָנֹכִי בְצָרָה, אֲחַלְּצֵהוּ וַאֲכַבְּדֵהוּ. ❖ אֹרֶךְ יָמִים אַשְׂבִּיעֵהוּ, וְאַרְאֵהוּ בִּישׁוּעָתִי.* אֹרֶךְ יָמִים אַשְׂבִּיעֵהוּ, וְאַרְאֵהוּ בִּישׁוּעָתִי.

תהלים קלה

הַלְלוּיָהּ הַלְלוּ אֶת שֵׁם יהוה, הַלְלוּ עַבְדֵי יהוה.* שֶׁעֹמְדִים בְּבֵית יהוה,* בְּחַצְרוֹת בֵּית אֱלֹהֵינוּ. הַלְלוּיָהּ כִּי טוֹב

---

the days You afflicted us. May our joy in the future be equal in intensity to our past suffering.

וִיהִי נֹעַם — *May the pleasantness.* When the Tabernacle was built, Moses uttered this prayer that it might endure and be blessed by God *(Midrash).* The term נֹעַם, *pleasantness,* refers to the bliss one feels when he has done something that achieved its purpose. When man has this feeling of accomplishment, God, too, feels satisfaction that His will has been done *(Malbim).*

וּמַעֲשֵׂה יָדֵינוּ — *Our handiwork.* Moses repeated the prayer for the success of *our handiwork,* once referring to the newly built Tabernacle and once referring to man's general activities *(Rashi).* This is a plea that we be independent of human pressures that interfere with our service of God *(R' Hirsch).*

⊱ יֹשֵׁב בְּסֵתֶר / Psalm 91

Moses continues his theme that man achieves fulfillment only through closeness to God. Moreover, God will rescue him from all danger. The Talmud *(Shavuos* 15b) calls this hymn *Song of Plagues,* [שִׁיר שֶׁל פְּגָעִים אוֹ שֶׁל נְגָעִים] because one who recites it with faith in God will be helped by Him in time of danger. In this psalm, Moses speaks of the faithful believer who finds refuge in *the shadow of the Almighty.* This is the true hero whom God promises long life and salvation.

According to the Midrash, Moses composed this work on the day he completed construction of the מִשְׁכָּן *[Mishkan], Tabernacle,* and these verses describe Moses himself, who entered the Divine clouds and was enveloped *in the shadow of the Almighty.* At that moment, a great question arose: How could a Tabernacle with walls and curtains contain the Presence of the Almighty? The Master of the Universe Himself explained, 'The entire world cannot contain My glory, yet when I wish, I can concentrate My entire essence into one small spot. Indeed, I am Most High, yet I sit in a [limited, constricted] refuge — in the shadow of the Tabernacle.' God's intention in removing the nation from the Egyptian slavery was, *'You shall serve God upon this mountain' (Exodus* 3:12). And it was to this service that the *Mishkan* was dedicated.

יֹשֵׁב בְּסֵתֶר עֶלְיוֹן — *Whoever sits in the refuge of the Most High.* The person who scorns conventional forms of protection and seeks only the refuge provided by the Most High will find his faith rewarded. He will be enveloped by God's

upon their children. Chazzan– *May the pleasantness* of my Lord, our God, be upon us — our handiwork, may He establish for us; our handiwork,* may He establish.*

Psalm 91

יֹשֵׁב *Whoever sits in the refuge of the Most High,* he shall dwell in the shadow of the Almighty. I will say of* HASHEM, *'He is my refuge and my fortress, my God, I will trust in Him.' For He will deliver you from the ensnaring trap, from devastating pestilence. With His pinion He will cover you, and beneath His wings you will be protected; shield and armor is His truth. You shall not fear the terror of night;* nor of the arrow that flies by day; nor the pestilence that walks in gloom; nor the destroyer who lays waste at noon. Let a thousand encamp at your side and a myriad at your right hand,* but to you they shall not approach. You will merely peer with your eyes and you will see the retribution of the wicked. Because [you said] 'You,* HASHEM, *are my refuge,' you have made the Most High your dwelling place. No evil will befall you, nor will any plague come near your tent.* He will charge His angels for you, to protect you in all your ways. On your palms they will carry you,* lest you strike your foot against a stone. Upon the lion and the viper* you will tread; you will trample the young lion and the serpent. For he has yearned for Me* and I will deliver him; I will elevate him because he knows My Name. He will call upon Me and I will answer him, I am with him in distress, I will release him and I will honor him.* Chazzan– *With long life will I satisfy him, and I will show him My salvation.* With long life will I satisfy him, and I will show him My salvation.*

Psalm 135

הַלְלוּיָהּ *Halleluyah! Praise the Name of* HASHEM*! Praise — you servants of* HASHEM*;* you who stand in the House of* HASHEM*,* in the courtyards of the House of our God — praise God, for*

---

providence so that he can continue to seek holiness and wisdom without fear of those who would seek to do him harm: *He shall dwell in the shadow of the Almighty (Rashi).*

לֹא תִירָא מִפַּחַד לָיְלָה — *You shall not fear the terror of night.* If you put your faith in God, fear will be banished from your heart *(Rashi).*

יִפֹּל מִצִּדְּךָ אֶלֶף וּרְבָבָה מִימִינֶךָ — *Let a thousand encamp at your side and a myriad at your right hand.* Thousands and myriads of demons may encamp around the man who is shielded by God's truth, but they will not be able to come near to harm him *(Rashi).*

וְנֶגַע לֹא יִקְרַב בְּאָהֳלֶךָ — *Nor will any plague come near your tent.* The Talmud *(Sanhedrin* 103a) perceives this as a blessing for domestic tranquillity and that one will have worthy children and students, who will not shame him.

עַל כַּפַּיִם יִשָּׂאוּנְךָ — *On [your] palms they will carry you.* The angels created by the *mitzvos* you perform with your *palms* [i.e., charity and other acts of kindness] will raise you above all dangers that lurk in your path *(Zera Yaakov).*

עַל שַׁחַל וָפֶתֶן — *Upon the lion and the viper.* Even when confronted by ferocious beasts and poisonous reptiles, you will simply tread on them and remain unharmed.

כִּי בִי חָשַׁק — *For he has yearned for Me.* From here to the end of the psalm, God praises and assures the person who has faith in Him.

וְאַרְאֵהוּ בִּישׁוּעָתִי — *And I will show him My salvation.* He will witness the salvation I will bring about at the advent of the Messiah, at the time of the revival of the dead, and at the salvation of the World to Come *(Radak).*

Indeed, it is not God who needs salvation, but Israel; yet God calls Israel's victory, 'My salvation,' to emphasize that Israel's salvation is His as well *(Midrash Shocher Tov).*

⸎ הַלְלוּיָהּ / Psalm 135

The Exodus from Egypt complements the Sabbath. While the Sabbath testifies that God created the universe, the miracles of the Exodus testify that He continues to supervise and guide history. This psalm recounts the miracles of the Exodus and Israel's trek through the Wilderness

יהוה, זַמְּרוּ לִשְׁמוֹ כִּי נָעִים. כִּי יַעֲקֹב בָּחַר לוֹ יָהּ, יִשְׂרָאֵל* לִסְגֻלָּתוֹ. כִּי אֲנִי יָדַעְתִּי כִּי גָדוֹל יהוה, וַאֲדֹנֵינוּ מִכָּל אֱלֹהִים. כֹּל אֲשֶׁר חָפֵץ יהוה עָשָׂה, בַּשָּׁמַיִם וּבָאָרֶץ, בַּיַּמִּים וְכָל תְּהֹמוֹת. מַעֲלֶה נְשִׂאִים מִקְצֵה הָאָרֶץ, בְּרָקִים לַמָּטָר עָשָׂה, מוֹצֵא רוּחַ מֵאוֹצְרוֹתָיו. שֶׁהִכָּה בְּכוֹרֵי מִצְרָיִם, מֵאָדָם עַד בְּהֵמָה. שָׁלַח אוֹתֹת וּמֹפְתִים בְּתוֹכֵכִי מִצְרָיִם, בְּפַרְעֹה וּבְכָל עֲבָדָיו. שֶׁהִכָּה גּוֹיִם רַבִּים, וְהָרַג מְלָכִים עֲצוּמִים. לְסִיחוֹן מֶלֶךְ הָאֱמֹרִי, וּלְעוֹג* מֶלֶךְ הַבָּשָׁן, וּלְכֹל מַמְלְכוֹת כְּנָעַן. וְנָתַן אַרְצָם נַחֲלָה, נַחֲלָה לְיִשְׂרָאֵל עַמּוֹ. יהוה שִׁמְךָ לְעוֹלָם,* יהוה זִכְרְךָ לְדֹר וָדֹר. כִּי יָדִין יהוה* עַמּוֹ, וְעַל עֲבָדָיו יִתְנֶחָם. עֲצַבֵּי הַגּוֹיִם כֶּסֶף וְזָהָב, מַעֲשֵׂה יְדֵי אָדָם. פֶּה לָהֶם וְלֹא יְדַבֵּרוּ,* עֵינַיִם לָהֶם וְלֹא יִרְאוּ. אָזְנַיִם לָהֶם וְלֹא יַאֲזִינוּ, אַף אֵין יֶשׁ רוּחַ בְּפִיהֶם. כְּמוֹהֶם יִהְיוּ עֹשֵׂיהֶם,* כֹּל אֲשֶׁר בֹּטֵחַ בָּהֶם. ❖ בֵּית יִשְׂרָאֵל בָּרְכוּ אֶת יהוה, בֵּית אַהֲרֹן בָּרְכוּ אֶת יהוה. בֵּית הַלֵּוִי* בָּרְכוּ אֶת יהוה, יִרְאֵי יהוה בָּרְכוּ אֶת יהוה. בָּרוּךְ יהוה מִצִּיּוֹן* שֹׁכֵן יְרוּשָׁלָיִם, הַלְלוּיָהּ.

Most congregations recite the following psalm while standing.

תהלים קלו

הוֹדוּ לַיהוה כִּי טוֹב,* כִּי לְעוֹלָם חַסְדּוֹ.*
הוֹדוּ לֵאלֹהֵי הָאֱלֹהִים,* כִּי לְעוֹלָם חַסְדּוֹ.
הוֹדוּ לַאֲדֹנֵי הָאֲדֹנִים,* כִּי לְעוֹלָם חַסְדּוֹ.

---

to *Eretz Yisrael*. It ends with the conclusion that it is worthless to worship anything except HASHEM.

הַלְלוּ עַבְדֵי ה׳ — *Praise — you servants of HASHEM.* You are free from the bonds of Pharaoh or any other human ruler — you owe allegiance only to God *(Sforno).*

שֶׁעֹמְדִים בְּבֵית ה׳ — *You who stand in the House of HASHEM.* The prime responsibility to lead Israel in God's praise falls upon the scholars and teachers in the synagogues and study halls *(Sforno).*

יַעֲקֹב . . . יִשְׂרָאֵל — *Jacob . . . Israel.* 'Jacob' represents the multitude of Jews while 'Israel' represents the great people among them. God chooses even ordinary Jews for His Own, but 'Israel' is His *treasure (Siach Yitzchak).*

לְסִיחוֹן . . . וּלְעוֹג — *Sichon . . . Og.* Upon coming to the part of *Eretz Yisrael* that lay east of the Jordan, the Jewish people encountered and defeated these two kings [*Numbers* 21:21-35]. Thus, they are symbolic of all the rulers whom Israel defeated. Also, they are singled out because of their unusual might *(Radak).*

ה׳ שִׁמְךָ לְעוֹלָם — *HASHEM is Your Name forever.* This Name symbolizes God's eternity. Just as He controlled history in the past, He continues to do so always *(Rashi).*

כִּי יָדִין ה׳ — *When HASHEM will judge.* Eventually, God will consider the plight of oppressed Israel, and then He will show mercy to His people.

פֶּה לָהֶם וְלֹא יְדַבֵּרוּ — *They have mouths, but they speak not.* Intelligent speech is man's greatest distinction, yet idolaters are foolish enough to worship mute idols! *(Ibn Ezra).*

כְּמוֹהֶם יִהְיוּ עֹשֵׂיהֶם — *Like them shall their makers become.* This can be taken as a prayer, or as a statement of fact that eventually idol worshipers will perish and be as lifeless as the clods they worship *(Radak).*

בֵּית יִשְׂרָאֵל . . . בֵּית אַהֲרֹן . . . בֵּית הַלֵּוִי — *House of*

HASHEM is good. Sing to His Name, for It is pleasant. For God selected Jacob for His own, Israel as His treasure. For I know that HASHEM is greater — our Lord — than all heavenly powers. Whatever HASHEM wished, He did, in heaven and on earth; in the seas and all the depths. He raises clouds from the end of the earth; He made lightning bolts for the rain; He brings forth wind from His treasuries. It was He who smote the firstborn of Egypt, from man to beast. He sent signs and wonders into your midst, O Egypt, upon Pharaoh and upon all of his servants. It was He who smote many nations, and slew mighty kings — Sichon, King of the Emorites, Og,* King of Bashan, and all the kingdoms of Canaan — and presented their land as a heritage, a heritage for Israel, His people. HASHEM is Your Name forever,* HASHEM is Your memorial throughout the generations. When HASHEM will judge* His people, He will relent concerning His servants. The idols of the nations are silver and gold, human handiwork. They have mouths, but they speak not;* they have eyes, but they see not; they have ears, but they heed not; neither is there any breath in their mouths. Like them shall their makers become,* everyone who trusts in them.* Chazzan– *O House of Israel, bless HASHEM; O House of Aaron, bless HASHEM. O House of Levi,* bless HASHEM; O those who fear HASHEM, bless HASHEM. Blessed is HASHEM from Zion,* He Who dwells in Jerusalem. Halleluyah!*

Most congregations recite the following psalm while standing.

Psalm 136

הודו *Give thanks to HASHEM for He is good,**
*for His kindness endures forever.**
*Give thanks to the God of the heavenly powers,**
for His kindness endures forever.
*Give thanks to the Lord of the lords,**
for His kindness endures forever.

Israel ... House of Aaron ... House of Levi. First comes the general call to all Jews, then the *Kohanim* [House of Aaron], who are privileged to perform the Temple service; the Levites, who sing and play the Temple songs; and finally the righteous people *who fear HASHEM.*

בָּרוּךְ ה׳ מִצִּיּוֹן — *Blessed is HASHEM from Zion.* May the end of the exile come soon — when we will be able to bless God from Zion, His holy mountain *(Sforno).*

◆§ הודו לה׳ / Psalm 136

The Talmud *(Pesachim* 118a) calls this psalm הַלֵּל הַגָּדוֹל, *the Great Song of Praise,* because it lauds God for giving sustenance to every living being. Thus, although it speaks of a multitude of mighty miracles, including the Creation of the universe and the Exodus from Egypt, the psalm concludes by saying נֹתֵן לֶחֶם לְכָל בָּשָׂר, *He gives nourishment* [lit., *bread*] *to all flesh,* because God's mercy upon every creature is equal to all the 'great' miracles. The twenty-six verses of the psalm are another allusion to God's mercy, for all twenty-six generations before the Torah was given, God provided for all living things out of His mercy. Once the Torah was given, man can *earn* his keep by performing the commandments.

כִּי טוֹב — *For He is good.* An aspect of His goodness is that He punishes man for his sins each according to his own level of prosperity. The rich man may lose an expensive bull while the pauper will be deprived of a crust of bread *(Pesachim* 118a).

כִּי לְעוֹלָם חַסְדּוֹ — *For His kindness endures forever.* Homiletically, this can be rendered: His kindness is for the *world.* Man's kindnesses can be prompted by selfish motives, but God acts for the sake of the *world,* not Himself *(Alshich).*

הָאֱלֹהִים — *The heavenly powers,* i.e., the angels *(Radak).*

הָאֲדֹנִים — *The lords,* i.e., the heavenly bodies *(Radak).*

לְעֹשֵׂה נִפְלָאוֹת גְּדֹלוֹת לְבַדּוֹ, כִּי לְעוֹלָם חַסְדּוֹ.
לְעֹשֵׂה הַשָּׁמַיִם בִּתְבוּנָה,* כִּי לְעוֹלָם חַסְדּוֹ.
לְרוֹקַע הָאָרֶץ עַל הַמָּיִם, כִּי לְעוֹלָם חַסְדּוֹ.
לְעֹשֵׂה אוֹרִים גְּדֹלִים, כִּי לְעוֹלָם חַסְדּוֹ.
אֶת הַשֶּׁמֶשׁ לְמֶמְשֶׁלֶת בַּיּוֹם, כִּי לְעוֹלָם חַסְדּוֹ.
אֶת הַיָּרֵחַ וְכוֹכָבִים לְמֶמְשְׁלוֹת בַּלָּיְלָה, כִּי לְעוֹלָם חַסְדּוֹ.
לְמַכֵּה מִצְרַיִם בִּבְכוֹרֵיהֶם,* כִּי לְעוֹלָם חַסְדּוֹ.
וַיּוֹצֵא יִשְׂרָאֵל מִתּוֹכָם, כִּי לְעוֹלָם חַסְדּוֹ.
בְּיָד חֲזָקָה וּבִזְרוֹעַ נְטוּיָה, כִּי לְעוֹלָם חַסְדּוֹ.
לְגֹזֵר יַם סוּף לִגְזָרִים,* כִּי לְעוֹלָם חַסְדּוֹ.
וְהֶעֱבִיר יִשְׂרָאֵל בְּתוֹכוֹ, כִּי לְעוֹלָם חַסְדּוֹ.
וְנִעֵר פַּרְעֹה וְחֵילוֹ בְיַם סוּף, כִּי לְעוֹלָם חַסְדּוֹ.
לְמוֹלִיךְ עַמּוֹ בַּמִּדְבָּר, כִּי לְעוֹלָם חַסְדּוֹ.
לְמַכֵּה מְלָכִים גְּדֹלִים,* כִּי לְעוֹלָם חַסְדּוֹ.
וַיַּהֲרֹג מְלָכִים אַדִּירִים,* כִּי לְעוֹלָם חַסְדּוֹ.
לְסִיחוֹן מֶלֶךְ הָאֱמֹרִי, כִּי לְעוֹלָם חַסְדּוֹ.
וּלְעוֹג מֶלֶךְ הַבָּשָׁן, כִּי לְעוֹלָם חַסְדּוֹ.
וְנָתַן אַרְצָם לְנַחֲלָה, כִּי לְעוֹלָם חַסְדּוֹ.
נַחֲלָה לְיִשְׂרָאֵל עַבְדּוֹ, כִּי לְעוֹלָם חַסְדּוֹ.
שֶׁבְּשִׁפְלֵנוּ* זָכַר לָנוּ, כִּי לְעוֹלָם חַסְדּוֹ.
וַיִּפְרְקֵנוּ מִצָּרֵינוּ, כִּי לְעוֹלָם חַסְדּוֹ.
❖ נֹתֵן לֶחֶם לְכָל בָּשָׂר, כִּי לְעוֹלָם חַסְדּוֹ.
הוֹדוּ לְאֵל הַשָּׁמָיִם, כִּי לְעוֹלָם חַסְדּוֹ.

בִּתְבוּנָה — *With understanding.* The solar system and the countless galaxies function with a complexity that is beyond human comprehension *(R' Hirsch).*

לְמַכֵּה מִצְרַיִם בִּבְכוֹרֵיהֶם — *Who smote Egypt through their firstborn.* Upon hearing that they would soon die, the firstborn Egyptians insisted that the Jews be set free. When their countrymen refused, the firstborn attacked and killed many of their fellow Egyptians. Thus, the plague of the firstborn was a double blow *(Midrash).*

יַם סוּף לִגְזָרִים — *The Sea of Reeds into parts.* The Midrash teaches that the sea was divided into twelve parts, one for each tribe. This shows that each tribe has its own mission and deserved the miracle for its own sake *(Sfas Emes).*

מְלָכִים גְּדֹלִים — *Great kings,* i.e., the thirty-one Canaanite kings *(Rashi).*

מְלָכִים אַדִּירִים — *Mighty kings,* i.e. Pharaoh and his legion, who were even mightier than the combined Canaanite nations *(Rashi).*

שֶׁבְּשִׁפְלֵנוּ — *In our lowliness,* i.e., during our Egyptian enslavement *(Rashi);* or this is a prophetic reference to Israel's downtrodden condition during the periods when the Temples were destroyed *(Radak).*

To Him Who alone performs great wonders,
for His kindness endures forever.
*To Him Who made the heavens with understanding,**
for His kindness endures forever.
To Him Who spread out the earth upon the waters,
for His kindness endures forever.
To Him Who made great lights,
for His kindness endures forever.
The sun for the reign of the day,
for His kindness endures forever.
The moon and the stars for the reign of the night,
for His kindness endures forever.
*To Him Who smote Egypt through their firstborn,**
for His kindness endures forever.
And brought Israel forth from their midst,
for His kindness endures forever.
With strong hand and outstretched arm,
for His kindness endures forever.
*To Him Who divided the Sea of Reeds into parts,**
for His kindness endures forever.
And caused Israel to pass through it,
for His kindness endures forever.
And threw Pharaoh and his army into the Sea of Reeds,
for His kindness endures forever.
To Him Who led His people through the wilderness,
for His kindness endures forever.
*To Him Who smote great kings,**
for His kindness endures forever.
*And slew mighty kings,**
for His kindness endures forever.
Sichon, king of the Emorites,
for His kindness endures forever.
And Og, king of Bashan,
for His kindness endures forever.
And presented their land as a heritage,
for His kindness endures forever.
A heritage for Israel, His servant,
for His kindness endures forever.
In our lowliness He remembered us,*
for His kindness endures forever.
And released us from our tormentors,
for His kindness endures forever.
Chazzan– *He gives nourishment to all flesh,*
for His kindness endures forever.
Give thanks to God of the heavens,
for His kindness endures forever.

תהלים לג

רַנְּנוּ צַדִּיקִים בַּיהוה, לַיְשָׁרִים נָאוָה תְהִלָּה. הוֹדוּ לַיהוה בְּכִנּוֹר, בְּנֵבֶל עָשׂוֹר זַמְּרוּ לוֹ. שִׁירוּ לוֹ שִׁיר חָדָשׁ, הֵיטִיבוּ נַגֵּן בִּתְרוּעָה. כִּי יָשָׁר דְּבַר יהוה, וְכָל מַעֲשֵׂהוּ בֶּאֱמוּנָה.* אֹהֵב צְדָקָה וּמִשְׁפָּט, חֶסֶד יהוה מָלְאָה הָאָרֶץ. בִּדְבַר יהוה שָׁמַיִם נַעֲשׂוּ, וּבְרוּחַ פִּיו כָּל צְבָאָם. כֹּנֵס כַּנֵּד מֵי הַיָּם, נֹתֵן בְּאוֹצָרוֹת תְּהוֹמוֹת. יִירְאוּ מֵיהוה כָּל הָאָרֶץ, מִמֶּנּוּ יָגוּרוּ כָּל יֹשְׁבֵי תֵבֵל. כִּי הוּא אָמַר וַיֶּהִי, הוּא צִוָּה וַיַּעֲמֹד.* יהוה הֵפִיר עֲצַת גּוֹיִם, הֵנִיא מַחְשְׁבוֹת עַמִּים. עֲצַת יהוה לְעוֹלָם תַּעֲמֹד, מַחְשְׁבוֹת לִבּוֹ לְדֹר וָדֹר. אַשְׁרֵי הַגּוֹי אֲשֶׁר יהוה אֱלֹהָיו, הָעָם בָּחַר לְנַחֲלָה לוֹ. מִשָּׁמַיִם הִבִּיט יהוה, רָאָה אֶת כָּל בְּנֵי הָאָדָם. מִמְּכוֹן שִׁבְתּוֹ הִשְׁגִּיחַ,* אֶל כָּל יֹשְׁבֵי הָאָרֶץ. הַיֹּצֵר יַחַד לִבָּם, הַמֵּבִין אֶל כָּל מַעֲשֵׂיהֶם. אֵין הַמֶּלֶךְ נוֹשָׁע בְּרָב חָיִל, גִּבּוֹר לֹא יִנָּצֵל בְּרָב כֹּחַ. שֶׁקֶר הַסּוּס לִתְשׁוּעָה, וּבְרֹב חֵילוֹ לֹא יְמַלֵּט. הִנֵּה עֵין יהוה אֶל יְרֵאָיו, לַמְיַחֲלִים לְחַסְדּוֹ. לְהַצִּיל מִמָּוֶת נַפְשָׁם, וּלְחַיּוֹתָם בָּרָעָב. ❖ נַפְשֵׁנוּ חִכְּתָה לַיהוה, עֶזְרֵנוּ וּמָגִנֵּנוּ הוּא. כִּי בוֹ יִשְׂמַח לִבֵּנוּ, כִּי בְשֵׁם קָדְשׁוֹ בָטָחְנוּ. יְהִי חַסְדְּךָ יהוה עָלֵינוּ, כַּאֲשֶׁר יִחַלְנוּ לָךְ.

תהלים צב

מִזְמוֹר שִׁיר לְיוֹם הַשַּׁבָּת.* טוֹב לְהֹדוֹת לַיהוה, וּלְזַמֵּר לְשִׁמְךָ עֶלְיוֹן. לְהַגִּיד בַּבֹּקֶר חַסְדֶּךָ, וֶאֱמוּנָתְךָ בַּלֵּילוֹת. עֲלֵי עָשׂוֹר וַעֲלֵי נָבֶל, עֲלֵי הִגָּיוֹן בְּכִנּוֹר. כִּי שִׂמַּחְתַּנִי יהוה בְּפָעֳלֶךָ בְּמַעֲשֵׂי יָדֶיךָ אֲרַנֵּן. מַה גָּדְלוּ מַעֲשֶׂיךָ יהוה, מְאֹד עָמְקוּ מַחְשְׁבֹתֶיךָ. אִישׁ בַּעַר לֹא יֵדָע, וּכְסִיל לֹא יָבִין אֶת זֹאת. בִּפְרֹחַ רְשָׁעִים כְּמוֹ עֵשֶׂב, וַיָּצִיצוּ כָּל פֹּעֲלֵי אָוֶן, לְהִשָּׁמְדָם עֲדֵי עַד. וְאַתָּה מָרוֹם לְעֹלָם יהוה. כִּי הִנֵּה אֹיְבֶיךָ יהוה, כִּי הִנֵּה אֹיְבֶיךָ יֹאבֵדוּ, יִתְפָּרְדוּ כָּל פֹּעֲלֵי אָוֶן. וַתָּרֶם כִּרְאֵים קַרְנִי, בַּלֹּתִי בְּשֶׁמֶן רַעֲנָן. וַתַּבֵּט עֵינִי בְּשׁוּרָי, בַּקָּמִים עָלַי מְרֵעִים, תִּשְׁמַעְנָה אָזְנָי. ❖ צַדִּיק כַּתָּמָר יִפְרָח, כְּאֶרֶז

☙ רַנְּנוּ צַדִּיקִים / Psalm 33

We turn now to the celebration of the World to Come when all will recognize that God controls events. The Sabbath represents awareness of this truth, and it calls upon us to *sing Him a new song.*

וְכָל מַעֲשֵׂהוּ בֶּאֱמוּנָה — *And all His deeds are done with faithfulness.* The natural forces are reliable and consistent. Otherwise we would be in constant fear of upheaval *(Malbim).*

הוּא צִוָּה וַיַּעֲמֹד — *He commanded and it stood firm.* When God ordered the world to come into being, it kept expanding until it reached the size He desired; then He commanded it to stand firm (*Chagigah* 12a).

הִבִּיט ה׳ . . . הִשְׁגִּיחַ — *HASHEM looks down . . . He oversees.* These expressions imply the two differing forms of God's הַשְׁגָּחָה, *supervision.*

Psalm 33

רַנְּנוּ *Sing joyfully, O righteous, before HASHEM; for the upright, praise is fitting. Give thanks to HASHEM with the harp, with the ten-stringed lyre make music to Him. Sing Him a new song, play well with sounds of deepest feeling. For upright is the word of HASHEM, and all His deeds are done with faithfulness.* He loves charity and justice, the kindness of HASHEM fills the earth. By the word of HASHEM the heavens were made, and by the breath of His mouth all their host. He assembles like a wall the waters of the sea, He places the deep waters in vaults. Fear HASHEM, all the earth; of Him be in dread, all inhabitants of the world. For He spoke and it came to be, He commanded and it stood firm.* HASHEM annuls the counsel of nations, He balks the designs of peoples. The counsel of HASHEM will endure forever, the designs of His heart throughout the generations. Praiseworthy is the nation whose God is HASHEM, the people He chose for His own heritage. From heaven HASHEM looks down, He sees all mankind. From His dwelling place He oversees* all inhabitants of earth. He fashions their hearts all together, He comprehends all their deeds. A king is not saved by a great army, nor is a hero rescued by great strength; sham is the horse for salvation; despite its great strength it provides no escape. Behold, the eye of HASHEM is on those who fear Him, upon those who await His kindness. To rescue their soul from death, and to sustain them in famine.* Chazzan— *Our soul longed for HASHEM — our help and our shield is He. For in Him will our hearts be glad, for in His Holy Name we trusted. May Your kindness, HASHEM, be upon us, just as we awaited You.*

Psalm 92

מִזְמוֹר שִׁיר *A psalm, a song for the Sabbath day.* It is good to thank HASHEM and to sing praise to Your Name, O Exalted One; to relate Your kindness in the dawn and Your faith in the nights. Upon ten-stringed instrument and lyre, with singing accompanied by a harp. For You have gladdened me, HASHEM, with Your deeds; at the works of Your Hands I sing glad song. How great are Your deeds, HASHEM; exceedingly profound are Your thoughts. A boor cannot know, nor can a fool understand this: when the wicked bloom like grass and all the doers of iniquity blossom — it is to destroy them till eternity. But You remain exalted forever, HASHEM. For behold! — Your enemies, HASHEM, for behold! — Your enemies shall perish, dispersed shall be all doers of iniquity. As exalted as a re'eim's shall be my pride, I will be saturated with ever-fresh oil. My eyes have seen my vigilant foes; when those who would harm me rise up against me, my ears have heard their doom.* Chazzan— *A righteous man will flourish like a date palm, like a cedar*

There is the general supervision [הַשְׁגָּחָה כְּלָלִית] of the laws of nature; in that sense, God seems to *look down* from a distance. But God also exercises close supervision [הַשְׁגָּחָה פְּרָטִית] — *He oversees* — over each person according to his own deeds (*Malbim*).

מִזְמוֹר שִׁיר לְיוֹם הַשַּׁבָּת / Psalm 92

מִזְמוֹר שִׁיר לְיוֹם הַשַּׁבָּת — *A psalm, a song for the Sabbath day*. This psalm is recited on Festivals as well as the Sabbath because they, too, are referred to as 'Sabbath' in the Torah. Although this psalm is identified as belonging particularly

בַּלְּבָנוֹן יִשְׂגֶּה. שְׁתוּלִים בְּבֵית יהוה, בְּחַצְרוֹת אֱלֹהֵינוּ יַפְרִיחוּ. עוֹד יְנוּבוּן בְּשֵׂיבָה, דְּשֵׁנִים וְרַעֲנַנִּים יִהְיוּ. לְהַגִּיד כִּי יָשָׁר יהוה, צוּרִי וְלֹא עַוְלָתָה בּוֹ.

תהלים צג

יהוה מָלָךְ גֵּאוּת לָבֵשׁ, לָבֵשׁ יהוה עֹז הִתְאַזָּר, אַף תִּכּוֹן תֵּבֵל בַּל תִּמּוֹט. נָכוֹן כִּסְאֲךָ מֵאָז, מֵעוֹלָם אָתָּה. נָשְׂאוּ נְהָרוֹת יהוה, נָשְׂאוּ נְהָרוֹת קוֹלָם, יִשְׂאוּ נְהָרוֹת דָּכְיָם. ❖ מִקֹּלוֹת מַיִם רַבִּים אַדִּירִים מִשְׁבְּרֵי יָם, אַדִּיר בַּמָּרוֹם יהוה. עֵדֹתֶיךָ נֶאֶמְנוּ מְאֹד לְבֵיתְךָ נַאֲוָה קֹדֶשׁ, יהוה לְאֹרֶךְ יָמִים.

The following prayer should be recited with special intensity.

יְהִי כְבוֹד יהוה* לְעוֹלָם, יִשְׂמַח יהוה בְּמַעֲשָׂיו.[1] יְהִי שֵׁם יהוה מְבֹרָךְ, מֵעַתָּה וְעַד עוֹלָם. מִמִּזְרַח שֶׁמֶשׁ עַד מְבוֹאוֹ, מְהֻלָּל שֵׁם יהוה. רָם עַל כָּל גּוֹיִם יהוה, עַל הַשָּׁמַיִם כְּבוֹדוֹ.[2] יהוה שִׁמְךָ לְעוֹלָם, יהוה זִכְרְךָ* לְדֹר וָדֹר.[3] יהוה בַּשָּׁמַיִם הֵכִין כִּסְאוֹ, וּמַלְכוּתוֹ בַּכֹּל מָשָׁלָה.[4] יִשְׂמְחוּ הַשָּׁמַיִם וְתָגֵל הָאָרֶץ,* וְיֹאמְרוּ בַגּוֹיִם יהוה מָלָךְ.[5] יהוה מֶלֶךְ,*[6] יהוה מָלָךְ,[7] יהוה יִמְלֹךְ לְעֹלָם וָעֶד.[8] יהוה מֶלֶךְ עוֹלָם וָעֶד, אָבְדוּ גוֹיִם* מֵאַרְצוֹ.[9] יהוה הֵפִיר עֲצַת גּוֹיִם, הֵנִיא מַחְשְׁבוֹת עַמִּים.[10] רַבּוֹת מַחֲשָׁבוֹת בְּלֶב אִישׁ, וַעֲצַת יהוה הִיא תָקוּם.[11] עֲצַת יהוה לְעוֹלָם תַּעֲמֹד, מַחְשְׁבוֹת לִבּוֹ לְדֹר וָדֹר.[12] כִּי הוּא אָמַר וַיֶּהִי, הוּא צִוָּה וַיַּעֲמֹד.[13] כִּי בָחַר יהוה בְּצִיּוֹן, אִוָּהּ לְמוֹשָׁב לוֹ.[14] כִּי יַעֲקֹב בָּחַר לוֹ יָהּ, יִשְׂרָאֵל לִסְגֻלָּתוֹ.[15] כִּי

---

to the theme of the Sabbath — indeed, it was the Levites' song for the Sabbath Temple service *(Rashi)* — the text contains not a single direct reference to the Sabbath. One explanation is that it refers not to the weekly Sabbath, but to the World to Come, when man will achieve the spiritual perfection we only glimpse during the Sabbath. The psalm is thus well suited to the Sabbath which is a semblance of that future spiritual perfection *(Rashi)*. Additional commentary to this psalm appears on p. 30.

⤛ ה׳ מָלָךְ / Psalm 93

This psalm is a direct continuation of the previous theme that God's greatness will be recognized by all in the Messianic era. It describes God in His full grandeur and power as He was when He completed the six days of Creation, and as 'donning' grandeur and 'girding' Himself like one dressing in his Sabbath finery. Additional commentary to this psalm appears on p. 32.

⤛ יְהִי כְבוֹד ה׳ — *May the glory of* HASHEM. This collection of verses, primarily from *Psalms*, revolves around two themes: the sovereignty of God and the role of Israel. Central to *tefillah* and to the purpose of creation is מַלְכוּת שָׁמַיִם, *Kingship of Heaven,* which means that every being exists as part of God's plan and is dedicated to His service. This idea is found in nature itself, for, as David says lyrically, man attains awareness of God when he contemplates the beauty and perfection of the universe. The Sages chose *Psalms* 104:31 to begin this prayer because it was the praise proclaimed by an angel when the newly created plant world developed according to God's wishes *(Chullin* 60a). In other words, the 'glory' of God is revealed on earth when His will is done. Most of this prayer deals with this idea of God's glory and Kingship. The last five verses speak of God's selection of the Jewish people and pleads for His mercy and attentiveness to their prayers (see *World of Prayer)*.

in the Lebanon he will grow tall. Planted in the house of HASHEM, in the courtyards of our God they will flourish. They will still be fruitful in old age, vigorous and fresh they will be — to declare that HASHEM is just, my Rock in Whom there is no wrong.

Psalm 93

יהוה מָלָךְ *HASHEM will have reigned, He will have donned grandeur; He will have donned might and girded Himself; even firmed the world that it should not falter. Your throne was established from of old; eternal are You. Like rivers they raised, O HASHEM, like rivers they raised their voice; like rivers they shall raise their destructiveness.* Chazzan– *More than the roars of many waters, mightier than the waves of the sea — You are mighty on high, HASHEM. Your testimonies are exceedingly trustworthy about Your House, the Sacred Dwelling — O HASHEM, may it be for long days.*

The following prayer should be recited with special intensity.

יְהִי כְבוֹד *May the glory of HASHEM* endure forever, let HASHEM rejoice in His works.*[1] *Blessed be the Name of HASHEM, from this time and forever. From the rising of the sun to its setting, HASHEM's Name is praised. High above all nations is HASHEM, above the heavens is His glory.*[2] *'HASHEM' is Your Name forever, 'HASHEM' is Your memorial* throughout the generations.*[3] *HASHEM has established His throne in the heavens, and His kingdom reigns over all.*[4] *The heavens will be glad and the earth will rejoice,* they will proclaim among the nations, 'HASHEM has reigned!'*[5] *HASHEM reigns,**[6] *HASHEM has reigned,*[7] *HASHEM shall reign for all eternity.*[8] *HASHEM reigns forever and ever, even when the nations will have perished* from His earth.*[9] *HASHEM annuls the counsel of nations, He balks the designs of peoples.*[10] *Many designs are in man's heart, but the counsel of HASHEM — only it will prevail.*[11] *The counsel of HASHEM will endure forever, the designs of His heart throughout the generations.*[12] *For He spoke and it came to be; He commanded and it stood firm.*[13] *For God selected Zion, He desired it for His dwelling place.*[14] *For God selected Jacob as His own, Israel as His treasure.*[15] *For*

(1) *Psalms* 104:31. (2) 113:2-4. (3) 135:13. (4) 103:19. (5) *I Chronicles* 16:31.
(6) *Psalms* 10:16. (7) 93:1 et al. (8) *Exodus* 15:18. (9) *Psalms* 10:16.
(10) 33:10. (11) *Proverbs* 19:21. (12) *Psalms* 33:11. (13) 33:9. (14) 132:13. (15) 135:4.

ה׳ שִׁמְךָ... וְזִכְרְךָ... — *'HASHEM' is Your Name ... Your memorial.* The *Name* of God represents what He truly is and implies a thorough understanding of His actions and the reasons for them. But because man's limited intelligence cannot reach this level of understanding, we do not pronounce the Name י־ה־ו־ה as it is spelled; thereby we symbolize our inability to know God as He truly is. In this sense, the pronunciation HASHEM is God's *memorial* (see *Pesachim* 50a).

יִשְׂמְחוּ הַשָּׁמַיִם וְתָגֵל הָאָרֶץ — *The heavens will be glad and the earth will rejoice.* The celestial and terrestrial parts of creation serve God. They will truly rejoice when all nations, too, acknowledge that *HASHEM has reigned.*

ה׳ מֶלֶךְ... — *HASHEM reigns ...* — This is one of the most familiar verses in the entire liturgy, but, surprisingly enough, it is not found in Scripture. Rather, each phrase comes from a different part of Scripture. In combination, the three phrases express the eternity of God's reign.

אָבְדוּ גוֹיִם — *Even when the nations will have perished.* The verse refers only to the *evil* people among the nations, for their deeds prevent others from acknowledging God *(Rashi, Radak).*

לֹא יִטֹּשׁ יהוה עַמּוֹ, וְנַחֲלָתוֹ לֹא יַעֲזֹב.[1] ❖ וְהוּא רַחוּם יְכַפֵּר עָוֹן
וְלֹא יַשְׁחִית, וְהִרְבָּה לְהָשִׁיב אַפּוֹ, וְלֹא יָעִיר כָּל חֲמָתוֹ.[2] יהוה
הוֹשִׁיעָה, הַמֶּלֶךְ יַעֲנֵנוּ בְיוֹם קָרְאֵנוּ.[3]

אַשְׁרֵי יוֹשְׁבֵי בֵיתֶךָ, עוֹד יְהַלְלוּךָ סֶּלָה.[4] אַשְׁרֵי הָעָם שֶׁכָּכָה לּוֹ,
אַשְׁרֵי הָעָם שֶׁיהוה אֱלֹהָיו.[5]

תהלים קמה

תְּהִלָּה לְדָוִד,
אֲרוֹמִמְךָ אֱלוֹהַי הַמֶּלֶךְ, וַאֲבָרְכָה שִׁמְךָ לְעוֹלָם וָעֶד.
בְּכָל יוֹם אֲבָרְכֶךָּ, וַאֲהַלְלָה שִׁמְךָ לְעוֹלָם וָעֶד.
גָּדוֹל יהוה וּמְהֻלָּל מְאֹד, וְלִגְדֻלָּתוֹ אֵין חֵקֶר.
דּוֹר לְדוֹר יְשַׁבַּח מַעֲשֶׂיךָ, וּגְבוּרֹתֶיךָ יַגִּידוּ.
הֲדַר כְּבוֹד הוֹדֶךָ, וְדִבְרֵי נִפְלְאֹתֶיךָ אָשִׂיחָה.
וֶעֱזוּז נוֹרְאוֹתֶיךָ יֹאמֵרוּ, וּגְדוּלָּתְךָ אֲסַפְּרֶנָּה.
זֵכֶר רַב טוּבְךָ יַבִּיעוּ, וְצִדְקָתְךָ יְרַנֵּנוּ.
חַנּוּן וְרַחוּם יהוה, אֶרֶךְ אַפַּיִם וּגְדָל חָסֶד.
טוֹב יהוה לַכֹּל, וְרַחֲמָיו עַל כָּל מַעֲשָׂיו.
יוֹדוּךָ יהוה כָּל מַעֲשֶׂיךָ, וַחֲסִידֶיךָ יְבָרְכוּכָה.
כְּבוֹד מַלְכוּתְךָ יֹאמֵרוּ, וּגְבוּרָתְךָ יְדַבֵּרוּ.
לְהוֹדִיעַ לִבְנֵי הָאָדָם גְּבוּרֹתָיו, וּכְבוֹד הֲדַר מַלְכוּתוֹ.
מַלְכוּתְךָ מַלְכוּת כָּל עֹלָמִים, וּמֶמְשַׁלְתְּךָ בְּכָל דּוֹר וָדֹר.
סוֹמֵךְ יהוה לְכָל הַנֹּפְלִים, וְזוֹקֵף לְכָל הַכְּפוּפִים.
עֵינֵי כֹל אֵלֶיךָ יְשַׂבֵּרוּ, וְאַתָּה נוֹתֵן לָהֶם אֶת אָכְלָם בְּעִתּוֹ.

While reciting the verse פּוֹתֵחַ, concentrate intently on its meaning.

פּוֹתֵחַ אֶת יָדֶךָ,
וּמַשְׂבִּיעַ לְכָל חַי רָצוֹן.
צַדִּיק יהוה בְּכָל דְּרָכָיו, וְחָסִיד בְּכָל מַעֲשָׂיו.

אַשְׁרֵי / Ashrei

Rambam writes: The Sages praised anyone who recites hymns from the Book of Psalms every day, from תְּהִלָּה לְדָוִד, *A psalm of praise by David* [145:1; the third verse of *Ashrei*] to the end of the Book [i.e., the six psalms including *Ashrei,* and the five familiarly known as the *Halleluyahs*]. It has become customary to recite other verses before and after these, and [the Sages] instituted a blessing, *Baruch She'amar,* before these psalms and a blessing, *Yishtabach,* after them (*Hil. Tefillah* 7:12).

From *Rambam's* formulation, it is clear that the six psalms beginning with *Ashrei* are the very essence of *Pesukei D'zimrah.* This is based on the Talmud (*Shabbos* 118b) which cites Rabbi Yose: 'May my share be with those who complete *Hallel* every day.' The Talmud explains that, in Rabbi Yose's context, *Hallel* means the six concluding chapters of *Psalms*

HASHEM will not cast off His people, nor will He forsake His heritage.[1] Chazzan– *He, the Merciful One, is forgiving of iniquity and does not destroy; frequently He withdraws His anger, not arousing His entire rage.*[2] *HASHEM, save! May the King answer us on the day we call.*[3]

אַשְׁרֵי *Praiseworthy are those who dwell in Your house; may they always praise You, Selah!*[4] *Praiseworthy is the people for whom this is so, praiseworthy is the people whose God is HASHEM.*[5]

Psalm 145

A psalm of praise by David:

א *I will exalt You, my God the King,*
and I will bless Your Name forever and ever.
ב *Every day I will bless You,*
and I will laud Your Name forever and ever.
ג *HASHEM is great and exceedingly lauded,*
and His greatness is beyond investigation.
ד *Each generation will praise Your deeds to the next*
and of Your mighty deeds they will tell.
ה *The splendrous glory of Your power*
and Your wondrous deeds I shall discuss.
ו *And of Your awesome power they will speak,*
and Your greatness I shall relate.
ז *A recollection of Your abundant goodness they will utter*
and of Your righteousness they will sing exultantly.
ח *Gracious and merciful is HASHEM,*
slow to anger, and great in [bestowing] kindness.
ט *HASHEM is good to all; His mercies are on all His works.*
י *All Your works shall thank You, HASHEM,*
and Your devout ones will bless You.
כ *Of the glory of Your kingdom they will speak,*
and of Your power they will tell;
ל *To inform human beings of His mighty deeds,*
and the glorious splendor of His kingdom.
מ *Your kingdom is a kingdom spanning all eternities,*
and Your dominion is throughout every generation.
ס *HASHEM supports all the fallen ones and straightens all the bent.*
ע *The eyes of all look to You with hope*
and You give them their food in its proper time;
פ *You open Your hand,*
and satisfy the desire
of every living thing.

While reciting the verse, *'You open . . .'* concentrate intently on its meaning.

צ *Righteous is HASHEM in all His ways*
and magnanimous in all His deeds.

(1) *Psalms* 94:14. (29 78:38. (3) 20:10. (4) 84:5. (5) 144:15.

that we are about to recite. [However, see *Rashi.*] *Ashrei* has a special significance of its own, because the Talmud *(Berachos* 4b) teaches that the Sages assured a share in the World to Come

קָרוֹב יהוה לְכָל קֹרְאָיו, לְכֹל אֲשֶׁר יִקְרָאֻהוּ בֶאֱמֶת.
רְצוֹן יְרֵאָיו יַעֲשֶׂה, וְאֶת שַׁוְעָתָם יִשְׁמַע וְיוֹשִׁיעֵם.
שׁוֹמֵר יהוה אֶת כָּל אֹהֲבָיו, וְאֵת כָּל הָרְשָׁעִים יַשְׁמִיד.
❖ תְּהִלַּת יהוה יְדַבֶּר פִּי, וִיבָרֵךְ כָּל בָּשָׂר שֵׁם קָדְשׁוֹ לְעוֹלָם וָעֶד.
וַאֲנַחְנוּ נְבָרֵךְ יָהּ, מֵעַתָּה וְעַד עוֹלָם, הַלְלוּיָהּ.[1]

תהלים קמו

הַלְלוּיָהּ, הַלְלִי נַפְשִׁי אֶת יהוה.* אֲהַלְלָה יהוה בְּחַיָּי, אֲזַמְּרָה לֵאלֹהַי בְּעוֹדִי. אַל תִּבְטְחוּ בִנְדִיבִים, בְּבֶן אָדָם* שֶׁאֵין לוֹ תְשׁוּעָה. תֵּצֵא רוּחוֹ, יָשֻׁב לְאַדְמָתוֹ, בַּיּוֹם הַהוּא אָבְדוּ עֶשְׁתֹּנֹתָיו. אַשְׁרֵי שֶׁאֵל יַעֲקֹב בְּעֶזְרוֹ, שִׂבְרוֹ עַל יהוה אֱלֹהָיו. עֹשֶׂה שָׁמַיִם וָאָרֶץ,* אֶת הַיָּם וְאֶת כָּל אֲשֶׁר בָּם, הַשֹּׁמֵר אֱמֶת לְעוֹלָם. עֹשֶׂה מִשְׁפָּט לָעֲשׁוּקִים, נֹתֵן לֶחֶם לָרְעֵבִים, יהוה מַתִּיר אֲסוּרִים. יהוה פֹּקֵחַ עִוְרִים, יהוה זֹקֵף כְּפוּפִים, יהוה אֹהֵב צַדִּיקִים. יהוה שֹׁמֵר אֶת גֵּרִים,* יָתוֹם וְאַלְמָנָה יְעוֹדֵד, וְדֶרֶךְ רְשָׁעִים יְעַוֵּת. ❖ יִמְלֹךְ יהוה לְעוֹלָם, אֱלֹהַיִךְ צִיּוֹן, לְדֹר וָדֹר, הַלְלוּיָהּ.

תהלים קמז

הַלְלוּיָהּ, כִּי טוֹב* זַמְּרָה אֱלֹהֵינוּ, כִּי נָעִים נָאוָה תְהִלָּה. בּוֹנֵה יְרוּשָׁלַיִם יהוה, נִדְחֵי יִשְׂרָאֵל יְכַנֵּס. הָרוֹפֵא לִשְׁבוּרֵי לֵב, וּמְחַבֵּשׁ לְעַצְּבוֹתָם. מוֹנֶה מִסְפָּר לַכּוֹכָבִים,* לְכֻלָּם שֵׁמוֹת יִקְרָא. גָּדוֹל אֲדוֹנֵינוּ וְרַב כֹּחַ, לִתְבוּנָתוֹ אֵין מִסְפָּר. מְעוֹדֵד עֲנָוִים יהוה, מַשְׁפִּיל רְשָׁעִים עֲדֵי אָרֶץ. עֱנוּ לַיהוה בְּתוֹדָה, זַמְּרוּ לֵאלֹהֵינוּ בְכִנּוֹר. הַמְּכַסֶּה שָׁמַיִם בְּעָבִים, הַמֵּכִין לָאָרֶץ מָטָר,

---

to anyone who recites it properly three times a day. It has this special status because no other psalm possesses both of its two virtues: (a) Beginning with the word אֲרוֹמִמְךָ (the first substantive word of the psalm), the initials of the psalm's respective verses follow the order of the *Aleph-Beis;* and (b) it contains inspiring and reassuring testimony to God's mercy, . . . פּוֹתֵחַ אֶת יָדֶךָ, *You open Your hand* . . . As *Zohar* teaches, the recitation of this verse in *Pesukei D'zimrah* is not considered a *request* that God open His hand for us; rather it is purely a recitation of praise. Similarly, the five psalms that follow are expressions of sublime ecstatic praise.

Commentary to *Ashrei* begins on page 7.

⊱ הַלְלוּיָהּ הַלְלִי נַפְשִׁי אֶת ה׳ — *Halleluyah! Praise HASHEM, O my soul! Radak* interprets this psalm as a hymn of encouragement for Jews in exile. It begins with the Psalmist insisting that he will praise God as long as he lives and warning his fellow Jews not to rely on human beings. After praising God as the One Who cares for the underprivileged and oppressed, the Psalmist concludes that God will reign forever — despite the current ascendancy of our enemies.

בְּבֶן אָדָם — *Nor on a human being.* Even when rulers help Israel, it is because God has influenced them to do so. So it will be when the nations seem to have a hand in the Messianic redemption *(Radak).*

עֹשֶׂה שָׁמַיִם וָאָרֶץ — *Maker of heaven and earth.* Unlike kings and rulers whose power is limited

ק *HASHEM is close to all who call upon Him — to all who call upon Him sincerely.*

ר *The will of those who fear Him He will do; and their cry He will hear, and save them.*

ש *HASHEM protects all who love Him; but all the wicked He will destroy.*

ת Chazzan– *May my mouth declare the praise of HASHEM and may all flesh bless His Holy Name forever and ever.*

We will bless God from this time and forever, Halleluyah![1]

Psalm 146

הַלְלוּיָהּ *Halleluyah! Praise HASHEM, O my Soul!* I will praise HASHEM while I live, I will make music to my God while I exist. Do not rely on nobles, nor on a human being* for he holds no salvation. When his spirit departs he returns to his earth, on that day his plans all perish. Praiseworthy is one whose help is Jacob's God, whose hope is in HASHEM, his God. He is the Maker of heaven and earth,* the sea and all that is in them, Who safeguards truth forever. He does justice for the exploited; He gives bread to the hungry; HASHEM releases the bound. HASHEM gives sight to the blind; HASHEM straightens the bent; HASHEM loves the righteous. HASHEM protects strangers;* orphan and widow He encourages; but the way of the wicked He contorts.* Chazzan– *HASHEM shall reign forever — your God, O Zion — from generation to generation. Halleluyah!*

Psalm 147

הַלְלוּיָהּ *Halleluyah! For it is good* to make music to our God, for praise is pleasant and befitting. The Builder of Jerusalem is HASHEM, the outcast of Israel He will gather in. He is the Healer of the broken-hearted, and the One Who binds up their sorrows. He counts the number of the stars,* to all of them He assigns names. Great is our Lord and abundant in strength, His understanding is beyond calculation. HASHEM encourages the humble, He lowers the wicked down to the ground. Call out to HASHEM with thanks, with the harp sing to our God — Who covers the heavens with clouds, Who prepares rain for the earth,*

(1) *Psalms* 115:18.

in both time and space, God is everywhere and all-powerful (*Yerushalmi Berachos* 9:1).

ה׳ שֹׁמֵר אֶת גֵּרִים — *HASHEM protects strangers.* God is the Protector of all weak and defenseless strangers, whether uprooted Jews or gentile converts (*Radak*).

☙ הַלְלוּיָהּ כִּי טוֹב — *Halleluyah! For it is good ...* Continuing the theme of redemption, this psalm places its primary focus on Jerusalem, the center from which holiness, redemption, and Torah will emanate. In this sense, Jerusalem cannot be considered rebuilt until the Redemption, because the city's spiritual grandeur cannot be recaptured by mere architecture and growing numbers of people.

מוֹנֶה מִסְפָּר לַכּוֹכָבִים — *He counts the number of the stars.* Having given the assurance that God will rebuild Jerusalem and gather in Israel in joy, the Psalmist goes on to illustrate God's ability to do so. The next series of verses catalogue His might, compassion and attention to individual needs.

The stars number in the billions, but God is aware of each one and gives it a 'name' that denotes its purpose in the universe. Thus, nothing goes unnoticed or unprovided for.

הַמַּצְמִיחַ הָרִים חָצִיר. נוֹתֵן לִבְהֵמָה לַחְמָהּ, לִבְנֵי עֹרֵב אֲשֶׁר יִקְרָאוּ. לֹא בִגְבוּרַת הַסּוּס יֶחְפָּץ, לֹא בְשׁוֹקֵי הָאִישׁ* יִרְצֶה. רוֹצֶה יהוה אֶת יְרֵאָיו, אֶת הַמְּיַחֲלִים לְחַסְדּוֹ. שַׁבְּחִי יְרוּשָׁלַיִם אֶת יהוה, הַלְלִי אֱלֹהַיִךְ צִיּוֹן. כִּי חִזַּק בְּרִיחֵי* שְׁעָרָיִךְ, בֵּרַךְ בָּנַיִךְ בְּקִרְבֵּךְ. הַשָּׂם גְּבוּלֵךְ שָׁלוֹם, חֵלֶב חִטִּים* יַשְׂבִּיעֵךְ. הַשֹּׁלֵחַ אִמְרָתוֹ אָרֶץ, עַד מְהֵרָה יָרוּץ דְּבָרוֹ. הַנֹּתֵן שֶׁלֶג כַּצָּמֶר, כְּפוֹר כָּאֵפֶר יְפַזֵּר. מַשְׁלִיךְ קַרְחוֹ כְפִתִּים, לִפְנֵי קָרָתוֹ מִי יַעֲמֹד. יִשְׁלַח דְּבָרוֹ וְיַמְסֵם,* יַשֵּׁב רוּחוֹ יִזְּלוּ מָיִם. ❖ מַגִּיד דְּבָרָיו לְיַעֲקֹב,* חֻקָּיו וּמִשְׁפָּטָיו לְיִשְׂרָאֵל. לֹא עָשָׂה כֵן לְכָל גּוֹי, וּמִשְׁפָּטִים בַּל יְדָעוּם, הַלְלוּיָהּ.

תהלים קמח

הַלְלוּיָהּ, הַלְלוּ אֶת יהוה* מִן הַשָּׁמַיִם,* הַלְלוּהוּ בַּמְּרוֹמִים. הַלְלוּהוּ כָל מַלְאָכָיו, הַלְלוּהוּ כָּל צְבָאָיו.* הַלְלוּהוּ שֶׁמֶשׁ וְיָרֵחַ, הַלְלוּהוּ כָּל כּוֹכְבֵי אוֹר. הַלְלוּהוּ שְׁמֵי הַשָּׁמָיִם, וְהַמַּיִם אֲשֶׁר מֵעַל הַשָּׁמָיִם. יְהַלְלוּ אֶת שֵׁם יהוה, כִּי הוּא צִוָּה וְנִבְרָאוּ. וַיַּעֲמִידֵם לָעַד לְעוֹלָם, חָק נָתַן* וְלֹא יַעֲבוֹר. הַלְלוּ אֶת יהוה מִן הָאָרֶץ, תַּנִּינִים וְכָל תְּהֹמוֹת. אֵשׁ וּבָרָד, שֶׁלֶג וְקִיטוֹר, רוּחַ סְעָרָה עֹשָׂה דְבָרוֹ. הֶהָרִים וְכָל גְּבָעוֹת, עֵץ פְּרִי וְכָל אֲרָזִים. הַחַיָּה וְכָל בְּהֵמָה, רֶמֶשׂ וְצִפּוֹר כָּנָף. מַלְכֵי אֶרֶץ וְכָל לְאֻמִּים, שָׂרִים וְכָל שֹׁפְטֵי אָרֶץ. בַּחוּרִים וְגַם בְּתוּלוֹת,* זְקֵנִים עִם נְעָרִים. ❖ יְהַלְלוּ אֶת שֵׁם יהוה, כִּי נִשְׂגָּב שְׁמוֹ לְבַדּוֹ, הוֹדוֹ עַל אֶרֶץ וְשָׁמָיִם. וַיָּרֶם קֶרֶן לְעַמּוֹ, תְּהִלָּה לְכָל חֲסִידָיו, לִבְנֵי יִשְׂרָאֵל עַם קְרֹבוֹ, הַלְלוּיָהּ.

בִגְבוּרַת הַסּוּס . . . בְשׁוֹקֵי הָאִישׁ — *In the strength of the horse . . . the legs of man.* The earlier verses spoke of God's compassion for helpless creatures. Now the Psalmist says in contrast, God is unimpressed with powerful battle horses or with the skill of the rider who controls the horse with his legs *(Radak; Ibn Ezra).*

כִּי חִזַּק בְּרִיחֵי — *For He has strengthened the bars.* The verse is figurative. The Jerusalem of the future will need no bars on its gates. The people will feel secure because God will protect their city *(Radak).*

חֵלֶב חִטִּים — *The cream of the wheat.* Wheat is a symbol of prosperity and, therefore, it is an omen of peace, because prosperous people are less contentious *(Berachos 57a).*

יִשְׁלַח דְּבָרוֹ וְיַמְסֵם — *He issues His command and it melts them.* The Psalmist had spoken of the many solid forms of moisture: snow, frost, ice — but at God's command, everything melts and flows like water. The Jew should emulate nature by conforming to the will of God *(R' Hirsch).*

מַגִּיד דְּבָרָיו לְיַעֲקֹב — *He relates His Word to Jacob.* God gave *His word,* the Torah, to *Jacob,* i.e., the entire Jewish nation, even those who are not capable of understanding its intricacies and mysteries. But to *Israel,* i.e., the greatest members of the nation, He made known the many variations and shadings of wisdom to be found within His statutes and judgments *(Zohar).*

Lest you wonder at the many centuries that have gone by without the redemption of Jerusalem and Israel, do not forget that the Torah itself — the very purpose of creation — was not given to man until 2448 years after Creation. That God sees fit to delay is no cause for despair *(Siach Yitzchak).*

Who makes mountains sprout with grass. He gives to an animal its food, to young ravens that cry out. Not in the strength of the horse does He desire, and not in the legs of man does He favor. HASHEM favors those who fear Him, those who hope for His kindness. Praise HASHEM, O Jerusalem, laud your God, O Zion. For He has strengthened the bars* of your gates, and blessed your children in your midst; He Who makes your borders peaceful, and with the cream of the wheat* He sates you; He Who dispatches His utterance earthward; how swiftly His commandment runs! He Who gives snow like fleece, He scatters frost like ashes. He hurls His ice like crumbs — before His cold, who can stand? He issues His command and it melts them,* He blows His wind — the waters flow.* Chazzan– *He relates His Word to Jacob,* His statutes and judgments to Israel. He did not do so for any other nation, such judgments — they know them not. Halleluyah!*

Psalm 148

הַלְלוּיָהּ *Halleluyah! Praise HASHEM* from the heavens;* praise Him in the heights. Praise Him, all His angels; praise Him, all His legions.* Praise Him, sun and moon; praise Him, all bright stars. Praise Him, the most exalted of the heavens and the waters that are above the heavens. Let them praise the Name of HASHEM, for He commanded and they were created. And He established them forever and ever, He issued a decree* that will not change. Praise HASHEM from the earth, sea giants and all watery depths. Fire and hail, snow and vapor, stormy wind fulfilling His word. Mountains and all hills, fruitful trees and all cedars. Beasts and all cattle, crawling things and winged fowl. Kings of the earth and all governments, princes and all judges on earth. Young men and also maidens,* old men together with youths.* Chazzan– *Let them praise the Name of HASHEM, for His Name alone will have been exalted; His glory is above earth and heaven. And He will have exalted the pride of His nation, causing praise for all His devout ones, for the Children of Israel, His intimate people. Halleluyah!*

⁂ הַלְלוּיָהּ הַלְלוּ אֶת ה׳ — *Halleluyah! Praise HASHEM.* Only after the Temple and Jerusalem are rebuilt will all the universe join in joyous songs of praise to God. Zion is the meeting point of heaven and earth, as it were, because it is from there that God's heavenly blessings emanate to the rest of the universe.

הַלְלוּ ... מִן הַשָּׁמַיִם — *Praise ... from the heavens.* The Psalmist begins by calling upon the heavenly beings to praise God, and then he directs his call to earthly beings. God's praises echo from the heavens and descend to earth, where the devout echo the heavenly songs with their own praises *(Sforno).*

מַלְאָכָיו ... צְבָאָיו — *His angels ... His legions.* The *angels* are spiritual beings without physical form while the *legions* are the heavenly bodies, which are so numerous that they are likened to legions *(Radak).*

חָק נָתַן — *He issued a decree.* God ordained that the sun shine by day and the moon by night, and this *decree* can never be violated *(Rashi).*

בַּחוּרִים וְגַם בְּתוּלוֹת — *Young men and also maidens.* The use here of the word וְגַם, *and also,* is noteworthy. The Psalmist does not say that young men *and* women will be together, because such mingling would be immodest. Only later, when he speaks of old men and youths, does the Psalmist say עִם, *with* — that they will be *together (Sefer Chassidim).*

תהלים קמט

הַלְלוּיָהּ, שִׁירוּ לַיהוה* שִׁיר חָדָשׁ, תְּהִלָּתוֹ בִּקְהַל חֲסִידִים. יִשְׂמַח יִשְׂרָאֵל בְּעֹשָׂיו,* בְּנֵי צִיּוֹן* יָגִילוּ בְמַלְכָּם. יְהַלְלוּ שְׁמוֹ בְמָחוֹל, בְּתֹף וְכִנּוֹר יְזַמְּרוּ לוֹ. כִּי רוֹצֶה יהוה בְּעַמּוֹ,* יְפָאֵר עֲנָוִים בִּישׁוּעָה. יַעְלְזוּ חֲסִידִים בְּכָבוֹד, יְרַנְּנוּ עַל מִשְׁכְּבוֹתָם.* רוֹמְמוֹת אֵל בִּגְרוֹנָם,* וְחֶרֶב פִּיפִיּוֹת בְּיָדָם. לַעֲשׂוֹת נְקָמָה בַּגּוֹיִם, תּוֹכֵחוֹת* בַּלְאֻמִּים. ❖ לֶאְסֹר מַלְכֵיהֶם בְּזִקִּים, וְנִכְבְּדֵיהֶם בְּכַבְלֵי בַרְזֶל. לַעֲשׂוֹת בָּהֶם מִשְׁפָּט כָּתוּב,* הָדָר הוּא לְכָל חֲסִידָיו, הַלְלוּיָהּ.

תהלים קנ

הַלְלוּיָהּ, הַלְלוּ אֵל* בְּקָדְשׁוֹ, הַלְלוּהוּ בִּרְקִיעַ עֻזּוֹ. הַלְלוּהוּ בִגְבוּרֹתָיו, הַלְלוּהוּ כְּרֹב גֻּדְלוֹ. הַלְלוּהוּ בְּתֵקַע שׁוֹפָר, הַלְלוּהוּ בְּנֵבֶל וְכִנּוֹר. הַלְלוּהוּ בְּתֹף וּמָחוֹל, הַלְלוּהוּ בְּמִנִּים וְעֻגָב. הַלְלוּהוּ בְצִלְצְלֵי שָׁמַע, הַלְלוּהוּ בְּצִלְצְלֵי תְרוּעָה. ❖ כֹּל הַנְּשָׁמָה תְּהַלֵּל* יָהּ, הַלְלוּיָהּ.* כֹּל הַנְּשָׁמָה תְּהַלֵּל יָהּ, הַלְלוּיָהּ.

בָּרוּךְ יהוה לְעוֹלָם,* אָמֵן וְאָמֵן.*[1] בָּרוּךְ יהוה מִצִּיּוֹן, שֹׁכֵן יְרוּשָׁלָיִם, הַלְלוּיָהּ.[2] בָּרוּךְ יהוה אֱלֹהִים אֱלֹהֵי יִשְׂרָאֵל, עֹשֵׂה נִפְלָאוֹת לְבַדּוֹ. ❖ וּבָרוּךְ שֵׁם כְּבוֹדוֹ לְעוֹלָם, וְיִמָּלֵא כְבוֹדוֹ אֶת כָּל הָאָרֶץ, אָמֵן וְאָמֵן.[3]

⚜ **הַלְלוּיָהּ שִׁירוּ לַה'** — *Halleluyah! Sing to* HASHEM. In every generation, God confronts us with new challenges and problems, yet He provides us with the opportunity to solve them. For this, our songs of praise never grow stale, because they are always infused with new meaning. But the greatest, newest song of all will spring from Israel's lips when history reaches its climax with the coming of the Messiah.

בְּעֹשָׂיו — *In its Maker.* Although God made *all* nations, only Israel is His Chosen People *(Sforno).*

בְּנֵי צִיּוֹן — *The Children of Zion.* The future holiness of Zion — the place from which the Torah's teachings will emanate — will be of a higher order than anything we now know. The Jews who benefit from this spiritual aura will be called *the Children of Zion.*

כִּי רוֹצֶה ה' בְּעַמּוֹ — *For* HASHEM *favors His nation.* God looks forward to Israel's praises *(Radak).*

עַל מִשְׁכְּבוֹתָם — *Upon their beds.* The righteous will thank God for allowing them to go to bed without fear of danger and attack *(Etz Yosef).*

רוֹמְמוֹת אֵל בִּגְרוֹנָם — *The lofty praises of God are in their throats.* Though Israel goes into battle holding its *double-edged sword,* it knows that its victory depends on the help of God to Whom it sings praises *(Rashi; Radak).* The expression *in their throats* symbolizes that the prayers are not merely mouthed, but are deeply felt internally *(Radak).*

תּוֹכֵחוֹת — *Rebukes.* Though Israel is forced to wage battle against its enemies, its primary goal is that they accept moral rebuke and mend their ways.

לַעֲשׂוֹת בָּהֶם מִשְׁפָּט כָּתוּב — *To execute upon them written judgment.* The future judgment upon the nations has been written in the Prophets. The execution of that judgment will bring the reign of justice to earth, and that will be the *splendor* — the pride and vindication — of the righteous who have always lived that way.

⚜ **הַלְלוּיָהּ הַלְלוּ אֵל** — *Halleluyah! Praise God.* In

Psalm 149

הַלְלוּיָהּ *Halleluyah! Sing to HASHEM* a new song, let His praise be in the congregation of the devout. Let Israel exult in its Maker,* let the Children of Zion* rejoice in their King. Let them praise His Name with dancing, with drums and harp let them make music to Him. For HASHEM favors His nation,* He adorns the humble with salvation. Let the devout exult in glory, let them sing joyously upon their beds.* The lofty praises of God are in their throats,* and a double-edged sword is in their hand — to execute vengeance among the nations, rebukes* among the governments.* Chazzan– *To bind their kings with chains, and their nobles with fetters of iron. To execute upon them written judgment* — that will be the splendor of all His devout ones. Halleluyah!*

Psalm 150

הַלְלוּיָהּ *Halleluyah! Praise God* in His Sanctuary; praise Him in the firmament of His power. Praise Him for His mighty acts; praise Him as befits His abundant greatness. Praise Him with the blast of the shofar; praise Him with lyre and harp. Praise Him with drum and dance; praise Him with organ and flute. Praise Him with clanging cymbals; praise Him with resonant trumpets.* Chazzan– *Let all souls praise* God, Halleluyah!* Let all souls praise God, Halleluyah!*

בָּרוּךְ *Blessed is HASHEM forever,* Amen and Amen.*[1] Blessed is HASHEM from Zion, Who dwells in Jerusalem, Halleluyah.[2] Blessed is HASHEM, God, the God of Israel, Who alone does wonders.* Chazzan– *Blessed is His glorious Name forever, and may all the earth be filled with His glory, Amen and Amen.[3]*

(1) *Psalms* 89:53. (2) 135:21. (3) 72:18-19.

this, the final psalm in the Book of *Psalms*, the Psalmist sums up his task by saying that man must enrich his spiritual self by recognizing God's greatness and kindness and by praising Him. The Psalmist's long list of musical instruments reflects the full spectrum of human emotions and spiritual potential, all of which can be aroused by music.

[A series of musical instruments is mentioned here. In many cases, we do not know the exact translations; those given here are based on the interpretations of various major commentators. A full exposition can be found in the ArtScroll *Tehillim/Psalms.*]

כֹּל הַנְּשָׁמָה תְּהַלֵּל — *Let all souls praise.* Far greater than the most sublime instrumental songs of praise is the song of the human soul. God's greatest praise is the soul that utilizes its full potential in His service *(Radak).*

Having now concluded the six psalms that are the main part of *Pesukei D'zimrah,* we repeat the last verse to signify that this section has come to an end *(Avudraham).*

הַלְלוּיָהּ — *Halleluyah.* The root הלל, *praise,* appears thirteen times in this psalm, an allusion to God's Thirteen Attributes of Mercy. [In counting the thirteen times, the repetition of the last verse is not included, since it appears only one time in *Psalms.*] *(Radak)*

☙ בָּרוּךְ ה׳ לְעוֹלָם — *Blessed is HASHEM forever.* This collection of verses, each of which begins with the word בָּרוּךְ, is in the nature of a blessing after the six psalms that, as noted above, are the very essence of *Pesukei D'zimrah (Etz Yosef).* The term בָּרוּךְ, which refers to God as the Source of all blessing, is particularly relevant to the just concluded psalms, since they describe God's kindness, power, and future redemption *(R' Munk).*

אָמֵן וְאָמֵן — *Amen and Amen.* The repetition is meant to re-emphasize the statement. A listener's *Amen* can have three connotations *(Shevuos* 29b): (a) to accept a vow upon oneself, (b) to acknowledge the truth of a statement, and (c) to express the hope that a statement come true. In our prayers, any or all are expressed by *Amen,* depending on the context *(Iyun Tefillah).*

One must stand from וַיְבָרֶךְ דָּוִיד, until after the phrase אַתָּה הוּא ה׳ הָאֱלֹהִים; however, there is a generally accepted custom to remain standing until after completing אָז יָשִׁיר (p. 208).

דברי הימים א כט:י-יג

וַיְבָֽרֶךְ דָּוִיד* אֶת יהוה לְעֵינֵי כָּל הַקָּהָל, וַיֹּאמֶר דָּוִיד: בָּרוּךְ אַתָּה יהוה, אֱלֹהֵי יִשְׂרָאֵל אָבִֽינוּ,* מֵעוֹלָם וְעַד עוֹלָם. לְךָ יהוה הַגְּדֻלָּה* וְהַגְּבוּרָה וְהַתִּפְאֶֽרֶת וְהַנֵּֽצַח וְהַהוֹד, כִּי כֹל בַּשָּׁמַֽיִם וּבָאָֽרֶץ; לְךָ יהוה הַמַּמְלָכָה וְהַמִּתְנַשֵּׂא לְכֹל לְרֹאשׁ. וְהָעֹֽשֶׁר וְהַכָּבוֹד מִלְּפָנֶֽיךָ, וְאַתָּה מוֹשֵׁל בַּכֹּל, וּבְיָדְךָ כֹּֽחַ וּגְבוּרָה, וּבְיָדְךָ לְגַדֵּל וּלְחַזֵּק לַכֹּל. וְעַתָּה אֱלֹהֵֽינוּ מוֹדִים אֲנַֽחְנוּ לָךְ, וּמְהַלְּלִים לְשֵׁם תִּפְאַרְתֶּֽךָ.

נחמיה ט:ו-יא

אַתָּה הוּא יהוה* לְבַדֶּֽךָ, אַתָּה עָשִֽׂיתָ אֶת הַשָּׁמַֽיִם, שְׁמֵי הַשָּׁמַֽיִם* וְכָל צְבָאָם, הָאָֽרֶץ וְכָל אֲשֶׁר עָלֶֽיהָ, הַיַּמִּים וְכָל אֲשֶׁר בָּהֶם, וְאַתָּה מְחַיֶּה אֶת כֻּלָּם,* וּצְבָא הַשָּׁמַֽיִם לְךָ מִשְׁתַּחֲוִים.* ❖ אַתָּה הוּא יהוה הָאֱלֹהִים אֲשֶׁר בָּחַֽרְתָּ בְּאַבְרָם,* וְהוֹצֵאתוֹ מֵאוּר כַּשְׂדִּים, וְשַֽׂמְתָּ שְּׁמוֹ אַבְרָהָם.* וּמָצָֽאתָ אֶת לְבָבוֹ נֶאֱמָן לְפָנֶֽיךָ — וְכָרוֹת* עִמּוֹ הַבְּרִית לָתֵת אֶת אֶֽרֶץ הַכְּנַעֲנִי הַחִתִּי הָאֱמֹרִי וְהַפְּרִזִּי וְהַיְבוּסִי וְהַגִּרְגָּשִׁי, לָתֵת* לְזַרְעוֹ, וַתָּֽקֶם אֶת דְּבָרֶֽיךָ, כִּי צַדִּיק אָֽתָּה.* וַתֵּֽרֶא אֶת עֳנִי אֲבֹתֵֽינוּ בְּמִצְרָֽיִם, וְאֶת זַעֲקָתָם שָׁמַֽעְתָּ עַל יַם סוּף. וַתִּתֵּן אֹתֹת וּמֹפְתִים* בְּפַרְעֹה וּבְכָל

☙ וַיְבָרֶךְ דָּוִיד — *And David blessed.* The following selections from the praises of David, Nehemiah, and Moses, in that order, were appended to *Pesukei D'zimrah* because the fifteen terms of praise used in *Yishtabach* are based on these selections *(Avudraham).*

The first four verses of this prayer were uttered by David at one of the supreme moments of his life: although he had been denied Divine permission to build the Holy Temple, he had assembled the necessary contributions and materials so that his heir, Solomon, could be ready to build immediately upon assuming the throne. In the presence of the assembled congregation, he thanked and blessed God for having allowed him to set aside resources for the Divine service (*I Chronicles* 29:10-13).

יִשְׂרָאֵל אָבִינוּ — *Israel our forefather.* David mentioned only Israel/Jacob, because he was the first to make a vow to contribute tithes for a holy cause as a source of merit in a time of distress (*Genesis* 28:20), an example followed by David (*Bereishis Rabbah* 70:1); and also because it was Jacob who first spoke of the Holy Temple *(Radak)* and designated Mount Moriah as its site [see ArtScroll *Bereishis* 28:16-19].

לְךָ ה׳ הַגְּדֻלָּה — *Yours, HASHEM, is the greatness.* In his moment of public glory, David scrupulously made clear that his every achievement was made possible by God and that it was meant to be utilized in His service. Lest anyone think that his attainments are to his *own* credit, David proclaims that God is Master of everything in heaven and earth and — because He has *sovereignty over every leader* — He decrees who shall gain high positions and who shall be toppled.

אַתָּה הוּא ה׳ — *It is You alone, HASHEM.* The next six verses were recited by the people, led by Ezra, Nehemiah, and the most distinguished Levites the day after Shemini Atzeres, when the newly returned Jews had completed their first festival season in Jerusalem after returning from their Babylonian exile. They gathered in devotion and repentance and echoed the resolve voiced by David nearly five hundred years earlier.

שְׁמֵי הַשָּׁמַיִם — *The most exalted heaven.* This refers either to the highest spiritual spheres or to the furthest reaches of space.

וְאַתָּה מְחַיֶּה אֶת כֻּלָּם — *And You give them all life.* Even inanimate objects have 'life' in the sense that they have whatever conditions are

One must stand from here until after the phrase *'It is You, HASHEM the God'*; however, there is a generally accepted custom to remain standing until after completing the Song at the Sea (p. 208).

I Chronicles 29:10-13

וַיְבָרֶךְ *And David blessed* HASHEM in the presence of the entire congregation; David said, 'Blessed are You, HASHEM, the God of Israel our forefather* from This World to the World to Come. Yours, HASHEM, is the greatness,* the strength, the splendor, the triumph, and the glory, even everything in heaven and earth; Yours, HASHEM, is the kingdom, and the sovereignty over every leader. Wealth and honor come from You and You rule everything — in Your hand is power and strength and it is in Your hand to make anyone great or strong. So now, our God, we thank You and praise Your splendrous Name.'*

Nehemiah 9:6-11

It is You alone, HASHEM, You have made the heaven, the most exalted heaven* and all their legions, the earth and everything upon it, the seas and everything in them and You give them all life;* the heavenly legions bow to You.** Chazzan– *It is You, HASHEM the God, Who selected Abram,* brought him out of Ur Kasdim and made his name Abraham.* You found his heart faithful before You —*

— and You established the covenant with him to give the land of the Canaanite, Hittite, Emorite, Perizzite, Jebusite, and Girgashite, to give* it to his offspring; and You affirmed Your word, for You are righteous.* You observed the suffering of our forefathers in Egypt, and their outcry You heard at the Sea of Reeds. You imposed signs and wonders**

---

necessary for their continued existence *(Iyun Tefillah)*.

לְךָ מִשְׁתַּחֲוִים — *Bow to You.* Despite their awesome size and power over other parts of the universe, the heavenly bodies *bow* in the sense that they exist totally to serve God *(Iyun Tefillah)*.

אֲשֶׁר בָּחַרְתָּ בְּאַבְרָם — *Who selected Abram.* After cataloguing the endless array of creation and its components, we acknowledge that from them all, God chose Abraham and his offspring as His chosen ones — an astonishing testimony to the Patriarch and the nation he founded *(Siach Yitzchak)*.

וְשַׂמְתָּ שְׁמוֹ אַבְרָהָם — *And made his name Abraham.* The change of name signified that Abram's mission had been changed and elevated. His original name was a contracted version of אַב אֲרָם, *father of Aram*, because he had been a spiritual father of his native Aram. The additional ה implies that he had become אַב הֲמוֹן גּוֹיִם, *father of a multitude of nations*, marking him as the spiritual mentor of all mankind (see *Genesis* 17:4-5).

וְכָרוֹת — *And You established* ... We have followed the virtually universal practice that *siddurim* begin a paragraph with וְכָרוֹת; however in the Book of *Nehemiah*, this is not the beginning of a new verse, but a continuation of the above; namely, that in reward for Abraham's faithfulness, God made a covenant with him.

In many congregations, the section beginning with וְכָרוֹת is chanted aloud when a circumcision is to be performed in the synagogue, because the circumcision sealed the covenant of which Abraham's new name was part. There are varying customs regarding reciting this section at a circumcision. In most of these congregations it is said by the *mohel*, in some by the rabbi. In some, all the verses from וְכָרוֹת until (but not including) יִשְׁתַּבַּח are recited responsively, with the *mohel* reciting the first aloud, the congregation the next, and so on. However, no verses are actually *omitted* by anyone; those not said aloud are said quietly. In some congregations, the *mohel* recites aloud only the verses from וְכָרוֹת until בְּמַיִם עַזִּים.

לָתֵת ... לָתֵת — *To give ... to give.* In effect, the Land was given twice: once it was pledged to Abraham, and centuries later it was ceded to his offspring *(Iyun Tefillah)*.

כִּי צַדִּיק אָתָּה — *For You are righteous.* God keeps His word even when Israel, on its own merits, would have been unworthy *(Iyun Tefillah)*.

אֹתֹת וּמֹפְתִים — *Signs and wonders. Signs* are miracles that were foretold by a prophet; *won-*

עֲבָדָיו וּבְכָל עַם אַרְצוֹ, כִּי יָדַעְתָּ כִּי הֵזִידוּ* עֲלֵיהֶם, וַתַּעַשׂ לְךָ שֵׁם כְּהַיּוֹם הַזֶּה.* ❖ וְהַיָּם בָּקַעְתָּ לִפְנֵיהֶם, וַיַּעַבְרוּ בְתוֹךְ הַיָּם בַּיַּבָּשָׁה, וְאֶת רֹדְפֵיהֶם הִשְׁלַכְתָּ בִמְצוֹלֹת, כְּמוֹ אֶבֶן בְּמַיִם עַזִּים.

שירת הים

שמות יד:ל-טו:יט

וַיּוֹשַׁע יהוה* בַּיּוֹם הַהוּא אֶת־יִשְׂרָאֵל מִיַּד מִצְרָיִם, וַיַּרְא יִשְׂרָאֵל אֶת־מִצְרַיִם מֵת עַל־שְׂפַת הַיָּם: ❖ וַיַּרְא יִשְׂרָאֵל אֶת־הַיָּד הַגְּדֹלָה אֲשֶׁר עָשָׂה יהוה בְּמִצְרַיִם, וַיִּירְאוּ הָעָם אֶת־יהוה, וַיַּאֲמִינוּ* בַּיהוה וּבְמֹשֶׁה עַבְדּוֹ:

אָז יָשִׁיר־מֹשֶׁה וּבְנֵי יִשְׂרָאֵל אֶת־הַשִּׁירָה הַזֹּאת לַיהוה, וַיֹּאמְרוּ
לֵאמֹר, אָשִׁירָה לַיהוה כִּי־גָאֹה גָּאָה, סוּס
וְרֹכְבוֹ רָמָה בַיָּם: עָזִּי וְזִמְרָת יָהּ* וַיְהִי־לִי
לִישׁוּעָה, זֶה אֵלִי* וְאַנְוֵהוּ,* אֱלֹהֵי
אָבִי וַאֲרֹמְמֶנְהוּ: יהוה אִישׁ מִלְחָמָה, יהוה
שְׁמוֹ:* מַרְכְּבֹת פַּרְעֹה וְחֵילוֹ יָרָה בַיָּם, וּמִבְחַר
שָׁלִשָׁיו טֻבְּעוּ בְיַם־סוּף: תְּהֹמֹת יְכַסְיֻמוּ, יָרְדוּ בִמְצוֹלֹת כְּמוֹ־
אָבֶן: יְמִינְךָ* יהוה נֶאְדָּרִי בַּכֹּחַ, יְמִינְךָ
יהוה תִּרְעַץ אוֹיֵב: וּבְרֹב גְּאוֹנְךָ תַּהֲרֹס
קָמֶיךָ, תְּשַׁלַּח חֲרֹנְךָ יֹאכְלֵמוֹ כַּקַּשׁ: וּבְרוּחַ

---

ders take place without prior announcement *(Rambam)*.

כִּי הֵזִידוּ — *That they sinned flagrantly* [lit., *willfully*]. The Egyptians sinned against the Jews by mistreating and enslaving them. Had the servitude not been so harsh and hatefully cruel, the Egyptians would not have suffered such devastation.

כְּהַיּוֹם הַזֶּה — *As [clear as] this very day*. The miracles of the Exodus were public and indisputable *(Etz Yosef)*.

⚜ שִׁירַת הַיָּם / The Song at the Sea

The early commentators note that the miracles of the Exodus, beginning with the Ten Plagues, illustrated that God controls every facet of nature at will. Thus, they remained the testimony to God as the all-powerful Creator: no human being saw the creation of the universe, but millions of Jews witnessed the Exodus. The climax of those miraculous events was the splitting of the sea; as the Passover *Haggadah* relates, the miracles at the sea were five times as great as those that took place in Egypt itself. That event was celebrated by Moses and the entire nation in the glorious Song of the Sea, a combination of praise and faith that fits in with the theme of *Pesukei D'zimrah*.

We have included the cantillation symbols *[trop]* for the convenience of those who recite the Song in the manner it is read from the Torah. Nevertheless, we have inserted commas for those unfamiliar with this notation. The basis for reciting the Song with this cantillation is found in Kabbalistic literature, which attaches great importance to the joyful, musical recitation of the Song, as if one were standing at the seashore witnessing the miracle. The *Zohar* states that one who recites the Song with the proper intent will merit to sing the praises of future miracles.

⚜ וַיּוֹשַׁע ה' — *HASHEM saved*. The Torah sums up the miracle at the sea as a prelude to Moses' song.

וַיִּירְאוּ . . . וַיַּאֲמִינוּ — *(They) feared . . . and they had faith*. The fact that God has the power to perform miracles is unimportant; the Creator of the universe has no difficulty in stopping the flow of a sea. What *did* matter was the effect the miracle had on Israel. The people felt a new and

upon Pharaoh and upon all his servants, and upon all the people of his land. For You knew that they sinned flagrantly against them, and You brought Yourself renown as [clear as] this very day.** Chazzan– *You split the Sea before them and they crossed in the midst of the Sea on dry land; but their pursuers You hurled into the depths, like a stone into turbulent waters.*

THE SONG AT THE SEA

Exodus 14:30-15:19

וַיּוֹשַׁע *HASHEM saved* — on that day — Israel from the hand of Egypt, and Israel saw the Egyptians dead on the seashore.* Chazzan– *Israel saw the great hand that HASHEM inflicted upon Egypt and the people feared HASHEM, and they had faith* in HASHEM and in Moses, His servant.*

Then Moses and the Children of Israel chose to sing this song to HASHEM, and they said the following:*

I shall sing to HASHEM for He is exalted above the arrogant, having hurled horse with its rider into the sea.

God is my might and my praise, and He was a salvation for me. This is my God,* and I will build Him a Sanctuary;* the God of my father, and I will exalt Him.*

*HASHEM is Master of war, through His Name HASHEM.**

Pharaoh's chariots and army He threw into the sea; and the pick of his officers were mired in the Sea of Reeds.

Deep waters covered them; they descended in the depths like stone.

Your right hand, HASHEM, is adorned with strength; Your right hand, HASHEM, smashes the enemy.*

In Your abundant grandeur You shatter Your opponents; You dispatch Your wrath, it consumes them like straw.

---

higher degree of *fear,* in the sense of awe and reverence. And their *faith* increased immeasurably, for they had seen that, through His prophet, God promised salvation from danger and had indeed saved them.

אָז יָשִׁיר מֹשֶׁה — *Then Moses . . . chose to sing.* Rather than שָׁר, *sang,* the Torah uses the verb יָשִׁיר, literally, *will sing.* In the simple sense, the verse means that upon seeing the miracle the people decided that they *would* sing. Midrashically, the verb implies the principle that God will bring the dead back to life in Messianic times — and then they *will* sing God's praises once again *(Rashi).*

עָזִּי וְזִמְרָת יָהּ — *God is my might and my praise.* The translation follows *Targum Onkelos.* According to *Rashi* the phrase is translated: *God's might and His cutting away [of the enemy] was a salvation for me.*

זֶה אֵלִי — *This is my God.* So obvious was God's Presence, that the Jews could point to it, as it were, and say 'This is my God.' As the Sages put it: 'A maidservant at the sea saw more than the prophet Yechezkel [saw in his heavenly prophecy]' *(Rashi).*

וְאַנְוֵהוּ — *And I will build Him a Sanctuary.* The root of the word is נָוֶה, *abode.* An alternative interpretation based on the same root: I will make myself into a Godly sanctuary *(Rashi)* — to remake oneself in God's image is to build the greatest of all sanctuaries.

Another translation is *I will beautify* or *glorify Him* [based on the root נאה, *fitting, beautiful*]. The Sages teach that this is done by performing the commandments in a beautiful manner, by having beautiful *tefillin,* a beautiful *succah,* a beautiful *esrog* and so on *(Shabbos* 133b).

ה׳ שְׁמוֹ — *Through His Name HASHEM.* Mortal kings require legions and armaments, but God overcomes His enemies with nothing more than His Name. Moreover, this Name of mercy applies to Him even when He is forced to vanquish the wicked *(Rashi).*

יְמִינְךָ — *Your right hand.* Of course God has no physical characteristics. All the many Scriptural references to physicality are allegorical.

אַפֶּיךָ נֶעֶרְמוּ מַיִם, נִצְּבוּ כְמוֹ־נֵד
נֹזְלִים, קָפְאוּ תְהֹמֹת בְּלֶב־יָם: אָמַר
אוֹיֵב,* אֶרְדֹּף אַשִּׂיג אֲחַלֵּק שָׁלָל, תִּמְלָאֵמוֹ
נַפְשִׁי, אָרִיק חַרְבִּי, תּוֹרִישֵׁמוֹ יָדִי: נָשַׁפְתָּ
בְרוּחֲךָ כִּסָּמוֹ יָם, צָלֲלוּ כַּעוֹפֶרֶת בְּמַיִם,
אַדִּירִים: מִי־כָמֹכָה בָּאֵלִם יהוה, מִי
כָּמֹכָה נֶאְדָּר בַּקֹּדֶשׁ, נוֹרָא תְהִלֹּת עֹשֵׂה
פֶלֶא: נָטִיתָ יְמִינְךָ, תִּבְלָעֵמוֹ אָרֶץ: נָחִיתָ
בְחַסְדְּךָ עַם־זוּ גָּאָלְתָּ, נֵהַלְתָּ בְעָזְּךָ אֶל־נְוֵה
קָדְשֶׁךָ:* שָׁמְעוּ עַמִּים יִרְגָּזוּן, חִיל
אָחַז יֹשְׁבֵי פְּלָשֶׁת: אָז נִבְהֲלוּ אַלּוּפֵי
אֱדוֹם,* אֵילֵי מוֹאָב יֹאחֲזֵמוֹ רָעַד, נָמֹגוּ
כֹּל יֹשְׁבֵי כְנָעַן: תִּפֹּל עֲלֵיהֶם אֵימָתָה
וָפַחַד, בִּגְדֹל זְרוֹעֲךָ יִדְּמוּ כָּאָבֶן, עַד־
יַעֲבֹר עַמְּךָ* יהוה, עַד־יַעֲבֹר עַם־זוּ
קָנִיתָ: תְּבִאֵמוֹ* וְתִטָּעֵמוֹ בְּהַר נַחֲלָתְךָ, מָכוֹן
לְשִׁבְתְּךָ פָּעַלְתָּ יהוה, מִקְּדָשׁ אֲדֹנָי כּוֹנְנוּ
יָדֶיךָ: יהוה ׀ יִמְלֹךְ* לְעֹלָם וָעֶד:

יהוה יִמְלֹךְ לְעֹלָם וָעֶד. (יהוה מַלְכוּתֵהּ קָאֵם, לְעָלַם וּלְעָלְמֵי עָלְמַיָּא.) כִּי בָא סוּס פַּרְעֹה בְּרִכְבּוֹ וּבְפָרָשָׁיו בַּיָּם, וַיָּשֶׁב יהוה עֲלֵהֶם אֶת מֵי הַיָּם, וּבְנֵי יִשְׂרָאֵל הָלְכוּ בַיַּבָּשָׁה בְּתוֹךְ הַיָּם. ❖ כִּי לַיהוה הַמְּלוּכָה,* וּמֹשֵׁל בַּגּוֹיִם.[1] וְעָלוּ מוֹשִׁעִים* בְּהַר צִיּוֹן, לִשְׁפֹּט אֶת הַר עֵשָׂו, וְהָיְתָה לַיהוה הַמְּלוּכָה.[2] וְהָיָה יהוה לְמֶלֶךְ* עַל כָּל הָאָרֶץ, בַּיּוֹם הַהוּא יִהְיֶה יהוה אֶחָד וּשְׁמוֹ אֶחָד.*[3] (וּבְתוֹרָתְךָ כָּתוּב לֵאמֹר: שְׁמַע יִשְׂרָאֵל יהוה אֱלֹהֵינוּ יהוה אֶחָד.[4])

אָמַר אוֹיֵב — *The enemy declared.* In order to coax his people to join him in pursuit of the Jews, Pharaoh *(the enemy)* spoke confidently of his ability to overtake and plunder them.

אֶל נְוֵה קָדְשֶׁךָ — *To Your holy abode,* i.e., the Holy Temple. Although the Temple would not be built for over four hundred years, prophetic song typically combines past with future, because in the Divine perception they are interrelated.

פְּלָשֶׁת . . . אֱדוֹם . . . — *Philistia . . . Edom . . .* Not all the nations were of equal status. Philistia and Canaan rightly feared conquest because their lands comprised *Eretz Yisrael.* Edom and Moab did not fear losing their land, but rather feared retribution because they did not and would not show compassion for Jewish suffering *(Rashi).*

עַד יַעֲבֹר עַמְּךָ — *Until Your people passes through.* This continues the previous thought; the terror of the nations would continue until Israel crossed into *Eretz Yisrael.* The term *passes through* is used twice: once in reference to the crossing of the Jordan and once in reference to the waters of the Arnon, on the border of Israel and Moab [see *Numbers* 21:13-20] *(Rashi).*

תְּבִאֵמוֹ — *You shall bring them.* Moses unconsciously prophesied that he would not enter the Land, for he said, 'You shall bring *them,*' and not 'You shall bring *us*' *(Rashi).*

At a blast from Your nostrils the waters were heaped up; straight as a wall stood the running water, the deep waters congealed in the heart of the sea.

The enemy declared: 'I will pursue, I will overtake, I will divide plunder; I will satisfy my lust with them; I will unsheathe my sword, my hand will impoverish them.'*

You blew with Your wind — the sea enshrouded them; the mighty ones sank like lead in the waters.

Who is like You among the heavenly powers, HASHEM! Who is like You, mighty in holiness, too awesome for praise, doing wonders!

You stretched out Your right hand — the earth swallowed them.

*You guided in Your kindness this people that You redeemed; You led with Your might to Your holy abode.**

Peoples heard — they were agitated; convulsive terror gripped the dwellers of Philistia.

Then the chieftains of Edom were confounded, trembling gripped the powers of Moab, all the dwellers of Canaan dissolved.*

May fear and terror befall them, at the greatness of Your arm may they be still as stone; until Your people passes through, HASHEM, until this people You have acquired passes through.*

You shall bring them and implant them on the mount of Your heritage, the foundation of Your dwelling-place, which You, HASHEM, have made: the Sanctuary, my Lord, that Your hands established.*

HASHEM shall reign for all eternity.*

HASHEM shall reign for all eternity. (HASHEM — His kingdom is established forever and ever.) When Pharaoh's cavalry came — with his chariots and horsemen — into the sea and HASHEM turned back the waters of the sea upon them, the Children of Israel walked on the dry bed amid the sea. Chazzan– *For the sovereignty is HASHEM's* and He rules over nations.*[1] *The saviors* will ascend Mount Zion to judge Esau's mountain, and the kingdom will be HASHEM's.*[2] *Then HASHEM will be King* over all the world, on that day HASHEM will be One and His Name will be One.**[3] *(And in Your Torah it is written: Hear O Israel: HASHEM is our God, HASHEM, the One and Only.*[4]*)*

(1) *Psalms* 22:29. (2) *Ovadiah* 1:21. (3) *Zechariah* 14:9. (4) *Deuteronomy* 6:4.

ה׳ יִמְלֹךְ — *HASHEM shall reign.* We repeat this verse to signify the climax of the Song — that God's sovereignty shall be recognized forever. Because this is so important, most congregations follow the *Arizal,* who taught that the Aramaic Targum of this verse also be recited.

כִּי לַה׳ הַמְּלוּכָה — *For the sovereignty is HASHEM's.* The collected verses attached to the Song are appropriate to the climactic verse that God will reign forever.

מוֹשִׁעִים — *The saviors.* Those who will in the future lead Israel out of exile will come to Mount Zion from which they will complete the conquest of the archenemy, Esau, whose descendants are responsible for our exile *(Rashi).*

וּמֹשֵׁל . . . לְמֶלֶךְ — *He rules . . . be King.* The term מוֹשֵׁל, *ruler,* refers to one who forces his subjects to obey him, while מֶלֶךְ, *king,* is one who is willingly accepted. Now God is *King* over Israel alone because only Israel acknowledges His sovereignty with love, but He *rules* the nations despite their unwillingness to accept Him as their God. In the future, however, all nations will proclaim Him as their King *(Vilna Gaon).*

ה׳ אֶחָד וּשְׁמוֹ אֶחָד — *HASHEM will be One and His Name will be One.* But does He not have One

לשני ימים הראשונים של סוכות

ON THE FIRST TWO DAYS OF SUCCOS CONTINUE HERE.
ON THE SABBATH OF CHOL HAMOED CONTINUE ON PAGE 454;
ON SHEMINI ATZERES, PAGE 882; ON SIMCHAS TORAH, PAGE 1108.

נִשְׁמַת כָּל חַי תְּבָרֵךְ אֶת שִׁמְךָ יהוה אֱלֹהֵינוּ, וְרְוּחַ* כָּל בָּשָׂר תְּפָאֵר וּתְרוֹמֵם זִכְרְךָ מַלְכֵּנוּ תָּמִיד. מִן הָעוֹלָם וְעַד הָעוֹלָם אַתָּה אֵל,[1] וּמִבַּלְעָדֶיךָ אֵין לָנוּ מֶלֶךְ[2] גּוֹאֵל וּמוֹשִׁיעַ. פּוֹדֶה וּמַצִּיל וּמְפַרְנֵס וּמְרַחֵם בְּכָל עֵת צָרָה וְצוּקָה,* אֵין לָנוּ מֶלֶךְ אֶלָּא אָתָּה. אֱלֹהֵי הָרִאשׁוֹנִים וְהָאַחֲרוֹנִים,* אֱלְוֹהַּ כָּל בְּרִיּוֹת, אֲדוֹן כָּל תּוֹלָדוֹת, הַמְּהֻלָּל בְּרֹב הַתִּשְׁבָּחוֹת, הַמְנַהֵג עוֹלָמוֹ בְּחֶסֶד וּבְרִיּוֹתָיו בְּרַחֲמִים. וַיהוה לֹא יָנוּם וְלֹא יִישָׁן.[3] הַמְּעוֹרֵר יְשֵׁנִים, וְהַמֵּקִיץ נִרְדָּמִים, וְהַמֵּשִׂיחַ אִלְּמִים, וְהַמַּתִּיר אֲסוּרִים,[4] וְהַסּוֹמֵךְ נוֹפְלִים, וְהַזּוֹקֵף כְּפוּפִים.[5] לְךָ לְבַדְּךָ אֲנַחְנוּ מוֹדִים. אִלּוּ פִינוּ* מָלֵא שִׁירָה כַּיָּם, וּלְשׁוֹנֵנוּ רִנָּה כַּהֲמוֹן גַּלָּיו, וְשִׂפְתוֹתֵינוּ שֶׁבַח כְּמֶרְחֲבֵי רָקִיעַ, וְעֵינֵינוּ מְאִירוֹת כַּשֶּׁמֶשׁ וְכַיָּרֵחַ,* וְיָדֵינוּ פְרוּשׂוֹת כְּנִשְׁרֵי שָׁמָיִם, וְרַגְלֵינוּ קַלּוֹת כָּאַיָּלוֹת, אֵין אֲנַחְנוּ מַסְפִּיקִים לְהוֹדוֹת לְךָ, יהוה אֱלֹהֵינוּ וֵאלֹהֵי אֲבוֹתֵינוּ, וּלְבָרֵךְ אֶת שְׁמֶךָ עַל אַחַת מֵאָלֶף אֶלֶף אַלְפֵי אֲלָפִים וְרִבֵּי רְבָבוֹת פְּעָמִים הַטּוֹבוֹת שֶׁעָשִׂיתָ עִם אֲבוֹתֵינוּ וְעִמָּנוּ.* מִמִּצְרַיִם גְּאַלְתָּנוּ יהוה אֱלֹהֵינוּ, וּמִבֵּית עֲבָדִים פְּדִיתָנוּ. בְּרָעָב זַנְתָּנוּ, וּבְשָׂבָע כִּלְכַּלְתָּנוּ, מֵחֶרֶב הִצַּלְתָּנוּ, וּמִדֶּבֶר מִלַּטְתָּנוּ, וּמֵחֳלָיִם רָעִים וְנֶאֱמָנִים דִּלִּיתָנוּ. עַד הֵנָּה עֲזָרוּנוּ רַחֲמֶיךָ, וְלֹא עֲזָבוּנוּ חֲסָדֶיךָ. וְאַל תִּטְּשֵׁנוּ יהוה אֱלֹהֵינוּ לָנֶצַח. עַל כֵּן אֵבָרִים שֶׁפִּלַּגְתָּ בָּנוּ, וְרוּחַ וּנְשָׁמָה שֶׁנָּפַחְתָּ בְּאַפֵּינוּ, וְלָשׁוֹן אֲשֶׁר

Name today? Rabbi Nachman bar Yitzchak taught: The world of the future will be unlike the world of today. In the world of today God's Name is spelled one way and pronounced differently, whereas in the world of the future all will be One — the spelling and pronunciation will both be י־ה־ו־ה (*Pesachim* 50a). Since we fail to perceive God's nature as it is expressed in the true pronunciation of His Name, we may not utter it. But in time to come, there will be no contradiction between perception and reality.

נִשְׁמַת / Nishmas

This beautiful and moving prayer is an outpouring of praise and gratitude to God. Lyrically, it depicts our utter dependency on God's mercy, our total inadequacy to laud Him properly, and our enthusiastic resolve to dedicate ourselves to His service. It is especially appropriate for recitation on the Sabbath and Festivals — although it contains no mention of the day — because the additional holiness of the Sabbath and the time it affords for extra contemplation make man better able to understand and express the message of the *Nishmas* prayer.

The Talmud (*Pesachim* 118a) calls this prayer בִּרְכַּת הַשִּׁיר, *the Blessing of the Song,* because it concludes the psalms and songs of *Pesukei D'zimrah,* and because it continues the theme of the Song of the Sea. In the Sabbath and Festival service as in the Passover *Haggadah, Nishmas* introduces the series of praises that culminate with יִשְׁתַּבַּח, *Yishtabach.* There, too, it climaxes the grateful narrative of the Exodus with an outpouring of dedication.

So highly was this prayer regarded that such great commentators as *Rabbi Yehudah HaLevi* and *Ibn Ezra* composed poetic introductions to *Nishmas.* That of *Ibn Ezra,* incidentally, צָמְאָה

THE FIRST TWO DAYS OF SUCCOS

ON THE FIRST TWO DAYS OF SUCCOS CONTINUE HERE.
ON THE SABBATH OF CHOL HAMOED CONTINUE ON PAGE 454;
ON SHEMINI ATZERES, PAGE 882; ON SIMCHAS TORAH, PAGE 1108.

נִשְׁמַת *The soul of every living being shall bless Your Name,* HASHEM, *our God; the spirit* of all flesh shall always glorify and exalt Your remembrance, our King. From This World to the World to Come, You are God,*[1] *and other than You we have no king,*[2] *redeemer or savior. Liberator, Rescuer, Sustainer and Merciful One in every time of distress and anguish,* we have no king but You! — God of the first and of the last,* God of all creatures, Master of all generations, Who is extolled through a multitude of praises, Who guides His world with kindness and His creatures with mercy.* HASHEM *neither slumbers nor sleeps.*[3] *He Who rouses the sleepers and awakens the slumberers, Who makes the mute speak and releases the bound;*[4] *Who supports the fallen and straightens the bent.*[5] *To You alone we give thanks. Were our mouth* as full of song as the sea, and our tongue as full of joyous song as its multitude of waves, and our lips as full of praise as the breadth of the heavens, and our eyes as brilliant as the sun and the moon,* and our hands as outspread as eagles of the sky and our feet as swift as hinds — we still could not thank You sufficiently,* HASHEM, *our God and God of our forefathers, and to bless Your Name for even one of the thousand thousand, thousands of thousands and myriad myriads of favors that You performed for our ancestors and for us.* You redeemed us from Egypt,* HASHEM, *our God, and liberated us from the house of bondage. In famine You nourished us and in plenty You sustained us. From sword You saved us; from plague You let us escape; and from severe and enduring diseases You spared us. Until now Your mercy has helped us, and Your kindness has not forsaken us. Do not abandon us,* HASHEM, *our God, forever. Therefore, the organs that You set within us, and the spirit and soul that You breathed into our nostrils, and the tongue that*

(1) Cf. *Psalms* 90:2. (2) Cf. *Isaiah* 44:6. (3) Cf. *Psalms* 121:4. (4) Cf. 146:7. (5) Cf. 145:14.

נַפְשִׁי לֵאלֹהִים, *My soul thirsts for God,* is sung by many in the Sabbath Eve *Zemiros* (see Artscroll *Zemiroth,* p. 118).

נִשְׁמַת ... רוּחַ — *The soul ... the spirit.* Essentially, these two concepts are similar, but נְשָׁמָה represents a higher degree of spiritual awareness than רוּחַ. Thus, on the Sabbath and Festivals when Jews are invested with a נְשָׁמָה יְתֵרָה, a higher degree of spiritual awareness, we dedicate that, too, to bless God.

בְּכָל עֵת צָרָה וְצוּקָה — *In every time of distress and anguish.* Commonly, people express gratitude in happy times and pray for salvation in hard times. We go further, however — even in times of distress and anguish, we express our gratitude to God for allowing us to survive the suffering.

אֱלֹהֵי הָרִאשׁוֹנִים וְהָאַחֲרוֹנִים — *God of the first and of the last.* When God initiates a course of action, He takes into account the results it will bring about centuries into the future. Thus He is the Master of the *first* set of events as well as of the *last (R' Moshe Cordevero).*

אִלּוּ פִינוּ — *Were our mouth ...* Having stated that God is All-powerful and All-merciful, and thus worthy of our grateful thanks, the liturgist now begins to explain that no creature could do justice to this task — even if he were endowed with superhuman qualities.

מְאִירוֹת כַּשֶּׁמֶשׁ וְכַיָּרֵחַ — *As brilliant as the sun and the moon,* which see everything on earth.

עִם אֲבוֹתֵינוּ וְעִמָּנוּ — *For our ancestors and for us.* Man does not live in a vacuum. The favors done for previous generations have lasting effects that benefit us as well.

שַׂמְתָּ בְּפִינוּ, הֵן הֵם יוֹדוּ וִיבָרְכוּ וִישַׁבְּחוּ וִיפָאֲרוּ וִירוֹמְמוּ וְיַעֲרִיצוּ וְיַקְדִּישׁוּ וְיַמְלִיכוּ אֶת שִׁמְךָ מַלְכֵּנוּ. כִּי כָל פֶּה לְךָ יוֹדֶה, וְכָל לָשׁוֹן לְךָ תִשָּׁבַע, וְכָל בֶּרֶךְ לְךָ תִכְרַע,[1] וְכָל קוֹמָה לְפָנֶיךָ תִשְׁתַּחֲוֶה,* וְכָל לְבָבוֹת יִירָאוּךָ, וְכָל קֶרֶב וּכְלָיוֹת יְזַמְּרוּ לִשְׁמֶךָ, כַּדָּבָר שֶׁכָּתוּב: כָּל עַצְמֹתַי תֹּאמַרְנָה,* יהוה מִי כָמוֹךָ, מַצִּיל עָנִי מֵחָזָק מִמֶּנּוּ, וְעָנִי וְאֶבְיוֹן מִגֹּזְלוֹ.[2] מִי יִדְמֶה לָּךְ, וּמִי יִשְׁוֶה לָּךְ, וּמִי יַעֲרָךְ לָךְ.[3] הָאֵל הַגָּדוֹל הַגִּבּוֹר וְהַנּוֹרָא, אֵל עֶלְיוֹן, קֹנֵה שָׁמַיִם וָאָרֶץ. ❖ נְהַלֶּלְךָ וּנְשַׁבֵּחֲךָ וּנְפָאֶרְךָ וּנְבָרֵךְ אֶת שֵׁם קָדְשֶׁךָ, כָּאָמוּר: לְדָוִד, בָּרְכִי נַפְשִׁי אֶת יהוה, וְכָל קְרָבַי אֶת שֵׁם קָדְשׁוֹ.[4]

The *chazzan* of *Shacharis* begins here.

הָאֵל* בְּתַעֲצֻמוֹת עֻזֶּךָ,* הַגָּדוֹל בִּכְבוֹד שְׁמֶךָ, הַגִּבּוֹר לָנֶצַח וְהַנּוֹרָא בְּנוֹרְאוֹתֶיךָ. הַמֶּלֶךְ הַיּוֹשֵׁב עַל כִּסֵּא רָם וְנִשָּׂא.[5]

שׁוֹכֵן עַד* מָרוֹם וְקָדוֹשׁ שְׁמוֹ.[6] וְכָתוּב: רַנְּנוּ צַדִּיקִים בַּיהוה לַיְשָׁרִים נָאוָה תְהִלָּה.[7]

❖ בְּפִי **יְ**שָׁרִים* תִּתְהַלָּל.
וּבְדִבְרֵי **צַ**דִּיקִים תִּתְבָּרַךְ.
וּבִלְשׁוֹן **חֲ**סִידִים תִּתְרוֹמָם.
וּבְקֶרֶב **קְ**דוֹשִׁים תִּתְקַדָּשׁ.

וְכָל קוֹמָה לְפָנֶיךָ תִשְׁתַּחֲוֶה — *Every erect spine shall prostrate itself before You.* One must bow to God even while he is standing erect. 'Bowing' is not only a physical action; it must also be done in the heart and mind *(R' Baruch of Mezhibozh).*

כָּל עַצְמוֹתַי תֹּאמַרְנָה — *All my bones shall say.* Having just described how each limb and organ will offer praise to God, we cite the Scriptural source for this obligation. The verse concludes with the inspiring praise that God's greatness is manifested in His rescue of the powerless from their oppressors. This is meant both literally and figuratively, for, as *Radak* explains, God rescues the seemingly overmatched good inclination from the seductions of the evil inclination.

☙ הָאֵל — *O God.* It is customary to divide the Sabbath and *Yom Tov* services among several *chazzanim:* one for *Pesukei D'zimrah;* another for *Shacharis;* and a third for *Mussaf.* On the Sabbath, the *chazzan* of *Shacharis* begins שׁוֹכֵן עַד, *He Who abides forever,* because the Sabbath was the climax of creation, when God had all of creation, including man, to acknowledge and praise Him.

On Pesach, Shavuos, and Succos, the *chazzan* of *Shacharis* begins הָאֵל בְּתַעֲצֻמוֹת, *O God, in the omnipotence,* because those three festivals testify to the Exodus, the great event when God revealed 'the omnipotence of His strength.' Thus the characteristics spoken of in this paragraph are fitting for the way in which God revealed Himself in bringing Israel to freedom and its new status as His people. However, on Rosh Hashanah and Yom Kippur when God is the 'King sitting in judgment,' the *chazzan* begins הַמֶּלֶךְ, *the King.*

הָאֵל בְּתַעֲצֻמוֹת עֻזֶּךָ — *O God, in the omnipotence of Your strength.* This and the following verses elaborate upon the themes of *Nishmas.* The last sentence of *Nishmas* containes the four terms הָאֵל הַגָּדוֹל הַגִּבּוֹר וְהַנּוֹרָא, *O great, mighty, and awesome God.* Now, each of those terms is used and elaborated upon in a phrase lauding God:

1. הָאֵל — *O God.* This Name refers to God as the All-Powerful. Thus, God's power is expressed by the idea that He does not depend on servants, armies, or the consent of His subjects. He is omnipotent in His strength without

You placed in our mouth — all of them shall thank and bless, praise and glorify, exalt and revere, sanctify and declare the sovereignty of Your Name, our King. For every mouth shall offer thanks to You; every tongue shall vow allegiance to You; every knee shall bend to You;[1] every erect spine shall prostrate itself before You; all hearts shall fear You, and all innermost feelings and thoughts shall sing praises to Your name, as it is written: "All my bones shall say:* 'HASHEM, who is like You?' You save the poor man from one stronger than he, the poor and destitute from one who would rob him."[2] Who is like unto You? Who is equal to You? Who can be compared to You?[3] O great, mighty, and awesome God, the supreme God, Creator of heaven and earth.* Chazzan– *We shall laud, praise, and glorify You and bless Your holy Name, as it is said 'Of David: Bless HASHEM, O my soul, and let all my innermost being bless His holy Name!'[4]*

The *chazzan* of *Shacharis* begins here:

הָאֵל *O God,* in the omnipotence of Your strength,* great in the glory of Your Name, mighty forever and awesome through Your awesome deeds. O King enthroned upon a high and lofty throne![5]*

שׁוֹכֵן עַד *He Who abides forever,* exalted and holy is His Name.[6] And it is written: 'Sing joyfully, O righteous, before HASHEM; for the upright, praise is fitting.'[7]*

Chazzan: *By the mouth of the upright* shall You be lauded;*
by the words of the righteous shall You be blessed;
by the tongue of the devout shall You be exalted;
and amid the holy shall You be sanctified.

(1) Cf. *Isaiah* 45:23. (2) *Psalms* 35:10. (3) Cf. 89:7; cf. *Isaiah* 40:25. (4) *Psalms* 103:1. (5) Cf. *Isaiah* 6:1. (6) Cf. 57:15. (7) *Psalms* 33:1.

---

reliance on anything else.

2. הַגָּדוֹל — *Great.* His greatness is signified by the fact that all creatures give honor to His Name.

3. הַגִּבּוֹר — *Mighty.* Unlike mighty human rulers, whose powers ebb as they grow old, God's majesty and strength are eternal and undiminished.

4. וְהַנּוֹרָא — *Awesome.* Unlike human kings who are held in awe only because they have the power to punish their detractors, God's awesomeness is obvious because the entire universe testifies to His greatness.

☙ שׁוֹכֵן עַד — *He Who abides forever.* Although God is *exalted and holy,* He nevertheless makes His abode on earth, for it is only here — through the deeds of the righteous — that His commandments can be carried out. Therefore, this paragraph goes on to say that the primary praise of God comes from such people. The key, however, is not in their rhetoric but in the 'song' of their good deeds.

בְּפִי יְשָׁרִים — *By the mouth of the upright.* Four categories of people are listed as praising God: יְשָׁרִים צַדִּיקִים חֲסִידִים קְדוֹשִׁים, *upright, righteous, devout,* and *holy.* The initials of these four words spell יִצְחָק, leading some to speculate that it is the signature of the unknown author of *Nishmas.*

Rabbi Shraga Feivel Mendlowitz noted that these four categories seem to be listed in ascending order of their spiritual accomplishment, the lowest being the upright, fair-minded people and the highest being the holy ones. The higher the level of the person, the more meaningful the manner in which he praises God. While the *upright* praises God with his *mouth,* the *righteous* uses articulated *words.* The *devout* uses his *tongue,* implying that the praise comes from deeper within himself. The *holy* person, however, praises God with his very *essence* [קֶרֶב, literally, *inner being*].

ובמקהלות רִבְבוֹת* עַמְּךָ בֵּית יִשְׂרָאֵל, בְּרִנָּה יִתְפָּאַר שִׁמְךָ מַלְכֵּנוּ בְּכָל דּוֹר וָדוֹר. ❖ שֶׁכֵּן חוֹבַת כָּל הַיְּצוּרִים,* לְפָנֶיךָ יהוה אֱלֹהֵינוּ וֵאלֹהֵי אֲבוֹתֵינוּ, לְהוֹדוֹת לְהַלֵּל לְשַׁבֵּחַ לְפָאֵר לְרוֹמֵם לְהַדֵּר לְבָרֵךְ לְעַלֵּה וּלְקַלֵּס, עַל כָּל דִּבְרֵי שִׁירוֹת וְתִשְׁבְּחוֹת דָּוִד* בֶּן יִשַׁי עַבְדְּךָ מְשִׁיחֶךָ.

Stand while reciting יִשְׁתַּבַּח . . . The fifteen expressions of praise — שִׁיר וּשְׁבָחָה . . . בְּרָכוֹת וְהוֹדָאוֹת — should be recited without pause, preferably in one breath.

ישתבח שִׁמְךָ לָעַד מַלְכֵּנוּ, הָאֵל הַמֶּלֶךְ הַגָּדוֹל וְהַקָּדוֹשׁ, בַּשָּׁמַיִם וּבָאָרֶץ. כִּי לְךָ נָאֶה יהוה אֱלֹהֵינוּ וֵאלֹהֵי אֲבוֹתֵינוּ, שִׁיר וּשְׁבָחָה, הַלֵּל וְזִמְרָה, עֹז וּמֶמְשָׁלָה, נֶצַח* גְּדֻלָּה וּגְבוּרָה, תְּהִלָּה וְתִפְאֶרֶת, קְדֻשָּׁה וּמַלְכוּת, בְּרָכוֹת וְהוֹדָאוֹת מֵעַתָּה וְעַד עוֹלָם. ❖ בָּרוּךְ אַתָּה יהוה, אֵל מֶלֶךְ גָּדוֹל בַּתִּשְׁבָּחוֹת,* אֵל הַהוֹדָאוֹת, אֲדוֹן הַנִּפְלָאוֹת, הַבּוֹחֵר בְּשִׁירֵי זִמְרָה,* מֶלֶךְ אֵל חֵי הָעוֹלָמִים.* (Cong. — אָמֵן.)

The *chazzan* recites חֲצִי קַדִּישׁ.

יתגדל וְיִתְקַדַּשׁ שְׁמֵהּ רַבָּא. (Cong. — אָמֵן.) בְּעָלְמָא דִּי בְרָא כִרְעוּתֵהּ. וְיַמְלִיךְ מַלְכוּתֵהּ, בְּחַיֵּיכוֹן וּבְיוֹמֵיכוֹן וּבְחַיֵּי דְכָל בֵּית יִשְׂרָאֵל, בַּעֲגָלָא וּבִזְמַן קָרִיב. וְאִמְרוּ: אָמֵן.

(Cong. — אָמֵן. יְהֵא שְׁמֵהּ רַבָּא מְבָרַךְ לְעָלַם וּלְעָלְמֵי עָלְמַיָּא.)

יְהֵא שְׁמֵהּ רַבָּא מְבָרַךְ לְעָלַם וּלְעָלְמֵי עָלְמַיָּא.

יִתְבָּרַךְ וְיִשְׁתַּבַּח וְיִתְפָּאַר וְיִתְרוֹמַם וְיִתְנַשֵּׂא וְיִתְהַדָּר וְיִתְעַלֶּה וְיִתְהַלָּל שְׁמֵהּ דְּקֻדְשָׁא בְּרִיךְ הוּא (Cong. — בְּרִיךְ הוּא) — לְעֵלָּא מִן כָּל בִּרְכָתָא וְשִׁירָתָא תֻּשְׁבְּחָתָא וְנֶחֱמָתָא, דַּאֲמִירָן בְּעָלְמָא. וְאִמְרוּ: אָמֵן. (Cong. — אָמֵן.)

⁂ וּבְמַקְהֲלוֹת רִבְבוֹת — *And in the assemblies of the myriads.* In future times, Jews will gather in their tens of thousands to glorify God.

שֶׁכֵּן חוֹבַת כָּל הַיְצוּרִים — *For such is the duty of all creatures.* It is their duty because of the simple fact that they are God's creatures; since He fashioned them, they must feel obligated to pay Him homage.

עַל כָּל דִּבְרֵי . . . דָּוִד — *Even beyond all expressions . . . of David.* Although David, the נְעִים זְמִרוֹת יִשְׂרָאֵל, *sweet singer of Israel* (*II Samuel* 23:1), is the quintessential composer of God's praises, even he could not nearly do justice to God's greatness. Therefore we now say that we are obligated to praise Him limitlessly — even beyond the songs of David.

⁂ **יִשְׁתַּבַּח / Yishtabach**

As noted in the commentary to בָּרוּךְ שֶׁאָמַר (p. 174), the יִשְׁתַּבַּח prayer ends the *Pesukei D'zimrah* section of *Shacharis*. The theme of fifteen is repeated twice in this prayer: there are fifteen expressions of praise in the first half of the paragraph, and after בָּרוּךְ אַתָּה ה׳, there are fifteen words. This number alludes to the fifteen שִׁיר הַמַּעֲלוֹת, *Songs of Ascents* [*Psalms* 120-134], composed by David. Also, fifteen is the numerical value of the Divine Name יָהּ, the letters of which were used by God to create heaven and earth; therefore, it alludes to the idea that everything is God's and He is its Creator. *Yishtabach* makes repeated use of this number to remind us to carry its message into our daily lives.

וּבְמַקְהֲלוֹת *And in the assemblies of the myriads* of Your people, the House of Israel, with joyous song shall Your Name be glorified, our King, throughout every generation.* Chazzan– *For such is the duty of all creatures* — before You, HASHEM, our God, God of our forefathers, to thank, laud, praise, glorify, exalt, adore, bless, raise high, and sing praises — even beyond all expressions of the songs and praises of David* the son of Jesse, Your servant, Your anointed.*

Stand while reciting *'May Your Name be praised . . .'*
The fifteen expressions of praise — *'song and praise. . .blessings and thanksgivings'* — should be recited without pause, preferably in one breath.

יִשְׁתַּבַּח *May Your Name be praised forever — our King, the God, the great and holy King — in heaven and on earth. Because for You is fitting — O HASHEM, our God, and the God of our forefathers — song and praise, lauding and hymns, power and dominion, triumph,* greatness and strength, praise and splendor, holiness and sovereignty, blessings and thanksgivings from this time and forever.* Chazzan– *Blessed are You, HASHEM, God, King exalted through praises,* God of thanksgivings, Master of wonders, Who chooses musical songs of praise* — King, God, Life-giver of the world.** (Cong.– *Amen.)*

The *chazzan* recites Half-*Kaddish.*

יִתְגַּדַּל *May His great Name grow exalted and sanctified* (Cong.– *Amen.) in the world that He created as He willed. May He give reign to His kingship in your lifetimes and in your days, and in the lifetimes of the entire Family of Israel, swiftly and soon. Now respond: Amen.*

(Cong.– *Amen. May His great Name be blessed forever and ever.)*
May His great Name be blessed forever and ever.

Blessed, praised, glorified, exalted, extolled, mighty, upraised, and lauded be the Name of the Holy One, Blessed is He (Cong.– *Blessed is He*) — *beyond any blessing and song, praise and consolation that are uttered in the world. Now respond: Amen.* (Cong.– *Amen.*)

עֹז וּמֶמְשָׁלָה נֶצַח ... — *Power and dominion, triumph* ... Although these qualities are attributed to God, we find them in people as well. When man uses them to further God's goals, they are praiseworthy. But if people seek power and pursue triumph for their own selfish ends, they bring destruction upon the world *(R' Gedaliah Schorr).*

גָּדוֹל בַּתִּשְׁבָּחוֹת — *Exalted through praises.* The implication is not that God requires our praises in order to become exalted; for His infinite greatness is beyond our capacity to comprehend, much less express. Rather, it is His will that we have the privilege of exalting Him, despite our inability to do so adequately. This is the implication of *Who chooses musical songs,* i.e., we praise Him because He wishes us to.

הַבּוֹחֵר בְּשִׁירֵי זִמְרָה — *Who chooses musical songs of praise. Rabbi Bunam of P'shis'cha* interpreted homiletically that the word שִׁירֵי can be translated *remnants* (from שִׁירַיִם, *leftovers).* God wishes to see how much of the lofty sentiments of our prayers remain with us after we close our *siddur.* Thus, He *chooses what is left over* after the Songs of Praise have been uttered.

חֵי הָעוֹלָמִים — *Life-giver of the world.* This essential principle of Jewish belief reiterates that creation is an ongoing process — God created and continues to create. Because He gives life constantly, our thanks and praise are likewise constant *(R' Munk).*

In some congregations the *chazzan* chants a melody during his recitation of בָּרְכוּ, so that the congregation can then recite יִתְבָּרַךְ.

Chazzan bows at בָּרְכוּ and straightens up at ה׳.

בָּרְכוּ אֶת יהוה הַמְּבֹרָךְ.

Congregation, followed by *chazzan*, responds, bowing at בָּרוּךְ and straightening up at ה׳.

בָּרוּךְ יהוה הַמְּבֹרָךְ לְעוֹלָם וָעֶד.

יִתְבָּרַךְ וְיִשְׁתַּבַּח וְיִתְפָּאַר וְיִתְרוֹמַם וְיִתְנַשֵּׂא שְׁמוֹ שֶׁל מֶלֶךְ מַלְכֵי הַמְּלָכִים, הַקָּדוֹשׁ בָּרוּךְ הוּא. שֶׁהוּא רִאשׁוֹן וְהוּא אַחֲרוֹן, וּמִבַּלְעָדָיו אֵין אֱלֹהִים.[1] סֹלּוּ, לָרֹכֵב בָּעֲרָבוֹת, בְּיָהּ שְׁמוֹ, וְעִלְזוּ לְפָנָיו.[2] וּשְׁמוֹ מְרוֹמַם עַל כָּל בְּרָכָה וּתְהִלָּה.[3] בָּרוּךְ שֵׁם כְּבוֹד מַלְכוּתוֹ לְעוֹלָם וָעֶד. יְהִי שֵׁם יהוה מְבֹרָךְ, מֵעַתָּה וְעַד עוֹלָם.[4]

ברכות קריאת שמע

It is preferable that one sit while reciting the following series of prayers — particularly the *Kedushah* verses, קָדוֹשׁ קָדוֹשׁ קָדוֹשׁ and בָּרוּךְ כְּבוֹד — until *Shemoneh Esrei.*

The following paragraph is recited aloud by the *chazzan,* then repeated by the congregation.

בָּרוּךְ אַתָּה יהוה אֱלֹהֵינוּ מֶלֶךְ הָעוֹלָם, יוֹצֵר אוֹר וּבוֹרֵא חֹשֶׁךְ,* עֹשֶׂה שָׁלוֹם וּבוֹרֵא אֶת הַכֹּל.[5]

Congregations that do not recite *Yotzros* continue on page 224.

Congregations that recite *Yotzros* continue:

אוֹר עוֹלָם בְּאוֹצַר חַיִּים, אוֹרוֹת מֵאֹפֶל אָמַר וַיֶּהִי.

◄ בִּרְכוֹת קְרִיאַת שְׁמַע / BLESSINGS OF THE SHEMA ►

◄§ בָּרְכוּ – *Bless.* Commentary to *Borchu* appears on page 34.

The third section of *Shacharis* is about to begin. Its central feature is the *Shema,* whose recitation is required by the Torah and which is the basic acknowledgment of God's sovereignty and Oneness. The *Shema* is accompanied by three blessings (two before it and one after it), which express God's mastery over nature, pray for intellectual and moral attainment through the study of Torah, and describe God's role in the flow of history *(R' Munk).*

◄§ יוֹצֵר אוֹר וּבוֹרֵא חֹשֶׁךְ — *Who forms light and creates darkness.* Since the beginning of time, the term 'light' has symbolized new life, wisdom, happiness — all the things associated with goodness. 'Darkness,' however, is associated with suffering, failure and death. The philosophers of idolatry claimed that the 'good' god who creates light cannot be the 'bad' one who creates darkness. Therefore, they reasoned, there must be at least two gods. In modern times, the same argument is presented in different terms: how can there be a God if He allows bad things to happen? This blessing refutes the argument

◄§ Interruptions During the Blessings of the Shema

As a general rule, no אָמֵן or other prayer response may be recited between בָּרְכוּ and *Shemoneh Esrei,* but there are exceptions. The main exception is 'between chapters' [בֵּין הַפְּרָקִים] of the *Shema* Blessings — i.e., after יוֹצֵר הַמְּאוֹרוֹת and הַבּוֹחֵר . . . בְּאַהֲבָה, and between the three chapters of *Shema.* At those points, אָמֵן (but not בָּרוּךְ הוּא וּבָרוּךְ שְׁמוֹ) may be responded to any blessing. Some responses, however, are so important that they are permitted at any point in the *Shema* blessings. They are:
(a) In Kaddish, אָמֵן יְהֵא שְׁמֵהּ רַבָּא . . . עָלְמַיָּא and the אָמֵן after דַּאֲמִירָן בְּעָלְמָא; (b) the response to בָּרְכוּ (even of one called to the Torah); and (c) during the *chazzan's* repetition of *Shemoneh Esrei* – 1) in *Kedushah,* the verses קָדוֹשׁ קָדוֹשׁ קָדוֹשׁ . . . כְּבוֹדוֹ and בָּרוּךְ כְּבוֹד ה׳ מִמְּקוֹמוֹ; 2) the אָמֵן after הָאֵל הַקָּדוֹשׁ; 3) the three words מוֹדִים אֲנַחְנוּ לָךְ.
During the recital of the two verses שְׁמַע and בָּרוּךְ שֵׁם, absolutely no interruptions are permitted.

In some congregations the *chazzan* chants a melody during his recitation of *Borchu,* so that the congregation can then recite *'Blessed, praised . . .'*

Chazzan bows at *'Bless,'* and straightens up at *'HASHEM.'*

Bless HASHEM, the blessed One.

Congregation, followed by *chazzan,* responds, bowing at *'Blessed'* and straightening up at *'HASHEM.'*

Blessed is HASHEM, the blessed One, for all eternity.

Blessed, praised, glorified, exalted and upraised is the Name of the King Who rules over kings — the Holy One, Blessed is He. For He is the First and He is the Last and aside from Him there is no god.[1] *Extol Him — Who rides the highest heavens — with His Name, YAH, and exult before Him.*[2] *His Name is exalted beyond every blessing and praise.*[3] *Blessed is the Name of His glorious kingdom for all eternity. Blessed be the Name of HASHEM from this time and forever.*[4]

BLESSINGS OF THE SHEMA

It is preferable that one sit while reciting the following series of prayers — particularly the *Kedushah* verses, *'Holy, holy, holy . . .'* and *'Blessed is the glory . . .'* — until *Shemoneh Esrei.*

The following paragraph is recited aloud by the *chazzan,* then repeated by the congregation.

בָּרוּךְ: *Blessed are You, HASHEM, our God, King of the universe, Who forms light and creates darkness,* makes peace and creates all.*[5]

Congregations that do not recite *Yotzros* continue on page 224.

Congregations that recite *Yotzros* continue:

The primeval light is in the treasury of eternal life;
'Let there be lights from the darkness,' He declared — and so it was!

(1) Cf. *Isaiah* 44:6. (2) *Psalms* 68:5. (3) Cf. *Nechemiah* 9:5. (4) *Psalms* 113:2. (5) Cf. *Isaiah* 45:7.

that anything people find unpleasant either is not an act of God or proves that He lacks power. To the contrary, we believe unequivocally that God is One; what appears to our limited human intelligence to be contradictory or evil is really part of the plan of the One Merciful God, despite our failure to understand it.

The 'light' of this blessing refers not merely to the newly dawned day, but to the physical forces of creation itself. Light is the energy-giving, life-giving force of the universe, and, in the words of the Psalmist (19:2): *The heavens declare the glory of God,* by functioning harmoniously and efficiently in accordance with His will (*R' Munk*).

◆§ Yotzros

Piyutim (liturgical poems) are inserted at various points in the synagogue service on the Festivals and on certain Sabbaths during the year. These prayers, which date back to ancient times (see page 35), are commonly known as *yotzer* or *yotzros,* but this is a misnomer. Depending upon the point at which it is recited, a *piyut* may be properly classified as an *ofan, me'orah, ahavah, zulas,* etc. Those *piyutim* recited at this point are correctly called *yotzros,* because they appear after the passage that begins יוֹצֵר, *[yotzer] Who forms. Piyutim* inserted during the *chazzan's Amidah* repetition are collectively called קְרוּבוֹת, *kerovos* [from קרב, *to draw near*], an allusion to 'the *chazzan* who presents the prayers.' These *piyutim* are sometimes called קְרוּבֶץ, *krovetz,* the acronym of קוֹל רִנָּה וִישׁוּעָה בְּאָהֳלֵי צַדִּיקִים, *The sound of rejoicing and salvation in the tents of the righteous* (*Psalms* 118:15), a verse that aptly describes these compositions. Again, the location of the *piyut* determines its proper name: *reshus, magen, mechayeh, meshalesh,* etc. Nevertheless, in common practice, all of the morning *piyutim* are known as *yotzros.*

The authorship of many *piyutim* may be indicated by the composer's signature, which is often woven into the initial letters of the verses of the *piyut.* Thus we know that the *kerovos* for both the first and second day of Succos were written by R' Elazar HaKalir (see p. 35). However, the Succos *yotzros* do not bear any signature. Based upon the style and age of these *piyutim,* they too were probably composed by R' Elazar HaKalir.

FIRST DAY

All:

אַכְתִּיר* זֵר תְּהִלָּה,*
לְנוֹרָא עֲלִילָה,
בְּמִי זֹאת עוֹלָה.*[1]
בְּאֶדֶר רְנָנִים אֶעֶלְסָה,
כְּנַף רְנָנִים נֶעֱלָסָה,[2]
לְמֶלֶךְ רָם וְנִשָּׂא.
גַּדְתִּי אַרְבַּע,
לְמִסְפַּר רֹבַע,
לְחָן עַל אַרְבַּע.*[3]

Chazzan, then congregation:

אֲסַלֵּד בְּשֶׁבַח וְתוֹדָה,
בְּתוֹךְ קָהָל וְעֵדָה,
בְּלָקְחִי לוּלָב וַאֲגֻדָּה, קָדוֹשׁ.

All:

דְּרוֹשׁ בָּמוֹ צֶדֶק,
לְשָׁפְטָם לְצֶדֶק,*
דִּינָם לְהוֹצִיא לְצֶדֶק.[4]
הַלֵּל בָּם אֶפְצֶה,
וּמְלִיצַי יַרְצֶה,
וְכַזָּהָב אֵצֵא.[5]
וְרוֹבֵץ בַּפֶּתַח* יֵבוֹשׁ,
וְחֵטְא בְּצוּל תִּכְבּוֹשׁ,[6]
קְרָאתִיךָ אַל אֵבוֹשׁ.[7]

SECOND DAY

All:

אַאֲמִיץ* לְנוֹרָא וְאָיוֹם,
בְּהִסְתּוֹפְפִי לְפָנָיו אֶמְצָא פִדְיוֹם,
אַךְ בַּחֲמִשָּׁה עָשָׂר יוֹם.*[8]
בְּלָקְחִי כַּף תֹּמֶר וּשְׁלֹשֶׁת מִינֵי קְבוּעִי,
בָּם אֲהַלֵּל לְאוֹרִי וְיִשְׁעִי, בַּחֹדֶשׁ הַשְּׁבִיעִי.[8]
גֵּאוּת אַלְבִּישׁ לְדָר בַּמְּרוֹמִים,
לְהַלְּלוֹ בְּמַרְבִּיּוֹת שְׁלֵמִים וְלֹא קְטוּמִים,
תָּחֹגּוּ אֶת חַג יהוה שִׁבְעַת יָמִים.[8]

Chazzan, then congregation:

אֲהַלֵּל בְּפֶה וְלָשׁוֹן, לְשׁוֹמֵעַ קוֹל לַחֲשׁוֹן,
כְּנָם וּלְקַחְתֶּם לָכֶם בַּיּוֹם הָרִאשׁוֹן,[9] קָדוֹשׁ.

All:

דָּגוּל מִקּוֹלוֹת מַיִם נֶאְדָּר,[10]
אֲאַפְּדֶנּוּ הוֹד וְהָדָר, בִּפְרִי עֵץ הָדָר.[9]
הַמְּרוֹמָם בִּקְהַל עַם נְצוּרִים,
בְּהִלּוּל וּפְאֵר אוֹתוֹ מַכְתִּירִים, בְּכַפּוֹת תְּמָרִים.[9]
וְיָרִיק רֹב בְּרָכוֹת מֵאֲרֻבּוֹת,
לְאוֹם מְהַלְּלוֹ מִסַּרְעַף וּמִקְּרָבוֹת,
בַּעֲנַף עֵץ עָבוֹת.[9]
זְכֻיּוֹת יִכְרְעוּ וְעָוֹן יִמְחַל,
מִלְּהִכָּווֹת בְּשַׁלְהֶבֶת רִשְׁפֵּי גַחַל,
תּוֹמְכֵי עַרְבֵי נָחַל.[9]

אַכְתִּיר ◆§ — *I shall fashion a crown.* The *paytan* follows the *aleph-beis* as he places himself in the *chazzan's* position and describes his task of leading the congregation in prayer and praise of God.

Some suggest that R' Elazar HaKalir's name appears in the first two verses: אַכְתִּיר זֵר תְּהִלָּה לְנוֹרָא עֲלִילָה בְּמִי זֹאת עוֹלָה בְּאֶדֶר רְנָנִים . . .

זֵר תְּהִלָּה — *A crown of praise.* The Midrash tells how the angel appointed over prayer weaves the prayers of Israel into wreaths with which he, so to speak, crowns God (*Shemos Rabbah* 21:4; *Chagigah* 13b).

בְּמִי זֹאת עוֹלָה — *Among [Israel,] 'She-that-rises.'* The gentile nations refer to Israel as, *'She that rises from the Wilderness like columns of smoke'* (*Song of Songs* 3:6), while the Heavenly Tribunal calls Israel, *'She that rises from the Wilderness, leaning upon her Beloved'* (ibid. 8:5).

לְחָן עַל אַרְבַּע — *In honor of Him of Him Who[se throne] rests upon four.* The first chapter of *Ezekiel* describes the prophet's *Merkavah* [Chariot] Vision in which he sees God's heavenly Throne [called the מֶרְכָּבָה, *Merkavah*] borne by four celestial beings. Presumably, the *paytan* finds an unspecified relationship between these four angels and the Four Species.

לְשָׁפְטָם לְצֶדֶק — *To judge them righteous.* On Succos God judges the world with respect to rainfall (*Rosh Hashanah* 1:2). Therefore we pray that by performing the *mitzvah* of the Four Species, Israel should be found meritorious and righteous.

וְרוֹבֵץ בַּפֶּתַח — *The [evil] one crouching at the door [lit., opening].* This expression, based on *Genesis* 4:7, means that the Evil Inclination always lurks nearby plotting to trap man into sin. Externally it waits at man's door to dog his every footstep, i.e., temptation is always present; internally it rests in his heart and mind waiting to find entrance into his emotions and thoughts.

אַאֲמִיץ ◆§ — *I shall powerfully praise.* The acrostic of this *piyut* forms the *aleph-beis*. Most *machzorim* have an introductory bibliographic note that the last verse contains the author's name שְׁלֹמֹה, *Shlomo*, but this is obviously a mistake.

At first glance this *piyut* is confusing for the author jumps back and forth between first,

FIRST DAY

All:

א *I shall fashion a crown* of praise,* for Him of awesome deed, among [Israel,] 'She-that-rises.'[1]**

ב *I shall rejoice with powerful glad song, we shall rejoice with the glad song of winged angels,[2] [sung] to the uplifted and exalted King.*

ג *I have gathered [the] Four [Species], the number [symbolic] of the four[-sided Israelite camp], in honor of Him Who[se throne] rests upon four.[3]**

Chazzan, then congregation:

I shall glorify with praise and thanksgiving, amidst congregation and flock, as I take the lulav and [its] bundle, O holy One!

All:

ד *Seek righteousness in them, to judge them righteous,* to bring forth their judgment in righteousness.[4]*

ה *As I recite Hallel with them [the Four Species], may my advocate angels [created by the mitzvah] find favor, and may I go forth [from my judgment as pure] as gold.[5]*

ו *May the [evil] one crouching at the door* be shamed, and may You suppress sin [and throw it] into the depths,[6] when I call upon You may I not be shamed.[7]*

SECOND DAY

All:

א *I shall powerfully praise* the Awesome and Fearful One, may I find redemption, as I stand before Him at the portal, on this fifteenth day.[8]**

ב *As I take the date-palm branch and the [other] three ordained species, with them to offer praise to my Light and my Salvation, in this seventh month.[8]*

ג *In grandeur shall I clothe Him Who dwells on high, praising Him with long branches, complete and unbroken, [as I fulfill,] 'You shall celebrate HASHEM's Festival for seven days.'[9]*

Chazzan, then congregation:

I shall offer praise with mouth and tongue, to Him Who hearkens to the sound of whispered prayer, as He has said, 'And you shall take for yourselves on the first day'[9] — O Holy One.

All:

ד *The Exalted One, stronger than rushing waters,[10] I shall adorn Him with majesty and splendor, [when I hold] the fruit of the esrog tree.[9]*

ה *He Who is exalted amid the congregation of [Israel] the guarded nation, they crown Him with praise and splendor, [when they hold] the date-palm branches.[9]*

ו *May He pour abundant blessings through the windows [of heaven], for the nation that praises Him with heart and innards, [when they hold] the branch of the plaited [myrtle] tree.[9]*

ז *May their merits be decisive and their sin forgiven, that they be not burned by flames of flashing coal, when they hold the brook willows.[9]*

(1) Cf. *Song of Songs* 3:6; 8:5. (2) *Job* 39:13. (3) Cf. *Ezekiel* ch. 1. (4) Cf. *Psalms* 37:6. (5) Cf. *Job* 23:10. (6) Cf. *Micah* 7:19. (7) Cf. *Psalms* 31:18. (8) Cf. *Leviticus* 23:9. (9) Cf. 23:40. (10) Cf. *Psalms* 93:4. (11) Cf. *Leviticus* 23:40.

second and third person, and between singular and plural. Moreover, the final stich of each verse quotes a Biblical verse from the portions of *Leviticus* (ch. 23) and *Deuteronomy* (ch. 16) that speak of Succos. In most cases the *paytan* has preserved the exact language of the verse, thus adding to the confusion. Careful examination will reveal, however, that the speaker of the verses is the *chazzan* sometimes speaking for himself, sometimes for the congregation. His words are directed either to the congregation or to God. Hopefully the translation has succeeded in eliminating the ambiguities and confusion.

בַּחֲמִשָּׁה עָשָׂר יוֹם — *On this fifteenth day.* Although the second day of Succos is the

FIRST DAY	SECOND DAY
זָכֹר סִכּוּךְ לְדוֹרוֹת, לָהֶם לְהוֹרוֹת, לְסַכֵּךְ וּלְקָרוֹת. חֲסוֹת בְּצֵל סֻכָּה, כְּחֹק נְסוּכָה, שִׁבְעָה לְהִסְתּוֹכְּכָה. טְלוּל עֲנָנִים אֶזְכְּרָה, בְּכָל דּוֹר וָדוֹר אַזְכִּירָה, לְחַסְדֵי דָוִד זָכְרָה.[1] יָקֵם סֻכָּתוֹ, וְתִכּוֹן מַלְכוּתוֹ, וְתֶרֶב גְּדֻלָּתוֹ. כִּימֵי עוֹלָם, וּמַלְכוּתוֹ עַד הָעוֹלָם,[2] לְדָוִד וּלְזַרְעוֹ עַד עוֹלָם.[3] לְדוֹר וָדוֹר תִּמְלֹךְ,[4] וְהוּא עֲדֵי עַד יִמְלֹךְ, מֶלֶךְ מַמְלִיךְ מְלֹךְ. מְהֵרָה לְהַצְמִיחַ זַרְעוֹ, עַל עַם מְשַׁוְּעוֹ, לַעֲבֹר עַל פִּשְׁעוֹ. נֶחֱזֶה בְּעָזְךָ, בְּשׁוּבְךָ לְגַן אֱגוֹזְךָ,* וְעַיִן בְּעַיִן נֶחֱזְךָ.[5] סֻכָּתְךָ עֲלֵיהֶם תִּמְתַּח, וּבְצֵל לְקוֹחֶיךָ יִמְתַּח, וְלֹא יַכֵּם מְרְתָּח.	חֶדְוַת רַב תִּמְצְאוּ בְּלַהֲקַתְכֶם, חֲסוּנִים בְּצִוּוּי דַּת מַלְכְּכֶם, וּשְׂמַחְתֶּם לִפְנֵי יהוה אֱלֹהֵיכֶם.[6] טָרְחֲכֶם יָפִיק נוֹהֵג לֵילוֹת וְיָמִים, גְּאוֹן נוֹגְשֵׂיכֶם יְגַדַּע וְיַדְמִים, לְבַל תֵּעָנְשׁוּ* בַּחֲגִיגַת שִׁבְעַת יָמִים.[6] יַסְכִּית אֵל פִּלּוּל וְיַאֲזִין הֶגְיוֹנַי, וִיקַבֵּל כְּקָרְבָּן רַחַשׁ עִנְיָנַי, וְחַגֹּתֶם אוֹתוֹ חַג לַיהוה.[7] כִּשְׁרוֹן כֹּחַ יַחֲלִיף לְשׁוֹשַׁנָּה, חוֹגֶגֶת וְעוֹצֶרֶת וְסוֹכֶכֶת בְּרִנָּנָה, שִׁבְעַת יָמִים בַּשָּׁנָה.[7] לְעֵת יָסִיר סֵבֶל מֵעַל שִׁכְמֵיכֶם, תָּרֹנּוּ וְתָחֹגּוּ בְּקִרְיַת מוֹעֲדֵיכֶם, חֻקַּת עוֹלָם לְדֹרֹתֵיכֶם.[7] מַשְׁגִּיחַ מֵחֶרֶךְ תְּהַלְלוּ בְּאִיּוּמִים, מַנְעִימִים קוֹל וְלֹא דוֹמִים, בַּסֻּכֹּת תֵּשְׁבוּ שִׁבְעַת יָמִים.[8] נְדִיבֵי עַמִּים סוֹדְרֵי עֲרָכוֹת, בְּאֶבְרָתוֹ לָעַד יָהוּ סְכוּכוֹת, כָּל הָאֶזְרָח בְּיִשְׂרָאֵל יֵשְׁבוּ בַּסֻּכֹּת.[8] סֹלּוּ בְּהִלּוּל לְשׁוֹכֵן בֵּינֵיכֶם, וְתָנוּחוּ בְּהַשְׁקֵט כָּל יְמֵיכֶם, לְמַעַן יֵדְעוּ דֹרֹתֵיכֶם.[9] עֶלְיוֹן הוֹדִיעַ פְּלָאָיו עַל יְדֵי גוֹאֵל, עֲמוּסָיו סִכֵּךְ בַּעֲנָנִים כְּהוֹאֵל, כִּי בַסֻּכּוֹת הוֹשַׁבְתִּי אֶת בְּנֵי יִשְׂרָאֵל.[9] פָּקַדְתִּי עַמִּי לָחוֹן שִׁירַיִם, מִשְׁפָּטָם לְהוֹצִיא כָּאוֹר וְכַצָּהֳרָיִם, בְּהוֹצִיאִי אוֹתָם מֵאֶרֶץ מִצְרָיִם.[9]

sixteenth of Tishrei, it must be remembered that in *Eretz Yisrael* there is only one *Yom Tov* day, the second day already being *Chol HaMoed*. The second *Yom Tov* day of the Diaspora was originally instituted when the exact day of *Yom Tov* was not known to those living outside of *Eretz Yisrael*. Hence, the *piyutim* often refer to the second day as the fifteenth of Tishrei.

לְגַן אֱגוֹזְךָ – *To Your orchard of nut-trees.* Israel is compared to an orchard of nut-trees. Upon looking at nuts one sees only shells, while the meat is hidden from view. When opened, however, the nut reveals its nutritious food. Similarly, Israel is modest and unpretentious. Her scholars are not conspicuous; they do not praise themselves publicly. But when examined, they are found to be full of wisdom.

Alternatively, when a nut falls to the muddy ground, its contents are not defiled because the shell protects it. So, too, although Israel, exiled among the nations, endures great tribulation, its actions are not defiled (*Rashi* to *Song of Songs* 6:11).

לְבַל תֵּעָנְשׁוּ – *That you not be punished.* During a long Festival of eating, drinking and merry-making, there is always a danger of one becom-

FIRST DAY

ז *A recollection for all generations of the [Wilderness] succos, in order to teach them to cover the succah with s'chach.*

ח *Take shelter in the succah's shade, as decreed in the chosen [Torah], [to dwell] seven days under its s'chach.*

ט *I shall recall the succah of clouds, I shall mention it in each generation. Remember the kindness of David[1] [and send the Messiah].*

י *Rebuild his [David's] succah, re-establish his kingship, and increase his greatness,*

כ *As in days of old; and may his kingdom be eternal,[2] to David and to his descendants forever.[3]*

ל *May You reign for all generations,[4] forever may he reign, O King Who gives sovereignty, let him rule.*

מ *Speedily cause his descendants to flourish, over the people of his salvation, to forgive their sin.*

נ *May we merit seeing Your might, when You return to Your orchard of nut-trees,* may every eye merit seeing You.[5]*

ס *May You spread Your succah over them, and let Your shade protect those whom You have taken, so that the heat will not smite them.*

SECOND DAY

ח *You [Israel] will find great delight in your assemblies, as you fulfill with power your King's decree, 'And you shall rejoice before* HASHEM, *your God.'[6]*

ט *May He Who controls the cycle of night and day put an end to your exertions, may He cut down and silence the power of your oppressors, that you not be punished* while celebrating for seven days.[6]*

י *May God listen to [my] prayer and harken to my words, and accept as an altar-offering the expression of my needs, [as I fulfill,] 'You shall celebrate it as a Festival to* HASHEM.*'[7]*

כ *May He rejuvenate the skillful strength of [Israel] the rose-like nation, as it celebrates, desists from labor and dwells in succah booths joyfully, for seven days in the year.[7]*

ל *When He will remove the burden [of exile] from upon your shoulders, you will sing joyfully and celebrate in [Jerusalem] the city of your assembly, it is an eternal decree for your generations.[7]*

מ *In awe you shall praise Him Who watches through the [heavenly] window, with sweetness of voice and not in silence, [while fulfilling] 'You shall dwell in succos for seven days.'[8]*

נ *The most noble of peoples, those who follow the order [of prayer], may they always be sheltered by Your pinion, [as they fulfill,] 'Every citizen of Israel is to dwell in succos.'[8]*

ס *Exalt with praise Him Who resides among you, and may you rest serenely all your days, so that your future generations may know.[9]*

ע *May the Supreme One let His wonders be known through the Redeemer, how He sheltered with clouds the nation He bore, as he desired, [as He has said,] 'For I caused the Children of Israel to dwell in succos.[9]*

פ *'I have ordered My community [of angels] to favor the remnants [of Israel], to exonerate them and clear them like the afternoon sun, [as I did] when I brought them out of the land of Egypt.[9]*

(1) Cf. *II Chronicles* 6:42. (2) Cf. *I Chronicles* 17:14.
(3) *II Samuel* 22:51; *Psalms* 18:51. (4) Cf. *Psalms* 146:10. (5) Cf. *Isaiah* 52:8.
(6) Cf. *Leviticus* 23:40. (7) Cf. 23:41. (8) Cf. 23:42. (9) Cf. 23:43.

FIRST DAY

עֵצִים בְּנָטְלָם אַרְבָּעָה,
לִמְזוּזַת רְבִעָה,[1]
לְזוֹכֵר בְּרִית וּשְׁבוּעָה.

פְּרִי עֵץ הָדָר,*[2]
אֶקַּח לְנֶאְדָּר,
כִּי כְבוֹדוֹ הוֹד וְהָדָר.

צֶמַח תֹּמֶר,
אֶשָּׂא לְהַאֲמֵר,
לְכֻלּוֹ כָּבוֹד אוֹמֵר.[3]

קִיחַת עֲנַף עֵץ עָבוֹת,
אֶאֱסוֹר בַּעֲבוֹת,
לְמַבִּיט בְּרִית אָבוֹת.

רַעֲנַנֵּי עֲרָבָה,
כְּצִמְחֵי רְבָבָה,
לְדָגוּל מֵרְבָבָה.

שְׁתוּלִים בַּחֲצֵרוֹת,
בָּם יְפַדּוּ מְצָרוֹת,
כִּבְזָכֵר חֲצוֹצְרוֹת.[4]

❖תְּכוּנִים לְכַפָּרָה,
לְסוֹרְרָה כְּפָרָה,
בְּלִי צֵאת* חֲפוּרָה,
מִפְּנֵי קָדוֹשׁ.

SECOND DAY

צְקוּן צַעֲקַתְכֶם הִסְכַּתִּי בְּאָזְנָי,
וּפְדוּת שָׁלַחְתִּי לְכָל הֲמוֹנָי,
וַיְדַבֵּר מֹשֶׁה אֶת מוֹעֲדֵי יהוה.[5]
קוֹרֵא דוֹרוֹת חַי עוֹלָמִים,
צִוָּה לְעַם שְׁמוֹ מַנְעִימִים,
חַג הַסֻּכֹּת תַּעֲשֶׂה לְךָ שִׁבְעַת יָמִים.[6]
רָם מִמְּעוֹנֶךָ הָסֵךְ מַקְהֲלוֹתֶיךָ,
לְרַחֵם וּלְהוֹשִׁיעַ כָּל לַהֲקוֹתֶיךָ,
וְשָׂמַחְתָּ בְּחַגֶּךָ אַתָּה וּבִנְךָ וּבִתֶּךָ.[7]
שׁוֹדֵד עוֹד לְבַל יְבַהִילֶךָ,
לָתֵת תִּקְוָה לִפְזוּרֵי כְמֵהֶיךָ,
שִׁבְעַת יָמִים תָּחֹג לַיהוה אֱלֹהֶיךָ.[8]
תְּקֶף הֲמוֹן קִרְיַת חָנָה,
בָּאִים לְהֵרָאוֹת פָּנָיו בַּחֲנִינָה,
שָׁלֹשׁ פְּעָמִים בַּשָּׁנָה.[9]
תְּאֵבֵי יִשְׁעוֹ לַחֲזוֹת כְּבוֹדוֹ,
לְהַתְשִׁירוֹ מִשֶּׁלוֹ וְהַכֹּל בְּיָדוֹ,[10]
אִישׁ כְּמַתְּנַת יָדוֹ.[11]
תּוֹמְכֵי סַנְסִנֵּי רְשָׁאִים,
מִשָּׂטָן וּמִמַּשְׁחִית יָהוּ חֲבוּאִים,
לַחֲזוֹת וּלְהַסְכִּית בִּבְשׂוֹרוֹת טוֹבוֹת,
לָכֵן הִנֵּה יָמִים בָּאִים.*[12]
❖אֲהַלֵּל בְּפֶה וְלָשׁוֹן, לְשׁוֹמֵעַ קוֹל לַחָשׁוֹן,
כְּנָם וּלְקַחְתֶּם לָכֶם בַּיּוֹם הָרִאשׁוֹן,[13] קָדוֹשׁ.

ing overly frivolous and even sinful.

This also refers to God's promise that nobody would burglarize the pilgrims' properties when they ascended to the Temple — even if they left their lands completely unprotected.

פְּרִי עֵץ הָדָר — *The fruit of the esrog [lit., splendrous] tree.* Each of the next four verses mentions one of the Four Species, and tells how Israel uses it in exalting God.

The Midrash explains that each of the Four Species symbolizes God. The *esrog* is called הָדָר, *splendrous,* and God is praised with הוֹד וְהָדָר לָבָשְׁתָּ, *You have donned majesty and splendor* (*Psalms* 104:1); the *lulav* is a branch of the תָּמָר, *date-palm,* and God is called צַדִּיק כַּתָּמָר יִפְרָח, *the Righteous One Who is like a flourishing date-palm* (ibid. 92:13); the third is the *haddasim,* and the prophet describes his vision of God עוֹמֵד בֵּין הַהֲדַסִּים, *standing among the haddasim* (*Zechariah* 1:8); the fourth is the *aravos,* and God רֹכֵב בָּעֲרָבוֹת, *rides upon the* [highest heaven; which is called] *aravos* (*Psalms* 68:5).

בְּלִי צֵאת — *That they not leave [the courtroom].* The *mitzvah* of the Four Species may be explained with a parable: Two people came to a judge to adjudicate their dispute. When they leave the courtroom, how can we know which one was victorious? If one of them raises his spear in triumph everyone knows he was victorious. So it is with Israel and the nations of the world. Each accuses the other on Rosh Hashanah and we do not know who won the dispute in the Heavenly Court. But when the Jews go out on Succos with *lulavim* and *esrogim* in their hands, this demonstrates Israel's victory (*Midrash Vayikra Rabbah* 30:2).

לָכֵן הִנֵּה יָמִים בָּאִים — *Therefore, behold! Days [of Redemption] are coming.* The prophet Jeremiah

FIRST DAY

ע *When they take [branches of] the four trees, to the [Temple that was built with] square doorposts,*[1] *in honor of Him Who remembers covenant and oath.*

פ *The fruit of the esrog tree,*[2]* *I shall take to [honor] the mighty One, for His honor is majesty and splendor.*

צ *The growth of the date palm, I shall raise in praise, to [honor] Him of Whom all proclaim, 'Glory!'*[3]

ק *Taking twigs of the myrtle tree, I shall bind them [to the lulav] with bands, to [honor] Him Who perceives the patriarchal covenant.*

ר *Fresh willow shoots [complete the bundle], [taken by the nation] that thrives like plants, to [honor] Him Who is surrounded by myriad [angels].*

ש *[Israel, the nation] planted in the [synagogue] courtyards, will be redeemed from troubles through them [Four Species], just as when they were remembered through the trumpets.*[4]

ת ∴*They [the Four Species] are prepared for atonement, [for those who have strayed] like a wayward cow, that they not leave [the courtroom]* in shame, from before the Holy One.*

SECOND DAY

צ *'My ears have heard the outpouring of their cries, and I have sent redemption for all My multitudes, [when] Moses declared the festive seasons of HASHEM.'*[5]

ק *The Caller to the generations, the Life-giver to the world, commanded the people who sing sweetly in His Name, 'Make yourself a Succos Festival for seven days.'*[6]

ר *O Exalted One, from Your heavenly abode protect Your assembly, be merciful and save Your entire congregation [as they fulfill], 'And you shall rejoice on your Festival — you, your son and daughter.'*[7]

ש *May [Satan] the pillager never again confound you, thus giving hope to your scattered yearners, [who fulfill,] 'For seven days you shall celebrate to HASHEM, your God.'*[8]

ת *The mighty multitude of [pilgrims to Jerusalem] the residential city, they come to appear before Him in supplication, three times each year.*[9] *Those who desire His salvation, to behold His honor, to present Him with His own, for all belongs to Him,*[10] *each person according to what has been given him.*[11]

Those who hold the branches of green plants, may they be hidden from Satan and Destroyer, may they see and hear the good tidings, 'Therefore, behold! Days [of Redemption] are coming!'[12]*

∴*I shall offer praise with mouth and tongue, to Him Who hearkens to the sound of whispered prayer, as He has said, 'And you shall take for yourself on the first day.'*[13]*— O Holy One.*

(1) Cf. *Ezekiel* 41:21. (2) *Leviticus* 23:40. (3) Cf. *Psalms* 29:9. (4) Cf. *Numbers* 10:9. (5) Cf. *Leviticus* 23:44. (6) *Deuteronomy* 16:13. (7) 16:14. (8) 16:15. (9) 16:16. (10) Cf. *I Chronicles* 29:14; see Mishnah *Avos* 3:8. (11) *Deuteronomy* 16:17. (12) *Jeremiah* 16:14; 23:7. (13) *Leviticus* 23:40.

uses this phrase to introduce seven of his prophecies. Some speak of the Destruction, others of the rebuilding in Messianic times. Assumedly, the *paytan,* having pleaded for salvation, redemption and the rebuilt *Beis HaMikdash,* means to cite the verse: *Therefore, behold! The days are coming — says HASHEM — when they will no longer say, 'By the life of HASHEM Who has removed the Children of Israel from the land of Egypt;' but, 'By the life of God Who has removed the Children of Israel from the land of the north [Babylon] and from all the lands to which they have been cast ...'* (*Jeremiah* 16:14-15). Thus, the phrase is a fitting conclusion to the *piyut.*

Additionally, the *Haftarah* for the first day of Succos begins הִנֵּה יוֹם בָּא, *Behold! A day is coming.* That phrase is the singular form of the phrase before us. Perhaps, the *paytan,* who lived in *Eretz Yisrael,* and celebrated only one day of *Yom Tov,* alludes to the day's *Haftarah* with this verse.

ON A WEEKDAY CONTINUE HERE:

הַמֵּאִיר לָאָרֶץ וְלַדָּרִים* עָלֶיהָ בְּרַחֲמִים, וּבְטוּבוֹ מְחַדֵּשׁ בְּכָל יוֹם תָּמִיד מַעֲשֵׂה בְרֵאשִׁית. מָה רַבּוּ מַעֲשֶׂיךָ* יהוה,

☙ הַמֵּאִיר לָאָרֶץ וְלַדָּרִים — *He Who illuminates the earth and those who dwell.* The earth's dwellers enjoy the light, but so does the earth itself, because sunlight makes vegetation possible.

ON THE SABBATH CONTINUE HERE:

הַכֹּל יוֹדוּךָ,* וְהַכֹּל יְשַׁבְּחוּךָ, וְהַכֹּל יֹאמְרוּ אֵין קָדוֹשׁ כַּיהוה.[1] הַכֹּל יְרוֹמְמְוּךָ סֶּלָה, יוֹצֵר הַכֹּל. הָאֵל הַפּוֹתֵחַ בְּכָל יוֹם דַּלְתוֹת שַׁעֲרֵי מִזְרָח, וּבוֹקֵעַ חַלּוֹנֵי רָקִיעַ,* מוֹצִיא חַמָּה מִמְּקוֹמָהּ וּלְבָנָה מִמְּכוֹן שִׁבְתָּהּ, וּמֵאִיר לָעוֹלָם כֻּלּוֹ וּלְיוֹשְׁבָיו, שֶׁבָּרָא בְּמִדַּת רַחֲמִים. הַמֵּאִיר לָאָרֶץ וְלַדָּרִים עָלֶיהָ בְּרַחֲמִים, וּבְטוּבוֹ מְחַדֵּשׁ בְּכָל יוֹם תָּמִיד מַעֲשֵׂה בְרֵאשִׁית. הַמֶּלֶךְ הַמְּרוֹמָם לְבַדּוֹ מֵאָז, הַמְּשֻׁבָּח וְהַמְּפֹאָר וְהַמִּתְנַשֵּׂא מִימוֹת עוֹלָם. אֱלֹהֵי עוֹלָם בְּרַחֲמֶיךָ הָרַבִּים, רַחֵם עָלֵינוּ, אֲדוֹן עֻזֵּנוּ, צוּר מִשְׂגַּבֵּנוּ, מָגֵן יִשְׁעֵנוּ, מִשְׂגָּב בַּעֲדֵנוּ. אֵין כְּעֶרְכֶּךָ,* וְאֵין זוּלָתֶךָ, אֶפֶס בִּלְתֶּךָ, וּמִי דּוֹמֶה לָּךְ. אֵין כְּעֶרְכְּךָ יהוה אֱלֹהֵינוּ בָּעוֹלָם הַזֶּה, וְאֵין זוּלָתְךָ מַלְכֵּנוּ לְחַיֵּי הָעוֹלָם הַבָּא. אֶפֶס בִּלְתְּךָ גּוֹאֲלֵנוּ לִימוֹת הַמָּשִׁיחַ, וְאֵין דּוֹמֶה לְּךָ מוֹשִׁיעֵנוּ לִתְחִיַּת הַמֵּתִים.

☙ The Sabbath Additions

Since the Sabbath is the weekly testimony to the fact that God created the world, the first blessing of the Shema, which deals with creation, is augmented on the Sabbath with three apt passages:

1. הַכֹּל יוֹדוּךָ, *All will thank You,* speaks of the Creator Who renews creation daily;

2. אֵל אָדוֹן, *God — The Master,* praises the glory of creation itself;

3. לָאֵל אֲשֶׁר שָׁבַת, *To the God Who rested,* celebrates the Sabbath. Thus, these three passages are appropriate only on the Sabbath, and are omitted on all weekday Festivals *(World of Prayer).*

☙ הַכֹּל יוֹדוּךָ — *All will thank You.* The word 'all' refers to the previous blessing, which ends וּבוֹרֵא אֶת הַכֹּל, *and creates all.* Thus, every facet of the universe will join in thanking and lauding God. Only man and the angels do this verbally; the rest of creation does so by carrying out its assigned tasks and inspiring man to recognize the Guiding Hand that created and orders everything.

דַּלְתוֹת שַׁעֲרֵי מִזְרָח ... חַלּוֹנֵי רָקִיעַ — *Doors of the gateways of the East ... windows of the firmament.* These expressions are given various interpretations. On the simple level, they refer poetically to the rising sun breaking through the portals of darkness. Alternatively, the phrase *doors of the gateways* refers to daybreak, which illuminates the sky long before sunrise. The *windows* are different points in the sky at which the sun rises as the seasons move to the longer days of summer and then back again to the shorter days of winter *(R' Hirsch; Iyun Tefillah).*

אֵין כְּעֶרְכֶּךָ — *There is no comparison to You.* This verse makes four statements about God that are explained in the next verse. Thus the two verses should be seen as a unit. As explained by *R'*

ON A WEEKDAY CONTINUE HERE:

הַמֵּאִיר *He Who illuminates the earth and those who dwell* upon it, with compassion; and in His goodness renews daily, perpetually, the work of Creation. How great are Your works,** HASHEM,

מָה רַבּוּ מַעֲשֶׂיךָ — *How great are Your works.* This refers to the heavenly bodies and other major forces in creation. Homiletically, the Talmud (*Chullin* 127a) interprets, *how diverse are Your works;* some can live only on land, others only in the sea, and so on.

ON THE SABBATH CONTINUE HERE:

הַכֹּל יוֹדְוּךָ *All will thank You* and all will praise You — and all will declare: 'Nothing is as holy as* HASHEM!'[1] *All will exalt You, Selah! — You Who forms everything. The God Who opens daily the doors of the gateways of the East, and splits the windows of the firmament,* Who removes the sun from its place and the moon from the site of its dwelling, and Who illuminates all the world and its inhabitants, which He created with the attribute of mercy. He Who illuminates the earth and those who dwell upon it, with compassion; and in His goodness renews daily, perpetually, the work of creation. The King Who was exalted in solitude from before creation, Who is praised, glorified, and extolled since days of old. Eternal God, with Your abundant compassion be compassionate to us — O Master of our power, our rocklike stronghold; O Shield of our salvation, be a stronghold for us. There is no comparison to You,* there is nothing except for You, there is nothing without You, for who is like You? There is no comparison to You,* HASHEM, *our God, in this world; and there will be nothing except for You, our King, in the life of the World to Come; there will be nothing without You, our Redeemer, in Messianic days; and there will be none like You, our Savior; at the Resuscitation of the Dead.*

(1) *I Samuel* 2:2.

Hirsch, the four statements are:

(a) אֵין כְּעֶרְכְּךָ — *There is no comparison to You.* Although we have expressed our gratitude for the heavenly bodies and the various forces of the universe, we hasten to affirm that none of them can even be compared to God's power on earth.

(b) וְאֵין זוּלָתְךָ — *There is nothing except for You.* In the World to Come, even the most beneficial aspects of life in this material world will not exist. In the blissful state of that world, nothing will exist except for God and those whose lives on earth have made them worthy of His spiritual grandeur.

(c) אֶפֶס בִּלְתְּךָ — *There is nothing without You.* On earth, too, there will be a state of bliss with the coming of the Messiah — but that redemption is impossible without God, despite the earthly factors that will seem to contribute to it.

(d) וּמִי דוֹמֶה לָּךְ — *For who is like You?* Nothing will so clearly reveal God's absolute mastery as the Resuscitation of the Dead. That is the ultimate redemption, for it will demonstrate that not only slavery and freedom, but even life and death, depend on Him.

ON A WEEKDAY

כֻּלָּם בְּחָכְמָה עָשִׂיתָ, מָלְאָה הָאָרֶץ קִנְיָנֶךָ.[1] הַמֶּלֶךְ הַמְּרוֹמָם לְבַדּוֹ* מֵאָז, הַמְּשֻׁבָּח וְהַמְּפֹאָר וְהַמִּתְנַשֵּׂא מִימוֹת עוֹלָם. אֱלֹהֵי עוֹלָם, בְּרַחֲמֶיךָ הָרַבִּים רַחֵם עָלֵינוּ, אֲדוֹן עֻזֵּנוּ, צוּר מִשְׂגַּבֵּנוּ, מָגֵן יִשְׁעֵנוּ, מִשְׂגָּב בַּעֲדֵנוּ. אֵל בָּרוּךְ* גְּדוֹל דֵּעָה, הֵכִין וּפָעַל

הַמֶּלֶךְ הַמְּרוֹמָם לְבַדּוֹ — *The King Who was exalted in solitude.* Before Creation, God was *exalted in solitude,* because there were no creatures to praise Him *(Etz Yosef).*

אֵל בָּרוּךְ — *The blessed God.* This begins a lyric praise consisting of twenty-two words following the order of the *Aleph-Beis.* As noted at the bottom of the page in the commentary to אֵל

ON THE SABBATH

The following liturgical song is recited responsively in most congregations.
In some congregations, the *chazzan* and congregation sing the stanzas together.

אֵל אָדוֹן* עַל כָּל הַמַּעֲשִׂים, בָּרוּךְ וּמְבֹרָךְ* בְּפִי כָּל נְשָׁמָה,
גָּדְלוֹ וְטוּבוֹ מָלֵא עוֹלָם, דַּעַת וּתְבוּנָה סוֹבְבִים אֹתוֹ.
הַמִּתְגָּאֶה* עַל חַיּוֹת הַקֹּדֶשׁ, וְנֶהְדָּר בְּכָבוֹד עַל הַמֶּרְכָּבָה,
זְכוּת וּמִישׁוֹר לִפְנֵי כִסְאוֹ, חֶסֶד וְרַחֲמִים לִפְנֵי כְבוֹדוֹ.
טוֹבִים מְאוֹרוֹת שֶׁבָּרָא אֱלֹהֵינוּ, יְצָרָם בְּדַעַת בְּבִינָה וּבְהַשְׂכֵּל,
כֹּחַ וּגְבוּרָה נָתַן בָּהֶם, לִהְיוֹת מוֹשְׁלִים בְּקֶרֶב תֵּבֵל.
מְלֵאִים זִיו וּמְפִיקִים נֹגַהּ, נָאֶה זִיוָם בְּכָל הָעוֹלָם,
שְׂמֵחִים בְּצֵאתָם* וְשָׂשִׂים בְּבוֹאָם, עוֹשִׂים בְּאֵימָה רְצוֹן קוֹנָם.
פְּאֵר וְכָבוֹד* נוֹתְנִים לִשְׁמוֹ, צָהֳלָה וְרִנָּה לְזֵכֶר מַלְכוּתוֹ,
קָרָא לַשֶּׁמֶשׁ וַיִּזְרַח אוֹר, רָאָה וְהִתְקִין צוּרַת הַלְּבָנָה.*
שֶׁבַח נוֹתְנִים לוֹ כָּל צְבָא מָרוֹם.
תִּפְאֶרֶת וּגְדֻלָּה, שְׂרָפִים וְאוֹפַנִּים וְחַיּוֹת הַקֹּדֶשׁ—

⊷ אֵל אָדוֹן — *God — the Master.* This poetic prayer comprises twenty-two phrases, the initial letters of which form the *Aleph-Beis.* It is parallel to the alphabetical prayer אֵל בָּרוּךְ גְּדוֹל דֵּעָה of the weekday *Shacharis;* but the weekday prayer contains only twenty-two words. The *Vilna Gaon* explains that the lesser holiness of the weekdays is expressed not only in the shorter version, but in the content. There, the praise concentrates on God's greatness as we perceive it in the form of the heavenly bodies. Here, the greater holiness of the Sabbath enables us to perceive more — though clearly not all — of His greatness.

בָּרוּךְ וּמְבֹרָךְ — *The Blessed One — and He is blessed,* i.e., God is the source of all blessing. In addition, His creatures bless Him in their prayers and through their obedience to His will *(Vilna Gaon).*

הַמִּתְגָּאֶה — *He Who exalts Himself.* The *Chayos* are the highest category of angels, and the Chariot [מֶרְכָּבָה] refers to the order of angelic praises of God. Both were seen by Ezekiel (ch. 1) in his *Ma'aseh Merkavah* prophecy. Thus, they represent the highest degree of holiness accessible to human understanding. Nevertheless, God is exalted far above even this.

שְׂמֵחִים בְּצֵאתָם — *Glad as they go forth.* The heavenly bodies are likened to a loyal servant

ON A WEEKDAY

You make them all with wisdom, the world is full of Your possessions.[1] *The King Who was exalted in solitude* before Creation, Who is praised, glorified, and upraised since days of old. Eternal God, with Your abundant compassion be compassionate to us — O Master of our power, our rocklike stronghold, O Shield of our salvation, be a stronghold for us. The blessed God,* Who is great in knowledge, prepared and worked on*

(1) *Psalms* 104:24.

אָדוֹן, *God — the Master,* which is recited on the Sabbath, this formula of an *Aleph-Beis* acrostic is followed on the Sabbath as well, except that on the Sabbath each letter introduces an entire

ON THE SABBATH

The following liturgical song is recited responsively in most congregations. In some congregations, the *chazzan* and congregation sing the stanzas together.

אֵל אָדוֹן *God — the Master* over all works;* ב *the Blessed One —*
and He is blessed by the mouth of every soul;*
ג *His greatness and goodness fill the world,*
ד *wisdom and insight surround Him.*
ה *He Who exalts Himself* over the holy Chayos*
ו *and is splendrous in glory above the Chariot;*
ז *Merit and fairness are before His throne,*
ח *kindness and mercy are before His glory.*
ט *Good are the luminaries that our God has created,*
י *He has fashioned them with wisdom,*
with insight and discernment;
כ *Strength and power has He granted them,*
ל *to be dominant within the world.*
מ *Filled with luster and radiating brightness,*
נ *their luster is beautiful throughout the world;*
ס *Glad as they go forth* and exultant as they return,*
ע *they do with awe their Creator's will.*
פ *Splendor and glory* they bestow upon His Name,*
צ *jubilation and glad song upon the mention of His reign —*
ק *He called out to the sun and it glowed with light,*
ר *He saw and fashioned the form of the moon.**
ש *All the host above bestows praise on Him,*
ת *splendor and greatness — the Seraphim, Ophanim,*
and holy Chayos —

entrusted with an important mission. He is proud and happy when he sets out, but is even more joyous when he returns to his master.

פְּאֵר וְכָבוֹד — *Splendor and glory.* The exact movements of the heavenly bodies inspire people to praise the One Who created them.

צוּרַת הַלְּבָנָה — *The form of the moon.* With insight, God shaped the phases of the moon so

ON A WEEKDAY

זָהֳרֵי חַמָּה, טוֹב יָצַר כָּבוֹד לִשְׁמוֹ,* מְאוֹרוֹת נָתַן סְבִיבוֹת עֻזּוֹ, פִּנּוֹת צְבָאָיו קְדוֹשִׁים רוֹמְמֵי שַׁדַּי, תָּמִיד מְסַפְּרִים כְּבוֹד אֵל וּקְדֻשָּׁתוֹ. תִּתְבָּרַךְ יהוה אֱלֹהֵינוּ עַל שֶׁבַח מַעֲשֵׂה יָדֶיךָ, וְעַל מְאוֹרֵי אוֹר שֶׁעָשִׂיתָ, יְפָאֲרוּךָ, סֶּלָה.

phrase. See commentary below for the significance of this difference.

As a general rule, the use of the *Aleph-Beis* acrostic in the prayers conveys the idea that we praise God with every available sound and that His greatness is absolutely complete and harmonious. Furthermore, the emphasis on the letters implies our acknowledgment that the Torah, whose words and thoughts are formed with the letters of the *Aleph-Beis,* is the very basis of the continued existence of heaven and earth. In the familiar teaching of the Sages (*Pesachim* 68b) R' Elazar expains: Were it not for the [constant study of] Torah, heaven and earth would not exist, as it is said, *Were it not for My covenant* [i.e., the Torah] *day and night, I would not have established the systematic function of heaven and earth (Jeremiah* 33:25). This concept of the letters of the Torah is further alluded to in the verse from *Song of Songs* (1:4) in which Israel allegorically says to God: נָגִילָה וְנִשְׂמְחָה בָּךְ *we will rejoice and be glad in You.* The word בָּךְ has the numerical value of twenty-two, an allusion to the twenty-two letters of the *Aleph-Beis*, as if

ON THE SABBATH

לָאֵל אֲשֶׁר שָׁבַת* מִכָּל הַמַּעֲשִׂים, בַּיּוֹם הַשְּׁבִיעִי הִתְעַלָּה וְיָשַׁב עַל כִּסֵּא כְבוֹדוֹ, תִּפְאֶרֶת עָטָה לְיוֹם הַמְּנוּחָה, עֹנֶג קָרָא לְיוֹם הַשַּׁבָּת. זֶה שֶׁבַח שֶׁל יוֹם הַשְּׁבִיעִי,* שֶׁבּוֹ שָׁבַת אֵל מִכָּל מְלַאכְתּוֹ. וְיוֹם הַשְּׁבִיעִי מְשַׁבֵּחַ וְאוֹמֵר: מִזְמוֹר שִׁיר לְיוֹם הַשַּׁבָּת, טוֹב לְהוֹדוֹת לַיהוה.[1] לְפִיכָךְ יְפָאֲרוּ* וִיבָרְכוּ לָאֵל כָּל יְצוּרָיו. שֶׁבַח יְקָר וּגְדֻלָּה יִתְּנוּ לָאֵל מֶלֶךְ יוֹצֵר כֹּל, הַמַּנְחִיל מְנוּחָה לְעַמּוֹ יִשְׂרָאֵל בִּקְדֻשָּׁתוֹ בְּיוֹם שַׁבַּת קֹדֶשׁ. שִׁמְךָ יהוה אֱלֹהֵינוּ יִתְקַדַּשׁ, וְזִכְרְךָ מַלְכֵּנוּ יִתְפָּאַר, בַּשָּׁמַיִם מִמַּעַל וְעַל הָאָרֶץ מִתָּחַת. תִּתְבָּרַךְ מוֹשִׁיעֵנוּ עַל שֶׁבַח מַעֲשֵׂה יָדֶיךָ, וְעַל מְאוֹרֵי אוֹר שֶׁעָשִׂיתָ, יְפָאֲרוּךָ, סֶּלָה.

that they would enable Israel to order the calendar as commanded by the Torah.

⋄§ לָאֵל אֲשֶׁר שָׁבַת — *To the God Who rested.* To Whom are directed the praises mentioned above? — to the God Who rested on the Sabbath from His six days of creation. We say that He 'ascended on the Seventh Day' in the sense that His Presence is no longer obvious on earth. Nevertheless, He left us with the Sabbath as an eternal testimony to His six days of activity and the Sabbath of His rest.

זֶה שֶׁבַח שֶׁל יוֹם הַשְּׁבִיעִי — *This is the praise of the Sabbath Day.* The glory of the Sabbath is not in the leisure it offers, but in its witness to the Creator and its stimulus to man to join it in praising God. In this sense, the very existence of

ON A WEEKDAY

the rays of the sun; the Beneficent One fashioned honor for His Name, emplaced luminaries all around His power; the leaders of His legions, holy ones, exalt the Almighty, constantly relate the honor of God and His sanctity. May You be blessed,* HASHEM, *our God, beyond the praises of Your handiwork and beyond the bright luminaries that You have made — may they glorify You — Selah!*

to say that we declare our joy in having been worthy to receive the Torah that is formed with the sacred letters (*Abudraham*). Since this portion of the liturgy focuses on the creation and functioning of heaven and earth, it is especially appropriate to insert this allusion to the primacy of Torah study.

According to a tradition cited by *Etz Yosef*, R' Elazar HaKalir, composer of this prayer, communicated with the angel Michael and asked him how the angels formulated their songs of praise. Michael told him that they based their praises on the *Aleph-Beis*. Accordingly, R' Elazar used that formulation in this and his many other *piyutim*. He alluded to the source of this knowledge, Michael, by inserting his name acrostically immediately after these twenty-two words: **מְסַפְּרִים כְּבוֹד אֵל**, *relate the honor of God.*

יָצַר כָּבוֹד לִשְׁמוֹ — *Fashioned honor for His Name.* The complexity and perfection of creation testifies to the fact that there must be a Creator. Consequently, by creating and emplacing the heavenly bodies, God fashioned the instruments that would bring honor to His Name.

ON THE SABBATH

לָאֵל *To the God Who rested* from all works, Who ascended on the Seventh Day and sat on the Throne of His Glory. With splendor He enwrapped the Day of Contentment — He declared the Sabbath day a delight! This is the praise of the Sabbath Day:* that on it God rested from all His work. And the Seventh Day gives praise saying: 'A psalm, a song for the Sabbath Day. It is good to thank* HASHEM *. . .'*[1] *Therefore let all that He has fashioned glorify* and bless God. Praise, honor, and greatness let them render to God, the King Who fashioned everything, Who gives a heritage of contentment to His People, Israel, in His holiness on the holy Sabbath Day. May Your Name,* HASHEM, *our God, be sanctified and may Your remembrance, Our King, be glorified in the heaven above and upon the earth below. May You be blessed, our Savior, beyond the praises of Your handiwork and beyond the brilliant luminaries that You have made — may they glorify You — Selah.*

(1) *Psalms* 92:1-2.

the Sabbath is a praise to God; alternatively, the 'praise' can be understood as the Song of the Day for the Sabbath.

לְפִיכָךְ יְפָאֲרוּ — *Therefore let all . . . glorify.* As the prayer goes on to say, the reason that Creation glorifies God is that He has given the Sabbath to Israel. By observing the Sabbath and absorbing its holiness, Israel brings a higher degree of fulfillment and holiness to the entire universe.

ON ALL DAYS CONTINUE HERE:

תִּתְבָּרַךְ צוּרֵנוּ* מַלְכֵּנוּ וְגֹאֲלֵנוּ,* בּוֹרֵא קְדוֹשִׁים. יִשְׁתַּבַּח שִׁמְךָ לָעַד מַלְכֵּנוּ, יוֹצֵר מְשָׁרְתִים,* וַאֲשֶׁר מְשָׁרְתָיו כֻּלָּם עוֹמְדִים בְּרוּם עוֹלָם, וּמַשְׁמִיעִים בְּיִרְאָה יַחַד בְּקוֹל דִּבְרֵי אֱלֹהִים חַיִּים וּמֶלֶךְ עוֹלָם.[1] כֻּלָּם אֲהוּבִים, כֻּלָּם בְּרוּרִים, כֻּלָּם גִּבּוֹרִים, וְכֻלָּם עֹשִׂים בְּאֵימָה וּבְיִרְאָה רְצוֹן קוֹנָם. ❖ וְכֻלָּם פּוֹתְחִים אֶת פִּיהֶם בִּקְדֻשָּׁה וּבְטָהֳרָה, בְּשִׁירָה וּבְזִמְרָה, וּמְבָרְכִים וּמְשַׁבְּחִים וּמְפָאֲרִים וּמַעֲרִיצִים וּמַקְדִּישִׁים וּמַמְלִיכִים —

אֶת שֵׁם הָאֵל הַמֶּלֶךְ הַגָּדוֹל הַגִּבּוֹר וְהַנּוֹרָא קָדוֹשׁ הוּא.[2] ❖ וְכֻלָּם מְקַבְּלִים עֲלֵיהֶם עֹל מַלְכוּת שָׁמַיִם זֶה מִזֶּה,* וְנוֹתְנִים רְשׁוּת זֶה לָזֶה, לְהַקְדִּישׁ לְיוֹצְרָם, בְּנַחַת רוּחַ בְּשָׂפָה בְרוּרָה וּבִנְעִימָה. קְדֻשָּׁה כֻּלָּם כְּאֶחָד עוֹנִים וְאוֹמְרִים בְּיִרְאָה:

Congregation recites aloud:

קָדוֹשׁ קָדוֹשׁ קָדוֹשׁ* יהוה צְבָאוֹת,*
מְלֹא כָל הָאָרֶץ כְּבוֹדוֹ.[3]

⚜ **תִּתְבָּרַךְ צוּרֵנוּ** — *May You be blessed, our Rock.* The previous paragraph expressed man's praise of God for having created the heavenly bodies. They are indeed outstanding manifestations of God's greatness, as the prophet Isaiah put it, *Raise your eyes up high and see Who created these (Isaiah* 40:26). The heavenly bodies, like the angels, are agents of God that carry out His will in conducting the universe. Thus, the sun's role in giving light, heat, and energy and the moon's role in causing the tides are in reality not demonstrations of their own power, but of the means God utilizes to carry out those functions of nature according to His will. If perceived accurately, such aspects of creation bear testimony to the existence of an omniscient, omnipotent Creator.

However, they can be understood perversely as well. *Rambam (Hil. Avodah Zarah* 1:1-2) notes that man began to view the heavenly bodies first as servants of God that should be honored and glorified for the sake of their Maker. Eventually they went further and built temples and brought offerings to them. All of this is forbidden idolatry, but at least the people guilty of these practices acknowledged that the objects of their homage were creatures of God. In time, the practice deteriorated to the point where false prophets and their followers went so far as to say that such objects and graven images of them and other creatures were actually gods with independent powers.

In contrast to such perversity and heresy, we now proclaim that the very bodies that man perceives as being so mighty — the sun and other heavenly bodies — are but part of the heavenly forces that themselves stand in awe before God and are privileged to proclaim His praises *(Kol Bo).*

צוּרֵנוּ מַלְכֵּנוּ וְגֹאֲלֵנוּ — *Our Rock, our King, and our Redeemer.* These three appellations for God allude to the three broad stages of creation as described by the Talmud *(Avodah Zarah* 9a): The world in its present form will endure for six thousand years including two thousand years of emptiness, two thousand years of Torah, and two thousand years of the days of Messiah. The first period continued until Abraham was fifty-two years old. In those days, the Torah had not yet been given nor were its teachings widespread. Those were days of emptiness, when God was צוּרֵנוּ, *our Rock,* in the sense that He was the Creator and Stronghold of the universe, but was not acknowledged. Then Abraham began to remake man's understanding of the world. Thus began the era of Torah and its teachings, a time during which the Jewish nation came into being to teach that God was מַלְכֵּנוּ, *our King,* to Whom we owe total allegiance. The final period of two

ON ALL DAYS CONTINUE HERE:

תִּתְבָּרַךְ *May You be blessed, our Rock,* our King and our Redeemer,* Creator of holy ones; may Your Name be praised forever, our King, O Fashioner of ministering angels;* all of Whose ministering angels stand at the summit of the universe and proclaim — with awe, together, loudly — the words of the living God and King of the universe.*[1] *They are all beloved; they are all flawless; they are all mighty; they all do the will of their Maker with dread and reverence.* Chazzan– *And they all open their mouth in holiness and purity, in song and hymn — and bless, praise, glorify, revere, sanctify and declare the kingship of —*

אֶת שֵׁם *The Name of God, the great, mighty, and awesome King; holy is He.*[2] Chazzan– *Then they all accept upon themselves the yoke of heavenly sovereignty from one another,* and grant permission to one another to sanctify the One Who formed them, with tranquillity, with clear articulation, and with sweetness. All of them as one proclaim His holiness and say with awe:*

Congregation recites aloud:

'Holy, holy, holy* is HASHEM, Master of Legions,* the whole world is filled with His glory.'[3]

(1) Cf. *Jeremiah* 10:10. (2) Cf. *Deuteronomy* 10:17; *Psalms* 99:3. (3) *Isaiah* 6:3.

thousand years began after the destruction of the Temple. Despite the chaos, hardship, persecution, and slaughters of these dark years of exile, it is a time when the conditions for the ultimate and final Redemption are being formed. Hard though it is to understand, these are the centuries when God will eventually come to be recognized as גֹּאֲלֵנוּ, *our Redeemer (Siddur Sha'ar HaRachamim).*

קְדוֹשִׁים ... מְשָׁרְתִים — *Holy ones ... ministering angels.* Generally speaking, there are two forms of angels. The first and holier kind never take physical form and have no part in controlling material existence. These *holy ones* are spiritual beings whose closeness to God is most intense. Below them are the *ministering angels,* who are charged with tasks relating to the universe and man. They 'minister' to such matters as health, rain, prosperity, punishment, and so on. These angels sometimes take human form as found in the narratives of Scriptures *(Iyun Tefillah).*

The creation of these heavenly beings is expressed in the present tense, because God constantly creates new angels as He desires and as they are needed to serve Him *(Etz Yosef).*

וְכֻלָּם מְקַבְּלִים ... זֶה מִזֶּה — *Then they all accept ... from one another. Tanna d'Bei Eliyahu* contrasts the behavior of the angels with that of human beings. Unlike people whose competitive jealousies cause them to thwart and outdo one another, the angels urge one another to take the initiative in serving and praising God. Conflict is the foe of perfection, harmony is its ally.

קָדוֹשׁ קָדוֹשׁ קָדוֹשׁ — *Holy, holy, holy. Targum Yonasan (Isaiah* 6:3) renders: *Holy* in the most exalted heaven, the abode of His Presence; *holy* on earth, product of His strength; *holy* forever and ever is HASHEM, Master of Legions ...

כָּבוֹד, *glory,* refers to the glory of God that is present *within* the material world; it is the degree of Godliness that man is capable of perceiving even within creation. קָדוֹשׁ, *holy,* on the other hand, refers to God's essence, which is beyond all comprehension.

צְבָאוֹת — *Master of Legions.* Although it is commonly translated simply as *hosts* or *legions,* the word צְבָאוֹת is a Name of God (see *Shevuos* 35a), which means that He is the *Master* of all the heavenly hosts. The word צָבָא is used to refer to an organized, disciplined group. Thus, an army is commonly called צָבָא. In the context of this Divine Name, it refers to the idea that the infinite heavenly bodies are organized according to God's will to do His service.

אַאֲמִיר* אוֹתְךָ סֶלָה, בְּהוֹד וְהָדָר וּתְהִלָּה,
גּוֹאֵל הַצְמִיחַ גְּאֻלָּה, דּוֹרֵשׁ אֱיֻמָּתְךָ לְשֵׁם וְלִתְהִלָּה.[1]

הַצָּגִים לְפָנֶיךָ בְּשִׂמְחָה, וּבְלוּלָבֵיהֶם אוֹתְךָ לְשַׂמְּחָה,
זוֹעֲקִים לְפָנֶיךָ שִׂיחָה, חֲמוֹל עֲלֵיהֶם הוֹשִׁיעָה וְהַצְלִיחָה.[2]

טוֹב בְּרַחֲמֶיךָ הָרַבִּים, יַקֵּר עֲדַת אֲהוּבִים,
כּוֹרְעִים וּמִשְׁתַּחֲוִים וּמוֹדִים בְּאַהֲבִים, לְשַׁעַר* בַּת רַבִּים.[3]

מַחֲמַדָּם תֵּן לָהֶם, נָא שְׂמַח עִמָּהֶם,
שָׂא נָא חַטֹּאתֵיהֶם, עֲבֹר עַל פִּשְׁעֵיהֶם.

פּוֹצְחִים הַלֵּל וְתוֹדוֹת, צוּר הַיּוֹדֵעַ עֲתִידוֹת,
קוֹל לְהַשְׁמִיעַ אוֹתָם לַחֲדוֹת, רַחֵם בְּנָשְׂאָם אֲגֻדּוֹת.

❖ שׁוֹקְדִים וְאוֹתְךָ מַקְדִּישִׁים,* שִׁבְחֲךָ בְּפִיהֶם רוֹחֲשִׁים,
תּוֹקְפִים בָּרוּךְ וְלוֹחֲשִׁים, תּוֹמְכִים כְּאֵילֵי תַרְשִׁישִׁים.

Congregation, followed by the *chazzan*, recites one of these versions, according to its tradition.

וְהָאוֹפַנִּים* וְחַיּוֹת הַקֹּדֶשׁ בְּרַעַשׁ גָּדוֹל מִתְנַשְּׂאִים לְעֻמַּת שְׂרָפִים. לְעֻמָּתָם מְשַׁבְּחִים וְאוֹמְרִים:

וְהַחַיּוֹת יְשׁוֹרֵרוּ,* וּכְרוּבִים יְפָאֵרוּ, וּשְׂרָפִים יָרֹנּוּ, וְאֶרְאֶלִּים יְבָרֵכוּ. פְּנֵי כָל חַיָּה וְאוֹפָן וּכְרוּב לְעֻמַּת שְׂרָפִים. לְעֻמָּתָם מְשַׁבְּחִים וְאוֹמְרִים:

Congregation recites aloud:

בָּרוּךְ כְּבוֹד יהוה מִמְּקוֹמוֹ.*[4]

אַאֲמִיר — *I shall exalt.* Composed anonymously, this *piyut* follows an alphabetical scheme.

לְשַׁעַר — *[Bring them] to the gate of ... [Jerusalem].* Some *machzorim* begin this stich with the word הֲבִיאֵם, *bring them.* However, that reading distorts the alphabetical acrostic of the verses.

An alternative rendering of לְשַׁעַר is, *facing the gate,* i.e., they bend their knees and bow in prayer while facing towards the direction of Jerusalem.

וְאוֹתְךָ מַקְדִּישִׁים — *And sanctify You,* with the verses of the angelic *Kedushah:* קָדוֹשׁ קָדוֹשׁ קָדוֹשׁ ..., *Holy, holy, holy ...,* and ... בָּרוּךְ כְּבוֹד, *Blessed is the glory ...*

וְהָאוֹפַנִּים — *Then the Ofanim.* The varieties of angels are not translated since we lack the vocabulary to define them. *Rambam (Yesodei HaTorah* 2:7) notes that there are ten levels of angels. Their names are *Chayos, Ofanim, Erelim, Chashmalim, Seraphim, Malachim, Elohim, Bnai Elohim, Cherubim,* and *Ishim.*

וְהַחַיּוֹת יְשׁוֹרֵרוּ — *Then the Chayos sing.* In keeping with the expanded liturgy of Rosh Hashanah, some congregations set forth lyrically how the various categories of angels render praise, each in its own way. Other congregations do not deviate from the text recited every day of the year.

בָּרוּךְ ... מִמְּקוֹמוֹ — *Blessed ... from His place.* 'Place' refers to a particular position or level of eminence. For example, we say that a person 'takes his father's place.' But in the case of God —

א *I shall exalt* You eternally,*
ב *with majesty, splendor and praise.*
ג *O Redeemer, make redemption flourish,*
ד *seek Your nation's renown and praise.*[1]

ה *They gather before You in joy,*
ו *with their lulavim they cause You to rejoice.*
ז *[As] they cry before You in prayer,*
ח *pity them, grant them salvation and success.*[2]

ט *O Beneficent One, in Your abundant compassion,*
י *honor Your beloved flock.*
כ *They bend their knees, bow and lovingly acknowledge their thanks,*
ל *[bring them] to the gate* of the many-peopled city [of Jerusalem].*[3]

מ *Grant them their desire,*
נ *please rejoice with them.*
ס *Forgive, please, their errors,*
ע *overlook their sins.*

פ *They burst out in praise and thanksgiving,*
צ *[to You,] O Rock, Who knows the future.*
ק *May they hear the voice that will gladden them,*
ר *be compassionate to them as they bear the [lulav-] bundles.*

ש ✣ *They hasten and sanctify You,**
Your praises teeming in their mouths.
ת *They recite 'Blessed' powerfully, then [continuing] in soft voice,*
they encourage each other as do the powerful crystal-pure angels.

Congregation, followed by the *chazzan,* recites one of these versions, according to its tradition.

Then the Ofanim and the holy Chayos, with great noise, raise themselves towards the Seraphim. Facing them they give praise saying:*

Then the Chayos sing, the Cherubim glorify, the Seraphim rejoice, and the Erelim bless, in the presence of every Chayah, Ofan, and Cherub towards the Seraphim. Facing them they give praise saying:*

Congregation recites aloud:

'Blessed is the glory of Hashem from His place.'*[4]

(1) Cf. *Deuteronomy* 26:19; *Jeremiah* 13:11. (2) Cf. *Psalms* 118:25.
(3) Cf. *Song of Songs* 7:6. (4) *Ezekiel* 3:12.

all we can do is bless His eminence as *we* perceive it coming to us *from* His place. In other words, we see Him acting as Sustainer, Healer, Judge, Life-giver and so on, but we don't know what He really is. Though the angels have a better knowledge of God than people, they too have no comprehension of His true essence *(Nefesh HaChaim).*

לְאֵל בָּרוּךְ* נְעִימוֹת יִתֵּנוּ. לְמֶלֶךְ* אֵל חַי וְקַיָּם, זְמִרוֹת יֹאמֵרוּ, וְתִשְׁבָּחוֹת יַשְׁמִיעוּ. כִּי הוּא לְבַדּוֹ פּוֹעֵל גְּבוּרוֹת, עֹשֶׂה חֲדָשׁוֹת, בַּעַל מִלְחָמוֹת, זוֹרֵעַ צְדָקוֹת,* מַצְמִיחַ יְשׁוּעוֹת, בּוֹרֵא רְפוּאוֹת, נוֹרָא תְהִלּוֹת, אֲדוֹן הַנִּפְלָאוֹת. הַמְּחַדֵּשׁ בְּטוּבוֹ בְּכָל יוֹם תָּמִיד מַעֲשֵׂה בְרֵאשִׁית. כָּאָמוּר: לְעֹשֵׂה אוֹרִים גְּדֹלִים, כִּי לְעוֹלָם חַסְדּוֹ.[1] ❖ אוֹר חָדָשׁ* עַל צִיּוֹן תָּאִיר, וְנִזְכֶּה כֻלָּנוּ מְהֵרָה לְאוֹרוֹ. בָּרוּךְ אַתָּה יהוה, יוֹצֵר הַמְּאוֹרוֹת. (.Cong.– אָמֵן)

אַהֲבָה רַבָּה* אֲהַבְתָּנוּ יהוה אֱלֹהֵינוּ, חֶמְלָה גְדוֹלָה וִיתֵרָה חָמַלְתָּ עָלֵינוּ. אָבִינוּ מַלְכֵּנוּ, בַּעֲבוּר אֲבוֹתֵינוּ שֶׁבָּטְחוּ בְךָ, וַתְּלַמְּדֵם חֻקֵּי חַיִּים, כֵּן תְּחָנֵּנוּ וּתְלַמְּדֵנוּ. אָבִינוּ הָאָב הָרַחֲמָן הַמְּרַחֵם, רַחֵם עָלֵינוּ, וְתֵן בְּלִבֵּנוּ לְהָבִין וּלְהַשְׂכִּיל, לִשְׁמוֹעַ לִלְמוֹד וּלְלַמֵּד, לִשְׁמֹר וְלַעֲשׂוֹת וּלְקַיֵּם אֶת כָּל דִּבְרֵי תַלְמוּד תּוֹרָתֶךָ בְּאַהֲבָה. וְהָאֵר עֵינֵינוּ* בְּתוֹרָתֶךָ,* וְדַבֵּק לִבֵּנוּ בְּמִצְוֹתֶיךָ, וְיַחֵד לְבָבֵנוּ* לְאַהֲבָה וּלְיִרְאָה אֶת שְׁמֶךָ,[2] וְלֹא נֵבוֹשׁ לְעוֹלָם וָעֶד.* כִּי בְשֵׁם קָדְשְׁךָ הַגָּדוֹל וְהַנּוֹרָא בָּטָחְנוּ, נָגִילָה וְנִשְׂמְחָה בִּישׁוּעָתֶךָ. וַהֲבִיאֵנוּ לְשָׁלוֹם מֵאַרְבַּע כַּנְפוֹת הָאָרֶץ, וְתוֹלִיכֵנוּ קוֹמְמִיּוּת לְאַרְצֵנוּ. כִּי אֵל פּוֹעֵל יְשׁוּעוֹת אָתָּה, וּבָנוּ בָחַרְתָּ מִכָּל עַם וְלָשׁוֹן. ❖ וְקֵרַבְתָּנוּ לְשִׁמְךָ הַגָּדוֹל סֶלָה בֶּאֱמֶת, לְהוֹדוֹת לְךָ וּלְיַחֶדְךָ בְּאַהֲבָה. בָּרוּךְ אַתָּה יהוה, הַבּוֹחֵר בְּעַמּוֹ יִשְׂרָאֵל בְּאַהֲבָה. (.Cong.– אָמֵן)

At this point, gather the four *tzitzis* between the fourth and fifth fingers of the left hand. Hold *tzitzis* in this manner throughout the *Shema*.

לְאֵל בָּרוּךְ — *To the blessed God.* Earlier in this *Shema* blessing (p. 226), we recited a twenty-two word *Aleph-Beis* acrostic that began with this same expression: אֵל בָּרוּךְ, *the blessed God.* Now, in keeping with the general principle regarding a long blessing, we conclude it by returning to the theme with which the blessing began. Thus, we return to the theme of *the blessed God,* Whom we gratefully praise for His works of creation in general and the heavenly luminaries in particular — upon which we will conclude by blessing Him as יוֹצֵר הַמְּאוֹרוֹת, *[God] Who fashions the luminaries.*

לְאֵל . . . לְמֶלֶךְ — *To the . . . God . . . to the King.* The commentators differ regarding the vocalization of these two words. Many hold that they are read לָאֵל and לַמֶּלֶךְ. We have followed the version of most *siddurim,* but every congregation should maintain its custom.

זוֹרֵעַ צְדָקוֹת — *Sows kindnesses.* God does not merely reward man for his good deeds; He rewards him even for the chain reaction that results from human kindness. Thus, an act of kindness is like a seed that can produce luxuriant vegetation *(Etz Yosef).*

אוֹר חָדָשׁ — *A new light.* The *new* light is actually a return of the original brilliance of creation. That light was concealed for the enjoyment of the righteous in the Messianic era. May it soon shine upon Zion *(Yaavetz).*

אַהֲבָה רַבָּה — *With an abundant love.* Up to now, we have blessed God for having created the luminaries, but there is a light even greater than that of the brightest stars and the sun — the light of the Torah. Now, in this second blessing before *Shema,* we thank God for the Torah and pray that He grant us the wisdom to understand it properly *(Yaavetz; R' Munk).*

וְהָאֵר עֵינֵינוּ — *Enlighten our eyes.* This begins a series of brief supplications with one general

לָאֵל *To the blessed God* they shall offer sweet melodies; to the King,* the living and enduring God, they shall sing hymns and proclaim praises. For He alone effects mighty deeds, makes new things, is Master of wars, sows kindnesses,* makes salvations flourish, creates cures, is too awesome for praise, is Lord of wonders. In His goodness He renews daily, perpetually, the work of creation. As it is said: '[Give thanks] to Him Who makes the great luminaries, for His kindness endures forever.'*[1] Chazzan– *May You shine a new light* on Zion, and may we all speedily merit its light. Blessed are You, HASHEM, Who fashions the luminaries.* (Cong.– *Amen.)*

אַהֲבָה *With an abundant love* have You loved us, HASHEM, our God; with exceedingly great pity have You pitied us. Our Father, our King, for the sake of our forefathers who trusted in You and whom You taught the decrees of life, may You be equally gracious to us and teach us. Our Father, the merciful Father, Who acts mercifully, have mercy upon us, instill in our hearts to understand and elucidate, to listen, learn, teach, safeguard, perform, and fulfill all the words of Your Torah's teaching with love. Enlighten our eyes* in Your Torah,* attach our hearts to Your commandments, and unify our hearts* to love and fear Your Name,*[2] *and may we not feel inner shame for all eternity.* Because we have trusted in Your great and awesome holy Name, may we exult and rejoice in Your salvation.*

At this point, gather the four *tzitzis* between the fourth and fifth fingers of the left hand. Hold *tzitzis* in this manner throughout the *Shema*.

Bring us in peacefulness from the four corners of the earth and lead us with upright pride to our land. For You effect salvations, O God; You have chosen us from among every people and tongue. Chazzan– *And You have brought us close to Your great Name forever in truth, to offer praiseful thanks to You, and proclaim Your Oneness with love. Blessed are You, HASHEM, Who chooses His people Israel with love.* (Cong.– *Amen.)*

(1) *Psalms* 136:7. (2) Cf. 86:11.

---

purpose: A Jew's involvement with Torah study and observance must saturate all his activities, even his business, leisure, and social life.

בְּתוֹרָתֶךָ — *In Your Torah.* Enlighten us so that we may understand all aspects of Your Torah.

וְיַחֵד לְבָבֵנוּ — *And unify our hearts.* Man's likes and needs propel him in many directions. We ask God to unify our emotions and wishes to serve Him in love and fear.

וְלֹא נֵבוֹשׁ לְעוֹלָם וָעֶד — *And may we not feel inner shame for all eternity.* Inner shame is the humiliation one feels deep within himself when he knows he has done wrong — even though the people around him may sing his praises. The cost of such shame is borne primarily in the World to Come, where it can diminish one's eternal bliss or even destroy it entirely. Therefore we pray that our eternity not be marred by inner shame.

שְׁמַע / THE SHEMA

The recitation of *Shema* is required by the Torah, and one must have in mind that he is about to fulfill this commandment. Although one should try to concentrate on the meaning of all three paragraphs, one must concentrate at least on the meaning of the first verse (שְׁמַע) and the second verse (בָּרוּךְ שֵׁם) because this represents fulfillment of the paramount *mitzvah* of acceptance of God's absolute sovereignty (קַבָּלַת עוֹל מַלְכוּת שָׁמַיִם). By declaring that God is One, Unique, and Indivisible, we subordinate every facet of our personalities, possessions — our very lives — to His will.

In the שְׁמַע we have included the cantillation symbols *(trop)* for the convenience of those who recite שְׁמַע in the manner it is read from the Torah. Nevertheless, to enable those unfamiliar with this notation to group the words properly,

שמע

Immediately before its recitation concentrate on fulfilling the positive commandment of reciting the *Shema* twice daily. It is important to enunciate each word clearly and not to run words together. For this reason, vertical lines have been placed between two words that are prone to be slurred into one and are not separated by a comma or a hyphen. See *Laws* §40-55.

When praying without a *minyan,* begin with the following three-word formula:

אֵל מֶלֶךְ נֶאֱמָן.

Recite the first verse aloud, with the right hand covering the eyes, and concentrate intently upon accepting God's absolute sovereignty.

שְׁמַע | יִשְׂרָאֵל, יהוה | אֱלֹהֵינוּ, יהוה | אֶחָד:

In an undertone – בָּרוּךְ שֵׁם כְּבוֹד מַלְכוּתוֹ לְעוֹלָם וָעֶד.

While reciting the first paragraph (דברים ו:ה-ט), concentrate on accepting the commandment to love God.

וְאָהַבְתָּ אֵת | יהוה | אֱלֹהֶיךָ, בְּכָל־לְבָבְךָ, וּבְכָל־נַפְשְׁךָ, וּבְכָל־מְאֹדֶךָ: וְהָיוּ הַדְּבָרִים הָאֵלֶּה, אֲשֶׁר | אָנֹכִי מְצַוְּךָ הַיּוֹם, עַל־לְבָבֶךָ: וְשִׁנַּנְתָּם לְבָנֶיךָ, וְדִבַּרְתָּ בָּם, בְּשִׁבְתְּךָ בְּבֵיתֶךָ, וּבְלֶכְתְּךָ בַדֶּרֶךְ, וּבְשָׁכְבְּךָ וּבְקוּמֶךָ: וּקְשַׁרְתָּם לְאוֹת | עַל־יָדֶךָ, וְהָיוּ לְטֹטָפֹת בֵּין | עֵינֶיךָ: וּכְתַבְתָּם | עַל־מְזֻזוֹת בֵּיתֶךָ, וּבִשְׁעָרֶיךָ:

While reciting the second paragraph (דברים יא:יג-כא), concentrate on accepting all the commandments and the concept of reward and punishment.

וְהָיָה, אִם־שָׁמֹעַ תִּשְׁמְעוּ אֶל־מִצְוֹתַי, אֲשֶׁר | אָנֹכִי מְצַוֶּה | אֶתְכֶם הַיּוֹם, לְאַהֲבָה אֶת־יהוה | אֱלֹהֵיכֶם וּלְעָבְדוֹ, בְּכָל־לְבַבְכֶם, וּבְכָל־נַפְשְׁכֶם: וְנָתַתִּי מְטַר־אַרְצְכֶם בְּעִתּוֹ, יוֹרֶה וּמַלְקוֹשׁ, וְאָסַפְתָּ דְגָנֶךָ וְתִירֹשְׁךָ וְיִצְהָרֶךָ: וְנָתַתִּי | עֵשֶׂב | בְּשָׂדְךָ לִבְהֶמְתֶּךָ, וְאָכַלְתָּ וְשָׂבָעְתָּ: הִשָּׁמְרוּ לָכֶם, פֶּן־יִפְתֶּה לְבַבְכֶם, וְסַרְתֶּם וַעֲבַדְתֶּם | אֱלֹהִים | אֲחֵרִים, וְהִשְׁתַּחֲוִיתֶם לָהֶם: וְחָרָה | אַף־יהוה בָּכֶם, וְעָצַר | אֶת־הַשָּׁמַיִם, וְלֹא־יִהְיֶה מָטָר, וְהָאֲדָמָה לֹא תִתֵּן אֶת־יְבוּלָהּ, וַאֲבַדְתֶּם | מְהֵרָה מֵעַל הָאָרֶץ הַטֹּבָה | אֲשֶׁר | יהוה נֹתֵן לָכֶם: וְשַׂמְתֶּם | אֶת־דְּבָרַי | אֵלֶּה, עַל־לְבַבְכֶם וְעַל־נַפְשְׁכֶם, וּקְשַׁרְתֶּם | אֹתָם לְאוֹת | עַל־יֶדְכֶם, וְהָיוּ לְטוֹטָפֹת בֵּין | עֵינֵיכֶם: וְלִמַּדְתֶּם | אֹתָם | אֶת־בְּנֵיכֶם, לְדַבֵּר בָּם, בְּשִׁבְתְּךָ בְּבֵיתֶךָ, וּבְלֶכְתְּךָ בַדֶּרֶךְ, וּבְשָׁכְבְּךָ וּבְקוּמֶךָ: וּכְתַבְתָּם | עַל־מְזוּזוֹת בֵּיתֶךָ, וּבִשְׁעָרֶיךָ: לְמַעַן | יִרְבּוּ | יְמֵיכֶם וִימֵי בְנֵיכֶם, עַל הָאֲדָמָה | אֲשֶׁר נִשְׁבַּע | יהוה לַאֲבֹתֵיכֶם לָתֵת לָהֶם, כִּימֵי הַשָּׁמַיִם | עַל־הָאָרֶץ:

THE SHEMA

Immediately before its recitation concentrate on fulfilling the positive commandment of reciting the *Shema* twice daily. It is important to enunciate each word clearly and not to run words together. See *Laws* §40-55.

When praying without a *minyan,* begin with the following three-word formula:
God, trustworthy King.

Recite the first verse aloud, with the right hand covering the eyes, and concentrate intently upon accepting God's absolute sovereignty.

Hear, O Israel: HASHEM is our God, HASHEM, the One and Only.[1]

In an undertone— *Blessed is the Name of His glorious kingdom for all eternity.*

While reciting the first paragraph (*Deuteronomy* 6:5-9), concentrate on accepting the commandment to love God.

וְאָהַבְתָּ *You shall love HASHEM, your God, with all your heart, with all your soul and with all your resources. Let these matters that I command you today be upon your heart. Teach them thoroughly to your children and speak of them while you sit in your home, while you walk on the way, when you retire and when you arise. Bind them as a sign upon your arm and let them be tefillin between your eyes. And write them on the doorposts of your house and upon your gates.*

While reciting the second paragraph (*Deuteronomy* 11:13-21), concentrate on accepting all the commandments and the concept of reward and punishment.

וְהָיָה *And it will come to pass that if you continually hearken to My commandments that I command you today, to love HASHEM, your God, and to serve Him, with all your heart and with all your soul — then I will provide rain for your land in its proper time, the early and late rains, that you may gather in your grain, your wine, and your oil. I will provide grass in your field for your cattle and you will eat and be satisfied. Beware lest your heart be seduced and you turn astray and serve gods of others and bow to them. Then the wrath of HASHEM will blaze against you. He will restrain the heaven so there will be no rain and the ground will not yield its produce. And you will swiftly be banished from the goodly land which HASHEM gives you. Place these words of Mine upon your heart and upon your soul; bind them for a sign upon your arm and let them be tefillin between your eyes. Teach them to your children, to discuss them, while you sit in your home, while you walk on the way, when you retire and when you arise. And write them on the doorposts of your house and upon your gates. In order to prolong your days and the days of your children upon the ground that HASHEM has sworn to your ancestors to give them, like the days of the heaven on the earth.*

---

(1) *Deuteronomy* 6:4.

---

commas have been inserted. Additionally, vertical lines have been placed between any two words that are prone to be slurred into one and are not separated by a comma or hyphen.

Before reciting the third paragraph (במדבר טו:לז-מא) the *tzitzis,* which have been held in the left hand, are taken in the right hand also. The *tzitzis* are kissed at each mention of the word and at the end of the paragraph, and are passed before the eyes at וּרְאִיתֶם אֹתוֹ.

וַיֹּאמֶר | יהוה | אֶל־מֹשֶׁה לֵּאמֹר: דַּבֵּר | אֶל־בְּנֵי | יִשְׂרָאֵל, וְאָמַרְתָּ אֲלֵהֶם, וְעָשׂוּ לָהֶם צִיצִת, עַל־כַּנְפֵי בִגְדֵיהֶם לְדֹרֹתָם, וְנָתְנוּ | עַל־צִיצִת הַכָּנָף, פְּתִיל תְּכֵלֶת: וְהָיָה לָכֶם לְצִיצִת, וּרְאִיתֶם | אֹתוֹ, וּזְכַרְתֶּם | אֶת־כָּל־מִצְוֺת | יהוה, וַעֲשִׂיתֶם | אֹתָם, וְלֹא תָתֻרוּ | אַחֲרֵי לְבַבְכֶם וְאַחֲרֵי | עֵינֵיכֶם, אֲשֶׁר־אַתֶּם זֹנִים | אַחֲרֵיהֶם: לְמַעַן תִּזְכְּרוּ, וַעֲשִׂיתֶם | אֶת־כָּל־מִצְוֺתָי, וִהְיִיתֶם קְדֹשִׁים לֵאלֹהֵיכֶם: אֲנִי יהוה | אֱלֹהֵיכֶם, אֲשֶׁר הוֹצֵאתִי | אֶתְכֶם | מֵאֶרֶץ מִצְרַיִם, לִהְיוֹת לָכֶם לֵאלֹהִים, אֲנִי | יהוה | אֱלֹהֵיכֶם: אֱמֶת —

Concentrate on fulfilling the commandment of remembering the Exodus from Egypt.

Although the word אֱמֶת belongs to the next paragraph, it is appended to the conclusion of the previous one, as explained in the commentary.

—*Chazzan* repeats **יהוה אֱלֹהֵיכֶם אֱמֶת.***

וְיַצִּיב* וְנָכוֹן וְקַיָּם וְיָשָׁר וְנֶאֱמָן וְאָהוּב וְחָבִיב וְנֶחְמָד וְנָעִים וְנוֹרָא וְאַדִּיר וּמְתֻקָּן וּמְקֻבָּל וְטוֹב וְיָפֶה הַדָּבָר הַזֶּה עָלֵינוּ לְעוֹלָם וָעֶד. אֱמֶת אֱלֹהֵי עוֹלָם מַלְכֵּנוּ צוּר יַעֲקֹב, מָגֵן יִשְׁעֵנוּ, לְדֹר וָדֹר הוּא קַיָּם, וּשְׁמוֹ קַיָּם, וְכִסְאוֹ נָכוֹן, וּמַלְכוּתוֹ וֶאֱמוּנָתוֹ לָעַד קַיֶּמֶת. וּדְבָרָיו חָיִים וְקַיָּמִים, נֶאֱמָנִים וְנֶחֱמָדִים לָעַד וּלְעוֹלְמֵי עוֹלָמִים. (kiss the tzitzis and release them) ❖ עַל אֲבוֹתֵינוּ וְעָלֵינוּ, עַל בָּנֵינוּ וְעַל דּוֹרוֹתֵינוּ, וְעַל כָּל דּוֹרוֹת זֶרַע יִשְׂרָאֵל עֲבָדֶיךָ.

עַל הָרִאשׁוֹנִים וְעַל הָאַחֲרוֹנִים, דָּבָר טוֹב וְקַיָּם לְעוֹלָם וָעֶד, אֱמֶת וֶאֱמוּנָה חֹק וְלֹא יַעֲבֹר. אֱמֶת שָׁאַתָּה הוּא יהוה אֱלֹהֵינוּ וֵאלֹהֵי אֲבוֹתֵינוּ, ❖ מַלְכֵּנוּ מֶלֶךְ אֲבוֹתֵינוּ, גֹּאֲלֵנוּ גֹּאֵל אֲבוֹתֵינוּ, יוֹצְרֵנוּ צוּר יְשׁוּעָתֵנוּ, פּוֹדֵנוּ וּמַצִּילֵנוּ מֵעוֹלָם שְׁמֶךָ, אֵין אֱלֹהִים זוּלָתֶךָ.

אֱמֶת ⌁ — *True.* The law that one may not interrupt between the last words of the *Shema* and אֱמֶת is of ancient origin. The reason for it is so that we may declare as did the prophet [*Jeremiah* 10:10] וַה׳ אֱלֹהִים אֱמֶת, *HASHEM, God, is true* (*Berachos* 14a).

אֱמֶת וְיַצִּיב — *True and certain.* This paragraph begins the third and final blessing of the *Shema,* which ends with גָּאַל יִשְׂרָאֵל, *Who redeemed Israel.* Like אֱמֶת וֶאֱמוּנָה, *True and faithful,* its counterpart in the Evening Service, this blessing continues our fulfillment of the requirement to recall the Exodus, morning and evening.

As the Sages teach (*Berachos* 12a), whoever omits either the morning or evening blessing has not properly discharged his obligation of reciting the *Shema* and its attendant prayers. Although both the morning and evening blessings of redemption refer to the Exodus, there is a basic difference between them. The Talmud (ibid.) teaches that the formulation of these blessings is based on the verse לְהַגִּיד בַּבֹּקֶר חַסְדֶּךָ וֶאֱמוּנָתְךָ

Before reciting the third paragraph (*Numbers* 15:37-41) the *tzitzis*, which have been held in the left hand, are taken in the right hand also. The *tzitzis* are kissed at each mention of the word and at the end of the paragraph, and are passed before the eyes at *'that you may see it.'*

וַיֹּאמֶר *And* HASHEM *said to Moses saying: Speak to the Children of Israel and say to them that they are to make themselves tzitzis on the corners of their garments, throughout their generations. And they are to place upon the tzitzis of each corner a thread of techeiles. And it shall constitute tzitzis for you, that you may see it and remember all the commandments of* HASHEM *and perform them; and not explore after your heart and after your eyes after which you stray. So that you may remember and perform all My commandments; and be holy to your God. I am* HASHEM, *your God, Who has removed you from the land of Egypt to be a God to you; I am* HASHEM *your God — it is true* —*

Concentrate on fulfilling the commandment of remembering the Exodus from Egypt.

Although the word אֱמֶת, *'it is true,'* belongs to the next paragraph, it is appended to the conclusion of the previous one, as explained in the commentary.

Chazzan repeats: **HASHEM, your God, is true.***

וְיַצִּיב *And certain,* established and enduring, fair and faithful, beloved and cherished, delightful and pleasant, awesome and powerful, correct and accepted, good and beautiful is this affirmation to us forever and ever. True — the God of the universe is our King; the Rock of Jacob is the Shield of our salvation. From generation to generation He endures and His Name endures and His throne is well established; His sovereignty and faithfulness endure forever. His words are living and enduring, faithful and delightful forever* (kiss the *tzitzis* and release them) *and to all eternity;* Chazzan– *for our forefathers and for us, for our children and for our generations, and for all the generations of Your servant Israel's offspring.*

עַל הָרִאשׁוֹנִים *Upon the earlier and upon the later generations, this affirmation is good and enduring forever. True and faithful, it is an unbreachable decree. It is true that You are* HASHEM, *our God and the God of our forefathers,* Chazzan– *our King and the King of our forefathers, our Redeemer, the Redeemer of our forefathers; our Molder, the Rock of our salvation; our Liberator and our Rescuer — this has ever been Your Name. There is no God but You.*

בַּלֵּילוֹת, *to relate Your kindness in the dawn and Your faithfulness in the nights* (*Psalms* 92:3). This implies that in the morning we express gratitude for already existing *kindness*, while in the evening we express our *faith* in something that has not yet taken place.

As *Rashi* and *Tosafos* explain, the morning blessing of אֱמֶת וְיַצִּיב, which is recited after *dawn*, concentrates on God's *kindness* in having redeemed us from Egypt, while אֱמֶת וֶאֱמוּנָה, which is recited at *night*, is based on the theme of our *faith* that God will redeem us in the future, just as He did at the time of Exodus.

Including the word אֱמֶת, *true*, there are sixteen adjectives describing הַדָּבָר הַזֶּה, *this affirmation* [lit., *this thing*]. What is this 'thing'? It is the total message contained in the sixteen verses of the first two paragraphs of the *Shema* (including בָּרוּךְ שֵׁם). Thus, it is as if we affirm each verse with an adjective acknowledging its truth. *Etz Yosef* and others show how each adjective is suited to the verse it affirms.

FIRST DAY

אָנָּא הוֹשִׁיעָה נָּא,*[1]
בְּנֵי עָפָר מִי מָנָה,[2]
גּוֹאֵל הַצְלִיחָה נָא,[1]
דּוֹרְשֶׁיךָ בְּכָל עוֹנָה.
הָקֵם סֻכַּת דָּוִד הַנּוֹפֶלֶת,[3]
וּבַל תְּהִי עוֹד מַשְׁפֶּלֶת,
זְכוֹר אֲיֻמָּה הַנִּקְהֶלֶת,
חוֹפְפָהּ וּבְצִלְּךָ נֶאֱהֶלֶת.
טוֹב הַצְמִיחַ שִׂמְחָתָם,
יָהּ כַּפֵּר אַשְׁמָתָם,
כַּלֵּה עַתָּה אַנְחוֹתָם,
לְמַעַנְךָ חִישׁ פְּדוּתָם.
מַלֵּא מִשְׁאֲלוֹת לִבָּם,
נוֹאֲקִים אֵלֶיךָ בְּכָל לְבָבָם,
סָמְכֵם וְרִיב רִיבָם,
עַתָּה תִּשְׁכֹּן בְּקִרְבָּם.
פְּנֵה תִפְנֶה לְפָאֳרָם,
צוּר אֱמֹר לְעָזְרָם,
קוֹמֵם בֵּית הֲדָרָם,
רְאוּתָם פִּתְאוֹם שִׁבְרָם.
שַׁלֵּם מְהֵרָה תִבָּנֶה
שְׁלֵמֶיךָ בְּכֵן תַּעֲנֶה,
תַּכֶּה* אוֹיְבֵינוּ
כְּמַכַּת בְּכוֹרִים וּתְעַנֶּה,
תִּקְרָעֵם כִּקְרִיעַת יַם סוּף
וְנִקְרָאֲךָ וְתַעֲנֶה.[4]

SECOND DAY

אָנָּא תֶּרֶב* עֲלִיצוּתֶךָ, לְקוֹוֵי יְשׁוּעָתֶךָ,
בָּאִים לְאַמֵּץ תְּהִלָּתֶךָ, בְּנוֹעַד בֵּית דְּגִילָתֶךָ,
גּוֹדְדֵם[5] לְבֵית בְּחִירָתֶךָ,[6] יֶשַׁע לְרֹאשָׁם בְּתִתֶּךָ,
דְּלֵם מִכְּשֶׁל תִּגְרָתֶךָ, וּתְסוֹכְכֵם בְּגִין אֶבְרָתֶךָ.[7]
הוֹשֵׁב עַל מִשְׁפָּטוֹ אַרְמוֹן,[8]
אֲשֶׁר שַׁתָּה יְלֵל יְשִׁמוֹן,[9]
וְכַנֵּס נִדְחֵי הֲמוֹן, זֶרַע תָּם פִּצֵּל לַח לוּז וְעַרְמוֹן,[10]
זֵדֵי רֶשַׁע עֲקַר אַדְמוֹן,* יְבוֹאוּם שְׁכוֹל וְאַלְמוֹן,[11]
חֲנוּנֶיךָ הוֹגֵי אָמוֹן, תִּטָּעֵם בְּהַר חֶרְמוֹן.
טוֹעֲנֵי עֻלְּךָ עַל גַּבָּם, יָהּ הַשְׁרֵה שְׁכִינָתְךָ בְּקִרְבָּם,
יַעֲלוּ לָחוֹג לְבֵית נָוָם, בְּהִכּוֹנֵן עִיר מוֹשָׁבָם,
כֹּחַ וְלָאֵל תְּשַׂגְּבָם, צוּר עֻזָּם וּמִשְׂגַּבָּם,[12]
לֹא לָנֶצַח תָּרִיבָם,[13] כִּי עָלֶיךָ מַשְׁלִיכִים יְהָבָם.[14]
מִקְדָּשְׁךָ הַשָּׁמֵם,[15] כִּימֵי עוֹלָם תְּרוֹמֵם,[16]
נֶצַח לְבַל יִשְׁתּוֹמֵם, תֵּת שִׁקּוּץ שׁוֹמֵם,[17]
סֻכַּת דָּוִד קוֹמֵם, וּפוֹרְצֵי גְּדֵרָהּ[18] הַשְׁמֵם,
עוּרָה כִּנּוֹרֵי הַדּוֹמֵם,[19] וְנִימָיו עוֹד לְבַל תְּנַמֵּם.
פִּנַּת מִגְדַּל עֵדֶר,[20] עֲפֵלָה[21] כְּשַׁחֲרוּרֵי קֵדֶר,
צַפֵּה לְהַדְרָהּ בְּהֶדֶר, הֱיוֹת סֻכָּה וְגָדֵר,[22]
קִנְיַן צֹאן דִּיר, אֲשֶׁר נִזְרָה לְהַעֲדֵר,
רְעֵה לְהִשָּׁמֵן וּלְהִפָּדֵר, כְּבַקָּרַת רוֹעֶה עֶדֶר.[23]
שַׁעַר בַּת רַבִּים,[24] מְקוֹם תְּמוֹרוֹת וּכְרוּבִים,[25]
תְּחַטְּבוֹ בְּחִטּוּבִים, בְּמִסְגְּרוֹת וּשְׁלַבִּים,[26]
תְּחַדֵּשׁ שִׁירִים עֲרֵבִים,
בְּפֶה מַשְׁכִּימִים וּמַעֲרִיבִים,
תִּפְדֵּנוּ בְּאֹמֶץ וְשִׂגּוּבִים, כְּאָז פָּדִיתָ גָּזֵי רְהָבִים.

(1) Cf. *Psalms* 118:25. (2) Cf. *Numbers* 23:10. (3) Cf. *Amos* 9:11. (4) Cf. *Isaiah* 58:9; 65:24. (5) Some *machzorim* read גָּרְרֵם, *draw them.* (6) Cf. *II Chronicles* 7:16. (7) Cf. *Psalms* 91:4. (8) Cf. *Jeremiah* 30:18. (9) *Deuteronomy* 32:10. (10) Cf. *Genesis* 30:37. (11) Cf. *Isaiah* 47:9. (12) Cf. *Psalms* 62:7-8. (13) Cf. 103:9. (14) Cf. 55:23. (15) *Daniel* 9:17. (12) Cf. *Amos* 9:11. (17) Cf. *Daniel* 12:11. (18) Cf. *Amos* 9:11. (19) Cf. *Psalms* 57:9. (20) *Micah* 4:8. (21) The word עֲפֵלָה means the same as אֲפֵלָה, *dark.* Indeed, many *machzorim read* אֲפֵלָה. (22) Cf. *Amos* 9:11. (23) Cf. *Ezekiel* 34:12. (24) *Song of Songs* 7:6. (25) Cf. *I Kings* 6:29. (26) Cf. 7:28-29.

אָנָּא הוֹשִׁיעָה נָּא – *Please save now.* Although this alphabetically arranged *piyut* is unsigned, it is generally attributed to R' Elazar HaKalir (see p. 270). [Some suggest that the author's name appears in the stich צוּר אֱמֹר לְעָזְרָם.]

תַּכֶּה – *Smite.* Some *machzorim* substitute the word קָמֶיךָ, *Your opponents,* for אוֹיְבֵינוּ, *our foes.* Many others change the last two stiches to read: חִישׁ מְהֵרָה אוֹתָנוּ תַּעֲנֶה, וְנִקְרָאֲךָ וְתַעֲנֶה, *Speedily, hurry, may You answer us; when we call to You, may You answer us.* Both of these emendations were obviously prompted by the gentile censors.

אָנָּא תֶּרֶב – *Please increase.* Alphabetically arranged and anonymously written, this *piyut* longs for the return to *Eretz Yisrael* and the rebuilt Temple. The theme is brought out with allusions to many passages from Scripture, while *Amos* 9:11 is cited repeatedly. That verse reads in its entirely: בַּיּוֹם הַהוּא אָקִים אֶת סֻכַּת דָּוִיד הַנֹּפֶלֶת, *on that day I shall re-establish David's fallen succah [the Temple],* וְגָדַרְתִּי אֶת פִּרְצֵיהֶן, *and I shall wall in their breaches,* וַהֲרִסֹתָיו אָקִים, *and I shall re-establish his ruins,* וּבְנִיתִיהָ כִּימֵי עוֹלָם, *and I shall rebuild it as in days of old.* The verse appears in many of the *piyutim* of the Succos *machzor,* and is alluded to in *Bircas HaMazon* (see p. 92).

FIRST DAY	SECOND DAY
א *Please save now,*[1]*	א *Please increase* Your exultation, for those who hope for Your salvation.*
ב *the children compared to the countless dust.*[2]	ב *They come to declare powerfully Your praises, among the assembly at Your bannered synagogues.*
ג *O Redeemer, bring success now,*[1]	ג *Gather them*[5] *to Your chosen Temple,*[6] *as You crown their heads with salvation.*
ד *for those who seek You at all times.*	ד *Raise them over the snare of the adversary [the Evil Inclination], and shelter them with Your protective pinion.*[7]
ה *Re-establish David's fallen succah,*[3]	ה *Re-establish the [Temple] Palace in its proper place,*[8] *which You have allowed to be made into a howling wilderness.*[9]
ו *may it never again be humbled.*	ו *And gather in the outcast multitude, seed of the wholesome [Jacob] who peeled poplar, hazel and chestnut rods.*[10]
ז *Remember the assembled nation,*	ז *Uproot the wanton, evil Edomite,* bring them to childlessness and widowhood.*[11]
ח *protect her and cover her with Your shelter.*	ח *[But] Your favored ones, who study [Torah] the nurturer, plant them upon Mount Hermon.*
ט *O Beneficent One, make their joy flourish,*	ט *Bearers of Your burden upon their backs, O God, let Your Presence rest among them.*
י *O God, forgive their guilt.*	י *May they ascend to the Temple of their abode to celebrate, when [Jerusalem] the city of their dwelling is restored.*
כ *End their groaning now,*	כ *Fortify them with power and might, O Rock, their Strength and their Fortification.*[12]
ל *for Your sake, hasten to redeem them.*	ל *Do not be at odds with them eternally,*[13] *for they cast their burden upon You.*[14]
מ *Fulfill their heart's desire,*	מ *Your desolate Sanctuary,*[15] *raise it up as in days of old.*[16]
נ *[for] they cry to You with all their hearts.*	נ *Never again allow it to become desolate, cause the abomination to be destroyed.*[17]
ס *Support them and take up their grievance,*	ס *Re-establish David's succah [Temple], and destroy those who would breach its walls.*[18]
ע *may You now dwell among them.*	ע *Arouse my silent harp,*[19] *may its strings never again be muted.*
פ *May You turn to them, to beautify them,*	פ *The cornerstone of the flock's [Temple] tower,*[20] *is now as dark*[21] *as the black tents of Kedar [bedouins].*
צ *O Rock, tell [the Messiah to come and] help them.*	צ *See to beautify her in splendor, that she be sheltered and walled in.*[22]
ק *Establish their splendid Temple,*	ק *[Your] possession, the sheep of the fold, who have been dispersed and have almost disappeared,*
ר *show them suddenly [the object of] their longing.*	ר *Graze [them — that they] become fattened and healthy — like a shepherd pasturing his flock.*[23]
ש *May Jerusalem speedily be rebuilt, thus to respond to Your wholesome ones.*	ש *The multi-peopled [Temple] gate,*[24] *a place [decorated] with [carved] palm trees and cherubim,*[25]
ת *Smite* our foes as at the Plague of the Firstborn and pain them; tear them apart as at the Splitting of the Sea; when we call to You, may You answer.*[4]	ת *Craft it skillfully, with [its] borders and ledges.*[26] *Renew the sweet songs, in the mouths of those who arrive early [at the synagogue] and stay late. May You powerfully redeem them and fortify them, as You redeemed those who hastened through the split sea.*

עֲקֹר אֲדְמוֹן – *Uproot ... the Edomite.* Some *machzorim* read: כְּפוֹף כְּאַגְמוֹן, *bend like an agmon* (see *Isaiah* 58:5). [According to *Rashi*, an *agmon* is a fish hook; *Ibn Ezra* translates, a supple reed.] This change was obviously introduced to appease the censors.

עֶזְרַת אֲבוֹתֵינוּ* אַתָּה הוּא מֵעוֹלָם, מָגֵן וּמוֹשִׁיעַ לִבְנֵיהֶם אַחֲרֵיהֶם בְּכָל דּוֹר וָדוֹר. בְּרוּם עוֹלָם מוֹשָׁבֶךָ, וּמִשְׁפָּטֶיךָ וְצִדְקָתְךָ עַד אַפְסֵי אָרֶץ. אַשְׁרֵי אִישׁ שֶׁיִּשְׁמַע לְמִצְוֹתֶיךָ, וְתוֹרָתְךָ וּדְבָרְךָ יָשִׂים עַל לִבּוֹ. אֱמֶת אַתָּה הוּא אָדוֹן לְעַמֶּךָ וּמֶלֶךְ גִּבּוֹר לָרִיב רִיבָם. אֱמֶת אַתָּה הוּא רִאשׁוֹן וְאַתָּה הוּא אַחֲרוֹן, וּמִבַּלְעָדֶיךָ אֵין לָנוּ מֶלֶךְ[1] גּוֹאֵל וּמוֹשִׁיעַ. מִמִּצְרַיִם גְּאַלְתָּנוּ יהוה אֱלֹהֵינוּ, וּמִבֵּית עֲבָדִים פְּדִיתָנוּ. כָּל בְּכוֹרֵיהֶם הָרָגְתָּ, וּבְכוֹרְךָ גָּאָלְתָּ, וְיַם סוּף בָּקַעְתָּ, וְזֵדִים טִבַּעְתָּ, וִידִידִים הֶעֱבַרְתָּ, וַיְכַסּוּ מַיִם צָרֵיהֶם, אֶחָד מֵהֶם לֹא נוֹתָר.[2] עַל זֹאת שִׁבְּחוּ אֲהוּבִים וְרוֹמְמוּ אֵל, וְנָתְנוּ יְדִידִים זְמִרוֹת שִׁירוֹת וְתִשְׁבָּחוֹת, בְּרָכוֹת וְהוֹדָאוֹת, לְמֶלֶךְ אֵל חַי וְקַיָּם, רָם וְנִשָּׂא, גָּדוֹל וְנוֹרָא, מַשְׁפִּיל גֵּאִים, וּמַגְבִּיהַּ שְׁפָלִים, מוֹצִיא אֲסִירִים, וּפוֹדֶה עֲנָוִים, וְעוֹזֵר דַּלִּים, וְעוֹנֶה לְעַמּוֹ בְּעֵת שַׁוְּעָם אֵלָיו.

Rise for *Shemoneh Esrei.* Some take three steps backward at this point; others do so before צוּר יִשְׂרָאֵל.

❖ תְּהִלּוֹת לְאֵל עֶלְיוֹן, בָּרוּךְ הוּא וּמְבֹרָךְ. מֹשֶׁה וּבְנֵי יִשְׂרָאֵל לְךָ עָנוּ שִׁירָה בְּשִׂמְחָה רַבָּה וְאָמְרוּ כֻלָּם:

מִי כָמֹכָה בָּאֵלִם יהוה, מִי כָּמֹכָה נֶאְדָּר בַּקֹּדֶשׁ, נוֹרָא תְהִלֹּת עֹשֵׂה פֶלֶא.[3] ❖ שִׁירָה חֲדָשָׁה שִׁבְּחוּ גְאוּלִים לְשִׁמְךָ עַל שְׂפַת הַיָּם, יַחַד כֻּלָּם הוֹדוּ וְהִמְלִיכוּ וְאָמְרוּ:

יהוה יִמְלֹךְ לְעֹלָם וָעֶד.[4]

It is forbidden to interrupt or pause between גָּאַל יִשְׂרָאֵל and *Shemoneh Esrei,* even for *Kaddish, Kedushah* or *Amen.*

❖ **צוּר יִשְׂרָאֵל,*** קוּמָה בְּעֶזְרַת יִשְׂרָאֵל, וּפְדֵה כִנְאֻמֶךָ יְהוּדָה וְיִשְׂרָאֵל. גֹּאֲלֵנוּ יהוה צְבָאוֹת שְׁמוֹ, קְדוֹשׁ יִשְׂרָאֵל.[5] בָּרוּךְ אַתָּה יהוה, גָּאַל יִשְׂרָאֵל.*

עֶזְרַת אֲבוֹתֵינוּ — *The Helper of our forefathers.* This passage elaborates upon the Exodus within the context of God's eternal supervision of Israel and mastery over its destiny.

צוּר יִשְׂרָאֵל — *Rock of Israel.* Since the end of *Shema,* we have concentrated on an elaboration of the miracles of the Exodus. We do not lose sight, however, of our faith that there is another, greater redemption yet to come. Thus we conclude with a plea that God rise up again to redeem Israel from this exile as He did in ancient Egypt.

גָּאַל יִשְׂרָאֵל — *Who redeemed Israel.* The text of the blessing is in keeping with the Talmudic

עֶזְרַת *The Helper of our forefathers* are You alone, forever, Shield and Savior for their children after them in every generation. At the zenith of the universe is Your dwelling, and Your justice and Your righteousness extend to the ends of the earth. Praiseworthy is the person who obeys Your commandments and takes to his heart Your teaching and Your word. True — You are the Master for Your people and a mighty King to take up their grievance. True — You are the First and You are the Last, and other than You we have no king,[1] redeemer, or savior. From Egypt You redeemed us, HASHEM, our God, and from the house of slavery You liberated us. All their firstborn You slew, but Your firstborn You redeemed; the Sea of Reeds You split; the wanton sinners You drowned; the dear ones You brought across; and the water covered their foes — not one of them was left.[2] For this, the beloved praised and exalted God; the dear ones offered hymns, songs, praises, blessings, and thanksgivings to the King, the living and enduring God — exalted and uplifted, great and awesome, Who humbles the haughty and lifts the lowly; withdraws the captive, liberates the humble, and helps the poor; Who responds to His people upon their outcry to Him.*

Rise for *Shemoneh Esrei.* Some take three steps backward at this point; others do so before צוּר יִשְׂרָאֵל, *'Rock of Israel.'*

Chazzan— *Praises to the Supreme God, the blessed One Who is blessed. Moses and the children of Israel exclaimed a song to You with great joy and they all said:*

'Who is like You among the heavenly powers, HASHEM! Who is like You, mighty in holiness, too awesome for praise, doing wonders.'[3]
Chazzan— *With a new song the redeemed ones praised Your Name at the seashore, all of them in unison gave thanks, acknowledged [Your] sovereignty, and said:*

'HASHEM shall reign for all eternity.'[4]

It is forbidden to interrupt or pause between *'Who redeemed Israel'* and *Shemoneh Esrei,* even for *Kaddish, Kedushah* or *Amen.*

צוּר יִשְׂרָאֵל Chazzan— *Rock of Israel,* arise to the aid of Israel and liberate, as You pledged, Judah and Israel. Our Redeemer — HASHEM, Master of Legions, is His Name — the Holy One of Israel.*[5] *Blessed are You, HASHEM, Who redeemed Israel.**

(1) Cf. *Isaiah* 44:6. (2) *Psalms* 106:11. (3) *Exodus* 15:11. (4) 15:18. (5) *Isaiah* 47:4.

---

dictum that prayer, i.e., *Shemoneh Esrei,* should follow mention of God's redemption of Israel. Only after we have set forth our faith in God as our Redeemer may we begin *Shemoneh Esrei,* in which we pray to Him for our personal and national needs *(R' Hirsch).*

שמונה עשרה – עמידה

Take three steps backward, then three steps forward. Remain standing with feet together while reciting *Shemoneh Esrei*. Recite it with quiet devotion and without interruption, verbal or otherwise. Although it should not be audible to others, one must pray loudly enough to hear himself.

אֲדֹנָי שְׂפָתַי תִּפְתָּח, וּפִי יַגִּיד תְּהִלָּתֶךָ.[1]

אבות

Bend the knees at בָּרוּךְ; bow at אַתָּה; straighten up at ה׳.

בָּרוּךְ אַתָּה יהוה אֱלֹהֵינוּ וֵאלֹהֵי אֲבוֹתֵינוּ, אֱלֹהֵי אַבְרָהָם, אֱלֹהֵי יִצְחָק, וֵאלֹהֵי יַעֲקֹב, הָאֵל הַגָּדוֹל הַגִּבּוֹר וְהַנּוֹרָא, אֵל עֶלְיוֹן, גּוֹמֵל חֲסָדִים טוֹבִים וְקוֹנֵה הַכֹּל, וְזוֹכֵר חַסְדֵי אָבוֹת, וּמֵבִיא גוֹאֵל לִבְנֵי בְנֵיהֶם, לְמַעַן שְׁמוֹ בְּאַהֲבָה. מֶלֶךְ עוֹזֵר וּמוֹשִׁיעַ וּמָגֵן.

Bend the knees at בָּרוּךְ; bow at אַתָּה; straighten up at ה׳.

בָּרוּךְ אַתָּה יהוה, מָגֵן אַבְרָהָם.

גבורות

אַתָּה גִּבּוֹר לְעוֹלָם אֲדֹנָי, מְחַיֵּה מֵתִים אַתָּה, רַב לְהוֹשִׁיעַ. מְכַלְכֵּל חַיִּים בְּחֶסֶד, מְחַיֵּה מֵתִים בְּרַחֲמִים רַבִּים, סוֹמֵךְ נוֹפְלִים, וְרוֹפֵא חוֹלִים, וּמַתִּיר אֲסוּרִים, וּמְקַיֵּם אֱמוּנָתוֹ לִישֵׁנֵי עָפָר. מִי כָמוֹךְ בַּעַל גְּבוּרוֹת, וּמִי דּוֹמֶה לָּךְ, מֶלֶךְ מֵמִית וּמְחַיֶּה וּמַצְמִיחַ יְשׁוּעָה. וְנֶאֱמָן אַתָּה לְהַחֲיוֹת מֵתִים. בָּרוּךְ אַתָּה יהוה, מְחַיֵּה הַמֵּתִים.

During the *chazzan's* repetition, *Kedushah* (below) is recited at this point.

קדושה

When reciting *Kedushah*, one must stand with his feet together and avoid any interruptions. One should rise on his toes when saying the words קָדוֹשׁ, קָדוֹשׁ, קָדוֹשׁ; בָּרוּךְ (of בָּרוּךְ כְּבוֹד); and יִמְלֹךְ.

Cong. then *Chazzan* – **נְקַדֵּשׁ** אֶת שִׁמְךָ בָּעוֹלָם, כְּשֵׁם שֶׁמַּקְדִּישִׁים אוֹתוֹ בִּשְׁמֵי מָרוֹם, כַּכָּתוּב עַל יַד נְבִיאֶךָ, וְקָרָא זֶה אֶל זֶה וְאָמַר:

All – קָדוֹשׁ קָדוֹשׁ קָדוֹשׁ יהוה צְבָאוֹת, מְלֹא כָל הָאָרֶץ כְּבוֹדוֹ.[2]

❖ אָז בְּקוֹל רַעַשׁ גָּדוֹל אַדִּיר וְחָזָק מַשְׁמִיעִים קוֹל, מִתְנַשְּׂאִים לְעֻמַּת שְׂרָפִים, לְעֻמָּתָם בָּרוּךְ יֹאמֵרוּ:

All – בָּרוּךְ כְּבוֹד יהוה, מִמְּקוֹמוֹ.[3] ❖ מִמְּקוֹמְךָ מַלְכֵּנוּ תוֹפִיעַ, וְתִמְלוֹךְ עָלֵינוּ, כִּי מְחַכִּים אֲנַחְנוּ לָךְ. מָתַי תִּמְלוֹךְ בְּצִיּוֹן, בְּקָרוֹב בְּיָמֵינוּ, לְעוֹלָם וָעֶד תִּשְׁכּוֹן. תִּתְגַּדַּל וְתִתְקַדַּשׁ בְּתוֹךְ יְרוּשָׁלַיִם עִירְךָ, לְדוֹר וָדוֹר וּלְנֵצַח נְצָחִים. וְעֵינֵינוּ תִרְאֶינָה מַלְכוּתֶךָ, כַּדָּבָר הָאָמוּר בְּשִׁירֵי עֻזֶּךָ, עַל יְדֵי דָוִד מְשִׁיחַ צִדְקֶךָ:

All – יִמְלֹךְ יהוה לְעוֹלָם, אֱלֹהַיִךְ צִיּוֹן לְדֹר וָדֹר, הַלְלוּיָהּ.[4]

Chazzan continues . . . לְדוֹר וָדוֹר (page 246).

SHEMONEH ESREI – AMIDAH

Take three steps backward, then three steps forward. Remain standing with feet together while reciting *Shemoneh Esrei.* Recite it with quiet devotion and without interruption, verbal or otherwise. Although it should not be audible to others, one must pray loudly enough to hear himself.

My Lord, open my lips, that my mouth may declare Your praise.[1]

PATRIARCHS

Bend the knees at *'Blessed'*; bow at *'You'*; straighten up at *'HASHEM.'*

בָּרוּךְ *Blessed are You, HASHEM, our God and the God of our forefathers, God of Abraham, God of Isaac, and God of Jacob; the great, mighty, and awesome God, the supreme God, Who bestows beneficial kindnesses and creates everything, Who recalls the kindnesses of the Patriarchs and brings a Redeemer to their children's children, for His Name's sake, with love. O King, Helper, Savior, and Shield.*

Bend the knees at *'Blessed'*; bow at *'You'*; straighten up at 'HASHEM.'

Blessed are You, HASHEM, Shield of Abraham.

GOD'S MIGHT

אַתָּה *You are eternally mighty, my Lord, the Resuscitator of the dead are You; abundantly able to save. He sustains the living with kindness, resuscitates the dead with abundant mercy, supports the fallen, heals the sick, releases the confined, and maintains His faith to those asleep in the dust. Who is like You, O Master of mighty deeds, and who is comparable to You, O King Who causes death and restores life and makes salvation sprout! And You are faithful to resuscitate the dead. Blessed are You, HASHEM, Who resuscitates the dead.*

During the *chazzan's* repetition, *Kedushah* (below) is recited at this point.

KEDUSHAH

When reciting *Kedushah*, one must stand with his feet together and avoid any interruptions. One should rise on his toes when saying the words *Holy, holy, holy; Blessed is;* and *HASHEM shall reign.*

Cong. then Chazzan – נְקַדֵּשׁ *We shall sanctify Your Name in this world, just as they sanctify it in heaven above, as it is written by Your prophet, "And one [angel] will call another and say:*

All – *'Holy, holy, holy is HASHEM, Master of Legions, the whole world is filled with His glory.'"*[2] ❖ *Then, with a sound of great noise, mighty and powerful, they make heard a voice, raising themselves toward the seraphim; those facing them say 'Blessed ...':*

All – *'Blessed is the glory of HASHEM from His place.'*[3] ❖ *From Your place, our King, You will appear and reign over us, for we await You. When will You reign in Zion? Soon, in our days — forever and ever — may You dwell there. May You be exalted and sanctified within Jerusalem, Your city, from generation to generation and for all eternity. May our eyes see Your kingdom, as it is expressed in the songs of Your might, written by David, Your righteous anointed:*

All – *'HASHEM shall reign forever — your God, O Zion — from generation to generation, Halleluyah!'*[4]

Chazzan continues לְדוֹר וָדוֹר, *From generation* ... (p. 246).

---

(1) *Psalms* 51:17. (2) *Isaiah* 6:3. (3) *Ezekiel* 3:12. (4) *Psalms* 146:10.

קדושת השם

INDIVIDUALS RECITE:

אַתָּה קָדוֹשׁ וְשִׁמְךָ קָדוֹשׁ, וּקְדוֹשִׁים בְּכָל יוֹם יְהַלְלְוּךָ סֶּלָה. בָּרוּךְ אַתָּה יהוה, הָאֵל הַקָּדוֹשׁ.

CHAZZAN RECITES DURING HIS REPETITION:

לְדוֹר וָדוֹר נַגִּיד גָּדְלֶךָ וּלְנֵצַח נְצָחִים קְדֻשָּׁתְךָ נַקְדִּישׁ, וְשִׁבְחֲךָ אֱלֹהֵינוּ מִפִּינוּ לֹא יָמוּשׁ לְעוֹלָם וָעֶד, כִּי אֵל מֶלֶךְ גָּדוֹל וְקָדוֹשׁ אָתָּה. בָּרוּךְ אַתָּה יהוה, הָאֵל הַקָּדוֹשׁ.

קדושת היום

אַתָּה בְחַרְתָּנוּ מִכָּל הָעַמִּים, אָהַבְתָּ אוֹתָנוּ, וְרָצִיתָ בָּנוּ, וְרוֹמַמְתָּנוּ מִכָּל הַלְּשׁוֹנוֹת, וְקִדַּשְׁתָּנוּ בְּמִצְוֹתֶיךָ, וְקֵרַבְתָּנוּ מַלְכֵּנוּ לַעֲבוֹדָתֶךָ, וְשִׁמְךָ הַגָּדוֹל וְהַקָּדוֹשׁ עָלֵינוּ קָרָאתָ.

On the Sabbath add the words in brackets. [If forgotten, see *Laws* §86-90.]

וַתִּתֶּן לָנוּ יהוה אֱלֹהֵינוּ בְּאַהֲבָה [שַׁבָּתוֹת לִמְנוּחָה וּ]מוֹעֲדִים לְשִׂמְחָה חַגִּים וּזְמַנִּים לְשָׂשׂוֹן, אֶת יוֹם [הַשַּׁבָּת הַזֶּה וְאֶת יוֹם] חַג הַסֻּכּוֹת הַזֶּה, זְמַן שִׂמְחָתֵנוּ [בְּאַהֲבָה] מִקְרָא קֹדֶשׁ, זֵכֶר לִיצִיאַת מִצְרָיִם.

During the *chazzan's* repetition, congregation responds אָמֵן as indicated.

אֱלֹהֵינוּ וֵאלֹהֵי אֲבוֹתֵינוּ, יַעֲלֶה, וְיָבֹא, וְיַגִּיעַ, וְיֵרָאֶה, וְיֵרָצֶה, וְיִשָּׁמַע, וְיִפָּקֵד, וְיִזָּכֵר זִכְרוֹנֵנוּ וּפִקְדוֹנֵנוּ, וְזִכְרוֹן אֲבוֹתֵינוּ, וְזִכְרוֹן מָשִׁיחַ בֶּן דָּוִד עַבְדֶּךָ, וְזִכְרוֹן יְרוּשָׁלַיִם עִיר קָדְשֶׁךָ, וְזִכְרוֹן כָּל עַמְּךָ בֵּית יִשְׂרָאֵל לְפָנֶיךָ, לִפְלֵיטָה לְטוֹבָה לְחֵן וּלְחֶסֶד וּלְרַחֲמִים, לְחַיִּים וּלְשָׁלוֹם בְּיוֹם חַג הַסֻּכּוֹת הַזֶּה. זָכְרֵנוּ יהוה אֱלֹהֵינוּ בּוֹ לְטוֹבָה (.Cong – אָמֵן), וּפָקְדֵנוּ בוֹ לִבְרָכָה (.Cong – אָמֵן), וְהוֹשִׁיעֵנוּ בוֹ לְחַיִּים (.Cong – אָמֵן). וּבִדְבַר יְשׁוּעָה וְרַחֲמִים, חוּס וְחָנֵּנוּ וְרַחֵם עָלֵינוּ וְהוֹשִׁיעֵנוּ, כִּי אֵלֶיךָ עֵינֵינוּ, כִּי אֵל מֶלֶךְ חַנּוּן וְרַחוּם אָתָּה.[1]

On the Sabbath add the words in brackets. [If forgotten, see *Laws* §86-90.]

וְהַשִּׂיאֵנוּ יהוה אֱלֹהֵינוּ אֶת בִּרְכַּת מוֹעֲדֶיךָ לְחַיִּים וּלְשָׁלוֹם, לְשִׂמְחָה וּלְשָׂשׂוֹן, כַּאֲשֶׁר רָצִיתָ וְאָמַרְתָּ לְבָרְכֵנוּ. [אֱלֹהֵינוּ וֵאלֹהֵי אֲבוֹתֵינוּ רְצֵה בִמְנוּחָתֵנוּ] קַדְּשֵׁנוּ בְּמִצְוֹתֶיךָ וְתֵן חֶלְקֵנוּ בְּתוֹרָתֶךָ, שַׂבְּעֵנוּ מִטּוּבֶךָ וְשַׂמְּחֵנוּ בִּישׁוּעָתֶךָ, וְטַהֵר לִבֵּנוּ

HOLINESS OF GOD'S NAME

INDIVIDUALS RECITE:

אַתָּה *You are holy and Your Name is holy, and holy ones praise You every day, forever. Blessed are You,* HASHEM, *the holy God.*

CHAZZAN RECITES DURING HIS REPETITION:

לְדוֹר *From generation to generation we shall relate Your greatness and for infinite eternities we shall proclaim Your holiness. Your praise, our God, shall not leave our mouth forever and ever, for You, O God, are a great and holy King. Blessed are You,* HASHEM, *the holy God.*

SANCTIFICATION OF THE DAY

אַתָּה בְחַרְתָּנוּ *You have chosen us from all the peoples; You loved us and found favor in us; You exalted us above all the tongues and You sanctified us with Your commandments. You drew us close, our King, to Your service and proclaimed Your great and Holy Name upon us.*

On the Sabbath add the words in brackets. [If forgotten, see *Laws* §86-90.]

וַתִּתֶּן לָנוּ *And You gave us,* HASHEM, *our God, with love [Sabbaths for rest], appointed festivals for gladness, Festivals and times for joy, [this day of Sabbath and] this day of the Festival of Succos, the time of our gladness [with love], a holy convocation, a memorial of the Exodus from Egypt.*

During the *chazzan's* repetition, congregation responds *Amen* as indicated.

אֱלֹהֵינוּ *Our God and God of our forefathers, may there rise, come, reach, be noted, be favored, be heard, be considered, and be remembered — the remembrance and consideration of ourselves; the remembrance of our forefathers; the remembrance of Messiah, son of David, Your servant; the remembrance of Jerusalem, the City of Your Holiness; the remembrance of Your entire people the Family of Israel — before You for deliverance, for goodness, for grace, for kindness, and for compassion, for life, and for peace on this day of the Festival of Succos. Remember us on it,* HASHEM, *our God, for goodness* (Cong. – *Amen*)*; consider us on it for blessing* (Cong. – *Amen*)*; and help us on it for life* (Cong. – *Amen*)*. In the matter of salvation and compassion, pity, be gracious and compassionate with us and help us, for our eyes are turned to You, because You are God, the gracious and compassionate King.*[1]

On the Sabbath add the words in brackets. [If forgotten, see *Laws* §86-90.]

וְהַשִּׂיאֵנוּ *Bestow upon us, O* HASHEM, *our God, the blessing of Your appointed Festivals for life and for peace, for gladness and for joy, as You desired and promised to bless us. [Our God and the God of our forefathers, may You be pleased with our rest.] Sanctify us withYour commandments and grant us our share in Your Torah; satisfy us from Your goodness and gladden us with Your salvation, and purify our heart*

(1) Cf. *Nechemiah* 9:31.

לְעָבְדְּךָ בֶּאֱמֶת, וְהַנְחִילֵנוּ יהוה אֱלֹהֵינוּ [בְּאַהֲבָה וּבְרָצוֹן] בְּשִׂמְחָה וּבְשָׂשׂוֹן [שַׁבָּת וּ]מוֹעֲדֵי קָדְשֶׁךָ, וְיִשְׂמְחוּ בְךָ יִשְׂרָאֵל מְקַדְּשֵׁי שְׁמֶךָ. בָּרוּךְ אַתָּה יהוה, מְקַדֵּשׁ [הַשַּׁבָּת וְ]יִשְׂרָאֵל וְהַזְּמַנִּים.

עבודה

רְצֵה יהוה אֱלֹהֵינוּ בְּעַמְּךָ יִשְׂרָאֵל וּבִתְפִלָּתָם, וְהָשֵׁב אֶת הָעֲבוֹדָה לִדְבִיר בֵּיתֶךָ. וְאִשֵּׁי יִשְׂרָאֵל וּתְפִלָּתָם בְּאַהֲבָה תְקַבֵּל בְּרָצוֹן, וּתְהִי לְרָצוֹן תָּמִיד עֲבוֹדַת יִשְׂרָאֵל עַמֶּךָ.

וְתֶחֱזֶינָה עֵינֵינוּ בְּשׁוּבְךָ לְצִיּוֹן בְּרַחֲמִים. בָּרוּךְ אַתָּה יהוה, הַמַּחֲזִיר שְׁכִינָתוֹ לְצִיּוֹן.

הודאה

Bow at מוֹדִים; straighten up at ה׳. In his repetition the *chazzan* should recite the entire מוֹדִים aloud, while the congregation recites מוֹדִים דְּרַבָּנָן softly.

מוֹדִים אֲנַחְנוּ לָךְ, שָׁאַתָּה הוּא יהוה אֱלֹהֵינוּ וֵאלֹהֵי אֲבוֹתֵינוּ לְעוֹלָם וָעֶד. צוּר חַיֵּינוּ, מָגֵן יִשְׁעֵנוּ אַתָּה הוּא לְדוֹר וָדוֹר. נוֹדֶה לְּךָ וּנְסַפֵּר תְּהִלָּתֶךָ[1] עַל חַיֵּינוּ הַמְּסוּרִים בְּיָדֶךָ, וְעַל נִשְׁמוֹתֵינוּ הַפְּקוּדוֹת לָךְ, וְעַל נִסֶּיךָ שֶׁבְּכָל יוֹם עִמָּנוּ, וְעַל נִפְלְאוֹתֶיךָ וְטוֹבוֹתֶיךָ שֶׁבְּכָל עֵת, עֶרֶב וָבֹקֶר וְצָהֳרָיִם. הַטּוֹב כִּי לֹא כָלוּ רַחֲמֶיךָ, וְהַמְרַחֵם כִּי לֹא תַמּוּ חֲסָדֶיךָ,[2] מֵעוֹלָם קִוִּינוּ לָךְ.

מודים דרבנן

מוֹדִים אֲנַחְנוּ לָךְ, שָׁאַתָּה הוּא יהוה אֱלֹהֵינוּ וֵאלֹהֵי אֲבוֹתֵינוּ, אֱלֹהֵי כָל בָּשָׂר, יוֹצְרֵנוּ, יוֹצֵר בְּרֵאשִׁית. בְּרָכוֹת וְהוֹדָאוֹת לְשִׁמְךָ הַגָּדוֹל וְהַקָּדוֹשׁ, עַל שֶׁהֶחֱיִיתָנוּ וְקִיַּמְתָּנוּ. כֵּן תְּחַיֵּנוּ וּתְקַיְּמֵנוּ, וְתֶאֱסוֹף גָּלֻיּוֹתֵינוּ לְחַצְרוֹת קָדְשֶׁךָ, לִשְׁמוֹר חֻקֶּיךָ וְלַעֲשׂוֹת רְצוֹנֶךָ, וּלְעָבְדְּךָ בְּלֵבָב שָׁלֵם, עַל שֶׁאֲנַחְנוּ מוֹדִים לָךְ. בָּרוּךְ אֵל הַהוֹדָאוֹת.

וְעַל כֻּלָּם יִתְבָּרַךְ וְיִתְרוֹמַם שִׁמְךָ מַלְכֵּנוּ תָּמִיד לְעוֹלָם וָעֶד.

Bend the knees at בָּרוּךְ; bow at אַתָּה; straighten up at ה׳.

וְכֹל הַחַיִּים יוֹדְוּךָ סֶּלָה, וִיהַלְלוּ אֶת שִׁמְךָ בֶּאֱמֶת, הָאֵל יְשׁוּעָתֵנוּ וְעֶזְרָתֵנוּ סֶלָה. בָּרוּךְ אַתָּה יהוה, הַטּוֹב שִׁמְךָ וּלְךָ נָאֶה לְהוֹדוֹת.

to serve You sincerely. And grant us a heritage, O HASHEM, our God — [with love and with favor] with gladness and with joy — [the Sabbath and] the appointed festivals of Your holiness, and may Israel, the sanctifiers of Your Name, rejoice in You. Blessed are You, HASHEM, Who sanctifies [the Sabbath,] Israel and the festive seasons.

TEMPLE SERVICE

רְצֵה *Be favorable, HASHEM, our God, toward Your people Israel and their prayer and restore the service to the Holy of Holies of Your Temple. The fire-offerings of Israel and their prayer accept with love and favor, and may the service of Your people Israel always be favorable to You.*

וְתֶחֱזֶינָה *May our eyes behold Your return to Zion in compassion. Blessed are You, HASHEM, Who restores His Presence to Zion.*

THANKSGIVING [MODIM]

Bow at *'We gratefully thank You'*; straighten up at *'HASHEM.'* In his repetition the *chazzan* should recite the entire *Modim* aloud, while the congregation recites *Modim of the Rabbis* softly.

מוֹדִים *We gratefully thank You, for it is You Who are HASHEM, our God and the God of our forefathers for all eternity; Rock of our lives, Shield of our salvation are You from generation to generation. We shall thank You and relate Your praise[1] — for our lives, which are committed to Your power and for our souls that are entrusted to You; for Your miracles that are with us every day; and for Your wonders and favors in every season — evening, morning, and afternoon. The Beneficent One, for Your compassions were never exhausted, and the Compassionate One, for Your kindnesses never ended[2] — always have we put our hope in You.*

MODIM OF THE RABBIS

מוֹדִים *We gratefully thank You, for it is You Who are HASHEM, our God and the God of our forefathers, the God of all flesh, our Molder, the Molder of the universe. Blessings and thanks are due Your great and holy Name for You have given us life and sustained us. So may You continue to give us life and sustain us and gather our exiles to the Courtyards of Your Sanctuary, to observe Your decrees, to do Your will and to serve You wholeheartedly. [We thank You] for inspiring us to thank You. Blessed is the God of thanksgivings.*

For all these, may Your Name be blessed and exalted, our King, continually forever and ever.

Bend the knees at *'Blessed'*; bow at *'You'*; straighten up at *'HASHEM.'*

Everything alive will gratefully acknowledge You, Selah! and praise Your Name sincerely, O God of our salvation and help, Selah! Blessed are You, HASHEM, Your Name is 'The Beneficent One' and to You it is fitting to give thanks.

(1) Cf. *Psalms* 79:13. (2) Cf. *Lamentations* 3:22.

ברכת כהנים

The *chazzan* recites בִּרְכַּת כֹּהֲנִים during his repetition. He faces right at וְיִשְׁמְרֶךָ; faces left at אֵלֶיךָ וִיחֻנֶּךָּ; faces the Ark for the rest of the blessings.

אֱלֹהֵינוּ, וֵאלֹהֵי אֲבוֹתֵינוּ, בָּרְכֵנוּ בַבְּרָכָה הַמְּשֻׁלֶּשֶׁת בַּתּוֹרָה הַכְּתוּבָה עַל יְדֵי מֹשֶׁה עַבְדֶּךָ, הָאֲמוּרָה מִפִּי אַהֲרֹן וּבָנָיו, כֹּהֲנִים עַם קְדוֹשֶׁךָ, כָּאָמוּר:

יְבָרֶכְךָ יהוה, וְיִשְׁמְרֶךָ. (Cong. – כֵּן יְהִי רָצוֹן.)

יָאֵר יהוה פָּנָיו אֵלֶיךָ וִיחֻנֶּךָּ. (Cong. – כֵּן יְהִי רָצוֹן.)

יִשָּׂא יהוה פָּנָיו אֵלֶיךָ וְיָשֵׂם לְךָ שָׁלוֹם.[1] (Cong. – כֵּן יְהִי רָצוֹן.)

שלום

שִׂים שָׁלוֹם, טוֹבָה, וּבְרָכָה, חֵן, וָחֶסֶד וְרַחֲמִים עָלֵינוּ וְעַל כָּל יִשְׂרָאֵל עַמֶּךָ. בָּרְכֵנוּ אָבִינוּ, כֻּלָּנוּ כְּאֶחָד בְּאוֹר פָּנֶיךָ, כִּי בְאוֹר פָּנֶיךָ נָתַתָּ לָּנוּ, יהוה אֱלֹהֵינוּ, תּוֹרַת חַיִּים וְאַהֲבַת חֶסֶד, וּצְדָקָה, וּבְרָכָה, וְרַחֲמִים, וְחַיִּים, וְשָׁלוֹם. וְטוֹב בְּעֵינֶיךָ לְבָרֵךְ אֶת עַמְּךָ יִשְׂרָאֵל, בְּכָל עֵת וּבְכָל שָׁעָה בִּשְׁלוֹמֶךָ. בָּרוּךְ אַתָּה יהוה, הַמְּבָרֵךְ אֶת עַמּוֹ יִשְׂרָאֵל בַּשָּׁלוֹם.

יִהְיוּ לְרָצוֹן אִמְרֵי פִי וְהֶגְיוֹן לִבִּי לְפָנֶיךָ, יהוה צוּרִי וְגֹאֲלִי.[2]

THE *CHAZZAN'S* REPETITION ENDS HERE; TURN TO PAGE 284. INDIVIDUALS CONTINUE:

אֱלֹהַי, נְצוֹר לְשׁוֹנִי מֵרָע, וּשְׂפָתַי מִדַּבֵּר מִרְמָה,[3] וְלִמְקַלְלַי נַפְשִׁי תִדּוֹם, וְנַפְשִׁי כֶּעָפָר לַכֹּל תִּהְיֶה. פְּתַח לִבִּי בְּתוֹרָתֶךָ, וּבְמִצְוֹתֶיךָ תִּרְדּוֹף נַפְשִׁי. וְכֹל הַחוֹשְׁבִים עָלַי רָעָה, מְהֵרָה הָפֵר עֲצָתָם וְקַלְקֵל מַחֲשַׁבְתָּם. עֲשֵׂה לְמַעַן שְׁמֶךָ, עֲשֵׂה לְמַעַן יְמִינֶךָ, עֲשֵׂה לְמַעַן קְדֻשָּׁתֶךָ, עֲשֵׂה לְמַעַן תּוֹרָתֶךָ. לְמַעַן יֵחָלְצוּן יְדִידֶיךָ, הוֹשִׁיעָה יְמִינְךָ וַעֲנֵנִי.[4]

Some recite verses pertaining to their names here. See page 1301.

יִהְיוּ לְרָצוֹן אִמְרֵי פִי וְהֶגְיוֹן לִבִּי לְפָנֶיךָ, יהוה צוּרִי וְגֹאֲלִי.[2] עֹשֶׂה שָׁלוֹם בִּמְרוֹמָיו, הוּא יַעֲשֶׂה שָׁלוֹם עָלֵינוּ, וְעַל כָּל יִשְׂרָאֵל. וְאִמְרוּ: אָמֵן.

Bow and take three steps back. Bow left and say . . . עֹשֶׂה, bow right and say . . . הוּא יַעֲשֶׂה; bow forward and say וְעַל כָּל . . . אָמֵן.

יְהִי רָצוֹן מִלְּפָנֶיךָ יהוה אֱלֹהֵינוּ וֵאלֹהֵי אֲבוֹתֵינוּ, שֶׁיִּבָּנֶה בֵּית הַמִּקְדָּשׁ בִּמְהֵרָה בְיָמֵינוּ, וְתֵן חֶלְקֵנוּ בְּתוֹרָתֶךָ. וְשָׁם נַעֲבָדְךָ בְּיִרְאָה, כִּימֵי עוֹלָם וּכְשָׁנִים קַדְמוֹנִיּוֹת. וְעָרְבָה לַיהוה מִנְחַת יְהוּדָה וִירוּשָׁלָיִם, כִּימֵי עוֹלָם וּכְשָׁנִים קַדְמוֹנִיּוֹת.[5]

THE INDIVIDUAL'S RECITATION OF *SHEMONEH ESREI* ENDS HERE.

The individual remain standing in place until the *chazzan* reaches *Kedushah* – or at least until the *chazzan* begins his repetition – then he takes three steps forward.

FOR THOSE CONGREGATIONS THAT RECITE *PIYUTIM*, THE *CHAZZAN'S* REPETITION FOR THE FIRST DAY BEGINS ON PAGE 252; FOR THE SECOND DAY, ON PAGE 268. IN CONGREGATIONS NOT RECITING *PIYUTIM*, THE REPETITION BEGINS ON PAGE 244.

THE PRIESTLY BLESSING

The chazzan recites the Priestly Blessing during his repetition.

אֱלֹהֵינוּ *Our God and the God of our forefathers, bless us with the three-verse blessing in the Torah that was written by the hand of Moses, Your servant, that was said by Aaron and his sons, the Kohanim, Your holy people, as it is said:*

May HASHEM bless you and safeguard you. (Cong.— *So may it be.*)

May HASHEM illuminate His countenance for you and be gracious to you. (Cong.— *So may it be.*)

May HASHEM turn His countenance to you and establish peace for you.[1] (Cong.— *So may it be.*)

PEACE

שִׂים *Establish peace, goodness, blessing, graciousness, kindness, and compassion upon us and upon all of Your people Israel. Bless us, our Father, all of us as one, with the light of Your countenance, for with the light of Your countenance You gave us, HASHEM, our God, the Torah of life and a love of kindness, righteousness, blessing, compassion, life, and peace. And may it be good in Your eyes to bless Your people Israel at every time and every hour with Your peace. Blessed are You, HASHEM, Who blesses His people Israel with peace.*

May the expressions of my mouth and the thoughts of my heart find favor before You, HASHEM, my Rock and my Redeemer.[2]

THE *CHAZZAN'S* REPETITION ENDS HERE; TURN TO PAGE 284. INDIVIDUALS CONTINUE:

אֱלֹהַי *My God, guard my tongue from evil and my lips from speaking deceitfully.*[3] *To those who curse me, let my soul be silent; and let my soul be like dust to everyone. Open my heart to Your Torah, then my soul will pursue Your commandments. As for all those who design evil against me, speedily nullify their counsel and disrupt their design. Act for Your Name's sake; act for Your right hand's sake; act for Your sanctity's sake; act for Your Torah's sake. That Your beloved ones may be given rest; let Your right hand save, and respond to me.*[4]

Some recite verses pertaining to their names at this point. See page 1301.

May the expressions of my mouth and the thoughts of my heart find favor before You, HASHEM, my Rock and my Redeemer.[2] *He Who makes peace in His heights, may He make peace upon us, and upon all Israel. Now respond: Amen.*

Bow and take three steps back. Bow left and say, *'He Who makes peace . . .'*; bow right and say, *'may He make peace . . .'*; bow forward and say, *'and upon . . . Amen.'*

יְהִי רָצוֹן *May it be Your will, HASHEM, our God and the God of our forefathers, that the Holy Temple be rebuilt, speedily in our days. Grant us our share in Your Torah, and may we serve You there with reverence, as in days of old and in former years. Then the offering of Judah and Jerusalem will be pleasing to HASHEM, as in days of old and in former years.*[5]

THE INDIVIDUAL'S RECITATION OF *SHEMONEH ESREI* ENDS HERE.

The individual remain standing in place until the *chazzan* reaches *Kedushah* — or at least until the *chazzan* begins his repetition — then he takes three steps forward. The *chazzan* himself, or one praying alone, should remain in place for a few moments before taking three steps forward.

FOR THOSE CONGREGATIONS THAT RECITE *PIYUTIM,* THE *CHAZZAN'S* REPETITION FOR THE FIRST DAY BEGINS ON PAGE 252; FOR THE SECOND DAY, ON PAGE 268. IN CONGREGATIONS NOT RECITING *PIYUTIM,* THE REPETITION BEGINS ON PAGE 244.

---

(1) *Numbers* 6:24-26. (2) *Psalms* 19:15. (3) Cf. 34:14. (4) 60:7; 108:7. (5) *Malachi* 3:4.

THE *CHAZZAN'S* REPETITION FOR THE SECOND DAY APPEARS ON PAGE 268.

חזרת הש״ץ ליום ראשון

WHEN THE FIRST DAY FALLS ON THE SABBATH, THE SECOND DAY'S REPETITION (P. 268) IS RECITED ON THE SABBATH, AND THE FIRST DAY'S REPETITION IS RECITED ON SUNDAY.

אֲדֹנָי שְׂפָתַי תִּפְתָּח, וּפִי יַגִּיד תְּהִלָּתֶךָ.[1]

אבות

The *chazzan* bends his knees at בָּרוּךְ; bows at אַתָּה; straightens up at ה׳.

בָּרוּךְ אַתָּה יהוה אֱלֹהֵינוּ וֵאלֹהֵי אֲבוֹתֵינוּ, אֱלֹהֵי אַבְרָהָם, אֱלֹהֵי יִצְחָק, וֵאלֹהֵי יַעֲקֹב, הָאֵל הַגָּדוֹל הַגִּבּוֹר וְהַנּוֹרָא, אֵל עֶלְיוֹן, גּוֹמֵל חֲסָדִים טוֹבִים וְקוֹנֵה הַכֹּל, וְזוֹכֵר חַסְדֵי אָבוֹת, וּמֵבִיא גּוֹאֵל לִבְנֵי בְנֵיהֶם, לְמַעַן שְׁמוֹ בְּאַהֲבָה. מֶלֶךְ עוֹזֵר וּמוֹשִׁיעַ וּמָגֵן.

מִסּוֹד* חֲכָמִים וּנְבוֹנִים, וּמִלֶּמֶד דַּעַת מְבִינִים, אֶפְתְּחָה פִּי בְּשִׁיר וּבִרְנָנִים, לְהוֹדוֹת וּלְהַלֵּל פְּנֵי שׁוֹכֵן מְעוֹנִים.

All:

אֵימָתִי* בְּחִיל כִּפּוּר, בְּעוּתָהּ בְּחֶשְׁבּוֹן הַסִּפּוּר,
גַּלְּתִי כְּהֻצְדַּק פּוּר, דּוֹלֵק* כְּנִמְצָא חָפוּר.
הֶדְרָאוּ מְתֵי הוֹלְלִים, וְצִמְּתוּ לְרֶגֶב חֲלָלִים,
זַכִּים כְּיָצְאוּ מְהֻלָּלִים, חָלִים* וְשָׁרִים כְּחוֹלְלִים.[2]
טִיעַת עֲצֵי עֵשֶׂב, יִשְׁאוּ הַיּוֹם מִזְבֵּחַ* לְהָסֵב,
❖ כְּתֶשֶׁר יְפַלְּסוּ בְּמֵסֵב, לְהֵרָצוֹת בְּשׁוֹר וָכֶשֶׂב.*

> This *Machzor* includes those *piyutim* that are commonly recited. A few *piyutim* that are omitted by a vast majority of congregations have been included in an appendix beginning on page 1262. The text will indicate where they may be recited.

חֲזָרַת הַשּׁ״ץ / CHAZZAN'S REPETITION

In ancient times, when *siddurim* were not available and many people did not know the text of *Shemoneh Esrei*, people could listen intently to the *chazzan's* repetition and respond *Amen* to the blessings, thereby fulfilling their own obligation to pray. Thus, the repetition has the status of a communal, rather than an individual, prayer.

On Rosh Hashanah and Yom Kippur — and, to a lesser extent, on other Festivals — *piyutim* are inserted in the *chazzan's* repetition. These *piyutim* [known as *kerovos*] express the mood and theme of the day, and many of them have become highlights of the day's service. Thus, the repetition is truly a communal prayer, for it involves the entire congregation.

The *kerovos* for the first two days of Succos were composed by R' Elazar HaKalir (see p. 35).

מִסּוֹד — *Based on the tradition.* Many prominent halachic authorities from medieval times onward have opposed the insertion of *piyutim* into the prayer order, primarily on the grounds that they are an interference with and a change in the words of the prayers as they were set forth by the Sages. Most congregations, though by no means all, follow *Rama* (*Orach Chaim* 68 and 112) who permits the recitation of *piyutim*. To justify our recitation of *piyutim* during the *chazzan's Shemoneh Esrei*, they are prefaced with the formula, מִסּוֹד חֲכָמִים וּנְבוֹנִים, *Based on the tradition of our wise and discerning teachers,* meaning that we dare to interrupt the prayer service only because these *piyutim* were transmitted to us by the wise and discerning teachers of yore, based on the 'foundation' of their great wisdom and piety.

אֵימָתִי — *I shuddered.* The first three sections of this *kerovos* contains an acrostic of the *aleph-beis.*

The *paytan* erects a bridge between the trepidation of Yom Kippur and the joy of Succos. Having been judged favorably on Yom Kippur,

THE *CHAZZAN'S* REPETITION FOR THE SECOND DAY APPEARS ON PAGE 268.

CHAZZAN'S REPETITION FOR THE FIRST DAY

WHEN THE FIRST DAY FALLS ON THE SABBATH, THE SECOND DAY'S REPETITION (P. 268) IS RECITED ON THE SABBATH, AND THE FIRST DAY'S REPETITION IS RECITED ON SUNDAY.

My Lord, open my lips, that my mouth may declare Your praise.[1]

PATRIARCHS

The *chazzan* bends his knees at *'Blessed'*; bows at *'You'*; straightens up at *'HASHEM.'*

בָּרוּךְ *Blessed are You, HASHEM, our God and the God of our forefathers, God of Abraham, God of Isaac, and God of Jacob; the great, mighty, and awesome God, the supreme God, Who bestows beneficial kindnesses and creates everything, Who recalls the kindnesses of the Patriarchs and brings a Redeemer to their children's children, for His Name's sake, with love. O King, Helper, Savior, and Shield.*

מְסוֹד *Based on the tradition* of our wise and discerning teachers, and the teaching derived from the knowledge of the discerning, I open my mouth in song and joyful praise, to give thanks and to offer praise before Him Who dwells in the heavens.*

All:

א *I shuddered* in awe on Yom Kippur,*
ב *terrified by the number [of sins] counted.*
ג *I rejoiced when my lot was judged righteous,*
ד *when [Satan] the pursuer* found himself shamed.*

ה *The sinful madmen were mortified,*
ו *and destroyed like clods in the bottomless pits.*
ז *[While] the pure ones went forth praising [God],*
ח *[with] flute* and song as they danced.*[2]

ט *Plantings of supple trees,*
י *they carry around the Altar today,**
כ ∴*May their circuit be reckoned as an offering,*
ל *finding favor as [if they offered] bull and sheep.**

(1) *Psalms* 51:17. (2) 87:7.

---

the righteous are given the Four Species to hold aloft as a sign of victory against Satan, the Accuser. Even more, the act of taking the Four Species is reckoned as a Temple offering, and is an additional merit for those who perform it.

The time frame of the *piyut* is ambiguous — it refers either to the Temple service or to the present day synagogue services — as the commentary will show.

דולק — *[Satan] the pursuer.* The Evil Inclination constantly pursues man, attempting to entice him into sin. Alternatively, דולק means *the kindler,* and refers to Satan's kindling of a person's passions, thereby inducing him to transgression.

חָלִים — *[With] flute.* On *Chol HaMoed,* an orchestra of many musical instruments played during the festivities in the Temple. Of these, the flute functioned as the primary instrument, and so the orchestra is called the 'flute.' See *Succah* 5:1-4 (p. 124), which describes the Temple festivities.

Alternatively, the word חָלִים comes from חִיל, *trembling* or *trepidation.* The verse then means, *the trepidation [of Yom Kippur turned into] song and dance [on Succos].*

הַיוֹם מִזְבֵּחַ — *The Altar today.* The *hakafah*-circuits that we make around the synagogue *bimah* as we hold the Four Species represent the circuits that were made around the great sacrificial Altar that stood in the Temple Courtyard (see *Succah* 4:5, p. 118).

בְּשׁוֹר וָכֶשֶׂב — *As [if they offered] bull and sheep.* Let our *hakafos* around the *bimah* be considered as if we had brought animal offerings upon the Altar.

Alternatively, this verse alludes to the day's Torah reading which begins: שׁוֹר אוֹ כֶשֶׂב, *A bull or a goat.* We pray that our reading of this passage be reckoned as if we had actually

All:

בָּךְ אָגִילָה וְאֶשְׂמְחָה,[1] בְּרִנָּה וְשִׂמְחָה,

❖ בְּאֵם הַבָּנִים שְׂמֵחָה,*[2] גּוֹנְנֵנוּ בְּפִדוּת צָמֵחָה.

Chazzan bends his knees at בָּרוּךְ; bows at אַתָּה; straightens up at ה׳.

בָּרוּךְ אַתָּה יהוה, מָגֵן אַבְרָהָם. (Cong.– אָמֵן.)

גבורות

אַתָּה גִּבּוֹר לְעוֹלָם אֲדֹנָי, מְחַיֵּה מֵתִים אַתָּה, רַב לְהוֹשִׁיעַ. מְכַלְכֵּל חַיִּים בְּחֶסֶד, מְחַיֵּה מֵתִים בְּרַחֲמִים רַבִּים, סוֹמֵךְ נוֹפְלִים, וְרוֹפֵא חוֹלִים, וּמַתִּיר אֲסוּרִים, וּמְקַיֵּם אֱמוּנָתוֹ לִישֵׁנֵי עָפָר. מִי כָמוֹךְ בַּעַל גְּבוּרוֹת, וּמִי דּוֹמֶה לָּךְ, מֶלֶךְ מֵמִית וּמְחַיֶּה וּמַצְמִיחַ יְשׁוּעָה. וְנֶאֱמָן אַתָּה לְהַחֲיוֹת מֵתִים.

All:

מְאַלְּמֵי מְגָדִים אַרְבָּעָה, מְשַׁמְּרֵי סֻכָּה שִׁבְעָה,

נוֹסְכֵי נֶזֶל שִׁבְעָה, נַהֲלֵם נְעִימוֹת שָׂבְעָה.[3]

שִׁיחִים בְּדֶרֶךְ מַטָּעָתָם,* סוֹלְלִים סְכוּת שַׁוְעָתָם,

עֲלֵי קָרִים נְטִיעָתָם, עֲלוֹת בָּמוֹ מִטְּבִיעָתָם.

פְּאוּרִים* לְשֵׁם יוֹם, פְּאֵר בָּם לְאָיוֹם,

❖ צִוּוּי קִיחָתָם הַיּוֹם, צַחֲצוּחַ בְּזֶה רִאשׁוֹן יוֹם.*

All:

בָּךְ אָגִילָה וְאֶשְׂמְחָה,[4] בְּגִילָה וְשִׂמְחָה,

❖ בְּאֵם הַבָּנִים שְׂמֵחָה,[5] טְלוּלִים בִּתְחִיָּה אֲשֶׁר צָמֵחָה.

Chazzan:

בָּרוּךְ אַתָּה יהוה, מְחַיֵּה הַמֵּתִים. (Cong.– אָמֵן.)

All:

קֹשֶׁט שְׁעִינַת עֵץ,* לְעוֹמְסֵי פְּרִי עֵץ,

---

performed its *mitzvah,* thus fulfilling the verse: *Let our lips compensate for the bulls (Hoshea* 14:3).

בְּאֵם הַבָּנִים שְׂמֵחָה — *Glad-mother-of-children.* In the future, Jerusalem will be teeming with inhabitants and the celebration in the city will resemble a joyful homecoming, as *Isaiah* 66:8 foretells: *For Zion has gone through travail and she has given birth to her sons* [who will return from the four corners of the earth].

בְּדֶרֶךְ מַטָּעָתָם — *In the direction of their growth.* The *mitzvah* of the Four Species requires that they be held upright as they grow from the tree. If one holds any of the species upside down, he has not fulfilled his obligation (see *Laws* §160).

פְּאוּרִים — *Adorned.* In Temple times, the people of Jerusalem would bind their *lulav*-bundles with strips of *lulav* leaves as we do today. They would then overlay the bindings with golden bands in order to adorn the *mitzvah (Succah* 3:8, see p. 110).

בְּזֶה רִאשׁוֹן יוֹם — *On this first day.* In the literal sense the phrase, *and you shall take for yourselves on the first day (Leviticus* 23:40), refers to the first day of Succos. Midrashically, *the first day* alludes to 'the first day for the calculation of sins.' That is, on Yom Kippur the penitent Jew was forgiven and cleansed of all his

All:

With You I shall rejoice and be glad,[1]
with joyous song and gladness,
∴ *In [the city called] 'Glad-mother-of-children,'*[2]*
O, shield us with flourishing redemption.

Chazzan bends his knees at *'Blessed'*; bows at *'You'*; straightens up at *'HASHEM.'*

Blessed are You, HASHEM, Shield of Abraham. (Cong.—*Amen.*)

GOD'S MIGHT

אַתָּה *You are eternally mighty, my Lord, the Resuscitator of the dead are You; abundantly able to save. He sustains the living with kindness, resuscitates the dead with abundant mercy, supports the fallen, heals the sick, releases the confined, and maintains His faith to those asleep in the dust. Who is like You, O Master of mighty deeds, and who is comparable to You, O King Who causes death and restores life and makes salvation sprout! And You are faithful to resuscitate the dead.*

All:

מ *They bind the four precious species,*
they observe the [mitzvah of] succah for seven [days];
נ *They pour the water-libation seven days,*
lead them to pleasant satiety.[3]
ס *[They hold the] tree-branches in the direction of their growth,**
exalting [You]; O hearken to their cries.
ע *[In the merit of the Four Species] which flourish near cool waters,*
raise them from the sinkholes [of their exile].
פ *Adorned** *in honor of the day,*
with them to glorify the Fearsome One,
צ ∴*The [reason for the] commandment to take them today,*
*is to cleanse Israel on this first day.**

All:

With You I shall rejoice and be glad,[4] *with joy and gladness,*
∴ *In [the city called] Glad-mother-of-children.*[5]
May the resuscitating dew cause [the dead] to arise like flourishing plants.

Chazzan:

Blessed are You, HASHEM, Who resuscitates the dead. (Cong.—*Amen.*)

All:

ק *Truthfully, the hospitality of 'reclining [beneath] the tree,'**
[should stand by] those who bear the [esrog] tree's fruit,

(1) Cf. *Song of Songs* 1:4. (2) Cf. *Psalms* 113:9. (3) Cf. *Psalms* 16:11. [Some *machzorim* read נְעִימוֹת שִׁבְעָה, *the pleasant seven,* an allusion to the seven *mitzvos* of Succos: the Four Species, the *succah,* the *chagigah*-offering and the peace-offering (see *Vayikra Rabbah* 30:2).]
(4) Cf. *Song of Songs* 1:4. (5) Cf. *Psalms* 113:9.

transgressions. After Yom Kippur, he was busy preparing for Succos — building a *succah,* obtaining the Four Species, etc. — and had no time to sin. But lest the period of leisure that begins with the prohibition against working on the Festival become a period of idleness that leads to sinning, the Torah forewarned that the first day of the Festival should not become 'the first day of sins.'

שְׁעִינַת עֵץ — *Reclining [beneath] the tree.* Seemingly trivial incidents often have cosmic implications that remain hidden for centuries before coming to light. The Midrash (*Bamidbar Rabbah* 14:2) shows how Abraham's every act of hospitality to his three angelic visitors [see *Genesis* 18:1-8] precipitated an act of kindness by God in later generations. Abraham offered shelter when he said, 'Recline beneath the tree.' In merit of this act, God sheltered the Jews in *succos* when they left Egypt.

זְכֹר נָא לְהִוָּעֵץ וּתְשׁוּעָה בְּרֹב יוֹעֵץ.[1]
רִבְבוֹת סָע סֻכּוֹתָה,* בְּלוּד[2] צִקְנָם הִסְכַּתָה,
בְּנֶשֶׁק לְרֹאשָׁם סַכּוֹתָה,[3] וּמֵאֱנֹף לַהֲקַם חֲשַׁכְתָּה.
שִׁבְעָה עֲנָנֵי מְשִׁי סִבַּבְתָּם, בַּעֲנִינַת פָּרֵס סִכַּכְתָּם,[4]
תָּעוּ כְּחֵדֶק מִמְּסוּכָתָם, בְּכֵן רִשְׁפָּה סֻכָּתָם.
תּוֹלְדוֹת כְּנַעַן* תְּאַבִּיד, גְּבִיר[5] לְבִלְתִּי לְהַעֲבִיד,
❖ תְּאַפְּדֵנוּ כְּאָז רְבִיד, בְּקוֹמְמָךְ סֻכַּת דָּוִד.[6]

Congregation aloud, then *chazzan:*

יִמְלֹךְ יהוה* לְעוֹלָם, אֱלֹהַיִךְ צִיּוֹן לְדֹר וָדֹר, הַלְלוּיָהּ.[7]
וְאַתָּה קָדוֹשׁ, יוֹשֵׁב תְּהִלּוֹת יִשְׂרָאֵל,[8] אֵל נָא.

Chazzan, then congregation:

אֲנוֹבֵב* בְּפֶה וְלָשׁוֹן, הַלֵּל בְּיוֹם רִאשׁוֹן,
לְהַעֲרִיץ לְאֵל אַחֲרוֹן וְרִאשׁוֹן,[9] קָדוֹשׁ.

Chazzan, then congregation:

שַׂגִּיא כֹחַ* לֹא נִמְצֵאתָ,[10] לְהַצְדִּיק עַם זוּ כְּחָפַצְתָּ,
בְּכֵן בְּאֵלֶּה נִרְצֵיתָ, קָדוֹשׁ.

All:

אֶקְחָה* פְּרִי עֵץ הָדָר,[11] בְּכָל שָׁנָה בִּתְדָר, מָקוֹם שֶׁהוּא מִתְדָּר.
לְהַלֵּל בּוֹ בֶּהָדָר, לְעָט הוֹד וְהָדָר,[12] עֲלֵי שִׁבְעָה דָּר.
עִזּוּז בַּקֹּדֶשׁ נֶאְדָּר, וּמִכָּל יְצִיר מְאֻדָּר, וְחָפֵץ זוּ לְהַדֵּר. אֲנוֹבֵב ...
זִמּוּן תְּמַר כַּף, אֶקְחָה הַיּוֹם בְּכַף, בָּם לְצוּר אִכַּף.

רִבְבוֹת סָע סֻכּוֹתָה — *The myriads who traveled to Succos.* A reference to the first leg of the journey out of Egypt: *And the Children of Israel traveled from Raamses to Succos* (*Exodus* 13:37).

Another interpretation: the myriad offspring of Jacob who had traveled to Succos where he had remained for eighteen months (see *Genesis* 33:17).

כְּנַעַן — *Canaan.* Some *machzorim* read צוֹר, *Tyre;* others read שֵׂעִיר, *Seir.* Presumably, the various versions were inspired by the gentile censors whose objections and emendations were inconsistent and varied from place to place and century to century.

☙ יִמְלֹךְ ה׳ — *HASHEM shall reign.* The *piyutim* that stress pleas for Israel are now interrupted with this stirring verse that speaks of the power and sovereignty of God. This underscores that all our prayers for forgiveness and success are intended so that we can serve Him better.

☙ אֲנוֹבֵב — *I shall recite.* This verse and the next are the refrains of the *piyut* אֶקְחָה, *I shall take,* which follows.

שַׂגִּיא כֹחַ — *Difficult feats.* Elihu, friend of Job, made two seemingly contradictory statements about God. First he said, *'Behold, God exalts Himself with His power'* (*Job* 36:22); then he said, *'We do not find God exalting Himself with power'* (*Job* 37:23). The Midrash (*Bamidbar Rabbah* 21:22) explains that when God gives something, He does so with great power, in full measure. But when He demands something, He does not demand difficult things. For example, He commanded: *You shall take yourselves . . . the fruit of the esrog tree . . .* (*Leviticus* 23:40), i.e., He demanded only the fruit or branches of the Four Species. But when giving He said: *I shall place in the Wilderness cedar, acacia, myrtle and olive-tree; I shall place on the plain cypress, box-tree and pine together* (*Isaiah* 41:19).

☙ אֶקְחָה — *I shall take.* The acrostic spells אֶלְעָזָר בִּירַבִּי קִילִיר, an alternate spelling often used by

please remember [them] — and offer [them] advice,
for [their] salvation is in [You,] O Great Advisor.[1]

ר *The myriads who traveled to Succos,**
You heard their entreaties in Lud [Egypt],[2]
You protected their heads in battle[3] *[in Canaan],*
You sheltered their congregation from burning anger.

ש *With seven silken clouds You surrounded them,*
with outspread clouds You sheltered them,[4]
[yet] they strayed like thorns [jutting] from [behind] their fence,
and so their Succah [Temple] was burned down.

ת *May You lay waste to the offspring of Canaan,**
that [Jacob] the master[5] *shall no longer serve [them].*
∴*adorn us as then with majestic jewelry,*
when You re-establish David's Succah [Temple].[6]

Congregation aloud, then *chazzan:*

HASHEM shall reign• forever — your God, O Zion — from generation to generation, Halleluyah![7]
You, O Holy One, are enthroned upon Israel's praises[8] **— please, O God.**

Chazzan, then congregation:

I shall recite• Hallel on the first day with mouth and tongue, to revere God Who is the Last and the First[9] **— O Holy One.**

Chazzan, then congregation:

Difficult feats• You do not demand [of them],[10]
to justify this people [Israel] as You desire,
therefore You find favor in these [readily available species]
— O Holy One.

All:

א *I shall take* the fruit of the esrog tree,*[11] *regularly each year,*
in the [synagogue, the] place where He permanently resides.
ל *There to praise with the esrog, Him Who is robed in majesty and splendor,*[12]
Who dwells upon seven [heavens].
ע *O powerful One, mighty in holiness, more majestic than all of Creation,*
Who desires to glorify this people [Israel]. *I shall recite ...*

ז *A date-palm branch prepared [with three other species],*
I shall take in hand today, with them to bow to the Rock.

---

(1) *Proverbs* 11:14; 24:6. (2) See *Genesis* 10:13. (3) Cf. *Psalms* 140:8. (4) Cf. 105:39. [Some *machzorim* have the words סִבַּבְתָּם, *You surrounded them,* and סִכַּכְתָּם, *You sheltered them,* reversed. If so, the stich is not based on the verse in *Psalms.*]
(5) Cf. *Genesis* 27:29. (6) Cf. *Amos* 9:11. (7) *Psalms* 146:10. (8) 22:4.
(9) Cf. *Isaiah* 44:6. (10) Cf. *Job* 37:23. (11) Cf. *Leviticus* 23:40. (12) Cf. *Psalms* 104:1-2.

R' Elazar HaKalir. In this *piyut,* R' Elazar expounds on various Midrashic explanations and allusions of the Four Species. A fuller discussion and additional interpretations are presented by the *paytan* in the *piyut* אֶקְחָה בָּרִאשׁוֹן, *I shall take on the first* (see p. 1262).

רָחַצְתִּי בְנִקָּיוֹן כַּפּוֹת,*[1] עָמוּס בְּמוֹ כַּפּוֹת, אַף וְאֶנֶף לִכְפּוֹת.
בְּלוּלַב שֹׁד חֲמָסִים, אֵיךְ אֶפְרֹט מַעֲשִׂים, פְּנֵי מַקְדִּיחַ הֲמָסִים.[2]

שַׁגִּיא ...

יְפִי שְׁלוֹשׁ הֲדַסִּים, בְּהוֹד טַעַם אָשִׁים, לְצַג בֵּין הַהֲדַסִּים.[3]
רְעוּלִים וְגַם מְתוּקִים,* אֲשַׁוֶּה כְּחֹק מְצוּקִים, לְחִכּוֹ מַמְתַקִּים.[4]
בְּעַנְפֵי עֵץ עָבוֹת,[5] שְׁעוּרִים לְבֵית אָבוֹת, אֶאֱסוֹר חַג בָּעֲבוֹת.[6]

אֲנוֹבֵב ...

יֹשֶׁר פְּאֵר עֲרָבוֹת, בָּמוֹ עֹז לְהַרְבּוֹת, לְרוֹכֵב בָּעֲרָבוֹת.
קְצוּבוֹת בַּדֵּי שְׁתַּיִם, כְּמוֹ עֲפִיפוֹת שְׁתַּיִם,* וּמְצָעוֹת בִּנְתָיִם.
יְעוּרוֹת בְּאַבֵּי הַנַּחַל, לְהַעֲרִיב בָּם מַחַל, לְיַעֲרֵי רְתוּמֵי גַחַל.*[7] שַׁגִּיא ...

לְכָל עֵץ תִּעַב, וּבְאַרְבַּעַת אֵלֶּה תָּאַב, לְהַלְּלוֹ בָם כְּאָב.
יַחַד בָּמוֹ לְהַלֵּל, שִׁבְעָה כְּבֵית הִלֵּל, בְּיוֹם וְלֹא בְלֵיל.
❖רוֹנְנִים מֵלִיץ בַּעֲדֵנוּ, לְהָחִישׁ נָא לְסַעֲדֵנוּ, עַתָּה לִקְרִיַת מוֹעֲדֵנוּ.

אֲנוֹבֵב ...

Congregation and *chazzan:*

וּבְכֵן וַיְהִי בְשָׁלֵם סֻכּוֹ.[8]*

Responsively:

אָז הָיְתָה חֲנָיַת סֻכּוֹ, בְּתַלְתַּלֵּי תֹקֶף, בְּשִׁנְאַנֵּי שֶׁקֶט,
בְּרֶכֶב רִבּוֹתַיִם,[9] בִּקְדוֹשֵׁי קֶדֶם, בְּסַפִּיר וְסֻכּוֹת.
וְהֵן בְּשָׁלֵם סֻכּוֹ, בִּצְנוּעֵי צֶדֶק, בִּפְאֵר פָּרֹכֶת,
בַּעֲבוֹדַת עֶרֶךְ, בְּסֻכַּת סְגֻלָּה, וְהִיא סֻכָּתוֹ.
אָז הָיְתָה חֲנָיַת סֻכּוֹ, בְּנוֹצְצֵי נֹגַהּ, בְּמַלְאֲכֵי מָרוֹם,
בְּלַהַט לוֹהֲטִים, בְּכַנְפֵי כְרוּבִים, בְּסַפִּיר וְסֻכּוֹת.

בְּנִקָּיוֹן כַּפּוֹת – *[My] hands in purity,* i.e., I have acquired the Four Species lawfully and not through theft, which would invalidate their use (see *Vayikra Rabbah* 30:5; *Succah* 3:1, p. 106).

רְעוּלִים וְגַם מְתוּקִים – *The bitter beside the sweet.* Among the Four Species, there is a combination of bitterness and sweetness. The willow and myrtle taste bitter, but the myrtle smells sweet. The esrog smells and tastes sweet, and dates, the fruit of the lulav tree, are sweet.

עֲפִיפוֹת שְׁתַּיִם – *The [angels'] two flight-wings.* In Isaiah's vision of the Heavenly Throne: *Seraphim stand above it, each with six wings; with two it covers its face, with two it covers its legs, and with two it flies (Isaiah* 6:2). The *paytan* relates the *aravos* to the angels' flight-wings in two ways. Firstly, they are both two in number; secondly, just as the flight-wings are between two other pairs of wings, so is the number of willow twigs the median between the three *haddasim* and the one *lulav.* [Alternatively, the *aravos* are held between the *lulav* and the *esrog.*]

רְתוּמֵי גַחַל – *[Gehinnom's] fiery coals.* Those who speak slanderously will be consigned to the fiery coals of *Gehinnom (Arachim* 15b). May the *mitzah* performed with the lip-shaped willow leaves atone for their sins and save them from the fire.

⊱ וּבְכֵן וַיְהִי בְשָׁלֵם סֻכּוֹ – *And so, His Succah [-Temple] was in Jerusalem.* God's Heavenly Throne [described as both sapphire-like (*Ezekiel* 1:26) and *succah*-like (*II Samuel* 22:12)] rests in the celestial Temple among pure, holy, fiery, sinless heavenly beings who constantly recite God's praises in reverential awe. Nevertheless, after King Solomon built the Temple in Jerusalem, God chose that site as His major residence. The *paytan* follows a reverse alpha-

ר *I have washed [my] hands in purity,*[1]*
to bear the [lulav-]bundle in them, to humble anger and wrath.
ב *For [were I to perform the mitzvah] with a lulav acquired by theft,*
how could I justify [my] deeds, before Him Who burns the dissolute.[2]
Difficult feats ...
י *Three beautiful haddasim with majestic aroma, I will place*
before Him Who stands among the myrtle[-like righteous ones].[3]
ר *The bitter beside the sweet,**
I shall hold together as decreed by the [Sages, the] foundations of the earth,
in [honor] of Him Whose palate is sweet.[4]
ב *In [merit of] the myrtle branches,*[5] *that symbolize the Patriarchs [three],*
May I bind the chagigah-offering in cords.[6] *I shall recite ...*
י *The proper splendor of the aravos, with them to increase in strength,*
to [honor] Him Who rides upon the highest heaven.
ק *Two is the set amount [of willow] twigs*
*the same as the [angels'] two flight-wings,**
and the median between both [the lulav and haddasim].
י *Rooted alongside watery brooks,*
[they] sweeten [strict justice allowing] for atonement,
for those consigned to [Gehinnom's] fiery coals.[7]* *Difficult feats ...*
ל *He disqualified every other tree, but longed for these four,*
to praise Him with them as a [son praises his] father.
י *Holding them together while reciting Hallel,*
for seven days; as Hillel's Academy rules, by day but not by night.
ר ∴*We pray that this [mitzvah] become for us an advocate [angel],*
to hasten now to our assistance,
now, to [bring us to Jerusalem] the city of our assembly.

Congregation and *chazzan:*

And so, His Succah[-Temple] was in Jerusalem.[8]*

Responsively:

Earlier His Succah rested among

ח *the lofty strong ones,*	ש *the serene angels,*
ר *the myriads of chariots,*[9]	ק *the ancient holy ones —*

a Succah of sapphire.

Then, He placed His Succah [in Jerusalem] among

צ *the righteous modest ones,*	פ *the splendid curtain,*
ע *the ordered service,*	ס *in a beloved Succah —*

and that is His Succah.

Earlier, His Succah rested among

נ *those sparkling aglow,*	מ *the heavenly angels,*
ל *the flashing fiery ones,*	כ *the winged cherubim —*

a Succah of sapphire.

(1) Cf. *Psalms* 26:6. (2) Cf. *Isaiah* 64:1. (3) Cf. *Zechariah* 1:8 [see *Sanhedrin* 93a]. (4) Cf. *Song of Songs* 5:16. (5) Cf. *Leviticus* 23:40. (6) Cf. *Psalms* 118:27. (7) Cf. 120:4. (8) *Psalms* 76:3. (9) Cf. 68:18.

betical pattern as he alternates between these two themes *earlier*, before the Temple was built, when God's Presence was among the angels, and *then* when it shifted to the Temple; four lines extolling the angels and then four describing the earthly Temple.

וְחָן בְּשָׁלֵם סֻכּוֹ, בִּידִידוּת יָעַר, בְּטִירַת טָהֳרָה,
בְּחֶפַּת חֶדְוָה, בְּזֵר זְמִירַת זְבוּל, וְהִיא סֻכָּתוֹ.
אָז הָיְתָה חֲנָיַת סֻכּוֹ, בְּוֹעוּדֵי וָעַד, בְּהוֹגֵי הַמֶּלָּה,
בְּדִמְוּמֵי דַקָּה, בְּדוֹהֲרֵי דוֹלְקִים, בְּסַפִּיר וְסֻכּוֹת.
וְחָן בְּשָׁלֵם סֻכּוֹ, בִּגְלוּמֵי גֵיא, בְּבֵית בְּחִירָתוֹ,
בְּאֹהֶל אִוּוּיוֹ, בְּאֶדֶר אַפַּדְנוֹ, וְהִיא סֻכָּתוֹ.

All:

וּבְכֵן וּלְךָ תַעֲלֶה קְדֻשָּׁה, כִּי אַתָּה קְדוֹשׁ יִשְׂרָאֵל וּמוֹשִׁיעַ.

Some congregations recite the prayer אָקְחָה (p. 1262) before *Kedushah*.
Most congregations recite the standard *Yom Tov Kedushah* (below).
Those who recite אָקְחָה omit the opening phrase in parentheses.

קדושה

When reciting *Kedushah,* one must stand with his feet together and avoid any interruptions. One should rise on his toes when saying the words קָדוֹשׁ, קָדוֹשׁ, קָדוֹשׁ; בָּרוּךְ (of בָּרוּךְ כְּבוֹד); and יִמְלֹךְ.

Cong. then *Chazzan* – **(נְקַדֵּשׁ** אֶת שִׁמְךָ בָּעוֹלָם, כְּשֵׁם שֶׁמַּקְדִּישִׁים אוֹתוֹ בִּשְׁמֵי מָרוֹם,) כַּכָּתוּב עַל יַד נְבִיאֶךָ, וְקָרָא זֶה אֶל זֶה וְאָמַר:

All – קָדוֹשׁ קָדוֹשׁ קָדוֹשׁ יהוה צְבָאוֹת, מְלֹא כָל הָאָרֶץ כְּבוֹדוֹ.[1]
❖ אָז בְּקוֹל* רַעַשׁ גָּדוֹל אַדִּיר וְחָזָק מַשְׁמִיעִים קוֹל, מִתְנַשְּׂאִים לְעֻמַּת שְׂרָפִים, לְעֻמָּתָם בָּרוּךְ יֹאמֵרוּ:

All – בָּרוּךְ כְּבוֹד יהוה, מִמְּקוֹמוֹ.*[2] ❖ מִמְּקוֹמְךָ* מַלְכֵּנוּ תוֹפִיעַ, וְתִמְלוֹךְ עָלֵינוּ, כִּי מְחַכִּים אֲנַחְנוּ לָךְ. מָתַי תִּמְלוֹךְ בְּצִיּוֹן, בְּקָרוֹב בְּיָמֵינוּ, לְעוֹלָם וָעֶד תִּשְׁכּוֹן. תִּתְגַּדַּל וְתִתְקַדַּשׁ בְּתוֹךְ יְרוּשָׁלַיִם עִירְךָ, לְדוֹר וָדוֹר וּלְנֵצַח נְצָחִים. וְעֵינֵינוּ תִרְאֶינָה מַלְכוּתֶךָ, כַּדָּבָר הָאָמוּר בְּשִׁירֵי עֻזֶּךָ, עַל יְדֵי דָוִד מְשִׁיחַ צִדְקֶךָ:

All – יִמְלֹךְ יהוה לְעוֹלָם, אֱלֹהַיִךְ צִיּוֹן לְדֹר וָדֹר, הַלְלוּיָהּ.[3]

קדושה / Kedushah

The *Kedushah* of the Sabbath is expanded to indicate the special significance of the Sabbath in attaining the goal of sanctification. The home of God's Presence was — and will be again — the Temple in Jerusalem. If we properly appreciate the great holiness of the Sabbath, we can better comprehend the song of the angels and elevate ourselves to the level where we are worthy for the coming of Messiah and the return of the Temple. Therefore, these two themes are stressed in the *Yom Tov* additions to *Kedushah*.

אָז בְּקוֹל — *Then with a sound.* This narrative describing the song of the angels is based on *Ezekiel* Ch. 1 and is also found in a different form in the morning Blessings of the *Shema* and *Uva Le'Tzion*. See pages 230 and 402.

מִמְּקוֹמוֹ — *From His place.* Rambam (*Moreh Nevuchim* 1:8) interprets *place* figuratively as meaning 'level' or 'degree,' in the sense that we say that someone takes his father's 'place.' However, even the angels do not know what God's 'place' really is — He is beyond all understanding. Therefore, when we say that God's glory comes *from His place,* we are purposely being vague because we cannot know the extent of His true glory. We are saying that whatever the true level of God's perfection may

Then, He placed His Succah among
י *the precious [wood from the Lebanon] forest,*
ט *the turret of purity.*
ח *the delightful canopy,* ז *the crown of Temple song —*
and that is His Succah.

Earlier, His Succah rested among
ו *those summoned to the gathering,* ה *those who call resoundingly,*
ד *the soft thin sound,* ד *the fiery flaming angels —*
a Succah of sapphire.

Then, He placed His Succah among
ג *those formed from the valley['s clay],*
ב *in His chosen Temple,*
א *in the Tent of His desire,* א *in His splendid palace —*
and that is His Succah.

All:

And so, the Kedushah prayer shall ascend to You,
for You are the Holy One of Israel, and its Savior.

Some congregations recite the prayer אֶקְחָה (p. 1262) before *Kedushah*.
Most congregations recite the standard *Yom Tov Kedushah* (below).
Those who recite אֶקְחָה omit the opening phrase in parentheses.

KEDUSHAH

When reciting *Kedushah*, one must stand with his feet together and avoid any interruptions. One should rise on his toes when saying the words *Holy, holy, holy; Blessed is;* and *HASHEM shall reign.*

Cong. then Chazzan — **נְקַדֵּשׁ** *(We shall sanctify Your Name in this world, just as they sanctify it in heaven above,) as it is written by Your prophet, "And one [angel] will call another and say:*

All— *'Holy, holy, holy is HASHEM, Master of Legions, the whole world is filled with His glory.' "*[1] ❖ *Then, with a sound* of great noise, mighty and powerful, they make heard a voice, raising themselves toward the seraphim; those facing them say 'Blessed ...':*

All— *'Blessed is the glory of HASHEM from His place.'*[2] ❖ *From Your place,* our King, You will appear and reign over us, for we await You. When will You reign in Zion? Soon, in our days — forever and ever — may You dwell there. May You be exalted and sanctified within Jerusalem, Your city, from generation to generation and for all eternity. May our eyes see Your kingdom, as it is expressed in the songs of Your might, written by David, Your righteous anointed:*

All— *'HASHEM shall reign forever — your God, O Zion — from generation to generation, Halleluyah!'*[3]

(1) *Isaiah* 6:3. (2) *Ezekiel* 3:12. (3) *Psalms* 146:10.

be, let it be implicit in the limited words with which we praise Him (*Nefesh HaChaim*).

מִמְּקוֹמְךָ — *From Your place.* As noted above, God's 'place' is the infinity of His perfection. We beg and confidently hope that He will reveal Himself to us by returning His Presence to Jerusalem with the final and eternal Redemption.

קדושת השם

Chazzan continues:

לְדוֹר וָדוֹר נַגִּיד גָּדְלֶךָ וּלְנֵצַח נְצָחִים קְדֻשָּׁתְךָ נַקְדִּישׁ, וְשִׁבְחֲךָ אֱלֹהֵינוּ מִפִּינוּ לֹא יָמוּשׁ לְעוֹלָם וָעֶד, כִּי אֵל מֶלֶךְ גָּדוֹל וְקָדוֹשׁ אָתָּה. בָּרוּךְ אַתָּה יהוה, הָאֵל הַקָּדוֹשׁ. (.Cong – אָמֵן.)

קדושת היום

אַתָּה בְחַרְתָּנוּ מִכָּל הָעַמִּים, אָהַבְתָּ אוֹתָנוּ, וְרָצִיתָ בָּנוּ, וְרוֹמַמְתָּנוּ מִכָּל הַלְּשׁוֹנוֹת, וְקִדַּשְׁתָּנוּ בְּמִצְוֹתֶיךָ, וְקֵרַבְתָּנוּ מַלְכֵּנוּ לַעֲבוֹדָתֶךָ, וְשִׁמְךָ הַגָּדוֹל וְהַקָּדוֹשׁ עָלֵינוּ קָרָאתָ.

On the Sabbath add the words in brackets. [If forgotten, see *Laws* §86-90.]

וַתִּתֶּן לָנוּ יהוה אֱלֹהֵינוּ בְּאַהֲבָה [שַׁבָּתוֹת לִמְנוּחָה וּ]מוֹעֲדִים לְשִׂמְחָה חַגִּים וּזְמַנִּים לְשָׂשׂוֹן, אֶת יוֹם [הַשַּׁבָּת הַזֶּה וְאֶת יוֹם] חַג הַסֻּכּוֹת הַזֶּה, זְמַן שִׂמְחָתֵנוּ [בְּאַהֲבָה] מִקְרָא קֹדֶשׁ, זֵכֶר לִיצִיאַת מִצְרָיִם.

During the *chazzan's* repetition, congregation responds אָמֵן as indicated.

אֱלֹהֵינוּ וֵאלֹהֵי אֲבוֹתֵינוּ, יַעֲלֶה, וְיָבֹא, וְיַגִּיעַ, וְיֵרָאֶה, וְיֵרָצֶה, וְיִשָּׁמַע, וְיִפָּקֵד, וְיִזָּכֵר זִכְרוֹנֵנוּ וּפִקְדוֹנֵנוּ, וְזִכְרוֹן אֲבוֹתֵינוּ, וְזִכְרוֹן מָשִׁיחַ בֶּן דָּוִד עַבְדֶּךָ, וְזִכְרוֹן יְרוּשָׁלַיִם עִיר קָדְשֶׁךָ, וְזִכְרוֹן כָּל עַמְּךָ בֵּית יִשְׂרָאֵל לְפָנֶיךָ, לִפְלֵיטָה לְטוֹבָה לְחֵן וּלְחֶסֶד וּלְרַחֲמִים, לְחַיִּים וּלְשָׁלוֹם בְּיוֹם חַג הַסֻּכּוֹת הַזֶּה. זָכְרֵנוּ יהוה אֱלֹהֵינוּ בּוֹ לְטוֹבָה (.Cong – אָמֵן), וּפָקְדֵנוּ בוֹ לִבְרָכָה (.Cong – אָמֵן), וְהוֹשִׁיעֵנוּ בוֹ לְחַיִּים (.Cong – אָמֵן). וּבִדְבַר יְשׁוּעָה וְרַחֲמִים, חוּס וְחָנֵּנוּ וְרַחֵם עָלֵינוּ וְהוֹשִׁיעֵנוּ, כִּי אֵלֶיךָ עֵינֵינוּ, כִּי אֵל מֶלֶךְ חַנּוּן וְרַחוּם אָתָּה.[1]

On the Sabbath add the words in brackets. [If forgotten, see *Laws* §86-90.]

וְהַשִּׂיאֵנוּ יהוה אֱלֹהֵינוּ אֶת בִּרְכַּת מוֹעֲדֶיךָ לְחַיִּים וּלְשָׁלוֹם, לְשִׂמְחָה וּלְשָׂשׂוֹן, כַּאֲשֶׁר רָצִיתָ וְאָמַרְתָּ לְבָרְכֵנוּ. [אֱלֹהֵינוּ וֵאלֹהֵי אֲבוֹתֵינוּ רְצֵה בִמְנוּחָתֵנוּ] קַדְּשֵׁנוּ בְּמִצְוֹתֶיךָ וְתֵן חֶלְקֵנוּ בְּתוֹרָתֶךָ, שַׂבְּעֵנוּ מִטּוּבֶךָ וְשַׂמְּחֵנוּ בִּישׁוּעָתֶךָ, וְטַהֵר לִבֵּנוּ

HOLINESS OF GOD'S NAME

Chazzan continues:

לְדוֹר *From generation to generation we shall relate Your greatness and for infinite eternities we shall proclaim Your holiness. Your praise, our God, shall not leave our mouth forever and ever, for You, O God, are a great and holy King. Blessed are You, HASHEM, the holy God.* (Cong. – *Amen.)*

SANCTIFICATION OF THE DAY

אַתָּה בְחַרְתָּנוּ *You have chosen us from all the peoples; You loved us and found favor in us; You exalted us above all the tongues and You sanctified us with Your commandments. You drew us close, our King, to Your service and proclaimed Your great and Holy Name upon us.*

On the Sabbath add the words in brackets. [If forgotten, see *Laws* §86-90.]

וַתִּתֶּן לָנוּ *And You gave us, HASHEM, our God, with love [Sabbaths for rest], appointed festivals for gladness, Festivals and times for joy, [this day of Sabbath and] this day of the Festival of Succos, the time of our gladness [with love], a holy convocation, a memorial of the Exodus from Egypt.*

During the *chazzan's* repetition, congregation responds *Amen* as indicated.

אֱלֹהֵינוּ *Our God and God of our forefathers, may there rise, come, reach, be noted, be favored, be heard, be considered, and be remembered — the remembrance and consideration of ourselves; the remembrance of our forefathers; the remembrance of Messiah, son of David, Your servant; the remembrance of Jerusalem, the City of Your Holiness; the remembrance of Your entire people the Family of Israel — before You for deliverance, for goodness, for grace, for kindness, and for compassion, for life, and for peace on this day of the Festival of Succos. Remember us on it, HASHEM, our God, for goodness* (Cong. – *Amen); consider us on it for blessing* (Cong. – *Amen); and help us on it for life* (Cong. – *Amen). In the matter of salvation and compassion, pity, be gracious and compassionate with us and help us, for our eyes are turned to You, because You are God, the gracious and compassionate King.*[1]

On the Sabbath add the words in brackets. [If forgotten, see *Laws* §86-90.]

וְהַשִּׂיאֵנוּ *Bestow upon us, O HASHEM, our God, the blessing of Your appointed Festivals for life and for peace, for gladness and for joy, as You desired and promised to bless us. [Our God and the God of our forefathers, may You be pleased with our rest.] Sanctify us withYour commandments and grant us our share in Your Torah; satisfy us from Your goodness and gladden us with Your salvation, and purify our heart*

(1) Cf. *Nechemiah* 9:31.

לְעָבְדְּךָ בֶּאֱמֶת, וְהַנְחִילֵנוּ יהוה אֱלֹהֵינוּ [בְּאַהֲבָה וּבְרָצוֹן] בְּשִׂמְחָה וּבְשָׂשׂוֹן [שַׁבָּת וּ]מוֹעֲדֵי קָדְשֶׁךָ, וְיִשְׂמְחוּ בְךָ יִשְׂרָאֵל מְקַדְּשֵׁי שְׁמֶךָ. בָּרוּךְ אַתָּה יהוה, מְקַדֵּשׁ [הַשַּׁבָּת וְ]יִשְׂרָאֵל וְהַזְּמַנִּים.

(Cong. – אָמֵן.)

עבודה

רְצֵה יהוה אֱלֹהֵינוּ בְּעַמְּךָ יִשְׂרָאֵל וּבִתְפִלָּתָם, וְהָשֵׁב אֶת הָעֲבוֹדָה לִדְבִיר בֵּיתֶךָ. וְאִשֵּׁי יִשְׂרָאֵל וּתְפִלָּתָם בְּאַהֲבָה תְקַבֵּל בְּרָצוֹן, וּתְהִי לְרָצוֹן תָּמִיד עֲבוֹדַת יִשְׂרָאֵל עַמֶּךָ.

וְתֶחֱזֶינָה עֵינֵינוּ בְּשׁוּבְךָ לְצִיּוֹן בְּרַחֲמִים. בָּרוּךְ אַתָּה יהוה, הַמַּחֲזִיר שְׁכִינָתוֹ לְצִיּוֹן. (Cong. – אָמֵן.)

הודאה

Bow at מוֹדִים; straighten up at 'ה. The *chazzan* should recite the entire מוֹדִים aloud, while the congregation recites מוֹדִים דְּרַבָּנָן softly.

מוֹדִים אֲנַחְנוּ לָךְ, שָׁאַתָּה הוּא יהוה אֱלֹהֵינוּ וֵאלֹהֵי אֲבוֹתֵינוּ לְעוֹלָם וָעֶד. צוּר חַיֵּינוּ, מָגֵן יִשְׁעֵנוּ אַתָּה הוּא לְדוֹר וָדוֹר. נוֹדֶה לְּךָ וּנְסַפֵּר תְּהִלָּתֶךָ[1] עַל חַיֵּינוּ הַמְּסוּרִים בְּיָדֶךָ, וְעַל נִשְׁמוֹתֵינוּ הַפְּקוּדוֹת לָךְ, וְעַל נִסֶּיךָ שֶׁבְּכָל יוֹם עִמָּנוּ, וְעַל נִפְלְאוֹתֶיךָ וְטוֹבוֹתֶיךָ שֶׁבְּכָל עֵת, עֶרֶב וָבֹקֶר וְצָהֳרָיִם. הַטּוֹב כִּי לֹא כָלוּ רַחֲמֶיךָ, וְהַמְרַחֵם כִּי לֹא תַמּוּ חֲסָדֶיךָ,[2] מֵעוֹלָם קִוִּינוּ לָךְ.

מודים דרבנן

מוֹדִים אֲנַחְנוּ לָךְ, שָׁאַתָּה הוּא יהוה אֱלֹהֵינוּ וֵאלֹהֵי אֲבוֹתֵינוּ, אֱלֹהֵי כָל בָּשָׂר, יוֹצְרֵנוּ, יוֹצֵר בְּרֵאשִׁית. בְּרָכוֹת וְהוֹדָאוֹת לְשִׁמְךָ הַגָּדוֹל וְהַקָּדוֹשׁ, עַל שֶׁהֶחֱיִיתָנוּ וְקִיַּמְתָּנוּ. כֵּן תְּחַיֵּנוּ וּתְקַיְּמֵנוּ, וְתֶאֱסוֹף גָּלֻיּוֹתֵינוּ לְחַצְרוֹת קָדְשֶׁךָ, לִשְׁמוֹר חֻקֶּיךָ וְלַעֲשׂוֹת רְצוֹנֶךָ, וּלְעָבְדְּךָ בְּלֵבָב שָׁלֵם, עַל שֶׁאֲנַחְנוּ מוֹדִים לָךְ. בָּרוּךְ אֵל הַהוֹדָאוֹת.

וְעַל כֻּלָּם יִתְבָּרַךְ וְיִתְרוֹמַם שִׁמְךָ מַלְכֵּנוּ תָּמִיד לְעוֹלָם וָעֶד.

The *chazzan* bends his knees at בָּרוּךְ; bows at אַתָּה; straightens up at 'ה.

וְכֹל הַחַיִּים יוֹדוּךָ סֶּלָה, וִיהַלְלוּ אֶת שִׁמְךָ בֶּאֱמֶת, הָאֵל יְשׁוּעָתֵנוּ וְעֶזְרָתֵנוּ סֶלָה. בָּרוּךְ אַתָּה יהוה, הַטּוֹב שִׁמְךָ וּלְךָ נָאֶה לְהוֹדוֹת. (Cong. – אָמֵן.)

to serve You sincerely. And grant us a heritage, O HASHEM, our God — [with love and with favor] with gladness and with joy — [the Sabbath and] the appointed festivals of Your holiness, and may Israel, the sanctifiers of Your Name, rejoice in You. Blessed are You, HASHEM, Who sanctifies [the Sabbath,] Israel and the festive seasons.

(Cong. – *Amen.*)

TEMPLE SERVICE

רְצֵה *Be favorable, HASHEM, our God, toward Your people Israel and their prayer and restore the service to the Holy of Holies of Your Temple. The fire-offerings of Israel and their prayer accept with love and favor, and may the service of Your people Israel always be favorable to You.*

וְתֶחֱזֶינָה *May our eyes behold Your return to Zion in compassion. Blessed are You, HASHEM, Who restores His Presence to Zion.*

(Cong. – *Amen.*)

THANKSGIVING [MODIM]

Bow at *'We gratefully thank You'*; straighten up at *'HASHEM.'* The *chazzan* should recite the entire *Modim* aloud, while the congregation recites *Modim of the Rabbis* softly.

מוֹדִים *We gratefully thank You, for it is You Who are HASHEM, our God and the God of our forefathers for all eternity; Rock of our lives, Shield of our salvation are You from generation to generation. We shall thank You and relate Your praise[1] — for our lives, which are committed to Your power and for our souls that are entrusted to You; for Your miracles that are with us every day; and for Your wonders and favors in every season — evening, morning, and afternoon. The Beneficent One, for Your compassions were never exhausted, and the Compassionate One, for Your kindnesses never ended[2] — always have we put our hope in You.*

MODIM OF THE RABBIS

מוֹדִים *We gratefully thank You, for it is You Who are HASHEM, our God and the God of our forefathers, the God of all flesh, our Molder, the Molder of the universe. Blessings and thanks are due Your great and holy Name for You have given us life and sustained us. So may You continue to give us life and sustain us and gather our exiles to the Courtyards of Your Sanctuary, to observe Your decrees, to do Your will and to serve You wholeheartedly. [We thank You] for inspiring us to thank You. Blessed is the God of thanksgivings.*

For all these, may Your Name be blessed and exalted, our King, continually forever and ever.

The *chazzan* bends his knees at *'Blessed'*; bows at *'You'*; straightens up at *'HASHEM.'*

Everything alive will gratefully acknowledge You, Selah! and praise Your Name sincerely, O God of our salvation and help, Selah! Blessed are You, HASHEM, Your Name is 'The Beneficent One' and to You it is fitting to give thanks.

(Cong. – *Amen.*)

(1) Cf. *Psalms* 79:13. (2) Cf. *Lamentations* 3:22.

ברכת כהנים

The *chazzan* recites בִּרְכַּת כֹּהֲנִים during his repetition. He faces right at וְיִשְׁמְרֶךָ; faces left at אֵלֶיךָ וִיחֻנֶּךָּ; faces the Ark for the rest of the blessings.

אֱלֹהֵינוּ, וֵאלֹהֵי אֲבוֹתֵינוּ, בָּרְכֵנוּ* בַבְּרָכָה הַמְּשֻׁלֶּשֶׁת* בַּתּוֹרָה הַכְּתוּבָה עַל יְדֵי מֹשֶׁה עַבְדֶּךָ, הָאֲמוּרָה מִפִּי אַהֲרֹן וּבָנָיו, כֹּהֲנִים עַם קְדוֹשֶׁךָ,* כָּאָמוּר:

יְבָרֶכְךָ יהוה,* וְיִשְׁמְרֶךָ.* (.Cong — כֵּן יְהִי רָצוֹן.)

יָאֵר יהוה פָּנָיו אֵלֶיךָ* וִיחֻנֶּךָּ.* (.Cong — כֵּן יְהִי רָצוֹן.)

יִשָּׂא יהוה פָּנָיו אֵלֶיךָ* וְיָשֵׂם לְךָ שָׁלוֹם.*[1] (.Cong — כֵּן יְהִי רָצוֹן.)

שלום

שִׂים שָׁלוֹם,* טוֹבָה, וּבְרָכָה, חֵן, וָחֶסֶד וְרַחֲמִים עָלֵינוּ וְעַל כָּל יִשְׂרָאֵל עַמֶּךָ. בָּרְכֵנוּ אָבִינוּ, כֻּלָּנוּ כְּאֶחָד בְּאוֹר פָּנֶיךָ, כִּי בְאוֹר פָּנֶיךָ נָתַתָּ לָּנוּ, יהוה אֱלֹהֵינוּ, תּוֹרַת חַיִּים וְאַהֲבַת חֶסֶד, וּצְדָקָה, וּבְרָכָה, וְרַחֲמִים, וְחַיִּים, וְשָׁלוֹם. וְטוֹב בְּעֵינֶיךָ לְבָרֵךְ אֶת עַמְּךָ יִשְׂרָאֵל, בְּכָל עֵת וּבְכָל שָׁעָה בִּשְׁלוֹמֶךָ. בָּרוּךְ אַתָּה יהוה, הַמְּבָרֵךְ אֶת עַמּוֹ יִשְׂרָאֵל בַּשָּׁלוֹם.

(.Cong — אָמֵן.)

Chazzan, in an undertone:

יִהְיוּ לְרָצוֹן אִמְרֵי פִי וְהֶגְיוֹן לִבִּי לְפָנֶיךָ, יהוה צוּרִי וְגֹאֲלִי.[2]

CHAZZAN'S REPETITION ENDS HERE; TURN TO PAGE 284.

⊲§ בִּרְכַּת כֹּהֲנִים / The Priestly Blessing

God commanded Aaron and his descendants to bless the Jewish people by pronouncing the blessings listed in the Torah (*Numbers* 6:22-27). Although in earlier times the *Kohanim* pronounced these blessings every day, a centuries-old custom has developed that they do so only on Festivals when the Jewish people still feel the joy that should accompany these blessings. Only in parts of *Eretz Yisrael* and in some Sephardic communities has the original practice of daily recitation been retained. Where the *Kohanim* do not bless the nation every day, the following prayer is recited by the *chazzan* at *Shacharis, Mussaf,* and at the *Minchah* of fast days. It contains the text of the Priestly Blessing and the prayer that God fulfill it upon us.

אֱלֹהֵינוּ . . . בָּרְכֵנוּ — *Our God . . . bless us.* Although the blessing is pronounced by the *Kohanim,* it is God who actually gives the blessing. This is made clear in the Scriptural commandment, which ends with God's pledge וַאֲנִי אֲבָרְכֵם, *and I will bless them* (*Numbers* 2:27)

בַּבְּרָכָה הַמְּשֻׁלֶּשֶׁת — *With the three-verse blessing.* The Priestly Blessing contains three verses, and it is found . . . בַּתּוֹרָה הַכְּתוּבָה, *in the Torah that was written by the hand of Moses.*

עַם קְדוֹשֶׁךָ — *Your holy people.* The *Kohanim* are described as a holy people (I *Chronicles* 23:13) because they were designated to serve God and bless Israel.

יְבָרֶכְךָ ה׳ — *May* HASHEM *bless you,* with increasing wealth (*Rashi*) and long lives (*Ibn Ezra*).

וְיִשְׁמְרֶךָ — *And safeguard you.* May the above blessing be preserved against loss or attack. Only God can guarantee that no one or nothing can tamper with the gifts He confers upon His loved ones (*Midrash Rabbah*).

THE PRIESTLY BLESSING

The *chazzan* recites the Priestly Blessing during his repetition.

אֱלֹהֵינוּ *Our God and the God of our forefathers, bless us* with the three-verse blessing* in the Torah that was written by the hand of Moses, Your servant, that was said by Aaron and his sons, the Kohanim, Your holy people,* as it is said:*

May HASHEM bless you and safeguard you.** (Cong.— *So may it be.*)

May HASHEM illuminate His countenance for you and be gracious to you.** (Cong.— *So may it be.*)

May HASHEM turn His countenance to you and establish peace for you.*[1]* (Cong.— *So may it be.*)

PEACE

שִׂים שָׁלוֹם *Establish peace,* goodness, blessing, graciousness, kindness, and compassion upon us and upon all of Your people Israel. Bless us, our Father, all of us as one, with the light of Your countenance, for with the light of Your countenance You gave us, HASHEM, our God, the Torah of life and a love of kindness, righteousness, blessing, compassion, life, and peace. And may it be good in Your eyes to bless Your people Israel at every time and every hour with Your peace. Blessed are You, HASHEM, Who blesses His people Israel with peace.*

(Cong.— *Amen.*)

Chazzan, in an undertone:

May the expressions of my mouth and the thoughts of my heart find favor before You, HASHEM, my Rock and my Redeemer.[2]

CHAZZAN'S REPETITION ENDS HERE; TURN TO PAGE 284.

(1) *Numbers* 6:24-26. (2) *Psalms* 19:15.

יָאֵר ה׳ פָּנָיו אֵלֶיךָ — *May HASHEM illuminate His countenance for you.* This is the blessing of spiritual growth, the light of Torah, which is symbolized by God's 'countenance' (*Sifre*).

וִיחֻנֶּךָּ — *And be gracious to you.* May you find favor in God's eyes (*Ramban*); or, may you find favor in the eyes of others, for all a person's talents and qualities will avail him little if others dislike him (*Ohr HaChaim*).

יִשָּׂא ה׳ פָּנָיו אֵלֶיךָ — *May HASHEM turn His countenance to you.* May He suppress His anger against you, even if you are sinful and deserve to be punished (*Rashi*). One's face is indicative of his attitude toward someone else. If he is angry, he will turn away from the one he dislikes. God 'turns His face' *toward* Israel to show that He loves them (*Maharzu*).

וְיָשֵׂם לְךָ שָׁלוֹם — *And establish peace for you.* Peace is the seal of all blessings, because without peace — prosperity, health, food, and drink are worthless (*Sifre*).

⁂ שָׁלוֹם / Peace

שִׂים שָׁלוֹם, *Establish peace,* is recited only at times when *Bircas Kohanim,* the Priestly Blessing, is pronounced (*Orach Chaim* 127:2). At other times, שָׁלוֹם רָב, *Abundant peace,* is recited instead. The text of שִׂים שָׁלוֹם contains allusions to the Priestly Blessing and the six forms of goodness listed here — peace, goodness, blessing, graciousness, kindness, and compasion — allude to the six blessings of *Bircas Kohanim* (*Etz Yosef*).

THE CHAZZAN'S REPETITION FOR THE FIRST DAY APPEARS ON PAGE 252.

חזרת הש"ץ ליום שני

IF THE FIRST DAY FALLS ON THE SABBATH, THE FOLLOWING REPETITION IS RECITED ON THE FIRST DAY. ON THE SECOND DAY, SUNDAY, THE REPETITION ON PAGE 252 IS RECITED.

אֲדֹנָי שְׂפָתַי תִּפְתָּח, וּפִי יַגִּיד תְּהִלָּתֶךָ.[1]

אבות

The *chazzan* bends his knees at בָּרוּךְ; bows at אַתָּה; straightens up at ה׳.

בָּרוּךְ אַתָּה יהוה אֱלֹהֵינוּ וֵאלֹהֵי אֲבוֹתֵינוּ, אֱלֹהֵי אַבְרָהָם, אֱלֹהֵי יִצְחָק, וֵאלֹהֵי יַעֲקֹב, הָאֵל הַגָּדוֹל הַגִּבּוֹר וְהַנּוֹרָא, אֵל עֶלְיוֹן, גּוֹמֵל חֲסָדִים טוֹבִים וְקוֹנֵה הַכֹּל, וְזוֹכֵר חַסְדֵי אָבוֹת, וּמֵבִיא גוֹאֵל לִבְנֵי בְנֵיהֶם, לְמַעַן שְׁמוֹ בְּאַהֲבָה. מֶלֶךְ עוֹזֵר וּמוֹשִׁיעַ וּמָגֵן.

מִסּוֹד חֲכָמִים וּנְבוֹנִים, וּמִלֶּמֶד דַּעַת מְבִינִים, אֶפְתְּחָה פִּי בְּשִׁיר וּבִרְנָנִים, לְהוֹדוֹת וּלְהַלֵּל פְּנֵי שׁוֹכֵן מְעוֹנִים.

All:

אֶרְחַץ* בְּנִקָּיוֹן כַּפּוֹת,*[2] בְּלִי חָמָס קַחַת סַנְסִנּוֹן כַּפּוֹת,
גְּמוּנֵי פַז לֶאֱגוֹד וְלִכְפּוֹת,[3] דְּשָׁאֵי אֶשְׁלִים[4] בָּם אַף לִכְפּוֹת.
הֵן מִבֶּעָשׂוֹר חֻקְקֵי לְחַיִּים, וְהוֹדִיעֲנִי אֹרַח חַיִּים,[5]
זַעַם מֵאָז תַּרְשִׁישׁ וְאִיִּים,* חָרָה אַפּוֹ בָּם מִהְיוֹת חַיִּים.
טָרְחִי נָשָׂא וְשָׁת לִי סְלִיחָה, יָצְתָה בַּת קוֹל לֵךְ אֱכֹל בְּשִׂמְחָה,*[6]
כְּאַרְבַּעַת יוֹם* שָׁת גְּבוּל שִׂיחָה, לְבַל לְעָרֵב שִׂמְחָה בְּשִׂמְחָה.[7]
מוֹעֵד רְאִיַּת חֲגִיגַת אָסֶף, נִתְמַךְ בְּחֶלְשִׁי לְחוֹגְגֵי בְּכֶסֶף,
סֻכָּה וּפוּר גֶּזֶל* לְהַעֲדִיף לִי בְּתוֹסֶף, עֲנָנֵי קְחוּ מוּסָרִי וְאַל כָּסֶף.[8]

This *Machzor* includes those *piyutim* that are commonly recited. A few *piyutim* that are omitted by a vast majority of congregations have been included in an appendix beginning on page 1262. The text will indicate where they may be recited.

אֶרְחַץ — *I shall wash.* The first *piyut* of the *kerovos* for the second day contains an acrostic of the *aleph-beis.* As in the opening *piyut* of the first day, the *paytan* builds a bridge connecting the awe of Yom Kippur with the rejoicing of Succos. He displays a faithful confidence that God granted forgiveness to Israel on the Day of Atonement, and describes how He rewarded Israel by bestowing the *mitzvos* of *Succos* and *Shemini Atzeres* upon them.

בְּנִקָּיוֹן כַּפּוֹת — *[My] hands in purity,* i.e., I have acquired the Four Species lawfully and not through thievery which would invalidate their use (see *Vayikra Rabbah* 30:5 and *Succah* 3:1, p. 106). This theme is mentioned at least three times in the *piyut.*

תַּרְשִׁישׁ וְאִיִּים — *Tarshish and the isles.* Based on *Psalms* 72:10, this phrase includes all the idolaters of the world.

לֵךְ אֱכֹל בְּשִׂמְחָה — *'Go eat with joy.'* The preceding stiches spoke of the forgiveness and atonement attained on Yom Kippur. The Midrash (*Koheles Rabbah* 9:9) states that when the nation fasts on Yom Kippur, God says, 'Let bygones be bygones! A new reckoning will commence now.' Then a voice enamating from heaven calls out, 'Go eat your bread with joy and drink your wine with a glad heart for God has accepted your prayers.'

THE CHAZZAN'S REPETITION FOR THE FIRST DAY APPEARS ON PAGE 252.

CHAZZAN'S REPETITION FOR THE SECOND DAY

IF THE FIRST DAY FALLS ON THE SABBATH, THE FOLLOWING REPETITION IS RECITED ON THE FIRST DAY. ON THE SECOND DAY, SUNDAY, THE REPETITION ON PAGE 252 IS RECITED.

My Lord, open my lips, that my mouth may declare Your praise.[1]

PATRIARCHS

The *chazzan* bends his knees at *'Blessed'*; bows at *'You'*; straightens up at *'HASHEM.'*

בָּרוּךְ *Blessed are You, HASHEM, our God and the God of our forefathers, God of Abraham, God of Isaac, and God of Jacob; the great, mighty, and awesome God, the supreme God, Who bestows beneficial kindnesses and creates everything, Who recalls the kindnesses of the Patriarchs and brings a Redeemer to their children's children, for His Name's sake, with love. O King, Helper, Savior, and Shield.*

מִסּוֹד *Based on the tradition of our wise and discerning teachers, and the teaching derived from the knowledge of the discerning, I open my mouth in song and joyful praise, to give thanks and to offer praise before Him Who dwells in the heavens.*

All:

א *I shall wash* [my] hands in purity,*[2]*
ב *without thievery to take the lulav branch.*
ג *Binding it and tying to it with golden bands,*[3]
ד *perfect greens*[4] *— to suppress anger through them.*

ה *Behold! On the tenth [of Tishrei — Yom Kippur] I was inscribed for life,*
ו *May He reveal to me the path of life.*[5]
ז *At that time He was wrathful with Tarshish and the isles,**
ח *His anger flared at them, that they not remain alive.*

ט *He bore my bothers, and granted me pardon,*
י *a heavenly voice emanated, 'Go eat with joy.'*[6]*
כ *He granted a four-day period* to procure the species,*
ל *so as not to mingle [the] joy [of atonement] with [the] joy [of Succos].*[7]

מ *To appear at the Festival of Ingathering [of crops],*
נ *fell to my lot to celebrate with desire.*
ס *Beside the [mitzvah of] succah He added more — lottery and prayer for rain.**
ע *He answered me, 'Choose My mitzvos instead of silver.'*[8]

(1) *Psalms* 51:17. (2) Cf. 26:6. (3) Mishnah, *Succah* 3:8. [see p. 110].
(4) Some *machzorim* read דִּשְׁאֵי אֲשָׁלִים, *greens of leafy trees.* (5) Cf. *Psalms* 16:11.
(6) *Ecclesiastes* 9:7. (7) Tractate *Moed Katan* 8b. (1) Cf. *Isaiah* 60:8.

כְּאַרְבַּעַת יוֹם — *A four-day period.* Four non-festive days intercede between Yom Kippur and Succos.

ופור נֶזֶל — *Lottery and prayer for rain.* This refers to Shemini Atzeres. In certain respects Shemini Atzeres is considered as a Festival unto itself. One distinction between it and the other seven days of Succos is the lottery discussed in Mishnah *Succah* 5:6 (see page 126). Another distinguishing feature is the prayer for rain (see page 980).

Another interpretation renders ופור as פּוּרָה, *the cistern into which the wine flows from the press,* and נֶזֶל as *poured water.* The phrase then refers to the special Succos water-libations on the Altar where only wine-libations are poured the rest of the year. Scripture sometimes refers to the Altar as יֶקֶב, *wine-press* (see *Isaiah* 5:2 where יֶקֶב is rendered מַדְבְּחִי, *my Altar,* by the *Targum*).

פְּרָחִים כְּנָטְעָם אֶעֶמְסָה לְאָיוֹם, צַחוֹת לְצַחְצֵחַ מְצוֹא בָם פִּדְיוֹם,
❖קִיחָתָם בְּדָמִים יָכְשְׁרוּ לְשֵׁם אָיוֹם,
רְאוּיִים לְהִנָּטֵל בְּזֶה רִאשׁוֹן יוֹם.*

All:

שִׁמְךָ מְשַׁתֵּף בִּשְׁמֵנוּ, שָׁקַדְתָּ מִכַּפּוּר מְחוֹת אֲשָׁמֵינוּ,
❖תְּסוֹכְכֵנוּ וְאַל תַּאֲשִׁימֵנוּ, תְּגוֹנְנֵנוּ וּתְרוֹמְמֵנוּ עַד מָרוֹם שִׂימֵנוּ.

Chazzan bends his knees at בָּרוּךְ; bows at אַתָּה; straightens up at ה׳.

בָּרוּךְ אַתָּה יהוה, מָגֵן אַבְרָהָם. (Cong.– אָמֵן.)

גבורות

אַתָּה גִּבּוֹר לְעוֹלָם אֲדֹנָי, מְחַיֵּה מֵתִים אַתָּה, רַב לְהוֹשִׁיעַ. מְכַלְכֵּל חַיִּים בְּחֶסֶד, מְחַיֵּה מֵתִים בְּרַחֲמִים רַבִּים, סוֹמֵךְ נוֹפְלִים, וְרוֹפֵא חוֹלִים, וּמַתִּיר אֲסוּרִים, וּמְקַיֵּם אֱמוּנָתוֹ לִישֵׁנֵי עָפָר. מִי כָמוֹךָ בַּעַל גְּבוּרוֹת, וּמִי דּוֹמֶה לָּךְ, מֶלֶךְ מֵמִית וּמְחַיֶּה וּמַצְמִיחַ יְשׁוּעָה. וְנֶאֱמָן אַתָּה לְהַחֲיוֹת מֵתִים.

All:

תְּשׁוּרַת שַׁי* אֲלָפִים שִׁבְעִים,* שִׁלַּמְתִּי בְּזֶה רֶגֶל עֲלֵי אֹם שִׁבְעִים,
רָצִיתִי שֵׂיִים שְׁמוֹנָה וְתִשְׁעִים, קְלֹעַ בָּם תּוֹכָחוֹת שְׁמוֹנָה וְתִשְׁעִים.*
צֵרַפְתִּי אֵלֶּה בְּאֵלֶּה* בְּאָסִיף, פְּדוּת וְגִילָה לִי לְהוֹסִיף,
עֹז וִישׁוּעָה לִי תוֹסִיף, סִכּוּךְ נֶשֶׁק זְרוֹעַ לְהַחֲשִׂיף.
נוֹצְרֵי כְּדַת יְמֵי חֲגִיגָתוֹ, מְלוֹן סֻכַּת עוֹר* תְּהֵא הַשָּׂגָתוֹ,
לְקַשֵּׁר לִוְיַת צִלְצַל דָּגָתוֹ, כְּגִבּוֹרֵי כֹחַ חֲזוֹת אֲפִיקֵי גַאֲוָתוֹ.
יוֹשֵׁב בְּסֻכָּה תָּמוּר נְוֵה אָהֳלוֹ, טְלוּל עֲצֵי עֵדֶן יַאֲהִילוֹ,
חֹם יוֹם הַבָּא בְּבוֹא לְהַבְהִילוֹ, זְכוּתוֹ תָּלִיף סֻכָּה לְנַהֲלוֹ.
וְשֹׂבַע שְׂמָחוֹת מְדֻשָּׁנָה, הֲלֹא בַּעֲדָהּ שֹׁבַע מְשַׁאֲנָנָה,
❖דָּגוּל לְהַנְזִיר שִׁבְעָה* שׁוֹשַׁנָּה, גָּזַר לְחוֹגְגָהּ שִׁבְעָה בַּשָּׁנָה.

בְּזֶה רִאשׁוֹן יוֹם – *On this first day [of Succos].* Rabbi Elazar HaKalir (see p. 35), composer of this *piyut,* lived in *Eretz Yisrael* where the second day of Succos is part of *Chol HaMoed,* the Intermediate Days. He often wrote a number of *piyutim* for the same occasion. In later centuries in the Diaspora, some of his compositions were instituted for the second day. The original wording, however, remained unchanged.

☙ תְּשׁוּרַת שַׁי – *With an offering.* The *paytan* uses a reverse alphabetical scheme [תַּשְׁרַ״ק]. First he explains the rationale for some of the animal offerings of Succos. He then describes the rewards in the World to Come for those who faithfully fulfill the *mitzvos* of Succos.

שִׁבְעִים – *Seventy.* On the first day of Succos thirteen bulls were offered. Each succeeding day one less bull was offered until the seventh day, on which seven bulls were used. The total number of bulls offered was seventy. See page 316.

שְׁמוֹנָה וְתִשְׁעִים – *Ninety-eight.* Each day fourteen lambs were offered. Over the seven days a total of ninety-eight lambs were used.

The verses of *Deuteronomy* 28:15-68 are collectively known as the תּוֹכָחוֹת, *admonitions.* They contain ninety-eight curses and threats of retribution for those who do not follow the Torah's laws. *Midrash Tadshei* teaches that the ninety-eight lambs of Succos are to protect

פ *I will hold branches in the direction of their growth*
to serve the Fearsome One,
צ *in purity, to utter pure words with which to attain redemption.*
ק ❖*Their purchase suits them to be used for the Fearsome One,*
ר *worthy of being taken on this first day [of Succos].**

All:

ש *Your Name [אֵל] is coupled to our name [יִשְׂרָאֵל].*
You were alacritous on [Yom] Kippur to erase our sins.
ת ❖*May You protect us and not treat us as guilty;*
may You shield us and elevate us until You place us on high.

Chazzan bends his knees at *'Blessed'*; bows at *'You'*; straightens up at *'HASHEM.'*

Blessed are You, HASHEM, Shield of Abraham. (Cong.—*Amen.*)

GOD'S MIGHT

אַתָּה *You are eternally mighty, my Lord, the Resuscitator of the dead are You; abundantly able to save. He sustains the living with kindness, resuscitates the dead with abundant mercy, supports the fallen, heals the sick, releases the confined, and maintains His faith to those asleep in the dust. Who is like You, O Master of mighty deeds, and who is comparable to You, O King Who causes death and restores life and makes salvation sprout! And You are faithful to resuscitate the dead.*

All:

ת *With an offering* of seventy* bulls,*
ש *I made peace on this Festival with the seventy nations.*
ר *To find favor I brought ninety-eight lambs,*
ק *with them to balance the ninety-eight* admonitions.*

צ *I have combined 'these' with 'these'* on [the Festival of] Ingathering,*
פ *thus to increase for myself redemption and glee.*
ע *Increase for me strength and salvation,*
ס *and protection from battle, by baring [Your] arm.*

נ *[Each of] those who properly observe His celebration days,*
מ *to dwell in the succah of [Leviathan's] skin* will be his attainment.*
ל *To bind a neckband [or a] covering from [the skin of] His fish,*
כ *like the strong [angelic] warriors to see the splendor of His pride.*
י *If one dwells in a succah instead of his permanent home,*
ט *the canopy of Eden's trees will shelter him,*
ח *When the [punitive] heat of the future will come to confound him.*
ז *May its merit be an advocate [angel]*
leading him to the succah [of Leviathan].
ו *And may those satiated with the joys [of Succos] be invigorated.*
ה *Will she not be rewarded for it by being sated with freshness?*
ד ❖*The exalted One has crowned rose[-like Israel] with seven;**
ג *He decreed that it be celebrated seven [days] each year.*

---

against the ninety-eight curses of *Deuteronomy.* Thus, by making the number of admonitions equal to the number of calf offerings, the Torah implies that they are related to one another.

צֵרַפְתִּי אֵלֶּה בְּאֵלֶּה — *I have combined 'these' with 'these.'* This is a continuation of the previous verse. The תּוֹכָחוֹת conclude with the verse: אֵלֶּה דִבְרֵי הַבְּרִית, **These** *are the words of the covenant* (*Deuteronomy* 28:69). The chapter regarding the Festival sacrificial offerings concludes with: אֵלֶּה תַּעֲשׂוּ לַה׳ בְּמוֹעֲדֵיכֶם, **These** *shall you offer to HASHEM on your Festivals* (*Numbers* 29:39).

סֻכַּת עוֹר — *A succah of [Leviathan's] skin.* In the World to Come, God will make a *succah* of the skin of Leviathan. In this *succah* a great feast will be served for the totally righteous. [That *succah* and feast are discussed on page 1020.] Those who are partially righteous will not sit in

All:

הַמִּזְבֵּחַ בְּכַפּוֹת וּבַעֲרָבוֹת, בָּאתִי לְסוֹבְבֶנְהוּ בְּשִׂיחוֹת עֲרֵבוֹת,*

❖אֲנִי וָהוֹ* הוֹשִׁיעָה נָּא, בְּנִיב לְהַרְבּוֹת, אוֹרוֹת טַל לְהַחֲיוֹת[1] יוֹנֵי אֲרֻבּוֹת.

Chazzan:

בָּרוּךְ אַתָּה יהוה, מְחַיֵּה הַמֵּתִים. (Cong.–אָמֵן.)

All:

אִוּוּי* סֻכַּת דָּוִד הַנּוֹפֶלֶת,[2] תָּקִים לְבַל תְּהִי עוֹד מֻשְׁפֶּלֶת,

בְּמִדּוֹתֶיהָ נוֹסֶבֶת וּמְכֻפֶּלֶת, שְׁלֹשִׁים וְשִׁשָּׁה* כְּמוֹ שֶׁהָיְתָה מִתְכַּפֶּלֶת.

גֹּרֶן שֶׁהָיְתָה בְּאֹרֶךְ חֲמֵשׁ מֵאוֹת, רְחָבָה עַל חֲמֵשׁ מֵאוֹת,

דּוֹד יִנְטֶה קַו שְׁלֹשֶׁת אַלְפֵי אַמּוֹת, קְצוּבָה עַל שְׁלֹשֶׁת אַלְפֵי אַמּוֹת.

הַסְּכוּכָה בְּעָנָן צֵל יוֹמָם, צְלָלֶיהָ מְסַכְּכִים כְּלֵיל צֵל יוֹמָם,

וְעַם אֲשֶׁר עַתָּה סֻכָּה מְקַיְּמִים, פָּרוֹחַ יִפְרְחוּ בָהּ* בְּסִיּוּמָם.

זָרִים* יְאֶתָיו לִשְׁמָהּ בְּחָסֶף, עֲשׂוֹת חֲגִיגָה לְהִשְׁתַּחֲווֹת בְּכֶסֶף,

חַרְבוֹנֵי קַיִץ יְלַהֲטֵם לְשַׁסֵּף, סְגוּרִים בְּמַסְגֵּר עַל חֲמִשִּׁים כֶּסֶף.

טָסִים וְעָפִים בִּקְצָווֹת יְקָרֶיהָ, נִסְכָּכִים בְּשֶׁבַע קְרָא מִקְרָאֶיהָ,

יֶאֱגְדוּ מִמֶּרְחָק כָּל קְרוּאֶיהָ, כְּתוֹרִים לִמְכוֹן הַר צִיּוֹן וְעַל מִקְרָאֶיהָ.

Congregation aloud, then *chazzan:*

יִמְלֹךְ יהוה לְעוֹלָם, אֱלֹהַיִךְ צִיּוֹן לְדֹר וָדֹר, הַלְלוּיָהּ.[3]
וְאַתָּה קָדוֹשׁ יוֹשֵׁב תְּהִלּוֹת יִשְׂרָאֵל,[4] אֵל נָא.

All:

כָּל תְּהִי מִצְוַת סֻכָּה בְּעֵינֶיךָ קַלָּה,*

כִּי כְּנֶגֶד כָּל מִצְוֹת דַּת כְּחֻקּוֹתֶיהָ שְׁקוּלָה.

---

the *succah* [i.e., four walls and a roof] of this skin, but will nevertheless sit in its shade [i.e., under a canopy without walls]. The still less righteous may be rewarded with a neckband or an amulet made from this skin (*Bava Basra* 75a, based on *Job* 40:31). Moreover, the skin of the Leviathan is so bright that even with only a small amulet one will be able to see from one end of the universe to the other. Thus, even the least righteous will be rewarded with vision comparable to that of the angels. The *paytan* alludes to all this in the next verses.

לְהַנְזִיר שִׁבְעָה – *Has crowned . . . with seven.* The seven *mitzvos* of Succos are: The *succah*, the *chagigah*-offering, the *simchah*-offering and the Four Species.

בְּשִׂיחוֹת עֲרֵבוֹת – *With these sweetening species.* This refers not to the taste or aroma of the species, for they are not all sweet, but to their *mitzvah's* ability to mitigate, or sweeten, harsh decrees.

אֲנִי וָהוֹ – *Ani Vaho.* This Divine Name is discussed in the commentary on page 365.

❧ אִוּוּי – *The coveted.* This *piyut* follows the א״ת ב״ש order of the alphabet, pairing the first letter, א, with the last letter, ת; the second, ב, with the second to last, ש; etc.

The first two stanzas contain a prayer for the rebuilt Temple that will be much larger than the previous two. The third and fifth stanzas speak of the reward awaiting those who yearn for the Temple, while the fourth tells of the retribution against those who destroyed it. Throughout, the *succah* is used as a metaphor for the Temple; and dwelling in the *succah* alludes to yearning for the re-establishment of the Temple.

שְׁלֹשִׁים וְשִׁשָּׁה – *Thirty-six.* King David purchased a piece of land for the Temple site. Previously this area was used as a granary by Ornan (also called Aravnah) the Jebusite. David paid Ornan fifty silver *shekalim* for the area (*II Samuel* 24:18-25). This granary measured five hundred cubits by five hundred cubits and that was the size of the Temple Mount (*Middos* 2:1). In relating his vision of the future Temple, *Ezekiel* 42:16-19 describes the Temple Mount as a square measuring five hundred six-cubit rods (i.e., 3000 cubits) on each side. Thus, the original

All:

The Altar with [palm] branches and with willows —
ב *I have come to encircle it with these sweetening species,**
א ❖*'ANI VAHO,* bring salvation now!' to utter repeatedly,*
with the sparkling dew to resuscitate[1] [Israel] the doves of the cote.

Chazzan:

Blessed are You, HASHEM, Who resuscitates the dead. (Cong.—*Amen.*)

All:

א *The coveted* fallen Succah [Temple] of David,[2]*
ת *re-establish it that it never again be humbled.*
ב *In its measure all around, it will be multiplied*
ש *thirty-six times* greater than before.*
ג *The granary was five hundred [cubits] long,*
ר *and five hundred [cubits] wide,*
ד *The Beloved will stretch a line of three thousand cubits,*
measured by three thousand cubits.
ה *The cloud-covered nation for shelter by day,*
צ *shaded by the succah, may the daytime shade make it feel like night,*
ו *And may the people who now fulfill [the laws of] succah,*
פ *blossom forth through it at the End of Days.*
ז *Strangers* will come to perform the mitzvah of succah openly,*
ע *to celebrate the Festival and to bow with desire.*
ח *But the summer sun will burn them, [causing them] to break [it],*
ס *may they be locked in prison for [destroying] the [Temple site*
purchased for] fifty silver [shekalim].
ט *But those who value it will fly, winging to it from far corners.*
נ *Those who call it a 'holy convocation' will sit under seven canopies.*
ימ *All who prepare [for the rebuilt Temple] will be gathered from afar,*
כל *to encircle the Temple on Mount Zion and to crown each of its invitees.*

Congregation aloud, then *chazzan:*

HASHEM shall reign forever — your God, O Zion — from generation to generation, Halleluyah![3]

You, O Holy One, are enthroned upon Israel's praises[4] — please, O God.

All:

בַּל תְּהִי *Let not the mitzvah of succah be light* in your eyes,*
for its laws are equal to all the mitzvos of the Torah.

(1) Cf. *Isaiah* 26:19. (2) Cf. *Amos* 9:11 [see comm. to אָנָּא תְּרַב, p. 240]. (3) *Psalms* 146:10. (4) 22:4.

Temple Mount contained 250,000 square cubits (500x500=250,000) while the enlarged Temple Mount of the future will be 9,000,000 square cubits (3,000x3,000=9,000,000) or thirty-six times as large (250,000x36=9,000,000).

Incidentally, *Rashi* to *Ezekiel* 42:20 cites our *piyut* in elucidating the verses there. This is another proof that the *piyutim* are much more than inspired poetry.

זָרִים – *Strangers.* The Talmud (*Avodah Zarah* 3a) records that in the World to Come, when God castigates the gentile nations for not accepting the Torah, they will reply, 'Offer us the Torah anew and we will obey it.'

To test them, God will say, 'I have an easy *mitzvah* called *succah;* go and perform it.' [This *mitzvah* is termed 'easy' because it is inexpensive to perform.]

Immediately, every gentile will go and make a *succah* on his roof, but God will cause the sun to blaze on them and each of them will kick over his *succah* and leave. [By kicking contemptuously, they will prove how insincere is their commitment to Torah.]

⚜ בַּל תְּהִי ... קַלָּה – *Let not the mitzvah of succah be light.* Although God calls *succah* an easy *mitzvah* (see preceding comment), nevertheless we must not make light of it. If the

הַמְעֻזָּקָה וְהַמְּסֻקָּלָה,*[1]
סֹלּוּ מְסִלָּה בְּסִלְסוּלֶיהָ מְסֻקָּלָה.*[2]
כִּי לְכָל שׁוֹמְרֶיהָ לֹא יֶאֱרַע תְּקָלָה.
וְכָל בּוֹגְדֶיהָ לֶעָתִיד לָבֹא לְקַח מֵהֶם קְלָלָה,[3]
בְּלַהַט הַיּוֹם הַבָּא קְלוֹנָם מַקְלָה.[4]
וְחוֹסֶיהָ לְצֶדֶק מַכְרִיעָה, וּבָם מִתְרוֹעֲעָה,
לְסוֹכְכָם מֵרָעָה, אוֹתָם לְהַרְעָה,
בְּסֻכַּת יְרִיעָה, לִהְיוֹת רוֹעָה,
שְׁאֵתָהּ בְּטוּב מִרְעָה, אֶתְנַנָּהּ לְפַרְעָה,

Chazzan, then congregation, aloud:

בְּסֻכַּת חַי וְקַיָּם נוֹרָא וּמָרוֹם וְקָדוֹשׁ.

All:

אֵלִים כְּהִשְׁעִין אָב* תַּחַת עֵץ סֻכָּה, וְנִצָּב לְהַאֲרִיחָם בְּנֶפֶשׁ חֲשֵׁכָה,
לְבַדָּיו שָׁמַר בְּלוּד קַו בְּקַו[5] לְמָשְׁכָה, וְעָמַד וָגָז וּפָסַח בַּעֲדָם לְסוֹכְכָה.
עַל כִּי תוֹעִים לִמֵּד תִּעוּב מַסֵּכָה, וּמָאַס רַהֲבֵי גְוִיָּה וְנֶעֶמְתָה לוֹ יִסְכָּה,
זָכָה בְּכֵן גִּזְעוֹ שְׁלֹל דָּת נְסוּכָה, בְּרוּחַ הַקֹּדֶשׁ סְכוּת כְּמוֹ הוֹרָם סָכָה.*
רֶגֶל גְּבִיר אַחִים וָסַע פַּעֲמַיִם סֻכּוֹתָה,* וּמֵאֲרַמִּי[6] וְשֵׂעִיר[7] בַּעֲדוֹ סַכּוֹתָה,
בְּכֵן חֲנִיטָיו סָעוּ רֵאשִׁית סֻכּוֹתָה,* וְשִׁבְעַת חֲזִיזֵי מֶשִׁי עָלֵימוֹ סִכַּכְתָּה.
יִדְאוּ חוֹרְבָה עֲדָיִם מְקֻשָּׁרִים, עֲנָנִים סְכוּכִים כְּעַל כַּנְפֵי נְשָׁרִים,
רֶגֶשׁ שַׁנְאַנִּים חָזוּ מְאֻשָּׁרִים, שֶׁבַע מְחִיצוֹת סוֹכְכוֹת וְלֶחֶם מְחַשְּׁרִים.
בְּטִלּוּל עֲנָנָיו הִרְכִּיבָן בֵּין סֹכֵךְ לְסָכָךְ,* וַיִּתְיַצְּבוּ תַחְתָּיו* כְּמִתַּחְתִּית סְכָךְ,
יִדְּעָם תַּבְנִית מִשְׁכָּן אֵיךְ יְהִי מְסֻכָּךְ, וּבְתַבְנִיתוֹ לְבָנוֹן מוּכָן לִסְכָךְ.
קָצַב בֵּין קֹדֶשׁ לְקֹדֶשׁ, תֵּת בְּדֵל מִמָּסָךְ, מְחִיצוֹת לְסַכֵּךְ, בְּפָרֹכֶת הַמָּסָךְ.
לִכְרוּבֵי סֹכְכִים, כַּפֹּרֶת סוֹכְכִים, מִשָּׁם רוּחַ סָכִים, וְצוּר עִמָּם מְסַכִּים.

---

mitzvah of *succah* will be used to test the gentiles, then it must be equal to the entire Torah. That is, if God tells the nations that their fulfillment of this one *mitzvah* will establish their desire and ability to perform the other 612 *mitzvos,* then this *mitzvah* must be equal to those 612 *mitzvos.*

וְהַמְּסֻקָּלָה — *And cleared of stones.* The *paytan* describes the *succah* in terms of a vineyard being readied for planting. The walls are represented by the fence around the yard, while the rule prohibiting certain utensils [e.g., pots and pans] from entering the *succah* is alluded to as clearing the stones from the area to be planted.

בְּסִלְסוּלֶיהָ מְסֻקָּלָה — *Cleared of stones by its laws.* In the merit of fulfilling the laws of dwelling in the *succah,* may we merit traveling unimpeded along the road to the rebuilt Temple.

☙ **אֵלִים כְּהִשְׁעִין אָב** — *When the Patriarch [Abraham] told the angels to recline.* The acrostic of this *piyut* spells the composer's name אֶלְעָזָר בִּירַבִּי קַלִּיר, *Elazar son of Rabbi Kalir.*

The *paytan* traces the roots of (a) the Clouds of Glory that protected the Jews in the Wilderness, (b) the *Mishkan* and Temple, and (c) the *mitzvah* of dwelling in the *succah,* to Abraham's hospitality with the three angels (see *Genesis* 18:1-8).

כְּמוֹ הוֹרָם סָכָה — *Just as their forebear saw.* Sarah was also called יִסְכָּה, *Iscah,* from the root סכה, *to see, to gaze,* because she was endowed with the holy spirit which allowed her to see the future (see *Rashi, Genesis* 11:29).

פַּעֲמַיִם סֻכּוֹתָה — *Twice-named Succos.* After emerging unharmed from his meeting with Esau, Jacob spent eighteen months in a place he called Succos. In later years the place was renamed in honor of the Clouds of Glory which surrounded the Jews in the Wilderness like a *succah* (see *Targum Yonasan* and *Baal HaTurim, Numbers* 33:5).

רֵאשִׁית סֻכּוֹתָה — *To Succos first.* Upon leaving

Walled in and cleared of stones,[1]
an unobstructed path cleared of stones by its laws.[2]
For to all who observe it, no stumbling block will appear;
but all who rebel against it will become the symbol of curse in the future,[3]
in the searing heat of the time to come their shame will be burned.[4]
While those who sit in its shade will be judged righteous,
and in it will be banded together,
to protect them from evil,
to nourish them,
in the succah of curtains [made of Leviathan's skin] to eat,
to carry them [from exile] to good pasture [in Eretz Yisrael],
to pay its reward,

Chazzan, then congregation, aloud:

In the Succah of the Living and Enduring One, Awesome, Exalted and Holy.

All:

א *When the Patriarch [Abraham] told the angels to recline* in the tree's shade,*
and stood over them serving their meal, with humility of soul,
ל *[G-d] observed [and repaid his offspring] measure for measure*[5]
in Lud [Egypt],
standing [watch], skipping and passing over [their homes] to protect them.
ע *Because he [Abraham] taught the wayward to despise molten idols,*
and loathed the haughty — he was given Iscah [Sarah] as a wife.
ז *Through her his offspring were given their reward — the chosen Torah,*
*and to see with the holy spirit [of prophecy] just as their forebear saw.**
ר *The lordly brother [Jacob] traveled to twice-named Succos,**
and He [God] protected him from the Aramean [Laban][6] *and Seir [Esau].*[7]
ב *Therefore his offspring traveled to Succos first,**
and seven silken clouds sheltered them.
י *They flew to Horeb [Sinai, where they were] adorned with crowns,*
sheltered and protected by clouds as if on eagle's wings.
ר *Gatherings of angels observed [Israel] the praiseworthy,*
protected by seven [cloud] curtains, [eating] bread that came [from heaven].
ב *In the tent of His clouds, He had them ride between clouds* [to Mount Sinai];*
they stood under it [Mount Sinai] as if under [a succah's] s'chach.*
י *He taught them the construction of the Tabernacle, how it should be covered,*
and [to erect] Lebanon [the Temple] in its form, prepared for protection.
ק *To delineate between the Holy and the Holy of Holies,*
place a separating curtain,
like walls to conceal [behind] the hanging Paroches.
ל *With covering Cherubim, spreading wing over the Ark-cover,*
from there [the holy] spirit can be seen, and the Rock meets with them.

(1) Cf. *Isaiah* 5:2. (2) Cf. 62:10. (3) Cf. *Jeremiah* 29:22. (4) Cf. *Malachi* 3:19.
(5) See Mishnah, *Sotah* 1:7. (6) See *Genesis* 31:24-30. (7) See 32:3.

Rameses [Egypt] the nation's first resting place was Succos (see *Exodus* 12:37).

בְּטְלוּל . . . לְסָכָךְ — *In the tent . . . between clouds.* Six clouds sheltered the Jews: four of them surrounded them on the four sides; one covered them overhead; the sixth was like a carpet under their feet. The seventh cloud mentioned above traveled before them, leading the way through the Wilderness.

וַיִּתְיַצְּבוּ תַּחְתָּיו — *They stood under it [Mount Sinai].* When the nation stood at Sinai, God lifted the mountain above their heads and said, 'If you accept the Torah, well and good! If not, here shall be your burial place' (*Shabbos* 88a).

יִקְרוּ שְׁמָהּ סֻכּוֹת, שָׁלֹשׁ פְּעָמִים בַּסֻּכּוֹת,*
רֶמֶז לְשַׁלֵּשׁ בְּכָל סֻכּוֹת, דְּפָנוֹת מְסֻכָּכוֹת.
❖ רְצוּיֵ דַּת הַשּׁוֹאֵבָה שָׁאֲבוּ, חָקוּק בָּהּ חָשָׁבוּ,
כְּמוֹ בְּסִין קָשְׁבוּ, בַּסֻּכּוֹת תֵּשְׁבוּ.

Chazzan continues:

אֵל נָא לְעוֹלָם* תֻּעֲרָץ, וּלְעוֹלָם תֻּקְדָּשׁ,[2] וּלְעוֹלְמֵי עוֹלָמִים תִּמְלוֹךְ וְתִתְנַשֵּׂא, הָאֵל מֶלֶךְ נוֹרָא מָרוֹם וְקָדוֹשׁ, כִּי אַתָּה הוּא מֶלֶךְ מַלְכֵי הַמְּלָכִים, מַלְכוּתוֹ נֶצַח. נוֹרְאוֹתָיו שִׂיחוּ, סַפְּרוּ עֻזּוֹ, פָּאֲרוּהוּ צְבָאָיו, קַדְּשׁוּהוּ רוֹמְמוּהוּ, רוֹן שִׁיר וָשֶׁבַח, תּוֹקֶף תְּהִלּוֹת תִּפְאַרְתּוֹ.

Chazzan, then congregation:

לְסוֹכְּבֵי לְמָסְכֵי, לְנַסְּכֵי בְנִסְכֵּי, בִּנְסִיכַת קָדוֹשׁ.

Chazzan, then congregation:

לְחַדְּשֵׁי רִאשׁוֹן כְּמֵרִאשׁוֹן, לִנְצוּרֵי כְאִישׁוֹן,
אֲהַלֵּל בְּפֶה וְלָשׁוֹן, לְמָרוֹם וְקָדוֹשׁ.

All:

אָמְנָם* מִצְוָה גּוֹרֶרֶת מִצְוֹת,[3]
בְּזֹאת אֲשֶׁר בְּאִבֶּיהָ תּוֹרוֹת קְצוּבוֹת, גְּזֵרוֹת חֻבְּרוּ לָהּ לְצַוּוֹת.
דָּרַשׁ יוֹם זֶה לְיַחֲסוֹ רִאשׁוֹן,[4]
הוּא חֲמִשָּׁה עָשָׂר וְהֻנְקַב רִאשׁוֹן, וּכְדֵי לְבַשְּׂרֵנוּ כִּי מָחַל רִאשׁוֹן.
זִכְרוֹן סוֹף שָׁנָה* וְהוּא תְּחִלַּת שָׁנָה,
חַג הָאָסִיף תְּקוּפַת הַשָּׁנָה, טוֹב יָדִין בּוֹ נִזְלֵי שָׁנָה.
יִקְחוּ לִשְׁמוֹ אַרְבַּעַת מִינִים,
כְּלוּלִים[5] כְּתוּרִים וּמְזֻמָּנִים, לְהַלֵּל בָּם כִּבְעֻגָב וּבְמִנִּים.[6]
מֵהוֹד הָדָר הַמְּהֻדָּר,
נֶאְדָּר וְנֶהְדָּר בַּהֲדָרוֹ לְהַדָּר, סוֹד אֶדֶר יְקַר בְּכֶתֶם פָּז לְאַדָּר.
עֲנַף עֵץ עָבֹת חֲפוּת מִבַּחוּץ,
פּוֹנוֹת לְכַוֵּן לֵב מִבַּיִת וּמִחוּץ, צָפוּי לְכַפֵּר בְּעַד לֵב שָׁחוּץ.
קִיחַת לוּלָב וְעַרְבֵי נְחָלִים,
רְגִילִים עֲנוֹת בָּם שִׁיר הִלּוּלִים, שְׁקוּלִים וְשָׁוִים כִּבְמְחוֹל חֲלִילִים.
תְּפִישַׂת שְׁלֹשָׁה הֲדַסִּים וּשְׁתֵּי עֲרָבוֹת,
שִׁיר לְהַסְלִיל לָרוֹכֵב בָּעֲרָבוֹת,
אֶתְרוֹג וְכַף תְּמָר יְחִידִים מִלְּהַמְעִיט וּמִלְּהַרְבּוֹת.

שָׁלֹשׁ פְּעָמִים בַּסֻּכּוֹת — *The thrice-written word 'basuccos.'* In *Leviticus* 23:42-43 the word בַּסֻּכֹּת, *in succos*, appears three times. From the spelling variants there, the Talmud deduces that a *succah* must have at least three walls (*Succah* 6b).

☙ אֵל נָא לְעוֹלָם — *O God, may You always.* This ancient *piyut* of anonymous authorship seems to be a fragment of a longer composition, perhaps even the fragments of two *piyutim* that have been merged into one. The first half contains no apparent acrostic scheme. It praises God and prays that we may always praise Him. The second half follows a repetitive alphabetical acrostic, beginning with the letter מ — two word phrases, the first with the initial letters מ״נ, the next with נ״ס, then ס״ע, etc; but with some phrases missing. In this second part the *chazzan* calls upon the congregation to sing God's praises.

☙ אָמְנָם — *Truly.* The *piyut* follows an alphabet-

י *There they [Israel] were honored by being allowed to understand,*
*the thrice-written word 'basuccos,'**
alluding to treble in all succos, the walls covered with s'chach.

ר ∴*The law of drawing [water] for the favor-finding [libation]*[1] *they elicited,*
they deduced it from what is inscribed [in the Torah],
and it is as valid as that which was heard at Sinai, 'In succos shall you dwell.'

Chazzan continues:

אֵל *O God, may You always* be lauded and always be sanctified,*[2] *and forever reign and be uplifted, the God, King, awesome, exalted, and holy, for You are the King Who reigns over kings, Whose sovereignty is eternal. Speak of His wonders, declare His stength, glorify Him, O His legions; sanctify Him, exalt Him. Sing song and praise, glorify Him with powerful psalms of praise.*

Chazzan, then congregation:

To shelter me, to conceal me; to enthrone my King [the Messiah], with the sovereignty of the Holy One.

Chazzan, then congregation:

That [God] the First One renew me
as the first time [at the Exodus],
the nation guarded as the pupil [of one's eye],
I shall offer praise with mouth and tongue,
to the Exalted and Holy One.

א *Truly,* one mitzvah leads to other mitzvos,*[3]
ב *in this [Torah] whose fruit-like mitzvos are dependent on each other,**
ג *thus many laws are connected to it [Succos].*
ד *This day is expounded upon to explain why it is dubbed 'the first.'*[4]
ה *Although it is [really] the fifteenth [of Tishrei] it is called 'first,'*
ו *to inform us that the First One has forgiven (our sins).*
ז *Mentioned as year's end* but it's at the beginning of the year,*
ח *the Festival of Ingathering at the tekufah of the year.*
ט *On it the Beneficent One will judge the rains of the year.*
י *They take — for His Name's sake — the Four Species,*
כ *adorned,*[5] *crowned and prepared,*
ל *to praise with them as with flute and organ.*[6]
מ *With the splendor of the beautiful esrog,*
נ *to praise and glorify the Mighty Splendrous One,*
ס *the secret of the valuable trees, contained in the golden [words of the Torah].*
ע *Branches of the plaited[-myrtle with] its wood covered [by its leaves],*
פ *[teach them] to align their heart, inside and out,*
צ *looking forward to atone for a haughty heart.*
ק *Taking the lulav and the brook willows,*
ר *they are wont to recite with them the Hallel song,*
ש *the same number [species] as the flutes played [during the Temple Service].*
ת *[While] holding three haddasim and two aravos,*
to praise with song Him Who rides on the highest heaven,
with one esrog and one lulav, no less and no more.

---

(1) See commentary to Mishnah, *Succah* 4:9, p. 120. (2) Cf. *Psalms* 89:8. (3) Cf. Mishnah, *Avos* 4:2. (4) See *Leviticus* 23:40.(5) See Mishnah *Succah* 3:8, p. 110. (6) Cf. *Psalms* 150:4.

---

ical acrostic as it discusses the Four Species and their midrashic allusions.

סוֹף שָׁנָה — *Year's end.* In *Exodus* 34:22 Succos is referred to as חַג הָאָסִיף תְּקוּפַת הַשָּׁנָה, *the Festival*

לְחַדְּשִׁי רִאשׁוֹן כְּמֵרִאשׁוֹן, לִנְצוּרֵי כְּאִישׁוֹן,
אֲהַלֵּל בְּפֶה וְלָשׁוֹן, לְמָרוֹם וְקָדוֹשׁ.

All:

וּבְכֵן וּלְךָ תַעֲלֶה קְדֻשָּׁה, כִּי אַתָּה קְדוֹשׁ יִשְׂרָאֵל וּמוֹשִׁיעַ.

Some congregations recite the prayer כִּי אֶקַּח (p. 1263) before *Kedushah.*
Most congregations recite the standard *Yom Tov Kedushah* (below).
Those who recite כִּי אֶקַּח omit the opening phrase in parentheses.

קדושה

When reciting *Kedushah,* one must stand with his feet together and avoid any interruptions. One should rise on his toes when saying the words קָדוֹשׁ, קָדוֹשׁ, קָדוֹשׁ; בָּרוּךְ (of בָּרוּךְ כְּבוֹד); and יִמְלֹךְ.

– Cong. then *Chazzan*: (נְקַדֵּשׁ אֶת שִׁמְךָ בָּעוֹלָם, כְּשֵׁם שֶׁמַּקְדִּישִׁים אוֹתוֹ בִּשְׁמֵי מָרוֹם,) כַּכָּתוּב עַל יַד נְבִיאֶךָ, וְקָרָא זֶה אֶל זֶה וְאָמַר:

– All: קָדוֹשׁ קָדוֹשׁ קָדוֹשׁ יהוה צְבָאוֹת, מְלֹא כָל הָאָרֶץ כְּבוֹדוֹ.[1]
❖ אָז בְּקוֹל* רַעַשׁ גָּדוֹל אַדִּיר וְחָזָק מַשְׁמִיעִים קוֹל, מִתְנַשְּׂאִים לְעֻמַּת שְׂרָפִים, לְעֻמָּתָם בָּרוּךְ יֹאמֵרוּ:

– All: בָּרוּךְ כְּבוֹד יהוה, מִמְּקוֹמוֹ.[2] ❖ מִמְּקוֹמְךָ מַלְכֵּנוּ תוֹפִיעַ, וְתִמְלֹךְ עָלֵינוּ, כִּי מְחַכִּים אֲנַחְנוּ לָךְ. מָתַי תִּמְלֹךְ בְּצִיּוֹן, בְּקָרוֹב בְּיָמֵינוּ, לְעוֹלָם וָעֶד תִּשְׁכּוֹן. תִּתְגַּדַּל וְתִתְקַדַּשׁ בְּתוֹךְ יְרוּשָׁלַיִם עִירְךָ, לְדוֹר וָדוֹר וּלְנֵצַח נְצָחִים. וְעֵינֵינוּ תִרְאֶינָה מַלְכוּתֶךָ, כַּדָּבָר הָאָמוּר בְּשִׁירֵי עֻזֶּךָ, עַל יְדֵי דָוִד מְשִׁיחַ צִדְקֶךָ:

– All: יִמְלֹךְ יהוה לְעוֹלָם, אֱלֹהַיִךְ צִיּוֹן לְדֹר וָדֹר, הַלְלוּיָהּ.[3]

קדושת השם

Chazzan continues:

לְדוֹר וָדוֹר נַגִּיד גָּדְלֶךָ וּלְנֵצַח נְצָחִים קְדֻשָּׁתְךָ נַקְדִּישׁ, וְשִׁבְחֲךָ אֱלֹהֵינוּ מִפִּינוּ לֹא יָמוּשׁ לְעוֹלָם וָעֶד, כִּי אֵל מֶלֶךְ גָּדוֹל וְקָדוֹשׁ אָתָּה. בָּרוּךְ אַתָּה יהוה, הָאֵל הַקָּדוֹשׁ. (Cong. – אָמֵן.)

קדושת היום

אַתָּה בְחַרְתָּנוּ מִכָּל הָעַמִּים, אָהַבְתָּ אוֹתָנוּ, וְרָצִיתָ בָּנוּ, וְרוֹמַמְתָּנוּ מִכָּל הַלְּשׁוֹנוֹת, וְקִדַּשְׁתָּנוּ בְּמִצְוֹתֶיךָ, וְקֵרַבְתָּנוּ מַלְכֵּנוּ לַעֲבוֹדָתֶךָ, וְשִׁמְךָ הַגָּדוֹל וְהַקָּדוֹשׁ עָלֵינוּ קָרָאתָ.

---

of the Ingathering at the 'tekufah' of the year. The word *'tekufah'* means a change of season. Thus, spring begins on the *tekufah* of Nissan [the vernal equinox]; summer, on the *tekufah* of Tammuz [the summer solstice]; fall, on the *tekufah* of Tishrei [the autumnal equinox]; and winter, on the *tekufah* of Teves [the winter solstice]. Since the Torah speaks of both in-

That [God] the First One renew me as the first time [at the Exodus],
the nation guarded as the pupil [of one's eye],
I shall offer praise with mouth and tongue, to the Exalted and Holy One.

All:

And so, the Kedushah prayer shall ascend to You,
for You are the Holy One of Israel, and Savior.

Some congregations recite the prayer כִּי אֶקַּח (p. 1263) before *Kedushah.*

Most congregations recite the standard *Yom Tov Kedushah* (below).
Those who recite כִּי אֶקַּח omit the opening phrase in parentheses.

KEDUSHAH

When reciting *Kedushah*, one must stand with his feet together and avoid any interruptions. One should rise on his toes when saying the words *Holy, holy, holy; Blessed is;* and *HASHEM shall reign.*

Cong. then Chazzan – **נְקַדֵּשׁ** *(We shall sanctify Your Name in this world, just as they sanctify it in heaven above,) as it is written by Your prophet, "And one [angel] will call another and say:*

All– *'Holy, holy, holy is HASHEM, Master of Legions, the whole world is filled with His glory.'"*[1] ❖ *Then, with a sound* of great noise, mighty and powerful, they make heard a voice, raising themselves toward the seraphim; those facing them say 'Blessed ...':*

All– *'Blessed is the glory of HASHEM from His place.'*[2] ❖ *From Your place, our King, You will appear and reign over us, for we await You. When will You reign in Zion? Soon, in our days — forever and ever — may You dwell there. May You be exalted and sanctified within Jerusalem, Your city, from generation to generation and for all eternity. May our eyes see Your kingdom, as it is expressed in the songs of Your might, written by David, Your righteous anointed:*

All– *'HASHEM shall reign forever — your God, O Zion — from generation to generation, Halleluyah!'*[3]

HOLINESS OF GOD'S NAME

Chazzan continues:

לְדוֹר *From generation to generation we shall relate Your greatness and for infinite eternities we shall proclaim Your holiness. Your praise, our God, shall not leave our mouth forever and ever, for You, O God, are a great and holy King. Blessed are You, HASHEM, the holy God.*

(Cong. – *Amen.)*

SANCTIFICATION OF THE DAY

אַתָּה בְחַרְתָּנוּ *You have chosen us from all the peoples; You loved us and found favor in us; You exalted us above all the tongues and You sanctified us with Your commandments. You drew us close, our King, to Your service and proclaimed Your great and Holy Name upon us.*

---

(1) *Isaiah* 6:3. (2) *Ezekiel* 3:12. (3) *Psalms* 146:10.

וַתִּתֶּן לָנוּ יהוה אֱלֹהֵינוּ בְּאַהֲבָה מוֹעֲדִים לְשִׂמְחָה חַגִּים וּזְמַנִּים לְשָׂשׂוֹן, אֶת יוֹם חַג הַסֻּכּוֹת הַזֶּה, זְמַן שִׂמְחָתֵנוּ מִקְרָא קֹדֶשׁ, זֵכֶר לִיצִיאַת מִצְרָיִם.

אֱלֹהֵינוּ וֵאלֹהֵי אֲבוֹתֵינוּ, יַעֲלֶה, וְיָבֹא, וְיַגִּיעַ, וְיֵרָאֶה, וְיֵרָצֶה, וְיִשָּׁמַע, וְיִפָּקֵד, וְיִזָּכֵר זִכְרוֹנֵנוּ וּפִקְדוֹנֵנוּ, וְזִכְרוֹן אֲבוֹתֵינוּ, וְזִכְרוֹן מָשִׁיחַ בֶּן דָּוִד עַבְדֶּךָ, וְזִכְרוֹן יְרוּשָׁלַיִם עִיר קָדְשֶׁךָ, וְזִכְרוֹן כָּל עַמְּךָ בֵּית יִשְׂרָאֵל לְפָנֶיךָ, לִפְלֵיטָה לְטוֹבָה לְחֵן וּלְחֶסֶד וּלְרַחֲמִים, לְחַיִּים וּלְשָׁלוֹם בְּיוֹם חַג הַסֻּכּוֹת הַזֶּה. זָכְרֵנוּ יהוה אֱלֹהֵינוּ בּוֹ לְטוֹבָה (.Cong – אָמֵן), וּפָקְדֵנוּ בוֹ לִבְרָכָה (.Cong – אָמֵן), וְהוֹשִׁיעֵנוּ בוֹ לְחַיִּים (.Cong – אָמֵן). וּבִדְבַר יְשׁוּעָה וְרַחֲמִים, חוּס וְחָנֵּנוּ וְרַחֵם עָלֵינוּ וְהוֹשִׁיעֵנוּ, כִּי אֵלֶיךָ עֵינֵינוּ, כִּי אֵל מֶלֶךְ חַנּוּן וְרַחוּם אָתָּה.[1]

וְהַשִּׂיאֵנוּ יהוה אֱלֹהֵינוּ אֶת בִּרְכַּת מוֹעֲדֶיךָ לְחַיִּים וּלְשָׁלוֹם, לְשִׂמְחָה וּלְשָׂשׂוֹן, כַּאֲשֶׁר רָצִיתָ וְאָמַרְתָּ לְבָרְכֵנוּ. קַדְּשֵׁנוּ בְּמִצְוֹתֶיךָ וְתֵן חֶלְקֵנוּ בְּתוֹרָתֶךָ, שַׂבְּעֵנוּ מִטּוּבֶךָ וְשַׂמְּחֵנוּ בִּישׁוּעָתֶךָ, וְטַהֵר לִבֵּנוּ לְעָבְדְּךָ בֶּאֱמֶת, וְהַנְחִילֵנוּ יהוה אֱלֹהֵינוּ בְּשִׂמְחָה וּבְשָׂשׂוֹן מוֹעֲדֵי קָדְשֶׁךָ, וְיִשְׂמְחוּ בְךָ יִשְׂרָאֵל מְקַדְּשֵׁי שְׁמֶךָ. בָּרוּךְ אַתָּה יהוה, מְקַדֵּשׁ יִשְׂרָאֵל וְהַזְּמַנִּים. (.Cong – אָמֵן.)

עבודה

רְצֵה יהוה אֱלֹהֵינוּ בְּעַמְּךָ יִשְׂרָאֵל וּבִתְפִלָּתָם, וְהָשֵׁב אֶת הָעֲבוֹדָה לִדְבִיר בֵּיתֶךָ. וְאִשֵּׁי יִשְׂרָאֵל וּתְפִלָּתָם בְּאַהֲבָה תְקַבֵּל בְּרָצוֹן, וּתְהִי לְרָצוֹן תָּמִיד עֲבוֹדַת יִשְׂרָאֵל עַמֶּךָ.

וְתֶחֱזֶינָה עֵינֵינוּ בְּשׁוּבְךָ לְצִיּוֹן בְּרַחֲמִים. בָּרוּךְ אַתָּה יהוה, הַמַּחֲזִיר שְׁכִינָתוֹ לְצִיּוֹן. (.Cong – אָמֵן.)

---

gathering the crops and a change of season, the month intended must be Tishrei.

However, another verse in Exodus (23:16) paraphrases this clause, חַג הָאָסִף בְּצֵאת הַשָּׁנָה, *the Festival of Ingathering at the departure* [i.e., end] *of the year*. But the year is counted either from Nissan, in which case Tishrei falls in the middle of the year, or from Tishrei, which places it at the beginning of the year. If so, why does the Torah call it the end of the year?

The *paytan* resolves this question by citing the second mishnah in tractate Rosh Hashanah where it is taught that on Succos the world is judged with respect to its annual rainfall. In

וַתִּתֶּן לָנוּ *And You gave us, HASHEM, our God, with love, appointed festivals for gladness, Festivals and times for joy, this day of the Festival of Succos, the time of our gladness, a holy convocation, a memorial of the Exodus from Egypt.*

אֱלֹהֵינוּ *Our God and God of our forefathers, may there rise, come, reach, be noted, be favored, be heard, be considered, and be remembered — the remembrance and consideration of ourselves; the remembrance of our forefathers; the remembrance of Messiah, son of David, Your servant; the remembrance of Jerusalem, the City of Your Holiness; the remembrance of Your entire people the Family of Israel — before You for deliverance, for goodness, for grace, for kindness, and for compassion, for life, and for peace on this day of the Festival of Succos. Remember us on it, HASHEM, our God, for goodness (*Cong. – *Amen); consider us on it for blessing (*Cong. – *Amen); and help us on it for life (*Cong. – *Amen). In the matter of salvation and compassion, pity, be gracious and compassionate with us and help us, for our eyes are turned to You, because You are God, the gracious and compassionate King.*[1]

וְהַשִּׂיאֵנוּ *Bestow upon us, O HASHEM, our God, the blessing of Your appointed Festivals for life and for peace, for gladness and for joy, as You desired and promised to bless us. Sanctify us with our commandments and grant us our share in Your Torah; satisfy us from Your goodness and gladden us with Your salvation, and purify our heart to serve You sincerely. And grant us a heritage, O HASHEM, our God — with gladness and with joy — the appointed festivals of Your holiness, and may Israel, the sanctifiers of Your Name, rejoice in You. Blessed are You, HASHEM, Who sanctifies Israel and the festive seasons.* (Cong. – *Amen.)*

TEMPLE SERVICE

רְצֵה *Be favorable, HASHEM, our God, toward Your people Israel and their prayer and restore the service to the Holy of Holies of Your Temple. The fire-offerings of Israel and their prayer accept with love and favor, and may the service of Your people Israel always be favorable to You.*

וְתֶחֱזֶינָה *May our eyes behold Your return to Zion in compassion. Blessed are You, HASHEM, Who restores His Presence to Zion.* (Cong. – *Amen.)*

(1) Cf. *Nechemiah* 9:31.

other words, Succos is a time when each day until 'the end of the year' is considered and judged. [See *Yerushalmi Rosh Hashanah* 1:2 which resolves this in a different manner.]

Bow at מוֹדִים; straighten up at 'ה. The *chazzan* should recite the entire מוֹדִים aloud, while the congregation recites מודים דְּרַבָּנָן softly.

מוֹדִים אֲנַחְנוּ לָךְ, שָׁאַתָּה הוּא יהוה אֱלֹהֵינוּ וֵאלֹהֵי אֲבוֹתֵינוּ לְעוֹלָם וָעֶד. צוּר חַיֵּינוּ, מָגֵן יִשְׁעֵנוּ אַתָּה הוּא לְדוֹר וָדוֹר. נוֹדֶה לְּךָ וּנְסַפֵּר תְּהִלָּתֶךָ[1] עַל חַיֵּינוּ הַמְּסוּרִים בְּיָדֶךָ, וְעַל נִשְׁמוֹתֵינוּ הַפְּקוּדוֹת לָךְ, וְעַל נִסֶּיךָ שֶׁבְּכָל יוֹם עִמָּנוּ, וְעַל נִפְלְאוֹתֶיךָ וְטוֹבוֹתֶיךָ שֶׁבְּכָל עֵת, עֶרֶב וָבֹקֶר וְצָהֳרָיִם. הַטּוֹב כִּי לֹא כָלוּ רַחֲמֶיךָ, וְהַמְּרַחֵם כִּי לֹא תַמּוּ חֲסָדֶיךָ,[2] מֵעוֹלָם קִוִּינוּ לָךְ.

מודים דרבנן

מוֹדִים אֲנַחְנוּ לָךְ, שָׁאַתָּה הוּא יהוה אֱלֹהֵינוּ וֵאלֹהֵי אֲבוֹתֵינוּ, אֱלֹהֵי כָל בָּשָׂר, יוֹצְרֵנוּ, יוֹצֵר בְּרֵאשִׁית. בְּרָכוֹת וְהוֹדָאוֹת לְשִׁמְךָ הַגָּדוֹל וְהַקָּדוֹשׁ, עַל שֶׁהֶחֱיִיתָנוּ וְקִיַּמְתָּנוּ. כֵּן תְּחַיֵּנוּ וּתְקַיְּמֵנוּ, וְתֶאֱסוֹף גָּלֻיּוֹתֵינוּ לְחַצְרוֹת קָדְשֶׁךָ, לִשְׁמוֹר חֻקֶּיךָ וְלַעֲשׂוֹת רְצוֹנֶךָ, וּלְעָבְדְּךָ בְּלֵבָב שָׁלֵם, עַל שֶׁאֲנַחְנוּ מוֹדִים לָךְ. בָּרוּךְ אֵל הַהוֹדָאוֹת.

וְעַל כֻּלָּם יִתְבָּרַךְ וְיִתְרוֹמַם שִׁמְךָ מַלְכֵּנוּ תָּמִיד לְעוֹלָם וָעֶד.

The *chazzan* bends his knees at בָּרוּךְ; bows at אַתָּה; straightens up at 'ה.

וְכֹל הַחַיִּים יוֹדְוּךָ סֶּלָה, וִיהַלְלוּ אֶת שִׁמְךָ בֶּאֱמֶת, הָאֵל יְשׁוּעָתֵנוּ וְעֶזְרָתֵנוּ סֶלָה. בָּרוּךְ אַתָּה יהוה, הַטּוֹב שִׁמְךָ וּלְךָ נָאֶה לְהוֹדוֹת. (.Cong – אָמֵן.)

The *chazzan* recites בִּרְכַּת כֹּהֲנִים during his repetition. He faces right at וְיִשְׁמְרֶךָ; faces left at אֵלֶיךָ וִיחֻנֶּךָּ; faces the Ark for the rest of the blessings.

אֱלֹהֵינוּ, וֵאלֹהֵי אֲבוֹתֵינוּ, בָּרְכֵנוּ בַבְּרָכָה הַמְּשֻׁלֶּשֶׁת בַּתּוֹרָה הַכְּתוּבָה עַל יְדֵי מֹשֶׁה עַבְדֶּךָ, הָאֲמוּרָה מִפִּי אַהֲרֹן וּבָנָיו, כֹּהֲנִים עַם קְדוֹשֶׁךָ, כָּאָמוּר: יְבָרֶכְךָ יהוה, וְיִשְׁמְרֶךָ. (.Cong – כֵּן יְהִי רָצוֹן.)

יָאֵר יהוה פָּנָיו אֵלֶיךָ וִיחֻנֶּךָּ. (.Cong – כֵּן יְהִי רָצוֹן.)

יִשָּׂא יהוה פָּנָיו אֵלֶיךָ וְיָשֵׂם לְךָ שָׁלוֹם.[3] (.Cong – כֵּן יְהִי רָצוֹן.)

שִׂים שָׁלוֹם, טוֹבָה, וּבְרָכָה, חֵן, וָחֶסֶד וְרַחֲמִים עָלֵינוּ וְעַל כָּל יִשְׂרָאֵל עַמֶּךָ. בָּרְכֵנוּ אָבִינוּ, כֻּלָּנוּ כְּאֶחָד בְּאוֹר פָּנֶיךָ, כִּי בְאוֹר פָּנֶיךָ נָתַתָּ לָּנוּ, יהוה אֱלֹהֵינוּ, תּוֹרַת חַיִּים וְאַהֲבַת חֶסֶד, וּצְדָקָה, וּבְרָכָה, וְרַחֲמִים, וְחַיִּים, וְשָׁלוֹם. וְטוֹב בְּעֵינֶיךָ לְבָרֵךְ אֶת עַמְּךָ יִשְׂרָאֵל, בְּכָל עֵת וּבְכָל שָׁעָה בִּשְׁלוֹמֶךָ. בָּרוּךְ אַתָּה יהוה, הַמְּבָרֵךְ אֶת עַמּוֹ יִשְׂרָאֵל בַּשָּׁלוֹם. (.Cong– אָמֵן.)

in an undertone— יִהְיוּ לְרָצוֹן אִמְרֵי פִי וְהֶגְיוֹן לִבִּי לְפָנֶיךָ, יהוה צוּרִי וְגֹאֲלִי.[4]

CHAZZAN'S REPETITION ENDS HERE; TURN TO PAGE 284.

Bow at *'We gratefully thank You';* straighten up at *'HASHEM.'* The *chazzan* should recite the entire *Modim* aloud, while congregation recites *Modim of the Rabbis* softly.

מוֹדִים *We gratefully thank You, for it is You Who are HASHEM, our God and the God of our forefathers for all eternity; Rock of our lives, Shield of our salvation are You from generation to generation. We shall thank You and relate Your praise[1] — for our lives, which are committed to Your power and for our souls that are entrusted to You; for Your miracles that are with us every day; and for Your wonders and favors in every season — evening, morning, and afternoon. The Beneficent One, for Your compassions were never exhausted, and the Compassionate One, for Your kindnesses never ended[2] — always have we put our hope in You.*

MODIM OF THE RABBIS

מוֹדִים *We gratefully thank You, for it is You Who are HASHEM, our God and the God of our forefathers, the God of all flesh, our Molder, the Molder of the universe. Blessings and thanks are due Your great and holy Name for You have given us life and sustained us. So may You continue to give us life and sustain us and gather our exiles to the Courtyards of Your Sanctuary, to observe Your decrees, to do Your will and to serve You wholeheartedly. [We thank You] for inspiring us to thank You. Blessed is the God of thanksgivings.*

For all these, may Your Name be blessed and exalted, our King, continually forever and ever.

The *chazzan* bends his knees at *'Blessed';* bows at *'You';* straightens up at *'HASHEM.'*

Everything alive will gratefully acknowledge You, Selah! and praise Your Name sincerely, O God of our salvation and help, Selah! Blessed are You, HASHEM, Your Name is 'The Beneficent One' and to You it is fitting to give thanks. (Cong.— *Amen.*)

THE PRIESTLY BLESSING

The *chazzan* recites the Priestly Blessing during his repetition.

אֱלֹהֵינוּ *Our God and the God of our forefathers, bless us with the three-verse blessing in the Torah that was written by the hand of Moses, Your servant, that was said by Aaron and his sons, the Kohanim, Your holy people, as it is said:*

May HASHEM bless you and safeguard you. (Cong.— *So may it be.*)

May HASHEM illuminate His countenance for you and be gracious to you. (Cong.— *So may it be.*)

May HASHEM turn His countenance to you and establish peace for you.[3] (Cong.— *So may it be.*)

שִׂים שָׁלוֹם *Establish peace, goodness, blessing, graciousness, kindness, and compassion upon us and upon all of Your people Israel. Bless us, our Father, all of us as one, with the light of Your countenance, for with the light of Your countenance You gave us, HASHEM, our God, the Torah of life and a love of kindness, righteousness, blessing, compassion, life, and peace. And may it be good in Your eyes to bless Your people Israel at every time and every hour with Your peace. Blessed are You, HASHEM, Who blesses His people Israel with peace.* (Cong.— *Amen.*)

May the expressions of my mouth and the thoughts of my heart find favor before You, HASHEM, my Rock and my Redeemer.[4]

CHAZZAN'S REPETITION ENDS HERE; TURN TO PAGE 284.

(1) Cf. *Psalms* 79:13. (2) Cf. *Lamentations* 3:22. (3) *Numbers* 6:24-26. (4) *Psalms* 19:15.

The Four Species and Hallel

◆§ Some Laws of the Four Species

If at all possible one should not eat or drink before taking the Four Species.

Most *siddurim* place the blessing of the Four Species just before *Hallel*, in accordance with the ruling of *Shulchan Aruch* (644:1) that the Four Species be taken between *Shemoneh Esrei* and *Hallel*. However, many follow *Arizal's* view that these blessings should be recited in the *succah*, and therefore, recite them before entering the synagogue for *Shacharis*.

The שֶׁהֶחֱיָנוּ blessing is recited on the first day that the Four Species are taken. Thus, if the first day of Succos coincides with the Sabbath, when the Four Species are not taken, this blessing is recited on Sunday. Additionally, if one was unable to take the Four Species on the first day of Succos, he recites this blessing the first time he is able to, regardless of which day of Succos it is. [A full exposition of the significance and laws of the *mitzvah* may be found in the ArtScroll *Succos*.]

In addition to holding the Four Species together — which is sufficient for performance of the commandment — one should also perform the *na'anu'im* or *waving* of the Four Species in six directions — the four points of the compass, up and down. It is preferable that one face east while waving the Four Species. The sequence followed in most Ashkenaz congregations is: straight ahead (i.e., east), right (south), back (west), left (north), up and down.

The generally followed manner of waving is to stretch out the arms and shake strongly enough to rustle the *lulav's* leaves, and then to draw the Species close to the chest and shake again. This is done three times in each direction *(Rama, Orach Chaim* 651:9).

The Four Species are also held during the recitation of *Hallel* and *Hoshanos*. During certain verses of *Hallel*, they are waved again in the manner described above. Although one should follow the custom of his own congregation, the customary rule is to wave the Species each time the verses הודו לַה׳ כִּי טוב and אָנָּא ה׳ הוֹשִׁיעָה נָּא are recited (ibid. 651:8).

For further details, see *Laws* §171-174.

◆§ Na'anu'im / The Waving of the Species

A Midrash is cited as the source for the practice of waving the Four Species that also explains why they are waved during *Hallel*.

Scripture states (*I Chronicles* 16:33-35): אָז יְרַנְּנוּ עֲצֵי הַיָּעַר מִלִּפְנֵי ה׳ כִּי בָא לִשְׁפּוֹט אֶת הָאָרֶץ. הוֹדוּ לַה׳ כִּי טוֹב כִּי לְעוֹלָם חַסְדּוֹ. וְאִמְרוּ הוֹשִׁיעֵנוּ אֱלֹהֵי יִשְׁעֵנוּ . . ., *Then shall the trees of the forest sing joyfully before* HASHEM *for He will have come to judge the earth. Give thanks to* HASHEM *for He is good; for His loving-kindness is eternal. And say, 'Save us, O God of our salvation . . .'*

The Midrash comments: When Israel and the nations are brought to trial on Rosh Hashanah it is not known who is found innocent and who is found guilty. Therefore, God granted this *mitzvah* to Israel — so that they rejoice with their *lulavim* as one who emerges innocent from before the judge.

This, then, is the meaning of the verse אָז יְרַנְּנוּ עֲצֵי הַיָּעַר, *then shall the trees of the forest sing*. The Jewish people will sing with the trees of the forest — i.e., holding their *lulavim* which came from date palms — by waving them when they emerge innocent [לִפְנֵי ה׳] *before God* [כִּי בָא לִשְׁפּוֹט הָאָרֶץ] *when He will have come to judge the earth*. And when do they wave? When they recite הודו

לַה׳, *Give thanks to HASHEM* . . . and when they recite אָנָּא ה׳ הוֹשִׁיעָה נָּא, *Please HASHEM bring salvation now* [which corresponds to וְאִמְרוּ הוֹשִׁיעֵנוּ אֱלֹהֵי יִשְׁעֵנוּ, *And say: 'Save us, O God of our Salvation'*] (*Tos.* 37b; *Rosh* 3:26).

The symbolism of these *na'anu'im* is given in the Talmud (ibid.) as follows: 'One waves them back and forth to Him Who is the Master of the four directions; up and down to Him Who is the Master of heaven and earth. Thus, the Four Species allude to God's creation of all existence, and testify that there is naught besides Him.'

The Talmud also states: 'One waves them back and forth to restrain harmful winds; up and down to restrain harmful dews.' Since Succos is the time of judgment for water and rain for the entire year, the nature of the Four Species symbolizes our prayer for water: the *esrog* tree requires more water than others; palm trees grow best in valleys that have abundant water; myrtles and willows grow near water. In waving the Four Species in all six directions, we therefore symbolically say to God: Just as these Four Species cannot exist without water, so can the world not exist without water. And when You give us water, let no harmful winds or dews negate Your blessing.

◆§ The Entire Hallel

On each of the seven days of Succos and on the concluding holiday, Shemini Atzeres, the entire *Hallel* (*Psalms* 113-118) is recited [see *Succah* 4:1,8]. This is in contrast to Pesach when the entire *Hallel* is recited only on the first day (in the Diaspora on the first two days). The Talmud (*Arachin* 10a-b) explains that this distinction between Succos and Pesach is based on the difference between their respective *mussaf* offerings (*Numbers* 28:19-25; 29:13-34). During Pesach the *mussaf* offering consists of the same number of bulls, rams, sheep, and goats for each day. On Succos, although the numbers of rams, sheep, and goats are the same every day, the amount of bulls is diminished by one on each successive day. *Rashi* (*Taanis* 28b, s.v. יחיד) and *Tosafos* (loc. cit., s.v. ויום) explain that this changing number of bulls offered indicates that Succos should be considered a set of separate one-day festivals, each of which requires its own recitation of *Hallel*, whereas all of Pesach should be regarded as a single festival spread out over a seven-day period, for which a single full *Hallel* at the beginning is sufficient.

Although the entire *Hallel* is not recited on the last six days of Pesach, an abridged version which omits the first eleven verses of Psalms 115 and of 116 is recited on these days. The same verses are omitted on Rosh Chodesh. This abridged form is popularly known as 'half' *Hallel*.

Another interpretation of why only 'half' *Hallel* is said on the intermediate and final day(s) of Pesach is that since the Egyptians drowned on the seventh day of Pesach it would be inappropriate to offer excessive praise to God on a day when so many people died — even though they were our enemies. As the Talmud [*Megillah* 10b] records, the angels wished to utter songs of praise to God upon the drowning of the Egyptians, but He rebuked them saying: 'My handiwork [the Egyptians] are drowning in the sea and you utter praise!' Accordingly, so as not to make the Intermediate Days of Pesach appear more important than the final day(s), we recite only 'half' *Hallel* throughout the Intermediate Days of Pesach as well (*Turei Zahav, Orach Chaim* 490:3; see *Beis Yosef* there). It is true that the entire Jewish people *did* sing praises to God at the Sea of Reeds, despite the fate of the Egyptians, but God did not object, because people whose own lives were in danger praise God for helping them.

נטילת לולב

Many recite the following declaration of intent before taking the Four Species:

יְהִי רָצוֹן* מִלְּפָנֶיךָ, יהוה אֱלֹהַי וֵאלֹהֵי אֲבוֹתַי, בִּפְרִי עֵץ הָדָר,* וְכַפּוֹת תְּמָרִים,* וַעֲנַף עֵץ עָבוֹת,* וְעַרְבֵי נָחַל,*[1] אוֹתִיּוֹת שִׁמְךָ הַמְּיֻחָד* תְּקָרֵב אֶחָד אֶל אֶחָד, וְהָיוּ לַאֲחָדִים בְּיָדִי, וְלֵידַע אֵיךְ שִׁמְךָ נִקְרָא עָלַי, וְיִירְאוּ מִגֶּשֶׁת אֵלָי. וּבְנַעֲנוּעִי אוֹתָם תַּשְׁפִּיעַ שֶׁפַע בְּרָכוֹת מִדַּעַת עֶלְיוֹן לִנְוֵה אַפִּרְיוֹן, לִמְכוֹן בֵּית אֱלֹהֵינוּ. וּתְהֵא חֲשׁוּבָה לְפָנֶיךָ מִצְוַת אַרְבָּעָה מִינִים אֵלּוּ, כְּאִלּוּ קִיַּמְתִּיהָ בְּכָל פְּרָטוֹתֶיהָ וְשָׁרָשֶׁיהָ וְתַרְיַ״ג מִצְוֹת הַתְּלוּיִם בָּהּ. כִּי כַוָּנָתִי* לְיַחֲדָא שְׁמָא דְקֻדְשָׁא בְּרִיךְ הוּא וּשְׁכִינְתֵּהּ, בִּדְחִילוּ וּרְחִימוּ, לְיַחֵד שֵׁם י״ה בְּו״ה בְּיִחוּדָא שְׁלִים, בְּשֵׁם כָּל יִשְׂרָאֵל. אָמֵן. בָּרוּךְ יהוה לְעוֹלָם, אָמֵן, וְאָמֵן.[2]

The Four Species — *lulav, haddasim, aravos, esrog* — are taken in hand every day of Succos — through *Hoshana Rabbah* — except on the Sabbath. The *lulav*-bundle is picked up with the right hand, then the *esrog* (with the *pitam* facing down) with the left. After the blessings are recited, the *esrog* is turned over and the Four Species are waved in the six directions. (See page 284).

בָּרוּךְ אַתָּה יהוה אֱלֹהֵינוּ מֶלֶךְ הָעוֹלָם, אֲשֶׁר קִדְּשָׁנוּ בְּמִצְוֹתָיו, וְצִוָּנוּ עַל נְטִילַת* לוּלָב.*

The following blessing is added only on the first day that the Four Species are taken.

בָּרוּךְ אַתָּה יהוה אֱלֹהֵינוּ מֶלֶךְ הָעוֹלָם, שֶׁהֶחֱיָנוּ וְקִיְּמָנוּ וְהִגִּיעָנוּ לַזְּמַן הַזֶּה.

נְטִילַת לוּלָב / THE FOUR SPECIES

The Torah commands the taking of the Four Species and concludes: *You shall be joyous before* HASHEM *... (Leviticus* 23:40). The Midrash explains the connection between this *mitzvah* and joyousness:

In earlier days if a litigant's claim before the royal court was decided in his favor, he would receive a spear from the king. When he left the palace holding the king's spear aloft all knew that he had been victorious in his suit. Similarly, during the Days of Awe, the Jewish people were on trial before the Heavenly Court. On Succos, 'the season of joy,' we celebrate our happiness that God has accepted our repentance — a confidence symbolized by the *lulav* held aloft.

יְהִי רָצוֹן — *May it be Your will.* This prayer, as well as many others that are heavy with kabbalistic impications, was introduced by the seventeenth-century master of kabbalah, R' Nassan of Hanover, and first appeared in his *Sha'arei Tzion* (Prague, 5422/1662).

בִּפְרִי עֵץ הָדָר — *Through the fruit of the esrog* [lit. *beautiful*] *tree.* The Torah does not specify the *esrog* by name, but uses this descriptive phrase. *Targum* renders הָדָר, *beautiful,* as אֶתְרוֹגִין, *esrogim.*

From the Torah's use of the word פְּרִי, *fruit* (in the singular), rather than פֵּרוֹת, *fruits,* the Talmud (*Succah* 34b) derives that only a single *esrog* is taken.

וְכַפּוֹת תְּמָרִים — *Date-palm branches,* i.e., *the lulav.* Although this term appears in *Leviticus* 23:40 in the plural form, branches, the Talmud understands the verse to indicate that only a single *lulav* be used. In the Torah, the word for branches is spelled כַּפֹּת with the letter ו omitted. Since the Torah is written without vowelpoints, it is possible to read the words as כַּפַּת תְּמָרִים, *a 'branch' of date-palms (Succah* 34b as explained by *Rashi).* Generally, a word written in the plural form is taken to mean exactly two; if more were required, the Torah should have specified how many (see below). In our case, however, the use of the deficient spelling implies that the word is to be understood in the singular.

In the Scriptural verse, the terms for *esrog* and *lulav* are not connected by the conjunctive ו, *and.* However, conjunctions do connect the terms for *lulav, haddasim* (myrtle), and *aravos* (willow). From this it is derived that the species are to be held in two groups: the *esrog* by itself; and a bundle containing the *lulav, haddasim* and *aravos (Succah* 24b).

וַעֲנַף עֵץ עָבוֹת — *Twigs of the myrtle tree,* i.e., *haddasim.* Literally, עֵץ עָבוֹת means a *thick* or *plaited* tree. The Talmud *(Succah* 32b) understands this to refer to a species whose leaf

THE FOUR SPECIES/LULAV AND ESROG

Many recite the following declaration of intent before taking the Four Species:

יְהִי רָצוֹן *May it be Your will,* HASHEM, my God and the God of my forefathers, that through the fruit of the esrog tree,* date-palm branches,* twigs of the myrtle tree,* and brook willows,[1]* the letters of Your unified Name* may become close to one another, that they may become united in my hand; and to make known that Your Name is called upon me, that [evil forces] may be fearful of approaching me. And when I wave them, may an abundant outpouring of blessings flow from the wisdom of the Most High to the abode of the tabernacle, to the prepared place of the House of our God. And may the mitzvah of these Four Species be reckoned before You as if I had fulfilled it with all its particulars, roots, and the six hundred thirteen mitzvos dependent on it. For my intention* is to unify the Name of the Holy One, Blessed is He, and His Presence, in awe and in love, to unify the Name Yud-Kei with Vav-Kei in perfect unity, in the name of all Israel; Amen. Blessed is HASHEM forever, Amen and Amen.[2]*

The Four Species — *lulav, haddasim, aravos, esrog* — are taken in hand every day of Succos — through *Hoshana Rabbah* — except on the Sabbath. The *lulav*-bundle is picked up with the right hand, then the *esrog* (with the *pitam* facing down) with the left. After the blessings are recited, the *esrog* is turned over and the Four Species are waved in the six directions. (See page 284).

בָּרוּךְ *Blessed are You, HASHEM, our God, King of the universe, Who has sanctified us with His commandments and has commanded us concerning the taking* of a palm branch.**

The following blessing is added only on the first day that the Four Species are taken.

בָּרוּךְ *Blessed are You, HASHEM, our God, King of the universe, Who has kept us alive, sustained us, and brought us to this season.*

(1) Cf. *Leviticus* 23:40. (2) *Psalms* 89:53.

---

coverage is thick, completely covering the twig, and whose leaves overlap each other, as if braided — and identify it as the הֲדַס, *myrtle.*

The fact that the Torah does not call the myrtle tree by name, but instead gives a three-word description, is taken to imply that three myrtle twigs should be included in the *lulav*-bundle (*Succah* 34b).

וְעַרְבֵי נָחַל— *And brook willows.* The unspecied plural is taken as meaning two, the least amount to which the plural form may be applied. If more than two were needed the number would have been given (*Succah* 34b).

Tosafos writes that although the verse implies three myrtle twigs and two willows, these numbers are given only as minimums. A larger number of either species may be taken. *Rambam* (*Lulav* 7:7), on the other hand, maintains that it is forbidden to take more or less than two willows, one *lulav* and one *esrog*. One may, however, adorn his *lulav*-bundle with additional myrtle twigs.

אוֹתִיּוֹת שִׁמְךָ הַמְיֻחָד — *The letters of Your unified Name.* Kabbalah teaches that each of the Four Species is identified with another of the letters of the Four-Letter Name of God. Rabbi Michael Ber Weissmandl (in *Toras Chemed*) adduces a complex series of calculations to prove that the *aravos, lulav, haddasim,* and *esrog* correspond, in that order, with the four letters of the Name.

כַּוָּנָתִי — *My intention.* Even one who has spent much time and money on perfect species should not taint the performance of his *mitzvah* by boasting about his acquisition. Rather, his intention in fulfilling the *mitzvah* should be above personal considerations. It is not coincidental that the initials of the verse (*Psalms* 36:12): אַל תְּבוֹאֵנִי רֶגֶל גַּאֲוָה, *Bring me not [to] the foot of arrogance,* form the word אֶתְרֹג (*Baal Shem Tov*).

☙ עַל נְטִילַת— *Concerning the taking.* In stating the *mitzvah* of *lulav,* the Torah uses the expression וּלְקַחְתֶּם, *and you shall take,* from the root לקח. Rabbinical literature, however, uses the word נְטִילָה, from the root נטל, almost exclusively when the Four Species are mentioned. Various reasons are given regarding the substitution of the Rabbinical form נְטִילָה for the Scriptural form לְקִיחָה in the blessing over the *lulav*-bundle. *Eliyah Rabbah* understands that the change is based on the desire to avoid a running together of the double ל in the two words עַל לְקִיחַת. Use of נְטִילַת prevents this corrupt pronunciation. [See *Tosafos* to *Berachos*

הלל

The *chazzan* recites the blessing. The congregation, after responding אָמֵן, repeats it, and continues with the first psalm.

בָּרוּךְ אַתָּה יהוה אֱלֹהֵינוּ מֶלֶךְ הָעוֹלָם, אֲשֶׁר קִדְּשָׁנוּ בְּמִצְוֹתָיו, וְצִוָּנוּ לִקְרוֹא אֶת הַהַלֵּל. (.Cong— אָמֵן.)

תהלים קיג

הַלְלוּיָהּ הַלְלוּ עַבְדֵי יהוה,* הַלְלוּ אֶת שֵׁם יהוה. יְהִי שֵׁם יהוה מְבֹרָךְ, מֵעַתָּה וְעַד עוֹלָם. מִמִּזְרַח שֶׁמֶשׁ עַד מְבוֹאוֹ, מְהֻלָּל שֵׁם יהוה. רָם עַל כָּל גּוֹיִם יהוה, עַל הַשָּׁמַיִם כְּבוֹדוֹ. מִי כַּיהוה אֱלֹהֵינוּ, הַמַּגְבִּיהִי לָשָׁבֶת. הַמַּשְׁפִּילִי לִרְאוֹת, בַּשָּׁמַיִם וּבָאָרֶץ.* ❖ מְקִימִי מֵעָפָר דָּל, מֵאַשְׁפֹּת יָרִים אֶבְיוֹן. לְהוֹשִׁיבִי עִם נְדִיבִים,* עִם נְדִיבֵי עַמּוֹ. מוֹשִׁיבִי עֲקֶרֶת הַבַּיִת,* אֵם הַבָּנִים שְׂמֵחָה, הַלְלוּיָהּ.

תהלים קיד

בְּצֵאת יִשְׂרָאֵל מִמִּצְרָיִם,* בֵּית יַעֲקֹב מֵעַם לֹעֵז.* הָיְתָה יְהוּדָה לְקָדְשׁוֹ,* יִשְׂרָאֵל מַמְשְׁלוֹתָיו. הַיָּם רָאָה וַיָּנֹס, הַיַּרְדֵּן יִסֹּב לְאָחוֹר. הֶהָרִים רָקְדוּ כְאֵילִים,* גְּבָעוֹת כִּבְנֵי צֹאן. ❖ מַה לְּךָ הַיָּם כִּי תָנוּס, הַיַּרְדֵּן תִּסֹּב לְאָחוֹר.* הֶהָרִים תִּרְקְדוּ כְאֵילִים, גְּבָעוֹת כִּבְנֵי צֹאן. מִלִּפְנֵי אָדוֹן חוּלִי אָרֶץ, מִלִּפְנֵי אֱלוֹהַּ יַעֲקֹב. הַהֹפְכִי הַצּוּר אֲגַם מָיִם,* חַלָּמִישׁ לְמַעְיְנוֹ מָיִם.

38b where a similar reason is given to explain the prefix הַ of the word הַמּוֹצִיא in the blessing over bread.]

Alternatively, the word לְקִיחָה has the additional meaning of *buying*, a connotation not shared by the word נְטִילָה. Lest one mistakenly think that he must purchase the Four Species, rather than use those grown in his field, the word נְטִילָה is used (*R' Munk*).

לוּלָב — *A palm branch.* The Talmud (*Succah* 37b) explains that only the *lulav* is mentioned in the benediction since the date-palm tree, of which the *lulav* is a branch, is taller than any of the other species.

הַלֵּל / HALLEL

The prophets ordained that the six psalms of *Hallel* [literally, *praise*] be recited on each Festival, and to commemorate times of national deliverance from peril. Moreover, before David redacted and incorporated these psalms into the Book of Psalms, *Hallel* was already known to the nation: Moses and Israel recited it after being saved from the Egyptians at the sea; Joshua, after defeating the Kings of Canaan; Deborah and Barak, after defeating Sisera. Later, Hezekiah recited it after defeating Sennacherib; Chananyah, Mishael and Azariah, after being saved from the wicked Nebuchadnezzar; and Mordechai and Esther, after the defeat of the wicked Haman (*Pesachim* 117a).

These psalms were singled out as the unit of praise because they contain five fundamental themes of Jewish faith: the Exodus, the Splitting of the Sea, the Giving of the Torah at Sinai, the future Resuscitation of the dead, and the coming of the Messiah (ibid. 118a).

הַלְלוּיָהּ הַלְלוּ עַבְדֵי ה׳ — *Halleluyah! Give praise, you servants of HASHEM.* Only after their liberation from Pharaoh's bondage could the Jews be considered the *servants of HASHEM,* because they no longer vowed allegiance to any other ruler.

הַמַּשְׁפִּילִי לִרְאוֹת בַּשָּׁמַיִם וּבָאָרֶץ — *Yet deigns to look* [lit., *bends low to see*] *upon the heaven and the earth?* This is the challenging and exciting aspect of God's relationship to man: As we act towards God, so does He react to us. If we ignore His presence, He withdraws high *above the*

HALLEL

The *chazzan* recites the blessing. The congregation, after responding *Amen,* repeats it, and continues with the first psalm.

בָּרוּךְ *Blessed are You,* HASHEM, *our God, King of the universe, Who has sanctified us with His commandments and has commanded us to read the Hallel.* (Cong.— *Amen.*)

Psalm 113

הַלְלוּיָהּ *Halleluyah! Give praise, you servants of* HASHEM;* *praise the Name of* HASHEM! *Blessed be the Name of* HASHEM, *from this time and forever. From the rising of the sun to its setting,* HASHEM's *Name is praised. High above all nations is* HASHEM, *above the heavens is His glory. Who is like* HASHEM, *our God, Who is enthroned on high — yet deigns to look upon the heaven and the earth?** Chazzan— *He raises the needy from the dust, from the trash heaps He lifts the destitute. To seat them with nobles,* with the nobles of His people. He transforms the barren wife* into a glad mother of children. Halleluyah!*

Psalm 114

בְּצֵאת *When Israel went out of Egypt,* Jacob's household from a people of alien tongue* — Judah became His sanctuary,* Israel His dominions. The sea saw and fled: the Jordan turned backward. The mountains skipped like rams,* the hills like young lambs.* Chazzan— *What ails you, O sea, that you flee? O Jordan, that you turn backward?* O mountains, that you skip like rams? O hills, like young lambs? Before the Lord's Presence — did I, the earth, tremble — before the presence of the God of Jacob, Who turns the rock into a pond of water,* the flint into a flowing fountain.*

---

heavens; but if we welcome His proximity, He lovingly involves Himself in every phase of our lives *(R' A.C. Feuer).*

לְהוֹשִׁיבִי עִם נְדִיבִים — *To seat them with nobles.* God does not merely lift the poor and needy out of degradation; He also elevates them to the highest ranks of nobility.

מוֹשִׁיבִי עֲקֶרֶת הַבַּיִת — *He transforms the barren wife.* The Creator exercises complete control over nature. This control is vividly demonstrated when God suddenly transforms a barren woman into a mother *(Radak).*

☙ **בְּצֵאת יִשְׂרָאֵל מִמִּצְרָיִם** — *When Israel went out of Egypt.* This second chapter of Hallel continues the theme of the first chapter, which praises God for raising up the needy and destitute. Israel was thus elevated when they left Egypt and risked their lives by entering the sea at God's command.

בֵּית יַעֲקֹב מֵעַם לֹעֵז — *Jacob's household from a people of alien tongue.* Even the Jews who were forced to communicate with the Egyptians in the language of the land did so only under duress. Among themselves, however, they spoke only the Holy Tongue and regarded Egyptian as a foreign language.

הָיְתָה יְהוּדָה לְקָדְשׁוֹ — *Judah became His sanctuary.* God singled out the tribe of Judah to be the family of royalty, because they sanctified God's Name at the Sea of Reeds. Led by their prince, Nachshon ben Aminadav, this tribe was the first to jump into the threatening waters *(Rosh).*

הֶהָרִים רָקְדוּ כְאֵילִים — *The mountains skipped like rams.* When Israel received the Torah, Sinai and the neighboring mountains and hills shook and trembled at the manifestation of God's Presence and the thunder and lightning that accompanied it.

מַה לְּךָ הַיָּם כִּי תָנוּס הַיַּרְדֵּן תִּסֹּב לְאָחוֹר — *What ails you, O sea, that you flee? O Jordan, that you turn backward?* The Psalmist captures the sense of awe and bewilderment which then seized mankind.

הַהֹפְכִי הַצּוּר אֲגַם מָיִם — *Who turns the rock into a pond of water.* When the Jews thirsted for water in the wilderness, God instructed Moses *(Exodus* 17:6), *'You shall smite the rock and water shall come out of it, so that the people may drink.'*

תהלים קטו:א-יא

לֹא לָנוּ* יהוה לֹא לָנוּ, כִּי לְשִׁמְךָ תֵּן כָּבוֹד,* עַל חַסְדְּךָ עַל אֲמִתֶּךָ. לָמָּה יֹאמְרוּ הַגּוֹיִם, אַיֵּה נָא אֱלֹהֵיהֶם. וֵאלֹהֵינוּ בַשָּׁמָיִם, כֹּל אֲשֶׁר חָפֵץ עָשָׂה. עֲצַבֵּיהֶם כֶּסֶף וְזָהָב, מַעֲשֵׂה יְדֵי אָדָם. פֶּה לָהֶם וְלֹא יְדַבֵּרוּ,* עֵינַיִם לָהֶם וְלֹא יִרְאוּ. אָזְנַיִם לָהֶם וְלֹא יִשְׁמָעוּ, אַף לָהֶם וְלֹא יְרִיחוּן. יְדֵיהֶם וְלֹא יְמִישׁוּן, רַגְלֵיהֶם וְלֹא יְהַלֵּכוּ, לֹא יֶהְגּוּ בִּגְרוֹנָם. כְּמוֹהֶם יִהְיוּ עֹשֵׂיהֶם, כֹּל אֲשֶׁר בֹּטֵחַ בָּהֶם. ❖ יִשְׂרָאֵל בְּטַח בַּיהוה,* עֶזְרָם וּמָגִנָּם הוּא.* בֵּית אַהֲרֹן בִּטְחוּ בַיהוה, עֶזְרָם וּמָגִנָּם הוּא. יִרְאֵי יהוה בִּטְחוּ בַיהוה, עֶזְרָם וּמָגִנָּם הוּא.

תהלים קטו:יב-יח

יהוה זְכָרָנוּ יְבָרֵךְ,* יְבָרֵךְ אֶת בֵּית יִשְׂרָאֵל, יְבָרֵךְ אֶת בֵּית אַהֲרֹן. יְבָרֵךְ יִרְאֵי יהוה, הַקְּטַנִּים עִם הַגְּדֹלִים. יֹסֵף יהוה עֲלֵיכֶם, עֲלֵיכֶם וְעַל בְּנֵיכֶם.* בְּרוּכִים אַתֶּם לַיהוה, עֹשֵׂה שָׁמַיִם וָאָרֶץ. ❖ הַשָּׁמַיִם שָׁמַיִם לַיהוה, וְהָאָרֶץ נָתַן לִבְנֵי אָדָם.* לֹא הַמֵּתִים יְהַלְלוּ יָהּ,* וְלֹא כָּל יֹרְדֵי דוּמָה. וַאֲנַחְנוּ נְבָרֵךְ יָהּ, מֵעַתָּה וְעַד עוֹלָם, הַלְלוּיָהּ.

תהלים קטז:א-יא

אָהַבְתִּי* כִּי יִשְׁמַע יהוה, אֶת קוֹלִי תַּחֲנוּנָי. כִּי הִטָּה אָזְנוֹ לִי,

---

⊱ **לֹא לָנוּ** ⊰ — *Not for our sake.* The preceding psalm depicts the awe inspired by God's miracles. Here the Psalmist describes the aftermath of that inspiration. Although Israel remained imbued with faith, our oppressors soon began to scoff, 'Where is their God?' We pray that God will intervene again in the affairs of man, not for our sake, but for His.

לֹא לָנוּ ה׳ . . . כִּי לְשִׁמְךָ תֵּן כָּבוֹד — *Not for our sake, HASHEM . . . but for Your Name's sake give glory.* We beg You to redeem us, but not because we are personally worthy, nor because of the merit of our forefathers *(Iyun Tefillah).* Rather we urgently strive to protect Your glorious Name, so that no one can deny Your mastery and dominion *(Radak).*

פֶּה לָהֶם וְלֹא יְדַבֵּרוּ — *They have a mouth, but cannot speak.* These illustrations emphasize the complete impotence of man-made idols, which even lack the senses that every ordinary man possesses.

יִשְׂרָאֵל בְּטַח בַּה׳ — *O Israel, trust in HASHEM.* The psalm now contrasts the Children of Israel, who trust in God alone, with those described in the previous verse, who trust in the lifeless and helpless idols *(Ibn Ezra).*

The Psalmist speaks of three kinds of Jews, each with a different motive for serving God. Some Jews cling to God simply because they feel that He is their Father, and they are His devoted sons. These are called יִשְׂרָאֵל, *Israel,* God's chosen, beloved nation. The second group serves God out of love. They resemble the *House of Aaron,* the *Kohanim*-priests who never betrayed God and were therefore designated to stand in His presence, in the Temple, for all time. Finally, *you who fear HASHEM* refers to a third group of Jews, who serve God out of fear and awe *(Maharal).*

עֶזְרָם וּמָגִנָּם הוּא — *Their help and their shield is He!* This is thrice repeated. Since each successive group possesses a different level of faith, it deserves a totally different degree of divine protection. Thus, God's reaction to each group is mentioned separately.

⊱ **ה׳ זְכָרָנוּ יְבָרֵךְ** ⊰ — *HASHEM Who has remembered us will bless.* The Psalmist expresses

Psalms 115:1-11

לֹא לָנוּ *Not for our sake,* HASHEM, not for our sake, but for Your Name's sake give glory,* for Your kindness and for Your truth! Why should the nations say, 'Where is their God now?' Our God is in the heavens; whatever He pleases, He does! Their idols are silver and gold, the handiwork of man. They have a mouth, but cannot speak;* they have eyes, but cannot see. They have ears, but cannot hear; they have a nose, but cannot smell. Their hands — they cannot feel; their feet — they cannot walk; they cannot utter a sound from their throat. Those who make them should become like them, whoever trusts in them!* Chazzan– *O Israel, trust in HASHEM;* — their help and their shield is He!* House of Aaron, trust in HASHEM; their help and their shield is He! You who fear HASHEM, trust in HASHEM; their help and their shield is He!*

Psalm 115:12-18

יהוה *HASHEM Who has remembered us will bless* — He will bless the House of Israel; He will bless the House of Aaron; He will bless those who fear HASHEM, the small as well as the great. May HASHEM increase upon you, upon you and upon your children!* You are blessed of HASHEM, maker of heaven and earth.* Chazzan– *As for the heavens — the heavens are HASHEM's, but the earth He has given to mankind.* Neither the dead can praise God,* nor any who descend into silence; but we will bless God from this time and forever. Halleluyah!*

Psalm 116:1-11

אָהַבְתִּי *I love Him,* for HASHEM hears my voice, my supplications. As He has inclined His ear to me, so in my days shall I*

---

confidence that just as God has blessed His people in the past, so He will bless them in the future.

יֹסֵף ה׳ עֲלֵיכֶם, עֲלֵיכֶם וְעַל בְּנֵיכֶם — *May HASHEM increase upon you, upon you and upon your children.* The true nature of בְּרָכָה, *blessing,* means increase and abundance *(Ibn Ezra).*

Abarbanel explains that the Psalmist foresaw that Israel would suffer from attrition in exile and they would fear eventual extinction. Therefore, he offers the assurance that, at the advent of the Messiah, they will increase dramatically.

הַשָּׁמַיִם שָׁמַיִם לַה׳, וְהָאָרֶץ נָתַן לִבְנֵי אָדָם — *As for the heavens — the heavens are HASHEM's, but the earth He has given to mankind.* Since the heavens remain under God's firm control, all celestial bodies are forced to act in accordance with His will without freedom of choice. On earth, however, man was granted the freedom to determine his own actions and beliefs *(Maharit).*

Many commentators explain this verse homiletically. Man need not perfect heaven because it is already dedicated to the holiness of God. But the earth is man's province. We are bidden to perfect it and transform its material nature into something spiritual. Indeed, we were created to make the earth heavenly.

לֹא הַמֵּתִים יְהַלְלוּ יָהּ — *Neither the dead can praise God.* The people who fail to recognize God's omnipresence and influence over the world resemble the dead, who are insensitive to all external stimuli and who are oblivious to reality *(R' Azariah Figo).* However, the souls of the righteous continue to praise God even after they depart from their bodies *(Ibn Ezra).*

A dried-out, bleached, or brittle *lulav* is invalid for use during the Festival of Succos, because the *lulav* symbolizes the human spine, which enables man to lead an active life. Thus the *lulav* must be fresh and supple, for the dead cannot praise God *(Yalkut Shimoni* 873).

☙ **אָהַבְתִּי** — *I love [Him].* The Psalmist foresaw that Israel would feel completely alone in exile. The nations would taunt them, 'Your prayers and pleas are worthless, because God has turned a deaf ear to you.' Therefore, he composed this

וּבְיָמַי אֶקְרָא. אֲפָפוּנִי חֶבְלֵי מָוֶת,* וּמְצָרֵי שְׁאוֹל מְצָאוּנִי, צָרָה וְיָגוֹן אֶמְצָא. וּבְשֵׁם יהוה אֶקְרָא, אָנָּה יהוה מַלְּטָה נַפְשִׁי. חַנּוּן יהוה וְצַדִּיק, וֵאלֹהֵינוּ מְרַחֵם. שֹׁמֵר פְּתָאִים יהוה, דַּלּוֹתִי וְלִי יְהוֹשִׁיעַ. שׁוּבִי נַפְשִׁי לִמְנוּחָיְכִי,* כִּי יהוה גָּמַל עָלָיְכִי. כִּי חִלַּצְתָּ נַפְשִׁי מִמָּוֶת, אֶת עֵינִי מִן דִּמְעָה, אֶת רַגְלִי מִדֶּחִי. ❖ אֶתְהַלֵּךְ לִפְנֵי יהוה, בְּאַרְצוֹת הַחַיִּים.* הֶאֱמַנְתִּי כִּי אֲדַבֵּר, אֲנִי עָנִיתִי מְאֹד. אֲנִי אָמַרְתִּי בְחָפְזִי, כָּל הָאָדָם כֹּזֵב.*

תהלים קטז:יב-יט

מָה אָשִׁיב לַיהוה,* כָּל תַּגְמוּלוֹהִי עָלָי. כּוֹס יְשׁוּעוֹת אֶשָּׂא,* וּבְשֵׁם יהוה אֶקְרָא. נְדָרַי לַיהוה אֲשַׁלֵּם,* נֶגְדָה נָּא לְכָל עַמּוֹ. יָקָר בְּעֵינֵי יהוה, הַמָּוְתָה לַחֲסִידָיו. אָנָּה יהוה כִּי אֲנִי עַבְדֶּךָ, אֲנִי עַבְדְּךָ, בֶּן אֲמָתֶךָ,* פִּתַּחְתָּ לְמוֹסֵרָי. ❖ לְךָ אֶזְבַּח זֶבַח תּוֹדָה, וּבְשֵׁם יהוה אֶקְרָא. נְדָרַי לַיהוה אֲשַׁלֵּם, נֶגְדָה נָּא לְכָל עַמּוֹ. בְּחַצְרוֹת בֵּית יהוה, בְּתוֹכֵכִי יְרוּשָׁלָיִם הַלְלוּיָהּ.

Congregation, then *chazzan:*

תהלים קיז

הַלְלוּ אֶת יהוה,* כָּל גּוֹיִם, שַׁבְּחוּהוּ כָּל הָאֻמִּים.* כִּי גָבַר עָלֵינוּ חַסְדּוֹ,* וֶאֱמֶת יהוה לְעוֹלָם, הַלְלוּיָהּ.

---

psalm to encourage the downcast exiles with the assurance that indeed: *HASHEM hears my voice, my supplications.*

The Talmud *(Rosh Hashanah* 16b-17a) explains that this psalm describes the day of Final Judgment at the time of תְּחִיַּת הַמֵּתִים, *the Resurrection of the Dead.* The average people, who are neither completely righteous nor completely wicked, will be saved from Gehinnom because God will hear their cries, and He will forgive them. In gratitude, they will sing, *'I love Him, for HASHEM hears my voice, my supplications.'*

חֶבְלֵי מָוֶת — *The pains of death.* This is an apt description of the exile, when Israel is encircled by violent enemies who seek to kill them *(Abarbanel).*

שׁוּבִי נַפְשִׁי לִמְנוּחָיְכִי — *Return, my soul, to your rest.* When misery and persecution upset me, I told my soul that it would find peace and comfort only if it would *return* to God *(Radak).*

אֶתְהַלֵּךְ לִפְנֵי ה׳ בְּאַרְצוֹת הַחַיִּים — *I shall walk before HASHEM in the lands of the living.* How I yearn to return to *Eretz Yisrael* where the very air makes men healthy and robust and the holy atmosphere grants the mind renewed vitality and alertness! *(Radak). Eretz Yisrael* is identified as the *land of the living* because the dead are destined to be resurrected there. This is why the Patriarchs and the righteous of all generations yearned to be buried there.

אֲנִי אָמַרְתִּי בְחָפְזִי כָּל הָאָדָם כֹּזֵב — *I said in my haste: 'All mankind is deceitful.'* This bitter comment was originally uttered by David when the people of Zif betrayed his hiding place to King Saul [see *I Samuel* 23:19-29] *(Rashi).* It is also a reference to the bleak, dismal exile [for the exile discourages the Jews and leads them to the hasty, premature conclusion that all the prophets' promises concerning redemption were *deceitful] (Abarbanel).*

❧ מָה אָשִׁיב לַה׳ — *How can I repay HASHEM?* What gift can I give to the King who owns everything? *(Ibn Ezra).* How can I possibly repay His acts of kindness, for they are too numerous to recount? *(Radak).* How can I even approach Him? He is eternal and I am finite; He is the highest, and I am the lowest! *(Ibn Yachya).*

call. The pains of death encircled me; the confines of the grave have found me; trouble and sorrow I would find. Then I would invoke the Name of HASHEM: 'Please, HASHEM, save my soul.' Gracious is HASHEM and righteous, our God is merciful. HASHEM protects the simple; I was brought low, but He saved me. Return, my soul, to your rest;* for HASHEM has been kind to you. For You have delivered my soul from death, my eyes from tears, my feet from stumbling.* Chazzan– *I shall walk before HASHEM in the lands of the living.* I have kept faith although I say: 'I suffer exceedingly.' I said in my haste: 'All mankind is deceitful.'**

Psalm 116:12-19

מָה אָשִׁיב *How can I repay HASHEM* for all His kindness to me? I will raise the cup of salvations* and the Name of HASHEM I will invoke. My vows to HASHEM I will pay,* in the presence, now, of His entire people. Difficult in the eyes of HASHEM is the death of His devout ones. Please, HASHEM — for I am Your servant, I am Your servant, son of Your handmaid* — You have released my bonds.* Chazzan– *To You I will sacrifice thanksgiving offerings, and the name of HASHEM I will invoke. My vows to HASHEM I will pay, in the presence, now, of His entire people. In the courtyards of the House of HASHEM, in your midst, O Jerusalem, Halleluyah!*

Congregation, then *chazzan:*

Psalm 117

הַלְלוּ *Praise HASHEM,* all nations; praise Him, all the states!* For His kindness has overwhelmed us,* and the truth of HASHEM is eternal, Halleluyah!*

כּוֹס יְשׁוּעוֹת אֶשָּׂא — *I will raise the cup of salvations.* This refers to the wine libations that will accompany the thanksgiving offerings of the returning exiles *(Rashi).*

נְדָרַי לַה׳ אֲשַׁלֵּם — *My vows to HASHEM I will pay.* As I was fleeing and wandering in exile, I vowed that if God would return me safely to *Eretz Yisrael,* I would render thanksgiving offerings to His Name; now I will make good on my vows *(Radak).*

אֲנִי עַבְדְּךָ בֶּן אֲמָתֶךָ — *I am Your servant, son of Your handmaid.* The slave who is born to a *handmaid* is far more submissive than a slave who was born free *(Rashi).* The former serves his master naturally and instinctively, whereas the latter serves him only in response to external threats *(Sforno).*

☙ הַלְלוּ אֶת ה׳ — *Praise HASHEM.* This psalm, containing only two verses, is the shortest chapter in all of Scripture. *Radak* explains that its brevity symbolizes the simplicity of the world order which will prevail after the advent of the Messiah.

גּוֹיִם . . . הָאֻמִּים — *Nations . . . the states.* הָאֻמִּים, *the states,* is written with the definite article, whereas גּוֹיִם, *nations,* is spelled without it. This teaches that הָאֻמִּים refers to large nations that are well known and powerful, whereas גּוֹיִם refers to small, backward nations that have no prominence *(Iyun Tefillah).*

כִּי גָבַר עָלֵינוּ חַסְדּוֹ — *For His kindness has overwhelmed us.* Why should non-Jewish peoples and nations praise God for overwhelming Israel with Divine kindness? Israel will merit God's kindness because of the extraordinary service they rendered to Him. Recognizing Israel's distinction, the nations will consider it a privilege to become subservient to God's chosen ones, and will praise Him for His kindness to the Jews *(Yaavetz Hadoresh).*

Congregation waves the Four Species as indicated above each word each time it recites the verse הודו. *Chazzan* waves the Four Species only when reciting the verses הודו and יאמר. (See *Laws* §171-174)

תהלים קיח

Chazzan – (FRONT) **הוֹדוּ** (RIGHT) לַיהוה (BACK) כִּי טוֹב,* (LEFT) כִּי (UP) לְעוֹלָם (DOWN) חַסְדּוֹ.

Cong. – (FRONT) הוֹדוּ (RIGHT) לַיהוה (BACK) כִּי טוֹב, (LEFT) כִּי (UP) לְעוֹלָם (DOWN) חַסְדּוֹ.
יֹאמַר נָא יִשְׂרָאֵל, כִּי לְעוֹלָם חַסְדּוֹ.

Chazzan – (FRONT) יֹאמַר (RIGHT) נָא (BACK) יִשְׂרָאֵל, (LEFT) כִּי (UP) לְעוֹלָם (DOWN) חַסְדּוֹ.

Cong. – (FRONT) הוֹדוּ (RIGHT) לַיהוה (BACK) כִּי טוֹב, (LEFT) כִּי (UP) לְעוֹלָם (DOWN) חַסְדּוֹ.
יֹאמְרוּ נָא בֵית אַהֲרֹן, כִּי לְעוֹלָם חַסְדּוֹ.

Chazzan – יֹאמְרוּ נָא בֵית אַהֲרֹן, כִּי לְעוֹלָם חַסְדּוֹ.

Cong. – (FRONT) הוֹדוּ (RIGHT) לַיהוה (BACK) כִּי טוֹב, (LEFT) כִּי (UP) לְעוֹלָם (DOWN) חַסְדּוֹ.
יֹאמְרוּ נָא יִרְאֵי יהוה, כִּי לְעוֹלָם חַסְדּוֹ.

Chazzan – יֹאמְרוּ נָא יִרְאֵי יהוה, כִּי לְעוֹלָם חַסְדּוֹ.

Cong. – (FRONT) הוֹדוּ (RIGHT) לַיהוה (BACK) כִּי טוֹב, (LEFT) כִּי (UP) לְעוֹלָם (DOWN) חַסְדּוֹ.

מִן הַמֵּצַר* קָרָאתִי יָּהּ, עָנָנִי בַמֶּרְחָב יָהּ. יהוה לִי לֹא אִירָא, מַה יַּעֲשֶׂה לִי אָדָם. יהוה לִי בְּעֹזְרָי,* וַאֲנִי אֶרְאֶה בְשֹׂנְאָי. טוֹב לַחֲסוֹת בַּיהוה, מִבְּטֹחַ בָּאָדָם.* טוֹב לַחֲסוֹת בַּיהוה, מִבְּטֹחַ בִּנְדִיבִים. כָּל גּוֹיִם סְבָבוּנִי, בְּשֵׁם יהוה כִּי אֲמִילַם. סַבּוּנִי גַם סְבָבוּנִי, בְּשֵׁם יהוה כִּי אֲמִילַם. סַבּוּנִי כִדְבֹרִים דֹּעֲכוּ כְּאֵשׁ קוֹצִים, בְּשֵׁם יהוה כִּי אֲמִילַם. דָּחֹה דְחִיתַנִי לִנְפֹּל, וַיהוה עֲזָרָנִי.* עָזִּי וְזִמְרָת יָהּ, וַיְהִי לִי לִישׁוּעָה. קוֹל רִנָּה וִישׁוּעָה, בְּאָהֳלֵי צַדִּיקִים,* יְמִין יהוה עֹשָׂה חָיִל. יְמִין יהוה רוֹמֵמָה, יְמִין יהוה עֹשָׂה חָיִל. לֹא

☙ **הודו לה׳ כי טוב** — *Give thanks to HASHEM, for He is good.* This is a general expression of thanks to God. No matter what occurs, God is always good and everything He does is for the best, even though this may not be immediately apparent to man *(Abarbanel).*

☙ **מן המצר** — *From the straits.* This psalm expresses gratitude and confidence. Just as David himself was catapulted from his personal straits to a reign marked by accomplishment and glory, so too Israel can look forward to Divine redemption from the straits of exile and oppression.

ה׳ לי בעזרי — *HASHEM is with me through my helpers.* I have many helpers, but I place confidence in them only because HASHEM is with them. If my helpers were not granted strength by God, their assistance would be futile *(Ibn Ezra; Radak).*

טוב לַחֲסוֹת בה׳ מִבְּטֹחַ בָּאָדָם — *It is better to take refuge in HASHEM than to rely on man.* חִסָּיוֹן, here translated *taking refuge,* denotes absolute confidence even though no guarantees have been given; בִּטָּחוֹן, *reliance,* however, presupposes a promise of protection. The Psalmist says that it is

Congregation waves the Four Species — FRONT, RIGHT, BACK, LEFT, UP, DOWN — each time it recites the verse *'Give thanks . . .'* (see *Laws* §171-174).

Psalm 118

Chazzan – *Give thanks to HASHEM for He is good;**
His kindness endures forever!
Cong. – *Give thanks to HASHEM, for He is good;*
His kindness endures forever!
Let Israel say now: His kindness endures forever!
Chazzan – *Let Israel say now: His kindness endures forever!*
Cong. – *Give thanks to HASHEM, for He is good;*
His kindness endures forever!
Let the House of Aaron say now:
His kindness endures forever!
Chazzan – *Let the House of Aaron say now:*
His kindness endures forever!
Cong. – *Give thanks to HASHEM, for He is good;*
His kindness endures forever!
Let those who fear HASHEM say now:
His kindness endures forever!
Chazzan – *Let those who fear HASHEM say now:*
His kindness endures forever!
Cong. – *Give thanks to HASHEM, for He is good;*
His kindness endures forever!

מִן הַמֵּצַר *From the straits* did I call upon God; God answered me with expansiveness. HASHEM is with me, I have no fear; how can man affect me? HASHEM is with me through my helpers;* therefore I can face my foes. It is better to take refuge in HASHEM than to rely on man.* It is better to take refuge in HASHEM than to rely on nobles. All the nations surround me; in the Name of HASHEM I cut them down! They encircle me, they also surround me; in the Name of HASHEM, I cut them down! They encircle me like bees, but they are extinguished as a fire does thorns; in the Name of HASHEM I cut them down! You pushed me hard that I might fall, but HASHEM assisted me.* God is my might and my praise, and He was a salvation for me. The sound of rejoicing and salvation is in the tents of the righteous:* 'HASHEM's right hand does valiantly. HASHEM's right hand is raised triumphantly; HASHEM's right hand does valiantly!' I shall not*

---

far better to put one's trust in God's protection, even without a pledge from Him, than to rely on the most profuse assurances of human beings *(R' Bachya; Vilna Gaon).*

דָּחֹה דְחִיתַנִי לִנְפֹּל וַה׳ עֲזָרָנִי — *You pushed me hard that I might fall, but HASHEM assisted me.* In the preceding verses, the Psalmist speaks of his enemy indirectly; now, however, he addresses the foe directly.

קוֹל רִנָּה וִישׁוּעָה בְּאָהֳלֵי צַדִּיקִים — *The sound of rejoicing and salvation is in the tents of the righteous.* When HASHEM's right hand does valiantly for the sake of His chosen people, then the righteous will respond by filling their tents with sounds of rejoicing over this salvation *(Radak).*

לֹא אָמוּת כִּי אֶחְיֶה וַאֲסַפֵּר מַעֲשֵׂי יָהּ — *I shall not die! But I shall live and relate the deeds of God.* I will survive the assassination attempts of my enemies and live to recount the deeds of God, Who saved me from my foes *(Radak).*

יַסֹּר יִסְּרַנִּי יָּהּ וְלַמָּוֶת לֹא נְתָנָנִי — *God has chastened me exceedingly, but He did not let me die.* Throughout the duration of the exile, I survived

אָמוּת כִּי אֶחְיֶה, וַאֲסַפֵּר מַעֲשֵׂי יָהּ.* יַסֹּר יִסְּרַנִּי יָּהּ, וְלַמָּוֶת לֹא נְתָנָנִי.* ❖ פִּתְחוּ לִי שַׁעֲרֵי צֶדֶק, אָבֹא בָם אוֹדֶה יָהּ. זֶה הַשַּׁעַר לַיהוה, צַדִּיקִים יָבֹאוּ בוֹ.* אוֹדְךָ* כִּי עֲנִיתָנִי, וַתְּהִי לִי לִישׁוּעָה. אוֹדְךָ כִּי עֲנִיתָנִי, וַתְּהִי לִי לִישׁוּעָה. אֶבֶן מָאֲסוּ הַבּוֹנִים, הָיְתָה לְרֹאשׁ פִּנָּה.* אֶבֶן מָאֲסוּ הַבּוֹנִים, הָיְתָה לְרֹאשׁ פִּנָּה. מֵאֵת יהוה הָיְתָה זֹּאת, הִיא נִפְלָאת בְּעֵינֵינוּ.* מֵאֵת יהוה הָיְתָה זֹּאת, הִיא נִפְלָאת בְּעֵינֵינוּ. זֶה הַיּוֹם עָשָׂה יהוה, נָגִילָה וְנִשְׂמְחָה בוֹ. זֶה הַיּוֹם עָשָׂה יהוה, נָגִילָה וְנִשְׂמְחָה בוֹ.

The next four lines are recited responsively — *chazzan,* then congregation. The Four Species are waved as indicated above each word.

FRONT-RIGHT   BACK-LEFT   UP-DOWN

אָנָּא יהוה הוֹשִׁיעָה נָּא.

FRONT-RIGHT   BACK-LEFT   UP-DOWN

אָנָּא יהוה הוֹשִׁיעָה נָּא.
אָנָּא יהוה הַצְלִיחָה נָּא.
אָנָּא יהוה הַצְלִיחָה נָּא.

בָּרוּךְ הַבָּא בְּשֵׁם יהוה, בֵּרַכְנוּכֶם מִבֵּית יהוה. בָּרוּךְ הַבָּא בְּשֵׁם יהוה, בֵּרַכְנוּכֶם מִבֵּית יהוה. אֵל יהוה וַיָּאֶר לָנוּ, אִסְרוּ חַג בַּעֲבֹתִים, עַד קַרְנוֹת הַמִּזְבֵּחַ. אֵל יהוה וַיָּאֶר לָנוּ, אִסְרוּ חַג בַּעֲבֹתִים, עַד קַרְנוֹת הַמִּזְבֵּחַ. אֵלִי אַתָּה וְאוֹדֶךָּ, אֱלֹהַי אֲרוֹמְמֶךָּ. אֵלִי אַתָּה וְאוֹדֶךָּ, אֱלֹהַי אֲרוֹמְמֶךָּ.

The Four Species are waved as indicated above each word.

FRONT   RIGHT   BACK   LEFT   UP   DOWN

הוֹדוּ לַיהוה כִּי טוֹב, כִּי לְעוֹלָם חַסְדּוֹ.

FRONT   RIGHT   BACK   LEFT   UP   DOWN

הוֹדוּ לַיהוה כִּי טוֹב, כִּי לְעוֹלָם חַסְדּוֹ

---

because whatever suffering God decreed was only to atone for my sins (*Rashi*).

זֶה הַשַּׁעַר לַה׳ צַדִּיקִים יָבֹאוּ בוֹ — *This is the gate of* H*ASHEM; the righteous shall enter through it.* This refers to the gate of the Temple. When the exile is over, the righteous will enter through this gate, and they will thank God for answering their plea for redemption (*Targum; Rashi*).

◆§ Repetition of Verses

אוֹדְךָ— *I thank You.* From this point until the end of the Scriptural part of *Hallel* — i.e., the nine verses until יְהַלְלוּךָ — each verse is recited twice. This entire psalm, which begins with הוֹדוּ לַה׳, *Give thanks to* H*ASHEM*, follows a pattern, namely, that each new theme is repeated in the next verse or two in the same or slightly different words. Therefore the custom was introduced to follow through on this repetition by repeating each of these verses as well (*Rashi* to *Succah* 38a).

Another reason for repeating each verse is based upon the Talmud (*Pesachim* 119a) which relates that these verses were recited in a responsive dialogue between Samuel, Jesse, David, and David's brothers when the prophet

die! But I shall live and relate the deeds of God. God has chastened me exceedingly, but He did not let me die.** Chazzan– *Open for me the gates of righteousness, I will enter them and thank God. This is the gate of* H*ASHEM; the righteous shall enter through it.* I thank You* for You have answered me and become my salvation. I thank You for You have answered me and become my salvation. The stone the builders despised has become the cornerstone.* The stone the builders despised has become the cornerstone. This emanated from* H*ASHEM; it is wondrous in our eyes.* This emanated from* H*ASHEM; it is wondrous in our eyes. This is the day* H*ASHEM has made; let us rejoice and be glad on it. This is the day* H*ASHEM has made; let us rejoice and be glad on it.*

The next four lines are recited responsively — *chazzan,* then congregation.
The Four Species are waved — FRONT, RIGHT, BACK, LEFT, UP, DOWN — during the next two verses.

אָנָּא *Please,* H*ASHEM, save now!*
Please, H*ASHEM, save now!*
Please, H*ASHEM, bring success now!*
Please, H*ASHEM, bring success now!*

בָּרוּךְ *Blessed is he who comes in the Name of* H*ASHEM; we bless you from the House of* H*ASHEM. Blessed is he who comes in the Name of* H*ASHEM; we bless you from the House of* H*ASHEM.* H*ASHEM is God, He illuminated for us; bind the festival offering with cords until the corners of the Altar.* H*ASHEM is God, He illuminated for us; bind the festival offering with cords until the corners of the Altar. You are my God, and I will thank You; my God, I will exalt You. You are my God, and I will thank You; my God, I will exalt You.*

The Four Species are waved — FRONT, RIGHT, BACK, LEFT, UP, DOWN — during the next two verses.

Give thanks to H*ASHEM, for He is good; His kindness endures forever.*
Give thanks to H*ASHEM, for He is good; His kindness endures forever.*

---

announced that the young shepherd would be the future king of Israel. To honor these distinguished personages, we repeat each one's statement, as if it were a full chapter.

אֶבֶן מָאֲסוּ הַבּוֹנִים הָיְתָה לְרֹאשׁ פִּנָּה — *The stone the builders despised has become the cornerstone.* This verse refers to David, who was rejected by his own father and brothers *(Targum).* When the prophet Samuel announced that one of Jesse's sons was to be anointed king, no one even thought of summoning David, who was out with the sheep [see *I Samuel* 16:4-13].

Israel too is called אֶבֶן, *stone (Genesis* 49:24), for Israel is the cornerstone of God's design for the world. The world endures only by virtue of Israel's observance of God's laws, a fact that has influenced all nations to appreciate and accept certain aspects of God's commands. If not for the order and meaning that Israel has brought to the world, it would long ago have sunk into chaos. But the builders, i.e., the rulers of the nations, despised the Jews, claiming that they were parasites who made no contribution to the common good. When the dawn of redemption arrives, however, all nations will realize that Israel is indeed the cornerstone of the world *(Radak).*

מֵאֵת ה׳ הָיְתָה זֹּאת הִיא נִפְלָאת בְּעֵינֵינוּ — *This emanated from* H*ASHEM; it is wondrous in our eyes.* When David was crowned, all were amazed. But David said, 'This is even more surprising and wondrous to me than it is to anyone else!'

Similarly, when Israel is catapulted to glory and tranquillity in the future, the nations who persecuted the Jews will ask in surprise, 'Aren't these the very Jews who were once despised and afflicted?'

The Jews will respond, 'We are even more amazed than you are, for only we know the depths of degradation we suffered!'

Then a heavenly voice will proclaim, 'This has emanated from HASHEM!'

יְהַלְלוּךָ יהוה אֱלֹהֵינוּ כָּל מַעֲשֶׂיךָ,* וַחֲסִידֶיךָ צַדִּיקִים* עוֹשֵׂי רְצוֹנֶךָ,* וְכָל עַמְּךָ בֵּית יִשְׂרָאֵל בְּרִנָּה יוֹדוּ וִיבָרְכוּ וִישַׁבְּחוּ וִיפָאֲרוּ וִירוֹמְמוּ וְיַעֲרִיצוּ וְיַקְדִּישׁוּ וְיַמְלִיכוּ אֶת שִׁמְךָ מַלְכֵּנוּ, ❖ כִּי לְךָ טוֹב לְהוֹדוֹת וּלְשִׁמְךָ נָאֶה לְזַמֵּר, כִּי מֵעוֹלָם וְעַד עוֹלָם אַתָּה אֵל. בָּרוּךְ אַתָּה יהוה, מֶלֶךְ מְהֻלָּל בַּתִּשְׁבָּחוֹת.

(.Cong. – אָמֵן)

SOME CONGREGATIONS RECITE הוֹשַׁעְנוֹת, *HOSHANOS,* (P. 362) AT THIS POINT.

קדיש שלם

The *chazzan* recites *Kaddish:*

יִתְגַּדַּל וְיִתְקַדַּשׁ שְׁמֵהּ רַבָּא. (.Cong. – אָמֵן.) בְּעָלְמָא דִּי בְרָא כִרְעוּתֵהּ. וְיַמְלִיךְ מַלְכוּתֵהּ, בְּחַיֵּיכוֹן וּבְיוֹמֵיכוֹן וּבְחַיֵּי דְכָל בֵּית יִשְׂרָאֵל, בַּעֲגָלָא וּבִזְמַן קָרִיב. וְאִמְרוּ: אָמֵן.

(.Cong. – אָמֵן. יְהֵא שְׁמֵהּ רַבָּא מְבָרַךְ לְעָלַם וּלְעָלְמֵי עָלְמַיָּא.)

יְהֵא שְׁמֵהּ רַבָּא מְבָרַךְ לְעָלַם וּלְעָלְמֵי עָלְמַיָּא.

יִתְבָּרַךְ וְיִשְׁתַּבַּח וְיִתְפָּאַר וְיִתְרוֹמַם וְיִתְנַשֵּׂא וְיִתְהַדָּר וְיִתְעַלֶּה וְיִתְהַלָּל שְׁמֵהּ דְּקֻדְשָׁא בְּרִיךְ הוּא (.Cong. – בְּרִיךְ הוּא) – לְעֵלָּא מִן כָּל בִּרְכָתָא וְשִׁירָתָא תֻּשְׁבְּחָתָא וְנֶחֱמָתָא, דַּאֲמִירָן בְּעָלְמָא. וְאִמְרוּ: אָמֵן. (.Cong. – אָמֵן.)

(.Cong. – קַבֵּל בְּרַחֲמִים וּבְרָצוֹן אֶת תְּפִלָּתֵנוּ.)

תִּתְקַבֵּל צְלוֹתְהוֹן וּבָעוּתְהוֹן דְּכָל בֵּית יִשְׂרָאֵל קֳדָם אֲבוּהוֹן דִּי בִשְׁמַיָּא. וְאִמְרוּ: אָמֵן. (.Cong. – אָמֵן.)

(.Cong. – יְהִי שֵׁם יהוה מְבֹרָךְ, מֵעַתָּה וְעַד עוֹלָם.[1])

יְהֵא שְׁלָמָא רַבָּא מִן שְׁמַיָּא, וְחַיִּים עָלֵינוּ וְעַל כָּל יִשְׂרָאֵל. וְאִמְרוּ: אָמֵן. (.Cong. – אָמֵן.)

(.Cong. – עֶזְרִי מֵעִם יהוה, עֹשֵׂה שָׁמַיִם וָאָרֶץ.[2])

Take three steps back. Bow left and say . . . עֹשֶׂה; bow right and say . . . הוּא; bow forward and say וְעַל כָּל . . . אָמֵן. Remain standing in place for a few moments, then take three steps forward.

עֹשֶׂה שָׁלוֹם בִּמְרוֹמָיו, הוּא יַעֲשֶׂה שָׁלוֹם עָלֵינוּ, וְעַל כָּל יִשְׂרָאֵל. וְאִמְרוּ: אָמֵן. (.Cong. – אָמֵן.)

☙ יְהַלְלוּךָ . . . כָּל מַעֲשֶׂיךָ — *All Your works shall praise You.* This paragraph is not part of Psalms, but is a concluding blessing that sums up the broad theme of *Hallel* — that Israel and the entire universe will join in praising God. *All Your works shall praise You* means that in the perfect world of the future, the entire universe, including the vast variety of human beings, will function harmoniously according to God's will. This is the highest form of praise, for without it all the beautiful spoken and sung words and songs of praise are insincere and meaningless.

וַחֲסִידֶיךָ צַדִּיקִים — *Your devout ones, the righteous.* The word חָסִיד, *devout one,* refers to one who serves God beyond the minimum require-

יְהַלְלְוּךָ *All Your works shall praise You,* HASHEM our God. And Your devout ones, the righteous,* who do Your will,* and Your entire people, the House of Israel, with glad song will thank, bless, praise, glorify, exalt, extol, sanctify, and proclaim the sovereignty of Your Name, our King.* Chazzan— *For to You it is fitting to give thanks, and unto Your Name it is proper to sing praises, for from This World to the World to Come You are God. Blessed are You, HASHEM, the King Who is lauded with praises.* (Cong.— *Amen.)*

SOME CONGREGATIONS RECITE *HOSHANOS* (P. 362) AT THIS POINT.

FULL KADDISH

The *chazzan* recites *Kaddish:*

יִתְגַּדַּל *May His great Name grow exalted and sanctified* (Cong.— *Amen.*) *in the world that He created as He willed. May He give reign to His kingship in your lifetimes and in your days, and in the lifetimes of the entire Family of Israel, swiftly and soon. Now respond: Amen.*

(Cong.— *Amen. May His great Name be blessed forever and ever.)*

May His great Name be blessed forever and ever.

Blessed, praised, glorified, exalted, extolled, mighty, upraised, and lauded be the Name of the Holy One, Blessed is He (Cong.— *Blessed is He*) — *beyond any blessing and song, praise and consolation that are uttered in the world. Now respond: Amen.* (Cong.— *Amen*).

(Cong.— *Accept our prayers with mercy and favor.*)

May the prayers and supplications of the entire Family of Israel be accepted before their Father Who is in Heaven. Now respond: Amen. (Cong.— *Amen.*)

(Cong.— *Blessed be the Name of HASHEM, from this time and forever.*[1])

May there be abundant peace from Heaven, and life, upon us and upon all Israel. Now respond: Amen. (Cong.— *Amen.*)

(Cong.— *My help is from HASHEM, Maker of heaven and earth.*[2])

Take three steps back. Bow left and say, *'He Who makes peace . . .';* bow right and say, *'may He . . .';* bow forward and say, *'and upon all Israel . . .'* Remain standing in place for a few moments, then take three steps forward.

He Who makes peace in His heights, may He make peace upon us, and upon all Israel. Now respond: Amen. (Cong.— *Amen.*)

---

(1) *Psalms* 113:2. (2) 121:2.

---

ment of the *Halachah.* The word is derived from חֶסֶד, *kindness,* as if to say that such people do acts of kindness for God's sake. They serve as an example for the *righteous* people, who fulfill all the requirements of the Law, and for the masses of Israel, whose goal is to serve God, even though they may not equal the spiritual accomplishments of the *devout* and the *righteous.*

עוֹשֵׂי רְצוֹנֶךָ — *Who do Your will.* In an inspiring homiletical interpretation, *Yismach Yisrael* interprets that the good deeds of the righteous can remake God's will, as it were. In other words, when Jews serve Him properly, God responds by lavishing kindness and a sense of fulfillment upon the world. Then, *Hallel* will become not only a song of praise for the miracles of the past, but also for the longed-for redemption.

הוצאת ספר תורה

From the moment the Ark is opened until the Torah is returned to it, one must conduct himself with the utmost respect, and avoid unnecessary conversation. It is commendable to kiss the Torah as it is carried to the *bimah* [reading table] and back to the Ark.

All rise and remain standing until the Torah is placed on the *bimah*. The congregation recites:

אֵין כָּמְוֹךָ* בָאֱלֹהִים אֲדֹנָי, וְאֵין כְּמַעֲשֶׂיךָ.*[1] מַלְכוּתְךָ מַלְכוּת כָּל עֹלָמִים, וּמֶמְשַׁלְתְּךָ בְּכָל דּוֹר וָדֹר.[2] יהוה מֶלֶךְ,[3] יהוה מָלָךְ,[4] יהוה יִמְלֹךְ לְעֹלָם וָעֶד.[5] יהוה עֹז לְעַמּוֹ יִתֵּן, יהוה יְבָרֵךְ אֶת עַמּוֹ בַשָּׁלוֹם.[6]

אַב הָרַחֲמִים, הֵיטִיבָה בִרְצוֹנְךָ אֶת צִיּוֹן,* תִּבְנֶה חוֹמוֹת יְרוּשָׁלָיִם.[7] כִּי בְךָ לְבַד בָּטָחְנוּ, מֶלֶךְ אֵל רָם וְנִשָּׂא, אֲדוֹן עוֹלָמִים.

THE ARK IS OPENED

Before the Torah is removed the congregation recites:

וַיְהִי בִּנְסֹעַ הָאָרֹן* וַיֹּאמֶר מֹשֶׁה, קוּמָה יהוה וְיָפֻצוּ אֹיְבֶיךָ וְיָנֻסוּ מְשַׂנְאֶיךָ מִפָּנֶיךָ.[8] כִּי מִצִּיּוֹן תֵּצֵא תוֹרָה, וּדְבַר יהוה מִירוּשָׁלָיִם.[9] בָּרוּךְ שֶׁנָּתַן תּוֹרָה לְעַמּוֹ יִשְׂרָאֵל בִּקְדֻשָּׁתוֹ.

ON THE SABBATH THE FOLLOWING PRAYERS ARE OMITTED AND THE SERVICE CONTINUES WITH בְּרִיךְ שְׁמֵהּ (P. 302).

The following paragraph [the Thirteen Attributes of Mercy] is recited three times:

יהוה, יהוה, אֵל, רַחוּם, וְחַנּוּן, אֶרֶךְ אַפַּיִם, וְרַב חֶסֶד, וֶאֱמֶת, נֹצֵר חֶסֶד לָאֲלָפִים, נֹשֵׂא עָוֹן, וָפֶשַׁע, וְחַטָּאָה, וְנַקֵּה.[10]

הוֹצָאַת סֵפֶר תּוֹרָה / Removal of the Torah

אֵין כָּמוֹךָ — *There is none like You.* On the Sabbath and Festivals, the service of removing the Torah from the Ark begins with an introductory series of verses that emphasize God's greatness and plead for the rebuilding of Zion and Jerusalem. Since we are about to read from God's word to Israel, it is fitting that we first call to mind that the One Who speaks to us is our All-powerful King.

וְאֵין כְּמַעֲשֶׂיךָ — *And there is nothing like Your works.* This refers to the work of creation. It follows, therefore, that since God is the Creator of the universe, He was and remains its King.

הֵיטִיבָה . . . אֶת צִיּוֹן — *Do good with Zion.* Only in God's chosen Sanctuary can His kingdom come to full flower among mankind. Only there can the Torah reading attain its greatest meaning.

וַיְהִי בִּנְסֹעַ הָאָרֹן — *When the Ark would travel.* When the Ark is opened we declare, as Moses did when the Ark traveled, that God's word is invincible. Having acknowledged this, we can read from the Torah with the proper awareness. We continue that it is God's will that the Torah's message go forth to the entire world, and by blessing Him for having given us the Torah, we accept our responsibility to carry out its commands and spread its message *(R' Hirsch).*

The Thirteen Attributes of Mercy

During Festivals a special prayer is inserted before בְּרִיךְ שְׁמֵהּ, *Blessed is the Name,* requesting God's help in attaining His goals for us. [Like all personal supplications, this is not recited on the Sabbath.] It is preceded by the י״ג מִדּוֹת הָרַחֲמִים, *Thirteen Attributes of Mercy,* the prayer that God Himself taught Moses after Israel worshiped the Golden Calf. Although Moses, quite understandably, thought that no prayers could help the nation that had bowed to and danced around an idol less than six weeks after hearing the Ten Commandments, God showed him that it was never too late for prayer and repentance. God made a Divine covenant with him that the prayerful, repentant recitation of the Thirteen Attributes of Mercy would never be turned back unanswered (*Rosh Hashanah* 17b).

There are various opinions among the com-

REMOVAL OF THE TORAH FROM THE ARK

From the moment the Ark is opened until the Torah is returned to it, one must conduct himself with the utmost respect, and avoid unnecessary conversation. It is commendable to kiss the Torah as it is carried to the *bimah* [reading table] and back to the Ark.

All rise and remain standing until the Torah is placed on the *bimah*. The congregation recites:

אֵין כָּמְוֹךָ *There is none like You* among the gods, my Lord, and there is nothing like Your works.*[1] Your kingdom is a kingdom spanning all eternities, and Your dominion is throughout every generation.[2] HASHEM reigns,[3] HASHEM has reigned,[4] HASHEM shall reign for all eternity.[5] HASHEM will give might to His people; HASHEM will bless His people with peace.[6]*

אַב הָרַחֲמִים *Father of compassion, do good with Zion* according to Your will; rebuild the walls of Jerusalem.[7] For we trust in You alone, O King, God, exalted and uplifted, Master of worlds.*

THE ARK IS OPENED

Before the Torah is removed the congregation recites:

וַיְהִי בִּנְסֹעַ *When the Ark would travel,* Moses would say, 'Arise, HASHEM, and let Your foes be scattered, let those who hate You flee from You.'[8] For from Zion the Torah will come forth and the word of HASHEM from Jerusalem.[9] Blessed is He Who gave the Torah to His people Israel in His holiness.*

ON THE SABBATH THE FOLLOWING PRAYERS ARE OMITTED AND THE SERVICE CONTINUES WITH בְּרִיךְ שְׁמֵהּ, *BLESSED IS THE NAME* (P. 302).

The following paragraph [the Thirteen Attributes of Mercy] is recited three times:

יהוה HASHEM, HASHEM, God, Compassionate and Gracious, Slow to anger, and Abundant in Kindness and Truth. Preserver of kindness for thousands of generations, Forgiver of iniquity, willful sin, and error, and Who cleanses.[10]

(1) *Psalms* 86:8. (2) 145:13. (3) 10:16. (4) 93:1 et al. (5) *Exodus* 15:18.
(6) *Psalms* 29:11. (7) 51:20. (8) *Numbers* 10:35. (9) *Isaiah* 2:3. (10) *Exodus* 34:6-7.

mentators regarding the precise enumeration of the Thirteen Attributes. The following is the opinion of *Rabbeinu Tam* (*Rosh Hashanah* 17b). For a fuller commentary, see the ArtScroll *Tashlich* and the *Yom Kippur Machzor*.

1. ה׳ — *HASHEM.* This Name denotes mercy. God is merciful before a person sins, though He knows that future evil lies dormant in him.

2. ה׳ — *HASHEM.* God is merciful after the sinner has gone astray.

3. אֵל — *God.* This Name denotes power: the force of God's mercy sometimes surpasses even that indicated by the Name *HASHEM.*

4. רַחוּם — *Compassionate.* God eases the punishment of the guilty; and He does not put people into extreme temptation.

5. וְחַנּוּן — *and Gracious,* even to the undeserving.

6. אֶרֶךְ אַפַּיִם — *Slow to anger,* so that the sinner can reconsider long before it is too late.

7. וְרַב חֶסֶד — *and Abundant in Kindness,* toward those who lack personal merits. Also, if the scales of good and evil are evenly balanced, He tips them to the good.

8. וֶאֱמֶת — *and Truth.* God never reneges on His word.

9. נֹצֵר חֶסֶד לָאֲלָפִים — *Preserver of kindness for thousands of generations.* The deeds of the righteous benefit their offspring far into the future.

10. נֹשֵׂא עָוֹן — *Forgiver of iniquity.* God forgives the intentional sinner, if he repents.

11. וָפֶשַׁע — *[Forgiver of] willful sin.* Even those who purposely anger God are allowed to repent.

12. וְחַטָּאָה — *and [Forgiver of] error.* This is a sin committed out of carelessness or apathy.

13. וְנַקֵּה — *and Who cleanses.* God wipes away the sins of those who repent.

רִבּוֹנוֹ שֶׁל עוֹלָם מַלֵּא מִשְׁאֲלוֹת לִבִּי לְטוֹבָה,* וְהָפֵק רְצוֹנִי, וְתֵן שְׁאֵלָתִי, לִי עַבְדְּךָ (name) בֶּן/בַּת (mother's name) אֲמָתֶךָ, וְזַכֵּנִי

Insert the appropriate phrase(s) — וְאֶת אִשְׁתִּי/בַּעְלִי, וּבְנִי/וּבָנַי, וּבִתִּי/וּבְנוֹתַי

וְכָל בְּנֵי בֵיתִי לַעֲשׂוֹת רְצוֹנְךָ בְּלֵבָב שָׁלֵם. וּמַלְּטֵנוּ מִיֵּצֶר הָרָע, וְתֵן חֶלְקֵנוּ בְּתוֹרָתֶךָ. וְזַכֵּנוּ שֶׁתִּשְׁרֶה שְׁכִינָתְךָ עָלֵינוּ, וְהוֹפַע עָלֵינוּ רוּחַ חָכְמָה וּבִינָה. וְיִתְקַיֵּם בָּנוּ מִקְרָא שֶׁכָּתוּב: וְנָחָה עָלָיו רוּחַ יהוה, רוּחַ חָכְמָה וּבִינָה, רוּחַ עֵצָה וּגְבוּרָה, רוּחַ דַּעַת וְיִרְאַת יהוה.[1] וְכֵן יְהִי רָצוֹן מִלְּפָנֶיךָ, יהוה אֱלֹהֵינוּ וֵאלֹהֵי אֲבוֹתֵינוּ, שֶׁתְּזַכֵּנוּ לַעֲשׂוֹת מַעֲשִׂים טוֹבִים בְּעֵינֶיךָ, וְלָלֶכֶת בְּדַרְכֵי יְשָׁרִים לְפָנֶיךָ. וְקַדְּשֵׁנוּ בְּמִצְוֹתֶיךָ כְּדֵי שֶׁנִּזְכֶּה לְחַיִּים טוֹבִים וַאֲרוּכִים לִימוֹת הַמָּשִׁיחַ וּלְחַיֵּי הָעוֹלָם הַבָּא. וְתִשְׁמְרֵנוּ מִמַּעֲשִׂים רָעִים, וּמִשָּׁעוֹת רָעוֹת הַמִּתְרַגְּשׁוֹת לָבֹא לָעוֹלָם. וְהַבּוֹטֵחַ בַּיהוה חֶסֶד יְסוֹבְבֶנְהוּ,[2] אָמֵן. יִהְיוּ לְרָצוֹן אִמְרֵי פִי וְהֶגְיוֹן לִבִּי לְפָנֶיךָ, יהוה צוּרִי וְגֹאֲלִי.[3]

Recite the following verse three times:

וַאֲנִי תְפִלָּתִי לְךָ* יהוה עֵת רָצוֹן, אֱלֹהִים בְּרָב חַסְדֶּךָ, עֲנֵנִי בֶּאֱמֶת יִשְׁעֶךָ.[4]

ON ALL DAYS CONTINUE:

זוהר ויקהל שסט:א

בְּרִיךְ שְׁמֵהּ* דְּמָרֵא עָלְמָא, בְּרִיךְ כִּתְרָךְ וְאַתְרָךְ. יְהֵא רְעוּתָךְ עִם עַמָּךְ יִשְׂרָאֵל לְעָלַם, וּפֻרְקַן יְמִינָךְ אַחֲזֵי לְעַמָּךְ בְּבֵית מַקְדְּשָׁךְ, וּלְאַמְטוּיֵי לָנָא מִטּוּב נְהוֹרָךְ, וּלְקַבֵּל צְלוֹתָנָא בְּרַחֲמִין. יְהֵא רַעֲוָא קֳדָמָךְ, דְּתוֹרִיךְ לָן חַיִּין בְּטִיבוּתָא, וְלֶהֱוֵי אֲנָא פְקִידָא בְּגוֹ צַדִּיקַיָּא, לְמִרְחַם עָלַי וּלְמִנְטַר יָתִי וְיַת כָּל דִּי לִי, וְדִי לְעַמָּךְ יִשְׂרָאֵל. אַנְתְּ הוּא זָן לְכֹלָּא, וּמְפַרְנֵס לְכֹלָּא, אַנְתְּ הוּא שַׁלִּיט עַל כֹּלָּא. אַנְתְּ הוּא דְּשַׁלִּיט עַל מַלְכַיָּא, וּמַלְכוּתָא דִּילָךְ הִיא. אֲנָא עַבְדָּא דְקֻדְשָׁא בְּרִיךְ הוּא, דְּסָגִידְנָא קַמֵּהּ וּמִקַּמָּא דִּיקַר אוֹרַיְתֵהּ בְּכָל עִדָּן וְעִדָּן. לָא עַל אֱנָשׁ רָחִיצְנָא, וְלָא עַל בַּר אֱלָהִין סָמִיכְנָא, אֶלָּא בֶּאֱלָהָא דִשְׁמַיָּא, דְּהוּא אֱלָהָא קְשׁוֹט, וְאוֹרַיְתֵהּ קְשׁוֹט, וּנְבִיאוֹהִי קְשׁוֹט, וּמַסְגֵּא לְמֶעְבַּד טַבְוָן וּקְשׁוֹט. בֵּהּ אֲנָא

⇐§ **רִבּוֹנוֹ שֶׁל עוֹלָם / Master of the Universe** מַלֵּא מִשְׁאֲלוֹת לִבִּי לְטוֹבָה — *Fulfill my heartfelt requests for good.* Often man's personal goals are not to his real benefit. May my requests be filled in a way that will be truly good.

⇐§ וַאֲנִי תְפִלָּתִי לְךָ — *As for me, may my prayer to You.* This verse makes three declarations: We pray to God alone; we hope that the time is proper in His eyes; and we know that only through His abundant kindness can we expect salvation.

רִבּוֹנוֹ *Master of the universe, fulfill my heartfelt requests for good,* satisfy my desire and grant my request, me—Your servant* (name) *son/daughter of* (mother's name) *Your maidservant—and privilege me*

Insert the appropriate phrase(s): *and my wife/husband, my son(s), my daughter(s)*

and everyone in my household to do Your will wholeheartedly. Rescue us from the Evil Inclination and grant our share in Your Torah. Privilege us that You may rest Your Presence upon us and radiate upon us a spirit of wisdom and insight. Let there be fulfilled in us the verse that is written: The spirit of HASHEM *shall rest upon him, the spirit of wisdom and insight, the spirit of counsel and strength, the spirit of knowledge and fear of* HASHEM.[1] *Similarly may it be Your will,* HASHEM, *our God and the God of our forefathers, that You privilege us to do deeds that are good in Your eyes and to walk before You in upright paths. Sanctify us with Your commandments so that we may be worthy of a good and long life, to the days of the Messiah and to the life of the World to Come. May You protect us against evil deeds and from bad times that surge upon the world. He who trusts in* HASHEM *— may kindness surround him.*[2] *Amen. May the expressions of my mouth and the thoughts of my heart find favor before You,* HASHEM, *my Rock and my Redeemer.*[3]

Recite the following verse three times:

וַאֲנִי תְפִלָּתִי *As for me, may my prayer to You,** HASHEM, *be at an opportune time; O God, in Your abundant kindness, answer me with the truth of Your salvation.*[4]

ON ALL DAYS CONTINUE:

Zohar, Vayakhel 369a

בְּרִיךְ שְׁמֵהּ *Blessed is the Name* of the Master of the universe, blessed is Your crown and Your place. May Your favor remain with Your people Israel forever; may You display the salvation of Your right hand to Your people in Your Holy Temple, to benefit us with the goodness of Your luminescence and to accept our prayers with mercy. May it be Your will that You extend our lives with goodness and that I be numbered among the righteous; that You have mercy on me and protect me, all that is mine and that is Your people Israel's. It is You Who nourishes all and sustains all; You control everything. It is You Who control kings, and kingship is Yours. I am a servant of the Holy One, Blessed is He, and I prostrate myself before Him and before the glory of His Torah at all times. Not in any man do I put trust, nor on any angel do I rely — only on the God of heaven Who is the God of truth, Whose Torah is truth and Whose prophets are true and Who acts liberally with kindness and truth. In Him do I*

(1) *Isaiah* 11:2. (2) Cf. *Psalms* 32:10. (3) 19:15. (4) 69:14.

בְּרִיךְ שְׁמֵהּ — *Blessed is the Name.* The *Zohar* declares that when the congregation prepares to read from the Torah, the heavenly gates of mercy are opened and God's love for Israel is aroused. Therefore, it is an auspicious occasion for the recital of this prayer which asks for God's compassion; pleads that He display His salvation in the finally rebuilt Holy Temple; declares our

רְחִיץ, וְלִשְׁמֵהּ קַדִּישָׁא יַקִּירָא אֲנָא אֵמַר תֻּשְׁבְּחָן. יְהֵא רַעֲוָא קֳדָמָךְ, דְּתִפְתַּח לִבָּאִי בְּאוֹרַיְתָא, וְתַשְׁלִים מִשְׁאֲלִין דְּלִבָּאִי, וְלִבָּא דְכָל עַמָּךְ יִשְׂרָאֵל, לְטָב וּלְחַיִּין וְלִשְׁלָם. (אָמֵן.)

Two Torah Scrolls are removed from the Ark; one for the main Torah reading and the second for *Maftir*. The first is presented to the *chazzan,* who accepts it in his right arm. Facing the congregation the *chazzan* raises the Torah and, followed by congregation, recites:

שְׁמַע יִשְׂרָאֵל• יהוה אֱלֹהֵינוּ יהוה אֶחָד.[1]

Still facing the congregation, the *chazzan* raises the Torah and, followed by congregation, recites:

אֶחָד (הוּא) אֱלֹהֵינוּ גָּדוֹל אֲדוֹנֵינוּ, קָדוֹשׁ שְׁמוֹ.

The *chazzan* turns to the Ark, bows while raising the Torah, and recites:

גַּדְּלוּ• לַיהוה אִתִּי וּנְרוֹמְמָה שְׁמוֹ יַחְדָּו.[2]

The *chazzan* turns to his right and carries the Torah to the *bimah,* as the congregation responds:

לְךָ יהוה הַגְּדֻלָּה• וְהַגְּבוּרָה וְהַתִּפְאֶרֶת וְהַנֵּצַח וְהַהוֹד כִּי כֹל בַּשָּׁמַיִם וּבָאָרֶץ, לְךָ יהוה הַמַּמְלָכָה וְהַמִּתְנַשֵּׂא לְכֹל לְרֹאשׁ.[3] רוֹמְמוּ יהוה אֱלֹהֵינוּ, וְהִשְׁתַּחֲווּ לַהֲדֹם רַגְלָיו,• קָדוֹשׁ הוּא. רוֹמְמוּ יהוה אֱלֹהֵינוּ, וְהִשְׁתַּחֲווּ לְהַר קָדְשׁוֹ, כִּי קָדוֹשׁ יהוה אֱלֹהֵינוּ.[4]

As the *chazzan* carries the Torah to the *bimah* the congregation recites:

עַל הַכֹּל,• יִתְגַּדַּל וְיִתְקַדַּשׁ וְיִשְׁתַּבַּח וְיִתְפָּאַר וְיִתְרוֹמַם וְיִתְנַשֵּׂא שְׁמוֹ שֶׁל מֶלֶךְ מַלְכֵי הַמְּלָכִים הַקָּדוֹשׁ בָּרוּךְ הוּא, בָּעוֹלָמוֹת שֶׁבָּרָא, הָעוֹלָם הַזֶּה וְהָעוֹלָם הַבָּא, כִּרְצוֹנוֹ,• וְכִרְצוֹן יְרֵאָיו, וְכִרְצוֹן כָּל בֵּית יִשְׂרָאֵל. צוּר הָעוֹלָמִים, אֲדוֹן כָּל הַבְּרִיּוֹת, אֱלוֹהַּ כָּל הַנְּפָשׁוֹת, הַיּוֹשֵׁב בְּמֶרְחֲבֵי מָרוֹם, הַשּׁוֹכֵן בִּשְׁמֵי שְׁמֵי קֶדֶם. קְדֻשָּׁתוֹ עַל הַחַיּוֹת, וּקְדֻשָּׁתוֹ עַל כִּסֵּא הַכָּבוֹד. וּבְכֵן יִתְקַדַּשׁ שִׁמְךָ בָּנוּ• יהוה אֱלֹהֵינוּ לְעֵינֵי כָּל חָי. וְנֹאמַר לְפָנָיו שִׁיר חָדָשׁ, כַּכָּתוּב: שִׁירוּ לֵאלֹהִים זַמְּרוּ שְׁמוֹ, סֹלּוּ לָרֹכֵב בָּעֲרָבוֹת

---

faith in Him and His Torah; and asks that He make us receptive to its wisdom.

שְׁמַע יִשְׂרָאֵל — *Hear, O Israel.* Holding the Torah Scroll the *chazzan* leads the congregation in reciting three verses that help set the majestic tone of reading publicly from the word of God. The verses form a logical progression: God is One; He is great and holy; therefore we join in declaring His greatness.

גַּדְּלוּ — *Declare the greatness.* Our rejoicing in the Torah manifests itself in praise of its Giver. The *chazzan* calls upon the congregation to join him in praising God.

לְךָ ה' הַגְּדֻלָּה — *Yours, HASHEM, is the greatness.* This praise was first uttered by David in his ecstasy at seeing how wholeheartedly the people contributed their riches toward the eventual building of the Temple. He ascribed the greatness of that and every other achievement to God's graciousness.

לַהֲדֹם רַגְלָיו — *At His footstool,* i.e., the Temple, as if to say that God's Heavenly Presence extends earthward, like a footstool that helps support a monarch sitting on his throne. In a further sense, this represents our resolve to live in such a way that we are worthy of His Presence resting upon us *(R' Hirsch).*

עַל הַכֹּל — *For all this.* All the praises that we

trust, and to His glorious and holy Name do I declare praises. May it be Your will that You open my heart to the Torah and that You fulfill the wishes of my heart and the heart of Your entire people Israel for good, for life, and for peace. (Amen.)

Two Torah Scrolls are removed from the Ark; one for the main Torah reading and the second for *Maftir*. The first is presented to the *chazzan*, who accepts it in his right arm. Facing the congregation the *chazzan* raises the Torah and, followed by congregation, recites:

Hear, O Israel:* HASHEM is our God, HASHEM, the One and Only.[1]

Still facing the congregation, the *chazzan* raises the Torah and, followed by congregation, recites:

One is our God, great is our Master, Holy is His Name.

The *chazzan* turns to the Ark, bows while raising the Torah, and recites:

Declare the greatness* of HASHEM with me, and let us exalt His Name together.[2]

The *chazzan* turns to his right and carries the Torah to the *bimah*, as the congregation responds:

לְךָ *Yours, HASHEM, is the greatness,* the strength, the splendor, the triumph, and the glory; even everything in heaven and earth; Yours, HASHEM, is the kingdom, and the sovereignty over every leader.*[3] *Exalt HASHEM, our God, and bow at His footstool;* He is Holy! Exalt HASHEM, our God, and bow to His holy mountain; for holy is HASHEM, our God.*[4]

As the *chazzan* carries the Torah to the *bimah* the congregation recites:

עַל הַכֹּל *For all this,* let the Name of the King of kings, the Holy One, Blessed is He, grow exalted, sanctified, praised, glorified, exalted, and extolled in the worlds that He has created — This World and the World to Come — according to His will,* the will of those who fear Him, and the will of the entire House of Israel. Rock of the eternities, Master of all creatures, God of all souls, He Who sits in the expanses on high, Who rests in the loftiest primeval heavens. His holiness is upon the Chayos; His holiness is upon the Throne of Glory. Similarly, may Your Name be sanctified within us,* HASHEM, our God, in the sight of all the living. May we chant before Him a new song as it is written: 'Sing to God, make music for His Name, extol the One Who*

(1) *Deuteronomy* 6:4. (2) *Psalms* 34:4. (3) *I Chronicles* 29:11. (4) *Psalms* 99:5,9.

---

have uttered heretofore are inadequate to describe God's greatness. May His Name continue to grow exalted (*Kol Bo*).

This paragraph is intended to express the majesty of God especially now that we are about to read from the Torah. We say that although He is sanctified in the heavens and by the spiritual beings, we long to become worthy vehicles through which His greatness can be manifested on earth, as well.

כִּרְצוֹנוֹ — *According to His will.* May He be *exalted, sanctified, praised ...* as He wishes to be. God created the universe so that His glory could be appreciated and emulated by man (see *Isaiah* 43:7). We now pray that this will indeed take place.

וּבְכֵן יִתְקַדַּשׁ שִׁמְךָ בָּנוּ — *Similarly, may Your Name be sanctified within us.* The goal of people should be to demonstrate that God's greatness should not be reserved for the 'higher, spiritual' spheres. Rather, the most noble purpose of life is for mortal man to become a bearer of Godliness.

בְּיָהּ שְׁמוֹ, וְעִלְזוּ לְפָנָיו.[1] וְנִרְאֵהוּ עַיִן בְּעַיִן בְּשׁוּבוֹ אֶל נָוֵהוּ, כַּכָּתוּב: כִּי עַיִן בְּעַיִן יִרְאוּ בְּשׁוּב יהוה צִיּוֹן.[2] וְנֶאֱמַר: וְנִגְלָה כְּבוֹד יהוה, וְרָאוּ כָל בָּשָׂר יַחְדָּו כִּי פִּי יהוה דִּבֵּר.[3]

אַב הָרַחֲמִים הוּא יְרַחֵם עַם עֲמוּסִים, וְיִזְכֹּר בְּרִית אֵיתָנִים, וְיַצִּיל נַפְשׁוֹתֵינוּ מִן הַשָּׁעוֹת הָרָעוֹת, וְיִגְעַר בְּיֵצֶר הָרָע מִן הַנְּשׂוּאִים, וְיָחֹן אוֹתָנוּ לִפְלֵיטַת עוֹלָמִים, וִימַלֵּא מִשְׁאֲלוֹתֵינוּ בְּמִדָּה טוֹבָה יְשׁוּעָה וְרַחֲמִים.

The Torah is placed on the *bimah* and prepared for reading.

The *gabbai* uses the following formula to call a *Kohen* to the Torah:

וְיַעֲזוֹר וְיָגֵן וְיוֹשִׁיעַ לְכֹל הַחוֹסִים בּוֹ, וְנֹאמַר, אָמֵן. הַכֹּל הָבוּ גֹדֶל לֵאלֹהֵינוּ וּתְנוּ כָבוֹד לַתּוֹרָה, כֹּהֵן° קְרָב, יַעֲמֹד (name) בֶּן (father's name) הַכֹּהֵן.

°If no *Kohen* is present, the *gabbai* says:
„אֵין כָּאן כֹּהֵן, יַעֲמֹד (insert name) יִשְׂרָאֵל (לֵוִי) בִּמְקוֹם כֹּהֵן.״

בָּרוּךְ שֶׁנָּתַן תּוֹרָה לְעַמּוֹ יִשְׂרָאֵל בִּקְדֻשָּׁתוֹ. (תּוֹרַת יהוה תְּמִימָה מְשִׁיבַת נָפֶשׁ, עֵדוּת יהוה נֶאֱמָנָה מַחְכִּימַת פֶּתִי. פִּקּוּדֵי יהוה יְשָׁרִים מְשַׂמְּחֵי לֵב, מִצְוַת יהוה בָּרָה מְאִירַת עֵינָיִם.[4] יהוה עֹז לְעַמּוֹ יִתֵּן, יהוה יְבָרֵךְ אֶת עַמּוֹ בַשָּׁלוֹם.[5] הָאֵל תָּמִים דַּרְכּוֹ, אִמְרַת יהוה צְרוּפָה, מָגֵן הוּא לְכֹל הַחוֹסִים בּוֹ.[6])

Congregation then *gabbai:*

וְאַתֶּם הַדְּבֵקִים בַּיהוה אֱלֹהֵיכֶם, חַיִּים כֻּלְּכֶם הַיּוֹם.[7]

קריאת התורה

The reader shows the *oleh* (person called to the Torah) the place in the Torah. The *oleh* touches the Torah with a corner of his *tallis,* or the belt or mantle of the Torah, and kisses it. He then begins the blessing, bowing at בָּרְכוּ, and straightening up at ה׳.

בָּרְכוּ אֶת יהוה הַמְּבֹרָךְ.

Congregation, followed by *oleh,* responds, bowing at בָּרוּךְ, and straightening up at ה׳.

בָּרוּךְ יהוה הַמְּבֹרָךְ לְעוֹלָם וָעֶד.

Oleh continues:

בָּרוּךְ אַתָּה יהוה אֱלֹהֵינוּ מֶלֶךְ הָעוֹלָם, אֲשֶׁר בָּחַר בָּנוּ מִכָּל הָעַמִּים, וְנָתַן לָנוּ אֶת תּוֹרָתוֹ. בָּרוּךְ אַתָּה יהוה, נוֹתֵן הַתּוֹרָה. (–Cong. אָמֵן.)

קְרִיאַת הַתּוֹרָה / Reading of the Torah

There is a basic difference between the reading of the Torah and the prayers. When we pray, *we* call upon *God;* that is why the *chazzan* stands in front of the congregation as its representative. But the Torah reading is reminiscent of God's revelation to Israel, when the nation gathered around Mount Sinai to hear Him communicate His word to Israel. That is why the Torah is read from a *bimah,* platform, in the center of the congregation and usually elevated, like the mountain around which Israel gathered.

The number of people called to the Torah varies in accordance with the sanctity of the day. Thus, on Monday and Thursday, fast days, Purim and Chanukah, three people are called; on Rosh Chodesh and Chol HaMoed, four are called; on Festivals and Rosh Hashanah, five; on

rides in the highest heavens with His Name YAH, *and exult before Him.'*[1] *May we see Him with a perceptive view upon His return to His Abode, as is written: 'For they shall see with a perceptive view as* HASHEM *returns to Zion.'*[2] *And it is said: 'The glory of* HASHEM *shall be revealed and all flesh together shall see that the mouth of* HASHEM *has spoken.'*[3]

אַב הָרַחֲמִים *May the Father of compassion have mercy on the nation that is borne by Him, and may He remember the covenant of the spiritually mighty. May He rescue our souls from the bad times, and upbraid the evil inclination to leave those borne by Him, graciously make us an eternal remnant, and fulfill our requests in good measure, for salvation and mercy.*

The Torah is placed on the *bimah* and prepared for reading.
The *gabbai* uses the following formula to call a *Kohen* to the Torah:

וְיַעֲזוֹר *May He help, shield, and save all who take refuge in Him — Now let us respond: Amen. All of you ascribe greatness to our God and give honor to the Torah. Kohen,*° *approach. Arise* (name) *son of* (father's name) *the Kohen.*

°If no *Kohen* is present, the *gabbai* says: *'There is no Kohen present, stand* (name) *son of* (father's name) *an Israelite (Levite) in place of the Kohen.'*

Blessed is He Who gave the Torah to His people Israel in His holiness. (The Torah of HASHEM *is perfect, restoring the soul; the testimony of* HASHEM *is trustworthy, making the simple one wise. The orders of* HASHEM *are upright, gladdening the heart; the command of* HASHEM *is clear, enlightening the eyes.*[4] HASHEM *will give might to His nation;* HASHEM *will bless His nation with peace.*[5] *The God Whose way is perfect, the promise of* HASHEM *is flawless, He is a shield for all who take refuge in Him.*[6]*)*

Congregation then *gabbai:*

You who cling to HASHEM, your God, you are all alive today.[7]

READING OF THE TORAH

The reader shows the *oleh* (person called to the Torah) the place in the Torah. The *oleh* touches the Torah with a corner of his *tallis,* or the belt or mantle of the Torah, and kisses it. He then begins the blessing, bowing at *'Bless,'* and straightening up at 'HASHEM.'

Bless HASHEM,* the blessed One.

Congregation, followed by *oleh,* responds, bowing at 'Blessed,' and straightening up at 'HASHEM.'

Blessed is HASHEM, *the blessed One, for all eternity.*

Oleh continues:

בָּרוּךְ *Blessed are You,* HASHEM, *our God, King of the universe, Who selected us from all the peoples and gave us His Torah. Blessed are You,* HASHEM, *Giver of the Torah.* (Cong.— *Amen.)*

(1) *Psalms* 68:5. (2) *Isaiah* 52:8. (3) 40:5. (4) *Psalms* 19:8-9. (5) 29:11. (6) 18:31. (7) *Deut.* 4:4.

Yom Kippur, six; and on the Sabbath [whether an ordinary Sabbath or a Festival that falls on the Sabbath], seven. (It should be noted that *Maftir* is not included in the above number since *Maftir* is attached to the *Haftarah* reading.) Only three are called on Sabbath afternoons since the Torah has already been read in the morning.

On most Festivals the Torah reading is a selection on either the historical narrative of the day or the commandment to observe the Festivals.

בָּרְכוּ אֶת ה' — *Bless* HASHEM. This call to the congregation to bless God prior to the Torah reading is based on the practice of Ezra (*Nechemiah* 8:6). Before he read from the Torah to the multitude, he blessed God and they responded in kind. Similarly, the Sages (*Berachos* 21a) derive the Scriptural requirement to recite a

After his Torah portion has been read, the *oleh* recites:

בָּרוּךְ אַתָּה יהוה אֱלֹהֵינוּ מֶלֶךְ הָעוֹלָם, אֲשֶׁר נָתַן לָנוּ תּוֹרַת אֱמֶת, וְחַיֵּי עוֹלָם* נָטַע בְּתוֹכֵנוּ. בָּרוּךְ אַתָּה יהוה, נוֹתֵן הַתּוֹרָה. (Cong. – אָמֵן.)

PRAYER FOR THE OLEH / מי שברך לעולה לתורה

After each *oleh* completes his concluding blessing, the *gabbai* calls the next *oleh* to the Torah, then blesses the one who has just concluded.

מִי שֶׁבֵּרַךְ אֲבוֹתֵינוּ אַבְרָהָם יִצְחָק וְיַעֲקֹב, הוּא יְבָרֵךְ אֶת (name) בֶּן (father's name) בַּעֲבוּר שֶׁעָלָה לִכְבוֹד הַמָּקוֹם, לִכְבוֹד הַתּוֹרָה, [On the Sabbath – לִכְבוֹד הַשַּׁבָּת,] לִכְבוֹד הָרֶגֶל. בִּשְׂכַר זֶה, הַקָּדוֹשׁ בָּרוּךְ הוּא יִשְׁמְּרֵהוּ וְיַצִּילֵהוּ מִכָּל צָרָה וְצוּקָה, וּמִכָּל נֶגַע וּמַחֲלָה, וְיִשְׁלַח בְּרָכָה וְהַצְלָחָה בְּכָל מַעֲשֵׂה יָדָיו, וְיִזְכֶּה לַעֲלוֹת לְרֶגֶל, עִם כָּל יִשְׂרָאֵל אֶחָיו. וְנֹאמַר: אָמֵן. (Cong. – אָמֵן.)

PRAYER FOR OTHERS / מי שברך לאחרים

It is customary that the following prayer be recited for the family members of the *oleh* and for anyone else that he may wish to include:

מִי שֶׁבֵּרַךְ אֲבוֹתֵינוּ אַבְרָהָם יִצְחָק וְיַעֲקֹב, הוּא יְבָרֵךְ אֶת (names of the recipients) בַּעֲבוּר שֶׁ(name of *oleh*) יִתֵּן לִצְדָקָה בַּעֲבוּרָם. בִּשְׂכַר זֶה, הַקָּדוֹשׁ בָּרוּךְ הוּא יִשְׁמְּרֵם וְיַצִּילֵם מִכָּל צָרָה וְצוּקָה, וּמִכָּל נֶגַע וּמַחֲלָה, וְיִשְׁלַח בְּרָכָה וְהַצְלָחָה בְּכָל מַעֲשֵׂה יְדֵיהֶם, וְיִזְכּוּ לַעֲלוֹת לְרֶגֶל, עִם כָּל יִשְׂרָאֵל אֲחֵיהֶם. וְנֹאמַר: אָמֵן. (Cong. – אָמֵן.)

PRAYER FOR A SICK PERSON / מי שברך לחולה

מִי שֶׁבֵּרַךְ אֲבוֹתֵינוּ אַבְרָהָם יִצְחָק וְיַעֲקֹב, מֹשֶׁה אַהֲרֹן דָּוִד וּשְׁלֹמֹה,

for a man

הוּא יְבָרֵךְ וִירַפֵּא אֶת הַחוֹלֶה (patient's name) בֶּן (mother's name) בַּעֲבוּר שֶׁ(supplicant's name) יִתֵּן לִצְדָקָה בַּעֲבוּרוֹ.°° בִּשְׂכַר זֶה, הַקָּדוֹשׁ בָּרוּךְ הוּא יִמָּלֵא רַחֲמִים עָלָיו, לְהַחֲלִימוֹ וּלְרַפְּאתוֹ וּלְהַחֲזִיקוֹ וּלְהַחֲיוֹתוֹ, וְיִשְׁלַח לוֹ מְהֵרָה רְפוּאָה שְׁלֵמָה מִן הַשָּׁמַיִם, לִרְמַ״ח אֵבָרָיו, וּשְׁסָ״ה גִּידָיו, בְּתוֹךְ

for a woman

הוּא יְבָרֵךְ וִירַפֵּא אֶת הַחוֹלָה (patient's name) בַּת (mother's name) בַּעֲבוּר שֶׁ(supplicant's name) יִתֵּן לִצְדָקָה בַּעֲבוּרָהּ.°° בִּשְׂכַר זֶה, הַקָּדוֹשׁ בָּרוּךְ הוּא יִמָּלֵא רַחֲמִים עָלֶיהָ, לְהַחֲלִימָהּ וּלְרַפְּאתָהּ וּלְהַחֲזִיקָהּ וּלְהַחֲיוֹתָהּ, וְיִשְׁלַח לָהּ מְהֵרָה רְפוּאָה שְׁלֵמָה מִן הַשָּׁמַיִם, לְכָל אֵבָרֶיהָ, וּלְכָל גִּידֶיהָ, בְּתוֹךְ

שְׁאָר חוֹלֵי יִשְׂרָאֵל, רְפוּאַת הַנֶּפֶשׁ, וּרְפוּאַת הַגּוּף, [On the Sabbath – שַׁבָּת וְ] יוֹם טוֹב הוּא מִלִּזְעֹק, וּרְפוּאָה קְרוֹבָה לָבֹא, הַשְׁתָּא, בַּעֲגָלָא וּבִזְמַן קָרִיב. וְנֹאמַר: אָמֵן. (Cong. – אָמֵן.)

°°Many congregations substitute:

בַּעֲבוּר שֶׁכָּל הַקָּהָל מִתְפַּלְּלִים בַּעֲבוּרוֹ (בַּעֲבוּרָהּ)

After his Torah portion has been read, the *oleh* recites:

בָּרוּךְ *Blessed are You, HASHEM, our God, King of the universe, Who gave us the Torah of truth and implanted eternal life* within us. Blessed are You, HASHEM, Giver of the Torah.* (Cong.— *Amen.)*

PRAYER FOR THE OLEH

After each *oleh* completes his concluding blessing, the *gabbai* calls the next *oleh* to the Torah, then blesses the one who has just concluded.

מִי שֶׁבֵּרַךְ *He Who blessed our forefathers Abraham, Isaac, and Jacob — may He bless (* Hebrew name*) son of (* father's Hebrew name*) because he has come up to the Torah in honor of the Omnipresent, in honor of the Torah, [in honor of the Sabbath] in honor of the pilgrimage festival. As reward for this, may the Holy One, Blessed is He, protect him and rescue him from every trouble and distress, from every plague and illness; may He send blessing and success in his every endeavor, and may he be privileged to ascend to Jerusalem for the pilgrimage, together with all Israel, his brethren. Now let us respond: Amen.* (Cong.— *Amen.)*

PRAYER FOR OTHERS

It is customary that the following prayer be recited for the family members of the *oleh* and for anyone else that he may wish to include:

מִי שֶׁבֵּרַךְ *He Who blessed our forefathers Abraham, Isaac, and Jacob — may He bless (* names of recipients*) for (* name of *oleh) will contribute to charity on their behalf. As reward for this, may the Holy One, Blessed is He, protect them and rescue them from every trouble and distress, from every plague and illness; may He send blessing and success in their every endeavor and may they be privileged to ascend to Jerusalem for the pilgrimage, together with all Israel, their brethren. Now let us respond: Amen.* (Cong.— *Amen.)*

PRAYER FOR A SICK PERSON

מִי שֶׁבֵּרַךְ *He Who blessed our forefathers Abraham, Isaac and Jacob, Moses and Aaron, David and Solomon — may He bless and heal the sick person (* patient's Hebrew name*) son/daughter of (* patient's mother's Hebrew name*) because (* name of supplicant*) will contribute to charity on his/her behalf.*°° *In reward for this, may the Holy One, Blessed is He, be filled with*

for a man

compassion for him to restore his health, to heal him, to strengthen him, and to revivify him. And may He send him speedily a complete recovery from heaven for his two hundred forty-eight organs and three hundred sixty-five blood vessels,

for a woman

compassion for her to restore her health, to heal her, to strengthen her, and to revivify her. And may He send her speedily a complete recovery from heaven for all her organs and all her blood vessels,

*among the other sick people of Israel, a recovery of the body and a recovery of the spirit though the [*on the Sabbath: *Sabbath and] Festival prohibit[s] us from crying out, may a recovery come speedily, swiftly and soon. Now let us respond: Amen.* (Cong.—*Amen.)*

°°Many congregations substitute:
because the entire congregation prays for him (her)

---

blessing before Torah study from the verse, *When I proclaim the Name of HASHEM, ascribe greatness to our God (Deuteronomy* 32:3). The implication is that the public study of Torah requires a blessing.

תּוֹרַת אֱמֶת וְחַיֵּי עוֹלָם — *The Torah of truth ... eternal life. Torah of truth* refers to the Written Torah, and *eternal life* to the Oral Law. The Oral Law is described as *implanted within us,* because Jews constantly expand their Torah knowledge through their personal study and analysis (*Tur Orach Chaim* 139).

קריאה לשני ימים הראשונים

ויקרא כב:כו־כג:מד

כהן–וַיְדַבֵּר יהוה אֶל־מֹשֶׁה לֵּאמֹר: שׁוֹר אוֹ־כֶשֶׂב אוֹ־עֵז כִּי יִוָּלֵד וְהָיָה שִׁבְעַת יָמִים תַּחַת אִמּוֹ וּמִיּוֹם הַשְּׁמִינִי וָהָלְאָה יֵרָצֶה לְקָרְבַּן אִשֶּׁה לַיהוה: וְשׁוֹר אוֹ־שֶׂה* אֹתוֹ וְאֶת־בְּנוֹ לֹא תִשְׁחֲטוּ בְּיוֹם אֶחָד: וְכִי־תִזְבְּחוּ זֶבַח־תּוֹדָה לַיהוה לִרְצֹנְכֶם* תִּזְבָּחוּ: בַּיּוֹם הַהוּא יֵאָכֵל לֹא־תוֹתִירוּ מִמֶּנּוּ עַד־בֹּקֶר אֲנִי יהוה: וּשְׁמַרְתֶּם מִצְוֹתַי וַעֲשִׂיתֶם* אֹתָם אֲנִי יהוה: וְלֹא תְחַלְּלוּ* אֶת־שֵׁם קָדְשִׁי וְנִקְדַּשְׁתִּי* בְּתוֹךְ בְּנֵי יִשְׂרָאֵל אֲנִי יהוה מְקַדִּשְׁכֶם: הַמּוֹצִיא אֶתְכֶם מֵאֶרֶץ מִצְרַיִם לִהְיוֹת לָכֶם לֵאלֹהִים אֲנִי יהוה:*

(בשבת לוי)–וַיְדַבֵּר יהוה אֶל־מֹשֶׁה לֵּאמֹר: דַּבֵּר אֶל־בְּנֵי יִשְׂרָאֵל וְאָמַרְתָּ אֲלֵהֶם מוֹעֲדֵי יהוה* אֲשֶׁר־תִּקְרְאוּ אֹתָם מִקְרָאֵי קֹדֶשׁ* אֵלֶּה הֵם מוֹעֲדָי:* שֵׁשֶׁת יָמִים תֵּעָשֶׂה מְלָאכָה וּבַיּוֹם הַשְּׁבִיעִי שַׁבַּת שַׁבָּתוֹן* מִקְרָא־קֹדֶשׁ כָּל־מְלָאכָה לֹא תַעֲשׂוּ שַׁבָּת הִוא לַיהוה בְּכֹל מוֹשְׁבֹתֵיכֶם:

לוי (בשבת שלישי)– אֵלֶּה מוֹעֲדֵי יהוה מִקְרָאֵי קֹדֶשׁ אֲשֶׁר־תִּקְרְאוּ* אֹתָם בְּמוֹעֲדָם: בַּחֹדֶשׁ הָרִאשׁוֹן בְּאַרְבָּעָה עָשָׂר לַחֹדֶשׁ בֵּין הָעַרְבָּיִם פֶּסַח לַיהוה: וּבַחֲמִשָּׁה עָשָׂר יוֹם לַחֹדֶשׁ הַזֶּה חַג הַמַּצּוֹת לַיהוה שִׁבְעַת יָמִים מַצּוֹת תֹּאכֵלוּ:* בַּיּוֹם הָרִאשׁוֹן מִקְרָא־קֹדֶשׁ יִהְיֶה לָכֶם כָּל־מְלֶאכֶת עֲבֹדָה* לֹא תַעֲשׂוּ: וְהִקְרַבְתֶּם אִשֶּׁה* לַיהוה שִׁבְעַת יָמִים בַּיּוֹם הַשְּׁבִיעִי מִקְרָא־קֹדֶשׁ כָּל־מְלֶאכֶת עֲבֹדָה לֹא תַעֲשׂוּ:

TORAH READING FOR FIRST TWO DAYS

Generally, the reading of the first day of a festival deals with the historical event being commemorated. Thus, on the first day of Passover, we read about the Exodus, and on the first day of Shavuos, we read about the Revelation at Sinai. Today, however, since there is no narrative dealing exclusively with Succos, we read a chapter that discusses all the festivals in general. The chapter is prefaced with seven verses that would seem to be unrelated to the festivals at hand. They are included for two reasons: Since Temple offerings are an integral part of every festival service, the requirements of these animals is logically appended to the festival reading. Secondly, these introductory verses conclude with an admonition not to desecrate the Name of Hashem Who liberated us from Egyptian bondage. Since all the festivals — and our very existence as a nation — flow from the Exodus, this section is used to introduce the festival portion.

וְשׁוֹר אוֹ שֶׂה – *But a cow or a ewe* [lit., a bull or a sheep]. According to the accepted Talmudic opinion, the prohibition applies only to the offspring (male or female) of the female, but not to the offspring of the male. However, if it is certain that a particular male is the sire of a calf or lamb, one should avoid slaughtering both on the same day (*Hil. Shechitah* 12:11).

לִרְצֹנְכֶם – *To gain acceptance for yourselves.* The one who slaughters an offering must have in mind that it will be eaten within the time frame the Torah prescribes. If his intention is that it will be eaten beyond the deadline, the offering becomes disqualified [פִּגּוּל] and does not *gain favor*.

וּשְׁמַרְתֶּם . . . וַעֲשִׂיתֶם – *You are to observe . . . and perform.* Study the laws [*observe*] so that you will be able to *perform* the *mitzvos* properly.

וְלֹא תְחַלְּלוּ – *You are not to desecrate.* If a Jew performs an act that the Torah forbids, he desecrates God's Name.

TORAH READING FOR FIRST TWO DAYS

Leviticus 22:26-23:44

Kohen – *HASHEM spoke to Moses saying: When a bull, a sheep, or a goat is born, it shall remain under its mother for seven days; and from the eighth day on it is acceptable for a fiery offering to HASHEM. But a cow or a ewe* — you may not slaughter it and its offspring on the same day. And when you slaughter a thanksgiving offering to HASHEM, slaughter it to gain acceptance for yourselves*: it must be eaten on that same day, you may not leave any of it until morning; I am HASHEM. You are to observe My commandments and perform* them; I am HASHEM. You are not to desecrate* My holy Name, rather I should be sanctified* among the children of Israel; I am HASHEM Who sanctifies you; Who took you out of the land of Egypt to be your God; I am HASHEM.**

(On the Sabbath – Levi) – *HASHEM spoke to Moses saying: Speak to the children of Israel and say to them: HASHEM's appointed festivals* that you are to proclaim as holy convocations* — these are My appointed festivals.* For six days labor may be done, and the seventh day is a day of complete rest,* a holy convocation, you may not do any work; it is a Sabbath for HASHEM in all your dwelling places.*

Levi (On the Sabbath – Third) – *These are the appointed festivals of HASHEM, the holy convocations, which you are to proclaim* in their appropriate time. In the first month on the fourteenth of the month in the afternoon is the time of the Pesach offering to HASHEM. And on the fifteenth day of this month is the festival of Matzos to HASHEM, you are to eat matzos* for seven days. On the first day is to be a holy convocation for you; you may do no laborious work.* You are to bring a fire-offering* to HASHEM for seven days; on the seventh day is to be a holy convocation, you may do no laborious work.*

וְנִקְדַּשְׁתִּי – *Rather I should be sanctified.* There are times when one must be ready to give up his life rather than transgresss a commandment, particularly in the presence of ten Jews [i.e., *among the children of Israel*]. To do so is a sanctification of God's Name.

אֲנִי ה׳ – *I am HASHEM.* I can be trusted to reward those who obey My commands.

מוֹעֲדֵי ה׳ – *HASHEM's appointed festivals.* This term for the festivals has the connotation of "meeting," i.e., God has designated these times when Israel can greet His Presence.

מִקְרָאֵי קֹדֶשׁ – *Holy convocations.* On these days, the nation is to gather for the pursuit of holiness, and to sanctify the festival through prayer and praise to God *(Ramban).*

מוֹעֲדָי – *My . . . festivals.* But holidays devoted to revelry, food, and pleasures are not *My* festivals (Sforno).

שַׁבַּת שַׁבָּתוֹן – *A day of complete rest.* This term differentiates the Sabbath, when all categories of work are forbidden, from the festivals, when certain kinds of work are permitted.

תִּקְרְאוּ – *You are to proclaim.* The nation, through its court, proclaims the New Moon, upon which the entire calendar — and, consequently, all the festivals — is based *(Ramban).*

מַצּוֹת תֹּאכֵלוּ – *You are to eat matzos.* Technically, the Scriptural requirement to eat matzah applies only to the Seder night. This verse means that whatever grain products one eats may not be leavened. Some hold that whenever one chooses to eat matzah during Pesach, it is a *mitzvah,* in the sense of a meritorious — but not required — deed.

מְלֶאכֶת עֲבֹדָה – *Laborious work.* But work performed for the preparation of food [except for kindling a fire and certain other restrictions] is permitted on the festivals, unlike the Sabbath *(Exodus* 12:16).

אִשֶּׁה – *Fire-offering,* i.e., the *Mussaf,* as described in *Numbers* 28:19-24. Similarly, the other

(בשבת רביעי)–וַיְדַבֵּר יהוה אֶל־מֹשֶׁה לֵּאמֹר: דַּבֵּר אֶל־בְּנֵי יִשְׂרָאֵל
וְאָמַרְתָּ אֲלֵהֶם כִּי־תָבֹאוּ אֶל־הָאָרֶץ אֲשֶׁר אֲנִי נֹתֵן לָכֶם וּקְצַרְתֶּם
אֶת־קְצִירָהּ וַהֲבֵאתֶם אֶת־עֹמֶר* רֵאשִׁית קְצִירְכֶם אֶל־הַכֹּהֵן:
וְהֵנִיף אֶת־הָעֹמֶר לִפְנֵי יהוה לִרְצֹנְכֶם מִמָּחֳרַת הַשַּׁבָּת* יְנִיפֶנּוּ
הַכֹּהֵן: וַעֲשִׂיתֶם בְּיוֹם הֲנִיפְכֶם אֶת־הָעֹמֶר כֶּבֶשׂ תָּמִים בֶּן־שְׁנָתוֹ
לְעֹלָה לַיהוה: וּמִנְחָתוֹ שְׁנֵי עֶשְׂרֹנִים סֹלֶת בְּלוּלָה בַשֶּׁמֶן אִשֶּׁה
לַיהוה רֵיחַ נִיחֹחַ וְנִסְכֹּה יַיִן רְבִיעִת הַהִין: וְלֶחֶם וְקָלִי וְכַרְמֶל לֹא
תֹאכְלוּ* עַד־עֶצֶם הַיּוֹם הַזֶּה עַד הֲבִיאֲכֶם אֶת־קָרְבַּן אֱלֹהֵיכֶם
חֻקַּת עוֹלָם לְדֹרֹתֵיכֶם בְּכֹל מֹשְׁבֹתֵיכֶם:

שלישי (בשבת חמישי)–וּסְפַרְתֶּם לָכֶם מִמָּחֳרַת הַשַּׁבָּת מִיּוֹם הֲבִיאֲכֶם
אֶת־עֹמֶר הַתְּנוּפָה שֶׁבַע שַׁבָּתוֹת תְּמִימֹת תִּהְיֶינָה:* עַד מִמָּחֳרַת
הַשַּׁבָּת הַשְּׁבִיעִת תִּסְפְּרוּ חֲמִשִּׁים יוֹם* וְהִקְרַבְתֶּם מִנְחָה חֲדָשָׁה
לַיהוה: מִמּוֹשְׁבֹתֵיכֶם תָּבִיאוּ ׀ לֶחֶם תְּנוּפָה שְׁתַּיִם שְׁנֵי עֶשְׂרֹנִים
סֹלֶת תִּהְיֶינָה חָמֵץ תֵּאָפֶינָה בִּכּוּרִים* לַיהוה: וְהִקְרַבְתֶּם עַל־הַלֶּחֶם
שִׁבְעַת כְּבָשִׂים תְּמִימִם בְּנֵי שָׁנָה וּפַר בֶּן־בָּקָר אֶחָד וְאֵילִם שְׁנָיִם
יִהְיוּ עֹלָה לַיהוה וּמִנְחָתָם וְנִסְכֵּיהֶם אִשֵּׁה רֵיחַ־נִיחֹחַ לַיהוה:
וַעֲשִׂיתֶם שְׂעִיר־עִזִּים אֶחָד לְחַטָּאת וּשְׁנֵי כְבָשִׂים בְּנֵי שָׁנָה לְזֶבַח
שְׁלָמִים: וְהֵנִיף הַכֹּהֵן ׀ אֹתָם* עַל לֶחֶם הַבִּכֻּרִים תְּנוּפָה לִפְנֵי יהוה
עַל־שְׁנֵי כְּבָשִׂים קֹדֶשׁ* יִהְיוּ לַיהוה לַכֹּהֵן: וּקְרָאתֶם בְּעֶצֶם ׀ הַיּוֹם
הַזֶּה מִקְרָא־קֹדֶשׁ יִהְיֶה לָכֶם כָּל־מְלֶאכֶת עֲבֹדָה לֹא תַעֲשׂוּ חֻקַּת
עוֹלָם בְּכָל־מוֹשְׁבֹתֵיכֶם לְדֹרֹתֵיכֶם: וּבְקֻצְרְכֶם* אֶת־קְצִיר אַרְצְכֶם
לֹא־תְכַלֶּה פְּאַת שָׂדְךָ בְּקֻצְרֶךָ וְלֶקֶט קְצִירְךָ לֹא תְלַקֵּט לֶעָנִי וְלַגֵּר
תַּעֲזֹב אֹתָם אֲנִי יהוה אֱלֹהֵיכֶם:

Mussaf offerings mentioned in this chapter are described in *Numbers* 28 and 29.

עֹמֶר – *An Omer.* The word *omer* is a dry measurement, which is the volume of approximately 43.2 average eggs; by extension, however, the entire offering is called *Omer*. Unlike all other meal-offerings, it is barley instead of wheat. The grain used in this offering should be the very first to be harvested. Indeed, it was cut the night before it was to be offered, and no species of grain products from the new crop may be eaten before the *Omer* is offered.

מִמָּחֳרַת הַשַּׁבָּת – *On the morrow of the rest-day.* The *rest-day* is the first day of Pesach. Thus, the *Omer* is offered on the morning of the second day of Pesach.

לֹא תֹאכְלוּ – *You may not eat.* The prohibition applies only to grain products from the new crop, but not to fruits and vegetables.

תְּמִימֹת תִּהְיֶינָה – *They are to be . . . complete.* The count must begin in the evening in order for it to be considered 'complete.'

חֲמִשִּׁים יוֹם – *Fifty days,* i.e., you are to count seven weeks until the fiftieth day, which is celebrated as Shavuos.

בִּכּוּרִים – *First-offerings.* Although it was permitted to use the new grain crop after the *Omer*-offering, none of it could be used as a Temple offering until this *new meal-offering* was brought on Shavuos.

אֹתָם – *Them.* Only the two peace-offering sheep

(On the Sabbath—Fourth) — *HASHEM spoke to Moses saying: Speak to the Children of Israel and say to them: When you arrive in the Land that I give you and you reap its harvest; you are to bring an Omer* from your first harvest to the Kohen. He is to wave the Omer before HASHEM to gain acceptance for you; on the morrow of the rest-day* the Kohen is to wave it. On the day when you wave the Omer you are to offer an unblemished lamb in its first year as an elevation-offering to HASHEM. And its meal-offering is to be two tenth-ephah of fine flour mixed with oil, a fire-offering to HASHEM, a satisfying aroma; and its wine-libation is to be a quarter-hin. You may not eat* bread nor roasted kernels, nor plump kernels until this very day, until you bring the offering of your God; it is an eternal decree for your generations in all your dwelling places.*

Third (on the Sabbath—Fifth) — *You are to count for yourselves — from the morrow of the rest-day, from the day when you bring the Omer of the waving — they are to be seven complete* weeks. Until the morrow of the seventh week you are to count, fifty days;* and then you are to offer a new meal-offering to HASHEM. From your dwelling places you are to bring bread which is to be waved, two loaves made from two tenth-ephah, they are to be fine flour, they are to be baked leavened; first-offerings* to HASHEM. With the bread you are to offer seven unblemished lambs within their first year, one young bull, and two rams; they are to be an elevation-offering to HASHEM, with their meal-offering and libations — a fire-offering, a satisfying aroma to HASHEM. You are to offer one he-goat as a sin-offering; and two lambs within their first year for peace-offerings. The Kohen is to wave them* with the first-offering breads as a waving before HASHEM — with the two sheep — they shall be most holy,* for HASHEM and for the Kohen. You are to proclaim on this very day that it is to be a holy convocation for yourselves, you are to do no laborious work, it is an eternal decree in your dwelling places for your generations.*

When you reap the harvest of your land you are not to remove completely the corners of your field as you reap, and also do not gather the gleanings of your harvest; for the poor and the stranger are you to leave them, I am HASHEM your God.*

— as specified later in this verse — are to be lifted up, while they are still alive, and waved together with the two breads.

קֹדֶשׁ — *Most holy.* This is the only case of *communal* peace-offerings. Therefore, they have the status of the holier offerings [קָדְשֵׁי קָדָשִׁים] and may be eaten only by *Kohanim,* unlike ordinary peace-offerings, which may be eaten by all Jews.

וּבְקֻצְרְכֶם — *When you reap.* The Jew who harvests his crop must leave a corner of his field for the poor, and if he drops one or two stalks at a time he must leave them as well. Why are these commandments inserted among the laws of the festivals? To teach that someone who obeys the Torah's injunction to share his crop with the poor is regarded as if he had built the Temple and performed the festival service of the offerings.

רביעי (בשבת ששי)–וַיְדַבֵּר יהוה אֶל־מֹשֶׁה לֵּאמֹר: דַּבֵּר אֶל־בְּנֵי יִשְׂרָאֵל
לֵאמֹר בַּחֹדֶשׁ הַשְּׁבִיעִי בְּאֶחָד לַחֹדֶשׁ יִהְיֶה לָכֶם שַׁבָּתוֹן זִכְרוֹן
תְּרוּעָה* מִקְרָא־קֹדֶשׁ: כָּל־מְלֶאכֶת עֲבֹדָה לֹא תַעֲשׂוּ וְהִקְרַבְתֶּם
אִשֶּׁה לַיהוה: וַיְדַבֵּר יהוה אֶל־מֹשֶׁה לֵּאמֹר: אַךְ* בֶּעָשׂוֹר לַחֹדֶשׁ
הַשְּׁבִיעִי הַזֶּה יוֹם הַכִּפֻּרִים הוּא מִקְרָא־קֹדֶשׁ יִהְיֶה לָכֶם וְעִנִּיתֶם*
אֶת־נַפְשֹׁתֵיכֶם וְהִקְרַבְתֶּם אִשֶּׁה לַיהוה: וְכָל־מְלָאכָה לֹא תַעֲשׂוּ*
בְּעֶצֶם הַיּוֹם הַזֶּה כִּי יוֹם כִּפֻּרִים הוּא לְכַפֵּר עֲלֵיכֶם לִפְנֵי יהוה
אֱלֹהֵיכֶם: כִּי כָל־הַנֶּפֶשׁ אֲשֶׁר לֹא־תְעֻנֶּה בְּעֶצֶם הַיּוֹם הַזֶּה וְנִכְרְתָה
מֵעַמֶּיהָ: וְכָל־הַנֶּפֶשׁ אֲשֶׁר תַּעֲשֶׂה כָּל־מְלָאכָה בְּעֶצֶם הַיּוֹם הַזֶּה
וְהַאֲבַדְתִּי אֶת־הַנֶּפֶשׁ הַהִוא מִקֶּרֶב עַמָּהּ: כָּל־מְלָאכָה לֹא תַעֲשׂוּ
חֻקַּת עוֹלָם לְדֹרֹתֵיכֶם בְּכֹל מֹשְׁבֹתֵיכֶם: שַׁבַּת שַׁבָּתוֹן הוּא לָכֶם
וְעִנִּיתֶם אֶת־נַפְשֹׁתֵיכֶם בְּתִשְׁעָה לַחֹדֶשׁ בָּעֶרֶב* מֵעֶרֶב עַד־עֶרֶב
תִּשְׁבְּתוּ שַׁבַּתְּכֶם:

חמישי (בשבת שביעי)–וַיְדַבֵּר יהוה אֶל־מֹשֶׁה לֵּאמֹר: דַּבֵּר אֶל־בְּנֵי יִשְׂרָאֵל
לֵאמֹר בַּחֲמִשָּׁה עָשָׂר יוֹם לַחֹדֶשׁ הַשְּׁבִיעִי הַזֶּה חַג הַסֻּכּוֹת שִׁבְעַת
יָמִים לַיהוה: בַּיּוֹם הָרִאשׁוֹן מִקְרָא־קֹדֶשׁ כָּל־מְלֶאכֶת עֲבֹדָה לֹא
תַעֲשׂוּ: שִׁבְעַת יָמִים תַּקְרִיבוּ אִשֶּׁה לַיהוה בַּיּוֹם הַשְּׁמִינִי מִקְרָא־
קֹדֶשׁ יִהְיֶה לָכֶם וְהִקְרַבְתֶּם אִשֶּׁה לַיהוה עֲצֶרֶת* הִוא כָּל־מְלֶאכֶת
עֲבֹדָה לֹא תַעֲשׂוּ: אֵלֶּה מוֹעֲדֵי יהוה אֲשֶׁר־תִּקְרְאוּ אֹתָם מִקְרָאֵי
קֹדֶשׁ לְהַקְרִיב אִשֶּׁה לַיהוה עֹלָה וּמִנְחָה זֶבַח וּנְסָכִים דְּבַר־יוֹם
בְּיוֹמוֹ: מִלְּבַד* שַׁבְּתֹת יהוה וּמִלְּבַד מַתְּנוֹתֵיכֶם וּמִלְּבַד כָּל־נִדְרֵיכֶם
וּמִלְּבַד כָּל־נִדְבֹתֵיכֶם אֲשֶׁר תִּתְּנוּ לַיהוה: אַךְ בַּחֲמִשָּׁה עָשָׂר יוֹם
לַחֹדֶשׁ הַשְּׁבִיעִי בְּאָסְפְּכֶם אֶת־תְּבוּאַת הָאָרֶץ תָּחֹגּוּ* אֶת־חַג־
יהוה שִׁבְעַת יָמִים בַּיּוֹם הָרִאשׁוֹן שַׁבָּתוֹן וּבַיּוֹם הַשְּׁמִינִי שַׁבָּתוֹן:

זִכְרוֹן תְּרוּעָה – *A remembrance with shofar blasts.* By reciting verses describing God's remembrance and the events associated with blasts of the *shofar*, a ram's horn, you will cause God to remember the *Akeidah* of Isaac, who was replaced on the altar by a ram *(Rashi). Ramban* comments that the *shofar* blast, coming in the month of repentance and atonement, reminds us that the first of the month is a Day of Judgment.

אַךְ – *However.* Although people are judged on Rosh Hashanah, God has set aside Yom Kippur for atonement and forgiveness *(Ramban).* The word אַךְ, *however,* always implies a limitation: the "atonement" is available only to those who repent, but not to those who ignore the opportunity to earn forgiveness through repentance.

וְעִנִּיתֶם – *You are to afflict,* i.e., fast.

וְכָל מְלָאכָה לֹא תַעֲשׂוּ – *You are not to do any work.* Unlike the other festivals, all work is forbidden on Yom Kippur, even food preparation.

בְּתִשְׁעָה לַחֹדֶשׁ בָּעֶרֶב – *On the ninth of the month in the evening.* The simple meaning is that the Yom Kippur fast begins in the evening after sunset of the ninth day. However, since the Torah specifies the ninth day, the Talmud finds support for the dictum that it is a *mitzvah* to eat on the ninth day [to be strong for the fast] just as it is a *mitzvah* to fast on the tenth, and that one who eats on the ninth day is reckoned as if he had fasted both days (*Yoma* 81b).

Fourth (On the Sabbath—Sixth) — *HASHEM spoke to Moses saying: Speak to the children of Israel saying: in the seventh month on the first of the month, it shall be a rest-day for you, a remembrance with shofar blasts,* a holy convocation. You are to do no laborious work; and you are to offer a fire-offering to HASHEM.*

HASHEM spoke to Moses saying: However, the tenth day of this seventh month is a Day of Atonement, it shall be a holy convocation for you and you are to afflict* yourselves; you are to offer a fire-offering to HASHEM. You are not to do any work* on this very day, for it is a Day of Atonement to atone for you before HASHEM your God. For any soul who will not be afflicted on this day will be excised from its people. And any soul who will perform work on this very day, I will destroy that soul from among its people. You are not to do any work; it is an eternal decree throughout your generations in all your dwelling places. It is a day of complete rest for you and you are to afflict yourselves; on the ninth of the month in the evening* — from evening to evening — you are to observe your rest day.*

Fifth (On the Sabbath—Seventh) — *HASHEM spoke to Moses saying: Speak to the children of Israel saying: on the fifteenth day of this seventh month is the Succos festival, for seven days to HASHEM. On the first day is a holy convocation; you are to do no laborious work. For seven days you are to offer a fire-offering to HASHEM; the eighth day shall be a holy convocation for you, and you are to offer a fire-offering to HASHEM, it shall be an assembly,* you may not do any laborious work.*

These are the convocations of HASHEM that you are to proclaim as holy convocations; to offer a fire-offering to HASHEM: an elevation-offering and its meal-offering; offering and its libation, each day what is required for that day. Aside from HASHEM's Sabbaths; aside from your gifts, aside from your vows, and aside from your free-will offerings, which you will present to HASHEM.*

However, on the fifteenth day of the seventh month when you gather in the crop of the land you are to celebrate HASHEM's festival for seven days; the first day is a rest-day and the eighth day is a rest-day.*

עֲצֶרֶת — *An assembly.* Known as Shemini Atzeres, the Eighth Day of Assembly, this day is treated as an independent festival, rather than part of Succos. On Shemini Atzeres, there is no requirement to eat in a *succah* or take the Four Species, and the *Mussaf* offering is of an entirely different nature from that of Succos.

Based on the Midrash, *Rashi* translates עֲצֶרֶת as an expression of *restraint.* God asks the Jewish people to restrain for one more day their desire to go back to their homes. The Midrash gives the parable of a king who invited his children to a week-long celebration. When the time was over, he asked them to stay for an extra day before leaving him. So, too, after the joyous week of Succos, God asks Israel to stay behind for one more festive day.

מִלְּבַד — *Aside from.* The previous verse refers only to the festivals; this one refers to the *Mussaf* of the Sabbath and to personal offerings that may be brought on the Intermediate Days of Pesach and Succos *(Or HaChaim).*

בַּחֲמִשָּׁה עָשָׂר ... תָּחֹגּוּ — *However, on the fifteenth ... you are to celebrate.* The 'celebration' of which the verse speaks refers to the *Chagigah* offering, which is a peace-offering that is brought by everyone who comes to celebrate a pilgrimage festival. The word אַךְ, *however,* is a limitation, implying that there are times when a *Chagigah* is *not* offered. In this case it teaches that the *Chagigah* offering may be brought only on a weekday. Were the festival to fall on the Sabbath, the offering would be deferred to a later day, because personal offerings may not be brought on the Sabbath.

וּלְקַחְתֶּם לָכֶם בַּיּוֹם הָרִאשׁוֹן* פְּרִי עֵץ הָדָר כַּפֹּת תְּמָרִים וַעֲנַף עֵץ־עָבֹת וְעַרְבֵי־נָחַל וּשְׂמַחְתֶּם לִפְנֵי יהוה אֱלֹהֵיכֶם שִׁבְעַת יָמִים: וְחַגֹּתֶם אֹתוֹ חַג לַיהוה שִׁבְעַת יָמִים בַּשָּׁנָה חֻקַּת עוֹלָם לְדֹרֹתֵיכֶם בַּחֹדֶשׁ הַשְּׁבִיעִי תָּחֹגּוּ אֹתוֹ: בַּסֻּכֹּת* תֵּשְׁבוּ שִׁבְעַת יָמִים כָּל־הָאֶזְרָח בְּיִשְׂרָאֵל יֵשְׁבוּ בַּסֻּכֹּת: לְמַעַן יֵדְעוּ דֹרֹתֵיכֶם כִּי בַסֻּכּוֹת הוֹשַׁבְתִּי אֶת־בְּנֵי יִשְׂרָאֵל בְּהוֹצִיאִי אוֹתָם מֵאֶרֶץ מִצְרָיִם אֲנִי יהוה אֱלֹהֵיכֶם: וַיְדַבֵּר מֹשֶׁה אֶת־מֹעֲדֵי יהוה אֶל־בְּנֵי יִשְׂרָאֵל:

חצי קדיש

After the last *oleh* has completed his closing blessing, the second Torah Scroll is placed on the *bimah* alongside the first, and the reader recites Half-*Kaddish*.

יִתְגַּדַּל וְיִתְקַדַּשׁ שְׁמֵהּ רַבָּא. (.Cong – אָמֵן.) בְּעָלְמָא דִּי בְרָא כִרְעוּתֵהּ. וְיַמְלִיךְ מַלְכוּתֵהּ, בְּחַיֵּיכוֹן וּבְיוֹמֵיכוֹן וּבְחַיֵּי דְכָל בֵּית יִשְׂרָאֵל, בַּעֲגָלָא וּבִזְמַן קָרִיב. וְאִמְרוּ: אָמֵן.

(.Cong – אָמֵן. יְהֵא שְׁמֵהּ רַבָּא מְבָרַךְ לְעָלַם וּלְעָלְמֵי עָלְמַיָּא.)

יְהֵא שְׁמֵהּ רַבָּא מְבָרַךְ לְעָלַם וּלְעָלְמֵי עָלְמַיָּא.

יִתְבָּרַךְ וְיִשְׁתַּבַּח וְיִתְפָּאַר וְיִתְרוֹמַם וְיִתְנַשֵּׂא וְיִתְהַדָּר וְיִתְעַלֶּה וְיִתְהַלָּל שְׁמֵהּ דְּקֻדְשָׁא בְּרִיךְ הוּא (.Cong – בְּרִיךְ הוּא) – לְעֵלָּא מִן כָּל בִּרְכָתָא וְשִׁירָתָא תֻּשְׁבְּחָתָא וְנֶחֱמָתָא, דַּאֲמִירָן בְּעָלְמָא. וְאִמְרוּ: אָמֵן. (.Cong – אָמֵן.)

הגבהה וגלילה

The first Torah is raised for all to see. Each person looks at the Torah and recites aloud:

וְזֹאת הַתּוֹרָה אֲשֶׁר שָׂם מֹשֶׁה לִפְנֵי בְּנֵי יִשְׂרָאֵל,[1] עַל פִּי יהוה בְּיַד מֹשֶׁה.[2]

Some add:

עֵץ חַיִּים הִיא לַמַּחֲזִיקִים בָּהּ, וְתֹמְכֶיהָ מְאֻשָּׁר.[3] דְּרָכֶיהָ דַרְכֵי נֹעַם, וְכָל נְתִיבוֹתֶיהָ שָׁלוֹם.[4] אֹרֶךְ יָמִים בִּימִינָהּ, בִּשְׂמֹאלָהּ עֹשֶׁר וְכָבוֹד.[5] יהוה חָפֵץ לְמַעַן צִדְקוֹ, יַגְדִּיל תּוֹרָה וְיַאְדִּיר.[6]

מפטיר

As the first Torah is wound, tied, and covered, the *oleh* for *Maftir* is called to the second Torah.

במדבר כט:יב־טז

וּבַחֲמִשָּׁה עָשָׂר יוֹם לַחֹדֶשׁ הַשְּׁבִיעִי מִקְרָא־קֹדֶשׁ יִהְיֶה לָכֶם כָּל־מְלֶאכֶת עֲבֹדָה לֹא תַעֲשׂוּ וְחַגֹּתֶם חַג לַיהוה שִׁבְעַת יָמִים: וְהִקְרַבְתֶּם עֹלָה אִשֵּׁה רֵיחַ נִיחֹחַ לַיהוה פָּרִים בְּנֵי־בָקָר שְׁלֹשָׁה עָשָׂר אֵילִם שְׁנָיִם כְּבָשִׂים בְּנֵי־שָׁנָה אַרְבָּעָה עָשָׂר תְּמִימִם יִהְיוּ:

(1) *Deuteronomy* 4:44. (2) *Numbers* 9:23. (3) *Proverbs* 3:18. (4) 3:17. (5) 3:16. (6) *Isaiah* 42:21.

On the first day you are to take for yourselves the fruit of a citron tree, the branches of date palms, twigs of a plaited tree, brook willows; and you are to rejoice before HASHEM your God for seven days. You are to dwell in booths for seven days; every citizen of Israel is to dwell in booths. So that your generations will know that I caused the Children of Israel to dwell in booths* when I took them from the land of Egypt; I am HASHEM your God.*

And Moses declared the appointed festivals of HASHEM to the Children of Israel.

HALF KADDISH

After the last *oleh* has completed his closing blessing, the second Torah Scroll is placed on the *bimah* alongside the first, and the reader recites Half-*Kaddish*.

יִתְגַּדַּל *May His great Name grow exalted and sanctified* (Cong.— *Amen.*) *in the world that He created as He willed. May He give reign to His kingship in your lifetimes and in your days, and in the lifetimes of the entire Family of Israel, swiftly and soon. Now respond: Amen.*

(Cong.— *Amen. May His great Name be blessed forever and ever.*)

May His great Name be blessed forever and ever.

Blessed, praised, glorified, exalted, extolled, mighty, upraised, and lauded be the Name of the Holy One, Blessed is He (Cong.— *Blessed is He*) — *beyond any blessing and song, praise and consolation that are uttered in the world. Now respond: Amen.* (Cong.— *Amen.*)

HAGBAHAH AND GELILAH

The first Torah is raised for all to see. Each person looks at the Torah and recites aloud:

This is the Torah that Moses placed before the Children of Israel,[1] upon the command of HASHEM, through Moses' hand.[2]

Some add:

עֵץ *It is a tree of life for those who grasp it, and its supporters are praiseworthy.[3] Its ways are ways of pleasantness and all its paths are peace.[4] Lengthy days are at its right; at its left are wealth and honor.[5] HASHEM desired, for the sake of its [Israel's] righteousness, that the Torah be made great and glorious.[6]*

MAFTIR

As the first Torah is wound, tied, and covered, the *oleh* for *Maftir* is called to the second Torah.

Numbers 29:12-16

Maftir – *The fifteenth day of the seventh month is to be a holy convocation for you, you may do no laborious work; you are to celebrate a festival to HASHEM for seven days. You are to offer an elevation-offering, a fire-offering, a satisfying aroma to HASHEM, thirteen young bulls, two rams, fourteen lambs within their first year; they are to be unblem-*

בְּיוֹם הָרִאשׁוֹן – *On the first day.* Torah law requires that the Four Species be taken only on the first day. The commandment that they be taken all seven days is of Rabbinic origin.

בַּסֻּכֹּת – *In booths.* The Sages disagree. Some hold that the 'booths' of the wilderness were figurative; they were actually the Clouds of Glory that God provided for Israel's protection. The other opinion is that the people literally built booths for shelter (*Succah* 11b).

⊲§ Maftir

On all festivals and Rosh Chodesh, the *Maftir* reading comes from the *Sidra Pinchas* (*Numbers* ch. 28 and 29) which sets forth the *Mussaf* offering of the respective days. Unlike Pesach, during which the same *Mussaf* is offered all seven days of the festival, every day of Succos has a slightly different *Mussaf*. Therefore, on

וּמִנְחָתָם סֹלֶת בְּלוּלָה בַשָּׁמֶן שְׁלֹשָׁה עֶשְׂרֹנִים לַפָּר הָאֶחָד לִשְׁלֹשָׁה עָשָׂר פָּרִים שְׁנֵי עֶשְׂרֹנִים לָאַיִל הָאֶחָד לִשְׁנֵי הָאֵילִם׃ וְעִשָּׂרוֹן עִשָּׂרוֹן לַכֶּבֶשׂ הָאֶחָד לְאַרְבָּעָה עָשָׂר כְּבָשִׂים׃ וּשְׂעִיר־עִזִּים אֶחָד חַטָּאת מִלְּבַד עֹלַת הַתָּמִיד מִנְחָתָהּ וְנִסְכָּהּ׃

הגבהה וגלילה

The *maftir* completes his closing blessing.
Then the second Torah Scroll is raised and each person looks at the Torah and recites aloud:

וְזֹאת הַתּוֹרָה אֲשֶׁר שָׂם מֹשֶׁה לִפְנֵי בְּנֵי יִשְׂרָאֵל,[1] עַל פִּי יהוה בְּיַד מֹשֶׁה.[2]

Some add:

עֵץ חַיִּים הִיא לַמַּחֲזִיקִים בָּהּ, וְתֹמְכֶיהָ מְאֻשָּׁר.[3] דְּרָכֶיהָ דַרְכֵי נֹעַם, וְכָל נְתִיבוֹתֶיהָ שָׁלוֹם.[4] אֹרֶךְ יָמִים בִּימִינָהּ, בִּשְׂמֹאלָהּ עֹשֶׁר וְכָבוֹד.[5] יהוה חָפֵץ לְמַעַן צִדְקוֹ, יַגְדִּיל תּוֹרָה וְיַאְדִּיר.[6]

After the Torah Scroll has been wound, tied and covered, the *maftir* recites the *Haftarah* blessings.

ברכה קודם ההפטרה

בָּרוּךְ אַתָּה יהוה אֱלֹהֵינוּ מֶלֶךְ הָעוֹלָם, אֲשֶׁר בָּחַר בִּנְבִיאִים טוֹבִים,* וְרָצָה בְדִבְרֵיהֶם* הַנֶּאֱמָרִים בֶּאֱמֶת, בָּרוּךְ אַתָּה יהוה,* הַבּוֹחֵר בַּתּוֹרָה וּבְמֹשֶׁה עַבְדּוֹ, וּבְיִשְׂרָאֵל עַמּוֹ, וּבִנְבִיאֵי הָאֱמֶת וָצֶדֶק׃ (Cong. – אָמֵן.)

---

each day we read the *Mussaf* of that particular day. In the Diaspora, each festival is celebrated for an extra day in commemoration of ancient times when people far from Jerusalem did not know the exact day of Rosh Chodesh. (See ArtScroll *Mishnah Rosh Hashanah* pp. 109-113.) Consequently, in the Diaspora each day's *Mussaf* is read for two days.

The 70 Oxen — Atonement for the 70 Nations

As part of the *Mussaf*, a different number of oxen was offered each day — thirteen on the first day, twelve on the second, with the total decreasing by one on each successive day. The total number of oxen offered throughout the festival (seven days) came to seventy, corresponding to the seventy nations who descended from Noah and who were the ancestors of all the nations of the world. The Temple in Jerusalem was perceived as 'a house of prayer for all the peoples' and these seventy oxen were sacrificed in atonement for these nations and in prayer for their well-being and peace (see *Rashi* to *Numbers* 29).

"Woe to the idolaters," moaned R' Yochanan (*Succah* 55b), "for they had a loss [by the destruction of the Temple] and they do not know what they have lost. When the Temple was in existence, the altar atoned for them, but now that it is no longer in existence who shall atone for them?"

The Midrash similarly expounds the verse in *Psalms* 109:4, תַּחַת אַהֲבָתִי יִשְׂטְנוּנִי וַאֲנִי תְפִלָּה, *In return for my love they hate me, and I am prayer.* — Notwithstanding Israel's love as manifested by their praying and sacrificing the seventy oxen during Succos as intercession on behalf of the seventy nations, the gentile nations hate them, instead of being grateful.

The Haftarah

The practice of reading from the Prophets — today known as the *Haftarah* — was introduced during the reign of the infamous Syrian-Greek King Antiochus, who ruled and persecuted Israel prior to the time of the Chanukah miracle [165 B.C.E.]. In his attempts to rid the Jewish people of their religion, he forbade the public reading from the Torah. Unable to refresh their spiritual thirst from the Torah itself, the people resorted to readings from the Prophets, calling seven people

ished. And their meal-offering shall be fine flour mixed with oil; three tenth-ephah for each bull of the thirteen bulls, two tenth-ephah for each ram of the two rams. And one tenth-ephah for each lamb of the fourteen lambs. And one he-goat for a sin-offering; aside from the continual elevation-offering with its meal-offering and its libation.

HAGBAHAH AND GELILAH

The *maftir* completes his closing blessing.
Then the second Torah Scroll is raised and each person looks at the Torah and recites aloud:

This is the Torah that Moses placed before the Children of Israel,[1] upon the command of HASHEM, through Moses' hand.[2]

Some add:

עֵץ *It is a tree of life for those who grasp it, and its supporters are praiseworthy.[3] Its ways are ways of pleasantness and all its paths are peace.[4] Lengthy days are at its right; at its left are wealth and honor.[5] HASHEM desired, for the sake of its [Israel's] righteousness, that the Torah be made great and glorious.[6]*

After the Torah Scroll has been wound, tied and covered, the *maftir* recites the *Haftarah* blessings.

BLESSING BEFORE THE HAFTARAH

בָּרוּךְ *Blessed are You, HASHEM, our God, King of the universe, Who has chosen good prophets* and was pleased with their words* that were uttered with truth. Blessed are You, HASHEM,* Who chooses the Torah; Moses, His servant; Israel, His nation; and the prophets of truth and righteousness.*

(Cong.— *Amen.*)

(1) *Deuteronomy* 4:44. (2) *Numbers* 9:23. (3) *Proverbs* 3:18. (4) 3:17. (5) 3:16. (6) *Isaiah* 42:21.

---

to read at least three verses each. Later, when the ban was lifted, the people retained their custom of having someone read from the Prophets. However, in order not to let it seem as though the reading from the Prophets had equal standing with the reading from the Torah, the Sages decreed that the person reading the *Haftarah* must first read a portion from the Torah.

Generally, the last group of verses from the week's Torah reading is read as the *Maftir* portion, and the *Haftarah* is on a subject related to the Torah portion. On Festivals, including Rosh Hashanah, the *Maftir* portion is from the verses in *Numbers* that describe the day's *Mussaf* offerings, and is read from a second Torah Scroll.

The word *Haftarah* comes from פטר, to *dismiss*, to *complete*. The dessert of a meal is known in the Talmud as *haftarah* because it is the end of the meal, just as the Prophetic reading completes the Torah-reading part of the service. The person doing this 'completing,' therefore, is called the *maftir*.

⋄§ Blessing before the Haftarah

בִּנְבִיאִים טוֹבִים — *Good prophets.* The theme of the *Haftarah* blessings is the integrity of the prophets and their teachings. They are good to the Jewish people, even when it is their mission to criticize and threaten. Also, they are chosen because they are good people: learned, righteous, impressive, and so on. Our tradition does not accept prophets who had been lacking in any of the attributes of Jewish greatness.

וְרָצָה בְדִבְרֵיהֶם — *And was pleased with their words.* There are a variety of interpretations:

— The words of the prophets are as authoritative to us as the Torah itself.

— God is especially pleased with the prophecies of Israel's future good.

— God is pleased even with what the prophets do on their own initiative.

— He is pleased that they adhere scrupulously to His mission.

בָּרוּךְ אַתָּה ה׳ — *Blessed are You, HASHEM.* Not a new blessing, this is a summing up of the previous points: God has chosen the Torah, which owes its authority to our absolute faith in the prophecy of Moses. The Torah was given to God's Chosen People, whom He instructs and chastises through His truthful and righteous prophets.

FIRST DAY

הפטרה ליום ראשון

זכריה יד:א־כא

הִנֵּה יוֹם־בָּא לַיהוָה* וְחֻלַּק שְׁלָלֵךְ בְּקִרְבֵּךְ: וְאָסַפְתִּי אֶת־כָּל־
הַגּוֹיִם ׀ אֶל־יְרוּשָׁלַםִ לַמִּלְחָמָה וְנִלְכְּדָה הָעִיר וְנָשַׁסּוּ הַבָּתִּים
וְהַנָּשִׁים תִּשָּׁכַבְנָה וְיָצָא חֲצִי הָעִיר בַּגּוֹלָה וְיֶתֶר הָעָם לֹא יִכָּרֵת
מִן־הָעִיר: וְיָצָא יהוה וְנִלְחַם בַּגּוֹיִם הָהֵם כְּיוֹם הִלָּחֲמוֹ בְּיוֹם קְרָב:*

HAFTARAH FOR THE FIRST DAY

Prominent in the *Haftarah* subjects of Succos is the War of Gog and Magog, the cataclysmic series of battles that will result in the final Redemption and the Messianic era. The *Haftarah* of the first day and that of the Sabbath of *Chol HaMoed* deal with this war. According to *Rashi*, this topic is related to Succos because of the prophecy that those nations who would survive the wars would join Israel every year in celebrating the Succos festival.

Nimukei Yosef to *Megillah* quotes a tradition from *R' Hai Gaon* that the victory over Gog and Magog will take place in the month of Tishrei — the month of Succos.

R' Hirsch (*Numbers* 29:13) discusses the inner connection between Gog and Magog and Succos. Following is a free rendition of his thesis:

In the name גוג, *Gog*, one recognizes the word גַּג, *roof*, and thereby at once sees the contrast to *succah*, the weak, unstable covering of foliage. Actually, the whole history of mankind consists of this contrast. Just as people have the power to make [themselves] safe and secure against their earthly contemporaries by sturdy walls, so they delude themselves into thinking that they can make themselves safe and secure against that which comes from above — against God and . . . His power to direct matters. They think that they can find security in the protection of their own might, take their fate in their own hands, and crown the building up of human greatness with gabled roofs, rendering them independent of God.

[The war of Gog and Magog] is the battle of גַּג, *roof*, against סוּכָּה, *succah*, the fight of the 'roof' illusion of human greatness which never allows rest, against the '*succah*' truth of cheerful confidence and serenity which comes of placing one's trust in God's protection.

R' Hirsch's exposition of the Gog-Magog relationship bases itself on the Hebrew grammatical rule that the prefix מ, *mem*, expresses the

SECOND DAY

הפטרה ליום שני

מלכים א׳ ח:ב־כא

וַיִּקָּהֲלוּ אֶל־הַמֶּלֶךְ שְׁלֹמֹה כָּל־אִישׁ יִשְׂרָאֵל בְּיֶרַח הָאֵתָנִים* בֶּחָג*
הוּא הַחֹדֶשׁ הַשְּׁבִיעִי: וַיָּבֹאוּ כֹּל זִקְנֵי יִשְׂרָאֵל וַיִּשְׂאוּ הַכֹּהֲנִים
אֶת־הָאָרוֹן: וַיַּעֲלוּ אֶת־אֲרוֹן יהוה* וְאֶת־אֹהֶל מוֹעֵד וְאֶת־כָּל־כְּלֵי
הַקֹּדֶשׁ אֲשֶׁר בָּאֹהֶל וַיַּעֲלוּ אֹתָם הַכֹּהֲנִים וְהַלְוִיִּם: וְהַמֶּלֶךְ שְׁלֹמֹה
וְכָל־עֲדַת יִשְׂרָאֵל הַנּוֹעָדִים עָלָיו אִתּוֹ לִפְנֵי הָאָרוֹן מְזַבְּחִים צֹאן
וּבָקָר אֲשֶׁר לֹא־יִסָּפְרוּ וְלֹא יִמָּנוּ מֵרֹב: וַיָּבִאוּ הַכֹּהֲנִים אֶת־אֲרוֹן

HAFTARAH FOR THE SECOND DAY

King Solomon and the people dedicated the First Temple in an ecstatic fourteen-day celebration, the last seven days of which were the Succos festival. Thus, Israel's joy in the Temple coincided with Succos, the season of joy.

בְּיֶרַח הָאֵתָנִים — *In the month of the mighty ones*, i.e., Tishrei. It is given this name because the spiritually mighty Patriarchs were born in Tishrei; because the festivals of judgment, atone-

FIRST DAY

HAFTARAH FOR THE FIRST DAY

Zechariah 14:1-21

Behold, God's awaited day is coming; and your spoils will be divided in your midst. I shall gather all the nations to Jerusalem to wage war, the city will be conquered, the home plundered and the women violated; half the city will go into exile, but the rest of the people will not be cut off from the city. Then* HASHEM *will go out and wage war against those nations as on the day He warred, the day of battle.**

idea of projecting something. For example, אור is *light;* מָאוֹר, *luminary,* is a heavenly body which projects light. So, too, גַּג means *roof* — in *R' Hirsch's* view, it represents the philosophy that man can insulate himself against the heavenly power of God — מָגוֹג is the attempt to project this philosophy on earth. (from ArtScroll *Ezekiel,* p. 580).

Zechariah's prophecies came at a critical juncture in Israel's history. Seventeen years after King Cyrus had given permission for the Second Temple to be built, construction had stopped upon orders of King Ahasuerus and after the harassment and slanders of the gentile nations who surrounded Jerusalem. Morale was low and despair was prevalent in the bedraggled Jewish settlement. Then, God sent Zechariah to command the people, under their leaders Zerubavel and Joshua, to ignore their fears and resume construction of the Temple. God promised them success and, indeed, soon after that King Darius of Persia sanctioned the undertaking. In the chapter which is today's *Haftarah,* Zechariah prophecies that the cataclysmic War of Gog and Magog will climax with the final redemption and the acknowledgment by the nations that HASHEM alone is King and that Israel is His people. This realization will be celebrated on Succos — for which reason it was chosen as the *Haftarah* for the first day of Succos. [For a discussion of the War of Gog and Magog, see ArtScroll commentary to *Ezekiel* ch. 38.]

יוֹם בָּא לַה׳ – *God's awaited day is coming,* i.e., the day when God and Magog will wage their great war will come one day. It will result in the revelation of God's greatness to the entire world, and the *spoils* that had been robbed from Israel will be returned to be divided among the newly triumphant Jews.

בְּיוֹם קְרָב – *The day of battle,* i.e., the day God intervened at the Sea of Reeds to save Israel from the pursuing Egyptians. Then as now, the Jewish people appeared to be in mortal danger.

SECOND DAY

HAFTARAH FOR THE SECOND DAY

I Kings 8:2-21

All the men of Israel gathered before King Solomon in the month of the mighty ones on the festival;* the seventh month. All the elders of Israel arrived; and the Kohanim bore the Ark. They brought up the Ark of* HASHEM,** the Tabernacle of the Meeting, and all the holy vessels that were in the Tabernacle; the Kohanim and the Levites brought them up.*

King Solomon and the entire Congregation of Israel that assembled by him, to join him before the Ark; were offering sheep and cattle too abundant to be counted or enumerated. The Kohanim brought the Ark

ment, and joy with their many commandments occur in Tishrei (*Talmud, Rosh Hashanah* 11a); or because the crops that are harvested in Tishrei give strength and health to the people (*Radak*).

בֶּחָג – *On the festival.* There was a seven-day inauguration festival immediately before Succos. Thus, there were a total of fourteen days of celebration.

אֲרוֹן ה׳ – *The Ark of* HASHEM. Until then, the Ark was in the threshing floor of Arnon the Jebusite, and the Tabernacle was in Gibeon (*I Chronicles* 21:29).

FIRST DAY

וְעָמְדוּ רַגְלָיו* בַּיּוֹם־הַהוּא עַל־הַר הַזֵּיתִים אֲשֶׁר עַל־פְּנֵי יְרוּשָׁלִַם
מִקֶּדֶם וְנִבְקַע הַר הַזֵּיתִים מֵחֶצְיוֹ מִזְרָחָה וָיָמָּה גֵּיא גְּדוֹלָה מְאֹד
וּמָשׁ חֲצִי הָהָר צָפוֹנָה וְחֶצְיוֹ־נֶגְבָּה׃ וְנַסְתֶּם גֵּיא־הָרַי כִּי־יַגִּיעַ
גֵּי־הָרִים אֶל־אָצַל וְנַסְתֶּם כַּאֲשֶׁר נַסְתֶּם מִפְּנֵי הָרַעַשׁ בִּימֵי עֻזִּיָּה
מֶלֶךְ־יְהוּדָה וּבָא יהוה אֱלֹהַי כָּל־קְדֹשִׁים עִמָּךְ׃ וְהָיָה בַּיּוֹם הַהוּא
לֹא־יִהְיֶה אוֹר יְקָרוֹת וְקִפָּאוֹן׃* וְהָיָה יוֹם־אֶחָד הוּא יִוָּדַע לַיהוה
לֹא־יוֹם וְלֹא־לָיְלָה וְהָיָה לְעֵת־עֶרֶב יִהְיֶה־אוֹר׃ וְהָיָה ׀ בַּיּוֹם הַהוּא
יֵצְאוּ מַיִם־חַיִּים מִירוּשָׁלִַם* חֶצְיָם אֶל־הַיָּם הַקַּדְמוֹנִי וְחֶצְיָם
אֶל־הַיָּם הָאַחֲרוֹן בַּקַּיִץ וּבָחֹרֶף יִהְיֶה׃ וְהָיָה יהוה לְמֶלֶךְ עַל־כָּל־
הָאָרֶץ בַּיּוֹם הַהוּא יִהְיֶה יהוה אֶחָד וּשְׁמוֹ אֶחָד׃ יִסּוֹב כָּל־הָאָרֶץ
כָּעֲרָבָה* מִגֶּבַע לְרִמּוֹן נֶגֶב יְרוּשָׁלִָם וְרָאֲמָה וְיָשְׁבָה תַחְתֶּיהָ
לְמִשַּׁעַר בִּנְיָמִן עַד־מְקוֹם שַׁעַר הָרִאשׁוֹן עַד־שַׁעַר הַפִּנִּים וּמִגְדַּל

וְעָמְדוּ רַגְלָיו — *His feet will stand astride.* God's intervention to perform miracles will be as plain as if He were seen standing on the mountain. The Mount of Olives will split as if through an earthquake, creating a ravine. The Jews endangered by Gog's invasion will flee through the ravine, and God will fight the adversary.

לֹא יִהְיֶה אוֹר יְקָרוֹת וְקִפָּאוֹן — *There will be neither clear light nor heavy darkness.* The passage is figurative. The Jewish people will be confused, not being sure whether they are seeing the light of salvation or the darkness of defeat.

יֵצְאוּ מַיִם חַיִּים מִירוּשָׁלִַם — *Fresh water will flow*

SECOND DAY

בְּרִית־יהוה אֶל־מְקוֹמוֹ אֶל־דְּבִיר הַבַּיִת אֶל־קֹדֶשׁ הַקֳּדָשִׁים
אֶל־תַּחַת כַּנְפֵי הַכְּרוּבִים׃* כִּי הַכְּרוּבִים פֹּרְשִׂים כְּנָפַיִם אֶל־מְקוֹם
הָאָרוֹן וַיָּסֹכּוּ הַכְּרֻבִים עַל־הָאָרוֹן וְעַל־בַּדָּיו מִלְמָעְלָה׃ וַיַּאֲרִכוּ
הַבַּדִּים וַיֵּרָאוּ רָאשֵׁי הַבַּדִּים* מִן־הַקֹּדֶשׁ עַל־פְּנֵי הַדְּבִיר וְלֹא יֵרָאוּ
הַחוּצָה וַיִּהְיוּ שָׁם עַד הַיּוֹם הַזֶּה׃ אֵין בָּאָרוֹן רַק שְׁנֵי לֻחוֹת הָאֲבָנִים
אֲשֶׁר הִנִּחַ שָׁם מֹשֶׁה בְּחֹרֵב אֲשֶׁר כָּרַת יהוה עִם־בְּנֵי יִשְׂרָאֵל
בְּצֵאתָם מֵאֶרֶץ מִצְרָיִם׃ וַיְהִי בְּצֵאת הַכֹּהֲנִים מִן־הַקֹּדֶשׁ וְהֶעָנָן
מָלֵא אֶת־בֵּית יהוה׃ וְלֹא־יָכְלוּ הַכֹּהֲנִים לַעֲמֹד לְשָׁרֵת מִפְּנֵי הֶעָנָן
כִּי־מָלֵא כְבוֹד־יהוה* אֶת־בֵּית יהוה׃ אָז אָמַר שְׁלֹמֹה יהוה אָמַר
לִשְׁכֹּן בָּעֲרָפֶל׃ בָּנֹה בָנִיתִי בֵּית זְבֻל לָךְ מָכוֹן לְשִׁבְתְּךָ עוֹלָמִים׃

תַּחַת כַּנְפֵי הַכְּרוּבִים — *Beneath the wings of the Cherubim.* These are not the Cherubim made under Moses's supervision in the Wilderness; those Cherubim were part of the Ark's cover. In addition to them, Solomon carved out Cherubim that were placed on the floor of the Holy of Holies. The Ark was brought in and placed beneath their outstretched wings.

רָאשֵׁי הַבַּדִּים — *The tips of the staves.* The staves

FIRST DAY

On that day His feet will stand astride the Mount of Olives, which faces Jerusalem on the east, and the Mount of Olives will split at its center, eastward and westward, making a huge ravine; half the mountain will move northward and half southward. Then you will flee, for the ravine will extend to Atzal; you will flee as you fled from the earthquake in the days of King Uzziah of Judah; then HASHEM my God will come with all the angels to your aid. And it will happen on that day that there will be neither clear light nor heavy darkness.* This will go on for a whole day — understood only by HASHEM — neither day nor night; but toward evening it will be perceived as light.*

It will be on that day that fresh water will flow from Jerusalem, half to the eastern sea and half backward to the west; in summer and winter the flow will continue. HASHEM will be King over all the world — on that day HASHEM will be One and His Name will be One. The entire area will be transformed to a plain,* from the hill of Rimmon south of Jerusalem; the City will rise high, on its original site, from the Gate of Benjamin until the place of the First Gate to the Inner Gate, and from the Tower of*

from Jerusalem. This will be a fulfillment of the prophecies in *Ezekiel* 47:12 and Joel 4:18, and it will be an indication of the great salvation. The *Eastern sea* is the Dead Sea and the *Western sea* is the Mediterranean. This fresh water, that will not dry out in summer or freeze in winter, will bring prosperity and happiness to the country.

כַּעֲרָבָה — *To a plain.* The entire topography of the Jerusalem area will change. The Judean hills will flatten and become a plain, with Jerusalem rising prominently and beautifully in its midst.

SECOND DAY

of HASHEM's covenant to its place, to the Sanctuary of the Temple, to the Holy of Holies; beneath the wings of the Cherubim. For the Cherubim spread their wings toward the place of the Ark; and the Cherubim sheltered the Ark and its staves from above. The staves extended so that the tips of the staves* could be noticed from the Holy, facing the Sanctuary, but could not be seen from outside; and they were to remain there to this very day. Nothing was in the Ark but the two stone tablets that Moses placed there in Horeb, when HASHEM covenanted with the Children of Israel when they left the land of Egypt.*

When the Kohanim left the Sanctuary, the cloud filled the Temple of HASHEM. The Kohanim could not stand and minister because of the cloud; for the glory of HASHEM filled the Temple of HASHEM.*

Then Solomon said, 'HASHEM pledged to dwell in the thick cloud. I have built You a habitation, an eternal foundation for Your dwelling.'

were connected to the Ark and had to remain there permanently. The outline of the tips could be noticed — but not actually seen — where they pressed against the curtain [פָּרוֹכֶת] that divided the Holy of Holies from the rest of the Temple.

כִּי מָלֵא כְבוֹד ה׳ — *For the glory of HASHEM filled.* The intensity of God's Presence, as represented by the cloud, proved that Solomon had carried out the hope of building a worthy Sanctuary, thus prompting his subsequent declaration.

FIRST DAY

חֲנַנְאֵל עַד יִקְבֵי הַמֶּלֶךְ: וְיָשְׁבוּ בָהּ וְחֵרֶם לֹא יִהְיֶה־עוֹד וְיָשְׁבָה יְרוּשָׁלַיִם לָבֶטַח: וְזֹאת ׀ תִּהְיֶה הַמַּגֵּפָה אֲשֶׁר יִגֹּף יהוה אֶת־כָּל־הָעַמִּים אֲשֶׁר צָבְאוּ עַל־יְרוּשָׁלָיִם הָמֵק ׀ בְּשָׂרוֹ וְהוּא עֹמֵד עַל־רַגְלָיו וְעֵינָיו תִּמַּקְנָה בְחֹרֵיהֶן וּלְשׁוֹנוֹ תִּמַּק בְּפִיהֶם: וְהָיָה בַּיּוֹם הַהוּא תִּהְיֶה מְהוּמַת־יהוה רַבָּה* בָּהֶם וְהֶחֱזִיקוּ אִישׁ יַד רֵעֵהוּ וְעָלְתָה יָדוֹ עַל־יַד רֵעֵהוּ: וְגַם־יְהוּדָה* תִּלָּחֵם בִּירוּשָׁלָיִם וְאֻסַּף חֵיל כָּל־הַגּוֹיִם סָבִיב זָהָב וָכֶסֶף וּבְגָדִים לָרֹב מְאֹד: וְכֵן תִּהְיֶה מַגֵּפַת הַסּוּס הַפֶּרֶד הַגָּמָל וְהַחֲמוֹר וְכָל־הַבְּהֵמָה אֲשֶׁר יִהְיֶה בַּמַּחֲנוֹת הָהֵמָּה כַּמַּגֵּפָה הַזֹּאת: וְהָיָה כָּל־הַנּוֹתָר מִכָּל־הַגּוֹיִם הַבָּאִים עַל־יְרוּשָׁלָיִם וְעָלוּ מִדֵּי שָׁנָה בְשָׁנָה לְהִשְׁתַּחֲוֹת לְמֶלֶךְ יהוה צְבָאוֹת וְלָחֹג אֶת־חַג הַסֻּכּוֹת:* וְהָיָה אֲשֶׁר לֹא־יַעֲלֶה מֵאֵת מִשְׁפְּחוֹת הָאָרֶץ אֶל־יְרוּשָׁלַיִם לְהִשְׁתַּחֲוֹת לְמֶלֶךְ יהוה צְבָאוֹת וְלֹא עֲלֵיהֶם יִהְיֶה הַגָּשֶׁם:* וְאִם־מִשְׁפַּחַת מִצְרַיִם לֹא־תַעֲלֶה וְלֹא בָאָה וְלֹא

מְהוּמַת ה׳ רַבָּה – *A great confusion from HASHEM.* In addition to the physical maladies of the previous verse, God will cause the nations to be confused, attacking one another and being suspicious and fearful of everyone. It will be every man for himself, as the verse continues, with people grasping, overpowering and killing those whom they fear.

וְגַם יְהוּדָה – *Even Judah.* The invading nations will force the inhabitants of the Judean hills to join in the attack on Jerusalem, but when the enemies are struck down by God's plague, these Jews will take the spoils.

לָחֹג אֶת חַג הַסֻּכּוֹת – *To celebrate the festival of Succos.* The defeat of Gog and its allies will be celebrated on Succos, the anniversary of its

SECOND DAY

וַיַּסֵּב הַמֶּלֶךְ אֶת־פָּנָיו וַיְבָרֶךְ אֵת כָּל־קְהַל יִשְׂרָאֵל וְכָל־קְהַל יִשְׂרָאֵל עֹמֵד: וַיֹּאמֶר בָּרוּךְ יהוה אֱלֹהֵי יִשְׂרָאֵל אֲשֶׁר דִּבֶּר בְּפִיו אֵת דָּוִד אָבִי וּבְיָדוֹ מִלֵּא לֵאמֹר: מִן־הַיּוֹם אֲשֶׁר הוֹצֵאתִי אֶת־עַמִּי אֶת־יִשְׂרָאֵל מִמִּצְרַיִם לֹא־בָחַרְתִּי בְעִיר מִכֹּל שִׁבְטֵי יִשְׂרָאֵל לִבְנוֹת בַּיִת לִהְיוֹת שְׁמִי שָׁם וָאֶבְחַר בְּדָוִד* לִהְיוֹת עַל־עַמִּי יִשְׂרָאֵל: וַיְהִי עִם־לְבַב דָּוִד אָבִי לִבְנוֹת בַּיִת לְשֵׁם יהוה אֱלֹהֵי יִשְׂרָאֵל: וַיֹּאמֶר יהוה אֶל־דָּוִד אָבִי יַעַן אֲשֶׁר הָיָה עִם־לְבָבְךָ לִבְנוֹת בַּיִת לִשְׁמִי הֱטִיבֹתָ כִּי הָיָה עִם־לְבָבֶךָ: רַק אַתָּה לֹא תִבְנֶה הַבָּיִת כִּי אִם־בִּנְךָ הַיֹּצֵא מֵחֲלָצֶיךָ הוּא־יִבְנֶה הַבַּיִת לִשְׁמִי: וַיָּקֶם יהוה אֶת־דְּבָרוֹ אֲשֶׁר דִּבֵּר וָאָקֻם תַּחַת דָּוִד אָבִי וָאֵשֵׁב עַל־כִּסֵּא יִשְׂרָאֵל

וָאֶבְחַר בְּדָוִד – *Then I chose David.* Only after David had been chosen would God make it known that Jerusalem would be the site of the Temple.

FIRST DAY

Chananel to the royal wine cellar. They will dwell within her and destruction shall be no more; Jerusalem shall dwell secure.

This will be the plague with which HASHEM *will smite all the nations that rallied against Jerusalem: their flesh will rot while they still stand erect, their eyes will rot in their sockets and their tongue will rot in their mouths. On that day there will be a great confusion from* HASHEM* *upon them; and when someone will seek to grasp his comrade's hand, he will overpower his comrade's hand. Even Judah* will be forced to attack Jerusalem; the wealth of all the surrounding nations will be gathered in a great abundance of gold, silver, and garments. Similar will be the plague against the horses, mules, camels, donkeys, and all the animals that will be in those camps; like the above plague.*

And it will happen that all who will be left from among all the nations that come upon Jerusalem; they will ascend every year to prostrate themselves before the King, HASHEM, *Master of Legions, and to celebrate the festival of Succos.* And any of the families of the Land that will not ascend to Jerusalem to prostrate themselves to the King,* HASHEM, *Master of Legions: the rain* will not fall upon them. And if the family of Egypt will not ascend and will not come — and the*

occurrence. Homiletically, the Sages (*Avodah Zarah* 3a) teach that, at the advent of the Messianic age, the nations will claim that they too would have wanted to accept the Torah. God will offer them the test of 'an easy *mitzvah,* known as *succah.*' They will rush to their roofs and build *succos,* but will leave in anger once the midday sun makes it uncomfortable. Thus, *succah* is the test of loyalty to God, and the nations will celebrate Succos as a symbol of their new-found allegiance to God.

הַגֶּשֶׁם — *The rain.* As punishment for their lack of allegiance to God, no rain will fall on the lands. As for Egypt (next verse), which does not

SECOND DAY

Then the King turned his face and blessed the entire Congregation of Israel; as the entire Congregation of Israel was standing. He said: 'Blessed is HASHEM, *the God of Israel, Who spoke directly to my father David; and with His power fulfilled it, saying: "From the day when I took My people Israel out of Egypt, I did not choose a city from among the tribes of Israel in which to build a Temple where My Name would be; then I chose David* to rule over My people Israel."*

'It was the desire of my father David to build a Temple for the sake of HASHEM, *the God of Israel. But* HASHEM *said to my father David, "Because you have desired to build a Temple for My sake, you did well to have so desired. But you shall not build the Temple — rather your son, who will emerge from your loins, he will build the Temple for My sake." Now* HASHEM *has fulfilled the word that He spoke, and I have risen to succeed my father David, and I have sat on the throne of Israel as*

עֲלֵיהֶם תִּהְיֶה הַמַּגֵּפָה אֲשֶׁר יִגֹּף יהוה אֶת־הַגּוֹיִם אֲשֶׁר לֹא יַעֲלוּ לָחֹג אֶת־חַג הַסֻּכּוֹת: זֹאת תִּהְיֶה חַטַּאת מִצְרָיִם וְחַטַּאת כָּל־הַגּוֹיִם אֲשֶׁר לֹא יַעֲלוּ לָחֹג אֶת־חַג הַסֻּכּוֹת: בַּיּוֹם הַהוּא יִהְיֶה עַל־מְצִלּוֹת הַסּוּס קֹדֶשׁ לַיהוה* וְהָיָה הַסִּירוֹת בְּבֵית יהוה כַּמִּזְרָקִים לִפְנֵי הַמִּזְבֵּחַ: וְהָיָה כָּל־סִיר בִּירוּשָׁלַיִם וּבִיהוּדָה קֹדֶשׁ לַיהוה צְבָאוֹת וּבָאוּ כָּל־הַזֹּבְחִים וְלָקְחוּ מֵהֶם וּבִשְּׁלוּ בָהֶם וְלֹא־יִהְיֶה כְנַעֲנִי עוֹד* בְּבֵית־יהוה צְבָאוֹת בַּיּוֹם הַהוּא:

THE MAFTIR CONTINUES WITH THE BLESSINGS BELOW

קֹדֶשׁ לַה׳ – *A sanctification of* HASHEM. The bells that decorated cavalry horses will be melted

require rain because of the Nile's overflow, they will be punished by a plague.

SECOND DAY

כַּאֲשֶׁר דִּבֶּר יהוה וָאֶבְנֶה הַבַּיִת לְשֵׁם יהוה אֱלֹהֵי יִשְׂרָאֵל: וָאָשִׂם שָׁם מָקוֹם לָאָרוֹן אֲשֶׁר־שָׁם בְּרִית יהוה אֲשֶׁר כָּרַת עִם־אֲבֹתֵינוּ בְּהוֹצִיאוֹ אֹתָם מֵאֶרֶץ מִצְרָיִם:

THE MAFTIR CONTINUES WITH THE BLESSINGS BELOW

ברכות לאחר ההפטרה

After the *Haftarah* is read, the *oleh* recites the following blessings.

בָּרוּךְ אַתָּה יהוה אֱלֹהֵינוּ מֶלֶךְ הָעוֹלָם, צוּר כָּל הָעוֹלָמִים,* צַדִּיק בְּכָל הַדּוֹרוֹת,* הָאֵל הַנֶּאֱמָן הָאוֹמֵר וְעֹשֶׂה,* הַמְדַבֵּר וּמְקַיֵּם,* שֶׁכָּל דְּבָרָיו אֱמֶת וָצֶדֶק.* נֶאֱמָן* אַתָּה הוּא יהוה אֱלֹהֵינוּ,

❧ Blessings after the Haftarah

צוּר כָּל הָעוֹלָמִים – *Rock of all eternities.* In its simple meaning this term describes God as all-powerful throughout the ages; therefore, only He is worthy of our trust. Nothing diminishes His power and nothing changes His sense of justice, fairness, and mercy. The *Zohar* interprets צוּר as צַיָּר, *Molder*. Thus, the term describes God as the One Who created and fashioned all the worlds and all ages. Both interpretations are especially apt with reference to the words of the prophets which we have read in the *Haftarah.* Because God is eternal, strong, and able to mold creation to suit His goal, we should have absolute faith in the prophecies He has communicated to us. This faith in the absolute truth and constancy of God's word is the theme of the first blessing.

צַדִּיק בְּכָל הַדּוֹרוֹת – *Righteous in all generations.* Whether a generation enjoys good fortune or suffers tragic oppression, God is righteous and His judgments are justified.

הָאוֹמֵר וְעֹשֶׂה – *Who says and does.* This term is found in *Baruch She'amar*, where it comes in

lack of rain does not affect them — they will suffer the plague with which HASHEM *will afflict the nations, because they will not have ascended to celebrate the festival of Succos. This will be the punishment of Egypt and the punishment of all the nations that will not ascend to celebrate the festival of Succos.*

On that day the bells on the horses will make a sanctification of HASHEM* *they will become cauldrons in the House of* HASHEM, *as numerous as the basins before the Altar. Every cauldron in Jerusalem and Judah will be sanctified to* HASHEM, *Master of Legions — and all who bring offerings will come and take from them to cook in them; and traders will no longer be* in the House of* HASHEM *on that day.*

THE MAFTIR CONTINUES WITH THE BLESSINGS BELOW

---

down and made into cauldrons for the Temple.

וְלֹא יִהְיֶה כְנַעֲנִי עוֹד – *And traders will no longer be.* There will be no need for the Temple to purchase supplies and vessels from traders, because the most distinguished people of all nations will deem it their privilege to contribute these necessities to the Temple.

SECOND DAY

HASHEM *spoke, and I have built the Temple for the sake of* HASHEM *the God of Israel.*

'And I have designated there a place for the Ark which contains the covenant of HASHEM, *which He made with our forefathers when He took them out of the land of Egypt.'*

THE MAFTIR CONTINUES WITH THE BLESSINGS BELOW

BLESSINGS AFTER THE HAFTARAH

After the *Haftarah* is read, the *oleh* recites the following blessings.

בָּרוּךְ *Blessed are You,* HASHEM, *King of the universe, Rock of all eternities,* Righteous in all generations,* the trustworthy God, Who says and does,* Who speaks and fulfills,* all of Whose words are true and righteous.* Trustworthy* are You,* HASHEM, *our God,*

---

conjunction with גּוֹזֵר וּמְקַיֵּם, *Who decrees* and *fulfills.* The connotation is that God brings His promise into being even when people no longer seem to deserve His generosity. Conversely, *He decrees and fulfills, i.e.,* when He warns of punishment, the sinner cannot escape unless he repents sincerely.

הַמְדַבֵּר וּמְקַיֵּם – *Who speaks and fulfills.* The allusion of speaking is to prophecy, by means of which God speaks to the prophets.

אֱמֶת וָצֶדֶק – *True and righteous.* The universe was established on God's commitment to *truth* and *righteousness.* Truth is the seal of God (*Shabbos* 55a), the theme underlying His guidance and control of the world. His truth endures because all those who violate it are brought to righteous judgment.

נֶאֱמָן – *Trustworthy.* Although in most *siddurim* this appears as a new paragraph, it does not begin a new blessing. Rather, in ancient times congregations would insert optional praises at this point *(Abudraham; Machzor Vitry).*

וְנֶאֱמָנִים דְּבָרֶיךָ, וְדָבָר אֶחָד מִדְּבָרֶיךָ אָחוֹר לֹא יָשׁוּב רֵיקָם, כִּי אֵל מֶלֶךְ נֶאֱמָן (וְרַחֲמָן) אָתָּה. בָּרוּךְ אַתָּה יהוה, הָאֵל הַנֶּאֱמָן בְּכָל דְּבָרָיו. (.Cong – אָמֵן.)

רַחֵם עַל צִיּוֹן* כִּי הִיא בֵּית חַיֵּינוּ, וְלַעֲלוּבַת נֶפֶשׁ תּוֹשִׁיעַ בִּמְהֵרָה בְיָמֵינוּ. בָּרוּךְ אַתָּה יהוה, מְשַׂמֵּחַ צִיּוֹן בְּבָנֶיהָ. (.Cong – אָמֵן.)

שַׂמְּחֵנוּ יהוה אֱלֹהֵינוּ בְּאֵלִיָּהוּ הַנָּבִיא עַבְדֶּךָ, וּבְמַלְכוּת בֵּית דָּוִד* מְשִׁיחֶךָ, בִּמְהֵרָה יָבֹא וְיָגֵל לִבֵּנוּ,* עַל כִּסְאוֹ לֹא יֵשֶׁב זָר וְלֹא יִנְחֲלוּ עוֹד אֲחֵרִים אֶת כְּבוֹדוֹ, כִּי בְשֵׁם קָדְשְׁךָ נִשְׁבַּעְתָּ לּוֹ, שֶׁלֹּא יִכְבֶּה נֵרוֹ לְעוֹלָם וָעֶד. בָּרוּךְ אַתָּה יהוה, מָגֵן דָּוִד.* (.Cong – אָמֵן.)

[On the Sabbath add the words in brackets.]

עַל הַתּוֹרָה,* וְעַל הָעֲבוֹדָה, וְעַל הַנְּבִיאִים, וְעַל יוֹם [הַשַּׁבָּת הַזֶּה, וְיוֹם] חַג הַסֻּכּוֹת הַזֶּה שֶׁנָּתַתָּ לָּנוּ יהוה אֱלֹהֵינוּ, [לִקְדֻשָּׁה וְלִמְנוּחָה,] לְשָׂשׂוֹן וּלְשִׂמְחָה, לְכָבוֹד וּלְתִפְאָרֶת.* עַל הַכֹּל יהוה אֱלֹהֵינוּ, אֲנַחְנוּ מוֹדִים לָךְ, וּמְבָרְכִים אוֹתָךְ, יִתְבָּרַךְ שִׁמְךָ בְּפִי כָּל חַי תָּמִיד לְעוֹלָם וָעֶד. בָּרוּךְ אַתָּה יהוה, מְקַדֵּשׁ [הַשַּׁבָּת וְ]יִשְׂרָאֵל וְהַזְּמַנִּים. (.Cong – אָמֵן.)

ON WEEKDAYS THE SERVICE CONTINUES ON PAGE 332;

ON THE SABBATH, PAGE 330.

רַחֵם עַל צִיּוֹן – *Have mercy on Zion.* The holiness of the Temple on Mount Zion is the source of our spiritual life. Exiled and without it, we are humiliated. Without her children, Zion, too, is despondent, as it is movingly described in the beginning of *Ecclesiastes.* Without her 'children' and Temple, Zion is likened by the prophets to a widow. The Torah warns repeatedly that one dare not wrong a widow because she feels her hurt so keenly. Similarly, in this blessing we plead with God to bring salvation to Zion because she is deeply humiliated.

בְּאֵלִיָּהוּ . . . בֵּית דָּוִד – *With Elijah . . . the House of David.* The prophets teach that the prophet Elijah will appear to the Jewish people before the coming of the Messiah to announce that redemption is imminent. Since the Messiah will be descended from David and will restore the Davidic dynasty to the throne of the Jewish people — its first undisputed reign since the days of Solomon — this blessing relates Elijah with the House of David.

and trustworthy are Your words, not one of Your words is turned back to its origin unfulfilled, for You are God, trustworthy (and compassionate) King. Blessed are You, HASHEM, the God Who is trustworthy in all His words. (Cong.— *Amen.*)

רַחֵם *Have mercy on Zion* for it is the source of our life; to the one who is deeply humiliated bring salvation speedily, in our days. Blessed are You, HASHEM, Who gladdens Zion through her children.* (Cong.— *Amen.*)

שַׂמְּחֵנוּ *Gladden us, HASHEM, our God, with Elijah the prophet, Your servant, and with the kingdom of the House of David,* Your anointed, may he come speedily and cause our heart to exult.* On his throne let no stranger sit nor let others continue to inherit his honor, for by Your holy Name You swore to him that his heir will not be extinguished forever and ever. Blessed are You, HASHEM, Shield of David.** (Cong.— *Amen.*)

[On the Sabbath add the words in brackets.]

עַל הַתּוֹרָה *For the Torah reading,* for the prayer service, for the reading from the Prophets [for this Sabbath day] and for this day of the Succos Festival that You, HASHEM, our God, have given us [for holiness and contentment,] for gladness and joy, for glory and splendor* — for all this, HASHEM, our God, we gratefully thank You and bless You. May Your Name be blessed by the mouth of all the living, always, for all eternity. Blessed are You, HASHEM, Who sanctifies [the Sabbath,] Israel and the festival seasons.* (Cong.— *Amen.*)

ON WEEKDAYS THE SERVICE CONTINUES ON PAGE 332;

ON THE SABBATH, PAGE 330.

וְיָגֵל לִבֵּנוּ – *Cause our heart to exult.* According to *Malbim,* the term גִּיל, *exultation,* refers to the feeling one has when he gets sudden, unexpected good news. Even though the Jewish people have always had full trust in God's promise of the Messianic salvation, nevertheless we do not take it for granted. We know we lack merit and therefore, when the hoped-for time comes, we will exult as if it were totally unexpected.

מָגֵן דָּוִד – *Shield of David.* In *II Samuel* (22:36) and *Psalms* (18:36), David praised God for shielding him against defeat.

עַל הַתּוֹרָה – *For the Torah [reading].* This final blessing sums up the entire service: not only the reading from the Prophets, but also the Torah reading, the prayers and the holiness of the Sabbath or Festival day.

וּלְתִפְאָרֶת – *And [for] splendor.* In Kabbalistic terminology, *splendor* refers to the perfect blend of truth and justice, kindness and strength.

יקום פרקן

On the Sabbath the following is recited. One praying alone omits the last two paragraphs.

יְקוּם פֻּרְקָן* מִן שְׁמַיָּא, חִנָּא וְחִסְדָּא וְרַחֲמֵי, וְחַיֵּי אֲרִיכֵי, וּמְזוֹנֵי רְוִיחֵי, וְסִיַּעְתָּא דִשְׁמַיָּא, וּבַרְיוּת גּוּפָא, וּנְהוֹרָא מַעַלְיָא, זַרְעָא חַיָּא וְקַיָּמָא, זַרְעָא דִּי לָא יִפְסוּק וְדִי לָא יִבְטוּל מִפִּתְגָּמֵי אוֹרַיְתָא. לְמָרָנָן וְרַבָּנָן חֲבוּרָתָא קַדִּישָׁתָא דִּי בְאַרְעָא דְיִשְׂרָאֵל וְדִי בְבָבֶל,* לְרֵישֵׁי כַלֵּי,* וּלְרֵישֵׁי גַלְוָתָא,* וּלְרֵישֵׁי מְתִיבָתָא, וּלְדַיָּנֵי דִי בָבָא, לְכָל תַּלְמִידֵיהוֹן, וּלְכָל תַּלְמִידֵי תַלְמִידֵיהוֹן, וּלְכָל מָן דְּעָסְקִין בְּאוֹרַיְתָא. מַלְכָּא דְעָלְמָא יְבָרֵךְ יַתְהוֹן, יַפִּישׁ חַיֵּיהוֹן, וְיַסְגֵּא יוֹמֵיהוֹן, וְיִתֵּן אַרְכָה לִשְׁנֵיהוֹן, וְיִתְפָּרְקוּן וְיִשְׁתֵּזְבוּן מִן כָּל עָקָא וּמִן כָּל מַרְעִין בִּישִׁין. מָרָן דִּי בִשְׁמַיָּא יְהֵא בְסַעְדְּהוֹן, כָּל זְמַן וְעִדָּן. וְנֹאמַר: אָמֵן.

(Cong. — אָמֵן.)

יְקוּם פֻּרְקָן* מִן שְׁמַיָּא, חִנָּא וְחִסְדָּא וְרַחֲמֵי, וְחַיֵּי אֲרִיכֵי, וּמְזוֹנֵי רְוִיחֵי, וְסִיַּעְתָּא דִשְׁמַיָּא, וּבַרְיוּת גּוּפָא, וּנְהוֹרָא מַעַלְיָא, זַרְעָא חַיָּא וְקַיָּמָא, זַרְעָא דִּי לָא יִפְסוּק וְדִי לָא יִבְטוּל מִפִּתְגָּמֵי אוֹרַיְתָא. לְכָל קְהָלָא קַדִּישָׁא הָדֵין, רַבְרְבַיָּא עִם זְעֵרַיָּא, טַפְלָא וּנְשַׁיָּא, מַלְכָּא דְעָלְמָא יְבָרֵךְ יַתְכוֹן, יַפִּישׁ חַיֵּיכוֹן, וְיַסְגֵּא יוֹמֵיכוֹן, וְיִתֵּן אַרְכָה לִשְׁנֵיכוֹן, וְתִתְפָּרְקוּן וְתִשְׁתֵּזְבוּן מִן כָּל עָקָא וּמִן כָּל מַרְעִין בִּישִׁין, מָרָן דִּי בִשְׁמַיָּא יְהֵא בְסַעְדְּכוֹן, כָּל זְמַן וְעִדָּן. וְנֹאמַר: אָמֵן. (Cong. — אָמֵן.)

מִי שֶׁבֵּרַךְ* אֲבוֹתֵינוּ אַבְרָהָם יִצְחָק וְיַעֲקֹב, הוּא יְבָרֵךְ אֶת כָּל הַקָּהָל הַקָּדוֹשׁ הַזֶּה, עִם כָּל קְהִלּוֹת הַקֹּדֶשׁ, הֵם, וּנְשֵׁיהֶם, וּבְנֵיהֶם, וּבְנוֹתֵיהֶם, וְכָל אֲשֶׁר לָהֶם. וּמִי שֶׁמְּיַחֲדִים בָּתֵּי כְנֵסִיּוֹת לִתְפִלָּה, וּמִי שֶׁבָּאִים בְּתוֹכָם לְהִתְפַּלֵּל, וּמִי שֶׁנּוֹתְנִים נֵר לַמָּאוֹר, וְיַיִן לְקִדּוּשׁ וּלְהַבְדָּלָה, וּפַת לָאוֹרְחִים, וּצְדָקָה לָעֲנִיִּים, וְכָל מִי שֶׁעוֹסְקִים בְּצָרְכֵי צִבּוּר בֶּאֱמוּנָה, הַקָּדוֹשׁ בָּרוּךְ הוּא יְשַׁלֵּם שְׂכָרָם, וְיָסִיר מֵהֶם כָּל מַחֲלָה, וְיִרְפָּא לְכָל גּוּפָם, וְיִסְלַח לְכָל עֲוֹנָם, וְיִשְׁלַח בְּרָכָה וְהַצְלָחָה בְּכָל מַעֲשֵׂה יְדֵיהֶם, עִם כָּל יִשְׂרָאֵל אֲחֵיהֶם. וְנֹאמַר: אָמֵן.

(Cong. — אָמֵן.)

In many congregations, a prayer for the welfare of the State is recited by the Rabbi, *chazzan*, or *gabbai* at this point.

יְקוּם פֻּרְקָן — *May salvation arise.* After reading from the Torah, a series of prayers is recited for those who teach, study, and support the Torah, and undertake the responsibilities of leadership. The first is a general prayer for all such people wherever they may be; consequently, it is recited even by people praying without a *minyan.* The second and third are prayers for the congregation with which one is praying; consequently, one praying alone omits them. The two יְקוּם פֻּרְקָן prayers were composed by the Babylonian *geonim* after the close of the Talmudic period, in Aramaic, the spoken language of that country. These prayers were instituted specifically for the Sabbath, not for Festivals, except those that fall on the Sabbath.

דִּי בְאַרְעָא דְיִשְׂרָאֵל וְדִי בְבָבֶל — *That are in Eretz Yisrael and that are in the Diaspora* [lit., *Babylonia*]. Although the Jewish community in *Eretz Yisrael* at that time was comparatively insignificant, the *geonim* gave honor and precedence to the Holy Land. Although the great

YEKUM PURKAN

On the Sabbath the following is recited. One praying alone omits the last two paragraphs.

יְקוּם פֻּרְקָן *May salvation arise* from heaven — grace, kindness, compassion, long life, abundant sustenance, heavenly assistance, physical health, lofty vision, living and surviving offspring, offspring who will neither interrupt nor cease from words of the Torah — for our masters and sages, the holy fellowships that are in Eretz Yisrael and that are in the Diaspora*: for the leaders of the Torah assemblages,* the leaders of the exile communities,* the leaders of the academies, the judges at the gateways, and all their students and to all the students of their students, and to everyone who engages in Torah study. May the King of the universe bless them, make their lives fruitful, increase their days and grant length to their years. May He save them and rescue them from every distress and from all serious ailments. May the Master in heaven come to their assistance at every season and time. Now let us respond: Amen.* (Cong.—*Amen.*)

יְקוּם פֻּרְקָן *May salvation arise* from heaven — grace, kindness, compassion, long life, abundant sustenance, heavenly assistance, physical health, lofty vision, living and surviving offspring, offspring who will neither interrupt nor cease from the words of the Torah — to this entire holy congregation, adults along with children, infants and women. May the King of the universe bless you, make your lives fruitful, increase your days, and grant length to your years. May He save you and rescue you from every distress and from all serious ailments. May the Master in heaven come to your assistance at every season and time. Now let us respond: Amen.* (Cong.—*Amen.*)

מִי שֶׁבֵּרַךְ *He Who blessed* our forefathers, Abraham, Isaac, and Jacob — may He bless this entire holy congregation along with all the holy congregations; them, their wives, sons, and daughters and all that is theirs; and those who dedicate synagogues for prayer and those who enter them to pray, and those who give lamps for illumination and wine for Kiddush and Havdalah, bread for guests and charity for the poor; and all who are involved faithfully in the needs of the community — may the Holy One, Blessed is He, pay their reward and remove from them every affliction, heal their entire body and forgive their every iniquity, and send blessing and success to all their handiwork, along with all Israel, their brethren. And let us say: Amen.* (Cong.—*Amen.*)

In many congregations, a prayer for the welfare of the State is recited by the Rabbi, *chazzan,* or *gabbai* at this point.

---

masses of Jewry no longer live in Babylonia, this timeless prayer refers to all Jewish communities; the word Babylonia is used as a general term for all Jewish communities outside of *Eretz Yisrael.*

לְרֵישֵׁי כַלֵּי — *For the leaders of the Torah assemblages.* These were the scholars who deliver Torah lectures on the Sabbath and Festivals to mass gatherings of the people.

וּלְרֵישֵׁי גַלְוָתָא — *The leaders of the exile communities.* The רֵישׁ גָלוּתָא, *Exilarch,* was the leader of the Jewish nation, equivalent to the *Nassi* in earlier times. His headquarters was in Babylonia.

☙ יְקוּם פֻּרְקָן — *May salvation arise.* This prayer refers to the congregation with which one is praying. Thus it omits mention of national teachers and leaders. It includes the entire congregation, young and old, men and women, because it prays for the welfare of each one.

☙ מִי שֶׁבֵּרַךְ — *He Who blessed.* This is a prayer for this and all other congregations, and singles out the people who provide the means and services for the general good. *Bais Yosef* (284) notes that these charitable causes are stressed so that the entire community will hear of the great reward of those who study and support Torah, and others will emulate their deeds.

יה אלי

Chazzan:

יָהּ אֵלִי* וְגוֹאֲלִי אֶתְיַצְּבָה לִקְרָאתֶךָ, הָיָה וְיִהְיֶה,* הָיָה וְהֹוֶה, כָּל גּוֹי אַדְמָתֶךָ.* וְתוֹדָה,* וְלָעוֹלָה, וְלַמִּנְחָה, וְלַחַטָּאת, וְלָאָשָׁם, וְלַשְּׁלָמִים, וְלַמִּלּוּאִים כָּל קָרְבָּנֶךָ. זְכוֹר נִלְאָה* אֲשֶׁר נָשְׂאָה וְהָשִׁיבָהּ לְאַדְמָתֶךָ. סֶלָה אֲהַלְלֶךָ,* בְּאַשְׁרֵי יוֹשְׁבֵי בֵיתֶךָ.

דַּק עַל דַּק,* עַד אֵין נִבְדָּק, וְלִתְבוּנָתוֹ אֵין חֵקֶר. הָאֵל נוֹרָא, בְּאַחַת סְקִירָה,* בֵּין טוֹב לָרַע יְבַקֵּר. וְתוֹדָה, וְלָעוֹלָה, וְלַמִּנְחָה, וְלַחַטָּאת, וְלָאָשָׁם, וְלַשְּׁלָמִים, וְלַמִּלּוּאִים כָּל קָרְבָּנֶךָ. זְכוֹר נִלְאָה אֲשֶׁר נָשְׂאָה וְהָשִׁיבָהּ לְאַדְמָתֶךָ. סֶלָה אֲהַלְלֶךָ, בְּאַשְׁרֵי יוֹשְׁבֵי בֵיתֶךָ.

אֲדוֹן צְבָאוֹת,* בְּרוֹב פְּלָאוֹת, חִבֵּר כָּל אָהֳלוֹ. בִּנְתִיבוֹת לֵב לְבָלֵב, הַצּוּר תָּמִים פָּעֳלוֹ. וְתוֹדָה, וְלָעוֹלָה, וְלַמִּנְחָה, וְלַחַטָּאת, וְלָאָשָׁם, וְלַשְּׁלָמִים, וְלַמִּלּוּאִים כָּל קָרְבָּנֶךָ. זְכוֹר נִלְאָה אֲשֶׁר נָשְׂאָה וְהָשִׁיבָהּ לְאַדְמָתֶךָ. סֶלָה אֲהַלְלֶךָ, בְּאַשְׁרֵי יוֹשְׁבֵי בֵיתֶךָ.

יָהּ אֵלִי — *O God, my God.* Since *Ashrei* is one of the most prominent of all the psalms (see p. 6), its recitation before the Festival *Mussaf* is introduced with a joyous prayer that longs for the opportunity to sing it before God in the rebuilt Temple, along with the order of sacrificial offerings. This is in keeping with the literal meaning of אַשְׁרֵי יוֹשְׁבֵי בֵיתֶךָ, *Praiseworthy are those who dwell in Your house.* Although, in the *Siddur,* God's 'house' has the broad meaning of the synagogue or any other place where one can serve God, it also refers specifically to the Temple, where the *Kohanim* and Levites have the good fortune to serve God (*Radak* and *Ibn Ezra* to *Psalms* 84:5). The spiritual elevation of the Festival, especially before *Mussaf* when we are about to cite the unique offering of the Festival, is a logical time for this prayer that combines joy in the Temple service and longing that we will soon be able to perform it in actuality as well as in aspiration. In view of the somber nature of *Yizkor,* this *piyut* is omitted on *Yizkor* days.

הָיָה וְיִהְיֶה — *Who was and Who will be.* God's Four-letter Name contains the letters that form the words indicating past, present, and future. Thus, this Name represents Him as the One Who creates and controls history — and Who will sooner or later return our service to the Temple.

כָּל גּוֹי אַדְמָתֶךָ — *With the entire nation on Your soil.* May all Israel be united in *Eretz Yisrael,* there to praise and thank God by offering all the prescribed offerings listed below.

וְתוֹדָה — *And the thanksgiving-offering.* We ask for the privilege of being in the Temple on God's soil so that we may bring Him all the offerings mentioned in the Torah.

The order of the offerings is difficult since the thanksgiving offering has less holiness than the next four on the list. Also, the meal offering consists of flour and oil, yet it is inserted between the animal offerings. Perhaps the order can be explained this way: first comes the thanksgiving offering because the very fact that we will have

PRE-MUSSAF PIYUT

Chazzan:

יָהּ אֵלִי *O God, my God* and Redeemer, I shall stand to greet You — Who was and Who will be,* Who was and Who is — with the entire nation on Your soil;* and the thanksgiving-,* elevation-, meal-, sin-, guilt-, peace-, and inauguration-offerings — Your every offering. Remember the exhausted [nation]* that won [Your favor], and return her to Your soil. Eternally will I laud You,* saying, 'Praiseworthy are those who dwell in Your House.'*

דַּק *Painstakingly exact,* beyond calculation — to His intelligence there is no limit. The awesome God — with a single stripe,* He differentiates the good from bad. And the thanksgiving-, elevation-, meal-, sin-, guilt-, peace-, and inauguration-offerings — Your every offering. Remember the exhausted [nation] that won [Your favor], and return her to Your soil. Eternally will I laud You, saying, 'Praiseworthy are those who dwell in Your House.'*

אֲדוֹן *The Lord of Legions,* with abundant miracles He connected His entire Tabernacle; in the paths of the heart may it blossom — the Rock, His work is perfect! And the thanksgiving-, elevation-, meal-, sin-, guilt-, peace-, and inauguration-offerings — Your every offering. Remember the exhausted [nation] that won [Your favor], and return her to Your soil. Eternally will I laud You, saying, 'Praiseworthy are those who dwell in Your House.'*

---

been returned to *Eretz Yisrael* and the rebuilt Temple will be cause for an enormous sense of thanksgiving. The elevation offering, which is consumed entirely on the altar, represents Israel's longing for elevation in God's service and dedication to Him; thus it takes precedence over offerings that come to atone for sin. Of the meal offering, the Sages derive from Scripture (see *Rashi, Leviticus* 2:1) that God heaps particular praise upon a poor man who can afford no more than a bit of flour and oil, yet wishes to bring an offering to express His dedication to God. The sin and guilt offerings are of greater holiness than the peace offering. The inauguration offerings are mentioned last because they will be offered only once — when the Temple is dedicated — and then will never be needed, because the Third Temple will be eternal.

זְכוֹר נִלְאָה — *Remember the exhausted [nation].* Israel has been exhausted by long exile and much travail, but she won God's favor long ago and therefore longs for her return from exile.

סֶלָה אֲהַלְלֶךָּ — *Eternally will I laud You.* This verse is a rearrangement of the first verse of *Ashrei.* It expresses our resolve to praise God by declaring our pride at being able to serve Him.

דַּק עַל דַּק — *Painstakingly exact.* This verse and the next describe the inscrutable greatness of God's awesome judgment.

בְּאַחַת סְקִירָה — *With a single stripe.* This phrase is based on the Talmudic expression that on the Day of Judgment, 'All who walk the earth pass before Him כִּבְנֵי מָרוֹן, *like young sheep*' (*Rosh Hashanah* 16a, 18a). When sheep were tithed, they were released one by one through a small opening in a corral. Each tenth one was marked with a single stripe, identifying it as a tithe animal that would become an Altar offering. In the context of this prayer, it refers to God differentiating between the sinful and the righteous.

צְבָאוֹת — *Legions.* God's Legions are the entire host of the universe's components. He weaves them together to create the complex harmony of Creation. We pray that realization of His greatness will blossom in our hearts so that we will recognize His greatness and be worthy to serve Him in the rebuilt Temple.

אַשְׁרֵי יוֹשְׁבֵי בֵיתֶךָ, עוֹד יְהַלְּלוּךָ סֶּלָה.[1] אַשְׁרֵי הָעָם שֶׁכָּכָה לּוֹ, אַשְׁרֵי הָעָם שֶׁיהוה אֱלֹהָיו.[2]

תהלים קמה

תְּהִלָּה לְדָוִד,

אֲרוֹמִמְךָ אֱלוֹהַי הַמֶּלֶךְ, וַאֲבָרְכָה שִׁמְךָ לְעוֹלָם וָעֶד.
בְּכָל יוֹם אֲבָרְכֶךָּ, וַאֲהַלְלָה שִׁמְךָ לְעוֹלָם וָעֶד.
גָּדוֹל יהוה וּמְהֻלָּל מְאֹד, וְלִגְדֻלָּתוֹ אֵין חֵקֶר.
דּוֹר לְדוֹר יְשַׁבַּח מַעֲשֶׂיךָ, וּגְבוּרֹתֶיךָ יַגִּידוּ.
הֲדַר כְּבוֹד הוֹדֶךָ, וְדִבְרֵי נִפְלְאֹתֶיךָ אָשִׂיחָה.
וֶעֱזוּז נוֹרְאוֹתֶיךָ יֹאמֵרוּ, וּגְדוּלָּתְךָ אֲסַפְּרֶנָּה.
זֵכֶר רַב טוּבְךָ יַבִּיעוּ, וְצִדְקָתְךָ יְרַנֵּנוּ.
חַנּוּן וְרַחוּם יהוה, אֶרֶךְ אַפַּיִם וּגְדָל חָסֶד.
טוֹב יהוה לַכֹּל, וְרַחֲמָיו עַל כָּל מַעֲשָׂיו.
יוֹדוּךָ יהוה כָּל מַעֲשֶׂיךָ, וַחֲסִידֶיךָ יְבָרְכוּכָה.
כְּבוֹד מַלְכוּתְךָ יֹאמֵרוּ, וּגְבוּרָתְךָ יְדַבֵּרוּ.
לְהוֹדִיעַ לִבְנֵי הָאָדָם גְּבוּרֹתָיו, וּכְבוֹד הֲדַר מַלְכוּתוֹ.
מַלְכוּתְךָ מַלְכוּת כָּל עֹלָמִים, וּמֶמְשַׁלְתְּךָ בְּכָל דּוֹר וָדֹר.
סוֹמֵךְ יהוה לְכָל הַנֹּפְלִים, וְזוֹקֵף לְכָל הַכְּפוּפִים.
עֵינֵי כֹל אֵלֶיךָ יְשַׂבֵּרוּ, וְאַתָּה נוֹתֵן לָהֶם אֶת אָכְלָם בְּעִתּוֹ.

While reciting the verse פּוֹתֵחַ, concentrate intently on its meaning.

פּוֹתֵחַ אֶת יָדֶךָ,
וּמַשְׂבִּיעַ לְכָל חַי רָצוֹן.
צַדִּיק יהוה בְּכָל דְּרָכָיו, וְחָסִיד בְּכָל מַעֲשָׂיו.
קָרוֹב יהוה לְכָל קֹרְאָיו, לְכֹל אֲשֶׁר יִקְרָאֻהוּ בֶאֱמֶת.
רְצוֹן יְרֵאָיו יַעֲשֶׂה, וְאֶת שַׁוְעָתָם יִשְׁמַע וְיוֹשִׁיעֵם.
שׁוֹמֵר יהוה אֶת כָּל אֹהֲבָיו, וְאֵת כָּל הָרְשָׁעִים יַשְׁמִיד.
❖ תְּהִלַּת יהוה יְדַבֶּר פִּי,
וִיבָרֵךְ כָּל בָּשָׂר שֵׁם קָדְשׁוֹ לְעוֹלָם וָעֶד.
וַאֲנַחְנוּ נְבָרֵךְ יָהּ, מֵעַתָּה וְעַד עוֹלָם, הַלְלוּיָהּ.[3]

(1) *Psalms* 84:5. (2) 144:15. (3) 115:18.

אַשְׁרֵי *Praiseworthy are those who dwell in Your house, may they always praise You, Selah![1] Praiseworthy is the people for whom this is so, praiseworthy is the people whose God is* HASHEM.[2]

Psalm 145

A psalm of praise by David:

א *I will exalt You, my God the King,*
and I will bless Your Name forever and ever.
ב *Every day I will bless You,*
and I will laud Your Name forever and ever.
ג HASHEM *is great and exceedingly lauded,*
and His greatness is beyond investigation.
ד *Each generation will praise Your deeds to the next*
and of Your mighty deeds they will tell;
ה *The splendrous glory of Your power*
and Your wondrous deeds I shall discuss.
ו *And of Your awesome power they will speak,*
and Your greatness I shall relate.
ז *A recollection of Your abundant goodness they will utter*
and of Your righteousness they will sing exultantly.
ח *Gracious and merciful is* HASHEM,
slow to anger, and great in [bestowing] kindness.
ט HASHEM *is good to all; His mercies are on all His works.*
י *All Your works shall thank You,* HASHEM,
and Your devout ones will bless You.
כ *Of the glory of Your kingdom they will speak,*
and of Your power they will tell;
ל *To inform human beings of His mighty deeds,*
and the glorious splendor of His kingdom.
מ *Your kingdom is a kingdom spanning all eternities,*
and Your dominion is throughout every generation.
ס HASHEM *supports all the fallen ones and straightens all the bent.*
ע *The eyes of all look to You with hope*
and You give them their food in its proper time;
פ *You open Your hand,* Concentrate intently while reciting the verse, *'You open. . .'*
and satisfy the desire of every living thing.
צ *Righteous is* HASHEM *in all His ways*
and magnanimous in all His deeds.
ק HASHEM *is close to all who call upon Him —*
to all who call upon Him sincerely.
ר *The will of those who fear Him He will do;*
and their cry He will hear, and save them.
ש HASHEM *protects all who love Him;*
but all the wicked He will destroy.
ת Chazzan— *May my mouth declare the praise of* HASHEM
and may all flesh bless His Holy Name forever and ever.
We will bless God from this time and forever, Halleluyah![3]

הכנסת ספר תורה

The *chazzan* takes the Torah in his right arm and recites:

יְהַלְלוּ אֶת שֵׁם יהוה, כִּי נִשְׂגָּב שְׁמוֹ לְבַדּוֹ –

Congregation responds:

– הוֹדוֹ עַל אֶרֶץ וְשָׁמָיִם. וַיָּרֶם קֶרֶן לְעַמּוֹ, תְּהִלָּה לְכָל חֲסִידָיו, לִבְנֵי יִשְׂרָאֵל עַם קְרֹבוֹ, הַלְלוּיָהּ.[1]

As the Torah is carried to the Ark the congregation recites the appropriate psalm.

ON A WEEKDAY:

תהלים כד

לְדָוִד מִזְמוֹר, לַיהוה הָאָרֶץ וּמְלוֹאָהּ, תֵּבֵל וְיֹשְׁבֵי בָהּ. כִּי הוּא עַל יַמִּים יְסָדָהּ, וְעַל נְהָרוֹת יְכוֹנְנֶהָ. מִי יַעֲלֶה בְהַר יהוה, וּמִי יָקוּם בִּמְקוֹם קָדְשׁוֹ. נְקִי כַפַּיִם וּבַר לֵבָב, אֲשֶׁר לֹא נָשָׂא לַשָּׁוְא נַפְשִׁי וְלֹא נִשְׁבַּע לְמִרְמָה. יִשָּׂא בְרָכָה מֵאֵת יהוה, וּצְדָקָה מֵאֱלֹהֵי יִשְׁעוֹ. זֶה דּוֹר דֹּרְשָׁיו, מְבַקְשֵׁי פָנֶיךָ, יַעֲקֹב, סֶלָה. שְׂאוּ שְׁעָרִים רָאשֵׁיכֶם, וְהִנָּשְׂאוּ פִּתְחֵי עוֹלָם, וְיָבוֹא מֶלֶךְ הַכָּבוֹד. מִי זֶה מֶלֶךְ הַכָּבוֹד, יהוה עִזּוּז וְגִבּוֹר, יהוה גִּבּוֹר מִלְחָמָה. שְׂאוּ שְׁעָרִים רָאשֵׁיכֶם, וּשְׂאוּ פִּתְחֵי עוֹלָם, וְיָבֹא מֶלֶךְ הַכָּבוֹד. מִי הוּא זֶה מֶלֶךְ הַכָּבוֹד, יהוה צְבָאוֹת הוּא מֶלֶךְ הַכָּבוֹד, סֶלָה.

ON THE SABBATH:

תהלים כט

מִזְמוֹר לְדָוִד, הָבוּ לַיהוה בְּנֵי אֵלִים, הָבוּ לַיהוה כָּבוֹד וָעֹז. הָבוּ לַיהוה כְּבוֹד שְׁמוֹ, הִשְׁתַּחֲווּ לַיהוה בְּהַדְרַת קֹדֶשׁ. קוֹל יהוה עַל הַמָּיִם, אֵל הַכָּבוֹד הִרְעִים, יהוה עַל מַיִם רַבִּים. קוֹל יהוה בַּכֹּחַ, קוֹל יהוה בֶּהָדָר. קוֹל יהוה שֹׁבֵר אֲרָזִים, וַיְשַׁבֵּר יהוה אֶת אַרְזֵי הַלְּבָנוֹן. וַיַּרְקִידֵם כְּמוֹ עֵגֶל, לְבָנוֹן וְשִׂרְיוֹן כְּמוֹ בֶן רְאֵמִים. קוֹל יהוה חֹצֵב לַהֲבוֹת אֵשׁ. קוֹל יהוה יָחִיל מִדְבָּר, יָחִיל יהוה מִדְבַּר קָדֵשׁ. קוֹל יהוה יְחוֹלֵל אַיָּלוֹת, וַיֶּחֱשֹׂף יְעָרוֹת, וּבְהֵיכָלוֹ, כֻּלּוֹ אֹמֵר כָּבוֹד. יהוה לַמַּבּוּל יָשָׁב, וַיֵּשֶׁב יהוה מֶלֶךְ לְעוֹלָם. יהוה עֹז לְעַמּוֹ יִתֵּן, יהוה יְבָרֵךְ אֶת עַמּוֹ בַשָּׁלוֹם.

Psalm 29 / מִזְמוֹר לְדָוִד ⊱

Tur (284) points out that the phrase *the voice of HASHEM* appears seven times in Psalm 29. This seven-fold mention alludes to: (a) the heavenly voice heard at Mount Sinai during the Giving of the Torah; and (b) the seven blessings contained in the *[Mussaf] Shemoneh Esrei* of

Psalm 24 / לְדָוִד מִזְמוֹר ⊱

This psalm is recited when the Torah is brought back to the Ark because its final verses: *Raise up your heads, O gates . . .* were recited when King Solomon brought the Ark into the newly built Temple. Commentary to this psalm appears on pages 388-389.

RETURNING THE TORAH

The *chazzan* takes the Torah in his right arm and recites:

Let them praise the Name of HASHEM, for His Name alone will have been exalted —

Congregation responds:

— His glory is above earth and heaven. And He will have exalted the pride of His people, causing praise for all His devout ones, for the Children of Israel, His intimate people. Halleluyah![1]

As the Torah is carried to the Ark the congregation recites the appropriate psalm.

ON A WEEKDAY:

Psalm 24

לְדָוִד *Of David a psalm. HASHEM's is the earth and its fullness, the inhabited land and those who dwell in it. For He founded it upon seas, and established it upon rivers. Who may ascend the mountain of HASHEM, and who may stand in the place of His sanctity? One with clean hands and pure heart, who has not sworn in vain by My soul and has not sworn deceitfully. He will receive a blessing from HASHEM and just kindness from the God of his salvation. This is the generation of those who seek Him, those who strive for Your Presence — Jacob, Selah. Raise up your heads, O gates, and be uplifted, you everlasting entrances, so that the King of Glory may enter. Who is this King of Glory? — HASHEM, the mighty and strong, HASHEM, the strong in battle. Raise up your heads, O gates, and raise up, you everlasting entrances, so that the King of Glory may enter. Who then is the King of Glory? HASHEM, Master of Legions, He is the King of Glory. Selah!*

ON THE SABBATH:

Psalm 29

מִזְמוֹר *A psalm of David. Render unto HASHEM, you sons of the powerful; render unto HASHEM, honor and might. Render unto HASHEM the honor worthy of His Name, prostrate yourselves before HASHEM in His intensely holy place. The voice of HASHEM is upon the waters, the God of Glory thunders, HASHEM is upon vast waters. The voice of HASHEM is in power! The voice of HASHEM is in majesty! The voice of HASHEM breaks the cedars, HASHEM shatters the cedars of Lebanon! He makes them prance about like a calf; Lebanon and Siryon like young re'eimim. The voice of HASHEM carves with shafts of fire. The voice of HASHEM convulses the wilderness. HASHEM convulses the wilderness of Kadesh. The voice of HASHEM frightens the hinds, and strips the forests bare; while in His Temple all proclaim, 'Glory!' HASHEM sat enthroned at the Deluge; HASHEM sits enthroned as King forever. HASHEM will give might to His people, HASHEM will bless His people with peace.*

(1) 148:13-14.

---

the Sabbath. Thus, it is appriopriate to recite this psalm at the time the Torah is returned to the Ark on the Sabbath just before the recitation of *Mussaf*.

As the Torah is placed into the Ark, the congregation recites the following verses:

וּבְנֻחֹה יֹאמַר,* שׁוּבָה יהוה רִבְבוֹת אַלְפֵי יִשְׂרָאֵל.[1] קוּמָה יהוה לִמְנוּחָתֶךָ, אַתָּה וַאֲרוֹן עֻזֶּךָ. כֹּהֲנֶיךָ יִלְבְּשׁוּ צֶדֶק, וַחֲסִידֶיךָ יְרַנֵּנוּ. בַּעֲבוּר דָּוִד עַבְדֶּךָ, אַל תָּשֵׁב פְּנֵי מְשִׁיחֶךָ.[2] כִּי לֶקַח טוֹב נָתַתִּי לָכֶם, תּוֹרָתִי אַל תַּעֲזֹבוּ.[3] ❖ עֵץ חַיִּים הִיא לַמַּחֲזִיקִים בָּהּ, וְתֹמְכֶיהָ מְאֻשָּׁר.[4] דְּרָכֶיהָ דַרְכֵי נֹעַם, וְכָל נְתִיבוֹתֶיהָ שָׁלוֹם.[5] הֲשִׁיבֵנוּ יהוה אֵלֶיךָ וְנָשׁוּבָה, חַדֵּשׁ יָמֵינוּ כְּקֶדֶם.[6]

The *chazzan* recites חֲצִי קַדִּישׁ.

יִתְגַּדַּל וְיִתְקַדַּשׁ שְׁמֵהּ רַבָּא. (.Cong — אָמֵן.) בְּעָלְמָא דִּי בְרָא כִרְעוּתֵהּ. וְיַמְלִיךְ מַלְכוּתֵהּ, בְּחַיֵּיכוֹן וּבְיוֹמֵיכוֹן וּבְחַיֵּי דְכָל בֵּית יִשְׂרָאֵל, בַּעֲגָלָא וּבִזְמַן קָרִיב. וְאִמְרוּ: אָמֵן.

(.Cong — אָמֵן. יְהֵא שְׁמֵהּ רַבָּא מְבָרַךְ לְעָלַם וּלְעָלְמֵי עָלְמַיָּא.)

יְהֵא שְׁמֵהּ רַבָּא מְבָרַךְ לְעָלַם וּלְעָלְמֵי עָלְמַיָּא.

יִתְבָּרַךְ וְיִשְׁתַּבַּח וְיִתְפָּאַר וְיִתְרוֹמַם וְיִתְנַשֵּׂא וְיִתְהַדָּר וְיִתְעַלֶּה וְיִתְהַלָּל שְׁמֵהּ דְּקֻדְשָׁא בְּרִיךְ הוּא (.Cong — בְּרִיךְ הוּא) — לְעֵלָּא מִן כָּל בִּרְכָתָא וְשִׁירָתָא תֻּשְׁבְּחָתָא וְנֶחֱמָתָא, דַּאֲמִירָן בְּעָלְמָא. וְאִמְרוּ: אָמֵן. (.Cong — אָמֵן.)

❦ מוסף לשני ימים הראשונים ❦

Take three steps backward, then three steps forward. Remain standing with the feet together while reciting *Shemoneh Esrei.* Recite it with quiet devotion and without interruption, verbal or otherwise. Although its recitation should not be audible to others, one must pray loudly enough to hear himself.

כִּי שֵׁם יהוה אֶקְרָא, הָבוּ גֹדֶל לֵאלֹהֵינוּ.[7]

אֲדֹנָי שְׂפָתַי תִּפְתָּח, וּפִי יַגִּיד תְּהִלָּתֶךָ.[8]

אבות

Bend the knees at בָּרוּךְ; bow at אַתָּה; straighten up at 'ה.

בָּרוּךְ אַתָּה יהוה אֱלֹהֵינוּ וֵאלֹהֵי אֲבוֹתֵינוּ, אֱלֹהֵי אַבְרָהָם, אֱלֹהֵי יִצְחָק, וֵאלֹהֵי יַעֲקֹב, הָאֵל הַגָּדוֹל הַגִּבּוֹר וְהַנּוֹרָא, אֵל עֶלְיוֹן, גּוֹמֵל חֲסָדִים טוֹבִים וְקוֹנֵה הַכֹּל, וְזוֹכֵר חַסְדֵי אָבוֹת, וּמֵבִיא גוֹאֵל לִבְנֵי בְנֵיהֶם, לְמַעַן שְׁמוֹ בְּאַהֲבָה. מֶלֶךְ עוֹזֵר וּמוֹשִׁיעַ וּמָגֵן.

Bend the knees at בָּרוּךְ; bow at אַתָּה; straighten up at 'ה.

בָּרוּךְ אַתָּה יהוה, מָגֵן אַבְרָהָם.

❧ **וּבְנֻחֹה יֹאמַר** — *And when it rested he would say.* This is the companion verse to וַיְהִי בִּנְסֹעַ הָאָרֹן, *When the Ark would travel,* above (p. 300), which Moses said when the Ark began to journey. When it came to rest, he expressed this hope that Israel should be worthy of being host to God's holiness.

❦ MUSSAF / מוסף ❦

Just as *Shacharis* and *Minchah* respectively correspond to the morning and afternoon continual offerings in the Temple, so does *Mussaf* correspond to the *mussaf,* or additional, offerings of the Festivals, Rosh Chodesh and the

As the Torah is placed into the Ark, the congregation recites the following verses:

ובְנֻחֹה *And when it rested he would say,* 'Return, HASHEM, to the myriad thousands of Israel.'*[1] *Arise, HASHEM, to Your resting place, You and the Ark of Your strength. Let Your priests be clothed in righteousness, and Your devout ones will sing joyously. For the sake of David, Your servant, turn not away the face of Your anointed.*[2] *For I have given you a good teaching, do not forsake My Torah.*[3] Chazzan– *It is a tree of life for those who grasp it, and its supporters are praiseworthy.*[4] *Its ways are ways of pleasantness and all its paths are peace.*[5] *Bring us back to You, HASHEM, and we shall return, renew our days as of old.*[6]

The *chazzan* recites Half-*Kaddish:*

יִתְגַּדַּל *May His great Name grow exalted and sanctified* (Cong.– *Amen.*) *in the world that He created as He willed. May He give reign to His kingship in your lifetimes and in your days, and in the lifetimes of the entire Family of Israel, swiftly and soon. Now respond: Amen.*

(Cong.– *Amen. May His great Name be blessed forever and ever.*)

May His great Name be blessed forever and ever.

Blessed, praised, glorified, exalted, extolled, mighty, upraised, and lauded be the Name of the Holy One, Blessed is He (Cong.– *Blessed is He*) — *beyond any blessing and song, praise and consolation that are uttered in the world. Now respond: Amen.* (Cong.– *Amen.*)

MUSSAF FOR THE FIRST TWO DAYS

Take three steps backward, then three steps forward. Remain standing with the feet together while reciting *Shemoneh Esrei.* Recite it with quiet devotion and without interruption, verbal or otherwise. Although its recitation should not be audible to others, one must pray loudly enough to hear himself.

When I call out the Name of HASHEM, ascribe greatness to our God.[7]

My Lord, open my lips, that my mouth may declare Your praise.[8]

PATRIARCHS

Bend the knees at *'Blessed'*; bow at *'You'*; straighten up at *'HASHEM.'*

בָּרוּךְ *Blessed are You, HASHEM, our God and the God of our forefathers, God of Abraham, God of Isaac, and God of Jacob; the great, mighty, and awesome God, the supreme God, Who bestows beneficial kindnesses and creates everything, Who recalls the kindnesses of the Patriarchs and brings a Redeemer to their children's children, for His Name's sake, with love. O King, Helper, Savior, and Shield.*

Bend the knees at *'Blessed'*; bow at *'You'*; straighten up at *'HASHEM.'*

Blessed are You, HASHEM, Shield of Abraham.

(1) *Numbers* 10:36. (2) *Psalms* 132:8-10. (3) *Proverbs* 4:2. (4) 3:18.
(5) 3:17. (6) *Lamentations* 5:21. (7) *Deuteronomy* 32:3. (8) *Psalms* 51:17.

Sabbath. Thus, it is natural that these offerings be enumerated in the *Shemoneh Esrei* of *Mussaf.* This is especially true in view of the fact that the Festivals do not all have identical *mussaf* offerings. Moreover, the additional offerings of Succos vary from day to day. This is because part of the Succos offerings symbolize the seventy primary nations of the world. Thus, thirteen bulls are offered on the first day of Succos; twelve on the second; and one less each day, until seven are offered on the last day, for a total of seventy bulls.

The necessity of enumerating the offerings of each day is the point of a halachic dispute between the *Rishonim* (medieval rabbinic authorities). In detailing the various offerings of each day, we follow the view of *Rabbeinu Tam* (*Rosh Hashanah* 35a). However, if one omitted

גבורות

אַתָּה גִּבּוֹר לְעוֹלָם אֲדֹנָי, מְחַיֵּה מֵתִים אַתָּה, רַב לְהוֹשִׁיעַ. מְכַלְכֵּל חַיִּים בְּחֶסֶד, מְחַיֵּה מֵתִים בְּרַחֲמִים רַבִּים, סוֹמֵךְ נוֹפְלִים, וְרוֹפֵא חוֹלִים, וּמַתִּיר אֲסוּרִים, וּמְקַיֵּם אֱמוּנָתוֹ לִישֵׁנֵי עָפָר. מִי כָמְוֹךָ בַּעַל גְּבוּרוֹת, וּמִי דּוֹמֶה לָּךְ, מֶלֶךְ מֵמִית וּמְחַיֶּה וּמַצְמִיחַ יְשׁוּעָה. וְנֶאֱמָן אַתָּה לְהַחֲיוֹת מֵתִים. בָּרוּךְ אַתָּה יהוה, מְחַיֵּה הַמֵּתִים.

During the *chazzan's* repetition, *Kedushah* (below) is recited at this point.

קדושה

When reciting *Kedushah,* one must stand with his feet together, and avoid any interruptions. One should rise on his toes when saying the words קָדוֹשׁ, קָדוֹשׁ, קָדוֹשׁ; בָּרוּךְ (of בָּרוּךְ כְּבוֹד); and יִמְלֹךְ.

Cong. then *chazzan*:

נַעֲרִיצְךָ וְנַקְדִּישְׁךָ* כְּסוֹד שִׂיחַ שַׂרְפֵי קֹדֶשׁ, הַמַּקְדִּישִׁים שִׁמְךָ בַּקֹּדֶשׁ, כַּכָּתוּב עַל יַד נְבִיאֶךָ, וְקָרָא זֶה אֶל זֶה וְאָמַר:

All – קָדוֹשׁ קָדוֹשׁ קָדוֹשׁ יהוה צְבָאוֹת, מְלֹא כָל הָאָרֶץ כְּבוֹדוֹ.[1] ❖ כְּבוֹדוֹ מָלֵא עוֹלָם,* מְשָׁרְתָיו שׁוֹאֲלִים זֶה לָזֶה, אַיֵּה מְקוֹם כְּבוֹדוֹ, לְעֻמָּתָם בָּרוּךְ יֹאמֵרוּ:

All – בָּרוּךְ כְּבוֹד יהוה, מִמְּקוֹמוֹ.[2] ❖ מִמְּקוֹמוֹ הוּא יִפֶן בְּרַחֲמִים,* וְיָחוֹן עַם הַמְיַחֲדִים שְׁמוֹ, עֶרֶב וָבֹקֶר בְּכָל יוֹם תָּמִיד, פַּעֲמַיִם בְּאַהֲבָה שְׁמַע אוֹמְרִים.*

All – שְׁמַע יִשְׂרָאֵל, יהוה אֱלֹהֵינוּ, יהוה אֶחָד.[3] ❖ הוּא אֱלֹהֵינוּ.* הוּא אָבִינוּ, הוּא מַלְכֵּנוּ, הוּא מוֹשִׁיעֵנוּ, וְהוּא יַשְׁמִיעֵנוּ בְּרַחֲמָיו שֵׁנִית,* לְעֵינֵי כָּל חָי, לִהְיוֹת לָכֶם לֵאלֹהִים,* אֲנִי יהוה אֱלֹהֵיכֶם.[4]

All – אַדִּיר אַדִּירֵנוּ,* יהוה אֲדֹנֵינוּ, מָה אַדִּיר שִׁמְךָ בְּכָל הָאָרֶץ.[5] וְהָיָה יהוה לְמֶלֶךְ עַל כָּל הָאָרֶץ, בַּיּוֹם הַהוּא יִהְיֶה יהוה אֶחָד וּשְׁמוֹ אֶחָד.[6]

Chazzan – וּבְדִבְרֵי קָדְשְׁךָ כָּתוּב לֵאמֹר:

All – יִמְלֹךְ יהוה לְעוֹלָם, אֱלֹהַיִךְ צִיּוֹן, לְדֹר וָדֹר, הַלְלוּיָהּ.[7]

---

the description of the offering, or recited the wrong day's offering, and has already completed the blessing . . . *Who sanctifies Israel and the seasons,* he may continue *Shemoneh Esrei* and is not required to rectify his error (*Mishnah Berurah* 488:13). This is in accord with *Rashi's* view that it is sufficient merely to recite the general statement, נַעֲשֶׂה וְנַקְרִיב . . . בְּתוֹרָתֶךָ, *We will perform and bring near to You, according to the commandment of Your will, as You have written for us in Your Torah,'* and the offerings need not be enumerated.

◆§ The commentary for the first section of *Shemoneh Esrei* and the shorter version of *Kedushah* may be found on pages 10- 12.

◆§ קְדוּשָׁה / Kedushah

The *Kedushah* of *Mussaf* is based on *Pirkei D'Rabbi Eliezer's* narrative of the angelic praises. Indicative of the higher spirituality of *Mussaf,* Israel joins the angels by proclaiming שְׁמַע יִשְׂרָאֵל, our own declaration of God's greatness.

נַעֲרִיצְךָ וְנַקְדִּישְׁךָ — *We will revere You and sanctify You. Revere* refers to our recognition of God's outward greatness as displayed in His deeds. *Sanctify* refers to our attempt to express the idea that God's essence is elevated beyond man's capacity to comprehend.

כְּבוֹדוֹ מָלֵא עוֹלָם — *His glory fills the world.* The material nature of the earth is no barrier to His glory; it is everywhere.

הוּא יִפֶן בְּרַחֲמִים — *May He turn with compassion.* God's mercy causes Him to move from the throne of judgment to the throne of compassion.

עִם הַמְיַחֲדִים שְׁמוֹ . . . שְׁמַע אוֹמְרִים — *The people who declare the Oneness of His Name . . . they proclaim 'Shema.'* With its twice-a-day declara-

GOD'S MIGHT

אַתָּה *You are eternally mighty, my Lord, the Resuscitator of the dead are You; abundantly able to save. He sustains the living with kindness, resuscitates the dead with abundant mercy, supports the fallen, heals the sick, releases the confined, and maintains His faith to those asleep in the dust. Who is like You, O Master of mighty deeds, and who is comparable to You, O King Who causes death and restores life and makes salvation sprout! And You are faithful to resuscitate the dead. Blessed are You, HASHEM, Who resuscitates the dead.*

During the *chazzan's* repetition, *Kedushah* (below) is recited at this point.

KEDUSHAH

When reciting *Kedushah*, one must stand with his feet together and avoid any interruptions. One should rise on his toes when saying the words *'Holy, holy, holy; Blessed is; HASHEM shall reign.'*

Cong. then *chazzan:*

נַעֲרִיצְךָ *We will revere You and sanctify You* according to the counsel of the holy Seraphim, who sanctify Your Name in the Sanctuary, as it is written by Your prophet: "And one [angel] will call another and say:*

All – *'Holy, holy, holy is HASHEM, Master of Legions, the whole world is filled with His glory.' "[1]* ⁘*His glory fills the world.* His ministering angels ask one another, 'Where is the place of His glory?' Those facing them say 'Blessed':*

All – *'Blessed is the glory of HASHEM from His place.'[2]* ⁘*From His place may He turn with compassion* and be gracious to the people who declare the Oneness of His Name; evening and morning, every day constantly, twice, with love, they proclaim 'Shema.'**

All – *'Hear O Israel: HASHEM is our God, HASHEM the One and Only.'[3]* ⁘*He is our God;* He is our Father; He is our King; He is our Savior; and He will let us hear, in His compassion, for a second time* in the presence of all the living,' . . . to be a God to you,* I am HASHEM, your God.'[4]*

All – *Mighty is our Mighty One,* HASHEM, our Master — how mighty is Your name throughout the earth![5] HASHEM will be King over all the world — on that day HASHEM will be One and His Name will be One.[6]*

Chazzan – *And in Your holy Writings the following is written:*

All – *'HASHEM shall reign forever — your God, O Zion — from generation to generation, Halleluyah!'[7]*

(1) *Isaiah* 6:3. (2) *Ezekiel* 3:12. (3) *Deuteronomy* 6:4.
(4) *Numbers* 15:41. (5) *Psalms* 8:2. (6) *Zechariah* 14:9. (7) *Psalms* 146:10.

---

tion of the *Shema,* Israel joins in the sacred chorus of the angels — and this is merit enough to win God's compassion.

As explained more fully in the commentary to קָרְבָּנוֹת (see p. 147), the fifth-century Persian king Yezdegerd forbade the recitation of *Shema.* They had to comply during the morning when guards were present, but the Jews partially circumvented the decree by incorporating *Shema* into the *Mussaf Kedushah.*

הוּא אֱלֹהֵינוּ — *He is our God,* i.e., He controls nature; He is our merciful Father, the Ruler of all peoples, and our only hope for salvation.

שֵׁנִית — *For a second time.* The prophet *Isaiah* (11:11) foretold that God would redeem Israel from its final exile in as miraculous a manner as He did at the time of the Exodus from Egypt. Thus, the *second time* refers to the concept of a complete and total redemption, unlike the limited one that ended the Babylonian exile and led to the building of the Second Temple

לִהְיוֹת לָכֶם לֵאלֹהִים — *To be a God to you.* When redeeming Israel from Egypt, God said that His purpose in doing so was to be a God to the Jewish people. The purpose of the *second* and ultimate redemption will be the same.

⁂ אַדִּיר אַדִּירֵנוּ — *Mighty is our Mighty One.* This brief selection is added to *Kedushah* only

קדושת השם

INDIVIDUALS RECITE:

אַתָּה קָדוֹשׁ וְשִׁמְךָ קָדוֹשׁ, וּקְדוֹשִׁים בְּכָל יוֹם יְהַלְלְוּךָ סֶּלָה. בָּרוּךְ אַתָּה יהוה, הָאֵל הַקָּדוֹשׁ.

CHAZZAN RECITES DURING HIS REPETITION:

לְדוֹר וָדוֹר נַגִּיד גָּדְלֶךָ וּלְנֵצַח נְצָחִים קְדֻשָּׁתְךָ נַקְדִּישׁ, וְשִׁבְחֲךָ אֱלֹהֵינוּ מִפִּינוּ לֹא יָמוּשׁ לְעוֹלָם וָעֶד, כִּי אֵל מֶלֶךְ גָּדוֹל וְקָדוֹשׁ אָתָּה. בָּרוּךְ אַתָּה יהוה, הָאֵל הַקָּדוֹשׁ.

קדושת היום

אַתָּה בְחַרְתָּנוּ מִכָּל הָעַמִּים, אָהַבְתָּ אוֹתָנוּ, וְרָצִיתָ בָּנוּ, וְרוֹמַמְתָּנוּ מִכָּל הַלְּשׁוֹנוֹת, וְקִדַּשְׁתָּנוּ בְּמִצְוֹתֶיךָ, וְקֵרַבְתָּנוּ מַלְכֵּנוּ לַעֲבוֹדָתֶךָ, וְשִׁמְךָ הַגָּדוֹל וְהַקָּדוֹשׁ עָלֵינוּ קָרָאתָ.

On the Sabbath add the words in brackets. [If forgotten, see *Laws* §86-90.]

וַתִּתֶּן לָנוּ יהוה אֱלֹהֵינוּ בְּאַהֲבָה [שַׁבָּתוֹת לִמְנוּחָה וּ]מוֹעֲדִים לְשִׂמְחָה חַגִּים וּזְמַנִּים לְשָׂשׂוֹן, אֶת יוֹם [הַשַּׁבָּת הַזֶּה וְאֶת יוֹם] חַג הַסֻּכּוֹת הַזֶּה, זְמַן שִׂמְחָתֵנוּ [בְּאַהֲבָה] מִקְרָא קֹדֶשׁ, זֵכֶר לִיצִיאַת מִצְרָיִם.

וּמִפְּנֵי חֲטָאֵינוּ* גָּלִינוּ מֵאַרְצֵנוּ, וְנִתְרַחַקְנוּ מֵעַל אַדְמָתֵנוּ.* וְאֵין אֲנַחְנוּ יְכוֹלִים לַעֲלוֹת וְלֵרָאוֹת וּלְהִשְׁתַּחֲוֹת לְפָנֶיךָ, וְלַעֲשׂוֹת חוֹבוֹתֵינוּ בְּבֵית בְּחִירָתֶךָ, בַּבַּיִת הַגָּדוֹל וְהַקָּדוֹשׁ שֶׁנִּקְרָא שִׁמְךָ עָלָיו, מִפְּנֵי הַיָּד שֶׁנִּשְׁתַּלְּחָה בְּמִקְדָּשֶׁךָ. יְהִי רָצוֹן מִלְּפָנֶיךָ יהוה אֱלֹהֵינוּ וֵאלֹהֵי אֲבוֹתֵינוּ, מֶלֶךְ רַחֲמָן, שֶׁתָּשׁוּב וּתְרַחֵם עָלֵינוּ וְעַל מִקְדָּשְׁךָ בְּרַחֲמֶיךָ הָרַבִּים, וְתִבְנֵהוּ מְהֵרָה וּתְגַדֵּל כְּבוֹדוֹ.* אָבִינוּ מַלְכֵּנוּ, גַּלֵּה כְּבוֹד מַלְכוּתְךָ

---

on Festivals, because, as discussed elsewhere, they are times of special closeness between God and Israel. In this brief prayer, we exclaim our confidence that God's absolute power will ultimately be recognized by the entire human race.

☙ **וּמִפְּנֵי חֲטָאֵינוּ** — *But because of our sins.* This is a cardinal principle of Jewish faith. History is not haphazard; Israel's exile and centuries-long distress is a result of its sins. It is axiomatic, therefore, that only repentance can reverse this process.

מֵאַרְצֵנוּ . . . מֵעַל אַדְמָתֵנוּ — *From our land . . . from our soil.* The term אֶרֶץ, *land,* refers to the entire country from which the nation as a whole was exiled; אֲדָמָה, *soil,* refers to the individual parcels of land. These two conditions involve halachic differences. Some commandments, such as the laws of the Jubilee Year and the laws of Jewish indentured servants, cannot be observed unless the nation as a whole lives in *Eretz Yisrael.* Other

HOLINESS OF GOD'S NAME

INDIVIDUALS RECITE:

אַתָּה *You are holy and Your Name is holy, and holy ones praise You every day, forever. Blessed are You,* HASHEM, *the holy God.*

CHAZZAN RECITES DURING HIS REPETITION:

לְדוֹר *From generation to generation we shall relate Your greatness and for infinite eternities we shall proclaim Your holiness. Your praise, our God, shall not leave our mouth forever and ever, for You, O God, are a great and holy King. Blessed are You,* HASHEM, *the holy God.*

SANCTIFICATION OF THE DAY

אַתָּה בְחַרְתָּנוּ *You have chosen us from all the peoples; You loved us and found favor in us; You exalted us above all the tongues and You sanctified us with Your commandments. You drew us close, our King, to Your service and proclaimed Your great and Holy Name upon us.*

On the Sabbath add the words in brackets. [If forgotten, see *Laws* §86-90.]

וַתִּתֶּן לָנוּ *And You gave us,* HASHEM, *our God, with love [Sabbaths for rest], appointed festivals for gladness, Festivals and times for joy, [this day of Sabbath and] this day of the Festival of Succos, the time of our gladness [with love], a holy convocation, a memorial of the Exodus from Egypt.*

וּמִפְּנֵי חֲטָאֵינוּ *But because of our sins* we have been exiled from our land and sent far from our soil.* We cannot ascend to appear and to prostrate ourselves before You, and to perform our obligations in the House of Your choice, in the great and holy House upon which Your Name was proclaimed, because of the hand that was dispatched against Your Sanctuary. May it be Your will,* HASHEM, *our God and the God of our forefathers, O merciful King, that You once more be compassionate upon us and upon Your Sanctuary in Your abundant mercy, and rebuild it soon and magnify its glory.* Our Father, our King, reveal the glory of Your Kingship*

---

commandments, such as those relating to tithes and the use of fruits during a tree's first four years, are observed by Jewish landowners in *Eretz Yisrael* even if the country is under foreign rule. We now say that the exile has deprived all or most of our people of these two categories of commandments. Then, we go on to mention a third category that we are deprived of in exile — the performance of the Temple service.

וְתִבְנֵהוּ מְהֵרָה וּתְגַדֵּל כְּבוֹדוֹ — *And rebuild it soon and magnify its glory. Eretz Yisrael* and the Temple are more than geographical or architectural concepts. There is a spiritual Presence that complements the material places on earth. When Israel sinned, the spiritual Presence withdrew because it could not tolerate the nearness of sinners. Consequently, the Jewish people were exiled from the land that they had spiritually contaminated. Conversely, Jewish return to the land is incomplete unless we can also bring about the return of the Divine holiness to the country and the Temple Mount. Thus we now pray that *God* rebuild the Temple in the sense that He return His Presence to the land, a condition that can come about only when God's sovereignty is accepted by all, and the Jews are returned to their land. Then will come the climax of our longing: that we will deserve to serve God in His Temple as He ordained in the Torah *(Sh'lah).*

עָלֵינוּ מְהֵרָה, וְהוֹפַע וְהִנָּשֵׂא עָלֵינוּ לְעֵינֵי כָּל חָי. וְקָרֵב פְּזוּרֵינוּ* מִבֵּין הַגּוֹיִם, וּנְפוּצוֹתֵינוּ כַּנֵּס מִיַּרְכְּתֵי אָרֶץ. וַהֲבִיאֵנוּ לְצִיּוֹן עִירְךָ בְּרִנָּה, וְלִירוּשָׁלַיִם בֵּית מִקְדָּשְׁךָ בְּשִׂמְחַת עוֹלָם. וְשָׁם נַעֲשֶׂה לְפָנֶיךָ אֶת קָרְבְּנוֹת חוֹבוֹתֵינוּ, תְּמִידִים כְּסִדְרָם, וּמוּסָפִים כְּהִלְכָתָם. וְאֶת [Weekdays– מוּסַף יוֹם] [Sabbath– מוּסְפֵי יוֹם הַשַּׁבָּת הַזֶּה וְיוֹם] חַג הַסֻּכּוֹת הַזֶּה נַעֲשֶׂה וְנַקְרִיב לְפָנֶיךָ בְּאַהֲבָה כְּמִצְוַת רְצוֹנֶךָ, כְּמוֹ שֶׁכָּתַבְתָּ עָלֵינוּ בְּתוֹרָתֶךָ, עַל יְדֵי מֹשֶׁה עַבְדֶּךָ, מִפִּי כְבוֹדֶךָ כָּאָמוּר:

On the Sabbath add. [If forgotten, do not repeat *Shemoneh Esrei*. See *Laws* §86.]

וּבְיוֹם הַשַּׁבָּת שְׁנֵי כְבָשִׂים בְּנֵי שָׁנָה תְּמִימִם, וּשְׁנֵי עֶשְׂרֹנִים סֹלֶת מִנְחָה בְּלוּלָה בַשֶּׁמֶן, וְנִסְכּוֹ. עֹלַת שַׁבַּת בְּשַׁבַּתּוֹ, עַל עֹלַת הַתָּמִיד וְנִסְכָּהּ.[1] (זֶה קָרְבַּן שַׁבָּת. וְקָרְבַּן הַיּוֹם כָּאָמוּר:)

וּבַחֲמִשָּׁה עָשָׂר יוֹם לַחֹדֶשׁ הַשְּׁבִיעִי, מִקְרָא קֹדֶשׁ יִהְיֶה לָכֶם, כָּל מְלֶאכֶת עֲבֹדָה לֹא תַעֲשׂוּ, וְחַגֹּתֶם חַג לַיהוה שִׁבְעַת יָמִים. וְהִקְרַבְתֶּם עֹלָה אִשֵּׁה רֵיחַ נִיחֹחַ לַיהוה, פָּרִים בְּנֵי בָקָר שְׁלֹשָׁה עָשָׂר, אֵילִם שְׁנָיִם, כְּבָשִׂים בְּנֵי שָׁנָה אַרְבָּעָה עָשָׂר, תְּמִימִם יִהְיוּ.[2] וּמִנְחָתָם וְנִסְכֵּיהֶם כִּמְדֻבָּר, שְׁלֹשָׁה עֶשְׂרֹנִים לַפָּר, וּשְׁנֵי עֶשְׂרֹנִים לָאָיִל, וְעִשָּׂרוֹן לַכֶּבֶשׂ, וְיַיִן כְּנִסְכּוֹ. וְשָׂעִיר לְכַפֵּר, וּשְׁנֵי תְמִידִים כְּהִלְכָתָם.

On the Sabbath add. [If forgotten, do not repeat *Shemoneh Esrei*. See *Laws* §86.]

יִשְׂמְחוּ בְמַלְכוּתְךָ שׁוֹמְרֵי שַׁבָּת וְקוֹרְאֵי עֹנֶג, עַם מְקַדְּשֵׁי שְׁבִיעִי, כֻּלָּם יִשְׂבְּעוּ וְיִתְעַנְּגוּ מִטּוּבֶךָ, וּבַשְּׁבִיעִי רָצִיתָ בּוֹ וְקִדַּשְׁתּוֹ, חֶמְדַּת יָמִים אוֹתוֹ קָרָאתָ, זֵכֶר לְמַעֲשֵׂה בְרֵאשִׁית.

On the Sabbath add the words in brackets. [If forgotten, see *Laws* §86-90.]

אֱלֹהֵינוּ וֵאלֹהֵי אֲבוֹתֵינוּ, [רְצֵה בִמְנוּחָתֵנוּ] מֶלֶךְ רַחֲמָן רַחֵם עָלֵינוּ, טוֹב וּמֵטִיב* הִדָּרֶשׁ לָנוּ, שׁוּבָה אֵלֵינוּ בַּהֲמוֹן רַחֲמֶיךָ, בִּגְלַל אָבוֹת שֶׁעָשׂוּ רְצוֹנֶךָ. בְּנֵה בֵיתְךָ כְּבַתְּחִלָּה, וְכוֹנֵן מִקְדָּשְׁךָ עַל מְכוֹנוֹ, וְהַרְאֵנוּ בְּבִנְיָנוֹ, וְשַׂמְּחֵנוּ בְּתִקּוּנוֹ.

וְקָרֵב פְּזוּרֵינוּ — *Draw our scattered ones near.* Israel's dispersion has created much dissension among Jews, because the communities in various lands have adopted different customs, languages, outlooks, etc. Sometimes it seems that unity could never be achieved. Therefore we pray not only for liberation, but that God bring us together in mutual understanding and a sharing of goals and aspirations *(Siach Yitzchak).*

⊱ אֱלֹהֵינוּ . . . טוֹב וּמֵטִיב — *Our God . . . O good and beneficent One.* In the case of human beings, one may be good, but not have the resources to

upon us, speedily; appear and be uplifted over us before the eyes of all the living. Draw our scattered ones near from among the nations, and bring in our dispersions from the ends of the earth. Bring us to Zion, Your City, in glad song, and to Jerusalem, home of Your Sanctuary, in eternal joy. There we will perform before You our obligatory offerings, the continual offerings according to their order and the additional offerings according to their law. And the additional offering[s of this day of Sabbath and] of this day of the Festival of Succos, we will perform and bring near to You with love, according to the commandment of Your will, as You have written for us in Your Torah, through Moses, Your servant, from Your glorious expression, as it is said:*

On the Sabbath add. [If forgotten, do not repeat *Shemoneh Esrei.* See *Laws* §86.]

וּבְיוֹם הַשַּׁבָּת *On the Sabbath day: two [male] first-year lambs, unblemished; and two tenth-ephah of fine flour for a meal-offering, mixed with olive oil, and its wine-libation. The elevation-offering of the Sabbath must be on its particular Sabbath, in addition to the continual elevation-offering and its wine-libation.*[1] *(This is the offering of the Sabbath. And the offering of the day is as it is said:)*

וּבַחֲמִשָּׁה עָשָׂר *And on the fifteenth day of the seventh month, there shall be a holy convocation for you; you may not do any laborious work; and you shall celebrate a festival to* HASHEM *for seven days. You are to bring an elevation-offering, a fire-offering, a satisfying aroma to* HASHEM*; thirteen young bulls, two rams, fourteen [male] first-year lambs, they are to be unblemished.*[2] *And their meal-offerings and their wine-libations as mentioned: three tenth-ephah for each bull; two tenth-ephah for each ram; one tenth-ephah for each lamb; and wine for its libation. A he-goat for atonement, and two continual offerings according to their law.*

On the Sabbath add. [If forgotten, do not repeat *Shemoneh Esrei.* See *Laws* §86.]

יִשְׂמְחוּ *They shall rejoice in Your Kingship — those who observe the Sabbath and call it a delight. The people that sanctifies the Seventh — they will all be satisfied and delighted from Your goodness. And the Seventh — You found favor in it and sanctified it. 'Most coveted of days' You called it, a remembrance of creation.*

On the Sabbath add the words in brackets. [If forgotten, see *Laws* §86-90.]

אֱלֹהֵינוּ *Our God and the God of our forefathers, [may You be pleased with our rest] O merciful King, have mercy on us; O good and beneficent One,* let Yourself be sought out by us; return to us in Your yearning mercy for the sake of the forefathers who did Your will. Rebuild Your House as it was at first, and establish Your Sanctuary on its prepared site; show us its rebuilding and gladden us in its perfection.*

(1) *Numbers* 28:9-10. (2) 29:12-13.

וְהָשֵׁב כֹּהֲנִים לַעֲבוֹדָתָם, וּלְוִיִּם לְשִׁירָם וּלְזִמְרָם, וְהָשֵׁב יִשְׂרָאֵל לִנְוֵיהֶם. וְשָׁם נַעֲלֶה וְנֵרָאֶה* וְנִשְׁתַּחֲוֶה לְפָנֶיךָ, בְּשָׁלֹשׁ פַּעֲמֵי רְגָלֵינוּ, כַּכָּתוּב בְּתוֹרָתֶךָ: שָׁלוֹשׁ פְּעָמִים בַּשָּׁנָה, יֵרָאֶה כָל זְכוּרְךָ אֶת פְּנֵי יהוה אֱלֹהֶיךָ, בַּמָּקוֹם אֲשֶׁר יִבְחָר, בְּחַג הַמַּצּוֹת, וּבְחַג הַשָּׁבֻעוֹת, וּבְחַג הַסֻּכּוֹת, וְלֹא יֵרָאֶה אֶת פְּנֵי יהוה רֵיקָם.* אִישׁ כְּמַתְּנַת יָדוֹ, כְּבִרְכַּת יהוה אֱלֹהֶיךָ, אֲשֶׁר נָתַן לָךְ.[1]

On the Sabbath add the words in brackets. [If forgotten, see *Laws* §86-90.]

וְהַשִּׂיאֵנוּ יהוה אֱלֹהֵינוּ אֶת בִּרְכַּת מוֹעֲדֶיךָ לְחַיִּים וּלְשָׁלוֹם, לְשִׂמְחָה וּלְשָׂשׂוֹן, כַּאֲשֶׁר רָצִיתָ וְאָמַרְתָּ לְבָרְכֵנוּ. [אֱלֹהֵינוּ וֵאלֹהֵי אֲבוֹתֵינוּ רְצֵה בִמְנוּחָתֵנוּ] קַדְּשֵׁנוּ בְּמִצְוֹתֶיךָ וְתֵן חֶלְקֵנוּ בְּתוֹרָתֶךָ, שַׂבְּעֵנוּ מִטּוּבֶךָ וְשַׂמְּחֵנוּ בִּישׁוּעָתֶךָ, וְטַהֵר לִבֵּנוּ לְעָבְדְּךָ בֶּאֱמֶת, וְהַנְחִילֵנוּ יהוה אֱלֹהֵינוּ [בְּאַהֲבָה וּבְרָצוֹן] בְּשִׂמְחָה וּבְשָׂשׂוֹן [שַׁבָּת וּ]מוֹעֲדֵי קָדְשֶׁךָ, וְיִשְׂמְחוּ בְךָ יִשְׂרָאֵל מְקַדְּשֵׁי שְׁמֶךָ. בָּרוּךְ אַתָּה יהוה, מְקַדֵּשׁ [הַשַּׁבָּת וְ]יִשְׂרָאֵל וְהַזְּמַנִּים.

עבודה

רְצֵה יהוה אֱלֹהֵינוּ בְּעַמְּךָ יִשְׂרָאֵל וּבִתְפִלָּתָם, וְהָשֵׁב אֶת הָעֲבוֹדָה לִדְבִיר בֵּיתֶךָ. וְאִשֵּׁי יִשְׂרָאֵל וּתְפִלָּתָם בְּאַהֲבָה תְקַבֵּל בְּרָצוֹן, וּתְהִי לְרָצוֹן תָּמִיד עֲבוֹדַת יִשְׂרָאֵל עַמֶּךָ.

WHEN THE *KOHANIM* ASCEND THE *DUCHAN*• TO PRONOUNCE *BIRCAS KOHANIM* [THE PRIESTLY BLESSING], THE *CHAZZAN'S* REPETITION CONTINUES ON PAGE 352.

If no *Kohen* is present, the *chazzan* continues here.

וְתֶחֱזֶינָה עֵינֵינוּ בְּשׁוּבְךָ לְצִיּוֹן בְּרַחֲמִים. בָּרוּךְ אַתָּה יהוה, הַמַּחֲזִיר שְׁכִינָתוֹ לְצִיּוֹן.

---

benefit others. On the other hand, one may benefit others by helping them do good deeds, but for himself he may prefer to indulge his sinful nature. God, however, is perfect — He is both good and beneficent *(Iyun Tefillah)*.

וְשָׁם נַעֲלֶה וְנֵרָאֶה — *And there we will ascend and appear.* Having been returned to *Eretz Yisrael*, we will be able to fulfill the commandment of going up to the Temple to appear before God.

ריקם — *Empty-handed.* During the pilgrimages, each Jew must offer elevation-offerings and peace-offerings in honor of the Festivals. However, though no one may come emptyhanded — without offerings — he should give only as much as he can afford, but not more, *according to the gift of his hand*, i.e., depending on how much God has blessed him with *(Rashi)*.

דוכן — *Duchan.* The Priestly Blessing is often

Restore the Kohanim to their service and the Levites to their song and music; and restore Israel to their dwellings. And there we will ascend and appear and prostrate ourselves before You, during our three pilgrimage seasons, as it is written in Your Torah: Three times a year all your males are to appear before HASHEM, your God, in the place He shall choose, on the Festival of Matzos, on the Festival of Shavuos, and on the Festival of Succos, and they shall not appear before HASHEM empty-handed.* Every man according to the gift of his hand, according to the blessing of HASHEM, your God, that He gave you.*[1]

On the Sabbath add the words in brackets. [If forgotten, see *Laws* §86-90.]

וְהַשִּׂיאֵנוּ *Bestow upon us, O HASHEM, our God, the blessing of Your appointed Festivals for life and for peace, for gladness and for joy, as You desired and promised to bless us. [Our God and the God of our forefathers, may You be pleased with our rest.] Sanctify us with Your commandments and grant us our share in Your Torah; satisfy us from Your goodness and gladden us with Your salvation, and purify our heart to serve You sincerely. And grant us a heritage, O HASHEM, our God — [with love and with favor] with gladness and with joy — [the Sabbath and] the appointed festivals of Your holiness, and may Israel, the sanctifiers of Your Name, rejoice in You. Blessed are You, HASHEM, Who sanctifies [the Sabbath] Israel and the festive seasons.*

TEMPLE SERVICE

רְצֵה *Be favorable, HASHEM, our God, toward Your people Israel and their prayer and restore the service to the Holy of Holies of Your Temple. The fire-offerings of Israel and their prayer accept with love and favor, and may the service of Your people Israel always be favorable to You.*

WHEN THE *KOHANIM* ASCEND THE *DUCHAN** TO PRONOUNCE *BIRCAS KOHANIM* [THE PRIESTLY BLESSING], THE *CHAZZAN'S* REPETITION CONTINUES ON PAGE 352.

If no *Kohen* is present, the *chazzan* continues here.

וְתֶחֱזֶינָה *May our eyes behold Your return to Zion in compassion. Blessed are You, HASHEM, Who restores His Presence to Zion.*

(1) *Deuteronomy* 16:16-17.

---

referred to as עֲלִיָּה לַדּוּכָן, *ascending the platform.* It refers to the location in the *Beis HaMikdash* from where the blessing was bestowed. The *Kohanim* stood on the stairs leading to the Temple proper as they raised their hands to pronounce *Bircas Kohanim (Tamid* 7:2). In most synagogues today the *Kohanim* stand on a *duchan,* or platform, in front of the Ark while they bestow the blessings on the congregation. Although the use of a *duchan* is not a necessary condition for *Bircas Kohanim,* use of a *duchan* is preferred.

הודאה

Bow at מוֹדִים; straighten up at ה'. In his repetition the *chazzan* should recite the entire מוֹדִים aloud, while the congregation recites מוֹדִים דְּרַבָּנָן softly.

מוֹדִים אֲנַחְנוּ לָךְ, שָׁאַתָּה הוּא יהוה אֱלֹהֵינוּ וֵאלֹהֵי אֲבוֹתֵינוּ לְעוֹלָם וָעֶד. צוּר חַיֵּינוּ, מָגֵן יִשְׁעֵנוּ אַתָּה הוּא לְדוֹר וָדוֹר. נוֹדֶה לְּךָ וּנְסַפֵּר תְּהִלָּתֶךָ[1] עַל חַיֵּינוּ הַמְּסוּרִים בְּיָדֶךָ, וְעַל נִשְׁמוֹתֵינוּ הַפְּקוּדוֹת לָךְ, וְעַל נִסֶּיךָ שֶׁבְּכָל יוֹם עִמָּנוּ, וְעַל נִפְלְאוֹתֶיךָ וְטוֹבוֹתֶיךָ שֶׁבְּכָל עֵת, עֶרֶב וָבֹקֶר וְצָהֳרָיִם. הַטּוֹב כִּי לֹא כָלוּ רַחֲמֶיךָ, וְהַמְּרַחֵם כִּי לֹא תַמּוּ חֲסָדֶיךָ,[2] מֵעוֹלָם קִוִּינוּ לָךְ.

מודים דרבנן

מוֹדִים אֲנַחְנוּ לָךְ, שָׁאַתָּה הוּא יהוה אֱלֹהֵינוּ וֵאלֹהֵי אֲבוֹתֵינוּ, אֱלֹהֵי כָל בָּשָׂר, יוֹצְרֵנוּ, יוֹצֵר בְּרֵאשִׁית. בְּרָכוֹת וְהוֹדָאוֹת לְשִׁמְךָ הַגָּדוֹל וְהַקָּדוֹשׁ, עַל שֶׁהֶחֱיִיתָנוּ וְקִיַּמְתָּנוּ. כֵּן תְּחַיֵּנוּ וּתְקַיְּמֵנוּ, וְתֶאֱסוֹף גָּלֻיּוֹתֵינוּ לְחַצְרוֹת קָדְשֶׁךָ, לִשְׁמוֹר חֻקֶּיךָ וְלַעֲשׂוֹת רְצוֹנֶךָ, וּלְעָבְדְּךָ בְּלֵבָב שָׁלֵם, עַל שֶׁאֲנַחְנוּ מוֹדִים לָךְ. בָּרוּךְ אֵל הַהוֹדָאוֹת.

וְעַל כֻּלָּם יִתְבָּרַךְ וְיִתְרוֹמַם שִׁמְךָ מַלְכֵּנוּ תָּמִיד לְעוֹלָם וָעֶד.

Bend the knees at בָּרוּךְ; bow at אַתָּה; straighten up at ה'.

וְכֹל הַחַיִּים יוֹדוּךָ סֶּלָה, וִיהַלְלוּ אֶת שִׁמְךָ בֶּאֱמֶת, הָאֵל יְשׁוּעָתֵנוּ וְעֶזְרָתֵנוּ סֶלָה. בָּרוּךְ אַתָּה יהוה, הַטּוֹב שִׁמְךָ וּלְךָ נָאֶה לְהוֹדוֹת.

ברכת כהנים

If the *Kohanim* do not ascend the *duchan,* the *chazzan* recites the following during his repetition. He faces right at וְיִשְׁמְרֶךָ; faces left at אֵלֶיךָ וִיחֻנֶּךָּ; faces the Ark for the rest of the blessings.

אֱלֹהֵינוּ, וֵאלֹהֵי אֲבוֹתֵינוּ, בָּרְכֵנוּ בַבְּרָכָה הַמְּשֻׁלֶּשֶׁת בַּתּוֹרָה הַכְּתוּבָה עַל יְדֵי מֹשֶׁה עַבְדֶּךָ, הָאֲמוּרָה מִפִּי אַהֲרֹן וּבָנָיו, כֹּהֲנִים עַם קְדוֹשֶׁךָ, כָּאָמוּר:

יְבָרֶכְךָ יהוה, וְיִשְׁמְרֶךָ. (Cong. – כֵּן יְהִי רָצוֹן.)

יָאֵר יהוה פָּנָיו אֵלֶיךָ וִיחֻנֶּךָּ. (Cong. – כֵּן יְהִי רָצוֹן.)

יִשָּׂא יהוה פָּנָיו אֵלֶיךָ וְיָשֵׂם לְךָ שָׁלוֹם.[3] (Cong. – כֵּן יְהִי רָצוֹן.)

THANKSGIVING [MODIM]

Bow at *'We gratefully thank You'*; straighten up at *'HASHEM.'* In his repetition the *chazzan* should recite the entire *Modim* aloud, while the congregation recites *Modim of the Rabbis* softly.

מוֹדִים *We gratefully thank You, for it is You Who are HASHEM, our God and the God of our forefathers for all eternity; Rock of our lives, Shield of our salvation are You from generation to generation. We shall thank You and relate Your praise*[1] *— for our lives, which are committed to Your power and for our souls that are entrusted to You; for Your miracles that are with us every day; and for Your wonders and favors in every season — evening, morning, and afternoon. The Beneficent One, for Your compassions were never exhausted, and the Compassionate One, for Your kindnesses never ended*[2] *— always have we put our hope in You.*

MODIM OF THE RABBIS

מוֹדִים *We gratefully thank You, for it is You Who are HASHEM, our God and the God of our forefathers, the God of all flesh, our Molder, the Molder of the universe. Blessings and thanks are due Your great and holy Name for You have given us life and sustained us. So may You continue to give us life and sustain us and gather our exiles to the Courtyards of Your Sanctuary, to observe Your decrees, to do Your will and to serve You wholeheartedly. [We thank You] for inspiring us to thank You. Blessed is the God of thanksgivings.*

For all these, may Your Name be blessed and exalted, our King, continually forever and ever.

Bend the knees at *'Blessed'*; bow at *'You'*; straighten up at *'HASHEM.'*

Everything alive will gratefully acknowledge You, Selah! and praise Your Name sincerely, O God of our salvation and help, Selah! Blessed are You, HASHEM, Your Name is 'The Beneficent One' and to You it is fitting to give thanks.

THE PRIESTLY BLESSING

If the *Kohanim* do not ascend the *duchan*, the *chazzan* recites the following during his repetition.

אֱלֹהֵינוּ *Our God and the God of our forefathers, bless us with the three-verse blessing in the Torah that was written by the hand of Moses, Your servant, that was said by Aaron and his sons, the Kohanim, Your holy people, as it is said:*

May HASHEM bless you and safeguard you. (Cong.— *So may it be.*)

May HASHEM illuminate His countenance for you and be gracious to you. (Cong.— *So may it be.*)

May HASHEM turn His countenance to you and establish peace for you.[3] (Cong.— *So may it be.*)

---

(1) Cf. *Psalms* 79:13. (2) Cf. *Lamentations* 3:22. (3) *Numbers* 6:24-26.

שלום

שִׂים שָׁלוֹם, טוֹבָה, וּבְרָכָה, חֵן, וָחֶסֶד וְרַחֲמִים עָלֵינוּ וְעַל כָּל יִשְׂרָאֵל עַמֶּךָ. בָּרְכֵנוּ אָבִינוּ, כֻּלָּנוּ כְּאֶחָד בְּאוֹר פָּנֶיךָ, כִּי בְאוֹר פָּנֶיךָ נָתַתָּ לָּנוּ, יהוה אֱלֹהֵינוּ, תּוֹרַת חַיִּים וְאַהֲבַת חֶסֶד, וּצְדָקָה, וּבְרָכָה, וְרַחֲמִים, וְחַיִּים, וְשָׁלוֹם. וְטוֹב בְּעֵינֶיךָ לְבָרֵךְ אֶת עַמְּךָ יִשְׂרָאֵל, בְּכָל עֵת וּבְכָל שָׁעָה בִּשְׁלוֹמֶךָ. בָּרוּךְ אַתָּה יהוה, הַמְּבָרֵךְ אֶת עַמּוֹ יִשְׂרָאֵל בַּשָּׁלוֹם.

יִהְיוּ לְרָצוֹן אִמְרֵי פִי וְהֶגְיוֹן לִבִּי לְפָנֶיךָ, יהוה צוּרִי וְגֹאֲלִי.[1]

The *chazzan's* repetition of *Shemoneh Esrei* ends here.
Individuals continue below:

אֱלֹהַי, נְצוֹר לְשׁוֹנִי מֵרָע, וּשְׂפָתַי מִדַּבֵּר מִרְמָה,[2] וְלִמְקַלְלַי נַפְשִׁי תִדּוֹם, וְנַפְשִׁי כֶּעָפָר לַכֹּל תִּהְיֶה. פְּתַח לִבִּי בְּתוֹרָתֶךָ, וּבְמִצְוֹתֶיךָ תִּרְדּוֹף נַפְשִׁי. וְכֹל הַחוֹשְׁבִים עָלַי רָעָה, מְהֵרָה הָפֵר עֲצָתָם וְקַלְקֵל מַחֲשַׁבְתָּם. עֲשֵׂה לְמַעַן שְׁמֶךָ, עֲשֵׂה לְמַעַן יְמִינֶךָ, עֲשֵׂה לְמַעַן קְדֻשָּׁתֶךָ, עֲשֵׂה לְמַעַן תּוֹרָתֶךָ. לְמַעַן יֵחָלְצוּן יְדִידֶיךָ, הוֹשִׁיעָה יְמִינְךָ וַעֲנֵנִי.[3]

Some recite verses pertaining to their names here. See page 1301.

יִהְיוּ לְרָצוֹן אִמְרֵי פִי וְהֶגְיוֹן לִבִּי לְפָנֶיךָ, יהוה צוּרִי וְגֹאֲלִי.[1]

Bow and take three steps back. Bow left and say . . . עֹשֶׂה, bow right and say . . . הוּא יַעֲשֶׂה; bow forward and say וְעַל כָּל . . . אָמֵן.

עֹשֶׂה שָׁלוֹם בִּמְרוֹמָיו, הוּא יַעֲשֶׂה שָׁלוֹם עָלֵינוּ, וְעַל כָּל יִשְׂרָאֵל. וְאִמְרוּ: אָמֵן.

יְהִי רָצוֹן מִלְּפָנֶיךָ יהוה אֱלֹהֵינוּ וֵאלֹהֵי אֲבוֹתֵינוּ, שֶׁיִּבָּנֶה בֵּית הַמִּקְדָּשׁ בִּמְהֵרָה בְיָמֵינוּ, וְתֵן חֶלְקֵנוּ בְּתוֹרָתֶךָ. וְשָׁם נַעֲבָדְךָ בְּיִרְאָה, כִּימֵי עוֹלָם וּכְשָׁנִים קַדְמוֹנִיּוֹת. וְעָרְבָה לַיהוה מִנְחַת יְהוּדָה וִירוּשָׁלָיִם, כִּימֵי עוֹלָם וּכְשָׁנִים קַדְמוֹנִיּוֹת.[4]

THE INDIVIDUAL'S RECITATION OF *SHEMONEH ESREI* ENDS HERE.

The invidual remains standing in place until the *chazzan* reaches *Kedushah* — or at least until the *chazzan* begins his repetition — then he takes three steps forward. The *chazzan* himself, or one praying alone, should remain in place for at least a few moments before taking three steps forward.

AT THE CONCLUSION OF THE *CHAZZAN' S* REPETITION, CONTINUE WITH HOSHANOS, P. 362.
[CONGREGATIONS THAT RECITED *HOSHANOS* EARLIER, CONTINUE WITH *KADDISH,* P. 374.]

PEACE

שִׂים שָׁלוֹם *Establish peace, goodness, blessing, graciousness, kindness, and compassion upon us and upon all of Your people Israel. Bless us, our Father, all of us as one, with the light of Your countenance, for with the light of Your countenance You gave us, HASHEM, our God, the Torah of life and a love of kindness, righteousness, blessing, compassion, life, and peace. And may it be good in Your eyes to bless Your people Israel at every time and every hour with Your peace. Blessed are You, HASHEM, Who blesses His people Israel with peace.*

May the expressions of my mouth and the thoughts of my heart find favor before You, HASHEM, my Rock and my Redeemer.[1]

The *chazzan's* repetition of *Shemoneh Esrei* ends here.
Individuals continue below:

אֱלֹהַי *My God, guard my tongue from evil and my lips from speaking deceitfully.*[2] *To those who curse me, let my soul be silent; and let my soul be like dust to everyone. Open my heart to Your Torah, then my soul will pursue Your commandments. As for all those who design evil against me, speedily nullify their counsel and disrupt their design. Act for Your Name's sake; act for Your right hand's sake; act for Your sanctity's sake; act for Your Torah's sake. That Your beloved ones may be given rest; let Your right hand save, and respond to me.*[3]

Some recite verses pertaining to their names at this point. See page 1301.

May the expressions of my mouth and the thoughts of my heart find favor before You, HASHEM, my Rock and my Redeemer.[1] *He Who makes peace in His heights, may He make peace upon us, and upon all Israel. Now respond: Amen.*

Bow and take three steps back. Bow left and say, *'He Who makes peace . . .'*; bow right and say, *'may He make peace . . .'*; bow forward and say, *'and upon . . . Amen.'*

יְהִי רָצוֹן *May it be Your will, HASHEM, our God and the God of our forefathers, that the Holy Temple be rebuilt, speedily in our days. Grant us our share in Your Torah, and may we serve You there with reverence, as in days of old and in former years. Then the offering of Judah and Jerusalem will be pleasing to HASHEM, as in days of old and in former years.*[4]

THE INDIVIDUAL'S RECITATION OF *SHEMONEH ESREI* ENDS HERE.

The invidual remains standing in place until the *chazzan* reaches *Kedushah* — or at least until the *chazzan* begins his repetition — then he takes three steps forward. The *chazzan* himself, or one praying alone, should remain in place for at least a few moments before taking three steps forward.

AT THE CONCLUSION OF THE *CHAZZAN'S* REPETITION, CONTINUE WITH HOSHANOS, P. 362.
[CONGREGATIONS THAT RECITED *HOSHANOS* EARLIER, CONTINUE WITH *KADDISH*, P. 374.]

(1) *Psalms* 19:15. (2) Cf. 34:14. (3) 60:7; 108:7. (4) *Malachi* 3:4.

ברכת כהנים

When the *Kohanim* ascend the *duchan* to pronounce *Bircas Kohanim* [the Priestly Blessing], the *chazzan's* repetition of *Shemoneh Esrei* continues here from page 346.

Congregation and *Kohanim*, then *chazzan*.

וְתֶעָרֵב לְפָנֶיךָ עֲתִירָתֵנוּ כְּעוֹלָה וּכְקָרְבָּן. אָנָּא, רַחוּם, בְּרַחֲמֶיךָ הָרַבִּים הָשֵׁב שְׁכִינָתְךָ לְצִיּוֹן עִירֶךָ, וְסֵדֶר הָעֲבוֹדָה לִירוּשָׁלָיִם. וְתֶחֱזֶינָה עֵינֵינוּ בְּשׁוּבְךָ לְצִיּוֹן בְּרַחֲמִים, וְשָׁם נַעֲבָדְךָ בְּיִרְאָה כִּימֵי עוֹלָם וּכְשָׁנִים קַדְמוֹנִיּוֹת.

Chazzan concludes – בָּרוּךְ אַתָּה יהוה, שֶׁאוֹתְךָ לְבַדְּךָ בְּיִרְאָה נַעֲבוֹד.

(Cong. and *Kohanim* – אָמֵן.)

The *chazzan* recites the entire מודים aloud, while the congregation recites מודים דְּרַבָּנָן softly. Bow at מוֹדִים; straighten up at ה׳.

מוֹדִים אֲנַחְנוּ לָךְ, שָׁאַתָּה הוּא יהוה אֱלֹהֵינוּ וֵאלֹהֵי אֲבוֹתֵינוּ לְעוֹלָם וָעֶד. צוּר חַיֵּינוּ, מָגֵן יִשְׁעֵנוּ אַתָּה הוּא לְדוֹר וָדוֹר. נוֹדֶה לְּךָ וּנְסַפֵּר תְּהִלָּתֶךָ[1] עַל חַיֵּינוּ הַמְּסוּרִים בְּיָדֶךָ, וְעַל נִשְׁמוֹתֵינוּ הַפְּקוּדוֹת לָךְ, וְעַל נִסֶּיךָ שֶׁבְּכָל יוֹם עִמָּנוּ, וְעַל נִפְלְאוֹתֶיךָ וְטוֹבוֹתֶיךָ שֶׁבְּכָל עֵת, עֶרֶב וָבֹקֶר וְצָהֳרָיִם. הַטּוֹב כִּי לֹא כָלוּ רַחֲמֶיךָ, וְהַמְּרַחֵם כִּי לֹא תַמּוּ חֲסָדֶיךָ,[2] מֵעוֹלָם קִוִּינוּ לָךְ.

מודים דרבנן

מוֹדִים אֲנַחְנוּ לָךְ, שָׁאַתָּה הוּא יהוה אֱלֹהֵינוּ וֵאלֹהֵי אֲבוֹתֵינוּ, אֱלֹהֵי כָל בָּשָׂר, יוֹצְרֵנוּ, יוֹצֵר בְּרֵאשִׁית. בְּרָכוֹת וְהוֹדָאוֹת לְשִׁמְךָ הַגָּדוֹל וְהַקָּדוֹשׁ, עַל שֶׁהֶחֱיִיתָנוּ וְקִיַּמְתָּנוּ. כֵּן תְּחַיֵּנוּ וּתְקַיְּמֵנוּ, וְתֶאֱסוֹף גָּלֻיּוֹתֵינוּ לְחַצְרוֹת קָדְשֶׁךָ, לִשְׁמוֹר חֻקֶּיךָ וְלַעֲשׂוֹת רְצוֹנֶךָ, וּלְעָבְדְּךָ בְּלֵבָב שָׁלֵם, עַל שֶׁאֲנַחְנוּ מוֹדִים לָךְ. בָּרוּךְ אֵל הַהוֹדָאוֹת.

וְעַל כֻּלָּם יִתְבָּרַךְ וְיִתְרוֹמַם שִׁמְךָ מַלְכֵּנוּ תָּמִיד לְעוֹלָם וָעֶד.

The *chazzan* bends his knees at בָּרוּךְ; bows at אַתָּה; and straightens up at ה׳. When the *chazzan* recites וְכֹל הַחַיִּים, the *Kohanim* recite יְהִי רָצוֹן.

וְכֹל הַחַיִּים יוֹדְוּךָ סֶּלָה, וִיהַלְלוּ אֶת שִׁמְךָ בֶּאֱמֶת, הָאֵל יְשׁוּעָתֵנוּ וְעֶזְרָתֵנוּ סֶלָה. בָּרוּךְ אַתָּה יהוה, הַטּוֹב שִׁמְךָ וּלְךָ נָאֶה לְהוֹדוֹת.

(Cong. and *Kohanim* – אָמֵן.)

יְהִי רָצוֹן מִלְּפָנֶיךָ, יהוה אֱלֹהֵינוּ וֵאלֹהֵי אֲבוֹתֵינוּ, שֶׁתְּהֵא הַבְּרָכָה הַזֹּאת שֶׁצִּוִּיתָנוּ לְבָרֵךְ אֶת עַמְּךָ יִשְׂרָאֵל בְּרָכָה שְׁלֵמָה, וְלֹא יִהְיֶה בָּהּ שׁוּם מִכְשׁוֹל וְעָוֹן מֵעַתָּה וְעַד עוֹלָם.

BIRCAS KOHANIM

When the *Kohanim* ascend the *duchan* to pronounce *Bircas Kohanim* [the Priestly Blessing], the *chazzan's* repetition of *Shemoneh Esrei* continues here from page 346.

Congregation and *Kohanim,* then *chazzan.*

וְתֶעָרֵב *May our entreaty be pleasing unto You as an elevation-offering and as a sacrifice. Please, O Merciful One, in Your abounding mercy return Your Shechinah to Zion, Your city, and the order of the Temple service to Jerusalem. And may our eyes behold when You return to Zion in mercy, that we may there serve You with awe as in days of old and as in earlier years.*

Chazzan concludes— *Blessed are You, HASHEM, for You alone do we serve, with awe.* (Cong. and *Kohanim*— *Amen.)*

Chazzan recites the entire *Modim* aloud, while the congregation recites *Modim of the Rabbis* softly. Bow at *'We gratefully thank You';* straighten up at *'HASHEM.'*

מוֹדִים *We gratefully thank You, for it is You Who are HASHEM, our God and the God of our forefathers for all eternity; Rock of our lives, Shield of our salvation are You from generation to generation. We shall thank You and relate Your praise*[1] *— for our lives, which are committed to Your power and for our souls that are entrusted to You; for Your miracles that are with us every day; and for Your wonders and favors in every season — evening, morning, and afternoon. The Beneficent One, for Your compassions were never exhausted, and the Compassionate One, for Your kindnesses never ended*[2] *— always have we put our hope in You.*

MODIM OF THE RABBIS

מוֹדִים *We gratefully thank You, for it is You Who are HASHEM, our God and the God of our forefathers, the God of all flesh, our Molder, the Molder of the universe. Blessings and thanks are due Your great and holy Name for You have given us life and sustained us. So may You continue to give us life and sustain us and gather our exiles to the Courtyards of Your Sanctuary, to observe Your decrees, to do Your will and to serve You wholeheartedly. [We thank You] for inspiring us to thank You. Blessed is the God of thanksgivings.*

For all these, may Your Name be blessed and exalted, our King, continually forever and ever.

When the *chazzan* recites וְכֹל הַחַיִּים, *Everything alive,* the *Kohanim* recite יְהִי רָצוֹן, *May it be Your will.*

וְכֹל *Everything alive will gratefully acknowledge You, Selah! and praise Your Name sincerely, O God of our salvation and help, Selah! Blessed are You, HASHEM, Your Name is 'The Beneficent One' and to You it is fitting to give thanks.*

(Cong. and *Kohanim*— *Amen.)*

יְהִי רָצוֹן *May it be Your will, HASHEM, our God and the God of our fathers, that this blessing which You have commanded us to bestow upon Your nation Israel be a full blessing, that there be in it neither stumbling block nor sin from now and forever.*

(1) Cf. *Psalms* 79:13. (2) Cf. *Lamentations* 3:22.

The *chazzan* recites the following in an undertone but says the word כֹּהֲנִים aloud as a formal summons to the *Kohanim*• to bless the people. In some communities the congregation, but not the *Kohanim,* responds עַם קְדוֹשֶׁךָ כָּאָמוּר, aloud.

אֱלֹהֵינוּ וֵאלֹהֵי אֲבוֹתֵינוּ, בָּרְכֵנוּ בַבְּרָכָה• הַמְּשֻׁלֶּשֶׁת• בַּתּוֹרָה הַכְּתוּבָה עַל יְדֵי מֹשֶׁה עַבְדֶּךָ, הָאֲמוּרָה מִפִּי אַהֲרֹן וּבָנָיו,

כֹּהֲנִים

עַם קְדוֹשֶׁךָ• — כָּאָמוּר:

The *Kohanim* recite the following blessing aloud, in unison, and the congregation, but not the *chazzan,* responds אָמֵן.

בָּרוּךְ אַתָּה יהוה, אֱלֹהֵינוּ מֶלֶךְ הָעוֹלָם, אֲשֶׁר קִדְּשָׁנוּ בִּקְדֻשָּׁתוֹ שֶׁל אַהֲרֹן,• וְצִוָּנוּ לְבָרֵךְ אֶת עַמּוֹ יִשְׂרָאֵל בְּאַהֲבָה.•

(–Cong. אָמֵן.)

See commentary regarding the related verses• in small print that appear beside the words of the *Kohanim's* blessing.

יְבָרֶכְךָ יְבָרֶכְךָ יהוה מִצִּיּוֹן, עֹשֵׂה שָׁמַיִם וָאָרֶץ.[1]

יהוה• יהוה אֲדוֹנֵינוּ, מָה אַדִּיר שִׁמְךָ בְּכָל הָאָרֶץ.[2]

וְיִשְׁמְרֶךָ.• שָׁמְרֵנִי, אֵל, כִּי חָסִיתִי בָךְ.[3]

THE PRISTLY BLESSING / בִּרְכַּת כֹּהֲנִים

The Midrash (*Bamidbar Rabbah* 11:2) teaches that until the time of the Patriarchs, God Himself retained the power to bless people. With the advent of the Patriarchs, He gave this

---

Laws of Bircas Kohanim

After *Kedushah,* a Levite pours water from a utensil over the *Kohen's* hands. When the *chazzan* begins רְצֵה the *Kohanim* slip off their shoes (the laces should be loosened before the hands are washed) and ascend the *duchan* [platform in front of the Ark] where they stand facing the Ark.

When the *chazzan* recites וְכֹל הַחַיִּים, the *Kohanim* quietly recite the יְהִי רָצוֹן supplication, concluding it to coincide with the ending of the *chazzan's* blessing, so that the congregational *Amen* will be in response to their prayer as well as the *chazzan's.*

In most congregations, the *chazzan* quietly recites, '. . . אֱלֹהֵינוּ וֵאלֹהֵי אֲבוֹתֵינוּ בָּרְכֵנוּ, *Our God . . . bless us . . .'* until the word כֹּהֲנִים, *Kohanim,* which he calls out in a loud voice. Then, resuming his undertone, he recites the next words, 'עַם קְדוֹשֶׁךָ כָּאָמוּר, *Your holy people, as it is said.'* Even if only one *Kohen* is present, the *chazzan* uses the word *Kohanim* in plural, since it is the established form of the prayer. In some congregations, however, the *chazzan* merely calls out *'Kohanim'* without reciting the introductory prayer. In these places the *chazzan* calls out the plural word *Kohanim* only if two or more *Kohanim* ascend the *duchan.* If only one *Kohen* is present, however, that *Kohen* does not wait for a call, but raises his hands and begins his blessing immediately.

From this point until the *chazzan* begins שִׂים שָׁלוֹם, the congregation stands, facing the *Kohanim* attentively. No one may gaze at the *Kohanim's* raised hands.

Those standing behind the *Kohanim* do not receive the benefits of the blessing. Therefore, people behind them should move up during *Bircas Kohanim.*

The *chazzan* reads each word of *Bircas Kohanim* aloud and the *Kohanim* repeat it after him. The congregation may not respond אָמֵן until the *Kohanim* have completed the initial blessing; the *chazzan* may not call out יְבָרֶכְךָ until the congregation has finished its אָמֵן; the *Kohanim* may not repeat יְבָרֶכְךָ until the *chazzan* has read the full word; etc., etc.

When the *chazzan* begins שִׂים שָׁלוֹם, the *Kohanim,* with hands still raised, turn to the Ark, then lower their hands. While the *chazzan* recites שִׂים שָׁלוֹם, the *Kohanim* recite רִבּוֹנוֹ שֶׁל עוֹלָם עָשִׂינוּ . . . and the congregation recites אַדִּיר בַּמָּרוֹם. All should conclude their respective prayers simultaneously with the *chazzan's* conclusion of שִׂים שָׁלוֹם.

It is preferable that the *Kohanim* not return to their seats until after the *chazzan* completes *Kaddish* (except on Succos when the *Hoshana* prayers are recited before *Kaddish).*

The *chazzan* recites the following in an undertone but says the word *'Kohanim'* aloud as a formal summons to the *Kohanim*• to bless the people. In some communities the congregation, but not the *Kohanim*, responds, *'Your holy people — as it is said,'* aloud.

אֱלֹהֵינוּ *Our God and the God of our forefathers, bless us with the three-verse* blessing* in the Torah that was written by the hand of Moses, Your servant, that was said by Aaron and his sons, the*

Kohanim,

Your holy people — as it is said:*

The *Kohanim* recite the following blessing aloud, in unison, and the congregation, but not the *chazzan,* responds *Amen.*

בָּרוּךְ *Blessed are You,* HASHEM, *our God, King of the universe, Who has sanctified us with the holiness of Aaron,* and has commanded us to bless His people Israel with love.** (Cong.– *Amen.*)

See commentary regarding the related verses• in small print that appear beside the words of the *Kohanim's* blessing.

May [He] bless you — *May* HASHEM *bless you from Zion, Maker of heaven and earth.*[1]

— HASHEM• — — HASHEM, *our Master, how mighty is Your Name throughout the earth!*[2]

and safeguard you.• — *Safeguard me, O God, for in You have I taken refuge.*[3]

(1) *Psalms* 134:3. (2) 8:10. (3) 16:1.

awesome power to them. After they died, God declared that henceforth the *Kohanim* would bless the Jewish people. Thus, the upraised hands of the *Kohanim* are the vehicle through which God's blessing flows upon His chosen people.

This section is abridged from ArtScroll's *Bircas Kohanim/The Priestly Blessings,* by Rabbi Avie Gold.

⊲§ **אֱלֹהֵינוּ . . . בָּרְכֵנוּ בַבְּרָכָה** — *Our God . . . bless us with the . . . blessing.* We ask God, not the *Kohanim,* to bless us, because, although the *Kohanim* pronounce the words, they are merely conduits through which the blessing descends from God to the nation below (*Chullin* 49a). This is made clear in the Scriptural commandment, which ends with God's pledge וַאֲנִי אֲבָרְכֵם, *and I will bless them* (*Numbers* 6:27).

הַמְשֻׁלֶּשֶׁת — *Three-verse.* The Priestly Blessing contains three Torah verses: *Numbers* 6:24-26.

עַם קְדוֹשֶׁךָ — *Your holy people.* The *Kohanim* are so described (*I Chronicles* 23:13) because they were designated to serve God and bless Israel.

⊲§ **בָּרוּךְ . . . בִּקְדֻשָּׁתוֹ שֶׁל אַהֲרֹן** — *Blessed . . . with the holiness of Aaron.* Just as the selection of Israel as the Holy Nation is not dependent solely upon the deeds of each individual member, but on the holiness of their forebears — indeed, it is the very sanctity of the Patriarchs which imbued their descendants with a capacity for holiness — so is the sanctity of the *Kehunah* [priesthood] unique among the descendants of Aaron.

בְּאַהֲבָה — *With love.* The *Kohanim* are to feel love for the congregation when they pronounce the blessing. The addition of this phrase is based upon *Zohar* (*Naso* 147b): 'Any *Kohen* who does not have love for the congregation or for whom the congregation has no love, may not raise his hands to bless the congregation . . .'

On his first day as *Kohen Gadol,* when he completed the service, *Aaron raised his hands toward the nation and blessed them* (*Leviticus* 9:22), but we are not told what he said (*Ramban*). This teaches that a person must rejoice in his fellow Jew's good fortune until his heart becomes filled with love, joy and blessing — a blessing so great that mere words cannot express it, so overflowing with love that the very movements of his hands express his joy and love.

Raising the hands is a symbol of a heart pouring forth blessing and joy from a treasure trove of happiness. Raising the hands is not a sterile act — it must be a wholehearted expression of the hope and blessing which are hidden in the soul. An ocean of inexpressible joy issues from a pure soul; and the purer the soul, the purer the blessing (*Ohr Chadash*).

⊲§ **יְבָרֶכְךָ ה׳** — *May* HASHEM *bless you,* with increasing wealth (*Rashi*) and long lives (*Ibn Ezra*).

וְיִשְׁמְרֶךָ — *And safeguard you.* May the above blessings be preserved against loss or attack. Only God can guarantee that no one or nothing can tamper with the gifts He confers upon His loved ones (*Midrash Rabbah*).

⊲§ **Related verses** appear alongside the fifteen words of *Bircas Kohanim* in most *Siddurim.* The function of these verses and the propriety of

The *Kohanim* sing an extended chant before saying וְיִשְׁמְרֶךָ, and the congregation recites the following supplication in an undertone. (On the Sabbath this supplication is omitted.) When the *Kohanim* conclude וְיִשְׁמְרֶךָ, the congregation and *chazzan* respond אָמֵן.

רִבּוֹנוֹ שֶׁל עוֹלָם, אֲנִי שֶׁלָּךְ וַחֲלוֹמוֹתַי שֶׁלָּךְ. חֲלוֹם חָלַמְתִּי וְאֵינִי יוֹדֵעַ מַה הוּא. יְהִי רָצוֹן מִלְּפָנֶיךָ, יהוה אֱלֹהַי וֵאלֹהֵי אֲבוֹתַי, שֶׁיִּהְיוּ כָּל חֲלוֹמוֹתַי עָלַי וְעַל כָּל יִשְׂרָאֵל לְטוֹבָה – בֵּין שֶׁחָלַמְתִּי עַל עַצְמִי, וּבֵין שֶׁחָלַמְתִּי עַל אֲחֵרִים, וּבֵין שֶׁחָלְמוּ אֲחֵרִים עָלָי. אִם טוֹבִים הֵם, חַזְּקֵם וְאַמְּצֵם, וְיִתְקַיְּמוּ בִי וּבָהֶם כַּחֲלוֹמוֹתָיו שֶׁל יוֹסֵף הַצַּדִּיק. וְאִם צְרִיכִים רְפוּאָה, רְפָאֵם כְּחִזְקִיָּהוּ מֶלֶךְ יְהוּדָה מֵחָלְיוֹ, וּכְמִרְיָם הַנְּבִיאָה מִצָּרַעְתָּהּ, וּכְנַעֲמָן מִצָּרַעְתּוֹ, וּכְמֵי מָרָה עַל יְדֵי מֹשֶׁה רַבֵּנוּ, וּכְמֵי יְרִיחוֹ עַל יְדֵי אֱלִישָׁע. וּכְשֵׁם שֶׁהָפַכְתָּ אֶת קִלְלַת בִּלְעָם הָרָשָׁע מִקְּלָלָה לִבְרָכָה, כֵּן תַּהֲפוֹךְ כָּל חֲלוֹמוֹתַי עָלַי וְעַל כָּל יִשְׂרָאֵל לְטוֹבָה, וְתִשְׁמְרֵנִי וּתְחָנֵּנִי וְתִרְצֵנִי. אָמֵן.

יָאֵר אֱלֹהִים יְחָנֵּנוּ וִיבָרְכֵנוּ, יָאֵר פָּנָיו אִתָּנוּ, סֶלָה.[1]

יהוה יהוה יהוה, אֵל רַחוּם וְחַנּוּן, אֶרֶךְ אַפַּיִם וְרַב חֶסֶד וֶאֱמֶת.[2]

פָּנָיו פְּנֵה אֵלַי וְחָנֵּנִי, כִּי יָחִיד וְעָנִי אָנִי.[3]

אֵלֶיךָ• אֵלֶיךָ יהוה נַפְשִׁי אֶשָּׂא.[4]

וִיחֻנֶּךָּ: הִנֵּה כְעֵינֵי עֲבָדִים אֶל יַד אֲדוֹנֵיהֶם, כְּעֵינֵי שִׁפְחָה אֶל יַד גְּבִרְתָּהּ, כֵּן עֵינֵינוּ אֶל יהוה אֱלֹהֵינוּ עַד שֶׁיְּחָנֵּנוּ.[5]

The *Kohanim* sing an extended chant before saying וִיחֻנֶּךָּ, and the congregation recites the supplication (above) in an undertone. (On the Sabbath this supplication is omitted.) When the *Kohanim* conclude וִיחֻנֶּךָּ, the congregation and *chazzan* respond אָמֵן.

יִשָּׂא יִשָּׂא בְרָכָה מֵאֵת יהוה, וּצְדָקָה מֵאֱלֹהֵי יִשְׁעוֹ.[6] וּמְצָא חֵן וְשֵׂכֶל טוֹב בְּעֵינֵי אֱלֹהִים וְאָדָם.[7]

יהוה יהוה, חָנֵּנוּ, לְךָ קִוִּינוּ, הֱיֵה זְרֹעָם לַבְּקָרִים, אַף יְשׁוּעָתֵנוּ בְּעֵת צָרָה.[8]

פָּנָיו אַל תַּסְתֵּר פָּנֶיךָ מִמֶּנִּי בְּיוֹם צַר לִי, הַטֵּה אֵלַי אָזְנֶךָ, בְּיוֹם אֶקְרָא מַהֵר עֲנֵנִי.[9]

אֵלֶיךָ• אֵלֶיךָ נָשָׂאתִי אֶת עֵינַי, הַיֹּשְׁבִי בַּשָּׁמָיִם.[10]

---

reciting them presents a difficulty already dealt with in the Talmud (*Sotah* 39b,40a). Most authorities agree that no verses should be recited at all. Some permit the verses to be read in an undertone while the *chazzan* calls out the words of the blessing. In any case, the practice of the masses who read these verses aloud—and especially of those who repeat the words of *Bircas Kohanim* after the *chazzan* — is wrong and has no halachic basis (*Mishnah Berurah* 128:103).

☙ **יָאֵר ה׳ פָּנָיו אֵלֶיךָ** — *May HASHEM illuminate His countenance for you.* This is the blessing of spiritual growth, the light of Torah, which is symbolized by God's 'countenance' (*Sifre*).

וִיחֻנֶּךָּ — *And be gracious to you.* May you find favor in God's eyes (*Ramban*); or, may you find favor in the eyes of others, for all a person's talents and qualities will avail him little if others dislike him (*Ohr HaChaim*).

☙ **יִשָּׂא ה׳ פָּנָיו אֵלֶיךָ** — *May [He] HASHEM turn His countenance to you.* May He suppress His anger against you, even if you are sinful and deserve to be punished (*Rashi*). One's face is indicative of his attitude toward someone else. If he is angry, he will turn away from the one he dislikes. God 'turns His face' *toward* Israel to show that He loves them (*Maharzu*).

The *Kohanim* sing an extended chant and the congregation recites the following supplication in an undertone. (On the Sabbath this supplication is omitted.) When the *Kohanim* conclude וְיִשְׁמְרֶךָ, *'and safeguard you,'* the congregation and *chazzan* respond *Amen.*

רִבּוֹנוֹ שֶׁל עוֹלָם *Master of the world, I am Yours and my dreams are Yours. I have dreamed a dream but I do not know what it indicates. May it be Your will,* HASHEM, *my God and the God of my fathers, that all my dreams regarding myself and regarding all of Israel be good ones — those I have dreamed about myself, those I have dreamed about others, and those that others dreamed about me. If they are good, strengthen them, fortify them, make them endure in me and in them like the dreams of the righteous Joseph. But if they require healing, heal them like Hezekiah, King of Judah, from his sickness; like Miriam the prophetess from her tzaraas; like Naaman from his tzaraas; like the waters of Marah through the hand of Moses our teacher; and like the waters of Jericho through the hand of Elisha. And just as You transformed the curse of the wicked Balaam from a curse to a blessing, so may You transform all of my dreams regarding myself and regarding all of Israel for goodness. May You protect me, may You be gracious to me, may You accept me. Amen.*

May [He] illuminate *May God favor us and bless us, may He illuminate His countenance with us, Selah.*[1]

HASHEM HASHEM, HASHEM, *God, Compassionate and Gracious, Slow to anger, and Abundant in Kindness and Truth.*[2]

His countenance *Turn Your face to me and be gracious to me, for alone and afflicted am I.*[3]

for you* *To You,* HASHEM, *I raise my soul.*[4]

and be gracious to you.* *Behold! Like the eyes of servants unto their master's hand, like the eyes of a maid unto her mistress's hand, so are our eyes unto* HASHEM, *our God, until He will favor us.*[5]

The *Kohanim* sing an extended chant and the congregation recites the supplication (above) in an undertone. (On the Sabbath this supplication is omitted.) When the *Kohanim* conclude וִיחֻנֶּךָּ, *'and be gracious to you,'* the congregation and *chazzan* respond *Amen.*

May [He] turn *May he receive a blessing from* HASHEM, *and just kindness from the God of his salvation.*[6] *And he will find favor and good understanding in the eyes of God and man.*[7]

— HASHEM — HASHEM, *find favor with us, for You have we hoped! Be their power in the mornings, and our salvation in times of distress.*[8]

His countenance *Do not hide Your countenance from me in a day that is distressing to me; lean Your ear toward me; in the day that I call, speedily answer me.*[9]

to you* *To You I raised my eyes, O You Who dwells in the Heavens.*[10]

---

(1) *Psalms* 67:2. (2) *Exodus* 34:6. (3) *Psalms* 25:16. (4) 25:1. (5) 123:2. (6) 24:5. (7) *Proverbs* 3:4. (8) *Isaiah* 33:2. (9) *Psalms* 102:3. (10) 123:1.

וְיָשֵׂם וְשָׂמוּ אֶת שְׁמִי עַל בְּנֵי יִשְׂרָאֵל, וַאֲנִי אֲבָרְכֵם.[1]

לְךָ לְךָ יהוה, הַגְּדֻלָּה וְהַגְּבוּרָה וְהַתִּפְאֶרֶת וְהַנֵּצַח וְהַהוֹד, כִּי כֹל בַּשָּׁמַיִם וּבָאָרֶץ, לְךָ יהוה, הַמַּמְלָכָה וְהַמִּתְנַשֵּׂא לְכֹל לְרֹאשׁ.[2]

שָׁלוֹם.* שָׁלוֹם שָׁלוֹם לָרָחוֹק וְלַקָּרוֹב, אָמַר יהוה, וּרְפָאתִיו.[3]

The *Kohanim* sing an extended chant before saying שָׁלוֹם, and the congregation recites the following supplication in an undertone. [The twenty-two-letter Divine Name appears here in brackets and bold type. This Name should be scanned with the eyes but not spoken.] (On the Sabbath this supplication is omitted.)
When the *Kohanim* conclude שָׁלוֹם, congregation and *chazzan* respond אָמֵן.

יְהִי רָצוֹן מִלְּפָנֶיךָ, יהוה אֱלֹהַי וֵאלֹהֵי אֲבוֹתַי, שֶׁתַּעֲשֶׂה לְמַעַן קְדֻשַּׁת חֲסָדֶיךָ וְגֹדֶל רַחֲמֶיךָ הַפְּשׁוּטִים, וּלְמַעַן טָהֳרַת שִׁמְךָ הַגָּדוֹל הַגִּבּוֹר וְהַנּוֹרָא, בֶּן עֶשְׂרִים וּשְׁתַּיִם אוֹתִיּוֹת* הַיּוֹצְאִים מִן הַפְּסוּקִים שֶׁל בִּרְכַּת כֹּהֲנִים **[אנקת״ם פסת״ם פספסי״ם דיונסי״ם]** הָאֲמוּרָה מִפִּי אַהֲרֹן וּבָנָיו עַם קְדוֹשֶׁךָ, שֶׁתִּהְיֶה קָרוֹב לִי בְּקָרְאִי לָךְ, וְתִשְׁמַע תְּפִלָּתִי נַאֲקָתִי וְאֶנְקָתִי תָּמִיד, כְּשֵׁם שֶׁשָּׁמַעְתָּ **אֶנְקַת** יַעֲקֹב תְּמִימֶךָ הַנִּקְרָא אִישׁ **תָּם**. וְתִתֶּן לִי וּלְכָל נַפְשׁוֹת בֵּיתִי מְזוֹנוֹתֵינוּ וּפַרְנָסָתֵנוּ – בְּרֶוַח וְלֹא בְצִמְצוּם, בְּהֶתֵּר וְלֹא בְאִסּוּר, בְּנַחַת וְלֹא בְצַעַר – מִתַּחַת יָדְךָ הָרְחָבָה, כְּשֵׁם שֶׁנָּתַתָּ **פַּת** לֶחֶם לֶאֱכוֹל וּבֶגֶד לִלְבּוֹשׁ לְיַעֲקֹב אָבִינוּ הַנִּקְרָא אִישׁ **תָּם**. וְתִתְּנֵנוּ לְאַהֲבָה, לְחֵן וּלְחֶסֶד וּלְרַחֲמִים בְּעֵינֶיךָ וּבְעֵינֵי כָל רוֹאֵינוּ, וְיִהְיוּ דְבָרַי נִשְׁמָעִים לַעֲבוֹדָתֶךָ, כְּשֵׁם שֶׁנָּתַתָּ אֶת יוֹסֵף צַדִּיקֶךָ – בְּשָׁעָה שֶׁהִלְבִּישׁוֹ אָבִיו כְּתֹנֶת **פַּסִּים** – לְחֵן וּלְחֶסֶד וּלְרַחֲמִים בְּעֵינֶיךָ וּבְעֵינֵי כָל רוֹאָיו. וְתַעֲשֶׂה עִמִּי נִפְלָאוֹת **וְנִסִּים**,* וּלְטוֹבָה אוֹת, וְתַצְלִיחֵנִי בִּדְרָכַי, וְתֵן בְּלִבִּי בִּינָה לְהָבִין וּלְהַשְׂכִּיל וּלְקַיֵּם אֶת כָּל דִּבְרֵי תַלְמוּד תּוֹרָתֶךָ וְסוֹדוֹתֶיהָ, וְתַצִּילֵנִי מִשְּׁגִיאוֹת, וּתְטַהֵר רַעְיוֹנַי וְלִבִּי לַעֲבוֹדָתֶךָ וּלְיִרְאָתֶךָ. וְתַאֲרִיךְ יָמַי (insert the appropriate words – וִימֵי אָבִי וְאִמִּי וְאִשְׁתִּי וּבָנַי וּבְנוֹתַי) בְּטוֹב וּבִנְעִימוּת, בְּרֹב עֹז וְשָׁלוֹם, אָמֵן סֶלָה.

וְיָשֵׂם לְךָ שָׁלוֹם — *And establish for you peace.* Peace is the seal of all blessings, because without peace — prosperity, health, food, and drink are worthless *(Sifre).*

יְהִי רָצוֹן / May it be Your Will

שִׁמְךָ . . . בֶּן עֶשְׂרִים וּשְׁתַּיִם אוֹתִיּוֹת — *Your Name . . . composed of twenty-two letters.* Scripture uses many appellations for God. Each of these Divine Names represents an attribute by which God allows man to perceive Him. י־ה־ו־ה represents the attribute of Divine Kindness. Since this Name is composed of the letters of הָיָה הֹוֶה יִהְיֶה, *He was, He is, He will be,* it is also an indication of God's Eternality. אֱלֹהִים, *ELOHIM,* represents Divine Justice. This word can also mean *judge* and *power.* Similarly, each Name found in Scripture is but an allusion to a different Divine attribute. Kabbalah records many Divine Names which are not found explicitly in Scripture but may be derived through various Kabbalistic principles. One of the Names is described in Kabballistic literature as the Twenty-two-Letter Name, and the letters of *Bircas Kohanim* are said to allude to it.

The well-known Kabbalist Rabbi Moshe Cordovero *[Ramak]* explains that this Twenty-two Letter Name comprises four individual Names [אנקת״ם פסת״ם פספסי״ם דיונסי״ם], each capable of effecting the fulfillment of a particular human need. The first Name, אנקת״ם, — a contraction of אֶנְקַת תָּמִים, literally *the cry of the perfect ones* — is efficacious in making one's prayer accepted in Heaven; the second, פסת״ם, is the Name

and establish *And they shall place My Name upon the Children of Israel, and I shall bless them.*[1]

for you *Yours, HASHEM, is the greatness, the strength, the splendor, the triumph, and the glory, even all that is in heaven and earth; Yours, HASHEM, is the kingdom and the sovereignty over every leader.*[2]

peace.* *'Peace, peace, for far and near,' says HASHEM, 'and I shall heal him.'*[3]

The *Kohanim* sing an extended chant and the congregation recites the following supplication in an undertone. [The twenty-two-letter Divine Name appears here in brackets and bold type. This Name should be scanned with the eyes but not spoken.] (On the Sabbath this supplication is omitted.)

When the *Kohanim* conclude שָׁלוֹם, *'peace,'* congregation and *chazzan* respond *Amen.*

יְהִי רָצוֹן *May it be Your will, HASHEM, my God and the God of my forefathers, that You act for the sake of the holiness of Your kindness and the greatness of Your mercies which reach out, and for the sake of the sanctity of Your Name — the great, the mighty and the awesome; composed of twenty-two letters* which derive from the verses of Bircas Kohanim* **[אנקת״ם פסת״ם פספסי״ם דיונסי״ם]** *spoken by Aaron and his sons, Your holy people — that You be near to me when I call to You; that You listen to my prayer, my plea and my cry at all times, just as You listened to the cry* **[אֶנְקַת]** *of Jacob, Your perfect one, who is called 'a wholesome man'* **[תָּם]**. *And may You bestow upon me and upon all the souls of my household, our food and our sustenance — generously and not sparsely, honestly and not in forbidden fashion, pleasurably and not in pain — from beneath Your generous hand, just as You gave a portion* **[פִּסַּת]** *of bread to eat and clothing to wear to our father Jacob who is called 'a wholesome man'* **[תָּם]**. *And may You grant that we find love, favor, kindness and mercy in Your eyes and in the eyes of all who behold us; and that my words in Your service be heard; just as You granted Joseph, Your righteous one — at the time that his father garbed him in a fine woolen tunic* **[פַּסִּים]** *— that he find favor, kindness and mercy in Your eyes and in the eyes of all who beheld him. May You perform wonders and miracles* **[וְנִסִּים]** *with me,* and a goodly sign; grant me success in my ways; place in my heart the power of understanding, to understand, to be wise, to fulfill all the words of Your Torah's teaching and its mysteries; save me from errors; and purify my thinking and my heart for Your service and Your awe. May You prolong my days [*insert the appropriate words— *and the days of my father, my mother, my wife, my son(s), my daughter(s)] with goodness, with sweetness, with an abundance of strength and peace. Amen: Selah.*

(1) *Numbers* 6:27. (2) *II Chronicles* 29:11. (3) *Isaiah* 57:19.

through which God distributes פִּסַּת בַּר, *portions of bread,* to the hungry; through the Name פספסי״ם — related to כְּתֹנֶת פַּסִּים, *woolen tunic,* that Jacob made for Joseph (*Genesis* 37:3) — He clothes the naked; and דיונסי״ם indicates that He performs נִסִּים, *miracles,* and wonders. These four Names were invoked by Jacob when he prayed (*Genesis* 28:21) that *God be with me and guard me on this way which I am going; and give me bread to eat and clothes to wear; and that I return in peace* ... (*Pardes,* cited in *Siddur Amudei Shamayim*).

וְתַעֲשֶׂה עִמִּי נִפְלָאוֹת וְנִסִּים — *May You perform wonders and miracles with me.* It is unseemly for an individual to request miraculous intervention in his personal affairs, for what assurance does he have that he is deserving?

There are two classifications of miracle — overt [e.g., the splitting of the Sea; Joshua's stopping the sun] and covert [e.g., the seeming historic simplicity of the Purim story]. One should not request *obvious* miracles, but he may pray for covert miracles, because they are disguised as natural phenomena (*Bechor Shor*).

The *chazzan* immediately begins שִׂים שָׁלוֹם; the *Kohanim* turn back to the Ark, lower their hands and recite their concluding prayer רִבּוֹנוֹ שֶׁל עוֹלָם; and the congregation recites אַדִּיר בַּמָּרוֹם. All should conclude their respective prayers simultaneously with the *chazzan's* conclusion of שִׂים שָׁלוֹם.

Kohanim:

רִבּוֹנוֹ שֶׁל עוֹלָם, עָשִׂינוּ מַה שֶׁגָּזַרְתָּ עָלֵינוּ, אַף אַתָּה עֲשֵׂה עִמָּנוּ כְּמָה שֶׁהִבְטַחְתָּנוּ: הַשְׁקִיפָה מִמְּעוֹן קָדְשְׁךָ, מִן הַשָּׁמַיִם, וּבָרֵךְ אֶת עַמְּךָ אֶת יִשְׂרָאֵל, וְאֵת הָאֲדָמָה אֲשֶׁר נָתַתָּה לָנוּ – כַּאֲשֶׁר נִשְׁבַּעְתָּ לַאֲבוֹתֵינוּ – אֶרֶץ זָבַת חָלָב וּדְבָשׁ.[1]

Congregation:

אַדִּיר בַּמָּרוֹם, שׁוֹכֵן בִּגְבוּרָה, אַתָּה שָׁלוֹם וְשִׁמְךָ שָׁלוֹם. יְהִי רָצוֹן שֶׁתָּשִׂים עָלֵינוּ וְעַל כָּל עַמְּךָ בֵּית יִשְׂרָאֵל חַיִּים וּבְרָכָה לְמִשְׁמֶרֶת שָׁלוֹם.

Chazzan:

שִׂים שָׁלוֹם, טוֹבָה וּבְרָכָה, חֵן, וָחֶסֶד וְרַחֲמִים עָלֵינוּ וְעַל כָּל יִשְׂרָאֵל עַמֶּךָ. בָּרְכֵנוּ אָבִינוּ, כֻּלָּנוּ כְּאֶחָד בְּאוֹר פָּנֶיךָ, כִּי בְאוֹר פָּנֶיךָ נָתַתָּ לָּנוּ, יהוה אֱלֹהֵינוּ, תּוֹרַת חַיִּים וְאַהֲבַת חֶסֶד, וּצְדָקָה, וּבְרָכָה, וְרַחֲמִים, וְחַיִּים, וְשָׁלוֹם. וְטוֹב בְּעֵינֶיךָ לְבָרֵךְ אֶת עַמְּךָ יִשְׂרָאֵל, בְּכָל עֵת וּבְכָל שָׁעָה בִּשְׁלוֹמֶךָ. בָּרוּךְ אַתָּה יהוה, הַמְּבָרֵךְ אֶת עַמּוֹ יִשְׂרָאֵל בַּשָּׁלוֹם. (–Cong. and *Kohanim* אָמֵן.)

Chazzan, in an undertone:

יִהְיוּ לְרָצוֹן אִמְרֵי פִי וְהֶגְיוֹן לִבִּי לְפָנֶיךָ, יהוה צוּרִי וְגֹאֲלִי.[2]

◆§ Hoshanos

Each day of Succos in the Holy Temple, the people in the Courtyard would hold their Four Species and make a circular procession [הַקָּפָה] around the Altar. During the procession they would pray for God's blessing, punctuating each phrase of the prayer with the word הוֹשַׁעְנָא, [*hoshana*], *Please save* (or, *Save now*)! Because of this constantly repeated word, the entire prayer came to be known as *Hoshanos.*

On each of the first six days of Succos there would be one circuit around the Altar, and on the seventh day there would be seven. For this reason the seventh day was called Hoshana Rabbah, or the Great Hoshana.

This *mitzvah,* which God commanded orally to Moses on Mount Sinai [הֲלָכָה לְמשֶׁה מִסִּינַי], applied only in the Temple. After the Destruction, however, the Jewish people universally adopted the custom to continue these circuits [הַקָּפוֹת] in their synagogues as an eternal remembrance of the Temple service. For the first six days, the role of the 'Altar' is played by a single member of the congregation standing at the *bimah* (Torah reading lectern), holding a Torah scroll, while the procession takes place around him. On Hoshana Rabbah, all the scrolls are removed from the Ark and those holding them gather at the *bimah.*

Since the Four Species are not taken on the Sabbath, there is no circuit around the synagogue because, in the Temple, the procession was made only by people holding the Four Species. However, the *Hoshana* service is recited on the Sabbath. Although the Ark is opened, a Torah Scroll is not removed from it.

There are two primary customs as to the part of the service when *Hoshanos* are recited.

The *chazzan* immediately begins שִׂים שָׁלוֹם, *Establish peace;* the *Kohanim* turn back to the Ark, lower their hands and recite their concluding prayer רִבּוֹנוֹ שֶׁל עוֹלָם, *Master of the World;* and the congregation recites אַדִּיר, *Mighty One.* All should conclude their respective prayers simultaneously with the *chazzan's* conclusion of שִׂים שָׁלוֹם.

Kohanim:

רִבּוֹנוֹ שֶׁל עוֹלָם *Master of the world, we have done what You have decreed upon us, now may You also do as You have promised us: Look down from Your sacred dwelling, from the heavens, and bless Your people, Israel, and the earth which You have given us — just as You have sworn to our fathers — a land that flows with milk and honey.*[1]

Congregation:

אַדִּיר *Mighty One on high, He Who dwells in power! You are Peace and Your Name is Peace! May it be acceptable that You grant us and all of Your people, the house of Israel, life and blessing for a safeguard of peace.*

Chazzan:

שִׂים שָׁלוֹם *Establish peace, goodness, blessing, graciousness, kindness, and compassion upon us and upon all of Your people Israel. Bless us, our Father, all of us as one, with the light of Your countenance, for with the light of Your countenance You gave us, HASHEM, our God, the Torah of life and a love of kindness, righteousness, blessing, compassion, life, and peace. And may it be good in Your eyes to bless Your people Israel, in every season and in every hour with Your Peace. Blessed are You, HASHEM, Who blesses His people Israel with peace.* (Cong. and *Kohanim*– *Amen.)*

Chazzan, in an undertone:

May the expressions of my mouth and the thoughts of my heart find favor before You, HASHEM, my Rock and my Redeemer.[2]

(1) *Deuteronomy* 26:15. (2) *Psalms* 19:15.

In most congregations that follow *Nusach Ashkenaz,* they are recited after *Mussaf,* because in the Temple the procession took place after the *Mussaf* offering. In *Nusach Sefard,* they are recited after *Hallel* because the congregation has its Four Species in hand at that point and it is inconvenient to put them away and then take them again for *Hoshanos.*

A mourner does not join the procession because the *Hoshanos* are prayers for mercy and he has been the object of Divine judgment.

☙ The Bimah

Vilna Gaon (*Orach Chaim* 660:1) explains the significance of the *bimah* during the *Hoshanos* procession. When the Temple stood, the Altar was the focus of the nation seeking God's help and His blessing of prosperity, for it was upon the Altar that the sacrifices were offered. Nowadays, the *bimah* upon which the Torah is read represents the Altar's extension into our daily personal lives, and the person holding the Torah is the representative of the nation displaying its loyalty to the Torah. The *Chofetz Chaim* broadens this explanation by referring to a reassurance given by God to Abraham. The Patriarch asked how Israel could merit God's blessings if they had no Temple in which to bring offerings. God responded that, when it is impossible to perform the Temple service, the study of the Torah's law about the offerings would be considered equivalent to the act of physically performing the service. Thus, the *bimah,* where the chapters of the offerings are read, is truly our substitute for the Altar.

סדר הושענות ליום ראשון ושני

IN SOME CONGREGATIONS, *HOSHANOS* ARE RECITED IMMEDIATELY AFTER *HALLEL*.

The *Hoshana* prayers are recited with the Four Species in hand. The Ark is opened; a Torah Scroll is removed and held at the *bimah*. The *chazzan* recites each line which is then repeated aloud by the congregation. [On the Sabbath, the Four Species are omitted and no Torah Scroll is removed.]

הוֹשַׁעְנָא, לְמַעַנְךָ* אֱלֹהֵינוּ, הוֹשַׁעְנָא.
הוֹשַׁעְנָא, לְמַעַנְךָ בּוֹרְאֵנוּ, הוֹשַׁעְנָא.
הוֹשַׁעְנָא, לְמַעַנְךָ גּוֹאֲלֵנוּ, הוֹשַׁעְנָא.
הוֹשַׁעְנָא, לְמַעַנְךָ דּוֹרְשֵׁנוּ,* הוֹשַׁעְנָא.

[When the first day falls on the Sabbath, אוֹם נְצוּרָה (page 368) is recited on the first day and לְמַעַן אֲמִתָּךְ is recited on the second day.]

The *chazzan* followed by every congregant that has the Four Species in hand, proceeds to walk around the *bimah*. He chants each stich of the appropriate *Hoshana* prayer (below) which is then repeated by the entire congregation.

FIRST DAY

לְמַעַן אֲמִתָּךְ.* לְמַעַן בְּרִיתָךְ. לְמַעַן גָּדְלָךְ וְתִפְאַרְתָּךְ. לְמַעַן דָּתָךְ. לְמַעַן הוֹדָךְ.* לְמַעַן וִעוּדָךְ.* לְמַעַן

SECOND DAY

אֶבֶן שְׁתִיָּה.* בֵּית הַבְּחִירָה. גֹּרֶן אָרְנָן.* דְּבִיר הַמֻּצְנָע.* הַר הַמּוֹרִיָּה. וְהַר יֵרָאֶה. זְבוּל תִּפְאַרְתֶּךָ.

לְמַעַנְךָ — *For Your sake.* Israel cries: '*Not for our sake,* HASHEM — not because our deeds make us deserving — *but for Your Name's sake give honor,*' (*Psalms* 115:1; *Targum Yonasan*).

God responds: 'לְמַעֲנִי לְמַעֲנִי אֶעֱשֶׂה, *For My sake, for My sake, shall I act . . .*' (*Isaiah* 48:11).

As long as Israel is in exile, the שְׁכִינָה *[Shechinah], manifestation of the Divine Presence,* is in exile with them, as God says: *I am with you in trouble* (*Psalms* 91:15).

The concept of *Shechinah* in exile, recurrent in the *Hoshana* liturgy, is also the theme of chapters 9-11 of *Ezekiel*. There, in response to Israel's idol-worship, the *Shechinah* withdraws, first from the Temple, then from Jerusalem, presaging the Temple's destruction and Israel's expulsion. Where sanctity is profaned, where purity is defiled, where wood, stone, and heavenly bodies replace their Creator as objects of worship, there the Divine Presence is not — indeed, cannot be — manifest. Gradually the *Shechinah* withdraws. For God's dwelling is not within buildings, but within hearts and minds. When they have no room for Him, He departs.

Yet, after the Divine Presence has completely departed from Jerusalem and the entire land, another facet of *Shechinah* in exile comes to light: *Thus says my Lord* HASHEM/ELOHIM, *Though I have removed them far off among the nations, and though I have scattered them among the countries, yet I have been for them a small sanctuary* (מִקְדָּשׁ מְעַט) *in the countries to which they came* (*Ezekiel* 11:16).

Despite everything, God's Presence remains מִקְדָּשׁ מְעַט, a term *Targum* renders *synagogue*. The synagogue is today's sanctuary of Divine worship, but it is מְעַט, *smaller, lesser,* than was Jerusalem's מִקְדָּשׁ, *Holy Temple*.

As we gather in the synagogue to recite the *hoshana* prayers, we ask for redemption of the *Shechinah* and the nation — for the sake of God, Himself — that we may once again worship not merely in the present small sanctuary, but in the בֵּית הַגָּדוֹל, *Great House* (see *II Chronicles* 3:5), may it be rebuilt speedily in our days, Amen.

דּוֹרְשֵׁנוּ — *Our Attender.* This ephithet for God was used by King David when He told his son: *You, Solomon my son, know your father's God and serve Him with a perfect heart . . . for* HASHEM *tends* (דּוֹרֵשׁ) *all hearts (I Chronicles* 28:9*).* The sense of the expression is that He takes an interest in His people and His land, never totally abandoning them to the vagaries of blind fate.

לְמַעַן אֲמִתָּךְ / For the Sake of Your Truth

Most of the *hoshanas* are composed around general motifs.

This *hoshana* records various attributes of God; accordingly, it may be considered an extension of the introductory stanza which directly precedes it (*Rashi*).

When reciting the *hoshana* prayers most congregations add the word הוֹשַׁעְנָא, *please save,*

HOSHANOS FOR THE FIRST TWO DAYS

IN SOME CONGREGATIONS, *HOSHANOS* ARE RECITED IMMEDIATELY AFTER *HALLEL*.

The *Hoshana* prayers are recited with the Four Species in hand. The Ark is opened; a Torah Scroll is removed and held at the *bimah*. The *chazzan* recites each line which is then repeated aloud by the congregation. [On the Sabbath, the Four Species are omitted and no Torah Scroll is removed.]

הוֹשַׁעְנָא *Please save — for Your sake,* our God! Please save!*
Please save — for Your sake, our Creator! Please save!
Please save — for Your sake, our Redeemer! Please save!
Please save — for Your sake, our Attender! Please save!*

[When the first day falls on the Sabbath, *Nation Protected* (page 368) is recited on the first day and *For the sake of Your Truth* is recited on the second day.]

The *chazzan* followed by every congregant that has the Four Species in hand, proceeds to walk around the *bimah*. He chants each stich of the appropriate *Hoshana* prayer (below) which is then repeated by the entire congregation.

FIRST DAY

לְמַעַן אֲמִתָּךְ *For the sake of Your Truth;** ב *for the sake of Your Covenant;* ג *for the sake of Your Greatness and Your Splendor;* ד *for the sake of Your Mandate;* ה *for the sake of Your Glory;** ו *for the sake of Your Meeting House;** ז *For the*

SECOND DAY

אֶבֶן שְׁתִיָּה *Foundation stone;** ב *chosen Temple;* ג *Arnan's granary;** ד *hidden rendezvous;** ה *Mount Moriah;* ו *Mount He-is-seen;* ז *residence of Your Splendor;* ח *where David resided;* ט *goodness of*

---

to each stich — either
(a) before it הוֹשַׁעְנָא לְמַעַן אֲמִתָּךְ;
or (b) after it לְמַעַן אֲמִתָּךְ הוֹשַׁעְנָא;
or (c) both הוֹשַׁעְנָא לְמַעַן אֲמִתָּךְ הוֹשַׁעְנָא.

Although omitted from the *machzor*, these interpolations are an intergral part of the *hoshana* liturgy.

אֲמִתָּךְ — *Your Truth.* During the long and difficult period of exile, we have seen the fulfillment of the prophecy: וְתַשְׁלֵךְ אֱמֶת אַרְצָה, *it will throw truth to the earth* (*Daniel* 8:12). Truth has become ridiculed and despised — therefore we pray: *for the sake of Your Truth.*

דָּתָךְ ... הוֹדָךְ — *Your Mandate ... Your Glory.* The *Zohar* relates the destruction of the Holy Temple to the defilement of God's הוד, *Glory.* Both blows, the destruction and the defilement, can be remedied through the same medium. Only through study of Torah can God's Glory be restored; and only through study of Torah can the Holy Temple be rebuilt. Thus the juxtaposition of דָּתָךְ, *Your Mandate,* i.e., the Torah, with הודָךְ, *Your Glory.* Only through Torah can Jerusalem be rebuilt and the Temple restored.

ועודך — *Your Meeting House.* This is an allusion to the Holy Temple where the *Shechinah* and Israel came together.

אֶבֶן שְׁתִיָּה / Foundation Stone

All twenty-two stiches of this prayer are allusions to either the *Beis HaMikdash* or the city of Jerusalem in which it was located. Most of the descriptive expressions are of Scriptural derivation; the remainder are of Talmudic origin.

The *kavanah, purposeful concentration,* of all these stiches is the same, namely: Please redeem the *Beis HaMikdash* from its present desolation and desecration; from the wild foxes that prowl over it (see *Lamentations* 5:18); that it may be rebuilt, speedily in our days.

אֶבֶן שְׁתִיָּה — *Foundation stone.* There was a stone in the center of the Holy of Holies (upon which stood the Ark of the Covenant) ... It was known from the days of the early prophets [Samuel and David (*Rashi*)] and was called Foundation Stone, ... for from this spot the world sprang forth [meaning that the stone was the first part of earth to be created by God; it grew into the planet as we know it] (*Yoma* 53b, 54b).

גֹּרֶן אָרְנָן — *Arnan's granary.* Upon the instruction of the prophet Gad, King David purchased Arnan's granary as the site for the erection of an altar (see *II Samuel* 24:18-25).

דְּבִיר הַמֻּצְנָע — *Hidden rendezvous.* This term refers to the Holy of Holies, in which stood the Ark, upon which the two *cherubim* were placed. From between them the voice of God issued when He summoned Moses (*Rashi* to *Leviticus* 1:1). The chamber was called דְּבִיר [from דבר, *to speak*], alluding to the דְּבַר ה', *word of* HASHEM, which issued from within, and was hidden from view by the curtain that separated it from the remainder of the *Mishkan.*

FIRST DAY

זִכְרָךְ.* לְמַעַן חַסְדָּךְ. לְמַעַן טוּבָךְ. לְמַעַן יִחוּדָךְ. לְמַעַן כְּבוֹדָךְ. לְמַעַן לִמּוּדָךְ. לְמַעַן מַלְכוּתָךְ. לְמַעַן נִצְחָךְ.* לְמַעַן סוֹדָךְ. לְמַעַן עֻזָּךְ. לְמַעַן פְּאֵרָךְ. לְמַעַן צִדְקָתָךְ. לְמַעַן קְדֻשָּׁתָךְ. לְמַעַן רַחֲמֶיךָ הָרַבִּים. לְמַעַן שְׁכִינָתָךְ. לְמַעַן תְּהִלָּתָךְ.

SECOND DAY

חָנָה דָוִד. טוּב הַלְּבָנוֹן.* יְפֵה נוֹף מְשׂוֹשׂ כָּל הָאָרֶץ.* כְּלִילַת יֹפִי.* לִינַת הַצֶּדֶק. מָכוֹן לְשִׁבְתֶּךָ. נָוֶה שַׁאֲנָן. סֻכַּת שָׁלֵם.* עֲלִיַּת שְׁבָטִים. פִּנַּת יִקְרַת.* צִיּוֹן הַמְּצֻיֶּנֶת. קֹדֶשׁ הַקֳּדָשִׁים. רָצוּף אַהֲבָה.* שְׁכִינַת כְּבוֹדֶךָ. תֵּל תַּלְפִּיּוֹת.*

ON BOTH DAYS

After each day's *hakafah*-circuit (except on the Sabbath), the following *Hoshana* is recited:

אֲנִי וָהוֹ הוֹשִׁיעָה נָּא.*

כְּהוֹשַׁעְתָּ אֵלִים* בְּלוּד עִמָּךְ,*
בְּצֵאתְךָ לְיֵשַׁע עַמָּךְ,
כְּהוֹשַׁעְתָּ גּוֹי וֵאלֹהִים,* כֵּן הוֹשַׁעְנָא.

זִכְרָךְ — *Your Mention* [lit. *memorial, remembrance*]. Moses asked of God: *"When I come to the children of Israel and say to them, 'The God of your ancestors has sent me to you,' and they will respond, 'What is His Name?' What shall shall I say to them?"*

God replied: *'HASHEM, God of Your ancestors* . . . זֶה שְּׁמִי, *This is My Name eternally,* וְזֶה זִכְרִי, *and this is My Mention in every generation'* (*Exodus* 3:13,15).

נִצְחָךְ — *Your Eternality.* The word has many meanings, several of which are possible in the sense of our verse: *strength, supervision, victory.*

טוּב הַלְּבָנוֹן — *Goodness of Lebanon.* The Temple is called 'goodness of Lebanon' because timber for the Temple was brought from the forest of Lebanon (see *I Kings* 5:20-28; *Song of Songs* 3:9). Since we may assume that only the best trees were felled for this purpose, 'goodness of Lebanon' is an apt description for the *Beis HaMikdash.*

יְפֵה נוֹף מְשׂוֹשׂ כָּל הָאָרֶץ — *Fairest of brides, joy of all the earth.* This description of the Temple Mount appears in *Psalms* 48:3. *Rashi* translates the obscure word נוֹף as *bride* based upon a statement of R' Shimon ben Lakish (*Rosh Hashanah* 26a): In the precinct of Ken Nesheraya a bride is called *nynph'e [=nymph,* Greek for bride]. Alternative interpretations of יְפֵה נוֹף are: *Fair as the spreading branches of a tree; fairest of sites; fairest of climates.*

כְּלִילַת יֹפִי — *Perfectly beautiful.* Jeremiah bewailed the destruction of Jerusalem: *Could this be the city of which they said,* כְּלִילַת יֹפִי, *perfectly beautiful, a joy to all the earth* (*Lamentations* 2:15). Strangely, this expression is also used to describe the city of Tyre: *Tyre, you have said, 'I am perfectly beautiful!'* (*Ezekiel* 27:3). But there is a difference. Tyre spoke these words in self-praise — *I am* — others did not praise her in this manner. But with Jerusalem such is not the case. It was, *The city of which* **they** *said, 'Perfectly beautiful!'*

סֻכַּת שָׁלֵם — *Tabernacle of Salem.* Salem was an ancient name of Jerusalem. Abraham called the city יִרְאֶה, *Yireh [=Jeru]* (*Genesis* 22:14). Shem [son of Noah, also known as Malchi-zedek] called the place שָׁלֵם, *Shalem [=Salem]* (ibid. 14:18).

God said, 'If I call it *Yireh* [=Jeru] as Abraham did, then the righteous Shem will be distraught; but if I call it *Shalem* [=Salem], then the righteous Abraham will be distraught. Instead I will satisfy both of these righteous men by calling it *Yireh-Shalem* [=Jeru-Salem] (*Bereishis Rabbah* 14:18).

פִּנַּת יִקְרַת — *Precious cornerstone.* The prophet *Isaiah* (28:16) uses this phrase to describe the building where the Sanhedrin sat. Its role was to engage in Torah study, which is more precious than pearls [a play on the similarity of sound between פִּנָּה, *cornerstone,* and פְּנִינָה, *pearl*] (*Rashi*).

רָצוּף אַהֲבָה — *Decked with love.* King Solomon

FIRST DAY

*sake of Your Mention;** ח *for the sake of Your Kindness;* ט *for the sake of Your Goodness;* י *for the sake of Your Oneness;* כ *for the sake of Your Honor;* ל *for the sake of Your Teaching;* מ *for the sake of Your Kingship;* נ *for the sake of Your Eternality;* ס *for the sake of Your Counsel;* ע *for the sake of Your Power;* פ *for the sake of Your Beauty;* צ *for the sake of Your Righteousness;* ק *for the sake of Your Sanctity;* ר *for the sake of Your numerous Mercies;* ש *for the sake of Your Shechinah;* ת *for the sake of Your Praise.*

SECOND DAY

*Lebanon;** י *fairest of brides; joy of all the earth;** כ *perfectly beautiful;** ל *lodge of righteousness;* מ *prepared for Your dwelling;* נ *tranquil abode;* ס *Tabernacle of Salem;** ע *pilgrimage of the tribes;* פ *valuable cornerstone;** צ *the distinguished Zion;* ק *Holy of Holies;* ר *decked with love;** ש *resting place of Your Honor;* ת *hill of Talpios.**

ON BOTH DAYS

After each day's *hakafah*-circuit (except on the Sabbath), the following *Hoshana* is recited:

ANI VAHO, bring salvation now.*

כְּהוֹשַׁעְתָּ אֵלִים *As You saved the terebinths* in Lud [Egypt] along with Yourself**

ב *when You went forth to save the nation — so save now.*

ג *As You saved a nation and its leaders**

describes the Temple that he built: *Its insides decked with love, for the daughters of Zion* (*Song of Songs* 3:9-10).

תֵּל תַּלְפִּיּוֹת — *Hill of Talpios.* The Temple was called *Talpios*, an adornment, because all gazed upon it to study its forms and the beautiful masterwork of its design (*Rashi*).

אֲנִי וָהוֹ הוֹשִׁיעָה נָּא — *ANI VAHO, bring salvation now.* The Talmud states: Every day [of Succos] they would circle the Altar one time saying: אָנָּא ה' הוֹשִׁיעָה נָּא, *Please, HASHEM, bring salvation now;* אָנָּא ה' הַצְלִיחָה נָּא, *please HASHEM grant success now* (*Psalms* 118:25). Rabbi Yehudah maintains [that they used the formula] אֲנִי וָהוֹ הוֹשִׁיעָה נָּא, *ANI VAHO, bring salvation now* (*Succah* 45a).

The obscure terms אֲנִי וָהוֹ, *ANI VAHO*, are identified by *Rashi* as two in a series of seventy-two Names of God, each containing three letters. The complete series is composed of the letters which make up three consecutive verses of *Exodus* (14:19-21), each containing exactly seventy-two letters. In the mystical formula by which these names are formed, *verses* 19 and 21 are read in their proper order, while *verse* 20 is read backwards. A table showing these groups of 72 letters is given below. The first group of letters gives the name והו, the thirty-seventh group yields the name אני.

The particular aptness of these two Names stems from their *gematria [numerical value]*, seventy-eight, which is equal to that of אָנָּא ה', *please, HASHEM* (*Rashi*).

◆ כְּהוֹשַׁעְתָּ אֵלִים / As You Saved the Terebinths

אֵלִים — *Terebinths.* Israel, staunch and firm in its faith in God, is compared to the oak-like terebinth tree. Alternatively, אֵלִים may be translated *powerful ones* (as in *Psalms* 29:1), and refers to the Patriarchs who were *powerful in their faith.*

עִמָּךְ — *Along with Yourself.* As long as Israel was enslaved in Egypt, God kept a brick under His feet [so to speak] as a constant reminder of the bricks that the enslaved Jews were forced to produce. When He redeemed them the brick turned to sapphire and emitted a joyful glow (*Rashi* to *Exodus* 24:10).

גּוֹי וֵאלֹהִים — *A nation and [its] leaders.* The

72	71	70	69	68	67	66	65	64	63	62	61	60	59	58	57	56	55	54	53	52	51	50	49	48	47	46	45	44	43	42	41	40	39	38	37	36	35	34	33	32	31	30	29	28	27	26	25	24	23	22	21	20	19	18	17	16	15	14	13	12	11	10	9	8	7	6	5	4	3	2	1
מ	ה	י	ר	ח	א	מ	ד	מ	ע	י	ו	מ	ה	י	נ	פ	מ	נ	נ	ע	ה	ד	ו	מ	ע	ע	ס	י	ו	מ	ה	י	ר	ח	**א**	מ	כ	ל	י	ו	ל	א	ר	ש	י	ה	נ	ח	מ	י	נ	פ	ל	כ	ל	ה	ה	מ	י	ה	ל	א	ה	כ	א	ל	מ	ע	ס	י	**ו**
ו	י	ב	א	ב	י	נ	מ	ח	נ	ה	מ	צ	ר	י	מ	ו	ב	י	נ	מ	ח	נ	ה	י	ש	ר	א	ל	ו	י	ה	י	ה	ע	**נ**	נ	ו	ה	ח	ש	כ	ו	י	א	ר	א	ת	ה	ל	י	ל	ה	ו	ל	א	ק	ר	ב	ז	ה	א	ל	ז	ה	כ	ל	ה	ל	י	ל	**ה**
מ	י	מ	ה	ו	ע	ק	ב	י	ו	ה	ב	ר	ח	ל	מ	י	ה	ת	א	מ	ש	י	ו	ה	ל	י	ל	ה	ל	כ	ה	ז	ע	מ	**י**	ד	ק	ח	ו	ר	ב	מ	י	ה	ת	א	ה	ו	ה	י	כ	ל	ו	י	ו	מ	י	ה	ל	ע	ו	ד	י	ת	א	ה	ש	מ	ט	י	**ו**

דְּרוּשִׁים לְיֵשַׁע אֱלֹהִים, כֵּן הוֹשַׁעְנָא.
כְּהוֹשַׁעְתָּ הֲמוֹן צְבָאוֹת,
וְעִמָּם מַלְאֲכֵי צְבָאוֹת,* כֵּן הוֹשַׁעְנָא.
כְּהוֹשַׁעְתָּ זַכִּים מִבֵּית עֲבָדִים,
חַנּוּן בְּיָדָם מַעֲבִידִים, כֵּן הוֹשַׁעְנָא.
כְּהוֹשַׁעְתָּ טְבוּעִים בְּצוּל גְּזָרִים,
יְקָרְךָ עִמָּם מַעֲבִירִים, כֵּן הוֹשַׁעְנָא.
כְּהוֹשַׁעְתָּ כַּנָּה* מְשׁוֹרֶרֶת וַיּוֹשַׁע,
לְגוֹחָה* מְצֻיֶּנֶת וַיִּוָּשַׁע,* כֵּן הוֹשַׁעְנָא.
כְּהוֹשַׁעְתָּ מַאֲמַר וְהוֹצֵאתִי אֶתְכֶם,
נָקוּב וְהוּצֵאתִי אִתְּכֶם,* כֵּן הוֹשַׁעְנָא.
כְּהוֹשַׁעְתָּ סוֹבְבֵי מִזְבֵּחַ,*
עוֹמְסֵי עֲרָבָה לְהַקִּיף מִזְבֵּחַ,* כֵּן הוֹשַׁעְנָא.
כְּהוֹשַׁעְתָּ פִּלְאֵי אָרוֹן* כְּהֻפְשַׁע,*
צִעֵר פְּלֶשֶׁת בַּחֲרוֹן אַף וְנוֹשַׁע, כֵּן הוֹשַׁעְנָא.
כְּהוֹשַׁעְתָּ קְהִלּוֹת בָּבֶלָה שִׁלַּחְתָּ,
רַחוּם לְמַעֲנָם שֻׁלַּחְתָּ, כֵּן הוֹשַׁעְנָא.
כְּהוֹשַׁעְתָּ שְׁבוּת שִׁבְטֵי יַעֲקֹב,
תָּשׁוּב וְתָשִׁיב שְׁבוּת אָהֳלֵי יַעֲקֹב, וְהוֹשִׁיעָה נָּא.
כְּהוֹשַׁעְתָּ שׁוֹמְרֵי מִצְוֹת,* וְחוֹכֵי יְשׁוּעוֹת,
אֵל לְמוֹשָׁעוֹת, וְהוֹשִׁיעָה נָּא.

---

translation follows *Rashi* who cites *Exodus* 7:1: *HASHEM said to Moses: See, I have made you a lord* (אֱלֹהִים) *over Pharaoh.* Thus *its leaders* means, Moses and Aaron. Alternatively, the stich refers to God and is another case of the recurring theme that God is exiled together with His people.

וְעִמָּם מַלְאֲכֵי צְבָאוֹת — *And with them hosts of angels.* The Midrash teaches that 900 million angels of destruction descended upon Egypt. All of them left together with Israel.

כַּנָּה — *The garden.* Israel is called the garden planted by God's right hand (*Psalms* 80:9).

גוֹחָה — *Him Who draws forth.* God draws the baby forth from the womb (see *Psalms* 22:10).

וַיּוֹשַׁע ... וַיִּוָּשַׁע — *He delivered ... He was delivered.* Torah Scrolls are written without the use of vowel points. The proper vowelization of each word has been handed down from generation to generation, dating from Moses who heard the words pronounced by God Himself. For midrashic and exegetical purposes, other pronunciations may be utilized, with the guidelines set by tradition.

The Song of the Sea, in which Moses led the nation after crossing the Sea of Reeds is introduced in Scripture with two verses [*Exodus* 14:30-31] beginning with the words וַיּוֹשַׁע ה׳, *HASHEM delivered* (or, *saved*). But with different vowels, these words could be read וַיִּוָּשַׁע ה׳, *HASHEM was delivered,* indicating the deliverance of the *Shechinah* from its Egyptian exile alongside of Israel.

וְהוֹצֵאתִי אֶתְכֶם ... וְהוּצֵאתִי אִתְּכֶם — *I shall bring you forth ... I shall be brought forth with you.* Another example of a word revowelized for homiletic purposes is given here. In commanding Moses to appear before Pharaoh to demand the release of Israel from bondage, God said: *I am HASHEM — I shall bring you forth* [וְהוֹצֵאתִי אֶתְכֶם] *from the Egyptian oppression* (*Exodus* 6:6). The vowels of this phrase, too, can be changed to yield an allusion to the redemption of

ד *who sought the salvations of God — so save now.*
ה *As You saved the multitudes of hosts*
ו *and with them the hosts of angels* — so save now.*
ז *As You saved pure ones from the house of slavery,*
ח *Gracious One, from those who forced manual labor upon them — so save now.*
ט *As You saved those sinking in the depths of the rifts,*
ט *Your honor was with them when they crossed — so save now.*
כ *As You saved the garden* which sang 'He delivered,'*
ל *regarding Him Who draws forth* it is pronounced 'He was delivered'* — so save now.*
מ *As You saved with the declaration 'I shall bring you forth,'*
נ *which may be interpreted, 'I shall be brought forth with you'* — so save now.*
ס *As You saved those who went roundabout with the Altar,**
ע *those who carry the willow to encircle the Altar* — so save now.*
פ *As You saved the Ark* of the Name, captured as a result of sin,**
צ *when you punished Philistia with flaming anger, and it was saved — so save now.*
ק *As You saved the congregations which You had sent to Babylon,*
ר *Merciful One, for their sake were You also sent — so save now.*
ש *As You saved the captivity of the tribes of Jacob,*
ת *return and restore the captivity of the tents of Jacob, and bring salvation now.*
As You saved those observant of mitzvos, and hopeful for salvation — O God Who brings about salvation, bring salvation now.*

God Himself. For וְהוֹצֵאתִי read וְהוּצֵאתִי, *I shall be brought forth,* and for אֶתְכֶם read אִתְּכֶם, *with you.* [For a full discussion of dual meanings based on revowelization, see *Minchas Shai* to *Isaiah* 43:14.]

סוֹבְבֵי מִזְבֵּחַ — *Those who went roundabout with the Altar.* When Joshua led the nation in the capture of Jericho, they circled the city one time on each of six consecutive days. On the seventh day they circled Jericho seven times after which its walls miraculously were destroyed, allowing Israel to enter [see *Joshua* chap. 6] (*Rashi*). Although Scripture mentions only that the Ark of the Covenant led the encircling procession, *Rashi* and the *paytan* probably assume that the other appurtenances of the Sanctuary, such as the Altar, followed behind the Ark.

מִזְבֵּחַ — *The Altar.* During the time of the Holy Temple the *hakafah*-circuits went around the sacrificial Altar. Today, the *bimah* is encircled as a reminder of those days.

אָרוֹן — *The Ark.* While still smarting from defeat by the Philistines, the elders of Israel took the Ark of the Covenant to lead their troops to battle. They were certain that the merit of the Ark and the Tablets and Torah Scroll it contained would protect them, but God willed otherwise and the Ark was captured by the Philistines. However, each city to which they brought the Ark was visited by a plague. Finally the elders of Philistia decided to return it to Israel (*I Samuel* chap. 5).

כְּהֻפְשַׁע — *As a result of sin.* This refers to Israel's sin of bringing the Ark to the battlefield without asking the consent of the prophet Samuel. This lack of respect for the prophet allowed the Ark to be captured.

שׁוֹמְרֵי מִצְוֹת — *Those observant of mitzvos.* Although the *hoshana* verses are generally attributed to R' Elazar HaKalir, this line was added at a later date by a *paytan* named שְׁמוּאֵל, *Shmuel,* as the acrostic clearly shows. That

אֲנִי וָהוֹ הוֹשִׁיעָה נָּא.

הוֹשִׁיעָה אֶת עַמֶּךָ, וּבָרֵךְ אֶת נַחֲלָתֶךָ, וּרְעֵם וְנַשְּׂאֵם עַד הָעוֹלָם.[1] וְיִהְיוּ דְבָרַי אֵלֶּה אֲשֶׁר הִתְחַנַּנְתִּי לִפְנֵי יהוה, קְרֹבִים אֶל יהוה אֱלֹהֵינוּ יוֹמָם וָלָיְלָה, לַעֲשׂוֹת מִשְׁפַּט עַבְדּוֹ וּמִשְׁפַּט עַמּוֹ יִשְׂרָאֵל, דְּבַר יוֹם בְּיוֹמוֹ. לְמַעַן דַּעַת כָּל עַמֵּי הָאָרֶץ, כִּי יהוה הוּא הָאֱלֹהִים, אֵין עוֹד.[2]

The Torah is returned to the Ark and the Ark is closed. The *chazzan* then recites קַדִּישׁ שָׁלֵם (p. 374).

THE SABBATH

On the Sabbath the following *Hoshana* is recited:

אוֹם נְצוּרָה כְּבָבַת. **בּ**וֹנֶנֶת בְּדָת נֶפֶשׁ מְשִׁיבַת. **ג**וֹמֶרֶת הִלְכוֹת שַׁבָּת. **ד**וֹרֶשֶׁת מַשְׂאַת שַׁבָּת.* **הַ**קּוֹבַעַת אַלְפַּיִם תְּחוּם* שַׁבָּת. **וּ**מְשִׁיבַת רֶגֶל* מִשַּׁבָּת. **זָ**כוֹר וְשָׁמוֹר* מְקַיֶּמֶת בַּשַּׁבָּת. **חָ**שָׁה לְמַהֵר בִּיאַת שַׁבָּת. **ט**וֹרַחַת כֹּל מִשְׁשָׁה לַשַּׁבָּת. **י**וֹשֶׁבֶת וּמַמְתֶּנֶת עַד כְּלוֹת שַׁבָּת. **כָּ**בוֹד וָעֹנֶג* קוֹרְאָה לַשַּׁבָּת. **לְ**בוּשׁ וּכְסוּת מְחַלֶּפֶת בַּשַּׁבָּת. **מַ**אֲכָל וּמִשְׁתֶּה מְכִינָה לַשַּׁבָּת. **נֹ**עַם מְגָדִים מַנְעֶמֶת לַשַּׁבָּת. **סְ**עוּדוֹת שָׁלֹשׁ מְקַיֶּמֶת בַּשַּׁבָּת. **עַ**ל שְׁתֵּי כִכָּרוֹת בּוֹצַעַת בַּשַּׁבָּת. **פּ**וֹרֶטֶת אַרְבַּע רְשֻׁיּוֹת* בַּשַּׁבָּת. **צִ**וּוּי הַדְלָקַת נֵר

Rashi, who comments on virtually every stich of the *hoshana* prayers, omits this stich from his *siddur* indicates that it was not yet written in *Rashi's* time [the eleventh century]. It is possible that observance of *mitzvos* and longing for the Messiah had ebbed during the time of the *paytan* Shmuel. Therefore, he found it necessary to strengthen these two basic tenets of Judaism by reminding his generation that all salvation comes in their merit.

הוֹשִׁיעָה אֶת עַמֶּךָ / Save Your Nation

Each day's *hoshana* service closes with these three verses which plea that God accept our just-concluded prayers.

אוֹם נְצוּרָה / Nation Protected

The Four Species are not taken on the Sabbath, because the Sages declare them to be מֻקְצֶה, *set apart*, thereby forbidding their use, or even their being moved from place to place. This decree was issued to prevent the unlearned from bringing their *lulav* and *esrog* to a learned neighbor's home for instruction in their use. Such carrying through a public thoroughfare would constitute a desecration of the Sabbath (*Succah* 42b, 43a).

Since the Four Species are not taken on the Sabbath, *hakafah*-circuits are omitted on that day (*Rashi*, responsum cited by *Tur* 660). A special *hoshana* prayer is recited, however. The Ark is opened but no Torah scroll is removed, and the *bimah* is not circled during the recital of this *hoshana*. As would be expected, the theme of this *hoshana* is the observance of the various *mitzvos* related to the Sabbath.

מַשְׂאַת שַׁבָּת — *The burdens of the Sabbath.* Transporting objects on the Sabbath is culpable under Torah law only if the item transported has a minimum value or utility. Accordingly, the dimensions may vary from object to object. The principles involved in determining these laws of *the burdens of the Sabbath* are discussed at length in the Talmud, primarily in *Shabbos* 76a-82a.

אַלְפַּיִם תְּחוּם — *Two thousand as the boundary.* Although the enactment of תְּחוּם שַׁבָּת, *the Sabbatical boundary*, is of Rabbinic origin, nevertheless, support for such a limitation is found in Scripture. אַל יֵצֵא אִישׁ מִמְּקֹמוֹ בַּיּוֹם הַשְּׁבִיעִי, *Let no man leave his place on the seventh day* (*Exodus* 16:29), alludes to the two-thousand-cubit limit past an inhabited area beyond which it is forbidden to walk on the Sabbath. *His place* refers to the city or town in which one spends the Sabbath, and includes a two-thousand-cubit-wide belt around it.

וּמְשִׁיבַת רֶגֶל — *And restrains her [lit. a] foot.* This

ANI VAHO, bring salvation now.

הוֹשִׁיעָה *Save Your people and bless Your heritage, tend them and elevate them forever.*[1] *May these words of mine, which I have supplicated before HASHEM, be near to HASHEM, our God, by day and by night; that He bring about justice for His servant and justice for His people, Israel, each day's need in its day. That all the peoples of the earth shall know that HASHEM is God — there is no other.*[2]

The Torah Scroll is returned to the Ark and the Ark is closed.

The *chazzan* then recites the *Full Kaddish* (page 374).

THE SABBATH

On the Sabbath the following *Hoshana* is recited:

אוֹם נְצוּרָה *Nation protected like the pupil of the eye —* ב *she seeks understanding of the law which restores the soul.* ג *She studies the laws of the Sabbath,* ד *explicates the burdens of the Sabbath,** ה *establishes two thousand as the boundary** *of the Sabbath,* ו *and restrains her foot** *because of the Sabbath.* ז *'Remember' and 'Safeguard'** *she fulfills on the Sabbath* ח *by rushing to hasten the onset of the Sabbath;* ט *by toiling throughout the six for the Sabbath;* י *by sitting, patiently waiting until the end of the Sabbath.* כ *'Honor' and 'Delight'** *she proclaims the Sabbath:* ל *clothing and raiment she changes for the Sabbath,* מ *food and drink she prepares for the Sabbath,* נ *of sweet, of delicate fruits she partakes on the Sabbath,* ס *three meals she fulfills on the Sabbath,* ע *over two loaves she breaks bread on the Sabbath.* פ *She distinguishes four domains** *on the Sabbath.* צ *The*

(1) *Psalms* 28:9. (2) *I Kings* 8:59-60.

---

is a continuation of the previous stich — after establishing the two-thousand-cubit limit, the people scrupulously adhere to it, restraining their feet from overstepping the boundary.

זָכוֹר וְשָׁמוֹר — *'Remember' and 'Safeguard.'* There are minor variations between the first and second versions of the Ten Commandments (*Exodus* 20:1-14 and *Deuteronomy* 5:5-18). The Sages explain that God spoke both versions simultaneously — a feat impossible for the human mouth to duplicate (*Shavuos* 20b), and that both versions are authoritative sources of halachic exegesis. The differences between the two are explicated and expounded upon. The *mitzvah* of Sabbath is expressed in the first Tablets as זָכוֹר אֶת יוֹם הַשַּׁבָּת, *'Remember' the day of Sabbath* (*Exodus* 20:8), while in the second Tablets it reads שָׁמוֹר אֶת יוֹם הַשַּׁבָּת, *'Safeguard' the day of Sabbath* (*Deuteronomy* 5:12). In *Mechilta*, many lessons are derived from this change of verb. Among them are those referred to in the following stiches: One must hasten the arrival of the Sabbath — 'remember' it before its onset; and delay its departure — 'safeguard' the Sabbath when it leaves.

Also, 'Remember' the day of Sabbath throughout the week. Whenever a goodly portion comes your way, set it aside, 'safeguard' it, for the Sabbath [see *Beitzah* 16a].

כָּבוֹד וָעֹנֶג — *'Honor' and 'Delight.'* The next six stiches are based on the verse, *if you proclaim the Sabbath* עֹנֶג, *'a delight,' the holy [day] of HASHEM* מְכֻבָּד, *'honored one' ... then you shall be granted pleasure with HASHEM ... (Isaiah* 58:13-14). כָּבוֹד, *honor*, refers to the special clothing worn in honor of the Sabbath. עֹנֶג, *delight*, refers to the Sabbath food, drink and meals.

אַרְבַּע רְשֻׁיּוֹת — *Four domains.* Regarding the prohibitions against transporting objects on the Sabbath, four distinct domains are recognized:
(a) רְשׁוּת הָרַבִּים, *public domain* — a non-enclosed area, sixteen or more cubits wide, used daily by vast numbers of people;
(b) רְשׁוּת הַיָּחִיד, *private domain* — an area enclosed for purposes of habitation;
(c) כַּרְמְלִית, *median domain* — property not meeting the halachic requirements of either a public domain or a private domain;
(d) מְקוֹם פָּטוּר, *free space* — certain well-defined areas which fall into none of the above categories.

מַדְלֶקֶת בַּשַּׁבָּת. קִדּוּשׁ הַיּוֹם מְקַדֶּשֶׁת בַּשַּׁבָּת. רֶנֶן שֶׁבַע* מְפַלֶּלֶת בַּשַּׁבָּת. שִׁבְעָה בְּדַת קוֹרְאָה בַּשַּׁבָּת. תַּנְחִילֶנָּה לְיוֹם שֶׁכֻּלּוֹ שַׁבָּת.*

אֲנִי וָהוּ הוֹשִׁיעָה נָּא:

כְּהוֹשַׁעְתָּ אָדָם יְצִיר כַּפֶּיךָ לְגוֹנְנָה,
בְּשַׁבַּת קֹדֶשׁ הִמְצֵאתוֹ כֹּפֶר* וַחֲנִינָה, כֵּן הוֹשַׁעְנָא.
כְּהוֹשַׁעְתָּ גּוֹי מְצֻיָּן מְקַוִּים חֹפֶשׁ,
דֵּעָה כִּוְּנוּ לָבוּר שְׁבִיעִי* לְנֹפֶשׁ, כֵּן הוֹשַׁעְנָא.
כְּהוֹשַׁעְתָּ הָעָם נִהַגְתָּ כַּצֹּאן לְהַנְחוֹת,
וְחֹק שַׂמְתָּ בְּמָרָה עַל מֵי מְנֻחוֹת, כֵּן הוֹשַׁעְנָא.
כְּהוֹשַׁעְתָּ זְבוּדֶיךָ בְּמִדְבַּר סִין* בַּמַּחֲנֶה,
חָכְמוּ וְלָקְטוּ בַּשִּׁשִּׁי לֶחֶם מִשְׁנֶה, כֵּן הוֹשַׁעְנָא.
כְּהוֹשַׁעְתָּ טְפוּלֶיךָ הוֹרוּ הֲכָנָה בְּמַדָּעָם,
יָשַׁר כֹּחָם וְהוֹדָה לָמוֹ רוֹעָם, כֵּן הוֹשַׁעְנָא.
כְּהוֹשַׁעְתָּ כָּלְכְּלוּ בְּעֹנֶג מָן הַמִּשְׁמָר,
לֹא הָפַךְ עֵינוֹ וְרֵיחוֹ לֹא נָמָר,* כֵּן הוֹשַׁעְנָא.
כְּהוֹשַׁעְתָּ מִשְׁפְּטֵי מַשָּׂאוֹת שַׁבָּת גָּמָרוּ,
נָחוּ וְשָׁבְתוּ רְשֻׁיּוֹת וּתְחוּמִים שָׁמָרוּ, כֵּן הוֹשַׁעְנָא.

Torah law forbids transport of objects between a public and a private domain, or for a distance of four cubits or more within a public domain. The movement of items between either of these locations and a median domain, or over four cubits within a median domain is forbidden by Rabbinic decree. Between any of these three domains and a free space, objects may be carried, providing four cubits are not traversed within a public or median domain. Within a private domain no restrictions exist.

רֶנֶן שֶׁבַע — *A seven-part prayer.* The weekday *Amidah* or *Shemoneh Esrei* comprises nineteen blessings. The *Amidah* of the Sabbath contains only seven. The first three and the last three blessings of the weekday *Shemoneh Esrei* are separated by one longer blessing relating to the sanctity of the day.

יוֹם שֶׁכֻּלּוֹ שַׁבָּת — *The day which will be [lit. is] completely a Sabbath.* Just as the Sabbath is described as מֵעֵין עוֹלָם הַבָּא, *a semblance of the World to Come* (Sabbath *Zemiroth;* see also *Berachos* 57b), so is the World to Come described as יוֹם שֶׁכֻּלּוֹ שַׁבָּת וּמְנוּחָה לְחַיֵּי הָעוֹלָמִים, *the day which will be completely a Sabbath and rest day for eternal life (Tamid* 7:4).

כְּהוֹשַׁעְתָּ אָדָם / As You Saved Adam

Unlike the other *hoshanas* which were composed by R' Elazar HaKalir, this *hoshana* is by R' Menachem ben R' Machir. Like the others it follows an alphabetical scheme, but then continues with an acrostic of the author's name, מְנַחֵם בְּרַבִּי מָכִיר, with a blessing appended to it, חֲזַק לָעַד אָמֵן, *may he be strengthened forever, amen,* in the style common to most *paytanim.* Like the preceding *hoshana* this one was written specifically for the Sabbath and contains many allusions to the *mitzvos* and customs of that day.

אָדָם . . . בְּשַׁבַּת קֹדֶשׁ הִמְצֵאתוֹ כֹּפֶר — *Adam . . . on the holy Sabbath You brought forth for him forgiveness.* When Adam ate from the Tree of Knowledge, he should have received the death sentence and been doomed to *Gehinnom* for eternity, as God Himself had forewarned: *For on the day you eat of it you shall surely die (Genesis* 2:17). By what merit was he spared?

Adam committed his sin on Friday afternoon, a short while before the onset of the Sabbath. Before his sentence was carried out, the holiness of the Sabbath descended. So Adam's death would in no small measure have marred the peacefulness and sanctity of the day. The Sabbath itself came to Adam's defense and cried, 'Master of the World, during the first six days no one died in all the universe. Do You want death to begin with me? Is this a display of my sanctity? Is this a display of my blessing?' So Adam was saved from *Gehinnom* in the merit of the Sabbath *(Midrash Shocher Tov* 92:1).

command of kindling the light she fulfills for the Sabbath. ק *The Sanctification of the day she recites on the Sabbath.* ר *A seven-part prayer* she prays on the Sabbath.* ש *Seven portions of the Torah she reads on the Sabbath.* ת *Cause her to inherit the day which will be completely a Sabbath.**

ANI VAHO, bring salvation now.

כְּהוֹשַׁעְתָּ אָדָם א *As You saved Adam, Your handiwork, to be his shield;*
ב *on the holy Sabbath You brought forth for him forgiveness* and grace — so save now.*

ג *As You saved the distinctive nation which sought freedom;*
ד *with wisdom they anticipated the choice of the seventh* for rest — so save now.*

ה *As You saved the people whom You guided like a flock to contentment;*
ו *and You issued a statute at Marah beside tranquil waters — so save now.*

ז *As You saved Your portion in the encampment at the Wilderness of Sin;**
ח *they acted wisely and gathered double bread on the sixth — so save now.*

ט *As You saved those who clung to You, who derived the rules of preparation through their wisdom;*
י *their shepherd blessed their talent and deferred to them — so save now.*

כ *As You saved those You sustained on the day of delight with the guarded manna,*
ל *whose appearance did not change and whose aroma did not sour* — so save now.*

מ *As You saved those who study the laws regarding the burdens of the Sabbath;*
נ *they are content and they rest, guarding domains and boundaries — so save now.*

כִּוְּנוּ לִבְחוֹר שְׁבִיעִי — *They anticipated the choice of the seventh.* Moses saw that the Jews in Egypt were allowed no time for rest from their labors. To ease their burdens, he suggested to Pharaoh that a worker who never rests is sure to die. 'Yet you, Pharaoh, have all these slaves working continuously. If they are not given one day's rest each week, they will not survive.'

'Go,' replied Pharaoh, 'and do as you suggest.' Moses went and ordained the seventh day as their day of rest, thus anticipating the commandment of Sabbath (*Shemos Rabbah* 1:28).

בְּמִדְבַּר סִין — *At the Wilderness of Sin.* [The name *Sin* is a transliterated Hebrew place name, and should not be confused with the English word 'sin.'] This was the place where the manna first fell. When the manna fell on the sixth day, there was a double portion, and *the elders of the congregation came and told Moses* (*Exodus* 16:22). But why just the elders — were the others not interested in discovering the reason for the double portion? The people presented this question before the elders who in their wisdom derived the rules of preparation of food for the Sabbath. These rules (see *Eruvin* 38b) taught that food for the Sabbath must be prepared beforehand, and that no food may be prepared on a Sabbath or Festival for another day. [The laws of *eruv tavshilin* are based on this rule; see page 2.] Although God had taught these laws to Moses (*Exodus* 16:5), he had not yet taught them to the nation. After deriving the rules of preparation, the elders presented their conclusions to Moses who admitted his error in not having taught the rules earlier, and he blessed them.

לֹא הָפַךְ עֵינוֹ וְרֵיחוֹ לֹא נָמַר — *Whose appearance*

כְּהוֹשַׁעְתָּ סִינַי הֻשְׁמְעוּ בְּדִבּוּר רְבִיעִי,*
עִנְיַן זָכוֹר וְשָׁמוֹר לְקַדֵּשׁ שְׁבִיעִי, כֵּן הוֹשַׁעְנָא.

כְּהוֹשַׁעְתָּ פְּקֻדוּ יְרִיחוֹ שֶׁבַע לְהַקֵּף,*
צָרוּ עַד רִדְתָּהּ בַּשַּׁבָּת לְתַקֵּף, כֵּן הוֹשַׁעְנָא.

כְּהוֹשַׁעְתָּ קֹהֶלֶת וְעַמּוֹ בְּבֵית עוֹלָמִים,
רְצוּךָ בְּחָגְגָם שִׁבְעָה וְשִׁבְעָה יָמִים,* כֵּן הוֹשַׁעְנָא.

כְּהוֹשַׁעְתָּ שָׁבִים עוֹלֵי גוֹלָה* לְפִדְיוֹם,
תּוֹרָתְךָ בְּקָרְאָם בֶּחָג יוֹם יוֹם, כֵּן הוֹשַׁעְנָא.

כְּהוֹשַׁעְתָּ מְשַׂמְּחֶיךָ בְּבִנְיַן שֵׁנִי הַמְּחֻדָּשׁ,
נוֹטְלִין לוּלָב* כָּל שִׁבְעָה בַּמִּקְדָּשׁ, כֵּן הוֹשַׁעְנָא.

כְּהוֹשַׁעְתָּ חִבּוּט עֲרָבָה שַׁבָּת מַדְחִים,
מֻרְבִּיּוֹת מוֹצָא לִיסוֹד מִזְבֵּחַ מַנִּיחִים, כֵּן הוֹשַׁעְנָא.

כְּהוֹשַׁעְתָּ בְּרַכּוֹת וַאֲרוּכוֹת וּגְבוֹהוֹת מְעַלְּסִים,
בִּפְטִירָתָן יֹפִי לְךָ מִזְבֵּחַ מְקַלְּסִים, כֵּן הוֹשַׁעְנָא.

כְּהוֹשַׁעְתָּ מוֹדִים וּמְיַחֲלִים וְלֹא מְשַׁנִּים,*
כֻּלָּנוּ אָנוּ לְיָהּ וְעֵינֵינוּ לְיָהּ שׁוֹנִים, כֵּן הוֹשַׁעְנָא.

כְּהוֹשַׁעְתָּ יֶקֶב מֵחֲצָבֶיךָ* סוֹבְבִים בְּרַעֲנָנָה,
רוֹנְנִים אֲנִי וָהוֹ הוֹשִׁיעָה נָּא, כֵּן הוֹשַׁעְנָא.

---

did not change and whose aroma did not sour. Unlike the manna of other days which *would became wormy and foul-smelling* (*Exodus* 16:20) if it were left overnight, the Sabbath manna remained absolutely fresh.

בְּדִבּוּר רְבִיעִי — *The fourth pronouncement.* The fourth of the Ten Commandments is the *mitzvah* of the Sabbath.

יְרִיחוֹ שֶׁבַע לְהַקֵּף — *At Jericho to encircle seven times.* Jericho was circled one time each day for six consecutive days. On the seventh day — the Sabbath — the city was circled seven times, after which the walls crumbled, allowing Jericho to be conquered by the Israelite army (see *Joshua* chap. 6 and *Rashi*).

The relationship between the encirclement of Jericho and the *hakafah*-circuits on Hoshana Rabbah is not coincidental. Twice the word וַאֲסוֹבְבָה, *I shall encircle,* appears in Scripture: וַאֲסֹבְבָה אֶת מִזְבַּחֲךָ ה׳, *I shall encircle Your Altar,* HASHEM (*Psalms* 26:6); and וַאֲסוֹבְבָה בָעִיר, *I shall encircle the city* (*Song of Songs* 3:2). The number of circuits around the Altar on Hoshana Rabbah is derived from the number of circuits around the city of Jericho. Just as Jericho was circuited once on each of the first six days, so the Altar is circuited once on each of the first six days of Succos. And just as Jericho was circuited seven times on the seventh day, so the Altar was circuited seven times on Hoshana Rabbah (see *Yalkut Shimoni* II, 703).

שִׁבְעָה וְשִׁבְעָה יָמִים — *Seven and another seven days.* The dedication of the Temple of Solomon began on the eighth day of Tishrei, and continued for seven days. Even though the third day of their feasting was Yom Kippur, the celebration continued and the fast was not observed. The next day a worried nation feared that it would be punished with excision (כָּרֵת) for having desecrated the sanctity of Yom Kippur, when a heavenly voice proclaimed, 'You are all eligible for the World to Come!' (*Moed Katan* 9a).

That seven-day celebration ended on the fourteenth of Tishrei, the eve of Succos. Instead of returning home, the nation celebrated for another seven days — their first pilgrimage festival in the Temple. Only after Succos did they take leave of Solomon and the Temple (see *I Kings* 8:65-66).

עוֹלֵי גוֹלָה — *Ascending from exile. Nehemiah* 8 relates that when the returnees from the Babylonian exile gathered before Ezra on the first day of the seventh month [Rosh Hashanah], he read the entire Torah to them. When they heard that

ס *As You saved those permitted to hear*
*the fourth pronouncement at Sinai;**
ע *the theme of 'Remember' and 'Safeguard'*
to sanctify the seventh — so save now.

פ *As You saved those bidden at Jericho to encircle seven times;**
צ *they besieged it until its downfall on the Sabbath,*
to strengthen them — so save now.

ק *As You saved Koheles [Solomon] and his nation in the eternal Temple,*
ר *they pleased You when they celebrated seven*
and another seven days — so save now.*

ש *As You saved those who returned, ascending from exile* to redemption;*
ת *as they read Your Torah every day of the Festival*
— so save now.

מ *As You saved those who brought You joy*
with the renewed Second Temple;
נ *who took up the lulav* all seven days in the Sanctuary*
— so save now.

ח *As You saved those for whom the beating of the willow*
overrode the Sabbath;
מ *those who placed Motza's branches*
at the base of the altar — so save now.

בר *As You saved those who praised with supple, long and tall willows;*
בי *who departed while extolling,*
'Beauty becomes you, O Altar' — so save now.

מ *As You saved those who thanked and hoped, but never exchanged;**
כ *like them we all cry out,*
'We are God's and our eyes are to God' — so save now.

י *As You saved those who encircled Your hewn wine cellar**
with greenery;
ר *singing, 'ANI VAHO, bring salvation now' — so save now.*

---

the fifteenth day of that month would be Succos they diligently prepared the Four Species and erected *succos.*

And he read in the Scroll of God's Torah each day, from the first day to the last (Nehemiah 8:18). In that year, Succos was celebrated in an unusually grand style and was accompanied by *very great joy* (ibid. 8:17).

נוטלין לולב — *Who took up the lulav.* The next five stanzas are based primarily on the narrative of the *aravah* ritual found in chapter 4 of *Succah* (see pp. 116-118). The *aravah* [willow] branches were used every day in the Temple, and the ritual of beating it on the ground was observed even on the Sabbath. Willows grew in abundance in a place near Jerusalem known as Motza. The people would pick eleven-cubit-long willows from Motza and stand them up around the ten-cubit-high Altar. They made daily circuits around the Altar and, as they completed the final circuit on Hoshana Rabbah, they would proclaim, 'Beauty becomes you, O Altar.'

וְלֹא מְשַׁנִּים — *But never exchanged.* Unlike the idol worshipers of the First Temple era (see *I Kings* 18:21), the people of the Second Temple never exchanged the God of their ancestors for the false gods of their neighbors.

יֶקֶב מֶחֱצָבֶיךָ — *Your hewn wine cellar.* The Altar is called a wine cellar. At the southwestern corner of the Altar roof were two funnel-shaped pipes which led deep into the ground under the altar. Into one were poured the wine-libations which accompanied each elevation-offering (עוֹלָה) and each peace-offering (שְׁלָמִים). Into the other were poured the water-libations which were exclusive to the Succos festival.

With this in mind the Talmud explains a verse in *Isaiah* (5:1-2): *I shall sing now for my beloved, my beloved's song of his vineyard. My beloved*

כְּהוֹשַׁעְתָּ חֵיל זְרִיזִים מְשָׁרְתִים בִּמְנוּחָה,
קָרְבַּן שַׁבָּת כָּפוּל* עוֹלָה וּמִנְחָה, כֵּן הוֹשַׁעְנָא.
כְּהוֹשַׁעְתָּ לְוִיֶּיךָ עַל דוּכָנָם לְהַרְבָּת,
אוֹמְרִים מִזְמוֹר שִׁיר לְיוֹם הַשַּׁבָּת, כֵּן הוֹשַׁעְנָא.
כְּהוֹשַׁעְתָּ נְחוּמֶיךָ בְּמִצְוֹתֶיךָ תָּמִיד יִשְׁתַּעְשְׁעוּן,
וּרְצֵם וְהַחֲלִיצֵם בְּשׁוּבָה וָנַחַת יִוָּשֵׁעוּן, כֵּן הוֹשַׁעְנָא.
כְּהוֹשַׁעְתָּ שְׁבוּת שִׁבְטֵי יַעֲקֹב,
תָּשׁוּב וְתָשִׁיב שְׁבוּת אָהֳלֵי יַעֲקֹב, וְהוֹשִׁיעָה נָּא.
כְּהוֹשַׁעְתָּ שׁוֹמְרֵי מִצְוֹת, וְחוֹכֵי יְשׁוּעוֹת,
אֵל לְמוֹשָׁעוֹת, וְהוֹשִׁיעָה נָּא.

אֲנִי וָהוֹ הוֹשִׁיעָה נָּא.

הוֹשִׁיעָה אֶת עַמֶּךָ, וּבָרֵךְ אֶת נַחֲלָתֶךָ, וּרְעֵם וְנַשְּׂאֵם עַד הָעוֹלָם.[1] וְיִהְיוּ דְבָרַי אֵלֶּה אֲשֶׁר הִתְחַנַּנְתִּי לִפְנֵי יהוה, קְרֹבִים אֶל יהוה אֱלֹהֵינוּ יוֹמָם וָלָיְלָה, לַעֲשׂוֹת מִשְׁפַּט עַבְדּוֹ וּמִשְׁפַּט עַמּוֹ יִשְׂרָאֵל, דְּבַר יוֹם בְּיוֹמוֹ. לְמַעַן דַּעַת כָּל עַמֵּי הָאָרֶץ, כִּי יהוה הוּא הָאֱלֹהִים, אֵין עוֹד.[2]

The Torah Scroll is returned to the Ark.

Congregations that recite *Hoshanos* after *Hallel,* return to page 298.

קדיש שלם

The *chazzan* recites קַדִּישׁ שָׁלֵם.

יִתְגַּדַּל וְיִתְקַדַּשׁ שְׁמֵהּ רַבָּא. (.Cong – אָמֵן.) בְּעָלְמָא דִּי בְרָא כִרְעוּתֵהּ. וְיַמְלִיךְ מַלְכוּתֵהּ, בְּחַיֵּיכוֹן וּבְיוֹמֵיכוֹן וּבְחַיֵּי דְכָל בֵּית יִשְׂרָאֵל, בַּעֲגָלָא וּבִזְמַן קָרִיב. וְאִמְרוּ: אָמֵן.

(.Cong – אָמֵן. יְהֵא שְׁמֵהּ רַבָּא מְבָרַךְ לְעָלַם וּלְעָלְמֵי עָלְמַיָּא.)

יְהֵא שְׁמֵהּ רַבָּא מְבָרַךְ לְעָלַם וּלְעָלְמֵי עָלְמַיָּא.

יִתְבָּרַךְ וְיִשְׁתַּבַּח וְיִתְפָּאַר וְיִתְרוֹמַם וְיִתְנַשֵּׂא וְיִתְהַדָּר וְיִתְעַלֶּה וְיִתְהַלָּל שְׁמֵהּ דְּקֻדְשָׁא בְּרִיךְ הוּא (.Cong – בְּרִיךְ הוּא) — לְעֵלָּא מִן כָּל בִּרְכָתָא וְשִׁירָתָא תֻּשְׁבְּחָתָא וְנֶחֱמָתָא, דַּאֲמִירָן בְּעָלְמָא. וְאִמְרוּ: אָמֵן. (.Cong – אָמֵן.)

(.Cong – קַבֵּל בְּרַחֲמִים וּבְרָצוֹן אֶת תְּפִלָּתֵנוּ.)

תִּתְקַבֵּל צְלוֹתְהוֹן וּבָעוּתְהוֹן דְּכָל בֵּית יִשְׂרָאֵל קֳדָם אֲבוּהוֹן דִּי בִשְׁמַיָּא. וְאִמְרוּ: אָמֵן. (.Cong – אָמֵן.)

He planted in it a vine refers to the Temple, *and built a tower in its midst* — to the Altar, *and also hewed a wine cellar within it* — to the pipes of the libations (*Succah* 49a).

had a vineyard atop a fertile hill. He fenced it, he stoned it, he planted in it a vine. He built a tower in its midst, and also hewed a wine cellar within it . . .

חז *As You saved the army of speedy ones*
who serve on the day of contentment,
ק *with the doubled Sabbath offering,*
of burnt and meal offering — so save now.

לעד *As You saved Your Levites who sang upon their platform,*
אמ *saying, 'A psalm, a song, for the Sabbath day' — so save now.*

נ *As You saved those whom You comforted,*
those who constantly find joy in Your mitzvos;
so may You favor them and give them rest,
and tranquility, and contentedly may they attain salvation — so save now.

As You saved the captivity of the tribes of Jacob,
return and restore the captivity of Jacob's tents
and bring salvation now.

As You saved those observing mitzvos, and hoping for salvation —
O God Who brings salvations bring salvation now.

ANI VAHO, bring salvation now.

הוֹשִׁיעָה *Save Your people and bless Your heritage, tend them and elevate them forever.*[1] *May these words of mine, which I have supplicated before* HASHEM, *be near to* HASHEM, *our God, by day and by night; that He bring about justice for His servant and justice for His people, Israel, each day's need in its day; that all the peoples of the earth shall know that* HASHEM *is God — there is no other.*[2]

The Torah Scroll is returned to the Ark and the Ark is closed.
Congregations that recite *Hoshanos* after *Hallel*, return to page 298.

FULL KADDISH

The *chazzan* recites the Full *Kaddish*.

יִתְגַּדַּל *May His great Name grow exalted and sanctified* (Cong.– *Amen.*) *in the world that He created as He willed. May He give reign to His kingship in your lifetimes and in your days, and in the lifetimes of the entire Family of Israel, swiftly and soon. Now respond: Amen.*

(Cong.– *Amen. May His great Name be blessed forever and ever.*)
May His great Name be blessed forever and ever.

Blessed, praised, glorified, exalted, extolled, mighty, upraised, and lauded be the Name of the Holy One, Blessed is He (Cong.– *Blessed is He*) *— beyond any blessing and song, praise and consolation that are uttered in the world. Now respond: Amen.* (Cong.– *Amen.*)

(Cong.– *Accept our prayers with mercy and favor.*)

May the prayers and supplications of the entire Family of Israel be accepted before their Father Who is in Heaven. Now respond: Amen. (Cong.– *Amen.*)

(1) *Psalms* 28:9. (2) *I Kings* 8:59-60.

קָרְבַּן שַׁבָּת כָּפוּל — *The doubled Sabbath offering.* Unlike the additional (מוּסָף) offerings of the festivals, which comprised varying numbers of bulls, rams, lambs, and goats with their accompanying meal offerings (see chapters 28-29 of *Numbers*), the Sabbath offering consisted of two lambs accompanied by two *esronim* of flour. Hence this sacrifice is called 'doubled.'

(Cong. –) יְהִי שֵׁם יהוה מְבֹרָךְ, מֵעַתָּה וְעַד עוֹלָם.[1]

יְהֵא שְׁלָמָא רַבָּא מִן שְׁמַיָּא, וְחַיִּים עָלֵינוּ וְעַל כָּל יִשְׂרָאֵל. וְאִמְרוּ: אָמֵן. (Cong. – אָמֵן.)

(Cong. –) עֶזְרִי מֵעִם יהוה, עֹשֵׂה שָׁמַיִם וָאָרֶץ.[2]

Take three steps back. Bow left and say . . . עֹשֶׂה; bow right and say . . . הוּא; bow forward and say וְעַל כָּל . . . אָמֵן. Remain standing in place for a few moments, then take three steps forward.

עֹשֶׂה שָׁלוֹם בִּמְרוֹמָיו, הוּא יַעֲשֶׂה שָׁלוֹם עָלֵינוּ, וְעַל כָּל יִשְׂרָאֵל. וְאִמְרוּ: אָמֵן. (Cong. – אָמֵן.)

קַוֵּה אֶל יהוה, חֲזַק וְיַאֲמֵץ לִבֶּךָ, וְקַוֵּה אֶל יהוה.[3] אֵין קָדוֹשׁ כַּיהוה, כִּי אֵין בִּלְתֶּךָ, וְאֵין צוּר כֵּאלֹהֵינוּ.[4] כִּי מִי אֱלוֹהַּ מִבַּלְעֲדֵי יהוה, וּמִי צוּר זוּלָתִי אֱלֹהֵינוּ.[5]

אֵין כֵּאלֹהֵינוּ,* אֵין כַּאדוֹנֵינוּ, אֵין כְּמַלְכֵּנוּ, אֵין כְּמוֹשִׁיעֵנוּ. מִי כֵאלֹהֵינוּ, מִי כַאדוֹנֵינוּ, מִי כְמַלְכֵּנוּ, מִי כְמוֹשִׁיעֵנוּ. נוֹדֶה לֵאלֹהֵינוּ, נוֹדֶה לַאדוֹנֵינוּ, נוֹדֶה לְמַלְכֵּנוּ, נוֹדֶה לְמוֹשִׁיעֵנוּ. בָּרוּךְ אֱלֹהֵינוּ, בָּרוּךְ אֲדוֹנֵינוּ, בָּרוּךְ מַלְכֵּנוּ, בָּרוּךְ מוֹשִׁיעֵנוּ. אַתָּה הוּא אֱלֹהֵינוּ, אַתָּה הוּא אֲדוֹנֵינוּ, אַתָּה הוּא מַלְכֵּנוּ, אַתָּה הוּא מוֹשִׁיעֵנוּ. אַתָּה הוּא שֶׁהִקְטִירוּ אֲבוֹתֵינוּ לְפָנֶיךָ אֶת קְטֹרֶת הַסַּמִּים.

כריתות ו.

פִּטּוּם הַקְּטֹרֶת:* (א) הַצֳּרִי, (ב) וְהַצִּפֹּרֶן, (ג) הַחֶלְבְּנָה, (ד) וְהַלְּבוֹנָה, מִשְׁקַל שִׁבְעִים שִׁבְעִים מָנֶה; (ה) מוֹר, (ו) וּקְצִיעָה, (ז) שִׁבֹּלֶת נֵרְדְּ, (ח) וְכַרְכֹּם, מִשְׁקַל שִׁשָּׁה עָשָׂר שִׁשָּׁה עָשָׂר מָנֶה; (ט) הַקֹּשְׁטְ שְׁנֵים עָשָׂר, (י) וְקִלּוּפָה שְׁלֹשָׁה, (יא) וְקִנָּמוֹן תִּשְׁעָה. בֹּרִית כַּרְשִׁינָה תִּשְׁעָה קַבִּין, יֵין קַפְרִיסִין סְאִין תְּלָתָא וְקַבִּין תְּלָתָא; וְאִם אֵין לוֹ יֵין קַפְרִיסִין, מֵבִיא חֲמַר חִוַּרְיָן עַתִּיק; מֶלַח סְדוֹמִית רֹבַע הַקָּב; מַעֲלֶה עָשָׁן כָּל שֶׁהוּא. רַבִּי נָתָן הַבַּבְלִי אוֹמֵר: אַף כִּפַּת הַיַּרְדֵּן כָּל שֶׁהוּא. וְאִם נָתַן בָּהּ דְּבַשׁ פְּסָלָהּ. וְאִם חִסַּר אַחַת מִכָּל סַמָּנֶיהָ, חַיָּב מִיתָה.

⚜ **אֵין כֵּאלֹהֵינוּ** — *There is none like our God.* The declaration of faith made in this hymn was formulated in response to a particular need of Sabbaths and Festivals. The Sages teach that it is meritorious to recite a hundred blessings every day. On weekdays, the bulk of this total is accounted for by the three-times-a-day recitation of *Shemoneh Esrei*, which contains nineteen blessings. On the Sabbath and Festivals, however, each *Shemoneh Esrei* contains only seven blessings. One means of filling this gap is the recitation of אֵין כֵּאלֹהֵינוּ, because each declaration of faith — *there is none like our God . . . who is like our God*, etc. — is regarded as a blessing of

(Cong.— *Blessed be the Name of* HASHEM, *from this time and forever.*[1])

May there be abundant peace from Heaven, and life, upon us and upon all Israel. Now respond: Amen. (Cong.— *Amen.*)

(Cong.— *My help is from* HASHEM, *Maker of heaven and earth.*[2])

Take three steps back. Bow left and say, *'He Who makes peace . . .'*; bow right and say, *'may He . . .'*; bow forward and say, *'and upon all Israel . . .'* Remain standing in place for a few moments, then take three steps forward.

He Who makes peace in His heights, may He make peace upon us, and upon all Israel. Now respond: Amen. (Cong.— *Amen.*)

קַוֵּה *Hope to* HASHEM, *strengthen yourself and He will give you courage; and hope to* HASHEM.[3] *There is none holy as* HASHEM, *for there is none beside You, and there is no Rock like our God.*[4] *For who is a god beside* HASHEM, *and who is a Rock except for our God.*[5]

אֵין *There is none like our God;* there is none like our Master;*
there is none like our King; there is none like our Savior.
Who is like our God? Who is like our Master?*
Who is like our King? Who is like our Savior?
Let us thank our God; let us thank our Master;
let us thank our King; let us thank our Savior.
Blessed is our God; blessed is our Master;
blessed is our King; blessed is our Savior.
It is You Who is our God; it is You Who is our Master;
it is You Who is our King; it is You Who is our Savior.
It is You before Whom our forefathers burned the spice-incense.

Talmud, *Kereisos* 6a

פִּטּוּם הַקְּטֹרֶת *The incense mixture* was formulated of [eleven spices]: (1) stacte, (2) onycha, (3) galbanum, (4) frankincense — each weighing seventy maneh; (5) myrrh, (6) cassia, (7) spikenard, (8) saffron — each weighing sixteen maneh; (9) costus — twelve [maneh]; (10) aromatic bark — three; and (11) cinnamon — nine. [Additionally] Carshina lye — nine kab; Cyprus wine, three se'ah and three kab — if he has no Cyprus wine, he brings old white wine; Sodom salt, a quarter kab; and a minute amount of smoke-raising herb. Rabbi Nassan the Babylonian says: Also a minute amount of Jordan amber. If he placed fruit-honey into it, he invalidated it. And if he left out any of its spices, he is liable to the death penalty.*

(1) *Psalms* 113:2. (2) 121:2. (3) *Psalms* 27:14. (4) *I Samuel* 2:2. (5) *Psalms* 18:32.

sorts. Furthermore, the initial letters of the words אֵין, מִי, and נוֹדֶה spell אָמֵן, a further allusion to the concept of blessing. Thus the recitation of this paragraph is equivalent to twenty blessings (*Kol Bo*).

Responsa Noda B'Yehudah (1:10) offers a novel reason for reciting אֵין כֵּאלֹהֵינוּ before the passage about the incense offering. The Talmud teaches that any *Kohen* who prepared the incense would become wealthy. Thus, before speaking about the incense ritual, we declare our absolute faith in God, acknowledging that wealth comes from Him, not through our own talent or effort.

אֵין . . . מִי — *There is none . . . Who is like?* First we declare unequivocally our recognition that nothing compares to our God. Then we ask the rhetorical question, can anyone or anything compare to Him?

פִּטּוּם הַקְּטֹרֶת — *The incense mixture.* Although the Temple incense was burned after the

רַבָּן שִׁמְעוֹן בֶּן גַּמְלִיאֵל אוֹמֵר: הַצֳּרִי אֵינוֹ אֶלָּא שְׂרָף הַנּוֹטֵף מֵעֲצֵי הַקְּטָף. בֹּרִית כַּרְשִׁינָה שֶׁשָּׁפִין בָּהּ אֶת הַצִּפֹּרֶן כְּדֵי שֶׁתְּהֵא נָאָה; יֵין קַפְרִיסִין שֶׁשּׁוֹרִין בּוֹ אֶת הַצִּפֹּרֶן כְּדֵי שֶׁתְּהֵא עַזָּה; וַהֲלֹא מֵי רַגְלַיִם יָפִין לָהּ, אֶלָּא שֶׁאֵין מַכְנִיסִין מֵי רַגְלַיִם בָּעֲזָרָה מִפְּנֵי הַכָּבוֹד.

משנה, תמיד ז:ד

הַשִּׁיר* שֶׁהַלְוִיִּם הָיוּ אוֹמְרִים בְּבֵית הַמִּקְדָּשׁ. בַּיּוֹם הָרִאשׁוֹן הָיוּ אוֹמְרִים: לַיהוה הָאָרֶץ וּמְלוֹאָהּ, תֵּבֵל וְיֹשְׁבֵי בָהּ.[1] בַּשֵּׁנִי הָיוּ אוֹמְרִים: גָּדוֹל יהוה וּמְהֻלָּל מְאֹד, בְּעִיר אֱלֹהֵינוּ הַר קָדְשׁוֹ.[2] בַּשְּׁלִישִׁי הָיוּ אוֹמְרִים: אֱלֹהִים נִצָּב בַּעֲדַת אֵל, בְּקֶרֶב אֱלֹהִים יִשְׁפֹּט.[3] בָּרְבִיעִי הָיוּ אוֹמְרִים: אֵל נְקָמוֹת יהוה, אֵל נְקָמוֹת הוֹפִיעַ.[4] בַּחֲמִישִׁי הָיוּ אוֹמְרִים: הַרְנִינוּ לֵאלֹהִים עוּזֵּנוּ, הָרִיעוּ לֵאלֹהֵי יַעֲקֹב.[5] בַּשִּׁשִּׁי הָיוּ אוֹמְרִים: יהוה מָלָךְ גֵּאוּת לָבֵשׁ, לָבֵשׁ יהוה עֹז הִתְאַזָּר, אַף תִּכּוֹן תֵּבֵל בַּל תִּמּוֹט.[6] בַּשַּׁבָּת הָיוּ אוֹמְרִים: מִזְמוֹר שִׁיר לְיוֹם הַשַּׁבָּת.[7] מִזְמוֹר שִׁיר לֶעָתִיד לָבֹא, לְיוֹם שֶׁכֻּלּוֹ שַׁבָּת וּמְנוּחָה לְחַיֵּי הָעוֹלָמִים.

מגילה כח:

תָּנָא דְבֵי אֵלִיָּהוּ:* כָּל הַשּׁוֹנֶה הֲלָכוֹת בְּכָל יוֹם, מֻבְטָח לוֹ שֶׁהוּא בֶּן עוֹלָם הַבָּא, שֶׁנֶּאֱמַר: הֲלִיכוֹת עוֹלָם לוֹ,[8] אַל תִּקְרֵי* הֲלִיכוֹת, אֶלָּא הֲלָכוֹת.

ברכות סד.

אָמַר רַבִּי אֶלְעָזָר* אָמַר רַבִּי חֲנִינָא: תַּלְמִידֵי חֲכָמִים מַרְבִּים שָׁלוֹם בָּעוֹלָם, שֶׁנֶּאֱמַר: וְכָל בָּנַיִךְ לִמּוּדֵי יהוה, וְרַב שְׁלוֹם בָּנָיִךְ,[9] אַל תִּקְרֵי* בָּנָיִךְ אֶלָּא בּוֹנָיִךְ. ❖ שָׁלוֹם רָב לְאֹהֲבֵי תוֹרָתֶךָ, וְאֵין לָמוֹ מִכְשׁוֹל.[10] יְהִי שָׁלוֹם בְּחֵילֵךְ, שַׁלְוָה בְּאַרְמְנוֹתָיִךְ. לְמַעַן אַחַי וְרֵעָי, אֲדַבְּרָה נָּא שָׁלוֹם בָּךְ. לְמַעַן בֵּית יהוה אֱלֹהֵינוּ, אֲבַקְשָׁה טוֹב לָךְ.[11] יהוה עֹז לְעַמּוֹ יִתֵּן, יהוה יְבָרֵךְ אֶת עַמּוֹ בַשָּׁלוֹם.[12]

---

morning *tamid*, before the *mussaf* offering, this passage describing the incense preparation is recited here so that a portion of Talmudic law will be studied at the conclusion of the service. It should be noted that we cannot be certain of the exact translation of the spices included in the incense.

☙ הַשִּׁיר — *The [daily] song.* This *mishnah* (*Tamid* 7:4) is recited here because the daily song was chanted by the Levites after the conclusion of the incense service. [See pages 388-394.]

☙ תָּנָא דְבֵי אֵלִיָּהוּ — *The Academy of Elijah taught.* This homiletical teaching likens the ways of the world to the laws that govern a Jew's life on earth. Only by studying, knowing and practicing the laws of the Torah can a Jew insure himself of ultimate success.

רַבָּן שִׁמְעוֹן *Rabban Shimon ben Gamliel says: The stacte is simply the sap that drips from balsam trees. Carshina lye is used to bleach the onycha to make it pleasing. Cyprus wine is used to soak the onycha to make it pungent. Even though urine is suitable for that, nevertheless they do not bring urine into the Temple out of respect.*

Mishnah, *Tamid* 7:4

הַשִּׁיר *The daily song* that the Levites would recite in the Temple was as follows: On the first day [of the week] they would say: 'HASHEM's is the earth and its fullness, the inhabited land and those who dwell in it.'[1] On the second day they would say: 'Great is HASHEM and much praised, in the city of our God, Mount of His Holiness.'[2] On the third day they would say: 'God stands in the Divine assembly, in the midst of judges shall He judge.'[3] On the fourth day they would say: 'O God of vengeance, HASHEM, O God of vengeance, appear.'[4] On the fifth day they would say: 'Sing joyously to the God of our might, call out to the God of Jacob.'[5] On the sixth day they would say: 'HASHEM will have reigned, He will have donned grandeur; He will have donned might and girded Himself; He even made the world firm so that it should not falter.'[6] On the Sabbath they would say: 'A psalm, a song for the Sabbath day.'[7] A psalm, a song for the time to come, to the day that will be entirely Sabbath and contentment for the eternal life.*

Talmud, *Megillah* 28b

תָּנָא *The Academy of Elijah taught:* He who studies Torah laws every day has the assurance that he will be in the World to Come, as it is said, 'The ways of the world are His'[8] — do not read** [הֲלִיכוֹת] *'ways,' but* [הֲלָכוֹת] *'laws.'*

Talmud, *Berachos* 64a

אָמַר *Rabbi Elazar said* on behalf of Rabbi Chanina: Torah scholars increase peace in the world, as it is said: 'And all your children will be students of HASHEM, and your children will have peace'[9] — do not read** [בָּנָיִךְ] *'your children,' but* [בּוֹנָיִךְ] *'your builders.'* Chazzan— *There is abundant peace for the lovers of Your Torah, and there is no stumbling block for them.[10] May there be peace within your wall, serenity within your palaces. For the sake of my brethren and comrades I shall speak of peace in your midst. For the sake of the House of HASHEM, our God, I will request your good.[11] HASHEM will give might to His people, HASHEM will bless His people with peace.[12]*

(1) *Psalms* 24:1. (2) 48:2. (3) 82:1. (4) 94:1. (5) 81:2. (6) 93:1. (7) 92:1.
(8) *Habakkuk* 3:6. (9) *Isaiah* 54:13. (10) *Psalms* 119:165. (11) 122:7-9. (12) 29:11.

◆§ **אָמַר רַבִּי אֶלְעָזָר** — *Rabbi Elazar said.* This famous teaching is the concluding statement of tractate *Berachos. Maharsha* there, in a comment that applies here as well, explains that the tractate dealt with prayers and blessings that had been instituted by the Sages. The reason they promulgated these expressions of devotion was to increase the harmony in the universe between man and his Maker.

אַל תִּקְרֵי — *Do not read.* The intention is not to change the accepted reading of Scripture. Whenever such a statement appears in Rabbinic literature it means that the verse contains an allusion in addition to its literal meaning, *as if* it were pronounced differently.

קדיש דרבנן

In the presence of a *minyan,* mourners recite קַדִּישׁ דְּרַבָּנָן (see *Laws* §84-85).

יִתְגַּדַּל וְיִתְקַדַּשׁ שְׁמֵהּ רַבָּא. (.Cong – אָמֵן.) בְּעָלְמָא דִּי בְרָא כִרְעוּתֵהּ. וְיַמְלִיךְ מַלְכוּתֵהּ, בְּחַיֵּיכוֹן וּבְיוֹמֵיכוֹן וּבְחַיֵּי דְכָל בֵּית יִשְׂרָאֵל, בַּעֲגָלָא וּבִזְמַן קָרִיב. וְאִמְרוּ: אָמֵן.

(.Cong – אָמֵן. יְהֵא שְׁמֵהּ רַבָּא מְבָרַךְ לְעָלַם וּלְעָלְמֵי עָלְמַיָּא.)

יְהֵא שְׁמֵהּ רַבָּא מְבָרַךְ לְעָלַם וּלְעָלְמֵי עָלְמַיָּא.

יִתְבָּרַךְ וְיִשְׁתַּבַּח וְיִתְפָּאַר וְיִתְרוֹמַם וְיִתְנַשֵּׂא וְיִתְהַדָּר וְיִתְעַלֶּה וְיִתְהַלָּל שְׁמֵהּ דְּקֻדְשָׁא בְּרִיךְ הוּא (.Cong – בְּרִיךְ הוּא) — לְעֵלָּא מִן כָּל בִּרְכָתָא וְשִׁירָתָא תֻּשְׁבְּחָתָא וְנֶחֱמָתָא, דַּאֲמִירָן בְּעָלְמָא. וְאִמְרוּ: אָמֵן. (.Cong – אָמֵן.)

עַל יִשְׂרָאֵל וְעַל רַבָּנָן, וְעַל תַּלְמִידֵיהוֹן וְעַל כָּל תַּלְמִידֵי תַלְמִידֵיהוֹן, וְעַל כָּל מָאן דְּעָסְקִין בְּאוֹרַיְתָא, דִּי בְאַתְרָא הָדֵין וְדִי בְכָל אֲתַר וַאֲתַר. יְהֵא לְהוֹן וּלְכוֹן שְׁלָמָא רַבָּא, חִנָּא וְחִסְדָּא וְרַחֲמִין, וְחַיִּין אֲרִיכִין, וּמְזוֹנֵי רְוִיחֵי, וּפֻרְקָנָא, מִן קֳדָם אֲבוּהוֹן דִּי בִשְׁמַיָּא (וְאַרְעָא). וְאִמְרוּ: אָמֵן. (.Cong – אָמֵן.)

יְהֵא שְׁלָמָא רַבָּא מִן שְׁמַיָּא, וְחַיִּים (טוֹבִים) עָלֵינוּ וְעַל כָּל יִשְׂרָאֵל. וְאִמְרוּ: אָמֵן. (.Cong – אָמֵן.)

Take three steps back. Bow left and say . . . עֹשֶׂה; bow right and say . . . הוּא; bow forward and say וְעַל כָּל . . . אָמֵן. Remain standing in place for a few moments, then take three steps forward.

עֹשֶׂה שָׁלוֹם בִּמְרוֹמָיו, הוּא בְּרַחֲמָיו יַעֲשֶׂה שָׁלוֹם עָלֵינוּ, וְעַל כָּל יִשְׂרָאֵל. וְאִמְרוּ: אָמֵן. (.Cong – אָמֵן.)

עלינו

Stand while reciting עָלֵינוּ.

עָלֵינוּ לְשַׁבֵּחַ לַאֲדוֹן הַכֹּל, לָתֵת גְּדֻלָּה לְיוֹצֵר בְּרֵאשִׁית, שֶׁלֹּא עָשָׂנוּ כְּגוֹיֵי הָאֲרָצוֹת, וְלֹא שָׂמָנוּ כְּמִשְׁפְּחוֹת הָאֲדָמָה. שֶׁלֹּא שָׂם חֶלְקֵנוּ כָּהֶם, וְגוֹרָלֵנוּ כְּכָל הֲמוֹנָם. (שֶׁהֵם מִשְׁתַּחֲוִים לְהֶבֶל וָרִיק, וּמִתְפַּלְּלִים אֶל אֵל לֹא יוֹשִׁיעַ.[1]) וַאֲנַחְנוּ כּוֹרְעִים וּמִשְׁתַּחֲוִים וּמוֹדִים, לִפְנֵי מֶלֶךְ מַלְכֵי הַמְּלָכִים הַקָּדוֹשׁ בָּרוּךְ הוּא. שֶׁהוּא נוֹטֶה שָׁמַיִם וְיֹסֵד אָרֶץ,[2] וּמוֹשַׁב יְקָרוֹ בַּשָּׁמַיִם מִמַּעַל, וּשְׁכִינַת עֻזּוֹ בְּגָבְהֵי מְרוֹמִים. הוּא אֱלֹהֵינוּ, אֵין עוֹד. אֱמֶת מַלְכֵּנוּ, אֶפֶס זוּלָתוֹ, כַּכָּתוּב בְּתוֹרָתוֹ: וְיָדַעְתָּ הַיּוֹם וַהֲשֵׁבֹתָ אֶל לְבָבֶךָ, כִּי יהוה הוּא הָאֱלֹהִים בַּשָּׁמַיִם מִמַּעַל וְעַל הָאָרֶץ מִתָּחַת, אֵין עוֹד.[3]

Bow while reciting וַאֲנַחְנוּ כּוֹרְעִים וּמִשְׁתַּחֲוִים.

THE RABBIS' KADDISH

In the presence of a *minyan,* mourners recite the Rabbis' *Kaddish* (see *Laws* §84-85).
[A transliteration of this *Kaddish* appears on p. 1304.]

יִתְגַּדַּל *May His great Name grow exalted and sanctified* (Cong.– *Amen.*) *in the world that He created as He willed. May He give reign to His kingship in your lifetimes and in your days, and in the lifetimes of the entire Family of Israel, swiftly and soon. Now respond: Amen.*

(Cong.– *Amen. May His great Name be blessed forever and ever.*)

May His great Name be blessed forever and ever.

Blessed, praised, glorified, exalted, extolled, mighty, upraised, and lauded be the Name of the Holy One, Blessed is He (Cong.– *Blessed is He*) *— beyond any blessing and song, praise and consolation that are uttered in the world. Now respond: Amen.* (Cong.– *Amen.*)

Upon Israel, upon the teachers, their disciples and all of their disciples and upon all those who engage in the study of Torah, who are here or anywhere else; may they and you have abundant peace, grace, kindness, and mercy, long life, ample nourishment, and salvation, from before their Father Who is in Heaven (and on earth). Now respond: Amen. (Cong. – *Amen.*)

May there be abundant peace from Heaven, and (good) life, upon us and upon all Israel. Now respond: Amen. (Cong.– *Amen.*)

Take three steps back. Bow left and say, *'He Who makes peace . . .';* bow right and say, *'may He . . .';* bow forward and say, *'and upon all Israel . . .'* Remain standing in place for a few moments, then take three steps forward.

He Who makes peace in His heights, may He, in His compassion, make peace upon us, and upon all Israel. Now respond: Amen. (Cong.– *Amen.*)

ALEINU

Stand while reciting עָלֵינוּ, *'It is our duty . . .'*

עָלֵינוּ *It is our duty to praise the Master of all, to ascribe greatness to the Molder of primeval creation, for He has not made us like the nations of the lands, and has not emplaced us like the families of the earth; for He has not assigned our portion like theirs nor our lot like all their multitudes. (For they bow to vanity and emptiness and pray to a god which helps not.*[1]*) But we bend our knees, bow, and acknowledge our thanks before the King Who reigns over kings, the Holy One, Blessed is He. He stretches out heaven and establishes earth's foundation,*[2] *the seat of His homage is in the heavens above and His powerful Presence is in the loftiest heights. He is our God and there is none other. True is our King, there is nothing beside Him, as it is written in His Torah: 'You are to know this day and take to your heart that* HASHEM *is the only God — in heaven above and on the earth below — there is none other.'*[3]

Bow while reciting *'But we bend our knees.'*

(1) *Isaiah* 45:20. (2) 51:13. (3) *Deuteronomy* 4:39.

עַל כֵּן נְקַוֶּה לְּךָ יהוה אֱלֹהֵינוּ לִרְאוֹת מְהֵרָה בְּתִפְאֶרֶת עֻזֶּךָ, לְהַעֲבִיר גִּלּוּלִים מִן הָאָרֶץ, וְהָאֱלִילִים כָּרוֹת יִכָּרֵתוּן, לְתַקֵּן עוֹלָם בְּמַלְכוּת שַׁדַּי. וְכָל בְּנֵי בָשָׂר יִקְרְאוּ בִשְׁמֶךָ, לְהַפְנוֹת אֵלֶיךָ כָּל רִשְׁעֵי אָרֶץ. יַכִּירוּ וְיֵדְעוּ כָּל יוֹשְׁבֵי תֵבֵל, כִּי לְךָ תִּכְרַע כָּל בֶּרֶךְ, תִּשָּׁבַע כָּל לָשׁוֹן.[1] לְפָנֶיךָ יהוה אֱלֹהֵינוּ יִכְרְעוּ וְיִפֹּלוּ, וְלִכְבוֹד שִׁמְךָ יְקָר יִתֵּנוּ. וִיקַבְּלוּ כֻלָּם אֶת עוֹל מַלְכוּתֶךָ, וְתִמְלֹךְ עֲלֵיהֶם מְהֵרָה לְעוֹלָם וָעֶד. כִּי הַמַּלְכוּת שֶׁלְּךָ הִיא וּלְעוֹלְמֵי עַד תִּמְלוֹךְ בְּכָבוֹד, כַּכָּתוּב בְּתוֹרָתֶךָ: יהוה יִמְלֹךְ לְעֹלָם וָעֶד.[2] ❖ וְנֶאֱמַר: וְהָיָה יהוה לְמֶלֶךְ עַל כָּל הָאָרֶץ, בַּיּוֹם הַהוּא יִהְיֶה יהוה אֶחָד וּשְׁמוֹ אֶחָד.[3]

Some congregations recite the following after עָלֵינוּ:

אַל תִּירָא מִפַּחַד פִּתְאֹם, וּמִשֹּׁאַת רְשָׁעִים כִּי תָבֹא.[4] עֻצוּ עֵצָה וְתֻפָר, דַּבְּרוּ דָבָר וְלֹא יָקוּם, כִּי עִמָּנוּ אֵל.[5] וְעַד זִקְנָה אֲנִי הוּא, וְעַד שֵׂיבָה אֲנִי אֶסְבֹּל, אֲנִי עָשִׂיתִי וַאֲנִי אֶשָּׂא, וַאֲנִי אֶסְבֹּל וַאֲמַלֵּט.[6]

קדיש יתום

In the presence of a *minyan,* mourners recite קַדִּישׁ יָתוֹם, the Mourner's *Kaddish* (see *Laws* §81-83):

יִתְגַּדַּל וְיִתְקַדַּשׁ שְׁמֵהּ רַבָּא. (.Cong – אָמֵן.) בְּעָלְמָא דִּי בְרָא כִרְעוּתֵהּ. וְיַמְלִיךְ מַלְכוּתֵהּ, בְּחַיֵּיכוֹן וּבְיוֹמֵיכוֹן וּבְחַיֵּי דְכָל בֵּית יִשְׂרָאֵל, בַּעֲגָלָא וּבִזְמַן קָרִיב. וְאִמְרוּ: אָמֵן.

(.Cong – אָמֵן. יְהֵא שְׁמֵהּ רַבָּא מְבָרַךְ לְעָלַם וּלְעָלְמֵי עָלְמַיָּא.)

יְהֵא שְׁמֵהּ רַבָּא מְבָרַךְ לְעָלַם וּלְעָלְמֵי עָלְמַיָּא.

יִתְבָּרַךְ וְיִשְׁתַּבַּח וְיִתְפָּאַר וְיִתְרוֹמַם וְיִתְנַשֵּׂא וְיִתְהַדָּר וְיִתְעַלֶּה וְיִתְהַלָּל שְׁמֵהּ דְּקֻדְשָׁא בְּרִיךְ הוּא (.Cong – בְּרִיךְ הוּא) — לְעֵלָּא מִן כָּל בִּרְכָתָא וְשִׁירָתָא תֻּשְׁבְּחָתָא וְנֶחֱמָתָא, דַּאֲמִירָן בְּעָלְמָא. וְאִמְרוּ: אָמֵן. (.Cong – אָמֵן.)

יְהֵא שְׁלָמָא רַבָּא מִן שְׁמַיָּא, וְחַיִּים עָלֵינוּ וְעַל כָּל יִשְׂרָאֵל. וְאִמְרוּ: אָמֵן. (.Cong – אָמֵן.)

Take three steps back. Bow left and say . . . עֹשֶׂה; bow right and say . . . הוּא; bow forward and say וְעַל כָּל . . . אָמֵן. Remain standing in place for a few moments, then take three steps forward.

עֹשֶׂה שָׁלוֹם בִּמְרוֹמָיו, הוּא יַעֲשֶׂה שָׁלוֹם עָלֵינוּ, וְעַל כָּל יִשְׂרָאֵל. וְאִמְרוּ: אָמֵן. (.Cong – אָמֵן.)

עַל כֵּן *Therefore we put our hope in You, HASHEM, our God, that we may soon see Your mighty splendor, to remove detestable idolatry from the earth, and false gods will be utterly cut off, to perfect the universe through the Almighty's sovereignty. Then all humanity will call upon Your Name, to turn all the earth's wicked toward You. All the world's inhabitants will recognize and know that to You every knee should bend, every tongue should swear.*[1] *Before You, HASHEM, our God, they will bend every knee and cast themselves down and to the glory of Your Name they will render homage, and they will all accept upon themselves the yoke of Your kingship that You may reign over them soon and eternally. For the kingdom is Yours and You will reign for all eternity in glory as it is written in Your Torah: HASHEM shall reign for all eternity.*[2] Chazzan– *And it is said: HASHEM will be King over all the world — on that day HASHEM will be One and His Name will be One.*[3]

Some congregations recite the following after *Aleinu.*

אַל תִּירָא *Do not fear sudden terror, or the holocaust of the wicked when it comes.*[4] *Plan a conspiracy and it will be annulled; speak your piece and it shall not stand, for God is with us.*[5] *Even till your seniority, I remain unchanged; and even till your ripe old age, I shall endure. I created you and I shall bear you; I shall endure and rescue.*[6]

MOURNER'S KADDISH

In the presence of a *minyan,* mourners recite קדיש יָתוֹם, the Mourner's *Kaddish* (see *Laws* §81-83).

[A transliteration of this *Kaddish* appears on p. 1305.]

יִתְגַּדַּל *May His great Name grow exalted and sanctified* (Cong.– *Amen.*) *in the world that He created as He willed. May He give reign to His kingship in your lifetimes and in your days, and in the lifetimes of the entire Family of Israel, swiftly and soon. Now respond: Amen.*

(Cong.– *Amen. May His great Name be blessed forever and ever.*)

May His great Name be blessed forever and ever.

Blessed, praised, glorified, exalted, extolled, mighty, upraised, and lauded be the Name of the Holy One, Blessed is He (Cong.– *Blessed is He*) *— beyond any blessing and song, praise and consolation that are uttered in the world. Now respond: Amen.* (Cong.– *Amen*).

May there be abundant peace from Heaven, and life, upon us and upon all Israel. Now respond: Amen. (Cong.– *Amen.*)

Take three steps back. Bow left and say, *'He Who makes peace . . .';* bow right and say, *'may He . . .';* bow forward and say, *'and upon all Israel . . .'* Remain standing in place for a few moments, then take three steps forward.

He Who makes peace in His heights, may He make peace upon us, and upon all Israel. Now respond: Amen. (Cong.– *Amen.*)

---

(1) Cf. *Isaiah* 45:23. (2) *Exodus* 15:18. (3) *Zechariah* 14:9.
(4) *Proverbs* 3:25. (5) *Isaiah* 8:10. (6) 46:4.

שיר הכבוד

The Ark is opened and שִׁיר הַכָּבוֹד, *The Song of Glory,* is recited responsively — the *chazzan* reciting the first verse, the congregation reciting the second and so on.

אַנְעִים זְמִירוֹת וְשִׁירִים אֶאֱרוֹג,* כִּי אֵלֶיךָ נַפְשִׁי תַעֲרוֹג.
נַפְשִׁי חָמְדָה בְּצֵל יָדֶךָ, לָדַעַת כָּל רָז סוֹדֶךָ.
❖ מִדֵּי דַבְּרִי בִּכְבוֹדֶךָ, הוֹמֶה לִבִּי אֶל דּוֹדֶיךָ.
עַל כֵּן אֲדַבֵּר בְּךָ נִכְבָּדוֹת, וְשִׁמְךָ אֲכַבֵּד בְּשִׁירֵי יְדִידוֹת.
❖ אֲסַפְּרָה כְבוֹדְךָ וְלֹא רְאִיתִיךָ,* אֲדַמְּךָ אֲכַנְּךָ וְלֹא יְדַעְתִּיךָ.
בְּיַד נְבִיאֶיךָ* בְּסוֹד עֲבָדֶיךָ, דִּמִּיתָ הֲדַר כְּבוֹד הוֹדֶךָ.
❖ גְּדֻלָּתְךָ וּגְבוּרָתֶךָ, כִּנּוּ לְתֹקֶף פְּעֻלָּתֶךָ.
דִּמּוּ אוֹתְךָ וְלֹא כְּפִי יֶשְׁךָ, וַיְשַׁוּוּךָ לְפִי מַעֲשֶׂיךָ.*
❖ הִמְשִׁילְוּךָ בְּרֹב חֶזְיוֹנוֹת, הִנְּךָ אֶחָד* בְּכָל דִּמְיוֹנוֹת.
וַיֶּחֱזוּ בְךָ זִקְנָה וּבַחֲרוּת, וּשְׂעַר רֹאשְׁךָ בְּשֵׂיבָה וְשַׁחֲרוּת.
❖ זִקְנָה* בְּיוֹם דִּין וּבַחֲרוּת בְּיוֹם קְרָב, כְּאִישׁ מִלְחָמוֹת יָדָיו לוֹ רָב.
חָבַשׁ כְּבַע יְשׁוּעָה בְּרֹאשׁוֹ, הוֹשִׁיעָה לּוֹ יְמִינוֹ* וּזְרוֹעַ קָדְשׁוֹ.
❖ טַלְלֵי אוֹרוֹת* רֹאשׁוֹ נִמְלָא, קְוֻצּוֹתָיו רְסִיסֵי לָיְלָה.
יִתְפָּאֵר בִּי כִּי חָפֵץ בִּי. וְהוּא יִהְיֶה לִּי לַעֲטֶרֶת צְבִי.
❖ כֶּתֶם טָהוֹר פָּז דְּמוּת רֹאשׁוֹ, וְחַק עַל מֵצַח כְּבוֹד שֵׁם קָדְשׁוֹ.*
לְחֵן וּלְכָבוֹד* צְבִי תִפְאָרָה, אֻמָּתוֹ לוֹ עִטְּרָה עֲטָרָה.
❖ מַחְלְפוֹת רֹאשׁוֹ* כְּבִימֵי בְחֻרוֹת, קְוֻצּוֹתָיו תַּלְתַּלִּים שְׁחוֹרוֹת.
נְוֵה הַצֶּדֶק צְבִי תִפְאַרְתּוֹ, יַעֲלֶה נָּא עַל רֹאשׁ שִׂמְחָתוֹ.
❖ סְגֻלָּתוֹ תְּהִי בְיָדוֹ עֲטֶרֶת, וּצְנִיף מְלוּכָה צְבִי תִפְאֶרֶת.
עֲמוּסִים נְשָׂאָם עֲטֶרֶת עִנְּדָם, מֵאֲשֶׁר יָקְרוּ בְעֵינָיו כִּבְּדָם.

שִׁיר הַכָּבוֹד / Song of Glory

This beautiful sacred song has been ascribed to R' Yehudah HaChassid, the twelfth century German scholar and Kabbalist. Due to the song's great holiness, the Ark is opened when it is recited, and it is not recited daily so that it not become too familiar *(Levush).* Most congregations recite it every Sabbath and on all Festivals. The *Vilna Gaon* held that it should be recited only on Festivals, and some congregations recite it only on Rosh Hashanah and Yom Kippur.

וְשִׁירִים אֶאֱרוֹג — *And weave hymns.* Just as a weaver unifies countless threads to make a finished garment, so does the *paytan* [liturgical poet] weave together words and phrases to compose beautiful songs of praise.

וְלֹא רְאִיתִיךָ — *Though I see You not.* This stich of the song introduces much of what comes later. We cannot see God, nor can we know His essence. The best we can do is to imagine and describe Him in human terms.

בְּיַד נְבִיאֶיךָ — *Through the hand of Your prophets.* The precedent for describing God in human, physical terminology comes from Him — for He described Himself to the prophets in such terms.

לְפִי מַעֲשֶׂיךָ — *According to Your deeds.* It is a familiar truth that we cannot conceive of what God *is;* we can only know something of Him through His deeds.

הִנְּךָ אֶחָד — *Yet You are a Unity.* God is One though He appears in many guises: merciful, judgmental, old, young, warrior and so on.

זִקְנָה — *Aged.* This stich expounds on the

SONG OF GLORY

The Ark is opened and the *Song of Glory* is recited responsively — the *chazzan* reciting the first verse, the congregation reciting the second and so on.

אַנְעִים זְמִירוֹת *I shall compose pleasant psalms and weave hymns,**
because for You shall my soul pine.
My soul desired the shelter of Your hand,
to know every mystery of Your secret.
∴ *As I speak of Your glory, my heart yearns for Your love.*
Therefore I shall speak of Your glories,
and Your Name I shall honor with loving songs.
∴ *I shall relate Your glory, though I see You not;**
I shall allegorize You, I shall describe You, though I know You not.
Through the hand of Your prophets, through the counsel of Your servants;*
You allegorized the splendrous glory of Your power.
∴ *Your greatness and Your strength,*
they described the might of Your works.
They allegorized You, but not according to Your reality,
*and they portrayed You according to Your deeds.**
∴ *They symbolized You in many varied visions;*
yet You are a Unity containing all the allegories.*
They envisioned in You agedness and virility,
and the hair of Your head as hoary and jet black.
∴ *Aged* on judgment day and virile on the day of battle,*
like a man of war whose powers are many.
The hat of salvation He put on His head;
salvation for Him, His right hand and His sacred arm.*
∴ *With illuminating dew drops* His head is filled,*
His locks are the rains of the night.
He shall glory in me for He desires me,
and He shall be for me a crown of pride.
∴ *A form of the very finest gold upon his head,*
*and carved on his forehead is His glorious, sacred Name.**
For grace and for glory the pride of His splendor;*
His nation crowns Him with its prayers.
∴ *The tresses of His head* are like His youthful days;*
His locks are jet-black ringlets.
The Abode of righteousness is the pride of His splendor;
may He elevate it to His foremost joy.
∴ *May His treasured nation be in His hand like a crown,*
and like a royal tiara the pride of His splendor.
From infancy He bore them and affixed them as a crown,
because they are precious in His eyes He honored them.

---

previous one. Since the song now begins an extensive discussion of God in human terms, it changes to third person out of respect.

הוֹשִׁיעָה לוֹ יְמִינוֹ — *Salvation for Him, His right hand.* God was like a warrior winning victory through his powerful arm.

טַלְלֵי אוֹרוֹת — *[With] illuminating dew drops. Dew* refers to the illumination of the Torah and the life-giving dew that resuscitates the dead. *Rain* refers to the flow of heavenly blessings.

כֶּתֶם ... שֵׁם קָדְשׁוֹ — *A form ... sacred Name.* A reference to the headplate of the *Kohen Gadol* [High Priest], upon which was inscribed God's sacred Name.

לְחֵן וּלְכָבוֹד — *... For grace and for glory.* It is a mark of God's esteem for Israel that He desires its prayers and that He takes them, as it were, as a crown on His head.

מַחְלְפוֹת רֹאשׁוֹ — *The tresses of His head.* God does not change with the passage of time. His

❖ פְּאֵרוֹ* עָלַי וּפְאֵרִי עָלָיו, וְקָרוֹב אֵלַי בְּקָרְאִי אֵלָיו.
צַח וְאָדוֹם* לִלְבוּשׁוֹ אָדוֹם, פּוּרָה בְדָרְכוֹ בְּבוֹאוֹ מֵאֱדוֹם.
❖ קֶשֶׁר תְּפִלִּין הֶרְאָה לֶעָנָו, תְּמוּנַת יהוה לְנֶגֶד עֵינָיו.
רוֹצֶה בְעַמּוֹ עֲנָוִים יְפָאֵר, יוֹשֵׁב תְּהִלּוֹת בָּם לְהִתְפָּאֵר.
❖ רֹאשׁ דְּבָרְךָ אֱמֶת קוֹרֵא מֵרֹאשׁ, דּוֹר וָדוֹר עַם דּוֹרֶשְׁךָ דְּרוֹשׁ.
שִׁית הֲמוֹן שִׁירַי נָא עָלֶיךָ, וְרִנָּתִי תִּקְרַב אֵלֶיךָ.
❖ תְּהִלָּתִי תְּהִי לְרֹאשְׁךָ עֲטֶרֶת, וּתְפִלָּתִי תִּכּוֹן קְטֹרֶת.
תִּיקַר שִׁירַת רָשׁ בְּעֵינֶיךָ, כַּשִּׁיר יוּשַׁר עַל קָרְבָּנֶיךָ.
❖ בִּרְכָתִי תַעֲלֶה לְרֹאשׁ מַשְׁבִּיר, מְחוֹלֵל וּמוֹלִיד צַדִּיק כַּבִּיר.
וּבְבִרְכָתִי תְנַעֲנַע לִי רֹאשׁ, וְאוֹתָהּ קַח לְךָ כִּבְשָׂמִים רֹאשׁ.
❖ יֶעֱרַב נָא שִׂיחִי עָלֶיךָ, כִּי נַפְשִׁי תַעֲרוֹג אֵלֶיךָ.

לְךָ יהוה הַגְּדֻלָּה וְהַגְּבוּרָה וְהַתִּפְאֶרֶת וְהַנֵּצַח וְהַהוֹד, כִּי כֹל בַּשָּׁמַיִם וּבָאָרֶץ; לְךָ יהוה הַמַּמְלָכָה וְהַמִּתְנַשֵּׂא לְכֹל לְרֹאשׁ.[1] מִי יְמַלֵּל גְּבוּרוֹת יהוה, יַשְׁמִיעַ כָּל תְּהִלָּתוֹ.[2]

קדיש יתום

In the presence of a *minyan,* mourners recite קַדִּישׁ יָתוֹם, the Mourner's *Kaddish* (see *Laws* §81-83):

יִתְגַּדַּל וְיִתְקַדַּשׁ שְׁמֵהּ רַבָּא. (.Cong – אָמֵן.) בְּעָלְמָא דִּי בְרָא כִרְעוּתֵהּ. וְיַמְלִיךְ מַלְכוּתֵהּ, בְּחַיֵּיכוֹן וּבְיוֹמֵיכוֹן וּבְחַיֵּי דְכָל בֵּית יִשְׂרָאֵל, בַּעֲגָלָא וּבִזְמַן קָרִיב. וְאִמְרוּ: אָמֵן.

(.Cong – אָמֵן. יְהֵא שְׁמֵהּ רַבָּא מְבָרַךְ לְעָלַם וּלְעָלְמֵי עָלְמַיָּא.)

יְהֵא שְׁמֵהּ רַבָּא מְבָרַךְ לְעָלַם וּלְעָלְמֵי עָלְמַיָּא.

יִתְבָּרַךְ וְיִשְׁתַּבַּח וְיִתְפָּאַר וְיִתְרוֹמַם וְיִתְנַשֵּׂא וְיִתְהַדָּר וְיִתְעַלֶּה וְיִתְהַלָּל שְׁמֵהּ דְּקֻדְשָׁא בְּרִיךְ הוּא (.Cong – בְּרִיךְ הוּא) — לְעֵלָּא מִן כָּל בִּרְכָתָא וְשִׁירָתָא תֻּשְׁבְּחָתָא וְנֶחֱמָתָא, דַּאֲמִירָן בְּעָלְמָא. וְאִמְרוּ: אָמֵן. (.Cong – אָמֵן.)

יְהֵא שְׁלָמָא רַבָּא מִן שְׁמַיָּא, וְחַיִּים עָלֵינוּ וְעַל כָּל יִשְׂרָאֵל. וְאִמְרוּ: אָמֵן. (.Cong – אָמֵן.)

Take three steps back. Bow left and say . . . עֹשֶׂה; bow right and say . . . הוּא; bow forward and say וְעַל כָּל . . . אָמֵן. Remain standing in place for a few moments, then take three steps forward.

עֹשֶׂה שָׁלוֹם בִּמְרוֹמָיו, הוּא יַעֲשֶׂה שָׁלוֹם עָלֵינוּ, וְעַל כָּל יִשְׂרָאֵל. וְאִמְרוּ: אָמֵן. (.Cong – אָמֵן.)

'youth' remains with Him, just as the 'maturity of age' was always with Him.

פְּאֵרוֹ — *His tefillin-splendor.* Just as Israel takes pride in God, so God takes pride in Israel. The Talmud (*Berachos* 6a) expresses this idea by saying that just as Israel wears *tefillin* in which are written the praises of God, so does God, as it were, wear *tefillin,* described as His *splendor,* which contain Scriptural verses that praise Israel.

צַח וְאָדוֹם — *He is white and crimson.* God is both

∴ *His tefillin-splendor* is upon me and my tefillin-splendor is upon Him, and He is near to me when I call to Him.*
He is white and crimson; His garment will be bloody red, when He tramples as in a press on His coming from Edom.*
∴ *He showed the tefillin-knot to the humble [Moses], the likeness of* HASHEM *before his eyes.*
He desires His people, He will glorify the humble; enthroned upon praises, He glories with them.
∴ *The very beginning of Your word is truth — one reads it from the Torah's start; the people that seeks You expounds each generation's fate.*
Place the multitude of my songs before You, please; and my glad song bring near to You.
∴ *May my praise be a crown for Your head, and may my prayer be accepted like incense.*
May the poor man's song be dear in Your eyes, like the song that is sung over Your offerings.
∴ *May my blessing rise up upon the head of the Sustainer — Creator, Giver of life, mighty Righteous One.*
And to my blessing, nod Your head to me, and take it to Yourself like the finest incense.
∴ *May my prayer be sweet to You, for my soul shall pine for You.*

לְךָ *Yours,* HASHEM, *is the greatness, the strength, the splendor, the triumph, and the glory; even everything in heaven and earth; Yours,* HASHEM, *is the kingdom, and the sovereignty over every leader.*[1] *Who can express the mighty acts of* HASHEM? *Who can declare all His praise?*[2]

MOURNER'S KADDISH

In the presence of a *minyan,* mourners recite the Mourner's *Kaddish* (see *Laws* §81-83).

יִתְגַּדַּל *May His great Name grow exalted and sanctified* (Cong.– *Amen.*) *in the world that He created as He willed. May He give reign to His kingship in your lifetimes and in your days, and in the lifetimes of the entire Family of Israel, swiftly and soon. Now respond: Amen.*

(Cong.– *Amen. May His great Name be blessed forever and ever.*)
May His great Name be blessed forever and ever.

Blessed, praised, glorified, exalted, extolled, mighty, upraised, and lauded be the Name of the Holy One, Blessed is He (Cong.– *Blessed is He*) — *beyond any blessing and song, praise and consolation that are uttered in the world. Now respond: Amen.* (Cong.– *Amen.*)

May there be abundant peace from Heaven, and life, upon us and upon all Israel. Now respond: Amen. (Cong.– *Amen.*)

Take three steps back. Bow left and say, *'He Who makes peace . . .';* bow right and say, *'may He . . .';* bow forward and say, *'and upon all Israel . . .'* Remain standing in place for a few moments, then take three steps forward.

He Who makes peace in His heights, may He make peace upon us, and upon all Israel. Now respond: Amen. (Cong.– *Amen.*)

(1) *I Chronicles* 29:11. (2) *Psalms* 106:2.

compassionate, symbolized by white, and strict, symbolized by crimson. He is kind or harsh, depending on the need. When the final Redemption comes, God will execute judgment against Edom for that nation's outrages against Israel. God is metaphorically portrayed as a warrior whose clothing becomes soaked with blood as he kills his adversary. [See *Isaiah* 63:1, *Rashi.*]

שיר של יום

A different psalm is assigned as the שִׁיר שֶׁל יוֹם, *Song of the Day,* for each day of the week.

SUNDAY

הַיּוֹם יוֹם רִאשׁוֹן בַּשַּׁבָּת, שֶׁבּוֹ הָיוּ הַלְוִיִּם אוֹמְרִים בְּבֵית הַמִּקְדָּשׁ:

תהלים כד

לְדָוִד מִזְמוֹר, לַיהוה הָאָרֶץ* וּמְלוֹאָהּ, תֵּבֵל וְיֹשְׁבֵי בָהּ. כִּי הוּא עַל יַמִּים יְסָדָהּ,* וְעַל נְהָרוֹת יְכוֹנְנֶהָ. מִי יַעֲלֶה* בְהַר יהוה, וּמִי יָקוּם בִּמְקוֹם קָדְשׁוֹ. נְקִי כַפַּיִם* וּבַר לֵבָב, אֲשֶׁר לֹא נָשָׂא לַשָּׁוְא נַפְשִׁי,* וְלֹא נִשְׁבַּע לְמִרְמָה. יִשָּׂא בְרָכָה* מֵאֵת יהוה, וּצְדָקָה מֵאֱלֹהֵי יִשְׁעוֹ. זֶה דּוֹר דֹּרְשָׁיו, מְבַקְשֵׁי פָנֶיךָ יַעֲקֹב סֶלָה. שְׂאוּ שְׁעָרִים* רָאשֵׁיכֶם, וְהִנָּשְׂאוּ פִּתְחֵי עוֹלָם,* וְיָבוֹא מֶלֶךְ הַכָּבוֹד.* מִי זֶה מֶלֶךְ הַכָּבוֹד, יהוה עִזּוּז וְגִבּוֹר, יהוה גִּבּוֹר מִלְחָמָה. ❖ שְׂאוּ שְׁעָרִים רָאשֵׁיכֶם, וּשְׂאוּ פִּתְחֵי עוֹלָם, וְיָבֹא מֶלֶךְ הַכָּבוֹד. מִי הוּא זֶה מֶלֶךְ הַכָּבוֹד, יהוה צְבָאוֹת, הוּא מֶלֶךְ הַכָּבוֹד סֶלָה.

The service continues with קַדִּישׁ יָתוֹם, *the Mourner's Kaddish* (page 396).

MONDAY

הַיּוֹם יוֹם שֵׁנִי בַּשַּׁבָּת, שֶׁבּוֹ הָיוּ הַלְוִיִּם אוֹמְרִים בְּבֵית הַמִּקְדָּשׁ:

תהלים מח

שִׁיר מִזְמוֹר לִבְנֵי קֹרַח. גָּדוֹל יהוה וּמְהֻלָּל מְאֹד, בְּעִיר אֱלֹהֵינוּ, הַר קָדְשׁוֹ. יְפֵה נוֹף, מְשׂוֹשׂ כָּל הָאָרֶץ,* הַר צִיּוֹן* יַרְכְּתֵי צָפוֹן,* קִרְיַת מֶלֶךְ רָב. אֱלֹהִים בְּאַרְמְנוֹתֶיהָ נוֹדַע לְמִשְׂגָּב. כִּי הִנֵּה הַמְּלָכִים נוֹעֲדוּ,* עָבְרוּ יַחְדָּו. הֵמָּה רָאוּ כֵּן תָּמָהוּ, נִבְהֲלוּ נֶחְפָּזוּ. רְעָדָה אֲחָזָתַם שָׁם, חִיל כַּיּוֹלֵדָה. בְּרוּחַ קָדִים תְּשַׁבֵּר אֳנִיּוֹת

שִׁיר שֶׁל יוֹם / SONG OF THE DAY

As part of the morning Temple service, the Levites chanted a psalm that was suited to the significance of that particular day of the week (*Tamid* 7:4). As a memorial to the Temple, these psalms have been incorporated into daily *Shacharis.* The Talmud (*Rosh Hashanah* 31a) explains how each psalm was appropriate to its respective day; we will note the reasons in the commentary. The introductory sentence, *'Today is the first day of the Sabbath ...,'* helps fulfill the Torah's command to remember the Sabbath always. By counting the days of the week with reference to the forthcoming Sabbath we tie our existence to the Sabbath. This is in sharp contrast to the non-Jewish custom of assigning names to the days in commemoration of events or gods, such as Sunday for the sun, Monday for the moon and so on (*Ramban, Exodus* 20:8).

יוֹם רִאשׁוֹן / The First Day

The first day's psalm teaches that everything belongs to God, because on the first day of creation, God was the sole Power — even the angels had not yet been created. He took possession of His newly created world with the intention of ceding it to man (*Rosh Hashanah* 31a).

לַה׳ הָאָרֶץ — *HASHEM's is the earth.* Since the world belongs to God, anyone who derives pleasure from His world without reciting the proper blessing expressing thanks to the Owner is regarded as a thief (*Berachos* 35a).

כִּי הוּא עַל יַמִּים יְסָדָהּ — *For He founded it upon seas.* The entire planet was covered with water until God commanded it to gather in seas and rivers and to expose the dry land (*Ibn Ezra*).

מִי יַעֲלֶה... — *Who may ascend* ... God's most intense Presence is in the Temple, so those who wish to draw near and to perceive His splendor must be especially worthy (*Rashi*). By extension, one who wishes to enjoy spiritual elevation must refine his behavior.

נְקִי כַפַּיִם — *One with clean hands.* This verse answers the previous questions. To 'ascend,' one's hands may not be soiled by dishonest gain. He must be honest in his dealings with man, and reverent in his attitude toward God.

נַפְשִׁי — *My soul.* God is the 'speaker.' He refers to

SONG OF THE DAY

A different psalm is assigned as the Song of the Day for each day of the week.

SUNDAY

Today is the first day of the Sabbath, on which the Levites would recite in the Holy Temple:

Psalm 24

לְדָוִד *Of David a psalm.* H*ASHEM's is the earth* and its fullness, the inhabited land and those who dwell in it. For He founded it upon seas,* and established it upon rivers. Who may ascend* the mountain of* H*ASHEM, and who may stand in the place of His sanctity? One with clean hands* and pure heart, who has not sworn in vain by My soul* and has not sworn deceitfully. He will receive a blessing* from* H*ASHEM and just kindness from the God of his salvation. This is the generation of those who seek Him, those who strive for Your Presence — Jacob, Selah. Raise up your heads, O gates,* and be uplifted, you everlasting entrances,* so that the King of Glory* may enter. Who is this King of Glory? —* H*ASHEM, the mighty and strong,* H*ASHEM, the strong in battle.* Chazzan— *Raise up your heads, O gates, and raise up, you everlasting entrances, so that the King of Glory may enter. Who then is the King of Glory?* H*ASHEM, Master of Legions, He is the King of Glory. Selah!*

The service continues with קַדִּישׁ יָתוֹם, *the Mourner's Kaddish* (p. 396).

MONDAY

Today is the second day of the Sabbath, on which the Levites would recite in the Holy Temple:

Psalm 48

שִׁיר מִזְמוֹר *A song, a psalm, by the sons of Korach. Great is* H*ASHEM and much praised, in the city of our God, Mount of His Holiness. Fairest of sites, joy of all the earth* is Mount Zion,* by the northern sides* of the great king's city. In her palaces God is known as the Stronghold. For behold — the kings assembled,* they came together. They saw and they were astounded, they were confounded and hastily fled. Trembling gripped them there, convulsions like a woman in birth travail. With an east wind You smashed the ships*

---

one who swears falsely as having treated God's 'soul,' as it were, with disrespect.

יִשָּׂא בְרָכָה . . . — *He will receive a blessing.* Because he honors God's Name in heart and behavior, such a person earns God's *blessing, kindness,* and *salvation (R' Hirsch).*

שְׂאוּ שְׁעָרִים — *Raise up ... O gates.* When Solomon sought to bring the Ark into the Temple, the gates remained shut despite all his pleas, until he prayed that God open the gates in the merit of David, who made all the preparations to build the Temple. Thus, this verse alludes to Solomon's future prayer *(Shabbos* 30a). The plea to the gates is repeated later to allude to the Ark's re-entry when the Third Temple will be built *(Ibn Ezra).*

פִּתְחֵי עוֹלָם — *Everlasting entrances,* i.e. the holiness of the Temple gates is eternal.

מֶלֶךְ הַכָּבוֹד — *The King of Glory.* God is given this title because He gives glory to those who revere Him *(Midrash).*

יוֹם שֵׁנִי / The Second Day

On this day, God separated between the heavenly and earthly components of the universe and ruled over both. Nevertheless, the psalm specifies Jerusalem because the seat of His holiness is Jerusalem *(Rosh Hashanah* 31a). *Resisei Laylah* comments that this day's separation between heaven and earth initiated the eternal strife between the spiritual and the physical. This is why the Levites recited a psalm composed by the sons of Korach, the man who instigated a quarrel against Moses.

מְשׂוֹשׂ כָּל הָאָרֶץ — *Joy of all the earth.* Jerusalem was given this title because the Holy City gave joy to the troubled who were atoned through the Temple service, and because the spiritual uplift of its holiness eased troubles *(Rashi).*

הַר צִיּוֹן — *Mount Zion.* The word Zion comes from צִיּוּן, a *monument.* The site of God's Sanctuary remains an eternal memorial to truth and sanctity *(R' Hirsch).*

יַרְכְּתֵי צָפוֹן — *The northern sides.* Mount Zion was north of the City of David, the *great king (Radak).*

הַמְּלָכִים נוֹעֲדוּ — *The kings assembled.* When

תַּרְשִׁישׁ.* כַּאֲשֶׁר שָׁמַעְנוּ* כֵּן רָאִינוּ בְּעִיר יהוה צְבָאוֹת, בְּעִיר אֱלֹהֵינוּ, אֱלֹהִים יְכוֹנְנֶהָ עַד עוֹלָם סֶלָה. דִּמִּינוּ אֱלֹהִים חַסְדֶּךָ, בְּקֶרֶב הֵיכָלֶךָ. כְּשִׁמְךָ אֱלֹהִים* כֵּן תְּהִלָּתְךָ, עַל קַצְוֵי אֶרֶץ, צֶדֶק מָלְאָה יְמִינֶךָ. יִשְׂמַח הַר צִיּוֹן, תָּגֵלְנָה בְּנוֹת יְהוּדָה, לְמַעַן מִשְׁפָּטֶיךָ. סֹבּוּ צִיּוֹן וְהַקִּיפוּהָ, סִפְרוּ מִגְדָּלֶיהָ. ❖ שִׁיתוּ לִבְּכֶם לְחֵילָה, פַּסְּגוּ אַרְמְנוֹתֶיהָ, לְמַעַן תְּסַפְּרוּ לְדוֹר אַחֲרוֹן. כִּי זֶה אֱלֹהִים אֱלֹהֵינוּ עוֹלָם וָעֶד, הוּא יְנַהֲגֵנוּ עַל־מוּת.*

The service continues with קַדִּישׁ יָתוֹם, *the Mourner's Kaddish* (page 396).

TUESDAY

הַיּוֹם יוֹם שְׁלִישִׁי בַּשַּׁבָּת, שֶׁבּוֹ הָיוּ הַלְוִיִּם אוֹמְרִים בְּבֵית הַמִּקְדָּשׁ:

תהלים פב

מִזְמוֹר לְאָסָף,* אֱלֹהִים נִצָּב בַּעֲדַת אֵל,* בְּקֶרֶב אֱלֹהִים יִשְׁפֹּט. עַד מָתַי* תִּשְׁפְּטוּ עָוֶל, וּפְנֵי רְשָׁעִים תִּשְׂאוּ סֶלָה. שִׁפְטוּ דָל וְיָתוֹם, עָנִי וָרָשׁ הַצְדִּיקוּ. פַּלְּטוּ דַל וְאֶבְיוֹן, מִיַּד רְשָׁעִים הַצִּילוּ. לֹא יָדְעוּ וְלֹא יָבִינוּ, בַּחֲשֵׁכָה יִתְהַלָּכוּ, יִמּוֹטוּ כָּל מוֹסְדֵי אָרֶץ. אֲנִי אָמַרְתִּי אֱלֹהִים אַתֶּם, וּבְנֵי עֶלְיוֹן כֻּלְּכֶם. אָכֵן כְּאָדָם תְּמוּתוּן, וּכְאַחַד הַשָּׂרִים תִּפֹּלוּ. ❖ קוּמָה אֱלֹהִים שָׁפְטָה הָאָרֶץ, כִּי אַתָּה תִנְחַל בְּכָל הַגּוֹיִם.

The service continues with קַדִּישׁ יָתוֹם, *the Mourner's Kaddish* (page 396).

WEDNESDAY

הַיּוֹם יוֹם רְבִיעִי בַּשַּׁבָּת, שֶׁבּוֹ הָיוּ הַלְוִיִּם אוֹמְרִים בְּבֵית הַמִּקְדָּשׁ:

תהלים צד:א-צה:ג

אֵל נְקָמוֹת יהוה, אֵל נְקָמוֹת הוֹפִיעַ. הִנָּשֵׂא שֹׁפֵט הָאָרֶץ, הָשֵׁב גְּמוּל עַל גֵּאִים. עַד מָתַי רְשָׁעִים, יהוה, עַד מָתַי רְשָׁעִים יַעֲלֹזוּ. יַבִּיעוּ יְדַבְּרוּ עָתָק, יִתְאַמְּרוּ כָּל פֹּעֲלֵי אָוֶן. עַמְּךָ יהוה יְדַכְּאוּ, וְנַחֲלָתְךָ יְעַנּוּ. אַלְמָנָה וְגֵר יַהֲרֹגוּ, וִיתוֹמִים יְרַצֵּחוּ. וַיֹּאמְרוּ לֹא יִרְאֶה יָּהּ,* וְלֹא יָבִין אֱלֹהֵי יַעֲקֹב. בִּינוּ* בֹּעֲרִים בָּעָם, וּכְסִילִים מָתַי תַּשְׂכִּילוּ. הֲנֹטַע

---

kings assembled at various times to attack Jerusalem, they saw that God was its *stronghold*. Seeing His miracles (next verse) they were astounded and fled *(Radak)*.

אֳנִיּוֹת תַּרְשִׁישׁ — *The ships of Tarshish.* A sea near Africa, Tarshish represents invading fleets that were dispatched against *Eretz Yisrael*.

כַּאֲשֶׁר שָׁמַעְנוּ — *As we heard.* From our ancestors we heard of God's miraculous salvations — but we will see similar wonders as well *(Rashi)*.

כְּשִׁמְךָ אֱלֹהִים — *Like Your Name, O God.* The prophets gave You exalted Names, but we can testify that *Your praise*, given You for actual deeds, justifies those glorious titles *(Radak)*.

עַל־מוּת — *Like children.* The two words are rendered as one: עַלְמוּת, *youth.* God will guide us like a father caring for his young *(Targum; Rashi)*; or He will preserve the enthusiasm and vigor of our youth *(Meiri)*. According to the Masoretic tradition that these are two words, they mean that God will continue to guide us *beyond death*, i.e., in the World to Come.

יוֹם שְׁלִישִׁי / The Third Day

On the third day, God caused the dry land to become visible and fit for habitation. He did so in order that man follow the Torah's laws and deal justly with other people. Therefore the psalm speaks of justice *(Rosh Hashanah* 31a). *Maharsha* explains that the theme of this psalm — the maintenance of equity and justice — is a prerequisite for the continued existence of the world that was revealed on the third day. But this message is not limited only to courts. In his own personal life, every Jew is a judge, for his opinions and decisions about people can affect their lives in a thousand different ways.

לְאָסָף — *Of Assaf.* A descendant of Korach, Assaf was one of the psalmists whose composi-

of Tarshish. As we heard,* so we saw in the city of* HASHEM, *Master of Legions, in the city of our God — may God establish it to eternity, Selah! We hoped, O God, for Your kindness, in the midst of Your Sanctuary. Like Your Name, O God,* so is Your praise — to the ends of the earth; righteousness fills Your right hand. May Mount Zion be glad, may the daughters of Judah rejoice, because of Your judgments. Walk about Zion and encircle her, count her towers.* Chazzan— *Mark well in your hearts her ramparts, raise up her palaces, that you may recount it to the succeeding generation: that this is God, our God, forever and ever, He will guide us like children.**

The service continues with קַדִּישׁ יָתוֹם, *the Mourner's Kaddish* (p. 396).

TUESDAY

Today is the third day of the Sabbath,
on which the Levites would recite in the Holy Temple:

Psalm 82

מִזְמוֹר *A psalm of Assaf:* God stands in the Divine assembly,* in the midst of judges shall He judge. Until when* will you judge lawlessly and favor the presence of the wicked, Selah? Judge the needy and the orphan, vindicate the poor and impoverished. Rescue the needy and destitute, from the hand of the wicked deliver them. They do not know nor do they understand, in darkness they walk; all foundations of the earth collapse. I said, 'You are angelic, sons of the Most High are you all.' But like men you shall die, and like one of the princes you shall fall.* Chazzan— *Arise, O God, judge the earth, for You allot the heritage among all the nations.*

The service continues with קַדִּישׁ יָתוֹם, *the Mourner's Kaddish* (p. 396).

WEDNESDAY

Today is the fourth day of the Sabbath,
on which the Levites would recite in the Holy Temple:

Psalm 94:1-95:3

אֵל נְקָמוֹת *O God of vengeance,* HASHEM; *O God of vengeance, appear! Arise, O Judge of the earth, render recompense to the haughty. How long shall the wicked — O* HASHEM *— how long shall the wicked exult? They speak freely, they utter malicious falsehood, they glorify themselves, all workers of iniquity. Your nation,* HASHEM, *they crush, and they afflict Your heritage. The widow and the stranger they slay, and the orphans they murder. And they say, 'God will not see,* nor will the God of Jacob understand.' Understand,* you boors among the people; and you fools, when will you gain wisdom? He Who implants*

---

tions David incorporated into the Book of Psalms.

בַּעֲדַת אֵל — *In the Divine assembly.* Judges who seek truth and justice are the *Divine assembly,* because they represent God's justice on earth. As a result of their sincerity, God Himself penetrates into their hearts — בְּקֶרֶב אֱלֹהִים, *in the midst of judges* — to assure them of reaching a just verdict *(Alshich).*

עַד מָתַי — *Until when . . .?* The next three verses address directly the judges who do not carry out their responsibilities. Included in this exhortation is the clear message for the judges to take the initiative in seeking out and correcting injustice.

יוֹם רְבִיעִי / The Fourth Day

On the fourth day, God created the sun, moon, and stars, but instead of recognizing them as God's servants, man eventually came to regard the luminaries as independent gods that should be worshiped. Because of this idolatry, God showed Himself to be, as this psalm describes Him, the *God of vengeance,* for despite His almost endless patience and mercy, He does not tolerate evil forever.

וַיֹּאמְרוּ לֹא יִרְאֶה יָּהּ — *And they say, 'God will not see . . .'* When the Temple was destroyed, it was as if God's power had been diminished and His Four-letter Name abbreviated to the two letters of יָהּ *(Eruvin* 18b). This gives evildoers the pretext to claim that God was detached from the world and unable to see the wickedness being done on earth *(Zera Yaakov).*

בִּינוּ — *Understand.* If only the boors would

אֹזֶן הֲלֹא יִשְׁמָע, אִם יֹצֵר עַיִן הֲלֹא יַבִּיט. הֲיֹסֵר גּוֹיִם הֲלֹא יוֹכִיחַ, הַמְלַמֵּד אָדָם דָּעַת. יהוה יֹדֵעַ מַחְשְׁבוֹת אָדָם, כִּי הֵמָּה הָבֶל. אַשְׁרֵי הַגֶּבֶר* אֲשֶׁר תְּיַסְּרֶנּוּ יָּהּ, וּמִתּוֹרָתְךָ תְלַמְּדֶנּוּ. לְהַשְׁקִיט לוֹ* מִימֵי רָע, עַד יִכָּרֶה לָרָשָׁע שָׁחַת. כִּי לֹא יִטֹּשׁ יהוה עַמּוֹ, וְנַחֲלָתוֹ* לֹא יַעֲזֹב. כִּי עַד צֶדֶק יָשׁוּב מִשְׁפָּט,* וְאַחֲרָיו כָּל יִשְׁרֵי לֵב. מִי יָקוּם לִי עִם מְרֵעִים, מִי יִתְיַצֵּב לִי עִם פֹּעֲלֵי אָוֶן. לוּלֵי יהוה עֶזְרָתָה לִּי, כִּמְעַט שָׁכְנָה דוּמָה נַפְשִׁי. אִם אָמַרְתִּי מָטָה רַגְלִי,* חַסְדְּךָ יהוה יִסְעָדֵנִי. בְּרֹב שַׂרְעַפַּי בְּקִרְבִּי, תַּנְחוּמֶיךָ יְשַׁעַשְׁעוּ נַפְשִׁי. הַיְחָבְרְךָ כִּסֵּא הַוּוֹת, יֹצֵר עָמָל* עֲלֵי חֹק. יָגוֹדּוּ עַל נֶפֶשׁ צַדִּיק, וְדָם נָקִי יַרְשִׁיעוּ. וַיְהִי יהוה לִי לְמִשְׂגָּב, וֵאלֹהַי לְצוּר מַחְסִי. וַיָּשֶׁב עֲלֵיהֶם אֶת אוֹנָם, וּבְרָעָתָם יַצְמִיתֵם, יַצְמִיתֵם יהוה אֱלֹהֵינוּ.

❖ לְכוּ נְרַנְּנָה* לַיהוה, נָרִיעָה לְצוּר יִשְׁעֵנוּ. נְקַדְּמָה פָנָיו בְּתוֹדָה, בִּזְמִרוֹת נָרִיעַ לוֹ. כִּי אֵל גָּדוֹל יהוה, וּמֶלֶךְ גָּדוֹל עַל כָּל אֱלֹהִים.

The service continues with קַדִּישׁ יָתוֹם, *the Mourner's Kaddish* (page 396).

THURSDAY

הַיּוֹם יוֹם חֲמִישִׁי בַּשַּׁבָּת, שֶׁבּוֹ הָיוּ הַלְוִיִּם אוֹמְרִים בְּבֵית הַמִּקְדָּשׁ:

תהלים פא

לַמְנַצֵּחַ עַל הַגִּתִּית* לְאָסָף. הַרְנִינוּ לֵאלֹהִים עוּזֵּנוּ, הָרִיעוּ לֵאלֹהֵי יַעֲקֹב.* שְׂאוּ זִמְרָה וּתְנוּ תֹף, כִּנּוֹר נָעִים עִם נָבֶל. תִּקְעוּ בַחֹדֶשׁ שׁוֹפָר,* בַּכֶּסֶה לְיוֹם חַגֵּנוּ. כִּי חֹק לְיִשְׂרָאֵל הוּא, מִשְׁפָּט* לֵאלֹהֵי יַעֲקֹב. עֵדוּת בִּיהוֹסֵף שָׂמוֹ,* בְּצֵאתוֹ עַל אֶרֶץ מִצְרָיִם, שְׂפַת לֹא יָדַעְתִּי אֶשְׁמָע. הֲסִירוֹתִי מִסֵּבֶל שִׁכְמוֹ, כַּפָּיו מִדּוּד תַּעֲבֹרְנָה. בַּצָּרָה קָרָאתָ, וָאֲחַלְּצֶךָּ, אֶעֶנְךָ בְּסֵתֶר רַעַם, אֶבְחָנְךָ עַל מֵי מְרִיבָה, סֶלָה. שְׁמַע עַמִּי וְאָעִידָה בָּךְ, יִשְׂרָאֵל אִם תִּשְׁמַע לִי. לֹא יִהְיֶה בְךָ אֵל זָר, וְלֹא תִשְׁתַּחֲוֶה לְאֵל נֵכָר.

---

realize that God cannot be fooled or ignored! *(Radak).*

אַשְׁרֵי הַגֶּבֶר — *Praiseworthy is the man.* The wicked ask why the righteous suffer, if God truly controls everything. The Psalmist answers that God afflicts the righteous only when it is to their benefit, to correct them, to make them realize the futility of physical pleasures, or to atone for their sins *(Radak; Meiri).*

לְהַשְׁקִיט לוֹ — *To give him rest.* The suffering of good people on earth spares them from the far worse *days of evil* in *Gehinnom,* but they will not suffer forever — only until evil is purged from the world and *a pit is dug for the wicked (Rashi).*

וְנַחֲלָתוֹ — *His heritage.* Even in exile, Israel knows it will survive, because it is God's *heritage (Radak).*

יָשׁוּב מִשְׁפָּט — *Shall revert to righteousness.* For the good person who has sinned, God's punishment will cause him to repent *(Rashi).*

מָטָה רַגְלִי — *'My foot falters.'* When Israel fears it will falter, God's goodness supports it *(Radak).*

יֹצֵר עָמָל . . . — *Those who fashion evil . . .* Would God associate with those who legitimize their evil by turning it into a code of law? *(Radak).*

לְכוּ נְרַנְּנָה — *Come — let us sing.* The next three verses are not part of the psalm of the day, and are not recited in all congregations. They are the beginning of the next psalm and are recited because of their inspiring message that is an apt climax to the song of the day.

❧ יוֹם חֲמִישִׁי / The Fifth Day

On the fifth day of creation, God made the birds and the fish, which bring joy to the world. When people observe the vast variety of colorful birds and fish, they are awed by the tremendous scope of God's creative ability, and they are stirred to praise Him with song *(Rosh Hashanah* 31a).

הַגִּתִּית — *The gittis.* A musical instrument named after the town of Gath, where it was made *(Rashi).*

הָרִיעוּ לֵאלֹהֵי יַעֲקֹב — *Call out to the God of Jacob.*

the ear, shall He not hear? He Who fashions the eye, shall He not see? He Who chastises nations, shall He not rebuke? — He Who teaches man knowledge. HASHEM knows the thoughts of man, that they are futile. Praiseworthy is the man whom God disciplines, and whom You teach from Your Torah. To give him rest* from the days of evil, until a pit is dug for the wicked. For HASHEM will not cast off His people, nor will He forsake His heritage.* For justice shall revert to righteousness,* and following it will be all of upright heart. Who will rise up for me against evildoers? Who will stand up for me against the workers of iniquity? Had HASHEM not been a help to me, my soul would soon have dwelt in silence. If I said, 'My foot falters,'* Your kindness, HASHEM, supported me. When my forebodings were abundant within me, Your comforts cheered my soul. Can the throne of destruction be associated with You? — those who fashion evil* into a way of life. They join together against the soul of the righteous, and the blood of the innocent they condemn. Then HASHEM became a stronghold for me, and my God, the Rock of my refuge. He turned upon them their own violence, and with their own evil He will cut them off, HASHEM, our God, will cut them off.*

Chazzan– *Come — let us sing* to HASHEM, let us call out to the Rock of our salvation. Let us greet Him with thanksgiving, with praiseful songs let us call out to Him. For a great God is HASHEM, and a great King above all heavenly powers.*

The service continues with קַדִּישׁ יָתוֹם, *the Mourner's Kaddish* (p. 396).

THURSDAY

Today is the fifth day of the Sabbath,
on which the Levites would recite in the Holy Temple:

Psalm 81

לַמְנַצֵּחַ *For the Conductor, upon the gittis,* by Assaf. Sing joyously to the God of our might, call out to the God of Jacob.* Raise a song and sound the drum, the sweet harp with the lyre. Blow the shofar at the moon's renewal,* at the time appointed for our festive day. Because it is a decree for Israel, a judgment day* for the God of Jacob. He imposed it as a testimony for Joseph* when he went forth over the land of Egypt — 'I understood a language I never knew!' I removed his shoulder from the burden, his hands let go of the kettle. In distress you called out, and I released you, I answered you with thunder when you hid, I tested you at the Waters of Strife, Selah. Listen, My nation, and I will attest to you; O Israel, if you would but listen to Me. There shall be no strange god within you, nor shall you bow before an alien god.*

The Patriarch Jacob is singled out because he went down to Egypt with his sons and their families. The two hundred and ten years of bondage are counted from the moment Jacob arrived in Egypt. During this period the children of Jacob called out to God in their distress (*Radak*).

תִּקְעוּ בַחֹדֶשׁ שׁוֹפָר — *Blow the shofar at the moon's renewal.* The *moon's renewal* is a poetic term for the first day of the lunar month, when the moon becomes visible again. This refers to Rosh Hashanah, the only Festival that occurs on the first day of the month and when the *shofar* is blown.

Homiletically Rosh Hashanah is the time for חֹדֶשׁ, *renewal,* of one's dedication and שׁוֹפָר [cognate with שִׁיפּוּר, *beautification*] *improvement,* of one's deeds (*Midrash Shocher Tov*).

חֹק . . . מִשְׁפָּט — *Decree . . . judgment [day].* It is a Divine decree that Israel blow the *shofar* on Rosh Hashanah, the day when God sits in judgment (*Rashi*).

The Talmud (*Beitzah* 16a) translates חֹק as a *fixed ration.* On Rosh Hashanah the heavenly tribunal fixes each person's sustenance for the coming year.

עֵדוּת בִּיהוֹסֵף שָׂמוֹ — *He imposed it as a testimony for Joseph.* This entire verse is based on the life of Joseph. The Talmud (*Rosh Hashanah* 10b) teaches that Joseph was released from prison and appointed viceroy of Egypt on Rosh Hashanah. In honor of that event, God ordained the *mitzvah* of shofar on Rosh Hashanah as a

אָנֹכִי יהוה אֱלֹהֶיךָ, הַמַּעַלְךָ מֵאֶרֶץ מִצְרָיִם, הַרְחֶב פִּיךָ* וַאֲמַלְאֵהוּ. וְלֹא שָׁמַע עַמִּי לְקוֹלִי, וְיִשְׂרָאֵל לֹא אָבָה לִי. וָאֲשַׁלְּחֵהוּ בִּשְׁרִירוּת לִבָּם, יֵלְכוּ בְּמוֹעֲצוֹתֵיהֶם. לוּ עַמִּי שֹׁמֵעַ לִי, יִשְׂרָאֵל בִּדְרָכַי יְהַלֵּכוּ. כִּמְעַט אוֹיְבֵיהֶם אַכְנִיעַ, וְעַל צָרֵיהֶם אָשִׁיב יָדִי. מְשַׂנְאֵי יהוה יְכַחֲשׁוּ לוֹ,* וִיהִי עִתָּם לְעוֹלָם.* ❖ וַיַּאֲכִילֵהוּ* מֵחֵלֶב חִטָּה, וּמִצּוּר דְּבַשׁ אַשְׂבִּיעֶךָ.

The service continues with קַדִּישׁ יָתוֹם, *the Mourner's Kaddish* (page 396).

FRIDAY

הַיּוֹם יוֹם שִׁשִּׁי בַּשַּׁבָּת, שֶׁבּוֹ הָיוּ הַלְוִיִּם אוֹמְרִים בְּבֵית הַמִּקְדָּשׁ:

תהלים צג

יהוה מָלָךְ, גֵּאוּת לָבֵשׁ, לָבֵשׁ יהוה עֹז הִתְאַזָּר, אַף תִּכּוֹן תֵּבֵל בַּל תִּמּוֹט. נָכוֹן כִּסְאֲךָ מֵאָז, מֵעוֹלָם אָתָּה. נָשְׂאוּ נְהָרוֹת יהוה, נָשְׂאוּ נְהָרוֹת קוֹלָם, יִשְׂאוּ נְהָרוֹת דָּכְיָם. מִקֹּלוֹת מַיִם רַבִּים, אַדִּירִים מִשְׁבְּרֵי יָם, אַדִּיר בַּמָּרוֹם יהוה. ❖ עֵדֹתֶיךָ נֶאֶמְנוּ מְאֹד לְבֵיתְךָ נַאֲוָה קֹדֶשׁ, יהוה לְאֹרֶךְ יָמִים.

The service continues with קַדִּישׁ יָתוֹם, *the Mourner's Kaddish* (page 396).

THE SABBATH

הַיּוֹם יוֹם שַׁבַּת קֹדֶשׁ שֶׁבּוֹ הָיוּ הַלְוִיִּם אוֹמְרִים בְּבֵית הַמִּקְדָּשׁ:

תהלים צב

מִזְמוֹר שִׁיר לְיוֹם הַשַּׁבָּת. טוֹב לְהֹדוֹת לַיהוה, וּלְזַמֵּר לְשִׁמְךָ עֶלְיוֹן. לְהַגִּיד בַּבֹּקֶר חַסְדֶּךָ, וֶאֱמוּנָתְךָ בַּלֵּילוֹת. עֲלֵי עָשׂוֹר וַעֲלֵי נָבֶל, עֲלֵי הִגָּיוֹן בְּכִנּוֹר. כִּי שִׂמַּחְתַּנִי יהוה בְּפָעֳלֶךָ, בְּמַעֲשֵׂי יָדֶיךָ אֲרַנֵּן. מַה גָּדְלוּ מַעֲשֶׂיךָ יהוה, מְאֹד עָמְקוּ מַחְשְׁבֹתֶיךָ. אִישׁ בַּעַר לֹא יֵדָע, וּכְסִיל לֹא יָבִין אֶת זֹאת. בִּפְרֹחַ רְשָׁעִים כְּמוֹ עֵשֶׂב, וַיָּצִיצוּ כָּל פֹּעֲלֵי אָוֶן, לְהִשָּׁמְדָם עֲדֵי עַד. וְאַתָּה מָרוֹם לְעֹלָם יהוה. כִּי הִנֵּה אֹיְבֶיךָ יהוה, כִּי הִנֵּה אֹיְבֶיךָ יֹאבֵדוּ, יִתְפָּרְדוּ כָּל פֹּעֲלֵי אָוֶן. וַתָּרֶם כִּרְאֵים קַרְנִי, בַּלֹּתִי בְּשֶׁמֶן רַעֲנָן. וַתַּבֵּט עֵינִי בְּשׁוּרָי, בַּקָּמִים עָלַי מְרֵעִים, תִּשְׁמַעְנָה אָזְנָי. ❖ צַדִּיק כַּתָּמָר יִפְרָח, כְּאֶרֶז בַּלְּבָנוֹן יִשְׂגֶּה. שְׁתוּלִים בְּבֵית יהוה, בְּחַצְרוֹת אֱלֹהֵינוּ יַפְרִיחוּ. עוֹד יְנוּבוּן בְּשֵׂיבָה, דְּשֵׁנִים וְרַעֲנַנִּים יִהְיוּ. לְהַגִּיד כִּי יָשָׁר יהוה, צוּרִי וְלֹא עַוְלָתָה בּוֹ.

---

testimony, i.e., a reminder of Joseph's freedom. In order to qualify as a ruler under Egyptian law, Joseph had to know all the languages — a requirement that was fulfilled when the angel Gabriel taught them to him. Thus Joseph exclaimed, *'I understood a language I never knew'* (*Rashi*).

הַרְחֶב פִּיךָ — *Open wide your mouth,* with requests, and I will fulfill them. God urges Israel to ask all that its heart desires (*Ibn Ezra*). By asking God for *everything* that he needs, a person demonstrates his faith that God's power and generosity know no bounds (*Taanis* 3:6).

מְשַׂנְאֵי ה' יְכַחֲשׁוּ לוֹ — *Those who hate* HASHEM [i.e., because Israel's enemies are God's as well] *lie to Him.* They deny that they ever harmed Israel (*Rashi*).

וִיהִי עִתָּם לְעוֹלָם — *So their destiny is eternal.* Israel's tormentors will be condemned to eternal suffering. In contrast, concerning Israel, God promises that:

וַיַּאֲכִילֵהוּ — *But He would feed him.* In the Wilderness, God provided Israel with manna that was finer than *the cream of the wheat* and with honey-sweet water from a rock (*Ibn Ezra*).

I am HASHEM, *your God, Who elevated you from the land of Egypt, open wide your mouth* and I will fill it. But My people did not heed My voice and Israel did not desire Me. So I let them follow their heart's fantasies, they follow their own counsels. If only My people would heed Me, if Israel would walk in My ways. In an instant I would subdue their foes, and against their tormentors turn My hand. Those who hate* HASHEM *lie to Him* — so their destiny is eternal.** Chazzan— *But He would feed him* with the cream of the wheat, and with honey from a rock sate you.*

The service continues with קַדִּישׁ יָתוֹם, *the Mourner's Kaddish* (p. 396).

FRIDAY

Today is the sixth day of the Sabbath,
on which the Levites would recite in the Holy Temple:

Psalm 93

יהוה מָלָךְ HASHEM *will have reigned, He will have donned grandeur; He will have donned might and girded Himself; He even made the world firm so that it should not falter. Your throne was established from of old, eternal are You. Like rivers they raised, O* HASHEM, *like rivers they raised their voice; like rivers they shall raise their destructiveness. More than the roars of many waters, mightier than the waves of the sea — You are mighty on high,* HASHEM. Chazzan— *Your testimonies are exceedingly trustworthy about Your House, the Sacred Dwelling — O* HASHEM, *may it be for long days.*

The service continues with קַדִּישׁ יָתוֹם, *the Mourner's Kaddish* (p. 396).

THE SABBATH

Today is the Holy Sabbath day,
on which the Levites would sing in the Holy Temple:

Psalm 92

מִזְמוֹר שִׁיר *A psalm, a song for the Sabbath day. It is good to thank* HASHEM *and to sing praise to Your Name, O Exalted One; to relate Your kindness in the dawn and Your faith in the nights. Upon ten-stringed instrument and lyre, with singing accompanied by a harp. For You have gladdened me,* HASHEM, *with Your deeds; at the works of Your Hands I sing glad song. How great are Your deeds,* HASHEM; *exceedingly profound are Your thoughts. A boor cannot know, nor can a fool understand this: when the wicked bloom like grass and all the doers of iniquity blossom — it is to destroy them till eternity. But You remain exalted forever,* HASHEM. *For behold! — Your enemies,* HASHEM, *for behold! — Your enemies shall perish, dispersed shall be all doers of iniquity. As exalted as a re'eim's shall be my pride, I will be saturated with ever-fresh oil. My eyes have seen my vigilant foes; when those who would harm me rise up against me, my ears have heard their doom.* Chazzan— *A righteous man will flourish like a date palm, like a cedar in the Lebanon he will grow tall. Planted in the house of* HASHEM, *in the courtyards of our God they will flourish. They will still be fruitful in old age, vigorous and fresh they will be — to declare that* HASHEM *is just, my Rock in Whom there is no wrong.*

יום שִׁשִּׁי / The Sixth Day

Because it describes God in His full grandeur and power as He was when He completed the six days of Creation, and because it describes Him as 'donning' grandeur and 'girding' Himself like one dressing in his Sabbath finery, this psalm was designated as the song of Friday, when the footsteps of the Sabbath begin to be heard.

שַׁבָּת / The Sabbath

Although this psalm is identified as belonging to the theme of the Sabbath and was the Levites' song for the Sabbath Temple service, the text contains not a single direct reference to the Sabbath. Among the explanations given are:

— The psalm refers not to the weekly Sabbath, but to the World to Come, when man

קדיש יתום

In the presence of a *minyan,* mourners recite קַדִּישׁ יָתוֹם, the Mourner's *Kaddish* (see *Laws* §81-83):

יִתְגַּדַּל וְיִתְקַדַּשׁ שְׁמֵהּ רַבָּא. (.Cong – אָמֵן.) בְּעָלְמָא דִּי בְרָא כִרְעוּתֵהּ. וְיַמְלִיךְ מַלְכוּתֵהּ, בְּחַיֵּיכוֹן וּבְיוֹמֵיכוֹן וּבְחַיֵּי דְכָל בֵּית יִשְׂרָאֵל, בַּעֲגָלָא וּבִזְמַן קָרִיב. וְאִמְרוּ: אָמֵן.

(.Cong – אָמֵן. יְהֵא שְׁמֵהּ רַבָּא מְבָרַךְ לְעָלַם וּלְעָלְמֵי עָלְמַיָּא.)

יְהֵא שְׁמֵהּ רַבָּא מְבָרַךְ לְעָלַם וּלְעָלְמֵי עָלְמַיָּא.

יִתְבָּרַךְ וְיִשְׁתַּבַּח וְיִתְפָּאַר וְיִתְרוֹמַם וְיִתְנַשֵּׂא וְיִתְהַדָּר וְיִתְעַלֶּה וְיִתְהַלָּל שְׁמֵהּ דְּקֻדְשָׁא בְּרִיךְ הוּא (.Cong – בְּרִיךְ הוּא) — לְעֵלָּא מִן כָּל בִּרְכָתָא וְשִׁירָתָא תֻּשְׁבְּחָתָא וְנֶחֱמָתָא, דַּאֲמִירָן בְּעָלְמָא. וְאִמְרוּ: אָמֵן. (.Cong – אָמֵן.)

יְהֵא שְׁלָמָא רַבָּא מִן שְׁמַיָּא, וְחַיִּים עָלֵינוּ וְעַל כָּל יִשְׂרָאֵל. וְאִמְרוּ: אָמֵן. (.Cong – אָמֵן.)

Take three steps back. Bow left and say . . . עֹשֶׂה; bow right and say . . . הוּא; bow forward and say וְעַל כָּל . . . אָמֵן. Remain standing in place for a few moments, then take three steps forward.

עֹשֶׂה שָׁלוֹם בִּמְרוֹמָיו, הוּא יַעֲשֶׂה שָׁלוֹם עָלֵינוּ, וְעַל כָּל יִשְׂרָאֵל. וְאִמְרוּ: אָמֵן. (.Cong – אָמֵן.)

תהלים כז

לְדָוִד, יהוה אוֹרִי וְיִשְׁעִי, מִמִּי אִירָא, יהוה מָעוֹז חַיַּי, מִמִּי אֶפְחָד. בִּקְרֹב עָלַי מְרֵעִים לֶאֱכֹל אֶת בְּשָׂרִי, צָרַי וְאֹיְבַי לִי, הֵמָּה כָּשְׁלוּ וְנָפָלוּ. אִם תַּחֲנֶה עָלַי מַחֲנֶה, לֹא יִירָא לִבִּי, אִם תָּקוּם עָלַי מִלְחָמָה, בְּזֹאת אֲנִי בוֹטֵחַ. אַחַת שָׁאַלְתִּי מֵאֵת יהוה, אוֹתָהּ אֲבַקֵּשׁ, שִׁבְתִּי בְּבֵית יהוה כָּל יְמֵי חַיַּי, לַחֲזוֹת בְּנֹעַם יהוה, וּלְבַקֵּר בְּהֵיכָלוֹ. כִּי יִצְפְּנֵנִי בְּסֻכֹּה בְּיוֹם רָעָה, יַסְתִּירֵנִי בְּסֵתֶר אָהֳלוֹ, בְּצוּר יְרוֹמְמֵנִי. וְעַתָּה יָרוּם רֹאשִׁי עַל אֹיְבַי סְבִיבוֹתַי, וְאֶזְבְּחָה בְאָהֳלוֹ זִבְחֵי תְרוּעָה, אָשִׁירָה וַאֲזַמְּרָה לַיהוה. שְׁמַע יהוה קוֹלִי אֶקְרָא, וְחָנֵּנִי וַעֲנֵנִי. לְךָ אָמַר לִבִּי בַּקְּשׁוּ פָנָי, אֶת פָּנֶיךָ יהוה אֲבַקֵּשׁ. אַל תַּסְתֵּר פָּנֶיךָ מִמֶּנִּי, אַל תַּט בְּאַף עַבְדֶּךָ, עֶזְרָתִי הָיִיתָ, אַל תִּטְּשֵׁנִי וְאַל תַּעַזְבֵנִי, אֱלֹהֵי יִשְׁעִי. כִּי אָבִי וְאִמִּי עֲזָבוּנִי, וַיהוה יַאַסְפֵנִי. הוֹרֵנִי יהוה דַּרְכֶּךָ, וּנְחֵנִי בְּאֹרַח מִישׁוֹר, לְמַעַן שֹׁרְרָי. אַל תִּתְּנֵנִי בְּנֶפֶשׁ צָרָי, כִּי קָמוּ בִי עֵדֵי שֶׁקֶר, וִיפֵחַ חָמָס. ❖ לוּלֵא הֶאֱמַנְתִּי לִרְאוֹת בְּטוּב יהוה בְּאֶרֶץ חַיִּים. קַוֵּה אֶל יהוה, חֲזַק וְיַאֲמֵץ לִבֶּךָ, וְקַוֵּה אֶל יהוה.

Mourners recite קַדִּישׁ יָתוֹם, the Mourner's *Kaddish* (above).

---

will achieve the spiritual perfection we only glimpse during the Sabbath. The psalm is thus well suited to the Sabbath which is a semblance of that future spiritual perfection *(Rashi).*

MOURNER'S KADDISH

In the presence of a *minyan,* mourners recite קַדִּישׁ יָתוֹם, the Mourner's *Kaddish* (see *Laws* §81-83):
[A transliteration of this *Kaddish* appears on p. 1305.]

יִתְגַּדַּל *May His great Name grow exalted and sanctified* (Cong.– *Amen.*) *in the world that He created as He willed. May He give reign to His kingship in your lifetimes and in your days, and in the lifetimes of the entire Family of Israel, swiftly and soon. Now respond: Amen.*

(Cong.– *Amen. May His great Name be blessed forever and ever.*)
May His great Name be blessed forever and ever.

Blessed, praised, glorified, exalted, extolled, mighty, upraised, and lauded be the Name of the Holy One, Blessed is He (Cong.– *Blessed is He*) — *beyond any blessing and song, praise and consolation that are uttered in the world. Now respond: Amen.* (Cong.– *Amen*).

May there be abundant peace from Heaven, and life, upon us and upon all Israel. Now respond: Amen. (Cong.– *Amen.*)

Take three steps back. Bow left and say, *'He Who makes peace . . .';* bow right and say, *'may He . . .';* bow forward and say, *'and upon all Israel . . .'* Remain standing in place for a few moments, then take three steps forward.

He Who makes peace in His heights, may He make peace upon us, and upon all Israel. Now respond: Amen. (Cong.– *Amen.*)

Psalm 27

לְדָוִד *Of David;* H*ASHEM is my light and my salvation, whom shall I fear?* H*ASHEM is my life's strength, whom shall I dread? When evildoers approach me to devour my flesh, my tormentors and my foes against me — it is they who stumble and fall. Though an army would besiege me, my heart would not fear; though war would arise against me, in this I trust. One thing I asked of* H*ASHEM, that shall I seek: That I dwell in the House of* H*ASHEM all the days of my life; to behold the sweetness of* H*ASHEM and to contemplate in His Sanctuary. Indeed, He will hide me in His Shelter on the day of evil; He will conceal me in the concealment of His Tent, He will lift me upon a rock. Now my head is raised above my enemies around me, and I will slaughter offerings in His Tent accompanied by joyous song; I will sing and make music to* H*ASHEM.* H*ASHEM, hear my voice when I call, be gracious toward me and answer me. In Your behalf, my heart has said, 'Seek My Presence'; Your Presence,* H*ASHEM, do I seek. Conceal not Your Presence from me, repel not Your servant in anger. You have been my Helper, abandon me not, forsake me not, O God of my salvation. Though my father and mother have forsaken me,* H*ASHEM will gather me in. Teach me Your way,* H*ASHEM, and lead me on the path of integrity, because of my watchful foes. Deliver me not to the wishes of my tormentors, for there have arisen against me false witnesses who breathe violence.* Chazzan– *Had I not trusted that I would see the goodness of* H*ASHEM in the land of life! Hope to* H*ASHEM, strengthen yourself and He will give you courage; and hope to* H*ASHEM.*

Mourners recite קַדִּישׁ יָתוֹם, the Mourner's *Kaddish* (above).

— Praise of God is necessary, but difficult on weekdays when people must struggle for a livelihood. On the Sabbath, free from the strictures of the week, Jews can turn their minds to the perception of God's ways and His praise — which are the topics of this psalm *(Radak).*

Additional commentary to this psalm appears on page 30.

קידושא רבא

Some recite the *Ushpizin* prayers (p. 74) each time they enter the Succah for a meal.

ON THE SABBATH BEGIN HERE.

Many omit some or all of these verses and begin with עַל כֵּן.

אִם תָּשִׁיב* מִשַּׁבָּת רַגְלֶךָ, עֲשׂוֹת חֲפָצֶךָ בְּיוֹם קָדְשִׁי, וְקָרָאתָ לַשַּׁבָּת עֹנֶג, לִקְדוֹשׁ יהוה מְכֻבָּד, וְכִבַּדְתּוֹ מֵעֲשׂוֹת דְּרָכֶיךָ, מִמְּצוֹא חֶפְצְךָ וְדַבֵּר דָּבָר. אָז תִּתְעַנַּג עַל יהוה, וְהִרְכַּבְתִּיךָ עַל בָּמֳתֵי אָרֶץ, וְהַאֲכַלְתִּיךָ נַחֲלַת יַעֲקֹב אָבִיךָ,* כִּי פִּי יהוה דִּבֵּר.[1]

וְשָׁמְרוּ בְנֵי יִשְׂרָאֵל אֶת הַשַּׁבָּת, לַעֲשׂוֹת אֶת הַשַּׁבָּת לְדֹרֹתָם בְּרִית עוֹלָם. בֵּינִי וּבֵין בְּנֵי יִשְׂרָאֵל אוֹת הִיא לְעֹלָם, כִּי שֵׁשֶׁת יָמִים עָשָׂה יהוה אֶת הַשָּׁמַיִם וְאֶת הָאָרֶץ, וּבַיּוֹם הַשְּׁבִיעִי שָׁבַת וַיִּנָּפַשׁ.[2]

זָכוֹר* אֶת יוֹם הַשַּׁבָּת לְקַדְּשׁוֹ. שֵׁשֶׁת יָמִים תַּעֲבֹד וְעָשִׂיתָ כָּל מְלַאכְתֶּךָ. וְיוֹם הַשְּׁבִיעִי שַׁבָּת לַיהוה אֱלֹהֶיךָ, לֹא תַעֲשֶׂה כָל מְלָאכָה, אַתָּה וּבִנְךָ וּבִתֶּךָ עַבְדְּךָ וַאֲמָתְךָ וּבְהֶמְתֶּךָ, וְגֵרְךָ אֲשֶׁר בִּשְׁעָרֶיךָ. כִּי שֵׁשֶׁת יָמִים עָשָׂה יהוה אֶת הַשָּׁמַיִם וְאֶת הָאָרֶץ אֶת הַיָּם וְאֶת כָּל אֲשֶׁר בָּם, וַיָּנַח בַּיּוֹם הַשְּׁבִיעִי –

עַל כֵּן בֵּרַךְ יהוה אֶת יוֹם הַשַּׁבָּת וַיְקַדְּשֵׁהוּ.[3]

(אֵלֶּה מוֹעֲדֵי יהוה מִקְרָאֵי קֹדֶשׁ אֲשֶׁר תִּקְרְאוּ אֹתָם בְּמוֹעֲדָם.[4])

וַיְדַבֵּר מֹשֶׁה* אֶת מֹעֲדֵי יהוה, אֶל בְּנֵי יִשְׂרָאֵל.[5]

סַבְרִי מָרָנָן וְרַבָּנָן וְרַבּוֹתַי:

בָּרוּךְ אַתָּה יהוה אֱלֹהֵינוּ מֶלֶךְ הָעוֹלָם, בּוֹרֵא פְּרִי הַגָּפֶן.

(All present – אָמֵן.)

If, for whatever reason, one does not recite *Kiddush* in a *succah,* the following blessing is omitted.

בָּרוּךְ אַתָּה יהוה אֱלֹהֵינוּ מֶלֶךְ הָעוֹלָם, אֲשֶׁר קִדְּשָׁנוּ בְּמִצְוֹתָיו וְצִוָּנוּ לֵישֵׁב בַּסֻּכָּה.

(All present – אָמֵן.)

עַל הַמִּחְיָה appears on page 92; בִּרְכַּת הַמָּזוֹן, on page 84.

קִידּוּשָׁא רַבָּא / The Morning Kiddush

The morning *Kiddush* was introduced by the Sages, and its status is thus inferior to the evening *Kiddush* which is Scriptural in origin (*Pesachim* 106b). Therefore, it is euphemistically called קִידּוּשָׁא רַבָּא, the *Great Kiddush.* Originally, the *Kiddush* consisted only of the blessing over wine (*Pesachim* 106b), the Scriptural verses having been added over the centuries. However, not everyone says all the verses.

אִם תָּשִׁיב – *If you restrain.* These verses from *Isaiah* conclude a chapter that urges a variety of good practices upon people and assures them of God's blessings in return for compliance.

נַחֲלַת יַעֲקֹב אָבִיךָ – *The heritage of your forefather Jacob.* The land promised Abraham and Isaac was delineated by borders, but Jacob's blessing had no limitation.

KIDDUSHA RABBA

Some recite the *Ushpizin* prayers (p. 74) each time they enter the Succah for a meal.

ON THE SABBATH BEGIN HERE.

Many omit some or all of these verses and begin with *'therefore HASHEM blessed.'*

אִם תָּשִׁיב *If you restrain,* because of the Sabbath, your feet, refrain from accomplishing your own needs on My holy day; if you proclaim the Sabbath 'a delight,' the holy one of HASHEM, 'honored one,' and you honor it by not doing your own ways, from seeking your needs or discussing the forbidden. Then you shall be granted pleasure with HASHEM and I shall mount you astride the heights of the world, and provide you the heritage of your forefather Jacob* — for the mouth of HASHEM has spoken.*[1]

וְשָׁמְרוּ *And the Children of Israel observed the Sabbath, to make the Sabbath for their generations an eternal covenant. Between Me and the Children of Israel it is a sign forever, that in six days did HASHEM make the heaven and the earth, and on the seventh day He rested and was refreshed.*[2]

זָכוֹר *Always remember* the Sabbath day to hallow it. For six days you may labor and do all your work. But the seventh day is the Sabbath for HASHEM, Your God; you may do no work — you, your son and your daughter, your slave and your maidservant, your animal, and the stranger who is in your gates. For in six days did HASHEM make the heaven and the earth, the sea and all that is in them and He rested on the seventh day;*

therefore HASHEM blessed the Sabbath day and sanctified it.[3]

(These are the appointed festivals of HASHEM, holy convocations, which you are to proclaim in their appointed times.[4]*)*

And Moses declared HASHEM's appointed festivals to the Children of Israel.*[5]

By your leave, my masters and teachers:

בָּרוּךְ *Blessed are You, HASHEM, our God, King of the universe, Who creates the fruit of the vine.* (All present – *Amen.*)

If, for whatever reason, one does not recite *Kiddush* in a *succah,* the following blessing is omitted.

בָּרוּךְ *Blessed are You, HASHEM, our God, King of the universe, Who has sanctified us with His commandments and has commanded us to dwell in the Succah.* (All present – *Amen.*)

The blessing after cake and wine appears on page 92; Grace after Meals, on page 84.

(1) *Isaiah* 58:13-14. (2) *Exodus* 31:16-17. (3) 20:8-11. (4) *Leviticus* 23:4. (5) 23:44.

זָכוֹר – *Always remember.* The fourth of the Ten Commandments, this passage implies the positive commandments of the day.

אֵלֶּה מוֹעֲדֵי . . . וַיְדַבֵּר מֹשֶׁה – *These are the appointed festivals ... And Moses declared.* These two verses bracket the Scriptural passage that delineates the laws pertaining to each Festival. Thus, they are an appropriate selection for the Festival *Kiddush.*

מנחה ליום ראשון ושני

אַשְׁרֵי יוֹשְׁבֵי בֵיתֶךָ, עוֹד יְהַלְלוּךָ סֶּלָה.[1] אַשְׁרֵי הָעָם שֶׁכָּכָה לּוֹ, אַשְׁרֵי הָעָם שֶׁיהוה אֱלֹהָיו.[2]

תהלים קמה

תְּהִלָּה לְדָוִד,

אֲרוֹמִמְךָ אֱלוֹהַי הַמֶּלֶךְ, וַאֲבָרְכָה שִׁמְךָ לְעוֹלָם וָעֶד.
בְּכָל יוֹם אֲבָרְכֶךָּ, וַאֲהַלְלָה שִׁמְךָ לְעוֹלָם וָעֶד.
גָּדוֹל יהוה וּמְהֻלָּל מְאֹד, וְלִגְדֻלָּתוֹ אֵין חֵקֶר.
דּוֹר לְדוֹר יְשַׁבַּח מַעֲשֶׂיךָ, וּגְבוּרֹתֶיךָ יַגִּידוּ.
הֲדַר כְּבוֹד הוֹדֶךָ, וְדִבְרֵי נִפְלְאֹתֶיךָ אָשִׂיחָה.
וֶעֱזוּז נוֹרְאוֹתֶיךָ יֹאמֵרוּ, וּגְדוּלָּתְךָ אֲסַפְּרֶנָּה.
זֵכֶר רַב טוּבְךָ יַבִּיעוּ, וְצִדְקָתְךָ יְרַנֵּנוּ.
חַנּוּן וְרַחוּם יהוה, אֶרֶךְ אַפַּיִם וּגְדָל חָסֶד.
טוֹב יהוה לַכֹּל, וְרַחֲמָיו עַל כָּל מַעֲשָׂיו.
יוֹדוּךָ יהוה כָּל מַעֲשֶׂיךָ, וַחֲסִידֶיךָ יְבָרְכוּכָה.
כְּבוֹד מַלְכוּתְךָ יֹאמֵרוּ, וּגְבוּרָתְךָ יְדַבֵּרוּ.
לְהוֹדִיעַ לִבְנֵי הָאָדָם גְּבוּרֹתָיו, וּכְבוֹד הֲדַר מַלְכוּתוֹ.
מַלְכוּתְךָ מַלְכוּת כָּל עֹלָמִים, וּמֶמְשַׁלְתְּךָ בְּכָל דּוֹר וָדֹר.
סוֹמֵךְ יהוה לְכָל הַנֹּפְלִים, וְזוֹקֵף לְכָל הַכְּפוּפִים.
עֵינֵי כֹל אֵלֶיךָ יְשַׂבֵּרוּ, וְאַתָּה נוֹתֵן לָהֶם אֶת אָכְלָם בְּעִתּוֹ.
פּוֹתֵחַ אֶת יָדֶךָ,
וּמַשְׂבִּיעַ לְכָל חַי רָצוֹן.

While reciting the verse פּוֹתֵחַ, concentrate intently on its meaning.

צַדִּיק יהוה בְּכָל דְּרָכָיו, וְחָסִיד בְּכָל מַעֲשָׂיו.
קָרוֹב יהוה לְכָל קֹרְאָיו, לְכֹל אֲשֶׁר יִקְרָאֻהוּ בֶאֱמֶת.
רְצוֹן יְרֵאָיו יַעֲשֶׂה, וְאֶת שַׁוְעָתָם יִשְׁמַע וְיוֹשִׁיעֵם.
שׁוֹמֵר יהוה אֶת כָּל אֹהֲבָיו, וְאֵת כָּל הָרְשָׁעִים יַשְׁמִיד.
❖ תְּהִלַּת יהוה יְדַבֶּר פִּי, וִיבָרֵךְ כָּל בָּשָׂר שֵׁם קָדְשׁוֹ לְעוֹלָם וָעֶד.
וַאֲנַחְנוּ נְבָרֵךְ יָהּ, מֵעַתָּה וְעַד עוֹלָם, הַלְלוּיָהּ.[3]

(1) *Psalms* 84:5. (2) 144:15. (3) 115:18.

MINCHAH / מִנְחָה

Minchah is usually recited in the late afternoon, a particularly apt time for prayer, for it is a time of Divine mercy. Thus, both Isaac (*Genesis* 24:63) and Elijah (*I Kings* 18:36) prayed in the afternoon. Prefatory remarks to *Minchah* and commentary to אַשְׁרֵי appear on pages 6-9.

MINCHAH FOR THE FIRST TWO DAYS

אַשְׁרֵי *Praiseworthy are those who dwell in Your house; may they always praise You, Selah!*[1] *Praiseworthy is the people for whom this is so, praiseworthy is the people whose God is* HASHEM.[2]

Psalm 145

A psalm of praise by David:

א *I will exalt You, my God the King,*
and I will bless Your Name forever and ever.

ב *Every day I will bless You,*
and I will laud Your Name forever and ever.

ג HASHEM *is great and exceedingly lauded,*
and His greatness is beyond investigation.

ד *Each generation will praise Your deeds to the next*
and of Your mighty deeds they will tell.

ה *The splendrous glory of Your power*
and Your wondrous deeds I shall discuss.

ו *And of Your awesome power they will speak,*
and Your greatness I shall relate.

ז *A recollection of Your abundant goodness they will utter*
and of Your righteousness they will sing exultantly.

ח *Gracious and merciful is* HASHEM,
slow to anger, and great in [bestowing] kindness.

ט HASHEM *is good to all; His mercies are on all His works.*

י *All Your works shall thank You,* HASHEM,
and Your devout ones will bless You.

כ *Of the glory of Your kingdom they will speak,*
and of Your power they will tell;

ל *To inform human beings of His mighty deeds,*
and the glorious splendor of His kingdom.

מ *Your kingdom is a kingdom spanning all eternities,*
and Your dominion is throughout every generation.

ס HASHEM *supports all the fallen ones and straightens all the bent.*

ע *The eyes of all look to You with hope*
and You give them their food in its proper time;

פ *You open Your hand,*
and satisfy the desire of every living thing.

While reciting the verse, *'You open . . .'* concentrate intently on its meaning

צ *Righteous is* HASHEM *in all His ways*
and magnanimous in all His deeds.

ק HASHEM *is close to all who call upon Him —*
to all who call upon Him sincerely.

ר *The will of those who fear Him He will do;*
and their cry He will hear, and save them.

ש HASHEM *protects all who love Him;*
but all the wicked He will destroy.

ת Chazzan– *May my mouth declare the praise of* HASHEM
and may all flesh bless His Holy Name forever and ever.

We will bless God from this time and forever, Halleluyah![3]

The primary part of וּבָא לְצִיּוֹן is the *Kedushah* recited by the angels. These verses are presented in bold type and it is preferable that the congregation recite them aloud and in unison. However, the interpretive translation in Aramaic (which follows the verses in bold type) should be recited softly.

וּבָא לְצִיּוֹן גּוֹאֵל,* וּלְשָׁבֵי פֶשַׁע בְּיַעֲקֹב, נְאֻם יהוה. וַאֲנִי, זֹאת בְּרִיתִי* אוֹתָם, אָמַר יהוה, רוּחִי אֲשֶׁר עָלֶיךָ, וּדְבָרַי אֲשֶׁר שַׂמְתִּי בְּפִיךָ, לֹא יָמוּשׁוּ מִפִּיךָ וּמִפִּי זַרְעֲךָ* וּמִפִּי זֶרַע זַרְעֲךָ, אָמַר יהוה, מֵעַתָּה וְעַד עוֹלָם:[1] ❖ וְאַתָּה קָדוֹשׁ יוֹשֵׁב תְּהִלּוֹת יִשְׂרָאֵל.*[2] וְקָרָא זֶה אֶל זֶה וְאָמַר:

קָדוֹשׁ, קָדוֹשׁ, קָדוֹשׁ יהוה צְבָאוֹת, מְלֹא כָל הָאָרֶץ כְּבוֹדוֹ.[3]

וּמְקַבְּלִין דֵּין מִן דֵּין וְאָמְרִין:

קַדִּישׁ בִּשְׁמֵי מְרוֹמָא עִלָּאָה בֵּית שְׁכִינְתֵּהּ,
קַדִּישׁ עַל אַרְעָא עוֹבַד גְּבוּרְתֵּהּ,
קַדִּישׁ לְעָלַם וּלְעָלְמֵי עָלְמַיָּא, יהוה צְבָאוֹת,
מַלְיָא כָל אַרְעָא זִיו יְקָרֵהּ.[4]

❖ וַתִּשָּׂאֵנִי רוּחַ,* וָאֶשְׁמַע אַחֲרַי קוֹל רַעַשׁ גָּדוֹל:

בָּרוּךְ כְּבוֹד יהוה מִמְּקוֹמוֹ.[5]

וּנְטָלַתְנִי רוּחָא, וְשִׁמְעֵת בַּתְרַי קָל זִיעַ סַגִּיא דִּמְשַׁבְּחִין וְאָמְרִין:

בְּרִיךְ יְקָרָא דַיהוה מֵאֲתַר בֵּית שְׁכִינְתֵּהּ.[6]

יהוה יִמְלֹךְ לְעֹלָם וָעֶד.[7]

יהוה מַלְכוּתֵהּ קָאֵם לְעָלַם וּלְעָלְמֵי עָלְמַיָּא.[8]

יהוה אֱלֹהֵי אַבְרָהָם יִצְחָק וְיִשְׂרָאֵל אֲבֹתֵינוּ, שָׁמְרָה זֹּאת* לְעוֹלָם, לְיֵצֶר מַחְשְׁבוֹת לְבַב עַמֶּךָ, וְהָכֵן לְבָבָם אֵלֶיךָ.[9] וְהוּא רַחוּם,

---

◆§ וּבָא לְצִיּוֹן / Uva Letzion

The most important part of the וּבָא לְצִיּוֹן prayer is the recitation of the angel's praises of God.

The Talmud *(Sotah* 49a) declares that since the destruction of the Temple, even the physical beauty and pleasures of the world began deteriorating. If so, by what merit does the world endure? Rava teaches: the *Kedushah* in the prayer *Uva Letzion,* and the recitation of *Kaddish* following the public study of Torah. *Rashi* explains that after the Destruction, the primary focus of holiness in the universe is Torah study. In *Uva Letzion,* the Sages combined the Scriptural verses containing the angel's praise of God with the interpretive translation of *Yonasan ben Uziel.* Thus, this prayer itself constitutes Torah study and its recitation involves the entire congregation in Torah study. This emphasis on Torah study is further stressed by the latter part of *Uva Letzion* which lauds the study and observance of the Torah. The *Kaddish* recited after public Torah study is a further affirmation of the Torah's central role in Jewish existence.

וּבָא לְצִיּוֹן גּוֹאֵל — *A redeemer shall come to Zion.* God pledges that the Messiah will come to redeem the city Zion and the people of Israel. Not only those who remained righteous throughout the ordeal of exile will be saved, but even those who had sinned will join in the glorious future, if they return to the ways of God *(Etz Yosef).*

בְּרִיתִי — *My covenant.* God affirms that His covenant, i.e., His *spirit* of prophecy and *words*

The primary part of וּבָא לְצִיּוֹן, *'A redeemer shall come . . .'*, is the *Kedushah* recited by the angels. These verses are presented in bold type and it is preferable that the congregation recite them aloud and in unison. However, the interpretive translation in Aramaic (which follows the verses in bold type) should be recited softly.

וּבָא לְצִיּוֹן *'A redeemer shall come to Zion* and to those of Jacob who repent from willful sin,' the words of HASHEM. 'And as for Me, this is My covenant* with them,' said HASHEM, 'My spirit that is upon you and My words that I have placed in your mouth shall not be withdrawn from your mouth, nor from the mouth of your offspring,* nor from the mouth of your offspring's offspring,' said HASHEM, 'from this moment and forever.'*[1] Chazzan– *You are the Holy One, enthroned upon the praises of Israel.**[2] *And one [angel] will call another and say:*

'Holy, holy, holy is HASHEM, Master of Legions, the whole world is filled with His glory.'[3]

And they receive permission from one another and say:
'Holy in the most exalted heaven, the abode of His Presence;
holy on earth, product of His strength;
holy forever and ever is HASHEM, Master of Legions —
the entire world is filled with the radiance of His glory.'[4]
Chazzan– *And a wind lifted me;* and I heard behind me the sound of a great noise:*

'Blessed is the glory of HASHEM from His place.'[5]

And a wind lifted me and I heard behind me the sound of the powerful movement of those who praised saying:
'Blessed is the honor of HASHEM
from the place of the abode of His Presence.'[6]

HASHEM shall reign for all eternity.[7]

HASHEM — His kingdom is established forever and ever.[8]

HASHEM, God of Abraham, Isaac, and Israel, our forefathers, may You preserve this forever as the realization of the thoughts in Your people's heart, and may You direct their heart to You.*[9] *He, the Merciful One,*

(1) *Isaiah* 59:20-21. (2) *Psalms* 22:4. (3) *Isaiah* 6:3. (4) *Targum Yonasan.* (5) *Ezekiel* 3:12. (6) *Targum Yonasan.* (7) *Exodus* 15:18. (8) *Targum Onkelos.* (9) *I Chronicles* 29:18.

of Torah, will remain with Israel forever (*Metzudos*).

מִפִּיךָ וּמִפִּי זַרְעֲךָ . . . — *From your mouth, nor from the mouth of your offspring . . .* This is a Divine assurance that if a family produces three consecutive generations of profound Torah scholars, the blessing of Torah knowledge will not be withdrawn from its posterity (*Bava Metzia* 85a). In a broader sense, we see the fulfillment of this blessing in the miracle that Torah greatness has remained with Israel throughout centuries of exile and flight from country to country and from continent to continent (*Siach Yitzchak*).

יוֹשֵׁב תְּהִלּוֹת יִשְׂרָאֵל — *Enthroned upon the praises of Israel.* Although God is praised by myriad angels, He values the praises of Israel above all; as the Sages teach (*Chullin* 90b), the angels are not permitted to sing their praises above until the Jews sing theirs below (*Abudraham*).

וַתִּשָּׂאֵנִי רוּחַ — *And a wind lifted me.* This was uttered by the prophet Ezekiel, who had just been commanded to undertake a difficult mission on behalf of the exiled Jews. God sent a wind to transport him to Babylon, and as he was lifted, he heard the song of the angels. This suggests that the person who ignores his own convenience in order to serve God can expect to climb spiritual heights beyond his normal capacity.

יְכַפֵּר עָוֹן וְלֹא יַשְׁחִית, וְהִרְבָּה לְהָשִׁיב אַפּוֹ, וְלֹא יָעִיר כָּל חֲמָתוֹ.[1] כִּי אַתָּה אֲדֹנָי טוֹב וְסַלָּח, וְרַב חֶסֶד לְכָל קֹרְאֶיךָ.[2] צִדְקָתְךָ צֶדֶק לְעוֹלָם, וְתוֹרָתְךָ אֱמֶת.[3] תִּתֵּן אֱמֶת לְיַעֲקֹב, חֶסֶד לְאַבְרָהָם, אֲשֶׁר נִשְׁבַּעְתָּ לַאֲבֹתֵינוּ מִימֵי קֶדֶם.[4] בָּרוּךְ אֲדֹנָי יוֹם יוֹם יַעֲמָס לָנוּ, הָאֵל יְשׁוּעָתֵנוּ סֶלָה.[5] יהוה צְבָאוֹת עִמָּנוּ, מִשְׂגָּב לָנוּ אֱלֹהֵי יַעֲקֹב סֶלָה.[6] יהוה צְבָאוֹת, אַשְׁרֵי אָדָם בֹּטֵחַ בָּךְ.[7] יהוה הוֹשִׁיעָה, הַמֶּלֶךְ יַעֲנֵנוּ בְיוֹם קָרְאֵנוּ.[8]

בָּרוּךְ הוּא אֱלֹהֵינוּ שֶׁבְּרָאָנוּ לִכְבוֹדוֹ, וְהִבְדִּילָנוּ מִן הַתּוֹעִים, וְנָתַן לָנוּ תּוֹרַת אֱמֶת, וְחַיֵּי עוֹלָם נָטַע בְּתוֹכֵנוּ. הוּא יִפְתַּח לִבֵּנוּ בְּתוֹרָתוֹ, וְיָשֵׂם בְּלִבֵּנוּ אַהֲבָתוֹ וְיִרְאָתוֹ וְלַעֲשׂוֹת רְצוֹנוֹ וּלְעָבְדוֹ בְּלֵבָב שָׁלֵם, לְמַעַן לֹא נִיגַע לָרִיק, וְלֹא נֵלֵד לַבֶּהָלָה.[9]

יְהִי רָצוֹן מִלְּפָנֶיךָ יהוה אֱלֹהֵינוּ וֵאלֹהֵי אֲבוֹתֵינוּ, שֶׁנִּשְׁמֹר חֻקֶּיךָ בָּעוֹלָם הַזֶּה, וְנִזְכֶּה וְנִחְיֶה וְנִרְאֶה וְנִירַשׁ טוֹבָה וּבְרָכָה לִשְׁנֵי יְמוֹת הַמָּשִׁיחַ וּלְחַיֵּי הָעוֹלָם הַבָּא. לְמַעַן יְזַמֶּרְךָ כָבוֹד וְלֹא יִדֹּם, יהוה אֱלֹהַי לְעוֹלָם אוֹדֶךָּ.[10] בָּרוּךְ הַגֶּבֶר אֲשֶׁר יִבְטַח בַּיהוה, וְהָיָה יהוה מִבְטַחוֹ.[11] בִּטְחוּ בַיהוה עֲדֵי עַד, כִּי בְּיָהּ יהוה צוּר עוֹלָמִים.[12] ❖ וְיִבְטְחוּ בְךָ יוֹדְעֵי שְׁמֶךָ, כִּי לֹא עָזַבְתָּ דֹּרְשֶׁיךָ, יהוה.[13] יהוה חָפֵץ לְמַעַן צִדְקוֹ, יַגְדִּיל תּוֹרָה וְיַאְדִּיר.[14]

חצי קדיש

Chazzan recites חֲצִי קַדִּישׁ.

יִתְגַּדַּל וְיִתְקַדַּשׁ שְׁמֵהּ רַבָּא. (Cong.– אָמֵן.) בְּעָלְמָא דִּי בְרָא כִרְעוּתֵהּ. וְיַמְלִיךְ מַלְכוּתֵהּ, בְּחַיֵּיכוֹן וּבְיוֹמֵיכוֹן וּבְחַיֵּי דְכָל בֵּית יִשְׂרָאֵל, בַּעֲגָלָא וּבִזְמַן קָרִיב. וְאִמְרוּ: אָמֵן.

(Cong.– אָמֵן. יְהֵא שְׁמֵהּ רַבָּא מְבָרַךְ לְעָלַם וּלְעָלְמֵי עָלְמַיָּא.)

יְהֵא שְׁמֵהּ רַבָּא מְבָרַךְ לְעָלַם וּלְעָלְמֵי עָלְמַיָּא.

יִתְבָּרַךְ וְיִשְׁתַּבַּח וְיִתְפָּאַר וְיִתְרוֹמַם וְיִתְנַשֵּׂא וְיִתְהַדָּר וְיִתְעַלֶּה וְיִתְהַלָּל שְׁמֵהּ דְּקֻדְשָׁא בְּרִיךְ הוּא (Cong.– בְּרִיךְ הוּא) – לְעֵלָּא מִן כָּל בִּרְכָתָא וְשִׁירָתָא תֻּשְׁבְּחָתָא וְנֶחֱמָתָא, דַּאֲמִירָן בְּעָלְמָא. וְאִמְרוּ: אָמֵן. (Cong.– אָמֵן.)

ON WEEKDAYS CONTINUE WITH *SHEMONEH ESREI,* PAGE 414.
ON THE SABBATH THE TORAH IS READ, PAGE 406.

שָׁמְרָה זֹאת — *May You preserve this.* May God help us remain permanently with the above fervent declaration of His holiness and kingship (*Abudraham*).

is forgiving of iniquity and does not destroy; frequently He withdraws His anger, not arousing His entire rage.[1] *For You, my Lord, are good and forgiving, and abundantly kind to all who call upon You.*[2] *Your righteousness remains righteous forever, and Your Torah is truth.*[3] *Grant truth to Jacob, kindness to Abraham, as You swore to our forefathers from ancient times.*[4] *Blessed is my Lord for every single day, He burdens us with blessings, the God of our salvation, Selah.*[5] *HASHEM, Master of Legions, is with us, a stronghold for us is the God of Jacob, Selah.*[6] *HASHEM, Master of Legions, praiseworthy is the man who trusts in You.*[7] *HASHEM, save! May the King answer us on the day we call.*[8]

Blessed is He, our God, Who created us for His glory, separated us from those who stray, gave us the Torah of truth and implanted eternal life within us. May He open our heart through His Torah and imbue our heart with love and awe of Him and that we may do His will and serve Him wholeheartedly, so that we do not struggle in vain nor produce for futility.[9]

May it be Your will, HASHEM, our God and the God of our forefathers, that we observe Your decrees in This World, and merit that we live and see and inherit goodness and blessing in the years of Messianic times and for the life of the World to Come. So that my soul might sing to You and not be stilled, HASHEM, my God, forever will I thank You.[10] *Blessed is the man who trusts in HASHEM, then HASHEM will be his security.*[11] *Trust in HASHEM forever, for in God, HASHEM, is the strength of the worlds.*[12] Chazzan– *Those knowing Your Name will trust in You, and You forsake not those Who seek You, HASHEM.*[13] *HASHEM desired, for the sake of its [Israel's] righteousness, that the Torah be made great and glorious.*[14]

HALF-KADDISH

Chazzan recites Half-*Kaddish*.

יִתְגַּדַּל *May His great Name grow exalted and sanctified* (Cong.– *Amen.*) *in the world that He created as He willed. May He give reign to His kingship in your lifetimes and in your days, and in the lifetimes of the entire Family of Israel, swiftly and soon. Now respond: Amen.*

(Cong.– *Amen. May His great Name be blessed forever and ever.*)

May His great Name be blessed forever and ever.

Blessed, praised, glorified, exalted, extolled, mighty, upraised, and lauded be the Name of the Holy One, Blessed is He (Cong.– *Blessed is He*) — *beyond any blessing and song, praise and consolation that are uttered in the world. Now respond: Amen.* (Cong.– *Amen*.)

ON WEEKDAYS CONTINUE WITH *SHEMONEH ESREI*, PAGE 414.

ON THE SABBATH THE TORAH IS READ, PAGE 406.

(1) *Psalms* 78:38. (2) 86:5. (3) 119:142. (4) *Micah* 7:20. (5) *Psalms* 68:20. (6) 46:8. (7) 84:13. (8) 20:10. (9) Cf. *Isaiah* 65:23. (10) *Psalms* 30:13. (11) *Jeremiah* 17:7. (12) *Isaiah* 26:4. (13) *Psalms* 9:11. (14) *Isaiah* 42:21.

Congregation, then *chazzan:*

וַאֲנִי תְפִלָּתִי לְךָ יהוה עֵת רָצוֹן, אֱלֹהִים בְּרָב חַסְדֶּךָ, עֲנֵנִי בֶּאֱמֶת יִשְׁעֶךָ.[1]

הוצאת ספר תורה

From the moment the Ark is opened until the Torah is returned to it, one must conduct himself with the utmost respect, and avoid unnecessary conversation. It is commendable to kiss the Torah as it is carried to the *bimah* [reading table] and back to the Ark.

All rise and remain standing until the Torah is placed on the *bimah.*
The Ark is opened; before the Torah is removed the congregation recites:

וַיְהִי בִּנְסֹעַ הָאָרֹן, וַיֹּאמֶר מֹשֶׁה, קוּמָה יהוה וְיָפֻצוּ אֹיְבֶיךָ, וְיָנֻסוּ מְשַׂנְאֶיךָ מִפָּנֶיךָ.[2] כִּי מִצִּיּוֹן תֵּצֵא תוֹרָה, וּדְבַר יהוה מִירוּשָׁלָיִם.[3] בָּרוּךְ שֶׁנָּתַן תּוֹרָה לְעַמּוֹ יִשְׂרָאֵל בִּקְדֻשָּׁתוֹ.

זוהר ויקהל שסט:א

בְּרִיךְ שְׁמֵהּ דְּמָרֵא עָלְמָא, בְּרִיךְ כִּתְרָךְ וְאַתְרָךְ. יְהֵא רְעוּתָךְ עִם עַמָּךְ יִשְׂרָאֵל לְעָלַם, וּפֻרְקַן יְמִינָךְ אַחֲזֵי לְעַמָּךְ בְּבֵית מַקְדְּשָׁךְ, וּלְאַמְטוּיֵי לָנָא מִטּוּב נְהוֹרָךְ, וּלְקַבֵּל צְלוֹתָנָא בְּרַחֲמִין. יְהֵא רַעֲוָא קֳדָמָךְ, דְּתוֹרִיךְ לָן חַיִּין בְּטִיבוּתָא, וְלֶהֱוֵי אֲנָא פְקִידָא בְּגוֹ צַדִּיקַיָּא, לְמִרְחַם עָלַי וּלְמִנְטַר יָתִי וְיַת כָּל דִּי לִי וְדִי לְעַמָּךְ יִשְׂרָאֵל. אַנְתְּ הוּא זָן לְכֹלָּא, וּמְפַרְנֵס לְכֹלָּא, אַנְתְּ הוּא שַׁלִּיט עַל כֹּלָּא. אַנְתְּ הוּא דְּשַׁלִּיט עַל מַלְכַיָּא, וּמַלְכוּתָא דִּילָךְ הִיא. אֲנָא עַבְדָּא דְקֻדְשָׁא בְּרִיךְ הוּא, דְּסָגִידְנָא קַמֵּהּ וּמִקַּמָּא דִּיקַר אוֹרַיְתֵהּ בְּכָל עִדָּן וְעִדָּן. לָא עַל אֱנָשׁ רָחִיצְנָא, וְלָא עַל בַּר אֱלָהִין סָמִיכְנָא, אֶלָּא בֶּאֱלָהָא דִשְׁמַיָּא, דְּהוּא אֱלָהָא קְשׁוֹט, וְאוֹרַיְתֵהּ קְשׁוֹט, וּנְבִיאוֹהִי קְשׁוֹט, וּמַסְגֵּא לְמֶעְבַּד טַבְוָן וּקְשׁוֹט. בֵּהּ אֲנָא רָחִיץ, וְלִשְׁמֵהּ קַדִּישָׁא יַקִּירָא אֲנָא אֵמַר תֻּשְׁבְּחָן. יְהֵא רַעֲוָא קֳדָמָךְ, דְּתִפְתַּח לִבָּאִי בְּאוֹרַיְתָא, וְתַשְׁלִים מִשְׁאֲלִין דְּלִבָּאִי, וְלִבָּא דְכָל עַמָּךְ יִשְׂרָאֵל, לְטַב וּלְחַיִּין וְלִשְׁלָם. (אָמֵן.)

The Torah is removed from the Ark and presented to the *chazzan,* who accepts it in his right arm. He then turns to the Ark and raises the Torah slightly as he bows and recites:

גַּדְּלוּ לַיהוה אִתִּי, וּנְרוֹמְמָה שְׁמוֹ יַחְדָּו.[4]

The *chazzan* turns to his right and carries the Torah to the *bimah,* as the congregation responds:

לְךָ יהוה הַגְּדֻלָּה וְהַגְּבוּרָה וְהַתִּפְאֶרֶת וְהַנֵּצַח וְהַהוֹד, כִּי כֹל בַּשָּׁמַיִם וּבָאָרֶץ, לְךָ יהוה הַמַּמְלָכָה וְהַמִּתְנַשֵּׂא לְכֹל לְרֹאשׁ.[5] רוֹמְמוּ יהוה אֱלֹהֵינוּ וְהִשְׁתַּחֲווּ לַהֲדֹם רַגְלָיו, קָדוֹשׁ הוּא. רוֹמְמוּ יהוה אֱלֹהֵינוּ וְהִשְׁתַּחֲווּ לְהַר קָדְשׁוֹ, כִּי קָדוֹשׁ יהוה אֱלֹהֵינוּ.[6]

Congregation, then *chazzan:*

וַאֲנִי תְפִלָּתִי *As for me, may my prayer to You, HASHEM, be at an opportune time; O God, in Your abundant kindness, answer me with the truth of Your salvation.*[1]

REMOVAL OF THE TORAH FROM THE ARK

From the moment the Ark is opened until the Torah is returned to it, one must conduct himself with the utmost respect, and avoid unnecessary conversation. It is commendable to kiss the Torah as it is carried to the *bimah* [reading table] and back to the Ark.

All rise and remain standing until the Torah is placed on the *bimah*.
The Ark is opened; before the Torah is removed the congregation recites:

וַיְהִי בִּנְסֹעַ *When the Ark would travel, Moses would say, 'Arise, HASHEM, and let Your foes be scattered, let those who hate You flee from You.'*[2] *For from Zion will the Torah come forth and the word of HASHEM from Jerusalem.*[3] *Blessed is He Who gave the Torah to His people Israel in His holiness.*

Zohar, Vayakhel 369a

בְּרִיךְ שְׁמֵהּ *Blessed is the Name of the Master of the universe, blessed is Your crown and Your place. May Your favor remain with Your people Israel forever; may You display the salvation of Your right hand to Your people in Your Holy Temple, to benefit us with the goodness of Your luminescence and to accept our prayers with mercy. May it be Your will that You extend our lives with goodness and that I be numbered among the righteous; that You have mercy on me and protect me, all that is mine and that is Your people Israel's. It is You Who nourishes all and sustains all, You control everything. It is You Who control kings, and Kingship is Yours. I am a servant of the Holy One, Blessed is He, and I prostrate myself before Him and before the glory of His Torah at all times. Not in any man do I put trust, nor on any angel do I rely — only on the God of heaven Who is the God of truth, Whose Torah is truth and Whose prophets are true and Who acts liberally with kindness and truth. In Him do I trust, and to His glorious and Holy Name do I declare praises. May it be Your will that You open my heart to the Torah and that You fulfill the wishes of my heart and the heart of Your entire people Israel for good, for life, and for peace. (Amen.)*

The Torah is removed from the Ark and presented to the *chazzan,* who accepts it in his right arm He then turns to the Ark and raises the Torah slightly as he bows and recites:

Declare the greatness of HASHEM with me, and let us exalt His Name together.[4]

The *chazzan* turns to his right and carries the Torah to the *bimah,* as the congregation responds:

לְךָ *Yours, HASHEM, is the greatness, the strength, the splendor, the triumph, and the glory; even everything in heaven and earth; Yours, HASHEM, is the kingdom, and the sovereignty over every leader.*[5] *Exalt HASHEM, our God, and bow at His footstool; He is Holy! Exalt HASHEM, our God, and bow at His holy mountain; for holy is HASHEM, our God.*[6]

---

(1) *Psalms* 69:14. (2) *Numbers* 10:35. (3) *Isaiah* 2:3.
(4) *Psalms* 34:4. (5) *I Chronicles* 29:11. (6) *Psalms* 99:5,9.

אַב הָרַחֲמִים הוּא יְרַחֵם עַם עֲמוּסִים, וְיִזְכֹּר בְּרִית אֵיתָנִים, וְיַצִּיל נַפְשׁוֹתֵינוּ מִן הַשָּׁעוֹת הָרָעוֹת, וְיִגְעַר בְּיֵצֶר הָרַע מִן הַנְּשׂוּאִים, וְיָחֹן אוֹתָנוּ לִפְלֵיטַת עוֹלָמִים, וִימַלֵּא מִשְׁאֲלוֹתֵינוּ בְּמִדָּה טוֹבָה יְשׁוּעָה וְרַחֲמִים.

The Torah is placed on the *bimah* and prepared for reading.

The *gabbai* uses the following formula to call a *Kohen* to the Torah:

וְתִגָּלֶה וְתֵרָאֶה מַלְכוּתוֹ עָלֵינוּ בִּזְמַן קָרוֹב, וְיָחֹן פְּלֵיטָתֵנוּ וּפְלֵיטַת עַמּוֹ בֵּית יִשְׂרָאֵל לְחֵן וּלְחֶסֶד וּלְרַחֲמִים וּלְרָצוֹן. וְנֹאמַר אָמֵן. הַכֹּל הָבוּ גֹדֶל לֵאלֹהֵינוּ וּתְנוּ כָבוֹד לַתּוֹרָה. כֹּהֵן° קְרָב, יַעֲמֹד (insert name) הַכֹּהֵן.

°If no *Kohen* is present, the *gabbai* says: "אֵין כָּאן כֹּהֵן, יַעֲמֹד (name) יִשְׂרָאֵל (לֵוִי) בִּמְקוֹם כֹּהֵן".

בָּרוּךְ שֶׁנָּתַן תּוֹרָה לְעַמּוֹ יִשְׂרָאֵל בִּקְדֻשָּׁתוֹ. (תּוֹרַת יהוה תְּמִימָה מְשִׁיבַת נָפֶשׁ, עֵדוּת יהוה נֶאֱמָנָה מַחְכִּימַת פֶּתִי. פִּקּוּדֵי יהוה יְשָׁרִים מְשַׂמְּחֵי לֵב, מִצְוַת יהוה בָּרָה מְאִירַת עֵינָיִם.[1] יהוה עֹז לְעַמּוֹ יִתֵּן, יהוה יְבָרֵךְ אֶת עַמּוֹ בַשָּׁלוֹם.[2] הָאֵל תָּמִים דַּרְכּוֹ, אִמְרַת יהוה צְרוּפָה, מָגֵן הוּא לְכֹל הַחֹסִים בּוֹ.[3])

Congregation, then *gabbai:*

וְאַתֶּם הַדְּבֵקִים בַּיהוה אֱלֹהֵיכֶם, חַיִּים כֻּלְּכֶם הַיּוֹם:[4]

קריאת התורה

The reader shows the *oleh* (person called to the Torah) the place in the Torah. The *oleh* touches the Torah with a corner of his *tallis,* or the belt or mantle of the Torah, and kisses it. He then begins the blessing, bowing at בָּרְכוּ, and straightening up at 'ה.

בָּרְכוּ אֶת יהוה הַמְּבֹרָךְ.

Congregation, followed by *oleh,* responds, bowing at בָּרוּךְ, and straightening up at 'ה:

בָּרוּךְ יהוה הַמְּבֹרָךְ לְעוֹלָם וָעֶד.

Oleh continues:

בָּרוּךְ אַתָּה יהוה אֱלֹהֵינוּ מֶלֶךְ הָעוֹלָם, אֲשֶׁר בָּחַר בָּנוּ מִכָּל הָעַמִּים, וְנָתַן לָנוּ אֶת תּוֹרָתוֹ. בָּרוּךְ אַתָּה יהוה, נוֹתֵן הַתּוֹרָה.

(–Cong. אָמֵן.)

After his Torah portion has been read, the *oleh* recites:

בָּרוּךְ אַתָּה יהוה אֱלֹהֵינוּ מֶלֶךְ הָעוֹלָם, אֲשֶׁר נָתַן לָנוּ תּוֹרַת אֱמֶת, וְחַיֵּי עוֹלָם נָטַע בְּתוֹכֵנוּ. בָּרוּךְ אַתָּה יהוה, נוֹתֵן הַתּוֹרָה.

(–Cong. אָמֵן.)

THE VARIOUS מִי שֶׁבֵּרַךְ PRAYERS APPEAR ON PAGE 308.

❧ THE TORAH READING ON THE SABBATH ❧

The Torah reading during the Sabbath *Minchah* includes the calling to the Torah of *Kohen,* Levite, and Israelite. The reading is the first section of the next *sidrah* in the regular order of weekly Torah reading. Thus, on the Sabbath of Succos, the first seventeen verses of *V'zos HaBerachah* are read.

The Torah reading just before the end of the

אַב הָרַחֲמִים *May the Father of mercy have mercy on the nation that is borne by Him, and may He remember the covenant of the spiritually mighty. May He rescue our souls from the bad times, and upbraid the evil inclination to leave those borne by Him, graciously make us an eternal remnant, and fulfill our requests in good measure, for salvation and mercy.*

The Torah is placed on the *bimah* and prepared for reading.
The *gabbai* uses the following formula to call a *Kohen* to the Torah:

וְתִגָּלֶה *And may His kingship over us be revealed and become visible soon, and may He be gracious to our remnant and the remnant of His people the Family of Israel, for graciousness, kindness, mercy, and favor. And let us respond, Amen. All of you ascribe greatness to our God and give honor to the Torah. Kohen,° approach. Stand* (name) *son of* (father's name) *the Kohen.*

°If no *Kohen* is present, the *gabbai* says: *'There is no Kohen present, stand* (name) *son of* (father's name) *an Israelite (Levite) in place of the Kohen.'*

Blessed is He Who gave the Torah to His people Israel in His holiness (The Torah of HASHEM is perfect, restoring the soul; the testimony of HASHEM is trustworthy, making the simple one wise. The orders of HASHEM are upright, gladdening the heart; the command of HASHEM is clear, enlightening the eyes.[1] HASHEM will give might to His people; HASHEM will bless His people with peace.[2] The God Whose way is perfect, the promise of HASHEM is flawless, He is a shield for all who take refuge in Him.[3])

Congregation, then *gabbai:*

You who cling to HASHEM your God—you are all alive today.[4]

READING OF THE TORAH

The reader shows the *oleh* (person called to the Torah) the place in the Torah. The *oleh* touches the Torah with a corner of his *tallis,* or the belt or mantle of the Torah, and kisses it. He then begins the blessing, bowing at *'Bless,'* and straightening up at 'HASHEM':

Bless HASHEM, the blessed One.

Congregation, followed by *oleh,* responds, bowing at 'Blessed,' and straightening up at 'HASHEM.'

Blessed is HASHEM, the blessed One, for all eternity.

Oleh continues:

בָּרוּךְ *Blessed are You, HASHEM, our God, King of the universe, Who selected us from all the peoples and gave us His Torah. Blessed are You, HASHEM, Giver of the Torah.* (Cong.— *Amen.)*

After his Torah portion has been read, the *oleh* recites:

בָּרוּךְ *Blessed are You, HASHEM, our God, King of the universe, Who gave us the Torah of truth and implanted eternal life within us. Blessed are You, HASHEM, Giver of the Torah.* (Cong.— *Amen.)*

THE VARIOUS *MI SHEBEIRACH* PRAYERS APPEAR ON PAGE 308.

(1) *Psalms* 19:8-9. (2) 29:11. (3) 18:31. (4) *Deuteronomy* 4:4.

Sabbath symbolizes that we will take the Torah-imbued spirit of the Sabbath with us into the next week. Commentary on this portion appears on page 1158.

דברים לג:א-כו (Commentary on page 1158.)

כהן – וְזֹאת הַבְּרָכָה אֲשֶׁר בֵּרַךְ מֹשֶׁה אִישׁ הָאֱלֹהִים אֶת־בְּנֵי יִשְׂרָאֵל לִפְנֵי מוֹתוֹ: וַיֹּאמַר יהוה מִסִּינַי בָּא וְזָרַח מִשֵּׂעִיר לָמוֹ הוֹפִיעַ מֵהַר פָּארָן וְאָתָה מֵרִבְבֹת קֹדֶשׁ מִימִינוֹ אֵשׁ דָּת לָמוֹ: אַף חֹבֵב עַמִּים כָּל־קְדֹשָׁיו בְּיָדֶךָ וְהֵם תֻּכּוּ לְרַגְלֶךָ יִשָּׂא מִדַּבְּרֹתֶיךָ: תּוֹרָה צִוָּה־לָנוּ מֹשֶׁה מוֹרָשָׁה קְהִלַּת יַעֲקֹב: וַיְהִי בִישֻׁרוּן מֶלֶךְ בְּהִתְאַסֵּף רָאשֵׁי עָם יַחַד שִׁבְטֵי יִשְׂרָאֵל: יְחִי רְאוּבֵן וְאַל־יָמֹת וִיהִי מְתָיו מִסְפָּר: וְזֹאת לִיהוּדָה וַיֹּאמַר שְׁמַע יהוה קוֹל יְהוּדָה וְאֶל־עַמּוֹ תְּבִיאֶנּוּ יָדָיו רָב לוֹ וְעֵזֶר מִצָּרָיו תִּהְיֶה:

לוי – וּלְלֵוִי אָמַר תֻּמֶּיךָ וְאוּרֶיךָ לְאִישׁ חֲסִידֶךָ אֲשֶׁר נִסִּיתוֹ בְּמַסָּה תְּרִיבֵהוּ עַל־מֵי מְרִיבָה: הָאֹמֵר לְאָבִיו וּלְאִמּוֹ לֹא רְאִיתִיו וְאֶת־אֶחָיו לֹא הִכִּיר וְאֶת־בָּנָו לֹא יָדָע כִּי שָׁמְרוּ אִמְרָתֶךָ וּבְרִיתְךָ יִנְצֹרוּ: יוֹרוּ מִשְׁפָּטֶיךָ לְיַעֲקֹב וְתוֹרָתְךָ לְיִשְׂרָאֵל יָשִׂימוּ קְטוֹרָה בְּאַפֶּךָ וְכָלִיל עַל־מִזְבְּחֶךָ: בָּרֵךְ יהוה חֵילוֹ וּפֹעַל יָדָיו תִּרְצֶה מְחַץ מָתְנַיִם קָמָיו וּמְשַׂנְאָיו מִן־יְקוּמוּן: לְבִנְיָמִן אָמַר יְדִיד יהוה יִשְׁכֹּן לָבֶטַח עָלָיו חֹפֵף עָלָיו כָּל־הַיּוֹם וּבֵין כְּתֵפָיו שָׁכֵן:

ישראל – וּלְיוֹסֵף אָמַר מְבֹרֶכֶת יהוה אַרְצוֹ מִמֶּגֶד שָׁמַיִם מִטָּל וּמִתְּהוֹם רֹבֶצֶת תָּחַת: וּמִמֶּגֶד תְּבוּאֹת שָׁמֶשׁ וּמִמֶּגֶד גֶּרֶשׁ יְרָחִים: וּמֵרֹאשׁ הַרְרֵי־קֶדֶם וּמִמֶּגֶד גִּבְעוֹת עוֹלָם: וּמִמֶּגֶד אֶרֶץ וּמְלֹאָהּ וּרְצוֹן שֹׁכְנִי סְנֶה תָּבוֹאתָה לְרֹאשׁ יוֹסֵף וּלְקָדְקֹד נְזִיר אֶחָיו: בְּכוֹר שׁוֹרוֹ הָדָר לוֹ וְקַרְנֵי רְאֵם קַרְנָיו בָּהֶם עַמִּים יְנַגַּח יַחְדָּו אַפְסֵי־אָרֶץ וְהֵם רִבְבוֹת אֶפְרַיִם וְהֵם אַלְפֵי מְנַשֶּׁה:

When the Torah reading has been completed, the Torah is raised for all to see. Each person looks at the Torah and recites aloud:

וְזֹאת הַתּוֹרָה אֲשֶׁר שָׂם מֹשֶׁה לִפְנֵי בְּנֵי יִשְׂרָאֵל,[1] עַל פִּי יהוה בְּיַד מֹשֶׁה.[2]

(1) *Deuteronomy* 4:44. (2) *Numbers* 9:23.

Deuteronomy 33:1-26 (Commentary on page 1158.)

Kohen – *This is the blessing that Moses, the man of God, bestowed upon the Children of Israel before his death.*

He said: H*ASHEM* *approached from Sinai — having shone forth to them from Seir, having appeared from Mount Paran, and then approached with some of the holy myriads — from His right hand He presented the fiery Torah to them. Indeed, You greatly loved the tribes, all their righteous ones were in Your hands; for they planted themselves at Your feet, accepting the burden of Your utterances: "The Torah which Moses charged us is the heritage of the Congregation of Jacob. He became King over Jeshurun when the leaders of the nation gathered — the tribes of Israel in unity."*

May Reuben live and not die, and may his population be counted among the others.

And this to Judah, and he said: Hear, O H*ASHEM*. *Judah's prayer, and return him safely to his people; may his hands gain him triumph and may You remain a helper against his enemies.*

Levi – *Of Levi he said: Your Tumim and your Urim befit Your devout one, whom You tested at Massah, and whom You challenged at the waters of Meribah. The one who said of his father and mother, "I have not favored him," he disregarded his brothers and ignored his own children; for they [i.e., the Levites] have observed Your word, and preserved Your covenant. Thus it is they who are worthy to teach Your law to Jacob and Your Torah to Israel; it is they who shall place incense before Your presence, and burnt offerings on Your altar. Bless, O* H*ASHEM*, *his resources, and favor his handiwork. Smash the loins of his foes, and his enemies that they may not rise again.*

Of Benjamin he said: May H*ASHEM's* *beloved dwell securely by Him; He hovers above him all day long; and rests His Presence among his hills.*

Third – *Of Joseph he said: His land is blessed by* H*ASHEM* *— with the heavenly bounty of dew, and with the deep waters crouching below: with the bounty of the sun's crops, and with the bounty of the moon's yield; with the quick-ripening crops of the ancient mountains, and with the bounty of eternally fertile hills; with the bounty of the land and its fullness, and by the favor of Him Who rested upon the thornbush. May this blessing rest upon Joseph's head, and upon the crown of him who was separated from his brothers. Sovereignty will go to his most distinguished, mighty descendant; and his glory will be like the horns of a re'eim; with both of them together he shall gore nations to the ends of the earth; they are the myriads of Ephraim's victims, and the thousands of Menashe's victims.*

When the Torah reading has been completed, the Torah is raised for all to see. Each person looks at the Torah and recites aloud:

This is the Torah that Moses placed
before the Children of Israel,[1]
upon the command of HASHEM, through Moses' hand.[2]

Some add the following verses:

עֵץ חַיִּים הִיא לַמַּחֲזִיקִים בָּהּ, וְתֹמְכֶיהָ מְאֻשָּׁר.[1] דְּרָכֶיהָ דַרְכֵי נֹעַם, וְכָל נְתִיבוֹתֶיהָ שָׁלוֹם.[2] אֹרֶךְ יָמִים בִּימִינָהּ, בִּשְׂמֹאלָהּ עֹשֶׁר וְכָבוֹד.[3] יהוה חָפֵץ לְמַעַן צִדְקוֹ, יַגְדִּיל תּוֹרָה וְיַאְדִּיר.[4]

Chazzan takes the Torah in his right arm and recites:

יְהַלְלוּ אֶת שֵׁם יהוה, כִּי נִשְׂגָּב שְׁמוֹ לְבַדּוֹ –

Congregation responds:

– הוֹדוֹ עַל אֶרֶץ וְשָׁמָיִם. וַיָּרֶם קֶרֶן לְעַמּוֹ, תְּהִלָּה לְכָל חֲסִידָיו, לִבְנֵי יִשְׂרָאֵל עַם קְרֹבוֹ, הַלְלוּיָהּ.[5]

As the Torah is carried to the Ark, congregation recites Psalm 24, לְדָוִד מִזְמוֹר.

לְדָוִד מִזְמוֹר, לַיהוה הָאָרֶץ וּמְלוֹאָהּ, תֵּבֵל וְיֹשְׁבֵי בָהּ. כִּי הוּא עַל יַמִּים יְסָדָהּ, וְעַל נְהָרוֹת יְכוֹנְנֶהָ. מִי יַעֲלֶה בְהַר יהוה, וּמִי יָקוּם בִּמְקוֹם קָדְשׁוֹ. נְקִי כַפַּיִם וּבַר לֵבָב, אֲשֶׁר לֹא נָשָׂא לַשָּׁוְא נַפְשִׁי וְלֹא נִשְׁבַּע לְמִרְמָה. יִשָּׂא בְרָכָה מֵאֵת יהוה, וּצְדָקָה מֵאֱלֹהֵי יִשְׁעוֹ. זֶה דּוֹר דֹּרְשָׁיו, מְבַקְשֵׁי פָנֶיךָ, יַעֲקֹב, סֶלָה. שְׂאוּ שְׁעָרִים רָאשֵׁיכֶם, וְהִנָּשְׂאוּ פִּתְחֵי עוֹלָם, וְיָבוֹא מֶלֶךְ הַכָּבוֹד. מִי זֶה מֶלֶךְ הַכָּבוֹד, יהוה עִזּוּז וְגִבּוֹר, יהוה גִּבּוֹר מִלְחָמָה. שְׂאוּ שְׁעָרִים רָאשֵׁיכֶם, וּשְׂאוּ פִּתְחֵי עוֹלָם, וְיָבֹא מֶלֶךְ הַכָּבוֹד. מִי הוּא זֶה מֶלֶךְ הַכָּבוֹד, יהוה צְבָאוֹת הוּא מֶלֶךְ הַכָּבוֹד, סֶלָה.

As the Torah is placed into the Ark, congregation recites the following verses:

וּבְנֻחֹה יֹאמַר, שׁוּבָה יהוה רִבְבוֹת אַלְפֵי יִשְׂרָאֵל.[6] קוּמָה יהוה לִמְנוּחָתֶךָ, אַתָּה וַאֲרוֹן עֻזֶּךָ. כֹּהֲנֶיךָ יִלְבְּשׁוּ צֶדֶק, וַחֲסִידֶיךָ יְרַנֵּנוּ. בַּעֲבוּר דָּוִד עַבְדֶּךָ אַל תָּשֵׁב פְּנֵי מְשִׁיחֶךָ.[7] כִּי לֶקַח טוֹב נָתַתִּי לָכֶם, תּוֹרָתִי אַל תַּעֲזֹבוּ.[8] ❖ עֵץ חַיִּים הִיא לַמַּחֲזִיקִים בָּהּ, וְתֹמְכֶיהָ מְאֻשָּׁר.[9] דְּרָכֶיהָ דַרְכֵי נֹעַם, וְכָל נְתִיבֹתֶיהָ שָׁלוֹם.[10] הֲשִׁיבֵנוּ יהוה אֵלֶיךָ וְנָשׁוּבָה, חַדֵּשׁ יָמֵינוּ כְּקֶדֶם.[11]

The Ark is closed and the *chazzan* recites חֲצִי קַדִּישׁ.

יִתְגַּדַּל וְיִתְקַדַּשׁ שְׁמֵהּ רַבָּא. (.Cong – אָמֵן.) בְּעָלְמָא דִּי בְרָא כִרְעוּתֵהּ. וְיַמְלִיךְ מַלְכוּתֵהּ, בְּחַיֵּיכוֹן וּבְיוֹמֵיכוֹן וּבְחַיֵּי דְכָל בֵּית יִשְׂרָאֵל, בַּעֲגָלָא וּבִזְמַן קָרִיב. וְאִמְרוּ: אָמֵן.

(.Cong – אָמֵן. יְהֵא שְׁמֵהּ רַבָּא מְבָרַךְ לְעָלַם וּלְעָלְמֵי עָלְמַיָּא.)

יְהֵא שְׁמֵהּ רַבָּא מְבָרַךְ לְעָלַם וּלְעָלְמֵי עָלְמַיָּא.

יִתְבָּרַךְ וְיִשְׁתַּבַּח וְיִתְפָּאַר וְיִתְרוֹמַם וְיִתְנַשֵּׂא וְיִתְהַדָּר וְיִתְעַלֶּה וְיִתְהַלָּל שְׁמֵהּ דְּקֻדְשָׁא בְּרִיךְ הוּא (.Cong – בְּרִיךְ הוּא) – לְעֵלָּא מִן כָּל בִּרְכָתָא וְשִׁירָתָא תֻּשְׁבְּחָתָא וְנֶחֱמָתָא, דַּאֲמִירָן בְּעָלְמָא. וְאִמְרוּ: אָמֵן. (.Cong – אָמֵן.)

(1) *Proverbs* 3:18. (2) 3:17. (3) 3:16. (4) *Isaiah* 42:21. (5) *Psalms* 148:13-14. (6) *Numbers* 10:36. (7) *Psalms* 132:8-10. (8) *Proverbs* 4:2. (9) 3:18. (10) 3:17. (11) *Lamentations* 5:21.

Some add the following verses:

עֵץ *It is a tree of life for those who grasp it, and its supporters are praiseworthy.*[1] *Its ways are ways of pleasantness and all its paths are peace.*[2] *Lengthy days are at its right; at its left are wealth and honor.*[3] *HASHEM desired, for the sake of its [Israel's] righteousness, that the Torah be made great and glorious.*[4]

Chazzan takes the Torah in his right arm and recites:

Let them praise the Name of HASHEM,
for His Name alone will have been exalted —

Congregation responds:

— His glory is above earth and heaven. And He will have exalted the pride of His people, causing praise for all His devout ones, for the Children of Israel, His intimate nation. Halleluyah![5]

As the Torah is carried to the Ark, congregation recites Psalm 24, *'Of David a psalm.'*

לְדָוִד *Of David a psalm. HASHEM's is the earth and its fullness, the inhabited land and those who dwell in it. For He founded it upon seas, and established it upon rivers. Who may ascend the mountain of HASHEM, and who may stand in the place of His sanctity? One with clean hands and pure heart, who has not sworn in vain by My soul and has not sworn deceitfully. He will receive a blessing from HASHEM and just kindness from the God of his salvation. This is the generation of those who seek Him, those who strive for Your Presence — Jacob, Selah. Raise up your heads, O gates, and be uplifted, you everlasting entrances, so that the King of Glory may enter. Who is this King of Glory? — HASHEM, the mighty and strong, HASHEM, the strong in battle. Raise up your heads, O gates, and raise up, you everlasting entrances, so that the King of Glory may enter. Who then is the King of Glory? HASHEM, Master of Legions, He is the King of Glory. Selah!*

As the Torah is placed into the Ark, congregation recites the following verses:

וּבְנֻחֹה *And when it rested he would say, 'Return, HASHEM, to the myriad thousands of Israel.'*[6] *Arise, HASHEM, to Your resting place, You and the Ark of Your strength. Let Your priests be clothed in righteousness, and Your devout ones will sing joyously. For the sake of David, Your servant, turn not away the face of Your anointed.*[7] *For I have given you a good teaching, do not forsake My Torah.*[8] Chazzan— *It is a tree of life for those who grasp it, and its supporters are praiseworthy.*[9] *Its ways are ways of pleasantness and all its paths are peace.*[10] *Bring us back to You, HASHEM, and we shall return, renew our days as of old.*[11]

The Ark is closed and the *chazzan* recites Half-*Kaddish*.

יִתְגַּדַּל *May His great Name grow exalted and sanctified* (Cong.— *Amen.*) *in the world that He created as He willed. May He give reign to His kingship in your lifetimes and in your days, and in the lifetimes of the entire Family of Israel, swiftly and soon. Now respond: Amen.*

(Cong.— *Amen. May His great Name be blessed forever and ever.*)
May His great Name be blessed forever and ever.

Blessed, praised, glorified, exalted, extolled, mighty, upraised, and lauded be the Name of the Holy One, Blessed is He (Cong.— *Blessed is He*) *— beyond any blessing and song, praise and consolation that are uttered in the world. Now respond: Amen.* (Cong.— *Amen.*)

שמונה עשרה – עמידה

Take three steps backward, then three steps forward. Remain standing with the feet together while reciting *Shemoneh Esrei.* Recite it with quiet devotion and without interruption, verbal or otherwise. Although its recitation should not be audible to others, one must pray loudly enough to hear himself.

כִּי שֵׁם יהוה אֶקְרָא,* הָבוּ גֹדֶל לֵאלֹהֵינוּ.[1]

אֲדֹנָי שְׂפָתַי תִּפְתָּח, וּפִי יַגִּיד תְּהִלָּתֶךָ.[2]

אבות

Bend the knees at בָּרוּךְ; bow at אַתָּה; straighten up at ה׳.

בָּרוּךְ אַתָּה יהוה אֱלֹהֵינוּ וֵאלֹהֵי אֲבוֹתֵינוּ, אֱלֹהֵי אַבְרָהָם, אֱלֹהֵי יִצְחָק, וֵאלֹהֵי יַעֲקֹב, הָאֵל הַגָּדוֹל הַגִּבּוֹר וְהַנּוֹרָא, אֵל עֶלְיוֹן, גּוֹמֵל חֲסָדִים טוֹבִים וְקוֹנֵה הַכֹּל, וְזוֹכֵר חַסְדֵי אָבוֹת, וּמֵבִיא גוֹאֵל לִבְנֵי בְנֵיהֶם, לְמַעַן שְׁמוֹ בְּאַהֲבָה. מֶלֶךְ עוֹזֵר וּמוֹשִׁיעַ וּמָגֵן.

Bend the knees at בָּרוּךְ; bow at אַתָּה; straighten up at ה׳.

בָּרוּךְ אַתָּה יהוה, מָגֵן אַבְרָהָם.

גבורות

אַתָּה גִּבּוֹר לְעוֹלָם אֲדֹנָי, מְחַיֵּה מֵתִים אַתָּה, רַב לְהוֹשִׁיעַ. מְכַלְכֵּל חַיִּים בְּחֶסֶד, מְחַיֵּה מֵתִים בְּרַחֲמִים רַבִּים, סוֹמֵךְ נוֹפְלִים, וְרוֹפֵא חוֹלִים, וּמַתִּיר אֲסוּרִים, וּמְקַיֵּם אֱמוּנָתוֹ לִישֵׁנֵי עָפָר. מִי כָמוֹךָ בַּעַל גְּבוּרוֹת, וּמִי דּוֹמֶה לָּךְ, מֶלֶךְ מֵמִית וּמְחַיֶּה וּמַצְמִיחַ יְשׁוּעָה. וְנֶאֱמָן אַתָּה לְהַחֲיוֹת מֵתִים. בָּרוּךְ אַתָּה יהוה, מְחַיֵּה הַמֵּתִים.

During the *chazzan's* repetition, *Kedushah* (below) is recited at this point.

קדושה

When reciting *Kedushah,* one must stand with his feet together and avoid any interruptions. One should rise on his toes when saying the words קָדוֹשׁ, קָדוֹשׁ, קָדוֹשׁ; בָּרוּךְ כְּבוֹד (of בָּרוּךְ); and יִמְלֹךְ.

Cong. then *Chazzan* – **נְקַדֵּשׁ** אֶת שִׁמְךָ בָּעוֹלָם, כְּשֵׁם שֶׁמַּקְדִּישִׁים אוֹתוֹ בִּשְׁמֵי מָרוֹם, כַּכָּתוּב עַל יַד נְבִיאֶךָ, וְקָרָא זֶה אֶל זֶה וְאָמַר:

All – קָדוֹשׁ קָדוֹשׁ קָדוֹשׁ יהוה צְבָאוֹת, מְלֹא כָל הָאָרֶץ כְּבוֹדוֹ.[3]

Chazzan – לְעֻמָּתָם בָּרוּךְ יֹאמֵרוּ:

All – בָּרוּךְ כְּבוֹד יהוה, מִמְּקוֹמוֹ.[4]

Chazzan – וּבְדִבְרֵי קָדְשְׁךָ כָּתוּב לֵאמֹר:

All – יִמְלֹךְ יהוה לְעוֹלָם, אֱלֹהַיִךְ צִיּוֹן לְדֹר וָדֹר, הַלְלוּיָהּ.[5]

Chazzan only concludes – לְדוֹר וָדוֹר נַגִּיד גָּדְלֶךָ וּלְנֵצַח נְצָחִים קְדֻשָּׁתְךָ נַקְדִּישׁ, וְשִׁבְחֲךָ אֱלֹהֵינוּ מִפִּינוּ לֹא יָמוּשׁ לְעוֹלָם וָעֶד, כִּי אֵל מֶלֶךְ גָּדוֹל וְקָדוֹשׁ אָתָּה. בָּרוּךְ אַתָּה יהוה, הָאֵל הַקָּדוֹשׁ.

Chazzan continues . . . אַתָּה בְחַרְתָּנוּ (page 416).

SHEMONEH ESREI – AMIDAH

Take three steps backward, then three steps forward. Remain standing with the feet together while reciting *Shemoneh Esrei.* Recite it with quiet devotion and without interruption, verbal or otherwise. Although its recitation should not be audible to others, one must pray loudly enough to hear himself.

When I call out the Name of HASHEM, ascribe greatness to our God.[1]

My Lord, open my lips, that my mouth may declare Your praise.[2]

PATRIARCHS

Bend the knees at *'Blessed'*; bow at *'You'*; straighten up at *'HASHEM.'*

בָּרוּךְ *Blessed are You, HASHEM, our God and the God of our forefathers, God of Abraham, God of Isaac, and God of Jacob; the great, mighty, and awesome God, the supreme God, Who bestows beneficial kindnesses and creates everything, Who recalls the kindnesses of the Patriarchs and brings a Redeemer to their children's children, for His Name's sake, with love.*

Bend the knees at *'Blessed'*; bow at *'You'*; straighten up at 'HASHEM.'

O King, Helper, Savior, and Shield. Blessed are You, HASHEM, Shield of Abraham.

GOD'S MIGHT

אַתָּה *You are eternally mighty, my Lord, the Resuscitator of the dead are You; abundantly able to save. He sustains the living with kindness, resuscitates the dead with abundant mercy, supports the fallen, heals the sick, releases the confined, and maintains His faith to those asleep in the dust. Who is like You, O Master of mighty deeds, and who is comparable to You, O King Who causes death and restores life and makes salvation sprout! And You are faithful to resuscitate the dead. Blessed are You, HASHEM, Who resuscitates the dead.*

During the *chazzan's* repetition, *Kedushah* (below) is recited at this point.

KEDUSHAH

When reciting *Kedushah*, one must stand with his feet together and avoid any interruptions. One should rise on his toes when saying the words *Holy, holy, holy; Blessed is;* and *HASHEM shall reign.*

Cong. then Chazzan – **נְקַדֵּשׁ** *We shall sanctify Your Name in this world, just as they sanctify it in heaven above, as it is written by Your prophet, "And one [angel] will call another and say:*

All – *'Holy, holy, holy is HASHEM, Master of Legions, the whole world is filled with His glory.'"*[3]

Chazzan – *Those facing them say 'Blessed':*

All – *'Blessed is the glory of HASHEM from His place.'*[4]

Chazzan – *And in Your holy Writings the following is written:*

All – *'HASHEM shall reign forever — your God, O Zion — from generation to generation, Halleluyah!'*[5]

Chazzan only concludes – *From generation to generation we shall relate Your greatness and for infinite eternities we shall proclaim Your holiness. Your praise, our God, shall not leave our mouth forever and ever, for You, O God, are a great and holy King. Blessed are You, HASHEM, the holy God.*

Chazzan continues אַתָּה בְחַרְתָּנוּ, *You have chosen us . . .* (page 416).

---

(1) *Deuteronomy* 32:3. (2) *Psalms* 51:17. (3) *Isaiah* 6:3. (4) *Ezekiel* 3:12. (5) *Psalms* 146:10.

קדושת השם

אַתָּה קָדוֹשׁ וְשִׁמְךָ קָדוֹשׁ, וּקְדוֹשִׁים בְּכָל יוֹם יְהַלְלוּךָ סֶּלָה. בָּרוּךְ אַתָּה יהוה, הָאֵל הַקָּדוֹשׁ.

קדושת היום

אַתָּה בְחַרְתָּנוּ מִכָּל הָעַמִּים, אָהַבְתָּ אוֹתָנוּ, וְרָצִיתָ בָּנוּ, וְרוֹמַמְתָּנוּ מִכָּל הַלְּשׁוֹנוֹת, וְקִדַּשְׁתָּנוּ בְּמִצְוֹתֶיךָ, וְקֵרַבְתָּנוּ מַלְכֵּנוּ לַעֲבוֹדָתֶךָ, וְשִׁמְךָ הַגָּדוֹל וְהַקָּדוֹשׁ עָלֵינוּ קָרָאתָ.

On the Sabbath add the words in brackets. [If forgotten, see *Laws* §86-90.]

וַתִּתֶּן לָנוּ יהוה אֱלֹהֵינוּ בְּאַהֲבָה [שַׁבָּתוֹת לִמְנוּחָה וּ]מוֹעֲדִים לְשִׂמְחָה חַגִּים וּזְמַנִּים לְשָׂשׂוֹן, אֶת יוֹם [הַשַּׁבָּת הַזֶּה וְאֶת יוֹם] חַג הַסֻּכּוֹת הַזֶּה, זְמַן שִׂמְחָתֵנוּ [בְּאַהֲבָה] מִקְרָא קֹדֶשׁ, זֵכֶר לִיצִיאַת מִצְרָיִם.

During the *chazzan's* repetition, congregation responds אָמֵן as indicated.

אֱלֹהֵינוּ וֵאלֹהֵי אֲבוֹתֵינוּ, יַעֲלֶה, וְיָבֹא, וְיַגִּיעַ, וְיֵרָאֶה, וְיֵרָצֶה, וְיִשָּׁמַע, וְיִפָּקֵד, וְיִזָּכֵר זִכְרוֹנֵנוּ וּפִקְדוֹנֵנוּ, וְזִכְרוֹן אֲבוֹתֵינוּ, וְזִכְרוֹן מָשִׁיחַ בֶּן דָּוִד עַבְדֶּךָ, וְזִכְרוֹן יְרוּשָׁלַיִם עִיר קָדְשֶׁךָ, וְזִכְרוֹן כָּל עַמְּךָ בֵּית יִשְׂרָאֵל לְפָנֶיךָ, לִפְלֵיטָה לְטוֹבָה לְחֵן וּלְחֶסֶד וּלְרַחֲמִים, לְחַיִּים וּלְשָׁלוֹם בְּיוֹם חַג הַסֻּכּוֹת הַזֶּה. זָכְרֵנוּ יהוה אֱלֹהֵינוּ בּוֹ לְטוֹבָה (Cong. – אָמֵן), וּפָקְדֵנוּ בוֹ לִבְרָכָה (Cong. – אָמֵן), וְהוֹשִׁיעֵנוּ בוֹ לְחַיִּים (Cong. – אָמֵן). וּבִדְבַר יְשׁוּעָה וְרַחֲמִים, חוּס וְחָנֵּנוּ וְרַחֵם עָלֵינוּ וְהוֹשִׁיעֵנוּ, כִּי אֵלֶיךָ עֵינֵינוּ, כִּי אֵל מֶלֶךְ חַנּוּן וְרַחוּם אָתָּה.[1]

On the Sabbath add the words in brackets. [If forgotten, see Laws §86-90.]

וְהַשִּׂיאֵנוּ יהוה אֱלֹהֵינוּ אֶת בִּרְכַּת מוֹעֲדֶיךָ לְחַיִּים וּלְשָׁלוֹם, לְשִׂמְחָה וּלְשָׂשׂוֹן, כַּאֲשֶׁר רָצִיתָ וְאָמַרְתָּ לְבָרְכֵנוּ. [אֱלֹהֵינוּ וֵאלֹהֵי אֲבוֹתֵינוּ רְצֵה בִמְנוּחָתֵנוּ] קַדְּשֵׁנוּ בְּמִצְוֹתֶיךָ וְתֵן חֶלְקֵנוּ בְּתוֹרָתֶךָ, שַׂבְּעֵנוּ מִטּוּבֶךָ וְשַׂמְּחֵנוּ בִּישׁוּעָתֶךָ, וְטַהֵר לִבֵּנוּ

HOLINESS OF GOD'S NAME

אַתָּה *You are holy and Your Name is holy, and holy ones praise You every day, forever. Blessed are You,* H*ASHEM, the holy God.*

SANCTIFICATION OF THE DAY

אַתָּה בְחַרְתָּנוּ *You have chosen us from all the peoples; You loved us and found favor in us; You exalted us above all the tongues and You sanctified us with Your commandments. You drew us close, our King, to Your service and proclaimed Your great and Holy Name upon us.*

On the Sabbath add the words in brackets. [If forgotten, see *Laws* §86-90.]

וַתִּתֶּן לָנוּ *And You gave us,* H*ASHEM, our God, with love [Sabbaths for rest], appointed festivals for gladness, Festivals and times for joy, [this day of Sabbath and] this day of the Festival of Succos, the time of our gladness [with love], a holy convocation, a memorial of the Exodus from Egypt.*

During the *chazzan's* repetition, congregation responds *Amen* as indicated.

אֱלֹהֵינוּ *Our God and God of our forefathers, may there rise, come, reach, be noted, be favored, be heard, be considered, and be remembered — the remembrance and consideration of ourselves; the remembrance of our forefathers; the remembrance of Messiah, son of David, Your servant; the remembrance of Jerusalem, the City of Your Holiness; the remembrance of Your entire people the Family of Israel — before You for deliverance, for goodness, for grace, for kindness, and for compassion, for life, and for peace on this day of the Festival of Succos. Remember us on it,* H*ASHEM, our God, for goodness (*Cong.*–Amen); consider us on it for blessing (*Cong.*–Amen); and help us on it for life (*Cong.*–Amen). In the matter of salvation and compassion, pity, be gracious and compassionate with us and help us, for our eyes are turned to You, because You are God, the gracious and compassionate King.*[1]

On the Sabbath add the words in brackets. [If forgotten, see *Laws* 86-90.]

וְהַשִּׂיאֵנוּ *Bestow upon us, O* H*ASHEM, our God, the blessing of Your appointed Festivals for life and for peace, for gladness and for joy, as You desired and promised to bless us. [Our God and the God of our forefathers, may You be pleased with our rest.] Sanctify us with Your commandments and grant us our share in Your Torah; satisfy us from Your goodness and gladden us with Your salvation, and purify our heart to serve You sincerely. And grant*

(1) Cf. *Nechemiah* 9:31.

לְעָבְדְּךָ בֶּאֱמֶת, וְהַנְחִילֵנוּ יהוה אֱלֹהֵינוּ [בְּאַהֲבָה וּבְרָצוֹן] בְּשִׂמְחָה וּבְשָׂשׂוֹן [שַׁבָּת וּ]מוֹעֲדֵי קָדְשֶׁךָ, וְיִשְׂמְחוּ בְךָ יִשְׂרָאֵל מְקַדְּשֵׁי שְׁמֶךָ. בָּרוּךְ אַתָּה יהוה, מְקַדֵּשׁ [הַשַּׁבָּת וְ]יִשְׂרָאֵל וְהַזְּמַנִּים.

עבודה

רְצֵה יהוה אֱלֹהֵינוּ בְּעַמְּךָ יִשְׂרָאֵל וּבִתְפִלָּתָם, וְהָשֵׁב אֶת הָעֲבוֹדָה לִדְבִיר בֵּיתֶךָ. וְאִשֵּׁי יִשְׂרָאֵל וּתְפִלָּתָם בְּאַהֲבָה תְקַבֵּל בְּרָצוֹן, וּתְהִי לְרָצוֹן תָּמִיד עֲבוֹדַת יִשְׂרָאֵל עַמֶּךָ.

וְתֶחֱזֶינָה עֵינֵינוּ בְּשׁוּבְךָ לְצִיּוֹן בְּרַחֲמִים. בָּרוּךְ אַתָּה יהוה, הַמַּחֲזִיר שְׁכִינָתוֹ לְצִיּוֹן.

הודאה

Bow at מוֹדִים; straighten up at 'ה. In his repetition the *chazzan* should recite the entire מוֹדִים aloud, while the congregation recites מוֹדִים דְּרַבָּנָן softly.

מוֹדִים אֲנַחְנוּ לָךְ, שָׁאַתָּה הוּא יהוה אֱלֹהֵינוּ וֵאלֹהֵי אֲבוֹתֵינוּ לְעוֹלָם וָעֶד. צוּר חַיֵּינוּ, מָגֵן יִשְׁעֵנוּ אַתָּה הוּא לְדוֹר וָדוֹר. נוֹדֶה לְּךָ וּנְסַפֵּר תְּהִלָּתֶךָ[1] עַל חַיֵּינוּ הַמְּסוּרִים בְּיָדֶךָ, וְעַל נִשְׁמוֹתֵינוּ הַפְּקוּדוֹת לָךְ, וְעַל נִסֶּיךָ שֶׁבְּכָל יוֹם עִמָּנוּ, וְעַל נִפְלְאוֹתֶיךָ וְטוֹבוֹתֶיךָ שֶׁבְּכָל עֵת, עֶרֶב וָבֹקֶר וְצָהֳרָיִם. הַטּוֹב כִּי לֹא כָלוּ רַחֲמֶיךָ, וְהַמְּרַחֵם כִּי לֹא תַמּוּ חֲסָדֶיךָ,[2] מֵעוֹלָם קִוִּינוּ לָךְ.

מודים דרבנן

מוֹדִים אֲנַחְנוּ לָךְ, שָׁאַתָּה הוּא יהוה אֱלֹהֵינוּ וֵאלֹהֵי אֲבוֹתֵינוּ, אֱלֹהֵי כָל בָּשָׂר, יוֹצְרֵנוּ, יוֹצֵר בְּרֵאשִׁית. בְּרָכוֹת וְהוֹדָאוֹת לְשִׁמְךָ הַגָּדוֹל וְהַקָּדוֹשׁ, עַל שֶׁהֶחֱיִיתָנוּ וְקִיַּמְתָּנוּ. כֵּן תְּחַיֵּנוּ וּתְקַיְּמֵנוּ, וְתֶאֱסוֹף גָּלֻיּוֹתֵינוּ לְחַצְרוֹת קָדְשֶׁךָ, לִשְׁמוֹר חֻקֶּיךָ וְלַעֲשׂוֹת רְצוֹנֶךָ, וּלְעָבְדְּךָ בְּלֵבָב שָׁלֵם, עַל שֶׁאֲנַחְנוּ מוֹדִים לָךְ. בָּרוּךְ אֵל הַהוֹדָאוֹת.

וְעַל כֻּלָּם יִתְבָּרַךְ וְיִתְרוֹמַם שִׁמְךָ מַלְכֵּנוּ תָּמִיד לְעוֹלָם וָעֶד.

Bend the knees at בָּרוּךְ; bow at אַתָּה; straighten up at 'ה.

וְכֹל הַחַיִּים יוֹדוּךָ סֶּלָה, וִיהַלְלוּ אֶת שִׁמְךָ בֶּאֱמֶת, הָאֵל יְשׁוּעָתֵנוּ וְעֶזְרָתֵנוּ סֶלָה. בָּרוּךְ אַתָּה יהוה, הַטּוֹב שִׁמְךָ וּלְךָ נָאֶה לְהוֹדוֹת.

us a heritage, O HASHEM, *our God — [with love and with favor] with gladness and with joy — [the Sabbath and] the appointed festivals of Your holiness, and may Israel, the sanctifiers of Your Name, rejoice in You. Blessed are You,* HASHEM, *Who sanctifies [the Sabbath] Israel and the festive seasons.*

TEMPLE SERVICE

רְצֵה *Be favorable,* HASHEM, *our God, toward Your people Israel and their prayer and restore the service to the Holy of Holies of Your Temple. The fire-offerings of Israel and their prayer accept with love and favor, and may the service of Your people Israel always be favorable to You.*

וְתֶחֱזֶינָה *May our eyes behold Your return to Zion in compassion. Blessed are You,* HASHEM, *Who restores His Presence to Zion.*

THANKSGIVING [MODIM]

Bow at *'We gratefully thank You'*; straighten up at *'HASHEM.'* In his repetition the *chazzan* should recite the entire *Modim* aloud, while the congregation recites *Modim of the Rabbis* softly.

מוֹדִים *We gratefully thank You, for it is You Who are* HASHEM, *our God and the God of our forefathers for all eternity; Rock of our lives, Shield of our salvation are You from generation to generation. We shall thank You and relate Your praise*[1] *— for our lives, which are committed to Your power and for our souls that are entrusted to You; for Your miracles that are with us every day; and for Your wonders and favors in every season — evening, morning, and afternoon. The Beneficent One, for Your compassions were never exhausted, and the Compassionate One, for Your kindnesses never ended*[2] *— always have we put our hope in You.*

MODIM OF THE RABBIS

מוֹדִים *We gratefully thank You, for it is You Who are* HASHEM, *our God and the God of our forefathers, the God of all flesh, our Molder, the Molder of the universe. Blessings and thanks are due Your great and holy Name for You have given us life and sustained us. So may You continue to give us life and sustain us and gather our exiles to the Courtyards of Your Sanctuary, to observe Your decrees, to do Your will and to serve You wholeheartedly. [We thank You] for inspiring us to thank You. Blessed is the God of thanksgivings.*

For all these, may Your Name be blessed and exalted, our King, continually forever and ever.

Bend the knees at *'Blessed'*; bow at *'You'*; straighten up at *'HASHEM.'*

Everything alive will gratefully acknowledge You, Selah! and praise Your Name sincerely, O God of our salvation and help, Selah! Blessed are You, HASHEM, *Your Name is 'The Beneficent One' and to You it is fitting to give thanks.*

(1) Cf. *Psalms* 79:13. (2) Cf. *Lamentations* 3:22.

שלום

שָׁלוֹם רָב עַל יִשְׂרָאֵל עַמְּךָ תָּשִׂים לְעוֹלָם, כִּי אַתָּה הוּא מֶלֶךְ אָדוֹן לְכָל הַשָּׁלוֹם. וְטוֹב בְּעֵינֶיךָ לְבָרֵךְ אֶת עַמְּךָ יִשְׂרָאֵל, בְּכָל עֵת וּבְכָל שָׁעָה בִּשְׁלוֹמֶךָ. בָּרוּךְ אַתָּה יהוה, הַמְּבָרֵךְ אֶת עַמּוֹ יִשְׂרָאֵל בַּשָּׁלוֹם.

יִהְיוּ לְרָצוֹן אִמְרֵי פִי וְהֶגְיוֹן לִבִּי לְפָנֶיךָ, יהוה צוּרִי וְגֹאֲלִי.[1]

Chazzan's repetition of *Shemoneh Esrei* ends here. Individuals continue below.

אֱלֹהַי, נְצוֹר לְשׁוֹנִי מֵרָע, וּשְׂפָתַי מִדַּבֵּר מִרְמָה,[2] וְלִמְקַלְלַי נַפְשִׁי תִדּוֹם, וְנַפְשִׁי כֶּעָפָר לַכֹּל תִּהְיֶה. פְּתַח לִבִּי בְּתוֹרָתֶךָ, וּבְמִצְוֹתֶיךָ תִּרְדּוֹף נַפְשִׁי. וְכֹל הַחוֹשְׁבִים עָלַי רָעָה, מְהֵרָה הָפֵר עֲצָתָם וְקַלְקֵל מַחֲשַׁבְתָּם. עֲשֵׂה לְמַעַן שְׁמֶךָ, עֲשֵׂה לְמַעַן יְמִינֶךָ, עֲשֵׂה לְמַעַן קְדֻשָּׁתֶךָ, עֲשֵׂה לְמַעַן תּוֹרָתֶךָ. לְמַעַן יֵחָלְצוּן יְדִידֶיךָ, הוֹשִׁיעָה יְמִינְךָ וַעֲנֵנִי.[3] Some recite verses pertaining to their names. See page 1301.

יִהְיוּ לְרָצוֹן אִמְרֵי פִי וְהֶגְיוֹן לִבִּי לְפָנֶיךָ, יהוה צוּרִי וְגֹאֲלִי.[1]

Bow and take three steps back. Bow left and say . . . עֹשֶׂה, bow right and say . . . הוּא יַעֲשֶׂה; bow forward and say וְעַל כָּל . . . אָמֵן.

עֹשֶׂה שָׁלוֹם בִּמְרוֹמָיו, הוּא יַעֲשֶׂה שָׁלוֹם עָלֵינוּ, וְעַל כָּל יִשְׂרָאֵל. וְאִמְרוּ: אָמֵן.

יְהִי רָצוֹן מִלְּפָנֶיךָ יהוה אֱלֹהֵינוּ וֵאלֹהֵי אֲבוֹתֵינוּ, שֶׁיִּבָּנֶה בֵּית הַמִּקְדָּשׁ בִּמְהֵרָה בְיָמֵינוּ, וְתֵן חֶלְקֵנוּ בְּתוֹרָתֶךָ. וְשָׁם נַעֲבָדְךָ בְּיִרְאָה, כִּימֵי עוֹלָם וּכְשָׁנִים קַדְמוֹנִיּוֹת. וְעָרְבָה לַיהוה מִנְחַת יְהוּדָה וִירוּשָׁלָיִם, כִּימֵי עוֹלָם וּכְשָׁנִים קַדְמוֹנִיּוֹת.[4]

THE INDIVIDUAL'S RECITATION OF שְׁמוֹנֶה עֶשְׂרֵה ENDS HERE.

The individual remains standing in place until the *chazzan* reaches *Kedushah* — or at least until the *chazzan* begins his repetition — then he takes three steps forward. The *chazzan* himself, or one praying alone, should remain in place for a few moments before taking three steps forward.

קדיש שלם

The *chazzan* recites קַדִּישׁ שָׁלֵם.

יִתְגַּדַּל וְיִתְקַדַּשׁ שְׁמֵהּ רַבָּא. (.Cong –אָמֵן.) בְּעָלְמָא דִּי בְרָא כִרְעוּתֵהּ. וְיַמְלִיךְ מַלְכוּתֵהּ, בְּחַיֵּיכוֹן וּבְיוֹמֵיכוֹן וּבְחַיֵּי דְכָל בֵּית יִשְׂרָאֵל, בַּעֲגָלָא וּבִזְמַן קָרִיב. וְאִמְרוּ: אָמֵן.

(.Cong– אָמֵן. יְהֵא שְׁמֵהּ רַבָּא מְבָרַךְ לְעָלַם וּלְעָלְמֵי עָלְמַיָּא.)

PEACE

שָׁלוֹם *Establish abundant peace upon Your people Israel forever, for You are King, Master of all peace. May it be good in Your eyes to bless Your people Israel at every time and every hour with Your peace. Blessed are You, HASHEM, Who blesses His people Israel with peace.*

May the expressions of my mouth and the thoughts of my heart find favor before You, HASHEM, my Rock and my Redeemer.[1]

Chazzan's repetition of *Shemoneh Esrei* ends here. Individuals continue below:

אֱלֹהַי *My God, guard my tongue from evil and my lips from speaking deceitfully.*[2] *To those who curse me, let my soul be silent; and let my soul be like dust to everyone. Open my heart to Your Torah, then my soul will pursue Your commandments. As for all those who design evil against me, speedily nullify their counsel and disrupt their design. Act for Your Name's sake; act for Your right hand's sake; act for Your sanctity's sake; act for Your Torah's sake. That Your beloved ones may be given rest; let Your right hand save, and respond to me.*[3]

Some recite verses pertaining to their names at this point. See page 1301.

May the expressions of my mouth and the thoughts of my heart find favor before You, HASHEM, my Rock and my Redeemer.[1] *He Who makes peace in His heights, may He make peace upon us, and upon all Israel. Now respond: Amen.*

Bow and take three steps back. Bow left and say, *'He Who makes peace . . .'*; bow right and say, *'may He make peace . . .'*; bow forward and say, *'and upon . . . Amen.'*

יְהִי רָצוֹן *May it be Your will, HASHEM, our God and the God of our forefathers, that the Holy Temple be rebuilt, speedily in our days. Grant us our share in Your Torah, and may we serve You there with reverence, as in days of old and in former years. Then the offering of Judah and Jerusalem will be pleasing to HASHEM, as in days of old and in former years.*[4]

THE INDIVIDUAL'S RECITATION OF *SHEMONEH ESREI* ENDS HERE.

The individual remains standing in place until the *chazzan* reaches *Kedushah* — or at least until the *chazzan* begins his repetition — then he takes three steps forward. The *chazzan* himself, or one praying alone, should remain in place for a few moments before taking three steps forward.

FULL KADDISH

The *chazzan* recites the Full *Kaddish.*

יִתְגַּדַּל *May His great Name grow exalted and sanctified* (Cong.— *Amen.*) *in the world that He created as He willed. May He give reign to His kingship in your lifetimes and in your days, and in the lifetimes of the entire Family of Israel, swiftly and soon. Now respond: Amen.*

(Cong.— *Amen. May His great Name be blessed forever and ever.)*

---

(1) *Psalms* 19:15. (2) Cf. 34:14. (3) 60:7; 108:7. (4) *Malachi* 3:4.

יְהֵא שְׁמֵהּ רַבָּא מְבָרַךְ לְעָלַם וּלְעָלְמֵי עָלְמַיָּא.

יִתְבָּרַךְ וְיִשְׁתַּבַּח וְיִתְפָּאַר וְיִתְרוֹמַם וְיִתְנַשֵּׂא וְיִתְהַדָּר וְיִתְעַלֶּה וְיִתְהַלָּל שְׁמֵהּ דְּקֻדְשָׁא בְּרִיךְ הוּא (.Cong – בְּרִיךְ הוּא) — לְעֵלָּא מִן כָּל בִּרְכָתָא וְשִׁירָתָא תֻּשְׁבְּחָתָא וְנֶחֱמָתָא, דַּאֲמִירָן בְּעָלְמָא. וְאִמְרוּ: אָמֵן. (.Cong – אָמֵן.)

(.Cong – קַבֵּל בְּרַחֲמִים וּבְרָצוֹן אֶת תְּפִלָּתֵנוּ.)

תִּתְקַבֵּל צְלוֹתְהוֹן וּבָעוּתְהוֹן דְּכָל בֵּית יִשְׂרָאֵל קֳדָם אֲבוּהוֹן דִּי בִשְׁמַיָּא. וְאִמְרוּ: אָמֵן. (.Cong – אָמֵן.)

(.Cong – יְהִי שֵׁם יהוה מְבֹרָךְ, מֵעַתָּה וְעַד עוֹלָם.[1])

יְהֵא שְׁלָמָא רַבָּא מִן שְׁמַיָּא, וְחַיִּים עָלֵינוּ וְעַל כָּל יִשְׂרָאֵל. וְאִמְרוּ: אָמֵן. (.Cong – אָמֵן.)

(.Cong – עֶזְרִי מֵעִם יהוה, עֹשֵׂה שָׁמַיִם וָאָרֶץ.[2])

Take three steps back. Bow left and say . . . עֹשֶׂה; bow right and say . . . הוּא; bow forward and say וְעַל כָּל . . . אָמֵן. Remain standing in place for a few moments, then take three steps forward.

עֹשֶׂה שָׁלוֹם בִּמְרוֹמָיו, הוּא יַעֲשֶׂה שָׁלוֹם עָלֵינוּ, וְעַל כָּל יִשְׂרָאֵל. וְאִמְרוּ: אָמֵן. (.Cong – אָמֵן.)

עלינו

Stand while reciting עָלֵינוּ.

עָלֵינוּ לְשַׁבֵּחַ לַאֲדוֹן הַכֹּל, לָתֵת גְּדֻלָּה לְיוֹצֵר בְּרֵאשִׁית, שֶׁלֹּא עָשָׂנוּ כְּגוֹיֵי הָאֲרָצוֹת, וְלֹא שָׂמָנוּ כְּמִשְׁפְּחוֹת הָאֲדָמָה. שֶׁלֹּא שָׂם חֶלְקֵנוּ כָּהֶם, וְגוֹרָלֵנוּ כְּכָל הֲמוֹנָם. (שֶׁהֵם מִשְׁתַּחֲוִים לְהֶבֶל וָרִיק, וּמִתְפַּלְּלִים אֶל אֵל לֹא יוֹשִׁיעַ.[3]) וַאֲנַחְנוּ כּוֹרְעִים וּמִשְׁתַּחֲוִים וּמוֹדִים, לִפְנֵי מֶלֶךְ מַלְכֵי הַמְּלָכִים הַקָּדוֹשׁ בָּרוּךְ הוּא. שֶׁהוּא נוֹטֶה שָׁמַיִם וְיֹסֵד אָרֶץ,[4] וּמוֹשַׁב יְקָרוֹ בַּשָּׁמַיִם מִמַּעַל, וּשְׁכִינַת עֻזּוֹ בְּגָבְהֵי מְרוֹמִים. הוּא אֱלֹהֵינוּ, אֵין עוֹד. אֱמֶת מַלְכֵּנוּ, אֶפֶס זוּלָתוֹ, כַּכָּתוּב בְּתוֹרָתוֹ: וְיָדַעְתָּ הַיּוֹם וַהֲשֵׁבֹתָ אֶל לְבָבֶךָ, כִּי יהוה הוּא הָאֱלֹהִים בַּשָּׁמַיִם מִמַּעַל וְעַל הָאָרֶץ מִתָּחַת, אֵין עוֹד.[5]

Bow while reciting וַאֲנַחְנוּ כּוֹרְעִים וּמִשְׁתַּחֲוִים.

עַל כֵּן נְקַוֶּה לְּךָ יהוה אֱלֹהֵינוּ לִרְאוֹת מְהֵרָה בְּתִפְאֶרֶת עֻזֶּךָ, לְהַעֲבִיר גִּלּוּלִים מִן הָאָרֶץ, וְהָאֱלִילִים כָּרוֹת יִכָּרֵתוּן, לְתַקֵּן עוֹלָם בְּמַלְכוּת שַׁדַּי. וְכָל בְּנֵי בָשָׂר יִקְרְאוּ בִשְׁמֶךָ, לְהַפְנוֹת אֵלֶיךָ כָּל רִשְׁעֵי אָרֶץ. יַכִּירוּ וְיֵדְעוּ כָּל יוֹשְׁבֵי תֵבֵל, כִּי לְךָ

May His great Name be blessed forever and ever.

Blessed, praised, glorified, exalted, extolled, mighty, upraised, and lauded be the Name of the Holy One, Blessed is He (Cong.– *Blessed is He*) *— beyond any blessing and song, praise and consolation that are uttered in the world. Now respond: Amen.* (Cong.– *Amen.*)

(Cong.– *Accept our prayers with mercy and favor.*)

May the prayers and supplications of the entire Family of Israel be accepted before their Father Who is in Heaven. Now respond: Amen. (Cong.– *Amen.*)

(Cong.– *Blessed be the Name of* HASHEM, *from this time and forever.*[1])

May there be abundant peace from Heaven, and life, upon us and upon all Israel. Now respond: Amen. (Cong.– *Amen.*)

(Cong.– *My help is from* HASHEM, *Maker of heaven and earth.*[2])

Take three steps back. Bow left and say, *'He Who makes peace . . .'*; bow right and say, *'may He . . .'*; bow forward and say, *'and upon all Israel . . .'* Remain standing in place for a few moments, then take three steps forward.

He Who makes peace in His heights, may He make peace upon us, and upon all Israel. Now respond: Amen. (Cong.– *Amen.*)

ALEINU

Stand while reciting עָלֵינוּ, *'It is our duty . . .'*

עָלֵינוּ *It is our duty to praise the Master of all, to ascribe greatness to the Molder of primeval creation, for He has not made us like the nations of the lands, and has not emplaced us like the families of the earth; for He has not assigned our portion like theirs nor our lot like all their multitudes. (For they bow to vanity and emptiness and pray to a god which helps not.*[3]*) But we bend our knees, bow, and acknowledge our thanks before the King Who reigns over kings, the Holy One, Blessed is He. He stretches out heaven and establishes earth's foundation,*[4] *the seat of His homage is in the heavens above and His powerful Presence is in the loftiest heights. He is our God and there is none other. True is our King, there is nothing beside Him, as it is written in His Torah: 'You are to know this day and take to your heart that* HASHEM *is the only God — in heaven above and on the earth below — there is none other.'*[5]

Bow while reciting *'But we bend our knees.'*

עַל כֵּן *Therefore we put our hope in You,* HASHEM, *our God, that we may soon see Your mighty splendor, to remove detestable idolatry from the earth, and false gods will be utterly cut off, to perfect the universe through the Almighty's sovereignty. Then all humanity will call upon Your Name, to turn all the earth's wicked toward You. All the world's inhabitants will recognize and know that to You*

(1) *Psalms* 113:2. (2) 121:2. (3) *Isaiah* 45:20. (4) 51:13. (5) *Deuteronomy* 4:39.

תִּכְרַע כָּל בֶּרֶךְ, תִּשָּׁבַע כָּל לָשׁוֹן.[1] לְפָנֶיךָ יהוה אֱלֹהֵינוּ יִכְרְעוּ וְיִפֹּלוּ, וְלִכְבוֹד שִׁמְךָ יְקָר יִתֵּנוּ. וִיקַבְּלוּ כֻלָּם אֶת עוֹל מַלְכוּתֶךָ, וְתִמְלֹךְ עֲלֵיהֶם מְהֵרָה לְעוֹלָם וָעֶד. כִּי הַמַּלְכוּת שֶׁלְּךָ הִיא וּלְעוֹלְמֵי עַד תִּמְלוֹךְ בְּכָבוֹד, כַּכָּתוּב בְּתוֹרָתֶךָ: יהוה יִמְלֹךְ לְעֹלָם וָעֶד.[2] ❖ וְנֶאֱמַר: וְהָיָה יהוה לְמֶלֶךְ עַל כָּל הָאָרֶץ, בַּיּוֹם הַהוּא יִהְיֶה יהוה אֶחָד וּשְׁמוֹ אֶחָד.[3]

Some congregations recite the following after עָלֵינוּ:

אַל תִּירָא מִפַּחַד פִּתְאֹם, וּמִשֹּׁאַת רְשָׁעִים כִּי תָבֹא.[4] עֻצוּ עֵצָה וְתֻפָר, דַּבְּרוּ דָבָר וְלֹא יָקוּם, כִּי עִמָּנוּ אֵל.[5] וְעַד זִקְנָה אֲנִי הוּא, וְעַד שֵׂיבָה אֲנִי אֶסְבֹּל, אֲנִי עָשִׂיתִי וַאֲנִי אֶשָּׂא, וַאֲנִי אֶסְבֹּל וַאֲמַלֵּט.[6]

קדיש יתום

In the presence of a *minyan,* mourners recite קַדִּישׁ יָתוֹם, the Mourner's *Kaddish* (see *Laws* §81-83).

יִתְגַּדַּל וְיִתְקַדַּשׁ שְׁמֵהּ רַבָּא. (.Cong – אָמֵן.) בְּעָלְמָא דִּי בְרָא כִרְעוּתֵהּ. וְיַמְלִיךְ מַלְכוּתֵהּ, בְּחַיֵּיכוֹן וּבְיוֹמֵיכוֹן וּבְחַיֵּי דְכָל בֵּית יִשְׂרָאֵל, בַּעֲגָלָא וּבִזְמַן קָרִיב. וְאִמְרוּ: אָמֵן.

(.Cong – אָמֵן. יְהֵא שְׁמֵהּ רַבָּא מְבָרַךְ לְעָלַם וּלְעָלְמֵי עָלְמַיָּא.)

יְהֵא שְׁמֵהּ רַבָּא מְבָרַךְ לְעָלַם וּלְעָלְמֵי עָלְמַיָּא.

יִתְבָּרַךְ וְיִשְׁתַּבַּח וְיִתְפָּאַר וְיִתְרוֹמַם וְיִתְנַשֵּׂא וְיִתְהַדָּר וְיִתְעַלֶּה וְיִתְהַלָּל שְׁמֵהּ דְּקֻדְשָׁא בְּרִיךְ הוּא (.Cong – בְּרִיךְ הוּא) — לְעֵלָּא מִן כָּל בִּרְכָתָא וְשִׁירָתָא תֻּשְׁבְּחָתָא וְנֶחֱמָתָא, דַּאֲמִירָן בְּעָלְמָא. וְאִמְרוּ: אָמֵן. (.Cong – אָמֵן.)

יְהֵא שְׁלָמָא רַבָּא מִן שְׁמַיָּא, וְחַיִּים עָלֵינוּ וְעַל כָּל יִשְׂרָאֵל. וְאִמְרוּ: אָמֵן. (.Cong – אָמֵן.)

Take three steps back. Bow left and say . . . עֹשֶׂה; bow right and say . . . הוּא; bow forward and say וְעַל כָּל . . . אָמֵן. Remain standing in place for a few moments, then take three steps forward.

עֹשֶׂה שָׁלוֹם בִּמְרוֹמָיו, הוּא יַעֲשֶׂה שָׁלוֹם עָלֵינוּ, וְעַל כָּל יִשְׂרָאֵל. וְאִמְרוּ: אָמֵן. (.Cong – אָמֵן.)

MAARIV FOR THE SECOND NIGHT BEGINS ON PAGE 34.
KABBALAS SHABBOS FOR THE SABBATH OF *CHOL HAMOED* BEGINS ON PAGE 426.
MAARIV FOR THE WEEKDAYS OF *CHOL HAMOED* BEGINS ON PAGE 612.

every knee should bend, every tongue should swear.[1] *Before You, HASHEM, our God, they will bend every knee and cast themselves down and to the glory of Your Name they will render homage, and they will all accept upon themselves the yoke of Your kingship that You may reign over them soon and eternally. For the kingdom is Yours and You will reign for all eternity in glory as it is written in Your Torah: HASHEM shall reign for all eternity.*[2] Chazzan– *And it is said: HASHEM will be King over all the world — on that day HASHEM will be One and His Name will be One.*[3]

Some congregations recite the following after *Aleinu.*

אַל תִּירָא *Do not fear sudden terror, or the holocaust of the wicked when it comes.*[4] *Plan a conspiracy and it will be annulled; speak your piece and it shall not stand, for God is with us.*[5] *Even till your seniority, I remain unchanged; and even till your ripe old age, I shall endure. I created you and I shall bear you; I shall endure and rescue.*[6]

MOURNER'S KADDISH

In the presence of a *minyan,* mourners recite קַדִּישׁ יָתוֹם, the Mourner's *Kaddish* (see *Laws* 81-83).

[A transliteration of this *Kaddish* appears on page 1305.]

יִתְגַּדַּל *May His great Name grow exalted and sanctified* (Cong.– *Amen.*) *in the world that He created as He willed. May He give reign to His kingship in your lifetimes and in your days, and in the lifetimes of the entire Family of Israel, swiftly and soon. Now respond: Amen.*

(Cong.– *Amen. May His great Name be blessed forever and ever.*)

May His great Name be blessed forever and ever.

Blessed, praised, glorified, exalted, extolled, mighty, upraised, and lauded be the Name of the Holy One, Blessed is He (Cong.– *Blessed is He*) *— beyond any blessing and song, praise and consolation that are uttered in the world. Now respond: Amen.* (Cong.– *Amen*).

May there be abundant peace from Heaven, and life, upon us and upon all Israel. Now respond: Amen. (Cong.– *Amen.*)

Take three steps back. Bow left and say, *'He Who makes peace . . .';* bow right and say, *'may He . . .';* bow forward and say, *'and upon all Israel . . .'* Remain standing in place for a few moments, then take three steps forward.

He Who makes peace in His heights, may He make peace upon us, and upon all Israel. Now respond: Amen. (Cong.– *Amen.*)

MAARIV FOR THE SECOND NIGHT BEGINS ON PAGE 34.
KABBALAS SHABBOS FOR THE SABBATH OF *CHOL HAMOED* BEGINS ON PAGE 426.
MAARIV FOR THE WEEKDAYS OF *CHOL HAMOED* BEGINS ON PAGE 612.

(1) Cf. *Isaiah* 45:23. (2) *Exodus* 15:18. (3) *Zechariah* 14:9. (4) *Proverbs* 3:25. (5) *Isaiah* 8:10. (6) 46:4.

◆ שבת חול המועד

◆ Sabbath of Chol HaMoed

הדלקת הנרות לשבת חול המועד

[It is forbidden to create a new flame — for example, by striking a match — on *Yom Tov*. Therefore, since when the first day of Chol HaMoed falls on the Sabbath, the Sabbath candles will be kindled during *Yom Tov,* the candles must be lit from a previously existing flame that has been burning from before *Yom Tov*.]

Light the candles, then cover the eyes and recite the blessing. Uncover the eyes and gaze briefly at the candles.

בָּרוּךְ אַתָּה יהוה אֱלֹהֵינוּ מֶלֶךְ הָעוֹלָם, אֲשֶׁר קִדְּשָׁנוּ בְּמִצְוֹתָיו, וְצִוָּנוּ לְהַדְלִיק נֵר שֶׁל שַׁבָּת.

It is customary to recite the following prayer after the kindling. The words in brackets are included as they apply.

יְהִי רָצוֹן לְפָנֶיךָ, יהוה אֱלֹהַי וֵאלֹהֵי אֲבוֹתַי, שֶׁתְּחוֹנֵן אוֹתִי [וְאֶת אִישִׁי, וְאֶת בָּנַי, וְאֶת בְּנוֹתַי, וְאֶת אָבִי, וְאֶת אִמִּי] וְאֶת כָּל קְרוֹבַי; וְתִתֶּן לָנוּ וּלְכָל יִשְׂרָאֵל חַיִּים טוֹבִים וַאֲרוּכִים; וְתִזְכְּרֵנוּ בְּזִכְרוֹן טוֹבָה וּבְרָכָה; וְתִפְקְדֵנוּ בִּפְקֻדַּת יְשׁוּעָה וְרַחֲמִים; וּתְבָרְכֵנוּ בְּרָכוֹת גְּדוֹלוֹת; וְתַשְׁלִים בָּתֵּינוּ; וְתַשְׁכֵּן שְׁכִינָתְךָ בֵּינֵינוּ. וְזַכֵּנִי לְגַדֵּל בָּנִים וּבְנֵי בָנִים חֲכָמִים וּנְבוֹנִים, אוֹהֲבֵי יהוה, יִרְאֵי אֱלֹהִים, אַנְשֵׁי אֱמֶת, זֶרַע קֹדֶשׁ, בַּיהוה דְּבֵקִים, וּמְאִירִים אֶת הָעוֹלָם בַּתּוֹרָה וּבְמַעֲשִׂים טוֹבִים, וּבְכָל מְלֶאכֶת עֲבוֹדַת הַבּוֹרֵא. אָנָּא שְׁמַע אֶת תְּחִנָּתִי בָּעֵת הַזֹּאת, בִּזְכוּת שָׂרָה וְרִבְקָה וְרָחֵל וְלֵאָה אִמּוֹתֵינוּ, וְהָאֵר נֵרֵנוּ שֶׁלֹּא יִכְבֶּה לְעוֹלָם וָעֶד, וְהָאֵר פָּנֶיךָ וְנִוָּשֵׁעָה. אָמֵן.

קבלת שבת לשבת חול המועד

תהלים צב

מִזְמוֹר שִׁיר לְיוֹם הַשַּׁבָּת. טוֹב לְהֹדוֹת לַיהוה, וּלְזַמֵּר לְשִׁמְךָ עֶלְיוֹן. לְהַגִּיד בַּבֹּקֶר חַסְדֶּךָ, וֶאֱמוּנָתְךָ בַּלֵּילוֹת. עֲלֵי עָשׂוֹר וַעֲלֵי נָבֶל, עֲלֵי הִגָּיוֹן בְּכִנּוֹר. כִּי שִׂמַּחְתַּנִי יהוה בְּפָעֳלֶךָ, בְּמַעֲשֵׂי יָדֶיךָ אֲרַנֵּן. מַה גָּדְלוּ מַעֲשֶׂיךָ יהוה, מְאֹד עָמְקוּ מַחְשְׁבֹתֶיךָ. אִישׁ בַּעַר לֹא יֵדָע, וּכְסִיל לֹא יָבִין אֶת זֹאת. בִּפְרֹחַ רְשָׁעִים כְּמוֹ עֵשֶׂב, וַיָּצִיצוּ כָּל פֹּעֲלֵי אָוֶן, לְהִשָּׁמְדָם עֲדֵי עַד. וְאַתָּה מָרוֹם לְעֹלָם יהוה. כִּי הִנֵּה אֹיְבֶיךָ יהוה, כִּי הִנֵּה אֹיְבֶיךָ יֹאבֵדוּ, יִתְפָּרְדוּ כָּל פֹּעֲלֵי אָוֶן. וַתָּרֶם כִּרְאֵים קַרְנִי, בַּלֹּתִי בְּשֶׁמֶן רַעֲנָן. וַתַּבֵּט עֵינִי בְּשׁוּרָי, בַּקָּמִים עָלַי מְרֵעִים, תִּשְׁמַעְנָה אָזְנָי. ❖ צַדִּיק כַּתָּמָר יִפְרָח, כְּאֶרֶז בַּלְּבָנוֹן יִשְׂגֶּה. שְׁתוּלִים בְּבֵית יהוה, בְּחַצְרוֹת אֱלֹהֵינוּ יַפְרִיחוּ. עוֹד יְנוּבוּן בְּשֵׂיבָה, דְּשֵׁנִים וְרַעֲנַנִּים יִהְיוּ. לְהַגִּיד כִּי יָשָׁר יהוה, צוּרִי וְלֹא עַוְלָתָה בּוֹ.

KINDLING LIGHTS FOR THE SABBATH OF CHOL HAMOED

[It is forbidden to create a new flame — for example, by striking a match — on *Yom Tov*. Therefore, since when the first day of Chol HaMoed falls on the Sabbath, the Sabbath candles will be kindled during *Yom Tov*, the candles must be lit from a previously existing flame that has been burning from before *Yom Tov*.]

Light the candles, then cover the eyes and recite the blessing.
Uncover the eyes and gaze briefly at the candles.

בָּרוּךְ *Blessed are You, HASHEM, our God, King of the universe, Who has sanctified us with His commandments, and has commanded us to kindle the light of the Sabbath.*

It is customary to recite the following prayer after the kindling.
The words in brackets are included as they apply.

יְהִי רָצוֹן *May it be Your will, HASHEM, my God and God of my forefathers, that You show favor to me [my husband, my sons, my daughters, my father, my mother] and all my relatives; and that You grant us and all Israel a good and long life; that You remember us with a beneficent memory and blessing; that You consider us with a consideration of salvation and compassion; that You bless us with great blessings; that You make our households complete; that You cause Your Presence to dwell among us. Privilege me to raise children and grandchildren who are wise and understanding, who love HASHEM and fear God, people of truth, holy offspring, attached to HASHEM, who illuminate the world with Torah and good deeds and with every labor in the service of the Creator. Please, hear my supplication at this time, in the merit of Sarah, Rebecca, Rachel, and Leah, our mothers, and cause our light to illuminate that it be not extinguished forever, and let Your countenance shine so that we are saved. Amen.*

KABBALAS SHABBOS

Psalm 92

מִזְמוֹר שִׁיר *A psalm, a song for the Sabbath day. It is good to thank HASHEM and to sing praise to Your Name, O Exalted One; to relate Your kindness in the dawn and Your faith in the nights. Upon ten-stringed instrument and lyre, with singing accompanied by a harp. For You have gladdened me, HASHEM, with Your deeds; at the works of Your Hands I sing glad song. How great are Your deeds, HASHEM; exceedingly profound are Your thoughts. A boor cannot know, nor can a fool understand this: when the wicked bloom like grass and all the doers of iniquity blossom — it is to destroy them till eternity. But You remain exalted forever, HASHEM. For behold! — Your enemies, HASHEM, for behold! — Your enemies shall perish, dispersed shall be all doers of iniquity. As exalted as a re'eim's shall be my pride, I will be saturated with ever-fresh oil. My eyes have seen my vigilant foes; when those who would harm me rise up against me, my ears have heard their doom.* Chazzan— *A righteous man will flourish like a date palm, like a cedar in the Lebanon he will grow tall. Planted in the house of HASHEM, in the courtyards of our God they will flourish. They will still be fruitful in old age, vigorous and fresh they will be — to declare that HASHEM is just, my Rock in Whom there is no wrong.*

תהלים צג

יהוה מָלָךְ גֵּאוּת לָבֵשׁ, לָבֵשׁ יהוה עֹז הִתְאַזָּר, אַף תִּכּוֹן תֵּבֵל בַּל תִּמּוֹט. נָכוֹן כִּסְאֲךָ מֵאָז, מֵעוֹלָם אָתָּה. נָשְׂאוּ נְהָרוֹת, יהוה, נָשְׂאוּ נְהָרוֹת קוֹלָם, יִשְׂאוּ נְהָרוֹת דָּכְיָם. ❖ מִקֹּלוֹת מַיִם רַבִּים אַדִּירִים מִשְׁבְּרֵי יָם, אַדִּיר בַּמָּרוֹם יהוה. עֵדֹתֶיךָ נֶאֶמְנוּ מְאֹד לְבֵיתְךָ נַאֲוָה קֹּדֶשׁ, יהוה, לְאֹרֶךְ יָמִים.

קדיש יתום

Mourners recite קַדִּישׁ יָתוֹם, the Mourner's *Kaddish* (see *Laws* 81-83).

יִתְגַּדַּל וְיִתְקַדַּשׁ שְׁמֵהּ רַבָּא. (.Cong – אָמֵן.) בְּעָלְמָא דִּי בְרָא כִרְעוּתֵהּ. וְיַמְלִיךְ מַלְכוּתֵהּ, בְּחַיֵּיכוֹן וּבְיוֹמֵיכוֹן וּבְחַיֵּי דְכָל בֵּית יִשְׂרָאֵל, בַּעֲגָלָא וּבִזְמַן קָרִיב. וְאִמְרוּ: אָמֵן.

(.Cong – אָמֵן. יְהֵא שְׁמֵהּ רַבָּא מְבָרַךְ לְעָלַם וּלְעָלְמֵי עָלְמַיָּא.)

יְהֵא שְׁמֵהּ רַבָּא מְבָרַךְ לְעָלַם וּלְעָלְמֵי עָלְמַיָּא.

יִתְבָּרַךְ וְיִשְׁתַּבַּח וְיִתְפָּאַר וְיִתְרוֹמַם וְיִתְנַשֵּׂא וְיִתְהַדָּר וְיִתְעַלֶּה וְיִתְהַלָּל שְׁמֵהּ דְּקֻדְשָׁא בְּרִיךְ הוּא (.Cong – בְּרִיךְ הוּא) – לְעֵלָּא מִן כָּל בִּרְכָתָא וְשִׁירָתָא תֻּשְׁבְּחָתָא וְנֶחֱמָתָא, דַּאֲמִירָן בְּעָלְמָא. וְאִמְרוּ: אָמֵן. (.Cong – אָמֵן.)

יְהֵא שְׁלָמָא רַבָּא מִן שְׁמַיָּא, וְחַיִּים עָלֵינוּ וְעַל כָּל יִשְׂרָאֵל. וְאִמְרוּ: אָמֵן. (.Cong – אָמֵן.)

Take three steps back. Bow left and say . . . עֹשֶׂה; bow right and say . . . הוּא; bow forward and say וְעַל כָּל . . . אָמֵן. Remain standing in place for a few moments, then take three steps forward.

עֹשֶׂה שָׁלוֹם בִּמְרוֹמָיו, הוּא יַעֲשֶׂה שָׁלוֹם עָלֵינוּ, וְעַל כָּל יִשְׂרָאֵל. וְאִמְרוּ: אָמֵן. (.Cong – אָמֵן.)

מעריב לשבת חול המועד

In some congregations the *chazzan* chants a melody during his recitation of בָּרְכוּ, so that the congregation can then recite יִתְבָּרַךְ.

Chazzan bows at בָּרְכוּ and straightens up at ה'.

בָּרְכוּ אֶת יהוה הַמְּבֹרָךְ.

Congregation, followed by *chazzan*, responds, bowing at בָּרוּךְ and straightening up at ה'.

בָּרוּךְ יהוה הַמְּבֹרָךְ לְעוֹלָם וָעֶד.

יִתְבָּרַךְ וְיִשְׁתַּבַּח וְיִתְפָּאַר וְיִתְרוֹמַם וְיִתְנַשֵּׂא שְׁמוֹ שֶׁל מֶלֶךְ מַלְכֵי הַמְּלָכִים, הַקָּדוֹשׁ בָּרוּךְ הוּא. שֶׁהוּא רִאשׁוֹן וְהוּא אַחֲרוֹן, וּמִבַּלְעָדָיו אֵין אֱלֹהִים.[1] סֹלּוּ, לָרֹכֵב בָּעֲרָבוֹת, בְּיָהּ שְׁמוֹ, וְעִלְזוּ לְפָנָיו.[2] וּשְׁמוֹ מְרוֹמָם עַל כָּל בְּרָכָה וּתְהִלָּה.[3] בָּרוּךְ שֵׁם כְּבוֹד מַלְכוּתוֹ לְעוֹלָם וָעֶד. יְהִי שֵׁם יהוה מְבֹרָךְ, מֵעַתָּה וְעַד עוֹלָם.[4]

Psalm 93

יהוה מָלָךְ *HASHEM will have reigned, He will have donned grandeur; He will have donned might and girded Himself; even firmed the world that it should not falter. Your throne was established from of old; eternal are You. Like rivers they raised, O HASHEM, like rivers they raised their voice; like rivers they shall raise their destructiveness.* Chazzan— *More than the roars of many waters, mightier than the waves of the sea — You are mighty on high, HASHEM. Your testimonies are exceedingly trustworthy about Your House, the Sacred Dwelling — O HASHEM, may it be for long days.*

MOURNER'S KADDISH

Mourners recite the Mourner's *Kaddish* (see *Laws* §81-83).

יִתְגַּדַּל *May His great Name grow exalted and sanctified* (Cong.— *Amen.*) *in the world that He created as He willed. May He give reign to His kingship in your lifetimes and in your days, and in the lifetimes of the entire Family of Israel, swiftly and soon. Now respond: Amen.*

(Cong.— *Amen. May His great Name be blessed forever and ever.*)

May His great Name be blessed forever and ever.

Blessed, praised, glorified, exalted, extolled, mighty, upraised, and lauded be the Name of the Holy One, Blessed is He (Cong.— *Blessed is He*) *— beyond any blessing and song, praise and consolation that are uttered in the world. Now respond: Amen.* (Cong. – *Amen*.)

May there be abundant peace from Heaven, and life, upon us and upon all Israel. Now respond: Amen. (Cong.— *Amen.*)

Take three steps back. Bow left and say, *'He Who makes peace . . .'*; bow right and say, *'may He . . .'*; bow forward and say, *'and upon all Israel . . .'* Remain standing in place for a few moments, then take three steps forward.

He Who makes peace in His heights, may He make peace upon us, and upon all Israel. Now respond: Amen. (Cong.— *Amen.*)

MAARIV FOR THE SABBATH OF CHOL HAMOED

In some congregations the *chazzan* chants a melody during his recitation of *Borchu*, so that the congregation can then recite *'Blessed, praised . . .'*

Chazzan bows at *'Bless,'* and straightens up at *'HASHEM.'*

Bless HASHEM, the blessed One.

Congregation, followed by *chazzan*, responds, bowing at *'Blessed'* and straightening up at *'HASHEM.'*

Blessed is HASHEM, the blessed One, for all eternity.

Blessed, praised, glorified, exalted and upraised is the Name of the King Who rules over kings — the Holy One, Blessed is He. For He is the First and He is the Last and aside from Him there is no god.[1] *Extol Him — Who rides the highest heavens — with His Name, YAH, and exult before Him.*[2] *His Name is exalted beyond every blessing and praise.*[3] *Blessed is the Name of His glorious kingdom for all eternity. Blessed be the Name of HASHEM from this time and forever.*[4]

(1) Cf. *Isaiah* 44:6. (2) *Psalms* 68:5. (3) Cf. *Nechemiah* 9:5. (4) *Psalms* 113:2.

ברכות קריאת שמע

בָּרוּךְ אַתָּה יהוה אֱלֹהֵינוּ מֶלֶךְ הָעוֹלָם, אֲשֶׁר בִּדְבָרוֹ מַעֲרִיב עֲרָבִים, בְּחָכְמָה פּוֹתֵחַ שְׁעָרִים, וּבִתְבוּנָה מְשַׁנֶּה עִתִּים, וּמַחֲלִיף אֶת הַזְּמַנִּים, וּמְסַדֵּר אֶת הַכּוֹכָבִים בְּמִשְׁמְרוֹתֵיהֶם בָּרָקִיעַ כִּרְצוֹנוֹ. בּוֹרֵא יוֹם וָלָיְלָה, גּוֹלֵל אוֹר מִפְּנֵי חֹשֶׁךְ וְחֹשֶׁךְ מִפְּנֵי אוֹר. וּמַעֲבִיר יוֹם וּמֵבִיא לָיְלָה, וּמַבְדִּיל בֵּין יוֹם וּבֵין לָיְלָה, יהוה צְבָאוֹת שְׁמוֹ. ❖ אֵל חַי וְקַיָּם, תָּמִיד יִמְלוֹךְ עָלֵינוּ, לְעוֹלָם וָעֶד. בָּרוּךְ אַתָּה יהוה, הַמַּעֲרִיב עֲרָבִים. (.Cong. – אָמֵן)

אַהֲבַת עוֹלָם בֵּית יִשְׂרָאֵל עַמְּךָ אָהָבְתָּ. תּוֹרָה וּמִצְוֹת, חֻקִּים וּמִשְׁפָּטִים, אוֹתָנוּ לִמַּדְתָּ. עַל כֵּן יהוה אֱלֹהֵינוּ, בְּשָׁכְבֵנוּ וּבְקוּמֵנוּ נָשִׂיחַ בְּחֻקֶּיךָ, וְנִשְׂמַח בְּדִבְרֵי תוֹרָתֶךָ, וּבְמִצְוֹתֶיךָ לְעוֹלָם וָעֶד. ❖ כִּי הֵם חַיֵּינוּ, וְאֹרֶךְ יָמֵינוּ, וּבָהֶם נֶהְגֶּה יוֹמָם וָלָיְלָה. וְאַהֲבָתְךָ, אַל תָּסִיר מִמֶּנּוּ לְעוֹלָמִים. בָּרוּךְ אַתָּה יהוה, אוֹהֵב עַמּוֹ יִשְׂרָאֵל. (.Cong. – אָמֵן)

שמע

Immediately before its recitation concentrate on fulfilling the positive commandment of reciting the *Shema* twice daily. It is important to enunciate each word clearly and not to run words together. For this reason, vertical lines have been placed between two words that are prone to be slurred into one and are not separated by a comma or a hyphen. See *Laws* §40-52.

When praying without a *minyan,* begin with the following three-word formula:

אֵל מֶלֶךְ נֶאֱמָן.

Recite the first verse aloud, with the right hand covering the eyes, and concentrate intently upon accepting God's absolute sovereignty.

שְׁמַע | יִשְׂרָאֵל, יהוה | אֱלֹהֵינוּ, יהוה | אֶחָד:

In an undertone – בָּרוּךְ שֵׁם כְּבוֹד מַלְכוּתוֹ לְעוֹלָם וָעֶד.

While reciting the first paragraph (דברים ו:ה-ט), concentrate on accepting the commandment to love God.

וְאָהַבְתָּ אֵת | יהוה | אֱלֹהֶיךָ, בְּכָל־לְבָבְךָ, וּבְכָל־נַפְשְׁךָ, וּבְכָל־מְאֹדֶךָ: וְהָיוּ הַדְּבָרִים הָאֵלֶּה, אֲשֶׁר | אָנֹכִי מְצַוְּךָ הַיּוֹם, עַל־לְבָבֶךָ: וְשִׁנַּנְתָּם לְבָנֶיךָ, וְדִבַּרְתָּ בָּם, בְּשִׁבְתְּךָ בְּבֵיתֶךָ, וּבְלֶכְתְּךָ בַדֶּרֶךְ, וּבְשָׁכְבְּךָ וּבְקוּמֶךָ: וּקְשַׁרְתָּם לְאוֹת | עַל־יָדֶךָ, וְהָיוּ לְטֹטָפֹת בֵּין | עֵינֶיךָ: וּכְתַבְתָּם | עַל־מְזֻזוֹת בֵּיתֶךָ, וּבִשְׁעָרֶיךָ:

While reciting the second paragraph (דברים יא:יג-כא), concentrate on accepting all the commandments and the concept of reward and punishment.

וְהָיָה, אִם־שָׁמֹעַ תִּשְׁמְעוּ אֶל־מִצְוֹתַי, אֲשֶׁר | אָנֹכִי מְצַוֶּה | אֶתְכֶם הַיּוֹם, לְאַהֲבָה אֶת־יהוה | אֱלֹהֵיכֶם וּלְעָבְדוֹ, בְּכָל־לְבַבְכֶם, וּבְכָל־נַפְשְׁכֶם: וְנָתַתִּי מְטַר־אַרְצְכֶם בְּעִתּוֹ, יוֹרֶה

BLESSINGS OF THE SHEMA

בָּרוּךְ *Blessed are You, HASHEM, our God, King of the universe, Who by His word brings on evenings, with wisdom opens gates, with understanding alters periods, changes the seasons, and orders the stars in their heavenly constellations as He wills. He creates day and night, removing light before darkness and darkness before light. He causes day to pass and brings night, and separates between day and night — HASHEM, Master of Legions, is His Name.* Chazzan— *May the living and enduring God continuously reign over us, for all eternity. Blessed are You, HASHEM, Who brings on evenings.* (Cong.— *Amen.*)

אַהֲבַת *With an eternal love have You loved the House of Israel, Your nation. Torah and commandments, decrees and ordinances have You taught us. Therefore HASHEM, our God, upon our retiring and arising, we will discuss Your decrees and we will rejoice with the words of Your Torah and with Your commandments for all eternity.* Chazzan— *For they are our life and the length of our days and about them we will meditate day and night. May You not remove Your love from us forever. Blessed are You, HASHEM, Who loves His nation Israel.* (Cong.— *Amen.*)

THE SHEMA

Immediately before its recitation concentrate on fulfilling the positive commandment of reciting the *Shema* twice daily. It is important to enunciate each word clearly and not to run words together. See *Laws* §40-52.

When praying without a *minyan,* begin with the following three-word formula:

God, trustworthy King.

Recite the first verse aloud, with the right hand covering the eyes, and concentrate intently upon accepting God's absolute sovereignty.

Hear, O Israel: HASHEM is our God, HASHEM, the One and Only.[1]

In an undertone— *Blessed is the Name of His glorious kingdom for all eternity.*

While reciting the first paragraph (*Deuteronomy* 6:5-9), concentrate on accepting the commandment to love God.

וְאָהַבְתָּ *You shall love HASHEM, your God, with all your heart, with all your soul and with all your resources. Let these matters that I command you today be upon your heart. Teach them thoroughly to your children and speak of them while you sit in your home, while you walk on the way, when you retire and when you arise. Bind them as a sign upon your arm and let them be tefillin between your eyes. And write them on the doorposts of your house and upon your gates.*

While reciting the second paragraph (*Deuteronomy* 11:13-21), concentrate on accepting all the commandments and the concept of reward and punishment.

וְהָיָה *And it will come to pass that if you continually hearken to My commandments that I command you today, to love HASHEM, your God, and to serve Him, with all your heart and with all your soul — then I will provide rain for your land in its proper time, the early*

(1) *Deuteronomy* 6:4.

וּמַלְקוֹשׁ, וְאָסַפְתָּ דְגָנֶךָ וְתִירֹשְׁךָ וְיִצְהָרֶךָ: וְנָתַתִּי | עֵשֶׂב | בְּשָׂדְךָ
לִבְהֶמְתֶּךָ, וְאָכַלְתָּ וְשָׂבָעְתָּ: הִשָּׁמְרוּ לָכֶם, פֶּן־יִפְתֶּה לְבַבְכֶם,
וְסַרְתֶּם וַעֲבַדְתֶּם | אֱלֹהִים | אֲחֵרִים, וְהִשְׁתַּחֲוִיתֶם לָהֶם: וְחָרָה |
אַף־יהוה בָּכֶם, וְעָצַר | אֶת־הַשָּׁמַיִם, וְלֹא־יִהְיֶה מָטָר, וְהָאֲדָמָה לֹא
תִתֵּן אֶת־יְבוּלָהּ, וַאֲבַדְתֶּם | מְהֵרָה מֵעַל הָאָרֶץ הַטֹּבָה | אֲשֶׁר |
יהוה נֹתֵן לָכֶם: וְשַׂמְתֶּם | אֶת־דְּבָרַי | אֵלֶּה, עַל־לְבַבְכֶם וְעַל־
נַפְשְׁכֶם, וּקְשַׁרְתֶּם | אֹתָם לְאוֹת | עַל־יֶדְכֶם, וְהָיוּ לְטוֹטָפֹת בֵּין |
עֵינֵיכֶם: וְלִמַּדְתֶּם | אֹתָם | אֶת־בְּנֵיכֶם, לְדַבֵּר בָּם, בְּשִׁבְתְּךָ בְּבֵיתֶךָ,
וּבְלֶכְתְּךָ בַדֶּרֶךְ, וּבְשָׁכְבְּךָ וּבְקוּמֶךָ: וּכְתַבְתָּם | עַל־מְזוּזוֹת בֵּיתֶךָ,
וּבִשְׁעָרֶיךָ: לְמַעַן | יִרְבּוּ | יְמֵיכֶם וִימֵי בְנֵיכֶם, עַל הָאֲדָמָה | אֲשֶׁר
נִשְׁבַּע | יהוה לַאֲבֹתֵיכֶם לָתֵת לָהֶם, כִּימֵי הַשָּׁמַיִם | עַל־הָאָרֶץ:

במדבר טו:לז-מא

וַיֹּאמֶר | יהוה | אֶל־מֹשֶׁה לֵּאמֹר: דַּבֵּר | אֶל־בְּנֵי | יִשְׂרָאֵל,
וְאָמַרְתָּ אֲלֵהֶם, וְעָשׂוּ לָהֶם צִיצִת, עַל־כַּנְפֵי בִגְדֵיהֶם
לְדֹרֹתָם, וְנָתְנוּ | עַל־צִיצִת הַכָּנָף, פְּתִיל תְּכֵלֶת: וְהָיָה לָכֶם לְצִיצִת,
וּרְאִיתֶם | אֹתוֹ, וּזְכַרְתֶּם | אֶת־כָּל־מִצְוֹת | יהוה, וַעֲשִׂיתֶם | אֹתָם,
וְלֹא תָתֻרוּ | אַחֲרֵי לְבַבְכֶם וְאַחֲרֵי | עֵינֵיכֶם, אֲשֶׁר־אַתֶּם זֹנִים |
אַחֲרֵיהֶם: לְמַעַן תִּזְכְּרוּ, וַעֲשִׂיתֶם | אֶת־כָּל־מִצְוֹתָי, וִהְיִיתֶם קְדֹשִׁים
לֵאלֹהֵיכֶם: אֲנִי יהוה | אֱלֹהֵיכֶם, אֲשֶׁר
הוֹצֵאתִי | אֶתְכֶם | מֵאֶרֶץ מִצְרַיִם, לִהְיוֹת
לָכֶם לֵאלֹהִים, אֲנִי | יהוה | אֱלֹהֵיכֶם: אֱמֶת —

Concentrate on fulfilling the commandment of remembering the Exodus from Egypt.

Although the word אֱמֶת belongs to the next paragraph, it is appended to the conclusion of the previous one, as explained in the commentary on page 42.

—*Chazzan* repeats **יהוה אֱלֹהֵיכֶם אֱמֶת.**

וֶאֱמוּנָה כָּל זֹאת, וְקַיָּם עָלֵינוּ, כִּי הוּא יהוה אֱלֹהֵינוּ וְאֵין
זוּלָתוֹ, וַאֲנַחְנוּ יִשְׂרָאֵל עַמּוֹ. הַפּוֹדֵנוּ מִיַּד מְלָכִים,
מַלְכֵּנוּ הַגּוֹאֲלֵנוּ מִכַּף כָּל הֶעָרִיצִים. הָאֵל הַנִּפְרָע לָנוּ מִצָּרֵינוּ,
וְהַמְשַׁלֵּם גְּמוּל לְכָל אֹיְבֵי נַפְשֵׁנוּ. הָעֹשֶׂה גְדֹלוֹת עַד אֵין חֵקֶר,
וְנִפְלָאוֹת עַד אֵין מִסְפָּר.[1] הַשָּׂם נַפְשֵׁנוּ בַּחַיִּים, וְלֹא נָתַן לַמּוֹט
רַגְלֵנוּ.[2] הַמַּדְרִיכֵנוּ עַל בָּמוֹת אוֹיְבֵינוּ, וַיָּרֶם קַרְנֵנוּ עַל כָּל שׂנְאֵינוּ.
הָעֹשֶׂה לָּנוּ נִסִּים וּנְקָמָה בְּפַרְעֹה, אוֹתוֹת וּמוֹפְתִים בְּאַדְמַת בְּנֵי חָם.
הַמַּכֶּה בְעֶבְרָתוֹ כָּל בְּכוֹרֵי מִצְרָיִם, וַיּוֹצֵא אֶת עַמּוֹ יִשְׂרָאֵל מִתּוֹכָם
לְחֵרוּת עוֹלָם. הַמַּעֲבִיר בָּנָיו בֵּין גִּזְרֵי יַם סוּף, אֶת רוֹדְפֵיהֶם וְאֶת

and late rains, that you may gather in your grain, your wine, and your oil. I will provide grass in your field for your cattle and you will eat and be satisfied. Beware lest your heart be seduced and you turn astray and serve gods of others and bow to them. Then the wrath of HASHEM *will blaze against you. He will restrain the heaven so there will be no rain and the ground will not yield its produce. And you will swiftly be banished from the goodly land which* HASHEM *gives you. Place these words of Mine upon your heart and upon your soul; bind them for a sign upon your arm and let them be tefillin between your eyes. Teach them to your children, to discuss them, while you sit in your home, while you walk on the way, when you retire and when you arise. And write them on the doorposts of your house and upon your gates. In order to prolong your days and the days of your children upon the ground that* HASHEM *has sworn to your ancestors to give them, like the days of the heaven on the earth.*

Numbers 15:37-41

וַיֹּאמֶר *And* HASHEM *said to Moses saying: Speak to the Children of Israel and say to them that they are to make themselves tzitzis on the corners of their garments, throughout their generations. And they are to place upon the tzitzis of each corner a thread of techeiles. And it shall constitute tzitzis for you, that you may see it and remember all the commandments of* HASHEM *and perform them; and not explore after your heart and after your eyes after which you stray. So that you may remember and perform all My commandments; and be holy to your God. I am* HASHEM*, your God, Who has removed you from the land of Egypt to be a God to you; I am* HASHEM *your God — it is true —*

Concentrate on fulfilling the commandment of remembering the Exodus from Egypt.

Although the word אֱמֶת, *'it is true,'* belongs to the next paragraph, it is appended to the conclusion of the previous one, as explained in the commentary on page 42.

Chazzan repeats: **HASHEM, your God, is true.**

וֶאֱמוּנָה *And faithful is all this, and it is firmly established for us that He is* HASHEM *our God, and there is none but Him, and we are Israel, His nation. He redeems us from the power of kings, our King Who delivers us from the hand of all the cruel tyrants. He is the God Who exacts vengeance for us from our foes and Who brings just retribution upon all enemies of our soul; Who performs great deeds that are beyond comprehension, and wonders beyond number.*[1] *Who set our soul in life and did not allow our foot to falter.*[2] *Who led us upon the heights of our enemies and raised our pride above all who hate us; Who wrought for us miracles and vengeance upon Pharaoh; signs and wonders on the land of the offspring of Ham; Who struck with His anger all the firstborn of Egypt and removed His nation Israel from their midst to eternal freedom; Who brought His children through the split parts of the Sea of Reeds while those who pursued them and*

(1) *Job* 9:10. (2) *Psalms* 66:9.

שׂוֹנְאֵיהֶם בִּתְהוֹמוֹת טִבַּע. וְרָאוּ בָנָיו גְּבוּרָתוֹ, שִׁבְּחוּ וְהוֹדוּ לִשְׁמוֹ. ❖ וּמַלְכוּתוֹ בְּרָצוֹן קִבְּלוּ עֲלֵיהֶם. מֹשֶׁה וּבְנֵי יִשְׂרָאֵל לְךָ עָנוּ שִׁירָה, בְּשִׂמְחָה רַבָּה, וְאָמְרוּ כֻלָּם:

מִי כָמֹכָה בָּאֵלִים יהוה, מִי כָּמֹכָה נֶאְדָּר בַּקֹּדֶשׁ, נוֹרָא תְהִלֹּת, עֹשֵׂה פֶלֶא.[1] ❖ מַלְכוּתְךָ רָאוּ בָנֶיךָ בּוֹקֵעַ יָם לִפְנֵי מֹשֶׁה, זֶה אֵלִי[2] עָנוּ וְאָמְרוּ:

יהוה יִמְלֹךְ לְעֹלָם וָעֶד.[3] ❖ וְנֶאֱמַר: כִּי פָדָה יהוה אֶת יַעֲקֹב, וּגְאָלוֹ מִיַּד חָזָק מִמֶּנּוּ.[4] בָּרוּךְ אַתָּה יהוה, גָּאַל יִשְׂרָאֵל.

(.Cong – אָמֵן.)

הַשְׁכִּיבֵנוּ יהוה אֱלֹהֵינוּ לְשָׁלוֹם, וְהַעֲמִידֵנוּ מַלְכֵּנוּ לְחַיִּים, וּפְרוֹשׂ עָלֵינוּ סֻכַּת שְׁלוֹמֶךָ, וְתַקְּנֵנוּ בְּעֵצָה טוֹבָה מִלְּפָנֶיךָ, וְהוֹשִׁיעֵנוּ לְמַעַן שְׁמֶךָ. וְהָגֵן בַּעֲדֵנוּ, וְהָסֵר מֵעָלֵינוּ אוֹיֵב, דֶּבֶר, וְחֶרֶב, וְרָעָב, וְיָגוֹן, וְהָסֵר שָׂטָן מִלְּפָנֵינוּ וּמֵאַחֲרֵינוּ, וּבְצֵל כְּנָפֶיךָ תַּסְתִּירֵנוּ,[5] כִּי אֵל שׁוֹמְרֵנוּ וּמַצִּילֵנוּ אָתָּה, כִּי אֵל מֶלֶךְ חַנּוּן וְרַחוּם אָתָּה.[6] ❖ וּשְׁמוֹר צֵאתֵנוּ וּבוֹאֵנוּ, לְחַיִּים וּלְשָׁלוֹם מֵעַתָּה וְעַד עוֹלָם.[7] וּפְרוֹשׂ עָלֵינוּ סֻכַּת שְׁלוֹמֶךָ. בָּרוּךְ אַתָּה יהוה, הַפּוֹרֵשׂ סֻכַּת שָׁלוֹם עָלֵינוּ וְעַל כָּל עַמּוֹ יִשְׂרָאֵל וְעַל יְרוּשָׁלָיִם. (.Cong – אָמֵן.)

Congregation rises and remains standing until after *Shemoneh Esrei.*
The congregation, followed by the *chazzan,* recites:

וְשָׁמְרוּ בְנֵי יִשְׂרָאֵל אֶת הַשַּׁבָּת, לַעֲשׂוֹת אֶת הַשַּׁבָּת לְדֹרֹתָם בְּרִית עוֹלָם. בֵּינִי וּבֵין בְּנֵי יִשְׂרָאֵל אוֹת הִיא לְעֹלָם, כִּי שֵׁשֶׁת יָמִים עָשָׂה יהוה אֶת הַשָּׁמַיִם וְאֶת הָאָרֶץ, וּבַיּוֹם הַשְּׁבִיעִי שָׁבַת וַיִּנָּפַשׁ.[8]

The *chazzan* recites חֲצִי קַדִּישׁ.

יִתְגַּדַּל וְיִתְקַדַּשׁ שְׁמֵהּ רַבָּא. (.Cong – אָמֵן.) בְּעָלְמָא דִּי בְרָא כִרְעוּתֵהּ, וְיַמְלִיךְ מַלְכוּתֵהּ, בְּחַיֵּיכוֹן וּבְיוֹמֵיכוֹן וּבְחַיֵּי דְכָל בֵּית יִשְׂרָאֵל, בַּעֲגָלָא וּבִזְמַן קָרִיב. וְאִמְרוּ: אָמֵן.

(.Cong – אָמֵן. יְהֵא שְׁמֵהּ רַבָּא מְבָרַךְ לְעָלַם וּלְעָלְמֵי עָלְמַיָּא.)

יְהֵא שְׁמֵהּ רַבָּא מְבָרַךְ לְעָלַם וּלְעָלְמֵי עָלְמַיָּא.

יִתְבָּרַךְ וְיִשְׁתַּבַּח וְיִתְפָּאַר וְיִתְרוֹמַם וְיִתְנַשֵּׂא וְיִתְהַדָּר וְיִתְעַלֶּה וְיִתְהַלָּל שְׁמֵהּ דְּקֻדְשָׁא בְּרִיךְ הוּא (.Cong – בְּרִיךְ הוּא) – לְעֵלָּא מִן כָּל בִּרְכָתָא וְשִׁירָתָא תֻּשְׁבְּחָתָא וְנֶחֱמָתָא, דַּאֲמִירָן בְּעָלְמָא. וְאִמְרוּ: אָמֵן. (.Cong – אָמֵן.)

hated them He caused to sink into the depths. When His children perceived His power, they lauded and gave grateful praise to His Name. Chazzan— *And His Kingship they accepted upon themselves willingly. Moses and the Children of Israel raised their voices to You in song with abundant gladness — and said unanimously:*

מִי כָמֹכָה *Who is like You among the heavenly powers, HASHEM! Who is like You, mighty in holiness, too awesome for praise, doing wonders!*[1] Chazzan— *Your children beheld Your majesty, as You split the sea before Moses: 'This is my God!'*[2] *they exclaimed, then they said:*

יהוה *'HASHEM shall reign for all eternity!'*[3] Chazzan— *And it is further said: 'For HASHEM has redeemed Jacob and delivered him from a power mightier than he.'*[4] *Blessed are You, HASHEM, Who redeemed Israel.*
(Cong.— *Amen.*)

הַשְׁכִּיבֵנוּ *Lay us down to sleep, HASHEM our God, in peace, raise us erect, our King, to life; and spread over us the shelter of Your peace. Set us aright with good counsel from before Your Presence, and save us for Your Name's sake. Shield us, remove from us foe, plague, sword, famine, and woe; and remove spiritual impediment from before us and behind us, and in the shadow of Your wings shelter us*[5] *— for God Who protects and rescues us are You; for God, the Gracious and Compassionate King, are You.*[6] Chazzan— *Safeguard our going and coming, for life and for peace from now to eternity.*[7] *And spread over us the shelter of Your peace. Blessed are You, HASHEM, Who spreads the shelter of peace upon us, upon all of His people Israel and upon Jerusalem.*
(Cong.— *Amen.*)

Congregation rises and remains standing until after *Shemoneh Esrei.*
The congregation, followed by the *chazzan,* recites:

וְשָׁמְרוּ *And the Children of Israel shall keep the Sabbath, to make the Sabbath an eternal covenant for their generations. Between Me and the Children of Israel it is a sign forever that in six days HASHEM made heaven and earth, and on the seventh day He rested and was refreshed.*[8]

The chazzan recites Half-*Kaddish.*

יִתְגַּדַּל *May His great Name grow exalted and sanctified* (Cong.— *Amen.*) *in the world that He created as He willed. May He give reign to His kingship in your lifetimes and in your days, and in the lifetimes of the entire Family of Israel, swiftly and soon. Now respond: Amen.*

(Cong.— *Amen. May His great Name be blessed forever and ever.*)
May His great Name be blessed forever and ever.

Blessed, praised, glorified, exalted, extolled, mighty, upraised, and lauded be the Name of the Holy One, Blessed is He (Cong.— *Blessed is He*) *— beyond any blessing and song, praise and consolation that are uttered in the world. Now respond: Amen.* (Cong.— *Amen.*)

---

(1) *Exodus* 15:11. (2) 15:2. (3) 15:18. (4) *Jeremiah* 31:10. (5) Cf. *Psalms* 17:8.
(6) Cf. *Nechemiah* 9:31. (7) Cf. *Psalms* 121:8. (8) *Exodus* 31:16-17.

❧ שמונה עשרה – עמידה ❧

Take three steps backward, then three steps forward. Remain standing with the feet together while reciting *Shemoneh Esrei*. Recite it with quiet devotion and without interruption, verbal or otherwise. Although its recitation should not be audible to others, one must pray loudly enough to hear himself.

אֲדֹנָי שְׂפָתַי תִּפְתָּח, וּפִי יַגִּיד תְּהִלָּתֶךָ.[1]

אבות

Bend the knees at בָּרוּךְ; bow at אַתָּה; straighten up at 'ה.

בָּרוּךְ אַתָּה יהוה אֱלֹהֵינוּ וֵאלֹהֵי אֲבוֹתֵינוּ, אֱלֹהֵי אַבְרָהָם, אֱלֹהֵי יִצְחָק, וֵאלֹהֵי יַעֲקֹב, הָאֵל הַגָּדוֹל הַגִּבּוֹר וְהַנּוֹרָא, אֵל עֶלְיוֹן, גּוֹמֵל חֲסָדִים טוֹבִים וְקוֹנֵה הַכֹּל, וְזוֹכֵר חַסְדֵי אָבוֹת, וּמֵבִיא גוֹאֵל לִבְנֵי בְנֵיהֶם, לְמַעַן שְׁמוֹ בְּאַהֲבָה. מֶלֶךְ עוֹזֵר וּמוֹשִׁיעַ וּמָגֵן.

Bend the knees at בָּרוּךְ; bow at אַתָּה; straighten up at 'ה.

בָּרוּךְ אַתָּה יהוה, מָגֵן אַבְרָהָם.

גבורות

אַתָּה גִּבּוֹר לְעוֹלָם אֲדֹנָי, מְחַיֵּה מֵתִים אַתָּה, רַב לְהוֹשִׁיעַ. מְכַלְכֵּל חַיִּים בְּחֶסֶד, מְחַיֵּה מֵתִים בְּרַחֲמִים רַבִּים, סוֹמֵךְ נוֹפְלִים, וְרוֹפֵא חוֹלִים, וּמַתִּיר אֲסוּרִים, וּמְקַיֵּם אֱמוּנָתוֹ לִישֵׁנֵי עָפָר. מִי כָמוֹךָ בַּעַל גְּבוּרוֹת, וּמִי דּוֹמֶה לָּךְ, מֶלֶךְ מֵמִית וּמְחַיֶּה וּמַצְמִיחַ יְשׁוּעָה. וְנֶאֱמָן אַתָּה לְהַחֲיוֹת מֵתִים. בָּרוּךְ אַתָּה יהוה, מְחַיֵּה הַמֵּתִים.

קדושת השם

אַתָּה קָדוֹשׁ וְשִׁמְךָ קָדוֹשׁ, וּקְדוֹשִׁים בְּכָל יוֹם יְהַלְלוּךָ סֶּלָה. בָּרוּךְ אַתָּה יהוה, הָאֵל הַקָּדוֹשׁ.

קדושת היום

אַתָּה קִדַּשְׁתָּ אֶת יוֹם הַשְּׁבִיעִי לִשְׁמֶךָ,* תַּכְלִית* מַעֲשֵׂה שָׁמַיִם וָאָרֶץ, וּבֵרַכְתּוֹ מִכָּל הַיָּמִים, וְקִדַּשְׁתּוֹ מִכָּל הַזְּמַנִּים, וְכֵן כָּתוּב* בְּתוֹרָתֶךָ:

❧ SHEMONEH ESREI OF SHABBOS / AMIDAH ❧

The *Amidah* of the Sabbath and *Yom Tov* should have been identical to the weekday one, with the inclusion of an appropriate paragraph indicating the holiness of the day, as is done on Rosh Chodesh and *Chol HaMoed*. The Sages, however, wished to make the Sabbath Festival prayers simpler and less burdensome than they would be if we had to beseech God for the entire catalogue of our personal and national needs. Therefore they omitted the middle thirteen blessings, and replaced them with a single blessing known as קְדוּשַּׁת הַיּוֹם, *Sanctity of the Day* (*Berachos* 21a).

Because of the fact that the entire weekday *Shemoneh Esrei* would have been appropriate for the holy days as well, in the event someone erred in his prayers and began to recite the weekday blessings on the Sabbath or *Yom Tov*, he should complete whatever blessing he has begun and then begin the appropriate blessing of קְדוּשַּׁת הַיּוֹם, *Sanctity of the Day* (*Orach Chaim* 268:2). In the case of the Sabbath eve *Maariv* this would be אַתָּה קִדַּשְׁתָּ.

❧ קְדוּשַּׁת הַיּוֹם / Sanctification of the Day

אַתָּה קִדַּשְׁתָּ . . . לִשְׁמֶךָ — *You sanctified . . . for*

SHEMONEH ESREI – AMIDAH

Take three steps backward, then three steps forward. Remain standing with the feet together while reciting *Shemoneh Esrei.* Recite it with quiet devotion and without interruption, verbal or otherwise. Although its recitation should not be audible to others, one must pray loudly enough to hear himself.

My Lord, open my lips, that my mouth may declare Your praise.[1]

PATRIARCHS

Bend the knees at *'Blessed'*; bow at *'You'*; straighten up at *'Hashem.'*

בָּרוּךְ *Blessed are You, Hashem, our God and the God of our forefathers, God of Abraham, God of Isaac, and God of Jacob; the great, mighty, and awesome God, the supreme God, Who bestows beneficial kindnesses and creates everything, Who recalls the kindnesses of the Patriarchs and brings a Redeemer to their children's children, for His Name's sake, with love. O King, Helper, Savior, and Shield.*

Bend the knees at *'Blessed'*; bow at *'You'*; straighten up at *'Hashem.'*

Blessed are You, Hashem, Shield of Abraham.

GOD'S MIGHT

אַתָּה *You are eternally mighty, my Lord, the Resuscitator of the dead are You; abundantly able to save. He sustains the living with kindness, resuscitates the dead with abundant mercy, supports the fallen, heals the sick, releases the confined, and maintains His faith to those asleep in the dust. Who is like You, O Master of mighty deeds, and who is comparable to You, O King Who causes death and restores life and makes salvation sprout! And You are faithful to resuscitate the dead. Blessed are You, Hashem, Who resuscitates the dead.*

HOLINESS OF GOD'S NAME

אַתָּה *You are holy and Your Name is holy, and holy ones praise You every day, forever. Blessed are You, Hashem, the holy God.*

SANCTIFICATION OF THE DAY

אַתָּה *You sanctified the seventh day for Your Name's sake,* the conclusion* of the creation of heaven and earth. Of all days, You blessed it; and of all seasons, You sanctified it — and so it is written* in Your Torah:*

(1) *Psalms* 51:17.

Your Name's sake. God sanctified the Sabbath as an eternal reminder that He rested on that day *(Abudraham);* and He made it clear that we are not to regard it as a humanly legislated day of rest for personal convenience, but are to dedicate it to His service, *for* [His] *Name's sake (R' Munk).*

תַּכְלִית — *The conclusion.* God's six days of labor ended on the Sabbath. The word תַּכְלִית has the secondary meaning of *purpose:* the purpose of Creation was so that God could allow people to enjoy the spiritual pleasure of His Presence. That will occur in its fullest sense only when the Messiah arrives; that era will be known as an unending Sabbath, because its holiness will be unlimited. Meanwhile, however, a taste of the spiritual bliss of the future is given Israel every week with the advent of the holy Sabbath. Accordingly, it is only on the Sabbath that Creation achieves its purpose *(Be'er Mayim Chaim).*

וְכֵן כָּתוּב — *And so it is written.* The passage about to be quoted proves that the Sabbath represents the *purpose of the creation (Tur).*

וַיְכֻלּוּ הַשָּׁמַיִם וְהָאָרֶץ* וְכָל צְבָאָם.* וַיְכַל אֱלֹהִים בַּיּוֹם הַשְּׁבִיעִי מְלַאכְתּוֹ אֲשֶׁר עָשָׂה, וַיִּשְׁבֹּת* בַּיּוֹם הַשְּׁבִיעִי מִכָּל מְלַאכְתּוֹ אֲשֶׁר עָשָׂה. וַיְבָרֶךְ אֱלֹהִים אֶת יוֹם הַשְּׁבִיעִי, וַיְקַדֵּשׁ אֹתוֹ, כִּי בוֹ שָׁבַת מִכָּל מְלַאכְתּוֹ, אֲשֶׁר בָּרָא אֱלֹהִים לַעֲשׂוֹת.*[1]

אֱלֹהֵינוּ וֵאלֹהֵי אֲבוֹתֵינוּ רְצֵה בִמְנוּחָתֵנוּ.* קַדְּשֵׁנוּ בְּמִצְוֹתֶיךָ,* וְתֵן חֶלְקֵנוּ בְּתוֹרָתֶךָ. שַׂבְּעֵנוּ מִטּוּבֶךָ, וְשַׂמְּחֵנוּ בִּישׁוּעָתֶךָ, וְטַהֵר לִבֵּנוּ לְעָבְדְּךָ בֶּאֱמֶת. וְהַנְחִילֵנוּ יהוה אֱלֹהֵינוּ בְּאַהֲבָה וּבְרָצוֹן שַׁבַּת קָדְשֶׁךָ, וְיָנוּחוּ בָהּ* יִשְׂרָאֵל מְקַדְּשֵׁי שְׁמֶךָ. בָּרוּךְ אַתָּה יהוה, מְקַדֵּשׁ הַשַּׁבָּת.

עבודה

רְצֵה יהוה אֱלֹהֵינוּ בְּעַמְּךָ יִשְׂרָאֵל וּבִתְפִלָּתָם, וְהָשֵׁב אֶת הָעֲבוֹדָה לִדְבִיר בֵּיתֶךָ. וְאִשֵּׁי יִשְׂרָאֵל וּתְפִלָּתָם בְּאַהֲבָה תְקַבֵּל בְּרָצוֹן, וּתְהִי לְרָצוֹן תָּמִיד עֲבוֹדַת יִשְׂרָאֵל עַמֶּךָ.

[If the following paragraph is forgotten, repeat *Shemoneh Esrei*. See *Laws* §56.]

אֱלֹהֵינוּ וֵאלֹהֵי אֲבוֹתֵינוּ, יַעֲלֶה, וְיָבֹא, וְיַגִּיעַ, וְיֵרָאֶה, וְיֵרָצֶה, וְיִשָּׁמַע, וְיִפָּקֵד, וְיִזָּכֵר זִכְרוֹנֵנוּ וּפִקְדוֹנֵנוּ, וְזִכְרוֹן אֲבוֹתֵינוּ, וְזִכְרוֹן מָשִׁיחַ בֶּן דָּוִד עַבְדֶּךָ, וְזִכְרוֹן יְרוּשָׁלַיִם עִיר קָדְשֶׁךָ, וְזִכְרוֹן כָּל עַמְּךָ בֵּית יִשְׂרָאֵל לְפָנֶיךָ, לִפְלֵיטָה לְטוֹבָה לְחֵן וּלְחֶסֶד וּלְרַחֲמִים, לְחַיִּים וּלְשָׁלוֹם בְּיוֹם חַג הַסֻּכּוֹת הַזֶּה. זָכְרֵנוּ יהוה אֱלֹהֵינוּ בּוֹ לְטוֹבָה, וּפָקְדֵנוּ בוֹ לִבְרָכָה, וְהוֹשִׁיעֵנוּ בוֹ לְחַיִּים. וּבִדְבַר יְשׁוּעָה וְרַחֲמִים, חוּס וְחָנֵּנוּ וְרַחֵם עָלֵינוּ וְהוֹשִׁיעֵנוּ, כִּי אֵלֶיךָ עֵינֵינוּ, כִּי אֵל מֶלֶךְ חַנּוּן וְרַחוּם אָתָּה.[2]

וְתֶחֱזֶינָה עֵינֵינוּ בְּשׁוּבְךָ לְצִיּוֹן בְּרַחֲמִים. בָּרוּךְ אַתָּה יהוה, הַמַּחֲזִיר שְׁכִינָתוֹ לְצִיּוֹן.

⁂ וַיְכֻלּוּ הַשָּׁמַיִם וְהָאָרֶץ — *Thus the heaven and the earth were finished*. The Talmud (*Shabbos* 119b) derives homiletically from this verse that whoever recites this passage is regarded as God's partner in Creation, because the word וַיְכֻלּוּ homiletically can be vocalized וַיְכַלּוּ, *and* **they** [i.e., God and everyone who acknowledges His Creation] *finished*. God's Creation would have fallen short of its purpose unless man acknowledged Him as the Creator (*Maharsha*).

וְכָל צְבָאָם — *And all their legion*. The word צָבָא, *array* or *legion*, refers to an organized, disciplined group acting in unison. The heavenly bodies and spiritual beings are a *legion* because they act only according to God's plan. On earth, it is the duty of Israel, by acting according to the Torah, to be His earthly legion (*R' Bunam of P'shis'cha*).

וַיְכַל ... וַיִּשְׁבֹּת — *Completed ... and He abstained*. These two words have different connotations. *He completed* [וַיְכַל] means that the task at hand was finished, with nothing left to be done; *He abstained* [וַיִּשְׁבֹּת] implies that more is to be done, but it is set aside for another day. The Torah uses both words to teach people that even though they are still in the middle of their work, when the Sabbath arrives they should consider it completed and not think about it (*Avnei Eliyahu*).

אֲשֶׁר בָּרָא אֱלֹהִים לַעֲשׂוֹת — *Which God created to*

וַיְכֻלּוּ *Thus the heaven and the earth were finished,* and all their legion.* On the seventh day God completed His work which He had done, and He abstained* on the seventh day from all His work which He had done. God blessed the seventh day and sanctified it, because on it He had abstained from all His work which God created to make.**[1]

אֱלֹהֵינוּ *Our God and the God of our forefathers, may You be pleased with our rest.* Sanctify us with Your commandments* and grant our share in Your Torah; satisfy us from Your goodness and gladden us with Your salvation, and purify our heart to serve You sincerely. O* HASHEM, *our God, with love and favor grant us Your holy Sabbath as a heritage and may Israel, the sanctifiers of Your Name, rest on it.* Blessed are You,* HASHEM, *Who sanctifies the Sabbath.*

TEMPLE SERVICE

רְצֵה *Be favorable,* HASHEM, *our God, toward Your people Israel and their prayer and restore the service to the Holy of Holies of Your Temple. The fire-offerings of Israel and their prayer accept with love and favor, and may the service of Your people Israel always be favorable to You.*

[If the following paragraph is forgotten, repeat *Shemoneh Esrei.* See *Laws* §56.]

אֱלֹהֵינוּ *Our God and God of our forefathers, may there rise, come, reach, be noted, be favored, be heard, be considered, and be remembered — the remembrance and consideration of ourselves; the remembrance of our forefathers; the remembrance of Messiah, son of David, Your servant; the remembrance of Jerusalem, the City of Your Holiness, the remembrance of Your entire people the Family of Israel — before You, for deliverance, for goodness, for grace, for kindness, and for compassion, for life, and for peace on this day of the Succos Festival. Remember us on it,* HASHEM, *our God, for goodness; consider us on it for blessing; and help us on it for life. In the matter of salvation and compassion, pity, be gracious and compassionate with us and help us, for our eyes are turned to You, because You are God, the gracious and compassionate King.*[2]

וְתֶחֱזֶינָה *May our eyes behold Your return to Zion in compassion. Blessed are You,* HASHEM, *Who restores His Presence to Zion.*

(1) *Genesis* 2:1-3. (2) Cf. *Nechemiah* 9:31.

---

make. People can labor long and hard to *create* something — whether it is a house, a tool, or a business. Then it is up to them to *use* it properly. God created the world for the use of humanity; the *completion* of Creation, however, He entrusted to mankind. Now it is up to *to us* to *use it* as He intended *(Chasam Sofer).*

⁂ אֱלֹהֵינוּ . . . רְצֵה בִמְנוּחָתֵנוּ — *O God . . . may You be pleased with our rest.* Even though we may concentrate more on relaxation and good food than we will on spiritual growth, we ask that You not be displeased by our human frailty *(Etz Yosef).*

קַדְּשֵׁנוּ בְּמִצְוֹתֶיךָ — *Sanctify us with Your commandments.* The *performance* of *mitzvos* in itself elevates a person and makes him more prone to absorb sanctity. Alternatively, the word קַדְּשֵׁנוּ can be related to קִדּוּשִׁין, *betrothal.* God has *betrothed* Israel, as it were, by allowing us to perform His commandments *(Abudraham).*

הודאה

Bow at מוֹדִים; straighten up at 'ה.

מוֹדִים אֲנַחְנוּ לָךְ שָׁאַתָּה הוּא יהוה אֱלֹהֵינוּ וֵאלֹהֵי אֲבוֹתֵינוּ לְעוֹלָם וָעֶד. צוּר חַיֵּינוּ, מָגֵן יִשְׁעֵנוּ אַתָּה הוּא לְדוֹר וָדוֹר. נוֹדֶה לְּךָ וּנְסַפֵּר תְּהִלָּתֶךָ[1] עַל חַיֵּינוּ הַמְּסוּרִים בְּיָדֶךָ, וְעַל נִשְׁמוֹתֵינוּ הַפְּקוּדוֹת לָךְ, וְעַל נִסֶּיךָ שֶׁבְּכָל יוֹם עִמָּנוּ, וְעַל נִפְלְאוֹתֶיךָ וְטוֹבוֹתֶיךָ שֶׁבְּכָל עֵת, עֶרֶב וָבֹקֶר וְצָהֳרָיִם. הַטּוֹב כִּי לֹא כָלוּ רַחֲמֶיךָ, וְהַמְּרַחֵם כִּי לֹא תַמּוּ חֲסָדֶיךָ,[2] מֵעוֹלָם קִוִּינוּ לָךְ.

וְעַל כֻּלָּם יִתְבָּרַךְ וְיִתְרוֹמַם שִׁמְךָ מַלְכֵּנוּ תָּמִיד לְעוֹלָם וָעֶד.

Bend the knees at בָּרוּךְ; bow at אַתָּה; straighten up at 'ה.

וְכֹל הַחַיִּים יוֹדוּךָ סֶּלָה, וִיהַלְלוּ אֶת שִׁמְךָ בֶּאֱמֶת, הָאֵל יְשׁוּעָתֵנוּ וְעֶזְרָתֵנוּ סֶלָה. בָּרוּךְ אַתָּה יהוה, הַטּוֹב שִׁמְךָ וּלְךָ נָאֶה לְהוֹדוֹת.

שלום

שָׁלוֹם רָב עַל יִשְׂרָאֵל עַמְּךָ תָּשִׂים לְעוֹלָם, כִּי אַתָּה הוּא מֶלֶךְ אָדוֹן לְכָל הַשָּׁלוֹם. וְטוֹב בְּעֵינֶיךָ לְבָרֵךְ אֶת עַמְּךָ יִשְׂרָאֵל, בְּכָל עֵת וּבְכָל שָׁעָה בִּשְׁלוֹמֶךָ. בָּרוּךְ אַתָּה יהוה, הַמְּבָרֵךְ אֶת עַמּוֹ יִשְׂרָאֵל בַּשָּׁלוֹם.

יִהְיוּ לְרָצוֹן אִמְרֵי פִי וְהֶגְיוֹן לִבִּי לְפָנֶיךָ, יהוה צוּרִי וְגֹאֲלִי.[3]

אֱלֹהַי, נְצוֹר לְשׁוֹנִי מֵרָע, וּשְׂפָתַי מִדַּבֵּר מִרְמָה,[4] וְלִמְקַלְלַי נַפְשִׁי תִדּוֹם, וְנַפְשִׁי כֶּעָפָר לַכֹּל תִּהְיֶה. פְּתַח לִבִּי בְּתוֹרָתֶךָ, וּבְמִצְוֹתֶיךָ תִּרְדּוֹף נַפְשִׁי. וְכֹל הַחוֹשְׁבִים עָלַי רָעָה, מְהֵרָה הָפֵר עֲצָתָם וְקַלְקֵל מַחֲשַׁבְתָּם. עֲשֵׂה לְמַעַן שְׁמֶךָ, עֲשֵׂה לְמַעַן יְמִינֶךָ, עֲשֵׂה לְמַעַן קְדֻשָּׁתֶךָ, עֲשֵׂה לְמַעַן תּוֹרָתֶךָ. לְמַעַן יֵחָלְצוּן יְדִידֶיךָ, הוֹשִׁיעָה יְמִינְךָ וַעֲנֵנִי.[5]

Some recite verses pertaining to their names here. See page 1301.

יִהְיוּ לְרָצוֹן אִמְרֵי פִי וְהֶגְיוֹן לִבִּי לְפָנֶיךָ, יהוה צוּרִי וְגֹאֲלִי.[3]

Bow and take three steps back. Bow left and say . . . עֹשֶׂה, bow right and say . . . הוּא יַעֲשֶׂה; bow forward and say וְעַל כָּל . . . אָמֵן.

עֹשֶׂה שָׁלוֹם בִּמְרוֹמָיו, הוּא יַעֲשֶׂה שָׁלוֹם עָלֵינוּ, וְעַל כָּל יִשְׂרָאֵל. וְאִמְרוּ: אָמֵן.

(1) Cf. *Psalms* 79:13. (2) Cf. *Lamentations* 3:22. (3) *Psalms* 19:15 (4) Cf. 34:14. (5) 60:7; 108:7.

THANKSGIVING [MODIM]

Bow at *'We gratefully thank You'*; straighten up at *'HASHEM.'*

מוֹדִים *We gratefully thank You, for it is You Who are HASHEM, our God and the God of our forefathers for all eternity; Rock of our lives, Shield of our salvation are You from generation to generation. We shall thank You and relate Your praise[1] — for our lives, which are committed to Your power and for our souls that are entrusted to You; for Your miracles that are with us every day; and for Your wonders and favors in every season — evening, morning, and afternoon. The Beneficent One, for Your compassions were never exhausted, and the Compassionate One, for Your kindnesses never ended[2] — always have we put our hope in You.*

For all these, may Your Name be blessed and exalted, our King, continually forever and ever.

Bend the knees at *'Blessed'*; bow at *'You'*; straighten up at *'HASHEM.'*

Everything alive will gratefully acknowledge You, Selah! and praise Your Name sincerely, O God of our salvation and help, Selah! Blessed are You, HASHEM, Your Name is 'The Beneficent One' and to You it is fitting to give thanks.

PEACE

שָׁלוֹם *Establish abundant peace upon Your people Israel forever, for You are King, Master of all peace. May it be good in Your eyes to bless Your people Israel at every time and every hour with Your peace. Blessed are You, HASHEM, Who blesses His people Israel with peace.*

May the expressions of my mouth and the thoughts of my heart find favor before You, HASHEM, my Rock and my Redeemer.[3]

אֱלֹהַי *My God, guard my tongue from evil and my lips from speaking deceitfully.[4] To those who curse me, let my soul be silent; and let my soul be like dust to everyone. Open my heart to Your Torah, then my soul will pursue Your commandments. As for all those who design evil against me, speedily nullify their counsel and disrupt their design. Act for Your Name's sake; act for Your right hand's sake; act for Your sanctity's sake; act for Your Torah's sake. That Your beloved ones may be given rest; let Your right hand save, and respond to me.[5]*

Some recite verses pertaining to their names at this point. See page 1301.

May the expressions of my mouth and the thoughts of my heart find favor before You, HASHEM, my Rock and my Redeemer.[3] He Who makes peace in His heights, may He make peace upon us, and upon all Israel. Now respond: Amen.

Bow and take three steps back. Bow left and say, *'He Who makes peace . . .'*; bow right and say, *'may He make peace . . .'*; bow forward and say, *'and upon . . . Amen.'*

יְהִי רָצוֹן מִלְּפָנֶיךָ יהוה אֱלֹהֵינוּ וֵאלֹהֵי אֲבוֹתֵינוּ, שֶׁיִּבָּנֶה בֵּית הַמִּקְדָּשׁ בִּמְהֵרָה בְיָמֵינוּ, וְתֵן חֶלְקֵנוּ בְּתוֹרָתֶךָ. וְשָׁם נַעֲבָדְךָ בְּיִרְאָה, כִּימֵי עוֹלָם וּכְשָׁנִים קַדְמוֹנִיּוֹת. וְעָרְבָה לַיהוה מִנְחַת יְהוּדָה וִירוּשָׁלָיִם, כִּימֵי עוֹלָם וּכְשָׁנִים קַדְמוֹנִיּוֹת.[1]

SHEMONEH ESREI ENDS HERE.

Remain standing in place for at least a few moments before taking three steps forward.

All present stand and recite וַיְכֻלּוּ aloud in unison.

Conversation is forbidden until after the אָמֵן response to the blessing מְקַדֵּשׁ הַשַּׁבָּת (below).

וַיְכֻלּוּ הַשָּׁמַיִם וְהָאָרֶץ וְכָל צְבָאָם. וַיְכַל אֱלֹהִים בַּיּוֹם הַשְּׁבִיעִי מְלַאכְתּוֹ אֲשֶׁר עָשָׂה, וַיִּשְׁבֹּת בַּיּוֹם הַשְּׁבִיעִי מִכָּל מְלַאכְתּוֹ אֲשֶׁר עָשָׂה. וַיְבָרֶךְ אֱלֹהִים אֶת יוֹם הַשְּׁבִיעִי, וַיְקַדֵּשׁ אֹתוֹ, כִּי בוֹ שָׁבַת מִכָּל מְלַאכְתּוֹ, אֲשֶׁר בָּרָא אֱלֹהִים לַעֲשׂוֹת.[2]

ברכה מעין שבע

Chazzan continues:

בָּרוּךְ אַתָּה יהוה אֱלֹהֵינוּ וֵאלֹהֵי אֲבוֹתֵינוּ, אֱלֹהֵי אַבְרָהָם, אֱלֹהֵי יִצְחָק, וֵאלֹהֵי יַעֲקֹב, הָאֵל הַגָּדוֹל הַגִּבּוֹר וְהַנּוֹרָא, אֵל עֶלְיוֹן, קוֹנֵה שָׁמַיִם וָאָרֶץ.

Congregation, then *chazzan:*

מָגֵן אָבוֹת בִּדְבָרוֹ, מְחַיֵּה מֵתִים בְּמַאֲמָרוֹ, הָאֵל הַקָּדוֹשׁ שֶׁאֵין כָּמוֹהוּ, הַמֵּנִיחַ לְעַמּוֹ בְּיוֹם שַׁבַּת קָדְשׁוֹ, כִּי בָם רָצָה לְהָנִיחַ לָהֶם. לְפָנָיו נַעֲבֹד בְּיִרְאָה וָפַחַד, וְנוֹדֶה לִשְׁמוֹ בְּכָל יוֹם תָּמִיד מֵעֵין הַבְּרָכוֹת. אֵל הַהוֹדָאוֹת, אֲדוֹן הַשָּׁלוֹם, מְקַדֵּשׁ הַשַּׁבָּת וּמְבָרֵךְ שְׁבִיעִי, וּמֵנִיחַ בִּקְדֻשָּׁה לְעַם מְדֻשְּׁנֵי עֹנֶג, זֵכֶר לְמַעֲשֵׂה בְרֵאשִׁית.

Chazzan continues:

אֱלֹהֵינוּ וֵאלֹהֵי אֲבוֹתֵינוּ רְצֵה בִמְנוּחָתֵנוּ. קַדְּשֵׁנוּ בְּמִצְוֹתֶיךָ, וְתֵן חֶלְקֵנוּ בְּתוֹרָתֶךָ. שַׂבְּעֵנוּ מִטּוּבֶךָ, וְשַׂמְּחֵנוּ בִּישׁוּעָתֶךָ, וְטַהֵר לִבֵּנוּ לְעָבְדְּךָ בֶּאֱמֶת. וְהַנְחִילֵנוּ יהוה אֱלֹהֵינוּ בְּאַהֲבָה וּבְרָצוֹן שַׁבַּת קָדְשֶׁךָ, וְיָנוּחוּ בָהּ יִשְׂרָאֵל מְקַדְּשֵׁי שְׁמֶךָ. בָּרוּךְ אַתָּה יהוה, מְקַדֵּשׁ הַשַּׁבָּת. (–Cong. אָמֵן.)

The *chazzan* recites קַדִּישׁ שָׁלֵם.

יִתְגַּדַּל וְיִתְקַדַּשׁ שְׁמֵהּ רַבָּא. (–Cong. אָמֵן.) בְּעָלְמָא דִּי בְרָא כִרְעוּתֵהּ. וְיַמְלִיךְ מַלְכוּתֵהּ, בְּחַיֵּיכוֹן וּבְיוֹמֵיכוֹן וּבְחַיֵּי דְכָל בֵּית יִשְׂרָאֵל, בַּעֲגָלָא וּבִזְמַן קָרִיב. וְאִמְרוּ: אָמֵן.

(–Cong. אָמֵן. יְהֵא שְׁמֵהּ רַבָּא מְבָרַךְ לְעָלַם וּלְעָלְמֵי עָלְמַיָּא.)

יְהִי רָצוֹן *May it be Your will,* HASHEM, *our God and the God of our forefathers, that the Holy Temple be rebuilt, speedily in our days. Grant us our share in Your Torah, and may we serve You there with reverence, as in days of old and in former years. Then the offering of Judah and Jerusalem will be pleasing to* HASHEM, *as in days of old and in former years.*[1]

SHEMONEH ESREI ENDS HERE.

Remain standing in place for at least a few moments before taking three steps forward.

All present stand and recite וַיְכֻלּוּ, *'Thus the heavens . . .,'* aloud in unison. Conversation is forbidden until after the *'Amen'* response to the blessing, *'Who sanctifies the Sabbath'* (below).

וַיְכֻלּוּ *Thus the heavens and the earth were finished, and all their legion. On the seventh day God completed His work which He had done, and He abstained on the seventh day from all His work which He had done. God blessed the seventh day and sanctified it, because on it He had abstained from all His work which God created to make.*[2]

THE SEVEN-FACETED BLESSING

Chazzan continues:

בָּרוּךְ *Blessed are You,* HASHEM, *our God and the God of our forefathers, God of Abraham, God of Isaac, and God of Jacob; the great, mighty, and awesome God, the supreme God, Creator of heaven and earth.*

Congregation, then *chazzan:*

מָגֵן *He Who was the shield of our forefathers with His word, Who resuscitates the dead with His utterance, the Holy God Who is unequalled, Who grants rest to His people on His holy Sabbath day, for He was pleased with them to grant them rest. Before Him we will serve with awe and dread and give thanks to His Name every day continually with appropriate blessings. God of grateful praise, Master of peace, Who sanctifies the Sabbath and blesses the seventh day, and gives rest with holiness to a people saturated with delight — in memory of the work of Creation.*

Chazzan continues:

אֱלֹהֵינוּ *Our God and the God of our forefathers, may You be pleased with our rest. Sanctify us with Your commandments and grant us our share in Your Torah; satisfy us from Your goodness and gladden us with Your salvation, and purify our heart to serve You sincerely. O* HASHEM, *our God, with love and favor grant us Your holy Sabbath as a heritage and may Israel, the sanctifiers of Your Name, rest on it. Blessed are You,* HASHEM, *Who sanctifies the Sabbath.*

(Cong.— *Amen.*)

The *chazzan* recites the Full *Kaddish.*

יִתְגַּדַּל *May His great Name grow exalted and sanctified* (Cong.— *Amen.*) *in the world that He created as He willed. May He give reign to His kingship in your lifetimes and in your days, and in the lifetimes of the entire Family of Israel, swiftly and soon. Now respond: Amen.*

(Cong.— *Amen. May His great Name be blessed forever and ever.*)

---

(1) *Malachi* 3:4. (2) *Genesis* 2:1-3.

יְהֵא שְׁמֵהּ רַבָּא מְבָרַךְ לְעָלַם וּלְעָלְמֵי עָלְמַיָּא.

יִתְבָּרַךְ וְיִשְׁתַּבַּח וְיִתְפָּאַר וְיִתְרוֹמַם וְיִתְנַשֵּׂא וְיִתְהַדָּר וְיִתְעַלֶּה וְיִתְהַלָּל שְׁמֵהּ דְּקֻדְשָׁא בְּרִיךְ הוּא (.Cong – בְּרִיךְ הוּא) – לְעֵלָּא מִן כָּל בִּרְכָתָא וְשִׁירָתָא תֻּשְׁבְּחָתָא וְנֶחֱמָתָא, דַּאֲמִירָן בְּעָלְמָא. וְאִמְרוּ: אָמֵן. (.Cong – אָמֵן.)

(.Cong – קַבֵּל בְּרַחֲמִים וּבְרָצוֹן אֶת תְּפִלָּתֵנוּ.)

תִּתְקַבֵּל צְלוֹתְהוֹן וּבָעוּתְהוֹן דְּכָל בֵּית יִשְׂרָאֵל קֳדָם אֲבוּהוֹן דִּי בִשְׁמַיָּא. וְאִמְרוּ: אָמֵן. (.Cong – אָמֵן.)

(.Cong – יְהִי שֵׁם יהוה מְבֹרָךְ, מֵעַתָּה וְעַד עוֹלָם.[1])

יְהֵא שְׁלָמָא רַבָּא מִן שְׁמַיָּא, וְחַיִּים עָלֵינוּ וְעַל כָּל יִשְׂרָאֵל. וְאִמְרוּ: אָמֵן. (.Cong – אָמֵן.)

(.Cong – עֶזְרִי מֵעִם יהוה, עֹשֵׂה שָׁמַיִם וָאָרֶץ.[2])

Take three steps back. Bow left and say . . . עֹשֶׂה; bow right and say . . . הוּא; bow forward and say וְעַל כָּל . . . אָמֵן. Remain standing in place for a few moments, then take three steps forward.

עֹשֶׂה שָׁלוֹם בִּמְרוֹמָיו, הוּא יַעֲשֶׂה שָׁלוֹם עָלֵינוּ, וְעַל כָּל יִשְׂרָאֵל. וְאִמְרוּ: אָמֵן. (.Cong – אָמֵן.)

קידוש בבית הכנסת

In some congregations, the *chazzan* recites *Kiddush* [although he will repeat *Kiddush* at home].

סַבְרִי מָרָנָן וְרַבָּנָן וְרַבּוֹתַי:

בָּרוּךְ אַתָּה יהוה אֱלֹהֵינוּ מֶלֶךְ הָעוֹלָם, בּוֹרֵא פְּרִי הַגָּפֶן. (.Cong – אָמֵן.)

בָּרוּךְ אַתָּה יהוה אֱלֹהֵינוּ מֶלֶךְ הָעוֹלָם, אֲשֶׁר קִדְּשָׁנוּ בְּמִצְוֹתָיו, וְרָצָה בָנוּ, וְשַׁבַּת קָדְשׁוֹ בְּאַהֲבָה וּבְרָצוֹן הִנְחִילָנוּ, זִכָּרוֹן לְמַעֲשֵׂה בְרֵאשִׁית. כִּי הוּא יוֹם תְּחִלָּה לְמִקְרָאֵי קֹדֶשׁ, זֵכֶר לִיצִיאַת מִצְרָיִם. כִּי בָנוּ בָחַרְתָּ, וְאוֹתָנוּ קִדַּשְׁתָּ, מִכָּל הָעַמִּים. וְשַׁבַּת קָדְשְׁךָ בְּאַהֲבָה וּבְרָצוֹן הִנְחַלְתָּנוּ. בָּרוּךְ אַתָּה יהוה, מְקַדֵּשׁ הַשַּׁבָּת. (.Cong – אָמֵן.)

The *chazzan* should not drink the *Kiddush* wine, but should give some to a child who has listened to *Kiddush* and responded אָמֵן. If no child is present, the *chazzan* himself should drink the wine. In either case, he should recite *Kiddush* again at home for the benefit of his family.

The congregation stands while reciting עָלֵינוּ.

עָלֵינוּ לְשַׁבֵּחַ לַאֲדוֹן הַכֹּל, לָתֵת גְּדֻלָּה לְיוֹצֵר בְּרֵאשִׁית, שֶׁלֹּא עָשָׂנוּ כְּגוֹיֵי הָאֲרָצוֹת, וְלֹא שָׂמָנוּ כְּמִשְׁפְּחוֹת הָאֲדָמָה. שֶׁלֹּא שָׂם חֶלְקֵנוּ כָּהֶם, וְגוֹרָלֵנוּ כְּכָל הֲמוֹנָם. (שֶׁהֵם מִשְׁתַּחֲוִים לְהֶבֶל וָרִיק, וּמִתְפַּלְלִים אֶל אֵל לֹא יוֹשִׁיעַ.[3]) וַאֲנַחְנוּ כּוֹרְעִים וּמִשְׁתַּחֲוִים וּמוֹדִים, לִפְנֵי מֶלֶךְ מַלְכֵי הַמְּלָכִים הַקָּדוֹשׁ בָּרוּךְ הוּא. שֶׁהוּא נוֹטֶה שָׁמַיִם וְיֹסֵד אָרֶץ,[4] וּמוֹשַׁב יְקָרוֹ בַּשָּׁמַיִם מִמַּעַל, וּשְׁכִינַת עֻזּוֹ בְּגָבְהֵי מְרוֹמִים. הוּא

Bow while reciting וַאֲנַחְנוּ כּוֹרְעִים וּמִשְׁתַּחֲוִים.

May His great Name be blessed forever and ever.

Blessed, praised, glorified, exalted, extolled, mighty, upraised, and lauded be the Name of the Holy One, Blessed is He (Cong.– *Blessed is He*) – *beyond any blessing and song, praise and consolation that are uttered in the world. Now respond: Amen.* (Cong.– *Amen.*)

(Cong.– *Accept our prayers with mercy and favor.*)

May the prayers and supplications of the entire Family of Israel be accepted before their Father Who is in Heaven. Now respond: Amen. (Cong.– *Amen.*)

(Cong.– *Blessed be the Name of* HASHEM, *from this time and forever.*[1])

May there be abundant peace from Heaven, and life, upon us and upon all Israel. Now respond: Amen. (Cong.– *Amen.*)

(Cong.– *My help is from* HASHEM, *Maker of heaven and earth.*[2])

Take three steps back. Bow left and say, *'He Who makes peace . . .'*; bow right and say, *'may He . . .'*; bow forward and say, *'and upon all Israel . . .'* Remain standing in place for a few moments, then take three steps forward.

He Who makes peace in His heights, may He make peace upon us, and upon all Israel. Now respond: Amen. (Cong.– *Amen.*)

KIDDUSH IN THE SYNAGOGUE

In some congregations, the *chazzan* recites *Kiddush* [although he will repeat *Kiddush* at home].

By your leave, my masters and teachers:

בָּרוּךְ *Blessed are You,* HASHEM, *our God, King of the universe, Who creates the fruit of the vine.* (Cong.– *Amen.*)

בָּרוּךְ *Blessed are You,* HASHEM, *our God, King of the universe, Who sanctified us with His commandments, took pleasure in us, and with love and favor gave us His holy Sabbath as a heritage, a remembrance of creation. For that day is the prologue to the holy convocations, a memorial of the Exodus from Egypt. For us did you choose and us did You sanctify from all the nations. And Your holy Sabbath, with love and favor did You give us as a heritage. Blessed are You,* HASHEM, *Who sanctifies the Sabbath.* (Cong.– *Amen.*)

The *chazzan* should not drink the *Kiddush* wine, but should give some to a child who has listened to *Kiddush* and responded, *'Amen'*. If no child is present, the *chazzan* himself should drink the wine. In either case, he should recite *Kiddush* again at home for the benefit of his family.

The congregation stands while reciting עָלֵינוּ, *'It is our duty . . .'*

עָלֵינוּ *It is our duty to praise the Master of all, to ascribe greatness to the Molder of primeval creation, for He has not made us like the nations of the lands, and has not emplaced us like the families of the earth; for He has not assigned our portion like theirs nor our lot like all their multitudes. (For they bow to vanity and emptiness and pray to a god which helps not.*[3]*) But we bend our knees, bow, and acknowledge our thanks before the King Who reigns over kings, the Holy One, Blessed is He. He stretches out heaven and establishes earth's foundation,*[4] *the seat of His homage is in the heavens above and His powerful Presence is in the loftiest heights. He is*

Bow while reciting *'But we bend our knees.'*

(1) *Psalms* 113:2. (2) 121:2. (3) *Isaiah* 45:20. (4) 51:13.

אֱלֹהֵינוּ, אֵין עוֹד. אֱמֶת מַלְכֵּנוּ, אֶפֶס זוּלָתוֹ, כַּכָּתוּב בְּתוֹרָתוֹ: וְיָדַעְתָּ הַיּוֹם וַהֲשֵׁבֹתָ אֶל לְבָבֶךָ, כִּי יהוה הוּא הָאֱלֹהִים בַּשָּׁמַיִם מִמַּעַל וְעַל הָאָרֶץ מִתָּחַת, אֵין עוֹד.[1]

עַל כֵּן נְקַוֶּה לְּךָ יהוה אֱלֹהֵינוּ לִרְאוֹת מְהֵרָה בְּתִפְאֶרֶת עֻזֶּךָ, לְהַעֲבִיר גִּלּוּלִים מִן הָאָרֶץ, וְהָאֱלִילִים כָּרוֹת יִכָּרֵתוּן, לְתַקֵּן עוֹלָם בְּמַלְכוּת שַׁדַּי. וְכָל בְּנֵי בָשָׂר יִקְרְאוּ בִשְׁמֶךָ, לְהַפְנוֹת אֵלֶיךָ כָּל רִשְׁעֵי אָרֶץ. יַכִּירוּ וְיֵדְעוּ כָּל יוֹשְׁבֵי תֵבֵל, כִּי לְךָ תִּכְרַע כָּל בֶּרֶךְ, תִּשָּׁבַע כָּל לָשׁוֹן.[2] לְפָנֶיךָ יהוה אֱלֹהֵינוּ יִכְרְעוּ וְיִפֹּלוּ, וְלִכְבוֹד שִׁמְךָ יְקָר יִתֵּנוּ. וִיקַבְּלוּ כֻלָּם אֶת עוֹל מַלְכוּתֶךָ, וְתִמְלֹךְ עֲלֵיהֶם מְהֵרָה לְעוֹלָם וָעֶד. כִּי הַמַּלְכוּת שֶׁלְּךָ הִיא וּלְעוֹלְמֵי עַד תִּמְלוֹךְ בְּכָבוֹד, כַּכָּתוּב בְּתוֹרָתֶךָ: יהוה יִמְלֹךְ לְעֹלָם וָעֶד.[3] ❖ וְנֶאֱמַר: וְהָיָה יהוה לְמֶלֶךְ עַל כָּל הָאָרֶץ, בַּיּוֹם הַהוּא יִהְיֶה יהוה אֶחָד וּשְׁמוֹ אֶחָד.[4]

Some recite the following after עָלֵינוּ:

אַל תִּירָא מִפַּחַד פִּתְאֹם, וּמִשֹּׁאַת רְשָׁעִים כִּי תָבֹא.[5] עֻצוּ עֵצָה וְתֻפָר, דַּבְּרוּ דָבָר וְלֹא יָקוּם, כִּי עִמָּנוּ אֵל.[6] וְעַד זִקְנָה אֲנִי הוּא, וְעַד שֵׂיבָה אֲנִי אֶסְבֹּל, אֲנִי עָשִׂיתִי וַאֲנִי אֶשָּׂא, וַאֲנִי אֶסְבֹּל וַאֲמַלֵּט.[7]

קדיש יתום

Mourners recite קַדִּישׁ יָתוֹם (see *Laws* §81-83.)

יִתְגַּדַּל וְיִתְקַדַּשׁ שְׁמֵהּ רַבָּא. (.Cong – אָמֵן.) בְּעָלְמָא דִּי בְרָא כִרְעוּתֵהּ. וְיַמְלִיךְ מַלְכוּתֵהּ, בְּחַיֵּיכוֹן וּבְיוֹמֵיכוֹן וּבְחַיֵּי דְכָל בֵּית יִשְׂרָאֵל, בַּעֲגָלָא וּבִזְמַן קָרִיב. וְאִמְרוּ: אָמֵן.

(.Cong – אָמֵן. יְהֵא שְׁמֵהּ רַבָּא מְבָרַךְ לְעָלַם וּלְעָלְמֵי עָלְמַיָּא.)

יְהֵא שְׁמֵהּ רַבָּא מְבָרַךְ לְעָלַם וּלְעָלְמֵי עָלְמַיָּא.

יִתְבָּרַךְ וְיִשְׁתַּבַּח וְיִתְפָּאַר וְיִתְרוֹמַם וְיִתְנַשֵּׂא וְיִתְהַדָּר וְיִתְעַלֶּה וְיִתְהַלָּל שְׁמֵהּ דְּקֻדְשָׁא בְּרִיךְ הוּא (.Cong – בְּרִיךְ הוּא) — לְעֵלָּא מִן כָּל בִּרְכָתָא וְשִׁירָתָא תֻּשְׁבְּחָתָא וְנֶחֱמָתָא, דַּאֲמִירָן בְּעָלְמָא. וְאִמְרוּ: אָמֵן. (.Cong – אָמֵן.)

יְהֵא שְׁלָמָא רַבָּא מִן שְׁמַיָּא, וְחַיִּים עָלֵינוּ וְעַל כָּל יִשְׂרָאֵל. וְאִמְרוּ: אָמֵן. (.Cong – אָמֵן.)

Take three steps back. Bow left and say . . . עֹשֶׂה; bow right and say . . . הוּא; bow forward and say וְעַל כָּל . . . אָמֵן. Remain standing in place for a few moments, then take three steps forward.

עֹשֶׂה שָׁלוֹם בִּמְרוֹמָיו, הוּא יַעֲשֶׂה שָׁלוֹם עָלֵינוּ, וְעַל כָּל יִשְׂרָאֵל וְאִמְרוּ: אָמֵן. (.Cong – אָמֵן.)

our God and there is none other. True is our King, there is nothing beside Him, as it is written in His Torah: 'You are to know this day and take to your heart that HASHEM *is the only God — in heaven above and on the earth below — there is none other.'*[1]

עַל כֵּן *Therefore we put our hope in You,* HASHEM, *our God, that we may soon see Your mighty splendor, to remove detestable idolatry from the earth, and false gods will be utterly cut off, to perfect the universe through the Almighty's sovereignty. Then all humanity will call upon Your Name, to turn all the earth's wicked toward You. All the world's inhabitants will recognize and know that to You every knee should bend, every tongue should swear.*[2] *Before You,* HASHEM, *our God, they will bend every knee and cast themselves down and to the glory of Your Name they will render homage, and they will all accept upon themselves the yoke of Your kingship that You may reign over them soon and eternally. For the kingdom is Yours and You will reign for all eternity in glory as it is written in Your Torah:* HASHEM *shall reign for all eternity.*[3] Chazzan– *And it is said:* HASHEM *will be King over all the world — on that day* HASHEM *will be One and His Name will be One.*[4]

Some recite the following after *Aleinu:*

אַל תִּירָא *Do not fear sudden terror, or the holocaust of the wicked when it comes.*[5] *Plan a conspiracy and it will be annulled; speak your piece and it shall not stand, for God is with us.*[6] *Even till your seniority, I remain unchanged; and even till your ripe old age, I shall endure. I created you and I shall bear you; I shall endure and rescue.*[7]

MOURNER'S KADDISH

Mourners recite the Mourner's *Kaddish* (see *Laws* §81-83).
[A transliteration of this *Kaddish* appears on page 1305.]

יִתְגַּדַּל *May His great Name grow exalted and sanctified* (Cong.– *Amen.*) *in the world that He created as He willed. May He give reign to His kingship in your lifetimes and in your days, and in the lifetimes of the entire Family of Israel, swiftly and soon. Now respond: Amen.*

(Cong.– *Amen. May His great Name be blessed forever and ever.*)
May His great Name be blessed forever and ever.

Blessed, praised, glorified, exalted, extolled, mighty, upraised, and lauded be the Name of the Holy One, Blessed is He (Cong.– *Blessed is He*) *— beyond any blessing and song, praise and consolation that are uttered in the world. Now respond: Amen.* (Cong.– *Amen.*)

May there be abundant peace from Heaven, and life, upon us and upon all Israel. Now respond: Amen. (Cong.– *Amen.*)

Take three steps back. Bow left and say, *'He Who makes peace . . .';* bow right and say, *'may He . . .';* bow forward and say, *'and upon all Israel . . .'* Remain standing in place for a few moments, then take three steps forward.

He Who makes peace in His heights, may He make peace upon us, and upon all Israel. Now respond: Amen. (Cong.– *Amen.*)

---

(1) *Deuteronomy* 4:39. (2) Cf. *Isaiah* 45:23. (3) *Exodus* 15:18.
(4) *Zechariah* 14:9. (5) *Proverbs* 3:25. (6) *Isaiah* 8:10. (7) 46:4.

תהלים כז

לְדָוִד, יהוה אוֹרִי וְיִשְׁעִי, מִמִּי אִירָא, יהוה מָעוֹז חַיַּי, מִמִּי אֶפְחָד. בִּקְרֹב עָלַי מְרֵעִים לֶאֱכֹל אֶת בְּשָׂרִי, צָרַי וְאֹיְבַי לִי, הֵמָּה כָשְׁלוּ וְנָפָלוּ. אִם תַּחֲנֶה עָלַי מַחֲנֶה, לֹא יִירָא לִבִּי, אִם תָּקוּם עָלַי מִלְחָמָה, בְּזֹאת אֲנִי בוֹטֵחַ. אַחַת שָׁאַלְתִּי מֵאֵת יהוה, אוֹתָהּ אֲבַקֵּשׁ, שִׁבְתִּי בְּבֵית יהוה כָּל יְמֵי חַיַּי, לַחֲזוֹת בְּנֹעַם יהוה, וּלְבַקֵּר בְּהֵיכָלוֹ. כִּי יִצְפְּנֵנִי בְּסֻכֹּה בְּיוֹם רָעָה, יַסְתִּירֵנִי בְּסֵתֶר אָהֳלוֹ, בְּצוּר יְרוֹמְמֵנִי. וְעַתָּה יָרוּם רֹאשִׁי עַל אֹיְבַי סְבִיבוֹתַי, וְאֶזְבְּחָה בְאָהֳלוֹ זִבְחֵי תְרוּעָה, אָשִׁירָה וַאֲזַמְּרָה לַיהוה. שְׁמַע יהוה קוֹלִי אֶקְרָא, וְחָנֵּנִי וַעֲנֵנִי. לְךָ אָמַר לִבִּי בַּקְּשׁוּ פָנָי, אֶת פָּנֶיךָ יהוה אֲבַקֵּשׁ. אַל תַּסְתֵּר פָּנֶיךָ מִמֶּנִּי, אַל תַּט בְּאַף עַבְדֶּךָ, עֶזְרָתִי הָיִיתָ, אַל תִּטְּשֵׁנִי וְאַל תַּעַזְבֵנִי, אֱלֹהֵי יִשְׁעִי. כִּי אָבִי וְאִמִּי עֲזָבוּנִי, וַיהוה יַאַסְפֵנִי. הוֹרֵנִי יהוה דַּרְכֶּךָ, וּנְחֵנִי בְּאֹרַח מִישׁוֹר, לְמַעַן שׁוֹרְרָי. אַל תִּתְּנֵנִי בְּנֶפֶשׁ צָרָי, כִּי קָמוּ בִי עֵדֵי שֶׁקֶר, וִיפֵחַ חָמָס. ❖ לוּלֵא הֶאֱמַנְתִּי לִרְאוֹת בְּטוּב יהוה בְּאֶרֶץ חַיִּים. קַוֵּה אֶל יהוה, חֲזַק וְיַאֲמֵץ לִבֶּךָ, וְקַוֵּה אֶל יהוה.

Mourners recite קַדִּישׁ יָתוֹם, the Mourner's *Kaddish* (p.446).
Many congregations recite either אֲדוֹן עוֹלָם or יִגְדַּל, or both, at this point.

אֲדוֹן עוֹלָם אֲשֶׁר מָלַךְ, בְּטֶרֶם כָּל יְצִיר נִבְרָא.
לְעֵת נַעֲשָׂה בְחֶפְצוֹ כֹּל, אֲזַי מֶלֶךְ שְׁמוֹ נִקְרָא.
וְאַחֲרֵי כִּכְלוֹת הַכֹּל, לְבַדּוֹ יִמְלוֹךְ נוֹרָא.
וְהוּא הָיָה וְהוּא הוֶֹה, וְהוּא יִהְיֶה בְּתִפְאָרָה.
וְהוּא אֶחָד וְאֵין שֵׁנִי, לְהַמְשִׁיל לוֹ לְהַחְבִּירָה.
בְּלִי רֵאשִׁית בְּלִי תַכְלִית, וְלוֹ הָעֹז וְהַמִּשְׂרָה.
וְהוּא אֵלִי וְחַי גֹּאֲלִי, וְצוּר חֶבְלִי בְּעֵת צָרָה.
וְהוּא נִסִּי וּמָנוֹס לִי, מְנָת כּוֹסִי בְּיוֹם אֶקְרָא.
בְּיָדוֹ אַפְקִיד רוּחִי, בְּעֵת אִישַׁן וְאָעִירָה.
וְעִם רוּחִי גְּוִיָּתִי, יהוה לִי וְלֹא אִירָא.

יִגְדַּל אֱלֹהִים חַי וְיִשְׁתַּבַּח, נִמְצָא וְאֵין עֵת אֶל מְצִיאוּתוֹ.
אֶחָד וְאֵין יָחִיד כְּיִחוּדוֹ, נֶעְלָם וְגַם אֵין סוֹף לְאַחְדוּתוֹ.
אֵין לוֹ דְמוּת הַגּוּף וְאֵינוֹ גוּף, לֹא נַעֲרוֹךְ אֵלָיו קְדֻשָּׁתוֹ.
קַדְמוֹן לְכָל דָּבָר אֲשֶׁר נִבְרָא, רִאשׁוֹן וְאֵין רֵאשִׁית לְרֵאשִׁיתוֹ.

Psalm 27

לְדָוִד *Of David; HASHEM is my light and my salvation, whom shall fear? HASHEM is my life's strength, whom shall I dread? When evildoers approach me to devour my flesh, my tormentors and my foes against me — it is they who stumble and fall. Though an army would besiege me, my heart would not fear; though war would arise against me, in this I trust. One thing I asked of HASHEM, that shall I seek: That I dwell in the House of HASHEM all the days of my life; to behold the sweetness of HASHEM and to contemplate in His Sanctuary. Indeed, He will hide me in His Shelter on the day of evil; He will conceal me in the concealment of His Tent, He will lift me upon a rock. Now my head is raised above my enemies around me, and I will slaughter offerings in His Tent accompanied by joyous song; I will sing and make music to HASHEM. HASHEM, hear my voice when I call, be gracious toward me and answer me. In Your behalf, my heart has said, 'Seek My Presence'; Your Presence, HASHEM, do I seek. Conceal not Your Presence from me, repel not Your servant in anger. You have been my Helper, abandon me not, forsake me not, O God of my salvation. Though my father and mother have forsaken me, HASHEM will gather me in. Teach me Your way, HASHEM, and lead me on the path of integrity, because of my watchful foes. Deliver me not to the wishes of my tormentors, for there have arisen against me false witnesses who breathe violence.* Chazzan– *Had I not trusted that I would see the goodness of HASHEM in the land of life! Hope to HASHEM, strengthen yourself and He will give you courage; and hope to HASHEM.*

Mourners recite קַדִּישׁ יָתוֹם, the Mourner's *Kaddish* (p. 446).

Many congregations recite either אֲדוֹן עוֹלָם, *Master of the universe,* or יִגְדַּל, *Exalted be,* or both.

אֲדוֹן עוֹלָם *Master of the universe, Who reigned*
before any form was created,
At the time when His will brought all into being —
then as 'King' was His Name proclaimed.
After all has ceased to be, He, the Awesome One, will reign alone.
It is He Who was, He Who is, and He Who shall remain, in splendor.
He is One — there is no second to compare to Him, to declare as His equal.
Without beginning, without conclusion — His is the power and dominion.
He is my God, my living Redeemer, Rock of my pain in time of distress.
He is my banner, a refuge for me, the portion in my cup on the day I call.
Into His hand I shall entrust my spirit when I go to sleep — and I shall awaken!
With my spirit shall my body remain. HASHEM is with me, I shall not fear.

יִגְדַּל *Exalted be the Living God and praised,*
He exists — unbounded by time is His existence.
He is One — and there is no unity like His Oneness.
Inscrutable and infinite is His Oneness.
He has no semblance of a body nor is He corporeal;
nor has His holiness any comparison.
He preceded every being that was created —
the First, and nothing precedes His precedence.

הִנּוֹ אֲדוֹן עוֹלָם לְכָל נוֹצָר, יוֹרֶה גְדֻלָּתוֹ וּמַלְכוּתוֹ.
שֶׁפַע נְבוּאָתוֹ נְתָנוֹ, אֶל אַנְשֵׁי סְגֻלָּתוֹ וְתִפְאַרְתּוֹ.
לֹא קָם בְּיִשְׂרָאֵל כְּמֹשֶׁה עוֹד, נָבִיא וּמַבִּיט אֶת תְּמוּנָתוֹ.
תּוֹרַת אֱמֶת נָתַן לְעַמּוֹ אֵל, עַל יַד נְבִיאוֹ נֶאֱמַן בֵּיתוֹ.
לֹא יַחֲלִיף הָאֵל וְלֹא יָמִיר דָּתוֹ, לְעוֹלָמִים לְזוּלָתוֹ.
צוֹפֶה וְיוֹדֵעַ סְתָרֵינוּ, מַבִּיט לְסוֹף דָּבָר בְּקַדְמָתוֹ.
גּוֹמֵל לְאִישׁ חֶסֶד כְּמִפְעָלוֹ, נוֹתֵן לְרָשָׁע רָע כְּרִשְׁעָתוֹ.
יִשְׁלַח לְקֵץ הַיָּמִין מְשִׁיחֵנוּ, לִפְדּוֹת מְחַכֵּי קֵץ יְשׁוּעָתוֹ.
מֵתִים יְחַיֶּה אֵל בְּרֹב חַסְדּוֹ, בָּרוּךְ עֲדֵי עַד שֵׁם תְּהִלָּתוֹ.

THE SYNAGOGUE SERVICE ENDS HERE.

The *Ushpizin* prayers begin on page 74.

Many recite the following before *Kiddush*. Each of the first four stanzas is recited three times.

שָׁלוֹם עֲלֵיכֶם, מַלְאֲכֵי הַשָּׁרֵת, מַלְאֲכֵי עֶלְיוֹן, מִמֶּלֶךְ מַלְכֵי הַמְּלָכִים הַקָּדוֹשׁ בָּרוּךְ הוּא.

בּוֹאֲכֶם לְשָׁלוֹם, מַלְאֲכֵי הַשָּׁלוֹם, מַלְאֲכֵי עֶלְיוֹן, מִמֶּלֶךְ מַלְכֵי הַמְּלָכִים הַקָּדוֹשׁ בָּרוּךְ הוּא.

בָּרְכוּנִי לְשָׁלוֹם, מַלְאֲכֵי הַשָּׁלוֹם, מַלְאֲכֵי עֶלְיוֹן, מִמֶּלֶךְ מַלְכֵי הַמְּלָכִים הַקָּדוֹשׁ בָּרוּךְ הוּא.

צֵאתְכֶם לְשָׁלוֹם, מַלְאֲכֵי הַשָּׁלוֹם, מַלְאֲכֵי עֶלְיוֹן, מִמֶּלֶךְ מַלְכֵי הַמְּלָכִים הַקָּדוֹשׁ בָּרוּךְ הוּא.

כִּי מַלְאָכָיו יְצַוֶּה לָּךְ, לִשְׁמָרְךָ בְּכָל דְּרָכֶיךָ.[1]
יהוה יִשְׁמָר צֵאתְךָ וּבוֹאֶךָ, מֵעַתָּה וְעַד עוֹלָם.[2]

(משלי לא:י-לא)

אֵשֶׁת חַיִל מִי יִמְצָא, וְרָחֹק מִפְּנִינִים מִכְרָהּ.
בָּטַח בָּהּ לֵב בַּעְלָהּ, וְשָׁלָל לֹא יֶחְסָר.
גְּמָלַתְהוּ טוֹב וְלֹא רָע, כֹּל יְמֵי חַיֶּיהָ.
דָּרְשָׁה צֶמֶר וּפִשְׁתִּים, וַתַּעַשׂ בְּחֵפֶץ כַּפֶּיהָ.
הָיְתָה כָּאֳנִיּוֹת סוֹחֵר, מִמֶּרְחָק תָּבִיא לַחְמָהּ.
וַתָּקָם בְּעוֹד לַיְלָה, וַתִּתֵּן טֶרֶף לְבֵיתָהּ, וְחֹק לְנַעֲרֹתֶיהָ.
זָמְמָה שָׂדֶה וַתִּקָּחֵהוּ, מִפְּרִי כַפֶּיהָ נָטְעָה כָּרֶם.
חָגְרָה בְעוֹז מָתְנֶיהָ, וַתְּאַמֵּץ זְרוֹעֹתֶיהָ.
טָעֲמָה כִּי טוֹב סַחְרָהּ, לֹא יִכְבֶּה בַלַּיְלָה נֵרָהּ.
יָדֶיהָ שִׁלְּחָה בַכִּישׁוֹר, וְכַפֶּיהָ תָּמְכוּ פָלֶךְ.

(1) *Psalms* 91:11. (2) 121:8.

Behold! He is Master of the universe to every creature,
He demonstrates His greatness and His sovereignty.
He granted His flow of prophecy
to His treasured splendrous people.
In Israel none like Moses arose again —
a prophet who perceived His vision clearly.
God gave His people a Torah of truth,
by means of His prophet, the most trusted of His household.
God will never amend nor exchange His law
for any other one, for all eternity.
He scrutinizes and knows our hiddenmost secrets;
He perceives a matter's outcome at its inception.
He recompenses man with kindness according to his deed;
He places evil on the wicked according to his wickedness.
By the End of Days He will send our Messiah,
to redeem those longing for His final salvation.
God will revive the dead in His abundant kindness —
Blessed forever is His praised Name.

THE SYNAGOGUE SERVICE ENDS HERE.

The *Ushpizin* prayers begin on page 74.

Many recite the following before *Kiddush*. Each of the first four stanzas is recited three times.

שָׁלוֹם עֲלֵיכֶם *Peace upon you, O ministering angels, angels of the Exalted One — from the King Who reigns over kings, the Holy One, Blessed is He.*

בּוֹאֲכֶם לְשָׁלוֹם *May your coming be for peace, O angels of peace, angels of the Exalted One — from the King Who reigns over kings, the Holy One, Blessed is He.*

בָּרְכוּנִי לְשָׁלוֹם *Bless me for peace, O angels of peace, angels of the Exalted One — from the King Who reigns over kings, the Holy One, Blessed is He.*

צֵאתְכֶם לְשָׁלוֹם *May your departure be to peace, O angels of peace, angels of the Exalted One — from the King Who reigns over kings, the Holy One, Blessed is He.*

He will charge His angels for you, to protect you in all your ways.[1]
May HASHEM *protect your going and returning, from this time and forever.*[2]

(*Proverbs* 31:10-31)

אֵשֶׁת חַיִל *An accomplished woman, who can find? —*
Far beyond pearls is her value.
ב *Her husband's heart relies on her and he shall lack no fortune.*
ג *She repays his good, but never his harm, all the days of her life.*
ד *She seeks out wool and linen, and her hands work willingly.*
ה *She is like a merchant's ships, from afar she brings her sustenance.*
ו *She arises while it is yet nighttime,*
and gives food to her household and a ration to her maidens.
ז *She envisions a field and buys it,*
from the fruit of her handiwork she plants a vineyard.
ח *With strength she girds her loins, and invigorates her arms.*
ט *She discerns that her enterprise is good —*
so her lamp is not snuffed out by night.
י *Her hands she stretches out to the distaff, and her palms support the spindle.*

כַּפָּהּ פָּרְשָׂה לֶעָנִי, וְיָדֶיהָ שִׁלְּחָה לָאֶבְיוֹן.
לֹא תִירָא לְבֵיתָהּ מִשָּׁלֶג, כִּי כָל בֵּיתָהּ לָבֻשׁ שָׁנִים.
מַרְבַדִּים עָשְׂתָה לָּהּ, שֵׁשׁ וְאַרְגָּמָן לְבוּשָׁהּ.
נוֹדָע בַּשְּׁעָרִים בַּעְלָהּ, בְּשִׁבְתּוֹ עִם זִקְנֵי אָרֶץ.
סָדִין עָשְׂתָה וַתִּמְכֹּר, וַחֲגוֹר נָתְנָה לַכְּנַעֲנִי.
עוֹז וְהָדָר לְבוּשָׁהּ, וַתִּשְׂחַק לְיוֹם אַחֲרוֹן.
פִּיהָ פָּתְחָה בְחָכְמָה, וְתוֹרַת חֶסֶד עַל לְשׁוֹנָהּ.
צוֹפִיָּה הֲלִיכוֹת בֵּיתָהּ, וְלֶחֶם עַצְלוּת לֹא תֹאכֵל.
קָמוּ בָנֶיהָ וַיְאַשְּׁרוּהָ, בַּעְלָהּ וַיְהַלְלָהּ.
רַבּוֹת בָּנוֹת עָשׂוּ חָיִל, וְאַתְּ עָלִית עַל כֻּלָּנָה.
שֶׁקֶר הַחֵן וְהֶבֶל הַיֹּפִי, אִשָּׁה יִרְאַת יהוה הִיא תִתְהַלָּל.
תְּנוּ לָהּ מִפְּרִי יָדֶיהָ, וִיהַלְלוּהָ בַשְּׁעָרִים מַעֲשֶׂיהָ.

קידוש לליל שבת חול המועד

(Recite silently — וַיְהִי עֶרֶב וַיְהִי בֹקֶר)

יוֹם הַשִּׁשִּׁי. וַיְכֻלּוּ הַשָּׁמַיִם וְהָאָרֶץ וְכָל צְבָאָם. וַיְכַל אֱלֹהִים בַּיּוֹם הַשְּׁבִיעִי מְלַאכְתּוֹ אֲשֶׁר עָשָׂה, וַיִּשְׁבֹּת בַּיּוֹם הַשְּׁבִיעִי מִכָּל מְלַאכְתּוֹ אֲשֶׁר עָשָׂה. וַיְבָרֶךְ אֱלֹהִים אֶת יוֹם הַשְּׁבִיעִי וַיְקַדֵּשׁ אֹתוֹ, כִּי בוֹ שָׁבַת מִכָּל מְלַאכְתּוֹ אֲשֶׁר בָּרָא אֱלֹהִים לַעֲשׂוֹת.[1]

סַבְרִי מָרָנָן וְרַבָּנָן וְרַבּוֹתַי:

בָּרוּךְ אַתָּה יהוה אֱלֹהֵינוּ מֶלֶךְ הָעוֹלָם, בּוֹרֵא פְּרִי הַגָּפֶן.

(All present respond — אָמֵן.)

בָּרוּךְ אַתָּה יהוה אֱלֹהֵינוּ מֶלֶךְ הָעוֹלָם, אֲשֶׁר קִדְּשָׁנוּ בְּמִצְוֹתָיו וְרָצָה בָנוּ, וְשַׁבַּת קָדְשׁוֹ בְּאַהֲבָה וּבְרָצוֹן הִנְחִילָנוּ, זִכָּרוֹן לְמַעֲשֵׂה בְרֵאשִׁית. כִּי הוּא יוֹם תְּחִלָּה לְמִקְרָאֵי קֹדֶשׁ, זֵכֶר לִיצִיאַת מִצְרָיִם. כִּי בָנוּ בָחַרְתָּ, וְאוֹתָנוּ קִדַּשְׁתָּ, מִכָּל הָעַמִּים. וְשַׁבַּת קָדְשְׁךָ בְּאַהֲבָה וּבְרָצוֹן הִנְחַלְתָּנוּ. בָּרוּךְ אַתָּה יהוה, מְקַדֵּשׁ הַשַּׁבָּת.

(All present respond — אָמֵן.)

If, for whatever the reason, one does not recite *Kiddush* in a *succah*, the following blessing is omitted.

בָּרוּךְ אַתָּה יהוה אֱלֹהֵינוּ מֶלֶךְ הָעוֹלָם, אֲשֶׁר קִדְּשָׁנוּ בְּמִצְוֹתָיו וְצִוָּנוּ לֵישֵׁב בַּסֻּכָּה.

(All present respond — אָמֵן.)

Bircas HaMazon appears on page 84.

כ *She spreads out her palm to the poor, and extends her hands to the destitute.*
ל *She fears not snow for her household,*
for her entire household is clothed with scarlet wool.
מ *Luxurious bedspreads she made herself, linen and purple wool are her clothing.*
נ *Distinctive in the councils is her husband,*
when he sits with the elders of the land.
ס *She makes a cloak to sell, and delivers a belt to the peddler.*
ע *Strength and majesty are her raiment, she joyfully awaits the last day.*
פ *She opens her mouth with wisdom, and a lesson of kindness is on her tongue.*
צ *She anticipates the ways of her household,*
and partakes not of the bread of laziness.
ק *Her children arise and praise her, her husband, and he lauds her:*
ר *'Many daughters have amassed achievement, but you surpassed them all.'*
ש *False is grace and vain is beauty,*
a God-fearing woman — she should be praised.
ת *Give her the fruits of her hand*
and let her be praised in the gates by her very own deeds.

KIDDUSH FOR THE SABBATH EVE OF CHOL HAMOED

(Recite silently— *And there was evening and there was morning*)

יוֹם הַשִּׁשִּׁי *The sixth day. Thus the heavens and earth were finished, and all their array. On the seventh day God completed His work which He had done, and He abstained on the seventh day from all His work which He had done. God blessed the seventh day and hallowed it, because on it He abstained from all His work which God created to make.*[1]

By your leave, my masters, rabbis and teachers,

בָּרוּךְ *Blessed are You, Hashem, our God, King of the universe, Who creates the fruit of the vine.* (All present respond— *Amen.*)

בָּרוּךְ *Blessed are You, Hashem, our God, King of the universe, Who has sanctified us with His commandments, took pleasure in us, and with love and favor gave us His holy Sabbath as a heritage, a remembrance of creation. For that day is the prologue to the holy convocations, a memorial of the Exodus from Egypt. For us did You choose and us did You sanctify from all the nations. And Your holy Sabbath, with love and favor did You give us as a heritage. Blessed are You, Hashem, Who sanctifies the Sabbath.* (All present respond— *Amen.*)

If, for whatever the reason, one does not recite *Kiddush* in a *succah*, the following blessing is omitted.

בָּרוּךְ *Blessed are You, Hashem, our God, King of the universe, Who has sanctified us with His commandments and has commanded us to dwell in the Succah.* (All present respond— *Amen.*)

Grace After Meals appears on page 84.

(1) *Genesis* 2:1-3.

❧ שחרית לשבת חול המועד ☙

THE MORNING SERVICE BEGINS WITH PAGES 130-208, THEN CONTINUES HERE.

נִשְׁמַת כָּל חַי תְּבָרֵךְ אֶת שִׁמְךָ יהוה אֱלֹהֵינוּ, וְרוּחַ כָּל בָּשָׂר תְּפָאֵר וּתְרוֹמֵם זִכְרְךָ מַלְכֵּנוּ תָּמִיד. מִן הָעוֹלָם וְעַד הָעוֹלָם אַתָּה אֵל,[1] וּמִבַּלְעָדֶיךָ אֵין לָנוּ מֶלֶךְ[2] גּוֹאֵל וּמוֹשִׁיעַ. פּוֹדֶה וּמַצִּיל וּמְפַרְנֵס וּמְרַחֵם בְּכָל עֵת צָרָה וְצוּקָה, אֵין לָנוּ מֶלֶךְ אֶלָּא אָתָּה. אֱלֹהֵי הָרִאשׁוֹנִים וְהָאַחֲרוֹנִים, אֱלוֹהַּ כָּל בְּרִיּוֹת, אֲדוֹן כָּל תּוֹלָדוֹת, הַמְּהֻלָּל בְּרֹב הַתִּשְׁבָּחוֹת, הַמְנַהֵג עוֹלָמוֹ בְּחֶסֶד וּבְרִיּוֹתָיו בְּרַחֲמִים. וַיהוה לֹא יָנוּם וְלֹא יִישָׁן.[3] הַמְּעוֹרֵר יְשֵׁנִים, וְהַמֵּקִיץ נִרְדָּמִים, וְהַמֵּשִׂיחַ אִלְּמִים, וְהַמַּתִּיר אֲסוּרִים,[4] וְהַסּוֹמֵךְ נוֹפְלִים, וְהַזּוֹקֵף כְּפוּפִים.[5] לְךָ לְבַדְּךָ אֲנַחְנוּ מוֹדִים. אִלּוּ פִינוּ מָלֵא שִׁירָה כַּיָּם, וּלְשׁוֹנֵנוּ רִנָּה כַּהֲמוֹן גַּלָּיו, וְשִׂפְתוֹתֵינוּ שֶׁבַח כְּמֶרְחֲבֵי רָקִיעַ, וְעֵינֵינוּ מְאִירוֹת כַּשֶּׁמֶשׁ וְכַיָּרֵחַ, וְיָדֵינוּ פְרוּשׂוֹת כְּנִשְׁרֵי שָׁמָיִם, וְרַגְלֵינוּ קַלּוֹת כָּאַיָּלוֹת, אֵין אֲנַחְנוּ מַסְפִּיקִים לְהוֹדוֹת לְךָ, יהוה אֱלֹהֵינוּ וֵאלֹהֵי אֲבוֹתֵינוּ, וּלְבָרֵךְ אֶת שְׁמֶךָ עַל אַחַת מֵאָלֶף אֶלֶף אַלְפֵי אֲלָפִים וְרִבֵּי רְבָבוֹת פְּעָמִים הַטּוֹבוֹת שֶׁעָשִׂיתָ עִם אֲבוֹתֵינוּ וְעִמָּנוּ. מִמִּצְרַיִם גְּאַלְתָּנוּ יהוה אֱלֹהֵינוּ, וּמִבֵּית עֲבָדִים פְּדִיתָנוּ. בְּרָעָב זַנְתָּנוּ, וּבְשָׂבָע כִּלְכַּלְתָּנוּ, מֵחֶרֶב הִצַּלְתָּנוּ, וּמִדֶּבֶר מִלַּטְתָּנוּ, וּמֵחֳלָיִם רָעִים וְנֶאֱמָנִים דִּלִּיתָנוּ. עַד הֵנָּה עֲזָרוּנוּ רַחֲמֶיךָ, וְלֹא עֲזָבוּנוּ חֲסָדֶיךָ. וְאַל תִּטְּשֵׁנוּ יהוה אֱלֹהֵינוּ לָנֶצַח. עַל כֵּן אֵבָרִים שֶׁפִּלַּגְתָּ בָּנוּ, וְרוּחַ וּנְשָׁמָה שֶׁנָּפַחְתָּ בְּאַפֵּינוּ, וְלָשׁוֹן אֲשֶׁר שַׂמְתָּ בְּפִינוּ, הֵן הֵם יוֹדוּ וִיבָרְכוּ וִישַׁבְּחוּ וִיפָאֲרוּ וִירוֹמְמוּ וְיַעֲרִיצוּ וְיַקְדִּישׁוּ וְיַמְלִיכוּ אֶת שִׁמְךָ מַלְכֵּנוּ. כִּי כָל פֶּה לְךָ יוֹדֶה, וְכָל לָשׁוֹן לְךָ תִשָּׁבַע, וְכָל בֶּרֶךְ לְךָ תִכְרַע,[6] וְכָל קוֹמָה לְפָנֶיךָ תִשְׁתַּחֲוֶה, וְכָל לְבָבוֹת יִירָאוּךָ, וְכָל קֶרֶב וּכְלָיוֹת יְזַמְּרוּ לִשְׁמֶךָ, כַּדָּבָר שֶׁכָּתוּב: כָּל עַצְמֹתַי תֹּאמַרְנָה, יהוה מִי כָמוֹךָ, מַצִּיל עָנִי מֵחָזָק מִמֶּנּוּ, וְעָנִי וְאֶבְיוֹן מִגֹּזְלוֹ.[7] מִי יִדְמֶה לָּךְ, וּמִי יִשְׁוֶה לָּךְ, וּמִי יַעֲרָךְ לָךְ.[8] הָאֵל הַגָּדוֹל הַגִּבּוֹר וְהַנּוֹרָא, אֵל עֶלְיוֹן, קֹנֵה שָׁמַיִם וָאָרֶץ. ❖ נְהַלֶּלְךָ וּנְשַׁבֵּחֲךָ וּנְפָאֶרְךָ וּנְבָרֵךְ אֶת שֵׁם קָדְשֶׁךָ, כָּאָמוּר: לְדָוִד, בָּרְכִי נַפְשִׁי אֶת יהוה, וְכָל קְרָבַי אֶת שֵׁם קָדְשׁוֹ.[9] הָאֵל בְּתַעֲצֻמוֹת

---

(1) Cf. *Psalms* 90:2. (2) Cf. *Isaiah* 44:6. (3) Cf. *Psalms* 121:4. (4) Cf. 146:7. (5) Cf. 145:14. (6) Cf. *Isaiah* 45:23. (7) *Psalms* 35:10. (8) Cf. 89:7. (9) *Psalms* 103:1.

SHACHARIS FOR THE SABBATH OF CHOL HAMOED

THE MORNING SERVICE BEGINS WITH PAGES 130-208, THEN CONTINUES HERE.

נִשְׁמַת *The soul of every living being shall bless Your Name,* HASHEM *our God; the spirit of all flesh shall always glorify and exalt Your remembrance, our King. From This World to the World to Come, You are God,[1] and other than You we have no king,[2] redeemer or savior. Liberator, Rescuer, Sustainer and Merciful One in every time of distress and anguish, we have no king but You! — God of the first and of the last, God of all creatures, Master of all generations, Who is extolled through a multitude of praises, Who guides His world with kindness and His creatures with mercy.* HASHEM *neither slumbers nor sleeps.[3] He Who rouses the sleepers and awakens the slumberers, Who makes the mute speak and releases the bound;[4] Who supports the fallen and straightens the bent.[5] To You alone we give thanks. Were our mouth as full of song as the sea, and our tongue as full of joyous song as its multitude of waves, and our lips as full of praise as the breadth of the heavens, and our eyes as brilliant as the sun and the moon, and our hands as outspread as eagles of the sky and our feet as swift as hinds — we still could not thank You sufficiently,* HASHEM *our God and God of our forefathers, and to bless Your Name for even one of the thousand thousand, thousands of thousands and myriad myriads of favors that You performed for our ancestors and for us. You redeemed us from Egypt,* HASHEM *our God, and liberated us from the house of bondage. In famine You nourished us and in plenty You sustained us. From sword You saved us; from plague You let us escape; and from severe and enduring diseases You spared us. Until now Your mercy has helped us, and Your kindness has not forsaken us. Do not abandon us,* HASHEM *our God, forever. Therefore, the organs that You set within us, and the spirit and soul that You breathed into our nostrils, and the tongue that You placed in our mouth — all of them shall thank and bless, praise and glorify, exalt and revere, sanctify and declare the sovereignty of Your Name, our King. For every mouth shall offer thanks to You; every tongue shall vow allegiance to You; every knee shall bend to You;[6] every erect spine shall prostrate itself before You; all hearts shall fear You, and all innermost feelings and thoughts shall sing praises to Your name, as it is written: "All my bones shall say: '*HASHEM*, who is like You?' You save the poor man from one stronger than he, the poor and destitute from one who would rob him."[7] Who is like unto You? Who is equal to You? Who can be compared to You?[8] O great, mighty, and awesome God, the supreme God, Creator of heaven and earth.* Chazzan– *We shall laud, praise, and glorify You and bless Your holy Name, as it is said 'Of David: Bless* HASHEM*, O my soul, and let all my innermost being bless His holy Name!'[9] O God, in the omnipotence of*

עֻזֶּךָ, הַגָּדוֹל בִּכְבוֹד שְׁמֶךָ, הַגִּבּוֹר לָנֶצַח וְהַנּוֹרָא בְּנוֹרְאוֹתֶיךָ. הַמֶּלֶךְ הַיּוֹשֵׁב עַל כִּסֵּא רָם וְנִשָּׂא.[1]

The *chazzan* of *Shacharis* begins here.

שׁוֹכֵן עַד מָרוֹם וְקָדוֹשׁ שְׁמוֹ.[2] וְכָתוּב: רַנְּנוּ צַדִּיקִים בַּיהוה לַיְשָׁרִים נָאוָה תְהִלָּה.[3]

❖ בְּפִי **יְ**שָׁרִים תִּתְהַלָּל.
וּבְדִבְרֵי **צַ**דִּיקִים תִּתְבָּרַךְ.
וּבִלְשׁוֹן **חֲ**סִידִים תִּתְרוֹמָם.
וּבְקֶרֶב **קְ**דוֹשִׁים תִּתְקַדָּשׁ.

וּבְמַקְהֲלוֹת רִבְבוֹת עַמְּךָ בֵּית יִשְׂרָאֵל, בְּרִנָּה יִתְפָּאַר שִׁמְךָ מַלְכֵּנוּ בְּכָל דּוֹר וָדוֹר. ❖ שֶׁכֵּן חוֹבַת כָּל הַיְצוּרִים, לְפָנֶיךָ יהוה אֱלֹהֵינוּ וֵאלֹהֵי אֲבוֹתֵינוּ, לְהוֹדוֹת לְהַלֵּל לְשַׁבֵּחַ לְפָאֵר לְרוֹמֵם לְהַדֵּר לְבָרֵךְ לְעַלֵּה וּלְקַלֵּס, עַל כָּל דִּבְרֵי שִׁירוֹת וְתִשְׁבְּחוֹת דָּוִד בֶּן יִשַׁי עַבְדְּךָ מְשִׁיחֶךָ.

Stand while reciting יִשְׁתַּבַּח . . .
The fifteen expressions of praise — שִׁיר וּשְׁבָחָה . . . בְּרָכוֹת וְהוֹדָאוֹת —
should be recited without pause, preferably in one breath.

יִשְׁתַּבַּח שִׁמְךָ לָעַד מַלְכֵּנוּ, הָאֵל הַמֶּלֶךְ הַגָּדוֹל וְהַקָּדוֹשׁ, בַּשָּׁמַיִם וּבָאָרֶץ. כִּי לְךָ נָאֶה יהוה אֱלֹהֵינוּ וֵאלֹהֵי אֲבוֹתֵינוּ, שִׁיר וּשְׁבָחָה, הַלֵּל וְזִמְרָה, עֹז וּמֶמְשָׁלָה, נֶצַח גְּדֻלָּה וּגְבוּרָה, תְּהִלָּה וְתִפְאֶרֶת, קְדֻשָּׁה וּמַלְכוּת, בְּרָכוֹת וְהוֹדָאוֹת מֵעַתָּה וְעַד עוֹלָם. ❖ בָּרוּךְ אַתָּה יהוה, אֵל מֶלֶךְ גָּדוֹל בַּתִּשְׁבָּחוֹת, אֵל הַהוֹדָאוֹת, אֲדוֹן הַנִּפְלָאוֹת, הַבּוֹחֵר בְּשִׁירֵי זִמְרָה, מֶלֶךְ אֵל חֵי הָעוֹלָמִים. (.Cong — אָמֵן.)

The *chazzan* recites חֲצִי קַדִּישׁ.

יִתְגַּדַּל וְיִתְקַדַּשׁ שְׁמֵהּ רַבָּא. (.Cong — אָמֵן.) בְּעָלְמָא דִּי בְרָא כִרְעוּתֵהּ. וְיַמְלִיךְ מַלְכוּתֵהּ, בְּחַיֵּיכוֹן וּבְיוֹמֵיכוֹן וּבְחַיֵּי דְכָל בֵּית יִשְׂרָאֵל, בַּעֲגָלָא וּבִזְמַן קָרִיב. וְאִמְרוּ: אָמֵן.

(.Cong — אָמֵן. יְהֵא שְׁמֵהּ רַבָּא מְבָרַךְ לְעָלַם וּלְעָלְמֵי עָלְמַיָּא.)
יְהֵא שְׁמֵהּ רַבָּא מְבָרַךְ לְעָלַם וּלְעָלְמֵי עָלְמַיָּא.

יִתְבָּרַךְ וְיִשְׁתַּבַּח וְיִתְפָּאַר וְיִתְרוֹמַם וְיִתְנַשֵּׂא וְיִתְהַדָּר וְיִתְעַלֶּה וְיִתְהַלָּל שְׁמֵהּ דְּקֻדְשָׁא בְּרִיךְ הוּא (.Cong — בְּרִיךְ הוּא) — לְעֵלָּא מִן כָּל בִּרְכָתָא וְשִׁירָתָא תֻּשְׁבְּחָתָא וְנֶחֱמָתָא, דַּאֲמִירָן בְּעָלְמָא. וְאִמְרוּ: אָמֵן. (.Cong — אָמֵן.)

Your strength, great in the glory of Your Name, mighty forever and awesome through Your awesome deeds. O King enthroned upon a high and lofty throne![1]

The *chazzan* of *Shacharis* begins here:

שׁוֹכֵן עַד *He Who abides forever, exalted and holy is His Name.*[2] *And it is written: 'Sing joyfully, O righteous, before* HASHEM*; for the upright, praise is fitting.'*[3]

Chazzan: *By the mouth of the upright shall You be lauded;*
by the words of the righteous shall You be blessed;
by the tongue of the devout shall You be exalted;
and amid the holy shall You be sanctified.

וּבְמַקְהֲלוֹת *And in the assemblies of the myriads of Your people, the House of Israel, with joyous song shall Your Name be glorified, our King, throughout every generation.* Chazzan– *For such is the duty of all creatures — before You,* HASHEM*, our God, God of our forefathers, to thank, laud, praise, glorify, exalt, adore, bless, raise high, and sing praises — even beyond all expressions of the songs and praises of David the son of Jesse, Your servant, Your anointed.*

Stand while reciting *'May Your Name be praised . . .'*
The fifteen expressions of praise — *'song and praise. . .blessings and thanksgivings'* — should be recited without pause, preferably in one breath.

יִשְׁתַּבַּח *May Your Name be praised forever — our King, the God, the great and holy King — in heaven and on earth. Because for You is fitting — O* HASHEM*, our God, and the God of our forefathers — song and praise, lauding and hymns, power and dominion, triumph, greatness and strength, praise and splendor, holiness and sovereignty, blessings and thanksgivings from this time and forever.* Chazzan– *Blessed are You,* HASHEM*, God, King exalted through praises, God of thanksgivings, Master of wonders, Who chooses musical songs of praise — King, God, Life-giver of the world.* (Cong.– *Amen.)*

The *chazzan* recites Half-*Kaddish.*

יִתְגַּדַּל *May His great Name grow exalted and sanctified* (Cong.– *Amen.) in the world that He created as He willed. May He give reign to His kingship in your lifetimes and in your days, and in the lifetimes of the entire Family of Israel, swiftly and soon. Now respond: Amen.*

(Cong.– *Amen. May His great Name be blessed forever and ever.)*
May His great Name be blessed forever and ever.

Blessed, praised, glorified, exalted, extolled, mighty, upraised, and lauded be the Name of the Holy One, Blessed is He (Cong.– *Blessed is He) — beyond any blessing and song, praise and consolation that are uttered in the world. Now respond: Amen.* (Cong.– *Amen.)*

---

(1) Cf. *Isaiah* 6:1. (2) Cf. 57:15. (3) *Psalms* 33:1.

In some congregations the *chazzan* chants a melody during his recitation of בָּרְכוּ, so that the congregation can then recite יִתְבָּרַךְ.

Chazzan bows at בָּרְכוּ and straightens up at 'ה.

בָּרְכוּ אֶת יהוה הַמְּבֹרָךְ.

Congregation, followed by *chazzan*, responds, bowing at בָּרוּךְ and straightening up at 'ה.

בָּרוּךְ יהוה הַמְּבֹרָךְ לְעוֹלָם וָעֶד.

יִתְבָּרַךְ וְיִשְׁתַּבַּח וְיִתְפָּאַר וְיִתְרוֹמַם וְיִתְנַשֵּׂא שְׁמוֹ שֶׁל מֶלֶךְ מַלְכֵי הַמְּלָכִים, הַקָּדוֹשׁ בָּרוּךְ הוּא. שֶׁהוּא רִאשׁוֹן וְהוּא אַחֲרוֹן, וּמִבַּלְעָדָיו אֵין אֱלֹהִים.[1] סֹלּוּ, לָרֹכֵב בָּעֲרָבוֹת, בְּיָהּ שְׁמוֹ, וְעִלְזוּ לְפָנָיו.[2] וּשְׁמוֹ מְרוֹמָם עַל כָּל בְּרָכָה וּתְהִלָּה.[3] בָּרוּךְ שֵׁם כְּבוֹד מַלְכוּתוֹ לְעוֹלָם וָעֶד. יְהִי שֵׁם יהוה מְבֹרָךְ, מֵעַתָּה וְעַד עוֹלָם.[4]

ברכות קריאת שמע

It is preferable that one sit while reciting the following series of prayers — particularly the *Kedushah* verses, קָדוֹשׁ קָדוֹשׁ קָדוֹשׁ and בָּרוּךְ כְּבוֹד — until *Shemoneh Esrei.*

The following paragraph is recited aloud by the *chazzan,* then repeated by the congregation.

בָּרוּךְ אַתָּה יהוה אֱלֹהֵינוּ מֶלֶךְ הָעוֹלָם, יוֹצֵר אוֹר וּבוֹרֵא חֹשֶׁךְ, עֹשֶׂה שָׁלוֹם וּבוֹרֵא אֶת הַכֹּל.[5]

Congregations that do not recite *Yotzros,* continue on page 462.

Congregations that recite *Yotzros* continue:

אוֹר עוֹלָם בְּאוֹצַר חַיִּים, אוֹרוֹת מֵאֹפֶל אָמַר וַיֶּהִי.

All:

אֲפָאֵר* לֵאלֹהֵי מַעֲרָכָה, אֲשֶׁר יָעַץ וּפָעַל בִּרְחָבָה וַאֲרֻכָּה,*
וְצִוָּנוּ לֵישֵׁב בַּסֻּכָּה.[6]

בֵּאֵר תּוֹרָתוֹ לִמְפַעְנְחִים* וְהִקְשִׁיבוּ, בְּסֵּסֵם לָנֶצַח תֶּאֱהָבוּ,
בַּסֻּכּוֹת תֵּשְׁבוּ.[7]

גִּלָּה שְׂכָרָהּ מִמְּרוֹמִים, וְהִנְחִילָם שְׁלֹשׁ מֵאוֹת וַעֲשָׂרָה עוֹלָמִים,*
בַּסֻּכּוֹת תֵּשְׁבוּ שִׁבְעַת יָמִים.[7]

❖ יְקַבְּצֵנוּ הָדוּר כְּמֵאָז בַּאֲרִיאֵל, דְּרָכֵינוּ הַיְשַׁר וְרַחֵם יִשְׁרֵי אֵל,
חַזְּקֵנוּ כְּעַל יַד יְקוּתִיאֵל,* קָדוֹשׁ.

אֲפָאֵר — *I shall glorify.* Written by the otherwise unknown *Yehudah* [his signature appears in the fourth and the final stiches], the *piyut* follows an alphabetical acrostic. The *paytan* describes and expounds on the various laws and details regarding the *mitzvah* of building and dwelling in the *succah;* the Feast of the Leviathan at which those who observed this *mitzvah* will receive eternal reward; the gentile nations' request for a second chance to receive the Torah; and finally a plea for the rebuilt Temple in Jerusalem. Many of the points covered have already been discussed in the commentary to the *piyutim* of the first two days.

בִּרְחָבָה וַאֲרֻכָּה — *With 'The Wide and the Long.'* The Torah is thus described: *Longer than the earth is its measure, and wider than the sea (Job* 11:9). Before creating the world, God took counsel [so to speak] with the Torah (*Pirkei d'R' Eliezer* 3), and then used it as a tool with which to create the world (*Bereishis Rabbah* 1:1).

In some congregations the *chazzan* chants a melody during his recitation of *Borchu*, so that the congregation can then recite *'Blessed, praised . . .'*

Chazzan bows at *'Bless,'* and straightens up at *'HASHEM.'*

Bless HASHEM, the blessed One.

Congregation, followed by *chazzan*, responds, bowing at *'Blessed'* and straightening up at *'HASHEM.'*

Blessed is HASHEM, the blessed One, for all eternity.

Blessed, praised, glorified, exalted and upraised is the Name of the King Who rules over kings — the Holy One, Blessed is He. For He is the First and He is the Last and aside from Him there is no god.[1] *Extol Him — Who rides the highest heavens — with His Name, YAH, and exult before Him.*[2] *His Name is exalted beyond every blessing and praise.*[3] *Blessed is the Name of His glorious kingdom for all eternity. Blessed be the Name of HASHEM from this time and forever.*[4]

BLESSINGS OF THE SHEMA

It is preferable that one sit while reciting the following series of prayers — particularly the *Kedushah* verses, *'Holy, holy, holy . . .'* and *'Blessed is the glory . . .'* — until *Shemoneh Esrei*.

The following paragraph is recited aloud by the *chazzan*, then repeated by the congregation.

בָּרוּךְ *Blessed are You, HASHEM, our God, King of the universe, Who forms light and creates darkness, makes peace and creates all.*[5]

Congregations that do not recite *Yotzros*, continue on page 462.

Congregations that recite *Yotzros* continue:

The primeval light is in the treasury of eternal life;
'Let there be lights from the darkness,' He declared — and so it was!

All:

א *I shall glorify* the God of the [heavenly] array,*
*Who took counsel and made [the world] with 'The Wide and the Long,'**
and commanded us to dwell in the succah.[6]

ב *He expounded His Torah to the discoverers* and they accepted,*
He established them forever [and commanded,] 'You shall love [the Torah],'
[in which it is written:] 'You shall dwell in succos.'[7]

ג *He revealed its reward from on high,*
*and He bequeathed them [a reward of] three hundred ten worlds,**
[for observing the mitzvos, including:]
'You shall dwell in succos for seven days.'[7]

∴ *May the Splendrous One gather us as of old in the Godly leonine Temple;*
align our paths and be compassionate to God's upright [nation];
strengthen us as [You did] through the hand of Yekusiel, O Holy One.*

---

(1) Cf. *Isaiah* 44:6. (2) *Psalms* 68:5. (3) Cf. *Nechemiah* 9:5. (4) *Psalms* 113:2. (5) Cf. *Isaiah* 45:7. (6) From the *succah* blessing, see p. 84. (7) *Leviticus* 23:42.

לַמְפַעְנְחִים – *To the discoverers,* i.e., the Sages who constantly seek and discover new insights and interpretations.

שְׁלֹשׁ מֵאוֹת וַעֲשָׂרָה עוֹלָמִים – *Three hundred ten worlds.* The final mishnah in the Talmud (*Uktzin* 3:12) teaches that this is the reward for the righteous in the World to Come.

יְקוּתִיאֵל – *Yekusiel.* The Talmud (*Megillah* 13a) and Midrash (*Vayikra Rabbah* 1:3) teach that the six names mentioned in *I Chronicles* 4:18 — Yered, Avigedor, Chever, Avisocho, Yekusiel, Avi Zanoach — all refer to Moses.

All:

דָּהֵר בְּנוֹף אוֹתוֹתָיו לְמַעַנְכֶם, וְסִכֵּךְ עֲנָנוֹ עֲלֵיכֶם,
לְמַעַן יֵדְעוּ דוֹרוֹתֵיכֶם.[1]
הֶאִירוּ מֻבְהָקִים בַּאֲמִירָה, שֶׁחַמָּתָהּ מְרֻבָּה מִצִּלָּתָהּ שֶׁלֹּא כַתּוֹרָה,[2]
וְאִם לָאו כְּשֵׁרָה.
וְעַטְּרָהּ בִּסְדִינִין וּבִקְרוּמִין הַמְּצֻיָּרִין, וְסִכְּכָהּ כְּהִלְכַת מוֹרִין,[3]
בִּגְזֵרַת קַדִּישִׁין וּמֵאמַר עִירִין.[4]
זָהֵר שְׁפוּדִין* חוּץ מִסֻּכָּה,[5] וַאֲכִילָה וּשְׁתִיָּה בְּתוֹךְ סֻכּוֹבָהּ,
וְהוּא מְטַיֵּל בַּסֻּכָּה.[6]
חִשְּׁבוּהָ אַרְבַּע אַמּוֹת עַל אַרְבַּע,* פְּסוּלָה פְּחוּתָה מֵאַרְבַּע,
כְּדֵי לִזַכּוֹת עַם רֹבַע.
טִכְּסוּ עֲדַת בְּחִירַי, כְּתִקּוּן דַּת מוֹרַי,
צֵא מִדִּירַת קֶבַע וְשֵׁב בְּדִירַת עֲרַאי.[7]
יָחִיד כְּשֶׁבָּרָא עוֹלָמוֹ, וְכִלְּלוֹ בְּזוּוּגִים בְּעִצּוּמוֹ,
שְׁנַיִם שְׁנַיִם כְּנָאֳמוֹ.
כְּשֶׁיָּצַר לִוְיָתָן* וְזוּגָתוֹ, כֵּן עָשׂ זִיז שָׂדַי וְהוֹרָתוֹ,
וּמִרְעֵהוּ אֶלֶף הָרִים וְאִשְׁתּוֹ.
לְשַׂחֶק בָּם[8] צִנֵּן הַזְּכָרִים בְּלִהוּקִים, וְהַנְּקֵבוֹת הָרַג בְּבִתּוּקִים,
וּמִלְּחָם לֶעָתִיד לָבֹא לַצַּדִּיקִים.
מוֹעֲדִים הֵכִין בְּגַן עֵדֶן בִּמְסִבָּה, וַיהוה עַל רֹאשָׁם[9] לְטוֹבָה,
וְהַמֶּלֶךְ הַמָּשִׁיחַ שַׂר הַצָּבָא.
נִכְנָסִין כָּל הָאֻמּוֹת לָדִין,[10] פְּנֵי יוֹשֵׁב עַל כִּסֵּא דִין,
בְּצֶדֶק אוֹתָם יָדִין.
סֵדֶר מִצְוֹתֶיךָ תֵּן לָנוּ וּנְקַיְּמָה, וְנִזְכֶּה עִם אֵלּוּ בְּנֶחָמָה,
שַׂגִּיא כֹּחַ שׁוֹכֵן רוּמָה.
עֶלְיוֹן הַשּׁוֹפֵט כֹּל בֶּאֱמוּנָה, יַשְׁמִיעַ לָהֶם בִּתְבוּנָה,
יֵשׁ לִי מִצְוָה קְטַנָּה.[11]
פֵּרוּשׁ סֻכָּה וּשְׁאֵלֶיהָ, אַרְבַּע דְּפָנוֹת וְצֵל עָלֶיהָ,
לֹא תִרְחֲקוּ מֵאֵלֶיהָ.
צְלָלִים לַעֲשׂוֹת בָּהּ יַעֲטוּ, וְחַמָּה תִּקְדַּח עֲלֵיהֶם וְלִהֲטוּ,
וּבְרַגְלֵיהֶם יְבַעֲטוּ.*

שְׁפוּדִין — *[Metal] spits.* The translation follows the major commentators. From the context, however, the stich may possibly refer to the prohibition against keeping cooking utensils in the succah. Thus, 'roasting spits should be kept outside the succah' [see *Succah* 29a].

אַרְבַּע אַמּוֹת עַל אַרְבַּע — *Four cubits by four.* This is the opinion of Rabbi [Yehudah HaNassi]. However, the *halachah* follows the view that seven fist-widths (or 1⅙ cubits) is the minimum for each side (*Succah* 3a).

לִוְיָתָן — *Leviathan.* The Midrashim regarding this monstrous fish and the giant of Behemoth are discussed on page 1020.

יְבַעֲטוּ — *They will kick [down the succah].* Instead of sheepishly leaving the *succah* in disappointment at not being able to fulfill the *mitzvah,* they will defiantly kick at the *succah,* thus venting their anger at the *mitzvah.*

All:

ד *He hurried through Noph [Egypt] with miraculous signs for your sake,*
and placed His sheltering clouds over you,
so that your future generations may know.[1]

ה *The bright [Sages] enlightened with their saying,*
'If its sunlight is more than its shade, it is outside of the law,[2]
but if not, then it is valid.'

ו *And it is decorated with curtains and pictorial tapestries,*
and covered with s'chach, as the ruling of the teachers,[3]
with the decree and the dictum of the holy and angelic Sages.[4]

ז *They cautioned not to use [metal] spits* for s'chach,*[5]
while eating and drinking within its covering;
and one should spend his leisure time in the succah.[6]

ח *They consider it valid if four cubits by four,**
but invalid if it is less than four,
in order to find merit for the four[-bannered nation].

ט *The congregation of my chosen [Sages] established,*
according to the decree of my Mentor's Torah,
'Leave [your] permanent residence and dwell in a temporary residence.'[7]

י *When the Unique One created His world,*
in His strength He crowned it with pairs,
two by two [male and female], as was His utterance.

כ *When He fashioned Leviathan* and his mate,*
He also made the Behemoth and its wife,
it and its mate each feed on the grass of one thousand hills [daily].

ל *[He created them] to sport with them;*[8]
and neutered the males to prevent them from mating,
while He slaughtered the females by stabbing,
and salted their meat for the righteous in the future.

מ *Prepared for the banquet in the Garden of Eden,*
with HASHEM *at their head,*[9] *for goodness,*
and the King Messiah as leader of the masses.

נ *All the nations will enter to be judged,*[10]
before Him Who sits on the Throne of Judgment,
and He will judge them righteously.

ס *'Give us a roster of mitzvos and we will fulfill them,*
so that we will earn assuagement along with these [Israel],
O You Who are of abundant strength, Who dwells on high.'

ע *The Exalted One Who faithfully judges all,*
will allow them to hear with understanding,
'I have a small mitzvah.'[11]

פ *He will explain the succah and its requisite details,*
four walls with a shade above it,
'Do not distance yourself from it.'

צ *They will make shelters in which to wrap themselves.*
The sun will burn down upon them and frustrate them,
*then with their feet they will kick [down the succah].**

(1) *Leviticus* 23:43. (2) Cf. Mishnah *Succah* 1:1, see p. 94. (3) Tractate *Succah* 10a. (4) Cf. *Daniel* 4:14. (5) Cf. Mishnah *Succah* 1:8, see p. 98. (6) See tractate *Succah* 28b. (7) 2a. (8) Cf. *Psalms* 104:26. (9) Cf. *Micah* 2:13. (10) See tractate *Avodah Zarah* 2a. (11) 3a.

קָדוֹשׁ יִשְׁפֹּךְ עֲלֵיהֶם חֵמָה, וְיַפִּילֵם בְּגֵיהִנֹּם בְּלִי רְחוּמָה,
בְּמַדְרֵגָה הַתַּחְתּוֹנָה בִּמְהוּמָה.
רָם רוֹכֵב עֲרָבוֹת, הִזְהִירָנוּ מִצְוֹת עֲרֵבוֹת,
וְתִתֵּן לְפָנָיו לְהַרְבּוֹת.
שָׁם יֶחֱזוּ וְיֵבֹשׁוּ קִנְאַת עָם, אַף אֵשׁ צָרֶיךָ תֹאכְלֵם[1] בְּמַסָּעָם,
בְּאַבְנֵי אֶלְגָּבִישׁ אֵשׁ וְגָפְרִית[2] וָזַעַם.
❖ תַּקִּיף יְחַיֵּינוּ מִיּוֹמָיִם,[3] **הוֹד** וְהָדָר תּוֹדִיעַ בְּכִפְלַיִם,
כְּהַיּוֹם הַזֶּה בְּהַר הַקֹּדֶשׁ וּבִירוּשָׁלַיִם, קָדוֹשׁ.

הַכֹּל יוֹדוּךָ, וְהַכֹּל יְשַׁבְּחוּךָ, וְהַכֹּל יֹאמְרוּ אֵין קָדוֹשׁ כַּיהוה.[4] הַכֹּל יְרוֹמְמוּךָ סֶּלָה, יוֹצֵר הַכֹּל. הָאֵל הַפּוֹתֵחַ בְּכָל יוֹם דַּלְתוֹת שַׁעֲרֵי מִזְרָח, וּבוֹקֵעַ חַלּוֹנֵי רָקִיעַ, מוֹצִיא חַמָּה מִמְּקוֹמָהּ וּלְבָנָה מִמְּכוֹן שִׁבְתָּהּ, וּמֵאִיר לָעוֹלָם כֻּלּוֹ וּלְיוֹשְׁבָיו, שֶׁבָּרָא בְּמִדַּת רַחֲמִים. הַמֵּאִיר לָאָרֶץ וְלַדָּרִים עָלֶיהָ בְּרַחֲמִים, וּבְטוּבוֹ מְחַדֵּשׁ בְּכָל יוֹם תָּמִיד מַעֲשֵׂה בְרֵאשִׁית. הַמֶּלֶךְ הַמְּרוֹמָם לְבַדּוֹ מֵאָז, הַמְּשֻׁבָּח וְהַמְּפֹאָר וְהַמִּתְנַשֵּׂא מִימוֹת עוֹלָם. אֱלֹהֵי עוֹלָם בְּרַחֲמֶיךָ הָרַבִּים, רַחֵם עָלֵינוּ, אֲדוֹן עֻזֵּנוּ, צוּר מִשְׂגַּבֵּנוּ, מָגֵן יִשְׁעֵנוּ, מִשְׂגָּב בַּעֲדֵנוּ. אֵין כְּעֶרְכֶּךָ, וְאֵין זוּלָתֶךָ, אֶפֶס בִּלְתֶּךָ, וּמִי דּוֹמֶה לָּךְ. אֵין כְּעֶרְכְּךָ יהוה אֱלֹהֵינוּ בָּעוֹלָם הַזֶּה, וְאֵין זוּלָתְךָ מַלְכֵּנוּ לְחַיֵּי הָעוֹלָם הַבָּא. אֶפֶס בִּלְתְּךָ גּוֹאֲלֵנוּ לִימוֹת הַמָּשִׁיחַ, וְאֵין דּוֹמֶה לְּךָ מוֹשִׁיעֵנוּ לִתְחִיַּת הַמֵּתִים.

The following liturgical song is recited responsively in most congregations.
In some congregations, the *chazzan* and congregation sing the stanzas together.

אֵל אָדוֹן עַל כָּל הַמַּעֲשִׂים, **בָּ**רוּךְ וּמְבֹרָךְ בְּפִי כָּל נְשָׁמָה,
גָּדְלוֹ וְטוּבוֹ מָלֵא עוֹלָם, **דַּ**עַת וּתְבוּנָה סוֹבְבִים אֹתוֹ.
הַמִּתְגָּאֶה עַל חַיּוֹת הַקֹּדֶשׁ, **וְ**נֶהְדָּר בְּכָבוֹד עַל הַמֶּרְכָּבָה,
זְכוּת וּמִישׁוֹר לִפְנֵי כִסְאוֹ, **חֶ**סֶד וְרַחֲמִים לִפְנֵי כְבוֹדוֹ.
טוֹבִים מְאוֹרוֹת שֶׁבָּרָא אֱלֹהֵינוּ, **יְ**צָרָם בְּדַעַת בְּבִינָה וּבְהַשְׂכֵּל,
כֹּחַ וּגְבוּרָה נָתַן בָּהֶם, **לִ**הְיוֹת מוֹשְׁלִים בְּקֶרֶב תֵּבֵל.

---

(1) *Isaiah* 26:11. (2) *Ezekiel* 38:22. (3) *Hoshea* 6:2. (4) *I Samuel* 2:2.

ק *May the Holy One pour wrath upon them,*
and lower them into Gehinnom without compassion,
confounded in the nether most depths.
ר *The Exalted One Who rides upon the highest heaven,*
has commanded us sweet mitzvos,
that we may pray before Him exceedingly.
ש *There they will see and be embarrassed with envy of the people [Israel],*
and your oppressors in their travels will be consumed by fiery wrath,[1]
with hailstones, sulphurous fire[2] *and anger.*
ת *O Powerful One, may You revive us after the two days*[3]
[of the Temples' destruction];
let us know [Your] majesty and splendor in double measure,
this very day on the holy mount and in Jerusalem, O Holy One.

הַכֹּל יוֹדוּךָ *All will thank You and all will praise You — and all will declare: 'Nothing is as holy as* HASHEM*!'*[4] *All will exalt You, Selah! — You Who forms everything. The God Who opens daily the doors of the gateways of the East, and splits the windows of the firmament, Who removes the sun from its place and the moon from the site of its dwelling, and Who illuminates all the world and its inhabitants, which He created with the attribute of mercy. He Who illuminates the earth and those who dwell upon it, with compassion; and in His goodness renews daily, perpetually, the work of creation. The King Who was exalted in solitude from before creation, Who is praised, glorified, and extolled since days of old. Eternal God, with Your abundant compassion be compassionate to us — O Master of our power, our rocklike stronghold; O Shield of our salvation, be a stronghold for us. There is no comparison to You, there is nothing except for You, there is nothing without You, for who is like You? There is no comparison to You,* HASHEM*, our God, in this world; and there will be nothing except for You, our King, in the life of the World to Come; there will be nothing without You, our Redeemer, in Messianic days; and there will be none like You, our Savior; at the Resuscitation of the Dead.*

The following liturgical song is recited responsively in most congregations.
In some congregations, the *chazzan* and congregation sing the stanzas together.

אֵל אָדוֹן *God — the Master over all works; the Blessed One —*
ב *and He is blessed by the mouth of every soul;*
ג *His greatness and goodness fill the world,*
ד *wisdom and insight surround Him.*
ה *He Who exalts Himself over the holy Chayos*
ו *and is splendrous in glory above the Chariot;*
ז *Merit and fairness are before His throne,*
ח *kindness and mercy are before His glory.*
ט *Good are the luminaries that our God has created,*
י *He has fashioned them with wisdom,*
with insight and discernment;
כ *Strength and power has He granted them,*
ל *to be dominant within the world.*

מְלֵאִים זִיו וּמְפִיקִים נֹגַהּ, נָאֶה זִיוָם בְּכָל הָעוֹלָם,
שְׂמֵחִים בְּצֵאתָם וְשָׂשִׂים בְּבוֹאָם, עוֹשִׂים בְּאֵימָה רְצוֹן קוֹנָם.
פְּאֵר וְכָבוֹד נוֹתְנִים לִשְׁמוֹ, צָהֳלָה וְרִנָּה לְזֵכֶר מַלְכוּתוֹ,
קָרָא לַשֶּׁמֶשׁ וַיִּזְרַח אוֹר, רָאָה וְהִתְקִין צוּרַת הַלְּבָנָה.
שֶׁבַח נוֹתְנִים לוֹ כָּל צְבָא מָרוֹם.
תִּפְאֶרֶת וּגְדֻלָּה, שְׂרָפִים וְאוֹפַנִּים וְחַיּוֹת הַקֹּדֶשׁ—

לָאֵל אֲשֶׁר שָׁבַת מִכָּל הַמַּעֲשִׂים, בַּיּוֹם הַשְּׁבִיעִי הִתְעַלָּה וְיָשַׁב עַל כִּסֵּא כְבוֹדוֹ, תִּפְאֶרֶת עָטָה לְיוֹם הַמְּנוּחָה, עֹנֶג קָרָא לְיוֹם הַשַּׁבָּת. זֶה שֶׁבַח שֶׁל יוֹם הַשְּׁבִיעִי, שֶׁבּוֹ שָׁבַת אֵל מִכָּל מְלַאכְתּוֹ. וְיוֹם הַשְּׁבִיעִי מְשַׁבֵּחַ וְאוֹמֵר: מִזְמוֹר שִׁיר לְיוֹם הַשַּׁבָּת, טוֹב לְהוֹדוֹת לַיהוה.[1] לְפִיכָךְ יְפָאֲרוּ וִיבָרְכוּ לָאֵל כָּל יְצוּרָיו. שֶׁבַח יְקָר וּגְדֻלָּה יִתְּנוּ לָאֵל מֶלֶךְ יוֹצֵר כֹּל, הַמַּנְחִיל מְנוּחָה לְעַמּוֹ יִשְׂרָאֵל בִּקְדֻשָּׁתוֹ בְּיוֹם שַׁבַּת קֹדֶשׁ. שִׁמְךָ יהוה אֱלֹהֵינוּ יִתְקַדַּשׁ, וְזִכְרְךָ מַלְכֵּנוּ יִתְפָּאַר, בַּשָּׁמַיִם מִמַּעַל וְעַל הָאָרֶץ מִתָּחַת. תִּתְבָּרַךְ מוֹשִׁיעֵנוּ עַל שֶׁבַח מַעֲשֵׂה יָדֶיךָ, וְעַל מְאוֹרֵי אוֹר שֶׁעָשִׂיתָ, יְפָאֲרוּךָ, סֶּלָה.

תִּתְבָּרַךְ צוּרֵנוּ מַלְכֵּנוּ וְגוֹאֲלֵנוּ, בּוֹרֵא קְדוֹשִׁים. יִשְׁתַּבַּח שִׁמְךָ לָעַד מַלְכֵּנוּ, יוֹצֵר מְשָׁרְתִים, וַאֲשֶׁר מְשָׁרְתָיו כֻּלָּם עוֹמְדִים בְּרוּם עוֹלָם, וּמַשְׁמִיעִים בְּיִרְאָה יַחַד בְּקוֹל דִּבְרֵי אֱלֹהִים חַיִּים וּמֶלֶךְ עוֹלָם.[2] כֻּלָּם אֲהוּבִים, כֻּלָּם בְּרוּרִים, כֻּלָּם גִּבּוֹרִים, וְכֻלָּם עֹשִׂים בְּאֵימָה וּבְיִרְאָה רְצוֹן קוֹנָם. ❖ וְכֻלָּם פּוֹתְחִים אֶת פִּיהֶם בִּקְדֻשָּׁה וּבְטָהֳרָה, בְּשִׁירָה וּבְזִמְרָה, וּמְבָרְכִים וּמְשַׁבְּחִים וּמְפָאֲרִים וּמַעֲרִיצִים וּמַקְדִּישִׁים וּמַמְלִיכִים —

אֶת שֵׁם הָאֵל הַמֶּלֶךְ הַגָּדוֹל הַגִּבּוֹר וְהַנּוֹרָא קָדוֹשׁ הוּא.[3] ❖ וְכֻלָּם מְקַבְּלִים עֲלֵיהֶם עֹל מַלְכוּת שָׁמַיִם זֶה מִזֶּה, וְנוֹתְנִים רְשׁוּת זֶה לָזֶה, לְהַקְדִּישׁ לְיוֹצְרָם, בְּנַחַת רוּחַ בְּשָׂפָה בְרוּרָה וּבִנְעִימָה. קְדֻשָּׁה כֻּלָּם כְּאֶחָד עוֹנִים וְאוֹמְרִים בְּיִרְאָה:

Congregation recites aloud:

קָדוֹשׁ קָדוֹשׁ קָדוֹשׁ יהוה צְבָאוֹת,
מְלֹא כָל הָאָרֶץ כְּבוֹדוֹ.[4]

---

(1) *Psalms* 92:1-2. (2) Cf. *Jeremiah* 10:10. (3) Cf. *Deuteronomy* 10:17; *Psalms* 99:3. (4) *Isaiah* 6:3.

מ *Filled with luster and radiating brightness,*
נ *their luster is beautiful throughout the world;*
ס *Glad as they go forth and exultant as they return,*
ע *they do with awe their Creator's will.*
פ *Splendor and glory they bestow upon His Name,*
צ *jubilation and glad song upon the mention of His reign —*
ק *He called out to the sun and it glowed with light,*
ר *He saw and fashioned the form of the moon.*
ש *All the host above bestows praise on Him,*
ת *splendor and greatness — the Seraphim, Ophanim, and holy Chayos —*

לָאֵל *To the God Who rested from all works, Who ascended on the Seventh Day and sat on the Throne of His Glory. With splendor He enwrapped the Day of Contentment — He declared the Sabbath day a delight! This is the praise of the Sabbath Day: that on it God rested from all His work. And the Seventh Day gives praise saying: 'A psalm, a song for the Sabbath Day. It is good to thank* HASHEM *. . .'*[1] *Therefore let all that He has fashioned glorify and bless God. Praise, honor, and greatness let them render to God, the King Who fashioned everything, Who gives a heritage of contentment to His People, Israel, in His holiness on the holy Sabbath Day. May Your Name,* HASHEM, *our God, be sanctified and may Your remembrance, our King, be glorified in the heaven above and upon the earth below. May You be blessed, our Savior, beyond the praises of Your handiwork and beyond the brilliant luminaries that You have made — may they glorify You — Selah.*

תִּתְבָּרַךְ *May You be blessed, our Rock, our King and our Redeemer, Creator of holy ones; may Your Name be praised forever, our King, O Fashioner of ministering angels; all of Whose ministering angels stand at the summit of the universe and proclaim — with awe, together, loudly — the words of the living God and King of the universe.*[2] *They are all beloved; they are all flawless; they are all mighty; they all do the will of their Maker with dread and reverence.* Chazzan– *And they all open their mouth in holiness and purity, in song and hymn — and bless, praise, glorify, revere, sanctify and declare the kingship of —*

אֶת שֵׁם *The Name of God, the great, mighty, and awesome King; holy is He.*[3] Chazzan– *Then they all accept upon themselves the yoke of heavenly sovereignty from one another, and grant permission to one another to sanctify the One Who formed them, with tranquillity, with clear articulation, and with sweetness. All of them as one proclaim His holiness and say with awe:*

Congregation recites aloud:

'Holy, holy, holy is HASHEM, Master of Legions, the whole world is filled with His glory.'[4]

Responsively:

יְרוּצְצוּ כִּבְרָקִים, יִשְׁתַּפְּכוּ כִּמְזֻרָקִים, יְשָׁרְתוּ לִפְרָקִים,
יְעוֹשׁוּ אִישׁ בְּאָחִיו וְלֹא נִזָּק. וְהַחַיּוֹת רָצוֹא וָשׁוֹב כְּמַרְאֵה הַבָּזָק.[1]
צָגִים בְּמִשְׁמָרוֹת, צְהַר וְאַשְׁמוּרוֹת, צִלְצוּל גַּם זְמִירוֹת,
צָהַל קוֹל יָרִיעוּ הוֹלֵךְ וְחָזָק. וְהַחַיּוֹת רָצוֹא וָשׁוֹב כְּמַרְאֵה הַבָּזָק.
חַשְׁמַלֵּי מֶרְכָּבָה, חֲשָׁשָׁם לֹא כָבָה, חָשִׁים בְּלִי עַכָּבָה,
חֲרֵדִים וּמְזִיעִים כְּצוּק מַיִם יְזָּק. וְהַחַיּוֹת רָצוֹא וָשׁוֹב כְּמַרְאֵה הַבָּזָק.
קַפְצִיאֵל הַשָּׂר, קוֹלוֹת יְבַשֵּׂר, קֶשֶׁת לֹא יֶחְסַר,*
קָרֵב לְהִסְתַּכֵּל יָרֵא פֶּן יִתְנַזָּק. וְהַחַיּוֹת רָצוֹא וָשׁוֹב כְּמַרְאֵה הַבָּזָק.*
הֲמוֹנֵי לִגְיוֹן, קוֹבְעִים הִגָּיוֹן, טוֹבְלִים בִּרְגִיוֹן,*
נוֹגְנִים בְּהֶקְדֵּשׁ גַּן נָעוּל וּמְעֻזָּק.* וְהַחַיּוֹת רָצוֹא וָשׁוֹב כְּמַרְאֵה הַבָּזָק.

Congregation, followed by the *chazzan,* recites one of these versions, according to its tradition.

וְהָאוֹפַנִּים וְחַיּוֹת הַקֹּדֶשׁ בְּרַעַשׁ גָּדוֹל מִתְנַשְּׂאִים לְעֻמַּת שְׂרָפִים. לְעֻמָּתָם מְשַׁבְּחִים וְאוֹמְרִים:

וְהַחַיּוֹת יְשׁוֹרֵרוּ, וּכְרוּבִים יְפָאֵרוּ, וּשְׂרָפִים יָרֹנּוּ, וְאֶרְאֶלִּים יְבָרֵכוּ. פְּנֵי כָל חַיָּה וְאוֹפָן וּכְרוּב לְעֻמַּת שְׂרָפִים. לְעֻמָּתָם מְשַׁבְּחִים וְאוֹמְרִים:

Congregation recites aloud:

בָּרוּךְ כְּבוֹד יהוה מִמְּקוֹמוֹ.[2]

יְרוּצְצוּ – *They run.* This piyut describes the Divine service of the celestial beings. Although there are ten categories of angels (see p. 232) only three are mentioned here: *Chayos, Chashmalim* and *Ishim.* The author signed his name יִצְחָק הַקָּטָן, *Yitzchak the Lesser,* in the acrostic, but nothing more is known of his identity.

From various Midrashim a picture emerges of the four *Chayos* that bear the *Merkavah* [lit., Chariot, a reference to God's Heavenly Throne (see *Ezekiel* ch. 1)] perspiring profusely in dread of God's majesty. As their perspiration flows it becomes the River of Fire [נְהַר דִּי נוּר]. This river serves many functions. Angels who have completed their mission and have become superfluous are destroyed in it; new angels are created from it; and angels preparing to recite *Kedushah* immerse in it as in a *mikveh.* The *paytan* makes several allusions to this scene.

קֶשֶׁת לֹא יֶחְסַר – *The 'bow' will not be diminished.* This is an allusion to the Messiah of the royal house of Judah. As the prophet Zechariah declares: *From him [Judah] the cornerstone; from him the spike; from him the bow of battle* (*Zechariah* 10:4). The *Targum* paraphrases: 'From him kingship; from him Messiah; from him strength in battle.' Thus, this angel informs the others that although he has not yet arrived, the Messiah's glory will not be diminished by the delay.

Alternatively, this alludes to the *Merkavah* vision in which Ezekiel describes his perception of God as *the appearance of a rainbow upon the cloud on a rainy day* (*Ezekiel* 1:28). That is, just as the colors of the rainbow are but the effect of the sunlight refracting through the atmosphere, so too, the Likeness of God's Glory which Ezekiel perceived is but the *effect* of His Intellectual Light [as distinguished from a physical light like that of the sun], the essence of which is indescribable in human terms *(Malbim).*

A third view interprets this as Noah's rainbow: the covenant that God made with Noah never again to flood the world is still in force (see *Genesis* 9:12-17).

רִגְיוֹן – *Rigyon.* This is another name for the River of Fire mentioned above. The *gematria* [numerical value] of רִגְיוֹן, *Rigyon,* is the same as that of דִּי נוּר, *of Fire.*

גַּן נָעוּל וּמְעֻזָּק – *[Israel] the locked and fenced-in garden [has begun].* Israel, the nation which retained the fence of moral purity and was free

Responsively:

י *They run* like lightning,*
they pour forth [their souls] as if from sprinkling vessels,
they serve at appointed intervals,
the Ishim hurry each other, yet none are harmed —
and the Chayos running to and fro like the appearance of a brilliant flash.[1]

צ *They stand at their watches,*
in [morning's] light and [evening's] watch,
resonantly singing out [praise],
cheer and trumpet-like voices growing ever stronger —
and the Chayos running to and fro like the appearance of a brilliant flash.

ח *Chashmalim of the Chariot*
not a trace of their fire extinguished,
they hurry unhindered,
in their awe they perspire like an outpouring of pure water —
and the Chayos running to and fro like the appearance of a brilliant flash.

ק *Kaftziel the master,*
sounds out the tidings,
*that the 'bow' will not be diminished,**
yet even he [Kaftziel] fears to approach and see, lest he be injured —
and the Chayos running to and fro like the appearance of a brilliant flash.

ה *The multitudinous legion,*
ק *establish a time [to recite God's praise],*
ט *they immerse in [the River] Rigyon,**
נ *to recite Kedushah after [Israel]*
the locked and fenced-in garden [has begun]—*
and the Chayos running to and fro like the appearance of a brilliant flash.

Congregation, followed by the *chazzan,* recites one of these versions, according to its tradition.

Then the Ofanim and the holy Chayos, with great noise raise themselves towards the Seraphim. Facing them they give praise saying:

Then the Chayos sing, the Cherubim glorify, the Seraphim rejoice, and the Erelim bless, in the presence of every Chayah, Ofan, and Cherub towards the Seraphim. Facing them they give praise saying:

Congregation recites aloud:

'Blessed is the glory of HASHEM from His place.'[2]

(1) *Ezekiel* 1:14. (2) 3:12.

of adulterous relationships during the entire period that it was locked in Egyptian slavery, is described in *Song of Songs* 4:12 as a 'locked garden,' i.e., it preserved its purity and spiritual beauty. The angels may not recite their praise of God until after Israel's *Kedushah.*

לְאֵל בָּרוּךְ נְעִימוֹת יִתֵּנוּ. לְמֶלֶךְ אֵל חַי וְקַיָּם, זְמִרוֹת יֹאמֵרוּ, וְתִשְׁבָּחוֹת יַשְׁמִיעוּ. כִּי הוּא לְבַדּוֹ פּוֹעֵל גְּבוּרוֹת, עֹשֶׂה חֲדָשׁוֹת, בַּעַל מִלְחָמוֹת, זוֹרֵעַ צְדָקוֹת, מַצְמִיחַ יְשׁוּעוֹת, בּוֹרֵא רְפוּאוֹת, נוֹרָא תְהִלּוֹת, אֲדוֹן הַנִּפְלָאוֹת. הַמְּחַדֵּשׁ בְּטוּבוֹ בְּכָל יוֹם תָּמִיד מַעֲשֵׂה בְרֵאשִׁית. כָּאָמוּר: לְעֹשֵׂה אוֹרִים גְּדֹלִים, כִּי לְעוֹלָם חַסְדּוֹ.[1] ❖ אוֹר חָדָשׁ עַל צִיּוֹן תָּאִיר, וְנִזְכֶּה כֻלָּנוּ מְהֵרָה לְאוֹרוֹ. בָּרוּךְ אַתָּה יהוה, יוֹצֵר הַמְּאוֹרוֹת. (.Cong. – אָמֵן)

אַהֲבָה רַבָּה אֲהַבְתָּנוּ יהוה אֱלֹהֵינוּ, חֶמְלָה גְדוֹלָה וִיתֵרָה חָמַלְתָּ עָלֵינוּ. אָבִינוּ מַלְכֵּנוּ, בַּעֲבוּר אֲבוֹתֵינוּ שֶׁבָּטְחוּ בְךָ, וַתְּלַמְּדֵם חֻקֵּי חַיִּים, כֵּן תְּחָנֵּנוּ וּתְלַמְּדֵנוּ. אָבִינוּ הָאָב הָרַחֲמָן הַמְּרַחֵם, רַחֵם עָלֵינוּ, וְתֵן בְּלִבֵּנוּ לְהָבִין וּלְהַשְׂכִּיל, לִשְׁמוֹעַ לִלְמוֹד וּלְלַמֵּד, לִשְׁמֹר וְלַעֲשׂוֹת וּלְקַיֵּם אֶת כָּל דִּבְרֵי תַלְמוּד תּוֹרָתֶךָ בְּאַהֲבָה. וְהָאֵר עֵינֵינוּ בְּתוֹרָתֶךָ, וְדַבֵּק לִבֵּנוּ בְּמִצְוֹתֶיךָ, וְיַחֵד לְבָבֵנוּ לְאַהֲבָה וּלְיִרְאָה אֶת שְׁמֶךָ,[2] וְלֹא נֵבוֹשׁ לְעוֹלָם וָעֶד. כִּי בְשֵׁם קָדְשְׁךָ הַגָּדוֹל וְהַנּוֹרָא בָּטָחְנוּ, נָגִילָה וְנִשְׂמְחָה בִּישׁוּעָתֶךָ.

At this point, gather the four *tzitzis* between the fourth and fifth fingers of the left hand. Hold *tzitzis* in this manner throughout the *Shema*.

וַהֲבִיאֵנוּ לְשָׁלוֹם מֵאַרְבַּע כַּנְפוֹת הָאָרֶץ, וְתוֹלִיכֵנוּ קוֹמְמִיּוּת לְאַרְצֵנוּ. כִּי אֵל פּוֹעֵל יְשׁוּעוֹת אָתָּה, וּבָנוּ בָחַרְתָּ מִכָּל עַם וְלָשׁוֹן. ❖ וְקֵרַבְתָּנוּ לְשִׁמְךָ הַגָּדוֹל סֶלָה בֶּאֱמֶת, לְהוֹדוֹת לְךָ וּלְיַחֶדְךָ בְּאַהֲבָה. בָּרוּךְ אַתָּה יהוה, הַבּוֹחֵר בְּעַמּוֹ יִשְׂרָאֵל בְּאַהֲבָה. (.Cong. – אָמֵן)

שמע

Immediately before its recitation concentrate on fulfilling the positive commandment of reciting the *Shema* twice daily. It is important to enunciate each word clearly and not to run words together. For this reason, vertical lines have been placed between two words that are prone to be slurred into one and are not separated by a comma or a hyphen. See *Laws* §40-55.

When praying without a *minyan,* begin with the following three-word formula:

אֵל מֶלֶךְ נֶאֱמָן.

Recite the first verse aloud, with the right hand covering the eyes, and concentrate intently upon accepting God's absolute sovereignty.

שְׁמַע | יִשְׂרָאֵל, יהוה | אֱלֹהֵינוּ, יהוה | אֶחָד:[3]

In an undertone – בָּרוּךְ שֵׁם כְּבוֹד מַלְכוּתוֹ לְעוֹלָם וָעֶד.

(1) *Psalms* 136:7. (2) Cf. 86:11. (3) *Deuteronomy* 6:4.

לָאֵל *To the blessed God they shall offer sweet melodies; to the King, the living and enduring God, they shall sing hymns and proclaim praises. For He alone effects mighty deeds, makes new things, is Master of wars, sows kindnesses, makes salvations flourish, creates cures, is too awesome for praise, is Lord of wonders. In His goodness He renews daily, perpetually, the work of creation. As it is said: '[Give thanks] to Him Who makes the great luminaries, for His kindness endures forever.'*[1] Chazzan– *May You shine a new light on Zion, and may we all speedily merit its light. Blessed are You,* HASHEM, *Who fashions the luminaries.* (Cong.– *Amen)*

אַהֲבָה *With an abundant love have You loved us,* HASHEM, *our God; with exceedingly great pity have You pitied us. Our Father, our King, for the sake of our forefathers who trusted in You and whom You taught the decrees of life, may You be equally gracious to us and teach us. Our Father, the merciful Father, Who acts mercifully, have mercy upon us, instill in our hearts to understand and elucidate, to listen, learn, teach, safeguard, perform, and fulfill all the words of Your Torah's teaching with love. Enlighten our eyes in Your Torah, attach our hearts to Your commandments, and unify our hearts to love and fear Your Name,*[2] *and may we not feel inner shame for all eternity. Because we have trusted in Your great and awesome holy Name, may we exult and rejoice in Your salvation.*

At this point, gather the four *tzitzis* between the fourth and fifth fingers of the left hand. Hold *tzitzis* in this manner throughout the *Shema.*

Bring us in peacefulness from the four corners of the earth and lead us with upright pride to our land. For You effect salvations O God; You have chosen us from among every people and tongue. Chazzan– *And You have brought us close to Your great Name forever in truth, to offer praiseful thanks to You, and proclaim Your Oneness with love. Blessed are You,* HASHEM, *Who chooses His people Israel with love.* (Cong.– *Amen.)*

THE SHEMA

Immediately before its recitation, concentrate on fulfilling the positive commandment of reciting the *Shema* twice daily. It is important to enunciate each word clearly and not to run words together. See *Laws* §40-55.

When praying without a *minyan,* begin with the following three-word formula:
God, trustworthy King.

Recite the first verse aloud, with the right hand covering the eyes, and concentrate intently upon accepting God's absolute sovereignty.

Hear, O Israel: HASHEM is our God, HASHEM, the One and Only.[3]

In an undertone– *Blessed is the Name of His glorious kingdom for all eternity.*

While reciting the first paragraph (דברים ו:ה-ט), concentrate on accepting the commandment to love God.

וְאָהַבְתָּ אֵת ׀ יהוה ׀ אֱלֹהֶיךָ, בְּכָל־לְבָבְךָ, וּבְכָל־נַפְשְׁךָ, וּבְכָל־
מְאֹדֶךָ: וְהָיוּ הַדְּבָרִים הָאֵלֶּה, אֲשֶׁר ׀ אָנֹכִי מְצַוְּךָ הַיּוֹם,
עַל־לְבָבֶךָ: וְשִׁנַּנְתָּם לְבָנֶיךָ, וְדִבַּרְתָּ בָּם, בְּשִׁבְתְּךָ בְּבֵיתֶךָ, וּבְלֶכְתְּךָ
בַדֶּרֶךְ, וּבְשָׁכְבְּךָ וּבְקוּמֶךָ: וּקְשַׁרְתָּם לְאוֹת ׀ עַל־יָדֶךָ, וְהָיוּ לְטֹטָפֹת
בֵּין ׀ עֵינֶיךָ: וּכְתַבְתָּם ׀ עַל־מְזֻזוֹת בֵּיתֶךָ, וּבִשְׁעָרֶיךָ:

While reciting the second paragraph (דברים יא:יג-כא), concentrate on accepting all the commandments and the concept of reward and punishment.

וְהָיָה, אִם־שָׁמֹעַ תִּשְׁמְעוּ אֶל־מִצְוֹתַי, אֲשֶׁר ׀ אָנֹכִי מְצַוֶּה ׀ אֶתְכֶם
הַיּוֹם, לְאַהֲבָה אֶת־יהוה ׀ אֱלֹהֵיכֶם וּלְעָבְדוֹ, בְּכָל־לְבַבְכֶם,
וּבְכָל־נַפְשְׁכֶם: וְנָתַתִּי מְטַר־אַרְצְכֶם בְּעִתּוֹ, יוֹרֶה וּמַלְקוֹשׁ, וְאָסַפְתָּ
דְגָנֶךָ וְתִירֹשְׁךָ וְיִצְהָרֶךָ: וְנָתַתִּי ׀ עֵשֶׂב ׀ בְּשָׂדְךָ לִבְהֶמְתֶּךָ, וְאָכַלְתָּ
וְשָׂבָעְתָּ: הִשָּׁמְרוּ לָכֶם, פֶּן־יִפְתֶּה לְבַבְכֶם, וְסַרְתֶּם וַעֲבַדְתֶּם ׀
אֱלֹהִים ׀ אֲחֵרִים, וְהִשְׁתַּחֲוִיתֶם לָהֶם: וְחָרָה ׀ אַף־יהוה בָּכֶם, וְעָצַר
׀ אֶת־הַשָּׁמַיִם, וְלֹא־יִהְיֶה מָטָר, וְהָאֲדָמָה לֹא תִתֵּן אֶת־יְבוּלָהּ,
וַאֲבַדְתֶּם ׀ מְהֵרָה מֵעַל הָאָרֶץ הַטֹּבָה ׀ אֲשֶׁר ׀ יהוה נֹתֵן לָכֶם:
וְשַׂמְתֶּם ׀ אֶת־דְּבָרַי ׀ אֵלֶּה, עַל־לְבַבְכֶם וְעַל־נַפְשְׁכֶם, וּקְשַׁרְתֶּם ׀
אֹתָם לְאוֹת ׀ עַל־יֶדְכֶם, וְהָיוּ לְטוֹטָפֹת בֵּין ׀ עֵינֵיכֶם: וְלִמַּדְתֶּם ׀
אֹתָם ׀ אֶת־בְּנֵיכֶם, לְדַבֵּר בָּם, בְּשִׁבְתְּךָ בְּבֵיתֶךָ, וּבְלֶכְתְּךָ בַדֶּרֶךְ,
וּבְשָׁכְבְּךָ וּבְקוּמֶךָ: וּכְתַבְתָּם ׀ עַל־מְזוּזוֹת בֵּיתֶךָ, וּבִשְׁעָרֶיךָ: לְמַעַן ׀
יִרְבּוּ ׀ יְמֵיכֶם וִימֵי בְנֵיכֶם, עַל הָאֲדָמָה ׀ אֲשֶׁר נִשְׁבַּע ׀ יהוה
לַאֲבֹתֵיכֶם לָתֵת לָהֶם, כִּימֵי הַשָּׁמַיִם ׀ עַל־הָאָרֶץ:

Before reciting the third paragraph (במדבר טו:לז-מא), the *tzitzis,* which have been held in the left hand, are taken in the right hand also. The *tzitzis* are kissed at each mention of the word and at the end of the paragraph, and are passed before the eyes at וּרְאִיתֶם אֹתוֹ.

וַיֹּאמֶר ׀ יהוה ׀ אֶל־מֹשֶׁה לֵּאמֹר: דַּבֵּר ׀ אֶל־בְּנֵי ׀ יִשְׂרָאֵל,
וְאָמַרְתָּ אֲלֵהֶם, וְעָשׂוּ לָהֶם צִיצִת, עַל־כַּנְפֵי בִגְדֵיהֶם
לְדֹרֹתָם, וְנָתְנוּ ׀ עַל־צִיצִת הַכָּנָף, פְּתִיל תְּכֵלֶת: וְהָיָה לָכֶם לְצִיצִת,
וּרְאִיתֶם ׀ אֹתוֹ, וּזְכַרְתֶּם ׀ אֶת־כָּל־מִצְוֹת ׀ יהוה, וַעֲשִׂיתֶם ׀ אֹתָם,
וְלֹא תָתוּרוּ ׀ אַחֲרֵי לְבַבְכֶם וְאַחֲרֵי ׀ עֵינֵיכֶם, אֲשֶׁר־אַתֶּם זֹנִים ׀
אַחֲרֵיהֶם: לְמַעַן תִּזְכְּרוּ, וַעֲשִׂיתֶם ׀ אֶת־כָּל־מִצְוֹתָי, וִהְיִיתֶם קְדֹשִׁים
לֵאלֹהֵיכֶם: אֲנִי יהוה ׀ אֱלֹהֵיכֶם, אֲשֶׁר
הוֹצֵאתִי ׀ אֶתְכֶם ׀ מֵאֶרֶץ מִצְרַיִם, לִהְיוֹת
לָכֶם לֵאלֹהִים, אֲנִי ׀ יהוה ׀ אֱלֹהֵיכֶם: אֱמֶת —

Concentrate on fulfilling the commandment of remembering the Exodus from Egypt.

While reciting the first paragraph (*Deuteronomy* 6:5-9), concentrate on accepting the commandment to love God.

וְאָהַבְתָּ *You shall love HASHEM, your God, with all your heart, with all your soul and with all your resources. Let these matters that I command you today be upon your heart. Teach them thoroughly to your children and speak of them while you sit in your home, while you walk on the way, when you retire and when you arise. Bind them as a sign upon your arm and let them be tefillin between your eyes. And write them on the doorposts of your house and upon your gates.*

While reciting the second paragraph (*Deuteronomy* 11:13-21), concentrate on accepting all the commandments and the concept of reward and punishment.

וְהָיָה *And it will come to pass that if you continually hearken to My commandments that I command you today, to love HASHEM, your God, and to serve Him, with all your heart and with all your soul — then I will provide rain for your land in its proper time, the early and late rains, that you may gather in your grain, your wine, and your oil. I will provide grass in your field for your cattle and you will eat and be satisfied. Beware lest your heart be seduced and you turn astray and serve gods of others and bow to them. Then the wrath of HASHEM will blaze against you. He will restrain the heaven so there will be no rain and the ground will not yield its produce. And you will swiftly be banished from the goodly land which HASHEM gives you. Place these words of Mine upon your heart and upon your soul; bind them for a sign upon your arm and let them be tefillin between your eyes. Teach them to your children, to discuss them, while you sit in your home, while you walk on the way, when you retire and when you arise. And write them on the doorposts of your house and upon your gates. In order to prolong your days and the days of your children upon the ground that HASHEM has sworn to your ancestors to give them, like the days of the heaven on the earth.*

Before reciting the third paragraph (*Numbers* 15:37-41), the *tzitzis,* which have been held in the left hand, are taken in the right hand also. The *tzitzis* are kissed at each mention of the word and at the end of the paragraph, and are passed before the eyes at *'that you may see it.'*

וַיֹּאמֶר *And HASHEM said to Moses saying: Speak to the Children of Israel and say to them that they are to make themselves tzitzis on the corners of their garments, throughout their generations. And they are to place upon the tzitzis of each corner a thread of techeiles. And it shall constitute tzitzis for you, that you may see it and remember all the commandments of HASHEM and perform them; and not explore after your heart and after your eyes after which you stray. So that you may remember and perform all My commandments; and be holy to your God. I am HASHEM, your God, Who has removed you from the land of Egypt to be a God to you; I am HASHEM your God — it is true —*

Concentrate on fulfilling the commandment of remembering the Exodus from Egypt.

Although the word אֱמֶת belongs to the next paragraph, it is appended to the conclusion of the previous one, as explained in the commentary on page 42.

—*Chazzan* repeats **יהוה אֱלֹהֵיכֶם אֱמֶת.***

וְיַצִּיב וְנָכוֹן וְקַיָּם וְיָשָׁר וְנֶאֱמָן וְאָהוּב וְחָבִיב וְנֶחְמָד וְנָעִים וְנוֹרָא וְאַדִּיר וּמְתֻקָּן וּמְקֻבָּל וְטוֹב וְיָפֶה הַדָּבָר הַזֶּה עָלֵינוּ לְעוֹלָם וָעֶד. אֱמֶת אֱלֹהֵי עוֹלָם מַלְכֵּנוּ צוּר יַעֲקֹב, מָגֵן יִשְׁעֵנוּ, לְדֹר וָדֹר הוּא קַיָּם, וּשְׁמוֹ קַיָּם, וְכִסְאוֹ נָכוֹן, וּמַלְכוּתוֹ וֶאֱמוּנָתוֹ לָעַד קַיֶּמֶת. וּדְבָרָיו חָיִים וְקַיָּמִים, נֶאֱמָנִים וְנֶחֱמָדִים לָעַד (kiss the *tzitzis* and release them) וּלְעוֹלְמֵי עוֹלָמִים. ❖ עַל אֲבוֹתֵינוּ וְעָלֵינוּ, עַל בָּנֵינוּ וְעַל דּוֹרוֹתֵינוּ, וְעַל כָּל דּוֹרוֹת זֶרַע יִשְׂרָאֵל עֲבָדֶיךָ.

עַל הָרִאשׁוֹנִים וְעַל הָאַחֲרוֹנִים, דָּבָר טוֹב וְקַיָּם לְעוֹלָם וָעֶד, אֱמֶת וֶאֱמוּנָה חֹק וְלֹא יַעֲבֹר. אֱמֶת שָׁאַתָּה הוּא יהוה אֱלֹהֵינוּ וֵאלֹהֵי אֲבוֹתֵינוּ, ❖ מַלְכֵּנוּ מֶלֶךְ אֲבוֹתֵינוּ, גֹּאֲלֵנוּ גֹּאֵל אֲבוֹתֵינוּ, יוֹצְרֵנוּ צוּר יְשׁוּעָתֵנוּ, פּוֹדֵנוּ וּמַצִּילֵנוּ מֵעוֹלָם שְׁמֶךָ, אֵין אֱלֹהִים זוּלָתֶךָ.

All:

יָפָה* וּבָרָה כְּרָדָה לְגֵיא פַּתְרוּסִים, יָהִיר חֲסַר לֵב הִכְבִּיד עֹל בְּשִׁנּוּסִים,
צָרְחָה וְקִבְּלָה לְמַעְתִּיק פְּלוּסִים, פִּקֵּד לָהּ סַרְסוּר לְהוֹצִיאָהּ בְּנִסִּים.
הִקְשָׁה עֲקַלָּתוֹן לְשַׁלֵּחַ אֹם עֲמוּסָה, הֵטִיחַ דְּבָרִים כְּמֶטֶל בַּעֲרִיסָה,
וּפָץ מִי יהוה[1] לְהַצִּיל אֲרוּסָה, וּבְסֵפֶר דָּתוֹתַי אֵין שְׁמוֹ בְּטִכְסִיסָה.
וֶהֱשִׁיבוֹ שָׁלִישׁ* בְּשֵׁם דַּר מְעוֹנִים, הִתְיַצֵּב וְהָכֵן לָךְ[2] מוּל נֶגֶף אֲבָנִים,
דָּם וּצְפַרְדְּעִים וְעָרוֹב עֵדִים נְכוֹנִים, וַחֲיָלִים קְטַנִּים הַמְּכֻנִּים כִּנִּים.
דִּבֵּר וְהִשְׁלִים מַכּוֹת עֲשָׂרָה, וְהוֹצִיאָהּ בְּתֻפִּים מֵאֲפֵלָה לְאוֹרָה,
וְהִכָּה עוֹיְנָהּ מַכָּה כְעוּרָה, וְהִנְחִילָהּ קְדוּמָה אַלְפַּיִם* סְתוּרָה.
הוֹשִׁיבָהּ בַּסֻּכָּה בְּאֶרֶץ מִדְבָּרִים, וְהִכְנִיסָהּ לְחֻפָּה בְּחַדְרֵי חֲדָרִים,
וַעֲנַף עֵץ עָבוֹת וּפְרִי עֵץ הֲדָרִים, וְעַרְבֵי נְחָלִים וְכַפּוֹת תְּמָרִים.[3]

(1) *Exodus* 5:2. (2) *Jeremiah* 46:14. (3) Cf. *Leviticus* 23:40.

☙ **יָפָה** – *[When] beautiful* ... The *piyut* describes Israel's suffering at the hands of Pharaoh, and its subsequent deliverance at the Exodus. The verses begin with the letters יְהוּדָה, *Yehudah*, the unknown author who also composed אֲפָאֵר, *I shall glorify* (p. 458).

שָׁלִישׁ – *The officer [Moses].* The word שָׁלִישׁ refers to a highly placed official (see e.g., *Exodus* 15:4). Alternatively, the word means the same as הַשְּׁלִישִׁי, *the third one*, and refers to Moses's being born third, after Miriam and Aaron.

אַלְפַּיִם – *Two thousand.* Although these terms are inexplicable to our limited minds, the Midrashim date God's writing of the Torah variously as 2,000 years before Creation, or 2,000 generations before it was given to Israel.

Although the word אֱמֶת, *'it is true,'* belongs to the next paragraph, it is appended to the conclusion of the previous one, as explained in the commentary on page 42.

Chazzan repeats: **HASHEM, your God, is true.**

וְיַצִּיב *And certain, established and enduring, fair and faithful, beloved and cherished, delightful and pleasant, awesome and powerful, correct and accepted, good and beautiful is this affirmation to us forever and ever. True — the God of the universe is our King; the Rock of Jacob is the Shield of our salvation. From generation to generation He endures and His Name endures and His throne is well established; His sovereignty and faithfulness endure forever. His words are living and enduring, faithful and delightful forever* (kiss the *tzitzis* and release them) *and to all eternity;* Chazzan– *for our forefathers and for us, for our children and for our generations, and for all the generations of Your servant Israel's offspring.*

עַל הָרִאשׁוֹנִים *Upon the earlier and upon the later generations, this affirmation is good and enduring forever. True and faithful, it is an unbreachable decree. It is true that You are HASHEM, our God and the God of our forefathers,* Chazzan– *our King and the King of our forefathers, our Redeemer, the Redeemer of our forefathers; our Molder, the Rock of our salvation; our Liberator and our Rescuer — this has ever been Your Name. There is no God but You.*

All:

י *[When] beautiful* and brilliant [Israel]*
descended to the Valley of Pasrosim [Egypt],
the haughty, heartless [Pharaoh] placed a heavy yoke
upon those who serve [God] with alacrity.
They cried and pleaded to the Crusher of mountains,
He appointed an agent [Moses] to bring them forth with miracles.

ה *[Pharaoh] the coiled serpent stubbornly refused to release*
the nation borne [by God],
he blasphemed, [mindlessly] as a baby in the crib.
He blurted out, 'Who is HASHEM,[1] *[Who desires] to save [Israel, His] betrothed?*
Yet in the annals of my religions His Name is not inscribed!'

ו *The officer [Moses]* responded in the name of Him Who dwells in heaven,*
'Stand by and prepare yourself[2] *for stone-like plagues:*
blood, frogs and wild beasts that are prepared to bear witness,
and tiny soldiers that are known as lice.'

ד *He spoke, and completed the Ten Plagues,*
and brought her [Israel] forth with drums, from darkness to light,
He smote her evil-eyed [oppressor] with humiliating plague,
and bequeathed to her [the Torah]
*that had been concealed since two thousand.**

ח *He placed her in the succah [of clouds] in the land of wilderness,*
and led her under the canopy, in this room of rooms,
with branch of the plaited-myrtle and fruit of the esrog tree,
with brook-willows and date-palm branch.[3]

❖ חִדְּשָׁה שִׁיר* וָזֶמֶר רְנָנוֹת וּרְנָנִים, זְכוּת אָבוֹת וּבָנִים יְמַלְּטֵם מֵאֲנוּנִים, כְּנִרְאָה בַּיָּם וּטְבִיעַת גְּאוֹנִים, חֲנָנָהּ מִמָּרוֹם עוֹזֵר אָבוֹת וּבָנִים.

עֶזְרַת אֲבוֹתֵינוּ אַתָּה הוּא מֵעוֹלָם, מָגֵן וּמוֹשִׁיעַ לִבְנֵיהֶם אַחֲרֵיהֶם בְּכָל דּוֹר וָדוֹר. בְּרוּם עוֹלָם מוֹשָׁבֶךָ, וּמִשְׁפָּטֶיךָ וְצִדְקָתְךָ עַד אַפְסֵי אָרֶץ. אַשְׁרֵי אִישׁ שֶׁיִּשְׁמַע לְמִצְוֹתֶיךָ, וְתוֹרָתְךָ וּדְבָרְךָ יָשִׂים עַל לִבּוֹ. אֱמֶת אַתָּה הוּא אָדוֹן לְעַמֶּךָ וּמֶלֶךְ גִּבּוֹר לָרִיב רִיבָם. אֱמֶת אַתָּה הוּא רִאשׁוֹן וְאַתָּה הוּא אַחֲרוֹן, וּמִבַּלְעָדֶיךָ אֵין לָנוּ מֶלֶךְ[1] גּוֹאֵל וּמוֹשִׁיעַ. מִמִּצְרַיִם גְּאַלְתָּנוּ יהוה אֱלֹהֵינוּ, וּמִבֵּית עֲבָדִים פְּדִיתָנוּ. כָּל בְּכוֹרֵיהֶם הָרָגְתָּ, וּבְכוֹרְךָ גָּאָלְתָּ, וְיַם סוּף בָּקַעְתָּ, וְזֵדִים טִבַּעְתָּ, וִידִידִים הֶעֱבַרְתָּ, וַיְכַסּוּ מַיִם צָרֵיהֶם, אֶחָד מֵהֶם לֹא נוֹתָר.[2] עַל זֹאת שִׁבְּחוּ אֲהוּבִים וְרוֹמְמוּ אֵל, וְנָתְנוּ יְדִידִים זְמִרוֹת שִׁירוֹת וְתִשְׁבָּחוֹת, בְּרָכוֹת וְהוֹדָאוֹת, לְמֶלֶךְ אֵל חַי וְקַיָּם, רָם וְנִשָּׂא, גָּדוֹל וְנוֹרָא, מַשְׁפִּיל גֵּאִים, וּמַגְבִּיהַּ שְׁפָלִים, מוֹצִיא אֲסִירִים, וּפוֹדֶה עֲנָוִים, וְעוֹזֵר דַּלִּים, וְעוֹנֶה לְעַמּוֹ בְּעֵת שַׁוְּעָם אֵלָיו.

Rise for *Shemoneh Esrei*. Some take three steps backward at this point; others do so before צוּר יִשְׂרָאֵל.

❖ תְּהִלּוֹת לְאֵל עֶלְיוֹן, בָּרוּךְ הוּא וּמְבֹרָךְ. מֹשֶׁה וּבְנֵי יִשְׂרָאֵל לְךָ עָנוּ שִׁירָה בְּשִׂמְחָה רַבָּה וְאָמְרוּ כֻלָּם:

מִי כָמֹכָה בָּאֵלִם יהוה, מִי כָּמֹכָה נֶאְדָּר בַּקֹּדֶשׁ, נוֹרָא תְהִלֹּת עֹשֵׂה פֶלֶא.[3] ❖ שִׁירָה חֲדָשָׁה שִׁבְּחוּ גְאוּלִים לְשִׁמְךָ עַל שְׂפַת הַיָּם, יַחַד כֻּלָּם הוֹדוּ וְהִמְלִיכוּ וְאָמְרוּ:

יהוה יִמְלֹךְ לְעֹלָם וָעֶד.[4]

It is forbidden to interrupt or pause between גָּאַל יִשְׂרָאֵל and *Shemoneh Esrei*, even for *Kaddish, Kedushah* or *Borchu*.

❖ **צוּר יִשְׂרָאֵל,** קוּמָה בְּעֶזְרַת יִשְׂרָאֵל, וּפְדֵה כִנְאֻמֶךָ יְהוּדָה וְיִשְׂרָאֵל. גֹּאֲלֵנוּ יהוה צְבָאוֹת שְׁמוֹ, קְדוֹשׁ יִשְׂרָאֵל.[5] בָּרוּךְ אַתָּה יהוה, גָּאַל יִשְׂרָאֵל.

(1) Cf. *Isaiah* 44:6. (2) *Psalms* 106:11. (3) *Exodus* 15:11. (4) 15:18. (5) *Isaiah* 47:4.

חִדְּשָׁה שִׁיר – *She composed new song.* This cryptic stanza seems to be a fragment of another *piyut* and not a continuation of the previous one. It is absent from the extant manuscript *machzorim* and from the early printed editions. Additionally, both the commentaries and the traditional Yiddish translation ignore it.

Chazzan – *She composed new song* and music, glad songs and paeans of joy. May the merit of the Patriarchs and their children protect them from bereavement. As it happened at the Sea, with the drowning of the haughty, be gracious to her from above, O You Who are Helper of father and sons.*

עֶזְרַת *The Helper of our forefathers are You alone, forever, Shield and Savior for their children after them in every generation. At the zenith of the universe is Your dwelling, and Your justice and Your righteousness extend to the ends of the earth. Praiseworthy is the person who obeys Your commandments and takes to his heart Your teaching and Your word. True — You are the Master for Your people and a mighty King to take up their grievance. True — You are the First and You are the Last, and other than You we have no king,*[1] *redeemer, or savior. From Egypt You redeemed us, HASHEM, our God, and from the house of slavery You liberated us. All their firstborn You slew, but Your firstborn You redeemed; the Sea of Reeds You split; the wanton sinners You drowned; the dear ones You brought across; and the water covered their foes — not one of them was left.*[2] *For this, the beloved praised and exalted God; the dear ones offered hymns, songs, praises, blessings, and thanksgivings to the King, the living and enduring God — exalted and uplifted, great and awesome, Who humbles the haughty and lifts the lowly; withdraws the captive, liberates the humble, and helps the poor; Who responds to His people upon their outcry to Him.*

Rise for *Shemoneh Esrei*. Some take three steps backward at this point; others do so before צוּר יִשְׂרָאֵל, *'Rock of Israel.'*

Chazzan – *Praises to the Supreme God, the blessed One Who is blessed. Moses and the children of Israel exclaimed a song to You with great joy and they all said:*

'Who is like You among the heavenly powers, HASHEM! Who is like You, mighty in holiness, too awesome for praise, doing wonders.'[3]

Chazzan – *With a new song the redeemed ones praised Your Name at the seashore, all of them in unison gave thanks, acknowledged [Your] sovereignty, and said:*

'HASHEM shall reign for all eternity.'[4]

It is forbidden to interrupt or pause between *'Who redeemed Israel'* and *Shemoneh Esrei*, even for *Kaddish, Kedushah* or *Borchu*.

צוּר יִשְׂרָאֵל Chazzan – *Rock of Israel, arise to the aid of Israel and liberate, as You pledged, Judah and Israel. Our Redeemer — HASHEM, Master of Legions, is His Name — the Holy One of Israel.*[5] *Blessed are You, HASHEM, Who redeemed Israel.*

שמונה עשרה – עמידה

Take three steps backward, then three steps forward. Remain standing with feet together while reciting *Shemoneh Esrei*. Recite it with quiet devotion and without interruption, verbal or otherwise. Although it should not be audible to others, one must pray loudly enough to hear himself.

אֲדֹנָי שְׂפָתַי תִּפְתָּח, וּפִי יַגִּיד תְּהִלָּתֶךָ.[1]

אבות

Bend the knees at בָּרוּךְ; bow at אַתָּה; straighten up at 'ה.

בָּרוּךְ אַתָּה יהוה אֱלֹהֵינוּ וֵאלֹהֵי אֲבוֹתֵינוּ, אֱלֹהֵי אַבְרָהָם, אֱלֹהֵי יִצְחָק, וֵאלֹהֵי יַעֲקֹב, הָאֵל הַגָּדוֹל הַגִּבּוֹר וְהַנּוֹרָא, אֵל עֶלְיוֹן, גּוֹמֵל חֲסָדִים טוֹבִים וְקוֹנֵה הַכֹּל, וְזוֹכֵר חַסְדֵי אָבוֹת, וּמֵבִיא גוֹאֵל לִבְנֵי בְנֵיהֶם, לְמַעַן שְׁמוֹ בְּאַהֲבָה. מֶלֶךְ עוֹזֵר וּמוֹשִׁיעַ וּמָגֵן.

Bend the knees at בָּרוּךְ; bow at אַתָּה; straighten up at 'ה.

בָּרוּךְ אַתָּה יהוה, מָגֵן אַבְרָהָם.

גבורות

אַתָּה גִּבּוֹר לְעוֹלָם אֲדֹנָי, מְחַיֵּה מֵתִים אַתָּה, רַב לְהוֹשִׁיעַ. מְכַלְכֵּל חַיִּים בְּחֶסֶד, מְחַיֵּה מֵתִים בְּרַחֲמִים רַבִּים, סוֹמֵךְ נוֹפְלִים, וְרוֹפֵא חוֹלִים, וּמַתִּיר אֲסוּרִים, וּמְקַיֵּם אֱמוּנָתוֹ לִישֵׁנֵי עָפָר. מִי כָמוֹךָ בַּעַל גְּבוּרוֹת, וּמִי דּוֹמֶה לָּךְ, מֶלֶךְ מֵמִית וּמְחַיֶּה וּמַצְמִיחַ יְשׁוּעָה. וְנֶאֱמָן אַתָּה לְהַחֲיוֹת מֵתִים. בָּרוּךְ אַתָּה יהוה, מְחַיֵּה הַמֵּתִים.

During the *chazzan's* repetition, *Kedushah* (below) is recited at this point.

קדושה

When reciting *Kedushah,* one must stand with his feet together and avoid any interruptions. One should rise on his toes when saying the words קָדוֹשׁ, קָדוֹשׁ, קָדוֹשׁ; בָּרוּךְ (of בָּרוּךְ כְּבוֹד); and יִמְלֹךְ.

Cong. then *Chazzan* – **נְקַדֵּשׁ** אֶת שִׁמְךָ בָּעוֹלָם, כְּשֵׁם שֶׁמַּקְדִּישִׁים אוֹתוֹ בִּשְׁמֵי מָרוֹם, כַּכָּתוּב עַל יַד נְבִיאֶךָ, וְקָרָא זֶה אֶל זֶה וְאָמַר:

All – קָדוֹשׁ קָדוֹשׁ קָדוֹשׁ יהוה צְבָאוֹת, מְלֹא כָל הָאָרֶץ כְּבוֹדוֹ.[2]
❖ אָז בְּקוֹל רַעַשׁ גָּדוֹל אַדִּיר וְחָזָק מַשְׁמִיעִים קוֹל, מִתְנַשְּׂאִים לְעֻמַּת שְׂרָפִים, לְעֻמָּתָם בָּרוּךְ יֹאמֵרוּ:

All – בָּרוּךְ כְּבוֹד יהוה, מִמְּקוֹמוֹ.[3] ❖ מִמְּקוֹמְךָ מַלְכֵּנוּ תוֹפִיעַ, וְתִמְלֹךְ עָלֵינוּ, כִּי מְחַכִּים אֲנַחְנוּ לָךְ. מָתַי תִּמְלֹךְ בְּצִיּוֹן, בְּקָרוֹב בְּיָמֵינוּ, לְעוֹלָם וָעֶד תִּשְׁכּוֹן. תִּתְגַּדַּל וְתִתְקַדַּשׁ בְּתוֹךְ יְרוּשָׁלַיִם עִירְךָ, לְדוֹר וָדוֹר וּלְנֵצַח נְצָחִים. וְעֵינֵינוּ תִרְאֶינָה מַלְכוּתֶךָ, כַּדָּבָר הָאָמוּר בְּשִׁירֵי עֻזֶּךָ, עַל יְדֵי דָוִד מְשִׁיחַ צִדְקֶךָ:

All – יִמְלֹךְ יהוה לְעוֹלָם, אֱלֹהַיִךְ צִיּוֹן לְדֹר וָדֹר, הַלְלוּיָהּ.[4]

Chazzan continues . . . לְדוֹר וָדוֹר (page 478).

SHEMONEH ESREI – AMIDAH

Take three steps backward, then three steps forward. Remain standing with feet together while reciting *Shemoneh Esrei*. Recite it with quiet devotion and without interruption, verbal or otherwise. Although it should not be audible to others, one must pray loudly enough to hear himself.

My Lord, open my lips, that my mouth may declare Your praise.[1]

PATRIARCHS

Bend the knees at *'Blessed'*; bow at *'You'*; straighten up at *'HASHEM.'*

בָּרוּךְ *Blessed are You, HASHEM, our God and the God of our forefathers, God of Abraham, God of Isaac, and God of Jacob; the great, mighty, and awesome God, the supreme God, Who bestows beneficial kindnesses and creates everything, Who recalls the kindnesses of the Patriarchs and brings a Redeemer to their children's children, for His Name's sake, with love. O King, Helper, Savior, and Shield.*

Bend the knees at *'Blessed'*; bow at *'You'*; straighten up at *'HASHEM.'*

Blessed are You, HASHEM, Shield of Abraham.

GOD'S MIGHT

אַתָּה *You are eternally mighty, my Lord, the Resuscitator of the dead are You; abundantly able to save. He sustains the living with kindness, resuscitates the dead with abundant mercy, supports the fallen, heals the sick, releases the confined, and maintains His faith to those asleep in the dust. Who is like You, O Master of mighty deeds, and who is comparable to You, O King Who causes death and restores life and makes salvation sprout! And You are faithful to resuscitate the dead. Blessed are You, HASHEM, Who resuscitates the dead.*

During the *chazzan's* repetition, *Kedushah* (below) is recited at this point.

KEDUSHAH

When reciting *Kedushah*, one must stand with his feet together and avoid any interruptions. One should rise on his toes when saying the words *Holy, holy, holy; Blessed is;* and *HASHEM shall reign.*

Cong. then Chazzan – נְקַדֵּשׁ *We shall sanctify Your Name in this world, just as they sanctify it in heaven above, as it is written by Your prophet, "And one [angel] will call another and say:*

All – *'Holy, holy, holy is HASHEM, Master of Legions, the whole world is filled with His glory.'"*[2] ∴ *Then, with a sound of great noise, mighty and powerful, they make heard a voice, raising themselves toward the seraphim; those facing them say 'Blessed ...':*

All – *'Blessed is the glory of HASHEM from His place.'*[3] ∴ *From Your place, our King, You will appear and reign over us, for we await You. When will You reign in Zion? Soon, in our days — forever and ever — may You dwell there. May You be exalted and sanctified within Jerusalem, Your city, from generation to generation and for all eternity. May our eyes see Your kingdom, as it is expressed in the songs of Your might, written by David, Your righteous anointed:*

All – *'HASHEM shall reign forever — your God, O Zion — from generation to generation, Halleluyah!'*[4]

Chazzan continues לְדוֹר וָדוֹר, *From generation* ... (p. 478).

---

(1) *Psalms* 51:17. (2) *Isaiah* 6:3. (3) *Ezekiel* 3:12. (4) *Psalms* 146:10.

קדושת השם

INDIVIDUALS RECITE:

אַתָּה קָדוֹשׁ וְשִׁמְךָ קָדוֹשׁ, וּקְדוֹשִׁים בְּכָל יוֹם יְהַלְּלוּךָ סֶּלָה. בָּרוּךְ אַתָּה יהוה, הָאֵל הַקָּדוֹשׁ.

CHAZZAN RECITES DURING HIS REPETITION:

לְדוֹר וָדוֹר נַגִּיד גָּדְלֶךָ וּלְנֵצַח נְצָחִים קְדֻשָּׁתְךָ נַקְדִּישׁ, וְשִׁבְחֲךָ אֱלֹהֵינוּ מִפִּינוּ לֹא יָמוּשׁ לְעוֹלָם וָעֶד, כִּי אֵל מֶלֶךְ גָּדוֹל וְקָדוֹשׁ אָתָּה. בָּרוּךְ אַתָּה יהוה, הָאֵל הַקָּדוֹשׁ.

קדושת היום

יִשְׂמַח מֹשֶׁה* בְּמַתְּנַת חֶלְקוֹ, כִּי עֶבֶד נֶאֱמָן קָרָאתָ לּוֹ. כְּלִיל תִּפְאֶרֶת* בְּרֹאשׁוֹ נָתַתָּ (לּוֹ), בְּעָמְדוֹ לְפָנֶיךָ עַל הַר סִינָי. וּשְׁנֵי לוּחוֹת אֲבָנִים הוֹרִיד בְּיָדוֹ,[1] וְכָתוּב בָּהֶם שְׁמִירַת שַׁבָּת. וְכֵן כָּתוּב בְּתוֹרָתֶךָ:

וְשָׁמְרוּ בְנֵי יִשְׂרָאֵל אֶת הַשַּׁבָּת, לַעֲשׂוֹת אֶת הַשַּׁבָּת לְדֹרֹתָם בְּרִית עוֹלָם. בֵּינִי וּבֵין בְּנֵי יִשְׂרָאֵל אוֹת הִיא לְעֹלָם, כִּי שֵׁשֶׁת יָמִים עָשָׂה יהוה אֶת הַשָּׁמַיִם וְאֶת הָאָרֶץ, וּבַיּוֹם הַשְּׁבִיעִי שָׁבַת וַיִּנָּפַשׁ.[2]

וְלֹא נְתַתּוֹ* יהוה אֱלֹהֵינוּ לְגוֹיֵי הָאֲרָצוֹת, וְלֹא הִנְחַלְתּוֹ מַלְכֵּנוּ לְעוֹבְדֵי פְסִילִים, וְגַם בִּמְנוּחָתוֹ לֹא יִשְׁכְּנוּ עֲרֵלִים. כִּי לְיִשְׂרָאֵל עַמְּךָ נְתַתּוֹ בְּאַהֲבָה, לְזֶרַע יַעֲקֹב אֲשֶׁר בָּם בָּחָרְתָּ. עַם מְקַדְּשֵׁי שְׁבִיעִי, כֻּלָּם יִשְׂבְּעוּ וְיִתְעַנְּגוּ מִטּוּבֶךָ. וּבַשְּׁבִיעִי רָצִיתָ בּוֹ וְקִדַּשְׁתּוֹ חֶמְדַּת יָמִים אוֹתוֹ קָרָאתָ, זֵכֶר לְמַעֲשֵׂה בְרֵאשִׁית.

אֱלֹהֵינוּ וֵאלֹהֵי אֲבוֹתֵינוּ, רְצֵה בִמְנוּחָתֵנוּ, קַדְּשֵׁנוּ בְּמִצְוֹתֶיךָ, וְתֵן חֶלְקֵנוּ בְּתוֹרָתֶךָ, שַׂבְּעֵנוּ מִטּוּבֶךָ, וְשַׂמְּחֵנוּ בִּישׁוּעָתֶךָ, וְטַהֵר לִבֵּנוּ לְעָבְדְּךָ בֶּאֱמֶת. וְהַנְחִילֵנוּ יהוה אֱלֹהֵינוּ בְּאַהֲבָה וּבְרָצוֹן שַׁבַּת קָדְשֶׁךָ, וְיָנוּחוּ בוֹ יִשְׂרָאֵל מְקַדְּשֵׁי שְׁמֶךָ. בָּרוּךְ אַתָּה יהוה, מְקַדֵּשׁ הַשַּׁבָּת.

⸎ **ישמח משה** — *Moses rejoiced* that God considered him a faithful servant [*Numbers* 12:7] and that, in reward for Moses' dedication, God chose him to receive the tablets of the Ten Commandments, which included the *mitzvah* of the Sabbath.

Why is Moses singled out for mention in connection with the Sabbath and why only in the morning *Amidah?* Among the reasons are:

— The Ten Commandments were given to Moses on the morning of the Sabbath.

— When he was still a child growing up in Pharaoh's palace, Moses asked the king to proclaim the Sabbath as a day of rest for the enslaved Jews.

— God told Moses in Marah, before Israel came to Mount Sinai, 'I have a precious gift called Sabbath. Teach the Jews about it.'

כְּלִיל תִּפְאֶרֶת — *A crown of splendor.* When Moses descended from Sinai, his face glowed

HOLINESS OF GOD'S NAME

INDIVIDUALS RECITE:

אַתָּה *You are holy and Your Name is holy, and holy ones praise You every day, forever. Blessed are You,* HASHEM, *the holy God.*

CHAZZAN RECITES DURING HIS REPETITION:

לְדוֹר *From generation to generation we shall relate Your greatness and for infinite eternities we shall proclaim Your holiness. Your praise, our God, shall not leave our mouth forever and ever, for You, O God, are a great and holy King. Blessed are You,* HASHEM, *the holy God.*

SANCTIFICATION OF THE DAY

יִשְׂמַח *Moses rejoiced* in the gift of his portion: that You called him a faithful servant. A crown of splendor* You placed on his head when he stood before You on Mount Sinai. He brought down two stone tablets in his hand,*[1] *on which is inscribed the observance of the Sabbath. So it is written in Your Torah:*

וְשָׁמְרוּ *And the Children of Israel shall keep the Sabbath, to make the Sabbath an eternal covenant for their generations. Between Me and the Children of Israel it is a sign forever that in six days* HASHEM *made heaven and earth, and on the seventh day He rested and was refreshed.*[2]

וְלֹא נְתַתּוֹ *You did not give it,** HASHEM, *our God, to the nations of the lands, nor did You make it the inheritance, our King, of the worshipers of graven idols. And in its contentment the uncircumcised shall not abide — for to Israel, Your people, have You given it in love, to the seed of Jacob, whom You have chosen. The people that sanctifies the Seventh — they will all be satisfied and delighted from Your goodness. And the Seventh — You found favor in it and sanctified it! 'Most coveted of days,' You called it, a remembrance of the act of creation.*

אֱלֹהֵינוּ *Our God and the God of our fathers, may You be pleased with our rest. Sanctify us with Your commandments and grant our share in Your Torah; satisfy us from Your goodness and gladden us with Your salvation, and purify our heart to serve You sincerely. O* HASHEM, *our God, with love and favor grant us Your holy Sabbath as a heritage, and may Israel, the sanctifiers of Your Name, rest on it. Blessed are You,* HASHEM, *Who sanctifies the Sabbath.*

(1) Cf. *Exodus* 32:15. (2) 31:16-17.

with a Divine radiance, signifying that he was worthy to be a bearer of God's splendor. [See *Exodus* 34:29.]

וְלֹא נְתַתּוֹ — *You did not give it.* If the Sabbath were nothing more than a day of rest, it could be the equal property of all nations. But the Sabbath is a day of holiness and, as such, it could be given only to the nation that accepts the mission of sanctity. God did not give the Sabbath to such unworthy nations as גּוֹיֵי הָאֲרָצוֹת, *nations of the lands,* who worship the 'land' and the power its possession implies; nor to עוֹבְדֵי פְסִילִים, *the worshipers of graven idols,* who ascribe mastery of the world to such natural forces as the heavenly bodies, fertility, nature and so on that they symbolize by means of idols; nor to עֲרֵלִים, *uncircumcised people,* who are unwilling to curb their lusts for the sake of a higher goal (*R' Hirsch*).

עבודה

רְצֵה יהוה אֱלֹהֵינוּ בְּעַמְּךָ יִשְׂרָאֵל וּבִתְפִלָּתָם, וְהָשֵׁב אֶת הָעֲבוֹדָה לִדְבִיר בֵּיתֶךָ. וְאִשֵּׁי יִשְׂרָאֵל וּתְפִלָּתָם בְּאַהֲבָה תְקַבֵּל בְּרָצוֹן, וּתְהִי לְרָצוֹן תָּמִיד עֲבוֹדַת יִשְׂרָאֵל עַמֶּךָ.

During the *chazzan's* repetition, congregation responds אָמֵן as indicated.
[If the following paragraph is forgotten, repeat *Shemoneh Esrei*. See *Laws* §56.]

אֱלֹהֵינוּ וֵאלֹהֵי אֲבוֹתֵינוּ, יַעֲלֶה, וְיָבֹא, וְיַגִּיעַ, וְיֵרָאֶה, וְיֵרָצֶה, וְיִשָּׁמַע, וְיִפָּקֵד, וְיִזָּכֵר זִכְרוֹנֵנוּ וּפִקְדוֹנֵנוּ, וְזִכְרוֹן אֲבוֹתֵינוּ, וְזִכְרוֹן מָשִׁיחַ בֶּן דָּוִד עַבְדֶּךָ, וְזִכְרוֹן יְרוּשָׁלַיִם עִיר קָדְשֶׁךָ, וְזִכְרוֹן כָּל עַמְּךָ בֵּית יִשְׂרָאֵל לְפָנֶיךָ, לִפְלֵיטָה לְטוֹבָה לְחֵן וּלְחֶסֶד וּלְרַחֲמִים, לְחַיִּים וּלְשָׁלוֹם בְּיוֹם חַג הַסֻּכּוֹת הַזֶּה. זָכְרֵנוּ יהוה אֱלֹהֵינוּ בּוֹ לְטוֹבָה (.Cong – אָמֵן), וּפָקְדֵנוּ בוֹ לִבְרָכָה (.Cong – אָמֵן), וְהוֹשִׁיעֵנוּ בוֹ לְחַיִּים (.Cong – אָמֵן). וּבִדְבַר יְשׁוּעָה וְרַחֲמִים, חוּס וְחָנֵּנוּ וְרַחֵם עָלֵינוּ וְהוֹשִׁיעֵנוּ, כִּי אֵלֶיךָ עֵינֵינוּ, כִּי אֵל מֶלֶךְ חַנּוּן וְרַחוּם אָתָּה.[1]

וְתֶחֱזֶינָה עֵינֵינוּ בְּשׁוּבְךָ לְצִיּוֹן בְּרַחֲמִים. בָּרוּךְ אַתָּה יהוה, הַמַּחֲזִיר שְׁכִינָתוֹ לְצִיּוֹן.

הודאה

Bow at מוֹדִים; straighten up at 'ה. In his repetition the *chazzan* should recite the entire מוֹדִים aloud, while the congregation recites מוֹדִים דְּרַבָּנָן softly.

מוֹדִים אֲנַחְנוּ לָךְ שָׁאַתָּה הוּא יהוה אֱלֹהֵינוּ וֵאלֹהֵי אֲבוֹתֵינוּ לְעוֹלָם וָעֶד. צוּר חַיֵּינוּ, מָגֵן יִשְׁעֵנוּ אַתָּה הוּא לְדוֹר וָדוֹר. נוֹדֶה לְּךָ וּנְסַפֵּר תְּהִלָּתֶךָ[2] עַל חַיֵּינוּ הַמְּסוּרִים בְּיָדֶךָ, וְעַל נִשְׁמוֹתֵינוּ הַפְּקוּדוֹת לָךְ, וְעַל נִסֶּיךָ שֶׁבְּכָל יוֹם עִמָּנוּ, וְעַל נִפְלְאוֹתֶיךָ וְטוֹבוֹתֶיךָ שֶׁבְּכָל עֵת, עֶרֶב וָבֹקֶר וְצָהֳרָיִם. הַטּוֹב כִּי לֹא כָלוּ רַחֲמֶיךָ, וְהַמְּרַחֵם כִּי לֹא תַמּוּ חֲסָדֶיךָ,[3] מֵעוֹלָם קִוִּינוּ לָךְ.

מודים דרבנן

מוֹדִים אֲנַחְנוּ לָךְ, שָׁאַתָּה הוּא יהוה אֱלֹהֵינוּ וֵאלֹהֵי אֲבוֹתֵינוּ, אֱלֹהֵי כָל בָּשָׂר, יוֹצְרֵנוּ, יוֹצֵר בְּרֵאשִׁית. בְּרָכוֹת וְהוֹדָאוֹת לְשִׁמְךָ הַגָּדוֹל וְהַקָּדוֹשׁ, עַל שֶׁהֶחֱיִיתָנוּ וְקִיַּמְתָּנוּ. כֵּן תְּחַיֵּנוּ וּתְקַיְּמֵנוּ, וְתֶאֱסוֹף גָּלֻיּוֹתֵינוּ לְחַצְרוֹת קָדְשֶׁךָ, לִשְׁמוֹר חֻקֶּיךָ וְלַעֲשׂוֹת רְצוֹנֶךָ, וּלְעָבְדְּךָ בְּלֵבָב שָׁלֵם, עַל שֶׁאֲנַחְנוּ מוֹדִים לָךְ. בָּרוּךְ אֵל הַהוֹדָאוֹת.

(1) Cf. *Nechemiah* 9:31. (2) Cf. *Psalms* 79:13. (3) Cf. *Lamentations* 3:22.

TEMPLE SERVICE

רְצֵה *Be favorable, HASHEM, our God, toward Your people Israel and their prayer and restore the service to the Holy of Holies of Your Temple. The fire-offerings of Israel and their prayer accept with love and favor, and may the service of Your people Israel always be favorable to You.*

During the *chazzan's* repetition, congregation responds *Amen* as indicated.
[If the following paragraph is forgotten, repeat *Shemoneh Esrei.* See *Laws* §56.]

אֱלֹהֵינוּ *Our God and God of our forefathers, may there rise, come, reach, be noted, be favored, be heard, be considered, and be remembered — the remembrance and consideration of ourselves; the remembrance of our forefathers; the remembrance of Messiah, son of David, Your servant; the remembrance of Jerusalem, the City of Your Holiness; the remembrance of Your entire people the Family of Israel — before You for deliverance, for goodness, for grace, for kindness, and for compassion, for life, and for peace on this day of the Festival of Succos. Remember us on it, HASHEM, our God, for goodness* (Cong.—*Amen*)*; consider us on it for blessing* (Cong.—*Amen*)*; and help us on it for life* (Cong.—*Amen*)*. In the matter of salvation and compassion, pity, be gracious and compassionate with us and help us, for our eyes are turned to You, because You are God, the gracious and compassionate King.*[1]

וְתֶחֱזֶינָה *May our eyes behold Your return to Zion in compassion. Blessed are You, HASHEM, Who restores His Presence to Zion.*

THANKSGIVING [MODIM]

Bow at *'We gratefully thank You'*; straighten up at *'HASHEM.'* In his repetition the *chazzan* should recite the entire *Modim* aloud, while the congregation recites *Modim of the Rabbis* softly.

מוֹדִים *We gratefully thank You, for it is You Who are HASHEM, our God and the God of our forefathers for all eternity; Rock of our lives, Shield of our salvation are You from generation to generation. We shall thank You and relate Your praise*[2] *— for our lives, which are committed to Your power and for our souls that are entrusted to You; for Your miracles that are with us every day; and for Your wonders and favors in every season — evening, morning, and afternoon. The Beneficent One, for Your compassions were never exhausted, and the Compassionate One, for Your kindnesses never ended*[3] *— always have we put our hope in You.*

MODIM OF THE RABBIS

מוֹדִים *We gratefully thank You, for it is You Who are HASHEM, our God and the God of our forefathers, the God of all flesh, our Molder, the Molder of the universe. Blessings and thanks are due Your great and holy Name for You have given us life and sustained us. So may You continue to give us life and sustain us and gather our exiles to the Courtyards of Your Sanctuary, to observe Your decrees, to do Your will and to serve You wholeheartedly. [We thank You] for inspiring us to thank You. Blessed is the God of thanksgivings.*

וְעַל כֻּלָּם יִתְבָּרַךְ וְיִתְרוֹמַם שִׁמְךָ מַלְכֵּנוּ תָּמִיד לְעוֹלָם וָעֶד.

Bend the knees at בָּרוּךְ; bow at אַתָּה; straighten up at ה׳.

וְכֹל הַחַיִּים יוֹדְוּךָ סֶּלָה, וִיהַלְלוּ אֶת שִׁמְךָ בֶּאֱמֶת, הָאֵל יְשׁוּעָתֵנוּ וְעֶזְרָתֵנוּ סֶלָה. בָּרוּךְ אַתָּה יהוה, הַטּוֹב שִׁמְךָ וּלְךָ נָאֶה לְהוֹדוֹת.

ברכת כהנים

The *chazzan* recites בִּרְכַּת כֹּהֲנִים during his repetition. He faces right at וְיִשְׁמְרֶךָ; faces left at אֵלֶיךָ וִיחֻנֶּךָּ; faces the Ark for the rest of the blessings.

אֱלֹהֵינוּ, וֵאלֹהֵי אֲבוֹתֵינוּ, בָּרְכֵנוּ בַבְּרָכָה הַמְּשֻׁלֶּשֶׁת בַּתּוֹרָה הַכְּתוּבָה עַל יְדֵי מֹשֶׁה עַבְדֶּךָ, הָאֲמוּרָה מִפִּי אַהֲרֹן וּבָנָיו, כֹּהֲנִים עַם קְדוֹשֶׁךָ, כָּאָמוּר:

יְבָרֶכְךָ יהוה, וְיִשְׁמְרֶךָ. (Cong. – כֵּן יְהִי רָצוֹן.)

יָאֵר יהוה פָּנָיו אֵלֶיךָ וִיחֻנֶּךָּ. (Cong. – כֵּן יְהִי רָצוֹן.)

יִשָּׂא יהוה פָּנָיו אֵלֶיךָ וְיָשֵׂם לְךָ שָׁלוֹם.[1] (Cong. – כֵּן יְהִי רָצוֹן.)

שלום

שִׂים שָׁלוֹם, טוֹבָה, וּבְרָכָה, חֵן, וָחֶסֶד וְרַחֲמִים עָלֵינוּ וְעַל כָּל יִשְׂרָאֵל עַמֶּךָ. בָּרְכֵנוּ אָבִינוּ, כֻּלָּנוּ כְּאֶחָד בְּאוֹר פָּנֶיךָ, כִּי בְאוֹר פָּנֶיךָ נָתַתָּ לָּנוּ, יהוה אֱלֹהֵינוּ, תּוֹרַת חַיִּים וְאַהֲבַת חֶסֶד, וּצְדָקָה, וּבְרָכָה, וְרַחֲמִים, וְחַיִּים, וְשָׁלוֹם. וְטוֹב בְּעֵינֶיךָ לְבָרֵךְ אֶת עַמְּךָ יִשְׂרָאֵל, בְּכָל עֵת וּבְכָל שָׁעָה בִּשְׁלוֹמֶךָ. בָּרוּךְ אַתָּה יהוה, הַמְּבָרֵךְ אֶת עַמּוֹ יִשְׂרָאֵל בַּשָּׁלוֹם.

יִהְיוּ לְרָצוֹן אִמְרֵי פִי וְהֶגְיוֹן לִבִּי לְפָנֶיךָ, יהוה צוּרִי וְגֹאֲלִי.[2]

Chazzan's repetition of *Shemoneh Esrei* ends here. Individuals continue:

אֱלֹהַי, נְצוֹר לְשׁוֹנִי מֵרָע, וּשְׂפָתַי מִדַּבֵּר מִרְמָה,[3] וְלִמְקַלְלַי נַפְשִׁי תִדּוֹם, וְנַפְשִׁי כֶּעָפָר לַכֹּל תִּהְיֶה. פְּתַח לִבִּי בְּתוֹרָתֶךָ, וּבְמִצְוֹתֶיךָ תִּרְדּוֹף נַפְשִׁי. וְכֹל הַחוֹשְׁבִים עָלַי רָעָה, מְהֵרָה הָפֵר עֲצָתָם וְקַלְקֵל מַחֲשַׁבְתָּם. עֲשֵׂה לְמַעַן שְׁמֶךָ, עֲשֵׂה לְמַעַן יְמִינֶךָ, עֲשֵׂה לְמַעַן קְדֻשָּׁתֶךָ, עֲשֵׂה לְמַעַן תּוֹרָתֶךָ. לְמַעַן יֵחָלְצוּן יְדִידֶיךָ, הוֹשִׁיעָה יְמִינְךָ וַעֲנֵנִי.[4]

Some recite verses pertaining to their names here. See page 1301.

יִהְיוּ לְרָצוֹן אִמְרֵי פִי וְהֶגְיוֹן לִבִּי לְפָנֶיךָ, יהוה צוּרִי וְגֹאֲלִי.[2]

Bow and take three steps back. Bow left and say . . . עֹשֶׂה; bow right and say . . . הוּא יַעֲשֶׂה; bow forward and say וְעַל כָּל . . . אָמֵן.

עֹשֶׂה שָׁלוֹם בִּמְרוֹמָיו, הוּא יַעֲשֶׂה שָׁלוֹם עָלֵינוּ, וְעַל כָּל יִשְׂרָאֵל. וְאִמְרוּ: אָמֵן.

For all these, may Your Name be blessed and exalted, our King, continually forever and ever.

Bend the knees at *'Blessed'*; bow at *'You'*; straighten up at *'HASHEM.'*

Everything alive will gratefully acknowledge You, Selah! and praise Your Name sincerely, O God of our salvation and help, Selah! Blessed are You, HASHEM, Your Name is 'The Beneficent One' and to You it is fitting to give thanks.

THE PRIESTLY BLESSING

The *chazzan* recites the Priestly Blessing during his repetition.

אֱלֹהֵינוּ *Our God and the God of our forefathers, bless us with the three-verse blessing in the Torah that was written by the hand of Moses, Your servant, that was said by Aaron and his sons, the Kohanim, Your holy people, as it is said:*

May HASHEM bless you and safeguard you. (Cong.— *So may it be.*)

May HASHEM illuminate His countenance for you and be gracious to you. (Cong.— *So may it be.*)

May HASHEM turn His countenance to you and establish peace for you.[1] (Cong.— *So may it be.*)

PEACE

שִׂים *Establish peace, goodness, blessing, graciousness, kindness, and compassion upon us and upon all of Your people Israel. Bless us, our Father, all of us as one, with the light of Your countenance, for with the light of Your countenance You gave us, HASHEM, our God, the Torah of life and a love of kindness, righteousness, blessing, compassion, life, and peace. And may it be good in Your eyes to bless Your people Israel at every time and every hour with Your peace. Blessed are You, HASHEM, Who blesses His people Israel with peace.*

May the expressions of my mouth and the thoughts of my heart find favor before You, HASHEM, my Rock and my Redeemer.[2]

Chazzan's repetition of *Shemoneh Esrei* ends here. Individuals continue:

אֱלֹהַי *My God, guard my tongue from evil and my lips from speaking deceitfully.*[3] *To those who curse me, let my soul be silent; and let my soul be like dust to everyone. Open my heart to Your Torah, then my soul will pursue Your commandments. As for all those who design evil against me, speedily nullify their counsel and disrupt their design. Act for Your Name's sake; act for Your right hand's sake; act for Your sanctity's sake; act for Your Torah's sake. That Your beloved ones may be given rest; let Your right hand save, and respond to me.*[4]

Some recite verses pertaining to their names at this point. See page 1301.

May the expressions of my mouth and the thoughts of my heart find favor before You, HASHEM, my Rock and my Redeemer.[2] *He Who makes peace in His heights, may He make peace upon us, and upon all Israel. Now respond: Amen.*

Bow and take three steps back. Bow left and say, *'He Who makes peace . . .'*; bow right and say, *'may He make peace . . .'*; bow forward and say, *'and upon . . . Amen.'*

---

(1) *Numbers* 6:24-26. (2) *Psalms* 19:15. (3) Cf. 34:14. (4) 60:7; 108:7.

יְהִי רָצוֹן מִלְּפָנֶיךָ יהוה אֱלֹהֵינוּ וֵאלֹהֵי אֲבוֹתֵינוּ, שֶׁיִּבָּנֶה בֵּית הַמִּקְדָּשׁ בִּמְהֵרָה בְיָמֵינוּ, וְתֵן חֶלְקֵנוּ בְּתוֹרָתֶךָ. וְשָׁם נַעֲבָדְךָ בְּיִרְאָה, כִּימֵי עוֹלָם וּכְשָׁנִים קַדְמוֹנִיּוֹת. וְעָרְבָה לַיהוה מִנְחַת יְהוּדָה וִירוּשָׁלָיִם, כִּימֵי עוֹלָם וּכְשָׁנִים קַדְמוֹנִיּוֹת.[1]

THE INDIVIDUAL'S RECITATION OF *SHEMONEH ESREI* ENDS HERE.

The individual remains standing in place until the *chazzan* reaches *Kedushah* — or at least until the *chazzan* begins his repetition — then he takes three steps forward. The *chazzan* himself, or one praying alone, should remain in place for a few moments before taking three steps forward.

הלל

The *chazzan* recites the blessing. The congregation, after responding אָמֵן, repeats it, and continues with the first psalm.

בָּרוּךְ אַתָּה יהוה אֱלֹהֵינוּ מֶלֶךְ הָעוֹלָם, אֲשֶׁר קִדְּשָׁנוּ בְּמִצְוֹתָיו, וְצִוָּנוּ לִקְרוֹא אֶת הַהַלֵּל. (Cong.— אָמֵן.)

תהלים קיג

הַלְלוּיָהּ הַלְלוּ עַבְדֵי יהוה, הַלְלוּ אֶת שֵׁם יהוה. יְהִי שֵׁם יהוה מְבֹרָךְ, מֵעַתָּה וְעַד עוֹלָם. מִמִּזְרַח שֶׁמֶשׁ עַד מְבוֹאוֹ, מְהֻלָּל שֵׁם יהוה. רָם עַל כָּל גּוֹיִם יהוה, עַל הַשָּׁמַיִם כְּבוֹדוֹ. מִי כַּיהוה אֱלֹהֵינוּ, הַמַּגְבִּיהִי לָשָׁבֶת. הַמַּשְׁפִּילִי לִרְאוֹת, בַּשָּׁמַיִם וּבָאָרֶץ. ❖ מְקִימִי מֵעָפָר דָּל, מֵאַשְׁפֹּת יָרִים אֶבְיוֹן. לְהוֹשִׁיבִי עִם נְדִיבִים, עִם נְדִיבֵי עַמּוֹ. מוֹשִׁיבִי עֲקֶרֶת הַבַּיִת, אֵם הַבָּנִים שְׂמֵחָה, הַלְלוּיָהּ.

תהלים קיד

בְּצֵאת יִשְׂרָאֵל מִמִּצְרָיִם, בֵּית יַעֲקֹב מֵעַם לֹעֵז. הָיְתָה יְהוּדָה לְקָדְשׁוֹ, יִשְׂרָאֵל מַמְשְׁלוֹתָיו. הַיָּם רָאָה וַיָּנֹס, הַיַּרְדֵּן יִסֹּב לְאָחוֹר. הֶהָרִים רָקְדוּ כְאֵילִים, גְּבָעוֹת כִּבְנֵי צֹאן. ❖ מַה לְּךָ הַיָּם כִּי תָנוּס, הַיַּרְדֵּן תִּסֹּב לְאָחוֹר. הֶהָרִים תִּרְקְדוּ כְאֵילִים, גְּבָעוֹת כִּבְנֵי צֹאן. מִלִּפְנֵי אָדוֹן חוּלִי אָרֶץ, מִלִּפְנֵי אֱלוֹהַּ יַעֲקֹב. הַהֹפְכִי הַצּוּר אֲגַם מָיִם, חַלָּמִישׁ לְמַעְיְנוֹ מָיִם.

תהלים קטו:א-יא

לֹא לָנוּ יהוה לֹא לָנוּ, כִּי לְשִׁמְךָ תֵּן כָּבוֹד, עַל חַסְדְּךָ עַל אֲמִתֶּךָ. לָמָּה יֹאמְרוּ הַגּוֹיִם, אַיֵּה נָא אֱלֹהֵיהֶם. וֵאלֹהֵינוּ בַשָּׁמָיִם, כֹּל אֲשֶׁר חָפֵץ עָשָׂה. עֲצַבֵּיהֶם כֶּסֶף וְזָהָב, מַעֲשֵׂה יְדֵי אָדָם. פֶּה לָהֶם וְלֹא יְדַבֵּרוּ, עֵינַיִם לָהֶם וְלֹא יִרְאוּ. אָזְנַיִם לָהֶם וְלֹא יִשְׁמָעוּ, אַף לָהֶם וְלֹא יְרִיחוּן. יְדֵיהֶם וְלֹא יְמִישׁוּן, רַגְלֵיהֶם וְלֹא יְהַלֵּכוּ, לֹא יֶהְגּוּ בִּגְרוֹנָם. כְּמוֹהֶם יִהְיוּ עֹשֵׂיהֶם,

יְהִי רָצוֹן *May it be Your will,* HASHEM, *our God and the God of our forefathers, that the Holy Temple be rebuilt, speedily in our days. Grant us our share in Your Torah, and may we serve You there with reverence, as in days of old and in former years. Then the offering of Judah and Jerusalem will be pleasing to* HASHEM, *as in days of old and in former years.*[1]

THE INDIVIDUAL'S RECITATION OF *SHEMONEH ESREI* ENDS HERE.

The individual remains standing in place until the *chazzan* reaches *Kedushah* — or at least until the *chazzan* begins his repetition — then he takes three steps forward. The *chazzan* himself, or one praying alone, should remain in place for a few moments before taking three steps forward.

HALLEL

The *chazzan* recites the blessing. The congregation, after responding *Amen,* repeats it, and continues with the first psalm.

בָּרוּךְ *Blessed are You,* HASHEM, *our God, King of the universe, Who has sanctified us with His commandments and has commanded us to read the Hallel.* (Cong.– *Amen.*)

Psalm 113

הַלְלוּיָהּ *Halleluyah! Give praise, you servants of* HASHEM; *praise the Name of* HASHEM! *Blessed be the Name of* HASHEM, *from this time and forever. From the rising of the sun to its setting,* HASHEM'*s Name is praised. High above all nations is* HASHEM, *above the heavens is His glory. Who is like* HASHEM, *our God, Who is enthroned on high — yet deigns to look upon the heaven and the earth?* Chazzan– *He raises the needy from the dust, from the trash heaps He lifts the destitute. To seat them with nobles, with the nobles of His people. He transforms the barren wife into a glad mother of children. Halleluyah!*

Psalm 114

בְּצֵאת *When Israel went out of Egypt, Jacob's household from a people of alien tongue — Judah became His sanctuary, Israel His dominions. The sea saw and fled: the Jordan turned backward. The mountains skipped like rams, the hills like young lambs.* Chazzan– *What ails you, O sea, that you flee? O Jordan, that you turn backward? O mountains, that you skip like rams? O hills, like young lambs? Before the Lord's Presence — did I, the earth, tremble — before the presence of the God of Jacob, Who turns the rock into a pond of water, the flint into a flowing fountain.*

Psalms 115:1-11

לֹא לָנוּ *Not for our sake,* HASHEM, *not for our sake, but for Your Name's sake give glory, for Your kindness and for Your truth! Why should the nations say, 'Where is their God now?' Our God is in the heavens; whatever He pleases, He does! Their idols are silver and gold, the handiwork of man. They have a mouth, but cannot speak; they have eyes, but cannot see. They have ears, but cannot hear; they have a nose, but cannot smell. Their hands — they cannot feel; their feet — they cannot walk; they cannot utter a sound from their throat. Those who make them should become like them,*

(1) *Malachi* 3:4.

כֹּל אֲשֶׁר בֹּטֵחַ בָּהֶם. ❖ יִשְׂרָאֵל בְּטַח בַּיהוה, עֶזְרָם וּמָגִנָּם הוּא. בֵּית אַהֲרֹן בִּטְחוּ בַיהוה, עֶזְרָם וּמָגִנָּם הוּא. יִרְאֵי יהוה בִּטְחוּ בַיהוה, עֶזְרָם וּמָגִנָּם הוּא.

תהלים קטו:יב-יח

יהוה זְכָרָנוּ יְבָרֵךְ, יְבָרֵךְ אֶת בֵּית יִשְׂרָאֵל, יְבָרֵךְ אֶת בֵּית אַהֲרֹן. יְבָרֵךְ יִרְאֵי יהוה, הַקְּטַנִּים עִם הַגְּדֹלִים. יֹסֵף יהוה עֲלֵיכֶם, עֲלֵיכֶם וְעַל בְּנֵיכֶם. בְּרוּכִים אַתֶּם לַיהוה, עֹשֵׂה שָׁמַיִם וָאָרֶץ. ❖ הַשָּׁמַיִם שָׁמַיִם לַיהוה, וְהָאָרֶץ נָתַן לִבְנֵי אָדָם. לֹא הַמֵּתִים יְהַלְּלוּ יָהּ, וְלֹא כָּל יֹרְדֵי דוּמָה. וַאֲנַחְנוּ נְבָרֵךְ יָהּ, מֵעַתָּה וְעַד עוֹלָם, הַלְּלוּיָהּ.

תהלים קטז:א-יא

אָהַבְתִּי כִּי יִשְׁמַע יהוה, אֶת קוֹלִי תַּחֲנוּנָי. כִּי הִטָּה אָזְנוֹ לִי, וּבְיָמַי אֶקְרָא. אֲפָפוּנִי חֶבְלֵי מָוֶת, וּמְצָרֵי שְׁאוֹל מְצָאוּנִי, צָרָה וְיָגוֹן אֶמְצָא. וּבְשֵׁם יהוה אֶקְרָא, אָנָּה יהוה מַלְּטָה נַפְשִׁי. חַנּוּן יהוה וְצַדִּיק, וֵאלֹהֵינוּ מְרַחֵם. שֹׁמֵר פְּתָאִים יהוה, דַּלּוֹתִי וְלִי יְהוֹשִׁיעַ. שׁוּבִי נַפְשִׁי לִמְנוּחָיְכִי, כִּי יהוה גָּמַל עָלָיְכִי. כִּי חִלַּצְתָּ נַפְשִׁי מִמָּוֶת, אֶת עֵינִי מִן דִּמְעָה, אֶת רַגְלִי מִדֶּחִי. ❖ אֶתְהַלֵּךְ לִפְנֵי יהוה, בְּאַרְצוֹת הַחַיִּים. הֶאֱמַנְתִּי כִּי אֲדַבֵּר, אֲנִי עָנִיתִי מְאֹד. אֲנִי אָמַרְתִּי בְחָפְזִי, כָּל הָאָדָם כֹּזֵב.

תהלים קטז:יב-יט

מָה אָשִׁיב לַיהוה, כָּל תַּגְמוּלוֹהִי עָלָי. כּוֹס יְשׁוּעוֹת אֶשָּׂא, וּבְשֵׁם יהוה אֶקְרָא. נְדָרַי לַיהוה אֲשַׁלֵּם, נֶגְדָה נָּא לְכָל עַמּוֹ. יָקָר בְּעֵינֵי יהוה, הַמָּוְתָה לַחֲסִידָיו. אָנָּה יהוה כִּי אֲנִי עַבְדֶּךָ, אֲנִי עַבְדְּךָ, בֶּן אֲמָתֶךָ, פִּתַּחְתָּ לְמוֹסֵרָי. ❖ לְךָ אֶזְבַּח זֶבַח תּוֹדָה, וּבְשֵׁם יהוה אֶקְרָא. נְדָרַי לַיהוה אֲשַׁלֵּם, נֶגְדָה נָּא לְכָל עַמּוֹ. בְּחַצְרוֹת בֵּית יהוה, בְּתוֹכֵכִי יְרוּשָׁלָיִם הַלְלוּיָהּ.

Congregation, then *chazzan:*

תהלים קיז

הַלְלוּ אֶת יהוה, כָּל גּוֹיִם, שַׁבְּחוּהוּ כָּל הָאֻמִּים. כִּי גָבַר עָלֵינוּ חַסְדּוֹ, וֶאֱמֶת יהוה לְעוֹלָם, הַלְלוּיָהּ.

whoever trusts in them! Chazzan– *O Israel, trust in* HASHEM; *— their help and their shield is He! House of Aaron, trust in* HASHEM; *their help and their shield is He! You who fear* HASHEM, *trust in* HASHEM; *their help and their shield is He!*

Psalm 115:12-18

יהוה *HASHEM Who has remembered us will bless — He will bless the House of Israel; He will bless the House of Aaron; He will bless those who fear* HASHEM, *the small as well as the great. May* HASHEM *increase upon you, upon you and upon your children! You are blessed of* HASHEM, *Maker of heaven and earth.* Chazzan– *As for the heavens — the heavens are* HASHEM*'s, but the earth He has given to mankind. Neither the dead can praise God, nor any who descend into silence; but we will bless God from this time and forever. Halleluyah!*

Psalm 116:1-11

אָהַבְתִּי *I love Him, for* HASHEM *hears my voice, my supplications. As He has inclined His ear to me, so in my days shall I call. The pains of death encircled me; the confines of the grave have found me; trouble and sorrow I would find. Then I would invoke the Name of* HASHEM: *'Please,* HASHEM, *save my soul.' Gracious is* HASHEM *and righteous, our God is merciful.* HASHEM *protects the simple; I was brought low, but He saved me. Return, my soul, to your rest; for* HASHEM *has been kind to you. For You have delivered my soul from death, my eyes from tears, my feet from stumbling.* Chazzan– *I shall walk before* HASHEM *in the lands of the living. I have kept faith although I say: 'I suffer exceedingly.' I said in my haste: 'All mankind is deceitful.'*

Psalm 116:12-19

מָה אָשִׁיב *How can I repay* HASHEM *for all His kindness to me? I will raise the cup of salvations and the Name of* HASHEM *I will invoke. My vows to* HASHEM *I will pay, in the presence, now, of His entire people. Difficult in the eyes of* HASHEM *is the death of His devout ones. Please,* HASHEM *— for I am Your servant, I am Your servant, son of Your handmaid — You have released my bonds.* Chazzan– *To You I will sacrifice thanksgiving offerings, and the name of* HASHEM *I will invoke. My vows to* HASHEM *I will pay, in the presence, now, of His entire people. In the courtyards of the House of* HASHEM, *in your midst, O Jerusalem, Halleluyah!*

Congregation, then *chazzan:*

Psalm 117

הַלְלוּ *Praise* HASHEM, *all nations; praise Him, all the states! For His kindness has overwhelmed us, and the truth of* HASHEM *is eternal, Halleluyah!*

תהלים קיח

Chazzan –	**הוֹדוּ** לַיהוה כִּי טוֹב,	כִּי לְעוֹלָם חַסְדּוֹ.
Cong. –	הוֹדוּ לַיהוה כִּי טוֹב,	כִּי לְעוֹלָם חַסְדּוֹ.
	יֹאמַר נָא יִשְׂרָאֵל,	כִּי לְעוֹלָם חַסְדּוֹ.
Chazzan –	יֹאמַר נָא יִשְׂרָאֵל,	כִּי לְעוֹלָם חַסְדּוֹ.
Cong. –	הוֹדוּ לַיהוה כִּי טוֹב,	כִּי לְעוֹלָם חַסְדּוֹ.
	יֹאמְרוּ נָא בֵית אַהֲרֹן,	כִּי לְעוֹלָם חַסְדּוֹ.
Chazzan –	יֹאמְרוּ נָא בֵית אַהֲרֹן,	כִּי לְעוֹלָם חַסְדּוֹ.
Cong. –	הוֹדוּ לַיהוה כִּי טוֹב,	כִּי לְעוֹלָם חַסְדּוֹ.
	יֹאמְרוּ נָא יִרְאֵי יהוה,	כִּי לְעוֹלָם חַסְדּוֹ.
Chazzan –	יֹאמְרוּ נָא יִרְאֵי יהוה,	כִּי לְעוֹלָם חַסְדּוֹ.
Cong. –	הוֹדוּ לַיהוה כִּי טוֹב,	כִּי לְעוֹלָם חַסְדּוֹ.

מִן הַמֵּצַר קָרָאתִי יָּהּ, עָנָנִי בַמֶּרְחָב יָהּ. יהוה לִי לֹא אִירָא, מַה יַּעֲשֶׂה לִי אָדָם. יהוה לִי בְּעֹזְרָי, וַאֲנִי אֶרְאֶה בְשֹׂנְאָי. טוֹב לַחֲסוֹת בַּיהוה, מִבְּטֹחַ בָּאָדָם. טוֹב לַחֲסוֹת בַּיהוה, מִבְּטֹחַ בִּנְדִיבִים. כָּל גּוֹיִם סְבָבוּנִי, בְּשֵׁם יהוה כִּי אֲמִילַם. סַבּוּנִי גַם סְבָבוּנִי, בְּשֵׁם יהוה כִּי אֲמִילַם. סַבּוּנִי כִדְבֹרִים דֹּעֲכוּ כְּאֵשׁ קוֹצִים, בְּשֵׁם יהוה כִּי אֲמִילַם. דָּחֹה דְחִיתַנִי לִנְפֹּל, וַיהוה עֲזָרָנִי. עָזִּי וְזִמְרָת יָהּ, וַיְהִי לִי לִישׁוּעָה. קוֹל רִנָּה וִישׁוּעָה, בְּאָהֳלֵי צַדִּיקִים, יְמִין יהוה עֹשָׂה חָיִל. יְמִין יהוה רוֹמֵמָה, יְמִין יהוה עֹשָׂה חָיִל. לֹא אָמוּת כִּי אֶחְיֶה, וַאֲסַפֵּר מַעֲשֵׂי יָהּ. יַסֹּר יִסְּרַנִּי יָּהּ, וְלַמָּוֶת לֹא נְתָנָנִי. ❖ פִּתְחוּ לִי שַׁעֲרֵי צֶדֶק, אָבֹא בָם אוֹדֶה יָהּ. זֶה הַשַּׁעַר לַיהוה, צַדִּיקִים יָבֹאוּ בוֹ. אוֹדְךָ כִּי עֲנִיתָנִי, וַתְּהִי לִי לִישׁוּעָה. אוֹדְךָ כִּי עֲנִיתָנִי, וַתְּהִי לִי לִישׁוּעָה. אֶבֶן מָאֲסוּ הַבּוֹנִים, הָיְתָה לְרֹאשׁ פִּנָּה. אֶבֶן מָאֲסוּ הַבּוֹנִים, הָיְתָה לְרֹאשׁ פִּנָּה. מֵאֵת יהוה הָיְתָה זֹּאת, הִיא נִפְלָאת בְּעֵינֵינוּ. מֵאֵת יהוה הָיְתָה זֹּאת, הִיא נִפְלָאת בְּעֵינֵינוּ. זֶה הַיּוֹם עָשָׂה יהוה, נָגִילָה וְנִשְׂמְחָה בוֹ. זֶה הַיּוֹם עָשָׂה יהוה, נָגִילָה וְנִשְׂמְחָה בוֹ.

The next four lines are recited responsively — *chazzan,* then congregation.

אָנָּא יהוה הוֹשִׁיעָה נָּא.
אָנָּא יהוה הוֹשִׁיעָה נָּא.
אָנָּא יהוה הַצְלִיחָה נָא.
אָנָּא יהוה הַצְלִיחָה נָא.

Psalm 118

Chazzan – **הוֹדוּ** *Give thanks to* HASHEM *for He is good;* *His kindness endures forever!*

Cong. – *Give thanks to* HASHEM*, for He is good;* *His kindness endures forever!*

Let Israel say now: *His kindness endures forever!*

Chazzan – *Let Israel say now:* *His kindness endures forever!*

Cong. – *Give thanks to* HASHEM*, for He is good;* *His kindness endures forever!*

Let the House of Aaron say now: *His kindness endures forever!*

Chazzan – *Let the House of Aaron say now:* *His kindness endures forever!*

Cong. – *Give thanks to* HASHEM*, for He is good;* *His kindness endures forever!*

Let those who fear HASHEM *say now:* *His kindness endures forever!*

Chazzan – *Let those who fear* HASHEM *say now:* *His kindness endures forever!*

Cong. – *Give thanks to* HASHEM*, for He is good;* *His kindness endures forever!*

מִן הַמֵּצַר *From the straits did I call upon God; God answered me with expansiveness.* HASHEM *is with me, I have no fear; how can man affect me?* HASHEM *is with me through my helpers; therefore I can face my foes. It is better to take refuge in* HASHEM *than to rely on man. It is better to take refuge in* HASHEM *than to rely on nobles. All the nations surround me; in the Name of* HASHEM *I cut them down! They encircle me, they also surround me; in the Name of* HASHEM*, I cut them down! They encircle me like bees, but they are extinguished as a fire does thorns; in the Name of* HASHEM *I cut them down! You pushed me hard that I might fall, but* HASHEM *assisted me. God is my might and my praise, and He was a salvation for me. The sound of rejoicing and salvation is in the tents of the righteous: '*HASHEM*'s right hand does valiantly.* HASHEM*'s right hand is raised triumphantly;* HASHEM*'s right hand does valiantly!' I shall not die! But I shall live and relate the deeds of God. God has chastened me exceedingly, but He did not let me die.* Chazzan– *Open for me the gates of righteousness, I will enter them and thank God. This is the gate of* HASHEM*; the righteous shall enter through it. I thank You for You have answered me and become my salvation. I thank You for You have answered me and become my salvation. The stone the builders despised has become the cornerstone. The stone the builders despised has become the cornerstone. This emanated from* HASHEM*; it is wondrous in our eyes. This emanated from* HASHEM*; it is wondrous in our eyes. This is the day* HASHEM *has made; let us rejoice and be glad on it. This is the day* HASHEM *has made; let us rejoice and be glad on it.*

The next four lines are recited responsively – *chazzan,* then congregation.

אָנָּא *Please,* HASHEM*, save now!*
Please, HASHEM*, save now!*
Please, HASHEM*, bring success now!*
Please, HASHEM*, bring success now!*

בָּרוּךְ הַבָּא בְּשֵׁם יהוה, בֵּרַכְנוּכֶם מִבֵּית יהוה. בָּרוּךְ הַבָּא בְּשֵׁם יהוה, בֵּרַכְנוּכֶם מִבֵּית יהוה. אֵל יהוה וַיָּאֶר לָנוּ, אִסְרוּ חַג בַּעֲבֹתִים, עַד קַרְנוֹת הַמִּזְבֵּחַ. אֵל יהוה וַיָּאֶר לָנוּ, אִסְרוּ חַג בַּעֲבֹתִים, עַד קַרְנוֹת הַמִּזְבֵּחַ. אֵלִי אַתָּה וְאוֹדֶךָּ, אֱלֹהַי אֲרוֹמְמֶךָּ. אֵלִי אַתָּה וְאוֹדֶךָּ, אֱלֹהַי אֲרוֹמְמֶךָּ. הוֹדוּ לַיהוה כִּי טוֹב, כִּי לְעוֹלָם חַסְדּוֹ. הוֹדוּ לַיהוה כִּי טוֹב, כִּי לְעוֹלָם חַסְדּוֹ.

יְהַלְלוּךָ יהוה אֱלֹהֵינוּ כָּל מַעֲשֶׂיךָ, וַחֲסִידֶיךָ צַדִּיקִים עוֹשֵׂי רְצוֹנֶךָ, וְכָל עַמְּךָ בֵּית יִשְׂרָאֵל בְּרִנָּה יוֹדוּ וִיבָרְכוּ וִישַׁבְּחוּ וִיפָאֲרוּ וִירוֹמְמוּ וְיַעֲרִיצוּ וְיַקְדִּישׁוּ וְיַמְלִיכוּ אֶת שִׁמְךָ מַלְכֵּנוּ. ❖ כִּי לְךָ טוֹב לְהוֹדוֹת וּלְשִׁמְךָ נָאֶה לְזַמֵּר, כִּי מֵעוֹלָם וְעַד עוֹלָם אַתָּה אֵל. בָּרוּךְ אַתָּה יהוה, מֶלֶךְ מְהֻלָּל בַּתִּשְׁבָּחוֹת.

(.Cong. – אָמֵן)

SOME CONGREGATIONS RECITE הוֹשַׁעְנוֹת, *HOSHANOS,* (P. 566) AT THIS POINT.

קדיש שלם

The *chazzan* recites *Kaddish:*

יִתְגַּדַּל וְיִתְקַדַּשׁ שְׁמֵהּ רַבָּא. (.Cong. – אָמֵן.) בְּעָלְמָא דִּי בְרָא כִרְעוּתֵהּ. וְיַמְלִיךְ מַלְכוּתֵהּ, בְּחַיֵּיכוֹן וּבְיוֹמֵיכוֹן וּבְחַיֵּי דְכָל בֵּית יִשְׂרָאֵל, בַּעֲגָלָא וּבִזְמַן קָרִיב. וְאִמְרוּ: אָמֵן.

(.Cong. – אָמֵן. יְהֵא שְׁמֵהּ רַבָּא מְבָרַךְ לְעָלַם וּלְעָלְמֵי עָלְמַיָּא.)

יְהֵא שְׁמֵהּ רַבָּא מְבָרַךְ לְעָלַם וּלְעָלְמֵי עָלְמַיָּא.

יִתְבָּרַךְ וְיִשְׁתַּבַּח וְיִתְפָּאַר וְיִתְרוֹמַם וְיִתְנַשֵּׂא וְיִתְהַדָּר וְיִתְעַלֶּה וְיִתְהַלָּל שְׁמֵהּ דְּקֻדְשָׁא בְּרִיךְ הוּא (.Cong. – בְּרִיךְ הוּא) – לְעֵלָּא מִן כָּל בִּרְכָתָא וְשִׁירָתָא תֻּשְׁבְּחָתָא וְנֶחֱמָתָא, דַּאֲמִירָן בְּעָלְמָא. וְאִמְרוּ: אָמֵן. (.Cong. – אָמֵן.)

(.Cong. – קַבֵּל בְּרַחֲמִים וּבְרָצוֹן אֶת תְּפִלָּתֵנוּ.)

תִּתְקַבֵּל צְלוֹתְהוֹן וּבָעוּתְהוֹן דְּכָל בֵּית יִשְׂרָאֵל קֳדָם אֲבוּהוֹן דִּי בִשְׁמַיָּא. וְאִמְרוּ: אָמֵן. (.Cong. – אָמֵן.)

(.Cong. – יְהִי שֵׁם יהוה מְבֹרָךְ, מֵעַתָּה וְעַד עוֹלָם.[1])

יְהֵא שְׁלָמָא רַבָּא מִן שְׁמַיָּא, וְחַיִּים עָלֵינוּ וְעַל כָּל יִשְׂרָאֵל. וְאִמְרוּ: אָמֵן. (.Cong. – אָמֵן.)

(.Cong. – עֶזְרִי מֵעִם יהוה, עֹשֵׂה שָׁמַיִם וָאָרֶץ.[2])

Take three steps back. Bow left and say . . . עֹשֶׂה; bow right and say . . . הוּא; bow forward and say וְעַל כָּל . . . אָמֵן. Remain standing in place for a few moments, then take three steps forward.

עֹשֶׂה שָׁלוֹם בִּמְרוֹמָיו, הוּא יַעֲשֶׂה שָׁלוֹם עָלֵינוּ, וְעַל כָּל יִשְׂרָאֵל. וְאִמְרוּ: אָמֵן. (.Cong. – אָמֵן.)

בָּרוּךְ *Blessed is he who comes in the Name of* HASHEM*; we bless you from the House of* HASHEM*. Blessed is he who comes in the Name of* HASHEM*; we bless you from the House of* HASHEM*.* HASHEM *is God, He illuminated for us; bind the festival offering with cords until the corners of the Altar.* HASHEM *is God, He illuminated for us; bind the festival offering with cords until the corners of the Altar. You are my God, and I will thank You; my God, I will exalt You. You are my God, and I will thank You; my God, I will exalt You. Give thanks to* HASHEM*, for He is good; His kindness endures forever. Give thanks to* HASHEM*, for He is good; His kindness endures forever.*

יְהַלְלוּךָ *All Your works shall praise You,* HASHEM *our God. And Your devout ones, the righteous, who do Your will, and Your entire people, the House of Israel, with glad song will thank, bless, praise, glorify, exalt, extol, sanctify, and proclaim the sovereignty of Your Name, our King.* Chazzan– *For to You it is fitting to give thanks, and unto Your Name it is proper to sing praises, for from This World to the World to Come You are God. Blessed are You,* HASHEM*, the King Who is lauded with praises.* (Cong.– *Amen.*)

SOME CONGREGATIONS RECITE *HOSHANOS* (P. 566) AT THIS POINT.

FULL KADDISH

The *chazzan* recites *Kaddish:*

יִתְגַּדַּל *May His great Name grow exalted and sanctified* (Cong.– *Amen.*) *in the world that He created as He willed. May He give reign to His kingship in your lifetimes and in your days, and in the lifetimes of the entire Family of Israel, swiftly and soon. Now respond: Amen.*

(Cong.– *Amen. May His great Name be blessed forever and ever.*)

May His great Name be blessed forever and ever.

Blessed, praised, glorified, exalted, extolled, mighty, upraised, and lauded be the Name of the Holy One, Blessed is He (Cong.– *Blessed is He*) *— beyond any blessing and song, praise and consolation that are uttered in the world. Now respond: Amen.* (Cong.– *Amen*).

(Cong.– *Accept our prayers with mercy and favor.*)

May the prayers and supplications of the entire Family of Israel be accepted before their Father Who is in Heaven. Now respond: Amen. (Cong.– *Amen.*)

(Cong.– *Blessed be the Name of* HASHEM*, from this time and forever.*[1])

May there be abundant peace from Heaven, and life, upon us and upon all Israel. Now respond: Amen. (Cong.– *Amen.*)

(Cong.– *My help is from* HASHEM*, Maker of heaven and earth.*[2])

Take three steps back. Bow left and say, *'He Who makes peace . . .';* bow right and say, *'may He . . .';* bow forward and say, *'and upon all Israel . . .'* Remain standing in place for a few moments, then take three steps forward.

He Who makes peace in His heights, may He make peace upon us, and upon all Israel. Now respond: Amen. (Cong.– *Amen.*)

(1) *Psalms* 113:2. (2) 121:2.

קהלת

Koheles is read before the Torah reading on the Sabbath of Chol HaMoed.
In the event there is no Sabbath during Chol HaMoed, it is read on Shemini Atzeres.

פרק א

א דִּבְרֵי קֹהֶלֶת בֶּן־דָּוִד מֶלֶךְ בִּירוּשָׁלָֽםִ׃ ב הֲבֵל הֲבָלִים אָמַר קֹהֶלֶת הֲבֵל
הֲבָלִים הַכֹּל הָֽבֶל׃ ג מַה־יִּתְרוֹן לָאָדָם בְּכָל־עֲמָלוֹ שֶׁיַּעֲמֹל תַּחַת הַשָּֽׁמֶשׁ׃
ד דּוֹר הֹלֵךְ וְדוֹר בָּא וְהָאָרֶץ לְעוֹלָם עֹמָֽדֶת׃ ה וְזָרַח הַשֶּׁמֶשׁ וּבָא הַשָּׁמֶשׁ
וְאֶל־מְקוֹמוֹ שׁוֹאֵף זוֹרֵחַ הוּא שָֽׁם׃ ו הוֹלֵךְ אֶל־דָּרוֹם וְסוֹבֵב אֶל־צָפוֹן
סוֹבֵב ׀ סֹבֵב הוֹלֵךְ הָרוּחַ וְעַל־סְבִיבֹתָיו שָׁב הָרֽוּחַ׃ ז כָּל־הַנְּחָלִים הֹלְכִים
אֶל־הַיָּם וְהַיָּם אֵינֶנּוּ מָלֵא אֶל־מְקוֹם שֶׁהַנְּחָלִים הֹלְכִים שָׁם הֵם שָׁבִים
לָלָֽכֶת׃ ח כָּל־הַדְּבָרִים יְגֵעִים לֹא־יוּכַל אִישׁ לְדַבֵּר לֹא־תִשְׂבַּע עַיִן
לִרְאוֹת וְלֹא־תִמָּלֵא אֹזֶן מִשְּׁמֹֽעַ׃ ט מַה־שֶּֽׁהָיָה הוּא שֶׁיִּהְיֶה וּמַה־

Koheles on Succos

Succos is זְמַן שִׂמְחָתֵנוּ, *the time of our gladness.* In *Eretz Yisrael,* the harvest is complete. For everyone, the stressful period of the Days of Awe is over and we prepare to celebrate and express our gratitude for God's blessing, bounty, and protection. Unfortunately unrestrained joy does not bring out the best in people. We may forget ourselves and fail to live up to our responsibilities as servants of God. To help us retain our perspectives during this season of happiness, major segments of the Jewish people have adopted the custom of reading the sobering Book of Koheles. Thinking people cannot be carried away to excess frivolity after listening carefully to Solomon, the wisest of men, proclaiming, 'Futility of futilities! All is futile!'

Indeed, *Avudraham* writes that Solomon first proclaimed Koheles to the Jewish people during Succos, precisely to serve as an antidote to the danger of light-headedness on Succos.

According to *Ramban* (*Sermon on Koheles*), the book has three main themes: 1. Man should not strive after the pleasures of this world, because — for all their allures — they are fleeting and without value. 2. Man's spiritual essence is eternal and he has a vital role in God's master plan. 3. Human intelligence cannot comprehend God's ways or assimilate all the situations and calculations upon which His justice is based. Only when the Messiah leads the world to perfection will we know why the righteous seem to suffer while the wicked seem to prosper.

Seen this way, *Koheles* hardly dampens the festivity of Succos; rather, it deepens our enjoyment of the festival because it helps us focus on what our goals in life should be. And, as in many areas, a clear knowledge of one's goal is half the job of getting there.

CHAPTER ONE

1. The *Talmud* notes that King Hezekiah and his colleagues committed themselves to writing the Books of *Isaiah, Proverbs, Song of Songs,* and *Koheles* (*Bava Basra* 15a).

Seder Olam Rabba [by the *Tanna,* Rabbi Yose ben Chalafta, student of Rabbi Akiva] mentions that: 'in Solomon's old age — shortly before his death — the Divine Spirit rested upon him and he "uttered" the three Books: *Proverbs, Song of Songs,* and *Koheles.*'

The Sages of the *Mishnah* (*Shabbos* 30b) considered whether to conceal [לִגְנוֹז] *Koheles* because it contained *apparent* contradictions [ibid.] and *seemingly* heretical statements (*Midrash*) [i.e., expressions which ignorant people might misinterpret (*Akeidas Yitzchak*)]. They decided to canonize it as part of the Scriptures because its beginning and conclusion indisputably demonstrate that the entire book is dedicated to the fear of God and is an expression of His Word. Thus the danger of misinterpretation is mitigated. (See *Overview to ArtScroll Koheles.*)

דִּבְרֵי – *The words of.* This expression always introduces דִּבְרֵי תוֹכָחָה, words of reproof or admonition (*Rashi*).

קֹהֶלֶת – *Koheles.* He was called by three names: Yedidyah [*II Samuel* 12:25], Koheles, and Solomon.

He was called '*Koheles*' because of the wisdom שֶׁנִּקְהֲלָה בּוֹ, 'which was assembled within him' (*Ibn Ezra*), or because שֶׁקִּיהֵל חָכְמוֹת הַרְבֵּה, 'he assembled many branches of wisdom' (*Rashi*).

מֶלֶךְ בִּירוּשָׁלָם – *King in Jerusalem.* The city of wisdom (*Rashi*). As King of an illustrious city famed for its wise men, Koheles had ample opportunity to delve deeply into the knowledge of the world and to investigate his theories first hand (*Sforno, Metzudos David*).

2. הֲבֵל הֲבָלִים – *Futility of futilities!* [lit., '*breath of breaths*'; '*vapor of vapors*', i.e., something empty of substance, utterly futile].

Koheles cries that everthing created during the seven days of creation is futile. The seven

KOHELES

Koheles is read before the Torah reading on the Sabbath of Chol HaMoed.
In the event there is no Sabbath during Chol HaMoed, it is read on Shemini Atzeres.

CHAPTER ONE

1 *The words of Koheles son of David, King in Jerusalem:*
2 *Futility of futilities! — said Koheles — Futility of futilities! All is futile!*
3 *What profit does man have for all his labor which he toils beneath the sun?* 4 *A*
generation goes and a generation comes, but the earth endures forever. 5 *And*
the sun rises and the sun sets — then to its place it rushes; there it rises again.
6 *It goes toward the south and veers toward the north; the wind goes round and*
round, and on its rounds the wind returns. 7 *All the rivers flow into the sea, yet*
the sea is not full; to the place where the rivers flow there they flow once more.
8 *All words are wearying, one becomes speechless; the eye is never sated with*
seeing, nor the ear filled with hearing. 9 *Whatever has been, is what will be, and*

---

references in this verse to הֶבֶל, *futility*, [the word הֶבֶל appears three times; and the plural הֲבָלִים, each of which connotes at least two, appears twice, making a total of seven] correspond to the seven days of creation (*Rashi; Midrash*).

All man's actions [see next verse] are futile and fruitless — unless they are motivated by lofty Torah ideals. Nothing will remain of his earthly labors; only his spiritual labor — his righteousness and Torah learning — will yield everlasting fruits (*Rabbeinu Yonah*).

3. מַה יִּתְרוֹן לָאָדָם – *What profit does man have . . .?* i.e., 'what reward or gains' (*Rashi*).

The verse does not read מַה יִּתְרוֹן לָעוֹלָם, 'what profit does the *world* have?' Indeed the world *does* gain from man's physical toil; as *Rambam* notes: 'Were it not for foolish people who hoard money and who build houses to last a hundred years, the earth would never be developed!' Rather, the verse questions what real gain does *man himself* have from such labor? (*Kol Yaakov*)

תַּחַת הַשָּׁמֶשׁ – *Beneath the sun.* The phrase means 'this earth where the sun shines' (*Metzudos David*).

4. וְהָאָרֶץ לְעוֹלָם עֹמָדֶת – *But the earth endures forever,* i.e., unlike man's temporary existence wherein one generation perishes and makes room for the next, the earth itself is enduring and unchanging (*Lekach Tov*).

5. וְזָרַח הַשֶּׁמֶשׁ וּבָא הַשָּׁמֶשׁ – *And the sun rises and the sun sets.* Verses 5-7 elaborate on the phrase 'but the earth endures forever' by citing the daily motions of the natural world. The sun follows a monotonously regular course in order to ensure the orderly continuity of life on earth.

The Midrash perceives a deeper meaning in this phrase: Rav Berachiah said in the name of Rav Abba bar Kahana: Do we not know that the sun rises and sets! Rather the verse [using the rising and setting sun to symbolize the life-death cycle] tells us that before the 'sun' of one righteous man sets, He causes the 'sun' of another righteous man to rise. On the day Rabbi Akiva died, Rabbi Yehudah haNasi was born . . . Before the sun of Sarah set, He caused the sun of Rebeccah to rise. Before the sun of Moses set, He caused the sun of Joshua to rise . . . and so on, generation after generation. [The same thought has been applied to the birth of Rashi which coincided with the death of Rabbeinu Gershom Meor HaGolah.]

Harav Mordechai Gifter adds that this concept is fundamental in Jewish life, and was apparent in the last generation, during the Holocaust. 'Before the sun of Europe set, He caused the sun of America to rise,' for God had prepared for the continuity of Torah.

6. This verse refers allegorically to the wicked. Although their 'sun' shines and they prosper — their 'sun' will ultimately set and they will return to their stench. 'From filth they come and to filth they shall return' (*Rashi*).

7. All physical endeavors are futile. Even primal elements engage in a constant, futile path, unable to break away from their monotonous course. Since there is no lasting value to toil in this world, why should man strive aimlessly for material gain? (*Ibn Ezra*).

8. כָּל־הַדְּבָרִים יְגֵעִים – *All words are wearying.* This translation follows *Rashi* who connects this verse to verse 3. If one gives up Torah study to engage in idle talk, such topics *are wearying,* and he will be unable to attain anything. If he seeks to indulge himself visually, his eyes will not be sated; if he seeks aural gratification, his ears will never be satisfied.

One who engages in idle talk transgresses a prohibition, for it is said, *all words are wearying, man cannot* [i.e., '*ought not*'] *speak.* (*Yoma* 19b).

9. מַה־שֶּׁהָיָה הוּא שֶׁיִּהְיֶה – *Whatever has been, is what will be,* etc. God's creation is perfect and complete, and lacks nothing. Whatever we view as new has already been provided for in His infinite wisdom. As part of Creation, God created the resources, conditions, and concepts for all discoveries and inventions until the end of

שֶׁנַּעֲשָׂה הוּא שֶׁיֵּעָשֶׂה וְאֵין כָּל־חָדָשׁ תַּחַת הַשָּׁמֶשׁ: י יֵשׁ דָּבָר שֶׁיֹּאמַר
רְאֵה־זֶה חָדָשׁ הוּא כְּבָר הָיָה לְעֹלָמִים אֲשֶׁר הָיָה מִלְּפָנֵנוּ: יא אֵין זִכְרוֹן
לָרִאשֹׁנִים וְגַם לָאַחֲרֹנִים שֶׁיִּהְיוּ לֹא־יִהְיֶה לָהֶם זִכָּרוֹן עִם שֶׁיִּהְיוּ
לָאַחֲרֹנָה: יב אֲנִי קֹהֶלֶת הָיִיתִי מֶלֶךְ עַל־יִשְׂרָאֵל בִּירוּשָׁלִָם: יג וְנָתַתִּי אֶת־
לִבִּי לִדְרוֹשׁ וְלָתוּר בַּחָכְמָה עַל כָּל־אֲשֶׁר נַעֲשָׂה תַּחַת הַשָּׁמָיִם הוּא ׀
עִנְיַן רָע נָתַן אֱלֹהִים לִבְנֵי הָאָדָם לַעֲנוֹת בּוֹ: יד רָאִיתִי אֶת־כָּל־הַמַּעֲשִׂים
שֶׁנַּעֲשׂוּ תַּחַת הַשָּׁמֶשׁ וְהִנֵּה הַכֹּל הֶבֶל וּרְעוּת רוּחַ: טו מְעֻוָּת לֹא־יוּכַל
לִתְקֹן וְחֶסְרוֹן לֹא־יוּכַל לְהִמָּנוֹת: טז דִּבַּרְתִּי אֲנִי עִם־לִבִּי לֵאמֹר אֲנִי הִנֵּה
הִגְדַּלְתִּי וְהוֹסַפְתִּי חָכְמָה עַל כָּל־אֲשֶׁר־הָיָה לְפָנַי עַל־יְרוּשָׁלִָם וְלִבִּי
רָאָה הַרְבֵּה חָכְמָה וָדָעַת: יז וָאֶתְּנָה לִבִּי לָדַעַת חָכְמָה וְדַעַת הוֹלֵלוֹת
וְשִׂכְלוּת יָדַעְתִּי שֶׁגַּם־זֶה הוּא רַעְיוֹן רוּחַ: יח כִּי בְּרֹב חָכְמָה רָב־כָּעַס
וְיוֹסִיף דַּעַת יוֹסִיף מַכְאוֹב:

פרק ב

א אָמַרְתִּי אֲנִי בְּלִבִּי לְכָה־נָּא אֲנַסְּכָה בְשִׂמְחָה וּרְאֵה בְטוֹב וְהִנֵּה גַם־הוּא
הָבֶל: ב לִשְׂחוֹק אָמַרְתִּי מְהוֹלָל וּלְשִׂמְחָה מַה־זֹּה עֹשָׂה: ג תַּרְתִּי בְלִבִּי
לִמְשׁוֹךְ בַּיַּיִן אֶת־בְּשָׂרִי וְלִבִּי נֹהֵג בַּחָכְמָה וְלֶאֱחֹז בְּסִכְלוּת עַד אֲשֶׁר־
אֶרְאֶה אֵי־זֶה טוֹב לִבְנֵי הָאָדָם אֲשֶׁר יַעֲשׂוּ תַּחַת הַשָּׁמַיִם מִסְפַּר יְמֵי
חַיֵּיהֶם: ד הִגְדַּלְתִּי מַעֲשָׂי בָּנִיתִי לִי בָּתִּים נָטַעְתִּי לִי כְּרָמִים: ה עָשִׂיתִי לִי

---

time. Therefore, when any generation witnesses an unusual phenomenon and takes it as 'new', they are mistaken; it is new only to them.

11. וְגַם לָאַחֲרֹנִים שֶׁיִּהְיוּ – *So too the latter ones that are yet to be.* Those who live after us will not be remembered by the generations that succeed them (*Rashi*).

Therefore, whatever 'profit' [verse 3] transient man thinks he has gained from his toil beneath the sun is only of temporal value and is in reality vanity and worthless (*Akeidas Yitzchak*).

15. לֹא יוּכַל לִתְקֹן – *Can not be made straight.* The Rabbis [*Chagigah* 9a] interpret this phrase as referring to the case of one who had illicit relations and begat a *mamzer.* The result of his sin lives on, unlike one who steals and can always return the theft. Alternately, the verse refers to a sage who abandoned the Torah — from a good beginning he became *'crooked'* (*Rashi*).

וְחֶסְרוֹן לֹא יוּכַל לְהִמָּנוֹת – *And what is not there cannot be numbered.* This refers to the case of one whose comrades formed a group to perform a *mitzvah* and he absented himself; once the *mitzvah* is performed he can not count himself among them to share their reward (*Rashi; Berachos* 26a).

18. כִּי בְּרֹב חָכְמָה רָב כָּעַס – *For with much wisdom comes much grief* [lit. *'anger'*]. *Rashi* explains that Solomon had always relied heavily on his exceptional wisdom to protect him from sin. He was confident that his amassing of horses would *not* cause the people to return to Egypt and that his many wives would *not* lead him astray as the Torah warns [comp. *Deut.* 17:16, 17]. But in the final analysis it is recorded of him (*I Kings* 11:3) *'and his wives turned away his heart'.* When one relies too much on his own wisdom and does not avoid prohibitions — *much grief comes to the Holy One blessed is He.* [Rashi thus interprets *God* as the subject of grief in this verse.]

A wise man perceives more than the ignorant man, and is more affected by it (*Lekach Tov*).

וְיוֹסִיף דַּעַת יוֹסִיף מַכְאוֹב – *And he who increases knowledge increases pain.* Similarly, the extra awareness caused by increased knowledge — of the futility of mankind's strivings — will only increase the wise man's pain at this realization (*Metzudos David*).

[Solomon is not advocating that 'ignorance is bliss'. He is acknowledging that the accumulation of רֹב חָכְמָה, *much* wisdom, is the main source of unhappiness (see verse 16). As the *Kotzker Rabbi* said, *'For with much wisdom comes much grief* — וְאַף עַל פִּי כֵן, but nevertheless, it is still man's obligation to acquire wisdom!']

CHAPTER TWO

1. אָמַרְתִּי אֲנִי בְּלִבִּי – *I [therefore] said to myself.* Having achieved little lasting satisfaction with

whatever has been done is what will be done. There is nothing new beneath the sun! 10 *Sometimes there is something of which one says: 'Look, this is new!' — It has already existed in the ages before us.* 11 *As there is no recollection of the former ones; so too, of the latter ones that are yet to be, there will be no recollection among those of a still later time.*

12 *I, Koheles, was King over Israel in Jerusalem.* 13 *I applied my mind to seek and probe by wisdom all that happens beneath the sky — it is a sorry task that God has given to the sons of man with which to be concerned.* 14 *I have seen all the deeds done beneath the sun, and behold all is futile and a vexation of the spirit.* 15 *A twisted thing can not be made straight; and what is not there cannot be numbered.*

16 *I said to myself: Here I have acquired great wisdom, more than any of my predecessors over Jerusalem, and my mind has had much experience with wisdom and knowledge.* 17 *I applied my mind to know wisdom and to know madness and folly. I perceived that this, too, is a vexation of the spirit.* 18 *For with much wisdom comes much grief, and he who increases knowledge increases pain.*

CHAPTER TWO

1 *I said to myself: Come, I will experiment with joy and enjoy pleasure. That, too, turned out to be futile.* 2 *I said of laughter, 'It is mad!' And of joy, 'what does it accomplish!'*

3 *I ventured to stimulate my body with wine — while my heart is involved with wisdom — and to grasp folly, until I can discern which is best for mankind to do under the heavens during the brief span of their lives.* 4 *I acted in grand style: I built myself houses, I planted vineyards;* 5 *I made for myself*

---

his previous pursuits, Solomon seeks new areas of experimentation.

וְהִנֵּה גַם הוּא הָבֶל – *That, too, turned out to be futile.* Because I saw prophetically that much evil is caused by light-hearted frivolity (*Rashi*); i.e., this obsession with worldly pleasure is itself futility (*Sforno; Metzudas David*).

2. לִשְׂחוֹק אָמַרְתִּי מְהוֹלָל – *I said of laughter, 'It is mad!'* i.e., I said of laughter born of joy that it is madness (*Metzudas David*); and it does not lead to worthwhile objectives (*Sforno*).

The *Talmud* relates the word to מְהוֹלָל, *praiseworthy,* and translates: *I said of laughter it is praiseworthy* — this refers to the mirth with which the Holy One, blessed is He, rejoices with the righteous in the World to Come. (*Shabbos* 30b).

וּלְשִׂמְחָה מַה זֹּה עֹשָׂה – *And of joy, 'What does it accomplish?' Taalumos Chachmah* comments that Solomon says: 'I never understood what harm could come from joy — until I indulged in it and found myself succumbing to temptations induced by light-headedness.'

The *Talmud* comments that joy is useless only if it is שִׂמְחָה שֶׁאֵינָהּ שֶׁל מִצְוָה, *joy not connected with a mitzvah.* This teaches that the *Shechinah* [Divine Presence] does not rest upon man through gloom, nor through sloth, nor through frivolity, nor through levity, nor through talk nor through vain pursuits, אֶלָּא מִתּוֹךְ דְּבַר שִׂמְחָה שֶׁל מִצְוָה, only as a result of a matter of joy connected with a mitzvah (*Shabbos* 30b).

3. תַּרְתִּי בְלִבִּי – *I ventured.* [lit., *'I probed my heart'* (as in 1:13 וְלָתוּר בַּחָכְמָה, *'and to probe wisdom'*)], i.e., I resolved to attempt to have everything: merry-making, wisdom, and folly, and to stimulate and pamper my flesh by imbibing wine (*Rashi*).

Having found pure wisdom a source of pain [1:18] and merriment futile [2:1], he resolves to explore a life of pleasure yet not remain neglectful of wisdom (*Ibn Ezra*).

וְלֶאֱחֹז בְּסִכְלוּת – *And to grasp folly,* i.e., the commandments of God that the heathens ridiculed as 'folly,' such as the prohibition against mixtures of wool and linen, and other Divine decrees for which we are not given a reason. Comp. 7:18 (*Rashi*).

Metzudas David explains 'folly' in this case as referring to the externalities that entice man: fine houses, musical instruments, etc. Since they do not enter the body [i.e., the body receives no direct nourishment from them], they are called *'folly'*.

4. In order to accomplish the experiment outlined in verses 1-3, Solomon not only 'lived like a king', he even exceeded the normal self-indulgence of royalty, as the following verses relate. [He bemoans the outcome in verse 11.]

גַּנּ֖וֹת וּפַרְדֵּסִ֑ים וְנָטַ֥עְתִּי בָהֶ֖ם עֵ֥ץ כָּל־פֶּֽרִי׃ ו עָשִׂ֥יתִי לִ֖י בְּרֵכ֣וֹת מָ֑יִם
לְהַשְׁק֣וֹת מֵהֶ֔ם יַ֖עַר צוֹמֵ֥חַ עֵצִֽים׃ ז קָנִ֙יתִי֙ עֲבָדִ֣ים וּשְׁפָח֔וֹת וּבְנֵי־בַ֖יִת
הָ֣יָה לִ֑י גַּ֣ם מִקְנֶה֩ בָקָ֨ר וָצֹ֤אן הַרְבֵּה֙ הָ֣יָה לִ֔י מִכֹּ֥ל שֶׁהָי֖וּ לְפָנַ֥י בִּירוּשָׁלִָֽם׃
ח כָּנַ֤סְתִּי לִי֙ גַּם־כֶּ֣סֶף וְזָהָ֔ב וּסְגֻלַּ֥ת מְלָכִ֖ים וְהַמְּדִינ֑וֹת עָשִׂ֨יתִי לִ֜י שָׁרִ֣ים
וְשָׁר֗וֹת וְתַעֲנֻג֛וֹת בְּנֵ֥י הָאָדָ֖ם שִׁדָּ֥ה וְשִׁדּֽוֹת׃ ט וְגָדַ֣לְתִּי וְהוֹסַ֔פְתִּי מִכֹּ֥ל
שֶׁהָיָ֖ה לְפָנַ֣י בִּירוּשָׁלִָ֑ם אַ֥ף חָכְמָתִ֖י עָ֥מְדָה לִּֽי׃ י וְכֹל֙ אֲשֶׁ֣ר שָׁאֲל֣וּ עֵינַ֔י לֹ֥א
אָצַ֖לְתִּי מֵהֶ֑ם לֹֽא־מָנַ֨עְתִּי אֶת־לִבִּ֜י מִכָּל־שִׂמְחָ֗ה כִּֽי־לִבִּ֤י שָׂמֵ֙חַ֙ מִכָּל־
עֲמָלִ֔י וְזֶה־הָיָ֥ה חֶלְקִ֖י מִכָּל־עֲמָלִֽי׃ יא וּפָנִ֣יתִֽי אֲנִ֗י בְּכָל־מַֽעֲשַׂי֙ שֶׁעָשׂ֣וּ יָדַ֔י
וּבֶֽעָמָ֖ל שֶׁעָמַ֣לְתִּי לַעֲשׂ֑וֹת וְהִנֵּ֨ה הַכֹּ֥ל הֶ֙בֶל֙ וּרְע֣וּת ר֔וּחַ וְאֵ֥ין יִתְר֖וֹן תַּ֥חַת
הַשָּֽׁמֶשׁ׃ יב וּפָנִ֤יתִֽי אֲנִי֙ לִרְא֣וֹת חָכְמָ֔ה וְהוֹלֵל֖וֹת וְסִכְל֑וּת כִּ֣י ׀ מֶ֣ה הָאָדָ֗ם
שֶׁיָּבוֹא֙ אַחֲרֵ֣י הַמֶּ֔לֶךְ אֵ֥ת אֲשֶׁר־כְּבָ֖ר עָשֽׂוּהוּ׃ יג וְרָאִ֣יתִֽי אָ֔נִי שֶׁיֵּ֥שׁ יִתְר֛וֹן
לַֽחָכְמָ֖ה מִן־הַסִּכְל֑וּת כִּֽיתְר֥וֹן הָא֖וֹר מִן־הַחֹֽשֶׁךְ׃ יד הֶֽחָכָם֙ עֵינָ֣יו בְּרֹאשׁ֔וֹ
וְהַכְּסִ֖יל בַּחֹ֣שֶׁךְ הוֹלֵ֑ךְ וְיָדַ֤עְתִּֽי גַם־אָ֔נִי שֶׁמִּקְרֶ֥ה אֶחָ֖ד יִקְרֶ֥ה אֶת־כֻּלָּֽם׃
טו וְאָמַ֨רְתִּי אֲנִ֜י בְּלִבִּ֗י כְּמִקְרֵ֤ה הַכְּסִיל֙ גַּם־אֲנִ֣י יִקְרֵ֔נִי וְלָ֧מָּה חָכַ֛מְתִּי אֲנִ֖י
אָ֣ז יֹתֵ֑ר וְדִבַּ֣רְתִּי בְלִבִּ֔י שֶׁגַּם־זֶ֖ה הָֽבֶל׃ טז כִּי֩ אֵ֨ין זִכְר֧וֹן לֶחָכָ֛ם עִֽם־
הַכְּסִ֖יל לְעוֹלָ֑ם בְּשֶׁכְּבָ֞ר הַיָּמִ֤ים הַבָּאִים֙ הַכֹּ֣ל נִשְׁכָּ֔ח וְאֵ֥יךְ יָמ֛וּת הֶחָכָ֖ם
עִֽם־הַכְּסִֽיל׃ יז וְשָׂנֵ֙אתִי֙ אֶת־הַֽחַיִּ֔ים כִּ֚י רַ֣ע עָלַ֔י הַֽמַּעֲשֶׂ֖ה שֶׁנַּעֲשָׂ֣ה תַּ֣חַת
הַשָּׁ֑מֶשׁ כִּֽי־הַכֹּ֥ל הֶ֖בֶל וּרְע֥וּת רֽוּחַ׃ יח וְשָׂנֵ֤אתִֽי אֲנִי֙ אֶת־כָּל־עֲמָלִ֔י שֶׁאֲנִ֥י
עָמֵ֖ל תַּ֣חַת הַשָּׁ֑מֶשׁ שֶׁאַנִּיחֶ֕נּוּ לָאָדָ֖ם שֶׁיִּהְיֶ֥ה אַחֲרָֽי׃ יט וּמִ֣י יוֹדֵ֗עַ הֶחָכָ֤ם יִֽהְיֶה֙
א֣וֹ סָכָ֔ל וְיִשְׁלַט֙ בְּכָל־עֲמָלִ֔י שֶׁעָמַ֥לְתִּי וְשֶׁחָכַ֖מְתִּי תַּ֣חַת הַשָּׁ֑מֶשׁ גַּם־זֶ֖ה
הָֽבֶל׃ כ וְסַבּ֥וֹתִֽי אֲנִ֖י לְיַאֵ֣שׁ אֶת־לִבִּ֑י עַ֚ל כָּל־הֶ֣עָמָ֔ל שֶׁעָמַ֖לְתִּי
תַּ֥חַת הַשָּֽׁמֶשׁ׃ כא כִּי־יֵ֣שׁ אָדָ֗ם שֶׁעֲמָל֛וֹ בְּחָכְמָ֥ה וּבְדַ֖עַת וּבְכִשְׁר֑וֹן וּלְאָדָ֞ם
שֶׁלֹּ֤א עָֽמַל־בּוֹ֙ יִתְּנֶ֣נּוּ חֶלְק֔וֹ גַּם־זֶ֥ה הֶ֖בֶל וְרָעָ֥ה רַבָּֽה׃ כב כִּ֤י מֶֽה־הֹוֶה֙
לָֽאָדָם֙ בְּכָל־עֲמָל֔וֹ וּבְרַעְי֖וֹן לִבּ֑וֹ שְׁה֥וּא עָמֵ֖ל תַּ֥חַת הַשָּֽׁמֶשׁ׃ כג כִּ֧י כָל־
יָמָ֣יו מַכְאֹבִ֗ים וָכַ֙עַס֙ עִנְיָנ֔וֹ גַּם־בַּלַּ֖יְלָה לֹא־שָׁכַ֣ב לִבּ֑וֹ גַּם־זֶ֖ה הֶ֥בֶל הֽוּא׃

---

10. [Determined to ensure the success of the experiment, Koheles catered to his every whim and desire, denying himself nothing.]

וְזֶה הָיָה חֶלְקִי מִכָּל עֲמָלִי – *And this was my reward for all my endeavors.* All these efforts yielded me nothing more than this (*Rashi*); i.e., this fleeting satisfaction, alone, was my only reward for all my endeavors (*Ibn Ezra*).

11. וְאֵין יִתְרוֹן תַּחַת הַשָּׁמֶשׁ – *And there is no real profit under the sun.* None of my endeavors was capable of yielding benefit *in this world beneath the sun* (*Metzudas David*). [The *Mishnah* in *Peah* lists good deeds for which there is some reward in This World, but in all cases the primary reward is bestowed in the World to Come.]

12. [Having realized the futility of all the above, Solomon sets out to establish whether there is an advantage to wisdom over folly and madness, and, as *Rashi* interprets, to contemplate the Torah and perceive madness and folly, i.e., the punishment of sins.]

כִּי מֶה הָאָדָם שֶׁיָּבוֹא אַחֲרֵי הַמֶּלֶךְ – *For what can man who comes after the king do?* Since God has created *folly,* how can man presume to detest it seeing that it already exists. Would, then, God have created it for naught? *(Metzudas David).*

What more could anyone hope to accomplish than the king has already done? (*Ibn Ezra*). [I.e., since the king is best equipped to institute the comparison between wisdom and folly on the basis of personal experience, there is no need for anyone to follow him and repeat the experiment.]

13. One can perceive the advantage of wisdom only by comparison with folly, just as one can

gardens and orchards and planted in them every kind of fruit tree; 6 I constructed pools from which to irrigate a grove of young trees; 7 I bought slaves — male and female — and I acquired stewards; I also owned more possessions, both cattle and sheep, than all of my predecessors in Jerusalem; 8 I amassed even silver and gold for myself, and the treasure of kings and the provinces; I provided myself with various musical instruments, and with every human luxury — chests and chests of them. 9 Thus, I grew and surpassed any of my predecessors in Jerusalem; still, my wisdom stayed with me. 10 Whatever my eyes desired I did not deny them; I did not deprive myself of any kind of joy. Indeed, my heart drew joy from all my activities, and this was my reward for all my endeavors.

11 Then I looked at all the things that I had done and the energy I had expended in doing them; it was clear that it was all futile and a vexation of the spirit — and there is no real profit under the sun.

12 Then I turned my attention to appraising wisdom with madness and folly — for what can man who comes after the king do? It has already been done. 13 And I perceived that wisdom excels folly as light excels darkness. 14 The wise man has his eyes in his head, whereas a fool walks in darkness. But I also realized that the same fate awaits them all. 15 So I said to myself: The fate of the fool will befall me also; to what advantage, then, have I become wise? But I concluded that this, too, was futility, 16 for there is no comparison between the remembrance of the wise man and of the fool at all, for as the succeeding days roll by, is all forgotten? How can the wise man die like the fool?

17 So I hated life, for I was depressed by all that goes on under the sun, because everything is futile and a vexation of the spirit.

18 Thus I hated all my achievements laboring under the sun, for I must leave it to the man who succeeds me. 19 — and who knows whether he will be wise or foolish? — and he will control of all my possessions for which I toiled and have shown myself wise beneath the sun. This, too, is futility. 20 So I turned my heart to despair of all that I had achieved by laboring under the sun, 21 for there is a man who labored with wisdom, knowledge and skill, yet he must hand on his portion to one who has not toiled for it. This, too, is futility and a great evil. 22 For what has a man of all his toil and his stress in which he labors beneath the sun? 23 For all his days are painful, and his business is a vexation; even at night his mind has no rest. This, too, is futility!

---

appreciate light only by comparison with darkness.

14. Solomon now elaborates on the factors that distinguish the sage from the fool.

בְּרֹאשׁוֹ – *In his head.* The wise man realizes that God put eyes high up on his body so he could see far and study his route well in advance. Figuratively, the wise man looks ahead to chart the proper course for himself (*Metzudas David*).

וְיָדַעְתִּי גַם אָנִי . . . אֶת כֻּלָּם – *But I also realized . . . them all.* Even though I praise the superiority of the wise man over the fool, nevertheless, I cannot overlook the fact that death will overtake אֶת כֻּלָּם, *them all,* i.e., the wise man and fool equally (*Rashi*).

16. The remembrance of a wise man is praised but that of the fool is degraded (*Metzudas David*) [as Solomon declared in *Proverbs* 10:7: '*The memory of the righteous is for a blessing, but the name of the wicked shall rot*'].

וְאֵיךְ יָמוּת הֶחָכָם עִם הַכְּסִיל – *How can the wise man die like the fool?* How can one even suggest that the deaths of the wise man and fool are similar! [The former's fame lives; the latter leaves nothing worth remembering.] (*Metzudas David; Alshich*)

18-23. Koheles is further distressed by the fact that even the fruits of man's strenuous *physical* efforts to accumulate wealth will ultimately go to heirs, whose prudence and wisdom are questionable.

כד אֵין־טוֹב בָּאָדָם שֶׁיֹּאכַל וְשָׁתָה וְהֶרְאָה אֶת־נַפְשׁוֹ טוֹב בַּעֲמָלוֹ גַּם־זֹה
רָאִיתִי אָנִי כִּי מִיַּד הָאֱלֹהִים הִיא׃ כה כִּי מִי יֹאכַל וּמִי יָחוּשׁ חוּץ מִמֶּנִּי׃
כו כִּי לְאָדָם שֶׁטּוֹב לְפָנָיו נָתַן חָכְמָה וְדַעַת וְשִׂמְחָה וְלַחוֹטֶא נָתַן עִנְיָן
לֶאֱסֹף וְלִכְנוֹס לָתֵת לְטוֹב לִפְנֵי הָאֱלֹהִים גַּם־זֶה הֶבֶל וּרְעוּת רוּחַ׃

פרק ג

א לַכֹּל זְמָן וְעֵת לְכָל־חֵפֶץ תַּחַת הַשָּׁמָיִם׃
ב עֵת לָלֶדֶת וְעֵת לָמוּת עֵת לָטַעַת וְעֵת לַעֲקוֹר נָטוּעַ׃
ג עֵת לַהֲרוֹג וְעֵת לִרְפּוֹא עֵת לִפְרוֹץ וְעֵת לִבְנוֹת׃
ד עֵת לִבְכּוֹת וְעֵת לִשְׂחוֹק עֵת סְפוֹד וְעֵת רְקוֹד׃
ה עֵת לְהַשְׁלִיךְ אֲבָנִים וְעֵת כְּנוֹס אֲבָנִים עֵת לַחֲבוֹק וְעֵת לִרְחֹק מֵחַבֵּק׃
ו עֵת לְבַקֵּשׁ וְעֵת לְאַבֵּד עֵת לִשְׁמוֹר וְעֵת לְהַשְׁלִיךְ׃
ז עֵת לִקְרוֹעַ וְעֵת לִתְפּוֹר עֵת לַחֲשׁוֹת וְעֵת לְדַבֵּר׃
ח עֵת לֶאֱהֹב וְעֵת לִשְׂנֹא עֵת מִלְחָמָה וְעֵת שָׁלוֹם׃
ט מַה־יִּתְרוֹן הָעוֹשֶׂה בַּאֲשֶׁר הוּא עָמֵל׃ י רָאִיתִי אֶת־הָעִנְיָן אֲשֶׁר נָתַן
אֱלֹהִים לִבְנֵי הָאָדָם לַעֲנוֹת בּוֹ׃ יא אֶת־הַכֹּל עָשָׂה יָפֶה בְעִתּוֹ גַּם אֶת־
הָעֹלָם נָתַן בְּלִבָּם מִבְּלִי אֲשֶׁר לֹא־יִמְצָא הָאָדָם אֶת־הַמַּעֲשֶׂה אֲשֶׁר־עָשָׂה
הָאֱלֹהִים מֵרֹאשׁ וְעַד־סוֹף׃ יב יָדַעְתִּי כִּי אֵין טוֹב בָּם כִּי אִם־לִשְׂמוֹחַ

---

24. אֵין טוֹב בָּאָדָם שֶׁיֹּאכַל וְשָׁתָה . . . — *Is it not good for man that he eats and drinks.* This translation follows *Rashi* who understands the phrase interrogatively, and according to whom the verse continues: 'and guides his soul to perform righteousness and charity with this food and drink?'

כִּי מִיַּד הָאֱלֹהִים הִיא — *That . . . is from the hand of God.* I perceived that he who accumulates wealth must view himself only as its guardian, who does not have permission to dispense it without Divine sanction. [Man must act only according to the ideals of charity and justice, because his wealth is not simply the result of his labor; it is a gift of God (*Kol Yaakov*).]

25. [This verse apparently modifies the previous one: If all my property will eventually pass on to strangers, is it not right that I should view my possessions as a Divine gift and perform lofty spiritual deeds with them while I am still alive? Why should only others benefit from my wealth (next verse)? This is all part of God's Master Plan.]

26. גַּם־זֶה הֶבֶל — *That, too, is futility.* Since God will, in any event, transfer the wealth to whomever pleases Him, it is futile to strive madly for its accumulation (*Ibn Ezra*).

CHAPTER THREE

1-15. Solomon elaborates on a theme that recurs throughout the Book: *'What profit does man have for all his labor which he toils beneath the sun'* — the sun symbolizes time which is governed by the rising and setting sun (see 1:3). Man has no power over the laws which control the world. Moreover, he cannot fathom God's scheme for the world, nor can he change the fixed order of natural phenomena. He can only live in awe of time, witnessing the endless procession of events following one another in an unbroken circle.

2. וְעֵת לָמוּת — *And a time to die.* The Midrash notes: Is then all the wisdom which Solomon uttered simply that there is *'A time to be born and a time to die?'* Rather, the meaning is: Happy is the man whose hour of death is like the hour of his birth; just as he was pure in the hour of his birth, so should he be pure in the hour of his death.

3. עֵת לַהֲרוֹג — *A time to kill.* The reference is to killing in war time (*Midrash*), or according to some, to the legal execution of criminals (*Michlol Yofi*).

4. עֵת לִבְכּוֹת — *A time to weep.* Tishah b'Av (*Rashi*).

וְעֵת לִשְׂחוֹק — *And a time to laugh* — in the time to come [when Israel is redeemed] as it is written (*Psalms* 126:2): אָז יִמָּלֵא שְׂחוֹק פִּינוּ, *Then our mouth will be filled with laughter* (*Midrash; Lekach Tov*).

5. עֵת לְהַשְׁלִיךְ אֲבָנִים — *A time to scatter stones. Midrash Lekach Tov* explains this as prophetic reference to the Destruction of the Temple, and

[24] *Is it not good for man that he eats and drinks and shows his soul satisfaction in his labor? And even that, I perceived, is from the hand of God. —*
[25] *For who should eat and who should make haste except me? —* [26]*To the man who pleases Him He has given wisdom, knowledge and joy; but to the sinner He has given the urge to gather and amass — that he may hand it on to one who is pleasing to God. That, too, is futility and a vexation of the spirit.*

CHAPTER THREE

[1]*Everything has its season, and there is a time for everything under the heaven:*
[2] *A time to be born — and a time to die;*
a time to plant — and a time to uproot the planted.
[3] *A time to kill — and a time to heal;*
a time to wreck — and a time to build.
[4] *A time to weep — and a time to laugh;*
a time to wail — and a time to dance.
[5] *A time to scatter stones — and a time to gather stones;*
a time to embrace — and a time to shun embraces.
[6] *A time to seek — and a time to lose;*
a time to keep — and a time to discard.
[7] *A time to rend — and a time to mend;*
a time to be silent — and a time to speak.
[8] *A time to love — and a time to hate;*
a time for war — and a time for peace.
[9] *What gain, then, has the worker by his toil?*
[10] *I have observed the task which God has given the sons of man to be*
concerned with: [11] *He made everything beautiful in its time; He has also put an enigma into their minds so that man cannot comprehend what God has done from beginning to end.*
[12] *Thus I perceived that there is nothing better for them than to rejoice and do*

---

to the ultimate Rebuilding.

7. עֵת לִקְרוֹעַ — *A time to rend* — garments over the dead; וְעֵת לִתְפּוֹר, *and a time to mend* — new clothes for a wedding (*R' Saadiah Gaon*).

8. עֵת לֶאֱהֹב וְעֵת לִשְׂנֹא — *A time to love and a time to hate.* Even *love/hate* is regulated by time (*Ibn Ezra*); one may love something today and detest that same object tomorrow (*Metzudas David*).

9. מַה יִּתְרוֹן — *What gain, then, has the worker?* Since all is governed by seasons and time — over which man has no control — what hope is there for him to retain mastery over his efforts? (*Ibn Ezra*) The *'time'* of the evildoer will come and all his ill-gotten gains will be forfeited (*Rashi*). [Solomon is not simply speaking rhetorically. Having himself amassed fortunes (2:4-11) and having concluded it was all *'futility'*, he includes his *personal* experiences in this query.]

10. לַעֲנוֹת בּוֹ — *To be concerned with.* [See 1:3.] *Sforno* translates: *'to be afflicted with'*: I perceive that God caused man to toil in order to keep him subservient lest he rebel against Him, as did Adam.

11. גַּם אֶת־הָעֹלָם נָתַן בְּלִבָּם — *He has also put an enigma into their minds.* This translation follows *Rashi:* Although God instilled worldly wisdom into the hearts of man, He did not instill all wisdom into all men. Rather, He dispensed small amounts to each person so no one would grasp fully the workings of God, or foresee the future. This is to ensure that, not knowing when they will die or what would befall them, people will indulge in repentance.

Therefore, continues Rashi: הָעֹלָם is spelled without a *vav*, so the word can be read as meaning הֶעֱלֵם, *hidden*, for if man knew that his day of death was near, he would neither build a house nor plant a vineyard. Thus Solomon exclaims that 'it is a good thing that . . . God has kept things hidden from man.'

מֵרֹאשׁ וְעַד־סוֹף — *From beginning to end*, i.e., the full plan and purpose of God.

12. בָּם — *For them*, i.e., for mankind. 'Since [as mentioned in the previous verse] people's 'time of remembrance' [i.e., day of death] is hidden, there is nothing better for them than to rejoice in their lot and do what is right in God's eyes while they are yet alive' (*Rashi*).

וְלַעֲשׂ֥וֹת ט֖וֹב בְּחַיָּֽיו׃ יג וְגַ֤ם כָּל־הָֽאָדָם֙ שֶׁיֹּאכַ֣ל וְשָׁתָ֔ה וְרָאָ֥ה ט֖וֹב
בְּכָל־עֲמָל֑וֹ מַתַּ֥ת אֱלֹהִ֖ים הִֽיא׃ יד יָדַ֗עְתִּי כִּ֣י כָּל־אֲשֶׁ֤ר יַעֲשֶׂה֙ הָֽאֱלֹהִ֔ים
ה֚וּא יִהְיֶ֣ה לְעוֹלָ֔ם עָלָיו֙ אֵ֣ין לְהוֹסִ֔יף וּמִמֶּ֖נּוּ אֵ֣ין לִגְרֹ֑עַ וְהָאֱלֹהִ֣ים עָשָׂ֔ה
שֶׁיִּֽרְא֖וּ מִלְּפָנָֽיו׃ טו מַה־שֶּֽׁהָיָה֙ כְּבָ֣ר ה֔וּא וַאֲשֶׁ֥ר לִהְי֖וֹת כְּבָ֣ר הָיָ֑ה וְהָאֱלֹהִ֖ים
יְבַקֵּ֥שׁ אֶת־נִרְדָּֽף׃ טז וְעוֹד֙ רָאִ֔יתִי תַּ֖חַת הַשָּׁ֑מֶשׁ מְק֤וֹם הַמִּשְׁפָּט֙ שָׁ֣מָּה
הָרֶ֔שַׁע וּמְק֥וֹם הַצֶּ֖דֶק שָׁ֥מָּה הָרָֽשַׁע׃ יז אָמַ֤רְתִּֽי אֲנִי֙ בְּלִבִּ֔י אֶת־הַצַּדִּיק֙
וְאֶת־הָ֣רָשָׁ֔ע יִשְׁפֹּ֖ט הָאֱלֹהִ֑ים כִּי־עֵ֣ת לְכָל־חֵ֔פֶץ וְעַ֥ל כָּל־הַֽמַּעֲשֶׂ֖ה שָֽׁם׃
יח אָמַ֤רְתִּֽי אֲנִי֙ בְּלִבִּ֔י עַל־דִּבְרַת֙ בְּנֵ֣י הָאָדָ֔ם לְבָרָ֖ם הָאֱלֹהִ֑ים וְלִרְא֕וֹת
שְׁהֶם־בְּהֵמָ֥ה הֵ֖מָּה לָהֶֽם׃ יט כִּי֩ מִקְרֶ֨ה בְנֵֽי־הָאָדָ֜ם וּמִקְרֶ֣ה הַבְּהֵמָ֗ה וּמִקְרֶ֤ה
אֶחָד֙ לָהֶ֔ם כְּמ֥וֹת זֶה֙ כֵּ֣ן מ֣וֹת זֶ֔ה וְר֥וּחַ אֶחָ֖ד לַכֹּ֑ל וּמוֹתַ֨ר הָאָדָ֤ם מִן־הַבְּהֵמָה֙
אָ֔יִן כִּ֥י הַכֹּ֖ל הָֽבֶל׃ כ הַכֹּ֥ל הוֹלֵ֖ךְ אֶל־מָק֣וֹם אֶחָ֑ד הַכֹּל֙ הָיָ֣ה מִן־הֶֽעָפָ֔ר וְהַכֹּ֖ל
שָׁ֥ב אֶל־הֶעָפָֽר׃ כא מִ֣י יוֹדֵ֗עַ ר֚וּחַ בְּנֵ֣י הָֽאָדָ֔ם הָעֹלָ֥ה הִ֖יא לְמָ֑עְלָה וְר֙וּחַ֙
הַבְּהֵמָ֔ה הַיֹּרֶ֥דֶת הִ֖יא לְמַ֥טָּה לָאָֽרֶץ׃ כב וְרָאִ֗יתִי כִּ֣י אֵ֥ין טוֹב֙ מֵאֲשֶׁ֨ר יִשְׂמַ֤ח
הָֽאָדָם֙ בְּמַ֣עֲשָׂ֔יו כִּי־ה֖וּא חֶלְק֑וֹ כִּ֣י מִ֤י יְבִיאֶ֙נּוּ֙ לִרְא֔וֹת בְּמֶ֖ה שֶׁיִּהְיֶ֥ה אַחֲרָֽיו׃

פרק ד

א וְשַׁ֣בְתִּֽי אֲנִ֗י וָאֶרְאֶה֙ אֶת־כָּל־הָ֣עֲשֻׁקִ֔ים אֲשֶׁ֥ר נַעֲשִׂ֖ים תַּ֣חַת הַשָּׁ֑מֶשׁ וְהִנֵּ֣ה
דִּמְעַ֣ת הָעֲשֻׁקִ֗ים וְאֵ֤ין לָהֶם֙ מְנַחֵ֔ם וּמִיַּ֤ד עֹֽשְׁקֵיהֶם֙ כֹּ֔חַ וְאֵ֥ין לָהֶ֖ם מְנַחֵֽם׃
ב וְשַׁבֵּ֥חַ אֲנִ֛י אֶת־הַמֵּתִ֖ים שֶׁכְּבָ֣ר מֵ֑תוּ מִן־הַ֣חַיִּ֔ים אֲשֶׁ֛ר הֵ֥מָּה חַיִּ֖ים עֲדֶֽנָה׃
ג וְטוֹב֙ מִשְּׁנֵיהֶ֔ם אֵ֥ת אֲשֶׁר־עֲדֶ֖ן לֹ֣א הָיָ֑ה אֲשֶׁ֤ר לֹֽא־רָאָה֙ אֶת־הַֽמַּעֲשֶׂ֣ה
הָרָ֔ע אֲשֶׁ֥ר נַעֲשָׂ֖ה תַּ֥חַת הַשָּֽׁמֶשׁ׃ ד וְרָאִ֨יתִי אֲנִ֜י אֶת־כָּל־עָמָ֗ל וְאֵת֙
כָּל־כִּשְׁר֣וֹן הַֽמַּעֲשֶׂ֔ה כִּ֛י הִ֥יא קִנְאַת־אִ֖ישׁ מֵרֵעֵ֑הוּ גַּם־זֶ֥ה הֶ֖בֶל וּרְע֥וּת רֽוּחַ׃

In this connection, *R' David Feinstein* points out that Jeremiah [9:22-23] prophesies that man should not praise himself for wisdom, strength, or wealth; but only for understanding and knowing God. This means that man's intelligence, strength, or wealth — which are unearned gifts of God — are not praiseworthy. Only for harnessing his ability and resources and turning them toward knowledge of God — achievements that he has *earned* — man is rightly praised.

14. Unlike man's actions, which are transient and vain, God's creation is eternal, except for those changes He purposely made to instill His fear in man.

15. מַה שֶּׁהָיָה כְּבָר הוּא – *What has been, already exists,* i.e., history repeats itself.

וְהָאֱלוֹהִים יְבַקֵּשׁ אֶת־נִרְדָּף – *And God always seeks* [i.e., to be on the side of] *the pursued*, and to exact retribution from the pursuer. Therefore, of what benefit are the evil ways in which one toils? Ultimately man will be held to account for his deeds (*Rashi*).

16-22. [Koheles now enters into a discussion on corruption in the administration of justice, eventual Divine retribution against the wicked, and the seeming similarity between man and beast.]

מְקוֹם הַמִּשְׁפָּט שָׁמָּה הָרֶשַׁע – *In the place of justice there is wickedness.* In the courts of law one expects to find justice; instead he finds injustice and perversion (*Alshich; Ibn Yachya*).

17. וְעַל כָּל הַמַּעֲשֶׂה – *And for every deed* — that man does on this world, שָׁם, *there,* will he be judged (*Ibn Yachya*).

Akeidas Yitzchak discusses the question of why, if certain evil acts are pre-ordained, man is punished for committing them, when, in effect, the perpetrator is merely carrying out God's will. He cites the example of the Egyptians who were punished for enslaving the Jews although it was the Jews' lot to be enslaved. He concludes that God reckons retribution *for every deed* because human beings possess free will. Neither the Egyptians nor other evildoers were motivated by the knowledge that they were carrying out God's will. The Divine plan had no effect on their actions; they committed evil because they wanted to.

*good in his life. 13 Indeed every man who eats and drinks and finds satisfaction
in all his labor — it is a gift of God.*
*14 I realized that whatever God does will endure forever: Nothing can be
added to it and nothing can be subtracted from it, and God has acted so that
[man] should stand in awe of Him. 15 What has been, already exists, and what
is still to be, has already been, and God always seeks the pursued.*
*16 Furthermore, I have observed beneath the sun: In the place of justice there
is wickedness, and in the place of righteousness there is wickedness. 17 I mused:
God will judge the righteous and the wicked, for there is a time for everything
and for every deed, there.*
*18 Then I said to myself concerning men: 'God has chosen them out, but only
to see that they themselves are as beasts.' 19 For the fate of men and the fate of
beast — they have one and the same fate: as one dies, so dies the other, and they
all have the same spirit. Man has no superiority over beast, for all is futile. 20 All
go to the same place; all originate from dust and all return to dust. 21 Who
perceives that the spirit of man is the one that ascends on high while the spirit
of the beast is the one that descends down into the earth? 22 I therefore observed
that there is nothing better for man than to be happy in what he is doing, for
that is his lot. For who can enable him to see what will be after him?*

CHAPTER FOUR

*1 I returned and contemplated all the acts of oppression that are committed
beneath the sun: Behold! Tears of the oppressed with none to comfort them, and
their oppressors have the power — with none to comfort them. 2 So I consider
more fortunate the dead who have already died, than the living who are still
alive; 3 but better than either of them is he who has not yet been, and has never
witnessed the evil that is committed beneath the sun.*
*4 And I saw that all labor and all skillful enterprise spring from man's
rivalry with his neighbor. This, too, is futility and a vexation of the spirit!*

---

18. שֶׁהֶם־בְּהֵמָה הֵמָּה לָהֶם – *That they themselves are as beasts.* [This is the general sense of this ambiguous phrase (lit., *'they are a beast, they are to them'*). The translation, rendering כִּבְהֵמָה as beasts, follows *Targum* and most commentators. The sense of the verse is clear. Although men are vain about their supposed superiority, God has selected the most eminent among them to demonstrate that they are not superior at all, that even kings and officers are as selfish and shortsighted as any other animal or beast.]

19. כִּי הַכֹּל הָבֶל – *For all is futile,* i.e., mankind perceives no difference between man and beast; or that the sin of Man has caused him to share the same physical death as the beast.

21. מִי יוֹדֵעַ – *Who perceives,* i.e., who is of sufficient intellect to grasp ... (*Akeidas Yitzchak*):

R' Saadiah comments that should anyone infer from these concluding verses of the chapter that Solomon truly doubts the superiority of man over beast or spirit over pleasure, his final certainty is made clear by his statement: *'And the spirit returns to God'* [12:7] and by his pronouncement: *'But know that for all these things God will bring you into judgment'* [11:9.]

הָעֹלָה הִיא לְמָעְלָה – *Is the one that ascends on high* — and, unlike the beast, must stand trial for his actions (*Rashi*).

CHAPTER FOUR

2-3. Koheles resolves, therefore, that the dead, who are no longer exposed to social injustices, are more fortunate than the living. But most fortunate of all are the unborn who were never exposed to any form of human cruelty (*R' Yosef Kara*).

4. Now Koheles turns to those whose toil is not motivated by criminal motives. He concludes that even though most people are basically sincere, they are impelled by competition, greed, and jealousy. These factors are themselves 'futility and a vexation of the spirit' (*Ibn Latif*).

כִּי הִיא קִנְאַת־אִישׁ מֵרֵעֵהוּ – *Spring from man's rivalry with his neighbor.* Everyone wants to outdo his neighbor in status, living quarters, clothing, children, food, wisdom, and reputation (*Ibn Ezra*).

ה הַכְּסִיל חֹבֵק אֶת־יָדָיו וְאֹכֵל אֶת־בְּשָׂרוֹ: ו טוֹב מְלֹא כַף נָחַת מִמְּלֹא
חָפְנַיִם עָמָל וּרְעוּת רוּחַ: ז וְשַׁבְתִּי אֲנִי וָאֶרְאֶה הֶבֶל תַּחַת הַשָּׁמֶשׁ: ח יֵשׁ
אֶחָד וְאֵין שֵׁנִי גַּם בֵּן וָאָח אֵין־לוֹ וְאֵין קֵץ לְכָל־עֲמָלוֹ גַּם־עֵינוֹ
לֹא־תִשְׂבַּע עֹשֶׁר וּלְמִי ׀ אֲנִי עָמֵל וּמְחַסֵּר אֶת־נַפְשִׁי מִטּוֹבָה גַּם־זֶה הֶבֶל
וְעִנְיַן רָע הוּא: ט טוֹבִים הַשְּׁנַיִם מִן־הָאֶחָד אֲשֶׁר יֵשׁ־לָהֶם שָׂכָר טוֹב
בַּעֲמָלָם: י כִּי אִם־יִפֹּלוּ הָאֶחָד יָקִים אֶת־חֲבֵרוֹ וְאִילוֹ הָאֶחָד שֶׁיִּפּוֹל וְאֵין
שֵׁנִי לַהֲקִימוֹ: יא גַּם אִם־יִשְׁכְּבוּ שְׁנַיִם וְחַם לָהֶם וּלְאֶחָד אֵיךְ יֵחָם:
יב וְאִם־יִתְקְפוֹ הָאֶחָד הַשְּׁנַיִם יַעַמְדוּ נֶגְדּוֹ וְהַחוּט הַמְשֻׁלָּשׁ לֹא בִמְהֵרָה
יִנָּתֵק: יג טוֹב יֶלֶד מִסְכֵּן וְחָכָם מִמֶּלֶךְ זָקֵן וּכְסִיל אֲשֶׁר לֹא־יָדַע לְהִזָּהֵר
עוֹד: יד כִּי־מִבֵּית הָסוּרִים יָצָא לִמְלֹךְ כִּי גַּם בְּמַלְכוּתוֹ נוֹלַד רָשׁ: טו רָאִיתִי
אֶת־כָּל־הַחַיִּים הַמְהַלְּכִים תַּחַת הַשָּׁמֶשׁ עִם הַיֶּלֶד הַשֵּׁנִי אֲשֶׁר יַעֲמֹד
תַּחְתָּיו: טז אֵין־קֵץ לְכָל־הָעָם לְכֹל אֲשֶׁר־הָיָה לִפְנֵיהֶם גַּם הָאַחֲרוֹנִים לֹא
יִשְׂמְחוּ־בוֹ כִּי־גַם־זֶה הֶבֶל וְרַעְיוֹן רוּחַ: יז שְׁמוֹר רַגְלְךָ כַּאֲשֶׁר תֵּלֵךְ
אֶל־בֵּית הָאֱלֹהִים וְקָרוֹב לִשְׁמֹעַ מִתֵּת הַכְּסִילִים זָבַח כִּי־אֵינָם יוֹדְעִים
לַעֲשׂוֹת רָע:

פרק ה

א אַל־תְּבַהֵל עַל־פִּיךָ וְלִבְּךָ אַל־יְמַהֵר לְהוֹצִיא דָבָר לִפְנֵי הָאֱלֹהִים
כִּי הָאֱלֹהִים בַּשָּׁמַיִם וְאַתָּה עַל־הָאָרֶץ עַל־כֵּן יִהְיוּ דְבָרֶיךָ מְעַטִּים:
ב כִּי בָּא הַחֲלוֹם בְּרֹב עִנְיָן וְקוֹל כְּסִיל בְּרֹב דְּבָרִים: ג כַּאֲשֶׁר תִּדֹּר נֶדֶר

---

5. הַכְּסִיל חֹבֵק אֶת־יָדָיו – *The fool folds* ['hugs'] *his hands.* The *fool* sits, *'with his arms folded,'* and eats what is readily available (*Ibn Ezra*).

וְאֹכֵל אֶת בְּשָׂרוֹ – *And eats his own flesh.* He destroys himself and eventually dies of starvation (*Ibn Ezra*). He allegorically 'lives off his fat' (*Metzudas David*).

6. טוֹב מְלֹא כַף נָחַת – *Better is one handful of pleasantness.* It is better for man to earn less, but with pleasantness and quiet, than to earn more — handfuls more — through difficult labor and aggravation (*Metzudas David*).

8. יֵשׁ אֶחָד וְאֵין שֵׁנִי – *A lone and solitary man.* He has no heirs (*Almosnino*).

Rashi interprets the verse [as a reference to people in varying situations who share the same flaw: they do not bring companionship into their lives]: He is utterly alone. If he is a scholar, he seeks no student to be like a son and no friend to be like a brother; if a bachelor, he seeks no wife; if an entrepreneur, no partner. He goes his way alone.

גַּם זֶה הֶבֶל – *This, too, is futility.* The indolent *'fool'* in verse 5, who folds his hands, and the miser who strives aimlessly — both are equally foolish. The proper approach is the middle path between laziness and over-aggressiveness (*R' Galico; Ibn Ezra; Metzudas David*).

9. In this verse, Koheles addresses the fool who toils utterly alone, and advises him of the advantages of companionship, someone with whom to toil and share (*Ibn Ezra*).

מִן־הָאֶחָד – *Than one.* Therefore man should find a comrade and get married (*Rashi*).

Two who study Torah are better than one who studies alone, for if one errs, his partner will correct him (*Midrash;* see also *Makkos* 10a). As the *Talmud* notes: 'Knowledge of Torah can be acquired only in association with others' (*Berachos* 63b).

10. כִּי אִם־יִפֹּלוּ – *For should they fall* — physically; or should one of them err in Torah learning or in judgment, his comrade will correct him and set him on the proper path (*R' Saadiah Gaon*).

11. Solomon cites another example of the benefits of association.

Alshich explains the verse in a spiritual sense: if two people fall into spiritual slumber and neglect their religious observances, their hearts will stir within them with the 'fire of God' and each one will 'warm the heart' of his comrade to 'awaken' and serve God in the proper manner.

12. [And the final example of mutual security:] וְהַחוּט הַמְשֻׁלָּשׁ לֹא בִמְהֵרָה יִנָּתֵק – *A three-ply*

5 The fool folds his hands and eats his own flesh. 6 Better is one handful of
pleasantness than two fistfuls of labor and vexation of the spirit.
7 Then I returned and contemplated [another] futility beneath the sun: 8 a
lone and solitary man who has neither son nor brother, yet there is no end to his
toil, nor is his eye ever sated with riches, [nor does he ask himself,] 'For whom
am I toiling and depriving myself of goodness.' This, too, is futility; indeed, it is
a sorry task.
9 Two are better than one, for they get a greater return for their labor. 10 For
should they fall, one can raise the other; but woe to him who is alone when he
falls and there is no one to raise him! 11 Also, if two sleep together they keep
warm, but how can one be warm alone? 12 Where one can be overpowered, two
can resist attack: A three-ply cord is not easily severed!
13 Better is a poor but wise youth than an old and foolish king who no longer
knows how to take care of himself; 14 because from the prison-house he emerged
to reign, while even in his reign he was born poor. 15 I saw all the living that
wander beneath the sun throng to the succeeding youth who steps into his place.
16 There is no end to the entire nation, to all that was before them; similarly the
ones that come later will not rejoice in him. For this, too, is futility and a
vexation of the spirit.
17 Guard your foot when you go to the House of God; better to draw near and
hearken than to offer the sacrifices of fools, for they do not consider that they
do evil.

CHAPTER FIVE

1 Be not rash with your mouth, and let not your heart be hasty to utter a word
before God; for God is in heaven and you are on earth, so let your words be few.
2 For a dream comes from much concern, and foolish talk from many words.

---

cord is not easily severed! If the companionship of one friend yields such benefits, (above, verse 10-11) imagine the value of *two* companions! A three-ply cord is stronger than one or two plies! [as if to say: *Two are better than one; but three are better than two.*]

Rashi refers to the Talmudic dictum [*Bava Metzia* 85a]: If someone is a scholar, and his son and grandson are scholars as well, the Torah will nevermore cease from his seed [see *Isaiah* 59:21]. These three generations of scholarship are alluded to by the strength of the *three-ply cord* in our verse. Henceforth, (*Kesubos* 62b) the Torah 'seeks its home' [i.e., the family which has been its host for three generations].

13. Solomon now proceeds to extol the reign of wisdom, but concludes that it, too, is impermanent and ultimately futile.

15-16. The structure of these two verses is difficult and ambiguous, but the theme emerges: Although droves of people flocked around this new young king, he himself ultimately fell into disfavor because popularity is short lived and is itself *futility and a vexation of the spirit.*

Solomon bemoans this series of events — commonplace even in our day, as *futility and a vexation of the spirit!*

17. Having stated the main theme of his philosophy and remonstrated against the futilities of life, *Koheles* now turns to a more optimistic series of thoughts: the proper path a man should take in this world. In the following verses he exhorts man to serve God with dignity and respect — even in such commonplace acts as walking and talking. He begins with prayer, man's most intimate form of communication with God, and concludes that hearkening to God's Word is preferable to insincere sacrifice.

CHAPTER FIVE

1. לְהוֹצִיא דָבָר לִפְנֵי הָאֱלֹהִים — *To utter a word before God,* i.e., to speak critically of Him (*Rashi*).

כִּי הָאֱלֹהִים בַּשָּׁמַיִם וְאַתָּה עַל־הָאָרֶץ — *For God is in heaven and you are on earth. Rashi* quotes the Midrash: 'If the weak one is above and the strong one below, the fear of the weak one is upon the strong one; how much more so when it is the strong One [God] Who is above and the weak one [mortal man] below [we should surely be in awe of Him and not speak rashly of Him.].'

2. כִּי בָא הַחֲלוֹם בְּרֹב עִנְיָן — *For a dream comes from much concern.* [Solomon employs the simile of dreams to lend cogency to the earlier

לֵאלֹהִים אַל־תְּאַחֵר לְשַׁלְּמוֹ כִּי אֵין חֵפֶץ בַּכְּסִילִים אֵת אֲשֶׁר־תִּדֹּר שַׁלֵּם:
ד טוֹב אֲשֶׁר לֹא־תִדֹּר מִשֶּׁתִּדּוֹר וְלֹא תְשַׁלֵּם: ה אַל־תִּתֵּן אֶת־פִּיךָ לַחֲטִיא
אֶת־בְּשָׂרֶךָ וְאַל־תֹּאמַר לִפְנֵי הַמַּלְאָךְ כִּי שְׁגָגָה הִיא לָמָּה יִקְצֹף הָאֱלֹהִים
עַל־קוֹלֶךָ וְחִבֵּל אֶת־מַעֲשֵׂה יָדֶיךָ: ו כִּי בְרֹב חֲלֹמוֹת וַהֲבָלִים וּדְבָרִים
הַרְבֵּה כִּי אֶת־הָאֱלֹהִים יְרָא: ז אִם־עֹשֶׁק רָשׁ וְגֵזֶל מִשְׁפָּט וָצֶדֶק תִּרְאֶה
בַמְּדִינָה אַל־תִּתְמַהּ עַל־הַחֵפֶץ כִּי גָבֹהַּ מֵעַל גָּבֹהַּ שֹׁמֵר וּגְבֹהִים עֲלֵיהֶם:
ח וְיִתְרוֹן אֶרֶץ בַּכֹּל הוּא מֶלֶךְ לְשָׂדֶה נֶעֱבָד: ט אֹהֵב כֶּסֶף לֹא־יִשְׂבַּע כֶּסֶף
וּמִי־אֹהֵב בֶּהָמוֹן לֹא תְבוּאָה גַּם־זֶה הָבֶל: י בִּרְבוֹת הַטּוֹבָה רַבּוּ אוֹכְלֶיהָ
וּמַה־כִּשְׁרוֹן לִבְעָלֶיהָ כִּי אִם־רְאוּת עֵינָיו: יא מְתוּקָה שְׁנַת הָעֹבֵד אִם־
מְעַט וְאִם־הַרְבֵּה יֹאכֵל וְהַשָּׂבָע לֶעָשִׁיר אֵינֶנּוּ מַנִּיחַ לוֹ לִישׁוֹן: יב יֵשׁ רָעָה
חוֹלָה רָאִיתִי תַּחַת הַשָּׁמֶשׁ עֹשֶׁר שָׁמוּר לִבְעָלָיו לְרָעָתוֹ: יג וְאָבַד הָעֹשֶׁר
הַהוּא בְּעִנְיַן רָע וְהוֹלִיד בֵּן וְאֵין בְּיָדוֹ מְאוּמָה: יד כַּאֲשֶׁר יָצָא מִבֶּטֶן אִמּוֹ
עָרוֹם יָשׁוּב לָלֶכֶת כְּשֶׁבָּא וּמְאוּמָה לֹא־יִשָּׂא בַעֲמָלוֹ שֶׁיֹּלֵךְ בְּיָדוֹ:

exhortation against excess verbiage.] Dreams reflect an overabundance of thoughts and preoccupation during the day. Similarly, excessive chatter [often as incoherent and unrelated as in a dream (*Akeidas Yitzchak*)] betrays the fool. Therefore 'let your words be few' (*Rashi*).

3. כַּאֲשֶׁר תִּדֹּר נֶדֶר לֵאלֹהִים — *When you make a vow to God*, to perform a righteous deed (*Metzudas David*). [Quoted almost verbatim from *Deut.* 23:22.]

Just as you are exhorted to guard your tongue in the House of God, and speak little, so should you exercise caution in every utterance you make before Him [as when you make vows] and not be like the fools for whom He has no use (*Ibn Ezra*).

אַל־תְּאַחֵר לְשַׁלְּמוֹ — *Do not delay paying it. Alshich* cautions that one, who made a vow to give charity as a result of being subjected to great suffering, should fulfill the vow immediately without waiting for the suffering to end. Proper belief in God dictates that the vow be discharged immediately.

4. טוֹב אֲשֶׁר לֹא־תִדֹּר — *Better that you do not vow at all*. Rav Meir said: It is preferable not to vow at all than to vow and not pay, or even to vow and pay. Rather let the man bring his lamb to the Temple [without previously making a vow to bring it], dedicate it, and then have it offered (*Midrash*).

If you don't have the money, why vow? Wait until the money is in your hand and give it then (*Ibn Yachya*).

[However, in time of trouble, it is commendable to make vows for charity, or vows to do good deeds, as we find *'and Jacob vowed a vow'* (*Genesis* 28:20; *Tosafos, Chullin* 2b). It is also commendable to made a vow to strengthen one's resolve to perform good deeds (*Nedarim* 8a).]

מִשֶּׁתִּדּוֹר וְלֹא תְשַׁלֵּם — *Than that you vow and not pay*. [Hence the praiseworthy custom of saying בְּלִי נֶדֶר, *'without a vow.'* Thereby, although the speaker still obligates himself to keep his word, he avoids the transgression of breaking a vow in the event he is unable to do so.]

5. וְאַל־תֹּאמַר לִפְנֵי הַמַּלְאָךְ — *And do not tell the messenger*. The representative of the congregation who comes to collect the proceeds of the vow (*Midrash; Rashi; Kara*).

6. כִּי בְרֹב חֲלֹמוֹת . . . — *In spite of all dreams, futility and idle chatter, rather: Fear God*. The verse is difficult in syntax and the translation follows most commentators who counsel that one should ignore all contrary influences (dreams, vain prophets and idle chatter) and, instead, *Fear God*.

7. בַמְּדִינָה — *In the State*., i.e., open and brazen oppression, rather than stealthy and clandestine (*Ibn Ezra*).

אַל־תִּתְמַהּ עַל־הַחֵפֶץ — *Do not be astonished at the fact* [or: *'at the will'*]. Do not be astonished that God *seems* to approve of this, and is *'slow'* in exacting retribution (*Almosnino*).

כִּי גָבֹהַּ מֵעַל גָּבֹהַּ — *For* [have faith that:] *there is One higher than high*, i.e., God. Do not despair at the impunity and freedom from retribution with which unscrupulous wielders of power oppress the helpless. Know that the most august of all beings, God, who is *Higher than High*, sees what they do and will avenge the victims when the proper time comes (*R' Saadiah Gaon; Sforno*).

8. וְיִתְרוֹן אֶרֶץ בַּכֹּל הִיא — *The advantage of land* [i.e., of agriculture] *is supreme; even a king is indebted* [i.e., subject] *to the soil*. The phrase is obscure and the translation follows *Ibn Ezra*, who comments: Having discoursed on the fear of God, Solomon reverts to the theme of which

3 *When you make a vow to God, do not delay paying it, for He has no liking*
for fools; what you vow, pay. 4 *Better that you do not vow at all than that you*
vow and not pay. 5 *Let not your mouth bring guilt on your flesh, and do not tell*
the messenger that it was an error. Why should God be angered by your speech
and destroy the work of your hands? 6 *In spite of all dreams, futility and idle*
chatter, rather: Fear God!
7 *If you see oppression of the poor, and the suppression of justice and right in*
the State, do not be astonished at the fact, for there is One higher than high Who
watches and there are high ones above them.
8 *The advantage of land is supreme; even a king is indebted to the soil.*
9 *A lover of money will never be satisfied with money; a lover of abundance*
has no wheat. This, too, is futility! 10 *As goods increase, so do those who consume*
them; what advantage, then, has the owner except what his eyes see? 11 *Sweet*
is the sleep of the laborer, whether he eats little or much; the satiety of the rich
does not let him sleep.
12 *There is a sickening evil which I have seen under the sun: riches hoarded*
by their owner to his misfortune, 13 *and he loses those riches in some bad vent-*
ure. If he begets a son, he has nothing in hand. 14 *As he had come from his*
mother's womb, naked will he return, as he had come; he can salvage nothing

---

occupation is best and most sin-free. Agriculture yields the most reward, for even a king is sustained by the soil...

And whoever tills the land, living a righteous life and providing honestly for his own sustenance, is assured a life of dignity likened to a king, who must himself by sustained by the produce of the earth. The miser in the next verse, however, loves money — rather than honest work — and steals to satisfy his lust for it. לֹא־יִשְׂבַּע כֶּסֶף – *he will never be* satisfied with money (*Alshich*).

9. אֹהֵב כֶּסֶף לֹא־יִשְׂבַּע כֶּסֶף – *A lover of money will never be satisfied with money.* Money will never still a rich man's hunger, for who can eat money? (*Akeidas Yitzchak*).

... וּמִי־אֹהֵב – *A lover of abundance has no wheat.* One who surrounds himself with an abundance of non-productive servants in order to impress his friends will *'have no wheat'*, i.e., will not be able to feed and sustain them and, what is more, he will have nothing left for himself as explained in the next verse (*Kara; Sforno*).

Rashi comments: he who loves to accumulate [inedible] money, rather than nourishing wheat, indulges in futility.

10. בִּרְבוֹת הַטּוֹבָה רַבּוּ אוֹכְלֶיהָ – *As goods increase, so do those who consume them.* A wealthier household acquires a larger stock of food and supplies and attracts more relatives, friends, and paupers. The owner sees before him a larger supply of provisions, speedily to be consumed. Thus, he is often in a worse position than he was before (*Ibn Yachya; Kara*).

11. מְתוּקָה שְׁנַת הָעֹבֵד – *Sweet is the sleep of the laborer.* This verse extols the man who is not indolent, and does not work only in order to hoard riches, but who tills the ground earnestly to support his family. Such a person has few concerns. He has no large estates or fortunes over which to worry constantly. Whether he eats little or much, he is able to sleep undisturbed by business worries (*Rav Yosef Kara*).

וְהַשָּׂבָע לֶעָשִׁיר אֵינֶנּוּ מַנִּיחַ לוֹ לִישׁוֹן – *The satiety of the rich does not let him sleep.* [Koheles does not refer to *physical* satiety; that would affect the rich and poor alike.] The reference is to the abundant *possessions* of the rich (*Ibn Ezra*): It fills him with worry and anxious cares which deprive him of his sleep (*Rashi; Lekach Tov*).

The Sages similarly expounded this concept in the *Mishnah* [*Avos* 2:7]: מַרְבֶּה נְכָסִים מַרְבֶּה דְאָגָה, *the more possessions the more worry* (*Rav Yosef Kara*).

12-13. רָעָה חוֹלָה – *A sickening evil* [i.e., an unusually grievous injustice]. This verse continues extolling the benefits of owning real property rather than hoarding money (*Ibn Ezra*).

וְהוֹלִיד בֵּן – *If he begets a son.* The further irony is that when he possessed the treasure he had no heir; only now that he is penniless is a child born (*Akeidas Yitzchak*).

14. וּמְאוּמָה לֹא־יִשָּׂא בַעֲמָלוֹ שֶׁיֹּלֵךְ בְּיָדוֹ – *He can salvage nothing from his labor to take with him.* When a person enters this world his hands are clenched as if to say: 'The whole world is mine, I shall inherit it'; but when he takes leave of the world, his hands are spread open as if to say: 'I have inherited nothing from the world' (*Midrash*).

טו וְגַם־זֹה֙ רָעָ֣ה חוֹלָ֔ה כָּל־עֻמַּ֥ת שֶׁבָּ֖א כֵּ֣ן יֵלֵ֑ךְ וּמַה־יִּתְר֣וֹן ל֔וֹ שֶֽׁיַּעֲמֹ֖ל
לָרֽוּחַ׃ טז גַּ֥ם כָּל־יָמָ֖יו בַּחֹ֣שֶׁךְ יֹאכֵ֑ל וְכָעַ֥ס הַרְבֵּ֖ה וְחָלְי֥וֹ וָקָֽצֶף׃ יז הִנֵּ֞ה
אֲשֶׁר־רָאִ֣יתִי אָ֗נִי ט֣וֹב אֲשֶׁר־יָפֶ֣ה לֶֽאֱכוֹל־וְ֠לִשְׁתּוֹת וְלִרְא֨וֹת טוֹבָ֜ה
בְּכָל־עֲמָל֣וֹ ׀ שֶֽׁיַּעֲמֹ֣ל תַּֽחַת־הַשֶּׁ֗מֶשׁ מִסְפַּ֛ר יְמֵי־חַיָּ֛ו אֲשֶׁר־נָֽתַן־ל֥וֹ
הָאֱלֹהִ֖ים כִּי־ה֥וּא חֶלְקֽוֹ׃ יח גַּ֣ם כָּל־הָאָדָ֡ם אֲשֶׁ֣ר נָֽתַן־ל֣וֹ הָאֱלֹהִים֩ עֹ֨שֶׁר
וּנְכָסִ֜ים וְהִשְׁלִיט֨וֹ לֶאֱכֹ֤ל מִמֶּ֙נּוּ֙ וְלָשֵׂ֣את אֶת־חֶלְק֔וֹ וְלִשְׂמֹ֖חַ בַּעֲמָל֑וֹ זֹ֕ה
מַתַּ֥ת אֱלֹהִ֖ים הִֽיא׃ יט כִּ֚י לֹ֣א הַרְבֵּ֔ה יִזְכֹּ֖ר אֶת־יְמֵ֣י חַיָּ֑יו כִּ֧י הָאֱלֹהִ֛ים מַעֲנֶ֖ה
בְּשִׂמְחַ֥ת לִבּֽוֹ׃

פרק ו

א יֵ֣שׁ רָעָ֔ה אֲשֶׁ֥ר רָאִ֖יתִי תַּ֣חַת הַשָּׁ֑מֶשׁ וְרַבָּ֥ה הִ֖יא עַל־הָאָדָֽם׃ ב אִ֣ישׁ
אֲשֶׁ֣ר יִתֶּן־ל֣וֹ הָאֱלֹהִ֡ים עֹשֶׁר֩ וּנְכָסִ֨ים וְכָב֜וֹד וְֽאֵינֶ֨נּוּ חָסֵ֥ר לְנַפְשׁ֣וֹ ׀ מִכֹּ֣ל
אֲשֶׁר־יִתְאַוֶּ֗ה וְלֹֽא־יַשְׁלִיטֶ֤נּוּ הָאֱלֹהִים֙ לֶאֱכֹ֣ל מִמֶּ֔נּוּ כִּ֛י אִ֥ישׁ נָכְרִ֖י
יֹאכְלֶ֑נּוּ זֶ֥ה הֶ֛בֶל וָחֳלִ֥י רָ֖ע הֽוּא׃ ג אִם־יוֹלִ֣יד אִ֣ישׁ מֵאָ֡ה וְשָׁנִ֣ים רַבּוֹת֩ יִֽחְיֶ֨ה
וְרַ֜ב ׀ שֶׁיִּהְי֣וּ יְמֵֽי־שָׁנָ֗יו וְנַפְשׁוֹ֙ לֹא־תִשְׂבַּ֣ע מִן־הַטּוֹבָ֔ה וְגַם־קְבוּרָ֖ה
לֹא־הָ֣יְתָה לּ֑וֹ אָמַ֕רְתִּי ט֥וֹב מִמֶּ֖נּוּ הַנָּֽפֶל׃ ד כִּֽי־בַהֶ֥בֶל בָּ֖א וּבַחֹ֣שֶׁךְ יֵלֵ֑ךְ
וּבַחֹ֖שֶׁךְ שְׁמ֥וֹ יְכֻסֶּֽה׃ ה גַּם־שֶׁ֥מֶשׁ לֹא־רָאָ֖ה וְלֹ֣א יָדָ֑ע נַ֥חַת לָזֶ֖ה מִזֶּֽה׃
ו וְאִלּ֣וּ חָיָ֗ה אֶ֤לֶף שָׁנִים֙ פַּעֲמַ֔יִם וְטוֹבָ֖ה לֹ֣א רָאָ֑ה הֲלֹ֛א אֶל־מָק֥וֹם אֶחָ֖ד
הַכֹּ֥ל הוֹלֵֽךְ׃ ז כָּל־עֲמַ֥ל הָאָדָ֖ם לְפִ֑יהוּ וְגַם־הַנֶּ֖פֶשׁ לֹ֥א תִמָּלֵֽא׃ ח כִּ֚י
מַה־יּוֹתֵ֣ר לֶחָכָ֔ם מִֽן־הַכְּסִ֑יל מַה־לֶּעָנִ֣י יוֹדֵ֔עַ לַהֲלֹ֖ךְ נֶ֥גֶד הַחַיִּֽים׃
ט ט֛וֹב מַרְאֵ֥ה עֵינַ֖יִם מֵֽהֲלָךְ־נָ֑פֶשׁ גַּם־זֶ֥ה הֶ֖בֶל וּרְע֥וּת רֽוּחַ׃ י מַה־שֶּֽׁהָיָ֗ה

---

16. גַּם כָּל־יָמָיו בַּחֹשֶׁךְ יֹאכֵל – *Indeed, all his life he eats in darkness.* Being obsessively overcome with accumulating riches, he sits down to eat only at night. He thus lives a life of rigorous self-denial, fear of robbery, and exposes himself to many trying experiences (*Ibn Ezra; Akeidas Yitzchak*).

17-18. These two verses are essentially a restatement of the conclusion Solomon reached in earlier discourses: (2:24; 3:12,22) Since man must depart exactly as he came, I concluded that financial pursuits are worthless. Let man rather involve himself in Torah pursuits (*Rashi*), and let him eat of God's bounty and be content (*Ibn Yachya; Ibn Ezra*).

לֶאֱכוֹל וְלִשְׁתּוֹת – *To eat and drink.* Note the *Midrash:* All the eating and drinking mentioned in this Book refers to Torah and good deeds. The most clear proof is in 8:15. Do, then, food and drink accompany men to the grave? What does accompany him? Torah and good deeds.

כִּי־הוּא חֶלְקוֹ – *For that is his lot.* God bequeathed these few pleasures to man, so it is only proper that man harness them and, by utilizing them for the proper spiritual goals, lift himself up to the greater service of God (*Almosnino*).

נָתַן־לוֹ הָאֱלֹהִים עֹשֶׁר וּנְכָסִים – *To whom God has given riches and possessions.* 'Why should God give you more than you need unless He intended to make you the administrator of this blessing for others; the treasurer of His treasures? Every penny you can spare is not yours, but should become a tool for bringing blessing to others. Would you close your hand on something that is not yours?' (Rabbi S. R. Hirsch, *Horeb*).

CHAPTER SIX

1. Solomon now bemoans those who have wealth, but whom God has denied the opportunity of enjoying it. In contrast to 5:12-14, which speaks of a man who begat children but lost his wealth, here the verse describes a man who has everything but is prevented by circumstances from enjoying it.

2. לֶאֱכֹל מִמֶּנּוּ – *The power to enjoy it.* Instead, He instilled in him miserly tendencies (*Metzudas David*) [in contrast to 5:18].

3. According to most commentators, this verse introduces a new case in distinction to the previous one of a childless person whom *'a stranger will inherit.'* Here Solomon describes the futility of someone blessed with a large family, longevity and every opportunity to

from his labor to take with him. 15*This, too, is a sickening evil: Exactly as he came he must depart, and what did he gain by toiling for the wind?* 16 *Indeed, all his life he eats in darkness; he is greatly grieved, and has illness and anger.*

17 *So what I have seen to be good is that it is suitable to eat and drink and enjoy pleasure with all one's labor that he toils beneath the sun during the brief span of his life that God has given him, for that is his lot.* 18 *Furthermore, every man to whom God has given riches and possessions and has given him the power to enjoy them, possess his share and be happy in his work: this is the gift of God.* 19 *For he shall remember that the days of his life are not many, while God provides him with the joy of his heart.*

CHAPTER SIX

1*There is an evil I have observed beneath the sun, and it is prevalent among mankind:* 2 *a man to whom God has given riches, wealth and honor, and he lacks nothing that the heart could desire, yet God did not give him the power to enjoy it; instead, a stranger will enjoy it. This is futility and an evil disease.* 3 *If a man begets a hundred children and lives many years — great being the days of his life — and his soul is not content with the good — and he even is deprived of burial; I say: the stillborn is better off than he.* 4 *Though its coming is futile and it departs in darkness, though its very name is enveloped in darkness,* 5 *though it never saw the sun nor knew it; it has more satisfaction than he.* 6 *Even if he should live a thousand years twice over, but find no contentment — do not all go to the same place?*

7 *All man's toil is for his mouth, yet his wants are never satisfied.* 8 *What advantage, then, has the wise man over the fool? What [less] has the pauper who knows how to conduct himself among the living?* 9 *Better is what the eyes see than what is imagined. That, too, is futility and a vexation of the spirit.*

---

enjoy goodness. But he lacks the capacity to derive joy from his blessings, and ultimately dies without even proper burial. A stillborn, declares Solomon, is better than he.

5. נַחַת לָזֶה מִזֶּה – *It has more satisfaction than he.* The stillborn does not anguish over what he never had, unlike the wealthy man who *'begat a hundred children,* etc.' but now grieves because everything was taken from him (*Metzudas David*).

6. [The subject of this verse is again the rich man described in verse 3.] Even if he lives to two thousand years, of what benefit is this longevity to him since וְטוֹבָה לֹא רָאָה, *'he found no contentment'?* Ultimately he will return to the dust, just like all paupers! (*Rashi*).

7-9. Man labors incessantly to satisfy his cravings, which, alas, remain unappeased. What, then, is the advantage of wisdom, especially when, despite intelligence and ability, one remains poor? It is of no advantage. It is better that we should enjoy the little we have than the futile quest of unsatisfied longing.

8. מַה־יּוֹתֵר לֶחָכָם – *What advantage then has the wise man* from his wisdom, מִן הַכְּסִיל – over what he would have if he were a fool? (*Rashi*). [A rhetorical question. There is no advantage to the wise. Both must toil for what they achieve. The difference lies in how the fruits of the labor are utilized and appreciated.]

מַה לֶּעָנִי יוֹדֵעַ לַהֲלֹךְ נֶגֶד הַחַיִּים – *What [less] has the pauper who knows how to conduct himself among the living?* A difficult phrase, the translation of which follows *Rashi, Kara, Ibn Ezra:* how is a pauper, who has the intelligence to get along in this world, worse off than the wise man who has wealth but finds no contentment?

The Midrash asks: What is a poor man to do regarding business transactions? Is he to sit idle? Let him learn a handicraft and the Holy One, blessed is He, will support him with a livelihood.

9. טוֹב מַרְאֵה עֵינַיִם מֵהֲלָךְ נָפֶשׁ – *Better is what the eyes see than what is imagined.* Man should utilize the little that is available to him (*'that which the eyes see'*), rather than yearn in vain for riches that may elude him (*R' Saadiah Gaon*).

R' Yosef Kara and *Rashi*, however, view this verse as the rationale of the miser: it is a great evil that many people would rather gaze upon a treasury full of gold and silver, enjoying *what the eyes see* and contenting themselves with that lustful vision, than to diminish their wealth by investing it to nourish their souls. Such a trait, is *'futility and a vexation of the spirit.'*

כְּבָר֙ נִקְרָ֣א שְׁמ֔וֹ וְנוֹדָ֖ע אֲשֶׁר־ה֣וּא אָדָ֑ם וְלֹא־יוּכַ֣ל לָדִ֔ין עִ֖ם שֶׁתַּקִּ֥יף מִמֶּֽנּוּ׃
יא כִּ֛י יֵשׁ־דְּבָרִ֥ים הַרְבֵּ֖ה מַרְבִּ֣ים הָ֑בֶל מַה־יֹּתֵ֖ר לָֽאָדָֽם׃ יב כִּ֣י מִֽי־יוֹדֵ֡עַ
מַה־טּ֨וֹב לָֽאָדָ֜ם בַּֽחַיִּ֗ים מִסְפַּ֛ר יְמֵֽי־חַיֵּ֥י הֶבְל֖וֹ וְיַעֲשֵׂ֣ם כַּצֵּ֑ל אֲשֶׁר֙ מִֽי־יַגִּ֣יד
לָֽאָדָ֔ם מַה־יִּהְיֶ֥ה אַחֲרָ֖יו תַּ֥חַת הַשָּֽׁמֶשׁ׃

פרק ז

א ט֥וֹב שֵׁ֖ם מִשֶּׁ֣מֶן ט֑וֹב וְי֥וֹם הַמָּ֖וֶת מִיּ֥וֹם הִוָּלְדֽוֹ׃ ב ט֞וֹב לָלֶ֣כֶת אֶל־בֵּֽית־
אֵ֗בֶל מִלֶּ֙כֶת֙ אֶל־בֵּ֣ית מִשְׁתֶּ֔ה בַּאֲשֶׁ֕ר ה֖וּא ס֣וֹף כָּל־הָאָדָ֑ם וְהַחַ֖י יִתֵּ֥ן
אֶל־לִבּֽוֹ׃ ג ט֥וֹב כַּ֖עַס מִשְּׂחֹ֑ק כִּֽי־בְרֹ֥עַ פָּנִ֖ים יִ֥יטַב לֵֽב׃ ד לֵ֤ב חֲכָמִים֙ בְּבֵ֣ית
אֵ֔בֶל וְלֵ֥ב כְּסִילִ֖ים בְּבֵ֥ית שִׂמְחָֽה׃ ה ט֕וֹב לִשְׁמֹ֖עַ גַּעֲרַ֣ת חָכָ֑ם מֵאִ֕ישׁ
שֹׁמֵ֖עַ שִׁ֥יר כְּסִילִֽים׃ ו כִּ֣י כְק֤וֹל הַסִּירִים֙ תַּ֣חַת הַסִּ֔יר כֵּ֖ן שְׂחֹ֣ק הַכְּסִ֑יל
וְגַם־זֶ֖ה הָֽבֶל׃ ז כִּ֥י הָעֹ֖שֶׁק יְהוֹלֵ֣ל חָכָ֑ם וִֽיאַבֵּ֥ד אֶת־לֵ֖ב מַתָּנָֽה׃ ח ט֛וֹב
אַחֲרִ֥ית דָּבָ֖ר מֵֽרֵאשִׁית֑וֹ ט֥וֹב אֶֽרֶךְ־ר֖וּחַ מִגְּבַהּ־רֽוּחַ׃ ט אַל־תְּבַהֵ֥ל
בְּרוּחֲךָ֖ לִכְע֑וֹס כִּ֣י כַ֔עַס בְּחֵ֥יק כְּסִילִ֖ים יָנֽוּחַ׃ י אַל־תֹּאמַר֙ מֶ֣ה הָיָ֔ה
שֶׁהַיָּמִים֙ הָרִ֣אשֹׁנִ֔ים הָי֥וּ טוֹבִ֖ים מֵאֵ֑לֶּה כִּ֛י לֹ֥א מֵחָכְמָ֖ה שָׁאַ֥לְתָּ עַל־זֶֽה׃

---

10. The verse cautions that man should perceive the limits of his essence as predetermined by God. He is אָדָם, *mortal man*, and his limitations as a human being have been imposed on him from Creation. He cannot contend with his Creator Who formed him thus (*Ibn Latif*). But he should be thankful for however God formed him (*Midrash Lekach Tov*). Nor can he hope to overpower the angel of death; he should submit to his mortality.

Rashi (as amplified by *Metzudas David*) explains the verse differently. Man's greatness was established and well known during his lifetime. His death, however, makes it manifestly clear that he is essentially אָדָם, *mortal*. Ultimately he dies, unable to resist the Angel of Death, who is more powerful than he.

11. כִּי יֵשׁ־דְּבָרִים הַרְבֵּה מַרְבִּים הָבֶל – *There are many things that increase futility.* Man becomes involved in many activities during his lifetime [such as the accumulation of wealth, power or pleasures (*Ibn Ezra*)]. Later he realizes that they were futile (*Kara; Rashi*).

12. מַה יִּהְיֶה אַחֲרָיו תַּחַת הַשָּׁמֶשׁ – *What will be after him beneath the sun.* Can anyone guarantee that the fortune which he accumulated unjustly will endure with his children on this world? (*Rashi*).

Koheles displays the same intellectual remorse which he developed in 2:3-21, and with which he culminated 3:22, regarding the uncertainty of the future. The best course, therefore, is to store up *spiritual fortunes* which will definitely live on beyond him (*Alshich*) — as the *Midrash* concludes: I will tell you what is best of all [next verse] טוֹב שֵׁם מִשֶּׁמֶן טוֹב, *a good name is better than good oil.*

CHAPTER SEVEN

1. טוֹב שֵׁם מִשֶּׁמֶן טוֹב – *A good name is better than good oil.* A fine reputation — acquired with diligence and good deeds (*Sforno*) — is a more valuable possession than precious oil (*Rashi*) [which was used in ancient times to preserve the body from disintegration]. Thus, notes the *Alshich*, a fine reputation will preserve a dead person's memory more effectively than precious oils will preserve his body.

It has been taught: A man is called by three names: one which his father and mother call him, a second which other persons call him, and a third which he gains for himself as the result of his conduct in life (*Midrash*).

וְיוֹם הַמָּוֶת מִיּוֹם הִוָּלְדוֹ – *And the day of death* [is better] *than the day of birth.* Because the man who has lived an exemplary life and acquired a *good name* views his death as a culmination of a life well spent and as a transition to the world of peace and reward, unlike the time of his birth, 'for man is born to toil' when he is uncertain of how his life will unfold (*Akeidas Yitzchak; Ibn Ezra*).

2. טוֹב לָלֶכֶת אֶל־בֵּית־אֵבֶל – *It is better to go to the house of mourning.* The commentators explain that by visiting the house of mourning and listening to the eulogies and lamentations, one will be stimulated to think about the beauty of life, and be inspired to repent and lead a religiously observant life. When the virtues of the deceased are recounted, the listener realizes that the only good thing of lasting value is a good reputation, and will resolve to assure himself an untarnished name by the time he dies and others visit *his* house of mourning.

בַּאֲשֶׁר הוּא סוֹף כָּל־הָאָדָם – *For that is the end*

*10 What has been was already named, and it is known that he is but a man. He
cannot contend with one who is mightier than he. 11 There are many things that
increase futility; how does it benefit man? 12 Who can possibly know what is
good for man in life, during the short span of his futile existence which he
should consider like a shadow; who can tell a man what will be after him
beneath the sun?*

CHAPTER SEVEN

*1 A good name is better than good oil, and the day of death than the day of
birth.
2 It is better to go to the house of mourning than to go to a house of feasting,
for that is the end of all man, and the living should take it to heart.
3 Grief is better than gaiety — for through a sad countenance the heart is
improved. 4 The thoughts of the wise turn to the house of mourning, but the
thoughts of a fool to the house of feasting.
5 It is better to listen to the rebuke of a wise man than for one to listen to the
song of fools, 6 for like the crackling of thorns under a pot, so is the laughter of
the fool; 7 for oppression makes the wise foolish, and a gift corrupts the heart.
8 The end of a matter is better than its beginning; patience is better than
pride. 9 Do not be hastily upset, for anger lingers in the bosom of fools.
10 Do not say, 'How was it that former times were better than these?' For that
is not a question prompted by wisdom.*

---

of all man. Death is the inevitable fate of everyone and if he does not attend the funeral now, when then? A feast is different — if a person could not attend one celebration, he will be able to attend another in that family at some later time (*Rashi*).

וְהַחַי יִתֵּן אֶל־לִבּוֹ – *And the living should take it to heart.* Do a kindness so that one will be done to you; attend a funeral so that people should attend your funeral; mourn for others so that others should mourn for you; bury others so that others should concern themselves with your burial; act benevolently so that benevolence should be done to you (*Midrash*).

3. טוֹב כַּעַס מִשְּׂחוֹק – *Grief is better than gaiety.* [In this context, many commentators understand כַּעַס not in its usual sense of *'anger'*, but as the *grief* aroused by the laments in the *'house of mourning.'*] Such 'grief' brings about רֹעַ פָּנִים, *a sad face,* i.e. a brooding, reflective countenance; which in turn יִיטַב לֵב, will cause *'his heart to be improved'*, i.e., turn his heart to try and better his ways — because such reflection will cause him to take stock of his own situation. He will repent and thus bring on his own redemption. שְׂחוֹק, *'gaiety'*, however, is not conducive to such serious contemplation (*Rav Yosef Kara*).

5. טוֹב לִשְׁמוֹעַ גַּעֲרַת חָכָם – *It is better to listen to the rebuke of a wise man* — although criticism hurts, it is beneficial because it brings about moral improvement (*Metzudas David*).

7. כִּי הָעֹשֶׁק יְהוֹלֵל חָכָם – *For oppression makes the wise foolish.* The provocations of fools cause the wise man's wisdom to depart from him — until even he may eventually provoke the Holy One, blessed is He (*Rashi; Midrash*).

8. טוֹב אַחֲרִית דָּבָר מֵרֵאשִׁיתוֹ – *The end of a matter is better than its beginning* — since only by the outcome can a matter be properly evaluated (*Rashi*). A wise man should always try to foresee any of the result of his every action and proceed accordingly (*Ibn Ezra*).

9. כִּי כַעַס בְּחֵיק כְּסִילִים יָנוּחַ – *For anger lingers in the bosom of fools* — eager to burst forth at the slightest provocation (*Sforno*).

10. This verse cautions the wise to be satisfied with their lot. If they suffer an adverse turn of fortune they should not complain about their lot and be jealous of those who are better and attribute their own decline to a changing world. Every understanding person is aware that life remains the same — man is given whatever has been ordained for him (*Ibn Ezra*).

The *Talmud* remarks that one should not deprecate the leaders of his time by comparing them to great personalities of the past. Rather Jerubaal in his generation is like Moses in his generation ... Yiftach in his generation is like Samuel in his ... one must be content with the judge who is in his days, and not look back at former times (*Rosh Hashanah* 25b).

The *Kobriner Rebbe* said: Some people feel that 'Nowadays it is difficult to serve God. In former times it was easier; there were more *tzadikim* whose example could be imitated.' This is absurd. Has anyone ever endeavored to seek God to no avail? Endeavor to seek Him in the manner of those in former days and you too will find Him, just as they did.

יא טוֹבָה חָכְמָה עִם־נַחֲלָה וְיֹתֵר לְרֹאֵי הַשָּׁמֶשׁ׃ יב כִּי בְּצֵל הַחָכְמָה בְּצֵל
הַכָּסֶף וְיִתְרוֹן דַּעַת הַחָכְמָה תְּחַיֶּה בְעָלֶיהָ׃ יג רְאֵה אֶת־מַעֲשֵׂה הָאֱלֹהִים
כִּי מִי יוּכַל לְתַקֵּן אֵת אֲשֶׁר עִוְּתוֹ׃ יד בְּיוֹם טוֹבָה הֱיֵה בְטוֹב וּבְיוֹם רָעָה רְאֵה
גַּם אֶת־זֶה לְעֻמַּת־זֶה עָשָׂה הָאֱלֹהִים עַל־דִּבְרַת שֶׁלֹּא יִמְצָא הָאָדָם
אַחֲרָיו מְאוּמָה׃ טו אֶת־הַכֹּל רָאִיתִי בִּימֵי הֶבְלִי יֵשׁ צַדִּיק אֹבֵד בְּצִדְקוֹ וְיֵשׁ
רָשָׁע מַאֲרִיךְ בְּרָעָתוֹ׃ טז אַל־תְּהִי צַדִּיק הַרְבֵּה וְאַל־תִּתְחַכַּם יוֹתֵר לָמָּה
תִּשּׁוֹמֵם׃ יז אַל־תִּרְשַׁע הַרְבֵּה וְאַל־תְּהִי סָכָל לָמָּה תָמוּת בְּלֹא עִתֶּךָ׃
יח טוֹב אֲשֶׁר תֶּאֱחֹז בָּזֶה וְגַם־מִזֶּה אַל־תַּנַּח אֶת־יָדֶךָ כִּי־יְרֵא אֱלֹהִים יֵצֵא
אֶת־כֻּלָּם׃ יט הַחָכְמָה תָּעֹז לֶחָכָם מֵעֲשָׂרָה שַׁלִּיטִים אֲשֶׁר הָיוּ בָּעִיר׃ כ כִּי
אָדָם אֵין צַדִּיק בָּאָרֶץ אֲשֶׁר יַעֲשֶׂה־טּוֹב וְלֹא יֶחֱטָא׃ כא גַּם לְכָל־הַדְּבָרִים
אֲשֶׁר יְדַבֵּרוּ אַל־תִּתֵּן לִבֶּךָ אֲשֶׁר לֹא־תִשְׁמַע אֶת־עַבְדְּךָ מְקַלְלֶךָ׃ כב כִּי
גַּם־פְּעָמִים רַבּוֹת יָדַע לִבֶּךָ אֲשֶׁר גַּם־אַתָּ קִלַּלְתָּ אֲחֵרִים׃ כג כָּל־זֹה נִסִּיתִי
בַחָכְמָה אָמַרְתִּי אֶחְכָּמָה וְהִיא רְחוֹקָה מִמֶּנִּי׃ כד רָחוֹק מַה־שֶּׁהָיָה וְעָמֹק
׀ עָמֹק מִי יִמְצָאֶנּוּ׃ כה סַבּוֹתִי אֲנִי וְלִבִּי לָדַעַת וְלָתוּר וּבַקֵּשׁ חָכְמָה וְחֶשְׁבּוֹן
וְלָדַעַת רֶשַׁע כֶּסֶל וְהַסִּכְלוּת הוֹלֵלוֹת׃ כו וּמוֹצֶא אֲנִי מַר מִמָּוֶת אֶת־הָאִשָּׁה
אֲשֶׁר־הִיא מְצוֹדִים וַחֲרָמִים לִבָּהּ אֲסוּרִים יָדֶיהָ טוֹב לִפְנֵי הָאֱלֹהִים יִמָּלֵט

---

11. טוֹבָה חָכְמָה עִם־נַחֲלָה — *Wisdom is good with an inheritance.* It is good for the scholar to be self-supporting and free from financial worries so he can immerse himself in his studies (*Alshich*).

וְיֹתֵר לְרֹאֵי הַשָּׁמֶשׁ — *And a boon to those who see the sun.* Such wisdom benefits all mankind. רֹאֵי הַשָּׁמֶשׁ, *'those who see the sun'*, is an all-encompassing phrase embracing all those who benefit from the sun and not only those with sight (*Rashi*).

13. Man must contemplate why God gave him life. Obviously, only to perform His commandments and act righteously — for who can right his wrongs after death? Therefore submit to God and accept the vicissitudes of life (*Tuv Taam*).

14. בְּיוֹם טוֹבָה הֱיֵה בְטוֹב — *Be pleased when things go well.* Enjoy the good that is granted you and derive pleasure to your heart's content (*Metzudas David*), seeking to acquire eternal perfection which is the greatest 'good' (*Sforno*). But while enjoying the good, וּבְיוֹם רָעָה רְאֵה, *anticipate the inevitability of bad times,* and act accordingly (*Ibn Ezra*).

Rashi interprets the phrase: when you are in a position to do good, be among those who do good — וּבְיוֹם רָעָה רְאֵה, and when evil comes upon the wicked, be among the observers only, not among the afflicted.

גַּם אֶת־זֶה לְעֻמַּת־זֶה עָשָׂה הָאֱלֹהִים — *God has made the one as well as the other* [i.e., one parallel to the other] — good with its reward, and evil with its ensuing punishment (*Rashi*).

שֶׁלֹּא יִמְצָא הָאָדָם אַחֲרָיו מְאוּמָה — *Man should find nothing after Him.* Man can have no just cause to complain to God because all punishment is clearly in response to man's deeds (*Rashi; Ibn Ezra; Alshich; Sforno*).

15. יֵשׁ צַדִּיק אֹבֵד בְּצִדְקוֹ — *Sometimes a righteous man perishes for all his righteousness.* In spite of his righteousness. God will be more exacting with him and punish him immediately for a minor infraction. Were he not righteous, he might not have been punished at all, because better behavior could not be expected of him (*Metzudas David*). [See *Overview* to ArtScroll edition of *Koheles*, and Overview to ArtScroll edition of *Ruth*, pp. 23-26.]

וְיֵשׁ רָשָׁע מַאֲרִיךְ בְּרָעָתוֹ — *And sometimes a wicked man endures for all his wickedness.* *Alshich* explains this as the paradox of צַדִּיק וְרַע לוֹ רָשָׁע וְטוֹב לוֹ — *righteous people who suffer while wicked are fortunate.* God deals strictly with the righteous to atone for their sins, so that they will not require punishment in the Hereafter, but He is seemingly lax in punishing the wicked. In reality, however, He is waiting for them to repent, or He may be rewarding their good deeds in This World so that they will not enjoy the bliss of the World to Come.

17. אַל תִּרְשַׁע הַרְבֵּה — *Be not overly wicked.* Even if you have done something wicked, do not persist in your wickedness [mistakenly thinking that there is no hope of repentance] (*Rashi*).

אַל תְּהִי סָכָל — *Nor be a fool.* Upon realizing that excessive wisdom is a cause of desolution, do

*11 Wisdom is good with an inheritance, and a boon to those who see the sun,
12 for to sit in the shelter of wisdom is to sit in the shelter of money, and the
advantage of knowledge is that wisdom preserves the life of its possessors.
13 Observe God's doing! For who can straighten what He has twisted? 14 Be
pleased when things go well, but in a time of misfortune reflect: God has made
the one as well as the other so that man should find nothing after Him.*

*15 I have seen everything during my futile existence: Sometimes a righteous
man perishes for all his righteousness, and sometimes a wicked man endures for
all his wickedness. 16 Do not be overly righteous or excessively wise: why be left
desolate? 17 Be not overly wicked nor be a fool: why die before your time? 18 It is
best to grasp the one and not let go of the other; he who fears God performs
them all. 19 Wisdom strengthens the wise more than ten rulers who are in the
city. 20 For there is no man so wholly righteous on earth that he [always] does
good and never sins.*

*21 Moreover, pay no attention to everything men say, lest you hear your own
servant disparaging you, 22 for your own conscience knows that many times you
yourself disparged others.*

*23 All this I tested with wisdom; I thought I could become wise, but it is
beyond me. 24 What existed is elusive; and so very deep, who can fathom it? 25 So
I turned my attention to study and probe and seek wisdom and reckoning, and
to know the wickedness of folly, and the foolishness which is madness:*

*26 And I have discovered more bitter than death: the woman whose heart
is snares and nets; her arms are chains. He who is pleasing to God escapes*

---

not take the opposite course and become a fool! (*Kara*).

18. טוֹב אֲשֶׁר תֶּאֱחֹז בָּזֶה וְגַם מִזֶּה ... — *It is best to grasp the one and not let go of the other. Ibn Ezra* comments that one should grasp both worlds — the spiritual and physical — and scrupulously follow the ideals of the Torah.

According to *R' Yosef Kara*, the verse refers to *'righteousness'* and *'wisdom'* in verse 16, and advises that one should tread a middle path between these two virtues and cling to both.

19. הַחָכְמָה תָּעֹז לֶחָכָם — *Wisdom strengthens the wise.* Having recommended that excessive, conceitful wisdom be shunned, Solomon adds that, nevertheless, wisdom in its proper measure — neither carried to extremes nor obsessive — is one's surest protection [because it leads him to repent (*Rashi*)] (*Ibn Ezra*).

20. אֲשֶׁר יַעֲשֶׂה טּוֹב וְלֹא יֶחֱטָא — *That he [always] does good and never sins.* Therefore the wise man should not be over confident. Even Moses sinned! (*Michlol Yofi*). Let him rather search out and improve his ways (*Rashi*).

Therefore, if you see a *righteous man who perishes notwithstanding all his righteousness* [verse 16], know that his punishment is probably the result of some infraction for which he received retribution in this world, because *no man is so righteous on earth that he never sinned* (*R' Saadiah Gaon*).

21-22. גַּם לְכָל־הַדְּבָרִים אֲשֶׁר יְדַבֵּרוּ — *Moreover, pay not attention to everything [men] say.* Do not be receptive to the evil talk of others about yourself (*Rashi*).

אֲשֶׁר לֹא־תִשְׁמַע אֶת־עַבְדְּךָ מְקַלְלֶךָ — *Lest you hear your [own] servant disparaging you.* If you pay attention to what others say about you, you will discover that even your own servant speaks disparagingly of you. Therefore, ignore such talk and spare yourself anger and vexation (*Ibn Ezra; Kehilas Yaakov*).

24. רָחוֹק מַה־שֶּׁהָיָה וְעָמֹק עָמֹק מִי יִמְצָאֶנּוּ — *What existed is elusive; so very deep, who can fathom it?* Everything is elusive: what pre-existed creation; what is above and below, who can fathom? Man is helpless — in his limited intellect — before the infinite greatness of God's Creation.

25. When it became clear to Koheles that comprehension of the deeper workings of the world was beyond his intellectual grasp, he shifted his attention to pursuing his observations on life as they flowed from his own practical wisdom. He tried to perceive which is the worst of all evils and most foolish of all follies, and he reveals them in the following verses (*Kara*).

26. וּמוֹצֶא אֲנִי מַר מִמָּוֶת — *And I have discovered more bitter than death.* Because she demands of man things which are beyond his power, such a woman ultimately kills him with a bitter death (*Midrash*). Given a choice, one should prefer death (*Metzudas David*).

[It is abundantly clear that Solomon refers

מִמֶּנָּה וְחוֹטֵא יִלָּכֶד בָּהּ: כז רְאֵה֙ זֶה מָצָאתִי אָמְרָה קֹהֶלֶת אַחַת לְאַחַת
לִמְצֹא חֶשְׁבּוֹן: כח אֲשֶׁר עוֹד־בִּקְשָׁה נַפְשִׁי וְלֹא מָצָאתִי אָדָם אֶחָד מֵאֶלֶף
מָצָאתִי וְאִשָּׁה בְכָל־אֵלֶּה לֹא מָצָאתִי: כט לְבַד רְאֵה־זֶה מָצָאתִי אֲשֶׁר
עָשָׂה הָאֱלֹהִים אֶת־הָאָדָם יָשָׁר וְהֵמָּה בִקְשׁוּ חִשְּׁבֹנוֹת רַבִּים:

פרק ח

א מִי כְּהֶחָכָם וּמִי יוֹדֵעַ פֵּשֶׁר דָּבָר חָכְמַת אָדָם תָּאִיר פָּנָיו וְעֹז פָּנָיו
יְשֻׁנֶּא: ב אֲנִי פִּי־מֶלֶךְ שְׁמֹר וְעַל דִּבְרַת שְׁבוּעַת אֱלֹהִים: ג אַל־תִּבָּהֵל
מִפָּנָיו תֵּלֵךְ אַל־תַּעֲמֹד בְּדָבָר רָע כִּי כָּל־אֲשֶׁר יַחְפֹּץ יַעֲשֶׂה: ד בַּאֲשֶׁר
דְּבַר־מֶלֶךְ שִׁלְטוֹן וּמִי יֹאמַר־לוֹ מַה־תַּעֲשֶׂה: ה שׁוֹמֵר מִצְוָה לֹא יֵדַע דָּבָר
רָע וְעֵת וּמִשְׁפָּט יֵדַע לֵב חָכָם: ו כִּי לְכָל־חֵפֶץ יֵשׁ עֵת וּמִשְׁפָּט כִּי־
רָעַת הָאָדָם רַבָּה עָלָיו: ז כִּי־אֵינֶנּוּ יֹדֵעַ מַה־שֶּׁיִּהְיֶה כִּי כַּאֲשֶׁר יִהְיֶה
מִי יַגִּיד לוֹ: ח אֵין אָדָם שַׁלִּיט בָּרוּחַ לִכְלוֹא אֶת־הָרוּחַ וְאֵין שִׁלְטוֹן בְּיוֹם
הַמָּוֶת וְאֵין מִשְׁלַחַת בַּמִּלְחָמָה וְלֹא־יְמַלֵּט רֶשַׁע אֶת־בְּעָלָיו: ט אֶת־
כָּל־זֶה רָאִיתִי וְנָתוֹן אֶת־לִבִּי לְכָל־מַעֲשֶׂה אֲשֶׁר נַעֲשָׂה תַּחַת הַשָּׁמֶשׁ
עֵת אֲשֶׁר שָׁלַט הָאָדָם בְּאָדָם לְרַע לוֹ: י וּבְכֵן רָאִיתִי רְשָׁעִים קְבֻרִים
וָבָאוּ וּמִמְּקוֹם קָדוֹשׁ יְהַלֵּכוּ וְיִשְׁתַּכְּחוּ בָעִיר אֲשֶׁר כֵּן־עָשׂוּ גַּם־זֶה הָבֶל:

---

only to evil, licentious women, who trap man into evil ways. This is not a wholesale condemnation of all woman. His praise of the God-fearing women in *Proverbs* 18:22 מָצָא אִשָּׁה מָצָא טוֹב, *he who has found a wife found good*; ibid. 31:10 ff (the famous *Aishes Chayil*); and his statement in 9:9 leave no room for doubt.]

27. [Solomon assures us that he formulated this discovery only after careful investigation.]

אָמְרָה קֹהֶלֶת — *Said Koheles.* The verb here is in the feminine form. *Rashi* explains that here *Koheles* means 'a collection of wisdom', rather than the name of Solomon. Thus, the noun *Koheles* is feminine in this sense.

28. אָדָם אֶחָד מֵאֶלֶף מָצָאתִי — *One man in a thousand I have found* — I was able to find a small number of worthy men, aloof from sin; who could collaborate in my investigation; *but one woman among them* — i.e., from all my thousand wives [700 wives, 300 concubines (*I Kings* 11:3)] *I could not find* (*Kara; Ralbag*) [because Solomon was ultimately led into sin by his wives (*Ibn Yachya*)].

[It is clear, as was pointed out earlier, that Solomon is not suggesting that righteous women did not exist at all — but, in his personal experience, they were even a greater rarity than righteous men.]

29. בִקְשׁוּ חִשְּׁבֹנוֹת רַבִּים — *Sought many intrigues.* Many commentators apply this verse to mankind as a whole: *God created mankind upright* — i.e., with a perfect nature capable of high attainments. Man's perversions spring from his own devices, which, in turn, cause his downfall (*Rambam*). [God has provided man with all his needs — but man is not satisfied; he always tries to 'improve' nature, thus causing his own complications].

CHAPTER EIGHT

1. מִי כְּהֶחָכָם — *Who is like the wise man?* [A rhetorical question:] Who in this world is as important as the man of wisdom (*Rashi*)?

חָכְמַת אָדָם תָּאִיר פָּנָיו — *A man's wisdom lights up his face.* Because of his wisdom man gains the admiration of all who know him. This gladdens one's heart and causes his countenance to beam (*Metzudas David*).

See the difference between wealth and wisdom. Wealth increases anxieties and robs one of his sleep [2:23]; wisdom, however, brightens up his face (*Kara*).

2. פִּי־מֶלֶךְ שְׁמֹר — *Obey the king's command.* [lit. *'guard the king's mouth'*]. The commentators differ regarding the identity of this *king:* the King of the Universe or a mortal king. *Rashi* offers both interpretations.

וְעַל דִּבְרַת שְׁבוּעַת אֱלֹהִים — *And that in the manner of an oath of God.* [An ambiguous phrase which can be variously interpreted:] Because of the oath of allegiance to God's commandments that we took at Horeb (*Rashi*).

Obey the king's orders if only because of the oath of allegiance taken in God's Name at the time of coronation (*Kara*).

The king's command must be obeyed — but only when his command is in consonance with

her but the sinner is caught by her.
27 *See, this is what I found, said Koheles, adding one to another to reach a*
conclusion, 28 *which yet my soul seeks but I have not found. One man in a*
thousand I have found, but one woman among them I have not found. 29 *But, see,*
this I did find: God has made man simple, but they sought many intrigues.

CHAPTER EIGHT

1 *Who is like the wise man? and who knows what things mean? A man's*
wisdom lights up his face, and the boldness of his face is transformed.
2 *I counsel you: Obey the king's command, and that in the manner of an oath*
of God. 3 *Do not hasten to leave his presence, do not persist in an evil thing; for*
he can do whatever he pleases. 4 *Since a king's word is law, who dare say to*
him, 'What are you doing?' 5 *He who obeys the commandment will know no*
evil; and a wise mind will know time and justice. 6 *For everything has its time*
and justice, for man's evil overwhelms him. 7 *Indeed, he does not know what*
will happen, for when it happens, who will tell him?
8 *Man is powerless over the spirit — to restrain the spirit; nor is there*
authority over the day of death; nor discharge in war; and wickedness cannot
save the wrongdoer.
9 *All this have I seen; and I applied my mind to every deed that is done under*
the sun: there is a time when one man rules over another to his detriment.
10 *And then I saw the wicked buried and newly come while those who had*
done right were gone from the Holy place and were forgotten in the city. This,
too, is futility! 11 *Because the sentence for wrong-doing is not executed quickly*
— that is why men are encouraged to do evil, 12 *because a sinner does what is*

---

the שְׁבוּעַת אֱלֹהִים, *the Oath to God*, i.e., that his requests are not contrary to the Laws of the Torah (*Metzudas David*).

3. אַל־תַּעֲמֹד בְּדָבָר רָע – *Do not persist* [lit., *'stand'*] *in an evil thing*, i.e., something that is evil in his eyes, for he can do as he pleases [and exact retribution] (*Ibn Ezra*).

This phrase is cited as the reason that in the synagogal reading of the Torah, the reader does not conclude an individual *aliyah* with an inauspicious phrase, because אַל תַּעֲמֹד בְּדָבָר רָע, 'Do not stand [i.e., pause] during a bad thing [an inauspicious verse]' (cf. *Midrash; Poras Yosef*).

5. וְעֵת וּמִשְׁפָּט יֵדַע לֵב חָכָם – *And a wise mind will know time and justice.* A wise man will perceive that there is a predetermined time during which God will exact justice from the wicked (*Rashi*). [לֵב, *heart*, is used interchangeably throughout Scriptures to represent both the seats of intellect and emotion.]

8. אֵין אָדָם שַׁלִּיט בָּרוּחַ – *Man is powerless over the spirit*. Even if man were to know his day of death, how would it avail him? He has no control over God's emissary [the Angel of Death who is referred to as a 'spirit' (*Midrash*)], לִכְלוֹא אֶת־הָרוּחַ, *to restrain the spirit*, i.e., to lock his soul within his body where it is 'imprisoned' and not release it (*Rashi, Ibn Ezra, Metzudas David*).

וְאֵין שִׁלְטוֹן בְּיוֹם הַמָּוֶת – *Nor is there authority over the day of death*, as the *Midrash* comments: A man cannot say to the Angel of Death, 'Wait until I finish my business and then I will come.'

Rashi and *Ibn Ezra* translate: Royalty is of no avail on the day of death [i.e., kings, too, are subject to death and their royalty is not recognized by the Angel of Death].

וְלֹא יְמַלֵּט רֶשַׁע אֶת־בְּעָלָיו – *And wickedness cannot save the wrongdoer*. Evildoers will not escape punishment for their deeds — their *wickedness* will not be their salvation (*Kara*).

10. וּבְכֵן רָאִיתִי – *And then I saw*. This is one of the most semantically difficult verses in the entire book and several interpretations are offered. Our translation, which follows the written text, is based on *Ibn Ezra*. The subject of the verse is the wicked of the previous verse 'who rule over their fellow man'. Those evildoers are קְבֻרִים, *buried* peacefully in their graves, i.e., they died without anguish. He understands וָבָאוּ as meaning "they came into the world a second time" (i.e., their children carry on after them) . . .

The phrase וּמִמְּקוֹם קָדוֹשׁ יְהַלֵּכוּ, *while those who . . . were gone from the holy place*, refers to the righteous, the holy ones who, because they die without children, become forgotten in the city where they were . . .

Ironically, these are the ones אֲשֶׁר כֵּן־עָשׂוּ, who

יא אֲשֶׁר֙ אֵין־נַעֲשָׂ֣ה פִתְגָ֔ם מַעֲשֵׂ֥ה הָרָעָ֖ה מְהֵרָ֑ה עַל־כֵּ֞ן מָלֵ֨א לֵ֧ב בְּנֵֽי־
הָאָדָ֛ם בָּהֶ֖ם לַעֲשׂ֥וֹת רָֽע׃ יב אֲשֶׁ֣ר חֹטֶ֗א עֹשֶׂ֥ה רָ֛ע מְאַ֖ת וּמַאֲרִ֣יךְ ל֑וֹ כִּ֚י
גַּם־יוֹדֵ֣עַ אָ֔נִי אֲשֶׁ֤ר יִֽהְיֶה־טּוֹב֙ לְיִרְאֵ֣י הָאֱלֹהִ֔ים אֲשֶׁ֥ר יִֽירְא֖וּ מִלְּפָנָֽיו׃ יג
וְטוֹב֙ לֹא־יִהְיֶ֣ה לָֽרָשָׁ֔ע וְלֹֽא־יַאֲרִ֥יךְ יָמִ֖ים כַּצֵּ֑ל אֲשֶׁ֛ר אֵינֶ֥נּוּ יָרֵ֖א מִלִּפְנֵ֥י
אֱלֹהִֽים׃ יד יֶשׁ־הֶ֘בֶל֮ אֲשֶׁ֣ר נַעֲשָׂ֣ה עַל־הָאָרֶץ֒ אֲשֶׁ֣ר ׀ יֵ֣שׁ צַדִּיקִ֗ים אֲשֶׁ֨ר
מַגִּ֤יעַ אֲלֵהֶם֙ כְּמַעֲשֵׂ֣ה הָרְשָׁעִ֔ים וְיֵ֣שׁ רְשָׁעִ֔ים שֶׁמַּגִּ֥יעַ אֲלֵהֶ֖ם כְּמַעֲשֵׂ֣ה
הַצַּדִּיקִ֑ים אָמַ֕רְתִּי שֶׁגַּם־זֶ֖ה הָֽבֶל׃ טו וְשִׁבַּ֤חְתִּֽי אֲנִי֙ אֶת־הַשִּׂמְחָ֔ה אֲשֶׁ֨ר
אֵין־ט֤וֹב לָֽאָדָם֙ תַּ֣חַת הַשֶּׁ֔מֶשׁ כִּ֛י אִם־לֶאֱכֹ֥ל וְלִשְׁתּ֖וֹת וְלִשְׂמ֑וֹחַ וְה֞וּא
יִלְוֶ֣נּוּ בַעֲמָל֗וֹ יְמֵ֛י חַיָּ֥יו אֲשֶׁר־נָֽתַן־ל֥וֹ הָאֱלֹהִ֖ים תַּ֥חַת הַשָּֽׁמֶשׁ׃ טז כַּאֲשֶׁ֨ר
נָתַ֤תִּי אֶת־לִבִּי֙ לָדַ֣עַת חָכְמָ֔ה וְלִרְאוֹת֙ אֶת־הָ֣עִנְיָ֔ן אֲשֶׁ֥ר נַעֲשָׂ֖ה עַל־הָאָ֑רֶץ
כִּ֣י גַ֤ם בַּיּוֹם֙ וּבַלַּ֔יְלָה שֵׁנָ֕ה בְּעֵינָ֖יו אֵינֶ֥נּוּ רֹאֶֽה׃ יז וְרָאִ֜יתִי אֶת־כָּל־מַעֲשֵׂ֣ה
הָאֱלֹהִ֗ים כִּי֩ לֹ֨א יוּכַ֜ל הָאָדָ֗ם לִמְצוֹא֙ אֶת־הַֽמַּעֲשֶׂה֙ אֲשֶׁ֣ר נַעֲשָׂ֣ה תַֽחַת־
הַשֶּׁ֔מֶשׁ בְּ֠שֶׁל אֲשֶׁ֨ר יַעֲמֹ֧ל הָאָדָ֛ם לְבַקֵּ֖שׁ וְלֹ֣א יִמְצָ֑א וְגַ֨ם אִם־יֹאמַ֤ר
הֶֽחָכָם֙ לָדַ֔עַת לֹ֥א יוּכַ֖ל לִמְצֹֽא׃

פרק ט

א כִּ֣י אֶת־כָּל־זֶ֞ה נָתַ֣תִּי אֶל־לִבִּי֮ וְלָב֣וּר אֶת־כָּל־זֶה֒ אֲשֶׁ֨ר הַצַּדִּיקִ֧ים
וְהַחֲכָמִ֛ים וַעֲבָדֵיהֶ֖ם בְּיַ֣ד הָאֱלֹהִ֑ים גַּם־אַהֲבָ֣ה גַם־שִׂנְאָ֗ה אֵ֤ין יוֹדֵ֙עַ֙ הָֽאָדָ֔ם
הַכֹּ֖ל לִפְנֵיהֶֽם׃ ב הַכֹּ֞ל כַּאֲשֶׁ֣ר לַכֹּ֗ל מִקְרֶ֨ה אֶחָ֜ד לַצַּדִּ֤יק וְלָרָשָׁע֙ לַטּוֹב֙
וְלַטָּה֣וֹר וְלַטָּמֵ֔א וְלַזֹּבֵ֔חַ וְלַאֲשֶׁ֖ר אֵינֶ֣נּוּ זֹבֵ֑חַ כַּטּוֹב֙ כַּֽחֹטֶ֔א הַנִּשְׁבָּ֕ע כַּאֲשֶׁ֖ר

---

had acted righteously (כֵּן meaning 'right' as in *Numbers* 27:7].

The anomaly is how the good deeds of the righteous are forgotten, but the wicked die peacefully and leave a legacy of evil behind them. This is a great futility.

11. Koheles attributes the flourishing of wickedness to the delay in retribution which tends to strengthen the tendency toward evil.

12-13. These verses continue the thought of the previous verse. They elaborate on what the wicked see that encourages them to sin with impunity. Nevertheless, Solomon disavows this evidence and affirms his faith in the Divine Justice which rewards the righteous and punishes the sinner.

כִּי גַם־יוֹדֵעַ אָנִי – *Yet, nevertheless, I am aware* [lit. *'for also I know'*]. Let no one think that I [Koheles] share the sinner's view. Just as every man of intellect perceives God's justice, so do I know that in the Eternal World it will go well only for those who fear Him, and that in the Hereafter the wicked will find no goodness, but their souls will be cut off (*Metzudas David*).

Even to the righteous God is 'patient' in granting his reward, but just as I believe that in the end the sinner will receive his due, I also believe that the righteous will ultimately receive his reward (*Tuv Taam*).

14. [The following verses until 9:12 form a cohesive unit discussing the dilemma presented by the prosperity of the wicked and the suffering of the righteous.]

שֶׁגַּם־זֶה הָבֶל – *This, too, is vanity.* The maintenance of Free Will — a necessary ingredient of God's plan — requires a certain amount of suffering for the righteous and prosperity for the wicked. For if all wickedness were to be punished immediately, there would be no room for choice and everyone would be righteous. Thus, the wicked often prosper, but they misinterpret this prosperity as sanction to continue their wicked ways. They should realize that it is futility — that in reality there is justice, but that God allows them to flourish in order to confuse mankind (*R' Saadiah Gaon*).

15. וְשִׁבַּחְתִּי אֲנִי אֶת הַשִּׂמְחָה – *So I praised enjoyment.* Not enjoyment for its own sake but שֶׁיְּהֵא שָׂמֵחַ בְּחֶלְקוֹ, that a person should be *satisfied with his lot* and be involved in performing 'righteous precepts which gladden the heart' [*Psalms* 19:9] from that which God has bestowed upon him (*Rashi*).

לֶאֱכֹל וְלִשְׁתּוֹת וְלִשְׂמֹחַ – *To eat, drink, and be*

wrong a hundred times and He is patient with him, yet nevertheless I am aware
that it will be well with those who fear God that they may fear Him, 13 *and that*
it will not be well with the wicked, and he will not long endure — like a shadow
— because he does not fear God.
14 *There is a futility that takes place on earth: Sometimes there are righteous*
men who are treated as if they had done the deeds of the wicked; and there are
wicked men who are treated as if they had done the deeds of the righteous. I
declared, this, too, is vanity.
15 *So I praised enjoyment, for man has no other goal under the sun but to eat,*
drink and be joyful; and this will accompany him in his toil during the days of
his life which God has given him beneath the sun.
16 *When I set my mind to know wisdom and to observe the activity which*
takes place on earth — for even day or night its eyes see no sleep. — 17 *And I*
perceived all the work of God. Indeed, man cannot fathom the events that occur
under the sun, inasmuch as man tries strenuously to search, but cannot fathom
it. And even though a wise man should presume to know, he cannot fathom it.

CHAPTER NINE

1 *For all this I noted and I sought to ascertain all this: that the righteous and*
the wise together with their actions are in the hand of God; whether love or hate
man does not know; all preceded them.
2 *All things come alike to all; the same fate awaits the righteous and the*
wicked, the good and the clean and the unclean, the one who brings a sacrifice
and the one who does not. As is the good man, so is the sinner; as is the one who
swears, so is the one who fears an oath.

---

joyful. The Midrash notes that all 'eating and drinking' mentioned in this Book signify Torah and good deeds. For just as eating and drinking sustain the body, Torah and good deeds sustain the soul (*Torah Temimah* based on *Zohar*).

The proof of this [continues the *Midrash*] is our verse: *this will accompany him in his toil during the days of his life* — to the grave. בַּעֲמָלוֹ, *in his toil* should be homiletically read בְּעָלְמוֹ, in his world. Are there, then, food and drink which accompany man to the grave? — It means Torah and good deeds that a man performs.

16-17. כַּאֲשֶׁר נָתַתִּי אֶת־לִבִּי. – *When I set my mind,* Solomon proceeds to explain why he came to the conclusion set forth in the last verse praising enjoyment: When I mustered up every ounce of my God-given superior wisdom to understand why the righteous suffer while the wicked prosper — even to the extent of going without sleep day and night — I became convinced that man cannot fathom these matters. Although he may feel he has nearly grasped it, he will ultimately fail in his quest. It is beyond the realm of his intellect. (*Divrei Chefetz; Kara; Rashi; Ralbag; Taalumos Chochmah*).

[Although Koheles opened this chapter implying that the wise man *'knows what all things mean,'* — he concludes that certain divine matters remain hidden even from the wisest of men.]

CHAPTER NINE

1. [Continuing his theme of the righteous and wicked, Divine Providence and Fate, Solomon affirms his conclusion that God's plan for the universe is unfathomable by mortal man, who bases his conclusions on empirical observations alone.]

גַּם־אַהֲבָה גַּם־שִׂנְאָה אֵין יוֹדֵעַ הָאָדָם – *Whether love or hate, man does not know.* Man cannot even comprehend what inspires him to love or hate something (*Metzudas David*). The execution of man's desire is in the realm of man's Free Will. However, the final determination of the true success of man's efforts is in God's hand: often one achieves what he seeks — only to find that the object of his love is detrimental to him, or that the object of his hate would have been beneficial to him.

2. מִקְרֶה אֶחָד – *The same fate awaits them all.* Everyone knows that death, the common equalizer, is the fate that awaits all men in this world. Nevertheless intelligent people choose the proper path because they realize that there is a distinction between good and evil people in the Hereafter (*Rashi*).

שְׁבוּעָה יָרֵא׃ ג זֶה ׀ רָע בְּכֹל אֲשֶׁר־נַעֲשָׂה תַּחַת הַשֶּׁמֶשׁ כִּי־מִקְרֶה אֶחָד
לַכֹּל וְגַם לֵב בְּנֵי־הָאָדָם מָלֵא־רָע וְהוֹלֵלוֹת בִּלְבָבָם בְּחַיֵּיהֶם וְאַחֲרָיו אֶל־
הַמֵּתִים׃ ד כִּי־מִי אֲשֶׁר יְחֻבַּר אֶל כָּל־הַחַיִּים יֵשׁ בִּטָּחוֹן כִּי־לְכֶלֶב חַי הוּא
טוֹב מִן־הָאַרְיֵה הַמֵּת׃ ה כִּי הַחַיִּים יוֹדְעִים שֶׁיָּמֻתוּ וְהַמֵּתִים אֵינָם יוֹדְעִים
מְאוּמָה וְאֵין־עוֹד לָהֶם שָׂכָר כִּי נִשְׁכַּח זִכְרָם׃ ו גַּם אַהֲבָתָם גַּם־שִׂנְאָתָם
גַּם־קִנְאָתָם כְּבָר אָבָדָה וְחֵלֶק אֵין־לָהֶם עוֹד לְעוֹלָם בְּכֹל אֲשֶׁר־נַעֲשָׂה
תַּחַת הַשָּׁמֶשׁ׃ ז לֵךְ אֱכֹל בְּשִׂמְחָה לַחְמֶךָ וּשְׁתֵה בְלֶב־טוֹב יֵינֶךָ כִּי כְבָר
רָצָה הָאֱלֹהִים אֶת־מַעֲשֶׂיךָ׃ ח בְּכָל־עֵת יִהְיוּ בְגָדֶיךָ לְבָנִים וְשֶׁמֶן עַל־
רֹאשְׁךָ אַל־יֶחְסָר׃ ט רְאֵה חַיִּים עִם־אִשָּׁה אֲשֶׁר־אָהַבְתָּ כָּל־יְמֵי חַיֵּי
הֶבְלֶךָ אֲשֶׁר נָתַן־לְךָ תַּחַת הַשֶּׁמֶשׁ כֹּל יְמֵי הֶבְלֶךָ כִּי הוּא חֶלְקְךָ בַּחַיִּים
וּבַעֲמָלְךָ אֲשֶׁר־אַתָּה עָמֵל תַּחַת הַשָּׁמֶשׁ׃ י כֹּל אֲשֶׁר תִּמְצָא יָדְךָ לַעֲשׂוֹת
בְּכֹחֲךָ עֲשֵׂה כִּי אֵין מַעֲשֶׂה וְחֶשְׁבּוֹן וְדַעַת וְחָכְמָה בִּשְׁאוֹל אֲשֶׁר אַתָּה
הֹלֵךְ שָׁמָּה׃ יא שַׁבְתִּי וְרָאֹה תַחַת־הַשֶּׁמֶשׁ כִּי לֹא לַקַּלִּים הַמֵּרוֹץ וְלֹא
לַגִּבּוֹרִים הַמִּלְחָמָה וְגַם לֹא לַחֲכָמִים לֶחֶם וְגַם לֹא לַנְּבֹנִים עֹשֶׁר וְגַם
לֹא לַיֹּדְעִים חֵן כִּי־עֵת וָפֶגַע יִקְרֶה אֶת־כֻּלָּם׃ יב כִּי גַּם לֹא־יֵדַע הָאָדָם
אֶת־עִתּוֹ כַּדָּגִים שֶׁנֶּאֱחָזִים בִּמְצוֹדָה רָעָה וְכַצִּפֳּרִים הָאֲחֻזוֹת בַּפָּח כָּהֵם
יוּקָשִׁים בְּנֵי הָאָדָם לְעֵת רָעָה כְּשֶׁתִּפּוֹל עֲלֵיהֶם פִּתְאֹם׃ יג גַּם־זֹה רָאִיתִי
חָכְמָה תַּחַת הַשָּׁמֶשׁ וּגְדוֹלָה הִיא אֵלָי׃ יד עִיר קְטַנָּה וַאֲנָשִׁים בָּהּ מְעָט

---

3. כִּי־מִקְרֶה אֶחָד לַכֹּל – *That the same fate awaits them all* [i.e., that תַּחַת הַשָּׁמֶשׁ, *in this world,* death comes to all, and no distinction is made 'beneath the sun' between the righteous and the wicked. All distinction comes in the Hereafter].

This is what confuses the wicked (*Taalumos Chochmah*).

4. כִּי־מִי אֲשֶׁר יְחֻבַּר . . . – *For he who is attached to all the living has hope.* As long as he lives, there is hope that even the sinner will repent (*Rashi*).

5. וְאֵין־עוֹד לָהֶם שָׂכָר – *There is no more reward for them.* Once they die they no longer perform *mitzvos* worthy of reward, and 'if one has not prepared on the eve of Sabbath, what shall he eat on Sabbath?' (*Rashi*).

6. [According to *Rashi* this verse refers to *the dead* who died without having repented, and who are forgotten.]

7-10. [There is a difference of opinion among the commentators concerning the interpretation of verses 3-10. In general, we follow the interpretation of *Rashi* and most commentators who understand these verses as describing the wicked man's inability to perceive beyond what his empirical experience allows him to comprehend. He therefore becomes a fatalist and feels that all is governed by chance. The wicked thus become emboldened to sin. Solomon bemoans this fact and praises life, for while life exists there is hope that the wicked will repent. Once they reach the grave, however, it is too late for regrets.

Now (in verses 7-10) Solomon advises the righteous — whose deeds God has already approved, and who are destined for the World to Come — to enjoy what God has granted them and not fear death but rather *'wear white'*, i.e., do good deeds and always stand in spiritual readiness for eventual death and their imminent reward, and in general, spend life in God's service.

8. בְּכָל־עֵת יִהְיוּ בְגָדֶיךָ לְבָנִים – *Let your garments always be white.* The Talmud interprets this verse allegorically that one should always be in a state of spiritual preparedness.

In a very beautiful homiletical interpretation of this verse, *Olelos Ephraim* comments that a white garment stains easily and even a small spot is readily noticeable, and hard to remove... Therefore, Solomon exhorts man to conduct his life constantly as if he were wearing white garments and carrying a full pitcher of oil on his head. He must concentrate on keeping his balance and not approach anything that can soil the whiteness of his garments. Man must live with spiritual and moral purity, always on guard lest he besmirch himself with a careless sin, for man, like a white garment, is easy to soil and hard to cleanse.

9. There is no contradiction between this verse

*[3] This is an evil about all things that go on under the sun: that the same fate
awaits all. Therefore, the heart of man is full of evil; and madness is in their
heart while they live; and after that, they go to the dead.*
*[4] For he who is attached to all the living has hope, a live dog being better than
a dead lion. [5] For the living know that they will die, but the dead know nothing
at all; there is no more reward for them, their memory is forgotten. [6] Their love,
their hate, their jealousy have already perished — nor will they ever again have
a share in whatever is done beneath the sun.*
*[7] Go, eat your bread with joy and drink your wine with a glad heart, for God
has already approved your deeds. [8] Let your garments always be white, and
your head never lack oil.*
*[9] Enjoy life with the wife you love through all the fleeting days of your life
that He has granted you beneath the sun, all of your futile existence; for that is
your compensation in life and in your toil which you exert beneath the sun.
[10] Whatever you are able to do with your might, do it. For there is neither doing
nor reckoning nor knowledge nor wisdom in the grave where you are going.*
*[11] Once more I saw under the sun that the race is not won by the swift; nor the
battle by the strong, nor does bread come to the wise, riches to the intelligent, nor
favor to the learned; but time and death will happen to them all. [12] For man does
not even know his hour: like fish caught in a fatal net, like birds seized in a
snare, so are men caught in the moment of disaster when it falls upon them
suddenly.*
*[13] This, too, have I observed [about] wisdom beneath the sun, and it affected
me profoundly:*
[14] There was a small town with only a few inhabitants; and a mighty king

---

and Solomon's harsh estimate of women in 7:26,28. There he condemns *the woman whose heart is snares and nets;* here his sober admonition is directed to *the wife you love.*

10. כֹּל אֲשֶׁר תִּמְצָא יָדְךָ לַעֲשׂוֹת בְּכֹחֲךָ עֲשֵׂה – *Whatever you are able to do with your might, do it.* In fulfilling the Will of your Creator do whatever you can; while you still possess your strength, use it properly (*Rashi*).

Repent while you have the ability. While the wick is still lit, add oil to keep it kindled. Once the light is extinguished, oil no longer helps (*Yalkut Shimoni*).

11. Solomon affirms his principles that this world is transitory and man is governed by God (*Rashi*).

וְגַם לֹא לַחֲכָמִים לֶחֶם – *Nor does bread come to the wise.* One would think that the wise man would rule over fools. But the matter is usually reversed (*Ibn Ezra*). Being wise does not guarantee one's food (*Metzudas David*).

וְגַם לֹא לַיֹּדְעִים חֵן – *Nor favor to the learned.* Knowledge does not always win one the acclaim of his fellow man (*Metzudas David*).

An example of unappreciated knowledge is given in verses 14-17 (*Kara*).

12. אֶת־עִתּוֹ – *His hour.* The time when misfortune suddenly descends upon him (*Rashbam*); so he can take precautions against it (*Sforno*).

This is a rebuke to men who always postpone repentance by rationalizing that death is far off, with the result that even if they live to seventy it does not suffice — death will still catch them unprepared (*Alshich*).

כָּהֵם יוּקָשִׁים בְּנֵי הָאָדָם לְעֵת רָעָה – *Like* (them)... *so are men caught in the moment of disaster.* Like fish who cause their own death, and later attribute it to the bait, not to the hook hidden within, so men attribute their death to sickness, not to their sins (*Alshich*).

[Thus, man — with all his intellect, power and skill — is not even superior to fish when it comes to knowing his life span; all Creation is subject to God's government of the Universe.]

13-14. גַּם־זֹה רָאִיתִי חָכְמָה תַּחַת הַשָּׁמֶשׁ – *This, too, have I observed [about] wisdom beneath the sun.* Having earlier deprecated wisdom [verse 11], Solomon now relates a story complimentary to wisdom (*Ibn Ezra; Sforno; Metzudas David*).

14. According to the *Talmud* [*Nedarim* 32b], *Midrash,* and many commentators, the story is an allegory:

There was a small town, refers to the body; *with only a few inhabitants:* the limbs; *and a mighty king ... surrounded it:* the יֵצֶר הָרָע, Evil Inclination; — Why is it called *'mighty'?* Because it is thirteen years older than the יֵצֶר הַטּוֹב, Good Inclination, since man is born with selfishness

וּבָא־אֵלֶיהָ מֶלֶךְ גָּדוֹל וְסָבַב אֹתָהּ וּבָנָה עָלֶיהָ מְצוֹדִים גְּדֹלִים׃ טו וּמָצָא
בָהּ אִישׁ מִסְכֵּן חָכָם וּמִלַּט־הוּא אֶת־הָעִיר בְּחָכְמָתוֹ וְאָדָם לֹא זָכַר
אֶת־הָאִישׁ הַמִּסְכֵּן הַהוּא׃ טז וְאָמַרְתִּי אָנִי טוֹבָה חָכְמָה מִגְּבוּרָה וְחָכְמַת
הַמִּסְכֵּן בְּזוּיָה וּדְבָרָיו אֵינָם נִשְׁמָעִים׃ יז דִּבְרֵי חֲכָמִים בְּנַחַת נִשְׁמָעִים
מִזַּעֲקַת מוֹשֵׁל בַּכְּסִילִים׃ יח טוֹבָה חָכְמָה מִכְּלֵי קְרָב וְחוֹטֶא אֶחָד יְאַבֵּד
טוֹבָה הַרְבֵּה׃

פרק י

א זְבוּבֵי מָוֶת יַבְאִישׁ יַבִּיעַ שֶׁמֶן רוֹקֵחַ יָקָר מֵחָכְמָה מִכָּבוֹד סִכְלוּת מְעָט׃
ב לֵב חָכָם לִימִינוֹ וְלֵב כְּסִיל לִשְׂמֹאלוֹ׃ ג וְגַם־בַּדֶּרֶךְ כְּשֶׁסָּכָל הֹלֵךְ לִבּוֹ
חָסֵר וְאָמַר לַכֹּל סָכָל הוּא׃ ד אִם־רוּחַ הַמּוֹשֵׁל תַּעֲלֶה עָלֶיךָ מְקוֹמְךָ אַל־
תַּנַּח כִּי מַרְפֵּא יַנִּיחַ חֲטָאִים גְּדוֹלִים׃ ה יֵשׁ רָעָה רָאִיתִי תַּחַת הַשָּׁמֶשׁ
כִּשְׁגָגָה שֶׁיֹּצָא מִלִּפְנֵי הַשַּׁלִּיט׃ ו נִתַּן הַסֶּכֶל בַּמְּרוֹמִים רַבִּים וַעֲשִׁירִים
בַּשֵּׁפֶל יֵשֵׁבוּ׃ ז רָאִיתִי עֲבָדִים עַל־סוּסִים וְשָׂרִים הֹלְכִים כַּעֲבָדִים עַל־
הָאָרֶץ׃ ח חֹפֵר גּוּמָּץ בּוֹ יִפּוֹל וּפֹרֵץ גָּדֵר יִשְּׁכֶנּוּ נָחָשׁ׃ ט מַסִּיעַ אֲבָנִים יֵעָצֵב
בָּהֶם בּוֹקֵעַ עֵצִים יִסָּכֶן בָּם׃ י אִם־קֵהָה הַבַּרְזֶל וְהוּא לֹא־פָנִים קִלְקַל
וַחֲיָלִים יְגַבֵּר וְיִתְרוֹן הַכְשֵׁיר חָכְמָה׃ יא אִם־יִשֹּׁךְ הַנָּחָשׁ בְּלוֹא־לָחַשׁ וְאֵין
יִתְרוֹן לְבַעַל הַלָּשׁוֹן׃ יב דִּבְרֵי פִי־חָכָם חֵן וְשִׂפְתוֹת כְּסִיל תְּבַלְּעֶנּוּ׃
יג תְּחִלַּת דִּבְרֵי־פִיהוּ סִכְלוּת וְאַחֲרִית פִּיהוּ הוֹלֵלוּת רָעָה׃ יד וְהַסָּכָל יַרְבֶּה
דְבָרִים לֹא־יֵדַע הָאָדָם מַה־שֶּׁיִּהְיֶה וַאֲשֶׁר יִהְיֶה מֵאַחֲרָיו מִי יַגִּיד לוֹ׃
טו עֲמַל הַכְּסִילִים תְּיַגְּעֶנּוּ אֲשֶׁר לֹא־יָדַע לָלֶכֶת אֶל־עִיר׃ טז אִי־לָךְ אֶרֶץ

---

and the makings of future greed, passion, and lust; *and built great siege works over it*: guiding it to do evil. The next verse continues, *Present was a poor wise man:* The Good Inclination — Why is it called *'poor'?* Because most people ignore it; *who by his wisdom saved the town:* for whoever obeys the Good Inclination escapes punishment; *yet no one remembers that poor man*: no one holds the Good Inclination in any kind of esteem, and when the Evil Inclination gains dominion, no one remembers the Good Inclination.

In the following verses, according to this interpretation, Solomon praises the Good Inclination as being superior to the Evil Inclination.

CHAPTER TEN

1. [This verse continues the theme of the last verse: *A single rogue can ruin a great deal of good.*]

יָקָר מֵחָכְמָה מִכָּבוֹד סִכְלוּת מְעָט — *A little folly outweighs wisdom and honor.* All of man's wisdom and honor can be nullified in the eyes of people by one foolish act, just as one sin can outweigh much good (*Ibn Ezra*)

2. [There follows a series of one sentence proverbs.]

לֵב חָכָם לִימִינוֹ — *A wise man's mind* [*tends*] *to his right.* His wisdom is always prepared to lead him in the correct path for his benefit (*Rashi*); and his intellect is always at hand when he needs it (*Metzudas David*).

4. כִּי מַרְפֵּא יַנִּיחַ חֲטָאִים גְּדוֹלִים — *For deference* ['weakness'] *appeases great offenses.* Deference to his rule — rather than flagrant flight from him — will make him more kindly disposed towards clemency and will avoid a penalty for great offenses (*Ibn Yachya*).

5. כִּשְׁגָגָה — *As if it were an error.* I.e., like a royal decree made in error, which is irreversible, so are the Heavenly decrees described in verses 6 and 7 (*Rashi*).

Ibn Ezra and *Metzudas David* comment that this verse continues the thought in verse 4 in describing the potential evils of a rise to power. A ruler sometimes finds it politically expedient to commit an injustice and say it was done in error.

6. נִתַּן הַסֶּכֶל בַּמְּרוֹמִים רַבִּים — *Folly is placed on lofty heights.* This is one of the evils referred to in the previous verse: The rich who presumably deserve honor are arbitrarily shunted, while fools are elevated to high positions. It appears to

came upon it and surrounded it, and built great siege works over it. [15] *Present in the city was a poor wise man who by his wisdom saved the town. Yet no one remembered that poor man.* [16] *So I said: Wisdom is better than might, although a poor man's wisdom is despised and his words go unheeded.*

[17] *The gentle words of the wise are heard above the shouts of a king over fools,* [18] *and wisdom is better than weapons, but a single rogue can ruin a great deal of good.*

CHAPTER TEN

[1] *Dead flies putrefy the perfumer's oil; a little folly outweighs wisdom and honor.*

[2] *A wise man's mind [tends] to his right; while a fool's mind [tends] to his left.* [3] *Even on the road as the fool walks, he lacks sense, and proclaims to all that he is a fool.*

[4] *If the anger of a ruler flares up against you, do not leave your place, for deference appeases great offenses.*

[5] *There is an evil which I have observed beneath the sun as if it were an error proceeding from the ruler:* [6] *Folly is placed on lofty heights, while rich men sit in low places.* [7] *I have seen slaves on horses and nobles walking on foot like slaves.*

[8] *He who digs a pit will fall into it, and he who breaks down a wall will be bitten by a snake.* [9] *He who moves about stones will be hurt by them; he who splits logs will be endangered by them.*

[10] *If an axe is blunt and one has not honed the edge, nevertheless it strengthens the warriors. Wisdom is a more powerful skill.*

[11] *If the snake bites because it was not charmed, then there is no advantage to the charmer's art.*

[12] *The words of a wise man win favor, but a fool's lips devour him.* [13] *His talk begins as foolishness and ends as evil madness.* [14] *The fool prates on and on, but man does not know what will be; and who can tell what will happen after him?*

[15] *The toil of fools exhaust them, as one who does not know the way to town.*

[16] *Woe to you, O land, whose king acts as an adolescent, and whose ministers*

---

be an error from On High, but it is no error [it is part of God's unrevealed plan of governing the Universe] (*Metzudas David*).

8. [In the following proverbs *Koheles* enjoins care in all undertakings. These verses may also be interpreted as additional examples of the 'evils' described in vss. 6-7, in the sense that man should not put faith in his control of events: Every act is the result, not of human planning, but of Divine Providence (*Alshich*)

חֹפֵר גּוּמָּץ בּוֹ יִפּוֹל – *He who digs a pit will fall into it*. He who plots against his fellow man, will himself fall into the trap (*Rashi*).

9. The fool will place himself in danger, while the wise man will guard himself. Also, nothing in this world is acquired without toil and some inherent danger (*Ibn Ezra*).

11. וְאֵין יִתְרוֹן לְבַעַל הַלָּשׁוֹן – *Then there is no advantage to the charmer's art,* There is no advantage in knowing how to exercise a charm and not making use of it (*Rashbam*).

Similarly, there is no advantage to wisdom if, while his fellow men sin, the wise man maintains his silence, and does not teach them Torah (*Rashi*).

14. לֹא־יֵדַע הָאָדָם מַה־שֶׁיִּהְיֶה – *But man does not know what will be*. Only a fool will presume to make irresponsible plans for the near or distant future.

15. A traveler could be guided properly were he to ask directions. Conversely, the fool persists in his folly to the point of exhaustion, because he refuses to consult with the wise and seek proper guidance.

16. וְשָׂרַיִךְ בַּבֹּקֶר יֹאכֵלוּ – *And whose ministers dine in the morning*. Because their prime concern is not the welfare of the State but their own satiety. They indulge in revelry when they should attend to the duties of the State (*Ibn Latif*).

שֶׁמַּלְכֵּךְ נָעַר וְשָׂרַיִךְ בַּבֹּקֶר יֹאכֵלוּ: יז אַשְׁרֵיךְ אֶרֶץ שֶׁמַּלְכֵּךְ בֶּן־חוֹרִים
וְשָׂרַיִךְ בָּעֵת יֹאכֵלוּ בִּגְבוּרָה וְלֹא בַשְּׁתִי: יח בַּעֲצַלְתַּיִם יִמַּךְ הַמְּקָרֶה
וּבְשִׁפְלוּת יָדַיִם יִדְלֹף הַבָּיִת: יט לִשְׂחוֹק עֹשִׂים לֶחֶם וְיַיִן יְשַׂמַּח חַיִּים
וְהַכֶּסֶף יַעֲנֶה אֶת־הַכֹּל: כ גַּם בְּמַדָּעֲךָ מֶלֶךְ אַל־תְּקַלֵּל וּבְחַדְרֵי מִשְׁכָּבְךָ
אַל־תְּקַלֵּל עָשִׁיר כִּי עוֹף הַשָּׁמַיִם יוֹלִיךְ אֶת־הַקּוֹל וּבַעַל כְּנָפַיִם יַגִּיד דָּבָר:

פרק יא

א שַׁלַּח לַחְמְךָ עַל־פְּנֵי הַמָּיִם כִּי־בְרֹב הַיָּמִים תִּמְצָאֶנּוּ: ב תֶּן־חֵלֶק
לְשִׁבְעָה וְגַם לִשְׁמוֹנָה כִּי לֹא תֵדַע מַה־יִּהְיֶה רָעָה עַל־הָאָרֶץ:
ג אִם־יִמָּלְאוּ הֶעָבִים גֶּשֶׁם עַל־הָאָרֶץ יָרִיקוּ וְאִם־יִפּוֹל עֵץ בַּדָּרוֹם וְאִם
בַּצָּפוֹן מְקוֹם שֶׁיִּפּוֹל הָעֵץ שָׁם יְהוּא: ד שֹׁמֵר רוּחַ לֹא יִזְרָע וְרֹאֶה בֶעָבִים
לֹא יִקְצוֹר: ה כַּאֲשֶׁר אֵינְךָ יוֹדֵעַ מַה־דֶּרֶךְ הָרוּחַ כַּעֲצָמִים בְּבֶטֶן הַמְּלֵאָה
כָּכָה לֹא תֵדַע אֶת־מַעֲשֵׂה הָאֱלֹהִים אֲשֶׁר יַעֲשֶׂה אֶת־הַכֹּל: ו בַּבֹּקֶר זְרַע
אֶת־זַרְעֶךָ וְלָעֶרֶב אַל־תַּנַּח יָדֶךָ כִּי אֵינְךָ יוֹדֵעַ אֵי זֶה יִכְשַׁר הֲזֶה אוֹ־זֶה
וְאִם־שְׁנֵיהֶם כְּאֶחָד טוֹבִים: ז וּמָתוֹק הָאוֹר וְטוֹב לַעֵינַיִם לִרְאוֹת
אֶת־הַשָּׁמֶשׁ: ח כִּי אִם־שָׁנִים הַרְבֵּה יִחְיֶה הָאָדָם בְּכֻלָּם יִשְׂמָח וְיִזְכֹּר
אֶת־יְמֵי הַחֹשֶׁךְ כִּי־הַרְבֵּה יִהְיוּ כָּל־שֶׁבָּא הָבֶל: ט שְׂמַח בָּחוּר בְּיַלְדוּתֶךָ
וִיטִיבְךָ לִבְּךָ בִּימֵי בְחוּרוֹתֶיךָ וְהַלֵּךְ בְּדַרְכֵי לִבְּךָ וּבְמַרְאֵה עֵינֶיךָ וְדָע כִּי
עַל־כָּל־אֵלֶּה יְבִיאֲךָ הָאֱלֹהִים בַּמִּשְׁפָּט: י וְהָסֵר כַּעַס מִלִּבֶּךָ וְהַעֲבֵר רָעָה
מִבְּשָׂרֶךָ כִּי־הַיַּלְדוּת וְהַשַּׁחֲרוּת הָבֶל:

---

19. וְהַכֶּסֶף יַעֲנֶה אֶת־הַכֹּל – *But money answers everything.* Money is needed by all and makes everything possible. In the previous verse slothfulness is deprecated; here man is encouraged toward industry. Lazy people do not earn the money required for living (*Rashi; Metzudas David*).

Yalkut HaGershuni comments that יַעֲנֶה can be related to עִינוּי, *affliction: 'money afflicts all.'* [Its abundance as well as its absence causes suffering.]

On an ethical level, the verse is interpreted: 'money makes everyone respond' — for money, people will accede to your every request (*Kedushas Levi*).

20. כִּי עוֹף הַשָּׁמַיִם יוֹלִיךְ אֶת הַקּוֹל – *For a bird of the skies may carry the sound.* An idiomatic phrase to imply that your utterance will quickly spread and reach the ears of government officials (*Metzudas David*).

CHAPTER ELEVEN

1. שַׁלַּח לַחְמְךָ עַל־פְּנֵי הַמָּיִם – *Send your bread upon the waters.* Most commentators explain this verse as urging that charity be given even to strangers who will never be seen again. The generosity will not go unrewarded; the favor will be repaid.

2. The commentators explain this verse also as referring to charity, specifically its wider distribution.

לְשִׁבְעָה וְגַם לִשְׁמוֹנָה – *To seven, or even to eight,* i.e., abundantly, without pause (*Ralbag*). Thus, the verse admonishes: Give charity constantly.

Avudraham quotes the Midrash that this verse alludes to *Succos*, a *seven*-day festival followed by *Shimini Atzeres*, the *eighth* festival day. This may be why Koheles is read on Succos.

כִּי לֹא תֵדַע – *For you never know what calamity* will strike the land. If you are thrust into poverty and require the assistance of others, you will be saved by virtue of your former charitable acts (*Rashi*).

3. אִם־יִמָּלְאוּ הֶעָבִים – *If the clouds are filled.* Clouds filled with rain-water do not keep it to themselves, but they beneficently pour it upon the earth. In turn, the earth receives moisture which, by the natural moisture-cycle, returns to the clouds [cf. 1:7]. Similarly, a man who is blessed by God and 'filled' with wealth is bidden not to hoard his wealth but should dispense a portion of it as charity to those less fortunate. If the wheel turns and he finds himself in need, he will be sustained by others (*Metzudas David*).

4. One must perform the tasks required of him

*dine in the morning. 17 Happy are you, O land, whose king is a man of dignity,
and whose ministers dine at the proper time — in strength and not in
drunkenness.*
*18 Through slothfulness the ceiling sags, and through idleness of the hands the
house leaks.*
*19 A feast is made for laughter, and wine gladdens life, but money answers
everything.*
*20 Even in your thoughts do not curse a king, and in your bed-chamber do not
curse the rich, for a bird of the skies may carry the sound, and some winged
creature may betray the matter.*

CHAPTER ELEVEN

*1 Send your bread upon the waters, for after many days you will find it.
2 Distribute portions to seven, or even to eight, for you never know what
calamity will strike the land.*
*3 If the clouds are filled they will pour down rain on the earth; if a tree falls
down in the south or the north, wherever the tree falls, there it remains. 4 One
who watches the wind will never sow, and one who keeps his eyes on the clouds
will never reap. 5 Just as you do not know the way of the wind, nor the nature
of the embryo in a pregnant stomach, so can you never know the work of God
Who makes everything. 6 In the morning sow your seed and in the evening do
not be idle, for you cannot know which will succeed: this or that; or whether
both are equally good.*
*7 Sweet is the light, and it is good for the eyes to behold the sun! 8 Even if a
man lives many years, let him rejoice in all of them, but let him remember that
the days of darkness will be many. All that comes is futility. 9 Rejoice, young
man, in your childhood; let your heart cheer you in the days of your youth;
follow the path of your heart and the sight of your eyes — but be aware that for
all these things God will call you to account. 10 Rather, banish anger from your
heart and remove evil from your flesh — for childhood and youth are futile.*

---

and have faith that God will bless his works.

שֹׁמֵר רוּחַ לֹא יִזְרָע — *One who watches the wind will never sow.* One who forever waits for ideal conditions will never get his work done (*Ibn Latif*). Similarly in matters of dispensing charity, one should not be over-suspicious and over-prudent; he should follow his inclination and dispense it as it is required (*Nachal Eshkol*).

5. אֶת־מַעֲשֵׂה הָאֱלֹהִים — *The work of God.* Similarly, God's decrees concerning wealth and poverty are sealed to man. Therefore, one must never recoil from charity out of fear that he will become poor; nor refrain from Torah study out of fear that he will neglect his business and grow poor; nor rationalize that he should not marry because he will then have to support children (*Rashi*).

7. וּמָתוֹק הָאוֹר — *Sweet is the light. Metzudas David* explains that 'light' refers metaphorically to life: Sweet is the life of man while he is still permitted to enjoy the light of day! In the second part of the verse, the thought is rephrased forming an effective parallel.

The Midrash explains 'light' as Torah: 'Sweet is the light of Torah ... and happy is he whose study enlightens him like the sun [leaving him free of doubts and perplexities.] ... Rav Acha said: Sweet is the light of the World to Come; happy is he who is worthy to behold that light!'

8. וְיִזְכֹּר אֶת־יְמֵי הַחֹשֶׁךְ — *But let him remember* [i.e., *ponder*] *the days of darkness.* But at the same time it is imperative that one keep in mind the transitory nature of this world and strive to improve his ways, for *the days of darkness* — an allusion to death and the judgment of the wicked — *will be many.* Those days are more eternal than the short duration of life on this world (*Rashi*).

This verse is reminiscent of an incident recorded in the *Talmud:* Rav Chisda's daughter asked him if he wished to take a nap. He answered: The time will come when there will be long days in the grave where Torah study and observance will be impossible. We will sleep much there. Meanwhile, we must exert ourselves and be involved with Torah and the commandments (*Eruvin* 65a).

9. שְׂמַח בָּחוּר בְּיַלְדוּתֶךָ — *Rejoice, young man, in your childhood.* [As evidenced by the end of the

פרק יב

א וּזְכֹר אֶת־בּוֹרְאֶיךָ בִּימֵי בְּחוּרֹתֶיךָ עַד אֲשֶׁר לֹא־יָבֹאוּ יְמֵי הָרָעָה וְהִגִּיעוּ
שָׁנִים אֲשֶׁר תֹּאמַר אֵין־לִי בָהֶם חֵפֶץ: ב עַד אֲשֶׁר לֹא־תֶחְשַׁךְ הַשֶּׁמֶשׁ
וְהָאוֹר וְהַיָּרֵחַ וְהַכּוֹכָבִים וְשָׁבוּ הֶעָבִים אַחַר הַגָּשֶׁם: ג בַּיּוֹם שֶׁיָּזֻעוּ שֹׁמְרֵי
הַבַּיִת וְהִתְעַוְּתוּ אַנְשֵׁי הֶחָיִל וּבָטְלוּ הַטֹּחֲנוֹת כִּי מִעֵטוּ וְחָשְׁכוּ הָרֹאוֹת
בָּאֲרֻבּוֹת: ד וְסֻגְּרוּ דְלָתַיִם בַּשּׁוּק בִּשְׁפַל קוֹל הַטַּחֲנָה וְיָקוּם לְקוֹל הַצִּפּוֹר
וְיִשַּׁחוּ כָּל־בְּנוֹת הַשִּׁיר: ה גַּם מִגָּבֹהַּ יִירָאוּ וְחַתְחַתִּים בַּדֶּרֶךְ וְיָנֵאץ הַשָּׁקֵד
וְיִסְתַּבֵּל הֶחָגָב וְתָפֵר הָאֲבִיּוֹנָה כִּי־הֹלֵךְ הָאָדָם אֶל־בֵּית עוֹלָמוֹ וְסָבְבוּ
בַשּׁוּק הַסֹּפְדִים: ו עַד אֲשֶׁר לֹא־יֵרָתֵק חֶבֶל הַכֶּסֶף וְתָרֻץ גֻּלַּת הַזָּהָב
וְתִשָּׁבֶר כַּד עַל־הַמַּבּוּעַ וְנָרֹץ הַגַּלְגַּל אֶל־הַבּוֹר: ז וְיָשֹׁב הֶעָפָר עַל־הָאָרֶץ
כְּשֶׁהָיָה וְהָרוּחַ תָּשׁוּב אֶל־הָאֱלֹהִים אֲשֶׁר נְתָנָהּ: ח הֲבֵל הֲבָלִים אָמַר
הַקּוֹהֶלֶת הַכֹּל הָבֶל: ט וְיֹתֵר שֶׁהָיָה קֹהֶלֶת חָכָם עוֹד לִמַּד־דַּעַת אֶת־
הָעָם וְאִזֵּן וְחִקֵּר תִּקֵּן מְשָׁלִים הַרְבֵּה: י בִּקֵּשׁ קֹהֶלֶת לִמְצֹא דִּבְרֵי־חֵפֶץ
וְכָתוּב יֹשֶׁר דִּבְרֵי אֱמֶת: יא דִּבְרֵי חֲכָמִים כַּדָּרְבֹנוֹת וּכְמַשְׂמְרוֹת נְטוּעִים

---

verse, this is in no way to be interpreted as a hedonistic *carte-blanche* to run amok with one's passion.] It is clearly to be understood as words of warning to those rebellious youths who wallow in sin [and who would not accept his words if they were said in such negative terms as: 'Do *not* rejoice . . . do *not* follow your heart']. Rather, Solomon said: I know full well that fools tend to sin in their youth, but beware! Judgment is forthcoming (*Midrash Lekach Tov*).

CHAPTER TWELVE

1. Having warned recalcitrant youth to *'be aware that for all these things God will call you to account'* (11:9) and that *'childhood and youth are futile,'* (11:10), Solomon continues that man should spend his vigorous youth in the service of his Creator.

וּזְכֹר אֶת־בּוֹרְאֶיךָ — *So remember your Creator,* and try — in spirit and deed — to honor Him (*Sforno*).

בִּימֵי בְּחוּרֹתֶיךָ — *In the days of your youth.* While in the possession of your strength (*Midrash*).

Man should take advantage of vigorous youth to serve God, before old age sets in and service becomes more difficult (*Metzudas David*).

יְמֵי הָרָעָה — *The evil days*, i.e., old age with its infirmities (*Rashi*).

2. [The following verses, as explained by the commentators, poetically conjure an image of the fading of life as old age approaches. The allegory refers to the waning powers of the organs of the body, as will be explained.

The Talmud relates an incident in which a man described his old age as follows: 'The mountain is snowy, it is surrounded by ice, the dog does not bark, and the grinders do not grind' [i.e., my head is snowy white, my beard likewise; my voice is feeble and my teeth do not function;] (*Shabbos* 152a).

הַשֶּׁמֶשׁ וְהָאוֹר וְהַיָּרֵחַ וְהַכּוֹכָבִים — *The sun, the light, the moon and the stars,* i.e., the forehead, the nose, the soul, and the cheeks (*Midrash*).

וְשָׁבוּ הֶעָבִים אַחַר הַגָּשֶׁם — *And the clouds return after the rain.* The eyesight which is weakened by weeping, i.e., the weeping of old age, caused by trouble and sickness, destroys the eyesight; crying, puffy eyes are compared to clouds (*Torah Temimah*)] (*Shabbos* 151b).

3. שֹׁמְרֵי הַבַּיִת — *The guards of the house.* [Koheles compares the aged human body to a house in ruins:] The 'guards of the house' are the hands and arms which protect the body from threat and injury (*Ibn Ezra*) [but now are enfeebled].

אַנְשֵׁי הֶחָיִל — *The powerful men,* i.e., the legs that support the bodily structure (*Rashi*); הַטֹּחֲנוֹת, *the grinders,* i.e., the teeth that have fallen out in old age (*Rashi*).

הָרֹאוֹת בָּאֲרֻבּוֹת — *The gazers through windows.* I.e., the eyes (*Talmud*, ibid.).

4. וְיָקוּם לְקוֹל הַצִּפּוֹר — *When one rises up at the voice of a bird.* Even the chirping of a bird will wake the aged from sleep (*Talmud* ibid.; *Rashi*, et al).

5. גַּם מִגָּבֹהַּ יִירָאוּ — [*When*] *they even fear a height.* Even a small knoll looks to him like the highest mountains (*Talmud* ibid.); and he is liable to stumble (*Rashi*).

CHAPTER TWELVE

1 So remember your Creator in the days of your youth, before the evil days
come, and those years arrive of which you will say, 'I have no pleasure in them;'
2 before the sun, the light, the moon and the stars grow dark, and the clouds
return after the rain; 3 in the day when the guards of the house will tremble, and
the powerful men will stoop, and the grinders are idle because they are few, and
the gazers through windows are dimmed; 4 when the doors in the street are
shut; when the sound of the grinding is low; when one rises up at the voice of the
bird, and all the daughters of song grow dim; 5 when they even fear a height and
terror in the road; and the almond tree blossoms and the grasshopper becomes
a burden and the desire fails — so man goes to his eternal home, while the
mourners go about the streets.

6 Before the silver cord snaps, and the golden bowl is shattered, and the
pitcher is broken at the fountain, and the wheel is smashed at the pit. 7 Thus the
dust returns to the ground, as it was, and the spirit returns to God Who gave it.
8 Futility of futilities — said Koheles — All is futile!

9 And besides being wise, Koheles also imparted knowledge to the people; he
listened, and sought out; and arranged many proverbs.

10 Koheles sought to find words of delight, and words of truth recorded
properly. 11 The words of the wise are like goads, and the nails well driven are the

---

הַשָּׁקֵד – *The almond tree.* The whiteness of the hair in old age (*Ibn Ezra*).

כִּי־הֹלֵךְ הָאָדָם אֶל־בֵּית עוֹלָמוֹ – *So man goes to his eternal home,* i.e., the grave where he will dwell forever (*Ibn Ezra*).

6. [The following verse also amplifies upon verse 1, exhorting man to repent before the arrival of old age, and offers another metaphor for the *final* dissolution of life.]

חֶבֶל הַכֶּסֶף – *The silver cord,* i.e., the spinal cord (*Rashi*). [The metaphor is as follows: The body — near death — is likened to the malfunctioning machinery of a well: cord, wheel and pitcher. The cord (spine) snaps; the skull shatters; the stomach breaks; and the body is smashed.]

7. וְיָשֹׁב הֶעָפָר – *Thus the dust returns. 'Dust'* refers to the body of man, which was formed from dust.

עַל־הָאָרֶץ כְּשֶׁהָיָה – *To the ground, as it was* [i.e., as it was at Creation]. The body rejoins the earth from which it was formed (*Almosnino*).

וְהָרוּחַ תָּשׁוּב אֶל־הָאֱלֹהִים – *And the spirit returns to God.* But the soul returns to its Source from which it was taken; unto God Who gave it at birth as it is written (*Gen.* 2:7); *'And [God] breathed into his nostrils the breath of life'*.

8. Epilogue

Thus begins the epilogue of the Book. Having discoursed on the life and trials of man, and described the vicissitudes that man experiences *'under the sun'* until death, Koheles reiterates the recurring refrain of his conclusions: *'All is futile'* (*Rashbam; Kehillas Yaakov*).

הַקּוֹהֶלֶת – *Koheles.* The Hebrew has the definite article ה, *'the'* Koheles, because, as pointed out, Koheles is not a proper name but a title [see *comm.* to 1.1] (*Ibn Ezra*).

9. עוֹד לִמַּד־דַּעַת אֶת הָעָם – *(He) also imparted knowledge to the people.* ... Unlike many geniuses who cannot distill their wisdom in a manner that the masses can comprehend, the verse stresses that Solomon, *'the wisest of all men'* [*I Kings* 5:11], was blessed with this ability, and he utilized it by publicly expounding his knowledge in popular form (*R' Yaakov Chagiz*).

10. בִּקֵּשׁ קֹהֶלֶת לִמְצֹא דִּבְרֵי־חֵפֶץ – *Koheles sought to find words of delight.* Koheles sought in his quests to achieve supreme wisdom; he exerted himself to find Truth (*Ibn Ezra; Metzudas David*).

The commentators explain that Solomon sought to comprehend God's government of the Universe.

וְכָתוּב יֹשֶׁר דִּבְרֵי אֱמֶת – *And words of truth recorded properly.* This refers to the Bible (*Rashi*).

He sought to insure that people would find his proverbs to be a 'delight of God', and he later discovered that all his thoughts were already recorded in the Word of Truth [i.e., that his wisdom reflected the Truth of Torah] (*Rashi*).

11. כַּדָּרְבֹנוֹת – *Like goads.* Used by shepherds to prod their animals (*Metzudas David*).

As *Rashi* explains: Just as the goad directs the heifer along its proper path, so do words of the wise lead men along the paths of life (*Chagigah* 3b).

בַּעֲלֵי אֲסֻפּוֹת נִתְּנוּ מֵרֹעֶה אֶחָד: יב וְיֹתֵר מֵהֵמָּה בְּנִי הִזָּהֵר עֲשׂוֹת סְפָרִים
הַרְבֵּה אֵין קֵץ וְלַהַג הַרְבֵּה יְגִעַת בָּשָׂר: יג סוֹף דָּבָר הַכֹּל נִשְׁמָע
אֶת־הָאֱלֹהִים יְרָא וְאֶת־מִצְוֹתָיו שְׁמוֹר כִּי־זֶה כָּל־הָאָדָם: יד כִּי אֶת־כָּל־
מַעֲשֶׂה הָאֱלֹהִים יָבִא בְמִשְׁפָּט עַל כָּל־נֶעְלָם אִם־טוֹב וְאִם־רָע:

סוֹף דָּבָר הַכֹּל נִשְׁמָע
אֶת־הָאֱלֹהִים יְרָא וְאֶת־מִצְוֹתָיו שְׁמוֹר
כִּי־זֶה כָּל־הָאָדָם:

קדיש יתום

Mourners recite קַדִּישׁ יָתוֹם, the Mourner's *Kaddish* (see *Laws* §81-83).

יִתְגַּדַּל וְיִתְקַדַּשׁ שְׁמֵהּ רַבָּא. (.Cong – אָמֵן.) בְּעָלְמָא דִּי בְרָא כִרְעוּתֵהּ. וְיַמְלִיךְ מַלְכוּתֵהּ, בְּחַיֵּיכוֹן וּבְיוֹמֵיכוֹן וּבְחַיֵּי דְכָל בֵּית יִשְׂרָאֵל, בַּעֲגָלָא וּבִזְמַן קָרִיב. וְאִמְרוּ: אָמֵן.

(.Cong – אָמֵן. יְהֵא שְׁמֵהּ רַבָּא מְבָרַךְ לְעָלַם וּלְעָלְמֵי עָלְמַיָּא.)

יְהֵא שְׁמֵהּ רַבָּא מְבָרַךְ לְעָלַם וּלְעָלְמֵי עָלְמַיָּא.

יִתְבָּרַךְ וְיִשְׁתַּבַּח וְיִתְפָּאַר וְיִתְרוֹמַם וְיִתְנַשֵּׂא וְיִתְהַדָּר וְיִתְעַלֶּה וְיִתְהַלָּל שְׁמֵהּ דְּקֻדְשָׁא בְּרִיךְ הוּא (.Cong – בְּרִיךְ הוּא) – לְעֵלָּא מִן כָּל בִּרְכָתָא וְשִׁירָתָא תֻּשְׁבְּחָתָא וְנֶחֱמָתָא, דַּאֲמִירָן בְּעָלְמָא. וְאִמְרוּ: אָמֵן. (.Cong – אָמֵן.)

יְהֵא שְׁלָמָא רַבָּא מִן שְׁמַיָּא, וְחַיִּים עָלֵינוּ וְעַל כָּל יִשְׂרָאֵל. וְאִמְרוּ: אָמֵן. (.Cong – אָמֵן.)

Take three steps back. Bow left and say . . . עֹשֶׂה; bow right and say . . . הוּא; bow forward and say וְעַל כָּל . . . אָמֵן. Remain standing in place for a few moments, then take three steps forward.

עֹשֶׂה שָׁלוֹם בִּמְרוֹמָיו, הוּא יַעֲשֶׂה שָׁלוֹם עָלֵינוּ, וְעַל כָּל יִשְׂרָאֵל. וְאִמְרוּ: אָמֵן. (.Cong – אָמֵן.)

On the Sabbath of Chol Hamoed continue on next page.
On Shemini Atzeres continue on page 928.

---

12. וְיֹתֵר מֵהֵמָּה בְּנִי הִזָּהֵר – *Beyond these, my son, beware.* The verse is couched in a term of endearment [as if addressing a pupil] (*Metzudas David*).

עֲשׂוֹת סְפָרִים הַרְבֵּה אֵין קֵץ – *The making of many books is without limit.* Lest you say, 'If it is necessary to obey wise men, why are their words not published?' The answer is — *'the making of many books is without limit;'* it is not possible to commit everything to writing (*Rashi*).

Rav Yisrael Salanter, when discussing publishing books, would homiletically cite this verse and say: King Solomon cautioned us that not everything that man thinks must he say; not everything he says must he write, but, most important, not everything that he has written must he publish.

וְלַהַג הַרְבֵּה יְגִעַת בָּשָׂר – *And much study is weariness of the flesh.* The total accumulation of Torah knowledge is more than man can absorb. If so, you may ask, 'Why indulge in so much wearying effort?' The answer is given in the following verse.

13. Solomon said: Although I have expounded many esoteric and difficult concepts in this Book, nevertheless סוֹף דָּבָר, *the summation of the*

sayings of the masters of collections, coming from one Shepherd.
12 *Beyond these, my son, beware: the making of many books is without limit, and much study is weariness of the flesh.*
13 *The sum of the matter, when all has been considered: Fear God and keep His commandments, for that is man's whole duty.* 14 *For God will judge every deed — even everything hidden — whether good or evil.*

The sum of the matter, when all has been considered:
fear God and keep His commandments,
for that is man's whole duty.

MOURNER'S KADDISH

Mourners recite the Mourner's *Kaddish* (see *Laws* §81-83).
[A transliteration of this *Kaddish* appears on page 1305.]

יִתְגַּדַּל *May His great Name grow exalted and sanctified* (Cong.– *Amen.*) *in the world that He created as He willed. May He give reign to His kingship in your lifetimes and in your days, and in the lifetimes of the entire Family of Israel, swiftly and soon. Now respond: Amen.*

(Cong.– *Amen. May His great Name be blessed forever and ever.*)

May His great Name be blessed forever and ever.

Blessed, praised, glorified, exalted, extolled, mighty, upraised, and lauded be the Name of the Holy One, Blessed is He (Cong.– *Blessed is He*) *— beyond any blessing and song, praise and consolation that are uttered in the world. Now respond: Amen.* (Cong.– *Amen.*)

May there be abundant peace from Heaven, and life, upon us and upon all Israel. Now respond: Amen. (Cong.– *Amen.*)

Take three steps back. Bow left and say, *'He Who makes peace . . .'*; bow right and say, *'may He . . .'*; bow forward and say, *'and upon all Israel . . .'* Remain standing in place for a few moments, then take three steps forward.

He Who makes peace in His heights, may He make peace upon us, and upon all Israel. Now respond: Amen. (Cong.– *Amen.*)

On the Sabbath of Chol Hamoed continue on next page.
On Shemini Atzeres continue on page 928.

---

matter, הַכֹּל נִשְׁמָע, *is obvious to all* and unquestionable: *Fear God* with your every limb and organ, *for this is all of man* (*Derech Chaim*).

אֶת־הָאֱלֹהִים יְרָא וְאֶת־מִצְוֹתָיו שְׁמוֹר – *Fear God and keep His commandments. 'Fear God'* in your heart; *'and keep His commandments'* by deed (*Ramban*).

Do your utmost [and direct] your heart to Heaven (*Rashi*).

כִּי־זֶה כָּל־הָאָדָם – *For that is man's whole duty.* It was for this that all men were created (*Rashi*).

This is the essence of man (*Ibn Ezra*); and 'the entire world was created only for such a man' (*Shabbos* 30b).

14. עַל כָּל־נֶעְלָם – *Even everything hidden* — even unwillful transgressions (*Rashi*).

Even transgressions done in privacy [concealed from your fellow man and hence not punishable by human courts of law] (*Ralbag*).

אִם־טוֹב וְאִם רָע – *Whether good or evil.* Whether the deed was good and deserving of reward; or evil and deserving of punishment (*Sforno*).

סוֹף דָּבָר – *The sum of the matter.* It is customary, during public-readings of Koheles, to repeat verse 13 rather than end with the word רָע, *evil,* in verse 14. We act similarly at the end of *Isaiah, Malachi* and *Lamentations,* and thus end these books on a positive note.

הוצאת ספר תורה לשבת חול המועד

From the moment the Ark is opened until the Torah is returned to it, one must conduct himself with the utmost respect, and avoid unnecessary conversation. It is commendable to kiss the Torah as it is carried to the *bimah* [reading table] and back to the Ark.

All rise and remain standing until the Torah is placed on the *bimah*. The congregation recites:

אֵין כָּמְוֹךָ בָאֱלֹהִים אֲדֹנָי, וְאֵין כְּמַעֲשֶׂיךָ.[1] מַלְכוּתְךָ מַלְכוּת כָּל עֹלָמִים, וּמֶמְשַׁלְתְּךָ בְּכָל דּוֹר וָדֹר.[2] יהוה מֶלֶךְ,[3] יהוה מָלָךְ,[4] יהוה יִמְלֹךְ לְעֹלָם וָעֶד.[5] יהוה עֹז לְעַמּוֹ יִתֵּן, יהוה יְבָרֵךְ אֶת עַמּוֹ בַשָּׁלוֹם.[6]

אַב הָרַחֲמִים, הֵיטִיבָה בִרְצוֹנְךָ אֶת צִיּוֹן, תִּבְנֶה חוֹמוֹת יְרוּשָׁלָיִם.[7] כִּי בְךָ לְבַד בָּטָחְנוּ, מֶלֶךְ אֵל רָם וְנִשָּׂא, אֲדוֹן עוֹלָמִים.

THE ARK IS OPENED

Before the Torah is removed the congregation recites:

וַיְהִי בִּנְסֹעַ הָאָרֹן וַיֹּאמֶר מֹשֶׁה, קוּמָה יהוה וְיָפֻצוּ אֹיְבֶיךָ וְיָנֻסוּ מְשַׂנְאֶיךָ מִפָּנֶיךָ.[8] כִּי מִצִּיּוֹן תֵּצֵא תוֹרָה, וּדְבַר יהוה מִירוּשָׁלָיִם.[9] בָּרוּךְ שֶׁנָּתַן תּוֹרָה לְעַמּוֹ יִשְׂרָאֵל בִּקְדֻשָּׁתוֹ.

זוהר ויקהל שסט:א

בְּרִיךְ שְׁמֵהּ דְּמָרֵא עָלְמָא, בְּרִיךְ כִּתְרָךְ וְאַתְרָךְ. יְהֵא רְעוּתָךְ עִם עַמָּךְ יִשְׂרָאֵל לְעָלַם, וּפֻרְקַן יְמִינָךְ אַחֲזֵי לְעַמָּךְ בְּבֵית מַקְדְּשָׁךְ, וּלְאַמְטוּיֵי לָנָא מִטּוּב נְהוֹרָךְ, וּלְקַבֵּל צְלוֹתָנָא בְּרַחֲמִין. יְהֵא רַעֲוָא קֳדָמָךְ, דְּתוֹרִיךְ לָן חַיִּין בְּטִיבוּתָא, וְלֶהֱוֵי אֲנָא פְקִידָא בְּגוֹ צַדִּיקַיָּא, לְמִרְחַם עָלַי וּלְמִנְטַר יָתִי וְיַת כָּל דִּי לִי, וְדִי לְעַמָּךְ יִשְׂרָאֵל. אַנְתְּ הוּא זָן לְכֹלָּא, וּמְפַרְנֵס לְכֹלָּא, אַנְתְּ הוּא שַׁלִּיט עַל כֹּלָּא. אַנְתְּ הוּא דְשַׁלִּיט עַל מַלְכַיָּא, וּמַלְכוּתָא דִּילָךְ הִיא. אֲנָא עַבְדָּא דְקֻדְשָׁא בְּרִיךְ הוּא, דְּסָגִידְנָא קַמֵּהּ וּמִקַּמָּא דִּיקַר אוֹרַיְתֵהּ בְּכָל עִדָּן וְעִדָּן. לָא עַל אֱנָשׁ רָחִיצְנָא, וְלָא עַל בַּר אֱלָהִין סָמִיכְנָא, אֶלָּא בֶּאֱלָהָא דִשְׁמַיָּא, דְּהוּא אֱלָהָא קְשׁוֹט, וְאוֹרַיְתֵהּ קְשׁוֹט, וּנְבִיאוֹהִי קְשׁוֹט, וּמַסְגֵּא לְמֶעְבַּד טַבְוָן וּקְשׁוֹט. בֵּהּ אֲנָא רָחִיץ, וְלִשְׁמֵהּ קַדִּישָׁא יַקִּירָא אֲנָא אֵמַר תֻּשְׁבְּחָן. יְהֵא רַעֲוָא קֳדָמָךְ, דְּתִפְתַּח לִבָּאִי בְּאוֹרַיְתָא, וְתַשְׁלִים מִשְׁאֲלִין דְּלִבָּאִי, וְלִבָּא דְכָל עַמָּךְ יִשְׂרָאֵל, לְטָב וּלְחַיִּין וְלִשְׁלָם. (אָמֵן.)

REMOVAL OF THE TORAH FROM THE ARK FOR SABBATH CHOL HAMOED

From the moment the Ark is opened until the Torah is returned to it, one must conduct himself with the utmost respect, and avoid unnecessary conversation. It is commendable to kiss the Torah as it is carried to the *bimah* [reading table] and back to the Ark.

All rise and remain standing until the Torah is placed on the *bimah*. The congregation recites:

אֵין כָּמְוֹךָ *There is none like You among the gods, my Lord, and there is nothing like Your works.*[1] *Your kingdom is a kingdom spanning all eternities, and Your dominion is throughout every generation.*[2] *HASHEM reigns,*[3] *HASHEM has reigned,*[4] *HASHEM shall reign for all eternity.*[5] *HASHEM will give might to His people; HASHEM will bless His people with peace.*[6]

אַב הָרַחֲמִים *Father of compassion, do good with Zion according to Your will; rebuild the walls of Jerusalem.*[7] *For we trust in You alone, O King, God, exalted and uplifted, Master of worlds.*

THE ARK IS OPENED

Before the Torah is removed the congregation recites:

וַיְהִי בִּנְסֹעַ *When the Ark would travel, Moses would say, 'Arise, HASHEM, and let Your foes be scattered, let those who hate You flee from You.'*[8] *For from Zion the Torah will come forth and the word of HASHEM from Jerusalem.*[9] *Blessed is He Who gave the Torah to His people Israel in His holiness.*

Zohar, Vayakhel 369a

בְּרִיךְ שְׁמֵהּ *Blessed is the Name of the Master of the universe, blessed is Your crown and Your place. May Your favor remain with Your people Israel forever; may You display the salvation of Your right hand to Your people in Your Holy Temple, to benefit us with the goodness of Your luminescence and to accept our prayers with mercy. May it be Your will that You extend our lives with goodness and that I be numbered among the righteous; that You have mercy on me and protect me, all that is mine and that is Your people Israel's. It is You Who nourishes all and sustains all; You control everything. It is You Who control kings, and kingship is Yours. I am a servant of the Holy One, Blessed is He, and I prostrate myself before Him and before the glory of His Torah at all times. Not in any man do I put trust, nor on any angel do I rely — only on the God of heaven Who is the God of truth, Whose Torah is truth and Whose prophets are true and Who acts liberally with kindness and truth. In Him do I trust, and to His glorious and holy Name do I declare praises. May it be Your will that You open my heart to the Torah and that You fulfill the wishes of my heart and the heart of Your entire people Israel for good, for life, and for peace. (Amen.)*

---

(1) *Psalms* 86:8. (2) 145:13. (3) 10:16. (4) 93:1 et al. (5) *Exodus* 15:18.
(6) *Psalms* 29:11. (7) 51:20. (8) *Numbers* 10:35. (9) *Isaiah* 2:3.

Two Torah Scrolls are removed from the Ark; the first for the main Torah reading and the second for *Maftir*. The first is presented to the *chazzan*, who accepts it in his right arm. Facing the congregation, the *chazzan* raises the Torah and, followed by congregation, recites:

שְׁמַע יִשְׂרָאֵל• יהוה אֱלֹהֵינוּ יהוה אֶחָד.[1]

Still facing the congregation, the *chazzan* raises the Torah and, followed by congregation, recites:

אֶחָד (הוּא) אֱלֹהֵינוּ גָּדוֹל אֲדוֹנֵינוּ, קָדוֹשׁ שְׁמוֹ.

The *chazzan* turns to the Ark, bows while raising the Torah, and recites:

גַּדְּלוּ• לַיהוה אִתִּי וּנְרוֹמְמָה שְׁמוֹ יַחְדָּו.[2]

The *chazzan* turns to his right and carries the Torah to the *bimah*, as the congregation responds:

לְךָ יהוה הַגְּדֻלָּה• וְהַגְּבוּרָה וְהַתִּפְאֶרֶת וְהַנֵּצַח וְהַהוֹד כִּי כֹל בַּשָּׁמַיִם וּבָאָרֶץ, לְךָ יהוה הַמַּמְלָכָה וְהַמִּתְנַשֵּׂא לְכֹל לְרֹאשׁ.[3] רוֹמְמוּ יהוה אֱלֹהֵינוּ, וְהִשְׁתַּחֲווּ לַהֲדֹם רַגְלָיו,• קָדוֹשׁ הוּא. רוֹמְמוּ יהוה אֱלֹהֵינוּ, וְהִשְׁתַּחֲווּ לְהַר קָדְשׁוֹ, כִּי קָדוֹשׁ יהוה אֱלֹהֵינוּ.[4]

As the *chazzan* carries the Torah to the *bimah* the congregation recites:

עַל הַכֹּל,• יִתְגַּדַּל וְיִתְקַדַּשׁ וְיִשְׁתַּבַּח וְיִתְפָּאַר וְיִתְרוֹמַם וְיִתְנַשֵּׂא שְׁמוֹ שֶׁל מֶלֶךְ מַלְכֵי הַמְּלָכִים הַקָּדוֹשׁ בָּרוּךְ הוּא, בָּעוֹלָמוֹת שֶׁבָּרָא, הָעוֹלָם הַזֶּה וְהָעוֹלָם הַבָּא, כִּרְצוֹנוֹ,• וְכִרְצוֹן יְרֵאָיו, וְכִרְצוֹן כָּל בֵּית יִשְׂרָאֵל. צוּר הָעוֹלָמִים, אֲדוֹן כָּל הַבְּרִיּוֹת, אֱלוֹהַּ כָּל הַנְּפָשׁוֹת, הַיּוֹשֵׁב בְּמֶרְחֲבֵי מָרוֹם, הַשּׁוֹכֵן בִּשְׁמֵי שְׁמֵי קֶדֶם. קְדֻשָּׁתוֹ עַל הַחַיּוֹת, וּקְדֻשָּׁתוֹ עַל כִּסֵּא הַכָּבוֹד. וּבְכֵן יִתְקַדַּשׁ שִׁמְךָ בָּנוּ יהוה אֱלֹהֵינוּ לְעֵינֵי כָּל חָי. וְנֹאמַר לְפָנָיו שִׁיר חָדָשׁ, כַּכָּתוּב: שִׁירוּ לֵאלֹהִים זַמְּרוּ שְׁמוֹ, סֹלּוּ לָרֹכֵב בָּעֲרָבוֹת בְּיָהּ שְׁמוֹ, וְעִלְזוּ לְפָנָיו.[5] וְנִרְאֵהוּ עַיִן בְּעַיִן בְּשׁוּבוֹ אֶל נָוֵהוּ, כַּכָּתוּב: כִּי עַיִן בְּעַיִן יִרְאוּ בְּשׁוּב יהוה צִיּוֹן.[6] וְנֶאֱמַר: וְנִגְלָה כְּבוֹד יהוה, וְרָאוּ כָל בָּשָׂר יַחְדָּו כִּי פִּי יהוה דִּבֵּר.[7]

שְׁמַע יִשְׂרָאֵל — *Hear, O Israel.* Holding the Torah Scroll the *chazzan* leads the congregation in reciting three verses that help set the majestic tone of reading publicly from the word of God. The verses form a logical progression: God is One; He is great and holy; therefore we join in declaring His greatness.

גַּדְּלוּ — *Declare the greatness.* Our rejoicing in the Torah manifests itself in praise of its Giver. The *chazzan* calls upon the congregation to join him in praising God.

לְךָ ה׳ הַגְּדֻלָּה — *Yours, HASHEM, is the greatness.* This praise was first uttered by David in his ecstasy at seeing how wholeheartedly the people contributed their riches toward the eventual building of the Temple. He ascribed the greatness of that and every other achievement to God's graciousness.

לַהֲדֹם רַגְלָיו — *At His footstool,* i.e., the Temple, as if to say that God's Heavenly Presence extends earthward, like a footstool that helps support a monarch sitting on his throne. In a further sense, this represents our resolve to live in such a way that we are worthy of His Presence resting upon us *(R' Hirsch).*

עַל הַכֹּל — *For all this.* All the praises that we

Two Torah Scrolls are removed from the Ark; the first for the main Torah reading and the second for *Maftir*. The first is presented to the *chazzan*, who accepts it in his right arm. Facing the congregation, the *chazzan* raises the Torah and, followed by congregation, recites:

Hear, O Israel:* HASHEM is our God, HASHEM, the One and Only.[1]

Still facing the congregation, the *chazzan* raises the Torah and, followed by congregation, recites:

One is our God, great is our Master, Holy is His Name.

The *chazzan* turns to the Ark, bows while raising the Torah, and recites:

Declare the greatness* of HASHEM with me, and let us exalt His Name together.[2]

The *chazzan* turns to his right and carries the Torah to the *bimah*, as the congregation responds:

לְךָ *Yours, HASHEM, is the greatness,* the strength, the splendor, the triumph, and the glory; even everything in heaven and earth; Yours, HASHEM, is the kingdom, and the sovereignty over every leader.*[3] *Exalt HASHEM, our God, and bow at His footstool;* He is Holy! Exalt HASHEM, our God, and bow to His holy mountain; for holy is HASHEM, our God.*[4]

As the *chazzan* carries the Torah to the *bimah*, the congregation recites:

עַל הַכֹּל *For all this,* let the Name of the King of kings, the Holy One, Blessed is He, grow exalted, sanctified, praised, glorified, exalted, and extolled in the worlds that He has created — This World and the World to Come — according to His will,* the will of those who fear Him, and the will of the entire House of Israel. Rock of the eternities, Master of all creatures, God of all souls, He Who sits in the expanses on high, Who rests in the loftiest primeval heavens. His holiness is upon the Chayos; His holiness is upon the Throne of Glory. Similarly, may Your Name be sanctified within us, HASHEM, our God, in the sight of all the living. May we chant before Him a new song as it is written: 'Sing to God, make music for His Name, extol the One Who rides in the highest heavens with His Name YAH, and exult before Him.'*[5] *May we see Him with a perceptive view upon His return to His Abode, as is written: 'For they shall see with a perceptive view as HASHEM returns to Zion.'*[6] *And it is said: 'The glory of HASHEM shall be revealed and all flesh together shall see that the mouth of HASHEM has spoken.'*[7]

(1) *Deuteronomy* 6:4. (2) *Psalms* 34:4. (3) *I Chronicles* 29:11.
(4) *Psalms* 99:5,9. (5) 68:5. (6) *Isaiah* 52:8. (7) 40:5.

have uttered heretofore are inadequate to describe God's greatness. May His Name continue to grow exalted (*Kol Bo*).

This paragraph is intended to express the majesty of God especially now that we are about to read from the Torah. We say that although He is sanctified in the heavens and by the spiritual beings, we long to become worthy vehicles through which His greatness can be manifested on earth, as well.

כִּרְצוֹנוֹ — *According to His will.* May He be *exalted, sanctified, praised* ... as He wishes to be. God created the universe so that His glory could be appreciated and emulated by man (see *Isaiah* 43:7). We now pray that this will indeed take place.

אַב הָרַחֲמִים הוּא יְרַחֵם עַם עֲמוּסִים, וְיִזְכֹּר בְּרִית אֵיתָנִים, וְיַצִּיל נַפְשׁוֹתֵינוּ מִן הַשָּׁעוֹת הָרָעוֹת, וְיִגְעַר בְּיֵצֶר הָרַע מִן הַנְּשׂוּאִים, וְיָחֹן אוֹתָנוּ לִפְלֵיטַת עוֹלָמִים, וִימַלֵּא מִשְׁאֲלוֹתֵינוּ בְּמִדָּה טוֹבָה יְשׁוּעָה וְרַחֲמִים.

The Torah is placed on the *bimah* and prepared for reading.

The *gabbai* uses the following formula to call a *Kohen* to the Torah:

וְיַעֲזוֹר וְיָגֵן וְיוֹשִׁיעַ לְכֹל הַחוֹסִים בּוֹ, וְנֹאמַר, אָמֵן. הַכֹּל הָבוּ גֹדֶל לֵאלֹהֵינוּ וּתְנוּ כָבוֹד לַתּוֹרָה, כֹּהֵן° קְרָב, יַעֲמֹד (name) בֶּן (father's name) הַכֹּהֵן.

°If no *Kohen* is present, the *gabbai* says:
"אֵין כַּאן כֹּהֵן, יַעֲמֹד (insert name) יִשְׂרָאֵל (לֵוִי) בִּמְקוֹם כֹּהֵן."

בָּרוּךְ שֶׁנָּתַן תּוֹרָה לְעַמּוֹ יִשְׂרָאֵל בִּקְדֻשָּׁתוֹ. (תּוֹרַת יהוה תְּמִימָה מְשִׁיבַת נָפֶשׁ, עֵדוּת יהוה נֶאֱמָנָה מַחְכִּימַת פֶּתִי. פִּקּוּדֵי יהוה יְשָׁרִים מְשַׂמְּחֵי לֵב, מִצְוַת יהוה בָּרָה מְאִירַת עֵינָיִם.[1] יהוה עֹז לְעַמּוֹ יִתֵּן, יהוה יְבָרֵךְ אֶת עַמּוֹ בַשָּׁלוֹם.[2] הָאֵל תָּמִים דַּרְכּוֹ, אִמְרַת יהוה צְרוּפָה, מָגֵן הוּא לְכֹל הַחוֹסִים בּוֹ.[3])

Congregation, then *gabbai:*

וְאַתֶּם הַדְּבֵקִים בַּיהוה אֱלֹהֵיכֶם, חַיִּים כֻּלְּכֶם הַיּוֹם.[4]

קריאת התורה

The reader shows the *oleh* (person called to the Torah) the place in the Torah. The *oleh* touches the Torah with a corner of his *tallis,* or the belt or mantle of the Torah, and kisses it. He then begins the blessing, bowing at בָּרְכוּ, and straightening up at 'ה.

בָּרְכוּ אֶת יהוה* הַמְבֹרָךְ.

Congregation, followed by *oleh,* responds, bowing at בָּרוּךְ, and straightening up at 'ה.

בָּרוּךְ יהוה הַמְבֹרָךְ לְעוֹלָם וָעֶד.

Oleh continues:

בָּרוּךְ אַתָּה יהוה אֱלֹהֵינוּ מֶלֶךְ הָעוֹלָם, אֲשֶׁר בָּחַר בָּנוּ מִכָּל הָעַמִּים, וְנָתַן לָנוּ אֶת תּוֹרָתוֹ. בָּרוּךְ אַתָּה יהוה, נוֹתֵן הַתּוֹרָה. (.Cong – אָמֵן.)

After his Torah portion has been read, the *oleh* recites:

בָּרוּךְ אַתָּה יהוה אֱלֹהֵינוּ מֶלֶךְ הָעוֹלָם, אֲשֶׁר נָתַן לָנוּ תּוֹרַת אֱמֶת, וְחַיֵּי עוֹלָם נָטַע בְּתוֹכֵנוּ. בָּרוּךְ אַתָּה יהוה, נוֹתֵן הַתּוֹרָה. (.Cong – אָמֵן.)

קְרִיאַת הַתּוֹרָה / Reading of the Torah

There is a basic difference between the reading of the Torah and the prayers. When we pray, *we* call upon *God;* that is why the *chazzan* stands in front of the congregation as its representative. But the Torah reading is reminiscent of God's revelation to Israel, when the nation gathered around Mount Sinai to hear Him communicate His word to Israel. That is why the Torah is read from a *bimah,* platform, in the center of the congregation and usually elevated, like the mountain around which Israel gathered.

The number of people called to the Torah varies in accordance with the sanctity of the day.

אַב הָרַחֲמִים *May the Father of compassion have mercy on the nation that is borne by Him, and may He remember the covenant of the spiritually mighty. May He rescue our souls from the bad times, and upbraid the evil inclination to leave those borne by Him, graciously make us an eternal remnant, and fulfill our requests in good measure, for salvation and mercy.*

The Torah is placed on the *bimah* and prepared for reading.

The *gabbai* uses the following formula to call a *Kohen* to the Torah:

וְיַעֲזוֹר *May He help, shield, and save all who take refuge in Him — Now let us respond: Amen. All of you ascribe greatness to our God and give honor to the Torah. Kohen,° approach. Arise* (name) *son of* (father's name) *the Kohen*

°If no *Kohen* is present, the *gabbai* says: *'There is no Kohen present, stand* (name) *son of* (father's name) *an Israelite (Levite) in place of the Kohen.'*

Blessed is He Who gave the Torah to His people Israel in His holiness. (The Torah of HASHEM is perfect, restoring the soul; the testimony of HASHEM is trustworthy, making the simple one wise. The orders of HASHEM are upright, gladdening the heart; the command of HASHEM is clear, enlightening the eyes.[1] *HASHEM will give might to His nation; HASHEM will bless His nation with peace.*[2] *The God Whose way is perfect, the promise of HASHEM is flawless, He is a shield for all who take refuge in Him.*[3]*)*

Congregation, then *gabbai:*

You who cling to HASHEM, your God, you are all alive today.[4]

❧ READING OF THE TORAH ❧

The reader shows the *oleh* (person called to the Torah) the place in the Torah. The *oleh* touches the Torah with a corner of his *tallis,* or the belt or mantle of the Torah, and kisses it. He then begins the blessing, bowing at *'Bless,'* and straightening up at 'HASHEM.'

Bless HASHEM,* the blessed One.

Congregation, followed by *oleh,* responds, bowing at 'Blessed,' and straightening up at 'HASHEM.'

Blessed is HASHEM, the blessed One, for all eternity.

Oleh continues:

בָּרוּךְ *Blessed are You, HASHEM, our God, King of the universe, Who selected us from all the peoples and gave us His Torah. Blessed are You, HASHEM, Giver of the Torah.* (Cong.– *Amen.)*

After his Torah portion has been read, the *oleh* recites:

בָּרוּךְ *Blessed are You, HASHEM, our God, King of the universe, Who gave us the Torah of truth and implanted eternal life within us. Blessed are You, HASHEM, Giver of the Torah.* (Cong.– *Amen.)*

(1) *Psalms* 19:8-9. (2) 29:11. (3) 18:31. (4) *Deuteronomy* 4:4.

Thus, on Monday and Thursday, fast days, Purim and Chanukah, three people are called; on Rosh Chodesh and Chol HaMoed, four; on Festivals and Rosh Hashanah, five; on Yom Kippur, six; and on the Sabbath [whether an ordinary Sabbath or a Festival that falls on the Sabbath], seven. (It should be noted that *Maftir* is not included in the above number since *Maftir* is attached to the *Haftarah* reading.) Only three are called on Sabbath afternoons since the Torah has already been read in the morning.

On most Festivals the Torah reading is a selection on either the historical narrative of the day or the commandment to observe the Festivals.

☙ בָּרְכוּ אֶת ה׳ — *Bless HASHEM.* This call to the congregation to bless God prior to the Torah reading is based on the practice of Ezra (*Nechemiah* 8:6). Before he read from the Torah to the multitude, he blessed God and they responded in kind. Similarly, the Sages (*Berachos* 21a) derive the Scriptural requirement to recite a

PRAYER FOR THE OLEH / מי שברך לעולה לתורה

After each *oleh* completes his concluding blessing, the *gabbai* calls the next *oleh* to the Torah, then blesses the one who has just concluded.

מִי שֶׁבֵּרַךְ אֲבוֹתֵינוּ אַבְרָהָם יִצְחָק וְיַעֲקֹב, הוּא יְבָרֵךְ אֶת (name) בֶּן (father's name) בַּעֲבוּר שֶׁעָלָה לִכְבוֹד הַמָּקוֹם, לִכְבוֹד הַתּוֹרָה, לִכְבוֹד הַשַּׁבָּת, לִכְבוֹד הָרֶגֶל. בִּשְׂכַר זֶה, הַקָּדוֹשׁ בָּרוּךְ הוּא יִשְׁמְּרֵהוּ וְיַצִּילֵהוּ מִכָּל צָרָה וְצוּקָה, וּמִכָּל נֶגַע וּמַחֲלָה, וְיִשְׁלַח בְּרָכָה וְהַצְלָחָה בְּכָל מַעֲשֵׂה יָדָיו, וְיִזְכֶּה לַעֲלוֹת לָרֶגֶל, עִם כָּל יִשְׂרָאֵל אֶחָיו. וְנֹאמַר: אָמֵן.

(.אָמֵן –Cong.)

PRAYER FOR OTHERS / מי שברך לאחרים

It is customary that the following prayer be recited for the family members of the *oleh* and for anyone else that he may wish to include:

מִי שֶׁבֵּרַךְ אֲבוֹתֵינוּ אַבְרָהָם יִצְחָק וְיַעֲקֹב, הוּא יְבָרֵךְ אֶת (names of the recipients) בַּעֲבוּר שֶׁ(name of *oleh*) יִתֵּן לִצְדָקָה בַּעֲבוּרָם. בִּשְׂכַר זֶה, הַקָּדוֹשׁ בָּרוּךְ הוּא יִשְׁמְּרֵם וְיַצִּילֵם מִכָּל צָרָה וְצוּקָה, וּמִכָּל נֶגַע וּמַחֲלָה, וְיִשְׁלַח בְּרָכָה וְהַצְלָחָה בְּכָל מַעֲשֵׂה יְדֵיהֶם, וְיִזְכּוּ לַעֲלוֹת לָרֶגֶל, עִם כָּל יִשְׂרָאֵל אֲחֵיהֶם. וְנֹאמַר: אָמֵן.

(.אָמֵן –Cong.)

PRAYER FOR A SICK PERSON / מי שברך לחולה

מִי שֶׁבֵּרַךְ אֲבוֹתֵינוּ אַבְרָהָם יִצְחָק וְיַעֲקֹב, מֹשֶׁה אַהֲרֹן דָּוִד וּשְׁלֹמֹה,

for a man

הוּא יְבָרֵךְ וִירַפֵּא אֶת הַחוֹלֶה (patient's name) בֶּן (mother's name) בַּעֲבוּר שֶׁ(supplicant's name) יִתֵּן לִצְדָקָה בַּעֲבוּרוֹ.°° בִּשְׂכַר זֶה, הַקָּדוֹשׁ בָּרוּךְ הוּא יִמָּלֵא רַחֲמִים עָלָיו, לְהַחֲלִימוֹ וּלְרַפְּאתוֹ לְהַחֲזִיקוֹ וּלְהַחֲיוֹתוֹ, וְיִשְׁלַח לוֹ מְהֵרָה רְפוּאָה שְׁלֵמָה מִן הַשָּׁמַיִם, לִרְמַ״ח אֵבָרָיו, וּשְׁסָ״ה גִּידָיו, בְּתוֹךְ

for a woman

הוּא יְבָרֵךְ וִירַפֵּא אֶת הַחוֹלָה (patient's name) בַּת (mother's name) בַּעֲבוּר שֶׁ(supplicant's name) יִתֵּן לִצְדָקָה בַּעֲבוּרָהּ.°° בִּשְׂכַר זֶה, הַקָּדוֹשׁ בָּרוּךְ הוּא יִמָּלֵא רַחֲמִים עָלֶיהָ, לְהַחֲלִימָהּ וּלְרַפְּאתָהּ וּלְהַחֲזִיקָהּ וּלְהַחֲיוֹתָהּ, וְיִשְׁלַח לָהּ מְהֵרָה רְפוּאָה שְׁלֵמָה מִן הַשָּׁמַיִם, לְכָל אֵבָרֶיהָ, וּלְכָל גִּידֶיהָ, בְּתוֹךְ

שְׁאָר חוֹלֵי יִשְׂרָאֵל, רְפוּאַת הַנֶּפֶשׁ, וּרְפוּאַת הַגּוּף, שַׁבָּת הִיא מִלִּזְעֹק, וּרְפוּאָה קְרוֹבָה לָבֹא, הַשְׁתָּא, בַּעֲגָלָא וּבִזְמַן קָרִיב. וְנֹאמַר: אָמֵן.

(.אָמֵן –Cong.)

°°Many congregations substitute:

בַּעֲבוּר שֶׁכָּל הַקָּהָל מִתְפַּלְּלִים בַּעֲבוּרוֹ (בַּעֲבוּרָהּ)

---

blessing before Torah study from the verse, *When I proclaim the Name of* HASHEM, *ascribe greatness to our God* (*Deuteronomy* 32:3). The implication is that the public study of Torah requires a blessing.

מִי שֶׁבֵּרַךְ / He Who blessed

בַּעֲבוּר שֶׁיִּתֵּן לִצְדָקָה — *For ... will contribute to charity.* The custom of blessing those called to the Torah is centuries old, and it has become

PRAYER FOR THE OLEH

After each *oleh* completes his concluding blessing, the *gabbai* calls the next *oleh* to the Torah, then blesses the one who has just concluded.

מִי שֶׁבֵּרַךְ *He Who blessed our forefathers Abraham, Isaac, and Jacob — may He bless (* Hebrew name*) son of (* father's Hebrew name*) because he has come up to the Torah in honor of the Omnipresent, in honor of the Torah, in honor of the Sabbath, in honor of the pilgrimage festival. As reward for this, may the Holy One, Blessed is He, protect him and rescue him from every trouble and distress, from every plague and illness; may He send blessing and success in his every endeavor, and may he be privileged to ascend to Jerusalem for the pilgrimage, together with all Israel, his brethren. Now let us respond: Amen.*

(Cong.— *Amen.)*

PRAYER FOR OTHERS

It is customary that the following prayer be recited for the family members of the *oleh* and for anyone else that he may wish to include:

מִי שֶׁבֵּרַךְ *He Who blessed our forefathers Abraham, Isaac, and Jacob — may He bless (* names of recipients*) for (* name of *oleh) will contribute to charity on their behalf. As reward for this, may the Holy One, Blessed is He, protect them and rescue them from every trouble and distress, from every plague and illness; may He send blessing and success in their every endeavor and may they be privileged to ascend to Jerusalem for the pilgrimage, together with all Israel, their brethren. Now let us respond: Amen.* (Cong.— *Amen.)*

PRAYER FOR A SICK PERSON

מִי שֶׁבֵּרַךְ *He Who blessed our forefathers Abraham, Isaac and Jacob, Moses and Aaron, David and Solomon — may He bless and heal the sick person (* patient's Hebrew name*) son/daughter of (* patient's mother's Hebrew name*) because (* name of supplicant*) will contribute to charity on his/her behalf.*°° *In reward for this, may the Holy One, Blessed is He, be filled with*

for a man	for a woman
compassion for him to restore his health, to heal him, to strengthen him, and to revivify him. And may He send him speedily a complete recovery from heaven for his two hundred forty-eight organs and three hundred sixty-five blood vessels,	*compassion for her to restore her health, to heal her, to strengthen her, and to revivify her. And may He send her speedily a complete recovery from heaven for all her organs and all her blood vessels,*

among the other sick people of Israel, a recovery of the body and a recovery of the spirit though the Sabbath prohibits us from crying out, may a recovery come speedily, swiftly and soon. Now let us respond: Amen. (Cong.—*Amen.)*

°°Many congregations substitute:
because the entire congregation prays for him (her)

---

customary for these blessings to include pledges to charitable causes. Although the formula most often used is בַּעֲבוּר שֶׁנָּדַר, *for he has pledged,* it is preferable to use the formula בַּעֲבוּר שֶׁיִּתֵּן, *for he will contribute.* This is based on the Talmudic teaching *(Beitzah* 36b) that it is improper to make certain types of monetary pledges on the Sabbath and Festivals, and this latter formula does not have the status of a vow. Variations of the מִי שֶׁבֵּרַךְ blessing express prayers for the congregation as a whole or individual members of it, sick people, or new mothers and their infants. In all cases, the concept behind the prayer is that the merit of the Torah reading and of the person who has read from it is a source of blessing.

❧ קריאת התורה לשבת חול המועד ☙

שמות לג:יב-לד:כו

כהן – וַיֹּאמֶר מֹשֶׁה* אֶל־יהוה רְאֵה אַתָּה אֹמֵר אֵלַי הַעַל אֶת־הָעָם הַזֶּה וְאַתָּה לֹא הוֹדַעְתַּנִי אֵת אֲשֶׁר־תִּשְׁלַח עִמִּי וְאַתָּה אָמַרְתָּ יְדַעְתִּיךָ בְשֵׁם* וְגַם־מָצָאתָ חֵן בְּעֵינָי: וְעַתָּה אִם־נָא מָצָאתִי חֵן בְּעֵינֶיךָ הוֹדִעֵנִי נָא אֶת־דְּרָכֶךָ וְאֵדָעֲךָ לְמַעַן אֶמְצָא־חֵן* בְּעֵינֶיךָ וּרְאֵה כִּי עַמְּךָ הַגּוֹי הַזֶּה: וַיֹּאמַר פָּנַי יֵלֵכוּ וַהֲנִחֹתִי לָךְ: וַיֹּאמֶר אֵלָיו אִם־אֵין פָּנֶיךָ הֹלְכִים* אַל־תַּעֲלֵנוּ מִזֶּה: וּבַמֶּה ׀ יִוָּדַע אֵפוֹא כִּי־מָצָאתִי חֵן בְּעֵינֶיךָ אֲנִי וְעַמֶּךָ הֲלוֹא בְּלֶכְתְּךָ עִמָּנוּ וְנִפְלֵינוּ אֲנִי וְעַמְּךָ מִכָּל־הָעָם אֲשֶׁר עַל־פְּנֵי הָאֲדָמָה:

לוי – וַיֹּאמֶר יהוה אֶל־מֹשֶׁה גַּם אֶת־הַדָּבָר הַזֶּה* אֲשֶׁר דִּבַּרְתָּ אֶעֱשֶׂה כִּי־מָצָאתָ חֵן בְּעֵינַי וָאֵדָעֲךָ בְּשֵׁם: וַיֹּאמַר הַרְאֵנִי נָא* אֶת־כְּבֹדֶךָ: וַיֹּאמֶר אֲנִי אַעֲבִיר כָּל־טוּבִי* עַל־פָּנֶיךָ וְקָרָאתִי בְשֵׁם יהוה* לְפָנֶיךָ וְחַנֹּתִי אֶת־אֲשֶׁר אָחֹן וְרִחַמְתִּי אֶת־אֲשֶׁר אֲרַחֵם:

שלישי – וַיֹּאמֶר לֹא תוּכַל לִרְאֹת* אֶת־פָּנָי כִּי לֹא־יִרְאַנִי הָאָדָם וָחָי: וַיֹּאמֶר יהוה הִנֵּה מָקוֹם אִתִּי* וְנִצַּבְתָּ עַל־הַצּוּר: וְהָיָה בַּעֲבֹר כְּבֹדִי וְשַׂמְתִּיךָ בְּנִקְרַת הַצּוּר וְשַׂכֹּתִי כַפִּי עָלֶיךָ עַד־עָבְרִי: וַהֲסִרֹתִי אֶת־כַּפִּי וְרָאִיתָ אֶת־אֲחֹרָי וּפָנַי לֹא יֵרָאוּ:

רביעי – וַיֹּאמֶר יהוה אֶל־מֹשֶׁה פְּסָל־לְךָ* שְׁנֵי־לֻחֹת אֲבָנִים כָּרִאשֹׁנִים וְכָתַבְתִּי עַל־הַלֻּחֹת אֶת־הַדְּבָרִים אֲשֶׁר הָיוּ עַל־

◆§ Torah Reading for the Sabbath of Chol HaMoed

וַיֹּאמֶר מֹשֶׁה – *Moses said.* After the sin of the Golden Calf, God commanded Moses to lead the Jews into *Eretz Yisrael,* but said that they would be accompanied by an angel, rather than by Hashem's Presence (*Exodus* 32:34). Now Moses came before God with three requests: (1) Moses could not accept the substitution of an angel for God Himself; he wanted God to promise that His own Divine Presence would accompany the people; (2) Moses wanted to understand God's ways of reward and punishment; (3) and he wanted to be sure that Israel would always remain God's people.

יְדַעְתִּיךָ בְשֵׁם – *I have distinguished you with high repute.* Prior to the Revelation at Sinai, God promised to appear personally to Moses and that the entire nation would always trust him.

לְמַעַן אֶמְצָא חֵן – *That I may find favor.* I wish to understand the rewards awaiting one who finds favor in Your eyes.

אִם אֵין פָּנֶיךָ הֹלְכִים – *If Your Presence does not go along.* Although God had already agreed to accompany Israel, Moses repeated this to stress how important it was to him and his people. In the next verse, Moses goes on to say that only if God does so will he and Israel know that God indeed loves them.

הַדָּבָר הַזֶּה – *This thing,* i.e., that Moses and Israel be distinguished from all other peoples in that God's Presence will rest on them alone.

הַרְאֵנִי נָא – *Show me now.* Seeing that God was receptive, Moses asked that he be permitted to perceive a deeper insight into God's glory than ever before *(Or HaChaim).*

כָּל טוּבִי – *All of My goodness.* The time had come when God would reveal to Moses the formula of prayer that Israel should employ whenever it is faced with impending catastrophe, as had now happened in the wake of the worship of the Golden Calf. Even if the merit of the Patriarchs can no longer suffice, this prayer would always awaken God's mercy.

וְקָרָאתִי בְשֵׁם ה׳ – *I will call out with the Name*

TORAH READING FOR THE SABBATH OF CHOL HAMOED

Exodus 33:12-34:26

Kohen – *Moses said* to HASHEM: "Look — You say to me, 'Take this people onward,' but You did not inform me whom You will send with me; and You had said, 'I have distinguished you with high repute* and you have also found favor in My eyes.' And now, if I have indeed found favor in Your eyes, let me know Your ways — that I may know You — in order that I may find favor* in Your eyes; but see to it that this nation remains Your people.'*

He said, 'My Own Presence will go along and provide you rest.'

He said to Him, 'If Your Presence does not go along, do not bring us onward from here. How, then will it be known that I have found favor in Your eyes — I and Your people — unless You accompany us, and thereby distinguish me and Your people from every people that is on the face of the earth?'*

Levi – *HASHEM said to Moses, 'I will even do this thing* of which you have spoken; for you have found favor in My eyes, and I have distinguished you with high repute.'*

He said, 'Show me now Your glory.'*

He said, 'I will cause all of My goodness to pass before you, and I will call out with the Name 'HASHEM'* before you; I will be gracious when I wish to be gracious, and I will be merciful when I wish to show mercy.'*

Third – *He said, 'You cannot see* My face; for no human can see My face and live. Then HASHEM said, 'Behold there is a place near Me;* you may stand on the rock. And when My Glory passes by, I shall place you in a cleft of the rock; I shall shield you with My hand until I have passed. Then I shall remove My hand, and You will see My back; but My face will not be seen.'*

Fourth – *HASHEM said to Moses, 'Carve yourself* two stone tablets, like the first ones; and I will inscribe upon the tablets the words that were on*

'HASHEM.' The prayer that God was about to teach Moses, the Thirteen Attributes of Mercy, begins with the word *HASHEM.*

לֹא תוּכַל לִרְאֹת – *You cannot see.* Although I am ready to reveal all of My glory, the flesh and blood nature of man makes it impossible for him to assimilate such holiness completely *(Sforno).*

הִנֵּה מָקוֹם אִתִּי – *Behold there is a place near Me.* In the next three verses, God speaks to Moses in figurative terms, telling him that a place has been prepared where he will be able to receive the new and higher degree of revelation, but that God would protect him from receiving a degree of prophecy that would be beyond human capacity. Thus, Moses would *see God's back,* i.e., a lower degree of revelation, but not His essence, for man cannot fully understand God's way, just as someone may recognize a person from behind, but, because he cannot see his eyes and expression, cannot be certain of his identity or mood.

פְּסָל לְךָ – *Carve yourself.* Moses' forty days of prayer have achieved their goal. God has consented to give the Ten Commandments once again to the Jewish people. This time, however, the stone tablets are to be carved by Moses, unlike the first tablets, which were hewn by God. The commandments, however, will be inscribed by God Himself. The fact that these tablets were not of Divine origin was proof that, despite Israel's repentance and Moses' prayers, the nation had not regained the spiritual pinnacle it had attained prior to the sin.

הַלֻּחֹת הָרִאשֹׁנִים אֲשֶׁר שִׁבַּרְתָּ: וֶהְיֵה נָכוֹן לַבֹּקֶר וְעָלִיתָ בַבֹּקֶר
אֶל־הַר סִינַי וְנִצַּבְתָּ לִי שָׁם עַל־רֹאשׁ הָהָר: וְאִישׁ לֹא־יַעֲלֶה עִמָּךְ*
וְגַם־אִישׁ אַל־יֵרָא בְּכָל־הָהָר גַּם־הַצֹּאן וְהַבָּקָר אַל־יִרְעוּ אֶל־מוּל
הָהָר הַהוּא:
חמישי – וַיִּפְסֹל שְׁנֵי־לֻחֹת אֲבָנִים כָּרִאשֹׁנִים וַיַּשְׁכֵּם מֹשֶׁה בַבֹּקֶר וַיַּעַל
אֶל־הַר סִינַי כַּאֲשֶׁר צִוָּה יהוה אֹתוֹ וַיִּקַּח בְּיָדוֹ שְׁנֵי לֻחֹת אֲבָנִים:
וַיֵּרֶד יהוה בֶּעָנָן וַיִּתְיַצֵּב עִמּוֹ שָׁם וַיִּקְרָא* בְשֵׁם יהוה: וַיַּעֲבֹר יהוה
| עַל־פָּנָיו וַיִּקְרָא יהוה | יהוה* אֵל רַחוּם וְחַנּוּן אֶרֶךְ אַפַּיִם
וְרַב־חֶסֶד וֶאֱמֶת: נֹצֵר חֶסֶד לָאֲלָפִים נֹשֵׂא עָוֹן וָפֶשַׁע וְחַטָּאָה וְנַקֵּה
לֹא יְנַקֶּה פֹּקֵד | עֲוֹן אָבוֹת עַל־בָּנִים* וְעַל־בְּנֵי בָנִים עַל־שִׁלֵּשִׁים
וְעַל־רִבֵּעִים: וַיְמַהֵר מֹשֶׁה וַיִּקֹּד אַרְצָה וַיִּשְׁתָּחוּ: וַיֹּאמֶר אִם־נָא
מָצָאתִי חֵן בְּעֵינֶיךָ אֲדֹנָי יֵלֶךְ־נָא אֲדֹנָי* בְּקִרְבֵּנוּ כִּי עַם־קְשֵׁה־עֹרֶף
הוּא וְסָלַחְתָּ לַעֲוֹנֵנוּ וּלְחַטָּאתֵנוּ וּנְחַלְתָּנוּ: וַיֹּאמֶר הִנֵּה אָנֹכִי כֹּרֵת
בְּרִית נֶגֶד כָּל־עַמְּךָ אֶעֱשֶׂה נִפְלָאֹת אֲשֶׁר לֹא־נִבְרְאוּ בְכָל־הָאָרֶץ
וּבְכָל־הַגּוֹיִם וְרָאָה כָל־הָעָם אֲשֶׁר־אַתָּה בְקִרְבּוֹ אֶת־מַעֲשֵׂה יהוה
כִּי־נוֹרָא הוּא אֲשֶׁר אֲנִי עֹשֶׂה עִמָּךְ:

וְאִישׁ לֹא יַעֲלֶה עִמָּךְ – *No man is to climb up with you.* There is nothing better than modesty. Moses' ascent for the first tablets was made with great pomp and in the presence of the entire nation. Those tablets were smashed. The ascent for the second tablets was made in complete privacy. Those tablets remained (*Tanchuma, Ki Sissa* 1:31).

וַיִּקְרָא – *And he called out.* According to *Rashi,* it was Moses who called out. Most other commentators, however, hold that God proclaimed His Own Name, meaning that He taught Moses His Attributes, as given in the next two verses.

ו״ג מדות / The Thirteen Attributes

R' Yehudah taught that God sealed a covenant with Moses and Israel that in any time of crisis or danger, they should pray for God's mercy by reciting these attributes, and God sealed a covenant that such a prayer would never be in vain (*Rosh Hashanah* 17b).

ה׳ ה׳ – *HASHEM, HASHEM.* There are various opinions regarding how to enumerate the Thirteen Attributes. We follow the view of *Rabbeinu Tam (Rosh Hashanah* 17b), which is generally accepted:

(1) ה׳ – *HASHEM.* This Name [containing the letters of הָיָה הֹוֶה יִהְיֶה, *He was, He is, He will be*] designates God as the מְהַוֶּה, *Prime Cause,* of everything. It is only natural that He wishes to assure the survival of all that He brought into being. Consequently, this Name represents the Attribute of Mercy. In addition, the Name's spelling implies God's timelessness. Though man may sin, he can repent and call upon the timeless God to restore him to his original innocent state. As the Talmud states: אֲנִי הוּא קוֹדֶם שֶׁיֶּחֱטָא הָאָדָם וַאֲנִי הוּא לְאַחַר שֶׁיֶּחֱטָא הָאָדָם, וְיַעֲשֶׂה תְּשׁוּבָה, *I am He* [i.e., the God of Mercy] *before a person sins, and I am He after a person sins and repents (Rosh Hashanah* 17b). Based on this dictum, *Rabbeinu Tam* counts the twin use of the Name *HASHEM* as two attributes. The first is that God is merciful before a person sins, even though He knows that the sin will be committed.

(2) ה׳ – *HASHEM.* God is merciful after the sin has been committed, by allowing the sinner time to repent, and by accepting his repentance, though it may be imperfect.

(3) **אֵל** – *God.* This Name denotes the power of God's mercy, which sometimes surpasses even the compassion indicated by the Name *HASHEM.* He displays this higher degree of mercy to genuinely righteous people who sin, but repent. In return for their previous behavior, God exerts Himself, as it were, to ensure their survival.

(4) **רַחוּם** – *Compassionate.* In response to pleas for mercy, God eases the suffering of those being punished for their sins. Another manifestation of compassion is that God does not confront deserving people with overpowering temptation.

(5) **וְחַנּוּן** – *And Gracious.* God is gracious even to those unworthy of His kindness. Also, if someone lacks the willpower to avoid sin, and he

the first tablets which you shattered. Be prepared in the morning; climb up Mount Sinai in the morning and stand by Me on the mountain top. No man is to climb up with you nor should anyone be seen on the entire mountain; even the sheep and cattle are not to graze facing that mountain.'*

Fifth – *So he carved two stone tablets like the first ones. Moses arose in the morning and climbed up Mount Sinai as HASHEM had commanded him; and he took the two stone tablets in his hand. HASHEM descended in a cloud and stood with him there, and he called out* with the Name — HASHEM.*

And HASHEM passed before him and proclaimed: HASHEM, HASHEM, God, Compassionate and Gracious, Slow to anger, and Abundant in Kindness and truth. Preserver of kindness for thousands of generations, Forgiver of iniquity, willful sin, and error — and who cleanses but does not cleanse completely — He recalls the sin of parents upon children* and grandchildren, for the third and fourth generations.'*

Moses hastened to kneel upon the ground and prostrate himself. He said, 'If I have found favor in Your eyes, my Lord, may my Lord go among us, for it is a stiff-necked people; so may You forgive our iniquity and our sin, and make us Your heritage.'*

He said, 'Behold, I seal a covenant before your entire nation I will make distinctions such as have never been created in the entire world and among all the nations; and the entire people among whom you are will see the work of HASHEM — which is awesome — that I am about to do with you.'*

---

seeks God's help, he will get it.

(6) אֶרֶךְ אַפַּיִם – *Slow to anger.* So that the sinner will have time to repent.

(7) וְרַב חֶסֶד – *And Abundant in Kindness.* God shows great kindness to those who lack personal merits. The Talmud teaches, as described above, that God exercises this attribute by removing sins from the scale of justice, thus tilting the scales in favor of merit.

(8) וֶאֱמֶת – *And Truth.* God never reneges; His promise to reward the deserving will be carried out unequivocally.

(9) נֹצֵר חֶסֶד לָאֲלָפִים – *Preserver of kindness for thousands [of generations].* The deeds of the righteous — especially those who serve Him out of intense love — bring benefits to their offspring far into the future.

(10) נֹשֵׂא עָוֹן – *Forgiver of iniquity.* God forgives the intentional sinner, if he repents.

(11) וָפֶשַׁע – *[Forgiver of] willful sin.* Even those who rebel against God and purposely seek to anger Him are given an opportunity to repent.

(12) וְחַטָּאָה – *And [Forgiver of] error.* God forgives those who repent of sins that are committed out of carelessness or apathy. Having already praised God as the forgiver of intentional sin and rebelliousness, why do we revert to praising Him for this seemingly lesser level of mercy? Because if someone repents out of fear rather than love, his intentional sins are reduced in severity and are treated by God as if they had been done in error. Thus, even after having partially forgiven the intentional sins by reducing their severity, God further forgives those who continue to repent for these lesser sins.

(13) וְנַקֵּה – *And Who cleanses.* God wipes away the sins of those who repent sincerely, as if they had never existed.

In the Torah the verse continues לֹא יְנַקֶּה, *He does not cleanse.* The simple interpretation of the verse is that God does not completely erase the sin, but He exacts retribution in minute stages. The Talmud *(Yoma* 86a), however, explains that *He cleanses* the sins of those who truly repent; but *He does not cleanse* the sins of those who do not repent.

פֹּקֵד עֲוֹן אָבוֹת עַל בָּנִים – *He recalls the sin of parents upon children.* As the Ten Commandments in *Exodus* 20:5,6 indicate, children may suffer for the sins of their elders only if the children consciously and willingly copy those sins. On the other hand, God spreads out reward for two thousand generations. The extent of His reward is five hundred times greater than the extent of His punishment.

יֵלֶךְ נָא אֲדֹנָי – *May my Lord go.* Having been taught God's attributes of Mercy, Moses reiterated his earlier plea that HASHEM Himself guide

ששי – שְׁמָר־לְךָ אֵת אֲשֶׁר אָנֹכִי מְצַוְּךָ הַיּוֹם הִנְנִי גֹרֵשׁ מִפָּנֶיךָ אֶת־הָאֱמֹרִי וְהַכְּנַעֲנִי וְהַחִתִּי וְהַפְּרִזִּי וְהַחִוִּי וְהַיְבוּסִי: הִשָּׁמֶר לְךָ פֶּן־תִּכְרֹת בְּרִית לְיוֹשֵׁב הָאָרֶץ אֲשֶׁר אַתָּה בָּא עָלֶיהָ פֶּן־יִהְיֶה לְמוֹקֵשׁ* בְּקִרְבֶּךָ: כִּי אֶת־מִזְבְּחֹתָם תִּתֹּצוּן וְאֶת־מַצֵּבֹתָם תְּשַׁבֵּרוּן וְאֶת־אֲשֵׁרָיו תִּכְרֹתוּן: כִּי לֹא תִשְׁתַּחֲוֶה לְאֵל אַחֵר כִּי יהוה קַנָּא* שְׁמוֹ אֵל קַנָּא הוּא: פֶּן*־תִּכְרֹת בְּרִית לְיוֹשֵׁב הָאָרֶץ וְזָנוּ ׀ אַחֲרֵי אֱלֹהֵיהֶם וְזָבְחוּ לֵאלֹהֵיהֶם וְקָרָא לְךָ וְאָכַלְתָּ מִזִּבְחוֹ: וְלָקַחְתָּ מִבְּנֹתָיו לְבָנֶיךָ וְזָנוּ בְנֹתָיו אַחֲרֵי אֱלֹהֵיהֶן וְהִזְנוּ אֶת־בָּנֶיךָ אַחֲרֵי אֱלֹהֵיהֶן: אֱלֹהֵי מַסֵּכָה לֹא תַעֲשֶׂה־לָּךְ:

שביעי – אֶת־חַג הַמַּצּוֹת תִּשְׁמֹר שִׁבְעַת יָמִים תֹּאכַל מַצּוֹת אֲשֶׁר צִוִּיתִךָ לְמוֹעֵד חֹדֶשׁ הָאָבִיב* כִּי בְּחֹדֶשׁ הָאָבִיב יָצָאתָ מִמִּצְרָיִם: כָּל־פֶּטֶר רֶחֶם* לִי וְכָל־מִקְנְךָ תִּזָּכָר פֶּטֶר שׁוֹר וָשֶׂה: וּפֶטֶר חֲמוֹר תִּפְדֶּה בְשֶׂה* וְאִם־לֹא תִפְדֶּה וַעֲרַפְתּוֹ כֹּל בְּכוֹר בָּנֶיךָ תִּפְדֶּה וְלֹא־יֵרָאוּ פָנַי רֵיקָם:* שֵׁשֶׁת יָמִים תַּעֲבֹד וּבַיּוֹם הַשְּׁבִיעִי תִּשְׁבֹּת בֶּחָרִישׁ וּבַקָּצִיר* תִּשְׁבֹּת: וְחַג שָׁבֻעֹת תַּעֲשֶׂה לְךָ בִּכּוּרֵי קְצִיר חִטִּים* וְחַג הָאָסִיף תְּקוּפַת הַשָּׁנָה:* שָׁלֹשׁ פְּעָמִים בַּשָּׁנָה יֵרָאֶה כָּל־זְכוּרְךָ אֶת־פְּנֵי הָאָדֹן ׀ יהוה אֱלֹהֵי יִשְׂרָאֵל: כִּי־אוֹרִישׁ גּוֹיִם מִפָּנֶיךָ וְהִרְחַבְתִּי אֶת־גְּבֻלֶךָ וְלֹא־יַחְמֹד אִישׁ* אֶת־אַרְצְךָ בַּעֲלֹתְךָ לֵרָאוֹת אֶת־פְּנֵי יהוה אֱלֹהֶיךָ שָׁלֹשׁ פְּעָמִים בַּשָּׁנָה: לֹא־תִשְׁחַט עַל־חָמֵץ* דַּם־זִבְחִי וְלֹא־יָלִין לַבֹּקֶר זֶבַח חַג הַפָּסַח: רֵאשִׁית בִּכּוּרֵי אַדְמָתְךָ תָּבִיא בֵּית יהוה אֱלֹהֶיךָ לֹא־תְבַשֵּׁל גְּדִי* בַּחֲלֵב אִמּוֹ:

---

the People. Precisely because Israel is *stiff-necked* and prone to sin, it must have God's ever-present mercy to preserve it.

לְמוֹקֵשׁ – *Be a snare.* Israel's fraternization with its gentile nations, in *Eretz Yisrael* or elsewhere, results in calamity.

קַנָּא – *'Jealous One.'* A jealous person does not permit another to take what is rightfully his. Similarly, God will not tolerate those who extend their reverence and worship to idols instead of (or in addition) to Him.

פֶּן – *Lest.* This verse and the next give a list of idolatrous practices that the Jewish people are warned not to do. The term *lest* implies that something dire will befall them if they do these things, but the punishment is not specified. It is similar, in the vernacular to saying, 'Do not do this — or else!'

חֹדֶשׁ הָאָבִיב – *The month of spring.* The requirement that Pesach be in the springtime is the basis for the addition (seven times every nineteen years) of a thirteenth month in the Jewish calendar. Only thereby can it be assured that the month of Passover will be in the spring.

פֶּטֶר רֶחֶם – *Opening issue of a womb.* The first male born normally from the womb must be redeemed, but not one born by Caesarian section (*Bechoros* 19a).

תִּפְדֶּה בְשֶׂה – *You are to redeem with a lamb or kid.* The donkey then loses its sanctity and the lamb or kid become the personal property of the *Kohen;* it is not an offering.

רֵיקָם – *Empty-handed.* This does not refer to the firstborn. It is a general commandment that people who come to Jerusalem for the three pilgrimage festivals should bring offerings.

בֶּחָרִישׁ וּבַקָּצִיר – *Plowing and harvest.* These are singled out because they are labors upon which

Sixth – *Be careful of what I command you today: behold I drive out before you the Emorite, the Canaanite, the Hittite, the Perizite, the Hivvite, and the Jebusite. Beware lest you seal a covenant with the inhabitants of the Land to which you come; lest it be a snare* among you. Rather you are to break apart their altars, smash their pillars and cut down their sacred trees. For you are not to prostrate yourselves to an alien god, for the very name of* HASHEM *is 'Jealous One,'* He is a jealous God. Lest* you seal a covenant with the inhabitants of the land and you stray after their gods, sacrifice to their gods, and they invite you and you eat from their offering! And you select their daughters for your sons; and their daughters stray after their gods and entice your sons to stray after their gods!*

Do not make yourselves molten gods.

Seventh – *You are to observe the Festival of Matzos: For seven days you are to eat matzos as I commanded you, at the appointed time in the month of spring;* for in the month of spring you went out of Egypt.*

Every opening issue of a womb is Mine; and all your flock that produces a male, the opening issue of cattle or sheep. The first issue of a donkey you are to redeem with a lamb or kid,* and if you do not redeem it, you are to axe the back of its neck; you are to redeem every firstborn of your sons; they may not appear before Me empty-handed.* Six days you are to work and on the seventh day you are to refrain from work; you are to refrain from plowing and harvest.* You are to mark the Festival of Shavuos with the first fruits of your wheat harvest;* and the Festival of the Harvest at the year's change of seasons.* Three times a year all your males are to appear before the Lord* HASHEM, *the God of Israel. For I shall banish nations before you and broaden your boundary; no man will covet* your land when you go up to appear before* HASHEM, *your God, three times a year.*

You may not slaughter My blood-offering while in possession of leavened food; nor may the offering of the Pesach festival be left overnight until morning. The first of your land's early produce you are to bring to the Temple of* HASHEM, *your God; do not cook a kid* in its mother's milk.*

---

human life depends; even such necessary work is forbidden on the Sabbath *(Ramban). Rashi* cites the Sages' halachic interpretations.

בִּכּוּרֵי קְצִיר חִטִּים – *The first fruits of your wheat harvest.* I.e., the two loaves of Shavuos, which are the first meal-offerings that may be offered from the new crop.

תְּקוּפַת הַשָּׁנָה – *At the change of the seasons.* Succos is the time when the agricultural year is over and the new plowing season begins.

לֹא יַחְמֹד אִישׁ – *No man will covet.* God promised a miracle: Multitudes of Jews would leave their homes and boundaries undefended to go to Jerusalem, but no enemy would sieze the opportunity to attack.

עַל חָמֵץ – *While in possession of leavened food.* All *chametz* must have been removed before the time when the Pesach offering may be brought.

לֹא תְבַשֵּׁל גְּדִי – *Do not cook a kid.* This is the general prohibition to cook meat in milk. It is included in the context of the first fruits because the Canaanites thought that cooking a kid in its mother's milk would result in bountiful crops *(Sforno).*

חצי קדיש

After the last *oleh* has completed his closing blessing, the second Torah Scroll is placed on the *bimah* alongside the first, and the reader recites Half *Kaddish*.

יִתְגַּדַּל וְיִתְקַדַּשׁ שְׁמֵהּ רַבָּא. (Cong.– אָמֵן.) בְּעָלְמָא דִּי בְרָא כִרְעוּתֵהּ. וְיַמְלִיךְ מַלְכוּתֵהּ, בְּחַיֵּיכוֹן וּבְיוֹמֵיכוֹן וּבְחַיֵּי דְכָל בֵּית יִשְׂרָאֵל, בַּעֲגָלָא וּבִזְמַן קָרִיב. וְאִמְרוּ: אָמֵן.

(Cong.– אָמֵן. יְהֵא שְׁמֵהּ רַבָּא מְבָרַךְ לְעָלַם וּלְעָלְמֵי עָלְמַיָּא.)

יְהֵא שְׁמֵהּ רַבָּא מְבָרַךְ לְעָלַם וּלְעָלְמֵי עָלְמַיָּא.

יִתְבָּרַךְ וְיִשְׁתַּבַּח וְיִתְפָּאַר וְיִתְרוֹמַם וְיִתְנַשֵּׂא וְיִתְהַדָּר וְיִתְעַלֶּה וְיִתְהַלָּל שְׁמֵהּ דְּקֻדְשָׁא בְּרִיךְ הוּא (Cong.– בְּרִיךְ הוּא) — לְעֵלָּא מִן כָּל בִּרְכָתָא וְשִׁירָתָא תֻּשְׁבְּחָתָא וְנֶחֱמָתָא, דַּאֲמִירָן בְּעָלְמָא. וְאִמְרוּ: אָמֵן. (Cong.– אָמֵן.)

הגבהה וגלילה

The first Torah is raised for all to see. Each person looks at the Torah and recites aloud:

וְזֹאת הַתּוֹרָה אֲשֶׁר שָׂם מֹשֶׁה לִפְנֵי בְּנֵי יִשְׂרָאֵל,[1] עַל פִּי יהוה בְּיַד מֹשֶׁה.[2]

Some add:

עֵץ חַיִּים הִיא לַמַּחֲזִיקִים בָּהּ, וְתֹמְכֶיהָ מְאֻשָּׁר.[3] דְּרָכֶיהָ דַרְכֵי נֹעַם, וְכָל נְתִיבוֹתֶיהָ שָׁלוֹם.[4] אֹרֶךְ יָמִים בִּימִינָהּ, בִּשְׂמֹאלָהּ עֹשֶׁר וְכָבוֹד.[5] יהוה חָפֵץ לְמַעַן צִדְקוֹ, יַגְדִּיל תּוֹרָה וְיַאְדִּיר.[6]

מפטיר לשבת חול המועד

As the first Torah is wound, tied, and covered, the *oleh* for *Maftir* is called to the second Torah. The Maftir of the Sabbath of Chol HaMoed varies with the day of Chol HaMoed on which it falls.

FIRST DAY OF CHOL HAMOED

במדבר כט:יז-כב

וּבַיּ֣וֹם הַשֵּׁנִ֗י פָּרִ֧ים בְּנֵי־בָקָ֛ר שְׁנֵ֥ים עָשָׂ֖ר אֵילִ֣ם שְׁנָ֑יִם כְּבָשִׂ֧ים בְּנֵי־שָׁנָ֛ה אַרְבָּעָ֥ה עָשָׂ֖ר תְּמִימִֽם׃ וּמִנְחָתָ֣ם וְנִסְכֵּיהֶ֡ם לַ֠פָּרִים לָאֵילִ֧ם וְלַכְּבָשִׂ֛ים בְּמִסְפָּרָ֖ם כַּמִּשְׁפָּֽט׃ וּשְׂעִיר־עִזִּ֥ים אֶחָ֖ד חַטָּ֑את מִלְּבַד֙ עֹלַ֣ת הַתָּמִ֔יד וּמִנְחָתָ֖הּ וְנִסְכֵּיהֶֽם׃ וּבַיּ֧וֹם הַשְּׁלִישִׁ֛י פָּרִ֥ים עַשְׁתֵּי־עָשָׂ֖ר אֵילִ֣ם שְׁנָ֑יִם כְּבָשִׂ֧ים בְּנֵי־שָׁנָ֛ה אַרְבָּעָ֥ה עָשָׂ֖ר תְּמִימִֽם׃ וּמִנְחָתָ֣ם וְנִסְכֵּיהֶ֡ם לַ֠פָּרִים לָאֵילִ֧ם וְלַכְּבָשִׂ֛ים בְּמִסְפָּרָ֖ם כַּמִּשְׁפָּֽט׃ וּשְׂעִ֥יר חַטָּ֖את אֶחָ֑ד מִלְּבַד֙ עֹלַ֣ת הַתָּמִ֔יד וּמִנְחָתָ֖הּ וְנִסְכָּֽהּ׃

THIRD DAY OF CHOL HAMOED

במדבר כט:כג-כח

וּבַיּ֧וֹם הָרְבִיעִ֛י פָּרִ֥ים עֲשָׂרָ֖ה אֵילִ֣ם שְׁנָ֑יִם כְּבָשִׂ֧ים בְּנֵי־שָׁנָ֛ה אַרְבָּעָ֥ה עָשָׂ֖ר תְּמִימִֽם׃ מִנְחָתָ֣ם וְנִסְכֵּיהֶ֡ם לַ֠פָּרִים לָאֵילִ֧ם וְלַכְּבָשִׂ֛ים

HALF KADDISH

After the last *oleh* has completed his closing blessing, the second Torah Scroll is placed on the *bimah* alongside the first, and the reader recites Half *Kaddish:*

יִתְגַּדַּל *May His great Name grow exalted and sanctified* (Cong.– *Amen.*) *in the world that He created as He willed. May He give reign to His kingship in your lifetimes and in your days, and in the lifetimes of the entire Family of Israel, swiftly and soon. Now respond: Amen.*

(Cong.– *Amen. May His great Name be blessed forever and ever.*)

May His great Name be blessed forever and ever.

Blessed, praised, glorified, exalted, extolled, mighty, upraised, and lauded be the Name of the Holy One, Blessed is He (Cong.– *Blessed is He*) *— beyond any blessing and song, praise and consolation that are uttered in the world. Now respond: Amen.* (Cong.– *Amen.*)

HAGBAHAH AND GELILAH

The first Torah is raised for all to see. Each person looks at the Torah and recites aloud:

This is the Torah that Moses placed before the Children of Israel,[1] upon the command of HASHEM, through Moses' hand.[2]

Some add:

עֵץ *It is a tree of life for those who grasp it, and its supporters are praiseworthy.[3] Its ways are ways of pleasantness and all its paths are peace.[4] Lengthy days are at its right; at its left are wealth and honor.[5] HASHEM desired, for the sake of its [Israel's] righteousness, that the Torah be made great and glorious.[6]*

MAFTIR FOR THE SABBATH OF CHOL HAMOED

As the first Torah is wound, tied, and covered, the *oleh* for *Maftir* is called to the second Torah. The Maftir of the Sabbath of Chol HaMoed varies with the day of Chol HaMoed on which it falls.

FIRST DAY OF CHOL HAMOED

Numbers 29:17-22

And on the second day: Twelve young bulls, two rams, fourteen lambs within their first year; they are to be unblemished. And their meal-offerings and their libations for the bulls, the rams, and the lambs, in their proper numbers as required. And one he-goat for a sin-offering; aside from the continual elevation-offering, its meal-offering and their libations. And on the third day: eleven bulls, two rams, fourteen lambs within their first year; they are to be unblemished. And their meal-offerings and their libations for the bulls, the rams, and the lambs, in their proper numbers as required. And one he-goat for a sin-offering; aside from the continual elevation-offering, its meal-offering and its libation.

THIRD DAY OF CHOL HAMOED

Numbers 29:23-28

And on the fourth day: Ten bulls, two rams, fourteen lambs within their first year; they are to be unblemished. And their meal-offerings and their libations for the bulls, the rams, and the lambs,

---

(1) *Deuteronomy* 4:44. (2) *Numbers* 9:23. (3) *Proverbs* 3:18. (4) 3:17. (5) 3:16. (6) *Isaiah* 42:21.

בְּמִסְפָּרָם כַּמִּשְׁפָּט: וּשְׂעִיר־עִזִּים אֶחָד חַטָּאת מִלְּבַד עֹלַת הַתָּמִיד
מִנְחָתָהּ וְנִסְכָּהּ: וּבַיּוֹם הַחֲמִישִׁי פָּרִים תִּשְׁעָה אֵילִם שְׁנָיִם כְּבָשִׂים
בְּנֵי־שָׁנָה אַרְבָּעָה עָשָׂר תְּמִימִם: וּמִנְחָתָם וְנִסְכֵּיהֶם לַפָּרִים לָאֵילִם
וְלַכְּבָשִׂים בְּמִסְפָּרָם כַּמִּשְׁפָּט: וּשְׂעִיר חַטָּאת אֶחָד מִלְּבַד עֹלַת
הַתָּמִיד וּמִנְחָתָהּ וְנִסְכָּהּ:

FOURTH DAY OF CHOL HAMOED

במדבר כט:כו-לא

וּבַיּוֹם הַחֲמִישִׁי פָּרִים תִּשְׁעָה אֵילִם שְׁנָיִם כְּבָשִׂים בְּנֵי־שָׁנָה
אַרְבָּעָה עָשָׂר תְּמִימִם: וּמִנְחָתָם וְנִסְכֵּיהֶם לַפָּרִים לָאֵילִם
וְלַכְּבָשִׂים בְּמִסְפָּרָם כַּמִּשְׁפָּט: וּשְׂעִיר חַטָּאת אֶחָד מִלְּבַד עֹלַת
הַתָּמִיד וּמִנְחָתָהּ וְנִסְכָּהּ: וּבַיּוֹם הַשִּׁשִּׁי פָּרִים שְׁמֹנָה אֵילִם שְׁנָיִם
כְּבָשִׂים בְּנֵי־שָׁנָה אַרְבָּעָה עָשָׂר תְּמִימִם: וּמִנְחָתָם וְנִסְכֵּיהֶם לַפָּרִים
לָאֵילִם וְלַכְּבָשִׂים בְּמִסְפָּרָם כַּמִּשְׁפָּט: וּשְׂעִיר חַטָּאת אֶחָד מִלְּבַד
עֹלַת הַתָּמִיד מִנְחָתָהּ וּנְסָכֶיהָ:

הגבהה וגלילה

The *Maftir* completes his closing blessing.
Then the second Torah Scroll is raised and each person looks at the Torah and recites aloud:

וְזֹאת הַתּוֹרָה אֲשֶׁר שָׂם מֹשֶׁה לִפְנֵי בְּנֵי יִשְׂרָאֵל,[1] עַל פִּי יהוה בְּיַד מֹשֶׁה.[2]

Some add:

עֵץ חַיִּים הִיא לַמַּחֲזִיקִים בָּהּ, וְתֹמְכֶיהָ מְאֻשָּׁר.[3] דְּרָכֶיהָ דַרְכֵי נֹעַם, וְכָל נְתִיבוֹתֶיהָ שָׁלוֹם.[4] אֹרֶךְ יָמִים בִּימִינָהּ, בִּשְׂמֹאלָהּ עֹשֶׁר וְכָבוֹד.[5] יהוה חָפֵץ לְמַעַן צִדְקוֹ, יַגְדִּיל תּוֹרָה וְיַאְדִּיר.[6]

After the Torah Scroll has been wound, tied and covered, the *maftir* recites the *Haftarah* blessings.

ברכה קודם ההפטרה

בָּרוּךְ אַתָּה יהוה אֱלֹהֵינוּ מֶלֶךְ הָעוֹלָם, אֲשֶׁר בָּחַר בִּנְבִיאִים טוֹבִים, וְרָצָה בְדִבְרֵיהֶם הַנֶּאֱמָרִים בֶּאֱמֶת, בָּרוּךְ אַתָּה יהוה, הַבּוֹחֵר בַּתּוֹרָה וּבְמֹשֶׁה עַבְדּוֹ, וּבְיִשְׂרָאֵל עַמּוֹ, וּבִנְבִיאֵי הָאֱמֶת וָצֶדֶק: (.Cong. – אָמֵן)

in their proper numbers as required. And one he-goat for a sin-offering; aside from the continual elevation-offering, its meal-offering, and its libation. And on the fifth day: nine bulls, two rams, fourteen lambs within their first year; they are to be unblemished. And their meal-offerings and their libations for the bulls, the rams, and the lambs, in their proper numbers as required. And one he-goat for a sin-offering; aside from the continual elevation-offering, its meal-offering, and its libation.

FOURTH DAY OF CHOL HAMOED

Numbers 29:26-31

And on the fifth day: nine bulls, two rams, fourteen lambs within their first year; they are to be unblemished. And their meal-offerings and their libations for the bulls, the rams, and the lambs, in their proper numbers as required. And one he-goat for a sin-offering; aside from the continual elevation-offering, its meal-offering, and its libation. And on the sixth day: eight bulls, two rams, fourteen lambs within their first year; they are to be unblemished. And their meal-offerings and their libations for the bulls, the rams and the lambs, in their proper numbers as required. And one he-goat for a sin-offering; aside from the continual elevation-offering, its meal-offering, and its libations.

HAGBAHAH AND GELILAH

The *Maftir* completes his closing blessing.
Then the second Torah Scroll is raised and each person looks at the Torah and recites aloud:

This is the Torah that Moses placed before the Children of Israel,[1] upon the command of HASHEM, through Moses' hand.[2]

Some add:

עֵץ *It is a tree of life for those who grasp it, and its supporters are praiseworthy.[3] Its ways are ways of pleasantness and all its paths are peace.[4] Lengthy days are at its right; at its left are wealth and honor.[5] HASHEM desired, for the sake of its [Israel's] righteousness, that the Torah be made great and glorious.[6]*

After the Torah Scroll has been wound, tied and covered, the *maftir* recites the *Haftarah* blessings.

BLESSING BEFORE THE HAFTARAH

בָּרוּךְ *Blessed are You, HASHEM, our God, King of the universe, Who has chosen good prophets and was pleased with their words that were uttered with truth. Blessed are You, HASHEM, Who chooses the Torah; Moses, His servant; Israel, His nation; and the prophets of truth and righteousness.* (Cong.— *Amen.*)

(1) *Deuteronomy* 4:44. (2) *Numbers* 9:23. (3) *Proverbs* 3:18. (4) 3:17. (5) 3:16. (6) *Isaiah* 42:21.

❧ הפטרה לשבת חול המועד ☙

[Although the Divine Name יהוה is pronounced as if it were spelled אֲדֹנָי, when it is vowelized יֱהֹוִה it is pronounced as if it were spelled אֱלֹהִים.]

יחזקאל לח:יח-לט:טז

וְהָיָה ׀ בַּיּוֹם הַהוּא* בְּיוֹם בּוֹא גוֹג עַל־אַדְמַת יִשְׂרָאֵל נְאֻם אֲדֹנָי
יֱהֹוִה תַּעֲלֶה חֲמָתִי בְּאַפִּי: וּבְקִנְאָתִי בְאֵשׁ־עֶבְרָתִי דִּבַּרְתִּי אִם־
לֹא ׀ בַּיּוֹם הַהוּא יִהְיֶה רַעַשׁ גָּדוֹל עַל אַדְמַת יִשְׂרָאֵל: וְרָעֲשׁוּ מִפָּנַי
דְּגֵי הַיָּם וְעוֹף הַשָּׁמַיִם וְחַיַּת הַשָּׂדֶה וְכָל־הָרֶמֶשׂ הָרֹמֵשׂ עַל־
הָאֲדָמָה וְכֹל הָאָדָם אֲשֶׁר עַל־פְּנֵי הָאֲדָמָה וְנֶהֶרְסוּ הֶהָרִים וְנָפְלוּ
הַמַּדְרֵגוֹת וְכָל־חוֹמָה לָאָרֶץ תִּפּוֹל: וְקָרָאתִי עָלָיו לְכָל־הָרַי
חֶרֶב* נְאֻם אֲדֹנָי יֱהֹוִה חֶרֶב אִישׁ בְּאָחִיו תִּהְיֶה: וְנִשְׁפַּטְתִּי אִתּוֹ
בְּדֶבֶר וּבְדָם* וְגֶשֶׁם שׁוֹטֵף וְאַבְנֵי אֶלְגָּבִישׁ אֵשׁ וְגָפְרִית אַמְטִיר
עָלָיו וְעַל־אֲגַפָּיו וְעַל־עַמִּים רַבִּים אֲשֶׁר אִתּוֹ: וְהִתְגַּדִּלְתִּי
וְהִתְקַדִּשְׁתִּי* וְנוֹדַעְתִּי לְעֵינֵי גּוֹיִם רַבִּים וְיָדְעוּ כִּי־אֲנִי יהוה: וְאַתָּה
בֶן־אָדָם הִנָּבֵא עַל־גּוֹג* וְאָמַרְתָּ כֹּה אָמַר אֲדֹנָי יֱהֹוִה הִנְנִי אֵלֶיךָ
גּוֹג נְשִׂיא רֹאשׁ מֶשֶׁךְ וְתֻבָל:* וְשֹׁבַבְתִּיךָ וְשִׁשֵּׁאתִיךָ* וְהַעֲלִיתִיךָ
מִיַּרְכְּתֵי צָפוֹן וַהֲבִאוֹתִךָ עַל־הָרֵי יִשְׂרָאֵל: וְהִכֵּיתִי קַשְׁתְּךָ מִיַּד
שְׂמֹאולֶךָ וְחִצֶּיךָ מִיַּד יְמִינְךָ אַפִּיל: עַל־הָרֵי יִשְׂרָאֵל תִּפּוֹל אַתָּה
וְכָל־אֲגַפֶּיךָ וְעַמִּים אֲשֶׁר אִתָּךְ לְעֵיט צִפּוֹר כָּל־כָּנָף וְחַיַּת הַשָּׂדֶה
נְתַתִּיךָ לְאָכְלָה: עַל־פְּנֵי הַשָּׂדֶה תִּפּוֹל כִּי אֲנִי דִבַּרְתִּי נְאֻם אֲדֹנָי
יֱהֹוִה: וְשִׁלַּחְתִּי־אֵשׁ בְּמָגוֹג וּבְיֹשְׁבֵי הָאִיִּים* לָבֶטַח וְיָדְעוּ כִּי־
אֲנִי יהוה: וְאֶת־שֵׁם קָדְשִׁי אוֹדִיעַ בְּתוֹךְ עַמִּי יִשְׂרָאֵל* וְלֹא־אַחֵל
אֶת־שֵׁם־קָדְשִׁי עוֹד וְיָדְעוּ הַגּוֹיִם כִּי־אֲנִי יהוה קָדוֹשׁ בְּיִשְׂרָאֵל:
הִנֵּה בָאָה* וְנִהְיָתָה נְאֻם אֲדֹנָי יֱהֹוִה הוּא הַיּוֹם אֲשֶׁר דִּבַּרְתִּי:

◆§ The Haftarah

As noted in the introduction to the *Haftarah* of the first day, this *Haftarah* was chosen because it deals with the war of Gog and Magog. The former *Haftarah* speaks briefly of an earthquake in *Eretz Yisrael*. This one describes it more fully. The commentary is based on the ArtScroll *Ezekiel* by Rabbi Moshe Eisemann.

בַּיּוֹם הַהוּא – *On that day.* This expression does not necessarily refer to a specific 'twenty-four-hour period'. The earthquake described below can occur at any point during the war.

וְקָרָאתִי עָלָיו . . . חֶרֶב – *I will summon the sword against him.* God will cause Gog's soldiers to panic and turn against one another.

בְּדֶבֶר וּבְדָם – *With pestilence and with blood.* The Midrash (*Tanchuma Bo* 4) relates the several plagues of this verse to the punishments that God brought upon the Egyptians. Thus, the Sages compare Pharaoh's intentions with Gog's. In the infancy of Israel, Pharaoh attempted to cripple the nation. At the end of time, Gog, in one last gigantic effort, tries to destroy the seemingly vulnerable nation. God responds to both by unleashing the forces of nature against them, proving that all power is in His hands.

וְהִתְגַּדִּלְתִּי וְהִתְקַדִּשְׁתִּי – *Thus will I be exalted and sanctified.* The purpose of Creation, and the goal of history, is the sanctification of God's Name and, as the verse concludes, that all nations will recognize God's omnipotence. This phrase is the source of the first words of *Kaddish.*

הִנָּבֵא עַל גּוֹג – *Prophesy against Gog.* Ezekiel is

HAFTARAH READING FOR THE SABBATH OF CHOL HAMOED

Ezekiel 38:18-39:16

It shall be on that day, on the day that Gog comes on the soil of Israel — the words of my Lord HASHEM/ELOHIM — My raging anger shall flare up. For in My indignation and in My blazing wrath I have spoken. I take an oath that on that day a great earthquake shall come upon the soil of Israel. And there shall quake before Me the fish of the sea, the birds of the sky, the beasts of the field, all creeping things that move on the ground, and every human being on the face of the earth. Mountains shall be overthrown, cliffs shall topple, and every wall shall topple to the ground. I will summon the sword against him* to all My mountains — the words of my Lord HASHEM/ELOHIM. Every man's sword shall be against his brother. I will punish him with pestilence and with blood;* torrential rain, hailstones, and sulfurous fire upon him and his cohorts, and the many peoples that are with him. Thus will I be exalted and sanctified,* and I will become known in the eyes of many nations, and they shall know that I am HASHEM.*

And you, Ben Adam, prophesy against Gog and say: Thus says my Lord HASHEM/ELOHIM: See I am against you Gog, prince, leader of Meshech and Tubal.* I shall lead you astray and seduce you,* and I shall cause you to advance from the farthest north and bring you to the mountains of Israel. I will strike your bow from your left hand, and I will cast down your arrows from your right hand. You shall fall upon Israel's mountains, you and all your cohorts and the nations that are with you; I will present you as carrion for every winged bird and beast of the field. You will fall upon the open field, for I have spoken — the words of my Lord HASHEM/ELOHIM.*

I will dispatch a fire against Magog and against those who dwell confidently in the islands, and they shall know that I am HASHEM. I will make known My holy Name among My people Israel,* and I will nevermore desecrate My holy Name, and the nations shall know that I am HASHEM, the holy One in Israel.*

Behold! it has come and happened — the words of my Lord HASHEM/ELOHIM; this is the day of which I have spoken. Then*

---

told to prophesy about the second of Gog's three wars against Israel.

מֶשֶׁךְ וְתֻבָל – *Meshech and Tubal.* There are traditions indicating that Meshech and Tubal were provinces in Russia (see ArtScroll *Ezekiel* 38:2).

וְשֹׁבַבְתִּיךָ וְשִׁשֵּׁאתִיךָ – *I shall lead you astray and seduce you.* Despite the imposing power of the nations, they are but tools in God's hand when He wishes to utilize them for His purposes.

בְּמָגוֹג וּבְיוֹשְׁבֵי הָאִיִּים – *Against Magog and against those who dwell ... in the islands.* See ArtScroll *Ezekiel* 38:2, which conjectures that Magog is the Russian Caucasus and the *islands* are those of the Aegean Sea.

בְּתוֹךְ עַמִּי יִשְׂרָאֵל – *Among My people Israel.* Even among the Jews, there will be doubt about God's supremacy, because Israel had been exiled and under the dominion of its enemies for so long. The defeat of Gog will renew Israel's faith and end the *desecration* caused by the ascendancy of the nations.

הִנֵּה בָאָה – *Behold! it has come.* I.e., the promised salvation will have taken place.

וְיָצְאוּ יֹשְׁבֵי ׀ עָרֵי יִשְׂרָאֵל וּבִעֲרוּ וְהִשִּׂיקוּ בְּנֶשֶׁק וּמָגֵן וְצִנָּה בְּקֶשֶׁת וּבְחִצִּים וּבְמַקֵּל יָד וּבְרֹמַח וּבִעֲרוּ בָהֶם אֵשׁ שֶׁבַע שָׁנִים: וְלֹא־יִשְׂאוּ עֵצִים מִן־הַשָּׂדֶה וְלֹא יַחְטְבוּ מִן־הַיְּעָרִים כִּי בַנֶּשֶׁק יְבַעֲרוּ־אֵשׁ וְשָׁלְלוּ אֶת־שֹׁלְלֵיהֶם וּבָזְזוּ אֶת־בֹּזְזֵיהֶם נְאֻם אֲדֹנָי יֱהוִֹה: וְהָיָה בַיּוֹם הַהוּא אֶתֵּן לְגוֹג ׀ מְקוֹם־שָׁם קֶבֶר* בְּיִשְׂרָאֵל גֵּי הָעֹבְרִים* קִדְמַת הַיָּם וְחֹסֶמֶת הִיא אֶת־הָעֹבְרִים* וְקָבְרוּ שָׁם אֶת־גּוֹג וְאֶת־כָּל־הֲמוֹנֹה וְקָרְאוּ גֵּיא הֲמוֹן גּוֹג: וּקְבָרוּם בֵּית יִשְׂרָאֵל לְמַעַן טַהֵר אֶת־הָאָרֶץ שִׁבְעָה חֳדָשִׁים: וְקָבְרוּ כָּל־עַם הָאָרֶץ וְהָיָה לָהֶם לְשֵׁם יוֹם הִכָּבְדִי נְאֻם אֲדֹנָי יֱהוִֹה: וְאַנְשֵׁי תָמִיד יַבְדִּילוּ עֹבְרִים בָּאָרֶץ מְקַבְּרִים אֶת־הָעֹבְרִים* אֶת־הַנּוֹתָרִים עַל־פְּנֵי הָאָרֶץ לְטַהֲרָהּ מִקְצֵה שִׁבְעָה־חֳדָשִׁים יַחְקֹרוּ: וְעָבְרוּ הָעֹבְרִים בָּאָרֶץ וְרָאָה עֶצֶם אָדָם וּבָנָה אֶצְלוֹ צִיּוּן עַד קָבְרוּ אֹתוֹ הַמְקַבְּרִים אֶל־גֵּיא הֲמוֹן גּוֹג: וְגַם שֶׁם־עִיר הֲמוֹנָה* וְטִהֲרוּ הָאָרֶץ:

ברכות לאחר ההפטרה

After the *Haftarah* is read, the *oleh* recites the following blessings.

בָּרוּךְ אַתָּה יהוה אֱלֹהֵינוּ מֶלֶךְ הָעוֹלָם, צוּר כָּל הָעוֹלָמִים, צַדִּיק בְּכָל הַדּוֹרוֹת, הָאֵל הַנֶּאֱמָן הָאוֹמֵר וְעֹשֶׂה, הַמְדַבֵּר וּמְקַיֵּם, שֶׁכָּל דְּבָרָיו אֱמֶת וָצֶדֶק. נֶאֱמָן אַתָּה הוּא יהוה אֱלֹהֵינוּ, וְנֶאֱמָנִים דְּבָרֶיךָ, וְדָבָר אֶחָד מִדְּבָרֶיךָ אָחוֹר לֹא יָשׁוּב רֵיקָם, כִּי אֵל מֶלֶךְ נֶאֱמָן (וְרַחֲמָן) אָתָּה. בָּרוּךְ אַתָּה יהוה, הָאֵל הַנֶּאֱמָן בְּכָל דְּבָרָיו.

(.Cong. — אָמֵן)

רַחֵם עַל צִיּוֹן כִּי הִיא בֵּית חַיֵּינוּ, וְלַעֲלוּבַת נֶפֶשׁ תּוֹשִׁיעַ בִּמְהֵרָה בְיָמֵינוּ. בָּרוּךְ אַתָּה יהוה, מְשַׂמֵּחַ צִיּוֹן בְּבָנֶיהָ.

(.Cong. — אָמֵן)

שַׂמְּחֵנוּ יהוה אֱלֹהֵינוּ בְּאֵלִיָּהוּ הַנָּבִיא עַבְדֶּךָ, וּבְמַלְכוּת בֵּית דָּוִד מְשִׁיחֶךָ, בִּמְהֵרָה יָבֹא וְיָגֵל לִבֵּנוּ, עַל כִּסְאוֹ לֹא יֵשֶׁב זָר וְלֹא יִנְחֲלוּ עוֹד אֲחֵרִים אֶת כְּבוֹדוֹ, כִּי בְשֵׁם קָדְשְׁךָ נִשְׁבַּעְתָּ לּוֹ, שֶׁלֹּא יִכְבֶּה נֵרוֹ לְעוֹלָם וָעֶד. בָּרוּךְ אַתָּה יהוה, מָגֵן דָּוִד.

(.Cong. — אָמֵן)

מְקוֹם שָׁם קֶבֶר — *A burial site there.* For a long time after Gog's disastrous defeat, the Jews will show that their innate compassion extends even to their mortal enemies. Thus, the Jewish people will carefully seek out and bury the remains of the fallen soldiers.

גֵּי הָעֹבְרִים — *The valley of the travelers.* I.e., the valley east of the Sea of Galilee, where people used to travel for the luscious fruits of Ginassar.

the inhabitants of Israel's cities will go out and make fires and feed them with weapons, shield and buckles, with bow and with arrows, with hand-club and spear — and shall fuel fire with them for seven years. They will not carry wood from the field, nor cut it from the forests, for with weapons they shall feed the fires. They will despoil those who despoiled them and plunder those who plunder them — the words of my Lord HASHEM/ELOHIM.

On that day I shall assign to Gog a burial site there in Israel — the valley of the travelers* — and there they will bury Gog and all his horde, and call it the Valley of Gog's Horde. The family of Israel will bury them for seven months, in order to cleanse the Land. All the people of the Land will bury, and it will cause them renown; the day I manifest My Glory — the words of my Lord HASHEM/ELOHIM. They will designate permanent officials passing through the Land, burying — with passersby* — those that remain upon the open field in order to cleanse it; after seven months, they are to seek out. As the passersby traverse the Land and see a human bone, then they shall build a marker near it, until the buriers bury it in the Valley of Gog's Horde. There shall also be a city called Hamonah*; thus will they cleanse the Land.*

BLESSINGS AFTER THE HAFTARAH

After the *Haftarah* is read, the *oleh* recites the following blessings.

בָּרוּךְ *Blessed are You, HASHEM, our God, King of the universe, Rock of all eternities, Righteous in all generations, the trustworthy God, Who says and does, Who speaks and fulfills, all of Whose words are true and righteous. Trustworthy are You, HASHEM, our God, and trustworthy are Your words, not one of Your words is turned back to its origin unfulfilled, for You are God, trustworthy (and compassionate) King. Blessed are You, HASHEM, the God Who is trustworthy in all His words.* (Cong. – *Amen.*)

רַחֵם *Have mercy on Zion for it is the source of our life; to the one who is deeply humiliated bring salvation speedily, in our days. Blessed are You, HASHEM, Who gladdens Zion through her children.* (Cong. – *Amen.*)

שַׂמְּחֵנוּ *Gladden us, HASHEM, our God, with Elijah the prophet, Your servant, and with the kingdom of the House of David, Your anointed, may he come speedily and cause our heart to exult. On his throne let no stranger sit nor let others continue to inherit his honor, for by Your holy Name You swore to him that his heir will not be extinguished forever and ever. Blessed are You, HASHEM, Shield of David.* (Cong. – *Amen.*)

אֶת הָעֹבְרִים – *With passersby.* People traveling through the Land will help bury the victims of the war.

הֲמוֹנָה – *Hamonah.* Just as the valley will be called the Valley of Gog's Horde, in commemoration of the miracle, so too the city near it

עַל הַתּוֹרָה, וְעַל הָעֲבוֹדָה, וְעַל הַנְּבִיאִים, וְעַל יוֹם הַשַּׁבָּת הַזֶּה, וְיוֹם חַג הַסֻּכּוֹת הַזֶּה שֶׁנָּתַתָּ לָּנוּ יהוה אֱלֹהֵינוּ, לִקְדֻשָּׁה וְלִמְנוּחָה, לְשָׂשׂוֹן וּלְשִׂמְחָה, לְכָבוֹד וּלְתִפְאָרֶת. עַל הַכֹּל יהוה אֱלֹהֵינוּ, אֲנַחְנוּ מוֹדִים לָךְ, וּמְבָרְכִים אוֹתָךְ, יִתְבָּרַךְ שִׁמְךָ בְּפִי כָּל חַי תָּמִיד לְעוֹלָם וָעֶד. בָּרוּךְ אַתָּה יהוה, מְקַדֵּשׁ הַשַּׁבָּת וְיִשְׂרָאֵל וְהַזְּמַנִּים. (Cong.— אָמֵן.)

❖ יקום פרקן ❖

One praying alone recites only the first paragraph and omits the following two paragraphs.

יְקוּם פֻּרְקָן מִן שְׁמַיָּא, חִנָּא וְחִסְדָּא וְרַחֲמֵי, וְחַיֵּי אֲרִיכֵי, וּמְזוֹנֵי רְוִיחֵי, וְסִיַּעְתָּא דִשְׁמַיָּא, וּבַרְיוּת גּוּפָא, וּנְהוֹרָא מַעַלְיָא, זַרְעָא חַיָּא וְקַיָּמָא, זַרְעָא דִּי לָא יִפְסוּק וְדִי לָא יִבְטוּל מִפִּתְגָמֵי אוֹרַיְתָא. לְמָרָנָן וְרַבָּנָן חֲבוּרָתָא קַדִּישָׁתָא דִּי בְאַרְעָא דְיִשְׂרָאֵל וְדִי בְבָבֶל, לְרֵישֵׁי כַלֵּי, וּלְרֵישֵׁי גַלְוָתָא, וּלְרֵישֵׁי מְתִיבָתָא, וּלְדַיָּנֵי דִי בָבָא, לְכָל תַּלְמִידֵיהוֹן, וּלְכָל תַּלְמִידֵי תַלְמִידֵיהוֹן, וּלְכָל מָן דְּעָסְקִין בְּאוֹרַיְתָא. מַלְכָּא דְעָלְמָא יְבָרֵךְ יַתְהוֹן, יַפִּישׁ חַיֵּיהוֹן, וְיַסְגֵּא יוֹמֵיהוֹן, וְיִתֵּן אַרְכָה לִשְׁנֵיהוֹן, וְיִתְפָּרְקוּן וְיִשְׁתֵּזְבוּן מִן כָּל עָקָא וּמִן כָּל מַרְעִין בִּישִׁין. מָרָן דִּי בִשְׁמַיָּא יְהֵא בְסַעְדְּהוֹן, כָּל זְמַן וְעִדָּן. וְנֹאמַר: אָמֵן. (Cong.— אָמֵן.)

יְקוּם פֻּרְקָן מִן שְׁמַיָּא, חִנָּא וְחִסְדָּא וְרַחֲמֵי, וְחַיֵּי אֲרִיכֵי, וּמְזוֹנֵי רְוִיחֵי, וְסִיַּעְתָּא דִשְׁמַיָּא, וּבַרְיוּת גּוּפָא, וּנְהוֹרָא מַעַלְיָא, זַרְעָא חַיָּא וְקַיָּמָא, זַרְעָא דִּי לָא יִפְסוּק וְדִי לָא יִבְטוּל מִפִּתְגָמֵי אוֹרַיְתָא. לְכָל קְהָלָא קַדִּישָׁא הָדֵין, רַבְרְבַיָּא עִם זְעֵרַיָּא, טַפְלָא וּנְשַׁיָּא, מַלְכָּא דְעָלְמָא יְבָרֵךְ יַתְכוֹן, יַפִּישׁ חַיֵּיכוֹן, וְיַסְגֵּא יוֹמֵיכוֹן, וְיִתֵּן אַרְכָה לִשְׁנֵיכוֹן, וְתִתְפָּרְקוּן וְתִשְׁתֵּזְבוּן מִן כָּל עָקָא וּמִן כָּל מַרְעִין בִּישִׁין, מָרָן דִּי בִשְׁמַיָּא יְהֵא בְסַעְדְּכוֹן, כָּל זְמַן וְעִדָּן. וְנֹאמַר: אָמֵן. (Cong.— אָמֵן.)

מִי שֶׁבֵּרַךְ אֲבוֹתֵינוּ אַבְרָהָם יִצְחָק וְיַעֲקֹב, הוּא יְבָרֵךְ אֶת כָּל הַקָּהָל הַקָּדוֹשׁ הַזֶּה, עִם כָּל קְהִלּוֹת הַקֹּדֶשׁ, הֵם, וּנְשֵׁיהֶם, וּבְנֵיהֶם, וּבְנוֹתֵיהֶם, וְכָל אֲשֶׁר לָהֶם. וּמִי שֶׁמְּיַחֲדִים בָּתֵּי כְנֵסִיּוֹת לִתְפִלָּה, וּמִי שֶׁבָּאִים בְּתוֹכָם לְהִתְפַּלֵּל, וּמִי שֶׁנּוֹתְנִים נֵר

---

should be called Hamonah, from הָמוֹן, *horde*, to recall Gog's hordes. This will help cleanse the Land since people from other parts of the Land will use it as a dumping ground for impurities.

עַל הַתּוֹרָה *For the Torah reading, for the prayer service, for the reading from the Prophets for this Sabbath day and for this day of the Succos Festival that You,* HASHEM, *our God, have given us for holiness and contentment, for gladness and joy, for glory and splendor — for all this,* HASHEM, *our God, we gratefully thank You and bless You. May Your Name be blessed by the mouth of all the living, always, for all eternity. Blessed are You,* HASHEM, *Who sanctifies the Sabbath, Israel and the festival seasons.* (Cong.– *Amen.)*

YEKUM PURKAN

One praying alone recites only the first paragraph and omits the following two paragraphs.

יְקוּם פֻּרְקָן *May salvation arise from heaven — grace, kindness, compassion, long life, abundant sustenance, heavenly assistance, physical health, lofty vision, living and surviving offspring, offspring who will neither interrupt nor cease from words of the Torah — for our masters and sages, the holy fellowships that are in Eretz Yisrael and that are in the Diaspora: for the leaders of the Torah assemblages, the leaders of the exile communities, the leaders of the academies, the judges at the gateways, and all their students and to all the students of their students, and to everyone who engages in Torah study. May the King of the universe bless them, make their lives fruitful, increase their days and grant length to their years. May He save them and rescue them from every distress and from all serious ailments. May the Master in heaven come to their assistance at every season and time. Now let us respond: Amen.* (Cong.–*Amen.)*

יְקוּם פֻּרְקָן *May salvation arise from heaven — grace, kindness, compassion, long life, abundant sustenance, heavenly assistance, physical health, lofty vision, living and surviving offspring, offspring who will neither interrupt nor cease from the words of the Torah — to this entire holy congregation, adults along with children, infants and women. May the King of the universe bless you, make your lives fruitful, increase your days, and grant length to your years. May He save you and rescue you from every distress and from all serious ailments. May the Master in heaven come to your assistance at every season and time. Now let us respond: Amen.* (Cong.–*Amen.)*

מִי שֶׁבֵּרַךְ *He Who blessed our forefathers, Abraham, Isaac, and Jacob — may He bless this entire holy congregation along with all the holy congregations; them, their wives, sons, and daughters and all that is theirs; and those who dedicate synagogues for prayer and those who enter them to pray, and those who give lamps for*

לַמָּאוֹר, וְיַיִן לְקִדּוּשׁ וּלְהַבְדָּלָה, וּפַת לָאוֹרְחִים, וּצְדָקָה לָעֲנִיִּים, וְכָל מִי שֶׁעוֹסְקִים בְּצָרְכֵי צִבּוּר בֶּאֱמוּנָה, הַקָּדוֹשׁ בָּרוּךְ הוּא יְשַׁלֵּם שְׂכָרָם, וְיָסִיר מֵהֶם כָּל מַחֲלָה, וְיִרְפָּא לְכָל גּוּפָם, וְיִסְלַח לְכָל עֲוֹנָם, וְיִשְׁלַח בְּרָכָה וְהַצְלָחָה בְּכָל מַעֲשֵׂה יְדֵיהֶם, עִם כָּל יִשְׂרָאֵל אֲחֵיהֶם. וְנֹאמַר: אָמֵן. (.Cong. – אָמֵן)

In many congregations, a prayer for the welfare of the State is recited by the Rabbi, *chazzan*, or *gabbai* at this point.

אַשְׁרֵי יוֹשְׁבֵי בֵיתֶךָ, עוֹד יְהַלְּלוּךָ סֶּלָה.[1] אַשְׁרֵי הָעָם שֶׁכָּכָה לּוֹ, אַשְׁרֵי הָעָם שֶׁיהוה אֱלֹהָיו.[2]

תהלים קמה

תְּהִלָּה לְדָוִד,

אֲרוֹמִמְךָ אֱלוֹהַי הַמֶּלֶךְ, וַאֲבָרְכָה שִׁמְךָ לְעוֹלָם וָעֶד.
בְּכָל יוֹם אֲבָרְכֶךָּ, וַאֲהַלְלָה שִׁמְךָ לְעוֹלָם וָעֶד.
גָּדוֹל יהוה וּמְהֻלָּל מְאֹד, וְלִגְדֻלָּתוֹ אֵין חֵקֶר.
דּוֹר לְדוֹר יְשַׁבַּח מַעֲשֶׂיךָ, וּגְבוּרֹתֶיךָ יַגִּידוּ.
הֲדַר כְּבוֹד הוֹדֶךָ, וְדִבְרֵי נִפְלְאֹתֶיךָ אָשִׂיחָה.
וֶעֱזוּז נוֹרְאוֹתֶיךָ יֹאמֵרוּ, וּגְדוּלָּתְךָ אֲסַפְּרֶנָּה.
זֵכֶר רַב טוּבְךָ יַבִּיעוּ, וְצִדְקָתְךָ יְרַנֵּנוּ.
חַנּוּן וְרַחוּם יהוה, אֶרֶךְ אַפַּיִם וּגְדָל חָסֶד.
טוֹב יהוה לַכֹּל, וְרַחֲמָיו עַל כָּל מַעֲשָׂיו.
יוֹדוּךָ יהוה כָּל מַעֲשֶׂיךָ, וַחֲסִידֶיךָ יְבָרְכוּכָה.
כְּבוֹד מַלְכוּתְךָ יֹאמֵרוּ, וּגְבוּרָתְךָ יְדַבֵּרוּ.
לְהוֹדִיעַ לִבְנֵי הָאָדָם גְּבוּרֹתָיו, וּכְבוֹד הֲדַר מַלְכוּתוֹ.
מַלְכוּתְךָ מַלְכוּת כָּל עֹלָמִים, וּמֶמְשַׁלְתְּךָ בְּכָל דּוֹר וָדֹר.
סוֹמֵךְ יהוה לְכָל הַנֹּפְלִים, וְזוֹקֵף לְכָל הַכְּפוּפִים.
עֵינֵי כֹל אֵלֶיךָ יְשַׂבֵּרוּ, וְאַתָּה נוֹתֵן לָהֶם אֶת אָכְלָם בְּעִתּוֹ.
פּוֹתֵחַ אֶת יָדֶךָ,
וּמַשְׂבִּיעַ לְכָל חַי רָצוֹן.
צַדִּיק יהוה בְּכָל דְּרָכָיו, וְחָסִיד בְּכָל מַעֲשָׂיו.

While reciting the verse פּוֹתֵחַ, concentrate intently on its meaning.

(1) *Psalms* 84:5. (2) 144:15.

illumination and wine for Kiddush and Havdalah, bread for guests and charity for the poor; and all who are involved faithfully in the needs of the community — may the Holy One, Blessed is He, pay their reward and remove from them every affliction, heal their entire body and forgive their every iniquity, and send blessing and success to all their handiwork, along with all Israel, their brethren. And let us say: Amen.

(Cong.—*Amen.*)

In many congregations, a prayer for the welfare of the State is recited by the Rabbi, *chazzan,* or *gabbai* at this point.

אַשְׁרֵי *Praiseworthy are those who dwell in Your house; may they always praise You, Selah!*[1] *Praiseworthy is the people for whom this is so, praiseworthy is the people whose God is* HASHEM.[2]

Psalm 145 *A psalm of praise by David:*

א *I will exalt You, my God the King,*
and I will bless Your Name forever and ever.
ב *Every day I will bless You,*
and I will laud Your Name forever and ever.
ג HASHEM *is great and exceedingly lauded,*
and His greatness is beyond investigation.
ד *Each generation will praise Your deeds to the next*
and of Your mighty deeds they will tell;
ה *The splendrous glory of Your power*
and Your wondrous deeds I shall discuss.
ו *And of Your awesome power they will speak,*
and Your greatness I shall relate.
ז *A recollection of Your abundant goodness they will utter*
and of Your righteousness they will sing exultantly.
ח *Gracious and merciful is* HASHEM,
slow to anger, and great in [bestowing] kindness.
ט HASHEM *is good to all; His mercies are on all His works.*
י *All Your works shall thank You,* HASHEM,
and Your devout ones will bless You.
כ *Of the glory of Your kingdom they will speak,*
and of Your power they will tell;
ל *To inform human beings of His mighty deeds,*
and the glorious splendor of His kingdom.
מ *Your kingdom is a kingdom spanning all eternities,*
and Your dominion is throughout every generation.
ס HASHEM *supports all the fallen ones and straightens all the bent.*
ע *The eyes of all look to You with hope*
and You give them their food in its proper time;
פ *You open Your hand,* Concentrate intently while reciting the verse, *'You open...'*
and satisfy the desire of every living thing.
צ *Righteous is* HASHEM *in all His ways*
and magnanimous in all His deeds.

קָרוֹב יהוה לְכָל קֹרְאָיו, לְכֹל אֲשֶׁר יִקְרָאֻהוּ בֶאֱמֶת.
רְצוֹן יְרֵאָיו יַעֲשֶׂה, וְאֶת שַׁוְעָתָם יִשְׁמַע וְיוֹשִׁיעֵם.
שׁוֹמֵר יהוה אֶת כָּל אֹהֲבָיו, וְאֵת כָּל הָרְשָׁעִים יַשְׁמִיד.
❖ תְּהִלַּת יהוה יְדַבֶּר פִּי, וִיבָרֵךְ כָּל בָּשָׂר שֵׁם קָדְשׁוֹ לְעוֹלָם וָעֶד.
וַאֲנַחְנוּ נְבָרֵךְ יָהּ, מֵעַתָּה וְעַד עוֹלָם, הַלְלוּיָהּ.[1]

הכנסת ספר תורה

The *chazzan* takes the Torah from which *Maftir* was read in his right arm and recites:

יְהַלְלוּ אֶת שֵׁם יהוה, כִּי נִשְׂגָּב שְׁמוֹ לְבַדּוֹ –

Congregation responds:

– הוֹדוֹ עַל אֶרֶץ וְשָׁמָיִם. וַיָּרֶם קֶרֶן לְעַמּוֹ, תְּהִלָּה לְכָל חֲסִידָיו, לִבְנֵי יִשְׂרָאֵל עַם קְרֹבוֹ, הַלְלוּיָהּ.[2]

As the Torah Scrolls are carried to the Ark the following psalm is recited.

תהלים כט

מִזְמוֹר לְדָוִד, הָבוּ לַיהוה בְּנֵי אֵלִים, הָבוּ לַיהוה כָּבוֹד וָעֹז. הָבוּ לַיהוה כְּבוֹד שְׁמוֹ, הִשְׁתַּחֲווּ לַיהוה בְּהַדְרַת קֹדֶשׁ. קוֹל יהוה עַל הַמָּיִם, אֵל הַכָּבוֹד הִרְעִים, יהוה עַל מַיִם רַבִּים. קוֹל יהוה בַּכֹּחַ, קוֹל יהוה בֶּהָדָר. קוֹל יהוה שֹׁבֵר אֲרָזִים, וַיְשַׁבֵּר יהוה אֶת אַרְזֵי הַלְּבָנוֹן. וַיַּרְקִידֵם כְּמוֹ עֵגֶל, לְבָנוֹן וְשִׂרְיוֹן כְּמוֹ בֶן רְאֵמִים. קוֹל יהוה חֹצֵב לַהֲבוֹת אֵשׁ. קוֹל יהוה יָחִיל מִדְבָּר, יָחִיל יהוה מִדְבַּר קָדֵשׁ. קוֹל יהוה יְחוֹלֵל אַיָּלוֹת, וַיֶּחֱשֹׂף יְעָרוֹת, וּבְהֵיכָלוֹ, כֻּלּוֹ אֹמֵר כָּבוֹד. יהוה לַמַּבּוּל יָשָׁב, וַיֵּשֶׁב יהוה מֶלֶךְ לְעוֹלָם. יהוה עֹז לְעַמּוֹ יִתֵּן, יהוה יְבָרֵךְ אֶת עַמּוֹ בַשָּׁלוֹם.

As the Torah Scrolls are placed into the Ark, the congregation recites the following verses:

וּבְנֻחֹה יֹאמַר, שׁוּבָה יהוה רִבְבוֹת אַלְפֵי יִשְׂרָאֵל.[3] קוּמָה יהוה לִמְנוּחָתֶךָ, אַתָּה וַאֲרוֹן עֻזֶּךָ. כֹּהֲנֶיךָ יִלְבְּשׁוּ צֶדֶק, וַחֲסִידֶיךָ יְרַנֵּנוּ. בַּעֲבוּר דָּוִד עַבְדֶּךָ, אַל תָּשֵׁב פְּנֵי מְשִׁיחֶךָ.[4] כִּי לֶקַח טוֹב נָתַתִּי לָכֶם, תּוֹרָתִי אַל תַּעֲזֹבוּ.[5] ❖ עֵץ חַיִּים הִיא לַמַּחֲזִיקִים בָּהּ, וְתֹמְכֶיהָ מְאֻשָּׁר.[6] דְּרָכֶיהָ דַרְכֵי נֹעַם, וְכָל נְתִיבוֹתֶיהָ שָׁלוֹם.[7] הֲשִׁיבֵנוּ יהוה אֵלֶיךָ וְנָשׁוּבָה, חַדֵּשׁ יָמֵינוּ כְּקֶדֶם.[8]

---

(1) *Psalms* 115:18. (2) 148:13-14. (3) *Numbers* 10:36. (4) *Psalms* 132:8-10.
(5) *Proverbs* 4:2. (6) 3:18. (7) 3:17. (8) *Lamentations* 5:21.

ק *HASHEM is close to all who call upon Him —*
to all who call upon Him sincerely.
ר *The will of those who fear Him He will do;*
and their cry He will hear, and save them.
ש *HASHEM protects all who love Him;*
but all the wicked He will destroy.
ת Chazzan– *May my mouth declare the praise of HASHEM*
and may all flesh bless His Holy Name forever and ever.
We will bless God from this time and forever, Halleluyah![1]

RETURNING THE TORAH

The *chazzan* takes the Torah from which *Maftir* was read in his right arm and recites:

Let them praise the Name of HASHEM,
for His Name alone will have been exalted –

Congregation responds:

— His glory is above earth and heaven. And He will have exalted the pride of His people, causing praise for all His devout ones, for the Children of Israel, His intimate people. Halleluyah![2]

As the Torah Scrolls are carried to the Ark the following psalm is recited:

Psalm 29

מִזְמוֹר *A psalm of David. Render unto HASHEM, you sons of the powerful; render unto HASHEM, honor and might. Render unto HASHEM the honor worthy of His Name, prostrate yourselves before HASHEM in His intensely holy place. The voice of HASHEM is upon the waters, the God of Glory thunders, HASHEM is upon vast waters. The voice of HASHEM is in power! The voice of HASHEM is in majesty! The voice of HASHEM breaks the cedars, HASHEM shatters the cedars of Lebanon! He makes them prance about like a calf; Lebanon and Siryon like young re'eimim. The voice of HASHEM carves with shafts of fire. The voice of HASHEM convulses the wilderness. HASHEM convulses the wilderness of Kadesh. The voice of HASHEM frightens the hinds, and strips the forests bare; while in His Temple all proclaim, 'Glory!' HASHEM sat enthroned at the Deluge; HASHEM sits enthroned as King forever. HASHEM will give might to His people, HASHEM will bless His people with peace.*

As the Torah Scrolls are placed into the Ark, the congregation recites the following verses:

וּבְנֻחֹה *And when it rested he would say, 'Return, HASHEM, to the myriad thousands of Israel.'*[3] *Arise, HASHEM, to Your resting place, You and the Ark of Your strength. Let Your priests be clothed in righteousness, and Your devout ones will sing joyously. For the sake of David, Your servant, turn not away the face of Your anointed.*[4] *For I have given you a good teaching, do not forsake My Torah.*[5] Chazzan– *It is a tree of life for those who grasp it, and its supporters are praiseworthy.*[6] *Its ways are ways of pleasantness and all its paths are peace.*[7] *Bring us back to You, HASHEM, and we shall return, renew our days as of old.*[8]

חצי קדיש

The *chazzan* recites חֲצִי קַדִּישׁ.

יִתְגַּדַּל וְיִתְקַדַּשׁ שְׁמֵהּ רַבָּא. (.Cong – אָמֵן.) בְּעָלְמָא דִּי בְרָא כִרְעוּתֵהּ. וְיַמְלִיךְ מַלְכוּתֵהּ, בְּחַיֵּיכוֹן וּבְיוֹמֵיכוֹן וּבְחַיֵּי דְכָל בֵּית יִשְׂרָאֵל, בַּעֲגָלָא וּבִזְמַן קָרִיב. וְאִמְרוּ: אָמֵן.

(.Cong – אָמֵן. יְהֵא שְׁמֵהּ רַבָּא מְבָרַךְ לְעָלַם וּלְעָלְמֵי עָלְמַיָּא.)

יְהֵא שְׁמֵהּ רַבָּא מְבָרַךְ לְעָלַם וּלְעָלְמֵי עָלְמַיָּא.

יִתְבָּרַךְ וְיִשְׁתַּבַּח וְיִתְפָּאַר וְיִתְרוֹמַם וְיִתְנַשֵּׂא וְיִתְהַדָּר וְיִתְעַלֶּה וְיִתְהַלָּל שְׁמֵהּ דְּקֻדְשָׁא בְּרִיךְ הוּא (.Cong – בְּרִיךְ הוּא) – לְעֵלָּא מִן כָּל בִּרְכָתָא וְשִׁירָתָא תֻּשְׁבְּחָתָא וְנֶחֱמָתָא, דַּאֲמִירָן בְּעָלְמָא. וְאִמְרוּ: אָמֵן. (.Cong – אָמֵן.)

מוסף לשבת חול המועד

Take three steps backward, then three steps forward. Remain standing with the feet together while reciting *Shemoneh Esrei*. Recite it with quiet devotion and without interruption, verbal or otherwise. Although its recitation should not be audible to others, one must pray loudly enough to hear himself.

כִּי שֵׁם יהוה אֶקְרָא, הָבוּ גֹדֶל לֵאלֹהֵינוּ.[1]

אֲדֹנָי שְׂפָתַי תִּפְתָּח, וּפִי יַגִּיד תְּהִלָּתֶךָ.[2]

אבות

Bend the knees at בָּרוּךְ; bow at אַתָּה; straighten up at 'ה.

בָּרוּךְ אַתָּה יהוה אֱלֹהֵינוּ וֵאלֹהֵי אֲבוֹתֵינוּ, אֱלֹהֵי אַבְרָהָם, אֱלֹהֵי יִצְחָק, וֵאלֹהֵי יַעֲקֹב, הָאֵל הַגָּדוֹל הַגִּבּוֹר וְהַנּוֹרָא, אֵל עֶלְיוֹן, גּוֹמֵל חֲסָדִים טוֹבִים וְקוֹנֵה הַכֹּל, וְזוֹכֵר חַסְדֵי אָבוֹת, וּמֵבִיא גוֹאֵל לִבְנֵי בְנֵיהֶם, לְמַעַן שְׁמוֹ בְּאַהֲבָה. מֶלֶךְ עוֹזֵר וּמוֹשִׁיעַ וּמָגֵן.

Bend the knees at בָּרוּךְ; bow at אַתָּה; straighten up at 'ה.

בָּרוּךְ אַתָּה יהוה, מָגֵן אַבְרָהָם.

גבורות

אַתָּה גִּבּוֹר לְעוֹלָם אֲדֹנָי, מְחַיֵּה מֵתִים אַתָּה, רַב לְהוֹשִׁיעַ. מְכַלְכֵּל חַיִּים בְּחֶסֶד, מְחַיֵּה מֵתִים בְּרַחֲמִים רַבִּים, סוֹמֵךְ נוֹפְלִים, וְרוֹפֵא חוֹלִים, וּמַתִּיר אֲסוּרִים, וּמְקַיֵּם אֱמוּנָתוֹ לִישֵׁנֵי עָפָר. מִי כָמוֹךָ בַּעַל גְּבוּרוֹת, וּמִי דּוֹמֶה לָּךְ, מֶלֶךְ מֵמִית וּמְחַיֶּה וּמַצְמִיחַ יְשׁוּעָה. וְנֶאֱמָן אַתָּה לְהַחֲיוֹת מֵתִים. בָּרוּךְ אַתָּה יהוה, מְחַיֵּה הַמֵּתִים.

During the *chazzan's* repetition, *Kedushah* (page 556) is recited at this point.

HALF KADDISH

The *chazzan* recites Half *Kaddish:*

יִתְגַּדַּל *May His great Name grow exalted and sanctified* (Cong.– *Amen.*) *in the world that He created as He willed. May He give reign to His kingship in your lifetimes and in your days, and in the lifetimes of the entire Family of Israel, swiftly and soon. Now respond: Amen.*

(Cong.– *Amen. May His great Name be blessed forever and ever.*)
May His great Name be blessed forever and ever.

Blessed, praised, glorified, exalted, extolled, mighty, upraised, and lauded be the Name of the Holy One, Blessed is He (Cong.– *Blessed is He*) — *beyond any blessing and song, praise and consolation that are uttered in the world. Now respond: Amen.* (Cong.– *Amen.*)

MUSSAF FOR THE SABBATH OF CHOL HAMOED

Take three steps backward, then three steps forward. Remain standing with the feet together while reciting *Shemoneh Esrei.* Recite it with quiet devotion and without interruption, verbal or otherwise. Although its recitation should not be audible to others, one must pray loudly enough to hear himself.

When I call out the Name of HASHEM, ascribe greatness to our God.[1]
My Lord, open my lips, that my mouth may declare Your praise.[2]

PATRIARCHS

Bend the knees at *'Blessed'*; bow at *'You'*; straighten up at *'HASHEM.'*

בָּרוּךְ *Blessed are You, HASHEM, our God and the God of our forefathers, God of Abraham, God of Isaac, and God of Jacob; the great, mighty, and awesome God, the supreme God, Who bestows beneficial kindnesses and creates everything, Who recalls the kindnesses of the Patriarchs and brings a Redeemer to their children's children, for His Name's sake, with love. O King, Helper, Savior, and Shield.*

Bend the knees at *'Blessed'*; bow at *'You'*; straighten up at *'HASHEM.'*

Blessed are You, HASHEM, Shield of Abraham.

GOD'S MIGHT

אַתָּה *You are eternally mighty, my Lord, the Resuscitator of the dead are You; abundantly able to save. He sustains the living with kindness, resuscitates the dead with abundant mercy, supports the fallen, heals the sick, releases the confined, and maintains His faith to those asleep in the dust. Who is like You, O Master of mighty deeds, and who is comparable to You, O King Who causes death and restores life and makes salvation sprout! And You are faithful to resuscitate the dead. Blessed are You, HASHEM, Who resuscitates the dead.*

During the *chazzan's* repetition, *Kedushah* (page 556) is recited at this point.

(1) *Deuteronomy* 32:3. (2) *Psalms* 51:17.

קדושת השם

INDIVIDUALS RECITE:

אַתָּה קָדוֹשׁ וְשִׁמְךָ קָדוֹשׁ, וּקְדוֹשִׁים בְּכָל יוֹם יְהַלְלוּךָ סֶּלָה. בָּרוּךְ אַתָּה יהוה, הָאֵל הַקָּדוֹשׁ.

CHAZZAN RECITES DURING HIS REPETITION:

לְדוֹר וָדוֹר נַגִּיד גָּדְלֶךָ וּלְנֵצַח נְצָחִים קְדֻשָּׁתְךָ נַקְדִּישׁ, וְשִׁבְחֲךָ אֱלֹהֵינוּ מִפִּינוּ לֹא יָמוּשׁ לְעוֹלָם וָעֶד, כִּי אֵל מֶלֶךְ גָּדוֹל וְקָדוֹשׁ אָתָּה. בָּרוּךְ אַתָּה יהוה, הָאֵל הַקָּדוֹשׁ.

קדושת היום

אַתָּה בְחַרְתָּנוּ מִכָּל הָעַמִּים, אָהַבְתָּ אוֹתָנוּ, וְרָצִיתָ בָּנוּ, וְרוֹמַמְתָּנוּ מִכָּל הַלְּשׁוֹנוֹת, וְקִדַּשְׁתָּנוּ בְּמִצְוֹתֶיךָ, וְקֵרַבְתָּנוּ מַלְכֵּנוּ לַעֲבוֹדָתֶךָ, וְשִׁמְךָ הַגָּדוֹל וְהַקָּדוֹשׁ עָלֵינוּ קָרָאתָ.

וַתִּתֶּן לָנוּ יהוה אֱלֹהֵינוּ בְּאַהֲבָה שַׁבָּתוֹת לִמְנוּחָה וּמוֹעֲדִים לְשִׂמְחָה חַגִּים וּזְמַנִּים לְשָׂשׂוֹן, אֶת יוֹם הַשַּׁבָּת הַזֶּה וְאֶת יוֹם חַג הַסֻּכּוֹת הַזֶּה, זְמַן שִׂמְחָתֵנוּ בְּאַהֲבָה מִקְרָא קֹדֶשׁ, זֵכֶר לִיצִיאַת מִצְרָיִם.

קדושה

When reciting *Kedushah,* one must stand with his feet together, and avoid any interruptions. One should rise on his toes when saying the words קָדוֹשׁ, קָדוֹשׁ, קָדוֹשׁ; בָּרוּךְ (of בָּרוּךְ כְּבוֹד); and יִמְלֹךְ.

Cong. then *chazzan*:

נַעֲרִיצְךָ וְנַקְדִּישְׁךָ כְּסוֹד שִׂיחַ שַׂרְפֵי קֹדֶשׁ, הַמַּקְדִּישִׁים שִׁמְךָ בַּקֹּדֶשׁ, כַּכָּתוּב עַל יַד נְבִיאֶךָ, וְקָרָא זֶה אֶל זֶה וְאָמַר:

All – קָדוֹשׁ קָדוֹשׁ קָדוֹשׁ יהוה צְבָאוֹת, מְלֹא כָל הָאָרֶץ כְּבוֹדוֹ.[1] ❖ כְּבוֹדוֹ מָלֵא עוֹלָם, מְשָׁרְתָיו שׁוֹאֲלִים זֶה לָזֶה, אַיֵּה מְקוֹם כְּבוֹדוֹ, לְעֻמָּתָם בָּרוּךְ יֹאמֵרוּ:

All – בָּרוּךְ כְּבוֹד יהוה, מִמְּקוֹמוֹ.[2] ❖ מִמְּקוֹמוֹ הוּא יִפֶן בְּרַחֲמִים, וְיָחֹן עַם הַמְּיַחֲדִים שְׁמוֹ, עֶרֶב וָבֹקֶר בְּכָל יוֹם תָּמִיד, פַּעֲמַיִם בְּאַהֲבָה שְׁמַע אוֹמְרִים.

All – שְׁמַע יִשְׂרָאֵל, יהוה אֱלֹהֵינוּ, יהוה אֶחָד.[3] ❖ הוּא אֱלֹהֵינוּ. הוּא אָבִינוּ, הוּא מַלְכֵּנוּ, הוּא מוֹשִׁיעֵנוּ, וְהוּא יַשְׁמִיעֵנוּ בְּרַחֲמָיו שֵׁנִית, לְעֵינֵי כָּל חָי, לִהְיוֹת לָכֶם לֵאלֹהִים, אֲנִי יהוה אֱלֹהֵיכֶם.[4]

In some congregations the following is added:

All – אַדִּיר אַדִּירֵנוּ, יהוה אֲדֹנֵינוּ, מָה אַדִּיר שִׁמְךָ בְּכָל הָאָרֶץ.[5] וְהָיָה יהוה לְמֶלֶךְ עַל כָּל הָאָרֶץ, בַּיּוֹם הַהוּא יִהְיֶה יהוה אֶחָד וּשְׁמוֹ אֶחָד.[6]

Chazzan – וּבְדִבְרֵי קָדְשְׁךָ כָּתוּב לֵאמֹר:

All – יִמְלֹךְ יהוה לְעוֹלָם, אֱלֹהַיִךְ צִיּוֹן, לְדֹר וָדֹר, הַלְלוּיָהּ.[7]

Chazzan continues לְדוֹר וָדוֹר (above).

HOLINESS OF GOD'S NAME

INDIVIDUALS RECITE:

אַתָּה *You are holy and Your Name is holy, and holy ones praise You every day, forever. Blessed are You,* HASHEM, *the holy God.*

CHAZZAN RECITES DURING HIS REPETITION:

לְדוֹר *From generation to generation we shall relate Your greatness and for infinite eternities we shall proclaim Your holiness. Your praise, our God, shall not leave our mouth forever and ever, for You, O God, are a great and holy King. Blessed are You,* HASHEM, *the holy God.*

SANCTIFICATION OF THE DAY

אַתָּה בְחַרְתָּנוּ *You have chosen us from all the peoples; You loved us and found favor in us; You exalted us above all the tongues and You sanctified us with Your commandments. You drew us close, our King, to Your service and proclaimed Your great and Holy Name upon us.*

וַתִּתֶּן לָנוּ *And You gave us,* HASHEM, *our God, with love Sabbaths for rest, appointed festivals for gladness, Festivals and times for joy, this day of Sabbath and this day of the Festival of Succos, the time of our gladness with love, a holy convocation, a memorial of the Exodus from Egypt.*

KEDUSHAH

When reciting *Kedushah*, one must stand with his feet together and avoid any interruptions. One should rise on his toes when saying the words *Holy, holy, holy; Blessed is;* HASHEM *shall reign.*

Cong. then *chazzan:*

נַעֲרִיצְךָ *We will revere You and sanctify You according to the counsel of the holy Seraphim, who sanctify Your Name in the Sanctuary, as it is written by Your prophet: "And one [angel] will call another and say:*

All — *'Holy, holy, holy is* HASHEM, *Master of Legions, the whole world is filled with His glory.'"*[1] ❖*His glory fills the world. His ministering angels ask one another, 'Where is the place of His glory?' Those facing them say 'Blessed':*

All — *'Blessed is the glory of* HASHEM *from His place.'*[2] ❖*From His place may He turn with compassion and be gracious to the people who declare the Oneness of His Name; evening and morning, every day constantly, twice, with love, they proclaim 'Shema.'*

All — *'Hear O Israel:* HASHEM *is our God,* HASHEM *the One and Only.'*[3] ❖*He is our God; He is our Father; He is our King; He is our Savior; and He will let us hear, in His compassion, for a second time in the presence of all the living,' . . . to be a God to you, I am* HASHEM, *your God.'*[4]

In some congregations the following is added:

All — *Mighty is our Mighty One,* HASHEM, *our Master — how mighty is Your name throughout the earth!*[5] HASHEM *will be King over all the world — on that day* HASHEM *will be One and His Name will be One.*[6]

Chazzan — And in Your holy Writings the following is written:

All — *'*HASHEM *shall reign forever — your God, O Zion — from generation to generation, Halleluyah!'*[7]

Chazzan continues לְדוֹר וָדוֹר, *From generation . . .* (above).

(1) *Isaiah* 6:3. (2) *Ezekiel* 3:12. (3) *Deuteronomy* 6:4.
(4) *Numbers* 15:41. (5) *Psalms* 8:2. (6) *Zechariah* 14:9. (7) *Psalms* 146:10.

וּמִפְּנֵי חֲטָאֵינוּ גָּלִינוּ מֵאַרְצֵנוּ, וְנִתְרַחַקְנוּ מֵעַל אַדְמָתֵנוּ. וְאֵין אֲנַחְנוּ יְכוֹלִים לַעֲלוֹת וְלֵרָאוֹת וּלְהִשְׁתַּחֲוֹת לְפָנֶיךָ, וְלַעֲשׂוֹת חוֹבוֹתֵינוּ בְּבֵית בְּחִירָתֶךָ, בַּבַּיִת הַגָּדוֹל וְהַקָּדוֹשׁ שֶׁנִּקְרָא שִׁמְךָ עָלָיו, מִפְּנֵי הַיָּד שֶׁנִּשְׁתַּלְּחָה בְּמִקְדָּשֶׁךָ. יְהִי רָצוֹן מִלְּפָנֶיךָ יהוה אֱלֹהֵינוּ וֵאלֹהֵי אֲבוֹתֵינוּ, מֶלֶךְ רַחֲמָן, שֶׁתָּשׁוּב וּתְרַחֵם עָלֵינוּ וְעַל מִקְדָּשְׁךָ בְּרַחֲמֶיךָ הָרַבִּים, וְתִבְנֵהוּ מְהֵרָה וּתְגַדֵּל כְּבוֹדוֹ. אָבִינוּ מַלְכֵּנוּ, גַּלֵּה כְּבוֹד מַלְכוּתְךָ עָלֵינוּ מְהֵרָה, וְהוֹפַע וְהִנָּשֵׂא עָלֵינוּ לְעֵינֵי כָּל חָי. וְקָרֵב פְּזוּרֵינוּ מִבֵּין הַגּוֹיִם, וּנְפוּצוֹתֵינוּ כַּנֵּס מִיַּרְכְּתֵי אָרֶץ. וַהֲבִיאֵנוּ לְצִיּוֹן עִירְךָ בְּרִנָּה, וְלִירוּשָׁלַיִם בֵּית מִקְדָּשְׁךָ בְּשִׂמְחַת עוֹלָם. וְשָׁם נַעֲשֶׂה לְפָנֶיךָ אֶת קָרְבְּנוֹת חוֹבוֹתֵינוּ, תְּמִידִים כְּסִדְרָם, וּמוּסָפִים כְּהִלְכָתָם. וְאֶת מוּסְפֵי יוֹם הַשַּׁבָּת הַזֶּה וְיוֹם חַג הַסֻּכּוֹת הַזֶּה נַעֲשֶׂה וְנַקְרִיב לְפָנֶיךָ בְּאַהֲבָה כְּמִצְוַת רְצוֹנֶךָ, כְּמוֹ שֶׁכָּתַבְתָּ עָלֵינוּ בְּתוֹרָתֶךָ, עַל יְדֵי מֹשֶׁה עַבְדֶּךָ, מִפִּי כְבוֹדֶךָ כָּאָמוּר:

וּבְיוֹם הַשַּׁבָּת שְׁנֵי כְבָשִׂים בְּנֵי שָׁנָה תְּמִימִם, וּשְׁנֵי עֶשְׂרֹנִים סֹלֶת מִנְחָה בְּלוּלָה בַשֶּׁמֶן, וְנִסְכּוֹ. עֹלַת שַׁבַּת בְּשַׁבַּתּוֹ, עַל עֹלַת הַתָּמִיד וְנִסְכָּהּ.[1] (זֶה קָרְבַּן שַׁבָּת. וְקָרְבַּן הַיּוֹם כָּאָמוּר:)

ON THE FIRST DAY CHOL HAMOED SUCCOS

וּבַיּוֹם הַשֵּׁנִי, פָּרִים בְּנֵי בָקָר שְׁנֵים עָשָׂר, אֵילִם שְׁנָיִם, כְּבָשִׂים בְּנֵי שָׁנָה אַרְבָּעָה עָשָׂר, תְּמִימִם.[2] וּמִנְחָתָם וְנִסְכֵּיהֶם כִּמְדֻבָּר, שְׁלֹשָׁה עֶשְׂרֹנִים לַפָּר, וּשְׁנֵי עֶשְׂרֹנִים לָאָיִל, וְעִשָּׂרוֹן לַכֶּבֶשׂ, וְיַיִן כְּנִסְכּוֹ. וְשָׂעִיר לְכַפֵּר, וּשְׁנֵי תְמִידִים כְּהִלְכָתָם. וּבַיּוֹם הַשְּׁלִישִׁי, פָּרִים עַשְׁתֵּי עָשָׂר, אֵילִם שְׁנָיִם, כְּבָשִׂים בְּנֵי שָׁנָה אַרְבָּעָה עָשָׂר, תְּמִימִם.[3] וּמִנְחָתָם וְנִסְכֵּיהֶם כִּמְדֻבָּר, שְׁלֹשָׁה עֶשְׂרֹנִים לַפָּר, וּשְׁנֵי עֶשְׂרֹנִים לָאָיִל, וְעִשָּׂרוֹן לַכֶּבֶשׂ, וְיַיִן כְּנִסְכּוֹ. וְשָׂעִיר לְכַפֵּר, וּשְׁנֵי תְמִידִים כְּהִלְכָתָם.

Continue . . . יִשְׂמְחוּ (page 560).

ON THE THIRD DAY CHOL HAMOED SUCCOS

וּבַיּוֹם הָרְבִיעִי פָּרִים עֲשָׂרָה, אֵילִם שְׁנָיִם, כְּבָשִׂים בְּנֵי שָׁנָה אַרְבָּעָה עָשָׂר, תְּמִימִם.[4] וּמִנְחָתָם וְנִסְכֵּיהֶם כִּמְדֻבָּר, שְׁלֹשָׁה עֶשְׂרֹנִים לַפָּר, וּשְׁנֵי עֶשְׂרֹנִים לָאָיִל, וְעִשָּׂרוֹן

וּמִפְּנֵי חֲטָאֵינוּ *But because of our sins we have been exiled from our land and sent far from our soil. We cannot ascend to appear and to prostrate ourselves before You, and to perform our obligations in the House of Your choice, in the great and holy House upon which Your Name was proclaimed, because of the hand that was dispatched against Your Sanctuary. May it be Your will,* HASHEM, *our God and the God of our forefathers, O merciful King, that You once more be compassionate upon us and upon Your Sanctuary in Your abundant mercy, and rebuild it soon and magnify its glory. Our Father, our King, reveal the glory of Your Kingship upon us, speedily; appear and be uplifted over us before the eyes of all the living. Draw our scattered ones near from among the nations, and bring in our dispersions from the ends of the earth. Bring us to Zion, Your City, in glad song, and to Jerusalem, home of Your Sanctuary, in eternal joy. There we will perform before You our obligatory offerings, the continual offerings according to their order and the additional offerings according to their law. And the additional offerings of this day of Sabbath and of this day of the Festival of Succos, we will perform and bring near to You with love, according to the commandment of Your will, as You have written for us in Your Torah, through Moses, Your servant, from Your glorious expression, as it is said:*

וּבְיוֹם הַשַּׁבָּת *On the Sabbath day: two [male] first-year lambs, unblemished; and two tenth-ephah of fine flour for a meal-offering, mixed with olive oil, and its wine-libation. The elevation-offering of the Sabbath must be on its particular Sabbath, in addition to the continual elevation-offering and its wine-libation.*[1] *(This is the offering of the Sabbath. And the offering of the day is as it is said:)*

ON THE FIRST DAY CHOL HAMOED SUCCOS

וּבַיּוֹם הַשֵּׁנִי *And on the second day: twelve young bulls, two rams, fourteen [male] first-year lambs, unblemished.*[2] *And their meal-offerings and their wine-libations as mentioned: three tenth-ephah for each bull; two tenth-ephah for each ram; one tenth-ephah for each lamb; and wine for its libation. A he-goat for atonement, and two continual offerings according to their law. And on the third day: eleven bulls, two rams, fourteen [male] first-year lambs, unblemished.*[3] *And their meal-offerings and their wine-libations as mentioned: three tenth-ephah for each bull; two tenth-ephah for each ram; one tenth-ephah for each lamb; and wine for its libation. A he-goat for atonement, and two continual offerings according to their law.* Continue, *'They shall rejoice. . .'* (page 561).

ON THE THIRD DAY CHOL HAMOED SUCCOS

וּבַיּוֹם הָרְבִיעִי *And on the fourth day: ten bulls, two rams, fourteen [male] first-year lambs, unblemished.*[4] *And their meal-offerings and their wine-libations as mentioned: three tenth-ephah*

(1) *Numbers* 28:9-10. (2) 29:17. (3) 29:20. (4) 29:23.

לַכֶּבֶשׂ, וְיַיִן כְּנִסְכּוֹ. וְשָׂעִיר לְכַפֵּר, וּשְׁנֵי תְמִידִים כְּהִלְכָתָם. וּבַיּוֹם הַחֲמִישִׁי, פָּרִים תִּשְׁעָה, אֵילִם שְׁנָיִם, כְּבָשִׂים בְּנֵי שָׁנָה אַרְבָּעָה עָשָׂר, תְּמִימִם.[1] וּמִנְחָתָם וְנִסְכֵּיהֶם כִּמְדֻבָּר, שְׁלֹשָׁה עֶשְׂרֹנִים לַפָּר, וּשְׁנֵי עֶשְׂרֹנִים לָאָיִל, וְעִשָּׂרוֹן לַכֶּבֶשׂ, וְיַיִן כְּנִסְכּוֹ. וְשָׂעִיר לְכַפֵּר, וּשְׁנֵי תְמִידִים כְּהִלְכָתָם.

Continue . . . יִשְׂמְחוּ (below).

ON THE FOURTH DAY CHOL HAMOED SUCCOS

וּבַיּוֹם הַחֲמִישִׁי פָּרִים תִּשְׁעָה, אֵילִם שְׁנָיִם, כְּבָשִׂים בְּנֵי שָׁנָה אַרְבָּעָה עָשָׂר, תְּמִימִם.[1] וּמִנְחָתָם וְנִסְכֵּיהֶם כִּמְדֻבָּר, שְׁלֹשָׁה עֶשְׂרֹנִים לַפָּר, וּשְׁנֵי עֶשְׂרֹנִים לָאָיִל, וְעִשָּׂרוֹן לַכֶּבֶשׂ, וְיַיִן כְּנִסְכּוֹ. וְשָׂעִיר לְכַפֵּר, וּשְׁנֵי תְמִידִים כְּהִלְכָתָם. וּבַיּוֹם הַשִּׁשִּׁי, פָּרִים שְׁמֹנָה, אֵילִם שְׁנָיִם, כְּבָשִׂים בְּנֵי שָׁנָה אַרְבָּעָה עָשָׂר, תְּמִימִם.[2] וּמִנְחָתָם וְנִסְכֵּיהֶם כִּמְדֻבָּר, שְׁלֹשָׁה עֶשְׂרֹנִים לַפָּר, וּשְׁנֵי עֶשְׂרֹנִים לָאָיִל, וְעִשָּׂרוֹן לַכֶּבֶשׂ, וְיַיִן כְּנִסְכּוֹ. וְשָׂעִיר לְכַפֵּר, וּשְׁנֵי תְמִידִים כְּהִלְכָתָם.

Continue . . . יִשְׂמְחוּ (below).

ON ALL DAYS CONTINUE HERE

יִשְׂמְחוּ בְמַלְכוּתְךָ שׁוֹמְרֵי שַׁבָּת וְקוֹרְאֵי עֹנֶג, עַם מְקַדְּשֵׁי שְׁבִיעִי, כֻּלָּם יִשְׂבְּעוּ וְיִתְעַנְּגוּ מִטּוּבֶךָ, וּבַשְּׁבִיעִי רָצִיתָ בּוֹ וְקִדַּשְׁתּוֹ, חֶמְדַּת יָמִים אוֹתוֹ קָרָאתָ, זֵכֶר לְמַעֲשֵׂה בְרֵאשִׁית.

אֱלֹהֵינוּ וֵאלֹהֵי אֲבוֹתֵינוּ, רְצֵה בִמְנוּחָתֵנוּ, מֶלֶךְ רַחֲמָן רַחֵם עָלֵינוּ, טוֹב וּמֵטִיב הִדָּרֶשׁ לָנוּ, שׁוּבָה אֵלֵינוּ בַּהֲמוֹן רַחֲמֶיךָ, בִּגְלַל אָבוֹת שֶׁעָשׂוּ רְצוֹנֶךָ. בְּנֵה בֵיתְךָ כְּבַתְּחִלָּה, וְכוֹנֵן מִקְדָּשְׁךָ עַל מְכוֹנוֹ, וְהַרְאֵנוּ בְּבִנְיָנוֹ, וְשַׂמְּחֵנוּ בְּתִקּוּנוֹ. וְהָשֵׁב כֹּהֲנִים לַעֲבוֹדָתָם, וּלְוִיִּם לְשִׁירָם וּלְזִמְרָם, וְהָשֵׁב יִשְׂרָאֵל לִנְוֵיהֶם. וְשָׁם נַעֲלֶה וְנֵרָאֶה וְנִשְׁתַּחֲוֶה לְפָנֶיךָ, בְּשָׁלֹשׁ פַּעֲמֵי רְגָלֵינוּ, כַּכָּתוּב בְּתוֹרָתֶךָ: שָׁלוֹשׁ פְּעָמִים בַּשָּׁנָה, יֵרָאֶה כָל זְכוּרְךָ אֶת פְּנֵי יהוה אֱלֹהֶיךָ, בַּמָּקוֹם אֲשֶׁר יִבְחָר, בְּחַג הַמַּצּוֹת, וּבְחַג הַשָּׁבֻעוֹת, וּבְחַג הַסֻּכּוֹת, וְלֹא יֵרָאֶה אֶת פְּנֵי יהוה רֵיקָם. אִישׁ כְּמַתְּנַת יָדוֹ, כְּבִרְכַּת יהוה אֱלֹהֶיךָ, אֲשֶׁר נָתַן לָךְ:[3]

for each bull; two tenth-ephah for each ram; one tenth-ephah for each lamb; and wine for its libation. A he-goat for atonement, and two continual offerings according to their law. And on the fifth day: nine bulls, two rams, fourteen [male] first-year lambs, unblemished.[1] *And their meal-offerings and their wine-libations as mentioned: three tenth-ephah for each bull; two tenth-ephah for each ram; one tenth-ephah for each lamb; and wine for its libation. A he-goat for atonement, and two continual offerings according to their law.*

Continue, *'They shall rejoice. . .'* (below).

ON THE FOURTH DAY CHOL HAMOED SUCCOS

וּבַיּוֹם הַחֲמִישִׁי *And on the fifth day: nine bulls, two rams, fourteen [male] first-year lambs, unblemished.*[1] *And their meal-offerings and their wine-libations as mentioned: three tenth-ephah for each bull; two tenth-ephah for each ram; one tenth-ephah for each lamb; and wine for its libation. A he-goat for atonement, and two continual offerings according to their law. And on the sixth day: eight bulls, two rams, fourteen [male] first-year lambs, unblemished.*[2] *And their meal-offerings and their wine-libations as mentioned: three tenth-ephah for each bull; two tenth-ephah for each ram; one tenth-ephah for each lamb; and wine for its libation. A he-goat for atonement, and two continual offerings according to their law.*

Continue, *'They shall rejoice. . .'* (below).

ON ALL DAYS CONTINUE HERE

יִשְׂמְחוּ *They shall rejoice in Your Kingship — those who observe the Sabbath and call it a delight. The people that sanctifies the Seventh — they will all be satisfied and delighted from Your goodness. And the Seventh — You found favor in it and sanctified it. 'Most coveted of days' You called it, a remembrance of creation.*

אֱלֹהֵינוּ *Our God and the God of our forefathers, may You be pleased with our rest, O merciful King, have mercy on us; O good and beneficent One, let Yourself be sought out by us; return to us in Your yearning mercy for the sake of the forefathers who did Your will. Rebuild Your House as it was at first, and establish Your Sanctuary on its prepared site; show us its rebuilding and gladden us in its perfection. Restore the Kohanim to their service and the Levites to their song and music; and restore Israel to their dwellings. And there we will ascend and appear and prostrate ourselves before You, during our three pilgrimage seasons, as it is written in Your Torah: Three times a year all your males are to appear before* HASHEM, *your God, in the place He shall choose, on the Festival of Matzos, on the Festival of Shavuos, and on the Festival of Succos, and they shall not appear before* HASHEM *empty-handed. Every man according to the gift of his hand, according to the blessing of* HASHEM, *your God, that He gave you.*[3]

(1) *Numbers* 29:26. (2) 29:29. (3) *Deuteronomy* 16:16-17.

וְהַשִּׂיאֵנוּ יהוה אֱלֹהֵינוּ אֶת בִּרְכַּת מוֹעֲדֶיךָ לְחַיִּים וּלְשָׁלוֹם, לְשִׂמְחָה וּלְשָׂשׂוֹן, כַּאֲשֶׁר רָצִיתָ וְאָמַרְתָּ לְבָרְכֵנוּ. אֱלֹהֵינוּ וֵאלֹהֵי אֲבוֹתֵינוּ רְצֵה בִמְנוּחָתֵנוּ קַדְּשֵׁנוּ בְּמִצְוֹתֶיךָ וְתֵן חֶלְקֵנוּ בְּתוֹרָתֶךָ, שַׂבְּעֵנוּ מִטּוּבֶךָ וְשַׂמְּחֵנוּ בִּישׁוּעָתֶךָ, וְטַהֵר לִבֵּנוּ לְעָבְדְּךָ בֶּאֱמֶת, וְהַנְחִילֵנוּ יהוה אֱלֹהֵינוּ בְּאַהֲבָה וּבְרָצוֹן בְּשִׂמְחָה וּבְשָׂשׂוֹן שַׁבָּת וּמוֹעֲדֵי קָדְשֶׁךָ, וְיִשְׂמְחוּ בְךָ יִשְׂרָאֵל מְקַדְּשֵׁי שְׁמֶךָ. בָּרוּךְ אַתָּה יהוה, מְקַדֵּשׁ הַשַּׁבָּת וְיִשְׂרָאֵל וְהַזְּמַנִּים.

עבודה

רְצֵה יהוה אֱלֹהֵינוּ בְּעַמְּךָ יִשְׂרָאֵל וּבִתְפִלָּתָם, וְהָשֵׁב אֶת הָעֲבוֹדָה לִדְבִיר בֵּיתֶךָ. וְאִשֵּׁי יִשְׂרָאֵל וּתְפִלָּתָם בְּאַהֲבָה תְקַבֵּל בְּרָצוֹן, וּתְהִי לְרָצוֹן תָּמִיד עֲבוֹדַת יִשְׂרָאֵל עַמֶּךָ.

וְתֶחֱזֶינָה עֵינֵינוּ בְּשׁוּבְךָ לְצִיּוֹן בְּרַחֲמִים. בָּרוּךְ אַתָּה יהוה, הַמַּחֲזִיר שְׁכִינָתוֹ לְצִיּוֹן.

הודאה

Bow at מוֹדִים; straighten up at 'ה. In his repetition the *chazzan* should recite the entire מוֹדִים aloud, while the congregation recites מוֹדִים דְּרַבָּנָן softly.

מוֹדִים אֲנַחְנוּ לָךְ, שָׁאַתָּה הוּא יהוה אֱלֹהֵינוּ וֵאלֹהֵי אֲבוֹתֵינוּ לְעוֹלָם וָעֶד. צוּר חַיֵּינוּ, מָגֵן יִשְׁעֵנוּ אַתָּה הוּא לְדוֹר וָדוֹר. נוֹדֶה לְּךָ וּנְסַפֵּר תְּהִלָּתֶךָ[1] עַל חַיֵּינוּ הַמְּסוּרִים בְּיָדֶךָ, וְעַל נִשְׁמוֹתֵינוּ הַפְּקוּדוֹת לָךְ, וְעַל נִסֶּיךָ שֶׁבְּכָל יוֹם עִמָּנוּ, וְעַל נִפְלְאוֹתֶיךָ וְטוֹבוֹתֶיךָ שֶׁבְּכָל עֵת, עֶרֶב וָבֹקֶר וְצָהֳרָיִם. הַטּוֹב כִּי לֹא כָלוּ רַחֲמֶיךָ, וְהַמְרַחֵם כִּי לֹא תַמּוּ חֲסָדֶיךָ,[2] מֵעוֹלָם קִוִּינוּ לָךְ.

מודים דרבנן

מוֹדִים אֲנַחְנוּ לָךְ, שָׁאַתָּה הוּא יהוה אֱלֹהֵינוּ וֵאלֹהֵי אֲבוֹתֵינוּ, אֱלֹהֵי כָל בָּשָׂר, יוֹצְרֵנוּ, יוֹצֵר בְּרֵאשִׁית. בְּרָכוֹת וְהוֹדָאוֹת לְשִׁמְךָ הַגָּדוֹל וְהַקָּדוֹשׁ, עַל שֶׁהֶחֱיִיתָנוּ וְקִיַּמְתָּנוּ. כֵּן תְּחַיֵּנוּ וּתְקַיְּמֵנוּ, וְתֶאֱסוֹף גָּלֻיּוֹתֵינוּ לְחַצְרוֹת קָדְשֶׁךָ, לִשְׁמוֹר חֻקֶּיךָ וְלַעֲשׂוֹת רְצוֹנֶךָ, וּלְעָבְדְּךָ בְּלֵבָב שָׁלֵם, עַל שֶׁאֲנַחְנוּ מוֹדִים לָךְ. בָּרוּךְ אֵל הַהוֹדָאוֹת.

וְעַל כֻּלָּם יִתְבָּרַךְ וְיִתְרוֹמַם שִׁמְךָ מַלְכֵּנוּ תָּמִיד לְעוֹלָם וָעֶד.

(1) Cf. *Psalms* 79:13. (2) Cf. *Lamentations* 3:22.

וְהַשִּׂיאֵנוּ *Bestow upon us, O* HASHEM, *our God, the blessing of Your appointed Festivals for life and for peace, for gladness and for joy, as You desired and promised to bless us. Our God and the God of our forefathers, may You be pleased with our rest. Sanctify us with Your commandments and grant us our share in Your Torah; satisfy us from Your goodness and gladden us with Your salvation, and purify our heart to serve You sincerely. And grant us a heritage, O* HASHEM, *our God — with love and with favor with gladness and with joy — the Sabbath and the appointed festivals of Your holiness, and may Israel, the sanctifiers of Your Name, rejoice in You. Blessed are You,* HASHEM, *Who sanctifies the Sabbath, Israel and the festive seasons.*

TEMPLE SERVICE

רְצֵה *Be favorable,* HASHEM, *our God, toward Your people Israel and their prayer and restore the service to the Holy of Holies of Your Temple. The fire-offerings of Israel and their prayer accept with love and favor, and may the service of Your people Israel always be favorable to You.*

וְתֶחֱזֶינָה *May our eyes behold Your return to Zion in compassion. Blessed are You,* HASHEM, *Who restores His Presence to Zion.*

THANKSGIVING [MODIM]

Bow at *'We gratefully thank You'*; straighten up at *'*HASHEM.*'* In his repetition the *chazzan* should recite the entire *Modim* aloud, while the congregation recites *Modim of the Rabbis* softly.

מוֹדִים *We gratefully thank You, for it is You Who are* HASHEM, *our God and the God of our forefathers for all eternity; Rock of our lives, Shield of our salvation are You from generation to generation. We shall thank You and relate Your praise*[1] *— for our lives, which are committed to Your power and for our souls that are entrusted to You; for Your miracles that are with us every day; and for Your wonders and favors in every season — evening, morning, and afternoon. The Beneficent One, for Your compassions were never exhausted, and the Compassionate One, for Your kindnesses never ended*[2] *— always have we put our hope in You.*

MODIM OF THE RABBIS

מוֹדִים *We gratefully thank You, for it is You Who are* HASHEM, *our God and the God of our forefathers, the God of all flesh, our Molder, the Molder of the universe. Blessings and thanks are due Your great and holy Name for You have given us life and sustained us. So may You continue to give us life and sustain us and gather our exiles to the Courtyards of Your Sanctuary, to observe Your decrees, to do Your will and to serve You wholeheartedly. [We thank You] for inspiring us to thank You. Blessed is the God of thanksgivings.*

For all these, may Your Name be blessed and exalted, our King, continually forever and ever.

Bend the knees at בָּרוּךְ; bow at אַתָּה; straighten up at 'ה.

וְכֹל הַחַיִּים יוֹדְוּךָ סֶּלָה, וִיהַלְּלוּ אֶת שִׁמְךָ בֶּאֱמֶת, הָאֵל יְשׁוּעָתֵנוּ וְעֶזְרָתֵנוּ סֶלָה. בָּרוּךְ אַתָּה יהוה, הַטּוֹב שִׁמְךָ וּלְךָ נָאֶה לְהוֹדוֹת.

ברכת כהנים

The *chazzan* recites the following during his repetition.
He faces right at וְיִשְׁמְרֶךָ; faces left at אֵלֶיךָ וִיחֻנֶּךָּ; faces the Ark for the rest of the blessings.

אֱלֹהֵינוּ, וֵאלֹהֵי אֲבוֹתֵינוּ, בָּרְכֵנוּ בַבְּרָכָה הַמְּשֻׁלֶּשֶׁת בַּתּוֹרָה הַכְּתוּבָה עַל יְדֵי מֹשֶׁה עַבְדֶּךָ, הָאֲמוּרָה מִפִּי אַהֲרֹן וּבָנָיו, כֹּהֲנִים עַם קְדוֹשֶׁךָ, כָּאָמוּר:

יְבָרֶכְךָ יהוה, וְיִשְׁמְרֶךָ. (Cong. – כֵּן יְהִי רָצוֹן.)

יָאֵר יהוה פָּנָיו אֵלֶיךָ וִיחֻנֶּךָּ. (Cong. – כֵּן יְהִי רָצוֹן.)

יִשָּׂא יהוה פָּנָיו אֵלֶיךָ וְיָשֵׂם לְךָ שָׁלוֹם.[1] (Cong. – כֵּן יְהִי רָצוֹן.)

שלום

שִׂים שָׁלוֹם, טוֹבָה, וּבְרָכָה, חֵן, וָחֶסֶד וְרַחֲמִים עָלֵינוּ וְעַל כָּל יִשְׂרָאֵל עַמֶּךָ. בָּרְכֵנוּ אָבִינוּ, כֻּלָּנוּ כְּאֶחָד בְּאוֹר פָּנֶיךָ, כִּי בְאוֹר פָּנֶיךָ נָתַתָּ לָּנוּ, יהוה אֱלֹהֵינוּ, תּוֹרַת חַיִּים וְאַהֲבַת חֶסֶד, וּצְדָקָה, וּבְרָכָה, וְרַחֲמִים, וְחַיִּים, וְשָׁלוֹם. וְטוֹב בְּעֵינֶיךָ לְבָרֵךְ אֶת עַמְּךָ יִשְׂרָאֵל, בְּכָל עֵת וּבְכָל שָׁעָה בִּשְׁלוֹמֶךָ. בָּרוּךְ אַתָּה יהוה, הַמְּבָרֵךְ אֶת עַמּוֹ יִשְׂרָאֵל בַּשָּׁלוֹם.

יִהְיוּ לְרָצוֹן אִמְרֵי פִי וְהֶגְיוֹן לִבִּי לְפָנֶיךָ, יהוה צוּרִי וְגֹאֲלִי.[2]

The *chazzan's* repetition of *Shemoneh Esrei* ends here. The individual continues below:

אֱלֹהַי, נְצוֹר לְשׁוֹנִי מֵרָע, וּשְׂפָתַי מִדַּבֵּר מִרְמָה,[3] וְלִמְקַלְלַי נַפְשִׁי תִדּוֹם, וְנַפְשִׁי כֶּעָפָר לַכֹּל תִּהְיֶה. פְּתַח לִבִּי בְּתוֹרָתֶךָ, וּבְמִצְוֹתֶיךָ תִּרְדּוֹף נַפְשִׁי. וְכֹל הַחוֹשְׁבִים עָלַי רָעָה, מְהֵרָה הָפֵר עֲצָתָם וְקַלְקֵל מַחֲשַׁבְתָּם. עֲשֵׂה לְמַעַן שְׁמֶךָ, עֲשֵׂה לְמַעַן יְמִינֶךָ, עֲשֵׂה לְמַעַן קְדֻשָּׁתֶךָ, עֲשֵׂה לְמַעַן תּוֹרָתֶךָ. לְמַעַן יֵחָלְצוּן יְדִידֶיךָ, הוֹשִׁיעָה יְמִינְךָ וַעֲנֵנִי.[4]

Some recite verses pertaining to their names here. See page 1301.

יִהְיוּ לְרָצוֹן אִמְרֵי פִי וְהֶגְיוֹן לִבִּי לְפָנֶיךָ, יהוה צוּרִי וְגֹאֲלִי.[2]

Bow and take three steps back. Bow left and say . . . עֹשֶׂה, bow right and say . . . הוּא יַעֲשֶׂה; bow forward and say וְעַל כָּל . . . אָמֵן.

עֹשֶׂה שָׁלוֹם בִּמְרוֹמָיו, הוּא יַעֲשֶׂה שָׁלוֹם עָלֵינוּ, וְעַל כָּל יִשְׂרָאֵל. וְאִמְרוּ: אָמֵן.

Bend the knees at *'Blessed'*; bow at *'You'*; straighten up at *'HASHEM.'*

Everything alive will gratefully acknowledge You, Selah! and praise Your Name sincerely, O God of our salvation and help, Selah! Blessed are You, HASHEM, Your Name is 'The Beneficent One' and to You it is fitting to give thanks.

THE PRIESTLY BLESSING

The *chazzan* recites the following during his repetition.

אֱלֹהֵינוּ *Our God and the God of our forefathers, bless us with the three-verse blessing in the Torah that was written by the hand of Moses, Your servant, that was said by Aaron and his sons, the Kohanim, Your holy people, as it is said:*

May HASHEM bless you and safeguard you. (Cong.— *So may it be.*)

May HASHEM illuminate His countenance for you and be gracious to you. (Cong.— *So may it be.*)

May HASHEM turn His countenance to you and establish peace for you.[1] (Cong.— *So may it be.*)

PEACE

שִׂים שָׁלוֹם *Establish peace, goodness, blessing, graciousness, kindness, and compassion upon us and upon all of Your people Israel. Bless us, our Father, all of us as one, with the light of Your countenance, for with the light of Your countenance You gave us, HASHEM, our God, the Torah of life and a love of kindness, righteousness, blessing, compassion, life, and peace. And may it be good in Your eyes to bless Your people Israel at every time and every hour with Your peace. Blessed are You, HASHEM, Who blesses His people Israel with peace.*

May the expressions of my mouth and the thoughts of my heart find favor before You, HASHEM, my Rock and my Redeemer.[2]

Chazzan's repetition of *Shemoneh Esrei* ends here. Individuals continue:

אֱלֹהַי *My God, guard my tongue from evil and my lips from speaking deceitfully.*[3] *To those who curse me, let my soul be silent; and let my soul be like dust to everyone. Open my heart to Your Torah, then my soul will pursue Your commandments. As for all those who design evil against me, speedily nullify their counsel and disrupt their design. Act for Your Name's sake; act for Your right hand's sake; act for Your sanctity's sake; act for Your Torah's sake. That Your beloved ones may be given rest; let Your right hand save, and respond to me.*[4]

Some recite verses pertaining to their names at this point. See page 1301.

May the expressions of my mouth and the thoughts of my heart find favor before You, HASHEM, my Rock and my Redeemer.[2] *He Who makes peace in His heights, may He make peace upon us, and upon all Israel. Now respond: Amen.*

Bow and take three steps back. Bow left and say, *'He Who makes peace ...'*; bow right and say, *'may He make peace ...'*; bow forward and say, *'and upon ... Amen.'*

---

(1) *Numbers* 6:24-26. (2) *Psalms* 19:15. (3) Cf. 34:14. (4) 60:7; 108:7.

יְהִי רָצוֹן מִלְּפָנֶיךָ יהוה אֱלֹהֵינוּ וֵאלֹהֵי אֲבוֹתֵינוּ, שֶׁיִּבָּנֶה בֵּית הַמִּקְדָּשׁ בִּמְהֵרָה בְיָמֵינוּ, וְתֵן חֶלְקֵנוּ בְּתוֹרָתֶךָ. וְשָׁם נַעֲבָדְךָ בְּיִרְאָה, כִּימֵי עוֹלָם וּכְשָׁנִים קַדְמוֹנִיּוֹת. וְעָרְבָה לַיהוה מִנְחַת יְהוּדָה וִירוּשָׁלָיִם, כִּימֵי עוֹלָם וּכְשָׁנִים קַדְמוֹנִיּוֹת.[1]

THE INDIVIDUAL'S RECITATION OF *SHEMONEH ESREI* ENDS HERE.

The individual remains standing in place until the *chazzan* reaches *Kedushah* — or at least until the *chazzan* begins his repetition — then he takes three steps forward. The *chazzan* himself, or one praying alone, should remain in place for a few moments before taking three steps forward.

סדר הושענות לשבת חול המועד

THE ARK IS OPENED, BUT THE TORAH SCROLL IS NOT REMOVED.

Each line is recited by *chazzan*, then repeated aloud by congregation. (Commentary on p. 368.)

הוֹשַׁעְנָא, לְמַעַנְךָ אֱלֹהֵינוּ, הוֹשַׁעְנָא.

הוֹשַׁעְנָא, לְמַעַנְךָ בּוֹרְאֵנוּ, הוֹשַׁעְנָא.

הוֹשַׁעְנָא, לְמַעַנְךָ גּוֹאֲלֵנוּ, הוֹשַׁעְנָא.

הוֹשַׁעְנָא, לְמַעַנְךָ דּוֹרְשֵׁנוּ, הוֹשַׁעְנָא.

All:

אוֹם נְצוּרָה כְּבָבַת. בּוֹנֶנֶת בְּדָת נֶפֶשׁ מְשִׁיבַת. גּוֹמֶרֶת הִלְכוֹת שַׁבָּת. דּוֹרֶשֶׁת מַשְׂאַת שַׁבָּת. הַקּוֹבַעַת אַלְפַּיִם תְּחוּם שַׁבָּת. וּמְשִׁיבַת רֶגֶל מִשַּׁבָּת. זָכוֹר וְשָׁמוֹר מְקַיֶּמֶת בַּשַּׁבָּת. חָשָׁה לְמַהֵר בִּיאַת שַׁבָּת. טוֹרַחַת כֹּל מִשִּׁשָּׁה לַשַּׁבָּת. יוֹשֶׁבֶת וּמַמְתֶּנֶת עַד כְּלוֹת שַׁבָּת. כָּבוֹד וָעֹנֶג קוֹרְאָה לַשַּׁבָּת. לְבוּשׁ וּכְסוּת מְחַלֶּפֶת בַּשַּׁבָּת. מַאֲכָל וּמִשְׁתֶּה מְכִינָה לַשַּׁבָּת. נֹעַם מְגָדִים מַנְעֶמֶת לַשַּׁבָּת. סְעוּדוֹת שָׁלֹשׁ מְקַיֶּמֶת בַּשַּׁבָּת. עַל שְׁתֵּי כִכָּרוֹת בּוֹצַעַת בַּשַּׁבָּת. פּוֹרֶטֶת אַרְבַּע רְשֻׁיּוֹת בַּשַּׁבָּת. צִוּוּי הַדְלָקַת נֵר מַדְלֶקֶת בַּשַּׁבָּת. קִדּוּשׁ הַיּוֹם מְקַדֶּשֶׁת בַּשַּׁבָּת. רֶנֶן שֶׁבַע מְפַלֶּלֶת בַּשַּׁבָּת. שִׁבְעָה בְּדָת קוֹרְאָה בַּשַּׁבָּת. תַּנְחִילֶנָּה לְיוֹם שֶׁכֻּלּוֹ שַׁבָּת.

אֲנִי וָהוֹ הוֹשִׁיעָה נָּא:

כְּהוֹשַׁעְתָּ אָדָם יְצִיר כַּפֶּיךָ לְגוֹנְנָה,
בְּשַׁבַּת קֹדֶשׁ הִמְצֵאתוֹ כֹּפֶר וַחֲנִינָה, כֵּן הוֹשַׁעְנָא.
כְּהוֹשַׁעְתָּ גּוֹי מְצֻיָּן מְקַוִּים חֹפֶשׁ,
דֵּעָה כִּוְּנוּ לָבוֹר שְׁבִיעִי לְנֹפֶשׁ, כֵּן הוֹשַׁעְנָא.
כְּהוֹשַׁעְתָּ הָעָם נִהַגְתָּ כַּצֹּאן לְהַנְחוֹת,
וְחֹק שַׂמְתָּ בְּמָרָה עַל מֵי מְנֻחוֹת, כֵּן הוֹשַׁעְנָא.

(1) *Malachi* 3:4.

יְהִי רָצוֹן *May it be Your will,* HASHEM, *our God and the God of our forefathers, that the Holy Temple be rebuilt, speedily in our days. Grant us our share in Your Torah, and may we serve You there with reverence, as in days of old and in former years. Then the offering of Judah and Jerusalem will be pleasing to* HASHEM, *as in days of old and in former years.*[1]

THE INDIVIDUAL'S RECITATION OF *SHEMONEH ESREI* ENDS HERE.

The individual remains standing in place until the *chazzan* reaches *Kedushah* — or at least until the *chazzan* begins his repetition — then he takes three steps forward. The *chazzan* himself, or one praying alone, should remain in place for a few moments before taking three steps forward.

HOSHANOS FOR THE SABBATH OF CHOL HAMOED

THE ARK IS OPENED, BUT THE TORAH SCROLL IS NOT REMOVED.

Each line is recited by *chazzan,* then repeated aloud by the congregation. (Commentary on p. 368.)

הוֹשַׁעְנָא *Please save — for Your sake, our God!* *Please save!*
Please save — for Your sake, our Creator! *Please save!*
Please save — for Your sake, our Redeemer! *Please save!*
Please save — for Your sake, our Attender! *Please save!*

All:

אוֹם נְצוּרָה *Nation protected like the pupil of the eye —* **ב** *she seeks understanding of the law which restores the soul.* **ג** *She studies the laws of the Sabbath,* **ד** *explicates the burdens of the Sabbath,* **ה** *establishes two thousand as the boundary, of the Sabbath,* **ו** *and restrains her foot because of the Sabbath.* **ז** *'Remember' and 'Safeguard' she fulfills on the Sabbath* **ח** *by rushing to hasten the onset of the Sabbath;* **ט** *by toiling throughout the six for the Sabbath;* **י** *by sitting, patiently waiting until the end of the Sabbath.* **כ** *'Honor' and 'Delight' she proclaims the Sabbath:* **ל** *clothing and raiment she changes for the Sabbath,* **מ** *food and drink she prepares for the Sabbath,* **נ** *of the sweetness of delicate fruits she partakes on the Sabbath,* **ס** *three meals she fulfills on the Sabbath,* **ע** *over two loaves she breaks bread on the Sabbath.* **פ** *She distinguishes four domains on the Sabbath.* **צ** *The command of kindling the light she fulfills for the Sabbath.* **ק** *The Sanctification of the day she recites on the Sabbath.* **ר** *A seven-part prayer she prays on the Sabbath.* **ש** *Seven portions of the Torah she reads on the Sabbath.* **ת** *Cause her to inherit the day which will be completely a Sabbath.*

ANI VAHO, bring salvation now.

כְּהוֹשַׁעְתָּ אָדָם **א** *As You saved Adam, Your handiwork, to be his shield;*
ב *on the holy Sabbath You brought forth for him forgiveness and grace* — *so save now.*
ג *As You saved the distinctive nation which sought freedom;*
ד *with wisdom they anticipated the choice of the seventh for rest* — *so save now.*
ה *As You saved the people whom You guided like a flock to contentment;*
ו *and You issued a statute at Marah beside tranquil waters* — *so save now.*

כְּהוֹשַׁעְתָּ זְבוּדֶיךָ בְּמִדְבַּר סִין בְּמַחֲנֶה,
חָכְמוּ וְלָקְטוּ בַּשִּׁשִּׁי לֶחֶם מִשְׁנֶה, כֵּן הוֹשַׁעְנָא.
כְּהוֹשַׁעְתָּ טְפוּלֶיךָ הוֹרוּ הֲכָנָה בְּמַדָּעָם,
יֹשֶׁר כֹּחָם וְהוֹדָה לָמוֹ רוֹעָם, כֵּן הוֹשַׁעְנָא.
כְּהוֹשַׁעְתָּ כֻּלְכְּלוּ בְּעֹנֶג מָן הַמִּשְׁמָר,
לֹא הָפַךְ עֵינוֹ וְרֵיחוֹ לֹא נָמָר, כֵּן הוֹשַׁעְנָא.
כְּהוֹשַׁעְתָּ מִשְׁפְּטֵי מַשְׂאוֹת שַׁבָּת גָּמָרוּ,
נָחוּ וְשָׁבְתוּ רְשׁוּיוֹת וּתְחוּמִים שָׁמָרוּ, כֵּן הוֹשַׁעְנָא.
כְּהוֹשַׁעְתָּ סִינַי הֻשְׁמְעוּ בְּדִבּוּר רְבִיעִי,
עִנְיַן זָכוֹר וְשָׁמוֹר לְקַדֵּשׁ שְׁבִיעִי, כֵּן הוֹשַׁעְנָא.
כְּהוֹשַׁעְתָּ פֻּקְּדוּ יְרִיחוֹ שֶׁבַע לְהַקֵּף,
צָרוּ עַד רִדְתָּהּ בַּשַּׁבָּת לְתַקֵּף, כֵּן הוֹשַׁעְנָא.
כְּהוֹשַׁעְתָּ קֹהֶלֶת וְעַמּוֹ בְּבֵית עוֹלָמִים,
רִצּוּךָ בְּחָגְגָם שִׁבְעָה וְשִׁבְעָה יָמִים, כֵּן הוֹשַׁעְנָא.
כְּהוֹשַׁעְתָּ שָׁבִים עוֹלֵי גוֹלָה לְפִדְיוֹם,
תּוֹרָתְךָ בְּקָרְאָם בֶּחָג יוֹם יוֹם, כֵּן הוֹשַׁעְנָא.
כְּהוֹשַׁעְתָּ מְשַׂמְּחֶיךָ בְּבִנְיַן שֵׁנִי הַמְּחֻדָּשׁ,
נוֹטְלִין לוּלָב כָּל שִׁבְעָה בַּמִּקְדָּשׁ, כֵּן הוֹשַׁעְנָא.
כְּהוֹשַׁעְתָּ חִבּוּט עֲרָבָה שַׁבָּת מַדְחִים,
מְרֻבִּיּוֹת מוֹצָא לִיסוֹד מִזְבֵּחַ מַנִּיחִים, כֵּן הוֹשַׁעְנָא.
כְּהוֹשַׁעְתָּ בְּרַכּוֹת וַאֲרוּכוֹת וּגְבוֹהוֹת מְעַלְּסִים,
בִּפְטִירָתָן יֹפִי לְךָ מִזְבֵּחַ מְקַלְּסִים, כֵּן הוֹשַׁעְנָא.
כְּהוֹשַׁעְתָּ מוֹדִים וּמְיַחֲלִים וְלֹא מְשַׁנִּים,
כֻּלָּנוּ אָנוּ לְיָהּ וְעֵינֵינוּ לְיָהּ שׁוֹנִים, כֵּן הוֹשַׁעְנָא.
כְּהוֹשַׁעְתָּ יֶקֶב מַחֲצָבֶיךָ סוֹבְבִים בִּרְנָנָה,
רוֹנְנִים אֲנִי וָהוֹ הוֹשִׁיעָה נָּא, כֵּן הוֹשַׁעְנָא.
כְּהוֹשַׁעְתָּ חֵיל זְרִיזִים מְשָׁרְתִים בִּמְנוּחָה,
קָרְבַּן שַׁבָּת כָּפוּל עוֹלָה וּמִנְחָה, כֵּן הוֹשַׁעְנָא.

ז *As You saved Your portion in the encampment at the Wilderness of Sin;*
ח *they acted wisely and gathered double bread on the sixth — so save now.*
ט *As You saved those who clung to You, who derived the rules of preparation through their wisdom;*
י *their shepherd blessed their talent and deferred to them — so save now.*
כ *As You saved those You sustained on the day of delight with the guarded manna,*
ל *whose appearance did not change and whose aroma did not sour — so save now.*
מ *As You saved those who study the laws regarding the burdens of the Sabbath;*
נ *they are content and they rest, guarding domains and boundaries — so save now.*
ס *As You saved those permitted to hear the fourth pronouncement at Sinai;*
ע *the theme of 'Remember' and 'Safeguard' to sanctify the seventh — so save now.*
פ *As You saved those bidden at Jericho to encircle seven times;*
צ *they besieged it until its downfall on the Sabbath, to strengthen them — so save now.*
ק *As You saved Koheles [Solomon] and his nation in the eternal Temple,*
ר *they pleased You when they celebrated seven and another seven days — so save now.*
ש *As You saved those who returned, ascending from exile to redemption;*
ת *as they read Your Torah every day of the Festival — so save now.*
מ *As You saved those who brought You joy with the renewed Second Temple;*
נ *who took up the lulav all seven days in the Sanctuary — so save now.*
ח *As You saved those for whom the beating of the willow overrode the Sabbath;*
מ *those who placed Motza's branches at the base of the altar — so save now.*
ב *As You saved those who praised with supple, long and tall willows;*
בי *who departed while extolling, 'Beauty becomes you, O Altar' — so save now.*
מ *As You saved those who thanked and hoped, but never exchanged;*
כ *like them we all cry out, 'We are God's and our eyes are to God' — so save now.*
י *As You saved those who encircled Your hewn wine cellar with greenery;*
ר *singing, 'ANI VAHO, bring salvation now' — so save now.*
חז *As You saved the army of speedy ones who serve on the day of contentment,*
ק *with the doubled Sabbath offering, of burnt and meal offering — so save now.*

כְּהוֹשַׁעְתָּ לְוִיֶּיךָ עַל דּוּכָנָם לְהַרְבָּת,
אוֹמְרִים מִזְמוֹר שִׁיר לְיוֹם הַשַּׁבָּת, כֵּן הוֹשַׁעְנָא.
כְּהוֹשַׁעְתָּ נְחוּמֶיךָ בְּמִצְוֹתֶיךָ תָּמִיד יִשְׁתַּעְשְׁעוּן,
וּרְצֵם וְהַחֲלִיצֵם בְּשׁוּבָה וָנַחַת יִוָּשֵׁעוּן, כֵּן הוֹשַׁעְנָא.
כְּהוֹשַׁעְתָּ שְׁבוּת שִׁבְטֵי יַעֲקֹב,
תָּשׁוּב וְתָשִׁיב שְׁבוּת אָהֳלֵי יַעֲקֹב, וְהוֹשִׁיעָה נָּא.
כְּהוֹשַׁעְתָּ שׁוֹמְרֵי מִצְוֹת, וְחוֹכֵי יְשׁוּעוֹת,
אֵל לְמוֹשָׁעוֹת, וְהוֹשִׁיעָה נָּא.

אֲנִי וָהוֹ הוֹשִׁיעָה נָּא.

הוֹשִׁיעָה אֶת עַמֶּךָ, וּבָרֵךְ אֶת נַחֲלָתֶךָ, וּרְעֵם וְנַשְּׂאֵם עַד הָעוֹלָם.[1] וְיִהְיוּ דְבָרַי אֵלֶּה אֲשֶׁר הִתְחַנַּנְתִּי לִפְנֵי יהוה, קְרֹבִים אֶל יהוה אֱלֹהֵינוּ יוֹמָם וָלָיְלָה, לַעֲשׂוֹת מִשְׁפַּט עַבְדּוֹ וּמִשְׁפַּט עַמּוֹ יִשְׂרָאֵל, דְּבַר יוֹם בְּיוֹמוֹ. לְמַעַן דַּעַת כָּל עַמֵּי הָאָרֶץ, כִּי יהוה הוּא הָאֱלֹהִים, אֵין עוֹד.[2]

Congregations that recite *Hoshanos* after *Hallel* turn to page 490.

קדיש שלם

The *chazzan* recites קַדִּישׁ שָׁלֵם.

יִתְגַּדַּל וְיִתְקַדַּשׁ שְׁמֵהּ רַבָּא. (.Cong — אָמֵן.) בְּעָלְמָא דִּי בְרָא כִרְעוּתֵהּ. וְיַמְלִיךְ מַלְכוּתֵהּ, בְּחַיֵּיכוֹן וּבְיוֹמֵיכוֹן וּבְחַיֵּי דְכָל בֵּית יִשְׂרָאֵל, בַּעֲגָלָא וּבִזְמַן קָרִיב. וְאִמְרוּ: אָמֵן.

(.Cong — אָמֵן. יְהֵא שְׁמֵהּ רַבָּא מְבָרַךְ לְעָלַם וּלְעָלְמֵי עָלְמַיָּא.)

יְהֵא שְׁמֵהּ רַבָּא מְבָרַךְ לְעָלַם וּלְעָלְמֵי עָלְמַיָּא.

יִתְבָּרַךְ וְיִשְׁתַּבַּח וְיִתְפָּאַר וְיִתְרוֹמַם וְיִתְנַשֵּׂא וְיִתְהַדָּר וְיִתְעַלֶּה וְיִתְהַלָּל שְׁמֵהּ דְּקֻדְשָׁא בְּרִיךְ הוּא (.Cong — בְּרִיךְ הוּא) — לְעֵלָּא מִן כָּל בִּרְכָתָא וְשִׁירָתָא תֻּשְׁבְּחָתָא וְנֶחֱמָתָא, דַּאֲמִירָן בְּעָלְמָא. וְאִמְרוּ: אָמֵן. (.Cong — אָמֵן.)

(.Cong — קַבֵּל בְּרַחֲמִים וּבְרָצוֹן אֶת תְּפִלָּתֵנוּ.)

תִּתְקַבֵּל צְלוֹתְהוֹן וּבָעוּתְהוֹן דְּכָל בֵּית יִשְׂרָאֵל קֳדָם אֲבוּהוֹן דִּי בִשְׁמַיָּא. וְאִמְרוּ: אָמֵן. (.Cong — אָמֵן.)

(.Cong — יְהִי שֵׁם יהוה מְבֹרָךְ, מֵעַתָּה וְעַד עוֹלָם.[3])

יְהֵא שְׁלָמָא רַבָּא מִן שְׁמַיָּא, וְחַיִּים עָלֵינוּ וְעַל כָּל יִשְׂרָאֵל. וְאִמְרוּ: אָמֵן. (.Cong — אָמֵן.)

(.Cong — עֶזְרִי מֵעִם יהוה, עֹשֵׂה שָׁמַיִם וָאָרֶץ.[4])

Take three steps back. Bow left and say . . . עֹשֶׂה; bow right and say . . . הוּא; bow forward and say וְעַל כָּל . . . אָמֵן. Remain standing in place for a few moments, then take three steps forward.

עֹשֶׂה שָׁלוֹם בִּמְרוֹמָיו, הוּא יַעֲשֶׂה שָׁלוֹם עָלֵינוּ, וְעַל כָּל יִשְׂרָאֵל. וְאִמְרוּ: אָמֵן. (.Cong — אָמֵן.)

לעד *As You saved Your Levites who sang upon their platform,*
אמ *saying, 'A psalm, a song, for the Sabbath day'*
— so save now.

נ *As You saved those whom You comforted,*
those who constantly find joy in Your mitzvos;
so may You favor them and give them rest,
and tranquility, and contentedly may they attain salvation
— so save now.

As You saved the captivity of the tribes of Jacob,
return and restore the captivity of Jacob's tents
and bring salvation now.

As You saved those observing mitzvos, and hoping for salvation —
O God Who brings salvations
bring salvation now.

ANI VAHO, bring salvation now.

הוֹשִׁיעָה *Save Your people and bless Your heritage, tend them and elevate them forever.*[1] *May these words of mine, which I have supplicated before* HASHEM, *be near to* HASHEM, *our God, by day and by night; that He bring about justice for His servant and justice for His people, Israel, each day's need in its day; that all the peoples of the earth shall know that* HASHEM *is God — there is no other.*[2]

Congregations that recite *Hoshanos* after *Hallel,* turn to page 490.

FULL KADDISH

The *chazzan* recites the Full *Kaddish.*

יִתְגַּדַּל *May His great Name grow exalted and sanctified* (Cong.— *Amen.*) *in the world that He created as He willed. May He give reign to His kingship in your lifetimes and in your days, and in the lifetimes of the entire Family of Israel, swiftly and soon. Now respond: Amen.*

(Cong.— *Amen. May His great Name be blessed forever and ever.*)
May His great Name be blessed forever and ever.

Blessed, praised, glorified, exalted, extolled, mighty, upraised, and lauded be the Name of the Holy One, Blessed is He (Cong.— *Blessed is He*) *— beyond any blessing and song, praise and consolation that are uttered in the world. Now respond: Amen.* (Cong.— *Amen.*)

(Cong.— *Accept our prayers with mercy and favor.*)

May the prayers and supplications of the entire Family of Israel be accepted before their Father Who is in Heaven. Now respond: Amen. (Cong.— *Amen.*)

(Cong.— *Blessed be the Name of* HASHEM, *from this time and forever.*[3])

May there be abundant peace from Heaven, and life, upon us and upon all Israel. Now respond: Amen. (Cong.— *Amen.*)

(Cong.— *My help is from* HASHEM, *Maker of heaven and earth.*[4])

Take three steps back. Bow left and say, *'He Who makes peace . . .';*
bow right and say, *'may He . . .';* bow forward and say, *'and upon all Israel . . .'*
Remain standing in place for a few moments, then take three steps forward.

He Who makes peace in His heights, may He make peace upon us, and upon all Israel. Now respond: Amen. (Cong.— *Amen.*)

---

(1) *Psalms* 28:9. (2) *I Kings* 8:59-60. (3) *Psalms* 113:2. (4) 121:2.

קַוֵּה אֶל יהוה, חֲזַק וְיַאֲמֵץ לִבֶּךָ, וְקַוֵּה אֶל יהוה.[1] אֵין קָדוֹשׁ כַּיהוה, כִּי אֵין בִּלְתֶּךָ, וְאֵין צוּר כֵּאלֹהֵינוּ.[2] כִּי מִי אֱלוֹהַּ מִבַּלְעֲדֵי יהוה, וּמִי צוּר זוּלָתִי אֱלֹהֵינוּ.[3]

אֵין כֵּאלֹהֵינוּ, אֵין כַּאדוֹנֵינוּ, אֵין כְּמַלְכֵּנוּ, אֵין כְּמוֹשִׁיעֵנוּ. מִי כֵאלֹהֵינוּ, מִי כַאדוֹנֵינוּ, מִי כְמַלְכֵּנוּ, מִי כְמוֹשִׁיעֵנוּ. נוֹדֶה לֵאלֹהֵינוּ, נוֹדֶה לַאדוֹנֵינוּ, נוֹדֶה לְמַלְכֵּנוּ, נוֹדֶה לְמוֹשִׁיעֵנוּ. בָּרוּךְ אֱלֹהֵינוּ, בָּרוּךְ אֲדוֹנֵינוּ, בָּרוּךְ מַלְכֵּנוּ, בָּרוּךְ מוֹשִׁיעֵנוּ. אַתָּה הוּא אֱלֹהֵינוּ, אַתָּה הוּא אֲדוֹנֵינוּ, אַתָּה הוּא מַלְכֵּנוּ, אַתָּה הוּא מוֹשִׁיעֵנוּ. אַתָּה הוּא שֶׁהִקְטִירוּ אֲבוֹתֵינוּ לְפָנֶיךָ אֶת קְטֹרֶת הַסַּמִּים.

כריתות ו.

פִּטּוּם הַקְּטֹרֶת: (א) הַצֳּרִי, (ב) וְהַצִּפֹּרֶן, (ג) הַחֶלְבְּנָה, (ד) וְהַלְּבוֹנָה, מִשְׁקַל שִׁבְעִים שִׁבְעִים מָנֶה; (ה) מוֹר, (ו) וּקְצִיעָה, (ז) שִׁבֹּלֶת נֵרְדְּ, (ח) וְכַרְכֹּם, מִשְׁקַל שִׁשָּׁה עָשָׂר שִׁשָּׁה עָשָׂר מָנֶה; (ט) הַקֹּשְׁטְ שְׁנֵים עָשָׂר, (י) וְקִלּוּפָה שְׁלֹשָׁה, (יא) וְקִנָּמוֹן תִּשְׁעָה. בֹּרִית כַּרְשִׁינָה תִּשְׁעָה קַבִּין, יֵין קַפְרִיסִין סְאִין תְּלָתָא וְקַבִּין תְּלָתָא; וְאִם אֵין לוֹ יֵין קַפְרִיסִין, מֵבִיא חֲמַר חִוַּרְיָן עַתִּיק; מֶלַח סְדוֹמִית רֹבַע הַקָּב; מַעֲלֶה עָשָׁן כָּל שֶׁהוּא. רַבִּי נָתָן הַבַּבְלִי אוֹמֵר: אַף כִּפַּת הַיַּרְדֵּן כָּל שֶׁהוּא. וְאִם נָתַן בָּהּ דְּבַשׁ פְּסָלָהּ. וְאִם חִסַּר אַחַת מִכָּל סַמָּנֶיהָ, חַיָּב מִיתָה.

רַבָּן שִׁמְעוֹן בֶּן גַּמְלִיאֵל אוֹמֵר: הַצֳּרִי אֵינוֹ אֶלָּא שְׂרָף הַנּוֹטֵף מֵעֲצֵי הַקְּטָף. בֹּרִית כַּרְשִׁינָה שֶׁשָּׁפִין בָּהּ אֶת הַצִּפֹּרֶן כְּדֵי שֶׁתְּהֵא נָאָה; יֵין קַפְרִיסִין שֶׁשּׁוֹרִין בּוֹ אֶת הַצִּפֹּרֶן כְּדֵי שֶׁתְּהֵא עַזָּה; וַהֲלֹא מֵי רַגְלַיִם יָפִין לָהּ, אֶלָּא שֶׁאֵין מַכְנִיסִין מֵי רַגְלַיִם בָּעֲזָרָה מִפְּנֵי הַכָּבוֹד.

משנה, תמיד ז:ד

הַשִּׁיר שֶׁהַלְוִיִּם הָיוּ אוֹמְרִים בְּבֵית הַמִּקְדָּשׁ. בַּיּוֹם הָרִאשׁוֹן הָיוּ אוֹמְרִים: לַיהוה הָאָרֶץ וּמְלוֹאָהּ, תֵּבֵל וְיֹשְׁבֵי בָהּ.[4] בַּשֵּׁנִי הָיוּ אוֹמְרִים: גָּדוֹל יהוה וּמְהֻלָּל מְאֹד, בְּעִיר אֱלֹהֵינוּ הַר קָדְשׁוֹ.[5] בַּשְּׁלִישִׁי הָיוּ אוֹמְרִים: אֱלֹהִים נִצָּב בַּעֲדַת אֵל, בְּקֶרֶב אֱלֹהִים יִשְׁפֹּט.[6] בָּרְבִיעִי הָיוּ אוֹמְרִים: אֵל נְקָמוֹת יהוה, אֵל נְקָמוֹת הוֹפִיעַ.[7] בַּחֲמִישִׁי הָיוּ אוֹמְרִים: הַרְנִינוּ לֵאלֹהִים עוּזֵּנוּ, הָרִיעוּ לֵאלֹהֵי

קַוֵּה *Hope to HASHEM, strengthen yourself and He will give you courage; and hope to HASHEM.[1] There is none holy as HASHEM, for there is none beside You, and there is no Rock like our God.[2] For who is a god beside HASHEM, and who is a Rock except for our God.[3]*

אֵין *There is none like our God; there is none like our Master;*
there is none like our King; there is none like our Savior.
Who is like our God? Who is like our Master?
Who is like our King? Who is like our Savior?
Let us thank our God; let us thank our Master;
let us thank our King; let us thank our Savior.
Blessed is our God; blessed is our Master;
blessed is our King; blessed is our Savior.
It is You Who is our God; it is You Who is our Master;
it is You Who is our King; it is You Who is our Savior.
It is You before Whom our forefathers burned the spice-incense.

Talmud, *Kereisos* 6a

פִּטּוּם הַקְּטֹרֶת *The incense mixture was formulated of [eleven spices]: (1) stacte, (2) onycha, (3) galbanum, (4) frankincense — each weighing seventy maneh; (5) myrrh, (6) cassia, (7) spikenard, (8) saffron — each weighing sixteen maneh; (9) costus — twelve [maneh]; (10) aromatic bark — three; and (11) cinnamon — nine. [Additionally] Carshina lye — nine kab; Cyprus wine, three se'ah and three kab — if he has no Cyprus wine, he brings old white wine; Sodom salt, a quarter kab; and a minute amount of smoke-raising herb. Rabbi Nassan the Babylonian says: Also a minute amount of Jordan amber. If he placed fruit-honey into it, he invalidated it. And if he left out any of its spices, he is liable to the death penalty.*

רַבָּן שִׁמְעוֹן *Rabban Shimon ben Gamliel says: The stacte is simply the sap that drips from balsam trees. Carshina lye is used to bleach the onycha to make it pleasing. Cyprus wine is used to soak the onycha to make it pungent. Even though urine is suitable for that, nevertheless they do not bring urine into the Temple out of respect.*

Mishnah, *Tamid* 7:4

הַשִּׁיר *The daily song that the Levites would recite in the Temple was as follows: On the first day [of the week] they would say: 'HASHEM's is the earth and its fullness, the inhabited land and those who dwell in it.'[4] On the second day they would say: 'Great is HASHEM and much praised, in the city of our God, Mount of His Holiness.'[5] On the third day they would say: 'God stands in the Divine assembly, in the midst of judges shall He judge.'[6] On the fourth day they would say: 'O God of vengeance, HASHEM, O God of vengeance, appear.'[7] On the fifth day they would say: 'Sing joyously to the God of our might, call out to*

(1) *Psalms* 27:14. (2) *I Samuel* 2:2. (3) *Psalms* 18:32. (4) 24:1. (5) 48:2. (6) 82:1. (7) 94:1.

יַעֲקֹב.[1] בַּשִּׁשִּׁי הָיוּ אוֹמְרִים: יהוה מָלָךְ גֵּאוּת לָבֵשׁ, לָבֵשׁ יהוה עֹז הִתְאַזָּר, אַף תִּכּוֹן תֵּבֵל בַּל תִּמּוֹט.[2] בַּשַּׁבָּת הָיוּ אוֹמְרִים: מִזְמוֹר שִׁיר לְיוֹם הַשַּׁבָּת.[3] מִזְמוֹר שִׁיר לֶעָתִיד לָבֹא, לְיוֹם שֶׁכֻּלּוֹ שַׁבָּת וּמְנוּחָה לְחַיֵּי הָעוֹלָמִים.

מגילה כח:

תָּנָא דְבֵי אֵלִיָּהוּ: כָּל הַשּׁוֹנֶה הֲלָכוֹת בְּכָל יוֹם, מֻבְטָח לוֹ שֶׁהוּא בֶּן עוֹלָם הַבָּא, שֶׁנֶּאֱמַר: הֲלִיכוֹת עוֹלָם לוֹ,[4] אַל תִּקְרֵי הֲלִיכוֹת, אֶלָּא הֲלָכוֹת.

ברכות סד.

אָמַר רַבִּי אֶלְעָזָר אָמַר רַבִּי חֲנִינָא: תַּלְמִידֵי חֲכָמִים מַרְבִּים שָׁלוֹם בָּעוֹלָם, שֶׁנֶּאֱמַר: וְכָל בָּנַיִךְ לִמּוּדֵי יהוה, וְרַב שְׁלוֹם בָּנָיִךְ,[5] אַל תִּקְרֵי בָּנָיִךְ אֶלָּא בּוֹנָיִךְ. ❖ שָׁלוֹם רָב לְאֹהֲבֵי תוֹרָתֶךָ, וְאֵין לָמוֹ מִכְשׁוֹל.[6] יְהִי שָׁלוֹם בְּחֵילֵךְ, שַׁלְוָה בְּאַרְמְנוֹתָיִךְ. לְמַעַן אַחַי וְרֵעָי, אֲדַבְּרָה נָּא שָׁלוֹם בָּךְ. לְמַעַן בֵּית יהוה אֱלֹהֵינוּ, אֲבַקְשָׁה טוֹב לָךְ.[7] יהוה עֹז לְעַמּוֹ יִתֵּן, יהוה יְבָרֵךְ אֶת עַמּוֹ בַשָּׁלוֹם.[8]

קדיש דרבנן

In the presence of a *minyan,* mourners recite קַדִּישׁ דְּרַבָּנָן (see *Laws* §84-85).

יִתְגַּדַּל וְיִתְקַדַּשׁ שְׁמֵהּ רַבָּא. (.Cong – אָמֵן.) בְּעָלְמָא דִּי בְרָא כִרְעוּתֵהּ. וְיַמְלִיךְ מַלְכוּתֵהּ, בְּחַיֵּיכוֹן וּבְיוֹמֵיכוֹן וּבְחַיֵּי דְכָל בֵּית יִשְׂרָאֵל, בַּעֲגָלָא וּבִזְמַן קָרִיב. וְאִמְרוּ: אָמֵן.

(.Cong – אָמֵן. יְהֵא שְׁמֵהּ רַבָּא מְבָרַךְ לְעָלַם וּלְעָלְמֵי עָלְמַיָּא.)

יְהֵא שְׁמֵהּ רַבָּא מְבָרַךְ לְעָלַם וּלְעָלְמֵי עָלְמַיָּא.

יִתְבָּרַךְ וְיִשְׁתַּבַּח וְיִתְפָּאַר וְיִתְרוֹמַם וְיִתְנַשֵּׂא וְיִתְהַדָּר וְיִתְעַלֶּה וְיִתְהַלָּל שְׁמֵהּ דְּקֻדְשָׁא בְּרִיךְ הוּא (.Cong – בְּרִיךְ הוּא) — לְעֵלָּא מִן כָּל בִּרְכָתָא וְשִׁירָתָא תֻּשְׁבְּחָתָא וְנֶחֱמָתָא, דַּאֲמִירָן בְּעָלְמָא. וְאִמְרוּ: אָמֵן. (.Cong – אָמֵן.)

עַל יִשְׂרָאֵל וְעַל רַבָּנָן, וְעַל תַּלְמִידֵיהוֹן וְעַל כָּל תַּלְמִידֵי תַלְמִידֵיהוֹן, וְעַל כָּל מָאן דְּעָסְקִין בְּאוֹרַיְתָא, דִּי בְאַתְרָא הָדֵין וְדִי בְכָל אֲתַר וַאֲתַר. יְהֵא לְהוֹן וּלְכוֹן שְׁלָמָא רַבָּא, חִנָּא וְחִסְדָּא וְרַחֲמִין, וְחַיִּין אֲרִיכִין, וּמְזוֹנֵי רְוִיחֵי, וּפֻרְקָנָא, מִן קֳדָם אֲבוּהוֹן דִּי בִשְׁמַיָּא (וְאַרְעָא). וְאִמְרוּ: אָמֵן. (.Cong – אָמֵן.)

יְהֵא שְׁלָמָא רַבָּא מִן שְׁמַיָּא, וְחַיִּים (טוֹבִים) עָלֵינוּ וְעַל כָּל יִשְׂרָאֵל. וְאִמְרוּ: אָמֵן. (.Cong – אָמֵן.)

Take three steps back. Bow left and say . . . עֹשֶׂה; bow right and say . . . הוּא; bow forward and say וְעַל כָּל . . . אָמֵן. Remain standing in place for a few moments, then take three steps forward.

עֹשֶׂה שָׁלוֹם בִּמְרוֹמָיו, הוּא בְּרַחֲמָיו יַעֲשֶׂה שָׁלוֹם עָלֵינוּ, וְעַל כָּל יִשְׂרָאֵל. וְאִמְרוּ: אָמֵן. (.Cong – אָמֵן.)

the God of Jacob.'[1] *On the sixth day they would say: 'HASHEM will have reigned, He will have donned grandeur; He will have donned might and girded Himself; He even made the world firm so that it should not falter.'*[2] *On the Sabbath they would say: 'A psalm, a song for the Sabbath day.'*[3] *A psalm, a song for the time to come, to the day that will be entirely Sabbath and contentment for the eternal life.*

Talmud, *Megillah* 28b

תָּנָא *The Academy of Elijah taught: He who studies Torah laws every day has the assurance that he will be in the World to Come, as it is said, 'The ways of the world are His'*[4] *— do not read* [הֲלִיכוֹת] *'ways,' but* [הֲלָכוֹת] *'laws.'*

Talmud, *Berachos* 64a

אָמַר *Rabbi Elazar said on behalf of Rabbi Chanina: Torah scholars increase peace in the world, as it is said: 'And all your children will be students of HASHEM, and your children will have peace'*[5] *— do not read** [בָּנָיִךְ] *'your children,' but* [בּוֹנָיִךְ] *'your builders.'* Chazzan– *There is abundant peace for the lovers of Your Torah, and there is no stumbling block for them.*[6] *May there be peace within your wall, serenity within your palaces. For the sake of my brethren and comrades I shall speak of peace in your midst. For the sake of the House of HASHEM, our God, I will request your good.*[7] *HASHEM will give might to His people, HASHEM will bless His people with peace.*[8]

THE RABBIS' KADDISH

In the presence of a *minyan,* mourners recite the Rabbis' *Kaddish* (see *Laws* §84-85).
[A transliteration of this *Kaddish* appears on p. 1304.]

יִתְגַּדַּל *May His great Name grow exalted and sanctified* (Cong.– *Amen.*) *in the world that He created as He willed. May He give reign to His kingship in your lifetimes and in your days, and in the lifetimes of the entire Family of Israel, swiftly and soon. Now respond: Amen.*

(Cong.– *Amen. May His great Name be blessed forever and ever.*)
May His great Name be blessed forever and ever.

Blessed, praised, glorified, exalted, extolled, mighty, upraised, and lauded be the Name of the Holy One, Blessed is He (Cong.– *Blessed is He*) *— beyond any blessing and song, praise and consolation that are uttered in the world. Now respond: Amen.* (Cong.– *Amen.*)

Upon Israel, upon the teachers, their disciples and all of their disciples and upon all those who engage in the study of Torah, who are here or anywhere else; may they and you have abundant peace, grace, kindness, and mercy, long life, ample nourishment, and salvation, from before their Father Who is in Heaven (and on earth). Now respond: Amen. (Cong. – *Amen.*)

May there be abundant peace from Heaven, and (good) life, upon us and upon all Israel. Now respond: Amen. (Cong.– *Amen.*)

Take three steps back. Bow left and say, *'He Who makes peace . . .';* bow right and say, *'may He . . .';* bow forward and say, *'and upon all Israel . . .'* Remain standing in place for a few moments, then take three steps forward.

He Who makes peace in His heights, may He, in His compassion, make peace upon us, and upon all Israel. Now respond: Amen. (Cong.– *Amen.*)

---

(1) *Psalms* 81:2. (2) 93:1. (3) 92:1. (4) *Habakkuk* 3:6.
(5) *Isaiah* 54:13. (6) *Psalms* 119:165. (7) 122:7-9. (8) 29:11.

Stand while reciting עָלֵינוּ.

עָלֵינוּ לְשַׁבֵּחַ לַאֲדוֹן הַכֹּל, לָתֵת גְּדֻלָּה לְיוֹצֵר בְּרֵאשִׁית, שֶׁלֹּא עָשָׂנוּ כְּגוֹיֵי הָאֲרָצוֹת, וְלֹא שָׂמָנוּ כְּמִשְׁפְּחוֹת הָאֲדָמָה. שֶׁלֹּא שָׂם חֶלְקֵנוּ כָּהֶם, וְגוֹרָלֵנוּ כְּכָל הֲמוֹנָם. (שֶׁהֵם מִשְׁתַּחֲוִים לְהֶבֶל וָרִיק, וּמִתְפַּלְלִים אֶל אֵל לֹא יוֹשִׁיעַ.[1]) וַאֲנַחְנוּ כּוֹרְעִים וּמִשְׁתַּחֲוִים וּמוֹדִים, לִפְנֵי מֶלֶךְ מַלְכֵי הַמְּלָכִים הַקָּדוֹשׁ בָּרוּךְ הוּא. שֶׁהוּא נוֹטֶה שָׁמַיִם וְיֹסֵד אָרֶץ,[2] וּמוֹשַׁב יְקָרוֹ בַּשָּׁמַיִם מִמַּעַל, וּשְׁכִינַת עֻזּוֹ בְּגָבְהֵי מְרוֹמִים. הוּא אֱלֹהֵינוּ, אֵין עוֹד. אֱמֶת מַלְכֵּנוּ, אֶפֶס זוּלָתוֹ, כַּכָּתוּב בְּתוֹרָתוֹ: וְיָדַעְתָּ הַיּוֹם וַהֲשֵׁבֹתָ אֶל לְבָבֶךָ, כִּי יהוה הוּא הָאֱלֹהִים בַּשָּׁמַיִם מִמַּעַל וְעַל הָאָרֶץ מִתָּחַת, אֵין עוֹד.[3]

Bow while reciting וַאֲנַחְנוּ כּוֹרְעִים וּמִשְׁתַּחֲוִים.

עַל כֵּן נְקַוֶּה לְּךָ יהוה אֱלֹהֵינוּ לִרְאוֹת מְהֵרָה בְּתִפְאֶרֶת עֻזֶּךָ, לְהַעֲבִיר גִּלּוּלִים מִן הָאָרֶץ, וְהָאֱלִילִים כָּרוֹת יִכָּרֵתוּן, לְתַקֵּן עוֹלָם בְּמַלְכוּת שַׁדַּי. וְכָל בְּנֵי בָשָׂר יִקְרְאוּ בִשְׁמֶךָ, לְהַפְנוֹת אֵלֶיךָ כָּל רִשְׁעֵי אָרֶץ. יַכִּירוּ וְיֵדְעוּ כָּל יוֹשְׁבֵי תֵבֵל, כִּי לְךָ תִּכְרַע כָּל בֶּרֶךְ, תִּשָּׁבַע כָּל לָשׁוֹן.[4] לְפָנֶיךָ יהוה אֱלֹהֵינוּ יִכְרְעוּ וְיִפֹּלוּ, וְלִכְבוֹד שִׁמְךָ יְקָר יִתֵּנוּ. וִיקַבְּלוּ כֻלָּם אֶת עוֹל מַלְכוּתֶךָ, וְתִמְלֹךְ עֲלֵיהֶם מְהֵרָה לְעוֹלָם וָעֶד. כִּי הַמַּלְכוּת שֶׁלְּךָ הִיא וּלְעוֹלְמֵי עַד תִּמְלוֹךְ בְּכָבוֹד, כַּכָּתוּב בְּתוֹרָתֶךָ: יהוה יִמְלֹךְ לְעֹלָם וָעֶד.[5] ❖ וְנֶאֱמַר: וְהָיָה יהוה לְמֶלֶךְ עַל כָּל הָאָרֶץ, בַּיּוֹם הַהוּא יִהְיֶה יהוה אֶחָד וּשְׁמוֹ אֶחָד.[6]

Some congregations recite the following after עָלֵינוּ:

אַל תִּירָא מִפַּחַד פִּתְאֹם, וּמִשֹּׁאַת רְשָׁעִים כִּי תָבֹא.[7] עֻצוּ עֵצָה וְתֻפָר, דַּבְּרוּ דָבָר וְלֹא יָקוּם, כִּי עִמָּנוּ אֵל.[8] וְעַד זִקְנָה אֲנִי הוּא, וְעַד שֵׂיבָה אֲנִי אֶסְבֹּל, אֲנִי עָשִׂיתִי וַאֲנִי אֶשָּׂא, וַאֲנִי אֶסְבֹּל וַאֲמַלֵּט.[9]

קדיש יתום

In the presence of a *minyan,* mourners recite קַדִּישׁ יָתוֹם, the Mourner's *Kaddish* (see *Laws* §81-83):

יִתְגַּדַּל וְיִתְקַדַּשׁ שְׁמֵהּ רַבָּא. (.Cong – אָמֵן.) בְּעָלְמָא דִּי בְרָא כִרְעוּתֵהּ. וְיַמְלִיךְ מַלְכוּתֵהּ, בְּחַיֵּיכוֹן וּבְיוֹמֵיכוֹן וּבְחַיֵּי דְכָל בֵּית יִשְׂרָאֵל, בַּעֲגָלָא וּבִזְמַן קָרִיב. וְאִמְרוּ: אָמֵן.

(.Cong – אָמֵן. יְהֵא שְׁמֵהּ רַבָּא מְבָרַךְ לְעָלַם וּלְעָלְמֵי עָלְמַיָּא.)

Stand while reciting עָלֵינוּ, *'It is our duty . . .'*

עָלֵינוּ *It is our duty to praise the Master of all, to ascribe greatness to the Molder of primeval creation, for He has not made us like the nations of the lands, and has not emplaced us like the families of the earth; for He has not assigned our portion like theirs nor our lot like all their multitudes. (For they bow to vanity and emptiness and pray to a god which helps not.*[1]*) But we bend our knees, bow, and acknowledge our thanks before the King Who reigns over kings, the Holy One, Blessed is He. He stretches out heaven and establishes earth's foundation,*[2] *the seat of His homage is in the heavens above and His powerful Presence is in the loftiest heights. He is our God and there is none other. True is our King, there is nothing beside Him, as it is written in His Torah: 'You are to know this day and take to your heart that* HASHEM *is the only God — in heaven above and on the earth below — there is none other.'*[3]

Bow while reciting *'But we bend our knees.'*

עַל כֵּן *Therefore we put our hope in You,* HASHEM, *our God, that we may soon see Your mighty splendor, to remove detestable idolatry from the earth, and false gods will be utterly cut off, to perfect the universe through the Almighty's sovereignty. Then all humanity will call upon Your Name, to turn all the earth's wicked toward You. All the world's inhabitants will recognize and know that to You every knee should bend, every tongue should swear.*[4] *Before You,* HASHEM, *our God, they will bend every knee and cast themselves down and to the glory of Your Name they will render homage, and they will all accept upon themselves the yoke of Your kingship that You may reign over them soon and eternally. For the kingdom is Yours and You will reign for all eternity in glory as it is written in Your Torah:* HASHEM *shall reign for all eternity.*[5] Chazzan– *And it is said:* HASHEM *will be King over all the world — on that day* HASHEM *will be One and His Name will be One.*[6]

Some congregations recite the following after *Aleinu.*

אַל תִּירָא *Do not fear sudden terror, or the holocaust of the wicked when it comes.*[7] *Plan a conspiracy and it will be annulled; speak your piece and it shall not stand, for God is with us.*[8] *Even till your seniority, I remain unchanged; and even till your ripe old age, I shall endure. I created you and I shall bear you; I shall endure and rescue.*[9]

MOURNER'S KADDISH

In the presence of a *minyan,* mourners recite קַדִּישׁ יָתוֹם, the Mourner's *Kaddish* (see *Laws* §81-83). [A transliteration of this *Kaddish* appears on p. 1305.]

יִתְגַּדַּל *May His great Name grow exalted and sanctified* (Cong.– *Amen.*) *in the world that He created as He willed. May He give reign to His kingship in your lifetimes and in your days, and in the lifetimes of the entire Family of Israel, swiftly and soon. Now respond: Amen.*

(Cong.– *Amen. May His great Name be blessed forever and ever.*)

---

(1) *Isaiah* 45:20. (2) 51:13. (3) *Deuteronomy* 4:39. (4) Cf. *Isaiah* 45:23. (5) *Exodus* 15:18. (6) *Zechariah* 14:9. (7) *Proverbs* 3:25. (8) *Isaiah* 8:10. (9) 46:4.

יְהֵא שְׁמֵהּ רַבָּא מְבָרַךְ לְעָלַם וּלְעָלְמֵי עָלְמַיָּא.

יִתְבָּרַךְ וְיִשְׁתַּבַּח וְיִתְפָּאַר וְיִתְרוֹמַם וְיִתְנַשֵּׂא וְיִתְהַדָּר וְיִתְעַלֶּה וְיִתְהַלָּל שְׁמֵהּ דְּקֻדְשָׁא בְּרִיךְ הוּא (.Cong – בְּרִיךְ הוּא) — לְעֵֽלָּא מִן כָּל בִּרְכָתָא וְשִׁירָתָא תֻּשְׁבְּחָתָא וְנֶחֱמָתָא, דַּאֲמִירָן בְּעָלְמָא. וְאִמְרוּ: אָמֵן. (.Cong – אָמֵן.)

יְהֵא שְׁלָמָא רַבָּא מִן שְׁמַיָּא, וְחַיִּים עָלֵינוּ וְעַל כָּל יִשְׂרָאֵל. וְאִמְרוּ: אָמֵן. (.Cong – אָמֵן.)

Take three steps back. Bow left and say . . . עֹשֶׂה; bow right and say . . . הוּא; bow forward and say וְעַל כָּל . . . אָמֵן. Remain standing in place for a few moments, then take three steps forward.

עֹשֶׂה שָׁלוֹם בִּמְרוֹמָיו, הוּא יַעֲשֶׂה שָׁלוֹם עָלֵינוּ, וְעַל כָּל יִשְׂרָאֵל. וְאִמְרוּ: אָמֵן. (.Cong – אָמֵן.)

שיר הכבוד

The Ark is opened and שִׁיר הַכָּבוֹד, *The Song of Glory,* is recited responsively — the *chazzan* reciting the first verse, the congregation reciting the second and so on.

אַנְעִים זְמִירוֹת וְשִׁירִים אֶאֱרוֹג, כִּי אֵלֶיךָ נַפְשִׁי תַעֲרוֹג.

נַפְשִׁי חָמְדָה בְּצֵל יָדֶךָ, לָדַעַת כָּל רָז סוֹדֶךָ.

❖ מִדֵּי דַבְּרִי בִּכְבוֹדֶךָ, הוֹמֶה לִבִּי אֶל דּוֹדֶיךָ.

עַל כֵּן אֲדַבֵּר בְּךָ נִכְבָּדוֹת, וְשִׁמְךָ אֲכַבֵּד בְּשִׁירֵי יְדִידוֹת.

❖ אֲסַפְּרָה כְבוֹדְךָ וְלֹא רְאִיתִיךָ, אֲדַמְּךָ אֲכַנְּךָ וְלֹא יְדַעְתִּיךָ.

בְּיַד נְבִיאֶיךָ בְּסוֹד עֲבָדֶיךָ, דִּמִּיתָ הֲדַר כְּבוֹד הוֹדֶךָ.

❖ גְּדֻלָּתְךָ וּגְבוּרָתֶךָ, כִּנּוּ לְתֹקֶף פְּעֻלָּתֶךָ.

דִּמּוּ אוֹתְךָ וְלֹא כְפִי יֶשְׁךָ, וַיַּשְׁווּךָ לְפִי מַעֲשֶׂיךָ.

❖ הִמְשִׁילוּךָ בְּרֹב חֶזְיוֹנוֹת, הִנְּךָ אֶחָד בְּכָל דִּמְיוֹנוֹת.

וַיֶּחֱזוּ בְךָ זִקְנָה וּבַחֲרוּת, וּשְׂעַר רֹאשְׁךָ בְּשֵׂיבָה וְשַׁחֲרוּת.

❖ זִקְנָה בְּיוֹם דִּין וּבַחֲרוּת בְּיוֹם קְרָב, כְּאִישׁ מִלְחָמוֹת יָדָיו לוֹ רָב.

חָבַשׁ כּוֹבַע יְשׁוּעָה בְּרֹאשׁוֹ, הוֹשִׁיעָה לּוֹ יְמִינוֹ וּזְרוֹעַ קָדְשׁוֹ.

❖ טַלְלֵי אוֹרוֹת רֹאשׁוֹ נִמְלָא, קְוֻצּוֹתָיו רְסִיסֵי לָיְלָה.

יִתְפָּאֵר בִּי כִּי חָפֵץ בִּי. וְהוּא יִהְיֶה לִּי לַעֲטֶרֶת צְבִי.

❖ כֶּתֶם טָהוֹר פָּז דְּמוּת רֹאשׁוֹ, וְחַק עַל מֵצַח כְּבוֹד שֵׁם קָדְשׁוֹ.

לְחֵן וּלְכָבוֹד צְבִי תִפְאָרָה, אֻמָּתוֹ לוֹ עִטְּרָה עֲטָרָה.

❖ מַחְלְפוֹת רֹאשׁוֹ כְּבִימֵי בְחֻרוֹת, קְוֻצּוֹתָיו תַּלְתַּלִּים שְׁחוֹרוֹת.

נְוֵה הַצֶּדֶק צְבִי תִפְאַרְתּוֹ, יַעֲלֶה נָּא עַל רֹאשׁ שִׂמְחָתוֹ.

May His great Name be blessed forever and ever.

Blessed, praised, glorified, exalted, extolled, mighty, upraised, and lauded be the Name of the Holy One, Blessed is He (Cong.– *Blessed is He*) — *beyond any blessing and song, praise and consolation that are uttered in the world. Now respond: Amen.* (Cong.– *Amen*).

May there be abundant peace from Heaven, and life, upon us and upon all Israel. Now respond: Amen. (Cong.– *Amen.*)

Take three steps back. Bow left and say, *'He Who makes peace . . .'*; bow right and say, *'may He . . .'*; bow forward and say, *'and upon all Israel . . .'* Remain standing in place for a few moments, then take three steps forward.

He Who makes peace in His heights, may He make peace upon us, and upon all Israel. Now respond: Amen. (Cong.– *Amen.*)

SONG OF GLORY

The Ark is opened and the *Song of Glory* is recited responsively — the *chazzan* reciting the first verse, the congregation reciting the second and so on.

אַנְעִים זְמִירוֹת *I shall compose pleasant psalms and weave hymns,*
because for You shall my soul pine.
My soul desired the shelter of Your hand,
to know every mystery of Your secret.
✣ *As I speak of Your glory, my heart yearns for Your love.*
Therefore I shall speak of Your glories,
and Your Name I shall honor with loving songs.
✣ *I shall relate Your glory, though I see You not;*
I shall allegorize You, I shall describe You, though I know You not.
Through the hand of Your prophets, through the counsel of Your servants;
You allegorized the splendrous glory of Your power.
✣ *Your greatness and Your strength,*
they described the might of Your works.
They allegorized You, but not according to Your reality,
and they portrayed You according to Your deeds.
✣ *They symbolized You in many varied visions;*
yet You are a Unity containing all the allegories.
They envisioned in You agedness and virility,
and the hair of Your head as hoary and jet black.
✣ *Aged on judgment day and virile on the day of battle,*
like a man of war whose powers are many.
The hat of salvation He put on His head;
salvation for Him, His right hand and His sacred arm.
✣ *With illuminating dew drops His head is filled,*
His locks are the rains of the night.
He shall glory in me for He desires me,
and He shall be for me a crown of pride.
✣ *A form of the very finest gold upon his head,*
and carved on his forehead is His glorious, sacred Name.
For grace and for glory the pride of His splendor;
His nation crowns Him with its prayers.
✣ *The tresses of His head are like His youthful days;*
His locks are jet-black ringlets.
The Abode of righteousness is the pride of His splendor;
may He elevate it to His foremost joy.

❖ סְגֻלָּתוֹ תְּהִי בְיָדוֹ עֲטֶרֶת, וּצְנִיף מְלוּכָה צְבִי תִפְאֶרֶת.
עֲמוּסִים נְשָׂאָם עֲטֶרֶת עִנְּדָם, מֵאֲשֶׁר יָקְרוּ בְעֵינָיו כִּבְּדָם.
❖ פְּאֵרוֹ עָלַי וּפְאֵרִי עָלָיו, וְקָרוֹב אֵלַי בְּקָרְאִי אֵלָיו.
צַח וְאָדוֹם לִלְבוּשׁוֹ אָדוֹם, פּוּרָה בְדָרְכוֹ בְּבוֹאוֹ מֵאֱדוֹם.
❖ קֶשֶׁר תְּפִלִּין הֶרְאָה לֶעָנָו, תְּמוּנַת יהוה לְנֶגֶד עֵינָיו.
רוֹצֶה בְעַמּוֹ עֲנָוִים יְפָאֵר, יוֹשֵׁב תְּהִלּוֹת בָּם לְהִתְפָּאֵר.
❖ רֹאשׁ דְּבָרְךָ אֱמֶת קוֹרֵא מֵרֹאשׁ, דּוֹר וָדוֹר עַם דּוֹרֶשְׁךָ דְּרוֹשׁ.
שִׁית הֲמוֹן שִׁירַי נָא עָלֶיךָ, וְרִנָּתִי תִּקְרַב אֵלֶיךָ.
❖ תְּהִלָּתִי תְּהִי לְרֹאשְׁךָ עֲטֶרֶת, וּתְפִלָּתִי תִּכּוֹן קְטֹרֶת.
תִּיקַר שִׁירַת רָשׁ בְּעֵינֶיךָ, כַּשִּׁיר יוּשַׁר עַל קָרְבָּנֶיךָ.
❖ בִּרְכָתִי תַעֲלֶה לְרֹאשׁ מַשְׁבִּיר, מְחוֹלֵל וּמוֹלִיד צַדִּיק כַּבִּיר.
וּבְבִרְכָתִי תְנַעֲנַע לִי רֹאשׁ, וְאוֹתָהּ קַח לְךָ כִּבְשָׂמִים רֹאשׁ.
❖ יֶעֱרַב נָא שִׂיחִי עָלֶיךָ, כִּי נַפְשִׁי תַעֲרוֹג אֵלֶיךָ.

לְךָ יהוה הַגְּדֻלָּה וְהַגְּבוּרָה וְהַתִּפְאֶרֶת וְהַנֵּצַח וְהַהוֹד, כִּי כֹל בַּשָּׁמַיִם וּבָאָרֶץ; לְךָ יהוה הַמַּמְלָכָה וְהַמִּתְנַשֵּׂא לְכֹל לְרֹאשׁ.[1] מִי יְמַלֵּל גְּבוּרוֹת יהוה, יַשְׁמִיעַ כָּל תְּהִלָּתוֹ.[2]

In the presence of a *minyan,* mourners recite קַדִּישׁ יָתוֹם (page 576).

שיר של יום

הַיּוֹם יוֹם שַׁבַּת קֹדֶשׁ שֶׁבּוֹ הָיוּ הַלְוִיִּם אוֹמְרִים בְּבֵית הַמִּקְדָּשׁ:

תהלים צב

מִזְמוֹר שִׁיר לְיוֹם הַשַּׁבָּת. טוֹב לְהֹדוֹת לַיהוה, וּלְזַמֵּר לְשִׁמְךָ עֶלְיוֹן. לְהַגִּיד בַּבֹּקֶר חַסְדֶּךָ, וֶאֱמוּנָתְךָ בַּלֵּילוֹת. עֲלֵי עָשׂוֹר וַעֲלֵי נָבֶל, עֲלֵי הִגָּיוֹן בְּכִנּוֹר. כִּי שִׂמַּחְתַּנִי יהוה בְּפָעֳלֶךָ, בְּמַעֲשֵׂי יָדֶיךָ אֲרַנֵּן. מַה גָּדְלוּ מַעֲשֶׂיךָ יהוה, מְאֹד עָמְקוּ מַחְשְׁבֹתֶיךָ. אִישׁ בַּעַר לֹא יֵדָע, וּכְסִיל לֹא יָבִין אֶת זֹאת. בִּפְרֹחַ רְשָׁעִים כְּמוֹ עֵשֶׂב, וַיָּצִיצוּ כָּל פֹּעֲלֵי אָוֶן, לְהִשָּׁמְדָם עֲדֵי עַד. וְאַתָּה מָרוֹם לְעֹלָם יהוה. כִּי הִנֵּה אֹיְבֶיךָ יהוה, כִּי הִנֵּה אֹיְבֶיךָ יֹאבֵדוּ, יִתְפָּרְדוּ כָּל פֹּעֲלֵי אָוֶן. וַתָּרֶם כִּרְאֵים קַרְנִי, בַּלֹּתִי בְּשֶׁמֶן רַעֲנָן. וַתַּבֵּט עֵינִי בְּשׁוּרָי,

(1) *I Chronicles* 29:11. (2) *Psalms* 106:2.

∴ *May His treasured nation be in His hand like a crown,*
and like a royal tiara the pride of His splendor.
From infancy He bore them and affixed them as a crown,
because they are precious in His eyes He honored them.
∴ *His tefillin-splendor is upon me and my tefillin-splendor is upon Him,*
and He is near to me when I call to Him.
He is white and crimson; His garment will be bloody red,
when He tramples as in a press on His coming from Edom.
∴ *He showed the tefillin-knot to the humble [Moses],*
the likeness of HASHEM *before his eyes.*
He desires His people, He will glorify the humble;
enthroned upon praises, He glories with them.
∴ *The very beginning of Your word is truth — one reads it from the*
Torah's start; the people that seeks You expounds each generation's fate.
Place the multitude of my songs before You, please;
and my glad song bring near to You.
∴ *May my praise be a crown for Your head,*
and may my prayer be accepted like incense.
May the poor man's song be dear in Your eyes,
like the song that is sung over Your offerings.
∴ *May my blessing rise up upon the head of the Sustainer —*
Creator, Giver of life, mighty Righteous One.
And to my blessing, nod Your head to me,
and take it to Yourself like the finest incense.
∴ *May my prayer be sweet to You, for my soul shall pine for You.*

לְךָ *Yours,* HASHEM, *is the greatness, the strength, the splendor, the triumph, and the glory; even everything in heaven and earth; Yours,* HASHEM, *is the kingdom, and the sovereignty over every leader.*[1] *Who can express the mighty acts of* HASHEM*? Who can declare all His praise?*[2]

In the presence of a *minyan,* mourners recite the Mourner's *Kaddish* (page 576.)

SONG OF THE DAY

Today is the Holy Sabbath day,
on which the Levites would sing in the Holy Temple:

Psalm 92

מִזְמוֹר שִׁיר *A psalm, a song for the Sabbath day. It is good to thank* HASHEM *and to sing praise to Your Name, O Exalted One; to relate Your kindness in the dawn and Your faith in the nights. Upon ten-stringed instrument and lyre, with singing accompanied by a harp. For You have gladdened me,* HASHEM, *with Your deeds; at the works of Your Hands I sing glad song. How great are Your deeds,* HASHEM*; exceedingly profound are Your thoughts. A boor cannot know, nor can a fool understand this: when the wicked bloom like grass and all the doers of iniquity blossom — it is to destroy them till eternity. But You remain exalted forever,* HASHEM. *For behold! — Your enemies,* HASHEM, *for behold! — Your enemies shall perish, dispersed shall be all doers of iniquity. As exalted as a re'eim's shall be my pride, I will be saturated with ever-fresh oil. My eyes have seen my vigilant foes;*

בְּקָמִים עָלַי מְרֵעִים, תִּשְׁמַעְנָה אָזְנָי. ❖ צַדִּיק כַּתָּמָר יִפְרָח, כְּאֶרֶז בַּלְּבָנוֹן יִשְׂגֶּה. שְׁתוּלִים בְּבֵית יהוה, בְּחַצְרוֹת אֱלֹהֵינוּ יַפְרִיחוּ. עוֹד יְנוּבוּן בְּשֵׂיבָה, דְּשֵׁנִים וְרַעֲנַנִּים יִהְיוּ. לְהַגִּיד כִּי יָשָׁר יהוה, צוּרִי וְלֹא עַוְלָתָה בּוֹ.

קדיש יתום

In the presence of a *minyan,* mourners recite קַדִּישׁ יָתוֹם, the Mourner's *Kaddish* (see *Laws* §81-83).

יִתְגַּדַּל וְיִתְקַדַּשׁ שְׁמֵהּ רַבָּא. (.Cong – אָמֵן.) בְּעָלְמָא דִּי בְרָא כִרְעוּתֵהּ. וְיַמְלִיךְ מַלְכוּתֵהּ, בְּחַיֵּיכוֹן וּבְיוֹמֵיכוֹן וּבְחַיֵּי דְכָל בֵּית יִשְׂרָאֵל, בַּעֲגָלָא וּבִזְמַן קָרִיב. וְאִמְרוּ: אָמֵן.

(.Cong – אָמֵן. יְהֵא שְׁמֵהּ רַבָּא מְבָרַךְ לְעָלַם וּלְעָלְמֵי עָלְמַיָּא.)

יְהֵא שְׁמֵהּ רַבָּא מְבָרַךְ לְעָלַם וּלְעָלְמֵי עָלְמַיָּא.

יִתְבָּרַךְ וְיִשְׁתַּבַּח וְיִתְפָּאַר וְיִתְרוֹמַם וְיִתְנַשֵּׂא וְיִתְהַדָּר וְיִתְעַלֶּה וְיִתְהַלָּל שְׁמֵהּ דְּקֻדְשָׁא בְּרִיךְ הוּא (.Cong – בְּרִיךְ הוּא) – לְעֵלָּא מִן כָּל בִּרְכָתָא וְשִׁירָתָא תֻּשְׁבְּחָתָא וְנֶחֱמָתָא, דַּאֲמִירָן בְּעָלְמָא. וְאִמְרוּ: אָמֵן. (.Cong – אָמֵן.)

יְהֵא שְׁלָמָא רַבָּא מִן שְׁמַיָּא, וְחַיִּים עָלֵינוּ וְעַל כָּל יִשְׂרָאֵל. וְאִמְרוּ: אָמֵן. (.Cong – אָמֵן.)

Take three steps back. Bow left and say . . . עֹשֶׂה; bow right and say . . . הוּא; bow forward and say וְעַל כָּל . . . אָמֵן. Remain standing in place for a few moments, then take three steps forward.

עֹשֶׂה שָׁלוֹם בִּמְרוֹמָיו, הוּא יַעֲשֶׂה שָׁלוֹם עָלֵינוּ, וְעַל כָּל יִשְׂרָאֵל. וְאִמְרוּ: אָמֵן. (.Cong – אָמֵן.)

תהלים כז

לְדָוִד, יהוה אוֹרִי וְיִשְׁעִי, מִמִּי אִירָא, יהוה מָעוֹז חַיַּי, מִמִּי אֶפְחָד. בִּקְרֹב עָלַי מְרֵעִים לֶאֱכֹל אֶת בְּשָׂרִי, צָרַי וְאֹיְבַי לִי, הֵמָּה כָּשְׁלוּ וְנָפָלוּ. אִם תַּחֲנֶה עָלַי מַחֲנֶה, לֹא יִירָא לִבִּי, אִם תָּקוּם עָלַי מִלְחָמָה, בְּזֹאת אֲנִי בוֹטֵחַ. אַחַת שָׁאַלְתִּי מֵאֵת יהוה, אוֹתָהּ אֲבַקֵּשׁ, שִׁבְתִּי בְּבֵית יהוה כָּל יְמֵי חַיַּי, לַחֲזוֹת בְּנֹעַם יהוה, וּלְבַקֵּר בְּהֵיכָלוֹ. כִּי יִצְפְּנֵנִי בְּסֻכֹּה בְּיוֹם רָעָה, יַסְתִּירֵנִי בְּסֵתֶר אָהֳלוֹ, בְּצוּר יְרוֹמְמֵנִי. וְעַתָּה יָרוּם רֹאשִׁי עַל אֹיְבַי סְבִיבוֹתַי, וְאֶזְבְּחָה בְאָהֳלוֹ זִבְחֵי תְרוּעָה, אָשִׁירָה וַאֲזַמְּרָה לַיהוה. שְׁמַע יהוה קוֹלִי אֶקְרָא, וְחָנֵּנִי וַעֲנֵנִי. לְךָ אָמַר לִבִּי בַּקְּשׁוּ פָנָי, אֶת פָּנֶיךָ יהוה אֲבַקֵּשׁ. אַל תַּסְתֵּר פָּנֶיךָ מִמֶּנִּי, אַל תַּט בְּאַף עַבְדֶּךָ, עֶזְרָתִי הָיִיתָ, אַל תִּטְּשֵׁנִי וְאַל תַּעַזְבֵנִי, אֱלֹהֵי יִשְׁעִי. כִּי אָבִי וְאִמִּי עֲזָבוּנִי, וַיהוה יַאַסְפֵנִי. הוֹרֵנִי יהוה דַּרְכֶּךָ, וּנְחֵנִי בְּאֹרַח מִישׁוֹר, לְמַעַן שׁוֹרְרָי.

when those who would harm me rise up against me, my ears have heard their doom. Chazzan– *A righteous man will flourish like a date palm, like a cedar in the Lebanon he will grow tall. Planted in the house of* HASHEM, *in the courtyards of our God they will flourish. They will still be fruitful in old age, vigorous and fresh they will be — to declare that* HASHEM *is just, my Rock in Whom there is no wrong.*

MOURNER'S KADDISH

In the presence of a *minyan,* mourners recite קַדִּישׁ יָתוֹם, the Mourner's *Kaddish* (see *Laws* 81-83).
[A transliteration of this *Kaddish* appears on page 1305.]

יִתְגַּדַּל *May His great Name grow exalted and sanctified* (Cong.– *Amen.*) *in the world that He created as He willed. May He give reign to His kingship in your lifetimes and in your days, and in the lifetimes of the entire Family of Israel, swiftly and soon. Now respond: Amen.*

(Cong.– *Amen. May His great Name be blessed forever and ever.)*
May His great Name be blessed forever and ever.

Blessed, praised, glorified, exalted, extolled, mighty, upraised, and lauded be the Name of the Holy One, Blessed is He (Cong.– *Blessed is He*) *— beyond any blessing and song, praise and consolation that are uttered in the world. Now respond: Amen.* (Cong.– *Amen.*)

May there be abundant peace from Heaven, and life, upon us and upon all Israel. Now respond: Amen. (Cong.– *Amen.*)

Take three steps back. Bow left and say, *'He Who makes peace . . .';* bow right and say, *'may He . . .';* bow forward and say, *'and upon all Israel . . .'* Remain standing in place for a few moments, then take three steps forward.

He Who makes peace in His heights, may He make peace upon us, and upon all Israel. Now respond: Amen. (Cong.– *Amen.*)

Psalm 27

לְדָוִד *Of David;* HASHEM *is my light and my salvation, whom shall I fear?* HASHEM *is my life's strength, whom shall I dread? When evildoers approach me to devour my flesh, my tormentors and my foes against me — it is they who stumble and fall. Though an army would besiege me, my heart would not fear; though war would arise against me, in this I trust. One thing I asked of* HASHEM, *that shall I seek: That I dwell in the House of* HASHEM *all the days of my life; to behold the sweetness of* HASHEM *and to contemplate in His Sanctuary. Indeed, He will hide me in His Shelter on the day of evil; He will conceal me in the concealment of His Tent, He will lift me upon a rock. Now my head is raised above my enemies around me, and I will slaughter offerings in His Tent accompanied by joyous song; I will sing and make music to* HASHEM. HASHEM, *hear my voice when I call, be gracious toward me and answer me. In Your behalf, my heart has said, 'Seek My Presence'; Your Presence,* HASHEM, *do I seek. Conceal not Your Presence from me, repel not Your servant in anger. You have been my Helper, abandon me not, forsake me not, O God of my salvation. Though my father and mother have forsaken me,* HASHEM *will gather me in. Teach me Your way,* HASHEM, *and lead me on the path of integrity, because of my watchful*

אַל תִּתְּנֵנִי בְּנֶפֶשׁ צָרָי, כִּי קָמוּ בִי עֵדֵי שֶׁקֶר, וִיפֵחַ חָמָס. ❖ לוּלֵא הֶאֱמַנְתִּי לִרְאוֹת בְּטוּב יהוה בְּאֶרֶץ חַיִּים. קַוֵּה אֶל יהוה, חֲזַק וְיַאֲמֵץ לִבֶּךָ, וְקַוֵּה אֶל יהוה.

In the presence of a *minyan,* mourners recite קַדִּישׁ יָתוֹם, the Mourner's *Kaddish* (page 582).

קידושא רבא

Some recite the *Ushpizin* prayers (p. 74) each time they enter the *Succah* for a meal. Many omit some or all of these verses and begin with עַל כֵּן.

אִם תָּשִׁיב מִשַּׁבָּת רַגְלֶךָ, עֲשׂוֹת חֲפָצֶךָ בְּיוֹם קָדְשִׁי, וְקָרָאתָ לַשַּׁבָּת עֹנֶג, לִקְדוֹשׁ יהוה מְכֻבָּד, וְכִבַּדְתּוֹ מֵעֲשׂוֹת דְּרָכֶיךָ, מִמְּצוֹא חֶפְצְךָ וְדַבֵּר דָּבָר. אָז תִּתְעַנַּג עַל יהוה, וְהִרְכַּבְתִּיךָ עַל בָּמֳתֵי אָרֶץ, וְהַאֲכַלְתִּיךָ נַחֲלַת יַעֲקֹב אָבִיךָ, כִּי פִּי יהוה דִּבֵּר.[1]

וְשָׁמְרוּ בְנֵי יִשְׂרָאֵל אֶת הַשַּׁבָּת, לַעֲשׂוֹת אֶת הַשַּׁבָּת לְדֹרֹתָם בְּרִית עוֹלָם. בֵּינִי וּבֵין בְּנֵי יִשְׂרָאֵל אוֹת הִיא לְעֹלָם, כִּי שֵׁשֶׁת יָמִים עָשָׂה יהוה אֶת הַשָּׁמַיִם וְאֶת הָאָרֶץ, וּבַיּוֹם הַשְּׁבִיעִי שָׁבַת וַיִּנָּפַשׁ.[2]

זָכוֹר אֶת יוֹם הַשַּׁבָּת לְקַדְּשׁוֹ. שֵׁשֶׁת יָמִים תַּעֲבֹד וְעָשִׂיתָ כָּל מְלַאכְתֶּךָ. וְיוֹם הַשְּׁבִיעִי שַׁבָּת לַיהוה אֱלֹהֶיךָ, לֹא תַעֲשֶׂה כָל מְלָאכָה, אַתָּה וּבִנְךָ וּבִתֶּךָ עַבְדְּךָ וַאֲמָתְךָ וּבְהֶמְתֶּךָ, וְגֵרְךָ אֲשֶׁר בִּשְׁעָרֶיךָ. כִּי שֵׁשֶׁת יָמִים עָשָׂה יהוה אֶת הַשָּׁמַיִם וְאֶת הָאָרֶץ אֶת הַיָּם וְאֶת כָּל אֲשֶׁר בָּם, וַיָּנַח בַּיּוֹם הַשְּׁבִיעִי –

עַל כֵּן בֵּרַךְ יהוה אֶת יוֹם הַשַּׁבָּת וַיְקַדְּשֵׁהוּ.[3]

סַבְרִי מָרָנָן וְרַבָּנָן וְרַבּוֹתַי:

בָּרוּךְ אַתָּה יהוה אֱלֹהֵינוּ מֶלֶךְ הָעוֹלָם, בּוֹרֵא פְּרִי הַגָּפֶן.

(All present – אָמֵן.)

If, for whatever reason, one does not recite *Kiddush* in a *succah,* the following blessing is omitted.

בָּרוּךְ אַתָּה יהוה אֱלֹהֵינוּ מֶלֶךְ הָעוֹלָם, אֲשֶׁר קִדְּשָׁנוּ בְּמִצְוֹתָיו וְצִוָּנוּ לֵישֵׁב בַּסֻּכָּה.

(All present – אָמֵן.)

עַל הַמִּחְיָה appears on page 92; בִּרְכַּת הַמָּזוֹן, on page 84.

foes. Deliver me not to the wishes of my tormentors, for there have arisen against me false witnesses who breathe violence. Chazzan– *Had I not trusted that I would see the goodness of* HASHEM *in the land of life! Hope to* HASHEM, *strengthen yourself and He will give you courage; and hope to* HASHEM.

In the presence of a *minyan*, mourners recite קַדִּישׁ יָתוֹם, the Mourner's *Kaddish* (page 582).

❧ KIDDUSHA RABBA ☙

Some recite the *Ushpizin* prayers (p. 74) each time they enter the *Succah* for a meal. Many omit some or all of these verses and begin with *'therefore* HASHEM *blessed.'*

אִם תָּשִׁיב *If you restrain, because of the Sabbath, your feet, refrain from accomplishing your own needs on My holy day; if you proclaim the Sabbath 'a delight,' the holy one of* HASHEM, *'honored one,' and you honor it by not doing your own ways, from seeking your needs or discussing the forbidden. Then you shall be granted pleasure with* HASHEM *and I shall mount you astride the heights of the world, and provide you the heritage of your forefather Jacob — for the mouth of* HASHEM *has spoken.*[1]

וְשָׁמְרוּ *And the Children of Israel observed the Sabbath, to make the Sabbath for their generations an eternal covenant. Between Me and the Children of Israel it is a sign forever, that in six days did* HASHEM *make the heaven and the earth, and on the seventh day He rested and was refreshed.*[2]

זָכוֹר *Always remember the Sabbath day to hallow it. For six days you may labor and do all your work. But the seventh day is the Sabbath for* HASHEM, *Your God; you may do no work — you, your son and your daughter, your slave and your maidservant, your animal, and the stranger who is in your gates. For in six days did* HASHEM *make the heaven and the earth, the sea and all that is in them and He rested on the seventh day;*

therefore HASHEM *blessed the Sabbath day and sanctified it.*[3]

By your leave, my masters and teachers:

בָּרוּךְ *Blessed are You,* HASHEM, *our God, King of the universe, Who creates the fruit of the vine.* (All present – *Amen.)*

If, for whatever reason, one does not recite *Kiddush* in a *succah,* the following blessing is omitted.

בָּרוּךְ *Blessed are You,* HASHEM, *our God, King of the universe, Who has sanctified us with His commandments and has commanded us to dwell in the Succah.* (All present – *Amen.)*

The blessing after cake and wine appears on page 92; Grace after Meals, on page 84.

(1) *Isaiah* 58:13-14. (2) *Exodus* 31:16-17. (3) 20:8-11.

מנחה לשבת חול המועד

אַשְׁרֵי יוֹשְׁבֵי בֵיתֶךָ, עוֹד יְהַלְלוּךָ סֶּלָה.[1] אַשְׁרֵי הָעָם שֶׁכָּכָה לּוֹ, אַשְׁרֵי הָעָם שֶׁיהוה אֱלֹהָיו.[2]

תהלים קמה

תְּהִלָּה לְדָוִד,

אֲרוֹמִמְךָ אֱלוֹהַי הַמֶּלֶךְ, וַאֲבָרְכָה שִׁמְךָ לְעוֹלָם וָעֶד.

בְּכָל יוֹם אֲבָרְכֶךָּ, וַאֲהַלְלָה שִׁמְךָ לְעוֹלָם וָעֶד.

גָּדוֹל יהוה וּמְהֻלָּל מְאֹד, וְלִגְדֻלָּתוֹ אֵין חֵקֶר.

דּוֹר לְדוֹר יְשַׁבַּח מַעֲשֶׂיךָ, וּגְבוּרֹתֶיךָ יַגִּידוּ.

הֲדַר כְּבוֹד הוֹדֶךָ, וְדִבְרֵי נִפְלְאֹתֶיךָ אָשִׂיחָה.

וֶעֱזוּז נוֹרְאוֹתֶיךָ יֹאמֵרוּ, וּגְדוּלָּתְךָ אֲסַפְּרֶנָּה.

זֵכֶר רַב טוּבְךָ יַבִּיעוּ, וְצִדְקָתְךָ יְרַנֵּנוּ.

חַנּוּן וְרַחוּם יהוה, אֶרֶךְ אַפַּיִם וּגְדָל חָסֶד.

טוֹב יהוה לַכֹּל, וְרַחֲמָיו עַל כָּל מַעֲשָׂיו.

יוֹדוּךָ יהוה כָּל מַעֲשֶׂיךָ, וַחֲסִידֶיךָ יְבָרְכוּכָה.

כְּבוֹד מַלְכוּתְךָ יֹאמֵרוּ, וּגְבוּרָתְךָ יְדַבֵּרוּ.

לְהוֹדִיעַ לִבְנֵי הָאָדָם גְּבוּרֹתָיו, וּכְבוֹד הֲדַר מַלְכוּתוֹ.

מַלְכוּתְךָ מַלְכוּת כָּל עֹלָמִים, וּמֶמְשַׁלְתְּךָ בְּכָל דּוֹר וָדֹר.

סוֹמֵךְ יהוה לְכָל הַנֹּפְלִים, וְזוֹקֵף לְכָל הַכְּפוּפִים.

עֵינֵי כֹל אֵלֶיךָ יְשַׂבֵּרוּ, וְאַתָּה נוֹתֵן לָהֶם אֶת אָכְלָם בְּעִתּוֹ.

While reciting the verse פּוֹתֵחַ, concentrate intently on its meaning.

פּוֹתֵחַ אֶת יָדֶךָ,

וּמַשְׂבִּיעַ לְכָל חַי רָצוֹן.

צַדִּיק יהוה בְּכָל דְּרָכָיו, וְחָסִיד בְּכָל מַעֲשָׂיו.

קָרוֹב יהוה לְכָל קֹרְאָיו, לְכֹל אֲשֶׁר יִקְרָאֻהוּ בֶאֱמֶת.

רְצוֹן יְרֵאָיו יַעֲשֶׂה, וְאֶת שַׁוְעָתָם יִשְׁמַע וְיוֹשִׁיעֵם.

שׁוֹמֵר יהוה אֶת כָּל אֹהֲבָיו, וְאֵת כָּל הָרְשָׁעִים יַשְׁמִיד.

❖ תְּהִלַּת יהוה יְדַבֶּר פִּי,

וִיבָרֵךְ כָּל בָּשָׂר שֵׁם קָדְשׁוֹ לְעוֹלָם וָעֶד.

וַאֲנַחְנוּ נְבָרֵךְ יָהּ, מֵעַתָּה וְעַד עוֹלָם, הַלְלוּיָהּ.[3]

---

(1) *Psalms* 84:5. (2) 144:15. (3) 115:18.

MINCHAH FOR THE SABBATH OF CHOL HAMOED

אַשְׁרֵי *Praiseworthy are those who dwell in Your house; may they always praise You, Selah![1] Praiseworthy is the people for whom this is so, praiseworthy is the people whose God is* HASHEM.[2]

Psalm 145 *A psalm of praise by David:*

א *I will exalt You, my God the King,*
and I will bless Your Name forever and ever.
ב *Every day I will bless You,*
and I will laud Your Name forever and ever.
ג HASHEM *is great and exceedingly lauded,*
and His greatness is beyond investigation.
ד *Each generation will praise Your deeds to the next*
and of Your mighty deeds they will tell.
ה *The splendrous glory of Your power*
and Your wondrous deeds I shall discuss.
ו *And of Your awesome power they will speak,*
and Your greatness I shall relate.
ז *A recollection of Your abundant goodness they will utter*
and of Your righteousness they will sing exultantly.
ח *Gracious and merciful is* HASHEM,
slow to anger, and great in [bestowing] kindness.
ט HASHEM *is good to all; His mercies are on all His works.*
י *All Your works shall thank You,* HASHEM,
and Your devout ones will bless You.
כ *Of the glory of Your kingdom they will speak,*
and of Your power they will tell;
ל *To inform human beings of His mighty deeds,*
and the glorious splendor of His kingdom.
מ *Your kingdom is a kingdom spanning all eternities,*
and Your dominion is throughout every generation.
ס HASHEM *supports all the fallen ones and straightens all the bent.*
ע *The eyes of all look to You with hope*
and You give them their food in its proper time;
פ *You open Your hand,*
and satisfy the desire of every living thing.

While reciting the verse, *'You open . . .'* concentrate intently on its meaning

צ *Righteous is* HASHEM *in all His ways*
and magnanimous in all His deeds.
ק HASHEM *is close to all who call upon Him —*
to all who call upon Him sincerely.
ר *The will of those who fear Him He will do;*
and their cry He will hear, and save them.
ש HASHEM *protects all who love Him;*
but all the wicked He will destroy.
ת Chazzan– *May my mouth declare the praise of* HASHEM
and may all flesh bless His Holy Name forever and ever.
We will bless God from this time and forever, Halleluyah![3]

The primary part of וּבָא לְצִיּוֹן is the *Kedushah* recited by the angels. These verses are presented in bold type and it is preferable that the congregation recite them aloud and in unison. However, the interpretive translation in Aramaic (which follows the verses in bold type) should be recited softly.

וּבָא לְצִיּוֹן גּוֹאֵל, וּלְשָׁבֵי פֶשַׁע בְּיַעֲקֹב, נְאֻם יהוה. וַאֲנִי, זֹאת בְּרִיתִי אוֹתָם, אָמַר יהוה, רוּחִי אֲשֶׁר עָלֶיךָ, וּדְבָרַי אֲשֶׁר שַׂמְתִּי בְּפִיךָ, לֹא יָמוּשׁוּ מִפִּיךָ וּמִפִּי זַרְעֲךָ וּמִפִּי זֶרַע זַרְעֲךָ, אָמַר יהוה, מֵעַתָּה וְעַד עוֹלָם:[1] ❖ וְאַתָּה קָדוֹשׁ יוֹשֵׁב תְּהִלּוֹת יִשְׂרָאֵל.[2] וְקָרָא זֶה אֶל זֶה וְאָמַר:

קָדוֹשׁ, קָדוֹשׁ, קָדוֹשׁ יהוה צְבָאוֹת, מְלֹא כָל הָאָרֶץ כְּבוֹדוֹ.[3]

וּמְקַבְּלִין דֵּין מִן דֵּין וְאָמְרִין:
קַדִּישׁ בִּשְׁמֵי מְרוֹמָא עִלָּאָה בֵּית שְׁכִינְתֵּהּ,
קַדִּישׁ עַל אַרְעָא עוֹבַד גְּבוּרְתֵּהּ,
קַדִּישׁ לְעָלַם וּלְעָלְמֵי עָלְמַיָּא, יהוה צְבָאוֹת,
מַלְיָא כָל אַרְעָא זִיו יְקָרֵהּ.[4]

❖ וַתִּשָּׂאֵנִי רוּחַ, וָאֶשְׁמַע אַחֲרַי קוֹל רַעַשׁ גָּדוֹל:

בָּרוּךְ כְּבוֹד יהוה מִמְּקוֹמוֹ.[5]

וּנְטָלַתְנִי רוּחָא, וְשִׁמְעֵת בַּתְרַי קָל זִיעַ סַגִּיא דִּמְשַׁבְּחִין וְאָמְרִין:
בְּרִיךְ יְקָרָא דַיהוה מֵאֲתַר בֵּית שְׁכִינְתֵּהּ.[6]

יהוה יִמְלֹךְ לְעֹלָם וָעֶד.[7]

יהוה מַלְכוּתֵהּ קָאֵם לְעָלַם וּלְעָלְמֵי עָלְמַיָּא.[8]

יהוה אֱלֹהֵי אַבְרָהָם יִצְחָק וְיִשְׂרָאֵל אֲבֹתֵינוּ, שָׁמְרָה זֹּאת לְעוֹלָם, לְיֵצֶר מַחְשְׁבוֹת לְבַב עַמֶּךָ, וְהָכֵן לְבָבָם אֵלֶיךָ.[9] וְהוּא רַחוּם, יְכַפֵּר עָוֹן וְלֹא יַשְׁחִית, וְהִרְבָּה לְהָשִׁיב אַפּוֹ, וְלֹא יָעִיר כָּל חֲמָתוֹ.[10] כִּי אַתָּה אֲדֹנָי טוֹב וְסַלָּח, וְרַב חֶסֶד לְכָל קֹרְאֶיךָ.[11] צִדְקָתְךָ צֶדֶק לְעוֹלָם, וְתוֹרָתְךָ אֱמֶת.[12] תִּתֵּן אֱמֶת לְיַעֲקֹב, חֶסֶד לְאַבְרָהָם, אֲשֶׁר נִשְׁבַּעְתָּ לַאֲבֹתֵינוּ מִימֵי קֶדֶם.[13] בָּרוּךְ אֲדֹנָי יוֹם יוֹם יַעֲמָס לָנוּ, הָאֵל יְשׁוּעָתֵנוּ סֶלָה.[14] יהוה צְבָאוֹת עִמָּנוּ, מִשְׂגָּב לָנוּ אֱלֹהֵי יַעֲקֹב סֶלָה.[15] יהוה צְבָאוֹת, אַשְׁרֵי אָדָם בֹּטֵחַ בָּךְ.[16] יהוה הוֹשִׁיעָה, הַמֶּלֶךְ יַעֲנֵנוּ בְיוֹם קָרְאֵנוּ.[17]

בָּרוּךְ הוּא אֱלֹהֵינוּ שֶׁבְּרָאָנוּ לִכְבוֹדוֹ, וְהִבְדִּילָנוּ מִן הַתּוֹעִים, וְנָתַן לָנוּ תּוֹרַת אֱמֶת, וְחַיֵּי עוֹלָם נָטַע בְּתוֹכֵנוּ. הוּא יִפְתַּח לִבֵּנוּ

(1) *Isaiah* 59:20-21. (2) *Psalms* 22:4. (3) *Isaiah* 6:3. (4) *Targum Yonasan.* (5) *Ezekiel* 3:12. (6) *Targum Yonasan.* (7) *Exodus* 15:18. (8) *Targum Onkelos.* (9) *I Chronicles* 29:18. (10) *Psalms* 78:38. (11) 86:5. (12) 119:142. (13) *Micah* 7:20. (14) *Psalms* 68:20. (15) 46:8. (16) 84:13. (17) 20:10.

The primary part of וּבָא לְצִיּוֹן, *'A redeemer shall come . . .'*, is the *Kedushah* recited by the angels. These verses are presented in bold type and it is preferable that the congregation recite them aloud and in unison. However, the interpretive translation in Aramaic (which follows the verses in bold type) should be recited softly.

וּבָא לְצִיּוֹן *'A redeemer shall come to Zion* and to those of Jacob who repent from willful sin,' the words of* HASHEM. *'And as for Me, this is My covenant* with them,' said* HASHEM, *'My spirit that is upon you and My words that I have placed in your mouth shall not be withdrawn from your mouth, nor from the mouth of your offspring,* nor from the mouth of your offspring's offspring,' said* HASHEM, *'from this moment and forever.'*[1] Chazzan– *You are the Holy One, enthroned upon the praises of Israel.**[2] *And one [angel] will call another and say:*

'Holy, holy, holy is HASHEM, Master of Legions, the whole world is filled with His glory.'[3]

And they receive permission from one another and say:
'Holy in the most exalted heaven, the abode of His Presence;
holy on earth, product of His strength;
holy forever and ever is HASHEM, *Master of Legions —*
the entire world is filled with the radiance of His glory.'[4]

Chazzan– *And a wind lifted me;* and I heard behind me the sound of a great noise:*

'Blessed is the glory of HASHEM from His place.'[5]

And a wind lifted me and I heard behind me the sound
of the powerful movement of those who praised saying:
'Blessed is the honor of HASHEM
from the place of the abode of His Presence.'[6]

HASHEM shall reign for all eternity.[7]

HASHEM *— His kingdom is established forever and ever.*[8]

HASHEM, *God of Abraham, Isaac, and Israel, our forefathers, may You preserve this* forever as the realization of the thoughts in Your people's heart, and may You direct their heart to You.*[9] *He, the Merciful One, is forgiving of iniquity and does not destroy; frequently He withdraws His anger, not arousing His entire rage.*[10] *For You, my Lord, are good and forgiving, and abundantly kind to all who call upon You.*[11] *Your righteousness remains righteous forever, and Your Torah is truth.*[12] *Grant truth to Jacob, kindness to Abraham, as You swore to our forefathers from ancient times.*[13] *Blessed is my Lord for every single day, He burdens us with blessings, the God of our salvation, Selah.*[14] HASHEM, *Master of Legions, is with us, a stronghold for us is the God of Jacob, Selah.*[15] HASHEM, *Master of Legions, praiseworthy is the man who trusts in You.*[16] HASHEM, *save! May the King answer us on the day we call.*[17]

Blessed is He, our God, Who created us for His glory, separated us from those who stray, gave us the Torah of truth and implanted eternal life within us. May He open our heart through His Torah and imbue our

בְּתוֹרָתוֹ, וְיָשֵׂם בְּלִבֵּנוּ אַהֲבָתוֹ וְיִרְאָתוֹ וְלַעֲשׂוֹת רְצוֹנוֹ וּלְעָבְדוֹ בְּלֵבָב שָׁלֵם, לְמַעַן לֹא נִיגַע לָרִיק, וְלֹא נֵלֵד לַבֶּהָלָה.[1]

יְהִי רָצוֹן מִלְּפָנֶיךָ יהוה אֱלֹהֵינוּ וֵאלֹהֵי אֲבוֹתֵינוּ, שֶׁנִּשְׁמֹר חֻקֶּיךָ בָּעוֹלָם הַזֶּה, וְנִזְכֶּה וְנִחְיֶה וְנִרְאֶה וְנִירַשׁ טוֹבָה וּבְרָכָה לִשְׁנֵי יְמוֹת הַמָּשִׁיחַ וּלְחַיֵּי הָעוֹלָם הַבָּא. לְמַעַן יְזַמֶּרְךָ כָבוֹד וְלֹא יִדֹּם, יהוה אֱלֹהַי לְעוֹלָם אוֹדֶךָּ.[2] בָּרוּךְ הַגֶּבֶר אֲשֶׁר יִבְטַח בַּיהוה, וְהָיָה יהוה מִבְטַחוֹ.[3] בִּטְחוּ בַיהוה עֲדֵי עַד, כִּי בְּיָהּ יהוה צוּר עוֹלָמִים.[4] ❖ וְיִבְטְחוּ בְךָ יוֹדְעֵי שְׁמֶךָ, כִּי לֹא עָזַבְתָּ דֹּרְשֶׁיךָ, יהוה.[5] יהוה חָפֵץ לְמַעַן צִדְקוֹ, יַגְדִּיל תּוֹרָה וְיַאְדִּיר.[6]

Chazzan recites חֲצִי קַדִּישׁ.

יִתְגַּדַּל וְיִתְקַדַּשׁ שְׁמֵהּ רַבָּא. (.Cong – אָמֵן.) בְּעָלְמָא דִּי בְרָא כִרְעוּתֵהּ. וְיַמְלִיךְ מַלְכוּתֵהּ, בְּחַיֵּיכוֹן וּבְיוֹמֵיכוֹן וּבְחַיֵּי דְכָל בֵּית יִשְׂרָאֵל, בַּעֲגָלָא וּבִזְמַן קָרִיב. וְאִמְרוּ: אָמֵן.

(.Cong – אָמֵן. יְהֵא שְׁמֵהּ רַבָּא מְבָרַךְ לְעָלַם וּלְעָלְמֵי עָלְמַיָּא.)

יְהֵא שְׁמֵהּ רַבָּא מְבָרַךְ לְעָלַם וּלְעָלְמֵי עָלְמַיָּא.

יִתְבָּרַךְ וְיִשְׁתַּבַּח וְיִתְפָּאַר וְיִתְרוֹמַם וְיִתְנַשֵּׂא וְיִתְהַדָּר וְיִתְעַלֶּה וְיִתְהַלָּל שְׁמֵהּ דְּקֻדְשָׁא בְּרִיךְ הוּא (.Cong – בְּרִיךְ הוּא) — לְעֵלָּא מִן כָּל בִּרְכָתָא וְשִׁירָתָא תֻּשְׁבְּחָתָא וְנֶחֱמָתָא, דַּאֲמִירָן בְּעָלְמָא. וְאִמְרוּ: אָמֵן. (.Cong – אָמֵן.)

Congregation, then *chazzan:*

וַאֲנִי תְפִלָּתִי לְךָ יהוה עֵת רָצוֹן, אֱלֹהִים בְּרָב חַסְדֶּךָ, עֲנֵנִי בֶּאֱמֶת יִשְׁעֶךָ.[7]

הוצאת ספר תורה

From the moment the Ark is opened until the Torah is returned to it, one must conduct himself with the utmost respect, and avoid unnecessary conversation. It is commendable to kiss the Torah as it is carried to the *bimah* [reading table] and back to the Ark.

All rise and remain standing until the Torah is placed on the *bimah*.
The Ark is opened; before the Torah is removed, the congregation recites:

וַיְהִי בִּנְסֹעַ הָאָרֹן, וַיֹּאמֶר מֹשֶׁה, קוּמָה יהוה וְיָפֻצוּ אֹיְבֶיךָ, וְיָנֻסוּ מְשַׂנְאֶיךָ מִפָּנֶיךָ.[8] כִּי מִצִּיּוֹן תֵּצֵא תוֹרָה, וּדְבַר יהוה מִירוּשָׁלָיִם.[9] בָּרוּךְ שֶׁנָּתַן תּוֹרָה לְעַמּוֹ יִשְׂרָאֵל בִּקְדֻשָּׁתוֹ.

זוהר ויקהל שסט:א

בְּרִיךְ שְׁמֵהּ דְּמָרֵא עָלְמָא, בְּרִיךְ כִּתְרָךְ וְאַתְרָךְ. יְהֵא רְעוּתָךְ עִם עַמָּךְ יִשְׂרָאֵל לְעָלַם, וּפֻרְקַן יְמִינָךְ אַחֲזֵי לְעַמָּךְ בְּבֵית מַקְדְּשָׁךְ, וּלְאַמְטוּיֵי לָנָא מִטּוּב נְהוֹרָךְ, וּלְקַבֵּל צְלוֹתָנָא בְּרַחֲמִין. יְהֵא רַעֲוָא קֳדָמָךְ, דְּתוֹרִיךְ לָן חַיִּין בְּטִיבוּתָא, וְלֶהֱוֵי אֲנָא פְקִידָא בְּגוֹ צַדִּיקַיָּא,

heart with love and awe of Him and that we may do His will and serve Him wholeheartedly, so that we do not struggle in vain nor produce for futility.[1]

May it be Your will, HASHEM, *our God and the God of our forefathers, that we observe Your decrees in This World, and merit that we live and see and inherit goodness and blessing in the years of Messianic times and for the life of the World to Come. So that my soul might sing to You and not be stilled,* HASHEM, *my God, forever will I thank You.*[2] *Blessed is the man who trusts in* HASHEM, *then* HASHEM *will be his security.*[3] *Trust in* HASHEM *forever, for in God,* HASHEM, *is the strength of the worlds.*[4] Chazzan– *Those knowing Your Name will trust in You, and You forsake not those Who seek You,* HASHEM.[5] HASHEM *desired, for the sake of its [Israel's] righteousness, that the Torah be made great and glorious.*[6]

Chazzan recites Half-*Kaddish*.

יִתְגַּדַּל *May His great Name grow exalted and sanctified* (Cong.– *Amen.*) *in the world that He created as He willed. May He give reign to His kingship in your lifetimes and in your days, and in the lifetimes of the entire Family of Israel, swiftly and soon. Now respond: Amen.*

(Cong.– *Amen. May His great Name be blessed forever and ever.*)
May His great Name be blessed forever and ever.

Blessed, praised, glorified, exalted, extolled, mighty, upraised, and lauded be the Name of the Holy One, Blessed is He (Cong.– *Blessed is He*) — *beyond any blessing and song, praise and consolation that are uttered in the world. Now respond: Amen.* (Cong.– *Amen*.)

Congregation, then *chazzan:*

וַאֲנִי תְפִלָּתִי *As for me, may my prayer to You,* HASHEM, *be at an opportune time; O God, in Your abundant kindness, answer me with the truth of Your salvation.*[7]

REMOVAL OF THE TORAH FROM THE ARK

From the moment the Ark is opened until the Torah is returned to it, one must conduct himself with the utmost respect, and avoid unnecessary conversation. It is commendable to kiss the Torah as it is carried to the *bimah* [reading table] and back to the Ark.

All rise and remain standing until the Torah is placed on the *bimah*.
The Ark is opened; before the Torah is removed, the congregation recites:

וַיְהִי בִּנְסֹעַ *When the Ark would travel, Moses would say, 'Arise,* HASHEM, *and let Your foes be scattered, let those who hate You flee from You.'*[8] *For from Zion will the Torah come forth and the word of* HASHEM *from Jerusalem.*[9] *Blessed is He Who gave the Torah to His people Israel in His holiness.*

Zohar, Vayakhel 369a

בְּרִיךְ שְׁמֵהּ *Blessed is the Name of the Master of the universe, blessed is Your crown and Your place. May Your favor remain with Your people Israel forever; may You display the salvation of Your right hand to Your people in Your Holy Temple, to benefit us with the goodness of Your luminescence and to accept our prayers with mercy. May it be Your will that You extend our lives with goodness and that I be numbered among the righteous; that*

---

(1) Cf. *Isaiah* 65:23. (2) *Psalms* 30:13. (3) *Jeremiah* 17:7. (4) *Isaiah* 26:4.
(5) *Psalms* 9:11. (6) *Isaiah* 42:21. (7) *Psalms* 69:14. (8) *Numbers* 10:35. (9) *Isaiah* 2:3.

לְמִרְחַם עָלַי וּלְמִנְטַר יָתִי וְיַת כָּל דִּי לִי וְדִי לְעַמָּךְ יִשְׂרָאֵל. אַנְתְּ הוּא זָן לְכֹלָּא, וּמְפַרְנֵס לְכֹלָּא, אַנְתְּ הוּא שַׁלִּיט עַל כֹּלָּא. אַנְתְּ הוּא דְּשַׁלִּיט עַל מַלְכַיָּא, וּמַלְכוּתָא דִּילָךְ הִיא. אֲנָא עַבְדָּא דְקֻדְשָׁא בְּרִיךְ הוּא, דְּסָגִידְנָא קַמֵּהּ וּמִקַּמָּא דִּיקַר אוֹרַיְתֵהּ בְּכָל עִדָּן וְעִדָּן. לָא עַל אֱנָשׁ רָחִיצְנָא, וְלָא עַל בַּר אֱלָהִין סָמִיכְנָא, אֶלָּא בֶּאֱלָהָא דִשְׁמַיָּא, דְּהוּא אֱלָהָא קְשׁוֹט, וְאוֹרַיְתֵהּ קְשׁוֹט, וּנְבִיאוֹהִי קְשׁוֹט, וּמַסְגֵּא לְמֶעְבַּד טַבְוָן וּקְשׁוֹט. בֵּהּ אֲנָא רָחִיץ, וְלִשְׁמֵהּ קַדִּישָׁא יַקִּירָא אֲנָא אֵמַר תֻּשְׁבְּחָן. יְהֵא רַעֲוָא קֳדָמָךְ, דְּתִפְתַּח לִבָּאִי בְּאוֹרַיְתָא, וְתַשְׁלִים מִשְׁאֲלִין דְּלִבָּאִי, וְלִבָּא דְכָל עַמָּךְ יִשְׂרָאֵל, לְטָב וּלְחַיִּין וְלִשְׁלָם. (אָמֵן.)

The Torah is removed from the Ark and presented to the *chazzan,* who accepts it in his right arm. He then turns to the Ark and raises the Torah slightly as he bows and recites:

גַּדְּלוּ לַיהוה אִתִּי, וּנְרוֹמְמָה שְׁמוֹ יַחְדָּו.[1]

The *chazzan* turns to his right and carries the Torah to the *bimah,* as the congregation responds:

לְךָ יהוה הַגְּדֻלָּה וְהַגְּבוּרָה וְהַתִּפְאֶרֶת וְהַנֵּצַח וְהַהוֹד, כִּי כֹל בַּשָּׁמַיִם וּבָאָרֶץ, לְךָ יהוה הַמַּמְלָכָה וְהַמִּתְנַשֵּׂא לְכֹל לְרֹאשׁ.[2] רוֹמְמוּ יהוה אֱלֹהֵינוּ וְהִשְׁתַּחֲווּ לַהֲדֹם רַגְלָיו, קָדוֹשׁ הוּא. רוֹמְמוּ יהוה אֱלֹהֵינוּ וְהִשְׁתַּחֲווּ לְהַר קָדְשׁוֹ, כִּי קָדוֹשׁ יהוה אֱלֹהֵינוּ.[3]

אַב הָרַחֲמִים הוּא יְרַחֵם עַם עֲמוּסִים, וְיִזְכֹּר בְּרִית אֵיתָנִים, וְיַצִּיל נַפְשׁוֹתֵינוּ מִן הַשָּׁעוֹת הָרָעוֹת, וְיִגְעַר בְּיֵצֶר הָרַע מִן הַנְּשׂוּאִים, וְיָחֹן אוֹתָנוּ לִפְלֵיטַת עוֹלָמִים, וִימַלֵּא מִשְׁאֲלוֹתֵינוּ בְּמִדָּה טוֹבָה יְשׁוּעָה וְרַחֲמִים.

The Torah is placed on the *bimah* and prepared for reading.

The *gabbai* uses the following formula to call a *Kohen* to the Torah:

וְתִגָּלֶה וְתֵרָאֶה מַלְכוּתוֹ עָלֵינוּ בִּזְמַן קָרוֹב, וְיָחֹן פְּלֵיטָתֵנוּ וּפְלֵיטַת עַמּוֹ בֵּית יִשְׂרָאֵל לְחֵן וּלְחֶסֶד וּלְרַחֲמִים וּלְרָצוֹן. וְנֹאמַר אָמֵן. הַכֹּל הָבוּ גֹדֶל לֵאלֹהֵינוּ וּתְנוּ כָבוֹד לַתּוֹרָה. כֹּהֵן° קְרָב, יַעֲמֹד (insert name) הַכֹּהֵן.

°If no *Kohen* is present, the *gabbai* says: "אֵין כָּאן כֹּהֵן, יַעֲמֹד (name) יִשְׂרָאֵל (לֵוִי) בִּמְקוֹם כֹּהֵן."

בָּרוּךְ שֶׁנָּתַן תּוֹרָה לְעַמּוֹ יִשְׂרָאֵל בִּקְדֻשָּׁתוֹ. (תּוֹרַת יהוה תְּמִימָה מְשִׁיבַת נָפֶשׁ, עֵדוּת יהוה נֶאֱמָנָה מַחְכִּימַת פֶּתִי. פִּקּוּדֵי יהוה יְשָׁרִים מְשַׂמְּחֵי לֵב, מִצְוַת יהוה בָּרָה מְאִירַת עֵינָיִם.[4] יהוה עֹז לְעַמּוֹ יִתֵּן, יהוה יְבָרֵךְ אֶת עַמּוֹ בַשָּׁלוֹם.[5] הָאֵל תָּמִים דַּרְכּוֹ, אִמְרַת יהוה צְרוּפָה, מָגֵן הוּא לְכֹל הַחֹסִים בּוֹ.[6])

Congregation, then *gabbai:*

וְאַתֶּם הַדְּבֵקִים בַּיהוה אֱלֹהֵיכֶם, חַיִּים כֻּלְּכֶם הַיּוֹם:[7]

You have mercy on me and protect me, all that is mine and that is Your people Israel's. It is You Who nourishes all and sustains all, You control everything. It is You Who control kings, and Kingship is Yours. I am a servant of the Holy One, Blessed is He, and I prostrate myself before Him and before the glory of His Torah at all times. Not in any man do I put trust, nor on any angel do I rely — only on the God of heaven Who is the God of truth, Whose Torah is truth and Whose prophets are true and Who acts liberally with kindness and truth. In Him do I trust, and to His glorious and Holy Name do I declare praises. May it be Your will that You open my heart to the Torah and that You fulfill the wishes of my heart and the heart of Your entire people Israel for good, for life, and for peace. (Amen.)

The Torah is removed from the Ark and presented to the *chazzan,* who accepts it in his right arm He then turns to the Ark and raises the Torah slightly as he bows and recites:

Declare the greatness of HASHEM with me, and let us exalt His Name together.[1]

The *chazzan* turns to his right and carries the Torah to the *bimah,* as the congregation responds:

לְךָ *Yours, HASHEM, is the greatness, the strength, the splendor, the triumph, and the glory; even everything in heaven and earth; Yours, HASHEM, is the kingdom, and the sovereignty over every leader.*[2] *Exalt HASHEM, our God, and bow at His footstool; He is Holy! Exalt HASHEM, our God, and bow at His holy mountain; for holy is HASHEM, our God.*[3]

אַב הָרַחֲמִים *May the Father of mercy have mercy on the nation that is borne by Him, and may He remember the covenant of the spiritually mighty. May He rescue our souls from the bad times, and upbraid the evil inclination to leave those borne by Him, graciously make us an eternal remnant, and fulfill our requests in good measure, for salvation and mercy.*

The Torah is placed on the *bimah* and prepared for reading.
The *gabbai* uses the following formula to call a *Kohen* to the Torah:

וְתִגָּלֶה *And may His kingship over us be revealed and become visible soon, and may He be gracious to our remnant and the remnant of His people the Family of Israel, for graciousness, kindness, mercy, and favor. And let us respond, Amen. All of you ascribe greatness to our God and give honor to the Torah. Kohen,° approach. Stand* (name) *son of* (father's name) *the Kohen.*

°If no *Kohen* is present, the *gabbai* says: *'There is no Kohen present, stand* (name) *son of* (father's name) *an Israelite (Levite) in place of the Kohen.'*

Blessed is He Who gave the Torah to His people Israel in His holiness (The Torah of HASHEM is perfect, restoring the soul; the testimony of HASHEM is trustworthy, making the simple one wise. The orders of HASHEM are upright, gladdening the heart; the command of HASHEM is clear, enlightening the eyes.[4] *HASHEM will give might to His people; HASHEM will bless His people with peace.*[5] *The God Whose way is perfect, the promise of HASHEM is flawless, He is a shield for all who take refuge in Him.*[6]*)*

Congregation, then *gabbai:*

You who cling to HASHEM your God—you are all alive today.[7]

---

(1) *Psalms* 34:4. (2) *I Chronicles* 29:11. (3) *Psalms* 99:5,9.
(4) 19:8-9. (5) 29:11. (6) 18:31. (7) *Deuteronomy* 4:4.

קריאת התורה

The reader shows the *oleh* (person called to the Torah) the place in the Torah. The *oleh* touches the Torah with a corner of his *tallis,* or the belt or mantle of the Torah, and kisses it. He then begins the blessing, bowing at בָּרְכוּ, and straightening up at 'ה.

בָּרְכוּ אֶת יהוה הַמְּבֹרָךְ.

Congregation, followed by *oleh,* responds, bowing at בָּרוּךְ, and straightening up at 'ה.

בָּרוּךְ יהוה הַמְּבֹרָךְ לְעוֹלָם וָעֶד.

Oleh continues:

בָּרוּךְ אַתָּה יהוה אֱלֹהֵינוּ מֶלֶךְ הָעוֹלָם, אֲשֶׁר בָּחַר בָּנוּ מִכָּל הָעַמִּים, וְנָתַן לָנוּ אֶת תּוֹרָתוֹ. בָּרוּךְ אַתָּה יהוה, נוֹתֵן הַתּוֹרָה.

(.Cong. – אָמֵן)

After his Torah portion has been read, the *oleh* recites:

בָּרוּךְ אַתָּה יהוה אֱלֹהֵינוּ מֶלֶךְ הָעוֹלָם, אֲשֶׁר נָתַן לָנוּ תּוֹרַת אֱמֶת, וְחַיֵּי עוֹלָם נָטַע בְּתוֹכֵנוּ. בָּרוּךְ אַתָּה יהוה, נוֹתֵן הַתּוֹרָה.

(.Cong. – אָמֵן)

THE VARIOUS מִי שֶׁבֵּרַךְ PRAYERS APPEAR ON PAGE 308.

דברים לג:א-יז (Commentary on page 1158.)

כהן – **וְזֹאת** הַבְּרָכָה אֲשֶׁר בֵּרַךְ מֹשֶׁה אִישׁ הָאֱלֹהִים אֶת־בְּנֵי יִשְׂרָאֵל לִפְנֵי מוֹתוֹ: וַיֹּאמַר יהוה מִסִּינַי בָּא וְזָרַח מִשֵּׂעִיר לָמוֹ הוֹפִיעַ מֵהַר פָּארָן וְאָתָה מֵרִבְבֹת קֹדֶשׁ מִימִינוֹ אֵשׁ דָּת לָמוֹ: אַף חֹבֵב עַמִּים כָּל־קְדֹשָׁיו בְּיָדֶךָ וְהֵם תֻּכּוּ לְרַגְלֶךָ יִשָּׂא מִדַּבְּרֹתֶיךָ: תּוֹרָה צִוָּה־לָנוּ מֹשֶׁה מוֹרָשָׁה קְהִלַּת יַעֲקֹב: וַיְהִי בִישֻׁרוּן מֶלֶךְ בְּהִתְאַסֵּף רָאשֵׁי עָם יַחַד שִׁבְטֵי יִשְׂרָאֵל: יְחִי רְאוּבֵן וְאַל־יָמֹת וִיהִי מְתָיו מִסְפָּר: וְזֹאת לִיהוּדָה וַיֹּאמַר שְׁמַע יהוה קוֹל יְהוּדָה וְאֶל־עַמּוֹ תְּבִיאֶנּוּ יָדָיו רָב לוֹ וְעֵזֶר מִצָּרָיו תִּהְיֶה:

לוי – **וּלְלֵוִי** אָמַר תֻּמֶּיךָ וְאוּרֶיךָ לְאִישׁ חֲסִידֶךָ אֲשֶׁר נִסִּיתוֹ בְּמַסָּה תְּרִיבֵהוּ עַל־מֵי מְרִיבָה: הָאֹמֵר לְאָבִיו וּלְאִמּוֹ לֹא רְאִיתִיו וְאֶת־אֶחָיו לֹא הִכִּיר וְאֶת־בָּנָו לֹא יָדָע כִּי שָׁמְרוּ אִמְרָתֶךָ וּבְרִיתְךָ יִנְצֹרוּ: יוֹרוּ מִשְׁפָּטֶיךָ לְיַעֲקֹב וְתוֹרָתְךָ לְיִשְׂרָאֵל יָשִׂימוּ קְטוֹרָה בְּאַפֶּךָ וְכָלִיל עַל־מִזְבְּחֶךָ: בָּרֵךְ יהוה חֵילוֹ וּפֹעַל יָדָיו תִּרְצֶה מְחַץ מָתְנַיִם קָמָיו וּמְשַׂנְאָיו מִן־יְקוּמוּן: לְבִנְיָמִן אָמַר יְדִיד יהוה יִשְׁכֹּן לָבֶטַח עָלָיו חֹפֵף עָלָיו כָּל־הַיּוֹם וּבֵין כְּתֵפָיו שָׁכֵן:

ישראל – **וּלְיוֹסֵף** אָמַר מְבֹרֶכֶת יהוה אַרְצוֹ מִמֶּגֶד שָׁמַיִם מִטָּל וּמִתְּהוֹם רֹבֶצֶת תָּחַת: וּמִמֶּגֶד תְּבוּאֹת שָׁמֶשׁ וּמִמֶּגֶד גֶּרֶשׁ יְרָחִים: וּמֵרֹאשׁ

READING OF THE TORAH

The reader shows the *oleh* (person called to the Torah) the place in the Torah. The *oleh* touches the Torah with a corner of his *tallis,* or the belt or mantle of the Torah, and kisses it. He then begins the blessing, bowing at *'Bless,'* and straightening up at 'HASHEM':

Bless HASHEM, the blessed One.

Congregation, followed by *oleh,* responds, bowing at 'Blessed,' and straightening up at 'HASHEM.'

Blessed is HASHEM, the blessed One, for all eternity.

Oleh continues:

בָּרוּךְ *Blessed are You, HASHEM, our God, King of the universe, Who selected us from all the peoples and gave us His Torah. Blessed are You, HASHEM, Giver of the Torah.* (Cong.— *Amen.)*

After his Torah portion has been read, the *oleh* recites:

בָּרוּךְ *Blessed are You, HASHEM, our God, King of the universe, Who gave us the Torah of truth and implanted eternal life within us. Blessed are You, HASHEM, Giver of the Torah.* (Cong.— *Amen.)*

THE VARIOUS *MI SHEBEIRACH* PRAYERS APPEAR ON PAGE 308.

Deuteronomy 33:1-17 (Commentary on page 1158.)

Kohen — *This is the blessing that Moses, the man of God, bestowed upon the Children of Israel before his death.*

He said: HASHEM approached from Sinai — having shone forth to them from Seir, having appeared from Mount Paran, and then approached with some of the holy myriads — from His right hand He presented the fiery Torah to them. Indeed, You greatly loved the tribes, all their righteous ones were in Your hands; for they planted themselves at Your feet, accepting the burden of Your utterances: "The Torah which Moses charged us is the heritage of the congregation of Jacob. He became King over Jeshurun when the leaders of the nation gathered — the tribes of Israel in unity."

May Reuben live and not die, and may his population be counted among the others.

And this to Judah, and he said: Hear, O HASHEM. Judah's prayer, and return him safely to his people; may his hands gain him triumph and may You remain a helper against his enemies.

Levi — *Of Levi he said: Your Tumim and Urim befit Your devout one, whom You tested at Massah, and whom You challenged at the waters of Meribah. The one who said of his father and mother, "I have not favored him," he disregarded his brothers and ignored his own children; for they [i.e., the Levites] have observed Your word, and preserved Your covenant. Thus it is they who are worthy to teach Your law to Jacob and Your Torah to Israel; it is they who shall place incense before Your presence, and burnt offerings on Your altar. Bless, O HASHEM, his resources, and favor his handiwork. Smash the loins of his foes, and his enemies that they may not rise again.*

Of Benjamin he said: May HASHEM's beloved dwell securely by Him; He hovers above him all day long; and rests His Presence among his hills.

Third — *Of Joseph he said: His land is blessed by HASHEM — with the heavenly bounty of dew, and with the deep waters crouching below: with the bounty of the sun's crops, and with the bounty of the moon's yield; with the quick-ripening crops of the ancient mountains, and with the bounty of eternally fertile*

הַרְרֵי־קֶדֶם וּמִמֶּגֶד גִּבְעוֹת עוֹלָם: וּמִמֶּגֶד אֶרֶץ וּמְלֹאָהּ וּרְצוֹן שֹׁכְנִי סְנֶה תָּבוֹאתָה לְרֹאשׁ יוֹסֵף וּלְקָדְקֹד נְזִיר אֶחָיו: בְּכוֹר שׁוֹרוֹ הָדָר לוֹ וְקַרְנֵי רְאֵם קַרְנָיו בָּהֶם עַמִּים יְנַגַּח יַחְדָּו אַפְסֵי־אָרֶץ וְהֵם רִבְבוֹת אֶפְרַיִם וְהֵם אַלְפֵי מְנַשֶּׁה:

When the Torah reading has been completed, the Torah is raised for all to see. Each person looks at the Torah and recites aloud:

וְזֹאת הַתּוֹרָה אֲשֶׁר שָׂם מֹשֶׁה לִפְנֵי בְּנֵי יִשְׂרָאֵל,[1] עַל פִּי יהוה בְּיַד מֹשֶׁה.[2]

Some add the following verses:

עֵץ חַיִּים הִיא לַמַּחֲזִיקִים בָּהּ, וְתֹמְכֶיהָ מְאֻשָּׁר.[3] דְּרָכֶיהָ דַרְכֵי נֹעַם, וְכָל נְתִיבוֹתֶיהָ שָׁלוֹם.[4] אֹרֶךְ יָמִים בִּימִינָהּ, בִּשְׂמֹאלָהּ עֹשֶׁר וְכָבוֹד.[5] יהוה חָפֵץ לְמַעַן צִדְקוֹ, יַגְדִּיל תּוֹרָה וְיַאְדִּיר.[6]

Chazzan takes the Torah in his right arm and recites:

יְהַלְלוּ אֶת שֵׁם יהוה, כִּי נִשְׂגָּב שְׁמוֹ לְבַדּוֹ –

Congregation responds:

– הוֹדוֹ עַל אֶרֶץ וְשָׁמָיִם. וַיָּרֶם קֶרֶן לְעַמּוֹ, תְּהִלָּה לְכָל חֲסִידָיו, לִבְנֵי יִשְׂרָאֵל עַם קְרֹבוֹ, הַלְלוּיָהּ.[7]

As the Torah is carried to the Ark, congregation recites Psalm 24, לְדָוִד מִזְמוֹר.

לְדָוִד מִזְמוֹר, לַיהוה הָאָרֶץ וּמְלוֹאָהּ, תֵּבֵל וְיֹשְׁבֵי בָהּ. כִּי הוּא עַל יַמִּים יְסָדָהּ, וְעַל נְהָרוֹת יְכוֹנְנֶהָ. מִי יַעֲלֶה בְהַר יהוה, וּמִי יָקוּם בִּמְקוֹם קָדְשׁוֹ. נְקִי כַפַּיִם וּבַר לֵבָב, אֲשֶׁר לֹא נָשָׂא לַשָּׁוְא נַפְשִׁי וְלֹא נִשְׁבַּע לְמִרְמָה. יִשָּׂא בְרָכָה מֵאֵת יהוה, וּצְדָקָה מֵאֱלֹהֵי יִשְׁעוֹ. זֶה דּוֹר דֹּרְשָׁיו, מְבַקְשֵׁי פָנֶיךָ, יַעֲקֹב, סֶלָה. שְׂאוּ שְׁעָרִים רָאשֵׁיכֶם, וְהִנָּשְׂאוּ פִּתְחֵי עוֹלָם, וְיָבוֹא מֶלֶךְ הַכָּבוֹד. מִי זֶה מֶלֶךְ הַכָּבוֹד, יהוה עִזּוּז וְגִבּוֹר, יהוה גִּבּוֹר מִלְחָמָה. שְׂאוּ שְׁעָרִים רָאשֵׁיכֶם, וּשְׂאוּ פִּתְחֵי עוֹלָם, וְיָבֹא מֶלֶךְ הַכָּבוֹד. מִי הוּא זֶה מֶלֶךְ הַכָּבוֹד, יהוה צְבָאוֹת הוּא מֶלֶךְ הַכָּבוֹד, סֶלָה.

As the Torah is placed into the Ark, congregation recites the following verses:

וּבְנֻחֹה יֹאמַר, שׁוּבָה יהוה רִבְבוֹת אַלְפֵי יִשְׂרָאֵל.[8] קוּמָה יהוה לִמְנוּחָתֶךָ, אַתָּה וַאֲרוֹן עֻזֶּךָ. כֹּהֲנֶיךָ יִלְבְּשׁוּ צֶדֶק, וַחֲסִידֶיךָ

hills; with the bounty of the land and its fullness, and by the favor of Him Who rested upon the thornbush. May this blessing rest upon Joseph's head, and upon the crown of him who was separated from his brothers. Sovereignty will go to his most distinguished, mighty descendant; and his glory will be like the horns of a re'eim; with both of them together he shall gore nations to the ends of the earth; they are the myriads of Ephraim's victims, and the thousands of Menashe's victims.

When the Torah reading has been completed, the Torah is raised for all to see. Each person looks at the Torah and recites aloud:

This is the Torah that Moses placed before the Children of Israel,[1] upon the command of HASHEM, through Moses' hand.[2]

Some add the following verses:

עֵץ *It is a tree of life for those who grasp it, and its supporters are praiseworthy.[3] Its ways are ways of pleasantness and all its paths are peace.[4] Lengthy days are at its right; at its left are wealth and honor.[5] HASHEM desired, for the sake of its [Israel's] righteousness, that the Torah be made great and glorious.[6]*

Chazzan takes the Torah in his right arm and recites:

Let them praise the Name of HASHEM, for His Name alone will have been exalted —

Congregation responds:

— His glory is above earth and heaven. And He will have exalted the pride of His people, causing praise for all His devout ones, for the Children of Israel, His intimate nation. Halleluyah![7]

As the Torah is carried to the Ark, congregation recites Psalm 24, *'Of David a psalm.'*

לְדָוִד *Of David a psalm. HASHEM's is the earth and its fullness, the inhabited land and those who dwell in it. For He founded it upon seas, and established it upon rivers. Who may ascend the mountain of HASHEM, and who may stand in the place of His sanctity? One with clean hands and pure heart, who has not sworn in vain by My soul and has not sworn deceitfully. He will receive a blessing from HASHEM and just kindness from the God of his salvation. This is the generation of those who seek Him, those who strive for Your Presence — Jacob, Selah. Raise up your heads, O gates, and be uplifted, you everlasting entrances, so that the King of Glory may enter. Who is this King of Glory? — HASHEM, the mighty and strong, HASHEM, the strong in battle. Raise up your heads, O gates, and raise up, you everlasting entrances, so that the King of Glory may enter. Who then is the King of Glory? HASHEM, Master of Legions, He is the King of Glory. Selah!*

As the Torah is placed into the Ark, the congregation recites the following verses:

וּבְנֻחֹה *And when it rested he would say, 'Return, HASHEM, to the myriad thousands of Israel.'[8] Arise, HASHEM, to Your resting place, You and the Ark of Your strength. Let Your priests be clothed in righteousness, and Your*

---

(1) *Deuteronomy* 4:44. (2) *Numbers* 9:23. (3) *Proverbs* 3:18. (4) 3:17.
(5) 3:16. (6) *Isaiah* 42:21. (7) *Psalms* 148:13-14. (8) *Numbers* 10:36.

יְרַנְּנוּ. בַּעֲבוּר דָּוִד עַבְדֶּךָ, אַל תָּשֵׁב פְּנֵי מְשִׁיחֶךָ.[1] כִּי לֶקַח טוֹב נָתַתִּי לָכֶם, תּוֹרָתִי אַל תַּעֲזֹבוּ.[2] ❖ עֵץ חַיִּים הִיא לַמַּחֲזִיקִים בָּהּ, וְתֹמְכֶיהָ מְאֻשָּׁר.[3] דְּרָכֶיהָ דַרְכֵי נֹעַם, וְכָל נְתִיבוֹתֶיהָ שָׁלוֹם.[4] הֲשִׁיבֵנוּ יהוה אֵלֶיךָ וְנָשׁוּבָה, חַדֵּשׁ יָמֵינוּ כְּקֶדֶם.[5]

The Ark is closed and the *chazzan* recites חֲצִי קַדִּישׁ.

יִתְגַּדַּל וְיִתְקַדַּשׁ שְׁמֵהּ רַבָּא. (.Cong – אָמֵן.) בְּעָלְמָא דִּי בְרָא כִרְעוּתֵהּ. וְיַמְלִיךְ מַלְכוּתֵהּ, בְּחַיֵּיכוֹן וּבְיוֹמֵיכוֹן וּבְחַיֵּי דְכָל בֵּית יִשְׂרָאֵל, בַּעֲגָלָא וּבִזְמַן קָרִיב. וְאִמְרוּ: אָמֵן.

(.Cong – אָמֵן. יְהֵא שְׁמֵהּ רַבָּא מְבָרַךְ לְעָלַם וּלְעָלְמֵי עָלְמַיָּא.)

יְהֵא שְׁמֵהּ רַבָּא מְבָרַךְ לְעָלַם וּלְעָלְמֵי עָלְמַיָּא.

יִתְבָּרַךְ וְיִשְׁתַּבַּח וְיִתְפָּאַר וְיִתְרוֹמַם וְיִתְנַשֵּׂא וְיִתְהַדָּר וְיִתְעַלֶּה וְיִתְהַלָּל שְׁמֵהּ דְּקֻדְשָׁא בְּרִיךְ הוּא (.Cong – בְּרִיךְ הוּא) — לְעֵלָּא מִן כָּל בִּרְכָתָא וְשִׁירָתָא תֻּשְׁבְּחָתָא וְנֶחֱמָתָא, דַּאֲמִירָן בְּעָלְמָא. וְאִמְרוּ: אָמֵן. (.Cong – אָמֵן.)

❧ שמונה עשרה ❧

Take three steps backward, then three steps forward. Remain standing with the feet together while reciting *Shemoneh Esrei*. Recite it with quiet devotion and without interruption, verbal or otherwise. Although its recitation should not be audible to others, one must pray loudly enough to hear himself.

כִּי שֵׁם יהוה אֶקְרָא, הָבוּ גֹדֶל לֵאלֹהֵינוּ.[6]

אֲדֹנָי שְׂפָתַי תִּפְתָּח, וּפִי יַגִּיד תְּהִלָּתֶךָ.[7]

אבות

Bend the knees at בָּרוּךְ; bow at אַתָּה; straighten up at 'ה.

בָּרוּךְ אַתָּה יהוה אֱלֹהֵינוּ וֵאלֹהֵי אֲבוֹתֵינוּ, אֱלֹהֵי אַבְרָהָם, אֱלֹהֵי יִצְחָק, וֵאלֹהֵי יַעֲקֹב, הָאֵל הַגָּדוֹל הַגִּבּוֹר וְהַנּוֹרָא, אֵל עֶלְיוֹן, גּוֹמֵל חֲסָדִים טוֹבִים וְקוֹנֵה הַכֹּל, וְזוֹכֵר חַסְדֵי אָבוֹת, וּמֵבִיא גוֹאֵל לִבְנֵי בְנֵיהֶם, לְמַעַן שְׁמוֹ בְּאַהֲבָה. מֶלֶךְ עוֹזֵר וּמוֹשִׁיעַ וּמָגֵן.

Bend the knees at בָּרוּךְ; bow at אַתָּה; straighten up at 'ה.

בָּרוּךְ אַתָּה יהוה, מָגֵן אַבְרָהָם.

גבורות

אַתָּה גִּבּוֹר לְעוֹלָם אֲדֹנָי, מְחַיֵּה מֵתִים אַתָּה, רַב לְהוֹשִׁיעַ. מְכַלְכֵּל חַיִּים בְּחֶסֶד, מְחַיֵּה מֵתִים בְּרַחֲמִים רַבִּים, סוֹמֵךְ נוֹפְלִים, וְרוֹפֵא חוֹלִים, וּמַתִּיר אֲסוּרִים, וּמְקַיֵּם אֱמוּנָתוֹ לִישֵׁנֵי עָפָר. מִי כָמוֹךָ בַּעַל גְּבוּרוֹת, וּמִי דּוֹמֶה לָּךְ, מֶלֶךְ מֵמִית וּמְחַיֶּה וּמַצְמִיחַ יְשׁוּעָה. וְנֶאֱמָן אַתָּה לְהַחֲיוֹת מֵתִים. בָּרוּךְ אַתָּה יהוה, מְחַיֵּה הַמֵּתִים.

During the *chazzan's* repetition, *Kedushah* (page 600) is recited at this point.

devout ones will sing joyously. For the sake of David, Your servant, turn not away the face of Your anointed.[1] *For I have given you a good teaching, do not forsake My Torah.*[2] Chazzan– *It is a tree of life for those who grasp it, and its supporters are praiseworthy.*[3] *Its ways are ways of pleasantness and all its paths are peace.*[4] *Bring us back to You, HASHEM, and we shall return, renew our days as of old.*[5]

The Ark is closed and the *chazzan* recites Half *Kaddish*.

יִתְגַּדַּל *May His great Name grow exalted and sanctified* (Cong.– *Amen.*) *in the world that He created as He willed. May He give reign to His kingship in your lifetimes and in your days, and in the lifetimes of the entire Family of Israel, swiftly and soon. Now respond: Amen.*

(Cong.– *Amen. May His great Name be blessed forever and ever.*)

May His great Name be blessed forever and ever.

Blessed, praised, glorified, exalted, extolled, mighty, upraised, and lauded be the Name of the Holy One, Blessed is He (Cong.– *Blessed is He*) *— beyond any blessing and song, praise and consolation that are uttered in the world. Now respond: Amen.* (Cong.– *Amen.*)

SHEMONEH ESREI – AMIDAH

Take three steps backward, then three steps forward. Remain standing with the feet together while reciting *Shemoneh Esrei.* Recite it with quiet devotion and without interruption, verbal or otherwise. Although its recitation should not be audible to others, one must pray loudly enough to hear himself.

When I call out the Name of HASHEM, ascribe greatness to our God.[6]
My Lord, open my lips, that my mouth may declare Your praise.[7]

PATRIARCHS

Bend the knees at *'Blessed'*; bow at *'You'*; straighten up at *'HASHEM.'*

בָּרוּךְ *Blessed are You, HASHEM, our God and the God of our forefathers, God of Abraham, God of Isaac, and God of Jacob; the great, mighty, and awesome God, the supreme God, Who bestows beneficial kindnesses and creates everything, Who recalls the kindnesses of the Patriarchs and brings a Redeemer to their children's children, for His Name's sake, with love. O King, Helper, Savior, and Shield.*

Bend the knees at *'Blessed'*; bow at *'You'*; straighten up at *'HASHEM.'*

Blessed are You, HASHEM, Shield of Abraham.

GOD'S MIGHT

אַתָּה *You are eternally mighty, my Lord, the Resuscitator of the dead are You; abundantly able to save. He sustains the living with kindness, resuscitates the dead with abundant mercy, supports the fallen, heals the sick, releases the confined, and maintains His faith to those asleep in the dust. Who is like You, O Master of mighty deeds, and who is comparable to You, O King Who causes death and restores life and makes salvation sprout! And You are faithful to resuscitate the dead. Blessed are You, HASHEM, Who resuscitates the dead.*

During the *chazzan's* repetition, *Kedushah* (page 600) is recited at this point.

---

(1) *Psalms* 132:8-10. (2) *Proverbs* 4:2. (3) 3:18. (4) 3:17.
(5) *Lamentations* 5:21. (6) *Deuteronomy* 32:3. (7) *Psalms* 51:17.

קדושת השם

אַתָּה קָדוֹשׁ וְשִׁמְךָ קָדוֹשׁ, וּקְדוֹשִׁים בְּכָל יוֹם יְהַלְּלוּךָ סֶּלָה. בָּרוּךְ אַתָּה יהוה, הָאֵל הַקָּדוֹשׁ.

קדושת היום

אַתָּה אֶחָד* וְשִׁמְךָ אֶחָד, וּמִי כְּעַמְּךָ יִשְׂרָאֵל* גּוֹי אֶחָד בָּאָרֶץ, תִּפְאֶרֶת גְּדֻלָּה,* וַעֲטֶרֶת יְשׁוּעָה, יוֹם מְנוּחָה וּקְדֻשָּׁה לְעַמְּךָ נָתָתָּ, אַבְרָהָם יָגֵל, יִצְחָק יְרַנֵּן, יַעֲקֹב וּבָנָיו יָנוּחוּ בוֹ,* מְנוּחַת אַהֲבָה וּנְדָבָה, מְנוּחַת אֱמֶת וֶאֱמוּנָה, מְנוּחַת שָׁלוֹם וְשַׁלְוָה וְהַשְׁקֵט וָבֶטַח, מְנוּחָה שְׁלֵמָה שֶׁאַתָּה רוֹצֶה בָּהּ, יַכִּירוּ בָנֶיךָ וְיֵדְעוּ כִּי מֵאִתְּךָ הִיא מְנוּחָתָם,* וְעַל מְנוּחָתָם יַקְדִּישׁוּ אֶת שְׁמֶךָ.

אֱלֹהֵינוּ וֵאלֹהֵי אֲבוֹתֵינוּ, רְצֵה בִמְנוּחָתֵנוּ, קַדְּשֵׁנוּ בְּמִצְוֹתֶיךָ, וְתֵן חֶלְקֵנוּ בְּתוֹרָתֶךָ, שַׂבְּעֵנוּ מִטּוּבֶךָ, וְשַׂמְּחֵנוּ בִּישׁוּעָתֶךָ, וְטַהֵר לִבֵּנוּ לְעָבְדְּךָ בֶּאֱמֶת. וְהַנְחִילֵנוּ יהוה אֱלֹהֵינוּ בְּאַהֲבָה וּבְרָצוֹן שַׁבַּת קָדְשֶׁךָ, וְיָנוּחוּ בָם יִשְׂרָאֵל מְקַדְּשֵׁי שְׁמֶךָ. בָּרוּךְ אַתָּה יהוה, מְקַדֵּשׁ הַשַּׁבָּת.

קדושה

When reciting *Kedushah,* one must stand with his feet together and avoid any interruptions. One should rise on his toes when saying the words קָדוֹשׁ, קָדוֹשׁ, קָדוֹשׁ; בָּרוּךְ (of בָּרוּךְ כְּבוֹד); and יִמְלֹךְ.

Cong. then *Chazzan* – **נְקַדֵּשׁ** אֶת שִׁמְךָ בָּעוֹלָם, כְּשֵׁם שֶׁמַּקְדִּישִׁים אוֹתוֹ בִּשְׁמֵי מָרוֹם, כַּכָּתוּב עַל יַד נְבִיאֶךָ, וְקָרָא זֶה אֶל זֶה וְאָמַר:

All – קָדוֹשׁ קָדוֹשׁ קָדוֹשׁ יהוה צְבָאוֹת, מְלֹא כָל הָאָרֶץ כְּבוֹדוֹ.[1]

Chazzan – לְעֻמָּתָם בָּרוּךְ יֹאמֵרוּ:

All – בָּרוּךְ כְּבוֹד יהוה, מִמְּקוֹמוֹ.[2]

Chazzan – וּבְדִבְרֵי קָדְשְׁךָ כָּתוּב לֵאמֹר:

All – יִמְלֹךְ יהוה לְעוֹלָם, אֱלֹהַיִךְ צִיּוֹן לְדֹר וָדֹר, הַלְלוּיָהּ.[3]

Chazzan only concludes – לְדוֹר וָדוֹר נַגִּיד גָּדְלֶךָ וּלְנֵצַח נְצָחִים קְדֻשָּׁתְךָ נַקְדִּישׁ, וְשִׁבְחֲךָ אֱלֹהֵינוּ מִפִּינוּ לֹא יָמוּשׁ לְעוֹלָם וָעֶד, כִּי אֵל מֶלֶךְ גָּדוֹל וְקָדוֹשׁ אָתָּה. בָּרוּךְ אַתָּה יהוה, הָאֵל הַקָּדוֹשׁ.

Chazzan continues . . . אַתָּה אֶחָד (above).

אַתָּה אֶחָד — *You are One.* The opening verse is a clear reference to the verse (*Zechariah* 14:9) stating that when the final redemption comes, all the world will recognize the Oneness of God, meaning that there are no contradictions in His behavior. As noted above, the Sabbath *Minchah* alludes to the long-awaited day when history will attain God's goal of perfection. Thus the *Minchah Shemoneh Esrei* directs our focus not only to the holiness of the Sabbath day, but to the spiritual bliss of the future.

וּמִי כְּעַמְּךָ יִשְׂרָאֵל — *And who is like Your people Israel.* Israel is unique because it alone accepted the Torah and dedicated itself to God's service.

HOLINESS OF GOD'S NAME

אַתָּה *You are holy and Your Name is holy, and holy ones praise You every day, forever. Blessed are You, HASHEM, the holy God.*

SANCTIFICATION OF THE DAY

אַתָּה אֶחָד *You are One* and Your Name is One; and who is like Your people Israel,* one nation on earth. The splendor of greatness* and the crown of salvation, the day of contentment and holiness have You given to Your people. Abraham would rejoice, Isaac would exult, Jacob and his children would rest on it,* a rest of love and magnanimity, a rest of truth and faith, a rest of peace and serenity and tranquility and security, a perfect rest in which You find favor. May Your children recognize and know that from You comes their rest,* and through their rest, they will sanctify Your Name.*

אֱלֹהֵינוּ *Our God and the God of our fathers, may You be pleased with our rest. Sanctify us with Your commandments and grant our share in Your Torah; satisfy us from Your goodness and gladden us with Your salvation, and purify our heart to serve You sincerely. O HASHEM, our God, with love and favor grant us Your holy Sabbath as a heritage, and may Israel, the sanctifiers of Your Name, rest on them. Blessed are You, HASHEM, Who sanctifies the Sabbath.*

KEDUSHAH

When reciting *Kedushah*, one must stand with his feet together and avoid any interruptions. One should rise on his toes when saying *Holy, holy, holy; Blessed is;* and *HASHEM shall reign.*

Cong. then Chazzan – **נְקַדֵּשׁ** *We shall sanctify Your Name in this world, just as they sanctify it in heaven above, as it is written by Your prophet, "And one [angel] will call another and say:*

All – *'Holy, holy, holy is HASHEM, Master of Legions, the whole world is filled with His glory.' "*[1]

Chazzan – *Those facing them say 'Blessed':*

All – *'Blessed is the glory of HASHEM from His place.'*[2]

Chazzan – *And in Your holy Writings the following is written:*

All – *'HASHEM shall reign forever — your God, O Zion — from generation to generation, Halleluyah!'*[3]

Chazzan only concludes – *From generation to generation we shall relate Your greatness and for infinite eternities we shall proclaim Your holiness. Your praise, our God, shall not leave our mouth forever and ever, for You, O God, are a great and holy King. Blessed are You, HASHEM, the holy God.*

Chazzan continues אַתָּה אֶחָד, *You are One* . . . (above).

(1) *Isaiah* 6:3. (2) *Ezekiel* 3:12. (3) *Psalms* 146:10.

Consequently, God awarded Israel the spiritual gifts cited in the next verse.

תִּפְאֶרֶת גְּדֻלָּה — *The splendor of greatness.* Some interpret this to mean the Temple. Others interpret this phrase and the others in this verse as references to various aspects of Messianic times.

יַעֲקֹב וּבָנָיו יָנוּחוּ בוֹ — *Jacob and his children would rest on it.* The Sages derive from Scriptural verses that all three Patriarchs observed the Sabbath, even before the Torah was given. Only of Jacob, however, could it be said that all his children joined him in observing the day, because Abraham's Ishmael and Isaac's Esau were not righteous.

כִּי מֵאִתְּךָ הִיא מְנוּחָתָם — *That from You comes their rest.* The quality of our Sabbath rest, as we have just described it, is God-given; and this is because God Himself rested on the Sabbath.

עבודה

רְצֵה יהוה אֱלֹהֵינוּ בְּעַמְּךָ יִשְׂרָאֵל וּבִתְפִלָּתָם, וְהָשֵׁב אֶת הָעֲבוֹדָה לִדְבִיר בֵּיתֶךָ. וְאִשֵּׁי יִשְׂרָאֵל וּתְפִלָּתָם בְּאַהֲבָה תְקַבֵּל בְּרָצוֹן, וּתְהִי לְרָצוֹן תָּמִיד עֲבוֹדַת יִשְׂרָאֵל עַמֶּךָ.

During the *chazzan's* repetition, congregation responds אָמֵן as indicated.
[If the following paragraph is forgotten, repeat *Shemoneh Esrei*. See *Laws* §56.]

אֱלֹהֵינוּ וֵאלֹהֵי אֲבוֹתֵינוּ, יַעֲלֶה, וְיָבֹא, וְיַגִּיעַ, וְיֵרָאֶה, וְיֵרָצֶה, וְיִשָּׁמַע, וְיִפָּקֵד, וְיִזָּכֵר זִכְרוֹנֵנוּ וּפִקְדּוֹנֵנוּ, וְזִכְרוֹן אֲבוֹתֵינוּ, וְזִכְרוֹן מָשִׁיחַ בֶּן דָּוִד עַבְדֶּךָ, וְזִכְרוֹן יְרוּשָׁלַיִם עִיר קָדְשֶׁךָ, וְזִכְרוֹן כָּל עַמְּךָ בֵּית יִשְׂרָאֵל לְפָנֶיךָ, לִפְלֵיטָה לְטוֹבָה לְחֵן וּלְחֶסֶד וּלְרַחֲמִים, לְחַיִּים וּלְשָׁלוֹם בְּיוֹם חַג הַסֻּכּוֹת הַזֶּה. זָכְרֵנוּ יהוה אֱלֹהֵינוּ בּוֹ לְטוֹבָה (.Cong – אָמֵן), וּפָקְדֵנוּ בוֹ לִבְרָכָה (.Cong – אָמֵן), וְהוֹשִׁיעֵנוּ בוֹ לְחַיִּים (.Cong – אָמֵן). וּבִדְבַר יְשׁוּעָה וְרַחֲמִים, חוּס וְחָנֵּנוּ וְרַחֵם עָלֵינוּ וְהוֹשִׁיעֵנוּ, כִּי אֵלֶיךָ עֵינֵינוּ, כִּי אֵל מֶלֶךְ חַנּוּן וְרַחוּם אָתָּה.[1]

וְתֶחֱזֶינָה עֵינֵינוּ בְּשׁוּבְךָ לְצִיּוֹן בְּרַחֲמִים. בָּרוּךְ אַתָּה יהוה, הַמַּחֲזִיר שְׁכִינָתוֹ לְצִיּוֹן.

הודאה

Bow at מוֹדִים; straighten up at 'ה. In his repetition the *chazzan* should recite the entire מוֹדִים aloud, while the congregation recites מוֹדִים דְּרַבָּנָן softly.

מוֹדִים אֲנַחְנוּ לָךְ שָׁאַתָּה הוּא יהוה אֱלֹהֵינוּ וֵאלֹהֵי אֲבוֹתֵינוּ לְעוֹלָם וָעֶד. צוּר חַיֵּינוּ, מָגֵן יִשְׁעֵנוּ אַתָּה הוּא לְדוֹר וָדוֹר. נוֹדֶה לְּךָ וּנְסַפֵּר תְּהִלָּתֶךָ[2] עַל חַיֵּינוּ הַמְּסוּרִים בְּיָדֶךָ, וְעַל נִשְׁמוֹתֵינוּ הַפְּקוּדוֹת לָךְ, וְעַל נִסֶּיךָ שֶׁבְּכָל יוֹם עִמָּנוּ, וְעַל נִפְלְאוֹתֶיךָ וְטוֹבוֹתֶיךָ שֶׁבְּכָל עֵת, עֶרֶב וָבֹקֶר וְצָהֳרָיִם. הַטּוֹב כִּי לֹא כָלוּ רַחֲמֶיךָ, וְהַמְּרַחֵם כִּי לֹא תַמּוּ חֲסָדֶיךָ,[3] מֵעוֹלָם קִוִּינוּ לָךְ.

מודים דרבנן

מוֹדִים אֲנַחְנוּ לָךְ, שָׁאַתָּה הוּא יהוה אֱלֹהֵינוּ וֵאלֹהֵי אֲבוֹתֵינוּ, אֱלֹהֵי כָל בָּשָׂר, יוֹצְרֵנוּ, יוֹצֵר בְּרֵאשִׁית. בְּרָכוֹת וְהוֹדָאוֹת לְשִׁמְךָ הַגָּדוֹל וְהַקָּדוֹשׁ, עַל שֶׁהֶחֱיִיתָנוּ וְקִיַּמְתָּנוּ. כֵּן תְּחַיֵּנוּ וּתְקַיְּמֵנוּ, וְתֶאֱסוֹף גָּלֻיּוֹתֵינוּ לְחַצְרוֹת קָדְשֶׁךָ, לִשְׁמוֹר חֻקֶּיךָ וְלַעֲשׂוֹת רְצוֹנֶךָ, וּלְעָבְדְּךָ בְּלֵבָב שָׁלֵם, עַל שֶׁאֲנַחְנוּ מוֹדִים לָךְ. בָּרוּךְ אֵל הַהוֹדָאוֹת.

(1) Cf. *Nechemiah* 9:31. (2) Cf. *Psalms* 79:13. (3) Cf. *Lamentations* 3:22.

TEMPLE SERVICE

רְצֵה *Be favorable, HASHEM, our God, toward Your people Israel and their prayer and restore the service to the Holy of Holies of Your Temple. The fire-offerings of Israel and their prayer accept with love and favor, and may the service of Your people Israel always be favorable to You.*

During the *chazzan's* repetition, congregation responds *Amen* as indicated.
[If the following paragraph is forgotten, repeat *Shemoneh Esrei.* See *Laws* §56.]

אֱלֹהֵינוּ *Our God and God of our forefathers, may there rise, come, reach, be noted, be favored, be heard, be considered, and be remembered — the remembrance and consideration of ourselves; the remembrance of our forefathers; the remembrance of Messiah, son of David, Your servant; the remembrance of Jerusalem, the City of Your Holiness; the remembrance of Your entire people the Family of Israel — before You for deliverance, for goodness, for grace, for kindness, and for compassion, for life, and for peace on this day of the Festival of Succos. Remember us on it, HASHEM, our God, for goodness (*Cong.*– Amen); consider us on it for blessing (*Cong.*– Amen); and help us on it for life (*Cong.*– Amen). In the matter of salvation and compassion, pity, be gracious and compassionate with us and help us, for our eyes are turned to You, because You are God, the gracious and compassionate King.*[1]

וְתֶחֱזֶינָה *May our eyes behold Your return to Zion in compassion. Blessed are You, HASHEM, Who restores His Presence to Zion.*

THANKSGIVING [MODIM]

Bow at *'We gratefully thank You'*; straighten up at *'HASHEM.'* In his repetition the *chazzan* should recite the entire *Modim* aloud, while the congregation recites *Modim of the Rabbis* softly.

מוֹדִים *We gratefully thank You, for it is You Who are HASHEM, our God and the God of our forefathers for all eternity; Rock of our lives, Shield of our salvation are You from generation to generation. We shall thank You and relate Your praise*[2] *— for our lives, which are committed to Your power and for our souls that are entrusted to You; for Your miracles that are with us every day; and for Your wonders and favors in every season — evening, morning, and afternoon. The Beneficent One, for Your compassions were never exhausted, and the Compassionate One, for Your kindnesses never ended*[3] *— always have we put our hope in You.*

MODIM OF THE RABBIS

מוֹדִים *We gratefully thank You, for it is You Who are HASHEM, our God and the God of our forefathers, the God of all flesh, our Molder, the Molder of the universe. Blessings and thanks are due Your great and holy Name for You have given us life and sustained us. So may You continue to give us life and sustain us and gather our exiles to the Courtyards of Your Sanctuary, to observe Your decrees, to do Your will and to serve You wholeheartedly. [We thank You] for inspiring us to thank You. Blessed is the God of thanksgivings.*

וְעַל כֻּלָּם יִתְבָּרַךְ וְיִתְרוֹמַם שִׁמְךָ מַלְכֵּנוּ תָּמִיד לְעוֹלָם וָעֶד.

Bend the knees at בָּרוּךְ; bow at אַתָּה; straighten up at ה׳.

וְכֹל הַחַיִּים יוֹדְוּךָ סֶּלָה, וִיהַלְלוּ אֶת שִׁמְךָ בֶּאֱמֶת, הָאֵל יְשׁוּעָתֵנוּ וְעֶזְרָתֵנוּ סֶלָה. בָּרוּךְ אַתָּה יהוה, הַטּוֹב שִׁמְךָ וּלְךָ נָאֶה לְהוֹדוֹת.

שלום

שָׁלוֹם רָב עַל יִשְׂרָאֵל עַמְּךָ תָּשִׂים לְעוֹלָם, כִּי אַתָּה הוּא מֶלֶךְ אָדוֹן לְכָל הַשָּׁלוֹם. וְטוֹב בְּעֵינֶיךָ לְבָרֵךְ אֶת עַמְּךָ יִשְׂרָאֵל, בְּכָל עֵת וּבְכָל שָׁעָה בִּשְׁלוֹמֶךָ. בָּרוּךְ אַתָּה יהוה, הַמְּבָרֵךְ אֶת עַמּוֹ יִשְׂרָאֵל בַּשָּׁלוֹם.

יִהְיוּ לְרָצוֹן אִמְרֵי פִי וְהֶגְיוֹן לִבִּי לְפָנֶיךָ, יהוה צוּרִי וְגֹאֲלִי.[1]

Chazzan's repetition of *Shemoneh Esrei* ends here. Individuals continue below.

אֱלֹהַי, נְצוֹר לְשׁוֹנִי מֵרָע, וּשְׂפָתַי מִדַּבֵּר מִרְמָה,[2] וְלִמְקַלְלַי נַפְשִׁי תִדּוֹם, וְנַפְשִׁי כֶּעָפָר לַכֹּל תִּהְיֶה. פְּתַח לִבִּי בְּתוֹרָתֶךָ, וּבְמִצְוֹתֶיךָ תִּרְדּוֹף נַפְשִׁי. וְכֹל הַחוֹשְׁבִים עָלַי רָעָה, מְהֵרָה הָפֵר עֲצָתָם וְקַלְקֵל מַחֲשַׁבְתָּם. עֲשֵׂה לְמַעַן שְׁמֶךָ, עֲשֵׂה לְמַעַן יְמִינֶךָ, עֲשֵׂה לְמַעַן קְדֻשָּׁתֶךָ, עֲשֵׂה לְמַעַן תּוֹרָתֶךָ. לְמַעַן יֵחָלְצוּן יְדִידֶיךָ, הוֹשִׁיעָה יְמִינְךָ וַעֲנֵנִי.[3]

Some recite verses pertaining to their names. See page 1301.

יִהְיוּ לְרָצוֹן אִמְרֵי פִי וְהֶגְיוֹן לִבִּי לְפָנֶיךָ, יהוה צוּרִי וְגֹאֲלִי.[1]

Bow and take three steps back. Bow left and say . . . עֹשֶׂה, bow right and say . . . הוּא יַעֲשֶׂה; bow forward and say וְעַל כָּל . . . אָמֵן.

עֹשֶׂה שָׁלוֹם בִּמְרוֹמָיו, הוּא יַעֲשֶׂה שָׁלוֹם עָלֵינוּ, וְעַל כָּל יִשְׂרָאֵל. וְאִמְרוּ: אָמֵן.

יְהִי רָצוֹן מִלְּפָנֶיךָ יהוה אֱלֹהֵינוּ וֵאלֹהֵי אֲבוֹתֵינוּ, שֶׁיִּבָּנֶה בֵּית הַמִּקְדָּשׁ בִּמְהֵרָה בְיָמֵינוּ, וְתֵן חֶלְקֵנוּ בְּתוֹרָתֶךָ. וְשָׁם נַעֲבָדְךָ בְּיִרְאָה, כִּימֵי עוֹלָם וּכְשָׁנִים קַדְמוֹנִיּוֹת. וְעָרְבָה לַיהוה מִנְחַת יְהוּדָה וִירוּשָׁלָיִם, כִּימֵי עוֹלָם וּכְשָׁנִים קַדְמוֹנִיּוֹת.[4]

THE INDIVIDUAL'S RECITATION OF שְׁמוֹנֶה עֶשְׂרֵה ENDS HERE.

The individual remains standing in place until the *chazzan* reaches *Kedushah* — or at least until the *chazzan* begins his repetition — then he takes three steps forward. The *chazzan* himself, or one praying alone, should remain in place for a few moments before taking three steps forward.

For all these, may Your Name be blessed and exalted, our King, continually forever and ever.

Bend the knees at *'Blessed'*; bow at *'You'*; straighten up at *'HASHEM.'*

Everything alive will gratefully acknowledge You, Selah! and praise Your Name sincerely, O God of our salvation and help, Selah! Blessed are You, HASHEM, Your Name is 'The Beneficent One' and to You it is fitting to give thanks.

PEACE

שָׁלוֹם *Establish abundant peace upon Your people Israel forever, for You are King, Master of all peace. May it be good in Your eyes to bless Your people Israel at every time and every hour with Your peace. Blessed are You, HASHEM, Who blesses His people Israel with peace.*

May the expressions of my mouth and the thoughts of my heart find favor before You, HASHEM, my Rock and my Redeemer.[1]

Chazzan's repetition of *Shemoneh Esrei* ends here. Individuals continue below:

אֱלֹהַי *My God, guard my tongue from evil and my lips from speaking deceitfully.*[2] *To those who curse me, let my soul be silent; and let my soul be like dust to everyone. Open my heart to Your Torah, then my soul will pursue Your commandments. As for all those who design evil against me, speedily nullify their counsel and disrupt their design. Act for Your Name's sake; act for Your right hand's sake; act for Your sanctity's sake; act for Your Torah's sake. That Your beloved ones may be given rest; let Your right hand save, and respond to me.*[3]

Some recite verses pertaining to their names at this point. See page 1301.

May the expressions of my mouth and the thoughts of my heart find favor before You, HASHEM, my Rock and my Redeemer.[1] *He Who makes peace in His heights, may He make peace upon us, and upon all Israel. Now respond: Amen.*

Bow and take three steps back. Bow left and say, *'He Who makes peace . . .'*; bow right and say, *'may He make peace . . .'*; bow forward and say, *'and upon . . . Amen.'*

יְהִי רָצוֹן *May it be Your will, HASHEM, our God and the God of our forefathers, that the Holy Temple be rebuilt, speedily in our days. Grant us our share in Your Torah, and may we serve You there with reverence, as in days of old and in former years. Then the offering of Judah and Jerusalem will be pleasing to HASHEM, as in days of old and in former years.*[4]

THE INDIVIDUAL'S RECITATION OF *SHEMONEH ESREI* ENDS HERE.

The individual remains standing in place until the *chazzan* reaches *Kedushah* — or at least until the *chazzan* begins his repetition — then he takes three steps forward. The *chazzan* himself, or one praying alone, should remain in place for a few moments before taking three steps forward.

---

(1) *Psalms* 19:15. (2) Cf. 34:14. (3) 60:7; 108:7. (4) *Malachi* 3:4.

קדיש שלם

The *chazzan* recites קַדִּישׁ שָׁלֵם.

יִתְגַּדַּל וְיִתְקַדַּשׁ שְׁמֵהּ רַבָּא. (.Cong – אָמֵן.) בְּעָלְמָא דִּי בְרָא כִרְעוּתֵהּ. וְיַמְלִיךְ מַלְכוּתֵהּ, בְּחַיֵּיכוֹן וּבְיוֹמֵיכוֹן וּבְחַיֵּי דְכָל בֵּית יִשְׂרָאֵל, בַּעֲגָלָא וּבִזְמַן קָרִיב. וְאִמְרוּ: אָמֵן.

(.Cong – אָמֵן. יְהֵא שְׁמֵהּ רַבָּא מְבָרַךְ לְעָלַם וּלְעָלְמֵי עָלְמַיָּא.)

יְהֵא שְׁמֵהּ רַבָּא מְבָרַךְ לְעָלַם וּלְעָלְמֵי עָלְמַיָּא.

יִתְבָּרַךְ וְיִשְׁתַּבַּח וְיִתְפָּאַר וְיִתְרוֹמַם וְיִתְנַשֵּׂא וְיִתְהַדָּר וְיִתְעַלֶּה וְיִתְהַלָּל שְׁמֵהּ דְּקֻדְשָׁא בְּרִיךְ הוּא (.Cong – בְּרִיךְ הוּא) — לְעֵלָּא מִן כָּל בִּרְכָתָא וְשִׁירָתָא תֻּשְׁבְּחָתָא וְנֶחֱמָתָא, דַּאֲמִירָן בְּעָלְמָא. וְאִמְרוּ: אָמֵן. (.Cong – אָמֵן.)

(.Cong – קַבֵּל בְּרַחֲמִים וּבְרָצוֹן אֶת תְּפִלָּתֵנוּ.)

תִּתְקַבֵּל צְלוֹתְהוֹן וּבָעוּתְהוֹן דְּכָל בֵּית יִשְׂרָאֵל קֳדָם אֲבוּהוֹן דִּי בִשְׁמַיָּא. וְאִמְרוּ: אָמֵן. (.Cong – אָמֵן.)

(.Cong – יְהִי שֵׁם יהוה מְבֹרָךְ, מֵעַתָּה וְעַד עוֹלָם.[1])

יְהֵא שְׁלָמָא רַבָּא מִן שְׁמַיָּא, וְחַיִּים עָלֵינוּ וְעַל כָּל יִשְׂרָאֵל. וְאִמְרוּ: אָמֵן. (.Cong – אָמֵן.)

(.Cong – עֶזְרִי מֵעִם יהוה, עֹשֵׂה שָׁמַיִם וָאָרֶץ.[2])

Take three steps back. Bow left and say . . . עֹשֶׂה; bow right and say . . . הוּא; bow forward and say וְעַל כָּל . . . אָמֵן. Remain standing in place for a few moments, then take three steps forward.

עֹשֶׂה שָׁלוֹם בִּמְרוֹמָיו, הוּא יַעֲשֶׂה שָׁלוֹם עָלֵינוּ, וְעַל כָּל יִשְׂרָאֵל. וְאִמְרוּ: אָמֵן. (.Cong – אָמֵן.)

עלינו

Stand while reciting עָלֵינוּ.

עָלֵינוּ לְשַׁבֵּחַ לַאֲדוֹן הַכֹּל, לָתֵת גְּדֻלָּה לְיוֹצֵר בְּרֵאשִׁית, שֶׁלֹּא עָשָׂנוּ כְּגוֹיֵי הָאֲרָצוֹת, וְלֹא שָׂמָנוּ כְּמִשְׁפְּחוֹת הָאֲדָמָה. שֶׁלֹּא שָׂם חֶלְקֵנוּ כָּהֶם, וְגוֹרָלֵנוּ כְּכָל הֲמוֹנָם. (שֶׁהֵם מִשְׁתַּחֲוִים לְהֶבֶל וָרִיק, וּמִתְפַּלְלִים אֶל אֵל לֹא יוֹשִׁיעַ.[3]) וַאֲנַחְנוּ כּוֹרְעִים וּמִשְׁתַּחֲוִים וּמוֹדִים, לִפְנֵי מֶלֶךְ מַלְכֵי הַמְּלָכִים הַקָּדוֹשׁ בָּרוּךְ הוּא. שֶׁהוּא נוֹטֶה שָׁמַיִם וְיֹסֵד אָרֶץ,[4] וּמוֹשַׁב יְקָרוֹ בַּשָּׁמַיִם מִמַּעַל, וּשְׁכִינַת עֻזּוֹ בְּגָבְהֵי מְרוֹמִים. הוּא אֱלֹהֵינוּ, אֵין עוֹד. אֱמֶת מַלְכֵּנוּ, אֶפֶס זוּלָתוֹ, כַּכָּתוּב בְּתוֹרָתוֹ: וְיָדַעְתָּ הַיּוֹם וַהֲשֵׁבֹתָ אֶל לְבָבֶךָ, כִּי יהוה הוּא הָאֱלֹהִים בַּשָּׁמַיִם מִמַּעַל וְעַל הָאָרֶץ מִתָּחַת, אֵין עוֹד.[5]

Bow while reciting וַאֲנַחְנוּ כּוֹרְעִים וּמִשְׁתַּחֲוִים.

FULL KADDISH

The *chazzan* recites the Full *Kaddish.*

יִתְגַּדַּל *May His great Name grow exalted and sanctified* (Cong.– *Amen.*) *in the world that He created as He willed. May He give reign to His kingship in your lifetimes and in your days, and in the lifetimes of the entire Family of Israel, swiftly and soon. Now respond: Amen.*

(Cong.– *Amen. May His great Name be blessed forever and ever.*)

May His great Name be blessed forever and ever.

Blessed, praised, glorified, exalted, extolled, mighty, upraised, and lauded be the Name of the Holy One, Blessed is He (Cong.– *Blessed is He*) — *beyond any blessing and song, praise and consolation that are uttered in the world. Now respond: Amen.* (Cong.– *Amen.*)

(Cong.– *Accept our prayers with mercy and favor.*)

May the prayers and supplications of the entire Family of Israel be accepted before their Father Who is in Heaven. Now respond: Amen. (Cong.– *Amen.*)

(Cong.– *Blessed be the Name of* HASHEM, *from this time and forever.*[1])

May there be abundant peace from Heaven, and life, upon us and upon all Israel. Now respond: Amen. (Cong.– *Amen.*)

(Cong.– *My help is from* HASHEM, *Maker of heaven and earth.*[2])

Take three steps back. Bow left and say, *'He Who makes peace . . .';* bow right and say, *'may He . . .';* bow forward and say, *'and upon all Israel . . .'* Remain standing in place for a few moments, then take three steps forward.

He Who makes peace in His heights, may He make peace upon us, and upon all Israel. Now respond: Amen. (Cong.– *Amen.*)

ALEINU

Stand while reciting עָלֵינוּ, *'It is our duty . . .'*

עָלֵינוּ *It is our duty to praise the Master of all, to ascribe greatness to the Molder of primeval creation, for He has not made us like the nations of the lands, and has not emplaced us like the families of the earth; for He has not assigned our portion like theirs nor our lot like all their multitudes. (For they bow to vanity and emptiness and pray to a god which helps not.*[3]*) But we bend our knees, bow, and acknowledge our thanks before the King Who reigns over kings, the Holy One, Blessed is He. He stretches out heaven and establishes earth's foundation,*[4] *the seat of His homage is in the heavens above and His powerful Presence is in the loftiest heights. He is our God and there is none other. True is our King, there is nothing beside Him, as it is written in His Torah: 'You are to know this day and take to your heart that* HASHEM *is the only God — in heaven above and on the earth below — there is none other.'*[5]

Bow while reciting *'But we bend our knees.'*

---

(1) *Psalms* 113:2. (2) 121:2. (3) *Isaiah* 45:20. (4) 51:13. (5) *Deuteronomy* 4:39.

עַל כֵּן נְקַוֶּה לְּךָ יהוה אֱלֹהֵינוּ לִרְאוֹת מְהֵרָה בְּתִפְאֶרֶת עֻזֶּךָ, לְהַעֲבִיר גִּלּוּלִים מִן הָאָרֶץ, וְהָאֱלִילִים כָּרוֹת יִכָּרֵתוּן, לְתַקֵּן עוֹלָם בְּמַלְכוּת שַׁדַּי. וְכָל בְּנֵי בָשָׂר יִקְרְאוּ בִשְׁמֶךָ, לְהַפְנוֹת אֵלֶיךָ כָּל רִשְׁעֵי אָרֶץ. יַכִּירוּ וְיֵדְעוּ כָּל יוֹשְׁבֵי תֵבֵל, כִּי לְךָ תִּכְרַע כָּל בֶּרֶךְ, תִּשָּׁבַע כָּל לָשׁוֹן.[1] לְפָנֶיךָ יהוה אֱלֹהֵינוּ יִכְרְעוּ וְיִפֹּלוּ, וְלִכְבוֹד שִׁמְךָ יְקָר יִתֵּנוּ. וִיקַבְּלוּ כֻלָּם אֶת עוֹל מַלְכוּתֶךָ, וְתִמְלֹךְ עֲלֵיהֶם מְהֵרָה לְעוֹלָם וָעֶד. כִּי הַמַּלְכוּת שֶׁלְּךָ הִיא וּלְעוֹלְמֵי עַד תִּמְלוֹךְ בְּכָבוֹד, כַּכָּתוּב בְּתוֹרָתֶךָ: יהוה יִמְלֹךְ לְעֹלָם וָעֶד.[2] ❖ וְנֶאֱמַר: וְהָיָה יהוה לְמֶלֶךְ עַל כָּל הָאָרֶץ, בַּיּוֹם הַהוּא יִהְיֶה יהוה אֶחָד וּשְׁמוֹ אֶחָד.[3]

Some congregations recite the following after עָלֵינוּ:

אַל תִּירָא מִפַּחַד פִּתְאֹם, וּמִשֹּׁאַת רְשָׁעִים כִּי תָבֹא.[4] עֻצוּ עֵצָה וְתֻפָר, דַּבְּרוּ דָבָר וְלֹא יָקוּם, כִּי עִמָּנוּ אֵל.[5] וְעַד זִקְנָה אֲנִי הוּא, וְעַד שֵׂיבָה אֲנִי אֶסְבֹּל, אֲנִי עָשִׂיתִי וַאֲנִי אֶשָּׂא, וַאֲנִי אֶסְבֹּל וַאֲמַלֵּט.[5]

קדיש יתום

In the presence of a *minyan,* mourners recite קַדִּישׁ יָתוֹם, the Mourner's *Kaddish* (see *Laws* §81-83).

יִתְגַּדַּל וְיִתְקַדַּשׁ שְׁמֵהּ רַבָּא. (.Cong – אָמֵן.) בְּעָלְמָא דִּי בְרָא כִרְעוּתֵהּ. וְיַמְלִיךְ מַלְכוּתֵהּ, בְּחַיֵּיכוֹן וּבְיוֹמֵיכוֹן וּבְחַיֵּי דְכָל בֵּית יִשְׂרָאֵל, בַּעֲגָלָא וּבִזְמַן קָרִיב. וְאִמְרוּ: אָמֵן.

(.Cong – אָמֵן. יְהֵא שְׁמֵהּ רַבָּא מְבָרַךְ לְעָלַם וּלְעָלְמֵי עָלְמַיָּא.)

יְהֵא שְׁמֵהּ רַבָּא מְבָרַךְ לְעָלַם וּלְעָלְמֵי עָלְמַיָּא.

יִתְבָּרַךְ וְיִשְׁתַּבַּח וְיִתְפָּאַר וְיִתְרוֹמַם וְיִתְנַשֵּׂא וְיִתְהַדָּר וְיִתְעַלֶּה וְיִתְהַלָּל שְׁמֵהּ דְּקֻדְשָׁא בְּרִיךְ הוּא (.Cong – בְּרִיךְ הוּא) — לְעֵלָּא מִן כָּל בִּרְכָתָא וְשִׁירָתָא תֻּשְׁבְּחָתָא וְנֶחֱמָתָא, דַּאֲמִירָן בְּעָלְמָא. וְאִמְרוּ: אָמֵן. (.Cong – אָמֵן.)

יְהֵא שְׁלָמָא רַבָּא מִן שְׁמַיָּא, וְחַיִּים עָלֵינוּ וְעַל כָּל יִשְׂרָאֵל. וְאִמְרוּ: אָמֵן. (.Cong – אָמֵן.)

Take three steps back. Bow left and say . . . עֹשֶׂה; bow right and say . . . הוּא; bow forward and say וְעַל כָּל . . . אָמֵן. Remain standing in place for a few moments, then take three steps forward.

עֹשֶׂה שָׁלוֹם בִּמְרוֹמָיו, הוּא יַעֲשֶׂה שָׁלוֹם עָלֵינוּ, וְעַל כָּל יִשְׂרָאֵל. וְאִמְרוּ: אָמֵן. (.Cong – אָמֵן.)

עַל כֵּן *Therefore we put our hope in You, HASHEM, our God, that we may soon see Your mighty splendor, to remove detestable idolatry from the earth, and false gods will be utterly cut off, to perfect the universe through the Almighty's sovereignty. Then all humanity will call upon Your Name, to turn all the earth's wicked toward You. All the world's inhabitants will recognize and know that to You every knee should bend, every tongue should swear.*[1] *Before You, HASHEM, our God, they will bend every knee and cast themselves down and to the glory of Your Name they will render homage, and they will all accept upon themselves the yoke of Your kingship that You may reign over them soon and eternally. For the kingdom is Yours and You will reign for all eternity in glory as it is written in Your Torah: HASHEM shall reign for all eternity.*[2] Chazzan– *And it is said: HASHEM will be King over all the world — on that day HASHEM will be One and His Name will be One.*[3]

Some congregations recite the following after *Aleinu.*

אַל תִּירָא *Do not fear sudden terror, or the holocaust of the wicked when it comes.*[4] *Plan a conspiracy and it will be annulled; speak your piece and it shall not stand, for God is with us.*[5] *Even till your seniority, I remain unchanged; and even till your ripe old age, I shall endure. I created you and I shall bear you; I shall endure and rescue.*[6]

MOURNER'S KADDISH

In the presence of a *minyan,* mourners recite קַדִּישׁ יָתוֹם, the Mourner's *Kaddish* (see *Laws* 81-83).
[A transliteration of this *Kaddish* appears on page 1305.]

יִתְגַּדַּל *May His great Name grow exalted and sanctified* (Cong.– *Amen.*) *in the world that He created as He willed. May He give reign to His kingship in your lifetimes and in your days, and in the lifetimes of the entire Family of Israel, swiftly and soon. Now respond: Amen.*

(Cong.– *Amen. May His great Name be blessed forever and ever.*)

May His great Name be blessed forever and ever.

Blessed, praised, glorified, exalted, extolled, mighty, upraised, and lauded be the Name of the Holy One, Blessed is He (Cong.– *Blessed is He*) *— beyond any blessing and song, praise and consolation that are uttered in the world. Now respond: Amen.* (Cong.– *Amen*).

May there be abundant peace from Heaven, and life, upon us and upon all Israel. Now respond: Amen. (Cong.– *Amen.*)

Take three steps back. Bow left and say, *'He Who makes peace . . .';* bow right and say, *'may He . . .';* bow forward and say, *'and upon all Israel . . .'* Remain standing in place for a few moments, then take three steps forward.

He Who makes peace in His heights, may He make peace upon us, and upon all Israel. Now respond: Amen. (Cong.– *Amen.*)

---

(1) Cf. *Isaiah* 45:23. (2) *Exodus* 15:18. (3) *Zechariah* 14:9. (4) *Proverbs* 3:25. (5) *Isaiah* 8:10. (6) 46:4.

חול המועד
והושענא רבה

Chol HaMoed
and Hoshana Rabbah

מעריב לחול המועד ולמוצאי שבת

ON ALL CHOL HAMOED NIGHTS OTHER THAN FRIDAY NIGHT BEGIN HERE.
ON FRIDAY NIGHT, TURN TO PAGE 426.

Congregation, then *chazzan:*

וְהוּא רַחוּם יְכַפֵּר עָוֹן וְלֹא יַשְׁחִית, וְהִרְבָּה לְהָשִׁיב אַפּוֹ, וְלֹא יָעִיר כָּל חֲמָתוֹ.[1] יהוה הוֹשִׁיעָה, הַמֶּלֶךְ יַעֲנֵנוּ בְיוֹם קָרְאֵנוּ.[2]

In some congregations the *chazzan* chants a melody during his recitation of בָּרְכוּ, so that the congregation can then recite יִתְבָּרַךְ.

Chazzan bows at בָּרְכוּ and straightens up at ה׳.

בָּרְכוּ אֶת יהוה הַמְּבֹרָךְ.

Congregation, followed by *chazzan,* responds, bowing at בָּרוּךְ and straightening up at ה׳.

בָּרוּךְ יהוה הַמְּבֹרָךְ לְעוֹלָם וָעֶד.

יִתְבָּרַךְ וְיִשְׁתַּבַּח וְיִתְפָּאַר וְיִתְרוֹמַם וְיִתְנַשֵּׂא שְׁמוֹ שֶׁל מֶלֶךְ מַלְכֵי הַמְּלָכִים, הַקָּדוֹשׁ בָּרוּךְ הוּא. שֶׁהוּא רִאשׁוֹן וְהוּא אַחֲרוֹן, וּמִבַּלְעָדָיו אֵין אֱלֹהִים.[3] סֹלּוּ, לָרֹכֵב בָּעֲרָבוֹת, בְּיָהּ שְׁמוֹ, וְעִלְזוּ לְפָנָיו.[4] וּשְׁמוֹ מְרוֹמָם עַל כָּל בְּרָכָה וּתְהִלָּה.[5] בָּרוּךְ שֵׁם כְּבוֹד מַלְכוּתוֹ לְעוֹלָם וָעֶד. יְהִי שֵׁם יהוה מְבֹרָךְ, מֵעַתָּה וְעַד עוֹלָם.[6]

ברכות קריאת שמע

בָּרוּךְ אַתָּה יהוה אֱלֹהֵינוּ מֶלֶךְ הָעוֹלָם, אֲשֶׁר בִּדְבָרוֹ מַעֲרִיב עֲרָבִים, בְּחָכְמָה פּוֹתֵחַ שְׁעָרִים, וּבִתְבוּנָה מְשַׁנֶּה עִתִּים, וּמַחֲלִיף אֶת הַזְּמַנִּים, וּמְסַדֵּר אֶת הַכּוֹכָבִים בְּמִשְׁמְרוֹתֵיהֶם בָּרָקִיעַ כִּרְצוֹנוֹ. בּוֹרֵא יוֹם וָלָיְלָה, גּוֹלֵל אוֹר מִפְּנֵי חֹשֶׁךְ וְחֹשֶׁךְ מִפְּנֵי אוֹר. וּמַעֲבִיר יוֹם וּמֵבִיא לָיְלָה, וּמַבְדִּיל בֵּין יוֹם וּבֵין לָיְלָה, יהוה צְבָאוֹת שְׁמוֹ. ❖ אֵל חַי וְקַיָּם, תָּמִיד יִמְלוֹךְ עָלֵינוּ, לְעוֹלָם וָעֶד. בָּרוּךְ אַתָּה יהוה, הַמַּעֲרִיב עֲרָבִים. (.Cong – אָמֵן.)

אַהֲבַת עוֹלָם בֵּית יִשְׂרָאֵל עַמְּךָ אָהָבְתָּ. תּוֹרָה וּמִצְוֹת, חֻקִּים וּמִשְׁפָּטִים, אוֹתָנוּ לִמַּדְתָּ. עַל כֵּן יהוה אֱלֹהֵינוּ, בְּשָׁכְבֵנוּ וּבְקוּמֵנוּ נָשִׂיחַ בְּחֻקֶּיךָ, וְנִשְׂמַח בְּדִבְרֵי תוֹרָתֶךָ, וּבְמִצְוֹתֶיךָ לְעוֹלָם וָעֶד. ❖ כִּי הֵם חַיֵּינוּ, וְאֹרֶךְ יָמֵינוּ, וּבָהֶם נֶהְגֶּה יוֹמָם וָלָיְלָה. וְאַהֲבָתְךָ, אַל תָּסִיר מִמֶּנּוּ לְעוֹלָמִים. בָּרוּךְ אַתָּה יהוה, אוֹהֵב עַמּוֹ יִשְׂרָאֵל. (.Cong – אָמֵן.)

MAARIV FOR CHOL HAMOED & CONCLUSION OF SABBATH

ON ALL CHOL HAMOED NIGHTS OTHER THAN FRIDAY NIGHT BEGIN HERE.
ON FRIDAY NIGHT, TURN TO PAGE 426.

Congregation, then *chazzan:*

וְהוּא רַחוּם *He, the Merciful One, is forgiving of iniquity and does not destroy. Frequently He withdraws His anger, not arousing His entire rage.*[1] *HASHEM, save! May the King answer us on the day we call.*[2]

In some congregations the *chazzan* chants a melody during his recitation of *Borchu* so that the congregation can then recite *'Blessed, praised . . .'*

Chazzan bows at *'Bless,'* and straightens up at *'HASHEM.'*

Bless HASHEM, the blessed One.

Congregation, followed by *chazzan,* responds, bowing at *'Blessed'* and straightening up at *'HASHEM.'*

Blessed is HASHEM, the blessed One, for all eternity.

Blessed, praised, glorified, exalted and upraised is the Name of the King Who rules over kings — the Holy One, Blessed is He. For He is the First and He is the Last and aside from Him there is no god.[3] *Extol Him — Who rides the highest heavens — with His Name, YAH, and exult before Him.*[4] *His Name is exalted beyond every blessing and praise.*[5] *Blessed is the Name of His glorious kingdom for all eternity. Blessed be the Name of HASHEM from this time and forever.*[6]

BLESSINGS OF THE SHEMA

בָּרוּךְ *Blessed are You, HASHEM, our God, King of the universe, Who by His word brings on evenings, with wisdom opens gates, with understanding alters periods, changes the seasons, and orders the stars in their heavenly constellations as He wills. He creates day and night, removing light before darkness and darkness before light. He causes day to pass and brings night, and separates between day and night — HASHEM, Master of Legions, is His Name.* Chazzan– *May the living and enduring God continuously reign over us, for all eternity. Blessed are You, HASHEM, Who brings on evenings.* (Cong.– *Amen.)*

אַהֲבַת *With an eternal love have You loved the House of Israel, Your nation. Torah and commandments, decrees and ordinances have You taught us. Therefore HASHEM, our God, upon our retiring and arising, we will discuss Your decrees and we will rejoice with the words of Your Torah and with Your commandments for all eternity.* Chazzan– *For they are our life and the length of our days and about them we will meditate day and night. May You not remove Your love from us forever. Blessed are You, HASHEM, Who loves His nation Israel.* (Cong.– *Amen.)*

(1) *Psalms* 78:38. (2) 20:10. (3) Cf. *Isaiah* 44:6. (4) *Psalms* 68:5.
(5) Cf. *Nechemiah* 9:5. (6) *Psalms* 113.2.

שמע

Immediately before its recitation, concentrate on fulfilling the positive commandment of reciting the *Shema* twice daily. It is important to enunciate each word clearly and not to run words together. For this reason, vertical lines have been placed between two words that are prone to be slurred into one and are not separated by a comma or a hyphen. See *Laws* §40-52.

When praying without a *minyan,* begin with the following three-word formula:

אֵל מֶלֶךְ נֶאֱמָן.

Recite the first verse aloud, with the right hand covering the eyes, and concentrate intently upon accepting God's absolute sovereignty.

שְׁמַע | יִשְׂרָאֵל, יְהֹוָה | אֱלֹהֵינוּ, יְהֹוָה | אֶחָד:

– In an undertone בָּרוּךְ שֵׁם כְּבוֹד מַלְכוּתוֹ לְעוֹלָם וָעֶד.

While reciting the first paragraph (דברים ו:ה-ט), concentrate on accepting the commandment to love God.

וְאָהַבְתָּ אֵת | יְהֹוָה | אֱלֹהֶיךָ, בְּכָל־לְבָבְךָ, וּבְכָל־נַפְשְׁךָ, וּבְכָל־
מְאֹדֶךָ: וְהָיוּ הַדְּבָרִים הָאֵלֶּה, אֲשֶׁר | אָנֹכִי מְצַוְּךָ הַיּוֹם,
עַל־לְבָבֶךָ: וְשִׁנַּנְתָּם לְבָנֶיךָ, וְדִבַּרְתָּ בָּם, בְּשִׁבְתְּךָ בְּבֵיתֶךָ, וּבְלֶכְתְּךָ
בַדֶּרֶךְ, וּבְשָׁכְבְּךָ וּבְקוּמֶךָ: וּקְשַׁרְתָּם לְאוֹת | עַל־יָדֶךָ, וְהָיוּ לְטֹטָפֹת
בֵּין | עֵינֶיךָ: וּכְתַבְתָּם | עַל־מְזֻזוֹת בֵּיתֶךָ, וּבִשְׁעָרֶיךָ:

While reciting the second paragraph (דברים יא:יג-כא), concentrate on accepting all the commandments and the concept of reward and punishment.

וְהָיָה, אִם־שָׁמֹעַ תִּשְׁמְעוּ אֶל־מִצְוֺתַי, אֲשֶׁר | אָנֹכִי מְצַוֶּה |
אֶתְכֶם הַיּוֹם, לְאַהֲבָה אֶת־יְהֹוָה | אֱלֹהֵיכֶם וּלְעָבְדוֹ,
בְּכָל־לְבַבְכֶם, וּבְכָל־נַפְשְׁכֶם: וְנָתַתִּי מְטַר־אַרְצְכֶם בְּעִתּוֹ, יוֹרֶה
וּמַלְקוֹשׁ, וְאָסַפְתָּ דְגָנֶךָ וְתִירֹשְׁךָ וְיִצְהָרֶךָ: וְנָתַתִּי | עֵשֶׂב | בְּשָׂדְךָ
לִבְהֶמְתֶּךָ, וְאָכַלְתָּ וְשָׂבָעְתָּ: הִשָּׁמְרוּ לָכֶם, פֶּן־יִפְתֶּה לְבַבְכֶם,
וְסַרְתֶּם וַעֲבַדְתֶּם | אֱלֹהִים | אֲחֵרִים, וְהִשְׁתַּחֲוִיתֶם לָהֶם: וְחָרָה |
אַף־יְהֹוָה בָּכֶם, וְעָצַר | אֶת־הַשָּׁמַיִם, וְלֹא־יִהְיֶה מָטָר, וְהָאֲדָמָה לֹא
תִתֵּן אֶת־יְבוּלָהּ, וַאֲבַדְתֶּם | מְהֵרָה מֵעַל הָאָרֶץ הַטֹּבָה | אֲשֶׁר |
יְהֹוָה נֹתֵן לָכֶם: וְשַׂמְתֶּם | אֶת־דְּבָרַי | אֵלֶּה, עַל־לְבַבְכֶם וְעַל־
נַפְשְׁכֶם, וּקְשַׁרְתֶּם | אֹתָם לְאוֹת | עַל־יֶדְכֶם, וְהָיוּ לְטוֹטָפֹת בֵּין |
עֵינֵיכֶם: וְלִמַּדְתֶּם | אֹתָם | אֶת־בְּנֵיכֶם, לְדַבֵּר בָּם, בְּשִׁבְתְּךָ
בְּבֵיתֶךָ, וּבְלֶכְתְּךָ בַדֶּרֶךְ, וּבְשָׁכְבְּךָ וּבְקוּמֶךָ: וּכְתַבְתָּם | עַל־מְזוּזוֹת
בֵּיתֶךָ, וּבִשְׁעָרֶיךָ: לְמַעַן | יִרְבּוּ | יְמֵיכֶם וִימֵי בְנֵיכֶם, עַל הָאֲדָמָה |
אֲשֶׁר נִשְׁבַּע | יְהֹוָה לַאֲבֹתֵיכֶם לָתֵת לָהֶם, כִּימֵי הַשָּׁמַיִם |
עַל־הָאָרֶץ:

THE SHEMA

Immediately before its recitation, concentrate on fulfilling the positive commandment of reciting the *Shema* twice daily. It is important to enunciate each word clearly and not to run words together. See *Laws* §40-52.

When praying without a *minyan*, begin with the following three-word formula:

God, trustworthy King.

Recite the first verse aloud, with the right hand covering the eyes, and concentrate intently upon accepting God's absolute sovereignty.

Hear, O Israel: HASHEM is our God, HASHEM, the One and Only.[1]

In an undertone— *Blessed is the Name of His glorious kingdom for all eternity.*

While reciting the first paragraph (*Deuteronomy* 6:5-9), concentrate on accepting the commandment to love God.

וְאָהַבְתָּ *You shall love HASHEM, your God, with all your heart, with all your soul and with all your resources. Let these matters that I command you today be upon your heart. Teach them thoroughly to your children and speak of them while you sit in your home, while you walk on the way, when you retire and when you arise. Bind them as a sign upon your arm and let them be tefillin between your eyes. And write them on the doorposts of your house and upon your gates.*

While reciting the second paragraph (*Deuteronomy* 11:13-21), concentrate on accepting all the commandments and the concept of reward and punishment.

וְהָיָה *And it will come to pass that if you continually hearken to My commandments that I command you today, to love HASHEM, your God, and to serve Him, with all your heart and with all your soul — then I will provide rain for your land in its proper time, the early and late rains, that you may gather in your grain, your wine, and your oil. I will provide grass in your field for your cattle and you will eat and be satisfied. Beware lest your heart be seduced and you turn astray and serve gods of others and bow to them. Then the wrath of HASHEM will blaze against you. He will restrain the heaven so there will be no rain and the ground will not yield its produce. And you will swiftly be banished from the goodly land which HASHEM gives you. Place these words of Mine upon your heart and upon your soul; bind them for a sign upon your arm and let them be tefillin between your eyes. Teach them to your children, to discuss them, while you sit in your home, while you walk on the way, when you retire and when you arise. And write them on the doorposts of your house and upon your gates. In order to prolong your days and the days of your children upon the ground that HASHEM has sworn to your ancestors to give them, like the days of the heaven on the earth.*

---

(1) *Deuteronomy* 6:4.

במדבר טו:לז-מא

וַיֹּאמֶר | יְהוָה | אֶל־מֹשֶׁה לֵּאמֹר: דַּבֵּר | אֶל־בְּנֵי | יִשְׂרָאֵל, וְאָמַרְתָּ אֲלֵהֶם, וְעָשׂוּ לָהֶם צִיצִת, עַל־כַּנְפֵי בִגְדֵיהֶם לְדֹרֹתָם, וְנָתְנוּ | עַל־צִיצִת הַכָּנָף, פְּתִיל תְּכֵלֶת: וְהָיָה לָכֶם לְצִיצִת, וּרְאִיתֶם | אֹתוֹ, וּזְכַרְתֶּם | אֶת־כָּל־מִצְוֹת | יְהוָה, וַעֲשִׂיתֶם | אֹתָם, וְלֹא תָתוּרוּ | אַחֲרֵי לְבַבְכֶם וְאַחֲרֵי | עֵינֵיכֶם, אֲשֶׁר־אַתֶּם זֹנִים | אַחֲרֵיהֶם: לְמַעַן תִּזְכְּרוּ, וַעֲשִׂיתֶם | אֶת־כָּל־מִצְוֹתָי, וִהְיִיתֶם קְדֹשִׁים לֵאלֹהֵיכֶם: אֲנִי יְהוָה | אֱלֹהֵיכֶם, אֲשֶׁר הוֹצֵאתִי | אֶתְכֶם | מֵאֶרֶץ מִצְרַיִם, לִהְיוֹת לָכֶם לֵאלֹהִים, אֲנִי | יְהוָה | אֱלֹהֵיכֶם: אֱמֶת —

Concentrate on fulfilling the commandment of remembering the Exodus from Egypt.

Although the word אֱמֶת belongs to the next paragraph, it is appended to the conclusion of the previous one, as explained in the commentary on page 42.

—*Chazzan* repeats **יהוה אֱלֹהֵיכֶם אֱמֶת.**

וֶאֱמוּנָה כָּל זֹאת, וְקַיָּם עָלֵינוּ, כִּי הוּא יהוה אֱלֹהֵינוּ וְאֵין זוּלָתוֹ, וַאֲנַחְנוּ יִשְׂרָאֵל עַמּוֹ. הַפּוֹדֵנוּ מִיַּד מְלָכִים, מַלְכֵּנוּ הַגּוֹאֲלֵנוּ מִכַּף כָּל הֶעָרִיצִים. הָאֵל הַנִּפְרָע לָנוּ מִצָּרֵינוּ, וְהַמְשַׁלֵּם גְּמוּל לְכָל אֹיְבֵי נַפְשֵׁנוּ. הָעֹשֶׂה גְדֹלוֹת עַד אֵין חֵקֶר, וְנִפְלָאוֹת עַד אֵין מִסְפָּר.[1] הַשָּׂם נַפְשֵׁנוּ בַּחַיִּים, וְלֹא נָתַן לַמּוֹט רַגְלֵנוּ.[2] הַמַּדְרִיכֵנוּ עַל בָּמוֹת אוֹיְבֵינוּ, וַיָּרֶם קַרְנֵנוּ עַל כָּל שֹׂנְאֵינוּ. הָעֹשֶׂה לָּנוּ נִסִּים וּנְקָמָה בְּפַרְעֹה, אוֹתוֹת וּמוֹפְתִים בְּאַדְמַת בְּנֵי חָם. הַמַּכֶּה בְעֶבְרָתוֹ כָּל בְּכוֹרֵי מִצְרָיִם, וַיּוֹצֵא אֶת עַמּוֹ יִשְׂרָאֵל מִתּוֹכָם לְחֵרוּת עוֹלָם. הַמַּעֲבִיר בָּנָיו בֵּין גִּזְרֵי יַם סוּף, אֶת רוֹדְפֵיהֶם וְאֶת שׂוֹנְאֵיהֶם בִּתְהוֹמוֹת טִבַּע. וְרָאוּ בָנָיו גְּבוּרָתוֹ, שִׁבְּחוּ וְהוֹדוּ לִשְׁמוֹ. ❖ וּמַלְכוּתוֹ בְּרָצוֹן קִבְּלוּ עֲלֵיהֶם. מֹשֶׁה וּבְנֵי יִשְׂרָאֵל לְךָ עָנוּ שִׁירָה, בְּשִׂמְחָה רַבָּה, וְאָמְרוּ כֻלָּם:

מִי כָמֹכָה בָּאֵלִם יהוה, מִי כָּמֹכָה נֶאְדָּר בַּקֹּדֶשׁ, נוֹרָא תְהִלֹּת, עֹשֵׂה פֶלֶא.[3] ❖ מַלְכוּתְךָ רָאוּ בָנֶיךָ בּוֹקֵעַ יָם לִפְנֵי מֹשֶׁה, זֶה אֵלִי[4] עָנוּ וְאָמְרוּ:

יהוה יִמְלֹךְ לְעֹלָם וָעֶד.[5] ❖ וְנֶאֱמַר: כִּי פָדָה יהוה אֶת יַעֲקֹב, וּגְאָלוֹ מִיַּד חָזָק מִמֶּנּוּ.[6] בָּרוּךְ אַתָּה יהוה, גָּאַל יִשְׂרָאֵל.

(—Cong. אָמֵן.)

(1) *Job* 9:10. (2) *Psalms* 66:9. (3) *Exodus* 15:11. (4) 15:2. (5) 15:18. (6) *Jeremiah* 31:10.

Numbers 15:37-41

וַיֹּאמֶר *And HASHEM said to Moses saying: Speak to the Children of Israel and say to them that they are to make themselves tzitzis on the corners of their garments, throughout their generations. And they are to place upon the tzitzis of each corner a thread of techeiles. And it shall constitute tzitzis for you, that you may see it and remember all the commandments of HASHEM and perform them; and not explore after your heart and after your eyes after which you stray. So that you may remember and perform all My commandments; and be holy to your God. I am HASHEM, your God, Who has removed you from the land of Egypt to be a God to you; I am HASHEM your God — it is true —*

Concentrate on fulfilling the commandment of remembering the Exodus from Egypt.

Although the word אֱמֶת, *'it is true,'* belongs to the next paragraph, it is appended to the conclusion of the previous one, as explained in the commentary on page 42.

Chazzan repeats: **HASHEM, your God, is true.**

וֶאֱמוּנָה *And faithful is all this, and it is firmly established for us that He is HASHEM our God, and there is none but Him, and we are Israel, His nation. He redeems us from the power of kings, our King Who delivers us from the hand of all the cruel tyrants. He is the God Who exacts vengeance for us from our foes and Who brings just retribution upon all enemies of our soul; Who performs great deeds that are beyond comprehension, and wonders beyond number.*[1] *Who set our soul in life and did not allow our foot to falter.*[2] *Who led us upon the heights of our enemies and raised our pride above all who hate us; Who wrought for us miracles and vengeance upon Pharaoh; signs and wonders on the land of the offspring of Ham; Who struck with His anger all the firstborn of Egypt and removed His nation Israel from their midst to eternal freedom; Who brought His children through the split parts of the Sea of Reeds while those who pursued them and hated them He caused to sink into the depths. When His children perceived His power, they lauded and gave grateful praise to His Name.* Chazzan– *And His Kingship they accepted upon themselves willingly. Moses and the Children of Israel raised their voices to You in song with abundant gladness — and said unanimously:*

מִי כָמֹכָה *Who is like You among the heavenly powers, HASHEM! Who is like You, mighty in holiness, too awesome for praise, doing wonders!*[3] Chazzan– *Your children beheld Your majesty, as You split the sea before Moses: 'This is my God!'*[4] *they exclaimed, then they said:*

יהוה *'HASHEM shall reign for all eternity!'*[5] Chazzan– *And it is further said: 'For HASHEM has redeemed Jacob and delivered him from a power mightier than he.'*[6] *Blessed are You, HASHEM, Who redeemed Israel.*

(Cong.– *Amen.*)

הַשְׁכִּיבֵנוּ יהוה אֱלֹהֵינוּ לְשָׁלוֹם, וְהַעֲמִידֵנוּ מַלְכֵּנוּ לְחַיִּים, וּפְרוֹשׂ עָלֵינוּ סֻכַּת שְׁלוֹמֶךָ, וְתַקְּנֵנוּ בְּעֵצָה טוֹבָה מִלְּפָנֶיךָ, וְהוֹשִׁיעֵנוּ לְמַעַן שְׁמֶךָ. וְהָגֵן בַּעֲדֵנוּ, וְהָסֵר מֵעָלֵינוּ אוֹיֵב, דֶּבֶר, וְחֶרֶב, וְרָעָב, וְיָגוֹן, וְהָסֵר שָׂטָן מִלְּפָנֵינוּ וּמֵאַחֲרֵינוּ, וּבְצֵל כְּנָפֶיךָ תַּסְתִּירֵנוּ,[1] כִּי אֵל שׁוֹמְרֵנוּ וּמַצִּילֵנוּ אָתָּה, כִּי אֵל מֶלֶךְ חַנּוּן וְרַחוּם אָתָּה.[2] ❖ וּשְׁמוֹר צֵאתֵנוּ וּבוֹאֵנוּ, לְחַיִּים וּלְשָׁלוֹם מֵעַתָּה וְעַד עוֹלָם.[3] בָּרוּךְ אַתָּה יהוה, שׁוֹמֵר עַמּוֹ יִשְׂרָאֵל לָעַד.

(.Cong. — אָמֵן)

Some congregations omit the following prayers and continue with Half-*Kaddish* (p. 620).

בָּרוּךְ יהוה לְעוֹלָם, אָמֵן וְאָמֵן.[4] בָּרוּךְ יהוה מִצִּיּוֹן, שֹׁכֵן יְרוּשָׁלָיִם, הַלְלוּיָהּ.[5] בָּרוּךְ יהוה אֱלֹהִים אֱלֹהֵי יִשְׂרָאֵל, עֹשֵׂה נִפְלָאוֹת לְבַדּוֹ. וּבָרוּךְ שֵׁם כְּבוֹדוֹ לְעוֹלָם, וְיִמָּלֵא כְבוֹדוֹ אֶת כָּל הָאָרֶץ, אָמֵן וְאָמֵן.[6] יְהִי כְבוֹד יהוה לְעוֹלָם, יִשְׂמַח יהוה בְּמַעֲשָׂיו.[7] יְהִי שֵׁם יהוה מְבֹרָךְ, מֵעַתָּה וְעַד עוֹלָם.[8] כִּי לֹא יִטֹּשׁ יהוה אֶת עַמּוֹ בַּעֲבוּר שְׁמוֹ הַגָּדוֹל, כִּי הוֹאִיל יהוה לַעֲשׂוֹת אֶתְכֶם לוֹ לְעָם.[9] וַיַּרְא כָּל הָעָם וַיִּפְּלוּ עַל פְּנֵיהֶם, וַיֹּאמְרוּ, יהוה הוּא הָאֱלֹהִים, יהוה הוּא הָאֱלֹהִים.[10] וְהָיָה יהוה לְמֶלֶךְ עַל כָּל הָאָרֶץ, בַּיּוֹם הַהוּא יִהְיֶה יהוה אֶחָד וּשְׁמוֹ אֶחָד.[11] יְהִי חַסְדְּךָ יהוה עָלֵינוּ, כַּאֲשֶׁר יִחַלְנוּ לָךְ.[12] הוֹשִׁיעֵנוּ יהוה אֱלֹהֵינוּ, וְקַבְּצֵנוּ מִן הַגּוֹיִם, לְהוֹדוֹת לְשֵׁם קָדְשֶׁךָ, לְהִשְׁתַּבֵּחַ בִּתְהִלָּתֶךָ.[13] כָּל גּוֹיִם אֲשֶׁר עָשִׂיתָ יָבוֹאוּ וְיִשְׁתַּחֲווּ לְפָנֶיךָ אֲדֹנָי, וִיכַבְּדוּ לִשְׁמֶךָ. כִּי גָדוֹל אַתָּה וְעֹשֵׂה נִפְלָאוֹת, אַתָּה אֱלֹהִים לְבַדֶּךָ.[14] וַאֲנַחְנוּ עַמְּךָ וְצֹאן מַרְעִיתֶךָ, נוֹדֶה לְּךָ לְעוֹלָם, לְדוֹר וָדֹר נְסַפֵּר תְּהִלָּתֶךָ.[15] בָּרוּךְ יהוה בַּיּוֹם. בָּרוּךְ יהוה בַּלָּיְלָה. בָּרוּךְ יהוה בְּשָׁכְבֵנוּ. בָּרוּךְ יהוה בְּקוּמֵנוּ. כִּי בְיָדְךָ נַפְשׁוֹת הַחַיִּים וְהַמֵּתִים. אֲשֶׁר בְּיָדוֹ נֶפֶשׁ כָּל חָי, וְרוּחַ כָּל בְּשַׂר אִישׁ.[16] בְּיָדְךָ אַפְקִיד רוּחִי, פָּדִיתָה אוֹתִי, יהוה אֵל אֱמֶת.[17] אֱלֹהֵינוּ שֶׁבַּשָּׁמַיִם יַחֵד שִׁמְךָ, וְקַיֵּם מַלְכוּתְךָ תָּמִיד, וּמְלוֹךְ עָלֵינוּ לְעוֹלָם וָעֶד.

יִרְאוּ עֵינֵינוּ וְיִשְׂמַח לִבֵּנוּ וְתָגֵל נַפְשֵׁנוּ בִּישׁוּעָתְךָ בֶּאֱמֶת, בֶּאֱמֹר לְצִיּוֹן מָלַךְ אֱלֹהָיִךְ.[18] יהוה מֶלֶךְ,[19] יהוה מָלָךְ,[20] יהוה יִמְלֹךְ לְעֹלָם וָעֶד.[21] ❖ כִּי הַמַּלְכוּת שֶׁלְּךָ הִיא, וּלְעוֹלְמֵי עַד

הַשְׁכִּיבֵנוּ *Lay us down to sleep, HASHEM our God, in peace, raise us erect, our King, to life; and spread over us the shelter of Your peace. Set us aright with good counsel from before Your Presence, and save us for Your Name's sake. Shield us, remove from us foe, plague, sword, famine, and woe; and remove spiritual impediment from before us and behind us, and in the shadow of Your wings shelter us*[1] *— for God Who protects and rescues us are You; for God, the Gracious and Compassionate King, are You.*[2] Chazzan– *Safeguard our going and coming, for life and for peace from now to eternity.*[3] *Blessed are You, HASHEM, Who protects His people Israel forever.* (Cong.– *Amen.*)

Some congregations omit the following prayers and continue with Half-*Kaddish* (p. 620).

בָּרוּךְ *Blessed is HASHEM forever, Amen and Amen.*[4] *Blessed is HASHEM from Zion, Who dwells in Jerusalem, Halleluyah!*[5] *Blessed is HASHEM, God, the God of Israel, Who alone does wondrous things. Blessed is His glorious Name forever, and may all the earth be filled with His glory, Amen and Amen.*[6] *May the glory of HASHEM endure forever, let HASHEM rejoice in His works.*[7] *Blessed be the Name of HASHEM from this time and forever.*[8] *For HASHEM will not cast off His nation for the sake of His Great Name, for HASHEM has vowed to make you His own people.*[9] *Then the entire nation saw and fell on their faces and said, 'HASHEM — only He is God! HASHEM — only He is God!'*[10] *Then HASHEM will be King over all the world, on that day HASHEM will be One and His Name will be One.*[11] *May Your kindness, HASHEM, be upon us, just as we awaited You.*[12] *Save us, HASHEM, our God, gather us from the nations, to thank Your Holy Name and to glory in Your praise!*[13] *All the nations that You made will come and bow before You, My Lord, and shall glorify Your Name. For You are great and work wonders; You alone, O God.*[14] *Then we, Your nation and the sheep of Your pasture, shall thank You forever; for generation after generation we will relate Your praise.*[15] *Blessed is HASHEM by day; Blessed is HASHEM by night; Blessed is HASHEM when we retire; Blessed is HASHEM when we arise. For in Your hand are the souls of the living and the dead. He in Whose hand is the soul of all the living and the spirit of every human being.*[16] *In Your hand I shall entrust my spirit, You redeemed me, HASHEM, God of truth.*[17] *Our God, Who is in heaven, bring unity to Your Name; establish Your kingdom forever and reign over us for all eternity.*

יִרְאוּ *May our eyes see, our heart rejoice and our soul exult in Your salvation in truth, when Zion is told, 'Your God has reigned!'*[18] *HASHEM reigns,*[19] *HASHEM has reigned,*[20] *HASHEM will reign for all eternity.*[21] Chazzan– *For the kingdom is Yours and for all eternity*

(1) Cf. *Psalms* 17:8. (2) Cf. *Nechemiah* 9:31. (3) Cf. *Psalms* 121:8. (4) *Psalms* 89:53. (5) 135:21. (6) 72:18-19. (7) 104:31. (8) 113:2. (9) *I Samuel* 12:22. (10) *I Kings* 18:39. (11) *Zechariah* 14:9. (12) *Psalms* 33:22. (13) 106:47. (14) 86:9-10. (15) 79:13. (16) *Job* 12:10. (17) *Psalms* 31:6. (18) Cf. *Isaiah* 52:7. (19) *Psalms* 10:16. (20) 93:1 et al. (21) *Exodus* 15:18.

תִּמְלוֹךְ בְּכָבוֹד, כִּי אֵין לָנוּ מֶלֶךְ אֶלָּא אָתָּה. בָּרוּךְ אַתָּה יהוה, הַמֶּלֶךְ בִּכְבוֹדוֹ תָּמִיד יִמְלוֹךְ עָלֵינוּ לְעוֹלָם וָעֶד, וְעַל כָּל מַעֲשָׂיו.
(.Cong. – אָמֵן)

The *chazzan* recites חֲצִי קַדִּישׁ.

יִתְגַּדַּל וְיִתְקַדַּשׁ שְׁמֵהּ רַבָּא. (.Cong. – אָמֵן.) בְּעָלְמָא דִּי בְרָא כִרְעוּתֵהּ, וְיַמְלִיךְ מַלְכוּתֵהּ, בְּחַיֵּיכוֹן וּבְיוֹמֵיכוֹן וּבְחַיֵּי דְכָל בֵּית יִשְׂרָאֵל, בַּעֲגָלָא וּבִזְמַן קָרִיב. וְאִמְרוּ: אָמֵן.

(.Cong. – אָמֵן. יְהֵא שְׁמֵהּ רַבָּא מְבָרַךְ לְעָלַם וּלְעָלְמֵי עָלְמַיָּא.)

יְהֵא שְׁמֵהּ רַבָּא מְבָרַךְ לְעָלַם וּלְעָלְמֵי עָלְמַיָּא.

יִתְבָּרַךְ וְיִשְׁתַּבַּח וְיִתְפָּאַר וְיִתְרוֹמַם וְיִתְנַשֵּׂא וְיִתְהַדָּר וְיִתְעַלֶּה וְיִתְהַלָּל שְׁמֵהּ דְּקֻדְשָׁא בְּרִיךְ הוּא (.Cong. – בְּרִיךְ הוּא) — לְעֵלָּא מִן כָּל בִּרְכָתָא וְשִׁירָתָא תֻּשְׁבְּחָתָא וְנֶחֱמָתָא, דַּאֲמִירָן בְּעָלְמָא. וְאִמְרוּ: אָמֵן.
(.Cong. – אָמֵן.)

שמונה עשרה – עמידה

Take three steps backward, then three steps forward. Remain standing with the feet together while reciting *Shemoneh Esrei*. Recite it with quiet devotion and without interruption, verbal or otherwise. Although its recitation should not be audible to others, one must pray loudly enough to hear himself.

אֲדֹנָי שְׂפָתַי תִּפְתָּח, וּפִי יַגִּיד תְּהִלָּתֶךָ.[1]

אבות

Bend the knees at בָּרוּךְ; bow at אַתָּה; straighten up at ה׳.

בָּרוּךְ אַתָּה יהוה אֱלֹהֵינוּ וֵאלֹהֵי אֲבוֹתֵינוּ, אֱלֹהֵי אַבְרָהָם, אֱלֹהֵי יִצְחָק, וֵאלֹהֵי יַעֲקֹב, הָאֵל הַגָּדוֹל הַגִּבּוֹר וְהַנּוֹרָא, אֵל עֶלְיוֹן, גּוֹמֵל חֲסָדִים טוֹבִים וְקוֹנֵה הַכֹּל, וְזוֹכֵר חַסְדֵי אָבוֹת, וּמֵבִיא גוֹאֵל לִבְנֵי בְנֵיהֶם, לְמַעַן שְׁמוֹ בְּאַהֲבָה. מֶלֶךְ עוֹזֵר וּמוֹשִׁיעַ וּמָגֵן.

Bend the knees at בָּרוּךְ; bow at אַתָּה; straighten up at ה׳.

בָּרוּךְ אַתָּה יהוה, מָגֵן אַבְרָהָם.

גבורות

אַתָּה גִּבּוֹר לְעוֹלָם אֲדֹנָי, מְחַיֵּה מֵתִים אַתָּה, רַב לְהוֹשִׁיעַ. מְכַלְכֵּל חַיִּים בְּחֶסֶד, מְחַיֵּה מֵתִים בְּרַחֲמִים רַבִּים, סוֹמֵךְ נוֹפְלִים, וְרוֹפֵא חוֹלִים, וּמַתִּיר אֲסוּרִים, וּמְקַיֵּם אֱמוּנָתוֹ לִישֵׁנֵי עָפָר. מִי כָמוֹךָ בַּעַל גְּבוּרוֹת, וּמִי דּוֹמֶה לָּךְ, מֶלֶךְ מֵמִית וּמְחַיֶּה וּמַצְמִיחַ יְשׁוּעָה. וְנֶאֱמָן אַתָּה לְהַחֲיוֹת מֵתִים. בָּרוּךְ אַתָּה יהוה, מְחַיֵּה הַמֵּתִים.

קדושת השם

אַתָּה קָדוֹשׁ וְשִׁמְךָ קָדוֹשׁ, וּקְדוֹשִׁים בְּכָל יוֹם יְהַלְלוּךָ סֶּלָה. בָּרוּךְ אַתָּה יהוה, הָאֵל הַקָּדוֹשׁ.

You will reign in glory, for we have no King but You. Blessed are You, HASHEM, the King in His glory — He shall constantly reign over us forever and ever, and over all His creatures. (Cong.— *Amen.*)

The chazzan recites Half-*Kaddish*.

יִתְגַּדַּל *May His great Name grow exalted and sanctified* (Cong.— *Amen.*) *in the world that He created as He willed. May He give reign to His kingship in your lifetimes and in your days, and in the lifetimes of the entire Family of Israel, swiftly and soon. Now respond: Amen.*

(Cong.— *Amen. May His great Name be blessed forever and ever.*)

May His great Name be blessed forever and ever.

Blessed, praised, glorified, exalted, extolled, mighty, upraised, and lauded be the Name of the Holy One, Blessed is He (Cong.— *Blessed is He*) *— beyond any blessing and song, praise and consolation that are uttered in the world. Now respond: Amen.* (Cong.— *Amen.*)

SHEMONEH ESREI – AMIDAH

Take three steps backward, then three steps forward. Remain standing with the feet together while reciting *Shemoneh Esrei*. Recite it with quiet devotion and without interruption, verbal or otherwise. Although its recitation should not be audible to others, one must pray loudly enough to hear himself.

My Lord, open my lips, that my mouth may declare Your praise.[1]

PATRIARCHS

Bend the knees at *'Blessed'*; bow at *'You'*; straighten up at *'HASHEM.'*

בָּרוּךְ *Blessed are You, HASHEM, our God and the God of our forefathers, God of Abraham, God of Isaac, and God of Jacob; the great, mighty, and awesome God, the supreme God, Who bestows beneficial kindnesses and creates everything, Who recalls the kindnesses of the Patriarchs and brings a Redeemer to their children's children, for His Name's sake, with love.*

Bend the knees at *'Blessed'*; bow at *'You'*; straighten up at *'HASHEM.'*

O King, Helper, Savior, and Shield. Blessed are You, HASHEM, Shield of Abraham.

GOD'S MIGHT

אַתָּה *You are eternally mighty, my Lord, the Resuscitator of the dead are You; abundantly able to save. He sustains the living with kindness, resuscitates the dead with abundant mercy, supports the fallen, heals the sick, releases the confined, and maintains His faith to those asleep in the dust. Who is like You, O Master of mighty deeds, and who is comparable to You, O King Who causes death and restores life and makes salvation sprout! And You are faithful to resuscitate the dead. Blessed are You, HASHEM, Who resuscitates the dead.*

HOLINESS OF GOD'S NAME

אַתָּה *You are holy and Your Name is holy, and holy ones praise You every day, forever. Blessed are You, HASHEM, the holy God.*

(1) *Psalms* 51:17.

בינה

אַתָּה חוֹנֵן לְאָדָם דַּעַת, וּמְלַמֵּד לֶאֱנוֹשׁ בִּינָה.

After the Sabbath or *Yom Tov*, add [if forgotten do not repeat *Shemoneh Esrei; see Laws* §93]:

אַתָּה חוֹנַנְתָּנוּ לְמַדַּע תּוֹרָתֶךָ, וַתְּלַמְּדֵנוּ לַעֲשׂוֹת חֻקֵּי רְצוֹנֶךָ וַתַּבְדֵּל יהוה אֱלֹהֵינוּ בֵּין קֹדֶשׁ לְחוֹל בֵּין אוֹר לְחוֹשֶׁךְ, בֵּין יִשְׂרָאֵל לָעַמִּים בֵּין יוֹם הַשְּׁבִיעִי לְשֵׁשֶׁת יְמֵי הַמַּעֲשֶׂה. אָבִינוּ מַלְכֵּנוּ הָחֵל עָלֵינוּ הַיָּמִים הַבָּאִים לִקְרָאתֵנוּ לְשָׁלוֹם חֲשׂוּכִים מִכָּל חֵטְא וּמְנֻקִּים מִכָּל עָוֹן וּמְדֻבָּקִים בְּיִרְאָתֶךָ. וְ...

חָנֵּנוּ מֵאִתְּךָ דֵּעָה בִּינָה וְהַשְׂכֵּל. בָּרוּךְ אַתָּה יהוה, חוֹנֵן הַדָּעַת.

תשובה

הֲשִׁיבֵנוּ אָבִינוּ לְתוֹרָתֶךָ, וְקָרְבֵנוּ מַלְכֵּנוּ לַעֲבוֹדָתֶךָ, וְהַחֲזִירֵנוּ בִּתְשׁוּבָה שְׁלֵמָה לְפָנֶיךָ. בָּרוּךְ אַתָּה יהוה, הָרוֹצֶה בִּתְשׁוּבָה.

סליחה

Strike the left side of the chest with the right fist while reciting the words חָטָאנוּ and פָּשָׁעְנוּ.

סְלַח לָנוּ אָבִינוּ כִּי חָטָאנוּ, מְחַל לָנוּ מַלְכֵּנוּ כִּי פָשָׁעְנוּ, כִּי מוֹחֵל וְסוֹלֵחַ אָתָּה. בָּרוּךְ אַתָּה יהוה, חַנּוּן הַמַּרְבֶּה לִסְלֹחַ.

גאולה

רְאֵה בְעָנְיֵנוּ, וְרִיבָה רִיבֵנוּ, וּגְאָלֵנוּ[1] מְהֵרָה לְמַעַן שְׁמֶךָ, כִּי גוֹאֵל חָזָק אָתָּה. בָּרוּךְ אַתָּה יהוה, גּוֹאֵל יִשְׂרָאֵל.

רפואה

רְפָאֵנוּ יהוה וְנֵרָפֵא, הוֹשִׁיעֵנוּ וְנִוָּשֵׁעָה, כִּי תְהִלָּתֵנוּ אָתָּה,[2] וְהַעֲלֵה רְפוּאָה שְׁלֵמָה לְכָל מַכּוֹתֵינוּ, °°כִּי אֵל מֶלֶךְ רוֹפֵא נֶאֱמָן וְרַחֲמָן אָתָּה. בָּרוּךְ אַתָּה יהוה, רוֹפֵא חוֹלֵי עַמּוֹ יִשְׂרָאֵל.

ברכת השנים

בָּרֵךְ עָלֵינוּ יהוה אֱלֹהֵינוּ אֶת הַשָּׁנָה הַזֹּאת וְאֶת כָּל מִינֵי תְבוּאָתָהּ לְטוֹבָה, וְתֵן בְּרָכָה עַל פְּנֵי הָאֲדָמָה, וְשַׂבְּעֵנוּ מִטּוּבֶךָ, וּבָרֵךְ שְׁנָתֵנוּ כַּשָּׁנִים הַטּוֹבוֹת. בָּרוּךְ אַתָּה יהוה, מְבָרֵךְ הַשָּׁנִים.

°°At this point one may interject a prayer for one who is ill:

יְהִי רָצוֹן מִלְּפָנֶיךָ יהוה אֱלֹהַי וֵאלֹהֵי אֲבוֹתַי, שֶׁתִּשְׁלַח מְהֵרָה רְפוּאָה שְׁלֵמָה מִן הַשָּׁמַיִם, רְפוּאַת הַנֶּפֶשׁ וּרְפוּאַת הַגּוּף

for a male—לַחוֹלֶה (patient's name) בֶּן (mother's name) בְּתוֹךְ שְׁאָר חוֹלֵי יִשְׂרָאֵל.

for a female—לַחוֹלָה (patient's name) בַּת (mother's name) בְּתוֹךְ שְׁאָר חוֹלֵי יִשְׂרָאֵל.

continue—כִּי אֵל . . .

INSIGHT

אַתָּה *You graciously endow man with wisdom and teach insight to a frail mortal.*

After the Sabbath or *Yom Tov*, add [if forgotten do not repeat *Shemoneh Esrei;* see *Laws* §93]:

אַתָּה *You have graced us with intelligence to study Your Torah and You have taught us to perform the decrees You have willed.* HASHEM, *our God, You have distinguished between the sacred and the secular, between light and darkness, between Israel and the peoples, between the seventh day and the six days of labor. Our Father, our King, begin for us the days approaching us for peace, free from all sin, cleansed from all iniquity and attached to fear of You. And ...*

Endow us graciously from Yourself with wisdom, insight, and discernment. Blessed are You, HASHEM, *gracious Giver of wisdom.*

REPENTANCE

הֲשִׁיבֵנוּ *Bring us back, our Father, to Your Torah, and bring us near, our King, to Your service, and influence us to return in perfect repentance before You. Blessed are You,* HASHEM, *Who desires repentance.*

FORGIVENESS

Strike the left side of the chest with the right fist while reciting the words *'erred'* and *'sinned.'*

סְלַח *Forgive us, our Father, for we have erred; pardon us, our King, for we have willfully sinned; for You pardon and forgive. Blessed are You,* HASHEM, *the gracious One Who pardons abundantly.*

REDEMPTION

רְאֵה *Behold our affliction, take up our grievance, and redeem us*[1] *speedily for Your Name's sake, for You are a powerful Redeemer. Blessed are You,* HASHEM, *Redeemer of Israel.*

HEALTH AND HEALING

רְפָאֵנוּ *Heal us,* HASHEM *— then we will be healed; save us — then we will be saved, for You are our praise.*[2] *Bring complete recovery for all our ailments,* °°*for You are God, King, the faithful and compassionate Healer. Blessed are You,* HASHEM, *Who heals the sick of His people Israel.*

YEAR OF PROSPERITY

בָּרֵךְ *Bless on our behalf — O* HASHEM, *our God — this year and all its kinds of crops for the best, and give a blessing on the face of the earth, and satisfy us from Your bounty, and bless our year like the best years. Blessed are You,* HASHEM, *Who blesses the years.*

°°At this point one may interject a prayer for one who is ill:

May it be Your will, HASHEM, *my God, and the God of my forefathers, that You quickly send a complete recovery from heaven, spiritual healing and physical healing to the patient* (name) *son/daughter of* (mother's name) *among the other patients of Israel.* Continue: *For You are God ...*

(1) Cf. *Psalms* 119:153-154. (2) Cf. *Jeremiah* 17:14.

קיבוץ גליות

תְּקַע בְּשׁוֹפָר גָּדוֹל לְחֵרוּתֵנוּ, וְשָׂא נֵס לְקַבֵּץ גָּלֻיּוֹתֵינוּ, וְקַבְּצֵנוּ יַחַד מֵאַרְבַּע כַּנְפוֹת הָאָרֶץ.[1] בָּרוּךְ אַתָּה יהוה, מְקַבֵּץ נִדְחֵי עַמּוֹ יִשְׂרָאֵל.

דין

הָשִׁיבָה שׁוֹפְטֵינוּ כְּבָרִאשׁוֹנָה, וְיוֹעֲצֵינוּ כְּבַתְּחִלָּה,[2] וְהָסֵר מִמֶּנּוּ יָגוֹן וַאֲנָחָה, וּמְלוֹךְ עָלֵינוּ אַתָּה יהוה לְבַדְּךָ בְּחֶסֶד וּבְרַחֲמִים, וְצַדְּקֵנוּ בַּמִּשְׁפָּט. בָּרוּךְ אַתָּה יהוה, מֶלֶךְ אוֹהֵב צְדָקָה וּמִשְׁפָּט.

ברכת המינים

וְלַמַּלְשִׁינִים אַל תְּהִי תִקְוָה, וְכָל הָרִשְׁעָה כְּרֶגַע תֹּאבֵד, וְכָל אֹיְבֶיךָ מְהֵרָה יִכָּרֵתוּ, וְהַזֵּדִים מְהֵרָה תְעַקֵּר וּתְשַׁבֵּר וּתְמַגֵּר וְתַכְנִיעַ בִּמְהֵרָה בְיָמֵינוּ. בָּרוּךְ אַתָּה יהוה, שׁוֹבֵר אֹיְבִים וּמַכְנִיעַ זֵדִים.

צדיקים

עַל הַצַּדִּיקִים וְעַל הַחֲסִידִים, וְעַל זִקְנֵי עַמְּךָ בֵּית יִשְׂרָאֵל, וְעַל פְּלֵיטַת סוֹפְרֵיהֶם, וְעַל גֵּרֵי הַצֶּדֶק וְעָלֵינוּ, יֶהֱמוּ רַחֲמֶיךָ יהוה אֱלֹהֵינוּ, וְתֵן שָׂכָר טוֹב לְכָל הַבּוֹטְחִים בְּשִׁמְךָ בֶּאֱמֶת, וְשִׂים חֶלְקֵנוּ עִמָּהֶם לְעוֹלָם, וְלֹא נֵבוֹשׁ כִּי בְךָ בָּטָחְנוּ. בָּרוּךְ אַתָּה יהוה, מִשְׁעָן וּמִבְטָח לַצַּדִּיקִים.

בנין ירושלים

וְלִירוּשָׁלַיִם עִירְךָ בְּרַחֲמִים תָּשׁוּב, וְתִשְׁכּוֹן בְּתוֹכָהּ כַּאֲשֶׁר דִּבַּרְתָּ, וּבְנֵה אוֹתָהּ בְּקָרוֹב בְּיָמֵינוּ בִּנְיַן עוֹלָם, וְכִסֵּא דָוִד מְהֵרָה לְתוֹכָהּ תָּכִין. בָּרוּךְ אַתָּה יהוה, בּוֹנֵה יְרוּשָׁלָיִם.

מלכות בית דוד

אֶת צֶמַח דָּוִד עַבְדְּךָ מְהֵרָה תַצְמִיחַ, וְקַרְנוֹ תָּרוּם בִּישׁוּעָתֶךָ, כִּי לִישׁוּעָתְךָ קִוִּינוּ כָּל הַיּוֹם. בָּרוּךְ אַתָּה יהוה, מַצְמִיחַ קֶרֶן יְשׁוּעָה.

קבלת תפלה

שְׁמַע קוֹלֵנוּ יהוה אֱלֹהֵינוּ, חוּס וְרַחֵם עָלֵינוּ, וְקַבֵּל בְּרַחֲמִים וּבְרָצוֹן אֶת תְּפִלָּתֵנוּ, כִּי אֵל שׁוֹמֵעַ תְּפִלּוֹת וְתַחֲנוּנִים אָתָּה. וּמִלְּפָנֶיךָ מַלְכֵּנוּ רֵיקָם אַל תְּשִׁיבֵנוּ,

INGATHERING OF EXILES

תְּקַע *Sound the great shofar for our freedom, raise the banner to gather our exiles and gather us together from the four corners of the earth.*[1] *Blessed are You,* HASHEM, *Who gathers in the dispersed of His people Israel.*

RESTORATION OF JUSTICE

הָשִׁיבָה *Restore our judges as in earliest times and our counselors as at first;*[2] *remove from us sorrow and groan; and reign over us — You,* HASHEM, *alone — with kindness and compassion, and justify us through judgment. Blessed are You,* HASHEM, *the King Who loves righteousness and judgment.*

AGAINST HERETICS

וְלַמַּלְשִׁינִים *And for slanderers let there be no hope; and may all wickedness perish in an instant; and may all Your enemies be cut down speedily. May You speedily uproot, smash, cast down, and humble the wanton sinners — speedily in our days. Blessed are You,* HASHEM, *Who breaks enemies and humbles wanton sinners.*

THE RIGHTEOUS

עַל הַצַּדִּיקִים *On the righteous, on the devout, on the elders of Your people the Family of Israel, on the remnant of their scholars, on the righteous converts and on ourselves — may Your compassion be aroused,* HASHEM, *our God, and give goodly reward to all who sincerely believe in Your Name. Put our lot with them forever, and we will not feel ashamed, for we trust in You. Blessed are You,* HASHEM, *Mainstay and Assurance of the righteous.*

REBUILDING JERUSALEM

וְלִירוּשָׁלַיִם *And to Jerusalem, Your city, may You return in compassion, and may You rest within it, as You have spoken. May You rebuild it soon in our days as an eternal structure, and may You speedily establish the throne of David within it. Blessed are You,* HASHEM, *the Builder of Jerusalem.*

DAVIDIC REIGN

אֶת צֶמַח *The offspring of Your servant David may You speedily cause to flourish, and enhance his pride through Your salvation, for we hope for Your salvation all day long. Blessed are You,* HASHEM, *Who causes the pride of salvation to flourish.*

ACCEPTANCE OF PRAYER

שְׁמַע *Hear our voice,* HASHEM *our God, pity and be compassionate to us, and accept — with compassion and favor — our prayer, for God Who hears prayers and supplications are You. From before Yourself, our King, turn us not away empty-handed,*

---

(1) Cf. *Isaiah* 11:12. (2) Cf. 1:26.

°°כִּי אַתָּה שׁוֹמֵעַ תְּפִלַּת עַמְּךָ יִשְׂרָאֵל בְּרַחֲמִים. בָּרוּךְ אַתָּה יהוה, שׁוֹמֵעַ תְּפִלָּה.

עבודה

רְצֵה יהוה אֱלֹהֵינוּ בְּעַמְּךָ יִשְׂרָאֵל וּבִתְפִלָּתָם, וְהָשֵׁב אֶת הָעֲבוֹדָה לִדְבִיר בֵּיתֶךָ. וְאִשֵּׁי יִשְׂרָאֵל וּתְפִלָּתָם בְּאַהֲבָה תְקַבֵּל בְּרָצוֹן, וּתְהִי לְרָצוֹן תָּמִיד עֲבוֹדַת יִשְׂרָאֵל עַמֶּךָ.

[If the following paragraph is forgotten, repeat *Shemoneh Esrei*. See *Laws* §56.]

אֱלֹהֵינוּ וֵאלֹהֵי אֲבוֹתֵינוּ, יַעֲלֶה, וְיָבֹא, וְיַגִּיעַ, וְיֵרָאֶה, וְיֵרָצֶה, וְיִשָּׁמַע, וְיִפָּקֵד, וְיִזָּכֵר זִכְרוֹנֵנוּ וּפִקְדוֹנֵנוּ, וְזִכְרוֹן אֲבוֹתֵינוּ, וְזִכְרוֹן מָשִׁיחַ בֶּן דָּוִד עַבְדֶּךָ, וְזִכְרוֹן יְרוּשָׁלַיִם עִיר קָדְשֶׁךָ, וְזִכְרוֹן כָּל עַמְּךָ בֵּית יִשְׂרָאֵל לְפָנֶיךָ, לִפְלֵיטָה לְטוֹבָה לְחֵן וּלְחֶסֶד וּלְרַחֲמִים, לְחַיִּים וּלְשָׁלוֹם בְּיוֹם חַג הַסֻּכּוֹת הַזֶּה. זָכְרֵנוּ יהוה אֱלֹהֵינוּ בּוֹ לְטוֹבָה, וּפָקְדֵנוּ בוֹ לִבְרָכָה, וְהוֹשִׁיעֵנוּ בוֹ לְחַיִּים. וּבִדְבַר יְשׁוּעָה וְרַחֲמִים, חוּס וְחָנֵּנוּ וְרַחֵם עָלֵינוּ וְהוֹשִׁיעֵנוּ, כִּי אֵלֶיךָ עֵינֵינוּ, כִּי אֵל מֶלֶךְ חַנּוּן וְרַחוּם אָתָּה.[1]

וְתֶחֱזֶינָה עֵינֵינוּ בְּשׁוּבְךָ לְצִיּוֹן בְּרַחֲמִים. בָּרוּךְ אַתָּה יהוה, הַמַּחֲזִיר שְׁכִינָתוֹ לְצִיּוֹן.

°°During the silent *shemoneh Esrei* one may insert either or both of these personal prayers.

For forgiveness:

אָנָּא יהוה, חָטָאתִי עָוִיתִי וּפָשַׁעְתִּי לְפָנֶיךָ, מִיּוֹם הֱיוֹתִי עַל הָאֲדָמָה עַד הַיּוֹם הַזֶּה (וּבִפְרַט בְּחֵטְא ....). אָנָּא יהוה, עֲשֵׂה לְמַעַן שִׁמְךָ הַגָּדוֹל, וּתְכַפֶּר לִי עַל עֲוֹנַי וַחֲטָאַי וּפְשָׁעַי שֶׁחָטָאתִי וְשֶׁעָוִיתִי וְשֶׁפָּשַׁעְתִּי לְפָנֶיךָ, מִנְּעוּרַי עַד הַיּוֹם הַזֶּה. וּתְמַלֵּא כָּל הַשֵּׁמוֹת שֶׁפָּגַמְתִּי בְּשִׁמְךָ הַגָּדוֹל.

For livelihood:

אַתָּה הוּא יהוה הָאֱלֹהִים, הַזָּן וּמְפַרְנֵס וּמְכַלְכֵּל מִקַּרְנֵי רְאֵמִים עַד בֵּיצֵי כִנִּים. הַטְרִיפֵנִי לֶחֶם חֻקִּי, וְהַמְצֵא לִי וּלְכָל בְּנֵי בֵיתִי מְזוֹנוֹתַי קוֹדֶם שֶׁאֶצְטָרֵךְ לָהֶם, בְּנַחַת וְלֹא בְצַעַר, בְּהֶתֵּר וְלֹא בְאִסּוּר, בְּכָבוֹד וְלֹא בְבִזָּיוֹן, לְחַיִּים וּלְשָׁלוֹם, מִשֶּׁפַע בְּרָכָה וְהַצְלָחָה, וּמִשֶּׁפַע בְּרֵכָה עֶלְיוֹנָה, כְּדֵי שֶׁאוּכַל לַעֲשׂוֹת רְצוֹנֶךָ וְלַעֲסוֹק בְּתוֹרָתֶךָ וּלְקַיֵּם מִצְוֹתֶיךָ. וְאַל תַּצְרִיכֵנִי לִידֵי מַתְּנַת בָּשָׂר וָדָם. וִיקֻיַּם בִּי מִקְרָא שֶׁכָּתוּב: פּוֹתֵחַ אֶת יָדֶךָ, וּמַשְׂבִּיעַ לְכָל חַי רָצוֹן.[2] וְכָתוּב: הַשְׁלֵךְ עַל יהוה יְהָבְךָ וְהוּא יְכַלְכְּלֶךָ.[3]

Continue — כִּי אַתָּה . . .

°° *for You hear the prayer of Your people Israel with compassion. Blessed are You,* HASHEM, *Who hears prayer.*

TEMPLE SERVICE

רְצֵה *Be favorable,* HASHEM, *our God, toward Your people Israel and their prayer and restore the service to the Holy of Holies of Your Temple. The fire-offerings of Israel and their prayer accept with love and favor, and may the service of Your people Israel always be favorable to You.*

[If the following paragraph is forgotten, repeat *Shemoneh Esrei.* See *Laws* §56.]

אֱלֹהֵינוּ *Our God and God of our forefathers, may there rise, come, reach, be noted, be favored, be heard, be considered, and be remembered — the remembrance and consideration of ourselves; the remembrance of our forefathers; the remembrance of Messiah, son of David, Your servant; the remembrance of Jerusalem, the City of Your Holiness; the remembrance of Your entire people the Family of Israel — before You for deliverance, for goodness, for grace, for kindness, and for compassion, for life, and for peace on this day of the Festival of Succos, Remember us on it,* HASHEM, *our God, for goodness, consider us on it for blessing, and help us on it for life. In the matter of salvation and compassion, pity, be gracious and compassionate with us and help us, for our eyes are turned to You, because You are God, the gracious and compassionate King.*[1]

וְתֶחֱזֶינָה *May our eyes behold Your return to Zion in compassion. Blessed are You,* HASHEM, *Who restores His Presence to Zion.*

°°During the silent *Shemoneh Esrei* one may insert either or both of these personal prayers.

For forgiveness:

אָנָּא *Please, O* HASHEM, *I have erred, been iniquitous, and willfully sinned before You, from the day I have existed on earth until this very day (and especially with the sin of . . .). Please,* HASHEM, *act for the sake of Your Great Name and grant me atonement for my iniquities, my errors, and my willful sins through which I have erred, been iniquitous, and willfully sinned before You, from my youth until this day. And make whole all the Names that I have blemished in Your Great Name.*

For livelihood:

אַתָּה *It is You,* HASHEM *the God, Who nourishes, sustains, and supports, from the horns of re'eimim to the eggs of lice. Provide me with my allotment of bread; and bring forth for me and all members of my household, my food, before I have need for it; in contentment but not in pain, in a permissible but not a forbidden manner, in honor but not in disgrace, for life and for peace; from the flow of blessing and success and from the flow of the Heavenly spring, so that I be enabled to do Your will and engage in Your Torah and fulfill Your commandments. Make me not needful of people's largesse; and may there be fulfilled in me the verse that states, 'You open Your hand and satisfy the desire of every living thing'*[2] *and that states, 'Cast Your burden upon* HASHEM *and He will support you.'*[3]

Continue: *For You hear the prayer . . .*

(1) Cf. *Nechemiah* 9:31. (2) *Psalms* 145:16. (3) 55:23.

הודאה

Bow at מוֹדִים; straighten up at ה׳.

מוֹדִים אֲנַחְנוּ לָךְ שָׁאַתָּה הוּא יהוה אֱלֹהֵינוּ וֵאלֹהֵי אֲבוֹתֵינוּ לְעוֹלָם וָעֶד. צוּר חַיֵּינוּ, מָגֵן יִשְׁעֵנוּ אַתָּה הוּא לְדוֹר וָדוֹר. נוֹדֶה לְּךָ וּנְסַפֵּר תְּהִלָּתֶךָ[1] עַל חַיֵּינוּ הַמְּסוּרִים בְּיָדֶךָ, וְעַל נִשְׁמוֹתֵינוּ הַפְּקוּדוֹת לָךְ, וְעַל נִסֶּיךָ שֶׁבְּכָל יוֹם עִמָּנוּ, וְעַל נִפְלְאוֹתֶיךָ וְטוֹבוֹתֶיךָ שֶׁבְּכָל עֵת, עֶרֶב וָבֹקֶר וְצָהֳרָיִם. הַטּוֹב כִּי לֹא כָלוּ רַחֲמֶיךָ, וְהַמְּרַחֵם כִּי לֹא תַמּוּ חֲסָדֶיךָ,[2] מֵעוֹלָם קִוִּינוּ לָךְ:

וְעַל כֻּלָּם יִתְבָּרַךְ וְיִתְרוֹמַם שִׁמְךָ מַלְכֵּנוּ תָּמִיד לְעוֹלָם וָעֶד.

Bend the knees at בָּרוּךְ; bow at אַתָּה; straighten up at ה׳.

וְכֹל הַחַיִּים יוֹדוּךָ סֶּלָה, וִיהַלְּלוּ אֶת שִׁמְךָ בֶּאֱמֶת, הָאֵל יְשׁוּעָתֵנוּ וְעֶזְרָתֵנוּ סֶלָה. בָּרוּךְ אַתָּה יהוה, הַטּוֹב שִׁמְךָ וּלְךָ נָאֶה לְהוֹדוֹת.

שלום

שָׁלוֹם רָב עַל יִשְׂרָאֵל עַמְּךָ תָּשִׂים לְעוֹלָם, כִּי אַתָּה הוּא מֶלֶךְ אָדוֹן לְכָל הַשָּׁלוֹם. וְטוֹב בְּעֵינֶיךָ לְבָרֵךְ אֶת עַמְּךָ יִשְׂרָאֵל, בְּכָל עֵת וּבְכָל שָׁעָה בִּשְׁלוֹמֶךָ. בָּרוּךְ אַתָּה יהוה, הַמְּבָרֵךְ אֶת עַמּוֹ יִשְׂרָאֵל בַּשָּׁלוֹם.

יִהְיוּ לְרָצוֹן אִמְרֵי פִי וְהֶגְיוֹן לִבִּי לְפָנֶיךָ, יהוה צוּרִי וְגֹאֲלִי.[3]

אֱלֹהַי, נְצוֹר לְשׁוֹנִי מֵרָע, וּשְׂפָתַי מִדַּבֵּר מִרְמָה,[4] וְלִמְקַלְלַי נַפְשִׁי תִדּוֹם, וְנַפְשִׁי כֶּעָפָר לַכֹּל תִּהְיֶה. פְּתַח לִבִּי בְּתוֹרָתֶךָ, וּבְמִצְוֹתֶיךָ תִּרְדּוֹף נַפְשִׁי. וְכֹל הַחוֹשְׁבִים עָלַי רָעָה, מְהֵרָה הָפֵר עֲצָתָם וְקַלְקֵל מַחֲשַׁבְתָּם. עֲשֵׂה לְמַעַן שְׁמֶךָ, עֲשֵׂה לְמַעַן יְמִינֶךָ, עֲשֵׂה לְמַעַן קְדֻשָּׁתֶךָ, עֲשֵׂה לְמַעַן תּוֹרָתֶךָ. לְמַעַן יֵחָלְצוּן יְדִידֶיךָ, הוֹשִׁיעָה יְמִינְךָ וַעֲנֵנִי.[5]

Some recite verses pertaining to their names here. See page 1301.

יִהְיוּ לְרָצוֹן אִמְרֵי פִי וְהֶגְיוֹן לִבִּי לְפָנֶיךָ, יהוה צוּרִי וְגֹאֲלִי.[3]

Bow and take three steps back. Bow left and say . . . עֹשֶׂה, bow right and say . . . הוּא יַעֲשֶׂה; bow forward and say וְעַל כָּל . . . אָמֵן.

עֹשֶׂה שָׁלוֹם בִּמְרוֹמָיו, הוּא יַעֲשֶׂה שָׁלוֹם עָלֵינוּ, וְעַל כָּל יִשְׂרָאֵל. וְאִמְרוּ: אָמֵן.

THANKSGIVING [MODIM]

Bow at *'We gratefully thank You'*; straighten up at *'HASHEM.'*

מוֹדִים *We gratefully thank You, for it is You Who are HASHEM, our God and the God of our forefathers for all eternity; Rock of our lives, Shield of our salvation are You from generation to generation. We shall thank You and relate Your praise*[1] *— for our lives, which are committed to Your power and for our souls that are entrusted to You; for Your miracles that are with us every day; and for Your wonders and favors in every season — evening, morning, and afternoon. The Beneficent One, for Your compassions were never exhausted, and the Compassionate One, for Your kindnesses never ended*[2] *— always have we put our hope in You.*

For all these, may Your Name be blessed and exalted, our King, continually forever and ever.

Bend the knees at *'Blessed'*; bow at *'You'*; straighten up at *'HASHEM.'*

Everything alive will gratefully acknowledge You, Selah! and praise Your Name sincerely, O God of our salvation and help, Selah! Blessed are You, HASHEM, Your Name is 'The Beneficent One' and to You it is fitting to give thanks.

PEACE

שָׁלוֹם *Establish abundant peace upon Your people Israel forever, for You are King, Master of all peace. May it be good in Your eyes to bless Your people Israel at every time and every hour with Your peace. Blessed are You, HASHEM, Who blesses His people Israel with peace.*

May the expressions of my mouth and the thoughts of my heart find favor before You, HASHEM, my Rock and my Redeemer.[3]

אֱלֹהַי *My God, guard my tongue from evil and my lips from speaking deceitfully.*[4] *To those who curse me, let my soul be silent; and let my soul be like dust to everyone. Open my heart to Your Torah, then my soul will pursue Your commandments. As for all those who design evil against me, speedily nullify their counsel and disrupt their design. Act for Your Name's sake; act for Your right hand's sake; act for Your sanctity's sake; act for Your Torah's sake. That Your beloved ones may be given rest; let Your right hand save, and respond to me.*[5]

Some recite verses pertaining to their names at this point. See page 1301.

May the expressions of my mouth and the thoughts of my heart find favor before You, HASHEM, my Rock and my Redeemer.[3] *He Who makes peace in His heights, may He make peace upon us, and upon all Israel. Now respond: Amen.*

Bow and take three steps back. Bow left and say, *'He Who makes peace . . .'*; bow right and say, *'may He make peace . . .'*; bow forward and say, *'and upon . . . Amen.'*

---

(1) Cf. *Psalms* 79:13. (2) Cf. *Lamentations* 3:22. (3) *Psalms* 19:15. (4) Cf. 34:14. (5) 60:7;108:7.

יְהִי רָצוֹן מִלְּפָנֶיךָ יהוה אֱלֹהֵינוּ וֵאלֹהֵי אֲבוֹתֵינוּ, שֶׁיִּבָּנֶה בֵּית הַמִּקְדָּשׁ בִּמְהֵרָה בְיָמֵינוּ, וְתֵן חֶלְקֵנוּ בְּתוֹרָתֶךָ. וְשָׁם נַעֲבָדְךָ בְּיִרְאָה, כִּימֵי עוֹלָם וּכְשָׁנִים קַדְמוֹנִיּוֹת. וְעָרְבָה לַיהוה מִנְחַת יְהוּדָה וִירוּשָׁלָיִם, כִּימֵי עוֹלָם וּכְשָׁנִים קַדְמוֹנִיּוֹת.[1]

SHEMONEH ESREI ENDS HERE.

Remain standing in place for at least a few moments before taking three steps forward.

קדיש שלם

The *chazzan* recites קַדִּישׁ שָׁלֵם.

יִתְגַּדַּל וְיִתְקַדַּשׁ שְׁמֵהּ רַבָּא. (Cong. – אָמֵן.) בְּעָלְמָא דִּי בְרָא כִרְעוּתֵהּ. וְיַמְלִיךְ מַלְכוּתֵהּ, בְּחַיֵּיכוֹן וּבְיוֹמֵיכוֹן וּבְחַיֵּי דְכָל בֵּית יִשְׂרָאֵל, בַּעֲגָלָא וּבִזְמַן קָרִיב. וְאִמְרוּ: אָמֵן.

(Cong. – אָמֵן. יְהֵא שְׁמֵהּ רַבָּא מְבָרַךְ לְעָלַם וּלְעָלְמֵי עָלְמַיָּא.)

יְהֵא שְׁמֵהּ רַבָּא מְבָרַךְ לְעָלַם וּלְעָלְמֵי עָלְמַיָּא.

יִתְבָּרַךְ וְיִשְׁתַּבַּח וְיִתְפָּאַר וְיִתְרוֹמַם וְיִתְנַשֵּׂא וְיִתְהַדָּר וְיִתְעַלֶּה וְיִתְהַלָּל שְׁמֵהּ דְּקֻדְשָׁא בְּרִיךְ הוּא (Cong. – בְּרִיךְ הוּא) — לְעֵלָּא מִן כָּל בִּרְכָתָא וְשִׁירָתָא תֻּשְׁבְּחָתָא וְנֶחֱמָתָא, דַּאֲמִירָן בְּעָלְמָא. וְאִמְרוּ: אָמֵן. (Cong. – אָמֵן.)

(Cong. – קַבֵּל בְּרַחֲמִים וּבְרָצוֹן אֶת תְּפִלָּתֵנוּ.)

תִּתְקַבֵּל צְלוֹתְהוֹן וּבָעוּתְהוֹן דְּכָל בֵּית יִשְׂרָאֵל קֳדָם אֲבוּהוֹן דִּי בִשְׁמַיָּא. וְאִמְרוּ: אָמֵן. (Cong. – אָמֵן.)

(Cong. – יְהִי שֵׁם יהוה מְבֹרָךְ, מֵעַתָּה וְעַד עוֹלָם.[2])

יְהֵא שְׁלָמָא רַבָּא מִן שְׁמַיָּא, וְחַיִּים עָלֵינוּ וְעַל כָּל יִשְׂרָאֵל. וְאִמְרוּ: אָמֵן. (Cong. – אָמֵן.)

(Cong. – עֶזְרִי מֵעִם יהוה, עֹשֵׂה שָׁמַיִם וָאָרֶץ.[3])

Take three steps back. Bow left and say . . . עֹשֶׂה; bow right and say . . . הוּא; bow forward and say וְעַל כָּל . . . אָמֵן. Remain standing in place for a few moments, then take three steps forward.

עֹשֶׂה שָׁלוֹם בִּמְרוֹמָיו, הוּא יַעֲשֶׂה שָׁלוֹם עָלֵינוּ, וְעַל כָּל יִשְׂרָאֵל. וְאִמְרוּ: אָמֵן. (Cong. – אָמֵן.)

ON THE NIGHT FOLLOWING *YOM TOV* THE SERVICE CONTINUES WITH *HAVDALAH,* P. 636;
AT THE CONCLUSION OF THE SABBATH THE SERVICE CONTINUES BELOW;
ON ALL OTHER NIGHTS THE SERVICE CONTINUES WITH *ALEINU,* PAGE 638.

פסוקי ברכה

וְיִתֶּן לְךָ הָאֱלֹהִים מִטַּל הַשָּׁמַיִם וּמִשְׁמַנֵּי הָאָרֶץ, וְרֹב דָּגָן וְתִירֹשׁ. יַעַבְדוּךָ עַמִּים, וְיִשְׁתַּחֲווּ לְךָ לְאֻמִּים, הֱוֵה גְבִיר לְאַחֶיךָ, וְיִשְׁתַּחֲווּ לְךָ בְּנֵי אִמֶּךָ, אֹרְרֶיךָ אָרוּר, וּמְבָרְכֶיךָ בָּרוּךְ.[4] וְאֵל שַׁדַּי יְבָרֵךְ אֹתְךָ וְיַפְרְךָ וְיַרְבֶּךָ, וְהָיִיתָ לִקְהַל עַמִּים. וְיִתֶּן לְךָ אֶת בִּרְכַּת אַבְרָהָם, לְךָ וּלְזַרְעֲךָ אִתָּךְ, לְרִשְׁתְּךָ אֶת אֶרֶץ מְגֻרֶיךָ, אֲשֶׁר נָתַן אֱלֹהִים לְאַבְרָהָם.[5] מֵאֵל אָבִיךָ וְיַעְזְרֶךָּ, וְאֵת שַׁדַּי וִיבָרְכֶךָּ, בִּרְכֹת שָׁמַיִם מֵעָל,

יְהִי רָצוֹן *May it be Your will,* HASHEM, *our God and the God of our forefathers, that the Holy Temple be rebuilt, speedily in our days. Grant us our share in Your Torah, and may we serve You there with reverence, as in days of old and in former years. Then the offering of Judah and Jerusalem will be pleasing to* HASHEM, *as in days of old and in former years.*[1]

SHEMONEH ESREI ENDS HERE.

Remain standing in place for a few moments before taking three steps forward.

FULL KADDISH

The *chazzan* recites the Full *Kaddish.*

יִתְגַּדַּל *May His great Name grow exalted and sanctified* (Cong.– *Amen.*) *in the world that He created as He willed. May He give reign to His kingship in your lifetimes and in your days, and in the lifetimes of the entire Family of Israel, swiftly and soon. Now respond: Amen.*

(Cong.– *Amen. May His great Name be blessed forever and ever.*)

May His great Name be blessed forever and ever.

Blessed, praised, glorified, exalted, extolled, mighty, upraised, and lauded be the Name of the Holy One, Blessed is He (Cong.– *Blessed is He*) — *beyond any blessing and song, praise and consolation that are uttered in the world. Now respond: Amen.* (Cong.– *Amen.*)

(Cong.– *Accept our prayers with mercy and favor.*)

May the prayers and supplications of the entire Family of Israel be accepted before their Father Who is in Heaven. Now respond: Amen. (Cong.– *Amen.*)

(Cong.– *Blessed be the Name of* HASHEM, *from this time and forever.*[2])

May there be abundant peace from Heaven, and life, upon us and upon all Israel. Now respond: Amen. (Cong.– *Amen.*)

(Cong.– *My help is from* HASHEM, *Maker of heaven and earth.*[3])

Take three steps back. Bow left and say, *'He Who makes peace . . .';* bow right and say, *'may He . . .';* bow forward and say, *'and upon all Israel . . .'* Remain standing in place for a few moments, then take three steps forward.

He Who makes peace in His heights, may He make peace upon us, and upon all Israel. Now respond: Amen. (Cong.– *Amen.*)

ON THE NIGHT FOLLOWING *YOM TOV* THE SERVICE CONTINUES WITH *HAVDALAH,* P. 636; AT THE CONCLUSION OF THE SABBATH THE SERVICE CONTINUES BELOW; ON ALL OTHER NIGHTS THE SERVICE CONTINUES WITH *ALEINU,* PAGE 638.

VERSES OF BLESSING

וְיִתֶּן *And may God give you of the dew of the heavens and of the fatness of the earth, and abundant grain and wine. Peoples will serve you, and regimes will prostrate themselves to you; be a lord to your kinsmen, and your mother's sons will prostrate themselves to you; they who curse you are cursed, and they who bless you are blessed.*[4] *And may El Shaddai bless you, make you fruitful and make you numerous, and may you be a congregation of peoples. May He grant you the blessing of Abraham, to you and to your offspring with you, that you may possess the land of your sojourns which God gave to Abraham.*[5] *It is from the God of your father and He will help you, and with Shaddai and He will bless you — blessings of heaven*

(1) *Malchi* 3:4. (2) *Psalms* 113:2. (3) 121:2. (4) *Genesis* 27:28-29. (5) 28:3-4.

בִּרְכֹת תְּהוֹם רֹבֶצֶת תָּחַת, בִּרְכֹת שָׁדַיִם וָרָחַם. בִּרְכֹת אָבִיךָ גָּבְרוּ עַל בִּרְכֹת הוֹרַי, עַד תַּאֲוַת גִּבְעֹת עוֹלָם, תִּהְיֶיןָ לְרֹאשׁ יוֹסֵף, וּלְקָדְקֹד נְזִיר אֶחָיו.[1] וַאֲהֵבְךָ וּבֵרַכְךָ וְהִרְבֶּךָ, וּבֵרַךְ פְּרִי בִטְנְךָ וּפְרִי אַדְמָתֶךָ, דְּגָנְךָ וְתִירֹשְׁךָ וְיִצְהָרֶךָ, שְׁגַר אֲלָפֶיךָ וְעַשְׁתְּרֹת צֹאנֶךָ, עַל הָאֲדָמָה אֲשֶׁר נִשְׁבַּע לַאֲבֹתֶיךָ לָתֶת לָךְ. בָּרוּךְ תִּהְיֶה מִכָּל הָעַמִּים, לֹא יִהְיֶה בְךָ עָקָר וַעֲקָרָה, וּבִבְהֶמְתֶּךָ. וְהֵסִיר יהוה מִמְּךָ כָּל חֹלִי, וְכָל מַדְוֵי מִצְרַיִם הָרָעִים אֲשֶׁר יָדַעְתָּ, לֹא יְשִׂימָם בָּךְ, וּנְתָנָם בְּכָל שֹׂנְאֶיךָ.[2]

הַמַּלְאָךְ הַגֹּאֵל אֹתִי מִכָּל רָע יְבָרֵךְ אֶת הַנְּעָרִים וְיִקָּרֵא בָהֶם שְׁמִי, וְשֵׁם אֲבֹתַי אַבְרָהָם וְיִצְחָק, וְיִדְגּוּ לָרֹב בְּקֶרֶב הָאָרֶץ.[3] יהוה אֱלֹהֵיכֶם הִרְבָּה אֶתְכֶם, וְהִנְּכֶם הַיּוֹם כְּכוֹכְבֵי הַשָּׁמַיִם לָרֹב. יהוה אֱלֹהֵי אֲבוֹתֵכֶם יֹסֵף עֲלֵיכֶם כָּכֶם אֶלֶף פְּעָמִים, וִיבָרֵךְ אֶתְכֶם כַּאֲשֶׁר דִּבֶּר לָכֶם.[4]

בָּרוּךְ אַתָּה בָּעִיר, וּבָרוּךְ אַתָּה בַּשָּׂדֶה. בָּרוּךְ אַתָּה בְּבֹאֶךָ, וּבָרוּךְ אַתָּה בְּצֵאתֶךָ. בָּרוּךְ טַנְאֲךָ וּמִשְׁאַרְתֶּךָ. בָּרוּךְ פְּרִי בִטְנְךָ וּפְרִי אַדְמָתְךָ וּפְרִי בְהֶמְתֶּךָ, שְׁגַר אֲלָפֶיךָ וְעַשְׁתְּרוֹת צֹאנֶךָ.[5] יְצַו יהוה אִתְּךָ אֶת הַבְּרָכָה בַּאֲסָמֶיךָ וּבְכֹל מִשְׁלַח יָדֶךָ, וּבֵרַכְךָ בָּאָרֶץ אֲשֶׁר יהוה אֱלֹהֶיךָ נֹתֵן לָךְ. יִפְתַּח יהוה לְךָ אֶת אוֹצָרוֹ הַטּוֹב, אֶת הַשָּׁמַיִם, לָתֵת מְטַר אַרְצְךָ בְּעִתּוֹ, וּלְבָרֵךְ אֵת כָּל מַעֲשֵׂה יָדֶךָ, וְהִלְוִיתָ גּוֹיִם רַבִּים, וְאַתָּה לֹא תִלְוֶה.[6] כִּי יהוה אֱלֹהֶיךָ בֵּרַכְךָ כַּאֲשֶׁר דִּבֶּר לָךְ, וְהַעֲבַטְתָּ גּוֹיִם רַבִּים, וְאַתָּה לֹא תַעֲבֹט, וּמָשַׁלְתָּ בְּגוֹיִם רַבִּים, וּבְךָ לֹא יִמְשֹׁלוּ.[7] אַשְׁרֶיךָ יִשְׂרָאֵל, מִי כָמוֹךָ, עַם נוֹשַׁע בַּיהוה, מָגֵן עֶזְרֶךָ, וַאֲשֶׁר חֶרֶב גַּאֲוָתֶךָ, וְיִכָּחֲשׁוּ אֹיְבֶיךָ לָךְ, וְאַתָּה עַל בָּמוֹתֵימוֹ תִדְרֹךְ.[8]

גאולה

מָחִיתִי כָעָב פְּשָׁעֶיךָ וְכֶעָנָן חַטֹּאתֶיךָ, שׁוּבָה אֵלַי כִּי גְאַלְתִּיךָ. רָנּוּ שָׁמַיִם, כִּי עָשָׂה יהוה, הָרִיעוּ תַּחְתִּיּוֹת אָרֶץ, פִּצְחוּ הָרִים רִנָּה, יַעַר וְכָל עֵץ בּוֹ, כִּי גָאַל יהוה יַעֲקֹב וּבְיִשְׂרָאֵל יִתְפָּאָר.[9] גֹּאֲלֵנוּ יהוה צְבָאוֹת שְׁמוֹ, קְדוֹשׁ יִשְׂרָאֵל.[10]

ישועה

יִשְׂרָאֵל נוֹשַׁע בַּיהוה תְּשׁוּעַת עוֹלָמִים, לֹא תֵבֹשׁוּ וְלֹא תִכָּלְמוּ עַד עוֹלְמֵי עַד.[11] וַאֲכַלְתֶּם אָכוֹל וְשָׂבוֹעַ, וְהִלַּלְתֶּם אֶת שֵׁם יהוה אֱלֹהֵיכֶם אֲשֶׁר עָשָׂה עִמָּכֶם לְהַפְלִיא, וְלֹא יֵבֹשׁוּ עַמִּי לְעוֹלָם. וִידַעְתֶּם כִּי בְקֶרֶב יִשְׂרָאֵל אָנִי, וַאֲנִי יהוה אֱלֹהֵיכֶם, וְאֵין

---

(1) *Genesis* 49:25-26. (2) *Deuteronomy* 7:13-15. (3) *Genesis* 48:16. (4) *Deuteronomy* 1:10-11. (5) 28:3,6,5,4. (6) 28:8,12. (7) 15:6. (8) 33:29. (9) *Isaiah* 44:22-23. (10) 47:4. (11) 45:17.

from above, blessings of the deep crouching below, blessings of the bosom and womb. The blessings of your father surpassed the blessings of my fathers, to the endless bounds of the world's hills; let them be upon Joseph's head and upon the head of the one separated from his brothers.[1] *And He shall love you, and He shall bless you, and He shall make you numerous; may He bless the fruit of your womb and the fruit of your land, your grain, your wine and your oil, the offspring of your cattle and the flocks of your sheep, on the land that He swore to your forefathers to give to you. Blessed shall you be above all peoples; there shall not be among you a barren man or woman, nor among your cattle.* HASHEM *shall remove from you all illness; and all the evil sufferings of Egypt that you knew, He will not place upon you, but He will set them upon all your enemies.*[2]

הַמַּלְאָךְ *May the angel who redeems me from all evil bless the lads, and may my name be declared upon them — and the names of my forefathers Abraham and Isaac — and may they proliferate abundantly like fish within the land.*[3] HASHEM, *your God, has made you numerous, and behold! you are today like the stars of heaven in abundance. May* HASHEM, *the God of your forefathers, increase you a thousandfold and bless you as He spoke to you.*[4]

בָּרוּךְ *Blessed are you in the city; blessed are you in the field. Blessed are you upon your arrival; blessed are you upon your departure. Blessed is your fruit basket and your kneading trough. Blessed is the fruit of your womb, the fruit of your land and the fruit of your animal, the offspring of your cattle and the flocks of your sheep.*[5] *May* HASHEM *command that the blessing accompany you in your storehouse and wherever you set your hand, and may He bless you in the land that* HASHEM, *your God, gives you. May* HASHEM *open for you His good treasury, the heaven, to give you rain for your land in its time and to bless your every handiwork; and may you lend many nations, but may you not borrow.*[6] *For* HASHEM, *your God, will have blessed you as He spoke to you; and may you make many nations indebted to you, but may you not become indebted; and you will dominate many nations, but they will not dominate you.*[7] *Praiseworthy are you, O Israel, who is like you! — a people saved by God, Who is the Shield of your help, and Who is the Sword of your majesty. Your enemies will be false with you, but you will tread upon their heights.*[8]

REDEMPTION

מָחִיתִי *I have blotted out your willful sins like a thick mist and your errors like a cloud — return to Me for I have redeemed you. Sing gladly, O heaven, for* HASHEM *has done so; exult O depths of the earth; break out, O mountains, in glad song, forest and every tree within it, for* HASHEM *has redeemed Jacob and will take pride in Israel.*[9] *Our Redeemer —* HASHEM, *Master of Legions, is His Name — is the Holy One of Israel.*[10]

SALVATION

יִשְׂרָאֵל *Israel is saved by God in an everlasting salvation; they will not be shamed nor humiliated forever and ever.*[11] *You shall eat food and be satisfied, and you shall praise the Name of* HASHEM, *your God, Who has done wondrously with you, and My people shall not be shamed forever. And you shall know that in the midst of Israel am I, and I am* HASHEM, *your God*

עוֹד, וְלֹא יֵבֹשׁוּ עַמִּי לְעוֹלָם.[1] כִּי בְשִׂמְחָה תֵצֵאוּ וּבְשָׁלוֹם תּוּבָלוּן, הֶהָרִים וְהַגְּבָעוֹת יִפְצְחוּ לִפְנֵיכֶם רִנָּה, וְכָל עֲצֵי הַשָּׂדֶה יִמְחֲאוּ כָף.[2] הִנֵּה אֵל יְשׁוּעָתִי, אֶבְטַח וְלֹא אֶפְחָד, כִּי עָזִּי וְזִמְרָת יָהּ יהוה וַיְהִי לִי לִישׁוּעָה. וּשְׁאַבְתֶּם מַיִם בְּשָׂשׂוֹן, מִמַּעַיְנֵי הַיְשׁוּעָה. וַאֲמַרְתֶּם בַּיּוֹם הַהוּא, הוֹדוּ לַיהוה קִרְאוּ בִשְׁמוֹ, הוֹדִיעוּ בָעַמִּים עֲלִילֹתָיו, הַזְכִּירוּ כִּי נִשְׂגָּב שְׁמוֹ. זַמְּרוּ יהוה כִּי גֵאוּת עָשָׂה, מוּדַעַת זֹאת בְּכָל הָאָרֶץ. צַהֲלִי וָרֹנִּי יוֹשֶׁבֶת צִיּוֹן, כִּי גָדוֹל בְּקִרְבֵּךְ קְדוֹשׁ יִשְׂרָאֵל.[3] וְאָמַר בַּיּוֹם הַהוּא, הִנֵּה אֱלֹהֵינוּ זֶה, קִוִּינוּ לוֹ וְיוֹשִׁיעֵנוּ, זֶה יהוה קִוִּינוּ לוֹ, נָגִילָה וְנִשְׂמְחָה בִּישׁוּעָתוֹ.[4]

דעת ה'

בֵּית יַעֲקֹב, לְכוּ וְנֵלְכָה בְּאוֹר יהוה.[5] וְהָיָה אֱמוּנַת עִתֶּיךָ חֹסֶן יְשׁוּעֹת חָכְמַת וָדָעַת, יִרְאַת יהוה הִיא אוֹצָרוֹ.[6] וַיְהִי דָוִד לְכָל דְּרָכָיו מַשְׂכִּיל, וַיהוה עִמּוֹ.[7]

פדיום

פָּדָה בְשָׁלוֹם נַפְשִׁי מִקְּרָב לִי, כִּי בְרַבִּים הָיוּ עִמָּדִי.[8] וַיֹּאמֶר הָעָם אֶל שָׁאוּל, הֲיוֹנָתָן יָמוּת אֲשֶׁר עָשָׂה הַיְשׁוּעָה הַגְּדוֹלָה הַזֹּאת בְּיִשְׂרָאֵל, חָלִילָה, חַי יהוה, אִם יִפֹּל מִשַּׂעֲרַת רֹאשׁוֹ אַרְצָה, כִּי עִם אֱלֹהִים עָשָׂה הַיּוֹם הַזֶּה, וַיִּפְדּוּ הָעָם אֶת יוֹנָתָן וְלֹא מֵת.[9] וּפְדוּיֵי יהוה יְשֻׁבוּן, וּבָאוּ צִיּוֹן בְּרִנָּה, וְשִׂמְחַת עוֹלָם עַל רֹאשָׁם, שָׂשׂוֹן וְשִׂמְחָה יַשִּׂיגוּ וְנָסוּ יָגוֹן וַאֲנָחָה.[10]

הפוך צרה

הָפַכְתָּ מִסְפְּדִי לְמָחוֹל לִי, פִּתַּחְתָּ שַׂקִּי, וַתְּאַזְּרֵנִי שִׂמְחָה.[11] וְלֹא אָבָה יהוה אֱלֹהֶיךָ לִשְׁמֹעַ אֶל בִּלְעָם, וַיַּהֲפֹךְ יהוה אֱלֹהֶיךָ לְּךָ אֶת הַקְּלָלָה לִבְרָכָה, כִּי אֲהֵבְךָ יהוה אֱלֹהֶיךָ.[12] אָז תִּשְׂמַח בְּתוּלָה בְּמָחוֹל, וּבַחֻרִים וּזְקֵנִים יַחְדָּו, וְהָפַכְתִּי אֶבְלָם לְשָׂשׂוֹן, וְנִחַמְתִּים וְשִׂמַּחְתִּים מִיגוֹנָם.[13]

שלום

בּוֹרֵא נִיב שְׂפָתָיִם, שָׁלוֹם שָׁלוֹם לָרָחוֹק וְלַקָּרוֹב, אָמַר יהוה וּרְפָאתִיו.[14] וְרוּחַ לָבְשָׁה אֶת עֲמָשַׂי, רֹאשׁ הַשָּׁלִישִׁים, לְךָ דָוִיד וְעִמְּךָ בֶן יִשַׁי שָׁלוֹם, שָׁלוֹם לְךָ, וְשָׁלוֹם לְעֹזְרֶךָ כִּי עֲזָרְךָ אֱלֹהֶיךָ וַיְקַבְּלֵם דָּוִיד וַיִּתְּנֵם בְּרָאשֵׁי הַגְּדוּד.[15] וַאֲמַרְתֶּם, כֹּה לֶחָי, וְאַתָּה שָׁלוֹם וּבֵיתְךָ שָׁלוֹם וְכֹל אֲשֶׁר לְךָ שָׁלוֹם.[16] יהוה עֹז לְעַמּוֹ יִתֵּן יהוה יְבָרֵךְ אֶת עַמּוֹ בַשָּׁלוֹם.[17]

---

(1) *Joel* 2:26-27. (2) *Isaiah* 55:12. (3) 12:2-6. (4) 25:9. (5) *Isaiah* 2:5. (6) 33:6. (7) *I Samuel* 18:14. (8) *Psalms* 55:19. (9) *I Samuel* 14:45. (10) *Isaiah* 35:10. (11) *Psalms* 30:12. (12) *Deuteronomy* 23:6. (13) *Jeremiah* 31:12. (14) *Isaiah* 57:19. (15) *I Chronicles* 12:19. (16) *I Samuel* 25:6. (17) *Psalms* 29:11.

— there is none other; and My people shall not be shamed forever.[1] *For in gladness shall you go out and in peace shall you arrive; the mountains and the hills will break out before you in glad song and all the trees of the field will clap hands.*[2] *Behold! God is my help, I shall trust and not fear — for God is my might and my praise — HASHEM — and He was a salvation to me. You can draw water in joy, from the springs of salvation. And you shall say on that day, 'Give thanks to HASHEM, declare His name, make His acts known among the peoples;' remind one another, for His Name is powerful. Make music to HASHEM for He has established grandeur — this is known throughout the earth. Exult and sing for joy, O inhabitant of Zion, for the Holy One of Israel has done greatly among you.*[3] *And he shall say on that day, 'Behold! this is our God, we have hoped for Him, that He would save us — this is HASHEM, we have hoped for Him, we shall rejoice and be glad at His salvation.*[4]

KNOWLEDGE OF GOD

בֵּית *O House of Jacob — come let us go by the light of HASHEM.*[5] *The stability of your times, the strength of your salvations shall be through knowledge and wisdom, fear of God — that is one's treasure.*[6] *And David was successful in all his ways, and HASHEM was with him.*[7]

RESCUE

פָּדָה *He redeemed my soul in peace from the battles that were upon me, for the sake of the multitudes who were with me.*[8] *And the people said to Saul, 'Shall Jonathan die, who performed this great salvation for Israel? A sacrilege! — as HASHEM lives, if a hair of his head falls to the ground, for with HASHEM has he acted this day!' And the people redeemed Jonathan and he did not die.*[9] *Those redeemed by God will return and arrive at Zion with glad song and eternal gladness on their heads; joy and gladness shall they attain, and sorrow and groan shall flee.*[10]

TRANSFORMATION OF DISTRESS TO RELIEF

הָפַכְתָּ *You have changed for me my lament into dancing; You undid my sackcloth and girded me with gladness.*[11] *HASHEM, your God, did not wish to pay heed to Balaam, and HASHEM, your God, transformed for you the curse to blessing, for HASHEM, your God, loves you.*[12] *Then the maiden shall rejoice in a dance, and lads and elders together; and I shall change their mourning to joy, and I shall console them and gladden them from their sorrow.*[13]

PEACE

בּוֹרֵא *I create fruit of the lips: 'Peace, peace, for far and near,' says HASHEM, 'and I shall heal him.'*[14] *A spirit clothed Amasai, head of the officers, 'For your sake, David, and to be with you, son of Jesse; peace, peace to you, and peace to him who helps you, for your God has helped you.' David accepted them and appointed them heads of the band.*[15] *And you shall say: 'So may it be as long as you live; peace for you, peace for your household and peace for all that is with you.'*[16] *HASHEM will give might to His people, HASHEM will bless His people with peace.*[17]

מסכת מגילה לא.

אָמַר רַבִּי יוֹחָנָן: בְּכָל מָקוֹם שֶׁאַתָּה מוֹצֵא גְדֻלָּתוֹ שֶׁל הַקָּדוֹשׁ בָּרוּךְ הוּא, שָׁם אַתָּה מוֹצֵא עַנְוְתָנוּתוֹ. דָּבָר זֶה כָּתוּב בַּתּוֹרָה, וְשָׁנוּי בַּנְּבִיאִים, וּמְשֻׁלָּשׁ בַּכְּתוּבִים. כָּתוּב בַּתּוֹרָה: כִּי יהוה אֱלֹהֵיכֶם הוּא אֱלֹהֵי הָאֱלֹהִים וַאֲדֹנֵי הָאֲדֹנִים, הָאֵל הַגָּדֹל הַגִּבֹּר וְהַנּוֹרָא אֲשֶׁר לֹא יִשָּׂא פָנִים וְלֹא יִקַּח שֹׁחַד.[1] וּכְתִיב בַּתְרֵהּ: עֹשֶׂה מִשְׁפַּט יָתוֹם וְאַלְמָנָה, וְאֹהֵב גֵּר לָתֶת לוֹ לֶחֶם וְשִׂמְלָה.[2] שָׁנוּי בַּנְּבִיאִים, דִּכְתִיב: כִּי כֹה אָמַר רָם וְנִשָּׂא שֹׁכֵן עַד וְקָדוֹשׁ שְׁמוֹ, מָרוֹם וְקָדוֹשׁ אֶשְׁכּוֹן, וְאֶת דַּכָּא וּשְׁפַל רוּחַ, לְהַחֲיוֹת רוּחַ שְׁפָלִים וּלְהַחֲיוֹת לֵב נִדְכָּאִים.[3] מְשֻׁלָּשׁ בַּכְּתוּבִים, דִּכְתִיב: שִׁירוּ לֵאלֹהִים, זַמְּרוּ שְׁמוֹ, סֹלּוּ לָרֹכֵב בָּעֲרָבוֹת, בְּיָהּ שְׁמוֹ, וְעִלְזוּ לְפָנָיו.[4] וּכְתִיב בַּתְרֵהּ: אֲבִי יְתוֹמִים וְדַיַּן אַלְמָנוֹת, אֱלֹהִים בִּמְעוֹן קָדְשׁוֹ.[5]

יְהִי יהוה אֱלֹהֵינוּ עִמָּנוּ כַּאֲשֶׁר הָיָה עִם אֲבֹתֵינוּ, אַל יַעַזְבֵנוּ וְאַל יִטְּשֵׁנוּ.[6] וְאַתֶּם הַדְּבֵקִים בַּיהוה אֱלֹהֵיכֶם חַיִּים כֻּלְּכֶם הַיּוֹם.[7] כִּי נִחַם יהוה צִיּוֹן, נִחַם כָּל חָרְבֹתֶיהָ, וַיָּשֶׂם מִדְבָּרָהּ כְּעֵדֶן וְעַרְבָתָהּ כְּגַן יהוה, שָׂשׂוֹן וְשִׂמְחָה יִמָּצֵא בָהּ, תּוֹדָה וְקוֹל זִמְרָה.[8] יהוה חָפֵץ לְמַעַן צִדְקוֹ, יַגְדִּיל תּוֹרָה וְיַאְדִּיר.[9]

תהלים קכח

שִׁיר הַמַּעֲלוֹת אַשְׁרֵי כָּל יְרֵא יהוה, הַהֹלֵךְ בִּדְרָכָיו. יְגִיעַ כַּפֶּיךָ כִּי תֹאכֵל, אַשְׁרֶיךָ וְטוֹב לָךְ. אֶשְׁתְּךָ כְּגֶפֶן פֹּרִיָּה בְּיַרְכְּתֵי בֵיתֶךָ, בָּנֶיךָ כִּשְׁתִלֵי זֵיתִים, סָבִיב לְשֻׁלְחָנֶךָ. הִנֵּה כִי כֵן יְבֹרַךְ גָּבֶר יְרֵא יהוה. יְבָרֶכְךָ יהוה מִצִּיּוֹן וּרְאֵה בְּטוּב יְרוּשָׁלָיִם, כֹּל יְמֵי חַיֶּיךָ. וּרְאֵה בָנִים לְבָנֶיךָ, שָׁלוֹם עַל יִשְׂרָאֵל.

In some congregations mourners recite קַדִּישׁ יָתוֹם (p. 640) at this point.

הבדלה בבית הכנסת

סַבְרִי מָרָנָן וְרַבָּנָן וְרַבּוֹתַי:

בָּרוּךְ אַתָּה יהוה אֱלֹהֵינוּ מֶלֶךְ הָעוֹלָם, בּוֹרֵא פְּרִי הַגָּפֶן.

(.Cong. – אָמֵן)

At the departure of the Sabbath the following two blessings are recited.

After the following blessing smell the spices.

בָּרוּךְ אַתָּה יהוה אֱלֹהֵינוּ מֶלֶךְ הָעוֹלָם, בּוֹרֵא מִינֵי בְשָׂמִים.

(.Cong. – אָמֵן)

After the following blessing hold fingers up to the flame to see the reflected light:

בָּרוּךְ אַתָּה יהוה אֱלֹהֵינוּ מֶלֶךְ הָעוֹלָם, בּוֹרֵא מְאוֹרֵי הָאֵשׁ.

(.Cong. – אָמֵן)

Talmud, Tractate *Megillah* 31a

אָמַר *Rabbi Yochanan said: Wherever you find the greatness of the Holy One, Blessed is He, there you find His humility. This phenomenon is written in the Torah, repeated in the Prophets and stated a third time in the Writings. It is written in the Torah: 'For* HASHEM, *your God, He is the God of heavenly forces and the Master of masters, the great, mighty and awesome God, Who shows no favoritism and accepts no bribe.'*[1] *Afterwards it is written: 'He performs justice for orphan and widow, and loves the stranger, to give him food and clothing.'*[2] *It is repeated in the Prophets, as it is written: "For so says the exalted and uplifted One, Who abides forever, and Whose Name is holy, 'I abide in exaltedness and holiness — but am with the contrite and lowly of spirit, to revive the spirit of the lowly and to revive the heart of the contrite.' "*[3] *And it is stated a third time in the Writings, as it is written: 'Sing to God, make music for His Name, extol Him Who rides in the highest heaven, with His Name — God — and exult before Him.'*[4] *Afterwards it is written: 'Father of orphans and Judge of widows, God in the habitation of His holiness.'*[5]

May HASHEM, *our God, be with us as He was with our forefathers, may He not forsake us nor cast us off.*[6] *You who cling to* HASHEM, *our God, are all alive today.*[7] *For* HASHEM *comforts Zion, He comforts all her ruins, He will make her wilderness like Eden and her wastes like a garden of* HASHEM *— joy and gladness will be found there, thanksgiving and the sound of music.*[8] HASHEM *desired, for the sake of its [Israel's] righteousness, that the Torah be made great and glorious.*[9]

Psalm 128

שִׁיר הַמַּעֲלוֹת *A song of ascents. Praiseworthy is each person who fears* HASHEM, *who walks in His paths. When you eat the labor of your hands, you are praiseworthy, and it is well with you. Your wife shall be like a fruitful vine in the inner chambers of your home; your children shall be like olive shoots surrounding your table. Behold! For so is blessed the man who fears* HASHEM. *May* HASHEM *bless you from Zion, and may you gaze upon the goodness of Jerusalem, all the days of your life. And may you see children born to children, peace upon Israel.*

In some congregations mourners recite the Mourner's *Kaddish* (page 640) at this point.

HAVDALAH IN THE SYNAGOGUE

By your leave, my masters and teachers:

בָּרוּךְ *Blessed are You,* HASHEM, *our God, King of the universe, Who creates the fruit of the vine.* (Cong. – *Amen.)*

At the departure of the Sabbath the following two blessings are recited.

After the following blessing smell the spices.

בָּרוּךְ *Blessed are You,* HASHEM, *our God, King of the universe, Who creates species of fragrance.* (Cong. – *Amen.)*

After the following blessing hold fingers up to the flame to see the reflected light:.

בָּרוּךְ *Blessed are You,* HASHEM, *our God, King of the universe, Who creates the illuminations of the fire.* (Cong.– *Amen.)*

---

(1) *Deuteronomy* 10:17. (2) 10:18. (3) *Isaiah* 57:15. (4) *Psalms* 68:5. (5) 68:6.
(6) *I Kings* 8:57. (7) *Deuteronomy* 4:4. (8) *Isaiah* 51:3. (9) 42:21.

בָּרוּךְ אַתָּה יהוה אֱלֹהֵינוּ מֶלֶךְ הָעוֹלָם, הַמַּבְדִּיל בֵּין קֹדֶשׁ לְחוֹל, בֵּין אוֹר לְחֹשֶׁךְ, בֵּין יִשְׂרָאֵל לָעַמִּים, בֵּין יוֹם הַשְּׁבִיעִי לְשֵׁשֶׁת יְמֵי הַמַּעֲשֶׂה. בָּרוּךְ אַתָּה יהוה, הַמַּבְדִּיל בֵּין קֹדֶשׁ לְחוֹל. (Cong. – אָמֵן.)

The *chazzan,* or someone else present for *Havdalah,* should drink most of the cup.

The congregation stands while reciting עָלֵינוּ.

עָלֵינוּ לְשַׁבֵּחַ לַאֲדוֹן הַכֹּל, לָתֵת גְּדֻלָּה לְיוֹצֵר בְּרֵאשִׁית, שֶׁלֹּא עָשָׂנוּ כְּגוֹיֵי הָאֲרָצוֹת, וְלֹא שָׂמָנוּ כְּמִשְׁפְּחוֹת הָאֲדָמָה. שֶׁלֹּא שָׂם חֶלְקֵנוּ כָּהֶם, וְגוֹרָלֵנוּ כְּכָל הֲמוֹנָם. (שֶׁהֵם מִשְׁתַּחֲוִים לְהֶבֶל וָרִיק, וּמִתְפַּלְלִים אֶל אֵל לֹא יוֹשִׁיעַ.[1]) וַאֲנַחְנוּ כּוֹרְעִים וּמִשְׁתַּחֲוִים וּמוֹדִים, לִפְנֵי מֶלֶךְ מַלְכֵי הַמְּלָכִים הַקָּדוֹשׁ בָּרוּךְ הוּא. שֶׁהוּא נוֹטֶה שָׁמַיִם וְיֹסֵד אָרֶץ,[2] וּמוֹשַׁב יְקָרוֹ בַּשָּׁמַיִם מִמַּעַל, וּשְׁכִינַת עֻזּוֹ בְּגָבְהֵי מְרוֹמִים. הוּא אֱלֹהֵינוּ, אֵין עוֹד. אֱמֶת מַלְכֵּנוּ, אֶפֶס זוּלָתוֹ, כַּכָּתוּב בְּתוֹרָתוֹ: וְיָדַעְתָּ הַיּוֹם וַהֲשֵׁבֹתָ אֶל לְבָבֶךָ, כִּי יהוה הוּא הָאֱלֹהִים בַּשָּׁמַיִם מִמַּעַל וְעַל הָאָרֶץ מִתָּחַת, אֵין עוֹד.[3]

Bow while reciting וַאֲנַחְנוּ כּוֹרְעִים וּמִשְׁתַּחֲוִים.

עַל כֵּן נְקַוֶּה לְּךָ יהוה אֱלֹהֵינוּ לִרְאוֹת מְהֵרָה בְּתִפְאֶרֶת עֻזֶּךָ, לְהַעֲבִיר גִּלּוּלִים מִן הָאָרֶץ, וְהָאֱלִילִים כָּרוֹת יִכָּרֵתוּן, לְתַקֵּן עוֹלָם בְּמַלְכוּת שַׁדַּי. וְכָל בְּנֵי בָשָׂר יִקְרְאוּ בִשְׁמֶךָ, לְהַפְנוֹת אֵלֶיךָ כָּל רִשְׁעֵי אָרֶץ. יַכִּירוּ וְיֵדְעוּ כָּל יוֹשְׁבֵי תֵבֵל, כִּי לְךָ תִּכְרַע כָּל בֶּרֶךְ, תִּשָּׁבַע כָּל לָשׁוֹן.[4] לְפָנֶיךָ יהוה אֱלֹהֵינוּ יִכְרְעוּ וְיִפֹּלוּ, וְלִכְבוֹד שִׁמְךָ יְקָר יִתֵּנוּ. וִיקַבְּלוּ כֻלָּם אֶת עוֹל מַלְכוּתֶךָ, וְתִמְלֹךְ עֲלֵיהֶם מְהֵרָה לְעוֹלָם וָעֶד. כִּי הַמַּלְכוּת שֶׁלְּךָ הִיא וּלְעוֹלְמֵי עַד תִּמְלוֹךְ בְּכָבוֹד, כַּכָּתוּב בְּתוֹרָתֶךָ: יהוה יִמְלֹךְ לְעֹלָם וָעֶד.[5] ❖ וְנֶאֱמַר: וְהָיָה יהוה לְמֶלֶךְ עַל כָּל הָאָרֶץ, בַּיּוֹם הַהוּא יִהְיֶה יהוה אֶחָד וּשְׁמוֹ אֶחָד.[6]

Some recite the following after עָלֵינוּ:

אַל תִּירָא מִפַּחַד פִּתְאֹם, וּמִשֹּׁאַת רְשָׁעִים כִּי תָבֹא.[7] עֻצוּ עֵצָה וְתֻפָר, דַּבְּרוּ דָבָר וְלֹא יָקוּם, כִּי עִמָּנוּ אֵל.[8] וְעַד זִקְנָה אֲנִי הוּא, וְעַד שֵׂיבָה אֲנִי אֶסְבֹּל, אֲנִי עָשִׂיתִי וַאֲנִי אֶשָּׂא, וַאֲנִי אֶסְבֹּל וַאֲמַלֵּט.[9]

בָּרוּךְ *Blessed are You,* HASHEM *our God, King of the universe, Who separates between holy and secular, between light and darkness, between Israel and the nations, between the seventh day and the six days of labor. Blessed are You,* HASHEM, *Who separates between holy and secular.* (Cong. – *Amen.*)

The *chazzan* or someone else present for *Havdalah,* should drink most of the cup.

Stand while reciting עָלֵינוּ, *'It is our duty . . .'*

עָלֵינוּ *It is our duty to praise the Master of all, to ascribe greatness to the Molder of primeval creation, for He has not made us like the nations of the lands, and has not emplaced us like the families of the earth; for He has not assigned our portion like theirs nor our lot like all their multitudes. (For they bow to vanity and emptiness and pray to a god which helps not.*[1]*) But we bend our knees, bow, and acknowledge our thanks before the King Who reigns over kings, the Holy One, Blessed is He. He stretches out heaven and establishes earth's foundation,*[2] *the seat of His homage is in the heavens above and His powerful Presence is in the loftiest heights. He is our God and there is none other. True is our King, there is nothing beside Him, as it is written in His Torah: 'You are to know this day and take to your heart that* HASHEM *is the only God — in heaven above and on the earth below — there is none other.'*[3]

Bow while reciting *'But we bend our knees.'*

עַל כֵּן *Therefore we put our hope in You,* HASHEM, *our God, that we may soon see Your mighty splendor, to remove detestable idolatry from the earth, and false gods will be utterly cut off, to perfect the universe through the Almighty's sovereignty. Then all humanity will call upon Your Name, to turn all the earth's wicked toward You. All the world's inhabitants will recognize and know that to You every knee should bend, every tongue should swear.*[4] *Before You,* HASHEM, *our God, they will bend every knee and cast themselves down and to the glory of Your Name they will render homage, and they will all accept upon themselves the yoke of Your kingship that You may reign over them soon and eternally. For the kingdom is Yours and You will reign for all eternity in glory as it is written in Your Torah:* HASHEM *shall reign for all eternity.*[5] Chazzan– *And it is said:* HASHEM *will be King over all the world — on that day* HASHEM *will be One and His Name will be One.*[6]

Some congregations recite the following after *Aleinu.*

אַל תִּירָא *Do not fear sudden terror, or the holocaust of the wicked when it comes.*[7] *Plan a conspiracy and it will be annulled; speak your piece and it shall not stand, for God is with us.*[8] *Even till your seniority, I remain unchanged; and even till your ripe old age, I shall endure. I created you and I shall bear you; I shall endure and rescue.*[9]

---

(1) *Isaiah* 45:20. (2) 51:13. (3) *Deuteronomy* 4:39. (4) Cf. *Isaiah* 45:23.
(5) *Exodus* 15:18. (6) *Zechariah* 14:9. (7) *Proverbs* 3:25. (8) *Isaiah* 8:10. (9) 46:4.

קדיש יתום

Mourners recite קַדִּישׁ יָתוֹם.

יִתְגַּדַּל וְיִתְקַדַּשׁ שְׁמֵהּ רַבָּא. (.Cong – אָמֵן.) בְּעָלְמָא דִּי בְרָא כִרְעוּתֵהּ. וְיַמְלִיךְ מַלְכוּתֵהּ, בְּחַיֵּיכוֹן וּבְיוֹמֵיכוֹן וּבְחַיֵּי דְכָל בֵּית יִשְׂרָאֵל, בַּעֲגָלָא וּבִזְמַן קָרִיב. וְאִמְרוּ: אָמֵן.

(.Cong – אָמֵן. יְהֵא שְׁמֵהּ רַבָּא מְבָרַךְ לְעָלַם וּלְעָלְמֵי עָלְמַיָּא.)

יְהֵא שְׁמֵהּ רַבָּא מְבָרַךְ לְעָלַם וּלְעָלְמֵי עָלְמַיָּא.

יִתְבָּרַךְ וְיִשְׁתַּבַּח וְיִתְפָּאַר וְיִתְרוֹמַם וְיִתְנַשֵּׂא וְיִתְהַדָּר וְיִתְעַלֶּה וְיִתְהַלָּל שְׁמֵהּ דְּקֻדְשָׁא בְּרִיךְ הוּא (.Cong – בְּרִיךְ הוּא) — לְעֵלָּא מִן כָּל בִּרְכָתָא וְשִׁירָתָא תֻּשְׁבְּחָתָא וְנֶחֱמָתָא, דַּאֲמִירָן בְּעָלְמָא. וְאִמְרוּ: אָמֵן. (.Cong – אָמֵן.)

יְהֵא שְׁלָמָא רַבָּא מִן שְׁמַיָּא, וְחַיִּים עָלֵינוּ וְעַל כָּל יִשְׂרָאֵל. וְאִמְרוּ: אָמֵן. (.Cong – אָמֵן.)

Take three steps back. Bow left and say . . . עֹשֶׂה; bow right and say . . . הוּא; bow forward and say וְעַל כָּל . . . אָמֵן. Remain standing in place for a few moments, then take three steps forward.

עֹשֶׂה שָׁלוֹם בִּמְרוֹמָיו, הוּא יַעֲשֶׂה שָׁלוֹם עָלֵינוּ, וְעַל כָּל יִשְׂרָאֵל. וְאִמְרוּ: אָמֵן. (.Cong – אָמֵן.)

תהלים כז

לְדָוִד, יהוה אוֹרִי וְיִשְׁעִי, מִמִּי אִירָא, יהוה מָעוֹז חַיַּי, מִמִּי אֶפְחָד. בִּקְרֹב עָלַי מְרֵעִים לֶאֱכֹל אֶת בְּשָׂרִי, צָרַי וְאֹיְבַי לִי, הֵמָּה כָשְׁלוּ וְנָפָלוּ. אִם תַּחֲנֶה עָלַי מַחֲנֶה, לֹא יִירָא לִבִּי, אִם תָּקוּם עָלַי מִלְחָמָה, בְּזֹאת אֲנִי בוֹטֵחַ. אַחַת שָׁאַלְתִּי מֵאֵת יהוה, אוֹתָהּ אֲבַקֵּשׁ, שִׁבְתִּי בְּבֵית יהוה כָּל יְמֵי חַיַּי, לַחֲזוֹת בְּנֹעַם יהוה, וּלְבַקֵּר בְּהֵיכָלוֹ. כִּי יִצְפְּנֵנִי בְּסֻכֹּה בְּיוֹם רָעָה, יַסְתִּירֵנִי בְּסֵתֶר אָהֳלוֹ, בְּצוּר יְרוֹמְמֵנִי. וְעַתָּה יָרוּם רֹאשִׁי עַל אֹיְבַי סְבִיבוֹתַי, וְאֶזְבְּחָה בְאָהֳלוֹ זִבְחֵי תְרוּעָה, אָשִׁירָה וַאֲזַמְּרָה לַיהוה. שְׁמַע יהוה קוֹלִי אֶקְרָא, וְחָנֵּנִי וַעֲנֵנִי. לְךָ אָמַר לִבִּי בַּקְּשׁוּ פָנָי, אֶת פָּנֶיךָ יהוה אֲבַקֵּשׁ. אַל תַּסְתֵּר פָּנֶיךָ מִמֶּנִּי, אַל תַּט בְּאַף עַבְדֶּךָ, עֶזְרָתִי הָיִיתָ, אַל תִּטְּשֵׁנִי וְאַל תַּעַזְבֵנִי, אֱלֹהֵי יִשְׁעִי. כִּי אָבִי וְאִמִּי עֲזָבוּנִי, וַיהוה יַאַסְפֵנִי. הוֹרֵנִי יהוה דַּרְכֶּךָ, וּנְחֵנִי בְּאֹרַח מִישׁוֹר, לְמַעַן שׁוֹרְרָי. אַל תִּתְּנֵנִי בְּנֶפֶשׁ צָרָי, כִּי קָמוּ בִי עֵדֵי שֶׁקֶר, וִיפֵחַ חָמָס. ❖ לוּלֵא הֶאֱמַנְתִּי לִרְאוֹת בְּטוּב יהוה בְּאֶרֶץ חַיִּים. קַוֵּה אֶל יהוה, חֲזַק וְיַאֲמֵץ לִבֶּךָ, וְקַוֵּה אֶל יהוה.

Mourners recite קַדִּישׁ יָתוֹם, the Mourner's *Kaddish* (above).

MOURNER'S KADDISH

Mourners recite קַדִּישׁ יָתוֹם, the Mourner's *Kaddish* (see *Laws* 81-83).

A transliteration of this *Kaddish* appears on page 1305.

יִתְגַּדַּל *May His great Name grow exalted and sanctified* (Cong.– *Amen.*) *in the world that He created as He willed. May He give reign to His kingship in your lifetimes and in your days, and in the lifetimes of the entire Family of Israel, swiftly and soon. Now respond: Amen.*

(Cong.– *Amen. May His great Name be blessed forever and ever.*)

May His great Name be blessed forever and ever.

Blessed, praised, glorified, exalted, extolled, mighty, upraised, and lauded be the Name of the Holy One, Blessed is He (Cong.– *Blessed is He*) — *beyond any blessing and song, praise and consolation that are uttered in the world. Now respond: Amen.* (Cong.– *Amen*).

May there be abundant peace from Heaven, and life, upon us and upon all Israel. Now respond: Amen. (Cong.– *Amen.*)

Take three steps back. Bow left and say, *'He Who makes peace . . .'*; bow right and say, *'may He . . .'*; bow forward and say, *'and upon all Israel . . .'* Remain standing in place for a few moments, then take three steps forward.

He Who makes peace in His heights, may He make peace upon us, and upon all Israel. Now respond: Amen. (Cong.– *Amen.*)

Psalm 27

לְדָוִד *Of David;* HASHEM *is my light and my salvation, whom shall I fear?* HASHEM *is my life's strength, whom shall I dread? When evildoers approach me to devour my flesh, my tormentors and my foes against me — it is they who stumble and fall. Though an army would besiege me, my heart would not fear; though war would arise against me, in this I trust. One thing I asked of* HASHEM, *that shall I seek: That I dwell in the House of* HASHEM *all the days of my life; to behold the sweetness of* HASHEM *and to contemplate in His Sanctuary. Indeed, He will hide me in His Shelter on the day of evil; He will conceal me in the concealment of His Tent, He will lift me upon a rock. Now my head is raised above my enemies around me, and I will slaughter offerings in His Tent accompanied by joyous song; I will sing and make music to* HASHEM. HASHEM, *hear my voice when I call, be gracious toward me and answer me. In Your behalf, my heart has said, 'Seek My Presence'; Your Presence,* HASHEM, *do I seek. Conceal not Your Presence from me, repel not Your servant in anger. You have been my Helper, abandon me not, forsake me not, O God of my salvation. Though my father and mother have forsaken me,* HASHEM *will gather me in. Teach me Your way,* HASHEM, *and lead me on the path of integrity, because of my watchful foes. Deliver me not to the wishes of my tormentors, for there have arisen against me false witnesses who breathe violence.* Chazzan– *Had I not trusted that I would see the goodness of* HASHEM *in the land of life! Hope to* HASHEM, *strengthen yourself and He will give you courage; and hope to* HASHEM.

Mourners recite the Mourner's *Kaddish* (above).

הבדלה

At the departure of the Sabbath begin here.

הִנֵּה אֵל יְשׁוּעָתִי אֶבְטַח וְלֹא אֶפְחָד, כִּי עָזִּי וְזִמְרָת יָהּ יהוה, וַיְהִי לִי לִישׁוּעָה. וּשְׁאַבְתֶּם מַיִם בְּשָׂשׂוֹן, מִמַּעַיְנֵי הַיְשׁוּעָה.[1] לַיהוה הַיְשׁוּעָה, עַל עַמְּךָ בִרְכָתֶךָ סֶּלָה.[2] יהוה צְבָאוֹת עִמָּנוּ, מִשְׂגָּב לָנוּ אֱלֹהֵי יַעֲקֹב סֶלָה.[3] יהוה צְבָאוֹת, אַשְׁרֵי אָדָם בֹּטֵחַ בָּךְ.[4] יהוה הוֹשִׁיעָה, הַמֶּלֶךְ יַעֲנֵנוּ בְיוֹם קָרְאֵנוּ.[5] לַיְּהוּדִים הָיְתָה אוֹרָה וְשִׂמְחָה, וְשָׂשֹׂן וִיקָר,[6] כֵּן תִּהְיֶה לָּנוּ. כּוֹס יְשׁוּעוֹת אֶשָּׂא, וּבְשֵׁם יהוה אֶקְרָא.[7]

סַבְרִי מָרָנָן וְרַבָּנָן וְרַבּוֹתַי:

בָּרוּךְ אַתָּה יהוה אֱלֹהֵינוּ מֶלֶךְ הָעוֹלָם, בּוֹרֵא פְּרִי הַגָּפֶן.

(all present respond— אָמֵן.)

At the departure of the Sabbath the following two blessings are recited.
After the following blessing smell the spices.

בָּרוּךְ אַתָּה יהוה אֱלֹהֵינוּ מֶלֶךְ הָעוֹלָם, בּוֹרֵא מִינֵי בְשָׂמִים.*

(all present respond— אָמֵן.)

After the following blessing hold fingers up to the flame to see the reflected light.

בָּרוּךְ אַתָּה יהוה אֱלֹהֵינוּ מֶלֶךְ הָעוֹלָם, בּוֹרֵא מְאוֹרֵי הָאֵשׁ.

(all present respond— אָמֵן.)

בָּרוּךְ אַתָּה יהוה אֱלֹהֵינוּ מֶלֶךְ הָעוֹלָם, הַמַּבְדִּיל בֵּין קֹדֶשׁ לְחוֹל,* בֵּין אוֹר לְחֹשֶׁךְ,* בֵּין יִשְׂרָאֵל לָעַמִּים, בֵּין יוֹם הַשְּׁבִיעִי לְשֵׁשֶׁת יְמֵי הַמַּעֲשֶׂה. בָּרוּךְ אַתָּה יהוה, הַמַּבְדִּיל בֵּין קֹדֶשׁ לְחוֹל.

(all present respond— אָמֵן.)

The one who recited *Havdalah,* or someone else present for *Havdalah,* should drink most of the wine from the cup.

At the departure of the Sabbath extinguish the flame by pouring leftover wine over it into a dish. It is customary to dip the fingers into the wine-dish and touch the eyelids and inner pockets with them. This symbolizes that the 'light of the *mitzvah*' will guide us and it invokes blessing for the week.

הַבְדָּלָה / HAVDALAH

The concluding moments of the Sabbath are a time of foreboding, as holiness wanes and travail looms. Consequently, the *Havdalah* after the Sabbath includes symbols of blessing. Among them are the optimistic verses of blessing that introduce the post-Sabbath *Havdalah* and the custom to fill the cup until it overflows.

The concept of *Havdalah,* literally, *distinction,* is ordained by the Torah as part of the general commandment to 'Remember the Sabbath,' implying that one must verbalize the differentiation between the Sabbath and other holy days, and the weekdays *(Rambam).*

With the departure of the Sabbath and the onset of the work week, it is essential to be conscious of the differences between sanctity and secularity. In explaining why the first mention of this separation is made in the *Shemoneh Esrei* blessing for wisdom, the Sages explain: אִם אֵין דֵּעָה הַבְדָּלָה מִנַּיִן, *If there is no wisdom, how can there be differentiation?* Clearly, then, to distinguish is a function of intelligent reasoning. It is incumbent, therefore, upon each Jew to be conscious of the sharp difference between the holiness he has just been experiencing and the sharply lower level of spirituality to which he is about to descend.

בּוֹרֵא מִינֵי בְשָׂמִים — *Who creates species of*

HAVDALAH

At the departure of the Sabbath begin here.

הִנֵּה *Behold! God is my salvation, I shall trust and not fear — for God is my might and my praise — HASHEM — and He was a salvation for me. You can draw water with joy, from the springs of salvation.*[1] *Salvation is HASHEM's, upon Your people is Your blessing, Selah.*[2] *HASHEM, Master of legions, is with us, a stronghold for us is the God of Jacob, Selah.*[3] *HASHEM, Master of legions, praised is the man who trusts in You.*[4] *HASHEM save! May the King answer us on the day we call.*[5] *For the Jews there was light, gladness, joy, and honor*[6] *— so may it be for us. I will raise the cup of salvations, and I shall invoke the Name of HASHEM.*[7]

By your leave, my masters and teachers:

בָּרוּךְ *Blessed are You, HASHEM, our God, King of the universe, Who creates the fruit of the vine.* (All present respond— *Amen.*)

At the departure of the Sabbath the following two blessings are recited.
After the following blessing smell the spices:

בָּרוּךְ *Blessed are You, HASHEM, our God, King of the universe, Who creates species of fragrance.* (All present respond— *Amen.*)

After the following blessing hold fingers up to the flame to see the reflected light.

בָּרוּךְ *Blessed are You, HASHEM, our God, King of the universe, Who creates the illuminations of the fire.* (All present respond— *Amen.*)

בָּרוּךְ *Blessed are You, HASHEM our God, King of the universe, Who separates between holy and secular,* between light and darkness,* between Israel and the nations, between the seventh day and the six days of labor. Blessed are You, HASHEM, Who separates between holy and secular.* (All present respond— *Amen.*)

The one who recited *Havdalah,* or someone else present for *Havdalah,* should drink most of the wine from the cup.

At the departure of the Sabbath extinguish the flame by pouring leftover wine over it into a dish. It is customary to dip the fingers into the wine-dish and touch the eyelids and inner pockets with them. This symbolizes that the 'light of the *mitzvah*' will guide us and it invokes blessing for the week.

(1) *Isaiah* 12:2-3. (2) *Psalms* 3:9. (3) 46:12. (4) 84:13. (5) 20:10. (6) *Esther* 8:16. (7) *Psalms* 116:13.

fragrance. The reason for smelling the pleasant odor of spices at the end of the Sabbath is to assuage oneself for the loss of the departing נְשָׁמָה יְתֵרָה, *additional* [Sabbath] *soul* [This explains why many authorities omit this blessing after Yom Kippur, when the additional soul is not present.] *(Abudraham).*

Additionally, the fires of *Gehinnom* begin to rage after having been dormant during the Sabbath. The pain of knowing that sinners are beginning to endure new punishments is eased by the spices *(Bach; Tosafos).*

חול — *Secular.* The more familiar translation, *profane,* has the general connotation of blasphemy and impurity. The message of Sabbath and Yom Kippur, however, goes further. It involves the need to recognize that even ordinary, *secular,* pursuits are deficient if they are not imbued with holiness.

בֵּין קֹדֶשׁ לְחוֹל בֵּין אוֹר לְחֹשֶׁךְ ... — *Between holy and secular, between light and darkness...* The *holy* represents sanctity, while חול is the קְלִפָּה, *shell,* i.e., the outer barrier that obscures holiness. By recognizing the difference between *light* and *darkness* one is able to discern God's wisdom, and thereby make one's own distinction between good, represented by light, and evil, represented by darkness. The awareness that God took Israel to Himself as His Chosen Nation should cause inexpressible joy. Finally, the last cause of intense joy is the realization that Sabbath is God's special day of holiness and, as the *Zohar* teaches, He presented it as a gift to Israel *(Yesod v'Shoresh Ha-Avodah).*

✧ שִׂמְחַת בֵּית הַשּׁוֹאֵבָה / The Water-Drawing Festivities ✧

☙§ Apart from the daily and festival sacrifices offered in the Temple during Succos — most of which were accompanied by an offering of fine flour mixed with oil, and a libation of wine — the height of the season's joy was expressed through and during נִיסּוּךְ הַמַּיִם, *a libation of water.*

Among the many reasons offered for this ceremony is that on Succos, which comes just prior to the rainy season in *Eretz Yisrael*, judgment is passed in regard to rainfall for the coming year (*Rosh Hashanah* 1:2). The Talmud notes that the water libation was performed only on Succos in order to invoke God's blessing on the year's rainfall in this time of judgment. "Pour out water before Me on the Festival," God is quoted, as it were, "in order that your rains for the year may be blessed."

All other libations in the Temple were of wine poured on the Altar, but during the seven days of Succos, water was poured simultaneously with the wine libation in conjunction with the morning offering (*Yoma* 26b).

☙§ The Festivities

The festivities associated with the drawing of the water were the highpoint of the festival, and fulfilled the verse וּשְׁאַבְתֶּם מַיִם בְּשָׂשׂוֹן, *and you shall draw forth water with gladness* (*Isaiah* 12:3). The name given to these festivities was שִׂמְחַת בֵּית הַשּׁוֹאֵבָה, *Simchas Beis HaSho'evah,* which according to the Babylonian Talmud, refers to the *she'ivah* (drawing up) of the water. The Jerusalem Talmud, interprets: 'Because from there they drew the spirit of holiness' (שֶׁמִּשָּׁם שׁוֹאֲבִים רוּחַ הַקֹּדֶשׁ). It is told that the prophet Yonah ben Amitai was one of those who made the pilgrimage on the Festivals; when he joined the rejoicing of *Beis HaSho'evah* the spirit of prophecy descended on him. This teaches us that the spirit of prophecy rests only on a joyous heart, as Scripture teaches: *And it came to pass, when the musician played, that the hand of God was upon him* (*II Kings* 3:15).

☙§ Preparation and Rejoicing

Imrei Emes asks: The essence of the *mitzvah* is the *libation* of the water; why, then, did the Sages place such emphasis on celebrating the *drawing* of the water? We learn from this that the preparation is sometimes greater than the *mitzvah* itself, because the effort and enthusiasm associated with the preparation instills a profound influence on a person.

So intense were the festivities associated with the water drawing that the Sages stated in the Mishnah: 'Whoever did not see the rejoicing of the *Beis HaSho'evah,* never saw rejoicing in his lifetime.'

This is how *Rambam* in *Hilchas Lulav* describes the festivities:

> Although it is a *mitzvah* to rejoice on all festivals, there was a day of special rejoicing in the Temple during the festival of Succos, in accordance with the verse, *And you shall rejoice before* HASHEM, *your God, seven days* (*Lev.* 23:40). What was the procedure? On the eve of the first day of the festival, an upper section was prepared in the Temple for women and a lower section for men to ensure that the sexes did not mix. Rejoicing began at the termination of the first day of the festival; on each day of *Chol Hamoed* it began after the regular afternoon *'tamid'* had been

offered, and went on for the rest of the day and all of the following night.

[The *mechitzah* or dividing wall currently separating the men and the women in synagogues is based on this separation of men and women in the Temple. The practice of building upper galleries in the large synagogues derives from the gallery built in the Temple Courtyard on Succos.]

What form did this rejoicing take? Fifes were sounded; they played harps, lyres, and cymbals; whoever could play a musical instrument did so, and whoever could sing, sang. Others would stamp their feet, slap their thighs, clap their hands, leap, or dances each one to the best of his ability, while they recited songs and hymns of praise. However, this rejoicing did not override the Sabbath or the first day of the Festival.

We read further in the Mishnah (*Succah* 5:4): "Men of piety and zeal (חֲסִידִים וְאַנְשֵׁי מַעֲשֶׂה) with fiery torches in their hands would dance in front [of the assemblage] reciting words of song and praise. And the Levites with harps, lutes, cymbals, trumpets and countless musical instruments [stood] on the fifteen steps that descend from the Courtyard of the Israelites to the Women's Court, corresponding to the fifteen Songs of Ascent [the fifteen Psalms beginning *Shir HaMaalos* (*Psalms* 120-134)], where Levites were stationed with musical instruments, singing songs of praise."

In commemoration of the Temple celebration, it is customary for people to gather in synagogues, yeshivos, and private homes beginning with the second evening of Succos to rejoice. Since part of the *Bais Hasho'evah* celebration involved the Levites' music as they stood on the fifteen steps, many congregations sing the fifteen שִׁיר הַמַּעֲלוֹת, *Song of Ascents*, psalms.

הוֹשַׁעְנָא רַבָּה / Hoshana Rabbah

The *Zohar* (*Tzav* 31b) describes Hoshana Rabbah as a judgment day akin to Yom Kippur itself, for on Hoshana Rabbah the parchments containing the Yom Kippur decrees are made final. Consequently, Hoshana Rabbah assumes special importance as a day of prayer and repentance. On Rosh Hashanah all people were judged. The righteous were given a favorable judgment, those found wanting — but not totally evil — were given until Yom Kippur to repent. If they failed to do so, the verdict against them was written and sealed, but not yet 'delivered.' That is not done until Hoshana Rabbah, a day when Jews assemble in prayer, dedication, and supplication. The joy of Succos reaches its climax not in revelry but in devotion. In His mercy, God finds ample reason to tear up the parchments bearing harsher sentences, as it were, and replace them with brighter tidings.

Various customs have arisen owing to the day's status as a time of Divine judgment. Among them:

Extra lights are lit in the synagogue.

It is customary to remain awake and spend the entire night of Hoshana Rabbah reading from the Torah and Psalms. The particular order to be followed is printed in a special volume called *Tikkun Leil Hoshana Rabbah*.

In some congregations, *Mishneh Torah*, i.e., the entire *Book of Deuteronomy*, is read from a Torah Scroll. [No blessing is recited over this reading.]

In some congregations the entire *Book of Psalms* is recited communally.

פסוקי דזמרה לחול המועד והושענא רבה

THE MORNING SERVICE BEGINS WITH PAGES 130-170, THEN CONTINUES HERE.

INTRODUCTORY PSALM TO PESUKEI D'ZIMRAH

תהלים ל

מִזְמוֹר שִׁיר חֲנֻכַּת הַבַּיִת לְדָוִד. אֲרוֹמִמְךָ יהוה כִּי דִלִּיתָנִי, וְלֹא שִׂמַּחְתָּ אֹיְבַי לִי. יהוה אֱלֹהָי, שִׁוַּעְתִּי אֵלֶיךָ וַתִּרְפָּאֵנִי. יהוה הֶעֱלִיתָ מִן שְׁאוֹל נַפְשִׁי, חִיִּיתַנִי מִיָּרְדִי בוֹר. זַמְּרוּ לַיהוה חֲסִידָיו, וְהוֹדוּ לְזֵכֶר קָדְשׁוֹ. כִּי רֶגַע בְּאַפּוֹ, חַיִּים בִּרְצוֹנוֹ, בָּעֶרֶב יָלִין בֶּכִי וְלַבֹּקֶר רִנָּה. וַאֲנִי אָמַרְתִּי בְשַׁלְוִי, בַּל אֶמּוֹט לְעוֹלָם. יהוה בִּרְצוֹנְךָ הֶעֱמַדְתָּה לְהַרְרִי עֹז, הִסְתַּרְתָּ פָנֶיךָ הָיִיתִי נִבְהָל. אֵלֶיךָ יהוה אֶקְרָא, וְאֶל אֲדֹנָי אֶתְחַנָּן. מַה בֶּצַע בְּדָמִי, בְּרִדְתִּי אֶל שָׁחַת, הֲיוֹדְךָ עָפָר, הֲיַגִּיד אֲמִתֶּךָ. שְׁמַע יהוה וְחָנֵּנִי, יהוה הֱיֵה עֹזֵר לִי. ❖ הָפַכְתָּ מִסְפְּדִי לְמָחוֹל לִי, פִּתַּחְתָּ שַׂקִּי, וַתְּאַזְּרֵנִי שִׂמְחָה. לְמַעַן יְזַמֶּרְךָ כָבוֹד וְלֹא יִדֹּם, יהוה אֱלֹהַי לְעוֹלָם אוֹדֶךָּ.

קדיש יתום

Mourners recite קַדִּישׁ יָתוֹם. See *Laws* §81-83.

יִתְגַּדַּל וְיִתְקַדַּשׁ שְׁמֵהּ רַבָּא. (.Cong. – אָמֵן) בְּעָלְמָא דִּי בְרָא כִרְעוּתֵהּ. וְיַמְלִיךְ מַלְכוּתֵהּ, בְּחַיֵּיכוֹן וּבְיוֹמֵיכוֹן וּבְחַיֵּי דְכָל בֵּית יִשְׂרָאֵל, בַּעֲגָלָא וּבִזְמַן קָרִיב. וְאִמְרוּ: אָמֵן.

(.Cong. – אָמֵן. יְהֵא שְׁמֵהּ רַבָּא מְבָרַךְ לְעָלַם וּלְעָלְמֵי עָלְמַיָּא.)

יְהֵא שְׁמֵהּ רַבָּא מְבָרַךְ לְעָלַם וּלְעָלְמֵי עָלְמַיָּא.

יִתְבָּרַךְ וְיִשְׁתַּבַּח וְיִתְפָּאַר וְיִתְרוֹמַם וְיִתְנַשֵּׂא וְיִתְהַדָּר וְיִתְעַלֶּה וְיִתְהַלָּל שְׁמֵהּ דְּקֻדְשָׁא בְּרִיךְ הוּא (.Cong. – בְּרִיךְ הוּא) — לְעֵלָּא מִן כָּל בִּרְכָתָא וְשִׁירָתָא תֻּשְׁבְּחָתָא וְנֶחֱמָתָא, דַּאֲמִירָן בְּעָלְמָא. וְאִמְרוּ: אָמֵן. (.Cong. – אָמֵן.)

יְהֵא שְׁלָמָא רַבָּא מִן שְׁמַיָּא, וְחַיִּים עָלֵינוּ וְעַל כָּל יִשְׂרָאֵל. וְאִמְרוּ: אָמֵן. (.Cong. – אָמֵן.)

Take three steps back. Bow left and say . . . עֹשֶׂה; bow right and say . . . הוּא; bow forward and say וְעַל כָּל . . . אָמֵן. Remain standing in place for a few moments, then take three steps forward.

עֹשֶׂה שָׁלוֹם בִּמְרוֹמָיו, הוּא יַעֲשֶׂה שָׁלוֹם עָלֵינוּ, וְעַל כָּל יִשְׂרָאֵל. וְאִמְרוּ: אָמֵן. (.Cong. – אָמֵן.)

(Some recite this short Kabbalistic declaration of intent before beginning *Pesukei D'zimrah:*)

(הֲרֵינִי מְזַמֵּן אֶת פִּי לְהוֹדוֹת וּלְהַלֵּל וּלְשַׁבֵּחַ אֶת בּוֹרְאִי. לְשֵׁם יִחוּד קוּדְשָׁא בְּרִיךְ הוּא וּשְׁכִינְתֵּיהּ עַל יְדֵי הַהוּא טָמִיר וְנֶעְלָם, בְּשֵׁם כָּל יִשְׂרָאֵל.)

PESUKEI D'ZIMRAH FOR CHOL HAMOED AND HOSHANA RABBAH

THE MORNING SERVICE BEGINS WITH PAGES 130-170, THEN CONTINUES HERE.

INTRODUCTORY PSALM TO PESUKEI D'ZIMRAH

Psalm 30

מִזְמוֹר *A psalm — a song for the inauguration of the Temple— by David. I will exalt You, HASHEM, for You have drawn me up and not let my foes rejoice over me. HASHEM, my God, I cried out to You and You healed me. HASHEM, You have raised my soul from the lower world, You have preserved me from my descent to the Pit. Make music to HASHEM, His devout ones, and give thanks to His Holy Name. For His anger endures but a moment; life results from His favor. In the evening one lies down weeping, but with dawn — a cry of joy! I had said in my serenity, 'I will never falter.' But, HASHEM, all is through Your favor — You supported my greatness with might; should You but conceal Your face, I would be confounded. To You, HASHEM, I would call and to my Lord I would appeal. What gain is there in my death, when I descend to the Pit? Will the dust acknowledge You? Will it declare Your truth? Hear, HASHEM, and favor me; HASHEM, be my Helper!* Chazzan– *You have changed for me my lament into dancing; You undid my sackcloth and girded me with gladness. So that my soul might make music to You and not be stilled, HASHEM my God, forever will I thank You.*

MOURNER'S KADDISH

Mourners recite the Mourners' *Kaddish. See Laws* §81-83.
[A transliteration of this *Kaddish* appears on page 1305.]

יִתְגַּדַּל *May His great Name grow exalted and sanctified* (Cong.– *Amen.*) *in the world that He created as He willed. May He give reign to His kingship in your lifetimes and in your days, and in the lifetimes of the entire Family of Israel, swiftly and soon. Now respond: Amen.*

(Cong.– *Amen. May His great Name be blessed forever and ever.*)

May His great Name be blessed forever and ever.

Blessed, praised, glorified, exalted, extolled, mighty, upraised, and lauded be the Name of the Holy One, Blessed is He (Cong.– *Blessed is He*) *— beyond any blessing and song, praise and consolation that are uttered in the world. Now respond: Amen.* (Cong.– *Amen*.)

May there be abundant peace from Heaven, and life, upon us and upon all Israel. Now respond: Amen. (Cong.– *Amen.*)

Take three steps back. Bow left and say, *'He Who makes peace . . .'*; bow right and say, *'may He . . .'*; bow forward and say, *'and upon all Israel . . .'* Remain standing in place for a few moments, then take three steps forward.

He Who makes peace in His heights, may He make peace upon us, and upon all Israel. Now respond: Amen. (Cong.– *Amen.*)

(Some recite this short Kabbalistic declaration of intent before beginning *Pesukei D'zimrah:*)

(I now prepare my mouth to thank, laud, and praise my Creator. For the sake of the unification of the Holy One, Blessed is He, and His Presence, through Him Who is hidden and inscrutable — [I pray] in the name of all Israel.)

Pesukei D'zimrah begins with the recital of בָּרוּךְ שֶׁאָמַר. Stand while reciting בָּרוּךְ שֶׁאָמַר. During its recitation, hold the two front *tzitzis* of the *tallis* (or *tallis kattan)* in the right hand, and at its conclusion kiss the *tzitzis* and release them. Conversation is forbidden from this point until after *Shemoneh Esrei,* except for certain prayer responses (see p. 175).

בָּרוּךְ שֶׁאָמַר וְהָיָה הָעוֹלָם, בָּרוּךְ הוּא. בָּרוּךְ עוֹשֶׂה בְרֵאשִׁית, בָּרוּךְ אוֹמֵר וְעוֹשֶׂה, בָּרוּךְ גּוֹזֵר וּמְקַיֵּם, בָּרוּךְ מְרַחֵם עַל הָאָרֶץ, בָּרוּךְ מְרַחֵם עַל הַבְּרִיּוֹת, בָּרוּךְ מְשַׁלֵּם שָׂכָר טוֹב לִירֵאָיו, בָּרוּךְ חַי לָעַד וְקַיָּם לָנֶצַח, בָּרוּךְ פּוֹדֶה וּמַצִּיל, בָּרוּךְ שְׁמוֹ. בָּרוּךְ אַתָּה יהוה אֱלֹהֵינוּ מֶלֶךְ הָעוֹלָם, הָאֵל הָאָב הָרַחֲמָן הַמְּהֻלָּל בְּפֶה עַמּוֹ, מְשֻׁבָּח וּמְפֹאָר בִּלְשׁוֹן חֲסִידָיו וַעֲבָדָיו, וּבְשִׁירֵי דָוִד עַבְדֶּךָ. נְהַלֶּלְךָ יהוה אֱלֹהֵינוּ, בִּשְׁבָחוֹת וּבִזְמִרוֹת. נְגַדֶּלְךָ וּנְשַׁבֵּחֲךָ וּנְפָאֶרְךָ וְנַזְכִּיר שִׁמְךָ וְנַמְלִיכְךָ, מַלְכֵּנוּ אֱלֹהֵינוּ. ❖ יָחִיד, חֵי הָעוֹלָמִים, מֶלֶךְ מְשֻׁבָּח וּמְפֹאָר עֲדֵי עַד שְׁמוֹ הַגָּדוֹל. בָּרוּךְ אַתָּה יהוה, מֶלֶךְ מְהֻלָּל בַּתִּשְׁבָּחוֹת. (Cong. – אָמֵן.)

דברי הימים א טז:ח-לו

הוֹדוּ לַיהוה קִרְאוּ בִשְׁמוֹ, הוֹדִיעוּ בָעַמִּים עֲלִילֹתָיו. שִׁירוּ לוֹ, זַמְּרוּ לוֹ, שִׂיחוּ בְּכָל נִפְלְאֹתָיו. הִתְהַלְּלוּ בְּשֵׁם קָדְשׁוֹ, יִשְׂמַח לֵב מְבַקְשֵׁי יהוה. דִּרְשׁוּ יהוה וְעֻזּוֹ, בַּקְּשׁוּ פָנָיו תָּמִיד. זִכְרוּ נִפְלְאֹתָיו אֲשֶׁר עָשָׂה, מֹפְתָיו וּמִשְׁפְּטֵי פִיהוּ. זֶרַע יִשְׂרָאֵל עַבְדּוֹ, בְּנֵי יַעֲקֹב בְּחִירָיו. הוּא יהוה אֱלֹהֵינוּ, בְּכָל הָאָרֶץ מִשְׁפָּטָיו. זִכְרוּ לְעוֹלָם בְּרִיתוֹ, דָּבָר צִוָּה לְאֶלֶף דּוֹר. אֲשֶׁר כָּרַת אֶת אַבְרָהָם, וּשְׁבוּעָתוֹ לְיִצְחָק. וַיַּעֲמִידֶהָ לְיַעֲקֹב לְחֹק, לְיִשְׂרָאֵל בְּרִית עוֹלָם. לֵאמֹר, לְךָ אֶתֵּן אֶרֶץ כְּנָעַן, חֶבֶל נַחֲלַתְכֶם. בִּהְיוֹתְכֶם מְתֵי מִסְפָּר, כִּמְעַט וְגָרִים בָּהּ. וַיִּתְהַלְּכוּ מִגּוֹי אֶל גּוֹי, וּמִמַּמְלָכָה אֶל עַם אַחֵר. לֹא הִנִּיחַ לְאִישׁ לְעָשְׁקָם, וַיּוֹכַח עֲלֵיהֶם מְלָכִים. אַל תִּגְּעוּ בִּמְשִׁיחָי, וּבִנְבִיאַי אַל תָּרֵעוּ. שִׁירוּ לַיהוה כָּל הָאָרֶץ, בַּשְּׂרוּ מִיּוֹם אֶל יוֹם יְשׁוּעָתוֹ. סַפְּרוּ בַגּוֹיִם אֶת כְּבוֹדוֹ, בְּכָל הָעַמִּים נִפְלְאוֹתָיו. כִּי גָדוֹל יהוה וּמְהֻלָּל מְאֹד, וְנוֹרָא הוּא עַל כָּל אֱלֹהִים. ❖ כִּי כָּל אֱלֹהֵי הָעַמִּים אֱלִילִים, (pause) וַיהוה שָׁמַיִם עָשָׂה.

הוֹד וְהָדָר לְפָנָיו, עֹז וְחֶדְוָה בִּמְקֹמוֹ. הָבוּ לַיהוה מִשְׁפְּחוֹת עַמִּים, הָבוּ לַיהוה כָּבוֹד וָעֹז. הָבוּ לַיהוה כְּבוֹד שְׁמוֹ, שְׂאוּ מִנְחָה וּבֹאוּ לְפָנָיו, הִשְׁתַּחֲווּ לַיהוה בְּהַדְרַת קֹדֶשׁ. חִילוּ מִלְּפָנָיו כָּל הָאָרֶץ, אַף תִּכּוֹן תֵּבֵל בַּל תִּמּוֹט. יִשְׂמְחוּ הַשָּׁמַיִם וְתָגֵל

Pesukei D'zimrah begins with the recital of בָּרוּךְ שֶׁאָמַר, *Blessed is He Who spoke . . .* Stand while reciting בָּרוּךְ שֶׁאָמַר. During its recitation, hold the two front *tzitzis* of the *tallis* (or *tallis kattan)* in the right hand, and at its conclusion kiss the *tzitzis* and release them. Conversation is forbidden from this point until after *Shemoneh Esrei,* except for certain prayer responses (see p. 175).

בָּרוּךְ שֶׁאָמַר *Blessed is He Who spoke, and the world came into being — blessed is He. Blessed is He Who maintains Creation; blessed is He Who speaks and does; blessed is He Who decrees and fulfills; blessed is He Who has mercy on the earth; blessed is He Who has mercy on the creatures; blessed is He Who gives goodly reward to those who fear Him; blessed is He Who lives forever and endures to eternity; blessed is He Who redeems and rescues — blessed is His Name! Blessed are You,* HASHEM, *our God, King of the universe, the God, the merciful Father, Who is lauded by the mouth of His people, praised and glorified by the tongue of His devout ones and His servants and through the psalms of David Your servant. We shall laud You,* HASHEM, *our God, with praises and songs. We shall exalt You, praise You, glorify You, mention Your Name and proclaim Your reign, our King, our God.* Chazzan– *O Unique One, Life-giver of the worlds, King Whose great Name is eternally praised and glorified. Blessed are You,* HASHEM, *the King Who is lauded with praises.* (Cong.– *Amen.)*

I Chronicles 16:8-36

הוֹדוּ *Give thanks to* HASHEM, *declare His Name, make His acts known among the peoples. Sing to Him, make music to Him, speak of all His wonders. Glory in His holy Name, be glad of heart, you who seek* HASHEM. *Search out* HASHEM *and His might, seek His Presence always. Remember His wonders that He wrought, His marvels and the judgments of His mouth. O seed of Israel, His servant, O children of Jacob, His chosen ones — He is* HASHEM, *our God, over all the earth are His judgments. Remember His covenant forever — the word He commanded for a thousand generations — that He made with Abraham and His vow to Isaac. Then He established it for Jacob as a statute, for Israel as an everlasting covenant; saying, 'To you I shall give the Land of Canaan, the lot of your heritage.' When you were but few in number, hardly dwelling there, and they wandered from nation to nation, from one kingdom to another people. He let no man rob them, and He rebuked kings for their sake: 'Dare not touch My anointed ones, and to My prophets do no harm.' Sing to* HASHEM, *everyone on earth, announce His salvation daily. Relate His glory among the nations, among all the peoples His wonders. That* HASHEM *is great and exceedingly lauded, and awesome is He above all heavenly powers.* Chazzan– *For all the gods of the peoples are nothings — but* HASHEM *made heaven!*

Glory and majesty are before Him, might and delight are in His place. Render to HASHEM, *O families of the peoples, render to* HASHEM *honor and might. Render to* HASHEM *honor worthy of His Name, take an offering and come before Him, prostrate yourselves before* HASHEM *in His intensely holy place. Tremble before Him, everyone on earth, indeed, the world is fixed so that it cannot falter. The heavens will be glad and*

הָאָֽרֶץ, וְיֹאמְרוּ בַגּוֹיִם, יהוה מָלָךְ. יִרְעַם הַיָּם וּמְלוֹאוֹ, יַעֲלֹץ הַשָּׂדֶה וְכָל אֲשֶׁר בּוֹ. אָז יְרַנְּנוּ עֲצֵי הַיָּֽעַר, מִלִּפְנֵי יהוה, כִּי בָא לִשְׁפּוֹט אֶת הָאָֽרֶץ. הוֹדוּ לַיהוה כִּי טוֹב, כִּי לְעוֹלָם חַסְדּוֹ. וְאִמְרוּ הוֹשִׁיעֵֽנוּ אֱלֹהֵי יִשְׁעֵֽנוּ, וְקַבְּצֵֽנוּ וְהַצִּילֵֽנוּ מִן הַגּוֹיִם, לְהֹדוֹת לְשֵׁם קָדְשֶֽׁךָ, לְהִשְׁתַּבֵּֽחַ בִּתְהִלָּתֶֽךָ. בָּרוּךְ יהוה אֱלֹהֵי יִשְׂרָאֵל מִן הָעוֹלָם וְעַד הָעֹלָם, וַיֹּאמְרוּ כָל הָעָם, אָמֵן, וְהַלֵּל לַיהוה.

❖ רוֹמְמוּ יהוה אֱלֹהֵֽינוּ וְהִשְׁתַּחֲווּ לַהֲדֹם רַגְלָיו, קָדוֹשׁ הוּא.[1] רוֹמְמוּ יהוה אֱלֹהֵֽינוּ וְהִשְׁתַּחֲווּ לְהַר קָדְשׁוֹ, כִּי קָדוֹשׁ יהוה אֱלֹהֵֽינוּ.[2]

וְהוּא רַחוּם יְכַפֵּר עָוֹן וְלֹא יַשְׁחִית, וְהִרְבָּה לְהָשִׁיב אַפּוֹ, וְלֹא יָעִיר כָּל חֲמָתוֹ.[3] אַתָּה יהוה, לֹא תִכְלָא רַחֲמֶֽיךָ מִמֶּֽנִּי, חַסְדְּךָ וַאֲמִתְּךָ תָּמִיד יִצְּרֽוּנִי.[4] זְכֹר רַחֲמֶֽיךָ יהוה וַחֲסָדֶֽיךָ, כִּי מֵעוֹלָם הֵֽמָּה.[5] תְּנוּ עֹז לֵאלֹהִים, עַל יִשְׂרָאֵל גַּאֲוָתוֹ, וְעֻזּוֹ בַּשְּׁחָקִים. נוֹרָא אֱלֹהִים מִמִּקְדָּשֶֽׁיךָ, אֵל יִשְׂרָאֵל הוּא נֹתֵן עֹז וְתַעֲצֻמוֹת לָעָם, בָּרוּךְ אֱלֹהִים.[6] אֵל נְקָמוֹת יהוה, אֵל נְקָמוֹת הוֹפִֽיעַ. הִנָּשֵׂא שֹׁפֵט הָאָֽרֶץ, הָשֵׁב גְּמוּל עַל גֵּאִים.[7] לַיהוה הַיְשׁוּעָה, עַל עַמְּךָ בִרְכָתֶֽךָ סֶּלָה.[8] ❖ יהוה צְבָאוֹת עִמָּֽנוּ, מִשְׂגָּב לָֽנוּ אֱלֹהֵי יַעֲקֹב סֶֽלָה.[9] יהוה צְבָאוֹת, אַשְׁרֵי אָדָם בֹּטֵֽחַ בָּךְ.[10] יהוה הוֹשִֽׁיעָה, הַמֶּֽלֶךְ יַעֲנֵֽנוּ בְיוֹם קָרְאֵֽנוּ.[11]

הוֹשִֽׁיעָה אֶת עַמֶּֽךָ, וּבָרֵךְ אֶת נַחֲלָתֶֽךָ, וּרְעֵם וְנַשְּׂאֵם עַד הָעוֹלָם.[12] נַפְשֵֽׁנוּ חִכְּתָה לַיהוה, עֶזְרֵֽנוּ וּמָגִנֵּֽנוּ הוּא. כִּי בוֹ יִשְׂמַח לִבֵּֽנוּ, כִּי בְשֵׁם קָדְשׁוֹ בָטָֽחְנוּ. יְהִי חַסְדְּךָ יהוה עָלֵֽינוּ, כַּאֲשֶׁר יִחַֽלְנוּ לָךְ.[13] הַרְאֵֽנוּ יהוה חַסְדֶּֽךָ, וְיֶשְׁעֲךָ תִּתֶּן לָֽנוּ.[14] קוּמָה עֶזְרָֽתָה לָּֽנוּ, וּפְדֵֽנוּ לְמַֽעַן חַסְדֶּֽךָ.[15] אָנֹכִי יהוה אֱלֹהֶֽיךָ הַמַּעַלְךָ מֵאֶֽרֶץ מִצְרָֽיִם, הַרְחֶב פִּֽיךָ וַאֲמַלְאֵֽהוּ.[16] אַשְׁרֵי הָעָם שֶׁכָּֽכָה לּוֹ, אַשְׁרֵי הָעָם שֶׁיהוה אֱלֹהָיו.[17] ❖ וַאֲנִי בְּחַסְדְּךָ בָטַֽחְתִּי, יָגֵל לִבִּי בִּישׁוּעָתֶֽךָ, אָשִֽׁירָה לַיהוה, כִּי גָמַל עָלָי.[18]

מִזְמוֹר לְתוֹדָה, *'A Psalm of thanksgiving'* (*Psalm* 100), is recited while standing.

מִזְמוֹר לְתוֹדָה, הָרִֽיעוּ לַיהוה כָּל הָאָֽרֶץ. עִבְדוּ אֶת יהוה בְּשִׂמְחָה, בֹּֽאוּ לְפָנָיו בִּרְנָנָה. דְּעוּ כִּי יהוה הוּא אֱלֹהִים, הוּא עָשָֽׂנוּ, וְלוֹ אֲנַֽחְנוּ, עַמּוֹ וְצֹאן מַרְעִיתוֹ. בֹּֽאוּ שְׁעָרָיו בְּתוֹדָה, חֲצֵרֹתָיו בִּתְהִלָּה, הוֹדוּ לוֹ, בָּרְכוּ שְׁמוֹ. ❖ כִּי טוֹב יהוה, לְעוֹלָם חַסְדּוֹ, וְעַד דֹּר וָדֹר אֱמוּנָתוֹ.

ON HOSHANAH CONTINUE ON PAGE 652; ON ALL OTHER DAYS CONTINUE ON PAGE 662.

(1) *Psalms* 99:5. (2) 99:9. (3) 78:38. (4) 40:12. (5) 25:6. (6) 68:35-36. (7) 94:1-2. (8) 3:9. (9) 46:8. (10) 84:13. (11) 20:10. (12) 28:9. (13) 33:20-22. (14) 85:8. (15) 44:27. (16) 81:11. (17) 144:15. (18) 13:6.

the earth will rejoice and say among the nations, 'HASHEM has reigned!' The sea and its fullness will roar, the field and everything in it will exult. Then the trees of the forest will sing with joy before HASHEM, for He will have arrived to judge the earth. Give thanks to HASHEM, for He is good, for His kindness endures forever. And say, 'Save us, O God of our salvation, gather us and rescue us from the nations, to thank Your Holy Name and to glory in Your praise!' Blessed is HASHEM, the God of Israel, from This World to the World to Come — and let the entire people say, 'Amen and praise to God!'

Chazzan– *Exalt HASHEM, our God, and bow at His footstool; He is holy![1] Exalt HASHEM, our God, and bow at His holy mountain; for holy is HASHEM, our God.[2]*

He, the Merciful One, is forgiving of iniquity and does not destroy; frequently, He withdraws His anger, not arousing His entire rage.[3] You, HASHEM — withhold not Your mercy from me; may Your kindness and Your truth always protect me.[4] Remember Your mercies, HASHEM, and Your kindnesses, for they are from the beginning of the world.[5] Render might to God, Whose majesty hovers over Israel and Whose might is in the clouds. You are awesome, O God, from Your sanctuaries, O God of Israel — it is He Who grants might and power to the people, blessed is God.[6] O God of vengeance, HASHEM, O God of vengeance, appear! Arise, O Judge of the earth, render recompense to the haughty.[7] Salvation is HASHEM's, upon Your people is Your blessing, Selah.[8] Chazzan– *HASHEM, Master of Legions, is with us, a stronghold for us is the God of Jacob, Selah.[9] HASHEM, Master of Legions, praiseworthy is the person who trusts in You.[10] HASHEM, save! May the King answer us on the day we call.[11]*

Save Your people and bless Your heritage, tend them and elevate them forever.[12] Our soul longed for HASHEM — our help and our shield is He. For in Him will our hearts be glad, for in His Holy Name we trusted. May Your kindness, HASHEM, be upon us, just as we awaited You.[13] Show us Your kindness, HASHEM, and grant us Your salvation.[14] Arise — assist us, and redeem us by virtue of Your kindness.[15] I am HASHEM, your God, Who raised you from the land of Egypt, open wide your mouth and I will fill it.[16] Praiseworthy is the people for whom this is so, praiseworthy is the people whose God is HASHEM.[17] Chazzan– *As for me, I trust in Your kindness; my heart will rejoice in Your salvation. I will sing to HASHEM, for He dealt kindly with me.[18]*

מִזְמוֹר לְתוֹדָה, *'A Psalm of thanksgiving'* (*Psalm* 100), is recited while standing.

מִזְמוֹר *A psalm of thanksgiving, call out to HASHEM, everyone on earth. Serve HASHEM with gladness, come before Him with joyous song. Know that HASHEM, He is God, it is He Who made us and we are His, His people and the sheep of His pasture. Enter His gates with thanksgiving, His courts with praise, give thanks to Him, bless His Name.* Chazzan– *For HASHEM is good, His kindness endures forever, and from generation to generation is His faithfulness.*

ON HOSHANAH CONTINUE ON PAGE 652; ON ALL OTHER DAYS CONTINUE ON PAGE 662.

ON HOSHANA RABBAH CONTINUE BELOW; ALL OTHER DAYS TURN TO PAGE 662.

תהלים יט

לַמְנַצֵּחַ מִזְמוֹר לְדָוִד. הַשָּׁמַיִם מְסַפְּרִים כְּבוֹד אֵל, וּמַעֲשֵׂה יָדָיו מַגִּיד הָרָקִיעַ. יוֹם לְיוֹם יַבִּיעַ אֹמֶר, וְלַיְלָה לְּלַיְלָה יְחַוֶּה דָּעַת. אֵין אֹמֶר וְאֵין דְּבָרִים, בְּלִי נִשְׁמָע קוֹלָם. בְּכָל הָאָרֶץ יָצָא קַוָּם, וּבִקְצֵה תֵבֵל מִלֵּיהֶם, לַשֶּׁמֶשׁ שָׂם אֹהֶל בָּהֶם. וְהוּא כְּחָתָן יֹצֵא מֵחֻפָּתוֹ, יָשִׂישׂ כְּגִבּוֹר לָרוּץ אֹרַח. מִקְצֵה הַשָּׁמַיִם מוֹצָאוֹ, וּתְקוּפָתוֹ עַל קְצוֹתָם, וְאֵין נִסְתָּר מֵחַמָּתוֹ. תּוֹרַת יהוה תְּמִימָה, מְשִׁיבַת נָפֶשׁ, עֵדוּת יהוה נֶאֱמָנָה, מַחְכִּימַת פֶּתִי. פִּקּוּדֵי יהוה יְשָׁרִים, מְשַׂמְּחֵי לֵב, מִצְוַת יהוה בָּרָה, מְאִירַת עֵינָיִם. יִרְאַת יהוה טְהוֹרָה, עוֹמֶדֶת לָעַד, מִשְׁפְּטֵי יהוה אֱמֶת, צָדְקוּ יַחְדָּו. הַנֶּחֱמָדִים מִזָּהָב וּמִפַּז רָב, וּמְתוּקִים מִדְּבַשׁ וְנֹפֶת צוּפִים. גַּם עַבְדְּךָ נִזְהָר בָּהֶם, בְּשָׁמְרָם עֵקֶב רָב. שְׁגִיאוֹת מִי יָבִין, מִנִּסְתָּרוֹת נַקֵּנִי. גַּם מִזֵּדִים חֲשֹׂךְ עַבְדֶּךָ, אַל יִמְשְׁלוּ בִי, אָז אֵיתָם, וְנִקֵּיתִי מִפֶּשַׁע רָב. ❖ יִהְיוּ לְרָצוֹן אִמְרֵי פִי, וְהֶגְיוֹן לִבִּי לְפָנֶיךָ, יהוה צוּרִי וְגֹאֲלִי.

תהלים לד

לְדָוִד, בְּשַׁנּוֹתוֹ אֶת טַעְמוֹ לִפְנֵי אֲבִימֶלֶךְ, וַיְגָרְשֵׁהוּ וַיֵּלַךְ.
אֲבָרְכָה אֶת יהוה בְּכָל עֵת, תָּמִיד תְּהִלָּתוֹ בְּפִי.
בַּיהוה תִּתְהַלֵּל נַפְשִׁי, יִשְׁמְעוּ עֲנָוִים וְיִשְׂמָחוּ.
גַּדְּלוּ לַיהוה אִתִּי, וּנְרוֹמְמָה שְׁמוֹ יַחְדָּו.
דָּרַשְׁתִּי אֶת יהוה וְעָנָנִי, וּמִכָּל מְגוּרוֹתַי הִצִּילָנִי.
הִבִּיטוּ אֵלָיו וְנָהָרוּ,
וּפְנֵיהֶם אַל יֶחְפָּרוּ.
זֶה עָנִי קָרָא וַיהוה שָׁמֵעַ, וּמִכָּל צָרוֹתָיו הוֹשִׁיעוֹ.
חֹנֶה מַלְאַךְ יהוה סָבִיב לִירֵאָיו, וַיְחַלְּצֵם.
טַעֲמוּ וּרְאוּ כִּי טוֹב יהוה, אַשְׁרֵי הַגֶּבֶר יֶחֱסֶה בּוֹ.
יְראוּ אֶת יהוה קְדֹשָׁיו, כִּי אֵין מַחְסוֹר לִירֵאָיו.
כְּפִירִים רָשׁוּ וְרָעֵבוּ, וְדֹרְשֵׁי יהוה לֹא יַחְסְרוּ כָל טוֹב.

ON HOSHANA RABBAH CONTINUE BELOW: ON ALL OTHER DAYS TURN TO PAGE 662.

Psalm 19

לַמְנַצֵּחַ *For the Conductor; a song of David. The heavens declare the glory of God, and the expanse of the sky tells of His handiwork. Day following day brings expressions of praise, and night following night bespeaks wisdom. There is no speech and there are no words; their sound is unheard. Their line goes forth throughout the earth, and their words reach the farthest ends of the land; He has set up a tent for the sun in their midst. And it is like a groom coming forth from his bridal chamber, rejoicing like a warrior to run the course. The end of the heavens is its source, and its circuit is to their other end; nothing is hidden from its heat. The Torah of HASHEM is perfect, restoring the soul; the testimony of HASHEM is trustworthy, making the simple one wise. The orders of HASHEM are upright, gladdening the heart; the command of HASHEM is clear, enlightening the eyes. The fear of HASHEM is pure, enduring forever; the judgments of HASHEM are true, altogether righteous. They are more desirable than gold, than even much fine gold; sweeter than honey and drippings from the combs. Even Your servant is careful of them, for in observing them there is great reward. Yet, who can discern mistakes? From unperceived faults cleanse me. Also from intentional sins, restrain Your servant; let them not rule me; then I shall be perfect and cleansed of great transgression.* Chazzan— *May the expressions of my mouth and the thoughts of my heart find favor before You, HASHEM, my Rock and my Redeemer.*

Psalm 34

לְדָוִד *Of David: When he disguised his sanity before Abimelech who drove him out and he left.*

א *I shall bless HASHEM at all times,*
always shall His praise be in my mouth.

ב *In HASHEM does my soul glory, may humble ones hear and be glad.*

ג *Declare the greatness of HASHEM with me,*
and let us exalt His Name together.

ד *I sought out HASHEM and He answered me,*
and from all my terror He delivered me.

ה *They look to Him and become radiant,*
ו *and their faces were not shamed.*

ז *This poor man calls and HASHEM hears —*
and from all his troubles He saved him.

ח *The angel of HASHEM encamps around His reverent ones*
and releases them.

ט *Contemplate and see that HASHEM is good —*
praiseworthy is the man who takes refuge in Him.

י *Fear HASHEM, you — His holy ones —*
for there is no deprivation for His reverent ones.

כ *Young lions may want and hunger,*
but those who seek HASHEM will not lack any good.

ON HOSHANA RABBAH

לְכוּ בָנִים שִׁמְעוּ לִי, יִרְאַת יהוה אֲלַמֶּדְכֶם.
מִי הָאִישׁ הֶחָפֵץ חַיִּים, אֹהֵב יָמִים לִרְאוֹת טוֹב.
נְצֹר לְשׁוֹנְךָ מֵרָע, וּשְׂפָתֶיךָ מִדַּבֵּר מִרְמָה.
סוּר מֵרָע וַעֲשֵׂה טוֹב, בַּקֵּשׁ שָׁלוֹם וְרָדְפֵהוּ.
עֵינֵי יהוה אֶל צַדִּיקִים, וְאָזְנָיו אֶל שַׁוְעָתָם.
פְּנֵי יהוה בְּעֹשֵׂי רָע, לְהַכְרִית מֵאֶרֶץ זִכְרָם.
צָעֲקוּ וַיהוה שָׁמֵעַ, וּמִכָּל צָרוֹתָם הִצִּילָם.
קָרוֹב יהוה לְנִשְׁבְּרֵי לֵב, וְאֶת דַּכְּאֵי רוּחַ יוֹשִׁיעַ.
רַבּוֹת רָעוֹת צַדִּיק, וּמִכֻּלָּם יַצִּילֶנּוּ יהוה.
שֹׁמֵר כָּל עַצְמוֹתָיו, אַחַת מֵהֵנָּה לֹא נִשְׁבָּרָה.
תְּמוֹתֵת רָשָׁע רָעָה, וְשֹׂנְאֵי צַדִּיק יֶאְשָׁמוּ.
❖ פּוֹדֶה יהוה נֶפֶשׁ עֲבָדָיו, וְלֹא יֶאְשְׁמוּ כָּל הַחֹסִים בּוֹ.

תהלים צ

תְּפִלָּה לְמשֶׁה אִישׁ הָאֱלֹהִים, אֲדֹנָי מָעוֹן אַתָּה הָיִיתָ לָּנוּ בְּדֹר וָדֹר. בְּטֶרֶם הָרִים יֻלָּדוּ וַתְּחוֹלֵל אֶרֶץ וְתֵבֵל, וּמֵעוֹלָם עַד עוֹלָם אַתָּה אֵל. תָּשֵׁב אֱנוֹשׁ עַד דַּכָּא, וַתֹּאמֶר שׁוּבוּ בְנֵי אָדָם. כִּי אֶלֶף שָׁנִים בְּעֵינֶיךָ כְּיוֹם אֶתְמוֹל כִּי יַעֲבֹר, וְאַשְׁמוּרָה בַלָּיְלָה. זְרַמְתָּם, שֵׁנָה יִהְיוּ, בַּבֹּקֶר כֶּחָצִיר יַחֲלֹף. בַּבֹּקֶר יָצִיץ וְחָלָף, לָעֶרֶב יְמוֹלֵל וְיָבֵשׁ. כִּי כָלִינוּ בְאַפֶּךָ, וּבַחֲמָתְךָ נִבְהָלְנוּ. שַׁתָּ עֲוֹנֹתֵינוּ לְנֶגְדֶּךָ, עֲלֻמֵנוּ לִמְאוֹר פָּנֶיךָ. כִּי כָל יָמֵינוּ פָּנוּ בְעֶבְרָתֶךָ, כִּלִּינוּ שָׁנֵינוּ כְמוֹ הֶגֶה. יְמֵי שְׁנוֹתֵינוּ בָהֶם שִׁבְעִים שָׁנָה, וְאִם בִּגְבוּרֹת שְׁמוֹנִים שָׁנָה, וְרָהְבָּם עָמָל וָאָוֶן, כִּי גָז חִישׁ וַנָּעֻפָה. מִי יוֹדֵעַ עֹז אַפֶּךָ, וּכְיִרְאָתְךָ עֶבְרָתֶךָ. לִמְנוֹת יָמֵינוּ כֵּן הוֹדַע, וְנָבִא לְבַב חָכְמָה. שׁוּבָה יהוה עַד מָתָי, וְהִנָּחֵם עַל עֲבָדֶיךָ. שַׂבְּעֵנוּ בַבֹּקֶר חַסְדֶּךָ, וּנְרַנְּנָה וְנִשְׂמְחָה בְּכָל יָמֵינוּ. שַׂמְּחֵנוּ כִּימוֹת עִנִּיתָנוּ, שְׁנוֹת רָאִינוּ רָעָה. יֵרָאֶה אֶל עֲבָדֶיךָ פָעֳלֶךָ, וַהֲדָרְךָ עַל בְּנֵיהֶם. ❖ וִיהִי נֹעַם אֲדֹנָי אֱלֹהֵינוּ עָלֵינוּ, וּמַעֲשֵׂה יָדֵינוּ כּוֹנְנָה עָלֵינוּ, וּמַעֲשֵׂה יָדֵינוּ כּוֹנְנֵהוּ.

ON HOSHANA RABBAH

ל *Go, O sons, heed me, the fear of* HASHEM *will I teach you.*
מ *Which man desires life, who loves days of seeing good?*
נ *Guard your tongue from evil, and your lips from speaking deceit.*
ס *Turn from evil and do good, seek peace and pursue it.*
ע *The eyes of* HASHEM *are toward the righteous, and His ears to their cry.*
פ *The face of* HASHEM *is against evildoers,*
to cut off their memory from earth.
צ *They cried out and* HASHEM *heeds,*
and from all their troubles He rescues them.
ק HASHEM *is close to the brokenhearted;*
and those crushed in spirit, He saves.
ר *Many are the mishaps of the righteous,*
but from them all HASHEM *rescues him.*
ש *He guards all his bones, even one of them was not broken.*
ת *The death blow of the wicked is evil,*
and the haters of the righteous will be condemned.
Chazzan— HASHEM *redeems the soul of His servants,*
and all those who take refuge in Him will not be condemned.

Psalm 90

תְּפִלָּה *A prayer by Moses, the man of God: My Lord, an abode have You been for us in all generations; before the mountains were born and You had not yet fashioned the earth and the inhabited land, and from This World to the World to Come You are God. You reduce man to pulp and You say, 'Repent, O sons of man.' For a thousand years in Your eyes are but a bygone yesterday, and like a watch in the night. You flood them away, they become sleeplike, by morning they are like grass that withers. In the morning it blossoms and is rejuvenated, by evening it is cut down and brittle. For we are consumed by Your fury; and we are confounded by Your wrath. You have set our iniquities before Yourself, our immaturity before the light of Your countenance. For all our days passed by because of Your anger, we consumed our years like a fleeting thought. The days of our years among them are seventy years, and if with strength, eighty years; their proudest success is but toil and pain, for it is cut off swiftly and we fly away. Who knows the power of Your fury? As You are feared, so is Your anger. According to the count of our days, so may You teach us; then we shall acquire a heart of wisdom. Return,* HASHEM, *how long? Relent concerning Your servants. Satisfy us in the morning with Your kindness, then we shall sing out and rejoice throughout our days. Gladden us according to the days You afflicted us, the years when we saw evil. May Your works be visible to Your servants, and Your majesty upon their children.* Chazzan— *May the pleasantness of my Lord, our God, be upon us — our handiwork, may He establish for us; our handiwork, may He establish.*

ON HOSHANA RABBAH

תהלים צא

יֹשֵׁב בְּסֵתֶר עֶלְיוֹן, בְּצֵל שַׁדַּי יִתְלוֹנָן. אֹמַר לַיהוה מַחְסִי וּמְצוּדָתִי, אֱלֹהַי אֶבְטַח בּוֹ. כִּי הוּא יַצִּילְךָ מִפַּח יָקוּשׁ, מִדֶּבֶר הַוּוֹת. בְּאֶבְרָתוֹ יָסֶךְ לָךְ, וְתַחַת כְּנָפָיו תֶּחְסֶה, צִנָּה וְסֹחֵרָה אֲמִתּוֹ. לֹא תִירָא מִפַּחַד לָיְלָה, מֵחֵץ יָעוּף יוֹמָם. מִדֶּבֶר בָּאֹפֶל יַהֲלֹךְ, מִקֶּטֶב יָשׁוּד צָהֳרָיִם. יִפֹּל מִצִּדְּךָ אֶלֶף, וּרְבָבָה מִימִינֶךָ, אֵלֶיךָ לֹא יִגָּשׁ. רַק בְּעֵינֶיךָ תַבִּיט, וְשִׁלֻּמַת רְשָׁעִים תִּרְאֶה. כִּי אַתָּה יהוה מַחְסִי, עֶלְיוֹן שַׂמְתָּ מְעוֹנֶךָ. לֹא תְאֻנֶּה אֵלֶיךָ רָעָה, וְנֶגַע לֹא יִקְרַב בְּאָהֳלֶךָ. כִּי מַלְאָכָיו יְצַוֶּה לָּךְ, לִשְׁמָרְךָ בְּכָל דְּרָכֶיךָ. עַל כַּפַּיִם יִשָּׂאוּנְךָ, פֶּן תִּגֹּף בָּאֶבֶן רַגְלֶךָ. עַל שַׁחַל וָפֶתֶן תִּדְרֹךְ, תִּרְמֹס כְּפִיר וְתַנִּין. כִּי בִי חָשַׁק וַאֲפַלְּטֵהוּ, אֲשַׂגְּבֵהוּ כִּי יָדַע שְׁמִי. יִקְרָאֵנִי וְאֶעֱנֵהוּ, עִמּוֹ אָנֹכִי בְצָרָה, אֲחַלְּצֵהוּ וַאֲכַבְּדֵהוּ. ❖ אֹרֶךְ יָמִים אַשְׂבִּיעֵהוּ, וְאַרְאֵהוּ בִּישׁוּעָתִי. אֹרֶךְ יָמִים אַשְׂבִּיעֵהוּ, וְאַרְאֵהוּ בִּישׁוּעָתִי.

תהלים קלה

הַלְלוּיָהּ הַלְלוּ אֶת שֵׁם יהוה, הַלְלוּ עַבְדֵי יהוה. שֶׁעֹמְדִים בְּבֵית יהוה, בְּחַצְרוֹת בֵּית אֱלֹהֵינוּ. הַלְלוּיָהּ כִּי טוֹב יהוה, זַמְּרוּ לִשְׁמוֹ כִּי נָעִים. כִּי יַעֲקֹב בָּחַר לוֹ יָהּ, יִשְׂרָאֵל לִסְגֻלָּתוֹ. כִּי אֲנִי יָדַעְתִּי כִּי גָדוֹל יהוה, וַאֲדֹנֵינוּ מִכָּל אֱלֹהִים. כֹּל אֲשֶׁר חָפֵץ יהוה עָשָׂה, בַּשָּׁמַיִם וּבָאָרֶץ, בַּיַּמִּים וְכָל תְּהֹמוֹת. מַעֲלֶה נְשִׂאִים מִקְצֵה הָאָרֶץ, בְּרָקִים לַמָּטָר עָשָׂה, מוֹצֵא רוּחַ מֵאוֹצְרוֹתָיו. שֶׁהִכָּה בְּכוֹרֵי מִצְרָיִם, מֵאָדָם עַד בְּהֵמָה. שָׁלַח אוֹתֹת וּמֹפְתִים בְּתוֹכֵכִי מִצְרָיִם, בְּפַרְעֹה וּבְכָל עֲבָדָיו. שֶׁהִכָּה גּוֹיִם רַבִּים, וְהָרַג מְלָכִים עֲצוּמִים. לְסִיחוֹן מֶלֶךְ הָאֱמֹרִי, וּלְעוֹג מֶלֶךְ הַבָּשָׁן, וּלְכֹל מַמְלְכוֹת כְּנָעַן. וְנָתַן אַרְצָם נַחֲלָה, נַחֲלָה לְיִשְׂרָאֵל עַמּוֹ. יהוה שִׁמְךָ לְעוֹלָם, יהוה זִכְרְךָ לְדֹר וָדֹר. כִּי יָדִין יהוה עַמּוֹ, וְעַל עֲבָדָיו יִתְנֶחָם. עֲצַבֵּי הַגּוֹיִם כֶּסֶף וְזָהָב, מַעֲשֵׂה יְדֵי אָדָם. פֶּה לָהֶם וְלֹא יְדַבֵּרוּ, עֵינַיִם לָהֶם וְלֹא יִרְאוּ. אָזְנַיִם לָהֶם וְלֹא יַאֲזִינוּ, אַף אֵין יֶשׁ רוּחַ בְּפִיהֶם. כְּמוֹהֶם יִהְיוּ עֹשֵׂיהֶם, כֹּל אֲשֶׁר בֹּטֵחַ בָּהֶם. ❖ בֵּית יִשְׂרָאֵל בָּרְכוּ אֶת יהוה, בֵּית אַהֲרֹן

ON HOSHANA RABBAH

Psalm 91

יֹשֵׁב *Whoever sits in the refuge of the Most High, he shall dwell in the shadow of the Almighty. I will say of* HASHEM, *'He is my refuge and my fortress, my God, I will trust in Him.' For He will deliver you from the ensnaring trap, from devastating pestilence. With His pinion He will cover you, and beneath His wings you will be protected; shield and armor is His truth. You shall not fear the terror of night; nor of the arrow that flies by day; nor the pestilence that walks in gloom; nor the destroyer who lays waste at noon. Let a thousand encamp at your side and a myriad at your right hand, but to you they shall not approach. You will merely peer with your eyes and you will see the retribution of the wicked. Because [you said], 'You,* HASHEM, *are my refuge,' you have made the Most High your dwelling place. No evil will befall you, nor will any plague come near your tent. He will charge His angels for you, to protect you in all your ways. On your palms they will carry you, lest you strike your foot against a stone. Upon the lion and the viper you will tread; you will trample the young lion and the serpent. For he has yearned for Me and I will deliver him; I will elevate him because he knows My Name. He will call upon Me and I will answer him, I am with him in distress, I will release him and I will honor him.* Chazzan– *With long life will I satisfy him, and I will show him My salvation. With long life will I satisfy him, and I will show him My salvation.*

Psalm 135

הַלְלוּיָהּ *Halleluyah! Praise the Name of* HASHEM! *Praise — you servants of* HASHEM; *you who stand in the House of* HASHEM, *in the courtyards of the House of our God — praise God, for* HASHEM *is good. Sing to His Name, for It is pleasant. For God selected Jacob for His own, Israel as His treasure. For I know that* HASHEM *is greater — our Lord — than all heavenly powers. Whatever* HASHEM *wished, He did, in heaven and on earth; in the seas and all the depths. He raises clouds from the end of the earth; He made lightning bolts for the rain; He brings forth wind from His treasuries. It was He who smote the firstborn of Egypt, from man to beast. He sent signs and wonders into your midst, O Egypt, upon Pharaoh and upon all of his servants. It was He who smote many nations, and slew mighty kings — Sichon, King of the Emorites, Og, King of Bashan, and all the kingdoms of Canaan — and presented their land as a heritage, a heritage for Israel, His people.* HASHEM *is Your Name forever,* HASHEM *is Your memorial throughout the generations. When* HASHEM *will judge His people, He will relent concerning His servants. The idols of the nations are silver and gold, human handiwork. They have mouths, but they speak not; they have eyes, but they see not; they have ears, but they heed not; neither is there any breath in their mouths. Like them shall their makers become, everyone who trusts in them.* Chazzan– *O House of Israel, bless* HASHEM; *O House of Aaron,*

ON HOSHANA RABBAH

בָּרְכוּ אֶת יהוה. בֵּית הַלֵּוִי בָּרְכוּ אֶת יהוה, יִרְאֵי יהוה בָּרְכוּ אֶת יהוה. בָּרוּךְ יהוה מִצִּיּוֹן שֹׁכֵן יְרוּשָׁלָיִם, הַלְלוּיָהּ.

Most congregations recite the following psalm (תהלים קלו) while standing.

הוֹדוּ לַיהוה כִּי טוֹב, כִּי לְעוֹלָם חַסְדּוֹ.
הוֹדוּ לֵאלֹהֵי הָאֱלֹהִים, כִּי לְעוֹלָם חַסְדּוֹ.
הוֹדוּ לַאֲדֹנֵי הָאֲדֹנִים, כִּי לְעוֹלָם חַסְדּוֹ.
לְעֹשֵׂה נִפְלָאוֹת גְּדֹלוֹת לְבַדּוֹ, כִּי לְעוֹלָם חַסְדּוֹ.
לְעֹשֵׂה הַשָּׁמַיִם בִּתְבוּנָה, כִּי לְעוֹלָם חַסְדּוֹ.
לְרוֹקַע הָאָרֶץ עַל הַמָּיִם, כִּי לְעוֹלָם חַסְדּוֹ.
לְעֹשֵׂה אוֹרִים גְּדֹלִים, כִּי לְעוֹלָם חַסְדּוֹ.
אֶת הַשֶּׁמֶשׁ לְמֶמְשֶׁלֶת בַּיּוֹם, כִּי לְעוֹלָם חַסְדּוֹ.
אֶת הַיָּרֵחַ וְכוֹכָבִים לְמֶמְשְׁלוֹת בַּלָּיְלָה, כִּי לְעוֹלָם חַסְדּוֹ.
לְמַכֵּה מִצְרַיִם בִּבְכוֹרֵיהֶם, כִּי לְעוֹלָם חַסְדּוֹ.
וַיּוֹצֵא יִשְׂרָאֵל מִתּוֹכָם, כִּי לְעוֹלָם חַסְדּוֹ.
בְּיָד חֲזָקָה וּבִזְרוֹעַ נְטוּיָה, כִּי לְעוֹלָם חַסְדּוֹ.
לְגֹזֵר יַם סוּף לִגְזָרִים, כִּי לְעוֹלָם חַסְדּוֹ.
וְהֶעֱבִיר יִשְׂרָאֵל בְּתוֹכוֹ, כִּי לְעוֹלָם חַסְדּוֹ.
וְנִעֵר פַּרְעֹה וְחֵילוֹ בְיַם סוּף, כִּי לְעוֹלָם חַסְדּוֹ.
לְמוֹלִיךְ עַמּוֹ בַּמִּדְבָּר, כִּי לְעוֹלָם חַסְדּוֹ.
לְמַכֵּה מְלָכִים גְּדֹלִים, כִּי לְעוֹלָם חַסְדּוֹ.
וַיַּהֲרֹג מְלָכִים אַדִּירִים, כִּי לְעוֹלָם חַסְדּוֹ.
לְסִיחוֹן מֶלֶךְ הָאֱמֹרִי, כִּי לְעוֹלָם חַסְדּוֹ.
וּלְעוֹג מֶלֶךְ הַבָּשָׁן, כִּי לְעוֹלָם חַסְדּוֹ.
וְנָתַן אַרְצָם לְנַחֲלָה, כִּי לְעוֹלָם חַסְדּוֹ.
נַחֲלָה לְיִשְׂרָאֵל עַבְדּוֹ, כִּי לְעוֹלָם חַסְדּוֹ.
שֶׁבְּשִׁפְלֵנוּ זָכַר לָנוּ, כִּי לְעוֹלָם חַסְדּוֹ.
וַיִּפְרְקֵנוּ מִצָּרֵינוּ, כִּי לְעוֹלָם חַסְדּוֹ.
❖ נֹתֵן לֶחֶם לְכָל בָּשָׂר, כִּי לְעוֹלָם חַסְדּוֹ.
הוֹדוּ לְאֵל הַשָּׁמָיִם, כִּי לְעוֹלָם חַסְדּוֹ.

ON HOSHANA RABBAH

bless HASHEM. O House of Levi, bless HASHEM; O those who fear HASHEM, bless HASHEM. Blessed is HASHEM from Zion, He Who dwells in Jerusalem. Halleluyah!

Most congregations recite the following psalm (Psalm 136) while standing.

הודו *Give thanks to HASHEM for He is good,*
for His kindness endures forever.
Give thanks to the God of the heavenly powers,
for His kindness endures forever.
Give thanks to the Lord of the lords, for His kindness endures forever.
To Him Who alone performs great wonders,
for His kindness endures forever.
To Him Who made the heavens with understanding,
for His kindness endures forever.
To Him Who spread out the earth upon the waters,
for His kindness endures forever.
To Him Who made great lights, for His kindness endures forever.
The sun for the reign of the day, for His kindness endures forever.
The moon and the stars for the reign of the night,
for His kindness endures forever.
To Him Who smote Egypt through their firstborn,
for His kindness endures forever.
And brought Israel forth from their midst,
for His kindness endures forever.
With strong hand and outstretched arm,
for His kindness endures forever.
To Him Who divided the Sea of Reeds into parts,
for His kindness endures forever.
And caused Israel to pass through it, for His kindness endures forever.
And threw Pharaoh and his army into the Sea of Reeds,
for His kindness endures forever.
To Him Who led His people through the wilderness,
for His kindness endures forever.
To Him Who smote great kings, for His kindness endures forever.
And slew mighty kings, for His kindness endures forever.
Sichon, king of the Emorites, for His kindness endures forever.
And Og, king of Bashan, for His kindness endures forever.
And presented their land as a heritage,
for His kindness endures forever.
A heritage for Israel, His servant, for His kindness endures forever.
In our lowliness He remembered us, for His kindness endures forever.
And released us from our tormentors, for His kindness endures forever.
Chazzan– *He gives nourishment to all flesh,*
for His kindness endures forever.
Give thanks to God of the heavens, for His kindness endures forever.

ON HOSHANA RABBAH

תהלים לג

רַנְּנוּ צַדִּיקִים בַּיהוה, לַיְשָׁרִים נָאוָה תְהִלָּה. הוֹדוּ לַיהוה בְּכִנּוֹר, בְּנֵבֶל עָשׂוֹר זַמְּרוּ לוֹ. שִׁירוּ לוֹ שִׁיר חָדָשׁ, הֵיטִיבוּ נַגֵּן בִּתְרוּעָה. כִּי יָשָׁר דְּבַר יהוה, וְכָל מַעֲשֵׂהוּ בֶּאֱמוּנָה. אֹהֵב צְדָקָה וּמִשְׁפָּט, חֶסֶד יהוה מָלְאָה הָאָרֶץ. בִּדְבַר יהוה שָׁמַיִם נַעֲשׂוּ, וּבְרוּחַ פִּיו כָּל צְבָאָם. כֹּנֵס כַּנֵּד מֵי הַיָּם, נֹתֵן בְּאוֹצָרוֹת תְּהוֹמוֹת. יִירְאוּ מֵיהוה כָּל הָאָרֶץ, מִמֶּנּוּ יָגוּרוּ כָּל יֹשְׁבֵי תֵבֵל. כִּי הוּא אָמַר וַיֶּהִי, הוּא צִוָּה וַיַּעֲמֹד. יהוה הֵפִיר עֲצַת גּוֹיִם, הֵנִיא מַחְשְׁבוֹת עַמִּים. עֲצַת יהוה לְעוֹלָם תַּעֲמֹד, מַחְשְׁבוֹת לִבּוֹ לְדֹר וָדֹר. אַשְׁרֵי הַגּוֹי אֲשֶׁר יהוה אֱלֹהָיו, הָעָם בָּחַר לְנַחֲלָה לוֹ. מִשָּׁמַיִם הִבִּיט יהוה, רָאָה אֶת כָּל בְּנֵי הָאָדָם. מִמְּכוֹן שִׁבְתּוֹ הִשְׁגִּיחַ, אֶל כָּל יֹשְׁבֵי הָאָרֶץ. הַיֹּצֵר יַחַד לִבָּם, הַמֵּבִין אֶל כָּל מַעֲשֵׂיהֶם. אֵין הַמֶּלֶךְ נוֹשָׁע בְּרָב חָיִל, גִּבּוֹר לֹא יִנָּצֵל בְּרָב כֹּחַ. שֶׁקֶר הַסּוּס לִתְשׁוּעָה, וּבְרֹב חֵילוֹ לֹא יְמַלֵּט. הִנֵּה עֵין יהוה אֶל יְרֵאָיו, לַמְיַחֲלִים לְחַסְדּוֹ. לְהַצִּיל מִמָּוֶת נַפְשָׁם, וּלְחַיּוֹתָם בָּרָעָב. ❖ נַפְשֵׁנוּ חִכְּתָה לַיהוה, עֶזְרֵנוּ וּמָגִנֵּנוּ הוּא. כִּי בוֹ יִשְׂמַח לִבֵּנוּ, כִּי בְשֵׁם קָדְשׁוֹ בָטָחְנוּ. יְהִי חַסְדְּךָ יהוה עָלֵינוּ, כַּאֲשֶׁר יִחַלְנוּ לָךְ.

תהלים צב

מִזְמוֹר שִׁיר לְיוֹם הַשַּׁבָּת. טוֹב לְהֹדוֹת לַיהוה, וּלְזַמֵּר לְשִׁמְךָ עֶלְיוֹן. לְהַגִּיד בַּבֹּקֶר חַסְדֶּךָ, וֶאֱמוּנָתְךָ בַּלֵּילוֹת. עֲלֵי עָשׂוֹר וַעֲלֵי נָבֶל, עֲלֵי הִגָּיוֹן בְּכִנּוֹר. כִּי שִׂמַּחְתַּנִי יהוה בְּפָעֳלֶךָ, בְּמַעֲשֵׂי יָדֶיךָ אֲרַנֵּן. מַה גָּדְלוּ מַעֲשֶׂיךָ יהוה, מְאֹד עָמְקוּ מַחְשְׁבֹתֶיךָ. אִישׁ בַּעַר לֹא יֵדָע, וּכְסִיל לֹא יָבִין אֶת זֹאת. בִּפְרֹחַ רְשָׁעִים כְּמוֹ עֵשֶׂב, וַיָּצִיצוּ כָּל פֹּעֲלֵי אָוֶן, לְהִשָּׁמְדָם עֲדֵי עַד. וְאַתָּה מָרוֹם לְעֹלָם יהוה. כִּי הִנֵּה אֹיְבֶיךָ יהוה, כִּי הִנֵּה אֹיְבֶיךָ יֹאבֵדוּ, יִתְפָּרְדוּ כָּל פֹּעֲלֵי אָוֶן. וַתָּרֶם כִּרְאֵים קַרְנִי, בַּלֹּתִי בְּשֶׁמֶן רַעֲנָן. וַתַּבֵּט עֵינִי בְּשׁוּרָי, בַּקָּמִים עָלַי מְרֵעִים, תִּשְׁמַעְנָה אָזְנָי. ❖ צַדִּיק כַּתָּמָר יִפְרָח, כְּאֶרֶז בַּלְּבָנוֹן יִשְׂגֶּה. שְׁתוּלִים בְּבֵית יהוה, בְּחַצְרוֹת אֱלֹהֵינוּ יַפְרִיחוּ. עוֹד יְנוּבוּן בְּשֵׂיבָה, דְּשֵׁנִים וְרַעֲנַנִּים יִהְיוּ. לְהַגִּיד כִּי יָשָׁר יהוה, צוּרִי וְלֹא עַוְלָתָה בּוֹ.

ON HOSHANA RABBAH

Psalm 33

רַנְּנוּ *Sing joyfully, O righteous, before* HASHEM*; for the upright, praise is fitting. Give thanks to* HASHEM *with the harp, with the ten-stringed lyre make music to Him. Sing Him a new song, play well with sounds of deepest feeling. For upright is the word of* HASHEM*, and all His deeds are done with faithfulness. He loves charity and justice, the kindness of* HASHEM *fills the earth. By the word of* HASHEM *the heavens were made, and by the breath of His mouth all their host. He assembles like a wall the waters of the sea, He places the deep waters in vaults. Fear* HASHEM*, all the earth; of Him be in dread, all inhabitants of the world. For He spoke and it came to be, He commanded and it stood firm.* HASHEM *annuls the counsel of nations, He balks the designs of peoples. The counsel of* HASHEM *will endure forever, the designs of His heart throughout the generations. Praiseworthy is the nation whose God is* HASHEM*, the people He chose for His own heritage. From heaven* HASHEM *looks down, He sees all mankind. From His dwelling place He oversees all inhabitants of earth. He fashions their hearts all together, He comprehends all their deeds. A king is not saved by a great army, nor is a hero rescued by great strength; sham is the horse for salvation; despite its great strength it provides no escape. Behold, the eye of* HASHEM *is on those who fear Him, upon those who await His kindness. To rescue their soul from death, and to sustain them in famine.* Chazzan– *Our soul longed for* HASHEM *— our help and our shield is He. For in Him will our hearts be glad, for in His Holy Name we trusted. May Your kindness,* HASHEM*, be upon us, just as we awaited You.*

Psalm 92

מִזְמוֹר שִׁיר *A psalm, a song for the Sabbath day. It is good to thank* HASHEM *and to sing praise to Your Name, O Exalted One; to relate Your kindness in the dawn and Your faith in the nights. Upon ten-stringed instrument and lyre, with singing accompanied by a harp. For You have gladdened me,* HASHEM*, with Your deeds; at the works of Your Hands I sing glad song. How great are Your deeds,* HASHEM*; exceedingly profound are Your thoughts. A boor cannot know, nor can a fool understand this: when the wicked bloom like grass and all the doers of iniquity blossom — it is to destroy them till eternity. But You remain exalted forever,* HASHEM*. For behold! — Your enemies,* HASHEM*, for behold! — Your enemies shall perish, dispersed shall be all doers of iniquity. As exalted as a re'eim's shall be my pride, I will be saturated with ever-fresh oil. My eyes have seen my vigilant foes; when those who would harm me rise up against me, my ears have heard their doom.* Chazzan– *A righteous man will flourish like a date palm, like a cedar in the Lebanon he will grow tall. Planted in the house of* HASHEM*, in the courtyards of our God they will flourish. They will still be fruitful in old age, vigorous and fresh they will be — to declare that* HASHEM *is just, my Rock in Whom there is no wrong.*

ON HOSHANA RABBAH

תהלים צג

יהוה מָלָךְ גֵּאוּת לָבֵשׁ, לָבֵשׁ יהוה עֹז הִתְאַזָּר, אַף תִּכּוֹן תֵּבֵל בַּל תִּמּוֹט. נָכוֹן כִּסְאֲךָ מֵאָז, מֵעוֹלָם אָתָּה. נָשְׂאוּ נְהָרוֹת יהוה, נָשְׂאוּ נְהָרוֹת קוֹלָם, יִשְׂאוּ נְהָרוֹת דָּכְיָם. ❖ מִקֹּלוֹת מַיִם רַבִּים אַדִּירִים מִשְׁבְּרֵי יָם, אַדִּיר בַּמָּרוֹם יהוה. עֵדֹתֶיךָ נֶאֶמְנוּ מְאֹד לְבֵיתְךָ נַאֲוָה קֹדֶשׁ, יהוה לְאֹרֶךְ יָמִים.

ON ALL DAYS CONTINUE HERE:

The following prayer should be recited with special intensity.

יְהִי כְבוֹד יהוה לְעוֹלָם, יִשְׂמַח יהוה בְּמַעֲשָׂיו.[1] יְהִי שֵׁם יהוה מְבֹרָךְ, מֵעַתָּה וְעַד עוֹלָם. מִמִּזְרַח שֶׁמֶשׁ עַד מְבוֹאוֹ, מְהֻלָּל שֵׁם יהוה. רָם עַל כָּל גּוֹיִם יהוה, עַל הַשָּׁמַיִם כְּבוֹדוֹ.[2] יהוה שִׁמְךָ לְעוֹלָם, יהוה זִכְרְךָ לְדֹר וָדֹר.[3] יהוה בַּשָּׁמַיִם הֵכִין כִּסְאוֹ, וּמַלְכוּתוֹ בַּכֹּל מָשָׁלָה.[4] יִשְׂמְחוּ הַשָּׁמַיִם וְתָגֵל הָאָרֶץ, וְיֹאמְרוּ בַגּוֹיִם יהוה מָלָךְ.[5] יהוה מֶלֶךְ,[6] יהוה מָלָךְ,[7] יהוה יִמְלֹךְ לְעֹלָם וָעֶד.[8] יהוה מֶלֶךְ עוֹלָם וָעֶד, אָבְדוּ גוֹיִם מֵאַרְצוֹ.[9] יהוה הֵפִיר עֲצַת גּוֹיִם, הֵנִיא מַחְשְׁבוֹת עַמִּים.[10] רַבּוֹת מַחֲשָׁבוֹת בְּלֶב אִישׁ, וַעֲצַת יהוה הִיא תָקוּם.[11] עֲצַת יהוה לְעוֹלָם תַּעֲמֹד, מַחְשְׁבוֹת לִבּוֹ לְדֹר וָדֹר.[12] כִּי הוּא אָמַר וַיֶּהִי, הוּא צִוָּה וַיַּעֲמֹד.[13] כִּי בָחַר יהוה בְּצִיּוֹן, אִוָּהּ לְמוֹשָׁב לוֹ.[14] כִּי יַעֲקֹב בָּחַר לוֹ יָהּ, יִשְׂרָאֵל לִסְגֻלָּתוֹ.[15] כִּי לֹא יִטֹּשׁ יהוה עַמּוֹ, וְנַחֲלָתוֹ לֹא יַעֲזֹב.[16] ❖ וְהוּא רַחוּם יְכַפֵּר עָוֹן וְלֹא יַשְׁחִית, וְהִרְבָּה לְהָשִׁיב אַפּוֹ, וְלֹא יָעִיר כָּל חֲמָתוֹ.[17] יהוה הוֹשִׁיעָה, הַמֶּלֶךְ יַעֲנֵנוּ בְיוֹם קָרְאֵנוּ.[18]

אַשְׁרֵי יוֹשְׁבֵי בֵיתֶךָ, עוֹד יְהַלְלוּךָ סֶּלָה.[19] אַשְׁרֵי הָעָם שֶׁכָּכָה לּוֹ, אַשְׁרֵי הָעָם שֶׁיהוה אֱלֹהָיו.[20]

תהלים קמה

תְּהִלָּה לְדָוִד,

אֲרוֹמִמְךָ אֱלוֹהַי הַמֶּלֶךְ, וַאֲבָרְכָה שִׁמְךָ לְעוֹלָם וָעֶד.
בְּכָל יוֹם אֲבָרְכֶךָּ, וַאֲהַלְלָה שִׁמְךָ לְעוֹלָם וָעֶד.
גָּדוֹל יהוה וּמְהֻלָּל מְאֹד, וְלִגְדֻלָּתוֹ אֵין חֵקֶר.

(1) *Psalms* 104:31. (2) 113:2-4. (3) 135:13. (4) 103:19. (5) *I Chronicles* 16:31. (6) *Psalms* 10:16. (7) 93:1 et al. (8) *Exodus* 15:18. (9) *Psalms* 10:16. (10) 33:10. (11) *Proverbs* 19:21. (12) *Psalms* 33:11. (13) 33:9. (14) 132:13. (15) 135:4. (16) 94:14. (17) 78:38. (18) 20:10. (19) 84:5. (20) 144:15.

ON HOSHANA RABBAH

Psalm 93

יהוה מָלָךְ *HASHEM will have reigned, He will have donned grandeur; He will have donned might and girded Himself; even firmed the world that it should not falter. Your throne was established from of old; eternal are You. Like rivers they raised, O HASHEM, like rivers they raised their voice; like rivers they shall raise their destructiveness.* Chazzan– *More than the roars of many waters, mightier than the waves of the sea — You are mighty on high, HASHEM. Your testimonies are exceedingly trustworthy about Your House, the Sacred Dwelling — O HASHEM, may it be for long days.*

ON ALL DAYS CONTINUE HERE:

The following prayer should be recited with special intensity.

יְהִי כְבוֹד *May the glory of HASHEM endure forever, let HASHEM rejoice in His works.[1] Blessed be the Name of HASHEM, from this time and forever. From the rising of the sun to its setting, HASHEM's Name is praised. High above all nations is HASHEM, above the heavens is His glory.[2] 'HASHEM' is Your Name forever, 'HASHEM' is Your memorial throughout the generations.[3] HASHEM has established His throne in the heavens, and His kingdom reigns over all.[4] The heavens will be glad and the earth will rejoice, they will proclaim among the nations, 'HASHEM has reigned!'[5] HASHEM reigns,[6] HASHEM has reigned,[7] HASHEM shall reign for all eternity.[8] HASHEM reigns forever and ever, even when the nations will have perished from His earth.[9] HASHEM annuls the counsel of nations, He balks the designs of peoples.[10] Many designs are in man's heart, but the counsel of HASHEM — only it will prevail.[11] The counsel of HASHEM will endure forever, the designs of His heart throughout the generations.[12] For He spoke and it came to be; He commanded and it stood firm.[13] For God selected Zion, He desired it for His dwelling place.[14] For God selected Jacob as His own, Israel as His treasure.[15] For HASHEM will not cast off His people, nor will He forsake His heritage.[16]* Chazzan– *He, the Merciful One, is forgiving of iniquity and does not destroy; frequently He withdraws His anger, not arousing His entire rage.[17] HASHEM, save! May the King answer us on the day we call.[18]*

אַשְׁרֵי *Praiseworthy are those who dwell in Your house; may they always praise You, Selah![19] Praiseworthy is the people for whom this is so, praiseworthy is the people whose God is HASHEM.[20]*

Psalm 145

A psalm of praise by David:

א *I will exalt You, my God the King,*
and I will bless Your Name forever and ever.

ב *Every day I will bless You,*
and I will laud Your Name forever and ever.

ג *HASHEM is great and exceedingly lauded,*
and His greatness is beyond investigation.

דּוֹר לְדוֹר יְשַׁבַּח מַעֲשֶׂיךָ, וּגְבוּרֹתֶיךָ יַגִּידוּ.
הֲדַר כְּבוֹד הוֹדֶךָ, וְדִבְרֵי נִפְלְאֹתֶיךָ אָשִׂיחָה.
וֶעֱזוּז נוֹרְאוֹתֶיךָ יֹאמֵרוּ, וּגְדוּלָּתְךָ אֲסַפְּרֶנָּה.
זֵכֶר רַב טוּבְךָ יַבִּיעוּ, וְצִדְקָתְךָ יְרַנֵּנוּ.
חַנּוּן וְרַחוּם יהוה, אֶרֶךְ אַפַּיִם וּגְדָל חָסֶד.
טוֹב יהוה לַכֹּל, וְרַחֲמָיו עַל כָּל מַעֲשָׂיו.
יוֹדוּךָ יהוה כָּל מַעֲשֶׂיךָ, וַחֲסִידֶיךָ יְבָרְכוּכָה.
כְּבוֹד מַלְכוּתְךָ יֹאמֵרוּ, וּגְבוּרָתְךָ יְדַבֵּרוּ.
לְהוֹדִיעַ לִבְנֵי הָאָדָם גְּבוּרֹתָיו, וּכְבוֹד הֲדַר מַלְכוּתוֹ.
מַלְכוּתְךָ מַלְכוּת כָּל עֹלָמִים, וּמֶמְשַׁלְתְּךָ בְּכָל דּוֹר וָדֹר.
סוֹמֵךְ יהוה לְכָל הַנֹּפְלִים, וְזוֹקֵף לְכָל הַכְּפוּפִים.
עֵינֵי כֹל אֵלֶיךָ יְשַׂבֵּרוּ, וְאַתָּה נוֹתֵן לָהֶם אֶת אָכְלָם בְּעִתּוֹ.
פּוֹתֵחַ אֶת יָדֶךָ,
וּמַשְׂבִּיעַ לְכָל חַי רָצוֹן.

While reciting the verse פּוֹתֵחַ, concentrate intently on its meaning.

צַדִּיק יהוה בְּכָל דְּרָכָיו, וְחָסִיד בְּכָל מַעֲשָׂיו.
קָרוֹב יהוה לְכָל קֹרְאָיו, לְכֹל אֲשֶׁר יִקְרָאֻהוּ בֶאֱמֶת.
רְצוֹן יְרֵאָיו יַעֲשֶׂה, וְאֶת שַׁוְעָתָם יִשְׁמַע וְיוֹשִׁיעֵם.
שׁוֹמֵר יהוה אֶת כָּל אֹהֲבָיו, וְאֵת כָּל הָרְשָׁעִים יַשְׁמִיד.
❖ תְּהִלַּת יהוה יְדַבֶּר פִּי, וִיבָרֵךְ כָּל בָּשָׂר שֵׁם קָדְשׁוֹ לְעוֹלָם וָעֶד.
וַאֲנַחְנוּ נְבָרֵךְ יָהּ, מֵעַתָּה וְעַד עוֹלָם, הַלְלוּיָהּ.[1]

תהלים קמו

הַלְלוּיָהּ, הַלְלִי נַפְשִׁי אֶת יהוה. אֲהַלְלָה יהוה בְּחַיָּי, אֲזַמְּרָה לֵאלֹהַי בְּעוֹדִי. אַל תִּבְטְחוּ בִנְדִיבִים, בְּבֶן אָדָם שֶׁאֵין לוֹ תְשׁוּעָה. תֵּצֵא רוּחוֹ, יָשֻׁב לְאַדְמָתוֹ, בַּיּוֹם הַהוּא אָבְדוּ עֶשְׁתֹּנֹתָיו. אַשְׁרֵי שֶׁאֵל יַעֲקֹב בְּעֶזְרוֹ, שִׂבְרוֹ עַל יהוה אֱלֹהָיו. עֹשֶׂה שָׁמַיִם וָאָרֶץ, אֶת הַיָּם וְאֶת כָּל אֲשֶׁר בָּם, הַשֹּׁמֵר אֱמֶת לְעוֹלָם. עֹשֶׂה מִשְׁפָּט לַעֲשׁוּקִים, נֹתֵן לֶחֶם לָרְעֵבִים, יהוה מַתִּיר אֲסוּרִים. יהוה פֹּקֵחַ עִוְרִים, יהוה זֹקֵף כְּפוּפִים, יהוה אֹהֵב צַדִּיקִים. יהוה שֹׁמֵר אֶת גֵּרִים, יָתוֹם וְאַלְמָנָה

(1) *Pslams* 115:8.

ד *Each generation will praise Your deeds to the next
and of Your mighty deeds they will tell.*
ה *The splendrous glory of Your power
and Your wondrous deeds I shall discuss.*
ו *And of Your awesome power they will speak,
and Your greatness I shall relate.*
ז *A recollection of Your abundant goodness they will utter
and of Your righteousness they will sing exultantly.*
ח *Gracious and merciful is HASHEM,
slow to anger, and great in [bestowing] kindness.*
ט *HASHEM is good to all; His mercies are on all His works.*
י *All Your works shall thank You, HASHEM,
and Your devout ones will bless You.*
כ *Of the glory of Your kingdom they will speak,
and of Your power they will tell;*
ל *To inform human beings of His mighty deeds,
and the glorious splendor of His kingdom.*
מ *Your kingdom is a kingdom spanning all eternities,
and Your dominion is throughout every generation.*
ס *HASHEM supports all the fallen ones and straightens all the bent.*
ע *The eyes of all look to You with hope
and You give them their food in its proper time;*
פ *You open Your hand, and satisfy
the desire of every living thing.*

While reciting the verse, *'You open . . .'* concentrate intently on its meaning.

צ *Righteous is HASHEM in all His ways
and magnanimous in all His deeds.*
ק *HASHEM is close to all who call upon Him —
to all who call upon Him sincerely.*
ר *The will of those who fear Him He will do;
and their cry He will hear, and save them.*
ש *HASHEM protects all who love Him;
but all the wicked He will destroy.*
ת Chazzan— *May my mouth declare the praise of HASHEM
and may all flesh bless His Holy Name forever and ever.
We will bless God from this time and forever, Halleluyah!*[1]

Psalm 146

הַלְלוּיָהּ *Halleluyah! Praise HASHEM, O my Soul! I will praise HASHEM while I live, I will make music to my God while I exist. Do not rely on nobles, nor on a human being for he holds no salvation. When his spirit departs he returns to his earth, on that day his plans all perish. Praiseworthy is one whose help is Jacob's God, whose hope is in HASHEM, his God. He is the Maker of heaven and earth, the sea and all that is in them, Who safeguards truth forever. He does justice for the exploited; He gives bread to the hungry; HASHEM releases the bound. HASHEM gives sight to the blind; HASHEM straightens the bent; HASHEM loves the righteous. HASHEM protects strangers; orphan and widow*

יְעוֹדֵד, וְדֶרֶךְ רְשָׁעִים יְעַוֵּת. ❖ יִמְלֹךְ יהוה לְעוֹלָם, אֱלֹהַיִךְ צִיּוֹן, לְדֹר וָדֹר, הַלְלוּיָהּ.

תהלים קמז

הַלְלוּיָהּ, כִּי טוֹב זַמְּרָה אֱלֹהֵינוּ, כִּי נָעִים נָאוָה תְהִלָּה. בּוֹנֵה יְרוּשָׁלַיִם יהוה, נִדְחֵי יִשְׂרָאֵל יְכַנֵּס. הָרוֹפֵא לִשְׁבְוּרֵי לֵב, וּמְחַבֵּשׁ לְעַצְּבוֹתָם. מוֹנֶה מִסְפָּר לַכּוֹכָבִים, לְכֻלָּם שֵׁמוֹת יִקְרָא. גָּדוֹל אֲדוֹנֵינוּ וְרַב כֹּחַ, לִתְבוּנָתוֹ אֵין מִסְפָּר. מְעוֹדֵד עֲנָוִים יהוה, מַשְׁפִּיל רְשָׁעִים עֲדֵי אָרֶץ. עֱנוּ לַיהוה בְּתוֹדָה, זַמְּרוּ לֵאלֹהֵינוּ בְכִנּוֹר. הַמְּכַסֶּה שָׁמַיִם בְּעָבִים, הַמֵּכִין לָאָרֶץ מָטָר, הַמַּצְמִיחַ הָרִים חָצִיר. נוֹתֵן לִבְהֵמָה לַחְמָהּ, לִבְנֵי עֹרֵב אֲשֶׁר יִקְרָאוּ. לֹא בִגְבוּרַת הַסּוּס יֶחְפָּץ, לֹא בְשׁוֹקֵי הָאִישׁ יִרְצֶה. רוֹצֶה יהוה אֶת יְרֵאָיו, אֶת הַמְיַחֲלִים לְחַסְדּוֹ. שַׁבְּחִי יְרוּשָׁלַיִם אֶת יהוה, הַלְלִי אֱלֹהַיִךְ צִיּוֹן. כִּי חִזַּק בְּרִיחֵי שְׁעָרָיִךְ, בֵּרַךְ בָּנַיִךְ בְּקִרְבֵּךְ. הַשָּׂם גְּבוּלֵךְ שָׁלוֹם, חֵלֶב חִטִּים יַשְׂבִּיעֵךְ. הַשֹּׁלֵחַ אִמְרָתוֹ אָרֶץ, עַד מְהֵרָה יָרוּץ דְּבָרוֹ. הַנֹּתֵן שֶׁלֶג כַּצָּמֶר, כְּפוֹר כָּאֵפֶר יְפַזֵּר. מַשְׁלִיךְ קַרְחוֹ כְפִתִּים, לִפְנֵי קָרָתוֹ מִי יַעֲמֹד. יִשְׁלַח דְּבָרוֹ וְיַמְסֵם, יַשֵּׁב רוּחוֹ יִזְּלוּ מָיִם. ❖ מַגִּיד דְּבָרָיו לְיַעֲקֹב, חֻקָּיו וּמִשְׁפָּטָיו לְיִשְׂרָאֵל. לֹא עָשָׂה כֵן לְכָל גּוֹי, וּמִשְׁפָּטִים בַּל יְדָעוּם, הַלְלוּיָהּ.

תהלים קמח

הַלְלוּיָהּ, הַלְלוּ אֶת יהוה מִן הַשָּׁמַיִם, הַלְלְוּהוּ בַּמְּרוֹמִים. הַלְלְוּהוּ כָל מַלְאָכָיו, הַלְלְוּהוּ כָּל צְבָאָיו. הַלְלְוּהוּ שֶׁמֶשׁ וְיָרֵחַ, הַלְלְוּהוּ כָּל כּוֹכְבֵי אוֹר. הַלְלְוּהוּ שְׁמֵי הַשָּׁמָיִם, וְהַמַּיִם אֲשֶׁר מֵעַל הַשָּׁמָיִם. יְהַלְלוּ אֶת שֵׁם יהוה, כִּי הוּא צִוָּה וְנִבְרָאוּ. וַיַּעֲמִידֵם לָעַד לְעוֹלָם, חָק נָתַן וְלֹא יַעֲבוֹר. הַלְלוּ אֶת יהוה מִן הָאָרֶץ, תַּנִּינִים וְכָל תְּהֹמוֹת. אֵשׁ וּבָרָד, שֶׁלֶג וְקִיטוֹר, רוּחַ סְעָרָה עֹשָׂה דְבָרוֹ. הֶהָרִים וְכָל גְּבָעוֹת, עֵץ פְּרִי וְכָל אֲרָזִים. הַחַיָּה וְכָל בְּהֵמָה, רֶמֶשׂ וְצִפּוֹר כָּנָף. מַלְכֵי אֶרֶץ וְכָל לְאֻמִּים, שָׂרִים וְכָל שֹׁפְטֵי אָרֶץ. בַּחוּרִים וְגַם בְּתוּלוֹת, זְקֵנִים עִם נְעָרִים. ❖ יְהַלְלוּ אֶת שֵׁם יהוה, כִּי נִשְׂגָּב שְׁמוֹ לְבַדּוֹ, הוֹדוֹ עַל אֶרֶץ וְשָׁמָיִם. וַיָּרֶם קֶרֶן לְעַמּוֹ, תְּהִלָּה לְכָל חֲסִידָיו, לִבְנֵי יִשְׂרָאֵל עַם קְרֹבוֹ, הַלְלוּיָהּ.

He encourages; but the way of the wicked He contorts. Chazzan– *HASHEM shall reign forever — your God, O Zion — from generation to generation. Halleluyah!*

Psalm 147

הַלְלוּיָהּ *Halleluyah! For it is good to make music to our God, for praise is pleasant and befitting. The Builder of Jerusalem is HASHEM, the outcast of Israel He will gather in. He is the Healer of the broken-hearted, and the One Who binds up their sorrows. He counts the number of the stars, to all of them He assigns names. Great is our Lord and abundant in strength, His understanding is beyond calculation. HASHEM encourages the humble, He lowers the wicked down to the ground. Call out to HASHEM with thanks, with the harp sing to our God — Who covers the heavens with clouds, Who prepares rain for the earth, Who makes mountains sprout with grass. He gives to an animal its food, to young ravens that cry out. Not in the strength of the horse does He desire, and not in the legs of man does He favor. HASHEM favors those who fear Him, those who hope for His kindness. Praise HASHEM, O Jerusalem, laud your God, O Zion. For He has strengthened the bars of your gates, and blessed your children in your midst; He Who makes your borders peaceful, and with the cream of the wheat He sates you; He Who dispatches His utterance earthward; how swiftly His commandment runs! He Who gives snow like fleece, He scatters frost like ashes. He hurls His ice like crumbs — before His cold, who can stand? He issues His command and it melts them, He blows His wind — the waters flow.* Chazzan– *He relates His Word to Jacob, His statutes and judgments to Israel. He did not do so for any other nation, such judgments — they know them not. Halleluyah!*

Psalm 148

הַלְלוּיָהּ *Halleluyah! Praise HASHEM from the heavens; praise Him in the heights. Praise Him, all His angels; praise Him, all His legions. Praise Him, sun and moon; praise Him, all bright stars. Praise Him, the most exalted of the heavens and the waters that are above the heavens. Let them praise the Name of HASHEM, for He commanded and they were created. And He established them forever and ever, He issued a decree that will not change. Praise HASHEM from the earth, sea giants and all watery depths. Fire and hail, snow and vapor, stormy wind fulfilling His word. Mountains and all hills, fruitful trees and all cedars. Beasts and all cattle, crawling things and winged fowl. Kings of the earth and all governments, princes and all judges on earth. Young men and also maidens, old men together with youths.* Chazzan– *Let them praise the Name of HASHEM, for His Name alone will have been exalted; His glory is above earth and heaven. And He will have exalted the pride of His nation, causing praise for all His devout ones, for the Children of Israel, His intimate people. Halleluyah!*

תהלים קמט

הַלְלוּיָהּ, שִׁירוּ לַיהוה שִׁיר חָדָשׁ, תְּהִלָּתוֹ בִּקְהַל חֲסִידִים. יִשְׂמַח יִשְׂרָאֵל בְּעֹשָׂיו, בְּנֵי צִיּוֹן יָגִילוּ בְמַלְכָּם. יְהַלְלוּ שְׁמוֹ בְמָחוֹל, בְּתֹף וְכִנּוֹר יְזַמְּרוּ לוֹ. כִּי רוֹצֶה יהוה בְּעַמּוֹ, יְפָאֵר עֲנָוִים בִּישׁוּעָה. יַעְלְזוּ חֲסִידִים בְּכָבוֹד, יְרַנְּנוּ עַל מִשְׁכְּבוֹתָם. רוֹמְמוֹת אֵל בִּגְרוֹנָם, וְחֶרֶב פִּיפִיּוֹת בְּיָדָם. לַעֲשׂוֹת נְקָמָה בַּגּוֹיִם, תּוֹכֵחוֹת בַּלְאֻמִּים. ❖ לֶאְסֹר מַלְכֵיהֶם בְּזִקִּים, וְנִכְבְּדֵיהֶם בְּכַבְלֵי בַרְזֶל. לַעֲשׂוֹת בָּהֶם מִשְׁפָּט כָּתוּב, הָדָר הוּא לְכָל חֲסִידָיו, הַלְלוּיָהּ.

תהלים קנ

הַלְלוּיָהּ, הַלְלוּ אֵל בְּקָדְשׁוֹ, הַלְלוּהוּ בִּרְקִיעַ עֻזּוֹ. הַלְלוּהוּ בִגְבוּרֹתָיו, הַלְלוּהוּ כְּרֹב גֻּדְלוֹ. הַלְלוּהוּ בְּתֵקַע שׁוֹפָר, הַלְלוּהוּ בְּנֵבֶל וְכִנּוֹר. הַלְלוּהוּ בְתֹף וּמָחוֹל, הַלְלוּהוּ בְּמִנִּים וְעוּגָב. הַלְלוּהוּ בְצִלְצְלֵי שָׁמַע, הַלְלוּהוּ בְּצִלְצְלֵי תְרוּעָה. ❖ כֹּל הַנְּשָׁמָה תְּהַלֵּל יָהּ, הַלְלוּיָהּ. כֹּל הַנְּשָׁמָה תְּהַלֵּל יָהּ, הַלְלוּיָהּ.

בָּרוּךְ יהוה לְעוֹלָם, אָמֵן וְאָמֵן.[1] בָּרוּךְ יהוה מִצִּיּוֹן, שֹׁכֵן יְרוּשָׁלָיִם, הַלְלוּיָהּ.[2] בָּרוּךְ יהוה אֱלֹהִים אֱלֹהֵי יִשְׂרָאֵל, עֹשֵׂה נִפְלָאוֹת לְבַדּוֹ. ❖ וּבָרוּךְ שֵׁם כְּבוֹדוֹ לְעוֹלָם, וְיִמָּלֵא כְבוֹדוֹ אֶת כָּל הָאָרֶץ, אָמֵן וְאָמֵן.[3]

One must stand from וַיְבָרֶךְ דָּוִיד, until after the phrase אַתָּה הוּא ה' הָאֱלֹהִים; however, there is a generally accepted custom to remain standing until after completing אָז יָשִׁיר (p. 670).

דברי הימים א כט:י-יג

וַיְבָרֶךְ דָּוִיד אֶת יהוה לְעֵינֵי כָּל הַקָּהָל, וַיֹּאמֶר דָּוִיד: בָּרוּךְ אַתָּה יהוה, אֱלֹהֵי יִשְׂרָאֵל אָבִינוּ, מֵעוֹלָם וְעַד עוֹלָם. לְךָ יהוה הַגְּדֻלָּה וְהַגְּבוּרָה וְהַתִּפְאֶרֶת וְהַנֵּצַח וְהַהוֹד, כִּי כֹל בַּשָּׁמַיִם וּבָאָרֶץ; לְךָ יהוה הַמַּמְלָכָה וְהַמִּתְנַשֵּׂא לְכֹל לְרֹאשׁ. וְהָעֹשֶׁר וְהַכָּבוֹד מִלְּפָנֶיךָ, וְאַתָּה מוֹשֵׁל בַּכֹּל, וּבְיָדְךָ כֹּחַ וּגְבוּרָה, וּבְיָדְךָ לְגַדֵּל וּלְחַזֵּק לַכֹּל. וְעַתָּה אֱלֹהֵינוּ מוֹדִים אֲנַחְנוּ לָךְ, וּמְהַלְלִים לְשֵׁם תִּפְאַרְתֶּךָ.

It is customary to set aside something for charity at this point.

נחמיה ט:ו-יא

אַתָּה הוּא יהוה לְבַדֶּךָ, אַתָּה עָשִׂיתָ אֶת הַשָּׁמַיִם, שְׁמֵי הַשָּׁמַיִם וְכָל צְבָאָם, הָאָרֶץ וְכָל אֲשֶׁר עָלֶיהָ, הַיַּמִּים וְכָל אֲשֶׁר בָּהֶם, וְאַתָּה מְחַיֶּה אֶת כֻּלָּם, וּצְבָא הַשָּׁמַיִם לְךָ מִשְׁתַּחֲוִים. ❖ אַתָּה הוּא יהוה הָאֱלֹהִים אֲשֶׁר בָּחַרְתָּ בְּאַבְרָם, וְהוֹצֵאתוֹ מֵאוּר כַּשְׂדִּים, וְשַׂמְתָּ שְׁמוֹ אַבְרָהָם. וּמָצָאתָ אֶת לְבָבוֹ נֶאֱמָן לְפָנֶיךָ —

Psalm 149

הַלְלוּיָהּ *Halleluyah! Sing to* HASHEM *a new song, let His praise be in the congregation of the devout. Let Israel exult in its Maker, let the Children of Zion rejoice in their King. Let them praise His Name with dancing, with drums and harp let them make music to Him. For* HASHEM *favors His nation, He adorns the humble with salvation. Let the devout exult in glory, let them sing joyously upon their beds. The lofty praises of God are in their throats, and a double-edged sword is in their hand — to execute vengeance among the nations, rebukes among the governments.* Chazzan– *To bind their kings with chains, and their nobles with fetters of iron. To execute upon them written judgment — that will be the splendor of all His devout ones. Halleluyah!*

Psalm 150

הַלְלוּיָהּ *Halleluyah! Praise God in His Sanctuary; praise Him in the firmament of His power. Praise Him for His mighty acts; praise Him as befits His abundant greatness. Praise Him with the blast of the shofar; praise Him with lyre and harp. Praise Him with drum and dance; praise Him with organ and flute. Praise Him with clanging cymbals; praise Him with resonant trumpets.* Chazzan– *Let all souls praise God, Halleluyah! Let all souls praise God, Halleluyah!*

בָּרוּךְ *Blessed is* HASHEM *forever, Amen and Amen.*[1] *Blessed is* HASHEM *from Zion, Who dwells in Jerusalem, Halleluyah.*[2] *Blessed is* HASHEM, *God, the God of Israel, Who alone does wonders.* Chazzan– *Blessed is His glorious Name forever, and may all the earth be filled with His glory, Amen and Amen.*[3]

One must stand from here until after the phrase *'It is You,* HASHEM *the God'*; however, there is a generally accepted custom to remain standing until after completing the Song at the Sea (p. 670).

I Chronicles 29:10-13

וַיְבָרֶךְ *And David blessed* HASHEM *in the presence of the entire congregation; David said, 'Blessed are You,* HASHEM, *the God of Israel our forefather from This World to the World to Come. Yours,* HASHEM, *is the greatness, the strength, the splendor, the triumph, and the glory, even everything in heaven and earth; Yours,* HASHEM, *is the kingdom, and the sovereignty over every leader.*

It is customary to set aside something for charity at this point.

Wealth and honor come from You and You rule everything — in Your hand is power and strength and it is in Your hand to make anyone great or strong. So now, our God, we thank You and praise Your splendrous Name.'

Nehemiah 9:6-11

It is You alone, HASHEM, *You have made the heaven, the most exalted heaven and all their legions, the earth and everything upon it, the seas and everything in them and You give them all life; the heavenly legions bow to You.* Chazzan– *It is You,* HASHEM *the God, Who selected Abram, brought him out of Ur Kasdim and made his name Abraham. You found his heart faithful before You —*

(1) *Psalms* 89:53. (2) 135:21. (3) 72:18-19.

— וְכָרוֹת עִמּוֹ הַבְּרִית לָתֵת אֶת אֶרֶץ הַכְּנַעֲנִי הַחִתִּי הָאֱמֹרִי וְהַפְּרִזִּי וְהַיְבוּסִי וְהַגִּרְגָּשִׁי, לָתֵת לְזַרְעוֹ, וַתָּקֶם אֶת דְּבָרֶיךָ, כִּי צַדִּיק אָתָּה. וַתֵּרֶא אֶת עֳנִי אֲבֹתֵינוּ בְּמִצְרָיִם, וְאֶת זַעֲקָתָם שָׁמַעְתָּ עַל יַם סוּף. וַתִּתֵּן אֹתֹת וּמֹפְתִים בְּפַרְעֹה וּבְכָל עֲבָדָיו וּבְכָל עַם אַרְצוֹ, כִּי יָדַעְתָּ כִּי הֵזִידוּ עֲלֵיהֶם, וַתַּעַשׂ לְךָ שֵׁם כְּהַיּוֹם הַזֶּה. ❖ וְהַיָּם בָּקַעְתָּ לִפְנֵיהֶם, וַיַּעַבְרוּ בְתוֹךְ הַיָּם בַּיַּבָּשָׁה, וְאֶת רֹדְפֵיהֶם הִשְׁלַכְתָּ בִמְצוֹלֹת, כְּמוֹ אֶבֶן בְּמַיִם עַזִּים.

שירת הים

שמות יד:ל–טו:יט

וַיּוֹשַׁע יהוה* בַּיּוֹם הַהוּא אֶת־יִשְׂרָאֵל מִיַּד מִצְרָיִם, וַיַּרְא
יִשְׂרָאֵל אֶת־מִצְרַיִם מֵת עַל־שְׂפַת הַיָּם: ❖ וַיַּרְא יִשְׂרָאֵל
אֶת־הַיָּד הַגְּדֹלָה אֲשֶׁר עָשָׂה יהוה בְּמִצְרַיִם, וַיִּירְאוּ הָעָם
אֶת־יהוה, וַיַּאֲמִינוּ* בַּיהוה וּבְמֹשֶׁה עַבְדּוֹ:

אָז יָשִׁיר־מֹשֶׁה וּבְנֵי יִשְׂרָאֵל אֶת־הַשִּׁירָה הַזֹּאת לַיהוה, וַיֹּאמְרוּ
לֵאמֹר, אָשִׁירָה לַיהוה כִּי־גָאֹה גָּאָה, סוּס
וְרֹכְבוֹ רָמָה בַיָּם: עָזִּי וְזִמְרָת יָהּ* וַיְהִי־לִי
לִישׁוּעָה, זֶה אֵלִי* וְאַנְוֵהוּ,* אֱלֹהֵי
אָבִי וַאֲרֹמְמֶנְהוּ: יהוה אִישׁ מִלְחָמָה, יהוה
שְׁמוֹ:* מַרְכְּבֹת פַּרְעֹה וְחֵילוֹ יָרָה בַיָּם, וּמִבְחַר
שָׁלִשָׁיו טֻבְּעוּ בְיַם־סוּף: תְּהֹמֹת יְכַסְיֻמוּ, יָרְדוּ בִמְצוֹלֹת כְּמוֹ־
אָבֶן: יְמִינְךָ* יהוה נֶאְדָּרִי בַּכֹּחַ, יְמִינְךָ
יהוה תִּרְעַץ אוֹיֵב: וּבְרֹב גְּאוֹנְךָ תַּהֲרֹס
קָמֶיךָ, תְּשַׁלַּח חֲרֹנְךָ יֹאכְלֵמוֹ כַּקַּשׁ: וּבְרוּחַ
אַפֶּיךָ נֶעֶרְמוּ מַיִם, נִצְּבוּ כְמוֹ־נֵד
נֹזְלִים, קָפְאוּ תְהֹמֹת בְּלֶב־יָם: אָמַר
אוֹיֵב,* אֶרְדֹּף אַשִּׂיג אֲחַלֵּק שָׁלָל, תִּמְלָאֵמוֹ
נַפְשִׁי, אָרִיק חַרְבִּי, תּוֹרִישֵׁמוֹ יָדִי: נָשַׁפְתָּ
בְרוּחֲךָ כִּסָּמוֹ יָם, צָלְלוּ כַּעוֹפֶרֶת בְּמַיִם
אַדִּירִים: מִי־כָמֹכָה בָּאֵלִם יהוה, מִי
כָּמֹכָה נֶאְדָּר בַּקֹּדֶשׁ, נוֹרָא תְהִלֹּת עֹשֵׂה
פֶלֶא: נָטִיתָ יְמִינְךָ, תִּבְלָעֵמוֹ אָרֶץ: נָחִיתָ
בְחַסְדְּךָ עַם־זוּ גָּאָלְתָּ, נֵהַלְתָּ בְעָזְּךָ אֶל־נְוֵה

— and You established the covenant with him to give the land of the Canaanite, Hittite, Emorite, Perizzite, Jebusite, and Girgashite, to give it to his offspring; and You affirmed Your word, for You are righteous. You observed the suffering of our forefathers in Egypt, and their outcry You heard at the Sea of Reeds. You imposed signs and wonders upon Pharaoh and upon all his servants, and upon all the people of his land. For You knew that they sinned flagrantly against them, and You brought Yourself renown as [clear as] this very day. Chazzan– *You split the Sea before them and they crossed in the midst of the Sea on dry land; but their pursuers You hurled into the depths, like a stone into turbulent waters.*

THE SONG AT THE SEA

Exodus 14:30-15:19

וַיּוֹשַׁע *HASHEM saved — on that day — Israel from the hand of Egypt, and Israel saw the Egyptians dead on the seashore.* Chazzan– *Israel saw the great hand that HASHEM inflicted upon Egypt and the people feared HASHEM, and they had faith in HASHEM and in Moses, His servant.*

Then Moses and the Children of Israel chose to sing this song to HASHEM, and they said the following:

I shall sing to HASHEM for He is exalted above the arrogant, having hurled horse with its rider into the sea.

God is my might and my praise, and He was a salvation for me. This is my God, and I will build Him a Sanctuary; the God of my father, and I will exalt Him.

HASHEM is Master of war, through His Name HASHEM.

Pharaoh's chariots and army He threw into the sea; and the pick of his officers were mired in the Sea of Reeds.

Deep waters covered them; they descended in the depths like stone.

Your right hand, HASHEM, is adorned with strength; Your right hand, HASHEM, smashes the enemy.

In Your abundant grandeur You shatter Your opponents; You dispatch Your wrath, it consumes them like straw.

At a blast from Your nostrils the waters were heaped up; straight as a wall stood the running water, the deep waters congealed in the heart of the sea.

The enemy declared: 'I will pursue, I will overtake, I will divide plunder; I will satisfy my lust with them; I will unsheathe my sword, my hand will impoverish them.'

You blew with Your wind — the sea enshrouded them; the mighty ones sank like lead in the waters.

Who is like You among the heavenly powers, HASHEM! Who is like You, mighty in holiness, too awesome for praise, doing wonders!

You stretched out Your right hand — the earth swallowed them.

You guided in Your kindness this people that You redeemed; You led with Your might to Your holy abode.

קָדְשֶׁךָ:* שָׁמְעוּ עַמִּים יִרְגָּזוּן, חִיל
אָחַז יֹשְׁבֵי פְּלָשֶׁת: אָז נִבְהֲלוּ אַלּוּפֵי
אֱדוֹם,* אֵילֵי מוֹאָב יֹאחֲזֵמוֹ רָעַד, נָמֹגוּ
כֹּל יֹשְׁבֵי כְנָעַן: תִּפֹּל עֲלֵיהֶם אֵימָתָה
וָפַחַד, בִּגְדֹל זְרוֹעֲךָ יִדְּמוּ כָּאָבֶן, עַד־
יַעֲבֹר עַמְּךָ* יהוה, עַד־יַעֲבֹר עַם־זוּ
קָנִיתָ: תְּבִאֵמוֹ* וְתִטָּעֵמוֹ בְּהַר נַחֲלָתְךָ, מָכוֹן
לְשִׁבְתְּךָ פָּעַלְתָּ יהוה, מִקְּדָשׁ אֲדֹנָי כּוֹנְנוּ
יָדֶיךָ: יהוה | יִמְלֹךְ* לְעֹלָם וָעֶד:

יהוה יִמְלֹךְ לְעֹלָם וָעֶד. (יהוה מַלְכוּתֵהּ קָאֵם, לְעָלַם וּלְעָלְמֵי עָלְמַיָּא.) כִּי בָא סוּס פַּרְעֹה בְּרִכְבּוֹ וּבְפָרָשָׁיו בַּיָּם, וַיָּשֶׁב יהוה עֲלֵהֶם אֶת מֵי הַיָּם, וּבְנֵי יִשְׂרָאֵל הָלְכוּ בַיַּבָּשָׁה בְּתוֹךְ הַיָּם. ❖ כִּי לַיהוה הַמְּלוּכָה,* וּמֹשֵׁל בַּגּוֹיִם.[1] וְעָלוּ מוֹשִׁעִים* בְּהַר צִיּוֹן, לִשְׁפֹּט אֶת הַר עֵשָׂו, וְהָיְתָה לַיהוה הַמְּלוּכָה.[2] וְהָיָה יהוה לְמֶלֶךְ* עַל כָּל הָאָרֶץ, בַּיּוֹם הַהוּא יִהְיֶה יהוה אֶחָד וּשְׁמוֹ אֶחָד.*[3] (וּבְתוֹרָתְךָ כָּתוּב לֵאמֹר: שְׁמַע יִשְׂרָאֵל יהוה אֱלֹהֵינוּ יהוה אֶחָד.[4])

Stand while reciting יִשְׁתַּבַּח . . . The fifteen expressions of praise — שִׁיר וּשְׁבָחָה . . . בְּרָכוֹת וְהוֹדָאוֹת — should be recited without pause, preferably in one breath.

יִשְׁתַּבַּח שִׁמְךָ לָעַד מַלְכֵּנוּ, הָאֵל הַמֶּלֶךְ הַגָּדוֹל וְהַקָּדוֹשׁ, בַּשָּׁמַיִם וּבָאָרֶץ. כִּי לְךָ נָאֶה יהוה אֱלֹהֵינוּ וֵאלֹהֵי אֲבוֹתֵינוּ, שִׁיר וּשְׁבָחָה, הַלֵּל וְזִמְרָה, עֹז וּמֶמְשָׁלָה, נֶצַח גְּדֻלָּה וּגְבוּרָה, תְּהִלָּה וְתִפְאֶרֶת, קְדֻשָּׁה וּמַלְכוּת, בְּרָכוֹת וְהוֹדָאוֹת מֵעַתָּה וְעַד עוֹלָם. ❖ בָּרוּךְ אַתָּה יהוה, אֵל מֶלֶךְ גָּדוֹל בַּתִּשְׁבָּחוֹת, אֵל הַהוֹדָאוֹת, אֲדוֹן הַנִּפְלָאוֹת, הַבּוֹחֵר בְּשִׁירֵי זִמְרָה, מֶלֶךְ אֵל חֵי הָעוֹלָמִים. (Cong. – אָמֵן.)

ON HOSHANA RABBAH

In many congregations the following psalm (*Psalm* 130) is recited. The Ark is opened and each verse is recited by the *chazzan,* then by the congregation.

שִׁיר הַמַּעֲלוֹת, מִמַּעֲמַקִּים קְרָאתִיךָ יהוה. אֲדֹנָי שִׁמְעָה בְקוֹלִי, תִּהְיֶינָה אָזְנֶיךָ קַשֻּׁבוֹת, לְקוֹל תַּחֲנוּנָי. אִם עֲוֹנוֹת תִּשְׁמָר יָהּ, אֲדֹנָי מִי יַעֲמֹד. כִּי עִמְּךָ הַסְּלִיחָה, לְמַעַן תִּוָּרֵא. קִוִּיתִי יהוה קִוְּתָה נַפְשִׁי, וְלִדְבָרוֹ הוֹחָלְתִּי. נַפְשִׁי לַאדֹנָי, מִשֹּׁמְרִים לַבֹּקֶר, שֹׁמְרִים לַבֹּקֶר. יַחֵל יִשְׂרָאֵל אֶל יהוה, כִּי עִם יהוה הַחֶסֶד, וְהַרְבֵּה עִמּוֹ פְדוּת. וְהוּא יִפְדֶּה אֶת יִשְׂרָאֵל, מִכֹּל עֲוֹנוֹתָיו.

Peoples heard — they were agitated; convulsive terror gripped the dwellers of Philistia.

Then the chieftains of Edom were confounded, trembling gripped the powers of Moab, all the dwellers of Canaan dissolved.

May fear and terror befall them, at the greatness of Your arm may they be still as stone; until Your people passes through, HASHEM, until this people You have acquired passes through.

You shall bring them and implant them on the mount of Your heritage, the foundation of Your dwelling-place, which You, HASHEM, have made: the Sanctuary, my Lord, that Your hands established.

HASHEM shall reign for all eternity.

HASHEM shall reign for all eternity. (HASHEM — His kingdom is established forever and ever.) When Pharaoh's cavalry came — with his chariots and horsemen — into the sea and HASHEM turned back the waters of the sea upon them, the Children of Israel walked on the dry bed amid the sea. Chazzan– *For the sovereignty is HASHEM's and He rules over nations.*[1] *The saviors will ascend Mount Zion to judge Esau's mountain, and the kingdom will be HASHEM's.*[2] *Then HASHEM will be King over all the world, on that day HASHEM will be One and His Name will be One.*[3] *(And in Your Torah it is written: Hear O Israel: HASHEM is our God, HASHEM, the One and Only.*[4]*)*

Stand while reciting *'May Your Name be praised . . .'*
The fifteen expressions of praise — *'song and praise. . .blessings and thanksgivings'* — should be recited without pause, preferably in one breath.

יִשְׁתַּבַּח *May Your Name be praised forever — our King, the God, the great and holy King — in heaven and on earth. Because for You is fitting — O HASHEM, our God, and the God of our forefathers — song and praise, lauding and hymns, power and dominion, triumph, greatness and strength, praise and splendor, holiness and sovereignty, blessings and thanksgivings from this time and forever.* Chazzan– *Blessed are You, HASHEM, God, King exalted through praises, God of thanksgivings, Master of wonders, Who chooses musical songs of praise — King, God, Life-giver of the world.* (Cong.– *Amen.)*

ON HOSHANA RABBAH

In many congregations the following psalm (*Psalm* 130) is recited.
The Ark is opened and each verse is recited by the *chazzan,* then by the congregation.

שִׁיר הַמַּעֲלוֹת *A song of ascents: From the depths I called You, HASHEM. My Lord, hear my voice, may Your ears be attentive to the sound of my pleas. If You preserve iniquities, O God, my Lord, who could survive? For with You is forgiveness, that You may be feared. I put confidence in HASHEM, my soul put confidence, and I hoped for His word. I yearn for my Lord, among those longing for the dawn, those longing for the dawn. Let Israel hope for HASHEM, for with HASHEM is kindness, and with Him is abundant redemption. And He shall redeem Israel from all its iniquities.*

(1) *Psalms* 22:29. (2) *Ovadiah* 1:21. (3) *Zechariah* 14:9.
(4) *Deuteronomy* 6:4.

The *chazzan* recites חֲצִי קַדִּישׁ.

יִתְגַּדַּל וְיִתְקַדַּשׁ שְׁמֵהּ רַבָּא. (.Cong – אָמֵן.) בְּעָלְמָא דִּי בְרָא כִרְעוּתֵהּ. וְיַמְלִיךְ מַלְכוּתֵהּ, בְּחַיֵּיכוֹן וּבְיוֹמֵיכוֹן וּבְחַיֵּי דְכָל בֵּית יִשְׂרָאֵל, בַּעֲגָלָא וּבִזְמַן קָרִיב. וְאִמְרוּ: אָמֵן.

(.Cong – אָמֵן. יְהֵא שְׁמֵהּ רַבָּא מְבָרַךְ לְעָלַם וּלְעָלְמֵי עָלְמַיָּא.)

יְהֵא שְׁמֵהּ רַבָּא מְבָרַךְ לְעָלַם וּלְעָלְמֵי עָלְמַיָּא.

יִתְבָּרַךְ וְיִשְׁתַּבַּח וְיִתְפָּאַר וְיִתְרוֹמַם וְיִתְנַשֵּׂא וְיִתְהַדָּר וְיִתְעַלֶּה וְיִתְהַלָּל שְׁמֵהּ דְּקֻדְשָׁא בְּרִיךְ הוּא (.Cong – בְּרִיךְ הוּא) – לְעֵלָּא מִן כָּל בִּרְכָתָא וְשִׁירָתָא תֻּשְׁבְּחָתָא וְנֶחֱמָתָא, דַּאֲמִירָן בְּעָלְמָא. וְאִמְרוּ: אָמֵן. (.Cong – אָמֵן.)

In some congregations the *chazzan* chants a melody during his recitation of בָּרְכוּ, so that the congregation can then recite יִתְבָּרַךְ.

Chazzan bows at בָּרְכוּ and straightens up at ה׳.

בָּרְכוּ אֶת יהוה הַמְּבֹרָךְ.

Congregation, followed by *chazzan*, responds, bowing at בָּרוּךְ and straightening up at ה׳.

בָּרוּךְ יהוה הַמְּבֹרָךְ לְעוֹלָם וָעֶד.

יִתְבָּרַךְ וְיִשְׁתַּבַּח וְיִתְפָּאַר וְיִתְרוֹמַם וְיִתְנַשֵּׂא שְׁמוֹ שֶׁל מֶלֶךְ מַלְכֵי הַמְּלָכִים, הַקָּדוֹשׁ בָּרוּךְ הוּא. שֶׁהוּא רִאשׁוֹן וְהוּא אַחֲרוֹן, וּמִבַּלְעָדָיו אֵין אֱלֹהִים.[1] סֹלּוּ, לָרֹכֵב בָּעֲרָבוֹת, בְּיָהּ שְׁמוֹ, וְעִלְזוּ לְפָנָיו.[2] וּשְׁמוֹ מְרוֹמָם עַל כָּל בְּרָכָה וּתְהִלָּה.[3] בָּרוּךְ שֵׁם כְּבוֹד מַלְכוּתוֹ לְעוֹלָם וָעֶד. יְהִי שֵׁם יהוה מְבֹרָךְ, מֵעַתָּה וְעַד עוֹלָם.[4]

ברכות קריאת שמע

It is preferable that one sit while reciting the following series of prayers — particularly the *Kedushah* verses, קָדוֹשׁ קָדוֹשׁ קָדוֹשׁ and בָּרוּךְ כְּבוֹד — until *Shemoneh Esrei*.

בָּרוּךְ אַתָּה יהוה אֱלֹהֵינוּ מֶלֶךְ הָעוֹלָם, יוֹצֵר אוֹר וּבוֹרֵא חֹשֶׁךְ, עֹשֶׂה שָׁלוֹם וּבוֹרֵא אֶת הַכֹּל.[5]

הַמֵּאִיר לָאָרֶץ וְלַדָּרִים עָלֶיהָ בְּרַחֲמִים, וּבְטוּבוֹ מְחַדֵּשׁ בְּכָל יוֹם תָּמִיד מַעֲשֵׂה בְרֵאשִׁית. מָה רַבּוּ מַעֲשֶׂיךָ יהוה, כֻּלָּם בְּחָכְמָה עָשִׂיתָ, מָלְאָה הָאָרֶץ קִנְיָנֶךָ.[6] הַמֶּלֶךְ הַמְּרוֹמָם לְבַדּוֹ מֵאָז, הַמְּשֻׁבָּח וְהַמְּפֹאָר וְהַמִּתְנַשֵּׂא מִימוֹת עוֹלָם. אֱלֹהֵי עוֹלָם, בְּרַחֲמֶיךָ הָרַבִּים רַחֵם עָלֵינוּ, אֲדוֹן עֻזֵּנוּ, צוּר מִשְׂגַּבֵּנוּ, מָגֵן יִשְׁעֵנוּ, מִשְׂגָּב בַּעֲדֵנוּ. אֵל בָּרוּךְ גְּדוֹל דֵּעָה, הֵכִין וּפָעַל זָהֳרֵי חַמָּה, טוֹב יָצַר כָּבוֹד לִשְׁמוֹ, מְאוֹרוֹת נָתַן סְבִיבוֹת עֻזּוֹ, פִּנּוֹת צְבָאָיו קְדוֹשִׁים רוֹמְמֵי שַׁדַּי, תָּמִיד מְסַפְּרִים כְּבוֹד אֵל וּקְדֻשָּׁתוֹ. תִּתְבָּרַךְ יהוה אֱלֹהֵינוּ עַל שֶׁבַח מַעֲשֵׂה יָדֶיךָ, וְעַל מְאוֹרֵי אוֹר שֶׁעָשִׂיתָ, יְפָאֲרוּךָ, סֶּלָה.

The *chazzan* recites Half-*Kaddish*.

יִתְגַּדַּל *May His great Name grow exalted and sanctified* (Cong.– *Amen.*) *in the world that He created as He willed. May He give reign to His kingship in your lifetimes and in your days, and in the lifetimes of the entire Family of Israel, swiftly and soon. Now respond: Amen.*

(Cong.– *Amen. May His great Name be blessed forever and ever.*)

May His great Name be blessed forever and ever.

Blessed, praised, glorified, exalted, extolled, mighty, upraised, and lauded be the Name of the Holy One, Blessed is He (Cong.– *Blessed is He*) — *beyond any blessing and song, praise and consolation that are uttered in the world. Now respond: Amen.* (Cong.– *Amen.*)

In some congregations the *chazzan* chants a melody during his recitation of *Borchu*, so that the congregation can then recite *'Blessed, praised . . .'*

Chazzan bows at *'Bless,'* and straightens up at *'HASHEM.'*

Bless HASHEM, the blessed One.

Congregation, followed by *chazzan*, responds, bowing at *'Blessed'* and straightening up at *'HASHEM.'*

Blessed is HASHEM, the blessed One, for all eternity.

Blessed, praised, glorified, exalted and upraised is the Name of the King Who rules over kings — the Holy One, Blessed is He. For He is the First and He is the Last and aside from Him there is no god.[1] *Extol Him — Who rides the highest heavens — with His Name, YAH, and exult before Him.*[2] *His Name is exalted beyond every blessing and praise.*[3] *Blessed is the Name of His glorious kingdom for all eternity. Blessed be the Name of HASHEM from this time and forever.*[4]

BLESSINGS OF THE SHEMA

It is preferable that one sit while reciting the following series of prayers — particularly the *Kedushah* verses, *'Holy, holy, holy . . .'* and *'Blessed is the glory . . .'* — until *Shemoneh Esrei*.

בָּרוּךְ *Blessed are You, HASHEM, our God, King of the universe, Who forms light and creates darkness, makes peace and creates all.*[5]

הַמֵּאִיר *He Who illuminates the earth and those who dwell upon it, with compassion; and in His goodness renews daily, perpetually, the work of Creation. How great are Your works, HASHEM, You make them all with wisdom, the world is full of Your possessions.*[6] *The King Who was exalted in solitude before Creation, Who is praised, glorified, and upraised since days of old. Eternal God, with Your abundant compassion be compassionate to us — O Master of our power, our rocklike stronghold, O Shield of our salvation, be a stronghold for us. The blessed God, Who is great in knowledge, prepared and worked on the rays of the sun; the Beneficent One fashioned honor for His Name, emplaced luminaries all around His power; the leaders of His legions, holy ones, exalt the Almighty, constantly relate the honor of God and His sanctity. May You be blessed, HASHEM, our God, beyond the praises of Your handiwork and beyond the bright luminaries that You have made — may they glorify You — Selah!*

(1) Cf. *Isaiah* 44:6. (2) *Psalms* 68:5. (3) Cf. *Nechemiah* 9:5.
(4) *Psalms* 113:2. (5) Cf. *Isaiah* 45:7. (6) *Psalms* 104:24.

תִּתְבָּרַךְ צוּרֵנוּ מַלְכֵּנוּ וְגֹאֲלֵנוּ, בּוֹרֵא קְדוֹשִׁים. יִשְׁתַּבַּח שִׁמְךָ לָעַד מַלְכֵּנוּ, יוֹצֵר מְשָׁרְתִים, וַאֲשֶׁר מְשָׁרְתָיו כֻּלָּם עוֹמְדִים בְּרוּם עוֹלָם, וּמַשְׁמִיעִים בְּיִרְאָה יַחַד בְּקוֹל דִּבְרֵי אֱלֹהִים חַיִּים וּמֶלֶךְ עוֹלָם.[1] כֻּלָּם אֲהוּבִים, כֻּלָּם בְּרוּרִים, כֻּלָּם גִּבּוֹרִים, וְכֻלָּם עֹשִׂים בְּאֵימָה וּבְיִרְאָה רְצוֹן קוֹנָם. ❖ וְכֻלָּם פּוֹתְחִים אֶת פִּיהֶם בִּקְדֻשָּׁה וּבְטָהֳרָה, בְּשִׁירָה וּבְזִמְרָה, וּמְבָרְכִים וּמְשַׁבְּחִים וּמְפָאֲרִים וּמַעֲרִיצִים וּמַקְדִּישִׁים וּמַמְלִיכִים —

אֶת שֵׁם הָאֵל הַמֶּלֶךְ הַגָּדוֹל הַגִּבּוֹר וְהַנּוֹרָא קָדוֹשׁ הוּא.[2] ❖ וְכֻלָּם מְקַבְּלִים עֲלֵיהֶם עֹל מַלְכוּת שָׁמַיִם זֶה מִזֶּה, וְנוֹתְנִים רְשׁוּת זֶה לָזֶה, לְהַקְדִּישׁ לְיוֹצְרָם, בְּנַחַת רוּחַ בְּשָׂפָה בְרוּרָה וּבִנְעִימָה. קְדֻשָּׁה כֻּלָּם כְּאֶחָד עוֹנִים וְאוֹמְרִים בְּיִרְאָה:

Congregation recites aloud:

קָדוֹשׁ קָדוֹשׁ קָדוֹשׁ יהוה צְבָאוֹת, מְלֹא כָל הָאָרֶץ כְּבוֹדוֹ.[3]

וְהָאוֹפַנִּים וְחַיּוֹת הַקֹּדֶשׁ בְּרַעַשׁ גָּדוֹל מִתְנַשְּׂאִים לְעֻמַּת שְׂרָפִים. לְעֻמָּתָם מְשַׁבְּחִים וְאוֹמְרִים:

Congregation recites aloud:

בָּרוּךְ כְּבוֹד יהוה מִמְּקוֹמוֹ.[4]

לְאֵל בָּרוּךְ נְעִימוֹת יִתֵּנוּ. לְמֶלֶךְ אֵל חַי וְקַיָּם, זְמִרוֹת יֹאמֵרוּ, וְתִשְׁבָּחוֹת יַשְׁמִיעוּ. כִּי הוּא לְבַדּוֹ פּוֹעֵל גְּבוּרוֹת, עֹשֶׂה חֲדָשׁוֹת, בַּעַל מִלְחָמוֹת, זוֹרֵעַ צְדָקוֹת, מַצְמִיחַ יְשׁוּעוֹת, בּוֹרֵא רְפוּאוֹת, נוֹרָא תְהִלּוֹת, אֲדוֹן הַנִּפְלָאוֹת. הַמְּחַדֵּשׁ בְּטוּבוֹ בְּכָל יוֹם תָּמִיד מַעֲשֵׂה בְרֵאשִׁית. כָּאָמוּר: לְעֹשֵׂה אוֹרִים גְּדֹלִים, כִּי לְעוֹלָם חַסְדּוֹ.[5] ❖ אוֹר חָדָשׁ עַל צִיּוֹן תָּאִיר, וְנִזְכֶּה כֻלָּנוּ מְהֵרָה לְאוֹרוֹ. בָּרוּךְ אַתָּה יהוה, יוֹצֵר הַמְּאוֹרוֹת. (Cong. – אָמֵן.)

אַהֲבָה רַבָּה אֲהַבְתָּנוּ יהוה אֱלֹהֵינוּ, חֶמְלָה גְדוֹלָה וִיתֵרָה חָמַלְתָּ עָלֵינוּ. אָבִינוּ מַלְכֵּנוּ, בַּעֲבוּר אֲבוֹתֵינוּ שֶׁבָּטְחוּ בְךָ, וַתְּלַמְּדֵם חֻקֵּי חַיִּים, כֵּן תְּחָנֵּנוּ וּתְלַמְּדֵנוּ. אָבִינוּ הָאָב הָרַחֲמָן הַמְּרַחֵם, רַחֵם עָלֵינוּ, וְתֵן בְּלִבֵּנוּ לְהָבִין וּלְהַשְׂכִּיל, לִשְׁמֹעַ לִלְמוֹד וּלְלַמֵּד, לִשְׁמֹר וְלַעֲשׂוֹת וּלְקַיֵּם אֶת כָּל דִּבְרֵי תַלְמוּד תּוֹרָתֶךָ בְּאַהֲבָה. וְהָאֵר עֵינֵינוּ בְּתוֹרָתֶךָ, וְדַבֵּק לִבֵּנוּ בְּמִצְוֹתֶיךָ, וְיַחֵד

תִּתְבָּרַךְ *May You be blessed, our Rock, our King and our Redeemer, Creator of holy ones; may Your Name be praised forever, our King, O Fashioner of ministering angels; all of Whose ministering angels stand at the summit of the universe and proclaim — with awe, together, loudly — the words of the living God and King of the universe.*[1] *They are all beloved; they are all flawless; they are all mighty; they all do the will of their Maker with dread and reverence.* Chazzan— *And they all open their mouth in holiness and purity, in song and hymn — and bless, praise, glorify, revere, sanctify and declare the kingship of —*

אֶת שֵׁם *The Name of God, the great, mighty, and awesome King; holy is He.*[2] Chazzan— *Then they all accept upon themselves the yoke of heavenly sovereignty from one another, and grant permission to one another to sanctify the One Who formed them, with tranquillity, with clear articulation, and with sweetness. All of them as one proclaim His holiness and say with awe:*

Congregation recites aloud:

'Holy, holy, holy is HASHEM, Master of Legions, the whole world is filled with His glory.'[3]

וְהָאוֹפַנִּים *Then the Ofanim and the holy Chayos, with great noise, raise themselves towards the Seraphim. Facing them they give praise saying:*

Congregation recites aloud:

'Blessed is the glory of HASHEM from His place.'[4]

לְאֵל *To the blessed God they shall offer sweet melodies; to the King, the living and enduring God, they shall sing hymns and proclaim praises. For He alone effects mighty deeds, makes new things, is Master of wars, sows kindnesses, makes salvations flourish, creates cures, is too awesome for praise, is Lord of wonders. In His goodness He renews daily, perpetually, the work of creation. As it is said: '[Give thanks] to Him Who makes the great luminaries, for His kindness endures forever.'*[5] Chazzan— *May You shine a new light on Zion, and may we all speedily merit its light. Blessed are You, HASHEM, Who fashions the luminaries.*

(Cong.— *Amen.*)

אַהֲבָה *With an abundant love have You loved us, HASHEM, our God; with exceedingly great pity have You pitied us. Our Father, our King, for the sake of our forefathers who trusted in You and whom You taught the decrees of life, may You be equally gracious to us and teach us. Our Father, the merciful Father, Who acts mercifully, have mercy upon us, instill in our hearts to understand and elucidate, to listen, learn, teach, safeguard, perform, and fulfill all the words of Your Torah's teaching with love. Enlighten our eyes in Your Torah, attach our hearts to Your commandments, and unify*

(1) Cf. *Jeremiah* 10:10. (2) Cf. *Deuteronomy* 10:17; *Psalms* 99:3.
(3) *Isaiah* 6:3. (4) *Ezekiel* 3:12. (5) *Psalms* 136:7.

לְבָבֵנוּ לְאַהֲבָה וּלְיִרְאָה אֶת שְׁמֶךָ,[1] וְלֹא נֵבוֹשׁ לְעוֹלָם וָעֶד. כִּי בְשֵׁם קָדְשְׁךָ הַגָּדוֹל וְהַנּוֹרָא בָּטָחְנוּ, נָגִילָה וְנִשְׂמְחָה בִּישׁוּעָתֶךָ. וַהֲבִיאֵנוּ לְשָׁלוֹם מֵאַרְבַּע כַּנְפוֹת הָאָרֶץ, וְתוֹלִיכֵנוּ קוֹמְמִיּוּת לְאַרְצֵנוּ. כִּי אֵל פּוֹעֵל יְשׁוּעוֹת אָתָּה, וּבָנוּ בָחַרְתָּ מִכָּל עַם וְלָשׁוֹן. ❖ וְקֵרַבְתָּנוּ לְשִׁמְךָ הַגָּדוֹל סֶלָה בֶּאֱמֶת, לְהוֹדוֹת לְךָ וּלְיַחֶדְךָ בְּאַהֲבָה. בָּרוּךְ אַתָּה יהוה, הַבּוֹחֵר בְּעַמּוֹ יִשְׂרָאֵל בְּאַהֲבָה.

At this point, gather the four *tzitzis* between the fourth and fifth fingers of the left hand. Hold *tzitzis* in this manner throughout the *Shema.*

(–Cong. אָמֵן.)

שמע

Immediately before its recitation concentrate on fulfilling the positive commandment of reciting the *Shema* twice daily. It is important to enunciate each word clearly and not to run words together. For this reason, vertical lines have been placed between two words that are prone to be slurred into one and are not separated by a comma or a hyphen. See *Laws* §40-55.

When praying without a *minyan,* begin with the following three-word formula:

אֵל מֶלֶךְ נֶאֱמָן.

Recite the first verse aloud, with the right hand covering the eyes, and concentrate intently upon accepting God's absolute sovereignty.

שְׁמַע | יִשְׂרָאֵל, יהוה | אֱלֹהֵינוּ, יהוה | אֶחָד:[2]

– In an undertone בָּרוּךְ שֵׁם כְּבוֹד מַלְכוּתוֹ לְעוֹלָם וָעֶד.

While reciting the first paragraph (דברים ו:ה-ט), concentrate on accepting the commandment to love God.

וְאָהַבְתָּ אֵת | יהוה | אֱלֹהֶיךָ, בְּכָל־לְבָבְךָ, וּבְכָל־נַפְשְׁךָ, וּבְכָל־מְאֹדֶךָ: וְהָיוּ הַדְּבָרִים הָאֵלֶּה, אֲשֶׁר | אָנֹכִי מְצַוְּךָ הַיּוֹם, עַל־לְבָבֶךָ: וְשִׁנַּנְתָּם לְבָנֶיךָ, וְדִבַּרְתָּ בָּם, בְּשִׁבְתְּךָ בְּבֵיתֶךָ, וּבְלֶכְתְּךָ בַדֶּרֶךְ, וּבְשָׁכְבְּךָ וּבְקוּמֶךָ: וּקְשַׁרְתָּם לְאוֹת | עַל־יָדֶךָ, וְהָיוּ לְטֹטָפֹת בֵּין | עֵינֶיךָ: וּכְתַבְתָּם | עַל־מְזֻזוֹת בֵּיתֶךָ, וּבִשְׁעָרֶיךָ:

While reciting the second paragraph (דברים יא:יג-כא), concentrate on accepting all the commandments and the concept of reward and punishment.

וְהָיָה, אִם־שָׁמֹעַ תִּשְׁמְעוּ אֶל־מִצְוֹתַי, אֲשֶׁר | אָנֹכִי מְצַוֶּה | אֶתְכֶם הַיּוֹם, לְאַהֲבָה אֶת־יהוה | אֱלֹהֵיכֶם וּלְעָבְדוֹ, בְּכָל־לְבַבְכֶם, וּבְכָל־נַפְשְׁכֶם: וְנָתַתִּי מְטַר־אַרְצְכֶם בְּעִתּוֹ, יוֹרֶה וּמַלְקוֹשׁ, וְאָסַפְתָּ דְגָנֶךָ וְתִירֹשְׁךָ וְיִצְהָרֶךָ: וְנָתַתִּי | עֵשֶׂב | בְּשָׂדְךָ לִבְהֶמְתֶּךָ, וְאָכַלְתָּ וְשָׂבָעְתָּ: הִשָּׁמְרוּ לָכֶם, פֶּן־יִפְתֶּה לְבַבְכֶם, וְסַרְתֶּם וַעֲבַדְתֶּם | אֱלֹהִים | אֲחֵרִים, וְהִשְׁתַּחֲוִיתֶם לָהֶם: וְחָרָה | אַף־יהוה בָּכֶם, וְעָצַר | אֶת־הַשָּׁמַיִם, וְלֹא־יִהְיֶה מָטָר, וְהָאֲדָמָה

our hearts to love and fear Your Name,[1] *and may we not feel inner shame for all eternity. Because we have trusted in Your great and awesome holy Name, may we exult and rejoice in Your salvation.*

At this point, gather the four *tzitzis* between the fourth and fifth fingers of the left hand. Hold *tzitzis* in this manner throughout the *Shema.*

Bring us in peacefulness from the four corners of the earth and lead us with upright pride to our land. For You effect salvations, O God; You have chosen us from among every people and tongue. Chazzan— *And You have brought us close to Your great Name forever in truth, to offer praiseful thanks to You, and proclaim Your Oneness with love. Blessed are You, HASHEM, Who chooses His people Israel with love.* (Cong.— *Amen.*)

THE SHEMA

Immediately before its recitation concentrate on fulfilling the positive commandment of reciting the *Shema* twice daily. It is important to enunciate each word clearly and not to run words together. See *Laws* §40-55.

When praying without a *minyan,* begin with the following three-word formula:

God, trustworthy King.

Recite the first verse aloud, with the right hand covering the eyes, and concentrate intently upon accepting God's absolute sovereignty.

Hear, O Israel: HASHEM is our God, HASHEM, the One and Only.[2]

In an undertone— *Blessed is the Name of His glorious kingdom for all eternity.*

While reciting the first paragraph (*Deuteronomy* 6:5-9), concentrate on accepting the commandment to love God.

וְאָהַבְתָּ *You shall love HASHEM, your God, with all your heart, with all your soul and with all your resources. Let these matters that I command you today be upon your heart. Teach them thoroughly to your children and speak of them while you sit in your home, while you walk on the way, when you retire and when you arise. Bind them as a sign upon your arm and let them be tefillin between your eyes. And write them on the doorposts of your house and upon your gates.*

While reciting the second paragraph (*Deuteronomy* 11:13-21), concentrate on accepting all the commandments and the concept of reward and punishment.

וְהָיָה *And it will come to pass that if you continually hearken to My commandments that I command you today, to love HASHEM, your God, and to serve Him, with all your heart and with all your soul — then I will provide rain for your land in its proper time, the early and late rains, that you may gather in your grain, your wine, and your oil. I will provide grass in your field for your cattle and you will eat and be satisfied. Beware lest your heart be seduced and you turn astray and serve gods of others and bow to them. Then the wrath of HASHEM will blaze against you. He will restrain the heaven so there will be no rain and the ground will not*

(1) Cf. *Psalms* 86:11. (2) *Deuteronomy* 6:4.

לֹא תִתֵּן אֶת־יְבוּלָהּ, וַאֲבַדְתֶּם | מְהֵרָה מֵעַל הָאָרֶץ הַטֹּבָה | אֲשֶׁר | יהוה נֹתֵן לָכֶם: וְשַׂמְתֶּם | אֶת־דְּבָרַי | אֵלֶּה, עַל־לְבַבְכֶם וְעַל־נַפְשְׁכֶם, וּקְשַׁרְתֶּם | אֹתָם לְאוֹת | עַל־יֶדְכֶם, וְהָיוּ לְטוֹטָפֹת בֵּין | עֵינֵיכֶם: וְלִמַּדְתֶּם | אֹתָם | אֶת־בְּנֵיכֶם, לְדַבֵּר בָּם, בְּשִׁבְתְּךָ בְּבֵיתֶךָ, וּבְלֶכְתְּךָ בַדֶּרֶךְ, וּבְשָׁכְבְּךָ וּבְקוּמֶךָ: וּכְתַבְתָּם | עַל־מְזוּזוֹת בֵּיתֶךָ, וּבִשְׁעָרֶיךָ: לְמַעַן | יִרְבּוּ | יְמֵיכֶם וִימֵי בְנֵיכֶם, עַל הָאֲדָמָה | אֲשֶׁר נִשְׁבַּע | יהוה לַאֲבֹתֵיכֶם לָתֵת לָהֶם, כִּימֵי הַשָּׁמַיִם | עַל־הָאָרֶץ:

Before reciting the third paragraph (במדבר טו:לז־מא) the *tzitzis,* which have been held in the left hand, are taken in the right hand also. The *tzitzis* are kissed at each mention of the word and at the end of the paragraph, and are passed before the eyes at וּרְאִיתֶם אֹתוֹ.

וַיֹּאמֶר | יהוה | אֶל־מֹשֶׁה לֵּאמֹר: דַּבֵּר | אֶל־בְּנֵי | יִשְׂרָאֵל, וְאָמַרְתָּ אֲלֵהֶם, וְעָשׂוּ לָהֶם צִיצִת, עַל־כַּנְפֵי בִגְדֵיהֶם לְדֹרֹתָם, וְנָתְנוּ | עַל־צִיצִת הַכָּנָף, פְּתִיל תְּכֵלֶת: וְהָיָה לָכֶם לְצִיצִת, וּרְאִיתֶם | אֹתוֹ, וּזְכַרְתֶּם | אֶת־כָּל־מִצְוֹת | יהוה, וַעֲשִׂיתֶם | אֹתָם, וְלֹא תָתוּרוּ | אַחֲרֵי לְבַבְכֶם וְאַחֲרֵי | עֵינֵיכֶם, אֲשֶׁר־אַתֶּם זֹנִים | אַחֲרֵיהֶם: לְמַעַן תִּזְכְּרוּ, וַעֲשִׂיתֶם | אֶת־כָּל־מִצְוֹתָי, וִהְיִיתֶם קְדֹשִׁים לֵאלֹהֵיכֶם: אֲנִי יהוה | אֱלֹהֵיכֶם, אֲשֶׁר הוֹצֵאתִי | אֶתְכֶם | מֵאֶרֶץ מִצְרַיִם, לִהְיוֹת לָכֶם לֵאלֹהִים, אֲנִי | יהוה | אֱלֹהֵיכֶם: אֱמֶת —

Concentrate on fulfilling the commandment of remembering the Exodus from Egypt.

Although the word אֱמֶת belongs to the next paragraph, it is appended to the conclusion of the previous one, as explained in the commentary.

—Chazzan repeats **יהוה אֱלֹהֵיכֶם אֱמֶת.**•

וְיַצִּיב וְנָכוֹן וְקַיָּם וְיָשָׁר וְנֶאֱמָן וְאָהוּב וְחָבִיב וְנֶחְמָד וְנָעִים וְנוֹרָא וְאַדִּיר וּמְתֻקָּן וּמְקֻבָּל וְטוֹב וְיָפֶה הַדָּבָר הַזֶּה עָלֵינוּ לְעוֹלָם וָעֶד. אֱמֶת אֱלֹהֵי עוֹלָם מַלְכֵּנוּ צוּר יַעֲקֹב, מָגֵן יִשְׁעֵנוּ, לְדֹר וָדֹר הוּא קַיָּם, וּשְׁמוֹ קַיָּם, וְכִסְאוֹ נָכוֹן, וּמַלְכוּתוֹ וֶאֱמוּנָתוֹ לָעַד קַיֶּמֶת. וּדְבָרָיו חָיִים וְקַיָּמִים, נֶאֱמָנִים וְנֶחֱמָדִים לָעַד (kiss the *tzitzis* and release them) וּלְעוֹלְמֵי עוֹלָמִים. ❖ עַל אֲבוֹתֵינוּ וְעָלֵינוּ, עַל בָּנֵינוּ וְעַל דּוֹרוֹתֵינוּ, וְעַל כָּל דּוֹרוֹת זֶרַע יִשְׂרָאֵל עֲבָדֶיךָ.

עַל הָרִאשׁוֹנִים וְעַל הָאַחֲרוֹנִים, דָּבָר טוֹב וְקַיָּם לְעוֹלָם וָעֶד, אֱמֶת וֶאֱמוּנָה חֹק וְלֹא יַעֲבֹר. אֱמֶת שָׁאַתָּה

yield its produce. And you will swiftly be banished from the goodly land which HASHEM gives you. Place these words of Mine upon your heart and upon your soul; bind them for a sign upon your arm and let them be tefillin between your eyes. Teach them to your children, to discuss them, while you sit in your home, while you walk on the way, when you retire and when you arise. And write them on the doorposts of your house and upon your gates. In order to prolong your days and the days of your children upon the ground that HASHEM has sworn to your ancestors to give them, like the days of the heaven on the earth.

Before reciting the third paragraph (*Numbers* 15:37-41) the *tzitzis,* which have been held in the left hand, are taken in the right hand also. The *tzitzis* are kissed at each mention of the word and at the end of the paragraph, and are passed before the eyes at *'that you may see it.'*

וַיֹּאמֶר *And HASHEM said to Moses saying: Speak to the Children of Israel and say to them that they are to make themselves tzitzis on the corners of their garments, throughout their generations. And they are to place upon the tzitzis of each corner a thread of techeiles. And it shall constitute tzitzis for you, that you may see it and remember all the commandments of HASHEM and perform them; and not explore after your heart and after your eyes after which you stray. So that you may remember and perform all My commandments; and be holy to your God. I am HASHEM, your God, Who has removed you from the land of Egypt to be a God to You; I am HASHEM your God — it is true —*

Concentrate on fulfilling the commandment of remembering the Exodus from Egypt.

Although the word אֱמֶת, *'it is true,'* belongs to the next paragraph, it is appended to the conclusion of the previous one, as explained in the commentary.

Chazzan repeats:

HASHEM, your God, is true.

וְיַצִּיב *And certain, established and enduring, fair and faithful, beloved and cherished, delightful and pleasant, awesome and powerful, correct and accepted, good and beautiful is this affirmation to us forever and ever. True — the God of the universe is our King; the Rock of Jacob is the Shield of our salvation. From generation to generation He endures and His Name endures and His throne is well established; His sovereignty and faithfulness endure forever. His words are living and enduring, faithful and delightful forever* (kiss the *tzitzis* and release them) *and to all eternity;* Chazzan— *for our forefathers and for us, for our children and for our generations, and for all the generations of Your servant Israel's offspring.*

עַל הָרִאשׁוֹנִים *Upon the earlier and upon the later generations, this affirmation is good and enduring forever. True and faithful, it is an unbreachable decree. It is true that You are*

הוּא יהוה אֱלֹהֵינוּ וֵאלֹהֵי אֲבוֹתֵינוּ, ❖ מַלְכֵּנוּ מֶלֶךְ אֲבוֹתֵינוּ, גֹּאֲלֵנוּ גֹּאֵל אֲבוֹתֵינוּ, יוֹצְרֵנוּ צוּר יְשׁוּעָתֵנוּ, פּוֹדֵנוּ וּמַצִּילֵנוּ מֵעוֹלָם שְׁמֶךָ, אֵין אֱלֹהִים זוּלָתֶךָ.

עֶזְרַת אֲבוֹתֵינוּ אַתָּה הוּא מֵעוֹלָם, מָגֵן וּמוֹשִׁיעַ לִבְנֵיהֶם אַחֲרֵיהֶם בְּכָל דּוֹר וָדוֹר. בְּרוּם עוֹלָם מוֹשָׁבֶךָ, וּמִשְׁפָּטֶיךָ וְצִדְקָתְךָ עַד אַפְסֵי אָרֶץ. אַשְׁרֵי אִישׁ שֶׁיִּשְׁמַע לְמִצְוֹתֶיךָ, וְתוֹרָתְךָ וּדְבָרְךָ יָשִׂים עַל לִבּוֹ. אֱמֶת אַתָּה הוּא אָדוֹן לְעַמֶּךָ וּמֶלֶךְ גִּבּוֹר לָרִיב רִיבָם. אֱמֶת אַתָּה הוּא רִאשׁוֹן וְאַתָּה הוּא אַחֲרוֹן, וּמִבַּלְעָדֶיךָ אֵין לָנוּ מֶלֶךְ[1] גּוֹאֵל וּמוֹשִׁיעַ. מִמִּצְרַיִם גְּאַלְתָּנוּ יהוה אֱלֹהֵינוּ, וּמִבֵּית עֲבָדִים פְּדִיתָנוּ. כָּל בְּכוֹרֵיהֶם הָרָגְתָּ, וּבְכוֹרְךָ גָּאָלְתָּ, וְיַם סוּף בָּקַעְתָּ, וְזֵדִים טִבַּעְתָּ, וִידִידִים הֶעֱבַרְתָּ, וַיְכַסּוּ מַיִם צָרֵיהֶם, אֶחָד מֵהֶם לֹא נוֹתָר.[2] עַל זֹאת שִׁבְּחוּ אֲהוּבִים וְרוֹמְמוּ אֵל, וְנָתְנוּ יְדִידִים זְמִרוֹת שִׁירוֹת וְתִשְׁבָּחוֹת, בְּרָכוֹת וְהוֹדָאוֹת, לְמֶלֶךְ אֵל חַי וְקַיָּם, רָם וְנִשָּׂא, גָּדוֹל וְנוֹרָא, מַשְׁפִּיל גֵּאִים, וּמַגְבִּיהַּ שְׁפָלִים, מוֹצִיא אֲסִירִים, וּפוֹדֶה עֲנָוִים, וְעוֹזֵר דַּלִּים, וְעוֹנֶה לְעַמּוֹ בְּעֵת שַׁוְּעָם אֵלָיו.

Rise for *Shemoneh Esrei.* Some take three steps backward at this point; others do so before צוּר יִשְׂרָאֵל.

❖ תְּהִלּוֹת לְאֵל עֶלְיוֹן, בָּרוּךְ הוּא וּמְבֹרָךְ. מֹשֶׁה וּבְנֵי יִשְׂרָאֵל לְךָ עָנוּ שִׁירָה בְּשִׂמְחָה רַבָּה וְאָמְרוּ כֻלָּם:

מִי כָמֹכָה בָּאֵלִם יהוה, מִי כָּמֹכָה נֶאְדָּר בַּקֹּדֶשׁ, נוֹרָא תְהִלֹּת עֹשֵׂה פֶלֶא.[3] ❖ שִׁירָה חֲדָשָׁה שִׁבְּחוּ גְאוּלִים לְשִׁמְךָ עַל שְׂפַת הַיָּם, יַחַד כֻּלָּם הוֹדוּ וְהִמְלִיכוּ וְאָמְרוּ:

יהוה יִמְלֹךְ לְעֹלָם וָעֶד.[4]

It is forbidden to interrupt or pause between גָּאַל יִשְׂרָאֵל and *Shemoneh Esrei,* even for *Kaddish, Kedushah* or *Borchu.*

❖ **צוּר יִשְׂרָאֵל,** קוּמָה בְּעֶזְרַת יִשְׂרָאֵל, וּפְדֵה כִנְאֻמֶךָ יְהוּדָה וְיִשְׂרָאֵל. גֹּאֲלֵנוּ יהוה צְבָאוֹת שְׁמוֹ, קְדוֹשׁ יִשְׂרָאֵל.[5] בָּרוּךְ אַתָּה יהוה, גָּאַל יִשְׂרָאֵל.

HASHEM, our God and the God of our forefathers, Chazzan– *our King and the King of our forefathers, our Redeemer, the Redeemer of our forefathers; our Molder, the Rock of our salvation; our Liberator and our Rescuer — this has ever been Your Name. There is no God but You.*

עֶזְרַת *The Helper of our forefathers are You alone, forever, Shield and Savior for their children after them in every generation. At the zenith of the universe is Your dwelling, and Your justice and Your righteousness extend to the ends of the earth. Praiseworthy is the person who obeys Your commandments and takes to his heart Your teaching and Your word. True — You are the Master for Your people and a mighty King to take up their grievance. True — You are the First and You are the Last, and other than You we have no king,*[1] *redeemer, or savior. From Egypt You redeemed us, HASHEM, our God, and from the house of slavery You liberated us. All their firstborn You slew, but Your firstborn You redeemed; the Sea of Reeds You split; the wanton sinners You drowned; the dear ones You brought across; and the water covered their foes — not one of them was left.*[2] *For this, the beloved praised and exalted God; the dear ones offered hymns, songs, praises, blessings, and thanksgivings to the King, the living and enduring God — exalted and uplifted, great and awesome, Who humbles the haughty and lifts the lowly; withdraws the captive, liberates the humble, and helps the poor; Who responds to His people upon their outcry to Him.*

Rise for *Shemoneh Esrei.* Some take three steps backward at this point; others do so before צוּר יִשְׂרָאֵל, *'Rock of Israel.'*

Chazzan– *Praises to the Supreme God, the blessed One Who is blessed. Moses and the children of Israel exclaimed a song to You with great joy and they all said:*

'Who is like You among the heavenly powers, HASHEM! Who is like You, mighty in holiness, too awesome for praise, doing wonders.'[3] Chazzan– *With a new song the redeemed ones praised Your Name at the seashore, all of them in unison gave thanks, acknowledged [Your] sovereignty, and said:*

'HASHEM shall reign for all eternity.'[4]

It is forbidden to interrupt or pause between *'Who redeemed Israel'* and *Shemoneh Esrei,* even for *Kaddish, Kedushah* or *Borchu*.

צוּר יִשְׂרָאֵל Chazzan– *Rock of Israel, arise to the aid of Israel and liberate, as You pledged, Judah and Israel. Our Redeemer — HASHEM, Master of Legions, is His Name — the Holy One of Israel.*[5] *Blessed are You, HASHEM, Who redeemed Israel.*

---

(1) Cf. *Isaiah* 44:6. (2) *Psalms* 106:11. (3) *Exodus* 15:11. (4) 15:18. (5) *Isaiah* 47:4.

שמונה עשרה – עמידה

Take three steps backward, then three steps forward. Remain standing with feet together while reciting *Shemoneh Esrei*. Recite it with quiet devotion and without interruption, verbal or otherwise. Although it should not be audible to others, one must pray loudly enough to hear himself.

אֲדֹנָי שְׂפָתַי תִּפְתָּח, וּפִי יַגִּיד תְּהִלָּתֶךָ.[1]

אבות

Bend the knees at בָּרוּךְ; bow at אַתָּה; straighten up at ה׳.

בָּרוּךְ אַתָּה יהוה אֱלֹהֵינוּ וֵאלֹהֵי אֲבוֹתֵינוּ, אֱלֹהֵי אַבְרָהָם, אֱלֹהֵי יִצְחָק, וֵאלֹהֵי יַעֲקֹב, הָאֵל הַגָּדוֹל הַגִּבּוֹר וְהַנּוֹרָא, אֵל עֶלְיוֹן, גּוֹמֵל חֲסָדִים טוֹבִים וְקוֹנֵה הַכֹּל, וְזוֹכֵר חַסְדֵי אָבוֹת, וּמֵבִיא גוֹאֵל לִבְנֵי בְנֵיהֶם, לְמַעַן שְׁמוֹ בְּאַהֲבָה. מֶלֶךְ עוֹזֵר וּמוֹשִׁיעַ וּמָגֵן.

Bend the knees at בָּרוּךְ; bow at אַתָּה; straighten up at ה׳.

בָּרוּךְ אַתָּה יהוה, מָגֵן אַבְרָהָם.

גבורות

אַתָּה גִּבּוֹר לְעוֹלָם אֲדֹנָי, מְחַיֵּה מֵתִים אַתָּה, רַב לְהוֹשִׁיעַ. מְכַלְכֵּל חַיִּים בְּחֶסֶד, מְחַיֵּה מֵתִים בְּרַחֲמִים רַבִּים, סוֹמֵךְ נוֹפְלִים, וְרוֹפֵא חוֹלִים, וּמַתִּיר אֲסוּרִים, וּמְקַיֵּם אֱמוּנָתוֹ לִישֵׁנֵי עָפָר. מִי כָמְוֹךָ בַּעַל גְּבוּרוֹת, וּמִי דּוֹמֶה לָּךְ, מֶלֶךְ מֵמִית וּמְחַיֶּה וּמַצְמִיחַ יְשׁוּעָה. וְנֶאֱמָן אַתָּה לְהַחֲיוֹת מֵתִים. בָּרוּךְ אַתָּה יהוה, מְחַיֵּה הַמֵּתִים.

During the *chazzan's* repetition, *Kedushah* (below) is recited at this point.

קדושה

When reciting *Kedushah*, one must stand with his feet together and avoid any interruptions. One should rise on his toes when saying the words קָדוֹשׁ, קָדוֹשׁ, קָדוֹשׁ; בָּרוּךְ (of בָּרוּךְ כְּבוֹד); and יִמְלֹךְ.

Cong. then *Chazzan* – **נְקַדֵּשׁ** אֶת שִׁמְךָ בָּעוֹלָם, כְּשֵׁם שֶׁמַּקְדִּישִׁים אוֹתוֹ בִּשְׁמֵי מָרוֹם, כַּכָּתוּב עַל יַד נְבִיאֶךָ, וְקָרָא זֶה אֶל זֶה וְאָמַר:

All – קָדוֹשׁ קָדוֹשׁ קָדוֹשׁ יהוה צְבָאוֹת, מְלֹא כָל הָאָרֶץ כְּבוֹדוֹ.[2]

Chazzan – לְעֻמָּתָם בָּרוּךְ יֹאמֵרוּ:

All – בָּרוּךְ כְּבוֹד יהוה, מִמְּקוֹמוֹ.[3]

Chazzan – וּבְדִבְרֵי קָדְשְׁךָ כָּתוּב לֵאמֹר:

All – יִמְלֹךְ יהוה לְעוֹלָם, אֱלֹהַיִךְ צִיּוֹן לְדֹר וָדֹר, הַלְלוּיָהּ.[4]

Chazzan only concludes – לְדוֹר וָדוֹר נַגִּיד גָּדְלֶךָ וּלְנֵצַח נְצָחִים קְדֻשָּׁתְךָ נַקְדִּישׁ, וְשִׁבְחֲךָ אֱלֹהֵינוּ מִפִּינוּ לֹא יָמוּשׁ לְעוֹלָם וָעֶד, כִּי אֵל מֶלֶךְ גָּדוֹל וְקָדוֹשׁ אָתָּה. בָּרוּךְ אַתָּה יהוה, הָאֵל הַקָּדוֹשׁ.

Chazzan continues . . . אַתָּה חוֹנֵן (p. 686).

SHEMONEH ESREI — AMIDAH

Take three steps backward, then three steps forward. Remain standing with feet together while reciting *Shemoneh Esrei.* Recite it with quiet devotion and without interruption, verbal or otherwise. Although it should not be audible to others, one must pray loudly enough to hear himself.

My Lord, open my lips, that my mouth may declare Your praise.[1]

PATRIARCHS

Bend the knees at *'Blessed'*; bow at *'You'*; straighten up at *'HASHEM.'*

בָּרוּךְ *Blessed are You, HASHEM, our God and the God of our forefathers, God of Abraham, God of Isaac, and God of Jacob; the great, mighty, and awesome God, the supreme God, Who bestows beneficial kindnesses and creates everything, Who recalls the kindnesses of the Patriarchs and brings a Redeemer to their children's children, for His Name's sake, with love.*

Bend the knees at *'Blessed'*; bow at *'You'*; straighten up at *'HASHEM.'*

O King, Helper, Savior, and Shield. Blessed are You, HASHEM, Shield of Abraham.

GOD'S MIGHT

אַתָּה *You are eternally mighty, my Lord, the Resuscitator of the dead are You; abundantly able to save. He sustains the living with kindness, resuscitates the dead with abundant mercy, supports the fallen, heals the sick, releases the confined, and maintains His faith to those asleep in the dust. Who is like You, O Master of mighty deeds, and who is comparable to You, O King Who causes death and restores life and makes salvation sprout! And You are faithful to resuscitate the dead. Blessed are You, HASHEM, Who resuscitates the dead.*

During the *chazzan's* repetition, *Kedushah* (below) is recited at this point.

KEDUSHAH

When reciting *Kedushah*, one must stand with his feet together and avoid any interruptions. One should rise on his toes when saying the words *Holy, holy, holy; Blessed is;* and *HASHEM shall reign.*

Cong. then Chazzan — **נְקַדֵּשׁ** *We shall sanctify Your Name in this world, just as they sanctify it in heaven above, as it is written by Your prophet, "And one [angel] will call another and say:*

All — *'Holy, holy, holy is HASHEM, Master of Legions, the whole world is filled with His glory.'"*[2]

Chazzan — *Those facing them say 'Blessed':*

All — *'Blessed is the glory of HASHEM from His place.'*[3]

Chazzan — *And in Your holy Writings the following is written:*

All — *'HASHEM shall reign forever — your God, O Zion — from generation to generation, Halleluyah!'*[4]

Chazzan only concludes — *From generation to generation we shall relate Your greatness and for infinite eternities we shall proclaim Your holiness. Your praise, our God, shall not leave our mouth forever and ever, for You, O God, are a great and holy King. Blessed are You, HASHEM, the holy God.*

Chazzan continues אַתָּה חוֹנֵן, *You graciously endow* . . . (p. 686).

---

(1) *Psalms* 51:17. (2) *Isaiah* 6:3. (3) *Ezekiel* 3:12. (4) *Psalms* 146:10.

קדושת השם

אַתָּה קָדוֹשׁ וְשִׁמְךָ קָדוֹשׁ, וּקְדוֹשִׁים בְּכָל יוֹם יְהַלְלוּךָ סֶּלָה. בָּרוּךְ אַתָּה יהוה, הָאֵל הַקָּדוֹשׁ.

בינה

אַתָּה חוֹנֵן לְאָדָם דַּעַת, וּמְלַמֵּד לֶאֱנוֹשׁ בִּינָה. חָנֵּנוּ מֵאִתְּךָ דֵּעָה בִּינָה וְהַשְׂכֵּל. בָּרוּךְ אַתָּה יהוה, חוֹנֵן הַדָּעַת.

תשובה

הֲשִׁיבֵנוּ אָבִינוּ לְתוֹרָתֶךָ, וְקָרְבֵנוּ מַלְכֵּנוּ לַעֲבוֹדָתֶךָ, וְהַחֲזִירֵנוּ בִּתְשׁוּבָה שְׁלֵמָה לְפָנֶיךָ. בָּרוּךְ אַתָּה יהוה, הָרוֹצֶה בִּתְשׁוּבָה.

סליחה

Strike the left side of the chest with the right fist while reciting the words חָטָאנוּ and פָּשָׁעְנוּ.

סְלַח לָנוּ אָבִינוּ כִּי חָטָאנוּ, מְחַל לָנוּ מַלְכֵּנוּ כִּי פָשָׁעְנוּ, כִּי מוֹחֵל וְסוֹלֵחַ אָתָּה. בָּרוּךְ אַתָּה יהוה, חַנּוּן הַמַּרְבֶּה לִסְלוֹחַ.

גאולה

רְאֵה בְעָנְיֵנוּ, וְרִיבָה רִיבֵנוּ, וּגְאָלֵנוּ[1] מְהֵרָה לְמַעַן שְׁמֶךָ, כִּי גוֹאֵל חָזָק אָתָּה. בָּרוּךְ אַתָּה יהוה, גּוֹאֵל יִשְׂרָאֵל.

רפואה

רְפָאֵנוּ יהוה וְנֵרָפֵא, הוֹשִׁיעֵנוּ וְנִוָּשֵׁעָה, כִּי תְהִלָּתֵנוּ אָתָּה,[2] וְהַעֲלֵה רְפוּאָה שְׁלֵמָה לְכָל מַכּוֹתֵינוּ, °°כִּי אֵל מֶלֶךְ רוֹפֵא נֶאֱמָן וְרַחֲמָן אָתָּה. בָּרוּךְ אַתָּה יהוה, רוֹפֵא חוֹלֵי עַמּוֹ יִשְׂרָאֵל.

ברכת השנים

בָּרֵךְ עָלֵינוּ יהוה אֱלֹהֵינוּ אֶת הַשָּׁנָה הַזֹּאת וְאֶת כָּל מִינֵי תְבוּאָתָהּ לְטוֹבָה, וְתֵן בְּרָכָה עַל פְּנֵי הָאֲדָמָה, וְשַׂבְּעֵנוּ מִטּוּבֶךָ, וּבָרֵךְ שְׁנָתֵנוּ כַּשָּׁנִים הַטּוֹבוֹת. בָּרוּךְ אַתָּה יהוה, מְבָרֵךְ הַשָּׁנִים.

°°At this point one may interject a prayer for one who is ill:

יְהִי רָצוֹן מִלְּפָנֶיךָ יהוה אֱלֹהַי וֵאלֹהֵי אֲבוֹתַי, שֶׁתִּשְׁלַח מְהֵרָה רְפוּאָה שְׁלֵמָה מִן הַשָּׁמַיִם, רְפוּאַת הַנֶּפֶשׁ וּרְפוּאַת הַגּוּף

for a male—לַחוֹלֶה (patient's name) בֶּן (mother's name) בְּתוֹךְ שְׁאָר חוֹלֵי יִשְׂרָאֵל.

for a female—לַחוֹלָה (patient's name) בַּת (mother's name) בְּתוֹךְ שְׁאָר חוֹלֵי יִשְׂרָאֵל.

Continue—כִּי אֵל . . .

HOLINESS OF GOD'S NAME

אַתָּה *You are holy and Your Name is holy, and holy ones praise You every day, forever. Blessed are You,* H*ASHEM*, *the holy God.*

INSIGHT

אַתָּה *You graciously endow man with wisdom and teach insight to a frail mortal. Endow us graciously from Yourself with wisdom, insight, and discernment. Blessed are You,* H*ASHEM*, *gracious Giver of wisdom.*

REPENTANCE

הֲשִׁיבֵנוּ *Bring us back, our Father, to Your Torah, and bring us near, our King, to Your service, and influence us to return in perfect repentance before You. Blessed are You,* H*ASHEM*, *Who desires repentance.*

FORGIVENESS

Strike the left side of the chest with the right fist while reciting the words *'erred'* and *'sinned.'*

סְלַח *Forgive us, our Father, for we have erred; pardon us, our King, for we have willfully sinned; for You pardon and forgive. Blessed are You,* H*ASHEM*, *the gracious One Who pardons abundantly.*

REDEMPTION

רְאֵה *Behold our affliction, take up our grievance, and redeem us*[1] *speedily for Your Name's sake, for You are a powerful Redeemer. Blessed are You,* H*ASHEM*, *Redeemer of Israel.*

HEALTH AND HEALING

רְפָאֵנוּ *Heal us,* H*ASHEM — then we will be healed; save us — then we will be saved, for You are our praise.*[2] *Bring complete recovery for all our ailments,* °°*for You are God, King, the faithful and compassionate Healer. Blessed are You,* H*ASHEM*, *Who heals the sick of His people Israel.*

YEAR OF PROSPERITY

בָּרֵךְ *Bless on our behalf — O* H*ASHEM*, *our God — this year and all its kinds of crops for the best, and give a blessing on the face of the earth, and satisfy us from Your bounty, and bless our year like the best years. Blessed are You,* H*ASHEM*, *Who blesses the years.*

°°At this point one may interject a prayer for one who is ill:

May it be Your will, H*ASHEM*, *my God, and the God of my forefathers, that You quickly send a complete recovery from heaven, spiritual healing and physical healing to the patient* (name) *son/daughter of* (mother's name) *among the other patients of Israel.* Continue: *For You are God ...*

(1) Cf. *Psalms* 119:153-154. (2) Cf. *Jeremiah* 17:14.

קיבוץ גליות

תְּקַע בְּשׁוֹפָר גָּדוֹל לְחֵרוּתֵנוּ, וְשָׂא נֵס לְקַבֵּץ גָּלֻיּוֹתֵינוּ, וְקַבְּצֵנוּ יַחַד מֵאַרְבַּע כַּנְפוֹת הָאָרֶץ.[1] בָּרוּךְ אַתָּה יהוה, מְקַבֵּץ נִדְחֵי עַמּוֹ יִשְׂרָאֵל.

דין

הָשִׁיבָה שׁוֹפְטֵינוּ כְּבָרִאשׁוֹנָה, וְיוֹעֲצֵינוּ כְּבַתְּחִלָּה,[2] וְהָסֵר מִמֶּנּוּ יָגוֹן וַאֲנָחָה, וּמְלוֹךְ עָלֵינוּ אַתָּה יהוה לְבַדְּךָ בְּחֶסֶד וּבְרַחֲמִים, וְצַדְּקֵנוּ בַּמִּשְׁפָּט. בָּרוּךְ אַתָּה יהוה, מֶלֶךְ אוֹהֵב צְדָקָה וּמִשְׁפָּט.

ברכת המינים

וְלַמַּלְשִׁינִים אַל תְּהִי תִקְוָה, וְכָל הָרִשְׁעָה כְּרֶגַע תֹּאבֵד, וְכָל אֹיְבֶיךָ מְהֵרָה יִכָּרֵתוּ, וְהַזֵּדִים מְהֵרָה תְעַקֵּר וּתְשַׁבֵּר וּתְמַגֵּר וְתַכְנִיעַ בִּמְהֵרָה בְיָמֵינוּ. בָּרוּךְ אַתָּה יהוה, שׁוֹבֵר אֹיְבִים וּמַכְנִיעַ זֵדִים.

צדיקים

עַל הַצַּדִּיקִים וְעַל הַחֲסִידִים, וְעַל זִקְנֵי עַמְּךָ בֵּית יִשְׂרָאֵל, וְעַל פְּלֵיטַת סוֹפְרֵיהֶם, וְעַל גֵּרֵי הַצֶּדֶק וְעָלֵינוּ, יֶהֱמוּ רַחֲמֶיךָ יהוה אֱלֹהֵינוּ, וְתֵן שָׂכָר טוֹב לְכָל הַבּוֹטְחִים בְּשִׁמְךָ בֶּאֱמֶת, וְשִׂים חֶלְקֵנוּ עִמָּהֶם לְעוֹלָם, וְלֹא נֵבוֹשׁ כִּי בְךָ בָּטָחְנוּ. בָּרוּךְ אַתָּה יהוה, מִשְׁעָן וּמִבְטָח לַצַּדִּיקִים.

בנין ירושלים

וְלִירוּשָׁלַיִם עִירְךָ בְּרַחֲמִים תָּשׁוּב, וְתִשְׁכּוֹן בְּתוֹכָהּ כַּאֲשֶׁר דִּבַּרְתָּ, וּבְנֵה אוֹתָהּ בְּקָרוֹב בְּיָמֵינוּ בִּנְיַן עוֹלָם, וְכִסֵּא דָוִד מְהֵרָה לְתוֹכָהּ תָּכִין. בָּרוּךְ אַתָּה יהוה, בּוֹנֵה יְרוּשָׁלָיִם.

מלכות בית דוד

אֶת צֶמַח דָּוִד עַבְדְּךָ מְהֵרָה תַצְמִיחַ, וְקַרְנוֹ תָּרוּם בִּישׁוּעָתֶךָ, כִּי לִישׁוּעָתְךָ קִוִּינוּ כָּל הַיּוֹם. בָּרוּךְ אַתָּה יהוה, מַצְמִיחַ קֶרֶן יְשׁוּעָה.

קבלת תפלה

שְׁמַע קוֹלֵנוּ יהוה אֱלֹהֵינוּ, חוּס וְרַחֵם עָלֵינוּ, וְקַבֵּל בְּרַחֲמִים וּבְרָצוֹן אֶת תְּפִלָּתֵנוּ, כִּי אֵל שׁוֹמֵעַ תְּפִלּוֹת וְתַחֲנוּנִים אָתָּה. וּמִלְּפָנֶיךָ מַלְכֵּנוּ רֵיקָם אַל תְּשִׁיבֵנוּ,

INGATHERING OF EXILES

תְּקַע *Sound the great shofar for our freedom, raise the banner to gather our exiles and gather us together from the four corners of the earth.*[1] *Blessed are You,* HASHEM, *Who gathers in the dispersed of His people Israel.*

RESTORATION OF JUSTICE

הָשִׁיבָה *Restore our judges as in earliest times and our counselors as at first;*[2] *remove from us sorrow and groan; and reign over us — You,* HASHEM, *alone — with kindness and compassion, and justify us through judgment. Blessed are You,* HASHEM, *the King Who loves righteousness and judgment.*

AGAINST HERETICS

וְלַמַּלְשִׁינִים *And for slanderers let there be no hope; and may all wickedness perish in an instant; and may all Your enemies be cut down speedily. May You speedily uproot, smash, cast down, and humble the wanton sinners — speedily in our days. Blessed are You,* HASHEM, *Who breaks enemies and humbles wanton sinners.*

THE RIGHTEOUS

עַל הַצַּדִּיקִים *On the righteous, on the devout, on the elders of Your people the Family of Israel, on the remnant of their scholars, on the righteous converts and on ourselves — may Your compassion be aroused,* HASHEM, *our God, and give goodly reward to all who sincerely believe in Your Name. Put our lot with them forever, and we will not feel ashamed, for we trust in You. Blessed are You,* HASHEM, *Mainstay and Assurance of the righteous.*

REBUILDING JERUSALEM

וְלִירוּשָׁלַיִם *And to Jerusalem, Your city, may You return in compassion, and may You rest within it, as You have spoken. May You rebuild it soon in our days as an eternal structure, and may You speedily establish the throne of David within it. Blessed are You,* HASHEM, *the Builder of Jerusalem.*

DAVIDIC REIGN

אֶת צֶמַח *The offspring of Your servant David may You speedily cause to flourish, and enhance his pride through Your salvation, for we hope for Your salvation all day long. Blessed are You,* HASHEM, *Who causes the pride of salvation to flourish.*

ACCEPTANCE OF PRAYER

שְׁמַע *Hear our voice,* HASHEM *our God, pity and be compassionate to us, and accept — with compassion and favor — our prayer, for God Who hears prayers and supplications are You. From before Yourself, our King, turn us not away empty-handed,*

(1) Cf. *Isaiah* 11:12. (2) Cf. 1:26.

°° כִּי אַתָּה שׁוֹמֵעַ תְּפִלַּת עַמְּךָ יִשְׂרָאֵל בְּרַחֲמִים. בָּרוּךְ אַתָּה יהוה, שׁוֹמֵעַ תְּפִלָּה.

עבודה

רְצֵה יהוה אֱלֹהֵינוּ בְּעַמְּךָ יִשְׂרָאֵל וּבִתְפִלָּתָם, וְהָשֵׁב אֶת הָעֲבוֹדָה לִדְבִיר בֵּיתֶךָ. וְאִשֵּׁי יִשְׂרָאֵל וּתְפִלָּתָם בְּאַהֲבָה תְקַבֵּל בְּרָצוֹן, וּתְהִי לְרָצוֹן תָּמִיד עֲבוֹדַת יִשְׂרָאֵל עַמֶּךָ.

During the *chazzan's* repetition, congregation responds אָמֵן as indicated.
[If paragraph is forgotten, repeat *Shemoneh Esrei*. See *Laws* §56.]

אֱלֹהֵינוּ וֵאלֹהֵי אֲבוֹתֵינוּ, יַעֲלֶה, וְיָבֹא, וְיַגִּיעַ, וְיֵרָאֶה, וְיֵרָצֶה, וְיִשָּׁמַע, וְיִפָּקֵד, וְיִזָּכֵר זִכְרוֹנֵנוּ וּפִקְדוֹנֵנוּ, וְזִכְרוֹן אֲבוֹתֵינוּ, וְזִכְרוֹן מָשִׁיחַ בֶּן דָּוִד עַבְדֶּךָ, וְזִכְרוֹן יְרוּשָׁלַיִם עִיר קָדְשֶׁךָ, וְזִכְרוֹן כָּל עַמְּךָ בֵּית יִשְׂרָאֵל לְפָנֶיךָ, לִפְלֵיטָה לְטוֹבָה לְחֵן וּלְחֶסֶד וּלְרַחֲמִים, לְחַיִּים וּלְשָׁלוֹם בְּיוֹם חַג הַסֻּכּוֹת הַזֶּה. זָכְרֵנוּ יהוה אֱלֹהֵינוּ בּוֹ לְטוֹבָה (Cong.– אָמֵן), וּפָקְדֵנוּ בוֹ לִבְרָכָה (Cong.– אָמֵן), וְהוֹשִׁיעֵנוּ בוֹ לְחַיִּים (Cong.– אָמֵן). וּבִדְבַר יְשׁוּעָה וְרַחֲמִים, חוּס וְחָנֵּנוּ וְרַחֵם עָלֵינוּ וְהוֹשִׁיעֵנוּ, כִּי אֵלֶיךָ עֵינֵינוּ, כִּי אֵל מֶלֶךְ חַנּוּן וְרַחוּם אָתָּה.[1]

וְתֶחֱזֶינָה עֵינֵינוּ בְּשׁוּבְךָ לְצִיּוֹן בְּרַחֲמִים. בָּרוּךְ אַתָּה יהוה, הַמַּחֲזִיר שְׁכִינָתוֹ לְצִיּוֹן.

°°During the silent *Shemoneh Esrei* one may insert either or both of these personal prayers.

For forgiveness:

אָנָּא יהוה, חָטָאתִי עָוִיתִי וּפָשַׁעְתִּי לְפָנֶיךָ, מִיּוֹם הֱיוֹתִי עַל הָאֲדָמָה עַד הַיּוֹם הַזֶּה (וּבִפְרַט בַּחֵטְא ....). אָנָּא יהוה, עֲשֵׂה לְמַעַן שִׁמְךָ הַגָּדוֹל, וּתְכַפֶּר לִי עַל עֲוֹנַי וַחֲטָאַי וּפְשָׁעַי שֶׁחָטָאתִי וְשֶׁעָוִיתִי וְשֶׁפָּשַׁעְתִּי לְפָנֶיךָ, מִנְּעוּרַי עַד הַיּוֹם הַזֶּה. וּתְמַלֵּא כָּל הַשֵּׁמוֹת שֶׁפָּגַמְתִּי בְּשִׁמְךָ הַגָּדוֹל.

For livelihood:

אַתָּה הוּא יהוה הָאֱלֹהִים, הַזָּן וּמְפַרְנֵס וּמְכַלְכֵּל מִקַּרְנֵי רְאֵמִים עַד בֵּיצֵי כִנִּים. הַטְרִיפֵנִי לֶחֶם חֻקִּי, וְהַמְצֵא לִי וּלְכָל בְּנֵי בֵיתִי מְזוֹנוֹתַי קוֹדֶם שֶׁאֶצְטָרֵךְ לָהֶם, בְּנַחַת וְלֹא בְצַעַר, בְּהֶתֵּר וְלֹא בְאִסּוּר, בְּכָבוֹד וְלֹא בְבִזָּיוֹן, לְחַיִּים וּלְשָׁלוֹם, מִשֶּׁפַע בְּרָכָה וְהַצְלָחָה, וּמִשֶּׁפַע בְּרֵכָה עֶלְיוֹנָה, כְּדֵי שֶׁאוּכַל לַעֲשׂוֹת רְצוֹנֶךָ וְלַעֲסוֹק בְּתוֹרָתֶךָ וּלְקַיֵּם מִצְוֹתֶיךָ. וְאַל תַּצְרִיכֵנִי לִידֵי מַתְּנַת בָּשָׂר וָדָם. וִיקֻיַּם בִּי מִקְרָא שֶׁכָּתוּב: פּוֹתֵחַ אֶת יָדֶךָ, וּמַשְׂבִּיעַ לְכָל חַי רָצוֹן.[2] וְכָתוּב: הַשְׁלֵךְ עַל יהוה יְהָבְךָ וְהוּא יְכַלְכְּלֶךָ.[3]

Continue — כִּי אַתָּה . . .

°° *for You hear the prayer of Your people Israel with compassion. Blessed are You, HASHEM, Who hears prayer.*

TEMPLE SERVICE

רְצֵה *Be favorable, HASHEM, our God, toward Your people Israel and their prayer and restore the service to the Holy of Holies of Your Temple. The fire-offerings of Israel and their prayer accept with love and favor, and may the service of Your people Israel always be favorable to You.*

During the *chazzan's* repetition, congregation responds *Amen* as indicated.
[If paragraph is forgotten, repeat *Shemoneh Esrei*. See *Laws* §56.]

אֱלֹהֵינוּ *Our God and God of our forefathers, may there rise, come, reach, be noted, be favored, be heard, be considered, and be remembered — the remembrance and consideration of ourselves; the remembrance of our forefathers; the remembrance of Messiah, son of David, Your servant; the remembrance of Jerusalem, the City of Your Holiness; the remembrance of Your entire people the Family of Israel — before You for deliverance, for goodness, for grace, for kindness, and for compassion, for life, and for peace on this day of the Festival of Succos. Remember us on it, HASHEM, our God, for goodness (*Cong.*–Amen); consider us on it for blessing (*Cong.*–Amen); and help us on it for life (*Cong.*–Amen). In the matter of salvation and compassion, pity, be gracious and compassionate with us and help us, for our eyes are turned to You, because You are God, the gracious and compassionate King.*[1]

וְתֶחֱזֶינָה *May our eyes behold Your return to Zion in compassion. Blessed are You, HASHEM, Who restores His Presence to Zion.*

°°During the silent *Shemoneh Esrei* one may insert either or both of these personal prayers.

For forgiveness:

אָנָּא *Please, O HASHEM, I have erred, been iniquitous, and willfully sinned before You, from the day I have existed on earth until this very day (and especially with the sin of . . .). Please, HASHEM, act for the sake of Your Great Name and grant me atonement for my iniquities, my errors, and my willful sins through which I have erred, been iniquitous, and willfully sinned before You, from my youth until this day. And make whole all the Names that I have blemished in Your Great Name.*

For livelihood:

אַתָּה *It is You, HASHEM the God, Who nourishes, sustains, and supports, from the horns of re'eimim to the eggs of lice. Provide me with my allotment of bread; and bring forth for me and all members of my household, my food, before I have need for it; in contentment but not in pain, in a permissible but not a forbidden manner, in honor but not in disgrace, for life and for peace; from the flow of blessing and success and from the flow of the Heavenly spring, so that I be enabled to do Your will and engage in Your Torah and fulfill Your commandments. Make me not needful of people's largesse; and may there be fulfilled in me the verse that states, 'You open Your hand and satisfy the desire of every living thing'*[2] *and that states, 'Cast Your burden upon HASHEM and He will support you.'*[3]

Continue: *For You hear the prayer . . .*

(1) Cf. *Nechemiah* 9:31. (2) *Psalms* 145:16. (3) 55:23.

הודאה

Bow at מודים; straighten up at ה׳. In his repetition the *chazzan* should recite the entire מודים aloud, while the congregation recites מודים דְּרַבָּנָן softly.

מוֹדִים אֲנַחְנוּ לָךְ, שָׁאַתָּה הוּא יהוה אֱלֹהֵינוּ וֵאלֹהֵי אֲבוֹתֵינוּ לְעוֹלָם וָעֶד. צוּר חַיֵּינוּ, מָגֵן יִשְׁעֵנוּ אַתָּה הוּא לְדוֹר וָדוֹר. נוֹדֶה לְּךָ וּנְסַפֵּר תְּהִלָּתֶךָ[1] עַל חַיֵּינוּ הַמְּסוּרִים בְּיָדֶךָ, וְעַל נִשְׁמוֹתֵינוּ הַפְּקוּדוֹת לָךְ, וְעַל נִסֶּיךָ שֶׁבְּכָל יוֹם עִמָּנוּ, וְעַל נִפְלְאוֹתֶיךָ וְטוֹבוֹתֶיךָ שֶׁבְּכָל עֵת, עֶרֶב וָבֹקֶר וְצָהֳרָיִם. הַטּוֹב כִּי לֹא כָלוּ רַחֲמֶיךָ, וְהַמְּרַחֵם כִּי לֹא תַמּוּ חֲסָדֶיךָ,[2] מֵעוֹלָם קִוִּינוּ לָךְ.

מודים דרבנן

מוֹדִים אֲנַחְנוּ לָךְ, שָׁאַתָּה הוּא יהוה אֱלֹהֵינוּ וֵאלֹהֵי אֲבוֹתֵינוּ, אֱלֹהֵי כָל בָּשָׂר, יוֹצְרֵנוּ, יוֹצֵר בְּרֵאשִׁית. בְּרָכוֹת וְהוֹדָאוֹת לְשִׁמְךָ הַגָּדוֹל וְהַקָּדוֹשׁ, עַל שֶׁהֶחֱיִיתָנוּ וְקִיַּמְתָּנוּ. כֵּן תְּחַיֵּנוּ וּתְקַיְּמֵנוּ, וְתֶאֱסוֹף גָּלֻיּוֹתֵינוּ לְחַצְרוֹת קָדְשֶׁךָ, לִשְׁמוֹר חֻקֶּיךָ וְלַעֲשׂוֹת רְצוֹנֶךָ, וּלְעָבְדְּךָ בְּלֵבָב שָׁלֵם, עַל שֶׁאֲנַחְנוּ מוֹדִים לָךְ. בָּרוּךְ אֵל הַהוֹדָאוֹת.

וְעַל כֻּלָּם יִתְבָּרַךְ וְיִתְרוֹמַם שִׁמְךָ מַלְכֵּנוּ תָּמִיד לְעוֹלָם וָעֶד.

Bend the knees at בָּרוּךְ; bow at אַתָּה; straighten up at ה׳.

וְכֹל הַחַיִּים יוֹדוּךָ סֶּלָה, וִיהַלְלוּ אֶת שִׁמְךָ בֶּאֱמֶת, הָאֵל יְשׁוּעָתֵנוּ וְעֶזְרָתֵנוּ סֶלָה. בָּרוּךְ אַתָּה יהוה, הַטּוֹב שִׁמְךָ וּלְךָ נָאֶה לְהוֹדוֹת.

ברכת כהנים

The *chazzan* recites בִּרְכַּת כֹּהֲנִים during his repetition. He faces right at וְיִשְׁמְרֶךָ; faces left at אֵלֶיךָ וִיחֻנֶּךָּ; faces the Ark for the rest of the blessings.

אֱלֹהֵינוּ, וֵאלֹהֵי אֲבוֹתֵינוּ, בָּרְכֵנוּ בַבְּרָכָה הַמְּשֻׁלֶּשֶׁת בַּתּוֹרָה הַכְּתוּבָה עַל יְדֵי מֹשֶׁה עַבְדֶּךָ, הָאֲמוּרָה מִפִּי אַהֲרֹן וּבָנָיו, כֹּהֲנִים עַם קְדוֹשֶׁךָ, כָּאָמוּר:

יְבָרֶכְךָ יהוה, וְיִשְׁמְרֶךָ. (Cong.–כֵּן יְהִי רָצוֹן.)

יָאֵר יהוה פָּנָיו אֵלֶיךָ וִיחֻנֶּךָּ. (Cong.–כֵּן יְהִי רָצוֹן.)

יִשָּׂא יהוה פָּנָיו אֵלֶיךָ וְיָשֵׂם לְךָ שָׁלוֹם.[3] (Cong.–כֵּן יְהִי רָצוֹן.)

שִׂים שָׁלוֹם, טוֹבָה, וּבְרָכָה, חֵן, וָחֶסֶד וְרַחֲמִים עָלֵינוּ וְעַל כָּל יִשְׂרָאֵל עַמֶּךָ. בָּרְכֵנוּ אָבִינוּ, כֻּלָּנוּ כְּאֶחָד בְּאוֹר פָּנֶיךָ, כִּי בְאוֹר פָּנֶיךָ נָתַתָּ לָּנוּ, יהוה אֱלֹהֵינוּ, תּוֹרַת חַיִּים וְאַהֲבַת חֶסֶד, וּצְדָקָה, וּבְרָכָה, וְרַחֲמִים, וְחַיִּים, וְשָׁלוֹם. וְטוֹב

THANKSGIVING [MODIM]

Bow at *'We gratefully thank You'*; straighten up at *'HASHEM.'* In his repetition the *chazzan* should recite the entire *Modim* aloud, while the congregation recites *Modim of the Rabbis* softly.

מוֹדִים *We gratefully thank You, for it is You Who are HASHEM, our God and the God of our forefathers for all eternity; Rock of our lives, Shield of our salvation are You from generation to generation. We shall thank You and relate Your praise[1] — for our lives, which are committed to Your power and for our souls that are entrusted to You; for Your miracles that are with us every day; and for Your wonders and favors in every season — evening, morning, and afternoon. The Beneficent One, for Your compassions were never exhausted, and the Compassionate One, for Your kindnesses never ended[2] — always have we put our hope in You.*

MODIM OF THE RABBIS

מוֹדִים *We gratefully thank You, for it is You Who are HASHEM, our God and the God of our forefathers, the God of all flesh, our Molder, the Molder of the universe. Blessings and thanks are due Your great and holy Name for You have given us life and sustained us. So may You continue to give us life and sustain us and gather our exiles to the Courtyards of Your Sanctuary, to observe Your decrees, to do Your will and to serve You wholeheartedly. [We thank You] for inspiring us to thank You. Blessed is the God of thanksgivings.*

For all these, may Your Name be blessed and exalted, our King, continually forever and ever.

Bend the knees at *'Blessed'*; bow at *'You'*; straighten up at *'HASHEM.'*

Everything alive will gratefully acknowledge You, Selah! and praise Your Name sincerely, O God of our salvation and help, Selah! Blessed are You, HASHEM, Your Name is 'The Beneficent One' and to You it is fitting to give thanks.

THE PRIESTLY BLESSING

The *chazzan* recites the Priestly Blessing during his repetition.

אֱלֹהֵינוּ *Our God and the God of our forefathers, bless us with the three-verse blessing in the Torah that was written by the hand of Moses, Your servant, that was said by Aaron and his sons, the Kohanim, Your holy people, as it is said:*

May HASHEM bless you and safeguard you. (Cong.— *So may it be.*)

May HASHEM illuminate His countenance for you and be gracious to you. (Cong.— *So may it be.*)

May HASHEM turn His countenance to you and establish peace for you.[3] (Cong.— *So may it be.*)

PEACE

שִׂים שָׁלוֹם *Establish peace, goodness, blessing, graciousness, kindness, and compassion upon us and upon all of Your people Israel. Bless us, our Father, all of us as one, with the light of Your countenance, for with the light of Your countenance You gave us, HASHEM, our God, the Torah of life and a love of kindness, righteousness, blessing, compassion, life, and peace. And may it be good*

---

(1) Cf. *Psalms* 79:13. (2) Cf. *Lamentations* 3:22. (3) *Numbers* 6:24-26.

בְּעֵינֶיךָ לְבָרֵךְ אֶת עַמְּךָ יִשְׂרָאֵל, בְּכָל עֵת וּבְכָל שָׁעָה בִּשְׁלוֹמֶךָ. בָּרוּךְ אַתָּה יהוה, הַמְּבָרֵךְ אֶת עַמּוֹ יִשְׂרָאֵל בַּשָּׁלוֹם.

יִהְיוּ לְרָצוֹן אִמְרֵי פִי וְהֶגְיוֹן לִבִּי לְפָנֶיךָ, יהוה צוּרִי וְגֹאֲלִי.[1]

Chazzan's repetition of *Shemoneh Esrei* ends here. Individuals continue below:

אֱלֹהַי, נְצוֹר לְשׁוֹנִי מֵרָע, וּשְׂפָתַי מִדַּבֵּר מִרְמָה,[2] וְלִמְקַלְלַי נַפְשִׁי תִדּוֹם, וְנַפְשִׁי כֶּעָפָר לַכֹּל תִּהְיֶה. פְּתַח לִבִּי בְּתוֹרָתֶךָ, וּבְמִצְוֹתֶיךָ תִּרְדּוֹף נַפְשִׁי. וְכֹל הַחוֹשְׁבִים עָלַי רָעָה, מְהֵרָה הָפֵר עֲצָתָם וְקַלְקֵל מַחֲשַׁבְתָּם. עֲשֵׂה לְמַעַן שְׁמֶךָ, עֲשֵׂה לְמַעַן יְמִינֶךָ, עֲשֵׂה לְמַעַן קְדֻשָּׁתֶךָ, עֲשֵׂה לְמַעַן תּוֹרָתֶךָ. לְמַעַן יֵחָלְצוּן יְדִידֶיךָ, הוֹשִׁיעָה יְמִינְךָ וַעֲנֵנִי.[3]

Some recite verses pertaining to their names here. See page 1301.

יִהְיוּ לְרָצוֹן אִמְרֵי פִי וְהֶגְיוֹן לִבִּי לְפָנֶיךָ, יהוה צוּרִי וְגֹאֲלִי.[1]

Bow and take three steps back. Bow left and say . . . עֹשֶׂה, bow right and say . . . הוּא יַעֲשֶׂה; bow forward and say וְעַל כָּל . . . אָמֵן.

עֹשֶׂה שָׁלוֹם בִּמְרוֹמָיו, הוּא יַעֲשֶׂה שָׁלוֹם עָלֵינוּ, וְעַל כָּל יִשְׂרָאֵל. וְאִמְרוּ: אָמֵן.

יְהִי רָצוֹן מִלְּפָנֶיךָ יהוה אֱלֹהֵינוּ וֵאלֹהֵי אֲבוֹתֵינוּ, שֶׁיִּבָּנֶה בֵּית הַמִּקְדָּשׁ בִּמְהֵרָה בְיָמֵינוּ, וְתֵן חֶלְקֵנוּ בְּתוֹרָתֶךָ. וְשָׁם נַעֲבָדְךָ בְּיִרְאָה, כִּימֵי עוֹלָם וּכְשָׁנִים קַדְמוֹנִיּוֹת. וְעָרְבָה לַיהוה מִנְחַת יְהוּדָה וִירוּשָׁלָיִם, כִּימֵי עוֹלָם וּכְשָׁנִים קַדְמוֹנִיּוֹת.[4]

THE INDIVIDUAL'S RECITATION OF *SHEMONEH ESREI* ENDS HERE.

Remain standing in place for at least a few moments before taking three steps forward.

נטילת לולב

For Laws, see page 284.

Many recite the following declaration of intent before taking the Four Species:

יְהִי רָצוֹן מִלְּפָנֶיךָ, יהוה אֱלֹהַי וֵאלֹהֵי אֲבוֹתַי, בִּפְרִי עֵץ הָדָר, וְכַפּוֹת תְּמָרִים, וַעֲנַף עֵץ עָבוֹת, וְעַרְבֵי נָחַל,[5] אוֹתִיּוֹת שִׁמְךָ הַמְּיֻחָד תְּקָרֵב אֶחָד אֶל אֶחָד, וְהָיוּ לַאֲחָדִים בְּיָדִי, וְלֵידַע אֵיךְ שִׁמְךָ נִקְרָא עָלַי, וְיִירְאוּ מִגֶּשֶׁת אֵלָי. וּבְנַעֲנוּעִי אוֹתָם תַּשְׁפִּיעַ שֶׁפַע בְּרָכוֹת מִדַּעַת עֶלְיוֹן לִנְוֵה אַפִּרְיוֹן, לִמְכוֹן בֵּית אֱלֹהֵינוּ. וּתְהֵא חֲשׁוּבָה לְפָנֶיךָ מִצְוַת אַרְבָּעָה מִינִים אֵלּוּ, כְּאִלּוּ קִיַּמְתִּיהָ בְּכָל פְּרָטוֹתֶיהָ וְשָׁרָשֶׁיהָ וְתַרְיַ״ג מִצְוֹת הַתְּלוּיִם בָּהּ. כִּי כַוָּנָתִי לְיַחֲדָא שְׁמָא דְקֻדְשָׁא בְּרִיךְ הוּא וּשְׁכִינְתֵּהּ, בִּדְחִילוּ וּרְחִימוּ, לְיַחֵד שֵׁם י״ה בְּו״ה בְּיִחוּדָא שְׁלִים, בְּשֵׁם כָּל יִשְׂרָאֵל. אָמֵן. בָּרוּךְ יהוה לְעוֹלָם, אָמֵן, וְאָמֵן.[6]

in Your eyes to bless Your people Israel at every time and every hour with Your peace. Blessed are You, HASHEM, Who blesses His people Israel with peace.

Chazzan's repetition of *Shemoneh Esrei* ends here. Individuals continue below:

May the expressions of my mouth and the thoughts of my heart find favor before You, HASHEM, my Rock and my Redeemer.[1]

אֱלֹהַי *My God, guard my tongue from evil and my lips from speaking deceitfully.*[2] *To those who curse me, let my soul be silent; and let my soul be like dust to everyone. Open my heart to Your Torah, then my soul will pursue Your commandments. As for all those who design evil against me, speedily nullify their counsel and disrupt their design. Act for Your Name's sake; act for Your right hand's sake; act for Your sanctity's sake; act for Your Torah's sake. That Your beloved ones may be given rest; let Your right hand save, and respond to me.*[3]

Some recite verses pertaining to their names at this point. See page 1301.

May the expressions of my mouth and the thoughts of my heart find favor before You, HASHEM, my Rock and my Redeemer.[1] °°*He Who makes peace in His heights, may He make peace upon us, and upon all Israel. Now respond: Amen.*

Bow and take three steps back. Bow left and say, *'He Who makes peace . . .'*; bow right and say, *'may He make peace . . .'*; bow forward and say, *'and upon . . . Amen.'*

יְהִי רָצוֹן *May it be Your will, HASHEM, our God and the God of our forefathers, that the Holy Temple be rebuilt, speedily in our days. Grant us our share in Your Torah, and may we serve You there with reverence, as in days of old and in former years. Then the offering of Judah and Jerusalem will be pleasing to HASHEM, as in days of old and in former years.*[4]

THE INDIVIDUAL'S RECITATION OF *SHEMONEH ESREI* ENDS HERE.

Remain standing in place for at least a few moments before taking three steps forward.

THE FOUR SPECIES/LULAV AND ESROG

For Laws see page 284.

Many recite the following declaration of intent before taking the Four Species:

יְהִי רָצוֹן *May it be Your will, HASHEM, my God and the God of my forefathers, that through the fruit of the esrog tree, date-palm branches, twigs of the myrtle tree, and brook willows,*[5] *the letters of Your unified Name may become close to one another, that they may become united in my hand; and to make known that Your Name is called upon me, that [evil forces] may be fearful of approaching me. And when I wave them, may an abundant outpouring of blessings flow from the wisdom of the Most High to the abode of the tabernacle, to the prepared place of the House of our God. And may the mitzvah of these Four Species be reckoned before You as if I had fulfilled it with all its particulars, roots, and the six hundred thirteen mitzvos dependent on it. For my intention is to unify the Name of the Holy One, Blessed is He, and His Presence, in awe and in love, to unify the Name Yud-Kei with Vav-Kei in perfect unity, in the name of all Israel; Amen. Blessed is HASHEM forever, Amen and Amen.*[6]

---

(1) *Psalms* 19:15. (2) Cf. 34:14. (3) 60:7; 108:7. (4) *Malachi* 3:4. (5) Cf. *Leviticus* 23:40. (6) *Psalms* 89:53.

The Four Species — *lulav, haddasim, aravos, esrog* — are taken in hand every day of Succos — through *Hoshana Rabbah* — except on the Sabbath. The *lulav*-bundle is picked up with the right hand, then the *esrog* (with the *pitam* facing down) with the left. After the blessings are recited, the *esrog* is turned over and the Four Species are waved in the six directions — front (east), right (south), back (west), left (north), up and down.

בָּרוּךְ אַתָּה יהוה אֱלֹהֵינוּ מֶלֶךְ הָעוֹלָם, אֲשֶׁר קִדְּשָׁנוּ בְּמִצְוֹתָיו, וְצִוָּנוּ עַל נְטִילַת לוּלָב.

הלל

Whenever possible, the *lulav*-bundle should be held during the recitation of *Hallel*, and waved as indicated in the text.

The *chazzan* recites the blessing. The congregation, after responding אָמֵן, repeats it, and continues with the first psalm.

בָּרוּךְ אַתָּה יהוה אֱלֹהֵינוּ מֶלֶךְ הָעוֹלָם, אֲשֶׁר קִדְּשָׁנוּ בְּמִצְוֹתָיו, וְצִוָּנוּ לִקְרוֹא אֶת הַהַלֵּל. (.Cong.– אָמֵן)

תהלים קיג

הַלְלוּיָהּ הַלְלוּ עַבְדֵי יהוה, הַלְלוּ אֶת שֵׁם יהוה. יְהִי שֵׁם יהוה מְבֹרָךְ, מֵעַתָּה וְעַד עוֹלָם. מִמִּזְרַח שֶׁמֶשׁ עַד מְבוֹאוֹ, מְהֻלָּל שֵׁם יהוה. רָם עַל כָּל גּוֹיִם יהוה, עַל הַשָּׁמַיִם כְּבוֹדוֹ. מִי כַּיהוה אֱלֹהֵינוּ, הַמַּגְבִּיהִי לָשָׁבֶת. הַמַּשְׁפִּילִי לִרְאוֹת, בַּשָּׁמַיִם וּבָאָרֶץ. ❖ מְקִימִי מֵעָפָר דָּל, מֵאַשְׁפֹּת יָרִים אֶבְיוֹן. לְהוֹשִׁיבִי עִם נְדִיבִים, עִם נְדִיבֵי עַמּוֹ. מוֹשִׁיבִי עֲקֶרֶת הַבַּיִת, אֵם הַבָּנִים שְׂמֵחָה, הַלְלוּיָהּ.

תהלים קיד

בְּצֵאת יִשְׂרָאֵל מִמִּצְרָיִם, בֵּית יַעֲקֹב מֵעַם לֹעֵז. הָיְתָה יְהוּדָה לְקָדְשׁוֹ, יִשְׂרָאֵל מַמְשְׁלוֹתָיו. הַיָּם רָאָה וַיָּנֹס, הַיַּרְדֵּן יִסֹּב לְאָחוֹר. הֶהָרִים רָקְדוּ כְאֵילִים, גְּבָעוֹת כִּבְנֵי צֹאן. ❖ מַה לְּךָ הַיָּם כִּי תָנוּס, הַיַּרְדֵּן תִּסֹּב לְאָחוֹר. הֶהָרִים תִּרְקְדוּ כְאֵילִים, גְּבָעוֹת כִּבְנֵי צֹאן. מִלִּפְנֵי אָדוֹן חוּלִי אָרֶץ, מִלִּפְנֵי אֱלוֹהַּ יַעֲקֹב. הַהֹפְכִי הַצּוּר אֲגַם מָיִם, חַלָּמִישׁ לְמַעְיְנוֹ מָיִם.

תהלים קטו:א-יא

לֹא לָנוּ יהוה לֹא לָנוּ, כִּי לְשִׁמְךָ תֵּן כָּבוֹד, עַל חַסְדְּךָ עַל אֲמִתֶּךָ. לָמָּה יֹאמְרוּ הַגּוֹיִם, אַיֵּה נָא אֱלֹהֵיהֶם. וֵאלֹהֵינוּ בַשָּׁמָיִם, כֹּל אֲשֶׁר חָפֵץ עָשָׂה. עֲצַבֵּיהֶם כֶּסֶף וְזָהָב, מַעֲשֵׂה יְדֵי אָדָם. פֶּה לָהֶם וְלֹא יְדַבֵּרוּ, עֵינַיִם לָהֶם וְלֹא יִרְאוּ. אָזְנַיִם לָהֶם

The Four Species — *lulav, haddasim, aravos, esrog* — are taken in hand every day of Succos — through *Hoshana Rabbah* — except on the Sabbath. The *lulav*-bundle is picked up with the right hand, then the *esrog* (with the *pitam* facing down) with the left. After the blessings are recited, the *esrog* is turned over and the Four Species are waved in the six directions — front (east), right (south), back (west), left (north), up and down.

בָּרוּךְ *Blessed are You, HASHEM, our God, King of the universe, Who has sanctified us with His commandments and has commanded us concerning the taking of a palm branch.*

HALLEL

Whenever possible, the *lulav*-bundle should be held during the recitation of *Hallel,* and waved as indicated in the text.

The *chazzan* recites the blessing. The congregation, after responding *Amen,* repeats it, and continues with the first psalm.

בָּרוּךְ *Blessed are You, HASHEM, our God, King of the universe, Who has sanctified us with His commandments and has commanded us to read the Hallel.* (Cong.— *Amen.)*

Psalm 113

הַלְלוּיָהּ *Halleluyah! Give praise, you servants of HASHEM; praise the Name of HASHEM! Blessed be the Name of HASHEM, from this time and forever. From the rising of the sun to its setting, HASHEM's Name is praised. High above all nations is HASHEM, above the heavens is His glory. Who is like HASHEM, our God, Who is enthroned on high — yet deigns to look upon the heaven and the earth?* Chazzan— *He raises the needy from the dust, from the trash heaps He lifts the destitute. To seat them with nobles, with the nobles of His people. He transforms the barren wife into a glad mother of children. Halleluyah!*

Psalm 114

בְּצֵאת *When Israel went out of Egypt, Jacob's household from a people of alien tongue — Judah became His sanctuary, Israel His dominions. The sea saw and fled: the Jordan turned backward. The mountains skipped like rams, the hills like young lambs.* Chazzan— *What ails you, O sea, that you flee? O Jordan, that you turn backward? O mountains, that you skip like rams? O hills, like young lambs? Before the Lord's Presence — did I, the earth, tremble — before the presence of the God of Jacob, Who turns the rock into a pond of water, the flint into a flowing fountain.*

Psalms 115:1-11

לֹא לָנוּ *Not for our sake, HASHEM, not for our sake, but for Your Name's sake give glory, for Your kindness and for Your truth! Why should the nations say, 'Where is their God now?' Our God is in the heavens; whatever He pleases, He does! Their idols are silver and gold, the handiwork of man. They have a mouth, but cannot speak; they have eyes, but cannot see. They have ears,*

וְלֹא יִשְׁמָעוּ, אַף לָהֶם וְלֹא יְרִיחוּן. יְדֵיהֶם וְלֹא יְמִישׁוּן, רַגְלֵיהֶם וְלֹא יְהַלֵּכוּ, לֹא יֶהְגּוּ בִּגְרוֹנָם. כְּמוֹהֶם יִהְיוּ עֹשֵׂיהֶם, כֹּל אֲשֶׁר בֹּטֵחַ בָּהֶם. ❖ יִשְׂרָאֵל בְּטַח בַּיהוה, עֶזְרָם וּמָגִנָּם הוּא. בֵּית אַהֲרֹן בִּטְחוּ בַיהוה, עֶזְרָם וּמָגִנָּם הוּא. יִרְאֵי יהוה בִּטְחוּ בַיהוה, עֶזְרָם וּמָגִנָּם הוּא.

תהלים קטו:יב-יח

יהוה זְכָרָנוּ יְבָרֵךְ, יְבָרֵךְ אֶת בֵּית יִשְׂרָאֵל, יְבָרֵךְ אֶת בֵּית אַהֲרֹן. יְבָרֵךְ יִרְאֵי יהוה, הַקְּטַנִּים עִם הַגְּדֹלִים. יֹסֵף יהוה עֲלֵיכֶם, עֲלֵיכֶם וְעַל בְּנֵיכֶם. בְּרוּכִים אַתֶּם לַיהוה, עֹשֵׂה שָׁמַיִם וָאָרֶץ. ❖ הַשָּׁמַיִם שָׁמַיִם לַיהוה, וְהָאָרֶץ נָתַן לִבְנֵי אָדָם. לֹא הַמֵּתִים יְהַלְלוּ יָהּ, וְלֹא כָּל יֹרְדֵי דוּמָה. וַאֲנַחְנוּ נְבָרֵךְ יָהּ, מֵעַתָּה וְעַד עוֹלָם, הַלְלוּיָהּ.

תהלים קטז:א-יא

אָהַבְתִּי כִּי יִשְׁמַע יהוה, אֶת קוֹלִי תַּחֲנוּנָי. כִּי הִטָּה אָזְנוֹ לִי, וּבְיָמַי אֶקְרָא. אֲפָפוּנִי חֶבְלֵי מָוֶת, וּמְצָרֵי שְׁאוֹל מְצָאוּנִי, צָרָה וְיָגוֹן אֶמְצָא. וּבְשֵׁם יהוה אֶקְרָא, אָנָּה יהוה מַלְּטָה נַפְשִׁי. חַנּוּן יהוה וְצַדִּיק, וֵאלֹהֵינוּ מְרַחֵם. שֹׁמֵר פְּתָאִים יהוה, דַּלּוֹתִי וְלִי יְהוֹשִׁיעַ. שׁוּבִי נַפְשִׁי לִמְנוּחָיְכִי, כִּי יהוה גָּמַל עָלָיְכִי. כִּי חִלַּצְתָּ נַפְשִׁי מִמָּוֶת, אֶת עֵינִי מִן דִּמְעָה, אֶת רַגְלִי מִדֶּחִי. ❖ אֶתְהַלֵּךְ לִפְנֵי יהוה, בְּאַרְצוֹת הַחַיִּים. הֶאֱמַנְתִּי כִּי אֲדַבֵּר, אֲנִי עָנִיתִי מְאֹד. אֲנִי אָמַרְתִּי בְחָפְזִי, כָּל הָאָדָם כֹּזֵב.

תהלים קטז:יב-יט

מָה אָשִׁיב לַיהוה, כָּל תַּגְמוּלוֹהִי עָלָי. כּוֹס יְשׁוּעוֹת אֶשָּׂא, וּבְשֵׁם יהוה אֶקְרָא. נְדָרַי לַיהוה אֲשַׁלֵּם, נֶגְדָה נָּא לְכָל עַמּוֹ. יָקָר בְּעֵינֵי יהוה, הַמָּוְתָה לַחֲסִידָיו. אָנָּה יהוה כִּי אֲנִי עַבְדֶּךָ, אֲנִי עַבְדְּךָ, בֶּן אֲמָתֶךָ, פִּתַּחְתָּ לְמוֹסֵרָי. ❖ לְךָ אֶזְבַּח זֶבַח תּוֹדָה, וּבְשֵׁם יהוה אֶקְרָא. נְדָרַי לַיהוה אֲשַׁלֵּם, נֶגְדָה נָּא לְכָל עַמּוֹ. בְּחַצְרוֹת בֵּית יהוה, בְּתוֹכֵכִי יְרוּשָׁלָיִם הַלְלוּיָהּ.

Congregation, then *chazzan:*

תהלים קיז

הַלְלוּ אֶת יהוה, כָּל גּוֹיִם, שַׁבְּחוּהוּ כָּל הָאֻמִּים. כִּי גָבַר עָלֵינוּ חַסְדּוֹ, וֶאֱמֶת יהוה לְעוֹלָם, הַלְלוּיָהּ.

but cannot hear; they have a nose, but cannot smell. Their hands — they cannot feel; their feet — they cannot walk; they cannot utter a sound from their throat. Those who make them should become like them, whoever trusts in them! Chazzan– *O Israel, trust in HASHEM; — their help and their shield is He! House of Aaron, trust in HASHEM; their help and their shield is He! You who fear HASHEM, trust in HASHEM; their help and their shield is He!*

Psalm 115:12-18

יהוה *HASHEM Who has remembered us will bless — He will bless the House of Israel; He will bless the House of Aaron; He will bless those who fear HASHEM, the small as well as the great. May HASHEM increase upon you, upon you and upon your children! You are blessed of HASHEM, maker of heaven and earth.* Chazzan– *As for the heavens — the heavens are HASHEM's, but the earth He has given to mankind. Neither the dead can praise God, nor any who descend into silence; but we will bless God from this time and forever. Halleluyah!*

Psalm 116:1-11

אָהַבְתִּי *I love Him, for HASHEM hears my voice, my supplications. As He has inclined His ear to me, so in my days shall I call. The pains of death encircled me; the confines of the grave have found me; trouble and sorrow I would find. Then I would invoke the Name of HASHEM: 'Please, HASHEM, save my soul.' Gracious is HASHEM and righteous, our God is merciful. HASHEM protects the simple; I was brought low, but He saved me. Return, my soul, to your rest; for HASHEM has been kind to you. For You have delivered my soul from death, my eyes from tears, my feet from stumbling.* Chazzan– *I shall walk before HASHEM in the lands of the living. I have kept faith although I say: 'I suffer exceedingly.' I said in my haste: 'All mankind is deceitful.'*

Psalm 116:12-19

מָה אָשִׁיב *How can I repay HASHEM for all His kindness to me? I will raise the cup of salvations and the Name of HASHEM I will invoke. My vows to HASHEM I will pay, in the presence, now, of His entire people. Difficult in the eyes of HASHEM is the death of His devout ones. Please, HASHEM — for I am Your servant, I am Your servant, son of Your handmaid — You have released my bonds.* Chazzan– *To You I will sacrifice thanksgiving offerings, and the name of HASHEM I will invoke. My vows to HASHEM I will pay, in the presence, now, of His entire people. In the courtyards of the House of HASHEM, in your midst, O Jerusalem, Halleluyah!*

Congregation, then *chazzan:*

Psalm 117

הַלְלוּ *Praise HASHEM, all nations; praise Him, all the states! For His kindness has overwhelmed us, and the truth of HASHEM is eternal, Halleluyah!*

Congregation waves the Four Species as indicated above each word each time it recites the verse הודו. *Chazzan* waves the Four Species only when reciting the verses הודו and יאמר (see *Laws* §171-174).

תהלים קיח

FRONT · RIGHT · BACK · LEFT · UP · DOWN

Chazzan – **הוֹדוּ** לַיהוה כִּי טוֹב, כִּי לְעוֹלָם חַסְדּוֹ.

FRONT · RIGHT · BACK · LEFT · UP · DOWN

Cong. – הוֹדוּ לַיהוה כִּי טוֹב, כִּי לְעוֹלָם חַסְדּוֹ.
יֹאמַר נָא יִשְׂרָאֵל, כִּי לְעוֹלָם חַסְדּוֹ.

FRONT · RIGHT · BACK · LEFT · UP · DOWN

Chazzan – יֹאמַר נָא יִשְׂרָאֵל, כִּי לְעוֹלָם חַסְדּוֹ

FRONT · RIGHT · BACK · LEFT · UP · DOWN

Cong. – הוֹדוּ לַיהוה כִּי טוֹב, כִּי לְעוֹלָם חַסְדּוֹ.
יֹאמְרוּ נָא בֵית אַהֲרֹן, כִּי לְעוֹלָם חַסְדּוֹ.

Chazzan – יֹאמְרוּ נָא בֵית אַהֲרֹן, כִּי לְעוֹלָם חַסְדּוֹ.

FRONT · RIGHT · BACK · LEFT · UP · DOWN

Cong. – הוֹדוּ לַיהוה כִּי טוֹב, כִּי לְעוֹלָם חַסְדּוֹ.
יֹאמְרוּ נָא יִרְאֵי יהוה, כִּי לְעוֹלָם חַסְדּוֹ.
Chazzan – יֹאמְרוּ נָא יִרְאֵי יהוה, כִּי לְעוֹלָם חַסְדּוֹ.

FRONT · RIGHT · BACK · LEFT · UP · DOWN

Cong. – הוֹדוּ לַיהוה כִּי טוֹב, כִּי לְעוֹלָם חַסְדּוֹ.

מִן הַמֵּצַר קָרָאתִי יָּהּ, עָנָנִי בַמֶּרְחָב יָהּ. יהוה לִי לֹא אִירָא, מַה יַּעֲשֶׂה לִי אָדָם. יהוה לִי בְּעֹזְרָי, וַאֲנִי אֶרְאֶה בְשֹׂנְאָי. טוֹב לַחֲסוֹת בַּיהוה, מִבְּטֹחַ בָּאָדָם. טוֹב לַחֲסוֹת בַּיהוה, מִבְּטֹחַ בִּנְדִיבִים. כָּל גּוֹיִם סְבָבוּנִי, בְּשֵׁם יהוה כִּי אֲמִילַם. סַבּוּנִי גַם סְבָבוּנִי, בְּשֵׁם יהוה כִּי אֲמִילַם. סַבּוּנִי כִדְבֹרִים דֹּעֲכוּ כְּאֵשׁ קוֹצִים, בְּשֵׁם יהוה כִּי אֲמִילַם. דָּחֹה דְחִיתַנִי לִנְפֹּל, וַיהוה עֲזָרָנִי. עָזִּי וְזִמְרָת יָהּ, וַיְהִי לִי לִישׁוּעָה. קוֹל רִנָּה וִישׁוּעָה, בְּאָהֳלֵי צַדִּיקִים, יְמִין יהוה עֹשָׂה חָיִל. יְמִין יהוה רוֹמֵמָה, יְמִין יהוה עֹשָׂה חָיִל. לֹא אָמוּת כִּי אֶחְיֶה, וַאֲסַפֵּר מַעֲשֵׂי יָהּ. יַסֹּר יִסְּרַנִּי יָּהּ, וְלַמָּוֶת לֹא נְתָנָנִי. ❖ פִּתְחוּ לִי שַׁעֲרֵי צֶדֶק, אָבֹא בָם אוֹדֶה יָהּ. זֶה הַשַּׁעַר לַיהוה, צַדִּיקִים יָבֹאוּ בוֹ. אוֹדְךָ כִּי עֲנִיתָנִי, וַתְּהִי לִי לִישׁוּעָה. אוֹדְךָ כִּי עֲנִיתָנִי, וַתְּהִי לִי לִישׁוּעָה. אֶבֶן מָאֲסוּ הַבּוֹנִים, הָיְתָה לְרֹאשׁ פִּנָּה. אֶבֶן מָאֲסוּ הַבּוֹנִים, הָיְתָה לְרֹאשׁ פִּנָּה. מֵאֵת יהוה הָיְתָה זֹּאת, הִיא נִפְלָאת בְּעֵינֵינוּ. מֵאֵת יהוה הָיְתָה זֹּאת, הִיא נִפְלָאת בְּעֵינֵינוּ. זֶה

Congregation waves the Four Species — FRONT, RIGHT, BACK, LEFT, UP, DOWN — each time it recites the verse *'Give thanks . . .'* (see *Laws* §171-174).

Psalm 118

Chazzan – *Give thanks to HASHEM for He is good;*
His kindness endures forever!

Cong. – *Give thanks to HASHEM, for He is good;*
His kindness endures forever!
Let Israel say now: His kindness endures forever!

Chazzan – *Let Israel say now: His kindness endures forever!*

Cong. – *Give thanks to HASHEM, for He is good;*
His kindness endures forever!
Let the House of Aaron say now:
His kindness endures forever!

Chazzan – *Let the House of Aaron say now:*
His kindness endures forever!

Cong. – *Give thanks to HASHEM, for He is good;*
His kindness endures forever!
Let those who fear HASHEM say now:
His kindness endures forever!

Chazzan – *Let those who fear HASHEM say now:*
His kindness endures forever!

Cong. – *Give thanks to HASHEM, for He is good;*
His kindness endures forever!

מִן הַמֵּצַר *From the straits did I call upon God; God answered me with expansiveness. HASHEM is with me, I have no fear; how can man affect me? HASHEM is with me through my helpers; therefore I can face my foes. It is better to take refuge in HASHEM than to rely on man. It is better to take refuge in HASHEM than to rely on nobles. All the nations surround me; in the Name of HASHEM I cut them down! They encircle me, they also surround me; in the Name of HASHEM, I cut them down! They encircle me like bees, but they are extinguished as a fire does thorns; in the Name of HASHEM I cut them down! You pushed me hard that I might fall, but HASHEM assisted me. God is my might and my praise, and He was a salvation for me. The sound of rejoicing and salvation is in the tents of the righteous: 'HASHEM's right hand does valiantly. HASHEM's right hand is raised triumphantly; HASHEM's right hand does valiantly!' I shall not die! But I shall live and relate the deeds of God. God has chastened me exceedingly, but He did not let me die.* Chazzan– *Open for me the gates of righteousness, I will enter them and thank God. This is the gate of HASHEM; the righteous shall enter through it. I thank You for You have answered me and become my salvation. I thank You for You have answered me and become my salvation. The stone the builders despised has become the cornerstone. The stone the builders despised has become the cornerstone. This emanated from HASHEM; it is wondrous in our eyes. This emanated from HASHEM; it is wondrous in our eyes. This is*

הַיּוֹם עָשָׂה יהוה, נָגִילָה וְנִשְׂמְחָה בוֹ. זֶה הַיּוֹם עָשָׂה יהוה, נָגִילָה וְנִשְׂמְחָה בוֹ.

The next four lines are recited responsively — *chazzan,* then congregation.
The Four Species are waved as indicated above each word.

FRONT-RIGHT — BACK-LEFT — UP-DOWN

אָנָּא יהוה הוֹשִׁיעָה נָּא.

FRONT-RIGHT — BACK-LEFT — UP-DOWN

אָנָּא יהוה הוֹשִׁיעָה נָּא.
אָנָּא יהוה הַצְלִיחָה נָא.
אָנָּא יהוה הַצְלִיחָה נָא.

בָּרוּךְ הַבָּא בְּשֵׁם יהוה, בֵּרַכְנוּכֶם מִבֵּית יהוה. בָּרוּךְ הַבָּא בְּשֵׁם יהוה, בֵּרַכְנוּכֶם מִבֵּית יהוה. אֵל יהוה וַיָּאֶר לָנוּ, אִסְרוּ חַג בַּעֲבֹתִים, עַד קַרְנוֹת הַמִּזְבֵּחַ. אֵל יהוה וַיָּאֶר לָנוּ, אִסְרוּ חַג בַּעֲבֹתִים, עַד קַרְנוֹת הַמִּזְבֵּחַ. אֵלִי אַתָּה וְאוֹדֶךָּ, אֱלֹהַי אֲרוֹמְמֶךָּ. אֵלִי אַתָּה וְאוֹדֶךָּ, אֱלֹהַי אֲרוֹמְמֶךָּ.

The Four Species are waved as indicated above each word.

FRONT — RIGHT — BACK — LEFT — UP — DOWN

הוֹדוּ לַיהוה כִּי טוֹב, כִּי לְעוֹלָם חַסְדּוֹ.

FRONT — RIGHT — BACK — LEFT — UP — DOWN

הוֹדוּ לַיהוה כִּי טוֹב, כִּי לְעוֹלָם חַסְדּוֹ.

יְהַלְלוּךָ יהוה אֱלֹהֵינוּ כָּל מַעֲשֶׂיךָ, וַחֲסִידֶיךָ צַדִּיקִים עוֹשֵׂי רְצוֹנֶךָ, וְכָל עַמְּךָ בֵּית יִשְׂרָאֵל בְּרִנָּה יוֹדוּ וִיבָרְכוּ וִישַׁבְּחוּ וִיפָאֲרוּ וִירוֹמְמוּ וְיַעֲרִיצוּ וְיַקְדִּישׁוּ וְיַמְלִיכוּ אֶת שִׁמְךָ מַלְכֵּנוּ, ❖ כִּי לְךָ טוֹב לְהוֹדוֹת וּלְשִׁמְךָ נָאֶה לְזַמֵּר, כִּי מֵעוֹלָם וְעַד עוֹלָם אַתָּה אֵל. בָּרוּךְ אַתָּה יהוה, מֶלֶךְ מְהֻלָּל בַּתִּשְׁבָּחוֹת. (.Cong — אָמֵן.)

SOME CONGREGATIONS RECITE *HOSHANOS* (CHOL HAMOED, P. 732; HOSHANA RABBAH, P. 776) AT THIS POINT.

קדיש שלם

The *chazzan* recites *Kaddish:*

יִתְגַּדַּל וְיִתְקַדַּשׁ שְׁמֵהּ רַבָּא. (.Cong — אָמֵן.) בְּעָלְמָא דִּי בְרָא כִרְעוּתֵהּ. וְיַמְלִיךְ מַלְכוּתֵהּ, בְּחַיֵּיכוֹן וּבְיוֹמֵיכוֹן וּבְחַיֵּי דְכָל בֵּית יִשְׂרָאֵל, בַּעֲגָלָא וּבִזְמַן קָרִיב. וְאִמְרוּ: אָמֵן.

(.Cong — אָמֵן. יְהֵא שְׁמֵהּ רַבָּא מְבָרַךְ לְעָלַם וּלְעָלְמֵי עָלְמַיָּא.)

יְהֵא שְׁמֵהּ רַבָּא מְבָרַךְ לְעָלַם וּלְעָלְמֵי עָלְמַיָּא.

יִתְבָּרַךְ וְיִשְׁתַּבַּח וְיִתְפָּאַר וְיִתְרוֹמַם וְיִתְנַשֵּׂא וְיִתְהַדָּר וְיִתְעַלֶּה וְיִתְהַלָּל שְׁמֵהּ דְּקֻדְשָׁא בְּרִיךְ הוּא (.Cong — בְּרִיךְ הוּא) — לְעֵלָּא מִן כָּל בִּרְכָתָא וְשִׁירָתָא תֻּשְׁבְּחָתָא וְנֶחֱמָתָא, דַּאֲמִירָן בְּעָלְמָא. וְאִמְרוּ: אָמֵן. (.Cong — אָמֵן.)

the day H*ASHEM* *has made; let us rejoice and be glad on it. This is the day* H*ASHEM* *has made; let us rejoice and be glad on it.*

The next four lines are recited responsively — *chazzan,* then congregation.
The Four Species are waved — FRONT, RIGHT, BACK, LEFT, UP, DOWN — during the next two verses.

אָנָּא *Please,* H*ASHEM, save now!*
Please, H*ASHEM, save now!*
Please, H*ASHEM, bring success now!*
Please, H*ASHEM, bring success now!*

בָּרוּךְ *Blessed is he who comes in the Name of* H*ASHEM; we bless you from the House of* H*ASHEM. Blessed is he who comes in the Name of* H*ASHEM; we bless you from the House of* H*ASHEM.* H*ASHEM is God, He illuminated for us; bind the festival offering with cords until the corners of the Altar.* H*ASHEM is God, He illuminated for us; bind the festival offering with cords until the corners of the Altar. You are my God, and I will thank You; my God, I will exalt You. You are my God, and I will thank You; my God, I will exalt You.*

The Four Species are waved — FRONT, RIGHT, BACK, LEFT, UP, DOWN — during the next two verses.

Give thanks to H*ASHEM, for He is good;*
His kindness endures forever.
Give thanks to H*ASHEM, for He is good;*
His kindness endures forever.

יְהַלְלוּךָ *All Your works shall praise You,* H*ASHEM our God. And Your devout ones, the righteous, who do Your will, and Your entire people, the House of Israel, with glad song will thank, bless, praise, glorify, exalt, extol, sanctify, and proclaim the sovereignty of Your Name, our King.* Chazzan— *For to You it is fitting to give thanks, and unto Your Name it is proper to sing praises, for from This World to the World to Come You are God. Blessed are You,* H*ASHEM, the King Who is lauded with praises.* (Cong.— *Amen.)*

SOME CONGREGATIONS RECITE *HOSHANOS* (CHOL HAMOED, P. 732; HOSHANA RABBAH, P. 776) AT THIS POINT.

FULL KADDISH

The *chazzan* recites *Kaddish:*

יִתְגַּדַּל *May His great Name grow exalted and sanctified* (Cong.— *Amen.) in the world that He created as He willed. May He give reign to His kingship in your lifetimes and in your days, and in the lifetimes of the entire Family of Israel, swiftly and soon. Now respond: Amen.*

(Cong.— *Amen. May His great Name be blessed forever and ever.)*

May His great Name be blessed forever and ever.

Blessed, praised, glorified, exalted, extolled, mighty, upraised, and lauded be the Name of the Holy One, Blessed is He (Cong.— *Blessed is He*) — *beyond any blessing and song, praise and consolation that are uttered in the world. Now respond: Amen.* (Cong.— *Amen*.)

(.Cong – קַבֵּל בְּרַחֲמִים וּבְרָצוֹן אֶת תְּפִלָּתֵנוּ.)

תִּתְקַבֵּל צְלוֹתְהוֹן וּבָעוּתְהוֹן דְּכָל בֵּית יִשְׂרָאֵל קֳדָם אֲבוּהוֹן דִּי בִשְׁמַיָּא. וְאִמְרוּ: אָמֵן. (.Cong – אָמֵן.)

(.Cong – יְהִי שֵׁם יהוה מְבֹרָךְ, מֵעַתָּה וְעַד עוֹלָם.[1])

יְהֵא שְׁלָמָא רַבָּא מִן שְׁמַיָּא, וְחַיִּים עָלֵינוּ וְעַל כָּל יִשְׂרָאֵל. וְאִמְרוּ: אָמֵן. (.Cong – אָמֵן.)

(.Cong – עֶזְרִי מֵעִם יהוה, עֹשֵׂה שָׁמַיִם וָאָרֶץ.[2])

Take three steps back. Bow left and say . . . עֹשֶׂה; bow right and say . . . הוּא; bow forward and say וְעַל כָּל . . . אָמֵן. Remain standing in place for a few moments, then take three steps forward.

עֹשֶׂה שָׁלוֹם בִּמְרוֹמָיו, הוּא יַעֲשֶׂה שָׁלוֹם עָלֵינוּ, וְעַל כָּל יִשְׂרָאֵל. וְאִמְרוּ: אָמֵן. (.Cong – אָמֵן.)

ON HOSHANA RABBAH TURN TO PAGE 750; ALL OTHER DAYS CONTINUE BELOW.

הוצאת ספר תורה לחול המועד

From the moment the Ark is opened until the Torah is returned to it, one must conduct himself with the utmost respect, and avoid unnecessary conversation. It is commendable to kiss the Torah as it is carried to the *bimah* [reading table] and back to the Ark.

All rise and remain standing until the Torah is placed on the *bimah*.

THE ARK IS OPENED

Before the Torah is removed the congregation recites:

וַיְהִי בִּנְסֹעַ הָאָרֹן וַיֹּאמֶר מֹשֶׁה, קוּמָה יהוה וְיָפֻצוּ אֹיְבֶיךָ וְיָנֻסוּ מְשַׂנְאֶיךָ מִפָּנֶיךָ.[3] כִּי מִצִּיּוֹן תֵּצֵא תוֹרָה, וּדְבַר יהוה מִירוּשָׁלָיִם.[4] בָּרוּךְ שֶׁנָּתַן תּוֹרָה לְעַמּוֹ יִשְׂרָאֵל בִּקְדֻשָּׁתוֹ.

זוהר ויקהל שסט:א

בְּרִיךְ שְׁמֵהּ דְּמָרֵא עָלְמָא, בְּרִיךְ כִּתְרָךְ וְאַתְרָךְ. יְהֵא רְעוּתָךְ עִם עַמָּךְ יִשְׂרָאֵל לְעָלַם, וּפֻרְקַן יְמִינָךְ אַחֲזֵי לְעַמָּךְ בְּבֵית מַקְדְּשָׁךְ, וּלְאַמְטוּיֵי לָנָא מִטּוּב נְהוֹרָךְ, וּלְקַבֵּל צְלוֹתָנָא בְּרַחֲמִין. יְהֵא רַעֲוָא קֳדָמָךְ, דְּתוֹרִיךְ לָן חַיִּין בְּטִיבוּתָא, וְלֶהֱוֵי אֲנָא פְקִידָא בְּגוֹ צַדִּיקַיָּא, לְמִרְחַם עָלַי וּלְמִנְטַר יָתִי וְיַת כָּל דִּי לִי, וְדִי לְעַמָּךְ יִשְׂרָאֵל. אַנְתְּ הוּא זָן לְכֹלָּא, וּמְפַרְנֵס לְכֹלָּא, אַנְתְּ הוּא שַׁלִּיט עַל כֹּלָּא. אַנְתְּ הוּא דְשַׁלִּיט עַל מַלְכַיָּא, וּמַלְכוּתָא דִּילָךְ הִיא. אֲנָא עַבְדָּא דְקֻדְשָׁא בְּרִיךְ הוּא, דְּסָגִידְנָא קַמֵּהּ וּמִקַּמָּא דִּיקַר אוֹרַיְתֵהּ בְּכָל עִדָּן וְעִדָּן. לָא עַל אֱנָשׁ רָחִיצְנָא, וְלָא עַל בַּר אֱלָהִין סָמִיכְנָא, אֶלָּא בֶּאֱלָהָא דִשְׁמַיָּא, דְּהוּא אֱלָהָא קְשׁוֹט, וְאוֹרַיְתֵהּ קְשׁוֹט, וּנְבִיאוֹהִי קְשׁוֹט, וּמַסְגֵּא לְמֶעְבַּד טַבְוָן וּקְשׁוֹט. בֵּהּ אֲנָא רָחִיץ, וְלִשְׁמֵהּ קַדִּישָׁא יַקִּירָא אֲנָא אֵמַר תֻּשְׁבְּחָן. יְהֵא רַעֲוָא קֳדָמָךְ, דְּתִפְתַּח לִבָּאִי בְּאוֹרַיְתָא, וְתַשְׁלִים מִשְׁאֲלִין דְּלִבָּאִי, וְלִבָּא דְכָל עַמָּךְ יִשְׂרָאֵל, לְטַב וּלְחַיִּין וְלִשְׁלָם. (אָמֵן.)

(Cong.— *Accept our prayers with mercy and favor.*)

May the prayers and supplications of the entire Family of Israel be accepted before their Father Who is in Heaven. Now respond: Amen. (Cong.— *Amen.*)

(Cong.— *Blessed be the Name of HASHEM, from this time and forever.*[1])

May there be abundant peace from Heaven, and life, upon us and upon all Israel. Now respond: Amen. (Cong.— *Amen.*)

(Cong.— *My help is from HASHEM, Maker of heaven and earth.*[2])

Take three steps back. Bow left and say, *'He Who makes peace . . .'*; bow right and say, *'may He . . .'*; bow forward and say, *'and upon all Israel . . .'* Remain standing in place for a few moments, then take three steps forward.

He Who makes peace in His heights, may He make peace upon us, and upon all Israel. Now respond: Amen. (Cong.— *Amen.*)

ON HOSHANA RABBAH TURN TO PAGE 750; ALL OTHER DAYS CONTINUE BELOW.

REMOVAL OF THE TORAH FROM THE ARK

From the moment the Ark is opened until the Torah is returned to it, one must conduct himself with the utmost respect, and avoid unnecessary conversation. It is commendable to kiss the Torah as it is carried to the *bimah* [reading table] and back to the Ark.

All rise and remain standing until the Torah is placed on the *bimah.*

THE ARK IS OPENED

Before the Torah is removed the congregation recites:

וַיְהִי בִּנְסֹעַ *When the Ark would travel, Moses would say, 'Arise, HASHEM, and let Your foes be scattered, let those who hate You flee from You.'*[3] *For from Zion the Torah will come forth and the word of HASHEM from Jerusalem.*[4] *Blessed is He Who gave the Torah to His people Israel in His holiness.*

Zohar, Vayakhel 369a

בְּרִיךְ שְׁמֵהּ *Blessed is the Name of the Master of the universe, blessed is Your crown and Your place. May Your favor remain with Your people Israel forever; may You display the salvation of Your right hand to Your people in Your Holy Temple, to benefit us with the goodness of Your luminescence and to accept our prayers with mercy. May it be Your will that You extend our lives with goodness and that I be numbered among the righteous; that You have mercy on me and protect me, all that is mine and that is Your people Israel's. It is You Who nourishes all and sustains all; You control everything. It is You Who control kings, and kingship is Yours. I am a servant of the Holy One, Blessed is He, and I prostrate myself before Him and before the glory of His Torah at all times. Not in any man do I put trust, nor on any angel do I rely — only on the God of heaven Who is the God of truth, Whose Torah is truth and Whose prophets are true and Who acts liberally with kindness and truth. In Him do I trust, and to His glorious and holy Name do I declare praises. May it be Your will that You open my heart to the Torah and that You fulfill the wishes of my heart and the heart of Your entire people Israel for good, for life, and for peace. (Amen.)*

(1) *Psalms* 113:2. (2) 121:2. (3) *Numbers* 10:35. (4) *Isaiah* 2:3.

The Torah is removed from the Ark and presented to the *chazzan,* who accepts it in his right arm. He then turns to the Ark, bows while raising the Torah, and recites:

גַּדְּלוּ לַיהוה אִתִּי וּנְרוֹמְמָה שְׁמוֹ יַחְדָּו.[1]

The *chazzan* turns to his right and carries the Torah to the *bimah,* as the congregation responds:

לְךָ יהוה הַגְּדֻלָּה וְהַגְּבוּרָה וְהַתִּפְאֶרֶת וְהַנֵּצַח וְהַהוֹד כִּי כֹל בַּשָּׁמַיִם וּבָאָרֶץ, לְךָ יהוה הַמַּמְלָכָה וְהַמִּתְנַשֵּׂא לְכֹל לְרֹאשׁ.[2] רוֹמְמוּ יהוה אֱלֹהֵינוּ, וְהִשְׁתַּחֲווּ לַהֲדֹם רַגְלָיו, קָדוֹשׁ הוּא. רוֹמְמוּ יהוה אֱלֹהֵינוּ, וְהִשְׁתַּחֲווּ לְהַר קָדְשׁוֹ, כִּי קָדוֹשׁ יהוה אֱלֹהֵינוּ.[3]

אַב הָרַחֲמִים הוּא יְרַחֵם עַם עֲמוּסִים, וְיִזְכֹּר בְּרִית אֵיתָנִים, וְיַצִּיל נַפְשׁוֹתֵינוּ מִן הַשָּׁעוֹת הָרָעוֹת, וְיִגְעַר בְּיֵצֶר הָרָע מִן הַנְּשׂוּאִים, וְיָחֹן אוֹתָנוּ לִפְלֵיטַת עוֹלָמִים, וִימַלֵּא מִשְׁאֲלוֹתֵינוּ בְּמִדָּה טוֹבָה יְשׁוּעָה וְרַחֲמִים.

The Torah is placed on the *bimah* and prepared for reading.
The *gabbai* uses the following formula to call a *Kohen* to the Torah:

וְתִגָּלֶה וְתֵרָאֶה מַלְכוּתוֹ עָלֵינוּ בִּזְמַן קָרוֹב, וְיָחֹן פְּלֵיטָתֵנוּ וּפְלֵיטַת עַמּוֹ בֵּית יִשְׂרָאֵל לְחֵן וּלְחֶסֶד וּלְרַחֲמִים וּלְרָצוֹן. וְנֹאמַר אָמֵן. הַכֹּל הָבוּ גֹדֶל לֵאלֹהֵינוּ וּתְנוּ כָבוֹד לַתּוֹרָה. כֹּהֵן° קְרָב, יַעֲמֹד (insert name) הַכֹּהֵן.

°If no *Kohen* is present, the *gabbai* says: "אֵין כָּאן כֹּהֵן, יַעֲמֹד (name) יִשְׂרָאֵל (לֵוִי) בִּמְקוֹם כֹּהֵן."

בָּרוּךְ שֶׁנָּתַן תּוֹרָה לְעַמּוֹ יִשְׂרָאֵל בִּקְדֻשָּׁתוֹ. (תּוֹרַת יהוה תְּמִימָה מְשִׁיבַת נָפֶשׁ, עֵדוּת יהוה נֶאֱמָנָה מַחְכִּימַת פֶּתִי. פִּקּוּדֵי יהוה יְשָׁרִים מְשַׂמְּחֵי לֵב, מִצְוַת יהוה בָּרָה מְאִירַת עֵינָיִם.[4] יהוה עֹז לְעַמּוֹ יִתֵּן, יהוה יְבָרֵךְ אֶת עַמּוֹ בַשָּׁלוֹם.[5] הָאֵל תָּמִים דַּרְכּוֹ, אִמְרַת יהוה צְרוּפָה, מָגֵן הוּא לְכֹל הַחוֹסִים בּוֹ.[6])

Congregation, then *gabbai:*

וְאַתֶּם הַדְּבֵקִים בַּיהוה אֱלֹהֵיכֶם, חַיִּים כֻּלְּכֶם הַיּוֹם.[7]

The reader shows the *oleh* (person called to the Torah) the place in the Torah. The *oleh* touches the Torah with a corner of his *tallis,* or the belt or mantle of the Torah, and kisses it. He then begins the blessing, bowing at בָּרְכוּ, and straightening up at 'ה.

בָּרְכוּ אֶת יהוה הַמְּבֹרָךְ.

Congregation, followed by *oleh,* responds, bowing at בָּרוּךְ, and straightening up at 'ה.

בָּרוּךְ יהוה הַמְּבֹרָךְ לְעוֹלָם וָעֶד.

Oleh continues:

בָּרוּךְ אַתָּה יהוה אֱלֹהֵינוּ מֶלֶךְ הָעוֹלָם, אֲשֶׁר בָּחַר בָּנוּ מִכָּל הָעַמִּים, וְנָתַן לָנוּ אֶת תּוֹרָתוֹ. בָּרוּךְ אַתָּה יהוה, נוֹתֵן הַתּוֹרָה. (Cong. – אָמֵן.)

The Torah is removed from the Ark and presented to the *chazzan,* who accepts it in his right arm. He turns to the Ark, bows while raising the Torah, and recites:

Declare the greatness of HASHEM with me, and let us exalt His Name together.[1]

The *chazzan* turns to his right and carries the Torah to the *bimah,* as the congregation responds:

לְךָ *Yours, HASHEM, is the greatness, the strength, the splendor, the triumph, and the glory; even everything in heaven and earth; Yours, HASHEM, is the kingdom, and the sovereignty over every leader.*[2] *Exalt HASHEM, our God, and bow at His footstool; He is Holy! Exalt HASHEM, our God, and bow to His holy mountain; for holy is HASHEM, our God.*[3]

אַב הָרַחֲמִים *May the Father of compassion have mercy on the nation that is borne by Him, and may He remember the covenant of the spiritually mighty. May He rescue our souls from the bad times, and upbraid the evil inclination to leave those borne by Him, graciously make us an eternal remnant, and fulfill our requests in good measure, for salvation and mercy.*

The Torah is placed on the *bimah* and prepared for reading.

The *gabbai* uses the following formula to call a *Kohen* to the Torah:

וְתִגָּלֶה *And may His kingship over us be revealed and become visible soon, and may He be gracious to our remnant and the remnant of His people the Family of Israel, for graciousness, kindness, mercy, and favor. And let us respond, Amen. All of you ascribe greatness to our God and give honor to the Torah. Kohen,° approach. Stand* (name) *son of* (father's name) *the Kohen.*

°If no *Kohen* is present, the *gabbai* says: *'There is no Kohen present, stand* (name) *son of* (father's name) *an Israelite (Levite) in place of the Kohen.'*

Blessed is He Who gave the Torah to His people Israel in His holiness. (The Torah of HASHEM is perfect, restoring the soul; the testimony of HASHEM is trustworthy, making the simple one wise. The orders of HASHEM are upright, gladdening the heart; the command of HASHEM is clear, enlightening the eyes.[4] *HASHEM will give might to His nation; HASHEM will bless His nation with peace.*[5] *The God Whose way is perfect, the promise of HASHEM is flawless, He is a shield for all who take refuge in Him.*[6]*)*

Congregation, then *gabbai:*

You who cling to HASHEM, your God, you are all alive today.[7]

The reader shows the *oleh* (person called to the Torah) the place in the Torah. The *oleh* touches the Torah with a corner of his *tallis,* or the belt or mantle of the Torah, and kisses it. He then begins the blessing, bowing at *'Bless,'* and straightening up at 'HASHEM.'

Bless HASHEM, the blessed One.

Congregation, followed by *oleh,* responds, bowing at 'Blessed,' and straightening up at 'HASHEM.'

Blessed is HASHEM, the blessed One, for all eternity.

Oleh continues:

בָּרוּךְ *Blessed are You, HASHEM, our God, King of the universe, Who selected us from all the peoples and gave us His Torah. Blessed are You, HASHEM, Giver of the Torah.* (Cong.– *Amen.)*

---

(1) *Psalms* 34:4. (2) *I Chronicles* 29:11. (3) *Psalms* 99:5,9. (4) *Psalms* 19:8-9. (5) 29:11. (6) 18:31. (7) *Deuteronomy* 4:4.

After his Torah portion has been read, the *oleh* recites:

בָּרוּךְ אַתָּה יהוה אֱלֹהֵינוּ מֶלֶךְ הָעוֹלָם, אֲשֶׁר נָתַן לָנוּ תּוֹרַת אֱמֶת, וְחַיֵּי עוֹלָם נָטַע בְּתוֹכֵנוּ. בָּרוּךְ אַתָּה יהוה, נוֹתֵן הַתּוֹרָה. (.Cong. – אָמֵן)

On each day of Chol HaMoed Succos (except on the Sabbath) one Torah scroll is removed from the Ark and four *olim* are called to the Torah.

FIRST DAY

במדבר כט:יז־כה

כהן – וּבַיּוֹם הַשֵּׁנִי פָּרִים בְּנֵי־בָקָר שְׁנֵים עָשָׂר אֵילִם שְׁנָיִם כְּבָשִׂים בְּנֵי־שָׁנָה אַרְבָּעָה עָשָׂר תְּמִימִם: וּמִנְחָתָם וְנִסְכֵּיהֶם לַפָּרִים לָאֵילִם וְלַכְּבָשִׂים בְּמִסְפָּרָם כַּמִּשְׁפָּט: וּשְׂעִיר־עִזִּים אֶחָד חַטָּאת מִלְּבַד עֹלַת הַתָּמִיד וּמִנְחָתָהּ וְנִסְכֵּיהֶם:

לוי – וּבַיּוֹם הַשְּׁלִישִׁי פָּרִים עַשְׁתֵּי־עָשָׂר אֵילִם שְׁנָיִם כְּבָשִׂים בְּנֵי־שָׁנָה אַרְבָּעָה עָשָׂר תְּמִימִם: וּמִנְחָתָם וְנִסְכֵּיהֶם לַפָּרִים לָאֵילִם וְלַכְּבָשִׂים בְּמִסְפָּרָם כַּמִּשְׁפָּט: וּשְׂעִיר חַטָּאת אֶחָד מִלְּבַד עֹלַת הַתָּמִיד וּמִנְחָתָהּ וְנִסְכָּהּ:

שלישי – וּבַיּוֹם הָרְבִיעִי פָּרִים עֲשָׂרָה אֵילִם שְׁנָיִם כְּבָשִׂים בְּנֵי־שָׁנָה אַרְבָּעָה עָשָׂר תְּמִימִם: מִנְחָתָם וְנִסְכֵּיהֶם לַפָּרִים לָאֵילִם וְלַכְּבָשִׂים בְּמִסְפָּרָם כַּמִּשְׁפָּט: וּשְׂעִיר־עִזִּים אֶחָד חַטָּאת מִלְּבַד עֹלַת הַתָּמִיד מִנְחָתָהּ וְנִסְכָּהּ:

רביעי – וּבַיּוֹם הַשֵּׁנִי פָּרִים בְּנֵי־בָקָר שְׁנֵים עָשָׂר אֵילִם שְׁנָיִם כְּבָשִׂים בְּנֵי־שָׁנָה אַרְבָּעָה עָשָׂר תְּמִימִם: וּמִנְחָתָם וְנִסְכֵּיהֶם לַפָּרִים לָאֵילִם וְלַכְּבָשִׂים בְּמִסְפָּרָם כַּמִּשְׁפָּט: וּשְׂעִיר־עִזִּים אֶחָד חַטָּאת מִלְּבַד עֹלַת הַתָּמִיד וּמִנְחָתָהּ וְנִסְכֵּיהֶם: וּבַיּוֹם הַשְּׁלִישִׁי פָּרִים עַשְׁתֵּי־עָשָׂר אֵילִם שְׁנָיִם כְּבָשִׂים בְּנֵי־שָׁנָה אַרְבָּעָה עָשָׂר תְּמִימִם: וּמִנְחָתָם וְנִסְכֵּיהֶם לַפָּרִים לָאֵילִם וְלַכְּבָשִׂים בְּמִסְפָּרָם כַּמִּשְׁפָּט: וּשְׂעִיר חַטָּאת אֶחָד מִלְּבַד עֹלַת הַתָּמִיד וּמִנְחָתָהּ וְנִסְכָּהּ:

Reader recites חֲצִי קַדִּישׁ, page 712.

SECOND DAY

במדבר כט:כ־כח

כהן – וּבַיּוֹם הַשְּׁלִישִׁי פָּרִים עַשְׁתֵּי־עָשָׂר אֵילִם שְׁנָיִם כְּבָשִׂים בְּנֵי־שָׁנָה אַרְבָּעָה עָשָׂר תְּמִימִם: וּמִנְחָתָם וְנִסְכֵּיהֶם לַפָּרִים לָאֵילִם וְלַכְּבָשִׂים בְּמִסְפָּרָם כַּמִּשְׁפָּט: וּשְׂעִיר חַטָּאת אֶחָד מִלְּבַד עֹלַת הַתָּמִיד וּמִנְחָתָהּ וְנִסְכָּהּ:

After his Torah portion has been read, the *oleh* recites:

בָּרוּךְ *Blessed are You,* HASHEM, *our God, King of the universe, Who gave us the Torah of truth and implanted eternal life within us. Blessed are You,* HASHEM, *Giver of the Torah.* (Cong.– *Amen.*)

THE VARIOUS *MI SHEBERACH* PRAYERS APPEAR ON PAGE 308.

On each day of Chol HaMoed Succos (except on the Sabbath) one Torah scroll is removed from the Ark and four *olim* are called to the Torah.

FIRST DAY

Numbers 29:17-25

Kohen – *And on the second day: Twelve bulls, two rams, fourteen lambs within their first year; they are to be unblemished. And their meal-offerings and their libations for the bulls, the rams, and the lambs, in their proper numbers as required. And one he-goat for a sin-offering; aside from the continual elevation-offering, its meal-offering and their libations.*

Levi – *And on the third day: eleven bulls, two rams, fourteen lambs within their first year; they are to be unblemished. And their meal-offerings and their libations for the bulls, the rams, and the lambs, in their proper numbers as required. And one he-goat for a sin-offering; aside from the continual elevation-offering, its meal-offering and its libation.*

Third – *And on the fourth day: Ten bulls, two rams, fourteen lambs within their first year; they are to be unblemished. And their meal-offerings and their libations for the bulls, the rams, and the lambs, in their proper numbers as required. And one he-goat for a sin-offering; aside from the continual elevation-offering, its meal-offering, and its libation.*

Fourth – *And on the second day: Twelve bulls, two rams, fourteen lambs within their first year; they are to be unblemished. And their meal-offerings and their libations for the bulls, the rams, and the lambs, in their proper numbers as required. And one he-goat for a sin-offering; aside from the continual elevation-offering, its meal-offering and their libations. And on the third day: eleven bulls, two rams, fourteen lambs within their first year; they are to be unblemished. And their meal-offerings and their libations for the bulls, the rams, and the lambs, in their proper numbers as required. And one he-goat for a sin-offering; aside from the continual elevation-offering, its meal-offering and its libation.*

Reader recites Half-*Kaddish,* page 712.

SECOND DAY

Numbers 29:20-28

Kohen – *And on the third day: eleven bulls, two rams, fourteen lambs within their first year; they are to be unblemished. And their meal-offerings and their libations for the bulls, the rams, and the lambs, in their proper numbers as required. And one he-goat for a sin-offering, aside from the continual elevation-offering, its meal-offering and its libation.*

לוי – וּבַיּוֹם הָרְבִיעִי פָּרִים עֲשָׂרָה אֵילִם שְׁנָיִם כְּבָשִׂים בְּנֵי־שָׁנָה אַרְבָּעָה עָשָׂר תְּמִימִם: מִנְחָתָם וְנִסְכֵּיהֶם לַפָּרִים לָאֵילִם וְלַכְּבָשִׂים בְּמִסְפָּרָם כַּמִּשְׁפָּט: וּשְׂעִיר־עִזִּים אֶחָד חַטָּאת מִלְּבַד עֹלַת הַתָּמִיד מִנְחָתָהּ וְנִסְכָּהּ:

שלישי – וּבַיּוֹם הַחֲמִישִׁי פָּרִים תִּשְׁעָה אֵילִם שְׁנָיִם כְּבָשִׂים בְּנֵי־שָׁנָה אַרְבָּעָה עָשָׂר תְּמִימִם: וּמִנְחָתָם וְנִסְכֵּיהֶם לַפָּרִים לָאֵילִם וְלַכְּבָשִׂים בְּמִסְפָּרָם כַּמִּשְׁפָּט: וּשְׂעִיר חַטָּאת אֶחָד מִלְּבַד עֹלַת הַתָּמִיד וּמִנְחָתָהּ וְנִסְכָּהּ:

רביעי – וּבַיּוֹם הַשְּׁלִישִׁי פָּרִים עַשְׁתֵּי־עָשָׂר אֵילִם שְׁנָיִם כְּבָשִׂים בְּנֵי־שָׁנָה אַרְבָּעָה עָשָׂר תְּמִימִם: וּמִנְחָתָם וְנִסְכֵּיהֶם לַפָּרִים לָאֵילִם וְלַכְּבָשִׂים בְּמִסְפָּרָם כַּמִּשְׁפָּט: וּשְׂעִיר חַטָּאת אֶחָד מִלְּבַד עֹלַת הַתָּמִיד וּמִנְחָתָהּ וְנִסְכָּהּ: וּבַיּוֹם הָרְבִיעִי פָּרִים עֲשָׂרָה אֵילִם שְׁנָיִם כְּבָשִׂים בְּנֵי־שָׁנָה אַרְבָּעָה עָשָׂר תְּמִימִם: מִנְחָתָם וְנִסְכֵּיהֶם לַפָּרִים לָאֵילִם וְלַכְּבָשִׂים בְּמִסְפָּרָם כַּמִּשְׁפָּט: וּשְׂעִיר־עִזִּים אֶחָד חַטָּאת מִלְּבַד עֹלַת הַתָּמִיד מִנְחָתָהּ וְנִסְכָּהּ:

Reader recites חֲצִי קַדִּישׁ, page 712.

THIRD DAY

במדבר כט:כג-לא

כהן – וּבַיּוֹם הָרְבִיעִי פָּרִים עֲשָׂרָה אֵילִם שְׁנָיִם כְּבָשִׂים בְּנֵי־שָׁנָה אַרְבָּעָה עָשָׂר תְּמִימִם: מִנְחָתָם וְנִסְכֵּיהֶם לַפָּרִים לָאֵילִם וְלַכְּבָשִׂים בְּמִסְפָּרָם כַּמִּשְׁפָּט: וּשְׂעִיר־עִזִּים אֶחָד חַטָּאת מִלְּבַד עֹלַת הַתָּמִיד מִנְחָתָהּ וְנִסְכָּהּ:

לוי – וּבַיּוֹם הַחֲמִישִׁי פָּרִים תִּשְׁעָה אֵילִם שְׁנָיִם כְּבָשִׂים בְּנֵי־שָׁנָה אַרְבָּעָה עָשָׂר תְּמִימִם: וּמִנְחָתָם וְנִסְכֵּיהֶם לַפָּרִים לָאֵילִם וְלַכְּבָשִׂים בְּמִסְפָּרָם כַּמִּשְׁפָּט: וּשְׂעִיר חַטָּאת אֶחָד מִלְּבַד עֹלַת הַתָּמִיד וּמִנְחָתָהּ וְנִסְכָּהּ:

שלישי – וּבַיּוֹם הַשִּׁשִּׁי פָּרִים שְׁמֹנָה אֵילִם שְׁנָיִם כְּבָשִׂים בְּנֵי־שָׁנָה אַרְבָּעָה עָשָׂר תְּמִימִם: וּמִנְחָתָם וְנִסְכֵּיהֶם לַפָּרִים לָאֵילִם וְלַכְּבָשִׂים בְּמִסְפָּרָם כַּמִּשְׁפָּט: וּשְׂעִיר חַטָּאת אֶחָד מִלְּבַד עֹלַת הַתָּמִיד מִנְחָתָהּ וּנְסָכֶיהָ:

רביעי – וּבַיּוֹם הָרְבִיעִי פָּרִים עֲשָׂרָה אֵילִם שְׁנָיִם כְּבָשִׂים בְּנֵי־שָׁנָה אַרְבָּעָה עָשָׂר תְּמִימִם: מִנְחָתָם וְנִסְכֵּיהֶם לַפָּרִים לָאֵילִם וְלַכְּבָשִׂים בְּמִסְפָּרָם כַּמִּשְׁפָּט: וּשְׂעִיר־עִזִּים אֶחָד חַטָּאת מִלְּבַד עֹלַת הַתָּמִיד מִנְחָתָהּ וְנִסְכָּהּ: וּבַיּוֹם הַחֲמִישִׁי פָּרִים תִּשְׁעָה אֵילִם שְׁנָיִם כְּבָשִׂים בְּנֵי־שָׁנָה אַרְבָּעָה עָשָׂר תְּמִימִם: וּמִנְחָתָם וְנִסְכֵּיהֶם לַפָּרִים לָאֵילִם

Levi – *And on the fourth day: Ten bulls, two rams, fourteen lambs within their first year; they are to be unblemished. And their meal-offerings and their libations for the bulls, the rams, and the lambs, in their proper numbers as required. And one he-goat for a sin-offering; aside from the continual elevation-offering, its meal-offering, and its libation.*

Third – *And on the fifth day: nine bulls, two rams, fourteen lambs within their first year; they are to be unblemished. And their meal-offerings and their libations for the bulls, the rams, and lambs, in their proper numbers as required. And one he-goat for a sin-offering; aside from the continual elevation-offering, its meal-offering, and its libation.*

Fourth – *And on the third day: eleven bulls, two rams, fourteen lambs within their first year; they are to be unblemished. And their meal-offerings and their libations for the bulls, the rams, and the lambs, in their proper numbers as required. And one he-goat for a sin-offering; aside from the continual elevation-offering, its meal-offering and its libation. And on the fourth day: Ten bulls, two rams, fourteen lambs within their first year; they are to be unblemished. And their meal-offerings and their libations for the bulls, the rams, and the lambs, in their proper numbers as required. And one he-goat for a sin-offering; aside from the continual elevation-offering, its meal-offering, and its libation.*

Reader recites Half-*Kaddish,* page 712.

THIRD DAY

Numbers 29:23-31

Kohen – *And on the fourth day: Ten bulls, two rams, fourteen lambs within their first year; they are to be unblemished. And their meal-offerings and their libations for the bulls, the rams, and the lambs, in their proper numbers as required. And one he-goat for a sin-offering; aside from the continual elevation-offering, its meal-offering, and its libation.*

Levi – *And on the fifth day: nine bulls, two rams, fourteen lambs within their first year; they are to be unblemished. And their meal-offerings and their libations for the bulls, the rams, and the lambs, in their proper numbers as required. And one he-goat for a sin-offering; aside from the continual elevation-offering, its meal-offering, and its libation.*

Third – *And on the sixth day: eight bulls, two rams, fourteen lambs within their first year; they are to be unblemished. And their meal-offerings and their libations for the bulls, the rams and the lambs, in their proper numbers as required. And one he-goat for a sin-offering; aside from the continual elevation-offering, its meal-offering, and its libations.*

Fourth – *And on the fourth day: Ten bulls, two rams, fourteen lambs within their first year; they are to be unblemished. And their meal-offerings and their libations for the bulls, the rams, and the lambs, in their proper numbers as required. And one he-goat for a sin-offering; aside from the continual elevation-offering, its meal-offering, and its libation. And on the fifth day: nine bulls, two rams, fourteen lambs within their first year; they are to be unblemished. And their meal-offerings and their libations for the bulls, the*

וְלַכְּבָשִׂים בְּמִסְפָּרָם כַּמִּשְׁפָּט: וּשְׂעִיר חַטָּאת אֶחָד מִלְּבַד עֹלַת הַתָּמִיד וּמִנְחָתָהּ וְנִסְכָּהּ:

Reader recites חֲצִי קַדִּישׁ, below.

FOURTH DAY

במדבר כט:כו-לד

כהן – וּבַיּוֹם הַחֲמִישִׁי פָּרִים תִּשְׁעָה אֵילִם שְׁנָיִם כְּבָשִׂים בְּנֵי־שָׁנָה אַרְבָּעָה עָשָׂר תְּמִימִם: וּמִנְחָתָם וְנִסְכֵּיהֶם לַפָּרִים לָאֵילִם וְלַכְּבָשִׂים בְּמִסְפָּרָם כַּמִּשְׁפָּט: וּשְׂעִיר חַטָּאת אֶחָד מִלְּבַד עֹלַת הַתָּמִיד וּמִנְחָתָהּ וְנִסְכָּהּ:

לוי – וּבַיּוֹם הַשִּׁשִּׁי פָּרִים שְׁמֹנָה אֵילִם שְׁנָיִם כְּבָשִׂים בְּנֵי־שָׁנָה אַרְבָּעָה עָשָׂר תְּמִימִם: וּמִנְחָתָם וְנִסְכֵּיהֶם לַפָּרִים לָאֵילִם וְלַכְּבָשִׂים בְּמִסְפָּרָם כַּמִּשְׁפָּט: וּשְׂעִיר חַטָּאת אֶחָד מִלְּבַד עֹלַת הַתָּמִיד מִנְחָתָהּ וּנְסָכֶיהָ:

שלישי – וּבַיּוֹם הַשְּׁבִיעִי פָּרִים שִׁבְעָה אֵילִם שְׁנָיִם כְּבָשִׂים בְּנֵי־שָׁנָה אַרְבָּעָה עָשָׂר תְּמִימִם: וּמִנְחָתָם וְנִסְכֵּהֶם לַפָּרִים לָאֵילִם וְלַכְּבָשִׂים בְּמִסְפָּרָם כְּמִשְׁפָּטָם: וּשְׂעִיר חַטָּאת אֶחָד מִלְּבַד עֹלַת הַתָּמִיד מִנְחָתָהּ וְנִסְכָּהּ:

רביעי – וּבַיּוֹם הַחֲמִישִׁי פָּרִים תִּשְׁעָה אֵילִם שְׁנָיִם כְּבָשִׂים בְּנֵי־שָׁנָה אַרְבָּעָה עָשָׂר תְּמִימִם: וּמִנְחָתָם וְנִסְכֵּיהֶם לַפָּרִים לָאֵילִם וְלַכְּבָשִׂים בְּמִסְפָּרָם כַּמִּשְׁפָּט: וּשְׂעִיר חַטָּאת אֶחָד מִלְּבַד עֹלַת הַתָּמִיד וּמִנְחָתָהּ וְנִסְכָּהּ: וּבַיּוֹם הַשִּׁשִּׁי פָּרִים שְׁמֹנָה אֵילִם שְׁנָיִם כְּבָשִׂים בְּנֵי־שָׁנָה אַרְבָּעָה עָשָׂר תְּמִימִם: וּמִנְחָתָם וְנִסְכֵּיהֶם לַפָּרִים לָאֵילִם וְלַכְּבָשִׂים בְּמִסְפָּרָם כַּמִּשְׁפָּט: וּשְׂעִיר חַטָּאת אֶחָד מִלְּבַד עֹלַת הַתָּמִיד מִנְחָתָהּ וּנְסָכֶיהָ:

After the Torah has been read, the reader recites חֲצִי קַדִּישׁ.

יִתְגַּדַּל וְיִתְקַדַּשׁ שְׁמֵהּ רַבָּא. (.Cong – אָמֵן.) בְּעָלְמָא דִּי בְרָא כִרְעוּתֵהּ. וְיַמְלִיךְ מַלְכוּתֵהּ, בְּחַיֵּיכוֹן וּבְיוֹמֵיכוֹן וּבְחַיֵּי דְכָל בֵּית יִשְׂרָאֵל, בַּעֲגָלָא וּבִזְמַן קָרִיב. וְאִמְרוּ: אָמֵן.

(.Cong – אָמֵן. יְהֵא שְׁמֵהּ רַבָּא מְבָרַךְ לְעָלַם וּלְעָלְמֵי עָלְמַיָּא.)

יְהֵא שְׁמֵהּ רַבָּא מְבָרַךְ לְעָלַם וּלְעָלְמֵי עָלְמַיָּא.

יִתְבָּרַךְ וְיִשְׁתַּבַּח וְיִתְפָּאַר וְיִתְרוֹמַם וְיִתְנַשֵּׂא וְיִתְהַדָּר וְיִתְעַלֶּה וְיִתְהַלָּל שְׁמֵהּ דְּקֻדְשָׁא בְּרִיךְ הוּא (.Cong – בְּרִיךְ הוּא) — לְעֵלָּא מִן כָּל בִּרְכָתָא וְשִׁירָתָא תֻּשְׁבְּחָתָא וְנֶחֱמָתָא, דַּאֲמִירָן בְּעָלְמָא. וְאִמְרוּ: אָמֵן.

(.Cong – אָמֵן.)

rams, and the lambs, in their proper numbers as required. And one he-goat for a sin-offering; aside from the continual elevation-offering, its meal-offering, and its libation.

Reader recites Half-*Kaddish,* below.

FOURTH DAY

Numbers 29:26-34

Kohen – *And on the fifth day: nine bulls, two rams, fourteen lambs within their first year; they are to be unblemished. And their meal-offerings and their libations for the bulls, the rams, and the lambs, in their proper numbers as required. And one he-goat for a sin-offering; aside from the continual elevation-offering, its meal-offering, and its libation.*

Levi – *And on the sixth day: eight bulls, two rams, fourteen lambs within their first year; they are to be unblemished. And their meal-offerings and their libations for the bulls, the rams and the lambs, in their proper numbers as required. And one he-goat for a sin-offering; aside from the continual elevation-offering, its meal-offering, and its libations.*

Third — *And on the seventh day: seven bulls, two rams, fourteen lambs within their first year; they are to be unblemished. And their meal-offerings and their libations for the bulls, the rams, and the lambs, in their proper numbers as required. And one he-goat for a sin offering; aside from the continual elevation-offering, its meal-offering, and its libation.*

Fourth – *And on the fifth day: nine bulls, two rams, fourteen lambs within their first year; they are to be unblemished. And their meal-offerings and their libations for the bulls, the rams, and the lambs, in their proper numbers as required. And one he-goat for a sin-offering; aside from the continual elevation-offering, its meal-offering, and its libation. And on the sixth day: eight bulls, two rams, fourteen lambs within their first year; they are to be unblemished. And their meal-offerings and their libations for the bulls, the rams and the lambs, in their proper numbers as required. And one he-goat for a sin-offering; aside from the continual elevation-offering, its meal-offering, and its libations.*

After the Torah has been read the reader recites Half-*Kaddish:*

יִתְגַּדַּל *May His great Name grow exalted and sanctified* (Cong.– *Amen.*) *in the world that He created as He willed. May He give reign to His kingship in your lifetimes and in your days, and in the lifetimes of the entire Family of Israel, swiftly and soon. Now respond: Amen.*

(Cong.– *Amen. May His great Name be blessed forever and ever.*)

May His great Name be blessed forever and ever.

Blessed, praised, glorified, exalted, extolled, mighty, upraised, and lauded be the Name of the Holy One, Blessed is He (Cong.– *Blessed is He*) — *beyond any blessing and song, praise and consolation that are uttered in the world. Now respond: Amen.* (Cong.– *Amen.*)

The Torah is raised for all to see. Each person looks at the Torah and recites aloud:

וְזֹאת הַתּוֹרָה אֲשֶׁר שָׂם מֹשֶׁה לִפְנֵי בְּנֵי יִשְׂרָאֵל,[1] עַל פִּי יהוה בְּיַד מֹשֶׁה.[2]

Some add:

עֵץ חַיִּים הִיא לַמַּחֲזִיקִים בָּהּ, וְתֹמְכֶיהָ מְאֻשָּׁר.[3] דְּרָכֶיהָ דַרְכֵי נֹעַם, וְכָל נְתִיבוֹתֶיהָ שָׁלוֹם.[4] אֹרֶךְ יָמִים בִּימִינָהּ, בִּשְׂמֹאלָהּ עֹשֶׁר וְכָבוֹד.[5] יהוה חָפֵץ לְמַעַן צִדְקוֹ, יַגְדִּיל תּוֹרָה וְיַאְדִּיר.[6]

הכנסת ספר תורה

The *chazzan* takes the Torah in his right arm and recites:

יְהַלְלוּ אֶת שֵׁם יהוה, כִּי נִשְׂגָּב שְׁמוֹ לְבַדּוֹ –

Congregation responds:

– הוֹדוֹ עַל אֶרֶץ וְשָׁמָיִם. וַיָּרֶם קֶרֶן לְעַמּוֹ, תְּהִלָּה לְכָל חֲסִידָיו, לִבְנֵי יִשְׂרָאֵל עַם קְרֹבוֹ, הַלְלוּיָהּ.[7]

As the Torah is carried to the Ark, the congregation recites the following psalm.

תהלים כד

לְדָוִד מִזְמוֹר, לַיהוה הָאָרֶץ וּמְלוֹאָהּ, תֵּבֵל וְיֹשְׁבֵי בָהּ. כִּי הוּא עַל יַמִּים יְסָדָהּ, וְעַל נְהָרוֹת יְכוֹנְנֶהָ. מִי יַעֲלֶה בְהַר יהוה, וּמִי יָקוּם בִּמְקוֹם קָדְשׁוֹ. נְקִי כַפַּיִם וּבַר לֵבָב, אֲשֶׁר לֹא נָשָׂא לַשָּׁוְא נַפְשִׁי וְלֹא נִשְׁבַּע לְמִרְמָה. יִשָּׂא בְרָכָה מֵאֵת יהוה, וּצְדָקָה מֵאֱלֹהֵי יִשְׁעוֹ. זֶה דּוֹר דֹּרְשָׁיו, מְבַקְשֵׁי פָנֶיךָ, יַעֲקֹב, סֶלָה. שְׂאוּ שְׁעָרִים רָאשֵׁיכֶם, וְהִנָּשְׂאוּ פִּתְחֵי עוֹלָם, וְיָבוֹא מֶלֶךְ הַכָּבוֹד. מִי זֶה מֶלֶךְ הַכָּבוֹד, יהוה עִזּוּז וְגִבּוֹר, יהוה גִּבּוֹר מִלְחָמָה. שְׂאוּ שְׁעָרִים רָאשֵׁיכֶם, וּשְׂאוּ פִּתְחֵי עוֹלָם, וְיָבֹא מֶלֶךְ הַכָּבוֹד. מִי הוּא זֶה מֶלֶךְ הַכָּבוֹד, יהוה צְבָאוֹת הוּא מֶלֶךְ הַכָּבוֹד, סֶלָה.

As the Torah is placed into the Ark, the congregation recites the following verses:

וּבְנֻחֹה יֹאמַר, שׁוּבָה יהוה רִבְבוֹת אַלְפֵי יִשְׂרָאֵל.[8] קוּמָה יהוה לִמְנוּחָתֶךָ, אַתָּה וַאֲרוֹן עֻזֶּךָ. כֹּהֲנֶיךָ יִלְבְּשׁוּ צֶדֶק, וַחֲסִידֶיךָ יְרַנֵּנוּ. בַּעֲבוּר דָּוִד עַבְדֶּךָ, אַל תָּשֵׁב פְּנֵי מְשִׁיחֶךָ.[9] כִּי לֶקַח טוֹב נָתַתִּי לָכֶם, תּוֹרָתִי אַל תַּעֲזֹבוּ.[10] ❖ עֵץ חַיִּים הִיא לַמַּחֲזִיקִים בָּהּ, וְתֹמְכֶיהָ מְאֻשָּׁר.[11] דְּרָכֶיהָ דַרְכֵי נֹעַם, וְכָל נְתִיבֹתֶיהָ שָׁלוֹם.[12] הֲשִׁיבֵנוּ יהוה אֵלֶיךָ וְנָשׁוּבָה, חַדֵּשׁ יָמֵינוּ כְּקֶדֶם.[13]

(1) *Deuteronomy* 4:4. (2) *Numbers* 9:23. (3) *Proverbs* 3:18. (4) 3:17.
(5) 3:16. (6) *Isaiah* 42:21. (7) *Psalms* 148:13-14. (8) *Numbers* 10:36.
(9) *Psalms* 132:8-10. (10) *Proverbs* 4:2. (11) 3:18. (12) 3:17. (13) *Lamentations* 5:21.

The Torah is raised for all to see. Each person looks at the Torah and recites aloud:

This is the Torah that Moses placed before the Children of Israel,[1] upon the command of HASHEM, through Moses' hand.[2]

Some add:

עֵץ *It is a tree of life for those who grasp it, and its supporters are praiseworthy.[3] Its ways are ways of pleasantness and all its paths are peace.[4] Lengthy days are at its right; at its left are wealth and honor.[5] HASHEM desired, for the sake of its [Israel's] righteousness, that the Torah be made great and glorious.[6]*

RETURNING THE TORAH

The *chazzan* takes the Torah in his right arm and recites:

Let them praise the Name of HASHEM, for His Name alone will have been exalted —

Congregation responds:

— His glory is above earth and heaven. And He will have exalted the pride of His people, causing praise for all His devout ones, for the Children of Israel, His intimate people. Halleluyah![7]

As the Torah is carried to the Ark, the congregation recites the following psalm.

Psalm 24

לְדָוִד *Of David a psalm. HASHEM's is the earth and its fullness, the inhabited land and those who dwell in it. For He founded it upon seas, and established it upon rivers. Who may ascend the mountain of HASHEM, and who may stand in the place of His sanctity? One with clean hands and pure heart, who has not sworn in vain by My soul and has not sworn deceitfully. He will receive a blessing from HASHEM and just kindness from the God of his salvation. This is the generation of those who seek Him, those who strive for Your Presence — Jacob, Selah. Raise up your heads, O gates, and be uplifted, you everlasting entrances, so that the King of Glory may enter. Who is this King of Glory? — HASHEM, the mighty and strong, HASHEM, the strong in battle. Raise up your heads, O gates, and raise up, you everlasting entrances, so that the King of Glory may enter. Who then is the King of Glory? HASHEM, Master of Legions, He is the King of Glory. Selah!*

As the Torah is placed into the Ark, the congregation recites the following verses:

וּבְנֻחֹה *And when it rested he would say, 'Return, HASHEM, to the myriad thousands of Israel.'[8] Arise, HASHEM, to Your resting place, You and the Ark of Your strength. Let Your priests be clothed in righteousness, and Your devout ones will sing joyously. For the sake of David, Your servant, turn not away the face of Your anointed.[9] For I have given you a good teaching, do not forsake My Torah.[10]* Chazzan— *It is a tree of life for those who grasp it, and its supporters are praiseworthy.[11] Its ways are ways of pleasantness and all its paths are peace.[12] Bring us back to You, HASHEM, and we shall return, renew our days as of old.[13]*

אַשְׁרֵי יוֹשְׁבֵי בֵיתֶךָ, עוֹד יְהַלְּלוּךָ סֶּלָה.[1] אַשְׁרֵי הָעָם שֶׁכָּכָה לּוֹ, אַשְׁרֵי הָעָם שֶׁיהוה אֱלֹהָיו.[2]

תהלים קמה

תְּהִלָּה לְדָוִד,

אֲרוֹמִמְךָ אֱלוֹהַי הַמֶּלֶךְ, וַאֲבָרְכָה שִׁמְךָ לְעוֹלָם וָעֶד.
בְּכָל יוֹם אֲבָרְכֶךָּ, וַאֲהַלְלָה שִׁמְךָ לְעוֹלָם וָעֶד.
גָּדוֹל יהוה וּמְהֻלָּל מְאֹד, וְלִגְדֻלָּתוֹ אֵין חֵקֶר.
דּוֹר לְדוֹר יְשַׁבַּח מַעֲשֶׂיךָ, וּגְבוּרֹתֶיךָ יַגִּידוּ.
הֲדַר כְּבוֹד הוֹדֶךָ, וְדִבְרֵי נִפְלְאֹתֶיךָ אָשִׂיחָה.
וֶעֱזוּז נוֹרְאוֹתֶיךָ יֹאמֵרוּ, וּגְדוּלָּתְךָ אֲסַפְּרֶנָּה.
זֵכֶר רַב טוּבְךָ יַבִּיעוּ, וְצִדְקָתְךָ יְרַנֵּנוּ.
חַנּוּן וְרַחוּם יהוה, אֶרֶךְ אַפַּיִם וּגְדָל חָסֶד.
טוֹב יהוה לַכֹּל, וְרַחֲמָיו עַל כָּל מַעֲשָׂיו.
יוֹדוּךָ יהוה כָּל מַעֲשֶׂיךָ, וַחֲסִידֶיךָ יְבָרְכוּכָה.
כְּבוֹד מַלְכוּתְךָ יֹאמֵרוּ, וּגְבוּרָתְךָ יְדַבֵּרוּ.
לְהוֹדִיעַ לִבְנֵי הָאָדָם גְּבוּרֹתָיו, וּכְבוֹד הֲדַר מַלְכוּתוֹ.
מַלְכוּתְךָ מַלְכוּת כָּל עֹלָמִים, וּמֶמְשַׁלְתְּךָ בְּכָל דּוֹר וָדֹר.
סוֹמֵךְ יהוה לְכָל הַנֹּפְלִים, וְזוֹקֵף לְכָל הַכְּפוּפִים.
עֵינֵי כֹל אֵלֶיךָ יְשַׂבֵּרוּ, וְאַתָּה נוֹתֵן לָהֶם אֶת אָכְלָם בְּעִתּוֹ.
פּוֹתֵחַ אֶת יָדֶךָ,
וּמַשְׂבִּיעַ לְכָל חַי רָצוֹן.

While reciting the verse פּוֹתֵחַ, concentrate intently on its meaning.

צַדִּיק יהוה בְּכָל דְּרָכָיו, וְחָסִיד בְּכָל מַעֲשָׂיו.
קָרוֹב יהוה לְכָל קֹרְאָיו, לְכֹל אֲשֶׁר יִקְרָאֻהוּ בֶאֱמֶת.
רְצוֹן יְרֵאָיו יַעֲשֶׂה, וְאֶת שַׁוְעָתָם יִשְׁמַע וְיוֹשִׁיעֵם.
שׁוֹמֵר יהוה אֶת כָּל אֹהֲבָיו, וְאֵת כָּל הָרְשָׁעִים יַשְׁמִיד.
❖ תְּהִלַּת יהוה יְדַבֶּר פִּי,
וִיבָרֵךְ כָּל בָּשָׂר שֵׁם קָדְשׁוֹ לְעוֹלָם וָעֶד.
וַאֲנַחְנוּ נְבָרֵךְ יָהּ, מֵעַתָּה וְעַד עוֹלָם, הַלְלוּיָהּ.[3]

(1) *Psalms* 84:5. (2) 144:15. (3) 115:18.

אַשְׁרֵי *Praiseworthy are those who dwell in Your house; may they always praise You, Selah![1] Praiseworthy is the people for whom this is so, praiseworthy is the people whose God is HASHEM.[2]*

Psalm 145 *A psalm of praise by David:*

א *I will exalt You, my God the King,*
and I will bless Your Name forever and ever.
ב *Every day I will bless You,*
and I will laud Your Name forever and ever.
ג *HASHEM is great and exceedingly lauded,*
and His greatness is beyond investigation.
ד *Each generation will praise Your deeds to the next*
and of Your mighty deeds they will tell.
ה *The splendrous glory of Your power*
and Your wondrous deeds I shall discuss.
ו *And of Your awesome power they will speak,*
and Your greatness I shall relate.
ז *A recollection of Your abundant goodness they will utter*
and of Your righteousness they will sing exultantly.
ח *Gracious and merciful is HASHEM,*
slow to anger, and great in [bestowing] kindness.
ט *HASHEM is good to all; His mercies are on all His works.*
י *All Your works shall thank You, HASHEM,*
and Your devout ones will bless You.
כ *Of the glory of Your kingdom they will speak,*
and of Your power they will tell;
ל *To inform human beings of His mighty deeds,*
and the glorious splendor of His kingdom.
מ *Your kingdom is a kingdom spanning all eternities,*
and Your dominion is throughout every generation.
ס *HASHEM supports all the fallen ones and straightens all the bent.*
ע *The eyes of all look to You with hope*
and You give them their food in its proper time;
פ *You open Your hand,*
and satisfy the desire of every living thing.

While reciting the verse, *'You open . . .'* concentrate intently on its meaning.

צ *Righteous is HASHEM in all His ways*
and magnanimous in all His deeds.
ק *HASHEM is close to all who call upon Him —*
to all who call upon Him sincerely.
ר *The will of those who fear Him He will do;*
and their cry He will hear, and save them.
ש *HASHEM protects all who love Him;*
but all the wicked He will destroy.
ת Chazzan— *May my mouth declare the praise of HASHEM*
and may all flesh bless His Holy Name forever and ever.
We will bless God from this time and forever, Halleluyah![3]

The primary part of וּבָא לְצִיּוֹן is the *Kedushah* recited by the angels. These verses are presented in bold type and it is preferable that the congregation recite them aloud and in unison. However, the interpretive translation in Aramaic (which follows the verses in bold type) should be recited softly.

וּבָא לְצִיּוֹן גּוֹאֵל, וּלְשָׁבֵי פֶשַׁע בְּיַעֲקֹב, נְאֻם יהוה. וַאֲנִי, זֹאת בְּרִיתִי אוֹתָם, אָמַר יהוה, רוּחִי אֲשֶׁר עָלֶיךָ, וּדְבָרַי אֲשֶׁר שַׂמְתִּי בְּפִיךָ, לֹא יָמוּשׁוּ מִפִּיךָ וּמִפִּי זַרְעֲךָ וּמִפִּי זֶרַע זַרְעֲךָ, אָמַר יהוה, מֵעַתָּה וְעַד עוֹלָם:[1] ❖ וְאַתָּה קָדוֹשׁ יוֹשֵׁב תְּהִלּוֹת יִשְׂרָאֵל.[2] וְקָרָא זֶה אֶל זֶה וְאָמַר:

קָדוֹשׁ, קָדוֹשׁ, קָדוֹשׁ יהוה צְבָאוֹת, מְלֹא כָל הָאָרֶץ כְּבוֹדוֹ.[3]

וּמְקַבְּלִין דֵּין מִן דֵּין וְאָמְרִין:
קַדִּישׁ בִּשְׁמֵי מְרוֹמָא עִלָּאָה בֵּית שְׁכִינְתֵּהּ,
קַדִּישׁ עַל אַרְעָא עוֹבַד גְּבוּרְתֵּהּ,
קַדִּישׁ לְעָלַם וּלְעָלְמֵי עָלְמַיָּא, יהוה צְבָאוֹת,
מַלְיָא כָל אַרְעָא זִיו יְקָרֵהּ.[4]

❖ וַתִּשָּׂאֵנִי רוּחַ, וָאֶשְׁמַע אַחֲרַי קוֹל רַעַשׁ גָּדוֹל:

בָּרוּךְ כְּבוֹד יהוה מִמְּקוֹמוֹ.[5]

וּנְטָלַתְנִי רוּחָא, וּשְׁמָעִית בַּתְרַי קָל זִיעַ סַגִּיא
דִּמְשַׁבְּחִין וְאָמְרִין:
בְּרִיךְ יְקָרָא דַיהוה מֵאֲתַר בֵּית שְׁכִינְתֵּהּ.[6]

יהוה יִמְלֹךְ לְעֹלָם וָעֶד.[7]

יהוה מַלְכוּתֵהּ קָאֵם לְעָלַם וּלְעָלְמֵי עָלְמַיָּא.[8]

יהוה אֱלֹהֵי אַבְרָהָם יִצְחָק וְיִשְׂרָאֵל אֲבֹתֵינוּ, שָׁמְרָה זֹּאת לְעוֹלָם, לְיֵצֶר מַחְשְׁבוֹת לְבַב עַמֶּךָ, וְהָכֵן לְבָבָם אֵלֶיךָ.[9] וְהוּא רַחוּם, יְכַפֵּר עָוֹן וְלֹא יַשְׁחִית, וְהִרְבָּה לְהָשִׁיב אַפּוֹ, וְלֹא יָעִיר כָּל חֲמָתוֹ.[10] כִּי אַתָּה אֲדֹנָי טוֹב וְסַלָּח, וְרַב חֶסֶד לְכָל קֹרְאֶיךָ.[11] צִדְקָתְךָ צֶדֶק לְעוֹלָם, וְתוֹרָתְךָ אֱמֶת.[12] תִּתֵּן אֱמֶת לְיַעֲקֹב, חֶסֶד לְאַבְרָהָם, אֲשֶׁר נִשְׁבַּעְתָּ לַאֲבֹתֵינוּ מִימֵי קֶדֶם.[13] בָּרוּךְ אֲדֹנָי יוֹם יוֹם יַעֲמָס לָנוּ, הָאֵל יְשׁוּעָתֵנוּ סֶלָה.[14] יהוה צְבָאוֹת עִמָּנוּ, מִשְׂגָּב לָנוּ אֱלֹהֵי יַעֲקֹב סֶלָה.[15] יהוה צְבָאוֹת, אַשְׁרֵי אָדָם בֹּטֵחַ בָּךְ.[16] יהוה הוֹשִׁיעָה, הַמֶּלֶךְ יַעֲנֵנוּ בְיוֹם קָרְאֵנוּ.[17]

בָּרוּךְ הוּא אֱלֹהֵינוּ שֶׁבְּרָאָנוּ לִכְבוֹדוֹ, וְהִבְדִּילָנוּ מִן הַתּוֹעִים, וְנָתַן לָנוּ תּוֹרַת אֱמֶת, וְחַיֵּי עוֹלָם נָטַע בְּתוֹכֵנוּ. הוּא יִפְתַּח לִבֵּנוּ

(1) *Isaiah* 59:20-21. (2) *Psalms* 22:4. (3) *Isaiah* 6:3. (4) *Targum Yonasan.* (5) *Ezekiel* 3:12. (6) *Targum Yonasan.* (7) *Exodus* 15:18. (8) *Targum Onkelos.* (9) *I Chronicles* 29:18. (10) *Psalms* 78:38. (11) 86:5. (12) 119:142. (13) *Micah* 7:20. (14) *Psalms* 68:20. (15) 46:8. (16) 84:13. (17) 20:10.

The primary part of וּבָא לְצִיּוֹן, *'A redeemer shall come . . .',* is the *Kedushah* recited by the angels. These verses are presented in bold type and it is preferable that the congregation recite them aloud and in unison. However, the interpretive translation in Aramaic (which follows the verses in bold type) should be recited softly.

וּבָא לְצִיּוֹן *'A redeemer shall come to Zion* and to those of Jacob who repent from willful sin,' the words of HASHEM. 'And as for Me, this is My covenant* with them,' said HASHEM, 'My spirit that is upon you and My words that I have placed in your mouth shall not be withdrawn from your mouth, nor from the mouth of your offspring,* nor from the mouth of your offspring's offspring,' said HASHEM, 'from this moment and forever.'*[1] Chazzan– *You are the Holy One, enthroned upon the praises of Israel.**[2] *And one [angel] will call another and say:*

'Holy, holy, holy is HASHEM, Master of Legions,
the whole world is filled with His glory.'[3]

And they receive permission from one another and say:
'Holy in the most exalted heaven, the abode of His Presence;
holy on earth, product of His strength;
holy forever and ever is HASHEM, Master of Legions —
the entire world is filled with the radiance of His glory.'[4]
Chazzan– *And a wind lifted me;* and I heard behind me*
the sound of a great noise:

'Blessed is the glory of HASHEM from His place.'[5]

And a wind lifted me and I heard behind me the sound
of the powerful movement of those who praised saying:
'Blessed is the honor of HASHEM
from the place of the abode of His Presence.'[6]

HASHEM shall reign for all eternity.[7]

HASHEM — His kingdom is established forever and ever.[8]

HASHEM, God of Abraham, Isaac, and Israel, our forefathers, may You preserve this forever as the realization of the thoughts in Your people's heart, and may You direct their heart to You.*[9] *He, the Merciful One, is forgiving of iniquity and does not destroy; frequently He withdraws His anger, not arousing His entire rage.*[10] *For You, my Lord, are good and forgiving, and abundantly kind to all who call upon You.*[11] *Your righteousness remains righteous forever, and Your Torah is truth.*[12] *Grant truth to Jacob, kindness to Abraham, as You swore to our forefathers from ancient times.*[13] *Blessed is my Lord for every single day, He burdens us with blessings, the God of our salvation, Selah.*[14] *HASHEM, Master of Legions, is with us, a stronghold for us is the God of Jacob, Selah.*[15] *HASHEM, Master of Legions, praiseworthy is the man who trusts in You.*[16] *HASHEM, save! May the King answer us on the day we call.*[17]

Blessed is He, our God, Who created us for His glory, separated us from those who stray, gave us the Torah of truth and implanted eternal life within us. May He open our heart through His Torah and imbue our

בְּתוֹרָתוֹ, וְיָשֵׂם בְּלִבֵּנוּ אַהֲבָתוֹ וְיִרְאָתוֹ וְלַעֲשׂוֹת רְצוֹנוֹ וּלְעָבְדוֹ בְּלֵבָב שָׁלֵם, לְמַעַן לֹא נִיגַע לָרִיק, וְלֹא נֵלֵד לַבֶּהָלָה.[1]

יְהִי רָצוֹן מִלְּפָנֶיךָ יהוה אֱלֹהֵינוּ וֵאלֹהֵי אֲבוֹתֵינוּ, שֶׁנִּשְׁמֹר חֻקֶּיךָ בָּעוֹלָם הַזֶּה, וְנִזְכֶּה וְנִחְיֶה וְנִרְאֶה וְנִירַשׁ טוֹבָה וּבְרָכָה לִשְׁנֵי יְמוֹת הַמָּשִׁיחַ וּלְחַיֵּי הָעוֹלָם הַבָּא. לְמַעַן יְזַמֶּרְךָ כָבוֹד וְלֹא יִדֹּם, יהוה אֱלֹהַי לְעוֹלָם אוֹדֶךָּ.[2] בָּרוּךְ הַגֶּבֶר אֲשֶׁר יִבְטַח בַּיהוה, וְהָיָה יהוה מִבְטַחוֹ.[3] בִּטְחוּ בַיהוה עֲדֵי עַד, כִּי בְּיָהּ יהוה צוּר עוֹלָמִים.[4] ❖ וְיִבְטְחוּ בְךָ יוֹדְעֵי שְׁמֶךָ, כִּי לֹא עָזַבְתָּ דֹּרְשֶׁיךָ, יהוה.[5] יהוה חָפֵץ לְמַעַן צִדְקוֹ, יַגְדִּיל תּוֹרָה וְיַאְדִּיר.[6]

Chazzan recites חֲצִי קַדִּישׁ.

יִתְגַּדַּל וְיִתְקַדַּשׁ שְׁמֵהּ רַבָּא. (.Cong – אָמֵן.) בְּעָלְמָא דִּי בְרָא כִרְעוּתֵהּ. וְיַמְלִיךְ מַלְכוּתֵהּ, בְּחַיֵּיכוֹן וּבְיוֹמֵיכוֹן וּבְחַיֵּי דְכָל בֵּית יִשְׂרָאֵל, בַּעֲגָלָא וּבִזְמַן קָרִיב. וְאִמְרוּ: אָמֵן.

(.Cong – אָמֵן. יְהֵא שְׁמֵהּ רַבָּא מְבָרַךְ לְעָלַם וּלְעָלְמֵי עָלְמַיָּא.)

יְהֵא שְׁמֵהּ רַבָּא מְבָרַךְ לְעָלַם וּלְעָלְמֵי עָלְמַיָּא.

יִתְבָּרַךְ וְיִשְׁתַּבַּח וְיִתְפָּאַר וְיִתְרוֹמַם וְיִתְנַשֵּׂא וְיִתְהַדָּר וְיִתְעַלֶּה וְיִתְהַלָּל שְׁמֵהּ דְּקֻדְשָׁא בְּרִיךְ הוּא (.Cong – בְּרִיךְ הוּא) – לְעֵלָּא מִן כָּל בִּרְכָתָא וְשִׁירָתָא תֻּשְׁבְּחָתָא וְנֶחֱמָתָא, דַּאֲמִירָן בְּעָלְמָא. וְאִמְרוּ: אָמֵן. (.Cong – אָמֵן.)

מוסף לחול המועד

MUSSAF FOR HOSHANA RABBAH APPEARS ON PAGE 766.

Take three steps backward, then three steps forward. Remain standing with the feet together while reciting *Shemoneh Esrei*. Recite it with quiet devotion and without interruption, verbal or otherwise. Although its recitation should not be audible to others, one must pray loudly enough to hear himself.

כִּי שֵׁם יהוה אֶקְרָא, הָבוּ גֹדֶל לֵאלֹהֵינוּ.[7]

אֲדֹנָי שְׂפָתַי תִּפְתָּח, וּפִי יַגִּיד תְּהִלָּתֶךָ.[8]

אבות

Bend the knees at בָּרוּךְ; bow at אַתָּה; straighten up at 'ה.

בָּרוּךְ אַתָּה יהוה אֱלֹהֵינוּ וֵאלֹהֵי אֲבוֹתֵינוּ, אֱלֹהֵי אַבְרָהָם, אֱלֹהֵי יִצְחָק, וֵאלֹהֵי יַעֲקֹב, הָאֵל הַגָּדוֹל הַגִּבּוֹר וְהַנּוֹרָא, אֵל עֶלְיוֹן, גּוֹמֵל חֲסָדִים טוֹבִים וְקוֹנֵה הַכֹּל, וְזוֹכֵר חַסְדֵי אָבוֹת, וּמֵבִיא גוֹאֵל לִבְנֵי בְנֵיהֶם, לְמַעַן שְׁמוֹ בְּאַהֲבָה. מֶלֶךְ עוֹזֵר וּמוֹשִׁיעַ וּמָגֵן.

Bend the knees at בָּרוּךְ; bow at אַתָּה; straighten up at 'ה.

בָּרוּךְ אַתָּה יהוה, מָגֵן אַבְרָהָם.

heart with love and awe of Him and that we may do His will and serve Him wholeheartedly, so that we do not struggle in vain nor produce for futility.[1]

May it be Your will, HASHEM, our God and the God of our forefathers, that we observe Your decrees in This World, and merit that we live and see and inherit goodness and blessing in the years of Messianic times and for the life of the World to Come. So that my soul might sing to You and not be stilled, HASHEM, my God, forever will I thank You.[2] *Blessed is the man who trusts in HASHEM, then HASHEM will be his security.*[3] *Trust in HASHEM forever, for in God, HASHEM, is the strength of the worlds.*[4] Chazzan– *Those knowing Your Name will trust in You, and You forsake not those Who seek You, HASHEM.*[5] *HASHEM desired, for the sake of its [Israel's] righteousness, that the Torah be made great and glorious.*[6]

Chazzan recites Half-*Kaddish.*

יִתְגַּדַּל *May His great Name grow exalted and sanctified* (Cong.– *Amen.*) *in the world that He created as He willed. May He give reign to His kingship in your lifetimes and in your days, and in the lifetimes of the entire Family of Israel, swiftly and soon. Now respond: Amen.*

(Cong.– *Amen. May His great Name be blessed forever and ever.*)

May His great Name be blessed forever and ever.

Blessed, praised, glorified, exalted, extolled, mighty, upraised, and lauded be the Name of the Holy One, Blessed is He (Cong.– *Blessed is He*) — *beyond any blessing and song, praise and consolation that are uttered in the world. Now respond: Amen.* (Cong.– *Amen.*)

MUSSAF FOR CHOL HAMOED

MUSSAF FOR HOSHANA RABBAH APPEARS ON PAGE 766.

Take three steps backward, then three steps forward. Remain standing with the feet together while reciting *Shemoneh Esrei.* Recite it with quiet devotion and without interruption, verbal or otherwise. Although its recitation should not be audible to others, one must pray loudly enough to hear himself.

When I call out the Name of HASHEM, ascribe greatness to our God.[7]

My Lord, open my lips, that my mouth may declare Your praise.[8]

PATRIARCHS

Bend the knees at *'Blessed'*; bow at *'You'*; straighten up at *'HASHEM.'*

בָּרוּךְ *Blessed are You, HASHEM, our God and the God of our forefathers, God of Abraham, God of Isaac, and God of Jacob; the great, mighty, and awesome God, the supreme God, Who bestows beneficial kindnesses and creates everything, Who recalls the kindnesses of the Patriarchs and brings a Redeemer to their children's children, for His Name's sake, with love. O King, Helper, Savior, and Shield.*

Bend the knees at *'Blessed'*; bow at *'You'*; straighten up at *'HASHEM.'*

Blessed are You, HASHEM, Shield of Abraham.

---

(1) Cf. *Isaiah* 65:23. (2) *Psalms* 30:13. (3) *Jeremiah* 17:7. (4) *Isaiah* 26:4.
(5) *Psalms* 9:11. (6) *Isaiah* 42:21. (7) *Deuteronomy* 32:3. (8) *Psalms* 51:17.

גבורות

אַתָּה גִּבּוֹר לְעוֹלָם אֲדֹנָי, מְחַיֵּה מֵתִים אַתָּה, רַב לְהוֹשִׁיעַ. מְכַלְכֵּל חַיִּים בְּחֶסֶד, מְחַיֵּה מֵתִים בְּרַחֲמִים רַבִּים, סוֹמֵךְ נוֹפְלִים, וְרוֹפֵא חוֹלִים, וּמַתִּיר אֲסוּרִים, וּמְקַיֵּם אֱמוּנָתוֹ לִישֵׁנֵי עָפָר. מִי כָמוֹךְ בַּעַל גְּבוּרוֹת, וּמִי דּוֹמֶה לָּךְ, מֶלֶךְ מֵמִית וּמְחַיֶּה וּמַצְמִיחַ יְשׁוּעָה. וְנֶאֱמָן אַתָּה לְהַחֲיוֹת מֵתִים. בָּרוּךְ אַתָּה יהוה, מְחַיֵּה הַמֵּתִים.

During the *chazzan's* repetition, *Kedushah* (below) is recited at this point.

קדושת השם

INDIVIDUALS RECITE:

אַתָּה קָדוֹשׁ וְשִׁמְךָ קָדוֹשׁ, וּקְדוֹשִׁים בְּכָל יוֹם יְהַלְלְוּךָ סֶּלָה. בָּרוּךְ אַתָּה יהוה, הָאֵל הַקָּדוֹשׁ.

CHAZZAN RECITES DURING HIS REPETITION:

לְדוֹר וָדוֹר נַגִּיד גָּדְלֶךָ וּלְנֵצַח נְצָחִים קְדֻשָּׁתְךָ נַקְדִּישׁ, וְשִׁבְחֲךָ אֱלֹהֵינוּ מִפִּינוּ לֹא יָמוּשׁ לְעוֹלָם וָעֶד, כִּי אֵל מֶלֶךְ גָּדוֹל וְקָדוֹשׁ אָתָּה. בָּרוּךְ אַתָּה יהוה, הָאֵל הַקָּדוֹשׁ.

קדושת היום

אַתָּה בְחַרְתָּנוּ מִכָּל הָעַמִּים, אָהַבְתָּ אוֹתָנוּ, וְרָצִיתָ בָּנוּ, וְרוֹמַמְתָּנוּ מִכָּל הַלְּשׁוֹנוֹת, וְקִדַּשְׁתָּנוּ בְּמִצְוֹתֶיךָ, וְקֵרַבְתָּנוּ מַלְכֵּנוּ לַעֲבוֹדָתֶךָ, וְשִׁמְךָ הַגָּדוֹל וְהַקָּדוֹשׁ עָלֵינוּ קָרָאתָ.

וַתִּתֶּן לָנוּ יהוה אֱלֹהֵינוּ בְּאַהֲבָה מוֹעֲדִים לְשִׂמְחָה חַגִּים וּזְמַנִּים לְשָׂשׂוֹן, אֶת יוֹם חַג הַסֻּכּוֹת הַזֶּה, זְמַן שִׂמְחָתֵנוּ מִקְרָא קֹדֶשׁ, זֵכֶר לִיצִיאַת מִצְרָיִם.

קדושה

When reciting *Kedushah,* one must stand with his feet together and avoid any interruptions. One should rise on his toes when saying the words קָדוֹשׁ, קָדוֹשׁ, קָדוֹשׁ; בָּרוּךְ (of בָּרוּךְ כְּבוֹד); and יִמְלֹךְ.

Cong. then *Chazzan* – **נְקַדֵּשׁ** אֶת שִׁמְךָ בָּעוֹלָם, כְּשֵׁם שֶׁמַּקְדִּישִׁים אוֹתוֹ בִּשְׁמֵי מָרוֹם, כַּכָּתוּב עַל יַד נְבִיאֶךָ, וְקָרָא זֶה אֶל זֶה וְאָמַר:

All – קָדוֹשׁ קָדוֹשׁ קָדוֹשׁ יהוה צְבָאוֹת, מְלֹא כָל הָאָרֶץ כְּבוֹדוֹ.[1]

Chazzan – לְעֻמָּתָם בָּרוּךְ יֹאמֵרוּ:

All – בָּרוּךְ כְּבוֹד יהוה, מִמְּקוֹמוֹ.[2]

Chazzan – וּבְדִבְרֵי קָדְשְׁךָ כָּתוּב לֵאמֹר:

All – יִמְלֹךְ יהוה לְעוֹלָם, אֱלֹהַיִךְ צִיּוֹן לְדֹר וָדֹר, הַלְלוּיָהּ.[3]

GOD'S MIGHT

אַתָּה *You are eternally mighty, my Lord, the Resuscitator of the dead are You; abundantly able to save. He sustains the living with kindness, resuscitates the dead with abundant mercy, supports the fallen, heals the sick, releases the confined, and maintains His faith to those asleep in the dust. Who is like You, O Master of mighty deeds, and who is comparable to You, O King Who causes death and restores life and makes salvation sprout! And You are faithful to resuscitate the dead. Blessed are You,* HASHEM, *Who resuscitates the dead.*

During the *chazzan's* repetition, *Kedushah* (below) is recited at this point.

HOLINESS OF GOD'S NAME

INDIVIDUALS RECITE:

אַתָּה *You are holy and Your Name is holy, and holy ones praise You every day, forever. Blessed are You,* HASHEM, *the holy God.*

CHAZZAN RECITES DURING HIS REPETITION:

לְדוֹר *From generation to generation we shall relate Your greatness and for infinite eternities we shall proclaim Your holiness. Your praise, our God, shall not leave our mouth forever and ever, for You, O God, are a great and holy King. Blessed are You,* HASHEM, *the holy God.*

SANCTIFICATION OF THE DAY

אַתָּה בְחַרְתָּנוּ *You have chosen us from all the peoples; You loved us and found favor in us; You exalted us above all the tongues and You sanctified us with Your commandments. You drew us close, our King, to Your service and proclaimed Your great and Holy Name upon us.*

וַתִּתֶּן לָנוּ *And You gave us,* HASHEM, *our God, with love, appointed festivals for gladness, Festivals and times for joy, this day of the Festival of Succos, the time of our gladness, a holy convocation, a memorial of the Exodus from Egypt.*

KEDUSHAH

When reciting *Kedushah*, one must stand with his feet together and avoid any interruptions. One should rise on his toes when saying the words *Holy, holy, holy; Blessed is;* and *HASHEM shall reign.*

Cong. then Chazzan – **נְקַדֵּשׁ** *We shall sanctify Your Name in this world, just as they sanctify it in heaven above, as it is written by Your prophet, "And one [angel] will call another and say:*

All – *'Holy, holy, holy is* HASHEM, *Master of Legions, the whole world is filled with His glory.' "*[1]

Chazzan – *Those facing them say 'Blessed':*

All – *'Blessed is the glory of* HASHEM *from His place.'*[2]

Chazzan – *And in Your holy Writings the following is written:*

All – *'*HASHEM *shall reign forever — your God, O Zion — from generation to generation, Halleluyah!'*[3]

---

(1) *Isaiah* 6:3. (2) *Ezekiel* 3:12. (3) *Psalms* 146:10.

וּמִפְּנֵי חֲטָאֵינוּ גָּלִינוּ מֵאַרְצֵנוּ, וְנִתְרַחַקְנוּ מֵעַל אַדְמָתֵנוּ. וְאֵין אֲנַחְנוּ יְכוֹלִים לַעֲלוֹת וְלֵרָאוֹת וּלְהִשְׁתַּחֲוֹת לְפָנֶיךָ, וְלַעֲשׂוֹת חוֹבוֹתֵינוּ בְּבֵית בְּחִירָתֶךָ, בַּבַּיִת הַגָּדוֹל וְהַקָּדוֹשׁ שֶׁנִּקְרָא שִׁמְךָ עָלָיו, מִפְּנֵי הַיָּד שֶׁנִּשְׁתַּלְּחָה בְּמִקְדָּשֶׁךָ. יְהִי רָצוֹן מִלְּפָנֶיךָ יהוה אֱלֹהֵינוּ וֵאלֹהֵי אֲבוֹתֵינוּ, מֶלֶךְ רַחֲמָן, שֶׁתָּשׁוּב וּתְרַחֵם עָלֵינוּ וְעַל מִקְדָּשְׁךָ בְּרַחֲמֶיךָ הָרַבִּים, וְתִבְנֵהוּ מְהֵרָה וּתְגַדֵּל כְּבוֹדוֹ. אָבִינוּ מַלְכֵּנוּ, גַּלֵּה כְּבוֹד מַלְכוּתְךָ עָלֵינוּ מְהֵרָה, וְהוֹפַע וְהִנָּשֵׂא עָלֵינוּ לְעֵינֵי כָּל חָי. וְקָרֵב פְּזוּרֵינוּ מִבֵּין הַגּוֹיִם, וּנְפוּצוֹתֵינוּ כַּנֵּס מִיַּרְכְּתֵי אָרֶץ. וַהֲבִיאֵנוּ לְצִיּוֹן עִירְךָ בְּרִנָּה, וְלִירוּשָׁלַיִם בֵּית מִקְדָּשְׁךָ בְּשִׂמְחַת עוֹלָם. וְשָׁם נַעֲשֶׂה לְפָנֶיךָ אֶת קָרְבְּנוֹת חוֹבוֹתֵינוּ, תְּמִידִים כְּסִדְרָם, וּמוּסָפִים כְּהִלְכָתָם. וְאֶת מוּסַף יוֹם חַג הַסֻּכּוֹת הַזֶּה נַעֲשֶׂה וְנַקְרִיב לְפָנֶיךָ בְּאַהֲבָה כְּמִצְוַת רְצוֹנֶךָ, כְּמוֹ שֶׁכָּתַבְתָּ עָלֵינוּ בְּתוֹרָתֶךָ, עַל יְדֵי מֹשֶׁה עַבְדֶּךָ, מִפִּי כְבוֹדֶךָ כָּאָמוּר:

ON THE FIRST DAY OF CHOL HAMOED

וּבַיּוֹם הַשֵּׁנִי, פָּרִים בְּנֵי בָקָר שְׁנֵים עָשָׂר, אֵילִם שְׁנָיִם, כְּבָשִׂים בְּנֵי שָׁנָה אַרְבָּעָה עָשָׂר, תְּמִימִם.[1] וּמִנְחָתָם וְנִסְכֵּיהֶם כִּמְדֻבָּר, שְׁלֹשָׁה עֶשְׂרֹנִים לַפָּר, וּשְׁנֵי עֶשְׂרֹנִים לָאָיִל, וְעִשָּׂרוֹן לַכֶּבֶשׂ, וְיַיִן כְּנִסְכּוֹ. וְשָׂעִיר לְכַפֵּר, וּשְׁנֵי תְמִידִים כְּהִלְכָתָם. וּבַיּוֹם הַשְּׁלִישִׁי, פָּרִים עַשְׁתֵּי עָשָׂר, אֵילִם שְׁנָיִם, כְּבָשִׂים בְּנֵי שָׁנָה אַרְבָּעָה עָשָׂר, תְּמִימִם.[2] וּמִנְחָתָם וְנִסְכֵּיהֶם כִּמְדֻבָּר, שְׁלֹשָׁה עֶשְׂרֹנִים לַפָּר, וּשְׁנֵי עֶשְׂרֹנִים לָאָיִל, וְעִשָּׂרוֹן לַכֶּבֶשׂ, וְיַיִן כְּנִסְכּוֹ. וְשָׂעִיר לְכַפֵּר, וּשְׁנֵי תְמִידִים כְּהִלְכָתָם.

Continue "אֱלֹהֵינוּ...," page 726.

ON THE SECOND DAY OF CHOL HAMOED

וּבַיּוֹם הַשְּׁלִישִׁי, פָּרִים עַשְׁתֵּי עָשָׂר, אֵילִם שְׁנָיִם, כְּבָשִׂים בְּנֵי שָׁנָה אַרְבָּעָה עָשָׂר, תְּמִימִם.[2] וּמִנְחָתָם וְנִסְכֵּיהֶם כִּמְדֻבָּר, שְׁלֹשָׁה עֶשְׂרֹנִים לַפָּר, וּשְׁנֵי עֶשְׂרֹנִים לָאָיִל, וְעִשָּׂרוֹן לַכֶּבֶשׂ, וְיַיִן כְּנִסְכּוֹ. וְשָׂעִיר לְכַפֵּר, וּשְׁנֵי תְמִידִים כְּהִלְכָתָם. וּבַיּוֹם הָרְבִיעִי פָּרִים עֲשָׂרָה, אֵילִם שְׁנָיִם, כְּבָשִׂים בְּנֵי שָׁנָה אַרְבָּעָה

(1) *Numbers* 29:17. (2) 29:20.

וּמִפְּנֵי חֲטָאֵינוּ *But because of our sins we have been exiled from our land and sent far from our soil. We cannot ascend to appear and to prostrate ourselves before You, and to perform our obligations in the House of Your choice, in the great and holy House upon which Your Name was proclaimed, because of the hand that was dispatched against Your Sanctuary. May it be Your will, HASHEM, our God and the God of our forefathers, O merciful King, that You once more be compassionate upon us and upon Your Sanctuary in Your abundant mercy, and rebuild it soon and magnify its glory. Our Father, our King, reveal the glory of Your Kingship upon us, speedily; appear and be uplifted over us before the eyes of all the living. Draw our scattered ones near from among the nations, and bring in our dispersions from the ends of the earth. Bring us to Zion, Your City, in glad song, and to Jerusalem, home of Your Sanctuary, in eternal joy. There we will perform before You our obligatory offerings, the continual offerings according to their order and the additional offerings according to their law. And the additional offering of this day of the Festival of Succos, we will perform and bring near to You with love, according to the commandment of Your will, as You have written for us in Your Torah, through Moses, Your servant, from Your glorious expression, as it is said:*

ON THE FIRST DAY OF CHOL HAMOED

וּבַיּוֹם הַשֵּׁנִי *And on the second day: twelve young bulls, two rams, fourteen [male] first-year lambs, unblemished.*[1] *And their meal-offerings and their wine-libations as mentioned: three tenth-ephah for each bull; two tenth-ephah for each ram; one tenth-ephah for each lamb; and wine for its libation. A he-goat for atonement, and two continual offerings according to their law. And on the third day: eleven bulls, two rams, fourteen [male] first-year lambs, unblemished.*[2] *And their meal-offerings and their wine-libations as mentioned: three tenth-ephah for each bull; two tenth-ephah for each ram; one tenth-ephah for each lamb; and wine for its libation. A he-goat for atonement, and two continual offerings according to their law.*

Continue – *'Our God. . .'*, page 726.

ON THE SECOND DAY OF CHOL HAMOED

וּבַיּוֹם הַשְּׁלִישִׁי *And on the third day: eleven bulls, two rams, fourteen [male] first-year lambs, unblemished.*[4] *And their meal-offerings and their wine-libations as mentioned: three tenth-ephah for each bull; two tenth-ephah for each ram; one tenth-ephah for each lamb; and wine for its libation. A he-goat for atonement, and two continual offerings according to their law. And on the fourth day: ten bulls, two rams, fourteen [male] first-year lambs,*

עָשָׂר, תְּמִימִם.[1] וּמִנְחָתָם וְנִסְכֵּיהֶם כִּמְדֻבָּר, שְׁלֹשָׁה עֶשְׂרֹנִים לַפָּר, וּשְׁנֵי עֶשְׂרֹנִים לָאָיִל, וְעִשָּׂרוֹן לַכֶּבֶשׂ, וְיַיִן כְּנִסְכּוֹ. וְשָׂעִיר לְכַפֵּר, וּשְׁנֵי תְמִידִים כְּהִלְכָתָם.

Continue "...אֱלֹהֵינוּ" below.

ON THE THIRD DAY OF CHOL HAMOED

וּבַיּוֹם הָרְבִיעִי פָּרִים עֲשָׂרָה, אֵילִם שְׁנָיִם, כְּבָשִׂים בְּנֵי שָׁנָה אַרְבָּעָה עָשָׂר, תְּמִימִם.[1] וּמִנְחָתָם וְנִסְכֵּיהֶם כִּמְדֻבָּר, שְׁלֹשָׁה עֶשְׂרֹנִים לַפָּר, וּשְׁנֵי עֶשְׂרֹנִים לָאָיִל, וְעִשָּׂרוֹן לַכֶּבֶשׂ, וְיַיִן כְּנִסְכּוֹ. וְשָׂעִיר לְכַפֵּר, וּשְׁנֵי תְמִידִים כְּהִלְכָתָם. וּבַיּוֹם הַחֲמִישִׁי, פָּרִים תִּשְׁעָה, אֵילִם שְׁנָיִם, כְּבָשִׂים בְּנֵי שָׁנָה אַרְבָּעָה עָשָׂר, תְּמִימִם.[2] וּמִנְחָתָם וְנִסְכֵּיהֶם כִּמְדֻבָּר, שְׁלֹשָׁה עֶשְׂרֹנִים לַפָּר, וּשְׁנֵי עֶשְׂרֹנִים לָאָיִל, וְעִשָּׂרוֹן לַכֶּבֶשׂ, וְיַיִן כְּנִסְכּוֹ. וְשָׂעִיר לְכַפֵּר, וּשְׁנֵי תְמִידִים כְּהִלְכָתָם.

Continue "...אֱלֹהֵינוּ" below.

ON THE FOURTH DAY OF CHOL HAMOED

וּבַיּוֹם הַחֲמִישִׁי פָּרִים תִּשְׁעָה, אֵילִם שְׁנָיִם, כְּבָשִׂים בְּנֵי שָׁנָה אַרְבָּעָה עָשָׂר, תְּמִימִם.[2] וּמִנְחָתָם וְנִסְכֵּיהֶם כִּמְדֻבָּר, שְׁלֹשָׁה עֶשְׂרֹנִים לַפָּר, וּשְׁנֵי עֶשְׂרֹנִים לָאָיִל, וְעִשָּׂרוֹן לַכֶּבֶשׂ, וְיַיִן כְּנִסְכּוֹ. וְשָׂעִיר לְכַפֵּר, וּשְׁנֵי תְמִידִים כְּהִלְכָתָם. וּבַיּוֹם הַשִּׁשִּׁי, פָּרִים שְׁמֹנָה, אֵילִם שְׁנָיִם, כְּבָשִׂים בְּנֵי שָׁנָה אַרְבָּעָה עָשָׂר, תְּמִימִם.[3] וּמִנְחָתָם וְנִסְכֵּיהֶם כִּמְדֻבָּר, שְׁלֹשָׁה עֶשְׂרֹנִים לַפָּר, וּשְׁנֵי עֶשְׂרֹנִים לָאָיִל, וְעִשָּׂרוֹן לַכֶּבֶשׂ, וְיַיִן כְּנִסְכּוֹ. וְשָׂעִיר לְכַפֵּר, וּשְׁנֵי תְמִידִים כְּהִלְכָתָם.

ON ALL DAYS CONTINUE:

אֱלֹהֵינוּ וֵאלֹהֵי אֲבוֹתֵינוּ, מֶלֶךְ רַחֲמָן רַחֵם עָלֵינוּ, טוֹב וּמֵטִיב הִדָּרֶשׁ לָנוּ, שׁוּבָה אֵלֵינוּ בַּהֲמוֹן רַחֲמֶיךָ, בִּגְלַל אָבוֹת שֶׁעָשׂוּ רְצוֹנֶךָ. בְּנֵה בֵיתְךָ כְּבַתְּחִלָּה, וְכוֹנֵן מִקְדָּשְׁךָ עַל מְכוֹנוֹ, וְהַרְאֵנוּ בְּבִנְיָנוֹ, וְשַׂמְּחֵנוּ בְּתִקּוּנוֹ. וְהָשֵׁב כֹּהֲנִים לַעֲבוֹדָתָם, וּלְוִיִּם לְשִׁירָם וּלְזִמְרָם, וְהָשֵׁב יִשְׂרָאֵל לִנְוֵיהֶם. וְשָׁם נַעֲלֶה וְנֵרָאֶה וְנִשְׁתַּחֲוֶה לְפָנֶיךָ, בְּשָׁלֹשׁ פַּעֲמֵי רְגָלֵינוּ, כַּכָּתוּב בְּתוֹרָתֶךָ: שָׁלוֹשׁ פְּעָמִים בַּשָּׁנָה, יֵרָאֶה כָל זְכוּרְךָ אֶת פְּנֵי יהוה אֱלֹהֶיךָ, בַּמָּקוֹם אֲשֶׁר

unblemished.[1] *And their meal-offerings and their wine-libations as mentioned: three tenth-ephah for each bull; two tenth-ephah for each ram; one tenth-ephah for each lamb; and wine for its libation. A he-goat for atonement, and two continual offerings according to their law.*

Continue — *'Our God. . .',* below.

ON THE THIRD DAY OF CHOL HAMOED

וּבַיּוֹם הָרְבִיעִי *And on the fourth day: ten bulls, two rams, fourteen [male] first-year lambs, unblemished.*[1] *And their meal-offerings and their wine-libations as mentioned: three tenth-ephah for each bull; two tenth-ephah for each ram; one tenth-ephah for each lamb; and wine for its libation. A he-goat for atonement, and two continual offerings according to their law. And on the fifth day: nine bulls, two rams, fourteen [male] first-year lambs, unblemished.*[2] *And their meal-offerings and their wine-libations as mentioned: three tenth-ephah for each bull; two tenth-ephah for each ram; one tenth-ephah for each lamb; and wine for its libation. A he-goat for atonement, and two continual offerings according to their law.*

Continue — *'Our God. . .',* below.

ON THE FOURTH DAY OF CHOL HAMOED

וּבַיּוֹם הַחֲמִישִׁי *And on the fifth day: nine bulls, two rams, fourteen [male] first-year lambs, unblemished.*[2] *And their meal-offerings and their wine-libations as mentioned: three tenth-ephah for each bull; two tenth-ephah for each ram; one tenth-ephah for each lamb; and wine for its libation. A he-goat for atonement, and two continual offerings according to their law. And on the sixth day: eight bulls, two rams, fourteen [male] first-year lambs, unblemished.*[3] *And their meal-offerings and their wine-libations as mentioned: three tenth-ephah for each bull; two tenth-ephah for each ram; one tenth-ephah for each lamb; and wine for its libation. A he-goat for atonement, and two continual offerings according to their law.*

ON ALL DAYS CONTINUE:

אֱלֹהֵינוּ *Our God and the God of our forefathers, O merciful King, have mercy on us; O good and beneficent One, let Yourself be sought out by us; return to us in Your yearning mercy for the sake of the forefathers who did Your will. Rebuild Your House as it was at first, and establish Your Sanctuary on its prepared site; show us its rebuilding and gladden us in its perfection. Restore the Kohanim to their service and the Levites to their song and music; and restore Israel to their dwellings. And there we will ascend and appear and prostrate ourselves before You, during our three pilgrimage seasons, as it is written in Your Torah: Three times a year all your males are to appear before* HASHEM,

(1) *Numbers* 29:23. (2) 29:26. (3) 29:29.

יִבְחָר, בְּחַג הַמַּצּוֹת, וּבְחַג הַשָּׁבֻעוֹת, וּבְחַג הַסֻּכּוֹת, וְלֹא יֵרָאֶה אֶת פְּנֵי יהוה רֵיקָם. אִישׁ כְּמַתְּנַת יָדוֹ, כְּבִרְכַּת יהוה אֱלֹהֶיךָ, אֲשֶׁר נָתַן לָךְ.[1]

וְהַשִּׂיאֵנוּ יהוה אֱלֹהֵינוּ אֶת בִּרְכַּת מוֹעֲדֶיךָ לְחַיִּים וּלְשָׁלוֹם, לְשִׂמְחָה וּלְשָׂשׂוֹן, כַּאֲשֶׁר רָצִיתָ וְאָמַרְתָּ לְבָרְכֵנוּ. קַדְּשֵׁנוּ בְּמִצְוֹתֶיךָ וְתֵן חֶלְקֵנוּ בְּתוֹרָתֶךָ, שַׂבְּעֵנוּ מִטּוּבֶךָ וְשַׂמְּחֵנוּ בִּישׁוּעָתֶךָ, וְטַהֵר לִבֵּנוּ לְעָבְדְּךָ בֶּאֱמֶת, וְהַנְחִילֵנוּ יהוה אֱלֹהֵינוּ בְּשִׂמְחָה וּבְשָׂשׂוֹן מוֹעֲדֵי קָדְשֶׁךָ, וְיִשְׂמְחוּ בְךָ יִשְׂרָאֵל מְקַדְּשֵׁי שְׁמֶךָ. בָּרוּךְ אַתָּה יהוה, מְקַדֵּשׁ יִשְׂרָאֵל וְהַזְּמַנִּים.

עבודה

רְצֵה יהוה אֱלֹהֵינוּ בְּעַמְּךָ יִשְׂרָאֵל וּבִתְפִלָּתָם, וְהָשֵׁב אֶת הָעֲבוֹדָה לִדְבִיר בֵּיתֶךָ. וְאִשֵּׁי יִשְׂרָאֵל וּתְפִלָּתָם בְּאַהֲבָה תְקַבֵּל בְּרָצוֹן, וּתְהִי לְרָצוֹן תָּמִיד עֲבוֹדַת יִשְׂרָאֵל עַמֶּךָ.

וְתֶחֱזֶינָה עֵינֵינוּ בְּשׁוּבְךָ לְצִיּוֹן בְּרַחֲמִים. בָּרוּךְ אַתָּה יהוה, הַמַּחֲזִיר שְׁכִינָתוֹ לְצִיּוֹן.

הודאה

Bow at מודים; straighten up at 'ה. In his repetition the *chazzan* should recite the entire מודים aloud, while the congregation recites מודים דְּרַבָּנָן softly.

מוֹדִים אֲנַחְנוּ לָךְ, שָׁאַתָּה הוּא יהוה אֱלֹהֵינוּ וֵאלֹהֵי אֲבוֹתֵינוּ לְעוֹלָם וָעֶד. צוּר חַיֵּינוּ, מָגֵן יִשְׁעֵנוּ אַתָּה הוּא לְדוֹר וָדוֹר. נוֹדֶה לְּךָ וּנְסַפֵּר תְּהִלָּתֶךָ[2] עַל חַיֵּינוּ הַמְּסוּרִים בְּיָדֶךָ, וְעַל נִשְׁמוֹתֵינוּ הַפְּקוּדוֹת לָךְ, וְעַל נִסֶּיךָ שֶׁבְּכָל יוֹם עִמָּנוּ, וְעַל נִפְלְאוֹתֶיךָ וְטוֹבוֹתֶיךָ שֶׁבְּכָל עֵת, עֶרֶב וָבֹקֶר וְצָהֳרָיִם. הַטּוֹב כִּי לֹא כָלוּ רַחֲמֶיךָ, וְהַמְרַחֵם כִּי לֹא תַמּוּ חֲסָדֶיךָ,[3] מֵעוֹלָם קִוִּינוּ לָךְ.

מודים דרבנן

מוֹדִים אֲנַחְנוּ לָךְ, שָׁאַתָּה הוּא יהוה אֱלֹהֵינוּ וֵאלֹהֵי אֲבוֹתֵינוּ, אֱלֹהֵי כָל בָּשָׂר, יוֹצְרֵנוּ, יוֹצֵר בְּרֵאשִׁית. בְּרָכוֹת וְהוֹדָאוֹת לְשִׁמְךָ הַגָּדוֹל וְהַקָּדוֹשׁ, עַל שֶׁהֶחֱיִיתָנוּ וְקִיַּמְתָּנוּ. כֵּן תְּחַיֵּנוּ וּתְקַיְּמֵנוּ, וְתֶאֱסוֹף גָּלֻיּוֹתֵינוּ לְחַצְרוֹת קָדְשֶׁךָ, לִשְׁמוֹר חֻקֶּיךָ וְלַעֲשׂוֹת רְצוֹנֶךָ, וּלְעָבְדְּךָ בְּלֵבָב שָׁלֵם, עַל שֶׁאֲנַחְנוּ מוֹדִים לָךְ. בָּרוּךְ אֵל הַהוֹדָאוֹת.

(1) *Deuteronomy* 16:16-17. (2) Cf. *Psalms* 79:13. (3) Cf. *Lamentations* 3:22.

your God, in the place He shall choose, on the Festival of Matzos, on the Festival of Shavuos, and on the Festival of Succos, and they shall not appear before HASHEM *empty-handed. Every man according to the gift of his hand, according to the blessing of* HASHEM, *your God, that He gave you.*[1]

וְהַשִּׂיאֵנוּ *Bestow upon us, O* HASHEM, *our God, the blessing of Your appointed Festivals for life and for peace, for gladness and for joy, as You desired and promised to bless us. Sanctify us with Your commandments and grant us our share in Your Torah; satisfy us from Your goodness and gladden us with Your salvation, and purify our heart to serve You sincerely. And grant us a heritage, O* HASHEM, *our God — with gladness and with joy — the appointed festivals of Your holiness, and may Israel, the sanctifiers of Your Name, rejoice in You. Blessed are You,* HASHEM, *Who sanctifies Israel and the festive seasons.*

TEMPLE SERVICE

רְצֵה *Be favorable,* HASHEM, *our God, toward Your people Israel and their prayer and restore the service to the Holy of Holies of Your Temple. The fire-offerings of Israel and their prayer accept with love and favor, and may the service of Your people Israel always be favorable to You.*

וְתֶחֱזֶינָה *May our eyes behold Your return to Zion in compassion. Blessed are You,* HASHEM, *Who restores His Presence to Zion.*

THANKSGIVING [MODIM]

Bow at *'We gratefully thank You'*; straighten up at *'HASHEM.'* In his repetition the *chazzan* should recite the entire *Modim* aloud, while the congregation recites *Modim of the Rabbis* softly.

מוֹדִים *We gratefully thank You, for it is You Who are* HASHEM, *our God and the God of our forefathers for all eternity; Rock of our lives, Shield of our salvation are You from generation to generation. We shall thank You and relate Your praise*[2] *— for our lives, which are committed to Your power and for our souls that are entrusted to You; for Your miracles that are with us every day; and for Your wonders and favors in every season — evening, morning, and afternoon. The Beneficent One, for Your compassions were never exhausted, and the Compassionate One, for Your kindnesses never ended*[3] *— always have we put our hope in You.*

MODIM OF THE RABBIS

מוֹדִים *We gratefully thank You, for it is You Who are* HASHEM, *our God and the God of our forefathers, the God of all flesh, our Molder, the Molder of the universe. Blessings and thanks are due Your great and holy Name for You have given us life and sustained us. So may You continue to give us life and sustain us and gather our exiles to the Courtyards of Your Sanctuary, to observe Your decrees, to do Your will and to serve You wholeheartedly. [We thank You] for inspiring us to thank You. Blessed is the God of thanksgivings.*

וְעַל כֻּלָּם יִתְבָּרַךְ וְיִתְרוֹמַם שִׁמְךָ מַלְכֵּנוּ תָּמִיד לְעוֹלָם וָעֶד.

Bend the knees at בָּרוּךְ; bow at אַתָּה; straighten up at 'ה.

וְכֹל הַחַיִּים יוֹדוּךָ סֶּלָה, וִיהַלְלוּ אֶת שִׁמְךָ בֶּאֱמֶת, הָאֵל יְשׁוּעָתֵנוּ וְעֶזְרָתֵנוּ סֶלָה. בָּרוּךְ אַתָּה יהוה, הַטּוֹב שִׁמְךָ וּלְךָ נָאֶה לְהוֹדוֹת.

ברכת כהנים

The *chazzan* recites the following during his repetition.
He faces right at וְיִשְׁמְרֶךָ; faces left at אֵלֶיךָ וִיחֻנֶּךָּ; faces the Ark for the rest of the blessings.

אֱלֹהֵינוּ, וֵאלֹהֵי אֲבוֹתֵינוּ, בָּרְכֵנוּ בַבְּרָכָה הַמְּשֻׁלֶּשֶׁת בַּתּוֹרָה הַכְּתוּבָה עַל יְדֵי מֹשֶׁה עַבְדֶּךָ, הָאֲמוּרָה מִפִּי אַהֲרֹן וּבָנָיו, כֹּהֲנִים עַם קְדוֹשֶׁךָ, כָּאָמוּר:

יְבָרֶכְךָ יהוה, וְיִשְׁמְרֶךָ. (Cong. – כֵּן יְהִי רָצוֹן.)

יָאֵר יהוה פָּנָיו אֵלֶיךָ וִיחֻנֶּךָּ. (Cong. – כֵּן יְהִי רָצוֹן.)

יִשָּׂא יהוה פָּנָיו אֵלֶיךָ וְיָשֵׂם לְךָ שָׁלוֹם.[1] (Cong. – כֵּן יְהִי רָצוֹן.)

שלום

שִׂים שָׁלוֹם, טוֹבָה, וּבְרָכָה, חֵן, וָחֶסֶד וְרַחֲמִים עָלֵינוּ וְעַל כָּל יִשְׂרָאֵל עַמֶּךָ. בָּרְכֵנוּ אָבִינוּ, כֻּלָּנוּ כְּאֶחָד בְּאוֹר פָּנֶיךָ, כִּי בְאוֹר פָּנֶיךָ נָתַתָּ לָּנוּ, יהוה אֱלֹהֵינוּ, תּוֹרַת חַיִּים וְאַהֲבַת חֶסֶד, וּצְדָקָה, וּבְרָכָה, וְרַחֲמִים, וְחַיִּים, וְשָׁלוֹם. וְטוֹב בְּעֵינֶיךָ לְבָרֵךְ אֶת עַמְּךָ יִשְׂרָאֵל, בְּכָל עֵת וּבְכָל שָׁעָה בִּשְׁלוֹמֶךָ. בָּרוּךְ אַתָּה יהוה, הַמְּבָרֵךְ אֶת עַמּוֹ יִשְׂרָאֵל בַּשָּׁלוֹם.

יִהְיוּ לְרָצוֹן אִמְרֵי פִי וְהֶגְיוֹן לִבִּי לְפָנֶיךָ, יהוה צוּרִי וְגֹאֲלִי.[2]

The *chazzan's* repetiiton of *Shemoneh Esrei* ends here. The individual continues below:

אֱלֹהַי, נְצוֹר לְשׁוֹנִי מֵרָע, וּשְׂפָתַי מִדַּבֵּר מִרְמָה,[3] וְלִמְקַלְלַי נַפְשִׁי תִדּוֹם, וְנַפְשִׁי כֶּעָפָר לַכֹּל תִּהְיֶה. פְּתַח לִבִּי בְּתוֹרָתֶךָ, וּבְמִצְוֹתֶיךָ תִּרְדּוֹף נַפְשִׁי. וְכֹל הַחוֹשְׁבִים עָלַי רָעָה, מְהֵרָה הָפֵר עֲצָתָם וְקַלְקֵל מַחֲשַׁבְתָּם. עֲשֵׂה לְמַעַן שְׁמֶךָ, עֲשֵׂה לְמַעַן יְמִינֶךָ, עֲשֵׂה לְמַעַן קְדֻשָּׁתֶךָ, עֲשֵׂה לְמַעַן תּוֹרָתֶךָ. לְמַעַן יֵחָלְצוּן יְדִידֶיךָ, הוֹשִׁיעָה יְמִינְךָ וַעֲנֵנִי.[4]

Some recite verses pertaining to their names here. See page 1301.

יִהְיוּ לְרָצוֹן אִמְרֵי פִי וְהֶגְיוֹן לִבִּי לְפָנֶיךָ, יהוה צוּרִי וְגֹאֲלִי.[2]

Bow and take three steps back. Bow left and say . . . עֹשֶׂה, bow right and say . . . הוּא יַעֲשֶׂה; bow forward and say וְעַל כָּל . . . אָמֵן.

עֹשֶׂה שָׁלוֹם בִּמְרוֹמָיו, הוּא יַעֲשֶׂה שָׁלוֹם עָלֵינוּ, וְעַל כָּל יִשְׂרָאֵל. וְאִמְרוּ: אָמֵן.

For all these, may Your Name be blessed and exalted, our King, continually forever and ever.

Bend the knees at *'Blessed'*; bow at *'You'*; straighten up at *'HASHEM.'*

Everything alive will gratefully acknowledge You, Selah! and praise Your Name sincerely, O God of our salvation and help, Selah! Blessed are You, HASHEM, Your Name is 'The Beneficent One' and to You it is fitting to give thanks.

THE PRIESTLY BLESSING

The *chazzan* recites the following during his repetition.

אֱלֹהֵינוּ *Our God and the God of our forefathers, bless us with the three-verse blessing in the Torah that was written by the hand of Moses, Your servant, that was said by Aaron and his sons, the Kohanim, Your holy people, as it is said:*

May HASHEM bless you and safeguard you. (Cong.— *So may it be.*)

May HASHEM illuminate His countenance for you and be gracious to you. (Cong.— *So may it be.*)

May HASHEM turn His countenance to you and establish peace for you.[1] (Cong.— *So may it be.*)

PEACE

שִׂים שָׁלוֹם *Establish peace, goodness, blessing, graciousness, kindness, and compassion upon us and upon all of Your people Israel. Bless us, our Father, all of us as one, with the light of Your countenance, for with the light of Your countenance You gave us, HASHEM, our God, the Torah of life and a love of kindness, righteousness, blessing, compassion, life, and peace. And may it be good in Your eyes to bless Your people Israel at every time and every hour with Your peace. Blessed are You, HASHEM, Who blesses His people Israel with peace.*

May the expressions of my mouth and the thoughts of my heart find favor before You, HASHEM, my Rock and my Redeemer.[2]

Chazzan's repetition of *Shemoneh Esrei* ends here. Individuals continue:

אֱלֹהַי *My God, guard my tongue from evil and my lips from speaking deceitfully.*[3] *To those who curse me, let my soul be silent; and let my soul be like dust to everyone. Open my heart to Your Torah, then my soul will pursue Your commandments. As for all those who design evil against me, speedily nullify their counsel and disrupt their design. Act for Your Name's sake; act for Your right hand's sake; act for Your sanctity's sake; act for Your Torah's sake. That Your beloved ones may be given rest; let Your right hand save, and respond to me.*[4]

Some recite verses pertaining to their names at this point. See page 1301.

May the expressions of my mouth and the thoughts of my heart find favor before You, HASHEM, my Rock and my Redeemer.[2] *He Who makes peace in His heights, may He make peace upon us, and upon all Israel. Now respond: Amen.*

Bow and take three steps back. Bow left and say, *'He Who makes peace . . .'*; bow right and say, *'may He make peace . . .'*; bow forward and say, *'and upon . . . Amen.'*

(1) *Numbers* 6:24-26. (2) *Psalms* 19:15. (3) Cf. 34:14. (4) 60:7; 108:7.

יְהִי רָצוֹן מִלְּפָנֶיךָ יהוה אֱלֹהֵינוּ וֵאלֹהֵי אֲבוֹתֵינוּ, שֶׁיִּבָּנֶה בֵּית הַמִּקְדָּשׁ בִּמְהֵרָה בְיָמֵינוּ, וְתֵן חֶלְקֵנוּ בְּתוֹרָתֶךָ. וְשָׁם נַעֲבָדְךָ בְּיִרְאָה, כִּימֵי עוֹלָם וּכְשָׁנִים קַדְמוֹנִיּוֹת. וְעָרְבָה לַיהוה מִנְחַת יְהוּדָה וִירוּשָׁלָיִם, כִּימֵי עוֹלָם וּכְשָׁנִים קַדְמוֹנִיּוֹת.[1]

THE INDIVIDUAL'S RECITATION OF *SHEMONEH ESREI* ENDS HERE.

The individual remains standing in place until the *chazzan* reaches *Kedushah* — or at least until the *chazzan* begins his repetition — then he takes three steps forward. The *chazzan* himself, or one praying alone, should remain in place for a few moments before taking three steps forward.

סדר הושענות לחול המועד

The *Hoshana* prayers are recited with the Four Species in hand.
The Ark is opened; a Torah Scroll is removed and held at the *bimah*.
The *chazzan* recites each line which is then repeated aloud by the congregation. (See page 362.)

הוֹשַׁעְנָא, לְמַעַנְךָ אֱלֹהֵינוּ, הוֹשַׁעְנָא.
הוֹשַׁעְנָא, לְמַעַנְךָ בּוֹרְאֵנוּ, הוֹשַׁעְנָא.
הוֹשַׁעְנָא, לְמַעַנְךָ גּוֹאֲלֵנוּ, הוֹשַׁעְנָא.
הוֹשַׁעְנָא, לְמַעַנְךָ דּוֹרְשֵׁנוּ, הוֹשַׁעְנָא.

The Ark remains open during the *Hoshana* prayers. The *chazzan,* followed by every congregant that has the Four Species in hand, proceeds to walk around the *bimah*. He chants each stich of the appropriate *Hoshana* prayer (below) which is then repeated by the entire congregation.

FIRST DAY CHOL HAMOED

אֶעֱרוֹךְ שׁוּעִי. בְּבֵית שַׁוְעִי. גִּלִּיתִי בַצּוֹם פִּשְׁעִי. דְּרַשְׁתִּיךָ בּוֹ לְהוֹשִׁיעִי. הַקְשִׁיבָה לְקוֹל שַׁוְעִי. וְקוּמָה וְהוֹשִׁיעִי. זְכוֹר וְרַחֵם מוֹשִׁיעִי. חַי כֵּן תְּשַׁעְשְׁעִי. טוֹב בְּאֶנֶק שְׁעִי. יָחִישׁ מוֹשִׁיעִי. כַּלֵּה מַרְשִׁיעִי. לְבַל עוֹד תַּרְשִׁיעִי. מַהֵר אֱלֹהֵי יִשְׁעִי. נֶצַח לְהוֹשִׁיעִי. שָׂא נָא עֲוֹן רִשְׁעִי. עֲבוֹר עַל פִּשְׁעִי. פְּנֵה נָא לְהוֹשִׁיעִי. צוּר צַדִּיק מוֹשִׁיעִי. קַבֵּל נָא שַׁוְעִי. רוֹמֵם קֶרֶן יִשְׁעִי. שַׁדַּי מוֹשִׁיעִי. תּוֹפִיעַ וְתוֹשִׁיעִי.

Continue אֲנִי וָהוֹ (page 736).

SECOND DAY CHOL HAMOED

If the second day of Chol HaMoed is Sunday: אֶעֱרוֹךְ שׁוּעִי (above), is recited.
If the second day of Chol HaMoed is Tuesday: אֶבֶן שְׁתִיָּה (page 734), is recited.
If the second day of Chol HaMoed is Thursday: אוֹם אֲנִי חוֹמָה (page 734), is recited.
If the second day of Chol HaMoed is Friday: אֵל לְמוֹשָׁעוֹת (page 734), is recited.

אֶעֱרוֹךְ שׁוּעִי / I Shall Arrange My Prayer

One must always anticipate troublesome situations and pray for salvation before oppressive times arrive. R' Elazar understood this lesson from the admonition of Job's friends (*Job* 36:19): הֲיַעֲרֹךְ שׁוּעֲךָ, *Have you arranged your prayer* [beforehand in order] *that oppression not overtake you?* (*Sanhedrin* 44b).

When is the opportune time for such prayer? *Seek* [דִּרְשׁוּ] *HASHEM when He may be found; call to Him when He is near* (*Isaiah* 55:6). The Talmud asks: When *may He be found?* When is

יְהִי רָצוֹן *May it be Your will, HASHEM, our God and the God of our forefathers, that the Holy Temple be rebuilt, speedily in our days. Grant us our share in Your Torah, and may we serve You there with reverence, as in days of old and in former years. Then the offering of Judah and Jerusalem will be pleasing to HASHEM, as in days of old and in former years.*[1]

THE INDIVIDUAL'S RECITATION OF *SHEMONEH ESREI* ENDS HERE.

The individual remains standing in place until the *chazzan* reaches *Kedushah* — or at least until the *chazzan* begins his repetition — then he takes three steps forward. The *chazzan* himself, or one praying alone, should remain in place for a few moments before taking three steps forward.

HOSHANOS FOR CHOL HAMOED

The *Hoshana* prayers are recited with the Four Species in hand.
The Ark is opened; a Torah Scroll is removed and held at the *bimah*.
The *chazzan* recites each line which is then repeated aloud by the congregation. (See page 362.)

הוֹשַׁעְנָא *Please save — for Your sake, our God! Please save!*
Please save — for Your sake, our Creator! Please save!
Please save — for Your sake, our Redeemer! Please save!
Please save — for Your sake, our Attender! Please save!

The Ark remains open during the *Hoshana* prayers. The *chazzan*, followed by every congregant that has the Four Species in hand, proceeds to walk around the *bimah*. He chants each stich of the appropriate *Hoshana* prayer (below) which is then repeated by the entire congregation.

FIRST DAY CHOL HAMOED

אֶעֱרוֹךְ שׁוּעִי *I shall arrange my prayer* ב *in the house of prayer:* ג *I have bared, on the fast day, my transgression;* ד *I have sought You on that day for salvation.* ה *Harken to the sound of my outcry;* ו *arise and save me;* ז *remember and be merciful, my Savior.* ח *Living God — in Your faithfulness let me rejoice.* ט *Goodly One — turn to my groan,* י *may my savior hasten.* כ *Destroy the one who tempts me to sin,* ל *that he may no longer incriminate me.* מ *Hasten, God of my salvation,* נ *eternally to save me.* ס *Please, pardon the iniquity of my wickedness,* ע *overlook my transgression,* פ *turn, now, and save me.* צ *Rock, Righteous One, You are my Savior —* ק *accept now my prayer,* ר *elevate the pride of my salvation.* ש *Almighty — my Savior,* ת *shine Your countenance upon me and save me.*

Continue *ANI VAHO* (page 736).

SECOND DAY CHOL HAMOED

If the second day of Chol HaMoed is Sunday: *'I shall arrange ...'* (above), is recited.
If the second day of Chol HaMoed is Tuesday: *'Foundation stone ...'* (page 734), is recited.
If the second day of Chol HaMoed is Thursday: *'Nation [that declares]...'* (page 734), is recited.
If the second day of Chol HaMoed is Friday: *'O God! Bring about salvations ...'* (page 734), is recited.

(1) *Malachi* 3:4.

He near? And answers: During the Ten Days [of Repentance] beginning with Rosh Hashanah and culminating with Yom Kippur (*Rosh Hashanah* 18a).

Now Israel prays that God recall its repentance during the period when God called for it. In response to my having *bared my transgression* before You on Yom Kippur, may You *pardon the iniquity of my wickedness and overlook my transgression.* Just as *I sought You on that day, for salvation,* You, in turn arise ... remember and be merciful, my Savior.

אֶבֶן שְׁתִיָּה. בֵּית הַבְּחִירָה. גֹּרֶן אָרְנָן. דְּבִיר הַמֻּצְנָע. הַר הַמּוֹרִיָּה. וְהַר יֵרָאֶה. זְבוּל תִּפְאַרְתֶּךָ. חָנָה דָוִד. טוֹב הַלְּבָנוֹן. יְפֵה נוֹף מְשׂוֹשׂ כָּל הָאָרֶץ. כְּלִילַת יֹפִי. לִינַת הַצֶּדֶק. מָכוֹן לְשִׁבְתֶּךָ. נָוֶה שַׁאֲנָן. סֻכַּת שָׁלֵם. עֲלִיַּת שְׁבָטִים. פִּנַּת יִקְרַת. צִיּוֹן הַמְּצֻיֶּנֶת. קֹדֶשׁ הַקֳּדָשִׁים. רָצוּף אַהֲבָה. שְׁכִינַת כְּבוֹדֶךָ. תֵּל תַּלְפִּיּוֹת.

Continue אֲנִי וָהוֹ (page 736).

אוֹם אֲנִי חוֹמָה.* בָּרָה כַּחַמָּה.* גּוֹלָה וְסוּרָה. דָּמְתָה לְתָמָר.* הַהֲרוּגָה עָלֶיךָ. וְנֶחְשֶׁבֶת כְּצֹאן טִבְחָה. זְרוּיָה בֵּין מַכְעִיסֶיהָ. חֲבוּקָה וּדְבוּקָה בָּךְ. טוֹעֶנֶת עֻלָּךְ. יְחִידָה לְיַחֲדָךְ. כְּבוּשָׁה בַּגּוֹלָה. לוֹמֶדֶת יִרְאָתָךְ. מְרוּטַת לֶחִי.* נְתוּנָה לְמַכִּים. סוֹבֶלֶת סִבְלָךְ. עֲנִיָּה סֹעֲרָה. פְּדוּיַת טוֹבִיָּה.* צֹאן קָדָשִׁים. קְהִלּוֹת יַעֲקֹב. רְשׁוּמִים בִּשְׁמֶךָ.* שׁוֹאֲגִים הוֹשַׁעְנָא. תְּמוּכִים עָלֶיךָ.

Continue אֲנִי וָהוֹ (page 736).

THIRD DAY CHOL HAMOED

אֵל לְמוֹשָׁעוֹת. בְּאַרְבַּע שְׁבֻעוֹת.* גָּשִׁים בְּשַׁוְעוֹת. דּוֹפְקֵי עֶרֶךְ שׁוּעוֹת.* הוֹגֵי שַׁעֲשֻׁעוֹת. וְחִידוֹתָם* מִשְׁתַּעַשְׁעוֹת. זֹעֲקִים לְהִשָּׁעוֹת. חוֹכֵי יְשׁוּעוֹת. טְפוּלִים בָּךְ שְׁעוֹת. יוֹדְעֵי בִּין שָׁעוֹת.* כּוֹרְעֶיךָ בְּשַׁוְעוֹת. לְהָבִין שְׁמוּעוֹת.* מֵפִיק נִשְׁמָעוֹת. נוֹתֵן תְּשׁוּעוֹת. סְפוּרוֹת מַשְׁמָעוֹת.* עֵדוּת מַשְׁמִיעוֹת. פּוֹעֵל יְשׁוּעוֹת. צַדִּיק נוֹשָׁעוֹת. קִרְיַת תְּשׁוּעוֹת. רֶגֶשׁ תְּשֻׁאוֹת. שָׁלֹשׁ שָׁעוֹת.* תָּחִישׁ לִתְשׁוּעוֹת.*

Continue אֲנִי וָהוֹ (page 736).

אֶבֶן שְׁתִיָּה – *Foundation stone.* Commentary to this *hoshana* appears on page 363.

אוֹם אֲנִי חוֹמָה – *Nation [that declares].* Commentary to this *hoshana* appears on page 776.

אֲדוֹן הַמּוֹשִׁיעַ – *Lord Who saves.* Commentary to this *hoshana* appears on page 778.

אֵל לְמוֹשָׁעוֹת / O God! Bring About Salvations

בְּאַרְבַּע שְׁבֻעוֹת — *Because of [the] four oaths.* Four times God turned to Israel and adjured them — as indicated by the four times *Song of Songs* uses the expression הִשְׁבַּעְתִּי אֶתְכֶם בְּנוֹת יְרוּשָׁלַיִם, *I have adjured you, O daughters of Jerusalem* (2:7; 3:5; 5:8; 8:4). R' Chelbo taught that God demanded four oaths of Israel regarding their exile: (a) That they not rebel against the governments [of the lands in which they are dispersed]; (b) that they not delay the end [i.e., by their sins *(Rashi)*]; (c) that they not reveal the mysteries [i.e., the depths of Torah knowledge *(Rashi)*] to the nations; and (d) that they not seek to end their exile by armed force or great masses. God adjured them for otherwise why should the Messiah come to gather in Israel from the Diaspora? *(Shir HaShirim Rabbah* 2:7). We follow the four oaths and rely on You alone. Therefore, O God! Bring about salvation.

A variant reading is בְּאַרְבָּעָה שָׁבוּעוֹת, *in four weeks,* and is a reference to the week before Rosh Hashanah, during which סְלִיחוֹת, *prayers for forgiveness,* are said each morning before daybreak, along with the first three weeks of Tishrei which end on Hoshana Rabbah, the day the final seal is placed on the verdict which had been written on Rosh Hashanah.

עֶרֶךְ שׁוּעוֹת — *Where prayers are arranged,* the synagogue (see *Job* 36:19).

וְחִידוֹתָם — *And their riddles.* This refers to the Oral Torah — the Talmud and its commentaries. Many of the teachings of the Talmudic Sages are terse and cryptic, requiring intense study to decipher them.

יוֹדְעֵי בִּין שָׁעוֹת — *They know the understanding of the hours* [i.e., times]. They know which hours and times are propitious for prayer. They know

אֶבֶן שְׁתִיָּה *Foundation stone;* ב *chosen Temple;* ג *Arnan's granary;* ד *hidden rendezvous;* ה *Mount Moriah;* ו *Mount He-is-seen;* ז *residence of Your Splendor;* ח *where David resided;* ט *goodness of Lebanon;* י *fairest of brides; joy of all the earth;* כ *perfectly beautiful;* ל *lodge of righteousness;* מ *prepared for Your dwelling;* נ *tranquil abode;* ס *Tabernacle of Salem;* ע *pilgrimage of the tribes;* פ *valuable cornerstone;* צ *the distinguished Zion;* ק *Holy of Holies;* ר *decked with love;* ש *resting place of Your Honor;* ת *hill of Talpios.*

Continue *ANI VAHO* (page 736).

אוֹם אֲנִי חוֹמָה *Nation [that declares], 'I am a wall!'* ב *Brilliant as the sun —* ג *yet exiled and displaced;* ד *likened to a palm tree —* ה *yet murdered for Your sake* ו *and regarded like a sheep for slaughter;* ז *although scattered among her provocateurs,* ח *she hugs and cleaves to You* ט *bearing Your yoke —* י *unique in declaring Your Oneness.* כ *While vanquished in exile,* ל *she learns Your awesomeness.* מ *Plucked of cheek,* נ *given over to the whippers,* ס *she shoulders Your burden.* ע *A storm-tossed pauper,* פ *she who was redeemed by Moses.* צ *Sacred sheep,* ק *congregations of Jacob,* ר *inscribed with Your Name,* ש *they cry, 'Please save us!' —* ת *they rely upon You!*

Continue *ANI VAHO* (page 736).

THIRD DAY CHOL HAMOED

אֵל לְמוֹשָׁעוֹת *O God! Bring about salvations* ב *because of the four oaths** ג *of those who approach with pleas.* ד *They knock on the doors where prayers are arranged;** ה *they meditate upon the beloved Torah* ו *and their riddles* are beloved;* ז *they cry for attention;* ח *they yearn for salvation;* ט *they cling to You, to You they turn.* י *They know the understanding of the hours,** כ *yet they kneel before You pleading* ל *that they may understand the lessons** מ *which were heard from Your mouth.* נ *O Grantor of salvations,* ס *gather the counters** ע *that teach the testimony.* פ *O Worker of salvations,* צ *send [the Messiah] the righteous one who will find salvation.* ק *For the city of salvations,* ר *swarming with masses,* ש *during the three hours,** ת *hasten the time of salvations.**

Continue *ANI VAHO* (page 736).

---

that the Ten Days of Awe are the days when Hashem may be found, when He is near to respond to prayers.

לְהָבִין שְׁמוּעוֹת — *That they understand the lessons.* Although they are well learned and wise in the intricacies of Halachah, nevertheless, they turn to You praying that You grant them an even deeper understanding of the Torah that they heard directly from Your mouth at Sinai.

סְפוּרוֹת מַשְׁמָעוֹת — *Gather the counters.* The sages are referred to as סוֹפְרִים, *counters,* for various reasons:

— They arrange the laws of the Torah into mnemonic groupings which are identified by number, e.g., there are four classifications of damage (*Bava Kama* 1:1).

— They study the verses which speak of the End of Days and attempt to calculate the date of Messiah's coming.

— They count every letter of the Torah [and explain its purpose and the lessons to be derived from it].

שָׁלֹשׁ שָׁעוֹת — *[During the] three hours.* God divided the twelve hours of daylight into four periods of three hours each. During the first of these periods, He sits and engages in Torah study. Another three hours He spends judging the world; should He see that strict justice demands the destruction of the world, He [so to speak] rises from the Throne of Justice and sits on the Throne of Mercy. For three more hours He supplies the entire universe with sustenance . . . (*Avodah Zarah* 3:2).

תָּחִישׁ לִתְשׁוּעוֹת — *Hasten the time of salvations.* We beseech God to hasten salvations during the three hours in which He judges His world (*Rashi*), and to support us during the three hours that he provides our means of sustenance.

FOURTH DAY CHOL HAMOED

אָדוֹן הַמּוֹשִׁיעַ. **בּ**ִלְתְּךָ אֵין לְהוֹשִׁיעַ. **ג**ִּבּוֹר וְרַב לְהוֹשִׁיעַ. **ד**ַּלּוֹתִי וְלִי יְהוֹשִׁיעַ. **ה**ָאֵל הַמּוֹשִׁיעַ. **וּ**מַצִּיל וּמוֹשִׁיעַ. **ז**וֹעֲקֶיךָ תּוֹשִׁיעַ. **ח**וֹכֶיךָ הוֹשִׁיעַ. **ט**ְלָאֶיךָ תַּשְׂבִּיעַ. **י**ְבוּל לְהַשְׁפִּיעַ. **כּ**ָל שִׂיחַ תַּדְשֵׁא וְתוֹשִׁיעַ. **ל**ְגֵיא בַּל תַּרְשִׁיעַ. **מ**ְגָדִים תַּמְתִּיק וְתוֹשִׁיעַ. **נ**ְשִׂיאִים לְהַסִּיעַ. **שׂ**ְעִירִים לְהָנִיעַ. **ע**ֲנָנִים מִלְּהַמְנִיעַ. **פּ**וֹתֵחַ יָד וּמַשְׂבִּיעַ. **צ**ְמֵאֶיךָ תַּשְׂבִּיעַ. **ק**וֹרְאֶיךָ תּוֹשִׁיעַ. **ר**ְחוּמֶיךָ תּוֹשִׁיעַ. **שׁ**וֹחֲרֶיךָ הוֹשִׁיעַ. **ת**ְּמִימֶיךָ תּוֹשִׁיעַ.

After each day's *hakafah*-circuit, the following *Hoshana* is recited:

אֲנִי וָהוֹ הוֹשִׁיעָה נָּא.

כְּהוֹשַׁעְתָּ אֵלִים בְּלוּד עִמָּךְ,
בְּצֵאתְךָ לְיֵשַׁע עַמָּךְ, כֵּן הוֹשַׁעְנָא.
כְּהוֹשַׁעְתָּ גּוֹי וֵאלֹהִים,
דְּרוּשִׁים לְיֵשַׁע אֱלֹהִים, כֵּן הוֹשַׁעְנָא.
כְּהוֹשַׁעְתָּ הֲמוֹן צְבָאוֹת,
וְעִמָּם מַלְאֲכֵי צְבָאוֹת, כֵּן הוֹשַׁעְנָא.
כְּהוֹשַׁעְתָּ זַכִּים מִבֵּית עֲבָדִים,
חַנּוּן בְּיָדָם מַעֲבִידִים, כֵּן הוֹשַׁעְנָא.
כְּהוֹשַׁעְתָּ טְבוּעִים בְּצוּל גְּזָרִים,
יְקָרְךָ עִמָּם מַעֲבִירִים, כֵּן הוֹשַׁעְנָא.
כְּהוֹשַׁעְתָּ כַּנָּה מְשׁוֹרֶרֶת וַיּוֹשַׁע,
לְגוֹחָהּ מְצֻיֶּנֶת וַיִּוָּשַׁע, כֵּן הוֹשַׁעְנָא.
כְּהוֹשַׁעְתָּ מַאֲמַר וְהוֹצֵאתִי אֶתְכֶם,
נָקוּב וְהוּצֵאתִי אִתְּכֶם, כֵּן הוֹשַׁעְנָא.
כְּהוֹשַׁעְתָּ סוֹבְבֵי מִזְבֵּחַ,
עוֹמְסֵי עֲרָבָה לְהַקִּיף מִזְבֵּחַ, כֵּן הוֹשַׁעְנָא.
כְּהוֹשַׁעְתָּ פִּלְאֵי אָרוֹן כְּהֻפְשַׁע,
צִעֵר פְּלֶשֶׁת בַּחֲרוֹן אַף וְנוֹשַׁע, כֵּן הוֹשַׁעְנָא.
כְּהוֹשַׁעְתָּ קְהִלּוֹת בָּבֶלָה שִׁלַּחְתָּ,
רַחוּם לְמַעֲנָם שֻׁלַּחְתָּ, כֵּן הוֹשַׁעְנָא.
כְּהוֹשַׁעְתָּ שְׁבוּת שִׁבְטֵי יַעֲקֹב,
תָּשׁוּב וְתָשִׁיב שְׁבוּת אָהֳלֵי יַעֲקֹב, וְהוֹשִׁיעָה נָּא.
כְּהוֹשַׁעְתָּ שׁוֹמְרֵי מִצְוֹת, וְחוֹכֵי יְשׁוּעוֹת,
אֵל לְמוֹשָׁעוֹת, וְהוֹשִׁיעָה נָּא.

FOURTH DAY CHOL HAMOED

אָדוֹן הַמּוֹשִׁיעַ *Lord Who saves, other than You there is no savior.* ג *You are powerful and abundantly able to save.* ד *I am impoverished, yet You shall save me.* ה *God is the Savior,* ו *He delivers and saves.* ז *Those who cry to You — save;* ח *those who yearn for You — save.* ט *Satiate Your lambs,* י *cause an abundance of crops,* כ *of trees, of vegetation — save.* ל *Do not condemn the ground,* מ *but sweeten the luscious fruits — save.* נ *Let the wind bring the soaring clouds,* ס *let the stormy rains be emplaced,* ע *let the clouds not be withheld,* פ *He Who opens a hand and satisfies,* צ *Your thirsty ones — satisfy;* ק *Your callers — save;* ר *Your beloved — save;* ש *Your seekers — save;* ת *Your wholesome ones — save.*

After each day's *hakafah*-circuit, the following *Hoshana* is recited:

ANI VAHO, bring salvation now.

כְּהוֹשַׁעְתָּ אֵלִים *As You saved the terebinths in Lud [Egypt] along with Yourself*
ב *when You went forth to save the nation — so save now.*

ג *As You saved the nation and its leaders*
ד *who sought the salvations of God — so save now.*

ה *As You saved the multitudes of hosts*
ו *and with them the hosts of angels — so save now.*

ז *As You saved pure ones from the house of slavery,*
ח *Gracious One, from those who forced manual labor upon them — so save now.*

ט *As You saved those sinking in the depths of the rifts,*
י *Your honor was with them when they crossed — so save now.*

כ *As You saved the garden which sang 'He delivered,'*
ל *regarding Him Who draws forth it is pronounced 'He was delivered' — so save now.*

מ *As You saved with the declaration 'I shall bring you forth,'*
נ *which may be interpreted, 'I shall be brought forth with you' — so save now.*

ס *As You saved those who went roundabout with the Altar,*
ע *those who carry the willow to encircle the Altar — so save now.*

פ *As You saved the Ark of the Name, captured as a result of sin,*
צ *when you punished Philistia with flaming anger, and it was saved — so save now.*

ק *As You saved the congregations which You had sent to Babylon,*
ר *Merciful One, for their sake were You also sent — so save now.*

ש *As You saved the captivity of the tribes of Jacob,*
ת *return and restore the captivity of the tents of Jacob, and bring salvation now.*

As You saved those observant of mitzvos, and hopeful for salvation — O God Who brings about salvation, bring salvation now.

אֲנִי וָהוֹ הוֹשִׁיעָה נָּא.

הוֹשִׁיעָה אֶת עַמֶּךָ, וּבָרֵךְ אֶת נַחֲלָתֶךָ, וּרְעֵם וְנַשְּׂאֵם עַד הָעוֹלָם.[1] וְיִהְיוּ דְבָרַי אֵלֶּה אֲשֶׁר הִתְחַנַּנְתִּי לִפְנֵי יהוה, קְרֹבִים אֶל יהוה אֱלֹהֵינוּ יוֹמָם וָלָיְלָה, לַעֲשׂוֹת מִשְׁפַּט עַבְדּוֹ וּמִשְׁפַּט עַמּוֹ יִשְׂרָאֵל, דְּבַר יוֹם בְּיוֹמוֹ. לְמַעַן דַּעַת כָּל עַמֵּי הָאָרֶץ, כִּי יהוה הוּא הָאֱלֹהִים, אֵין עוֹד.[2]

Congregations that recite *Hoshanos* after *Hallel* turn to page 702.

קדיש שלם

The *chazzan* recites קַדִּישׁ שָׁלֵם.

יִתְגַּדַּל וְיִתְקַדַּשׁ שְׁמֵהּ רַבָּא. (.Cong – אָמֵן.) בְּעָלְמָא דִּי בְרָא כִרְעוּתֵהּ. וְיַמְלִיךְ מַלְכוּתֵהּ, בְּחַיֵּיכוֹן וּבְיוֹמֵיכוֹן וּבְחַיֵּי דְכָל בֵּית יִשְׂרָאֵל, בַּעֲגָלָא וּבִזְמַן קָרִיב. וְאִמְרוּ: אָמֵן.

(.Cong – אָמֵן. יְהֵא שְׁמֵהּ רַבָּא מְבָרַךְ לְעָלַם וּלְעָלְמֵי עָלְמַיָּא.)

יְהֵא שְׁמֵהּ רַבָּא מְבָרַךְ לְעָלַם וּלְעָלְמֵי עָלְמַיָּא.

יִתְבָּרַךְ וְיִשְׁתַּבַּח וְיִתְפָּאַר וְיִתְרוֹמַם וְיִתְנַשֵּׂא וְיִתְהַדָּר וְיִתְעַלֶּה וְיִתְהַלָּל שְׁמֵהּ דְּקֻדְשָׁא בְּרִיךְ הוּא (.Cong – בְּרִיךְ הוּא) — לְעֵלָּא מִן כָּל בִּרְכָתָא וְשִׁירָתָא תֻּשְׁבְּחָתָא וְנֶחֱמָתָא, דַּאֲמִירָן בְּעָלְמָא. וְאִמְרוּ: אָמֵן. (.Cong – אָמֵן.)

(.Cong – קַבֵּל בְּרַחֲמִים וּבְרָצוֹן אֶת תְּפִלָּתֵנוּ.)

תִּתְקַבֵּל צְלוֹתְהוֹן וּבָעוּתְהוֹן דְּכָל בֵּית יִשְׂרָאֵל קֳדָם אֲבוּהוֹן דִּי בִשְׁמַיָּא. וְאִמְרוּ: אָמֵן. (.Cong – אָמֵן.)

(.Cong – יְהִי שֵׁם יהוה מְבֹרָךְ, מֵעַתָּה וְעַד עוֹלָם.[3])

יְהֵא שְׁלָמָא רַבָּא מִן שְׁמַיָּא, וְחַיִּים עָלֵינוּ וְעַל כָּל יִשְׂרָאֵל. וְאִמְרוּ: אָמֵן. (.Cong – אָמֵן.)

(.Cong – עֶזְרִי מֵעִם יהוה, עֹשֵׂה שָׁמַיִם וָאָרֶץ.[4])

Take three steps back. Bow left and say . . . עֹשֶׂה; bow right and say . . . הוּא; bow forward and say וְעַל כָּל . . . אָמֵן. Remain standing in place for a few moments, then take three steps forward.

עֹשֶׂה שָׁלוֹם בִּמְרוֹמָיו, הוּא יַעֲשֶׂה שָׁלוֹם עָלֵינוּ, וְעַל כָּל יִשְׂרָאֵל. וְאִמְרוּ: אָמֵן. (.Cong – אָמֵן.)

Stand while reciting עָלֵינוּ.

עָלֵינוּ לְשַׁבֵּחַ לַאֲדוֹן הַכֹּל, לָתֵת גְּדֻלָּה לְיוֹצֵר בְּרֵאשִׁית, שֶׁלֹּא עָשָׂנוּ כְּגוֹיֵי הָאֲרָצוֹת, וְלֹא שָׂמָנוּ כְּמִשְׁפְּחוֹת הָאֲדָמָה. שֶׁלֹּא שָׂם חֶלְקֵנוּ כָּהֶם, וְגוֹרָלֵנוּ כְּכָל הֲמוֹנָם. (שֶׁהֵם מִשְׁתַּחֲוִים לְהֶבֶל וָרִיק, וּמִתְפַּלְלִים אֶל אֵל לֹא יוֹשִׁיעַ.[5]) וַאֲנַחְנוּ כּוֹרְעִים וּמִשְׁתַּחֲוִים וּמוֹדִים, לִפְנֵי מֶלֶךְ מַלְכֵי הַמְּלָכִים הַקָּדוֹשׁ בָּרוּךְ הוּא. שֶׁהוּא נוֹטֶה שָׁמַיִם וְיֹסֵד אָרֶץ,[6] וּמוֹשַׁב יְקָרוֹ בַּשָּׁמַיִם מִמַּעַל, וּשְׁכִינַת עֻזּוֹ בְּגָבְהֵי מְרוֹמִים.

Bow while reciting וַאֲנַחְנוּ כּוֹרְעִים וּמִשְׁתַּחֲוִים.

ANI VAHO, bring salvation now.

הוֹשִׁיעָה *Save Your people and bless Your heritage, tend them and elevate them forever.*[1] *May these words of mine, which I have supplicated before* HASHEM, *be near to* HASHEM, *our God, by day and by night; that He bring about justice for His servant and justice for His people, Israel, each day's need in its day; that all the peoples of the earth shall know that* HASHEM *is God — there is no other.*[2]

The Torah is returned to the Ark.

Congregations that recite *Hoshanos* after *Hallel,* turn to page 702.

FULL KADDISH

The *chazzan* recites the Full *Kaddish.*

יִתְגַּדַּל *May His great Name grow exalted and sanctified* (Cong.– *Amen.*) *in the world that He created as He willed. May He give reign to His kingship in your lifetimes and in your days, and in the lifetimes of the entire Family of Israel, swiftly and soon. Now respond: Amen.*

(Cong.– *Amen. May His great Name be blessed forever and ever.*)

May His great Name be blessed forever and ever.

Blessed, praised, glorified, exalted, extolled, mighty, upraised, and lauded be the Name of the Holy One, Blessed is He (Cong.– *Blessed is He*) *— beyond any blessing and song, praise and consolation that are uttered in the world. Now respond: Amen.* (Cong.– *Amen.*)

(Cong.– *Accept our prayers with mercy and favor.*)

May the prayers and supplications of the entire Family of Israel be accepted before their Father Who is in Heaven. Now respond: Amen. (Cong.– *Amen.*)

(Cong.– *Blessed be the Name of* HASHEM, *from this time and forever.*[3])

May there be abundant peace from Heaven, and life, upon us and upon all Israel. Now respond: Amen. (Cong.– *Amen.*)

(Cong.– *My help is from* HASHEM, *Maker of heaven and earth.*[4])

Take three steps back. Bow left and say, *'He Who makes peace . . .';* bow right and say, *'may He . . .';* bow forward and say, *'and upon all Israel . . .'* Remain standing in place for a few moments, then take three steps forward.

He Who makes peace in His heights, may He make peace upon us, and upon all Israel. Now respond: Amen. (Cong.– *Amen.*)

Stand while reciting עָלֵינוּ, *'It is our duty . . .'*

עָלֵינוּ *It is our duty to praise the Master of all, to ascribe greatness to the Molder of primeval creation, for He has not made us like the nations of the lands, and has not emplaced us like the families of the earth; for He has not assigned our portion like theirs nor our lot like all their multitudes. (For they bow to vanity and emptiness and pray to a god which helps not.*[5]*) But we bend our knees, bow, and acknowledge our thanks before the King Who reigns over kings, the Holy One, Blessed is He. He stretches out heaven and establishes earth's foundation,*[6] *the seat of His homage is in the heavens above and His powerful Presence is in the loftiest heights.*

Bow while reciting *'But we bend our knees.'*

(1) *Psalms* 28:9. (2) *I Kings* 8:59-60. (3) *Psalms* 113:2. (4) 121:2. (5) *Isaiah* 45:20. (6) 51:13.

הוּא אֱלֹהֵינוּ, אֵין עוֹד. אֱמֶת מַלְכֵּנוּ, אֶפֶס זוּלָתוֹ, כַּכָּתוּב בְּתוֹרָתוֹ: וְיָדַעְתָּ הַיּוֹם וַהֲשֵׁבֹתָ אֶל לְבָבֶךָ, כִּי יהוה הוּא הָאֱלֹהִים בַּשָּׁמַיִם מִמַּעַל וְעַל הָאָרֶץ מִתָּחַת, אֵין עוֹד.[1]

עַל כֵּן נְקַוֶּה לְּךָ יהוה אֱלֹהֵינוּ לִרְאוֹת מְהֵרָה בְּתִפְאֶרֶת עֻזֶּךָ, לְהַעֲבִיר גִּלּוּלִים מִן הָאָרֶץ, וְהָאֱלִילִים כָּרוֹת יִכָּרֵתוּן, לְתַקֵּן עוֹלָם בְּמַלְכוּת שַׁדַּי. וְכָל בְּנֵי בָשָׂר יִקְרְאוּ בִשְׁמֶךָ, לְהַפְנוֹת אֵלֶיךָ כָּל רִשְׁעֵי אָרֶץ. יַכִּירוּ וְיֵדְעוּ כָּל יוֹשְׁבֵי תֵבֵל, כִּי לְךָ תִּכְרַע כָּל בֶּרֶךְ, תִּשָּׁבַע כָּל לָשׁוֹן.[2] לְפָנֶיךָ יהוה אֱלֹהֵינוּ יִכְרְעוּ וְיִפֹּלוּ, וְלִכְבוֹד שִׁמְךָ יְקָר יִתֵּנוּ. וִיקַבְּלוּ כֻלָּם אֶת עוֹל מַלְכוּתֶךָ, וְתִמְלֹךְ עֲלֵיהֶם מְהֵרָה לְעוֹלָם וָעֶד. כִּי הַמַּלְכוּת שֶׁלְּךָ הִיא וּלְעוֹלְמֵי עַד תִּמְלוֹךְ בְּכָבוֹד, כַּכָּתוּב בְּתוֹרָתֶךָ: יהוה יִמְלֹךְ לְעֹלָם וָעֶד.[3] ❖ וְנֶאֱמַר: וְהָיָה יהוה לְמֶלֶךְ עַל כָּל הָאָרֶץ, בַּיּוֹם הַהוּא יִהְיֶה יהוה אֶחָד וּשְׁמוֹ אֶחָד.[4]

Some congregations recite the following after עָלֵינוּ:

אַל תִּירָא מִפַּחַד פִּתְאֹם, וּמִשֹּׁאַת רְשָׁעִים כִּי תָבֹא.[5] עֻצוּ עֵצָה וְתֻפָר, דַּבְּרוּ דָבָר וְלֹא יָקוּם, כִּי עִמָּנוּ אֵל.[6] וְעַד זִקְנָה אֲנִי הוּא, וְעַד שֵׂיבָה אֲנִי אֶסְבֹּל, אֲנִי עָשִׂיתִי וַאֲנִי אֶשָּׂא, וַאֲנִי אֶסְבֹּל וַאֲמַלֵּט.[7]

קדיש יתום

In the presence of a *minyan,* mourners recite קַדִּישׁ יָתוֹם, the Mourner's *Kaddish* (see *Laws* §81-83):

יִתְגַּדַּל וְיִתְקַדַּשׁ שְׁמֵהּ רַבָּא. (.Cong – אָמֵן.) בְּעָלְמָא דִּי בְרָא כִרְעוּתֵהּ. וְיַמְלִיךְ מַלְכוּתֵהּ, בְּחַיֵּיכוֹן וּבְיוֹמֵיכוֹן וּבְחַיֵּי דְכָל בֵּית יִשְׂרָאֵל, בַּעֲגָלָא וּבִזְמַן קָרִיב. וְאִמְרוּ: אָמֵן.

(.Cong – אָמֵן. יְהֵא שְׁמֵהּ רַבָּא מְבָרַךְ לְעָלַם וּלְעָלְמֵי עָלְמַיָּא.)

יְהֵא שְׁמֵהּ רַבָּא מְבָרַךְ לְעָלַם וּלְעָלְמֵי עָלְמַיָּא.

יִתְבָּרַךְ וְיִשְׁתַּבַּח וְיִתְפָּאַר וְיִתְרוֹמַם וְיִתְנַשֵּׂא וְיִתְהַדָּר וְיִתְעַלֶּה וְיִתְהַלָּל שְׁמֵהּ דְּקֻדְשָׁא בְּרִיךְ הוּא (.Cong – בְּרִיךְ הוּא) — לְעֵלָּא מִן כָּל בִּרְכָתָא וְשִׁירָתָא תֻּשְׁבְּחָתָא וְנֶחֱמָתָא, דַּאֲמִירָן בְּעָלְמָא. וְאִמְרוּ: אָמֵן. (.Cong – אָמֵן.)

יְהֵא שְׁלָמָא רַבָּא מִן שְׁמַיָּא, וְחַיִּים עָלֵינוּ וְעַל כָּל יִשְׂרָאֵל. וְאִמְרוּ: אָמֵן. (.Cong – אָמֵן.)

Take three steps back. Bow left and say . . . עֹשֶׂה; bow right and say . . . הוּא; bow forward and say וְעַל כָּל . . . אָמֵן. Remain standing in place for a few moments, then take three steps forward.

עֹשֶׂה שָׁלוֹם בִּמְרוֹמָיו, הוּא יַעֲשֶׂה שָׁלוֹם עָלֵינוּ, וְעַל כָּל יִשְׂרָאֵל. וְאִמְרוּ: אָמֵן. (.Cong – אָמֵן.)

He is our God and there is none other. True is our King, there is nothing beside Him, as it is written in His Torah: 'You are to know this day and take to your heart that HASHEM is the only God — in heaven above and on the earth below — there is none other.'[1]

עַל כֵּן *Therefore we put our hope in You, HASHEM, our God, that we may soon see Your mighty splendor, to remove detestable idolatry from the earth, and false gods will be utterly cut off, to perfect the universe through the Almighty's sovereignty. Then all humanity will call upon Your Name, to turn all the earth's wicked toward You. All the world's inhabitants will recognize and know that to You every knee should bend, every tongue should swear.*[2] *Before You, HASHEM, our God, they will bend every knee and cast themselves down and to the glory of Your Name they will render homage, and they will all accept upon themselves the yoke of Your kingship that You may reign over them soon and eternally. For the kingdom is Yours and You will reign for all eternity in glory as it is written in Your Torah: HASHEM shall reign for all eternity.*[3] Chazzan– *And it is said: HASHEM will be King over all the world — on that day HASHEM will be One and His Name will be One.*[4]

Some congregations recite the following after *Aleinu.*

אַל תִּירָא *Do not fear sudden terror, or the holocaust of the wicked when it comes.*[5] *Plan a conspiracy and it will be annulled; speak your piece and it shall not stand, for God is with us.*[6] *Even till your seniority, I remain unchanged; and even till your ripe old age, I shall endure. I created you and I shall bear you; I shall endure and rescue.*[7]

MOURNER'S KADDISH

In the presence of a *minyan,* mourners recite קַדִּישׁ יָתוֹם, the Mourner's *Kaddish* (see *Laws* §81-83).
[A transliteration of this *Kaddish* appears on p. 1305.]

יִתְגַּדַּל *May His great Name grow exalted and sanctified* (Cong.– *Amen.*) *in the world that He created as He willed. May He give reign to His kingship in your lifetimes and in your days, and in the lifetimes of the entire Family of Israel, swiftly and soon. Now respond: Amen.*

(Cong.– *Amen. May His great Name be blessed forever and ever.*)
May His great Name be blessed forever and ever.

Blessed, praised, glorified, exalted, extolled, mighty, upraised, and lauded be the Name of the Holy One, Blessed is He (Cong.– *Blessed is He*) *— beyond any blessing and song, praise and consolation that are uttered in the world. Now respond: Amen.* (Cong.– *Amen*).

May there be abundant peace from Heaven, and life, upon us and upon all Israel. Now respond: Amen. (Cong.– *Amen.*)

Take three steps back. Bow left and say, *'He Who makes peace . . .';* bow right and say, *'may He . . .';* bow forward and say, *'and upon all Israel . . .'* Remain standing in place for a few moments, then take three steps forward.

He Who makes peace in His heights, may He make peace upon us, and upon all Israel. Now respond: Amen. (Cong.– *Amen.*)

---

(1) *Deuteronomy* 4:39. (2) Cf. *Isaiah* 45:23. (3) *Exodus* 15:18.
(4) *Zechariah* 14:9. (5) *Proverbs* 3:25. (6) *Isaiah* 8:10. (7) 46:4.

שיר של יום

A different apsalm is assigned as the *Song of the Day* for each day of the week (see p. 388).

SUNDAY

הַיּוֹם יוֹם רִאשׁוֹן בַּשַּׁבָּת, שֶׁבּוֹ הָיוּ הַלְוִיִּם אוֹמְרִים בְּבֵית הַמִּקְדָּשׁ:

תהלים כד

לְדָוִד מִזְמוֹר, לַיהוה הָאָרֶץ וּמְלוֹאָהּ, תֵּבֵל וְיֹשְׁבֵי בָהּ. כִּי הוּא עַל יַמִּים יְסָדָהּ, וְעַל נְהָרוֹת יְכוֹנְנֶהָ. מִי יַעֲלֶה בְהַר יהוה, וּמִי יָקוּם בִּמְקוֹם קָדְשׁוֹ. נְקִי כַפַּיִם וּבַר לֵבָב, אֲשֶׁר לֹא נָשָׂא לַשָּׁוְא נַפְשִׁי, וְלֹא נִשְׁבַּע לְמִרְמָה. יִשָּׂא בְרָכָה מֵאֵת יהוה, וּצְדָקָה מֵאֱלֹהֵי יִשְׁעוֹ. זֶה דּוֹר דֹּרְשָׁיו, מְבַקְשֵׁי פָנֶיךָ יַעֲקֹב סֶלָה. שְׂאוּ שְׁעָרִים רָאשֵׁיכֶם, וְהִנָּשְׂאוּ פִּתְחֵי עוֹלָם, וְיָבוֹא מֶלֶךְ הַכָּבוֹד. מִי זֶה מֶלֶךְ הַכָּבוֹד, יהוה עִזּוּז וְגִבּוֹר, יהוה גִּבּוֹר מִלְחָמָה. ❖ שְׂאוּ שְׁעָרִים רָאשֵׁיכֶם, וּשְׂאוּ פִּתְחֵי עוֹלָם, וְיָבֹא מֶלֶךְ הַכָּבוֹד. מִי הוּא זֶה מֶלֶךְ הַכָּבוֹד, יהוה צְבָאוֹת, הוּא מֶלֶךְ הַכָּבוֹד סֶלָה.

The service continues with קַדִּישׁ יָתוֹם, *the Mourner's Kaddish* (page 746).

MONDAY

הַיּוֹם יוֹם שֵׁנִי בַּשַּׁבָּת, שֶׁבּוֹ הָיוּ הַלְוִיִּם אוֹמְרִים בְּבֵית הַמִּקְדָּשׁ:

תהלים מח

שִׁיר מִזְמוֹר לִבְנֵי קֹרַח. גָּדוֹל יהוה וּמְהֻלָּל מְאֹד, בְּעִיר אֱלֹהֵינוּ, הַר קָדְשׁוֹ. יְפֵה נוֹף, מְשׂוֹשׂ כָּל הָאָרֶץ, הַר צִיּוֹן יַרְכְּתֵי צָפוֹן, קִרְיַת מֶלֶךְ רָב. אֱלֹהִים בְּאַרְמְנוֹתֶיהָ נוֹדַע לְמִשְׂגָּב. כִּי הִנֵּה הַמְּלָכִים נוֹעֲדוּ, עָבְרוּ יַחְדָּו. הֵמָּה רָאוּ כֵּן תָּמָהוּ, נִבְהֲלוּ נֶחְפָּזוּ. רְעָדָה אֲחָזָתַם שָׁם, חִיל כַּיּוֹלֵדָה. בְּרוּחַ קָדִים תְּשַׁבֵּר אֳנִיּוֹת תַּרְשִׁישׁ. כַּאֲשֶׁר שָׁמַעְנוּ כֵּן רָאִינוּ בְּעִיר יהוה צְבָאוֹת, בְּעִיר אֱלֹהֵינוּ, אֱלֹהִים יְכוֹנְנֶהָ עַד עוֹלָם סֶלָה. דִּמִּינוּ אֱלֹהִים חַסְדֶּךָ, בְּקֶרֶב הֵיכָלֶךָ. כְּשִׁמְךָ אֱלֹהִים כֵּן תְּהִלָּתְךָ, עַל קַצְוֵי אֶרֶץ, צֶדֶק מָלְאָה יְמִינֶךָ. יִשְׂמַח הַר צִיּוֹן, תָּגֵלְנָה בְּנוֹת יְהוּדָה, לְמַעַן מִשְׁפָּטֶיךָ. סֹבּוּ צִיּוֹן וְהַקִּיפוּהָ, סִפְרוּ מִגְדָּלֶיהָ. ❖ שִׁיתוּ לִבְּכֶם לְחֵילָה, פַּסְּגוּ אַרְמְנוֹתֶיהָ, לְמַעַן תְּסַפְּרוּ לְדוֹר אַחֲרוֹן. כִּי זֶה אֱלֹהִים אֱלֹהֵינוּ עוֹלָם וָעֶד, הוּא יְנַהֲגֵנוּ עַל־מוּת.

The service continues with קַדִּישׁ יָתוֹם, *the Mourner's Kaddish* (page 746).

TUESDAY

הַיּוֹם יוֹם שְׁלִישִׁי בַּשַּׁבָּת, שֶׁבּוֹ הָיוּ הַלְוִיִּם אוֹמְרִים בְּבֵית הַמִּקְדָּשׁ:

תהלים פב

מִזְמוֹר לְאָסָף, אֱלֹהִים נִצָּב בַּעֲדַת אֵל, בְּקֶרֶב אֱלֹהִים יִשְׁפֹּט. עַד מָתַי תִּשְׁפְּטוּ עָוֶל, וּפְנֵי רְשָׁעִים תִּשְׂאוּ סֶלָה. שִׁפְטוּ דָל וְיָתוֹם, עָנִי וָרָשׁ הַצְדִּיקוּ. פַּלְּטוּ דַל וְאֶבְיוֹן, מִיַּד רְשָׁעִים הַצִּילוּ. לֹא יָדְעוּ וְלֹא יָבִינוּ, בַּחֲשֵׁכָה יִתְהַלָּכוּ, יִמּוֹטוּ כָּל מוֹסְדֵי אָרֶץ. אֲנִי אָמַרְתִּי אֱלֹהִים אַתֶּם,

SONG OF THE DAY

A different psalm is assigned as the Song of the Day for each day of the week.

SUNDAY

Today is the first day of the Sabbath,
on which the Levites would recite in the Holy Temple:

Psalm 24

לְדָוִד *Of David a psalm.* HASHEM*'s is the earth and its fullness, the inhabited land and those who dwell in it. For He founded it upon seas, and established it upon rivers. Who may ascend the mountain of* HASHEM*, and who may stand in the place of His sanctity? One with clean hands and pure heart, who has not sworn in vain by My soul and has not sworn deceitfully. He will receive a blessing from* HASHEM *and just kindness from the God of his salvation. This is the generation of those who seek Him, those who strive for Your Presence — Jacob, Selah. Raise up your heads, O gates, and be uplifted, you everlasting entrances, so that the King of Glory may enter. Who is this King of Glory? —* HASHEM*, the mighty and strong,* HASHEM*, the strong in battle.* Chazzan– *Raise up your heads, O gates, and raise up, you everlasting entrances, so that the King of Glory may enter. Who then is the King of Glory?* HASHEM*, Master of Legions, He is the King of Glory. Selah!*

The service continues with קַדִּישׁ יָתוֹם, *the Mourner's Kaddish* (p. 746).

MONDAY

Today is the second day of the Sabbath,
on which the Levites would recite in the Holy Temple:

Psalm 48

שִׁיר מִזְמוֹר *A song, a psalm, by the sons of Korach. Great is* HASHEM *and much praised, in the city of our God, Mount of His Holiness. Fairest of sites, joy of all the earth is Mount Zion, by the northern sides of the great king's city. In her palaces God is known as the Stronghold. For behold — the kings assembled, they came together. They saw and they were astounded, they were confounded and hastily fled. Trembling gripped them there, convulsions like a woman in birth travail. With an east wind You smashed the ships of Tarshish. As we heard, so we saw in the city of* HASHEM*, Master of Legions, in the city of our God — may God establish it to eternity, Selah! We hoped, O God, for Your kindness, in the midst of Your Sanctuary. Like Your Name, O God, so is Your praise — to the ends of the earth; righteousness fills Your right hand. May Mount Zion be glad, may the daughters of Judah rejoice, because of Your judgments. Walk about Zion and encircle her, count her towers.* Chazzan– *Mark well in your hearts her ramparts, raise up her palaces, that you may recount it to the succeeding generation: that this is God, our God, forever and ever, He will guide us like children.*

The service continues with קַדִּישׁ יָתוֹם, *the Mourner's Kaddish* (p. 746).

TUESDAY

Today is the third day of the Sabbath,
on which the Levites would recite in the Holy Temple:

Psalm 82

מִזְמוֹר *A psalm of Assaf: God stands in the Divine assembly, in the midst of judges shall He judge. Until when will you judge lawlessly and favor the presence of the wicked, Selah? Judge the needy and the orphan, vindicate the poor and impoverished. Rescue the needy and destitute, from the hand of the wicked deliver them. They do not know nor do they understand, in darkness they walk; all foundations of the earth collapse. I said, 'You are angelic,*

וּבְנֵי עֶלְיוֹן כֻּלְּכֶם. אָכֵן כְּאָדָם תְּמוּתוּן, וּכְאַחַד הַשָּׂרִים תִּפֹּלוּ. ❖ קוּמָה אֱלֹהִים שָׁפְטָה הָאָרֶץ, כִּי אַתָּה תִנְחַל בְּכָל הַגּוֹיִם.

The service continues with קַדִּישׁ יָתוֹם, *the Mourner's Kaddish* (page 746).

WEDNESDAY

הַיּוֹם יוֹם רְבִיעִי בַּשַּׁבָּת, שֶׁבּוֹ הָיוּ הַלְוִיִּם אוֹמְרִים בְּבֵית הַמִּקְדָּשׁ:

תהלים צד:א-צה:ג

אֵל נְקָמוֹת יהוה, אֵל נְקָמוֹת הוֹפִיעַ. הִנָּשֵׂא שֹׁפֵט הָאָרֶץ, הָשֵׁב גְּמוּל עַל גֵּאִים. עַד מָתַי רְשָׁעִים, יהוה, עַד מָתַי רְשָׁעִים יַעֲלֹזוּ. יַבִּיעוּ יְדַבְּרוּ עָתָק, יִתְאַמְּרוּ כָּל פֹּעֲלֵי אָוֶן. עַמְּךָ יהוה יְדַכְּאוּ, וְנַחֲלָתְךָ יְעַנּוּ. אַלְמָנָה וְגֵר יַהֲרֹגוּ, וִיתוֹמִים יְרַצֵּחוּ. וַיֹּאמְרוּ לֹא יִרְאֶה יָּהּ, וְלֹא יָבִין אֱלֹהֵי יַעֲקֹב. בִּינוּ בֹּעֲרִים בָּעָם, וּכְסִילִים מָתַי תַּשְׂכִּילוּ. הֲנֹטַע אֹזֶן הֲלֹא יִשְׁמָע, אִם יֹצֵר עַיִן הֲלֹא יַבִּיט. הֲיֹסֵר גּוֹיִם הֲלֹא יוֹכִיחַ, הַמְלַמֵּד אָדָם דָּעַת. יהוה יֹדֵעַ מַחְשְׁבוֹת אָדָם, כִּי הֵמָּה הָבֶל. אַשְׁרֵי הַגֶּבֶר אֲשֶׁר תְּיַסְּרֶנּוּ יָּהּ, וּמִתּוֹרָתְךָ תְלַמְּדֶנּוּ. לְהַשְׁקִיט לוֹ מִימֵי רָע, עַד יִכָּרֶה לָרָשָׁע שָׁחַת. כִּי לֹא יִטֹּשׁ יהוה עַמּוֹ, וְנַחֲלָתוֹ לֹא יַעֲזֹב. כִּי עַד צֶדֶק יָשׁוּב מִשְׁפָּט, וְאַחֲרָיו כָּל יִשְׁרֵי לֵב. מִי יָקוּם לִי עִם מְרֵעִים, מִי יִתְיַצֵּב לִי עִם פֹּעֲלֵי אָוֶן. לוּלֵי יהוה עֶזְרָתָה לִּי, כִּמְעַט שָׁכְנָה דוּמָה נַפְשִׁי. אִם אָמַרְתִּי מָטָה רַגְלִי, חַסְדְּךָ יהוה יִסְעָדֵנִי. בְּרֹב שַׂרְעַפַּי בְּקִרְבִּי, תַּנְחוּמֶיךָ יְשַׁעַשְׁעוּ נַפְשִׁי. הַיְחָבְרְךָ כִּסֵּא הַוּוֹת, יֹצֵר עָמָל עֲלֵי חֹק. יָגוֹדּוּ עַל נֶפֶשׁ צַדִּיק, וְדָם נָקִי יַרְשִׁיעוּ. וַיְהִי יהוה לִי לְמִשְׂגָּב, וֵאלֹהַי לְצוּר מַחְסִי. וַיָּשֶׁב עֲלֵיהֶם אֶת אוֹנָם, וּבְרָעָתָם יַצְמִיתֵם, יַצְמִיתֵם יהוה אֱלֹהֵינוּ.

❖ לְכוּ נְרַנְּנָה לַיהוה, נָרִיעָה לְצוּר יִשְׁעֵנוּ. נְקַדְּמָה פָנָיו בְּתוֹדָה, בִּזְמִרוֹת נָרִיעַ לוֹ. כִּי אֵל גָּדוֹל יהוה, וּמֶלֶךְ גָּדוֹל עַל כָּל אֱלֹהִים.

The service continues with קַדִּישׁ יָתוֹם, *the Mourner's Kaddish* (page 746).

THURSDAY

הַיּוֹם יוֹם חֲמִישִׁי בַּשַּׁבָּת, שֶׁבּוֹ הָיוּ הַלְוִיִּם אוֹמְרִים בְּבֵית הַמִּקְדָּשׁ:

תהלים פא

לַמְנַצֵּחַ עַל הַגִּתִּית לְאָסָף. הַרְנִינוּ לֵאלֹהִים עוּזֵּנוּ, הָרִיעוּ לֵאלֹהֵי יַעֲקֹב. שְׂאוּ זִמְרָה וּתְנוּ תֹף, כִּנּוֹר נָעִים עִם נָבֶל. תִּקְעוּ בַחֹדֶשׁ שׁוֹפָר, בַּכֵּסֶה לְיוֹם חַגֵּנוּ. כִּי חֹק לְיִשְׂרָאֵל הוּא, מִשְׁפָּט לֵאלֹהֵי יַעֲקֹב. עֵדוּת בִּיהוֹסֵף שָׂמוֹ, בְּצֵאתוֹ עַל אֶרֶץ מִצְרָיִם, שְׂפַת לֹא יָדַעְתִּי אֶשְׁמָע. הֲסִירוֹתִי מִסֵּבֶל שִׁכְמוֹ, כַּפָּיו מִדּוּד תַּעֲבֹרְנָה. בַּצָּרָה קָרָאתָ, וָאֲחַלְּצֶךָּ, אֶעֶנְךָ בְּסֵתֶר רַעַם, אֶבְחָנְךָ עַל מֵי מְרִיבָה, סֶלָה. שְׁמַע עַמִּי וְאָעִידָה בָּךְ,

sons of the Most High are you all.' But like men you shall die, and like one of the princes you shall fall. Chazzan– *Arise, O God, judge the earth, for You allot the heritage among all the nations.*

The service continues with קַדִּישׁ יָתוֹם, *the Mourner's Kaddish* (p. 746).

WEDNESDAY

Today is the fourth day of the Sabbath,
on which the Levites would recite in the Holy Temple:

Psalm 94:1-95:3

אֵל נְקָמוֹת *O God of vengeance, HASHEM; O God of vengeance, appear! Arise, O Judge of the earth, render recompense to the haughty. How long shall the wicked — O HASHEM — how long shall the wicked exult? They speak freely, they utter malicious falsehood, they glorify themselves, all workers of iniquity. Your nation, HASHEM, they crush, and they afflict Your heritage. The widow and the stranger they slay, and the orphans they murder. And they say, 'God will not see, nor will the God of Jacob understand.' Understand, you boors among the people; and you fools, when will you gain wisdom? He Who implants the ear, shall He not hear? He Who fashions the eye, shall He not see? He Who chastises nations, shall He not rebuke? — He Who teaches man knowledge. HASHEM knows the thoughts of man, that they are futile. Praiseworthy is the man whom God disciplines, and whom You teach from Your Torah. To give him rest from the days of evil, until a pit is dug for the wicked. For HASHEM will not cast off His people, nor will He forsake His heritage. For justice shall revert to righteousness, and following it will be all of upright heart. Who will rise up for me against evildoers? Who will stand up for me against the workers of iniquity? Had HASHEM not been a help to me, my soul would soon have dwelt in silence. If I said, 'My foot falters,' Your kindness, HASHEM, supported me. When my forebodings were abundant within me, Your comforts cheered my soul. Can the throne of destruction be associated with You? — those who fashion evil into a way of life. They join together against the soul of the righteous, and the blood of the innocent they condemn. Then HASHEM became a stronghold for me, and my God, the Rock of my refuge. He turned upon them their own violence, and with their own evil He will cut them off, HASHEM, our God, will cut them off.*

Chazzan– *Come — let us sing to HASHEM, let us call out to the Rock of our salvation. Let us greet Him with thanksgiving, with praiseful songs let us call out to Him. For a great God is HASHEM, and a great King above all heavenly powers.*

The service continues with קַדִּישׁ יָתוֹם, *the Mourner's Kaddish* (p. 746).

THURSDAY

Today is the fifth day of the Sabbath,
on which the Levites would recite in the Holy Temple:

Psalm 81

לַמְנַצֵּחַ *For the Conductor, upon the gittis, by Assaf. Sing joyously to the God of our might, call out to the God of Jacob. Raise a song and sound the drum, the sweet harp with the lyre. Blow the shofar at the moon's renewal, at the time appointed for our festive day. Because it is a decree for Israel, a judgment day for the God of Jacob. He imposed it as a testimony for Joseph when he went forth over the land of Egypt — 'I understood a language I never knew!' I removed his shoulder from the burden, his hands let go of the kettle. In distress you called out, and I released you, I answered you with thunder when you hid, I tested you at the Waters of Strife, Selah. Listen,*

יִשְׂרָאֵל אִם תִּשְׁמַע לִי. לֹא יִהְיֶה בְךָ אֵל זָר, וְלֹא תִשְׁתַּחֲוֶה לְאֵל נֵכָר. אָנֹכִי יהוה אֱלֹהֶיךָ, הַמַּעַלְךָ מֵאֶרֶץ מִצְרָיִם, הַרְחֶב פִּיךָ וַאֲמַלְאֵהוּ. וְלֹא שָׁמַע עַמִּי לְקוֹלִי, וְיִשְׂרָאֵל לֹא אָבָה לִי. וָאֲשַׁלְּחֵהוּ בִּשְׁרִירוּת לִבָּם, יֵלְכוּ בְּמוֹעֲצוֹתֵיהֶם. לוּ עַמִּי שֹׁמֵעַ לִי, יִשְׂרָאֵל בִּדְרָכַי יְהַלֵּכוּ. כִּמְעַט אוֹיְבֵיהֶם אַכְנִיעַ, וְעַל צָרֵיהֶם אָשִׁיב יָדִי. מְשַׂנְאֵי יהוה יְכַחֲשׁוּ לוֹ, וִיהִי עִתָּם לְעוֹלָם. ❖ וַיַּאֲכִילֵהוּ מֵחֵלֶב חִטָּה, וּמִצּוּר דְּבַשׁ אַשְׂבִּיעֶךָ.

The service continues with קַדִּישׁ יָתוֹם, *the Mourner's Kaddish* (below).

FRIDAY

הַיּוֹם יוֹם שִׁשִּׁי בַּשַּׁבָּת, שֶׁבּוֹ הָיוּ הַלְוִיִּם אוֹמְרִים בְּבֵית הַמִּקְדָּשׁ:

תהלים צג

יהוה מָלָךְ, גֵּאוּת לָבֵשׁ, לָבֵשׁ יהוה עֹז הִתְאַזָּר, אַף תִּכּוֹן תֵּבֵל בַּל תִּמּוֹט. נָכוֹן כִּסְאֲךָ מֵאָז, מֵעוֹלָם אָתָּה. נָשְׂאוּ נְהָרוֹת יהוה, נָשְׂאוּ נְהָרוֹת קוֹלָם, יִשְׂאוּ נְהָרוֹת דָּכְיָם. מִקֹּלוֹת מַיִם רַבִּים, אַדִּירִים מִשְׁבְּרֵי יָם, אַדִּיר בַּמָּרוֹם יהוה. ❖ עֵדֹתֶיךָ נֶאֶמְנוּ מְאֹד לְבֵיתְךָ נַאֲוָה קֹדֶשׁ, יהוה לְאֹרֶךְ יָמִים.

The service continues with קַדִּישׁ יָתוֹם, *the Mourner's Kaddish* (below).

קדיש יתום

In the presence of a *minyan,* mourners recite קַדִּישׁ יָתוֹם, the Mourner's *Kaddish* (see *Laws* §81-83):

יִתְגַּדַּל וְיִתְקַדַּשׁ שְׁמֵהּ רַבָּא. (Cong. – אָמֵן.) בְּעָלְמָא דִּי בְרָא כִרְעוּתֵהּ. וְיַמְלִיךְ מַלְכוּתֵהּ, בְּחַיֵּיכוֹן וּבְיוֹמֵיכוֹן וּבְחַיֵּי דְכָל בֵּית יִשְׂרָאֵל, בַּעֲגָלָא וּבִזְמַן קָרִיב. וְאִמְרוּ: אָמֵן.

(Cong. – אָמֵן. יְהֵא שְׁמֵהּ רַבָּא מְבָרַךְ לְעָלַם וּלְעָלְמֵי עָלְמַיָּא.)

יְהֵא שְׁמֵהּ רַבָּא מְבָרַךְ לְעָלַם וּלְעָלְמֵי עָלְמַיָּא.

יִתְבָּרַךְ וְיִשְׁתַּבַּח וְיִתְפָּאַר וְיִתְרוֹמַם וְיִתְנַשֵּׂא וְיִתְהַדָּר וְיִתְעַלֶּה וְיִתְהַלָּל שְׁמֵהּ דְּקֻדְשָׁא בְּרִיךְ הוּא (Cong. – בְּרִיךְ הוּא) — לְעֵלָּא מִן כָּל בִּרְכָתָא וְשִׁירָתָא תֻּשְׁבְּחָתָא וְנֶחֱמָתָא, דַּאֲמִירָן בְּעָלְמָא. וְאִמְרוּ: אָמֵן. (Cong. – אָמֵן.)

יְהֵא שְׁלָמָא רַבָּא מִן שְׁמַיָּא, וְחַיִּים עָלֵינוּ וְעַל כָּל יִשְׂרָאֵל. וְאִמְרוּ: אָמֵן. (Cong. – אָמֵן.)

Take three steps back. Bow left and say . . . עֹשֶׂה; bow right and say . . . הוּא; bow forward and say וְעַל כָּל . . . אָמֵן. Remain standing in place for a few moments, then take three steps forward.

עֹשֶׂה שָׁלוֹם בִּמְרוֹמָיו, הוּא יַעֲשֶׂה שָׁלוֹם עָלֵינוּ, וְעַל כָּל יִשְׂרָאֵל. וְאִמְרוּ: אָמֵן. (Cong. – אָמֵן.)

My nation, and I will attest to you; O Israel, if you would but listen to Me. There shall be no strange god within you, nor shall you bow before an alien god. I am HASHEM, your God, who elevated you from the land of Egypt, open wide your mouth and I will fill it. But My people did not heed My voice and Israel did not desire Me. So I let them follow their heart's fantasies, they follow their own counsels. If only My people would heed Me, if Israel would walk in My ways. In an instant I would subdue their foes, and against their tormentors turn My hand. Those who hate HASHEM lie to Him — so their destiny is eternal. Chazzan— *But He would feed him with the cream of the wheat, and with honey from a rock sate you.*

The service continues with קַדִּישׁ יָתוֹם, *the Mourner's Kaddish* (below).

FRIDAY

Today is the sixth day of the Sabbath,
on which the Levites would recite in the Holy Temple:

Psalm 93

יהוה מָלָךְ *HASHEM will have reigned, He will have donned grandeur; He will have donned might and girded Himself; He even made the world firm so that it should not falter. Your throne was established from of old, eternal are You. Like rivers they raised, O HASHEM, like rivers they raised their voice; like rivers they shall raise their destructiveness. More than the roars of many waters, mightier than the waves of the sea — You are mighty on high, HASHEM.* Chazzan— *Your testimonies are exceedingly trustworthy about Your House, the Sacred Dwelling — O HASHEM, may it be for long days.*

The service continues with קַדִּישׁ יָתוֹם, *the Mourner's Kaddish* (below).

MOURNER'S KADDISH

In the presence of a *minyan,* mourners recite קַדִּישׁ יָתוֹם, the Mourner's *Kaddish* (see *Laws* §81-83):

[A transliteration of this *Kaddish* appears on p. 1305.]

יִתְגַּדַּל *May His great Name grow exalted and sanctified* (Cong.— *Amen.*) *in the world that He created as He willed. May He give reign to His kingship in your lifetimes and in your days, and in the lifetimes of the entire Family of Israel, swiftly and soon. Now respond: Amen.*

(Cong.— *Amen. May His great Name be blessed forever and ever.*)

May His great Name be blessed forever and ever.

Blessed, praised, glorified, exalted, extolled, mighty, upraised, and lauded be the Name of the Holy One, Blessed is He (Cong.— *Blessed is He*) *— beyond any blessing and song, praise and consolation that are uttered in the world. Now respond: Amen.* (Cong.— *Amen*).

May there be abundant peace from Heaven, and life, upon us and upon all Israel. Now respond: Amen. (Cong.— *Amen.*)

Take three steps back. Bow left and say, *'He Who makes peace . . .';* bow right and say, *'may He . . .';* bow forward and say, *'and upon all Israel . . .'* Remain standing in place for a few moments, then take three steps forward.

He Who makes peace in His heights, may He make peace upon us, and upon all Israel. Now respond: Amen. (Cong.— *Amen.*)

תהלים כז

לְדָוִד, יהוה אוֹרִי וְיִשְׁעִי, מִמִּי אִירָא, יהוה מָעוֹז חַיַּי, מִמִּי אֶפְחָד. בִּקְרֹב עָלַי מְרֵעִים לֶאֱכֹל אֶת בְּשָׂרִי, צָרַי וְאֹיְבַי לִי, הֵמָּה כָשְׁלוּ וְנָפָלוּ. אִם תַּחֲנֶה עָלַי מַחֲנֶה, לֹא יִירָא לִבִּי, אִם תָּקוּם עָלַי מִלְחָמָה, בְּזֹאת אֲנִי בוֹטֵחַ. אַחַת שָׁאַלְתִּי מֵאֵת יהוה, אוֹתָהּ אֲבַקֵּשׁ, שִׁבְתִּי בְּבֵית יהוה כָּל יְמֵי חַיַּי, לַחֲזוֹת בְּנֹעַם יהוה, וּלְבַקֵּר בְּהֵיכָלוֹ. כִּי יִצְפְּנֵנִי בְּסֻכֹּה בְּיוֹם רָעָה, יַסְתִּירֵנִי בְּסֵתֶר אָהֳלוֹ, בְּצוּר יְרוֹמְמֵנִי. וְעַתָּה יָרוּם רֹאשִׁי עַל אֹיְבַי סְבִיבוֹתַי, וְאֶזְבְּחָה בְאָהֳלוֹ זִבְחֵי תְרוּעָה, אָשִׁירָה וַאֲזַמְּרָה לַיהוה. שְׁמַע יהוה קוֹלִי אֶקְרָא, וְחָנֵּנִי וַעֲנֵנִי. לְךָ אָמַר לִבִּי בַּקְּשׁוּ פָנָי, אֶת פָּנֶיךָ יהוה אֲבַקֵּשׁ. אַל תַּסְתֵּר פָּנֶיךָ מִמֶּנִּי, אַל תַּט בְּאַף עַבְדֶּךָ, עֶזְרָתִי הָיִיתָ, אַל תִּטְּשֵׁנִי וְאַל תַּעַזְבֵנִי, אֱלֹהֵי יִשְׁעִי. כִּי אָבִי וְאִמִּי עֲזָבוּנִי, וַיהוה יַאַסְפֵנִי. הוֹרֵנִי יהוה דַּרְכֶּךָ, וּנְחֵנִי בְּאֹרַח מִישׁוֹר, לְמַעַן שׁוֹרְרָי. אַל תִּתְּנֵנִי בְּנֶפֶשׁ צָרָי, כִּי קָמוּ בִי עֵדֵי שֶׁקֶר, וִיפֵחַ חָמָס. ❖ לוּלֵא הֶאֱמַנְתִּי לִרְאוֹת בְּטוּב יהוה בְּאֶרֶץ חַיִּים. קַוֵּה אֶל יהוה, חֲזַק וְיַאֲמֵץ לִבֶּךָ, וְקַוֵּה אֶל יהוה.

קדיש יתום

In the presence of a *minyan,* mourners recite קַדִּישׁ יָתוֹם, the Mourner's *Kaddish* (see *Laws* §81-83):

יִתְגַּדַּל וְיִתְקַדַּשׁ שְׁמֵהּ רַבָּא. (.Cong – אָמֵן.) בְּעָלְמָא דִּי בְרָא כִרְעוּתֵהּ. וְיַמְלִיךְ מַלְכוּתֵהּ, בְּחַיֵּיכוֹן וּבְיוֹמֵיכוֹן וּבְחַיֵּי דְכָל בֵּית יִשְׂרָאֵל, בַּעֲגָלָא וּבִזְמַן קָרִיב. וְאִמְרוּ: אָמֵן.

(.Cong – אָמֵן. יְהֵא שְׁמֵהּ רַבָּא מְבָרַךְ לְעָלַם וּלְעָלְמֵי עָלְמַיָּא.)

יְהֵא שְׁמֵהּ רַבָּא מְבָרַךְ לְעָלַם וּלְעָלְמֵי עָלְמַיָּא.

יִתְבָּרַךְ וְיִשְׁתַּבַּח וְיִתְפָּאַר וְיִתְרוֹמַם וְיִתְנַשֵּׂא וְיִתְהַדָּר וְיִתְעַלֶּה וְיִתְהַלָּל שְׁמֵהּ דְּקֻדְשָׁא בְּרִיךְ הוּא (.Cong – בְּרִיךְ הוּא) – לְעֵלָּא מִן כָּל בִּרְכָתָא וְשִׁירָתָא תֻּשְׁבְּחָתָא וְנֶחֱמָתָא, דַּאֲמִירָן בְּעָלְמָא. וְאִמְרוּ: אָמֵן. (.Cong – אָמֵן.)

יְהֵא שְׁלָמָא רַבָּא מִן שְׁמַיָּא, וְחַיִּים עָלֵינוּ וְעַל כָּל יִשְׂרָאֵל. וְאִמְרוּ: אָמֵן. (.Cong – אָמֵן.)

Take three steps back. Bow left and say . . . עֹשֶׂה; bow right and say . . . הוּא; bow forward and say וְעַל כָּל . . . אָמֵן. Remain standing in place for a few moments, then take three steps forward.

עֹשֶׂה שָׁלוֹם בִּמְרוֹמָיו, הוּא יַעֲשֶׂה שָׁלוֹם עָלֵינוּ, וְעַל כָּל יִשְׂרָאֵל. וְאִמְרוּ: אָמֵן. (.Cong – אָמֵן.)

Psalm 27

לְדָוִד *Of David; HASHEM is my light and my salvation, whom shall I fear? HASHEM is my life's strength, whom shall I dread? When evildoers approach me to devour my flesh, my tormentors and my foes against me — it is they who stumble and fall. Though an army would besiege me, my heart would not fear; though war would arise against me, in this I trust. One thing I asked of HASHEM, that shall I seek: That I dwell in the House of HASHEM all the days of my life; to behold the sweetness of HASHEM and to contemplate in His Sanctuary. Indeed, He will hide me in His Shelter on the day of evil; He will conceal me in the concealment of His Tent, He will lift me upon a rock. Now my head is raised above my enemies around me, and I will slaughter offerings in His Tent accompanied by joyous song; I will sing and make music to HASHEM. HASHEM, hear my voice when I call, be gracious toward me and answer me. In Your behalf, my heart has said, 'Seek My Presence'; Your Presence, HASHEM, do I seek. Conceal not Your Presence from me, repel not Your servant in anger. You have been my Helper, abandon me not, forsake me not, O God of my salvation. Though my father and mother have forsaken me, HASHEM will gather me in. Teach me Your way, HASHEM, and lead me on the path of integrity, because of my watchful foes. Deliver me not to the wishes of my tormentors, for there have arisen against me false witnesses who breathe violence.* Chazzan— *Had I not trusted that I would see the goodness of HASHEM in the land of life! Hope to HASHEM, strengthen yourself and He will give you courage; and hope to HASHEM.*

MOURNER'S KADDISH

In the presence of a *minyan,* mourners recite קַדִּישׁ יָתוֹם, the Mourner's *Kaddish* (see *Laws* §81-83):

[A transliteration of this *Kaddish* appears on p. 1305.]

יִתְגַּדַּל *May His great Name grow exalted and sanctified* (Cong.— *Amen.*) *in the world that He created as He willed. May He give reign to His kingship in your lifetimes and in your days, and in the lifetimes of the entire Family of Israel, swiftly and soon. Now respond: Amen.*

(Cong.— *Amen. May His great Name be blessed forever and ever.*)

May His great Name be blessed forever and ever.

Blessed, praised, glorified, exalted, extolled, mighty, upraised, and lauded be the Name of the Holy One, Blessed is He (Cong.— *Blessed is He*) — *beyond any blessing and song, praise and consolation that are uttered in the world. Now respond: Amen.* (Cong.— *Amen*).

May there be abundant peace from Heaven, and life, upon us and upon all Israel. Now respond: Amen. (Cong.— *Amen.*)

Take three steps back. Bow left and say, *'He Who makes peace . . .';* bow right and say, *'may He . . .';* bow forward and say, *'and upon all Israel . . .'* Remain standing in place for a few moments, then take three steps forward.

He Who makes peace in His heights, may He make peace upon us, and upon all Israel. Now respond: Amen. (Cong.— *Amen.*)

THE MORNING SERVICE FOR HOSHANA RABBAH BEGINS ON PAGES 130-170 AND 646-702, THEN CONTINUES HERE.

הוצאת ספר תורה להושענא רבה

From the moment the Ark is opened until the Torah is returned to it, one must conduct himself with the utmost respect, and avoid unnecessary conversation. It is commendable to kiss the Torah as it is carried to the *bimah* [reading table] and back to the Ark.

All rise and remain standing until the Torah is placed on the *bimah*. The congregation recites:

אֵין כָּמְוֹךָ בָאֱלֹהִים אֲדֹנָי, וְאֵין כְּמַעֲשֶׂיךָ[1] מַלְכוּתְךָ מַלְכוּת כָּל עֹלָמִים, וּמֶמְשַׁלְתְּךָ בְּכָל דּוֹר וָדֹר.[2] יהוה מֶלֶךְ,[3] יהוה מָלָךְ,[4] יהוה יִמְלֹךְ לְעֹלָם וָעֶד.[5] יהוה עֹז לְעַמּוֹ יִתֵּן, יהוה יְבָרֵךְ אֶת עַמּוֹ בַשָּׁלוֹם.[6]

אַב הָרַחֲמִים, הֵיטִיבָה בִרְצוֹנְךָ אֶת צִיּוֹן, תִּבְנֶה חוֹמוֹת יְרוּשָׁלָיִם.[7] כִּי בְךָ לְבַד בָּטָחְנוּ, מֶלֶךְ אֵל רָם וְנִשָּׂא, אֲדוֹן עוֹלָמִים.

THE ARK IS OPENED

Before the Torah is removed the congregation recites:

וַיְהִי בִּנְסֹעַ הָאָרֹן וַיֹּאמֶר מֹשֶׁה, קוּמָה יהוה וְיָפֻצוּ אֹיְבֶיךָ וְיָנֻסוּ מְשַׂנְאֶיךָ מִפָּנֶיךָ.[8] כִּי מִצִּיּוֹן תֵּצֵא תוֹרָה, וּדְבַר יהוה מִירוּשָׁלָיִם.[9] בָּרוּךְ שֶׁנָּתַן תּוֹרָה לְעַמּוֹ יִשְׂרָאֵל בִּקְדֻשָּׁתוֹ.

The following paragraph [the Thirteen Attributes of Mercy] is recited three times:

יהוה, יהוה, אֵל, רַחוּם, וְחַנּוּן, אֶרֶךְ אַפַּיִם, וְרַב חֶסֶד, וֶאֱמֶת, נֹצֵר חֶסֶד לָאֲלָפִים, נֹשֵׂא עָוֹן, וָפֶשַׁע, וְחַטָּאָה, וְנַקֵּה.[10]

רִבּוֹנוֹ שֶׁל עוֹלָם, מַלֵּא מִשְׁאֲלוֹתַי לְטוֹבָה, וְהָפֵק רְצוֹנִי, וְתֵן שְׁאֵלָתִי, וּמְחוֹל לִי עַל כָּל עֲוֹנוֹתַי, וְעַל כָּל עֲוֹנוֹת אַנְשֵׁי בֵיתִי, מְחִילָה בְּחֶסֶד, מְחִילָה בְּרַחֲמִים, וְטַהֲרֵנִי מֵחֲטָאַי וּמֵעֲוֹנוֹתַי וּמִפְּשָׁעַי. וְזָכְרֵנִי בְּזִכָּרוֹן טוֹב לְפָנֶיךָ, וּפָקְדֵנִי בִּפְקֻדַּת יְשׁוּעָה וְרַחֲמִים, וְזָכְרֵנִי לְחַיִּים אֲרוּכִים לְחַיִּים טוֹבִים וּלְשָׁלוֹם, וּפַרְנָסָה טוֹבָה וְכַלְכָּלָה, וְלֶחֶם לֶאֱכוֹל, וּבֶגֶד לִלְבּוֹשׁ, וְעֹשֶׁר וְכָבוֹד וַאֲרִיכוּת יָמִים לַהֲגוֹת בְּתוֹרָתֶךָ וּבְמִצְוֹתֶיךָ, וְשֵׂכֶל וּבִינָה לְהָבִין וּלְהַשְׂכִּיל עִמְקֵי סוֹדוֹתֶיךָ. וְהָפֵק רְפוּאָה שְׁלֵמָה לְכָל מַכְאוֹבֵינוּ, וּתְבָרֵךְ אֶת כָּל מַעֲשֵׂה יָדֵינוּ. וְתִגְזוֹר עָלֵינוּ גְּזֵרוֹת טוֹבוֹת יְשׁוּעוֹת וְנֶחָמוֹת. וּתְבַטֵּל מֵעָלֵינוּ כָּל גְּזֵרוֹת קָשׁוֹת וְרָעוֹת,

THE MORNING SERVICE FOR HOSHANA RABBAH BEGINS ON PAGES 130-170 AND 646-702, THEN CONTINUES HERE.

REMOVAL OF THE TORAH ON HOSHANA RABBAH

From the moment the Ark is opened until the Torah is returned to it, one must conduct himself with the utmost respect, and avoid unnecessary conversation. It is commendable to kiss the Torah as it is carried to the *bimah* [reading table] and back to the Ark.

All rise and remain standing until the Torah is placed on the *bimah*. The congregation recites:

אֵין כָּמְוֹךָ *There is none like You among the gods, my Lord, and there is nothing like Your works.*[1] *Your kingdom is a kingdom spanning all eternities, and Your dominion is throughout every generation.*[2] *HASHEM reigns,*[3] *HASHEM has reigned,*[4] *HASHEM shall reign for all eternity.*[5] *HASHEM will give might to His people; HASHEM will bless His people with peace.*[6]

אַב הָרַחֲמִים *Father of compassion, do good with Zion according to Your will; rebuild the walls of Jerusalem.*[7] *For we trust in You alone, O King, God, exalted and uplifted, Master of worlds.*

THE ARK IS OPENED

Before the Torah is removed the congregation recites:

וַיְהִי בִּנְסֹעַ *When the Ark would travel, Moses would say, 'Arise, HASHEM, and let Your foes be scattered, let those who hate You flee from You.'*[8] *For from Zion the Torah will come forth and the word of HASHEM from Jerusalem.*[9] *Blessed is He Who gave the Torah to His people Israel in His holiness.*

The following paragraph [the Thirteen Attributes of Mercy] is recited three times:

יהוה HASHEM, HASHEM, God, Compassionate and Gracious, Slow to anger, and Abundant in Kindness and Truth. Preserver of kindness for thousands of generations, Forgiver of iniquity, willful sin, and error, and Who cleanses.[10]

רִבּוֹנוֹ *Master of the universe, fulfill my requests for good, satisfy my desire and grant my request. Pardon all my iniquities and all the iniquities of my household — a pardon of kindness, a pardon of compassion — and purify me of my errors, my iniquities, and my willful sins. Remember me with a favorable memory before You and consider me for salvation and compassion. Remember me for long life, for good life and for peace, good livelihood and sustenance, bread to eat, clothes to wear, wealth, honor, a long life engaged in Your Torah and Your commandments; and intelligence and insight to understand and discern the depths of Your mysteries. Grant a complete recovery to all our sufferings and bless all our handiwork. Decree upon us good decrees, salvations and consolations. Nullify all harsh and evil decrees against*

---

(1) *Psalms* 86:8. (2) 145:13. (3) 10:16. (4) 93:1 et al. (5) *Exodus* 15:18.
(6) *Psalms* 29:11. (7) 51:20. (8) *Numbers* 10:35. (9) *Isaiah* 2:3. (10) *Exodus* 34:6-7.

וְתֵן בְּלֵב מַלְכוּת וְיוֹעֲצָיו וְשָׂרָיו עָלֵינוּ לְטוֹבָה. אָמֵן וְכֵן יְהִי רָצוֹן. יִהְיוּ לְרָצוֹן אִמְרֵי פִי, וְהֶגְיוֹן לִבִּי לְפָנֶיךָ, יהוה צוּרִי וְגוֹאֲלִי.[1]

Recite the following verse three times:

וַאֲנִי תְפִלָּתִי לְךָ יהוה עֵת רָצוֹן, אֱלֹהִים בְּרָב חַסְדֶּךָ, עֲנֵנִי בֶּאֱמֶת יִשְׁעֶךָ.[2]

זוהר ויקהל שסט:א

בְּרִיךְ שְׁמֵהּ דְּמָרֵא עָלְמָא, בְּרִיךְ כִּתְרָךְ וְאַתְרָךְ. יְהֵא רְעוּתָךְ עִם עַמָּךְ יִשְׂרָאֵל לְעָלַם, וּפֻרְקַן יְמִינָךְ אַחֲזֵי לְעַמָּךְ בְּבֵית מַקְדְּשָׁךְ, וּלְאַמְטוּיֵי לָנָא מִטּוּב נְהוֹרָךְ, וּלְקַבֵּל צְלוֹתָנָא בְּרַחֲמִין. יְהֵא רַעֲוָא קֳדָמָךְ, דְּתוֹרִיךְ לָן חַיִּין בְּטִיבוּתָא, וְלֶהֱוֵי אֲנָא פְקִידָא בְּגוֹ צַדִּיקַיָּא, לְמִרְחַם עָלַי וּלְמִנְטַר יָתִי וְיַת כָּל דִּי לִי, וְדִי לְעַמָּךְ יִשְׂרָאֵל. אַנְתְּ הוּא זָן לְכֹלָּא, וּמְפַרְנֵס לְכֹלָּא, אַנְתְּ הוּא שַׁלִּיט עַל כֹּלָּא. אַנְתְּ הוּא דְּשַׁלִּיט עַל מַלְכַיָּא, וּמַלְכוּתָא דִּילָךְ הִיא. אֲנָא עַבְדָּא דְקֻדְשָׁא בְּרִיךְ הוּא, דְּסָגִידְנָא קַמֵּהּ וּמִקַּמָּא דִּיקַר אוֹרַיְתֵהּ בְּכָל עִדָּן וְעִדָּן. לָא עַל אֱנָשׁ רָחִיצְנָא, וְלָא עַל בַּר אֱלָהִין סָמִיכְנָא, אֶלָּא בֶּאֱלָהָא דִשְׁמַיָּא, דְּהוּא אֱלָהָא קְשׁוֹט, וְאוֹרַיְתֵהּ קְשׁוֹט, וּנְבִיאוֹהִי קְשׁוֹט, וּמַסְגֵּא לְמֶעְבַּד טַבְוָן וּקְשׁוֹט. בֵּהּ אֲנָא רָחִיץ, וְלִשְׁמֵהּ קַדִּישָׁא יַקִּירָא אֲנָא אֵמַר תֻּשְׁבְּחָן. יְהֵא רַעֲוָא קֳדָמָךְ, דְּתִפְתַּח לִבָּאִי בְּאוֹרַיְתָא, וְתַשְׁלִים מִשְׁאֲלִין דְּלִבָּאִי, וְלִבָּא דְכָל עַמָּךְ יִשְׂרָאֵל, לְטַב וּלְחַיִּין וְלִשְׁלָם. (אָמֵן.)

A Torah Scroll is removed from the Ark and presented to the *chazzan*, who accepts it in his right arm. Facing the congregation the *chazzan* raises the Torah and, followed by congregation, recites:

שְׁמַע יִשְׂרָאֵל יהוה אֱלֹהֵינוּ יהוה אֶחָד.[3]

Still facing the congregation, the *chazzan* raises the Torah and, followed by congregation, recites:

אֶחָד (הוּא) אֱלֹהֵינוּ גָּדוֹל אֲדוֹנֵינוּ, קָדוֹשׁ וְנוֹרָא שְׁמוֹ.

The *chazzan* turns to the Ark, bows while raising the Torah, and recites:

גַּדְּלוּ לַיהוה אִתִּי וּנְרוֹמְמָה שְׁמוֹ יַחְדָּו.[4]

us and dispose the feelings of the government, its counselors and ministers upon us for good. Amen, and so be Your will. May the expressions of my mouth and the thoughts of my heart find favor before You, HASHEM*, my Rock and my Redeemer.*[1]

Recite the following verse three times:

וַאֲנִי תְפִלָּתִי *As for me, may my prayer to You,* HASHEM*, be at an opportune time; O God, in Your abundant kindness, answer me with the truth of Your salvation.*[2]

Zohar, Vayakhel 369a

בְּרִיךְ שְׁמֵהּ *Blessed is the Name of the Master of the universe, blessed is Your crown and Your place. May Your favor remain with Your people Israel forever; may You display the salvation of Your right hand to Your people in Your Holy Temple, to benefit us with the goodness of Your luminescence and to accept our prayers with mercy. May it be Your will that You extend our lives with goodness and that I be numbered among the righteous; that You have mercy on me and protect me, all that is mine and that is Your people Israel's. It is You Who nourishes all and sustains all; You control everything. It is You Who control kings, and kingship is Yours. I am a servant of the Holy One, Blessed is He, and I prostrate myself before Him and before the glory of His Torah at all times. Not in any man do I put trust, nor on any angel do I rely — only on the God of heaven Who is the God of truth, Whose Torah is truth and Whose prophets are true and Who acts liberally with kindness and truth. In Him do I trust, and to His glorious and holy Name do I declare praises. May it be Your will that You open my heart to the Torah and that You fulfill the wishes of my heart and the heart of Your entire people Israel for good, for life, and for peace. (Amen.)*

A Torah Scroll is removed from the Ark and presented to the *chazzan,* who accepts it in his right arm. Facing the congregation the *chazzan* raises the Torah and, followed by congregation, recites:

Hear, O Israel: HASHEM is our God, HASHEM, the One and Only.[3]

Still facing the congregation, the *chazzan* raises the Torah and, followed by congregation, recites:

One is our God, great is our Master, Holy and awesome is His Name.

The *chazzan* turns to the Ark, bows while raising the Torah, and recites:

Declare the greatness of HASHEM with me, and let us exalt His Name together.[4]

---

(1) *Psalms* 19:15. (2) 69:14. (3) *Deuteronomy* 6:4. (4) *Psalms* 34:4.

The *chazzan* turns to his right and carries the Torah to the *bimah,* as the congregation responds:

לְךָ יהוה הַגְּדֻלָּה וְהַגְּבוּרָה וְהַתִּפְאֶרֶת וְהַנֵּצַח וְהַהוֹד כִּי כֹל בַּשָּׁמַיִם וּבָאָרֶץ, לְךָ יהוה הַמַּמְלָכָה וְהַמִּתְנַשֵּׂא לְכֹל לְרֹאשׁ.[1] רוֹמְמוּ יהוה אֱלֹהֵינוּ, וְהִשְׁתַּחֲווּ לַהֲדֹם רַגְלָיו, קָדוֹשׁ הוּא. רוֹמְמוּ יהוה אֱלֹהֵינוּ, וְהִשְׁתַּחֲווּ לְהַר קָדְשׁוֹ, כִּי קָדוֹשׁ יהוה אֱלֹהֵינוּ.[2]

As the *chazzan* carries the Torah to the *bimah* the congregation recites:

עַל הַכֹּל, יִתְגַּדַּל וְיִתְקַדַּשׁ וְיִשְׁתַּבַּח וְיִתְפָּאַר וְיִתְרוֹמַם וְיִתְנַשֵּׂא שְׁמוֹ שֶׁל מֶלֶךְ מַלְכֵי הַמְּלָכִים הַקָּדוֹשׁ בָּרוּךְ הוּא, בָּעוֹלָמוֹת שֶׁבָּרָא, הָעוֹלָם הַזֶּה וְהָעוֹלָם הַבָּא, כִּרְצוֹנוֹ, וְכִרְצוֹן יְרֵאָיו, וְכִרְצוֹן כָּל בֵּית יִשְׂרָאֵל. צוּר הָעוֹלָמִים, אֲדוֹן כָּל הַבְּרִיּוֹת, אֱלוֹהַּ כָּל הַנְּפָשׁוֹת, הַיּוֹשֵׁב בְּמֶרְחֲבֵי מָרוֹם, הַשּׁוֹכֵן בִּשְׁמֵי שְׁמֵי קֶדֶם. קְדֻשָּׁתוֹ עַל הַחַיּוֹת, וּקְדֻשָּׁתוֹ עַל כִּסֵּא הַכָּבוֹד. וּבְכֵן יִתְקַדַּשׁ שִׁמְךָ בָּנוּ יהוה אֱלֹהֵינוּ לְעֵינֵי כָּל חָי. וְנֹאמַר לְפָנָיו שִׁיר חָדָשׁ, כַּכָּתוּב: שִׁירוּ לֵאלֹהִים זַמְּרוּ שְׁמוֹ, סֹלּוּ לָרֹכֵב בָּעֲרָבוֹת בְּיָהּ שְׁמוֹ, וְעִלְזוּ לְפָנָיו.[3] וְנִרְאֵהוּ עַיִן בְּעַיִן בְּשׁוּבוֹ אֶל נָוֵהוּ, כַּכָּתוּב: כִּי עַיִן בְּעַיִן יִרְאוּ בְּשׁוּב יהוה צִיּוֹן.[4] וְנֶאֱמַר: וְנִגְלָה כְּבוֹד יהוה, וְרָאוּ כָל בָּשָׂר יַחְדָּו כִּי פִּי יהוה דִּבֵּר.[5]

אַב הָרַחֲמִים הוּא יְרַחֵם עַם עֲמוּסִים, וְיִזְכֹּר בְּרִית אֵיתָנִים, וְיַצִּיל נַפְשׁוֹתֵינוּ מִן הַשָּׁעוֹת הָרָעוֹת, וְיִגְעַר בְּיֵצֶר הָרָע מִן הַנְּשׂוּאִים, וְיָחֹן אוֹתָנוּ לִפְלֵיטַת עוֹלָמִים, וִימַלֵּא מִשְׁאֲלוֹתֵינוּ בְּמִדָּה טוֹבָה יְשׁוּעָה וְרַחֲמִים.

The Torah is placed on the *bimah* and prepared for reading.
The *gabbai* uses the following formula to call a *Kohen* to the Torah:

וְיַעֲזוֹר וְיָגֵן וְיוֹשִׁיעַ לְכֹל הַחוֹסִים בּוֹ, וְנֹאמַר, אָמֵן. הַכֹּל הָבוּ גֹדֶל לֵאלֹהֵינוּ וּתְנוּ כָבוֹד לַתּוֹרָה, כֹּהֵן° קְרָב, יַעֲמֹד (name) בֶּן (father's name) הַכֹּהֵן.

°If no *Kohen* is present, the *gabbai* says:
„אֵין כַּאן כֹּהֵן, יַעֲמֹד (insert name) יִשְׂרָאֵל (לֵוִי) בִּמְקוֹם כֹּהֵן.״

בָּרוּךְ שֶׁנָּתַן תּוֹרָה לְעַמּוֹ יִשְׂרָאֵל בִּקְדֻשָּׁתוֹ. (תּוֹרַת יהוה תְּמִימָה מְשִׁיבַת נָפֶשׁ, עֵדוּת יהוה נֶאֱמָנָה מַחְכִּימַת פֶּתִי. פִּקּוּדֵי יהוה יְשָׁרִים מְשַׂמְּחֵי לֵב, מִצְוַת יהוה בָּרָה מְאִירַת עֵינָיִם.[6] יהוה עֹז לְעַמּוֹ יִתֵּן, יהוה יְבָרֵךְ אֶת עַמּוֹ בַשָּׁלוֹם.[7] הָאֵל תָּמִים דַּרְכּוֹ, אִמְרַת יהוה צְרוּפָה, מָגֵן הוּא לְכֹל הַחוֹסִים בּוֹ.[8])

Congregation, then *gabbai:*

וְאַתֶּם הַדְּבֵקִים בַּיהוה אֱלֹהֵיכֶם, חַיִּים כֻּלְּכֶם הַיּוֹם.[9]

(1) *I Chronicles* 29:11. (2) *Psalms* 99:5,9. (3) 68:5. (4) *Isaiah* 52:8.
(5) 40:5. (6) *Psalms* 19:8-9.(7) 29:11. (8) 18:31. (9) *Deuteronomy* 4:4.

The *chazzan* turns to his right and carries the Torah to the *bimah,* as the congregation responds:

לְךָ *Yours, HASHEM, is the greatness, the strength, the splendor, the triumph, and the glory; even everything in heaven and earth; Yours, HASHEM, is the kingdom, and the sovereignty over every leader.*[1] *Exalt HASHEM, our God, and bow at His footstool; He is Holy! Exalt HASHEM, our God, and bow to His holy mountain; for holy is HASHEM, our God.*[2]

As the *chazzan* carries the Torah to the *bimah* the congregation recites:

עַל הַכֹּל *For all this, let the Name of the King of kings, the Holy One, Blessed is He, grow exalted, sanctified, praised, glorified, exalted, and extolled in the worlds that He has created — This World and the World to Come — according to His will, the will of those who fear Him, and the will of the entire House of Israel. Rock of the eternities, Master of all creatures, God of all souls, He Who sits in the expanses on high, Who rests in the loftiest primeval heavens. His holiness is upon the Chayos; His holiness is upon the Throne of Glory. Similarly, may Your Name be sanctified within us, HASHEM, our God, in the sight of all the living. May we chant before Him a new song as it is written: 'Sing to God, make music for His Name, extol the One Who rides in the highest heavens with His Name YAH, and exult before Him.'*[3] *May we see Him with a perceptive view upon His return to His Abode, as is written: 'For they shall see with a perceptive view as HASHEM returns to Zion.'*[4] *And it is said: 'The glory of HASHEM shall be revealed and all flesh together shall see that the mouth of HASHEM has spoken.'*[5]

אַב הָרַחֲמִים *May the Father of compassion have mercy on the nation that is borne by Him, and may He remember the covenant of the spiritually mighty. May He rescue our souls from the bad times, and upbraid the evil inclination to leave those borne by Him, graciously make us an eternal remnant, and fulfill our requests in good measure, for salvation and mercy.*

The Torah is placed on the *bimah* and prepared for reading.

The *gabbai* uses the following formula to call a *Kohen* to the Torah:

וְיַעֲזוֹר *May He help, shield, and save all who take refuge in Him — Now let us respond: Amen. All of you ascribe greatness to our God and give honor to the Torah. Kohen,° approach. Arise* (name) *son of* (father's name) *the Kohen*

°If no *Kohen* is present, the *gabbai* says: *'There is no Kohen present, stand* (name) *son of* (father's name) *an Israelite (Levite) in place of the Kohen.'*

Blessed is He Who gave the Torah to His people Israel in His holiness. (The Torah of HASHEM is perfect, restoring the soul; the testimony of HASHEM is trustworthy, making the simple one wise. The orders of HASHEM are upright, gladdening the heart; the command of HASHEM is clear, enlightening the eyes.[6] *HASHEM will give might to His nation; HASHEM will bless His nation with peace.*[7] *The God Whose way is perfect, the promise of HASHEM is flawless, He is a shield for all who take refuge in Him.*[8]*)*

Congregation then *gabbai:*

You who cling to HASHEM, your God, you are all alive today.[9]

קריאת התורה להושענא רבה

The reader shows the *oleh* (person called to the Torah) the place in the Torah. The *oleh* touches the Torah with a corner of his *tallis,* or the belt or mantle of the Torah, and kisses it. He then begins the blessing, bowing at בָּרְכוּ, and straightening up at ה׳.

בָּרְכוּ אֶת יהוה הַמְּבֹרָךְ.

Congregation, followed by *oleh,* responds, bowing at בָּרוּךְ, and straightening up at ה׳.

בָּרוּךְ יהוה הַמְּבֹרָךְ לְעוֹלָם וָעֶד.

Oleh continues:

בָּרוּךְ אַתָּה יהוה אֱלֹהֵינוּ מֶלֶךְ הָעוֹלָם, אֲשֶׁר בָּחַר בָּנוּ מִכָּל הָעַמִּים, וְנָתַן לָנוּ אֶת תּוֹרָתוֹ. בָּרוּךְ אַתָּה יהוה, נוֹתֵן הַתּוֹרָה. (–Cong. אָמֵן.)

After his Torah portion has been read, the *oleh* recites:

בָּרוּךְ אַתָּה יהוה אֱלֹהֵינוּ מֶלֶךְ הָעוֹלָם, אֲשֶׁר נָתַן לָנוּ תּוֹרַת אֱמֶת, וְחַיֵּי עוֹלָם נָטַע בְּתוֹכֵנוּ. בָּרוּךְ אַתָּה יהוה, נוֹתֵן הַתּוֹרָה. (–Cong. אָמֵן.)

במדבר כט:כו-לד

כהן – וּבַיּ֧וֹם הַחֲמִישִׁ֛י פָּרִ֥ים תִּשְׁעָ֖ה אֵילִ֣ם שְׁנָ֑יִם כְּבָשִׂ֧ים בְּנֵי־שָׁנָ֛ה אַרְבָּעָ֥ה עָשָׂ֖ר תְּמִימִֽם׃ וּמִנְחָתָ֣ם וְנִסְכֵּיהֶ֡ם לַפָּרִ֡ים לָֽאֵילִ֧ם וְלַכְּבָשִׂ֛ים בְּמִסְפָּרָ֖ם כַּמִּשְׁפָּֽט׃ וּשְׂעִ֥יר חַטָּ֖את אֶחָ֑ד מִלְּבַד֙ עֹלַ֣ת הַתָּמִ֔יד וּמִנְחָתָ֖הּ וְנִסְכָּֽהּ׃

לוי – וּבַיּ֧וֹם הַשִּׁשִּׁ֛י פָּרִ֥ים שְׁמֹנָ֖ה אֵילִ֣ם שְׁנָ֑יִם כְּבָשִׂ֧ים בְּנֵי־שָׁנָ֛ה אַרְבָּעָ֥ה עָשָׂ֖ר תְּמִימִֽם׃ וּמִנְחָתָ֣ם וְנִסְכֵּיהֶ֡ם לַפָּרִ֡ים לָֽאֵילִ֧ם וְלַכְּבָשִׂ֛ים בְּמִסְפָּרָ֖ם כַּמִּשְׁפָּֽט׃ וּשְׂעִ֥יר חַטָּ֖את אֶחָ֑ד מִלְּבַד֙ עֹלַ֣ת הַתָּמִ֔יד מִנְחָתָ֖הּ וּנְסָכֶֽיהָ׃

שלישי – וּבַיּ֧וֹם הַשְּׁבִיעִ֛י פָּרִ֥ים שִׁבְעָ֖ה אֵילִ֣ם שְׁנָ֑יִם כְּבָשִׂ֧ים בְּנֵי־שָׁנָ֛ה אַרְבָּעָ֥ה עָשָׂ֖ר תְּמִימִֽם׃ וּמִנְחָתָ֣ם וְנִסְכֵּהֶ֡ם לַפָּרִ֡ים לָֽאֵילִ֧ם וְלַכְּבָשִׂ֛ים בְּמִסְפָּרָ֖ם כְּמִשְׁפָּטָֽם׃ וּשְׂעִ֥יר חַטָּ֖את אֶחָ֑ד מִלְּבַד֙ עֹלַ֣ת הַתָּמִ֔יד מִנְחָתָ֖הּ וְנִסְכָּֽהּ׃

רביעי – וּבַיּ֧וֹם הַשִּׁשִּׁ֛י פָּרִ֥ים שְׁמֹנָ֖ה אֵילִ֣ם שְׁנָ֑יִם כְּבָשִׂ֧ים בְּנֵי־שָׁנָ֛ה אַרְבָּעָ֥ה עָשָׂ֖ר תְּמִימִֽם׃ וּמִנְחָתָ֣ם וְנִסְכֵּיהֶ֡ם לַפָּרִ֡ים לָֽאֵילִ֧ם וְלַכְּבָשִׂ֛ים בְּמִסְפָּרָ֖ם כַּמִּשְׁפָּֽט׃ וּשְׂעִ֥יר חַטָּ֖את אֶחָ֑ד מִלְּבַד֙ עֹלַ֣ת הַתָּמִ֔יד מִנְחָתָ֖הּ וּנְסָכֶֽיהָ׃ וּבַיּ֧וֹם הַשְּׁבִיעִ֛י פָּרִ֥ים שִׁבְעָ֖ה אֵילִ֣ם שְׁנָ֑יִם כְּבָשִׂ֧ים בְּנֵי־שָׁנָ֛ה אַרְבָּעָ֥ה עָשָׂ֖ר תְּמִימִֽם׃ וּמִנְחָתָ֣ם וְנִסְכֵּהֶ֡ם לַפָּרִ֡ים לָֽאֵילִ֧ם וְלַכְּבָשִׂ֛ים בְּמִסְפָּרָ֖ם כְּמִשְׁפָּטָֽם׃ וּשְׂעִ֥יר חַטָּ֖את אֶחָ֑ד מִלְּבַד֙ עֹלַ֣ת הַתָּמִ֔יד מִנְחָתָ֖הּ וְנִסְכָּֽהּ׃

⁂ READING OF THE TORAH ⁂

The reader shows the *oleh* (person called to the Torah) the place in the Torah. The *oleh* touches the Torah with a corner of his *tallis,* or the belt or mantle of the Torah, and kisses it. He then begins the blessing, bowing at *'Bless,'* and straightening up at 'HASHEM.'

Bless HASHEM, the blessed One.

Congregation, followed by *oleh,* responds, bowing at 'Blessed,' and straightening up at 'HASHEM.'

Blessed is HASHEM, the blessed One, for all eternity.

Oleh continues:

בָּרוּךְ *Blessed are You, HASHEM, our God, King of the universe, Who selected us from all the peoples and gave us His Torah. Blessed are You, HASHEM, Giver of the Torah.* (Cong.– *Amen.)*

After his Torah portion has been read, the *oleh* recites:

בָּרוּךְ *Blessed are You, HASHEM, our God, King of the universe, Who gave us the Torah of truth and implanted eternal life within us. Blessed are You, HASHEM, Giver of the Torah.* (Cong.– *Amen.)*

Numbers 29:26-34

Kohen – *And on the fifth day: nine bulls, two rams, fourteen lambs within their first year; they are to be unblemished. And their meal-offerings and their libations for the bulls, the rams, and the lambs, in their proper numbers as required. And one he-goat for a sin-offering; aside from the continual elevation-offering, its meal-offering, and its libation.*

Levi – *And on the sixth day: eight bulls, two rams, fourteen lambs within their first year; they are to be unblemished. And their meal-offerings and their libations for the bulls, the rams and the lambs, in their proper numbers as required. And one he-goat for a sin-offering; aside from the continual elevation-offering, its meal-offering, and its libations.*

Third – *And on the seventh day: seven bulls, two rams, fourteen lambs within their first year; they are to be unblemished. And their meal-offerings and their libations for the bulls, the rams, and the lambs, in their proper numbers as required. And one he-goat for a sin offering; aside from the continual elevation-offering, its meal-offering, and its libation.*

Fourth – *And on the sixth day: eight bulls, two rams, fourteen lambs within their first year; they are to be unblemished. And their meal-offerings and their libations for the bulls, the rams and the lambs, in their proper numbers as required. And one he-goat for a sin-offering; aside from the continual elevation-offering, its meal-offering, and its libations. And on the seventh day: seven bulls, two rams, fourteen lambs within their first year; they are to be unblemished. And their meal-offerings and their libations for the bulls, the rams, and the lambs, in their proper numbers as required. And one he-goat for a sin offering; aside from the continual elevation-offering, its meal-offering, and its libation.*

חצי קדיש

After the last *oleh* has completed his closing blessing, the reader recites Half-*Kaddish*.

יִתְגַּדַּל וְיִתְקַדַּשׁ שְׁמֵהּ רַבָּא. (.Cong – אָמֵן.) בְּעָלְמָא דִּי בְרָא כִרְעוּתֵהּ. וְיַמְלִיךְ מַלְכוּתֵהּ, בְּחַיֵּיכוֹן וּבְיוֹמֵיכוֹן וּבְחַיֵּי דְכָל בֵּית יִשְׂרָאֵל, בַּעֲגָלָא וּבִזְמַן קָרִיב. וְאִמְרוּ: אָמֵן.

(.Cong – אָמֵן. יְהֵא שְׁמֵהּ רַבָּא מְבָרַךְ לְעָלַם וּלְעָלְמֵי עָלְמַיָּא.)

יְהֵא שְׁמֵהּ רַבָּא מְבָרַךְ לְעָלַם וּלְעָלְמֵי עָלְמַיָּא.

יִתְבָּרַךְ וְיִשְׁתַּבַּח וְיִתְפָּאַר וְיִתְרוֹמַם וְיִתְנַשֵּׂא וְיִתְהַדָּר וְיִתְעַלֶּה וְיִתְהַלָּל שְׁמֵהּ דְּקֻדְשָׁא בְּרִיךְ הוּא (.Cong – בְּרִיךְ הוּא) – לְעֵלָּא מִן כָּל בִּרְכָתָא וְשִׁירָתָא תֻּשְׁבְּחָתָא וְנֶחֱמָתָא, דַּאֲמִירָן בְּעָלְמָא. וְאִמְרוּ: אָמֵן. (.Cong – אָמֵן.)

The Torah is raised for all to see. Each person looks at the Torah and recites aloud:

וְזֹאת הַתּוֹרָה אֲשֶׁר שָׂם מֹשֶׁה לִפְנֵי בְּנֵי יִשְׂרָאֵל,[1] עַל פִּי יהוה בְּיַד מֹשֶׁה.[2]

Some add:

עֵץ חַיִּים הִיא לַמַּחֲזִיקִים בָּהּ, וְתֹמְכֶיהָ מְאֻשָּׁר.[3] דְּרָכֶיהָ דַרְכֵי נֹעַם, וְכָל נְתִיבוֹתֶיהָ שָׁלוֹם.[4] אֹרֶךְ יָמִים בִּימִינָהּ, בִּשְׂמֹאלָהּ עֹשֶׁר וְכָבוֹד.[5] יהוה חָפֵץ לְמַעַן צִדְקוֹ, יַגְדִּיל תּוֹרָה וְיַאְדִּיר.[6]

הכנסת ספר תורה

The *chazzan* takes the Torah in his right arm and recites:

יְהַלְלוּ אֶת שֵׁם יהוה, כִּי נִשְׂגָּב שְׁמוֹ לְבַדּוֹ –

Congregation responds:

– הוֹדוֹ עַל אֶרֶץ וְשָׁמָיִם. וַיָּרֶם קֶרֶן לְעַמּוֹ, תְּהִלָּה לְכָל חֲסִידָיו, לִבְנֵי יִשְׂרָאֵל עַם קְרֹבוֹ, הַלְלוּיָהּ.[7]

As the Torah is carried to the Ark the congregation recites the following psalm.

תהלים כד

לְדָוִד מִזְמוֹר, לַיהוה הָאָרֶץ וּמְלוֹאָהּ, תֵּבֵל וְיֹשְׁבֵי בָהּ. כִּי הוּא עַל יַמִּים יְסָדָהּ, וְעַל נְהָרוֹת יְכוֹנְנֶהָ. מִי יַעֲלֶה בְהַר יהוה, וּמִי יָקוּם בִּמְקוֹם קָדְשׁוֹ. נְקִי כַפַּיִם וּבַר לֵבָב, אֲשֶׁר לֹא נָשָׂא לַשָּׁוְא נַפְשִׁי וְלֹא נִשְׁבַּע לְמִרְמָה. יִשָּׂא בְרָכָה מֵאֵת יהוה, וּצְדָקָה מֵאֱלֹהֵי יִשְׁעוֹ. זֶה דּוֹר דֹּרְשָׁיו, מְבַקְשֵׁי פָנֶיךָ, יַעֲקֹב, סֶלָה. שְׂאוּ שְׁעָרִים רָאשֵׁיכֶם, וְהִנָּשְׂאוּ פִּתְחֵי עוֹלָם, וְיָבוֹא מֶלֶךְ הַכָּבוֹד. מִי זֶה מֶלֶךְ הַכָּבוֹד, יהוה עִזּוּז וְגִבּוֹר, יהוה גִּבּוֹר מִלְחָמָה. שְׂאוּ

HALF KADDISH

After the last *oleh* has completed his closing blessing, the reader recites Half-*Kaddish:*

יִתְגַּדַּל *May His great Name grow exalted and sanctified* (Cong.– *Amen.*) *in the world that He created as He willed. May He give reign to His kingship in your lifetimes and in your days, and in the lifetimes of the entire Family of Israel, swiftly and soon. Now respond: Amen.*

(Cong.– *Amen. May His great Name be blessed forever and ever.*)
May His great Name be blessed forever and ever.

Blessed, praised, glorified, exalted, extolled, mighty, upraised, and lauded be the Name of the Holy One, Blessed is He (Cong.– *Blessed is He*) *— beyond any blessing and song, praise and consolation that are uttered in the world. Now respond: Amen.* (Cong.– *Amen.*)

The Torah is raised for all to see. Each person looks at the Torah and recites aloud:

This is the Torah that Moses placed before the Children of Israel,[1] upon the command of HASHEM, through Moses' hand.[2]

Some add:

עֵץ *It is a tree of life for those who grasp it, and its supporters are praiseworthy.[3] Its ways are ways of pleasantness and all its paths are peace.[4] Lengthy days are at its right; at its left are wealth and honor.[5] HASHEM desired, for the sake of its [Israel's] righteousness, that the Torah be made great and glorious.[6]*

RETURNING THE TORAH

The *chazzan* takes the Torah in his right arm and recites:

Let them praise the Name of HASHEM,
for His Name alone will have been exalted –

Congregation responds:

— His glory is above earth and heaven. And He will have exalted the pride of His people, causing praise for all His devout ones, for the Children of Israel, His intimate people. Halleluyah![7]

As the Torah is carried to the Ark the congregation recites the following psalm.

Psalm 24

לְדָוִד *Of David a psalm. HASHEM's is the earth and its fullness, the inhabited land and those who dwell in it. For He founded it upon seas, and established it upon rivers. Who may ascend the mountain of HASHEM, and who may stand in the place of His sanctity? One with clean hands and pure heart, who has not sworn in vain by My soul and has not sworn deceitfully. He will receive a blessing from HASHEM and just kindness from the God of his salvation. This is the generation of those who seek Him, those who strive for Your Presence — Jacob, Selah. Raise up your heads, O gates, and be uplifted, you everlasting entrances, so that the King of Glory may enter. Who is this King of Glory? — HASHEM, the mighty and strong, HASHEM, the strong in battle.*

---

(1) *Deuteronomy* 4:44. (2) *Numbers* 9:23. (3) *Proverbs* 3:18. (4) 3:17.
(5) 3:16. (6) *Isaiah* 42:21. (7) *Psalms* 148:13-14.

שְׂעָרִים רָאשֵׁיכֶם, וּשְׂאוּ פִּתְחֵי עוֹלָם, וְיָבֹא מֶלֶךְ הַכָּבוֹד. מִי הוּא זֶה מֶלֶךְ הַכָּבוֹד, יהוה צְבָאוֹת הוּא מֶלֶךְ הַכָּבוֹד, סֶלָה.

As the Torah is placed into the Ark, the congregation recites the following verses:

וּבְנֻחֹה יֹאמַר, שׁוּבָה יהוה רִבְבוֹת אַלְפֵי יִשְׂרָאֵל.[1] קוּמָה יהוה לִמְנוּחָתֶךָ, אַתָּה וַאֲרוֹן עֻזֶּךָ. כֹּהֲנֶיךָ יִלְבְּשׁוּ צֶדֶק, וַחֲסִידֶיךָ יְרַנֵּנוּ. בַּעֲבוּר דָּוִד עַבְדֶּךָ, אַל תָּשֵׁב פְּנֵי מְשִׁיחֶךָ.[2] כִּי לֶקַח טוֹב נָתַתִּי לָכֶם, תּוֹרָתִי אַל תַּעֲזֹבוּ.[3] ❖ עֵץ חַיִּים הִיא לַמַּחֲזִיקִים בָּהּ, וְתֹמְכֶיהָ מְאֻשָּׁר.[4] דְּרָכֶיהָ דַרְכֵי נֹעַם, וְכָל נְתִיבוֹתֶיהָ שָׁלוֹם.[5] הֲשִׁיבֵנוּ יהוה אֵלֶיךָ וְנָשׁוּבָה, חַדֵּשׁ יָמֵינוּ כְּקֶדֶם.[6]

אַשְׁרֵי יוֹשְׁבֵי בֵיתֶךָ, עוֹד יְהַלְלוּךָ סֶּלָה.[7] אַשְׁרֵי הָעָם שֶׁכָּכָה לּוֹ, אַשְׁרֵי הָעָם שֶׁיהוה אֱלֹהָיו.[8]

תהלים קמה

תְּהִלָּה לְדָוִד,

אֲרוֹמִמְךָ אֱלוֹהַי הַמֶּלֶךְ, וַאֲבָרְכָה שִׁמְךָ לְעוֹלָם וָעֶד.
בְּכָל יוֹם אֲבָרְכֶךָּ, וַאֲהַלְלָה שִׁמְךָ לְעוֹלָם וָעֶד.
גָּדוֹל יהוה וּמְהֻלָּל מְאֹד, וְלִגְדֻלָּתוֹ אֵין חֵקֶר.
דּוֹר לְדוֹר יְשַׁבַּח מַעֲשֶׂיךָ, וּגְבוּרֹתֶיךָ יַגִּידוּ.
הֲדַר כְּבוֹד הוֹדֶךָ, וְדִבְרֵי נִפְלְאוֹתֶיךָ אָשִׂיחָה.
וֶעֱזוּז נוֹרְאוֹתֶיךָ יֹאמֵרוּ, וּגְדוּלָּתְךָ אֲסַפְּרֶנָּה.
זֵכֶר רַב טוּבְךָ יַבִּיעוּ, וְצִדְקָתְךָ יְרַנֵּנוּ.
חַנּוּן וְרַחוּם יהוה, אֶרֶךְ אַפַּיִם וּגְדָל חָסֶד.
טוֹב יהוה לַכֹּל, וְרַחֲמָיו עַל כָּל מַעֲשָׂיו.
יוֹדוּךָ יהוה כָּל מַעֲשֶׂיךָ, וַחֲסִידֶיךָ יְבָרְכוּכָה.
כְּבוֹד מַלְכוּתְךָ יֹאמֵרוּ, וּגְבוּרָתְךָ יְדַבֵּרוּ.
לְהוֹדִיעַ לִבְנֵי הָאָדָם גְּבוּרֹתָיו, וּכְבוֹד הֲדַר מַלְכוּתוֹ.
מַלְכוּתְךָ מַלְכוּת כָּל עֹלָמִים, וּמֶמְשַׁלְתְּךָ בְּכָל דּוֹר וָדֹר.
סוֹמֵךְ יהוה לְכָל הַנֹּפְלִים, וְזוֹקֵף לְכָל הַכְּפוּפִים.

---

(1) *Numbers* 10:36. (2) *Psalms* 132:8-10. (3) *Proverbs* 4:2. (4) 3:18.
(5) 3:17. (6) *Lamentations* 5:21. (7) Psalms 84:5. (8) 144:15.

Raise up your heads, O gates, and raise up, you everlasting entrances, so that the King of Glory may enter. Who then is the King of Glory? HASHEM, Master of Legions, He is the King of Glory. Selah!

As the Torah is placed into the Ark, the congregation recites the following verses:

וּבְנֻחֹה *And when it rested he would say, 'Return HASHEM to the myriad thousands of Israel.'*[1] *Arise, HASHEM, to Your resting place, You and the Ark of Your strength. Let Your priests be clothed in righteousness, and Your devout ones will sing joyously. For the sake of David, Your servant, turn not away the face of Your anointed.*[2] *For I have given you a good teaching, do not forsake My Torah.*[3] Chazzan– *It is a tree of life for those who grasp it, and its supporters are praiseworthy.*[4] *Its ways are ways of pleasantness and all its paths are peace.*[5] *Bring us back to You, HASHEM, and we shall return, renew our days as of old.*[6]

אַשְׁרֵי *Praiseworthy are those who dwell in Your house; may they always praise You, Selah!*[7] *Praiseworthy is the people for whom this is so, praiseworthy is the people whose God is HASHEM.*[8]

Psalm 145 — *A psalm of praise by David:*

א *I will exalt You, my God the King,*
and I will bless Your Name forever and ever.
ב *Every day I will bless You,*
and I will laud Your Name forever and ever.
ג *HASHEM is great and exceedingly lauded,*
and His greatness is beyond investigation.
ד *Each generation will praise Your deeds to the next*
and of Your mighty deeds they will tell.
ה *The splendrous glory of Your power*
and Your wondrous deeds I shall discuss.
ו *And of Your awesome power they will speak,*
and Your greatness I shall relate.
ז *A recollection of Your abundant goodness they will utter*
and of Your righteousness they will sing exultantly.
ח *Gracious and merciful is HASHEM,*
slow to anger, and great in [bestowing] kindness.
ט *HASHEM is good to all; His mercies are on all His works.*
י *All Your works shall thank You, HASHEM,*
and Your devout ones will bless You.
כ *Of the glory of Your kingdom they will speak,*
and of Your power they will tell;
ל *To inform human beings of His mighty deeds,*
and the glorious splendor of His kingdom.
מ *Your kingdom is a kingdom spanning all eternities,*
and Your dominion is throughout every generation.
ס *HASHEM supports all the fallen ones and straightens all the bent.*

עֵינֵי כֹל אֵלֶיךָ יְשַׂבֵּרוּ, וְאַתָּה נוֹתֵן לָהֶם אֶת אָכְלָם בְּעִתּוֹ.

While reciting the verse פּוֹתֵחַ, concentrate intently on its meaning.

פּוֹתֵחַ אֶת יָדֶךָ,
וּמַשְׂבִּיעַ לְכָל חַי רָצוֹן.
צַדִּיק יהוה בְּכָל דְּרָכָיו, וְחָסִיד בְּכָל מַעֲשָׂיו.
קָרוֹב יהוה לְכָל קֹרְאָיו, לְכֹל אֲשֶׁר יִקְרָאֻהוּ בֶאֱמֶת.
רְצוֹן יְרֵאָיו יַעֲשֶׂה, וְאֶת שַׁוְעָתָם יִשְׁמַע וְיוֹשִׁיעֵם.
שׁוֹמֵר יהוה אֶת כָּל אֹהֲבָיו, וְאֵת כָּל הָרְשָׁעִים יַשְׁמִיד.
❖ תְּהִלַּת יהוה יְדַבֶּר פִּי,
וִיבָרֵךְ כָּל בָּשָׂר שֵׁם קָדְשׁוֹ לְעוֹלָם וָעֶד.
וַאֲנַחְנוּ נְבָרֵךְ יָהּ, מֵעַתָּה וְעַד עוֹלָם, הַלְלוּיָהּ.[1]

The primary part of וּבָא לְצִיּוֹן is the *Kedushah* recited by the angels. These verses are presented in bold type and it is preferable that the congregation recite them aloud and in unison. However, the interpretive translation in Aramaic (which follows the verses in bold type) should be recited softly.

וּבָא לְצִיּוֹן גּוֹאֵל, וּלְשָׁבֵי פֶשַׁע בְּיַעֲקֹב, נְאֻם יהוה. וַאֲנִי, זֹאת בְּרִיתִי אוֹתָם, אָמַר יהוה, רוּחִי אֲשֶׁר עָלֶיךָ, וּדְבָרַי אֲשֶׁר שַׂמְתִּי בְּפִיךָ, לֹא יָמוּשׁוּ מִפִּיךָ וּמִפִּי זַרְעֲךָ וּמִפִּי זֶרַע זַרְעֲךָ, אָמַר יהוה, מֵעַתָּה וְעַד עוֹלָם:[2] ❖ וְאַתָּה קָדוֹשׁ יוֹשֵׁב תְּהִלּוֹת יִשְׂרָאֵל.[3] וְקָרָא זֶה אֶל זֶה וְאָמַר:

קָדוֹשׁ, קָדוֹשׁ, קָדוֹשׁ יהוה צְבָאוֹת, מְלֹא כָל הָאָרֶץ כְּבוֹדוֹ.[4]

וּמְקַבְּלִין דֵּין מִן דֵּין וְאָמְרִין:
קַדִּישׁ בִּשְׁמֵי מְרוֹמָא עִלָּאָה בֵּית שְׁכִינְתֵּהּ,
קַדִּישׁ עַל אַרְעָא עוֹבַד גְּבוּרְתֵּהּ,
קַדִּישׁ לְעָלַם וּלְעָלְמֵי עָלְמַיָּא, יהוה צְבָאוֹת,
מַלְיָא כָל אַרְעָא זִיו יְקָרֵהּ.[5]

❖ וַתִּשָּׂאֵנִי רוּחַ, וָאֶשְׁמַע אַחֲרַי קוֹל רַעַשׁ גָּדוֹל:

בָּרוּךְ כְּבוֹד יהוה מִמְּקוֹמוֹ.[6]

וּנְטָלַתְנִי רוּחָא, וּשְׁמִעֵת בַּתְרַי קָל זִיעַ סַגִּיא דִּמְשַׁבְּחִין וְאָמְרִין:
בְּרִיךְ יְקָרָא דַיהוה מֵאֲתַר בֵּית שְׁכִינְתֵּהּ.[7]

יהוה יִמְלֹךְ לְעֹלָם וָעֶד.[8]

יהוה מַלְכוּתֵהּ קָאֵם לְעָלַם וּלְעָלְמֵי עָלְמַיָּא.[9]

---

(1) *Psalms* 115:18. (2) *Isaiah* 59:20-21. (3) *Psalms* 22:4. (4) *Isaiah* 6:3. (5) *Targum Yonasan.* (6) *Ezekiel* 3:12. (7) *Targum Yonasan.* (8) *Exodus* 15:18. (9) *Targum Onkelos.*

ע *The eyes of all look to You with hope*
and You give them their food in its proper time;
פ *You open Your hand,*
and satisfy the desire of every living thing.

While reciting the verse, *'You open . . .'* concentrate intently on its meaning.

צ *Righteous is HASHEM in all His ways*
and magnanimous in all His deeds.
ק *HASHEM is close to all who call upon Him —*
to all who call upon Him sincerely.
ר *The will of those who fear Him He will do;*
and their cry He will hear, and save them.
ש *HASHEM protects all who love Him;*
but all the wicked He will destroy.
ת Chazzan– *May my mouth declare the praise of HASHEM*
and may all flesh bless His Holy Name forever and ever.
We will bless God from this time and forever, Halleluyah![1]

The primary part of וּבָא לְצִיּוֹן, *'A redeemer shall come . . .',* is the *Kedushah* recited by the angels. These verses are presented in bold type and it is preferable that the congregation recite them aloud and in unison. However, the interpretive translation in Aramaic (which follows the verses in bold type) should be recited softly.

וּבָא לְצִיּוֹן *'A redeemer shall come to Zion* and to those of Jacob who repent from willful sin,' the words of HASHEM. 'And as for Me, this is My covenant* with them,' said HASHEM, 'My spirit that is upon you and My words that I have placed in your mouth shall not be withdrawn from your mouth, nor from the mouth of your offspring,* nor from the mouth of your offspring's offspring,' said HASHEM, 'from this moment and forever.'*[2]

Chazzan– *You are the Holy One, enthroned upon the praises of Israel.**[3]
And one [angel] will call another and say:

'Holy, holy, holy is HASHEM, Master of Legions,
the whole world is filled with His glory.'[4]

And they receive permission from one another and say:
'Holy in the most exalted heaven, the abode of His Presence;
holy on earth, product of His strength;
holy forever and ever is HASHEM, Master of Legions —
the entire world is filled with the radiance of His glory.'[5]

Chazzan– *And a wind lifted me;* and I heard behind me*
the sound of a great noise:

'Blessed is the glory of HASHEM from His place.'[6]

And a wind lifted me and I heard behind me the sound
of the powerful movement of those who praised saying:
'Blessed is the honor of HASHEM
from the place of the abode of His Presence.'[7]

HASHEM shall reign for all eternity.[8]

HASHEM — His kingdom is established forever and ever.[9]

יהוה אֱלֹהֵי אַבְרָהָם יִצְחָק וְיִשְׂרָאֵל אֲבֹתֵינוּ, שָׁמְרָה זֹּאת לְעוֹלָם, לְיֵצֶר מַחְשְׁבוֹת לְבַב עַמֶּךָ, וְהָכֵן לְבָבָם אֵלֶיךָ.[1] וְהוּא רַחוּם, יְכַפֵּר עָוֹן וְלֹא יַשְׁחִית, וְהִרְבָּה לְהָשִׁיב אַפּוֹ, וְלֹא יָעִיר כָּל חֲמָתוֹ.[2] כִּי אַתָּה אֲדֹנָי טוֹב וְסַלָּח, וְרַב חֶסֶד לְכָל קֹרְאֶיךָ.[3] צִדְקָתְךָ צֶדֶק לְעוֹלָם, וְתוֹרָתְךָ אֱמֶת.[4] תִּתֵּן אֱמֶת לְיַעֲקֹב, חֶסֶד לְאַבְרָהָם, אֲשֶׁר נִשְׁבַּעְתָּ לַאֲבֹתֵינוּ מִימֵי קֶדֶם.[5] בָּרוּךְ אֲדֹנָי יוֹם יוֹם יַעֲמָס לָנוּ, הָאֵל יְשׁוּעָתֵנוּ סֶלָה.[6] יהוה צְבָאוֹת עִמָּנוּ, מִשְׂגָּב לָנוּ אֱלֹהֵי יַעֲקֹב סֶלָה.[7] יהוה צְבָאוֹת, אַשְׁרֵי אָדָם בֹּטֵחַ בָּךְ.[8] יהוה הוֹשִׁיעָה, הַמֶּלֶךְ יַעֲנֵנוּ בְיוֹם קָרְאֵנוּ.[9]

בָּרוּךְ הוּא אֱלֹהֵינוּ שֶׁבְּרָאָנוּ לִכְבוֹדוֹ, וְהִבְדִּילָנוּ מִן הַתּוֹעִים, וְנָתַן לָנוּ תּוֹרַת אֱמֶת, וְחַיֵּי עוֹלָם נָטַע בְּתוֹכֵנוּ. הוּא יִפְתַּח לִבֵּנוּ בְּתוֹרָתוֹ, וְיָשֵׂם בְּלִבֵּנוּ אַהֲבָתוֹ וְיִרְאָתוֹ וְלַעֲשׂוֹת רְצוֹנוֹ וּלְעָבְדוֹ בְּלֵבָב שָׁלֵם, לְמַעַן לֹא נִיגַע לָרִיק, וְלֹא נֵלֵד לַבֶּהָלָה.[10]

יְהִי רָצוֹן מִלְּפָנֶיךָ יהוה אֱלֹהֵינוּ וֵאלֹהֵי אֲבוֹתֵינוּ, שֶׁנִּשְׁמֹר חֻקֶּיךָ בָּעוֹלָם הַזֶּה, וְנִזְכֶּה וְנִחְיֶה וְנִרְאֶה וְנִירַשׁ טוֹבָה וּבְרָכָה לִשְׁנֵי יְמוֹת הַמָּשִׁיחַ וּלְחַיֵּי הָעוֹלָם הַבָּא. לְמַעַן יְזַמֶּרְךָ כָבוֹד וְלֹא יִדֹּם, יהוה אֱלֹהַי לְעוֹלָם אוֹדֶךָּ.[11] בָּרוּךְ הַגֶּבֶר אֲשֶׁר יִבְטַח בַּיהוה, וְהָיָה יהוה מִבְטַחוֹ.[12] בִּטְחוּ בַיהוה עֲדֵי עַד, כִּי בְּיָהּ יהוה צוּר עוֹלָמִים.[13] ❖ וְיִבְטְחוּ בְךָ יוֹדְעֵי שְׁמֶךָ, כִּי לֹא עָזַבְתָּ דֹּרְשֶׁיךָ, יהוה.[14] יהוה חָפֵץ לְמַעַן צִדְקוֹ, יַגְדִּיל תּוֹרָה וְיַאְדִּיר.[15]

Chazzan recites חֲצִי קַדִּישׁ.

יִתְגַּדַּל וְיִתְקַדַּשׁ שְׁמֵהּ רַבָּא. (.Cong – אָמֵן.) בְּעָלְמָא דִּי בְרָא כִרְעוּתֵהּ. וְיַמְלִיךְ מַלְכוּתֵהּ, בְּחַיֵּיכוֹן וּבְיוֹמֵיכוֹן וּבְחַיֵּי דְכָל בֵּית יִשְׂרָאֵל, בַּעֲגָלָא וּבִזְמַן קָרִיב. וְאִמְרוּ: אָמֵן.

(.Cong – אָמֵן. יְהֵא שְׁמֵהּ רַבָּא מְבָרַךְ לְעָלַם וּלְעָלְמֵי עָלְמַיָּא.)

יְהֵא שְׁמֵהּ רַבָּא מְבָרַךְ לְעָלַם וּלְעָלְמֵי עָלְמַיָּא.

יִתְבָּרַךְ וְיִשְׁתַּבַּח וְיִתְפָּאַר וְיִתְרוֹמַם וְיִתְנַשֵּׂא וְיִתְהַדָּר וְיִתְעַלֶּה וְיִתְהַלָּל שְׁמֵהּ דְּקֻדְשָׁא בְּרִיךְ הוּא (.Cong – בְּרִיךְ הוּא) — לְעֵלָּא מִן כָּל בִּרְכָתָא וְשִׁירָתָא תֻּשְׁבְּחָתָא וְנֶחֱמָתָא, דַּאֲמִירָן בְּעָלְמָא. וְאִמְרוּ: אָמֵן. (.Cong – אָמֵן.)

---

(1) *I Chronicles* 29:18. (2) *Psalms* 78:38. (3) 86:5. (4) 119:142. (5) *Micah* 7:20. (6) *Psalms* 68:20. (7) 46:8. (8) 84:13. (9) 20:10. (10) Cf. *Isaiah* 65:23. (11) *Psalms* 30:13. (12) *Jeremiah* 17:7. (13) *Isaiah* 26:4. (14) *Psalms* 9:11. (15) *Isaiah* 42:21.

HASHEM, God of Abraham, Isaac, and Israel, our forefathers, may You preserve this forever as the realization of the thoughts in Your people's heart, and may You direct their heart to You.*[1] *He, the Merciful One, is forgiving of iniquity and does not destroy; frequently He withdraws His anger, not arousing His entire rage.*[2] *For You, my Lord, are good and forgiving, and abundantly kind to all who call upon You.*[3] *Your righteousness remains righteous forever, and Your Torah is truth.*[4] *Grant truth to Jacob, kindness to Abraham, as You swore to our forefathers from ancient times.*[5] *Blessed is my Lord for every single day, He burdens us with blessings, the God of our salvation, Selah.*[6] *HASHEM, Master of Legions, is with us, a stronghold for us is the God of Jacob, Selah.*[7] *HASHEM, Master of Legions, praiseworthy is the man who trusts in You.*[8] *HASHEM, save! May the King answer us on the day we call.*[9]

Blessed is He, our God, Who created us for His glory, separated us from those who stray, gave us the Torah of truth and implanted eternal life within us. May He open our heart through His Torah and imbue our heart with love and awe of Him and that we may do His will and serve Him wholeheartedly, so that we do not struggle in vain nor produce for futility.[10]

May it be Your will, HASHEM, our God and the God of our forefathers, that we observe Your decrees in This World, and merit that we live and see and inherit goodness and blessing in the years of Messianic times and for the life of the World to Come. So that my soul might sing to You and not be stilled, HASHEM, my God, forever will I thank You.[11] *Blessed is the man who trusts in HASHEM, then HASHEM will be his security.*[12] *Trust in HASHEM forever, for in God, HASHEM, is the strength of the worlds.*[13] Chazzan– *Those knowing Your Name will trust in You, and You forsake not those Who seek You, HASHEM.*[14] *HASHEM desired, for the sake of its [Israel's] righteousness, that the Torah be made great and glorious.*[15]

Chazzan recites Half-*Kaddish*.

יִתְגַּדַּל *May His great Name grow exalted and sanctified* (Cong.– *Amen.*) *in the world that He created as He willed. May He give reign to His kingship in your lifetimes and in your days, and in the lifetimes of the entire Family of Israel, swiftly and soon. Now respond: Amen.*

(Cong.– *Amen. May His great Name be blessed forever and ever.*)

May His great Name be blessed forever and ever.

Blessed, praised, glorified, exalted, extolled, mighty, upraised, and lauded be the Name of the Holy One, Blessed is He (Cong.– *Blessed is He*) — *beyond any blessing and song, praise and consolation that are uttered in the world. Now respond: Amen.* (Cong.– *Amen.*)

מוסף להושענא רבה

Take three steps backward, then three steps forward. Remain standing with the feet together while reciting *Shemoneh Esrei.* Recite it with quiet devotion and without interruption, verbal or otherwise. Although its recitation should not be audible to others, one must pray loudly enough to hear himself.

כִּי שֵׁם יהוה אֶקְרָא, הָבוּ גֹדֶל לֵאלֹהֵינוּ.[1]
אֲדֹנָי שְׂפָתַי תִּפְתָּח, וּפִי יַגִּיד תְּהִלָּתֶךָ.[2]

Bend the knees at בָּרוּךְ; bow at אַתָּה; straighten up at ה׳.

בָּרוּךְ אַתָּה יהוה אֱלֹהֵינוּ וֵאלֹהֵי אֲבוֹתֵינוּ, אֱלֹהֵי אַבְרָהָם, אֱלֹהֵי יִצְחָק, וֵאלֹהֵי יַעֲקֹב, הָאֵל הַגָּדוֹל הַגִּבּוֹר וְהַנּוֹרָא, אֵל עֶלְיוֹן, גּוֹמֵל חֲסָדִים טוֹבִים וְקוֹנֵה הַכֹּל, וְזוֹכֵר חַסְדֵי אָבוֹת, וּמֵבִיא גוֹאֵל לִבְנֵי בְנֵיהֶם, לְמַעַן שְׁמוֹ בְּאַהֲבָה. מֶלֶךְ עוֹזֵר וּמוֹשִׁיעַ וּמָגֵן.

Bend the knees at בָּרוּךְ; bow at אַתָּה; straighten up at ה׳.

בָּרוּךְ אַתָּה יהוה, מָגֵן אַבְרָהָם.

אַתָּה גִּבּוֹר לְעוֹלָם אֲדֹנָי, מְחַיֵּה מֵתִים אַתָּה, רַב לְהוֹשִׁיעַ. מְכַלְכֵּל חַיִּים בְּחֶסֶד, מְחַיֵּה מֵתִים בְּרַחֲמִים רַבִּים, סוֹמֵךְ נוֹפְלִים, וְרוֹפֵא חוֹלִים, וּמַתִּיר אֲסוּרִים, וּמְקַיֵּם אֱמוּנָתוֹ לִישֵׁנֵי עָפָר. מִי כָמוֹךָ בַּעַל גְּבוּרוֹת, וּמִי דּוֹמֶה לָּךְ, מֶלֶךְ מֵמִית וּמְחַיֶּה וּמַצְמִיחַ יְשׁוּעָה. וְנֶאֱמָן אַתָּה לְהַחֲיוֹת מֵתִים. בָּרוּךְ אַתָּה יהוה, מְחַיֵּה הַמֵּתִים.

During the *chazzan's* repetition, *Kedushah* (below) is recited at this point.

קדושה

When reciting *Kedushah,* one must stand with his feet together, and avoid any interruptions. One should rise on his toes when saying the words קָדוֹשׁ, קָדוֹשׁ, קָדוֹשׁ; בָּרוּךְ (of בָּרוּךְ כְּבוֹד); and יִמְלֹךְ.

Cong. then *chazzan*:

נַעֲרִיצְךָ וְנַקְדִּישְׁךָ כְּסוֹד שִׂיחַ שַׂרְפֵי קֹדֶשׁ, הַמַּקְדִּישִׁים שִׁמְךָ בַּקֹּדֶשׁ, כַּכָּתוּב עַל יַד נְבִיאֶךָ, וְקָרָא זֶה אֶל זֶה וְאָמַר:

All – קָדוֹשׁ קָדוֹשׁ קָדוֹשׁ יהוה צְבָאוֹת, מְלֹא כָל הָאָרֶץ כְּבוֹדוֹ.[3] ❖ כְּבוֹדוֹ מָלֵא עוֹלָם, מְשָׁרְתָיו שׁוֹאֲלִים זֶה לָזֶה, אַיֵּה מְקוֹם כְּבוֹדוֹ, לְעֻמָּתָם בָּרוּךְ יֹאמֵרוּ:

All – בָּרוּךְ כְּבוֹד יהוה, מִמְּקוֹמוֹ.[4] ❖ מִמְּקוֹמוֹ הוּא יִפֶן בְּרַחֲמִים, וְיָחוֹן עַם הַמְיַחֲדִים שְׁמוֹ, עֶרֶב וָבֹקֶר בְּכָל יוֹם תָּמִיד, פַּעֲמַיִם בְּאַהֲבָה שְׁמַע אוֹמְרִים.

All – שְׁמַע יִשְׂרָאֵל, יהוה אֱלֹהֵינוּ, יהוה אֶחָד.[5] ❖ הוּא אֱלֹהֵינוּ. הוּא אָבִינוּ, הוּא מַלְכֵּנוּ, הוּא מוֹשִׁיעֵנוּ, וְהוּא יַשְׁמִיעֵנוּ בְּרַחֲמָיו שֵׁנִית, לְעֵינֵי כָּל חָי, לִהְיוֹת לָכֶם לֵאלֹהִים, אֲנִי יהוה אֱלֹהֵיכֶם.[6]

All – אַדִּיר אַדִּירֵנוּ, יהוה אֲדֹנֵינוּ, מָה אַדִּיר שִׁמְךָ בְּכָל הָאָרֶץ.[7] וְהָיָה יהוה לְמֶלֶךְ עַל כָּל הָאָרֶץ, בַּיּוֹם הַהוּא יִהְיֶה יהוה אֶחָד וּשְׁמוֹ אֶחָד.[8]

Chazzan – וּבְדִבְרֵי קָדְשְׁךָ כָּתוּב לֵאמֹר:

All – יִמְלֹךְ יהוה לְעוֹלָם, אֱלֹהַיִךְ צִיּוֹן, לְדֹר וָדֹר, הַלְלוּיָהּ.[9]

MUSSAF FOR HOSHANA RABBAH

Take three steps backward, then three steps forward. Remain standing with the feet together while reciting *Shemoneh Esrei*. Recite it with quiet devotion and without interruption, verbal or otherwise. Although its recitation should not be audible to others, one must pray loudly enough to hear himself.

When I call out the Name of HASHEM, ascribe greatness to our God.[1]
My Lord, open my lips, that my mouth may declare Your praise.[2]

Bend the knees at *'Blessed'*; bow at *'You'*; straighten up at *'HASHEM.'*

בָּרוּךְ *Blessed are You, HASHEM, our God and the God of our forefathers, God of Abraham, God of Isaac, and God of Jacob; the great, mighty, and awesome God, the supreme God, Who bestows beneficial kindnesses and creates everything, Who recalls the kindnesses of the Patriarchs and brings a Redeemer to their children's children, for His Name's sake, with love. O King, Helper, Savior, and Shield.*

Bend the knees at *'Blessed'*; bow at *'You'*; straighten up at *'HASHEM.'*

Blessed are You, HASHEM, Shield of Abraham.

אַתָּה *You are eternally mighty, my Lord, the Resuscitator of the dead are You; abundantly able to save. He sustains the living with kindness, resuscitates the dead with abundant mercy, supports the fallen, heals the sick, releases the confined, and maintains His faith to those asleep in the dust. Who is like You, O Master of mighty deeds, and who is comparable to You, O King Who causes death and restores life and makes salvation sprout! And You are faithful to resuscitate the dead. Blessed are You, HASHEM, Who resuscitates the dead.*

During the *chazzan's* repetition, *Kedushah* (below) is recited at this point.

KEDUSHAH

When reciting *Kedushah*, one must stand with his feet together and avoid any interruptions. One should rise on his toes when saying the words *Holy, holy, holy; Blessed is; HASHEM shall reign.*

Cong. then *chazzan:*

נַעֲרִיצְךָ *We will revere You and sanctify You according to the counsel of the holy Seraphim, who sanctify Your Name in the Sanctuary, as it is written by Your prophet: "And one [angel] will call another and say:*

All — *'Holy, holy, holy is HASHEM, Master of Legions, the whole world is filled with His glory.' "*[3] ❖*His glory fills the world. His ministering angels ask one another, 'Where is the place of His glory?' Those facing them say 'Blessed':*

All — *'Blessed is the glory of HASHEM from His place.'*[4] ❖*From His place may He turn with compassion and be gracious to the people who declare the Oneness of His Name; evening and morning, every day constantly, twice, with love, they proclaim 'Shema.'*

All — *'Hear O Israel: HASHEM is our God, HASHEM the One and Only.'*[5] ❖*He is our God; He is our Father; He is our King; He is our Savior; and He will let us hear, in His compassion, for a second time in the presence of all the living,' . . . to be a God to you, I am HASHEM, your God.'*[6]

All — *Mighty is our Mighty One, HASHEM, our Master — how mighty is Your name throughout the earth!*[7] *HASHEM will be King over all the world — on that day HASHEM will be One and His Name will be One.*[8]

Chazzan — *And in Your holy Writings the following is written:*

All — *'HASHEM shall reign forever — your God, O Zion — from generation to generation, Halleluyah!'*[9]

---

(1) *Deuteronomy* 32:3. (2) *Psalms* 51:17. (3) *Isaiah* 6:3. (4) *Ezekiel* 3:12. (5) *Deuteronomy* 6:4. (6) *Numbers* 15:41. (7) *Psalms* 8:2. (8) *Zechariah* 14:9. (9) *Psalms* 146:10.

קדושת השם

INDIVIDUALS RECITE:

אַתָּה קָדוֹשׁ וְשִׁמְךָ קָדוֹשׁ, וּקְדוֹשִׁים בְּכָל יוֹם יְהַלְלוּךָ סֶּלָה. בָּרוּךְ אַתָּה יהוה, הָאֵל הַקָּדוֹשׁ.

CHAZZAN RECITES DURING HIS REPETITION:

לְדוֹר וָדוֹר נַגִּיד גָּדְלֶךָ וּלְנֵצַח נְצָחִים קְדֻשָּׁתְךָ נַקְדִּישׁ, וְשִׁבְחֲךָ אֱלֹהֵינוּ מִפִּינוּ לֹא יָמוּשׁ לְעוֹלָם וָעֶד, כִּי אֵל מֶלֶךְ גָּדוֹל וְקָדוֹשׁ אָתָּה. בָּרוּךְ אַתָּה יהוה, הָאֵל הַקָּדוֹשׁ.

קדושת היום

אַתָּה בְחַרְתָּנוּ מִכָּל הָעַמִּים, אָהַבְתָּ אוֹתָנוּ, וְרָצִיתָ בָּנוּ, וְרוֹמַמְתָּנוּ מִכָּל הַלְּשׁוֹנוֹת, וְקִדַּשְׁתָּנוּ בְּמִצְוֹתֶיךָ, וְקֵרַבְתָּנוּ מַלְכֵּנוּ לַעֲבוֹדָתֶךָ, וְשִׁמְךָ הַגָּדוֹל וְהַקָּדוֹשׁ עָלֵינוּ קָרָאתָ.

וַתִּתֶּן לָנוּ יהוה אֱלֹהֵינוּ בְּאַהֲבָה מוֹעֲדִים לְשִׂמְחָה חַגִּים וּזְמַנִּים לְשָׂשׂוֹן, אֶת יוֹם חַג הַסֻּכּוֹת הַזֶּה, זְמַן שִׂמְחָתֵנוּ מִקְרָא קֹדֶשׁ, זֵכֶר לִיצִיאַת מִצְרָיִם.

וּמִפְּנֵי חֲטָאֵינוּ גָּלִינוּ מֵאַרְצֵנוּ, וְנִתְרַחַקְנוּ מֵעַל אַדְמָתֵנוּ. וְאֵין אֲנַחְנוּ יְכוֹלִים לַעֲלוֹת וְלֵרָאוֹת וּלְהִשְׁתַּחֲוֹת לְפָנֶיךָ, וְלַעֲשׂוֹת חוֹבוֹתֵינוּ בְּבֵית בְּחִירָתֶךָ, בַּבַּיִת הַגָּדוֹל וְהַקָּדוֹשׁ שֶׁנִּקְרָא שִׁמְךָ עָלָיו, מִפְּנֵי הַיָּד שֶׁנִּשְׁתַּלְּחָה בְּמִקְדָּשֶׁךָ. יְהִי רָצוֹן מִלְּפָנֶיךָ יהוה אֱלֹהֵינוּ וֵאלֹהֵי אֲבוֹתֵינוּ, מֶלֶךְ רַחֲמָן, שֶׁתָּשׁוּב וּתְרַחֵם עָלֵינוּ וְעַל מִקְדָּשְׁךָ בְּרַחֲמֶיךָ הָרַבִּים, וְתִבְנֵהוּ מְהֵרָה וּתְגַדֵּל כְּבוֹדוֹ. אָבִינוּ מַלְכֵּנוּ, גַּלֵּה כְּבוֹד מַלְכוּתְךָ עָלֵינוּ מְהֵרָה, וְהוֹפַע וְהִנָּשֵׂא עָלֵינוּ לְעֵינֵי כָּל חָי. וְקָרֵב פְּזוּרֵינוּ מִבֵּין הַגּוֹיִם, וּנְפוּצוֹתֵינוּ כַּנֵּס מִיַּרְכְּתֵי אָרֶץ. וַהֲבִיאֵנוּ לְצִיּוֹן עִירְךָ בְּרִנָּה, וְלִירוּשָׁלַיִם בֵּית מִקְדָּשְׁךָ בְּשִׂמְחַת עוֹלָם. וְשָׁם נַעֲשֶׂה לְפָנֶיךָ אֶת קָרְבְּנוֹת חוֹבוֹתֵינוּ, תְּמִידִים כְּסִדְרָם, וּמוּסָפִים כְּהִלְכָתָם. וְאֶת מוּסַף יוֹם חַג הַסֻּכּוֹת הַזֶּה נַעֲשֶׂה וְנַקְרִיב לְפָנֶיךָ בְּאַהֲבָה כְּמִצְוַת רְצוֹנֶךָ, כְּמוֹ שֶׁכָּתַבְתָּ עָלֵינוּ בְּתוֹרָתֶךָ, עַל יְדֵי מֹשֶׁה עַבְדֶּךָ, מִפִּי כְבוֹדֶךָ כָּאָמוּר:

HOLINESS OF GOD'S NAME

INDIVIDUALS RECITE:

אַתָּה *You are holy and Your Name is holy, and holy ones praise You every day, forever. Blessed are You,* HASHEM, *the holy God.*

CHAZZAN RECITES DURING HIS REPETITION:

לְדוֹר *From generation to generation we shall relate Your greatness and for infinite eternities we shall proclaim Your holiness. Your praise, our God, shall not leave our mouth forever and ever, for You, O God, are a great and holy King. Blessed are You,* HASHEM, *the holy God.*

SANCTIFICATION OF THE DAY

אַתָּה בְחַרְתָּנוּ *You have chosen us from all the peoples; You loved us and found favor in us; You exalted us above all the tongues and You sanctified us with Your commandments. You drew us close, our King, to Your service and proclaimed Your great and Holy Name upon us.*

וַתִּתֶּן לָנוּ *And You gave us,* HASHEM, *our God, with love appointed festivals for gladness, Festivalsand times for joy, this day of the Festival of Succos, the time of our gladness, a holy convocation, a memorial of the Exodus from Egypt.*

וּמִפְּנֵי חֲטָאֵינוּ *But because of our sins we have been exiled from our land and sent far from our soil. We cannot ascend to appear and to prostrate ourselves before You, and to perform our obligations in the House of Your choice, in the great and holy House upon which Your Name was proclaimed, because of the hand that was dispatched against Your Sanctuary. May it be Your will,* HASHEM, *our God and the God of our forefathers, O merciful King, that You once more be compassionate upon us and upon Your Sanctuary in Your abundant mercy, and rebuild it soon and magnify its glory. Our Father, our King, reveal the glory of Your Kingship upon us, speedily; appear and be uplifted over us before the eyes of all the living. Draw our scattered ones near, from among the nations, and bring in our dispersions from the ends of the earth. Bring us to Zion, Your City, in glad song, and to Jerusalem, home of Your Sanctuary, in eternal joy. There we will perform before You our obligatory offerings, the continual offerings according to their order and the additional offerings according to their law. And the additional offering*[s of this day of Sabbath and] *of this day of the Festival of Succos, we will perform and bring near to You with love, according to the commandment of Your will, as You have written for us in Your Torah, through Moses, Your servant, from Your glorious expression, as it is said:*

וּבַיּוֹם הַשִּׁשִּׁי פָּרִים שְׁמֹנָה, אֵילִם שְׁנָיִם, כְּבָשִׂים בְּנֵי שָׁנָה אַרְבָּעָה עָשָׂר, תְּמִימִם.[1] וּמִנְחָתָם וְנִסְכֵּיהֶם כִּמְדֻבָּר, שְׁלֹשָׁה עֶשְׂרֹנִים לַפָּר, וּשְׁנֵי עֶשְׂרֹנִים לָאָיִל, וְעִשָּׂרוֹן לַכֶּבֶשׂ, וְיַיִן כְּנִסְכּוֹ. וְשָׂעִיר לְכַפֵּר, וּשְׁנֵי תְמִידִים כְּהִלְכָתָם. וּבַיּוֹם הַשְּׁבִיעִי, פָּרִים שִׁבְעָה, אֵילִם שְׁנָיִם, כְּבָשִׂים בְּנֵי שָׁנָה אַרְבָּעָה עָשָׂר, תְּמִימִם.[2] וּמִנְחָתָם וְנִסְכֵּיהֶם כִּמְדֻבָּר, שְׁלֹשָׁה עֶשְׂרֹנִים לַפָּר, וּשְׁנֵי עֶשְׂרֹנִים לָאָיִל, וְעִשָּׂרוֹן לַכֶּבֶשׂ, וְיַיִן כְּנִסְכּוֹ. וְשָׂעִיר לְכַפֵּר, וּשְׁנֵי תְמִידִים כְּהִלְכָתָם.

אֱלֹהֵינוּ וֵאלֹהֵי אֲבוֹתֵינוּ, מֶלֶךְ רַחֲמָן רַחֵם עָלֵינוּ, טוֹב וּמֵטִיב הִדָּרֶשׁ לָנוּ, שׁוּבָה אֵלֵינוּ בַּהֲמוֹן רַחֲמֶיךָ, בִּגְלַל אָבוֹת שֶׁעָשׂוּ רְצוֹנֶךָ. בְּנֵה בֵיתְךָ כְּבַתְּחִלָּה, וְכוֹנֵן מִקְדָּשְׁךָ עַל מְכוֹנוֹ, וְהַרְאֵנוּ בְּבִנְיָנוֹ, וְשַׂמְּחֵנוּ בְּתִקּוּנוֹ. וְהָשֵׁב כֹּהֲנִים לַעֲבוֹדָתָם, וּלְוִיִּם לְשִׁירָם וּלְזִמְרָם, וְהָשֵׁב יִשְׂרָאֵל לִנְוֵיהֶם. וְשָׁם נַעֲלֶה וְנֵרָאֶה וְנִשְׁתַּחֲוֶה לְפָנֶיךָ, בְּשָׁלֹשׁ פַּעֲמֵי רְגָלֵינוּ, כַּכָּתוּב בְּתוֹרָתֶךָ: שָׁלוֹשׁ פְּעָמִים בַּשָּׁנָה, יֵרָאֶה כָל זְכוּרְךָ אֶת פְּנֵי יהוה אֱלֹהֶיךָ, בַּמָּקוֹם אֲשֶׁר יִבְחָר, בְּחַג הַמַּצּוֹת, וּבְחַג הַשָּׁבֻעוֹת, וּבְחַג הַסֻּכּוֹת, וְלֹא יֵרָאֶה אֶת פְּנֵי יהוה רֵיקָם. אִישׁ כְּמַתְּנַת יָדוֹ, כְּבִרְכַּת יהוה אֱלֹהֶיךָ, אֲשֶׁר נָתַן לָךְ.[3]

וְהַשִּׂיאֵנוּ יהוה אֱלֹהֵינוּ אֶת בִּרְכַּת מוֹעֲדֶיךָ לְחַיִּים וּלְשָׁלוֹם, לְשִׂמְחָה וּלְשָׂשׂוֹן, כַּאֲשֶׁר רָצִיתָ וְאָמַרְתָּ לְבָרְכֵנוּ. קַדְּשֵׁנוּ בְּמִצְוֹתֶיךָ וְתֵן חֶלְקֵנוּ בְּתוֹרָתֶךָ, שַׂבְּעֵנוּ מִטּוּבֶךָ וְשַׂמְּחֵנוּ בִּישׁוּעָתֶךָ, וְטַהֵר לִבֵּנוּ לְעָבְדְּךָ בֶּאֱמֶת, וְהַנְחִילֵנוּ יהוה אֱלֹהֵינוּ בְּשִׂמְחָה וּבְשָׂשׂוֹן מוֹעֲדֵי קָדְשֶׁךָ, וְיִשְׂמְחוּ בְךָ יִשְׂרָאֵל מְקַדְּשֵׁי שְׁמֶךָ. בָּרוּךְ אַתָּה יהוה, מְקַדֵּשׁ יִשְׂרָאֵל וְהַזְּמַנִּים.

עבודה

רְצֵה יהוה אֱלֹהֵינוּ בְּעַמְּךָ יִשְׂרָאֵל וּבִתְפִלָּתָם, וְהָשֵׁב אֶת הָעֲבוֹדָה לִדְבִיר בֵּיתֶךָ. וְאִשֵּׁי יִשְׂרָאֵל וּתְפִלָּתָם בְּאַהֲבָה תְקַבֵּל בְּרָצוֹן, וּתְהִי לְרָצוֹן תָּמִיד עֲבוֹדַת יִשְׂרָאֵל עַמֶּךָ.

וּבַיּוֹם הַשִּׁשִּׁי *And on the sixth day: eight bulls, two rams, fourteen [male] first-year lambs, unblemished.*[1] *And their meal-offerings and their wine-libations as mentioned: three tenth-ephah for each bull; two tenth-ephah for each ram; one tenth-ephah for each lamb; and wine for its libation. A he-goat for atonement, and two continual offerings according to their law. And on the seventh day: seven bulls, two rams, fourteen [male] first-year lambs, unblemished.*[2] *And their meal-offerings and their wine-libations as mentioned: three tenth-ephah for each bull; two tenth-ephah for each ram; one tenth-ephah for each lamb; and wine for its libation. A he-goat for atonement, and two continual offerings according to their law.*

אֱלֹהֵינוּ *Our God and the God of our forefathers, O merciful King, have mercy on us; O good and beneficent One, let Yourself be sought out by us; return to us in Your yearning mercy for the sake of the forefathers who did Your will. Rebuild Your House as it was at first, and establish Your Sanctuary on its prepared site; show us its rebuilding and gladden us in its perfection. Restore the Kohanim to their service and the Levites to their song and music; and restore Israel to their dwellings. And there we will ascend and appear and prostrate ourselves before You, during our three pilgrimage seasons, as it is written in Your Torah: Three times a year all your males are to appear before* HASHEM, *your God, in the place He shall choose, on the Festival of Matzos, on the Festival of Shavuos, and on the Festival of Succos, and they shall not appear before* HASHEM *empty-handed. Every man according to the gift of his hand, according to the blessing of* HASHEM, *your God, that He gave you.*[3]

וְהַשִּׂיאֵנוּ *Bestow upon us, O* HASHEM, *our God, the blessing of Your appointed Festivals for life and for peace, for gladness and for joy, as You desired and promised to bless us. Sanctify us with Your commandments and grant us our share in Your Torah; satisfy us from Your goodness and gladden us with Your salvation, and purify our heart to serve You sincerely. And grant us a heritage, O* HASHEM, *our God — with gladness and with joy — the appointed festivals of Your holiness, and may Israel, the sanctifiers of Your Name, rejoice in You. Blessed are You,* HASHEM, *Who sanctifies Israel and the festive seasons.*

TEMPLE SERVICE

רְצֵה *Be favorable,* HASHEM, *our God, toward Your people Israel and their prayer and restore the service to the Holy of Holies of Your Temple. The fire-offerings of Israel and their prayer accept with love and favor, and may the service of Your people Israel always be favorable to You.*

---

(1) *Numbers* 29:29. (2) 29:32. (3) *Deuteronomy* 16:16-17.

וְתֶחֱזֶינָה עֵינֵינוּ בְּשׁוּבְךָ לְצִיּוֹן בְּרַחֲמִים. בָּרוּךְ אַתָּה יהוה, הַמַּחֲזִיר שְׁכִינָתוֹ לְצִיּוֹן.

הודאה

Bow at מוֹדִים; straighten up at ה׳. In his repetition the *chazzan* should recite the entire מוֹדִים aloud, while the congregation recites מוֹדִים דְּרַבָּנָן softly.

מוֹדִים אֲנַחְנוּ לָךְ, שָׁאַתָּה הוּא יהוה אֱלֹהֵינוּ וֵאלֹהֵי אֲבוֹתֵינוּ לְעוֹלָם וָעֶד. צוּר חַיֵּינוּ, מָגֵן יִשְׁעֵנוּ אַתָּה הוּא לְדוֹר וָדוֹר. נוֹדֶה לְּךָ וּנְסַפֵּר תְּהִלָּתֶךָ[1] עַל חַיֵּינוּ הַמְּסוּרִים בְּיָדֶךָ, וְעַל נִשְׁמוֹתֵינוּ הַפְּקוּדוֹת לָךְ, וְעַל נִסֶּיךָ שֶׁבְּכָל יוֹם עִמָּנוּ, וְעַל נִפְלְאוֹתֶיךָ וְטוֹבוֹתֶיךָ שֶׁבְּכָל עֵת, עֶרֶב וָבֹקֶר וְצָהֳרָיִם. הַטּוֹב כִּי לֹא כָלוּ רַחֲמֶיךָ, וְהַמְּרַחֵם כִּי לֹא תַמּוּ חֲסָדֶיךָ,[2] מֵעוֹלָם קִוִּינוּ לָךְ.

מודים דרבנן

מוֹדִים אֲנַחְנוּ לָךְ, שָׁאַתָּה הוּא יהוה אֱלֹהֵינוּ וֵאלֹהֵי אֲבוֹתֵינוּ, אֱלֹהֵי כָל בָּשָׂר, יוֹצְרֵנוּ, יוֹצֵר בְּרֵאשִׁית. בְּרָכוֹת וְהוֹדָאוֹת לְשִׁמְךָ הַגָּדוֹל וְהַקָּדוֹשׁ, עַל שֶׁהֶחֱיִיתָנוּ וְקִיַּמְתָּנוּ. כֵּן תְּחַיֵּנוּ וּתְקַיְּמֵנוּ, וְתֶאֱסוֹף גָּלֻיּוֹתֵינוּ לְחַצְרוֹת קָדְשֶׁךָ, לִשְׁמוֹר חֻקֶּיךָ וְלַעֲשׂוֹת רְצוֹנֶךָ, וּלְעָבְדְּךָ בְּלֵבָב שָׁלֵם, עַל שֶׁאֲנַחְנוּ מוֹדִים לָךְ. בָּרוּךְ אֵל הַהוֹדָאוֹת.

וְעַל כֻּלָּם יִתְבָּרַךְ וְיִתְרוֹמַם שִׁמְךָ מַלְכֵּנוּ תָּמִיד לְעוֹלָם וָעֶד.

Bend the knees at בָּרוּךְ; bow at אַתָּה; straighten up at ה׳.

וְכֹל הַחַיִּים יוֹדוּךָ סֶּלָה, וִיהַלְלוּ אֶת שִׁמְךָ בֶּאֱמֶת, הָאֵל יְשׁוּעָתֵנוּ וְעֶזְרָתֵנוּ סֶלָה. בָּרוּךְ אַתָּה יהוה, הַטּוֹב שִׁמְךָ וּלְךָ נָאֶה לְהוֹדוֹת.

ברכת כהנים

The *chazzan* recites the following during his repetition. He faces right at וְיִשְׁמְרֶךָ; faces left at אֵלֶיךָ וִיחֻנֶּךָּ; faces the Ark for the rest of the blessings.

אֱלֹהֵינוּ, וֵאלֹהֵי אֲבוֹתֵינוּ, בָּרְכֵנוּ בַבְּרָכָה הַמְּשֻׁלֶּשֶׁת בַּתּוֹרָה הַכְּתוּבָה עַל יְדֵי מֹשֶׁה עַבְדֶּךָ, הָאֲמוּרָה מִפִּי אַהֲרֹן וּבָנָיו, כֹּהֲנִים עַם קְדוֹשֶׁךָ, כָּאָמוּר:

יְבָרֶכְךָ יהוה, וְיִשְׁמְרֶךָ. (.Cong – כֵּן יְהִי רָצוֹן.)

יָאֵר יהוה פָּנָיו אֵלֶיךָ וִיחֻנֶּךָּ. (.Cong – כֵּן יְהִי רָצוֹן.)

יִשָּׂא יהוה פָּנָיו אֵלֶיךָ וְיָשֵׂם לְךָ שָׁלוֹם.[3] (.Cong – כֵּן יְהִי רָצוֹן.)

וְתֶחֱזֶינָה *May our eyes behold Your return to Zion in compassion. Blessed are You, HASHEM, Who restores His Presence to Zion.*

THANKSGIVING [MODIM]

Bow at *'We gratefully thank You'*; straighten up at *'HASHEM.'* In his repetition the *chazzan* should recite the entire *Modim* aloud, while the congregation recites *Modim of the Rabbis* softly.

מוֹדִים *We gratefully thank You, for it is You Who are HASHEM, our God and the God of our forefathers for all eternity; Rock of our lives, Shield of our salvation are You from generation to generation. We shall thank You and relate Your praise*[1] *— for our lives, which are committed to Your power and for our souls that are entrusted to You; for Your miracles that are with us every day; and for Your wonders and favors in every season — evening, morning, and afternoon. The Beneficent One, for Your compassions were never exhausted, and the Compassionate One, for Your kindnesses never ended*[2] *— always have we put our hope in You.*

MODIM OF THE RABBIS

מוֹדִים *We gratefully thank You, for it is You Who are HASHEM, our God and the God of our forefathers, the God of all flesh, our Molder, the Molder of the universe. Blessings and thanks are due Your great and holy Name for You have given us life and sustained us. So may You continue to give us life and sustain us and gather our exiles to the Courtyards of Your Sanctuary, to observe Your decrees, to do Your will and to serve You wholeheartedly. [We thank You] for inspiring us to thank You. Blessed is the God of thanksgivings.*

For all these, may Your Name be blessed and exalted, our King, continually forever and ever.

Bend the knees at *'Blessed'*; bow at *'You'*; straighten up at *'HASHEM.'*

Everything alive will gratefully acknowledge You, Selah! and praise Your Name sincerely, O God of our salvation and help, Selah! Blessed are You, HASHEM, Your Name is 'The Beneficent One' and to You it is fitting to give thanks.

THE PRIESTLY BLESSING

The *chazzan* recites the following during his repetition.

אֱלֹהֵינוּ *Our God and the God of our forefathers, bless us with the three-verse blessing in the Torah that was written by the hand of Moses, Your servant, that was said by Aaron and his sons, the Kohanim, Your holy people, as it is said:*

May HASHEM bless you and safeguard you. (Cong.— *So may it be.*)

May HASHEM illuminate His countenance for you and be gracious to you. (Cong.— *So may it be.*)

May HASHEM turn His countenance to you and establish peace for you.[3] (Cong.— *So may it be.*)

(1) Cf. *Psalms* 79:13. (2) Cf. *Lamentations* 3:22. (3) *Numbers* 6:24-26.

שלום

שִׂים שָׁלוֹם, טוֹבָה, וּבְרָכָה, חֵן, וָחֶסֶד וְרַחֲמִים עָלֵינוּ וְעַל כָּל יִשְׂרָאֵל עַמֶּךָ. בָּרְכֵנוּ אָבִינוּ, כֻּלָּנוּ כְּאֶחָד בְּאוֹר פָּנֶיךָ, כִּי בְאוֹר פָּנֶיךָ נָתַתָּ לָּנוּ, יהוה אֱלֹהֵינוּ, תּוֹרַת חַיִּים וְאַהֲבַת חֶסֶד, וּצְדָקָה, וּבְרָכָה, וְרַחֲמִים, וְחַיִּים, וְשָׁלוֹם. וְטוֹב בְּעֵינֶיךָ לְבָרֵךְ אֶת עַמְּךָ יִשְׂרָאֵל, בְּכָל עֵת וּבְכָל שָׁעָה בִּשְׁלוֹמֶךָ. בָּרוּךְ אַתָּה יהוה, הַמְּבָרֵךְ אֶת עַמּוֹ יִשְׂרָאֵל בַּשָּׁלוֹם.

יִהְיוּ לְרָצוֹן אִמְרֵי פִי וְהֶגְיוֹן לִבִּי לְפָנֶיךָ, יהוה צוּרִי וְגוֹאֲלִי.[1]

The *chazzan's* repetition of *Shemoneh Esrei* ends here. The individual continues below:

אֱלֹהַי, נְצוֹר לְשׁוֹנִי מֵרָע, וּשְׂפָתַי מִדַּבֵּר מִרְמָה,[2] וְלִמְקַלְלַי נַפְשִׁי תִדּוֹם, וְנַפְשִׁי כֶּעָפָר לַכֹּל תִּהְיֶה. פְּתַח לִבִּי בְּתוֹרָתֶךָ, וּבְמִצְוֹתֶיךָ תִּרְדּוֹף נַפְשִׁי. וְכֹל הַחוֹשְׁבִים עָלַי רָעָה, מְהֵרָה הָפֵר עֲצָתָם וְקַלְקֵל מַחֲשַׁבְתָּם. עֲשֵׂה לְמַעַן שְׁמֶךָ, עֲשֵׂה לְמַעַן יְמִינֶךָ, עֲשֵׂה לְמַעַן קְדֻשָּׁתֶךָ, עֲשֵׂה לְמַעַן תּוֹרָתֶךָ. לְמַעַן יֵחָלְצוּן יְדִידֶיךָ, הוֹשִׁיעָה יְמִינְךָ וַעֲנֵנִי.[3]

Some recite verses pertaining to their names here. See page 1301.

יִהְיוּ לְרָצוֹן אִמְרֵי פִי וְהֶגְיוֹן לִבִּי לְפָנֶיךָ, יהוה צוּרִי וְגוֹאֲלִי.[1]

Bow and take three steps back. Bow left and say ... עֹשֶׂה, bow right and say ... הוּא יַעֲשֶׂה; bow forward and say וְעַל כָּל ... אָמֵן.

עֹשֶׂה שָׁלוֹם בִּמְרוֹמָיו, הוּא יַעֲשֶׂה שָׁלוֹם עָלֵינוּ, וְעַל כָּל יִשְׂרָאֵל. וְאִמְרוּ: אָמֵן.

יְהִי רָצוֹן מִלְּפָנֶיךָ יהוה אֱלֹהֵינוּ וֵאלֹהֵי אֲבוֹתֵינוּ, שֶׁיִּבָּנֶה בֵּית הַמִּקְדָּשׁ בִּמְהֵרָה בְיָמֵינוּ, וְתֵן חֶלְקֵנוּ בְּתוֹרָתֶךָ. וְשָׁם נַעֲבָדְךָ בְּיִרְאָה, כִּימֵי עוֹלָם וּכְשָׁנִים קַדְמוֹנִיּוֹת. וְעָרְבָה לַיהוה מִנְחַת יְהוּדָה וִירוּשָׁלָיִם, כִּימֵי עוֹלָם וּכְשָׁנִים קַדְמוֹנִיּוֹת.[4]

THE INDIVIDUAL'S RECITATION OF *SHEMONEH ESREI* ENDS HERE.

The individual remains standing in place until the *chazzan* reaches *Kedushah* — or at least until the *chazzan* begins his repetition — then he takes three steps forward. The *chazzan* himself, or one praying alone, should remain in place for a few moments before taking three steps forward.

☙ Hoshanos on Hoshana Rabbah

Unlike the other days of Succos when only one Torah Scroll is removed from the Ark for the *Hoshana* prayers, on Hoshana Rabbah every Torah Scroll is removed and held at the *bimah*. Many congregations place a burning candle — symbolic of אוֹר תּוֹרָה, *the Torah's light* — in the empty Ark until the Scrolls are returned.

Instead of the usual single *Hoshana* circuit of the previous days, on Hoshana Rabbah seven circuits are made as seven *Hoshana* prayers are recited. This recalls the procedure followed by Joshua when he led the nation in the victory against Jericho. For six days the nation circled the city one time each day. But on the seventh day they circled the city seven times [see *Joshua* ch. 8].

PEACE

שִׂים שָׁלוֹם *Establish peace, goodness, blessing, graciousness, kindness, and compassion upon us and upon all of Your people Israel. Bless us, our Father, all of us as one, with the light of Your countenance, for with the light of Your countenance You gave us,* HASHEM, *our God, the Torah of life and a love of kindness, righteousness, blessing, compassion, life, and peace. And may it be good in Your eyes to bless Your people Israel at every time and every hour with Your peace. Blessed are You,* HASHEM, *Who blesses His people Israel with peace.*

May the expressions of my mouth and the thoughts of my heart find favor before You, HASHEM, *my Rock and my Redeemer.*[1]

The *chazzan's* repetition of *Shemoneh Esrei* ends here. Individuals continue:

אֱלֹהַי *My God, guard my tongue from evil and my lips from speaking deceitfully.*[2] *To those who curse me, let my soul be silent; and let my soul be like dust to everyone. Open my heart to Your Torah, then my soul will pursue Your commandments. As for all those who design evil against me, speedily nullify their counsel and disrupt their design. Act for Your Name's sake; act for Your right hand's sake; act for Your sanctity's sake; act for Your Torah's sake. That Your beloved ones may be given rest; let Your right hand save, and respond to me.*[3]

Some recite verses pertaining to their names at this point. See page 1301.

May the expressions of my mouth and the thoughts of my heart find favor before You, HASHEM, *my Rock and my Redeemer.*[1] *He Who makes peace in His heights, may He make peace upon us, and upon all Israel. Now respond: Amen.*

Bow and take three steps back. Bow left and say, *'He Who makes peace . . .'*; bow right and say, *'may He make peace . . .'*; bow forward and say, *'and upon . . . Amen.'*

יְהִי רָצוֹן *May it be Your will,* HASHEM, *our God and the God of our forefathers, that the Holy Temple be rebuilt, speedily in our days. Grant us our share in Your Torah, and may we serve You there with reverence, as in days of old and in former years. Then the offering of Judah and Jerusalem will be pleasing to* HASHEM, *as in days of old and in former years.*[4]

THE INDIVIDUAL'S RECITATION OF *SHEMONEH ESREI* ENDS HERE.

The individual remains standing in place until the *chazzan* reaches *Kedushah* — or at least until the *chazzan* begins his repetition — then he takes three steps forward. The *chazzan* himself, or one praying alone, should remain in place for a few moments before taking three steps forward.

---

(1) *Psalms* 19:15. (2) Cf. 34:14. (3) 60:7; 108:7. (4) *Malachi* 3:4.

In some congregations the *shofar* is blown after each of the seven circuits.

After the circuits, seven additional prayers — for salvation, for abundant rainfall during the coming rainy season, for the Messiah — are recited.

At some point during the service (depending upon local custom; see p. 798) the Four Species are put down and the *hoshana*-bundle consisting of five *aravos* (willow twigs) is taken in hand. The *Hoshana* service concludes with the beating of the *Hoshana*-bundle, marking the end of the repentance and judgment period that began on Rosh Hashanah.

סדר הושענות להושענא רבה

For the ways in which the *Hoshana* service of Hoshana Rabbah differs from that of the earlier days of Succos, see page 774.

הוֹשַׁעְנָא, לְמַעַנְךָ אֱלֹהֵינוּ, הוֹשַׁעְנָא.
הוֹשַׁעְנָא, לְמַעַנְךָ בּוֹרְאֵנוּ, הוֹשַׁעְנָא.
הוֹשַׁעְנָא, לְמַעַנְךָ גּוֹאֲלֵנוּ, הוֹשַׁעְנָא.
הוֹשַׁעְנָא, לְמַעַנְךָ דּוֹרְשֵׁנוּ, הוֹשַׁעְנָא.

FIRST HAKAFAH CIRCUIT

לְמַעַן אֲמִתָּךְ. לְמַעַן בְּרִיתָךְ. לְמַעַן גָּדְלָךְ וְתִפְאַרְתָּךְ. לְמַעַן דָּתָךְ. לְמַעַן הוֹדָךְ. לְמַעַן וִעוּדָךְ. לְמַעַן זִכְרָךְ. לְמַעַן חַסְדָּךְ. לְמַעַן טוּבָךְ. לְמַעַן יִחוּדָךְ. לְמַעַן כְּבוֹדָךְ. לְמַעַן לִמּוּדָךְ. לְמַעַן מַלְכוּתָךְ. לְמַעַן נִצְחָךְ. לְמַעַן סוֹדָךְ. לְמַעַן עֻזָּךְ. לְמַעַן פְּאֵרָךְ. לְמַעַן צִדְקָתָךְ. לְמַעַן קְדֻשָּׁתָךְ. לְמַעַן רַחֲמֶיךָ הָרַבִּים. לְמַעַן שְׁכִינָתָךְ. לְמַעַן תְּהִלָּתָךְ.

כִּי אָמַרְתִּי עוֹלָם חֶסֶד יִבָּנֶה.[1]

SECOND HAKAFAH CIRCUIT

אֶבֶן שְׁתִיָּה. בֵּית הַבְּחִירָה. גֹּרֶן אָרְנָן. דְּבִיר הַמֻּצְנָע. הַר הַמּוֹרִיָּה. וְהַר יֵרָאֶה. זְבוּל תִּפְאַרְתֶּךָ. חָנָה דָוִד. טוֹב הַלְּבָנוֹן. יְפֵה נוֹף מְשׂוֹשׂ כָּל הָאָרֶץ. כְּלִילַת יֹפִי. לִינַת הַצֶּדֶק. מָכוֹן לְשִׁבְתֶּךָ. נָוֶה שַׁאֲנָן. סֻכַּת שָׁלֵם. עֲלִיַּת שְׁבָטִים. פִּנַּת יִקְרַת. צִיּוֹן הַמְּצֻיֶּנֶת. קֹדֶשׁ הַקֳּדָשִׁים. רָצוּף אַהֲבָה. שְׁכִינַת כְּבוֹדֶךָ. תֵּל תַּלְפִּיּוֹת.

לְךָ זְרוֹעַ עִם גְּבוּרָה, תָּעֹז יָדְךָ תָּרוּם יְמִינֶךָ.[2]

THIRD HAKAFAH CIRCUIT

אוֹם אֲנִי חוֹמָה.* בָּרָה כַּחַמָּה.* גּוֹלָה וְסוּרָה. דָּמְתָה לְתָמָר.* הַהֲרוּגָה עָלֶיךָ. וְנֶחֱשֶׁבֶת כְּצֹאן טִבְחָה. זְרוּיָה בֵּין

HOSHANOS FOR HOSHANA RABBAH

Commentary on the first two *Hoshanos* appears on page 362.

אוֹם אֲנִי חוֹמָה / Nation that Declares

Many metaphors are used in Scripture and Rabbinic writing to describe the nation of Israel. This *Hoshana* contains an alphabetical catalogue of such metaphors, chanted in prayer for the nation's redemption and salvation. Most of the epithets in this *Hoshana* are particularly applicable to Israel during its decline and exile. Material poverty is juxtaposed with spiritual wealth as the *paytan* paints a word-picture depicting the firm faith of God's chosen people.

אוֹם אֲנִי חוֹמָה — *Nation [that declares], 'I am a wall!'* The Heavenly Tribunal asks Israel: 'Are you steadfast in your faith as a wall of the strongest metal? Or are you influenced by every alien culture like a door swinging on its hinges this way and that?'

And Israel responds: 'אֲנִי חוֹמָה, *I am a wall*, strong and stalwart in my love for God!' (*Song of Songs* 8:9,10).

בָּרָה כַּחַמָּה — *Brilliant as the sun.* Israel is compared to the heavenly bodies — יָפָה כַלְּבָנָה,

HOSHANOS FOR HOSHANAH RABBAH

For the ways in which the *Hoshana* service of Hoshana Rabbah differs from that of the earlier days of Succos, see page 774.

הוֹשַׁעְנָא *Please save — for Your sake, our God! Please save!*
Please save — for Your sake, our Creator! Please save!
Please save — for Your sake, our Redeemer! Please save!
Please save — for Your sake, our Attender! Please save!

FIRST HAKAFAH CIRCUIT

לְמַעַן אֲמִתָּךְ *For the sake of Your Truth;* ב *for the sake of Your Covenant;* ג *for the sake of Your Greatness and Your Splendor;* ד *for the sake of Your Mandate;* ה *for the sake of Your Glory;* ו *for the sake of Your Meeting House;* ז *For the sake of Your Mention;* ח *for the sake of Your Kindness;* ט *for the sake of Your Goodness;* י *for the sake of Your Oneness;* כ *for the sake of Your Honor;* ל *for the sake of Your Teaching;* מ *for the sake of Your Kingship;* נ *for the sake of Your Eternality;* ס *for the sake of Your Counsel;* ע *for the sake of Your Power;* פ *for the sake of Your Beauty;* צ *for the sake of Your Righteousness;* ק *for the sake of Your Sanctity;* ר *for the sake of Your numerous Mercies;* ש *for the sake of Your Shechinah;* ת *for the sake of Your Praise.*

For I have said: 'The world shall be built with kindness.'[1]

SECOND HAKAFAH CIRCUIT

אֶבֶן שְׁתִיָּה *Foundation stone;* ב *chosen Temple;* ג *Arnan's granary;* ד *hidden rendezvous;* ה *Mount Moriah;* ו *Mount He-is-seen;* ז *residence of Your Splendor;* ח *where David resided;* ט *goodness of Lebanon;* י *fairest of brides, joy of all the earth;* כ *perfectly beautiful;* ל *lodge of righteousness;* מ *prepared for Your dwelling;* נ *tranquil abode;* ס *Tabernacle of Salem;* ע *pilgrimage of the tribes;* פ *valuable cornerstone;* צ *the distinguished Zion;* ק *Holy of Holies;* ר *decked with love;* ש *resting place of Your Honor;* ת *hill of Talpios.*

Yours is the arm with strength, show us the power of Your hand, raise high Your right hand.[2]

THIRD HAKAFAH CIRCUIT

אוֹם אֲנִי חוֹמָה *Nation [that declares], 'I am a wall!'** ב *Brilliant as the sun** — ג *yet exiled and displaced;* ד *likened to a palm tree** — ה *yet murdered for Your sake* ו *and regarded like a sheep for slaughter;* ז *although*

(1) *Psalms* 89:3. (2) 89:14.

beautiful as the moon, בָּרָה כַּחַמָּה, *brilliant as the sun (Song of Songs* 6:10). The dawn is preceded by darkness. Whatever light there is comes from the moon, itself but a small reflection of the sun's brilliance. Gradually, as the sun rises, darkness gives way to light; the moon's reflected splendor fades as the sun dazzles the earth in its full majesty. So it was during the era of the Second Temple. When the rebuilt *Beis HaMikdash* first gazed down upon the world from its lofty mountain, Israel was ruled by Zerubavel, an appointed governor — a mere reflection of majesty — serving at the pleasure of King Cyrus. Nevertheless, Israel was *beautiful as the moon.* But in later years, when the Hasmoneans rid the land of the alien Hellenist culture and established their own Jewish dynasty, the nation became בָּרָה כַּחַמָּה, *brilliant as the sun (Rashi).*

O return us to those days, not when we were merely a moonlike reflection of beauty, but when our brilliance rivaled even that of the sun.

דָּמְתָה לְתָמָר — *(She is) likened to a palm tree.* While every other nation prostrated itself before Nebuchadnezzar's statue, only Israel refused to

מַכְעִיסֶיהָ. חֲבוּקָה וּדְבוּקָה בָּךְ. טוֹעֶנֶת עֻלָּךְ. יְחִידָה לְיַחֲדָךְ. כְּבוּשָׁה בַּגּוֹלָה. לוֹמֶדֶת יִרְאָתָךְ. מְרוּטַת לֶחִי.* נְתוּנָה לְמַכִּים. סוֹבֶלֶת סִבְלָךְ. עֲנִיָּה סֹעֲרָה. פְּדוּיַת טוֹבִיָּה.* צֹאן קָדָשִׁים. קְהִלּוֹת יַעֲקֹב. רְשׁוּמִים בִּשְׁמֶךָ.* שׁוֹאֲגִים הוֹשַׁעְנָא. תְּמוּכִים עָלֶיךָ.

תִּתֵּן אֱמֶת לְיַעֲקֹב, חֶסֶד לְאַבְרָהָם.[1]

FOURTH HAKAFAH CIRCUIT

אָדוֹן הַמּוֹשִׁיעַ. בִּלְתְּךָ אֵין לְהוֹשִׁיעַ. גִּבּוֹר וְרַב לְהוֹשִׁיעַ. דַּלּוֹתִי וְלִי יְהוֹשִׁיעַ. הָאֵל הַמּוֹשִׁיעַ. וּמַצִּיל וּמוֹשִׁיעַ. זוֹעֲקֶיךָ תּוֹשִׁיעַ. חוֹכֶיךָ הוֹשִׁיעַ. טְלָאֶיךָ תַּשְׂבִּיעַ. יְבוּל לְהַשְׁפִּיעַ. כָּל שִׂיחַ תַּדְשֵׁא וְתוֹשִׁיעַ. לְגֵיא בַּל תַּרְשִׁיעַ. מְגָדִים תַּמְתִּיק וְתוֹשִׁיעַ. נְשִׂיאִים לְהַסִּיעַ. שְׂעִירִים לְהָנִיעַ. עֲנָנִים מִלְּהַמְנִיעַ. פּוֹתֵחַ יָד וּמַשְׂבִּיעַ. צְמֵאֶיךָ תַּשְׂבִּיעַ. קוֹרְאֶיךָ תּוֹשִׁיעַ. רְחוּמֶיךָ תּוֹשִׁיעַ. שׁוֹחֲרֶיךָ הוֹשִׁיעַ. תְּמִימֶיךָ תּוֹשִׁיעַ.

נְעִמוֹת בִּימִינְךָ נֶצַח.[2]

FIFTH HAKAFAH CIRCUIT

אָדָם וּבְהֵמָה. בָּשָׂר וְרוּחַ וּנְשָׁמָה. גִּיד וְעֶצֶם וְקָרְמָה. דְּמוּת וְצֶלֶם וְרִקְמָה. הוֹד לַהֶבֶל דָּמָה. וְנִמְשַׁל כַּבְּהֵמוֹת נִדְמָה.* זִיו וְתֹאַר וְקוֹמָה.* חִדּוּשׁ פְּנֵי אֲדָמָה.* טִיעַת עֲצֵי נְשַׁמָּה. יְקָבִים וְקָמָה. כְּרָמִים וְשִׁקְמָה. לְתֵבֵל הַמְּסֻיָּמָה.* מִטְרוֹת עֹז לְסַמְּמָה. נְשִׁיָּה לְקַיְּמָה. שִׂיחִים לְקוֹמְמָה. עֲדָנִים לְעָצְמָה. פְּרָחִים לְהַעֲצִימָה. צְמָחִים לְגָשְׁמָה. קָרִים לְזָרְמָה. רְבִיבִים לְשַׁלְּמָה. שְׁתִיָּה לְרוֹמְמָה. תְּלוּיָה עַל בְּלִימָה.

יהוה אֲדֹנֵינוּ מָה אַדִּיר שִׁמְךָ בְּכָל הָאָרֶץ, אֲשֶׁר תְּנָה הוֹדְךָ עַל הַשָּׁמָיִם.[3]

---

pay tribute to an idol (see *Daniel* ch. 3). Her posture remained upright like a stately palm tree (*Rashi* to *Song of Songs* 7:8).

מְרוּטַת לֶחִי — *Plucked of cheek.* Beards are torn from cheeks, not to inflict pain, but to insult and embarrass the victim (*Tosefta Bava Kama* 9:11). [It is noteworthy that one of the favorite tactics of Jew-baiters through the centuries, and especially the Nazis, שר״י, was to make sport of defenseless Jews by plucking their beards.]

טוֹבִיָּה — *Moses.* The Torah describes Yocheved's first vision of her new-born baby Moses: *And she saw that he was* טוֹב, *good* (*Exodus* 2:2). This teaches that she named him טוֹבִיָּה, *Toviah* [lit., *God is good*] (*Sotah* 12a).

רְשׁוּמִים בִּשְׁמֶךָ — *Inscribed with Your Name.* This alludes to the covenant of circumcision which is inscribed — i.e., carved — from their very flesh. The next stich — שׁוֹאֲגִים הוֹשַׁעְנָא, *they cry, 'Please save us!'* — recalls the custom [not found in the Ashkenazic rite, but retained in some Sephardic rites] that those gathered at a circumcision call out in unison: אָנָּא ה׳ הוֹשִׁיעָה נָּא, *Please, HASHEM, save now!*

אָדוֹן הַמּוֹשִׁיעַ / Lord Who Saves

Every part of Creation may be assigned to one of four kingdoms or categories of existence. In ascending spiritual order they are: דּוֹמֵם, *silent* or *mineral;* צוֹמֵחַ, *sprouting* or *vegetable;* חַי, *living* or *animal;* and מְדַבֵּר, *speaking* or *human.*

In the Divine plan for the world, each member of one realm is capable of becoming elevated to a higher one. Indeed, this is the purpose of its existence. The soil, water, and air of the Mineral Kingdom are the nutrients which are absorbed by, and become one with, the plant life of the Vegetable Kingdom. Plants, in turn, serve as food and building blocks for the creatures of the Animal Kingdom. Finally, these become the fare of Man, subject of the Human Kingdom. The Torah alludes to this system of elevation: וְנָתַתִּי עֵשֶׂב בְּשָׂדְךָ לִבְהֶמְתֶּךָ וְאָכַלְתָּ וְשָׂבָעְתָּ, *And I shall*

scattered among her provocateurs, ח *she hugs and cleaves to You* ט *bearing Your yoke —* י *unique in declaring Your Oneness.* כ *While vanquished in exile,* ל *she learns Your awesomeness.* מ *Plucked of cheek,** נ *given over to the whippers,* ס *she shoulders Your burden.* ע *A storm-tossed pauper,* פ *she who was redeemed by Moses.** צ *Sacred sheep,* ק *congregations of Jacob,* ר *inscribed with Your Name,** ש *they cry, 'Please save us!' —* ת *they rely upon You!*

Grant truth to Jacob, kindness to Abraham.[1]

FOURTH HAKAFAH CIRCUIT

אָדוֹן הַמּוֹשִׁיעַ *Lord Who saves,* ב *other than You there is no savior.* ג *You are powerful and abundantly able to save.* ד *I am impoverished, yet You shall save me.* ה *God is the Savior,* ו *He delivers and saves.* ז *Those who cry to You — save;* ח *those who yearn for You — save.* ט *Satiate Your lambs,* י *cause an abundance of crops,* כ *of trees, of vegetation — save.* ל *Do not condemn the ground,* מ *but sweeten the luscious fruits — save.* נ *Let the wind bring the soaring clouds,* ס *let the stormy rains be emplaced,* ע *let the clouds not be withheld,* פ *He Who opens a hand and satisfies,* צ *Your thirsty ones — satisfy;* ק *Your callers — save;* ר *Your beloved — save;* ש *Your seekers — save;* ת *Your wholesome ones — save.*

There is delight at Your right hand for triumph.[2]

FIFTH HAKAFAH CIRCUIT

אָדָם וּבְהֵמָה *Man and beast:* ב *Flesh, spirit and soul;* ג *sinew, bone and skin;* ד *likeness and image — a tapestry;* ה *splendor resembling futility,* ו *compared to the likeness of beasts** — ז *luster, figure and stature.** ח *Renew the face of the earth** — ט *planting trees in desolate lands,* י *winepresses and stands of grain,* כ *vineyards and sycamores.* ל *To the demarcated land** — מ *to heal with powerful rains,* נ *to give life to forsaken wastes,* ס *to sustain with trees,* ע *to enhance with sweet fruits,* פ *to invigorate with flowers.* צ *To rain on the sproutings —* ק *to pour a stream of cool waters,* ר *to cloak with droplets,* ש *to elevate the thirsty earth* ת *which is suspended upon silence.*

HASHEM, our Lord, how mighty is Your Name throughout the earth;
for it were fit that You place Your splendor above the heavens.[3]

(1) *Michah* 7:20. (2) *Psalms* 16:11. (3) 8:2.

give grass [vegetable] in your field [mineral] for your cattle [animal], and you [Man] shall eat and be sated (*Deuteronomy* 11:15).

In the next three *Hoshanos* we invoke Divine protection for the animal, vegetable and mineral realms, and we pray for our own welfare — *Lord Who saves . . . save now man and beast . . . (and) the ground from accursedness.*

אָדָם וּבְהֵמָה / Man and Beast

וְנִמְשַׁל כַּבְּהֵמוֹת נִדְמָה — *Compared to the likeness of beasts.* Man's splendor is so futile that it is not even compared to a living beast, but to a mere wall-painting of animals (*Iggeres HaTiyul, Psalms* 49:13).

זִיו וְתֹאַר וְקוֹמָה — *Luster, figure, and stature.* Continuing the thought of the preceding two stiches — as Man's splendor is futile and beast-like, so are his luster, figure and stature.

חִדּוּשׁ פְּנֵי אֲדָמָה — *Renew the face of the earth.* This expresses the concept that life is in a constant state of renewal — an old man expires, a baby is born; one life ends, another begins. *A generation goes and a generation comes, but the earth endures forever* (*Ecclesiastes* 1:4). Although individuals die, the species endures (*Radak*).

לְתֵבֵל הַמְסֻיָּמָה — *To the demarcated land.* The extent to which Man may use the soil is demarcated by the many land-related *mitzvos* — e.g., כִּלְאַיִם, *forbidden mixtures* (*Leviticus* 19:19); שְׁמִיטָּה, *Sabbatical Year* (ibid. 25:1-7); בַּל תַּשְׁחִית, *destruction of fruit trees* (*Deut.* 20:19-20).

SIXTH HAKAFAH CIRCUIT

אֲדָמָה מֵאֵרֶר. בְּהֵמָה מִמְּשַׁכֶּלֶת. גֹּרֶן מִגָּזָם.* דָּגָן מִדַּלֶּקֶת. הוֹן מִמְּאֵרָה. וְאֹכֶל מִמְּהוּמָה.* זַיִת מִנֶּשֶׁל. חִטָּה מֵחָגָב. טֶרֶף מִגּוֹבַי. יֶקֶב מִיֶּלֶק. כֶּרֶם מִתּוֹלַעַת. לֶקֶשׁ מֵאַרְבֶּה. מֶגֶד מִצְּלָצַל. נֶפֶשׁ מִבֶּהָלָה. שֹׂבַע מִסָּלְעָם. עֲדָרִים מִדַּלּוּת. פֵּרוֹת מִשִּׁדָּפוֹן.* צֹאן מִצְּמִיתוּת. קָצִיר מִקְּלָלָה. רֹב מֵרָזוֹן. שִׁבֹּלֶת מִצִּנָּמוֹן. תְּבוּאָה מֵחָסִיל.

צַדִּיק יהוה בְּכָל דְּרָכָיו, וְחָסִיד בְּכָל מַעֲשָׂיו.[1]

SEVENTH HAKAFAH CIRCUIT

לְמַעַן אֵיתָן הַנִּזְרָק בְּלַהַב אֵשׁ.
לְמַעַן בֵּן הַנֶּעֱקַד עַל עֵצִים וָאֵשׁ.
לְמַעַן גִּבּוֹר הַנֶּאֱבַק עִם שַׂר אֵשׁ.
לְמַעַן דְּגָלִים נָחִיתָ בְּאוֹר וַעֲנַן אֵשׁ.
לְמַעַן הָעֲלָה לַמָּרוֹם וְנִתְעַלָּה כְּמַלְאֲכֵי אֵשׁ.
לְמַעַן וְהוּא לָךְ כְּסֶגֶן בְּאֶרְאֶלֵּי אֵשׁ.
לְמַעַן זֶבֶד דִּבְּרוֹת הַנִּתוּנוֹת מֵאֵשׁ.
לְמַעַן חִפּוּי יְרִיעוֹת עֲנַן אֵשׁ.
לְמַעַן טֶכֶס הַר יָרַדְתָּ עָלָיו בָּאֵשׁ.
לְמַעַן יְדִידוּת בַּיִת אֲשֶׁר אָהַבְתָּ מִשְּׁמֵי אֵשׁ.

אֲדָמָה מֵאֵרֶר / Ground from Accursedness

When Adam sinned, his punishment was indirect: אֲרוּרָה הָאֲדָמָה בַּעֲבוּרֶךָ, *accursed is the ground because of you; through suffering shall you eat (Genesis* 3:17). No longer will you, Adam, be nurtured by the bosom of your mother, the earth from which you were created. *Accursed is the ground because it bore you.* Henceforth, seed shall no longer sprout and trees shall no longer bear fruit on the day they are planted *(Tanchuma). By the sweat of your brow shall you get bread to eat (Genesis* 3:19). No longer will the earth's produce nourish you immediately and directly. Before you can partake of your bread you must till, sow, and reap. But still the harvest will be in scant measure *(Ibn Ezra).* All sorts of destructive, accursed insects will spring forth from the earth *(Rashi).*

What hope has Man? How can he hope to relieve the accursedness which he brought to the earth? The Torah reveals the way: *And it shall come to pass, when you will heed, observe and fulfill all of these laws, that HASHEM, your God, will . . . bless the fruit of your womb, the produce of your earth, your grain, your wine and your oil, the offspring of your cattle and the flocks of your sheep (Deuteronomy* 7:12-13). Fulfillment of God's will as expressed in His Torah is the redemption and salvation of Man. Such service can ameliorate the accursedness of the earth. On Hoshana Rabbah, and during this entire festival period, the Jew proclaims to God: We have used the produce of the earth in the ways prescribed by your Torah — we have dwelt in the *succah* with its covering *(s'chach)* of plant material; we have taken the Four Species; we have read from the Torah which is written on animal skin; we have blown the *shofar* made from the ram's horn. We have heeded Your laws, fulfilled Your commands. Now, our God, may You fulfill the second part of the verse — undo the curse which You pronounced upon the earth.

מִגָּזָם — *From gazam.* The accursedness caused by Adam's sin caused the earth to give forth various destructive insects *(Rashi* to *Genesis* 3:17). For this reason the *paytan* mentions no less than eight species of locusts: *gazam, chagav, govai, yelek, arbeh, tz'latzal, salam* and *chasil.* Perhaps each variety attacks the particular crop with which the *paytan* associates it *(Kol Bo).*

וְאֹכֶל מִמְּהוּמָה — *Food from confusion.* This is an allusion to the confusion and panic caused by the sounds of an attacking army. During times of

SIXTH HAKAFAH CIRCUIT

אֲדָמָה מֵאֶרֶר *Ground from accursedness;* **ב** *beast from aborting;* **ג** *granary from gazam;** **ד** *grain from scorch;* **ה** *wealth from affliction;* **ו** *food from confusion;** **ז** *olives from dropping;* **ח** *wheat from chagav;* **ט** *nourishment from govai;* **י** *wine-press from yelek;* **כ** *vineyard from worms;* **ל** *late crop from arbeh;* **מ** *fruit from tz'latzal;* **נ** *soul from panic;* **ס** *satiety from salam;* **ע** *flocks from leanness;* **פ** *fruits from the east wind;** **צ** *sheep from extermination;* **ק** *harvest from curse;* **ר** *abundance from emaciation;* **ש** *grain spikes from withering;* **ת** *crops from chasil.*

HASHEM is righteous in all His ways; virtuous in all His deeds.[1]

SEVENTH HAKAFAH CIRCUIT

לְמַעַן אֵיתָן *In the merit of the courageous one [Abraham] who was hurled into flaming fire.*
ב *In the merit of the son [Isaac] who was bound upon the wood near the fire.*
ג *In the merit of the strong one [Jacob] who wrestled with a prince of fire.*
ד *In the merit of the tribal banners which You guided with a light — and a cloud — of fire.*
ה *In the merit of him [Moses] who was raised to the heavens and became as exalted as angels of fire.*
ו *In the merit of him [Aaron] who was to You like a deputy at the Altars of fire.*
ז *In the merit of the gift of Commandments presented from a fire.*
ח *In the merit of the canopy of curtains — a cloud of fire.*
ט *In the merit of the array at the mountain upon which You descended in fire.*
י *In the merit of the love of the Temple which You adored beyond heavens made of fire.*

(1) *Psalms* 145:17.

war, foodstuffs become scarce, inflation sets in, and food prices soar.

Alternatively, this refers to gluttonous repasts eaten in vast banquet halls among throngs of people. Invariably there is insurmountable difficulty in accommodating the entire assemblage. The resulting confusion causes ill will and physical discomfort. King Solomon taught: *Better to have little with fear of HASHEM, than a vast treasure accompanied by confusion. Better a meal of vegetables in a place of love, than a fatted bull, imbued with hatred* (*Proverbs* 15:16-17).

מִשְּׁדָּפוֹן — *From the east wind.* The east wind is the strongest of all winds; it is the wind with which God punishes the wicked (*Rashi* to *Exodus* 14:21).

◆§ לְמַעַן אֵיתָן / In the Merit of the Courageous One

Who planted the seeds of superhuman fortitude and dignity with which millennia of Jews have endured hardship and privation? From whom did Israel inherit the ability to remain holy even amid holocaust? *Ramban* provides the answer: כָּל מַה שֶׁאֵירַע לְאָבוֹת סִמָּן לְבָנִים, *all that happened to the Patriarchs is of prophetic significance to their descendants.* For this reason, too, the Torah often relates seemingly unimportant events in the lives of our forebears.

Not only did the deeds of the Patriarchs insure the posterity of Israel, but they also inculcated the traits which engendered those deeds into the nation's fiber. The Talmud teaches: תַּמָּה זְכוּת אָבוֹת, *the merits of the Patriarchs have expired* (*Shabbos* 55a); nevertheless, the qualities of character with which their merits have imbued their offspring have not expired. Because we still exhibit Abraham's loving-kindness, Isaac's courage, and Jacob's adherence to truth, because we follow the trails blazed by Moses and Aaron, Joshua and Samuel, David and Solomon, because we maintain and display the unwavering faith of Daniel and his companions, we are able to pray for salvation.

This *Hoshana* traces the achievements of our

לְמַעַן כָּמַה עַד שָׁקְעָה הָאֵשׁ.*
לְמַעַן לָקַח מַחְתַּת אֵשׁ וְהֵסִיר חָרוֹן אֵשׁ.
לְמַעַן מְקַנֵּא קִנְאָה גְדוֹלָה בָּאֵשׁ.
לְמַעַן נָף יָדוֹ וְיָרְדוּ אַבְנֵי אֵשׁ.
לְמַעַן שָׂם טְלֵה חָלָב כְּלִיל אֵשׁ.
לְמַעַן עָמַד בַּגֹּרֶן וְנִתְרַצָּה בָּאֵשׁ.
לְמַעַן פִּלֵּל בָּעֲזָרָה וְיָרְדָה הָאֵשׁ.
לְמַעַן צִיר עָלָה וְנִתְעַלָּה בְּרֶכֶב וְסוּסֵי אֵשׁ.
לְמַעַן קְדוֹשִׁים מֻשְׁלָכִים בָּאֵשׁ.
לְמַעַן רִבּוֹ רִבְבָן חָז וְנַהֲרֵי אֵשׁ.
לְמַעַן שְׁמֻמוֹת עִירְךָ הַשְּׂרוּפָה בָּאֵשׁ.
לְמַעַן תּוֹלְדוֹת אַלּוּפֵי יְהוּדָה תָּשִׂים כְּכִיּוֹר אֵשׁ.

לְךָ יהוה הַגְּדֻלָּה וְהַגְּבוּרָה וְהַתִּפְאֶרֶת וְהַנֵּצַח וְהַהוֹד כִּי כֹל בַּשָּׁמַיִם וּבָאָרֶץ, לְךָ יהוה הַמַּמְלָכָה וְהַמִּתְנַשֵּׂא לְכֹל לְרֹאשׁ.[1] וְהָיָה יהוה לְמֶלֶךְ עַל כָּל הָאָרֶץ, בַּיּוֹם הַהוּא יִהְיֶה יהוה אֶחָד וּשְׁמוֹ אֶחָד.[2] וּבְתוֹרָתְךָ כָּתוּב לֵאמֹר: שְׁמַע יִשְׂרָאֵל יהוה אֱלֹהֵינוּ יהוה אֶחָד.[3] בָּרוּךְ שֵׁם כְּבוֹד מַלְכוּתוֹ לְעוֹלָם וָעֶד.

אֲנִי וָהוֹ הוֹשִׁיעָה נָּא.

כְּהוֹשַׁעְתָּ אֵלִים בְּלוּד עִמָּךְ,
בְּצֵאתְךָ לְיֵשַׁע עַמָּךְ, כֵּן הוֹשַׁעְנָא.
כְּהוֹשַׁעְתָּ גּוֹי וֵאלֹהִים,
דְּרוּשִׁים לְיֵשַׁע אֱלֹהִים, כֵּן הוֹשַׁעְנָא.
כְּהוֹשַׁעְתָּ הֲמוֹן צְבָאוֹת,
וְעִמָּם מַלְאֲכֵי צְבָאוֹת, כֵּן הוֹשַׁעְנָא.
כְּהוֹשַׁעְתָּ זַכִּים מִבֵּית עֲבָדִים,
חַנּוּן בְּיָדָם מַעֲבִידִים, כֵּן הוֹשַׁעְנָא.
כְּהוֹשַׁעְתָּ טְבוּעִים בְּצוּל גְּזָרִים,
יְקָרְךָ עִמָּם מַעֲבִירִים, כֵּן הוֹשַׁעְנָא.
כְּהוֹשַׁעְתָּ כַּנָּה מְשׁוֹרֶרֶת וַיּוֹשַׁע,
לְגוֹחָהּ מְצֻיֶּנֶת וַיִּוָּשַׁע, כֵּן הוֹשַׁעְנָא.
כְּהוֹשַׁעְתָּ מַאֲמַר וְהוֹצֵאתִי אֶתְכֶם,
נָקוּב וְהוּצֵאתִי אִתְּכֶם, כֵּן הוֹשַׁעְנָא.

---

spiritual models, and appeals for salvation in the merit of their indelible imprint upon Israel's national character.

כָּמַה עַד שָׁקְעָה הָאֵשׁ — *Him [Moses] who yearned [for forgiveness] until the sinking of the fire.* During the Wilderness wanderings, many Israelites chose to complain about imagined future difficulties. *HASHEM heard and His anger was kindled. The fire of HASHEM burned within them and consumed the lowly ones of the camp ... Moses prayed to HASHEM* וַתִּשְׁקַע הָאֵשׁ, *and the fire sank* [it was swallowed up by the ground *(Rashi)*] *(Numbers* 11:1-2).

כ *In the merit of him [Moses] who yearned until the sinking of the fire.*
ל *In the merit of him [Aaron] who took a fire pan and removed an anger burning like fire.*
מ *In the merit of him [Elijah] who zealously took great vengeance with fire.*
נ *In the merit of him [Joshua] who raised his hand in prayer — and down came stones of fire.*
ס *In the merit of him [Samuel] who offered a nursing ewe to be completely consumed by fire.*
ע *In the merit of him [David] who stood in the granary and was shown favor with fire.*
פ *In the merit of him [Solomon] who prayed in the Courtyard and down came fire.*
צ *In the merit of the agent [Elijah] who ascended to heaven and was exalted, through a chariot and horses of fire.*
ק *In the merit of holy ones [Chananiah, Mishael, and Azariah] who were cast into the fire.*
ר *In the merit of him [Daniel] who saw myriad myriads and streams of fire.*
ש *In the merit of the ruins of Your city which was devoured in fire.*
ת *In the merit of the descendants of Judah's princes whom You will set as a flaming fire.*

לְךָ *Yours, HASHEM, is the greatness, the strength, the splendor, the triumph, and the glory, even everything in heaven and earth; Yours, HASHEM, is the kingdom, and the sovereignty over every leader.*[1] *HASHEM will be King over all the earth, on that day HASHEM will be One and His Name will be One.*[2] *And in Your Torah is written as follows: Hear, O Israel, HASHEM is our God, HASHEM is the One and Only.*[3] *Blessed is the Name of His glorious kingdom for all eternity.*

ANI VAHO, bring salvation now.

כְּהוֹשַׁעְתָּ אֵלִים *As You saved the terebinths in Lud [Egypt] along with Yourself*
ב *when You went forth to save the nation — so save now.*
ג *As You saved the nation and its leaders*
ד *who sought the salvations of God — so save now.*
ה *As You saved the multitudes of hosts*
ו *and with them the hosts of angels — so save now.*
ז *As You saved pure ones from the house of slavery,*
ח *Gracious One, from those who forced manual labor upon them — so save now.*
ט *As You saved those sinking in the depths of the rifts,*
י *Your honor was with them when they crossed — so save now.*
כ *As You saved the garden which sang 'He delivered,'*
ל *regarding Him Who draws forth it is pronounced 'He was delivered' — so save now.*
מ *As You saved with the declaration 'I shall bring you forth,'*
נ *which may be interpreted, 'I shall be brought forth with you' — so save now.*

(1) *II Chronicles* 29:11. (2) *Zechariah* 14:9. (3) *Deuteronomy* 6:4.

כְּהוֹשַֽׁעְתָּ סוֹבְבֵי מִזְבֵּחַ,
עוֹמְסֵי עֲרָבָה לְהַקִּיף מִזְבֵּחַ, כֵּן הוֹשַׁעְנָא.
כְּהוֹשַֽׁעְתָּ פְּלְאֵי אָרוֹן כְּהֻפְשַׁע,
צִעֵר פְּלֶשֶׁת בַּחֲרוֹן אַף וְנוֹשַׁע, כֵּן הוֹשַׁעְנָא.
כְּהוֹשַֽׁעְתָּ קְהִלּוֹת בָּבֶֽלָה שִׁלַּֽחְתָּ,
רַחוּם לְמַעֲנָם שֻׁלַּֽחְתָּ, כֵּן הוֹשַׁעְנָא.
כְּהוֹשַֽׁעְתָּ שְׁבוּת שִׁבְטֵי יַעֲקֹב,
תָּשׁוּב וְתָשִׁיב שְׁבוּת אָהֳלֵי יַעֲקֹב, וְהוֹשִֽׁיעָה נָּא.
כְּהוֹשַֽׁעְתָּ שׁוֹמְרֵי מִצְוֹת, וְחוֹכֵי יְשׁוּעוֹת,
אֵל לְמוֹשָׁעוֹת, וְהוֹשִֽׁיעָה נָּא.

אֲנִי וָהוֹ הוֹשִֽׁיעָה נָּא.

תִּתְּנֵנוּ לְשֵׁם וְלִתְהִלָּה. תְּשִׁיתֵנוּ אֶל הַחֶבֶל וְאֶל הַנַּחֲלָה. תְּרוֹמְמֵנוּ לְמַעְלָה לְמָעְלָה. תְּקַבְּצֵנוּ לְבֵית הַתְּפִלָּה. תַּצִּיבֵנוּ כְּעֵץ עַל פַּלְגֵי מַיִם שְׁתוּלָה. תִּפְדֵּנוּ מִכָּל נֶגַע וּמַחֲלָה. תְּעַטְּרֵנוּ בְּאַהֲבָה כְלוּלָה. תְּשַׂמְּחֵנוּ בְּבֵית הַתְּפִלָּה. תְּנַהֲלֵנוּ עַל מֵי מְנוּחוֹת סֶלָה. תְּמַלְּאֵנוּ חָכְמָה וְשִׂכְלָה. תַּלְבִּישֵׁנוּ עֹז וּגְדֻלָּה. תַּכְתִּירֵנוּ בְּכֶתֶר כְּלוּלָה. תְּיַשְּׁרֵנוּ בְּאֹרַח סְלוּלָה. תִּטָּעֵנוּ בְּיֹשֶׁר מְסִלָּה. תְּחָנֵּנוּ בְּרַחֲמִים וּבְחֶמְלָה. תַּזְכִּירֵנוּ בְּמִי זֹאת עוֹלָה.* תּוֹשִׁיעֵנוּ לְקֵץ* הַגְּאֻלָּה. תְּהַדְּרֵנוּ בְּזִיו הֲמוּלָּה. תַּדְבִּיקֵנוּ כְּאֵזוֹר חֲתוּלָה. תְּגַדְּלֵנוּ בְּיָד הַגְּדוֹלָה. תְּבִיאֵנוּ לְבֵיתְךָ בְּרִנָּה וְצָהֳלָה. תְּאַמְּצֵנוּ בְּרֶוַח וְהַצָּלָה. תְּאַדְּרֵנוּ בְּאֶבֶן תְּלוּלָה.* תְּלַבְּבֵנוּ בְּבִנְיַן עִירָךְ כְּבַתְּחִלָּה. תְּעוֹרְרֵנוּ לְצִיּוֹן בְּשִׁכְלוּלָהּ. תְּזַכֵּנוּ בְּנִבְנָתָה הָעִיר עַל תִּלָּהּ. תַּרְבִּיצֵנוּ בְּשָׂשׂוֹן וְגִילָה. תְּחַזְּקֵנוּ אֱלֹהֵי יַעֲקֹב סֶלָה.

Chazzan, then congregation:

אָנָּא הוֹשִֽׁיעָה נָּא.

All:

אָנָּא אֱזוֹן חִין תְּאֵבֵי יִשְׁעָךְ,
בְּעַרְבֵי נַֽחַל* לְשַׁעְשְׁעָךְ, וְהוֹשִֽׁיעָה נָּא.
אָנָּא גְּאַל כַּנַּת נִטְעָךְ,

☙§ תִּתְּנֵנוּ / Establish Us

Although all the *Hoshanos* are attributed to R' Elazar HaKalir, only this one bears his signature. The second letters of each verse form the twenty-two letters of the *aleph-beis* in reverse order, followed by אֶלְעָזָר חָזָק, *Elazar Chazak* [lit., *Elazar, may he be strengthened*].

מִי זֹאת עוֹלָה — *How worthy is she!* [lit., *Who is this who rises?*]. The translation follows *Rashi* to *Song of Songs* 8:5 where these words are spoken by God and His Heavenly Tribunal with reference to the still-exiled Community of Israel (see p. 218).

קֵץ — *[Final] End. Daniel* (11:40) refers to the final redemption as עֵת קֵץ, *the time of the End*, and (12:13) קֵץ הַיָּמִין, *the End of Days.*

אֶבֶן תְּלוּלָה — *The elevated stone.* אֶבֶן, *stone*, refers to the Temple which contained the אֶבֶן שְׁתִיָּה, *foundation stone.* תָּלוּל, an intensified form of תֵּל, *hill*, means a lofty mountain (see *Ezekiel* 17:22). Thus אֶבֶן תְּלוּלָה is the Temple which stood on a lofty mount.

ס *As You saved those who went roundabout with the Altar,*
ע *those who carry the willow to encircle the Altar*
— so save now.
פ *As You saved the Ark of the Name, captured as a result of sin,*
צ *when you punished Philistia with flaming anger,*
and it was saved — so save now.
ק *As You saved the congregations which You had sent to Babylon,*
ר *Merciful One, for their sake were You also sent*
— so save now.
ש *As You saved the captivity of the tribes of Jacob,*
ת *return and restore the captivity of the tents of Jacob,*
and bring salvation now.
As You saved those observant of mitzvos, and hopeful for salvation
— O God Who brings about salvation, bring salvation now.

ANI VAHO, bring salvation now.

תִּתְּנֵנוּ *Establish us for fame and renown;* ש *place us upon our measured heritage;* ר *raise us ever higher;* ק *gather us to the House of Prayer;* צ *stand us erect, like a tree embedded by streams of water;* פ *redeem us from every plague and sickness;* ע *envelop us with perfect love;* ס *gladden us in the House of Prayer;* נ *lead us beside tranquil waters, forever;* מ *fill us with wisdom and sense;* ל *clothe us with strength and greatness;* כ *crown us with the perfect crown;* י *set us right on the level road;* ט *plant us on the straight path;* ח *grace us with mercy and pity;* ז *remember us with 'How worthy is she!';* ו *save us for the final End* of Redemption;* ה *beautify us with the radiance of angels;* ד *cause us to cleave to You like a tightly wrapped sash;* ג *make us great with Your great hand;* ב *bring us to Your Temple with joyous song and cheer;* א *strengthen us with relief and rescue;* א *adorn us with the elevated stone;** ל *hearten us with the rebuilding of Your city as of old;* ע *awaken us to Zion in its completeness;* ז *let us merit the rebuilding of the City on its hill;* ר *let us recline with joy and gladness; strengthen us, O God of Jacob, Selah.*

Chazzan, then congregation:

Please bring salvation now.

All:

אָנָּא אֱזוֹן *Please hearken to the plea of those*
who long for Your salvation;
ב *with brook willows* they bring You joy — and bring salvation now.*
ג *Please redeem the garden of Your planting,*

אָנָּא אֱזוֹן / Please Hearken

The rainy season in *Eretz Yisrael* begins almost immediately after Succos. For this reason special prayers for rain (p. 980) are recited on Shemini Atzeres. Additionally, the *Hoshanos* service of Hoshana Rabbah centers on the *aravos,* or brook willows, a species which both depends upon and is identified with water.

The Talmud teaches that during Succos the Heavenly Tribunal judges the world with regard to its water supply for the following year. God ordained the water-libations of Succos as a source of merit; as if He said, 'Pour water before Me on this Festival, that you be blessed with the year's rains' *(Rosh Hashanah* 16a). These prayers for rain are not recited until the last day of the festival because 'rain is but a symptom of curse during Succos,' for it makes it impossible to sit in the *succah (Taanis* 2a).

עַרְבֵי נַחַל *— Brook willows.* The Talmud offers two explanations of this term: (1) willows which grow by the side of a brook; and (2) willows whose leaves are elongated like a brook. Although willows growing in the fields or on mountaintops are also acceptable for the fulfillment of this *mitzvah (Succah* 33b), it is

דּוּמָה* בְּטַאטְאָךְ, וְהוֹשִׁיעָה נָּא.
אָנָּא הַבֵּט לַבְּרִית* טִבְעָךְ,
וּמַחֲשַׁכֵּי אֶרֶץ* בְּהַטְבִּיעָךְ, וְהוֹשִׁיעָה נָּא.
אָנָּא זְכָר לָנוּ אָב יְדָעָךְ,
חַסְדְּךָ לָמוֹ בְּהוֹדִיעָךְ, וְהוֹשִׁיעָה נָּא.
אָנָּא טְהוֹרֵי לֵב בְּהַפְלִיאָךְ,
יוֹדֵעַ כִּי הוּא פִלְאָךְ, וְהוֹשִׁיעָה נָּא.
אָנָּא כַּבִּיר כֹּחַ תֵּן לָנוּ יִשְׁעָךְ,
לַאֲבוֹתֵינוּ כְּהִשָּׁבְעָךְ, וְהוֹשִׁיעָה נָּא.
אָנָּא מַלֵּא מִשְׁאֲלוֹת עַם מְשַׁוְּעָךְ,
נֶעֱקַד בְּהַר מוֹר כְּמוֹ שׁוֹעָךְ, וְהוֹשִׁיעָה נָּא.
אָנָּא סַגֵּב אֶשְׁלֵי נִטְעָךְ,
עֲרִיצִים בְּהַנִיעָךְ, וְהוֹשִׁיעָה נָּא.
אָנָּא פְּתַח לָנוּ אוֹצְרוֹת רִבְעָךְ,
צִיָּה מֵהֶם בְּהַרְבִּיעָךְ, וְהוֹשִׁיעָה נָּא.
אָנָּא קוֹרְאֶיךָ אֶרֶץ בְּרוֹעֲעָךְ,
רְעֵם בְּטוּב מִרְעָךְ, וְהוֹשִׁיעָה נָּא.
אָנָּא שְׁעָרֶיךָ תַּעַל מִמַּשּׁוֹאָךְ,
תֵּל תַּלְפִּיּוֹת בְּהַשִּׂיאָךְ, וְהוֹשִׁיעָה נָּא.

Chazzan, then congregation:

אָנָּא אֵל נָא, הוֹשַׁעְנָא וְהוֹשִׁיעָה נָּא.

All:

אֵל נָא תָּעִינוּ כְּשֶׂה אֹבֵד,
שְׁמֵנוּ מִסִּפְרְךָ אַל תְּאַבֵּד, הוֹשַׁעְנָא וְהוֹשִׁיעָה נָּא.
אֵל נָא רְעֵה אֶת צֹאן הַהֲרֵגָה,
קְצוּפָה וְעָלֶיךָ הֲרוּגָה, הוֹשַׁעְנָא וְהוֹשִׁיעָה נָּא.
אֵל נָא צֹאנְךָ וְצֹאן מַרְעִיתֶךָ,
פְּעֻלָּתְךָ וְרַעְיָתֶךָ, הוֹשַׁעְנָא וְהוֹשִׁיעָה נָּא.
אֵל נָא עֲנִיֵּי הַצֹּאן,
שִׂיחָם עֲנֵה בְּעֵת רָצוֹן, הוֹשַׁעְנָא וְהוֹשִׁיעָה נָּא.
אֵל נָא נוֹשְׂאֵי לְךָ עַיִן,
מִתְקוֹמְמֵיהֶם יִהְיוּ כְאַיִן, הוֹשַׁעְנָא וְהוֹשִׁיעָה נָּא.
אֵל נָא לִמְנַסְּכֵי לְךָ מַיִם,
כְּמִמַּעַיְנֵי הַיְשׁוּעָה יִשְׁאֲבוּן מַיִם, הוֹשַׁעְנָא וְהוֹשִׁיעָה נָּא.

---

preferable to use willows which grew alongside a stream.

דּוּמָה — *Dumah. Isaiah* 21:11 prophesies the doom of דּוּמָה, *Dumah,* a name which *Rashi* understands to be synonymous with אֱדוֹם, *Edom. Ibn Ezra* and *Radak* trace *Dumah* to the descendants of Ishmael (see *Genesis* 25:14).

הַבֵּט לַבְּרִית . . . — *Gaze upon the covenant . . .*

ד *as You sweep away Dumah* — and bring salvation now.*
ה *Please gaze upon the covenant* of Your signet ring,*
ו *even as You sink the ones who darken the earth**
— and bring salvation now.
ז *Please recall on our behalf the Patriarch [Abraham] who perceived You;*
ח *may Your loving-kindness be upon them, for he made You known*
— and bring salvation now.
ט *Please when you set aside the pure of heart,*
י *let it be known that this is Your wonder — and bring salvation now.*
כ *Please Almighty One, grant us Your salvation,*
ל *as You swore to our fathers — and bring salvation now.*
מ *Please fulfill the requests of Your entreating nation,*
נ *as [Isaac] the one bound on the myrrh mountain entreated You*
— and bring salvation now.
ס *Please strengthen [Israel] the tamarisks of Your planting,*
ע *as You cause the idolaters to wander — and bring salvation now.*
פ *Please open the treasure troves of Your rains for us,*
צ *as You water the parched earth from them — and bring salvation now.*
ק *Please — those who call to You, when You bring the earth destruction,*
ר *shepherd them in Your goodly pastures — and bring salvation now.*
ש *Please raise Your gates in the wake of Your desolation,*
ת *when You exalt the Hill of Talpios — and bring salvation now.*

Chazzan, then congregation:

Please God, please! Save now and bring salvation now.

All:

אֵל נָא *Please God! We have strayed like lost sheep;*
ש *do not cause our name to be lost from Your Book*
— save now and bring salvation now.
ר *Please God! Graze the sheep of the slaughter,*
ק *who are the victims of wrath*
and are killed for Your sake — save now and bring salvation now.
צ *Please God! Your sheep and the sheep of Your pasture,*
פ *Your accomplishment and Your beloved*
— save now and bring salvation now.
ע *Please God! The poorest of the sheep,*
ס *answer their prayers at an opportune time*
— save now and bring salvation now.
נ *Please God! Those who raise their eyes to You,*
מ *may those who rise against them be as naught*
— save now and bring salvation now.
ל *Please God! Those who pour water before You,*
כ *from the springs of salvation may they draw water*
— save now and bring salvation now.

Paraphrased from *Psalms* 74:20, these stiches allude to the covenant of circumcision which is likened to the embossed image caused by a signet ring because it is indelibly inscribed, so to speak, in the flesh of each male Jew. He is thus 'stamped' with the King's signet ring.

מַחֲשַׁכֵּי אֶרֶץ — *The ones who darken the earth,* i.e., the idolaters who darken the earth with their sinfulness, and who will one day sink into *Gehinnom.*

אֵל נָא יַעֲלוּ לְצִיּוֹן מוֹשִׁיעִים,
טְפוּלִים בָּךְ וּבְשִׁמְךָ נוֹשָׁעִים, הוֹשַׁעְנָא וְהוֹשִׁיעָה נָּא.
אֵל נָא חֲמוּץ בְּגָדִים,*
זְעוֹם לְנַעֵר כָּל בּוֹגְדִים, הוֹשַׁעְנָא וְהוֹשִׁיעָה נָּא.
אֵל נָא וְזָכוֹר תִּזְכּוֹר,
הַנְּכוּרֵי בְּלֶתֶךְ וָכוֹר,* הוֹשַׁעְנָא וְהוֹשִׁיעָה נָּא.
אֵל נָא דּוֹרְשֶׁיךָ בְּעַנְפֵי עֲרָבוֹת,
גֹּעִים שְׁעֵה מֵעֲרָבוֹת, הוֹשַׁעְנָא וְהוֹשִׁיעָה נָּא.
אֵל נָא בָּרֵךְ בְּעִטּוּר שָׁנָה,
אֲמָרֵי רְצֵה בְּפִלּוּלִי בְּיוֹם הוֹשַׁעְנָא, הוֹשַׁעְנָא וְהוֹשִׁיעָה נָּא.

Chazzan, then congregation:

אָנָּא אֵל נָא, הוֹשַׁעְנָא וְהוֹשִׁיעָה נָּא, אָבִינוּ אָתָּה.

All:

לְמַעַן תָּמִים בְּדוֹרוֹתָיו,* הַנִּמְלָט בְּרוֹב צִדְקוֹתָיו,
מֻצָּל מִשֶּׁטֶף בְּבֹא מַבּוּל מַיִם.
לְאוֹם אֲנִי חוֹמָה,* הוֹשַׁעְנָא וְהוֹשִׁיעָה נָּא, אָבִינוּ אָתָּה.
לְמַעַן שָׁלֵם* בְּכָל מַעֲשִׂים, הַמְּנֻסֶּה בַּעֲשָׂרָה נִסִּים,*
בְּשֶׂר מַלְאָכִים* נָם יֻקַּח נָא מְעַט מַיִם.

⇐§ תָּעִינוּ / We Have Strayed

חֲמוּץ בְּגָדִים — *With bloodied clothes.* When the proper time comes, God will avenge Himself against Edom for its outrages against Israel. In the manner common to prophecy, God is metaphorically portrayed as a warrior who becomes soiled by the blood of his slain foe. The Sages teach that no nation can be defeated on earth until its heavenly guardian angel is stripped of his power above. When the End of Days comes, therefore, God will destroy the angel of Edom, which is also the angel of evil, and His clothing will become bloodied, as it were. (See *Rashi* to *Isaiah* 63:1.)

הַנְּכוּרֵי בְּלֶתֶךְ וָכוֹר — *Those purchased for a lesech and a kor.* The prophet Hoshea declared: *I have bought her* [=Israel] *for Myself for fifteen pieces of silver, a chomer of barley and a lesech of barley* (*Hosea* 3:2). Of what significance are these figures of speech?

Rashi interprets: The *gematria* [numerical value] of כֶּסֶף, *silver,* is 160, the same as the *gematria* of נִסָּן, *Nissan.* Thus *fifteen pieces of silver* is an allusion to the fifteenth day of Nissan, the day of the Exodus from Egypt.

The *chomer* (or *kor* which is equal to it) contains thirty *s'ah,* and the *lesech* has half the volume, fifteen *s'ah.* Together these two measures hold forty-five *s'ah. Chomer* and *lesech,* then, are an allusion to the forty-five days which began on the fifteenth of Nissan until the nation reached Sinai. There Israel made the final preparations to receive the Torah and become the 'possession' of God (*Rashi* to *Hosea* 3:2).

⇐§ לְמַעַן תָּמִים / In the Merit of Him who was Perfect

In a style reminiscent of the *Hoshana* beginning לְמַעַן אֵיתָן, *In the merit of the courageous one* (p. 780), this *Hoshana* recounts the love for God which was the hallmark of the righteous people of old. Since that *Hoshana* was a prayer for an end to Israel's suffering in exile, it mentioned an incident involving fire in the life of each Patriarch. This *Hoshana* is a prayer for rain, so the biographical events are related to water.

A double acrostic is used by the *paytan.* Each stanza is divided into four parts. The first word of each stanza is לְמַעַן, *In the merit of,* followed by an allusion to the righteousness of one of Israel's progenitors. These allusions are contained in the first two verses of each stanza and form a reverse alphabetical acrostic going from ת to א. The third verse of each stanza refers to a water-related incident. The final verses form a straight alphabetical acrostic, beginning with א, and listing praises of Israel, the nation, or of *Eretz Yisrael.*

תָּמִים בְּדוֹרוֹתָיו — *The one who was perfect in his generations.* Scripture (*Genesis* 6:9) describes

י *Please God! May saviors arise from Zion;*
ט *those who cling to You and are saved in Your Name*
— save now and bring salvation now.
ח *Please God! With bloodied clothes,**
ז *be enraged to shake out all the rebels — save now and bring salvation now.*
ו *Please God! Remember may You remember,*
ה *those purchased for a lesech and a kor**
— save now and bring salvation now.
ד *Please God! Those who seek You with willow branches,*
ג *to their cries turn, from Aravos — save now and bring salvation now.*
ב *Please God! With a crown bless this year.*
א *May you find my words favorable as I pray on this day of Hoshana*
— save now and bring salvation now.

Chazzan, then congregation:

Please God, please! Save now and bring salvation now, for You are our Father.

All:

ת *In the merit of [Noah] the one who was perfect in his generations,**
he escaped by his abundant righteousness,
and was rescued from inundation upon the arrival of the Flood of water
א *for [the nation that declares,] 'I am a wall,'**
may You save now and bring salvation now,
for You are our Father.

ש *In the merit of [Abraham] the one who was perfect* in all deeds,*
who was proven through ten trials; upon seeing the angels**
he said, 'Let there be brought some water.'

Noah this way. For the story of the Flood see *Genesis* 6:9 — 9:17.

אום אֲנִי חוֹמָה — *The nation that declares, 'I am a wall.'* Israel declares its faith in God to be as sturdy as a wall. The term 'wall' is also used in Scripture's description of the waters of the Sea after they were split. They stood up strong and straight: וְהַמַּיִם לָהֶם חוֹמָה, *the waters were a wall for them (Exodus* 14:22, 29). Thus, in coupling Israel with the merit of Noah, the *paytan* alludes to the protection given both of them from destructive waters.

שָׁלֵם — *Perfect.* God told Abraham, *'Walk before me and be perfect' (Genesis* 17:1).

בַּעֲשָׂרָה נִסִּים — *Through ten trials.* God tested Abraham with ten trials of faith, all of which he withstood. The commentators differ on the precise identity of the 'ten trials,' for more than ten incidents in Abraham's life could be so designated.

According to *Avos d'Rabbi Nosson* 33 he was tested (all verses are in *Genesis):*

— *Twice* when he had to move [once in 12:1, and again in 12:10 when, after God's glowing promise of a good life in Canaan, Abraham was forced to go to Egypt in the face of a famine].

— *Twice* in connection with his two sons [the difficult decision to heed Sarah's insistence that he drive away Ishmael (21:10); and second, in the supreme test of binding his beloved son Isaac to the altar in preparation to sacrifice him (22:1-2)];

— *Twice* with his two wives [when Sarah was taken from him to Pharaoh's palace (12:15); and when he was required to drive Hagar from his home (21:10). An alternate interpretation includes the banishment of Hagar with that of Ishmael as a single test. In its place among the list of the trials is the abduction of Sarah to the palace of Abimelech (20:2)];

— *Once* on the occasion of his war with the kings (14:14);

— *Once* at the Covenant between the Parts [(15:7ff) when he was told that his descendants would be enslaved and exiled for four hundred years];

— *Once* in Ur Kasdim [where he was thrown into a fiery furnace by Nimrod; and

— *Once* at the covenant of Circumcision (17:9) [which was an unprecedented act and, at his advanced age, a dangerous operation].

מַלְאָכִים — *Angels.* Abraham's encounter with the angels is recorded in *Genesis* 18:1-15.

לְבָרָה כַּחַמָּה,* הוֹשַׁעְנָא וְהוֹשִׁיעָה נָּא, אָבִינוּ אָתָּה.
לְמַעַן רַךְ וְיָחִיד* נֶחֱנַט פְּרִי לְמֵאָה,* וָעַק אַיֵּה הַשֶּׂה* לְעוֹלָה,
בִּשְּׂרוּהוּ עֲבָדָיו מָצָאנוּ מַיִם.*
לְגוֹלָה וְסוּרָה,* הוֹשַׁעְנָא וְהוֹשִׁיעָה נָּא, אָבִינוּ אָתָּה.
לְמַעַן קָדַם* שְׂאֵת בְּרָכָה, הַנִּשְׂטַם וּלְשִׁמְךָ חִכָּה,
מִיַּחֵם* בְּמַקְלוֹת בְּשִׁקְתוֹת הַמָּיִם.
לְדָמְתָה לְתָמָר,* הוֹשַׁעְנָא וְהוֹשִׁיעָה נָּא, אָבִינוּ אָתָּה.
לְמַעַן צֶדֶק הֱיוֹת לְךָ לְכֹהֵן,* כֶּחָתָן פְּאֵר יְכַהֵן,
מְנֻסֶּה בְּמַסָּה* בְּמֵי מְרִיבַת מַיִם.
לְהָהָר הַטּוֹב,* הוֹשַׁעְנָא וְהוֹשִׁיעָה נָּא, אָבִינוּ אָתָּה.
לְמַעַן פְּאַר הֱיוֹת גְּבִיר לְאֶחָיו, יְהוּדָה* אֲשֶׁר גָּבַר בְּאֶחָיו,
מִסְפַּר רֹבַע מִדָּלְיָו יִזַּל מַיִם.*
לוֹא לָנוּ כִּי אִם לְמַעַנְךָ, הוֹשַׁעְנָא וְהוֹשִׁיעָה נָּא, אָבִינוּ אָתָּה.
לְמַעַן עָנָיו מִכֹּל וְנֶאֱמָן,* אֲשֶׁר בְּצִדְקוֹ כִּלְכֵּל הַמָּן,*
מָשׁוּךְ* לְגוֹאֵל וּמָשׁוּי מִמַּיִם.*
לְזֹאת הַנִּשְׁקָפָה,* הוֹשַׁעְנָא וְהוֹשִׁיעָה נָּא, אָבִינוּ אָתָּה.

בָּרָה כַּחַמָּה — *Brilliant as the sun.* Scripture describes Abraham's performance of *mitzvos* as taking place in broad daylight. Circumcision was done בְּעֶצֶם הַיּוֹם, *in the strength of the day* [i.e., at midday when the sun is at its strongest *(Genesis* 17:23); his search for wayfarers to whom he may offer hospitality was כְּחֹם הַיּוֹם, *in the heat of the day (Genesis* 18:1). For this reason his offspring are called *brilliant as the sun.*

רַךְ וְיָחִיד — *Tender and only.* Isaac was *tender* in the sense that he was Abraham's younger son. When God told Abraham to sacrifice his son, He described Isaac as בִּנְךָ . . . יְחִידְךָ, *your son, your only son (Genesis* 22:2; *Rashi).*

Alternatively, Isaac was יָחִיד, *the only son,* of Sarah who had no other children; but Abraham had other children *(Beis Avraham).*

נֶחֱנַט פְּרִי לְמֵאָה — *[The] fruit which blossomed at one hundred.* Abraham was one hundred years old at Isaac's birth *(Genesis* 21:5).

אַיֵּה הַשֶּׂה — *Where is the lamb?* Upon realizing that he was to be offered as a sacrifice, Isaac asked this question.

מָצָאנוּ מַיִם — *We have found water. Genesis* 26:12-33 relates Isaac's difficulties at the hands of his Philistine neighbors. Jealous of his wealth, they continually stuffed his wells and disputed his ownership of them. His servants kept digging wells until the Philistines stopped disputing his right to them.

גּוֹלָה וְסוּרָה — *Exiled and displaced.* This reference to Israel is an apt description of the nation descended from Isaac, who was banished by Abimelech *(Genesis* 26:16) because of the Philistine's jealousy of his success *(Rashi).*

קָדַם — *The first.* Jacob preceded Esau in bringing delicacies to Isaac. The blessings which he received in return became the excuse for an eternal hatred which Esau harbored against him.

מִיַּחֵם — *He stimulated.* The devices to which Jacob resorted to obtain his rightful share of the flocks are described in *Genesis* 30:37-43.

דָּמְתָה לְתָמָר — *Likened to a palm tree.* Just as the palm tree has a single heart, which is directed upward [i.e., its trunk does not branch out in many directions]; so Israel has a single heart directed only to God.

צֶדֶק הֱיוֹת לְךָ לְכֹהֵן — *The one worthy of being Your Kohen.* Levi, son of Jacob, was the progenitor of the priestly tribe from which sprang Aaron the *Kohen.*

מְנֻסֶּה בְּמַסָּה — *He was proven at Massah.* In his blessing of the Levites, Moses praised them as the tribe whom God *proved at Massah . . . at Merivah's water (Deuteronomy* 33:8). *Sforno* explains that the Levites never joined Israel in any of the ten times the nation questioned God's ability to sustain them in the Wilderness (see *Numbers* 14:22).

הָהָר הַטּוֹב — *The good mountain.* Moses referred to the Temple Mount by this name *(Deuteronomy* 3:25). In the verse which speaks of the righteousness of the Levites, it is proper that we pray for the return of the Holy Temple in which they served.

יְהוּדָה — *Judah.* From among the twelve sons of Jacob [who were all equally righteous (see *Rashi* to *Genesis* 35:22)], the *paytan* mentions only

ב *for [the people] brilliant as the sun,**
may You save now and bring salvation now,
for You are our Father.

ר *In the merit of [Isaac] the tender and only* fruit*
*which blossomed at one hundred,**
who cried, 'Where is the lamb for the offering?'*
*His servants informed him, 'We have found water'**

ג *for the exiled and displaced,**
may You save now and bring salvation now,
for You are our Father.

ק *In the merit of [Jacob] the first* with a gift for the blessing,*
who was hated but who yearned for Your Name,
he stimulated with rods at the troughs of water*

ד *for those likened to a palm tree,**
may You save now and bring salvation now,
for You are our Father.

צ *In the merit of [Levi] the one worthy of being Your Kohen,**
adorned like a bridegroom he would serve,
he was proven at Massah, at Merivah's water*

ה *for the good mountain,**
may You save now and bring salvation now,
for You are our Father.

פ *In the merit of the splendrous one who would be master over his brothers,*
Judah who ruled over his brothers though he was fourth,*
*from his buckets shall pour water**

ו *not for our sake but for Yours,*
may You save now and bring salvation now,
for You are our Father.

ע *In the merit of [Moses] the humblest of all and the most trusted,**
for whose righteousness He supplied manna, he was drawn**
*to be a redeemer and pulled from the water**

ז *for the one who gazes down,**
may You save now and bring salvation now,
for You are our Father.

Levi and Judah because (a) Scripture relates incidents in their lives relating to water, and (b) priesthood and royalty were granted them respectively.

מִדָּלְיָו יִזַּל מַיִם — *From his buckets shall pour water.* A paraphrase of Balaam's third blessing to Israel *(Numbers* 24:7), the use of this phrase is an allusion to Judah based on the end of the verse: *And may his kingdom be extended. Rashi* there interprets: May Jacob's royal line be extended with the reigns of David and his son Solomon [who are descended from Judah].

עָנָיו מִכֹּל וְנֶאֱמָן — *The humblest of all and the most trusted.* In *Numbers* 12:3,7 Moses is referred to as עָנָו מְאֹד מִכֹּל הָאָדָם, *the very humblest of all men,* and בְּכָל בֵּיתִי נֶאֱמָן הוּא, *in My entire house he is trusted.*

כִּלְכֵּל הַמָּן — *He supplied manna.* Three good shepherds arose among the Israelites: Moses, Aaron, and Miriam. God presented the nation with three gifts in their respective merit: the well in Miriam's merit [see below]; the protective clouds [which surrounded the nation in the Wilderness] in Aaron's; and the manna in Moses' *(Taanis* 9a).

מָשׁוּךְ — *He was drawn.* Against his will, God drew Moses into the role of leadership (see *Exodus* 3:11-13; 14:13).

מָשׁוּי מִמַּיִם — *Pulled from the water.* The name Moses means *pulled from the water (Exodus* 2:10).

וֹאת הַנִּשְׁקָפָה — *The one who gazes down.* Israel is described as: *She gazes down like the dawn; she is beautiful as the moon, brilliant as the sun (Song of Songs* 6:10). This verse alluding to Israel is especially apt to the stiches which speak of Moses and his disciple Joshua (see below). The Talmud *(Bava Basra* 75a) compares the leader-

לְמַעַן שַׂמְתּוֹ כְּמַלְאֲכֵי מְרוֹמִים,* הַלּוֹבֵשׁ אוּרִים וְתֻמִּים,*
מְצֻוֶּה* לָבֹא בַּמִּקְדָּשׁ בְּקִדּוּשׁ יָדַיִם וְרַגְלַיִם וּרְחִיצַת מַיִם.
לְחוֹלַת אַהֲבָה, הוֹשַׁעְנָא וְהוֹשִׁיעָה נָּא, אָבִינוּ אָתָּה.
לְמַעַן נְבִיאָה מְחוֹלַת מַחֲנַיִם, לְכַמְהֵי לֵב הוּשְׂמָה עֵינַיִם,
לְרַגְלָהּ רָצָה עֲלוֹת וָרֶדֶת בְּאֵר מַיִם.*
לְטוֹבוּ אֹהָלָיו,* הוֹשַׁעְנָא וְהוֹשִׁיעָה נָּא, אָבִינוּ אָתָּה.
לְמַעַן מְשָׁרֵת* לֹא מָשׁ מֵאֹהֶל, וְרוּחַ הַקֹּדֶשׁ עָלָיו אֹהֶל,
בְּעָבְרוֹ בַּיַּרְדֵּן* נִכְרְתוּ הַמַּיִם.
לְיָפָה וּבָרָה,* הוֹשַׁעְנָא וְהוֹשִׁיעָה נָּא, אָבִינוּ אָתָּה.
לְמַעַן לִמֵּד רְאוֹת לְטוֹבָה אוֹת,* זָעַק אַיֵּה נִפְלָאוֹת,
מִצָּה טַל מִגִּזָּה מְלֹא הַסֵּפֶל מַיִם.
לְכַלַּת לְבָנוֹן,* הוֹשַׁעְנָא וְהוֹשִׁיעָה נָּא, אָבִינוּ אָתָּה.
לְמַעַן כְּלוּלֵי עֲשׂוֹת מִלְחַמְתֶּךָ, אֲשֶׁר בְּיָדָם תַּתָּה יְשׁוּעָתֶךָ,
צְרוּפֵי מִגּוֹי בְּלָקְקָם בְּיָדָם* מַיִם.
לְלֹא בָגְדוּ בָךְ,* הוֹשַׁעְנָא וְהוֹשִׁיעָה נָּא, אָבִינוּ אָתָּה.

---

ship of Joshua to that of Moses and finds that, great though he was, the disciple was a mere reflection of the master. In the Talmud's words: The face of Moses was like the sun; the face of Joshua was like the moon.

כְּמַלְאֲכֵי מְרוֹמִים — *Like exalted angels.* Aaron's holiness is described by the prophet (*Malachi* 2:7): *For the Kohen's lips shall safeguard knowledge; and Torah shall they seek from his mouth, for he is an angel of HASHEM of hosts.*

אוּרִים וְתֻמִּים — *The Urim and Tumim.* The *Kohen Gadol's* breastplate consisted of twelve precious stones, each inscribed with the name of one tribe.

Contained in the fold of the breastplate was a parchment upon which the Ineffable Name of God was written. When Israel required prophetic advice, the *Kohen Gadol* clad in his sacred garments would be presented with the question, which he would repeat. Through the power of the Ineffable Name, various letters of the tribal names would light up, spelling the answer to the question (see *Yoma* 73a).

The parchment on which the Ineffable Name was written was called the *Urim* and *Tumim* (*Rashi* to *Exodus* 28:30). The name אוּרִים, *Urim* [lit., *lights*], is an allusion to the illumination of the letters on the breastplate; תֻּמִּים, *Tumim* [lit., *perfect ones*], refers to the perfect advice which it rendered (based on a marginal gloss to *Berachos* 4a).

מְצֻוֶּה ... — *Is commanded ...* No one may enter the Temple Courtyard without prior immersion (*Yoma* 30a). A *Kohen* is forbidden to perform the Temple service unless he has sanctified his hands and feet in the waters of the כִּיּוֹר, *laver*, which stood in the Courtyard (*Exodus* 30:17-21).

בְּאֵר מַיִם — *The well of water.* The well which accompanied the Israelites through the Wilderness was granted them in the merit of Miriam.

טוֹבוּ אֹהָלָיו — *The one of goodly tests.* Another paraphrase of Balaam's blessing (*Numbers* 24:5). The relationship of this reference to Israel and Miriam's well may be understood from the Midrash (*Bamidbar Rabbah* 19:26). When the nation camped in the Wilderness, the leader of each tribe would take his staff and draw a line from the well through his tribe's encampment. The water would then flow along these twelve paths so that each person had water without exertion. The waters of Miriam's well thus came right to *the goodly tents of Israel.*

מְשָׁרֵת — *The servant.* Joshua's loyalty to Moses is described in *Exodus* 33:11: *But his [Moses'] servant Joshua ... did not move from the tent.* This dedication enabled Joshua to assume the leadership of Israel after Moses' death. For as the Talmud teaches (*Berachos* 7b): A disciple's service is more significant than his studies.

בְּעָבְרוֹ בַּיַּרְדֵּן — *When he crossed the Jordan.* Israel's entry into the Land of Canaan under Joshua's leadership is recounted in *Joshua* 3:9-4:24.

יָפָה וּבָרָה — *Beautiful and brilliant.* This abridgment of the verse *beautiful as the moon, brilliant as the sun,* alludes to Joshua's command to the heavenly bodies: *Sun in Gibeon remain still, also the moon in the valley of Ayalon* (*Joshua* 10:12).

אוֹת — *Omen.* Gideon was visited by an angel

ס *In the merit of [Aaron] the one You emplaced like exalted angels,**
*he who, wearing the Urim and Tumim,**
is commanded to come to the Temple with sanctified hands and feet, and an immersion in water*
ח *for the one sick with love,*
may You save now and bring salvation now,
for You are our Father.

נ *In the merit of [Miriam] the prophetess of the dance of the camps,*
to those of thirsting heart she was an inspiration,
*at her feet ran, rising and descending, the well of water**
ט *for the one of goodly tents,**
may You save now and bring salvation now,
for You are our Father.

מ *In the merit of [Joshua] the servant* who moved not from the tent,*
upon him the Holy Spirit rested,
when he crossed the Jordan, cut was the water*
י *for the beautiful and brilliant,**
may You save now and bring salvation now,
for You are our Father.

ל *In the merit of [Gideon] the one who showed how to perceive a good omen,**
he cried, 'Where are Your wonders,'
from a fleece he pressed, a bowl full of water
כ *for the bride of Lebanon,**
may You save now and bring salvation now,
for You are our Father.

כ *In the merit of [Gideon's army] the dedicated fighters in Your war,*
into whose hands You placed Your salvation, proven purest of the nation by having lapped from their hand water*
ל *for those that did not rebel against You,**
may You save now and bring salvation now,
for You are our Father.

---

when Israel was subjugated by Midian. He asked the angel, *'Where are His wonders which our fathers have recounted about Him ...?'* In response, God Himself (see *Rashi*) told Gideon to save the nation from the Midianites. Gideon asked for omens which would prove that his mission would be successful, and a sign was given him (see *Judges* 6:1-38 for the complete narrative). He asked for a second sign, one which he specified: *I shall spread a fleece on the threshing floor, if dew falls only on the fleece, and the earth shall all be dry, then I shall know that through my hands will Israel be saved, as You have spoken. And so it was, he awoke in the morning and squeezed the fleece; he pressed dew from the fleece — a full bowl of water (Judges* 6:37-38). He subsequently asked for a third sign, that the fleece remain dry while the earth surrounding it becomes wet with dew. This sign was also granted him.

כַּלַּת לְבָנוֹן — *The bride of Lebanon.* Lebanon is a reference to the Holy Temple, so called because the [blood-like] sins of the nation are cleansed there [a play on the words לְבָנוֹן, *Lebanon,* and לָבָן, *white*] (*Yoma* 39b).

בְּלָקְקָם בְּיָדָם — *Having lapped from their hand.* When Gideon's thirty-two thousand man army prepared for battle with Midian, God told him that the army was too large — Israel would claim that its victory was due to its superior forces. The army was reduced to ten thousand men, but still God demanded a much smaller band. To select only those who were completely loyal to God, the troops were marched to the water where they were told to drink. Those who fell to their knees and brought their faces down to the water were judged unsuitable to serve in God's army [for they were wont to fall on their knees and prostrate themselves before idols (*Rashi*)]. Those who scooped up water and lapped it from their hands were allowed to remain. They numbered only three hundred men (see *Judges* 7:1-8).

לֹא בָגְדוּ בָךְ — *Those that did not rebel against You.* The connection between this allusion to Israel from *Isaiah* 33:1 and the loyal troops of Gideon's army is obvious.

לְמַעַן יָחִיד* צוֹרְרִים דָּשׁ, אֲשֶׁר מֵרֶחֶם לְנָזִיר* הֻקְדַּשׁ,
מִמַּכְתֵּשׁ לֶחִי* הִבְקַעְתָּ לוֹ מַיִם.
לְמַעַן שֵׁם קָדְשֶׁךָ, הוֹשַׁעְנָא וְהוֹשִׁיעָה נָּא, אָבִינוּ אָתָּה.
לְמַעַן טוֹב הוֹלֵךְ וְגָדֵל,* אֲשֶׁר מֵעֹשֶׁק עֵדָה חָדֵל,*
בְּשׁוּב עָם מֵחֵטְא צָו שְׁאָב מַיִם.*
לְנָאוָה כִּירוּשָׁלָיִם,* הוֹשַׁעְנָא וְהוֹשִׁיעָה נָּא, אָבִינוּ אָתָּה.
לְמַעַן חַיָּךְ מְכַרְכֵּר בְּשִׁיר,* הַמְּלַמֵּד תּוֹרָה בְּכָל כְּלֵי שִׁיר,*
מְנַסֵּךְ לְפָנָיו* כְּתָאֵב שְׁתוֹת מַיִם.
לְשָׁמוּ בְךָ סִבְרָם, הוֹשַׁעְנָא וְהוֹשִׁיעָה נָּא, אָבִינוּ אָתָּה.
לְמַעַן זָךְ עָלָה* בַּסְּעָרָה, הַמְּקַנֵּא וּמֵשִׁיב עֶבְרָה,
לְפִלּוּלוֹ יָרְדָה אֵשׁ וְלִחֲכָה עָפָר וּמַיִם.*
לְעֵינֶיהָ בְּרֵכוֹת,* הוֹשַׁעְנָא וְהוֹשִׁיעָה נָּא, אָבִינוּ אָתָּה.
לְמַעַן וְשֵׁרֵת בֶּאֱמֶת לְרַבּוֹ,* פִּי שְׁנַיִם* בְּרוּחוֹ נֶאֱצַל בּוֹ,
בְּקַחְתּוֹ מְנַגֵּן* נִתְמַלְּאוּ גֵּבִים מַיִם.

יָחִיד — *The only child* [lit., *single one*]. Samson's parents had only one child.

מֵרֶחֶם לְנָזִיר — *From the womb as a Nazir.* The circumstances preceding Samson's miraculous birth and the instructions given his mother to consecrate him as a Nazir even before he was born are recounted in *Judges* chap. 13.

מִמַּכְתֵּשׁ לֶחִי — *From the hollow of a jawbone.* After slaying a thousand Philistines with the jawbone of a donkey, Samson was stricken with an unslakable thirst. HASHEM split the hollow of the jawbone and water flowed out from it; and he drank. His spirit was refreshed (Judges 15:18-19).

טוֹב הוֹלֵךְ וְגָדֵל — *The good and increasingly exalted one.* This description of the young Samuel is paraphrased from *I Samuel* 2:26.

חָדֵל — *Who restrained himself.* Samuel gathered the nation asking them to testify whether, at any time during his tenure as judge and prophet, he accepted a bribe or even took the wages to which he was legitimately entitled. None came forward (see *I Samuel* 12:35).

שְׁאָב מַיִם — *Draw water. I Samuel* 7:5-6 describes how Samuel gathered the nation in prayer and repentance. *They drew water and poured it before HASHEM. Targum* renders: 'They poured out their hearts before HASHEM as if it were water.'

נָאוָה כִּירוּשָׁלָיִם — *Beautiful as Jerusalem.* Israel is so designated in *Song of Songs* 6:4. Samuel's gathering for repentance took place after the destruction of the Tabernacle of Shiloh. *Psalms* 78:60-68 teaches that Jerusalem was selected after the destruction of Shiloh, hence this epithet for Israel is used here.

מְכַרְכֵּר בְּשִׁיר — *Dancing with song.* The Ark of the Mishkan had been captured by the Philistines but they could not hold on to it. Wherever they brought it, an epidemic would break out. After seven months they finally returned it to Israel. It was brought to the house of Avinadav in Givah where it remained for twenty years *(I Samuel* 7:1-2).

When David attempted to bring the Ark to Jerusalem, tragedy struck. Uzzah inadvertently stretched out his hand, touched the Ark, and died. The festivities ended in mourning and the Ark was left at the house of Oved-edom the Levite for the next three months. At the end of this period it was removed to Jerusalem with great festivities. *And David danced with all [his] strength before HASHEM (II Samuel* 6:1-14).

הַמְּלַמֵּד תּוֹרָה בְּכָל כְּלֵי שִׁיר — *Who teaches Torah accompanied by every sort of instrument.* David taught Torah joyously, as if he were listening to a full orchestra.

מְנַסֵּךְ לְפָנָיו — *He poured libations before Him.* When David thirsted for water in the thick of battle he cried, *'Who will give me water to drink from the cistern at the gate of Bethlehem?'*

Three bold warriors broke through the Philistine camp and drew water . . . When he was given the water, David said that to drink water obtained with such potential danger was like drinking the blood of the bold warriors who risked their lives to get it. Such water can only be consecrated to God. And David poured the water as a libation before God *(II Samuel* 23:15-17).

זָךְ עָלָה — *The pure one who ascended.* Elijah and his disciple Elisha were taking their final leave of each other before the master would be summoned to his heavenly abode. *Suddenly, a fiery chariot with fiery horses separated the two of them and Elijah ascended to the heavens in a storm wind (II Kings* 2:11).

י *In the merit of [Samson] the only child,* who thrashed the oppressors,*
*sanctified from the womb as a Nazir;**
from the hollow of a jawbone You brought him water*
מ *for the sake of Your Holy Name,*
may You save now and bring salvation now,
for You are our Father.

ט *In the merit of [Samuel] the good and increasingly exalted one**
who restrained himself from robbing the flock,*
*when the nation repented he bade them draw water**
נ *for the one as beautiful as Jerusalem,**
may You save now and bring salvation now,
for You are our Father.

ח *In the merit of [David] the one who caused You joy, dancing with song,* who*
*teaches Torah accompanied by every sort of instrument,**
*he poured libations before Him**
though he thirsted to drink water
ס *for those who place their hope in You,*
may You save now and bring salvation now,
for You are our Father.

ז *In the merit of [Elijah] the pure one who ascended* in a storm wind,*
who avenged and turned back fury, at his prayer
*there descended fire which consumed dust and water**
ע *for the one whose eyes are [like] pools,**
may You save now and bring salvation now,
for You are our Father.

ו *In the merit of [Elisha] the one who served his master earnestly,**
a double measure of his spirit was vested in him,*
when he summoned a musician the cisterns*
were filled with water

וְלִחֲכָה עָפָר וּמַיִם — *Which consumed dust and water.* Ahab, the wicked king of the Ten Tribes, and Jezebel, his even more wicked queen, had long led the nation along the road to idolatry. But Elijah knew that the people inwardly resented the alien culture being pressed upon them. He challenged Ahab and the prophets of Baal into invoking their god to send a heavenly fire which would consume their offering to him. Elijah would offer an animal to the true God of Israel, and summon a fire from heaven to consume it.

When the priests of Baal were unsuccessful after an entire day's efforts, Elijah flooded his offering and altar with barrels of water and called out, *'Answer me, HASHEM, answer me.'* A fire descended, consumed the animal, the wood, the stones, the earth and even the water which had been poured over them.

The people subsequently carried the false prophets to the stream of Kishon where they were executed for practicing idolatry — the 'zealous vengeance' for which Elijah was responsible (*I Kings* ch. 18).

עֵינֶיהָ בְּרֵכוֹת — *(Whose) eyes are [like] pools.* This description of Israel is paraphrased from *Song of Songs* 7:5. The members of Sanhedrin are called *the eyes of the congregation* (*Leviticus* 4:17; *Numbers* 15:24). Just as the Sanhedrin issued definitive judgment in matters of dispute, so will Elijah, when he arrives to herald the Messiah and resolve the questions whose solutions escaped the Sages of each generation.

שֵׁרֵת בֶּאֱמֶת לְרַבּוֹ — *(The one who) served his master earnestly.* Elisha served Elijah faithfully and was therefore worthy to succeed him. The Talmud explains the verse (*II Kings* 3:11), *here is Elisha ben Shafat who poured water at the feet of Elijah:* Scripture does not say 'he studied' at the feet of Elijah, but 'he poured water.' This teaches that a disciple gains more by serving his master than by studying his words (*Berachos* 7b).

פִּי שְׁנַיִם — *A double measure.* Before Elijah was taken to heaven he allowed Elisha one request. Elisha asked that *'there rest upon me a double portion of your spirit'* (*II Kings* 2:9).

Rashi (ibid. v. 14) notes that when Elijah and Elisha were walking together, the Jordan split to let them pass. On the return trip Elisha was alone, yet the water split for him. Thus, Elisha's double portion was granted, for Elisha's own merit accomplished what had earlier required the merit of both.

בְּקַחְתּוֹ מְנַגֵּן — *When he summoned a musician.* The kings of Judea, Israel and Edom formed an

לְפָצוּ מִי כָמְכָה,* הוֹשַׁעְנָא וְהוֹשִׁיעָה נָּא, אָבִינוּ אָתָּה.

לְמַעַן הִרְהֵר עֲשׂוֹת רְצוֹנֶךָ,* הַמַּכְרִיז תְּשׁוּבָה* לְצֹאנֶךָ,
אָז בְּבֹא מְחָרֵף* סָתַם עֵינוֹת מַיִם.*
לְצִיּוֹן מִכְלַל יֹפִי, הוֹשַׁעְנָא וְהוֹשִׁיעָה נָּא, אָבִינוּ אָתָּה.

לְמַעַן דְּרָשׁוּךָ בְּתוֹךְ הַגּוֹלָה,* וְסוֹדְךָ לָמוֹ נִגְלָה,*
בְּלִי לְהִתְגָּאֵל דָּרְשׁוּ זֵרְעוֹנִים וּמַיִם.
לְקוֹרְאֶיךָ בַּצָּר,* הוֹשַׁעְנָא וְהוֹשִׁיעָה נָּא, אָבִינוּ אָתָּה.

לְמַעַן גְּמַר חָכְמָה וּבִינָה, סוֹפֵר מָהִיר מְפַלֵּשׁ אֲמָנָה,
מְחַכְּמֵנוּ* אֲמָרִים הַמְּשׁוּלִים בְּרַחֲבֵי מַיִם.*
לְרַבָּתִי עָם,* הוֹשַׁעְנָא וְהוֹשִׁיעָה נָּא, אָבִינוּ אָתָּה.

לְמַעַן בָּאֵי לְךָ הַיּוֹם* בְּכָל לֵב, שׁוֹפְכִים לְךָ שִׂיחַ בְּלֹא לֵב וָלֵב,*
שׁוֹאֲלִים מִמְּךָ עוֹז מִטְרוֹת מַיִם.
לְשׁוֹרְרוּךָ בַּיָּם, הוֹשַׁעְנָא וְהוֹשִׁיעָה נָּא, אָבִינוּ אָתָּה.

לְמַעַן אוֹמְרֵי יִגְדַּל שְׁמֶךָ, וְהֵם נַחֲלָתְךָ וְעַמֶּךָ,*
צְמֵאִים לְיֶשְׁעֲךָ. כְּאֶרֶץ עֲיֵפָה לַמַּיִם.
לְתַרְתָּ לָמוֹ מְנוּחָה, הוֹשַׁעְנָא וְהוֹשִׁיעָה נָּא, אָבִינוּ אָתָּה.

---

alliance against Moab. After their armies had marched seven-days' journey into the wilderness they ran out of water. Jehosaphat, king of Judea, summoned Elisha who said: *'Now bring me a musician.' As the musician played, the Hand of HASHEM came upon him [Elisha] and he said, 'So says HASHEM: This valley shall be filled with cisterns, cisterns. For thus says HASHEM: You shall not see wind, you shall not see rain, but this valley shall be full of water. You shall drink — you, your cattle and your pack-animals* (*II Kings* 3:9-17).

פָּצוּ מִי כָמְכָה — *Those who exclaimed, 'Who is like You?'* Israel sang these words twice in the Song of the Sea (*Exodus* 15:11). The Sea of Reeds split for Israel, the Jordan twice split for Elisha.

הִרְהֵר עֲשׂוֹת רְצוֹנֶךָ — *Who meant to do Your will.* Hezekiah, king of Judea, committed six halachically questionable acts. Of three of them, the Sages approved; of the other three, they disapproved (*Pesachim* 56a; *Berachos* 10b). Although they did not consent to all of Hezekiah's actions, they repudiated only the particular acts, not the man, for they knew that (*II Kings* 18:5) *he had faith in HASHEM, God of Israel.*

הַמַּכְרִיז תְּשׁוּבָה — *He cried out, 'Repentance.'* Hezekiah sent runners throughout Israel, *and in accordance with the king's order they said: 'Children of Israel! Return to HASHEM, God of Abraham, Isaac and Israel!'* (*II Chronicles* 30:6).

מְחָרֵף — *The blasphemer.* Ravshakeh, the Assyrian general, cried out blasphemously to the Jewish king and army to abandon their faith in God (*II Kings* 18:19-35).

סָתַם עֵינוֹת מַיִם — *He sealed the springs of water.* When Sennacherib's army, led by Ravshakeh, threatened, Hezekiah ordered that the springs which supplied Jerusalem with water be sealed. *'Why should the Assyrian kings come and find abundant water?'* Hezekiah contended (*I Chronicles* 32:4).

בְּתוֹךְ הַגּוֹלָה — *In midst of the exile.* Daniel, Chananiah, Mishael, and Azariah were taken from among the exiles of Judah (*Daniel* 2:25) to live in Nebuchadnezzar's palace. Their refusal to partake of the conqueror's food, their insistence on eating a vegetarian diet of pulse and water (ibid. 1:8-16), and their prayers to God (ibid. 2:18 and 6:11-12) are sure signs that they sought closeness to God even in the midst of the exile.

וְסוֹדְךָ לָמוֹ נִגְלָה — *Your secret was uncovered to them.* This refers to Daniel's interpretation of Nebuchadnezzar's dream recounted in chapter two of *Daniel.*

לְקוֹרְאֶיךָ בַּצָּר — *For those who call in distress.* Israel cries to God when in distress just as did Daniel and his companions.

מְחַכְּמֵנוּ — *He made us wise.* Ezra was worthy enough that the Torah could have been given

פ *for those who exclaimed, 'Who is like You?',**
may You save now and bring salvation now,
for You are our Father.

ה *In the merit [Hezekiah] of the one who meant to do Your will,**
he cried out, 'Repentance,' to Your sheep, then when*
the blasphemer came he sealed the springs of water**
צ *for Zion, perfect in beauty,*
may You save now and bring salvation now,
for You are our Father.

ד *In the merit of [Daniel, Chananiah, Mishael, and Azariah]*
*those who sought You in midst of the exile,**
*Your secret was uncovered to them.**
Not to defile themselves they requested pulse and water
ק *for those who call in distress,**
may You save now and bring salvation now,
for You are our Father.

ג *In the merit of [Ezra] the one who studied wisdom and understanding,*
*a skillful scribe, expounder of faith, he made us wise**
*with sayings that are likened to expanses of water**
ר *for [the city] great with people,**
may You save now and bring salvation now,
for You are our Father.

ב *For the sake of [the present congregation] those who come to You today**
with all their heart, pouring prayer before You with
undivided heart, asking You for powerful rains of water*
ש *for those who sang to You at the Sea,*
may You save now and bring salvation now,
for You are our Father.

א *For the sake of those [Israel] who say, 'May Your Name be exalted!'*
they are Your heritage and Your people; they thirst for*
Your salvation as does a land that thirsts for water
ת *for those for whom You scouted a resting place,*
may You save now and bring salvation now,
for You are our Father.

---

through him, had not Moses preceded him (*Sanhedrin* 21b). When the Torah was almost forgotten by Israel, Ezra came up from Babylon and re-established it (*Succah* 20a).

הַמְּשׁוּלִים בְּרַחֲבֵי מָיִם — *That are likened to expanses of water.* King Solomon compares the Torah to water: *May your wellsprings burst forth outwardly, in broad channels of water* (*Proverbs* 5:16).

רַבָּתִי עָם — *[The city] great with people.* The translation of this description of Jerusalem is based on its use in *Lamentations* 1:1 where the phrase is preceded by the word הָעִיר, *the city.* Just as Ezra led Israel back to Jerusalem from the exile, so may we merit to see Jerusalem once again *great with people.*

Alternatively, רַבָּתִי עָם alludes to Israel and means *the greatest of peoples.*

הַיּוֹם — *Today.* This stich refers to the congregants who are reciting the *Hoshana* prayers.

בְּלֹא לֵב וָלֵב — *With undivided heart* [lit., *without heart and heart*]. This phrase is synonymous with לֵב אֶחָד, *one heart* (*Radak* to *I Chronicles* 12:33).

נַחֲלָתְךָ וְעַמֶּךָ — *Your heritage and Your people.* Israel is God's *heritage* by virtue of its Patriarchs; and His *people,* for He freed it from Egyptian slavery (*Ibn Ezra* to *Deuteronomy* 9:29).

Some put aside the *lulav* and *esrog* and take up the *Hoshana*-bundle of five willow twigs. This is held until it is beaten at the end of the service. Others retain the *lulav* and *esrog* and do not take up the *Hoshana*-bundle until it is to be beaten.

Chazzan, then congregation:

הוֹשַׁעְנָא, אֵל נָא, אָנָּא הוֹשִׁיעָה נָא, הוֹשַׁעְנָא, סְלַח נָא וְהַצְלִיחָה נָא, וְהוֹשִׁיעֵנוּ אֵל מָעֻזֵּנוּ.

All:

תַּעֲנֶה אֱמוּנִים שׁוֹפְכִים לְךָ לֵב כַּמַּיִם, וְהוֹשִׁיעָה נָּא,
לְמַעַן בָּא בָאֵשׁ וּבַמַּיִם,*
גָּזַר וְנָם יֻקַּח נָא* מְעַט מַיִם, וְהַצְלִיחָה נָא, וְהוֹשִׁיעֵנוּ אֵל מָעֻזֵּנוּ.
תַּעֲנֶה דְגָלִים* גָּזוּ גִּזְרֵי מַיִם,* וְהוֹשִׁיעָה נָּא,
לְמַעַן הַנֶּעֱקַד בְּשַׁעַר הַשָּׁמַיִם,
וְשָׁב וְחָפַר* בְּאֵרוֹת מַיִם, וְהַצְלִיחָה נָא, וְהוֹשִׁיעֵנוּ אֵל מָעֻזֵּנוּ.
תַּעֲנֶה זַכִּים חוֹנִים עֲלֵי מַיִם, וְהוֹשִׁיעָה נָּא,
לְמַעַן חָלָק* מְפַצֵּל מַקְלוֹת* בְּשִׁקְתוֹת הַמַּיִם,
טָעַן וְגָל* אֶבֶן מִבְּאֵר מַיִם, וְהַצְלִיחָה נָא, וְהוֹשִׁיעֵנוּ אֵל מָעֻזֵּנוּ.
תַּעֲנֶה יְדִידִים נוֹחֲלֵי דָּת מְשׁוּלַת מַיִם,* וְהוֹשִׁיעָה נָּא,
לְמַעַן כָּרוּ בְּמִשְׁעֲנוֹתָם* מַיִם.
לְהָכִין לָמוֹ וּלְצֶאֱצָאֵימוֹ מַיִם, וְהַצְלִיחָה נָא, וְהוֹשִׁיעֵנוּ אֵל מָעֻזֵּנוּ.
תַּעֲנֶה מִתְחַנְּנִים כְּבִישִׁימוֹן עֲלֵי מַיִם, וְהוֹשִׁיעָה נָּא,
לְמַעַן נֶאֱמַן בַּיִת מַסְפִּיק לָעָם מַיִם,
סֶלַע הָךְ* וַיָּזוּבוּ מַיִם, וְהַצְלִיחָה נָא, וְהוֹשִׁיעֵנוּ אֵל מָעֻזֵּנוּ.

תַּעֲנֶה אֱמוּנִים / Answer the Faithful

At this point, *Maharam* would lay aside the Four Species and pick up the *Hoshana*-bundle, consisting of five willow twigs, and hold it until the end of the service. *Arizal* would hold the Four Species until the end of the service; only then would he lay them aside and pick up the *Hoshana*-bundle until the end of the service. Both *Maharam* and *Arizal* agree that the Four Species and the *Hoshana*-bundle should not be held simultaneously.

Shelah reconciles the two opinions: Those who say the *Hoshana* prayers after *Mussaf,* as did *Maharam,* should follow his view and take up the *Hoshana*-bundle here; those who say the *Hoshana* prayers immediately after *Hallel,* as did *Arizal,* should not take up the *Hoshana*-bundle until the end of the service. Both customs are valid and have profound Kabbalistic implications.

Following the theme of the preceding *Hoshana,* we again ask for rain in the merit of our righteous forebears. The Talmud teaches that during Succos the Heavenly Tribunal judges the world with regard to its water supply for the following year. God ordained the water libations of Succos as a source of merit; as if He said, 'Pour water before Me on this festival, that you be blessed with the year's rains' (*Rosh Hashanah* 16a). These prayers for rain are not recited until the last day of the festival because 'rain is but a symptom of curse during Succos,' for it makes it impossible to sit in the *succah* (*Taanis* 2a).

בָּא בָאֵשׁ וּבַמַּיִם — *The one who entered fire and water.* Abraham allowed himself to be thrown by Nimrod into a blazing furnace. When Abraham was on the way to the *Akeidah* with Isaac, Satan appeared in the form of a wide, deep river, attempting to block their path. They braved the obstacle and plunged into the water until it was up to their necks — then the river was removed and they proceeded on their mission undeterred (*Tanchuma, Vayeira* 22).

יֻקַּח נָא — *Let there now be taken.* This is an allusion to Abraham's hospitality to the angels (see *Genesis* 18:1-15).

דְּגָלִים — *The bannered.* The Israelite tribes in the Wilderness were distinguished by the colors and emblems of their banners.

גִּזְרֵי מַיִם — *Divisions of water.* A reference to the Splitting of the Sea.

Some put aside the *lulav* and *esrog* and take up the *Hoshana*-bundle of five willow twigs. This is held until it is beaten at the end of the service. Others retain the *lulav* and *esrog* and do not take up the *Hoshana*-bundle until it is to be beaten.

Chazzan, then congregation:

Save now, please God, please bring salvation now; save now, forgive now, bring success now, and save us, God, our Fortress.

All:

א *Answer the faithful who pour out their heart to You like water — and bring salvation now,*
ב *in the merit of [Abraham] the one who entered fire and water* —*
ג *who decreed saying, 'Let there now be taken* some water;' and bring success now and save us, God, our Fortress.*

ד *Answer the [Twelve] bannered* [Tribes] who passed through divisions of water;* — and bring salvation now,*
ה *in the merit of [Isaac] the one bound at the gateway of Heaven,*
ו *who returned and dug* wells of water; and bring success now and save us, God, our Fortress.*

ז *Answer [the Israelites] the pure ones who encamped near the water* — and bring salvation now,*
ח *in the merit of [Jacob] the smooth-skinned one* who peeled rods* at the trough of water,*
ט *who lifted and rolled away* a boulder from a well of water; and bring success now and save us, God, our Fortress.*

י *Answer the beloved heirs of the mandate likened to water* — and bring salvation now,*
כ *in the merit of those who dug with their staffs* for water,*
ל *to prepare, for themselves and for their offspring, water; and bring success now and save us, God, our Fortress.*

מ *Answer those who beseech as in the Wilderness for water — and bring salvation now,*
נ *in the merit of [Moses] the most trusted of the household, who supplied the people with water,*
ס *who struck the rock* and there flowed water,*
and bring success now and save us, God, our Fortress.

הַנֶּעֱקַד . . . וְחָפַר — *The one bound . . . who . . . dug.* These references to Isaac are discussed earlier; see page 790.

חוֹנִים עֲלֵי מַיִם — *Who encamped near the water.* After leaving Marah where it was taught a number of *mitzvos,* the nation arrived at Eilim. There the people found twelve wells and seventy date trees. The seventy elders each sat under one of the trees and expounded the Torah to the twelve tribes, each of which encamped around one of the wells. *And the nation rested there near the water (Exodus* 15:27).

חָלָק — *The smooth-skinned one.* Jacob called himself smooth-skinned in comparison to his hairy brother Esau (*Genesis* 27:11).

מְפַצֵּל מַקְלוֹת — *Who peeled rods.* This was one of the devices to which Jacob resorted to gain a just share of the flocks from Laban (*Genesis* 30:37-43).

טָעַן וְגָל — *Who lifted and rolled away.* Upon meeting Rachel, Jacob displayed his strength by rolling a huge stone from the mouth of a well (*Genesis* 29:7-10).

דָּת מְשׁוּלַת מַיִם — *The mandate likened to water.* The Torah is compared to water: just as water runs from a high to a low place, so does Torah run from the haughty and find its place with the humble of spirit (*Taanis* 7a).

כָּרוּ בְּמִשְׁעֲנוֹתָם — *Those who dug with their staffs.* This refers to the tribal princes who drew the water to their respective tribes.

סֶלַע הָךְ — *Who struck the rock.* Soon after the

תַּעֲנֶה עוֹנִים עֲלִי בְאֵר* מַיִם, וְהוֹשִׁיעָה נָּא,
לְמַעַן פֻּקַּד בְּמֵי מְרִיבַת מַיִם,*
צְמֵאִים לְהַשְׁקוֹתָם מַיִם, וְהַצְלִיחָה נָא, וְהוֹשִׁיעֵנוּ אֵל מָעֻזֵּנוּ.
תַּעֲנֶה קְדוֹשִׁים מְנַסְּכִים לְךָ מַיִם,* וְהוֹשִׁיעָה נָּא,
לְמַעַן רֹאשׁ מְשׁוֹרְרִים כְּתָאֵב שְׁתוֹת* מַיִם,
שָׁב וְנָסַךְ לְךָ מַיִם, וְהַצְלִיחָה נָא, וְהוֹשִׁיעֵנוּ אֵל מָעֻזֵּנוּ.
תַּעֲנֶה שׁוֹאֲלִים בְּרִבּוּעַ אֶשְׁלֵי מַיִם,* וְהוֹשִׁיעָה נָּא,
לְמַעַן תֵּל תַּלְפִּיּוֹת מוֹצָא מַיִם,
תִּפְתַּח אֶרֶץ וְתַרְעִיף שָׁמַיִם, וְהַצְלִיחָה נָא, וְהוֹשִׁיעֵנוּ אֵל מָעֻזֵּנוּ.

Chazzan, then congregation:

רַחֵם נָא קְהַל עֲדַת יְשֻׁרוּן, סְלַח וּמְחַל עֲוֹנָם, וְהוֹשִׁיעֵנוּ אֱלֹהֵי יִשְׁעֵנוּ.

All:

אָז* כְּעֵינֵי עֲבָדִים* אֶל יַד אֲדוֹנִים,
בָּאנוּ לְפָנֶיךָ נְדוֹנִים, וְהוֹשִׁיעֵנוּ אֱלֹהֵי יִשְׁעֵנוּ.
גֵּאָה אֲדוֹנֵי הָאֲדוֹנִים, נִתְגָּרוּ בָנוּ מְדָנִים,
דְּשׁוּנוּ וּבְעָלוּנוּ זוּלָתְךָ אֲדוֹנִים*, וְהוֹשִׁיעֵנוּ אֱלֹהֵי יִשְׁעֵנוּ.
הֵן גַּשְׁנוּ הַיּוֹם בְּתַחֲנוּן, עָדֶיךָ רַחוּם וְחַנּוּן,
וְסִפַּרְנוּ נִפְלְאוֹתֶיךָ בְּשִׁנּוּן, וְהוֹשִׁיעֵנוּ אֱלֹהֵי יִשְׁעֵנוּ.
זָבַת חָלָב וּדְבָשׁ,* נָא אַל תִּיבָשׁ,
חַשְׁרַת מַיִם בְּאִבֶּיהָ תְּחֻבָּשׁ, וְהוֹשִׁיעֵנוּ אֱלֹהֵי יִשְׁעֵנוּ.
טָעֲנוּ בִשְׁמֹנָה, בְּיַד שִׁבְעָה וּשְׁמוֹנָה,*
יָשָׁר צַדִּיק אֵל אֱמוּנָה, וְהוֹשִׁיעֵנוּ אֱלֹהֵי יִשְׁעֵנוּ.

Exodus, the people were without water. God commanded Moses to strike a rock, whereupon water would gush forth (*Exodus* 17:6). Although Moses struck a rock to bring water on a second occasion (*Numbers* 20:11), it is unlikely that the *paytan* refers to that incident, because there Moses was commanded to *speak*, not strike, and he was punished for not doing so.

עֲלִי בְאֵר — *Ascend, O well.* The song of the well is found in *Numbers* 21:17-20. It thanks God for miracles through which He saved Israel from death, among which is the well which followed them throughout their wanderings.

מְרִיבַת מַיִם — *Merivah's waters.* Moses was given the assignment of supplying water to the thirsty nation at a place called מַסָּה וּמְרִיבָה, *Massah and Merivah,* literally, *trial and dispute.* It was so named *because of the dispute of the Children of Israel and their testing of HASHEM in that place* (*Exodus* 17:7).

מְנַסְּכִים לְךָ מַיִם — *Who pour before You libations of water.* I.e., the special water libations of Succos.

כְּתָאֵב שְׁתוֹת — *Though thirsting to drink.* When three of his bravest warriors risked their lives to bring him water from the cistern in Bethlehem, David refused to drink water purchased at such danger. Instead, he used the water for a libation to God (see *II Samuel* 23:15-17).

בְּרִבּוּעַ אֶשְׁלֵי מַיִם — *With a quartet of species planted near water.* A reference to the Four Species held while the *Hoshana* prayers are uttered.

אָז כְּעֵינֵי עֲבָדִים / Then, like the Eyes of Slaves

אָז — *Then.* In bygone days, when the Temple stood in all its glory, the nation turned only to You.

כְּעֵינֵי עֲבָדִים — *Like the eyes of slaves.* Slaves have no avenues of support other than the largesse of their master. Likewise, Israel has no

ע *Answer those who responded, 'Ascend, O well* of water'*
— and bring salvation now,
פ *in the merit of[Aaron] the one assigned at Merivah's waters,**
צ *to give drink to those thirsting for water;*
and bring success now and save us, God, our Fortress.
ק *Answer the holy ones who pour before You libations of water**
— and bring salvation now,
ר *in the merit of[David] the foremost singer who,*
though thirsting to drink water, poured before You a libation of water;*
and bring success now and save us, God, our Fortress.
ש *Answer those who ask with a quartet of species planted near water**
— and bring salvation now,
ת *in the merit of the Hill of Talpios [the Temple], source of water, may the earth open wide and the heavens give rain;*
and bring success now and save us, God, our Fortress.

Chazzan, then congregation:

Be merciful, please, with the congregation of Jeshurun's flock; forgive and pardon their iniquities; and save us, God of our salvation.

All:

א *Then,* like the eyes of slaves* looking to their master's hand,*
ב *so did we come before You for judgment*
— so save us, God of our salvation.
ג *Proud One, Lord of lords, they have stirred up strife within us;*
ד *lords have trodden upon us and become our masters, excluding You**
— so save us, God of our salvation.
ה *Indeed we have approached with supplication today,*
before You, O merciful and gracious One.
ו *And we have recounted, and repeated Your wonders*
— so save us, God of our salvation.
ז *Where milk and honey flow* please make not arid.*
ח *With watering clouds clothe her produce*
— and save us, God of our salvation.
ט *Plant us in the fertile land, by the hand of seven and eight;**
י *O just and righteous One, O trustworthy God*
— and save us, God of our salvation.

---

source of sustenance other than its faith in God to whom it turns its eyes.

וּבְעָלוּנוּ זוּלָתְךָ אֲדוֹנִים — *Lords have . . . become our masters, excluding You.* This is not to say that something can be done against God's will. It is God's will that a sinful Israel be punished by exile and subjugation to human masters. However, the ultimate purpose of creation is that Israel bring holiness into a sin-free world. In attaining this perfect state Israel, and each of its members, is free to choose between right and wrong.

זָבַת חָלָב וּדְבַשׁ — *Where milk and honey flow.* This description of *Eretz Yisrael* appears no less than twenty times in Scripture. It is first mentioned to Moses in his initial contact with God at the Burning Bush *(Exodus* 3:8). *Sforno* there explains it as a promise of a fertile land where herds of cattle will thrive [milk] and bumper crops will grow [honey refers to the sweetness of dates].

שִׁבְעָה וּשְׁמֹנָה — *Seven and eight.* In prophesying about Messianic times, *Michah* 5:4 speaks of *seven shepherds and eight chiefs of humanity.* The Talmud *(Succah* 52b) identifies the seven shepherds as: David in the center, Adam, Seth and Methuselah to his right, Abraham, Jacob and Moses to his left. The eight chiefs of humanity are: Jesse, Saul, Samuel, Amos,

כָּרַתָּ בְּרִית לָאָרֶץ, עַד כָּל יְמֵי הָאָרֶץ,*
לְבִלְתִּי פְרָץ בָּהּ פֶּרֶץ, וְהוֹשִׁיעֵנוּ אֱלֹהֵי יִשְׁעֵנוּ.
מִתְחַנְּנִים עֲלֵי מַיִם, כַּעֲרָבִים עַל יִבְלֵי מַיִם,
נָא זְכָר לָמוֹ נִסּוּךְ הַמַּיִם, וְהוֹשִׁיעֵנוּ אֱלֹהֵי יִשְׁעֵנוּ.
שִׂיחִים בְּדֶרֶךְ מַטָּעָתָם,* עוֹמְסִים בְּשַׁוְעָתָם,
עֲנֵם בְּקוֹל פְּגִיעָתָם, וְהוֹשִׁיעֵנוּ אֱלֹהֵי יִשְׁעֵנוּ.
פּוֹעֵל יְשׁוּעוֹת, פְּנֵה לְפִלּוּלָם שְׁעוֹת,
צַדְּקֵם אֵל לְמוֹשָׁעוֹת, וְהוֹשִׁיעֵנוּ אֱלֹהֵי יִשְׁעֵנוּ.
קוֹל רִגְשָׁם תֶּשַׁע, תִּפְתַּח אֶרֶץ וְיִפְרוּ יֶשַׁע,
רַב לְהוֹשִׁיעַ וְלֹא חָפֵץ רֶשַׁע,* וְהוֹשִׁיעֵנוּ אֱלֹהֵי יִשְׁעֵנוּ.

Chazzan, then congregation:

שַׁעֲרֵי שָׁמַיִם פְּתַח,* וְאוֹצָרְךָ הַטּוֹב לָנוּ תִפְתַּח, תּוֹשִׁיעֵנוּ וְרִיב אַל תִּמְתַּח, וְהוֹשִׁיעֵנוּ אֱלֹהֵי יִשְׁעֵנוּ.

Chazzan, then congregation:

קוֹל מְבַשֵּׂר* מְבַשֵּׂר וְאוֹמֵר:

All:

אֹמֶץ יֶשְׁעֲךָ בָּא, קוֹל דּוֹדִי הִנֵּה זֶה בָּא, מְבַשֵּׂר וְאוֹמֵר.
קוֹל בָּא בְּרִבְבוֹת כִּתִּים, לַעֲמוֹד עַל הַר הַזֵּיתִים,* מְבַשֵּׂר וְאוֹמֵר.
קוֹל גִּשְׁתּוֹ בַּשּׁוֹפָר* לִתְקַע, תַּחְתָּיו הַר יִבָּקַע, מְבַשֵּׂר וְאוֹמֵר.

Zephaniah, Zidkiyahu (an alternate reading has Hezekiah), Elijah and the Messiah. *Rashi* comments that he does not know from where the Talmud derives these particular lists.

Alternatively, *seven and eight* alludes to the Talmud's interpretation of the verse in *Ecclesiastes* 11:2: *Give a portion to seven and also to eight.* Seven are the days of Pesach, eight are the days of Succos [including Shemini Atzeres] *(Eruvin* 40b). Thus we ask for salvation in the merit of our observance of these two Festivals.

עַד כָּל יְמֵי הָאָרֶץ — *Continuously, all the days of the earth.* After inhaling, so to speak, the sweet smell of Noah's sacrifice, God used these words in declaring that He would never again cause a cessation of the normal rotation of the seasons (see *Genesis* 8:21-22).

בְּדֶרֶךְ מַטָּעָתָם — *In the direction of their growth.* Every *mitzvah* prescribed with a specific type of plant must be performed in the direction of that plant's natural growth *(Succah* 45b). For example, the Four Species must be held with their lower parts down and their upper parts up, just as they grew on their respective trees.

וְלֹא חָפֵץ רֶשַׁע — *And desires not wickedness. Rashi* interprets *Psalms* 5:5, from which this stich is paraphrased, as a call to rid the world of evildoers.

שַׁעֲרֵי שָׁמַיִם פְּתַח — *Open the gates of heaven.* As can readily be seen from the acrostic, these next two lines are actually the final two stiches of the *Hoshana.* However, they are set off from the others to be read responsively with the *chazzan.* Since these lines have been borrowed from this *Hoshana* for use in the Yom Kippur *Neilah* service, where they stand alone, they are accorded the same honor here *(Beis Yaakov).*

Arizal explains the divergent liturgies which have arisen among the Jews: There are twelve gateways in heaven, corresponding to the twelve tribes. These are the gateways referred to in *Ezekiel* (48:31-34). *Arizal* teaches that each of these gateways differs from the others, therefore the prayers of each tribe [entering through these gateways] are different *(Pri Etz Chaim).* It is these gateways that we ask God to open, that our prayers may enter.

קוֹל מְבַשֵּׂר / The Voice of the Herald

Upon concluding the prayers for rain we proclaim our faith in תְּחִיַּת הַמֵּתִים, *the resurrection of the dead,* which will follow the coming of the Messiah. The connection between these events and the rain can be seen in the Talmud and Midrash:

כ *You have made a covenant with the earth, continuously, all the days of the earth,**
ל *not to cause a breach in it — so save us, God of our salvation.*
מ *Those who supplicate for water like willows alongside streams of water;*
נ *please, remember for their sake the libations of water — and save us, God of our salvation.*
ס *Trees, in the direction of their growth,* they carry as they supplicate —*
ע *respond to the sound of their entreaties — and save us, God of our salvation.*
פ *Worker of salvations, heed their prayers and turn to them,*
צ *adjudge them righteous, O God of salvations — and save us, God of our salvation.*
ק *To the voices of their multitudes turn, open the earth and let salvation sprout,*
ר *O He Who is bounteous in salvation, and desires not wickedness* — and save us, God of our salvation.*

Chazzan, then congregation:

Open the gates of heaven,*
and Your goodly treasure trove may You open for us.
Save us, do not let accusations be drawn out,
and save us, God of our salvation.

Chazzan, then congregation:

The voice of the herald* heralds and proclaims:

All:

א *The strength of Your salvations comes, a voice — my Beloved, behold He comes — heralds and proclaims.*
ב *A voice — He comes among myriad bands, to stand upon the Mount of Olives* — heralds and proclaims.*
ג *A voice — To the blast of the shofar,* He draws near, beneath Him the mountain shall be split — heralds and proclaims.*

R' Abuhu teaches: Greater is the day of the rains than the resurrection of the dead. The resurrection will benefit only the righteous, while the rains benefit both the righteous and the wicked (*Taanis* 7a).

R' Chiyah bar Abba adds: The resurrection will benefit only man, while the rains benefit both man and beast (*Bereishi Rabbah* 13:6).

מְבַשֵּׂר — *The herald.* The Talmud (*Pesachim* 5a) teaches that the Messiah is alluded to in the verse (*Isaiah* 41:27): *The first [to come] to Zion will say, 'Behold! Here they are!' And to Jerusalem, 'I shall dispatch* מְבַשֵּׂר*, a herald.'* Based on the verse (*Malachi* 3:23): *Behold! I send you Elijah the prophet, before the arrival of the great and awesome day of* HASHEM, the herald is identified as Elijah.

The voice of this 'herald' will proclaim many things about the coming of the Messiah and the subsequent resurrection. The *paytan* constructs each line (except the first) of this *Hoshana* similarly — first comes the word קוֹל, *a voice;* then a parenthetical stich, and finally מְבַשֵּׂר וְאוֹמֵר, *heralds and proclaims* [lit., *says*]. These three words קוֹל מְבַשֵּׂר וְאוֹמֵר, *a voice heralds and proclaims,* should be treated as one phrase despite the intervening words of the stich (*Avodas Yisrael*).

הַר הַזֵּיתִים — *The Mount of Olives.* The next four stiches are based on *Zechariah* 14:4-5, which reads: *His feet shall stand that day upon the Mount of Olives, which is to the east of Jerusalem, and the Mount of Olives shall be split in half, along the east-west line, a very great rift. Half the mountain shall move northward, and its other half, southward . . .* HASHEM, *my God, has come, all His holy ones with Him.*

שׁוֹפָר — *Shofar.* As the prophet teaches: *And it will come to pass on that day, a great shofar will be blown; those lost in the land of Assyria will come, and those ousted to the land of Egypt; and they will bow to* HASHEM *upon the holy mountain in Jerusalem* (*Isaiah* 27:13).

קוֹל דָּפַק וְהֵצִיץ וְזָרַח, וּמָשׁ חֲצִי הָהָר מִמִּזְרָח, מְבַשֵּׂר וְאוֹמֵר.
קוֹל הֵקִים מִלּוּל נְאֻמוֹ, וּבָא הוּא וְכָל קְדוֹשָׁיו עִמּוֹ, מְבַשֵּׂר וְאוֹמֵר.
קוֹל וּלְכָל בָּאֵי הָעוֹלָם, בַּת קוֹל יִשָּׁמַע בָּעוֹלָם, מְבַשֵּׂר וְאוֹמֵר.
קוֹל זֶרַע עֲמוּסֵי רַחֲמוֹ,* נוֹלְדוּ כְּיֶלֶד מִמְּעֵי אִמּוֹ, מְבַשֵּׂר וְאוֹמֵר.
קוֹל חָלָה* וְיָלְדָה מִי זֹאת, מִי שָׁמַע כָּזֹאת, מְבַשֵּׂר וְאוֹמֵר.
קוֹל טָהוֹר פָּעַל כָּל אֵלֶּה, וּמִי רָאָה כָּאֵלֶּה, מְבַשֵּׂר וְאוֹמֵר.
קוֹל יֶשַׁע וּזְמַן הוּחַד, הֲיוּחַל אֶרֶץ בְּיוֹם אֶחָד, מְבַשֵּׂר וְאוֹמֵר.
קוֹל כַּבִּיר רוֹם וָתַחַת, אִם יִוָּלֵד גּוֹי פַּעַם אֶחָת, מְבַשֵּׂר וְאוֹמֵר.
קוֹל לְעֵת יִגְאַל עַמּוֹ נָאוֹר, וְהָיָה לְעֵת עֶרֶב יִהְיֶה אוֹר,* מְבַשֵּׂר וְאוֹמֵר.
קוֹל מוֹשִׁיעִים* יַעֲלוּ לְהַר צִיּוֹן, כִּי חָלָה גַּם יָלְדָה צִיּוֹן, מְבַשֵּׂר וְאוֹמֵר.
קוֹל נִשְׁמַע בְּכָל גְּבוּלֵךְ, הַרְחִיבִי מְקוֹם אָהֳלֵךְ, מְבַשֵּׂר וְאוֹמֵר.
קוֹל שִׂימִי עַד דַּמֶּשֶׂק* מִשְׁכְּנוֹתַיִךְ, קַבְּלִי בָנַיִךְ וּבְנוֹתַיִךְ, מְבַשֵּׂר וְאוֹמֵר.
קוֹל עִלְזִי חֲבַצֶּלֶת הַשָּׁרוֹן, כִּי קָמוּ יְשֵׁנֵי חֶבְרוֹן,* מְבַשֵּׂר וְאוֹמֵר.
קוֹל פְּנוּ אֵלַי וְהִוָּשְׁעוּ,* הַיּוֹם אִם בְּקוֹלִי תִשְׁמָעוּ, מְבַשֵּׂר וְאוֹמֵר.
קוֹל צֶמַח אִישׁ צֶמַח שְׁמוֹ,* הוּא דָוִד בְּעַצְמוֹ,* מְבַשֵּׂר וְאוֹמֵר.
קוֹל קוּמוּ כְּפוּשֵׁי עָפָר, הָקִיצוּ וְרַנְּנוּ שׁוֹכְנֵי עָפָר, מְבַשֵּׂר וְאוֹמֵר.
קוֹל רַבָּתִי עָם בְּהַמְלִיכוֹ, מִגְדּוֹל יְשׁוּעוֹת מַלְכּוֹ, מְבַשֵּׂר וְאוֹמֵר.
קוֹל שֵׁם רְשָׁעִים לְהַאֲבִיד, עֹשֶׂה חֶסֶד לִמְשִׁיחוֹ לְדָוִד, מְבַשֵּׂר וְאוֹמֵר.
קוֹל תְּנָה יְשׁוּעוֹת לְעַם עוֹלָם, לְדָוִד וּלְזַרְעוֹ עַד עוֹלָם, מְבַשֵּׂר וְאוֹמֵר.

Chazzan calls out loudly three times, followed by the congregation:

קוֹל מְבַשֵּׂר מְבַשֵּׂר וְאוֹמֵר.
קוֹל מְבַשֵּׂר מְבַשֵּׂר וְאוֹמֵר.
קוֹל מְבַשֵּׂר מְבַשֵּׂר וְאוֹמֵר.

עֲמוּסֵי רַחֲמוֹ — *Borne [by Him] from the womb.* God has carried the Jewish nation since its inception, unlike the false gods which are borne by their adherents' animals (see *Isaiah* 46:3).

חָלָה — *She delivered.* The next four stiches are based on the verse: *Who has heard the like of this? Who has seen the like of these? Can the earth deliver issue in but one day? Can a nation be born in a trice? For Zion has delivered and borne her children* (*Isaiah* 66:8). Can it be imagined that the complete nation would arise from the exile in one day to populate the desolate land of Israel?

וְהָיָה לְעֵת עֶרֶב יִהְיֶה אוֹר — *At evening time there will be light.* R' Elazar cites *Zechariah* 14:7 from which this stich is taken verbatim, to prove that the entire duration of Israel's exile under the Four Kingdoms is but one day in the eyes of God. And before that day ends the radiance of the redemption will shine for Israel, and *at evening time there will be light* (*Yalkut Shimoni II*, 585).

מוֹשִׁיעִים — *Saviors.* This stich is based upon *Obadiah* 1:21: *And saviors shall go up upon Mount Zion to punish Mount Esau, then, unto HASHEM shall be the kingdom.* The word *saviors* is variously explained as the princes of Israel (*Rashi*); the judges of Israel (*Ibn Ezra*); or the Messiah together with the seven shepherds and eight officers (see *Micah* 5:4) who will accompany him (*Radak*).

הַרְחִיבִי מְקוֹם אָהֳלֵךְ . . . עַד דַּמֶּשֶׂק — *Expand the area of your tents ... until Damasek.* The prophet (*Isaiah* 54:2) calls upon the desolate Jerusalem to expand its boundaries to enable it to accommodate all those returning from the exile. *Zechariah* 9:1 prophesies that these new boundaries will reach all the way to Damasek (see *Rashi* there).

יְשֵׁנֵי חֶבְרוֹן — *Those sleeping in Hebron.* This refers to the Patriarchs and Matriarchs of the nation [Adam and Eve, Abraham and Sarah, Isaac and Rebecca, Jacob and Leah], who are

ד *A voice — He knocks, He peers and He shines, and half the mountain moves from the east — heralds and proclaims.*

ה *A voice — He has verified the words of His utterance, He has come, and all His holy ones with Him — heralds and proclaims.*

ו *A voice — To all who walk the earth, a heavenly voice is heard on the earth — heralds and proclaims.*

ז *A voice — The seed borne [by Him] from the womb,* born like a child from its mother's innards — heralds and proclaims.*

ח *A voice — She delivered* and gave birth: 'Who is this? Who has heard the likes of this?' — heralds and proclaims.*

ט *A voice — The pure One has done all these; and who has seen the likes of these? — heralds and proclaims.*

י *A voice — Salvation and its moment were ordained. Can the earth deliver issue in a single day? — heralds and proclaims.*

כ *A voice — He Who is mighty above and below, can a nation be born in a trice? — heralds and proclaims.*

ל *A voice — When the resplendent One redeems His nation, at evening time there will be light* — heralds and proclaims.*

מ *A voice — Saviors* shall ascend upon Mount Zion, for Zion has delivered and given birth — heralds and proclaims.*

נ *A voice — It is heard within all your boundaries, 'Expand the area of your tents!' — heralds and proclaims.*

ס *A voice — Set up your dwellings until Damasek,* receive your sons and your daughters — heralds and proclaims.*

ע *A voice — Be joyous, O rose of Sharon, for those sleeping in Hebron* have arisen — heralds and proclaims.*

פ *A voice — Turn to Me and you shall be saved* — this very day, if you will but heed My voice — heralds and proclaims.*

צ *A voice — A man has sprouted, Tzemach is his name,* He is David himself* — heralds and proclaims.*

ק *A voice — Arise, you who are covered with dust; awake and sing, you who lie in the dust — heralds and proclaims.*

ר *A voice — When He rules the city great with people, His king shall be a tower of salvations — heralds and proclaims.*

ש *A voice — The name of the wicked He will cause to be lost, but He will show kindness to His anointed, to David — heralds and proclaims.*

ת *A voice — Grant salvations to the eternal people, to David and to his descendants, forever — heralds and proclaims.*

Chazzan, then congregation, loudly.

The voice of the herald heralds and proclaims.
The voice of the herald heralds and proclaims.
The voice of the herald heralds and proclaims.

---

buried in the Cave of Machpelah in Hebron.

פְּנוּ אֵלַי וְהִוָּשְׁעוּ — *Turn to Me and you shall be saved.* This verse from *Isaiah* 45:22 reads in full: *Turn to Me and you shall be saved, all who dwell at the ends of the earth, for I am God, there is no other.*

צֶמַח שְׁמוֹ — *Tzemach is his name.* In *Zechariah* 6:12 (see commentaries there) this phrase refers to both Zerubavel, builder of the Second Temple, and his descendant, the Messiah, who will build the Third Temple.

הוּא דָוִד בְּעַצְמוֹ — *He is David himself.* David's pure soul will be reincarnated in the body of the Messiah so that he is truly David himself.

All:

הוֹשִׁיעָה אֶת עַמֶּךָ וּבָרֵךְ אֶת נַחֲלָתֶךָ, וּרְעֵם וְנַשְּׂאֵם עַד הָעוֹלָם.[1] וְיִהְיוּ דְבָרַי אֵלֶּה אֲשֶׁר הִתְחַנַּנְתִּי לִפְנֵי יהוה, קְרֹבִים אֶל יהוה אֱלֹהֵינוּ יוֹמָם וָלָיְלָה, לַעֲשׂוֹת מִשְׁפַּט עַבְדּוֹ וּמִשְׁפַּט עַמּוֹ יִשְׂרָאֵל, דְּבַר יוֹם בְּיוֹמוֹ. לְמַעַן דַּעַת כָּל עַמֵּי הָאָרֶץ, כִּי יהוה הוּא הָאֱלֹהִים, אֵין עוֹד.[2]

חביטת הערבה

The Torah Scrolls are returned to the Ark and it is closed. The *Hoshana*-bundle is beaten on the ground (five times according to some), after which the יְהִי רָצוֹן prayer is recited, followed by קַדִּישׁ שָׁלֵם. In some congregations the order is reversed, with *Kaddish* being recited before the *Hoshana*-bundle is beaten.

יְהִי רָצוֹן מִלְּפָנֶיךָ יהוה אֱלֹהֵינוּ וֵאלֹהֵי אֲבוֹתֵינוּ, הַבּוֹחֵר בִּנְבִיאִים טוֹבִים וּבְמִנְהֲגֵיהֶם הַטּוֹבִים,* שֶׁתְּקַבֵּל בְּרַחֲמִים וּבְרָצוֹן אֶת תְּפִלָּתֵנוּ וְהַקָּפוֹתֵינוּ, וּזְכָר לָנוּ זְכוּת שִׁבְעַת תְּמִימֶיךָ,* וְתָסִיר מְחִיצַת הַבַּרְזֶל* הַמַּפְסֶקֶת בֵּינֵינוּ וּבֵינֶיךָ, וְתַאֲזִין שַׁוְעָתֵנוּ, וְתֵיטִיב לָנוּ הַחֲתִימָה,* תֹּלֶה אֶרֶץ עַל בְּלִימָה.* וְחָתְמֵנוּ בְּסֵפֶר חַיִּים טוֹבִים.* וְהַיּוֹם הַזֶּה תִּתֵּן בִּשְׁכִינַת עֻזֶּךָ חֲמִשָּׁה גְבוּרוֹת* מְמֻתָּקוֹת עַל יְדֵי חֲבִיטַת עֲרָבָה מִנְהַג נְבִיאֶיךָ הַקְּדוֹשִׁים. וְתִתְעוֹרֵר הָאַהֲבָה בֵּינֵיהֶם, וּתְנַשְּׁקֵנוּ מִנְּשִׁיקוֹת פִּיךָ,* מַמְתֶּקֶת כָּל הַגְּבוּרוֹת וְכָל הַדִּינִין, וְתָאִיר לִשְׁכִינַת עֻזֶּךָ בְּשֵׁם יו״ד הֵ״א וָא״ו* שֶׁהוּא טַל* אוֹרֹת טַלֶּךָ,* וּמִשָּׁם תַּשְׁפִּיעַ שֶׁפַע לְעַבְדְּךָ הַמִּתְנַפֵּל

יְהִי רָצוֹן / May it be Favorable

וּבְמִנְהֲגֵיהֶם הַטּוֹבִים — *And their good customs.* The beating of the willow is a custom ordained by the prophets.

שִׁבְעַת תְּמִימֶיךָ — *Your seven perfect ones.* This is an allusion to the seven patriarchs: Abraham, Isaac, Jacob, Moses, Aaron, Joseph, and David.

מְחִיצַת הַבַּרְזֶל — *The iron partition.* Sinful acts build and maintain partitions between the sinner and the spark of holiness which is his source of spiritual life. As one gets deeper and deeper into the ways of evil the partition built by his actions is strengthened until it has the strength of iron, while the prison in which his spark of holiness is confined becomes more and more impermeable. Only repentance can breach the partition and extricate that spark of holiness (see *Tanya* 1:17).

הַחֲתִימָה — *The . . . seal.* On Hoshana Rabbah the final seal is placed on the verdict issued on Rosh Hashanah and tentatively sealed on Yom Kippur.

תֹּלֶה אֶרֶץ עַל בְּלִימָה — *He Who suspends the earth upon silence.* The word בְּלִימָה, here translated *silence,* is a combination of two words בְּלִי, *without,* and מָה, *anything.*

בְּסֵפֶר חַיִּים טוֹבִים — *In the Book of Good Life.* Three books are opened by the Heavenly Tribunal on Rosh Hashanah: one for the totally wicked, one for the perfectly righteous and one for those between these extremes. The perfectly righteous are inscribed and immediately sealed with a verdict of life. The totally wicked are inscribed and immediately sealed with a verdict of death. The judgment of those in between stands suspended from Rosh Hashanah until Yom Kippur. If [during that period] they prove worthy they are inscribed for life. If they are not found worthy they are inscribed for death *(Rosh Hashanah* 16b).

חֲמִשָּׁה גְבוּרוֹת — *Five strict powers.* Five of the twenty-two letters of the *aleph-beis* have two forms: כְּפוּפָה, *bent,* and פְּשׁוּטָה, *straight.* They are the letters מנצפ״כ. Their straight forms [םןץףך] are usually called סוֹפִית, *concluding* [letters], because they are used at the end of a word. Since these letters are in a sense restraining forces which force a halt in speaking they are called גְּבוּרוֹת, *strict powers.* These letters are the כֵּלִים, *vessels,* within which are contained that minute portion of God's infinite being which can be conceived by finite people *(Tanya* 2:4).

The five-time beating of the *aravah* branches symbolizes the breaking of the five vessels which restrain the revelation of the full force of holiness. The beating of the branches thus causes a 'sweetening' of the strict powers.

נְשִׁיקוֹת פִּיךָ — *The kisses of Your mouth.* God's love for Israel is expressed in terms of embrace *(Song of Songs* 2:6) and kisses (ibid. 1:2). Embrace is an action and refers to the coupling of acts of

All:

הוֹשִׁיעָה *Save Your nation and bless Your heritage, tend them and elevate them forever.*[1] *May these words of mine, which I have supplicated before HASHEM, be near to HASHEM, our God, by day and by night; that He bring about justice for His servant and justice for His people, Israel, each day's need in its day; that all the peoples of the earth shall know that HASHEM is God, there is no other.*[2]

BEATING THE HOSHANA-BUNDLE

The Torah Scrolls are returned to the Ark and it is closed. The *Hoshana*-bundle is beaten on the ground (five times according to some), after which the יְהִי רָצוֹן prayer is recited, followed by the Full *Kaddish*. In some congregations the order is reversed, with *Kaddish* being recited before the *Hoshana*-bundle is beaten.

יְהִי רָצוֹן *May it be favorable before You, HASHEM, our God and God of our fathers, He Who opts for good prophets and their good customs,* that You accept with mercy and favor our prayers and our hakafah-circuits. Remember for our sake the merit of Your seven perfect ones.* Remove the iron partition* separating us from You. Hearken to our pleas and grant us the good seal,* He Who suspends the earth upon silence.* Seal us in the Book of Good Life.* Today may You place, with the manifestation of Your strength, five strict powers* which have been sweetened through the beating of willows, the custom ordained by Your holy prophets. May You awaken love among them and kiss us with the kisses of Your mouth,* which sweeten all the strict powers and all the harsh judgments. May You illuminate the manifestation of Your strength with the Name Yud-Kei-Vav* which corresponds to the dew* — Your dew is the dew of lights.* From there endow Your servant, who prostrates himself*

(1) *Psalms* 28:9. (2) *I Kings* 8:59-60.

man with acts of God through the performance of *mitzvos* and deeds of kindness. Such action brings God to embrace Israel. Kissing brings mouth to mouth — the word of man unites with the word of God through the study of the holy Torah (*Tanya* 1:45).

Torah study is the superior method by which the vessels containing the contracted Divine manifestation may be broken, that the full glory of the *Shechinah* may be revealed.

יו״ד הֵ״א נָא״ו — *Yud-Kei-Vav. [Arizal* teaches that when spelling the Divine Name, the letter ה should not be pronounced *hei,* but *kei.]* These three letters are the beginning of the Ineffable Name of God and represent the descent of the Divine to the corporeal. The fourth letter ׳ה represents the *Shechinah.*

More specifically, the ׳י, *yud,* is a mere dot, symbolizing Divine Wisdom. As this seminal wisdom expands, it develops into a revelation which the human intellect can grasp and understand. This expansion is represented by the letter ה. The top of the ה resembles a widened ׳י, indicating a broadening of understanding, while the legs extending downward indicate a downward flow of this wisdom. The continued downward flow is represented by the shape of the ו. The numerical value of ו is six, alluding to the first six of the *sefirah*-emanations. The seventh *sefirah,* מַלְכוּת, *Kingship,* is represented by the final ה of the Holy Name (*Tanya* 3:4). God's Kingship on earth is manifested through the *Shechinah* which represented His Presence in a perceptible manner. Thus we pray that the *Shechinah,* represented by the final *hei,* be illuminated by the Divine Wisdom represented by the ה and ו of the Ineffable Name, thus bringing about a perfect unification of the Holy Name.

טַל — *Dew.* The numerical value of יו״ד הֵ״א נָא״ו is thirty-nine, the same as the value of טַל, *dew.*

טַל אוֹרֹת טַלֶּךָ — *Your dew is the dew of lights.* This phrase is borrowed from *Isaiah* 26:19. *Rashi* there explains: It is fitting that the dew given as a reward for Torah study and performance of *mitzvos* be an illuminating dew.

Radak, however, translates אורת as a species of vegetable. Thus טַל אורת is *dew capable of sustaining vegetables.* Just as the dew brings the plants to life so does God awaken the dead to eternal life.

לְפָנֶיךָ, מְחִילָה, שֶׁתַּאֲרִיךְ יָמַי וְתִמְחָל לִי חֲטָאַי וַעֲוֹנוֹתַי וּפְשָׁעַי, וְתִפְשׁוֹט יְמִינְךָ וְיָדְךָ לְקַבְּלֵנִי בִּתְשׁוּבָה שְׁלֵמָה לְפָנֶיךָ, וְאוֹצָרְךָ הַטּוֹב תִּפְתַּח לְהַשְׂבִּיעַ מַיִם נֶפֶשׁ שׁוֹקֵקָה,* כְּמוֹ שֶׁכָּתוּב: יִפְתַּח יהוה לְךָ* אֶת אוֹצָרוֹ הַטּוֹב אֶת הַשָּׁמַיִם, לָתֵת מְטַר אַרְצְךָ בְּעִתּוֹ וּלְבָרֵךְ אֵת כָּל מַעֲשֵׂה יָדֶךָ.[1] אָמֵן.

קדיש שלם

The *chazzan* recites קַדִּישׁ שָׁלֵם.

יִתְגַּדַּל וְיִתְקַדַּשׁ שְׁמֵהּ רַבָּא. (.Cong – אָמֵן.) בְּעָלְמָא דִּי בְרָא כִרְעוּתֵהּ. וְיַמְלִיךְ מַלְכוּתֵהּ, בְּחַיֵּיכוֹן וּבְיוֹמֵיכוֹן וּבְחַיֵּי דְכָל בֵּית יִשְׂרָאֵל, בַּעֲגָלָא וּבִזְמַן קָרִיב. וְאִמְרוּ: אָמֵן.

(.Cong – אָמֵן. יְהֵא שְׁמֵהּ רַבָּא מְבָרַךְ לְעָלַם וּלְעָלְמֵי עָלְמַיָּא.)

יְהֵא שְׁמֵהּ רַבָּא מְבָרַךְ לְעָלַם וּלְעָלְמֵי עָלְמַיָּא.

יִתְבָּרַךְ וְיִשְׁתַּבַּח וְיִתְפָּאַר וְיִתְרוֹמַם וְיִתְנַשֵּׂא וְיִתְהַדָּר וְיִתְעַלֶּה וְיִתְהַלָּל שְׁמֵהּ דְּקֻדְשָׁא בְּרִיךְ הוּא (.Cong – בְּרִיךְ הוּא) – לְעֵלָּא מִן כָּל בִּרְכָתָא וְשִׁירָתָא תֻּשְׁבְּחָתָא וְנֶחֱמָתָא, דַּאֲמִירָן בְּעָלְמָא. וְאִמְרוּ: אָמֵן. (.Cong – אָמֵן.)

(.Cong – קַבֵּל בְּרַחֲמִים וּבְרָצוֹן אֶת תְּפִלָּתֵנוּ.)

תִּתְקַבֵּל צְלוֹתְהוֹן וּבָעוּתְהוֹן דְּכָל בֵּית יִשְׂרָאֵל קֳדָם אֲבוּהוֹן דִּי בִשְׁמַיָּא. וְאִמְרוּ: אָמֵן. (.Cong – אָמֵן.)

(.Cong – יְהִי שֵׁם יהוה מְבֹרָךְ, מֵעַתָּה וְעַד עוֹלָם.[2])

יְהֵא שְׁלָמָא רַבָּא מִן שְׁמַיָּא, וְחַיִּים עָלֵינוּ וְעַל כָּל יִשְׂרָאֵל. וְאִמְרוּ: אָמֵן. (.Cong – אָמֵן.)

(.Cong – עֶזְרִי מֵעִם יהוה, עֹשֵׂה שָׁמַיִם וָאָרֶץ.[3])

Take three steps back. Bow left and say . . . עֹשֶׂה; bow right and say . . . הוּא; bow forward and say וְעַל כָּל . . . אָמֵן. Remain standing in place for a few moments, then take three steps forward.

עֹשֶׂה שָׁלוֹם בִּמְרוֹמָיו, הוּא יַעֲשֶׂה שָׁלוֹם עָלֵינוּ, וְעַל כָּל יִשְׂרָאֵל. וְאִמְרוּ: אָמֵן. (.Cong – אָמֵן.)

לְהַשְׂבִּיעַ מַיִם נֶפֶשׁ שׁוֹקֵקָה — *To satisfy with water a thirsty soul.* שׁוֹקֵקָה is an intensified form of שׁוֹק, which means *desire.* Our translation of *thirsty* is based on the reference to water here, and on the use of this word in *Psalms* 107:9 where נֶפֶשׁ שׁוֹקֵקָה, *a thirsty soul,* appears in apposition to נֶפֶשׁ רְעֵבָה, *a hungry soul.*

Although on a simple level this part of the prayer must be taken in its obvious meaning as a prayer for rain, if the tenor of this prayer, which until this point has dealt exclusively with spiritual matters, is to continue on that lofty plane, then the reference to thirst and water must be seen as more than of just material nature.

My soul thirsts for God, the living God (*Psalms* 42:3). The prophet compares the perception of God achieved through Torah study to the satisfaction derived by a thirsty man drinking water: הוֹי כָּל צָמֵא לְכוּ לַמַּיִם, *Ho, everyone who thirsts, go to water* (*Isaiah* 55:1). *Radak* explains

before You, with forgiveness, that my days may be lengthened. Forgive me my sins, my iniquities, and my transgressions. Spread wide Your right arm and Your hand to accept me, with my whole-hearted repentance before You. Open Your goodly treasure trove to satisfy with water a thirsty soul — as it is written: May HASHEM open for you* His goodly treasure trove, the heavens, to give your land rain in its season and to bless all of your handiwork.*[1] *Amen.*

FULL KADDISH

The *chazzan* recites the Full *Kaddish.*

יִתְגַּדַּל *May His great Name grow exalted and sanctified* (Cong.– *Amen.*) *in the world that He created as He willed. May He give reign to His kingship in your lifetimes and in your days, and in the lifetimes of the entire Family of Israel, swiftly and soon. Now respond: Amen.*

(Cong.– *Amen. May His great Name be blessed forever and ever.*)

May His great Name be blessed forever and ever.

Blessed, praised, glorified, exalted, extolled, mighty, upraised, and lauded be the Name of the Holy One, Blessed is He (Cong.– *Blessed is He*) *— beyond any blessing and song, praise and consolation that are uttered in the world. Now respond: Amen.* (Cong.– *Amen.*)

(Cong.– *Accept our prayers with mercy and favor.*)

May the prayers and supplications of the entire Family of Israel be accepted before their Father Who is in Heaven. Now respond: Amen. (Cong.– *Amen.*)

(Cong.– *Blessed be the Name of HASHEM, from this time and forever.*[2])

May there be abundant peace from Heaven, and life, upon us and upon all Israel. Now respond: Amen. (Cong.– *Amen.*)

(Cong.– *My help is from HASHEM, Maker of heaven and earth.*[3])

Take three steps back. Bow left and say, *'He Who makes peace . . .';* bow right and say, *'may He . . .';* bow forward and say, *'and upon all Israel . . .'* Remain standing in place for a few moments, then take three steps forward.

He Who makes peace in His heights, may He make peace upon us, and upon all Israel. Now respond: Amen. (Cong.– *Amen.*)

---

(1) *Deuteronomy* 28:12. (2) *Psalms* 113:2. (3) 121:2.

---

that just as the world cannot exist without water, so it cannot exist without Torah.

Amos 8:11 is even more specific. *'Behold, days are coming,' says HASHEM/ELOHIM, 'when I shall send a hunger upon the land; neither a hunger for bread nor a thirst for water, but only to hear the words of HASHEM.'*

. . . יִפְתַּח ה׳ לְךָ — *May HASHEM open for you . . .* This verse *(Deuteronomy* 28:12) is elucidated in the Talmud: Only God Himself can open the floodgates of rain. Three keys were not given over to the angels but are held in God's hand, so to speak. One of these is the key to the storehouse of rain, as it is written: *May HASHEM [*personally, not His emissary *(Rashi)] open for you His goodly treasure trove . . . to give your land rain in its season (Taanis* 2a).

קַוֵּה אֶל יהוה, חֲזַק וְיַאֲמֵץ לִבֶּךָ, וְקַוֵּה אֶל יהוה.[1] אֵין קָדוֹשׁ כַּיהוה, כִּי אֵין בִּלְתֶּךָ, וְאֵין צוּר כֵּאלֹהֵינוּ.[2] כִּי מִי אֱלוֹהַּ מִבַּלְעֲדֵי יהוה, וּמִי צוּר זוּלָתִי אֱלֹהֵינוּ.[3]

אֵין כֵּאלֹהֵינוּ, אֵין כַּאדוֹנֵינוּ, אֵין כְּמַלְכֵּנוּ, אֵין כְּמוֹשִׁיעֵנוּ. מִי כֵאלֹהֵינוּ, מִי כַאדוֹנֵינוּ, מִי כְמַלְכֵּנוּ, מִי כְמוֹשִׁיעֵנוּ. נוֹדֶה לֵאלֹהֵינוּ, נוֹדֶה לַאדוֹנֵינוּ, נוֹדֶה לְמַלְכֵּנוּ, נוֹדֶה לְמוֹשִׁיעֵנוּ. בָּרוּךְ אֱלֹהֵינוּ, בָּרוּךְ אֲדוֹנֵינוּ, בָּרוּךְ מַלְכֵּנוּ, בָּרוּךְ מוֹשִׁיעֵנוּ. אַתָּה הוּא אֱלֹהֵינוּ, אַתָּה הוּא אֲדוֹנֵינוּ, אַתָּה הוּא מַלְכֵּנוּ, אַתָּה הוּא מוֹשִׁיעֵנוּ. אַתָּה הוּא שֶׁהִקְטִירוּ אֲבוֹתֵינוּ לְפָנֶיךָ אֶת קְטֹרֶת הַסַּמִּים.

כריתות ו.

פִּטּוּם הַקְּטֹרֶת: (א) הַצֳּרִי, (ב) וְהַצִּפֹּרֶן, (ג) הַחֶלְבְּנָה, (ד) וְהַלְּבוֹנָה, מִשְׁקַל שִׁבְעִים שִׁבְעִים מָנֶה; (ה) מוֹר, (ו) וּקְצִיעָה, (ז) שִׁבֹּלֶת נֵרְדְּ, (ח) וְכַרְכֹּם, מִשְׁקַל שִׁשָּׁה עָשָׂר שִׁשָּׁה עָשָׂר מָנֶה; (ט) הַקֹּשְׁטְ שְׁנֵים עָשָׂר, (י) וְקִלּוּפָה שְׁלֹשָׁה, (יא) וְקִנָּמוֹן תִּשְׁעָה. בֹּרִית כַּרְשִׁינָה תִּשְׁעָה קַבִּין, יֵין קַפְרִיסִין סְאִין תְּלָתָא וְקַבִּין תְּלָתָא; וְאִם אֵין לוֹ יֵין קַפְרִיסִין, מֵבִיא חֲמַר חִוַּרְיָן עַתִּיק; מֶלַח סְדוֹמִית רֹבַע הַקָּב; מַעֲלֶה עָשָׁן כָּל שֶׁהוּא. רַבִּי נָתָן הַבַּבְלִי אוֹמֵר: אַף כִּפַּת הַיַּרְדֵּן כָּל שֶׁהוּא. וְאִם נָתַן בָּהּ דְּבַשׁ פְּסָלָהּ. וְאִם חִסַּר אַחַת מִכָּל סַמָּנֶיהָ, חַיָּב מִיתָה.

רַבָּן שִׁמְעוֹן בֶּן גַּמְלִיאֵל אוֹמֵר: הַצֳּרִי אֵינוֹ אֶלָּא שְׂרָף הַנּוֹטֵף מֵעֲצֵי הַקְּטָף. בֹּרִית כַּרְשִׁינָה שֶׁשָּׁפִין בָּהּ אֶת הַצִּפֹּרֶן כְּדֵי שֶׁתְּהֵא נָאָה; יֵין קַפְרִיסִין שֶׁשּׁוֹרִין בּוֹ אֶת הַצִּפֹּרֶן כְּדֵי שֶׁתְּהֵא עַזָּה; וַהֲלֹא מֵי רַגְלַיִם יָפִין לָהּ, אֶלָּא שֶׁאֵין מַכְנִיסִין מֵי רַגְלַיִם בָּעֲזָרָה מִפְּנֵי הַכָּבוֹד.

משנה, תמיד ז:ד

הַשִּׁיר שֶׁהַלְוִיִּם הָיוּ אוֹמְרִים בְּבֵית הַמִּקְדָּשׁ. בַּיּוֹם הָרִאשׁוֹן הָיוּ אוֹמְרִים: לַיהוה הָאָרֶץ וּמְלוֹאָהּ, תֵּבֵל וְיֹשְׁבֵי בָהּ.[4] בַּשֵּׁנִי הָיוּ אוֹמְרִים: גָּדוֹל יהוה וּמְהֻלָּל מְאֹד, בְּעִיר אֱלֹהֵינוּ הַר קָדְשׁוֹ.[5] בַּשְּׁלִישִׁי הָיוּ אוֹמְרִים: אֱלֹהִים נִצָּב בַּעֲדַת אֵל, בְּקֶרֶב אֱלֹהִים יִשְׁפֹּט.[6] בָּרְבִיעִי הָיוּ אוֹמְרִים: אֵל נְקָמוֹת יהוה, אֵל נְקָמוֹת הוֹפִיעַ.[7] בַּחֲמִישִׁי הָיוּ אוֹמְרִים: הַרְנִינוּ לֵאלֹהִים עוּזֵּנוּ, הָרִיעוּ לֵאלֹהֵי

קַוֵּה *Hope to* H*ASHEM, strengthen yourself and He will give you courage; and hope to* H*ASHEM.*[1] *There is none holy as* H*ASHEM, for there is none beside You, and there is no Rock like our God.*[2] *For who is a god beside* H*ASHEM, and who is a Rock except for our God.*[3]

אֵין *There is none like our God; there is none like our Master;*
there is none like our King; there is none like our Savior.
Who is like our God? Who is like our Master?
Who is like our King? Who is like our Savior?
Let us thank our God; let us thank our Master;
let us thank our King; let us thank our Savior.
Blessed is our God; blessed is our Master;
blessed is our King; blessed is our Savior.
It is You Who is our God; it is You Who is our Master;
it is You Who is our King; it is You Who is our Savior.
It is You before Whom our forefathers burned the spice-incense.

Talmud, *Kereisos 6a*

פִּטּוּם הַקְּטֹרֶת *The incense mixture was formulated of [eleven spices]: (1) stacte, (2) onycha, (3) galbanum, (4) frankincense — each weighing seventy maneh; (5) myrrh, (6) cassia, (7) spikenard, (8) saffron — each weighing sixteen maneh; (9) costus — twelve [maneh]; (10) aromatic bark — three; and (11) cinnamon — nine. [Additionally] Carshina lye — nine kab; Cyprus wine, three se'ah and three kab — if he has no Cyprus wine, he brings old white wine; Sodom salt, a quarter kab; and a minute amount of smoke-raising herb. Rabbi Nassan the Babylonian says: Also a minute amount of Jordan amber. If he placed fruit-honey into it, he invalidated it. And if he left out any of its spices, he is liable to the death penalty.*

רַבָּן שִׁמְעוֹן *Rabban Shimon ben Gamliel says: The stacte is simply the sap that drips from balsam trees. Carshina lye is used to bleach the onycha to make it pleasing. Cyprus wine is used to soak the onycha to make it pungent. Even though urine is suitable for that, nevertheless they do not bring urine into the Temple out of respect.*

Mishnah, *Tamid 7:4*

הַשִּׁיר *The daily song that the Levites would recite in the Temple was as follows: On the first day [of the week] they would say: '*H*ASHEM's is the earth and its fullness, the inhabited land and those who dwell in it.'*[4] *On the second day they would say: 'Great is* H*ASHEM and much praised, in the city of our God, Mount of His Holiness.'*[5] *On the third day they would say: 'God stands in the Divine assembly, in the midst of judges shall He judge.'*[6] *On the fourth day they would say: 'O God of vengeance,* H*ASHEM, O God of vengeance, appear.'*[7] *On the fifth day they would say: 'Sing joyously to the God of our might, call out to*

---

(1) *Psalms* 27:14. (2) *I Samuel* 2:2. (3) *Psalms* 18:32. (4) 24:1. (5) 48:2. (6) 82:1. (7) 94:1.

יַעֲקֹב.[1] בַּשִּׁשִּׁי הָיוּ אוֹמְרִים: יהוה מָלָךְ גֵּאוּת לָבֵשׁ, לָבֵשׁ יהוה עֹז הִתְאַזָּר, אַף תִּכּוֹן תֵּבֵל בַּל תִּמּוֹט.[2] בַּשַּׁבָּת הָיוּ אוֹמְרִים: מִזְמוֹר שִׁיר לְיוֹם הַשַּׁבָּת.[3] מִזְמוֹר שִׁיר לֶעָתִיד לָבֹא, לְיוֹם שֶׁכֻּלּוֹ שַׁבָּת וּמְנוּחָה לְחַיֵּי הָעוֹלָמִים.

מגילה כח:

תָּנָא דְבֵי אֵלִיָּהוּ: כָּל הַשּׁוֹנֶה הֲלָכוֹת בְּכָל יוֹם, מֻבְטָח לוֹ שֶׁהוּא בֶּן עוֹלָם הַבָּא, שֶׁנֶּאֱמַר: הֲלִיכוֹת עוֹלָם לוֹ,[4] אַל תִּקְרֵי הֲלִיכוֹת, אֶלָּא הֲלָכוֹת.

ברכות סד.

אָמַר רַבִּי אֶלְעָזָר אָמַר רַבִּי חֲנִינָא: תַּלְמִידֵי חֲכָמִים מַרְבִּים שָׁלוֹם בָּעוֹלָם, שֶׁנֶּאֱמַר: וְכָל בָּנַיִךְ לִמּוּדֵי יהוה, וְרַב שְׁלוֹם בָּנָיִךְ,[5] אַל תִּקְרֵי בָּנָיִךְ אֶלָּא בּוֹנָיִךְ. ❖ שָׁלוֹם רָב לְאֹהֲבֵי תוֹרָתֶךָ, וְאֵין לָמוֹ מִכְשׁוֹל.[6] יְהִי שָׁלוֹם בְּחֵילֵךְ, שַׁלְוָה בְּאַרְמְנוֹתָיִךְ. לְמַעַן אַחַי וְרֵעָי, אֲדַבְּרָה נָּא שָׁלוֹם בָּךְ. לְמַעַן בֵּית יהוה אֱלֹהֵינוּ, אֲבַקְשָׁה טוֹב לָךְ.[7] יהוה עֹז לְעַמּוֹ יִתֵּן, יהוה יְבָרֵךְ אֶת עַמּוֹ בַשָּׁלוֹם.[8]

קדיש דרבנן

In the presence of a *minyan,* mourners recite קַדִּישׁ דְּרַבָּנָן (see *Laws* §84-85).

יִתְגַּדַּל וְיִתְקַדַּשׁ שְׁמֵהּ רַבָּא. (.Cong – אָמֵן.) בְּעָלְמָא דִּי בְרָא כִרְעוּתֵהּ. וְיַמְלִיךְ מַלְכוּתֵהּ, בְּחַיֵּיכוֹן וּבְיוֹמֵיכוֹן וּבְחַיֵּי דְכָל בֵּית יִשְׂרָאֵל, בַּעֲגָלָא וּבִזְמַן קָרִיב. וְאִמְרוּ: אָמֵן.

(.Cong – אָמֵן. יְהֵא שְׁמֵהּ רַבָּא מְבָרַךְ לְעָלַם וּלְעָלְמֵי עָלְמַיָּא.)

יְהֵא שְׁמֵהּ רַבָּא מְבָרַךְ לְעָלַם וּלְעָלְמֵי עָלְמַיָּא.

יִתְבָּרַךְ וְיִשְׁתַּבַּח וְיִתְפָּאַר וְיִתְרוֹמַם וְיִתְנַשֵּׂא וְיִתְהַדָּר וְיִתְעַלֶּה וְיִתְהַלָּל שְׁמֵהּ דְּקֻדְשָׁא בְּרִיךְ הוּא (.Cong – בְּרִיךְ הוּא) – לְעֵלָּא מִן כָּל בִּרְכָתָא וְשִׁירָתָא תֻּשְׁבְּחָתָא וְנֶחֱמָתָא, דַּאֲמִירָן בְּעָלְמָא. וְאִמְרוּ: אָמֵן. (.Cong – אָמֵן.)

עַל יִשְׂרָאֵל וְעַל רַבָּנָן, וְעַל תַּלְמִידֵיהוֹן וְעַל כָּל תַּלְמִידֵי תַלְמִידֵיהוֹן, וְעַל כָּל מָאן דְּעָסְקִין בְּאוֹרַיְתָא, דִּי בְאַתְרָא הָדֵין וְדִי בְכָל אֲתַר וַאֲתַר. יְהֵא לְהוֹן וּלְכוֹן שְׁלָמָא רַבָּא, חִנָּא וְחִסְדָּא וְרַחֲמִין, וְחַיִּין אֲרִיכִין, וּמְזוֹנֵי רְוִיחֵי, וּפֻרְקָנָא, מִן קֳדָם אֲבוּהוֹן דִּי בִשְׁמַיָּא (וְאַרְעָא). וְאִמְרוּ: אָמֵן. (.Cong – אָמֵן.)

יְהֵא שְׁלָמָא רַבָּא מִן שְׁמַיָּא, וְחַיִּים (טוֹבִים) עָלֵינוּ וְעַל כָּל יִשְׂרָאֵל. וְאִמְרוּ: אָמֵן. (.Cong – אָמֵן.)

Take three steps back. Bow left and say . . . עֹשֶׂה; bow right and say . . . הוּא; bow forward and say וְעַל כָּל . . . אָמֵן. Remain standing in place for a few moments, then take three steps forward.

עֹשֶׂה שָׁלוֹם בִּמְרוֹמָיו, הוּא בְּרַחֲמָיו יַעֲשֶׂה שָׁלוֹם עָלֵינוּ, וְעַל כָּל יִשְׂרָאֵל. וְאִמְרוּ: אָמֵן. (.Cong – אָמֵן.)

the God of Jacob.'[1] *On the sixth day they would say: 'HASHEM will have reigned, He will have donned grandeur; He will have donned might and girded Himself; He even made the world firm so that it should not falter.'*[2] *On the Sabbath they would say: 'A psalm, a song for the Sabbath day.'*[3] *A psalm, a song for the time to come, to the day that will be entirely Sabbath and contentment for the eternal life.*

Talmud, *Megillah* 28b

תָּנָא *The Academy of Elijah taught: He who studies Torah laws every day has the assurance that he will be in the World to Come, as it is said, 'The ways of the world are His'*[4] *— do not read* [הֲלִיכוֹת] *'ways,' but* [הֲלָכוֹת] *'laws.'*

Talmud, *Berachos* 64a

אָמַר *Rabbi Elazar said on behalf of Rabbi Chanina: Torah scholars increase peace in the world, as it is said: 'And all your children will be students of HASHEM, and your children will have peace'*[5] *— do not read* [בָּנָיִךְ] *'your children,' but* [בּוֹנָיִךְ] *'your builders.'* Chazzan– *There is abundant peace for the lovers of Your Torah, and there is no stumbling block for them.*[6] *May there be peace within your wall, serenity within your palaces. For the sake of my brethren and comrades I shall speak of peace in your midst. For the sake of the House of HASHEM, our God, I will request your good.*[7] *HASHEM will give might to His people, HASHEM will bless His people with peace.*[8]

THE RABBIS' KADDISH

In the presence of a *minyan,* mourners recite the Rabbis' *Kaddish* (see *Laws* §84-85).
[A transliteration of this *Kaddish* appears on p. 1304.]

יִתְגַּדַּל *May His great Name grow exalted and sanctified* (Cong.– *Amen.*) *in the world that He created as He willed. May He give reign to His kingship in your lifetimes and in your days, and in the lifetimes of the entire Family of Israel, swiftly and soon. Now respond: Amen.*

(Cong.– *Amen. May His great Name be blessed forever and ever.*)
May His great Name be blessed forever and ever.

Blessed, praised, glorified, exalted, extolled, mighty, upraised, and lauded be the Name of the Holy One, Blessed is He (Cong.– *Blessed is He*) *— beyond any blessing and song, praise and consolation that are uttered in the world. Now respond: Amen.* (Cong.– *Amen.*)

Upon Israel, upon the teachers, their disciples and all of their disciples and upon all those who engage in the study of Torah, who are here or anywhere else; may they and you have abundant peace, grace, kindness, and mercy, long life, ample nourishment, and salvation, from before their Father Who is in Heaven (and on earth). Now respond: Amen. (Cong. – *Amen.*)

May there be abundant peace from Heaven, and (good) life, upon us and upon all Israel. Now respond: Amen. (Cong.– *Amen.*)

Take three steps back. Bow left and say, *'He Who makes peace . . .';* bow right and say, *'may He . . .';* bow forward and say, *'and upon all Israel . . .'* Remain standing in place for a few moments, then take three steps forward.

He Who makes peace in His heights, may He, in His compassion, make peace upon us, and upon all Israel. Now respond: Amen. (Cong.– *Amen.*)

---

(1) *Psalms* 81:2. (2) 93:1. (3) 92:1. (4) *Habakkuk* 3:6.
(5) *Isaiah* 54:13. (6) *Psalms* 119:165. (7) 122:7-9. (8) 29:11.

Stand while reciting עָלֵינוּ.

עָלֵינוּ לְשַׁבֵּחַ לַאֲדוֹן הַכֹּל, לָתֵת גְּדֻלָּה לְיוֹצֵר בְּרֵאשִׁית, שֶׁלֹּא עָשָׂנוּ כְּגוֹיֵי הָאֲרָצוֹת, וְלֹא שָׂמָנוּ כְּמִשְׁפְּחוֹת הָאֲדָמָה. שֶׁלֹּא שָׂם חֶלְקֵנוּ כָּהֶם, וְגוֹרָלֵנוּ כְּכָל הֲמוֹנָם. (שֶׁהֵם מִשְׁתַּחֲוִים לְהֶבֶל וָרִיק, וּמִתְפַּלְּלִים אֶל אֵל לֹא יוֹשִׁיעַ.[1]) וַאֲנַחְנוּ כּוֹרְעִים וּמִשְׁתַּחֲוִים וּמוֹדִים, לִפְנֵי מֶלֶךְ מַלְכֵי הַמְּלָכִים הַקָּדוֹשׁ בָּרוּךְ הוּא. שֶׁהוּא נוֹטֶה שָׁמַיִם וְיֹסֵד אָרֶץ,[2] וּמוֹשַׁב יְקָרוֹ בַּשָּׁמַיִם מִמַּעַל, וּשְׁכִינַת עֻזּוֹ בְּגָבְהֵי מְרוֹמִים. הוּא אֱלֹהֵינוּ, אֵין עוֹד. אֱמֶת מַלְכֵּנוּ, אֶפֶס זוּלָתוֹ, כַּכָּתוּב בְּתוֹרָתוֹ: וְיָדַעְתָּ הַיּוֹם וַהֲשֵׁבֹתָ אֶל לְבָבֶךָ, כִּי יהוה הוּא הָאֱלֹהִים בַּשָּׁמַיִם מִמַּעַל וְעַל הָאָרֶץ מִתָּחַת, אֵין עוֹד.[3]

Bow while reciting וַאֲנַחְנוּ כּוֹרְעִים וּמִשְׁתַּחֲוִים.

עַל כֵּן נְקַוֶּה לְּךָ יהוה אֱלֹהֵינוּ לִרְאוֹת מְהֵרָה בְּתִפְאֶרֶת עֻזֶּךָ, לְהַעֲבִיר גִּלּוּלִים מִן הָאָרֶץ, וְהָאֱלִילִים כָּרוֹת יִכָּרֵתוּן, לְתַקֵּן עוֹלָם בְּמַלְכוּת שַׁדַּי. וְכָל בְּנֵי בָשָׂר יִקְרְאוּ בִשְׁמֶךָ, לְהַפְנוֹת אֵלֶיךָ כָּל רִשְׁעֵי אָרֶץ. יַכִּירוּ וְיֵדְעוּ כָּל יוֹשְׁבֵי תֵבֵל, כִּי לְךָ תִּכְרַע כָּל בֶּרֶךְ, תִּשָּׁבַע כָּל לָשׁוֹן.[4] לְפָנֶיךָ יהוה אֱלֹהֵינוּ יִכְרְעוּ וְיִפֹּלוּ, וְלִכְבוֹד שִׁמְךָ יְקָר יִתֵּנוּ. וִיקַבְּלוּ כֻלָּם אֶת עוֹל מַלְכוּתֶךָ, וְתִמְלֹךְ עֲלֵיהֶם מְהֵרָה לְעוֹלָם וָעֶד. כִּי הַמַּלְכוּת שֶׁלְּךָ הִיא וּלְעוֹלְמֵי עַד תִּמְלוֹךְ בְּכָבוֹד, כַּכָּתוּב בְּתוֹרָתֶךָ: יהוה יִמְלֹךְ לְעֹלָם וָעֶד.[5] ❖ וְנֶאֱמַר: וְהָיָה יהוה לְמֶלֶךְ עַל כָּל הָאָרֶץ, בַּיּוֹם הַהוּא יִהְיֶה יהוה אֶחָד וּשְׁמוֹ אֶחָד.[6]

Some congregations recite the following after עָלֵינוּ.

אַל תִּירָא מִפַּחַד פִּתְאֹם, וּמִשֹּׁאַת רְשָׁעִים כִּי תָבֹא.[7] עֻצוּ עֵצָה וְתֻפָר, דַּבְּרוּ דָבָר וְלֹא יָקוּם, כִּי עִמָּנוּ אֵל.[8] וְעַד זִקְנָה אֲנִי הוּא, וְעַד שֵׂיבָה אֲנִי אֶסְבֹּל, אֲנִי עָשִׂיתִי וַאֲנִי אֶשָּׂא, וַאֲנִי אֶסְבֹּל וַאֲמַלֵּט.[9]

קדיש יתום

In the presence of a *minyan,* mourners recite קַדִּישׁ יָתוֹם, the Mourner's *Kaddish* (see *Laws* §81-83):

יִתְגַּדַּל וְיִתְקַדַּשׁ שְׁמֵהּ רַבָּא. (.Cong – אָמֵן.) בְּעָלְמָא דִּי בְרָא כִרְעוּתֵהּ. וְיַמְלִיךְ מַלְכוּתֵהּ, בְּחַיֵּיכוֹן וּבְיוֹמֵיכוֹן וּבְחַיֵּי דְכָל בֵּית יִשְׂרָאֵל, בַּעֲגָלָא וּבִזְמַן קָרִיב. וְאִמְרוּ: אָמֵן.

(.Cong – אָמֵן. יְהֵא שְׁמֵהּ רַבָּא מְבָרַךְ לְעָלַם וּלְעָלְמֵי עָלְמַיָּא.)

Stand while reciting עָלֵינוּ, *'It is our duty . . .'*

עָלֵינוּ *It is our duty to praise the Master of all, to ascribe greatness to the Molder of primeval creation, for He has not made us like the nations of the lands, and has not emplaced us like the families of the earth; for He has not assigned our portion like theirs nor our lot like all their multitudes. (For they bow to vanity and emptiness and pray to a god which helps not.*[1]*) But we bend our knees, bow, and acknowledge our thanks before the King Who reigns over kings, the Holy One, Blessed is He. He stretches out heaven and establishes earth's foundation,*[2] *the seat of His homage is in the heavens above and His powerful Presence is in the loftiest heights. He is our God and there is none other. True is our King, there is nothing beside Him, as it is written in His Torah: 'You are to know this day and take to your heart that* HASHEM *is the only God — in heaven above and on the earth below — there is none other.'*[3]

Bow while reciting 'But we bend our knees.'

עַל כֵּן *Therefore we put our hope in You,* HASHEM, *our God, that we may soon see Your mighty splendor, to remove detestable idolatry from the earth, and false gods will be utterly cut off, to perfect the universe through the Almighty's sovereignty. Then all humanity will call upon Your Name, to turn all the earth's wicked toward You. All the world's inhabitants will recognize and know that to You every knee should bend, every tongue should swear.*[4] *Before You,* HASHEM, *our God, they will bend every knee and cast themselves down and to the glory of Your Name they will render homage, and they will all accept upon themselves the yoke of Your kingship that You may reign over them soon and eternally. For the kingdom is Yours and You will reign for all eternity in glory as it is written in Your Torah:* HASHEM *shall reign for all eternity.*[5] Chazzan– *And it is said:* HASHEM *will be King over all the world — on that day* HASHEM *will be One and His Name will be One.*[6]

Some congregations recite the following after *Aleinu.*

אַל תִּירָא *Do not fear sudden terror, or the holocaust of the wicked when it comes.*[7] *Plan a conspiracy and it will be annulled; speak your piece and it shall not stand, for God is with us.*[8] *Even till your seniority, I remain unchanged; and even till your ripe old age, I shall endure. I created you and I shall bear you; I shall endure and rescue.*[9]

MOURNER'S KADDISH

In the presence of a *minyan,* mourners recite קַדִּישׁ יָתוֹם, the Mourner's *Kaddish* (see *Laws* §81-83). [A transliteration of this *Kaddish* appears on p. 1305.]

יִתְגַּדַּל *May His great Name grow exalted and sanctified* (Cong.– *Amen.*) *in the world that He created as He willed. May He give reign to His kingship in your lifetimes and in your days, and in the lifetimes of the entire Family of Israel, swiftly and soon. Now respond: Amen.*

(Cong.– *Amen. May His great Name be blessed forever and ever.*)

---

(1) *Isaiah* 45:20. (2) 51:13. (3) *Deuteronomy* 4:39. (4) Cf. *Isaiah* 45:23. (5) *Exodus* 15:18. (6) *Zechariah* 14:9. (7) *Proverbs* 3:25. (8) *Isaiah* 8:10. (9) 46:4.

יְהֵא שְׁמֵהּ רַבָּא מְבָרַךְ לְעָלַם וּלְעָלְמֵי עָלְמַיָּא.

יִתְבָּרַךְ וְיִשְׁתַּבַּח וְיִתְפָּאַר וְיִתְרוֹמַם וְיִתְנַשֵּׂא וְיִתְהַדָּר וְיִתְעַלֶּה וְיִתְהַלָּל שְׁמֵהּ דְּקֻדְשָׁא בְּרִיךְ הוּא (.Cong – בְּרִיךְ הוּא) – לְעֵלָּא מִן כָּל בִּרְכָתָא וְשִׁירָתָא תֻּשְׁבְּחָתָא וְנֶחֱמָתָא, דַּאֲמִירָן בְּעָלְמָא. וְאִמְרוּ: אָמֵן. (.Cong – אָמֵן.)

יְהֵא שְׁלָמָא רַבָּא מִן שְׁמַיָּא, וְחַיִּים עָלֵינוּ וְעַל כָּל יִשְׂרָאֵל. וְאִמְרוּ: אָמֵן. (.Cong – אָמֵן.)

Take three steps back. Bow left and say . . . עֹשֶׂה; bow right and say . . . הוּא; bow forward and say וְעַל כָּל . . . אָמֵן. Remain standing in place for a few moments, then take three steps forward.

עֹשֶׂה שָׁלוֹם בִּמְרוֹמָיו, הוּא יַעֲשֶׂה שָׁלוֹם עָלֵינוּ, וְעַל כָּל יִשְׂרָאֵל. וְאִמְרוּ: אָמֵן. (.Cong – אָמֵן.)

שיר הכבוד

The Ark is opened and שִׁיר הַכָּבוֹד, *The Song of Glory,* is recited responsively – the *chazzan* reciting the first verse, the congregation reciting the second and so on.

אַנְעִים זְמִירוֹת וְשִׁירִים אֶאֱרוֹג, כִּי אֵלֶיךָ נַפְשִׁי תַעֲרוֹג.

נַפְשִׁי חָמְדָה בְּצֵל יָדֶךָ, לָדַעַת כָּל רָז סוֹדֶךָ.

❖ מִדֵּי דַבְּרִי בִּכְבוֹדֶךָ, הוֹמֶה לִבִּי אֶל דּוֹדֶיךָ.

עַל כֵּן אֲדַבֵּר בְּךָ נִכְבָּדוֹת, וְשִׁמְךָ אֲכַבֵּד בְּשִׁירֵי יְדִידוֹת.

❖ אֲסַפְּרָה כְבוֹדְךָ וְלֹא רְאִיתִיךָ, אֲדַמְּךָ אֲכַנְּךָ וְלֹא יְדַעְתִּיךָ.

בְּיַד נְבִיאֶיךָ בְּסוֹד עֲבָדֶיךָ, דִּמִּיתָ הֲדַר כְּבוֹד הוֹדֶךָ.

❖ גְּדֻלָּתְךָ וּגְבוּרָתֶךָ, כִּנּוּ לְתֹקֶף פְּעֻלָּתֶךָ.

דִּמּוּ אוֹתְךָ וְלֹא כְפִי יֶשְׁךָ, וַיְשַׁוּוּךָ לְפִי מַעֲשֶׂיךָ.

❖ הִמְשִׁילוּךָ בְּרֹב חֶזְיוֹנוֹת, הִנְּךָ אֶחָד בְּכָל דִּמְיוֹנוֹת.

וַיֶּחֱזוּ בְךָ זִקְנָה וּבַחֲרוּת, וּשְׂעַר רֹאשְׁךָ בְּשֵׂיבָה וְשַׁחֲרוּת.

❖ זִקְנָה בְּיוֹם דִּין וּבַחֲרוּת בְּיוֹם קְרָב, כְּאִישׁ מִלְחָמוֹת יָדָיו לוֹ רָב.

חָבַשׁ כּוֹבַע יְשׁוּעָה בְּרֹאשׁוֹ, הוֹשִׁיעָה לּוֹ יְמִינוֹ וּזְרוֹעַ קָדְשׁוֹ.

❖ טַלְלֵי אוֹרוֹת רֹאשׁוֹ נִמְלָא, קְוֻצּוֹתָיו רְסִיסֵי לָיְלָה.

יִתְפָּאֵר בִּי כִּי חָפֵץ בִּי. וְהוּא יִהְיֶה לִּי לַעֲטֶרֶת צְבִי.

❖ כֶּתֶם טָהוֹר פָּז דְּמוּת רֹאשׁוֹ, וְחַק עַל מֵצַח כְּבוֹד שֵׁם קָדְשׁוֹ.

לְחֵן וּלְכָבוֹד צְבִי תִפְאָרָה, אֻמָּתוֹ לוֹ עִטְּרָה עֲטָרָה.

❖ מַחְלְפוֹת רֹאשׁוֹ כְּבִימֵי בְחֻרוֹת, קְוֻצּוֹתָיו תַּלְתַּלִּים שְׁחוֹרוֹת.

נְוֵה הַצֶּדֶק צְבִי תִפְאַרְתּוֹ, יַעֲלֶה נָּא עַל רֹאשׁ שִׂמְחָתוֹ.

May His great Name be blessed forever and ever.

Blessed, praised, glorified, exalted, extolled, mighty, upraised, and lauded be the Name of the Holy One, Blessed is He (Cong.– *Blessed is He*) — *beyond any blessing and song, praise and consolation that are uttered in the world. Now respond: Amen.* (Cong.– *Amen*).

May there be abundant peace from Heaven, and life, upon us and upon all Israel. Now respond: Amen. (Cong.– *Amen.*)

Take three steps back. Bow left and say, *'He Who makes peace . . .';* bow right and say, *'may He . . .';* bow forward and say, *'and upon all Israel . . .'* Remain standing in place for a few moments, then take three steps forward.

He Who makes peace in His heights, may He make peace upon us, and upon all Israel. Now respond: Amen. (Cong.– *Amen.*)

SONG OF GLORY

The Ark is opened and the *Song of Glory* is recited responsively — the *chazzan* reciting the first verse, the congregation reciting the second and so on.

אַנְעִים זְמִירוֹת *I shall compose pleasant psalms and weave hymns,*
because for You shall my soul pine.

My soul desired the shelter of Your hand,
to know every mystery of Your secret.
∴ *As I speak of Your glory, my heart yearns for Your love.*
Therefore I shall speak of Your glories,
and Your Name I shall honor with loving songs.
∴ *I shall relate Your glory, though I see You not;*
I shall allegorize You, I shall describe You, though I know You not.
Through the hand of Your prophets, through the counsel of Your servants;
You allegorized the splendrous glory of Your power.
∴ *Your greatness and Your strength,*
they described the might of Your works.
They allegorized You, but not according to Your reality,
and they portrayed You according to Your deeds.
∴ *They symbolized You in many varied visions;*
yet You are a Unity containing all the allegories.
They envisioned in You agedness and virility,
and the hair of Your head as hoary and jet black.
∴ *Aged on judgment day and virile on the day of battle,*
like a man of war whose powers are many.
The hat of salvation He put on His head;
salvation for Him, His right hand and His sacred arm.
∴ *With illuminating dew drops His head is filled,*
His locks are the rains of the night.
He shall glory in me for He desires me,
and He shall be for me a crown of pride.
∴ *A form of the very finest gold upon his head,*
and carved on his forehead is His glorious, sacred Name.
For grace and for glory the pride of His splendor;
His nation crowns Him with its prayers.
∴ *The tresses of His head are like His youthful days;*
His locks are jet-black ringlets.
The Abode of righteousness is the pride of His splendor;
may He elevate it to His foremost joy.

❖ סְגֻלָּתוֹ תְּהִי בְיָדוֹ עֲטֶרֶת, וּצְנִיף מְלוּכָה צְבִי תִפְאֶרֶת.
עֲמוּסִים נְשָׂאָם עֲטֶרֶת עִנְּדָם, מֵאֲשֶׁר יָקְרוּ בְעֵינָיו כִּבְּדָם.
❖ פְּאֵרוֹ עָלַי וּפְאֵרִי עָלָיו, וְקָרוֹב אֵלַי בְּקָרְאִי אֵלָיו.
צַח וְאָדוֹם לִלְבוּשׁוֹ אָדוֹם, פּוּרָה בְדָרְכוֹ בְּבוֹאוֹ מֵאֱדוֹם.
❖ קֶשֶׁר תְּפִלִּין הֶרְאָה לֶעָנָו, תְּמוּנַת יהוה לְנֶגֶד עֵינָיו.
רוֹצֶה בְעַמּוֹ עֲנָוִים יְפָאֵר, יוֹשֵׁב תְּהִלּוֹת בָּם לְהִתְפָּאֵר.
❖ רֹאשׁ דְּבָרְךָ אֱמֶת קוֹרֵא מֵרֹאשׁ, דּוֹר וָדוֹר עַם דּוֹרֶשְׁךָ דְּרוֹשׁ.
שִׁית הֲמוֹן שִׁירַי נָא עָלֶיךָ, וְרִנָּתִי תִּקְרַב אֵלֶיךָ.
❖ תְּהִלָּתִי תְּהִי לְרֹאשְׁךָ עֲטֶרֶת, וּתְפִלָּתִי תִּכּוֹן קְטֹרֶת.
תִּיקַר שִׁירַת רָשׁ בְּעֵינֶיךָ, כַּשִּׁיר יוּשַׁר עַל קָרְבָּנֶיךָ.
❖ בִּרְכָתִי תַעֲלֶה לְרֹאשׁ מַשְׁבִּיר, מְחוֹלֵל וּמוֹלִיד צַדִּיק כַּבִּיר.
וּבְבִרְכָתִי תְנַעֲנַע לִי רֹאשׁ, וְאוֹתָהּ קַח לְךָ כִּבְשָׂמִים רֹאשׁ.
❖ יֶעֱרַב נָא שִׂיחִי עָלֶיךָ, כִּי נַפְשִׁי תַעֲרוֹג אֵלֶיךָ.

לְךָ יהוה הַגְּדֻלָּה וְהַגְּבוּרָה וְהַתִּפְאֶרֶת וְהַנֵּצַח וְהַהוֹד, כִּי כֹל בַּשָּׁמַיִם וּבָאָרֶץ; לְךָ יהוה הַמַּמְלָכָה וְהַמִּתְנַשֵּׂא לְכֹל לְרֹאשׁ.[1] מִי יְמַלֵּל גְּבוּרוֹת יהוה, יַשְׁמִיעַ כָּל תְּהִלָּתוֹ.[2]

קדיש יתום

In the presence of a *minyan,* mourners recite קַדִּישׁ יָתוֹם, the Mourner's *Kaddish* (see *Laws* §81-83):

יִתְגַּדַּל וְיִתְקַדַּשׁ שְׁמֵהּ רַבָּא. (.Cong – אָמֵן.) בְּעָלְמָא דִּי בְרָא כִרְעוּתֵהּ. וְיַמְלִיךְ מַלְכוּתֵהּ, בְּחַיֵּיכוֹן וּבְיוֹמֵיכוֹן וּבְחַיֵּי דְכָל בֵּית יִשְׂרָאֵל, בַּעֲגָלָא וּבִזְמַן קָרִיב. וְאִמְרוּ: אָמֵן.

(.Cong – אָמֵן. יְהֵא שְׁמֵהּ רַבָּא מְבָרַךְ לְעָלַם וּלְעָלְמֵי עָלְמַיָּא.)
יְהֵא שְׁמֵהּ רַבָּא מְבָרַךְ לְעָלַם וּלְעָלְמֵי עָלְמַיָּא.

יִתְבָּרַךְ וְיִשְׁתַּבַּח וְיִתְפָּאַר וְיִתְרוֹמַם וְיִתְנַשֵּׂא וְיִתְהַדָּר וְיִתְעַלֶּה וְיִתְהַלָּל שְׁמֵהּ דְּקֻדְשָׁא בְּרִיךְ הוּא (.Cong – בְּרִיךְ הוּא) — לְעֵלָּא מִן כָּל בִּרְכָתָא וְשִׁירָתָא תֻּשְׁבְּחָתָא וְנֶחֱמָתָא, דַּאֲמִירָן בְּעָלְמָא. וְאִמְרוּ: אָמֵן. (.Cong – אָמֵן.)

יְהֵא שְׁלָמָא רַבָּא מִן שְׁמַיָּא, וְחַיִּים עָלֵינוּ וְעַל כָּל יִשְׂרָאֵל. וְאִמְרוּ: אָמֵן. (.Cong – אָמֵן.)

Take three steps back. Bow left and say . . . עֹשֶׂה; bow right and say . . . הוּא; bow forward and say וְעַל כָּל . . . אָמֵן. Remain standing in place for a few moments, then take three steps forward.

עֹשֶׂה שָׁלוֹם בִּמְרוֹמָיו, הוּא יַעֲשֶׂה שָׁלוֹם עָלֵינוּ, וְעַל כָּל יִשְׂרָאֵל. וְאִמְרוּ: אָמֵן. (.Cong – אָמֵן.)

∴ *May His treasured nation be in His hand like a crown,*
and like a royal tiara the pride of His splendor.
From infancy He bore them and affixed them as a crown,
because they are precious in His eyes He honored them.
∴ *His tefillin-splendor is upon me and my tefillin-splendor is upon Him,*
and He is near to me when I call to Him.
He is white and crimson; His garment will be bloody red,
when He tramples as in a press on His coming from Edom.
∴ *He showed the tefillin-knot to the humble [Moses],*
the likeness of HASHEM *before his eyes.*
He desires His people, He will glorify the humble;
enthroned upon praises, He glories with them.
∴ *The very beginning of Your word is truth — one reads it from the Torah's start; the people that seeks You expounds each generation's fate.*
Place the multitude of my songs before You, please;
and my glad song bring near to You.
∴ *May my praise be a crown for Your head,*
and may my prayer be accepted like incense.
May the poor man's song be dear in Your eyes,
like the song that is sung over Your offerings.
∴ *May my blessing rise up upon the head of the Sustainer —*
Creator, Giver of life, mighty Righteous One.
And to my blessing, nod Your head to me,
and take it to Yourself like the finest incense.
∴ *May my prayer be sweet to You, for my soul shall pine for You.*

לְךָ *Yours,* HASHEM, *is the greatness, the strength, the splendor, the triumph, and the glory; even everything in heaven and earth; Yours,* HASHEM, *is the kingdom, and the sovereignty over every leader.*[1] *Who can express the mighty acts of* HASHEM? *Who can declare all His praise?*[2]

MOURNER'S KADDISH

In the presence of a *minyan,* mourners recite קַדִּישׁ יָתוֹם, the Mourner's *Kaddish* (see *Laws* §81-83). [A transliteration of this *Kaddish* appears on p. 1305.]

יִתְגַּדַּל *May His great Name grow exalted and sanctified* (Cong.— *Amen.*) *in the world that He created as He willed. May He give reign to His kingship in your lifetimes and in your days, and in the lifetimes of the entire Family of Israel, swiftly and soon. Now respond: Amen.*

(Cong.— *Amen. May His great Name be blessed forever and ever.*)
May His great Name be blessed forever and ever.

Blessed, praised, glorified, exalted, extolled, mighty, upraised, and lauded be the Name of the Holy One, Blessed is He (Cong.— *Blessed is He*) *— beyond any blessing and song, praise and consolation that are uttered in the world. Now respond: Amen.* (Cong.— *Amen*).

May there be abundant peace from Heaven, and life, upon us and upon all Israel. Now respond: Amen. (Cong.— *Amen.*)

Take three steps back. Bow left and say, *'He Who makes peace . . .';* bow right and say, *'may He . . .';* bow forward and say, *'and upon all Israel . . .'* Remain standing in place for a few moments, then take three steps forward.

He Who makes peace in His heights, may He make peace upon us, and upon all Israel. Now respond: Amen. (Cong.— *Amen.*)

(1) *I Chronicles* 29:11. (2) *Psalms* 106:2.

שיר של יום

A different psalm is assigned as the שִׁיר שֶׁל יוֹם, *Song of the Day,* for each day of the week (see p. 388).

SUNDAY

הַיּוֹם יוֹם רִאשׁוֹן בַּשַּׁבָּת, שֶׁבּוֹ הָיוּ הַלְוִיִּם אוֹמְרִים בְּבֵית הַמִּקְדָּשׁ:

לְדָוִד מִזְמוֹר, לַיהוה הָאָרֶץ וּמְלוֹאָהּ, תֵּבֵל וְיֹשְׁבֵי בָהּ. כִּי הוּא עַל יַמִּים יְסָדָהּ, וְעַל נְהָרוֹת יְכוֹנְנֶהָ. מִי יַעֲלֶה בְהַר יהוה, וּמִי יָקוּם בִּמְקוֹם קָדְשׁוֹ. נְקִי כַפַּיִם וּבַר לֵבָב, אֲשֶׁר לֹא נָשָׂא לַשָּׁוְא נַפְשִׁי, וְלֹא נִשְׁבַּע לְמִרְמָה. יִשָּׂא בְרָכָה מֵאֵת יהוה, וּצְדָקָה מֵאֱלֹהֵי יִשְׁעוֹ. זֶה דּוֹר דֹּרְשָׁיו, מְבַקְשֵׁי פָנֶיךָ יַעֲקֹב סֶלָה. שְׂאוּ שְׁעָרִים רָאשֵׁיכֶם, וְהִנָּשְׂאוּ פִּתְחֵי עוֹלָם, וְיָבוֹא מֶלֶךְ הַכָּבוֹד. מִי זֶה מֶלֶךְ הַכָּבוֹד, יהוה עִזּוּז וְגִבּוֹר, יהוה גִּבּוֹר מִלְחָמָה. ❖ שְׂאוּ שְׁעָרִים רָאשֵׁיכֶם, וּשְׂאוּ פִּתְחֵי עוֹלָם, וְיָבֹא מֶלֶךְ הַכָּבוֹד. מִי הוּא זֶה מֶלֶךְ הַכָּבוֹד, יהוה צְבָאוֹת, הוּא מֶלֶךְ הַכָּבוֹד סֶלָה.

Mourners recite the Mourner's *Kaddish* (p. 818) and the service continues with Psalm 27 (p. 822).

MONDAY

הַיּוֹם יוֹם שֵׁנִי בַּשַּׁבָּת, שֶׁבּוֹ הָיוּ הַלְוִיִּם אוֹמְרִים בְּבֵית הַמִּקְדָּשׁ:

שִׁיר מִזְמוֹר לִבְנֵי קֹרַח. גָּדוֹל יהוה וּמְהֻלָּל מְאֹד, בְּעִיר אֱלֹהֵינוּ, הַר קָדְשׁוֹ. יְפֵה נוֹף, מְשׂוֹשׂ כָּל הָאָרֶץ, הַר צִיּוֹן יַרְכְּתֵי צָפוֹן, קִרְיַת מֶלֶךְ רָב. אֱלֹהִים בְּאַרְמְנוֹתֶיהָ נוֹדַע לְמִשְׂגָּב. כִּי הִנֵּה הַמְּלָכִים נוֹעֲדוּ, עָבְרוּ יַחְדָּו. הֵמָּה רָאוּ כֵּן תָּמָהוּ, נִבְהֲלוּ נֶחְפָּזוּ. רְעָדָה אֲחָזָתַם שָׁם, חִיל כַּיּוֹלֵדָה. בְּרוּחַ קָדִים תְּשַׁבֵּר אֳנִיּוֹת תַּרְשִׁישׁ. כַּאֲשֶׁר שָׁמַעְנוּ כֵּן רָאִינוּ בְּעִיר יהוה צְבָאוֹת, בְּעִיר אֱלֹהֵינוּ, אֱלֹהִים יְכוֹנְנֶהָ עַד עוֹלָם סֶלָה. דִּמִּינוּ אֱלֹהִים חַסְדֶּךָ, בְּקֶרֶב הֵיכָלֶךָ. כְּשִׁמְךָ אֱלֹהִים כֵּן תְּהִלָּתְךָ, עַל קַצְוֵי אֶרֶץ, צֶדֶק מָלְאָה יְמִינֶךָ. יִשְׂמַח הַר צִיּוֹן, תָּגֵלְנָה בְּנוֹת יְהוּדָה, לְמַעַן מִשְׁפָּטֶיךָ. סֹבּוּ צִיּוֹן וְהַקִּיפוּהָ, סִפְרוּ מִגְדָּלֶיהָ. ❖ שִׁיתוּ לִבְּכֶם לְחֵילָה, פַּסְּגוּ אַרְמְנוֹתֶיהָ, לְמַעַן תְּסַפְּרוּ לְדוֹר אַחֲרוֹן. כִּי זֶה אֱלֹהִים אֱלֹהֵינוּ עוֹלָם וָעֶד, הוּא יְנַהֲגֵנוּ עַל־מוּת.

Mourners recite the Mourner's *Kaddish* (p. 818) and the service continues with Psalm 27 (p. 822).

WEDNESDAY

הַיּוֹם יוֹם רְבִיעִי בַּשַּׁבָּת, שֶׁבּוֹ הָיוּ הַלְוִיִּם אוֹמְרִים בְּבֵית הַמִּקְדָּשׁ:

אֵל נְקָמוֹת יהוה, אֵל נְקָמוֹת הוֹפִיעַ. הִנָּשֵׂא שֹׁפֵט הָאָרֶץ, הָשֵׁב גְּמוּל עַל גֵּאִים. עַד מָתַי רְשָׁעִים, יהוה, עַד מָתַי רְשָׁעִים יַעֲלֹזוּ. יַבִּיעוּ יְדַבְּרוּ עָתָק, יִתְאַמְּרוּ כָּל פֹּעֲלֵי אָוֶן. עַמְּךָ יהוה יְדַכְּאוּ, וְנַחֲלָתְךָ יְעַנּוּ. אַלְמָנָה וְגֵר יַהֲרֹגוּ, וִיתוֹמִים יְרַצֵּחוּ. וַיֹּאמְרוּ לֹא יִרְאֶה יָּהּ, וְלֹא יָבִין אֱלֹהֵי יַעֲקֹב. בִּינוּ בֹּעֲרִים בָּעָם, וּכְסִילִים מָתַי תַּשְׂכִּילוּ. הֲנֹטַע אֹזֶן הֲלֹא יִשְׁמָע, אִם יֹצֵר עַיִן הֲלֹא יַבִּיט. הֲיֹסֵר גּוֹיִם הֲלֹא יוֹכִיחַ, הַמְלַמֵּד אָדָם דָּעַת. יהוה יֹדֵעַ מַחְשְׁבוֹת אָדָם, כִּי הֵמָּה הָבֶל. אַשְׁרֵי הַגֶּבֶר אֲשֶׁר תְּיַסְּרֶנּוּ יָּהּ, וּמִתּוֹרָתְךָ תְלַמְּדֶנּוּ. לְהַשְׁקִיט לוֹ מִימֵי רָע, עַד יִכָּרֶה לָרָשָׁע שָׁחַת.

SONG OF THE DAY

A different psalm is assigned as the Song of the Day for each day of the week.

SUNDAY

Today is the first day of the Sabbath,
on which the Levites would recite in the Holy Temple:

לְדָוִד *Of David a psalm.* HASHEM'*s is the earth and its fullness, the inhabited land and those who dwell in it. For He founded it upon seas, and established it upon rivers. Who may ascend the mountain of* HASHEM, *and who may stand in the place of His sanctity? One with clean hands and pure heart, who has not sworn in vain by My soul and has not sworn deceitfully. He will receive a blessing from* HASHEM *and just kindness from the God of his salvation. This is the generation of those who seek Him, those who strive for Your Presence — Jacob, Selah. Raise up your heads, O gates, and be uplifted, you everlasting entrances, so that the King of Glory may enter. Who is this King of Glory? —* HASHEM, *the mighty and strong,* HASHEM, *the strong in battle.* Chazzan— *Raise up your heads, O gates, and raise up, you everlasting entrances, so that the King of Glory may enter. Who then is the King of Glory?* HASHEM, *Master of Legions, He is the King of Glory. Selah!*

Mourners recite the Mourner's *Kaddish* (p. 818) and the service continues with Psalm 27 (p. 822).

MONDAY

Today is the second day of the Sabbath,
on which the Levites would recite in the Holy Temple:

שִׁיר מִזְמוֹר *A song, a psalm, by the sons of Korach. Great is* HASHEM *and much praised, in the city of our God, Mount of His Holiness. Fairest of sites, joy of all the earth is Mount Zion, by the northern sides of the great king's city. In her palaces God is known as the Stronghold. For behold — the kings assembled, they came together. They saw and they were astounded, they were confounded and hastily fled. Trembling gripped them there, convulsions like a woman in birth travail. With an east wind You smashed the ships of Tarshish. As we heard, so we saw in the city of* HASHEM, *Master of Legions, in the city of our God — may God establish it to eternity, Selah! We hoped, O God, for Your kindness, in the midst of Your Sanctuary. Like Your Name, O God, so is Your praise — to the ends of the earth; righteousness fills Your right hand. May Mount Zion be glad, may the daughters of Judah rejoice, because of Your judgments. Walk about Zion and encircle her, count her towers.* Chazzan— *Mark well in your hearts her ramparts, raise up her palaces, that you may recount it to the succeeding generation: that this is God, our God, forever and ever, He will guide us like children.*

Mourners recite the Mourner's *Kaddish* (p. 818) and the service continues with Psalm 27 (p. 822).

WEDNESDAY

Today is the fourth day of the Sabbath,
on which the Levites would recite in the Holy Temple:

אֵל נְקָמוֹת *O God of vengeance,* HASHEM; *O God of vengeance, appear! Arise, O Judge of the earth, render recompense to the haughty. How long shall the wicked — O* HASHEM *— how long shall the wicked exult? They speak freely, they utter malicious falsehood, they glorify themselves, all workers of iniquity. Your nation,* HASHEM, *they crush, and they afflict Your heritage. The widow and the stranger they slay, and the orphans they murder. And they say, 'God will not see, nor will the God of Jacob understand.' Understand, you boors among the people; and you fools, when will you gain wisdom? He Who implants the ear, shall He not hear? He Who fashions the eye, shall He not see? He Who chastises nations, shall He not rebuke? — He Who teaches man knowledge.* HASHEM *knows the thoughts of man, that they are futile. Praiseworthy is the man whom God disciplines, and whom You teach from Your Torah. To give him rest from the days of evil, until a pit is dug for the wicked.*

כִּי לֹא יִטֹּשׁ יהוה עַמּוֹ, וְנַחֲלָתוֹ לֹא יַעֲזֹב. כִּי עַד צֶדֶק יָשׁוּב מִשְׁפָּט, וְאַחֲרָיו כָּל יִשְׁרֵי לֵב. מִי יָקוּם לִי עִם מְרֵעִים, מִי יִתְיַצֵּב לִי עִם פֹּעֲלֵי אָוֶן. לוּלֵי יהוה עֶזְרָתָה לִּי, כִּמְעַט שָׁכְנָה דוּמָה נַפְשִׁי. אִם אָמַרְתִּי מָטָה רַגְלִי, חַסְדְּךָ יהוה יִסְעָדֵנִי. בְּרֹב שַׂרְעַפַּי בְּקִרְבִּי, תַּנְחוּמֶיךָ יְשַׁעַשְׁעוּ נַפְשִׁי. הַיְחָבְרְךָ כִּסֵּא הַוּוֹת, יֹצֵר עָמָל עֲלֵי חֹק. יָגוֹדּוּ עַל נֶפֶשׁ צַדִּיק, וְדָם נָקִי יַרְשִׁיעוּ. וַיְהִי יהוה לִי לְמִשְׂגָּב, וֵאלֹהַי לְצוּר מַחְסִי. וַיָּשֶׁב עֲלֵיהֶם אֶת אוֹנָם, וּבְרָעָתָם יַצְמִיתֵם, יַצְמִיתֵם יהוה אֱלֹהֵינוּ.

❖ לְכוּ נְרַנְּנָה לַיהוה, נָרִיעָה לְצוּר יִשְׁעֵנוּ. נְקַדְּמָה פָנָיו בְּתוֹדָה, בִּזְמִרוֹת נָרִיעַ לוֹ. כִּי אֵל גָּדוֹל יהוה, וּמֶלֶךְ גָּדוֹל עַל כָּל אֱלֹהִים.

Mourners recite the Mourner's *Kaddish* (p. 818) and the service continues with Psalm 27 (p. 822).

FRIDAY

הַיּוֹם יוֹם שִׁשִּׁי בַּשַּׁבָּת, שֶׁבּוֹ הָיוּ הַלְוִיִּם אוֹמְרִים בְּבֵית הַמִּקְדָּשׁ:

יהוה מָלָךְ, גֵּאוּת לָבֵשׁ, לָבֵשׁ יהוה עֹז הִתְאַזָּר, אַף תִּכּוֹן תֵּבֵל בַּל תִּמּוֹט. נָכוֹן כִּסְאֲךָ מֵאָז, מֵעוֹלָם אָתָּה. נָשְׂאוּ נְהָרוֹת יהוה, נָשְׂאוּ נְהָרוֹת קוֹלָם, יִשְׂאוּ נְהָרוֹת דָּכְיָם. מִקֹּלוֹת מַיִם רַבִּים, אַדִּירִים מִשְׁבְּרֵי יָם, אַדִּיר בַּמָּרוֹם יהוה. ❖ עֵדֹתֶיךָ נֶאֶמְנוּ מְאֹד לְבֵיתְךָ נַאֲוָה קֹדֶשׁ, יהוה לְאֹרֶךְ יָמִים.

Mourners recite the Mourner's *Kaddish* (p. 818) and the service continues below.

תהלים כז

לְדָוִד, יהוה אוֹרִי וְיִשְׁעִי, מִמִּי אִירָא, יהוה מָעוֹז חַיַּי, מִמִּי אֶפְחָד. בִּקְרֹב עָלַי מְרֵעִים לֶאֱכֹל אֶת בְּשָׂרִי, צָרַי וְאֹיְבַי לִי, הֵמָּה כָשְׁלוּ וְנָפָלוּ. אִם תַּחֲנֶה עָלַי מַחֲנֶה, לֹא יִירָא לִבִּי, אִם תָּקוּם עָלַי מִלְחָמָה, בְּזֹאת אֲנִי בוֹטֵחַ. אַחַת שָׁאַלְתִּי מֵאֵת יהוה, אוֹתָהּ אֲבַקֵּשׁ, שִׁבְתִּי בְּבֵית יהוה כָּל יְמֵי חַיַּי, לַחֲזוֹת בְּנֹעַם יהוה, וּלְבַקֵּר בְּהֵיכָלוֹ. כִּי יִצְפְּנֵנִי בְּסֻכֹּה בְּיוֹם רָעָה, יַסְתִּרֵנִי בְּסֵתֶר אָהֳלוֹ, בְּצוּר יְרוֹמְמֵנִי. וְעַתָּה יָרוּם רֹאשִׁי עַל אֹיְבַי סְבִיבוֹתַי, וְאֶזְבְּחָה בְאָהֳלוֹ זִבְחֵי תְרוּעָה, אָשִׁירָה וַאֲזַמְּרָה לַיהוה. שְׁמַע יהוה קוֹלִי אֶקְרָא, וְחָנֵּנִי וַעֲנֵנִי. לְךָ אָמַר לִבִּי בַּקְּשׁוּ פָנָי, אֶת פָּנֶיךָ יהוה אֲבַקֵּשׁ. אַל תַּסְתֵּר פָּנֶיךָ מִמֶּנִּי, אַל תַּט בְּאַף עַבְדֶּךָ, עֶזְרָתִי הָיִיתָ, אַל תִּטְּשֵׁנִי וְאַל תַּעַזְבֵנִי, אֱלֹהֵי יִשְׁעִי. כִּי אָבִי וְאִמִּי עֲזָבוּנִי, וַיהוה יַאַסְפֵנִי. הוֹרֵנִי יהוה דַּרְכֶּךָ, וּנְחֵנִי בְּאֹרַח מִישׁוֹר, לְמַעַן שֹׁרְרָי. אַל תִּתְּנֵנִי בְּנֶפֶשׁ צָרָי, כִּי קָמוּ בִי עֵדֵי שֶׁקֶר, וִיפֵחַ חָמָס. ❖ לוּלֵא הֶאֱמַנְתִּי לִרְאוֹת בְּטוּב יהוה בְּאֶרֶץ חַיִּים. קַוֵּה אֶל יהוה, חֲזַק וְיַאֲמֵץ לִבֶּךָ, וְקַוֵּה אֶל יהוה.

Mourners recite the Mourner's *Kaddish* (p. 818) and the service is concluded.

For HASHEM will not cast off His people, nor will He forsake His heritage. For justice shall revert to righteousness, and following it will be all of upright heart. Who will rise up for me against evildoers? Who will stand up for me against the workers of iniquity? Had HASHEM not been a help to me, my soul would soon have dwelt in silence. If I said, 'My foot falters,' Your kindness, HASHEM, supported me. When my forebodings were abundant within me, Your comforts cheered my soul. Can the throne of destruction be associated with You? — those who fashion evil into a way of life. They join together against the soul of the righteous, and the blood of the innocent they condemn. Then HASHEM became a stronghold for me, and my God, the Rock of my refuge. He turned upon them their own violence, and with their own evil He will cut them off, HASHEM, our God, will cut them off. Chazzan– *Come — let us sing to HASHEM, let us call out to the Rock of our salvation. Let us greet Him with thanksgiving, with praiseful songs let us call out to Him. For a great God is HASHEM, and a great King above all heavenly powers.*

Mourners recite the Mourner's *Kaddish* (p. 818) and the service continues with Psalm 27 (p. 822).

FRIDAY

Today is the sixth day of the Sabbath,
on which the Levites would recite in the Holy Temple:

יהוה מָלָךְ *HASHEM will have reigned, He will have donned grandeur; He will have donned might and girded Himself; He even made the world firm so that it should not falter. Your throne was established from of old, eternal are You. Like rivers they raised, O HASHEM, like rivers they raised their voice; like rivers they shall raise their destructiveness. More than the roars of many waters, mightier than the waves of the sea — You are mighty on high, HASHEM.* Chazzan– *Your testimonies are exceedingly trustworthy about Your House, the Sacred Dwelling — O HASHEM, may it be for long days.*

Mourners recite the Mourner's *Kaddish* (p. 818) and the service continues below.

Psalm 27

לְדָוִד *Of David; HASHEM is my light and my salvation, whom shall I fear? HASHEM is my life's strength, whom shall I dread? When evildoers approach me to devour my flesh, my tormentors and my foes against me — it is they who stumble and fall. Though an army would besiege me, my heart would not fear; though war would arise against me, in this I trust. One thing I asked of HASHEM, that shall I seek: That I dwell in the House of HASHEM all the days of my life; to behold the sweetness of HASHEM and to contemplate in His Sanctuary. Indeed, He will hide me in His Shelter on the day of evil; He will conceal me in the concealment of His Tent, He will lift me upon a rock. Now my head is raised above my enemies around me, and I will slaughter offerings in His Tent accompanied by joyous song; I will sing and make music to HASHEM. HASHEM, hear my voice when I call, be gracious toward me and answer me. In Your behalf, my heart has said, 'Seek My Presence'; Your Presence, HASHEM, do I seek. Conceal not Your Presence from me, repel not Your servant in anger. You have been my Helper, abandon me not, forsake me not, O God of my salvation. Though my father and mother have forsaken me, HASHEM will gather me in. Teach me Your way, HASHEM, and lead me on the path of integrity, because of my watchful foes. Deliver me not to the wishes of my tormentors, for there have arisen against me false witnesses who breathe violence.* Chazzan– *Had I not trusted that I would see the goodness of HASHEM in the land of life! Hope to HASHEM, strengthen yourself and He will give you courage; and hope to HASHEM.*

Mourners recite the Mourner's *Kaddish* (p. 818) and the service is concluded.

מנחה לחול המועד ולהושענא רבה

אַשְׁרֵי יוֹשְׁבֵי בֵיתֶךָ, עוֹד יְהַלְלְוּךָ סֶּלָה.[1] אַשְׁרֵי הָעָם שֶׁכָּכָה לּוֹ, אַשְׁרֵי הָעָם שֶׁיהוה אֱלֹהָיו.[2]

תהלים קמה

תְּהִלָּה לְדָוִד,

אֲרוֹמִמְךָ אֱלוֹהַי הַמֶּלֶךְ, וַאֲבָרְכָה שִׁמְךָ לְעוֹלָם וָעֶד.
בְּכָל יוֹם אֲבָרְכֶךָּ, וַאֲהַלְלָה שִׁמְךָ לְעוֹלָם וָעֶד.
גָּדוֹל יהוה וּמְהֻלָּל מְאֹד, וְלִגְדֻלָּתוֹ אֵין חֵקֶר.
דּוֹר לְדוֹר יְשַׁבַּח מַעֲשֶׂיךָ, וּגְבוּרֹתֶיךָ יַגִּידוּ.
הֲדַר כְּבוֹד הוֹדֶךָ, וְדִבְרֵי נִפְלְאֹתֶיךָ אָשִׂיחָה.
וֶעֱזוּז נוֹרְאוֹתֶיךָ יֹאמֵרוּ, וּגְדוּלָּתְךָ אֲסַפְּרֶנָּה.
זֵכֶר רַב טוּבְךָ יַבִּיעוּ, וְצִדְקָתְךָ יְרַנֵּנוּ.
חַנּוּן וְרַחוּם יהוה, אֶרֶךְ אַפַּיִם וּגְדָל חָסֶד.
טוֹב יהוה לַכֹּל, וְרַחֲמָיו עַל כָּל מַעֲשָׂיו.
יוֹדְוּךָ יהוה כָּל מַעֲשֶׂיךָ, וַחֲסִידֶיךָ יְבָרְכוּכָה.
כְּבוֹד מַלְכוּתְךָ יֹאמֵרוּ, וּגְבוּרָתְךָ יְדַבֵּרוּ.
לְהוֹדִיעַ לִבְנֵי הָאָדָם גְּבוּרֹתָיו, וּכְבוֹד הֲדַר מַלְכוּתוֹ.
מַלְכוּתְךָ מַלְכוּת כָּל עֹלָמִים, וּמֶמְשַׁלְתְּךָ בְּכָל דּוֹר וָדֹר.
סוֹמֵךְ יהוה לְכָל הַנֹּפְלִים, וְזוֹקֵף לְכָל הַכְּפוּפִים.
עֵינֵי כֹל אֵלֶיךָ יְשַׂבֵּרוּ, וְאַתָּה נוֹתֵן לָהֶם אֶת אָכְלָם בְּעִתּוֹ.
פּוֹתֵחַ אֶת יָדֶךָ,
וּמַשְׂבִּיעַ לְכָל חַי רָצוֹן.

While reciting the verse פּוֹתֵחַ, concentrate intently on its meaning.

צַדִּיק יהוה בְּכָל דְּרָכָיו, וְחָסִיד בְּכָל מַעֲשָׂיו.
קָרוֹב יהוה לְכָל קֹרְאָיו, לְכֹל אֲשֶׁר יִקְרָאֻהוּ בֶאֱמֶת.
רְצוֹן יְרֵאָיו יַעֲשֶׂה, וְאֶת שַׁוְעָתָם יִשְׁמַע וְיוֹשִׁיעֵם.
שׁוֹמֵר יהוה אֶת כָּל אֹהֲבָיו, וְאֵת כָּל הָרְשָׁעִים יַשְׁמִיד.
❖ תְּהִלַּת יהוה יְדַבֶּר פִּי, וִיבָרֵךְ כָּל בָּשָׂר שֵׁם קָדְשׁוֹ לְעוֹלָם וָעֶד.
וַאֲנַחְנוּ נְבָרֵךְ יָהּ, מֵעַתָּה וְעַד עוֹלָם, הַלְלוּיָהּ.[3]

---

(1) *Psalms* 84:5. (2) 144:15. (3) 115:18.

MINCHAH FOR CHOL HAMOED AND HOSHANA RABBAH

אַשְׁרֵי *Praiseworthy are those who dwell in Your house; may they always praise You, Selah!*[1] *Praiseworthy is the people for whom this is so, praiseworthy is the people whose God is* HASHEM.[2]

Psalm 145

A psalm of praise by David:

א *I will exalt You, my God the King,*
and I will bless Your Name forever and ever.
ב *Every day I will bless You,*
and I will laud Your Name forever and ever.
ג HASHEM *is great and exceedingly lauded,*
and His greatness is beyond investigation.
ד *Each generation will praise Your deeds to the next*
and of Your mighty deeds they will tell.
ה *The splendrous glory of Your power*
and Your wondrous deeds I shall discuss.
ו *And of Your awesome power they will speak,*
and Your greatness I shall relate.
ז *A recollection of Your abundant goodness they will utter*
and of Your righteousness they will sing exultantly.
ח *Gracious and merciful is* HASHEM,
slow to anger, and great in [bestowing] kindness.
ט HASHEM *is good to all; His mercies are on all His works.*
י *All Your works shall thank You,* HASHEM,
and Your devout ones will bless You.
כ *Of the glory of Your kingdom they will speak,*
and of Your power they will tell;
ל *To inform human beings of His mighty deeds,*
and the glorious splendor of His kingdom.
מ *Your kingdom is a kingdom spanning all eternities,*
and Your dominion is throughout every generation.
ס HASHEM *supports all the fallen ones and straightens all the bent.*
ע *The eyes of all look to You with hope*
and You give them their food in its proper time;
פ *You open Your hand,*
and satisfy the desire of every living thing.

While reciting the verse *'You open . . .,'* concentrate intently on its meaning.

צ *Righteous is* HASHEM *in all His ways*
and magnanimous in all His deeds.
ק HASHEM *is close to all who call upon Him —*
to all who call upon Him sincerely.
ר *The will of those who fear Him He will do;*
and their cry He will hear, and save them.
ש HASHEM *protects all who love Him;*
but all the wicked He will destroy.
ת Chazzan– *May my mouth declare the praise of* HASHEM
and may all flesh bless His Holy Name forever and ever.
We will bless God from this time and forever, Halleluyah![3]

חצי קדיש

The *chazzan* recites חֲצִי קַדִּישׁ.

יִתְגַּדַּל וְיִתְקַדַּשׁ שְׁמֵהּ רַבָּא. (.Cong – אָמֵן.) בְּעָלְמָא דִּי בְרָא כִרְעוּתֵהּ. וְיַמְלִיךְ מַלְכוּתֵהּ, בְּחַיֵּיכוֹן וּבְיוֹמֵיכוֹן וּבְחַיֵּי דְכָל בֵּית יִשְׂרָאֵל, בַּעֲגָלָא וּבִזְמַן קָרִיב. וְאִמְרוּ: אָמֵן.

(.Cong – אָמֵן. יְהֵא שְׁמֵהּ רַבָּא מְבָרַךְ לְעָלַם וּלְעָלְמֵי עָלְמַיָּא.)

יְהֵא שְׁמֵהּ רַבָּא מְבָרַךְ לְעָלַם וּלְעָלְמֵי עָלְמַיָּא.

יִתְבָּרַךְ וְיִשְׁתַּבַּח וְיִתְפָּאַר וְיִתְרוֹמַם וְיִתְנַשֵּׂא וְיִתְהַדָּר וְיִתְעַלֶּה וְיִתְהַלָּל שְׁמֵהּ דְּקֻדְשָׁא בְּרִיךְ הוּא (.Cong – בְּרִיךְ הוּא) – לְעֵלָּא מִן כָּל בִּרְכָתָא וְשִׁירָתָא תֻּשְׁבְּחָתָא וְנֶחֱמָתָא, דַּאֲמִירָן בְּעָלְמָא. וְאִמְרוּ: אָמֵן. (.Cong – אָמֵן.)

שמונה עשרה – עמידה

Take three steps backward, then three steps forward. Remain standing with the feet together while reciting *Shemoneh Esrei*. Recite it with quiet devotion and without interruption, verbal or otherwise. Although its recitation should not be audible to others, one must pray loudly enough to hear himself.

כִּי שֵׁם יהוה אֶקְרָא, הָבוּ גֹדֶל לֵאלֹהֵינוּ.[1]

אֲדֹנָי שְׂפָתַי תִּפְתָּח, וּפִי יַגִּיד תְּהִלָּתֶךָ.[2]

אבות

Bend the knees at בָּרוּךְ; bow at אַתָּה; straighten up at ה׳.

בָּרוּךְ אַתָּה יהוה אֱלֹהֵינוּ וֵאלֹהֵי אֲבוֹתֵינוּ, אֱלֹהֵי אַבְרָהָם, אֱלֹהֵי יִצְחָק, וֵאלֹהֵי יַעֲקֹב, הָאֵל הַגָּדוֹל הַגִּבּוֹר וְהַנּוֹרָא, אֵל עֶלְיוֹן, גּוֹמֵל חֲסָדִים טוֹבִים וְקוֹנֵה הַכֹּל, וְזוֹכֵר חַסְדֵי אָבוֹת, וּמֵבִיא גוֹאֵל לִבְנֵי בְנֵיהֶם, לְמַעַן שְׁמוֹ בְּאַהֲבָה. מֶלֶךְ עוֹזֵר וּמוֹשִׁיעַ וּמָגֵן.

Bend the knees at בָּרוּךְ; bow at אַתָּה; straighten up at ה׳.

בָּרוּךְ אַתָּה יהוה, מָגֵן אַבְרָהָם.

גבורות

אַתָּה גִּבּוֹר לְעוֹלָם אֲדֹנָי, מְחַיֵּה מֵתִים אַתָּה, רַב לְהוֹשִׁיעַ. מְכַלְכֵּל חַיִּים בְּחֶסֶד, מְחַיֵּה מֵתִים בְּרַחֲמִים רַבִּים, סוֹמֵךְ נוֹפְלִים, וְרוֹפֵא חוֹלִים, וּמַתִּיר אֲסוּרִים, וּמְקַיֵּם אֱמוּנָתוֹ לִישֵׁנֵי עָפָר. מִי כָמוֹךָ בַּעַל גְּבוּרוֹת, וּמִי דּוֹמֶה לָּךְ, מֶלֶךְ מֵמִית וּמְחַיֶּה וּמַצְמִיחַ יְשׁוּעָה. וְנֶאֱמָן אַתָּה לְהַחֲיוֹת מֵתִים. בָּרוּךְ אַתָּה יהוה, מְחַיֵּה הַמֵּתִים.

During the *chazzan's* repetition, *Kedushah* (page 828) is recited at this point.

HALF KADDISH

The *chazzan* recites Half *Kaddish:*

יִתְגַּדַּל *May His great Name grow exalted and sanctified* (Cong.– *Amen.*) *in the world that He created as He willed. May He give reign to His kingship in your lifetimes and in your days, and in the lifetimes of the entire Family of Israel, swiftly and soon. Now respond: Amen.*

(Cong.– *Amen. May His great Name be blessed forever and ever.*)

May His great Name be blessed forever and ever.

Blessed, praised, glorified, exalted, extolled, mighty, upraised, and lauded be the Name of the Holy One, Blessed is He (Cong.– *Blessed is He*) *— beyond any blessing and song, praise and consolation that are uttered in the world. Now respond: Amen.* (Cong.– *Amen.*)

❧ SHEMONEH ESREI – AMIDAH ☙

Take three steps backward, then three steps forward. Remain standing with the feet together while reciting *Shemoneh Esrei.* Recite it with quiet devotion and without interruption, verbal or otherwise. Although its recitation should not be audible to others, one must pray loudly enough to hear himself.

When I call out the Name of HASHEM, ascribe greatness to our God.[1]
My Lord, open my lips, that my mouth may declare Your praise.[2]

PATRIARCHS

Bend the knees at *'Blessed'*; bow at *'You'*; straighten up at *'HASHEM.'*

בָּרוּךְ *Blessed are You, HASHEM, our God and the God of our forefathers, God of Abraham, God of Isaac, and God of Jacob; the great, mighty, and awesome God, the supreme God, Who bestows beneficial kindnesses and creates everything, Who recalls the kindnesses of the Patriarchs and brings a Redeemer to their children's children, for His Name's sake, with love. O King, Helper, Savior, and Shield.*

Bend the knees at *'Blessed'*; bow at *'You'*; straighten up at *'HASHEM.'*

Blessed are You, HASHEM, Shield of Abraham.

GOD'S MIGHT

אַתָּה *You are eternally mighty, my Lord, the Resuscitator of the dead are You; abundantly able to save. He sustains the living with kindness, resuscitates the dead with abundant mercy, supports the fallen, heals the sick, releases the confined, and maintains His faith to those asleep in the dust. Who is like You, O Master of mighty deeds, and who is comparable to You, O King Who causes death and restores life and makes salvation sprout! And You are faithful to resuscitate the dead. Blessed are You, HASHEM, Who resuscitates the dead.*

During the *chazzan's* repetition, *Kedushah* (page 828) is recited at this point.

---

(1) *Deuteronomy* 32:3. (2) *Psalms* 51:17.

קדושת השם

אַתָּה קָדוֹשׁ וְשִׁמְךָ קָדוֹשׁ, וּקְדוֹשִׁים בְּכָל יוֹם יְהַלְּלוּךָ סֶּלָה. בָּרוּךְ אַתָּה יהוה, הָאֵל הַקָּדוֹשׁ.

בינה

אַתָּה חוֹנֵן לְאָדָם דַּעַת, וּמְלַמֵּד לֶאֱנוֹשׁ בִּינָה. חָנֵּנוּ מֵאִתְּךָ דֵּעָה בִּינָה וְהַשְׂכֵּל. בָּרוּךְ אַתָּה יהוה, חוֹנֵן הַדָּעַת.

תשובה

הֲשִׁיבֵנוּ אָבִינוּ לְתוֹרָתֶךָ, וְקָרְבֵנוּ מַלְכֵּנוּ לַעֲבוֹדָתֶךָ, וְהַחֲזִירֵנוּ בִּתְשׁוּבָה שְׁלֵמָה לְפָנֶיךָ. בָּרוּךְ אַתָּה יהוה, הָרוֹצֶה בִּתְשׁוּבָה.

סליחה

Strike the left side of the chest with the right fist while reciting the words חָטָאנוּ and פָּשָׁעְנוּ.

סְלַח לָנוּ אָבִינוּ כִּי חָטָאנוּ, מְחַל לָנוּ מַלְכֵּנוּ כִּי פָשָׁעְנוּ, כִּי מוֹחֵל וְסוֹלֵחַ אָתָּה. בָּרוּךְ אַתָּה יהוה, חַנּוּן הַמַּרְבֶּה לִסְלוֹחַ.

גאולה

רְאֵה בְעָנְיֵנוּ, וְרִיבָה רִיבֵנוּ, וּגְאָלֵנוּ[1] מְהֵרָה לְמַעַן שְׁמֶךָ, כִּי גוֹאֵל חָזָק אָתָּה. בָּרוּךְ אַתָּה יהוה, גּוֹאֵל יִשְׂרָאֵל.

קדושה

When reciting *Kedushah,* one must stand with his feet together and avoid any interruptions. One should rise on his toes when saying the words קָדוֹשׁ, קָדוֹשׁ, קָדוֹשׁ; בָּרוּךְ (of בָּרוּךְ כְּבוֹד); and יִמְלֹךְ.

– Cong. then *Chazzan* **נְקַדֵּשׁ** אֶת שִׁמְךָ בָּעוֹלָם, כְּשֵׁם שֶׁמַּקְדִּישִׁים אוֹתוֹ בִּשְׁמֵי מָרוֹם, כַּכָּתוּב עַל יַד נְבִיאֶךָ, וְקָרָא זֶה אֶל זֶה וְאָמַר:

– All קָדוֹשׁ קָדוֹשׁ קָדוֹשׁ יהוה צְבָאוֹת, מְלֹא כָל הָאָרֶץ כְּבוֹדוֹ.[2]

– *Chazzan* לְעֻמָּתָם בָּרוּךְ יֹאמֵרוּ:

– All בָּרוּךְ כְּבוֹד יהוה, מִמְּקוֹמוֹ.[3]

– *Chazzan* וּבְדִבְרֵי קָדְשְׁךָ כָּתוּב לֵאמֹר:

– All יִמְלֹךְ יהוה לְעוֹלָם, אֱלֹהַיִךְ צִיּוֹן לְדֹר וָדֹר, הַלְלוּיָהּ.[4]

– *Chazzan* only concludes לְדוֹר וָדוֹר נַגִּיד גָּדְלֶךָ וּלְנֵצַח נְצָחִים קְדֻשָּׁתְךָ נַקְדִּישׁ, וְשִׁבְחֲךָ אֱלֹהֵינוּ מִפִּינוּ לֹא יָמוּשׁ לְעוֹלָם וָעֶד, כִּי אֵל מֶלֶךְ גָּדוֹל וְקָדוֹשׁ אָתָּה. בָּרוּךְ אַתָּה יהוה, הָאֵל הַקָּדוֹשׁ.

Chazzan continues . . . אַתָּה חוֹנֵן (above).

HOLINESS OF GOD'S NAME

אַתָּה *You are holy and Your Name is holy, and holy ones praise You every day, forever. Blessed are You,* HASHEM, *the holy God.*

INSIGHT

אַתָּה *You graciously endow man with wisdom and teach insight to a frail mortal. Endow us graciously from Yourself with wisdom, insight, and discernment. Blessed are You,* HASHEM, *gracious Giver of wisdom.*

REPENTANCE

הֲשִׁיבֵנוּ *Bring us back, our Father, to Your Torah, and bring us near, our King, to Your service, and influence us to return in perfect repentance before You. Blessed are You,* HASHEM, *Who desires repentance.*

FORGIVENESS

Strike the left side of the chest with the right fist while reciting the words *'erred'* and *'sinned.'*

סְלַח *Forgive us, our Father, for we have erred; pardon us, our King, for we have willfully sinned; for You pardon and forgive. Blessed are You,* HASHEM, *the gracious One Who pardons abundantly.*

REDEMPTION

רְאֵה *Behold our affliction, take up our grievance, and redeem us*[1] *speedily for Your Name's sake, for You are a powerful Redeemer. Blessed are You,* HASHEM, *Redeemer of Israel.*

KEDUSHAH

When reciting *Kedushah*, one must stand with his feet together and avoid any interruptions. One should rise on his toes when saying the words *Holy, holy, holy; Blessed is;* and *HASHEM shall reign.*

Cong. then Chazzan – **נְקַדֵּשׁ** *We shall sanctify Your Name in this world, just as they sanctify it in heaven above, as it is written by Your prophet, "And one [angel] will call another and say:*

All – *'Holy, holy, holy is* HASHEM, *Master of Legions, the whole world is filled with His glory.'"*[2]

Chazzan – *Those facing them say 'Blessed':*

All – *'Blessed is the glory of* HASHEM *from His place.'*[3]

Chazzan – *And in Your holy Writings the following is written:*

All – *'*HASHEM *shall reign forever — your God, O Zion — from generation to generation, Halleluyah!'*[4]

Chazzan only concludes – *From generation to generation we shall relate Your greatness and for infinite eternities we shall proclaim Your holiness. Your praise, our God, shall not leave our mouth forever and ever, for You, O God, are a great and holy King. Blessed are You,* HASHEM, *the holy God.*

Chazzan continues אַתָּה חוֹנֵן, *You graciously endow . . .* (above).

---

(1) Cf. *Psalms* 119:153-154. (2) *Isaiah* 6:3. (3) *Ezekiel* 3:12. (4) *Psalms* 146:10.

רפואה

רְפָאֵנוּ יהוה וְנֵרָפֵא, הוֹשִׁיעֵנוּ וְנִוָּשֵׁעָה, כִּי תְהִלָּתֵנוּ אָתָּה,[1] וְהַעֲלֵה רְפוּאָה שְׁלֵמָה לְכָל מַכּוֹתֵינוּ, °°כִּי אֵל מֶלֶךְ רוֹפֵא נֶאֱמָן וְרַחֲמָן אָתָּה. בָּרוּךְ אַתָּה יהוה, רוֹפֵא חוֹלֵי עַמּוֹ יִשְׂרָאֵל.

ברכת השנים

בָּרֵךְ עָלֵינוּ יהוה אֱלֹהֵינוּ אֶת הַשָּׁנָה הַזֹּאת וְאֶת כָּל מִינֵי תְבוּאָתָהּ לְטוֹבָה, וְתֵן בְּרָכָה עַל פְּנֵי הָאֲדָמָה, וְשַׂבְּעֵנוּ מִטּוּבֶךָ, וּבָרֵךְ שְׁנָתֵנוּ כַּשָּׁנִים הַטּוֹבוֹת. בָּרוּךְ אַתָּה יהוה, מְבָרֵךְ הַשָּׁנִים.

קיבוץ גליות

תְּקַע בְּשׁוֹפָר גָּדוֹל לְחֵרוּתֵנוּ, וְשָׂא נֵס לְקַבֵּץ גָּלֻיּוֹתֵינוּ, וְקַבְּצֵנוּ יַחַד מֵאַרְבַּע כַּנְפוֹת הָאָרֶץ.[2] בָּרוּךְ אַתָּה יהוה, מְקַבֵּץ נִדְחֵי עַמּוֹ יִשְׂרָאֵל.

דין

הָשִׁיבָה שׁוֹפְטֵינוּ כְּבָרִאשׁוֹנָה, וְיוֹעֲצֵינוּ כְּבַתְּחִלָּה,[3] וְהָסֵר מִמֶּנּוּ יָגוֹן וַאֲנָחָה, וּמְלוֹךְ עָלֵינוּ אַתָּה יהוה לְבַדְּךָ בְּחֶסֶד וּבְרַחֲמִים, וְצַדְּקֵנוּ בַּמִּשְׁפָּט. בָּרוּךְ אַתָּה יהוה, מֶלֶךְ אוֹהֵב צְדָקָה וּמִשְׁפָּט.

ברכת המינים

וְלַמַּלְשִׁינִים אַל תְּהִי תִקְוָה, וְכָל הָרִשְׁעָה כְּרֶגַע תֹּאבֵד, וְכָל אֹיְבֶיךָ מְהֵרָה יִכָּרֵתוּ, וְהַזֵּדִים מְהֵרָה תְעַקֵּר וּתְשַׁבֵּר וּתְמַגֵּר וְתַכְנִיעַ בִּמְהֵרָה בְיָמֵינוּ. בָּרוּךְ אַתָּה יהוה, שׁוֹבֵר אֹיְבִים וּמַכְנִיעַ זֵדִים.

צדיקים

עַל הַצַּדִּיקִים וְעַל הַחֲסִידִים, וְעַל זִקְנֵי עַמְּךָ בֵּית יִשְׂרָאֵל, וְעַל פְּלֵיטַת סוֹפְרֵיהֶם, וְעַל גֵּרֵי הַצֶּדֶק וְעָלֵינוּ, יֶהֱמוּ רַחֲמֶיךָ יהוה אֱלֹהֵינוּ, וְתֵן שָׂכָר טוֹב לְכָל

°°At this point one may interject a prayer for one who is ill:

יְהִי רָצוֹן מִלְּפָנֶיךָ יהוה אֱלֹהַי וֵאלֹהֵי אֲבוֹתַי, שֶׁתִּשְׁלַח מְהֵרָה רְפוּאָה שְׁלֵמָה מִן הַשָּׁמַיִם, רְפוּאַת הַנֶּפֶשׁ וּרְפוּאַת הַגּוּף

לַחוֹלֶה (patient's name) בֶּן (mother's name) בְּתוֹךְ שְׁאָר חוֹלֵי יִשְׂרָאֵל. —for a male

לַחוֹלָה (patient's name) בַּת (mother's name) בְּתוֹךְ שְׁאָר חוֹלֵי יִשְׂרָאֵל. —for a female

Continue—כִּי אֵל . . .

HEALTH AND HEALING

רְפָאֵנוּ *Heal us,* H*ASHEM — then we will be healed; save us — then we will be saved, for You are our praise.*[1] *Bring complete recovery for all our ailments,* °°*for You are God, King, the faithful and compassionate Healer. Blessed are You,* H*ASHEM, Who heals the sick of His people Israel.*

YEAR OF PROSPERITY

בָּרֵךְ *Bless on our behalf — O* H*ASHEM, our God — this year and all its kinds of crops for the best, and give a blessing on the face of the earth, and satisfy us from Your bounty, and bless our year like the best years. Blessed are You,* H*ASHEM, Who blesses the years.*

INGATHERING OF EXILES

תְּקַע *Sound the great shofar for our freedom, raise the banner to gather our exiles and gather us together from the four corners of the earth.*[2] *Blessed are You,* H*ASHEM, Who gathers in the dispersed of His people Israel.*

RESTORATION OF JUSTICE

הָשִׁיבָה *Restore our judges as in earliest times and our counselors as at first;*[3] *remove from us sorrow and groan; and reign over us — You,* H*ASHEM, alone — with kindness and compassion, and justify us through judgment. Blessed are You,* H*ASHEM, the King Who loves righteousness and judgment.*

AGAINST HERETICS

וְלַמַּלְשִׁינִים *And for slanderers let there be no hope; and may all wickedness perish in an instant; and may all Your enemies be cut down speedily. May You speedily uproot, smash, cast down, and humble the wanton sinners — speedily in our days. Blessed are You,* H*ASHEM, Who breaks enemies and humbles wanton sinners.*

THE RIGHTEOUS

עַל הַצַּדִּיקִים *On the righteous, on the devout, on the elders of Your people the Family of Israel, on the remnant of their scholars, on the righteous converts and on ourselves — may Your compassion be aroused,* H*ASHEM, our God, and give goodly reward to all*

°°At this point one may interject a prayer for one who is ill:

May it be Your will, H*ASHEM, my God, and the God of my forefathers, that You quickly send a complete recovery from heaven, spiritual healing and physical healing to the patient* (name) *son/daughter of* (mother's name) *among the other patients of Israel.* Continue: *For You are God . . .*

---

(1) Cf. *Jeremiah* 17:14. (2) Cf. *Isaiah* 11:12. (3) Cf. 1:26.

הַבּוֹטְחִים בְּשִׁמְךָ בֶּאֱמֶת, וְשִׂים חֶלְקֵנוּ עִמָּהֶם לְעוֹלָם, וְלֹא נֵבוֹשׁ כִּי בְךָ בָּטָחְנוּ. בָּרוּךְ אַתָּה יהוה, מִשְׁעָן וּמִבְטָח לַצַּדִּיקִים.

בנין ירושלים

וְלִירוּשָׁלַיִם עִירְךָ בְּרַחֲמִים תָּשׁוּב, וְתִשְׁכּוֹן בְּתוֹכָהּ כַּאֲשֶׁר דִּבַּרְתָּ, וּבְנֵה אוֹתָהּ בְּקָרוֹב בְּיָמֵינוּ בִּנְיַן עוֹלָם, וְכִסֵּא דָוִד מְהֵרָה לְתוֹכָהּ תָּכִין. בָּרוּךְ אַתָּה יהוה, בּוֹנֵה יְרוּשָׁלָיִם.

מלכות בית דוד

אֶת צֶמַח דָּוִד עַבְדְּךָ מְהֵרָה תַצְמִיחַ, וְקַרְנוֹ תָּרוּם בִּישׁוּעָתֶךָ, כִּי לִישׁוּעָתְךָ קִוִּינוּ כָּל הַיּוֹם. בָּרוּךְ אַתָּה יהוה, מַצְמִיחַ קֶרֶן יְשׁוּעָה.

קבלת תפלה

שְׁמַע קוֹלֵנוּ יהוה אֱלֹהֵינוּ, חוּס וְרַחֵם עָלֵינוּ, וְקַבֵּל בְּרַחֲמִים וּבְרָצוֹן אֶת תְּפִלָּתֵנוּ, כִּי אֵל שׁוֹמֵעַ תְּפִלּוֹת וְתַחֲנוּנִים אָתָּה. וּמִלְּפָנֶיךָ מַלְכֵּנוּ רֵיקָם אַל תְּשִׁיבֵנוּ, °° כִּי אַתָּה שׁוֹמֵעַ תְּפִלַּת עַמְּךָ יִשְׂרָאֵל בְּרַחֲמִים. בָּרוּךְ אַתָּה יהוה, שׁוֹמֵעַ תְּפִלָּה.

עבודה

רְצֵה יהוה אֱלֹהֵינוּ בְּעַמְּךָ יִשְׂרָאֵל וּבִתְפִלָּתָם, וְהָשֵׁב אֶת הָעֲבוֹדָה לִדְבִיר בֵּיתֶךָ. וְאִשֵּׁי יִשְׂרָאֵל וּתְפִלָּתָם בְּאַהֲבָה תְקַבֵּל בְּרָצוֹן, וּתְהִי לְרָצוֹן תָּמִיד עֲבוֹדַת יִשְׂרָאֵל עַמֶּךָ.

°°During the silent *Shemoneh Esrei* one may insert either or both of these personal prayers.

For forgiveness:

אָנָּא יהוה, חָטָאתִי עָוִיתִי וּפָשַׁעְתִּי לְפָנֶיךָ, מִיּוֹם הֱיוֹתִי עַל הָאֲדָמָה עַד הַיּוֹם הַזֶּה (וּבִפְרַט בַּחֵטְא ....). אָנָּא יהוה, עֲשֵׂה לְמַעַן שִׁמְךָ הַגָּדוֹל, וּתְכַפֶּר לִי עַל עֲוֹנַי וַחֲטָאַי וּפְשָׁעַי שֶׁחָטָאתִי וְשֶׁעָוִיתִי וְשֶׁפָּשַׁעְתִּי לְפָנֶיךָ, מִנְּעוּרַי עַד הַיּוֹם הַזֶּה. וּתְמַלֵּא כָּל הַשֵּׁמוֹת שֶׁפָּגַמְתִּי בְּשִׁמְךָ הַגָּדוֹל.

For livelihood:

אַתָּה הוּא יהוה הָאֱלֹהִים, הַזָּן וּמְפַרְנֵס וּמְכַלְכֵּל מִקַּרְנֵי רְאֵמִים עַד בֵּיצֵי כִנִּים. הַטְרִיפֵנִי לֶחֶם חֻקִּי, וְהַמְצֵא לִי וּלְכָל בְּנֵי בֵיתִי מְזוֹנוֹתַי קוֹדֶם שֶׁאֶצְטָרֵךְ לָהֶם, בְּנַחַת וְלֹא בְצַעַר, בְּהֶתֵּר וְלֹא בְאִסּוּר, בְּכָבוֹד וְלֹא בְבִזָּיוֹן, לְחַיִּים וּלְשָׁלוֹם, מִשֶּׁפַע בְּרָכָה וְהַצְלָחָה, וּמִשֶּׁפַע בְּרֵכָה עֶלְיוֹנָה, כְּדֵי שֶׁאוּכַל לַעֲשׂוֹת רְצוֹנֶךָ וְלַעֲסוֹק בְּתוֹרָתֶךָ וּלְקַיֵּם מִצְוֹתֶיךָ. וְאַל תַּצְרִיכֵנִי לִידֵי מַתְּנַת בָּשָׂר וָדָם. וִיקֻיַּם בִּי מִקְרָא שֶׁכָּתוּב: פּוֹתֵחַ אֶת יָדֶךָ, וּמַשְׂבִּיעַ לְכָל חַי רָצוֹן.[1] וְכָתוּב: הַשְׁלֵךְ עַל יהוה יְהָבְךָ וְהוּא יְכַלְכְּלֶךָ.[2]

Continue — כִּי אַתָּה . . .

who sincerely believe in Your Name. Put our lot with them forever, and we will not feel ashamed, for we trust in You. Blessed are You, HASHEM, Mainstay and Assurance of the righteous.

REBUILDING JERUSALEM

וְלִירוּשָׁלַיִם *And to Jerusalem, Your city, may You return in compassion, and may You rest within it, as You have spoken. May You rebuild it soon in our days as an eternal structure, and may You speedily establish the throne of David within it. Blessed are You, HASHEM, the Builder of Jerusalem.*

DAVIDIC REIGN

אֶת צֶמַח *The offspring of Your servant David may You speedily cause to flourish, and enhance his pride through Your salvation, for we hope for Your salvation all day long. Blessed are You, HASHEM, Who causes the pride of salvation to flourish.*

ACCEPTANCE OF PRAYER

שְׁמַע *Hear our voice, HASHEM our God, pity and be compassionate to us, and accept — with compassion and favor — our prayer, for God Who hears prayers and supplications are You. From before Yourself, our King, turn us not away empty-handed,* °° *for You hear the prayer of Your people Israel with compassion. Blessed are You, HASHEM, Who hears prayer.*

TEMPLE SERVICE

רְצֵה *Be favorable, HASHEM, our God, toward Your people Israel and their prayer and restore the service to the Holy of Holies of Your Temple. The fire-offerings of Israel and their prayer accept with love and favor, and may the service of Your people Israel always be favorable to You.*

°°During the silent *Shemoneh Esrei* one may insert either or both of these personal prayers.

For forgiveness:

אָנָּא *Please, O HASHEM, I have erred, been iniquitous, and willfully sinned before You, from the day I have existed on earth until this very day (and especially with the sin of . . .). Please, HASHEM, act for the sake of Your Great Name and grant me atonement for my iniquities, my errors, and my willful sins through which I have erred, been iniquitous, and willfully sinned before You, from my youth until this day. And make whole all the Names that I have blemished in Your Great Name.*

For livelihood:

אַתָּה *It is You, HASHEM the God, Who nourishes, sustains, and supports, from the horns of re'eimim to the eggs of lice. Provide me with my allotment of bread; and bring forth for me and all members of my household, my food, before I have need for it; in contentment but not in pain, in a permissible but not a forbidden manner, in honor but not in disgrace, for life and for peace; from the flow of blessing and success and from the flow of the Heavenly spring, so that I be enabled to do Your will and engage in Your Torah and fulfill Your commandments. Make me not needful of people's largesse; and may there be fulfilled in me the verse that states, 'You open Your hand and satisfy the desire of every living thing'[1] and that states, 'Cast Your burden upon HASHEM and He will support you.'[2]*

Continue: *For You hear the prayer . . .*

---

(1) *Psalms* 145:16. (2) 55:23.

During the *chazzan's* repetition, congregation responds אָמֵן as indicated.
[If paragraph is forgotten, repeat *Shemoneh Esrei*. See *Laws* §56.]

אֱלֹהֵינוּ וֵאלֹהֵי אֲבוֹתֵינוּ, יַעֲלֶה, וְיָבֹא, וְיַגִּיעַ, וְיֵרָאֶה, וְיֵרָצֶה, וְיִשָּׁמַע, וְיִפָּקֵד, וְיִזָּכֵר זִכְרוֹנֵנוּ וּפִקְדוֹנֵנוּ, וְזִכְרוֹן אֲבוֹתֵינוּ, וְזִכְרוֹן מָשִׁיחַ בֶּן דָּוִד עַבְדֶּךָ, וְזִכְרוֹן יְרוּשָׁלַיִם עִיר קָדְשֶׁךָ, וְזִכְרוֹן כָּל עַמְּךָ בֵּית יִשְׂרָאֵל לְפָנֶיךָ, לִפְלֵיטָה לְטוֹבָה לְחֵן וּלְחֶסֶד וּלְרַחֲמִים, לְחַיִּים וּלְשָׁלוֹם בְּיוֹם חַג הַסֻּכּוֹת הַזֶּה. זָכְרֵנוּ יהוה אֱלֹהֵינוּ בּוֹ לְטוֹבָה (.Cong – אָמֵן), וּפָקְדֵנוּ בוֹ לִבְרָכָה (.Cong – אָמֵן), וְהוֹשִׁיעֵנוּ בוֹ לְחַיִּים (.Cong – אָמֵן). וּבִדְבַר יְשׁוּעָה וְרַחֲמִים, חוּס וְחָנֵּנוּ וְרַחֵם עָלֵינוּ וְהוֹשִׁיעֵנוּ, כִּי אֵלֶיךָ עֵינֵינוּ, כִּי אֵל מֶלֶךְ חַנּוּן וְרַחוּם אָתָּה.[1]

וְתֶחֱזֶינָה עֵינֵינוּ בְּשׁוּבְךָ לְצִיּוֹן בְּרַחֲמִים. בָּרוּךְ אַתָּה יהוה, הַמַּחֲזִיר שְׁכִינָתוֹ לְצִיּוֹן.

הודאה

Bow at מוֹדִים; straighten up at 'ה. In his repetition the *chazzan* should recite the entire מוֹדִים aloud, while the congregation recites מוֹדִים דְּרַבָּנָן softly.

מוֹדִים אֲנַחְנוּ לָךְ, שָׁאַתָּה הוּא יהוה אֱלֹהֵינוּ וֵאלֹהֵי אֲבוֹתֵינוּ לְעוֹלָם וָעֶד. צוּר חַיֵּינוּ, מָגֵן יִשְׁעֵנוּ אַתָּה הוּא לְדוֹר וָדוֹר. נוֹדֶה לְּךָ וּנְסַפֵּר תְּהִלָּתֶךָ[2] עַל חַיֵּינוּ הַמְּסוּרִים בְּיָדֶךָ, וְעַל נִשְׁמוֹתֵינוּ הַפְּקוּדוֹת לָךְ, וְעַל נִסֶּיךָ שֶׁבְּכָל יוֹם עִמָּנוּ, וְעַל נִפְלְאוֹתֶיךָ וְטוֹבוֹתֶיךָ שֶׁבְּכָל עֵת, עֶרֶב וָבֹקֶר וְצָהֳרָיִם. הַטּוֹב כִּי לֹא כָלוּ רַחֲמֶיךָ, וְהַמְּרַחֵם כִּי לֹא תַמּוּ חֲסָדֶיךָ,[3] מֵעוֹלָם קִוִּינוּ לָךְ.

מודים דרבנן

מוֹדִים אֲנַחְנוּ לָךְ, שָׁאַתָּה הוּא יהוה אֱלֹהֵינוּ וֵאלֹהֵי אֲבוֹתֵינוּ, אֱלֹהֵי כָל בָּשָׂר, יוֹצְרֵנוּ, יוֹצֵר בְּרֵאשִׁית. בְּרָכוֹת וְהוֹדָאוֹת לְשִׁמְךָ הַגָּדוֹל וְהַקָּדוֹשׁ, עַל שֶׁהֶחֱיִיתָנוּ וְקִיַּמְתָּנוּ. כֵּן תְּחַיֵּנוּ וּתְקַיְּמֵנוּ, וְתֶאֱסוֹף גָּלֻיּוֹתֵינוּ לְחַצְרוֹת קָדְשֶׁךָ, לִשְׁמוֹר חֻקֶּיךָ וְלַעֲשׂוֹת רְצוֹנֶךָ, וּלְעָבְדְּךָ בְּלֵבָב שָׁלֵם, עַל שֶׁאֲנַחְנוּ מוֹדִים לָךְ. בָּרוּךְ אֵל הַהוֹדָאוֹת.

During the *chazzan's* repetition, congregation responds *Amen* as indicated.
[If paragraph is forgotten, repeat *Shemoneh Esrei*. See *Laws* §56.]

אֱלֹהֵינוּ *Our God and God of our forefathers, may there rise, come, reach, be noted, be favored, be heard, be considered, and be remembered — the remembrance and consideration of ourselves; the remembrance of our forefathers; the remembrance of Messiah, son of David, Your servant; the remembrance of Jerusalem, the City of Your Holiness; the remembrance of Your entire people the Family of Israel — before You for deliverance, for goodness, for grace, for kindness, and for compassion, for life, and for peace on this day of the Festival of Succos. Remember us on it,* HASHEM, *our God, for goodness* (Cong.—*Amen*)*; consider us on it for blessing* (Cong.—*Amen*)*; and help us on it for life* (Cong.—*Amen*)*. In the matter of salvation and compassion, pity, be gracious and compassionate with us and help us, for our eyes are turned to You, because You are God, the gracious and compassionate King.*[1]

וְתֶחֱזֶינָה *May our eyes behold Your return to Zion in compassion. Blessed are You,* HASHEM, *Who restores His Presence unto Zion.*

THANKSGIVING [MODIM]

Bow at *'We gratefully thank You'*; straighten up at *'HASHEM.'* In his repetition the *chazzan* should recite the entire *Modim* aloud, while the congregation recites *Modim of the Rabbis* softly.

מוֹדִים *We gratefully thank You, for it is You Who are* HASHEM, *our God and the God of our forefathers for all eternity; Rock of our lives, Shield of our salvation are You from generation to generation. We shall thank You and relate Your praise*[2] *— for our lives, which are committed to Your power and for our souls that are entrusted to You; for Your miracles that are with us every day; and for Your wonders and favors in every season — evening, morning, and afternoon. The Beneficent One, for Your compassions were never exhausted, and the Compassionate One, for Your kindnesses never ended*[3] *— always have we put our hope in You.*

MODIM OF THE RABBIS

מוֹדִים *We gratefully thank You, for it is You Who are* HASHEM, *our God and the God of our forefathers, the God of all flesh, our Molder, the Molder of the universe. Blessings and thanks are due Your great and holy Name for You have given us life and sustained us. So may You continue to give us life and sustain us and gather our exiles to the Courtyards of Your Sanctuary, to observe Your decrees, to do Your will and to serve You wholeheartedly. [We thank You] for inspiring us to thank You. Blessed is the God of thanksgivings.*

(1) Cf. *Nechemiah* 9:31. (2) Cf. *Psalms* 79:13. (3) Cf. *Lamentations* 3:22.

וְעַל כֻּלָּם יִתְבָּרַךְ וְיִתְרוֹמַם שִׁמְךָ מַלְכֵּנוּ תָּמִיד לְעוֹלָם וָעֶד.

Bend the knees at בָּרוּךְ; bow at אַתָּה; straighten up at ה׳.

וְכֹל הַחַיִּים יוֹדוּךָ סֶּלָה, וִיהַלְלוּ אֶת שִׁמְךָ בֶּאֱמֶת, הָאֵל יְשׁוּעָתֵנוּ וְעֶזְרָתֵנוּ סֶלָה. בָּרוּךְ אַתָּה יהוה, הַטּוֹב שִׁמְךָ וּלְךָ נָאֶה לְהוֹדוֹת.

שלום

שָׁלוֹם רָב עַל יִשְׂרָאֵל עַמְּךָ תָּשִׂים לְעוֹלָם, כִּי אַתָּה הוּא מֶלֶךְ אָדוֹן לְכָל הַשָּׁלוֹם. וְטוֹב בְּעֵינֶיךָ לְבָרֵךְ אֶת עַמְּךָ יִשְׂרָאֵל, בְּכָל עֵת וּבְכָל שָׁעָה בִּשְׁלוֹמֶךָ. בָּרוּךְ אַתָּה יהוה, הַמְּבָרֵךְ אֶת עַמּוֹ יִשְׂרָאֵל בַּשָּׁלוֹם.

יִהְיוּ לְרָצוֹן אִמְרֵי פִי וְהֶגְיוֹן לִבִּי לְפָנֶיךָ, יהוה צוּרִי וְגֹאֲלִי.[1]

Chazzan's repetition of *Shemoneh Esrei* ends here. Individuals continue below.

אֱלֹהַי, נְצוֹר לְשׁוֹנִי מֵרָע, וּשְׂפָתַי מִדַּבֵּר מִרְמָה,[2] וְלִמְקַלְלַי נַפְשִׁי תִדּוֹם, וְנַפְשִׁי כֶּעָפָר לַכֹּל תִּהְיֶה. פְּתַח לִבִּי בְּתוֹרָתֶךָ, וּבְמִצְוֹתֶיךָ תִּרְדּוֹף נַפְשִׁי. וְכֹל הַחוֹשְׁבִים עָלַי רָעָה, מְהֵרָה הָפֵר עֲצָתָם וְקַלְקֵל מַחֲשַׁבְתָּם. עֲשֵׂה לְמַעַן שְׁמֶךָ, עֲשֵׂה לְמַעַן יְמִינֶךָ, עֲשֵׂה לְמַעַן קְדֻשָּׁתֶךָ, עֲשֵׂה לְמַעַן תּוֹרָתֶךָ. לְמַעַן יֵחָלְצוּן יְדִידֶיךָ, הוֹשִׁיעָה יְמִינְךָ וַעֲנֵנִי.[3]

Some recite verses pertaining to their names. See page 1301.

יִהְיוּ לְרָצוֹן אִמְרֵי פִי וְהֶגְיוֹן לִבִּי לְפָנֶיךָ, יהוה צוּרִי וְגֹאֲלִי.[1]

Bow and take three steps back. Bow left and say . . . עֹשֶׂה, bow right and say . . . הוּא יַעֲשֶׂה; bow forward and say וְעַל כָּל . . . אָמֵן.

עֹשֶׂה שָׁלוֹם בִּמְרוֹמָיו, הוּא יַעֲשֶׂה שָׁלוֹם עָלֵינוּ, וְעַל כָּל יִשְׂרָאֵל. וְאִמְרוּ: אָמֵן.

יְהִי רָצוֹן מִלְּפָנֶיךָ יהוה אֱלֹהֵינוּ וֵאלֹהֵי אֲבוֹתֵינוּ, שֶׁיִּבָּנֶה בֵּית הַמִּקְדָּשׁ בִּמְהֵרָה בְיָמֵינוּ, וְתֵן חֶלְקֵנוּ בְּתוֹרָתֶךָ. וְשָׁם נַעֲבָדְךָ בְּיִרְאָה, כִּימֵי עוֹלָם וּכְשָׁנִים קַדְמוֹנִיּוֹת. וְעָרְבָה לַיהוה מִנְחַת יְהוּדָה וִירוּשָׁלָיִם, כִּימֵי עוֹלָם וּכְשָׁנִים קַדְמוֹנִיּוֹת.[4]

THE INDIVIDUAL'S RECITATION OF שְׁמוֹנֶה עֶשְׂרֵה ENDS HERE.

The individual remains standing in place until the *chazzan* reaches *Kedushah* — or at least until the *chazzan* begins his repetition — then he takes three steps forward. The *chazzan* himself, or one praying alone, should remain in place for a few moments before taking three steps forward.

For all these, may Your Name be blessed and exalted, our King, continually forever and ever.

Bend the knees at *'Blessed'*; bow at *'You'*; straighten up at *'HASHEM.'*

Everything alive will gratefully acknowledge You, Selah! and praise Your Name sincerely, O God of our salvation and help, Selah! Blessed are You, HASHEM, Your Name is 'The Beneficent One' and to You it is fitting to give thanks.

PEACE

שָׁלוֹם *Establish abundant peace upon Your people Israel forever, for You are King, Master of all peace. May it be good in Your eyes to bless Your people Israel at every time and every hour with Your peace. Blessed are You, HASHEM, Who blesses His people Israel with peace.*

May the expressions of my mouth and the thoughts of my heart find favor before You, HASHEM, my Rock and my Redeemer.[1]

Chazzan's repetition of *Shemoneh Esrei* ends here. Individuals continue below.

אֱלֹהַי *My God, guard my tongue from evil and my lips from speaking deceitfully.*[2] *To those who curse me, let my soul be silent; and let my soul be like dust to everyone. Open my heart to Your Torah, then my soul will pursue Your commandments. As for all those who design evil against me, speedily nullify their counsel and disrupt their design. Act for Your Name's sake; act for Your right hand's sake; act for Your sanctity's sake; act for Your Torah's sake. That Your beloved ones may be given rest; let Your right hand save, and respond to me.*[3]

Some recite verses pertaining to their names at this point. See page 1301.

May the expressions of my mouth and the thoughts of my heart find favor before You, HASHEM, my Rock and my Redeemer.[1] *He Who makes peace in His heights, may He make peace upon us, and upon all Israel. Now respond: Amen.*

Bow and take three steps back. Bow left and say, *'He Who makes peace . . .'*; bow right and say, *'may He make peace . . .'*; bow forward and say, *'and upon . . . Amen.'*

יְהִי רָצוֹן *May it be Your will, HASHEM, our God and the God of our forefathers, that the Holy Temple be rebuilt, speedily in our days. Grant us our share in Your Torah, and may we serve You there with reverence, as in days of old and in former years. Then the offering of Judah and Jerusalem will be pleasing to HASHEM, as in days of old and in former years.*[4]

THE INDIVIDUAL'S RECITATION OF *SHEMONEH ESREI* ENDS HERE.

The individual remains standing in place until the *chazzan* reaches *Kedushah* – or at least until the *chazzan* begins his repetition – then he takes three steps forward. The *chazzan* himself, or one praying alone, should remain in place for a few moments before taking three steps forward.

---

(1) *Psalms* 19:15. (2) Cf. 34:14. (3) 60:7;108:7. (4) *Malachi* 3:4.

קדיש שלם

The *chazzan* recites קַדִּישׁ שָׁלֵם.

יִתְגַּדַּל וְיִתְקַדַּשׁ שְׁמֵהּ רַבָּא. (.Cong – אָמֵן.) בְּעָלְמָא דִּי בְרָא כִרְעוּתֵהּ. וְיַמְלִיךְ מַלְכוּתֵהּ, בְּחַיֵּיכוֹן וּבְיוֹמֵיכוֹן וּבְחַיֵּי דְכָל בֵּית יִשְׂרָאֵל, בַּעֲגָלָא וּבִזְמַן קָרִיב. וְאִמְרוּ: אָמֵן.

(.Cong – אָמֵן. יְהֵא שְׁמֵהּ רַבָּא מְבָרַךְ לְעָלַם וּלְעָלְמֵי עָלְמַיָּא.)

יְהֵא שְׁמֵהּ רַבָּא מְבָרַךְ לְעָלַם וּלְעָלְמֵי עָלְמַיָּא.

יִתְבָּרַךְ וְיִשְׁתַּבַּח וְיִתְפָּאַר וְיִתְרוֹמַם וְיִתְנַשֵּׂא וְיִתְהַדָּר וְיִתְעַלֶּה וְיִתְהַלָּל שְׁמֵהּ דְּקֻדְשָׁא בְּרִיךְ הוּא (.Cong – בְּרִיךְ הוּא) – לְעֵלָּא מִן כָּל בִּרְכָתָא וְשִׁירָתָא תֻּשְׁבְּחָתָא וְנֶחֱמָתָא, דַּאֲמִירָן בְּעָלְמָא. וְאִמְרוּ: אָמֵן. (.Cong – אָמֵן.)

(.Cong – קַבֵּל בְּרַחֲמִים וּבְרָצוֹן אֶת תְּפִלָּתֵנוּ.)

תִּתְקַבֵּל צְלוֹתְהוֹן וּבָעוּתְהוֹן דְּכָל בֵּית יִשְׂרָאֵל קֳדָם אֲבוּהוֹן דִּי בִשְׁמַיָּא. וְאִמְרוּ: אָמֵן. (.Cong – אָמֵן.)

(.Cong – יְהִי שֵׁם יהוה מְבֹרָךְ, מֵעַתָּה וְעַד עוֹלָם.[1])

יְהֵא שְׁלָמָא רַבָּא מִן שְׁמַיָּא, וְחַיִּים עָלֵינוּ וְעַל כָּל יִשְׂרָאֵל. וְאִמְרוּ: אָמֵן. (.Cong – אָמֵן.)

(.Cong – עֶזְרִי מֵעִם יהוה, עֹשֵׂה שָׁמַיִם וָאָרֶץ.[2])

Take three steps back. Bow left and say . . . עֹשֶׂה; bow right and say . . . הוּא; bow forward and say וְעַל כָּל . . . אָמֵן. Remain standing in place for a few moments, then take three steps forward.

עֹשֶׂה שָׁלוֹם בִּמְרוֹמָיו, הוּא יַעֲשֶׂה שָׁלוֹם עָלֵינוּ, וְעַל כָּל יִשְׂרָאֵל. וְאִמְרוּ: אָמֵן. (.Cong – אָמֵן.)

עלינו

Stand while reciting עָלֵינוּ.

עָלֵינוּ לְשַׁבֵּחַ לַאֲדוֹן הַכֹּל, לָתֵת גְּדֻלָּה לְיוֹצֵר בְּרֵאשִׁית, שֶׁלֹּא עָשָׂנוּ כְּגוֹיֵי הָאֲרָצוֹת, וְלֹא שָׂמָנוּ כְּמִשְׁפְּחוֹת הָאֲדָמָה. שֶׁלֹּא שָׂם חֶלְקֵנוּ כָּהֶם, וְגוֹרָלֵנוּ כְּכָל הֲמוֹנָם. (שֶׁהֵם מִשְׁתַּחֲוִים לְהֶבֶל וָרִיק, וּמִתְפַּלְּלִים אֶל אֵל לֹא יוֹשִׁיעַ.[3]) וַאֲנַחְנוּ כּוֹרְעִים וּמִשְׁתַּחֲוִים וּמוֹדִים, לִפְנֵי מֶלֶךְ מַלְכֵי הַמְּלָכִים הַקָּדוֹשׁ בָּרוּךְ הוּא. שֶׁהוּא נוֹטֶה שָׁמַיִם וְיֹסֵד אָרֶץ,[4] וּמוֹשַׁב יְקָרוֹ בַּשָּׁמַיִם מִמַּעַל, וּשְׁכִינַת עֻזּוֹ בְּגָבְהֵי מְרוֹמִים. הוּא אֱלֹהֵינוּ, אֵין עוֹד. אֱמֶת מַלְכֵּנוּ, אֶפֶס זוּלָתוֹ, כַּכָּתוּב בְּתוֹרָתוֹ: וְיָדַעְתָּ הַיּוֹם וַהֲשֵׁבֹתָ אֶל לְבָבֶךָ, כִּי יהוה הוּא הָאֱלֹהִים בַּשָּׁמַיִם מִמַּעַל וְעַל הָאָרֶץ מִתָּחַת, אֵין עוֹד.[5]

Bow while reciting וַאֲנַחְנוּ כּוֹרְעִים וּמִשְׁתַּחֲוִים.

FULL KADDISH

The *chazzan* recites the Full *Kaddish*.

יִתְגַּדַּל *May His great Name grow exalted and sanctified* (Cong.– *Amen.*) *in the world that He created as He willed. May He give reign to His kingship in your lifetimes and in your days, and in the lifetimes of the entire Family of Israel, swiftly and soon. Now respond: Amen.*

(Cong.– *Amen. May His great Name be blessed forever and ever.*)
May His great Name be blessed forever and ever.

Blessed, praised, glorified, exalted, extolled, mighty, upraised, and lauded be the Name of the Holy One, Blessed is He (Cong.– *Blessed is He*) *— beyond any blessing and song, praise and consolation that are uttered in the world. Now respond: Amen.* (Cong.– *Amen.*)

(Cong.– *Accept our prayers with mercy and favor.*)

May the prayers and supplications of the entire Family of Israel be accepted before their Father Who is in Heaven. Now respond: Amen. (Cong.– *Amen.*)

(Cong.– *Blessed be the Name of* HASHEM, *from this time and forever.*[1])

May there be abundant peace from Heaven, and life, upon us and upon all Israel. Now respond: Amen. (Cong.– *Amen.*)

(Cong.– *My help is from* HASHEM, *Maker of heaven and earth.*[2])

Take three steps back. Bow left and say, *'He Who makes peace . . .'*; bow right and say, *'may He . . .'*; bow forward and say, *'and upon all Israel . . .'* Remain standing in place for a few moments, then take three steps forward.

He Who makes peace in His heights, may He make peace upon us, and upon all Israel. Now respond: Amen. (Cong.– *Amen.*)

ALEINU

Stand while reciting עָלֵינוּ, *'It is our duty . . .'*

עָלֵינוּ *It is our duty to praise the Master of all, to ascribe greatness to the Molder of primeval creation, for He has not made us like the nations of the lands, and has not emplaced us like the families of the earth; for He has not assigned our portion like theirs nor our lot like all their multitudes. (For they bow to vanity and emptiness and pray to a god which helps not.*[3]*) But we bend our knees, bow, and acknowledge our thanks before the King Who reigns over kings, the Holy One, Blessed is He. He stretches out heaven and establishes earth's foundation,*[4] *the seat of His homage is in the heavens above and His powerful Presence is in the loftiest heights. He is our God and there is none other. True is our King, there is nothing beside Him, as it is written in His Torah: 'You are to know this day and take to your heart that* HASHEM *is the only God — in heaven above and on the earth below — there is none other.'*[5]

Bow while reciting *'But we bend our knees.'*

(1) *Psalms* 113:2. (2) 121:2. (3) *Isaiah* 45:20. (4) 51:13. (5) *Deuteronomy* 4:39.

עַל כֵּן נְקַוֶּה לְּךָ יהוה אֱלֹהֵינוּ לִרְאוֹת מְהֵרָה בְּתִפְאֶרֶת עֻזֶּךָ, לְהַעֲבִיר גִּלּוּלִים מִן הָאָרֶץ, וְהָאֱלִילִים כָּרוֹת יִכָּרֵתוּן, לְתַקֵּן עוֹלָם בְּמַלְכוּת שַׁדַּי. וְכָל בְּנֵי בָשָׂר יִקְרְאוּ בִשְׁמֶךָ, לְהַפְנוֹת אֵלֶיךָ כָּל רִשְׁעֵי אָרֶץ. יַכִּירוּ וְיֵדְעוּ כָּל יוֹשְׁבֵי תֵבֵל, כִּי לְךָ תִּכְרַע כָּל בֶּרֶךְ, תִּשָּׁבַע כָּל לָשׁוֹן.[1] לְפָנֶיךָ יהוה אֱלֹהֵינוּ יִכְרְעוּ וְיִפֹּלוּ, וְלִכְבוֹד שִׁמְךָ יְקָר יִתֵּנוּ. וִיקַבְּלוּ כֻלָּם אֶת עוֹל מַלְכוּתֶךָ, וְתִמְלֹךְ עֲלֵיהֶם מְהֵרָה לְעוֹלָם וָעֶד. כִּי הַמַּלְכוּת שֶׁלְּךָ הִיא וּלְעוֹלְמֵי עַד תִּמְלוֹךְ בְּכָבוֹד, כַּכָּתוּב בְּתוֹרָתֶךָ: יהוה יִמְלֹךְ לְעֹלָם וָעֶד.[2] ❖ וְנֶאֱמַר: וְהָיָה יהוה לְמֶלֶךְ עַל כָּל הָאָרֶץ, בַּיּוֹם הַהוּא יִהְיֶה יהוה אֶחָד וּשְׁמוֹ אֶחָד.[3]

Some congregations recite the following after עָלֵינוּ.

אַל תִּירָא מִפַּחַד פִּתְאֹם, וּמִשֹּׁאַת רְשָׁעִים כִּי תָבֹא.[4] עֻצוּ עֵצָה וְתֻפָר, דַּבְּרוּ דָבָר וְלֹא יָקוּם, כִּי עִמָּנוּ אֵל.[5] וְעַד זִקְנָה אֲנִי הוּא, וְעַד שֵׂיבָה אֲנִי אֶסְבֹּל, אֲנִי עָשִׂיתִי וַאֲנִי אֶשָּׂא, וַאֲנִי אֶסְבֹּל וַאֲמַלֵּט.[6]

קדיש יתום

In the presence of a *minyan*, mourners recite קַדִּישׁ יָתוֹם, the Mourner's *Kaddish* (see *Laws* §81-83).

יִתְגַּדַּל וְיִתְקַדַּשׁ שְׁמֵהּ רַבָּא. (.Cong. – אָמֵן) בְּעָלְמָא דִּי בְרָא כִרְעוּתֵהּ. וְיַמְלִיךְ מַלְכוּתֵהּ, בְּחַיֵּיכוֹן וּבְיוֹמֵיכוֹן וּבְחַיֵּי דְכָל בֵּית יִשְׂרָאֵל, בַּעֲגָלָא וּבִזְמַן קָרִיב. וְאִמְרוּ: אָמֵן.

(.Cong. – אָמֵן. יְהֵא שְׁמֵהּ רַבָּא מְבָרַךְ לְעָלַם וּלְעָלְמֵי עָלְמַיָּא.)

יְהֵא שְׁמֵהּ רַבָּא מְבָרַךְ לְעָלַם וּלְעָלְמֵי עָלְמַיָּא.

יִתְבָּרַךְ וְיִשְׁתַּבַּח וְיִתְפָּאַר וְיִתְרוֹמַם וְיִתְנַשֵּׂא וְיִתְהַדָּר וְיִתְעַלֶּה וְיִתְהַלָּל שְׁמֵהּ דְּקֻדְשָׁא בְּרִיךְ הוּא (.Cong. – בְּרִיךְ הוּא) – לְעֵלָּא מִן כָּל בִּרְכָתָא וְשִׁירָתָא תֻּשְׁבְּחָתָא וְנֶחֱמָתָא, דַּאֲמִירָן בְּעָלְמָא. וְאִמְרוּ: אָמֵן. (.Cong. – אָמֵן)

יְהֵא שְׁלָמָא רַבָּא מִן שְׁמַיָּא, וְחַיִּים עָלֵינוּ וְעַל כָּל יִשְׂרָאֵל. וְאִמְרוּ: אָמֵן. (.Cong. – אָמֵן)

Take three steps back. Bow left and say . . . עֹשֶׂה; bow right and say . . . הוּא; bow forward and say וְעַל כָּל . . . אָמֵן. Remain standing in place for a few moments, then take three steps forward.

עֹשֶׂה שָׁלוֹם בִּמְרוֹמָיו, הוּא יַעֲשֶׂה שָׁלוֹם עָלֵינוּ, וְעַל כָּל יִשְׂרָאֵל. וְאִמְרוּ: אָמֵן. (.Cong. – אָמֵן)

עַל כֵּן *Therefore we put our hope in You, HASHEM, our God, that we may soon see Your mighty splendor, to remove detestable idolatry from the earth, and false gods will be utterly cut off, to perfect the universe through the Almighty's sovereignty. Then all humanity will call upon Your Name, to turn all the earth's wicked toward You. All the world's inhabitants will recognize and know that to You every knee should bend, every tongue should swear.*[1] *Before You, HASHEM, our God, they will bend every knee and cast themselves down and to the glory of Your Name they will render homage, and they will all accept upon themselves the yoke of Your kingship that You may reign over them soon and eternally. For the kingdom is Yours and You will reign for all eternity in glory as it is written in Your Torah: HASHEM shall reign for all eternity.*[2] Chazzan– *And it is said: HASHEM will be King over all the world — on that day HASHEM will be One and His Name will be One.*[3]

Some congregations recite the following after *Aleinu.*

אַל תִּירָא *Do not fear sudden terror, or the holocaust of the wicked when it comes.*[4] *Plan a conspiracy and it will be annulled; speak your piece and it shall not stand, for God is with us.*[5] *Even till your seniority, I remain unchanged; and even till your ripe old age, I shall endure. I created you and I shall bear you; I shall endure and rescue.*[6]

MOURNER'S KADDISH

In the presence of a *minyan,* mourners recite קַדִּישׁ יָתוֹם, the Mourner's *Kaddish* (see *Laws* 81-83).
[A transliteration of this *Kaddish* appears on page 1305.]

יִתְגַּדַּל *May His great Name grow exalted and sanctified* (Cong.– *Amen.*) *in the world that He created as He willed. May He give reign to His kingship in your lifetimes and in your days, and in the lifetimes of the entire Family of Israel, swiftly and soon. Now respond: Amen.*

(Cong.– *Amen. May His great Name be blessed forever and ever.*)

May His great Name be blessed forever and ever.

Blessed, praised, glorified, exalted, extolled, mighty, upraised, and lauded be the Name of the Holy One, Blessed is He (Cong.– *Blessed is He*) *— beyond any blessing and song, praise and consolation that are uttered in the world. Now respond: Amen.* (Cong.– *Amen*).

May there be abundant peace from Heaven, and life, upon us and upon all Israel. Now respond: Amen. (Cong.– *Amen.*)

Take three steps back. Bow left and say, *'He Who makes peace . . .';* bow right and say, *'may He . . .';* bow forward and say, *'and upon all Israel . . .'* Remain standing in place for a few moments, then take three steps forward.

He Who makes peace in His heights, may He make peace upon us, and upon all Israel. Now respond: Amen. (Cong.– *Amen.*)

---

(1) Cf. *Isaiah* 45:23. (2) *Exodus* 15:18. (3) *Zechariah* 14:9.
(4) *Proverbs* 3:25. (5) *Isaiah* 8:10. (6) 46:4.

◈ שמיני עצרת

◈ Shemini Atzeres

ערוב תבשילין

When Shemini Atzeres and Simchas Torah fall on Thursday and Friday, an *eruv tavshilin* is made on Wednesday Hoshana Rabbah [see commentary]. The *eruv*-foods are held while the following blessing and declaration are recited.

בָּרוּךְ אַתָּה יהוה אֱלֹהֵינוּ מֶלֶךְ הָעוֹלָם, אֲשֶׁר קִדְּשָׁנוּ בְּמִצְוֹתָיו, וְצִוָּנוּ עַל מִצְוַת עֵרוּב.

בַּהֲדֵין עֵרוּבָא יְהֵא שָׁרֵא לָנָא לַאֲפוּיֵי וּלְבַשּׁוּלֵי וּלְאַטְמוּנֵי וּלְאַדְלוּקֵי שְׁרָגָא וּלְתַקָּנָא וּלְמֶעְבַּד כָּל צָרְכָּנָא, מִיּוֹמָא טָבָא לְשַׁבְּתָא [לָנָא וּלְכָל יִשְׂרָאֵל* הַדָּרִים בָּעִיר הַזֹּאת].

ערובי תחומין

The *eruv*-food is put in a safe place [see commentary] and the following blessing and declaration are recited. The appropriate bracketed phrases should be added.

בָּרוּךְ אַתָּה יהוה אֱלֹהֵינוּ מֶלֶךְ הָעוֹלָם, אֲשֶׁר קִדְּשָׁנוּ בְּמִצְוֹתָיו, וְצִוָּנוּ עַל מִצְוַת עֵרוּב.

בְּזֶה הָעֵרוּב יְהֵא מֻתָּר [לִי/לָנוּ] לֵילֵךְ מִמָּקוֹם זֶה אַלְפַּיִם אַמָּה לְכָל רוּחַ בְּ[שַׁבָּת וּבְ]יוֹם טוֹב זֶה.

ערובי חצרות

This *eruv* is required for the Sabbath, but not for a weekday Festival [see commentary]. The *eruv*-foods are held while the following blessing and declaration are recited. [If the *eruv* is made for the entire year, the bracketed passage is added.]

בָּרוּךְ אַתָּה יהוה אֱלֹהֵינוּ מֶלֶךְ הָעוֹלָם, אֲשֶׁר קִדְּשָׁנוּ בְּמִצְוֹתָיו, וְצִוָּנוּ עַל מִצְוַת עֵרוּב.

בַּהֲדֵין עֵרוּבָא יְהֵא שָׁרֵא לָנָא לְאַפּוּקֵי וּלְעַיּוּלֵי מִן הַבָּתִּים לֶחָצֵר, וּמִן הֶחָצֵר לְבָתִּים, וּמִבַּיִת לְבַיִת, וּמֵחָצֵר לְחָצֵר, וּמִגַּג לְגַג, כָּל מַאי דִצְרִיךְ לָן, וּלְכָל יִשְׂרָאֵל הַדָּרִים בַּשְּׁכוּנָה זוּ [וּלְכָל מִי שֶׁיִּתּוֹסֵף בָּהּ, לְכָל שַׁבְּתוֹת הַשָּׁנָה, וּלְכָל יָמִים טוֹבִים].

עֵרוּב תַּבְשִׁילִין / ERUV TAVSHILIN

The Biblical prohibition against labor on the Festivals *(Exodus* 12:16) specifically excludes preparation of food. Still, it is forbidden to prepare food on a Festival for use on another day. When a Festival falls on Friday, however, it is permitted to prepare food needed for the Sabbath. But since this may lead people to think that they may even cook in preparation for a weekday, the Rabbis attached a condition to the preparation of Sabbath meals on a Festival — i.e., such preparations must be started before the Festival *(Pesachim* 46b). Thus, when *Yom Tov* falls on Thursday and Friday, preparations for the Sabbath meal must begin on Wednesday. This enactment is called *eruv tavshilin,* literally, *mingling of cooked foods.* It consists of a *challah, matzah,* or loaf of bread, along with any other cooked food (such as fish, meat or an egg), set aside on the day before the Festival to be eaten on the Sabbath. The *eruv*-foods are held in the hand *(Orach Chaim* 527:2) and a blessing is recited. Since the person setting the *eruv* must understand its purpose, the accompanying declaration [beginning בַּהֲדֵין, *'Through this . . .'*] must be said in a language he understands.

וּלְכָל יִשְׂרָאֵל — *And for all Jews.* The bracketed phrase is recited only if the maker of the *eruv*

ERUV TAVSHILIN

When Shemini Atzeres and Simchas Torah fall on Thursday and Friday, an *eruv tavshilin* is made on Wednesday Hoshana Rabbah [see commentary]. The *eruv*-foods are held while the following blessing and declaration are recited.

בָּרוּךְ *Blessed are You, HASHEM, our God, King of the universe, Who has sanctified us with His commandments and has commanded us concerning the mitzvah of eruv.*

בַּהֲדֵין *Through this eruv may we be permitted to bake, cook, insulate, kindle flame, prepare, and do anything necessary on the Festival for the sake of the Sabbath [for ourselves and for all Jews* who live in this city].*

ERUVEI TECHUMIN

The *eruv*-food is put in a safe place [see commentary] and the following blessing and declaration are recited. The appropriate bracketed phrases should be added.

בָּרוּךְ *Blessed are You, HASHEM, our God, King of the universe, Who has sanctified us with His commandments and has commanded us concerning the mitzvah of eruv.*

בְּזֶה *Through this eruv may [I/we] be permitted to walk two thousand cubits in every direction from this place during this [Sabbath and] Festival.*

ERUVEI CHATZEIROS

This *eruv* is required for the Sabbath, but not for a weekday Festival [see commentary]. The *eruv*-foods are held while the following blessing and declaration are recited. [If the *eruv* is made for the entire year, the bracketed passage is added.]

בָּרוּךְ *Blessed are You, HASHEM, our God, King of the universe, Who has sanctified us with His commandments and has commanded us concerning the mitzvah of eruv.*

בַּהֲדֵין *Through this eruv may we be permitted to carry out or to carry in from the houses to the courtyard, and from the courtyard to the houses, from house to house, from courtyard to courtyard, and from roof to roof, all that we require, for ourselves and for all Jews who live in this area [and to all who will move into this area, for all the Sabbaths and Festivals of the year].*

---

wishes to include those who may not have made an *eruv* for themselves. If so, a second person (not the minor child of the maker) must act as agent for the townspeople and take possession of the *eruv*-foods on their behalf.

עֵרוּבֵי תְחוּמִין / MERGING OF BOUNDARIES

On the Sabbath and Festivals, one is forbidden to go more than 2,000 cubits from his halachically defined dwelling. This limit is called his תְּחוּם, *boundary*. Ordinarily, this 'dwelling' is the town in which one resides, but one has the option of establishing his dwelling elsewhere. By placing a sufficient amount of food for two Sabbath meals in a place as much as 2,000 cubits from his 'dwelling', one establishes *that* place as his 'dwelling', and his 2,000-cubit radius is reckoned from there. [For a full discussion of *eruvei chatzeiros* and *techumin*, see the Introduction to the ArtScroll Mishnah *Eruvin.*]

עֵרוּבֵי חֲצֵרוֹת / MERGING OF COURTYARDS

The Sages forbade carrying from the private domain of one person to that of another on the Sabbath. Similarly a courtyard, hall, or staircase shared by the residents of houses or apartments is regarded as a separate domain, and it is forbidden to carry from the private dwellings into the shared area. The Sages also provided a procedure to remove this prohibition against carrying. Known as *eruvei chatzeiros*, or the

⁂ הדלקת הנרות ⁂

On Shemini Atzeres and Simchas Torah two blessings are recited. When *Yom Tov* coincides with the Sabbath, light the candles, then cover the eyes and recite the blessings. Uncover the eyes and gaze briefly at the candles. When *Yom Tov* falls on a weekday, some follow the above procedure, while others recite the blessings before lighting the candles. When *Yom Tov* coincides with the Sabbath, the words in brackets are added.

[It is forbidden to create a new flame — for example, by striking a match — on *Yom Tov*. Therefore, on the second night the candles must be lit from a flame that has been burning from before *Yom Tov*.]

בָּרוּךְ אַתָּה יהוה אֱלֹהֵינוּ מֶלֶךְ הָעוֹלָם, אֲשֶׁר קִדְּשָׁנוּ בְּמִצְוֹתָיו, וְצִוָּנוּ לְהַדְלִיק נֵר* שֶׁל [שַׁבָּת וְשֶׁל] יוֹם טוֹב.*

בָּרוּךְ אַתָּה יהוה אֱלֹהֵינוּ מֶלֶךְ הָעוֹלָם, שֶׁהֶחֱיָנוּ* וְקִיְּמָנוּ וְהִגִּיעָנוּ לַזְּמַן הַזֶּה.

It is customary to recite the following prayer after the kindling. The words in brackets are included as they apply.

יְהִי רָצוֹן* לְפָנֶיךָ, יהוה אֱלֹהַי וֵאלֹהֵי אֲבוֹתַי, שֶׁתְּחוֹנֵן אוֹתִי [וְאֶת אִישִׁי, וְאֶת בָּנַי, וְאֶת בְּנוֹתַי, וְאֶת אָבִי, וְאֶת אִמִּי] וְאֶת כָּל קְרוֹבַי; וְתִתֶּן לָנוּ וּלְכָל יִשְׂרָאֵל חַיִּים טוֹבִים וַאֲרוּכִים; וְתִזְכְּרֵנוּ בְּזִכְרוֹן טוֹבָה וּבְרָכָה; וְתִפְקְדֵנוּ בִּפְקֻדַּת יְשׁוּעָה וְרַחֲמִים; וּתְבָרְכֵנוּ בְּרָכוֹת גְּדוֹלוֹת; וְתַשְׁלִים בָּתֵּינוּ; וְתַשְׁכֵּן שְׁכִינָתְךָ בֵּינֵינוּ. וְזַכֵּנִי לְגַדֵּל בָּנִים וּבְנֵי בָנִים חֲכָמִים וּנְבוֹנִים, אוֹהֲבֵי יהוה, יִרְאֵי אֱלֹהִים, אַנְשֵׁי אֱמֶת, זֶרַע קֹדֶשׁ, בַּיהוה דְּבֵקִים, וּמְאִירִים אֶת הָעוֹלָם בַּתּוֹרָה וּבְמַעֲשִׂים טוֹבִים, וּבְכָל מְלֶאכֶת עֲבוֹדַת הַבּוֹרֵא. אָנָּא שְׁמַע אֶת תְּחִנָּתִי בָּעֵת הַזֹּאת, בִּזְכוּת שָׂרָה וְרִבְקָה וְרָחֵל וְלֵאָה אִמּוֹתֵינוּ, וְהָאֵר נֵרֵנוּ שֶׁלֹּא יִכְבֶּה לְעוֹלָם וָעֶד, וְהָאֵר פָּנֶיךָ וְנִוָּשֵׁעָה. אָמֵן.

'merging of courtyards,' this procedure considers all houses opening into the shared area as owned by a single consortium. This is done by collecting bread or *matzah* from each of the families and placing all the loaves in one of the dwelling units. [Even if only one person supplies the bread, it is still possible to make an *eruv*. In this case, a second person (not the minor child of the donor) must act as agent for all those involved and take possession of the bread on their behalf.] This symbolizes that all the contributors are legal residents of the unit where they have deposited their bread, and the entire area is regarded as a single dwelling. All the residents may carry in all its parts on the Sabbath, as long as the breads were intact and edible at the onset of the Sabbath. [The declaration as given here may not be used if the *eruv* area includes a public thoroughfare. Such an area requires complex additional procedures which should not be undertaken by a layman.]

The restrictions on carrying apply only to the Sabbath and not to the Festivals. Thus, *eruvei chatzeiros* is only necessary for *Yom Tov* that falls on the Sabbath but not for the other days of the Festival.

⁂ הַדְלָקַת הַנֵּרוֹת / KINDLING LIGHTS ⁂

Since women generally look after household matters, the *mitzvah* of kindling the lights has devolved upon the mistress of the house *(Rambam)*. Nevertheless, a man living alone is required to kindle the lights and recite the proper blessing. Similarly, if a woman is too ill to light, her husband should light the candles and recite the blessing *(Magen Avraham)*.

KINDLING LIGHTS

On Shemini Atzeres and Simchas Torah two blessings are recited. When *Yom Tov* coincides with the Sabbath, light the candles, then cover the eyes and recite the blessings. Uncover the eyes and gaze briefly at the candles. When *Yom Tov* falls on a weekday, some follow the above procedure, while others recite the blessings before lighting the candles. When *Yom Tov* coincides with the Sabbath, the words in brackets are added.

[It is forbidden to create a new flame — for example, by striking a match — on *Yom Tov*. Therefore, on the second night the candles must be lit from a flame that has been burning from before *Yom Tov*.]

בָּרוּךְ *Blessed are You, HASHEM, our God, King of the universe, Who has sanctified us with His commandments, and has commanded us to kindle the light* of [the Sabbath and of] the Festival.**

בָּרוּךְ *Blessed are You, HASHEM, our God, King of the universe, Who has kept us alive,* sustained us, and brought us to this season.*

It is customary to recite the following prayer after the kindling. The words in brackets are included as they apply.

יְהִי רָצוֹן *May it be Your will,* HASHEM, my God and God of my forefathers, that You show favor to me [my husband, my sons, my daughters, my father, my mother] and all my relatives; and that You grant us and all Israel a good and long life; that You remember us with a beneficent memory and blessing; that You consider us with a consideration of salvation and compassion; that You bless us with great blessings; that You make our households complete; that You cause Your Presence to dwell among us. Privilege me to raise children and grandchildren who are wise and understanding, who love HASHEM and fear God, people of truth, holy offspring, attached to HASHEM, who illuminate the world with Torah and good deeds and with every labor in the service of the Creator. Please, hear my supplication at this time, in the merit of Sarah, Rebecca, Rachel, and Leah, our mothers, and cause our light to illuminate that it be not extinguished forever, and let Your countenance shine so that we are saved. Amen.*

There should be some light in every room where it will be needed—and indeed this is a halachic requirement—nevertheless, the blessing is recited upon the flames that are kindled in the dining room (*Mishnah Berurah*). The lights honor the Sabbath and Festival by brightening and dignifying the festive meal (*Rashi*).

נֵר — *The light.* Prevalent custom calls for at least two candles. According to *Eliyah Rabbah,* they symbolize man and wife. Nevertheless, since one can fulfill the *mitzvah* with a single candle [indeed, *Mishnah Berurah* advises one with extremely limited means to purchase one good candle rather than two inferior ones] the blessing is couched in the singular form, נֵר, *light,* and not נֵרוֹת, *lights.*

שֶׁל [שַׁבָּת וְשֶׁל] יוֹם טוֹב — *Of [the Sabbath and of] the Festival.* The Sabbath is mentioned first, following the Talmudic rule that a more frequently performed *mitzvah* takes precedence over a less frequent one.

שֶׁהֶחֱיָנוּ — *Who has kept us alive.* Some authorities rule that women should not recite the שֶׁהֶחֱיָנוּ blessing at this point, but instead should listen to the blessing during *Kiddush,* as does the rest of the family. However, it is a virtually universal custom that women do recite the blessing when kindling the lights.

יְהִי רָצוֹן — *May it be Your will.* It is customary to recite this prayer after the kindling. Because of the Talmudic declaration, 'One who is scrupulous in the kindling of lights will be blessed with children who are Torah scholars' (*Shabbos* 23b), the prayer stresses the supplication that the children of the home grow up learned and righteous.

WHEN SHEMINI ATZERES FALLS ON A WEEKDAY, TURN TO *MAARIV,* PAGE 850.

❀ קבלת שבת ❀

When Shemini Atzeres coincides with the Sabbath, *Kabbalas Shabbos* [our acceptance upon ourselves of the holiness of the Sabbath] consists of Psalms 92 and 93.

תהלים צב

מִזְמוֹר שִׁיר לְיוֹם הַשַּׁבָּת. טוֹב לְהֹדוֹת לַיהוה, וּלְזַמֵּר לְשִׁמְךָ עֶלְיוֹן. לְהַגִּיד בַּבֹּקֶר חַסְדֶּךָ, וֶאֱמוּנָתְךָ בַּלֵּילוֹת. עֲלֵי עָשׂוֹר וַעֲלֵי נָבֶל, עֲלֵי הִגָּיוֹן בְּכִנּוֹר. כִּי שִׂמַּחְתַּנִי יהוה בְּפָעֳלֶךָ, בְּמַעֲשֵׂי יָדֶיךָ אֲרַנֵּן. מַה גָּדְלוּ מַעֲשֶׂיךָ יהוה, מְאֹד עָמְקוּ מַחְשְׁבֹתֶיךָ. אִישׁ בַּעַר לֹא יֵדָע, וּכְסִיל לֹא יָבִין אֶת זֹאת. בִּפְרֹחַ רְשָׁעִים כְּמוֹ עֵשֶׂב, וַיָּצִיצוּ כָּל פֹּעֲלֵי אָוֶן, לְהִשָּׁמְדָם עֲדֵי עַד. וְאַתָּה מָרוֹם לְעֹלָם יהוה. כִּי הִנֵּה אֹיְבֶיךָ יהוה, כִּי הִנֵּה אֹיְבֶיךָ יֹאבֵדוּ, יִתְפָּרְדוּ כָּל פֹּעֲלֵי אָוֶן. וַתָּרֶם כִּרְאֵים קַרְנִי, בַּלֹּתִי בְּשֶׁמֶן רַעֲנָן. וַתַּבֵּט עֵינִי בְּשׁוּרָי, בַּקָּמִים עָלַי מְרֵעִים, תִּשְׁמַעְנָה אָזְנָי. ❖ צַדִּיק כַּתָּמָר יִפְרָח, כְּאֶרֶז בַּלְּבָנוֹן יִשְׂגֶּה. שְׁתוּלִים בְּבֵית יהוה, בְּחַצְרוֹת אֱלֹהֵינוּ יַפְרִיחוּ. עוֹד יְנוּבוּן בְּשֵׂיבָה, דְּשֵׁנִים וְרַעֲנַנִּים יִהְיוּ. לְהַגִּיד כִּי יָשָׁר יהוה, צוּרִי וְלֹא עַוְלָתָה בּוֹ.

תהלים צג

יהוה מָלָךְ גֵּאוּת לָבֵשׁ, לָבֵשׁ יהוה עֹז הִתְאַזָּר, אַף תִּכּוֹן תֵּבֵל בַּל תִּמּוֹט. נָכוֹן כִּסְאֲךָ מֵאָז, מֵעוֹלָם אָתָּה. נָשְׂאוּ נְהָרוֹת, יהוה, נָשְׂאוּ נְהָרוֹת קוֹלָם, יִשְׂאוּ נְהָרוֹת דָּכְיָם. ❖ מִקֹּלוֹת מַיִם רַבִּים אַדִּירִים מִשְׁבְּרֵי יָם, אַדִּיר בַּמָּרוֹם יהוה. עֵדֹתֶיךָ נֶאֶמְנוּ מְאֹד לְבֵיתְךָ נַאֲוָה קֹדֶשׁ, יהוה, לְאֹרֶךְ יָמִים.

Mourners recite קַדִּישׁ יָתוֹם, the Mourner's *Kaddish* (see *Laws* §81-83).

יִתְגַּדַּל וְיִתְקַדַּשׁ שְׁמֵהּ רַבָּא. (.Cong – אָמֵן.) בְּעָלְמָא דִּי בְרָא כִרְעוּתֵהּ. וְיַמְלִיךְ מַלְכוּתֵהּ, בְּחַיֵּיכוֹן וּבְיוֹמֵיכוֹן וּבְחַיֵּי דְכָל בֵּית יִשְׂרָאֵל, בַּעֲגָלָא וּבִזְמַן קָרִיב. וְאִמְרוּ: אָמֵן.

(.Cong – אָמֵן. יְהֵא שְׁמֵהּ רַבָּא מְבָרַךְ לְעָלַם וּלְעָלְמֵי עָלְמַיָּא.)

יְהֵא שְׁמֵהּ רַבָּא מְבָרַךְ לְעָלַם וּלְעָלְמֵי עָלְמַיָּא.

יִתְבָּרַךְ וְיִשְׁתַּבַּח וְיִתְפָּאַר וְיִתְרוֹמַם וְיִתְנַשֵּׂא וְיִתְהַדָּר וְיִתְעַלֶּה וְיִתְהַלָּל שְׁמֵהּ דְּקֻדְשָׁא בְּרִיךְ הוּא (.Cong – בְּרִיךְ הוּא) — לְעֵלָּא מִן כָּל בִּרְכָתָא וְשִׁירָתָא תֻּשְׁבְּחָתָא וְנֶחֱמָתָא, דַּאֲמִירָן בְּעָלְמָא. וְאִמְרוּ: אָמֵן. (.Cong – אָמֵן.)

יְהֵא שְׁלָמָא רַבָּא מִן שְׁמַיָּא, וְחַיִּים עָלֵינוּ וְעַל כָּל יִשְׂרָאֵל. וְאִמְרוּ: אָמֵן. (.Cong – אָמֵן.)

Take three steps back. Bow left and say . . . עֹשֶׂה; bow right and say . . . הוּא; bow forward and say וְעַל כָּל . . . אָמֵן. Remain standing in place for a few moments, then take three steps forward.

עֹשֶׂה שָׁלוֹם בִּמְרוֹמָיו, הוּא יַעֲשֶׂה שָׁלוֹם עָלֵינוּ, וְעַל כָּל יִשְׂרָאֵל. וְאִמְרוּ: אָמֵן. (.Cong – אָמֵן.)

WHEN SHEMINI ATZERES FALLS ON A WEEKDAY, TURN TO *MAARIV*, PAGE 850.

KABBALAS SHABBOS

When Shemini Atzeres coincides with the Sabbath, *Kabbalas Shabbos* [our acceptance upon ourselves of the holiness of the Sabbath] consists of Psalms 92 and 93.

Psalm 92

מִזְמוֹר שִׁיר *A psalm, a song for the Sabbath day. It is good to thank HASHEM and to sing praise to Your Name, O Exalted One; to relate Your kindness in the dawn and Your faith in the nights. Upon ten-stringed instrument and lyre, with singing accompanied by a harp. For You have gladdened me, HASHEM, with Your deeds; at the works of Your Hands I sing glad song. How great are Your deeds, HASHEM; exceedingly profound are Your thoughts. A boor cannot know, nor can a fool understand this: when the wicked bloom like grass and all the doers of iniquity blossom — it is to destroy them till eternity. But You remain exalted forever, HASHEM. For behold! — Your enemies, HASHEM, for behold! — Your enemies shall perish, dispersed shall be all doers of iniquity. As exalted as a re'eim's shall be my pride, I will be saturated with ever-fresh oil. My eyes have seen my vigilant foes; when those who would harm me rise up against me, my ears have heard their doom.* Chazzan– *A righteous man will flourish like a date palm, like a cedar in the Lebanon he will grow tall. Planted in the house of HASHEM, in the courtyards of our God they will flourish. They will still be fruitful in old age, vigorous and fresh they will be — to declare that HASHEM is just, my Rock in Whom there is no wrong.*

Psalm 93

יהוה מָלָךְ *HASHEM will have reigned, He will have donned grandeur; He will have donned might and girded Himself; even firmed the world that it should not falter. Your throne was established from of old; eternal are You. Like rivers they raised, O HASHEM, like rivers they raised their voice; like rivers they shall raise their destructiveness.* Chazzan– *More than the roars of many waters, mightier than the waves of the sea — You are mighty on high, HASHEM. Your testimonies about Your House, the Sacred Dwelling are exceedingly trustworthy — O HASHEM, may it be for lengthy days.*

Mourners recite the Mourner's *Kaddish* (see *Laws* §81-83).
[A transliteration of this *Kaddish* appears on page 1305.]

יִתְגַּדַּל *May His great Name grow exalted and sanctified* (Cong.– *Amen.*) *in the world that He created as He willed. May He give reign to His kingship in your lifetimes and in your days, and in the lifetimes of the entire Family of Israel, swiftly and soon. Now respond: Amen.*

(Cong.– *Amen. May His great Name be blessed forever and ever.*)

May His great Name be blessed forever and ever.

Blessed, praised, glorified, exalted, extolled, mighty, upraised, and lauded be the Name of the Holy One, Blessed is He (Cong.– *Blessed is He*) *— beyond any blessing and song, praise and consolation that are uttered in the world. Now respond: Amen.* (Cong. – *Amen.*)

May there be abundant peace from Heaven, and life, upon us and upon all Israel. Now respond: Amen. (Cong.– *Amen.*)

Take three steps back. Bow left and say, *'He Who makes peace . . .'*; bow right and say, *'may He . . .'*; bow forward and say, *'and upon all Israel . . .'* Remain standing in place for a few moments, then take three steps forward.

He Who makes peace in His heights, may He make peace upon us, and upon all Israel. Now respond: Amen. (Cong.– *Amen.*)

מעריב לשמיני עצרת

In some congregations the *chazzan* chants a melody during his recitation of בָּרְכוּ so that the congregation can then recite יִתְבָּרַךְ.

Chazzan bows at בָּרְכוּ and straightens up at ה׳.

בָּרְכוּ אֶת יהוה הַמְּבֹרָךְ.

Congregation, followed by *chazzan,* responds, bowing at בָּרוּךְ and straightening up at ה׳.

בָּרוּךְ יהוה הַמְּבֹרָךְ לְעוֹלָם וָעֶד.

יִתְבָּרַךְ[1] וְיִשְׁתַּבַּח וְיִתְפָּאַר וְיִתְרוֹמַם וְיִתְנַשֵּׂא שְׁמוֹ שֶׁל מֶלֶךְ מַלְכֵי הַמְּלָכִים, הַקָּדוֹשׁ בָּרוּךְ הוּא. שֶׁהוּא רִאשׁוֹן וְהוּא אַחֲרוֹן, וּמִבַּלְעָדָיו אֵין אֱלֹהִים.[2] סֹלּוּ, לָרֹכֵב בָּעֲרָבוֹת, בְּיָהּ שְׁמוֹ, וְעִלְזוּ לְפָנָיו.[3] וּשְׁמוֹ מְרוֹמַם עַל כָּל בְּרָכָה וּתְהִלָּה.[4] בָּרוּךְ שֵׁם כְּבוֹד מַלְכוּתוֹ לְעוֹלָם וָעֶד. יְהִי שֵׁם יהוה מְבֹרָךְ, מֵעַתָּה וְעַד עוֹלָם.[5]

ברכות קריאת שמע

בָּרוּךְ אַתָּה יהוה אֱלֹהֵינוּ מֶלֶךְ הָעוֹלָם, אֲשֶׁר בִּדְבָרוֹ מַעֲרִיב עֲרָבִים, בְּחָכְמָה פּוֹתֵחַ שְׁעָרִים, וּבִתְבוּנָה מְשַׁנֶּה עִתִּים, וּמַחֲלִיף אֶת הַזְּמַנִּים, וּמְסַדֵּר אֶת הַכּוֹכָבִים בְּמִשְׁמְרוֹתֵיהֶם בָּרָקִיעַ כִּרְצוֹנוֹ. בּוֹרֵא יוֹם וָלָיְלָה, גּוֹלֵל אוֹר מִפְּנֵי חֹשֶׁךְ וְחֹשֶׁךְ מִפְּנֵי אוֹר. וּמַעֲבִיר יוֹם וּמֵבִיא לָיְלָה, וּמַבְדִּיל בֵּין יוֹם וּבֵין לָיְלָה, יהוה צְבָאוֹת שְׁמוֹ. ❖ אֵל חַי וְקַיָּם, תָּמִיד יִמְלוֹךְ עָלֵינוּ, לְעוֹלָם וָעֶד.

אַעֲנִיד* לְךָ תִּפְאָרָה וְהַלֵּל, **בְּ**יוֹם שְׁמִינִי הָעֲצֶרֶת בְּלֵיל,
גְּבוּרוֹתֶיךָ בְּרָב עָם אֲמַלֵּל,[6] **ד**וֹד מַעֲבִיר יוֹם וּמֵבִיא לֵיל.

בָּרוּךְ אַתָּה יהוה, הַמַּעֲרִיב עֲרָבִים. (Cong.— אָמֵן.)

אַהֲבַת עוֹלָם בֵּית יִשְׂרָאֵל עַמְּךָ אָהָבְתָּ. תּוֹרָה וּמִצְוֹת, חֻקִּים וּמִשְׁפָּטִים, אוֹתָנוּ לִמַּדְתָּ. עַל כֵּן יהוה אֱלֹהֵינוּ, בְּשָׁכְבֵנוּ וּבְקוּמֵנוּ נָשִׂיחַ בְּחֻקֶּיךָ, וְנִשְׂמַח בְּדִבְרֵי תוֹרָתֶךָ, וּבְמִצְוֹתֶיךָ לְעוֹלָם וָעֶד. ❖ כִּי הֵם חַיֵּינוּ, וְאֹרֶךְ יָמֵינוּ, וּבָהֶם נֶהְגֶּה יוֹמָם וָלָיְלָה. וְאַהֲבָתְךָ, אַל תָּסִיר מִמֶּנּוּ לְעוֹלָמִים.

הַזָּכֵר* לְעַטְּרֵנוּ בִּשְׁנַת טוֹבוֹתֶיךָ,[7] **וְ**נִרְוֶה מִדֶּשֶׁן בֵּיתֶךָ,[8]
זְכֹר לְדוֹרְשֶׁיךָ יוֹשְׁבֵי בֵיתֶךָ, **חֶ**סֶד נְעוּרִים* וְכְלוּל אַהֲבָתֶךָ.[9]

בָּרוּךְ אַתָּה יהוה, אוֹהֵב עַמּוֹ יִשְׂרָאֵל. (Cong.— אָמֵן.)

(1) See *Orach Chaim* 57:1 (2) Cf. *Isaiah* 44:6. (3) *Psalms* 68:5. (4) Cf. *Nechemiah* 9:5. (5) *Psalms* 113:2. (6) Cf. 106:2. (7) Cf. 65:12. (8) Cf. 36:9. (9) Cf. *Jeremiah* 2:2.

אַעֲנִיד — *I shall crown.* The *piyutim* for *Maariv* of Shemini Atzeres were composed by R' Daniel bar Yaakov, an otherwise unknown *paytan* who wrote early in the thirteenth century. As expected, they discuss the day itself as well as the preceding days of Succos. Additionally, correlations are drawn between this *mitzvah* of שְׁמִינִי, *the eighth,* and other *mitzvos* involving the number eight.

The *piyut* contains five short stanzas that are

MAARIV FOR SHEMINI ATZERES

In some congregations the *chazzan* chants a melody during his recitation of *Borchu* so that the congregation can then recite *'Blessed, praised . . .'*

Chazzan bows at *'Bless'* and straightens up at *'HASHEM.'*

Bless HASHEM, the blessed One.

Congregation, followed by *chazzan*, responds, bowing at *'Blessed'* and straightening up at *'HASHEM.'*

Blessed is HASHEM, the blessed One, for all eternity.

Blessed,[1] *praised, glorified, exalted and upraised is the Name of the King Who rules over kings — the Holy One, Blessed is He. For He is the First and He is the Last and aside from Him there is no god.*[2] *Extol Him — Who rides the highest heavens — with His Name, YAH, and exult before Him.*[3] *His Name is exalted beyond every blessing and praise.*[4] *Blessed is the Name of His glorious kingdom for all eternity. Blessed be the Name of HASHEM from this time and forever.*[5]

BLESSINGS OF THE SHEMA

בָּרוּךְ *Blessed are You, HASHEM, our God, King of the universe, Who by His word brings on evenings, with wisdom opens gates, with understanding alters periods, changes the seasons, and orders the stars in their heavenly constellations as He wills. He creates day and night, removing light before darkness and darkness before light. He causes day to pass and brings night, and separates between day and night — HASHEM, Master of Legions, is His Name.* Chazzan– *May the living and enduring God continuously reign over us, for all eternity.*

א *I shall crown* You with glory and praise,*
ב *In the evening of the eighth day of assembly,*
ג *Your strength I shall relate*[6] *among the multitude of people;*
ד *O Beloved, Who causes day to pass and brings night.*

Blessed are You, HASHEM, Who brings on evenings. (Cong.– *Amen.*)

אַהֲבַת *With an eternal love have You loved the House of Israel, Your nation. Torah and commandments, decrees and ordinances have You taught us. Therefore HASHEM, our God, upon our retiring and arising, we will discuss Your decrees and we will rejoice with the words of Your Torah and with Your commandments for all eternity.* Chazzan– *For they are our life and the length of our days and about them we will meditate day and night. May You not remove Your love from us forever.*

ה *Remember* to crown us in this year of Your goodness,*[7]
ו *Sate us with the abundance of Your house.*[8]
ז *For those who seek You, those who dwell in Your house, remember*
ח *The kindness of youth,* and the nuptials of Your love.*[9]

Blessed are You, HASHEM, Who loves His nation Israel. (Cong.– *Amen.*)

---

distributed through the regular *Maariv* service. The initial letters of their verses form an *aleph-beis* acrostic. A longer piece of twenty-three verses is interposed in the paragraph beginning אֱמֶת וֶאֱמוּנָה, *True and faithful.*

הִזָּכֵר – *Remember.* this stanza paraphrases two verse from *Psalms* that speak of the heavenly blessing of rain. Thus, it alludes to the prayer for rain recited at this point during the *Mussaf* service of Shemini Atzeres (see p. 980).

שמע

Immediately before its recitation concentrate on fulfilling the positive commandment of reciting the *Shema* twice daily. It is important to enunciate each word clearly and not to run words together. For this reason, vertical lines have been placed between two words that are prone to be slurred into one and are not separated by a comma or a hyphen. See *Laws* §40-52.

When praying without a *minyan,* begin with the following three-word formula:

אֵל מֶלֶךְ נֶאֱמָן.

Recite the first verse aloud, with the right hand covering the eyes, and concentrate intently upon accepting God's absolute sovereignty.

שְׁמַע ׀ יִשְׂרָאֵל, יהוה ׀ אֱלֹהֵינוּ, יהוה ׀ אֶחָד:

In an undertone – בָּרוּךְ שֵׁם כְּבוֹד מַלְכוּתוֹ לְעוֹלָם וָעֶד.

While reciting the first paragraph (דברים ו:ה-ט), concentrate on accepting the commandment to love God.

וְאָהַבְתָּ אֵת ׀ יהוה ׀ אֱלֹהֶיךָ, בְּכָל-לְבָבְךָ, וּבְכָל-נַפְשְׁךָ, וּבְכָל-מְאֹדֶךָ: וְהָיוּ הַדְּבָרִים הָאֵלֶּה, אֲשֶׁר ׀ אָנֹכִי מְצַוְּךָ הַיּוֹם, עַל-לְבָבֶךָ: וְשִׁנַּנְתָּם לְבָנֶיךָ, וְדִבַּרְתָּ בָּם, בְּשִׁבְתְּךָ בְּבֵיתֶךָ, וּבְלֶכְתְּךָ בַדֶּרֶךְ, וּבְשָׁכְבְּךָ וּבְקוּמֶךָ: וּקְשַׁרְתָּם לְאוֹת ׀ עַל-יָדֶךָ, וְהָיוּ לְטֹטָפֹת בֵּין ׀ עֵינֶיךָ: וּכְתַבְתָּם ׀ עַל-מְזֻזוֹת בֵּיתֶךָ, וּבִשְׁעָרֶיךָ:

While reciting the second paragraph (דברים יא:יג-כא), concentrate on accepting all the commandments and the concept of reward and punishment.

וְהָיָה, אִם-שָׁמֹעַ תִּשְׁמְעוּ אֶל-מִצְוֹתַי, אֲשֶׁר ׀ אָנֹכִי מְצַוֶּה ׀ אֶתְכֶם הַיּוֹם, לְאַהֲבָה אֶת-יהוה ׀ אֱלֹהֵיכֶם וּלְעָבְדוֹ, בְּכָל-לְבַבְכֶם, וּבְכָל-נַפְשְׁכֶם: וְנָתַתִּי מְטַר-אַרְצְכֶם בְּעִתּוֹ, יוֹרֶה וּמַלְקוֹשׁ, וְאָסַפְתָּ דְגָנֶךָ וְתִירֹשְׁךָ וְיִצְהָרֶךָ: וְנָתַתִּי ׀ עֵשֶׂב ׀ בְּשָׂדְךָ לִבְהֶמְתֶּךָ, וְאָכַלְתָּ וְשָׂבָעְתָּ: הִשָּׁמְרוּ לָכֶם, פֶּן-יִפְתֶּה לְבַבְכֶם, וְסַרְתֶּם וַעֲבַדְתֶּם ׀ אֱלֹהִים ׀ אֲחֵרִים, וְהִשְׁתַּחֲוִיתֶם לָהֶם: וְחָרָה ׀ אַף-יהוה בָּכֶם, וְעָצַר ׀ אֶת-הַשָּׁמַיִם, וְלֹא-יִהְיֶה מָטָר, וְהָאֲדָמָה לֹא תִתֵּן אֶת-יְבוּלָהּ, וַאֲבַדְתֶּם ׀ מְהֵרָה מֵעַל הָאָרֶץ הַטֹּבָה ׀ אֲשֶׁר ׀ יהוה נֹתֵן לָכֶם: וְשַׂמְתֶּם ׀ אֶת-דְּבָרַי ׀ אֵלֶּה, עַל-לְבַבְכֶם וְעַל-נַפְשְׁכֶם, וּקְשַׁרְתֶּם ׀ אֹתָם לְאוֹת ׀ עַל-יֶדְכֶם, וְהָיוּ לְטוֹטָפֹת בֵּין ׀ עֵינֵיכֶם: וְלִמַּדְתֶּם ׀ אֹתָם ׀ אֶת-בְּנֵיכֶם, לְדַבֵּר בָּם, בְּשִׁבְתְּךָ בְּבֵיתֶךָ, וּבְלֶכְתְּךָ בַדֶּרֶךְ, וּבְשָׁכְבְּךָ וּבְקוּמֶךָ: וּכְתַבְתָּם ׀ עַל-מְזוּזוֹת בֵּיתֶךָ, וּבִשְׁעָרֶיךָ: לְמַעַן ׀ יִרְבּוּ ׀ יְמֵיכֶם וִימֵי בְנֵיכֶם, עַל הָאֲדָמָה ׀ אֲשֶׁר נִשְׁבַּע ׀ יהוה לַאֲבֹתֵיכֶם לָתֵת לָהֶם, כִּימֵי הַשָּׁמַיִם ׀ עַל-הָאָרֶץ:

במדבר טו:לז-מא

וַיֹּאמֶר ׀ יהוה ׀ אֶל-מֹשֶׁה לֵּאמֹר: דַּבֵּר ׀ אֶל-בְּנֵי ׀ יִשְׂרָאֵל, וְאָמַרְתָּ אֲלֵהֶם, וְעָשׂוּ לָהֶם צִיצִת, עַל-כַּנְפֵי בִגְדֵיהֶם

THE SHEMA

Immediately before its recitation concentrate on fulfilling the positive commandment of reciting the *Shema* twice daily. It is important to enunciate each word clearly and not to run words together. See *Laws* §40-52.

When praying without a *minyan,* begin with the following three-word formula:

God, trustworthy King.

Recite the first verse aloud, with the right hand covering the eyes, and concentrate intently upon accepting God's absolute sovereignty.

Hear, O Israel: HASHEM is our God, HASHEM, the One and Only.[1]

In an undertone— *Blessed is the Name of His glorious kingdom for all eternity.*

While reciting the first paragraph (*Deuteronomy* 6:5-9) concentrate on accepting the commandment to love God.

וְאָהַבְתָּ *You shall love HASHEM, your God, with all your heart, with all your soul and with all your resources. Let these matters that I command you today be upon your heart. Teach them thoroughly to your children and speak of them while you sit in your home, while you walk on the way, when you retire and when you arise. Bind them as a sign upon your arm and let them be tefillin between your eyes. And write them on the doorposts of your house and upon your gates.*

While reciting the second paragraph (*Deuteronomy* 11:13-21), concentrate on accepting all the commandments and the concept of reward and punishment.

וְהָיָה *And it will come to pass that if you continually hearken to My commandments that I command you today, to love HASHEM, your God, and to serve Him, with all your heart and with all your soul — then I will provide rain for your land in its proper time, the early and late rains, that you may gather in your grain, your wine, and your oil. I will provide grass in your field for your cattle and you will eat and be satisfied. Beware lest your heart be seduced and you turn astray and serve gods of others and bow to them. Then the wrath of HASHEM will blaze against you. He will restrain the heaven so there will be no rain and the ground will not yield its produce. And you will swiftly be banished from the goodly land which HASHEM gives you. Place these words of Mine upon your heart and upon your soul; bind them for a sign upon your arm and let them be tefillin between your eyes. Teach them to your children, to discuss them, while you sit in your home, while you walk on the way, when you retire and when you arise. And write them on the doorposts of your house and upon your gates. In order to prolong your days and the days of your children upon the ground that HASHEM has sworn to your ancestors to give them, like the days of the heaven on the earth.*

Numbers 15:37-41

וַיֹּאמֶר *And HASHEM said to Moses saying: Speak to the Children of Israel and say to them that they are to make themselves tzitzis*

(1) *Deuteronomy* 6:4.

לְדֹרֹתָם, וְנָתְנוּ | עַל־צִיצִת הַכָּנָף, פְּתִיל תְּכֵלֶת: וְהָיָה לָכֶם לְצִיצִת, וּרְאִיתֶם | אֹתוֹ, וּזְכַרְתֶּם | אֶת־כָּל־מִצְוֹת | יהוה, וַעֲשִׂיתֶם | אֹתָם, וְלֹא תָתוּרוּ | אַחֲרֵי לְבַבְכֶם וְאַחֲרֵי | עֵינֵיכֶם, אֲשֶׁר־אַתֶּם זֹנִים | אַחֲרֵיהֶם: לְמַעַן תִּזְכְּרוּ, וַעֲשִׂיתֶם | אֶת־כָּל־מִצְוֹתָי, וִהְיִיתֶם קְדֹשִׁים לֵאלֹהֵיכֶם: אֲנִי יהוה | אֱלֹהֵיכֶם, אֲשֶׁר הוֹצֵאתִי | אֶתְכֶם | מֵאֶרֶץ מִצְרַיִם, לִהְיוֹת לָכֶם לֵאלֹהִים, אֲנִי | יהוה | אֱלֹהֵיכֶם: אֱמֶת —

Concentrate on fulfilling the commandment of remembering the Exodus from Egypt.

Although the word אֱמֶת belongs to the next paragraph, it is appended to the conclusion of the previous one, as explained in the commentary.

Chazzan repeats — **יהוה אֱלֹהֵיכֶם אֱמֶת.**

וֶאֱמוּנָה כָּל זֹאת, וְקַיָּם עָלֵינוּ, כִּי הוּא יהוה אֱלֹהֵינוּ וְאֵין זוּלָתוֹ, וַאֲנַחְנוּ יִשְׂרָאֵל עַמּוֹ. הַפּוֹדֵנוּ מִיַּד מְלָכִים, מַלְכֵּנוּ הַגּוֹאֲלֵנוּ מִכַּף כָּל הֶעָרִיצִים. הָאֵל הַנִּפְרָע לָנוּ מִצָּרֵינוּ, וְהַמְשַׁלֵּם גְּמוּל לְכָל אֹיְבֵי נַפְשֵׁנוּ. הָעֹשֶׂה גְדֹלוֹת עַד אֵין חֵקֶר, וְנִפְלָאוֹת עַד אֵין מִסְפָּר.[1] הַשָּׂם נַפְשֵׁנוּ בַּחַיִּים, וְלֹא נָתַן לַמּוֹט רַגְלֵנוּ.[2] הַמַּדְרִיכֵנוּ עַל בָּמוֹת אוֹיְבֵינוּ, וַיָּרֶם קַרְנֵנוּ עַל כָּל שׂנְאֵינוּ. הָעֹשֶׂה לָּנוּ נִסִּים וּנְקָמָה בְּפַרְעֹה, אוֹתוֹת וּמוֹפְתִים בְּאַדְמַת בְּנֵי חָם. הַמַּכֶּה בְעֶבְרָתוֹ כָּל בְּכוֹרֵי מִצְרָיִם, וַיּוֹצֵא אֶת עַמּוֹ יִשְׂרָאֵל מִתּוֹכָם לְחֵרוּת עוֹלָם. הַמַּעֲבִיר בָּנָיו בֵּין גִּזְרֵי יַם סוּף, אֶת רוֹדְפֵיהֶם וְאֶת שׂוֹנְאֵיהֶם בִּתְהוֹמוֹת טִבַּע. וְרָאוּ בָנָיו גְּבוּרָתוֹ, שִׁבְּחוּ וְהוֹדוּ לִשְׁמוֹ. ❖ וּמַלְכוּתוֹ בְּרָצוֹן קִבְּלוּ עֲלֵיהֶם. מֹשֶׁה וּבְנֵי יִשְׂרָאֵל לְךָ עָנוּ שִׁירָה,

שְׁמִינִי אֶשְׁפֹּךְ* לֵב וָנֶפֶשׁ כַּמַּיִם,[3] לִפְנֵי רוֹכֵב בְּגַאֲוָתוֹ שָׁמַיִם,[4]
בַּיּוֹם הַשְּׁמִינִי.
שְׁמִינִי בִּכְהֻנָּה לְשָׁרֵת מְשָׁרֵת וְנִינָיו, קָרָא מֹשֶׁה לְאַהֲרֹן וּלְבָנָיו,[5]
בַּיּוֹם הַשְּׁמִינִי.
שְׁמִינִי גְּזֵרַת דַּת גְּשָׁמִים, אִם רַב וְאִם מְעַט נִרְשָׁמִים, בַּיּוֹם הַשְּׁמִינִי.
שְׁמִינִי דּוֹרֵשׁ לְאוֹת בְּרִית,* לְהִנָּצֵל בּוֹ מֵאַף שְׁאֵרִית, בַּיּוֹם הַשְּׁמִינִי.
שְׁמִינִי הוּכַן לְנֶאֱמָנָה, תֶּן חֵלֶק לְשִׁבְעָה וְגַם לִשְׁמוֹנָה,[6] בַּיּוֹם הַשְּׁמִינִי.

⤜ שְׁמִינִי אֶשְׁפֹּךְ — *The eighth I pour forth.* The themes of this *piyut* are: (a) the Shemini Atzeres prayers for rain; (b) the transition from Succos to Shemini Atzeres; (c) allusions to other *mitzvos* and events involving the number eight; and (d) the day itself. Each stanza begins with the word שְׁמִינִי, *eighth,* and ends with בַּיּוֹם הַשְּׁמִינִי, *on the eighth day.* The initial letters of the second word of each stanza follow the *aleph-beis.* And the final stanza bears the acrostic דָּנִיאֵל בַּר יַעֲקֹב, *Daniel bar Yaakov.*

אוֹת בְּרִית — *The sign of the covenant* (of circumcision). When Moses returned to Egypt from Midian he had not yet circumcised his son. Moses was engulfed by Wrath and Anger which almost swallowed him alive. His wife Zipporah quickly circumcised their son, and

on the corners of their garments, throughout their generations. And they are to place upon the tzitzis of each corner a thread of techeiles. And it shall constitute tzitzis for you, that you may see it and remember all the commandments of HASHEM and perform them; and not explore after your heart and after your eyes after which you stray. So that you may remember and perform all My commandments; and be holy to your God. I am HASHEM, your God, Who has removed you from the land of Egypt to be a God to you; I am HASHEM your God — it is true —

Concentrate on fulfilling the commandment of remembering the Exodus from Egypt.

Although the word אֱמֶת, *'it is true,'* belongs to the next paragraph, it is appended to the conclusion of the previous one, as explained in the commentary.

Chazzan repeats: **HASHEM, your God, is true.**

וֶאֱמוּנָה *And faithful is all this, and it is firmly established for us that He is HASHEM our God, and there is none but Him, and we are Israel, His nation. He redeems us from the power of kings, our King Who delivers us from the hand of all the cruel tyrants. He is the God Who exacts vengeance for us from our foes and Who brings just retribution upon all enemies of our soul; Who performs great deeds that are beyond comprehension, and wonders beyond number.[1] Who set our soul in life and did not allow our foot to falter.[2] Who led us upon the heights of our enemies and raised our pride above all who hate us; Who wrought for us miracles and vengeance upon Pharaoh; signs and wonders on the land of the offspring of Ham; Who struck with His anger all the firstborn of Egypt and removed His nation Israel from their midst to eternal freedom; Who brought His children through the split parts of the Sea of Reeds while those who pursued them and hated them He caused to sink into the depths. When His children perceived His power, they lauded and gave grateful praise to His Name.* Chazzan– *And His Kingship they accepted upon themselves willingly. Moses and the Children of Israel raised their voices to You in song,*

א *The eighth, I pour forth heart and soul like water,[3]*
before Him Who rides in His grandeur upon the heavens[4] —
on the eighth day.

ב *The eighth [day of the Mishkan's inauguration], [so that Aaron]*
the minister and his offspring may serve in the priesthood,
Moses called to Aaron and his sons[5] — on the eighth day.

ג *The eighth, the decree of the amount of rain,*
whether abundant or scarce, is recorded — on the eighth day.

ד *The eighth, He sought the sign of the covenant,**
to save the remnant [nation] from wrath — on the eighth day.

ה *The eighth, [the Festival] prepared for the faithful [nation],*
set a portion for [the] seven [days of Succos]
and also for [the] eight[h day][6] — on the eighth day.

---

(1) *Job* 9:10. (2) *Psalms* 66:9. (3) Cf. *Lamentations* 2:19.
(4) Cf. *Deuteronomy* 33:26. (5) *Leviticus* 9:1. (6) *Ecclesiastes* 11:2.

שְׁמִינִי וִתֵּר לְסֻכָּה עוֹצְרִים, לֵישֵׁב בְּבָתִּים וּבַחֲצֵרִים, בַּיּוֹם הַשְּׁמִינִי.
שְׁמִינִי זִמֵּן לִבְהֵמָה,* לְהֵרָצוֹת[1] פְּנֵי שׁוֹכֵן רוּמָה, בַּיּוֹם הַשְּׁמִינִי.
שְׁמִינִי חָקַר לְאָסְפוֹ עִם שִׁבְעָה, מִפְּנֵי טֹרַח יוֹלֶדֶת הַשִּׁבְעָה,*
בַּיּוֹם הַשְּׁמִינִי.
שְׁמִינִי טֻכַּס לְבָרֵךְ קְהַל מַלְכָּם, בְּשַׁלַּח הָעָם לְדַרְכָּם,[2] בַּיּוֹם הַשְּׁמִינִי.
שְׁמִינִי יִחֵד אוֹר עֵט, לְקָרְבָּן טוֹב מְעַט,* בַּיּוֹם הַשְּׁמִינִי.
שְׁמִינִי כִּפּוּר וּמָנוֹחַ דּוֹחֶה, לְקַיֵּם צִוּוּי עֲוֹנוֹת מוֹחֶה, בַּיּוֹם הַשְּׁמִינִי.
שְׁמִינִי לְעֹדֶף שִׂמְחָה* לִרְאוֹת, לְנַעֲנֵעַ שְׁמִינִי בַּעֲשׂוֹתוֹ נוֹרָאוֹת,
בַּיּוֹם הַשְּׁמִינִי.
שְׁמִינִי מְזֻמָּן לֶעָתִיד לָבוֹא, לְשַׂמֵּחַ בּוֹ עַם קְרוֹבוֹ, בַּיּוֹם הַשְּׁמִינִי.
שְׁמִינִי נִקְרָא עֲצֶרֶת, לְאֹם כְּאִישׁוֹן נִנְצֶרֶת, בַּיּוֹם הַשְּׁמִינִי.
שְׁמִינִי סְדוּרָה בְּדָתוֹת, וּבוֹ נִכְרְתוּ שְׁלֹשׁ עֶשְׂרֵה בְרִיתוֹת,*
בַּיּוֹם הַשְּׁמִינִי.
שְׁמִינִי עָרוּךְ הַחֲתוּמִים בּוֹ לְהַצִּיל, מִפּוֹעֶרֶת גָּנוֹן וְהִצִּיל,* בַּיּוֹם הַשְּׁמִינִי.
שְׁמִינִי פַּיִס* בּוֹ לְהִתְכֵּן, לִטְבֹחַ טֶבַח וְהָכֵן,[3] בַּיּוֹם הַשְּׁמִינִי.
שְׁמִינִי צִוּוּי לוֹמַר זְמָן, לְבָרֵךְ הָאֵל הַנֶּאֱמָן בַּיּוֹם הַשְּׁמִינִי.
שְׁמִינִי קָבוּעַ רֶגֶל בִּפְנֵי עַצְמוֹ, לִשְׂמֹחַ בּוֹ עַמּוֹ, בַּיּוֹם הַשְּׁמִינִי.
שְׁמִינִי רָצוּי לְהַקְרִיב קָרְבָּן בּוֹ לְבַדּוֹ, לִמְלֹא כָל הָאָרֶץ כְּבוֹדוֹ,[4]
בַּיּוֹם הַשְּׁמִינִי.
שְׁמִינִי שִׁיר בּוֹ לְבַדּוֹ לְמַלֵּל, לִגְמֹר בּוֹ אֶת הַהַלֵּל, בַּיּוֹם הַשְּׁמִינִי.
שְׁמִינִי תֵּת בְּרָכָה בִּפְנֵי עַצְמָהּ, לַנּוֹתֵן לַיָּעֵף כֹּחַ[5] וְעָצְמָה, בַּיּוֹם הַשְּׁמִינִי.
שְׁמִינִי דּוֹרְשֵׁי נִצּוּחַ יִחוּדֶךָ, אָנָּא לְהִשְׁתַּחֲווֹת בָּאִים בְּרֹב חֲסָדֶיךָ,[6]
יוּחַשׁ עֶזְרָם מִקְּדֶשׁ בִּזְכוּת חֲסִידֶיךָ,
בְּעֶזְרַת שׁוֹרְרוּ עַל הַיָּם סַהֲדֶיךָ. בְּגִילָה, בְּרִנָּה,

(1) See *Leviticus* 22:27. (2) See *I Kings* 8:66. (3) Cf. *Genesis* 43:16.
(4) Cf. *Isaiah* 6:3. (5) Cf. 40:29. (6) Cf. *Psalms* 5:8.

Moses' life was spared (*Exodus* 4:24-26; *Nedarim* 32a). Thus the *paytan* relates circumcision to protection against wrath.

לְאָסְפוֹ עִם שִׁבְעָה – *To attach it to the seven.* According to the Midrash, Shemini Atzeres is to Succos as Shavuos is to Pesach. And just as Shavuos follows fifty days after Pesach, so should Shemini Atzeres have been fifty days after Succos, in the month of Kislev. However, since Kislev is a month of heavy rains, God advanced its date and attached it to Succos. Thus, the people need not make a pilgrimage during the rainy season (*Pesikta deR' Kahana*).

יוֹלֶדֶת הַשִּׁבְעָה – *She-who-bore-the-seven.* This appellation for Israel is variously explained by the commentaries to *Jeremiah* 15:9. According to *Radak*, the number 'seven' is used throughout Scripture as a synonym for 'many.' Thus, *She-Who-bore-the-seven* means 'the fruitful nations.' [See also *I Samuel* 2:5.]

לְעֹדֶף שִׂמְחָה – *Increased joyfulness.* Regarding Shemini Atzeres the Torah states, וְהָיִיתָ אַךְ שָׂמֵחַ, *And you shall be nothing but joyous* (*Deuteronomy* 16:15). This indicates an increased measure of the joy attendant to other festivals.

שְׁלֹשׁ עֶשְׂרֵה בְרִיתוֹת – *Thirteen covenants.* In the Biblical section containing the commandment of circumcision, the word בְּרִית, *covenant*, appears thirteen times (*Nedarim* 3:11).

פַּיִס – *Lots.* In regard to six laws, Shemini Atzeres is considered a festival unto itself unrelated to Succos. The Talmud (*Succah* 48a,

ו *The eighth, [when] those assembled in the succah are released,*
to dwell in [their] houses and courtyards — on the eighth day.
ז *The eighth [day of its life] is the time set for an animal,*
to be acceptable [for sacrifice][1] before Him Who dwells on high — on the eighth day.
ח *The eighth, He decided to attach it to the seven,**
not to overburden [Israel, the nation called] She-who-bore-the-seven — on the eighth day.*
ט *The eighth was established for the congregation to bless their king,*
when he sent the people on their way[2] — on the eighth day.
י *The eighth [day] was set aside by Him Who is cloaked in light,*
for a small but goodly sacrificial offering — on the eighth day.
כ *The eighth [day's circumcision] overrides [Yom] Kippur*
and [the Sabbath] contentment,
to fulfill the commandment of Him Who forgives iniquity — on the eighth day.
ל *The eighth indicates increased joyfulness,**
to strum the eighth [string] when He performs wonders — on the eighth day.
מ *The eighth [string] is prepared for the Time to Come,*
to rejoice on it with His intimate people — on the eighth day.
נ *The eighth is called Atzeres [Day of Assembly],*
for the nation guarded like the pupil [of the eye] — on the eighth day.
ס *The eighth [day of circumcision] is established in the Torah,*
and on it thirteen covenants were made — on the eighth day.*
ע *The eighth [day of circumcision] is prepared to save those sealed by it,*
to shield [them] and protect [them] from Gehinnom — on the eighth day.
פ *The eighth, to cast lots* on it,*
to slaughter the sacrificial offering and to prepare it[3] — on the eighth day.
צ *The eighth, He commanded to recite the Shehecheyanu,*
to bless God, the Faithful One — on the eighth day.
ק *The eighth, established as a festival unto itself,*
that His people may rejoice on it — on the eighth day.
ר *The eighth, favor is to be found in the bringing of its unique offering,*
to Him Whose glory fills the entire earth[4] — on the eighth day.
ש *The eighth, a special song to recite on it alone,*
and to complete Hallel on it — on the eighth day.
ת *The eighth, gives a blessing of its own,*
to Him Who gives strength and power to the weary[5] — on the eighth day.

דני *The eighth, those who foster the praise of Your Oneness,*
אלבר *please, they come to bow to Your abundant kindness.[6]*
יעקב *Hurry, help them from Your holy place,*
in the merit of Your devout ones,
with the aid [of the merit] of those who sang Your witness at the Sea.
with mirth, with glad song,

בְּשִׂמְחָה רַבָּה וְאָמְֽרוּ כֻלָּם:

מִי כָמֹֽכָה בָּאֵלִם יהוה, מִי כָּמֹֽכָה נֶאְדָּר בַּקֹּֽדֶשׁ, נוֹרָא תְהִלֹּת, עֹֽשֵׂה פֶֽלֶא.[1] ❖ מַלְכוּתְךָ רָאוּ בָנֶֽיךָ בּוֹקֵֽעַ יָם לִפְנֵי מֹשֶׁה,

טוֹעֲנֵי עֹל מֶֽלֶךְ אֵל אֱמוּנָה,
יָֽשְׁבוּ בַּסֻּכָּה שִׁבְעָה בֶּאֱמוּנָה,
כְּנָתְנוּ חֵֽלֶק לְשִׁבְעָה וְגַם לִשְׁמוֹנָה,[2]
לִקְרָאתָם זֶה יִשְׁעֵנוּ לְהָחִישׁ שִׁבְעָה וּשְׁמוֹנָה.*
זֶה צוּר יִשְׁעֵנוּ פָּֽצוּ פֶה וְאָמְֽרוּ:

Continue: ה׳ יִמְלֹךְ . . .

זֶה אֵלִי[3] עָנוּ וְאָמְֽרוּ:

יהוה יִמְלֹךְ לְעֹלָם וָעֶד.[4] ❖ וְנֶאֱמַר: כִּי פָדָה יהוה אֶת יַעֲקֹב, וּגְאָלוֹ מִיַּד חָזָק מִמֶּֽנּוּ.[5]

מְחַיִל אֵל חַיִל הוֹלְכִים,[6]
נָסְעוּ מִסֻּכָּה וְלִשְׂמֹחַ בַּשְּׁמִינִי נִמְלָכִים,
סֵבֶר יְהָבָם עָלֶֽיךָ מַשְׁלִיכִים,[7]
עוֹזֵר יִשְׂרָאֵל וְגוֹאֲלוֹ מַמְלִיכִים.

[Some conclude the blessing as follows; others conclude with בָּרוּךְ . . . גָּאַל יִשְׂרָאֵל.]

בָּרוּךְ אַתָּה יהוה, מֶֽלֶךְ צוּר יִשְׂרָאֵל וְגוֹאֲלוֹ. (Cong. — אָמֵן.)

בָּרוּךְ אַתָּה יהוה, גָּאַל יִשְׂרָאֵל. (Cong. — אָמֵן.)

הַשְׁכִּיבֵֽנוּ יהוה אֱלֹהֵֽינוּ לְשָׁלוֹם, וְהַעֲמִידֵֽנוּ מַלְכֵּֽנוּ לְחַיִּים, וּפְרוֹשׂ עָלֵֽינוּ סֻכַּת שְׁלוֹמֶֽךָ, וְתַקְּנֵֽנוּ בְּעֵצָה טוֹבָה מִלְּפָנֶֽיךָ, וְהוֹשִׁיעֵֽנוּ לְמַֽעַן שְׁמֶֽךָ. וְהָגֵן בַּעֲדֵֽנוּ, וְהָסֵר מֵעָלֵֽינוּ אוֹיֵב, דֶּֽבֶר, וְחֶֽרֶב, וְרָעָב, וְיָגוֹן, וְהָסֵר שָׂטָן מִלְּפָנֵֽינוּ וּמֵאַחֲרֵֽינוּ, וּבְצֵל כְּנָפֶֽיךָ תַּסְתִּירֵֽנוּ,[8] כִּי אֵל שׁוֹמְרֵֽנוּ וּמַצִּילֵֽנוּ אָֽתָּה, כִּי אֵל מֶֽלֶךְ חַנּוּן

---

see *Rashi* there) lists them under the mnemonic פז״ר קש״ב. They are:

(a) פַּיִס, *lots.* During Succos the twenty-four watches of *Kohanim* rotated the sacrificial offerings among them. This rotation did not continue on Shemini Atzeres when a lot was cast to determine which watch would serve at the Altar (*Succah* 5:6; see p. 126).

(b) זְמַן, *season.* Unlike the last days of Pesach on which the *Shehecheyanu* blessing ('. . . Who has kept us alive, sustained us, and brought us — לַזְּמַן הַזֶּה — to this season') is omitted, on Shemini Atzeres that blessing is recited.

(c) רֶגֶל, *festival.* The festival laws are different from those of Succos. On Shemini Atzeres [in *Eretz Yisrael* where it is only a one-day festival] we do not eat in the *succah.* [Even outside of *Eretz Yisrael* the *succah* blessing is omitted when eating in the *succah* on Shemini Atzeres; and the *succah* is not used on Simchas

with abundant gladness — and said unanimously:

מִי כָמֹכָה *Who is like You among the heavenly powers,* HASHEM*! Who is like You, mighty in holiness, too awesome for praise, doing wonders!*[1] Chazzan– *Your children beheld Your majesty, as You split the sea before Moses,*

ה *Those who bear the yoke of the faithful God.*
י *Sat faithfully in the succah for seven [days],*
כ *As they set a portion for [the] seven [days of Succos] and also for the eight[h day],*[2]
ל *In return for this, cause our salvation to come speedily, seven and eight.**
'He is the Rock of our salvation!' they opened their mouths and said:

Continue: *'*HASHEM *shall reign . . .'*

'This is my God!'[3] *they exclaimed, then they said:*

יהוה *'*HASHEM *shall reign for all eternity!'*[4] Chazzan– *And it is further said: 'For* HASHEM *has redeemed Jacob and delivered him from a power mightier than he.'*[5]

מ *They advance from strength to strength,*[6]
נ *[When] they move from the succah and take counsel to rejoice on the eighth,*
ס *They cast the weight of their burden upon You,*[7]
ע *They coronate the Helper and Redeemer of Israel.*

Some conclude the blessing as follows; others conclude with *'Blessed . . . Who redeemed Israel'.*

Blessed are You, HASHEM, *King, Rock of Israel and its Redeemer.*

(Cong.– *Amen.*)

Blessed are You, HASHEM, *Who redeemed Israel.* (Cong.– *Amen.*)

הַשְׁכִּיבֵנוּ *Lay us down to sleep,* HASHEM *our God, in peace, raise us erect, our King, to life; and spread over us the shelter of Your peace. Set us aright with good counsel from before Your Presence, and save us for Your Name's sake. Shield us, remove from us foe, plague, sword, famine, and woe; and remove spiritual impediment from before us and behind us, and in the shadow of Your wings shelter us*[8] *— for God Who protects and rescues us are You; for God, the Gracious*

(1) *Exodus* 15:1. (2) Cf. *Ecclesiastes* 11:2. (3) *Exodus* 15:2. (4) 15:18.
(5) *Jeremiah* 31:10. (6) Cf. *Psalms* 84:8. (7) Cf. 55:23. (8) Cf. *Psalms* 17:18.

Torah.]

(d) קָרְבָּן, *offering.* As noted above, the order of Altar offerings does not follow that of Succos.

(e) שִׁיר, *song.* The Levites' song that accompanied the sacrificial service on Shemini Atzeres was one especially suited to the day — לַמְנַצֵּחַ עַל הַשְּׁמִינִית, *A song on the eighth* (*Psalms* ch. 12).

(f) בְּרָכָה, *blessing.* In the *Amidah* and in *the Bircas Hamazon* blessings the festival is called by the name Shemini Atzeres and not Succos.

In the next six stanzas the *paytan* alludes to these six laws, respectively.

שִׁבְעָה וּשְׁמוֹנָה – *Seven and eight.* In prophesying about Messianic times, *Micha* 5:4 speaks of *seven shepherds and eight chiefs of humanity.* The Talmud (*Succah* 52b) identifies the seven shepherds as: David in the center, Adam, Seth and Methuselah to his right, Abraham, Jacob

וְרַחוּם אָתָּה.[1] ❖ וּשְׁמוֹר צֵאתֵנוּ וּבוֹאֵנוּ, לְחַיִּים וּלְשָׁלוֹם מֵעַתָּה וְעַד עוֹלָם.[2] וּפְרוֹשׂ עָלֵינוּ סֻכַּת שְׁלוֹמֶךָ.

פּוֹנִים מִסֻּכָּה לְבֵיתָם לֵישֵׁב,
צָקוּן לַחֲשָׁם הַקְּשֵׁב,
קוֹרְאֵי רוֹמְמוֹתֶיךָ שִׁמְךָ לְחַשֵּׁב,
תִּפְרֹשׂ עָלֵימוֹ סֻכַּת שְׁלוֹמֶךָ תְּהִלּוֹת יוֹשֵׁב.[3]

בָּרוּךְ אַתָּה יהוה, הַפּוֹרֵשׂ סֻכַּת שָׁלוֹם עָלֵינוּ וְעַל כָּל עַמּוֹ יִשְׂרָאֵל וְעַל יְרוּשָׁלָיִם. (Cong.– אָמֵן.)

Congregation rises and remains standing until after *Shemoneh Esrei.*

On the Sabbath, the congregation, followed by the *chazzan,* recites:

וְשָׁמְרוּ* בְנֵי יִשְׂרָאֵל אֶת הַשַּׁבָּת, לַעֲשׂוֹת אֶת הַשַּׁבָּת* לְדֹרֹתָם בְּרִית עוֹלָם. בֵּינִי וּבֵין בְּנֵי יִשְׂרָאֵל* אוֹת הִיא לְעֹלָם, כִּי שֵׁשֶׁת יָמִים עָשָׂה יהוה אֶת הַשָּׁמַיִם וְאֶת הָאָרֶץ, וּבַיּוֹם הַשְּׁבִיעִי שָׁבַת וַיִּנָּפַשׁ.*[4]

Congregation, then *chazzan:*

וַיְדַבֵּר מֹשֶׁה* אֶת מֹעֲדֵי יהוה, אֶל בְּנֵי יִשְׂרָאֵל.[5]

The *chazzan* recites חֲצִי קַדִּישׁ.

יִתְגַּדַּל וְיִתְקַדַּשׁ שְׁמֵהּ רַבָּא. (Cong.– אָמֵן.) בְּעָלְמָא דִּי בְרָא כִרְעוּתֵהּ, וְיַמְלִיךְ מַלְכוּתֵהּ, בְּחַיֵּיכוֹן וּבְיוֹמֵיכוֹן וּבְחַיֵּי דְכָל בֵּית יִשְׂרָאֵל, בַּעֲגָלָא וּבִזְמַן קָרִיב. וְאִמְרוּ: אָמֵן.

(Cong.– אָמֵן. יְהֵא שְׁמֵהּ רַבָּא מְבָרַךְ לְעָלַם וּלְעָלְמֵי עָלְמַיָּא.)

יְהֵא שְׁמֵהּ רַבָּא מְבָרַךְ לְעָלַם וּלְעָלְמֵי עָלְמַיָּא.

יִתְבָּרַךְ וְיִשְׁתַּבַּח וְיִתְפָּאַר וְיִתְרוֹמַם וְיִתְנַשֵּׂא וְיִתְהַדָּר וְיִתְעַלֶּה וְיִתְהַלָּל שְׁמֵהּ דְּקֻדְשָׁא בְּרִיךְ הוּא (Cong.– בְּרִיךְ הוּא) – לְעֵלָּא מִן כָּל בִּרְכָתָא וְשִׁירָתָא תֻּשְׁבְּחָתָא וְנֶחֱמָתָא, דַּאֲמִירָן בְּעָלְמָא. וְאִמְרוּ: אָמֵן. (Cong.– אָמֵן.)

---

and Moses to his left. The eight chiefs of humanity are: Jesse, Saul, Samuel, Amos, Zephaniah, Zidkiyahu (an alternate reading has Hezekiah), Elijah and the Messiah. *Rashi* comments that he does not know from where the Talmud derives these particular lists.

וְשָׁמְרוּ — *And . . . shall keep.* As noted above, there should be no interruption between the theme of redemption and *Shemoneh Esrei.* However, this Scriptural statement of Israel's Sabbath observance is related to the theme of redemption, because Israel will be redeemed from exile in the merit of Sabbath observance (*Abudraham*).

This chapter of Sabbath observance appears in the Torah immediately after the commandment to commence the construction of the Tabernacle. This teaches that even for the sake of building the Temple, one may not desecrate

and Compassionate King, are You.[1] Chazzan— *Safeguard our going and coming, for life and for peace from now to eternity.*[2] *And spread over us the shelter of Your peace.*

פ *They turn from the succah to dwell in their house,*
צ *Hearken to the outpouring of their whispered prayer,*
קרש *They declare Your exaltedness, and give thought to Your Name,*
ת *Spread over them the succah of Your peace,*
O You Who are enthroned upon the prayers [of Israel].[3]

Blessed are You, HASHEM, Who spreads the shelter of peace upon us, upon all of His people Israel and upon Jerusalem. (Cong.— *Amen.*)

Congregation rises and remains standing until after *Shemoneh Esrei.*

On the Sabbath, the congregation, followed by the chazzan, recites:

וְשָׁמְרוּ *And the Children of Israel shall keep* the Sabbath, to make the Sabbath* an eternal covenant for their generations. Between Me and the Children of Israel* it is a sign forever that in six days HASHEM made heaven and earth, and on the seventh day He rested and was refreshed.**[4]

Congregation, then *chazzan:*

And Moses declared* HASHEM's appointed festivals to the Children of Israel.[5]

The *chazzan* recites Half-*Kaddish.*

יִתְגַּדַּל *May His great Name grow exalted and sanctified* (Cong.— *Amen.*) *in the world that He created as He willed. May He give reign to His kingship in your lifetimes and in your days, and in the lifetimes of the entire Family of Israel, swiftly and soon. Now respond: Amen.*

(Cong.— *Amen. May His great Name be blessed forever and ever.*)
May His great Name be blessed forever and ever.

Blessed, praised, glorified, exalted, extolled, mighty, upraised, and lauded be the Name of the Holy One, Blessed is He (Cong.— *Blessed is He*) — *beyond any blessing and song, praise and consolation that are uttered in the world. Now respond: Amen.* (Cong.— *Amen.*)

(1) Cf. *Nechemiah* 9:31. (2) Cf. *Psalms* 121:8. (3) Cf. 22:4. (4) *Exodus* 31:16-17. (5) *Leviticus* 23:44.

the Sabbath (*Rashi* to *Exodus* 31:13). [By logical extension, this concept refutes those who may tend to relax the observance of the Sabbath or other *mitzvos* for the sake of what they consider to be noble spiritual causes.]

לַעֲשׂוֹת אֶת הַשַּׁבָּת — *To make the Sabbath.* Each generation must *'make' the Sabbath,* by teaching its importance and holiness to those who are lax in sanctifying it because they fail to appreciate its importance (*Maor VaShemesh*).

בֵּינִי וּבֵין בְּנֵי יִשְׂרָאֵל — *Between Me and the Children of Israel.* Only Israel is commanded to observe the Sabbath, thereby bearing witness to God's creation of heaven and earth in six days. Consequently, the Sabbath is a *sign* of God's special relationship with Israel.

וַיִּנָּפַשׁ — *And was refreshed.* The translation follows *Rashi* who comments that this is an example of how God is described in human terms: God, of course, cannot become tired or refreshed, but a man would need a day of rest to refresh himself after six days of labor.

Other commentators, *Ramban* and *R' Yehudah HaChassid* among them, derive this word from נֶפֶשׁ, *soul.* They render וַיִּנָּפַשׁ, *and He gave them a soul,* i.e., the heaven and earth just mentioned *were given a soul,* as if to say that the creation of the Sabbath gave a new spiritual dimension to the universe.

⇐§ וַיְדַבֵּר משֶׁה — *And Moses declared.* This verse concludes a chapter that discusses the festivals. Thus, the verse alludes to all the specific laws and teachings of each of the festivals.

❦ שמונה עשרה – עמידה ❧

Take three steps backward, then three steps forward. Remain standing with the feet together while reciting *Shemoneh Esrei*. Recite it with quiet devotion and without interruption, verbal or otherwise. Although its recitation should not be audible to others, one must pray loudly enough to hear himself.

אֲדֹנָי שְׂפָתַי תִּפְתָּח, וּפִי יַגִּיד תְּהִלָּתֶךָ.[1]

אבות

Bend the knees at בָּרוּךְ; bow at אַתָּה; straighten up at 'ה.

בָּרוּךְ אַתָּה יהוה אֱלֹהֵינוּ וֵאלֹהֵי אֲבוֹתֵינוּ, אֱלֹהֵי אַבְרָהָם, אֱלֹהֵי יִצְחָק, וֵאלֹהֵי יַעֲקֹב, הָאֵל הַגָּדוֹל הַגִּבּוֹר וְהַנּוֹרָא, אֵל עֶלְיוֹן, גּוֹמֵל חֲסָדִים טוֹבִים וְקוֹנֵה הַכֹּל, וְזוֹכֵר חַסְדֵי אָבוֹת, וּמֵבִיא גוֹאֵל לִבְנֵי בְנֵיהֶם, לְמַעַן שְׁמוֹ בְּאַהֲבָה. מֶלֶךְ עוֹזֵר וּמוֹשִׁיעַ וּמָגֵן.

Bend the knees at בָּרוּךְ; bow at אַתָּה; straighten up at 'ה.

בָּרוּךְ אַתָּה יהוה, מָגֵן אַבְרָהָם.

גבורות

אַתָּה גִּבּוֹר לְעוֹלָם אֲדֹנָי, מְחַיֵּה מֵתִים אַתָּה, רַב לְהוֹשִׁיעַ. מְכַלְכֵּל חַיִּים בְּחֶסֶד, מְחַיֵּה מֵתִים בְּרַחֲמִים רַבִּים, סוֹמֵךְ נוֹפְלִים, וְרוֹפֵא חוֹלִים, וּמַתִּיר אֲסוּרִים, וּמְקַיֵּם אֱמוּנָתוֹ לִישֵׁנֵי עָפָר. מִי כָמוֹךָ בַּעַל גְּבוּרוֹת, וּמִי דּוֹמֶה לָּךְ, מֶלֶךְ מֵמִית וּמְחַיֶּה וּמַצְמִיחַ יְשׁוּעָה. וְנֶאֱמָן אַתָּה לְהַחֲיוֹת מֵתִים. בָּרוּךְ אַתָּה יהוה, מְחַיֵּה הַמֵּתִים.

קדושת השם

אַתָּה קָדוֹשׁ וְשִׁמְךָ קָדוֹשׁ, וּקְדוֹשִׁים בְּכָל יוֹם יְהַלְלוּךָ סֶּלָה. בָּרוּךְ אַתָּה יהוה, הָאֵל הַקָּדוֹשׁ.

קדושת היום

אַתָּה בְחַרְתָּנוּ מִכָּל הָעַמִּים, אָהַבְתָּ אוֹתָנוּ, וְרָצִיתָ בָּנוּ, וְרוֹמַמְתָּנוּ מִכָּל הַלְּשׁוֹנוֹת, וְקִדַּשְׁתָּנוּ בְּמִצְוֹתֶיךָ, וְקֵרַבְתָּנוּ מַלְכֵּנוּ לַעֲבוֹדָתֶךָ, וְשִׁמְךָ הַגָּדוֹל וְהַקָּדוֹשׁ עָלֵינוּ קָרָאתָ.

On the Sabbath add the words in brackets. [If forgotten, see *Laws* §86-90.]

וַתִּתֶּן לָנוּ יהוה אֱלֹהֵינוּ בְּאַהֲבָה [שַׁבָּתוֹת לִמְנוּחָה וּ]מוֹעֲדִים לְשִׂמְחָה חַגִּים וּזְמַנִּים לְשָׂשׂוֹן, אֶת יוֹם [הַשַּׁבָּת הַזֶּה וְאֶת יוֹם] הַשְּׁמִינִי חַג הָעֲצֶרֶת הַזֶּה, זְמַן שִׂמְחָתֵנוּ [בְּאַהֲבָה] מִקְרָא קֹדֶשׁ, זֵכֶר לִיצִיאַת מִצְרָיִם.

SHEMONEH ESREI – AMIDAH

Take three steps backward, then three steps forward. Remain standing with the feet together while reciting *Shemoneh Esrei.* Recite it with quiet devotion and without interruption, verbal or otherwise. Although its recitation should not be audible to others, one must pray loudly enough to hear himself

My Lord, open my lips, that my mouth may declare Your praise.[1]

PATRIARCHS

Bend the knees at *'Blessed'*; bow at *'You'*; straighten up at *'HASHEM.'*

בָּרוּךְ *Blessed are You, HASHEM, our God and the God of our forefathers, God of Abraham, God of Isaac, and God of Jacob; the great, mighty, and awesome God, the supreme God, Who bestows beneficial kindnesses and creates everything, Who recalls the kindnesses of the Patriarchs and brings a Redeemer to their children's children, for His Name's sake, with love. O King, Helper, Savior, and Shield.*

Bend the knees at *'Blessed'*; bow at *'You'*; straighten up at *'HASHEM.'*

Blessed are You, HASHEM, Shield of Abraham.

GOD'S MIGHT

אַתָּה *You are eternally mighty, my Lord, the Resuscitator of the dead are You; abundantly able to save. He sustains the living with kindness, resuscitates the dead with abundant mercy, supports the fallen, heals the sick, releases the confined, and maintains His faith to those asleep in the dust. Who is like You, O Master of mighty deeds, and who is comparable to You, O King Who causes death and restores life and makes salvation sprout! And You are faithful to resuscitate the dead. Blessed are You, HASHEM, Who resuscitates the dead.*

HOLINESS OF GOD'S NAME

אַתָּה *You are holy and Your Name is holy, and holy ones praise You every day, forever. Blessed are You, HASHEM, the holy God.*

SANCTIFICATION OF THE DAY

אַתָּה בְחַרְתָּנוּ *You have chosen us from all the peoples; You loved us and found favor in us; You exalted us above all the tongues and You sanctified us with Your commandments. You drew us close, our King, to Your service and proclaimed Your great and Holy Name upon us.*

On the Sabbath add the words in brackets. [If forgotten, see *Laws* 86-90.]

וַתִּתֶּן לָנוּ *And You gave us, HASHEM, our God, with love [Sabbaths for rest], appointed festivals for gladness, Festivals and times for joy, [this day of Sabbath and] this day of the Shemini Atzeres Festival, the time of our gladness [with love], a holy convocation, a memorial of the Exodus from Egypt.*

(1) *Psalms* 51:17.

אֱלֹהֵינוּ וֵאלֹהֵי אֲבוֹתֵינוּ, יַעֲלֶה, וְיָבֹא, וְיַגִּיעַ, וְיֵרָאֶה, וְיֵרָצֶה, וְיִשָּׁמַע, וְיִפָּקֵד, וְיִזָּכֵר זִכְרוֹנֵנוּ וּפִקְדוֹנֵנוּ, וְזִכְרוֹן אֲבוֹתֵינוּ, וְזִכְרוֹן מָשִׁיחַ בֶּן דָּוִד עַבְדֶּךָ, וְזִכְרוֹן יְרוּשָׁלַיִם עִיר קָדְשֶׁךָ, וְזִכְרוֹן כָּל עַמְּךָ בֵּית יִשְׂרָאֵל לְפָנֶיךָ, לִפְלֵיטָה לְטוֹבָה לְחֵן וּלְחֶסֶד וּלְרַחֲמִים, לְחַיִּים וּלְשָׁלוֹם בְּיוֹם הַשְּׁמִינִי חַג הָעֲצֶרֶת הַזֶּה. זָכְרֵנוּ יהוה אֱלֹהֵינוּ בּוֹ לְטוֹבָה, וּפָקְדֵנוּ בוֹ לִבְרָכָה, וְהוֹשִׁיעֵנוּ בוֹ לְחַיִּים. וּבִדְבַר יְשׁוּעָה וְרַחֲמִים, חוּס וְחָנֵּנוּ וְרַחֵם עָלֵינוּ וְהוֹשִׁיעֵנוּ, כִּי אֵלֶיךָ עֵינֵינוּ, כִּי אֵל מֶלֶךְ חַנּוּן וְרַחוּם אָתָּה.[1]

On the Sabbath add the words in brackets. [If forgotten, see *Laws* §86-90.]

וְהַשִּׂיאֵנוּ יהוה אֱלֹהֵינוּ אֶת בִּרְכַּת מוֹעֲדֶיךָ לְחַיִּים וּלְשָׁלוֹם, לְשִׂמְחָה וּלְשָׂשׂוֹן, כַּאֲשֶׁר רָצִיתָ וְאָמַרְתָּ לְבָרְכֵנוּ. [אֱלֹהֵינוּ וֵאלֹהֵי אֲבוֹתֵינוּ רְצֵה בִמְנוּחָתֵנוּ] קַדְּשֵׁנוּ בְּמִצְוֹתֶיךָ וְתֵן חֶלְקֵנוּ בְּתוֹרָתֶךָ, שַׂבְּעֵנוּ מִטּוּבֶךָ וְשַׂמְּחֵנוּ בִּישׁוּעָתֶךָ, וְטַהֵר לִבֵּנוּ לְעָבְדְּךָ בֶּאֱמֶת, וְהַנְחִילֵנוּ יהוה אֱלֹהֵינוּ [בְּאַהֲבָה וּבְרָצוֹן] בְּשִׂמְחָה וּבְשָׂשׂוֹן [שַׁבָּת וּ]מוֹעֲדֵי קָדְשֶׁךָ, וְיִשְׂמְחוּ בְךָ יִשְׂרָאֵל מְקַדְּשֵׁי שְׁמֶךָ. בָּרוּךְ אַתָּה יהוה, מְקַדֵּשׁ [הַשַּׁבָּת וְ]יִשְׂרָאֵל וְהַזְּמַנִּים.

עבודה

רְצֵה יהוה אֱלֹהֵינוּ בְּעַמְּךָ יִשְׂרָאֵל וּבִתְפִלָּתָם, וְהָשֵׁב אֶת הָעֲבוֹדָה לִדְבִיר בֵּיתֶךָ. וְאִשֵּׁי יִשְׂרָאֵל וּתְפִלָּתָם בְּאַהֲבָה תְקַבֵּל בְּרָצוֹן, וּתְהִי לְרָצוֹן תָּמִיד עֲבוֹדַת יִשְׂרָאֵל עַמֶּךָ.

וְתֶחֱזֶינָה עֵינֵינוּ בְּשׁוּבְךָ לְצִיּוֹן בְּרַחֲמִים. בָּרוּךְ אַתָּה יהוה, הַמַּחֲזִיר שְׁכִינָתוֹ לְצִיּוֹן.

הודאה

Bow at מוֹדִים; straighten up at ה׳.

מוֹדִים אֲנַחְנוּ לָךְ, שָׁאַתָּה הוּא יהוה אֱלֹהֵינוּ וֵאלֹהֵי אֲבוֹתֵינוּ לְעוֹלָם וָעֶד. צוּר חַיֵּינוּ, מָגֵן יִשְׁעֵנוּ אַתָּה הוּא לְדוֹר וָדוֹר. נוֹדֶה לְּךָ וּנְסַפֵּר תְּהִלָּתֶךָ[2] עַל חַיֵּינוּ הַמְּסוּרִים בְּיָדֶךָ, וְעַל

(1) Cf. *Nechemiah* 9:31. (2) Cf. *Psalms* 79:13.

אֱלֹהֵינוּ *Our God and God of our forefathers, may there rise, come, reach, be noted, be favored, be heard, be considered, and be remembered — the remembrance and consideration of ourselves; the remembrance of our forefathers; the remembrance of Messiah, son of David, Your servant; the remembrance of Jerusalem, the City of Your Holiness; the remembrance of Your entire people the Family of Israel — before You for deliverance, for goodness, for grace, for kindness, and for compassion, for life, and for peace on this day of the Shemini Atzeres Festival. Remember us on it,* HASHEM, *our God, for goodness, consider us on it for blessing, and help us on it for life. In the matter of salvation and compassion, pity, be gracious and compassionate with us and help us, for our eyes are turned to You, because You are God, the gracious and compassionate King.*[1]

On the Sabbath add the words in brackets. [If forgotten, see *Laws* §86-90.]

וְהַשִּׂיאֵנוּ *Bestow upon us, O* HASHEM, *our God, the blessing of Your appointed Festivals for life and for peace, for gladness and for joy, as You desired and promised to bless us. [Our God and the God of our forefathers, may You be pleased with our rest.] Sanctify us with Your commandments and grant us our share in Your Torah; satisfy us from Your goodness and gladden us with Your salvation, and purify our heart to serve You sincerely. And grant us a heritage, O* HASHEM, *our God — [with love and with favor] with gladness and with joy — [the Sabbath and] the appointed festivals of Your holiness, and may Israel, the sanctifiers of Your Name, rejoice in You. Blessed are You,* HASHEM, *Who sanctifies [the Sabbath] Israel and the festive seasons.*

TEMPLE SERVICE

רְצֵה *Be favorable,* HASHEM, *our God, toward Your people Israel and their prayer and restore the service to the Holy of Holies of Your Temple. The fire-offerings of Israel and their prayer accept with love and favor, and may the service of Your people Israel always be favorable to You.*

וְתֶחֱזֶינָה *May our eyes behold Your return to Zion in compassion. Blessed are You,* HASHEM, *Who restores His Presence to Zion.*

THANKSGIVING [MODIM]

Bow at *'We gratefully thank You'*; straighten up at *'*HASHEM.*'*

מוֹדִים *We gratefully thank You, for it is You Who are* HASHEM, *our God and the God of our forefathers for all eternity; Rock of our lives, Shield of our salvation are You from generation to generation. We shall thank You and relate Your praise*[2] *— for our lives, which*

נִשְׁמוֹתֵינוּ הַפְּקוּדוֹת לָךְ, וְעַל נִסֶּיךָ שֶׁבְּכָל יוֹם עִמָּנוּ, וְעַל נִפְלְאוֹתֶיךָ וְטוֹבוֹתֶיךָ שֶׁבְּכָל עֵת, עֶרֶב וָבֹקֶר וְצָהֳרָיִם. הַטּוֹב כִּי לֹא כָלוּ רַחֲמֶיךָ, וְהַמְּרַחֵם כִּי לֹא תַמּוּ חֲסָדֶיךָ,[1] מֵעוֹלָם קִוִּינוּ לָךְ.

וְעַל כֻּלָּם יִתְבָּרַךְ וְיִתְרוֹמַם שִׁמְךָ מַלְכֵּנוּ תָּמִיד לְעוֹלָם וָעֶד.

Bend the knees at בָּרוּךְ; bow at אַתָּה; straighten up at ה׳.

וְכֹל הַחַיִּים יוֹדְוּךָ סֶּלָה, וִיהַלְלוּ אֶת שִׁמְךָ בֶּאֱמֶת, הָאֵל יְשׁוּעָתֵנוּ וְעֶזְרָתֵנוּ סֶלָה. בָּרוּךְ אַתָּה יהוה, הַטּוֹב שִׁמְךָ וּלְךָ נָאֶה לְהוֹדוֹת.

שלום

שָׁלוֹם רָב עַל יִשְׂרָאֵל עַמְּךָ תָּשִׂים לְעוֹלָם, כִּי אַתָּה הוּא מֶלֶךְ אָדוֹן לְכָל הַשָּׁלוֹם. וְטוֹב בְּעֵינֶיךָ לְבָרֵךְ אֶת עַמְּךָ יִשְׂרָאֵל, בְּכָל עֵת וּבְכָל שָׁעָה בִּשְׁלוֹמֶךָ. בָּרוּךְ אַתָּה יהוה, הַמְּבָרֵךְ אֶת עַמּוֹ יִשְׂרָאֵל בַּשָּׁלוֹם.

יִהְיוּ לְרָצוֹן אִמְרֵי פִי וְהֶגְיוֹן לִבִּי לְפָנֶיךָ, יהוה צוּרִי וְגֹאֲלִי.[2]

אֱלֹהַי, נְצוֹר לְשׁוֹנִי מֵרָע, וּשְׂפָתַי מִדַּבֵּר מִרְמָה,[3] וְלִמְקַלְלַי נַפְשִׁי תִדּוֹם, וְנַפְשִׁי כֶּעָפָר לַכֹּל תִּהְיֶה. פְּתַח לִבִּי בְּתוֹרָתֶךָ, וּבְמִצְוֹתֶיךָ תִּרְדּוֹף נַפְשִׁי. וְכֹל הַחוֹשְׁבִים עָלַי רָעָה, מְהֵרָה הָפֵר עֲצָתָם וְקַלְקֵל מַחֲשַׁבְתָּם. עֲשֵׂה לְמַעַן שְׁמֶךָ, עֲשֵׂה לְמַעַן יְמִינֶךָ, עֲשֵׂה לְמַעַן קְדֻשָּׁתֶךָ, עֲשֵׂה לְמַעַן תּוֹרָתֶךָ. לְמַעַן יֵחָלְצוּן יְדִידֶיךָ, הוֹשִׁיעָה יְמִינְךָ וַעֲנֵנִי.[4]

Some recite verses pertaining to their names. See page 1301.

יִהְיוּ לְרָצוֹן אִמְרֵי פִי וְהֶגְיוֹן לִבִּי לְפָנֶיךָ, יהוה צוּרִי וְגֹאֲלִי.[2]

Bow and take three steps back. Bow left and say ... עֹשֶׂה, bow right and say ... הוּא יַעֲשֶׂה; bow forward and say וְעַל כָּל ... אָמֵן.

עֹשֶׂה שָׁלוֹם בִּמְרוֹמָיו, הוּא יַעֲשֶׂה שָׁלוֹם עָלֵינוּ, וְעַל כָּל יִשְׂרָאֵל. וְאִמְרוּ: אָמֵן.

יְהִי רָצוֹן מִלְּפָנֶיךָ יהוה אֱלֹהֵינוּ וֵאלֹהֵי אֲבוֹתֵינוּ, שֶׁיִּבָּנֶה בֵּית הַמִּקְדָּשׁ בִּמְהֵרָה בְיָמֵינוּ, וְתֵן חֶלְקֵנוּ בְּתוֹרָתֶךָ. וְשָׁם נַעֲבָדְךָ בְּיִרְאָה, כִּימֵי עוֹלָם וּכְשָׁנִים קַדְמוֹנִיּוֹת. וְעָרְבָה לַיהוה מִנְחַת יְהוּדָה וִירוּשָׁלָיִם, כִּימֵי עוֹלָם וּכְשָׁנִים קַדְמוֹנִיּוֹת.[5]

ON FRIDAY NIGHT, THE SERVICE CONTINUES ON P. 868; ON OTHER NIGHTS, ON P. 870.

are committed to Your power and for our souls that are entrusted to You; for Your miracles that are with us every day; and for Your wonders and favors in every season — evening, morning, and afternoon. The Beneficent One, for Your compassions were never exhausted, and the Compassionate One, for Your kindnesses never ended[1] *— always have we put our hope in You.*

For all these, may Your Name be blessed and exalted, our King, continually forever and ever.

Bend the knees at *'Blessed'*; bow at *'You'*; straighten up at *'HASHEM.'*

Everything alive will gratefully acknowledge You, Selah! and praise Your Name sincerely, O God of our salvation and help, Selah! Blessed are You, HASHEM, Your Name is 'The Beneficent One' and to You it is fitting to give thanks.

PEACE

שָׁלוֹם *Establish abundant peace upon Your people Israel forever, for You are King, Master of all peace. May it be good in Your eyes to bless Your people Israel at every time and every hour with Your peace. Blessed are You, HASHEM, Who blesses His people Israel with peace.*

May the expressions of my mouth and the thoughts of my heart find favor before You, HASHEM, my Rock and my Redeemer.[2]

אֱלֹהַי *My God, guard my tongue from evil and my lips from speaking deceitfully.*[3] *To those who curse me, let my soul be silent; and let my soul be like dust to everyone. Open my heart to Your Torah, then my soul will pursue Your commandments. As for all those who design evil against me, speedily nullify their counsel and disrupt their design. Act for Your Name's sake; act for Your right hand's sake; act for Your sanctity's sake; act for Your Torah's sake. That Your beloved ones may be given rest; let Your right hand save, and respond to me.*[4]

Some recite verses pertaining to their names at this point. See page 1301.

May the expressions of my mouth and the thoughts of my heart find favor before You, HASHEM, my Rock and my Redeemer.[2] *He Who makes peace in His heights, may He make peace upon us, and upon all Israel. Now respond: Amen.*

Bow and take three steps back. Bow left and say, *'He Who makes peace . . .'*; bow right and say, *'may He make peace . . .'*; bow forward and say, *'and upon . . . Amen.'*

יְהִי רָצוֹן *May it be Your will, HASHEM, our God and the God of our forefathers, that the Holy Temple be rebuilt, speedily in our days. Grant us our share in Your Torah, and may we serve You there with reverence, as in days of old and in former years. Then the offering of Judah and Jerusalem will be pleasing to HASHEM, as in days of old and in former years.*[5]

ON FRIDAY NIGHT, THE SERVICE CONTINUES ON P. 868; ON OTHER NIGHTS, ON P. 870.

---

(1) Cf. *Lamentations* 3:22. (2) *Psalms* 19:15. (3) Cf. 34:14. (4) 60:7;108:7. (5) *Malachi* 3:4.

On Friday night, all present stand and recite וַיְכֻלּוּ aloud in unison. Conversation is forbidden until after the אָמֵן response to the blessing מְקַדֵּשׁ הַשַּׁבָּת (below).

וַיְכֻלּוּ* הַשָּׁמַיִם וְהָאָרֶץ וְכָל צְבָאָם. וַיְכַל אֱלֹהִים בַּיּוֹם הַשְּׁבִיעִי מְלַאכְתּוֹ אֲשֶׁר עָשָׂה, וַיִּשְׁבֹּת בַּיּוֹם הַשְּׁבִיעִי מִכָּל מְלַאכְתּוֹ אֲשֶׁר עָשָׂה. וַיְבָרֶךְ אֱלֹהִים אֶת יוֹם הַשְּׁבִיעִי, וַיְקַדֵּשׁ אֹתוֹ, כִּי בוֹ שָׁבַת מִכָּל מְלַאכְתּוֹ, אֲשֶׁר בָּרָא אֱלֹהִים לַעֲשׂוֹת.[1]

ברכה מעין שבע

Chazzan continues:

בָּרוּךְ אַתָּה יהוה אֱלֹהֵינוּ וֵאלֹהֵי אֲבוֹתֵינוּ, אֱלֹהֵי אַבְרָהָם, אֱלֹהֵי יִצְחָק, וֵאלֹהֵי יַעֲקֹב, הָאֵל הַגָּדוֹל הַגִּבּוֹר וְהַנּוֹרָא, אֵל עֶלְיוֹן, קוֹנֵה שָׁמַיִם וָאָרֶץ.

Congregation, then *chazzan:*

מָגֵן אָבוֹת בִּדְבָרוֹ, מְחַיֵּה מֵתִים בְּמַאֲמָרוֹ, הָאֵל הַקָּדוֹשׁ שֶׁאֵין כָּמוֹהוּ, הַמֵּנִיחַ לְעַמּוֹ בְּיוֹם שַׁבַּת קָדְשׁוֹ, כִּי בָם רָצָה לְהָנִיחַ לָהֶם. לְפָנָיו נַעֲבֹד בְּיִרְאָה וָפַחַד, וְנוֹדֶה לִשְׁמוֹ בְּכָל יוֹם תָּמִיד מֵעֵין הַבְּרָכוֹת. אֵל הַהוֹדָאוֹת, אֲדוֹן הַשָּׁלוֹם, מְקַדֵּשׁ הַשַּׁבָּת וּמְבָרֵךְ שְׁבִיעִי, וּמֵנִיחַ בִּקְדֻשָּׁה לְעַם מְדֻשְּׁנֵי עֹנֶג, זֵכֶר לְמַעֲשֵׂה בְרֵאשִׁית.

Chazzan continues:

אֱלֹהֵינוּ וֵאלֹהֵי אֲבוֹתֵינוּ רְצֵה בִמְנוּחָתֵנוּ. קַדְּשֵׁנוּ בְּמִצְוֹתֶיךָ, וְתֵן חֶלְקֵנוּ בְּתוֹרָתֶךָ. שַׂבְּעֵנוּ מִטּוּבֶךָ, וְשַׂמְּחֵנוּ בִּישׁוּעָתֶךָ, וְטַהֵר לִבֵּנוּ לְעָבְדְּךָ בֶּאֱמֶת. וְהַנְחִילֵנוּ יהוה אֱלֹהֵינוּ בְּאַהֲבָה וּבְרָצוֹן שַׁבַּת קָדְשֶׁךָ, וְיָנוּחוּ בָהּ יִשְׂרָאֵל מְקַדְּשֵׁי שְׁמֶךָ. בָּרוּךְ אַתָּה יהוה, מְקַדֵּשׁ הַשַּׁבָּת.* (—Cong. אָמֵן.)

וַיְכֻלּוּ — ... *were finished.* We stand and recite this paragraph aloud because it is a form of testimony that God created heaven and earth — and witnesses must give their testimony while standing and in a loud, clear voice *(Ibn Yarchi).*

Because of this paragraph's status as a testimony, it should preferably be said with the congregation, or at least in the company of one other person. However, it may be recited by an individual as well *(Orach Chaim* 268).

Tur (ibid.) notes that it is especially important not to speak during וַיְכֻלּוּ or during the recitation of the seven-faceted blessing.

בְּרָכָה מֵעֵין שֶׁבַע / The Seven-faceted Blessing

In Talmudic times, the synagogues were generally located outside town limits, in open fields. Since it was dangerous to walk home alone in the dark after *Maariv,* the Sages instituted an extra prayer for the congregation so that everyone would stay a little longer, in case someone was slow in finishing his own *Maariv (Shabbos* 24b). On weekdays, the prayer בָּרוּךְ ה׳ לְעוֹלָם, *Blessed is HASHEM forever,* alludes to the number of blessings in the weekday *Shemoneh Esrei.* On the eve of the Sabbath, this extra prayer was formulated as a synopsis of the

On Friday night, all present stand and recite וַיְכֻלּוּ, *'Thus the heavens . . .,'* aloud in unison. Conversation is forbidden until after the *'Amen'* response to the blessing, *'Who sanctifies the Sabbath'* (below).

וַיְכֻלּוּ *Thus the heavens and the earth were finished,* and all their legion. On the seventh day God completed His work which He had done, and He abstained on the seventh day from all His work which He had done. God blessed the seventh day and sanctified it, because on it He had abstained from all His work which God created to make.*[1]

THE SEVEN-FACETED BLESSING

Chazzan continues:

בָּרוּךְ *Blessed are You, HASHEM, our God and the God of our forefathers, God of Abraham, God of Isaac, and God of Jacob; the great, mighty, and awesome God, the supreme God, Creator of heaven and earth.*

Congregation, then *chazzan:*

מָגֵן *He Who was the shield of our forefathers with His word, Who resuscitates the dead with His utterance, the Holy God Who is unequalled, Who grants rest to His people on His holy Sabbath day, for He was pleased with them to grant them rest. Before Him we will serve with awe and dread and give thanks to His Name every day continually with appropriate blessings. God of grateful praise, Master of peace, Who sanctifies the Sabbath and blesses the seventh day, and gives rest with holiness to a people saturated with delight — in memory of the work of Creation.*

Chazzan continues:

אֱלֹהֵינוּ *Our God and the God of our forefathers, may You be pleased with our rest. Sanctify us with Your commandments and grant us our share in Your Torah; satisfy us from Your goodness and gladden us with Your salvation, and purify our heart to serve You sincerely. O HASHEM, our God, with love and favor grant us Your holy Sabbath as a heritage and may Israel, the sanctifiers of Your Name, rest on it. Blessed are You, HASHEM, Who sanctifies the Sabbath.** (Cong.— *Amen.*)

(1) *Genesis* 2:1-3.

seven blessings of the *Shemoneh Esrei.* It begins בָּרוּךְ אַתָּה ה׳, which is very similar to the beginning of *Shemoneh Esrei.* Then it continues with מָגֵן אָבוֹת, which has seven parts, as follows:

(1) מָגֵן אָבוֹת, *Shield of our forefathers* = the blessing of אָבוֹת, *forefathers;*

(2) מְחַיֵּה מֵתִים, *Who resuscitates the dead* = the blessing of resuscitation;

(3) הָאֵל הַקָּדוֹשׁ, *The Holy God* = the blessing of His holiness;

(4) הַמֵּנִיחַ לְעַמּוֹ, *Who grants rest to His people* = קְדוּשַּׁת הַיּוֹם, the intermediate blessing, which discusses the Sabbath;

(5) לְפָנָיו נַעֲבוֹד, *Before Him we serve* = רְצֵה, which appeals for acceptance of our service;

(6) וְנוֹדֶה לִשְׁמוֹ, *And give thanks to His Name* = the blessing of מוֹדִים, which thanks God for His many favors;

(7) אֲדוֹן הַשָּׁלוֹם, *Master of peace* = שָׁלוֹם רָב, the last blessing, which speaks of peace.

מְקַדֵּשׁ הַשַּׁבָּת – *Who sanctifies the Sabbath.* When a Festival falls on the Sabbath, this prayer is recited without any mention of the Festival, because the Sages did not compose a separate Seven-faceted Blessing for Festivals.

The *chazzan* recites קַדִּישׁ שָׁלֵם.

יִתְגַּדַּל וְיִתְקַדַּשׁ שְׁמֵהּ רַבָּא. (.Cong – אָמֵן.) בְּעָלְמָא דִּי בְרָא כִרְעוּתֵהּ. וְיַמְלִיךְ מַלְכוּתֵהּ, בְּחַיֵּיכוֹן וּבְיוֹמֵיכוֹן וּבְחַיֵּי דְכָל בֵּית יִשְׂרָאֵל, בַּעֲגָלָא וּבִזְמַן קָרִיב. וְאִמְרוּ: אָמֵן.

(.Cong – אָמֵן. יְהֵא שְׁמֵהּ רַבָּא מְבָרַךְ לְעָלַם וּלְעָלְמֵי עָלְמַיָּא.)

יְהֵא שְׁמֵהּ רַבָּא מְבָרַךְ לְעָלַם וּלְעָלְמֵי עָלְמַיָּא.

יִתְבָּרַךְ וְיִשְׁתַּבַּח וְיִתְפָּאַר וְיִתְרוֹמַם וְיִתְנַשֵּׂא וְיִתְהַדָּר וְיִתְעַלֶּה וְיִתְהַלָּל שְׁמֵהּ דְּקֻדְשָׁא בְּרִיךְ הוּא (.Cong – בְּרִיךְ הוּא) – לְעֵלָּא מִן כָּל בִּרְכָתָא וְשִׁירָתָא תֻּשְׁבְּחָתָא וְנֶחֱמָתָא, דַּאֲמִירָן בְּעָלְמָא. וְאִמְרוּ: אָמֵן. (.Cong – אָמֵן.)

(.Cong – קַבֵּל בְּרַחֲמִים וּבְרָצוֹן אֶת תְּפִלָּתֵנוּ.)

תִּתְקַבֵּל צְלוֹתְהוֹן וּבָעוּתְהוֹן דְּכָל בֵּית יִשְׂרָאֵל קֳדָם אֲבוּהוֹן דִּי בִשְׁמַיָּא. וְאִמְרוּ: אָמֵן. (.Cong – אָמֵן.)

(.Cong – יְהִי שֵׁם יהוה מְבֹרָךְ, מֵעַתָּה וְעַד עוֹלָם.[1])

יְהֵא שְׁלָמָא רַבָּא מִן שְׁמַיָּא, וְחַיִּים עָלֵינוּ וְעַל כָּל יִשְׂרָאֵל. וְאִמְרוּ: אָמֵן. (.Cong – אָמֵן.)

(.Cong – עֶזְרִי מֵעִם יהוה, עֹשֵׂה שָׁמַיִם וָאָרֶץ.[2])

Take three steps back. Bow left and say . . . עֹשֶׂה; bow right and say . . . הוּא; bow forward and say וְעַל כָּל . . . אָמֵן. Remain standing in place for a few moments, then take three steps forward.

עֹשֶׂה שָׁלוֹם בִּמְרוֹמָיו, הוּא יַעֲשֶׂה שָׁלוֹם עָלֵינוּ, וְעַל כָּל יִשְׂרָאֵל. וְאִמְרוּ: אָמֵן. (.Cong – אָמֵן.)

קידוש בבית הכנסת

In some congregations, the *chazzan* recites *Kiddush* [although he will repeat *Kiddush* at home]. *Chazzan's Kiddush* consists of the blessings over wine, the holiness of the day, and *Shehecheyanu*.

סַבְרִי מָרָנָן וְרַבָּנָן וְרַבּוֹתַי:

בָּרוּךְ אַתָּה יהוה אֱלֹהֵינוּ מֶלֶךְ הָעוֹלָם, בּוֹרֵא פְּרִי הַגָּפֶן. (.Cong – אָמֵן.)

On Friday night, the words in brackets are included.

בָּרוּךְ אַתָּה יהוה אֱלֹהֵינוּ מֶלֶךְ הָעוֹלָם, אֲשֶׁר בָּחַר בָּנוּ מִכָּל עָם, וְרוֹמְמָנוּ מִכָּל לָשׁוֹן, וְקִדְּשָׁנוּ בְּמִצְוֹתָיו. וַתִּתֶּן לָנוּ יהוה אֱלֹהֵינוּ בְּאַהֲבָה [שַׁבָּתוֹת לִמְנוּחָה וּ]מוֹעֲדִים לְשִׂמְחָה חַגִּים וּזְמַנִּים לְשָׂשׂוֹן, אֶת יוֹם [הַשַּׁבָּת הַזֶּה וְאֶת יוֹם] הַשְּׁמִינִי חַג הָעֲצֶרֶת הַזֶּה, זְמַן שִׂמְחָתֵנוּ [בְּאַהֲבָה] מִקְרָא קֹדֶשׁ, זֵכֶר לִיצִיאַת מִצְרָיִם. כִּי בָנוּ בָחַרְתָּ וְאוֹתָנוּ קִדַּשְׁתָּ מִכָּל הָעַמִּים, [וְשַׁבָּת] וּמוֹעֲדֵי קָדְשֶׁךָ [בְּאַהֲבָה וּבְרָצוֹן] בְּשִׂמְחָה וּבְשָׂשׂוֹן הִנְחַלְתָּנוּ. בָּרוּךְ אַתָּה יהוה, מְקַדֵּשׁ [הַשַּׁבָּת וְ]יִשְׂרָאֵל וְהַזְּמַנִּים. (.Cong – אָמֵן.)

KIDDUSH CONTINUES ON NEXT PAGE.

The *chazzan* recites the Full *Kaddish.*

יִתְגַּדַּל *May His great Name grow exalted and sanctified* (Cong.— *Amen.*) *in the world that He created as He willed. May He give reign to His kingship in your lifetimes and in your days, and in the lifetimes of the entire Family of Israel, swiftly and soon. Now respond: Amen.*

(Cong.— *Amen. May His great Name be blessed forever and ever.*)

May His great Name be blessed forever and ever.

Blessed, praised, glorified, exalted, extolled, mighty, upraised, and lauded be the Name of the Holy One, Blessed is He (Cong.— *Blessed is He*) *— beyond any blessing and song, praise and consolation that are uttered in the world. Now respond: Amen.* (Cong.— *Amen.*)

(Cong.— *Accept our prayers with mercy and favor.*)

May the prayers and supplications of the entire Family of Israel be accepted before their Father Who is in Heaven. Now respond: Amen. (Cong.— *Amen.*)

(Cong.— *Blessed be the Name of* HASHEM, *from this time and forever.*[1])

May there be abundant peace from Heaven, and life, upon us and upon all Israel. Now respond: Amen. (Cong.— *Amen.*)

(Cong.— *My help is from* HASHEM, *Maker of heaven and earth.*[2])

Take three steps back. Bow left and say, *'He Who makes peace . . .';* bow right and say, *'may He . . .';* bow forward and say, *'and upon all Israel . . .'* Remain standing in place for a few moments, then take three steps forward.

He Who makes peace in His heights, may He make peace upon us, and upon all Israel. Now respond: Amen. (Cong.— *Amen.*)

KIDDUSH IN THE SYNAGOGUE

In some congregations, the *chazzan* recites *Kiddush* [although he will repeat *Kiddush* at home]. *Chazzan's Kiddush* consists of the blessings over wine,the holiness of the day, and *Shehecheyanu.*

By your leave, my masters and teachers:

בָּרוּךְ *Blessed are You,* HASHEM, *our God, King of the universe, Who creates the fruit of the vine.* (Cong.— *Amen.*)

On Friday night, the words in brackets are included.

בָּרוּךְ *Blessed are You,* HASHEM, *our God, King of the universe, Who has chosen us from every people, exalted us above every tongue, and sanctified us with His commandments. And You gave us,* HASHEM, *our God, with love, [Sabbaths for rest], appointed festivals for gladness, festivals and times of joy, [this day of Sabbath and] this day of the Shemini Atzeres Festival, the time of our gladness [with love], a holy convocation, a memorial of the Exodus from Egypt. For You have chosen us and You have sanctified us above all the peoples, [and the Sabbath] and Your holy festivals [in love and in favor] in gladness and in joy have You granted us as a heritage. Blessed are You,* HASHEM, *Who sanctifies [the Sabbath and] Israel and the seasons.*

(Cong.— *Amen.*)

KIDDUSH CONTINUES ON NEXT PAGE.

(1) *Psalms* 113:2. (2) 121:2.

⁂ Kiddush in the Synagogue

The custom of reciting *Kiddush* in the synagogue dates back to very early times. It was instituted for the benefit of homeless people or travelers who often ate and slept in the synagogue. They were thus able to discharge their obligation of *Kiddush* by listening to the *chazzan's* recitation. Although the need for this *Kiddush* ceased to exist as even people without homes would be invited home by other congregants, the custom is maintained by

בָּרוּךְ אַתָּה יהוה אֱלֹהֵינוּ מֶלֶךְ הָעוֹלָם, שֶׁהֶחֱיָנוּ וְקִיְּמָנוּ וְהִגִּיעָנוּ לַזְּמַן הַזֶּה. (Cong. – אָמֵן.)

A child who listened to the *Kiddush* and responded אָמֵן is given some of the wine.
[If no child is present, the *chazzan* drinks the required amount; see commentary below.]

The congregation stands while reciting עָלֵינוּ.

עָלֵינוּ לְשַׁבֵּחַ לַאֲדוֹן הַכֹּל, לָתֵת גְּדֻלָּה לְיוֹצֵר בְּרֵאשִׁית, שֶׁלֹּא עָשָׂנוּ כְּגוֹיֵי הָאֲרָצוֹת, וְלֹא שָׂמָנוּ כְּמִשְׁפְּחוֹת הָאֲדָמָה. שֶׁלֹּא שָׂם חֶלְקֵנוּ כָּהֶם, וְגוֹרָלֵנוּ כְּכָל הֲמוֹנָם. (שֶׁהֵם מִשְׁתַּחֲוִים לְהֶבֶל וָרִיק, וּמִתְפַּלְלִים אֶל אֵל לֹא יוֹשִׁיעַ.[1]) וַאֲנַחְנוּ כּוֹרְעִים וּמִשְׁתַּחֲוִים וּמוֹדִים, לִפְנֵי מֶלֶךְ מַלְכֵי הַמְּלָכִים הַקָּדוֹשׁ בָּרוּךְ הוּא. שֶׁהוּא נוֹטֶה שָׁמַיִם וְיֹסֵד אָרֶץ,[2] וּמוֹשַׁב יְקָרוֹ בַּשָּׁמַיִם מִמַּעַל, וּשְׁכִינַת עֻזּוֹ בְּגָבְהֵי מְרוֹמִים. הוּא אֱלֹהֵינוּ, אֵין עוֹד. אֱמֶת מַלְכֵּנוּ, אֶפֶס זוּלָתוֹ, כַּכָּתוּב בְּתוֹרָתוֹ: וְיָדַעְתָּ הַיּוֹם וַהֲשֵׁבֹתָ אֶל לְבָבֶךָ, כִּי יהוה הוּא הָאֱלֹהִים בַּשָּׁמַיִם מִמַּעַל וְעַל הָאָרֶץ מִתָּחַת, אֵין עוֹד.[3]

Bow while reciting וַאֲנַחְנוּ כּוֹרְעִים וּמִשְׁתַּחֲוִים.

עַל כֵּן נְקַוֶּה לְּךָ יהוה אֱלֹהֵינוּ לִרְאוֹת מְהֵרָה בְּתִפְאֶרֶת עֻזֶּךָ, לְהַעֲבִיר גִּלּוּלִים מִן הָאָרֶץ, וְהָאֱלִילִים כָּרוֹת יִכָּרֵתוּן, לְתַקֵּן עוֹלָם בְּמַלְכוּת שַׁדַּי. וְכָל בְּנֵי בָשָׂר יִקְרְאוּ בִשְׁמֶךָ, לְהַפְנוֹת אֵלֶיךָ כָּל רִשְׁעֵי אָרֶץ. יַכִּירוּ וְיֵדְעוּ כָּל יוֹשְׁבֵי תֵבֵל, כִּי לְךָ תִּכְרַע כָּל בֶּרֶךְ, תִּשָּׁבַע כָּל לָשׁוֹן.[4] לְפָנֶיךָ יהוה אֱלֹהֵינוּ יִכְרְעוּ וְיִפֹּלוּ, וְלִכְבוֹד שִׁמְךָ יְקָר יִתֵּנוּ. וִיקַבְּלוּ כֻלָּם אֶת עוֹל מַלְכוּתֶךָ, וְתִמְלֹךְ עֲלֵיהֶם מְהֵרָה לְעוֹלָם וָעֶד. כִּי הַמַּלְכוּת שֶׁלְּךָ הִיא וּלְעוֹלְמֵי עַד תִּמְלוֹךְ בְּכָבוֹד, כַּכָּתוּב בְּתוֹרָתֶךָ: יהוה יִמְלֹךְ לְעֹלָם וָעֶד.[5] ❖ וְנֶאֱמַר: וְהָיָה יהוה לְמֶלֶךְ עַל כָּל הָאָרֶץ, בַּיּוֹם הַהוּא יִהְיֶה יהוה אֶחָד וּשְׁמוֹ אֶחָד.[6]

Some recite the following after עָלֵינוּ:

אַל תִּירָא מִפַּחַד פִּתְאֹם, וּמִשֹּׁאַת רְשָׁעִים כִּי תָבֹא.[7] עֻצוּ עֵצָה וְתֻפָר, דַּבְּרוּ דָבָר וְלֹא יָקוּם, כִּי עִמָּנוּ אֵל.[8] וְעַד זִקְנָה אֲנִי הוּא, וְעַד שֵׂיבָה אֲנִי אֶסְבֹּל, אֲנִי עָשִׂיתִי וַאֲנִי אֶשָּׂא, וַאֲנִי אֶסְבֹּל וַאֲמַלֵּט.[9]

---

virtually all Ashkenaz synagogues. Since the person reciting this *Kiddush* will be reciting *Kiddush* at home for the benefit of his family — and for himself, as well, since that is where he will have his *Yom Tov* meal — he should have in mind that he will not discharge his own

בָּרוּךְ *Blessed are You, HASHEM, our God, King of the universe, Who has kept us alive, sustained us, and brought us to this season.* (Cong.– *Amen.)*

A child who listened to the *Kiddush* and responded *Amen* is given some of the wine. [If no child is present, the *chazzan* drinks the required amount; see commentary below.]

The congregation stands while reciting עָלֵינוּ, *'It is our duty . . .'*

עָלֵינוּ *It is our duty to praise the Master of all, to ascribe greatness to the Molder of primeval creation, for He has not made us like the nations of the lands, and has not emplaced us like the families of the earth; for He has not assigned our portion like theirs nor our lot like all their multitudes. (For they bow to vanity and emptiness and pray to a god which helps not.*[1]*) But we bend our knees, bow, and acknowledge our thanks before the King Who reigns over kings, the Holy One, Blessed is He. He stretches out heaven and establishes earth's foundation,*[2] *the seat of His homage is in the heavens above and His powerful Presence is in the loftiest heights. He is our God and there is none other. True is our King, there is nothing beside Him, as it is written in His Torah: 'You are to know this day and take to your heart that HASHEM is the only God — in heaven above and on the earth below — there is none other.'*[3]

Bow while reciting 'But we bend our knees.'

עַל כֵּן *Therefore we put our hope in You, HASHEM, our God, that we may soon see Your mighty splendor, to remove detestable idolatry from the earth, and false gods will be utterly cut off, to perfect the universe through the Almighty's sovereignty. Then all humanity will call upon Your Name, to turn all the earth's wicked toward You. All the world's inhabitants will recognize and know that to You every knee should bend, every tongue should swear.*[4] *Before You, HASHEM, our God, they will bend every knee and cast themselves down and to the glory of Your Name they will render homage, and they will all accept upon themselves the yoke of Your kingship that You may reign over them soon and eternally. For the kingdom is Yours and You will reign for all eternity in glory as it is written in Your Torah: HASHEM shall reign for all eternity.*[5] *And it is said: HASHEM will be King over all the world — on that day HASHEM will be One and His Name will be One.*[6]

Some recite the following after *Aleinu:*

אַל תִּירָא *Do not fear sudden terror, or the holocaust of the wicked when it comes.*[7] *Plan a conspiracy and it will be annulled; speak your piece and it shall not stand, for God is with us.*[8] *Even till your seniority, I remain unchanged; and even till your ripe old age, I shall endure. I created you and I shall bear you; I shall endure and rescue.*[9]

---

(1) *Isaiah* 45:20. (2) 51:13. (3) *Deuteronomy* 4:39. (4) Cf. *Isaiah* 45:23.
(5) *Exodus* 15:18. (6) *Zechariah* 14:9. (7) *Proverbs* 3:25. (8) *Isaiah* 8:10. (9) 46:4.

---

obligation in the synagogue. Therefore, he should not drink from the wine, but instead give some to one or more young children who listened to the *Kiddush* and responded אָמֵן.

קדיש יתום

Mourners recite קַדִּישׁ יָתוֹם (see *Laws* §81-83).

יִתְגַּדַּל וְיִתְקַדַּשׁ שְׁמֵהּ רַבָּא. (.Cong – אָמֵן.) בְּעָלְמָא דִּי בְרָא כִרְעוּתֵהּ. וְיַמְלִיךְ מַלְכוּתֵהּ, בְּחַיֵּיכוֹן וּבְיוֹמֵיכוֹן וּבְחַיֵּי דְכָל בֵּית יִשְׂרָאֵל, בַּעֲגָלָא וּבִזְמַן קָרִיב. וְאִמְרוּ: אָמֵן.

(.Cong – אָמֵן. יְהֵא שְׁמֵהּ רַבָּא מְבָרַךְ לְעָלַם וּלְעָלְמֵי עָלְמַיָּא.)

יְהֵא שְׁמֵהּ רַבָּא מְבָרַךְ לְעָלַם וּלְעָלְמֵי עָלְמַיָּא.

יִתְבָּרַךְ וְיִשְׁתַּבַּח וְיִתְפָּאַר וְיִתְרוֹמַם וְיִתְנַשֵּׂא וְיִתְהַדָּר וְיִתְעַלֶּה וְיִתְהַלָּל שְׁמֵהּ דְּקֻדְשָׁא בְּרִיךְ הוּא (.Cong – בְּרִיךְ הוּא) — לְעֵלָּא מִן כָּל בִּרְכָתָא וְשִׁירָתָא תֻּשְׁבְּחָתָא וְנֶחֱמָתָא, דַּאֲמִירָן בְּעָלְמָא. וְאִמְרוּ: אָמֵן. (.Cong – אָמֵן.)

יְהֵא שְׁלָמָא רַבָּא מִן שְׁמַיָּא, וְחַיִּים עָלֵינוּ וְעַל כָּל יִשְׂרָאֵל. וְאִמְרוּ: אָמֵן. (.Cong – אָמֵן.)

Take three steps back. Bow left and say . . . עֹשֶׂה; bow right and say . . . הוּא; bow forward and say וְעַל כָּל . . . אָמֵן. Remain standing in place for a few moments, then take three steps forward.

עֹשֶׂה שָׁלוֹם בִּמְרוֹמָיו, הוּא יַעֲשֶׂה שָׁלוֹם עָלֵינוּ, וְעַל כָּל יִשְׂרָאֵל. וְאִמְרוּ: אָמֵן. (.Cong – אָמֵן.)

תהלים כז

לְדָוִד, יהוה אוֹרִי וְיִשְׁעִי, מִמִּי אִירָא, יהוה מָעוֹז חַיַּי, מִמִּי אֶפְחָד. בִּקְרֹב עָלַי מְרֵעִים לֶאֱכֹל אֶת בְּשָׂרִי, צָרַי וְאֹיְבַי לִי, הֵמָּה כָּשְׁלוּ וְנָפָלוּ. אִם תַּחֲנֶה עָלַי מַחֲנֶה, לֹא יִירָא לִבִּי, אִם תָּקוּם עָלַי מִלְחָמָה, בְּזֹאת אֲנִי בוֹטֵחַ. אַחַת שָׁאַלְתִּי מֵאֵת יהוה, אוֹתָהּ אֲבַקֵּשׁ, שִׁבְתִּי בְּבֵית יהוה כָּל יְמֵי חַיַּי, לַחֲזוֹת בְּנֹעַם יהוה, וּלְבַקֵּר בְּהֵיכָלוֹ. כִּי יִצְפְּנֵנִי בְּסֻכֹּה בְּיוֹם רָעָה, יַסְתִּירֵנִי בְּסֵתֶר אָהֳלוֹ, בְּצוּר יְרוֹמְמֵנִי. וְעַתָּה יָרוּם רֹאשִׁי עַל אֹיְבַי סְבִיבוֹתַי, וְאֶזְבְּחָה בְאָהֳלוֹ זִבְחֵי תְרוּעָה, אָשִׁירָה וַאֲזַמְּרָה לַיהוה. שְׁמַע יהוה קוֹלִי אֶקְרָא, וְחָנֵּנִי וַעֲנֵנִי. לְךָ אָמַר לִבִּי בַּקְּשׁוּ פָנָי, אֶת פָּנֶיךָ יהוה אֲבַקֵּשׁ. אַל תַּסְתֵּר פָּנֶיךָ מִמֶּנִּי, אַל תַּט בְּאַף עַבְדֶּךָ, עֶזְרָתִי הָיִיתָ, אַל תִּטְּשֵׁנִי וְאַל תַּעַזְבֵנִי, אֱלֹהֵי יִשְׁעִי. כִּי אָבִי וְאִמִּי עֲזָבוּנִי, וַיהוה יַאַסְפֵנִי. הוֹרֵנִי יהוה דַּרְכֶּךָ, וּנְחֵנִי בְּאֹרַח מִישׁוֹר, לְמַעַן שׁוֹרְרָי. אַל תִּתְּנֵנִי בְּנֶפֶשׁ צָרָי, כִּי קָמוּ בִי עֵדֵי שֶׁקֶר, וִיפֵחַ חָמָס. ❖ לוּלֵא הֶאֱמַנְתִּי לִרְאוֹת בְּטוּב יהוה בְּאֶרֶץ חַיִּים. קַוֵּה אֶל יהוה, חֲזַק וְיַאֲמֵץ לִבֶּךָ, וְקַוֵּה אֶל יהוה.

Mourners recite קַדִּישׁ יָתוֹם, the Mourner's *Kaddish* (above).

MOURNER'S KADDISH

Mourners recite the Mourner's *Kaddish* (see *Laws* §81-83).
[A transliteration of this *Kaddish* appears on page 1301.]

יִתְגַּדַּל *May His great Name grow exalted and sanctified* (Cong.– *Amen.*) *in the world that He created as He willed. May He give reign to His kingship in your lifetimes and in your days, and in the lifetimes of the entire Family of Israel, swiftly and soon. Now respond: Amen.*

(Cong.– *Amen. May His great Name be blessed forever and ever.*)
May His great Name be blessed forever and ever.

Blessed, praised, glorified, exalted, extolled, mighty, upraised, and lauded be the Name of the Holy One, Blessed is He (Cong.– *Blessed is He*) — *beyond any blessing and song, praise and consolation that are uttered in the world. Now respond: Amen.* (Cong.– *Amen.*)

May there be abundant peace from Heaven, and life, upon us and upon all Israel. Now respond: Amen. (Cong.– *Amen.*)

Take three steps back. Bow left and say, *'He Who makes peace . . .'*; bow right and say, *'may He . . .'*; bow forward and say, *'and upon all Israel . . .'* Remain standing in place for a few moments, then take three steps forward.

He Who makes peace in His heights, may He make peace upon us, and upon all Israel. Now respond: Amen. (Cong.– *Amen.*)

Psalm 27

לְדָוִד *Of David;* HASHEM *is my light and my salvation, whom shall I fear?* HASHEM *is my life's strength, whom shall I dread? When evildoers approach me to devour my flesh, my tormentors and my foes against me — it is they who stumble and fall. Though an army would besiege me, my heart would not fear; though war would arise against me, in this I trust. One thing I asked of* HASHEM, *that shall I seek: That I dwell in the House of* HASHEM *all the days of my life; to behold the sweetness of* HASHEM *and to contemplate in His Sanctuary. Indeed, He will hide me in His Shelter on the day of evil; He will conceal me in the concealment of His Tent, He will lift me upon a rock. Now my head is raised above my enemies around me, and I will slaughter offerings in His Tent accompanied by joyous song; I will sing and make music to* HASHEM. HASHEM, *hear my voice when I call, be gracious toward me and answer me. In Your behalf, my heart has said, 'Seek My Presence'; Your Presence,* HASHEM, *do I seek. Conceal not Your Presence from me, repel not Your servant in anger. You have been my Helper, abandon me not, forsake me not, O God of my salvation. Though my father and mother have forsaken me,* HASHEM *will gather me in. Teach me Your way,* HASHEM, *and lead me on the path of integrity, because of my watchful foes. Deliver me not to the wishes of my tormentors, for there have arisen against me false witnesses who breathe violence.* Chazzan– *Had I not trusted that I would see the goodness of* HASHEM *in the land of life! Hope to* HASHEM, *strengthen yourself and He will give you courage; and hope to* HASHEM.

Mourners recite קַדִּישׁ יָתוֹם, the Mourner's *Kaddish* (above).

Many congregations recite either אֲדוֹן עוֹלָם or יִגְדַּל, or both, at this point.

אֲדוֹן עוֹלָם* אֲשֶׁר מָלַךְ, בְּטֶרֶם כָּל יְצִיר נִבְרָא.
לְעֵת נַעֲשָׂה בְחֶפְצוֹ כֹּל, אֲזַי מֶלֶךְ שְׁמוֹ נִקְרָא.
וְאַחֲרֵי כִּכְלוֹת הַכֹּל, לְבַדּוֹ יִמְלוֹךְ נוֹרָא.
וְהוּא הָיָה וְהוּא הֹוֶה, וְהוּא יִהְיֶה בְּתִפְאָרָה.
וְהוּא אֶחָד וְאֵין שֵׁנִי, לְהַמְשִׁיל לוֹ לְהַחְבִּירָה.
בְּלִי רֵאשִׁית בְּלִי תַכְלִית, וְלוֹ הָעֹז וְהַמִּשְׂרָה.
וְהוּא אֵלִי וְחַי גֹּאֲלִי, וְצוּר חֶבְלִי בְּעֵת צָרָה.
וְהוּא נִסִּי וּמָנוֹס לִי, מְנָת כּוֹסִי בְּיוֹם אֶקְרָא.
בְּיָדוֹ אַפְקִיד רוּחִי, בְּעֵת אִישַׁן וְאָעִירָה.
וְעִם רוּחִי גְּוִיָּתִי, יהוה לִי וְלֹא אִירָא.

יִגְדַּל אֱלֹהִים חַי* וְיִשְׁתַּבַּח, נִמְצָא וְאֵין עֵת אֶל מְצִיאוּתוֹ.
אֶחָד וְאֵין יָחִיד כְּיִחוּדוֹ, נֶעְלָם וְגַם אֵין סוֹף לְאַחְדוּתוֹ.
אֵין לוֹ דְּמוּת הַגּוּף וְאֵינוֹ גוּף, לֹא נַעֲרוֹךְ אֵלָיו קְדֻשָּׁתוֹ.
קַדְמוֹן לְכָל דָּבָר אֲשֶׁר נִבְרָא, רִאשׁוֹן וְאֵין רֵאשִׁית לְרֵאשִׁיתוֹ.
הִנּוֹ אֲדוֹן עוֹלָם לְכָל נוֹצָר, יוֹרֶה גְדֻלָּתוֹ וּמַלְכוּתוֹ.
שֶׁפַע נְבוּאָתוֹ נְתָנוֹ, אֶל אַנְשֵׁי סְגֻלָּתוֹ וְתִפְאַרְתּוֹ.
לֹא קָם בְּיִשְׂרָאֵל כְּמשֶׁה עוֹד, נָבִיא וּמַבִּיט אֶת תְּמוּנָתוֹ.
תּוֹרַת אֱמֶת נָתַן לְעַמּוֹ אֵל, עַל יַד נְבִיאוֹ נֶאֱמַן בֵּיתוֹ.
לֹא יַחֲלִיף הָאֵל וְלֹא יָמִיר דָּתוֹ, לְעוֹלָמִים לְזוּלָתוֹ.
צוֹפֶה וְיוֹדֵעַ סְתָרֵינוּ, מַבִּיט לְסוֹף דָּבָר בְּקַדְמָתוֹ.
גּוֹמֵל לְאִישׁ חֶסֶד כְּמִפְעָלוֹ, נוֹתֵן לְרָשָׁע רָע כְּרִשְׁעָתוֹ.
יִשְׁלַח לְקֵץ הַיָּמִין מְשִׁיחֵנוּ, לִפְדּוֹת מְחַכֵּי קֵץ יְשׁוּעָתוֹ.
מֵתִים יְחַיֶּה אֵל בְּרֹב חַסְדּוֹ, בָּרוּךְ עֲדֵי עַד שֵׁם תְּהִלָּתוֹ.

☙ **אֲדוֹן עוֹלָם** — *Master of the universe.* This inspiring song of praise is attributed to R' Shlomo ibn Gabirol, one of the greatest early *paytanim* [liturgical poets], who flourished in the eleventh century. The daily prayer service is inaugurated with the Name אָדוֹן to recall the merit of Abraham, the first one to address God with this title [*Genesis* 15:2] *(Etz Yosef),* and the one who instituted the morning prayers [*Berachos* 26b] *(Vilna Gaon).*

The song emphasizes that God is timeless, infinite and omnipotent. Mankind can offer Him only one thing: to proclaim Him as King, by doing His will and praising Him. Despite God's greatness, however, He involves Himself with man's personal needs in time of pain and distress. The prayer concludes on the inspiring note that, lofty though He is, *HASHEM is with me, I shall not fear.*

☙ **יִגְדַּל אֱלֹהִים חַי** — *Exalted be the Living God.* This song of uncertain authorship summarizes the 'Thirteen Principles of Faith' expounded by *Rambam* [Maimonides] in his *Commentary to Mishnah, Sanhedrin,* ch. 10, and stated succinctly in the famous *Ani Maamin* prayer. They comprise the basic principles that every Jew is required to believe. In *Rambam's* view, to deny any of them constitutes heresy.

Many congregations recite either אֲדוֹן עוֹלָם, *Master of the universe,* or יִגְדַּל, *Exalted be,* or both.

אֲדוֹן עוֹלָם *Master of the universe,* Who reigned*
before any form was created,
At the time when His will brought all into being —
then as 'King' was His Name proclaimed.
After all has ceased to be,
He, the Awesome One, will reign alone.
It is He Who was, He Who is,
and He Who shall remain, in splendor.
He is One — there is no second
to compare to Him, to declare as His equal.
Without beginning, without conclusion —
His is the power and dominion.
He is my God, my living Redeemer,
Rock of my pain in time of distress.
He is my banner, a refuge for me,
the portion in my cup on the day I call.
Into His hand I shall entrust my spirit
when I go to sleep — and I shall awaken!
With my spirit shall my body remain.
HASHEM is with me, I shall not fear.

יִגְדַּל *Exalted be the Living God* and praised,*
He exists — unbounded by time is His existence.
He is One — and there is no unity like His Oneness.
Inscrutable and infinite is His Oneness.
He has no semblance of a body nor is He corporeal;
nor has His holiness any comparison.
He preceded every being that was created —
the First, and nothing precedes His precedence.
Behold! He is Master of the universe to every creature,
He demonstrates His greatness and His sovereignty.
He granted His flow of prophecy
to His treasured splendrous people.
In Israel none like Moses arose again —
a prophet who perceived His vision clearly.
God gave His people a Torah of truth,
by means of His prophet, the most trusted of His household.
God will never amend nor exchange His law
for any other one, for all eternity.
He scrutinizes and knows our hiddenmost secrets;
He perceives a matter's outcome at its inception.
He recompenses man with kindness according to his deed;
He places evil on the wicked according to his wickedness.
By the End of Days He will send our Messiah,
to redeem those longing for His final salvation.
God will revive the dead in His abundant kindness —
Blessed forever is His praised Name.

On Friday night, some recite the following before *Kiddush*.
Each of the first four stanzas is recited three times.

שָׁלוֹם עֲלֵיכֶם, מַלְאֲכֵי הַשָּׁרֵת, מַלְאֲכֵי עֶלְיוֹן, מִמֶּלֶךְ מַלְכֵי הַמְּלָכִים הַקָּדוֹשׁ בָּרוּךְ הוּא.

בּוֹאֲכֶם לְשָׁלוֹם, מַלְאֲכֵי הַשָּׁלוֹם, מַלְאֲכֵי עֶלְיוֹן, מִמֶּלֶךְ מַלְכֵי הַמְּלָכִים הַקָּדוֹשׁ בָּרוּךְ הוּא.

בָּרְכוּנִי לְשָׁלוֹם, מַלְאֲכֵי הַשָּׁלוֹם, מַלְאֲכֵי עֶלְיוֹן, מִמֶּלֶךְ מַלְכֵי הַמְּלָכִים הַקָּדוֹשׁ בָּרוּךְ הוּא.

צֵאתְכֶם לְשָׁלוֹם, מַלְאֲכֵי הַשָּׁלוֹם, מַלְאֲכֵי עֶלְיוֹן, מִמֶּלֶךְ מַלְכֵי הַמְּלָכִים הַקָּדוֹשׁ בָּרוּךְ הוּא.

כִּי מַלְאָכָיו יְצַוֶּה לָּךְ, לִשְׁמָרְךָ בְּכָל דְּרָכֶיךָ.[1]
יהוה יִשְׁמָר צֵאתְךָ וּבוֹאֶךָ, מֵעַתָּה וְעַד עוֹלָם.[2]

(משלי לא:י-לא)

אֵשֶׁת חַיִל מִי יִמְצָא, וְרָחֹק מִפְּנִינִים מִכְרָהּ.
בָּטַח בָּהּ לֵב בַּעְלָהּ, וְשָׁלָל לֹא יֶחְסָר.
גְּמָלַתְהוּ טוֹב וְלֹא רָע, כֹּל יְמֵי חַיֶּיהָ.
דָּרְשָׁה צֶמֶר וּפִשְׁתִּים, וַתַּעַשׂ בְּחֵפֶץ כַּפֶּיהָ.
הָיְתָה כָּאֳנִיּוֹת סוֹחֵר, מִמֶּרְחָק תָּבִיא לַחְמָהּ.
וַתָּקָם בְּעוֹד לַיְלָה, וַתִּתֵּן טֶרֶף לְבֵיתָהּ, וְחֹק לְנַעֲרֹתֶיהָ.
זָמְמָה שָׂדֶה וַתִּקָּחֵהוּ, מִפְּרִי כַפֶּיהָ נָטְעָה כָּרֶם.
חָגְרָה בְעוֹז מָתְנֶיהָ, וַתְּאַמֵּץ זְרוֹעֹתֶיהָ.
טָעֲמָה כִּי טוֹב סַחְרָהּ, לֹא יִכְבֶּה בַלַּיְלָה נֵרָהּ.
יָדֶיהָ שִׁלְּחָה בַכִּישׁוֹר, וְכַפֶּיהָ תָּמְכוּ פָלֶךְ.
כַּפָּהּ פָּרְשָׂה לֶעָנִי, וְיָדֶיהָ שִׁלְּחָה לָאֶבְיוֹן.
לֹא תִירָא לְבֵיתָהּ מִשָּׁלֶג, כִּי כָל בֵּיתָהּ לָבֻשׁ שָׁנִים.
מַרְבַדִּים עָשְׂתָה לָּהּ, שֵׁשׁ וְאַרְגָּמָן לְבוּשָׁהּ.
נוֹדָע בַּשְּׁעָרִים בַּעְלָהּ, בְּשִׁבְתּוֹ עִם זִקְנֵי אָרֶץ.
סָדִין עָשְׂתָה וַתִּמְכֹּר, וַחֲגוֹר נָתְנָה לַכְּנַעֲנִי.
עוֹז וְהָדָר לְבוּשָׁהּ, וַתִּשְׂחַק לְיוֹם אַחֲרוֹן.
פִּיהָ פָּתְחָה בְחָכְמָה, וְתוֹרַת חֶסֶד עַל לְשׁוֹנָהּ.
צוֹפִיָּה הֲלִיכוֹת בֵּיתָהּ, וְלֶחֶם עַצְלוּת לֹא תֹאכֵל.
קָמוּ בָנֶיהָ וַיְאַשְּׁרוּהָ, בַּעְלָהּ וַיְהַלְלָהּ.
רַבּוֹת בָּנוֹת עָשׂוּ חָיִל, וְאַתְּ עָלִית עַל כֻּלָּנָה.
שֶׁקֶר הַחֵן וְהֶבֶל הַיֹּפִי, אִשָּׁה יִרְאַת יהוה הִיא תִתְהַלָּל.
תְּנוּ לָהּ מִפְּרִי יָדֶיהָ, וִיהַלְלוּהָ בַשְּׁעָרִים מַעֲשֶׂיהָ.

On Friday night, some recite the following before *Kiddush*.
Each of the first four stanzas is recited three times.

שָׁלוֹם עֲלֵיכֶם *Peace upon you, O ministering angels, angels of the Exalted One — from the King Who reigns over kings, the Holy One, Blessed is He.*

בּוֹאֲכֶם לְשָׁלוֹם *May your coming be for peace, O angels of peace, angels of the Exalted One — from the King Who reigns over kings, the Holy One, Blessed is He.*

בָּרְכוּנִי לְשָׁלוֹם *Bless me for peace, O angels of peace, angels of the Exalted One — from the King Who reigns over kings, the Holy One, Blessed is He.*

צֵאתְכֶם לְשָׁלוֹם *May your departure be to peace, O angels of peace, angels of the Exalted One — from the King Who reigns over kings, the Holy One, Blessed is He.*

He will charge His angels for you, to protect you in all your ways.[1]
May H*ASHEM protect your going and returning, from this time and forever.*[2]

(*Proverbs* 31:10-31)

אֵשֶׁת חַיִל *An accomplished woman, who can find? —*
Far beyond pearls is her value.
ב *Her husband's heart relies on her and he shall lack no fortune.*
ג *She repays his good, but never his harm, all the days of her life.*
ד *She seeks out wool and linen, and her hands work willingly.*
ה *She is like a merchant's ships, from afar she brings her sustenance.*
ו *She arises while it is yet nighttime,*
and gives food to her household and a ration to her maidens.
ז *She envisions a field and buys it,*
from the fruit of her handiwork she plants a vineyard.
ח *With strength she girds her loins, and invigorates her arms.*
ט *She discerns that her enterprise is good —*
so her lamp is not snuffed out by night.
י *Her hands she stretches out to the distaff, and her palms support the spindle.*
כ *She spreads out her palm to the poor, and extends her hands to the destitute.*
ל *She fears not snow for her household,*
for her entire household is clothed with scarlet wool.
מ *Luxurious bedspreads she made herself, linen and purple wool are her clothing.*
נ *Distinctive in the councils is her husband,*
when he sits with the elders of the land.
ס *She makes a cloak to sell, and delivers a belt to the peddler.*
ע *Strength and majesty are her raiment, she joyfully awaits the last day.*
פ *She opens her mouth with wisdom, and a lesson of kindness is on her tongue.*
צ *She anticipates the ways of her household,*
and partakes not of the bread of laziness.
ק *Her children arise and praise her, her husband, and he lauds her:*
ר *'Many daughters have amassed achievement, but you surpassed them all.'*
ש *False is grace and vain is beauty,*
a God-fearing woman — she should be praised.
ת *Give her the fruits of her hand*
and let her be praised in the gates by her very own deeds.

(1) *Psalms* 91:11. (2) 121:8.

קידוש לליל שמיני עצרת

When the Festival falls on Friday night, begin here:

(וַיְהִי עֶרֶב* וַיְהִי בֹקֶר –Recite silently)

יוֹם הַשִּׁשִּׁי. וַיְכֻלּוּ* הַשָּׁמַיִם וְהָאָרֶץ* וְכָל צְבָאָם. וַיְכַל אֱלֹהִים בַּיּוֹם הַשְּׁבִיעִי מְלַאכְתּוֹ אֲשֶׁר עָשָׂה, וַיִּשְׁבֹּת בַּיּוֹם הַשְּׁבִיעִי מִכָּל מְלַאכְתּוֹ אֲשֶׁר עָשָׂה. וַיְבָרֶךְ אֱלֹהִים אֶת יוֹם הַשְּׁבִיעִי וַיְקַדֵּשׁ אֹתוֹ, כִּי בוֹ שָׁבַת מִכָּל מְלַאכְתּוֹ אֲשֶׁר בָּרָא אֱלֹהִים לַעֲשׂוֹת.[1]

On all nights other than Friday begin here (on Friday night include all words in brackets):

סַבְרִי מָרָנָן וְרַבָּנָן וְרַבּוֹתַי:

בָּרוּךְ אַתָּה יהוה אֱלֹהֵינוּ מֶלֶךְ הָעוֹלָם, בּוֹרֵא* פְּרִי הַגָּפֶן.

(אָמֵן. –All present respond)

בָּרוּךְ אַתָּה יהוה אֱלֹהֵינוּ מֶלֶךְ הָעוֹלָם, אֲשֶׁר בָּחַר בָּנוּ מִכָּל עָם,* וְרוֹמְמָנוּ מִכָּל לָשׁוֹן, וְקִדְּשָׁנוּ בְּמִצְוֹתָיו. וַתִּתֶּן לָנוּ יהוה אֱלֹהֵינוּ בְּאַהֲבָה [שַׁבָּתוֹת לִמְנוּחָה וּ]מוֹעֲדִים לְשִׂמְחָה חַגִּים וּזְמַנִּים לְשָׂשׂוֹן, אֶת יוֹם [הַשַּׁבָּת הַזֶּה וְאֶת יוֹם] הַשְּׁמִינִי חַג הָעֲצֶרֶת הַזֶּה, זְמַן שִׂמְחָתֵנוּ [בְּאַהֲבָה] מִקְרָא קֹדֶשׁ, זֵכֶר לִיצִיאַת מִצְרָיִם. כִּי בָנוּ בָחַרְתָּ וְאוֹתָנוּ קִדַּשְׁתָּ מִכָּל הָעַמִּים, [וְשַׁבָּת] וּמוֹעֲדֵי קָדְשֶׁךָ [בְּאַהֲבָה וּבְרָצוֹן] בְּשִׂמְחָה וּבְשָׂשׂוֹן הִנְחַלְתָּנוּ. בָּרוּךְ אַתָּה יהוה, מְקַדֵּשׁ [הַשַּׁבָּת וְ]יִשְׂרָאֵל וְהַזְּמַנִּים.

(אָמֵן. –All present respond)

בָּרוּךְ אַתָּה יהוה אֱלֹהֵינוּ מֶלֶךְ הָעוֹלָם, שֶׁהֶחֱיָנוּ וְקִיְּמָנוּ וְהִגִּיעָנוּ לַזְּמַן הַזֶּה.

(אָמֵן. –All present respond)

Bircas HaMazon appears on page 84.

Kiddush

Every Sabbath and *Yom Tov* is ushered in by *Kiddush*, a declaration of the day's sanctity. Even though we have already proclaimed the holiness of the day in our evening prayers, its proper celebration belongs in the home (tonight, of course, home is in the *succah*), where we usually pursue our weekday activities. As we begin our festive meal, therefore, we dedicate ourselves to the special message of the day.

וַיְהִי עֶרֶב – *And there was evening.* When *Yom Tov* falls on the Sabbath, we preface the *Kiddush* with the same verses that we recite every Friday night, and which describe the Sabbath of the week of creation, to remind us of the profound purpose of the Sabbath.

וַיְכֻלּוּ – *Were finished.* The Midrash interprets וַיְכַל and וַיְכֻלּוּ homiletically as *longing,* as we find כָּלְתָה נַפְשִׁי, *my soul longed (Psalms* 84:3). Heaven and earth, and God Himself, long for the coming of the Sabbath, because it infuses all of creation with holiness *(Tzror HaMor).*

וַיְכֻלּוּ הַשָּׁמַיִם וְהָאָרֶץ – *Thus the heavens and the earth were finished.* The verse uses the passive form *were finished* rather than the active *and* HASHEM *finished.* This implies that, despite the magnitude of the task, God expended only minimum effort in the creation of the universe *(Tzror HaMor).*

KIDDUSH FOR THE NIGHT OF SHEMINI ATZERES

When the Festival falls on Friday night, begin here:

(Recite silently— *And there was evening* and there was morning)*

יוֹם הַשִּׁשִּׁי *The sixth day. Thus the heavens and the earth were finished,* and all their array. On the seventh day God completed His work which He had done, and He abstained on the seventh day from all His work which He had done. God blessed the seventh day and hallowed it, because on it He abstained from all His work which God created to make.*[1]

On all nights other than Friday begin here (on Friday night include all words in brackets):

By your leave, my masters, rabbis and teachers:

בָּרוּךְ *Blessed are You, HASHEM, our God, King of the universe, Who creates* the fruit of the vine.* (All present respond— *Amen.)*

בָּרוּךְ *Blessed are You, HASHEM, our God, King of the universe, Who has chosen us from every people,* exalted us above every tongue, and sanctified us with His commandments. And You gave us, HASHEM, our God, with love [Sabbaths for rest], appointed festivals for gladness, festivals and times for joy, [this day of Sabbath and] this day of the Shemini Atzeres Festival, the time of our gladness [with love], a holy convocation, a memorial of the Exodus from Egypt. For You have chosen us and You have sanctified us above all the peoples, [and the Sabbath] and Your holy festivals [in love and in favor] in gladness and in joy have You granted us as a heritage. Blessed are You, HASHEM, Who sanctifies [the Sabbath and] Israel and the seasons.* (All present respond— *Amen.)*

בָּרוּךְ *Blessed are You, HASHEM, our God, King of the universe, Who has kept us alive, sustained us, and brought us to this season.* (All present respond— *Amen.)*

Grace After Meals appears on page 84.

(1) *Genesis* 1:31-2:3.

בָּרוּךְ אַתָּה ... בּוֹרֵא — *Blessed are You ... Who creates.* The blessing begins by addressing God directly in second person — אַתָּה, *You* — it then reverts to third person, בּוֹרֵא, *(He) Who creates.* This is also true of all blessings. They begin by addressing God in second person because prayer is so exalted that it enables mortal man to turn directly to God, so to speak. Then the blessings change to third person because the balance of the blessing speaks of His outward manifestations as He guides and controls the universe. Of that aspect of God, we have no direct understanding — only an imperfect perception of outward appearances *(Michtav MeEliyahu).*

אֲשֶׁר בָּחַר בָּנוּ מִכָּל עָם ... — *Who has chosen us from every people ...* The wording of *Kiddush* is reminiscent of the Festival *Shemoneh Esrei* (see page 54).

⋖§ Shehecheyanu

שֶׁהֶחֱיָנוּ — *Who has kept us alive.* This blessing is called בִּרְכַּת הַזְּמַן, *the blessing of the time,* or simply זְמַן, *time.* It is recited: on the festivals; over fruits of a new season, provided they ripen at recurring intervals and are not always available; upon *mitzvos* that are performed at seasonal interval such as *succah, lulav,* and others connected with the annual festivals; upon seeing a friend whom one has not seen for a significant interval; upon purchasing a new garment of significance; and upon benefiting from a significant event [see *Orach Chaim* 225].

This blessing is technically in the category of בִּרְכוֹת הוֹדָאָה, *blessings of thanksgiving.* It expresses our gratitude to God for having granted us the life and sustenance to celebrate another festive season.

שחרית לשמיני עצרת

THE MORNING SERVICE BEGINS WITH PAGES 130-208, THEN CONTINUES HERE.

נִשְׁמַת כָּל חַי תְּבָרֵךְ אֶת שִׁמְךָ יהוה אֱלֹהֵינוּ, וְרוּחַ כָּל בָּשָׂר תְּפָאֵר וּתְרוֹמֵם זִכְרְךָ מַלְכֵּנוּ תָּמִיד. מִן הָעוֹלָם וְעַד הָעוֹלָם אַתָּה אֵל,[1] וּמִבַּלְעָדֶיךָ אֵין לָנוּ מֶלֶךְ[2] גּוֹאֵל וּמוֹשִׁיעַ. פּוֹדֶה וּמַצִּיל וּמְפַרְנֵס וּמְרַחֵם בְּכָל עֵת צָרָה וְצוּקָה, אֵין לָנוּ מֶלֶךְ אֶלָּא אָתָּה. אֱלֹהֵי הָרִאשׁוֹנִים וְהָאַחֲרוֹנִים, אֱלוֹהַּ כָּל בְּרִיּוֹת, אֲדוֹן כָּל תּוֹלָדוֹת, הַמְּהֻלָּל בְּרֹב הַתִּשְׁבָּחוֹת, הַמְּנַהֵג עוֹלָמוֹ בְּחֶסֶד וּבְרִיּוֹתָיו בְּרַחֲמִים. וַיהוה לֹא יָנוּם וְלֹא יִישָׁן.[3] הַמְּעוֹרֵר יְשֵׁנִים, וְהַמֵּקִיץ נִרְדָּמִים, וְהַמֵּשִׂיחַ אִלְּמִים, וְהַמַּתִּיר אֲסוּרִים,[4] וְהַסּוֹמֵךְ נוֹפְלִים, וְהַזּוֹקֵף כְּפוּפִים.[5] לְךָ לְבַדְּךָ אֲנַחְנוּ מוֹדִים. אִלּוּ פִינוּ מָלֵא שִׁירָה כַּיָּם, וּלְשׁוֹנֵנוּ רִנָּה כַּהֲמוֹן גַּלָּיו, וְשִׂפְתוֹתֵינוּ שֶׁבַח כְּמֶרְחֲבֵי רָקִיעַ, וְעֵינֵינוּ מְאִירוֹת כַּשֶּׁמֶשׁ וְכַיָּרֵחַ, וְיָדֵינוּ פְרוּשׂוֹת כְּנִשְׁרֵי שָׁמָיִם, וְרַגְלֵינוּ קַלּוֹת כָּאַיָּלוֹת, אֵין אֲנַחְנוּ מַסְפִּיקִים לְהוֹדוֹת לְךָ, יהוה אֱלֹהֵינוּ וֵאלֹהֵי אֲבוֹתֵינוּ, וּלְבָרֵךְ אֶת שְׁמֶךָ עַל אַחַת מֵאָלֶף אֶלֶף אַלְפֵי אֲלָפִים וְרִבֵּי רְבָבוֹת פְּעָמִים הַטּוֹבוֹת שֶׁעָשִׂיתָ עִם אֲבוֹתֵינוּ וְעִמָּנוּ. מִמִּצְרַיִם גְּאַלְתָּנוּ יהוה אֱלֹהֵינוּ, וּמִבֵּית עֲבָדִים פְּדִיתָנוּ. בְּרָעָב זַנְתָּנוּ, וּבְשָׂבָע כִּלְכַּלְתָּנוּ, מֵחֶרֶב הִצַּלְתָּנוּ, וּמִדֶּבֶר מִלַּטְתָּנוּ, וּמֵחֳלָיִם רָעִים וְנֶאֱמָנִים דִּלִּיתָנוּ. עַד הֵנָּה עֲזָרוּנוּ רַחֲמֶיךָ, וְלֹא עֲזָבוּנוּ חֲסָדֶיךָ. וְאַל תִּטְּשֵׁנוּ יהוה אֱלֹהֵינוּ לָנֶצַח. עַל כֵּן אֵבָרִים שֶׁפִּלַּגְתָּ בָּנוּ, וְרוּחַ וּנְשָׁמָה שֶׁנָּפַחְתָּ בְּאַפֵּינוּ, וְלָשׁוֹן אֲשֶׁר שַׂמְתָּ בְּפִינוּ, הֵן הֵם יוֹדוּ וִיבָרְכוּ וִישַׁבְּחוּ וִיפָאֲרוּ וִירוֹמְמוּ וְיַעֲרִיצוּ וְיַקְדִּישׁוּ וְיַמְלִיכוּ אֶת שִׁמְךָ מַלְכֵּנוּ. כִּי כָל פֶּה לְךָ יוֹדֶה, וְכָל לָשׁוֹן לְךָ תִשָּׁבַע, וְכָל בֶּרֶךְ לְךָ תִכְרַע,[6] וְכָל קוֹמָה לְפָנֶיךָ תִשְׁתַּחֲוֶה, וְכָל לְבָבוֹת יִירָאוּךָ, וְכָל קֶרֶב וּכְלָיוֹת יְזַמְּרוּ לִשְׁמֶךָ, כַּדָּבָר שֶׁכָּתוּב: כָּל עַצְמֹתַי תֹּאמַרְנָה, יהוה מִי כָמוֹךָ, מַצִּיל עָנִי מֵחָזָק מִמֶּנּוּ, וְעָנִי וְאֶבְיוֹן מִגֹּזְלוֹ.[7] מִי יִדְמֶה לָּךְ, וּמִי יִשְׁוֶה לָּךְ, וּמִי יַעֲרָךְ לָךְ.[8] הָאֵל הַגָּדוֹל הַגִּבּוֹר וְהַנּוֹרָא, אֵל עֶלְיוֹן, קֹנֵה שָׁמַיִם וָאָרֶץ. ❖ נְהַלֶּלְךָ וּנְשַׁבֵּחֲךָ וּנְפָאֶרְךָ וּנְבָרֵךְ אֶת שֵׁם קָדְשֶׁךָ, כָּאָמוּר: לְדָוִד, בָּרְכִי נַפְשִׁי אֶת יהוה, וְכָל קְרָבַי אֶת שֵׁם קָדְשׁוֹ.[9]

---

(1) Cf. *Psalms* 90:2. (2) Cf. *Isaiah* 44:6. (3) Cf. *Psalms* 121:4. (4) Cf. 146:7. (5) Cf. 145:14. (6) Cf. *Isaiah* 45:23. (7) *Psalms* 35:10. (8) Cf. 89:7; cf. *Isaiah* 40:25. (9) *Psalms* 103:1.

SHACHARIS FOR SHEMINI ATZERES

THE MORNING SERVICE BEGINS WITH PAGES 130-208, THEN CONTINUES HERE.

נִשְׁמַת *The soul of every living being shall bless Your Name, HASHEM our God; the spirit of all flesh shall always glorify and exalt Your remembrance, our King. From This World to the World to Come, You are God,[1] and other than You we have no king,[2] redeemer or savior. Liberator, Rescuer, Sustainer and Merciful One in every time of distress and anguish, we have no king but You! — God of the first and of the last, God of all creatures, Master of all generations, Who is extolled through a multitude of praises, Who guides His world with kindness and His creatures with mercy. HASHEM neither slumbers nor sleeps.[3] He Who rouses the sleepers and awakens the slumberers, Who makes the mute speak and releases the bound;[4] Who supports the fallen and straightens the bent.[5] To You alone we give thanks. Were our mouth as full of song as the sea, and our tongue as full of joyous song as its multitude of waves, and our lips as full of praise as the breadth of the heavens, and our eyes as brilliant as the sun and the moon, and our hands as outspread as eagles of the sky and our feet as swift as hinds — we still could not thank You sufficiently, HASHEM our God and God of our forefathers, and to bless Your Name for even one of the thousand thousand, thousands of thousands and myriad myriads of favors that You performed for our ancestors and for us. You redeemed us from Egypt, HASHEM our God, and liberated us from the house of bondage. In famine You nourished us and in plenty You sustained us. From sword You saved us; from plague You let us escape; and from severe and enduring diseases You spared us. Until now Your mercy has helped us, and Your kindness has not forsaken us. Do not abandon us, HASHEM our God, forever. Therefore, the organs that You set within us, and the spirit and soul that You breathed into our nostrils, and the tongue that You placed in our mouth — all of them shall thank and bless, praise and glorify, exalt and revere, sanctify and declare the sovereignty of Your Name, our King. For every mouth shall offer thanks to You; every tongue shall vow allegiance to You; every knee shall bend to You;[6] every erect spine shall prostrate itself before You; all hearts shall fear You, and all innermost feelings and thoughts shall sing praises to Your name, as it is written: "All my bones shall say: 'HASHEM, who is like You?' You save the poor man from one stronger than he, the poor and destitute from one who would rob him."[7] Who is like unto You? Who is equal to You? Who can be compared to You?[8] O great, mighty, and awesome God, the supreme God, Creator of heaven and earth.* Chazzan– *We shall laud, praise, and glorify You and bless Your holy Name, as it is said 'Of David: Bless HASHEM, O my soul, and let all my innermost being bless His holy Name!'[9]*

The *chazzan* of *Shacharis* begins here.

הָאֵל בְּתַעֲצֻמוֹת עֻזֶּךָ, הַגָּדוֹל בִּכְבוֹד שְׁמֶךָ, הַגִּבּוֹר לָנֶצַח וְהַנּוֹרָא בְּנוֹרְאוֹתֶיךָ. הַמֶּלֶךְ הַיּוֹשֵׁב עַל כִּסֵּא רָם וְנִשָּׂא.[1]

שׁוֹכֵן עַד מָרוֹם וְקָדוֹשׁ שְׁמוֹ.[2] וְכָתוּב: רַנְּנוּ צַדִּיקִים בַּיהוה לַיְשָׁרִים נָאוָה תְהִלָּה.[3]

❖ בְּפִי **יְ**שָׁרִים תִּתְהַלָּל.
וּבְדִבְרֵי **צַ**דִּיקִים תִּתְבָּרַךְ.
וּבִלְשׁוֹן **חֲ**סִידִים תִּתְרוֹמָם.
וּבְקֶרֶב **קְ**דוֹשִׁים תִּתְקַדָּשׁ.

וּבְמַקְהֲלוֹת רִבְבוֹת עַמְּךָ בֵּית יִשְׂרָאֵל, בְּרִנָּה יִתְפָּאַר שִׁמְךָ מַלְכֵּנוּ בְּכָל דּוֹר וָדוֹר. ❖ שֶׁכֵּן חוֹבַת כָּל הַיְצוּרִים, לְפָנֶיךָ יהוה אֱלֹהֵינוּ וֵאלֹהֵי אֲבוֹתֵינוּ, לְהוֹדוֹת לְהַלֵּל לְשַׁבֵּחַ לְפָאֵר לְרוֹמֵם לְהַדֵּר לְבָרֵךְ לְעַלֵּה וּלְקַלֵּס, עַל כָּל דִּבְרֵי שִׁירוֹת וְתִשְׁבְּחוֹת דָּוִד בֶּן יִשַׁי עַבְדְּךָ מְשִׁיחֶךָ.

Stand while reciting יִשְׁתַּבַּח . . .
The fifteen expressions of praise — שִׁיר וּשְׁבָחָה . . . בְּרָכוֹת וְהוֹדָאוֹת —
should be recited without pause, preferably in one breath.

יִשְׁתַּבַּח שִׁמְךָ לָעַד מַלְכֵּנוּ, הָאֵל הַמֶּלֶךְ הַגָּדוֹל וְהַקָּדוֹשׁ, בַּשָּׁמַיִם וּבָאָרֶץ. כִּי לְךָ נָאֶה יהוה אֱלֹהֵינוּ וֵאלֹהֵי אֲבוֹתֵינוּ, שִׁיר וּשְׁבָחָה, הַלֵּל וְזִמְרָה, עֹז וּמֶמְשָׁלָה, נֶצַח גְּדֻלָּה וּגְבוּרָה, תְּהִלָּה וְתִפְאֶרֶת, קְדֻשָּׁה וּמַלְכוּת, בְּרָכוֹת וְהוֹדָאוֹת מֵעַתָּה וְעַד עוֹלָם. ❖ בָּרוּךְ אַתָּה יהוה, אֵל מֶלֶךְ גָּדוֹל בַּתִּשְׁבָּחוֹת, אֵל הַהוֹדָאוֹת, אֲדוֹן הַנִּפְלָאוֹת, הַבּוֹחֵר בְּשִׁירֵי זִמְרָה, מֶלֶךְ אֵל חֵי הָעוֹלָמִים. (.Cong – אָמֵן.)

The *chazzan* recites חֲצִי קַדִּישׁ.

יִתְגַּדַּל וְיִתְקַדַּשׁ שְׁמֵהּ רַבָּא. (.Cong – אָמֵן.) בְּעָלְמָא דִּי בְרָא כִרְעוּתֵהּ. וְיַמְלִיךְ מַלְכוּתֵהּ, בְּחַיֵּיכוֹן וּבְיוֹמֵיכוֹן וּבְחַיֵּי דְכָל בֵּית יִשְׂרָאֵל, בַּעֲגָלָא וּבִזְמַן קָרִיב. וְאִמְרוּ: אָמֵן.

(.Cong – אָמֵן. יְהֵא שְׁמֵהּ רַבָּא מְבָרַךְ לְעָלַם וּלְעָלְמֵי עָלְמַיָּא.)

יְהֵא שְׁמֵהּ רַבָּא מְבָרַךְ לְעָלַם וּלְעָלְמֵי עָלְמַיָּא.

יִתְבָּרַךְ וְיִשְׁתַּבַּח וְיִתְפָּאַר וְיִתְרוֹמַם וְיִתְנַשֵּׂא וְיִתְהַדָּר וְיִתְעַלֶּה וְיִתְהַלָּל שְׁמֵהּ דְּקֻדְשָׁא בְּרִיךְ הוּא (.Cong – בְּרִיךְ הוּא) – לְעֵלָּא מִן כָּל בִּרְכָתָא וְשִׁירָתָא תֻּשְׁבְּחָתָא וְנֶחֱמָתָא, דַּאֲמִירָן בְּעָלְמָא. וְאִמְרוּ: אָמֵן. (.Cong – אָמֵן.)

The chazzan of *Shacharis* begins here:

הָאֵל *O God, in the omnipotence of Your strength, great in the glory of Your Name, mighty forever and awesome through Your awesome deeds. O King enthroned upon a high and lofty throne!*[1]

שׁוֹכֵן עַד *He Who abides forever, exalted and holy is His Name.*[2] *And it is written: 'Sing joyfully, O righteous, before* HASHEM*; for the upright, praise is fitting.'*[3]

Chazzan: *By the mouth of the upright shall You be lauded;*
by the words of the righteous shall You be blessed;
by the tongue of the devout shall You be exalted;
and amid the holy shall You be sanctified.

וּבְמַקְהֲלוֹת *And in the assemblies of the myriads of Your people, the House of Israel, with joyous song shall Your Name be glorified, our King, throughout every generation.* Chazzan– *For such is the duty of all creatures — before You,* HASHEM, *our God, God of our forefathers, to thank, laud, praise, glorify, exalt, adore, bless, raise high, and sing praises — even beyond all expressions of the songs and praises of David the son of Jesse, Your servant, Your anointed.*

Stand while reciting *'May Your Name be praised . . .'*
The fifteen expressions of praise — *'song and praise. . .blessings and thanksgivings'* — should be recited without pause, preferably in one breath.

יִשְׁתַּבַּח *May Your Name be praised forever — our King, the God, the great and holy King — in heaven and on earth. Because for You is fitting — O* HASHEM, *our God, and the God of our forefathers — song and praise, lauding and hymns, power and dominion, triumph, greatness and strength, praise and splendor, holiness and sovereignty, blessings and thanksgivings from this time and forever.* Chazzan– *Blessed are You,* HASHEM, *God, King exalted through praises, God of thanksgivings, Master of wonders, Who chooses musical songs of praise — King, God, Life-giver of the world.* (Cong.– *Amen.*)

The *chazzan* recites Half-*Kaddish*.

יִתְגַּדַּל *May His great Name grow exalted and sanctified* (Cong.– *Amen.*) *in the world that He created as He willed. May He give reign to His kingship in your lifetimes and in your days, and in the lifetimes of the entire Family of Israel, swiftly and soon. Now respond: Amen.*

(Cong.– *Amen. May His great Name be blessed forever and ever.*)
May His great Name be blessed forever and ever.

Blessed, praised, glorified, exalted, extolled, mighty, upraised, and lauded be the Name of the Holy One, Blessed is He (Cong.– *Blessed is He*) — *beyond any blessing and song, praise and consolation that are uttered in the world. Now respond: Amen.* (Cong.– *Amen.*)

---

(1) Cf. *Isaiah* 6:1. (2) Cf. 57:15. (3) *Psalms* 33:1.

In some congregations the *chazzan* chants a melody during his recitation of בָּרְכוּ, so that the congregation can then recite יִתְבָּרַךְ.

Chazzan bows at בָּרְכוּ and straightens up at ה'.

בָּרְכוּ אֶת יהוה הַמְּבֹרָךְ.

Congregation, followed by *chazzan*, responds, bowing at בָּרוּךְ and straightening up at ה'.

בָּרוּךְ יהוה הַמְּבֹרָךְ לְעוֹלָם וָעֶד.

יִתְבָּרַךְ וְיִשְׁתַּבַּח וְיִתְפָּאַר וְיִתְרוֹמַם וְיִתְנַשֵּׂא שְׁמוֹ שֶׁל מֶלֶךְ מַלְכֵי הַמְּלָכִים, הַקָּדוֹשׁ בָּרוּךְ הוּא. שֶׁהוּא רִאשׁוֹן וְהוּא אַחֲרוֹן, וּמִבַּלְעָדָיו אֵין אֱלֹהִים.[1] סֹלּוּ, לָרֹכֵב בָּעֲרָבוֹת, בְּיָהּ שְׁמוֹ, וְעִלְזוּ לְפָנָיו.[2] וּשְׁמוֹ מְרוֹמָם עַל כָּל בְּרָכָה וּתְהִלָּה.[3] בָּרוּךְ שֵׁם כְּבוֹד מַלְכוּתוֹ לְעוֹלָם וָעֶד. יְהִי שֵׁם יהוה מְבֹרָךְ, מֵעַתָּה וְעַד עוֹלָם.[4]

ברכות קריאת שמע

It is preferable that one sit while reciting the following series of prayers — particularly the *Kedushah* verses, קָדוֹשׁ קָדוֹשׁ קָדוֹשׁ and בָּרוּךְ כְּבוֹד — until *Shemoneh Esrei*.

The following paragraph is recited aloud by the *chazzan*, then repeated by the congregation.

בָּרוּךְ אַתָּה יהוה אֱלֹהֵינוּ מֶלֶךְ הָעוֹלָם, יוֹצֵר אוֹר וּבוֹרֵא חֹשֶׁךְ, עֹשֶׂה שָׁלוֹם וּבוֹרֵא אֶת הַכֹּל.[5]

Congregations that do not recite *yotzros,* continue on page 890.

Congregations that recite *yotzros* continue:

אוֹר עוֹלָם בְּאוֹצַר חַיִּים, אוֹרוֹת מֵאֹפֶל אָמַר וַיֶּהִי.

All:

אֵם* כְּאִישׁוֹן נִנְצֶרֶת,[6] חָשַׁךְ אוֹתָהּ מִבַּצְּרֶת, בַּיּוֹם הַשְּׁמִינִי עֲצֶרֶת.
בָּאָה בְתַחֲנוּן לְפָנֶיךָ, לְחַלּוֹת אֶת פָּנֶיךָ, בִּיטָה וּפְקַח עֵינֶיךָ.
גַּלֵּה לָהּ יוֹמָךְ, נַחֵמוֹל עַל עַמָּךְ, וְשִׂמְחָה יַשִּׂיגוּ מֵעִמָּךְ.
בַּיּוֹם הַשְּׁמִינִי, שְׂמָחוֹת הַזְמִינִי, וּסְכוֹת נָא מַעֲנִי, קָדוֹשׁ.

דּוֹרְשִׁים בְּתַכְלִית מוֹעֲדָם, גִּשְׁמֵי נְדָבוֹת בְּמַעֲמָדָם, צְפֵה נָא לְעוֹרְדָם.
הַשְׁקִיפָה עֲלֵיהֶם מִמְּרוֹמִים, וּזְכֹר בְּרִית שְׁלֹשֶׁת קְדוּמִים,
וְהִמָּלֵא עַל צֶאֱצָאֵימוֹ רַחֲמִים.

◆§ Interruptions During the Blessings of the Shema

As a general rule, no אָמֵן or other prayer response may be recited between בָּרְכוּ and *Shemoneh Esrei,* but there are exceptions. The main exception is 'between chapters' [בֵּין הַפְּרָקִים] of the *Shema* Blessings — i.e., after יוֹצֵר הַמְּאוֹרוֹת and הַבּוֹחֵר ... בְּאַהֲבָה, and between the three chapters of *Shema.* At those points, אָמֵן (but not בָּרוּךְ הוּא וּבָרוּךְ שְׁמוֹ) may be responded to any blessing. Some responses, however, are so important that they are permitted at any point in the *Shema* blessings. They are:

(a) In Kaddish, דַּאֲמִירָן בְּעָלְמָא ... אָמֵן יְהֵא שְׁמֵהּ רַבָּא עָלְמַיָּא and the אָמֵן after; (b) the response to בָּרְכוּ (even of one called to the Torah); and (c) during the *chazzan's* repetition of *Shemoneh Esrei* — 1) in *Kedushah,* the verses קָדוֹשׁ קָדוֹשׁ קָדוֹשׁ ... כְּבוֹדוֹ and בָּרוּךְ כְּבוֹד ה' מִמְּקוֹמוֹ; 2) the אָמֵן after הָאֵל הַקָּדוֹשׁ; 3) the three words מוֹדִים אֲנַחְנוּ לָךְ.

During the recital of the two verses שְׁמַע and בָּרוּךְ שֵׁם, absolutely no interruptions are permitted.

In some congregations the *chazzan* chants a melody during his recitation of *Borchu*, so that the congregation can then recite *'Blessed, praised . . .'*

Chazzan bows at *'Bless'* and straightens up at *'HASHEM.'*

Bless HASHEM, the blessed One.

Congregation, followed by *chazzan*, responds, bowing at *'Blessed'* and straightening up at *'HASHEM.'*

Blessed is HASHEM, the blessed One, for all eternity.

Blessed, praised, glorified, exalted and upraised is the Name of the King Who rules over kings — the Holy One, Blessed is He. For He is the First and He is the Last and aside from Him there is no god.[1] *Extol Him — Who rides the highest heavens — with His Name, YAH, and exult before Him.*[2] *His Name is exalted beyond every blessing and praise.*[3] *Blessed is the Name of His glorious kingdom for all eternity. Blessed be the Name of HASHEM from this time and forever.*[4]

BLESSINGS OF THE SHEMA

It is preferable that one sit while reciting the following series of prayers — particularly the *Kedushah* verses, *'Holy, holy, holy . . .'* and *'Blessed is the glory . . .'* — until *Shemoneh Esrei*.

The following paragraph is recited aloud by the *chazzan*, then repeated by the congregation.

בָּרוּךְ *Blessed are You, HASHEM, our God, King of the universe, Who forms light and creates darkness, makes peace and creates all.*[5]

Congregations that do not recite *yotzros* continue on page 890.

Congregations that recite *yotzros* continue:

The primeval light is in the treasury of eternal life;
'Let there be lights from the darkness,' He declared — and so it was!

All:

א *The nation* that is guarded like the pupil of the eye,*[6]
protect her from [a decree of] insufficient rainfall,
on this day of Shemini Atzeres.

ב *She comes before You in supplication,*
to entreat before Your countenance,
O look, and open Your eyes.

ג *Reveal to her Your day [of redemption],*
and have pity upon Your people,
may they achieve joy from You.

On the eighth day prepare joys for me,
and please hear my prayer, O Holy One.

ד *At the end of their festival season they request from You,*
generous rains — in their Amidah prayers,
please see to strengthen them.

ה *Peer down upon them from on high,*
remember the covenant of the three Patriarchs,
and fill Yourself with compassion for their offspring.

---

(1) Cf. *Isaiah* 44:6. (2) *Psalms* 68:5. (3) Cf. *Nechemiah* 9:5.
(4) *Psalms* 113:2. (5) Cf. *Isaiah* 45:7. (6) Cf. *Deuteronomy* 32:10.

אום —*The nation.* This anonymous *piyut* follows the *aleph-beis*. It begins with a plea that God accept the nation's prayers for rain and concludes with a petition for the Messianic redemption, destruction of our fore, and rebuilding of the Temple.

וְאִם עִקְּלוּ בְּרֶשַׁע, חוּסָה וַעֲבֹר עַל פֶּשַׁע, וְהַצְמַח לָמוֹ יֶשַׁע.

זוֹעֲקִים אֵלֶיךָ בְּכָל לֵב, הָרוֹפֵא לִשְׁבוּרֵי לֵב,[1] כּוֹנֵן מְקוֹם עַיִן וָלֵב.*

חֶטְאָם תְּנְאֹם לְכַפֵּר, וּבְרִית אַל תָּפֵר, בִּזְכוּת אִמְרֵי שָׁפֶר.[2]

טוֹב הַשּׁוֹכֵן רוּמָה, קָרֵב קֵץ נֶחָמָה, וְעוֹרֵר יְשֵׁנֵי אֲדָמָה.*

יָהּ שׁוֹכֵן עֲלִיּוֹת, וְרַב הָעֲלִילִיּוֹת,[3] עַתָּה כַּנֵּס גָּלִיּוֹת.

כָּל אוֹיְבֶיךָ לְהַאֲבִיד, וְאוֹהֲבֶיךָ שְׂמָחוֹת לְהַרְבִּיד,
בְּמַלְכוּת מָשִׁיחַ בֶּן דָּוִד.

לְמַעְלָה לְמַעְלָה לְרוֹמֵם, בֵּית מִקְדָּשְׁךָ הַשָּׁמֵם, צָרִים מֶנּוּ לְהַדְמֵם.

מְהַלְּלִים לְךָ בַּחֲגִיגָתָם, שׁוּר קְהַל עֲדָתָם, וּשְׁמַע קוֹל זַעֲקָתָם.

נֶגְדְּךָ בְּתַחַן עוֹמְדִים, וְעַל דַּלְתוֹתֶיךָ שׁוֹקְדִים,
וְאוֹתְךָ בְּהַתְמֵד מְיַחֲדִים.

שִׂיחָם לְפָנֶיךָ יֶעֱרַב,[4] וְחָשְׁכֵם מִיּוֹם קְרָב, וּמִמְּחִתָּה כִּי לֹא תִקְרַב.[5]

עַטְּרֵם רֹב בְּרָכוֹת, וְחַיִּים אֲרֻכוֹת, עֲדֵי עַד מַאֲרִיכוֹת.

פְּתַח לָמוֹ אוֹצָרֶךָ,[6] וְקַיֵּם עָלֵימוֹ אֲמָרֶךָ, וְאַל יֵבֹשׁוּ מִשִּׂבְרֶךָ.[7]

צְקוֹן לַחֲשָׁם תִּשְׁמַע, וְקוֹל מְבַשֵּׂר לְהַשְׁמַע, טוֹבוֹת וְנֶחָמוֹת בְּמַשְׁמָע.

קוֹלוֹת אַרְבָּעָה* לְהָחִישָׁה, וּלְעֶזְרָתֵנוּ חוּשָׁה, וּלְצוֹרְרֶיךָ תַּכְחִישָׁה.

רָם עַל רָמִים, שַׂמַּח נֶפֶשׁ עֲגוּמִים, בְּבָנוּי כְּמוֹ רָמִים.[8]

שִׁבְחֲךָ בְּפִימוֹ מְתַנִּים, וְגָדְלְךָ בְּלִבָּם מְשַׁנְּנִים, וְיִחוּדְךָ בְּכָל יוֹם עוֹנִים.

❖ תּוֹקְפִים שֶׁבַח וְהוֹדָיָה רוֹחֲשִׁים, רוֹנְנִים רוֹעֲשִׁים וְלֹא חָשִׁים,
וְאוֹתְךָ מַעֲרִיצִים וּמַקְדִּישִׁים, קָדוֹשׁ.

(1) *Psalms* 147:3. (2) Cf. *Genesis* 49:21. (3) *Jeremiah* 32:19. (4) Cf. *Psalms* 104:34. (5) *Isaiah* 54:14. (6) Cf. *Deuteronomy* 28:12. (7) Cf. *Psalms* 119:116. (8) Cf. 78:69.

מְקוֹם עַיִן וָלֵב — *A place [the Temple] for eye and heart.* After King Solomon completed the First Temple, he recited a long prayer asking God to make the Temple His dwelling. God answered: *I have heard your prayer ... and My eyes and heart shall be there for all time (I Kings 9:3).*

וְעוֹרֵר יְשֵׁנֵי אֲדָמָה — *And arouse those asleep in the earth.* This is a prayer of תְּחִיַּת הַמֵּתִים, *the Ressuscitation of the dead.*

קוֹלוֹת אַרְבָּעָה — *Four voices.* In prophesying about the destruction of Jerusalem, the prophet declared: *I shall destroy from the cities of Judah and the streets of Jerusalem the voice of joy and the voice of gladness, the voice of the groom and the voice of the bride (Jeremiah 7:34).* Later when foretelling of the return to Jerusalem in Messianic times, the prophet returns these same four voices to the city: *There will again be heard in this place — about which you say, 'It is destroyed; there is no person there is no animal in the cities of Judah or in the streets of Jerusalem, they are desolate ...' — the voice of joy and the voice of gladness, the voice of the groom and the voice of the bride ...* (ibid. 33:10-11). Now we pray that the fulfillment of the second prophecy should come speedily.

ו *But if they have strayed with wickedness,*
pity them and overlook their sin,
and cause salvation to flourish for them.
ז *They cry wholeheartedly to You, 'O Healer of the broken-hearted,*[1]
*Prepare a place [the Temple] for eye and heart.'**
ח *Speak out to atone for their sins, and do not revoke the covenant,*
in the merit of the beautiful sayings [of the Torah].[2]
ט *O Beneficent One Who dwells on high,*
bring near the comfort of the End [of Days],
*and arouse those asleep in the earth.**
י *God Who dwells in the heights, Whose works are abundant,*[3]
may You now bring back our exiles.
כ *To destroy all Your enemies, to adorn Your beloved [nation] with joy,*
with the kingdom of Messiah, son of David.
ל *To exalt higher and higher,*
Your desolate Holy Temple,
[and] to silence our oppressors.
מ *They praise You on their festivals,*
look upon the congregation of their flock,
and hear the sound of their cry.
נ *They stand facing You in supplication,*
they arrive early at Your [synagogue's] doors,
and continually declare Your Oneness.
ס *May their words be sweet before You,*[4]
may You protect them on the day of battle,
that their doom shall not come near.[5]
ע *Crown them with abundant blessing.*
and with long life [in the World to Come],
stretching across all eternity.
פ *Open Your treasure trove for them,*[6]
and fulfill Your words for them,
do not cause them disgrace in hoping to You.[7]
צ *Listen to the outpouring of their whispered prayer,*
and let the voice of the Herald be heard,
as he proclaims good [tidings] and consolations.
ק *Hurrying the four voices,**
may You rush to help us,
and may You halt Your enemies.
ר *O [You Who are] exalted over the exalted ones,*
gladden the depressed of spirit,
with the [Temple] rebuilt like the high heavens.[8]
ש *They speak Your praises with their mouths,*
they relate Your greatness with their hearts,
and they proclaim Your Oneness each day.

ת ∴*They strengthen themselves in praise and bestir [their hearts] in thanksgiving,*
they recite glad song, they call out aloud, they are not silent,
as they revere You and sanctify You, O Holy One.

ON A WEEKDAY CONTINUE HERE:

הַמֵּאִיר לָאָרֶץ וְלַדָּרִים* עָלֶיהָ בְּרַחֲמִים, וּבְטוּבוֹ מְחַדֵּשׁ בְּכָל יוֹם תָּמִיד מַעֲשֵׂה בְרֵאשִׁית. מָה רַבּוּ מַעֲשֶׂיךָ* יהוה,

הַמֵּאִיר לָאָרֶץ וְלַדָּרִים — *He Who illuminates the earth and those who dwell.* The earth's dwellers enjoy the light, but so does the earth itself, because sunlight makes vegetation possible.

ON THE SABBATH CONTINUE HERE:

הַכֹּל יוֹדְוּךָ,* וְהַכֹּל יְשַׁבְּחְוּךָ, וְהַכֹּל יֹאמְרוּ אֵין קָדוֹשׁ כַּיהוה.[1] הַכֹּל יְרוֹמְמְוּךָ סֶּלָה, יוֹצֵר הַכֹּל. הָאֵל הַפּוֹתֵחַ בְּכָל יוֹם דַּלְתוֹת שַׁעֲרֵי מִזְרָח, וּבוֹקֵעַ חַלּוֹנֵי רָקִיעַ,* מוֹצִיא חַמָּה מִמְּקוֹמָהּ וּלְבָנָה מִמְּכוֹן שִׁבְתָּהּ, וּמֵאִיר לָעוֹלָם כֻּלּוֹ וּלְיוֹשְׁבָיו, שֶׁבָּרָא בְּמִדַּת רַחֲמִים. הַמֵּאִיר לָאָרֶץ וְלַדָּרִים עָלֶיהָ בְּרַחֲמִים, וּבְטוּבוֹ מְחַדֵּשׁ בְּכָל יוֹם תָּמִיד מַעֲשֵׂה בְרֵאשִׁית. הַמֶּלֶךְ הַמְּרוֹמָם לְבַדּוֹ מֵאָז, הַמְּשֻׁבָּח וְהַמְּפֹאָר וְהַמִּתְנַשֵּׂא מִימוֹת עוֹלָם. אֱלֹהֵי עוֹלָם בְּרַחֲמֶיךָ הָרַבִּים, רַחֵם עָלֵינוּ, אֲדוֹן עֻזֵּנוּ, צוּר מִשְׂגַּבֵּנוּ, מָגֵן יִשְׁעֵנוּ, מִשְׂגָּב בַּעֲדֵנוּ. אֵין כְּעֶרְכֶּךָ,* וְאֵין זוּלָתֶךָ, אֶפֶס בִּלְתֶּךָ, וּמִי דּוֹמֶה לָּךְ. אֵין כְּעֶרְכְּךָ יהוה אֱלֹהֵינוּ בָּעוֹלָם הַזֶּה, וְאֵין זוּלָתְךָ מַלְכֵּנוּ לְחַיֵּי הָעוֹלָם הַבָּא. אֶפֶס בִּלְתְּךָ גּוֹאֲלֵנוּ לִימוֹת הַמָּשִׁיחַ, וְאֵין דּוֹמֶה לְּךָ מוֹשִׁיעֵנוּ לִתְחִיַּת הַמֵּתִים.

The Sabbath Additions

Since the Sabbath is the weekly testimony to the fact that God created the world, the first blessing of the Shema, which deals with creation, is augmented on the Sabbath with three apt passages:

1. הַכֹּל יוֹדְוּךָ, *All will thank You,* speaks of the Creator Who renews creation daily;

2. אֵל אָדוֹן, *God — The Master,* praises the glory of creation itself;

3. לָאֵל אֲשֶׁר שָׁבַת, *To the God Who rested,* celebrates the Sabbath. Thus, these three passages are appropriate only on the Sabbath, and are omitted on all weekday Festivals *(World of Prayer)*.

הַכֹּל יוֹדְוּךָ — *All will thank You.* The word 'all' refers to the previous blessing, which ends וּבוֹרֵא אֶת הַכֹּל, *and creates all.* Thus, every facet of the universe will join in thanking and lauding God. Only man and the angels do this verbally; the rest of creation does so by carrying out its assigned tasks and inspiring man to recognize the Guiding Hand that created and orders everything.

דַּלְתוֹת שַׁעֲרֵי מִזְרָח ... חַלּוֹנֵי רָקִיעַ — *Doors of the gateways of the East ... windows of the firmament.* These expressions are given various interpretations. On the simple level, they refer poetically to the rising sun breaking through the portals of darkness. Alternatively, the phrase *doors of the gateways* refers to daybreak, which illuminates the sky long before sunrise. The *windows* are different points in the sky at which the sun rises as the seasons move to the longer days of summer and then back again to the shorter days of winter *(R' Hirsch; Iyun Tefillah)*.

אֵין כְּעֶרְכְּךָ — *There is no comparison to You.* This verse makes four statements about God that are explained in the next verse. Thus the two verses should be seen as a unit. As explained by *R'*

ON A WEEKDAY CONTINUE HERE:

הַמֵּאִיר *He Who illuminates the earth and those who dwell* upon it, with compassion; and in His goodness renews daily, perpetually, the work of Creation. How great are Your works,* HASHEM,*

מָה רַבּוּ מַעֲשֶׂיךָ — *How great are Your works.* This refers to the heavenly bodies and other major forces in creation. Homiletically, the Talmud (*Chullin* 127a) interprets, *how diverse are Your works;* some can live only on land, others only in the sea, and so on.

ON THE SABBATH CONTINUE HERE:

הַכֹּל יוֹדְוּךָ *All will thank You* and all will praise You — and all will declare: 'Nothing is as holy as HASHEM!'[1] All will exalt You, Selah! — You Who forms everything. The God Who opens daily the doors of the gateways of the East, and splits the windows of the firmament,* Who removes the sun from its place and the moon from the site of its dwelling, and Who illuminates all the world and its inhabitants, which He created with the attribute of mercy. He Who illuminates the earth and those who dwell upon it, with compassion; and in His goodness renews daily, perpetually, the work of creation. The King Who was exalted in solitude from before creation, Who is praised, glorified, and extolled since days of old. Eternal God, with Your abundant compassion be compassionate to us — O Master of our power, our rocklike stronghold; O Shield of our salvation, be a stronghold for us. There is no comparison to You,* there is nothing except for You, there is nothing without You, for who is like You? There is no comparison to You, HASHEM, our God, in this world; and there will be nothing except for You, our King, in the life of the World to Come; there will be nothing without You, our Redeemer, in Messianic days; and there will be none like You, our Savior; at the Resuscitation of the Dead.*

(1) *I Samuel* 2:2.

Hirsch, the four statements are:

(a) אֵין כְּעֶרְכֶּךָ — *There is no comparison to You.* Although we have expressed our gratitude for the heavenly bodies and the various forces of the universe, we hasten to affirm that none of them can even be compared to God's power on earth.

(b) וְאֵין זוּלָתֶךָ — *There is nothing except for You.* In the World to Come, even the most beneficial aspects of life in this material world will not exist. In the blissful state of that world, nothing will exist except for God and those whose lives on earth have made them worthy of His spiritual grandeur.

(c) אֶפֶס בִּלְתֶּךָ — *There is nothing without You.* On earth, too, there will be a state of bliss with the coming of the Messiah — but that redemption is impossible without God, despite the earthly factors that will seem to contribute to it.

(d) וּמִי דּוֹמֶה לָּךְ — *For who is like You?* Nothing will so clearly reveal God's absolute mastery as the Resuscitation of the Dead. That is the ultimate redemption, for it will demonstrate that not only slavery and freedom, but even life and death, depend on Him.

ON A WEEKDAY

כֻּלָּם בְּחָכְמָה עָשִׂיתָ, מָלְאָה הָאָרֶץ קִנְיָנֶךָ.[1] הַמֶּלֶךְ הַמְּרוֹמָם לְבַדּוֹ* מֵאָז, הַמְּשֻׁבָּח וְהַמְּפֹאָר וְהַמִּתְנַשֵּׂא מִימוֹת עוֹלָם. אֱלֹהֵי עוֹלָם, בְּרַחֲמֶיךָ הָרַבִּים רַחֵם עָלֵינוּ, אֲדוֹן עֻזֵּנוּ, צוּר מִשְׂגַּבֵּנוּ, מָגֵן יִשְׁעֵנוּ, מִשְׂגָּב בַּעֲדֵנוּ. אֵל בָּרוּךְ* גְּדוֹל דֵּעָה, הֵכִין וּפָעַל

הַמֶּלֶךְ הַמְּרוֹמָם לְבַדּוֹ — *The King Who was exalted in solitude.* Before Creation, God was *exalted in solitude,* because there were no creatures to praise Him *(Etz Yosef).*

אֵל בָּרוּךְ — *The blessed God.* This begins a lyric praise consisting of twenty-two words following the order of the *Aleph-Beis.* As noted at the bottom of the page in the commentary to אֵל

ON THE SABBATH

The following liturgical song is recited responsively in most congregations. In some congregations, the *chazzan* and congregation sing the stanzas together.

אֵל אָדוֹן* עַל כָּל הַמַּעֲשִׂים, **בָּ**רוּךְ וּמְבֹרָךְ* בְּפִי כָּל נְשָׁמָה,
גָּדְלוֹ וְטוּבוֹ מָלֵא עוֹלָם, **דַּ**עַת וּתְבוּנָה סוֹבְבִים אֹתוֹ.
הַמִּתְגָּאֶה* עַל חַיּוֹת הַקֹּדֶשׁ, **וְ**נֶהְדָּר בְּכָבוֹד עַל הַמֶּרְכָּבָה,
זְכוּת וּמִישׁוֹר לִפְנֵי כִסְאוֹ, **חֶ**סֶד וְרַחֲמִים לִפְנֵי כְבוֹדוֹ.
טוֹבִים מְאוֹרוֹת שֶׁבָּרָא אֱלֹהֵינוּ, **יְ**צָרָם בְּדַעַת בְּבִינָה וּבְהַשְׂכֵּל,
כֹּחַ וּגְבוּרָה נָתַן בָּהֶם, **לִ**הְיוֹת מוֹשְׁלִים בְּקֶרֶב תֵּבֵל.
מְלֵאִים זִיו וּמְפִיקִים נֹגַהּ, **נָ**אֶה זִיוָם בְּכָל הָעוֹלָם,
שְׂמֵחִים בְּצֵאתָם* וְשָׂשִׂים בְּבוֹאָם, **עוֹ**שִׂים בְּאֵימָה רְצוֹן קוֹנָם.
פְּאֵר וְכָבוֹד* נוֹתְנִים לִשְׁמוֹ, **צָ**הֳלָה וְרִנָּה לְזֵכֶר מַלְכוּתוֹ,
קָרָא לַשֶּׁמֶשׁ וַיִּזְרַח אוֹר, **רָ**אָה וְהִתְקִין צוּרַת הַלְּבָנָה.*
שֶׁבַח נוֹתְנִים לוֹ כָּל צְבָא מָרוֹם.
תִּפְאֶרֶת וּגְדֻלָּה, שְׂרָפִים וְאוֹפַנִּים וְחַיּוֹת הַקֹּדֶשׁ—

אֵל אָדוֹן — *God — the Master.* This poetic prayer comprises twenty-two phrases, the initial letters of which form the *Aleph-Beis.* It is parallel to the alphabetical prayer אֵל בָּרוּךְ גְּדוֹל דֵּעָה of the weekday *Shacharis;* but the weekday prayer contains only twenty-two words. The *Vilna Gaon* explains that the lesser holiness of the weekdays is expressed not only in the shorter version, but in the content. There, the praise concentrates on God's greatness as we perceive it in the form of the heavenly bodies. Here, the greater holiness of the Sabbath enables us to perceive more — though clearly not all — of His greatness.

בָּרוּךְ וּמְבֹרָךְ — *The blessed One — and He is blessed,* i.e., God is the source of all blessing. In addition, His creatures bless Him in their prayers and through their obedience to His will *(Vilna Gaon).*

הַמִּתְגָּאֶה — *He Who exalts Himself.* The *Chayos* are the highest category of angels, and the Chariot [מֶרְכָּבָה] refers to the order of angelic praises of God. Both were seen by Ezekiel (ch. 1) in his *Ma'aseh Merkavah* prophecy. Thus, they represent the highest degree of holiness accessible to human understanding. Nevertheless, God is exalted far above even this.

שְׂמֵחִים בְּצֵאתָם — *Glad as they go forth.* The heavenly bodies are likened to a loyal servant

ON A WEEKDAY

You make them all with wisdom, the world is full of Your possessions.[1] *The King Who was exalted in solitude* before Creation, Who is praised, glorified, and upraised since days of old. Eternal God, with Your abundant compassion be compassionate to us — O Master of our power, our rocklike stronghold, O Shield of our salvation, be a stronghold for us. The blessed God,* Who is great in knowledge, prepared and worked on*

(1) *Psalms* 104:24.

אדון, *God — the Master,* which is recited on the Sabbath, this formula of an *Aleph-Beis* acrostic is followed on the Sabbath as well, except that on the Sabbath each letter introduces an entire

ON THE SABBATH

The following liturgical song is recited responsively in most congregations. In some congregations, the *chazzan* and congregation sing the stanzas together.

אֵל אָדוֹן *God — the Master* over all works; the Blessed One —*
ב *and He is blessed* by the mouth of every soul;*
ג *His greatness and goodness fill the world,*
ד *wisdom and insight surround Him.*
ה *He Who exalts Himself* over the holy Chayos*
ו *and is splendrous in glory above the Chariot;*
ז *Merit and fairness are before His throne,*
ח *kindness and mercy are before His glory.*
ט *Good are the luminaries that our God has created,*
י *He has fashioned them with wisdom,*
with insight and discernment;
כ *Strength and power has He granted them,*
ל *to be dominant within the world.*
מ *Filled with luster and radiating brightness,*
נ *their luster is beautiful throughout the world;*
ס *Glad as they go forth* and exultant as they return,*
ע *they do with awe their Creator's will.*
פ *Splendor and glory* they bestow upon His Name,*
צ *jubilation and glad song upon the mention of His reign —*
ק *He called out to the sun and it glowed with light,*
ר *He saw and fashioned the form of the moon.**
ש *All the host above bestows praise on Him,*
ת *splendor and greatness — the Seraphim, Ophanim,*
and holy Chayos —

entrusted with an important mission. He is proud and happy when he sets out, but is even more joyous when he returns to his master.

פְּאֵר וְכָבוֹד — *Splendor and glory.* The exact movements of the heavenly bodies inspire people to praise the One Who created them.

צוּרַת הַלְּבָנָה — *The form of the moon.* With insight, God shaped the phases of the moon so

ON A WEEKDAY

זָהֳרֵי חַמָּה, טוֹב יָצַר כָּבוֹד לִשְׁמוֹ,* מְאוֹרוֹת נָתַן סְבִיבוֹת עֻזּוֹ, פִּנּוֹת צְבָאָיו קְדוֹשִׁים רוֹמְמֵי שַׁדַּי, תָּמִיד מְסַפְּרִים כְּבוֹד אֵל וּקְדֻשָּׁתוֹ. תִּתְבָּרַךְ יהוה אֱלֹהֵינוּ עַל שֶׁבַח מַעֲשֵׂה יָדֶיךָ, וְעַל מְאוֹרֵי אוֹר שֶׁעָשִׂיתָ, יְפָאֲרוּךָ, סֶּלָה.

phrase. See commentary below for the significance of this difference.

As a general rule, the use of the *Aleph-Beis* acrostic in the prayers conveys the idea that we praise God with every available sound and that His greatness is absolutely complete and harmonious. Furthermore, the emphasis on the letters implies our acknowledgment that the Torah, whose words and thoughts are formed with the letters of the *Aleph-Beis*, is the very basis of the continued existence of heaven and earth. In the familiar teaching of the Sages (*Pesachim* 68b) R' Elazar expains: Were it not for the [constant study of] Torah, heaven and earth would not exist, as it is said, *Were it not for My covenant* [i.e., the Torah] *day and night, I would not have established the systematic function of heaven and earth* (*Jeremiah* 33:25). This concept of the letters of the Torah is further alluded to in the verse from *Song of Songs* (1:4) in which Israel allegorically says to God: נָגִילָה וְנִשְׂמְחָה בָּךְ, *we will rejoice and be glad in You*. The word בָּךְ has the numerical value of twenty-two, an allusion to the twenty-two letters of the *Aleph-Beis*, as if

ON THE SABBATH

לָאֵל אֲשֶׁר שָׁבַת* מִכָּל הַמַּעֲשִׂים, בַּיּוֹם הַשְּׁבִיעִי הִתְעַלָּה וְיָשַׁב עַל כִּסֵּא כְבוֹדוֹ, תִּפְאֶרֶת עָטָה לְיוֹם הַמְּנוּחָה, עֹנֶג קָרָא לְיוֹם הַשַּׁבָּת. זֶה שֶׁבַח שֶׁל יוֹם הַשְּׁבִיעִי,* שֶׁבּוֹ שָׁבַת אֵל מִכָּל מְלַאכְתּוֹ. וְיוֹם הַשְּׁבִיעִי מְשַׁבֵּחַ וְאוֹמֵר: מִזְמוֹר שִׁיר לְיוֹם הַשַּׁבָּת, טוֹב לְהוֹדוֹת לַיהוה.[1] לְפִיכָךְ יְפָאֲרוּ* וִיבָרְכוּ לָאֵל כָּל יְצוּרָיו. שֶׁבַח יְקָר וּגְדֻלָּה יִתְּנוּ לָאֵל מֶלֶךְ יוֹצֵר כֹּל, הַמַּנְחִיל מְנוּחָה לְעַמּוֹ יִשְׂרָאֵל בִּקְדֻשָּׁתוֹ בְּיוֹם שַׁבַּת קֹדֶשׁ. שִׁמְךָ יהוה אֱלֹהֵינוּ יִתְקַדַּשׁ, וְזִכְרְךָ מַלְכֵּנוּ יִתְפָּאַר, בַּשָּׁמַיִם מִמַּעַל וְעַל הָאָרֶץ מִתָּחַת. תִּתְבָּרַךְ מוֹשִׁיעֵנוּ עַל שֶׁבַח מַעֲשֵׂה יָדֶיךָ, וְעַל מְאוֹרֵי אוֹר שֶׁעָשִׂיתָ, יְפָאֲרוּךָ, סֶּלָה.

that they would enable Israel to order the calendar as commanded by the Torah.

לָאֵל אֲשֶׁר שָׁבַת ◆§ — *To the God Who rested.* To Whom are directed the praises mentioned above? — to the God Who rested on the Sabbath from His six days of creation. We say that He 'ascended on the Seventh Day' in the sense that His Presence is no longer obvious on earth. Nevertheless, He left us with the Sabbath as an eternal testimony to His six days of activity and the Sabbath of His rest.

זֶה שֶׁבַח שֶׁל יוֹם הַשְּׁבִיעִי — *This is the praise of the Sabbath Day.* The glory of the Sabbath is not in the leisure it offers, but in its witness to the Creator and its stimulus to man to join it in praising God. In this sense, the very existence of

ON A WEEKDAY

the rays of the sun; the Beneficent One fashioned honor for His Name, emplaced luminaries all around His power; the leaders of His legions, holy ones, exalt the Almighty, constantly relate the honor of God and His sanctity. May You be blessed,* HASHEM, *our God, beyond the praises of Your handiwork and beyond the bright luminaries that You have made — may they glorify You — Selah!*

to say that we declare our joy in having been worthy to receive the Torah that is formed with the sacred letters (*Abudraham*). Since this portion of the liturgy focuses on the creation and functioning of heaven and earth, it is especially appropriate to insert this allusion to the primacy of Torah study.

According to a tradition cited by *Etz Yosef*, R' Elazar HaKalir, composer of this prayer, communicated with the angel Michael and asked him how the angels formulated their songs of praise. Michael told him that they based their praises on the *Aleph-Beis*. Accordingly, R' Elazar used that formulation in this and his many other *piyutim*. He alluded to the source of this knowledge, Michael, by inserting his name acrostically immediately after these twenty-two words: מְסַפְּרִים כְּבוֹד אֵל, *relate the honor of God.*

יָצַר כָּבוֹד לִשְׁמוֹ — *Fashioned honor for His Name.* The complexity and perfection of creation testifies to the fact that there must be a Creator. Consequently, by creating and emplacing the heavenly bodies, God fashioned the instruments that would bring honor to His Name.

ON THE SABBATH

לָאֵל *To the God Who rested* from all works, Who ascended on the Seventh Day and sat on the Throne of His Glory. With splendor He enwrapped the Day of Contentment — He declared the Sabbath day a delight! This is the praise of the Sabbath Day:* that on it God rested from all His work. And the Seventh Day gives praise saying: 'A psalm, a song for the Sabbath Day. It is good to thank* HASHEM *. . .'*[1] *Therefore let all that He has fashioned glorify* and bless God. Praise, honor, and greatness let them render to God, the King Who fashioned everything, Who gives a heritage of contentment to His People, Israel, in His holiness on the holy Sabbath Day. May Your Name,* HASHEM, *our God, be sanctified and may Your remembrance, Our King, be glorified in the heaven above and upon the earth below. May You be blessed, our Savior, beyond the praises of Your handiwork and beyond the brilliant luminaries that You have made — may they glorify You — Selah.*

(1) *Psalms* 92:1-2.

the Sabbath is a praise to God; alternatively, the 'praise' can be understood as the Song of the Day for the Sabbath.

לְפִיכָךְ יְפָאֲרוּ — *Therefore let all . . . glorify.* As the prayer goes on to say, the reason that Creation glorifies God is that He has given the Sabbath to Israel. By observing the Sabbath and absorbing its holiness, Israel brings a higher degree of fulfillment and holiness to the entire universe.

ON ALL DAYS CONTINUE HERE:

תִּתְבָּרַךְ צוּרֵנוּ* מַלְכֵּנוּ וְגֹאֲלֵנוּ,* בּוֹרֵא קְדוֹשִׁים. יִשְׁתַּבַּח שִׁמְךָ לָעַד מַלְכֵּנוּ, יוֹצֵר מְשָׁרְתִים,* וַאֲשֶׁר מְשָׁרְתָיו כֻּלָּם עוֹמְדִים בְּרוּם עוֹלָם, וּמַשְׁמִיעִים בְּיִרְאָה יַחַד בְּקוֹל דִּבְרֵי אֱלֹהִים חַיִּים וּמֶלֶךְ עוֹלָם.[1] כֻּלָּם אֲהוּבִים, כֻּלָּם בְּרוּרִים, כֻּלָּם גִּבּוֹרִים, וְכֻלָּם עֹשִׂים בְּאֵימָה וּבְיִרְאָה רְצוֹן קוֹנָם. ❖ וְכֻלָּם פּוֹתְחִים אֶת פִּיהֶם בִּקְדֻשָּׁה וּבְטָהֳרָה, בְּשִׁירָה וּבְזִמְרָה, וּמְבָרְכִים וּמְשַׁבְּחִים וּמְפָאֲרִים וּמַעֲרִיצִים וּמַקְדִּישִׁים וּמַמְלִיכִים —

אֶת שֵׁם הָאֵל הַמֶּלֶךְ הַגָּדוֹל הַגִּבּוֹר וְהַנּוֹרָא קָדוֹשׁ הוּא.[2] ❖ וְכֻלָּם מְקַבְּלִים עֲלֵיהֶם עֹל מַלְכוּת שָׁמַיִם זֶה מִזֶּה,* וְנוֹתְנִים רְשׁוּת זֶה לָזֶה, לְהַקְדִּישׁ לְיוֹצְרָם, בְּנַחַת רוּחַ בְּשָׂפָה בְרוּרָה וּבִנְעִימָה. קְדֻשָּׁה כֻּלָּם כְּאֶחָד עוֹנִים וְאוֹמְרִים בְּיִרְאָה:

Congregation recites aloud:

קָדוֹשׁ קָדוֹשׁ קָדוֹשׁ* יהוה צְבָאוֹת,* מְלֹא כָל הָאָרֶץ כְּבוֹדוֹ.[3]

⊱ **תִּתְבָּרַךְ צוּרֵנוּ** — *May You be blessed, our Rock.* The previous paragraph expressed man's praise of God for having created the heavenly bodies. They are indeed outstanding manifestations of God's greatness, as the prophet Isaiah put it, *Raise your eyes up high and see Who created these (Isaiah* 40:26). The heavenly bodies, like the angels, are agents of God that carry out His will in conducting the universe. Thus, the sun's role in giving light, heat, and energy and the moon's role in causing the tides are in reality not demonstrations of their own power, but of the means God utilizes to carry out those functions of nature according to His will. If perceived accurately, such aspects of creation bear testimony to the existence of an omniscient, omnipotent Creator.

However, they can be understood perversely as well. *Rambam (Hil. Avodah Zarah* 1:1-2) notes that man began to view the heavenly bodies first as servants of God that should be honored and glorified for the sake of their Maker. Eventually they went further and built temples and brought offerings to them. All of this is forbidden idolatry, but at least the people guilty of these practices acknowledged that the objects of their homage were creatures of God. In time, the practice deteriorated to the point where false prophets and their followers went so far as to say that such objects and graven images of them and other creatures were actually gods with independent powers.

In contrast to such perversity and heresy, we now proclaim that the very bodies that man perceives as being so mighty — the sun and other heavenly bodies — are but part of the heavenly forces that themselves stand in awe before God and are privileged to proclaim His praises *(Kol Bo).*

צוּרֵנוּ מַלְכֵּנוּ וְגֹאֲלֵנוּ — *Our Rock, our King, and our Redeemer.* These three appellations for God allude to the three broad stages of creation as described by the Talmud *(Avodah Zarah* 9a): The world in its present form will endure for six thousand years including two thousand years of emptiness, two thousand years of Torah, and two thousand years of the days of Messiah. The first period continued until Abraham was fifty-two years old. In those days, the Torah had not yet been given nor were its teachings widespread. Those were days of emptiness, when God was צוּרֵנוּ, *our Rock,* in the sense that He was the Creator and Stronghold of the universe, but was not acknowledged. Then Abraham began to remake man's understanding of the world. Thus began the era of Torah and its teachings, a time during which the Jewish nation came into being to teach that God was מַלְכֵּנוּ, *our King,* to Whom we owe total allegiance. The final period of two

ON ALL DAYS CONTINUE HERE:

תִּתְבָּרַךְ *May You be blessed, our Rock,* our King and our Redeemer,* Creator of holy ones; may Your Name be praised forever, our King, O Fashioner of ministering angels;* all of Whose ministering angels stand at the summit of the universe and proclaim — with awe, together, loudly — the words of the living God and King of the universe.*[1] *They are all beloved; they are all flawless; they are all mighty; they all do the will of their Maker with dread and reverence.* Chazzan– *And they all open their mouth in holiness and purity, in song and hymn — and bless, praise, glorify, revere, sanctify and declare the kingship of —*

אֶת שֵׁם *The Name of God, the great, mighty, and awesome King; holy is He.*[2] Chazzan– *Then they all accept upon themselves the yoke of heavenly sovereignty from one another,* and grant permission to one another to sanctify the One Who formed them, with tranquillity, with clear articulation, and with sweetness. All of them as one proclaim His holiness and say with awe:*

Congregation recites aloud:

'Holy, holy, holy* is HASHEM, Master of Legions,* the whole world is filled with His glory.'[3]

(1) Cf. *Jeremiah* 10:10. (2) Cf. *Deuteronomy* 10:17; *Psalms* 99:3. (3) *Isaiah* 6:3.

thousand years began after the destruction of the Temple. Despite the chaos, hardship, persecution, and slaughters of these dark years of exile, it is a time when the conditions for the ultimate and final Redemption are being formed. Hard though it is to understand, these are the centuries when God will eventually come to be recognized as גֹּאֲלֵנוּ, *our Redeemer (Siddur Sha'ar HaRachamim).*

קְדוֹשִׁים . . . מְשָׁרְתִים — *Holy ones . . . ministering angels.* Generally speaking, there are two forms of angels. The first and holier kind never take physical form and have no part in controlling material existence. These *holy ones* are spiritual beings whose closeness to God is most intense. Below them are the *ministering angels,* who are charged with tasks relating to the universe and man. They 'minister' to such matters as health, rain, prosperity, punishment, and so on. These angels sometimes take human form as found in the narratives of Scriptures *(Iyun Tefillah).*

The creation of these heavenly beings is expressed in the present tense, because God constantly creates new angels as He desires and as they are needed to serve Him *(Etz Yosef).*

וְכֻלָּם מְקַבְּלִים . . . זֶה מִזֶּה — *Then they all accept . . . from one another. Tanna d'Bei Eliyahu* contrasts the behavior of the angels with that of human beings. Unlike people whose competitive jealousies cause them to thwart and outdo one another, the angels urge one another to take the initiative in serving and praising God. Conflict is the foe of perfection, harmony is its ally.

קָדוֹשׁ קָדוֹשׁ קָדוֹשׁ — *Holy, holy, holy. Targum Yonasan (Isaiah* 6:3) renders: *Holy* in the most exalted heaven, the abode of His Presence; *holy* on earth, product of His strength; *holy* forever and ever is HASHEM, Master of Legions . . .

כָּבוֹד, *glory,* refers to the glory of God that is present *within* the material world; it is the degree of Godliness that man is capable of perceiving even within creation. קָדוֹשׁ, *holy,* on the other hand, refers to God's essence, which is beyond all comprehension.

צְבָאוֹת — *Master of Legions.* Although it is commonly translated simply as *hosts* or *legions,* the word צְבָאוֹת is a Name of God (see *Shevuos* 35a), which means that He is the *Master* of all the heavenly hosts. The word צָבָא is used to refer to an organized, disciplined group. Thus, an army is commonly called צָבָא. In the context of this Divine Name, it refers to the idea that the infinite heavenly bodies are organized according to God's will to do His service.

All:

אֶרְאֶלִּים* וּמַלְאָכִים, מַקְדִּישִׁים וּמְבָרְכִים, לְמֶלֶךְ מַלְכֵי הַמְּלָכִים.
מוּכָנִים וַעֲרוּכִים, בְּכַנְפֵיהֶם סוֹכְכִים, יוֹם יוֹם מַמְלִיכִים,
לְמֶלֶךְ מַלְכֵי הַמְּלָכִים.
תַּקִּיפֵי שְׂרָפִים, תִּשְׁבָּחוֹת מְיַפִּים, לְמֶלֶךְ מַלְכֵי הַמְּלָכִים.
יְקַר אַלְפֵי אֲלָפִים, וְרִבֵּי רִבְבָן צְפוּפִים,[1] רָאשֵׁיהֶם כּוֹפְפִים,
לְמֶלֶךְ מַלְכֵי הַמְּלָכִים.
בַּחוּרֵי מֶרְכָּבָה, מְרַנְּנִים בְּאַהֲבָה, לְמֶלֶךְ מַלְכֵי הַמְּלָכִים.
יְדוֹדוּן יֶצְבָּא, בְּהוֹד שִׁירָה עֲרֵבָה, לְשׁוֹרֵר בְּחִבָּה,
לְמֶלֶךְ מַלְכֵי הַמְּלָכִים.
רִגְיוֹן הַנָּהָר,[2] מְאֹד חָשׁ וִיוּמְהָר, לְמֶלֶךְ מַלְכֵי הַמְּלָכִים.
בּוֹ לְהִטָּהֵר, חַשְׁמַלֵּי זֹהַר, בְּחִדּוּשׁ שִׁיר לְהַגְהַר,
לְמֶלֶךְ מַלְכֵי הַמְּלָכִים.
יְשׁוֹרֵר מִיכָאֵל, וִיזַמֵּר גַּבְרִיאֵל, לְמֶלֶךְ מַלְכֵי הַמְּלָכִים.
שׁוֹאֵג קְמוּאֵל, וְגוֹעֶה רְפָאֵל, וּמְהַדֵּר הֲדַרְנִיאֵל, לְמֶלֶךְ מַלְכֵי הַמְּלָכִים.
פּוֹחֵד סַנְדַּלְפוֹן, לְצַד דֹּפֶן יִדְפֹּן, לְמֶלֶךְ מַלְכֵי הַמְּלָכִים.
טַעֲמֵי חִין יַחְפֹּן, כֶּתֶר מֵהֶם לִסְפֹּן,[3] וּמַשְׁבִּיעַ לֶאֱפוֹן, עַל רֹאשׁ
מֶלֶךְ מַלְכֵי הַמְּלָכִים.
יְקַדֵּשׁ גַּלִּיצוּר, הַמְּגַלֶּה* טַעֲמֵי צוּר, מִפִּי מֶלֶךְ מַלְכֵי הַמְּלָכִים.
הַמַּשְׁמִיעַ לְכָל יְצוּר, שְׁנַת שְׂבַע וּבִצּוּר,
וְכָל דָּבָר הָאָצוּר, בִּרְצוֹן מֶלֶךְ מַלְכֵי הַמְּלָכִים.
חַיּוֹת אַרְבַּעְתָּן, מְשַׁלְּשׁוֹת קְדֻשָּׁתָן, לְמֶלֶךְ מַלְכֵי הַמְּלָכִים.
❖ זוֹעוֹת מֵאֵימָתָן, קוֹפְצוֹת בְּנַהֲמָתָן, קוֹרְאוֹת לְעֻמָּתָן,
לְמֶלֶךְ מַלְכֵי הַמְּלָכִים.

(1) Cf. *Daniel* 7:10. (2) See commentary on p. 466. (3) See commentary on p. 218.

אֶרְאֶלִּים — *Erelim.* R' Shephatiah, a distinguished scholar and kabbalist, established a yeshivah and headed the local *beis din* in Oria, Italy in the mid-ninth century. When the Byzantine emperor Basil I issued anti-Jewish decrees (about 873), R' Shephatiah traveled to Constantinople in an attempt to convince the emperor to annul his decrees. Although unsuccessful in his overall mission, while in Basil's court R' Shephatiah was able to effect a miraculous cure for the emperor's deathly ill daughter. He asked that as his reward Basil annul his decrees, but his request was only granted in part. The Jews of Oria and four other cities were released from the decrees. R' Shephatiah and his son and successor, R' Amittai, were both accomplished *paytanim* whose works occupy an important place in the *Selichos* liturgy. In their compositions they often allude to the persecutions and forced conversions that Basil inflicted upon the Jews.

The present *piyut* contains the acrostic אֲמִתַּי בְּרַבִּי שְׁפַטְיָה חֲזַק, *Amittai son of Rabbi Shephatiah, may he be strong.* It describes the angels in their recitation of the *Kedushah* verses. *Rambam*

All:

א *Erelim* and Malachim recite Kedushah and blessings*
to the King Who reigns over kings.

מ *Prepared and ordered, their wings outspread,*
each day they proclaim the kingdom of the King Who reigns over kings.

ח *The mighty Seraphim recite beautiful praises*
to the King Who reigns over kings.

י *The worthy thousands of thousands and myriads of myriads crowding,*[1]
their heads bowed to the King Who reigns over kings.

ב *The chosen [bearers] of the Chariot, sing glad song with love,*
for the King Who reigns over kings.

י *Moving in legions, with the majesty of sweet song,*
to be sung with affection to the King Who reigns over kings.

ר *The river Rigyon*[2] *very speedily hurries*
to the King Who reigns over kings.

ב *In it to purify the shining Chashmalim,*
with renewed song to bow to the King Who reigns over kings.

י *Michael would sing, Gabriel would recite praise*
to the King Who reigns over kings.

ש *Kemuel would roar, Refael would call out,*
Hadarniel would glorify the King Who reigns over kings.

פ *Sandalfon would tremble and edge towards the wall, [in fear]*
of the King Who reigns over kings.

ט *He [Sandalfon] gathers in hand the tasteful prayers,*
to weave them into a crown,[3]
in a most satisfying manner, [to be placed] upon the head
of the King Who reigns over kings.

י *Galitzur would sanctify, it is he who reveals* the Rock's reason,*
from the mouth of the King Who reigns over kings.

ה *He lets every creature hear whether [the year's rain will be]*
plentiful or scarce,
and everything [else that is] hidden, when it is the will
to the King Who reigns over kings.

ח *The foursome of Chayos treble their Kedushah*
of the King Who reigns over kings.

זק ❖*They perspire in fear, they spring with their cries,*
they call to those facing them [the praises]
of the King Who reigns over kings.

(*Yesodei HaTorah* 2:7) notes ten levels of angels: *Chayos, Ofanim, Erelim, Chashmalim, Seraphim, Malachim, Elohim, B'nai Elohim, Cherubim* and *Ishim*. Five of these categories are mentioned in the *piyut*, along with the names of at least seven angels.

הַמְגַלֶּה — *He who reveals.* The Midrash teaches that since the Destruction of the Temple, God would speak to no angel but Galitzur, who would in turn reveal God's message to the other angels. Hence the name גַּלִיצוּר, lit., *revealer of the Rock* (*Pesikta* 97).

Congregation, followed by the *chazzan*, recites one of these versions, according to its tradition.

וְהָאוֹפַנִּים וְחַיּוֹת הַקֹּדֶשׁ בְּרַעַשׁ גָּדוֹל מִתְנַשְּׂאִים לְעֻמַּת שְׂרָפִים. לְעֻמָּתָם מְשַׁבְּחִים וְאוֹמְרִים:

וְהַחַיּוֹת יְשׁוֹרֵרוּ, וּכְרוּבִים יְפָאֵרוּ, וּשְׂרָפִים יָרֹנּוּ, וְאֶרְאֶלִּים יְבָרֵכוּ. פְּנֵי כָל חַיָּה וְאוֹפָן וּכְרוּב לְעֻמַּת שְׂרָפִים. לְעֻמָּתָם מְשַׁבְּחִים וְאוֹמְרִים:

Congregation recites aloud:

בָּרוּךְ כְּבוֹד יהוה מִמְּקוֹמוֹ.[1]

לְאֵל בָּרוּךְ נְעִימוֹת יִתֵּנוּ. לְמֶלֶךְ אֵל חַי וְקַיָּם, זְמִרוֹת יֹאמֵרוּ, וְתִשְׁבָּחוֹת יַשְׁמִיעוּ. כִּי הוּא לְבַדּוֹ פּוֹעֵל גְּבוּרוֹת, עֹשֶׂה חֲדָשׁוֹת, בַּעַל מִלְחָמוֹת, זוֹרֵעַ צְדָקוֹת, מַצְמִיחַ יְשׁוּעוֹת, בּוֹרֵא רְפוּאוֹת, נוֹרָא תְהִלּוֹת, אֲדוֹן הַנִּפְלָאוֹת. הַמְּחַדֵּשׁ בְּטוּבוֹ בְּכָל יוֹם תָּמִיד מַעֲשֵׂה בְרֵאשִׁית. כָּאָמוּר: לְעֹשֵׂה אוֹרִים גְּדֹלִים, כִּי לְעוֹלָם חַסְדּוֹ.[2] ❖ אוֹר חָדָשׁ עַל צִיּוֹן תָּאִיר, וְנִזְכֶּה כֻלָּנוּ מְהֵרָה לְאוֹרוֹ. בָּרוּךְ אַתָּה יהוה, יוֹצֵר הַמְּאוֹרוֹת. (Cong. – אָמֵן.)

אַהֲבָה רַבָּה אֲהַבְתָּנוּ יהוה אֱלֹהֵינוּ, חֶמְלָה גְדוֹלָה וִיתֵרָה חָמַלְתָּ עָלֵינוּ. אָבִינוּ מַלְכֵּנוּ, בַּעֲבוּר אֲבוֹתֵינוּ שֶׁבָּטְחוּ בְךָ, וַתְּלַמְּדֵם חֻקֵּי חַיִּים, כֵּן תְּחָנֵּנוּ וּתְלַמְּדֵנוּ. אָבִינוּ הָאָב הָרַחֲמָן הַמְּרַחֵם, רַחֵם עָלֵינוּ, וְתֵן בְּלִבֵּנוּ לְהָבִין וּלְהַשְׂכִּיל, לִשְׁמֹעַ לִלְמוֹד וּלְלַמֵּד, לִשְׁמֹר וְלַעֲשׂוֹת וּלְקַיֵּם אֶת כָּל דִּבְרֵי תַלְמוּד תּוֹרָתֶךָ בְּאַהֲבָה. וְהָאֵר עֵינֵינוּ בְּתוֹרָתֶךָ, וְדַבֵּק לִבֵּנוּ בְּמִצְוֹתֶיךָ, וְיַחֵד לְבָבֵנוּ לְאַהֲבָה וּלְיִרְאָה אֶת שְׁמֶךָ,[3] וְלֹא נֵבוֹשׁ לְעוֹלָם וָעֶד. כִּי בְשֵׁם קָדְשְׁךָ הַגָּדוֹל וְהַנּוֹרָא בָּטָחְנוּ, נָגִילָה וְנִשְׂמְחָה בִּישׁוּעָתֶךָ.

At this point, gather the four *tzitzis* between the fourth and fifth fingers of the left hand. Hold *tzitzis* in this manner throughout the *Shema*.

וַהֲבִיאֵנוּ לְשָׁלוֹם מֵאַרְבַּע כַּנְפוֹת הָאָרֶץ, וְתוֹלִיכֵנוּ קוֹמְמִיּוּת לְאַרְצֵנוּ. כִּי אֵל פּוֹעֵל יְשׁוּעוֹת אָתָּה, וּבָנוּ בָחַרְתָּ מִכָּל עַם וְלָשׁוֹן. ❖ וְקֵרַבְתָּנוּ לְשִׁמְךָ הַגָּדוֹל סֶלָה בֶּאֱמֶת, לְהוֹדוֹת לְךָ וּלְיַחֶדְךָ בְּאַהֲבָה. בָּרוּךְ אַתָּה יהוה, הַבּוֹחֵר בְּעַמּוֹ יִשְׂרָאֵל בְּאַהֲבָה. (Cong. – אָמֵן.)

(1) *Ezekiel* 3:12.(2) *Psalms* 136:7. (3) Cf. 86:11.

Congregation, followed by the *chazzan,* recites one of these versions, according to its tradition.

Then the Ofanim and the holy Chayos, with great noise raise themselves towards the Seraphim. Facing them they give praise saying:

Then the Chayos sing, the Cherubim glorify, the Seraphim rejoice, and the Erelim bless, in the presence of every Chayah, Ofan, and Cherub towards the Seraphim. Facing them they give praise saying:

Congregation recites aloud:

'Blessed is the glory of HASHEM from His place.'[1]

לְאֵל *To the blessed God they shall offer sweet melodies; to the King, the living and enduring God, they shall sing hymns and proclaim praises. For He alone effects mighty deeds, makes new things, is Master of wars, sows kindnesses, makes salvations flourish, creates cures, is too awesome for praise, is Lord of wonders. In His goodness He renews daily, perpetually, the work of creation. As it is said: '[Give thanks] to Him Who makes the great luminaries, for His kindness endures forever.'*[2] Chazzan– *May You shine a new light on Zion, and may we all speedily merit its light. Blessed are You, HASHEM, Who fashions the luminaries.* (Cong.– *Amen.)*

אַהֲבָה *With an abundant love have You loved us, HASHEM, our God; with exceedingly great pity have You pitied us. Our Father, our King, for the sake of our forefathers who trusted in You and whom You taught the decrees of life, may You be equally gracious to us and teach us. Our Father, the merciful Father, Who acts mercifully, have mercy upon us, instill in our hearts to understand and elucidate, to listen, learn, teach, safeguard, perform, and fulfill all the words of Your Torah's teaching with love. Enlighten our eyes in Your Torah, attach our hearts to Your commandments, and unify our hearts to love and fear Your Name,*[3] *and may we not feel inner shame for all eternity. Because we have trusted in Your great and awesome holy Name, may we exult and rejoice in Your salvation.*

At this point, gather the four *tzitzis* between the fourth and fifth fingers of the left hand. Hold *tzitzis* in this manner throughout the *Shema.*

Bring us in peacefulness from the four corners of the earth and lead us with upright pride to our land. For You effect salvations O God; You have chosen us from among every people and tongue. Chazzan– *And You have brought us close to Your great Name forever in truth, to offer praiseful thanks to You, and proclaim Your Oneness with love. Blessed are You, HASHEM, Who chooses His people Israel with love.* (Cong.– *Amen.)*

שמע

Immediately before its recitation concentrate on fulfilling the positive commandment of reciting the *Shema* twice daily. It is important to enunciate each word clearly and not to run words together. For this reason, vertical lines have been placed between two words that are prone to be slurred into one and are not separated by a comma or a hyphen. See *Laws* §40-55.

When praying without a *minyan,* begin with the following three-word formula:

אֵל מֶלֶךְ נֶאֱמָן.

Recite the first verse aloud, with the right hand covering the eyes, and concentrate intently upon accepting God's absolute sovereignty.

שְׁמַע | יִשְׂרָאֵל, יהוה | אֱלֹהֵינוּ, יהוה | אֶחָד:

In an undertone – בָּרוּךְ שֵׁם כְּבוֹד מַלְכוּתוֹ לְעוֹלָם וָעֶד.

While reciting the first paragraph (דברים ו:ה-ט), concentrate on accepting the commandment to love God.

וְאָהַבְתָּ אֵת | יהוה | אֱלֹהֶיךָ, בְּכָל־לְבָבְךָ, וּבְכָל־נַפְשְׁךָ, וּבְכָל־מְאֹדֶךָ: וְהָיוּ הַדְּבָרִים הָאֵלֶּה, אֲשֶׁר | אָנֹכִי מְצַוְּךָ הַיּוֹם, עַל־לְבָבֶךָ: וְשִׁנַּנְתָּם לְבָנֶיךָ, וְדִבַּרְתָּ בָּם, בְּשִׁבְתְּךָ בְּבֵיתֶךָ, וּבְלֶכְתְּךָ בַדֶּרֶךְ, וּבְשָׁכְבְּךָ וּבְקוּמֶךָ: וּקְשַׁרְתָּם לְאוֹת | עַל־יָדֶךָ, וְהָיוּ לְטֹטָפֹת בֵּין | עֵינֶיךָ: וּכְתַבְתָּם | עַל־מְזֻזוֹת בֵּיתֶךָ, וּבִשְׁעָרֶיךָ:

While reciting the second paragraph (דברים יא:יג-כא), concentrate on accepting all the commandments and the concept of reward and punishment.

וְהָיָה, אִם־שָׁמֹעַ תִּשְׁמְעוּ אֶל־מִצְוֺתַי, אֲשֶׁר | אָנֹכִי מְצַוֶּה | אֶתְכֶם הַיּוֹם, לְאַהֲבָה אֶת־יהוה | אֱלֹהֵיכֶם וּלְעָבְדוֹ, בְּכָל־לְבַבְכֶם, וּבְכָל־נַפְשְׁכֶם: וְנָתַתִּי מְטַר־אַרְצְכֶם בְּעִתּוֹ, יוֹרֶה וּמַלְקוֹשׁ, וְאָסַפְתָּ דְגָנֶךָ וְתִירֹשְׁךָ וְיִצְהָרֶךָ: וְנָתַתִּי | עֵשֶׂב | בְּשָׂדְךָ לִבְהֶמְתֶּךָ, וְאָכַלְתָּ וְשָׂבָעְתָּ: הִשָּׁמְרוּ לָכֶם, פֶּן־יִפְתֶּה לְבַבְכֶם, וְסַרְתֶּם וַעֲבַדְתֶּם | אֱלֹהִים | אֲחֵרִים, וְהִשְׁתַּחֲוִיתֶם לָהֶם: וְחָרָה | אַף־יהוה בָּכֶם, וְעָצַר | אֶת־הַשָּׁמַיִם, וְלֹא־יִהְיֶה מָטָר, וְהָאֲדָמָה לֹא תִתֵּן אֶת־יְבוּלָהּ, וַאֲבַדְתֶּם | מְהֵרָה מֵעַל הָאָרֶץ הַטֹּבָה | אֲשֶׁר | יהוה נֹתֵן לָכֶם: וְשַׂמְתֶּם | אֶת־דְּבָרַי | אֵלֶּה, עַל־לְבַבְכֶם וְעַל־נַפְשְׁכֶם, וּקְשַׁרְתֶּם | אֹתָם לְאוֹת | עַל־יֶדְכֶם, וְהָיוּ לְטוֹטָפֹת בֵּין | עֵינֵיכֶם: וְלִמַּדְתֶּם | אֹתָם | אֶת־בְּנֵיכֶם, לְדַבֵּר בָּם, בְּשִׁבְתְּךָ בְּבֵיתֶךָ, וּבְלֶכְתְּךָ בַדֶּרֶךְ, וּבְשָׁכְבְּךָ וּבְקוּמֶךָ: וּכְתַבְתָּם | עַל־מְזוּזוֹת בֵּיתֶךָ, וּבִשְׁעָרֶיךָ: לְמַעַן | יִרְבּוּ | יְמֵיכֶם וִימֵי בְנֵיכֶם, עַל הָאֲדָמָה | אֲשֶׁר נִשְׁבַּע | יהוה לַאֲבֹתֵיכֶם לָתֵת לָהֶם, כִּימֵי הַשָּׁמַיִם | עַל־הָאָרֶץ:

THE SHEMA

Immediately before its recitation concentrate on fulfilling the positive commandment of reciting the *Shema* twice daily. It is important to enunciate each word clearly and not to run words together. See *Laws* §40-55.

When praying without a *minyan,* begin with the following three-word formula:

God, trustworthy King.

Recite the first verse aloud, with the right hand covering the eyes, and concentrate intently upon accepting God's absolute sovereignty.

Hear, O Israel: HASHEM is our God, HASHEM, the One and Only.[1]

In an undertone— *Blessed is the Name of His glorious kingdom for all eternity.*

While reciting the first paragraph (*Deuteronomy* 6:5-9), concentrate on accepting the commandment to love God.

וְאָהַבְתָּ *You shall love HASHEM, your God, with all your heart, with all your soul and with all your resources. Let these matters that I command you today be upon your heart. Teach them thoroughly to your children and speak of them while you sit in your home, while you walk on the way, when you retire and when you arise. Bind them as a sign upon your arm and let them be tefillin between your eyes. And write them on the doorposts of your house and upon your gates.*

While reciting the second paragraph (*Deuteronomy* 11:13-21), concentrate on accepting all the commandments and the concept of reward and punishment.

וְהָיָה *And it will come to pass that if you continually hearken to My commandments that I command you today, to love HASHEM, your God, and to serve Him, with all your heart and with all your soul — then I will provide rain for your land in its proper time, the early and late rains, that you may gather in your grain, your wine, and your oil. I will provide grass in your field for your cattle and you will eat and be satisfied. Beware lest your heart be seduced and you turn astray and serve gods of others and bow to them. Then the wrath of HASHEM will blaze against you. He will restrain the heaven so there will be no rain and the ground will not yield its produce. And you will swiftly be banished from the goodly land which HASHEM gives you. Place these words of Mine upon your heart and upon your soul; bind them for a sign upon your arm and let them be tefillin between your eyes. Teach them to your children, to discuss them, while you sit in your home, while you walk on the way, when you retire and when you arise. And write them on the doorposts of your house and upon your gates. In order to prolong your days and the days of your children upon the ground that HASHEM has sworn to your ancestors to give them, like the days of the heaven on the earth.*

---

(1) *Deuteronomy* 6:4.

Before reciting the third paragraph (במדבר טו:לז-מא), the *tzitzis*, which have been held in the left hand, are taken in the right hand also. The *tzitzis* are kissed at each mention of the word and at the end of the paragraph, and are passed before the eyes at וּרְאִיתֶם אֹתוֹ.

וַיֹּ֣אמֶר ׀ יהוָ֖ה ׀ אֶל־מֹשֶׁ֥ה לֵּאמֹֽר: דַּבֵּ֞ר ׀ אֶל־בְּנֵ֤י ׀ יִשְׂרָאֵל֙, וְאָמַרְתָּ֣ אֲלֵהֶ֔ם, וְעָשׂ֨וּ לָהֶ֥ם צִיצִ֛ת, עַל־כַּנְפֵ֥י בִגְדֵיהֶ֖ם לְדֹרֹתָ֑ם, וְנָֽתְנ֛וּ ׀ עַל־צִיצִ֥ת הַכָּנָ֖ף, פְּתִ֥יל תְּכֵֽלֶת: וְהָיָ֣ה לָכֶם֮ לְצִיצִת֒, וּרְאִיתֶ֣ם ׀ אֹת֗וֹ, וּזְכַרְתֶּם֙ ׀ אֶת־כָּל־מִצְוֹ֣ת ׀ יהוָ֔ה, וַעֲשִׂיתֶ֖ם ׀ אֹתָ֑ם, וְלֹֽא־תָת֜וּרוּ ׀ אַחֲרֵ֤י לְבַבְכֶם֙ וְאַחֲרֵ֣י ׀ עֵֽינֵיכֶ֔ם, אֲשֶׁר־אַתֶּ֥ם זֹנִ֖ים ׀ אַחֲרֵיהֶֽם: לְמַ֣עַן תִּזְכְּר֔וּ, וַעֲשִׂיתֶ֖ם ׀ אֶת־כָּל־מִצְוֹתָ֑י, וִהְיִיתֶ֥ם קְדֹשִׁ֖ים לֵאלֹֽהֵיכֶֽם: אֲנִ֞י יהוָ֣ה ׀ אֱלֹֽהֵיכֶ֗ם, אֲשֶׁ֨ר הוֹצֵ֤אתִי ׀ אֶתְכֶם֙ ׀ מֵאֶ֣רֶץ מִצְרַ֔יִם, לִהְי֥וֹת לָכֶ֖ם לֵאלֹהִ֑ים, אֲנִ֖י ׀ יהוָ֥ה אֱלֹֽהֵיכֶֽם: אֱמֶת —

Concentrate on fulfilling the commandment of remembering the Exodus from Egypt.

Although the word אֱמֶת belongs to the next paragraph, it is appended to the conclusion of the previous one, as explained in the commentary.

Chazzan repeats — **יהוה אֱלֹהֵיכֶם אֱמֶת.**

וְיַצִּיב וְנָכוֹן וְקַיָּם וְיָשָׁר וְנֶאֱמָן וְאָהוּב וְחָבִיב וְנֶחְמָד וְנָעִים וְנוֹרָא וְאַדִּיר וּמְתֻקָּן וּמְקֻבָּל וְטוֹב וְיָפֶה הַדָּבָר הַזֶּה עָלֵינוּ לְעוֹלָם וָעֶד. אֱמֶת אֱלֹהֵי עוֹלָם מַלְכֵּנוּ צוּר יַעֲקֹב, מָגֵן יִשְׁעֵנוּ, לְדֹר וָדֹר הוּא קַיָּם, וּשְׁמוֹ קַיָּם, וְכִסְאוֹ נָכוֹן, וּמַלְכוּתוֹ וֶאֱמוּנָתוֹ לָעַד קַיֶּמֶת. וּדְבָרָיו חָיִים וְקַיָּמִים, נֶאֱמָנִים וְנֶחֱמָדִים לָעַד (kiss the tzitzis and release them) וּלְעוֹלְמֵי עוֹלָמִים. ❖ עַל אֲבוֹתֵינוּ וְעָלֵינוּ, עַל בָּנֵינוּ וְעַל דּוֹרוֹתֵינוּ, וְעַל כָּל דּוֹרוֹת זֶרַע יִשְׂרָאֵל עֲבָדֶיךָ.

עַל הָרִאשׁוֹנִים וְעַל הָאַחֲרוֹנִים, דָּבָר טוֹב וְקַיָּם לְעוֹלָם וָעֶד, אֱמֶת וֶאֱמוּנָה חֹק וְלֹא יַעֲבֹר. אֱמֶת שָׁאַתָּה הוּא יהוה אֱלֹהֵינוּ וֵאלֹהֵי אֲבוֹתֵינוּ, ❖ מַלְכֵּנוּ מֶלֶךְ אֲבוֹתֵינוּ, גֹּאֲלֵנוּ גֹּאֵל אֲבוֹתֵינוּ, יוֹצְרֵנוּ צוּר יְשׁוּעָתֵנוּ, פּוֹדֵנוּ וּמַצִּילֵנוּ מֵעוֹלָם שְׁמֶךָ, אֵין אֱלֹהִים זוּלָתֶךָ.

אֱמוּנִים* אֲשֶׁר נֶאֱסָפוּ, בְּרָכוֹת נִכְסָפוּ,
גַּם קוֹמָתָם כָּפָפוּ, דְּבַר חִנּוּנָם הֶעֱדִיפוּ.
הוֹבִילָם לְאָהֳלֵיהֶם לְשָׁלוֹם, וְיִמְצְאוּ שָׁם שָׁלוֹם,
זֶרַע הַשָּׁלוֹם, חַסְּנֵם בְּצֶדֶק וְשָׁלוֹם. טוֹבוֹת לְכַלְּלָם, יְקָר לְהַכְלִילָם,

כ *to bequeathe their honor,* ל *to elevate them on high.*
מ *Fulfill their requests,* נ *lead their celebration,*
ס *rejoice with their flock,* ע *arouse their redemption.*
פ *Turn to their supplication,* צ *cut down those who pain them,*
ק *accept their prayers,* ר *exalt their multitudes.*
ש *Guard the splendrous ones,* *cause the accursed to be forgotten,*
ת *re-establish the flocks,*
and we shall exalt You as when You split the Sea.

עֶזְרַת *The Helper of our forefathers are You alone, forever, Shield and Savior for their children after them in every generation. At the zenith of the universe is Your dwelling, and Your justice and Your righteousness extend to the ends of the earth. Praiseworthy is the person who obeys Your commandments and takes to his heart Your teaching and Your word. True — You are the Master for Your people and a mighty King to take up their grievance. True — You are the First and You are the Last, and other than You we have no king,*[1] *redeemer, or savior. From Egypt You redeemed us,* HASHEM, *our God, and from the house of slavery You liberated us. All their firstborn You slew, but Your firstborn You redeemed; the Sea of Reeds You split; the wanton sinners You drowned; the dear ones You brought across; and the water covered their foes — not one of them was left.*[2] *For this, the beloved praised and exalted God; the dear ones offered hymns, songs, praises, blessings, and thanksgivings to the King, the living and enduring God — exalted and uplifted, great and awesome, Who humbles the haughty and lifts the lowly; withdraws the captive, liberates the humble, and helps the poor; Who responds to His people upon their outcry to Him.*

Rise for *Shemoneh Esrei.* Some take three steps backward at this point; others do so before צוּר יִשְׂרָאֵל, *'Rock of Israel.'*

Chazzan— *Praises to the Supreme God, the blessed One Who is blessed. Moses and the Children of Israel exclaimed a song to You with great joy and they all said:*

'Who is like You among the heavenly powers, HASHEM! *Who is like You, mighty in holiness, too awesome for praise, doing wonders.'*[3]
Chazzan— *With a new song the redeemed ones praised Your Name at the seashore, all of them in unison gave thanks, acknowledged [Your] sovereignty, and said:*

'HASHEM shall reign for all eternity.'[4]

It is forbidden to interrupt or pause between *'Who redeemed Israel'* and *Shemoneh Esrei,* even for *Kaddish, Kedushah* or *Borchu.*

צוּר יִשְׂרָאֵל Chazzan— *Rock of Israel, arise to the aid of Israel and liberate, as You pledged, Judah and Israel. Our Redeemer —* HASHEM, *Master of Legions, is His Name — the Holy One of Israel.*[5] *Blessed are You,* HASHEM, *Who redeemed Israel.*

שמונה עשרה – עמידה

Take three steps backward, then three steps forward. Remain standing with feet together while reciting *Shemoneh Esrei.* Recite it with quiet devotion and without interruption, verbal or otherwise. Although it should not be audible to others, one must pray loudly enough to hear himself.

אֲדֹנָי שְׂפָתַי תִּפְתָּח, וּפִי יַגִּיד תְּהִלָּתֶךָ.[1]

אבות

Bend the knees at בָּרוּךְ; bow at אַתָּה; straighten up at ה׳.

בָּרוּךְ אַתָּה יהוה אֱלֹהֵינוּ וֵאלֹהֵי אֲבוֹתֵינוּ, אֱלֹהֵי אַבְרָהָם, אֱלֹהֵי יִצְחָק, וֵאלֹהֵי יַעֲקֹב, הָאֵל הַגָּדוֹל הַגִּבּוֹר וְהַנּוֹרָא, אֵל עֶלְיוֹן, גּוֹמֵל חֲסָדִים טוֹבִים וְקוֹנֵה הַכֹּל, וְזוֹכֵר חַסְדֵי אָבוֹת, וּמֵבִיא גוֹאֵל לִבְנֵי בְנֵיהֶם, לְמַעַן שְׁמוֹ בְּאַהֲבָה. מֶלֶךְ עוֹזֵר וּמוֹשִׁיעַ וּמָגֵן.

Bend the knees at בָּרוּךְ; bow at אַתָּה; straighten up at ה׳.

בָּרוּךְ אַתָּה יהוה, מָגֵן אַבְרָהָם.

גבורות

אַתָּה גִּבּוֹר לְעוֹלָם אֲדֹנָי, מְחַיֵּה מֵתִים אַתָּה, רַב לְהוֹשִׁיעַ. מְכַלְכֵּל חַיִּים בְּחֶסֶד, מְחַיֵּה מֵתִים בְּרַחֲמִים רַבִּים, סוֹמֵךְ נוֹפְלִים, וְרוֹפֵא חוֹלִים, וּמַתִּיר אֲסוּרִים, וּמְקַיֵּם אֱמוּנָתוֹ לִישֵׁנֵי עָפָר. מִי כָמוֹךָ בַּעַל גְּבוּרוֹת, וּמִי דּוֹמֶה לָּךְ, מֶלֶךְ מֵמִית וּמְחַיֶּה וּמַצְמִיחַ יְשׁוּעָה. וְנֶאֱמָן אַתָּה לְהַחֲיוֹת מֵתִים. בָּרוּךְ אַתָּה יהוה, מְחַיֵּה הַמֵּתִים.

During the *chazzan's* repetition, *Kedushah* (below) is recited at this point.

קדושה

When reciting *Kedushah,* one must stand with his feet together and avoid any interruptions. One should rise on his toes when saying the words קָדוֹשׁ, קָדוֹשׁ, קָדוֹשׁ; בָּרוּךְ (of בָּרוּךְ כְּבוֹד); and יִמְלֹךְ.

Cong. then *Chazzan* – **נְקַדֵּשׁ** אֶת שִׁמְךָ בָּעוֹלָם, כְּשֵׁם שֶׁמַּקְדִּישִׁים אוֹתוֹ בִּשְׁמֵי מָרוֹם, כַּכָּתוּב עַל יַד נְבִיאֶךָ, וְקָרָא זֶה אֶל זֶה וְאָמַר:

All – קָדוֹשׁ קָדוֹשׁ קָדוֹשׁ יהוה צְבָאוֹת, מְלֹא כָל הָאָרֶץ כְּבוֹדוֹ.[2]

❖ אָז בְּקוֹל רַעַשׁ גָּדוֹל אַדִּיר וְחָזָק מַשְׁמִיעִים קוֹל, מִתְנַשְּׂאִים לְעֻמַּת שְׂרָפִים, לְעֻמָּתָם בָּרוּךְ יֹאמֵרוּ:

All – בָּרוּךְ כְּבוֹד יהוה, מִמְּקוֹמוֹ.[3] ❖ מִמְּקוֹמְךָ מַלְכֵּנוּ תוֹפִיעַ, וְתִמְלֹךְ עָלֵינוּ, כִּי מְחַכִּים אֲנַחְנוּ לָךְ. מָתַי תִּמְלֹךְ בְּצִיּוֹן, בְּקָרוֹב בְּיָמֵינוּ, לְעוֹלָם וָעֶד תִּשְׁכּוֹן. תִּתְגַּדַּל וְתִתְקַדַּשׁ בְּתוֹךְ יְרוּשָׁלַיִם עִירְךָ, לְדוֹר וָדוֹר וּלְנֵצַח נְצָחִים. וְעֵינֵינוּ תִרְאֶינָה מַלְכוּתֶךָ, כַּדָּבָר הָאָמוּר בְּשִׁירֵי עֻזֶּךָ, עַל יְדֵי דָוִד מְשִׁיחַ צִדְקֶךָ:

All – יִמְלֹךְ יהוה לְעוֹלָם, אֱלֹהַיִךְ צִיּוֹן לְדֹר וָדֹר, הַלְלוּיָהּ.[4]

Chazzan continues . . . לְדוֹר וָדוֹר (page 910).

SHEMONEH ESREI – AMIDAH

Take three steps backward, then three steps forward. Remain standing with feet together while reciting *Shemoneh Esrei.* Recite it with quiet devotion and without interruption, verbal or otherwise. Although it should not be audible to others, one must pray loudly enough to hear himself.

My Lord, open my lips, that my mouth may declare Your praise.[1]

PATRIARCHS

Bend the knees at *'Blessed'*; bow at *'You'*; straighten up at *'HASHEM.'*

בָּרוּךְ *Blessed are You, HASHEM, our God and the God of our forefathers, God of Abraham, God of Isaac, and God of Jacob; the great, mighty, and awesome God, the supreme God, Who bestows beneficial kindnesses and creates everything, Who recalls the kindnesses of the Patriarchs and brings a Redeemer to their children's children, for His Name's sake, with love. O King, Helper, Savior, and Shield.*

Bend the knees at *'Blessed'*; bow at *'You'*; straighten up at 'HASHEM.'

Blessed are You, HASHEM, Shield of Abraham.

GOD'S MIGHT

אַתָּה *You are eternally mighty, my Lord, the Resuscitator of the dead are You; abundantly able to save. He sustains the living with kindness, resuscitates the dead with abundant mercy, supports the fallen, heals the sick, releases the confined, and maintains His faith to those asleep in the dust. Who is like You, O Master of mighty deeds, and who is comparable to You, O King Who causes death and restores life and makes salvation sprout! And You are faithful to resuscitate the dead. Blessed are You, HASHEM, Who resuscitates the dead.*

During the *chazzan's* repetition, *Kedushah* (below) is recited at this point.

KEDUSHAH

When reciting ***Kedushah***, one must stand with his feet together and avoid any interruptions. One should rise on his toes when saying the words *Holy, holy, holy; Blessed is;* and *HASHEM shall reign.*

Cong. then Chazzan – **נְקַדֵּשׁ** *We shall sanctify Your Name in this world, just as they sanctify it in heaven above, as it is written by Your prophet, "And one [angel] will call another and say:*

All – *'Holy, holy, holy is HASHEM, Master of Legions, the whole world is filled with His glory.'"*[2] ❖ *Then, with a sound of great noise, mighty and powerful, they make heard a voice, raising themselves toward the seraphim; those facing them say 'Blessed ...':*

All – *'Blessed is the glory of HASHEM from His place.'*[3] ❖ *From Your place, our King, You will appear and reign over us, for we await You. When will You reign in Zion? Soon, in our days — forever and ever — may You dwell there. May You be exalted and sanctified within Jerusalem, Your city, from generation to generation and for all eternity. May our eyes see Your kingdom, as it is expressed in the songs of Your might, written by David, Your righteous anointed:*

All – *'HASHEM shall reign forever — your God, O Zion — from generation to generation, Halleluyah!'*[4]

Chazzan continues לְדוֹר וָדוֹר, *From generation* ... (p. 910).

(1) *Psalms* 51:17. (2) *Isaiah* 6:3. (3) *Ezekiel* 3:12. (4) *Psalms* 146:10.

קדושת השם

INDIVIDUALS RECITE:

אַתָּה קָדוֹשׁ וְשִׁמְךָ קָדוֹשׁ, וּקְדוֹשִׁים בְּכָל יוֹם יְהַלְלְוּךָ סֶּלָה. בָּרוּךְ אַתָּה יהוה, הָאֵל הַקָּדוֹשׁ.

CHAZZAN RECITES DURING HIS REPETITION:

לְדוֹר וָדוֹר נַגִּיד גָּדְלֶךָ וּלְנֵצַח נְצָחִים קְדֻשָּׁתְךָ נַקְדִּישׁ, וְשִׁבְחֲךָ אֱלֹהֵינוּ מִפִּינוּ לֹא יָמוּשׁ לְעוֹלָם וָעֶד, כִּי אֵל מֶלֶךְ גָּדוֹל וְקָדוֹשׁ אָתָּה. בָּרוּךְ אַתָּה יהוה, הָאֵל הַקָּדוֹשׁ.

קדושת היום

אַתָּה בְחַרְתָּנוּ מִכָּל הָעַמִּים, אָהַבְתָּ אוֹתָנוּ, וְרָצִיתָ בָּנוּ, וְרוֹמַמְתָּנוּ מִכָּל הַלְּשׁוֹנוֹת, וְקִדַּשְׁתָּנוּ בְּמִצְוֹתֶיךָ, וְקֵרַבְתָּנוּ מַלְכֵּנוּ לַעֲבוֹדָתֶךָ, וְשִׁמְךָ הַגָּדוֹל וְהַקָּדוֹשׁ עָלֵינוּ קָרָאתָ.

On the Sabbath add the words in brackets. [If forgotten, see *Laws* §86-90.]

וַתִּתֶּן לָנוּ יהוה אֱלֹהֵינוּ בְּאַהֲבָה [שַׁבָּתוֹת לִמְנוּחָה וּ]מוֹעֲדִים לְשִׂמְחָה חַגִּים וּזְמַנִּים לְשָׂשׂוֹן, אֶת יוֹם [הַשַּׁבָּת הַזֶּה וְאֶת יוֹם] הַשְּׁמִינִי חַג הָעֲצֶרֶת הַזֶּה, זְמַן שִׂמְחָתֵנוּ [בְּאַהֲבָה] מִקְרָא קֹדֶשׁ, זֵכֶר לִיצִיאַת מִצְרָיִם.

During the *chazzan's* repetition, congregation responds אָמֵן as indicated.

אֱלֹהֵינוּ וֵאלֹהֵי אֲבוֹתֵינוּ, יַעֲלֶה, וְיָבֹא, וְיַגִּיעַ, וְיֵרָאֶה, וְיֵרָצֶה, וְיִשָּׁמַע, וְיִפָּקֵד, וְיִזָּכֵר זִכְרוֹנֵנוּ וּפִקְדוֹנֵנוּ, וְזִכְרוֹן אֲבוֹתֵינוּ, וְזִכְרוֹן מָשִׁיחַ בֶּן דָּוִד עַבְדֶּךָ, וְזִכְרוֹן יְרוּשָׁלַיִם עִיר קָדְשֶׁךָ, וְזִכְרוֹן כָּל עַמְּךָ בֵּית יִשְׂרָאֵל לְפָנֶיךָ, לִפְלֵיטָה לְטוֹבָה לְחֵן וּלְחֶסֶד וּלְרַחֲמִים, לְחַיִּים וּלְשָׁלוֹם בְּיוֹם הַשְּׁמִינִי חַג הָעֲצֶרֶת הַזֶּה. זָכְרֵנוּ יהוה אֱלֹהֵינוּ בּוֹ לְטוֹבָה (.Cong – אָמֵן), וּפָקְדֵנוּ בוֹ לִבְרָכָה (.Cong – אָמֵן), וְהוֹשִׁיעֵנוּ בוֹ לְחַיִּים (.Cong – אָמֵן). וּבִדְבַר יְשׁוּעָה וְרַחֲמִים, חוּס וְחָנֵּנוּ וְרַחֵם עָלֵינוּ וְהוֹשִׁיעֵנוּ, כִּי אֵלֶיךָ עֵינֵינוּ, כִּי אֵל מֶלֶךְ חַנּוּן וְרַחוּם אָתָּה.[1]

On the Sabbath add the words in brackets. [If forgotten, see *Laws* §86-90.]

וְהַשִּׂיאֵנוּ יהוה אֱלֹהֵינוּ אֶת בִּרְכַּת מוֹעֲדֶיךָ לְחַיִּים וּלְשָׁלוֹם, לְשִׂמְחָה וּלְשָׂשׂוֹן, כַּאֲשֶׁר רָצִיתָ וְאָמַרְתָּ לְבָרְכֵנוּ. [אֱלֹהֵינוּ וֵאלֹהֵי אֲבוֹתֵינוּ רְצֵה בִמְנוּחָתֵנוּ] קַדְּשֵׁנוּ בְּמִצְוֹתֶיךָ וְתֵן חֶלְקֵנוּ בְּתוֹרָתֶךָ, שַׂבְּעֵנוּ מִטּוּבֶךָ וְשַׂמְּחֵנוּ בִּישׁוּעָתֶךָ, וְטַהֵר לִבֵּנוּ

HOLINESS OF GOD'S NAME

INDIVIDUALS RECITE:

אַתָּה *You are holy and Your Name is holy, and holy ones praise You every day, forever. Blessed are You, HASHEM, the holy God.*

CHAZZAN RECITES DURING HIS REPETITION:

לְדוֹר *From generation to generation we shall relate Your greatness and for infinite eternities we shall proclaim Your holiness. Your praise, our God, shall not leave our mouth forever and ever, for You, O God, are a great and holy King. Blessed are You, HASHEM, the holy God.*

SANCTIFICATION OF THE DAY

אַתָּה בְחַרְתָּנוּ *You have chosen us from all the peoples; You loved us and found favor in us; You exalted us above all the tongues and You sanctified us with Your commandments. You drew us close, our King, to Your service and proclaimed Your great and Holy Name upon us.*

On the Sabbath add the words in brackets. [If forgotten, see *Laws* §86-90.]

וַתִּתֶּן לָנוּ *And You gave us, HASHEM, our God, with love [Sabbaths for rest], appointed festivals for gladness, Festivals and times for joy, [this day of Sabbath and] this day of the Shemini Atzeres Festival, the time of our gladness [with love], a holy convocation, a memorial of the Exodus from Egypt.*

During the *chazzan's* repetition, congregation responds *Amen* as indicated.

אֱלֹהֵינוּ *Our God and God of our forefathers, may there rise, come, reach, be noted, be favored, be heard, be considered, and be remembered — the remembrance and consideration of ourselves; the remembrance of our forefathers; the remembrance of Messiah, son of David, Your servant; the remembrance of Jerusalem, the City of Your Holiness; the remembrance of Your entire people the Family of Israel — before You for deliverance, for goodness, for grace, for kindness, and for compassion, for life, and for peace on this day of the Shemini Atzeres Festival. Remember us on it, HASHEM, our God, for goodness (*Cong. – *Amen); consider us on it for blessing (*Cong. – *Amen); and help us on it for life (*Cong. – *Amen). In the matter of salvation and compassion, pity, be gracious and compassionate with us and help us, for our eyes are turned to You, because You are God, the gracious and compassionate King.*[1]

On the Sabbath add the words in brackets. [If forgotten, see *Laws* §86-90.]

וְהַשִּׂיאֵנוּ *Bestow upon us, O HASHEM, our God, the blessing of Your appointed Festivals for life and for peace, for gladness and for joy, as You desired and promised to bless us. [Our God and the God of our forefathers, may You be pleased with our rest.] Sanctify us with Your commandments and grant us our share in Your Torah; satisfy us from Your goodness and gladden us with Your salvation, and purify our heart*

(1) Cf. *Nechemiah* 9:31.

לְעָבְדְּךָ בֶּאֱמֶת, וְהַנְחִילֵנוּ יהוה אֱלֹהֵינוּ [בְּאַהֲבָה וּבְרָצוֹן] בְּשִׂמְחָה וּבְשָׂשׂוֹן [שַׁבָּת וּ]מוֹעֲדֵי קָדְשֶׁךָ, וְיִשְׂמְחוּ בְךָ יִשְׂרָאֵל מְקַדְּשֵׁי שְׁמֶךָ. בָּרוּךְ אַתָּה יהוה, מְקַדֵּשׁ [הַשַּׁבָּת וְ]יִשְׂרָאֵל וְהַזְּמַנִּים.

עבודה

רְצֵה יהוה אֱלֹהֵינוּ בְּעַמְּךָ יִשְׂרָאֵל וּבִתְפִלָּתָם, וְהָשֵׁב אֶת הָעֲבוֹדָה לִדְבִיר בֵּיתֶךָ. וְאִשֵּׁי יִשְׂרָאֵל וּתְפִלָּתָם בְּאַהֲבָה תְקַבֵּל בְּרָצוֹן, וּתְהִי לְרָצוֹן תָּמִיד עֲבוֹדַת יִשְׂרָאֵל עַמֶּךָ.

וְתֶחֱזֶינָה עֵינֵינוּ בְּשׁוּבְךָ לְצִיּוֹן בְּרַחֲמִים. בָּרוּךְ אַתָּה יהוה, הַמַּחֲזִיר שְׁכִינָתוֹ לְצִיּוֹן.

הודאה

Bow at מוֹדִים; straighten up at ה׳. In his repetition the *chazzan* should recite the entire מוֹדִים aloud, while the congregation recites מוֹדִים דְּרַבָּנָן softly.

מוֹדִים אֲנַחְנוּ לָךְ, שָׁאַתָּה הוּא יהוה אֱלֹהֵינוּ וֵאלֹהֵי אֲבוֹתֵינוּ לְעוֹלָם וָעֶד. צוּר חַיֵּינוּ, מָגֵן יִשְׁעֵנוּ אַתָּה הוּא לְדוֹר וָדוֹר. נוֹדֶה לְּךָ וּנְסַפֵּר תְּהִלָּתֶךָ[1] עַל חַיֵּינוּ הַמְּסוּרִים בְּיָדֶךָ, וְעַל נִשְׁמוֹתֵינוּ הַפְּקוּדוֹת לָךְ, וְעַל נִסֶּיךָ שֶׁבְּכָל יוֹם עִמָּנוּ, וְעַל נִפְלְאוֹתֶיךָ וְטוֹבוֹתֶיךָ שֶׁבְּכָל עֵת, עֶרֶב וָבֹקֶר וְצָהֳרָיִם. הַטּוֹב כִּי לֹא כָלוּ רַחֲמֶיךָ, וְהַמְרַחֵם כִּי לֹא תַמּוּ חֲסָדֶיךָ,[2] מֵעוֹלָם קִוִּינוּ לָךְ.

מודים דרבנן

מוֹדִים אֲנַחְנוּ לָךְ, שָׁאַתָּה הוּא יהוה אֱלֹהֵינוּ וֵאלֹהֵי אֲבוֹתֵינוּ, אֱלֹהֵי כָל בָּשָׂר, יוֹצְרֵנוּ, יוֹצֵר בְּרֵאשִׁית. בְּרָכוֹת וְהוֹדָאוֹת לְשִׁמְךָ הַגָּדוֹל וְהַקָּדוֹשׁ, עַל שֶׁהֶחֱיִיתָנוּ וְקִיַּמְתָּנוּ. כֵּן תְּחַיֵּנוּ וּתְקַיְּמֵנוּ, וְתֶאֱסוֹף גָּלֻיּוֹתֵינוּ לְחַצְרוֹת קָדְשֶׁךָ, לִשְׁמוֹר חֻקֶּיךָ וְלַעֲשׂוֹת רְצוֹנֶךָ, וּלְעָבְדְּךָ בְּלֵבָב שָׁלֵם, עַל שֶׁאֲנַחְנוּ מוֹדִים לָךְ. בָּרוּךְ אֵל הַהוֹדָאוֹת.

וְעַל כֻּלָּם יִתְבָּרַךְ וְיִתְרוֹמַם שִׁמְךָ מַלְכֵּנוּ תָּמִיד לְעוֹלָם וָעֶד.

Bend the knees at בָּרוּךְ; bow at אַתָּה; straighten up at ה׳.

וְכֹל הַחַיִּים יוֹדוּךָ סֶּלָה, וִיהַלְלוּ אֶת שִׁמְךָ בֶּאֱמֶת, הָאֵל יְשׁוּעָתֵנוּ וְעֶזְרָתֵנוּ סֶלָה. בָּרוּךְ אַתָּה יהוה, הַטּוֹב שִׁמְךָ וּלְךָ נָאֶה לְהוֹדוֹת.

to serve You sincerely. And grant us a heritage, O HASHEM, our God — [with love and with favor] with gladness and with joy — [the Sabbath and] the appointed festivals of Your holiness, and may Israel, the sanctifiers of Your Name, rejoice in You. Blessed are You, HASHEM, Who sanctifies [the Sabbath,] Israel and the festive seasons.

TEMPLE SERVICE

רְצֵה *Be favorable, HASHEM, our God, toward Your people Israel and their prayer and restore the service to the Holy of Holies of Your Temple. The fire-offerings of Israel and their prayer accept with love and favor, and may the service of Your people Israel always be favorable to You.*

וְתֶחֱזֶינָה *May our eyes behold Your return to Zion in compassion. Blessed are You, HASHEM, Who restores His Presence to Zion.*

THANKSGIVING [MODIM]

Bow at *'We gratefully thank You'*; straighten up at *'HASHEM.'* In his repetition the *chazzan* should recite the entire *Modim* aloud, while the congregation recites *Modim of the Rabbis* softly.

מוֹדִים *We gratefully thank You, for it is You Who are HASHEM, our God and the God of our forefathers for all eternity; Rock of our lives, Shield of our salvation are You from generation to generation. We shall thank You and relate Your praise[1] — for our lives, which are committed to Your power and for our souls that are entrusted to You; for Your miracles that are with us every day; and for Your wonders and favors in every season — evening, morning, and afternoon. The Beneficent One, for Your compassions were never exhausted, and the Compassionate One, for Your kindnesses never ended[2] — always have we put our hope in You.*

MODIM OF THE RABBIS

מודים *We gratefully thank You, for it is You Who are HASHEM, our God and the God of our forefathers, the God of all flesh, our Molder, the Molder of the universe. Blessings and thanks are due Your great and holy Name for You have given us life and sustained us. So may You continue to give us life and sustain us and gather our exiles to the Courtyards of Your Sanctuary, to observe Your decrees, to do Your will and to serve You wholeheartedly. [We thank You] for inspiring us to thank You. Blessed is the God of thanksgivings.*

For all these, may Your Name be blessed and exalted, our King, continually forever and ever.

Bend the knees at *'Blessed'*; bow at *'You'*; straighten up at *'HASHEM.'*

Everything alive will gratefully acknowledge You, Selah! and praise Your Name sincerely, O God of our salvation and help, Selah! Blessed are You, HASHEM, Your Name is 'The Beneficent One' and to You it is fitting to give thanks.

(1) Cf. *Psalms* 79:13. (2) Cf. *Lamentations* 3:22.

ברכת כהנים

The *chazzan* recites בִּרְכַּת כֹּהֲנִים during his repetition. He faces right at וְיִשְׁמְרֶךָ; faces left at אֵלֶיךָ וִיחֻנֶּךָּ; faces the Ark for the rest of the blessings.

אֱלֹהֵינוּ, וֵאלֹהֵי אֲבוֹתֵינוּ, בָּרְכֵנוּ בַבְּרָכָה הַמְּשֻׁלֶּשֶׁת בַּתּוֹרָה הַכְּתוּבָה עַל יְדֵי מֹשֶׁה עַבְדֶּךָ, הָאֲמוּרָה מִפִּי אַהֲרֹן וּבָנָיו, כֹּהֲנִים עַם קְדוֹשֶׁךָ, כָּאָמוּר:

יְבָרֶכְךָ יהוה, וְיִשְׁמְרֶךָ. (–Cong. כֵּן יְהִי רָצוֹן.)

יָאֵר יהוה פָּנָיו אֵלֶיךָ וִיחֻנֶּךָּ. (–Cong. כֵּן יְהִי רָצוֹן.)

יִשָּׂא יהוה פָּנָיו אֵלֶיךָ וְיָשֵׂם לְךָ שָׁלוֹם.[1] (–Cong. כֵּן יְהִי רָצוֹן.)

שלום

שִׂים שָׁלוֹם, טוֹבָה, וּבְרָכָה, חֵן, וָחֶסֶד וְרַחֲמִים עָלֵינוּ וְעַל כָּל יִשְׂרָאֵל עַמֶּךָ. בָּרְכֵנוּ אָבִינוּ, כֻּלָּנוּ כְּאֶחָד בְּאוֹר פָּנֶיךָ, כִּי בְאוֹר פָּנֶיךָ נָתַתָּ לָּנוּ, יהוה אֱלֹהֵינוּ, תּוֹרַת חַיִּים וְאַהֲבַת חֶסֶד, וּצְדָקָה, וּבְרָכָה, וְרַחֲמִים, וְחַיִּים, וְשָׁלוֹם. וְטוֹב בְּעֵינֶיךָ לְבָרֵךְ אֶת עַמְּךָ יִשְׂרָאֵל, בְּכָל עֵת וּבְכָל שָׁעָה בִּשְׁלוֹמֶךָ. בָּרוּךְ אַתָּה יהוה, הַמְּבָרֵךְ אֶת עַמּוֹ יִשְׂרָאֵל בַּשָּׁלוֹם.

יִהְיוּ לְרָצוֹן אִמְרֵי פִי וְהֶגְיוֹן לִבִּי לְפָנֶיךָ, יהוה צוּרִי וְגֹאֲלִי.[2]

THE *CHAZZAN*'S REPETITION ENDS HERE; TURN TO PAGE 916.
INDIVIDUALS CONTINUE TO END OF THIS PAGE.

אֱלֹהַי, נְצוֹר לְשׁוֹנִי מֵרָע, וּשְׂפָתַי מִדַּבֵּר מִרְמָה,[3] וְלִמְקַלְלַי נַפְשִׁי תִדּוֹם, וְנַפְשִׁי כֶּעָפָר לַכֹּל תִּהְיֶה. פְּתַח לִבִּי בְּתוֹרָתֶךָ, וּבְמִצְוֹתֶיךָ תִּרְדּוֹף נַפְשִׁי. וְכֹל הַחוֹשְׁבִים עָלַי רָעָה, מְהֵרָה הָפֵר עֲצָתָם וְקַלְקֵל מַחֲשַׁבְתָּם. עֲשֵׂה לְמַעַן שְׁמֶךָ, עֲשֵׂה לְמַעַן יְמִינֶךָ, עֲשֵׂה לְמַעַן קְדֻשָּׁתֶךָ, עֲשֵׂה לְמַעַן תּוֹרָתֶךָ. לְמַעַן יֵחָלְצוּן יְדִידֶיךָ, הוֹשִׁיעָה יְמִינְךָ וַעֲנֵנִי.[4]

Some recite verses pertaining to their names here. See page 1301.

יִהְיוּ לְרָצוֹן אִמְרֵי פִי וְהֶגְיוֹן לִבִּי לְפָנֶיךָ, יהוה צוּרִי וְגֹאֲלִי.[2] עֹשֶׂה שָׁלוֹם בִּמְרוֹמָיו, הוּא יַעֲשֶׂה שָׁלוֹם עָלֵינוּ, וְעַל כָּל יִשְׂרָאֵל. וְאִמְרוּ: אָמֵן.

Bow and take three steps back. Bow left and say ... עֹשֶׂה, bow right and say ... הוּא יַעֲשֶׂה; bow forward and say וְעַל כָּל ... אָמֵן.

יְהִי רָצוֹן מִלְּפָנֶיךָ יהוה אֱלֹהֵינוּ וֵאלֹהֵי אֲבוֹתֵינוּ, שֶׁיִּבָּנֶה בֵּית הַמִּקְדָּשׁ בִּמְהֵרָה בְיָמֵינוּ, וְתֵן חֶלְקֵנוּ בְּתוֹרָתֶךָ. וְשָׁם נַעֲבָדְךָ בְּיִרְאָה, כִּימֵי עוֹלָם וּכְשָׁנִים קַדְמוֹנִיּוֹת. וְעָרְבָה לַיהוה מִנְחַת יְהוּדָה וִירוּשָׁלָיִם, כִּימֵי עוֹלָם וּכְשָׁנִים קַדְמוֹנִיּוֹת.[5]

THE INDIVIDUAL'S RECITATION OF *SHEMONEH ESREI* ENDS HERE.

The individual remains standing in place until the *chazzan* reaches *Kedushah* — or at least until the *chazzan* begins his repetition — then he takes three steps forward. The *chazzan* himself, or one praying alone, should remain in place for a few moments before taking three steps forward.

THE PRIESTLY BLESSING

The *chazzan* recites the Priestly Blessing during his repetition.

אֱלֹהֵינוּ *Our God and the God of our forefathers, bless us with the three-verse blessing in the Torah that was written by the hand of Moses, Your servant, that was said by Aaron and his sons, the Kohanim, Your holy people, as it is said:*

May HASHEM bless you and safeguard you. (Cong.— *So may it be.*)

May HASHEM illuminate His countenance for you and be gracious to you. (Cong.— *So may it be.*)

May HASHEM turn His countenance to you and establish peace for you.[1] (Cong.— *So may it be.*)

PEACE

שִׂים *Establish peace, goodness, blessing, graciousness, kindness, and compassion upon us and upon all of Your people Israel. Bless us, our Father, all of us as one, with the light of Your countenance, for with the light of Your countenance You gave us, HASHEM, our God, the Torah of life and a love of kindness, righteousness, blessing, compassion, life, and peace. And may it be good in Your eyes to bless Your people Israel at every time and every hour with Your peace. Blessed are You, HASHEM, Who blesses His people Israel with peace.*

May the expressions of my mouth and the thoughts of my heart find favor before You, HASHEM, my Rock and my Redeemer.[2]

THE *CHAZZAN'S* REPETITION ENDS HERE; TURN TO PAGE 916.

INDIVIDUALS CONTINUE TO END OF THIS PAGE.

אֱלֹהַי *My God, guard my tongue from evil and my lips from speaking deceitfully.*[3] *To those who curse me, let my soul be silent; and let my soul be like dust to everyone. Open my heart to Your Torah, then my soul will pursue Your commandments. As for all those who design evil against me, speedily nullify their counsel and disrupt their design. Act for Your Name's sake; act for Your right hand's sake; act for Your sanctity's sake; act for Your Torah's sake. That Your beloved ones may be given rest; let Your right hand save, and respond to me.*[4]

Some recite verses pertaining to their names at this point. See page 1301.

May the expressions of my mouth and the thoughts of my heart find favor before You, HASHEM, my Rock and my Redeemer.[2] *He Who makes peace in His heights, may He make peace upon us, and upon all Israel. Now respond: Amen.*

Bow and take three steps back. Bow left and say, *'He Who makes peace . . .'*; bow right and say, *'may He make peace . . .'*; bow forward and say, *'and upon . . . Amen.'*

יְהִי רָצוֹן *May it be Your will, HASHEM, our God and the God of our forefathers, that the Holy Temple be rebuilt, speedily in our days. Grant us our share in Your Torah, and may we serve You there with reverence, as in days of old and in former years. Then the offering of Judah and Jerusalem will be pleasing to HASHEM, as in days of old and in former years.*[5]

THE INDIVIDUAL'S RECITATION OF *SHEMONEH ESREI* ENDS HERE.

The individual remains standing in place until the *chazzan* reaches *Kedushah* — or at least until the *chazzan* begins his repetition — then he takes three steps forward. The *chazzan* himself, or one praying alone, should remain in place for a few moments before taking three steps forward.

---

(1) *Numbers* 6:24-26. (2) *Psalms* 19:15. (3) Cf. 34:14. (4) 60:7; 108:7. (5) *Malachi* 3:4.

הלל

The *chazzan* recites the blessing. The congregation, after responding אָמֵן, repeats it, and continues with the first psalm.

בָּרוּךְ אַתָּה יהוה אֱלֹהֵינוּ מֶלֶךְ הָעוֹלָם, אֲשֶׁר קִדְּשָׁנוּ בְּמִצְוֹתָיו, וְצִוָּנוּ לִקְרוֹא אֶת הַהַלֵּל. (.Cong – אָמֵן)

תהלים קיג

הַלְלוּיָהּ הַלְלוּ עַבְדֵי יהוה,* הַלְלוּ אֶת שֵׁם יהוה. יְהִי שֵׁם יהוה מְבֹרָךְ, מֵעַתָּה וְעַד עוֹלָם. מִמִּזְרַח שֶׁמֶשׁ עַד מְבוֹאוֹ, מְהֻלָּל שֵׁם יהוה. רָם עַל כָּל גּוֹיִם יהוה, עַל הַשָּׁמַיִם כְּבוֹדוֹ. מִי כַּיהוה אֱלֹהֵינוּ, הַמַּגְבִּיהִי לָשָׁבֶת. הַמַּשְׁפִּילִי לִרְאוֹת, בַּשָּׁמַיִם וּבָאָרֶץ.* ❖ מְקִימִי מֵעָפָר דָּל, מֵאַשְׁפֹּת יָרִים אֶבְיוֹן. לְהוֹשִׁיבִי עִם נְדִיבִים,* עִם נְדִיבֵי עַמּוֹ. מוֹשִׁיבִי עֲקֶרֶת הַבַּיִת,* אֵם הַבָּנִים שְׂמֵחָה, הַלְלוּיָהּ.

תהלים קיד

בְּצֵאת יִשְׂרָאֵל מִמִּצְרָיִם,* בֵּית יַעֲקֹב מֵעַם לֹעֵז.* הָיְתָה יְהוּדָה לְקָדְשׁוֹ,* יִשְׂרָאֵל מַמְשְׁלוֹתָיו. הַיָּם רָאָה וַיָּנֹס, הַיַּרְדֵּן יִסֹּב לְאָחוֹר. הֶהָרִים רָקְדוּ כְאֵילִים,* גְּבָעוֹת כִּבְנֵי צֹאן. ❖ מַה לְּךָ הַיָּם כִּי תָנוּס, הַיַּרְדֵּן תִּסֹּב לְאָחוֹר.* הֶהָרִים תִּרְקְדוּ כְאֵילִים, גְּבָעוֹת כִּבְנֵי צֹאן. מִלִּפְנֵי אָדוֹן חוּלִי אָרֶץ, מִלִּפְנֵי אֱלוֹהַּ יַעֲקֹב. הַהֹפְכִי הַצּוּר אֲגַם מָיִם,* חַלָּמִישׁ לְמַעְיְנוֹ מָיִם.

הַלֵּל / HALLEL

The prophets ordained that the six psalms of *Hallel* [literally, *praise*] be recited on each Festival, and to commemorate times of national deliverance from peril. Moreover, before David redacted and incorporated these psalms into the Book of Psalms, *Hallel* was already known to the nation: Moses and Israel recited it after being saved from the Egyptians at the sea; Joshua, after defeating the Kings of Canaan; Deborah and Barak, after defeating Sisera. Later, Hezekiah recited it after defeating Sennacherib; Chananyah, Mishael and Azariah, after being saved from the wicked Nebuchadnezzar; and Mordechai and Esther, after the defeat of the wicked Haman *(Pesachim* 117a).

These psalms were singled out as the unit of praise because they contain five fundamental themes of Jewish faith: the Exodus, the Splitting of the Sea, the Giving of the Torah at Sinai, the future Resuscitation of the dead, and the coming of the Messiah (ibid. 118a).

הַלְלוּיָהּ הַלְלוּ עַבְדֵי ה׳ — *Halleluyah! Give praise, you servants of HASHEM.* Only after their liberation from Pharaoh's bondage could the Jews be considered the *servants of HASHEM,* because they no longer vowed allegiance to any other ruler.

הַמַּשְׁפִּילִי לִרְאוֹת בַּשָּׁמַיִם וּבָאָרֶץ — *Yet deigns to look* [lit., *bends low to see*] *upon the heaven and the earth?* This is the challenging and exciting aspect of God's relationship to man: as we act towards God, so does He react to us. If we ignore His presence, He withdraws high *above the heavens;* but if we welcome His proximity, He lovingly involves Himself in every phase of our lives *(R' A.C. Feuer).*

לְהוֹשִׁיבִי עִם נְדִיבִים — *To seat them with nobles.* God does not merely lift the poor and needy out

HALLEL

The *chazzan* recites the blessing. The congregation, after responding *Amen,* repeats it, and continues with the first psalm.

בָּרוּךְ *Blessed are You,* HASHEM, *our God, King of the universe, Who has sanctified us with His commandments and has commanded us to read the Hallel.* (Cong.— *Amen.)*

Psalm 113

הַלְלוּיָהּ *Halleluyah! Give praise, you servants of* HASHEM;* *praise the Name of* HASHEM! *Blessed be the Name of* HASHEM, *from this time and forever. From the rising of the sun to its setting,* HASHEM'*s Name is praised. High above all nations is* HASHEM, *above the heavens is His glory. Who is like* HASHEM, *our God, Who is enthroned on high — yet deigns to look upon the heaven and the earth?** Chazzan— *He raises the needy from the dust, from the trash heaps He lifts the destitute. To seat them with nobles,* with the nobles of His people. He transforms the barren wife* into a glad mother of children. Halleluyah!*

Psalm 114

בְּצֵאת *When Israel went out of Egypt,* Jacob's household from a people of alien tongue* — Judah became His sanctuary,* Israel His dominions. The sea saw and fled: the Jordan turned backward. The mountains skipped like rams,* the hills like young lambs.* Chazzan— *What ails you, O sea, that you flee? O Jordan, that you turn backward?* O mountains, that you skip like rams? O hills, like young lambs? Before the Lord's Presence — did I, the earth, tremble — before the presence of the God of Jacob, Who turns the rock into a pond of water,* the flint into a flowing fountain.*

---

of degradation; He also elevates them to the highest ranks of nobility.

מוֹשִׁיבִי עֲקֶרֶת הַבַּיִת — *He transforms the barren wife.* The Creator exercises complete control over nature. This control is vividly demonstrated when God suddenly transforms a barren woman into a mother *(Radak).*

בְּצֵאת יִשְׂרָאֵל מִמִּצְרָיִם ◆§ — *When Israel went out of Egypt.* This second chapter of Hallel continues the theme of the first chapter, which praises God for raising up the needy and destitute. Israel was thus elevated when they left Egypt and risked their lives by entering the sea at God's command.

בֵּית יַעֲקֹב מֵעַם לֹעֵז — *Jacob's household from a people of alien tongue.* Even the Jews who were forced to communicate with the Egyptians in the language of the land did so only under duress. Among themselves, however, they spoke only the Holy Tongue and regarded Egyptian as a foreign language.

הָיְתָה יְהוּדָה לְקָדְשׁוֹ — *Judah became His sanctuary.* God singled out the tribe of Judah to be the family of royalty, because they sanctified God's Name at the Sea of Reeds. Led by their prince, Nachshon ben Aminadav, this tribe was the first to jump into the threatening waters *(Rosh).*

הֶהָרִים רָקְדוּ כְאֵילִים — *The mountains skipped like rams.* When Israel received the Torah, Sinai and the neighboring mountains and hills shook and trembled at the manifestation of God's Presence and the thunder and lightning that accompanied it.

מַה לְּךָ הַיָּם כִּי תָנוּס הַיַּרְדֵּן תִּסֹּב לְאָחוֹר — *What ails you, O sea, that you flee? O Jordan, that you turn backward?* The Psalmist captures the sense of awe and bewilderment which then seized mankind.

הַהֹפְכִי הַצּוּר אֲגַם מָיִם — *Who turns the rock into a pond of water.* When the Jews thirsted for water in the wilderness, God instructed Moses *(Exodus* 17:6), *'You shall smite the rock and water shall come out of it, so that the people may drink.'*

תהלים קטו:א-יא

לֹא לָנוּ יהוה לֹא לָנוּ, כִּי לְשִׁמְךָ תֵּן כָּבוֹד,* עַל חַסְדְּךָ עַל אֲמִתֶּךָ. לָמָּה יֹאמְרוּ הַגּוֹיִם, אַיֵּה נָא אֱלֹהֵיהֶם. וֵאלֹהֵינוּ בַשָּׁמָיִם, כֹּל אֲשֶׁר חָפֵץ עָשָׂה. עֲצַבֵּיהֶם כֶּסֶף וְזָהָב, מַעֲשֵׂה יְדֵי אָדָם. פֶּה לָהֶם וְלֹא יְדַבֵּרוּ,* עֵינַיִם לָהֶם וְלֹא יִרְאוּ. אָזְנַיִם לָהֶם וְלֹא יִשְׁמָעוּ, אַף לָהֶם וְלֹא יְרִיחוּן. יְדֵיהֶם וְלֹא יְמִישׁוּן, רַגְלֵיהֶם וְלֹא יְהַלֵּכוּ, לֹא יֶהְגּוּ בִּגְרוֹנָם. כְּמוֹהֶם יִהְיוּ עֹשֵׂיהֶם, כֹּל אֲשֶׁר בֹּטֵחַ בָּהֶם. ❖ יִשְׂרָאֵל בְּטַח בַּיהוה,* עֶזְרָם וּמָגִנָּם הוּא.* בֵּית אַהֲרֹן בִּטְחוּ בַיהוה, עֶזְרָם וּמָגִנָּם הוּא. יִרְאֵי יהוה בִּטְחוּ בַיהוה, עֶזְרָם וּמָגִנָּם הוּא.

תהלים קטו:יב-יח

יהוה זְכָרָנוּ יְבָרֵךְ,* יְבָרֵךְ אֶת בֵּית יִשְׂרָאֵל, יְבָרֵךְ אֶת בֵּית אַהֲרֹן. יְבָרֵךְ יִרְאֵי יהוה, הַקְּטַנִּים עִם הַגְּדֹלִים. יֹסֵף יהוה עֲלֵיכֶם, עֲלֵיכֶם וְעַל בְּנֵיכֶם.* בְּרוּכִים אַתֶּם לַיהוה, עֹשֵׂה שָׁמַיִם וָאָרֶץ. ❖ הַשָּׁמַיִם שָׁמַיִם לַיהוה, וְהָאָרֶץ נָתַן לִבְנֵי אָדָם.* לֹא הַמֵּתִים יְהַלְּלוּ יָהּ,* וְלֹא כָּל יֹרְדֵי דוּמָה. וַאֲנַחְנוּ נְבָרֵךְ יָהּ, מֵעַתָּה וְעַד עוֹלָם, הַלְלוּיָהּ.

תהלים קטז:א-יא

אָהַבְתִּי כִּי יִשְׁמַע יהוה, אֶת קוֹלִי תַּחֲנוּנָי. כִּי הִטָּה אָזְנוֹ לִי,

---

⌘ **לֹא לָנוּ** — *Not for our sake.* The preceding psalm depicts the awe inspired by God's miracles. Here the Psalmist describes the aftermath of that inspiration. Although Israel remained imbued with faith, our oppressors soon began to scoff, 'Where is their God?' We pray that God will intervene again in the affairs of man, not for our sake, but for His.

לֹא לָנוּ ה׳ . . . כִּי לְשִׁמְךָ תֵּן כָּבוֹד — *Not for our sake, HASHEM . . . but for Your Name's sake give glory.* We beg You to redeem us, but not because we are personally worthy, nor because of the merit of our forefathers *(Iyun Tefillah)*. Rather we urgently strive to protect Your glorious Name, so that no one can deny Your mastery and dominion *(Radak)*.

פֶּה לָהֶם וְלֹא יְדַבֵּרוּ — *They have a mouth, but cannot speak.* These illustrations emphasize the complete impotence of man-made idols, which even lack the senses that every ordinary man possesses.

יִשְׂרָאֵל בְּטַח בַּה׳ — *O Israel, trust in HASHEM.* The psalm now contrasts the Children of Israel, who trust in God alone, with those described in the previous verse, who trust in the lifeless and helpless idols *(Ibn Ezra)*.

The Psalmist speaks of three kinds of Jews, each with a different motive for serving God. Some Jews cling to God simply because they feel that He is their Father, and they are His devoted sons. These are called יִשְׂרָאֵל, *Israel,* God's chosen, beloved nation. The second group serves God out of love. They resemble the *House of Aaron,* the *Kohanim*-priests who never betrayed God and were therefore designated to stand in His presence, in the Temple, for all time. Finally, *you who fear HASHEM* refers to a third group of Jews, who serve God out of fear and awe *(Maharal)*.

עֶזְרָם וּמָגִנָּם הוּא — *Their help and their shield is He!* This is thrice repeated. Since each successive group possesses a different level of faith, it deserves a totally different degree of divine protection. Thus, God's reaction to each group is mentioned separately.

⌘ **ה׳ זְכָרָנוּ יְבָרֵךְ** — *HASHEM Who has remembered us will bless.* The Psalmist expresses

Psalms 115:1-11

לֹא לָנוּ *Not for our sake,* HASHEM, not for our sake, but for Your Name's sake give glory,* for Your kindness and for Your truth! Why should the nations say, 'Where is their God now?' Our God is in the heavens; whatever He pleases, He does! Their idols are silver and gold, the handiwork of man. They have a mouth, but cannot speak;* they have eyes, but cannot see. They have ears, but cannot hear; they have a nose, but cannot smell. Their hands — they cannot feel; their feet — they cannot walk; they cannot utter a sound from their throat. Those who make them should become like them, whoever trusts in them!* Chazzan— *O Israel, trust in HASHEM;* — their help and their shield is He!* House of Aaron, trust in HASHEM; their help and their shield is He! You who fear HASHEM, trust in HASHEM; their help and their shield is He!*

Psalm 115:12-18

יהוה *HASHEM Who has remembered us will bless* — He will bless the House of Israel; He will bless the House of Aaron; He will bless those who fear HASHEM, the small as well as the great. May HASHEM increase upon you, upon you and upon your children!* You are blessed of HASHEM, maker of heaven and earth.* Chazzan— *As for the heavens — the heavens are HASHEM's, but the earth He has given to mankind.* Neither the dead can praise God,* nor any who descend into silence; but we will bless God from this time and forever. Halleluyah!*

Psalm 116:1-11

אָהַבְתִּי *I love Him,* for HASHEM hears my voice, my supplications. As He has inclined His ear to me, so in my days shall I*

---

confidence that just as God has blessed His people in the past, so He will bless them in the future.

יֹסֵף ה' עֲלֵיכֶם, עֲלֵיכֶם וְעַל בְּנֵיכֶם — *May HASHEM increase upon you, upon you and upon your children.* The true nature of בְּרָכָה, *blessing,* means increase and abundance *(Ibn Ezra).*

Abarbanel explains that the Psalmist foresaw that Israel would suffer from attrition in exile and they would fear eventual extinction. Therefore, he offers the assurance that, at the advent of the Messiah, they will increase dramatically.

הַשָּׁמַיִם שָׁמַיִם לַה', וְהָאָרֶץ נָתַן לִבְנֵי אָדָם — *As for the heavens — the heavens are HASHEM's, but the earth He has given to mankind.* Since the heavens remain under God's firm control, all celestial bodies are forced to act in accordance with His will without freedom of choice. On earth, however, man was granted the freedom to determine his own actions and beliefs *(Maharit).*

Many commentators explain this verse homiletically. Man need not perfect heaven because it is already dedicated to the holiness of God. But the earth is man's province. We are bidden to perfect it and transform its material nature into something spiritual. Indeed, we were created to make the earth heavenly.

לֹא הַמֵּתִים יְהַלְלוּ יָהּ — *Neither the dead can praise God.* The people who fail to recognize God's omnipresence and influence over the world resemble the dead, who are insensitive to all external stimuli and who are oblivious to reality *(R' Azariah Figo).* However, the souls of the righteous continue to praise God even after they depart from their bodies *(Ibn Ezra).*

A dried-out, bleached, or brittle *lulav* is invalid for use during the Festival of Succos, because the *lulav* symbolizes the human spine, which enables man to lead an active life. Thus the *lulav* must be fresh and supple, for the dead cannot praise God *(Yalkut Shimoni* 873).

☙ אָהַבְתִּי — *I love [Him].* The Psalmist foresaw that Israel would feel completely alone in exile. The nations would taunt them, 'Your prayers and pleas are worthless, because God has turned a deaf ear to you.' Therefore, he composed this

וּבְיָמַי אֶקְרָא. אֲפָפוּנִי חֶבְלֵי מָוֶת,* וּמְצָרֵי שְׁאוֹל מְצָאוּנִי, צָרָה וְיָגוֹן אֶמְצָא. וּבְשֵׁם יהוה אֶקְרָא, אָנָּה יהוה מַלְּטָה נַפְשִׁי. חַנּוּן יהוה וְצַדִּיק, וֵאלֹהֵינוּ מְרַחֵם. שֹׁמֵר פְּתָאִים יהוה, דַּלּוֹתִי וְלִי יְהוֹשִׁיעַ. שׁוּבִי נַפְשִׁי לִמְנוּחָיְכִי,* כִּי יהוה גָּמַל עָלָיְכִי. כִּי חִלַּצְתָּ נַפְשִׁי מִמָּוֶת, אֶת עֵינִי מִן דִּמְעָה, אֶת רַגְלִי מִדֶּחִי. ❖ אֶתְהַלֵּךְ לִפְנֵי יהוה, בְּאַרְצוֹת הַחַיִּים.* הֶאֱמַנְתִּי כִּי אֲדַבֵּר, אֲנִי עָנִיתִי מְאֹד. אֲנִי אָמַרְתִּי בְחָפְזִי, כָּל הָאָדָם כֹּזֵב.*

תהלים קטז:יב-יט

מָה אָשִׁיב לַיהוה,* כָּל תַּגְמוּלוֹהִי עָלָי. כּוֹס יְשׁוּעוֹת אֶשָּׂא,* וּבְשֵׁם יהוה אֶקְרָא. נְדָרַי לַיהוה אֲשַׁלֵּם,* נֶגְדָה נָּא לְכָל עַמּוֹ. יָקָר בְּעֵינֵי יהוה, הַמָּוְתָה לַחֲסִידָיו. אָנָּה יהוה כִּי אֲנִי עַבְדֶּךָ, אֲנִי עַבְדְּךָ, בֶּן אֲמָתֶךָ,* פִּתַּחְתָּ לְמוֹסֵרָי. ❖ לְךָ אֶזְבַּח זֶבַח תּוֹדָה, וּבְשֵׁם יהוה אֶקְרָא. נְדָרַי לַיהוה אֲשַׁלֵּם, נֶגְדָה נָּא לְכָל עַמּוֹ. בְּחַצְרוֹת בֵּית יהוה, בְּתוֹכֵכִי יְרוּשָׁלָיִם הַלְלוּיָהּ.

Congregation, then *chazzan:*

תהלים קיז

הַלְלוּ אֶת יהוה,* כָּל גּוֹיִם, שַׁבְּחוּהוּ כָּל הָאֻמִּים.* כִּי גָבַר עָלֵינוּ חַסְדּוֹ,* וֶאֱמֶת יהוה לְעוֹלָם, הַלְלוּיָהּ.

---

psalm to encourage the downcast exiles with the assurance that indeed: *HASHEM hears my voice, my supplications.*

The Talmud (*Rosh Hashanah* 16b-17a) explains that this psalm describes the day of Final Judgment at the time of תְּחִיַּת הַמֵּתִים, *the Resurrection of the Dead*. The average people, who are neither completely righteous nor completely wicked, will be saved from Gehinnom because God will hear their cries, and He will forgive them. In gratitude, they will sing, *'I love Him, for HASHEM hears my voice, my supplications.'*

חֶבְלֵי מָוֶת — *The pains of death.* This is an apt description of the exile, when Israel is encircled by violent enemies who seek to kill them (*Abarbanel*).

שׁוּבִי נַפְשִׁי לִמְנוּחָיְכִי — *Return, my soul, to your rest.* When misery and persecution upset me, I told my soul that it would find peace and comfort only if it would *return* to God (*Radak*).

אֶתְהַלֵּךְ לִפְנֵי ה׳ בְּאַרְצוֹת הַחַיִּים — *I shall walk before HASHEM in the lands of the living.* How I yearn to return to *Eretz Yisrael* where the very air makes men healthy and robust and the holy atmosphere grants the mind renewed vitality and alertness! (*Radak*). *Eretz Yisrael* is identified as the *land of the living* because the dead are destined to be resurrected there. This is why the Patriarchs and the righteous of all generations yearned to be buried there.

אֲנִי אָמַרְתִּי בְחָפְזִי כָּל הָאָדָם כֹּזֵב — *I said in my haste: 'All mankind is deceitful.'* This bitter comment was originally uttered by David when the people of Zif betrayed his hiding place to King Saul [see *I Samuel* 23:19-29] (*Rashi*). It is also a reference to the bleak, dismal exile [for the exile discourages the Jews and leads them to the hasty, premature conclusion that all the prophets' promises concerning redemption were *deceitful*] (*Abarbanel*).

⋄ **מָה אָשִׁיב לַה׳** — *How can I repay HASHEM?* What gift can I give to the King who owns everything? (*Ibn Ezra*). How can I possibly repay His acts of kindness, for they are too numerous to recount? (*Radak*). How can I even approach Him? He is eternal and I am finite; He is the highest, and I am the lowest! (*Ibn Yachya*).

call. The pains of death encircled me; the confines of the grave have found me; trouble and sorrow I would find. Then I would invoke the Name of HASHEM: 'Please, HASHEM, save my soul.' Gracious is HASHEM and righteous, our God is merciful. HASHEM protects the simple; I was brought low, but He saved me. Return, my soul, to your rest;* for HASHEM has been kind to you. For You have delivered my soul from death, my eyes from tears, my feet from stumbling.* Chazzan– *I shall walk before HASHEM in the lands of the living.* I have kept faith although I say: 'I suffer exceedingly.' I said in my haste: 'All mankind is deceitful.'**

Psalm 116:12-19

מָה אָשִׁיב *How can I repay HASHEM* for all His kindness to me? I will raise the cup of salvations* and the Name of HASHEM I will invoke. My vows to HASHEM I will pay,* in the presence, now, of His entire people. Difficult in the eyes of HASHEM is the death of His devout ones. Please, HASHEM — for I am Your servant, I am Your servant, son of Your handmaid* — You have released my bonds.* Chazzan– *To You I will sacrifice thanksgiving offerings, and the name of HASHEM I will invoke. My vows to HASHEM I will pay, in the presence, now, of His entire people. In the courtyards of the House of HASHEM, in your midst, O Jerusalem, Halleluyah!*

Congregation, then *chazzan:*

Psalm 117

הַלְלוּ *Praise HASHEM,* all nations; praise Him, all the states!* For His kindness has overwhelmed us,* and the truth of HASHEM is eternal, Halleluyah!*

כּוֹס יְשׁוּעוֹת אֶשָּׂא — *I will raise the cup of salvations.* This refers to the wine libations that will accompany the thanksgiving offerings of the returning exiles (*Rashi*).

נְדָרַי לַה׳ אֲשַׁלֵּם — *My vows to HASHEM I will pay.* As I was fleeing and wandering in exile, I vowed that if God would return me safely to *Eretz Yisrael,* I would render thanksgiving offerings to His Name; now I will make good on my vows (*Radak*).

אֲנִי עַבְדְּךָ בֶּן אֲמָתֶךָ — *I am Your servant, son of Your handmaid.* The slave who is born to a *handmaid* is far more submissive than a slave who was born free (*Rashi*). The former serves his master naturally and instinctively, whereas the latter serves him only in response to external threats (*Sforno*).

☙ **הַלְלוּ אֶת ה׳** — *Praise HASHEM.* This psalm, containing only two verses, is the shortest chapter in all of Scripture. *Radak* explains that its brevity symbolizes the simplicity of the world order which will prevail after the advent of the Messiah.

גּוֹיִם ... הָאֻמִּים — *Nations ... the states.* הָאֻמִּים, *the states,* is written with the definite article, whereas גוֹיִם, *nations,* is spelled without it. This teaches that הָאֻמִּים refers to large nations that are well known and powerful, whereas גוֹיִם refers to small, backward nations that have no prominence (*Iyun Tefillah*).

כִּי גָבַר עָלֵינוּ חַסְדּוֹ — *For His kindness has overwhelmed us.* Why should non-Jewish peoples and nations praise God for overwhelming Israel with Divine kindness? Israel will merit God's kindness because of the extraordinary service they rendered to Him. Recognizing Israel's distinction, the nations will consider it a privilege to become subservient to God's chosen ones, and will praise Him for His kindness to the Jews (*Yaavetz Hadoresh*).

תהלים קיח

Chazzan – **הוֹדוּ** לַיהוה כִּי טוֹב,* כִּי לְעוֹלָם חַסְדּוֹ.
Cong. – הוֹדוּ לַיהוה כִּי טוֹב, כִּי לְעוֹלָם חַסְדּוֹ.
יֹאמַר נָא יִשְׂרָאֵל, כִּי לְעוֹלָם חַסְדּוֹ.
Chazzan – יֹאמַר נָא יִשְׂרָאֵל, כִּי לְעוֹלָם חַסְדּוֹ.
Cong. – הוֹדוּ לַיהוה כִּי טוֹב, כִּי לְעוֹלָם חַסְדּוֹ.
יֹאמְרוּ נָא בֵית אַהֲרֹן, כִּי לְעוֹלָם חַסְדּוֹ.
Chazzan – יֹאמְרוּ נָא בֵית אַהֲרֹן, כִּי לְעוֹלָם חַסְדּוֹ.
Cong. – הוֹדוּ לַיהוה כִּי טוֹב, כִּי לְעוֹלָם חַסְדּוֹ.
יֹאמְרוּ נָא יִרְאֵי יהוה, כִּי לְעוֹלָם חַסְדּוֹ.
Chazzan – יֹאמְרוּ נָא יִרְאֵי יהוה, כִּי לְעוֹלָם חַסְדּוֹ.
Cong. – הוֹדוּ לַיהוה כִּי טוֹב, כִּי לְעוֹלָם חַסְדּוֹ.

מִן הַמֵּצַר* קָרָאתִי יָּהּ, עָנָנִי בַמֶּרְחָב יָהּ. יהוה לִי לֹא אִירָא, מַה יַּעֲשֶׂה לִי אָדָם. יהוה לִי בְּעֹזְרָי,* וַאֲנִי אֶרְאֶה בְשֹׂנְאָי. טוֹב לַחֲסוֹת בַּיהוה, מִבְּטֹחַ בָּאָדָם.* טוֹב לַחֲסוֹת בַּיהוה, מִבְּטֹחַ בִּנְדִיבִים. כָּל גּוֹיִם סְבָבוּנִי, בְּשֵׁם יהוה כִּי אֲמִילַם. סַבּוּנִי גַם סְבָבוּנִי, בְּשֵׁם יהוה כִּי אֲמִילַם. סַבּוּנִי כִדְבֹרִים דֹּעֲכוּ כְּאֵשׁ קוֹצִים, בְּשֵׁם יהוה כִּי אֲמִילַם. דָּחֹה דְחִיתַנִי לִנְפֹּל, וַיהוה עֲזָרָנִי.* עָזִּי וְזִמְרָת יָהּ, וַיְהִי לִי לִישׁוּעָה. קוֹל רִנָּה וִישׁוּעָה, בְּאָהֳלֵי צַדִּיקִים,* יְמִין יהוה עֹשָׂה חָיִל. יְמִין יהוה רוֹמֵמָה, יְמִין יהוה עֹשָׂה חָיִל. לֹא אָמוּת כִּי אֶחְיֶה, וַאֲסַפֵּר מַעֲשֵׂי יָהּ.* יַסֹּר יִסְּרַנִּי יָּהּ,

---

⁂ **הוֹדוּ לַה׳ כִּי טוֹב** — *Give thanks to HASHEM, for He is good.* This is a general expression of thanks to God. No matter what occurs, God is always good and everything He does is for the best, even though this may not be immediately apparent to man *(Abarbanel).*

⁂ **מִן הַמֵּצַר** — *From the straits.* This psalm expresses gratitude and confidence. Just as David himself was catapulted from his personal straits to a reign marked by accomplishment and glory, so too Israel can look forward to Divine redemption from the straits of exile and oppression.

ה׳ לִי בְּעֹזְרָי — *HASHEM is with me through my helpers.* I have many helpers, but I place confidence in them only because HASHEM is with them. If my helpers were not granted strength by God, their assistance would be futile *(Ibn Ezra; Radak).*

טוֹב לַחֲסוֹת בַּה׳ מִבְּטֹחַ בָּאָדָם — *It is better to take refuge in HASHEM than to rely on man.* חִסָּיוֹן, here translated *taking refuge,* denotes absolute confidence even though no guarantees have been given; בִּטָּחוֹן, *reliance,* however, presupposes a promise of protection. The Psalmist says that it is far better to put one's trust in God's protection, even without a pledge from Him, than to rely on the most profuse assurances of human beings *(R' Bachya; Vilna Gaon).*

דָּחֹה דְחִיתַנִי לִנְפֹּל וַה׳ עֲזָרָנִי — *You pushed me hard that I might fall, but HASHEM assisted me.* In the preceding verses, the Psalmist speaks of his enemy indirectly; now, however, he addresses

Psalm 118

Chazzan – *Give thanks to* HASHEM *for He is good;**
His kindness endures forever!

Cong. – *Give thanks to* HASHEM, *for He is good;*
His kindness endures forever!
Let Israel say now: *His kindness endures forever!*

Chazzan – *Let Israel say now:* *His kindness endures forever!*

Cong. – *Give thanks to* HASHEM, *for He is good;*
His kindness endures aforever!
Let the House of Aaron say now:
His kindness endures forever!

Chazzan – *Let the House of Aaron say now:*
His kindness endures forever!

Cong. – *Give thanks to* HASHEM, *for He is good;*
His kindness endures forever!
Let those who fear HASHEM *say now:*
His kindness endures forever!

Chazzan – *Let those who fear* HASHEM *say now:*
His kindness endures forever!

Cong. – *Give thanks to* HASHEM, *for He is good;*
His kindness endures forever!

מִן הַמֵּצַר *From the straits* did I call upon God; God answered me with expansiveness.* HASHEM *is with me, I have no fear; how can man affect me?* HASHEM *is with me through my helpers;* therefore I can face my foes. It is better to take refuge in* HASHEM *than to rely on man.* It is better to take refuge in* HASHEM *than to rely on nobles. All the nations surround me; in the Name of* HASHEM *I cut them down! They encircle me, they also surround me; in the Name of* HASHEM, *I cut them down! They encircle me like bees, but they are extinguished as a fire does thorns; in the Name of* HASHEM *I cut them down! You pushed me hard that I might fall, but* HASHEM *assisted me.* God is my might and my praise, and He was a salvation for me. The sound of rejoicing and salvation is in the tents of the righteous:* '*HASHEM*'s right hand does valiantly.* HASHEM*'s right hand is raised triumphantly;* HASHEM*'s right hand does valiantly!' I shall not die! But I shall live and relate the deeds of God.* God has chastened me*

---

the foe directly.

קוֹל רִנָּה וִישׁוּעָה בְּאָהֳלֵי צַדִּיקִים — *The sound of rejoicing and salvation is in the tents of the righteous.* When HASHEM's right hand does valiantly for the sake of His chosen people, then the righteous will respond by filling their tents with sounds of rejoicing over this salvation (*Radak*).

לֹא אָמוּת כִּי אֶחְיֶה וַאֲסַפֵּר מַעֲשֵׂי יָהּ — *I shall not die! But I shall live and relate the deeds of God.* I will

וְלַמָּוֶת לֹא נְתָנָנִי.* ❖ פִּתְחוּ לִי שַׁעֲרֵי צֶדֶק, אָבֹא בָם אוֹדֶה יָהּ. זֶה הַשַּׁעַר לַיהוה, צַדִּיקִים יָבֹאוּ בוֹ.* אוֹדְךָ* כִּי עֲנִיתָנִי, וַתְּהִי לִי לִישׁוּעָה. אוֹדְךָ כִּי עֲנִיתָנִי, וַתְּהִי לִי לִישׁוּעָה. אֶבֶן מָאֲסוּ הַבּוֹנִים, הָיְתָה לְרֹאשׁ פִּנָּה.* אֶבֶן מָאֲסוּ הַבּוֹנִים, הָיְתָה לְרֹאשׁ פִּנָּה. מֵאֵת יהוה הָיְתָה זֹּאת, הִיא נִפְלָאת בְּעֵינֵינוּ.* מֵאֵת יהוה הָיְתָה זֹּאת, הִיא נִפְלָאת בְּעֵינֵינוּ. זֶה הַיּוֹם עָשָׂה יהוה, נָגִילָה וְנִשְׂמְחָה בוֹ. זֶה הַיּוֹם עָשָׂה יהוה, נָגִילָה וְנִשְׂמְחָה בוֹ.

The next four lines are recited responsively — *chazzan,* then congregation.

אָנָּא יהוה הוֹשִׁיעָה נָּא.
אָנָּא יהוה הוֹשִׁיעָה נָּא.
אָנָּא יהוה הַצְלִיחָה נָא.
אָנָּא יהוה הַצְלִיחָה נָא.

בָּרוּךְ הַבָּא בְּשֵׁם יהוה, בֵּרַכְנוּכֶם מִבֵּית יהוה. בָּרוּךְ הַבָּא בְּשֵׁם יהוה, בֵּרַכְנוּכֶם מִבֵּית יהוה. אֵל יהוה וַיָּאֶר לָנוּ, אִסְרוּ חַג בַּעֲבֹתִים, עַד קַרְנוֹת הַמִּזְבֵּחַ. אֵל יהוה וַיָּאֶר לָנוּ, אִסְרוּ חַג בַּעֲבֹתִים, עַד קַרְנוֹת הַמִּזְבֵּחַ. אֵלִי אַתָּה וְאוֹדֶךָּ, אֱלֹהַי אֲרוֹמְמֶךָּ. אֵלִי אַתָּה וְאוֹדֶךָּ, אֱלֹהַי אֲרוֹמְמֶךָּ. הוֹדוּ לַיהוה כִּי טוֹב, כִּי לְעוֹלָם חַסְדּוֹ. הוֹדוּ לַיהוה כִּי טוֹב, כִּי לְעוֹלָם חַסְדּוֹ.

---

survive the assassination attempts of my enemies and live to recount the deeds of God, Who saved me from my foes *(Radak).*

יַסֹּר יִסְּרַנִּי יָּהּ וְלַמָּוֶת לֹא נְתָנָנִי — *God has chastened me exceedingly, but He did not let me die.* Throughout the duration of the exile, I survived because whatever suffering God decreed was only to atone for my sins *(Rashi).*

זֶה הַשַּׁעַר לַה׳ צַדִּיקִים יָבֹאוּ בוֹ — *This is the gate of* HASHEM; *the righteous shall enter through it.* This refers to the gate of the Temple. When the exile is over, the righteous will enter through this gate, and they will thank God for answering their plea for redemption *(Targum; Rashi).*

⁂ Repetition of Verses

אוֹדְךָ— *I thank You.* From this point until the end of the Scriptural part of *Hallel* — i.e., the nine verses until יְהַלְלוּךָ — each verse is recited twice.

This entire psalm, which begins with הוֹדוּ לַה׳, *Give thanks to* HASHEM, follows a pattern, namely, that each new theme is repeated in the next verse or two in the same or slightly different words. Therefore the custom was introduced to follow through on this repetition by repeating each of these verses as well *(Rashi* to *Succah* 38a).

Another reason for repeating each verse is based upon the Talmud *(Pesachim* 119a) which relates that these verses were recited in a responsive dialogue between Samuel, Jesse, David, and David's brothers when the prophet announced that the young shepherd would be the future king of Israel. To honor these distinguished personages, we repeat each one's statement, as if it were a full chapter.

אֶבֶן מָאֲסוּ הַבּוֹנִים הָיְתָה לְרֹאשׁ פִּנָּה — *The stone the*

*exceedingly, but He did not let me die.** Chazzan– *Open for me the gates of righteousness, I will enter them and thank God. This is the gate of HASHEM; the righteous shall enter through it.* I thank You* for You have answered me and become my salvation. I thank You for You have answered me and become my salvation. The stone the builders despised has become the cornerstone.* The stone the builders despised has become the cornerstone. This emanated from HASHEM; it is wondrous in our eyes.* This emanated from HASHEM; it is wondrous in our eyes. This is the day HASHEM has made; let us rejoice and be glad on it. This is the day HASHEM has made; let us rejoice and be glad on it.*

The next four lines are recited responsively — *chazzan,* then congregation.

אָנָּא *Please, HASHEM, save now!*
Please, HASHEM, save now!
Please, HASHEM, bring success now!
Please, HASHEM, bring success now!

בָּרוּךְ *Blessed is he who comes in the Name of HASHEM; we bless you from the House of HASHEM. Blessed is he who comes in the Name of HASHEM; we bless you from the House of HASHEM. HASHEM is God, He illuminated for us; bind the festival offering with cords until the corners of the Altar. HASHEM is God, He illuminated for us; bind the festival offering with cords until the corners of the Altar. You are my God, and I will thank You; my God, I will exalt You. You are my God, and I will thank You; my God, I will exalt You. Give thanks to HASHEM, for He is good; His kindness endures forever. Give thanks to HASHEM, for He is good; His kindness endures forever.*

---

builders despised has become the cornerstone. This verse refers to David, who was rejected by his own father and brothers *(Targum).* When the prophet Samuel announced that one of Jesse's sons was to be anointed king, no one even thought of summoning David, who was out with the sheep [see *I Samuel* 16:4-13].

Israel too is called אֶבֶן, *stone (Genesis* 49:24), for Israel is the cornerstone of God's design for the world. The world endures only by virtue of Israel's observance of God's laws, a fact that has influenced all nations to appreciate and accept certain aspects of God's commands. If not for the order and meaning that Israel has brought to the world, it would long ago have sunk into chaos. But the builders, i.e., the rulers of the nations, despised the Jews, claiming that they were parasites who made no contribution to the common good. When the dawn of redemption arrives, however, all nations will realize that Israel is indeed the cornerstone of the world *(Radak).*

מֵאֵת ה׳ הָיְתָה זֹּאת הִיא נִפְלָאת בְּעֵינֵינוּ — *This emanated from HASHEM; it is wondrous in our eyes.* When David was crowned, all were amazed. But David said, 'This is even more surprising and wondrous to me than it is to anyone else!'

Similarly, when Israel is catapulted to glory and tranquillity in the future, the nations who persecuted the Jews will ask in surprise, 'Aren't these the very Jews who were once despised and afflicted?'

The Jews will respond, 'We are even more amazed than you are, for only we know the depths of degradation we suffered!'

Then a heavenly voice will proclaim, 'This has emanated from HASHEM!'

יְהַלְלוּךָ יהוה אֱלֹהֵינוּ כָּל מַעֲשֶׂיךָ,* וַחֲסִידֶיךָ צַדִּיקִים* עוֹשֵׂי רְצוֹנֶךָ,* וְכָל עַמְּךָ בֵּית יִשְׂרָאֵל בְּרִנָּה יוֹדוּ וִיבָרְכוּ וִישַׁבְּחוּ וִיפָאֲרוּ וִירוֹמְמוּ וְיַעֲרִיצוּ וְיַקְדִּישׁוּ וְיַמְלִיכוּ אֶת שִׁמְךָ מַלְכֵּנוּ, ❖ כִּי לְךָ טוֹב לְהוֹדוֹת וּלְשִׁמְךָ נָאֶה לְזַמֵּר, כִּי מֵעוֹלָם וְעַד עוֹלָם אַתָּה אֵל. בָּרוּךְ אַתָּה יהוה, מֶלֶךְ מְהֻלָּל בַּתִּשְׁבָּחוֹת.

(.Cong. – אָמֵן)

קדיש שלם

The *chazzan* recites *Kaddish:*

יִתְגַּדַּל וְיִתְקַדַּשׁ שְׁמֵהּ רַבָּא. (.Cong. – אָמֵן.) בְּעָלְמָא דִּי בְרָא כִרְעוּתֵהּ. וְיַמְלִיךְ מַלְכוּתֵהּ, בְּחַיֵּיכוֹן וּבְיוֹמֵיכוֹן וּבְחַיֵּי דְכָל בֵּית יִשְׂרָאֵל, בַּעֲגָלָא וּבִזְמַן קָרִיב. וְאִמְרוּ: אָמֵן.

(.Cong. – אָמֵן. יְהֵא שְׁמֵהּ רַבָּא מְבָרַךְ לְעָלַם וּלְעָלְמֵי עָלְמַיָּא.)

יְהֵא שְׁמֵהּ רַבָּא מְבָרַךְ לְעָלַם וּלְעָלְמֵי עָלְמַיָּא.

יִתְבָּרַךְ וְיִשְׁתַּבַּח וְיִתְפָּאַר וְיִתְרוֹמַם וְיִתְנַשֵּׂא וְיִתְהַדָּר וְיִתְעַלֶּה וְיִתְהַלָּל שְׁמֵהּ דְּקֻדְשָׁא בְּרִיךְ הוּא (.Cong. – בְּרִיךְ הוּא) — לְעֵלָּא מִן כָּל בִּרְכָתָא וְשִׁירָתָא תֻּשְׁבְּחָתָא וְנֶחֱמָתָא, דַּאֲמִירָן בְּעָלְמָא. וְאִמְרוּ: אָמֵן. (.Cong. – אָמֵן.)

(.Cong. – קַבֵּל בְּרַחֲמִים וּבְרָצוֹן אֶת תְּפִלָּתֵנוּ.)

תִּתְקַבֵּל צְלוֹתְהוֹן וּבָעוּתְהוֹן דְּכָל בֵּית יִשְׂרָאֵל קֳדָם אֲבוּהוֹן דִּי בִשְׁמַיָּא. וְאִמְרוּ: אָמֵן. (.Cong. – אָמֵן.)

(.Cong. – יְהִי שֵׁם יהוה מְבֹרָךְ, מֵעַתָּה וְעַד עוֹלָם.[1])

יְהֵא שְׁלָמָא רַבָּא מִן שְׁמַיָּא, וְחַיִּים עָלֵינוּ וְעַל כָּל יִשְׂרָאֵל. וְאִמְרוּ: אָמֵן. (.Cong. – אָמֵן.)

(.Cong. – עֶזְרִי מֵעִם יהוה, עֹשֵׂה שָׁמַיִם וָאָרֶץ.[2])

Take three steps back. Bow left and say . . . עֹשֶׂה; bow right and say . . . הוּא; bow forward and say וְעַל כָּל . . . אָמֵן. Remain standing in place for a few moments, then take three steps forward.

עֹשֶׂה שָׁלוֹם בִּמְרוֹמָיו, הוּא יַעֲשֶׂה שָׁלוֹם עָלֵינוּ, וְעַל כָּל יִשְׂרָאֵל. וְאִמְרוּ: אָמֵן. (.Cong. – אָמֵן.)

⋞§ יְהַלְלוּךָ . . . כָּל מַעֲשֶׂיךָ — *All Your works shall praise You.* This paragraph is not part of Psalms, but is a concluding blessing that sums up the broad theme of *Hallel* — that Israel and the entire universe will join in praising God. *All Your works shall praise You* means that in the perfect world of the future, the entire universe, including the vast variety of human beings, will function harmoniously according to God's will. This is the highest form of praise, for without it all the beautiful spoken and sung words and songs of praise are insincere and meaningless.

וַחֲסִידֶיךָ צַדִּיקִים — *Your devout ones, the righteous.* The word חָסִיד, *devout one,* refers to one who serves God beyond the minimum require-

יְהַלְלוּךָ *All Your works shall praise You,* HASHEM our God. And Your devout ones, the righteous,* who do Your will,* and Your entire people, the House of Israel, with glad song will thank, bless, praise, glorify, exalt, extol, sanctify, and proclaim the sovereignty of Your Name, our King.* Chazzan— *For to You it is fitting to give thanks, and unto Your Name it is proper to sing praises, for from This World to the World to Come You are God. Blessed are You, HASHEM, the King Who is lauded with praises.* (Cong.— *Amen.)*

FULL KADDISH

The *chazzan* recites *Kaddish:*

יִתְגַּדַּל *May His great Name grow exalted and sanctified* (Cong.— *Amen.) in the world that He created as He willed. May He give reign to His kingship in your lifetimes and in your days, and in the lifetimes of the entire Family of Israel, swiftly and soon. Now respond: Amen.*

(Cong.— *Amen. May His great Name be blessed forever and ever.)*

May His great Name be blessed forever and ever.

Blessed, praised, glorified, exalted, extolled, mighty, upraised, and lauded be the Name of the Holy One, Blessed is He (Cong.— *Blessed is He) — beyond any blessing and song, praise and consolation that are uttered in the world. Now respond: Amen.* (Cong.— *Amen.)*

(Cong.— *Accept our prayers with mercy and favor.)*

May the prayers and supplications of the entire Family of Israel be accepted before their Father Who is in Heaven. Now respond: Amen. (Cong.— *Amen.)*

(Cong.— *Blessed be the Name of HASHEM, from this time and forever.*[1])

May there be abundant peace from Heaven, and life, upon us and upon all Israel. Now respond: Amen. (Cong.— *Amen.)*

(Cong.— *My help is from HASHEM, Maker of heaven and earth.*[2])

Take three steps back. Bow left and say, *'He Who makes peace . . .';* bow right and say, *'may He . . .';* bow forward and say, *'and upon all Israel . . .'* Remain standing in place for a few moments, then take three steps forward.

He Who makes peace in His heights, may He make peace upon us, and upon all Israel. Now respond: Amen. (Cong.— *Amen.)*

(1) *Psalms* 113:2. (2) 121:2.

ment of the *Halachah.* The word is derived from חֶסֶד, *kindness,* as if to say that such people do acts of kindness for God's sake. They serve as an example for the *righteous* people, who fulfill all the requirements of the Law, and for the masses of Israel, whose goal is to serve God, even though they may not equal the spiritual accomplishments of the *devout* and the *righteous.*

עוֹשֵׂי רְצוֹנֶךָ — *Who do Your will.* In an inspiring homiletical interpretation, *Yismach Yisrael* interprets that the good deeds of the righteous can remake God's will, as it were. In other words, when Jews serve Him properly, God responds by lavishing kindness and a sense of fulfillment upon the world. Then, *Hallel* will become not only a song of praise for the miracles of the past, but also for the longed-for redemption.

⊰ הוצאת ספר תורה ⊱

From the moment the Ark is opened until the Torah is returned to it, one must conduct himself with the utmost respect, and avoid unnecessary conversation. It is commendable to kiss the Torah as it is carried to the *bimah* [reading table] and back to the Ark.

All rise and remain standing until the Torah is placed on the *bimah*. The congregation recites:

אֵין כָּמְוֹךָ* בָאֱלֹהִים אֲדֹנָי, וְאֵין כְּמַעֲשֶׂיךָ.*[1] מַלְכוּתְךָ מַלְכוּת כָּל עֹלָמִים, וּמֶמְשַׁלְתְּךָ בְּכָל דּוֹר וָדֹר.[2] יהוה מֶלֶךְ,[3] יהוה מָלָךְ,[4] יהוה יִמְלֹךְ לְעֹלָם וָעֶד.[5] יהוה עֹז לְעַמּוֹ יִתֵּן, יהוה יְבָרֵךְ אֶת עַמּוֹ בַשָּׁלוֹם.[6]

אַב הָרַחֲמִים, הֵיטִיבָה בִרְצוֹנְךָ אֶת צִיּוֹן,* תִּבְנֶה חוֹמוֹת יְרוּשָׁלָיִם.[7] כִּי בְךָ לְבַד בָּטָחְנוּ, מֶלֶךְ אֵל רָם וְנִשָּׂא, אֲדוֹן עוֹלָמִים.

THE ARK IS OPENED

Before the Torah is removed the congregation recites:

וַיְהִי בִּנְסֹעַ הָאָרֹן* וַיֹּאמֶר מֹשֶׁה, קוּמָה יהוה וְיָפֻצוּ אֹיְבֶיךָ וְיָנֻסוּ מְשַׂנְאֶיךָ מִפָּנֶיךָ.[8] כִּי מִצִּיּוֹן תֵּצֵא תוֹרָה, וּדְבַר יהוה מִירוּשָׁלָיִם.[9] בָּרוּךְ שֶׁנָּתַן תּוֹרָה לְעַמּוֹ יִשְׂרָאֵל בִּקְדֻשָּׁתוֹ.

ON THE SABBATH THE FOLLOWING PRAYERS ARE OMITTED AND THE SERVICE CONTINUES WITH בְּרִיךְ שְׁמֵהּ (P. 930).

The following paragraph [the Thirteen Attributes of Mercy] is recited three times:

יהוה, יהוה, אֵל, רַחוּם, וְחַנּוּן, אֶרֶךְ אַפַּיִם, וְרַב חֶסֶד, וֶאֱמֶת, נֹצֵר חֶסֶד לָאֲלָפִים, נֹשֵׂא עָוֹן, וָפֶשַׁע, וְחַטָּאָה, וְנַקֵּה.[10]

⊰ **הוֹצָאַת סֵפֶר תּוֹרָה / Removal of the Torah**

⊰ אֵין כָּמוֹךָ — *There is none like You.* On the Sabbath and Festivals, the service of removing the Torah from the Ark begins with an introductory series of verses that emphasize God's greatness and plead for the rebuilding of Zion and Jerusalem. Since we are about to read from God's word to Israel, it is fitting that we first call to mind that the One Who speaks to us is our All-powerful King.

וְאֵין כְּמַעֲשֶׂיךָ — *And there is nothing like Your works.* This refers to the work of creation. It follows, therefore, that since God is the Creator of the universe, He was and remains its King.

הֵיטִיבָה . . . אֶת צִיּוֹן — *Do good with Zion.* Only in God's chosen Sanctuary can His kingdom come to full flower among mankind. Only there can the Torah reading attain its greatest meaning.

⊰ וַיְהִי בִּנְסֹעַ הָאָרֹן — *When the Ark would travel.* When the Ark is opened we declare, as Moses did when the Ark traveled, that God's word is invincible. Having acknowledged this, we can read from the Torah with the proper awareness. We continue that it is God's will that the Torah's message go forth to the entire world, and by blessing Him for having given us the Torah, we accept our responsibility to carry out its commands and spread its message *(R' Hirsch).*

⊰ **The Thirteen Attributes of Mercy**

During Festivals a special prayer is inserted before בְּרִיךְ שְׁמֵהּ, *Blessed is the Name,* requesting God's help in attaining His goals for us. [Like all personal supplications, this is not recited on the Sabbath.] It is preceded by the י״ג מִדּוֹת הָרַחֲמִים, *Thirteen Attributes of Mercy,* the prayer that God Himself taught Moses after Israel worshiped the Golden Calf. Although Moses, quite understandably, thought that no prayers could help the nation that had bowed to and danced around an idol less than six weeks after hearing the Ten Commandments, God showed him that it was never too late for prayer and repentance. God made a Divine covenant with him that the prayerful, repentant recitation of the Thirteen Attributes of Mercy would never be turned back unanswered (*Rosh Hashanah* 17b).

There are various opinions among the com-

REMOVAL OF THE TORAH FROM THE ARK

From the moment the Ark is opened until the Torah is returned to it, one must conduct himself with the utmost respect, and avoid unnecessary conversation. It is commendable to kiss the Torah as it is carried to the *bimah* [reading table] and back to the Ark.

All rise and remain standing until the Torah is placed on the *bimah*. The congregation recites:

אֵין כָּמוֹךָ *There is none like You* among the gods, my Lord, and there is nothing like Your works.*[1] Your kingdom is a kingdom spanning all eternities, and Your dominion is throughout every generation.[2] HASHEM reigns,[3] HASHEM has reigned,[4] HASHEM shall reign for all eternity.[5] HASHEM will give might to His people; HASHEM will bless His people with peace.[6]*

אַב הָרַחֲמִים *Father of compassion, do good with Zion* according to Your will; rebuild the walls of Jerusalem.[7] For we trust in You alone, O King, God, exalted and uplifted, Master of worlds.*

THE ARK IS OPENED

Before the Torah is removed the congregation recites:

וַיְהִי בִּנְסֹעַ *When the Ark would travel,* Moses would say, 'Arise, HASHEM, and let Your foes be scattered, let those who hate You flee from You.'[8] For from Zion the Torah will come forth and the word of HASHEM from Jerusalem.[9] Blessed is He Who gave the Torah to His people Israel in His holiness.*

ON THE SABBATH THE FOLLOWING PRAYERS ARE OMITTED AND THE SERVICE CONTINUES WITH בְּרִיךְ שְׁמֵהּ, *BLESSED IS THE NAME* (P. 930).

The following paragraph [the Thirteen Attributes of Mercy] is recited three times:

יהוה HASHEM, HASHEM, God, Compassionate and Gracious, Slow to anger, and Abundant in Kindness and Truth. Preserver of kindness for thousands of generations, Forgiver of iniquity, willful sin, and error, and Who cleanses.[10]

(1) *Psalms* 86:8. (2) 145:13. (3) 10:16. (4) 93:1 et al. (5) *Exodus* 15:18.
(6) *Psalms* 29:11. (7) 51:20. (8) *Numbers* 10:35. (9) *Isaiah* 2:3. (10) *Exodus* 34:6-7.

---

mentators regarding the precise enumeration of the Thirteen Attributes. The following is the opinion of *Rabbeinu Tam* (*Rosh Hashanah* 17b). For a fuller commentary, see the ArtScroll *Tashlich* and the *Yom Kippur Machzor*.

1. ה׳ — *HASHEM.* This Name denotes mercy. God is merciful before a person sins, though He knows that future evil lies dormant in him.

2. ה׳ — *HASHEM.* God is merciful after the sinner has gone astray.

3. אֵל — *God.* This Name denotes power: the force of God's mercy sometimes surpasses even that indicated by the Name *HASHEM.*

4. רַחוּם — *Compassionate.* God eases the punishment of the guilty; and He does not put people into extreme temptation.

5. וְחַנּוּן — *and Gracious,* even to the undeserving.

6. אֶרֶךְ אַפַּיִם — *Slow to anger,* so that the sinner can reconsider long before it is too late.

7. וְרַב חֶסֶד — *and Abundant in Kindness,* toward those who lack personal merits. Also, if the scales of good and evil are evenly balanced, He tips them to the good.

8. וֶאֱמֶת — *and Truth.* God never reneges on His word.

9. נֹצֵר חֶסֶד לָאֲלָפִים — *Preserver of kindness for thousands of generations.* The deeds of the righteous benefit their offspring far into the future.

10. נֹשֵׂא עָוֹן — *Forgiver of iniquity.* God forgives the intentional sinner, if he repents.

11. וָפֶשַׁע — *[Forgiver of] willful sin.* Even those who purposely anger God are allowed to repent.

12. וְחַטָּאָה — *and [Forgiver of] error.* This is a sin committed out of carelessness or apathy.

13. וְנַקֵּה — *and Who cleanses.* God wipes away the sins of those who repent.

רִבּוֹנוֹ שֶׁל עוֹלָם מַלֵּא מִשְׁאֲלוֹת לִבִּי לְטוֹבָה,* וְהָפֵק רְצוֹנִי, וְתֵן שְׁאֵלָתִי, לִי עַבְדְּךָ (name) בֶּן/בַּת (mother's name) אֲמָתֶךָ, וְזַכֵּנִי

Insert the appropriate phrase(s) – וְאֶת אִשְׁתִּי/בַּעְלִי, וּבְנִי/וּבָנַי, וּבִתִּי/וּבְנוֹתַי

וְכָל בְּנֵי בֵיתִי לַעֲשׂוֹת רְצוֹנְךָ בְּלֵבָב שָׁלֵם. וּמַלְּטֵנוּ מִיֵּצֶר הָרָע, וְתֵן חֶלְקֵנוּ בְּתוֹרָתֶךָ. וְזַכֵּנוּ שֶׁתִּשְׁרֶה שְׁכִינָתְךָ עָלֵינוּ, וְהוֹפַע עָלֵינוּ רוּחַ חָכְמָה וּבִינָה. וְיִתְקַיֵּם בָּנוּ מִקְרָא שֶׁכָּתוּב: וְנָחָה עָלָיו רוּחַ יהוה, רוּחַ חָכְמָה וּבִינָה, רוּחַ עֵצָה וּגְבוּרָה, רוּחַ דַּעַת וְיִרְאַת יהוה.[1] וְכֵן יְהִי רָצוֹן מִלְּפָנֶיךָ, יהוה אֱלֹהֵינוּ וֵאלֹהֵי אֲבוֹתֵינוּ, שֶׁתְּזַכֵּנוּ לַעֲשׂוֹת מַעֲשִׂים טוֹבִים בְּעֵינֶיךָ, וְלָלֶכֶת בְּדַרְכֵי יְשָׁרִים לְפָנֶיךָ. וְקַדְּשֵׁנוּ בְּמִצְוֹתֶיךָ כְּדֵי שֶׁנִּזְכֶּה לְחַיִּים טוֹבִים וַאֲרוּכִים לִימוֹת הַמָּשִׁיחַ וּלְחַיֵּי הָעוֹלָם הַבָּא. וְתִשְׁמְרֵנוּ מִמַּעֲשִׂים רָעִים, וּמִשָּׁעוֹת רָעוֹת הַמִּתְרַגְּשׁוֹת לָבֹא לָעוֹלָם. וְהַבּוֹטֵחַ בַּיהוה חֶסֶד יְסוֹבְבֶנְהוּ,[2] אָמֵן. יִהְיוּ לְרָצוֹן אִמְרֵי פִי וְהֶגְיוֹן לִבִּי לְפָנֶיךָ, יהוה צוּרִי וְגֹאֲלִי.[3]

Recite the following verse three times:

וַאֲנִי תְפִלָּתִי לְךָ* יהוה עֵת רָצוֹן, אֱלֹהִים בְּרָב חַסְדֶּךָ, עֲנֵנִי בֶּאֱמֶת יִשְׁעֶךָ.[4]

ON ALL DAYS CONTINUE:

זוהר ויקהל שסט:א

בְּרִיךְ שְׁמֵהּ* דְּמָרֵא עָלְמָא, בְּרִיךְ כִּתְרָךְ וְאַתְרָךְ. יְהֵא רְעוּתָךְ עִם עַמָּךְ יִשְׂרָאֵל לְעָלַם, וּפֻרְקַן יְמִינָךְ אַחֲזֵי לְעַמָּךְ בְּבֵית מַקְדְּשָׁךְ, וּלְאַמְטוּיֵי לָנָא מִטּוּב נְהוֹרָךְ, וּלְקַבֵּל צְלוֹתָנָא בְּרַחֲמִין. יְהֵא רַעֲוָא קֳדָמָךְ, דְּתוֹרִיךְ לָן חַיִּין בְּטִיבוּתָא, וְלֶהֱוֵי אֲנָא פְקִידָא בְּגוֹ צַדִּיקַיָּא, לְמִרְחַם עָלַי וּלְמִנְטַר יָתִי וְיַת כָּל דִּי לִי, וְדִי לְעַמָּךְ יִשְׂרָאֵל. אַנְתְּ הוּא זָן לְכֹלָּא, וּמְפַרְנֵס לְכֹלָּא, אַנְתְּ הוּא שַׁלִּיט עַל כֹּלָּא. אַנְתְּ הוּא דְשַׁלִּיט עַל מַלְכַיָּא, וּמַלְכוּתָא דִּילָךְ הִיא. אֲנָא עַבְדָּא דְקֻדְשָׁא בְּרִיךְ הוּא, דְּסָגִידְנָא קַמֵּהּ וּמִקַּמָּא דִּיקַר אוֹרַיְתֵהּ בְּכָל עִדָּן וְעִדָּן. לָא עַל אֱנָשׁ רָחִיצְנָא, וְלָא עַל בַּר אֱלָהִין סָמִיכְנָא, אֶלָּא בֶּאֱלָהָא דִשְׁמַיָּא, דְּהוּא אֱלָהָא קְשׁוֹט, וְאוֹרַיְתֵהּ קְשׁוֹט, וּנְבִיאוֹהִי קְשׁוֹט, וּמַסְגֵּא לְמֶעְבַּד טַבְוָן וּקְשׁוֹט. בֵּהּ אֲנָא

רִבּוֹנוֹ שֶׁל עוֹלָם / Master of the Universe

מַלֵּא מִשְׁאֲלוֹת לִבִּי לְטוֹבָה — *Fulfill my heartfelt requests for good.* Often man's personal goals are not to his real benefit. May my requests be filled in a way that will be truly good.

וַאֲנִי תְפִלָּתִי לְךָ — *As for me, may my prayer to You.* This verse makes three declarations: We pray to God alone; we hope that the time is proper in His eyes; and we know that only through His abundant kindness can we expect salvation.

רִבּוֹנוֹ *Master of the universe, fulfill my heartfelt requests for good,* satisfy my desire and grant my request, me—Your servant* (name) *son/daughter of* (mother's name) *Your maidservant—and privilege me*

Insert the appropriate phrase(s): *and my wife/husband, my son(s), my daughter(s)*

and everyone in my household to do Your will wholeheartedly. Rescue us from the Evil Inclination and grant our share in Your Torah. Privilege us that You may rest Your Presence upon us and radiate upon us a spirit of wisdom and insight. Let there be fulfilled in us the verse that is written: The spirit of HASHEM *shall rest upon him, the spirit of wisdom and insight, the spirit of counsel and strength, the spirit of knowledge and fear of* HASHEM.[1] *Similarly may it be Your will,* HASHEM, *our God and the God of our forefathers, that You privilege us to do deeds that are good in Your eyes and to walk before You in upright paths. Sanctify us with Your commandments so that we may be worthy of a good and long life, to the days of the Messiah and to the life of the World to Come. May You protect us against evil deeds and from bad times that surge upon the world. He who trusts in* HASHEM *— may kindness surround him.*[2] *Amen. May the expressions of my mouth and the thoughts of my heart find favor before You,* HASHEM, *my Rock and my Redeemer.*[3]

Recite the following verse three times:

וַאֲנִי תְפִלָּתִי *As for me, may my prayer to You,** HASHEM, *be at an opportune time; O God, in Your abundant kindness, answer me with the truth of Your salvation.*[4]

ON ALL DAYS CONTINUE:

Zohar, Vayakhel 369a

בְּרִיךְ שְׁמֵהּ *Blessed is the Name* of the Master of the universe, blessed is Your crown and Your place. May Your favor remain with Your people Israel forever; may You display the salvation of Your right hand to Your people in Your Holy Temple, to benefit us with the goodness of Your luminescence and to accept our prayers with mercy. May it be Your will that You extend our lives with goodness and that I be numbered among the righteous; that You have mercy on me and protect me, all that is mine and that is Your people Israel's. It is You Who nourishes all and sustains all; You control everything. It is You Who control kings, and kingship is Yours. I am a servant of the Holy One, Blessed is He, and I prostrate myself before Him and before the glory of His Torah at all times. Not in any man do I put trust, nor on any angel do I rely — only on the God of heaven Who is the God of truth, Whose Torah is truth and Whose prophets are true and Who acts liberally with kindness and truth. In Him do I*

(1) *Isaiah* 11:2. (2) Cf. *Psalms* 32:10. (3) 19:15. (4) 69:14.

☙ בְּרִיךְ שְׁמֵהּ — *Blessed is the Name.* The *Zohar* declares that when the congregation prepares to read from the Torah, the heavenly gates of mercy are opened and God's love for Israel is aroused. Therefore, it is an auspicious occasion for the recital of this prayer which asks for God's compassion; pleads that He display His salvation in the finally rebuilt Holy Temple; declares our

רָחִיץ, וְלִשְׁמֵהּ קַדִּישָׁא יַקִּירָא אֲנָא אֵמַר תֻּשְׁבְּחָן. יְהֵא רַעֲוָא קֳדָמָךְ, דְּתִפְתַּח לִבָּאִי בְּאוֹרַיְתָא, וְתַשְׁלִים מִשְׁאֲלִין דְּלִבָּאִי, וְלִבָּא דְכָל עַמָּךְ יִשְׂרָאֵל, לְטַב וּלְחַיִּין וְלִשְׁלָם. (אָמֵן.)

Two Torah Scrolls are removed from the Ark; one for the main Torah reading and the second for *Maftir*. The first is presented to the *chazzan*, who accepts it in his right arm. Facing the congregation, the *chazzan* raises the Torah and, followed by congregation, recites:

שְׁמַע יִשְׂרָאֵל• יהוה אֱלֹהֵינוּ יהוה אֶחָד.[1]

Still facing the congregation, the *chazzan* raises the Torah and, followed by congregation, recites:

אֶחָד (הוּא) אֱלֹהֵינוּ גָּדוֹל אֲדוֹנֵינוּ, קָדוֹשׁ שְׁמוֹ.

The *chazzan* turns to the Ark, bows while raising the Torah, and recites:

גַּדְּלוּ• לַיהוה אִתִּי וּנְרוֹמְמָה שְׁמוֹ יַחְדָּו.[2]

The *chazzan* turns to his right and carries the Torah to the *bimah*, as the congregation responds:

לְךָ יהוה הַגְּדֻלָּה• וְהַגְּבוּרָה וְהַתִּפְאֶרֶת וְהַנֵּצַח וְהַהוֹד כִּי כֹל בַּשָּׁמַיִם וּבָאָרֶץ, לְךָ יהוה הַמַּמְלָכָה וְהַמִּתְנַשֵּׂא לְכֹל לְרֹאשׁ.[3] רוֹמְמוּ יהוה אֱלֹהֵינוּ, וְהִשְׁתַּחֲווּ לַהֲדֹם רַגְלָיו,• קָדוֹשׁ הוּא. רוֹמְמוּ יהוה אֱלֹהֵינוּ, וְהִשְׁתַּחֲווּ לְהַר קָדְשׁוֹ, כִּי קָדוֹשׁ יהוה אֱלֹהֵינוּ.[4]

As the *chazzan* carries the Torah to the *bimah* the congregation recites:

עַל הַכֹּל,• יִתְגַּדַּל וְיִתְקַדַּשׁ וְיִשְׁתַּבַּח וְיִתְפָּאַר וְיִתְרוֹמַם וְיִתְנַשֵּׂא שְׁמוֹ שֶׁל מֶלֶךְ מַלְכֵי הַמְּלָכִים הַקָּדוֹשׁ בָּרוּךְ הוּא, בָּעוֹלָמוֹת שֶׁבָּרָא, הָעוֹלָם הַזֶּה וְהָעוֹלָם הַבָּא, כִּרְצוֹנוֹ,• וְכִרְצוֹן יְרֵאָיו, וְכִרְצוֹן כָּל בֵּית יִשְׂרָאֵל. צוּר הָעוֹלָמִים, אֲדוֹן כָּל הַבְּרִיּוֹת, אֱלוֹהַּ כָּל הַנְּפָשׁוֹת, הַיּוֹשֵׁב בְּמֶרְחֲבֵי מָרוֹם, הַשּׁוֹכֵן בִּשְׁמֵי שְׁמֵי קֶדֶם. קְדֻשָּׁתוֹ עַל הַחַיּוֹת, וּקְדֻשָּׁתוֹ עַל כִּסֵּא הַכָּבוֹד. וּבְכֵן יִתְקַדַּשׁ שִׁמְךָ בָּנוּ• יהוה אֱלֹהֵינוּ לְעֵינֵי כָּל חָי. וְנֹאמַר לְפָנָיו שִׁיר חָדָשׁ, כַּכָּתוּב: שִׁירוּ לֵאלֹהִים זַמְּרוּ שְׁמוֹ, סֹלּוּ לָרֹכֵב בָּעֲרָבוֹת

---

faith in Him and His Torah; and asks that He make us receptive to its wisdom.

שְׁמַע יִשְׂרָאֵל — *Hear, O Israel.* Holding the Torah Scroll the *chazzan* leads the congregation in reciting three verses that help set the majestic tone of reading publicly from the word of God. The verses form a logical progression: God is One; He is great and holy; therefore we join in declaring His greatness.

גַּדְּלוּ — *Declare the greatness.* Our rejoicing in the Torah manifests itself in praise of its Giver. The *chazzan* calls upon the congregation to join him in praising God.

לְךָ ה׳ הַגְּדֻלָּה — *Yours, HASHEM, is the greatness.* This praise was first uttered by David in his ecstasy at seeing how wholeheartedly the people contributed their riches toward the eventual building of the Temple. He ascribed the greatness of that and every other achievement to God's graciousness.

לַהֲדֹם רַגְלָיו — *At His footstool,* i.e., the Temple, as if to say that God's Heavenly Presence extends earthward, like a footstool that helps support a monarch sitting on his throne. In a further sense, this represents our resolve to live in such a way that we are worthy of His Presence resting upon us *(R' Hirsch).*

עַל הַכֹּל — *For all this.* All the praises that we

trust, and to His glorious and holy Name do I declare praises. May it be Your will that You open my heart to the Torah and that You fulfill the wishes of my heart and the heart of Your entire people Israel for good, for life, and for peace. (Amen.)

Two Torah Scrolls are removed from the Ark; one for the main Torah reading and the second for *Maftir.* The first is presented to the *chazzan,* who accepts it in his right arm. Facing the congregation, the *chazzan* raises the Torah and, followed by congregation, recites:

Hear, O Israel:* HASHEM is our God, HASHEM, the One and Only.[1]

Still facing the congregation, the *chazzan* raises the Torah and, followed by congregation, recites:

One is our God, great is our Master, Holy is His Name.

The *chazzan* turns to the Ark, bows while raising the Torah, and recites:

Declare the greatness* of HASHEM with me, and let us exalt His Name together.[2]

The *chazzan* turns to his right and carries the Torah to the *bimah,* as the congregation responds:

לְךָ *Yours, HASHEM, is the greatness,* the strength, the splendor, the triumph, and the glory; even everything in heaven and earth; Yours, HASHEM, is the kingdom, and the sovereignty over every leader.*[3] *Exalt HASHEM, our God, and bow at His footstool;* He is Holy! Exalt HASHEM, our God, and bow to His holy mountain; for holy is HASHEM, our God.*[4]

As the *chazzan* carries the Torah to the *bimah* the congregation recites:

עַל הַכֹּל *For all this,* let the Name of the King of kings, the Holy One, Blessed is He, grow exalted, sanctified, praised, glorified, exalted, and extolled in the worlds that He has created — This World and the World to Come — according to His will,* the will of those who fear Him, and the will of the entire House of Israel. Rock of the eternities, Master of all creatures, God of all souls, He Who sits in the expanses on high, Who rests in the loftiest primeval heavens. His holiness is upon the Chayos; His holiness is upon the Throne of Glory. Similarly, may Your Name be sanctified within us,* HASHEM, our God, in the sight of all the living. May we chant before Him a new song as it is written: 'Sing to God, make music for His Name, extol the One Who*

(1) *Deuteronomy* 6:4. (2) *Psalms* 34:4. (3) *I Chronicles* 29:11. (4) *Psalms* 99:5,9.

---

have uttered heretofore are inadequate to describe God's greatness. May His Name continue to grow exalted (*Kol Bo*).

This paragraph is intended to express the majesty of God especially now that we are about to read from the Torah. We say that although He is sanctified in the heavens and by the spiritual beings, we long to become worthy vehicles through which His greatness can be manifested on earth, as well.

כִּרְצוֹנוֹ — *According to His will.* May He be *exalted, sanctified, praised ...* as He wishes to be. God created the universe so that His glory could be appreciated and emulated by man (see *Isaiah* 43:7). We now pray that this will indeed take place.

וּבְכֵן יִתְקַדַּשׁ שִׁמְךָ בָּנוּ — *Similarly, may Your Name be sanctified within us.* The goal of people should be to demonstrate that God's greatness should not be reserved for the 'higher, spiritual' spheres. Rather, the most noble purpose of life is for mortal man to become a bearer of Godliness.

בְּיָהּ שְׁמוֹ, וְעִלְזוּ לְפָנָיו.[1] וְנִרְאֵהוּ עַיִן בְּעַיִן בְּשׁוּבוֹ אֶל נָוֵהוּ, כַּכָּתוּב: כִּי עַיִן בְּעַיִן יִרְאוּ בְּשׁוּב יהוה צִיּוֹן.[2] וְנֶאֱמַר: וְנִגְלָה כְּבוֹד יהוה, וְרָאוּ כָל בָּשָׂר יַחְדָּו כִּי פִּי יהוה דִּבֵּר.[3]

אַב הָרַחֲמִים הוּא יְרַחֵם עַם עֲמוּסִים, וְיִזְכֹּר בְּרִית אֵיתָנִים, וְיַצִּיל נַפְשׁוֹתֵינוּ מִן הַשָּׁעוֹת הָרָעוֹת, וְיִגְעַר בְּיֵצֶר הָרָע מִן הַנְּשׂוּאִים, וְיָחֹן אוֹתָנוּ לִפְלֵיטַת עוֹלָמִים, וִימַלֵּא מִשְׁאֲלוֹתֵינוּ בְּמִדָּה טוֹבָה יְשׁוּעָה וְרַחֲמִים.

The Torah is placed on the *bimah* and prepared for reading.

The *gabbai* uses the following formula to call a *Kohen* to the Torah:

וְיַעֲזוֹר וְיָגֵן וְיוֹשִׁיעַ לְכֹל הַחוֹסִים בּוֹ, וְנֹאמַר, אָמֵן. הַכֹּל הָבוּ גֹדֶל לֵאלֹהֵינוּ וּתְנוּ כָבוֹד לַתּוֹרָה, כֹּהֵן° קְרָב, יַעֲמֹד (name) בֶּן (father's name) הַכֹּהֵן.

°If no *Kohen* is present, the *gabbai* says:
„אֵין כָּאן כֹּהֵן, יַעֲמֹד (insert name) יִשְׂרָאֵל (לֵוִי) בִּמְקוֹם כֹּהֵן.״

בָּרוּךְ שֶׁנָּתַן תּוֹרָה לְעַמּוֹ יִשְׂרָאֵל בִּקְדֻשָּׁתוֹ. (תּוֹרַת יהוה תְּמִימָה מְשִׁיבַת נָפֶשׁ, עֵדוּת יהוה נֶאֱמָנָה מַחְכִּימַת פֶּתִי. פִּקּוּדֵי יהוה יְשָׁרִים מְשַׂמְּחֵי לֵב, מִצְוַת יהוה בָּרָה מְאִירַת עֵינָיִם.[4] יהוה עֹז לְעַמּוֹ יִתֵּן, יהוה יְבָרֵךְ אֶת עַמּוֹ בַשָּׁלוֹם.[5] הָאֵל תָּמִים דַּרְכּוֹ, אִמְרַת יהוה צְרוּפָה, מָגֵן הוּא לְכֹל הַחוֹסִים בּוֹ.[6])

Congregation then *gabbai:*

וְאַתֶּם הַדְּבֵקִים בַּיהוה אֱלֹהֵיכֶם, חַיִּים כֻּלְּכֶם הַיּוֹם.[7]

קריאת התורה

The reader shows the *oleh* (person called to the Torah) the place in the Torah. The *oleh* touches the Torah with a corner of his *tallis,* or the belt or mantle of the Torah, and kisses it. He then begins the blessing, bowing at בָּרְכוּ, and straightening up at ה׳.

בָּרְכוּ אֶת יהוה* הַמְּבֹרָךְ.

Congregation, followed by *oleh,* responds, bowing at בָּרוּךְ, and straightening up at ה׳.

בָּרוּךְ יהוה הַמְּבֹרָךְ לְעוֹלָם וָעֶד.

Oleh continues:

בָּרוּךְ אַתָּה יהוה אֱלֹהֵינוּ מֶלֶךְ הָעוֹלָם, אֲשֶׁר בָּחַר בָּנוּ מִכָּל הָעַמִּים, וְנָתַן לָנוּ אֶת תּוֹרָתוֹ. בָּרוּךְ אַתָּה יהוה, נוֹתֵן הַתּוֹרָה. (Cong. – אָמֵן.)

קְרִיאַת הַתּוֹרָה / Reading of the Torah

There is a basic difference between the reading of the Torah and the prayers. When we pray, *we* call upon *God;* that is why the *chazzan* stands in front of the congregation as its representative. But the Torah reading is reminiscent of God's revelation to Israel, when the nation gathered around Mount Sinai to hear Him communicate His word to Israel. That is why the Torah is read from a *bimah,* platform, in the center of the congregation and usually elevated, like Israel gathered around the mountain.

The number of people called to the Torah varies in accordance with the sanctity of the day. Thus, on Monday and Thursday, fast days, Purim and Chanukah, three people are called; on Rosh Chodesh and Chol HaMoed, four are called; on Festivals and Rosh Hashanah, five; on

rides in the highest heavens with His Name YAH, and exult before Him.'[1] *May we see Him with a perceptive view upon His return to His Abode, as is written: 'For they shall see with a perceptive view as HASHEM returns to Zion.'*[2] *And it is said: 'The glory of HASHEM shall be revealed and all flesh together shall see that the mouth of HASHEM has spoken.'*[3]

אַב הָרַחֲמִים *May the Father of compassion have mercy on the nation that is borne by Him, and may He remember the covenant of the spiritually mighty. May He rescue our souls from the bad times, and upbraid the evil inclination to leave those borne by Him, graciously make us an eternal remnant, and fulfill our requests in good measure, for salvation and mercy.*

The Torah is placed on the *bimah* and prepared for reading.
The *gabbai* uses the following formula to call a *Kohen* to the Torah:

וְיַעֲזוֹר *May He help, shield, and save all who take refuge in Him — Now let us respond: Amen. All of you ascribe greatness to our God and give honor to the Torah. Kohen,° approach. Arise* (name) *son of* (father's name) *the Kohen.*

°If no *Kohen* is present, the *gabbai* says: *'There is no Kohen present, stand* (name) *son of* (father's name) *an Israelite (Levite) in place of the Kohen.'*

Blessed is He Who gave the Torah to His people Israel in His holiness. (The Torah of HASHEM is perfect, restoring the soul; the testimony of HASHEM is trustworthy, making the simple one wise. The orders of HASHEM are upright, gladdening the heart; the command of HASHEM is clear, enlightening the eyes.[4] *HASHEM will give might to His nation; HASHEM will bless His nation with peace.*[5] *The God Whose way is perfect, the promise of HASHEM is flawless, He is a shield for all who take refuge in Him.*[6]*)*

Congregation then *gabbai:*

You who cling to HASHEM, your God, you are all alive today.[7]

READING OF THE TORAH

The reader shows the *oleh* (person called to the Torah) the place in the Torah. The *oleh* touches the Torah with a corner of his *tallis,* or the belt or mantle of the Torah, and kisses it. He then begins the blessing, bowing at *'Bless,'* and straightening up at 'HASHEM.'

Bless HASHEM,* the blessed One.

Congregation, followed by *oleh,* responds, bowing at 'Blessed,' and straightening up at 'HASHEM.'

Blessed is HASHEM, the blessed One, for all eternity.

Oleh continues:

בָּרוּךְ *Blessed are You, HASHEM, our God, King of the universe, Who selected us from all the peoples and gave us His Torah. Blessed are You, HASHEM, Giver of the Torah.* (Cong.— *Amen.)*

(1) *Psalms* 68:5. (2) *Isaiah* 52:8. (3) 40:5. (4) *Psalms* 19:8-9. (5) 29:11. (6) 18:31. (7) *Deut.* 4:4.

Yom Kippur, six; and on the Sabbath [whether an ordinary Sabbath or a Festival that falls on the Sabbath], seven. (It should be noted that *Maftir* is not included in the above number since *Maftir* is attached to the *Haftarah* reading.) Only three are called on Sabbath afternoons since the Torah has already been read in the morning.

On most Festivals the Torah reading is a selection on either the historical narrative of the day or the commandment to observe the Festivals.

☙ בָּרְכוּ אֶת ה׳ — *Bless HASHEM.* This call to the congregation to bless God prior to the Torah reading is based on the practice of Ezra (*Nechemiah* 8:6). Before he read from the Torah to the multitude, he blessed God and they responded in kind. Similarly, the Sages (*Berachos* 21a) derive the Scriptural requirement to recite a

After his Torah portion has been read, the *oleh* recites:

בָּרוּךְ אַתָּה יהוה אֱלֹהֵינוּ מֶלֶךְ הָעוֹלָם, אֲשֶׁר נָתַן לָנוּ תּוֹרַת אֱמֶת, וְחַיֵּי עוֹלָם* נָטַע בְּתוֹכֵנוּ. בָּרוּךְ אַתָּה יהוה, נוֹתֵן הַתּוֹרָה. (Cong. – אָמֵן.)

PRAYER FOR THE OLEH / מי שברך לעולה לתורה

After each *oleh* completes his concluding blessing, the *gabbai* calls the next *oleh* to the Torah, then blesses the one who has just concluded.

מִי שֶׁבֵּרַךְ אֲבוֹתֵינוּ אַבְרָהָם יִצְחָק וְיַעֲקֹב, הוּא יְבָרֵךְ אֶת (name) בֶּן (father's name) בַּעֲבוּר שֶׁעָלָה לִכְבוֹד הַמָּקוֹם, לִכְבוֹד הַתּוֹרָה, [On the Sabbath – לִכְבוֹד הַשַּׁבָּת,] לִכְבוֹד הָרֶגֶל. בִּשְׂכַר זֶה, הַקָּדוֹשׁ בָּרוּךְ הוּא יִשְׁמְּרֵהוּ וְיַצִּילֵהוּ מִכָּל צָרָה וְצוּקָה, וּמִכָּל נֶגַע וּמַחֲלָה, וְיִשְׁלַח בְּרָכָה וְהַצְלָחָה בְּכָל מַעֲשֵׂה יָדָיו, וְיִזְכֶּה לַעֲלוֹת לָרֶגֶל, עִם כָּל יִשְׂרָאֵל אֶחָיו. וְנֹאמַר: אָמֵן. (Cong. – אָמֵן.)

PRAYER FOR OTHERS / מי שברך לאחרים

It is customary that the following prayer be recited for the family members of the *oleh* and for anyone else that he may wish to include:

מִי שֶׁבֵּרַךְ אֲבוֹתֵינוּ אַבְרָהָם יִצְחָק וְיַעֲקֹב, הוּא יְבָרֵךְ אֶת (names of the recipients) בַּעֲבוּר שֶׁ(name of *oleh*) יִתֵּן לִצְדָקָה בַּעֲבוּרָם. בִּשְׂכַר זֶה, הַקָּדוֹשׁ בָּרוּךְ הוּא יִשְׁמְּרֵם וְיַצִּילֵם מִכָּל צָרָה וְצוּקָה, וּמִכָּל נֶגַע וּמַחֲלָה, וְיִשְׁלַח בְּרָכָה וְהַצְלָחָה בְּכָל מַעֲשֵׂה יְדֵיהֶם, וְיִזְכּוּ לַעֲלוֹת לָרֶגֶל, עִם כָּל יִשְׂרָאֵל אֲחֵיהֶם. וְנֹאמַר: אָמֵן. (Cong. – אָמֵן.)

PRAYER FOR A SICK PERSON / מי שברך לחולה

מִי שֶׁבֵּרַךְ אֲבוֹתֵינוּ אַבְרָהָם יִצְחָק וְיַעֲקֹב, מֹשֶׁה אַהֲרֹן דָּוִד וּשְׁלֹמֹה,

for a man

הוּא יְבָרֵךְ וִירַפֵּא אֶת הַחוֹלֶה (patient's name) בֶּן (mother's name) בַּעֲבוּר שֶׁ(supplicant's name) יִתֵּן לִצְדָקָה בַּעֲבוּרוֹ.°° בִּשְׂכַר זֶה, הַקָּדוֹשׁ בָּרוּךְ הוּא יִמָּלֵא רַחֲמִים עָלָיו, לְהַחֲלִימוֹ וּלְרַפֹּאתוֹ וּלְהַחֲזִיקוֹ וּלְהַחֲיוֹתוֹ, וְיִשְׁלַח לוֹ מְהֵרָה רְפוּאָה שְׁלֵמָה מִן הַשָּׁמַיִם, לִרְמַ״ח אֵבָרָיו, וּשְׁסָ״ה גִּידָיו, בְּתוֹךְ

for a woman

הוּא יְבָרֵךְ וִירַפֵּא אֶת הַחוֹלָה (patient's name) בַּת (mother's name) בַּעֲבוּר שֶׁ(supplicant's name) יִתֵּן לִצְדָקָה בַּעֲבוּרָהּ.°° בִּשְׂכַר זֶה, הַקָּדוֹשׁ בָּרוּךְ הוּא יִמָּלֵא רַחֲמִים עָלֶיהָ, לְהַחֲלִימָהּ וּלְרַפֹּאתָהּ וּלְהַחֲזִיקָהּ וּלְהַחֲיוֹתָהּ, וְיִשְׁלַח לָהּ מְהֵרָה רְפוּאָה שְׁלֵמָה מִן הַשָּׁמַיִם, לְכָל אֵבָרֶיהָ, וּלְכָל גִּידֶיהָ, בְּתוֹךְ

שְׁאָר חוֹלֵי יִשְׂרָאֵל, רְפוּאַת הַנֶּפֶשׁ, וּרְפוּאַת הַגּוּף, [On the Sabbath – שַׁבָּת וְ] יוֹם טוֹב הוּא מִלִּזְעֹק, וּרְפוּאָה קְרוֹבָה לָבֹא, הַשְׁתָּא, בַּעֲגָלָא וּבִזְמַן קָרִיב. וְנֹאמַר: אָמֵן. (Cong. – אָמֵן.)

°°Many congregations substitute:

בַּעֲבוּר שֶׁכָּל הַקָּהָל מִתְפַּלְּלִים בַּעֲבוּרוֹ (בַּעֲבוּרָהּ)

After his Torah portion has been read, the *oleh* recites:

בָּרוּךְ *Blessed are You, HASHEM, our God, King of the universe, Who gave us the Torah of truth and implanted eternal life* within us. Blessed are You, HASHEM, Giver of the Torah.* (Cong.– *Amen.)*

PRAYER FOR THE OLEH

After each *oleh* completes his concluding blessing, the *gabbai* calls the next *oleh* to the Torah, then blesses the one who has just concluded.

מִי שֶׁבֵּרַךְ *He Who blessed our forefathers Abraham, Isaac, and Jacob — may He bless (*Hebrew name*) son of (*father's Hebrew name*) because he has come up to the Torah in honor of the Omnipresent, in honor of the Torah, [in honor of the Sabbath] in honor of the pilgrimage festival. As reward for this, may the Holy One, Blessed is He, protect him and rescue him from every trouble and distress, from every plague and illness; may He send blessing and success in his every endeavor, and may he be privileged to ascend to Jerusalem for the pilgrimage, together with all Israel, his brethren. Now let us respond: Amen.* (Cong.– *Amen.)*

PRAYER FOR OTHERS

It is customary that the following prayer be recited for the family members of the *oleh* and for anyone else that he may wish to include:

מִי שֶׁבֵּרַךְ *He Who blessed our forefathers Abraham, Isaac, and Jacob — may He bless (*names of recipients*) for (*name of *oleh) will contribute to charity on their behalf. As reward for this, may the Holy One, Blessed is He, protect them and rescue them from every trouble and distress, from every plague and illness; may He send blessing and success in their every endeavor and may they be privileged to ascend to Jerusalem for the pilgrimage, together with all Israel, their brethren. Now let us respond: Amen.* (Cong.– *Amen.)*

PRAYER FOR A SICK PERSON

מִי שֶׁבֵּרַךְ *He Who blessed our forefathers Abraham, Isaac and Jacob, Moses and Aaron, David and Solomon — may He bless and heal the sick person (*patient's Hebrew name*) son/daughter of (*patient's mother's Hebrew name*) because (*name of supplicant*) will contribute to charity on his/her behalf.*°° *In reward for this, may the Holy One, Blessed is He, be filled with*

for a man	for a woman
compassion for him to restore his health, to heal him, to strengthen him, and to revivify him. And may He send him speedily a complete recovery from heaven for his two hundred forty-eight organs and three hundred sixty-five blood vessels,	*compassion for her to restore her health, to heal her, to strengthen her, and to revivify her. And may He send her speedily a complete recovery from heaven for all her organs and all her blood vessels,*

*among the other sick people of Israel, a recovery of the body and a recovery of the spirit though the [*on the Sabbath: *Sabbath and] Festival prohibit[s] us from crying out, may a recovery come speedily, swiftly and soon. Now let us respond: Amen.* (Cong.–*Amen.)*

°°Many congregations substitute:
because the entire congregation prays for him (her)

---

blessing before Torah study from the verse, *When I proclaim the Name of HASHEM, ascribe greatness to our God* (*Deuteronomy* 32:3). The implication is that the public study of Torah requires a blessing.

תּוֹרַת אֱמֶת וְחַיֵּי עוֹלָם — *The Torah of truth ... eternal life. Torah of truth* refers to the Written Torah, and *eternal life* to the Oral Law. The Oral Law is described as *implanted within us,* because Jews constantly expand their Torah knowledge through their personal study and analysis *(Tur Orach Chaim* 139).

קריאת התורה לשמיני עצרת

דברים יד:כב-טז:יז

כהן – עַשֵּׂר תְּעַשֵּׂר* אֵת כָּל־תְּבוּאַת זַרְעֶךָ הַיֹּצֵא הַשָּׂדֶה שָׁנָה שָׁנָה:
וְאָכַלְתָּ לִפְנֵי | יהוה* אֱלֹהֶיךָ בַּמָּקוֹם אֲשֶׁר־יִבְחַר לְשַׁכֵּן שְׁמוֹ שָׁם
מַעְשַׂר דְּגָנְךָ תִּירֹשְׁךָ וְיִצְהָרֶךָ וּבְכֹרֹת בְּקָרְךָ וְצֹאנֶךָ לְמַעַן תִּלְמַד
לְיִרְאָה* אֶת־יהוה אֱלֹהֶיךָ כָּל־הַיָּמִים: וְכִי־יִרְבֶּה מִמְּךָ הַדֶּרֶךְ כִּי
לֹא תוּכַל שְׂאֵתוֹ כִּי־יִרְחַק מִמְּךָ הַמָּקוֹם אֲשֶׁר יִבְחַר יהוה אֱלֹהֶיךָ
לָשׂוּם שְׁמוֹ שָׁם כִּי יְבָרֶכְךָ* יהוה אֱלֹהֶיךָ: וְנָתַתָּה בַּכָּסֶף* וְצַרְתָּ
הַכֶּסֶף בְּיָדְךָ וְהָלַכְתָּ אֶל־הַמָּקוֹם אֲשֶׁר יִבְחַר יהוה אֱלֹהֶיךָ בּוֹ:
וְנָתַתָּה הַכֶּסֶף בְּכֹל אֲשֶׁר־תְּאַוֶּה נַפְשְׁךָ בַּבָּקָר וּבַצֹּאן וּבַיַּיִן וּבַשֵּׁכָר
וּבְכֹל אֲשֶׁר תִּשְׁאָלְךָ נַפְשֶׁךָ וְאָכַלְתָּ שָּׁם לִפְנֵי יהוה אֱלֹהֶיךָ וְשָׂמַחְתָּ
אַתָּה וּבֵיתֶךָ: וְהַלֵּוִי אֲשֶׁר־בִּשְׁעָרֶיךָ לֹא תַעַזְבֶנּוּ* כִּי אֵין לוֹ חֵלֶק
וְנַחֲלָה עִמָּךְ: מִקְצֵה | שָׁלֹשׁ שָׁנִים* תּוֹצִיא אֶת־כָּל־מַעְשַׂר
תְּבוּאָתְךָ בַּשָּׁנָה הַהִוא וְהִנַּחְתָּ בִּשְׁעָרֶיךָ: וּבָא הַלֵּוִי* כִּי אֵין־לוֹ חֵלֶק
וְנַחֲלָה עִמָּךְ וְהַגֵּר וְהַיָּתוֹם וְהָאַלְמָנָה אֲשֶׁר בִּשְׁעָרֶיךָ וְאָכְלוּ וְשָׂבֵעוּ
לְמַעַן יְבָרֶכְךָ יהוה אֱלֹהֶיךָ בְּכָל־מַעֲשֵׂה יָדְךָ אֲשֶׁר תַּעֲשֶׂה:
(בשבת לוי) – מִקֵּץ שֶׁבַע־שָׁנִים תַּעֲשֶׂה שְׁמִטָּה:* וְזֶה דְּבַר הַשְּׁמִטָּה
שָׁמוֹט כָּל־בַּעַל מַשֵּׁה יָדוֹ אֲשֶׁר יַשֶּׁה בְּרֵעֵהוּ לֹא־יִגֹּשׂ אֶת־רֵעֵהוּ
וְאֶת־אָחִיו כִּי־קָרָא שְׁמִטָּה לַיהוה: אֶת־הַנָּכְרִי תִּגֹּשׂ* וַאֲשֶׁר יִהְיֶה
לְךָ אֶת־אָחִיךָ תַּשְׁמֵט יָדֶךָ: אֶפֶס כִּי לֹא יִהְיֶה־בְּךָ אֶבְיוֹן* כִּי־בָרֵךְ

⊰§ Torah Reading for Shemini Atzeres

This portion is read on the last days of Pesach and Shavuos as well on Shemini Atzeres, but there is a difference. If those days of Pesach and Shavuos fall on weekdays, the reading begins at 15:9, with כָּל הַבְּכוֹר, *Every firstborn.* Only on the Sabbath, when seven people instead of five are called to the Torah and more verses are needed, do we begin from עַשֵּׂר תְּעַשֵּׂר, *you are to take tithes.* On Shemini Atzeres, however, the reading always begins with the passage on tithes, because this is the time when people are enjoined to deliver their tithes to the needy. As the season when crops are gathered in, Shemini Atzeres is the time when it is especially important for all Jews to share their prosperity with the less fortunate.

עַשֵּׂר תְּעַשֵּׂר — *You are to take tithes.* The Sages expound homiletically עַשֵּׂר בִּשְׁבִיל שֶׁתִּתְעַשֵּׁר, *give tithes in order that you should become wealthy,* i.e., God rewards charitable people with prosperity far beyond their contributions (*Shabbos* 119a).

וְאָכַלְתָּ לִפְנֵי ה׳ — *And you are to eat it before* HASHEM. This commandment applies to מַעְשַׂר שֵׁנִי, the *second tithe,* which is brought to Jerusalem and eaten there.

לְמַעַן תִּלְמַד לְיִרְאָה — *So that you will learn to fear.* One who comes to Jerusalem, which is saturated with holiness, learns יִרְאַת שָׁמַיִם, *fear of Heaven.*

כִּי יְבָרֶכְךָ — *For . . . will have blessed you.* God has blessed you with such abundant crops that you cannot carry all your tithes to Jerusalem, even though you are going there anyway.

וְנָתַתָּה בַּכָּסֶף — *Then you may exchange it for money.* When the crops of the tithe are exchanged for coins, the crops lose their sanctity and the money gets the status of the second tithe. The money is brought to Jerusalem and must be used to buy food, which must then be eaten in the city.

TORAH READING FOR SHEMINI ATZERES

Deuteronomy 14:22-16:17

Kohen – *You are to take tithes* from the entire crop of your planting; what is produced by the field year in, year out. And you are to eat it before* HASHEM,* *your God — in the place in which He will have chosen to rest His Name — the tithe of your grain, wine and oil, and the firstborn of your cattle and sheep; so that you will learn to fear** HASHEM, *your God, throughout the years. If the distance is too great for you so that you cannot carry it, because far from you is the place that* HASHEM, *your God, will have chosen to place His Name there; for* HASHEM, *your God, will have blessed you.* Then you may exchange it for money,* wrap up the money and hold it in hand, and go to the place that* HASHEM, *your God, will have chosen. You may spend the money for anything that your soul desires — for cattle, sheep, wine, or alchoholic beverage — or for anything that your soul wishes; eat it there before* HASHEM, *your God, and rejoice — you and your household. And do not forsake the Levite* who is in your own gates, for he has no portion or heritage as you do.*

At the end of three years, you are to take out every tithe of your crop in that year and set it down within your gates. Then the Levite can come* — for he has no portion or heritage as you do — and the stranger, the orphan and the widow, who are in your gates, and they can eat and be satisfied; in order that* HASHEM, *your God, will bless you in all of your handiwork that you may undertake.*

(On the Sabbath – Levi) *At the end of seven years you are to institute a remission year.* This is the function of the remission: every creditor remits his authority over what he has lent to his neighbor; he may not press his neighbor or brother, for the remission-time in honor of* HASHEM *has arrived. You may press the gentile;* but you must remit the authority that you have over your kinsman. Then there will be no destitute among you;* rather* HASHEM *will surely bless you*

וְהַלֵּוִי . . . לֹא תַעַזְבֶנּוּ – *Do not forsake the Levite.* When you go to Jerusalem with your second tithe, do not forget to give your מַעֲשֵׂר רִאשׁוֹן, *first tithe,* to the Levite whom you leave behind *in your own gates,* i.e., your home town.

מִקְצֵה שָׁלֹשׁ שָׁנִים – *At the end of three years.* Each three years is a tithe-cycle: in addition to the Levite's tithe, which must be given every year, the first tithe is taken from the crops of the first two years and in the third year, a tithe is given to the poor [מַעְשַׂר עָנִי]. When the three years are over, each householder is commanded to give to the proper parties any tithes that he may have held back up to then.

וּבָא הַלֵּוִי – *Then the Levite can come.* This verse describes all those who are entitled to receive the various tithes. The Levite gets the first tithe, the others are frequently poor and are entitled to the tithe of the poor, and all of them, including the first Levite, should be invited to share the second tithe in Jerusalem with its owner.

שְׁמִטָּה – *A remission year [Shemittah].* The laws of the Sabbatical year that relate to crops and farming are given in *Leviticus* ch. 25. This chapter deals with the law that all debts are forgiven in the seventh year.

אֶת הַנָּכְרִי תִּגֹּשׂ – *You may press the gentile.* The commandments of the seventh year do not apply to non-Jews. Just as they may work the land and collect debts from Jews, so may Jews collect their debts from gentiles.

כִּי לֹא יִהְיֶה בְּךָ אֶבְיוֹן – *There will be no destitute among you.* Even though, in observance of the

יְבָרֶכְךָ יהוה בָּאָרֶץ אֲשֶׁר יהוה אֱלֹהֶיךָ נֹתֵן־לְךָ נַחֲלָה לְרִשְׁתָּהּ:
רַק אִם־שָׁמוֹעַ תִּשְׁמַע* בְּקוֹל יהוה אֱלֹהֶיךָ לִשְׁמֹר לַעֲשׂוֹת אֶת־
כָּל־הַמִּצְוָה הַזֹּאת אֲשֶׁר אָנֹכִי מְצַוְּךָ הַיּוֹם: כִּי־יהוה אֱלֹהֶיךָ בֵּרַכְךָ
כַּאֲשֶׁר דִּבֶּר־לָךְ וְהַעֲבַטְתָּ גּוֹיִם רַבִּים וְאַתָּה לֹא תַעֲבֹט וּמָשַׁלְתָּ
בְּגוֹיִם רַבִּים וּבְךָ לֹא יִמְשֹׁלוּ: כִּי־יִהְיֶה בְךָ אֶבְיוֹן מֵאַחַד אַחֶיךָ*
בְּאַחַד שְׁעָרֶיךָ בְּאַרְצְךָ אֲשֶׁר־יהוה אֱלֹהֶיךָ נֹתֵן לָךְ לֹא תְאַמֵּץ
אֶת־לְבָבְךָ וְלֹא תִקְפֹּץ אֶת־יָדְךָ מֵאָחִיךָ הָאֶבְיוֹן: כִּי־פָתֹחַ תִּפְתַּח
אֶת־יָדְךָ לוֹ וְהַעֲבֵט תַּעֲבִיטֶנּוּ דֵּי מַחְסֹרוֹ אֲשֶׁר יֶחְסַר לוֹ:* הִשָּׁמֶר
לְךָ פֶּן־יִהְיֶה דָבָר עִם־לְבָבְךָ בְלִיַּעַל לֵאמֹר קָרְבָה שְׁנַת־הַשֶּׁבַע
שְׁנַת הַשְּׁמִטָּה וְרָעָה עֵינְךָ בְּאָחִיךָ הָאֶבְיוֹן וְלֹא תִתֵּן לוֹ* וְקָרָא
עָלֶיךָ* אֶל־יהוה וְהָיָה בְךָ חֵטְא: נָתוֹן תִּתֵּן לוֹ וְלֹא־יֵרַע לְבָבְךָ
בְּתִתְּךָ לוֹ כִּי בִּגְלַל ׀ הַדָּבָר הַזֶּה יְבָרֶכְךָ יהוה אֱלֹהֶיךָ בְּכָל־מַעֲשֶׂךָ
וּבְכֹל מִשְׁלַח יָדֶךָ: כִּי לֹא־יֶחְדַּל אֶבְיוֹן* מִקֶּרֶב הָאָרֶץ עַל־כֵּן אָנֹכִי
מְצַוְּךָ לֵאמֹר פָּתֹחַ תִּפְתַּח אֶת־יָדְךָ לְאָחִיךָ לַעֲנִיֶּךָ וּלְאֶבְיֹנְךָ
בְּאַרְצֶךָ: כִּי־יִמָּכֵר לְךָ אָחִיךָ הָעִבְרִי אוֹ הָעִבְרִיָּה וַעֲבָדְךָ שֵׁשׁ שָׁנִים
וּבַשָּׁנָה הַשְּׁבִיעִת תְּשַׁלְּחֶנּוּ חָפְשִׁי מֵעִמָּךְ: וְכִי־תְשַׁלְּחֶנּוּ חָפְשִׁי
מֵעִמָּךְ לֹא תְשַׁלְּחֶנּוּ רֵיקָם: הַעֲנֵיק תַּעֲנִיק לוֹ* מִצֹּאנְךָ וּמִגָּרְנְךָ
וּמִיִּקְבֶךָ אֲשֶׁר בֵּרַכְךָ יהוה אֱלֹהֶיךָ תִּתֶּן־לוֹ: וְזָכַרְתָּ כִּי עֶבֶד
הָיִיתָ בְּאֶרֶץ מִצְרַיִם וַיִּפְדְּךָ יהוה אֱלֹהֶיךָ עַל־כֵּן אָנֹכִי מְצַוְּךָ
אֶת־הַדָּבָר הַזֶּה הַיּוֹם: וְהָיָה כִּי־יֹאמַר אֵלֶיךָ לֹא אֵצֵא מֵעִמָּךְ כִּי
אֲהֵבְךָ וְאֶת־בֵּיתֶךָ כִּי־טוֹב לוֹ עִמָּךְ: וְלָקַחְתָּ אֶת־הַמַּרְצֵעַ* וְנָתַתָּה
בְאָזְנוֹ וּבַדֶּלֶת וְהָיָה לְךָ עֶבֶד עוֹלָם* וְאַף לַאֲמָתְךָ* תַּעֲשֶׂה־כֵּן:

Shemittah laws, you forgo the opportunity to collect enormous debts, God promises you that you will not suffer poverty. He will bless you with wealth and power.

רק אם שמוע תשמע — *Only if you continually hearken.* Logic might dictate that you cannot be prosperous if you make loans and don't collect them or own farms and don't work them. However, the contrary is true. Only if you obey God's laws will He give you the blessings of prosperity.

מאחד אחיך — *Any of your brethren.* From this verse, the Sages derive the priorities of charity giving: first come close relatives (*brethren*), then neighbors and townspeople (*your gates*), then countrymen (*the land . . .*).

די מחסרו אשר יחסר לו — *His requirement, whatever he lacks.* Give him what he requires, but don't make him rich. On the other hand, if someone grew up in luxury, do not begrudge him more than minimum needs — to him a degree of elegance is a necessity.

ולא תתן לו — *And you will refuse to give him,* i.e., you will refuse to lend him money, because you are afraid that the seventh year will render your loan worthless.

וקרא עליך — *Then he may appeal against you.* Even if he does not appeal against you, you will be punished for your sin, but if your victim feels aggrieved, you will be punished sooner.

כי לא יחדל אביון — *For destitute people will not*

in the Land that HASHEM, your God, gives you as a heritage, for a possession. Only if you continually hearken to the voice of HASHEM, your God; to observe, to perform this entire commandment that I command you today. For HASHEM, your God, will bless you as He has told you; you will lend to many nations, but you will not borrow; and you will dominate many nations, but they will not dominate you.*

If there is to be a destitute person among you, any of your brethren in any of your gates, in the Land that HASHEM, your God, gives you, do not harden your heart or close your hand against your destitute brother. Instead, you shall surely open your hand to him; you shall surely lend him his requirement, whatever he lacks.* Beware, lest there be a lawless thought in your heart, saying, the seventh year approaches, the remission year, and you will look malevolently upon your destitute brother, and you will refuse to give him;* then he may appeal against you* to HASHEM — and the sin will rest upon you. Give him always, and let your heart not feel bad when you give him, for in return for this, HASHEM, your God, will bless you in all your deeds and wherever you send your hand. For destitute people will not cease to exist* within your land, therefore I command you, 'Always open your hand to your brother, your poor, and your destitute in your land.'*

If your brother, a Hebrew man or woman, is sold to you, he is to serve you for six years; and in the seventh year you are to send him away free. But when you send him away free, do not send him empty-handed. Adorn him generously from your sheep, your threshing floor, and your wine-cellar; as HASHEM, your God, has blessed you, so shall you give him. You must remember that you were a slave in the land of Egypt, and HASHEM, your God, redeemed you; therefore, I command you today regarding this matter.*

And in the event he will say to you, 'I will not leave you,' for he loves you and your household, for it goes well for him with you. Then take the awl and put it through his ear and the door, and he shall be for you an eternal slave;* and do the same for your maidservant.**

---

cease to exist. Let no one think he is immune from poverty or tragedy. To the extent that someone has pity on others, God will be compassionate with him when he suffers misfortune.

הַעֲנֵיק תַּעֲנִיק לוֹ – *Adorn him generously.* Do not simply set him free with gifts; present them generously and ceremoniously so that it will be clear to him and to the public that you appreciate his years of service.

וְלָקַחְתָּ אֶת הַמַּרְצֵעַ – *Then take the awl.* Every Jewish ear heard at Sinai that we are servants of God, not man. And in Egypt, it was the doorpost that we daubed with blood from the Pesach offering, and the Jewish doorposts over which God passed when He took the lives of the Egyptian firstborn. Thus the ear and the doorpost are symbols of our freedom from every master except God. Consequently, a Jew who has tasted slavery and still consciously prefers it to freedom, is stood at the doorpost and has his ear punctured.

עֶבֶד עוֹלָם – *An eternal slave,* i.e., until the next יוֹבֵל, *Jubilee year,* which comes every fifty years. When that year arrives, all Jewish slaves go free, even if they prefer to remain with their masters.

לַאֲמָתְךָ – *For your maidservant.* This applies only to the owner's requirement to give gifts at the end of the servitude. However, a maidservant is not permitted to remain enslaved until the Jubilee year.

לֹא־יִקְשֶׁה בְעֵינֶךָ* בְּשַׁלֵּחֲךָ אֹתוֹ חָפְשִׁי מֵעִמָּךְ כִּי מִשְׁנֶה שְׂכַר שָׂכִיר* עֲבָדְךָ שֵׁשׁ שָׁנִים וּבֵרַכְךָ יהוה אֱלֹהֶיךָ בְּכֹל אֲשֶׁר תַּעֲשֶׂה:

(בשבת שלישי) – כָּל־הַבְּכוֹר* אֲשֶׁר יִוָּלֵד בִּבְקָרְךָ וּבְצֹאנְךָ הַזָּכָר תַּקְדִּישׁ לַיהוה אֱלֹהֶיךָ לֹא תַעֲבֹד בִּבְכֹר שׁוֹרֶךָ וְלֹא תָגֹז בְּכוֹר צֹאנֶךָ: לִפְנֵי יהוה אֱלֹהֶיךָ תֹאכְלֶנּוּ* שָׁנָה בְשָׁנָה בַּמָּקוֹם אֲשֶׁר־יִבְחַר יהוה אַתָּה וּבֵיתֶךָ: וְכִי־יִהְיֶה בוֹ מוּם פִּסֵּחַ אוֹ עִוֵּר כֹּל מוּם רָע לֹא תִזְבָּחֶנּוּ לַיהוה אֱלֹהֶיךָ: בִּשְׁעָרֶיךָ תֹּאכְלֶנּוּ הַטָּמֵא וְהַטָּהוֹר יַחְדָּו כַּצְּבִי וְכָאַיָּל: רַק אֶת־דָּמוֹ לֹא תֹאכֵל עַל־הָאָרֶץ תִּשְׁפְּכֶנּוּ כַּמָּיִם:*

לוי (בשבת רביעי) – שָׁמוֹר אֶת־חֹדֶשׁ הָאָבִיב* וְעָשִׂיתָ פֶּסַח לַיהוה אֱלֹהֶיךָ כִּי בְּחֹדֶשׁ הָאָבִיב הוֹצִיאֲךָ יהוה אֱלֹהֶיךָ מִמִּצְרַיִם לָיְלָה:* וְזָבַחְתָּ פֶּסַח לַיהוה אֱלֹהֶיךָ צֹאן וּבָקָר* בַּמָּקוֹם אֲשֶׁר יִבְחַר יהוה לְשַׁכֵּן שְׁמוֹ שָׁם: לֹא־תֹאכַל עָלָיו חָמֵץ שִׁבְעַת יָמִים תֹּאכַל־עָלָיו מַצּוֹת לֶחֶם עֹנִי* כִּי בְחִפָּזוֹן יָצָאתָ מֵאֶרֶץ מִצְרַיִם לְמַעַן תִּזְכֹּר אֶת־יוֹם צֵאתְךָ מֵאֶרֶץ מִצְרַיִם כֹּל יְמֵי חַיֶּיךָ:

שלישי (בשבת חמישי) – וְלֹא־יֵרָאֶה לְךָ שְׂאֹר בְּכָל־גְּבֻלְךָ שִׁבְעַת יָמִים וְלֹא־יָלִין מִן־הַבָּשָׂר אֲשֶׁר תִּזְבַּח בָּעֶרֶב בַּיּוֹם הָרִאשׁוֹן* לַבֹּקֶר: לֹא תוּכַל לִזְבֹּחַ אֶת־הַפָּסַח בְּאַחַד שְׁעָרֶיךָ אֲשֶׁר־יהוה אֱלֹהֶיךָ

לֹא יִקְשֶׁה בְעֵינֶךָ — *Do not feel distressed.* Although his purchase price was for only six years of work, your may feel distressed that you are being forced to give him substantial gifts when you free him. Bear in mind, however, that he worked hard for you and that God's blessing will more than compensate you for your losses.

מִשְׁנֶה שְׂכַר שָׂכִיר — *Double the wages of a hired hand.* From this expression the Sages derive that a Jewish slave serves his master not only during the regular workday, but also at night. How so? Because his owner may require him to live with a gentile maidservant, whose children will belong to the master.

כָּל הַבְּכוֹר — *Every firstborn male.* The previous chapter has outlined a series of commandments requiring us to be kind, from tithes to the need to give gifts to freed slaves. This chapter includes commandments that express our gratitude for God's kindness to us, from the consecration of our firstborn to the various festivals that symbolize gratitude for God's gifts of sustenance and prosperity *(Sforno).* The sanctification of first fruits and the gift to the Kohen of *terumah* before crops or dough may be eaten demonstrates our acknowledgment that the ultimate Owner and Giver is God.

תֹאכְלֶנּוּ — *Eat it.* Elsewhere (*Numbers* 18:17) the Torah tells us that the owner presents the firstborn animal to the *Kohen* of his choice. If it is unblemished, the *Kohen* brings it as an offering within the first year of its life, and he may invite anyone, including non-*Kohanim,* to share its meat. If the animal is blemished and not fit for an offering, it becomes the *Kohen's* personal property; he may slaughter it wherever he wishes, sell it, or share its meat with non-*Kohanim* or even non-Jews.

תִּשְׁפְּכֶנּוּ כַּמָּיִם — *You are to pour it . . . like water.* From the comparison of blood to water, the Sages derive two laws. First, just as it is permitted to use and derive benefit from water, so one may sell or use blood as he wishes, even though it is forbidden to drink it. Second, even though the blood of fowl, harts, and gazelles must be covered after slaughter (*Leviticus* 17:13), this does not

Do not feel distressed when you send him away free, for he has earned you double the wages of a hired hand* in six years; and may HASHEM, your God, bless you in all that you do.*

(On the Sabbath–Third) *Every firstborn male* that is born in your cattle and flock you are to sanctify to HASHEM, your God; you may not work with the firstborn of your bull and you may not shear the firstborn of your sheep. Eat it* before HASHEM, your God, year in, year out, in the place that HASHEM will choose; you and your household. If it has a blemish — lameness or blindness — or any serious blemish, do not offer it to HASHEM, your God. You may eat it within your gates, clean and unclean people alike, like the gazelle and the hart. However you may not eat the blood; you are to pour it upon the ground like water.**

Levi (on the Sabbath–Fourth) *Observe the month of springtime* and perform the Pesach service to HASHEM, your God, for in the month of springtime HASHEM, your God, took you out of Egypt at night.* You are to slaughter the Pesach offering to HASHEM, your God, from the flock — and also offer bulls* — in the place where HASHEM will choose to rest His Name. Do not eat leavened food with it, for seven days you are to eat matzos, bread of affliction,* for you departed from Egypt in haste — so that you will remember the day of your departure from Egypt all the days of your life.*

Third(on the Sabbath–Fifth) *No leaven of yours may be seen throughout your boundary for seven days; nor may any of the meat you have offered on the afternoon before the first day* remain until morning. You may not bring the Pesach offering in one of your private gates that HASHEM, your*

---

apply to cattle, sheep and goats. Their blood is likened to water, and need not be covered.

חֹדֶשׁ הָאָבִיב – *The month of springtime.* Since the Torah requires that Nissan, the month of Pesach, must fall in the springtime, the court adds a thirteenth month to the calendar at regular intervals. Since the twelve-month lunar year is about eleven days shorter than the solar year, the month of Nissan would become progressively earlier unless these months were added.

לָיְלָה – *At night.* The actual march out of Egypt took place in the morning, but Pharaoh freed the people in the middle of the night.

צֹאן וּבָקָר – *From the flock — and also offer bulls.* The Pesach offering comes *from the flock,* i.e. lambs or kids; the קָרְבַּן חֲגִיגָה [Chagigah], *festival peace-offerings,* may come from bulls as well. From the juxtaposition of *flock* and *bulls,* the Sages derive the law of an animal designated for a Pesach-offering that had not been offered on the fourteenth of Nissan, or money designated to purchase a Pesach offering, which was not used for that purpose. This animal or money should be used for the sort of offering that can come from both the *flock* and *bulls,* meaning peace-offerings [מוֹתַר פֶּסַח קָרֵב שְׁלָמִים].

מַצּוֹת לֶחֶם עֹנִי – *Matzos, bread of affliction.* If you wish to eat grain products during the seven days of Pesach, they must be matzah, i.e. unleavened bread. Matzah reminds us of the *affliction* of Egyptian slavery, because it is made of unadorned, unflavored, and unleavened flour and water — the sort of food that harried, poverty-stricken slaves would prepare for themselves.

בָּעֶרֶב בַּיּוֹם הָרִאשׁוֹן – *On the afternoon before the first day.* I.e., the Pesach offering, which comes the afternoon before the first Seder night.

Three time periods are mentioned here: (1) the Pesach offering is offered *in the afternoon;* (2) it is eaten after *the sun sets;* and (3) if any of its meat has not been eaten by morning, i.e., *the time of your departure from Egypt,* the leftovers must be burned.

נֹתֵ֥ן לָֽךְ׃ כִּ֠י אִֽם־אֶל־הַמָּק֞וֹם אֲשֶׁר־יִבְחַ֞ר יְהוָ֣ה אֱלֹהֶ֗יךָ לְשַׁכֵּ֣ן שְׁמ֔וֹ שָׁ֛ם תִּזְבַּ֥ח אֶת־הַפֶּ֖סַח בָּעָ֑רֶב כְּב֣וֹא הַשֶּׁ֔מֶשׁ מוֹעֵ֖ד צֵאתְךָ֥ מִמִּצְרָֽיִם׃ וּבִשַּׁלְתָּ֙ וְאָ֣כַלְתָּ֔ בַּמָּק֕וֹם אֲשֶׁ֥ר יִבְחַ֛ר יְהוָ֥ה אֱלֹהֶ֖יךָ בּ֑וֹ וּפָנִ֣יתָ בַבֹּ֔קֶר* וְהָלַכְתָּ֖ לְאֹהָלֶֽיךָ׃ שֵׁ֥שֶׁת יָמִ֖ים* תֹּאכַ֣ל מַצּ֑וֹת וּבַיּ֣וֹם הַשְּׁבִיעִ֗י עֲצֶ֙רֶת֙* לַיהוָ֣ה אֱלֹהֶ֔יךָ לֹ֥א תַעֲשֶׂ֖ה מְלָאכָֽה׃

רביעי (בשבת ששי) – שִׁבְעָ֥ה שָׁבֻעֹ֖ת תִּסְפָּר־לָ֑ךְ מֵהָחֵ֤ל חֶרְמֵשׁ֙* בַּקָּמָ֔ה תָּחֵ֣ל לִסְפֹּ֔ר שִׁבְעָ֖ה שָׁבֻעֽוֹת׃ וְעָשִׂ֜יתָ חַ֤ג שָׁבֻעוֹת֙ לַיהוָ֣ה אֱלֹהֶ֔יךָ מִסַּ֛ת* נִדְבַ֥ת יָדְךָ֖ אֲשֶׁ֣ר תִּתֵּ֑ן כַּאֲשֶׁ֥ר יְבָרֶכְךָ֖ יְהוָ֥ה אֱלֹהֶֽיךָ׃ וְשָׂמַחְתָּ֞ לִפְנֵ֣י ׀ יְהוָ֣ה אֱלֹהֶ֗יךָ אַתָּ֨ה וּבִנְךָ֣* וּבִתֶּךָ֮ וְעַבְדְּךָ֣ וַאֲמָתֶךָ֒ וְהַלֵּוִי֙ אֲשֶׁ֣ר בִּשְׁעָרֶ֔יךָ וְהַגֵּ֛ר וְהַיָּת֥וֹם וְהָאַלְמָנָ֖ה אֲשֶׁ֣ר בְּקִרְבֶּ֑ךָ בַּמָּק֗וֹם אֲשֶׁ֤ר יִבְחַר֙ יְהוָ֣ה אֱלֹהֶ֔יךָ לְשַׁכֵּ֥ן שְׁמ֖וֹ שָֽׁם׃ וְזָ֣כַרְתָּ֔ כִּי־עֶ֥בֶד הָיִ֖יתָ בְּמִצְרָ֑יִם וְשָׁמַרְתָּ֣ וְעָשִׂ֔יתָ אֶת־הַחֻקִּ֖ים הָאֵֽלֶּה׃

חמישי (בשבת שביעי) – חַ֧ג הַסֻּכֹּ֛ת תַּעֲשֶׂ֥ה לְךָ֖ שִׁבְעַ֣ת יָמִ֑ים בְּאָ֨סְפְּךָ֔ מִגָּרְנְךָ֖ וּמִיִּקְבֶֽךָ׃ וְשָׂמַחְתָּ֖* בְּחַגֶּ֑ךָ אַתָּ֨ה וּבִנְךָ֤ וּבִתֶּ֙ךָ֙ וְעַבְדְּךָ֣ וַאֲמָתֶ֔ךָ וְהַלֵּוִ֗י וְהַגֵּ֛ר וְהַיָּת֥וֹם וְהָאַלְמָנָ֖ה אֲשֶׁ֥ר בִּשְׁעָרֶֽיךָ׃ שִׁבְעַ֣ת יָמִ֗ים תָּחֹג֙ לַיהוָ֣ה אֱלֹהֶ֔יךָ בַּמָּק֖וֹם אֲשֶׁר־יִבְחַ֣ר יְהוָ֑ה כִּ֣י יְבָרֶכְךָ֞ יְהוָ֣ה אֱלֹהֶ֗יךָ בְּכֹ֤ל תְּבוּאָֽתְךָ֙ וּבְכֹל֙ מַעֲשֵׂ֣ה יָדֶ֔יךָ וְהָיִ֖יתָ אַ֥ךְ שָׂמֵֽחַ׃* שָׁל֣וֹשׁ פְּעָמִ֣ים ׀ בַּשָּׁנָ֡ה יֵרָאֶ֨ה כָל־זְכוּרְךָ֜ אֶת־פְּנֵ֣י ׀ יְהוָ֣ה אֱלֹהֶ֗יךָ בַּמָּקוֹם֙ אֲשֶׁ֣ר יִבְחָ֔ר בְּחַ֧ג הַמַּצּ֛וֹת וּבְחַ֥ג הַשָּׁבֻע֖וֹת וּבְחַ֣ג הַסֻּכּ֑וֹת וְלֹ֧א יֵרָאֶ֛ה אֶת־פְּנֵ֥י יְהוָ֖ה רֵיקָֽם׃* אִ֖ישׁ כְּמַתְּנַ֣ת יָד֑וֹ* כְּבִרְכַּ֛ת יְהוָ֥ה אֱלֹהֶ֖יךָ אֲשֶׁ֥ר נָֽתַן־לָֽךְ׃

וּפָנִיתָ בַבֹּקֶר – *In the morning you may turn back.* Whenever someone brings an offering, he is required to spend the following night in Jerusalem, and may not return home until morning. In the case of the Pesach offering, since the following morning is the first festival day of Pesach when it is forbidden to travel, he may not return home until the morning of the first Intermediate Day.

שֵׁשֶׁת יָמִים – *For six days.* But earlier we were told that matzos are eaten for *seven* days? Through hermeneutical means, the Sages derive that only on the Seder night is one *required* to eat matzah. During the rest of Passover, there is no positive commandment to eat matzah; only a prohibition against eating *chometz.*

עֲצֶרֶת – *An assembly.* Since the seventh day should be dedicated to service of God, work is prohibited.

מֵהָחֵל חֶרְמֵשׁ – *From when the sickle is first put.* The first grain to be cut is the barley for the Omer offering, which is brought on the second day of Pesach. The seven-week count is begun from that day.

מִסַּת – *Commensurate with.* On festivals, one is required to bring peace- and elevation-offerings. The number and value of such offerings depends on the wealth with which God has blessed him.

אַתָּה וּבִנְךָ – *You, your son.* Just as you will surely rejoice with your own family and servants, you should also see to it that the Levites, the poor and lonely are provided for. Your joy is incomplete unless you share it with others.

God, gives you. Only at the place that HASHEM will choose to rest His Name, there are you to slaughter the Pesach offering in the afternoon, when the sun descends, the appointed time of your departure from Egypt. You are to cook and eat it in the place that HASHEM will choose; and in the morning you may turn back and go to your shelters. For six days* you are to eat matzos and the seventh day shall be an assembly* to HASHEM, your God, you may not perform labor.*

Fourth (on the Sabbath – Sixth) *You are to count for yourselves seven weeks; from when the sickle is first put* to the standing crop, you are to begin counting seven weeks. Then you are to observe the festival of Shavuos for HASHEM, your God; the voluntary offerings that you give should be commensurate with* how much HASHEM, your God, will have blessed you. You are to rejoice before HASHEM, your God — you, your son,* your daughter, your slave, your maidservant, the Levite who is in your gates, the stranger, the orphan, and the widow who are among you — in the place where HASHEM, your God, will choose to rest His Name. And you are to remember that you were a slave in Egypt; and you are to observe and perform these decrees.*

Fifth (on the Sabbath – Seventh) *You are to observe the festival of Succos for seven days, when you gather in from your threshing floor and your wine cellar. You are to rejoice* on your festival — you, your son, your daughter, your slave, your maidservant, the Levite, the stranger, the orphan, and the widow who are in your gates. For seven days you are to celebrate to HASHEM, your God, in the place that HASHEM will choose; for HASHEM, your God, will have blessed you in all your crop and in all your handiwork, and you will be completely joyful.**

Three times a year all your males should appear before HASHEM, your God, in the place that He will choose: on the festival of Matzos, the festival of Shavuos, and the festival of Succos; and you are not to appear before HASHEM empty-handed. Everyone according to what he can give,* according to the blessing that HASHEM, your God, gives you.*

וְשָׂמַחְתָּ — *You are to rejoice.* Succos is the time of year when the crops are gathered in from the fields and the success of the past agricultural year is apparent. This makes it a time of great joy. In a deeper sense, Succos follows the season of repentance and atonement, when people 'gather in' their spiritual harvest. This commandment to rejoice on Succos is expressed in the prayers, in which Succos is described as זְמַן שִׂמְחָתֵנוּ, *the time of our gladness.*

אַךְ שָׂמֵחַ — *Completely joyful.* In its simple meaning, rather than a *mitzvah,* this is a Divine promise that we will be joyful. The Sages also derive from this phrase that Shemini Atzeres is included in the earlier commandment to rejoice on this festival.

רֵיקָם — *Empty-handed.* I.e, do not make your pilgrimage without bringing burnt and peace-offerings.

אִישׁ כְּמַתְּנַת יָדוֹ — *Everyone according to what he can give.* A person should give generously but not excessively, lest he become poor and require the charity of others. As the Sages say, one should not spend more than a fifth of his resources for the performance of a *mitzvah* (*Sforno*).

חצי קדיש

After the last *oleh* has completed his closing blessing, the second Torah Scroll is placed on the *bimah* alongside the first, and the reader recites Half-*Kaddish*.

יִתְגַּדַּל וְיִתְקַדַּשׁ שְׁמֵהּ רַבָּא. (.Cong – אָמֵן.) בְּעָלְמָא דִּי בְרָא כִרְעוּתֵהּ. וְיַמְלִיךְ מַלְכוּתֵהּ, בְּחַיֵּיכוֹן וּבְיוֹמֵיכוֹן וּבְחַיֵּי דְכָל בֵּית יִשְׂרָאֵל, בַּעֲגָלָא וּבִזְמַן קָרִיב. וְאִמְרוּ: אָמֵן.

(.Cong – אָמֵן. יְהֵא שְׁמֵהּ רַבָּא מְבָרַךְ לְעָלַם וּלְעָלְמֵי עָלְמַיָּא.)

יְהֵא שְׁמֵהּ רַבָּא מְבָרַךְ לְעָלַם וּלְעָלְמֵי עָלְמַיָּא.

יִתְבָּרַךְ וְיִשְׁתַּבַּח וְיִתְפָּאַר וְיִתְרוֹמַם וְיִתְנַשֵּׂא וְיִתְהַדָּר וְיִתְעַלֶּה וְיִתְהַלָּל שְׁמֵהּ דְּקֻדְשָׁא בְּרִיךְ הוּא (.Cong – בְּרִיךְ הוּא) – לְעֵלָּא מִן כָּל בִּרְכָתָא וְשִׁירָתָא תֻּשְׁבְּחָתָא וְנֶחֱמָתָא, דַּאֲמִירָן בְּעָלְמָא. וְאִמְרוּ: אָמֵן. (.Cong – אָמֵן.)

הגבהה וגלילה

The first Torah is raised. Each person looks at the Torah and recites aloud:

וְזֹאת הַתּוֹרָה אֲשֶׁר שָׂם מֹשֶׁה לִפְנֵי בְּנֵי יִשְׂרָאֵל,[1] עַל פִּי יהוה בְּיַד מֹשֶׁה.[2]

Some add:

עֵץ חַיִּים הִיא לַמַּחֲזִיקִים בָּהּ, וְתֹמְכֶיהָ מְאֻשָּׁר.[3] דְּרָכֶיהָ דַרְכֵי נֹעַם, וְכָל נְתִיבוֹתֶיהָ שָׁלוֹם.[4] אֹרֶךְ יָמִים בִּימִינָהּ, בִּשְׂמֹאלָהּ עֹשֶׁר וְכָבוֹד.[5] יהוה חָפֵץ לְמַעַן צִדְקוֹ, יַגְדִּיל תּוֹרָה וְיַאְדִּיר.[6]

מפטיר

As the first Torah is wound, tied, and covered, the *oleh* for *maftir* is called to the second Torah.

במדבר כט:לה-ל:א

בַּיּוֹם֙ הַשְּׁמִינִ֔י עֲצֶ֖רֶת* תִּהְיֶ֣ה לָכֶ֑ם כָּל־מְלֶ֥אכֶת עֲבֹדָ֖ה לֹ֥א תַעֲשֽׂוּ׃ וְהִקְרַבְתֶּ֨ם עֹלָ֜ה אִשֵּׁ֨ה רֵ֤יחַ נִיחֹ֙חַ֙ לַֽיהוָ֔ה פַּ֥ר אֶחָ֖ד אַ֣יִל אֶחָ֑ד* כְּבָשִׂ֧ים בְּנֵי־שָׁנָ֛ה שִׁבְעָ֖ה תְּמִימִֽם׃ מִנְחָתָ֣ם וְנִסְכֵּיהֶ֗ם לַפָּ֞ר לָאַ֧יִל וְלַכְּבָשִׂ֛ים בְּמִסְפָּרָ֖ם כַּמִּשְׁפָּֽט׃ וּשְׂעִ֥יר חַטָּ֖את אֶחָ֑ד מִלְּבַד֙ עֹלַ֣ת הַתָּמִ֔יד וּמִנְחָתָ֖הּ וְנִסְכָּֽהּ׃ אֵ֛לֶּה תַּעֲשׂ֥וּ לַֽיהוָ֖ה בְּמוֹעֲדֵיכֶ֑ם* לְבַ֨ד מִנִּדְרֵיכֶ֜ם וְנִדְבֹתֵיכֶ֗ם לְעֹלֹֽתֵיכֶם֙ וּלְמִנְחֹ֣תֵיכֶ֔ם וּלְנִסְכֵּיכֶ֖ם וּלְשַׁלְמֵיכֶֽם׃ וַיֹּ֥אמֶר מֹשֶׁ֖ה אֶל־בְּנֵ֣י יִשְׂרָאֵ֑ל כְּכֹ֛ל אֲשֶׁר־צִוָּ֥ה יְהוָ֖ה אֶת־מֹשֶֽׁה׃

⁂ Maftir

בַּיּוֹם הַשְּׁמִינִי עֲצֶרֶת – *The eighth day ... an assembly. Rashi* comments that the word עֲצֶרֶת derives from עצר, to *restrain*, and offers three interpretations based on this translation: (1) restrain yourselves from work; (2) restrain yourselves from leaving Jerusalem, because one must remain at least overnight after a festival; and (3) after a festival during which *Mussaf* offerings were brought daily to invoke God's protection for the seventy nations, God asks us to remain for one day that is devoted solely to the unique relationship of God and Israel.

HALF KADDISH

After the last *oleh* has completed his closing blessing, the second Torah Scroll is placed on the *bimah* alongside the first, and the reader recites Half-*Kaddish:*

יִתְגַּדַּל *May His great Name grow exalted and sanctified* (Cong.– *Amen.*) *in the world that He created as He willed. May He give reign to His kingship in your lifetimes and in your days, and in the lifetimes of the entire Family of Israel, swiftly and soon. Now respond: Amen.*

(Cong.– *Amen. May His great Name be blessed forever and ever.*)
May His great Name be blessed forever and ever.

Blessed, praised, glorified, exalted, extolled, mighty, upraised, and lauded be the Name of the Holy One, Blessed is He (Cong.– *Blessed is He*) — *beyond any blessing and song, praise and consolation that are uttered in the world. Now respond: Amen.* (Cong.– *Amen.*)

HAGBAHAH AND GELILAH

The first Torah is raised. Each person looks at the Torah and recites aloud:

This is the Torah that Moses placed before the Children of Israel,[1] upon the command of HASHEM, through Moses' hand.[2]

Some add:

עֵץ *It is a tree of life for those who grasp it, and its supporters are praiseworthy.[3] Its ways are ways of pleasantness and all its paths are peace.[4] Lengthy days are at its right; at its left are wealth and honor.[5] HASHEM desired, for the sake of its [Israel's] righteousness, that the Torah be made great and glorious.[6]*

MAFTIR

As the first Torah is wound, tied, and covered, the *oleh* for *maftir* is called to the second Torah.

Numbers 29:35-30:1

The eighth day shall be an assembly for you; you may not do any laborious work. You are to offer an elevation-offering, a fire-offering, a satisfying aroma to HASHEM; one bull, one ram,* seven lambs within their first years; they are all to be unblemished. Their meal-offerings and libations for the bull, the ram, and the lambs are to be in their proper numbers as required. And one he-goat for a sin-offering; aside from the continual elevation-offering, and its meal-offering and its libation. These are what you should offer to HASHEM on your appointed festivals;* aside from your vows and your free-will offerings for your elevation-offerings, your meal-offerings, your libations, and your peace-offerings.*

Moses spoke to the Children of Israel; according to everything that HASHEM commanded Moses.

(1) *Deuteronomy* 4:44. (2) *Numbers* 9:23. (3) *Proverbs* 3:18. (4) 3:17. (5) 3:16. (6) *Isaiah* 42:21.

פַּר אֶחָד אַיִל אֶחָד — *One bull, one ram.* Unlike Succos when the *Mussaf* offerings symbolize the seventy national groups, on Shemini Atzeres, the *Mussaf* symbolizes God's one, Chosen nation.

בְּמוֹעֲדֵיכֶם — *On your appointed festivals.* This verse sums up the list of *Mussaf* offerings for all the respective festival days. The above list is required of the nation; individuals may make private *vows* and bring *free-willed offerings* as they see fit.

הגבהה וגלילה

The *maftir* completes his closing blessing.
Then the second Torah Scroll is raised and each person looks at the Torah and recites aloud:

וְזֹאת הַתּוֹרָה אֲשֶׁר שָׂם מֹשֶׁה לִפְנֵי בְּנֵי יִשְׂרָאֵל,[1] עַל פִּי יהוה בְּיַד מֹשֶׁה.[2]

Some add:

עֵץ חַיִּים הִיא לַמַּחֲזִיקִים בָּהּ, וְתֹמְכֶיהָ מְאֻשָּׁר.[3] דְּרָכֶיהָ דַרְכֵי נֹעַם, וְכָל נְתִיבוֹתֶיהָ שָׁלוֹם.[4] אֹרֶךְ יָמִים בִּימִינָהּ, בִּשְׂמֹאלָהּ עֹשֶׁר וְכָבוֹד.[5] יהוה חָפֵץ לְמַעַן צִדְקוֹ, יַגְדִּיל תּוֹרָה וְיַאְדִּיר.[6]

After the Torah Scroll has been wound, tied and covered, the *maftir* recites the *Haftarah* blessings.

ברכה קודם ההפטרה

בָּרוּךְ אַתָּה יהוה אֱלֹהֵינוּ מֶלֶךְ הָעוֹלָם, אֲשֶׁר בָּחַר בִּנְבִיאִים טוֹבִים, וְרָצָה בְדִבְרֵיהֶם הַנֶּאֱמָרִים בֶּאֱמֶת, בָּרוּךְ אַתָּה יהוה, הַבּוֹחֵר בַּתּוֹרָה וּבְמֹשֶׁה עַבְדּוֹ, וּבְיִשְׂרָאֵל עַמּוֹ, וּבִנְבִיאֵי הָאֱמֶת וָצֶדֶק: (Cong. – אָמֵן.)

הפטרה לשמיני עצרת

מלכים א ח:נד-ט:א

וַיְהִי ׀ כְּכַלּוֹת שְׁלֹמֹה לְהִתְפַּלֵּל אֶל־יהוה אֵת כָּל־הַתְּפִלָּה וְהַתְּחִנָּה* הַזֹּאת קָם מִלִּפְנֵי מִזְבַּח יהוה מִכְּרֹעַ עַל־בִּרְכָּיו וְכַפָּיו פְּרֻשׂוֹת הַשָּׁמָיִם:* וַיַּעֲמֹד וַיְבָרֶךְ אֵת כָּל־קְהַל יִשְׂרָאֵל קוֹל גָּדוֹל לֵאמֹר: בָּרוּךְ יהוה אֲשֶׁר נָתַן מְנוּחָה לְעַמּוֹ יִשְׂרָאֵל כְּכֹל אֲשֶׁר דִּבֵּר* לֹא־נָפַל דָּבָר אֶחָד מִכֹּל דְּבָרוֹ הַטּוֹב אֲשֶׁר דִּבֶּר בְּיַד מֹשֶׁה עַבְדּוֹ: יְהִי יהוה אֱלֹהֵינוּ עִמָּנוּ כַּאֲשֶׁר הָיָה עִם־אֲבֹתֵינוּ אַל־יַעַזְבֵנוּ וְאַל־יִטְּשֵׁנוּ: לְהַטּוֹת לְבָבֵנוּ אֵלָיו לָלֶכֶת בְּכָל־דְּרָכָיו

Haftarah for Shemini Atzeres

The *Haftarah* of the second day was the beginning of Solomon's dedication of the new Temple; today's *Haftarah* is its conclusion. As noted above, the celebration extended throughout Succos. In the selection for today's *Haftarah*, Solomon gave his blessing to the people and finally, on the eighth day of Succos — Shemini Atzeres — he told the people that they were free to depart.

כָּל הַתְּפִלָּה וְהַתְּחִנָּה – *This entire prayer and supplication.* In a long and moving prayer, Solomon had asked God to maintain His Presence on the Temple and accept the prayers and offerings of all who would come there. Generally the difference between תְּפִלָּה, *prayer;* and תְּחִנָּה, *supplication,* is as follows: In *prayer,* one follows a standard formula, as in our regular prayers, and seeks to achieve a closeness to God by means of which he will be blessed with his needs. Thus, in prayer we begin by praising Him, then list our requests, and close by praising Him. If someone is successful in achieving a degree of closeness to God, it is natural that his requests will be granted, because their achievement will provide him with the peace of mind and the means with which to further his service of God. *Supplication,* on the other hand, is a plea for gifts and grace that the supplicant cannot justify through

HAGBAHAH AND GELILAH

The *maftir* completes his closing blessing.
Then the second Torah Scroll is raised and each person looks at the Torah and recites aloud:

This is the Torah that Moses placed before the Children of Israel,[1] upon the command of HASHEM, through Moses' hand.[2]

Some add:

עֵץ *It is a tree of life for those who grasp it, and its supporters are praiseworthy.[3] Its ways are ways of pleasantness and all its paths are peace.[4] Lengthy days are at its right; at its left are wealth and honor.[5] HASHEM desired, for the sake of its [Israel's] righteousness, that the Torah be made great and glorious.[6]*

After the Torah Scroll has been wound, tied and covered, the *maftir* recites the *Haftarah* blessings.

BLESSING BEFORE THE HAFTARAH

בָּרוּךְ *Blessed are You, HASHEM, our God, King of the universe, Who has chosen good prophets* and was pleased with their words* that were uttered with truth. Blessed are You, HASHEM,* Who chooses the Torah; Moses, His servant; Israel, His nation; and the prophets of truth and righteousness.* (Cong.— *Amen.*)

HAFTARAH FOR SHEMINI ATZERES

I Kings 8:54-9:1

When Solomon had finished praying to HASHEM this entire prayer and supplication, he stood up from having knealt on his knees with his hands spread out heavanward before the Altar of HASHEM. He stood and blessed the entire congregation of Israel in a loud voice, saying: 'Blessed is HASHEM Who has granted rest to His people Israel according to all that He has spoken;* not one word has been defaulted from the entire gracious promise that He pronounced through His servant Moses. May HASHEM, our God, be with us, as He was with our forefathers, may He not forsake us nor cast us off. To turn our hearts to Him, to walk in all*

(1) *Deuteronomy* 4:44. (2) *Numbers* 9:23. (3) *Proverbs* 3:18. (4) 3:17. (5) 3:16. (6) *Isaiah* 42:21.

any merits or good deeds of his own. In Solomon's prayer, for example, he asks God to grant his supplication on behalf of the Jewish people, indicating that his pleas could be granted only for the sake of the nation, not because he personally deserves it.

וְכַפָּיו פְּרֻשׂוֹת הַשָּׁמָיִם — *With his hands spread out heavenward.* Solomon held up his hands to signify that just as his hands were empty at that moment, so, too, they had never taken anything from the funds or precious materials that had been assembled for the construction of the Temple (*Yerushalmi Berachos* 1:5). At that moment of national rejoicing Solomon demonstrated publicly that no accomplishment justifies negligence of honesty. People engaged in God's work must be able to account for every penny that has passed through their hands. Moses, too, upon completion of the Tabernacle, made a full accounting of all the funds and materials that had been collected under his supervision.

כְּכֹל אֲשֶׁר דִּבֵּר — *According to all that He had spoken.* God had promised that the Jewish people would cross the Jordan and settle the land finding peace and security (*Deuteronomy* 12:10). The first three centuries after Joshua led the people into *Eretz Yisrael* were marked by constant foreign incursions because, as the books of *Joshua* and *Judges* make plain, the people failed to purge the land of all the Canaanite

וְלִשְׁמֹר מִצְוֺתָיו וְחֻקָּיו וּמִשְׁפָּטָיו אֲשֶׁר צִוָּה אֶת־אֲבֹתֵינוּ: וְיִהְיוּ
דְבָרַי אֵלֶּה אֲשֶׁר הִתְחַנַּנְתִּי לִפְנֵי יהוה קְרֹבִים אֶל־יהוה אֱלֹהֵינוּ
יוֹמָם וָלָיְלָה לַעֲשׂוֹת | מִשְׁפַּט עַבְדּוֹ* וּמִשְׁפַּט עַמּוֹ יִשְׂרָאֵל דְּבַר־יוֹם
בְּיוֹמוֹ: לְמַעַן דַּעַת כָּל־עַמֵּי הָאָרֶץ כִּי יהוה הוּא הָאֱלֹהִים אֵין עוֹד:
וְהָיָה לְבַבְכֶם שָׁלֵם עִם יהוה אֱלֹהֵינוּ לָלֶכֶת בְּחֻקָּיו וְלִשְׁמֹר מִצְוֺתָיו
כַּיּוֹם הַזֶּה: וְהַמֶּלֶךְ וְכָל־יִשְׂרָאֵל עִמּוֹ זֹבְחִים זֶבַח לִפְנֵי יהוה: וַיִּזְבַּח
שְׁלֹמֹה אֵת זֶבַח הַשְּׁלָמִים אֲשֶׁר זָבַח לַיהוה בָּקָר עֶשְׂרִים וּשְׁנַיִם
אֶלֶף וְצֹאן מֵאָה וְעֶשְׂרִים אָלֶף וַיַּחְנְכוּ אֶת־בֵּית יהוה הַמֶּלֶךְ
וְכָל־בְּנֵי יִשְׂרָאֵל: בַּיּוֹם הַהוּא קִדַּשׁ הַמֶּלֶךְ* אֶת־תּוֹךְ הֶחָצֵר אֲשֶׁר
לִפְנֵי בֵית־יהוה כִּי־עָשָׂה שָׁם אֶת־הָעֹלָה וְאֶת־הַמִּנְחָה וְאֵת חֶלְבֵי
הַשְּׁלָמִים כִּי־מִזְבַּח הַנְּחֹשֶׁת* אֲשֶׁר לִפְנֵי יהוה קָטֹן מֵהָכִיל
אֶת־הָעֹלָה וְאֶת־הַמִּנְחָה וְאֵת חֶלְבֵי הַשְּׁלָמִים: וַיַּעַשׂ שְׁלֹמֹה
בָעֵת־הַהִיא | אֶת־הֶחָג וְכָל־יִשְׂרָאֵל עִמּוֹ קָהָל גָּדוֹל מִלְּבוֹא
חֲמָת* | עַד־נַחַל מִצְרַיִם לִפְנֵי יהוה אֱלֹהֵינוּ שִׁבְעַת יָמִים וְשִׁבְעַת
יָמִים* אַרְבָּעָה עָשָׂר יוֹם: בַּיּוֹם הַשְּׁמִינִי* שִׁלַּח אֶת־הָעָם וַיְבָרְכוּ
אֶת־הַמֶּלֶךְ וַיֵּלְכוּ לְאָהֳלֵיהֶם שְׂמֵחִים וְטוֹבֵי לֵב עַל כָּל־הַטּוֹבָה
אֲשֶׁר עָשָׂה יהוה לְדָוִד עַבְדּוֹ וּלְיִשְׂרָאֵל עַמּוֹ: וַיְהִי כְּכַלּוֹת שְׁלֹמֹה
לִבְנוֹת אֶת־בֵּית־יהוה וְאֶת־בֵּית הַמֶּלֶךְ וְאֵת כָּל־חֵשֶׁק שְׁלֹמֹה
אֲשֶׁר חָפֵץ לַעֲשׂוֹת:

---

nations. Only under David and Solomon was the entire country won by the Jewish people. When they did so and when they remained loyal to God and the Torah, they were no longer threatened by enemy invaders.

מִשְׁפַּט עַבְדּוֹ — *The just due of His servant.* As noted above, *supplication* implies a plea for an unearned, undeserved gift. Here, where Solomon asks that he be given what he personally requires, he joins his request with that of the national need. The individual's shortcomings can be submerged in the general merit. We find often that the Jewish people is treated kindly by God if they are unified and care about one another.

לְמַעַן דַּעַת כָּל עַמֵּי הָאָרֶץ — *That all the peoples of the earth shall know.* When God provides the needs of the Jewish people, everyone realizes that only He is the Master of the universe. Similarly, when Moses told the people of the momentous blessings that would be theirs if they heeded God's commandments, he said, *All the peoples of the world will see that God's Name has been proclaimed upon you — and they will be in awe of you* (*Deuteronomy* 28:10).

וְהָיָה לְבַבְכֶם שָׁלֵם — *May your heart remain wholesome.* Only if Israel remains loyal to God and His commandments can it hope that God will fulfill Solomon's blessing.

קִדַּשׁ הַמֶּלֶךְ — *The King sanctified.* According to R' Yehudah, King Solomon sanctified the stone floor of the Courtyard so that offerings could be burned upon it, since the Altar was not big enough for the enormous number of offerings that were brought during the dedication. R' Yose

His ways and to observe His commandments, decrees, and statutes that He commanded our forefathers. May these words of mine which I have supplicated before HASHEM, *be near to* HASHEM, *our God, by day and by night; that He may provide the just due of His servant* and the just due of His people Israel, each day's need in its day. That all the peoples of the earth shall know* that* HASHEM *is God — there is no other. May your heart remain wholesome* with* HASHEM, *our God, to follow His decrees and to observe His commandments as on this very day.'*

The King and all Israel with him were bringing an offering before HASHEM. *Solomon brought this peace-offering that he offered to* HASHEM: *twenty-two thousand cattle and one hundred twenty thousand sheep; and the King and all the Children of Israel dedicated the Temple of* HASHEM.

On that day the King sanctified the interior of the Courtyard that was before the Temple of* HASHEM, *for there he performed the service of the elevation-offering, the meal-offering, and the fats of the peace-offering; for the Copper Altar* that was before* HASHEM *was too small to contain the burnt-offering, the meal-offering, and the fats of the peace-offerings.*

At that time Solomon instituted the celebration — and all Israel was with him, a huge congregation from the approach to Chamos until the Brook of Egypt — before* HASHEM, *our God, seven days and then seven days* — totaling fourteen days. On the eighth day,* he released the people and they blessed the King; they went to their tents, joyous and good-hearted over all the good that* HASHEM *did for His servant David and His people Israel.*

And thus it was that Solomon had finished building the Temple of HASHEM *and the palace of the King, and everything that he had longed to make.*

---

disagrees. He holds that Solomon's Altar, which was many times the size of the one that had been used up to then, was big enough to accommodate the offerings of the dedication. Accordingly, Solomon sanctified the *new* Altar, not the floor of the Courtyard (*Zevachim* 59a-b).

מִזְבַּח הַנְּחֹשֶׁת — *The Copper Altar*. The original Altar built by Moses in the Wilderness was made of copper, while Solomon's was of stone. However, Solomon's was usually called the Copper Altar, because that was the commonly used name for hundreds of years. According to R' Yehudah (see above), the 'Copper' Altar now described as *too small* was actually Solomon's stone Altar. According to R' Yose, however, the original Altar, actually made of copper, was too small (ibid.).

חֲמָת — *Chamos*. Chamos was north of Jerusalem and the *Brook of Egypt* was to the south.

שִׁבְעַת יָמִים וְשִׁבְעַת יָמִים — *Seven days and then seven days*. The celebration began on the eighth of Tishrei and included Yom Kippur; that year, in deference to the joy of the Temple dedication, the Sages permitted the people to eat and drink on Yom Kippur. Then came the seven days of Succos, when the celebration continued.

בַּיּוֹם הַשְּׁמִינִי — *On the eighth day*. On Shemini Atzeres, Solomon gave the people permission to return home, although they could not actually begin the trip until the festival was over.

ברכות לאחר ההפטרה

After the *Haftarah* is read, the *oleh* recites the following blessings.

בָּרוּךְ אַתָּה יהוה אֱלֹהֵינוּ מֶלֶךְ הָעוֹלָם, צוּר כָּל הָעוֹלָמִים, צַדִּיק בְּכָל הַדּוֹרוֹת, הָאֵל הַנֶּאֱמָן הָאוֹמֵר וְעֹשֶׂה, הַמְּדַבֵּר וּמְקַיֵּם, שֶׁכָּל דְּבָרָיו אֱמֶת וָצֶדֶק. נֶאֱמָן אַתָּה הוּא יהוה אֱלֹהֵינוּ, וְנֶאֱמָנִים דְּבָרֶיךָ, וְדָבָר אֶחָד מִדְּבָרֶיךָ אָחוֹר לֹא יָשׁוּב רֵיקָם, כִּי אֵל מֶלֶךְ נֶאֱמָן (וְרַחֲמָן) אָתָּה. בָּרוּךְ אַתָּה יהוה, הָאֵל הַנֶּאֱמָן בְּכָל דְּבָרָיו. (Cong.– אָמֵן.)

רַחֵם עַל צִיּוֹן כִּי הִיא בֵּית חַיֵּינוּ, וְלַעֲלוּבַת נֶפֶשׁ תּוֹשִׁיעַ בִּמְהֵרָה בְיָמֵינוּ. בָּרוּךְ אַתָּה יהוה, מְשַׂמֵּחַ צִיּוֹן בְּבָנֶיהָ. (Cong.– אָמֵן.)

שַׂמְּחֵנוּ יהוה אֱלֹהֵינוּ בְּאֵלִיָּהוּ הַנָּבִיא עַבְדֶּךָ, וּבְמַלְכוּת בֵּית דָּוִד מְשִׁיחֶךָ, בִּמְהֵרָה יָבֹא וְיָגֵל לִבֵּנוּ, עַל כִּסְאוֹ לֹא יֵשֶׁב זָר וְלֹא יִנְחֲלוּ עוֹד אֲחֵרִים אֶת כְּבוֹדוֹ, כִּי בְשֵׁם קָדְשְׁךָ נִשְׁבַּעְתָּ לוֹ, שֶׁלֹּא יִכְבֶּה נֵרוֹ לְעוֹלָם וָעֶד. בָּרוּךְ אַתָּה יהוה, מָגֵן דָּוִד. (Cong.– אָמֵן.)

[On the Sabbath add the words in brackets.]

עַל הַתּוֹרָה, וְעַל הָעֲבוֹדָה, וְעַל הַנְּבִיאִים, וְעַל יוֹם [הַשַּׁבָּת הַזֶּה, וְיוֹם] הַשְּׁמִינִי חַג הָעֲצֶרֶת הַזֶּה שֶׁנָּתַתָּ לָנוּ יהוה אֱלֹהֵינוּ, [לִקְדֻשָּׁה וְלִמְנוּחָה,] לְשָׂשׂוֹן וּלְשִׂמְחָה, לְכָבוֹד וּלְתִפְאָרֶת. עַל הַכֹּל יהוה אֱלֹהֵינוּ, אֲנַחְנוּ מוֹדִים לָךְ, וּמְבָרְכִים אוֹתָךְ, יִתְבָּרַךְ שִׁמְךָ בְּפִי כָּל חַי תָּמִיד לְעוֹלָם וָעֶד. בָּרוּךְ אַתָּה יהוה, מְקַדֵּשׁ [הַשַּׁבָּת וְ]יִשְׂרָאֵל וְהַזְּמַנִּים. (Cong.– אָמֵן.)

ON WEEKDAYS THE SERVICE CONTINUES ON PAGE 956;

ON THE SABBATH, PAGE 954.

BLESSINGS AFTER THE HAFTARAH

After the *Haftarah* is read, the *oleh* recites the following blessings.

בָּרוּךְ *Blessed are You,* HASHEM, *King of the universe, Rock of all eternities, Righteous in all generations, the trustworthy God, Who says and does, Who speaks and fulfills, all of Whose words are true and righteous. Trustworthy are You,* HASHEM, *our God, and trustworthy are Your words, not one of Your words is turned back to its origin unfulfilled, for You are God, trustworthy (and compassionate) King. Blessed are You,* HASHEM, *the God Who is trustworthy in all His words.*

(Cong.— *Amen.)*

רַחֵם *Have mercy on Zion for it is the source of our life; to the one who is deeply humiliated bring salvation speedily, in our days. Blessed are You,* HASHEM, *Who gladdens Zion through her children.*

(Cong.— *Amen.)*

שַׂמְּחֵנוּ *Gladden us,* HASHEM, *our God, with Elijah the prophet, Your servant, and with the kingdom of the House of David, Your anointed, may he come speedily and cause our heart to exult. On his throne let no stranger sit nor let others continue to inherit his honor, for by Your holy Name You swore to him that his heir will not be extinguished forever and ever. Blessed are You,* HASHEM, *Shield of David.*

(Cong.— *Amen.)*

[On the Sabbath add the words in brackets.]

עַל הַתּוֹרָה *For the Torah reading, for the prayer service, for the reading from the Prophets [and for this day of Sabbath] and for this day of the Shemini Atzeres Festival that You,* HASHEM, *our God, have given us [for holiness and contentment,] for gladness and joy, for glory and splendor — for all this,* HASHEM, *our God, we gratefully thank You and bless You. May Your Name be blessed by the mouth of all the living, always, for all eternity. Blessed are You,* HASHEM, *Who sanctifies [the Sabbath,] Israel and the festival seasons.*

(Cong.— *Amen.)*

ON WEEKDAYS THE SERVICE CONTINUES ON PAGE 956;
ON THE SABBATH, PAGE 954.

יקום פרקן

On the Sabbath the following is recited. One praying alone omits the last two paragraphs.

יְקוּם פֻּרְקָן* מִן שְׁמַיָּא, חִנָּא וְחִסְדָּא וְרַחֲמֵי, וְחַיֵּי אֲרִיכֵי, וּמְזוֹנֵי רְוִיחֵי, וְסִיַּעְתָּא דִשְׁמַיָּא, וּבַרְיוּת גּוּפָא, וּנְהוֹרָא מַעַלְיָא, זַרְעָא חַיָּא וְקַיָּמָא, זַרְעָא דִּי לָא יִפְסוּק וְדִי לָא יִבְטוּל מִפִּתְגָּמֵי אוֹרַיְתָא. לְמָרָנָן וְרַבָּנָן חֲבוּרָתָא קַדִּישָׁתָא דִּי בְאַרְעָא דְיִשְׂרָאֵל וְדִי בְּבָבֶל,* לְרֵישֵׁי כַלֵּי,* וּלְרֵישֵׁי גַלְוָתָא,* וּלְרֵישֵׁי מְתִיבָתָא, וּלְדַיָּנֵי דִי בָבָא, לְכָל תַּלְמִידֵיהוֹן, וּלְכָל תַּלְמִידֵי תַלְמִידֵיהוֹן, וּלְכָל מָן דְּעָסְקִין בְּאוֹרַיְתָא. מַלְכָּא דְעָלְמָא יְבָרֵךְ יַתְהוֹן, יַפִּישׁ חַיֵּיהוֹן, וְיַסְגֵּא יוֹמֵיהוֹן, וְיִתֵּן אַרְכָה לִשְׁנֵיהוֹן, וְיִתְפָּרְקוּן וְיִשְׁתֵּזְבוּן מִן כָּל עָקָא וּמִן כָּל מַרְעִין בִּישִׁין. מָרַן דִּי בִשְׁמַיָּא יְהֵא בְסַעְדְּהוֹן, כָּל זְמַן וְעִדָּן. וְנֹאמַר: אָמֵן.

(.Cong. – אָמֵן)

יְקוּם פֻּרְקָן* מִן שְׁמַיָּא, חִנָּא וְחִסְדָּא וְרַחֲמֵי, וְחַיֵּי אֲרִיכֵי, וּמְזוֹנֵי רְוִיחֵי, וְסִיַּעְתָּא דִשְׁמַיָּא, וּבַרְיוּת גּוּפָא, וּנְהוֹרָא מַעַלְיָא, זַרְעָא חַיָּא וְקַיָּמָא, זַרְעָא דִּי לָא יִפְסוּק וְדִי לָא יִבְטוּל מִפִּתְגָּמֵי אוֹרַיְתָא. לְכָל קְהָלָא קַדִּישָׁא הָדֵין, רַבְרְבַיָּא עִם זְעֵרַיָּא, טַפְלָא וּנְשַׁיָּא, מַלְכָּא דְעָלְמָא יְבָרֵךְ יַתְכוֹן, יַפִּישׁ חַיֵּיכוֹן, וְיַסְגֵּא יוֹמֵיכוֹן, וְיִתֵּן אַרְכָה לִשְׁנֵיכוֹן, וְתִתְפָּרְקוּן וְתִשְׁתֵּזְבוּן מִן כָּל עָקָא וּמִן כָּל מַרְעִין בִּישִׁין, מָרַן דִּי בִשְׁמַיָּא יְהֵא בְסַעְדְּכוֹן, כָּל זְמַן וְעִדָּן. וְנֹאמַר: אָמֵן. (.Cong. – אָמֵן)

מִי שֶׁבֵּרַךְ* אֲבוֹתֵינוּ אַבְרָהָם יִצְחָק וְיַעֲקֹב, הוּא יְבָרֵךְ אֶת כָּל הַקָּהָל הַקָּדוֹשׁ הַזֶּה, עִם כָּל קְהִלּוֹת הַקֹּדֶשׁ, הֵם, וּנְשֵׁיהֶם, וּבְנֵיהֶם, וּבְנוֹתֵיהֶם, וְכָל אֲשֶׁר לָהֶם. וּמִי שֶׁמְּיַחֲדִים בָּתֵּי כְנֵסִיּוֹת לִתְפִלָּה, וּמִי שֶׁבָּאִים בְּתוֹכָם לְהִתְפַּלֵּל, וּמִי שֶׁנּוֹתְנִים נֵר לַמָּאוֹר, וְיַיִן לְקִדּוּשׁ וּלְהַבְדָּלָה, וּפַת לָאוֹרְחִים, וּצְדָקָה לָעֲנִיִּים, וְכָל מִי שֶׁעוֹסְקִים בְּצָרְכֵי צִבּוּר בֶּאֱמוּנָה, הַקָּדוֹשׁ בָּרוּךְ הוּא יְשַׁלֵּם שְׂכָרָם, וְיָסִיר מֵהֶם כָּל מַחֲלָה, וְיִרְפָּא לְכָל גּוּפָם, וְיִסְלַח לְכָל עֲוֹנָם, וְיִשְׁלַח בְּרָכָה וְהַצְלָחָה בְּכָל מַעֲשֵׂה יְדֵיהֶם, עִם כָּל יִשְׂרָאֵל אֲחֵיהֶם. וְנֹאמַר: אָמֵן.

(.Cong. – אָמֵן)

In many congregations, a prayer for the welfare of the State is recited by the Rabbi, *chazzan*, or *gabbai* at this point.

יקום פֻּרקן — *May salvation arise.* After reading from the Torah, a series of prayers is recited for those who teach, study, and support the Torah, and undertake the responsibilities of leadership. The first is a general prayer for all such people wherever they may be; consequently, it is recited even by people praying without a *minyan.* The second and third are prayers for the congregation with which one is praying; consequently, one praying alone omits them. The two יקום פֻּרקן prayers were composed by the Babylonian *geonim* after the close of the Talmudic period, in Aramaic, the spoken language of that country. These prayers were instituted specifically for the Sabbath, not for Festivals, except those that fall on the Sabbath.

דִּי בְאַרְעָא דְיִשְׂרָאֵל וְדִי בְּבָבֶל — *That are in Eretz Yisrael and that are in the Diaspora* [lit., *Babylonia*]. Although the Jewish community in *Eretz Yisrael* at that time was comparatively insignificant, the *geonim* gave honor and precedence to the Holy Land. Although the great

YEKUM PURKAN

On the Sabbath the following is recited. One praying alone omits the last two paragraphs.

יְקוּם פֻּרְקָן *May salvation arise* from heaven — grace, kindness, compassion, long life, abundant sustenance, heavenly assistance, physical health, lofty vision, living and surviving offspring, offspring who will neither interrupt nor cease from words of the Torah — for our masters and sages, the holy fellowships that are in Eretz Yisrael and that are in the Diaspora*: for the leaders of the Torah assemblages,* the leaders of the exile communities,* the leaders of the academies, the judges at the gateways, and all their students and to all the students of their students, and to everyone who engages in Torah study. May the King of the universe bless them, make their lives fruitful, increase their days and grant length to their years. May He save them and rescue them from every distress and from all serious ailments. May the Master in heaven come to their assistance at every season and time. Now let us respond: Amen.* (Cong.—*Amen.*)

יְקוּם פֻּרְקָן *May salvation arise* from heaven — grace, kindness, compassion, long life, abundant sustenance, heavenly assistance, physical health, lofty vision, living and surviving offspring, offspring who will neither interrupt nor cease from the words of the Torah — to this entire holy congregation, adults along with children, infants and women. May the King of the universe bless you, make your lives fruitful, increase your days, and grant length to your years. May He save you and rescue you from every distress and from all serious ailments. May the Master in heaven come to your assistance at every season and time. Now let us respond: Amen.* (Cong.—*Amen.*)

מִי שֶׁבֵּרַךְ *He Who blessed* our forefathers, Abraham, Isaac, and Jacob — may He bless this entire holy congregation along with all the holy congregations; them, their wives, sons, and daughters and all that is theirs; and those who dedicate synagogues for prayer and those who enter them to pray, and those who give lamps for illumination and wine for Kiddush and Havdalah, bread for guests and charity for the poor; and all who are involved faithfully in the needs of the community — may the Holy One, Blessed is He, pay their reward and remove from them every affliction, heal their entire body and forgive their every iniquity, and send blessing and success to all their handiwork, along with all Israel, their brethren. And let us say: Amen.* (Cong.—*Amen.*)

In many congregations, a prayer for the welfare of the State is recited by the Rabbi, *chazzan,* or *gabbai* at this point.

---

masses of Jewry no longer live in Babylonia, this timeless prayer refers to all Jewish communities; the word Babylonia is used as a general term for all Jewish communities outside of *Eretz Yisrael.*

לְרֵישֵׁי כַלֵּי — *For the leaders of the Torah assemblages.* These were the scholars who deliver Torah lectures on the Sabbath and Festivals to mass gatherings of the people.

וּלְרֵישֵׁי גַלְוָתָא — *The leaders of the exile communities.* The רֵישׁ גָּלוּתָא, *Exilarch,* was the leader of the Jewish nation, equivalent to the *Nassi* in earlier times. His headquarters was in Babylonia.

יְקוּם פֻּרְקָן ❧ — *May salvation arise.* This prayer refers to the congregation with which one is praying. Thus it omits mention of national teachers and leaders. It includes the entire congregation, young and old, men and women, because it prays for the welfare of each one.

מִי שֶׁבֵּרַךְ ❧ — *He Who blessed.* This is a prayer for this and all other congregations, and singles out the people who provide the means and services for the general good. *Bais Yosef* (284) notes that these charitable causes are stressed so that the entire community will hear of the great reward of those who study and support Torah, and others will emulate their deeds.

סדר הזכרת נשמות — יזכור

Those congregants whose parents are both living do not participate in the *Yizkor* service, but leave the synagogue and return when the congregation begins אַב הָרַחֲמִים (p. 962) after *Yizkor*.

Although the following verses are not part of the traditional *Yizkor* service, some congregations have adopted the custom of reciting them responsively before *Yizkor*.

יהוה, מָה אָדָם וַתֵּדָעֵהוּ, בֶּן אֱנוֹשׁ וַתְּחַשְּׁבֵהוּ.
אָדָם לַהֶבֶל דָּמָה, יָמָיו כְּצֵל עוֹבֵר.[1]
בַּבֹּקֶר יָצִיץ וְחָלָף, לָעֶרֶב יְמוֹלֵל וְיָבֵשׁ.[2]
לִמְנוֹת יָמֵינוּ כֵּן הוֹדַע, וְנָבִא לְבַב חָכְמָה.[3]
שְׁמָר תָּם וּרְאֵה יָשָׁר, כִּי אַחֲרִית לְאִישׁ שָׁלוֹם.[4]
אַךְ אֱלֹהִים יִפְדֶּה נַפְשִׁי מִיַּד שְׁאוֹל, כִּי יִקָּחֵנִי סֶלָה.[5]
כָּלָה שְׁאֵרִי וּלְבָבִי, צוּר לְבָבִי וְחֶלְקִי אֱלֹהִים לְעוֹלָם.[6]
וְיָשֹׁב הֶעָפָר עַל הָאָרֶץ כְּשֶׁהָיָה,
וְהָרוּחַ תָּשׁוּב אֶל הָאֱלֹהִים אֲשֶׁר נְתָנָהּ.[7]

תהלים צא

יֹשֵׁב בְּסֵתֶר עֶלְיוֹן, בְּצֵל שַׁדַּי יִתְלוֹנָן. אֹמַר לַיהוה, מַחְסִי וּמְצוּדָתִי, אֱלֹהַי אֶבְטַח בּוֹ. כִּי הוּא יַצִּילְךָ מִפַּח יָקוּשׁ, מִדֶּבֶר הַוּוֹת. בְּאֶבְרָתוֹ יָסֶךְ לָךְ, וְתַחַת כְּנָפָיו תֶּחְסֶה, צִנָּה וְסֹחֵרָה אֲמִתּוֹ. לֹא תִירָא מִפַּחַד לָיְלָה, מֵחֵץ יָעוּף יוֹמָם. מִדֶּבֶר בָּאֹפֶל יַהֲלֹךְ, מִקֶּטֶב יָשׁוּד צָהֳרָיִם. יִפֹּל מִצִּדְּךָ אֶלֶף, וּרְבָבָה מִימִינֶךָ, אֵלֶיךָ לֹא יִגָּשׁ. רַק בְּעֵינֶיךָ תַבִּיט, וְשִׁלֻּמַת רְשָׁעִים תִּרְאֶה. כִּי אַתָּה יהוה מַחְסִי, עֶלְיוֹן שַׂמְתָּ מְעוֹנֶךָ. לֹא תְאֻנֶּה אֵלֶיךָ רָעָה, וְנֶגַע לֹא יִקְרַב בְּאָהֳלֶךָ. כִּי מַלְאָכָיו יְצַוֶּה לָּךְ, לִשְׁמָרְךָ בְּכָל דְּרָכֶיךָ. עַל כַּפַּיִם יִשָּׂאוּנְךָ, פֶּן תִּגֹּף בָּאֶבֶן רַגְלֶךָ. עַל שַׁחַל וָפֶתֶן תִּדְרֹךְ, תִּרְמֹס כְּפִיר וְתַנִּין. כִּי בִי חָשַׁק וַאֲפַלְּטֵהוּ, אֲשַׂגְּבֵהוּ, כִּי יָדַע שְׁמִי. יִקְרָאֵנִי וְאֶעֱנֵהוּ, עִמּוֹ אָנֹכִי בְצָרָה, אֲחַלְּצֵהוּ וַאֲכַבְּדֵהוּ. אֹרֶךְ יָמִים אַשְׂבִּיעֵהוּ, וְאַרְאֵהוּ בִּישׁוּעָתִי. אֹרֶךְ יָמִים אַשְׂבִּיעֵהוּ, וְאַרְאֵהוּ בִּישׁוּעָתִי.

YIZKOR / יִזְכֹּר

The ancient custom of recalling the souls of the departed and contributing to charity in their memory is rooted in the fundamental Jewish belief in the eternity of the soul. When physical life ends, only the body dies, but the soul ascends to the realm of the spirit where it regularly attains higher levels of purity and holiness.

When this life is over, the soul can no longer perform good deeds; that method of attaining merit is the sole province of mortal man who must struggle with the baseness and selfishness of his animal nature. But there is a way that the disembodied soul can derive new sources of merit. History is a continuum. If we, the living, give charity or do good deeds due to the lasting influence or in memory of a departed parent or other loved one, the merit is truly that of the soul in its spiritual realm. Moreover, God in His mercy credits our deeds to the departed one because he or she would have done the same were it possible. Even if the departed one was too poor to have made contributions to charity, the soul benefits nonetheless, because it may be assumed that he or she would have been charitable, had sufficient means been available. But mere intentions do not suffice; only accomplishment can achieve this purpose. The intention to give and the fulfillment of that intention are both necessary; consequently, the pledges to charity should be redeemed as soon as possible after Yom Kippur.

It should be noted that a נֶדֶר, *vow*, is a very serious matter in Jewish law, and one must be scrupulous in fulfilling his vows. In order to avoid the possibility that one may make a pledge to charity and then forget to redeem it, we follow the practice of many *machzorim* in not using the word נֶדֶר, *vow*, in the *Yizkor* text. Instead we use

YIZKOR

Those congregants whose parents are both living do not participate in the *Yizkor* service, but leave the synagogue and return when the congregation begins אַב הָרַחֲמִים (p. 962) after *Yizkor*.

Although the following verses are not part of the traditional *Yizkor* service, some congregations have adopted the custom of reciting them responsively before *Yizkor*.

יהוה *HASHEM, what is man that You recognize him? The son of a frail human that You reckon with him?*
Man is like a breath, his days are like a passing shadow.[1]
In the morning it blossoms and is rejuvenated, by evening it is cut down and brittle.[2]
According to the count of our days, so may You teach us;
then we shall acquire a heart of wisdom.[3]
Safeguard the perfect and watch the upright, for the destiny of that man is peace.[4]
But God will redeem my soul from the grip of the Lower World,
for He will take me, Selah![5]
My flesh and my heart yearn — Rock of my heart, and my portion is God, forever.[6]
Thus the dust returns to the ground as it was, and the spirit returns to God who gave it.[7]

Psalm 91

יֹשֵׁב *Whoever sits in the refuge of the Most High, he shall dwell in the shadow of the Almighty. I will say of HASHEM, 'He is my refuge and my fortress, my God, I will trust in Him.' That He will deliver you from the ensnaring trap and from devastating pestilence. With His pinion He will cover you, and beneath His wings you will be protected; shield and armor is His truth. You shall not be afraid of the terror of night, nor of the arrow that flies by day; nor the pestilence that walks in gloom, nor the destroyer who lays waste at noon. Let a thousand encamp at your side and a myriad at your right hand, but to you they shall not approach. You will merely peer with your eyes and you will see the retribution of the wicked. Because [you said], 'You, HASHEM, are my refuge'; you have made the Most High your dwelling place. No evil will befall you, nor will any plague come near your tent. He will charge His angels for you, to protect you in all your ways. On their palms they will carry you, lest you strike your foot against a stone. Upon the lion and the viper you will tread; you will trample the young lion and the serpent. For he has yearned for Me and I will deliver him; I will elevate him because he knows My Name. He will call upon Me and I will answer him, I am with him in distress, I will release him and I will honor him. I will satisfy him with long life and show him My salvation. I will satisfy him with long life and show him My salvation.*

(1) *Psalms* 144:3-4. (2) 90:6. (3) 90:12. (4) 37:37. (5) 49:16. (6) 73:26. (7) *Ecclesiastes* 12:7.

the form שֶׁבְּלִי נֶדֶר אֶתֵּן, *without making a vow I shall give.*

It is virtually a universal custom that those whose parents are still living leave the synagogue during *Yizkor*. This is done to avoid the 'evil eye,' i.e., the resentment that might be felt by those without parents toward those whose parents are still living. *R' Elie Munk* suggests a further reason: we wish to avoid the possibility that people with living parents may mistakenly join in reciting *Yizkor*.

In most congregations children do not recite *Yizkor* in the first year after their parent's death, because they may become very emotional and disturb the prayers of others.

The earliest source of the custom to recite *Yizkor* is *Midrash Tanchuma, Haazinu,* which cites the rite of recalling the departed and pledging to contribute to charity on their behalf on Yom Kippur. In *Shulchan Aruch (Orach Chaim* 621:6), *Bais Yosef* records that on Yom Kippur it is customary to pledge to charity as a merit to the departed; and *Rama* adds the Ashkenazic custom of reciting Yizkor. However there is no mention in *Shulchan Aruch* of Yizkor on other days.

Ashkenazic Jewry's custom of reciting *Yizkor* on the last days of Pesach and Shavuos and on Shemini Atzeres may have begun at the time of the Crusades, when bloody massacres by the 'holy' warriors wiped out many Jewish communities, and seriously depleted many others. The general rule is that *Yizkor* is recited when the Torah portion of כָּל הַבְּכוֹר, *Every firstborn,* is read, because this portion includes the exhortation that everyone should give to charity according to the degree with which God has blessed him. Since the charity of their children and other close relatives is a source of merit for the departed, it is natural that the charity commanded by the Torah reading should be coupled with a prayer for their souls.

In addition to *Yizkor* for parents, it is also recited for other close relatives and for martyrs who have perished עַל קִדּוּשׁ הַשֵּׁם, *in sanctification of God's Name.*

Whenever the name of the deceased is mentioned in the *Yizkor* service, it is given in the following form: the Hebrew name of the deceased followed by the word בֶּן, *son of* — or, בַּת, *daughter of* — and then the deceased's father's Hebrew name.

FOR ONE'S FATHER

יִזְכֹּר אֱלֹהִים* נִשְׁמַת אָבִי מוֹרִי (name of the deceased) שֶׁהָלַךְ לְעוֹלָמוֹ, בַּעֲבוּר שֶׁבְּלִי נֶדֶר אֶתֵּן צְדָקָה בַּעֲדוֹ. בִּשְׂכַר זֶה תְּהֵא נַפְשׁוֹ צְרוּרָה בִּצְרוֹר הַחַיִּים* עִם נִשְׁמוֹת אַבְרָהָם יִצְחָק וְיַעֲקֹב, שָׂרָה רִבְקָה רָחֵל וְלֵאָה, וְעִם שְׁאָר צַדִּיקִים וְצִדְקָנִיּוֹת שֶׁבְּגַן עֵדֶן.* וְנֹאמַר: אָמֵן.

FOR ONE'S MOTHER

יִזְכֹּר אֱלֹהִים* נִשְׁמַת אִמִּי מוֹרָתִי (name of the deceased) שֶׁהָלְכָה לְעוֹלָמָהּ, בַּעֲבוּר שֶׁבְּלִי נֶדֶר אֶתֵּן צְדָקָה בַּעֲדָהּ. בִּשְׂכַר זֶה תְּהֵא נַפְשָׁהּ צְרוּרָה בִּצְרוֹר הַחַיִּים* עִם נִשְׁמוֹת אַבְרָהָם יִצְחָק וְיַעֲקֹב, שָׂרָה רִבְקָה רָחֵל וְלֵאָה, וְעִם שְׁאָר צַדִּיקִים וְצִדְקָנִיּוֹת שֶׁבְּגַן עֵדֶן.* וְנֹאמַר: אָמֵן.

FOR A RELATIVE

יִזְכֹּר אֱלֹהִים* נִשְׁמַת

wife	husband	daughter	son	sister	brother	aunt	uncle	grandmother	grandfather
אִשְׁתִּי	בַּעְלִי	בִּתִּי	בְּנִי	אֲחוֹתִי	אָחִי	דּוֹדָתִי	דּוֹדִי	זְקֶנְתִּי	זְקֵנִי

for a man

(name of the deceased) שֶׁהָלַךְ לְעוֹלָמוֹ, בַּעֲבוּר שֶׁבְּלִי נֶדֶר אֶתֵּן צְדָקָה בַּעֲדוֹ. בִּשְׂכַר זֶה תְּהֵא נַפְשׁוֹ צְרוּרָה בִּצְרוֹר הַחַיִּים* עִם נִשְׁמוֹת אַבְרָהָם יִצְחָק וְיַעֲקֹב, שָׂרָה רִבְקָה רָחֵל וְלֵאָה, וְעִם שְׁאָר צַדִּיקִים וְצִדְקָנִיּוֹת שֶׁבְּגַן עֵדֶן.* וְנֹאמַר: אָמֵן.

for a woman

(name of the deceased) שֶׁהָלְכָה לְעוֹלָמָהּ, בַּעֲבוּר שֶׁבְּלִי נֶדֶר אֶתֵּן צְדָקָה בַּעֲדָהּ. בִּשְׂכַר זֶה תְּהֵא נַפְשָׁהּ צְרוּרָה בִּצְרוֹר הַחַיִּים* עִם נִשְׁמוֹת אַבְרָהָם יִצְחָק וְיַעֲקֹב, שָׂרָה רִבְקָה רָחֵל וְלֵאָה, וְעִם שְׁאָר צַדִּיקִים וְצִדְקָנִיּוֹת שֶׁבְּגַן עֵדֶן.* וְנֹאמַר: אָמֵן.

FOR ONE'S EXTENDED FAMILY

יִזְכֹּר אֱלֹהִים* נִשְׁמוֹת זְקֵנַי וּזְקֵנוֹתַי, דּוֹדַי וְדוֹדוֹתַי, אַחַי וְאַחְיוֹתַי, הֵן מִצַּד אָבִי, הֵן מִצַּד אִמִּי, שֶׁהָלְכוּ לְעוֹלָמָם, בַּעֲבוּר שֶׁבְּלִי נֶדֶר אֶתֵּן צְדָקָה בַּעֲדָם. בִּשְׂכַר זֶה תִּהְיֶינָה נַפְשׁוֹתֵיהֶם צְרוּרוֹת בִּצְרוֹר הַחַיִּים* עִם נִשְׁמוֹת אַבְרָהָם יִצְחָק וְיַעֲקֹב, שָׂרָה רִבְקָה רָחֵל וְלֵאָה, וְעִם שְׁאָר צַדִּיקִים וְצִדְקָנִיּוֹת שֶׁבְּגַן עֵדֶן.* וְנֹאמַר: אָמֵן.

FOR MARTYRS

יִזְכֹּר אֱלֹהִים* נִשְׁמוֹת (כָּל קְרוֹבַי וּקְרוֹבוֹתַי, הֵן מִצַּד אָבִי, הֵן מִצַּד אִמִּי) הַקְּדוֹשִׁים וְהַטְּהוֹרִים שֶׁהוּמְתוּ וְשֶׁנֶּהֶרְגוּ וְשֶׁנִּשְׁחֲטוּ וְשֶׁנִּשְׂרְפוּ וְשֶׁנִּטְבְּעוּ וְשֶׁנֶּחְנְקוּ עַל קִדּוּשׁ הַשֵּׁם, בַּעֲבוּר שֶׁבְּלִי נֶדֶר אֶתֵּן צְדָקָה בְּעַד הַזְכָּרַת נִשְׁמוֹתֵיהֶם. בִּשְׂכַר זֶה תִּהְיֶינָה נַפְשׁוֹתֵיהֶם צְרוּרוֹת בִּצְרוֹר הַחַיִּים* עִם נִשְׁמוֹת אַבְרָהָם יִצְחָק וְיַעֲקֹב, שָׂרָה רִבְקָה רָחֵל וְלֵאָה, וְעִם שְׁאָר צַדִּיקִים וְצִדְקָנִיּוֹת שֶׁבְּגַן עֵדֶן.* וְנֹאמַר: אָמֵן.

Whenever the name of the deceased is mentioned in the *Yizkor* service, it is given in the following form: the Hebrew name of the deceased followed by בֶּן, *son of* — or, בַּת, *daughter of* — and then the deceased's father's Hebrew name.

FOR ONE'S FATHER

יִזְכֹּר *May God remember* the soul of my father, my teacher,* (name of the deceased) *who has gone on to his world, because, without making a vow, I shall give to charity on his behalf. As reward for this, may his soul be bound in the Bond of Life,* together with the souls of Abraham, Isaac, and Jacob; Sarah, Rebecca, Rachel, and Leah; and together with the other righteous men and women in the Garden of Eden.* Now let us respond: Amen.*

FOR ONE'S MOTHER

יִזְכֹּר *May God remember* the soul of my mother, my teacher,* (name of the deceased) *who has gone on to her world, because, without making a vow, I shall give to charity on her behalf. As reward for this, may her soul be bound in the Bond of Life,* together with the souls of Abraham, Isaac, and Jacob; Sarah, Rebecca, Rachel, and Leah; and together with the other righteous men and women in the Garden of Eden.* Now let us respond: Amen.*

FOR A RELATIVE

יִזְכֹּר *May God remember* the soul of my grandfather/grandmother/uncle/aunt/brother/sister/son/daughter/husband/wife* (name of the deceased) *who has gone on to his/her world, because, without making a vow, I shall give to charity on his/her behalf. As reward for this, may his/her soul be bound in the Bond of Life,* together with the souls of Abraham, Isaac, and Jacob; Sarah, Rebecca, Rachel, and Leah; and together with the other righteous men and women in the Garden of Eden.* Now let us respond: Amen.*

FOR ONE'S EXTENDED FAMILY

יִזְכֹּר *May God remember* the souls of my grandfathers and grandmothers, uncles and aunts, brothers and sisters both on my father's side and on my mother's side, who went on to their world, because, without making a vow, I shall give to charity on their behalf. As reward for this, may their souls be bound in the Bond of Life,* together with the souls of Abraham, Isaac, and Jacob; Sarah, Rebecca, Rachel, and Leah; and together with the other righteous men and women in the Garden of Eden.* Now let us respond: Amen.*

FOR MARTYRS

יִזְכֹּר *May God remember* the souls of (all my relatives, both on my father's side and on my mother's side), the holy and pure ones who were killed, murdered, slaughtered, burned, drowned and strangled for the sanctification of the Name, because, without making a vow, I shall give to charity on their behalf. As reward for this, may their souls be bound in the Bond of Life,* together with the souls of Abraham, Isaac, and Jacob; Sarah, Rebecca, Rachel, and Leah; and together with the other righteous men and women in the Garden of Eden.* Now let us respond: Amen.*

יִזְכֹּר אֱלֹהִים — *May God remember.* In calling upon God to 'remember' the soul of the departed, we do not suggest that the possibility of forgetting exists before the All-Knowing One. Rather we pray that in return for our devotion and generosity, God should take cognizance of the new source of merit for the soul whose memory is now influencing our conduct.

בִּצְרוֹר הַחַיִּים — *In the Bond of Life.* The ultimate which is unlimited by the constraints of time and space and the weakness of flesh. The greater the merit achieved by a soul during its time on earth — or as a result of our good deeds in its memory — the more it is bound together with the souls of the Patriarchs and Matriarchs.

בְּגַן עֵדֶן — *In the Garden of Eden.* Although literally this is the place where Adam and Eve lived until their sin caused them to be driven out,

FOR MEMBERS OF THE ISRAEL DEFENSE FORCE

[The following text is taken from the *Minchas Yerushalayim Siddur.*]

יִזְכֹּר אֱלֹהִים אֶת נִשְׁמוֹת חַיָּלֵי צְבָא הַהֲגָנָּה לְיִשְׂרָאֵל שֶׁמָּסְרוּ נַפְשָׁם עַל קְדֻשַּׁת הַשֵּׁם, הָעָם וְהָאָרֶץ, וְנָפְלוּ מוֹת גִּבּוֹרִים בְּמִלְחֶמֶת הַשִּׁחְרוּר, וּבְמַעַרְכוֹת סִינַי בְּתַפְקִידֵי הֲגָנָּה וּבִטָּחוֹן. מִנְּשָׁרִים קַלּוּ, וּמֵאֲרָיוֹת גָּבֵרוּ, בְּהֵחָלְצָם לְעֶזְרַת הָעָם, וְהִרְווּ בְּדָמָם הַטָּהוֹר אֶת רִגְבֵי אַדְמַת קָדְשֵׁנוּ וּמִדְבְּרוֹת סִינָי. זֵכֶר עֲקֵדָתָם וּמַעֲשֵׂי גְבוּרָתָם לֹא יָסוּפוּ מֵאִתָּנוּ לְעוֹלָמִים. תִּהְיֶינָה נִשְׁמוֹתֵיהֶם צְרוּרוֹת בִּצְרוֹר הַחַיִּים עִם נִשְׁמוֹת אַבְרָהָם יִצְחָק וְיַעֲקֹב, וְעִם נִשְׁמוֹת שְׁאָר גִּבּוֹרֵי יִשְׂרָאֵל וּקְדוֹשָׁיו שֶׁבְּגַן עֵדֶן. אָמֵן.

After reciting *Yizkor* it is customary to recite the following prayers. It is permitted to mention many names in this prayer, but it is preferable to recite separate prayers for men and women.

FOR AN INDIVIDUAL

אֵל מָלֵא רַחֲמִים, שׁוֹכֵן בַּמְּרוֹמִים, הַמְצֵא מְנוּחָה נְכוֹנָה* עַל כַּנְפֵי הַשְּׁכִינָה,* בְּמַעֲלוֹת קְדוֹשִׁים וּטְהוֹרִים* כְּזֹהַר הָרָקִיעַ מַזְהִירִים,

for a man

אֶת נִשְׁמַת (name of the deceased) שֶׁהָלַךְ לְעוֹלָמוֹ, בַּעֲבוּר שֶׁבְּלִי נֶדֶר אֶתֵּן צְדָקָה בְּעַד הַזְכָּרַת נִשְׁמָתוֹ, בְּגַן עֵדֶן תְּהֵא מְנוּחָתוֹ, לָכֵן בַּעַל הָרַחֲמִים יַסְתִּירֵהוּ בְּסֵתֶר כְּנָפָיו לְעוֹלָמִים, וְיִצְרוֹר בִּצְרוֹר הַחַיִּים אֶת נִשְׁמָתוֹ, יהוה הוּא נַחֲלָתוֹ, וְיָנוּחַ בְּשָׁלוֹם עַל מִשְׁכָּבוֹ. וְנֹאמַר: אָמֵן.

for a woman

אֶת נִשְׁמַת (name of the deceased) שֶׁהָלְכָה לְעוֹלָמָהּ, בַּעֲבוּר שֶׁבְּלִי נֶדֶר אֶתֵּן צְדָקָה בְּעַד הַזְכָּרַת נִשְׁמָתָהּ, בְּגַן עֵדֶן תְּהֵא מְנוּחָתָהּ, לָכֵן בַּעַל הָרַחֲמִים יַסְתִּירֶהָ בְּסֵתֶר כְּנָפָיו לְעוֹלָמִים, וְיִצְרוֹר בִּצְרוֹר הַחַיִּים אֶת נִשְׁמָתָהּ, יהוה הוּא נַחֲלָתָהּ, וְתָנוּחַ בְּשָׁלוֹם עַל מִשְׁכָּבָהּ. וְנֹאמַר: אָמֵן.

FOR A GROUP

אֵל מָלֵא רַחֲמִים, שׁוֹכֵן בַּמְּרוֹמִים, הַמְצֵא מְנוּחָה נְכוֹנָה* עַל כַּנְפֵי הַשְּׁכִינָה,* בְּמַעֲלוֹת קְדוֹשִׁים וּטְהוֹרִים* כְּזֹהַר הָרָקִיעַ מַזְהִירִים,

for men

אֶת נִשְׁמוֹת (names of the deceased) שֶׁהָלְכוּ לְעוֹלָמָם, בַּעֲבוּר שֶׁבְּלִי נֶדֶר אֶתֵּן צְדָקָה בְּעַד הַזְכָּרַת נִשְׁמוֹתֵיהֶם, בְּגַן עֵדֶן תְּהֵא מְנוּחָתָם, לָכֵן בַּעַל הָרַחֲמִים יַסְתִּירֵם בְּסֵתֶר כְּנָפָיו לְעוֹלָמִים, וְיִצְרוֹר בִּצְרוֹר הַחַיִּים אֶת נִשְׁמוֹתֵיהֶם, יהוה הוּא נַחֲלָתָם, וְיָנוּחוּ בְּשָׁלוֹם עַל מִשְׁכְּבוֹתֵיהֶם. וְנֹאמַר: אָמֵן.

for women

אֶת נִשְׁמוֹת (names of the deceased) שֶׁהָלְכוּ לְעוֹלָמָן, בַּעֲבוּר שֶׁבְּלִי נֶדֶר אֶתֵּן צְדָקָה בְּעַד הַזְכָּרַת נִשְׁמוֹתֵיהֶן, בְּגַן עֵדֶן תְּהֵא מְנוּחָתָן, לָכֵן בַּעַל הָרַחֲמִים יַסְתִּירֵן בְּסֵתֶר כְּנָפָיו לְעוֹלָמִים, וְיִצְרוֹר בִּצְרוֹר הַחַיִּים אֶת נִשְׁמוֹתֵיהֶן, יהוה הוּא נַחֲלָתָן, וְתָנוּחוּ בְּשָׁלוֹם עַל מִשְׁכְּבוֹתֵיהֶן. וְנֹאמַר: אָמֵן.

FOR MEMBERS OF THE ISRAEL DEFENSE FORCE
[The following text is translated from the *Minchas Yerushalayim Siddur.*]

יִזְכֹּר *May God remember the souls of the fighters of the Israel Defense Force who gave their lives for the sanctification of the Name, the People and the Land; who died a heroic death in the War of Independence and the battlefields of Sinai in missions of defense and safety. They were quicker than eagles and stronger than lions as they volunteered to assist the people and with their pure blood soaked the clods of our holy earth and the deserts of Sinai. The memory of their self-sacrifice and heroic deeds will never perish from us. May their souls be bound in the Bond of Life with the souls of Abraham, Isaac and Jacob, and with the souls of the other Jewish heroes and martyrs who are in the Garden of Eden. Amen.*

After reciting *Yizkor* it is customary to recite the following prayers. It is permitted to mention many names in this prayer, but it is preferable to recite separate prayers for men and women.

FOR AN INDIVIDUAL

אֵל *O God, full of mercy, Who dwells on high, grant proper rest* on the wings of the Divine Presence* — in the lofty levels of the holy and the pure ones,* who shine like the glow of the firmament — for the soul of*

for a man

(name of the deceased) *who went on to his world, because, without making a vow, I will contribute to charity in remembrance of his soul. May his resting place be in the Garden of Eden — therefore may the Master of mercy shelter him in the shelter of His wings for eternity; and may He bind his soul in the Bond of Life. HASHEM is his heritage, and may he repose in peace on his resting place. Now let us respond: Amen.*

for a woman

(name of the deceased) *who went on to her world, because, without making a vow, I will contribute to charity in remembrance of her soul. May her resting place be in the Garden of Eden — therefore may the Master of mercy shelter her in the shelter of His wings for eternity; and may He bind her soul in the Bond of Life. HASHEM is her heritage, and may she repose in peace on her resting place. Now let us respond: Amen.*

FOR A GROUP

אֵל *O God, full of mercy, Who dwells on high, grant proper rest* on the wings of the Divine Presence* — in the lofty levels of the holy and the pure ones,* who shine like the glow of the firmament — for the souls of* (names of the deceased) *who went on to their world, because, without making a vow, I will contribute to charity in remembrance of their souls. May their resting place be in the Garden of Eden — therefore may the Master of mercy shelter them in the shelter of His wings for eternity; and may He bind their souls in the Bond of Life. HASHEM is their heritage, and may they repose in peace on their resting places. Now let us respond: Amen.*

---

it is also used to refer to the spiritual paradise because it implies spiritual perfection and bliss.

⊱ **אֵל ... הַמְצֵא מְנוּחָה נְכוֹנָה** — *O God, ... grant proper rest.* The fact that a soul is in Paradise does not guarantee it complete contentment. Its level there depends on its prior achievements here on earth; consequently, there are as many degrees there as there are degrees of righteousness on earth. Through our prayers and deeds, we hope to earn God's compassion upon the departed soul.

עַל כַּנְפֵי הַשְּׁכִינָה — *On the wings of the Divine Presence.* When this term is used to mean Heavenly protection from danger, we say **תַּחַת**, *under,* the wings, using the analogy of a bird spreading its protective wings over its young. In this prayer, where we speak of spiritual elevation, we reverse the analogy, comparing God's Presence to a soaring eagle that puts its young on top of its wings and carries them aloft.

קְדוֹשִׁים וּטְהוֹרִים — *The holy and the pure ones,* a reference to the angels.

FOR MARTYRS

אֵל מָלֵא רַחֲמִים, שׁוֹכֵן בַּמְּרוֹמִים, הַמְצֵא מְנוּחָה נְכוֹנָה* עַל כַּנְפֵי הַשְּׁכִינָה,* בְּמַעֲלוֹת קְדוֹשִׁים וּטְהוֹרִים* כְּזֹהַר הָרָקִיעַ מַזְהִירִים, אֶת נִשְׁמוֹת (כָּל קְרוֹבַי וּקְרוֹבוֹתַי, הֵן מִצַּד אָבִי, הֵן מִצַּד אִמִּי) הַקְּדוֹשִׁים וְהַטְּהוֹרִים שֶׁהוּמְתוּ וְשֶׁנֶּהֶרְגוּ וְשֶׁנִּשְׁחֲטוּ וְשֶׁנִּשְׂרְפוּ וְשֶׁנִּטְבְּעוּ וְשֶׁנֶּחְנְקוּ עַל קִדּוּשׁ הַשֵּׁם, (עַל יְדֵי הַצּוֹרְרִים הַגֶּרְמָנִים, יִמַּח שְׁמָם וְזִכְרָם) בַּעֲבוּר שֶׁבְּלִי נֶדֶר אֶתֵּן צְדָקָה בְּעַד הַזְכָּרַת נִשְׁמוֹתֵיהֶם, בְּגַן עֵדֶן תְּהֵא מְנוּחָתָם, לָכֵן בַּעַל הָרַחֲמִים יַסְתִּירֵם בְּסֵתֶר כְּנָפָיו לְעוֹלָמִים, וְיִצְרוֹר בִּצְרוֹר הַחַיִּים אֶת נִשְׁמוֹתֵיהֶם, יהוה הוּא נַחֲלָתָם, וְיָנוּחוּ בְּשָׁלוֹם עַל מִשְׁכְּבוֹתֵיהֶם. וְנֹאמַר: אָמֵן.

מי שברך להרב

At the conclusion of the *Yizkor* service, it is customary for the *gabbai* to recite a prayer on behalf of the rabbi of the congregation.

מִי שֶׁבֵּרַךְ אֲבוֹתֵינוּ אַבְרָהָם יִצְחָק וְיַעֲקֹב, מֹשֶׁה וְאַהֲרֹן, דָּוִד וּשְׁלֹמֹה, הוּא יְבָרֵךְ אֶת רַבִּי (name) בֶּן (father's name) שֶׁיִּתֵּן לִצְדָקָה בְּעַד הַנְּשָׁמוֹת שֶׁהִזְכִּיר הַיּוֹם, לִכְבוֹד הַמָּקוֹם, לִכְבוֹד הַתּוֹרָה, בִּשְׂכַר זֶה, הַקָּדוֹשׁ בָּרוּךְ הוּא יִשְׁמְרֵהוּ וְיַצִּילֵהוּ מִכָּל צָרָה וְצוּקָה, וּמִכָּל נֶגַע וּמַחֲלָה, וְיִשְׁלַח בְּרָכָה וְהַצְלָחָה בְּכָל מַעֲשֵׂה יָדָיו, וְיִזְכֶּה לַעֲלוֹת לָרֶגֶל, עִם כָּל יִשְׂרָאֵל אֶחָיו. וְנֹאמַר: אָמֵן. (Cong. – אָמֵן.)

Congregation and *chazzan:*

אַב הָרַחֲמִים,* שׁוֹכֵן מְרוֹמִים, בְּרַחֲמָיו הָעֲצוּמִים הוּא יִפְקוֹד בְּרַחֲמִים, הַחֲסִידִים וְהַיְשָׁרִים וְהַתְּמִימִים, קְהִלּוֹת הַקֹּדֶשׁ שֶׁמָּסְרוּ נַפְשָׁם עַל קְדֻשַּׁת הַשֵּׁם, הַנֶּאֱהָבִים וְהַנְּעִימִים בְּחַיֵּיהֶם, וּבְמוֹתָם לֹא נִפְרָדוּ. מִנְּשָׁרִים קַלּוּ, וּמֵאֲרָיוֹת גָּבֵרוּ, לַעֲשׂוֹת רְצוֹן קוֹנָם וְחֵפֶץ צוּרָם. יִזְכְּרֵם אֱלֹהֵינוּ לְטוֹבָה, עִם שְׁאָר צַדִּיקֵי עוֹלָם, וְיִנְקוֹם* לְעֵינֵינוּ נִקְמַת דַּם עֲבָדָיו הַשָּׁפוּךְ, כַּכָּתוּב בְּתוֹרַת מֹשֶׁה אִישׁ הָאֱלֹהִים: הַרְנִינוּ גוֹיִם עַמּוֹ כִּי דַם עֲבָדָיו יִקּוֹם, וְנָקָם יָשִׁיב לְצָרָיו, וְכִפֶּר אַדְמָתוֹ עַמּוֹ.[1] וְעַל יְדֵי עֲבָדֶיךָ הַנְּבִיאִים כָּתוּב לֵאמֹר: וְנִקֵּיתִי דָּמָם לֹא נִקֵּיתִי, וַיהוה שֹׁכֵן בְּצִיּוֹן.[2] וּבְכִתְבֵי הַקֹּדֶשׁ נֶאֱמַר: לָמָּה יֹאמְרוּ הַגּוֹיִם, אַיֵּה אֱלֹהֵיהֶם, יִוָּדַע בַּגּוֹיִם לְעֵינֵינוּ, נִקְמַת דַּם עֲבָדֶיךָ הַשָּׁפוּךְ.[3] וְאוֹמֵר: כִּי דֹרֵשׁ דָּמִים אוֹתָם זָכָר, לֹא שָׁכַח צַעֲקַת עֲנָוִים.[4] וְאוֹמֵר: יָדִין בַּגּוֹיִם* מָלֵא גְוִיּוֹת, מָחַץ רֹאשׁ עַל אֶרֶץ רַבָּה. מִנַּחַל בַּדֶּרֶךְ יִשְׁתֶּה, עַל כֵּן יָרִים רֹאשׁ.[5]

THE *YIZKOR* SERVICE ENDS HERE.

(1) *Deuteronomy* 32:43. (2) *Joel* 4:21. (3) *Psalms* 79:10. (4) 9:13. (5) 110:6-7.

⊛ **אַב הָרַחֲמִים** — *Father of compassion.* This is a memorial prayer, as the text makes clear, for the martyrs who died to sanctify God's Name.

וְיִנְקוֹם — *May He ... exact retribution.* We do not pray that we be strong enough to avenge our martyrs; Jews are not motivated by a lust to repay violence and murder with violence and murder. Rather we pray that God choose how and when to atone for the blood of His fallen martyrs. For the living, decency and integrity remain the primary goals of social life *(R' Hirsch).*

יָדִין בַּגּוֹיִם — *He will judge the ... nations.* God intervenes against the nations who seek to

FOR MARTYRS

אֵל *O God, full of mercy, Who dwells on high, grant proper rest* on the wings of the Divine Presence* — in the lofty levels of the holy and the pure ones,* who shine like the glow of the firmament — for the souls of (all my relatives, both on my father's side and on my mother's side,) the holy and pure ones who were killed, murdered, slaughtered, burned, drowned and strangled for the sanctification of the Name, (through the hands of the German oppressors, may their name and memory be obliterated) because, without making a vow, I will contribute to charity in remembrance of their souls. May their resting place be in the Garden of Eden — therefore may the Master of mercy shelter them in the shelter of His wings for eternity; and may He bind their souls in the Bond of Life.* HASHEM *is their heritage, and may they repose in peace on their resting places. Now let us respond: Amen.*

PRAYER FOR THE RABBI

At the conclusion of the *Yizkor* service, it is customary for the *gabbai* to recite a prayer on behalf of the rabbi of the congregation.

מִי שֶׁבֵּרַךְ *He Who blessed our forefathers Abraham, Isaac and Jacob, Moses and Aaron, David and Solomon — may He bless Rabbi (*Hebrew name*) son of (*father's Hebrew name*) because he shall contribute to charity on behalf of the souls remembered today, in honor of the Omnipresent, in honor of the Torah, in honor of the Day of Judgment. As reward for this, may the Holy One, Blessed is He, protect him and rescue him from every trouble and distress, from every plague and illness; and may He send blessing and success in his every endeavor, and may he be privileged to ascend to Jerusalem for the pilgrimage, together with all Israel, his brethren. Now let us respond: Amen.*

(Cong. – *Amen)*

Congregation and *chazzan:*

אַב הָרַחֲמִים *Father of compassion,* Who dwells on high, in His powerful compassion may He recall with compassion the devout, the upright, and the perfect ones; the holy congregations who gave their lives for the Sanctification of the Name — who were beloved and pleasant in their lifetime and in their death were not parted [from God]. They were quicker than eagles and stronger than lions to do their Creator's will and their Rock's desire. May our God remember them for good with the other righteous of the world. May He, before our eyes, exact retribution* for the spilled blood of His servants, as is written in the Torah of Moses, the man of God: O nations, sing the praise of His people for He will avenge the blood of His servants and He will bring retribution upon His foes; and He will appease His land and His people.[1] And by Your servants, the prophets, it is written saying: Though I cleanse [the enemy] — their bloodshed I will not cleanse when* HASHEM *dwells in Zion.[2] And in the Holy Writings it is said: Why should the nations say, 'Where is their God?' Let there be known among the nations, before our eyes, revenge for Your servants' spilled blood.[3] And it says: For the Avenger of blood has remembered them; He has not forgotten the cry of the humble.[4] And it says: He will judge the corpse-filled nations,* He will crush the leader of the mighty land. From a river along the way he shall drink — therefore he may proudly lift his head.[5]*

THE *YIZKOR* SERVICE ENDS HERE.

---

slaughter the Jews. He turns their army into a mass of corpses and crushes their leader. Figuratively, enemy blood flows like a river from which the rescued fugitives can 'drink.' Spared from danger and shame, Israel 'may proudly lift his head.'

In view of the somber nature of *Yizkor*, most congregations omit the following *piyut* whenever *Yizkor* is recited.

יה אלי

Chazzan:

יָהּ אֵלִי* וְגוֹאֲלִי אֶתְיַצְּבָה לִקְרָאתֶךָ, הָיָה וְיִהְיֶה,* הָיָה וְהֹוֶה, כָּל גּוֹי אַדְמָתֶךָ.* וְתוֹדָה,* וְלָעוֹלָה, וְלַמִּנְחָה, וְלַחַטָּאת, וְלָאָשָׁם, וְלַשְּׁלָמִים, וְלַמִּלּוּאִים כָּל קָרְבָּנֶךָ. זְכוֹר נִלְאָה* אֲשֶׁר נָשְׂאָה וְהָשִׁיבָהּ לְאַדְמָתֶךָ. סֶלָה אֲהַלְלֶךָּ,* בְּאַשְׁרֵי יוֹשְׁבֵי בֵיתֶךָ.

דַּק עַל דַּק,* עַד אֵין נִבְדָּק, וְלִתְבוּנָתוֹ אֵין חֵקֶר. הָאֵל נוֹרָא, בְּאַחַת סְקִירָה,* בֵּין טוֹב לָרַע יְבַקֵּר. וְתוֹדָה, וְלָעוֹלָה, וְלַמִּנְחָה, וְלַחַטָּאת, וְלָאָשָׁם, וְלַשְּׁלָמִים, וְלַמִּלּוּאִים כָּל קָרְבָּנֶךָ. זְכוֹר נִלְאָה אֲשֶׁר נָשְׂאָה וְהָשִׁיבָהּ לְאַדְמָתֶךָ. סֶלָה אֲהַלְלֶךָּ, בְּאַשְׁרֵי יוֹשְׁבֵי בֵיתֶךָ.

אֲדוֹן צְבָאוֹת,* בְּרוֹב פְּלָאוֹת, חִבֵּר כָּל אָהֳלוֹ. בִּנְתִיבוֹת לֵב לִבְלֵב, הַצּוּר תָּמִים פָּעֳלוֹ. וְתוֹדָה, וְלָעוֹלָה, וְלַמִּנְחָה, וְלַחַטָּאת, וְלָאָשָׁם, וְלַשְּׁלָמִים, וְלַמִּלּוּאִים כָּל קָרְבָּנֶךָ. זְכוֹר נִלְאָה אֲשֶׁר נָשְׂאָה וְהָשִׁיבָהּ לְאַדְמָתֶךָ. סֶלָה אֲהַלְלֶךָּ, בְּאַשְׁרֵי יוֹשְׁבֵי בֵיתֶךָ.

יָהּ אֵלִי — *O God, my God.* Since *Ashrei* is one of the most prominent of all the psalms (see p. 6), its recitation before the Festival *Mussaf* is introduced with a joyous prayer that longs for the opportunity to sing it before God in the rebuilt Temple, along with the order of sacrificial offerings. This is in keeping with the literal meaning of אַשְׁרֵי יוֹשְׁבֵי בֵיתֶךָ, *Praiseworthy are those who dwell in Your house.* Although, in the *Siddur*, God's 'house' has the broad meaning of the synagogue or any other place where one can serve God, it also refers specifically to the Temple, where the *Kohanim* and Levites have the good fortune to serve God (*Radak* and *Ibn Ezra* to *Psalms* 84:5). The spiritual elevation of the Festival, especially before *Mussaf* when we are about to cite the unique offering of the Festival, is a logical time for this prayer that combines joy in the Temple service and longing that we will soon be able to perform it in actuality as well as in aspiration. In view of the somber nature of *Yizkor*, this *piyut* is omitted on *Yizkor* days in most congregations.

הָיָה וְיִהְיֶה — *Who was and Who will be.* God's Four-letter Name contains the letters that form the words indicating past, present, and future. Thus, this Name represents Him as the One Who creates and controls history — and Who will sooner or later return our service to the Temple.

כָּל גּוֹי אַדְמָתֶךָ — *With the entire nation on Your soil.* May all Israel be united in *Eretz Yisrael*, there to praise and thank God by offering all the prescribed offerings listed below.

וְתוֹדָה — *And the thanksgiving-offering.* We ask for the privilege of being in the Temple on God's soil so that we may bring Him all the offerings mentioned in the Torah.

The order of the offerings is difficult since the thanksgiving-offering has less holiness than the next four on the list. Also, the meal-offering consists of flour and oil, yet it is inserted between the animal offerings. Perhaps the order can be explained this way: first comes the thanksgiving-offering because the very fact that we will have been returned to *Eretz Yisrael* and the rebuilt Temple will be cause for an enormous sense of thanksgiving. The elevation-offering, which is consumed entirely on the altar, represents Israel's

In view of the somber nature of *Yizkor*, most congregations omit the following *piyut* whenever *Yizkor* is recited.

PRE-MUSSAF PIYUT

Chazzan:

יָהּ אֵלִי *O God, my God* and Redeemer, I shall stand to greet You — Who was and Who will be,* Who was and Who is — with the entire nation on Your soil;* and the thanksgiving-,* elevation-, meal-, sin-, guilt-, peace-, and inauguration-offerings — Your every offering. Remember the exhausted [nation] that won [Your favor], and return her to Your soil. Eternally will I laud You,* saying, 'Praiseworthy are those who dwell in Your House.'*

דַּק *Painstakingly exact,* beyond calculation — to His intelligence there is no limit. The awesome God — with a single stripe,* He differentiates the good from bad. And the thanksgiving-, elevation-, meal-, sin-, guilt-, peace-, and inauguration-offerings — Your every offering. Remember the exhausted [nation] that won [Your favor], and return her to Your soil. Eternally will I laud You, saying, 'Praiseworthy are those who dwell in Your House.'*

אֲדוֹן *The Lord of Legions,* with abundant miracles He connected His entire Tabernacle; in the paths of the heart may it blossom — the Rock, His work is perfect! And the thanksgiving-, elevation-, meal-, sin-, guilt-, peace-, and inauguration-offerings — Your every offering. Remember the exhausted [nation] that won [Your favor], and return her to Your soil. Eternally will I laud You, saying, 'Praiseworthy are those who dwell in Your House.'*

---

longing for elevation in God's service and dedication to Him; thus it takes precedence over offerings that come to atone for sin. Of the meal offering, the Sages derive from Scripture (see *Rashi, Leviticus* 2:1) that God heaps particular praise upon a poor man who can afford no more than a bit of flour and oil, yet wishes to bring an offering to express His dedication to God. The sin- and guilt-offerings are of greater holiness than the peace-offering. The inauguration offerings are mentioned last because they will be offered only once — when the Temple is dedicated — and then will never be needed, because the Third Temple will be eternal.

זְכוֹר נִלְאָה — *Remember the exhausted [nation].* Israel has been exhausted by long exile and much travail, but she won God's favor long ago and therefore longs for her return from exile.

סֶלָה אֲהַלְלֶךָּ — *Eternally will I laud You.* This verse is a rearrangement of the first verse of *Ashrei.* It expresses our resolve to praise God by declaring our pride at being able to serve Him.

דַּק עַל דַּק — *Painstakingly exact.* This verse and the next describe the inscrutable greatness of God's awesome judgment.

בְּאַחַת סְקִירָה — *With a single stripe.* This phrase is based on the Talmudic expression that on the Day of Judgment, 'All who walk the earth pass before Him כִּבְנֵי מָרוֹן, *like young sheep' (Rosh Hashanah* 16a, 18a). When sheep were tithed, they were released one by one through a small opening in a corral. Each tenth one was marked with a single stripe, identifying it as a tithe animal that would become an Altar offering. In the context of this prayer, it refers to God differentiating between the sinful and the righteous.

צְבָאוֹת — *Legions.* God's Legions are the entire host of the universe's components. He weaves them together to create the complex harmony of Creation. We pray that realization of His greatness will blossom in our hearts so that we will recognize His greatness and be worthy to serve Him in the rebuilt Temple.

אַשְׁרֵי יוֹשְׁבֵי בֵיתֶךָ, עוֹד יְהַלְלוּךָ סֶּלָה.[1] אַשְׁרֵי הָעָם שֶׁכָּכָה לּוֹ, אַשְׁרֵי הָעָם שֶׁיהוה אֱלֹהָיו.[2]

תהלים קמה

תְּהִלָּה לְדָוִד,

אֲרוֹמִמְךָ אֱלוֹהַי הַמֶּלֶךְ, וַאֲבָרְכָה שִׁמְךָ לְעוֹלָם וָעֶד.
בְּכָל יוֹם אֲבָרְכֶךָּ, וַאֲהַלְלָה שִׁמְךָ לְעוֹלָם וָעֶד.
גָּדוֹל יהוה וּמְהֻלָּל מְאֹד, וְלִגְדֻלָּתוֹ אֵין חֵקֶר.
דּוֹר לְדוֹר יְשַׁבַּח מַעֲשֶׂיךָ, וּגְבוּרֹתֶיךָ יַגִּידוּ.
הֲדַר כְּבוֹד הוֹדֶךָ, וְדִבְרֵי נִפְלְאֹתֶיךָ אָשִׂיחָה.
וֶעֱזוּז נוֹרְאוֹתֶיךָ יֹאמֵרוּ, וּגְדוּלָּתְךָ אֲסַפְּרֶנָּה.
זֵכֶר רַב טוּבְךָ יַבִּיעוּ, וְצִדְקָתְךָ יְרַנֵּנוּ.
חַנּוּן וְרַחוּם יהוה, אֶרֶךְ אַפַּיִם וּגְדָל חָסֶד.
טוֹב יהוה לַכֹּל, וְרַחֲמָיו עַל כָּל מַעֲשָׂיו.
יוֹדוּךָ יהוה כָּל מַעֲשֶׂיךָ, וַחֲסִידֶיךָ יְבָרְכוּכָה.
כְּבוֹד מַלְכוּתְךָ יֹאמֵרוּ, וּגְבוּרָתְךָ יְדַבֵּרוּ.
לְהוֹדִיעַ לִבְנֵי הָאָדָם גְּבוּרֹתָיו, וּכְבוֹד הֲדַר מַלְכוּתוֹ.
מַלְכוּתְךָ מַלְכוּת כָּל עֹלָמִים, וּמֶמְשַׁלְתְּךָ בְּכָל דּוֹר וָדֹר.
סוֹמֵךְ יהוה לְכָל הַנֹּפְלִים, וְזוֹקֵף לְכָל הַכְּפוּפִים.
עֵינֵי כֹל אֵלֶיךָ יְשַׂבֵּרוּ, וְאַתָּה נוֹתֵן לָהֶם אֶת אָכְלָם בְּעִתּוֹ.
פּוֹתֵחַ אֶת יָדֶךָ,
וּמַשְׂבִּיעַ לְכָל חַי רָצוֹן.

While reciting the verse פּוֹתֵחַ, concentrate intently on its meaning.

צַדִּיק יהוה בְּכָל דְּרָכָיו, וְחָסִיד בְּכָל מַעֲשָׂיו.
קָרוֹב יהוה לְכָל קֹרְאָיו, לְכֹל אֲשֶׁר יִקְרָאֻהוּ בֶאֱמֶת.
רְצוֹן יְרֵאָיו יַעֲשֶׂה, וְאֶת שַׁוְעָתָם יִשְׁמַע וְיוֹשִׁיעֵם.
שׁוֹמֵר יהוה אֶת כָּל אֹהֲבָיו, וְאֵת כָּל הָרְשָׁעִים יַשְׁמִיד.
❖ תְּהִלַּת יהוה יְדַבֶּר פִּי,
וִיבָרֵךְ כָּל בָּשָׂר שֵׁם קָדְשׁוֹ לְעוֹלָם וָעֶד.
וַאֲנַחְנוּ נְבָרֵךְ יָהּ, מֵעַתָּה וְעַד עוֹלָם, הַלְלוּיָהּ.[3]

---

(1) *Psalms* 84:5. (2) 144:15. (3) 115:18.

אַשְׁרֵי *Praiseworthy are those who dwell in Your house, may they always praise You, Selah![1] Praiseworthy is the people for whom this is so, praiseworthy is the people whose God is HASHEM.[2]*

Psalm 145

A psalm of praise by David:

א *I will exalt You, my God the King,*
and I will bless Your Name forever and ever.
ב *Every day I will bless You,*
and I will laud Your Name forever and ever.
ג *HASHEM is great and exceedingly lauded,*
and His greatness is beyond investigation.
ד *Each generation will praise Your deeds to the next*
and of Your mighty deeds they will tell;
ה *The splendrous glory of Your power*
and Your wondrous deeds I shall discuss.
ו *And of Your awesome power they will speak,*
and Your greatness I shall relate.
ז *A recollection of Your abundant goodness they will utter*
and of Your righteousness they will sing exultantly.
ח *Gracious and merciful is HASHEM,*
slow to anger, and great in [bestowing] kindness.
ט *HASHEM is good to all; His mercies are on all His works.*
י *All Your works shall thank You, HASHEM,*
and Your devout ones will bless You.
כ *Of the glory of Your kingdom they will speak,*
and of Your power they will tell;
ל *To inform human beings of His mighty deeds,*
and the glorious splendor of His kingdom.
מ *Your kingdom is a kingdom spanning all eternities,*
and Your dominion is throughout every generation.
ס *HASHEM supports all the fallen ones and straightens all the bent.*
ע *The eyes of all look to You with hope*
and You give them their food in its proper time;
פ *You open Your hand,* Concentrate intently while reciting the verse, *'You open. . .'*
and satisfy the desire of every living thing.
צ *Righteous is HASHEM in all His ways*
and magnanimous in all His deeds.
ק *HASHEM is close to all who call upon Him —*
to all who call upon Him sincerely.
ר *The will of those who fear Him He will do;*
and their cry He will hear, and save them.
ש *HASHEM protects all who love Him;*
but all the wicked He will destroy.
ת Chazzan– *May my mouth declare the praise of HASHEM*
and may all flesh bless His Holy Name forever and ever.
We will bless God from this time and forever, Halleluyah![3]

הכנסת ספר תורה

The *chazzan* takes the Torah in his right arm and recites:

יְהַלְלוּ אֶת שֵׁם יהוה, כִּי נִשְׂגָּב שְׁמוֹ לְבַדּוֹ –

Congregation responds:

– הוֹדוֹ עַל אֶרֶץ וְשָׁמָיִם. וַיָּרֶם קֶרֶן לְעַמּוֹ, תְּהִלָּה לְכָל חֲסִידָיו, לִבְנֵי יִשְׂרָאֵל עַם קְרֹבוֹ, הַלְלוּיָהּ.[1]

As the Torah is carried to the Ark the congregation recites the appropriate psalm.

ON A WEEKDAY:

תהלים כד

לְדָוִד מִזְמוֹר, לַיהוה הָאָרֶץ וּמְלוֹאָהּ, תֵּבֵל וְיֹשְׁבֵי בָהּ. כִּי הוּא עַל יַמִּים יְסָדָהּ, וְעַל נְהָרוֹת יְכוֹנְנֶהָ. מִי יַעֲלֶה בְהַר יהוה, וּמִי יָקוּם בִּמְקוֹם קָדְשׁוֹ. נְקִי כַפַּיִם וּבַר לֵבָב, אֲשֶׁר לֹא נָשָׂא לַשָּׁוְא נַפְשִׁי וְלֹא נִשְׁבַּע לְמִרְמָה. יִשָּׂא בְרָכָה מֵאֵת יהוה, וּצְדָקָה מֵאֱלֹהֵי יִשְׁעוֹ. זֶה דּוֹר דֹּרְשָׁיו, מְבַקְשֵׁי פָנֶיךָ, יַעֲקֹב, סֶלָה. שְׂאוּ שְׁעָרִים רָאשֵׁיכֶם, וְהִנָּשְׂאוּ פִּתְחֵי עוֹלָם, וְיָבוֹא מֶלֶךְ הַכָּבוֹד. מִי זֶה מֶלֶךְ הַכָּבוֹד, יהוה עִזּוּז וְגִבּוֹר, יהוה גִּבּוֹר מִלְחָמָה. שְׂאוּ שְׁעָרִים רָאשֵׁיכֶם, וּשְׂאוּ פִּתְחֵי עוֹלָם, וְיָבֹא מֶלֶךְ הַכָּבוֹד. מִי הוּא זֶה מֶלֶךְ הַכָּבוֹד, יהוה צְבָאוֹת הוּא מֶלֶךְ הַכָּבוֹד, סֶלָה.

ON THE SABBATH:

תהלים כט

מִזְמוֹר לְדָוִד, הָבוּ לַיהוה בְּנֵי אֵלִים, הָבוּ לַיהוה כָּבוֹד וָעֹז. הָבוּ לַיהוה כְּבוֹד שְׁמוֹ, הִשְׁתַּחֲווּ לַיהוה בְּהַדְרַת קֹדֶשׁ. קוֹל יהוה עַל הַמָּיִם, אֵל הַכָּבוֹד הִרְעִים, יהוה עַל מַיִם רַבִּים. קוֹל יהוה בַּכֹּחַ, קוֹל יהוה בֶּהָדָר. קוֹל יהוה שֹׁבֵר אֲרָזִים, וַיְשַׁבֵּר יהוה אֶת אַרְזֵי הַלְּבָנוֹן. וַיַּרְקִידֵם כְּמוֹ עֵגֶל, לְבָנוֹן וְשִׂרְיוֹן כְּמוֹ בֶן רְאֵמִים. קוֹל יהוה חֹצֵב לַהֲבוֹת אֵשׁ. קוֹל יהוה יָחִיל מִדְבָּר, יָחִיל יהוה מִדְבַּר קָדֵשׁ. קוֹל יהוה יְחוֹלֵל אַיָּלוֹת, וַיֶּחֱשֹׂף יְעָרוֹת, וּבְהֵיכָלוֹ, כֻּלּוֹ אֹמֵר כָּבוֹד. יהוה לַמַּבּוּל יָשָׁב, וַיֵּשֶׁב יהוה מֶלֶךְ לְעוֹלָם. יהוה עֹז לְעַמּוֹ יִתֵּן, יהוה יְבָרֵךְ אֶת עַמּוֹ בַשָּׁלוֹם.

לְדָוִד מִזְמוֹר / Psalm 24

This psalm is recited when the Torah is brought back to the Ark because its final verses: *Raise up your heads, O gates ...* were recited when King Solomon brought the Ark into the newly built Temple. Commentary to this psalm appears on pages 388-389.

מִזְמוֹר לְדָוִד / Psalm 29

Tur (284) points out that the phrase *the voice of HASHEM* appears seven times in Psalm 29. This seven-fold mention alludes to: (a) the heavenly voice heard at Mount Sinai during the Giving of the Torah; and (b) the seven blessings contained in the *[Mussaf] Shemoneh Esrei* of

RETURNING THE TORAH

The *chazzan* takes the Torah in his right arm and recites:

Let them praise the Name of HASHEM, for His Name alone will have been exalted —

Congregation responds:

— His glory is above earth and heaven. And He will have exalted the pride of His people, causing praise for all His devout ones, for the Children of Israel, His intimate people. Halleluyah![1]

As the Torah is carried to the Ark the congregation recites the appropriate psalm.

ON A WEEKDAY:

Psalm 24

לְדָוִד *Of David a psalm. HASHEM's is the earth and its fullness, the inhabited land and those who dwell in it. For He founded it upon seas, and established it upon rivers. Who may ascend the mountain of HASHEM, and who may stand in the place of His sanctity? One with clean hands and pure heart, who has not sworn in vain by My soul and has not sworn deceitfully. He will receive a blessing from HASHEM and just kindness from the God of his salvation. This is the generation of those who seek Him, those who strive for Your Presence — Jacob, Selah. Raise up your heads, O gates, and be uplifted, you everlasting entrances, so that the King of Glory may enter. Who is this King of Glory? — HASHEM, the mighty and strong, HASHEM, the strong in battle. Raise up your heads, O gates, and raise up, you everlasting entrances, so that the King of Glory may enter. Who then is the King of Glory? HASHEM, Master of Legions, He is the King of Glory. Selah!*

ON THE SABBATH:

Psalm 29

מִזְמוֹר *A psalm of David. Render unto HASHEM, you sons of the powerful; render unto HASHEM, honor and might. Render unto HASHEM the honor worthy of His Name, prostrate yourselves before HASHEM in His intensely holy place. The voice of HASHEM is upon the waters, the God of Glory thunders, HASHEM is upon vast waters. The voice of HASHEM is in power! The voice of HASHEM is in majesty! The voice of HASHEM breaks the cedars, HASHEM shatters the cedars of Lebanon! He makes them prance about like a calf; Lebanon and Siryon like young re'eimim. The voice of HASHEM carves with shafts of fire. The voice of HASHEM convulses the wilderness. HASHEM convulses the wilderness of Kadesh. The voice of HASHEM frightens the hinds, and strips the forests bare; while in His Temple all proclaim, 'Glory!' HASHEM sat enthroned at the Deluge; HASHEM sits enthroned as King forever. HASHEM will give might to His people, HASHEM will bless His people with peace.*

(1) 148:13-14.

the Sabbath. Thus, it is appropriate to recite this psalm at the time the Torah is returned to the Ark on the Sabbath just before the recitation of *Mussaf*.

As the Torah is placed into the Ark, the congregation recites the following verses:

וּבְנֻחֹה יֹאמַר,* שׁוּבָה יהוה רִבְבוֹת אַלְפֵי יִשְׂרָאֵל.[1] קוּמָה יהוה לִמְנוּחָתֶךָ, אַתָּה וַאֲרוֹן עֻזֶּךָ. כֹּהֲנֶיךָ יִלְבְּשׁוּ צֶדֶק, וַחֲסִידֶיךָ יְרַנֵּנוּ. בַּעֲבוּר דָּוִד עַבְדֶּךָ, אַל תָּשֵׁב פְּנֵי מְשִׁיחֶךָ.[2] כִּי לֶקַח טוֹב נָתַתִּי לָכֶם, תּוֹרָתִי אַל תַּעֲזֹבוּ.[3] ❖ עֵץ חַיִּים הִיא לַמַּחֲזִיקִים בָּהּ, וְתֹמְכֶיהָ מְאֻשָּׁר.[4] דְּרָכֶיהָ דַרְכֵי נֹעַם, וְכָל נְתִיבֹתֶיהָ שָׁלוֹם.[5] הֲשִׁיבֵנוּ יהוה אֵלֶיךָ וְנָשׁוּבָה, חַדֵּשׁ יָמֵינוּ כְּקֶדֶם.[6]

Some *chazzanim* silently add the following personal prayer.

[The Divine Names that appear in brackets should be scanned with the eyes but not spoken.]

אֵל מֶלֶךְ נֶאֱמָן שַׁדַּי מֶלֶךְ עֶלְיוֹן, קַבֵּל שַׁוְעָתִי בְּרָצוֹן. אֱמוֹץ לְבָבִי, **[כוזו במוכסז כוזו]** אֵל חַי, דַּיָּן אֱמֶת. שׁוֹפֵט צֶדֶק. רַחוּם וְחַנּוּן, רַחֲמֵעָלַי וּשְׁמַע הַיּוֹם אֲשֶׁר אַעְתִּיר בַּעֲדִי, וּבְעַד בֵּיתִי, וּבְעַד עֲדָתִי, הַמַּסְכִּימִים עִמִּי בִּתְפִלָּתִי. וְתִכְלוֹל תְּפִלָּתֵנוּ עִם כָּל תְּפִלּוֹת הַיְּשָׁרוֹת וְהַנְּקִיּוֹת שֶׁיַּעֲשׂוּ הַיּוֹם בְּעַמְּךָ יִשְׂרָאֵל. וְתַחְתּוֹר תַּחַת כִּסֵּא כְבוֹדֶךָ כְּמוֹ שֶׁחָתַרְתָּ לִתְפִלַּת מֹשֶׁה, שֶׁלֹּא יֵבוֹשׁוּ שׁוֹלְחַי בִּי, וְלֹא אֲנִי בָּהֶם. יִהְיוּ לְרָצוֹן אִמְרֵי פִי וְהֶגְיוֹן לִבִּי לְפָנֶיךָ, יהוה צוּרִי וְגוֹאֲלִי.[7] אָמֵן, סֶלָה. יְהִי רָצוֹן לְפָנֶיךָ, אָיוֹם וְנוֹרָא, שֶׁתִּתֵּן לִי קוֹל עָרֵב וְנָעִים הַיּוֹם; וְאַל יִפָּסֵק קוֹלִי, וְאַל יֵחַר גְּרוֹנִי, וִיהֵא קוֹלִי נָעִים וְחָזָק כְּמוֹ שֶׁנֶּאֱמַר: וַיְהִי קוֹל הַשֹּׁפָר הוֹלֵךְ וְחָזֵק מְאֹד.[8] אָמֵן, סֶלָה.

The *chazzan* recites חֲצִי קַדִּישׁ.

יִתְגַּדַּל וְיִתְקַדַּשׁ שְׁמֵהּ רַבָּא. (.Cong – אָמֵן.) בְּעָלְמָא דִּי בְרָא כִרְעוּתֵהּ. וְיַמְלִיךְ מַלְכוּתֵהּ, בְּחַיֵּיכוֹן וּבְיוֹמֵיכוֹן וּבְחַיֵּי דְכָל בֵּית יִשְׂרָאֵל, בַּעֲגָלָא וּבִזְמַן קָרִיב. וְאִמְרוּ: אָמֵן.

(.Cong – אָמֵן. יְהֵא שְׁמֵהּ רַבָּא מְבָרַךְ לְעָלַם וּלְעָלְמֵי עָלְמַיָּא.)

יְהֵא שְׁמֵהּ רַבָּא מְבָרַךְ לְעָלַם וּלְעָלְמֵי עָלְמַיָּא.

יִתְבָּרַךְ וְיִשְׁתַּבַּח וְיִתְפָּאַר וְיִתְרוֹמַם וְיִתְנַשֵּׂא וְיִתְהַדָּר וְיִתְעַלֶּה וְיִתְהַלָּל שְׁמֵהּ דְּקֻדְשָׁא בְּרִיךְ הוּא (.Cong – בְּרִיךְ הוּא) – לְעֵלָּא מִן כָּל בִּרְכָתָא וְשִׁירָתָא תֻּשְׁבְּחָתָא וְנֶחֱמָתָא, דַּאֲמִירָן בְּעָלְמָא. וְאִמְרוּ: אָמֵן. (.Cong – אָמֵן.)

AN OFFICER OF THE CONGREGATION MUST ANNOUNCE THAT מַשִּׁיב הָרוּחַ וּמוֹרִיד הַגֶּשֶׁם IS RECITED DURING MUSSAF. IT IS IMPORTANT THAT THIS ANNOUNCEMENT BE MADE: OTHERWISE THE CONGREGATION DOES NOT BEGIN THIS ADDITION DURING THE SILENT SHEMONEH ESREI.

As the Torah is placed into the Ark, the congregation recites the following verses:

וּבְנֻחֹה *And when it rested he would say,* 'Return, HASHEM, to the myriad thousands of Israel.'[1] Arise, HASHEM, to Your resting place, You and the Ark of Your strength. Let Your priests be clothed in righteousness, and Your devout ones will sing joyously. For the sake of David, Your servant, turn not away the face of Your anointed.[2] For I have given you a good teaching, do not forsake My Torah.[3]* Chazzan– *It is a tree of life for those who grasp it, and its supporters are praiseworthy.[4] Its ways are ways of pleasantness and all its paths are peace.[5] Bring us back to You, HASHEM, and we shall return, renew our days as of old.[6]*

Some *chazzanim* silently add the following personal prayer.
[The Divine Names that appear in brackets should be scanned with the eyes but not spoken.]

אֵל *O God, trustworthy King, Almighty Supreme King, accept my outcry with favor. Give my heart courage,* [כוזו במוכסז כוזו] *O Living God, true Judge, righteous Magistrate. O Merciful and Gracious One, have mercy on me and hear today what I shall entreat for myself, for my household, and for my congregation, who join with me in my prayer. And may our prayers be included with all the upright and pure prayers that will be rendered today among Your people, Israel. Tunnel under Your Throne of Glory as You tunneled for the prayer of Moses, so that those who send me should not be ashamed of me, nor I of them. May the expressions of my mouth and the thoughts of my heart find favor before You, HASHEM, my Rock and my Redeemer.[7] Amen, Selah! May it be Your will, Frightening and Awesome One, that You give me a sweet and pleasant voice today; may my voice not be interrupted, may my throat not become sore, and may my voice remain pleasant and strong, as it is said: And the sound of the shofar kept becoming exceedingly stronger.[8] Amen, Selah!*

The *chazzan* recites Half-*Kaddish:*

יִתְגַּדַּל *May His great Name grow exalted and sanctified* (Cong.– *Amen.*) *in the world that He created as He willed. May He give reign to His kingship in your lifetimes and in your days, and in the lifetimes of the entire Family of Israel, swiftly and soon. Now respond: Amen.*

(Cong.– *Amen. May His great Name be blessed forever and ever.*)

May His great Name be blessed forever and ever.

Blessed, praised, glorified, exalted, extolled, mighty, upraised, and lauded be the Name of the Holy One, Blessed is He (Cong.– *Blessed is He*) — *beyond any blessing and song, praise and consolation that are uttered in the world. Now respond: Amen.* (Cong.– *Amen.*)

AN OFFICER OF THE CONGREGATION MUST ANNOUNCE THAT מַשִּׁיב הָרוּחַ וּמוֹרִיד הַגָּשֶׁם IS RECITED DURING MUSSAF.
IT IS IMPORTANT THAT THIS ANNOUNCEMENT BE MADE: OTHERWISE THE CONGREGATION DOES NOT BEGIN THIS ADDITION DURING THE SILENT SHEMONEH ESREI.

---

(1) *Numbers* 10:36. (2) *Psalms* 132:8-10. (3) *Proverbs* 4:2. (4) 3:18.
(5) 3:17. (6) *Lamentations* 5:21. (7) *Psalms* 19:15. (8) *Exodus* 19:19.

❧ מוסף לשמיני עצרת ☙

Take three steps backward, then three steps forward. Remain standing with the feet together while reciting *Shemoneh Esrei.* Recite it with quiet devotion and without interruption, verbal or otherwise. Although its recitation should not be audible to others, one must pray loudly enough to hear himself.

כִּי שֵׁם יהוה אֶקְרָא, הָבוּ גֹדֶל לֵאלֹהֵינוּ.[1]

אֲדֹנָי שְׂפָתַי תִּפְתָּח, וּפִי יַגִּיד תְּהִלָּתֶךָ.[2]

אבות

Bend the knees at בָּרוּךְ; bow at אַתָּה; straighten up at 'ה.

בָּרוּךְ אַתָּה יהוה אֱלֹהֵינוּ וֵאלֹהֵי אֲבוֹתֵינוּ, אֱלֹהֵי אַבְרָהָם, אֱלֹהֵי יִצְחָק, וֵאלֹהֵי יַעֲקֹב, הָאֵל הַגָּדוֹל הַגִּבּוֹר וְהַנּוֹרָא, אֵל עֶלְיוֹן, גּוֹמֵל חֲסָדִים טוֹבִים וְקוֹנֵה הַכֹּל, וְזוֹכֵר חַסְדֵי אָבוֹת, וּמֵבִיא גוֹאֵל לִבְנֵי בְנֵיהֶם, לְמַעַן שְׁמוֹ בְּאַהֲבָה. מֶלֶךְ עוֹזֵר וּמוֹשִׁיעַ וּמָגֵן.

Bend the knees at בָּרוּךְ; bow at אַתָּה; straighten up at 'ה.

בָּרוּךְ אַתָּה יהוה, מָגֵן אַבְרָהָם.

גבורות

אַתָּה גִּבּוֹר לְעוֹלָם אֲדֹנָי, מְחַיֵּה מֵתִים אַתָּה, רַב לְהוֹשִׁיעַ.

מַשִּׁיב הָרְוּחַ וּמוֹרִיד הַגֶּשֶׁם.

מְכַלְכֵּל חַיִּים בְּחֶסֶד, מְחַיֵּה מֵתִים בְּרַחֲמִים רַבִּים, סוֹמֵךְ נוֹפְלִים, וְרוֹפֵא חוֹלִים, וּמַתִּיר אֲסוּרִים, וּמְקַיֵּם אֱמוּנָתוֹ לִישֵׁנֵי עָפָר. מִי כָמְוֹךָ בַּעַל גְּבוּרוֹת, וּמִי דְּוֹמֶה לָּךְ, מֶלֶךְ מֵמִית וּמְחַיֶּה וּמַצְמִיחַ יְשׁוּעָה. וְנֶאֱמָן אַתָּה לְהַחֲיוֹת מֵתִים. בָּרוּךְ אַתָּה יהוה, מְחַיֵּה הַמֵּתִים.

קדושת השם

אַתָּה קָדוֹשׁ וְשִׁמְךָ קָדוֹשׁ, וּקְדוֹשִׁים בְּכָל יוֹם יְהַלְלְוּךָ סֶּלָה. בָּרוּךְ אַתָּה יהוה, הָאֵל הַקָּדוֹשׁ.

קדושת היום

אַתָּה בְחַרְתָּנוּ מִכָּל הָעַמִּים, אָהַבְתָּ אוֹתָנוּ, וְרָצִיתָ בָּנוּ, וְרוֹמַמְתָּנוּ מִכָּל הַלְּשׁוֹנוֹת, וְקִדַּשְׁתָּנוּ בְּמִצְוֹתֶיךָ, וְקֵרַבְתָּנוּ מַלְכֵּנוּ לַעֲבוֹדָתֶךָ, וְשִׁמְךָ הַגָּדוֹל וְהַקָּדוֹשׁ עָלֵינוּ קָרָאתָ.

On the Sabbath add the words in brackets. [If forgotten, see *Laws* §86-90.]

וַתִּתֶּן לָנוּ יהוה אֱלֹהֵינוּ בְּאַהֲבָה [שַׁבָּתוֹת לִמְנוּחָה וּ]מוֹעֲדִים לְשִׂמְחָה חַגִּים וּזְמַנִּים לְשָׂשׂוֹן, אֶת יוֹם [הַשַּׁבָּת הַזֶּה וְאֶת יוֹם] הַשְּׁמִינִי חַג הָעֲצֶרֶת הַזֶּה, זְמַן שִׂמְחָתֵנוּ [בְּאַהֲבָה] מִקְרָא קֹדֶשׁ, זֵכֶר לִיצִיאַת מִצְרָיִם.

MUSSAF FOR SHEMINI ATZERES

Take three steps backward, then three steps forward. Remain standing with the feet together while reciting *Shemoneh Esrei*. Recite it with quiet devotion and without interruption, verbal or otherwise. Although its recitation should not be audible to others, one must pray loudly enough to hear himself.

When I call out the Name of HASHEM, ascribe greatness to our God.[1]
My Lord, open my lips, that my mouth may declare Your praise.[2]

PATRIARCHS

Bend the knees at *'Blessed'*; bow at *'You'*; straighten up at *'HASHEM.'*

בָּרוּךְ *Blessed are You, HASHEM, our God and the God of our forefathers, God of Abraham, God of Isaac, and God of Jacob; the great, mighty, and awesome God, the supreme God, Who bestows beneficial kindnesses and creates everything, Who recalls the kindnesses of the Patriarchs and brings a Redeemer to their children's children, for His Name's sake, with love. O King, Helper, Savior, and Shield.*

Bend the knees at *'Blessed'*; bow at *'You'*; straighten up at *'HASHEM.'*

Blessed are You, HASHEM, Shield of Abraham.

GOD'S MIGHT

אַתָּה *You are eternally mighty, my Lord, the Resuscitator of the dead are You; abundantly able to save.*

He makes the wind blow and He makes the rain descend.

He sustains the living with kindness, resuscitates the dead with abundant mercy, supports the fallen, heals the sick, releases the confined, and maintains His faith to those asleep in the dust. Who is like You, O Master of mighty deeds, and who is comparable to You, O King Who causes death and restores life and makes salvation sprout! And You are faithful to resuscitate the dead. Blessed are You, HASHEM, Who resuscitates the dead.

אַתָּה *You are holy and Your Name is holy, and holy ones praise You every day, forever. Blessed are You, HASHEM, the holy God.*

SANCTIFICATION OF THE DAY

אַתָּה בְחַרְתָּנוּ *You have chosen us from all the peoples; You loved us and found favor in us; You exalted us above all the tongues and You sanctified us with Your commandments. You drew us close, our King, to Your service and proclaimed Your great and Holy Name upon us.*

On the Sabbath add the words in brackets. [If forgotten, see *Laws* §86-90.]

וַתִּתֶּן לָנוּ *And You gave us, HASHEM, our God, with love [Sabbaths for rest], appointed festivals for gladness, Festivals and times for joy, [this day of Sabbath and] this day of the Shemini Atzeres Festival, the time of our gladness [with love], a holy convocation, a memorial of the Exodus from Egypt.*

---

(1) *Deuteronomy* 32:3. (2) *Psalms* 51:17.

וּמִפְּנֵי חֲטָאֵינוּ גָּלִינוּ מֵאַרְצֵנוּ, וְנִתְרַחַקְנוּ מֵעַל אַדְמָתֵנוּ. וְאֵין אֲנַחְנוּ יְכוֹלִים לַעֲלוֹת וְלֵרָאוֹת וּלְהִשְׁתַּחֲוֹת לְפָנֶיךָ, וְלַעֲשׂוֹת חוֹבוֹתֵינוּ בְּבֵית בְּחִירָתֶךָ, בַּבַּיִת הַגָּדוֹל וְהַקָּדוֹשׁ שֶׁנִּקְרָא שִׁמְךָ עָלָיו, מִפְּנֵי הַיָּד שֶׁנִּשְׁתַּלְּחָה בְּמִקְדָּשֶׁךָ. יְהִי רָצוֹן מִלְּפָנֶיךָ יהוה אֱלֹהֵינוּ וֵאלֹהֵי אֲבוֹתֵינוּ, מֶלֶךְ רַחֲמָן, שֶׁתָּשׁוּב וּתְרַחֵם עָלֵינוּ וְעַל מִקְדָּשְׁךָ בְּרַחֲמֶיךָ הָרַבִּים, וְתִבְנֵהוּ מְהֵרָה וּתְגַדֵּל כְּבוֹדוֹ. אָבִינוּ מַלְכֵּנוּ, גַּלֵּה כְּבוֹד מַלְכוּתְךָ עָלֵינוּ מְהֵרָה, וְהוֹפַע וְהִנָּשֵׂא עָלֵינוּ לְעֵינֵי כָּל חָי. וְקָרֵב פְּזוּרֵינוּ מִבֵּין הַגּוֹיִם, וּנְפוּצוֹתֵינוּ כַּנֵּס מִיַּרְכְּתֵי אָרֶץ. וַהֲבִיאֵנוּ לְצִיּוֹן עִירְךָ בְּרִנָּה, וְלִירוּשָׁלַיִם בֵּית מִקְדָּשְׁךָ בְּשִׂמְחַת עוֹלָם. וְשָׁם נַעֲשֶׂה לְפָנֶיךָ אֶת קָרְבְּנוֹת חוֹבוֹתֵינוּ, תְּמִידִים כְּסִדְרָם, וּמוּסָפִים כְּהִלְכָתָם. וְאֶת [Weekdays– מוּסַף יוֹם] [Sabbath– מוּסְפֵי יוֹם הַשַּׁבָּת הַזֶּה וְיוֹם] הַשְּׁמִינִי חַג הָעֲצֶרֶת הַזֶּה נַעֲשֶׂה וְנַקְרִיב לְפָנֶיךָ בְּאַהֲבָה כְּמִצְוַת רְצוֹנֶךָ, כְּמוֹ שֶׁכָּתַבְתָּ עָלֵינוּ בְּתוֹרָתֶךָ, עַל יְדֵי מֹשֶׁה עַבְדֶּךָ, מִפִּי כְבוֹדֶךָ כָּאָמוּר:

On the Sabbath add. [If forgotten, do not repeat *Shemoneh Esrei*. See *Laws* §86.]

וּבְיוֹם הַשַּׁבָּת שְׁנֵי כְבָשִׂים בְּנֵי שָׁנָה תְּמִימִם, וּשְׁנֵי עֶשְׂרֹנִים סֹלֶת מִנְחָה בְּלוּלָה בַשֶּׁמֶן, וְנִסְכּוֹ. עֹלַת שַׁבַּת בְּשַׁבַּתּוֹ, עַל עֹלַת הַתָּמִיד וְנִסְכָּהּ.[1] (זֶה קָרְבַּן שַׁבָּת. וְקָרְבַּן הַיּוֹם כָּאָמוּר:)

בַּיּוֹם הַשְּׁמִינִי, עֲצֶרֶת תִּהְיֶה לָכֶם, כָּל מְלֶאכֶת עֲבֹדָה לֹא תַעֲשׂוּ. וְהִקְרַבְתֶּם עֹלָה אִשֵּׁה רֵיחַ נִיחֹחַ לַיהוה, פַּר אֶחָד, אַיִל אֶחָד, כְּבָשִׂים בְּנֵי שָׁנָה שִׁבְעָה, תְּמִימִם.[2] וּמִנְחָתָם וְנִסְכֵּיהֶם כִּמְדֻבָּר, שְׁלֹשָׁה עֶשְׂרֹנִים לַפָּר, וּשְׁנֵי עֶשְׂרֹנִים לָאָיִל, וְעִשָּׂרוֹן לַכֶּבֶשׂ, וְיַיִן כְּנִסְכּוֹ. וְשָׂעִיר לְכַפֵּר, וּשְׁנֵי תְמִידִים כְּהִלְכָתָם.

On the Sabbath add. [If forgotten, do not repeat *Shemoneh Esrei*. See *Laws* §86.]

יִשְׂמְחוּ בְמַלְכוּתְךָ שׁוֹמְרֵי שַׁבָּת וְקוֹרְאֵי עֹנֶג, עַם מְקַדְּשֵׁי שְׁבִיעִי, כֻּלָּם יִשְׂבְּעוּ וְיִתְעַנְּגוּ מִטּוּבֶךָ, וּבַשְּׁבִיעִי רָצִיתָ בּוֹ וְקִדַּשְׁתּוֹ, חֶמְדַּת יָמִים אֹתוֹ קָרָאתָ, זֵכֶר לְמַעֲשֵׂה בְרֵאשִׁית.

וּמִפְּנֵי חֲטָאֵינוּ *But because of our sins we have been exiled from our land and sent far from our soil. We cannot ascend to appear and to prostrate ourselves before You, and to perform our obligations in the House of Your choice, in the great and holy House upon which Your Name was proclaimed, because of the hand that was dispatched against Your Sanctuary. May it be Your will, HASHEM, our God and the God of our forefathers, O merciful King, that You once more be compassionate upon us and upon Your Sanctuary in Your abundant mercy, and rebuild it soon and magnify its glory. Our Father, our King, reveal the glory of Your Kingship upon us, speedily; appear and be uplifted over us before the eyes of all the living. Draw our scattered ones near from among the nations, and bring in our dispersions from the ends of the earth. Bring us to Zion, Your City, in glad song, and to Jerusalem, home of Your Sanctuary, in eternal joy. There we will perform before You our obligatory offerings, the continual offerings according to their order and the additional offerings according to their law. And the additional offering[s of this day of Sabbath and] of this day of the Shemini Atzeres Festival, we will perform and bring near to You with love, according to the commandment of Your will, as You have written for us in Your Torah, through Moses, Your servant, from Your glorious expression, as it is said:*

On the Sabbath add. [If forgotten, do not repeat *Shemoneh Esrei*. See *Laws* §86.]

וּבְיוֹם הַשַּׁבָּת *On the Sabbath day: two [male] first-year lambs, unblemished; and two tenth-ephah of fine flour for a meal-offering, mixed with olive oil, and its wine-libation. The elevation-offering of the Sabbath must be on its particular Sabbath, in addition to the continual elevation-offering and its wine-libation.*[1] *(This is the offering of the Sabbath. And the offering of the day is as it is said:)*

בַּיּוֹם הַשְּׁמִינִי *On the eighth day, there shall be an Assembly for you, you may not do any laborious work. You are to bring an elevation-offering, a fire-offering, a satisfying aroma to HASHEM, one bull, one ram, seven [male] first-year lambs, unblemished.*[1] *And their meal-offerings and their wine-libations as mentioned: three tenth-ephah for each bull; two tenth-ephah for each ram; one tenth-ephah for each lamb; and wine for its libation. A he-goat for atonement, and two continual offerings according to their law.*

On the Sabbath add. [If forgotten, do not repeat *Shemoneh Esrei*. See *Laws* §86.]

יִשְׂמְחוּ *They shall rejoice in Your Kingship — those who observe the Sabbath and call it a delight. The people that sanctifies the Seventh — they will all be satisfied and delighted from Your goodness. And the Seventh — You found favor in it and sanctified it. 'Most coveted of days' You called it, a remembrance of creation.*

---

(1) *Numbers* 29:35:36. (2) 29:12-13.

On the Sabbath add the words in brackets. [If forgotten, see *Laws* §86-90.]

אֱלֹהֵינוּ וֵאלֹהֵי אֲבוֹתֵינוּ, [רְצֵה בִמְנוּחָתֵנוּ] מֶלֶךְ רַחֲמָן רַחֵם עָלֵינוּ, טוֹב וּמֵטִיב הִדָּרֶשׁ לָנוּ, שׁוּבָה אֵלֵינוּ בַּהֲמוֹן רַחֲמֶיךָ, בִּגְלַל אָבוֹת שֶׁעָשׂוּ רְצוֹנֶךָ. בְּנֵה בֵיתְךָ כְּבַתְּחִלָּה, וְכוֹנֵן מִקְדָּשְׁךָ עַל מְכוֹנוֹ, וְהַרְאֵנוּ בְּבִנְיָנוֹ, וְשַׂמְּחֵנוּ בְּתִקּוּנוֹ. וְהָשֵׁב כֹּהֲנִים לַעֲבוֹדָתָם, וּלְוִיִּם לְשִׁירָם וּלְזִמְרָם, וְהָשֵׁב יִשְׂרָאֵל לִנְוֵיהֶם. וְשָׁם נַעֲלֶה וְנֵרָאֶה וְנִשְׁתַּחֲוֶה לְפָנֶיךָ, בְּשָׁלֹשׁ פַּעֲמֵי רְגָלֵינוּ, כַּכָּתוּב בְּתוֹרָתֶךָ: שָׁלוֹשׁ פְּעָמִים בַּשָּׁנָה, יֵרָאֶה כָל זְכוּרְךָ אֶת פְּנֵי יהוה אֱלֹהֶיךָ, בַּמָּקוֹם אֲשֶׁר יִבְחָר, בְּחַג הַמַּצּוֹת, וּבְחַג הַשָּׁבֻעוֹת, וּבְחַג הַסֻּכּוֹת, וְלֹא יֵרָאֶה אֶת פְּנֵי יהוה רֵיקָם. אִישׁ כְּמַתְּנַת יָדוֹ, כְּבִרְכַּת יהוה אֱלֹהֶיךָ, אֲשֶׁר נָתַן לָךְ.[1]

וְהַשִּׂיאֵנוּ יהוה אֱלֹהֵינוּ אֶת בִּרְכַּת מוֹעֲדֶיךָ לְחַיִּים וּלְשָׁלוֹם, לְשִׂמְחָה וּלְשָׂשׂוֹן, כַּאֲשֶׁר רָצִיתָ וְאָמַרְתָּ לְבָרְכֵנוּ. [אֱלֹהֵינוּ וֵאלֹהֵי אֲבוֹתֵינוּ רְצֵה בִמְנוּחָתֵנוּ] קַדְּשֵׁנוּ בְּמִצְוֹתֶיךָ וְתֵן חֶלְקֵנוּ בְּתוֹרָתֶךָ, שַׂבְּעֵנוּ מִטּוּבֶךָ וְשַׂמְּחֵנוּ בִּישׁוּעָתֶךָ, וְטַהֵר לִבֵּנוּ לְעָבְדְּךָ בֶּאֱמֶת, וְהַנְחִילֵנוּ יהוה אֱלֹהֵינוּ [בְּאַהֲבָה וּבְרָצוֹן] בְּשִׂמְחָה וּבְשָׂשׂוֹן [שַׁבָּת וּ]מוֹעֲדֵי קָדְשֶׁךָ, וְיִשְׂמְחוּ בְךָ יִשְׂרָאֵל מְקַדְּשֵׁי שְׁמֶךָ. בָּרוּךְ אַתָּה יהוה, מְקַדֵּשׁ [הַשַּׁבָּת וְ]יִשְׂרָאֵל וְהַזְּמַנִּים.

עבודה

רְצֵה יהוה אֱלֹהֵינוּ בְּעַמְּךָ יִשְׂרָאֵל וּבִתְפִלָּתָם, וְהָשֵׁב אֶת הָעֲבוֹדָה לִדְבִיר בֵּיתֶךָ. וְאִשֵּׁי יִשְׂרָאֵל וּתְפִלָּתָם בְּאַהֲבָה תְקַבֵּל בְּרָצוֹן, וּתְהִי לְרָצוֹן תָּמִיד עֲבוֹדַת יִשְׂרָאֵל עַמֶּךָ.

וְתֶחֱזֶינָה עֵינֵינוּ בְּשׁוּבְךָ לְצִיּוֹן בְּרַחֲמִים. בָּרוּךְ אַתָּה יהוה, הַמַּחֲזִיר שְׁכִינָתוֹ לְצִיּוֹן.

הודאה

Bow at מוֹדִים; straighten up at 'ה.

מוֹדִים אֲנַחְנוּ לָךְ, שָׁאַתָּה הוּא יהוה אֱלֹהֵינוּ וֵאלֹהֵי אֲבוֹתֵינוּ לְעוֹלָם וָעֶד. צוּר חַיֵּינוּ, מָגֵן יִשְׁעֵנוּ אַתָּה הוּא לְדוֹר וָדוֹר. נוֹדֶה לְּךָ וּנְסַפֵּר תְּהִלָּתֶךָ[2] עַל חַיֵּינוּ הַמְּסוּרִים בְּיָדֶךָ, וְעַל נִשְׁמוֹתֵינוּ הַפְּקוּדוֹת לָךְ, וְעַל נִסֶּיךָ שֶׁבְּכָל יוֹם עִמָּנוּ, וְעַל נִפְלְאוֹתֶיךָ

(1) *Deuteronomy* 16:16-17. (2) Cf. *Psalms* 79:13.

On the Sabbath add the words in brackets. [If forgotten, see *Laws* §86-90.]

אֱלֹהֵינוּ *Our God and the God of our forefathers, [may You be pleased with our rest] O merciful King, have mercy on us; O good and beneficent One, let Yourself be sought out by us; return to us in Your yearning mercy for the sake of the forefathers who did Your will. Rebuild Your House as it was at first, and establish Your Sanctuary on its prepared site; show us its rebuilding and gladden us in its perfection. Restore the Kohanim to their service and the Levites to their song and music; and restore Israel to their dwellings. And there we will ascend and appear and prostrate ourselves before You, during our three pilgrimage seasons, as it is written in Your Torah: Three times a year all your males are to appear before HASHEM, your God, in the place He shall choose, on the Festival of Matzos, on the Festival of Shavuos, and on the Festival of Succos, and they shall not appear before HASHEM empty-handed. Every man according to the gift of his hand, according to the blessing of HASHEM, your God, that He gave you.*[1]

וְהַשִּׂיאֵנוּ *Bestow upon us, O HASHEM, our God, the blessing of Your appointed Festivals for life and for peace, for gladness and for joy, as You desired and promised to bless us. [Our God and the God of our forefathers, may You be pleased with our rest.] Sanctify us with Your commandments and grant us our share in Your Torah; satisfy us from Your goodness and gladden us with Your salvation, and purify our heart to serve You sincerely. And grant us a heritage, O HASHEM, our God — [with love and with favor] with gladness and with joy — [the Sabbath and] the appointed festivals of Your holiness, and may Israel, the sanctifiers of Your Name, rejoice in You. Blessed are You, HASHEM, Who sanctifies [the Sabbath] Israel and the festive seasons.*

TEMPLE SERVICE

רְצֵה *Be favorable, HASHEM, our God, toward Your people Israel and their prayer and restore the service to the Holy of Holies of Your Temple. The fire-offerings of Israel and their prayer accept with love and favor, and may the service of Your people Israel always be favorable to You.*

וְתֶחֱזֶינָה *May our eyes behold Your return to Zion in compassion. Blessed are You, HASHEM, Who restores His Presence to Zion.*

THANKSGIVING [MODIM]

Bow at *'We gratefully thank You'.*

מוֹדִים *We gratefully thank You, for it is You Who are HASHEM, our God and the God of our forefathers for all eternity; Rock of our lives, Shield of our salvation are You from generation to generation. We shall thank You and relate Your praise*[2] *— for our lives, which are committed to Your power and for our souls that are entrusted to You; for Your miracles that are with us every day; and for Your wonders and*

וְטוֹבוֹתֶיךָ שֶׁבְּכָל עֵת, עֶרֶב וָבֹקֶר וְצָהֳרָיִם. הַטּוֹב כִּי לֹא כָלוּ רַחֲמֶיךָ, וְהַמְּרַחֵם כִּי לֹא תַמּוּ חֲסָדֶיךָ,[1] מֵעוֹלָם קִוִּינוּ לָךְ.

וְעַל כֻּלָּם יִתְבָּרַךְ וְיִתְרוֹמַם שִׁמְךָ מַלְכֵּנוּ תָּמִיד לְעוֹלָם וָעֶד.

Bend the knees at בָּרוּךְ; bow at אַתָּה; straighten up at ה׳.

וְכֹל הַחַיִּים יוֹדְוּךָ סֶּלָה, וִיהַלְּלוּ אֶת שִׁמְךָ בֶּאֱמֶת, הָאֵל יְשׁוּעָתֵנוּ וְעֶזְרָתֵנוּ סֶלָה. בָּרוּךְ אַתָּה יהוה, הַטּוֹב שִׁמְךָ וּלְךָ נָאֶה לְהוֹדוֹת.

שלום

שִׂים שָׁלוֹם, טוֹבָה, וּבְרָכָה, חֵן, וָחֶסֶד וְרַחֲמִים עָלֵינוּ וְעַל כָּל יִשְׂרָאֵל עַמֶּךָ. בָּרְכֵנוּ אָבִינוּ, כֻּלָּנוּ כְּאֶחָד בְּאוֹר פָּנֶיךָ, כִּי בְאוֹר פָּנֶיךָ נָתַתָּ לָּנוּ, יהוה אֱלֹהֵינוּ, תּוֹרַת חַיִּים וְאַהֲבַת חֶסֶד, וּצְדָקָה, וּבְרָכָה, וְרַחֲמִים, וְחַיִּים, וְשָׁלוֹם. וְטוֹב בְּעֵינֶיךָ לְבָרֵךְ אֶת עַמְּךָ יִשְׂרָאֵל, בְּכָל עֵת וּבְכָל שָׁעָה בִּשְׁלוֹמֶךָ. בָּרוּךְ אַתָּה יהוה, הַמְּבָרֵךְ אֶת עַמּוֹ יִשְׂרָאֵל בַּשָּׁלוֹם.

יִהְיוּ לְרָצוֹן אִמְרֵי פִי וְהֶגְיוֹן לִבִּי לְפָנֶיךָ, יהוה צוּרִי וְגֹאֲלִי.[2]

אֱלֹהַי, נְצוֹר לְשׁוֹנִי מֵרָע, וּשְׂפָתַי מִדַּבֵּר מִרְמָה,[3] וְלִמְקַלְּלַי נַפְשִׁי תִדּוֹם, וְנַפְשִׁי כֶּעָפָר לַכֹּל תִּהְיֶה. פְּתַח לִבִּי בְּתוֹרָתֶךָ, וּבְמִצְוֹתֶיךָ תִּרְדּוֹף נַפְשִׁי. וְכֹל הַחוֹשְׁבִים עָלַי רָעָה, מְהֵרָה הָפֵר עֲצָתָם וְקַלְקֵל מַחֲשַׁבְתָּם. עֲשֵׂה לְמַעַן שְׁמֶךָ, עֲשֵׂה לְמַעַן יְמִינֶךָ, עֲשֵׂה לְמַעַן קְדֻשָּׁתֶךָ, עֲשֵׂה לְמַעַן תּוֹרָתֶךָ. לְמַעַן יֵחָלְצוּן יְדִידֶיךָ, הוֹשִׁיעָה יְמִינְךָ וַעֲנֵנִי.[4]

Some recite verses pertaining to their names here. See page 1301.

יִהְיוּ לְרָצוֹן אִמְרֵי פִי וְהֶגְיוֹן לִבִּי לְפָנֶיךָ, יהוה צוּרִי וְגֹאֲלִי.[2] עֹשֶׂה שָׁלוֹם בִּמְרוֹמָיו, הוּא יַעֲשֶׂה שָׁלוֹם עָלֵינוּ, וְעַל כָּל יִשְׂרָאֵל. וְאִמְרוּ: אָמֵן.

Bow and take three steps back. Bow left and say . . . עֹשֶׂה, bow right and say . . . הוּא יַעֲשֶׂה; bow forward and say וְעַל כָּל . . . אָמֵן.

יְהִי רָצוֹן מִלְּפָנֶיךָ יהוה אֱלֹהֵינוּ וֵאלֹהֵי אֲבוֹתֵינוּ, שֶׁיִּבָּנֶה בֵּית הַמִּקְדָּשׁ בִּמְהֵרָה בְיָמֵינוּ, וְתֵן חֶלְקֵנוּ בְּתוֹרָתֶךָ. וְשָׁם נַעֲבָדְךָ בְּיִרְאָה, כִּימֵי עוֹלָם וּכְשָׁנִים קַדְמוֹנִיּוֹת. וְעָרְבָה לַיהוה מִנְחַת יְהוּדָה וִירוּשָׁלָיִם, כִּימֵי עוֹלָם וּכְשָׁנִים קַדְמוֹנִיּוֹת.[5]

THE INDIVIDUAL'S RECITATION OF *SHEMONEH ESREI* ENDS HERE.

The individual remains standing in place until the *chazzan* reaches *Kedushah* — or at least until the *chazzan* begins his repetition — then he takes three steps forward. The *chazzan* himself, or one praying alone, should remain in place for a few moments before taking three steps forward.

---

(1) Cf. *Lamentations* 3:22. (2) *Psalms* 19:15. (3) Cf. 34:14. (4) 60:7; 108:7. (5) *Malachi* 3:4.

favors in every season — evening, morning, and afternoon. The Beneficent One, for Your compassions were never exhausted, and the Compassionate One, for Your kindnesses never ended[1] — always have we put our hope in You.

For all these, may Your Name be blessed and exalted, our King, continually forever and ever.

Bend the knees at *'Blessed'*; bow at *'You'*; straighten up at *'HASHEM.'*

Everything alive will gratefully acknowledge You, Selah! and praise Your Name sincerely, O God of our salvation and help, Selah! Blessed are You, HASHEM, Your Name is 'The Beneficent One' and to You it is fitting to give thanks.

PEACE

שִׂים שָׁלוֹם *Establish peace, goodness, blessing, graciousness, kindness, and compassion upon us and upon all of Your people Israel. Bless us, our Father, all of us as one, with the light of Your countenance, for with the light of Your countenance You gave us, HASHEM, our God, the Torah of life and a love of kindness, righteousness, blessing, compassion, life, and peace. And may it be good in Your eyes to bless Your people Israel at every time and every hour with Your peace. Blessed are You, HASHEM, Who blesses His people Israel with peace.*

May the expressions of my mouth and the thoughts of my heart find favor before You, HASHEM, my Rock and my Redeemer.[2]

אֱלֹהַי *My God, guard my tongue from evil and my lips from speaking deceitfully.[3] To those who curse me, let my soul be silent; and let my soul be like dust to everyone. Open my heart to Your Torah, then my soul will pursue Your commandments. As for all those who design evil against me, speedily nullify their counsel and disrupt their design. Act for Your Name's sake; act for Your right hand's sake; act for Your sanctity's sake; act for Your Torah's sake. That Your beloved ones may be given rest; let Your right hand save, and respond to me.[4]*

Some recite verses pertaining to their names at this point. See page1301.

May the expressions of my mouth and the thoughts of my heart find favor before You, HASHEM, my Rock and my Redeemer.[2] He Who makes peace in His heights, may He make peace upon us, and upon all Israel. Now respond: Amen.

Bow and take three steps back. Bow left and say, *'He Who makes peace . . .'*; bow right and say, *'may He make peace . . .'*; bow forward and say, *'and upon . . . Amen.'*

יְהִי רָצוֹן *May it be Your will, HASHEM, our God and the God of our forefathers, that the Holy Temple be rebuilt, speedily in our days. Grant us our share in Your Torah, and may we serve You there with reverence, as in days of old and in former years. Then the offering of Judah and Jerusalem will be pleasing to HASHEM, as in days of old and in former years.[5]*

THE INDIVIDUAL'S RECITATION OF *SHEMONEH ESREI* ENDS HERE.

The individual remains standing in place until the *chazzan* reaches *Kedushah* — or at least until the *chazzan* begins his repetition — then he takes three steps forward. The *chazzan* himself, or one praying alone, should remain in place for a few moments before taking three steps forward.

חזרת הש״ץ – תפלת גשם

THE ARK IS OPENED AND THE CONGREGATION STANDS.

כִּי שֵׁם יהוה אֶקְרָא, הָבוּ גֹדֶל לֵאלֹהֵינוּ.[1]
אֲדֹנָי שְׂפָתַי תִּפְתָּח,* וּפִי יַגִּיד תְּהִלָּתֶךָ.[2]

אבות

Chazzan bends his knees at בָּרוּךְ; bows at אַתָּה; straightens up at ה׳.

בָּרוּךְ אַתָּה יהוה אֱלֹהֵינוּ וֵאלֹהֵי אֲבוֹתֵינוּ, אֱלֹהֵי אַבְרָהָם, אֱלֹהֵי יִצְחָק, וֵאלֹהֵי יַעֲקֹב, הָאֵל הַגָּדוֹל הַגִּבּוֹר וְהַנּוֹרָא, אֵל עֶלְיוֹן, גּוֹמֵל חֲסָדִים טוֹבִים וְקוֹנֵה הַכֹּל, וְזוֹכֵר חַסְדֵי אָבוֹת, וּמֵבִיא גוֹאֵל לִבְנֵי בְנֵיהֶם, לְמַעַן שְׁמוֹ בְּאַהֲבָה. מֶלֶךְ עוֹזֵר וּמוֹשִׁיעַ וּמָגֵן.

אַף־בְּרִי* אֻתַּת שֵׁם שַׂר מָטָר,
לְהַעֲבִיב וּלְהַעֲנִין לְהָרִיק לְהַמְטַר,
מַיִם אִבִּים בָּם גֵּיא לַעֲטַר, לְבַל יֵעָצְרוּ בְּנִשְׁיוֹן שְׁטָר,*
אֱמוּנִים גְּנוֹן בָּם שׁוֹאֲלֵי מָטָר.

Chazzan bends his knees at בָּרוּךְ; bows at אַתָּה; straightens up at ה׳.

בָּרוּךְ אַתָּה יהוה, מָגֵן אַבְרָהָם. (Cong. – אָמֵן.)

גבורות

אַתָּה גִּבּוֹר לְעוֹלָם אֲדֹנָי, מְחַיֵּה מֵתִים אַתָּה, רַב לְהוֹשִׁיעַ.

יַטְרִיחַ לְפַלֵּג מִפֶּלֶג גֶּשֶׁם,*
לְמוֹגֵג פְּנֵי נֶשִׁי בְּצַחוֹת לֶשֶׁם,
מַיִם לְאַדְּרָךְ כִּנִּיתָ בְּרֶשֶׁם,* לְהַרְגִּיעַ בְּרַעֲפָם לְנִפּוּחֵי נֶשֶׁם,
לְהַחֲיוֹת מַזְכִּירִים גְּבוּרוֹת הַגֶּשֶׁם.

[In some congregations the Ark is closed while additional prayers (p. 1265) are recited at this point.]

תְּפִלַּת גֶּשֶׁם / PRAYER FOR RAIN

Since the fall and winter are the rainy season in *Eretz Yisrael,* and it is a country that depends on rainfall more than most, the Sages ordained that the prayer for rain be recited on Succos, the pilgrimage festival closest to the rainy season. Because the festival itself is spent primarily in the *succah,* and it is regarded as a symbol of Divine displeasure for rain to prevent people from eating and living there, it would be incongruous to pray for rain at a time when we do not want it to fall. Therefore, the prayer is recited on Shemini Atzeres, after the Scriptural commandment of *succah*-dwelling is over.

אַף־בְּרִי — *Af-Bri,* the name of the angel appointed over the rainclouds *(Rashi* to *Job* 37:11), is formed from the two words אַף, *anger,* and בְּרִי, *health.* This name alludes to the two ways in which rain may fall. Sometimes it comes in harsh torrents and is a sign of Divine anger (אַף); at other times it falls in a beneficial manner and brings health (בְּרִי) and prosperity in its

CHAZZAN'S REPETITION – PRAYER FOR RAIN

THE ARK IS OPENED AND THE CONGREGATION STANDS.

When I call out the Name of HASHEM, ascribe greatness to our God.[1]
My Lord, open my lips, that my mouth may declare Your praise.[2]

PATRIARCHS

Chazzan bends his knees at *'Blessed'*; bows at *'You'*; straightens up at *'HASHEM.'*

בָּרוּךְ *Blessed are You, HASHEM, our God and the God of our forefathers, God of Abraham, God of Isaac, and God of Jacob; the great, mighty, and awesome God, the supreme God, Who bestows beneficial kindnesses and creates everything, Who recalls the kindnesses of the Patriarchs and brings a Redeemer to their children's children, for His Name's sake, with love. O King, Helper, Savior, and Shield.*

אַף־בְּרִי *Af-Bri* is designated as the name of the angel of rain;*
to thicken and to form clouds,
to empty them and to cause rain.
Water with which to crown the valley's vegetation
*— may it not be withheld because of our unredeemed debt.**
In the merit of the faithful Patriarchs protect the ones who pray for rain.

Chazzan bends his knees at *'Blessed'*; bows at *'You'*; straightens up at *'HASHEM.'*

Blessed are You, HASHEM, Shield of Abraham. (Cong. – *Amen.*)

GOD'S MIGHT

אַתָּה *You are eternally mighty, my Lord, the Resuscitator of the dead are You; abundantly able to save.*

יַטְרִיחַ *May He obligate [the Angel Af-Bri]*
*to give us portions of the segregated rain,**
to soften the wasteland's face when it is dry as rock.
*With water You symbolized Your might in Scripture,**
to soothe with its drops those in whom was blown a soul,
to keep alive the ones who recall the strengths of the rain.

[In some congregations the Ark is closed while additional prayers (p. 1265) are recited at this point.]

(1) *Deuteronomy* 32:3. (2) *Psalms* 51:17.

wake (*Mateh Levi*). The responsibilities of this angel are described in the first two stanzas of this prayer.

נְשִׁיוֹן שְׁטָר — *Unredeemed debt* [lit., *document*]. A long list of our sins is recorded in God's ledger.

מִפֶּלֶג גֶּשֶׁם — *Of the segregated rain.* God separated between the heavenly water and the earthly water (*Genesis* 1:6). Here the segregated rain, i.e., the heavenly water, is used as a metaphor for the spiritual flow of blessing from on high.

מַיִם לְאַדְּרָךְ כִּנִּיתָ בְּרֶשֶׁם — *With water You symbolized Your might in Scripture.* The Prophet (*Ezekiel* 43:2) compares God's voice to *the sound of great waters* (*Maaseh Oreg*).

אֱלֹהֵינוּ וֵאלֹהֵי אֲבוֹתֵינוּ,

זְכוֹר* אָב* נִמְשַׁךְ אַחֲרֶיךָ כַּמַּיִם,
בֵּרַכְתּוֹ כְּעֵץ שָׁתוּל עַל פַּלְגֵי מָיִם,
גְּנַנְתּוֹ, הִצַּלְתּוֹ מֵאֵשׁ וּמִמַּיִם,*
דְּרַשְׁתּוֹ בְּזָרְעוֹ עַל כָּל מָיִם.*

Cong.– בַּעֲבוּרוֹ אַל תִּמְנַע מָיִם.

זְכוֹר הַנּוֹלָד בִּבְשׂוֹרַת* יֻקַּח נָא מְעַט מַיִם,
וְשַׁחְתָּ לְהוֹרוֹ לְשָׁחֲטוֹ, לִשְׁפּוֹךְ דָּמוֹ כַּמַּיִם,
זְהֵר גַּם הוּא לִשְׁפּוֹךְ לֵב כַּמַּיִם,
חָפַר וּמָצָא בְּאֵרוֹת מָיִם.*

Cong.– בְּצִדְקוֹ חֹן חַשְׁרַת מָיִם.

זְכוֹר טָעַן מַקְלוֹ* וְעָבַר יַרְדֵּן מַיִם,
יִחַד לֵב* וְגָל אֶבֶן מִפִּי בְּאֵר מַיִם,
כְּנֶאֱבַק לוֹ שַׂר בָּלוּל מֵאֵשׁ וּמִמַּיִם,*
לָכֵן הִבְטַחְתּוֹ הֱיוֹת עִמּוֹ בָּאֵשׁ וּבַמָּיִם.*

Cong.– בַּעֲבוּרוֹ אַל תִּמְנַע מָיִם.

זְכוֹר מָשׁוּי* בְּתֵבַת גֹּמֶא מִן הַמַּיִם,
נָמוּ* דָּלֹה דָלָה וְהִשְׁקָה צֹאן מָיִם,
סְגוּלֶיךָ עֵת צָמְאוּ לַמַּיִם,
עַל הַסֶּלַע הָךְ* וַיֵּצְאוּ מָיִם.

Cong.– בְּצִדְקוֹ חֹן חַשְׁרַת מָיִם.

☙ זְכוֹר — *Remember.* The next six stanzas respectively speak of Abraham, Isaac, Jacob, Moses, Aaron and the twelve tribes. Each stanza is followed by a prayer that for their sake water not be withheld; instead abundant rain should fall in their righteous merit.

אָב — *The Patriarch.* Abraham was called אַב הֲמוֹן גּוֹיִם, *the father* [or, *Patriarch*] *of a multitude of nations (Genesis* 17:5).

מֵאֵשׁ וּמִמַּיִם — *From fire and from water.* The Talmud *(Pesachim* 118a) and Midrash *(Bereishis Rabbah* 38) relate how Abraham allowed himself to be thrown into a fiery furnace when he refused to bow before Nimrod's idols. Another Midrash *(Tanchuma)* describes how Satan, in the guise of a wide and deep river, attempted to drown Abraham and Isaac on their way to the *Akeidah* (see p. 142) on Mount Moriah *(Maaseh Oreg).*

בְּזָרְעוֹ עַל כָּל מָיִם — *When he sowed upon all waters.* The Talmud *(Bava Kamma* 17a) applies the words of the Prophet — *Praiseworthy are those who sow upon all waters (Isaiah* 32:20) — to those who perform kind and charitable deeds *(Maaseh Oreg).* Abraham is the epitome of kindness and his generosity was based on the rules of the Torah, which is likened to water.

הַנּוֹלָד בִּבְשׂוֹרַת — *The one born with the tidings of . . .* The birth of Isaac was prophesied to Abraham after he began his hospitality to the three angels by saying, *'Let some water be brought and wash your feet . . .' (Genesis* 18:4).

Our God and the God of our forefathers:

זְכוֹר *Remember** א *the Patriarch [Abraham],**
who was drawn behind You like water.
ב *You blessed him like a tree replanted alongside streams of water.*
ג *You shielded him, You rescued him from fire and from water.**
ד *You tested him when he sowed upon all waters.**
Cong.— *For his sake, do not hold water back!*

זְכוֹר *Remember* ה *the one [Isaac] born with the tidings of,**
'Let some water be brought.'
ו *You told his father to slaughter him — to spill his blood like water.*
ז *He too was scrupulous to pour his heart like water.*
ח *He dug and discovered wells of water.**
Cong.— *For the sake of his righteousness, grant abundant water!*

זְכוֹר *Remember* ט *the one [Jacob] who carried his staff**
and crossed the Jordan's water.
י *He dedicated his heart* and rolled a stone*
off the mouth of a well of water,
כ *as when he was wrestled by an angel composed of fire and water.**
ל *Therefore You pledged to remain with him through fire and water.**
Cong.— *For his sake, do not hold water back!*

זְכוֹר *Remember* מ *the one [Moses] drawn forth**
in a bulrush basket from the water.
נ *They said,* 'He drew water and provided the sheep with water.'*
ס *At the time Your treasured people thirsted for water,*
ע *he struck the rock* and out came water.*
Cong.— *For the sake of his righteousness, grant abundant water!*

בְּאֵרוֹת מָיִם — *Wells of water.* Scripture (*Genesis* 26:18-22) relates that Isaac dug no less than five wells.

טְעַן מַקְלוֹ... — *The one who carried his staff ...* Upon returning to Canaan from Aram, Jacob offered a prayer in which he declared, *'For with my staff I crossed this Jordan'* (*Genesis* 32:11). *Rashi* cites the Midrashic teaching that when Jacob had reached the Jordan River, he had placed his staff in the waters of the river and it split for him, allowing him to pass through.

יִחֵד לֵב — *He dedicated his heart.* Jacob's steadfast faith in God enabled him singlehandedly to roll a huge boulder off the mouth of the well — a chore that usually required the cooperative efforts of a large number of shepherds — in order to water Laban's sheep (see *Genesis* 29:11).

בָּלוּל מֵאֵשׁ וּמִמַּיִם — *Composed of fire and water.* Angels are composed of fire and water (*Yerushalmi, Rosh Hashanah* 2:5). The episode of Jacob's wrestling with an angel is told in *Genesis* (32:25-31).

הִבְטַחְתּוֹ ... בָּאֵשׁ וּבַמָּיִם — *You pledged ... fire and water.* The Prophet (*Isaiah* 43:1-2) proclaimed: *'And now,' so said* HASHEM, *your Creator ... 'when you pass through water, I am with you ... when you go through fire, you shall not be burned ...'*

מָשׁוּי — *The one drawn forth.* When Pharaoh's daughter found a Jewish baby among the reeds, she named him מֹשֶׁה, *Moses,* because מִן הַמַּיִם מְשִׁיתִהוּ, *'I have drawn him from the water'* (*Exodus* 2:10).

נָמוּ — *They said.* The daughters of Jethro reported to their father how 'an Egyptian man' [Moses] drew water for them (see *Exodus* 2:16-19).

עַל הַסֶּלַע הָךְ... — *He struck the rock ...* When Israel cried for water in the Wilderness, God ordered Moses to smite a stone from which water would issue forth (see *Exodus* 17:6).

זְכוֹר פָּקִיד* שָׁתוֹת* טוֹבֵל חָמֵשׁ טְבִילוֹת* בַּמַּיִם,
צוֹעֶה וּמַרְחִיץ כַּפָּיו בְּקִדּוּשׁ מַיִם,
קוֹרֵא וּמַזֶּה* טָהֳרַת מַיִם,
רֻחַק* מֵעַם פַּחַז כַּמָּיִם.

–Cong. בַּעֲבוּרוֹ אַל תִּמְנַע מָיִם.

זְכוֹר שְׁנֵים עָשָׂר שְׁבָטִים שֶׁהֶעֱבַרְתָּ בְּגִזְרַת מַיִם,*
שֶׁהִמְתַּקְתָּ לָמוֹ מְרִירוּת מַיִם,
תּוֹלְדוֹתָם* נִשְׁפַּךְ דָּמָם עָלֶיךָ כַּמַּיִם,
תֵּפֶן כִּי נַפְשֵׁנוּ אָפְפוּ מָיִם.

–Cong. בְּצִדְקָם חֹן חַשְׁרַת מָיִם.

Chazzan:

שָׁאַתָּה הוּא יהוה אֱלֹהֵינוּ, מַשִּׁיב הָרוּחַ וּמוֹרִיד הַגָּשֶׁם.

–Cong. then *chazzan* **לִבְרָכָה וְלֹא לִקְלָלָה.** (–Cong. אָמֵן.)

–Cong. then *chazzan* **לְחַיִּים וְלֹא לַמָּוֶת.** (–Cong. אָמֵן.)

–Cong. then *chazzan* **לְשׂוֹבַע וְלֹא לְרָזוֹן.** (–Cong. אָמֵן.)

THE ARK IS CLOSED.

[The congregation may sit]; the *chazzan* continues:

מְכַלְכֵּל חַיִּים בְּחֶסֶד, מְחַיֵּה מֵתִים בְּרַחֲמִים רַבִּים, סוֹמֵךְ נוֹפְלִים, וְרוֹפֵא חוֹלִים, וּמַתִּיר אֲסוּרִים, וּמְקַיֵּם אֱמוּנָתוֹ לִישֵׁנֵי עָפָר. מִי כָמוֹךָ בַּעַל גְּבוּרוֹת, וּמִי דוֹמֶה לָּךְ, מֶלֶךְ מֵמִית וּמְחַיֶּה וּמַצְמִיחַ יְשׁוּעָה. וְנֶאֱמָן אַתָּה לְהַחֲיוֹת מֵתִים. בָּרוּךְ אַתָּה יהוה, מְחַיֵּה הַמֵּתִים. (–Cong. אָמֵן)

פָּקִיד — *The appointee.* This word refers to the holder of a high office, in this case, Aaron, the first *Kohen Gadol (Mateh Levi).*

שָׁתוֹת — *The Temple.* The Holy Temple is called the אֶבֶן שְׁתִיָּה, *Foundation Stone,* after a stone located at the center of the Holy of Holies upon which stood the Ark of the Covenant. According to the Talmud *(Yoma* 53b) this stone was the first part of the earth to be created by God, and from it the planet as we know it expanded.

חָמֵשׁ טְבִילוֹת . . . — *Five immersions.* The Mishnah *(Yoma* 3:3, based on *Leviticus,* ch. 16) teaches that the *Kohen Gadol* must immerse himself five times during the Yom Kippur Temple service. Before and after each immersion he would wash his hands and feet in a ritually prescribed manner with water that had been sanctified in a sacred vessel.

זְכוֹר *Remember* פ *the appointee* [Aaron] over the Temple,* who made five immersions* in the water.*

צ *He went to cleanse his hands through sanctification with water.*

ק *He called out and sprinkled* [blood bringing] purity as with water.*

ר *He remained apart* from a people of waterlike impetuosity.*

Cong.– *For his sake, do not hold water back!*

זְכוֹר *Remember* שׁ *the twelve tribes You caused to cross through the split waters,**

שׁ *for whom You sweetened the water's bitter taste.*

ת *Their offspring* whose blood was spilt for You like water.*

ת *Turn to us — for woes engulf our souls like water.*

Cong.– *For the sake of their righteousness, grant abundant water!*

Chazzan:

For You are HASHEM, our God, Who makes the wind blow and makes the rain descend.

Cong. then *chazzan* – **For blessing and not for curse.** (Cong.– *Amen.)*

Cong. then *chazzan* – **For life and not for death.** (Cong.– *Amen.)*

Cong. then *chazzan* – **For plenty and not for scarcity.** (Cong.– *Amen.)*

THE ARK IS CLOSED.

[The congregation may sit]; the *chazzan* continues:

He sustains the living with kindness, resuscitates the dead with abundant mercy, supports the fallen, heals the sick, releases the confined, and maintains His faith to those asleep in the dust. Who is like You, O Master of mighty deeds, and who is comparable to You, O King Who causes death and restores life and makes salvation sprout! And You are faithful to resuscitate the dead. Blessed are You, HASHEM, Who resuscitates the dead. (Cong.– *Amen.)*

קוֹרֵא וּמַזֶּה — *He called out and sprinkled.* During the Yom Kippur service, the *Kohen Gadol* would sprinkle the blood of various offerings in various parts of the Temple (see *Leviticus* 16:14-18). To ensure that the proper number of sprinklings was performed, the *Kohen Gadol* would count aloud as he sprinkled the blood (see *Yoma* 5:3-4).

רָחַק — *He remained apart.* Aaron's personal sanctity was much greater than that of the rest of Israel, as Scripture states: *And Aaron was set apart that he be sanctified [as] holy of holies . . . (I Chronicles* 23:13).

שֶׁהֶעֱבַרְתָּ בְּגִזְרַת מַיִם — *You caused to cross through the split waters . . .* The Splitting of the Sea and the Song at the Sea are described in *Exodus* (14:15-15:21). This is followed by the story of the sweetening of the waters of Marah (15:22-26).

תּוֹלְדוֹתָם — *Their offspring,* i.e., the generations of Jews whose blood has been spilled in Sanctification of the Holy Name. Alternatively, this refers to the supplicants, the descendants of the twelve tribes, who pour out their hearts in prayer.

קדושה

When reciting *Kedushah,* one must stand with his feet together and avoid any interruptions. One should rise on his toes when saying the words קָדוֹשׁ, קָדוֹשׁ, קָדוֹשׁ; בָּרוּךְ (of בָּרוּךְ כְּבוֹד); and יִמְלֹךְ.

Cong. then *chazzan*:

נַעֲרִיצְךָ וְנַקְדִּישְׁךָ כְּסוֹד שִׂיחַ שַׂרְפֵי קֹדֶשׁ, הַמַּקְדִּישִׁים שִׁמְךָ בַּקֹּדֶשׁ, כַּכָּתוּב עַל יַד נְבִיאֶךָ, וְקָרָא זֶה אֶל זֶה וְאָמַר:

All– קָדוֹשׁ קָדוֹשׁ קָדוֹשׁ יהוה צְבָאוֹת, מְלֹא כָל הָאָרֶץ כְּבוֹדוֹ.[1] ❖ כְּבוֹדוֹ מָלֵא עוֹלָם, מְשָׁרְתָיו שׁוֹאֲלִים זֶה לָזֶה, אַיֵּה מְקוֹם כְּבוֹדוֹ, לְעֻמָּתָם בָּרוּךְ יֹאמֵרוּ:

All– בָּרוּךְ כְּבוֹד יהוה, מִמְּקוֹמוֹ.[2] ❖ מִמְּקוֹמוֹ הוּא יִפֶן בְּרַחֲמִים, וְיָחוֹן עַם הַמְיַחֲדִים שְׁמוֹ, עֶרֶב וָבֹקֶר בְּכָל יוֹם תָּמִיד, פַּעֲמַיִם בְּאַהֲבָה שְׁמַע אוֹמְרִים.

All– שְׁמַע יִשְׂרָאֵל, יהוה אֱלֹהֵינוּ, יהוה אֶחָד.[3] ❖ הוּא אֱלֹהֵינוּ. הוּא אָבִינוּ, הוּא מַלְכֵּנוּ, הוּא מוֹשִׁיעֵנוּ, וְהוּא יַשְׁמִיעֵנוּ בְּרַחֲמָיו שֵׁנִית, לְעֵינֵי כָּל חָי, לִהְיוֹת לָכֶם לֵאלֹהִים, אֲנִי יהוה אֱלֹהֵיכֶם.[4]

All– אַדִּיר אַדִּירֵנוּ, יהוה אֲדֹנֵינוּ, מָה אַדִּיר שִׁמְךָ בְּכָל הָאָרֶץ.[5] וְהָיָה יהוה לְמֶלֶךְ עַל כָּל הָאָרֶץ, בַּיּוֹם הַהוּא יִהְיֶה יהוה אֶחָד וּשְׁמוֹ אֶחָד.[6]

Chazzan– וּבְדִבְרֵי קָדְשְׁךָ כָּתוּב לֵאמֹר:

All– יִמְלֹךְ יהוה לְעוֹלָם, אֱלֹהַיִךְ צִיּוֹן, לְדֹר וָדֹר, הַלְלוּיָהּ.[7]

קדושת השם

Chazzan continues:

לְדוֹר וָדוֹר נַגִּיד גָּדְלֶךָ וּלְנֵצַח נְצָחִים קְדֻשָּׁתְךָ נַקְדִּישׁ, וְשִׁבְחֲךָ אֱלֹהֵינוּ מִפִּינוּ לֹא יָמוּשׁ לְעוֹלָם וָעֶד, כִּי אֵל מֶלֶךְ גָּדוֹל וְקָדוֹשׁ אָתָּה. בָּרוּךְ אַתָּה יהוה, הָאֵל הַקָּדוֹשׁ. (Cong. – אָמֵן.)

קדושת היום

אַתָּה בְחַרְתָּנוּ מִכָּל הָעַמִּים, אָהַבְתָּ אוֹתָנוּ, וְרָצִיתָ בָּנוּ, וְרוֹמַמְתָּנוּ מִכָּל הַלְּשׁוֹנוֹת, וְקִדַּשְׁתָּנוּ בְּמִצְוֹתֶיךָ, וְקֵרַבְתָּנוּ מַלְכֵּנוּ לַעֲבוֹדָתֶךָ, וְשִׁמְךָ הַגָּדוֹל וְהַקָּדוֹשׁ עָלֵינוּ קָרָאתָ.

On the Sabbath add the words in brackets. [If forgotten, see *Laws* §86-90.]

וַתִּתֶּן לָנוּ יהוה אֱלֹהֵינוּ בְּאַהֲבָה [שַׁבָּתוֹת לִמְנוּחָה וּ]מוֹעֲדִים לְשִׂמְחָה חַגִּים וּזְמַנִּים לְשָׂשׂוֹן, אֶת יוֹם [הַשַּׁבָּת הַזֶּה וְאֶת יוֹם] הַשְּׁמִינִי חַג הָעֲצֶרֶת הַזֶּה, זְמַן שִׂמְחָתֵנוּ [בְּאַהֲבָה] מִקְרָא קֹדֶשׁ, זֵכֶר לִיצִיאַת מִצְרָיִם.

KEDUSHAH

When reciting *Kedushah,* one must stand with his feet together and avoid any interruptions. One should rise on his toes when saying the words *Holy, holy, holy; Blessed is; HASHEM shall reign.*

Cong. then *chazzan:*

נַעֲרִיצְךָ *We will revere You and sanctify You according to the counsel of the holy Seraphim, who sanctify Your Name in the Sanctuary, as it is written by Your prophet: "And one [angel] will call another and say:*

All – *'Holy, holy, holy is HASHEM, Master of Legions, the whole world is filled with His glory.' "*[1] ∴*His glory fills the world. His ministering angels ask one another, 'Where is the place of His glory?' Those facing them say 'Blessed':*

All – *'Blessed is the glory of HASHEM from His place.'*[2] ∴*From His place may He turn with compassion and be gracious to the people who declare the Oneness of His Name; evening and morning, every day constantly, twice, with love, they proclaim 'Shema.'*

All – *'Hear O Israel: HASHEM is our God, HASHEM the One and Only.'*[3] ∴*He is our God; He is our Father; He is our King; He is our Savior; and He will let us hear, in His compassion, for a second time in the presence of all the living,' . . . to be a God to you, I am HASHEM, your God.'*[4]

All – *Mighty is our Mighty One, HASHEM, our Master — how mighty is Your name throughout the earth!*[5] *HASHEM will be King over all the world — on that day HASHEM will be One and His Name will be One.*[6]

Chazzan – *And in Your holy Writings the following is written:*

All – *'HASHEM shall reign forever — your God, O Zion — from generation to generation, Halleluyah!'*[7]

HOLINESS OF GOD'S NAME

Chazzan continues:

לְדוֹר *From generation to generation we shall relate Your greatness and for infinite eternities we shall proclaim Your holiness. Your praise, our God, shall not leave our mouth forever and ever, for You, O God, are a great and holy King. Blessed are You, HASHEM, the holy God.*

(Cong. – *Amen.*)

SANCTIFICATION OF THE DAY

אַתָּה בְחַרְתָּנוּ *You have chosen us from all the peoples; You loved us and found favor in us; You exalted us above all the tongues and You sanctified us with Your commandments. You drew us close, our King, to Your service and proclaimed Your great and Holy Name upon us.*

On the Sabbath add the words in brackets. [If forgotten, see *Laws* §86-90.]

וַתִּתֶּן לָנוּ *And You gave us, HASHEM, our God, with love [Sabbaths for rest], appointed festivals for gladness, Festivals and times for joy, [this day of Sabbath and] this day of the Shemini Atzeres Festival, the time of our gladness [with love], a holy convocation, a memorial of the Exodus from Egypt.*

---

(1) *Isaiah* 6:3. (2) *Ezekiel* 3:12. (3) *Deuteronomy* 6:4.
(4) *Numbers* 15:41. (5) *Psalms* 8:2. (6) *Zechariah* 14:9. (7) *Psalms* 146:10.

וּמִפְּנֵי חֲטָאֵינוּ גָּלִינוּ מֵאַרְצֵנוּ, וְנִתְרַחַקְנוּ מֵעַל אַדְמָתֵנוּ. וְאֵין אֲנַחְנוּ יְכוֹלִים לַעֲלוֹת וְלֵרָאוֹת וּלְהִשְׁתַּחֲוֹת לְפָנֶיךָ, וְלַעֲשׂוֹת חוֹבוֹתֵינוּ בְּבֵית בְּחִירָתֶךָ, בַּבַּיִת הַגָּדוֹל וְהַקָּדוֹשׁ שֶׁנִּקְרָא שִׁמְךָ עָלָיו, מִפְּנֵי הַיָּד שֶׁנִּשְׁתַּלְּחָה בְּמִקְדָּשֶׁךָ. יְהִי רָצוֹן מִלְּפָנֶיךָ יהוה אֱלֹהֵינוּ וֵאלֹהֵי אֲבוֹתֵינוּ, מֶלֶךְ רַחֲמָן, שֶׁתָּשׁוּב וּתְרַחֵם עָלֵינוּ וְעַל מִקְדָּשְׁךָ בְּרַחֲמֶיךָ הָרַבִּים, וְתִבְנֵהוּ מְהֵרָה וּתְגַדֵּל כְּבוֹדוֹ. אָבִינוּ מַלְכֵּנוּ, גַּלֵּה כְּבוֹד מַלְכוּתְךָ עָלֵינוּ מְהֵרָה, וְהוֹפַע וְהִנָּשֵׂא עָלֵינוּ לְעֵינֵי כָּל חָי. וְקָרֵב פְּזוּרֵינוּ מִבֵּין הַגּוֹיִם, וּנְפוּצוֹתֵינוּ כַּנֵּס מִיַּרְכְּתֵי אָרֶץ. וַהֲבִיאֵנוּ לְצִיּוֹן עִירְךָ בְּרִנָּה, וְלִירוּשָׁלַיִם בֵּית מִקְדָּשְׁךָ בְּשִׂמְחַת עוֹלָם. וְשָׁם נַעֲשֶׂה לְפָנֶיךָ אֶת קָרְבְּנוֹת חוֹבוֹתֵינוּ, תְּמִידִים כְּסִדְרָם, וּמוּסָפִים כְּהִלְכָתָם. וְאֶת [—Weekdays מוּסַף יוֹם] [—Sabbath מוּסְפֵי יוֹם הַשַּׁבָּת הַזֶּה וְיוֹם] הַשְּׁמִינִי חַג הָעֲצֶרֶת הַזֶּה נַעֲשֶׂה וְנַקְרִיב לְפָנֶיךָ בְּאַהֲבָה כְּמִצְוַת רְצוֹנֶךָ, כְּמוֹ שֶׁכָּתַבְתָּ עָלֵינוּ בְּתוֹרָתֶךָ, עַל יְדֵי מֹשֶׁה עַבְדֶּךָ, מִפִּי כְבוֹדֶךָ כָּאָמוּר:

On the Sabbath add. [If forgotten, do not repeat *Shemoneh Esrei*. See *Laws* §86.]

וּבְיוֹם הַשַּׁבָּת שְׁנֵי כְבָשִׂים בְּנֵי שָׁנָה תְּמִימִם, וּשְׁנֵי עֶשְׂרֹנִים סֹלֶת מִנְחָה בְּלוּלָה בַשֶּׁמֶן, וְנִסְכּוֹ. עֹלַת שַׁבַּת בְּשַׁבַּתּוֹ, עַל עֹלַת הַתָּמִיד וְנִסְכָּהּ.[1] (זֶה קָרְבַּן שַׁבָּת. וְקָרְבַּן הַיּוֹם כָּאָמוּר:)

בַּיּוֹם הַשְּׁמִינִי, עֲצֶרֶת תִּהְיֶה לָכֶם, כָּל מְלֶאכֶת עֲבֹדָה לֹא תַעֲשׂוּ. וְהִקְרַבְתֶּם עֹלָה אִשֵּׁה רֵיחַ נִיחֹחַ לַיהוה, פַּר אֶחָד, אַיִל אֶחָד, כְּבָשִׂים בְּנֵי שָׁנָה שִׁבְעָה, תְּמִימִם.[2] וּמִנְחָתָם וְנִסְכֵּיהֶם כִּמְדֻבָּר, שְׁלֹשָׁה עֶשְׂרֹנִים לַפָּר, וּשְׁנֵי עֶשְׂרֹנִים לָאָיִל, וְעִשָּׂרוֹן לַכֶּבֶשׂ, וְיַיִן כְּנִסְכּוֹ. וְשָׂעִיר לְכַפֵּר, וּשְׁנֵי תְמִידִים כְּהִלְכָתָם.

On the Sabbath add. [If forgotten, do not repeat *Shemoneh Esrei*. See *Laws* §86.]

יִשְׂמְחוּ בְמַלְכוּתְךָ שׁוֹמְרֵי שַׁבָּת וְקוֹרְאֵי עֹנֶג, עַם מְקַדְּשֵׁי שְׁבִיעִי, כֻּלָּם יִשְׂבְּעוּ וְיִתְעַנְּגוּ מִטּוּבֶךָ, וּבַשְּׁבִיעִי רָצִיתָ בּוֹ וְקִדַּשְׁתּוֹ, חֶמְדַּת יָמִים אוֹתוֹ קָרָאתָ, זֵכֶר לְמַעֲשֵׂה בְרֵאשִׁית.

וּמִפְּנֵי חֲטָאֵינוּ *But because of our sins we have been exiled from our land and sent far from our soil. We cannot ascend to appear and to prostrate ourselves before You, and to perform our obligations in the House of Your choice, in the great and holy House upon which Your Name was proclaimed, because of the hand that was dispatched against Your Sanctuary. May it be Your will,* HASHEM, *our God and the God of our forefathers, O merciful King, that You once more be compassionate upon us and upon Your Sanctuary in Your abundant mercy, and rebuild it soon and magnify its glory. Our Father, our King, reveal the glory of Your Kingship upon us, speedily; appear and be uplifted over us before the eyes of all the living. Draw our scattered ones near, from among the nations, and bring in our dispersions from the ends of the earth. Bring us to Zion, Your City, in glad song, and to Jerusalem, home of Your Sanctuary, in eternal joy. There we will perform before You our obligatory offerings, the continual offerings according to their order and the additional offerings according to their law. And the additional offering[s of this day of Sabbath and] of this day of the Shemini Atzeres Festival, we will perform and bring near to You with love, according to the commandment of Your will, as You have written for us in Your Torah, through Moses, Your servant, from Your glorious expression, as it is said:*

On the Sabbath add. [If forgotten, do not repeat *Shemoneh Esrei.* See *Laws* §86.]

וּבְיוֹם הַשַּׁבָּת *On the Sabbath day: two [male] first-year lambs, unblemished; and two tenth-ephah of fine flour for a meal-offering, mixed with olive oil, and its wine-libation. The elevation-offering of the Sabbath must be on its particular Sabbath, in addition to the continual elevation-offering and its wine-libation.*[1] *(This is the offering of the Sabbath. And the offering of the day is as it is said:)*

בַּיּוֹם הַשְּׁמִינִי *On the eighth day, there shall be an Assembly for you, you may not do any laborious work. You are to bring an elevation-offering, a fire-offering, a satisfying aroma to* HASHEM, *one bull, one ram, seven [male] first-year lambs, unblemished.*[2] *And their meal-offerings and their wine-libations as mentioned: three tenth-ephah for each bull; two tenth-ephah for each ram; one tenth-ephah for each lamb; and wine for its libation. A he-goat for atonement, and two continual offerings according to their law.*

On the Sabbath add. [If forgotten, do not repeat *Shemoneh Esrei.* See *Laws* §86.]

יִשְׂמְחוּ *They shall rejoice in Your Kingship — those who observe the Sabbath and call it a delight. The people that sanctifies the Seventh — they will all be satisfied and delighted from Your goodness. And the Seventh — You found favor in it and sanctified it. 'Most coveted of days' You called it, a remembrance of creation.*

(1) *Numbers* 28:9-10. (2) 29:35-39.

On the Sabbath add the words in brackets. [If forgotten, see *Laws* §86-90.]

אֱלֹהֵינוּ וֵאלֹהֵי אֲבוֹתֵינוּ, [רְצֵה בִמְנוּחָתֵנוּ] מֶלֶךְ רַחֲמָן רַחֵם עָלֵינוּ, טוֹב וּמֵטִיב הִדָּרֶשׁ לָנוּ, שׁוּבָה אֵלֵינוּ בַּהֲמוֹן רַחֲמֶיךָ, בִּגְלַל אָבוֹת שֶׁעָשׂוּ רְצוֹנֶךָ. בְּנֵה בֵיתְךָ כְּבַתְּחִלָּה, וְכוֹנֵן מִקְדָּשְׁךָ עַל מְכוֹנוֹ, וְהַרְאֵנוּ בְּבִנְיָנוֹ, וְשַׂמְּחֵנוּ בְּתִקּוּנוֹ. וְהָשֵׁב כֹּהֲנִים לַעֲבוֹדָתָם, וּלְוִיִּם לְשִׁירָם וּלְזִמְרָם, וְהָשֵׁב יִשְׂרָאֵל לִנְוֵיהֶם. וְשָׁם נַעֲלֶה וְנֵרָאֶה וְנִשְׁתַּחֲוֶה לְפָנֶיךָ, בְּשָׁלֹשׁ פַּעֲמֵי רְגָלֵינוּ, כַּכָּתוּב בְּתוֹרָתֶךָ: שָׁלוֹשׁ פְּעָמִים בַּשָּׁנָה, יֵרָאֶה כָל זְכוּרְךָ אֶת פְּנֵי יהוה אֱלֹהֶיךָ, בַּמָּקוֹם אֲשֶׁר יִבְחָר, בְּחַג הַמַּצּוֹת, וּבְחַג הַשָּׁבֻעוֹת, וּבְחַג הַסֻּכּוֹת, וְלֹא יֵרָאֶה אֶת פְּנֵי יהוה רֵיקָם. אִישׁ כְּמַתְּנַת יָדוֹ, כְּבִרְכַּת יהוה אֱלֹהֶיךָ, אֲשֶׁר נָתַן לָךְ.

וְהַשִּׂיאֵנוּ יהוה אֱלֹהֵינוּ אֶת בִּרְכַּת מוֹעֲדֶיךָ לְחַיִּים וּלְשָׁלוֹם, לְשִׂמְחָה וּלְשָׂשׂוֹן, כַּאֲשֶׁר רָצִיתָ וְאָמַרְתָּ לְבָרְכֵנוּ. [אֱלֹהֵינוּ וֵאלֹהֵי אֲבוֹתֵינוּ רְצֵה בִמְנוּחָתֵנוּ] קַדְּשֵׁנוּ בְּמִצְוֹתֶיךָ וְתֵן חֶלְקֵנוּ בְּתוֹרָתֶךָ, שַׂבְּעֵנוּ מִטּוּבֶךָ וְשַׂמְּחֵנוּ בִּישׁוּעָתֶךָ, וְטַהֵר לִבֵּנוּ לְעָבְדְּךָ בֶּאֱמֶת, וְהַנְחִילֵנוּ יהוה אֱלֹהֵינוּ [בְּאַהֲבָה וּבְרָצוֹן] בְּשִׂמְחָה וּבְשָׂשׂוֹן [שַׁבָּת וּ]מוֹעֲדֵי קָדְשֶׁךָ, וְיִשְׂמְחוּ בְךָ יִשְׂרָאֵל מְקַדְּשֵׁי שְׁמֶךָ. בָּרוּךְ אַתָּה יהוה, מְקַדֵּשׁ [הַשַּׁבָּת וְ]יִשְׂרָאֵל וְהַזְּמַנִּים. (Cong. – אָמֵן.)

עבודה

רְצֵה יהוה אֱלֹהֵינוּ בְּעַמְּךָ יִשְׂרָאֵל וּבִתְפִלָּתָם, וְהָשֵׁב אֶת הָעֲבוֹדָה לִדְבִיר בֵּיתֶךָ. וְאִשֵּׁי יִשְׂרָאֵל וּתְפִלָּתָם בְּאַהֲבָה תְקַבֵּל בְּרָצוֹן, וּתְהִי לְרָצוֹן תָּמִיד עֲבוֹדַת יִשְׂרָאֵל עַמֶּךָ.

When the *Kohanim* ascend the *duchan* to pronounce *Bircas Kohanim* [the Priestly Blessing], the *chazzan's* repetition of *Shemoneh Esrei* continues below.
If no *Kohanim* are present, *chazzan* continues with וְתֶחֱזֶינָה, p. 992.

Congregation and *Kohanim,* then *chazzan.*

וְתֶעָרֵב לְפָנֶיךָ עֲתִירָתֵנוּ כְּעוֹלָה וּכְקָרְבָּן. אָנָּא, רַחוּם, בְּרַחֲמֶיךָ הָרַבִּים הָשֵׁב שְׁכִינָתְךָ לְצִיּוֹן עִירֶךָ, וְסֵדֶר הָעֲבוֹדָה לִירוּשָׁלָיִם. וְתֶחֱזֶינָה עֵינֵינוּ בְּשׁוּבְךָ לְצִיּוֹן בְּרַחֲמִים, וְשָׁם נַעֲבָדְךָ בְּיִרְאָה כִּימֵי עוֹלָם וּכְשָׁנִים קַדְמוֹנִיּוֹת.

On the Sabbath add the words in brackets. [If forgotten, see *Laws* §86-90.]

אֱלֹהֵינוּ *Our God and the God of our forefathers, [may You be pleased with our rest] O merciful King, have mercy on us; O good and beneficent One, let Yourself be sought out by us; return to us in Your yearning mercy for the sake of the forefathers who did Your will. Rebuild Your House as it was at first, and establish Your Sanctuary on its prepared site; show us its rebuilding and gladden us in its perfection. Restore the Kohanim to their service and the Levites to their song and music; and restore Israel to their dwellings. And there we will ascend and appear and prostrate ourselves before You, during our three pilgrimage seasons, as it is written in Your Torah: Three times a year all your males are to appear before* HASHEM, *your God, in the place He shall choose, on the Festival of Matzos, on the Festival of Shavuos, and on the Festival of Succos, and they shall not appear before* HASHEM *empty-handed. Every man according to the gift of his hand, according to the blessing of* HASHEM, *your God, that He gave you.*[1]

וְהַשִּׂיאֵנוּ *Bestow upon us, O* HASHEM, *our God, the blessing of Your appointed Festivals for life and for peace, for gladness and for joy, as You desired and promised to bless us. [Our God and the God of our forefathers, may You be pleased with our rest.] Sanctify us with Your commandments and grant us our share in Your Torah; satisfy us from Your goodness and gladden us with Your salvation, and purify our heart to serve You sincerely. And grant us a heritage, O* HASHEM, *our God — [with love and with favor] with gladness and with joy — [the Sabbath and] the appointed festivals of Your holiness, and may Israel, the sanctifiers of Your Name, rejoice in You. Blessed are You,* HASHEM, *Who sanctifies [the Sabbath] Israel and the festive seasons.* (Cong.— *Amen.)*

TEMPLE SERVICE

רְצֵה *Be favorable,* HASHEM, *our God, toward Your people Israel and their prayer and restore the service to the Holy of Holies of Your Temple. The fire-offerings of Israel and their prayer accept with love and favor, and may the service of Your people Israel always be favorable to You.*

When the *Kohanim* ascend the *duchan* to pronounce *Bircas Kohanim* [the Priestly Blessing], the *chazzan's* repetition of *Shemoneh Esrei* continues below.
If no *Kohanim* are present, *chazzan* continues with וְתֶחֱזֶינָה, p. 992.

Congregation and *Kohanim,* then *chazzan.*

וְתֶעָרֵב *May our entreaty be pleasing unto You as an elevation-offering and as a sacrifice. Please, O Merciful One, in Your abounding mercy return Your Shechinah to Zion, Your city, and the order of the Temple service to Jerusalem. And may our eyes behold when You return to Zion in mercy, that we may there serve You with awe as in days of old and as in earlier years.*

(1) *Deuteronomy* 16:16-17.

Chazzan concludes:

When וְתֶעֱרַב is recited

בָּרוּךְ אַתָּה יהוה, שֶׁאוֹתְךָ לְבַדְּךָ בְּיִרְאָה נַעֲבוֹד.

When וְתֶעֱרַב is not recited

וְתֶחֱזֶינָה עֵינֵינוּ בְּשׁוּבְךָ לְצִיּוֹן בְּרַחֲמִים. בָּרוּךְ אַתָּה יהוה, הַמַּחֲזִיר שְׁכִינָתוֹ לְצִיּוֹן.

(.אָמֵן — Cong. and *Kohanim*)

הודאה

The *chazzan* recites the entire מוֹדִים aloud, while the congregation recites מוֹדִים דְּרַבָּנָן softly. Bow at מוֹדִים; straighten up at ה׳.

מוֹדִים אֲנַחְנוּ לָךְ, שָׁאַתָּה הוּא יהוה אֱלֹהֵינוּ וֵאלֹהֵי אֲבוֹתֵינוּ לְעוֹלָם וָעֶד. צוּר חַיֵּינוּ, מָגֵן יִשְׁעֵנוּ אַתָּה הוּא לְדוֹר וָדוֹר. נוֹדֶה לְּךָ וּנְסַפֵּר תְּהִלָּתֶךָ[1] עַל חַיֵּינוּ הַמְּסוּרִים בְּיָדֶךָ, וְעַל נִשְׁמוֹתֵינוּ הַפְּקוּדוֹת לָךְ, וְעַל נִסֶּיךָ שֶׁבְּכָל יוֹם עִמָּנוּ, וְעַל נִפְלְאוֹתֶיךָ וְטוֹבוֹתֶיךָ שֶׁבְּכָל עֵת, עֶרֶב וָבֹקֶר וְצָהֳרָיִם. הַטּוֹב כִּי לֹא כָלוּ רַחֲמֶיךָ, וְהַמְּרַחֵם כִּי לֹא תַמּוּ חֲסָדֶיךָ,[2] מֵעוֹלָם קִוִּינוּ לָךְ.

מודים דרבנן

מוֹדִים אֲנַחְנוּ לָךְ, שָׁאַתָּה הוּא יהוה אֱלֹהֵינוּ וֵאלֹהֵי אֲבוֹתֵינוּ, אֱלֹהֵי כָל בָּשָׂר, יוֹצְרֵנוּ, יוֹצֵר בְּרֵאשִׁית. בְּרָכוֹת וְהוֹדָאוֹת לְשִׁמְךָ הַגָּדוֹל וְהַקָּדוֹשׁ, עַל שֶׁהֶחֱיִיתָנוּ וְקִיַּמְתָּנוּ. כֵּן תְּחַיֵּנוּ וּתְקַיְּמֵנוּ, וְתֶאֱסוֹף גָּלֻיּוֹתֵינוּ לְחַצְרוֹת קָדְשֶׁךָ, לִשְׁמוֹר חֻקֶּיךָ וְלַעֲשׂוֹת רְצוֹנֶךָ, וּלְעָבְדְּךָ בְּלֵבָב שָׁלֵם, עַל שֶׁאֲנַחְנוּ מוֹדִים לָךְ. בָּרוּךְ אֵל הַהוֹדָאוֹת.

וְעַל כֻּלָּם יִתְבָּרַךְ וְיִתְרוֹמַם שִׁמְךָ מַלְכֵּנוּ תָּמִיד לְעוֹלָם וָעֶד.

The *chazzan* bends his knees at בָּרוּךְ; bows at אַתָּה; and straightens up at ה׳. When the *chazzan* recites וְכֹל הַחַיִּים, the *Kohanim* recite יְהִי רָצוֹן.

וְכֹל הַחַיִּים יוֹדְוּךָ סֶּלָה, וִיהַלְּלוּ אֶת שִׁמְךָ בֶּאֱמֶת, הָאֵל יְשׁוּעָתֵנוּ וְעֶזְרָתֵנוּ סֶלָה. בָּרוּךְ אַתָּה יהוה, הַטּוֹב שִׁמְךָ וּלְךָ נָאֶה לְהוֹדוֹת.

(.אָמֵן — Cong. and *Kohanim*)

יְהִי רָצוֹן מִלְּפָנֶיךָ, יהוה אֱלֹהֵינוּ וֵאלֹהֵי אֲבוֹתֵינוּ, שֶׁתְּהֵא הַבְּרָכָה הַזֹּאת שֶׁצִּוִּיתָנוּ לְבָרֵךְ אֶת עַמְּךָ יִשְׂרָאֵל בְּרָכָה שְׁלֵמָה, וְלֹא יִהְיֶה בָּהּ שׁוּם מִכְשׁוֹל וְעָוֹן מֵעַתָּה וְעַד עוֹלָם.

IF NO *KOHANIM* ARE PRESENT THE *CHAZZAN* CONTINUES WITH אֱלֹהֵינוּ ON PAGE 1000.

Chazzan concludes:

When וְתֶעֱרַב is recited

בָּרוּךְ *Blessed are You,* HASHEM, *for You alone do we serve, with awe.*

When וְתֶעֱרַב is not recited

וְתֶחֱזֶינָה *May our eyes behold Your return to Zion in compassion. Blessed are You,* HASHEM, *Who restores His Presence to Zion.*

(Cong. and *Kohanim*— *Amen.*)

THANKSGIVING [MODIM]

Chazzan recites the entire *Modim* aloud, while the congregation recites *Modim of the Rabbis* softly. Bow at *'We gratefully thank You'*; straighten up at *'HASHEM.'*

מוֹדִים *We gratefully thank You, for it is You Who are* HASHEM, *our God and the God of our forefathers for all eternity; Rock of our lives, Shield of our salvation are You from generation to generation. We shall thank You and relate Your praise*[1] *— for our lives, which are committed to Your power and for our souls that are entrusted to You; for Your miracles that are with us every day; and for Your wonders and favors in every season — evening, morning, and afternoon. The Beneficent One, for Your compassions were never exhausted, and the Compassionate One, for Your kindnesses never ended*[2] *— always have we put our hope in You.*

MODIM OF THE RABBIS

מוֹדִים *We gratefully thank You, for it is You Who are* HASHEM, *our God and the God of our forefathers, the God of all flesh, our Molder, the Molder of the universe. Blessings and thanks are due Your great and holy Name for You have given us life and sustained us. So may You continue to give us life and sustain us and gather our exiles to the Courtyards of Your Sanctuary, to observe Your decrees, to do Your will and to serve You wholeheartedly. [We thank You] for inspiring us to thank You. Blessed is the God of thanksgivings.*

For all these, may Your Name be blessed and exalted, our King, continually forever and ever.

When the *chazzan* recites וְכֹל הַחַיִּים, *Everything alive,* the *Kohanim* recite יְהִי רָצוֹן, *May it be Your will.*

וְכֹל *Everything alive will gratefully acknowledge You, Selah! and praise Your Name sincerely, O God of our salvation and help, Selah! Blessed are You,* HASHEM, *Your Name is 'The Beneficent One' and to You it is fitting to give thanks.*

(Cong. and *Kohanim*— *Amen.*)

יְהִי רָצוֹן *May it be Your will,* HASHEM, *our God and the God of our fathers, that this blessing which You have commanded us to bestow upon Your nation Israel be a full blessing, that there be in it neither stumbling block nor sin from now and forever.*

IF NO *KOHANIM* ARE PRESENT THE *CHAZZAN* CONTINUES WITH אֱלֹהֵינוּ ON PAGE 1000.

(1) Cf. *Psalms* 79:13. (2) Cf. *Lamentations* 3:22.

The *chazzan* recites the following in an undertone but says the word כֹּהֲנִים aloud as a formal summons to the *Kohanim** to bless the people. In some communities the congregation, but not the *Kohanim,* responds עַם קְדוֹשֶׁךָ כָּאָמוּר, aloud.

אֱלֹהֵינוּ וֵאלֹהֵי אֲבוֹתֵינוּ, בָּרְכֵנוּ בַבְּרָכָה* הַמְּשֻׁלֶּשֶׁת* בַּתּוֹרָה הַכְּתוּבָה עַל יְדֵי מֹשֶׁה עַבְדֶּךָ, הָאֲמוּרָה מִפִּי אַהֲרֹן וּבָנָיו,

כֹּהֲנִים

עַם קְדוֹשֶׁךָ* — כָּאָמוּר:

The *Kohanim* recite the following blessing aloud, in unison, and the congregation, but not the *chazzan,* responds אָמֵן.

בָּרוּךְ אַתָּה יהוה, אֱלֹהֵינוּ מֶלֶךְ הָעוֹלָם, אֲשֶׁר קִדְּשָׁנוּ בִּקְדֻשָּׁתוֹ שֶׁל אַהֲרֹן,* וְצִוָּנוּ לְבָרֵךְ אֶת עַמּוֹ יִשְׂרָאֵל בְּאַהֲבָה.*

(Cong. – אָמֵן.)

See commentary regarding the related verses* in small print that appear beside the words of the *Kohanim's* blessing.

יְבָרֶכְךָ יְבָרֶכְךָ יהוה מִצִּיּוֹן, עֹשֵׂה שָׁמַיִם וָאָרֶץ.[1]

יהוה* יהוה אֲדוֹנֵינוּ, מָה אַדִּיר שִׁמְךָ בְּכָל הָאָרֶץ.[2]

וְיִשְׁמְרֶךָ.* שָׁמְרֵנִי, אֵל, כִּי חָסִיתִי בָךְ.[3]

בִּרְכַּת כֹּהֲנִים / THE PRIESTLY BLESSING

The Midrash (*Bamidbar Rabbah* 11:2) teaches that until the time of the Patriarchs, God Himself retained the power to bless people. With the advent of the Patriarchs, He gave this

---

Laws of Bircas Kohanim

After *Kedushah,* a Levite pours water from a utensil over the *Kohen's* hands. When the *chazzan* begins רְצֵה the *Kohanim* slip off their shoes (the laces should be loosened before the hands are washed) and ascend the *duchan* [platform in front of the Ark] where they stand facing the Ark.

When the *chazzan* recites וְכֹל הַחַיִּים, the *Kohanim* quietly recite the יְהִי רָצוֹן supplication, concluding it to coincide with the ending of the *chazzan's* blessing, so that the congregational *Amen* will be in response to their prayer as well as the *chazzan's.*

In most congregations, the *chazzan* quietly recites, '. . . אֱלֹהֵינוּ וֵאלֹהֵי אֲבוֹתֵינוּ בָּרְכֵנוּ, *Our God . . . bless us . . .*' until the word כֹּהֲנִים, *Kohanim,* which he calls out in a loud voice. Then, resuming his undertone, he recites the next words, ' עַם קְדוֹשֶׁךָ כָּאָמוּר, *Your holy people, as it is said.*' Even if only one *Kohen* is present, the *chazzan* uses the word *Kohanim* in plural, since it is the established form of the prayer. In some congregations, however, the *chazzan* merely calls out *'Kohanim'* without reciting the introductory prayer. In these places the *chazzan* calls out the plural word *Kohanim* only if two or more *Kohanim* ascend the *duchan.* If only one *Kohen* is present, however, that *Kohen* does not wait for a call, but raises his hands and begins his blessing immediately.

From this point until the *chazzan* begins שִׂים שָׁלוֹם, the congregation stands, facing the *Kohanim* attentively. No one may gaze at the *Kohanim's* raised hands.

Those standing behind the *Kohanim* do not receive the benefits of the blessing. Therefore, people behind them should move up during *Bircas Kohanim.*

The *chazzan* reads each word of *Bircas Kohanim* aloud and the *Kohanim* repeat it after him. The congregation may not respond אָמֵן until the *Kohanim* have completed the initial blessing; the *chazzan* may not call out יְבָרֶכְךָ until the congregation has finished its אָמֵן; the *Kohanim* may not repeat יְבָרֶכְךָ until the *chazzan* has read the full word; etc., etc.

When the *chazzan* begins שִׂים שָׁלוֹם, the *Kohanim,* with hands still raised, turn to the Ark, then lower their hands. While the *chazzan* recites שִׂים שָׁלוֹם, the *Kohanim* recite רִבּוֹנוֹ שֶׁל עוֹלָם עָשִׂינוּ . . . and the congregation recites אַדִּיר בַּמָּרוֹם. All should conclude their respective prayers simultaneously with the *chazzan's* conclusion of שִׂים שָׁלוֹם.

It is preferable that the *Kohanim* not return to their seats until after the *chazzan* completes *Kaddish* (except on Succos when the *Hoshana* prayers are recited before *Kaddish).*

The *chazzan* recites the following in an undertone but says the word *'Kohanim'* aloud as a formal summons to the *Kohanim*• to bless the people. In some communities the congregation, but not the *Kohanim*, responds, *'Your holy people — as it is said,'* aloud.

אֱלֹהֵינוּ *Our God and the God of our forefathers, bless us with the three-verse* blessing* in the Torah that was written by the hand of Moses, Your servant, that was said by Aaron and his sons, the*

Kohanim,

Your holy people — as it is said:*

The *Kohanim* recite the following blessing aloud, in unison, and the congregation, but not the *chazzan*, respond *Amen*.

בָּרוּךְ *Blessed are You, HASHEM, our God, King of the universe, Who has sanctified us with the holiness of Aaron,* and has commanded us to bless His people Israel with love.** (Cong.— *Amen.)*

See commentary regarding the related verses• in small print that appear beside the words of the *Kohanim's* blessing.

May [He] bless you	*May HASHEM bless you from Zion, Maker of heaven and earth.*[1]
— HASHEM• —	*HASHEM, our Master, how mighty is Your Name throughout the earth!*[2]
and safeguard you.•	*Safeguard me, O God, for in You have I taken refuge.*[3]

(1) *Psalms* 134:3. (2) 8:10. (3) 16:1.

---

awesome power to them. After they died, God declared that henceforth the *Kohanim* would bless the Jewish people. Thus, the upraised hands of the *Kohanim* are the vehicle through which God's blessing flows upon His chosen people.

This section is abridged from ArtScroll's *Bircas Kohanim/The Priestly Blessings*, by Rabbi Avie Gold.

☙ אֱלֹהֵינוּ . . . בָּרְכֵנוּ בַבְּרָכָה — *Our God . . . bless us with the . . . blessing.* We ask God, not the *Kohanim*, to bless us, because, although the *Kohanim* pronounce the words, they are merely conduits through which the blessing descends from God to the nation below (*Chullin* 49a). This is made clear in the Scriptural commandment, which ends with God's pledge וַאֲנִי אֲבָרְכֵם, *and I will bless them* (*Numbers* 6:27).

הַמְשֻׁלֶּשֶׁת — *Three-verse.* The Priestly Blessing contains three Torah verses: *Numbers* 6:24-26.

עַם קְדוֹשֶׁךָ — *Your holy people.* The *Kohanim* are so described (*I Chronicles* 23:13) because they were designated to serve God and bless Israel.

☙ בָּרוּךְ . . . בִּקְדֻשָּׁתוֹ שֶׁל אַהֲרֹן — *Blessed . . . with the holiness of Aaron.* Just as the selection of Israel as the Holy Nation is not dependent solely upon the deeds of each individual member, but on the holiness of their forebears — indeed, it is the very sanctity of the Patriarchs which imbued their descendants with a capacity for holiness — so is the sanctity of the *Kehunah* [priesthood] unique among the descendants of Aaron.

בְּאַהֲבָה — *With love.* The *Kohanim* are to feel love for the congregation when they pronounce the blessing. The addition of this phrase is based upon *Zohar* (*Naso* 147b): 'Any *Kohen* who does not have love for the congregation or for whom the congregation has no love, may not raise his hands to bless the congregation . . .'

On his first day as *Kohen Gadol*, when he completed the service, *Aaron raised his hands toward the nation and blessed them* (*Leviticus* 9:22), but we are not told what he said (*Ramban*). This teaches that a person must rejoice in his fellow Jew's good fortune until his heart becomes filled with love, joy and blessing — a blessing so great that mere words cannot express it, so overflowing with love that the very movements of his hands express his joy and love.

Raising the hands is a symbol of a heart pouring forth blessing and joy from a treasure trove of happiness. Raising the hands is not a sterile act — it must be a wholehearted expression of the hope and blessing which are hidden in the soul. An ocean of inexpressible joy issues from a pure soul; and the purer the soul, the purer the blessing (*Ohr Chadash*).

☙ יְבָרֶכְךָ ה׳ — *May HASHEM bless you,* with increasing wealth (*Rashi*) and long lives (*Ibn Ezra*).

וְיִשְׁמְרֶךָ — *And safeguard you.* May the above blessings be preserved against loss or attack. Only God can guarantee that no one or nothing can tamper with the gifts He confers upon His loved ones (*Midrash Rabbah*).

☙ **Related verses** appear alongside the fifteen words of *Bircas Kohanim* in most *Siddurim*. The function of these verses and the propriety of

The *Kohanim* sing an extended chant before saying וְיִשְׁמְרֶךָ, and the congregation recites the following supplication in an undertone. (On the Sabbath this supplication is omitted.) When the *Kohanim* conclude וְיִשְׁמְרֶךָ, the congregation and *chazzan* respond אָמֵן.

רִבּוֹנוֹ שֶׁל עוֹלָם,* אֲנִי שֶׁלָּךְ וַחֲלוֹמוֹתַי שֶׁלָּךְ. חֲלוֹם חָלַמְתִּי וְאֵינִי יוֹדֵעַ מַה הוּא.* יְהִי רָצוֹן מִלְּפָנֶיךָ, יהוה אֱלֹהַי וֵאלֹהֵי אֲבוֹתַי, שֶׁיִּהְיוּ כָּל חֲלוֹמוֹתַי עָלַי וְעַל כָּל יִשְׂרָאֵל לְטוֹבָה – בֵּין שֶׁחָלַמְתִּי עַל עַצְמִי, וּבֵין שֶׁחָלַמְתִּי עַל אֲחֵרִים, וּבֵין שֶׁחָלְמוּ אֲחֵרִים עָלָי. אִם טוֹבִים הֵם, חַזְּקֵם וְאַמְּצֵם, וְיִתְקַיְּמוּ בִי וּבָהֶם כַּחֲלוֹמוֹתָיו שֶׁל יוֹסֵף הַצַּדִּיק. וְאִם צְרִיכִים רְפוּאָה, רְפָאֵם כְּחִזְקִיָּהוּ מֶלֶךְ יְהוּדָה מֵחָלְיוֹ, וּכְמִרְיָם הַנְּבִיאָה מִצָּרַעְתָּהּ, וּכְנַעֲמָן מִצָּרַעְתּוֹ, וּכְמֵי מָרָה עַל יְדֵי מֹשֶׁה רַבֵּנוּ, וּכְמֵי יְרִיחוֹ עַל יְדֵי אֱלִישָׁע. וּכְשֵׁם שֶׁהָפַכְתָּ אֶת קִלְלַת בִּלְעָם הָרָשָׁע מִקְּלָלָה לִבְרָכָה, כֵּן תַּהֲפוֹךְ כָּל חֲלוֹמוֹתַי עָלַי וְעַל כָּל יִשְׂרָאֵל לְטוֹבָה, וְתִשְׁמְרֵנִי וּתְחָנֵּנִי וְתִרְצֵנִי. אָמֵן.

יָאֵר אֱלֹהִים יְחָנֵּנוּ וִיבָרְכֵנוּ, יָאֵר פָּנָיו אִתָּנוּ, סֶלָה.[1]

יהוה יהוה יהוה, אֵל רַחוּם וְחַנּוּן, אֶרֶךְ אַפַּיִם וְרַב חֶסֶד וֶאֱמֶת.[2]

פָּנָיו פְּנֵה אֵלַי וְחָנֵּנִי, כִּי יָחִיד וְעָנִי אָנִי.[3]

אֵלֶיךָ* אֵלֶיךָ יהוה נַפְשִׁי אֶשָּׂא.[4]

וִיחֻנֶּךָּ* הִנֵּה כְעֵינֵי עֲבָדִים אֶל יַד אֲדוֹנֵיהֶם, כְּעֵינֵי שִׁפְחָה אֶל יַד גְּבִרְתָּהּ, כֵּן עֵינֵינוּ אֶל יהוה אֱלֹהֵינוּ עַד שֶׁיְּחָנֵּנוּ.[5]

The *Kohanim* sing an extended chant before saying וִיחֻנֶּךָּ, and the congregation recites the supplication (above) in an undertone. (On the Sabbath this supplication is omitted.) When the *Kohanim* conclude וִיחֻנֶּךָּ, the congregation and *chazzan* respond אָמֵן.

יִשָּׂא יִשָּׂא בְרָכָה מֵאֵת יהוה, וּצְדָקָה מֵאֱלֹהֵי יִשְׁעוֹ.[6] וּמְצָא חֵן וְשֵׂכֶל טוֹב בְּעֵינֵי אֱלֹהִים וְאָדָם.[7]

יהוה יהוה, חָנֵּנוּ, לְךָ קִוִּינוּ, הֱיֵה זְרֹעָם לַבְּקָרִים, אַף יְשׁוּעָתֵנוּ בְּעֵת צָרָה.[8]

פָּנָיו אַל תַּסְתֵּר פָּנֶיךָ מִמֶּנִּי בְּיוֹם צַר לִי, הַטֵּה אֵלַי אָזְנֶךָ, בְּיוֹם אֶקְרָא מַהֵר עֲנֵנִי.[9]

אֵלֶיךָ* אֵלֶיךָ נָשָׂאתִי אֶת עֵינַי, הַיֹּשְׁבִי בַּשָּׁמָיִם.[10]

---

reciting them presents a difficulty already dealt with in the Talmud (*Sotah* 39b,40a). Most authorities agree that no verses should be recited at all. Some permit the verses to be read in an undertone while the *chazzan* calls out the words of the blessing. In any case, the practice of the masses who read these verses aloud—and especially of those who repeat the words of *Bircas Kohanim* after the *chazzan* — is wrong and has no halachic basis (*Mishnah Berurah* 128:103).

☙ **יָאֵר ה' פָּנָיו אֵלֶיךָ** — *May HASHEM illuminate His countenance for you.* This is the blessing of spiritual growth, the light of Torah, which is symbolized by God's 'countenance' (*Sifre*).

וִיחֻנֶּךָּ — *And be gracious to you.* May you find favor in God's eyes (*Ramban*); or, may you find favor in the eyes of others, for all a person's talents and qualities will avail him little if others dislike him (*Ohr HaChaim*).

☙ **יִשָּׂא ה' פָּנָיו אֵלֶיךָ** — *May [He] HASHEM turn His countenance to you.* May He suppress His anger against you, even if you are sinful and deserve to be punished (*Rashi*). One's face is indicative of his attitude toward someone else. If he is angry, he will turn away from the one he dislikes. God 'turns His face' *toward* Israel to show that He loves them (*Maharzu*).

The *Kohanim* sing an extended chant and the congregation recites the following supplication in an undertone. (On the Sabbath this supplication is omitted.) When the *Kohanim* conclude וְיִשְׁמְרֶךָ, *'and safeguard you,'* the congregation and *chazzan* respond *Amen.*

רִבּוֹנוֹ שֶׁל עוֹלָם *Master of the world,* I am Yours and my dreams are Yours. I have dreamed a dream but I do not know what it indicates.* May it be Your will, HASHEM, my God and the God of my fathers, that all my dreams regarding myself and regarding all of Israel be good ones — those I have dreamed about myself, those I have dreamed about others, and those that others dreamed about me. If they are good, strengthen them, fortify them, make them endure in me and in them like the dreams of the righteous Joseph. But if they require healing, heal them like Hezekiah, King of Judah, from his sickness; like Miriam the prophetess from her tzaraas; like Naaman from his tzaraas; like the waters of Marah through the hand of Moses our teacher; and like the waters of Jericho through the hand of Elisha. And just as You transformed the curse of the wicked Balaam from a curse to a blessing, so may You transform all of my dreams regarding myself and regarding all of Israel for goodness. May You protect me, may You be gracious to me, may You accept me. Amen.*

May [He] illuminate *May God favor us and bless us, may He illuminate His countenance with us, Selah.*[1]

HASHEM *HASHEM, HASHEM, God, Compassionate and Gracious, Slow to anger, and Abundant in Kindness and Truth.*[2]

His countenance *Turn Your face to me and be gracious to me, for alone and afflicted am I.*[3]

for you* *To You, HASHEM, I raise my soul.*[4]

and be gracious to you.* *Behold! Like the eyes of servants unto their master's hand, like the eyes of a maid unto her mistress's hand, so are our eyes unto HASHEM, our God, until He will favor us.*[5]

The *Kohanim* sing an extended chant and the congregation recites the supplication (above) in an undertone. (On the Sabbath this supplication is omitted.) When the *Kohanim* conclude וִיחֻנֶּךָּ, *'and be gracious to you,'* the congregation and *chazzan* respond *Amen.*

May [He] turn *May he receive a blessing from HASHEM, and just kindness from the God of his salvation.*[6] *And he will find favor and good understanding in the eyes of God and man.*[7]

— HASHEM — *HASHEM, find favor with us, for You have we hoped! Be their power in the mornings, and our salvation in times of distress.*[8]

His countenance *Do not hide Your countenance from me in a day that is distressing to me; lean Your ear toward me; in the day that I call, speedily answer me.*[9]

to you* *To You I raised my eyes, O You Who dwells in the Heavens.*[10]

(1) *Psalms* 67:2. (2) *Exodus* 34:6. (3) *Psalms* 25:16. (4) 25:1. (5) 123:2.
(6) 24:5. (7) *Proverbs* 3:4. (8) *Isaiah* 33:2. (9) *Psalms* 102:3. (10) 123:1.

וְיָשֵׂם וְשָׂמוּ אֶת שְׁמִי עַל בְּנֵי יִשְׂרָאֵל, וַאֲנִי אֲבָרְכֵם.[1]

לְךָ לְךָ יהוה, הַגְּדֻלָּה וְהַגְּבוּרָה וְהַתִּפְאֶרֶת וְהַנֵּצַח וְהַהוֹד, כִּי כֹל בַּשָּׁמַיִם וּבָאָרֶץ, לְךָ יהוה, הַמַּמְלָכָה וְהַמִּתְנַשֵּׂא לְכֹל לְרֹאשׁ.[2]

שָׁלוֹם.* שָׁלוֹם שָׁלוֹם לָרָחוֹק וְלַקָּרוֹב, אָמַר יהוה, וּרְפָאתִיו.[3]

The *Kohanim* sing an extended chant before saying שָׁלוֹם, and the congregation recites the following supplication in an undertone. [The twenty-two letter Divine Name appears here in brackets and bold type. This Name should be scanned with the eyes but not spoken.] (On the Sabbath this supplication is omitted.) When the *Kohanim* conclude שָׁלוֹם, congregation and *chazzan* respond אָמֵן.

יְהִי רָצוֹן מִלְּפָנֶיךָ, יהוה אֱלֹהַי וֵאלֹהֵי אֲבוֹתַי, שֶׁתַּעֲשֶׂה לְמַעַן קְדֻשַּׁת חֲסָדֶיךָ וְגֹדֶל רַחֲמֶיךָ הַפְּשׁוּטִים, וּלְמַעַן טָהֳרַת שִׁמְךָ הַגָּדוֹל הַגִּבּוֹר וְהַנּוֹרָא, בֶּן עֶשְׂרִים וּשְׁתַּיִם אוֹתִיּוֹת* הַיּוֹצְאִים מִן הַפְּסוּקִים שֶׁל בִּרְכַּת כֹּהֲנִים [**אנקת״ם פסת״ם פספסי״ם דיונסי״ם**] הָאֲמוּרָה מִפִּי אַהֲרֹן וּבָנָיו עַם קְדוֹשֶׁךָ, שֶׁתִּהְיֶה קָרוֹב לִי בְּקָרְאִי לָךְ, וְתִשְׁמַע תְּפִלָּתִי נַאֲקָתִי וְאֶנְקָתִי תָּמִיד, כְּשֵׁם שֶׁשָּׁמַעְתָּ **אֶנְקַת** יַעֲקֹב תְּמִימֶךָ הַנִּקְרָא אִישׁ **תָּם**. וְתִתֶּן לִי וּלְכָל נַפְשׁוֹת בֵּיתִי מְזוֹנוֹתֵינוּ וּפַרְנָסָתֵנוּ — בְּרֶוַח וְלֹא בְצִמְצוּם, בְּהֶתֵּר וְלֹא בְאִסּוּר, בְּנַחַת וְלֹא בְצַעַר, — מִתַּחַת יָדְךָ הָרְחָבָה, כְּשֵׁם שֶׁנָּתַתָּ **פַּת** לֶחֶם לֶאֱכוֹל וּבֶגֶד לִלְבּוֹשׁ לְיַעֲקֹב אָבִינוּ הַנִּקְרָא אִישׁ **תָּם**. וְתִתְּנֵנוּ לְאַהֲבָה, לְחֵן וּלְחֶסֶד וּלְרַחֲמִים בְּעֵינֶיךָ וּבְעֵינֵי כָל רוֹאֵינוּ, וְיִהְיוּ דְבָרַי נִשְׁמָעִים לַעֲבוֹדָתֶךָ, כְּשֵׁם שֶׁנָּתַתָּ אֶת יוֹסֵף צַדִּיקֶךָ — בְּשָׁעָה שֶׁהִלְבִּישׁוֹ אָבִיו כְּתֹנֶת **פַּסִּים** — לְחֵן וּלְחֶסֶד וּלְרַחֲמִים בְּעֵינֶיךָ וּבְעֵינֵי כָל רוֹאָיו. וְתַעֲשֶׂה עִמִּי נִפְלָאוֹת **וְנִסִּים**,* וּלְטוֹבָה אוֹת, וְתַצְלִיחֵנִי בִּדְרָכַי, וְתֵן בְּלִבִּי בִּינָה לְהָבִין וּלְהַשְׂכִּיל וּלְקַיֵּם אֶת כָּל דִּבְרֵי תַלְמוּד תּוֹרָתֶךָ וְסוֹדוֹתֶיהָ, וְתַצִּילֵנִי מִשְּׁגִיאוֹת, וּתְטַהֵר רַעְיוֹנַי וְלִבִּי לַעֲבוֹדָתֶךָ וּלְיִרְאָתֶךָ. וְתַאֲרִיךְ יָמַי (insert the appropriate words— וִימֵי אָבִי וְאִמִּי וְאִשְׁתִּי וּבָנַי וּבְנוֹתַי) בְּטוֹב וּבִנְעִימוֹת, בְּרֹב עֹז וְשָׁלוֹם, אָמֵן סֶלָה.

וְיָשֵׂם לְךָ שָׁלוֹם — *And establish for you peace.* Peace is the seal of all blessings, because without peace — prosperity, health, food, and drink are worthless *(Sifre)*.

יְהִי רָצוֹן / May it be Your Will

שִׁמְךָ . . . בֶּן עֶשְׂרִים וּשְׁתַּיִם אוֹתִיּוֹת — *Your Name . . . composed of twenty-two letters.* Scripture uses many appellations for God. Each of these Divine Names represents an attribute by which God allows man to perceive Him. י־ה־ו־ה represents the attribute of Divine Kindness. Since this Name is composed of the letters of הָיָה הֹוֶה יִהְיֶה, *He was, He is, He will be,* it is also an indication of God's Eternality. אֱלֹהִים, *ELOHIM,* represents Divine Justice. This word can also mean *judge* and *power*. Similarly, each Name found in Scripture is but an allusion to a different Divine attribute. Kaballah records many Divine Names which are not found explicitly in Scripture but may be derived through various Kaballistic principles. One of the Names is described in Kabballistic literature as the Twenty-two Letter Name, and the letters of *Bircas Kohanim* are said to allude to it.

The well-known Kabbalist Rabbi Moshe Cordovero *[Ramak]* explains that this Twenty-two Letter Name comprises four individual Names [אנקת״ם פסת״ם פספסי״ם דיונסי״ם], each capable of effecting the fulfillment of a particular human need. The first Name, אנקת״ם, — a contraction of אֶנְקַת תָּמִים, literally *the cry of the perfect ones* — is efficacious in making one's prayer accepted in Heaven; the second, פסת״ם, is the Name

and establish *And they shall place My Name upon the Children of Israel, and I shall bless them.*[1]

for you *Yours, HASHEM, is the greatness, the strength, the splendor, the triumph, and the glory, even all that is in heaven and earth; Yours, HASHEM, is the kingdom and the sovereignty over every leader.*[2]

peace.* *'Peace, peace, for far and near,' says HASHEM, 'and I shall heal him.'*[3]

The *Kohanim* sing an extended chant and the congregation recites the following supplication in an undertone. [The twenty-two letter Divine Name appears here in brackets and bold type. This Name should be scanned with the eyes but not spoken.] (On the Sabbath this supplication is omitted.) When the *Kohanim* conclude שָׁלוֹם, *'peace,'* congregation and *chazzan* respond *Amen.*

יְהִי רָצוֹן *May it be Your will, HASHEM, my God and the God of my forefathers, that You act for the sake of the holiness of Your kindness and the greatness of Your mercies which reach out, and for the sake of the sanctity of Your Name — the great, the mighty and the awesome; composed of twenty-two letters* which derive from the verses of Bircas Kohanim* [**אנקת״ם פסת״ם פספסי״ם דיונסי״ם**]*; spoken by Aaron and his sons, Your holy people — that You be near to me when I call to You; that You listen to my prayer, my plea and my cry at all times, just as You listened to the cry* [**אֶנְקַת**] *of Jacob, Your perfect one, who is called 'a wholesome man'* [**תָּם**]. *And may You bestow upon me and upon all the souls of my household, our food and our sustenance — generously and not sparsely, honestly and not in forbidden fashion, pleasurably and not in pain — from beneath Your generous hand, just as You gave a portion* [**פִּסַּת**] *of bread to eat and clothing to wear to our father Jacob who is called 'a wholesome man'* [**תָּם**]. *And may You grant that we find love, favor, kindness and mercy in Your eyes and in the eyes of all who behold us; and that my words in Your service be heard; just as You granted Joseph, Your righteous one — at the time that his father garbed him in a fine woolen tunic* [**פַּסִּים**] *— that he find favor, kindness and mercy in Your eyes and in the eyes of all who beheld him. May You perform wonders and miracles* [**וְנִיסִּים**] *with me,* and a goodly sign; grant me success in my ways; place in my heart the power of understanding, to understand, to be wise, to fulfill all the words of Your Torah's teaching and its mysteries; save me from errors; and purify my thinking and my heart for Your service and Your awe. May You prolong my days [*insert the appropriate words— *and the days of my father, my mother, my wife, my son(s), my daughter(s)] with goodness, with sweetness, with an abundance of strength and peace. Amen: Selah.*

(1) *Numbers* 6:27. (2) *II Chronicles* 29:11. (3) *Isaiah* 57:19.

through which God distributes פַּת בַּר, *portions of bread,* to the hungry; through the Name פספסי״ם — related to כְּתֹנֶת פַּסִּים, *woolen tunic,* that Jacob made for Joseph (*Genesis* 37:3) — He clothes the naked; and דיונסי״ם indicates that He performs נִסִּים, *miracles,* and wonders. These four Names were invoked by Jacob when he prayed (*Genesis* 28:21) that *God be with me and guard me on this way which I am going; and give me bread to eat and clothes to wear; and that I return in peace ...* (*Pardes,* cited in *Siddur Amudei Shamayim*).

וְתַעֲשֶׂה עִמִּי נִפְלָאוֹת וְנִסִּית — *May You perform wonders and miracles with me.* It is unseemly for an individual to request miraculous intervention in his personal affairs, for what assurance does he have that he is deserving?

There are two classifications of miracle — overt [e.g., the splitting of the Sea; Joshua's stopping the sun] and covert [e.g., the seeming historic simplicity of the Purim story]. One should not request *obvious* miracles, but he may pray for covert miracles, because they are disguised as natural phenomena (*Bechor Shor*).

The *chazzan* immediately begins שִׂים שָׁלוֹם; the *Kohanim* turn back to the Ark, lower their hands and recite their concluding prayer רִבּוֹנוֹ שֶׁל עוֹלָם; and the congregation recites אַדִּיר בַּמָּרוֹם. All should conclude their respective prayers simultaneously with the *chazzan's* conclusion of שִׂים שָׁלוֹם.

Kohanim:

רִבּוֹנוֹ שֶׁל עוֹלָם, עָשִׂינוּ מַה שֶּׁגָּזַרְתָּ עָלֵינוּ, אַף אַתָּה עֲשֵׂה עִמָּנוּ כְּמָה שֶׁהִבְטַחְתָּנוּ: הַשְׁקִיפָה מִמְּעוֹן קָדְשְׁךָ, מִן הַשָּׁמַיִם, וּבָרֵךְ אֶת עַמְּךָ אֶת יִשְׂרָאֵל, וְאֵת הָאֲדָמָה אֲשֶׁר נָתַתָּה לָנוּ — כַּאֲשֶׁר נִשְׁבַּעְתָּ לַאֲבוֹתֵינוּ — אֶרֶץ זָבַת חָלָב וּדְבָשׁ.[1]

Congregation:

אַדִּיר בַּמָּרוֹם, שׁוֹכֵן בִּגְבוּרָה, אַתָּה שָׁלוֹם וְשִׁמְךָ שָׁלוֹם. יְהִי רָצוֹן שֶׁתָּשִׂים עָלֵינוּ וְעַל כָּל עַמְּךָ בֵּית יִשְׂרָאֵל חַיִּים וּבְרָכָה לְמִשְׁמֶרֶת שָׁלוֹם.

If the *Kohanim* do not ascend the *duchan, t*he *chazzan* recites the following. He faces right at וְיִשְׁמְרֶךָ; faces left at אֵלֶיךָ וִיחֻנֶּךָּ; faces the Ark for the rest of the blessings.

אֱלֹהֵינוּ, וֵאלֹהֵי אֲבוֹתֵינוּ, בָּרְכֵנוּ בַבְּרָכָה הַמְּשֻׁלֶּשֶׁת בַּתּוֹרָה הַכְּתוּבָה עַל יְדֵי מֹשֶׁה עַבְדֶּךָ, הָאֲמוּרָה מִפִּי אַהֲרֹן וּבָנָיו, כֹּהֲנִים עַם קְדוֹשֶׁךָ, כָּאָמוּר:

יְבָרֶכְךָ יהוה, וְיִשְׁמְרֶךָ. (.Cong – כֵּן יְהִי רָצוֹן.)

יָאֵר יהוה פָּנָיו אֵלֶיךָ וִיחֻנֶּךָּ. (.Cong – כֵּן יְהִי רָצוֹן.)

יִשָּׂא יהוה פָּנָיו אֵלֶיךָ וְיָשֵׂם לְךָ שָׁלוֹם.[2] (.Cong – כֵּן יְהִי רָצוֹן.)

Chazzan:

שִׂים שָׁלוֹם, טוֹבָה וּבְרָכָה, חֵן, וָחֶסֶד וְרַחֲמִים עָלֵינוּ וְעַל כָּל יִשְׂרָאֵל עַמֶּךָ. בָּרְכֵנוּ אָבִינוּ, כֻּלָּנוּ כְּאֶחָד בְּאוֹר פָּנֶיךָ, כִּי בְאוֹר פָּנֶיךָ נָתַתָּ לָּנוּ, יהוה אֱלֹהֵינוּ, תּוֹרַת חַיִּים וְאַהֲבַת חֶסֶד, וּצְדָקָה, וּבְרָכָה, וְרַחֲמִים, וְחַיִּים, וְשָׁלוֹם. וְטוֹב בְּעֵינֶיךָ לְבָרֵךְ אֶת עַמְּךָ יִשְׂרָאֵל, בְּכָל עֵת וּבְכָל שָׁעָה בִּשְׁלוֹמֶךָ. בָּרוּךְ אַתָּה יהוה, הַמְּבָרֵךְ אֶת עַמּוֹ יִשְׂרָאֵל בַּשָּׁלוֹם. (Cong. and *Kohanim* – אָמֵן.)

Chazzan, in an undertone:

יִהְיוּ לְרָצוֹן אִמְרֵי פִי וְהֶגְיוֹן לִבִּי לְפָנֶיךָ, יהוה צוּרִי וְגֹאֲלִי.[3]

קדיש שלם

The *chazzan* recites קַדִּישׁ שָׁלֵם.

יִתְגַּדַּל וְיִתְקַדַּשׁ שְׁמֵהּ רַבָּא. (.Cong – אָמֵן.) בְּעָלְמָא דִּי בְרָא כִרְעוּתֵהּ. וְיַמְלִיךְ מַלְכוּתֵהּ, בְּחַיֵּיכוֹן וּבְיוֹמֵיכוֹן וּבְחַיֵּי דְכָל בֵּית יִשְׂרָאֵל, בַּעֲגָלָא וּבִזְמַן קָרִיב. וְאִמְרוּ: אָמֵן.

(.Cong – אָמֵן. יְהֵא שְׁמֵהּ רַבָּא מְבָרַךְ לְעָלַם וּלְעָלְמֵי עָלְמַיָּא.)

יְהֵא שְׁמֵהּ רַבָּא מְבָרַךְ לְעָלַם וּלְעָלְמֵי עָלְמַיָּא.

The *chazzan* immediately begins שִׂים שָׁלוֹם, *Establish peace;* the *Kohanim* turn back to the Ark, lower their hands and recite their concluding prayer רִבּוֹנוֹ שֶׁל עוֹלָם, *Master of the World;* and the congregation recites אַדִּיר, *Mighty One.* All should conclude their respective prayers simultaneously with the *chazzan's* conclusion of שִׂים שָׁלוֹם.

Kohanim:

רִבּוֹנוֹ שֶׁל עוֹלָם *Master of the world, we have done what You have decreed upon us, now may You also do as You have promised us: Look down from Your sacred dwelling, from the heavens, and bless Your people, Israel, and the earth which You have given us — just as You have sworn to our fathers — a land that flows with milk and honey.*[1]

Congregation:

אַדִּיר *Mighty One on high, He Who dwells in power! You are Peace and Your Name is Peace! May it be acceptable that You grant us and all of Your people, the house of Israel, life and blessing for a safeguard of peace.*

If the *Kohanim* do not ascend the *duchan,* the *chazzan* recites the following:

אֱלֹהֵינוּ *Our God and the God of our forefathers, bless us with the three-verse blessing in the Torah that was written by the hand of Moses, Your servant, that was said by Aaron and his sons, the Kohanim, Your holy people, as it is said:*

May HASHEM *bless you and safeguard you.* (Cong.— *So may it be.*)

May HASHEM *illuminate His countenance for you and be gracious to you.* (Cong.— *So may it be.*)

May HASHEM *turn His countenance to you and establish peace for you.*[2] (Cong.— *So may it be.*)

Chazzan:

שִׂים שָׁלוֹם *Establish peace, goodness, blessing, graciousness, kindness, and compassion upon us and upon all of Your people Israel. Bless us, our Father, all of us as one, with the light of Your countenance, for with the light of Your countenance You gave us,* HASHEM, *our God, the Torah of life and a love of kindness, righteousness, blessing, compassion, life, and peace. And may it be good in Your eyes to bless Your people Israel, in every season and in every hour with Your Peace. Blessed are You,* HASHEM, *Who blesses His people Israel with peace.*

(Cong. and *Kohanim*— *Amen.*)

Chazzan, in an undertone:

May the expressions of my mouth and the thoughts of my heart find favor before You, HASHEM, *my Rock and my Redeemer.*[3]

FULL KADDISH

The *chazzan* recites the Full *Kaddish.*

יִתְגַּדַּל *May His great Name grow exalted and sanctified* (Cong.— *Amen.*) *in the world that He created as He willed. May He give reign to His kingship in your lifetimes and in your days, and in the lifetimes of the entire Family of Israel, swiftly and soon. Now respond: Amen.*

(Cong.— *Amen. May His great Name be blessed forever and ever.*)

May His great Name be blessed forever and ever.

---

(1) *Deuteronomy* 26:15. (2) *Numbers* 6:24-26. (3) *Psalms* 19:15.

יִתְבָּרַךְ וְיִשְׁתַּבַּח וְיִתְפָּאַר וְיִתְרוֹמַם וְיִתְנַשֵּׂא וְיִתְהַדָּר וְיִתְעַלֶּה וְיִתְהַלָּל שְׁמֵהּ דְּקֻדְשָׁא בְּרִיךְ הוּא (.Cong — בְּרִיךְ הוּא) — לְעֵלָּא מִן כָּל בִּרְכָתָא וְשִׁירָתָא תֻּשְׁבְּחָתָא וְנֶחֱמָתָא, דַּאֲמִירָן בְּעָלְמָא. וְאִמְרוּ: אָמֵן. (.Cong — אָמֵן.)

(.Cong — קַבֵּל בְּרַחֲמִים וּבְרָצוֹן אֶת תְּפִלָּתֵנוּ.)

תִּתְקַבֵּל צְלוֹתְהוֹן וּבָעוּתְהוֹן דְּכָל בֵּית יִשְׂרָאֵל קֳדָם אֲבוּהוֹן דִּי בִשְׁמַיָּא. וְאִמְרוּ: אָמֵן. (.Cong — אָמֵן.)

(.Cong — יְהִי שֵׁם יהוה מְבֹרָךְ, מֵעַתָּה וְעַד עוֹלָם.[1])

יְהֵא שְׁלָמָא רַבָּא מִן שְׁמַיָּא, וְחַיִּים עָלֵינוּ וְעַל כָּל יִשְׂרָאֵל. וְאִמְרוּ: אָמֵן. (.Cong — אָמֵן.)

(.Cong — עֶזְרִי מֵעִם יהוה, עֹשֵׂה שָׁמַיִם וָאָרֶץ.[2])

Take three steps back. Bow left and say . . . עֹשֶׂה; bow right and say . . . הוּא; bow forward and say וְעַל כָּל . . . אָמֵן. Remain standing in place for a few moments, then take three steps forward.

עֹשֶׂה שָׁלוֹם בִּמְרוֹמָיו, הוּא יַעֲשֶׂה שָׁלוֹם עָלֵינוּ, וְעַל כָּל יִשְׂרָאֵל. וְאִמְרוּ: אָמֵן. (.Cong — אָמֵן.)

קַוֵּה אֶל יהוה, חֲזַק וְיַאֲמֵץ לִבֶּךָ, וְקַוֵּה אֶל יהוה.[3] אֵין קָדוֹשׁ כַּיהוה, כִּי אֵין בִּלְתֶּךָ, וְאֵין צוּר כֵּאלֹהֵינוּ.[4] כִּי מִי אֱלוֹהַּ מִבַּלְעֲדֵי יהוה, וּמִי צוּר זוּלָתִי אֱלֹהֵינוּ.[5]

אֵין כֵּאלֹהֵינוּ, אֵין כַּאדוֹנֵינוּ, אֵין כְּמַלְכֵּנוּ, אֵין כְּמוֹשִׁיעֵנוּ. מִי כֵאלֹהֵינוּ, מִי כַאדוֹנֵינוּ, מִי כְמַלְכֵּנוּ, מִי כְמוֹשִׁיעֵנוּ. נוֹדֶה לֵאלֹהֵינוּ, נוֹדֶה לַאדוֹנֵינוּ, נוֹדֶה לְמַלְכֵּנוּ, נוֹדֶה לְמוֹשִׁיעֵנוּ. בָּרוּךְ אֱלֹהֵינוּ, בָּרוּךְ אֲדוֹנֵינוּ, בָּרוּךְ מַלְכֵּנוּ, בָּרוּךְ מוֹשִׁיעֵנוּ. אַתָּה הוּא אֱלֹהֵינוּ, אַתָּה הוּא אֲדוֹנֵינוּ, אַתָּה הוּא מַלְכֵּנוּ, אַתָּה הוּא מוֹשִׁיעֵנוּ. אַתָּה הוּא שֶׁהִקְטִירוּ אֲבוֹתֵינוּ לְפָנֶיךָ אֶת קְטֹרֶת הַסַּמִּים.

כריתות ו.

פִּטּוּם הַקְּטֹרֶת: (א) הַצֳּרִי, (ב) וְהַצִּפֹּרֶן, (ג) הַחֶלְבְּנָה, (ד) וְהַלְּבוֹנָה, מִשְׁקַל שִׁבְעִים שִׁבְעִים מָנֶה; (ה) מוֹר, (ו) וּקְצִיעָה, (ז) שִׁבֹּלֶת נֵרְדְּ, (ח) וְכַרְכֹּם, מִשְׁקַל שִׁשָּׁה עָשָׂר שִׁשָּׁה עָשָׂר מָנֶה; (ט) הַקֹּשְׁטְ שְׁנֵים עָשָׂר, (י) וְקִלּוּפָה שְׁלֹשָׁה, (יא) וְקִנָּמוֹן תִּשְׁעָה. בֹּרִית כַּרְשִׁינָה תִּשְׁעָה קַבִּין, יֵין קַפְרִיסִין סְאִין תְּלָתָא וְקַבִּין תְּלָתָא; וְאִם אֵין לוֹ יֵין קַפְרִיסִין, מֵבִיא חֲמַר חִוַּרְיָן עַתִּיק; מֶלַח סְדוֹמִית רֹבַע הַקָּב; מַעֲלֶה עָשָׁן כָּל שֶׁהוּא. רַבִּי נָתָן הַבַּבְלִי אוֹמֵר: אַף כִּפַּת הַיַּרְדֵּן כָּל שֶׁהוּא. וְאִם נָתַן בָּהּ דְּבַשׁ פְּסָלָהּ. וְאִם חִסַּר אַחַת מִכָּל סַמָּנֶיהָ, חַיָּב מִיתָה.

Blessed, praised, glorified, exalted, extolled, mighty, upraised, and lauded be the Name of the Holy One, Blessed is He (Cong.– *Blessed is He*) — *beyond any blessing and song, praise and consolation that are uttered in the world. Now respond: Amen.* (Cong.– *Amen.*)

(Cong.– *Accept our prayers with mercy and favor.*)

May the prayers and supplications of the entire Family of Israel be accepted before their Father Who is in Heaven. Now respond: Amen. (Cong.– *Amen.*)

(Cong.– *Blessed be the Name of* HASHEM, *from this time and forever.*[1])

May there be abundant peace from Heaven, and life, upon us and upon all Israel. Now respond: Amen. (Cong.– *Amen.*)

(Cong.– *My help is from* HASHEM, *Maker of heaven and earth.*[2])

Take three steps back. Bow left and say, *'He Who makes peace . . .'*; bow right and say, *'may He . . .'*; bow forward and say, *'and upon all Israel . . .'* Remain standing in place for a few moments, then take three steps forward.

He Who makes peace in His heights, may He make peace upon us, and upon all Israel. Now respond: Amen. (Cong.– *Amen.*)

קַוֵּה *Hope to* HASHEM, *strengthen yourself and He will give you courage; and hope to* HASHEM.[3] *There is none holy as* HASHEM, *for there is none beside You, and there is no Rock like our God.*[4] *For who is a god beside* HASHEM, *and who is a Rock except for our God.*[5]

אֵין *There is none like our God; there is none like our Master;*
there is none like our King; there is none like our Savior.
Who is like our God? Who is like our Master?
Who is like our King? Who is like our Savior?
Let us thank our God; let us thank our Master;
let us thank our King; let us thank our Savior.
Blessed is our God; blessed is our Master;
blessed is our King; blessed is our Savior.
It is You Who is our God; it is You Who is our Master;
it is You Who is our King; it is You Who is our Savior.
It is You before Whom our forefathers burned the spice-incense.

Talmud, *Kereisos* 6a

פִּטּוּם הַקְּטֹרֶת *The incense mixture was formulated of [eleven spices]:* (1) *stacte,* (2) *onycha,* (3) *galbanum,* (4) *frankincense — each weighing seventy maneh;* (5) *myrrh,* (6) *cassia,* (7) *spikenard,* (8) *saffron — each weighing sixteen maneh;* (9) *costus — twelve [maneh];* (10) *aromatic bark — three; and* (11) *cinnamon — nine. [Additionally] Carshina lye — nine kab; Cyprus wine, three se'ah and three kab — if he has no Cyprus wine, he brings old white wine; Sodom salt, a quarter kab; and a minute amount of smoke-raising herb. Rabbi Nassan the Babylonian says: Also a minute amount of Jordan amber. If he placed fruit-honey into it, he invalidated it. And if he left out any of its spices, he is liable to the death penalty.*

---

(1) *Psalms* 113:2. (2) 121:2. (3) 27:14. (4) *I Samuel* 2:2. (5) *Psalms* 18:32.

רַבָּן שִׁמְעוֹן בֶּן גַּמְלִיאֵל אוֹמֵר: הַצֳּרִי אֵינוֹ אֶלָּא שְׂרָף הַנּוֹטֵף מֵעֲצֵי הַקְּטָף. בֹּרִית כַּרְשִׁינָה שֶׁשָּׁפִין בָּהּ אֶת הַצִּפֹּרֶן כְּדֵי שֶׁתְּהֵא נָאָה; יֵין קַפְרִיסִין שֶׁשּׁוֹרִין בּוֹ אֶת הַצִּפֹּרֶן כְּדֵי שֶׁתְּהֵא עַזָּה; וַהֲלֹא מֵי רַגְלַיִם יָפִין לָהּ, אֶלָּא שֶׁאֵין מַכְנִיסִין מֵי רַגְלַיִם בָּעֲזָרָה מִפְּנֵי הַכָּבוֹד.

משנה, תמיד ז:ד

הַשִּׁיר* שֶׁהַלְוִיִּם הָיוּ אוֹמְרִים בְּבֵית הַמִּקְדָּשׁ. בַּיּוֹם הָרִאשׁוֹן הָיוּ אוֹמְרִים: לַיהוה הָאָרֶץ וּמְלוֹאָהּ, תֵּבֵל וְיֹשְׁבֵי בָהּ.[1] בַּשֵּׁנִי הָיוּ אוֹמְרִים: גָּדוֹל יהוה וּמְהֻלָּל מְאֹד, בְּעִיר אֱלֹהֵינוּ הַר קָדְשׁוֹ.[2] בַּשְּׁלִישִׁי הָיוּ אוֹמְרִים: אֱלֹהִים נִצָּב בַּעֲדַת אֵל, בְּקֶרֶב אֱלֹהִים יִשְׁפֹּט.[3] בָּרְבִיעִי הָיוּ אוֹמְרִים: אֵל נְקָמוֹת יהוה, אֵל נְקָמוֹת הוֹפִיעַ.[4] בַּחֲמִישִׁי הָיוּ אוֹמְרִים: הַרְנִינוּ לֵאלֹהִים עוּזֵּנוּ, הָרִיעוּ לֵאלֹהֵי יַעֲקֹב.[5] בַּשִּׁשִּׁי הָיוּ אוֹמְרִים: יהוה מָלָךְ גֵּאוּת לָבֵשׁ, לָבֵשׁ יהוה עֹז הִתְאַזָּר, אַף תִּכּוֹן תֵּבֵל בַּל תִּמּוֹט.[6] בַּשַּׁבָּת הָיוּ אוֹמְרִים: מִזְמוֹר שִׁיר לְיוֹם הַשַּׁבָּת.[7] מִזְמוֹר שִׁיר לֶעָתִיד לָבֹא, לְיוֹם שֶׁכֻּלּוֹ שַׁבָּת וּמְנוּחָה לְחַיֵּי הָעוֹלָמִים.

מגילה כח:

תָּנָא דְבֵי אֵלִיָּהוּ:* כָּל הַשּׁוֹנֶה הֲלָכוֹת בְּכָל יוֹם, מֻבְטָח לוֹ שֶׁהוּא בֶּן עוֹלָם הַבָּא, שֶׁנֶּאֱמַר: הֲלִיכוֹת עוֹלָם לוֹ,[8] אַל תִּקְרֵי הֲלִיכוֹת, אֶלָּא הֲלָכוֹת.

ברכות סד.

אָמַר רַבִּי אֶלְעָזָר* אָמַר רַבִּי חֲנִינָא: תַּלְמִידֵי חֲכָמִים מַרְבִּים שָׁלוֹם בָּעוֹלָם, שֶׁנֶּאֱמַר: וְכָל בָּנַיִךְ לִמּוּדֵי יהוה, וְרַב שְׁלוֹם בָּנָיִךְ,[9] אַל תִּקְרֵי* בָּנָיִךְ אֶלָּא בּוֹנָיִךְ. ❖ שָׁלוֹם רָב לְאֹהֲבֵי תוֹרָתֶךָ, וְאֵין לָמוֹ מִכְשׁוֹל.[10] יְהִי שָׁלוֹם בְּחֵילֵךְ, שַׁלְוָה בְּאַרְמְנוֹתָיִךְ. לְמַעַן אַחַי וְרֵעָי, אֲדַבְּרָה נָּא שָׁלוֹם בָּךְ. לְמַעַן בֵּית יהוה אֱלֹהֵינוּ, אֲבַקְשָׁה טוֹב לָךְ.[11] יהוה עֹז לְעַמּוֹ יִתֵּן, יהוה יְבָרֵךְ אֶת עַמּוֹ בַשָּׁלוֹם.[12]

---

§ **הַשִּׁיר** — *The [daily] song.* This *mishnah* (*Tamid* 7:4) is recited here because the daily song was chanted by the Levites at the conclusion of the incense service. [See pages 388-394.]

§ **תָּנָא דְבֵי אֵלִיָּהוּ** — *The Academy of Elijah taught.* This homiletical teaching likens the ways of the world to the laws that govern a Jew's life on earth. Only by studying, knowing and practicing the laws of the Torah can a Jew insure himself of ultimate success.

§ **אָמַר רַבִּי אֶלְעָזָר** — *Rabbi Elazar said.* This famous teaching is the concluding statement of tractate *Berachos.*

Maharsha there, in a comment that applies here as well, explains that the tractate dealt with prayers and blessings that had been instituted by

רַבָּן שִׁמְעוֹן *Rabban Shimon ben Gamliel says: The stacte is simply the sap that drips from balsam trees. Carshina lye is used to bleach the onycha to make it pleasing. Cyprus wine is used to soak the onycha to make it pungent. Even though urine is suitable for that, nevertheless they do not bring urine into the Temple out of respect.*

Mishnah, *Tamid* 7:4

הַשִּׁיר *The daily song* that the Levites would recite in the Temple was as follows: On the first day [of the week] they would say: 'HASHEM's is the earth and its fullness, the inhabited land and those who dwell in it.'*[1] *On the second day they would say: 'Great is HASHEM and much praised, in the city of our God, Mount of His Holiness.'*[2] *On the third day they would say: 'God stands in the Divine assembly, in the midst of judges shall He judge.'*[3] *On the fourth day they would say: 'O God of vengeance, HASHEM, O God of vengeance, appear.'*[4] *On the fifth day they would say: 'Sing joyously to the God of our might, call out to the God of Jacob.'*[5] *On the sixth day they would say: 'HASHEM will have reigned, He will have donned grandeur; He will have donned might and girded Himself; He even made the world firm so that it should not falter.'*[6] *On the Sabbath they would say: 'A psalm, a song for the Sabbath day.'*[7] *A psalm, a song for the time to come, to the day that will be entirely Sabbath and contentment for the eternal life.*

Talmud, *Megillah* 28b

תָּנָא *The Academy of Elijah taught:* He who studies Torah laws every day, has the assurance that he will be in the World to Come, as it is said, 'The ways of the world are His'*[8] *— do not read* [הֲלִיכוֹת] *'ways,' but* [הֲלָכוֹת] *'laws.'*

Talmud, *Berachos* 64a

אָמַר *Rabbi Elazar said* on behalf of Rabbi Chanina: Torah scholars increase peace in the world, as it is said: 'And all your children will be students of HASHEM, and your children will have peace'*[9] *— do not read* [בָּנָיִךְ] *'your children,' but* [בּוֹנָיִךְ] *'your builders.'* Chazzan– *There is abundant peace for the lovers of Your Torah, and there is no stumbling block for them.*[10] *May there be peace within your wall, serenity within your palaces. For the sake of my brethren and comrades I shall speak of peace in your midst. For the sake of the House of HASHEM, our God, I will request your good.*[11] *HASHEM will give might to His people, HASHEM will bless His people with peace.*[12]

(1) *Psalms* 24:1. (2) 48:2. (3) 82:1. (4) 94:1. (5) 81:2. (6) 93:1. (7) 92:1.
(8) *Habakkuk* 3:6. (9) *Isaiah* 54:13. (10) *Psalms* 119:165. (11) 122:7-9. (12) 29:11.

the Sages. The reason they promulgated these expressions of devotion was to increase the harmony in the universe between man and his Maker.

קדיש דרבנן

In the presence of a *minyan,* mourners recite קַדִּישׁ דְּרַבָּנָן (see *Laws* §84-85).

יִתְגַּדַּל וְיִתְקַדַּשׁ שְׁמֵהּ רַבָּא. (.Cong – אָמֵן.) בְּעָלְמָא דִּי בְרָא כִרְעוּתֵהּ. וְיַמְלִיךְ מַלְכוּתֵהּ, בְּחַיֵּיכוֹן וּבְיוֹמֵיכוֹן וּבְחַיֵּי דְכָל בֵּית יִשְׂרָאֵל, בַּעֲגָלָא וּבִזְמַן קָרִיב. וְאִמְרוּ: אָמֵן.

(.Cong – אָמֵן. יְהֵא שְׁמֵהּ רַבָּא מְבָרַךְ לְעָלַם וּלְעָלְמֵי עָלְמַיָּא.)

יְהֵא שְׁמֵהּ רַבָּא מְבָרַךְ לְעָלַם וּלְעָלְמֵי עָלְמַיָּא.

יִתְבָּרַךְ וְיִשְׁתַּבַּח וְיִתְפָּאַר וְיִתְרוֹמַם וְיִתְנַשֵּׂא וְיִתְהַדָּר וְיִתְעַלֶּה וְיִתְהַלָּל שְׁמֵהּ דְּקֻדְשָׁא בְּרִיךְ הוּא (.Cong – בְּרִיךְ הוּא) — לְעֵלָּא מִן כָּל בִּרְכָתָא וְשִׁירָתָא תֻּשְׁבְּחָתָא וְנֶחֱמָתָא, דַּאֲמִירָן בְּעָלְמָא. וְאִמְרוּ: אָמֵן. (.Cong – אָמֵן.)

עַל יִשְׂרָאֵל וְעַל רַבָּנָן, וְעַל תַּלְמִידֵיהוֹן וְעַל כָּל תַּלְמִידֵי תַלְמִידֵיהוֹן, וְעַל כָּל מָאן דְּעָסְקִין בְּאוֹרַיְתָא, דִּי בְאַתְרָא הָדֵין וְדִי בְכָל אֲתַר וַאֲתַר. יְהֵא לְהוֹן וּלְכוֹן שְׁלָמָא רַבָּא, חִנָּא וְחִסְדָּא וְרַחֲמִין, וְחַיִּין אֲרִיכִין, וּמְזוֹנֵי רְוִיחֵי, וּפֻרְקָנָא, מִן קֳדָם אֲבוּהוֹן דִּי בִשְׁמַיָּא (וְאַרְעָא). וְאִמְרוּ: אָמֵן. (.Cong – אָמֵן.)

יְהֵא שְׁלָמָא רַבָּא מִן שְׁמַיָּא, וְחַיִּים (טוֹבִים) עָלֵינוּ וְעַל כָּל יִשְׂרָאֵל. וְאִמְרוּ: אָמֵן. (.Cong – אָמֵן.)

Take three steps back. Bow left and say . . . עֹשֶׂה; bow right and say . . . הוּא; bow forward and say וְעַל כָּל . . . אָמֵן. Remain standing in place for a few moments, then take three steps forward.

עֹשֶׂה שָׁלוֹם בִּמְרוֹמָיו, הוּא בְּרַחֲמָיו יַעֲשֶׂה שָׁלוֹם עָלֵינוּ, וְעַל כָּל יִשְׂרָאֵל. וְאִמְרוּ: אָמֵן. (.Cong – אָמֵן.)

Stand while reciting עָלֵינוּ.

עָלֵינוּ לְשַׁבֵּחַ לַאֲדוֹן הַכֹּל, לָתֵת גְּדֻלָּה לְיוֹצֵר בְּרֵאשִׁית, שֶׁלֹּא עָשָׂנוּ כְּגוֹיֵי הָאֲרָצוֹת, וְלֹא שָׂמָנוּ כְּמִשְׁפְּחוֹת הָאֲדָמָה. שֶׁלֹּא שָׂם חֶלְקֵנוּ כָּהֶם, וְגוֹרָלֵנוּ כְּכָל הֲמוֹנָם. (שֶׁהֵם מִשְׁתַּחֲוִים לְהֶבֶל וָרִיק, וּמִתְפַּלְּלִים אֶל אֵל לֹא יוֹשִׁיעַ.[1]) וַאֲנַחְנוּ כּוֹרְעִים וּמִשְׁתַּחֲוִים וּמוֹדִים, לִפְנֵי מֶלֶךְ מַלְכֵי הַמְּלָכִים הַקָּדוֹשׁ בָּרוּךְ הוּא. שֶׁהוּא נוֹטֶה שָׁמַיִם וְיֹסֵד אָרֶץ,[2] וּמוֹשַׁב יְקָרוֹ בַּשָּׁמַיִם מִמַּעַל, וּשְׁכִינַת עֻזּוֹ בְּגָבְהֵי מְרוֹמִים. הוּא אֱלֹהֵינוּ, אֵין עוֹד. אֱמֶת מַלְכֵּנוּ, אֶפֶס זוּלָתוֹ, כַּכָּתוּב בְּתוֹרָתוֹ: וְיָדַעְתָּ הַיּוֹם וַהֲשֵׁבֹתָ אֶל לְבָבֶךָ, כִּי יהוה הוּא הָאֱלֹהִים בַּשָּׁמַיִם מִמַּעַל וְעַל הָאָרֶץ מִתָּחַת, אֵין עוֹד.[3]

Bow while reciting וַאֲנַחְנוּ כּוֹרְעִים וּמִשְׁתַּחֲוִים.

THE RABBIS' KADDISH

In the presence of a *minyan,* mourners recite the Rabbis' *Kaddish* (see *Laws* §84-85). [A transliteration of this *Kaddish* appears on p. 1304.]

יִתְגַּדַּל *May His great Name grow exalted and sanctified* (Cong.– *Amen.*) *in the world that He created as He willed. May He give reign to His kingship in your lifetimes and in your days, and in the lifetimes of the entire Family of Israel, swiftly and soon. Now respond: Amen.*

(Cong.– *Amen. May His great Name be blessed forever and ever.)*

May His great Name be blessed forever and ever.

Blessed, praised, glorified, exalted, extolled, mighty, upraised, and lauded be the Name of the Holy One, Blessed is He (Cong.– *Blessed is He*) — *beyond any blessing and song, praise and consolation that are uttered in the world. Now respond: Amen.* (Cong.– *Amen.*)

Upon Israel, upon the teachers, their disciples and all of their disciples and upon all those who engage in the study of Torah, who are here or anywhere else; may they and you have abundant peace, grace, kindness, and mercy, long life, ample nourishment, and salvation, from before their Father Who is in Heaven (and on earth). Now respond: Amen. (Cong. – *Amen.*)

May there be abundant peace from Heaven, and (good) life, upon us and upon all Israel. Now respond: Amen. (Cong.– *Amen.*)

Take three steps back. Bow left and say, *'He Who makes peace . . .';* bow right and say, *'may He . . .';* bow forward and say, *'and upon all Israel . . .'* Remain standing in place for a few moments, then take three steps forward.

He Who makes peace in His heights, may He, in His compassion, make peace upon us, and upon all Israel. Now respond: Amen. (Cong.– *Amen.*)

ALEINU

Stand while reciting עָלֵינוּ, *'It is our duty . . .'*

עָלֵינוּ *It is our duty to praise the Master of all, to ascribe greatness to the Molder of primeval creation, for He has not made us like the nations of the lands, and has not emplaced us like the families of the earth; for He has not assigned our portion like theirs nor our lot like all their multitudes. (For they bow to vanity and emptiness and pray to a god which helps not.*[1]*) But we bend our knees, bow, and acknowledge our thanks before the King Who reigns over kings, the Holy One, Blessed is He. He stretches out heaven and establishes earth's foundation,*[2] *the seat of His homage is in the heavens above and His powerful Presence is in the loftiest heights. He is our God and there is none other. True is our King, there is nothing beside Him, as it is written in His Torah: 'You are to know this day and take to your heart that* HASHEM *is the only God — in heaven above and on the earth below — there is none other.'*[3]

Bow while reciting *'But we bend our knees.'*

---

(1) *Isaiah* 45:20. (2) 51:13. (3) *Deuteronomy* 4:39.

עַל כֵּן נְקַוֶּה לְּךָ יהוה אֱלֹהֵינוּ לִרְאוֹת מְהֵרָה בְּתִפְאֶרֶת עֻזֶּךָ, לְהַעֲבִיר גִּלּוּלִים מִן הָאָרֶץ, וְהָאֱלִילִים כָּרוֹת יִכָּרֵתוּן, לְתַקֵּן עוֹלָם בְּמַלְכוּת שַׁדַּי. וְכָל בְּנֵי בָשָׂר יִקְרְאוּ בִשְׁמֶךָ, לְהַפְנוֹת אֵלֶיךָ כָּל רִשְׁעֵי אָרֶץ. יַכִּירוּ וְיֵדְעוּ כָּל יוֹשְׁבֵי תֵבֵל, כִּי לְךָ תִּכְרַע כָּל בֶּרֶךְ, תִּשָּׁבַע כָּל לָשׁוֹן.[1] לְפָנֶיךָ יהוה אֱלֹהֵינוּ יִכְרְעוּ וְיִפֹּלוּ, וְלִכְבוֹד שִׁמְךָ יְקָר יִתֵּנוּ. וִיקַבְּלוּ כֻלָּם אֶת עוֹל מַלְכוּתֶךָ, וְתִמְלֹךְ עֲלֵיהֶם מְהֵרָה לְעוֹלָם וָעֶד. כִּי הַמַּלְכוּת שֶׁלְּךָ הִיא וּלְעוֹלְמֵי עַד תִּמְלוֹךְ בְּכָבוֹד, כַּכָּתוּב בְּתוֹרָתֶךָ: יהוה יִמְלֹךְ לְעֹלָם וָעֶד.[2] ❖ וְנֶאֱמַר: וְהָיָה יהוה לְמֶלֶךְ עַל כָּל הָאָרֶץ, בַּיּוֹם הַהוּא יִהְיֶה יהוה אֶחָד וּשְׁמוֹ אֶחָד.[3]

Some congregations recite the following after עָלֵינוּ.

אַל תִּירָא מִפַּחַד פִּתְאֹם, וּמִשֹּׁאַת רְשָׁעִים כִּי תָבֹא.[4] עֻצוּ עֵצָה וְתֻפָר, דַּבְּרוּ דָבָר וְלֹא יָקוּם, כִּי עִמָּנוּ אֵל.[5] וְעַד זִקְנָה אֲנִי הוּא, וְעַד שֵׂיבָה אֲנִי אֶסְבֹּל, אֲנִי עָשִׂיתִי וַאֲנִי אֶשָּׂא, וַאֲנִי אֶסְבֹּל וַאֲמַלֵּט.[6]

קדיש יתום

In the presence of a *minyan,* mourners recite קַדִּישׁ יָתוֹם, the Mourner's *Kaddish* (see *Laws* §81-83):

יִתְגַּדַּל וְיִתְקַדַּשׁ שְׁמֵהּ רַבָּא. (.Cong – אָמֵן.) בְּעָלְמָא דִּי בְרָא כִרְעוּתֵהּ. וְיַמְלִיךְ מַלְכוּתֵהּ, בְּחַיֵּיכוֹן וּבְיוֹמֵיכוֹן וּבְחַיֵּי דְכָל בֵּית יִשְׂרָאֵל, בַּעֲגָלָא וּבִזְמַן קָרִיב. וְאִמְרוּ: אָמֵן.

(.Cong – אָמֵן. יְהֵא שְׁמֵהּ רַבָּא מְבָרַךְ לְעָלַם וּלְעָלְמֵי עָלְמַיָּא.)

יְהֵא שְׁמֵהּ רַבָּא מְבָרַךְ לְעָלַם וּלְעָלְמֵי עָלְמַיָּא.

יִתְבָּרַךְ וְיִשְׁתַּבַּח וְיִתְפָּאַר וְיִתְרוֹמַם וְיִתְנַשֵּׂא וְיִתְהַדָּר וְיִתְעַלֶּה וְיִתְהַלָּל שְׁמֵהּ דְּקֻדְשָׁא בְּרִיךְ הוּא (.Cong – בְּרִיךְ הוּא) — לְעֵלָּא מִן כָּל בִּרְכָתָא וְשִׁירָתָא תֻּשְׁבְּחָתָא וְנֶחֱמָתָא, דַּאֲמִירָן בְּעָלְמָא. וְאִמְרוּ: אָמֵן. (.Cong – אָמֵן.)

יְהֵא שְׁלָמָא רַבָּא מִן שְׁמַיָּא, וְחַיִּים עָלֵינוּ וְעַל כָּל יִשְׂרָאֵל. וְאִמְרוּ: אָמֵן. (.Cong – אָמֵן.)

Take three steps back. Bow left and say . . . עֹשֶׂה; bow right and say . . . הוּא; bow forward and say וְעַל כָּל . . . אָמֵן. Remain standing in place for a few moments, then take three steps forward.

עֹשֶׂה שָׁלוֹם בִּמְרוֹמָיו, הוּא יַעֲשֶׂה שָׁלוֹם עָלֵינוּ, וְעַל כָּל יִשְׂרָאֵל. וְאִמְרוּ: אָמֵן. (.Cong – אָמֵן.)

עַל כֵּן *Therefore we put our hope in You, HASHEM, our God, that we may soon see Your mighty splendor, to remove detestable idolatry from the earth, and false gods will be utterly cut off, to perfect the universe through the Almighty's sovereignty. Then all humanity will call upon Your Name, to turn all the earth's wicked toward You. All the world's inhabitants will recognize and know that to You every knee should bend, every tongue should swear.*[1] *Before You, HASHEM, our God, they will bend every knee and cast themselves down and to the glory of Your Name they will render homage, and they will all accept upon themselves the yoke of Your kingship that You may reign over them soon and eternally. For the kingdom is Yours and You will reign for all eternity in glory as it is written in Your Torah: HASHEM shall reign for all eternity.*[2] Chazzan– *And it is said: HASHEM will be King over all the world — on that day HASHEM will be One and His Name will be One.*[3]

Some congregations recite the following after *Aleinu.*

אַל תִּירָא *Do not fear sudden terror, or the holocaust of the wicked when it comes.*[4] *Plan a conspiracy and it will be annulled; speak your piece and it shall not stand, for God is with us.*[5] *Even till your seniority, I remain unchanged; and even till your ripe old age, I shall endure. I created you and I shall bear you; I shall endure and rescue.*[6]

MOURNER'S KADDISH

In the presence of a *minyan,* mourners recite קַדִּישׁ יָתוֹם, the Mourner's *Kaddish* (see *Laws* §81-83).
[A transliteration of this *Kaddish* appears on p. 1305.]

יִתְגַּדַּל *May His great Name grow exalted and sanctified* (Cong.– *Amen.*) *in the world that He created as He willed. May He give reign to His kingship in your lifetimes and in your days, and in the lifetimes of the entire Family of Israel, swiftly and soon. Now respond: Amen.*

(Cong.– *Amen. May His great Name be blessed forever and ever.*)

May His great Name be blessed forever and ever.

Blessed, praised, glorified, exalted, extolled, mighty, upraised, and lauded be the Name of the Holy One, Blessed is He (Cong.– *Blessed is He*) *— beyond any blessing and song, praise and consolation that are uttered in the world. Now respond: Amen.* (Cong.– *Amen*).

May there be abundant peace from Heaven, and life, upon us and upon all Israel. Now respond: Amen. (Cong.– *Amen.*)

Take three steps back. Bow left and say, *'He Who makes peace . . .';* bow right and say, *'may He . . .';* bow forward and say, *'and upon all Israel . . .'* Remain standing in place for a few moments, then take three steps forward.

He Who makes peace in His heights, may He make peace upon us, and upon all Israel. Now respond: Amen. (Cong.– *Amen.*)

---

(1) Cf. *Isaiah* 45:23. (2) *Exodus* 15:18. (3) *Zechariah* 14:9.
(4) *Proverbs* 3:25. (5) *Isaiah* 8:10. (6) 46:4.

שיר הכבוד

The Ark is opened and שִׁיר הַכָּבוֹד, *The Song of Glory,* is recited responsively — the *chazzan* reciting the first verse, the congregation reciting the second and so on.

אַנְעִים זְמִירוֹת וְשִׁירִים אֶאֱרוֹג, כִּי אֵלֶיךָ נַפְשִׁי תַעֲרוֹג.
נַפְשִׁי חָמְדָה בְּצֵל יָדֶךָ, לָדַעַת כָּל רָז סוֹדֶךָ.
❖ מִדֵּי דַבְּרִי בִּכְבוֹדֶךָ, הוֹמֶה לִבִּי אֶל דּוֹדֶיךָ.
עַל כֵּן אֲדַבֵּר בְּךָ נִכְבָּדוֹת, וְשִׁמְךָ אֲכַבֵּד בְּשִׁירֵי יְדִידוֹת.
❖ אֲסַפְּרָה כְבוֹדְךָ וְלֹא רְאִיתִיךָ, אֲדַמְּךָ אֲכַנְּךָ וְלֹא יְדַעְתִּיךָ.
בְּיַד נְבִיאֶיךָ בְּסוֹד עֲבָדֶיךָ, דִּמִּיתָ הֲדַר כְּבוֹד הוֹדֶךָ.
❖ גְּדֻלָּתְךָ וּגְבוּרָתֶךָ, כִּנּוּ לְתֹקֶף פְּעֻלָּתֶךָ.
דִּמּוּ אוֹתְךָ וְלֹא כְּפִי יֶשְׁךָ, וַיַּשְׁווּךָ לְפִי מַעֲשֶׂיךָ.
❖ הִמְשִׁילוּךָ בְּרֹב חֶזְיוֹנוֹת, הִנְּךָ אֶחָד בְּכָל דִּמְיוֹנוֹת.
וַיֶּחֱזוּ בְךָ זִקְנָה וּבַחֲרוּת, וּשְׂעַר רֹאשְׁךָ בְּשֵׂיבָה וְשַׁחֲרוּת.
❖ זִקְנָה בְּיוֹם דִּין וּבַחֲרוּת בְּיוֹם קְרָב, כְּאִישׁ מִלְחָמוֹת יָדָיו לוֹ רָב.
חָבַשׁ כּוֹבַע יְשׁוּעָה בְּרֹאשׁוֹ, הוֹשִׁיעָה לּוֹ יְמִינוֹ וּזְרוֹעַ קָדְשׁוֹ.
❖ טַלְלֵי אוֹרוֹת רֹאשׁוֹ נִמְלָא, קְוֻצּוֹתָיו רְסִיסֵי לָיְלָה.
יִתְפָּאֵר בִּי כִּי חָפֵץ בִּי. וְהוּא יִהְיֶה לִּי לַעֲטֶרֶת צְבִי.
❖ כֶּתֶם טָהוֹר פָּז דְּמוּת רֹאשׁוֹ, וְחַק עַל מֵצַח כְּבוֹד שֵׁם קָדְשׁוֹ.
לְחֵן וּלְכָבוֹד צְבִי תִפְאָרָה, אֻמָּתוֹ לוֹ עִטְּרָה עֲטָרָה.
❖ מַחְלְפוֹת רֹאשׁוֹ כְּבִימֵי בְחֻרוֹת, קְוֻצּוֹתָיו תַּלְתַּלִּים שְׁחוֹרוֹת.
נְוֵה הַצֶּדֶק צְבִי תִפְאַרְתּוֹ, יַעֲלֶה נָּא עַל רֹאשׁ שִׂמְחָתוֹ.
❖ סְגֻלָּתוֹ תְּהִי בְיָדוֹ עֲטֶרֶת, וּצְנִיף מְלוּכָה צְבִי תִפְאֶרֶת.
עֲמוּסִים נְשָׂאָם עֲטֶרֶת עִנְּדָם, מֵאֲשֶׁר יָקְרוּ בְעֵינָיו כִּבְּדָם.
❖ פְּאֵרוֹ עָלַי וּפְאֵרִי עָלָיו, וְקָרוֹב אֵלַי בְּקָרְאִי אֵלָיו.
צַח וְאָדוֹם לִלְבוּשׁוֹ אָדוֹם, פּוּרָה בְּדָרְכוֹ בְּבוֹאוֹ מֵאֱדוֹם.
❖ קֶשֶׁר תְּפִלִּין הֶרְאָה לֶעָנָו, תְּמוּנַת יהוה לְנֶגֶד עֵינָיו.
רוֹצֶה בְעַמּוֹ עֲנָוִים יְפָאֵר, יוֹשֵׁב תְּהִלּוֹת בָּם לְהִתְפָּאֵר.
❖ רֹאשׁ דְּבָרְךָ אֱמֶת קוֹרֵא מֵרֹאשׁ, דּוֹר וָדוֹר עַם דּוֹרֶשְׁךָ דְּרוֹשׁ.

SONG OF GLORY

The Ark is opened and the *Song of Glory* is recited responsively — the *chazzan* reciting the first verse, the congregation reciting the second and so on.

אַנְעִים זְמִירוֹת *I shall compose pleasant psalms and weave hymns,*
because for You shall my soul pine.
My soul desired the shelter of Your hand,
to know every mystery of Your secret.
✣ *As I speak of Your glory, my heart yearns for Your love.*
Therefore I shall speak of Your glories,
and Your Name I shall honor with loving songs.
✣ *I shall relate Your glory, though I see You not;*
I shall allegorize You, I shall describe You, though I know You not.
Through the hand of Your prophets, through the counsel of Your servants;
You allegorized the splendrous glory of Your power.
✣ *Your greatness and Your strength,*
they described the might of Your works.
They allegorized You, but not according to Your reality,
and they portrayed You according to Your deeds.
✣ *They symbolized You in many varied visions;*
yet You are a Unity containing all the allegories.
They envisioned in You agedness and virility,
and the hair of Your head as hoary and jet black.
✣ *Aged on judgment day and virile on the day of battle,*
like a man of war whose powers are many.
The hat of salvation He put on His head;
salvation for Him, His right hand and His sacred arm.
✣ *With illuminating dew drops His head is filled,*
His locks are the rains of the night.
He shall glory in me for He desires me,
and He shall be for me a crown of pride.
✣ *A form of the very finest gold upon his head,*
and carved on his forehead is His glorious, sacred Name.
For grace and for glory the pride of His splendor;
His nation crowns Him with its prayers.
✣ *The tresses of His head are like His youthful days;*
His locks are jet-black ringlets.
The Abode of righteousness is the pride of His splendor;
may He elevate it to His foremost joy.
✣ *May His treasured nation be in His hand like a crown,*
and like a royal tiara the pride of His splendor.
From infancy He bore them and affixed them as a crown,
because they are precious in His eyes He honored them.
✣ *His tefillin-splendor is upon me and my tefillin-splendor is upon Him,*
and He is near to me when I call to Him.
He is white and crimson; His garment will be bloody red,
when He tramples as in a press on His coming from Edom.
✣ *He showed the tefillin-knot to the humble [Moses],*
the likeness of HASHEM *before his eyes.*
He desires His people, He will glorify the humble;
enthroned upon praises, He glories with them.
✣ *The very beginning of Your word is truth — one reads it from the*
Torah's start; the people that seeks You expounds each generation's fate.

שִׁית הֲמוֹן שִׁירַי נָא עָלֶיךָ, וְרִנָּתִי תִּקְרַב אֵלֶיךָ.
❖ תְּהִלָּתִי תְּהִי לְרֹאשְׁךָ עֲטֶרֶת, וּתְפִלָּתִי תִּכּוֹן קְטֹרֶת.
תִּיקַר שִׁירַת רָשׁ בְּעֵינֶיךָ, כַּשִּׁיר יוּשַׁר עַל קָרְבָּנֶיךָ.
❖ בִּרְכָתִי תַעֲלֶה לְרֹאשׁ מַשְׁבִּיר, מְחוֹלֵל וּמוֹלִיד צַדִּיק כַּבִּיר.
וּבְבִרְכָתִי תְנַעֲנַע לִי רֹאשׁ, וְאוֹתָהּ קַח לְךָ כִּבְשָׂמִים רֹאשׁ.
יֶעֱרַב נָא שִׂיחִי עָלֶיךָ, כִּי נַפְשִׁי תַעֲרוֹג אֵלֶיךָ.

לְךָ יהוה הַגְּדֻלָּה וְהַגְּבוּרָה וְהַתִּפְאֶרֶת וְהַנֵּצַח וְהַהוֹד, כִּי כֹל בַּשָּׁמַיִם וּבָאָרֶץ; לְךָ יהוה הַמַּמְלָכָה וְהַמִּתְנַשֵּׂא לְכֹל לְרֹאשׁ.[1] מִי יְמַלֵּל גְּבוּרוֹת יהוה, יַשְׁמִיעַ כָּל תְּהִלָּתוֹ.[2]

קדיש יתום

In the presence of a *minyan,* mourners recite קַדִּישׁ יָתוֹם, the Mourner's *Kaddish* (see *Laws* §81-83).

יִתְגַּדַּל וְיִתְקַדַּשׁ שְׁמֵהּ רַבָּא. (.Cong – אָמֵן.) בְּעָלְמָא דִּי בְרָא כִרְעוּתֵהּ. וְיַמְלִיךְ מַלְכוּתֵהּ, בְּחַיֵּיכוֹן וּבְיוֹמֵיכוֹן וּבְחַיֵּי דְכָל בֵּית יִשְׂרָאֵל, בַּעֲגָלָא וּבִזְמַן קָרִיב. וְאִמְרוּ: אָמֵן.

(.Cong – אָמֵן. יְהֵא שְׁמֵהּ רַבָּא מְבָרַךְ לְעָלַם וּלְעָלְמֵי עָלְמַיָּא.)

יְהֵא שְׁמֵהּ רַבָּא מְבָרַךְ לְעָלַם וּלְעָלְמֵי עָלְמַיָּא.

יִתְבָּרַךְ וְיִשְׁתַּבַּח וְיִתְפָּאַר וְיִתְרוֹמַם וְיִתְנַשֵּׂא וְיִתְהַדָּר וְיִתְעַלֶּה וְיִתְהַלָּל שְׁמֵהּ דְּקֻדְשָׁא בְּרִיךְ הוּא (.Cong – בְּרִיךְ הוּא) – לְעֵלָּא מִן כָּל בִּרְכָתָא וְשִׁירָתָא תֻּשְׁבְּחָתָא וְנֶחֱמָתָא, דַּאֲמִירָן בְּעָלְמָא. וְאִמְרוּ: אָמֵן. (.Cong – אָמֵן.)

יְהֵא שְׁלָמָא רַבָּא מִן שְׁמַיָּא, וְחַיִּים עָלֵינוּ וְעַל כָּל יִשְׂרָאֵל. וְאִמְרוּ: אָמֵן. (.Cong – אָמֵן.)

Take three steps back. Bow left and say . . . עֹשֶׂה; bow right and say . . . הוּא; bow forward and say וְעַל כָּל . . . אָמֵן. Remain standing in place for a few moments, then take three steps forward.

עֹשֶׂה שָׁלוֹם בִּמְרוֹמָיו, הוּא יַעֲשֶׂה שָׁלוֹם עָלֵינוּ, וְעַל כָּל יִשְׂרָאֵל. וְאִמְרוּ: אָמֵן. (.Cong – אָמֵן.)

❧ שיר של יום ❧

A different psalm is assigned as the שִׁיר שֶׁל יוֹם, *Song of the Day,* for each day of the week.

MONDAY

הַיּוֹם יוֹם שֵׁנִי בַּשַּׁבָּת, שֶׁבּוֹ הָיוּ הַלְוִיִּם אוֹמְרִים בְּבֵית הַמִּקְדָּשׁ:

תהלים מח

שִׁיר מִזְמוֹר לִבְנֵי קֹרַח. גָּדוֹל יהוה וּמְהֻלָּל מְאֹד, בְּעִיר אֱלֹהֵינוּ, הַר קָדְשׁוֹ. יְפֵה נוֹף, מְשׂוֹשׂ כָּל הָאָרֶץ, הַר צִיּוֹן יַרְכְּתֵי צָפוֹן, קִרְיַת מֶלֶךְ רָב. אֱלֹהִים בְּאַרְמְנוֹתֶיהָ נוֹדַע לְמִשְׂגָּב. כִּי הִנֵּה

Place the multitude of my songs before You, please;
and my glad song bring near to You.
∴ *May my praise be a crown for Your head,*
and may my prayer be accepted like incense.
May the poor man's song be dear in Your eyes,
like the song that is sung over Your offerings.
∴ *May my blessing rise up upon the head of the Sustainer —*
Creator, Giver of life, mighty Righteous One.
And to my blessing, nod Your head to me,
and take it to Yourself like the finest incense.
∴ *May my prayer be sweet to You, for my soul shall pine for You.*

לְךָ *Yours,* H*ASHEM, is the greatness, the strength, the splendor, the triumph, and the glory; even everything in heaven and earth; Yours,* H*ASHEM, is the kingdom, and the sovereignty over every leader.*[1] *Who can express the mighty acts of* H*ASHEM? Who can declare all His praise?*[2]

MOURNER'S KADDISH

Mourners recite the Mourner's *Kaddish* (see *Laws* §81-83).

יִתְגַּדַּל *May His great Name grow exalted and sanctified* (Cong.– *Amen.*) *in the world that He created as He willed. May He give reign to His kingship in your lifetimes and in your days, and in the lifetimes of the entire Family of Israel, swiftly and soon. Now respond: Amen.*

(Cong.– *Amen. May His great Name be blessed forever and ever.*)

May His great Name be blessed forever and ever.

Blessed, praised, glorified, exalted, extolled, mighty, upraised, and lauded be the Name of the Holy One, Blessed is He (Cong.– *Blessed is He*) *— beyond any blessing and song, praise and consolation that are uttered in the world. Now respond: Amen.* (Cong.– *Amen.*)

May there be abundant peace from Heaven, and life, upon us and upon all Israel. Now respond: Amen. (Cong.– *Amen.*)

Take three steps back. Bow left and say, *'He Who makes peace . . .'*; bow right and say, *'may He . . .'*; bow forward and say, *'and upon all Israel . . .'* Remain standing in place for a few moments, then take three steps forward.

He Who makes peace in His heights, may He make peace upon us, and upon all Israel. Now respond: Amen. (Cong.– *Amen.*)

SONG OF THE DAY

A different psalm is assigned as the Song of the Day for each day of the week.

MONDAY

Today is the second day of the Sabbath,
on which the Levites would recite in the Holy Temple:

Psalm 48

שִׁיר מִזְמוֹר *A song, a psalm, by the sons of Korach. Great is* H*ASHEM and much praised, in the city of our God, Mount of His Holiness. Fairest of sites, joy of all the earth is Mount Zion, by the northern sides of the great king's city. In her palaces God is known as the Stronghold. For behold —*

(1) *I Chronicles* 29:11. (2) *Psalms* 106:2.

הַמְּלָכִים נוֹעֲדוּ, עָבְרוּ יַחְדָּו. הֵמָּה רָאוּ כֵּן תָּמָהוּ, נִבְהֲלוּ נֶחְפָּזוּ. רְעָדָה אֲחָזָתַם שָׁם, חִיל כַּיּוֹלֵדָה. בְּרוּחַ קָדִים תְּשַׁבֵּר אֳנִיּוֹת תַּרְשִׁישׁ. כַּאֲשֶׁר שָׁמַעְנוּ כֵּן רָאִינוּ בְּעִיר יהוה צְבָאוֹת, בְּעִיר אֱלֹהֵינוּ, אֱלֹהִים יְכוֹנְנֶהָ עַד עוֹלָם סֶלָה. דִּמִּינוּ אֱלֹהִים חַסְדֶּךָ, בְּקֶרֶב הֵיכָלֶךָ. כְּשִׁמְךָ אֱלֹהִים כֵּן תְּהִלָּתְךָ, עַל קַצְוֵי אֶרֶץ, צֶדֶק מָלְאָה יְמִינֶךָ. יִשְׂמַח הַר צִיּוֹן, תָּגֵלְנָה בְּנוֹת יְהוּדָה, לְמַעַן מִשְׁפָּטֶיךָ. סֹבּוּ צִיּוֹן וְהַקִּיפוּהָ, סִפְרוּ מִגְדָּלֶיהָ. ❖ שִׁיתוּ לִבְּכֶם לְחֵילָה, פַּסְּגוּ אַרְמְנוֹתֶיהָ, לְמַעַן תְּסַפְּרוּ לְדוֹר אַחֲרוֹן. כִּי זֶה אֱלֹהִים אֱלֹהֵינוּ עוֹלָם וָעֶד, הוּא יְנַהֲגֵנוּ עַל־מוּת.

The service continues with קַדִּישׁ יָתוֹם, *the Mourner's Kaddish* (page 1016).

TUESDAY

הַיּוֹם יוֹם שְׁלִישִׁי בַּשַּׁבָּת, שֶׁבּוֹ הָיוּ הַלְוִיִּם אוֹמְרִים בְּבֵית הַמִּקְדָּשׁ:

תהלים פב

מִזְמוֹר לְאָסָף, אֱלֹהִים נִצָּב בַּעֲדַת אֵל, בְּקֶרֶב אֱלֹהִים יִשְׁפֹּט. עַד מָתַי תִּשְׁפְּטוּ עָוֶל, וּפְנֵי רְשָׁעִים תִּשְׂאוּ סֶלָה. שִׁפְטוּ דַל וְיָתוֹם, עָנִי וָרָשׁ הַצְדִּיקוּ. פַּלְּטוּ דַל וְאֶבְיוֹן, מִיַּד רְשָׁעִים הַצִּילוּ. לֹא יָדְעוּ וְלֹא יָבִינוּ, בַּחֲשֵׁכָה יִתְהַלָּכוּ, יִמּוֹטוּ כָּל מוֹסְדֵי אָרֶץ. אֲנִי אָמַרְתִּי אֱלֹהִים אַתֶּם, וּבְנֵי עֶלְיוֹן כֻּלְּכֶם. אָכֵן כְּאָדָם תְּמוּתוּן, וּכְאַחַד הַשָּׂרִים תִּפֹּלוּ. ❖ קוּמָה אֱלֹהִים שָׁפְטָה הָאָרֶץ, כִּי אַתָּה תִנְחַל בְּכָל הַגּוֹיִם.

The service continues with קַדִּישׁ יָתוֹם, *the Mourner's Kaddish* (page 1016).

THURSDAY

הַיּוֹם יוֹם חֲמִישִׁי בַּשַּׁבָּת, שֶׁבּוֹ הָיוּ הַלְוִיִּם אוֹמְרִים בְּבֵית הַמִּקְדָּשׁ:

תהלים פא

לַמְנַצֵּחַ עַל הַגִּתִּית לְאָסָף. הַרְנִינוּ לֵאלֹהִים עוּזֵּנוּ, הָרִיעוּ לֵאלֹהֵי יַעֲקֹב. שְׂאוּ זִמְרָה וּתְנוּ תֹף, כִּנּוֹר נָעִים עִם נָבֶל. תִּקְעוּ בַחֹדֶשׁ שׁוֹפָר, בַּכֶּסֶה לְיוֹם חַגֵּנוּ. כִּי חֹק לְיִשְׂרָאֵל הוּא, מִשְׁפָּט לֵאלֹהֵי יַעֲקֹב. עֵדוּת בִּיהוֹסֵף שָׂמוֹ, בְּצֵאתוֹ עַל אֶרֶץ מִצְרָיִם, שְׂפַת לֹא יָדַעְתִּי אֶשְׁמָע. הֲסִירוֹתִי מִסֵּבֶל שִׁכְמוֹ, כַּפָּיו מִדּוּד תַּעֲבֹרְנָה. בַּצָּרָה קָרָאתָ, וָאֲחַלְּצֶךָּ, אֶעֶנְךָ בְּסֵתֶר רַעַם, אֶבְחָנְךָ עַל מֵי מְרִיבָה, סֶלָה. שְׁמַע עַמִּי וְאָעִידָה בָּךְ, יִשְׂרָאֵל אִם תִּשְׁמַע לִי. לֹא יִהְיֶה בְךָ אֵל זָר, וְלֹא תִשְׁתַּחֲוֶה לְאֵל נֵכָר. אָנֹכִי יהוה אֱלֹהֶיךָ, הַמַּעַלְךָ מֵאֶרֶץ מִצְרָיִם, הַרְחֶב פִּיךָ וַאֲמַלְאֵהוּ. וְלֹא שָׁמַע עַמִּי לְקוֹלִי, וְיִשְׂרָאֵל לֹא אָבָה לִי. וָאֲשַׁלְּחֵהוּ בִּשְׁרִירוּת לִבָּם, יֵלְכוּ בְּמוֹעֲצוֹתֵיהֶם. לוּ עַמִּי שֹׁמֵעַ לִי, יִשְׂרָאֵל בִּדְרָכַי יְהַלֵּכוּ. כִּמְעַט אוֹיְבֵיהֶם אַכְנִיעַ, וְעַל צָרֵיהֶם אָשִׁיב יָדִי. מְשַׂנְאֵי יהוה יְכַחֲשׁוּ לוֹ, וִיהִי עִתָּם לְעוֹלָם. ❖ וַיַּאֲכִילֵהוּ מֵחֵלֶב חִטָּה, וּמִצּוּר דְּבַשׁ אַשְׂבִּיעֶךָ.

The service continues with קַדִּישׁ יָתוֹם, *the Mourner's Kaddish* (page 1016).

the kings assembled, they came together. They saw and they were astounded, they were confounded and hastily fled. Trembling gripped them there, convulsions like a woman in birth travail. With an east wind You smashed the ships of Tarshish. As we heard, so we saw in the city of HASHEM, Master of Legions, in the city of our God — may God establish it to eternity, Selah! We hoped, O God, for Your kindness, in the midst of Your Sanctuary. Like Your Name, O God, so is Your praise — to the ends of the earth; righteousness fills Your right hand. May Mount Zion be glad, may the daughters of Judah rejoice, because of Your judgments. Walk about Zion and encircle her, count her towers. Chazzan– *Mark well in your hearts her ramparts, raise up her palaces, that you may recount it to the succeeding generation: that this is God, our God, forever and ever, He will guide us like children.*

The service continues with קַדִּישׁ יָתוֹם, *the Mourner's Kaddish* (p. 1016).

TUESDAY

Today is the third day of the Sabbath,
on which the Levites would recite in the Holy Temple:

Psalm 82

מִזְמוֹר *A psalm of Assaf: God stands in the Divine assembly, in the midst of judges shall He judge. Until when will you judge lawlessly and favor the presence of the wicked, Selah? Judge the needy and the orphan, vindicate the poor and impoverished. Rescue the needy and destitute, from the hand of the wicked deliver them. They do not know nor do they understand, in darkness they walk; all foundations of the earth collapse. I said, 'You are angelic, sons of the Most High are you all.' But like men you shall die, and like one of the princes you shall fall.* Chazzan– *Arise, O God, judge the earth, for You allot the heritage among all the nations.*

The service continues with קַדִּישׁ יָתוֹם, *the Mourner's Kaddish* (p. 1016).

THURSDAY

Today is the fifth day of the Sabbath,
on which the Levites would recite in the Holy Temple:

Psalm 81

לַמְנַצֵּחַ *For the Conductor, upon the gittis, by Assaf. Sing joyously to the God of our might, call out to the God of Jacob. Raise a song and sound the drum, the sweet harp with the lyre. Blow the shofar at the moon's renewal, at the time appointed for our festive day. Because it is a decree for Israel, a judgment day for the God of Jacob. He imposed it as a testimony for Joseph when he went forth over the land of Egypt — 'I understood a language I never knew!' I removed his shoulder from the burden, his hands let go of the kettle. In distress you called out, and I released you, I answered you with thunder when you hid, I tested you at the Waters of Strife, Selah. Listen, My nation, and I will attest to you; O Israel, if you would but listen to Me. There shall be no strange god within you, nor shall you bow before an alien god. I am HASHEM, your God, who elevated you from the land of Egypt, open wide your mouth and I will fill it. But My people did not heed My voice and Israel did not desire Me. So I let them follow their heart's fantasies, they follow their own counsels. If only My people would heed Me, if Israel would walk in My ways. In an instant I would subdue their foes, and against their tormentors turn My hand. Those who hate HASHEM lie to Him — so their destiny is eternal.* Chazzan– *But He would feed him with the cream of the wheat, and with honey from a rock sate you.*

The service continues with קַדִּישׁ יָתוֹם, *the Mourner's Kaddish* (p. 1016).

THE SABBATH

הַיּוֹם יוֹם שַׁבַּת קֹדֶשׁ שֶׁבּוֹ הָיוּ הַלְוִיִּם אוֹמְרִים בְּבֵית הַמִּקְדָּשׁ:

תהלים צב

מִזְמוֹר שִׁיר לְיוֹם הַשַּׁבָּת. טוֹב לְהֹדוֹת לַיהוה, וּלְזַמֵּר לְשִׁמְךָ עֶלְיוֹן. לְהַגִּיד בַּבֹּקֶר חַסְדֶּךָ, וֶאֱמוּנָתְךָ בַּלֵּילוֹת. עֲלֵי עָשׂוֹר וַעֲלֵי נָבֶל, עֲלֵי הִגָּיוֹן בְּכִנּוֹר. כִּי שִׂמַּחְתַּנִי יהוה בְּפָעֳלֶךָ, בְּמַעֲשֵׂי יָדֶיךָ אֲרַנֵּן. מַה גָּדְלוּ מַעֲשֶׂיךָ יהוה, מְאֹד עָמְקוּ מַחְשְׁבֹתֶיךָ. אִישׁ בַּעַר לֹא יֵדָע, וּכְסִיל לֹא יָבִין אֶת זֹאת. בִּפְרֹחַ רְשָׁעִים כְּמוֹ עֵשֶׂב, וַיָּצִיצוּ כָּל פֹּעֲלֵי אָוֶן, לְהִשָּׁמְדָם עֲדֵי עַד. וְאַתָּה מָרוֹם לְעֹלָם יהוה. כִּי הִנֵּה אֹיְבֶיךָ יהוה, כִּי הִנֵּה אֹיְבֶיךָ יֹאבֵדוּ, יִתְפָּרְדוּ כָּל פֹּעֲלֵי אָוֶן. וַתָּרֶם כִּרְאֵים קַרְנִי, בַּלֹּתִי בְּשֶׁמֶן רַעֲנָן. וַתַּבֵּט עֵינִי בְּשׁוּרָי, בַּקָּמִים עָלַי מְרֵעִים, תִּשְׁמַעְנָה אָזְנָי. ❖ צַדִּיק כַּתָּמָר יִפְרָח, כְּאֶרֶז בַּלְּבָנוֹן יִשְׂגֶּה. שְׁתוּלִים בְּבֵית יהוה, בְּחַצְרוֹת אֱלֹהֵינוּ יַפְרִיחוּ. עוֹד יְנוּבוּן בְּשֵׂיבָה, דְּשֵׁנִים וְרַעֲנַנִּים יִהְיוּ. לְהַגִּיד כִּי יָשָׁר יהוה, צוּרִי וְלֹא עַוְלָתָה בּוֹ.

קדיש יתום

In the presence of a *minyan,* mourners recite קַדִּישׁ יָתוֹם, the Mourner's *Kaddish* (see *Laws* §81-83):

יִתְגַּדַּל וְיִתְקַדַּשׁ שְׁמֵהּ רַבָּא. (.Cong – אָמֵן.) בְּעָלְמָא דִּי בְרָא כִרְעוּתֵהּ. וְיַמְלִיךְ מַלְכוּתֵהּ, בְּחַיֵּיכוֹן וּבְיוֹמֵיכוֹן וּבְחַיֵּי דְכָל בֵּית יִשְׂרָאֵל, בַּעֲגָלָא וּבִזְמַן קָרִיב. וְאִמְרוּ: אָמֵן.

(.Cong – אָמֵן. יְהֵא שְׁמֵהּ רַבָּא מְבָרַךְ לְעָלַם וּלְעָלְמֵי עָלְמַיָּא.)

יְהֵא שְׁמֵהּ רַבָּא מְבָרַךְ לְעָלַם וּלְעָלְמֵי עָלְמַיָּא.

יִתְבָּרַךְ וְיִשְׁתַּבַּח וְיִתְפָּאַר וְיִתְרוֹמַם וְיִתְנַשֵּׂא וְיִתְהַדָּר וְיִתְעַלֶּה וְיִתְהַלָּל שְׁמֵהּ דְּקֻדְשָׁא בְּרִיךְ הוּא (.Cong – בְּרִיךְ הוּא) — לְעֵלָּא מִן כָּל בִּרְכָתָא וְשִׁירָתָא תֻּשְׁבְּחָתָא וְנֶחֱמָתָא, דַּאֲמִירָן בְּעָלְמָא. וְאִמְרוּ: אָמֵן. (.Cong – אָמֵן.)

יְהֵא שְׁלָמָא רַבָּא מִן שְׁמַיָּא, וְחַיִּים עָלֵינוּ וְעַל כָּל יִשְׂרָאֵל. וְאִמְרוּ: אָמֵן. (.Cong – אָמֵן.)

Take three steps back. Bow left and say . . . עֹשֶׂה; bow right and say . . . הוּא; bow forward and say וְעַל כָּל . . . אָמֵן. Remain standing in place for a few moments, then take three steps forward.

עֹשֶׂה שָׁלוֹם בִּמְרוֹמָיו, הוּא יַעֲשֶׂה שָׁלוֹם עָלֵינוּ, וְעַל כָּל יִשְׂרָאֵל. וְאִמְרוּ: אָמֵן. (.Cong – אָמֵן.)

תהלים כז

לְדָוִד, יהוה אוֹרִי וְיִשְׁעִי, מִמִּי אִירָא, יהוה מָעוֹז חַיַּי, מִמִּי אֶפְחָד. בִּקְרֹב עָלַי מְרֵעִים לֶאֱכֹל אֶת בְּשָׂרִי, צָרַי וְאֹיְבַי לִי, הֵמָּה כָּשְׁלוּ וְנָפָלוּ. אִם תַּחֲנֶה עָלַי מַחֲנֶה, לֹא יִירָא לִבִּי, אִם תָּקוּם עָלַי מִלְחָמָה, בְּזֹאת אֲנִי בוֹטֵחַ. אַחַת שָׁאַלְתִּי מֵאֵת יהוה, אוֹתָהּ אֲבַקֵּשׁ, שִׁבְתִּי בְּבֵית יהוה כָּל יְמֵי חַיַּי, לַחֲזוֹת בְּנֹעַם יהוה, וּלְבַקֵּר בְּהֵיכָלוֹ.

THE SABBATH

Today is the Holy Sabbath day,
on which the Levites would sing in the Holy Temple:

Psalm 92

מִזְמוֹר שִׁיר *A psalm, a song for the Sabbath day. It is good to thank* HASHEM *and to sing praise to Your Name, O Exalted One; to relate Your kindness in the dawn and Your faith in the nights. Upon ten-stringed instrument and lyre, with singing accompanied by a harp. For You have gladdened me,* HASHEM, *with Your deeds; at the works of Your Hands I sing glad song. How great are Your deeds,* HASHEM; *exceedingly profound are Your thoughts. A boor cannot know, nor can a fool understand this: when the wicked bloom like grass and all the doers of iniquity blossom — it is to destroy them till eternity. But You remain exalted forever,* HASHEM. *For behold! — Your enemies,* HASHEM, *for behold! — Your enemies shall perish, dispersed shall be all doers of iniquity. As exalted as a re'eim's shall be my pride, I will be saturated with ever-fresh oil. My eyes have seen my vigilant foes; when those who would harm me rise up against me, my ears have heard their doom.* Chazzan– *A righteous man will flourish like a date palm, like a cedar in the Lebanon he will grow tall. Planted in the house of* HASHEM, *in the courtyards of our God they will flourish. They will still be fruitful in old age, vigorous and fresh they will be — to declare that* HASHEM *is just, my Rock in Whom there is no wrong.*

MOURNER'S KADDISH

In the presence of a *minyan,* mourners recite קַדִּישׁ יָתוֹם, the Mourner's *Kaddish* (see *Laws* §81-83):
[A transliteration of this *Kaddish* appears on p. 1305.]

יִתְגַּדַּל *May His great Name grow exalted and sanctified* (Cong.– *Amen.*) *in the world that He created as He willed. May He give reign to His kingship in your lifetimes and in your days, and in the lifetimes of the entire Family of Israel, swiftly and soon. Now respond: Amen.*

(Cong.– *Amen. May His great Name be blessed forever and ever.*)
May His great Name be blessed forever and ever.

Blessed, praised, glorified, exalted, extolled, mighty, upraised, and lauded be the Name of the Holy One, Blessed is He (Cong.– *Blessed is He*) *— beyond any blessing and song, praise and consolation that are uttered in the world. Now respond: Amen.* (Cong.– *Amen*).

May there be abundant peace from Heaven, and life, upon us and upon all Israel. Now respond: Amen. (Cong.– *Amen.*)

Take three steps back. Bow left and say, *'He Who makes peace . . .'*;
bow right and say, *'may He . . .'*; bow forward and say, *'and upon all Israel . . .'*
Remain standing in place for a few moments, then take three steps forward.

He Who makes peace in His heights, may He make peace upon us, and upon all Israel. Now respond: Amen. (Cong.– *Amen.*)

Psalm 27

לְדָוִד *Of David;* HASHEM *is my light and my salvation, whom shall I fear?* HASHEM *is my life's strength, whom shall I dread? When evildoers approach me to devour my flesh, my tormentors and my foes against me — it is they who stumble and fall. Though an army would besiege me, my heart would not fear; though war would arise against me, in this I trust. One thing I asked of* HASHEM, *that shall I seek: That I dwell in the House of* HASHEM *all the days of my life; to behold the sweetness of* HASHEM *and to contemplate in His*

כִּי יִצְפְּנֵנִי בְּסֻכֹּה בְּיוֹם רָעָה, יַסְתִּירֵנִי בְּסֵתֶר אָהֳלוֹ, בְּצוּר יְרוֹמְמֵנִי. וְעַתָּה יָרוּם רֹאשִׁי עַל אֹיְבַי סְבִיבוֹתַי, וְאֶזְבְּחָה בְאָהֳלוֹ זִבְחֵי תְרוּעָה, אָשִׁירָה וַאֲזַמְּרָה לַיהוה. שְׁמַע יהוה קוֹלִי אֶקְרָא, וְחָנֵּנִי וַעֲנֵנִי. לְךָ אָמַר לִבִּי בַּקְּשׁוּ פָנָי, אֶת פָּנֶיךָ יהוה אֲבַקֵּשׁ. אַל תַּסְתֵּר פָּנֶיךָ מִמֶּנִּי, אַל תַּט בְּאַף עַבְדֶּךָ, עֶזְרָתִי הָיִיתָ, אַל תִּטְּשֵׁנִי וְאַל תַּעַזְבֵנִי, אֱלֹהֵי יִשְׁעִי. כִּי אָבִי וְאִמִּי עֲזָבוּנִי, וַיהוה יַאַסְפֵנִי. הוֹרֵנִי יהוה דַּרְכֶּךָ, וּנְחֵנִי בְּאֹרַח מִישׁוֹר, לְמַעַן שׁוֹרְרָי. אַל תִּתְּנֵנִי בְּנֶפֶשׁ צָרָי, כִּי קָמוּ בִי עֵדֵי שֶׁקֶר, וִיפֵחַ חָמָס. ❖ לוּלֵא הֶאֱמַנְתִּי לִרְאוֹת בְּטוּב יהוה בְּאֶרֶץ חַיִּים. קַוֵּה אֶל יהוה, חֲזַק וְיַאֲמֵץ לִבֶּךָ, וְקַוֵּה אֶל יהוה.

Mourners recite קַדִּישׁ יָתוֹם, the Mourner's *Kaddish* (p. 1016).

קידושא רבא

ON THE SABBATH BEGIN HERE.

Many omit some or all of these verses and begin with עַל כֵּן.

אִם תָּשִׁיב מִשַּׁבָּת רַגְלֶךָ, עֲשׂוֹת חֲפָצֶךָ בְּיוֹם קָדְשִׁי, וְקָרָאתָ לַשַּׁבָּת עֹנֶג, לִקְדוֹשׁ יהוה מְכֻבָּד, וְכִבַּדְתּוֹ מֵעֲשׂוֹת דְּרָכֶיךָ, מִמְּצוֹא חֶפְצְךָ וְדַבֵּר דָּבָר. אָז תִּתְעַנַּג עַל יהוה, וְהִרְכַּבְתִּיךָ עַל בָּמֳתֵי אָרֶץ, וְהַאֲכַלְתִּיךָ נַחֲלַת יַעֲקֹב אָבִיךָ, כִּי פִּי יהוה דִּבֵּר.[1]

וְשָׁמְרוּ בְנֵי יִשְׂרָאֵל אֶת הַשַּׁבָּת, לַעֲשׂוֹת אֶת הַשַּׁבָּת לְדֹרֹתָם בְּרִית עוֹלָם. בֵּינִי וּבֵין בְּנֵי יִשְׂרָאֵל אוֹת הִיא לְעֹלָם, כִּי שֵׁשֶׁת יָמִים עָשָׂה יהוה אֶת הַשָּׁמַיִם וְאֶת הָאָרֶץ, וּבַיּוֹם הַשְּׁבִיעִי שָׁבַת וַיִּנָּפַשׁ.[2]

זָכוֹר אֶת יוֹם הַשַּׁבָּת לְקַדְּשׁוֹ. שֵׁשֶׁת יָמִים תַּעֲבֹד וְעָשִׂיתָ כָּל מְלַאכְתֶּךָ. וְיוֹם הַשְּׁבִיעִי שַׁבָּת לַיהוה אֱלֹהֶיךָ, לֹא תַעֲשֶׂה כָל מְלָאכָה, אַתָּה וּבִנְךָ וּבִתֶּךָ עַבְדְּךָ וַאֲמָתְךָ וּבְהֶמְתֶּךָ, וְגֵרְךָ אֲשֶׁר בִּשְׁעָרֶיךָ. כִּי שֵׁשֶׁת יָמִים עָשָׂה יהוה אֶת הַשָּׁמַיִם וְאֶת הָאָרֶץ אֶת הַיָּם וְאֶת כָּל אֲשֶׁר בָּם, וַיָּנַח בַּיּוֹם הַשְּׁבִיעִי –

עַל כֵּן בֵּרַךְ יהוה אֶת יוֹם הַשַּׁבָּת וַיְקַדְּשֵׁהוּ.[3]

(אֵלֶּה מוֹעֲדֵי יהוה מִקְרָאֵי קֹדֶשׁ אֲשֶׁר תִּקְרְאוּ אֹתָם בְּמוֹעֲדָם.[4])

וַיְדַבֵּר מֹשֶׁה אֶת מֹעֲדֵי יהוה, אֶל בְּנֵי יִשְׂרָאֵל.[5]

סַבְרִי מָרָנָן וְרַבָּנָן וְרַבּוֹתַי:

בָּרוּךְ אַתָּה יהוה אֱלֹהֵינוּ מֶלֶךְ הָעוֹלָם, בּוֹרֵא פְּרִי הַגָּפֶן.

(All present – אָמֵן.)

עַל הַמִּחְיָה appears on page 92; בִּרְכַּת הַמָּזוֹן, on page 84.

Sanctuary. Indeed, He will hide me in His Shelter on the day of evil; He will conceal me in the concealment of His Tent, He will lift me upon a rock. Now my head is raised above my enemies around me, and I will slaughter offerings in His Tent accompanied by joyous song; I will sing and make music to HASHEM. HASHEM, *hear my voice when I call, be gracious toward me and answer me. In Your behalf, my heart has said, 'Seek My Presence'; Your Presence,* HASHEM, *do I seek. Conceal not Your Presence from me, repel not Your servant in anger. You have been my Helper, abandon me not, forsake me not, O God of my salvation. Though my father and mother have forsaken me,* HASHEM *will gather me in. Teach me Your way,* HASHEM, *and lead me on the path of integrity, because of my watchful foes. Deliver me not to the wishes of my tormentors, for there have arisen against me false witnesses who breathe violence.* Chazzan— *Had I not trusted that I would see the goodness of* HASHEM *in the land of life! Hope to* HASHEM, *strengthen yourself and He will give you courage; and hope to* HASHEM.

Mourners recite קַדִּישׁ יָתוֹם, the Mourner's *Kaddish* (p. 1016).

KIDDUSHA RABBA

ON THE SABBATH BEGIN HERE.

Many omit some or all of these verses and begin with *'therefore* HASHEM *blessed.'*

אִם תָּשִׁיב *If you restrain, because of the Sabbath, your feet, refrain from accomplishing your own needs on My holy day; if you proclaim the Sabbath 'a delight,' the holy one of* HASHEM, *'honored one,' and you honor it by not doing your own ways, from seeking your needs or discussing the forbidden. Then you shall be granted pleasure with* HASHEM *and I shall mount you astride the heights of the world, and provide you the heritage of your forefather Jacob — for the mouth of* HASHEM *has spoken.*[1]

וְשָׁמְרוּ *And the Children of Israel observed the Sabbath, to make the Sabbath for their generations an eternal covenant. Between Me and the Children of Israel it is a sign forever, that in six days did* HASHEM *make the heaven and the earth, and on the seventh day He rested and was refreshed.*[2]

זָכוֹר *Always remember the Sabbath day to hallow it. For six days you may labor and do all your work. But the seventh day is the Sabbath for* HASHEM, *Your God; you may do no work — you, your son and your daughter, your slave and your maidservant, your animal, and the stranger who is in your gates. For in six days did* HASHEM *make the heaven and the earth, the sea and all that is in them and He rested on the seventh day;*

therefore HASHEM *blessed the Sabbath day and sanctified it.*[3]

(These are the appointed festivals of HASHEM, *holy convocations, which you are to proclaim in their appointed times.*[4]*)*

And Moses declared HASHEM*'s appointed festivals to the Children of Israel.*[5]

By your leave, my masters and teachers:

בָּרוּךְ *Blessed are You,* HASHEM, *our God, King of the universe, Who creates the fruit of the vine.* (All present – *Amen.*)

The blessing after cake and wine appears on page 92; Grace after Meals, on page 84.

(1) *Isaiah* 58:13-14. (2) *Exodus* 31:16-17. (3) 20:8-11. (4) *Leviticus* 23:4. (5) 23:44.

❧ יציאה מן הסוכה ☙

During the afternoon of Shemini Atzeres, before leaving the *succah* for the last time, it is customary to recite the following prayers:

יְהִי רָצוֹן מִלְּפָנֶיךָ, יהוה אֱלֹהֵינוּ וֵאלֹהֵי אֲבוֹתֵינוּ, כְּשֵׁם שֶׁקִּיַּמְתִּי וְיָשַׁבְתִּי בְּסֻכָּה זוּ, כֵּן אֶזְכֶּה לְשָׁנָה הַבָּאָה לֵישֵׁב בְּסֻכַּת עוֹרוֹ שֶׁל לִוְיָתָן.*

לְשָׁנָה הַבָּאָה בִּירוּשָׁלָיִם.

Some add:

רִבּוֹנָא דְעָלְמָא, יְהֵא רַעֲוָה מִן קֳדָמָךְ שֶׁאוֹתָן מַלְאָכִים הַקְּדוֹשִׁים הַשַּׁיָּכִים לְמִצְוַת סֻכָּה, וּלְמִצְוַת אַרְבָּעָה מִינִים – לוּלָב וְאֶתְרוֹג, הֲדַס וַעֲרָבָה – הַנּוֹהֲגִים בְּחַג הַסֻּכּוֹת, הֵם יִתְלַווּ עִמָּנוּ בְּצֵאתֵנוּ מִן הַסֻּכָּה וְיִכָּנְסוּ עִמָּנוּ לְבָתֵּינוּ לְחַיִּים וּלְשָׁלוֹם. וְלִהְיוֹת תָּמִיד עָלֵינוּ שְׁמִירָה עֶלְיוֹנָה מִמְּעוֹן קָדְשֶׁךָ, וּלְהַצִּילֵנוּ מִכָּל חֵטְא וְעָוֹן, וּמִכָּל פְּגָעִים רָעִים, וּמִכָּל שָׁעוֹת רָעוֹת הַמִּתְרַגְּשׁוֹת לָבֹא לָעוֹלָם. וְתַעֲרֶה עָלֵינוּ רוּחַ מִמָּרוֹם; וְחַדֵּשׁ כִּלְיוֹתֵינוּ לְעָבְדְּךָ בֶּאֱמֶת, בְּאַהֲבָה וּבְיִרְאָה; וְנִתְמִיד מְאֹד בְּלִמּוּד תּוֹרָתְךָ הַקְּדוֹשָׁה, לִלְמוֹד וּלְלַמֵּד. וּזְכוּת אַרְבָּעָה מִינִים וּמִצְוַת סֻכָּה תַּעֲמֹד לָנוּ, שֶׁתַּאֲרִיךְ אַפְּךָ עַד שׁוּבֵנוּ אֵלֶיךָ בִּתְשׁוּבָה שְׁלֵמָה לְפָנֶיךָ; וּנְתַקֵּן כָּל אֲשֶׁר פָּגַמְנוּ; וְנִזְכֶּה לִשְׁתֵּי שֻׁלְחָנוֹת, בְּלִי צַעַר וְיָגוֹן – אֲנִי וּבְנֵי בֵיתִי וְיוֹצְאֵי חֲלָצַי – וְנִהְיֶה כֻּלָּנוּ שְׁקֵטִים וּשְׁלֵוִים, דְּשֵׁנִים וְרַעֲנַנִּים, וְעוֹבְדֵי יהוה בֶּאֱמֶת לַאֲמִתּוֹ כִּרְצוֹנְךָ הַטּוֹב, בִּכְלַל כָּל בְּנֵי יִשְׂרָאֵל; אָמֵן. יִהְיוּ לְרָצוֹן אִמְרֵי פִי, וְהֶגְיוֹן לִבִּי לְפָנֶיךָ, יהוה צוּרִי וְגוֹאֲלִי.[1]

❧ FAREWELL TO THE SUCCAH ☙

בְּסֻכַּת עוֹרוֹ שֶׁל לִוְיָתָן – *In the succah of the skin of Leviathan.* According to the Aggadah of the Talmud and Midrash, the לִוְיָתָן, *Leviathan,* is a giant fish created on the fifth day of Creation and who rules all the creatures of the sea.

Originally, two were created, a male and a female, as with all other species. However, God saw that if these two fish were allowed to mate and multiply, they would destroy the entire world by dint of their great strength and numbers, for the Leviathan is so enormous that all the waters that flow from the Jordan river into the sea can scarcely quench its thirst. God, therefore, killed the female and preserved it in brine, to be eaten by the righteous at the banquet prepared for them in the Time to Come. Additionally, the Leviathan is very beautiful. Its fins are so radiant that they outshine the sun. Its eyes are so bright that they sometimes illuminate the entire sea (*Bava Basra* 74b).

Another huge beast whose flesh will be served to the righteous in the World to Come is the בְּהֵמוֹת, *Behemoth,* created on the sixth day of the creation of the world. The Behemoth is a gigantic ox, and, like the Leviathan, possesses enormous strength. It, too, was created male and female, and, like the Leviathan, had to be prevented from multiplying, lest the world be destroyed. God therefore neutered the male and eliminated the female's desire to propagate (*Bava Basra* 74b).

When the Messiah comes, God will summon the angels to enter into battle against the Leviathan, for the amusement of the righteous. But the Leviathan will cast one glance upon them, and the angels will run in fear and dismay from the field of battle. They will return to attack him with swords, spears and stones, but to no avail, since steel is like straw against his scales (*Bava Basra* 74b). Disheartened, the angels will give up the battle, and God will signal to the Leviathan and the Behemoth to fight one another. The result will be that the Leviathan will slaughter the Behemoth with a cut from his very sharp fins. Simultaneously the Behemoth will kill

FAREWELL TO THE SUCCAH

During the afternoon of Shemini Atzeres, before leaving the *succah* for the last time, it is customary to recite the following prayers:

יְהִי רָצוֹן *May it be Your will, HASHEM, our God and the God of our forefathers, that just as I have fulfilled [the mitzvah] and dwelled in this succah, so may I merit in the coming year to dwell in the succah of the skin of Leviathan.**

Next year in Jerusalem.*

Some add:

רִבּוֹנָא *Master of the universe, may it be Your will that the holy angels connected with the mitzvah of succah and the mitzvah of the Four Species — lulav, esrog, hadas, aravah — that are performed during the Festival of Succos, accompany us when we leave the succah, and may they enter our homes with us in life and in peace. May there always be upon us a heavenly protection from Your holy abode, to save us from all sin and iniquity, from evil occurrences, from malevolent periods that are stirring to come upon the world. Arouse upon us a spirit from above; rejuvenate our inner source of counsel that we may serve You in truth, in love and in awe; that we may be diligent in the study of Your holy Torah, to study and to teach. May the merit of the Four Species and the mitzvah of succah stand by us, that You act with forbearance until we have returned to You in full repentance before You; may we rectify all that we have destroyed; may we merit both tables, with neither pain nor grief — myself, my household and my offspring — may we all dwell placid and serene, vigorous and fresh, serving HASHEM in utmost truthfulness according to Your benevolent will, among all the Children of Israel; Amen. May the expression of my mouth and the thoughts of my heart find favor before You, HASHEM, my Rock and my Redeemer.*[1]

(1) *Psalms* 19:15.

---

the Leviathan with a blow from his horns (*Leviticus Rabbah* 13:3).

From the beautiful skin of the Leviathan, God will construct canopies to shelter the righteous from the sun (*Bava Basra* 75a). These canopies are referred to in our prayer as סֻכַּת עוֹרוֹ שֶׁל לִוְיָתָן, *the succah of the skin of Leviathan.* Under these canopies they will eat the meat of the Leviathan and the Behemoth, amid great joy and merriment (ibid. 74b). Although the Talmud does not specify this banquet as a reward for fulfillment of the *mitzvah* of dwelling in the *succah,* an introduction in *Pesikta d'R' Eliezer* reads: R' Levi taught that God will seat all who fulfill the *mitzvah* of *succah* in This World in a *succah* of the skin of the Leviathan in the World to Come.

[The above is but a very brief synopsis of the Aggadah on Leviathan, Behemoth, and the banquet. See ArtScroll *Akdamus,* pp. 127-139, for a fuller account.]

לְשָׁנָה הַבָּאָה בִּירוּשָׁלָיִם — *Next year in Jerusalem.* This terse prayer is usually taken as an expression of faith and hope that during the next year the Messiah will arrive to redeem Israel from its exile and lead the nation back to the Holy Land, to a rebuilt Temple in Jerusalem. When viewed in this light, however, it seems to conflict with one of the Thirteen Articles of Faith formulated by *Rambam* (see p. 72). For the twelfth of those articles states: 'I believe with perfect faith in the advent of the Messiah, and even though he may tarry, nevertheless, I hope, *each day,* for his arrival.' Why, then, do we pray for his arrival during the coming year and not during the present one? R' Yoel of Satmar offers the following solution. If accented on its first syllable, the word בָּאָה means *had come,* in the past tense. If accented on the second syllable, בָּאָה means *is coming,* in the present tense (see *Rashi* to Genesis 29:7,9). Based upon these two possible meanings, we may retranslate our prayer: *The year that* **has come** [הַבָּאָה in the present tense] *in Jerusalem,* i.e., may we be in Jerusalem even during the current year, for Messiah can come at any moment.

מנחה לשמיני עצרת

אַשְׁרֵי יוֹשְׁבֵי בֵיתֶךָ, עוֹד יְהַלְלוּךָ סֶּלָה.[1] אַשְׁרֵי הָעָם שֶׁכָּכָה לּוֹ, אַשְׁרֵי הָעָם שֶׁיהוה אֱלֹהָיו.[2]

תהלים קמה

תְּהִלָּה לְדָוִד,

אֲרוֹמִמְךָ אֱלוֹהַי הַמֶּלֶךְ, וַאֲבָרְכָה שִׁמְךָ לְעוֹלָם וָעֶד.
בְּכָל יוֹם אֲבָרְכֶךָּ, וַאֲהַלְלָה שִׁמְךָ לְעוֹלָם וָעֶד.
גָּדוֹל יהוה וּמְהֻלָּל מְאֹד, וְלִגְדֻלָּתוֹ אֵין חֵקֶר.
דּוֹר לְדוֹר יְשַׁבַּח מַעֲשֶׂיךָ, וּגְבוּרֹתֶיךָ יַגִּידוּ.
הֲדַר כְּבוֹד הוֹדֶךָ, וְדִבְרֵי נִפְלְאֹתֶיךָ אָשִׂיחָה.
וֶעֱזוּז נוֹרְאוֹתֶיךָ יֹאמֵרוּ, וּגְדוּלָּתְךָ אֲסַפְּרֶנָּה.
זֵכֶר רַב טוּבְךָ יַבִּיעוּ, וְצִדְקָתְךָ יְרַנֵּנוּ.
חַנּוּן וְרַחוּם יהוה, אֶרֶךְ אַפַּיִם וּגְדָל חָסֶד.
טוֹב יהוה לַכֹּל, וְרַחֲמָיו עַל כָּל מַעֲשָׂיו.
יוֹדוּךָ יהוה כָּל מַעֲשֶׂיךָ, וַחֲסִידֶיךָ יְבָרְכוּכָה.
כְּבוֹד מַלְכוּתְךָ יֹאמֵרוּ, וּגְבוּרָתְךָ יְדַבֵּרוּ.
לְהוֹדִיעַ לִבְנֵי הָאָדָם גְּבוּרֹתָיו, וּכְבוֹד הֲדַר מַלְכוּתוֹ.
מַלְכוּתְךָ מַלְכוּת כָּל עֹלָמִים, וּמֶמְשַׁלְתְּךָ בְּכָל דּוֹר וָדֹר.
סוֹמֵךְ יהוה לְכָל הַנֹּפְלִים, וְזוֹקֵף לְכָל הַכְּפוּפִים.
עֵינֵי כֹל אֵלֶיךָ יְשַׂבֵּרוּ, וְאַתָּה נוֹתֵן לָהֶם אֶת אָכְלָם בְּעִתּוֹ.

While reciting the verse פּוֹתֵחַ, concentrate intently on its meaning.

פּוֹתֵחַ אֶת יָדֶךָ,
וּמַשְׂבִּיעַ לְכָל חַי רָצוֹן.
צַדִּיק יהוה בְּכָל דְּרָכָיו, וְחָסִיד בְּכָל מַעֲשָׂיו.
קָרוֹב יהוה לְכָל קֹרְאָיו, לְכֹל אֲשֶׁר יִקְרָאֻהוּ בֶאֱמֶת.
רְצוֹן יְרֵאָיו יַעֲשֶׂה, וְאֶת שַׁוְעָתָם יִשְׁמַע וְיוֹשִׁיעֵם.
שׁוֹמֵר יהוה אֶת כָּל אֹהֲבָיו, וְאֵת כָּל הָרְשָׁעִים יַשְׁמִיד.
❖ תְּהִלַּת יהוה יְדַבֶּר פִּי, וִיבָרֵךְ כָּל בָּשָׂר שֵׁם קָדְשׁוֹ לְעוֹלָם וָעֶד.
וַאֲנַחְנוּ נְבָרֵךְ יָהּ, מֵעַתָּה וְעַד עוֹלָם, הַלְלוּיָהּ.[3]

(1) *Psalms* 84:5. (2) 144:15. (3) 115:18.

MINCHAH / מִנְחָה

Minchah is usually recited in the late afternoon, a particularly apt time for prayer, for it is a time of Divine mercy. Thus, both Isaac (*Genesis* 24:63) and Elijah (*I Kings* 18:36) prayed in the afternoon. Prefatory remarks to *Minchah* and commentary to אַשְׁרֵי appear on pages 6-9.

MINCHAH FOR SHEMINI ATZERES

אַשְׁרֵי *Praiseworthy are those who dwell in Your house; may they always praise You, Selah!*[1] *Praiseworthy is the people for whom this is so, praiseworthy is the people whose God is* HASHEM.[2]

Psalm 145

A psalm of praise by David:

א *I will exalt You, my God the King,*
and I will bless Your Name forever and ever.

ב *Every day I will bless You,*
and I will laud Your Name forever and ever.

ג HASHEM *is great and exceedingly lauded,*
and His greatness is beyond investigation.

ד *Each generation will praise Your deeds to the next*
and of Your mighty deeds they will tell.

ה *The splendrous glory of Your power*
and Your wondrous deeds I shall discuss.

ו *And of Your awesome power they will speak,*
and Your greatness I shall relate.

ז *A recollection of Your abundant goodness they will utter*
and of Your righteousness they will sing exultantly.

ח *Gracious and merciful is* HASHEM,
slow to anger, and great in [bestowing] kindness.

ט HASHEM *is good to all; His mercies are on all His works.*

י *All Your works shall thank You,* HASHEM,
and Your devout ones will bless You.

כ *Of the glory of Your kingdom they will speak,*
and of Your power they will tell;

ל *To inform human beings of His mighty deeds,*
and the glorious splendor of His kingdom.

מ *Your kingdom is a kingdom spanning all eternities,*
and Your dominion is throughout every generation.

ס HASHEM *supports all the fallen ones and straightens all the bent.*

ע *The eyes of all look to You with hope*
and You give them their food in its proper time;

פ *You open Your hand,*
and satisfy the desire of every living thing.

While reciting the verse *'You open . . .,'* concentrate intently on its meaning

צ *Righteous is* HASHEM *in all His ways*
and magnanimous in all His deeds.

ק HASHEM *is close to all who call upon Him —*
to all who call upon Him sincerely.

ר *The will of those who fear Him He will do;*
and their cry He will hear, and save them.

ש HASHEM *protects all who love Him;*
but all the wicked He will destroy.

ת Chazzan– *May my mouth declare the praise of* HASHEM
and may all flesh bless His Holy Name forever and ever.

We will bless God from this time and forever, Halleluyah![3]

The primary part of וּבָא לְצִיּוֹן is the *Kedushah* recited by the angels. These verses are presented in bold type and it is preferable that the congregation recite them aloud and in unison. However, the interpretive translation in Aramaic (which follows the verses in bold type) should be recited softly.

וּבָא לְצִיּוֹן גּוֹאֵל,* וּלְשָׁבֵי פֶשַׁע בְּיַעֲקֹב, נְאֻם יהוה. וַאֲנִי, זֹאת בְּרִיתִי* אוֹתָם, אָמַר יהוה, רוּחִי אֲשֶׁר עָלֶיךָ, וּדְבָרַי אֲשֶׁר שַׂמְתִּי בְּפִיךָ, לֹא יָמוּשׁוּ מִפִּיךָ וּמִפִּי זַרְעֲךָ* וּמִפִּי זֶרַע זַרְעֲךָ, אָמַר יהוה, מֵעַתָּה וְעַד עוֹלָם:[1] ❖ וְאַתָּה קָדוֹשׁ יוֹשֵׁב תְּהִלּוֹת יִשְׂרָאֵל.*[2] וְקָרָא זֶה אֶל זֶה וְאָמַר:

קָדוֹשׁ, קָדוֹשׁ, קָדוֹשׁ יהוה צְבָאוֹת, מְלֹא כָל הָאָרֶץ כְּבוֹדוֹ.[3]

וּמְקַבְּלִין דֵּין מִן דֵּין וְאָמְרִין:
קַדִּישׁ בִּשְׁמֵי מְרוֹמָא עִלָּאָה בֵּית שְׁכִינְתֵּהּ,
קַדִּישׁ עַל אַרְעָא עוֹבַד גְּבוּרְתֵּהּ,
קַדִּישׁ לְעָלַם וּלְעָלְמֵי עָלְמַיָּא, יהוה צְבָאוֹת,
מַלְיָא כָל אַרְעָא זִיו יְקָרֵהּ.[4]

❖ וַתִּשָּׂאֵנִי רוּחַ,* וָאֶשְׁמַע אַחֲרַי קוֹל רַעַשׁ גָּדוֹל:

בָּרוּךְ כְּבוֹד יהוה מִמְּקוֹמוֹ.[5]

וּנְטָלַתְנִי רוּחָא, וּשְׁמָעִית בַּתְרַי קָל זִיעַ סַגִּיא
דִּמְשַׁבְּחִין וְאָמְרִין:
בְּרִיךְ יְקָרָא דַיהוה מֵאֲתַר בֵּית שְׁכִינְתֵּהּ.[6]

יהוה יִמְלֹךְ לְעֹלָם וָעֶד.[7]

יהוה מַלְכוּתֵהּ קָאֵם לְעָלַם וּלְעָלְמֵי עָלְמַיָּא.[8]

יהוה אֱלֹהֵי אַבְרָהָם יִצְחָק וְיִשְׂרָאֵל אֲבֹתֵינוּ, שָׁמְרָה זֹּאת* לְעוֹלָם, לְיֵצֶר מַחְשְׁבוֹת לְבַב עַמֶּךָ, וְהָכֵן לְבָבָם אֵלֶיךָ.[9] וְהוּא רַחוּם,

---

וּבָא לְצִיּוֹן / Uva Letzion

The most important part of the וּבָא לְצִיּוֹן prayer is the recitation of the angel's praises of God.

The Talmud (*Sotah* 49a) declares that since the destruction of the Temple, even the physical beauty and pleasures of the world began deteriorating. If so, by what merit does the world endure? Rava teaches: the *Kedushah* in the prayer *Uva Letzion,* and the recitation of *Kaddish* following the public study of Torah. *Rashi* explains that after the Destruction, the primary focus of holiness in the universe is Torah study. In *Uva Letzion,* the Sages combined the Scriptural verses containing the angel's praise of God with the interpretive translation of *Yonasan ben Uziel.* Thus, this prayer itself constitutes Torah study and its recitation involves the entire congregation in Torah study. This emphasis on Torah study is further stressed by the latter part of *Uva Letzion* which lauds the study and observance of the Torah. The *Kaddish* recited after public Torah study is a further affirmation of the Torah's central role in Jewish existence.

וּבָא לְצִיּוֹן גּוֹאֵל — *A redeemer shall come to Zion.* God pledges that the Messiah will come to redeem the city Zion and the people of Israel. Not only

The primary part of וּבָא לְצִיּוֹן, *'A redeemer shall come . . .'*, is the *Kedushah* recited by the angels. These verses are presented in bold type and it is preferable that the congregation recite them aloud and in unison. However, the interpretive translation in Aramaic (which follows the verses in bold type) should be recited softly.

וּבָא לְצִיּוֹן *'A redeemer shall come to Zion* and to those of Jacob who repent from willful sin,' the words of* HASHEM. *'And as for Me, this is My covenant* with them,' said* HASHEM, *'My spirit that is upon you and My words that I have placed in your mouth shall not be withdrawn from your mouth, nor from the mouth of your offspring,* nor from the mouth of your offspring's offspring,' said* HASHEM, *'from this moment and forever.'*[1] Chazzan– *You are the Holy One, enthroned upon the praises of Israel.**[2] *And one [angel] will call another and say:*

'Holy, holy, holy is HASHEM, Master of Legions,
the whole world is filled with His glory.'[3]

And they receive permission from one another and say:
'Holy in the most exalted heaven, the abode of His Presence;
holy on earth, product of His strength;
holy forever and ever is HASHEM, *Master of Legions —*
the entire world is filled with the radiance of His glory.'[4]
Chazzan– *And a wind lifted me;* and I heard behind me*
the sound of a great noise:

'Blessed is the glory of HASHEM from His place.'[5]

And a wind lifted me and I heard behind me the sound
of the powerful movement of those who praised saying:
'Blessed is the honor of HASHEM
from the place of the abode of His Presence.'[6]

HASHEM shall reign for all eternity.[7]

HASHEM *— His kingdom is established forever and ever.*[8]

HASHEM, *God of Abraham, Isaac, and Israel, our forefathers, may You preserve this* forever as the realization of the thoughts in Your people's heart, and may You direct their heart to You.*[9] *He, the Merciful One,*

(1) *Isaiah* 59:20-21. (2) *Psalms* 22:4. (3) *Isaiah* 6:3. (4) *Targum Yonasan.* (5) *Ezekiel* 3:12. (6) *Targum Yonasan.* (7) *Exodus* 15:18. (8) *Targum Onkelos.* (9) *I Chronicles* 29:18.

those who remained righteous throughout the ordeal of exile will be saved, but even those who had sinned will join in the glorious future, if they return to the ways of God *(Etz Yosef).*

בְּרִיתִי — *My covenant.* God affirms that His covenant, i.e., His *spirit* of prophecy and *words* of Torah, will remain with Israel forever *(Metzudos).*

מִפִּיךָ וּמִפִּי זַרְעֲךָ . . . — *From your mouth, nor from the mouth of your offspring . . .* This is a Divine assurance that if a family produces three consecutive generations of profound Torah scholars, the blessing of Torah knowledge will not be withdrawn from its posterity *(Bava Metzia* 85a). In a broader sense, we see the fulfillment of this blessing in the miracle that Torah greatness has remained with Israel throughout centuries of exile and flight from country to country and from continent to continent *(Siach Yitzchak).*

יוֹשֵׁב תְּהִלּוֹת יִשְׂרָאֵל — *Enthroned upon the praises of Israel.* Although God is praised by myriad angels, He values the praises of Israel above all; as the Sages teach *(Chullin* 90b), the angels are not permitted to sing their praises above until the Jews sing theirs below *(Abudraham).*

וַתִּשָּׂאֵנִי רוּחַ — *And a wind lifted me.* These words were uttered by the prophet Ezekiel, who had just been commanded to undertake a difficult mission

יְכַפֵּר עָוֹן וְלֹא יַשְׁחִית, וְהִרְבָּה לְהָשִׁיב אַפּוֹ, וְלֹא יָעִיר כָּל חֲמָתוֹ.[1] כִּי אַתָּה אֲדֹנָי טוֹב וְסַלָּח, וְרַב חֶסֶד לְכָל קֹרְאֶיךָ.[2] צִדְקָתְךָ צֶדֶק לְעוֹלָם, וְתוֹרָתְךָ אֱמֶת.[3] תִּתֵּן אֱמֶת לְיַעֲקֹב, חֶסֶד לְאַבְרָהָם, אֲשֶׁר נִשְׁבַּעְתָּ לַאֲבֹתֵינוּ מִימֵי קֶדֶם.[4] בָּרוּךְ אֲדֹנָי יוֹם יוֹם יַעֲמָס לָנוּ, הָאֵל יְשׁוּעָתֵנוּ סֶלָה.[5] יהוה צְבָאוֹת עִמָּנוּ, מִשְׂגָּב לָנוּ אֱלֹהֵי יַעֲקֹב סֶלָה.[6] יהוה צְבָאוֹת, אַשְׁרֵי אָדָם בֹּטֵחַ בָּךְ.[7] יהוה הוֹשִׁיעָה, הַמֶּלֶךְ יַעֲנֵנוּ בְיוֹם קָרְאֵנוּ.[8]

בָּרוּךְ הוּא אֱלֹהֵינוּ שֶׁבְּרָאָנוּ לִכְבוֹדוֹ, וְהִבְדִּילָנוּ מִן הַתּוֹעִים, וְנָתַן לָנוּ תּוֹרַת אֱמֶת, וְחַיֵּי עוֹלָם נָטַע בְּתוֹכֵנוּ. הוּא יִפְתַּח לִבֵּנוּ בְּתוֹרָתוֹ, וְיָשֵׂם בְּלִבֵּנוּ אַהֲבָתוֹ וְיִרְאָתוֹ וְלַעֲשׂוֹת רְצוֹנוֹ וּלְעָבְדוֹ בְּלֵבָב שָׁלֵם, לְמַעַן לֹא נִיגַע לָרִיק, וְלֹא נֵלֵד לַבֶּהָלָה.[9]

יְהִי רָצוֹן מִלְּפָנֶיךָ יהוה אֱלֹהֵינוּ וֵאלֹהֵי אֲבוֹתֵינוּ, שֶׁנִּשְׁמֹר חֻקֶּיךָ בָּעוֹלָם הַזֶּה, וְנִזְכֶּה וְנִחְיֶה וְנִרְאֶה וְנִירַשׁ טוֹבָה וּבְרָכָה לִשְׁנֵי יְמוֹת הַמָּשִׁיחַ וּלְחַיֵּי הָעוֹלָם הַבָּא. לְמַעַן יְזַמֶּרְךָ כָבוֹד וְלֹא יִדֹּם, יהוה אֱלֹהַי לְעוֹלָם אוֹדֶךָּ.[10] בָּרוּךְ הַגֶּבֶר אֲשֶׁר יִבְטַח בַּיהוה, וְהָיָה יהוה מִבְטַחוֹ.[11] בִּטְחוּ בַיהוה עֲדֵי עַד, כִּי בְּיָהּ יהוה צוּר עוֹלָמִים.[12] ❖ וְיִבְטְחוּ בְךָ יוֹדְעֵי שְׁמֶךָ, כִּי לֹא עָזַבְתָּ דֹּרְשֶׁיךָ, יהוה.[13] יהוה חָפֵץ לְמַעַן צִדְקוֹ, יַגְדִּיל תּוֹרָה וְיַאְדִּיר.[14]

חצי קדיש

Chazzan recites חֲצִי קַדִּישׁ.

יִתְגַּדַּל וְיִתְקַדַּשׁ שְׁמֵהּ רַבָּא. (.Cong – אָמֵן.) בְּעָלְמָא דִּי בְרָא כִרְעוּתֵהּ. וְיַמְלִיךְ מַלְכוּתֵהּ, בְּחַיֵּיכוֹן וּבְיוֹמֵיכוֹן וּבְחַיֵּי דְכָל בֵּית יִשְׂרָאֵל, בַּעֲגָלָא וּבִזְמַן קָרִיב. וְאִמְרוּ: אָמֵן.

(.Cong – אָמֵן. יְהֵא שְׁמֵהּ רַבָּא מְבָרַךְ לְעָלַם וּלְעָלְמֵי עָלְמַיָּא.)

יְהֵא שְׁמֵהּ רַבָּא מְבָרַךְ לְעָלַם וּלְעָלְמֵי עָלְמַיָּא.

יִתְבָּרַךְ וְיִשְׁתַּבַּח וְיִתְפָּאַר וְיִתְרוֹמַם וְיִתְנַשֵּׂא וְיִתְהַדָּר וְיִתְעַלֶּה וְיִתְהַלָּל שְׁמֵהּ דְּקֻדְשָׁא בְּרִיךְ הוּא (.Cong – בְּרִיךְ הוּא) — לְעֵלָּא מִן כָּל בִּרְכָתָא וְשִׁירָתָא תֻּשְׁבְּחָתָא וְנֶחֱמָתָא, דַּאֲמִירָן בְּעָלְמָא. וְאִמְרוּ: אָמֵן. (.Cong – אָמֵן.)

ON WEEKDAYS CONTINUE WITH *SHEMONEH ESREI*, PAGE 1036.

ON THE SABBATH THE TORAH IS READ, PAGE 1028.

---

on behalf of the exiled Jews. God sent a wind to transport him to Babylon, and as he was lifted, he heard the angels' song. This suggests that the person who ignores his own convenience in order to serve God can expect to climb spiritual heights beyond his normal capacity.

שָׁמְרָה זֹּאת — *May You preserve this.* May God help us remain permanently with the above fervent declaration of His holiness and kingship (*Abudraham*).

is forgiving of iniquity and does not destroy; frequently He withdraws His anger, not arousing His entire rage.[1] *For You, my Lord, are good and forgiving, and abundantly kind to all who call upon You.*[2] *Your righteousness remains righteous forever, and Your Torah is truth.*[3] *Grant truth to Jacob, kindness to Abraham, as You swore to our forefathers from ancient times.*[4] *Blessed is my Lord for every single day, He burdens us with blessings, the God of our salvation, Selah.*[5] *HASHEM, Master of Legions, is with us, a stronghold for us is the God of Jacob, Selah.*[6] *HASHEM, Master of Legions, praiseworthy is the man who trusts in You.*[7] *HASHEM, save! May the King answer us on the day we call.*[8]

Blessed is He, our God, Who created us for His glory, separated us from those who stray, gave us the Torah of truth and implanted eternal life within us. May He open our heart through His Torah and imbue our heart with love and awe of Him and that we may do His will and serve Him wholeheartedly, so that we do not struggle in vain nor produce for futility.[9]

May it be Your will, HASHEM, our God and the God of our forefathers, that we observe Your decrees in This World, and merit that we live and see and inherit goodness and blessing in the years of Messianic times and for the life of the World to Come. So that my soul might sing to You and not be stilled, HASHEM, my God, forever will I thank You.[10] *Blessed is the man who trusts in HASHEM, then HASHEM will be his security.*[11] *Trust in HASHEM forever, for in God, HASHEM, is the strength of the worlds.*[12] Chazzan– *Those knowing Your Name will trust in You, and You forsake not those Who seek You, HASHEM.*[13] *HASHEM desired, for the sake of its [Israel's] righteousness, that the Torah be made great and glorious.*[14]

HALF-KADDISH

Chazzan recites Half-*Kaddish.*

יִתְגַּדַּל *May His great Name grow exalted and sanctified* (Cong.– *Amen.*) *in the world that He created as He willed. May He give reign to His kingship in your lifetimes and in your days, and in the lifetimes of the entire Family of Israel, swiftly and soon. Now respond: Amen.*

(Cong.– *Amen. May His great Name be blessed forever and ever.*)

May His great Name be blessed forever and ever.

Blessed, praised, glorified, exalted, extolled, mighty, upraised, and lauded be the Name of the Holy One, Blessed is He (Cong.– *Blessed is He*) — *beyond any blessing and song, praise and consolation that are uttered in the world. Now respond: Amen.* (Cong.– *Amen.*)

ON WEEKDAYS CONTINUE WITH *SHEMONEH ESREI,* PAGE 1036.
ON THE SABBATH THE TORAH IS READ, PAGE 1028.

(1) *Psalms* 78:38. (2) 86:5. (3) 119:142. (4) *Micah* 7:20. (5) *Psalms* 68:20. (6) 46:8. (7) 84:13. (8) 20:10. (9) Cf. *Isaiah* 65:23. (10) *Psalms* 30:13. (11) *Jeremiah* 17:7. (12) *Isaiah* 26:4. (13) *Psalms* 9:11. (14) *Isaiah* 42:21.

Congregation, then *chazzan:*

וַאֲנִי תְפִלָּתִי לְךָ יהוה עֵת רָצוֹן, אֱלֹהִים בְּרָב חַסְדֶּךָ, עֲנֵנִי בֶּאֱמֶת יִשְׁעֶךָ.[1]

הוצאת ספר תורה

From the moment the Ark is opened until the Torah is returned to it, one must conduct himself with the utmost respect, and avoid unnecessary conversation. It is commendable to kiss the Torah as it is carried to the *bimah* [reading table] and back to the Ark.

All rise and remain standing until the Torah is placed on the *bimah*.
The Ark is opened; before the Torah is removed the congregation recites:

וַיְהִי בִּנְסֹעַ הָאָרֹן, וַיֹּאמֶר מֹשֶׁה, קוּמָה יהוה וְיָפֻצוּ אֹיְבֶיךָ, וְיָנֻסוּ מְשַׂנְאֶיךָ מִפָּנֶיךָ.[2] כִּי מִצִּיּוֹן תֵּצֵא תוֹרָה, וּדְבַר יהוה מִירוּשָׁלָיִם.[3] בָּרוּךְ שֶׁנָּתַן תּוֹרָה לְעַמּוֹ יִשְׂרָאֵל בִּקְדֻשָּׁתוֹ.

זוהר ויקהל שסט:א

בְּרִיךְ שְׁמֵהּ דְּמָרֵא עָלְמָא, בְּרִיךְ כִּתְרָךְ וְאַתְרָךְ. יְהֵא רְעוּתָךְ עִם עַמָּךְ יִשְׂרָאֵל לְעָלַם, וּפֻרְקַן יְמִינָךְ אַחֲזֵי לְעַמָּךְ בְּבֵית מַקְדְּשָׁךְ, וּלְאַמְטוּיֵי לָנָא מִטּוּב נְהוֹרָךְ, וּלְקַבֵּל צְלוֹתָנָא בְּרַחֲמִין. יְהֵא רַעֲוָא קֳדָמָךְ, דְּתוֹרִיךְ לָן חַיִּין בְּטִיבוּתָא, וְלֶהֱוֵי אֲנָא פְּקִידָא בְּגוֹ צַדִּיקַיָּא, לְמִרְחַם עָלַי וּלְמִנְטַר יָתִי וְיַת כָּל דִּי לִי וְדִי לְעַמָּךְ יִשְׂרָאֵל. אַנְתְּ הוּא זָן לְכֹלָּא, וּמְפַרְנֵס לְכֹלָּא, אַנְתְּ הוּא שַׁלִּיט עַל כֹּלָּא. אַנְתְּ הוּא דְּשַׁלִּיט עַל מַלְכַיָּא, וּמַלְכוּתָא דִּילָךְ הִיא. אֲנָא עַבְדָּא דְקֻדְשָׁא בְּרִיךְ הוּא, דְּסָגִידְנָא קַמֵּהּ וּמִקַּמָּא דִּיקַר אוֹרַיְתֵהּ בְּכָל עִדָּן וְעִדָּן. לָא עַל אֱנָשׁ רָחִיצְנָא, וְלָא עַל בַּר אֱלָהִין סָמֵיכְנָא, אֶלָּא בֶּאֱלָהָא דִשְׁמַיָּא, דְּהוּא אֱלָהָא קְשׁוֹט, וְאוֹרַיְתֵהּ קְשׁוֹט, וּנְבִיאוֹהִי קְשׁוֹט, וּמַסְגֵּא לְמֶעְבַּד טַבְוָן וּקְשׁוֹט. בֵּהּ אֲנָא רָחִיץ, וְלִשְׁמֵהּ קַדִּישָׁא יַקִּירָא אֲנָא אֵמַר תֻּשְׁבְּחָן. יְהֵא רַעֲוָא קֳדָמָךְ, דְּתִפְתַּח לִבָּאִי בְּאוֹרַיְתָא, וְתַשְׁלִים מִשְׁאֲלִין דְּלִבָּאִי, וְלִבָּא דְכָל עַמָּךְ יִשְׂרָאֵל, לְטַב וּלְחַיִּין וְלִשְׁלָם. (אָמֵן.)

The Torah is removed from the Ark and presented to the *chazzan,* who accepts it in his right arm. He then turns to the Ark and raises the Torah slightly as he bows and recites:

גַּדְּלוּ לַיהוה אִתִּי, וּנְרוֹמְמָה שְׁמוֹ יַחְדָּו.[4]

The *chazzan* turns to his right and carries the Torah to the *bimah,* as the congregation responds:

לְךָ יהוה הַגְּדֻלָּה וְהַגְּבוּרָה וְהַתִּפְאֶרֶת וְהַנֵּצַח וְהַהוֹד, כִּי כֹל בַּשָּׁמַיִם וּבָאָרֶץ, לְךָ יהוה הַמַּמְלָכָה וְהַמִּתְנַשֵּׂא לְכֹל לְרֹאשׁ.[5] רוֹמְמוּ יהוה אֱלֹהֵינוּ וְהִשְׁתַּחֲווּ לַהֲדֹם רַגְלָיו, קָדוֹשׁ הוּא. רוֹמְמוּ יהוה אֱלֹהֵינוּ וְהִשְׁתַּחֲווּ לְהַר קָדְשׁוֹ, כִּי קָדוֹשׁ יהוה אֱלֹהֵינוּ.[6]

Congregation, then *chazzan:*

וַאֲנִי תְפִלָּתִי *As for me, may my prayer to You, HASHEM, be at an opportune time; O God, in Your abundant kindness, answer me with the truth of Your salvation.*[1]

REMOVAL OF THE TORAH FROM THE ARK

From the moment the Ark is opened until the Torah is returned to it, one must conduct himself with the utmost respect, and avoid unnecessary conversation. It is commendable to kiss the Torah as it is carried to the *bimah* [reading table] and back to the Ark.

All rise and remain standing until the Torah is placed on the *bimah.*
The Ark is opened; before the Torah is removed the congregation recites:

וַיְהִי בִּנְסֹעַ *When the Ark would travel, Moses would say, 'Arise, HASHEM, and let Your foes be scattered, let those who hate You flee from You.'*[2] *For from Zion will the Torah come forth and the word of HASHEM from Jerusalem.*[3] *Blessed is He Who gave the Torah to His people Israel in His holiness.*

Zohar, Vayakhel 369a

בְּרִיךְ שְׁמֵהּ *Blessed is the Name of the Master of the universe, blessed is Your crown and Your place. May Your favor remain with Your people Israel forever; may You display the salvation of Your right hand to Your people in Your Holy Temple, to benefit us with the goodness of Your luminescence and to accept our prayers with mercy. May it be Your will that You extend our lives with goodness and that I be numbered among the righteous; that You have mercy on me and protect me, all that is mine and that is Your people Israel's. It is You Who nourishes all and sustains all, You control everything. It is You Who control kings, and Kingship is Yours. I am a servant of the Holy One, Blessed is He, and I prostrate myself before Him and before the glory of His Torah at all times. Not in any man do I put trust, nor on any angel do I rely — only on the God of heaven Who is the God of truth, Whose Torah is truth and Whose prophets are true and Who acts liberally with kindness and truth. In Him do I trust, and to His glorious and Holy Name do I declare praises. May it be Your will that You open my heart to the Torah and that You fulfill the wishes of my heart and the heart of Your entire people Israel for good, for life, and for peace. (Amen.)*

The Torah is removed from the Ark and presented to the *chazzan,* who accepts it in his right arm. He then turns to the Ark and raises the Torah slightly as he bows and recites:

Declare the greatness of HASHEM with me, and let us exalt His Name together.[4]

The *chazzan* turns to his right and carries the Torah to the *bimah,* as the congregation responds:

לְךָ *Yours, HASHEM, is the greatness, the strength, the splendor, the triumph, and the glory; even everything in heaven and earth; Yours, HASHEM, is the kingdom, and the sovereignty over every leader.*[5] *Exalt HASHEM, our God, and bow at His footstool; He is Holy! Exalt HASHEM, our God, and bow at His holy mountain; for holy is HASHEM, our God.*[6]

(1) *Psalms* 69:14. (2) *Numbers* 10:35. (3) *Isaiah* 2:3.
(4) *Psalms* 34:4. (5) *I Chronicles* 29:11. (6) *Psalms* 99:5,9.

אַב הָרַחֲמִים הוּא יְרַחֵם עַם עֲמוּסִים, וְיִזְכֹּר בְּרִית אֵיתָנִים, וְיַצִּיל נַפְשׁוֹתֵינוּ מִן הַשָּׁעוֹת הָרָעוֹת, וְיִגְעַר בְּיֵצֶר הָרַע מִן הַנְּשׂוּאִים, וְיָחֹן אוֹתָנוּ לִפְלֵיטַת עוֹלָמִים, וִימַלֵּא מִשְׁאֲלוֹתֵינוּ בְּמִדָּה טוֹבָה יְשׁוּעָה וְרַחֲמִים.

The Torah is placed on the *bimah* and prepared for reading.

The *gabbai* uses the following formula to call a *Kohen* to the Torah:

וְתִגָּלֶה וְתֵרָאֶה מַלְכוּתוֹ עָלֵינוּ בִּזְמַן קָרוֹב, וְיָחֹן פְּלֵיטָתֵנוּ וּפְלֵיטַת עַמּוֹ בֵּית יִשְׂרָאֵל לְחֵן וּלְחֶסֶד וּלְרַחֲמִים וּלְרָצוֹן. וְנֹאמַר אָמֵן. הַכֹּל הָבוּ גֹדֶל לֵאלֹהֵינוּ וּתְנוּ כָבוֹד לַתּוֹרָה. כֹּהֵן° קְרָב, יַעֲמֹד (insert name) הַכֹּהֵן.

°If no *Kohen* is present, the *gabbai* says: "אֵין כָּאן כֹּהֵן, יַעֲמֹד (name) יִשְׂרָאֵל (לֵוִי) בִּמְקוֹם כֹּהֵן."

בָּרוּךְ שֶׁנָּתַן תּוֹרָה לְעַמּוֹ יִשְׂרָאֵל בִּקְדֻשָּׁתוֹ. (תּוֹרַת יהוה תְּמִימָה מְשִׁיבַת נָפֶשׁ, עֵדוּת יהוה נֶאֱמָנָה מַחְכִּימַת פֶּתִי. פִּקּוּדֵי יהוה יְשָׁרִים מְשַׂמְּחֵי לֵב, מִצְוַת יהוה בָּרָה מְאִירַת עֵינָיִם.[1] יהוה עֹז לְעַמּוֹ יִתֵּן, יהוה יְבָרֵךְ אֶת עַמּוֹ בַשָּׁלוֹם.[2] הָאֵל תָּמִים דַּרְכּוֹ, אִמְרַת יהוה צְרוּפָה, מָגֵן הוּא לְכֹל הַחֹסִים בּוֹ.[3])

Congregation, then *gabbai*:

וְאַתֶּם הַדְּבֵקִים בַּיהוה אֱלֹהֵיכֶם, חַיִּים כֻּלְּכֶם הַיּוֹם:[4]

קריאת התורה

The reader shows the *oleh* (person called to the Torah) the place in the Torah. The *oleh* touches the Torah with a corner of his *tallis*, or the belt or mantle of the Torah, and kisses it. He then begins the blessing, bowing at בָּרְכוּ, and straightening up at ה׳.

בָּרְכוּ אֶת יהוה הַמְּבֹרָךְ.

Congregation, followed by *oleh*, responds, bowing at בָּרוּךְ, and straightening up at ה׳:

בָּרוּךְ יהוה הַמְּבֹרָךְ לְעוֹלָם וָעֶד.

Oleh continues:

בָּרוּךְ אַתָּה יהוה אֱלֹהֵינוּ מֶלֶךְ הָעוֹלָם, אֲשֶׁר בָּחַר בָּנוּ מִכָּל הָעַמִּים, וְנָתַן לָנוּ אֶת תּוֹרָתוֹ. בָּרוּךְ אַתָּה יהוה, נוֹתֵן הַתּוֹרָה.

(Cong. – אָמֵן.)

After his Torah portion has been read, the *oleh* recites:

בָּרוּךְ אַתָּה יהוה אֱלֹהֵינוּ מֶלֶךְ הָעוֹלָם, אֲשֶׁר נָתַן לָנוּ תּוֹרַת אֱמֶת, וְחַיֵּי עוֹלָם נָטַע בְּתוֹכֵנוּ. בָּרוּךְ אַתָּה יהוה, נוֹתֵן הַתּוֹרָה.

(Cong. – אָמֵן.)

THE VARIOUS מִי שֶׁבֵּרַךְ PRAYERS APPEAR ON PAGE 308.

THE TORAH READING ON THE SABBATH

The Torah reading during the Sabbath *Minchah* includes the calling to the Torah of *Kohen*, Levite, and Israelite. The reading is the first section of the next *sidrah* in the regular order of weekly Torah reading. Thus, on the Sabbath of Succos, the first seventeen verses of *V'zos HaBerachah* are read. The Torah reading just before the end of the Sabbath symbolizes that we will take the Torah-imbued spirit of the Sabbath with us into the next week. Commentary on this portion appears on page 1158.

אַב הָרַחֲמִים *May the Father of mercy have mercy on the nation that is borne by Him, and may He remember the covenant of the spiritually mighty. May He rescue our souls from the bad times, and upbraid the evil inclination to leave those borne by Him, graciously make us an eternal remnant, and fulfill our requests in good measure, for salvation and mercy.*

The Torah is placed on the *bimah* and prepared for reading.
The *gabbai* uses the following formula to call a *Kohen* to the Torah:

וְתִגָּלֶה *And may His kingship over us be revealed and become visible soon, and may He be gracious to our remnant and the remnant of His people the Family of Israel, for graciousness, kindness, mercy, and favor. And let us respond, Amen. All of you ascribe greatness to our God and give honor to the Torah. Kohen,° approach. Stand* (name) *son of* (father's name) *the Kohen.*

°If no *Kohen* is present, the *gabbai* says: *'There is no Kohen present, stand* (name) *son of* (father's name) *an Israelite (Levite) in place of the Kohen.'*

Blessed is He Who gave the Torah to His people Israel in His holiness. (The Torah of HASHEM is perfect, restoring the soul; the testimony of HASHEM is trustworthy, making the simple one wise. The orders of HASHEM are upright, gladdening the heart; the command of HASHEM is clear, enlightening the eyes.[1] *HASHEM will give might to His people; HASHEM will bless His people with peace.*[2] *The God Whose way is perfect, the promise of HASHEM is flawless, He is a shield for all who take refuge in Him.*[3]*)*

Congregation, then *gabbai:*

You who cling to HASHEM your God—you are all alive today.[4]

READING OF THE TORAH

The reader shows the *oleh* (person called to the Torah) the place in the Torah. The *oleh* touches the Torah with a corner of his *tallis,* or the belt or mantle of the Torah, and kisses it. He then begins the blessing, bowing at *'Bless,'* and straightening up at 'HASHEM':

Bless HASHEM, the blessed One.

Congregation, followed by *oleh,* responds, bowing at 'Blessed,' and straightening up at 'HASHEM.'

Blessed is HASHEM, the blessed One, for all eternity.

Oleh continues:

בָּרוּךְ *Blessed are You, HASHEM, our God, King of the universe, Who selected us from all the peoples and gave us His Torah. Blessed are You, HASHEM, Giver of the Torah.* (Cong.— *Amen.)*

After his Torah portion has been read, the *oleh* recites:

בָּרוּךְ *Blessed are You, HASHEM, our God, King of the universe, Who gave us the Torah of truth and implanted eternal life within us. Blessed are You, HASHEM, Giver of the Torah.* (Cong.— *Amen.)*

THE VARIOUS *MI SHEBEIRACH* PRAYERS APPEAR ON PAGE 308.

---

(1) *Psalms* 19:8-9. (2) 29:11. (3) 18:31. (4) *Deuteronomy* 4:4.

דברים לג:א-יז (Commentary on page 1158.)

כהן – וְזֹאת הַבְּרָכָה אֲשֶׁר בֵּרַךְ מֹשֶׁה אִישׁ הָאֱלֹהִים אֶת־בְּנֵי יִשְׂרָאֵל לִפְנֵי מוֹתוֹ: וַיֹּאמַר יהוה מִסִּינַי בָּא וְזָרַח מִשֵּׂעִיר לָמוֹ הוֹפִיעַ מֵהַר פָּארָן וְאָתָה מֵרִבְבֹת קֹדֶשׁ מִימִינוֹ אֵשׁ דָּת לָמוֹ: אַף חֹבֵב עַמִּים כָּל־קְדֹשָׁיו בְּיָדֶךָ וְהֵם תֻּכּוּ לְרַגְלֶךָ יִשָּׂא מִדַּבְּרֹתֶיךָ: תּוֹרָה צִוָּה־לָנוּ מֹשֶׁה מוֹרָשָׁה קְהִלַּת יַעֲקֹב: וַיְהִי בִישֻׁרוּן מֶלֶךְ בְּהִתְאַסֵּף רָאשֵׁי עָם יַחַד שִׁבְטֵי יִשְׂרָאֵל: יְחִי רְאוּבֵן וְאַל־יָמֹת וִיהִי מְתָיו מִסְפָּר: וְזֹאת לִיהוּדָה וַיֹּאמַר שְׁמַע יהוה קוֹל יְהוּדָה וְאֶל־עַמּוֹ תְּבִיאֶנּוּ יָדָיו רָב לוֹ וְעֵזֶר מִצָּרָיו תִּהְיֶה:

לוי – וּלְלֵוִי אָמַר תֻּמֶּיךָ וְאוּרֶיךָ לְאִישׁ חֲסִידֶךָ אֲשֶׁר נִסִּיתוֹ בְּמַסָּה תְּרִיבֵהוּ עַל־מֵי מְרִיבָה: הָאֹמֵר לְאָבִיו וּלְאִמּוֹ לֹא רְאִיתִיו וְאֶת־אֶחָיו לֹא הִכִּיר וְאֶת־בָּנָו לֹא יָדָע כִּי שָׁמְרוּ אִמְרָתֶךָ וּבְרִיתְךָ יִנְצֹרוּ: יוֹרוּ מִשְׁפָּטֶיךָ לְיַעֲקֹב וְתוֹרָתְךָ לְיִשְׂרָאֵל יָשִׂימוּ קְטוֹרָה בְּאַפֶּךָ וְכָלִיל עַל־מִזְבְּחֶךָ: בָּרֵךְ יהוה חֵילוֹ וּפֹעַל יָדָיו תִּרְצֶה מְחַץ מָתְנַיִם קָמָיו וּמְשַׂנְאָיו מִן־יְקוּמוּן: לְבִנְיָמִן אָמַר יְדִיד יהוה יִשְׁכֹּן לָבֶטַח עָלָיו חֹפֵף עָלָיו כָּל־הַיּוֹם וּבֵין כְּתֵפָיו שָׁכֵן:

ישראל – וּלְיוֹסֵף אָמַר מְבֹרֶכֶת יהוה אַרְצוֹ מִמֶּגֶד שָׁמַיִם מִטָּל וּמִתְּהוֹם רֹבֶצֶת תָּחַת: וּמִמֶּגֶד תְּבוּאֹת שָׁמֶשׁ וּמִמֶּגֶד גֶּרֶשׁ יְרָחִים: וּמֵרֹאשׁ הַרְרֵי־קֶדֶם וּמִמֶּגֶד גִּבְעוֹת עוֹלָם: וּמִמֶּגֶד אֶרֶץ וּמְלֹאָהּ וּרְצוֹן שֹׁכְנִי סְנֶה תָּבוֹאתָה לְרֹאשׁ יוֹסֵף וּלְקָדְקֹד נְזִיר אֶחָיו: בְּכוֹר שׁוֹרוֹ הָדָר לוֹ וְקַרְנֵי רְאֵם קַרְנָיו בָּהֶם עַמִּים יְנַגַּח יַחְדָּו אַפְסֵי־אָרֶץ וְהֵם רִבְבוֹת אֶפְרַיִם וְהֵם אַלְפֵי מְנַשֶּׁה:

הגבהה וגלילה

When the Torah reading has been completed, the Torah is raised for all to see. Each person looks at the Torah and recites aloud:

וְזֹאת הַתּוֹרָה אֲשֶׁר שָׂם מֹשֶׁה לִפְנֵי בְּנֵי יִשְׂרָאֵל,[1] עַל פִּי יהוה בְּיַד מֹשֶׁה.[2]

Deuteronomy 33:1-17 (Commentary on page 1158.)

Kohen – *This is the blessing that Moses, the man of God, bestowed upon the Children of Israel before his death.*

He said: HASHEM *approached from Sinai — having shone forth to them from Seir, having appeared from Mount Paran, and then approached with some of the holy myriads — from His right hand He presented the fiery Torah to them. Indeed, You greatly loved the tribes, all His righteous ones were in Your hands; for they planted themselves at Your feet, accepting the burden of Your utterances: "The Torah which Moses charged us is the heritage of the Congregation of Jacob. He became King over Jeshurun when the leaders of the nation gathered — the tribes of Israel in unity."*

May Reuben live and not die, and may his population be counted among the others.

And this to Judah, and he said: Hear, O HASHEM. *Judah's prayer, and return him safely to his people; may his hands gain him triumph and may You remain a helper against his enemies.*

Levi – *Of Levi he said: Your Tumim and Your Urim befit Your devout one, whom You tested at Massah, and whom You challenged at the waters of Meribah. The one who said of his father and mother, "I have not favored him," he disregarded his brothers and ignored his own children; for they [i.e., the Levites] have observed Your word, and preserved Your covenant. Thus it is they who are worthy to teach Your law to Jacob and Your Torah to Israel; it is they who shall place incense before Your presence, and burnt offerings on Your altar. Bless, O* HASHEM, *his resources, and favor his handiwork. Smash the loins of his foes, and his enemies that they may not rise again.*

Of Benjamin he said: May HASHEM's *beloved dwell securely by Him; He hovers above him all day long; and rests His Presence among his hills.*

Third – *Of Joseph he said: His land is blessed by* HASHEM *— with the heavenly bounty of dew, and with the deep waters crouching below: with the bounty of the sun's crops, and with the bounty of the moon's yield; with the quick-ripening crops of the ancient mountains, and with the bounty of eternally fertile hills; with the bounty of the land and its fullness, and by the favor of Him Who rested upon the thornbush. May this blessing rest upon Joseph's head, and upon the crown of him who was separated from his brothers. Sovereignty will go to his most distinguished, mighty descendant; and his glory will be like the horns of a re'eim; with both of them together he shall gore nations to the ends of the earth; they are the myriads of Ephraim's victims, and the thousands of Menashe's victims.*

HAGBAHAH AND GELILAH

When the Torah reading has been completed, the Torah is raised for all to see. Each person looks at the Torah and recites aloud:

This is the Torah that Moses placed before the Children of Israel,[1] upon the command of HASHEM, through Moses' hand.[2]

(1) *Deuteronomy* 4:44. (2) *Numbers* 9:23.

Some add the following verses:

עֵץ חַיִּים הִיא לַמַּחֲזִיקִים בָּהּ, וְתֹמְכֶיהָ מְאֻשָּׁר.[1] דְּרָכֶיהָ דַרְכֵי נֹעַם, וְכָל נְתִיבוֹתֶיהָ שָׁלוֹם.[2] אֹרֶךְ יָמִים בִּימִינָהּ, בִּשְׂמֹאלָהּ עֹשֶׁר וְכָבוֹד.[3] יהוה חָפֵץ לְמַעַן צִדְקוֹ, יַגְדִּיל תּוֹרָה וְיַאְדִּיר.[4]

Chazzan takes the Torah in his right arm and recites:

יְהַלְּלוּ אֶת שֵׁם יהוה, כִּי נִשְׂגָּב שְׁמוֹ לְבַדּוֹ —

Congregation responds:

— הוֹדוֹ עַל אֶרֶץ וְשָׁמָיִם. וַיָּרֶם קֶרֶן לְעַמּוֹ, תְּהִלָּה לְכָל חֲסִידָיו, לִבְנֵי יִשְׂרָאֵל עַם קְרֹבוֹ, הַלְלוּיָהּ.[5]

As the Torah is carried to the Ark, congregation recites Psalm 24, לְדָוִד מִזְמוֹר.

לְדָוִד מִזְמוֹר, לַיהוה הָאָרֶץ וּמְלוֹאָהּ, תֵּבֵל וְיֹשְׁבֵי בָהּ. כִּי הוּא עַל יַמִּים יְסָדָהּ, וְעַל נְהָרוֹת יְכוֹנְנֶהָ. מִי יַעֲלֶה בְהַר יהוה, וּמִי יָקוּם בִּמְקוֹם קָדְשׁוֹ. נְקִי כַפַּיִם וּבַר לֵבָב, אֲשֶׁר לֹא נָשָׂא לַשָּׁוְא נַפְשִׁי וְלֹא נִשְׁבַּע לְמִרְמָה. יִשָּׂא בְרָכָה מֵאֵת יהוה, וּצְדָקָה מֵאֱלֹהֵי יִשְׁעוֹ. זֶה דּוֹר דֹּרְשָׁיו, מְבַקְשֵׁי פָנֶיךָ, יַעֲקֹב, סֶלָה. שְׂאוּ שְׁעָרִים רָאשֵׁיכֶם, וְהִנָּשְׂאוּ פִּתְחֵי עוֹלָם, וְיָבוֹא מֶלֶךְ הַכָּבוֹד. מִי זֶה מֶלֶךְ הַכָּבוֹד, יהוה עִזּוּז וְגִבּוֹר, יהוה גִּבּוֹר מִלְחָמָה. שְׂאוּ שְׁעָרִים רָאשֵׁיכֶם, וּשְׂאוּ פִּתְחֵי עוֹלָם, וְיָבֹא מֶלֶךְ הַכָּבוֹד. מִי הוּא זֶה מֶלֶךְ הַכָּבוֹד, יהוה צְבָאוֹת הוּא מֶלֶךְ הַכָּבוֹד, סֶלָה.

As the Torah is placed into the Ark, congregation recites the following verses:

וּבְנֻחֹה יֹאמַר, שׁוּבָה יהוה רִבְבוֹת אַלְפֵי יִשְׂרָאֵל.[6] קוּמָה יהוה לִמְנוּחָתֶךָ, אַתָּה וַאֲרוֹן עֻזֶּךָ. כֹּהֲנֶיךָ יִלְבְּשׁוּ צֶדֶק, וַחֲסִידֶיךָ יְרַנֵּנוּ. בַּעֲבוּר דָּוִד עַבְדֶּךָ אַל תָּשֵׁב פְּנֵי מְשִׁיחֶךָ.[7] כִּי לֶקַח טוֹב נָתַתִּי לָכֶם, תּוֹרָתִי אַל תַּעֲזֹבוּ.[8] ❖ עֵץ חַיִּים הִיא לַמַּחֲזִיקִים בָּהּ, וְתֹמְכֶיהָ מְאֻשָּׁר.[9] דְּרָכֶיהָ דַרְכֵי נֹעַם, וְכָל נְתִיבֹתֶיהָ שָׁלוֹם.[10] הֲשִׁיבֵנוּ יהוה אֵלֶיךָ וְנָשׁוּבָה, חַדֵּשׁ יָמֵינוּ כְּקֶדֶם.[11]

The Ark is closed and the *chazzan* recites חֲצִי קַדִּישׁ.

יִתְגַּדַּל וְיִתְקַדַּשׁ שְׁמֵהּ רַבָּא. (.Cong — אָמֵן.) בְּעָלְמָא דִּי בְרָא כִרְעוּתֵהּ. וְיַמְלִיךְ מַלְכוּתֵהּ, בְּחַיֵּיכוֹן וּבְיוֹמֵיכוֹן וּבְחַיֵּי דְכָל בֵּית יִשְׂרָאֵל, בַּעֲגָלָא וּבִזְמַן קָרִיב. וְאִמְרוּ: אָמֵן.

(.Cong — אָמֵן. יְהֵא שְׁמֵהּ רַבָּא מְבָרַךְ לְעָלַם וּלְעָלְמֵי עָלְמַיָּא.)

יְהֵא שְׁמֵהּ רַבָּא מְבָרַךְ לְעָלַם וּלְעָלְמֵי עָלְמַיָּא.

יִתְבָּרַךְ וְיִשְׁתַּבַּח וְיִתְפָּאַר וְיִתְרוֹמַם וְיִתְנַשֵּׂא וְיִתְהַדָּר וְיִתְעַלֶּה וְיִתְהַלָּל שְׁמֵהּ דְּקֻדְשָׁא בְּרִיךְ הוּא (.Cong — בְּרִיךְ הוּא) — לְעֵלָּא מִן כָּל בִּרְכָתָא וְשִׁירָתָא תֻּשְׁבְּחָתָא וְנֶחֱמָתָא, דַּאֲמִירָן בְּעָלְמָא. וְאִמְרוּ: אָמֵן. (.Cong — אָמֵן.)

Some add the following verses:

עֵץ *It is a tree of life for those who grasp it, and its supporters are praiseworthy.*[1] *Its ways are ways of pleasantness and all its paths are peace.*[2] *Lengthy days are at its right; at its left are wealth and honor.*[3] *HASHEM desired, for the sake of its [Israel's] righteousness, that the Torah be made great and glorious.*[4]

Chazzan takes the Torah in his right arm and recites:

Let them praise the Name of HASHEM, for His Name alone will have been exalted —

Congregation responds:

— His glory is above earth and heaven. And He will have exalted the pride of His people, causing praise for all His devout ones, for the Children of Israel, His intimate nation. Halleluyah![5]

As the Torah is carried to the Ark, congregation recites Psalm 24, *'Of David a psalm.'*

לְדָוִד *Of David a psalm. HASHEM's is the earth and its fullness, the inhabited land and those who dwell in it. For He founded it upon seas, and established it upon rivers. Who may ascend the mountain of HASHEM, and who may stand in the place of His sanctity? One with clean hands and pure heart, who has not sworn in vain by My soul and has not sworn deceitfully. He will receive a blessing from HASHEM and just kindness from the God of his salvation. This is the generation of those who seek Him, those who strive for Your Presence — Jacob, Selah. Raise up your heads, O gates, and be uplifted, you everlasting entrances, so that the King of Glory may enter. Who is this King of Glory? — HASHEM, the mighty and strong, HASHEM, the strong in battle. Raise up your heads, O gates, and raise up, you everlasting entrances, so that the King of Glory may enter. Who then is the King of Glory? HASHEM, Master of Legions, He is the King of Glory. Selah!*

As the Torah is placed into the Ark, congregation recites the following verses:

וּבְנֻחֹה *And when it rested he would say, 'Return, HASHEM, to the myriad thousands of Israel.'*[6] *Arise, HASHEM, to Your resting place, You and the Ark of Your strength. Let Your priests be clothed in righteousness, and Your devout ones will sing joyously. For the sake of David, Your servant, turn not away the face of Your anointed.*[7] *For I have given you a good teaching, do not forsake My Torah.*[8] Chazzan — *It is a tree of life for those who grasp it, and its supporters are praiseworthy.*[9] *Its ways are ways of pleasantness and all its paths are peace.*[10] *Bring us back to You, HASHEM, and we shall return, renew our days as of old.*[11]

The Ark is closed and the *chazzan* recites Half-*Kaddish.*

יִתְגַּדַּל *May His great Name grow exalted and sanctified* (Cong.— *Amen.*) *in the world that He created as He willed. May He give reign to His kingship in your lifetimes and in your days, and in the lifetimes of the entire Family of Israel, swiftly and soon. Now respond: Amen.*

(Cong.— *Amen. May His great Name be blessed forever and ever.*)

May His great Name be blessed forever and ever.

Blessed, praised, glorified, exalted, extolled, mighty, upraised, and lauded be the Name of the Holy One, Blessed is He (Cong.— *Blessed is He*) *— beyond any blessing and song, praise and consolation that are uttered in the world. Now respond: Amen.* (Cong.— *Amen.*)

---

(1) *Proverbs* 3:18. (2) 3:17. (3) 3:16. (4) *Isaiah* 42:21. (5) *Psalms* 148:13-14. (6) *Numbers* 10:36. (7) *Psalms* 132:8-10. (8) *Proverbs* 4:2. (9) 3:18. (10) 3:17. (11) *Lamentations* 5:21.

שמונה עשרה – עמידה

Take three steps backward, then three steps forward. Remain standing with the feet together while reciting *Shemoneh Esrei*. Recite it with quiet devotion and without interruption, verbal or otherwise. Although its recitation should not be audible to others, one must pray loudly enough to hear himself.

כִּי שֵׁם יהוה אֶקְרָא, הָבוּ גֹדֶל לֵאלֹהֵינוּ.[1]

אֲדֹנָי שְׂפָתַי תִּפְתָּח, וּפִי יַגִּיד תְּהִלָּתֶךָ.[2]

אבות

Bend the knees at בָּרוּךְ; bow at אַתָּה; straighten up at ה׳.

בָּרוּךְ אַתָּה יהוה אֱלֹהֵינוּ וֵאלֹהֵי אֲבוֹתֵינוּ, אֱלֹהֵי אַבְרָהָם, אֱלֹהֵי יִצְחָק, וֵאלֹהֵי יַעֲקֹב, הָאֵל הַגָּדוֹל הַגִּבּוֹר וְהַנּוֹרָא, אֵל עֶלְיוֹן, גּוֹמֵל חֲסָדִים טוֹבִים וְקוֹנֵה הַכֹּל, וְזוֹכֵר חַסְדֵי אָבוֹת, וּמֵבִיא גוֹאֵל לִבְנֵי בְנֵיהֶם, לְמַעַן שְׁמוֹ בְּאַהֲבָה. מֶלֶךְ עוֹזֵר וּמוֹשִׁיעַ וּמָגֵן.

Bend the knees at בָּרוּךְ; bow at אַתָּה; straighten up at ה׳.

בָּרוּךְ אַתָּה יהוה, מָגֵן אַבְרָהָם.

גבורות

אַתָּה גִּבּוֹר לְעוֹלָם אֲדֹנָי, מְחַיֵּה מֵתִים אַתָּה, רַב לְהוֹשִׁיעַ.

מַשִּׁיב הָרְוּחַ וּמוֹרִיד הַגֶּשֶׁם.

מְכַלְכֵּל חַיִּים בְּחֶסֶד, מְחַיֵּה מֵתִים בְּרַחֲמִים רַבִּים, סוֹמֵךְ נוֹפְלִים, וְרוֹפֵא חוֹלִים, וּמַתִּיר אֲסוּרִים, וּמְקַיֵּם אֱמוּנָתוֹ לִישֵׁנֵי עָפָר. מִי כָמוֹךָ בַּעַל גְּבוּרוֹת, וּמִי דּוֹמֶה לָּךְ, מֶלֶךְ מֵמִית וּמְחַיֶּה וּמַצְמִיחַ יְשׁוּעָה. וְנֶאֱמָן אַתָּה לְהַחֲיוֹת מֵתִים. בָּרוּךְ אַתָּה יהוה, מְחַיֵּה הַמֵּתִים.

During the *chazzan's* repetition, *Kedushah* (below) is recited at this point.

קדושה

When reciting *Kedushah,* one must stand with his feet together and avoid any interruptions. One should rise on his toes when saying the words קָדוֹשׁ, קָדוֹשׁ, קָדוֹשׁ; בָּרוּךְ (of בָּרוּךְ כְּבוֹד); and יִמְלֹךְ.

Cong. then *Chazzan* – **נְקַדֵּשׁ** אֶת שִׁמְךָ בָּעוֹלָם, כְּשֵׁם שֶׁמַּקְדִּישִׁים אוֹתוֹ בִּשְׁמֵי מָרוֹם, כַּכָּתוּב עַל יַד נְבִיאֶךָ, וְקָרָא זֶה אֶל זֶה וְאָמַר:

All – קָדוֹשׁ קָדוֹשׁ קָדוֹשׁ יהוה צְבָאוֹת, מְלֹא כָל הָאָרֶץ כְּבוֹדוֹ.[3]

Chazzan – לְעֻמָּתָם בָּרוּךְ יֹאמֵרוּ:

All – בָּרוּךְ כְּבוֹד יהוה, מִמְּקוֹמוֹ.[4]

Chazzan – וּבְדִבְרֵי קָדְשְׁךָ כָּתוּב לֵאמֹר:

All – יִמְלֹךְ יהוה לְעוֹלָם, אֱלֹהַיִךְ צִיּוֹן לְדֹר וָדֹר, הַלְלוּיָהּ.[5]

Chazzan only concludes – לְדוֹר וָדוֹר נַגִּיד גָּדְלֶךָ וּלְנֵצַח נְצָחִים קְדֻשָּׁתְךָ נַקְדִּישׁ, וְשִׁבְחֲךָ אֱלֹהֵינוּ מִפִּינוּ לֹא יָמוּשׁ לְעוֹלָם וָעֶד, כִּי אֵל מֶלֶךְ גָּדוֹל וְקָדוֹשׁ אָתָּה. בָּרוּךְ אַתָּה יהוה, הָאֵל הַקָּדוֹשׁ.

Chazzan continues . . . אַתָּה בְחַרְתָּנוּ (page 1038).

SHEMONEH ESREI — AMIDAH

Take three steps backward, then three steps forward. Remain standing with the feet together while reciting *Shemoneh Esrei*. Recite it with quiet devotion and without interruption, verbal or otherwise. Although its recitation should not be audible to others, one must pray loudly enough to hear himself.

When I call out the Name of HASHEM, ascribe greatness to our God.[1]
My Lord, open my lips, that my mouth may declare Your praise.[2]

PATRIARCHS

Bend the knees at *'Blessed'*; bow at *'You'*; straighten up at *'HASHEM.'*

בָּרוּךְ *Blessed are You, HASHEM, our God and the God of our forefathers, God of Abraham, God of Isaac, and God of Jacob; the great, mighty, and awesome God, the supreme God, Who bestows beneficial kindnesses and creates everything, Who recalls the kindnesses of the Patriarchs and brings a Redeemer to their children's children, for His Name's sake, with love. O King, Helper, Savior, and Shield.*

Bend the knees at *'Blessed'*; bow at *'You'*; straighten up at *'HASHEM.'*

Blessed are You, HASHEM, Shield of Abraham.

GOD'S MIGHT

אַתָּה *You are eternally mighty, my Lord, the Resuscitator of the dead are You; abundantly able to save.*

He makes the wind blow and He makes the rain descend.

He sustains the living with kindness, resuscitates the dead with abundant mercy, supports the fallen, heals the sick, releases the confined, and maintains His faith to those asleep in the dust. Who is like You, O Master of mighty deeds, and who is comparable to You, O King Who causes death and restores life and makes salvation sprout! And You are faithful to resuscitate the dead. Blessed are You, HASHEM, Who resuscitates the dead.

During the *chazzan's* repetition, *Kedushah* (below) is recited at this point.

KEDUSHAH

When reciting *Kedushah*, one must stand with his feet together and avoid any interruptions. One should rise on his toes when saying the words *Holy, holy, holy; Blessed is;* and *HASHEM shall reign.*

Cong. then Chazzan — **נְקַדֵּשׁ** *We shall sanctify Your Name in this world, just as they sanctify it in heaven above, as it is written by Your prophet, "And one [angel] will call another and say:*

All — *'Holy, holy, holy is HASHEM, Master of Legions, the whole world is filled with His glory.'"*[3]

Chazzan — *Those facing them say 'Blessed':*

All — *'Blessed is the glory of HASHEM from His place.'*[4]

Chazzan — *And in Your holy Writings the following is written:*

All — *'HASHEM shall reign forever — your God, O Zion — from generation to generation, Halleluyah!'*[5]

Chazzan only concludes — *From generation to generation we shall relate Your greatness and for infinite eternities we shall proclaim Your holiness. Your praise, our God, shall not leave our mouth forever and ever, for You, O God, are a great and holy King. Blessed are You HASHEM, the holy God.*

Chazzan continues אַתָּה בְחַרְתָּנוּ, *You have chosen us . . .* (page 1038).

---

(1) *Deuteronomy* 32:3. (2) *Psalms* 51:17. (3) *Isaiah* 6:3. (4) *Ezekiel* 3:12. (5) *Psalms* 146:10.

קדושת השם

אַתָּה קָדוֹשׁ וְשִׁמְךָ קָדוֹשׁ, וּקְדוֹשִׁים בְּכָל יוֹם יְהַלְּלוּךָ סֶּלָה. בָּרוּךְ אַתָּה יהוה, הָאֵל הַקָּדוֹשׁ.

קדושת היום

אַתָּה בְחַרְתָּנוּ מִכָּל הָעַמִּים, אָהַבְתָּ אוֹתָנוּ, וְרָצִיתָ בָּנוּ, וְרוֹמַמְתָּנוּ מִכָּל הַלְּשׁוֹנוֹת, וְקִדַּשְׁתָּנוּ בְּמִצְוֹתֶיךָ, וְקֵרַבְתָּנוּ מַלְכֵּנוּ לַעֲבוֹדָתֶךָ, וְשִׁמְךָ הַגָּדוֹל וְהַקָּדוֹשׁ עָלֵינוּ קָרָאתָ.

On the Sabbath add the words in brackets. [If forgotten, see *Laws* §86-90.]

וַתִּתֶּן לָנוּ יהוה אֱלֹהֵינוּ בְּאַהֲבָה [שַׁבָּתוֹת לִמְנוּחָה וּ]מוֹעֲדִים לְשִׂמְחָה חַגִּים וּזְמַנִּים לְשָׂשׂוֹן, אֶת יוֹם [הַשַּׁבָּת הַזֶּה וְאֶת יוֹם] הַשְּׁמִינִי חַג הָעֲצֶרֶת הַזֶּה, זְמַן שִׂמְחָתֵנוּ [בְּאַהֲבָה] מִקְרָא קֹדֶשׁ, זֵכֶר לִיצִיאַת מִצְרָיִם.

During the *chazzan's* repetition, congregation responds אָמֵן as indicated.

אֱלֹהֵינוּ וֵאלֹהֵי אֲבוֹתֵינוּ, יַעֲלֶה, וְיָבֹא, וְיַגִּיעַ, וְיֵרָאֶה, וְיֵרָצֶה, וְיִשָּׁמַע, וְיִפָּקֵד, וְיִזָּכֵר זִכְרוֹנֵנוּ וּפִקְדוֹנֵנוּ, וְזִכְרוֹן אֲבוֹתֵינוּ, וְזִכְרוֹן מָשִׁיחַ בֶּן דָּוִד עַבְדֶּךָ, וְזִכְרוֹן יְרוּשָׁלַיִם עִיר קָדְשֶׁךָ, וְזִכְרוֹן כָּל עַמְּךָ בֵּית יִשְׂרָאֵל לְפָנֶיךָ, לִפְלֵיטָה לְטוֹבָה לְחֵן וּלְחֶסֶד וּלְרַחֲמִים, לְחַיִּים וּלְשָׁלוֹם בְּיוֹם הַשְּׁמִינִי חַג הָעֲצֶרֶת הַזֶּה. זָכְרֵנוּ יהוה אֱלֹהֵינוּ בּוֹ לְטוֹבָה (.Cong – אָמֵן), וּפָקְדֵנוּ בוֹ לִבְרָכָה (.Cong – אָמֵן), וְהוֹשִׁיעֵנוּ בוֹ לְחַיִּים (.Cong – אָמֵן). וּבִדְבַר יְשׁוּעָה וְרַחֲמִים, חוּס וְחָנֵּנוּ וְרַחֵם עָלֵינוּ וְהוֹשִׁיעֵנוּ, כִּי אֵלֶיךָ עֵינֵינוּ, כִּי אֵל מֶלֶךְ חַנּוּן וְרַחוּם אָתָּה.[1]

Add the words in brackets on the Sabbath. [If forgotten, see *Laws* §86-90.]

וְהַשִּׂיאֵנוּ יהוה אֱלֹהֵינוּ אֶת בִּרְכַּת מוֹעֲדֶיךָ לְחַיִּים וּלְשָׁלוֹם, לְשִׂמְחָה וּלְשָׂשׂוֹן, כַּאֲשֶׁר רָצִיתָ וְאָמַרְתָּ לְבָרְכֵנוּ. [אֱלֹהֵינוּ וֵאלֹהֵי אֲבוֹתֵינוּ רְצֵה בִמְנוּחָתֵנוּ] קַדְּשֵׁנוּ בְּמִצְוֹתֶיךָ וְתֵן חֶלְקֵנוּ בְּתוֹרָתֶךָ, שַׂבְּעֵנוּ מִטּוּבֶךָ וְשַׂמְּחֵנוּ בִּישׁוּעָתֶךָ, וְטַהֵר לִבֵּנוּ לְעָבְדְּךָ בֶּאֱמֶת, וְהַנְחִילֵנוּ יהוה אֱלֹהֵינוּ [בְּאַהֲבָה וּבְרָצוֹן] בְּשִׂמְחָה וּבְשָׂשׂוֹן [שַׁבָּת וּ]מוֹעֲדֵי קָדְשֶׁךָ, וְיִשְׂמְחוּ בְךָ יִשְׂרָאֵל מְקַדְּשֵׁי שְׁמֶךָ. בָּרוּךְ אַתָּה יהוה, מְקַדֵּשׁ [הַשַּׁבָּת וְ]יִשְׂרָאֵל וְהַזְּמַנִּים.

HOLINESS OF GOD'S NAME

אַתָּה *You are holy and Your Name is holy, and holy ones praise You every day, forever. Blessed are You,* HASHEM, *the holy God.*

SANCTIFICATION OF THE DAY

אַתָּה בְחַרְתָּנוּ *You have chosen us from all the peoples; You loved us and found favor in us; You exalted us above all the tongues and You sanctified us with Your commandments. You drew us close, our King, to Your service and proclaimed Your great and Holy Name upon us.*

On the Sabbath add the words in brackets. [If forgotten, see *Laws* 86-90.]

וַתִּתֶּן לָנוּ *And You gave us,* HASHEM, *our God, with love [Sabbaths for rest], appointed festivals for gladness, Festivals and times for joy, [this day of Sabbath and] this day of the Shemini Atzeres Festival, the time of our gladness [with love], a holy convocation, a memorial of the Exodus from Egypt.*

During the *chazzan's* repetition, congregation responds *Amen* as indicated.

אֱלֹהֵינוּ *Our God and God of our forefathers, may there rise, come, reach, be noted, be favored, be heard, be considered, and be remembered — the remembrance and consideration of ourselves; the remembrance of our forefathers; the remembrance of Messiah, son of David, Your servant; the remembrance of Jerusalem, the City of Your Holiness; the remembrance of Your entire people the Family of Israel — before You for deliverance, for goodness, for grace, for kindness, and for compassion, for life, and for peace on this day of the Shemini Atzeres Festival. Remember us on it,* HASHEM, *our God, for goodness* (Cong.–*Amen*)*; consider us on it for blessing* (Cong.–*Amen*)*; and help us on it for life* (Cong.–*Amen*)*. In the matter of salvation and compassion, pity, be gracious and compassionate with us and help us, for our eyes are turned to You, because You are God, the gracious and compassionate King.*[1]

Add the words in brackets on the Sabbath. [If forgotten, see *Laws* 86-90.]

וְהַשִּׂיאֵנוּ *Bestow upon us, O* HASHEM, *our God, the blessing of Your appointed Festivals for life and for peace, for gladness and for joy, as You desired and promised to bless us. [Our God and the God of our forefathers, may You be pleased with our rest.] Sanctify us with Your commandments and grant us our share in Your Torah; satisfy us from Your goodness and gladden us with Your salvation, and purify our heart to serve You sincerely. And grant us a heritage, O* HASHEM, *our God — [with love and with favor] with gladness and with joy — [the Sabbath and] the appointed festivals of Your holiness, and may Israel, the sanctifiers of Your Name, rejoice in You. Blessed are You,* HASHEM, *Who sanctifies [the Sabbath] Israel and the festive seasons.*

---

(1) Cf. *Nechemiah* 9:31.

עבודה

רְצֵה יהוה אֱלֹהֵינוּ בְּעַמְּךָ יִשְׂרָאֵל וּבִתְפִלָּתָם, וְהָשֵׁב אֶת הָעֲבוֹדָה לִדְבִיר בֵּיתֶךָ. וְאִשֵּׁי יִשְׂרָאֵל וּתְפִלָּתָם בְּאַהֲבָה תְקַבֵּל בְּרָצוֹן, וּתְהִי לְרָצוֹן תָּמִיד עֲבוֹדַת יִשְׂרָאֵל עַמֶּךָ.

וְתֶחֱזֶינָה עֵינֵינוּ בְּשׁוּבְךָ לְצִיּוֹן בְּרַחֲמִים. בָּרוּךְ אַתָּה יהוה, הַמַּחֲזִיר שְׁכִינָתוֹ לְצִיּוֹן.

הודאה

Bow at מוֹדִים; straighten up at ה'. In his repetition the *chazzan* should recite the entire מוֹדִים aloud, while the congregation recites מוֹדִים דְּרַבָּנָן softly.

מוֹדִים אֲנַחְנוּ לָךְ, שָׁאַתָּה הוּא יהוה אֱלֹהֵינוּ וֵאלֹהֵי אֲבוֹתֵינוּ לְעוֹלָם וָעֶד. צוּר חַיֵּינוּ, מָגֵן יִשְׁעֵנוּ אַתָּה הוּא לְדוֹר וָדוֹר. נוֹדֶה לְּךָ וּנְסַפֵּר תְּהִלָּתֶךָ[1] עַל חַיֵּינוּ הַמְּסוּרִים בְּיָדֶךָ, וְעַל נִשְׁמוֹתֵינוּ הַפְּקוּדוֹת לָךְ, וְעַל נִסֶּיךָ שֶׁבְּכָל יוֹם עִמָּנוּ, וְעַל נִפְלְאוֹתֶיךָ וְטוֹבוֹתֶיךָ שֶׁבְּכָל עֵת, עֶרֶב וָבֹקֶר וְצָהֳרָיִם. הַטּוֹב כִּי לֹא כָלוּ רַחֲמֶיךָ, וְהַמְּרַחֵם כִּי לֹא תַמּוּ חֲסָדֶיךָ,[2] מֵעוֹלָם קִוִּינוּ לָךְ.

מודים דרבנן

מוֹדִים אֲנַחְנוּ לָךְ, שָׁאַתָּה הוּא יהוה אֱלֹהֵינוּ וֵאלֹהֵי אֲבוֹתֵינוּ, אֱלֹהֵי כָל בָּשָׂר, יוֹצְרֵנוּ, יוֹצֵר בְּרֵאשִׁית. בְּרָכוֹת וְהוֹדָאוֹת לְשִׁמְךָ הַגָּדוֹל וְהַקָּדוֹשׁ, עַל שֶׁהֶחֱיִיתָנוּ וְקִיַּמְתָּנוּ. כֵּן תְּחַיֵּנוּ וּתְקַיְּמֵנוּ, וְתֶאֱסוֹף גָּלֻיּוֹתֵינוּ לְחַצְרוֹת קָדְשֶׁךָ, לִשְׁמוֹר חֻקֶּיךָ וְלַעֲשׂוֹת רְצוֹנֶךָ, וּלְעָבְדְּךָ בְּלֵבָב שָׁלֵם, עַל שֶׁאֲנַחְנוּ מוֹדִים לָךְ. בָּרוּךְ אֵל הַהוֹדָאוֹת.

וְעַל כֻּלָּם יִתְבָּרַךְ וְיִתְרוֹמַם שִׁמְךָ מַלְכֵּנוּ תָּמִיד לְעוֹלָם וָעֶד.

Bend the knees at בָּרוּךְ; bow at אַתָּה; straighten up at ה'.

וְכֹל הַחַיִּים יוֹדוּךָ סֶּלָה, וִיהַלְלוּ אֶת שִׁמְךָ בֶּאֱמֶת, הָאֵל יְשׁוּעָתֵנוּ וְעֶזְרָתֵנוּ סֶלָה. בָּרוּךְ אַתָּה יהוה, הַטּוֹב שִׁמְךָ וּלְךָ נָאֶה לְהוֹדוֹת.

TEMPLE SERVICE

רְצֵה *Be favorable, HASHEM, our God, toward Your people Israel and their prayer and restore the service to the Holy of Holies of Your Temple. The fire-offerings of Israel and their prayer accept with love and favor, and may the service of Your people Israel always be favorable to You.*

וְתֶחֱזֶינָה *May our eyes behold Your return to Zion in compassion. Blessed are You, HASHEM, Who restores His Presence to Zion.*

THANKSGIVING [MODIM]

Bow at *'We gratefully thank You';* straighten up at *'HASHEM.'* In his repetition the *chazzan* should recite the entire *Modim* aloud, while the congregation recites *Modim of the Rabbis* softly.

מוֹדִים *We gratefully thank You, for it is You Who are HASHEM, our God and the God of our forefathers for all eternity; Rock of our lives, Shield of our salvation are You from generation to generation. We shall thank You and relate Your praise*[1] *— for our lives, which are committed to Your power and for our souls that are entrusted to You; for Your miracles that are with us every day; and for Your wonders and favors in every season — evening, morning, and afternoon. The Beneficent One, for Your compassions were never exhausted, and the Compassionate One, for Your kindnesses never ended*[2] *— always have we put our hope in You.*

MODIM OF THE RABBIS

מוֹדִים *We gratefully thank You, for it is You Who are HASHEM, our God and the God of our forefathers, the God of all flesh, our Molder, the Molder of the universe. Blessings and thanks are due Your great and holy Name for You have given us life and sustained us. So may You continue to give us life and sustain us and gather our exiles to the Courtyards of Your Sanctuary, to observe Your decrees, to do Your will and to serve You wholeheartedly. [We thank You] for inspiring us to thank You. Blessed is the God of thanksgivings.*

For all these, may Your Name be blessed and exalted, our King, continually forever and ever.

Bend the knees at *'Blessed';* bow at *'You';* straighten up at *'HASHEM.'*

Everything alive will gratefully acknowledge You, Selah! and praise Your Name sincerely, O God of our salvation and help, Selah! Blessed are You, HASHEM, Your Name is 'The Beneficent One' and to You it is fitting to give thanks.

---

(1) Cf. *Psalms* 79:13. (2) Cf. *Lamentations* 3:22.

שלום

שָׁלוֹם רָב עַל יִשְׂרָאֵל עַמְּךָ תָּשִׂים לְעוֹלָם, כִּי אַתָּה הוּא מֶלֶךְ אָדוֹן לְכָל הַשָּׁלוֹם. וְטוֹב בְּעֵינֶיךָ לְבָרֵךְ אֶת עַמְּךָ יִשְׂרָאֵל, בְּכָל עֵת וּבְכָל שָׁעָה בִּשְׁלוֹמֶךָ. בָּרוּךְ אַתָּה יהוה, הַמְּבָרֵךְ אֶת עַמּוֹ יִשְׂרָאֵל בַּשָּׁלוֹם.

יִהְיוּ לְרָצוֹן אִמְרֵי פִי וְהֶגְיוֹן לִבִּי לְפָנֶיךָ, יהוה צוּרִי וְגֹאֲלִי.[1]

Chazzan's repetition of *Shemoneh Esrei* ends here. Individuals continue below.

אֱלֹהַי, נְצוֹר לְשׁוֹנִי מֵרָע, וּשְׂפָתַי מִדַּבֵּר מִרְמָה,[2] וְלִמְקַלְלַי נַפְשִׁי תִדּוֹם, וְנַפְשִׁי כֶּעָפָר לַכֹּל תִּהְיֶה. פְּתַח לִבִּי בְּתוֹרָתֶךָ, וּבְמִצְוֹתֶיךָ תִּרְדּוֹף נַפְשִׁי. וְכֹל הַחוֹשְׁבִים עָלַי רָעָה, מְהֵרָה הָפֵר עֲצָתָם וְקַלְקֵל מַחֲשַׁבְתָּם. עֲשֵׂה לְמַעַן שְׁמֶךָ, עֲשֵׂה לְמַעַן יְמִינֶךָ, עֲשֵׂה לְמַעַן קְדֻשָּׁתֶךָ, עֲשֵׂה לְמַעַן תּוֹרָתֶךָ. לְמַעַן יֵחָלְצוּן יְדִידֶיךָ, הוֹשִׁיעָה יְמִינְךָ וַעֲנֵנִי.[3] Some recite verses pertaining to their names. See page 1301.

יִהְיוּ לְרָצוֹן אִמְרֵי פִי וְהֶגְיוֹן לִבִּי לְפָנֶיךָ, יהוה צוּרִי וְגֹאֲלִי.[1]

Bow and take three steps back. Bow left and say . . . עֹשֶׂה, bow right and say . . . הוּא יַעֲשֶׂה; bow forward and say וְעַל כָּל . . . אָמֵן.

עֹשֶׂה שָׁלוֹם בִּמְרוֹמָיו, הוּא יַעֲשֶׂה שָׁלוֹם עָלֵינוּ, וְעַל כָּל יִשְׂרָאֵל. וְאִמְרוּ: אָמֵן.

יְהִי רָצוֹן מִלְּפָנֶיךָ יהוה אֱלֹהֵינוּ וֵאלֹהֵי אֲבוֹתֵינוּ, שֶׁיִּבָּנֶה בֵּית הַמִּקְדָּשׁ בִּמְהֵרָה בְיָמֵינוּ, וְתֵן חֶלְקֵנוּ בְּתוֹרָתֶךָ. וְשָׁם נַעֲבָדְךָ בְּיִרְאָה, כִּימֵי עוֹלָם וּכְשָׁנִים קַדְמוֹנִיּוֹת. וְעָרְבָה לַיהוה מִנְחַת יְהוּדָה וִירוּשָׁלָיִם, כִּימֵי עוֹלָם וּכְשָׁנִים קַדְמוֹנִיּוֹת.[4]

THE INDIVIDUAL'S RECITATION OF שְׁמוֹנֶה עֶשְׂרֵה ENDS HERE.

The individual remains standing in place until the *chazzan* reaches *Kedushah* — or at least until the *chazzan* begins his repetition — then he takes three steps forward. The *chazzan* himself, or one praying alone, should remain in place for a few moments before taking three steps forward.

קדיש שלם

The *chazzan* recites קַדִּישׁ שָׁלֵם.

יִתְגַּדַּל וְיִתְקַדַּשׁ שְׁמֵהּ רַבָּא. (.Cong – אָמֵן.) בְּעָלְמָא דִּי בְרָא כִרְעוּתֵהּ. וְיַמְלִיךְ מַלְכוּתֵהּ, בְּחַיֵּיכוֹן וּבְיוֹמֵיכוֹן וּבְחַיֵּי דְכָל בֵּית יִשְׂרָאֵל, בַּעֲגָלָא וּבִזְמַן קָרִיב. וְאִמְרוּ: אָמֵן.

(.Cong – אָמֵן. יְהֵא שְׁמֵהּ רַבָּא מְבָרַךְ לְעָלַם וּלְעָלְמֵי עָלְמַיָּא.)

PEACE

שָׁלוֹם *Establish abundant peace upon Your people Israel forever, for You are King, Master of all peace. May it be good in Your eyes to bless Your people Israel at every time and every hour with Your peace. Blessed are You, HASHEM, Who blesses His people Israel with peace.*

May the expressions of my mouth and the thoughts of my heart find favor before You, HASHEM, my Rock and my Redeemer.[1]

Chazzan's repetition of *Shemoneh Esrei* ends here. Individuals continue below:

אֱלֹהַי *My God, guard my tongue from evil and my lips from speaking deceitfully.*[2] *To those who curse me, let my soul be silent; and let my soul be like dust to everyone. Open my heart to Your Torah, then my soul will pursue Your commandments. As for all those who design evil against me, speedily nullify their counsel and disrupt their design. Act for Your Name's sake; act for Your right hand's sake; act for Your sanctity's sake; act for Your Torah's sake. That Your beloved ones may be given rest; let Your right hand save, and respond to me.*[3]

Some recite verses pertaining to their names at this point. See page 1301.

May the expressions of my mouth and the thoughts of my heart find favor before You, HASHEM, my Rock and my Redeemer.[1] *He Who makes peace in His heights, may He make peace upon us, and upon all Israel. Now respond: Amen.*

Bow and take three steps back. Bow left and say, *'He Who makes peace . . .'*; bow right and say, *'may He make peace . . .'*; bow forward and say, *'and upon . . . Amen.'*

יְהִי רָצוֹן *May it be Your will, HASHEM, our God and the God of our forefathers, that the Holy Temple be rebuilt, speedily in our days. Grant us our share in Your Torah, and may we serve You there with reverence, as in days of old and in former years. Then the offering of Judah and Jerusalem will be pleasing to HASHEM, as in days of old and in former years.*[4]

THE INDIVIDUAL'S RECITATION OF *SHEMONEH ESREI* ENDS HERE.

The individual remains standing in place until the *chazzan* reaches *Kedushah* — or at least until the *chazzan* begins his repetition — then he takes three steps forward. The *chazzan* himself, or one praying alone, should remain in place for a few moments before taking three steps forward.

FULL KADDISH

The *chazzan* recites the Full *Kaddish*.

יִתְגַּדַּל *May His great Name grow exalted and sanctified* (Cong.— *Amen.*) *in the world that He created as He willed. May He give reign to His kingship in your lifetimes and in your days, and in the lifetimes of the entire Family of Israel, swiftly and soon. Now respond: Amen.*

(Cong.— *Amen. May His great Name be blessed forever and ever.)*

---

(1) *Psalms* 19:15. (2) Cf. 34:14. (3) 60:7;108:7. (4) *Malachi* 3:4.

יְהֵא שְׁמֵהּ רַבָּא מְבָרַךְ לְעָלַם וּלְעָלְמֵי עָלְמַיָּא.

יִתְבָּרַךְ וְיִשְׁתַּבַּח וְיִתְפָּאַר וְיִתְרוֹמַם וְיִתְנַשֵּׂא וְיִתְהַדָּר וְיִתְעַלֶּה וְיִתְהַלָּל שְׁמֵהּ דְּקֻדְשָׁא בְּרִיךְ הוּא (.Cong — בְּרִיךְ הוּא) — לְעֵלָּא מִן כָּל בִּרְכָתָא וְשִׁירָתָא תֻּשְׁבְּחָתָא וְנֶחֱמָתָא, דַּאֲמִירָן בְּעָלְמָא. וְאִמְרוּ: אָמֵן. (.Cong — אָמֵן.)

(.Cong — קַבֵּל בְּרַחֲמִים וּבְרָצוֹן אֶת תְּפִלָּתֵנוּ.)

תִּתְקַבֵּל צְלוֹתְהוֹן וּבָעוּתְהוֹן דְּכָל בֵּית יִשְׂרָאֵל קֳדָם אֲבוּהוֹן דִּי בִשְׁמַיָּא. וְאִמְרוּ: אָמֵן. (.Cong — אָמֵן.)

(.Cong — יְהִי שֵׁם יהוה מְבֹרָךְ, מֵעַתָּה וְעַד עוֹלָם.[1])

יְהֵא שְׁלָמָא רַבָּא מִן שְׁמַיָּא, וְחַיִּים עָלֵינוּ וְעַל כָּל יִשְׂרָאֵל. וְאִמְרוּ: אָמֵן. (.Cong — אָמֵן.)

(.Cong — עֶזְרִי מֵעִם יהוה, עֹשֵׂה שָׁמַיִם וָאָרֶץ.[2])

Take three steps back. Bow left and say . . . עֹשֶׂה; bow right and say . . . הוּא; bow forward and say וְעַל כָּל . . . אָמֵן. Remain standing in place for a few moments, then take three steps forward.

עֹשֶׂה שָׁלוֹם בִּמְרוֹמָיו, הוּא יַעֲשֶׂה שָׁלוֹם עָלֵינוּ, וְעַל כָּל יִשְׂרָאֵל. וְאִמְרוּ: אָמֵן. (.Cong — אָמֵן.)

עלינו

Stand while reciting עָלֵינוּ.

עָלֵינוּ לְשַׁבֵּחַ לַאֲדוֹן הַכֹּל, לָתֵת גְּדֻלָּה לְיוֹצֵר בְּרֵאשִׁית, שֶׁלֹּא עָשָׂנוּ כְּגוֹיֵי הָאֲרָצוֹת, וְלֹא שָׂמָנוּ כְּמִשְׁפְּחוֹת הָאֲדָמָה. שֶׁלֹּא שָׂם חֶלְקֵנוּ כָּהֶם, וְגוֹרָלֵנוּ כְּכָל הֲמוֹנָם. (שֶׁהֵם מִשְׁתַּחֲוִים לְהֶבֶל וָרִיק, וּמִתְפַּלְלִים אֶל אֵל לֹא יוֹשִׁיעַ.[3]) וַאֲנַחְנוּ כּוֹרְעִים וּמִשְׁתַּחֲוִים וּמוֹדִים, לִפְנֵי מֶלֶךְ מַלְכֵי הַמְּלָכִים הַקָּדוֹשׁ בָּרוּךְ הוּא. שֶׁהוּא נוֹטֶה שָׁמַיִם וְיֹסֵד אָרֶץ,[4] וּמוֹשַׁב יְקָרוֹ בַּשָּׁמַיִם מִמַּעַל, וּשְׁכִינַת עֻזּוֹ בְּגָבְהֵי מְרוֹמִים. הוּא אֱלֹהֵינוּ, אֵין עוֹד. אֱמֶת מַלְכֵּנוּ, אֶפֶס זוּלָתוֹ, כַּכָּתוּב בְּתוֹרָתוֹ: וְיָדַעְתָּ הַיּוֹם וַהֲשֵׁבֹתָ אֶל לְבָבֶךָ, כִּי יהוה הוּא הָאֱלֹהִים בַּשָּׁמַיִם מִמַּעַל וְעַל הָאָרֶץ מִתָּחַת, אֵין עוֹד.[5]

Bow while reciting וַאֲנַחְנוּ כּוֹרְעִים וּמִשְׁתַּחֲוִים.

עַל כֵּן נְקַוֶּה לְּךָ יהוה אֱלֹהֵינוּ לִרְאוֹת מְהֵרָה בְּתִפְאֶרֶת עֻזֶּךָ, לְהַעֲבִיר גִּלּוּלִים מִן הָאָרֶץ, וְהָאֱלִילִים כָּרוֹת יִכָּרֵתוּן, לְתַקֵּן עוֹלָם בְּמַלְכוּת שַׁדַּי. וְכָל בְּנֵי בָשָׂר יִקְרְאוּ בִשְׁמֶךָ, לְהַפְנוֹת אֵלֶיךָ כָּל רִשְׁעֵי אָרֶץ. יַכִּירוּ וְיֵדְעוּ כָּל יוֹשְׁבֵי תֵבֵל, כִּי לְךָ

May His great Name be blessed forever and ever.

Blessed, praised, glorified, exalted, extolled, mighty, upraised, and lauded be the Name of the Holy One, Blessed is He (Cong.— *Blessed is He*) — *beyond any blessing and song, praise and consolation that are uttered in the world. Now respond: Amen.* (Cong.— *Amen*.)

(Cong.— *Accept our prayers with mercy and favor.*)

May the prayers and supplications of the entire Family of Israel be accepted before their Father Who is in Heaven. Now respond: Amen. (Cong.— *Amen.*)

(Cong.— *Blessed be the Name of* HASHEM, *from this time and forever.*[1])

May there be abundant peace from Heaven, and life, upon us and upon all Israel. Now respond: Amen. (Cong.— *Amen.*)

(Cong.— *My help is from* HASHEM, *Maker of heaven and earth.*[2])

Take three steps back. Bow left and say, *'He Who makes peace . . .'*; bow right and say, *'may He . . .'*; bow forward and say, *'and upon all Israel . . .'* Remain standing in place for a few moments, then take three steps forward.

He Who makes peace in His heights, may He make peace upon us, and upon all Israel. Now respond: Amen. (Cong.— *Amen.*)

ALEINU

Stand while reciting עָלֵינוּ, *'It is our duty . . .'*

עָלֵינוּ *It is our duty to praise the Master of all, to ascribe greatness to the Molder of primeval creation, for He has not made us like the nations of the lands, and has not emplaced us like the families of the earth; for He has not assigned our portion like theirs nor our lot like all their multitudes. (For they bow to vanity and emptiness and pray to a god which helps not.*[3]*) But we bend our knees, bow, and acknowledge our thanks before the King Who reigns over kings, the Holy One, Blessed is He. He stretches out heaven and establishes earth's foundation,*[4] *the seat of His homage is in the heavens above and His powerful Presence is in the loftiest heights. He is our God and there is none other. True is our King, there is nothing beside Him, as it is written in His Torah: 'You are to know this day and take to your heart that* HASHEM *is the only God — in heaven above and on the earth below — there is none other.'*[5]

Bow while reciting *'But we bend our knees.'*

עַל כֵּן *Therefore we put our hope in You,* HASHEM, *our God, that we may soon see Your mighty splendor, to remove detestable idolatry from the earth, and false gods will be utterly cut off, to perfect the universe through the Almighty's sovereignty. Then all humanity will call upon Your Name, to turn all the earth's wicked toward You. All the world's inhabitants will recognize and know that to You*

---

(1) *Psalms* 113:2. (2) 121:2. (3) *Isaiah* 45:20. (4) 51:13. (5) *Deuteronomy* 4:39.

תִּכְרַע כָּל בֶּרֶךְ, תִּשָּׁבַע כָּל לָשׁוֹן.[1] לְפָנֶיךָ יהוה אֱלֹהֵינוּ יִכְרְעוּ וְיִפֹּלוּ, וְלִכְבוֹד שִׁמְךָ יְקָר יִתֵּנוּ. וִיקַבְּלוּ כֻלָּם אֶת עוֹל מַלְכוּתֶךָ, וְתִמְלֹךְ עֲלֵיהֶם מְהֵרָה לְעוֹלָם וָעֶד. כִּי הַמַּלְכוּת שֶׁלְּךָ הִיא וּלְעוֹלְמֵי עַד תִּמְלוֹךְ בְּכָבוֹד, כַּכָּתוּב בְּתוֹרָתֶךָ: יהוה יִמְלֹךְ לְעֹלָם וָעֶד.[2] ❖ וְנֶאֱמַר: וְהָיָה יהוה לְמֶלֶךְ עַל כָּל הָאָרֶץ, בַּיּוֹם הַהוּא יִהְיֶה יהוה אֶחָד וּשְׁמוֹ אֶחָד.[3]

Some congregations recite the following after עָלֵינוּ.

אַל תִּירָא מִפַּחַד פִּתְאֹם, וּמִשֹּׁאַת רְשָׁעִים כִּי תָבֹא.[4] עֻצוּ עֵצָה וְתֻפָר, דַּבְּרוּ דָבָר וְלֹא יָקוּם, כִּי עִמָּנוּ אֵל.[5] וְעַד זִקְנָה אֲנִי הוּא, וְעַד שֵׂיבָה אֲנִי אֶסְבֹּל, אֲנִי עָשִׂיתִי וַאֲנִי אֶשָּׂא, וַאֲנִי אֶסְבֹּל וַאֲמַלֵּט.[5]

קדיש יתום

In the presence of a *minyan,* mourners recite קַדִּישׁ יָתוֹם, the Mourner's *Kaddish* (see *Laws* §81-83).

יִתְגַּדַּל וְיִתְקַדַּשׁ שְׁמֵהּ רַבָּא. (Cong. – אָמֵן.) בְּעָלְמָא דִּי בְרָא כִרְעוּתֵהּ. וְיַמְלִיךְ מַלְכוּתֵהּ, בְּחַיֵּיכוֹן וּבְיוֹמֵיכוֹן וּבְחַיֵּי דְכָל בֵּית יִשְׂרָאֵל, בַּעֲגָלָא וּבִזְמַן קָרִיב. וְאִמְרוּ: אָמֵן.

(Cong. – אָמֵן. יְהֵא שְׁמֵהּ רַבָּא מְבָרַךְ לְעָלַם וּלְעָלְמֵי עָלְמַיָּא.)

יְהֵא שְׁמֵהּ רַבָּא מְבָרַךְ לְעָלַם וּלְעָלְמֵי עָלְמַיָּא.

יִתְבָּרַךְ וְיִשְׁתַּבַּח וְיִתְפָּאַר וְיִתְרוֹמַם וְיִתְנַשֵּׂא וְיִתְהַדָּר וְיִתְעַלֶּה וְיִתְהַלָּל שְׁמֵהּ דְּקֻדְשָׁא בְּרִיךְ הוּא (Cong. – בְּרִיךְ הוּא) — לְעֵלָּא מִן כָּל בִּרְכָתָא וְשִׁירָתָא תֻּשְׁבְּחָתָא וְנֶחֱמָתָא, דַּאֲמִירָן בְּעָלְמָא. וְאִמְרוּ: אָמֵן. (Cong. – אָמֵן.)

יְהֵא שְׁלָמָא רַבָּא מִן שְׁמַיָּא, וְחַיִּים עָלֵינוּ וְעַל כָּל יִשְׂרָאֵל. וְאִמְרוּ: אָמֵן. (Cong. – אָמֵן.)

Take three steps back. Bow left and say . . . עֹשֶׂה; bow right and say . . . הוּא; bow forward and say וְעַל כָּל . . . אָמֵן. Remain standing in place for a few moments, then take three steps forward.

עֹשֶׂה שָׁלוֹם בִּמְרוֹמָיו, הוּא יַעֲשֶׂה שָׁלוֹם עָלֵינוּ, וְעַל כָּל יִשְׂרָאֵל. וְאִמְרוּ: אָמֵן. (Cong. – אָמֵן.)

THE BLESSINGS UPON KINDLING THE YOM TOV LIGHTS APPEAR ON PAGE 846.

every knee should bend, every tongue should swear.[1] *Before You, HASHEM, our God, they will bend every knee and cast themselves down and to the glory of Your Name they will render homage, and they will all accept upon themselves the yoke of Your kingship that You may reign over them soon and eternally. For the kingdom is Yours and You will reign for all eternity in glory as it is written in Your Torah: HASHEM shall reign for all eternity.*[2] Chazzan– *And it is said: HASHEM will be King over all the world — on that day HASHEM will be One and His Name will be One.*[3]

Some congregations recite the following after *Aleinu.*

אַל תִּירָא *Do not fear sudden terror, or the holocaust of the wicked when it comes.*[4] *Plan a conspiracy and it will be annulled; speak your piece and it shall not stand, for God is with us.*[5] *Even till your seniority, I remain unchanged; and even till your ripe old age, I shall endure. I created you and I shall bear you; I shall endure and rescue.*[6]

MOURNER'S KADDISH

In the presence of a *minyan,* mourners recite קַדִּישׁ יָתוֹם, the Mourner's *Kaddish* (see *Laws* 81-83).
[A transliteration of this *Kaddish* appears on page 1305.]

יִתְגַּדַּל *May His great Name grow exalted and sanctified* (Cong.– *Amen.*) *in the world that He created as He willed. May He give reign to His kingship in your lifetimes and in your days, and in the lifetimes of the entire Family of Israel, swiftly and soon. Now respond: Amen.*

(Cong.– *Amen. May His great Name be blessed forever and ever.*)

May His great Name be blessed forever and ever.

Blessed, praised, glorified, exalted, extolled, mighty, upraised, and lauded be the Name of the Holy One, Blessed is He (Cong.– *Blessed is He*) *— beyond any blessing and song, praise and consolation that are uttered in the world. Now respond: Amen.* (Cong.– *Amen*).

May there be abundant peace from Heaven, and life, upon us and upon all Israel. Now respond: Amen. (Cong.– *Amen.*)

Take three steps back. Bow left and say, *'He Who makes peace . . .';*
bow right and say, *'may He . . .';* bow forward and say, *'and upon all Israel . . .'*
Remain standing in place for a few moments, then take three steps forward.

He Who makes peace in His heights, may He make peace upon us, and upon all Israel. Now respond: Amen. (Cong.– *Amen.*)

THE BLESSINGS UPON KINDLING THE YOM TOV LIGHTS APPEAR ON PAGE 846.

---

(1) Cf. *Isaiah* 45:23. (2) *Exodus* 15:18. (3) *Zechariah* 14:9. (4) *Proverbs* 3:25. (5) *Isaiah* 8:10. (6) 46:4.

◈ שמחת תורה

◈ Simchas Torah

מעריב לשמחת תורה

In some congregations the *chazzan* chants a melody during his recitation of בָּרְכוּ so that the congregation can then recite יִתְבָּרַךְ.

Chazzan bows at בָּרְכוּ and straightens up at ה׳.

בָּרְכוּ אֶת יהוה הַמְּבֹרָךְ.

Congregation, followed by *chazzan*, responds, bowing at בָּרוּךְ and straightening up at ה׳.

בָּרוּךְ יהוה הַמְּבֹרָךְ לְעוֹלָם וָעֶד.

יִתְבָּרַךְ[1] וְיִשְׁתַּבַּח וְיִתְפָּאַר וְיִתְרוֹמַם וְיִתְנַשֵּׂא שְׁמוֹ שֶׁל מֶלֶךְ מַלְכֵי הַמְּלָכִים, הַקָּדוֹשׁ בָּרוּךְ הוּא. שֶׁהוּא רִאשׁוֹן וְהוּא אַחֲרוֹן, וּמִבַּלְעָדָיו אֵין אֱלֹהִים.[2] סֹלּוּ, לָרֹכֵב בָּעֲרָבוֹת, בְּיָהּ שְׁמוֹ, וְעִלְזוּ לְפָנָיו.[3] וּשְׁמוֹ מְרוֹמָם עַל כָּל בְּרָכָה וּתְהִלָּה.[4] בָּרוּךְ שֵׁם כְּבוֹד מַלְכוּתוֹ לְעוֹלָם וָעֶד. יְהִי שֵׁם יהוה מְבֹרָךְ, מֵעַתָּה וְעַד עוֹלָם.[5]

ברכות קריאת שמע

בָּרוּךְ אַתָּה יהוה אֱלֹהֵינוּ מֶלֶךְ הָעוֹלָם, אֲשֶׁר בִּדְבָרוֹ מַעֲרִיב עֲרָבִים, בְּחָכְמָה פּוֹתֵחַ שְׁעָרִים, וּבִתְבוּנָה מְשַׁנֶּה עִתִּים, וּמַחֲלִיף אֶת הַזְּמַנִּים, וּמְסַדֵּר אֶת הַכּוֹכָבִים בְּמִשְׁמְרוֹתֵיהֶם בָּרָקִיעַ כִּרְצוֹנוֹ. בּוֹרֵא יוֹם וָלָיְלָה, גּוֹלֵל אוֹר מִפְּנֵי חֹשֶׁךְ וְחֹשֶׁךְ מִפְּנֵי אוֹר. וּמַעֲבִיר יוֹם וּמֵבִיא לָיְלָה, וּמַבְדִּיל בֵּין יוֹם וּבֵין לָיְלָה, יהוה צְבָאוֹת שְׁמוֹ. ❖ אֵל חַי וְקַיָּם, תָּמִיד יִמְלוֹךְ עָלֵינוּ, לְעוֹלָם וָעֶד.

אֶת יוֹם הַשְּׁמִינִי,* בְּטוֹב יַזְמִינִי,
רָנֵּי פַלֵּט יְסוֹבְבֵנִי,[6] לְעֵת עֶרֶב בְּצִלּוֹ יְלוֹנְנִי.

בָּרוּךְ אַתָּה יהוה, הַמַּעֲרִיב עֲרָבִים. (Cong. – אָמֵן.)

אַהֲבַת עוֹלָם בֵּית יִשְׂרָאֵל עַמְּךָ אָהָבְתָּ. תּוֹרָה וּמִצְוֹת, חֻקִּים וּמִשְׁפָּטִים, אוֹתָנוּ לִמַּדְתָּ. עַל כֵּן יהוה אֱלֹהֵינוּ, בְּשָׁכְבֵנוּ וּבְקוּמֵנוּ נָשִׂיחַ בְּחֻקֶּיךָ, וְנִשְׂמַח בְּדִבְרֵי תוֹרָתֶךָ, וּבְמִצְוֹתֶיךָ לְעוֹלָם וָעֶד. ❖ כִּי הֵם חַיֵּינוּ, וְאֹרֶךְ יָמֵינוּ, וּבָהֶם נֶהְגֶּה יוֹמָם וָלָיְלָה. וְאַהֲבָתְךָ, אַל תָּסִיר מִמֶּנּוּ לְעוֹלָמִים.

אֲיֻמָּה אָהַב בֵּרַךְ בְּכֶסֶף, בְּמִדָּה מְרֻבָּה מֵרֹאשׁ בְּתוֹסֶף,
בְּזֶה עֲצֶרֶת חַג אֹסֶף, אוֹהֲבָיו יְקָרֵב אֵלָיו לְהֵאָסֵף.

בָּרוּךְ אַתָּה יהוה, אוֹהֵב עַמּוֹ יִשְׂרָאֵל. (Cong. – אָמֵן.)

Many congregations recite *piyutim* (liturgical poems) that are inserted at various points in the synagogue service, often in the middle of a paragraph. Those who do not recite *piyutim* should not assume their appearance to indicate a stop, but should continue to the next new paragraph as indicated by bold type for the first word.

אֶת יוֹם הַשְּׁמִינִי – *On the eight day.* The *piyutim* for Simchas Torah make repeated reference to Shemini Atzeres. It must be remembered that in *Eretz Yisrael* Shemini Atzeres / Simchas Torah is a one-day festival. The second day has been given the name

MAARIV FOR SIMCHAS TORAH

In some congregations the *chazzan* chants a melody during his recitation of *Borchu* so that the congregation can then recite *'Blessed, praised . . .'*

Chazzan bows at *'Bless'* and straightens up at *'HASHEM.'*

Bless HASHEM, the blessed One.

Congregation, followed by *chazzan*, responds, bowing at *'Blessed'* and straightening up at *'HASHEM.'*

Blessed is HASHEM, the blessed One, for all eternity.

Blessed,[1] praised, glorified, exalted and upraised is the Name of the King Who rules over kings — the Holy One, Blessed is He. For He is the First and He is the Last and aside from Him there is no god.[2] Extol Him — Who rides the highest heavens — with His Name, YAH, and exult before Him.[3] His Name is exalted beyond every blessing and praise.[4] Blessed is the Name of His glorious kingdom for all eternity. Blessed be the Name of HASHEM from this time and forever.[5]

BLESSINGS OF THE SHEMA

בָּרוּךְ *Blessed are You, HASHEM, our God, King of the universe, Who by His word brings on evenings, with wisdom opens gates, with understanding alters periods, changes the seasons, and orders the stars in their heavenly constellations as He wills. He creates day and night, removing light before darkness and darkness before light. He causes day to pass and brings night, and separates between day and night — HASHEM, Master of Legions, is His Name.* Chazzan— *May the living and enduring God continuously reign over us, for all eternity.*

*On the eighth day,**
may He prepare goodness for me,
may He surround me with glad song of rescue,[6]
at evening time may He cause me to dwell in His shelter.

Blessed are You, HASHEM, Who brings on evenings. (Cong.— *Amen.)*

אַהֲבַת *With an eternal love have You loved the House of Israel, Your nation. Torah and commandments, decrees and ordinances have You taught us. Therefore HASHEM, our God, upon our retiring and arising, we will discuss Your decrees and we will rejoice with the words of Your Torah and with Your commandments for all eternity.* Chazzan— *For they are our life and the length of our days and about them we will meditate day and night. May You not remove Your love from us forever.*

[Israel] the nation He loved, He blessed with desire,
in greater measure than before [on Succos], this added day,
on this the Day of Assembly of the Ingathering Festival,
may He draw His beloved [Israel] and gather them to Him.

Blessed are You, HASHEM, Who loves His nation Israel. (Cong.— *Amen.)*

(1) See *Orach Chaim* 57:1 (2) Cf. *Isaiah* 44:6. (3) *Psalms* 68:5. (4) Cf. *Nechemiah* 9:5. (5) *Psalms* 113:2. (6) Cf. *Psalms* 32:7.

Simchas Torah [lit., rejoicing of the Torah] because the annual Torah-reading cycle ends and starts anew on that day. Nevertheless, it is just as much a part of Shemini Atzeres as the second day of Shavuos is a part of that festival.

The unknown composer of these *piyutim* followed an alphabetical scheme and signed his name in the last four stanzas: יִצְחָק הַקָּטָן חֲזַק אָמֵן,

שמע

Immediately before its recitation concentrate on fulfilling the positive commandment of reciting the *Shema* twice daily. It is important to enunciate each word clearly and not to run words together. For this reason, vertical lines have been placed between two words that are prone to be slurred into one and are not separated by a comma or a hyphen. See *Laws* §40-52.

When praying without a *minyan,* begin with the following three-word formula:

אֵל מֶלֶךְ נֶאֱמָן.

Recite the first verse aloud, with the right hand covering the eyes, and concentrate intently upon accepting God's absolute sovereignty.

שְׁמַע ׀ יִשְׂרָאֵל, יהוה ׀ אֱלֹהֵינוּ, יהוה ׀ אֶחָד:

In an undertone – בָּרוּךְ שֵׁם כְּבוֹד מַלְכוּתוֹ לְעוֹלָם וָעֶד.

While reciting the first paragraph (דברים ו:ה-ט), concentrate on accepting the commandment to love God.

וְאָהַבְתָּ אֵת ׀ יהוה ׀ אֱלֹהֶיךָ, בְּכָל־לְבָבְךָ, וּבְכָל־נַפְשְׁךָ, וּבְכָל־מְאֹדֶךָ: וְהָיוּ הַדְּבָרִים הָאֵלֶּה, אֲשֶׁר ׀ אָנֹכִי מְצַוְּךָ הַיּוֹם, עַל־לְבָבֶךָ: וְשִׁנַּנְתָּם לְבָנֶיךָ, וְדִבַּרְתָּ בָּם, בְּשִׁבְתְּךָ בְּבֵיתֶךָ, וּבְלֶכְתְּךָ בַדֶּרֶךְ, וּבְשָׁכְבְּךָ וּבְקוּמֶךָ: וּקְשַׁרְתָּם לְאוֹת ׀ עַל־יָדֶךָ, וְהָיוּ לְטֹטָפֹת בֵּין ׀ עֵינֶיךָ: וּכְתַבְתָּם ׀ עַל־מְזֻזוֹת בֵּיתֶךָ, וּבִשְׁעָרֶיךָ:

While reciting the second paragraph (דברים יא:יג-כא), concentrate on accepting all the commandments and the concept of reward and punishment.

וְהָיָה, אִם־שָׁמֹעַ תִּשְׁמְעוּ אֶל־מִצְוֹתַי, אֲשֶׁר ׀ אָנֹכִי מְצַוֶּה ׀ אֶתְכֶם הַיּוֹם, לְאַהֲבָה אֶת־יהוה ׀ אֱלֹהֵיכֶם וּלְעָבְדוֹ, בְּכָל־לְבַבְכֶם, וּבְכָל־נַפְשְׁכֶם: וְנָתַתִּי מְטַר־אַרְצְכֶם בְּעִתּוֹ, יוֹרֶה וּמַלְקוֹשׁ, וְאָסַפְתָּ דְגָנֶךָ וְתִירֹשְׁךָ וְיִצְהָרֶךָ: וְנָתַתִּי ׀ עֵשֶׂב ׀ בְּשָׂדְךָ לִבְהֶמְתֶּךָ, וְאָכַלְתָּ וְשָׂבָעְתָּ: הִשָּׁמְרוּ לָכֶם, פֶּן־יִפְתֶּה לְבַבְכֶם, וְסַרְתֶּם וַעֲבַדְתֶּם ׀ אֱלֹהִים ׀ אֲחֵרִים, וְהִשְׁתַּחֲוִיתֶם לָהֶם: וְחָרָה ׀ אַף־יהוה בָּכֶם, וְעָצַר ׀ אֶת־הַשָּׁמַיִם, וְלֹא־יִהְיֶה מָטָר, וְהָאֲדָמָה לֹא תִתֵּן אֶת־יְבוּלָהּ, וַאֲבַדְתֶּם ׀ מְהֵרָה מֵעַל הָאָרֶץ הַטֹּבָה ׀ אֲשֶׁר ׀ יהוה נֹתֵן לָכֶם: וְשַׂמְתֶּם ׀ אֶת־דְּבָרַי ׀ אֵלֶּה, עַל־לְבַבְכֶם וְעַל־נַפְשְׁכֶם, וּקְשַׁרְתֶּם ׀ אֹתָם לְאוֹת ׀ עַל־יֶדְכֶם, וְהָיוּ לְטוֹטָפֹת בֵּין ׀ עֵינֵיכֶם: וְלִמַּדְתֶּם ׀ אֹתָם ׀ אֶת־בְּנֵיכֶם, לְדַבֵּר בָּם, בְּשִׁבְתְּךָ בְּבֵיתֶךָ, וּבְלֶכְתְּךָ בַדֶּרֶךְ, וּבְשָׁכְבְּךָ וּבְקוּמֶךָ: וּכְתַבְתָּם ׀ עַל־מְזוּזוֹת בֵּיתֶךָ, וּבִשְׁעָרֶיךָ: לְמַעַן ׀ יִרְבּוּ ׀ יְמֵיכֶם וִימֵי בְנֵיכֶם, עַל הָאֲדָמָה ׀ אֲשֶׁר נִשְׁבַּע ׀ יהוה לַאֲבֹתֵיכֶם לָתֵת לָהֶם, כִּימֵי הַשָּׁמַיִם ׀ עַל־הָאָרֶץ:

Yitzchak the lesser, may he be strong, amen. Most of the allusions to the day and to the number eight also appear in the *piyutim* for Shemini Atzeres with commentary.

THE SHEMA

Immediately before its recitation concentrate on fulfilling the positive commandment of reciting the *Shema* twice daily. It is important to enunciate each word clearly and not to run words together. See *Laws* §40-52.

When praying without a *minyan,* begin with the following three-word formula:
God, trustworthy King.

Recite the first verse aloud, with the right hand covering the eyes, and concentrate intently upon accepting God's absolute sovereignty.

Hear, O Israel: HASHEM is our God, HASHEM, the One and Only.[1]

In an undertone— *Blessed is the Name of His glorious kingdom for all eternity.*

While reciting the first paragraph (*Deuteronomy* 6:5-9), concentrate on accepting the commandment to love God.

וְאָהַבְתָּ *You shall love HASHEM, your God, with all your heart, with all your soul and with all your resources. Let these matters that I command you today be upon your heart. Teach them thoroughly to your children and speak of them while you sit in your home, while you walk on the way, when you retire and when you arise. Bind them as a sign upon your arm and let them be tefillin between your eyes. And write them on the doorposts of your house and upon your gates.*

While reciting the second paragraph (*Deuteronomy* 11:13-21), concentrate on accepting all the commandments and the concept of reward and punishment.

וְהָיָה *And it will come to pass that if you continually hearken to My commandments that I command you today, to love HASHEM, your God, and to serve Him, with all your heart and with all your soul — then I will provide rain for your land in its proper time, the early and late rains, that you may gather in your grain, your wine, and your oil. I will provide grass in your field for your cattle and you will eat and be satisfied. Beware lest your heart be seduced and you turn astray and serve gods of others and bow to them. Then the wrath of HASHEM will blaze against you. He will restrain the heaven so there will be no rain and the ground will not yield its produce. And you will swiftly be banished from the goodly land which HASHEM gives you. Place these words of Mine upon your heart and upon your soul; bind them for a sign upon your arm and let them be tefillin between your eyes. Teach them to your children, to discuss them, while you sit in your home, while you walk on the way, when you retire and when you arise. And write them on the doorposts of your house and upon your gates. In order to prolong your days and the days of your children upon the ground that HASHEM has sworn to your ancestors to give them, like the days of the heaven on the earth.*

---

(1) *Deuteronomy* 6:4.

במדבר טו:לז-מא

וַיְּאמֶר ׀ יהוה ׀ אֶל־מֹשֶׁה לֵּאמֹר: דַּבֵּר ׀ אֶל־בְּנֵי ׀ יִשְׂרָאֵל, וְאָמַרְתָּ אֲלֵהֶם, וְעָשׂוּ לָהֶם צִיצִת, עַל־כַּנְפֵי בִגְדֵיהֶם לְדֹרֹתָם, וְנָתְנוּ ׀ עַל־צִיצִת הַכָּנָף, פְּתִיל תְּכֵלֶת: וְהָיָה לָכֶם לְצִיצִת, וּרְאִיתֶם ׀ אֹתוֹ, וּזְכַרְתֶּם ׀ אֶת־כָּל־מִצְוֹת ׀ יהוה, וַעֲשִׂיתֶם ׀ אֹתָם, וְלֹא תָתוּרוּ ׀ אַחֲרֵי לְבַבְכֶם וְאַחֲרֵי ׀ עֵינֵיכֶם, אֲשֶׁר־אַתֶּם זֹנִים ׀ אַחֲרֵיהֶם: לְמַעַן תִּזְכְּרוּ, וַעֲשִׂיתֶם ׀ אֶת־כָּל־מִצְוֹתָי, וִהְיִיתֶם קְדֹשִׁים לֵאלֹהֵיכֶם: אֲנִי יהוה ׀ אֱלֹהֵיכֶם, אֲשֶׁר הוֹצֵאתִי ׀ אֶתְכֶם ׀ מֵאֶרֶץ מִצְרַיִם, לִהְיוֹת לָכֶם לֵאלֹהִים, אֲנִי ׀ יהוה ׀ אֱלֹהֵיכֶם: אֱמֶת —

Concentrate on fulfilling the commandment of remembering the Exodus from Egypt.

Although the word אֱמֶת belongs to the next paragraph, it is appended to the conclusion of the previous one, as explained in the commentary.

—*Chazzan* repeats **יהוה אֱלֹהֵיכֶם אֱמֶת.**

וֶאֱמוּנָה כָּל זֹאת, וְקַיָּם עָלֵינוּ, כִּי הוּא יהוה אֱלֹהֵינוּ וְאֵין זוּלָתוֹ, וַאֲנַחְנוּ יִשְׂרָאֵל עַמּוֹ. הַפּוֹדֵנוּ מִיַּד מְלָכִים, מַלְכֵּנוּ הַגּוֹאֲלֵנוּ מִכַּף כָּל הֶעָרִיצִים. הָאֵל הַנִּפְרָע לָנוּ מִצָּרֵינוּ, וְהַמְשַׁלֵּם גְּמוּל לְכָל אֹיְבֵי נַפְשֵׁנוּ. הָעֹשֶׂה גְדֹלוֹת עַד אֵין חֵקֶר, וְנִפְלָאוֹת עַד אֵין מִסְפָּר.[1] הַשָּׂם נַפְשֵׁנוּ בַּחַיִּים, וְלֹא נָתַן לַמּוֹט רַגְלֵנוּ.[2] הַמַּדְרִיכֵנוּ עַל בָּמוֹת אוֹיְבֵינוּ, וַיָּרֶם קַרְנֵנוּ עַל כָּל שֹׂנְאֵינוּ. הָעֹשֶׂה לָּנוּ נִסִּים וּנְקָמָה בְּפַרְעֹה, אוֹתוֹת וּמוֹפְתִים בְּאַדְמַת בְּנֵי חָם. הַמַּכֶּה בְעֶבְרָתוֹ כָּל בְּכוֹרֵי מִצְרָיִם, וַיּוֹצֵא אֶת עַמּוֹ יִשְׂרָאֵל מִתּוֹכָם לְחֵרוּת עוֹלָם. הַמַּעֲבִיר בָּנָיו בֵּין גִּזְרֵי יַם סוּף, אֶת רוֹדְפֵיהֶם וְאֶת שׂוֹנְאֵיהֶם בִּתְהוֹמוֹת טִבַּע. וְרָאוּ בָנָיו גְּבוּרָתוֹ, שִׁבְּחוּ וְהוֹדוּ לִשְׁמוֹ. ❖ וּמַלְכוּתוֹ בְרָצוֹן קִבְּלוּ עֲלֵיהֶם. מֹשֶׁה וּבְנֵי יִשְׂרָאֵל לְךָ עָנוּ שִׁירָה,

שְׁמִינִי **אִ**מֵּץ בִּפְנֵי עַצְמוֹ,
בְּחוֹב קָבוּעַ לִשְׁמוֹ, בַּיּוֹם הַשְּׁמִינִי.
שְׁמִינִי **גְּ**מָרוֹ בְּפַיֵּס רֶגֶל וּזְמָן,
דְּבַר שִׁיר וְקָרְבָּן מְזֻמָּן, בַּיּוֹם הַשְּׁמִינִי.
שְׁמִינִי **הוֹ**סִיף לְגוֹי נִכְבָּד,[3]
וּבְמוּסְפֵי קֹדֶשׁ מְכֻבָּד, בַּיּוֹם הַשְּׁמִינִי.
שְׁמִינִי **זְ**מָן וְהֻקְבַּע לְרַצּוֹת,
חֹק נוֹלַד בּוֹ לְהֵרָצוֹת,[4] בַּיּוֹם הַשְּׁמִינִי.

(1) *Job* 9:10. (2) *Psalms* 66:9. (3) Cf. *Isaiah* 26:15 [*Pesikta d'Rav Kahana* interprets this verse as an allusion to Shemini Atzeres.] (4) Cf. *Leviticus* 22:27.

Numbers 15:37-41

וַיֹּאמֶר *And* HASHEM *said to Moses saying: Speak to the Children of Israel and say to them that they are to make themselves tzitzis on the corners of their garments, throughout their generations. And they are to place upon the tzitzis of each corner a thread of techeiles. And it shall constitute tzitzis for you, that you may see it and remember all the commandments of* HASHEM *and perform them; and not explore after your heart and after your eyes after which you stray. So that you may remember and perform all My commandments; and be holy to your God. I am* HASHEM, *your God, Who has removed you from the land of Egypt to be a God to you; I am* HASHEM *your God — it is true —*

Concentrate on fulfilling the commandment of remembering the Exodus from Egypt.

Although the word אֱמֶת, *'it is true,'* belongs to the next paragraph, it is appended to the conclusion of the previous one, as explained in the commentary.

Chazzan repeats: **HASHEM, your God, is true.**

וֶאֱמוּנָה *And faithful is all this, and it is firmly established for us that He is* HASHEM *our God, and there is none but Him, and we are Israel, His nation. He redeems us from the power of kings, our King Who delivers us from the hand of all the cruel tyrants. He is the God Who exacts vengeance for us from our foes and Who brings just retribution upon all enemies of our soul; Who performs great deeds that are beyond comprehension, and wonders beyond number.*[1] *Who set our soul in life and did not allow our foot to falter.*[2] *Who led us upon the heights of our enemies and raised our pride above all who hate us; Who wrought for us miracles and vengeance upon Pharaoh; signs and wonders on the land of the offspring of Ham; Who struck with His anger all the firstborn of Egypt and removed His nation Israel from their midst to eternal freedom; Who brought His children through the split parts of the Sea of Reeds while those who pursued them and hated them He caused to sink into the depths. When His children perceived His power, they lauded and gave grateful praise to His Name.* Chazzan– *And His Kingship they accepted upon themselves willingly. Moses and the Children of Israel raised their voices to You in song,*

א *The eighth has been exalted unto itself,*
ב *with obligation established uniquely for it — on the eighth day.*
ג *The eighth He completed with lots, festival and season,*
ד *uttered blessings, song and prepared offering — on the eighth day.*
ה *The eighth He added for the honored nation,*[3]
ו *and honored it with sanctified mussaf-offerings — on the eighth day.*
ז *The eighth [day of an animal's life] is established and set to find favor,*
ח *the law is that a newborn may find favor on it*[4] *— on the eighth day.*

מִכְתָּם – *Abraham.* In *Psalms* the word מִכְתָּם often introduces a psalm. The word is variously interpreted as: a song, a crown, the finest gold. The Talmud (*Sotah* 10b) explains the word as an allusion to מַכָּה תָּם, *the wound of perfection,* i.e., circumcision, about which God said to Abraham, *'Walk before Me and perfect'* (*Genesis* 17:1).

שְׁמִינִי טִבַּע חֲתוּמִים חוֹתָם,
יְדִידוּת נֵצֶר מִכְתָּם,* בַּיּוֹם הַשְּׁמִינִי.
שְׁמִינִי כָּלוּל לְשִׂמְחָה גְדוֹלָה,
לִמְכַהֵן בְּחִנּוּךְ עוֹלָה, בַּיּוֹם הַשְּׁמִינִי.
שְׁמִינִי מִלִּפְנֵי פְּנֵי פָנָיו,[1]
נֶחֱלָק בְּכָל עִנְיָנָיו, בַּיּוֹם הַשְּׁמִינִי.
שְׁמִינִי סְכַם לְשִׁלּוּחַ מֶלֶךְ,
עֵת וַיְבָרְכוּ אֶת הַמֶּלֶךְ,[2] בַּיּוֹם הַשְּׁמִינִי.
שְׁמִינִי פְּנוֹת בֹּקֶר הֲלָנָתוֹ,[3]
צֶדֶק יָלִין מְעוֹנָתוֹ,[4] בַּיּוֹם הַשְּׁמִינִי.
שְׁמִינִי קוֹל שֶׁמַע בְּאַהֲבָה,
רִנַּת בֵּית הַשּׁוֹאֵבָה,* בַּיּוֹם הַשְּׁמִינִי.
שְׁמִינִי שָׁלוֹם שׁוֹמֵר אָהֳלוֹ,
תּוֹךְ יְמֵי עֲלִיַּת רַגְלוֹ,* בַּיּוֹם הַשְּׁמִינִי.
שְׁמִינִי יְצַוֶּה חַסְדּוֹ קָדוֹשׁ לְעַמּוֹ, וּבַלַּיְלָה* שִׁירֹה עִמּוֹ,[5]
מוֹשֵׁל הַשַּׁלִּיט בְּעוֹלָמוֹ, עָלֵינוּ כִּמְאָז יְהִי נָעֳמוֹ.[6]
בְּגִילָה, בְּרִנָּה,

בְּשִׂמְחָה רַבָּה וְאָמְרוּ כֻלָּם:

מִי כָמֹכָה בָּאֵלִים יהוה, מִי כָּמֹכָה נֶאְדָּר בַּקֹּדֶשׁ, נוֹרָא תְהִלֹּת, עֹשֵׂה פֶלֶא.[7] ❖ מַלְכוּתְךָ רָאוּ בָנֶיךָ בּוֹקֵעַ יָם לִפְנֵי מֹשֶׁה,

שְׁמִינִי הֵיטִיבָה יהוה לַטּוֹבִים,[8] קוֹרְאֶיךָ בִּדְבָרִים עֲרֵבִים,
טוֹבוֹת יַשְׁמִיעַ לַאֲהוּבִים, נֹעַם מַלְכוּתְךָ עֲנוֹת תְּאֵבִים.
זֶה צוּר יִשְׁעֵנוּ פָּצוּ פֶה וְאָמְרוּ:

Continue: ... ה׳ יִמְלֹךְ

זֶה אֵלִי[9] עָנוּ וְאָמְרוּ:

יהוה יִמְלֹךְ לְעֹלָם וָעֶד.[10] ❖ וְנֶאֱמַר: כִּי פָדָה יהוה אֶת יַעֲקֹב, וּגְאָלוֹ מִיַּד חָזָק מִמֶּנּוּ.[11]

הַשּׁוֹאֵבָה – *The water-drawing.* Although the *halachah* follows the view that the water-libations were made only on the seven days of Succos and not on Shemini Atzeres, the *paytan* presumably alludes to the rejected minority opinion that on Shemini Atzeres there was a water-libation (see *Succah* 47a).

עֲלִיַּת רַגְלוֹ – *He makes the pilgrimage.* The Talmud (*Pesachim* 8b) interprets the verse as follows: *In the morning you may turn back and go to your tents (Deuteronomy* 16:7), as a blessing. While you are on your pilgrimage God will protect your property until your return home.

ט *The eighth [day of circumcision], when those sealed [in the covenant] set the seal,*
י *beloved offspring of Abraham* — on the eighth day.*
כ *The eighth [day of the Mishkan's inauguration] was crowned with great rejoicing,*
ל *the investiture of the Kohanim with the elevation-offering — on the eighth day.*
מ *The eighth, from that [Festival of Succos] which precedes it,*[1]
נ *is different in all its aspects — on the eighth day.*
ס *The eighth, on it the king [Solomon] agreed to dismiss [the nation],*
ע *at the time that they blessed the king*[2] *— on the eighth day.*
פ *The eighth, you may return [home] in the morning after spending the night,*[3]
צ *righteousness lodges in His dwelling [Jerusalem]*[4] *— on the eighth day.*
ק *The eighth, the sound is lovingly heard,*
ר *the glad song of the water-drawing* — on the eighth day.*
ש *The eighth, may Shalom [God] guard his tent,*
ת *during the days he makes the pilgrimage* — on the eighth day.*
י *The eighth, may the Holy One command His kindness to His people [by day], and at night* may His resting place be with them.*[5]
The Sovereign Who rules in His world, may His pleasantness be upon us,[6] *as in the past.*
with mirth, with glad song,

with abundant gladness — and said unanimously:

מִי כָמֹכָה *Who is like You among the heavenly powers, HASHEM! Who is like You, mighty in holiness, too awesome for praise, doing wonders!*[7] Chazzan– *Your children beheld Your majesty, as You split the sea before Moses,*

ה *The eighth, do good, O HASHEM, to good people,*[8]
ק *Those who call to You with sweet words.*
ט *May He cause His beloved ones to hear good tidings,*
נ *Those who long to retell the sweetness of Your Kingship.*
'He is the Rock of our salvation!' they opened their mouths and said:
Continue: *'HASHEM shall reign . . .'*

'This is my God!'[9] *they exclaimed, then they said:*

יהוה *'HASHEM shall reign for all eternity!'*[10] Chazzan– *And it is further said: 'For HASHEM has redeemed Jacob and delivered him from a power mightier than he.'*[11]

(1) See tractate *Succah* 47a. (2) Cf. *I Kings* 8:66. (3) Cf. *Deuteronomy* 16:7. (4) Cf. *Isaiah* 1:21. (5) Cf. *Psalms* 42:9. (6) Cf. 90:17. (7) *Exodus* 15:11. (8) *Psalms* 125:4. (9) *Exodus* 15:2. (10) 15:18. (11) *Jeremiah* 31:10.

וּבַלַּיְלָה – *And at night*. The terrors and dangers of night are often used as metaphors for exile, while the brightness of day symbolizes the redemption.

שְׁמִינִי חֵלֶק לְשִׁבְעָה וְגַם לִשְׁמוֹנָה,[1] מִצְוָה עָלֵינוּ לָתֵת מָנָה,
זְכוּת אָבוֹת יִזְכָּר בָּם שׁוֹכֵן מְעוֹנָה, קְנוֹת שֵׁנִית עֲדַת מִי מָנָה.

[Some conclude the blessing as follows; others conclude with בָּרוּךְ . . . גָּאַל יִשְׂרָאֵל.]

בָּרוּךְ אַתָּה יהוה, מֶלֶךְ צוּר יִשְׂרָאֵל וְגוֹאֲלוֹ. (Cong. – אָמֵן.)

בָּרוּךְ אַתָּה יהוה, גָּאַל יִשְׂרָאֵל. (Cong. – אָמֵן.)

הַשְׁכִּיבֵנוּ יהוה אֱלֹהֵינוּ לְשָׁלוֹם, וְהַעֲמִידֵנוּ מַלְכֵּנוּ לְחַיִּים, וּפְרוֹשׂ עָלֵינוּ סֻכַּת שְׁלוֹמֶךָ, וְתַקְּנֵנוּ בְּעֵצָה טוֹבָה מִלְּפָנֶיךָ, וְהוֹשִׁיעֵנוּ לְמַעַן שְׁמֶךָ. וְהָגֵן בַּעֲדֵנוּ, וְהָסֵר מֵעָלֵינוּ אוֹיֵב, דֶּבֶר, וְחֶרֶב, וְרָעָב, וְיָגוֹן, וְהָסֵר שָׂטָן מִלְּפָנֵינוּ וּמֵאַחֲרֵינוּ, וּבְצֵל כְּנָפֶיךָ תַּסְתִּירֵנוּ,[2] כִּי אֵל שׁוֹמְרֵנוּ וּמַצִּילֵנוּ אָתָּה, כִּי אֵל מֶלֶךְ חַנּוּן וְרַחוּם אָתָּה.[3] ❖ וּשְׁמוֹר צֵאתֵנוּ וּבוֹאֵנוּ, לְחַיִּים וּלְשָׁלוֹם מֵעַתָּה וְעַד עוֹלָם.[4] וּפְרוֹשׂ עָלֵינוּ סֻכַּת שְׁלוֹמֶךָ.

שְׁמִינִי אֱלֹהִים יְחָנֵּנוּ, מִמְּעוֹן קָדְשׁוֹ לְבָרְכֵנוּ,[5]
נָאֳמוֹ יָקֵם מַלְכֵּנוּ, בִּפְרִיסַת שְׁלוֹמוֹ לְסוֹכְכֵנוּ.

בָּרוּךְ אַתָּה יהוה, הַפּוֹרֵשׂ סֻכַּת שָׁלוֹם עָלֵינוּ וְעַל כָּל עַמּוֹ יִשְׂרָאֵל וְעַל יְרוּשָׁלָיִם. (Cong. – אָמֵן.)

Congregation rises and remains standing until after *Shemoneh Esrei.*

Congregation, then *chazzan:*

וַיְדַבֵּר מֹשֶׁה אֶת מֹעֲדֵי יהוה, אֶל בְּנֵי יִשְׂרָאֵל.[6]

The *chazzan* recites חֲצִי קַדִּישׁ.

יִתְגַּדַּל וְיִתְקַדַּשׁ שְׁמֵהּ רַבָּא. (Cong. – אָמֵן.) בְּעָלְמָא דִּי בְרָא כִרְעוּתֵהּ, וְיַמְלִיךְ מַלְכוּתֵהּ, בְּחַיֵּיכוֹן וּבְיוֹמֵיכוֹן וּבְחַיֵּי דְכָל בֵּית יִשְׂרָאֵל, בַּעֲגָלָא וּבִזְמַן קָרִיב. וְאִמְרוּ: אָמֵן.

(Cong. – אָמֵן. יְהֵא שְׁמֵהּ רַבָּא מְבָרַךְ לְעָלַם וּלְעָלְמֵי עָלְמַיָּא.)

יְהֵא שְׁמֵהּ רַבָּא מְבָרַךְ לְעָלַם וּלְעָלְמֵי עָלְמַיָּא.

יִתְבָּרַךְ וְיִשְׁתַּבַּח וְיִתְפָּאַר וְיִתְרוֹמַם וְיִתְנַשֵּׂא וְיִתְהַדָּר וְיִתְעַלֶּה וְיִתְהַלָּל שְׁמֵהּ דְּקֻדְשָׁא בְּרִיךְ הוּא (Cong. – בְּרִיךְ הוּא) — לְעֵלָּא מִן כָּל בִּרְכָתָא וְשִׁירָתָא תֻּשְׁבְּחָתָא וְנֶחֱמָתָא, דַּאֲמִירָן בְּעָלְמָא. וְאִמְרוּ: אָמֵן. (Cong. – אָמֵן.)

ח *The eighth, a share for seven and also for eight,*[1]
if it is incumbent upon us to set aside a portion.
ז *May He Who dwells in heaven remember the merit of the Patriarchs,*
ק *once again to take possession of the uncountable flock.*

Some conclude the blessing as follows; others conclude with *'Blessed . . . Who redeemed Israel'.*

Blessed are You, HASHEM, King, Rock of Israel and its Redeemer.

Blessed are You, HASHEM, Who redeemed Israel. (Cong.– *Amen.)*

הַשְׁכִּיבֵנוּ *Lay us down to sleep, HASHEM our God, in peace, raise us erect, our King, to life; and spread over us the shelter of Your peace. Set us aright with good counsel from before Your Presence, and save us for Your Name's sake. Shield us, remove from us foe, plague, sword, famine, and woe; and remove spiritual impediment from before us and behind us, and in the shadow of Your wings shelter us*[2] *— for God Who protects and rescues us are You; for God, the Gracious and Compassionate King, are You.*[3] Chazzan– *Safeguard our going and coming, for life and for peace from now to eternity.*[4] *And spread over us the shelter of Your peace.*

א *The eighth, may God favor us,*
מ *to bless us from His holy dwellings.*[5]
נ *May our King fulfill His word,*
by spreading His peace to shelter us.

Blessed are You, HASHEM, Who spreads the shelter of peace upon us, upon all of His people Israel and upon Jerusalem. (Cong.– *Amen.)*

Congregation rises and remains standing until after *Shemoneh Esrei.*

Congregation, then *chazzan:*

And Moses declared HASHEM's appointed festivals to the Children of Israel.[6]

The *chazzan* recites Half-*Kaddish.*

יִתְגַּדַּל *May His great Name grow exalted and sanctified* (Cong.– *Amen.) in the world that He created as He willed. May He give reign to His kingship in your lifetimes and in your days, and in the lifetimes of the entire Family of Israel, swiftly and soon. Now respond: Amen.*

(Cong.– *Amen. May His great Name be blessed forever and ever.)*

May His great Name be blessed forever and ever.

Blessed, praised, glorified, exalted, extolled, mighty, upraised, and lauded be the Name of the Holy One, Blessed is He (Cong.– *Blessed is He) — beyond any blessing and song, praise and consolation that are uttered in the world. Now respond: Amen.* (Cong.– *Amen.)*

---

(1) Cf. *Ecclesiastes* 11:2. (2) Cf. *Psalms* 17:8. (3) Cf. *Nechemiah* 9:31.
(4) Cf. *Psalms* 121:8. (5) Cf. *Deuteronomy* 26:15. (6) *Leviticus* 23:44.

שמונה עשרה – עמידה

Take three steps backward, then three steps forward. Remain standing with the feet together while reciting *Shemoneh Esrei*. Recite it with quiet devotion and without interruption, verbal or otherwise. Although its recitation should not be audible to others, one must pray loudly enough to hear himself.

אֲדֹנָי שְׂפָתַי תִּפְתָּח, וּפִי יַגִּיד תְּהִלָּתֶךָ.[1]

אבות

Bend the knees at בָּרוּךְ; bow at אַתָּה; straighten up at ה׳.

בָּרוּךְ אַתָּה יהוה אֱלֹהֵינוּ וֵאלֹהֵי אֲבוֹתֵינוּ, אֱלֹהֵי אַבְרָהָם, אֱלֹהֵי יִצְחָק, וֵאלֹהֵי יַעֲקֹב, הָאֵל הַגָּדוֹל הַגִּבּוֹר וְהַנּוֹרָא, אֵל עֶלְיוֹן, גּוֹמֵל חֲסָדִים טוֹבִים וְקוֹנֵה הַכֹּל, וְזוֹכֵר חַסְדֵי אָבוֹת, וּמֵבִיא גוֹאֵל לִבְנֵי בְנֵיהֶם, לְמַעַן שְׁמוֹ בְּאַהֲבָה. מֶלֶךְ עוֹזֵר וּמוֹשִׁיעַ וּמָגֵן.

Bend the knees at בָּרוּךְ; bow at אַתָּה; straighten up at ה׳.

בָּרוּךְ אַתָּה יהוה, מָגֵן אַבְרָהָם.

גבורות

אַתָּה גִּבּוֹר לְעוֹלָם אֲדֹנָי, מְחַיֵּה מֵתִים אַתָּה, רַב לְהוֹשִׁיעַ.

מַשִּׁיב הָרְוּחַ וּמוֹרִיד הַגֶּשֶׁם.

מְכַלְכֵּל חַיִּים בְּחֶסֶד, מְחַיֵּה מֵתִים בְּרַחֲמִים רַבִּים, סוֹמֵךְ נוֹפְלִים, וְרוֹפֵא חוֹלִים, וּמַתִּיר אֲסוּרִים, וּמְקַיֵּם אֱמוּנָתוֹ לִישֵׁנֵי עָפָר. מִי כָמְוֹךָ בַּעַל גְּבוּרוֹת, וּמִי דּוֹמֶה לָּךְ, מֶלֶךְ מֵמִית וּמְחַיֶּה וּמַצְמִיחַ יְשׁוּעָה. וְנֶאֱמָן אַתָּה לְהַחֲיוֹת מֵתִים. בָּרוּךְ אַתָּה יהוה, מְחַיֵּה הַמֵּתִים.

קדושת השם

אַתָּה קָדוֹשׁ וְשִׁמְךָ קָדוֹשׁ, וּקְדוֹשִׁים בְּכָל יוֹם יְהַלְּלְוּךָ סֶּלָה. בָּרוּךְ אַתָּה יהוה, הָאֵל הַקָּדוֹשׁ.

קדושת היום

אַתָּה בְחַרְתָּנוּ מִכָּל הָעַמִּים, אָהַבְתָּ אוֹתָנוּ, וְרָצִיתָ בָּנוּ, וְרוֹמַמְתָּנוּ מִכָּל הַלְּשׁוֹנוֹת, וְקִדַּשְׁתָּנוּ בְּמִצְוֹתֶיךָ, וְקֵרַבְתָּנוּ מַלְכֵּנוּ לַעֲבוֹדָתֶךָ, וְשִׁמְךָ הַגָּדוֹל וְהַקָּדוֹשׁ עָלֵינוּ קָרָאתָ.

SHEMONEH ESREI – AMIDAH

Take three steps backward, then three steps forward. Remain standing with the feet together while reciting *Shemoneh Esrei*. Recite it with quiet devotion and without interruption, verbal or otherwise. Although its recitation should not be audible to others, one must pray loudly enough to hear himself.

My Lord, open my lips, that my mouth may declare Your praise.[1]

PATRIARCHS

Bend the knees at *'Blessed'*; bow at *'You'*; straighten up at *'HASHEM.'*

בָּרוּךְ *Blessed are You, HASHEM, our God and the God of our forefathers, God of Abraham, God of Isaac, and God of Jacob; the great, mighty, and awesome God, the supreme God, Who bestows beneficial kindnesses and creates everything, Who recalls the kindnesses of the Patriarchs and brings a Redeemer to their children's children, for His Name's sake, with love. O King, Helper, Savior, and Shield.*

Bend the knees at *'Blessed'*; bow at *'You'*; straighten up at 'HASHEM.'

Blessed are You, HASHEM, Shield of Abraham.

GOD'S MIGHT

אַתָּה *You are eternally mighty, my Lord, the Resuscitator of the dead are You; abundantly able to save.*

He makes the wind blow and He makes the rain descend.

He sustains the living with kindness, resuscitates the dead with abundant mercy, supports the fallen, heals the sick, releases the confined, and maintains His faith to those asleep in the dust. Who is like You, O Master of mighty deeds, and who is comparable to You, O King Who causes death and restores life and makes salvation sprout! And You are faithful to resuscitate the dead. Blessed are You, HASHEM, Who resuscitates the dead.

HOLINESS OF GOD'S NAME

אַתָּה *You are holy and Your Name is holy, and holy ones praise You every day, forever. Blessed are You, HASHEM, the holy God.*

SANCTIFICATION OF THE DAY

אַתָּה בְחַרְתָּנוּ *You have chosen us from all the peoples; You loved us and found favor in us; You exalted us above all the tongues and You sanctified us with Your commandments. You drew us close, our King, to Your service and proclaimed Your great and Holy Name upon us.*

---

(1) *Psalms* 51:17.

On Saturday night add. [If forgotten, do not repeat *Shemoneh Esrei.* See *Laws* §91.]

וַתּוֹדִיעֵנוּ יהוה אֱלֹהֵינוּ אֶת מִשְׁפְּטֵי צִדְקֶךָ, וַתְּלַמְּדֵנוּ לַעֲשׂוֹת (בָּהֶם) חֻקֵּי רְצוֹנֶךָ. וַתִּתֶּן לָנוּ יהוה אֱלֹהֵינוּ מִשְׁפָּטִים יְשָׁרִים וְתוֹרוֹת אֱמֶת חֻקִּים וּמִצְוֹת טוֹבִים. וַתַּנְחִילֵנוּ זְמַנֵּי שָׂשׂוֹן וּמוֹעֲדֵי קֹדֶשׁ וְחַגֵּי נְדָבָה. וַתּוֹרִישֵׁנוּ קְדֻשַּׁת שַׁבָּת וּכְבוֹד מוֹעֵד וַחֲגִיגַת הָרֶגֶל. וַתַּבְדֵּל יהוה אֱלֹהֵינוּ בֵּין קֹדֶשׁ לְחוֹל, בֵּין אוֹר לְחֹשֶׁךְ, בֵּין יִשְׂרָאֵל לָעַמִּים, בֵּין יוֹם הַשְּׁבִיעִי לְשֵׁשֶׁת יְמֵי הַמַּעֲשֶׂה. בֵּין קְדֻשַּׁת שַׁבָּת לִקְדֻשַּׁת יוֹם טוֹב הִבְדַּלְתָּ, וְאֶת יוֹם הַשְּׁבִיעִי מִשֵּׁשֶׁת יְמֵי הַמַּעֲשֶׂה קִדַּשְׁתָּ, הִבְדַּלְתָּ וְקִדַּשְׁתָּ אֶת עַמְּךָ יִשְׂרָאֵל בִּקְדֻשָּׁתֶךָ.

וַתִּתֶּן לָנוּ יהוה אֱלֹהֵינוּ בְּאַהֲבָה מוֹעֲדִים לְשִׂמְחָה חַגִּים וּזְמַנִּים לְשָׂשׂוֹן, אֶת יוֹם הַשְּׁמִינִי חַג הָעֲצֶרֶת הַזֶּה, זְמַן שִׂמְחָתֵנוּ מִקְרָא קֹדֶשׁ, זֵכֶר לִיצִיאַת מִצְרָיִם.

אֱלֹהֵינוּ וֵאלֹהֵי אֲבוֹתֵינוּ, יַעֲלֶה, וְיָבֹא, וְיַגִּיעַ, וְיֵרָאֶה, וְיֵרָצֶה, וְיִשָּׁמַע, וְיִפָּקֵד, וְיִזָּכֵר זִכְרוֹנֵנוּ וּפִקְדוֹנֵנוּ, וְזִכְרוֹן אֲבוֹתֵינוּ, וְזִכְרוֹן מָשִׁיחַ בֶּן דָּוִד עַבְדֶּךָ, וְזִכְרוֹן יְרוּשָׁלַיִם עִיר קָדְשֶׁךָ, וְזִכְרוֹן כָּל עַמְּךָ בֵּית יִשְׂרָאֵל לְפָנֶיךָ, לִפְלֵיטָה לְטוֹבָה לְחֵן וּלְחֶסֶד וּלְרַחֲמִים, לְחַיִּים וּלְשָׁלוֹם בְּיוֹם הַשְּׁמִינִי חַג הָעֲצֶרֶת הַזֶּה. זָכְרֵנוּ יהוה אֱלֹהֵינוּ בּוֹ לְטוֹבָה, וּפָקְדֵנוּ בוֹ לִבְרָכָה, וְהוֹשִׁיעֵנוּ בוֹ לְחַיִּים. וּבִדְבַר יְשׁוּעָה וְרַחֲמִים, חוּס וְחָנֵּנוּ וְרַחֵם עָלֵינוּ וְהוֹשִׁיעֵנוּ, כִּי אֵלֶיךָ עֵינֵינוּ, כִּי אֵל מֶלֶךְ חַנּוּן וְרַחוּם אָתָּה.

וְהַשִּׂיאֵנוּ יהוה אֱלֹהֵינוּ אֶת בִּרְכַּת מוֹעֲדֶיךָ לְחַיִּים וּלְשָׁלוֹם, לְשִׂמְחָה וּלְשָׂשׂוֹן, כַּאֲשֶׁר רָצִיתָ וְאָמַרְתָּ לְבָרְכֵנוּ. קַדְּשֵׁנוּ בְּמִצְוֹתֶיךָ וְתֵן חֶלְקֵנוּ בְּתוֹרָתֶךָ, שַׂבְּעֵנוּ מִטּוּבֶךָ וְשַׂמְּחֵנוּ בִּישׁוּעָתֶךָ, וְטַהֵר לִבֵּנוּ לְעָבְדְּךָ בֶּאֱמֶת, וְהַנְחִילֵנוּ יהוה אֱלֹהֵינוּ בְּשִׂמְחָה וּבְשָׂשׂוֹן מוֹעֲדֵי קָדְשֶׁךָ, וְיִשְׂמְחוּ בְךָ יִשְׂרָאֵל מְקַדְּשֵׁי שְׁמֶךָ. בָּרוּךְ אַתָּה יהוה, מְקַדֵּשׁ יִשְׂרָאֵל וְהַזְּמַנִּים.

On Saturday night add. [If forgotten, do not repeat *Shemoneh Esrei*. See *Laws* §91.]

וַתּוֹדִיעֵנוּ *You made known to us,* HASHEM, *our God, Your righteous ordinances, and You taught us to do the decrees of Your will. You gave us,* HASHEM, *our God, fair laws and true teachings, good decrees and commandments. As a heritage You gave us seasons of joy, appointed festivals of holiness, and free-willed festive offerings. You made us heir to the Sabbath holiness, the appointed festival glory, and festive offering of the pilgrimage. You distinguished, O* HASHEM, *our God, between the sacred and secular, between light and darkness, between Israel and the peoples, between the seventh day and the six days of labor. Between the sanctity of the Sabbath and the sanctity of the holiday You have distinguished, and the seventh day, from among the six days of labor You have sanctified. You have distinguished and You have sanctified Your people Israel with Your holiness.*

וַתִּתֶּן לָנוּ *And You gave us,* HASHEM, *our God, with love, appointed festivals for gladness, Festivals and times for joy, this day of the Shemini Atzeres Festival, the time of our gladness, a holy convocation, a memorial of the Exodus from Egypt.*

אֱלֹהֵינוּ *Our God and God of our forefathers, may there rise, come, reach, be noted, be favored, be heard, be considered, and be remembered — the remembrance and consideration of ourselves; the remembrance of our forefathers; the remembrance of Messiah, son of David, Your servant; the remembrance of Jerusalem, the City of Your Holiness; the remembrance of Your entire people the Family of Israel — before You for deliverance, for goodness, for grace, for kindness, and for compassion, for life, and for peace on this day of the Shemini Atzeres Festival. Remember us on it,* HASHEM, *our God, for goodness, consider us on it for blessing, and help us on it for life. In the matter of salvation and compassion, pity, be gracious and compassionate with us and help us, for our eyes are turned to You, because You are God, the gracious and compassionate King.*[1]

וְהַשִּׂיאֵנוּ *Bestow upon us, O* HASHEM, *our God, the blessing of Your appointed Festivals for life and for peace, for gladness and for joy, as You desired and promised to bless us. Sanctify us with Your commandments and grant us our share in Your Torah; satisfy us from Your goodness and gladden us with Your salvation, and purify our heart to serve You sincerely. And grant us a heritage, O* HASHEM, *our God — with gladness and with joy — the appointed festivals of Your holiness, and may Israel, the sanctifiers of Your Name, rejoice in You. Blessed are You,* HASHEM, *Who sanctifies Israel and the festive seasons.*

---

(1) Cf. *Nechemiah* 9:31.

עבודה

רְצֵה יהוה אֱלֹהֵינוּ בְּעַמְּךָ יִשְׂרָאֵל וּבִתְפִלָּתָם, וְהָשֵׁב אֶת הָעֲבוֹדָה לִדְבִיר בֵּיתֶךָ. וְאִשֵּׁי יִשְׂרָאֵל וּתְפִלָּתָם בְּאַהֲבָה תְקַבֵּל בְּרָצוֹן, וּתְהִי לְרָצוֹן תָּמִיד עֲבוֹדַת יִשְׂרָאֵל עַמֶּךָ.

וְתֶחֱזֶינָה עֵינֵינוּ בְּשׁוּבְךָ לְצִיּוֹן בְּרַחֲמִים. בָּרוּךְ אַתָּה יהוה, הַמַּחֲזִיר שְׁכִינָתוֹ לְצִיּוֹן.

הודאה

Bow at מוֹדִים; straighten up at 'ה.

מוֹדִים אֲנַחְנוּ לָךְ, שָׁאַתָּה הוּא יהוה אֱלֹהֵינוּ וֵאלֹהֵי אֲבוֹתֵינוּ לְעוֹלָם וָעֶד. צוּר חַיֵּינוּ, מָגֵן יִשְׁעֵנוּ אַתָּה הוּא לְדוֹר וָדוֹר. נוֹדֶה לְּךָ וּנְסַפֵּר תְּהִלָּתֶךָ[1] עַל חַיֵּינוּ הַמְּסוּרִים בְּיָדֶךָ, וְעַל נִשְׁמוֹתֵינוּ הַפְּקוּדוֹת לָךְ, וְעַל נִסֶּיךָ שֶׁבְּכָל יוֹם עִמָּנוּ, וְעַל נִפְלְאוֹתֶיךָ וְטוֹבוֹתֶיךָ שֶׁבְּכָל עֵת, עֶרֶב וָבֹקֶר וְצָהֳרָיִם. הַטּוֹב כִּי לֹא כָלוּ רַחֲמֶיךָ, וְהַמְרַחֵם כִּי לֹא תַמּוּ חֲסָדֶיךָ,[2] מֵעוֹלָם קִוִּינוּ לָךְ.

וְעַל כֻּלָּם יִתְבָּרַךְ וְיִתְרוֹמַם שִׁמְךָ מַלְכֵּנוּ תָּמִיד לְעוֹלָם וָעֶד.

Bend the knees at בָּרוּךְ; bow at אַתָּה; straighten up at 'ה.

וְכֹל הַחַיִּים יוֹדוּךָ סֶּלָה, וִיהַלְלוּ אֶת שִׁמְךָ בֶּאֱמֶת, הָאֵל יְשׁוּעָתֵנוּ וְעֶזְרָתֵנוּ סֶלָה. בָּרוּךְ אַתָּה יהוה, הַטּוֹב שִׁמְךָ וּלְךָ נָאֶה לְהוֹדוֹת.

שלום

שָׁלוֹם רָב עַל יִשְׂרָאֵל עַמְּךָ תָּשִׂים לְעוֹלָם, כִּי אַתָּה הוּא מֶלֶךְ אָדוֹן לְכָל הַשָּׁלוֹם. וְטוֹב בְּעֵינֶיךָ לְבָרֵךְ אֶת עַמְּךָ יִשְׂרָאֵל, בְּכָל עֵת וּבְכָל שָׁעָה בִּשְׁלוֹמֶךָ. בָּרוּךְ אַתָּה יהוה, הַמְבָרֵךְ אֶת עַמּוֹ יִשְׂרָאֵל בַּשָּׁלוֹם.

יִהְיוּ לְרָצוֹן אִמְרֵי פִי וְהֶגְיוֹן לִבִּי לְפָנֶיךָ, יהוה צוּרִי וְגֹאֲלִי.[3]

אֱלֹהַי, נְצוֹר לְשׁוֹנִי מֵרָע, וּשְׂפָתַי מִדַּבֵּר מִרְמָה,[4] וְלִמְקַלְלַי נַפְשִׁי תִדּוֹם, וְנַפְשִׁי כֶּעָפָר לַכֹּל תִּהְיֶה. פְּתַח לִבִּי בְּתוֹרָתֶךָ, וּבְמִצְוֹתֶיךָ תִּרְדּוֹף נַפְשִׁי. וְכֹל הַחוֹשְׁבִים עָלַי רָעָה, מְהֵרָה הָפֵר עֲצָתָם וְקַלְקֵל מַחֲשַׁבְתָּם. עֲשֵׂה לְמַעַן שְׁמֶךָ, עֲשֵׂה לְמַעַן יְמִינֶךָ,

TEMPLE SERVICE

רְצֵה *Be favorable, HASHEM, our God, toward Your people Israel and their prayer and restore the service to the Holy of Holies of Your Temple. The fire-offerings of Israel and their prayer accept with love and favor, and may the service of Your people Israel always be favorable to You.*

וְתֶחֱזֶינָה *May our eyes behold Your return to Zion in compassion. Blessed are You, HASHEM, Who restores His Presence to Zion.*

THANKSGIVING [MODIM]

Bow at *'We gratefully thank You'*; straighten up at *'HASHEM.'*

מוֹדִים *We gratefully thank You, for it is You Who are HASHEM, our God and the God of our forefathers for all eternity; Rock of our lives, Shield of our salvation are You from generation to generation. We shall thank You and relate Your praise*[1] *— for our lives, which are committed to Your power and for our souls that are entrusted to You; for Your miracles that are with us every day; and for Your wonders and favors in every season — evening, morning, and afternoon. The Beneficent One, for Your compassions were never exhausted, and the Compassionate One, for Your kindnesses never ended*[2] *— always have we put our hope in You.*

For all these, may Your Name be blessed and exalted, our King, continually forever and ever.

Bend the knees at *'Blessed'*; bow at *'You'*; straighten up at *'HASHEM.'*

Everything alive will gratefully acknowledge You, Selah! and praise Your Name sincerely, O God of our salvation and help, Selah! Blessed are You, HASHEM, Your Name is 'The Beneficent One' and to You it is fitting to give thanks.

PEACE

שָׁלוֹם *Establish abundant peace upon Your people Israel forever, for You are King, Master of all peace. May it be good in Your eyes to bless Your people Israel at every time and every hour with Your peace. Blessed are You, HASHEM, Who blesses His people Israel with peace.*

May the expressions of my mouth and the thoughts of my heart
find favor before You, HASHEM, my Rock and my Redeemer.[3]

אֱלֹהַי *My God, guard my tongue from evil and my lips from speaking deceitfully.*[4] *To those who curse me, let my soul be silent; and let my soul be like dust to everyone. Open my heart to Your Torah, then my soul will pursue Your commandments. As for all those who design evil against me, speedily nullify their counsel and disrupt their design. Act for Your Name's sake; act for Your right hand's sake; act*

(1) Cf. *Psalms* 79:13. (2) Cf. *Lamentations* 3:22. (3) *Psalms* 19:15. (4) Cf. 34:14.

עֲשֵׂה לְמַעַן קְדֻשָּׁתֶךָ, עֲשֵׂה לְמַעַן תּוֹרָתֶךָ. לְמַעַן יֵחָלְצוּן יְדִידֶיךָ, הוֹשִׁיעָה יְמִינְךָ וַעֲנֵנִי.[1] Some recite verses pertaining to their names. See page 1301.

יִהְיוּ לְרָצוֹן אִמְרֵי פִי וְהֶגְיוֹן לִבִּי לְפָנֶיךָ, יהוה צוּרִי וְגֹאֲלִי.[2] עֹשֶׂה שָׁלוֹם בִּמְרוֹמָיו, הוּא יַעֲשֶׂה שָׁלוֹם עָלֵינוּ, וְעַל כָּל יִשְׂרָאֵל. וְאִמְרוּ: אָמֵן.

Bow and take three steps back. Bow left and say . . . עֹשֶׂה, bow right and say . . . הוּא יַעֲשֶׂה; bow forward and say וְעַל כָּל . . . אָמֵן.

יְהִי רָצוֹן מִלְּפָנֶיךָ יהוה אֱלֹהֵינוּ וֵאלֹהֵי אֲבוֹתֵינוּ, שֶׁיִּבָּנֶה בֵּית הַמִּקְדָּשׁ בִּמְהֵרָה בְיָמֵינוּ, וְתֵן חֶלְקֵנוּ בְּתוֹרָתֶךָ. וְשָׁם נַעֲבָדְךָ בְּיִרְאָה, כִּימֵי עוֹלָם וּכְשָׁנִים קַדְמוֹנִיּוֹת. וְעָרְבָה לַיהוה מִנְחַת יְהוּדָה וִירוּשָׁלָיִם, כִּימֵי עוֹלָם וּכְשָׁנִים קַדְמוֹנִיּוֹת.[3]

SHEMONEH ESREI ENDS HERE.

Remain standing in place for a few moments before taking three steps forward.

קדיש שלם

The *chazzan* recites קַדִּישׁ שָׁלֵם.

יִתְגַּדַּל וְיִתְקַדַּשׁ שְׁמֵהּ רַבָּא. (.Cong – אָמֵן.) בְּעָלְמָא דִּי בְרָא כִרְעוּתֵהּ. וְיַמְלִיךְ מַלְכוּתֵהּ, בְּחַיֵּיכוֹן וּבְיוֹמֵיכוֹן וּבְחַיֵּי דְכָל בֵּית יִשְׂרָאֵל, בַּעֲגָלָא וּבִזְמַן קָרִיב. וְאִמְרוּ: אָמֵן.

(.Cong – אָמֵן. יְהֵא שְׁמֵהּ רַבָּא מְבָרַךְ לְעָלַם וּלְעָלְמֵי עָלְמַיָּא.)

יְהֵא שְׁמֵהּ רַבָּא מְבָרַךְ לְעָלַם וּלְעָלְמֵי עָלְמַיָּא.

יִתְבָּרַךְ וְיִשְׁתַּבַּח וְיִתְפָּאַר וְיִתְרוֹמַם וְיִתְנַשֵּׂא וְיִתְהַדָּר וְיִתְעַלֶּה וְיִתְהַלָּל שְׁמֵהּ דְּקֻדְשָׁא בְּרִיךְ הוּא (.Cong – בְּרִיךְ הוּא) – לְעֵלָּא מִן כָּל בִּרְכָתָא וְשִׁירָתָא תֻּשְׁבְּחָתָא וְנֶחֱמָתָא, דַּאֲמִירָן בְּעָלְמָא. וְאִמְרוּ: אָמֵן. (.Cong – אָמֵן.)

(.Cong – קַבֵּל בְּרַחֲמִים וּבְרָצוֹן אֶת תְּפִלָּתֵנוּ.)

תִּתְקַבֵּל צְלוֹתְהוֹן וּבָעוּתְהוֹן דְּכָל בֵּית יִשְׂרָאֵל קֳדָם אֲבוּהוֹן דִּי בִשְׁמַיָּא. וְאִמְרוּ: אָמֵן. (.Cong – אָמֵן.)

(.Cong – יְהִי שֵׁם יהוה מְבֹרָךְ, מֵעַתָּה וְעַד עוֹלָם.[4])

יְהֵא שְׁלָמָא רַבָּא מִן שְׁמַיָּא, וְחַיִּים עָלֵינוּ וְעַל כָּל יִשְׂרָאֵל. וְאִמְרוּ: אָמֵן. (.Cong – אָמֵן.)

(.Cong – עֶזְרִי מֵעִם יהוה, עֹשֵׂה שָׁמַיִם וָאָרֶץ.[5])

Take three steps back. Bow left and say . . . עֹשֶׂה; bow right and say . . . הוּא; bow forward and say וְעַל כָּל . . . אָמֵן. Remain standing in place for a few moments, then take three steps forward.

עֹשֶׂה שָׁלוֹם בִּמְרוֹמָיו, הוּא יַעֲשֶׂה שָׁלוֹם עָלֵינוּ, וְעַל כָּל יִשְׂרָאֵל. וְאִמְרוּ: אָמֵן. (.Cong – אָמֵן.)

IN SOME CONGREGATIONS *KIDDUSH* (P. 1100) IS RECITED AT THIS POINT AND THE CONGREGATION PARTAKES OF REFRESHMENTS BEFORE THE *HAKAFOS*.

for Your sanctity's sake; act for Your Torah's sake. That Your beloved ones may be given rest; let Your right hand save, and respond to me.[1]

Some recite verses pertaining to their names at this point. See page 1301.

May the expressions of my mouth and the thoughts of my heart find favor before You, HASHEM, my Rock and my Redeemer.[2] *He Who makes peace in His heights, may He make peace upon us, and upon all Israel. Now respond: Amen.*

Bow and take three steps back. Bow left and say, *'He Who makes peace . . .'*; bow right and say, *'may He make peace . . .'*; bow forward and say, *'and upon . . . Amen.'*

יְהִי רָצוֹן *May it be Your will, HASHEM, our God and the God of our forefathers, that the Holy Temple be rebuilt, speedily in our days. Grant us our share in Your Torah, and may we serve You there with reverence, as in days of old and in former years. Then the offering of Judah and Jerusalem will be pleasing to HASHEM, as in days of old and in former years.*[3]

SHEMONEH ESREI ENDS HERE.

Remain standing in place for a few moments before taking three steps forward.

FULL KADDISH

The *chazzan* recites the Full *Kaddish.*

יִתְגַּדַּל *May His great Name grow exalted and sanctified* (Cong.– *Amen.*) *in the world that He created as He willed. May He give reign to His kingship in your lifetimes and in your days, and in the lifetimes of the entire Family of Israel, swiftly and soon. Now respond: Amen.*

(Cong.– *Amen. May His great Name be blessed forever and ever.*)

May His great Name be blessed forever and ever.

Blessed, praised, glorified, exalted, extolled, mighty, upraised, and lauded be the Name of the Holy One, Blessed is He (Cong.– *Blessed is He*) — *beyond any blessing and song, praise and consolation that are uttered in the world. Now respond: Amen.* (Cong.– *Amen.*)

(Cong.– *Accept our prayers with mercy and favor.*)

May the prayers and supplications of the entire Family of Israel be accepted before their Father Who is in Heaven. Now respond: Amen. (Cong.– *Amen.*)

(Cong.– *Blessed be the Name of HASHEM, from this time and forever.*[4])

May there be abundant peace from Heaven, and life, upon us and upon all Israel. Now respond: Amen. (Cong.– *Amen.*)

(Cong.– *My help is from HASHEM, Maker of heaven and earth.*[5])

Take three steps back. Bow left and say, *'He Who makes peace . . .'*; bow right and say, *'may He . . .'*; bow forward and say, *'and upon all Israel . . .'* Remain standing in place for a few moments, then take three steps forward.

He Who makes peace in His heights, may He make peace upon us, and upon all Israel. Now respond: Amen. (Cong.– *Amen.*)

IN SOME CONGREGATIONS *KIDDUSH* (P. 1100) IS RECITED AT THIS POINT AND THE CONGREGATION PARTAKES OF REFRESHMENTS BEFORE THE *HAKAFOS.*

---

(1) *Psalms* 60:7;108:7. (2) 19:15. (3) *Malachi* 3:4. (4) *Psalms* 113:2. (5) 121:2.

הקפות לשמחת תורה

Before the Ark is opened for the *Hakafos,* the following selection of verses is recited responsively:

אַתָּה הָרְאֵתָ* לָדַעַת, כִּי יהוה הוּא הָאֱלֹהִים, אֵין עוֹד מִלְּבַדּוֹ.[1]
לְעֹשֵׂה נִפְלָאוֹת גְּדֹלוֹת לְבַדּוֹ,* כִּי לְעוֹלָם חַסְדּוֹ.[2]
אֵין כָּמוֹךָ בָאֱלֹהִים,* אֲדֹנָי, וְאֵין כְּמַעֲשֶׂיךָ.[3]
יְהִי כְבוֹד יהוה לְעוֹלָם, יִשְׂמַח יהוה בְּמַעֲשָׂיו.[4]
יְהִי שֵׁם* יהוה מְבֹרָךְ, מֵעַתָּה וְעַד עוֹלָם.[5]
יְהִי יהוה* אֱלֹהֵינוּ עִמָּנוּ, כַּאֲשֶׁר הָיָה עִם אֲבֹתֵינוּ,
אַל יַעַזְבֵנוּ וְאַל יִטְּשֵׁנוּ.[6]
וְאִמְרוּ, הוֹשִׁיעֵנוּ, אֱלֹהֵי יִשְׁעֵנוּ, וְקַבְּצֵנוּ וְהַצִּילֵנוּ מִן הַגּוֹיִם,*
לְהֹדוֹת לְשֵׁם קָדְשֶׁךָ, לְהִשְׁתַּבֵּחַ בִּתְהִלָּתֶךָ.[7]
יהוה מֶלֶךְ,[8] יהוה מָלָךְ,[9] יהוה יִמְלֹךְ לְעוֹלָם וָעֶד.[10]
יהוה עֹז לְעַמּוֹ יִתֵּן, יהוה יְבָרֵךְ אֶת עַמּוֹ בַשָּׁלוֹם.*[11]
וְיִהְיוּ נָא אֲמָרֵינוּ לְרָצוֹן,* לִפְנֵי אֲדוֹן כֹּל.[12]

The Ark is opened and the responsive recitation continues:

וַיְהִי בִּנְסֹעַ הָאָרֹן,* וַיֹּאמֶר מֹשֶׁה, קוּמָה יהוה, וְיָפֻצוּ אֹיְבֶיךָ,
וְיָנֻסוּ מְשַׂנְאֶיךָ מִפָּנֶיךָ.[13]
קוּמָה יהוה לִמְנוּחָתֶךָ,* אַתָּה וַאֲרוֹן עֻזֶּךָ.

הקפות לשמחת תורה / HAKAFOS FOR SIMCHAS TORAH

אַתָּה הָרְאֵתָ – *You have been shown.* Before the Torah Scrolls are removed from the Ark for the *Hakafos,* the congregation recites this collection of verses. Since it is the introduction to the *Hakafos,* it is recited in a particularly joyous and festive manner. In most congregations, the honor of reciting אַתָּה הָרְאֵתָ is auctioned off, with the proceeds going to the synagogue or some other charitable cause. Often, the winner of the auction will honor the rabbi or some other prominent member of the congregation, or many different persons, with chanting the verses aloud.

Essentially, this collection consists of all the verses that are recited when the Torah scrolls are removed from the Ark for the regular Sabbath or Festival Torah reading. In honor of the *Hakafos,* however, the regular service is augmented with many additional verses. The general themes of this selection are praise of God's greatness and plea for the rebuilding of Zion and Jerusalem.

הָרְאֵתָ – *You have been shown.* When God gave Israel the Torah, He revealed to them all the celestial beings and forces and He let them understand all the powers of nature. After all this, they could see clearly that there is only one Creator and one All-Powerful Being. Thus, the verse states, *'You have been shown to know'* that God is One and incomparable.

לְבַדּוֹ – *Alone.* Although God has delegated some of His power to intermediaries, they are not His equals or His partners. The idolaters who worship these forces imagine that they have independent strength, but in reality they are merely God's agent without any power to act on their own.

כִּי לְעוֹלָם חַסְדּוֹ – *For His kindness endures forever.* The good works accomplished by intermediaries are of limited duration, because the agents themselves are finite. But God's works endure forever.

בָאֱלֹהִים – *Among the gods.* This refers to the seemingly godlike intermediaries, such as the angels and the planets, mentioned in the preceding verse.

יְהִי כְבוֹד . . . יְהִי שֵׁם . . . – *May the glory . . . Blessed be the Name . . .* Since His works endure forever, it is fitting that we glorify Him and recite His blessings at all times, and that we rejoice in His works eternally.

יְהִי ה' – *May HASHEM . . . be.* Having declared His greatness we pray that He not forsake us.

THE HAKAFAH-CIRCUITS OF SIMCHAS TORAH

Before the Ark is opened for the *Hakafos,* the following selection of verses is recited responsively:

אַתָּה הָרְאֵתָ *You have been shown* to know, that HASHEM, He is the God, there is none beside Him.*[1]

To Him Who alone performs great wonders, for His kindness endures forever.*[2]*

There is none like You among the gods, my Lord, and there is nothing like Your works.*[3]

May the glory of HASHEM endure forever, let HASHEM rejoice in His works.[4]

Blessed be the Name of HASHEM, from this time and forever.*[5]

May HASHEM, our God, be with us, as He was with our forefathers, may He not forsake us nor cast us off.*[6]

Say: 'Save us, O God of our salvation, gather us and rescue us from the nations, to thank Your Holy Name and to glory in Your praise.'*[7]

HASHEM reigns,[8] *HASHEM has reigned,*[9] *HASHEM shall reign for all eternity.*[10]

HASHEM will give might to His people, HASHEM will bless His people with peace.[11]*

May our words find favor, we pray, before the Lord of everything.*[12]

The Ark is opened and the responsive recitation continues:

When the Ark would travel, Moses would say, 'Arise, HASHEM, and let Your foes be scattered; let those who hate You flee from You.'*[13]

Arise, HASHEM, to Your resting place, You and the Ark of Your strength.*

(1) *Deuteronomy* 4:35. (2) *Psalms* 136:4. (3) 86:8. (4) 104:31. (5) 113:2. (6) *I Kings* 8:57. (7) *I Chronicles* 16:35. (8) *Psalms* 10:16. (9) 93:1 et al. (10) *Exodus* 15:18. (11) *Psalms* 29:11. (12) Cf. 19:15. (13) *Numbers* 10:35.

Just as His Presence constantly accompanied our forefathers during their forty years in the Wilderness, so may He always be with us. This verse was recited by King Solomon at the dedication of the Temple; Solomon asked that the Divine Presence never leave the *Beis HaMikdash.*

וְהַצִּילֵנוּ מִן הַגּוֹיִם – *And rescue us from the nations.* Having alluded to the *Beis HaMikdash,* we pray for our release from exile, that we may rebuild the Temple. There we will thank Him and glory in His praise.

בַשָּׁלוֹם – *With peace.* The last *mishnah* of the Talmud states: Rabbi Shimon ben Chalafta said, 'God could find no vessel that could contain blessings better than peace; as it says, *HASHEM . . . will bless His people with peace'* (Uktzin 3:12). This concept is so vital and precious that the word **שָׁלוֹם**, *peace,* is the concluding word of the Oral Torah (ibid.), the *Shemoneh Esrei* blessings, the Priestly Blessings and *Bircas HaMazon.*

לְרָצוֹן – *(To) find favor.* Just as we conclude the *Shemoneh Esrei* blessings with the word **שָׁלוֹם**, *peace,* followed by a short prayer that our words find favor before God, so do our introductory verses to the *Hakafos* close with **שָׁלוֹם**, followed by a plea that our words find favor. After *Shemoneh Esrei,* recited by each individual, we use the singular (**אִמְרֵי פִי**, *the words of my mouth*). Here, however, where the verses are recited in unison, we use the plural (**אֲמָרֵינוּ**, *our words*).

וַיְהִי בִּנְסֹעַ הָאָרֹן – *When the Ark would travel.* As we open the Ark, we pray, as Moses did when the Ark traveled through the Wilderness towards *Eretz Yisrael,* that the enemies who would prevent us from entering the Land and from studying the Torah be dispersed and scattered.

קוּמָה ה׳ לִמְנוּחָתֶךָ – *Arise, HASHEM, to Your resting place.* The next three verses, by David, were repeated by Solomon, with minor variations, when he dedicated the Temple (*II Chroni-*

כֹּהֲנֶיךָ יִלְבְּשׁוּ צֶדֶק, וַחֲסִידֶיךָ יְרַנֵּנוּ.
בַּעֲבוּר דָּוִד עַבְדֶּךָ, אַל תָּשֵׁב פְּנֵי מְשִׁיחֶךָ.[1]
וְאָמַר בַּיּוֹם הַהוּא, הִנֵּה אֱלֹהֵינוּ זֶה, קִוִּינוּ לוֹ וְיוֹשִׁיעֵנוּ,
זֶה יהוה קִוִּינוּ לוֹ, נָגִילָה וְנִשְׂמְחָה בִּישׁוּעָתוֹ.[2]
מַלְכוּתְךָ מַלְכוּת כָּל עֹלָמִים, וּמֶמְשַׁלְתְּךָ בְּכָל דּוֹר וָדֹר.[3]
כִּי מִצִּיּוֹן תֵּצֵא תוֹרָה,* וּדְבַר יהוה מִירוּשָׁלָיִם.[4]

All, in unison:

אַב הָרַחֲמִים, הֵיטִיבָה בִרְצוֹנְךָ אֶת צִיּוֹן,* תִּבְנֶה חוֹמוֹת יְרוּשָׁלָיִם.[5] כִּי בְךָ לְבַד בָּטָחְנוּ, מֶלֶךְ אֵל רָם וְנִשָּׂא, אֲדוֹן עוֹלָמִים.

All the Torah scrolls are removed from the Ark and members of the congregation are given the honor of carrying them during the procession. In some congregations, a lit candle, symbolizing the light of Torah, is placed in the Ark while it is empty.

Some recite a kabbalistic prayer (p.1272) as the Torah Scrolls are removed from the Ark.

FIRST *HAKAFAH*-CIRCUIT

As the Torah Scrolls are carried around the *bimah,* each of the following verses is recited by the *chazzan* or *Hakafah* leader and is then repeated by the congregation:

אָנָּא יהוה,* הוֹשִׁיעָה נָּא.
אָנָּא יהוה, הַצְלִיחָה נָא.[6]
אָנָּא יהוה, עֲנֵנוּ בְיוֹם קָרְאֵנוּ.[7]
אֱלֹהֵי הָרוּחוֹת,*[8] הוֹשִׁיעָה נָּא.
בּוֹחֵן לְבָבוֹת,[9] הַצְלִיחָה נָא.
גּוֹאֵל חָזָק,[10] עֲנֵנוּ בְיוֹם קָרְאֵנוּ.

---

cles 6:41-42). The first verse asks that God establish His resting place among Israel. The next verse refers to the priests, who dedicate themselves to God's service, and the Levites, whose song accompanies the Temple ritual. Finally, David prayed that the site chosen for the Temple — a choice that was made by David and the prophet Nathan — not be spurned, but that it remain eternally holy. With these words, God was invited, so to speak, to move from His temporary abode in the *Mishkan* to His permanent resting place in the *Beis HaMikdash.*

Our recitation of these verses indicates our desire to celebrate Simchas Torah in the rebuilt Temple. There we will recognize the Divine Presence and declare, '*Behold — this our God . . .*' This also fulfills: *I shall bring Jerusalem to mind at the onset of my rejoicing* (*Psalms* 137:6).

כִּי מִצִּיּוֹן תֵּצֵא תוֹרָה — *For from Zion the Torah will come forth.* Having expressed our hopes for God's redemption, we explain that Jerusalem is the primary source of the Torah's most profound wisdom.

הֵיטִיבָה בִרְצוֹנְךָ אֶת צִיּוֹן — *Do good to Zion according to Your will.* Only in God's chosen Sanctuary can study of the Torah and rejoicing at the completion of its annual reading attain their greatest heights.

⊷ אָנָּא ה׳ — *Please,* HASHEM. Each of the *Hakafos* starts with three Scriptural verses beginning אָנָּא ה׳, *Please,* HASHEM. This signifies that even while we celebrate joyously with the Torah, we nevertheless remember that we are in exile. These three verses contain the prayers *save . . . bring success . . .* and *answer . . .* These same prayers are repeated in the next three verses — and in each of the seven *Hakafos* — but they are introduced by different titles for God, in the order of the *aleph-beis,* i.e., אֱלֹהֵי הָרוּחוֹת הוֹשִׁיעָה נָּא, *God of the spirits, save now,* and so on.

Let Your priests be clothed in righteousness,
*and Your devout ones will sing joyously.**
For the sake of David, Your servant,
turn not away the face of Your anointed.[1]
He shall say on that day, 'Behold! — this is our God,
we hoped to Him and He saved us; this is HASHEM to whom we hoped,
let us exult and be glad in His salvation.'[2]
Your kingdom is a kingdom spanning all eternities,
and Your dominion is throughout every generation.[3]
*For from Zion the Torah will come forth,**
and the word of HASHEM from Jerusalem.[4]

All, in unison:

אַב הָרַחֲמִים *Father of compassion, do good to Zion according to Your will;* rebuild the walls of Jerusalem.*[5] *For we trust in You alone, O King, God, exalted and uplifted, Master of worlds.*

All the Torah scrolls are removed from the Ark and members of the congregation are given the honor of carrying them during the procession. In some congregations, a lit candle, symbolizing the light of Torah, is placed in the Ark while it is empty.

Some recite a kabbalistic prayer (p. 1272) as the Torah Scrolls are removed from the Ark.

FIRST *HAKAFAH*-CIRCUIT

As the Torah Scrolls are carried around the *bimah,* each of the following verses is recited by the *chazzan* or *Hakafah* leader and is then repeated by the congregation:

Please, HASHEM, save now!*
Please, HASHEM, bring success now![6]
Please, HASHEM, answer us on the day we call.[7]
God of the spirits,[8]** save now!*
Tester of hearts,[9] *bring success now!*
O Powerful Redeemer,[10] *answer us on the day we call!*

(1) *Psalms* 132:8-10. (2) *Isaiah* 25:9. (3) *Psalms* 145:13. (4) *Isaiah* 2:3; *Micah* 4:2. (5) *Psalms* 51:20. (6) 118:25. (7) Cf. 20:10. (8) *Numbers* 27:16. (9) Cf. *Psalms* 7:10. (10) Cf. *Jeremiah* 50:34.

The *piyut* was composed anonymously, probably before the fourteenth century, and was recited as the Torah Scrolls were brought to the *bimah.* Some scholars surmise that it was originally intended as a *hoshana* prayer. Most of its stanzas are examples of the Talmudic dictum (*Megillah* 31a): 'Wherever you find God's greatness, there you find His humility.' Thus, we find His awesome majesty contrasted with His care and protection of the lowly.

In many congregations these verses are followed by verses that declare God's Oneness, His eternality, and His choice of Israel to receive His Torah and His blessings of peace.

These verses are recited loudly and responsively by the *chazzan* and congregation. Then, after each of the seven *Hakafos,* many individuals recite series of verses that allude to the respective *Hakafos.* Each series comprises verses taken from five sources:
(a) *Psalms* 18:8-11, which enumerates seven benefits of Torah study;
(b) *Psalms* 29, which contains the expression קוֹל ה׳, *the voice of HASHEM,* seven times;
(c) *Psalms* 67, which contains seven verses (excluding the introductory verse);
(d) the mystic prayer אָנָּא בְּכֹחַ, *We beg You, with the strength,* which is composed of seven stanzas; and
(e) the verses recited after each of the Hoshana Rabbah *Hakafos.*

In most *machzorim* these verses are followed by a *piyut* which is either unique to Simchas Torah or borrowed from elsewhere in the prayers.

Each *Hakafah's* liturgy concludes with a reference to the Patriarch associated with it and a kabbalistic prayer that alludes to that Patriarch and to the relevant *sefirah*-emanation.

FIRST HAKAFAH

⊸§ אֱלֹהֵי הָרוּחוֹת – *God of the spirits.* Moses used

In some congregations the responsive recitation continues:

שְׁמַע יִשְׂרָאֵל, יהוה אֱלֹהֵינוּ יהוה אֶחָד.[1]

יהוה מֶלֶךְ,[2] יהוה מָלָךְ,[3] יהוה יִמְלֹךְ לְעוֹלָם וָעֶד.[4]

יהוה מֶלֶךְ, יהוה מָלָךְ, יהוה יִמְלֹךְ לְעוֹלָם וָעֶד.

יהוה עֹז לְעַמּוֹ יִתֵּן, יהוה יְבָרֵךְ אֶת עַמּוֹ בַשָּׁלוֹם.[5]

Some individuals recite all or some of the following paragraphs:

תּוֹרַת יהוה תְּמִימָה,* מְשִׁיבַת נָפֶשׁ.[6] מִזְמוֹר לְדָוִד, הָבוּ לַיהוה בְּנֵי אֵלִים,* הָבוּ לַיהוה כָּבוֹד וָעֹז. הָבוּ לַיהוה כְּבוֹד שְׁמוֹ, הִשְׁתַּחֲווּ לַיהוה בְּהַדְרַת קֹדֶשׁ. קוֹל יהוה עַל הַמָּיִם. אֵל הַכָּבוֹד הִרְעִים, יהוה עַל מַיִם רַבִּים.[7] לַמְנַצֵּחַ בִּנְגִינֹת מִזְמוֹר שִׁיר. אֱלֹהִים יְחָנֵּנוּ וִיבָרְכֵנוּ, יָאֵר פָּנָיו אִתָּנוּ* סֶלָה.[8] אָנָּא, בְּכֹחַ גְּדֻלַּת יְמִינְךָ, תַּתִּיר צְרוּרָה. כִּי אָמַרְתִּי, עוֹלָם חֶסֶד יִבָּנֶה.[9]

יְדִיד נֶפֶשׁ* אָב הָרַחֲמָן, מְשׁוֹךְ עַבְדְּךָ* אֶל רְצוֹנֶךָ, יָרוּץ עַבְדְּךָ כְּמוֹ אַיָּל, יִשְׁתַּחֲוֶה אֶל מוּל הֲדָרֶךָ, יֶעֱרַב לוֹ יְדִידוֹתֶיךָ, מִנֹּפֶת צוּף* וְכָל טָעַם.

הָדוּר נָאֶה זִיו הָעוֹלָם, נַפְשִׁי חוֹלַת אַהֲבָתֶךָ,* אָנָּא אֵל נָא רְפָא נָא לָהּ, בְּהַרְאוֹת לָהּ נֹעַם זִיוֶךָ, אָז תִּתְחַזֵּק וְתִתְרַפֵּא,* וְהָיְתָה לָהּ שִׂמְחַת עוֹלָם.

וָתִיק יֶהֱמוּ נָא רַחֲמֶיךָ, וְחוּסָה נָּא עַל בֵּן אֲהוּבֶךָ, כִּי זֶה כַּמָּה נִכְסֹף נִכְסַפְתִּי, לִרְאוֹת מְהֵרָה בְּתִפְאֶרֶת עֻזֶּךָ, אֵלֶּה חָמְדָה לִבִּי, וְחוּסָה נָּא וְאַל תִּתְעַלָּם.

הִגָּלֶה נָּא וּפְרוֹשׂ חֲבִיבִי עָלַי, אֶת סֻכַּת שְׁלוֹמֶךָ, תָּאִיר אֶרֶץ מִכְּבוֹדֶךָ, נָגִילָה וְנִשְׂמְחָה בָּךְ. מַהֵר אֱהֹב* כִּי בָא מוֹעֵד, וְחָנֵּנוּ כִּימֵי עוֹלָם.

שְׁכִינָה הַקְּדוֹשָׁה בְּתוֹכֵנוּ, וְכוּתֵהּ **דְּאַבְרָהָם** עִמָּנוּ,
וְשָׁם נִשְׂמַח כֻּלָּנוּ, בְּבוֹא לְצִיּוֹן בְּרִנָּה.
רַחֲמָנָא אִדְכַּר לָן זְכוּתֵהּ **דְּאַבְרָהָם** רְחִימָא.

Some recite a kabbalistic prayer at this point (see p. 1273).

---

this title (*Numbers* 27:16), which means that God knows each person's *spirit* and tests every heart to determine one's innermost thoughts. Man, however, cannot judge his fellow by anything other than external actions.

תּוֹרַת ה׳ תְּמִימָה — *The Torah of* HASHEM *is perfect.* When is the Torah of HASHEM perfect? When it comes from the mouths of those who are perfect [i.e., when it is studied sincerely and unselfishly] (*Midrash Shocher Tov*).

בְּנֵי אֵלִים — *Sons of the powerful.* I.e., the descendants of Abraham, Isaac, and Jacob, the *powerful* men of the spirit.

יָאֵר פָּנָיו אִתָּנוּ — *May He illuminate His countenance with us.* May God illuminate our minds so that we may perceive the wondrous lessons of the Torah.

§ יְדִיד נֶפֶשׁ — *Beloved of the soul.* The composer of this *piyut* is R' Eliezer Azikri, one of the great kabbalists and halachists of the sixteenth century in *Eretz Yisrael*, whose major work was *Sefer Charedim.* A central theme of his moral and liturgical writings was the intense love one must feel for God. This theme is readily apparent

In some congregations the responsive recitation continues:

Hear, O Israel: HASHEM is our God, HASHEM the One and Only.[1]
HASHEM reigns,[2] *HASHEM has reigned,*[3] *HASHEM shall reign for all eternity.*[4]
HASHEM reigns, HASHEM has reigned, HASHEM shall reign for all eternity.
HASHEM will give might to His people,
HASHEM will bless His people with peace.[5]

Some individuals recite all or some of the following paragraphs:

תּוֹרַת *The Torah of HASHEM is perfect,* restoring the soul.*[6] *A psalm of David. Render unto HASHEM, you sons of the powerful,* render unto HASHEM honor and might. Render unto HASHEM honor worthy of His Name; prostrate yourselves before HASHEM in His intensely holy place. The voice of HASHEM is upon the waters, the God of Glory thunders, HASHEM is upon vast waters.*[7] *For the conductor, upon Neginos, a psalm, a song. May God favor us and bless us, may He illuminate His countenance with us,* Selah.*[8] *We beg you! With the strength of Your right hand's greatness, untie the bundled sins. For I have said: The world shall be built with kindness.*[9]

יְדִיד נֶפֶשׁ *Beloved of the soul,* Compassionate Father, draw Your servant* to Your will. Then Your servant will hurry like a hart to bow before Your majesty. To him Your friendship will be sweeter than the dripping of the honeycomb* and any taste.*

ה *Majestic, Beautiful, Radiance of the universe — my soul pines for Your love.* Please, O God, heal her now by showing her the pleasantness of Your radiance. Then she will be strengthened and healed,* and eternal gladness will be hers.*

ו *All-worthy One — may Your mercy be aroused and please take pity on the son of Your beloved, because it is so very long that I have yearned intensely to see the splendor of Your strength. Only these my heart desired, so please take pity and do not conceal Yourself.*

ה *Please be revealed and spread upon me, my Beloved, the shelter of Your peace. Illuminate the world with Your glory that we may rejoice and be glad with You. Hasten, show love,* for the time has come, and show us grace as in days of old.*

The holy Shechinah is among us, the merit of **Abraham** *is with us;*
May we all rejoice there upon arriving at Zion with glad song.
O Merciful One, remember for our sake the merit of beloved **Abraham.**

Some recite a kabbalistic prayer at this point (see p. 1273).

(1) *Deuteronomy* 6:4. (2) *Psalms* 10:16. (3) 93:1 et al. (4) *Exodus* 15:18.
(5) *Psalms* 29:11. (6) 19:8. (7) 29:1-3. (8) 67:1-2. (9) 89:3.

in the *piyut*. The acrostic of the four verses forms the Four-Letter Divine Name.

מְשֹׁךְ עַבְדְּךָ — *Draw Your servant.* We plead with God to take the first step toward bringing us closer to His Will. We assure Him that if He takes such an initiative, then we will continue with the alacrity of a swift hart.

יֶעֱרַב לוֹ יְדִידוֹתֶיךָ מִנֹּפֶת צוּף — *To him Your friendship will be sweeter than the dripping of the honeycomb.* To the human taste, honey is the sweetest of delicacies. Nevertheless, its taste lingers for only a brief while, and too much of it can cause discomfort. God's friendship, however, endures forever and it becomes more beneficial the more one draws closer to Him (*Radak* to *Psalms* 19:11).

נַפְשִׁי חוֹלַת אַהֲבָתֶךָ — *My soul pines for Your love.* The soul that yearns for God's closeness grows lovesick, much like a person who is denied the closeness of his beloved.

אָז תִּתְחַזֵּק וְתִתְרַפֵּא — *Then she will be strengthened and healed.* Generally, a patient is healed first, and later regains his strength. In this case, however, the illness came about only because the spiritual level of the soul was weakened. Once that holiness is strengthened again, the healing will come naturally (*Ahavas Shalom*).

מַהֵר אֱהֹב — *Hasten, show love.* That God retains His love for Israel is unquestioned, but in the length and severity of the exile, this love is

SECOND *HAKAFAH*-CIRCUIT

אָנָּא יהוה, הוֹשִׁיעָה נָּא.
אָנָּא יהוה, הַצְלִיחָה נָא.
אָנָּא יהוה, עֲנֵנוּ בְיוֹם קָרְאֵנוּ.

דּוֹבֵר צְדָקוֹת, הוֹשִׁיעָה נָּא.
הָדוּר בִּלְבוּשׁוֹ,[1] הַצְלִיחָה נָא.
וָתִיק וְחָסִיד, עֲנֵנוּ בְיוֹם קָרְאֵנוּ.

In some congregations the responsive recitation continues:

שְׁמַע יִשְׂרָאֵל, יהוה אֱלֹהֵינוּ יהוה אֶחָד.
יהוה מֶלֶךְ, יהוה מָלָךְ, יהוה יִמְלֹךְ לְעוֹלָם וָעֶד.
יהוה מֶלֶךְ, יהוה מָלָךְ, יהוה יִמְלֹךְ לְעוֹלָם וָעֶד.
יהוה עֹז לְעַמּוֹ יִתֵּן, יהוה יְבָרֵךְ אֶת עַמּוֹ בַשָּׁלוֹם.

Some individuals recite all or some of the following paragraphs:

עֵדוּת יהוה נֶאֱמָנָה, מַחְכִּימַת פֶּתִי.[2] קוֹל יהוה, בַּכֹּחַ.[3] לָדַעַת בָּאָרֶץ דַּרְכֶּךָ, בְּכָל גּוֹיִם יְשׁוּעָתֶךָ.[4] קַבֵּל רִנַּת עַמְּךָ, שַׂגְּבֵנוּ, טַהֲרֵנוּ, נוֹרָא. לְךָ זְרוֹעַ עִם גְּבוּרָה, תָּעֹז יָדְךָ, תָּרוּם יְמִינֶךָ.[5]

אֵל מִסְתַּתֵּר* בְּשַׁפְרִיר חֶבְיוֹן, הַשֵּׂכֶל הַנֶּעְלָם מִכָּל רַעְיוֹן,
עִלַּת הָעִלּוֹת* מֻכְתָּר בְּכֶתֶר עֶלְיוֹן,* כֶּתֶר יִתְּנוּ לְךָ יהוה.
בְּרֵאשִׁית תּוֹרָתְךָ הַקְּדוּמָה, רְשׁוּמָה חָכְמָתְךָ הַסְּתוּמָה,
מֵאַיִן תִּמָּצֵא וְהִיא נֶעְלָמָה, רֵאשִׁית חָכְמָה יִרְאַת יהוה.*[6]
רְחוֹבוֹת הַנָּהָר נַחֲלֵי אֱמוּנָה, מַיִם עֲמוּקִים יִדְלֵם אִישׁ תְּבוּנָה,
תּוֹצְאוֹתֶיהָ חֲמִשִּׁים שַׁעֲרֵי בִינָה,* אֱמוּנִים נֹצֵר יהוה.[7]

---

barely perceptible. Therefore, we ask God to make His love manifest.

SECOND HAKAFAH

This stanza is based on the Sages' interpretation of *Isaiah* 63:1, which says that "someone" with bloodied clothes will come from Edom. In a manner common to prophecy, it is God Who is metaphorically portrayed as a warrior who becomes soiled by the blood of his slain foe.

The Jews will then ask, 'Who is this Whose clothes are stained with blood? He has always been majestic in His garb!'

And God will reply, 'It is I, the Speaker of righteousness, abundantly able to save.'

When the proper time comes, God will avenge Himself against Edom for its outrages against Israel. However, as the Sages teach, no nation can be defeated on earth until its heavenly guardian angel is stripped of his power above. Consequently, when the End of Days comes, God will destroy the angel of Edom, which is also the angel of evil.

אֵל מִסְתַּתֵּר – *God conceals Himself.* This mystical *piyut* was composed by *Avraham Maimin* whose name is formed by the acrostic. He lived from 5282-5330 (1522-1570 C.E.) and was a student of the famed Kabbalist Rabbi Moshe Kordevero. The eleven stanzas of this *zemer* are often sung during the third meal of the Sabbath. For the *Hakafos,* five stanzas are recited for the second *Hakafah* and six for the third.

מִסְתַּתֵּר – *Conceals Himself.* Man can have no conception of God Himself, for His true Being is beyond human intelligence. We can know Him only by the way He reveals His behavior to us: with mercy, power, judgment, and so on. Given

SECOND *HAKAFAH*-CIRCUIT

Please, HASHEM, save now!
Please, HASHEM, bring success now!
Please, HASHEM, answer us on the day we call.

Speaker of righteousness, save now!
Majestic One in His garb,[1] bring success now!
Faithful and Devout One, answer us on the day we call!

In some congregations the responsive recitation continues:

Hear, O Israel: HASHEM is our God, HASHEM the One and Only.
HASHEM reigns, HASHEM has reigned, HASHEM shall reign for all eternity.
HASHEM reigns, HASHEM has reigned, HASHEM shall reign for all eternity.
HASHEM will give might to His people, HASHEM will bless His people with peace.

Some individuals recite all or some of the following paragraphs:

עֵדוּת *The testimony of HASHEM is trustworthy, making the simple one wise.[2] The voice of HASHEM is in power![3] To make known Your way on earth, among all the nations Your salvation.[4] Accept the prayer of Your nation; strengthen us, purify us, O awesome One. Yours is the arm with strength, show us the power of Your hand, raise high Your right hand.[5]*

א *God conceals Himself* in the beauty of secrecy,*
the wisdom hidden from all conception,
Primary Cause, crowned with the most exalted crown* —*
They give You a crown, O HASHEM!

ב *In the beginning there was Your pre-existing Torah*
Inscribed with Your mysterious wisdom.
From the Invisible One it derives, but it is hidden —
*The source of wisdom is awe of HASHEM![6]**

ר *Like a broad flowing river, like faithful streams,*
deep waters drawn by the most understanding man.
Its outflows are the fifty gates of understanding —*
Faithful ones are guarded by HASHEM[7]

(1) Cf. *Isaiah* 63:1. (2) *Psalms* 19:8. (3) 29:4. (4) 67:3. (5) *Psalms* 89:14. (6) 111:10. (7) 31:24.

that we are incapable of perceiving God directly, these manifestations can come to us only through intermediaries. In kabbalistic literature, these intermediaries are called *Sefiros,* generally translated *emanations.*

Although many *Sefiros*-related *mitzvos* follow a cycle of seven [e.g., the seven *ushpizin/* guests of the seven days of Succos; the seven *Hakafah/*circuits of Hoshana Rabbah; the seven *Hakafos* of Simchas Torah], there are actually ten *Sefiros.* However, the first three are considered to be on a higher plane than the remaining seven. Thus, the seven are often viewed independently of the others. This *piyut* speaks of all ten *Sefiros* respectively.

עִלַּת הָעִלּוֹת – *Primary Cause.* Human intelligence finds causes for everything that happens, but the fact is that it is God Who makes the 'causes' happen.

בְּכֶתֶר עֶלְיוֹן – *With the most exalted crown.* In the terminology of the *Sefiros,* כֶּתֶר, *the Crown,* is first and is above all the others. Like a crown that rests above the head, the כֶּתֶר is higher than the others.

רֵאשִׁית חָכְמָה יִרְאַת ה׳ – *The source* [lit., *beginning*] *of wisdom is awe of HASHEM.* The person who feels *awe of HASHEM* recognizes that he is completely insignificant in relation to God. He is ready to negate himself to God's will — as a result he is fit to receive Divine wisdom. חָכְמָה, *Wisdom,* is the second *Sefirah.*

חֲמִשִּׁים שַׁעֲרֵי בִינָה – *The fifty gates of understanding.* The third of the *Sefiros* is בִּינָה, *Understanding.* A person begins with חָכְמָה, *wisdom,* the inspiration that is the father of knowledge. But that first spark of knowledge must be developed and applied properly — that is *understanding.*

הָאֵל הַגָּדוֹל עֵינֵי כֹל נֶגְדֶּךָ, רַב חֶסֶד גָּדוֹל עַל הַשָּׁמַיִם חַסְדֶּךָ,
אֱלֹהֵי אַבְרָהָם* זְכֹר לְעַבְדֶּךָ, חַסְדֵי יהוה אַזְכִּיר תְּהִלּוֹת יהוה.[1]
מָרוֹם נֶאְדָּר בְּכֹחַ וּגְבוּרָה, מוֹצִיא אוֹרָה מֵאֵין תְּמוּרָה,
פַּחַד יִצְחָק מִשְׁפָּטֵנוּ הָאִירָה, אַתָּה גִבּוֹר* לְעוֹלָם יהוה.

שְׁכִינָה הַקְּדוֹשָׁה בְּתוֹכֵנוּ, זְכוּתֵהּ דַּעֲקֵדַת **יִצְחָק** עִמָּנוּ,
וְשָׁם נִשְׂמַח כֻּלָּנוּ, בְּבוֹא לְצִיּוֹן בְּרִנָּה.
רַחֲמָנָא אִדְכַּר לָן זְכוּתֵהּ **דְּיִצְחָק** עֲקֵדְתָּא.

Some recite a kabbalistic prayer at this point (p. 1273).

THIRD *HAKAFAH*-CIRCUIT

אָנָּא יהוה, הוֹשִׁיעָה נָּא
אָנָּא יהוה, הַצְלִיחָה נָא.
אָנָּא יהוה, עֲנֵנוּ בְיוֹם קָרְאֵנוּ.

זַךְ וְיָשָׁר, הוֹשִׁיעָה נָּא.
חוֹמֵל דַּלִּים, הַצְלִיחָה נָא.
טוֹב וּמֵטִיב,[2] עֲנֵנוּ בְיוֹם קָרְאֵנוּ.

In some congregations the responsive recitation continues:

שְׁמַע יִשְׂרָאֵל, יהוה אֱלֹהֵינוּ יהוה אֶחָד.
יהוה מֶלֶךְ, יהוה מָלָךְ, יהוה יִמְלֹךְ לְעוֹלָם וָעֶד.
יהוה מֶלֶךְ, יהוה מָלָךְ, יהוה יִמְלֹךְ לְעוֹלָם וָעֶד.
יהוה עֹז לְעַמּוֹ יִתֵּן, יהוה יְבָרֵךְ אֶת עַמּוֹ בַשָּׁלוֹם.

Some individuals recite all or some of the following paragraphs:

פִּקּוּדֵי יהוה יְשָׁרִים, מְשַׂמְּחֵי לֵב.[3] קוֹל יהוה, בֶּהָדָר.[4] יוֹדְוּךָ עַמִּים אֱלֹהִים, יוֹדְוּךָ עַמִּים כֻּלָּם.[5] נָא גִּבּוֹר, דּוֹרְשֵׁי יִחוּדָךְ, כְּבָבַת שָׁמְרֵם. תִּתֵּן אֱמֶת לְיַעֲקֹב, חֶסֶד לְאַבְרָהָם.[6]

מִי אֵל כָּמְוֹךָ עוֹשֶׂה גְדוֹלוֹת, אֲבִיר יַעֲקֹב נוֹרָא תְהִלּוֹת,
תִּפְאֶרֶת* יִשְׂרָאֵל שׁוֹמֵעַ תְּפִלּוֹת, כִּי שֹׁמֵעַ אֶל אֶבְיוֹנִים יהוה.[7]
יָהּ זְכוּת אָבוֹת יָגֵן עָלֵינוּ, נֶצַח יִשְׂרָאֵל מִצָּרוֹתֵינוּ גְּאָלֵנוּ,
וּמִבּוֹר גָּלוּת דְּלֵנוּ וְהַעֲלֵנוּ, לְנַצֵּחַ עַל מְלֶאכֶת בֵּית יהוה.[8]

חַסְדֶּךָ ... אַבְרָהָם — *Your kindness ... Abraham.* Abraham was the embodiment of kindness. In his merit, we beseech God to be kind to us. חֶסֶד, *Kindness,* is the fourth *Sefirah.*

פַּחַד יִצְחָק ... אַתָּה גִבּוֹר — *O Awesome One of Isaac ... You are the mightiest.* Isaac represents the attribute of strict judgment and the exercise of extreme caution lest one transgress God's will.

ה *O great God, all eyes look toward You,*
O great One of abundant kindness,
higher than heaven is Your kindness.
O God of Abraham, recall upon Your servant —*
HASHEM's kindness shall I proclaim as praises of HASHEM![1]

מ *The lofty One adorned with strength and power,*
He draws forth light from the unequalled Torah.
O Awesome One of Isaac, illuminate our judgment —
You are the mightiest forever, HASHEM!*

The holy Shechinah is among us, the merit of the binding of **Isaac** *is with us;*
May we all rejoice there, upon arriving at Zion with glad song.
O Merciful One, remember for our sake the merit of **Isaac** *who was bound on the altar.*

Some recite a kabbalistic prayer at this point (see p. 1273).

THIRD *HAKAFAH*-CIRCUIT

Please, HASHEM, save now!
Please, HASHEM, bring success now!
Please, HASHEM, answer us on the day we call.

Pure and Just One, save now!
He Who pities the poor, bring success now!
Good and Beneficent One,[2] *answer us on the day we call!*

In some congregations the responsive recitation continues:

Hear, O Israel: HASHEM is our God, HASHEM the One and Only.
HASHEM reigns, HASHEM has reigned, HASHEM shall reign for all eternity.
HASHEM reigns, HASHEM has reigned, HASHEM shall reign for all eternity.
HASHEM will give might to His people, HASHEM will bless His people with peace.

Some individuals recite all or some of the following paragraphs:

פִּקּוּדֵי *The orders of HASHEM are upright, gladdening the heart.*[3] *the voice of HASHEM is in majesty!*[4] *The peoples will acknowledge You, O God, the peoples will acknowledge You, all of them.*[5] *Please, O strong One — those who foster Your Oneness, guard them like the pupil of an eye. Grant truth to Jacob, kindness to Abraham.*[6]

מ *What power can match You, O Doer of great deeds,*
Champion of Jacob, too awesome to praise,
Splendor of Israel Who hearkens to prayers —*
For attentive to the needy is HASHEM![7]

י *O God, may the Patriarch's merit shield us.*
Eternal One of Israel, from our torments redeem us,
And from the pit of exile, draw and raise us —
To sing mightily at the service of the House of HASHEM![8]

(1) *Isaiah* 63:7. (2) Cf. *Psalms* 119:68. (3) 19:9. (4) 29:4. (5) 67:4.
(6) *Micah* 7:20. (7) *Psalms* 69:34. (8) *Ezra* 3:8; *I Chronicles* 23:4.

גְּבוּרָה, *Might* or *Power*, is the fifth *Sefirah*.

THIRD HAKAFAH

God is intrinsically pure and just; thus He pities the poor and provides for them.

יַעֲקֹב ... תִּפְאֶרֶת — *Jacob ... Splendor.* Jacob represents the attribute תִּפְאֶרֶת, *Splendor*, which is the proper blend of חֶסֶד, *Kindness*, (Abraham's primary characteristic) and גְּבוּרָה, *Strength* (Isaac's primary characteristic). Because Jacob was able to unify kindness and strength in the best proportion, he is described by the Sages as the best of the Patriarchs. תִּפְאֶרֶת, *Splendor*, is the sixth *Sefirah*.

מִיָּמִין וּמִשְּׂמֹאל יְנִיקַת הַנְּבִיאִים, נֶצַח וָהוֹד* מֵהֶם נִמְצָאִים,
יָכִין וּבוֹעַז בְּשֵׁם נִקְרָאִים, וְכָל בָּנַיִךְ לִמּוּדֵי יהוה.[1]
יְסוֹד צַדִּיק* בְּשִׁבְעָה נֶעְלָם, אוֹת בְּרִית הוּא לְעוֹלָם,
מַעְיַן הַבְּרָכָה צַדִּיק יְסוֹד עוֹלָם, צַדִּיק אַתָּה יהוה.[2]
נָא הָקֵם מַלְכוּת דָּוִד* וּשְׁלֹמֹה, בָּעֲטָרָה שֶׁעִטְּרָה לוֹ אִמּוֹ,[3]
כְּנֶסֶת יִשְׂרָאֵל כַּלָּה קְרוּאָה בִנְעִימָה, עֲטֶרֶת תִּפְאֶרֶת בְּיַד יהוה.[4]
חָזָק מְיַחֵד כְּאֶחָד, עֶשֶׂר סְפִירוֹת, וּמַפְרִיד אַלּוּף* לֹא יִרְאֶה מְאוֹרוֹת,
סַפִּיר גִּזְרָתָם יַחַד מְאִירוֹת, תִּקְרַב רִנָּתִי לְפָנֶיךָ יהוה.[5]

שְׁכִינָה הַקְּדוֹשָׁה בְּתוֹכֵנוּ, זְכוּתָא דִתְמִימַת **יַעֲקֹב** עִמָּנוּ,
וְשָׁם נִשְׂמַח כֻּלָּנוּ, בְּבוֹא לְצִיּוֹן בְּרִנָּה.
רַחֲמָנָא אִדְכַּר לָן זְכוּתֵהּ דְּ**יַעֲקֹב** שְׁלֵמְתָּא.

Some recite a kabbalistic prayer at this point (p. 1273).

FOURTH *HAKAFAH*-CIRCUIT

אָנָּא יהוה, הוֹשִׁיעָה נָּא.
אָנָּא יהוה, הַצְלִיחָה נָא.
אָנָּא יהוה, עֲנֵנוּ בְיוֹם קָרְאֵנוּ.

יוֹדֵעַ מַחֲשָׁבוֹת,[6] הוֹשִׁיעָה נָּא.
כַּבִּיר וְנָאוֹר, הַצְלִיחָה נָא.
לוֹבֵשׁ צְדָקוֹת, עֲנֵנוּ בְיוֹם קָרְאֵנוּ.

In some congregations the responsive recitation continues:

שְׁמַע יִשְׂרָאֵל, יהוה אֱלֹהֵינוּ יהוה אֶחָד.
יהוה מֶלֶךְ, יהוה מָלָךְ, יהוה יִמְלֹךְ לְעוֹלָם וָעֶד.
יהוה מֶלֶךְ, יהוה מָלָךְ, יהוה יִמְלֹךְ לְעוֹלָם וָעֶד.
יהוה עֹז לְעַמּוֹ יִתֵּן, יהוה יְבָרֵךְ אֶת עַמּוֹ בַשָּׁלוֹם.

Some individuals recite all or some of the following paragraphs:

מִצְוַת יהוה בָּרָה, מְאִירַת עֵינָיִם.[7] קוֹל יהוה שֹׁבֵר אֲרָזִים, וַיְשַׁבֵּר יהוה אֶת אַרְזֵי הַלְּבָנוֹן. וַיַּרְקִידֵם* כְּמוֹ עֵגֶל, לְבָנוֹן וְשִׂרְיוֹן כְּמוֹ בֶן רְאֵמִים.[8] יִשְׂמְחוּ וִירַנְּנוּ לְאֻמִּים, כִּי תִשְׁפֹּט עַמִּים מִישֹׁר, וּלְאֻמִּים בָּאָרֶץ

יְנִיקַת הַנְּבִיאִים, נֶצַח וָהוֹד — *The nurture of the prophets, Eternity and Glory*. The reference is to Moses and Aaron who represent respectively the attributes of נֶצַח, *Eternity* or *Triumph*, and הוֹד, *Glory*, the seventh and eight *Sefirah*, respectively.

The term יְנִיקָה, literally *suckling*, suggests a mother nursing her child. The prophets are likened to a mother because they provide spiritual nourishment for the people.

יְסוֹד צַדִּיק — *The foundation — the righteous one.* The truly righteous person is the *foundation* of the universe because he is the one who carries out God's will and, therefore, as *Rambam* explains, the creation of the entire universe was worth-

מ *From the right and left is the nurture of the prophets,*
'Eternity' and 'Glory' are found with them.*
Yachin and Boaz are the names they are given —
And all Your children will be students of HASHEM![1]

י *The foundation — the righteous one* — is shrouded in Seven Attributes.*
he is the world's symbol of the covenant
A spring of blessing is the Tzaddik, foundation of the world —
The ultimate Tzaddik are You, HASHEM![2]

נ *Please establish the kingship of David* and Solomon*
with the crown with which his nation encrowned him.[3]
The community of Israel is fondly called a bride —
She is a crown of splendor in the hand of HASHEM![4]

ח *O Mighty One — unite as one the Ten Emanations,*
and remove the chief who will see no luminaries.*
Those emanations hewn from sapphire, may they illuminate together —
Bringing my glad song near You, HASHEM![5]

The holy Shechinah is among us, the merit of **Jacob***'s wholesomeness is with us;*
May we all rejoice there, upon arriving at Zion with glad song.
O Merciful One, remember for our sake the merit of wholesome **Jacob.**

Some recite a kabbalistic prayer at this point (see p. 1273).

FOURTH *HAKAFAH*-CIRCUIT

Please, HASHEM, save now!
Please, HASHEM, bring success now!
Please, HASHEM, answer us on the day we call.

Knower of thoughts,[6] *save now!*
Powerful and Illustrious One, bring success now!
He who garbs Himself in righteousness,
answer us on the day we call!

In some congregations the responsive recitation continues:

Hear, O Israel: HASHEM is our God, HASHEM the One and Only.
HASHEM reigns, HASHEM has reigned, HASHEM shall reign for all eternity.
HASHEM reigns, HASHEM has reigned, HASHEM shall reign for all eternity.
HASHEM will give might to His people, HASHEM will bless His people with peace.

Some individuals recite all or some of the following paragraphs:

מִצְוַת *The command of HASHEM is clear, enlightening the eyes.*[7] *The voice of HASHEM breaks the cedars, HASHEM shatters the cedars of Lebanon! He makes them prance about* like a calf; Lebanon and Siryon like young re'eimim.*[8] *Nations will be glad and sing for joy, because You will judge the peoples fairly and guide the nations on earth,*

(1) *Isaiah* 54:13. (2) *Jeremiah* 12:1. (3) *Song of Songs* 3:11. (4) *Isaiah* 62:3.
(5) *Psalms* 119:169. (6) 94:11. (7) 19:9. (8) 29:5-6.

while for the sake of even a single *tzaddik.* יְסוֹד, *Foundation,* is the ninth *Sefirah.*

נָא הָקֵם מַלְכוּת דָּוִד — *Please establish the kingship of David.* The tenth *Sefirah* — מַלְכוּת, *Kingship* — is the revelation of God's sovereignty over the universe. This Divine royalty is symbolized by King David.

וּמַפְרִיד אַלּוּף — *And remove the chief.* This refers to the destruction of Esau and his guardian angel, who are the *chief* embodiments of evil in the world. The Torah refers to Esau's most prominent offspring as 'chiefs' (*Gen.* 36:15-19).

FOURTH HAKAFAH

As mentioned earlier in the first *Hakafah,* God knows man's innermost thoughts. Moreover, He is all powerful. Nevertheless, He is righteous and

תַּנְחֵם סֶלָה.[1] בָּרְכֵם, טַהֲרֵם, רַחֲמֵם, צִדְקָתְךָ תָּמִיד גָּמְלֵם. נְעִמוֹת בִּימִינְךָ נֶצַח.[2]

אֵין אַדִּיר* כַּיהוה, אֵין בָּרוּךְ כְּבֶן עַמְרָם,
אֵין גְּדֻלָּה כַּתּוֹרָה, אֵין דּוֹרְשֶׁיהָ כְּיִשְׂרָאֵל.
מִפִּי אֵל, מִפִּי אֵל, יְבֹרַךְ יִשְׂרָאֵל.

אֵין הָדוּר כַּיהוה, אֵין וָתִיק כְּבֶן עַמְרָם,
אֵין זְכִיָּה כַּתּוֹרָה, אֵין חֲכָמֶיהָ כְּיִשְׂרָאֵל.
מִפִּי אֵל, מִפִּי אֵל, יְבֹרַךְ יִשְׂרָאֵל.

אֵין טָהוֹר כַּיהוה, אֵין יָשָׁר כְּבֶן עַמְרָם,
אֵין כָּבוֹד כַּתּוֹרָה, אֵין לוֹמְדֶיהָ כְּיִשְׂרָאֵל.
מִפִּי אֵל, מִפִּי אֵל, יְבֹרַךְ יִשְׂרָאֵל.

אֵין מֶלֶךְ כַּיהוה, אֵין נָבִיא כְּבֶן עַמְרָם,
אֵין סְגֻלָּה כַּתּוֹרָה, אֵין עוֹסְקֶיהָ כְּיִשְׂרָאֵל.
מִפִּי אֵל, מִפִּי אֵל, יְבֹרַךְ יִשְׂרָאֵל.

אֵין פּוֹדֶה כַּיהוה, אֵין צַדִּיק כְּבֶן עַמְרָם,
אֵין קְדֻשָּׁה כַּתּוֹרָה, אֵין רוֹמְמֶיהָ כְּיִשְׂרָאֵל.
מִפִּי אֵל, מִפִּי אֵל, יְבֹרַךְ יִשְׂרָאֵל.

אֵין קָדוֹשׁ כַּיהוה, אֵין רַחוּם כְּבֶן עַמְרָם,
אֵין שְׁמִירָה כַּתּוֹרָה, אֵין תּוֹמְכֶיהָ כְּיִשְׂרָאֵל.
מִפִּי אֵל, מִפִּי אֵל, יְבֹרַךְ יִשְׂרָאֵל.

וְיֶאֱתָיוּ כֹּל* לְעָבְדֶךָ. וִיבָרְכוּ שֵׁם כְּבוֹדֶךָ.
וְיַגִּידוּ בָאִיִּים צִדְקֶךָ. וְיִדְרְשׁוּךָ עַמִּים לֹא יְדָעוּךָ.
וִיהַלְלוּךָ כָּל אַפְסֵי אָרֶץ. וְיֹאמְרוּ תָמִיד יִגְדַּל יהוה.
(וְיִזְבְּחוּ לְךָ אֶת זִבְחֵיהֶם.)
וְיִזְנְחוּ אֶת עֲצַבֵּיהֶם. וְיַחְפְּרוּ עִם פְּסִילֵיהֶם.
וְיַטּוּ שְׁכֶם אֶחָד לְעָבְדֶךָ. וְיִירָאוּךָ עִם שֶׁמֶשׁ מְבַקְשֵׁי פָנֶיךָ.
וְיַכִּירוּ כֹּחַ מַלְכוּתֶךָ. וִילַמְּדוּ תוֹעִים בִּינָה.
וִימַלְּלוּ אֶת גְּבוּרָתֶךָ. וִינַשְּׂאוּךָ מִתְנַשֵּׂא לְכֹל לְרֹאשׁ.
וִיסַלְּדוּ בְחִילָה פָּנֶיךָ. וִיעַטְּרוּךָ נֵזֶר תִּפְאָרָה.
וְיִפְצְחוּ הָרִים רִנָּה. וְיִצְהֲלוּ אִיִּים בְּמָלְכֶךָ.
וִיקַבְּלוּ עֹל מַלְכוּתְךָ עֲלֵיהֶם. וִירוֹמְמוּךָ בִּקְהַל עָם.
וְיִשְׁמְעוּ רְחוֹקִים וְיָבֹאוּ. וְיִתְּנוּ לְךָ כֶּתֶר מְלוּכָה.

---

charitable to every one.

וַיַּרְקִידֵם – *He makes them prance about.* This is an allusion to the leaders of Israel and the nations who will come to serve God. They will dance for joy like lively young calves and *re'eimim.* The exact translation of *re'eim* is unknown, but it is an animal with a prominent horn.

אֵין אַדִּיר – *There is none as powerful.*

Selah.[1] *Bless them, purify them, show them pity, may Your righteousness always recompense them. There is delight at Your right hand for triumph.*[2]

א *There is none as powerful* as* HASHEM.	ב *There is none as blessed as Amram's son.*
ג *There is no greatness like the Torah;*	ד *no one expounds it like Israel.*

From God's mouth, from God's mouth, may Israel be blessed!

ה *There is none as majestic as* HASHEM.	ו *There is none as worthy as Amram's son.*
ז *There is no merit like the Torah;*	ח *it has no scholars like Israel.*

From God's mouth, from God's mouth, may Israel be blessed!

ט *There is none as pure as* HASHEM.	י *There is none as straight as Amram's son.*
כ *There is no honor like the Torah;*	ל *it has no students like Israel.*

From God's mouth, from God's mouth, may Israel be blessed!

מ *There is no king like* HASHEM.	נ *There is no prophet like Amram's son.*
ס *There is no treasure like the Torah;*	ע *it has none involved with it like Israel.*

From God's mouth, from God's mouth, may Israel be blessed!

פ *There is none who redeems like* HASHEM.	צ *There is none as righteous as Amram's son.*
ק *There is no holiness like the Torah;*	ר *it has none who exalt it like Israel.*

From God's mouth, from God's mouth, may Israel be blessed!

ק *There is none as holy as* HASHEM.	ר *There is none as merciful as Amram's son.*
ש *There is no protection like the Torah;*	ת *it has none who support it like Israel.*

From God's mouth, from God's mouth, may Israel be blessed!

וְיֶאֱתָיוּ *Then all shall come* to serve You;*
ב *they shall bless Your glorious Name*
ג *and declare Your righteousness in far-flung lands.*
ד *Peoples that knew You not will seek You out;*
ה *all ends of the earth will laud You*
ו *and always say, 'May* HASHEM *be exalted.'*
ז *They will reject their idols,*
ח *be mortified with their status,*
ט *and turn unanimously to serve You.*
י *Those who seek Your presence will revere You as long as the sun exists;*
כ *they will recognize the power of Your sovereignty,*
ל *and teach understanding to those gone astray.*
מ *They shall speak of Your strength,*
נ *they shall extol You, Who are sovereign over every leader.*
ס *In Your Presence they will pray with trepidation,*
ע *and crown You with a corona of splendor.*
פ *The mountains will burst forth with glad song,*
צ *far-flung lands will exult in Your Kingship,*
ק *they shall accept the yoke of Your Kingship upon themselves,*
ר *and exalt You among the assembled people.*
ש *Distant ones will hear and come,*
ת *and they will present You with a crown of Kingship.*

(1) *Psalms* 67:5. (2) 16:11.

Ascribed to the Maggid of Koznitz, Rabbi Yisrael ben Shabsei Hapstein (1733-1814), one of the earliest chassidic masters in Poland, this *piyut* follows the *aleph-beis*. Each of its six stanzas praises God, Moses (Amram's son), the Torah, and its students and supporters. This *piyut* is one of the few written specifically for the Simchas Torah *Hakafos*.

וְיֶאֱתָיוּ כֹּל — *Then all shall come.* This joyous and lyrical *piyut* sets forth the manner in which all people will cast off their erroneous creeds, and flock to the service of God. Each stich in this *piyut* of anonymous authorship begins with the prefix וי, *they will,* followed by the letters of the *aleph-beis* respectively. It is taken from the *Mussaf* of Rosh Hashanah and Yom Kippur.

שְׁכִינָה הַקְּדוֹשָׁה בְּתוֹכֵנוּ, זְכוּתֵהּ דְּמֹשֶׁה רַעְיָא מְהֵימְנָא עִמָּנוּ,
וְשָׁם נִשְׂמַח כֻּלָּנוּ, בְּבוֹא לְצִיּוֹן בְּרִנָּה.
רַחֲמָנָא אִדְכַּר לָן זְכוּתֵהּ דְּמֹשֶׁה רַעְיָא מְהֵימְנָא.

Some recite a kabbalistic prayer at this point (see p. 1274).

FIFTH *HAKAFAH*-CIRCUIT

אָנָּא יהוה, הוֹשִׁיעָה נָּא.
אָנָּא יהוה, הַצְלִיחָה נָא.
אָנָּא יהוה, עֲנֵנוּ בְיוֹם קָרְאֵנוּ.

מֶלֶךְ עוֹלָמִים,[1] הוֹשִׁיעָה נָּא.
נָאוֹר וְאַדִּיר,[2] הַצְלִיחָה נָא.
סוֹמֵךְ נוֹפְלִים,[3] עֲנֵנוּ בְיוֹם קָרְאֵנוּ.

In some congregations the responsive recitation continues:

שְׁמַע יִשְׂרָאֵל, יהוה אֱלֹהֵינוּ יהוה אֶחָד.
יהוה מֶלֶךְ, יהוה מָלָךְ, יהוה יִמְלֹךְ לְעוֹלָם וָעֶד.
יהוה מֶלֶךְ, יהוה מָלָךְ, יהוה יִמְלֹךְ לְעוֹלָם וָעֶד.
יהוה עֹז לְעַמּוֹ יִתֵּן, יהוה יְבָרֵךְ אֶת עַמּוֹ בַשָּׁלוֹם.

Some individuals recite all or some of the following paragraphs:

יִרְאַת יהוה טְהוֹרָה, עוֹמֶדֶת לָעַד.[4] קוֹל יהוה חֹצֵב לַהֲבוֹת אֵשׁ.[5] יוֹדוּךָ עַמִּים אֱלֹהִים, יוֹדוּךָ עַמִּים כֻּלָּם.[6] חֲסִין קָדוֹשׁ, בְּרֹב טוּבְךָ, נַהֵל עֲדָתֶךָ. יהוה אֲדֹנֵינוּ מָה אַדִּיר שִׁמְךָ בְּכָל הָאָרֶץ, אֲשֶׁר תְּנָה הוֹדְךָ עַל הַשָּׁמָיִם.[7]

הָאַדֶּרֶת וְהָאֱמוּנָה* לְחַי עוֹלָמִים. הַבִּינָה וְהַבְּרָכָה* לְחַי עוֹלָמִים.
הַגַּאֲוָה וְהַגְּדֻלָּה לְחַי עוֹלָמִים. הַדֵּעָה וְהַדִּבּוּר לְחַי עוֹלָמִים.
הַהוֹד וְהֶהָדָר לְחַי עוֹלָמִים. הַוַּעַד וְהַוָּתִיקוּת* לְחַי עוֹלָמִים.
הַזִּיו וְהַזֹּהַר לְחַי עוֹלָמִים. הַחַיִל וְהַחֹסֶן לְחַי עוֹלָמִים.
הַטֶּכֶס וְהַטֹּהַר לְחַי עוֹלָמִים. הַיִּחוּד וְהַיִּרְאָה לְחַי עוֹלָמִים.
הַכֶּתֶר וְהַכָּבוֹד לְחַי עוֹלָמִים. הַלֶּקַח וְהַלִּבּוּב* לְחַי עוֹלָמִים.

FIFTH HAKAFAH

Once again the *paytan* contrasts God's awesomeness with His care for each individual. Although He is eternal, illustrious and mighty, He still stoops to support the fallen.

הָאַדֶּרֶת וְהָאֱמוּנָה – *Strength and faithfulness.* With some variations, this song is found in *Heichalos Rabbasi*, ch. 26. It is recited by the angels at the time when Israel recites *Baruch She'amar;* therefore it is recited before *Baruch She'amar* on the Sabbath and Festivals, and, by

The holy Shechinah is among us, the merit of **Moses** *the faithful shepherd;*
May we all rejoice there, upon arriving at Zion with glad song.
O Merciful One, remember for our sake
the merit of **Moses** *the faithful shepherd.*

Some recite a kabbalistic prayer at this point (see p. 1274).

FIFTH *HAKAFAH*-CIRCUIT

Please, HASHEM, save now!
Please, HASHEM, bring success now!
Please, HASHEM, answer us on the day we call.

Eternal King,[1] save now!
Illustrious and Mighty One,[2] bring success now!
Supporter of the fallen,[3] answer us on the day we call!

In some congregations the responsive recitation continues:

Hear, O Israel: HASHEM is our God, HASHEM the One and Only.
HASHEM reigns, HASHEM has reigned, HASHEM shall reign for all eternity.
HASHEM reigns, HASHEM has reigned, HASHEM shall reign for all eternity.
HASHEM will give might to His people, HASHEM will bless His people with peace.

Some individuals recite all or some of the following paragraphs:

יִרְאַת *The fear of HASHEM is pure, enduring forever.[4] The voice of HASHEM cleaves with shafts of fire.[5] The peoples will acknowledge You, O God, the peoples will acknowledge You, all of them.[6] Powerful Holy One, with Your abundant goodness guide Your congregation. HASHEM, our Lord, how mighty is Your Name throughout the earth; for it were fit that You place Your splendor above the heavens.[7]*

הָאַדֶּרֶת *Strength and faithfulness** — *are His Who lives eternally;**
ב *Discernment and blessing** — *are His Who lives eternally;*
ג *Grandeur and greatness* — *are His Who lives eternally;*
ד *Wisdom and speech* — *are His Who lives eternally;*
ה *Glory and majesty* — *are His Who lives eternally;*
ו *Convocation and authority** — *are His Who lives eternally;*
ז *Refinement and radiance* — *are His Who lives eternally;*
ח *Accomplishment and power* — *are His Who lives eternally;*
ט *Adornment and purity* — *are His Who lives eternally;*
י *Oneness and reverence* — *are His Who lives eternally;*
כ *Crown and honor* — *are His Who lives eternally;*
ל *Study and insight** — *are His Who lives eternally;*

(1) Cf. *Daniel* 3:33; *Psalms* 245:13. (2) Cf. 76:5. (3) Cf. 145:14. (4) 19:10. (5) 29:7. (6) 67:6. (7) 8:2.

---

some, every day before *Hodu*. In *Nusach Ashkenaz* it is recited on Yom Kippur when Israel rises to the level of the angels.

הָאַדֶּרֶת ... לְחַי עוֹלָמִים — *Strength ... are His Who lives eternally.* The sense of all twenty-two verses is that since God is eternal — and He is the Creator and Life-Giver of all worlds — it is to Him that all praises and attributes should be ascribed.

הַבִּינָה וְהַבְּרָכָה — *Discernment and blessing.* Because God understands the essence of every human being, He knows who is worthy of blessing.

הַוַּעַד וְהַוָּתִיקוּת — *Convocation and authority.* Human judges can die or become ill before the court convenes or hands down its decision, but there is no limit on God's power to convoke the Heavenly Court.

הַלֶּקַח וְהַלִּבּוּב — *Study and insight*, i.e., the study of the Torah and the ability to comprehend it fully.

הַמְּלוּכָה וְהַמֶּמְשָׁלָה* לְחַי עוֹלָמִים. הַנּוֹי וְהַנֵּצַח לְחַי עוֹלָמִים.
הַסִּגּוּי וְהַשֶּׂגֶב לְחַי עוֹלָמִים. הָעֹז וְהָעֲנָוָה לְחַי עוֹלָמִים.
הַפְּדוּת וְהַפְּאֵר לְחַי עוֹלָמִים. הַצְּבִי וְהַצֶּדֶק* לְחַי עוֹלָמִים.
הַקְּרִיאָה וְהַקְּדֻשָּׁה לְחַי עוֹלָמִים. הָרֹן וְהָרוֹמֵמוּת לְחַי עוֹלָמִים.
הַשִּׁיר וְהַשֶּׁבַח לְחַי עוֹלָמִים. הַתְּהִלָּה וְהַתִּפְאֶרֶת לְחַי עוֹלָמִים.

שְׁכִינָה הַקְּדוֹשָׁה בְּתוֹכֵנוּ, זְכוּתֵהּ דְּאַהֲרֹן כַּהֲנָא עִמָּנוּ,
וְשָׁם נִשְׂמַח כֻּלָּנוּ, בְּבוֹא לְצִיּוֹן בְּרִנָּה.
רַחֲמָנָא אִדְכַּר לָן זְכוּתֵהּ דְּאַהֲרֹן כַּהֲנָא קַדִּישָׁא.

Some recite a kabbalistic prayer at this point (see p. 1274).

SIXTH *HAKAFAH*-CIRCUIT

אָנָּא יהוה, הוֹשִׁיעָה נָּא.
אָנָּא יהוה, הַצְלִיחָה נָא.
אָנָּא יהוה, עֲנֵנוּ בְיוֹם קָרְאֵנוּ.

עוֹזֵר דַּלִּים, הוֹשִׁיעָה נָּא.
פּוֹדֶה וּמַצִּיל, הַצְלִיחָה נָא.
צוּר עוֹלָמִים,*[1] עֲנֵנוּ בְיוֹם קָרְאֵנוּ.

In some congregations the responsive recitation continues:

שְׁמַע יִשְׂרָאֵל, יהוה אֱלֹהֵינוּ יהוה אֶחָד.
יהוה מֶלֶךְ, יהוה מָלָךְ, יהוה יִמְלֹךְ לְעוֹלָם וָעֶד.
יהוה מֶלֶךְ, יהוה מָלָךְ, יהוה יִמְלֹךְ לְעוֹלָם וָעֶד.
יהוה עֹז לְעַמּוֹ יִתֵּן, יהוה יְבָרֵךְ אֶת עַמּוֹ בַשָּׁלוֹם.

Some individuals recite all or some of the following paragraphs:

מִשְׁפְּטֵי יהוה אֱמֶת, צָדְקוּ יַחְדָּו.[2] קוֹל יהוה יָחִיל מִדְבָּר, יָחִיל יהוה מִדְבַּר קָדֵשׁ.[3] אֶרֶץ נָתְנָה יְבוּלָהּ, יְבָרְכֵנוּ אֱלֹהִים אֱלֹהֵינוּ.[4] יָחִיד גֵּאֶה, לְעַמְּךָ פְּנֵה, זוֹכְרֵי קְדֻשָּׁתֶךָ. צַדִּיק יהוה בְּכָל דְּרָכָיו, וְחָסִיד בְּכָל מַעֲשָׂיו.[5]

עַל יִשְׂרָאֵל אֱמוּנָתוֹ* עַל יִשְׂרָאֵל בִּרְכָתוֹ.
עַל יִשְׂרָאֵל גַּאֲוָתוֹ. עַל יִשְׂרָאֵל דִּבְרָתוֹ.*

הַמְּלוּכָה וְהַמֶּמְשָׁלָה — *Kingship and dominion.* A 'king' has the respect and consent of the governed, but even if people refuse to recognize God, as their king, He dominates, nonetheless.

הַצְּבִי וְהַצֶּדֶק — *Desire and righteousness.* Though God is beholden to no one, He desires to be righteous.

הַקְּרִיאָה וְהַקְּדֻשָּׁה — *Summons and sanctity.* The angels summon one another to sanctify God.

SIXTH HAKAFAH

This *Hakafah* offers yet another comparison between God's eternal strength with its cosmic implications, and His humility in helping, re-

מ *Kingship and dominion** are His Who lives eternally;
נ *Beauty and triumph* are His Who lives eternally;
ס *Eminence and supremacy* are His Who lives eternally;
ע *Might and modesty* are His Who lives eternally;
פ *Redemption and splendor* are His Who lives eternally;
צ *Desire and righteousness** are His Who lives eternally;
ק *Summons and sanctity** are His Who lives eternally;
ר *Exultation and exaltation* are His Who lives eternally;
ש *Song and praise* are His Who lives eternally;
ת *Lauding and magnificence* are His Who lives eternally;

The holy Shechinah is among us, the merit of **Aaron** *the Kohen;*
May we all rejoice there, Upon arriving at Zion with glad song.
O Merciful One, remember for our sake the merit of **Aaron** *the holy Kohen.*

Some recite a kabbalistic prayer at this point (see p. 1274).

SIXTH *HAKAFAH*-CIRCUIT

Please, HASHEM, save now!
Please, HASHEM, bring success now!
Please, HASHEM, answer us on the day we call.

Helper of the destitute, save now!
Redeemer and rescuer, bring success now!
Eternal Rock,[1] answer us on the day we call!*

In some congregations the responsive recitation continues:

Hear, O Israel: HASHEM is our God, HASHEM the One and Only.
HASHEM reigns, HASHEM has reigned, HASHEM shall reign for all eternity.
HASHEM reigns, HASHEM has reigned, HASHEM shall reign for all eternity.
HASHEM will give might to His people, HASHEM will bless His people with peace.

Some individuals recite all or some of the following paragraphs:

מִשְׁפְּטֵי *The judgments of HASHEM are true, altogether righteous.*[2] *The voice of HASHEM convulses the wilderness; HASHEM convulses the wilderness of Kadesh.*[3] *The earth has yielded its produce, may God, our own God, bless us.*[4] *One and only Exalted One, turn to Your nation which proclaims Your holiness. HASHEM is righteous in all His ways; virtuous in all His deeds.*[5]

א *Upon Israel is His faithfulness.** ב *Upon Israel is His blessing.*
ג *Upon Israel is His pride.* ד *Upon Israel is His word.**

(1) *Isaiah* 26:4. (2) *Psalms* 19:10. (3) 29:8. (4) 67:7. (5) 145:17.

deeming, and rescuing the destitute.

צוּר עוֹלָמִים — *Eternal Rock.* In the simple sense, this term refers to God's rock-like constancy and impregnability. The Sages also render the word צוּר homiletically as if it were צָיָר, an *artisan,* who fashions or molds. Thus, *God is The One Who fashioned* עוֹלָמִים, *the worlds above and below.*

☙ עַל יִשְׂרָאֵל אֱמוּנָתוֹ — *Upon Israel is His faithfulness.* Based upon the phrase in *Psalms* 68:35 that God takes special pride in the Jewish people, this *piyut* follows the *aleph-beis* in depicting God's special relationship to Israel in all areas. In some verses the *piyut* describes how God gives something (majesty; purity; pleasantness) to Israel. In others, it describes how certain characteristics of the world (His Kingdom; His Presence) depend upon Israel's performance of the commandments.

אֱמוּנָתוֹ — *His faithfulness.* Faith in God is found primarily among the Jewish people; similarly, in the next stich, the Jewish people are the ones who bless Him.

דִּבְרָתוֹ — *His word.* God gave the gift of prophecy for the sake of Israel.

עַל יִשְׂרָאֵל הַדְרָתוֹ. עַל יִשְׂרָאֵל וְעִידָתוֹ.
עַל יִשְׂרָאֵל זְכִירָתוֹ.* עַל יִשְׂרָאֵל חֶמְלָתוֹ
עַל יִשְׂרָאֵל טָהֳרָתוֹ.* עַל יִשְׂרָאֵל יִשְׁרָתוֹ.
עַל יִשְׂרָאֵל כַּנָּתוֹ.* עַל יִשְׂרָאֵל לְאֻמָּתוֹ.
עַל יִשְׂרָאֵל מַלְכוּתוֹ. עַל יִשְׂרָאֵל נְעִימָתוֹ.
עַל יִשְׂרָאֵל סְגֻלָּתוֹ.* עַל יִשְׂרָאֵל עֲדָתוֹ.*
עַל יִשְׂרָאֵל פְּעֻלָּתוֹ. עַל יִשְׂרָאֵל צִדְקָתוֹ.
עַל יִשְׂרָאֵל קְדֻשָּׁתוֹ. עַל יִשְׂרָאֵל רוֹמְמוּתוֹ.
עַל יִשְׂרָאֵל שְׁכִינָתוֹ. עַל יִשְׂרָאֵל תִּפְאַרְתּוֹ.

שְׁכִינָה הַקְּדוֹשָׁה בְּתוֹכֵנוּ, זְכוּתֵהּ דְּ**יוֹסֵף** צַדִּיקָא עִמָּנוּ,
וְשָׁם נִשְׂמַח כֻּלָּנוּ, בְּבוֹא לְצִיּוֹן בְּרִנָּה.
רַחֲמָנָא אִדְכַּר לָן זְכוּתֵהּ דְּ**יוֹסֵף** צַדִּיקָא.

Some recite a kabbalistic prayer at this point (see p. 1275).

SEVENTH *HAKAFAH*-CIRCUIT

אָנָּא יהוה, הוֹשִׁיעָה נָּא.
אָנָּא יהוה, הַצְלִיחָה נָא.
אָנָּא יהוה, עֲנֵנוּ בְיוֹם קָרְאֵנוּ.

קָדוֹשׁ וְנוֹרָא,[1] הוֹשִׁיעָה נָּא.
רַחוּם וְחַנּוּן,[2] הַצְלִיחָה נָא.
שׁוֹמֵר הַבְּרִית, עֲנֵנוּ בְיוֹם קָרְאֵנוּ.

תּוֹמֵךְ תְּמִימִים, הוֹשִׁיעָה נָּא.
תַּקִּיף לָעַד, הַצְלִיחָה נָא.
תָּמִים בְּמַעֲשָׂיו, עֲנֵנוּ בְיוֹם קָרְאֵנוּ.

In some congregations the responsive recitation continues:

שְׁמַע יִשְׂרָאֵל, יהוה אֱלֹהֵינוּ יהוה אֶחָד.
יהוה מֶלֶךְ, יהוה מָלָךְ, יהוה יִמְלֹךְ לְעוֹלָם וָעֶד.
יהוה מֶלֶךְ, יהוה מָלָךְ, יהוה יִמְלֹךְ לְעוֹלָם וָעֶד.
יהוה עֹז לְעַמּוֹ יִתֵּן, יהוה יְבָרֵךְ אֶת עַמּוֹ בַשָּׁלוֹם.

Some individuals recite all or some of the following paragraphs:

הַנֶּחֱמָדִים מִזָּהָב וּמִפָּז רָב, וּמְתוּקִים מִדְּבַשׁ וְנֹפֶת צוּפִים.[3] קוֹל יהוה יְחוֹלֵל אַיָּלוֹת, וַיֶּחֱשֹׂף יְעָרוֹת, וּבְהֵיכָלוֹ, כֻּלּוֹ אֹמֵר כָּבוֹד. יהוה לַמַּבּוּל יָשָׁב, וַיֵּשֶׁב יהוה מֶלֶךְ לְעוֹלָם. יהוה עֹז לְעַמּוֹ יִתֵּן,

ה *Upon Israel is His majesty.* ו *Upon Israel is His convocation.*
ז *Upon Israel is His remembrance.** ח *Upon Israel is His compassion.*
ט *Upon Israel is His purity.** י *Upon Israel is His uprightness.*
כ *Upon Israel is His foundation.** ל *Upon Israel is His nationhood.*
מ *Upon Israel is His kingdom.* נ *Upon Israel is His pleasantness.*
ס *Upon Israel is His treasured status.** ע *Upon Israel is His congregation.**
פ *Upon Israel is His handiwork.* צ *Upon Israel is His righteousness.*
ק *Upon Israel is His holiness.* ר *Upon Israel is His exaltation.*
ש *Upon Israel is His Presence.* ת *Upon Israel is His splendor.*

The holy Shechinah is among us, the merit of the righteous **Joseph***;*
May we all rejoice there, upon arriving at Zion with glad song.
O Merciful One, remember for our sake the merit of the righteous **Joseph.**

Some recite a kabbalistic prayer at this point (see p. 1275).

SEVENTH *HAKAFAH*-CIRCUIT

Please, HASHEM, save now!
Please, HASHEM, bring success now!
Please, HASHEM, answer us on the day we call.

Holy and awesome One,[1] save now!
Merciful and gracious One,[2] bring success now!
Keeper of the covenant, answer us on the day we call!

Supporter of the wholesome, save now!
Eternally strong One, bring success now!
Perfect in His deeds, answer us on the day we call!

In some congregations the responsive recitation continues:

Hear, O Israel: HASHEM is our God, HASHEM the One and Only.
HASHEM reigns, HASHEM has reigned, HASHEM shall reign for all eternity.
HASHEM reigns, HASHEM has reigned, HASHEM shall reign for all eternity.
HASHEM will give might to His people, HASHEM will bless His people with peace.

Some individuals recite all or some of the following paragraphs:

הַנֶּחֱמָדִים *They are more desirable than gold, than even much fine gold; sweeter than honey and drippings from the combs.[3] The voice of HASHEM frightens the hinds, and strips the forests bare; while in His Temple all proclaim, 'Glory!' HASHEM sat enthroned at the Deluge; HASHEM sits enthroned as King forever. HASHEM will give might*

(1) *Psalms* 111:9. (2) 103:8. (3) 19:11.

זְכִירָתוֹ – *His remembrance.* God says that despite Israel's sinfulness and disloyalty, He always remembers His people fondly and longs for the time when He will redeem them *(Jeremiah* 31;19).

טָהֳרָתוֹ – *His purity.* God purifies Israel.

כַּנָּתוֹ – *His foundation.* God created the universe as a vehicle for spiritual growth and accomplishment. The *foundation* upon which this spiritual greatness would be built is the Jewish people (*R' Hirsch, Psalms* 80:16).

סְגֻלָּתוֹ – *His treasured status.* God says to Israel וִהְיִיתֶם לִי סְגֻלָּה, *you shall be My treasure (Exodus* 19:5).

עֲדָתוֹ – *His congregation.* Scripture says that God stands בַּעֲדַת אֵל, in *the Divine assembly* [or congregation] *(Psalms* 82:1).

SEVENTH HAKAFAH

Seven three-verse *Hakafos* would use twenty-one of the twenty-two letters of the *aleph-beis.* In order to use the twenty-second letter — ת — and at the same time maintain the style of

יהוה יְבָרֵךְ אֶת עַמּוֹ בַשָּׁלוֹם.[1] יְבָרְכֵנוּ אֱלֹהִים, וְיִירְאוּ אוֹתוֹ כָּל אַפְסֵי אָרֶץ.[2] שַׁוְעָתֵנוּ קַבֵּל, וּשְׁמַע צַעֲקָתֵנוּ, יוֹדֵעַ תַּעֲלוּמוֹת. לְךָ יהוה הַגְּדֻלָּה וְהַגְּבוּרָה וְהַתִּפְאֶרֶת וְהַנֵּצַח וְהַהוֹד, כִּי כֹל בַּשָּׁמַיִם וּבָאָרֶץ, לְךָ יהוה הַמַּמְלָכָה, וְהַמִּתְנַשֵּׂא לְכֹל לְרֹאשׁ.[3] וְהָיָה יהוה לְמֶלֶךְ עַל כָּל הָאָרֶץ, בַּיּוֹם הַהוּא יִהְיֶה יהוה אֶחָד וּשְׁמוֹ אֶחָד.[4] וּבְתוֹרָתְךָ, כָּתוּב לֵאמֹר: שְׁמַע יִשְׂרָאֵל, יהוה אֱלֹהֵינוּ, יהוה אֶחָד.[5] בָּרוּךְ שֵׁם כְּבוֹד מַלְכוּתוֹ לְעוֹלָם וָעֶד.

אֵין כֵּאלֹהֵינוּ,* אֵין כַּאדוֹנֵינוּ, אֵין כְּמַלְכֵּנוּ, אֵין כְּמוֹשִׁיעֵנוּ.
מִי כֵאלֹהֵינוּ, מִי כַאדוֹנֵינוּ, מִי כְמַלְכֵּנוּ, מִי כְמוֹשִׁיעֵנוּ.
נוֹדֶה לֵאלֹהֵינוּ, נוֹדֶה לַאדוֹנֵינוּ, נוֹדֶה לְמַלְכֵּנוּ, נוֹדֶה לְמוֹשִׁיעֵנוּ.
בָּרוּךְ אֱלֹהֵינוּ, בָּרוּךְ אֲדוֹנֵינוּ, בָּרוּךְ מַלְכֵּנוּ, בָּרוּךְ מוֹשִׁיעֵנוּ.
אַתָּה הוּא אֱלֹהֵינוּ, אַתָּה הוּא אֲדוֹנֵינוּ,
אַתָּה הוּא מַלְכֵּנוּ, אַתָּה הוּא מוֹשִׁיעֵנוּ.

שְׁכִינָה הַקְּדוֹשָׁה בְּתוֹכֵנוּ, וְכוּתֵהּ דְּדָוִד מַלְכָּא מְשִׁיחָא עִמָּנוּ,
וְשָׁם נִשְׂמַח כֻּלָּנוּ, בְּבוֹא לְצִיּוֹן בְּרִנָּה.
רַחֲמָנָא אִדְכַּר לָן זְכוּתֵהּ דְּדָוִד מַלְכָּא מְשִׁיחָא.

The following is recited at the daytime *Hakafos* only.
In the evening, continue דָּוִד מַלְכָּא מְשִׁיחָא (p. 1088).

יָבוֹא אַדִּיר* בִּמְהֵרָה, יָבוֹא בָּחוּר בְּיָמֵינוּ,
יָבוֹא אֵלִיָּהוּ לְבַשְּׂרֵנוּ, יָבוֹא מָשִׁיחַ צִדְקֵנוּ,
בֶּן דָּוִד גּוֹאֲלֵנוּ, יוֹם גִּילָה, יוֹם רִנָּה, יוֹם דִּיצָה, יוֹם חֶדְוָה, יָבוֹא אֵלֵינוּ.
יָבוֹא גָּדוֹל בִּמְהֵרָה, יָבוֹא דָּגוּל בְּיָמֵינוּ,
יָבוֹא אֵלִיָּהוּ לְבַשְּׂרֵנוּ, יָבוֹא מָשִׁיחַ צִדְקֵנוּ,
בֶּן דָּוִד גּוֹאֲלֵנוּ, יוֹם גִּילָה, יוֹם רִנָּה, יוֹם דִּיצָה, יוֹם חֶדְוָה, יָבוֹא אֵלֵינוּ.
יָבוֹא הָדוּר בִּמְהֵרָה, יָבוֹא וָתִיק בְּיָמֵינוּ,
יָבוֹא אֵלִיָּהוּ לְבַשְּׂרֵנוּ, יָבוֹא מָשִׁיחַ צִדְקֵנוּ,
בֶּן דָּוִד גּוֹאֲלֵנוּ, יוֹם גִּילָה, יוֹם רִנָּה, יוֹם דִּיצָה, יוֹם חֶדְוָה, יָבוֹא אֵלֵינוּ.
יָבוֹא זַכַּאי בִּמְהֵרָה, יָבוֹא חָסִיד בְּיָמֵינוּ,
יָבוֹא אֵלִיָּהוּ לְבַשְּׂרֵנוּ, יָבוֹא מָשִׁיחַ צִדְקֵנוּ,
בֶּן דָּוִד גּוֹאֲלֵנוּ, יוֹם גִּילָה, יוֹם רִנָּה, יוֹם דִּיצָה, יוֹם חֶדְוָה, יָבוֹא אֵלֵינוּ.
יָבוֹא טָהוֹר בִּמְהֵרָה, יָבוֹא יָשָׁר בְּיָמֵינוּ,
יָבוֹא אֵלִיָּהוּ לְבַשְּׂרֵנוּ, יָבוֹא מָשִׁיחַ צִדְקֵנוּ,
בֶּן דָּוִד גּוֹאֲלֵנוּ, יוֹם גִּילָה, יוֹם רִנָּה, יוֹם דִּיצָה, יוֹם חֶדְוָה, יָבוֹא אֵלֵינוּ.

three-verse stanzas, two stanzas are recited during this final *Hakafah*. The last letter is used for all three stiches of the additional stanza.

⊱ **אֵין כֵּאלֹהֵינוּ** – *There is none like our God.* First we must declare unequivocally our recognition that nothing and no one compares to our God. Then we may ask the rhetorical question, 'Does anyone or anything compare to Him?' The recitation of this famous hymn is particulary apt

to His people, HASHEM will bless His people with peace.[1] May God bless us, and may all the ends of the earth fear Him.[2] Accept our entreaty and hear our cry, O knower of mysteries. Yours HASHEM, is the greatness, the strength, the splendor, the triumph, and the glory, even everything in heaven and earth; Yours, HASHEM, is the kingdom and the sovereignty over every leader.[3] HASHEM will be king over all the world — on that day HASHEM will be One and His Name will be One.[4] And in Your Torah it is written: Hear O Israel, HASHEM is our God, HASHEM, the One and Only.[5] Blessed is the Name of His glorious kingdom for all eternity.

א *There is none like our God;* there is none like our Master;*
there is none like our King; there is none like our Savior.
מ *Who is like our God? Who is like our Master?*
Who is like our King? Who is like our Master?
נ *Let us thank our God; let us thank our Master;*
let us thank our King; let us thank our Saviour
Blessed is our God; blessed is our Master;
blessed is our King; blessed is our Saviour.
It is You Who is our God; it is You Who is our Master;
it is You Who is our King; it is You Who is our Saviour.

The holy Shechinah is among us, the merit of **David** *the anointed King;*
May we all rejoice there, upon arriving at Zion with glad song.
O Merciful One, remember for our sake the merit of **David** *the anointed King.*

The following is recited at the daytime *Hakafos* only.
In the evening, continue *'May David the Anointed king . . .'* (p. 1088).

א *May the mighty one come* speedily,*
ב *May the excellent one come in our days,*
May Elijah come to bring us good tidings, may our righteous Messiah come,
The offspring of David, our redeemer; may the day of mirth,
the day of glad song, the day of pleasure, the day of delight come to us.
ג *May the great one come speedily,*
ד *May the supreme one come in our days,*
May Elijah come to bring us good tidings, may our righteous Messiah come,
The offspring of David, our redeemer; may the day of mirth,
the day of glad song, the day of pleasure, the day of delight come to us.
ה *May the glorious one come speedily,*
ו *May the faithful one come in our days,*
May Elijah come to bring us good tidings, may our righteous Messiah come,
The offspring of David, our redeemer; may the day of mirth,
the day of glad song, the day of pleasure, the day of delight come to us.
ז *May the worthy one come speedily*
ח *the devout one come in our days,*
May Elijah come to bring us good tidings, may our righteous Messiah come,
The offspring of David, our redeemer; may the day of mirth,
the day of glad song, the day of pleasure, the day of delight come to us.
ט *May the pure one come speedily*
י *May the just one come in our days,*
May Elijah come to bring us good tidings, may our righteous Messiah come,
The offspring of David, our redeemer; may the day of mirth,
the day of glad song, the day of pleasure, the day of delight come to us.

(1) 29:9-11. (2) 67:8. (3) *II Chronicles* 29:11. (4) *Zechariah* 14:9. (5) *Deuteronomy* 6:4.

---

at the end of the *Hakafos*, for it is a declaration of our loyalty to God and the Torah, with which we are rejoicing.

☙ יָבוֹא אַדִּיר – *May the mighty one come.* This is a lyrical prayer for the coming of Messiah, whose advent will be heralded by Elijah the

יָבוֹא כַּבִּיר בִּמְהֵרָה, יָבוֹא לָמוּד בְּיָמֵינוּ,
יָבוֹא אֵלִיָּהוּ לְבַשְּׂרֵנוּ, יָבוֹא מָשִׁיחַ צִדְקֵנוּ,
בֶּן דָּוִד גּוֹאֲלֵנוּ, יוֹם גִּילָה, יוֹם רִנָּה, יוֹם דִּיצָה, יוֹם חֶדְוָה, יָבוֹא אֵלֵינוּ.
יָבוֹא מוֹשִׁיעַ בִּמְהֵרָה, יָבוֹא נוֹרָא בְּיָמֵינוּ,
יָבוֹא אֵלִיָּהוּ לְבַשְּׂרֵנוּ, יָבוֹא מָשִׁיחַ צִדְקֵנוּ,
בֶּן דָּוִד גּוֹאֲלֵנוּ, יוֹם גִּילָה, יוֹם רִנָּה, יוֹם דִּיצָה, יוֹם חֶדְוָה, יָבוֹא אֵלֵינוּ.
יָבוֹא סַגִּיב בִּמְהֵרָה, יָבוֹא עִזּוּז בְּיָמֵינוּ,
יָבוֹא אֵלִיָּהוּ לְבַשְּׂרֵנוּ, יָבוֹא מָשִׁיחַ צִדְקֵנוּ,
בֶּן דָּוִד גּוֹאֲלֵנוּ, יוֹם גִּילָה, יוֹם רִנָּה, יוֹם דִּיצָה, יוֹם חֶדְוָה, יָבוֹא אֵלֵינוּ.
יָבוֹא פּוֹדֶה בִּמְהֵרָה, יָבוֹא צַדִּיק בְּיָמֵינוּ,
יָבוֹא אֵלִיָּהוּ לְבַשְּׂרֵנוּ, יָבוֹא מָשִׁיחַ צִדְקֵנוּ,
בֶּן דָּוִד גּוֹאֲלֵנוּ, יוֹם גִּילָה, יוֹם רִנָּה, יוֹם דִּיצָה, יוֹם חֶדְוָה, יָבוֹא אֵלֵינוּ.
יָבוֹא קָדוֹשׁ בִּמְהֵרָה, יָבוֹא רַחוּם בְּיָמֵינוּ,
יָבוֹא אֵלִיָּהוּ לְבַשְּׂרֵנוּ, יָבוֹא מָשִׁיחַ צִדְקֵנוּ,
בֶּן דָּוִד גּוֹאֲלֵנוּ, יוֹם גִּילָה, יוֹם רִנָּה, יוֹם דִּיצָה, יוֹם חֶדְוָה, יָבוֹא אֵלֵינוּ.
יָבוֹא שַׁדַּי בִּמְהֵרָה, יָבוֹא תַּקִּיף בְּיָמֵינוּ,
יָבוֹא אֵלִיָּהוּ לְבַשְּׂרֵנוּ, יָבוֹא מָשִׁיחַ צִדְקֵנוּ,
בֶּן דָּוִד גּוֹאֲלֵנוּ, יוֹם גִּילָה, יוֹם רִנָּה, יוֹם דִּיצָה, יוֹם חֶדְוָה, יָבוֹא אֵלֵינוּ.

יְצַוֶּה צוּר חַסְדּוֹ קְהִלּוֹתָיו לְקַבֵּץ, מֵאַרְבַּע רוּחוֹת עָדָיו לְהִקָּבֵץ, וּבְהַר מְרוֹם הָרִים אוֹתָנוּ לְהַרְבֵּץ, וְאִתָּנוּ יָשׁוּב נִדָּחִים קוֹבֵץ. יָשִׁיב לֹא נֶאֱמַר, כִּי אִם וְשָׁב וְקִבֵּץ.

בָּרוּךְ הוּא אֱלֹהֵינוּ אֲשֶׁר טוֹב גְּמָלָנוּ, כְּרַחֲמָיו וּכְרֹב חֲסָדָיו הִגְדִּיל לָנוּ, אֵלֶּה וְכָאֵלֶּה יוֹסֵף עִמָּנוּ, לְהַגְדִּיל שְׁמוֹ הַגָּדוֹל הַגִּבּוֹר וְהַנּוֹרָא שֶׁנִּקְרָא עָלֵינוּ.

בָּרוּךְ הוּא אֱלֹהֵינוּ שֶׁבְּרָאָנוּ לִכְבוֹדוֹ, לְהַלְּלוֹ וּלְשַׁבְּחוֹ וּלְסַפֵּר הוֹדוֹ, מִכָּל אֹם גָּבַר עָלֵינוּ חַסְדּוֹ, לָכֵן בְּכָל לֵב וּבְכָל נֶפֶשׁ וּבְכָל מְאוֹדוֹ, נַמְלִיכוֹ וּנְיַחֲדוֹ.[1]

שֶׁהַשָּׁלוֹם שֶׁלּוֹ יָשִׂים עָלֵינוּ בְּרָכָה וְשָׁלוֹם, מִשְּׂמֹאל וּמִיָּמִין עַל יִשְׂרָאֵל שָׁלוֹם, הָרַחֲמָן הוּא יְבָרֵךְ אֶת עַמּוֹ בַשָּׁלוֹם,[2] וְיִזְכּוּ לִרְאוֹת בָּנִים וּבְנֵי בָנִים עוֹסְקִים בַּתּוֹרָה וּבְמִצְוֹת, עַל יִשְׂרָאֵל שָׁלוֹם. יוֹעֵץ אֵל גִּבּוֹר אֲבִי עַד שַׂר שָׁלוֹם.[3]

דָּוִד מַלְכָּא מְשִׁיחָא יִשְׂמַח עִמָּנוּ. —Three times

לְשָׁנָה הַבָּאָה בִּירוּשָׁלָיִם. —Three times

Some recite a kabbalistic prayer at this point (see p. 1275).

Prophet. Messiah is lauded with twenty-two praises according to the *aleph-beis*. Finally, the day of his eventual arrival is described in terms of great joy.

כ *May the grand one come speedily*
ל *May the learned one come in our days,*
May Elijah come to bring us good tidings, may our righteous Messiah come,
The offspring of David, our redeemer; may the day of mirth,
the day of glad song, the day of pleasure, the day of delight come to us.

מ *May the saviour come speedily*
נ *May the awesome one come in our days,*
May Elijah come to bring us good tidings, may our righteous Messiah come,
The offspring of David, our redeemer; may the day of mirth,
the day of glad song, the day of pleasure, the day of delight come to us.

ס *May the strong one come speedily*
ע *May the all-powerful come in our days,*
May Elijah come to bring us good tidings, may our righteous Messiah come,
The offspring of David, our redeemer; may the day of mirth,
the day of glad song, the day of pleasure, the day of delight come to us.

פ *May the redeemer come speedily*
צ *May the righteous one come in our days,*
May Elijah come to bring us good tidings, may our righteous Messiah come,
The offspring of David, our redeemer; may the day of mirth,
the day of glad song, the day of pleasure, the day of delight come to us.

ק *May the holy one come speedily*
ר *May the merciful one come in our days,*
May Elijah come to bring us good tidings, may our righteous Messiah come,
The offspring of David, our redeemer; may the day of mirth,
the day of glad song, the day of pleasure, the day of delight come to us.

ש *May the Almighty come speedily*
ת *May the powerful one come in our days,*
May Elijah come to bring us good tidings, may our righteous Messiah come,
The offspring of David, our redeemer; may the day of mirth,
the day of glad song, the day of pleasure, the day of delight come to us.

יְצַוֶּה *May the Rock command His kindness to gather in His congregations; from the four winds to be gathered up to Him, upon the loftiest mountain to set us down. He shall return with us, the Gatherer of outcasts — 'He shall bring back' is not said, but 'He shall return' and gather in.*

Blessed is our God Who did us good. According to His mercy and His abundant kindness He did great things for us. Both these and those may He increase with us — to magnify His great, mighty, and awesome Name Which was proclaimed upon us.

Blessed is our God Who created us for His glory; to praise Him, laud Him and relate His majesty. More than any nation He strengthened His kindness over us. Therefore with complete heart, with complete soul, and with complete resources, let us proclaim Him King and proclaim Him Unique.[1]

May He to Whom peace belongs set upon us blessing and peace — from left and from right, peace upon Israel. May the Merciful One bless His people with peace;[2] *and may they merit to see children and grandchildren engaging in Torah and precepts, bringing peace upon Israel. Advisor, Mighty God, Eternal Father, Prince of Peace.*[3]

Three times – **May David the anointed king rejoice with us.**

Three times – **Next year in Jerusalem.**

Some recite a kabbalistic prayer at this point (see p. 1275).

---

(1) Cf. *Deuteronomy* 6:4-5. (2) *Psalms* 29:11. (3) *Isaiah* 9:5.

After the end of the seven *Hakafah*-circuits, all the Torah Scrolls except one are returned to the Ark.
Some congregations return all the Scrolls and continue with with קִדּוּשׁ, *Kiddush*, p. 1100.
The Torah Scroll which will now be read from is then presented to the *chazzan*, who accepts it in his right arm. Facing the congregation, he raises the Torah and, followed by congregation, recites:

שְׁמַע יִשְׂרָאֵל יהוה אֱלֹהֵינוּ יהוה אֶחָד.[1]

Still facing the congregation, the *chazzan* raises the Torah and, followed by congregation, recites:

אֶחָד (הוּא) אֱלֹהֵינוּ גָּדוֹל אֲדוֹנֵינוּ, קָדוֹשׁ שְׁמוֹ.

The *chazzan* turns to the Ark, bows while raising the Torah, and recites:

גַּדְּלוּ לַיהוה אִתִּי וּנְרוֹמְמָה שְׁמוֹ יַחְדָּו.[2]

The *chazzan* turns to his right and carries the Torah to the *bimah*, as the congregation responds:

לְךָ יהוה הַגְּדֻלָּה וְהַגְּבוּרָה וְהַתִּפְאֶרֶת וְהַנֵּצַח וְהַהוֹד כִּי כֹל בַּשָּׁמַיִם וּבָאָרֶץ, לְךָ יהוה הַמַּמְלָכָה וְהַמִּתְנַשֵּׂא לְכֹל לְרֹאשׁ.[3] רוֹמְמוּ יהוה אֱלֹהֵינוּ, וְהִשְׁתַּחֲווּ לַהֲדֹם רַגְלָיו, קָדוֹשׁ הוּא. רוֹמְמוּ יהוה אֱלֹהֵינוּ, וְהִשְׁתַּחֲווּ לְהַר קָדְשׁוֹ, כִּי קָדוֹשׁ יהוה אֱלֹהֵינוּ.[4]

As the *chazzan* carries the Torah to the *bimah* the congregation recites:

עַל הַכֹּל, יִתְגַּדַּל וְיִתְקַדַּשׁ וְיִשְׁתַּבַּח וְיִתְפָּאַר וְיִתְרוֹמַם וְיִתְנַשֵּׂא שְׁמוֹ שֶׁל מֶלֶךְ מַלְכֵי הַמְּלָכִים הַקָּדוֹשׁ בָּרוּךְ הוּא, בָּעוֹלָמוֹת שֶׁבָּרָא, הָעוֹלָם הַזֶּה וְהָעוֹלָם הַבָּא, כִּרְצוֹנוֹ, וְכִרְצוֹן יְרֵאָיו, וְכִרְצוֹן כָּל בֵּית יִשְׂרָאֵל. צוּר הָעוֹלָמִים, אֲדוֹן כָּל הַבְּרִיּוֹת, אֱלוֹהַּ כָּל הַנְּפָשׁוֹת, הַיּוֹשֵׁב בְּמֶרְחֲבֵי מָרוֹם, הַשּׁוֹכֵן בִּשְׁמֵי שְׁמֵי קֶדֶם. קְדֻשָּׁתוֹ עַל הַחַיּוֹת, וּקְדֻשָּׁתוֹ עַל כִּסֵּא הַכָּבוֹד. וּבְכֵן יִתְקַדַּשׁ שִׁמְךָ בָּנוּ יהוה אֱלֹהֵינוּ לְעֵינֵי כָּל חָי. וְנֹאמַר לְפָנָיו שִׁיר חָדָשׁ, כַּכָּתוּב: שִׁירוּ לֵאלֹהִים זַמְּרוּ שְׁמוֹ, סֹלּוּ לָרֹכֵב בָּעֲרָבוֹת בְּיָהּ שְׁמוֹ, וְעִלְזוּ לְפָנָיו.[5] וְנִרְאֵהוּ עַיִן בְּעַיִן בְּשׁוּבוֹ אֶל נָוֵהוּ, כַּכָּתוּב: כִּי עַיִן בְּעַיִן יִרְאוּ בְּשׁוּב יהוה צִיּוֹן.[6] וְנֶאֱמַר: וְנִגְלָה כְּבוֹד יהוה, וְרָאוּ כָל בָּשָׂר יַחְדָּו כִּי פִּי יהוה דִּבֵּר.[7]

אַב הָרַחֲמִים הוּא יְרַחֵם עַם עֲמוּסִים, וְיִזְכֹּר בְּרִית אֵיתָנִים, וְיַצִּיל נַפְשׁוֹתֵינוּ מִן הַשָּׁעוֹת הָרָעוֹת, וְיִגְעַר בְּיֵצֶר הָרָע מִן הַנְּשׂוּאִים, וְיָחֹן אוֹתָנוּ לִפְלֵיטַת עוֹלָמִים, וִימַלֵּא מִשְׁאֲלוֹתֵינוּ בְּמִדָּה טוֹבָה יְשׁוּעָה וְרַחֲמִים.

The Torah is placed on the *bimah* and prepared for reading.

---

(1) *Deuteronomy* 6:4. (2) *Psalms* 34:4. (3) *I Chronicles* 29:11.
(4) *Psalms* 99:5,9. (5) 68:5. (6) *Isaiah* 52:8. (7) 40:5.

After the end of the seven *Hakafah*-circuits, all the Torah Scrolls except one are returned to the Ark. Some congregations return all the Scrolls and continue with with קִדּוּשׁ, *Kiddush*, p. 1100. The Torah Scroll which will now be read from is then presented to the *chazzan,* who accepts it in his right arm. Facing the congregation, he raises the Torah and, followed by congregation, recites:

Hear, O Israel: HASHEM is our God, HASHEM, the One and Only.[1]

Still facing the congregation, the *chazzan* raises the Torah and, followed by congregation, recites:

One is our God, great is our Master, Holy is His Name.

The *chazzan* turns to the Ark, bows while raising the Torah, and recites:

Declare the greatness of HASHEM with me, and let us exalt His Name together.[2]

The *chazzan* turns to his right and carries the Torah to the *bimah,* as the congregation responds:

לְךָ *Yours, HASHEM, is the greatness, the strength, the splendor, the triumph, and the glory; even everything in heaven and earth; Yours, HASHEM, is the kingdom, and the sovereignty over every leader.*[3] *Exalt HASHEM, our God, and bow at His footstool; He is Holy! Exalt HASHEM, our God, and bow to His holy mountain; for holy is HASHEM, our God.*[4]

As the *chazzan* carries the Torah to the *bimah* the congregation recites:

עַל הַכֹּל *For all this, let the Name of the King of kings, the Holy One, Blessed is He, grow exalted, sanctified, praised, glorified, exalted, and extolled in the worlds that He has created — This World and the World to Come — according to His will, the will of those who fear Him, and the will of the entire House of Israel. Rock of the eternities, Master of all creatures, God of all souls, He Who sits in the expanses on high, Who rests in the loftiest primeval heavens. His holiness is upon the Chayos; His holiness is upon the Throne of Glory. Similarly, may Your Name be sanctified within us, HASHEM, our God, in the sight of all the living. May we chant before Him a new song as it is written: 'Sing to God, make music for His Name, extol the One Who rides in the highest heavens with His Name YAH, and exult before Him.'*[5] *May we see Him with a perceptive view upon His return to His Abode, as is written: 'For they shall see with a perceptive view as HASHEM returns to Zion.'*[6] *And it is said: 'The glory of HASHEM shall be revealed and all flesh together shall see that the mouth of HASHEM has spoken.'*[7]

אַב הָרַחֲמִים *May the Father of compassion have mercy on the nation that is borne by Him, and may He remember the covenant of the spiritually mighty. May He rescue our souls from the bad times, and upbraid the evil inclination to leave those borne by Him, graciously make us an eternal remnant, and fulfill our requests in good measure, for salvation and mercy.*

The Torah is placed on the *bimah* and prepared for reading.

The *gabbai* uses the following formula to call a *Kohen* to the Torah:

וְיַעֲזוֹר וְיָגֵן וְיוֹשִׁיעַ לְכֹל הַחוֹסִים בּוֹ, וְנֹאמַר, אָמֵן. הַכֹּל הָבוּ גֹדֶל לֵאלֹהֵינוּ וּתְנוּ כָבוֹד לַתּוֹרָה, כֹּהֵן° קְרָב, יַעֲמֹד (name) בֶּן (father's name) הַכֹּהֵן.

°If no *Kohen* is present, the *gabbai* says:
"אֵין כַּאן כֹּהֵן, יַעֲמֹד (insert name) יִשְׂרָאֵל (לֵוִי) בִּמְקוֹם כֹּהֵן."

בָּרוּךְ שֶׁנָּתַן תּוֹרָה לְעַמּוֹ יִשְׂרָאֵל בִּקְדֻשָּׁתוֹ. (תּוֹרַת יהוה תְּמִימָה מְשִׁיבַת נָפֶשׁ, עֵדוּת יהוה נֶאֱמָנָה מַחְכִּימַת פֶּתִי. פִּקּוּדֵי יהוה יְשָׁרִים מְשַׂמְּחֵי לֵב, מִצְוַת יהוה בָּרָה מְאִירַת עֵינָיִם.[1] יהוה עֹז לְעַמּוֹ יִתֵּן, יהוה יְבָרֵךְ אֶת עַמּוֹ בַשָּׁלוֹם.[2] הָאֵל תָּמִים דַּרְכּוֹ, אִמְרַת יהוה צְרוּפָה, מָגֵן הוּא לְכֹל הַחוֹסִים בּוֹ.[3])

Congregation then *gabbai*:

וְאַתֶּם הַדְּבֵקִים בַּיהוה אֱלֹהֵיכֶם, חַיִּים כֻּלְּכֶם הַיּוֹם.[4]

❧ קריאת התורה ❧

The reader shows the *oleh* (person called to the Torah) the place in the Torah. The *oleh* touches the Torah with a corner of his *tallis,* or the belt or mantle of the Torah, and kisses it. He then begins the blessing, bowing at בָּרְכוּ, and straightening up at ה׳.

בָּרְכוּ אֶת יהוה הַמְּבֹרָךְ.

Congregation, followed by *oleh*, responds, bowing at בָּרוּךְ, and straightening up at ה׳.

בָּרוּךְ יהוה הַמְּבֹרָךְ לְעוֹלָם וָעֶד.

Oleh continues:

בָּרוּךְ אַתָּה יהוה אֱלֹהֵינוּ מֶלֶךְ הָעוֹלָם, אֲשֶׁר בָּחַר בָּנוּ מִכָּל הָעַמִּים, וְנָתַן לָנוּ אֶת תּוֹרָתוֹ. בָּרוּךְ אַתָּה יהוה, נוֹתֵן הַתּוֹרָה. (Cong. – אָמֵן.)

After his Torah portion has been read, the *oleh* recites:

בָּרוּךְ אַתָּה יהוה אֱלֹהֵינוּ מֶלֶךְ הָעוֹלָם, אֲשֶׁר נָתַן לָנוּ תּוֹרַת אֱמֶת, וְחַיֵּי עוֹלָם נָטַע בְּתוֹכֵנוּ. בָּרוּךְ אַתָּה יהוה, נוֹתֵן הַתּוֹרָה. (Cong. – אָמֵן.)

דברים לג:א-כו

כהן – וְזֹ֣את הַבְּרָכָ֗ה אֲשֶׁ֨ר בֵּרַ֥ךְ מֹשֶׁ֛ה אִ֥ישׁ הָאֱלֹהִ֖ים אֶת־בְּנֵ֣י יִשְׂרָאֵ֑ל לִפְנֵ֖י מוֹתֽוֹ: וַיֹּאמַ֗ר יהו֞ה מִסִּינַ֥י בָּא֙ וְזָרַ֤ח מִשֵּׂעִיר֙ לָ֔מוֹ הוֹפִ֙יעַ֙ מֵהַ֣ר פָּארָ֔ן וְאָתָ֖ה מֵרִבְבֹ֣ת קֹ֑דֶשׁ מִֽימִינ֕וֹ אֵ֥שׁ דָּ֖ת לָֽמוֹ: אַ֚ף חֹבֵ֣ב עַמִּ֔ים כָּל־קְדֹשָׁ֖יו בְּיָדֶ֑ךָ וְהֵם֙ תֻּכּ֣וּ לְרַגְלֶ֔ךָ יִשָּׂ֖א מִדַּבְּרֹתֶֽיךָ: תּוֹרָ֥ה צִוָּה־לָ֖נוּ מֹשֶׁ֑ה מוֹרָשָׁ֖ה קְהִלַּ֥ת יַעֲקֹֽב: וַיְהִ֥י בִישֻׁר֖וּן מֶ֑לֶךְ בְּהִתְאַסֵּף֙ רָ֣אשֵׁי עָ֔ם יַ֖חַד שִׁבְטֵ֥י יִשְׂרָאֵֽל: יְחִ֥י רְאוּבֵ֖ן וְאַל־יָמֹ֑ת וִיהִ֥י מְתָ֖יו מִסְפָּֽר: וְזֹ֣את לִֽיהוּדָה֮ וַיֹּאמַר֒ שְׁמַ֤ע יהוה֙ ק֣וֹל יְהוּדָ֔ה וְאֶל־עַמּ֖וֹ תְּבִיאֶ֑נּוּ יָדָיו֙ רָ֣ב ל֔וֹ וְעֵ֥זֶר מִצָּרָ֖יו תִּֽהְיֶֽה:

The *gabbai* uses the following formula to call a *Kohen* to the Torah:

וְיַעֲזוֹר *May He help, shield, and save all who take refuge in Him — Now let us respond: Amen. All of you ascribe greatness to our God and give honor to the Torah. Kohen,° approach. Arise* (name) *son of* (father's name) *the Kohen.*

°If no *Kohen* is present, the *gabbai* says: *'There is no Kohen present, stand* (name) *son of* (father's name) *an Israelite (Levite) in place of the Kohen.'*

Blessed is He Who gave the Torah to His people Israel in His holiness. (The Torah of HASHEM is perfect, restoring the soul; the testimony of HASHEM is trustworthy, making the simple one wise. The orders of HASHEM are upright, gladdening the heart; the command of HASHEM is clear, enlightening the eyes.[1] HASHEM will give might to His nation; HASHEM will bless His nation with peace.[2] The God Whose way is perfect, the promise of HASHEM is flawless, He is a shield for all who take refuge in Him.[3])

Congregation then *gabbai:*

You who cling to HASHEM, your God, you are all alive today.[4]

READING OF THE TORAH

The reader shows the *oleh* (person called to the Torah) the place in the Torah. The *oleh* touches the Torah with a corner of his *tallis,* or the belt or mantle of the Torah, and kisses it. He then begins the blessing, bowing at *'Bless,'* and straightening up at 'HASHEM.'

Bless HASHEM, the blessed One.

Congregation, followed by *oleh,* responds, bowing at 'Blessed,' and straightening up at 'HASHEM.'

Blessed is HASHEM, the blessed One, for all eternity.

Oleh continues:

בָּרוּךְ *Blessed are You, HASHEM, our God, King of the universe, Who selected us from all the peoples and gave us His Torah. Blessed are You, HASHEM, Giver of the Torah.* (Cong.– *Amen.)*

After his Torah portion has been read, the *oleh* recites:

בָּרוּךְ *Blessed are You, HASHEM, our God, King of the universe, Who gave us the Torah of truth and implanted eternal life within us. Blessed are You, HASHEM, Giver of the Torah.* (Cong.– *Amen.)*

Deuteronomy 33:1-26

Kohen – *This is the blessing that Moses, the man of God, bestowed upon the Children of Israel before his death.*

He said: HASHEM approached from Sinai — having shone forth to them from Seir, having appeared from Mount Paran, and then approached with some of the holy myriads — from His right hand He presented the fiery Torah to them. Indeed, You greatly loved the tribes, all His righteous ones were in Your hands; for they planted themselves at Your feet, accepting the burden of Your utterances: "The Torah which Moses charged us is the heritage of the Congregation of Jacob. He became King over Jeshurun when the leaders of the nation gathered — the tribes of Israel in unity."

May Reuben live and not die, and may his population be counted among the others.

And this to Judah, and he said: Hear, O HASHEM. Judah's prayer, and return him safely to his people; may his hands gain him triumph and may You remain a helper against his enemies.

(1) *Psalms* 19:8-9. (2) 29:11. (3) 18:31. (4) *Deuteronomy* 4:4.

לוי – וּלְלֵוִי אָמַר תֻּמֶּיךָ וְאוּרֶיךָ לְאִישׁ חֲסִידֶךָ אֲשֶׁר נִסִּיתוֹ בְּמַסָּה תְּרִיבֵהוּ עַל־מֵי מְרִיבָה: הָאֹמֵר לְאָבִיו וּלְאִמּוֹ לֹא רְאִיתִיו וְאֶת־אֶחָיו לֹא הִכִּיר וְאֶת־בָּנָו לֹא יָדָע כִּי שָׁמְרוּ אִמְרָתֶךָ וּבְרִיתְךָ יִנְצֹרוּ: יוֹרוּ מִשְׁפָּטֶיךָ לְיַעֲקֹב וְתוֹרָתְךָ לְיִשְׂרָאֵל יָשִׂימוּ קְטוֹרָה בְּאַפֶּךָ וְכָלִיל עַל־מִזְבְּחֶךָ: בָּרֵךְ יהוה חֵילוֹ וּפֹעַל יָדָיו תִּרְצֶה מְחַץ מָתְנַיִם קָמָיו וּמְשַׂנְאָיו מִן־יְקוּמוּן: לְבִנְיָמִן אָמַר יְדִיד יהוה יִשְׁכֹּן לָבֶטַח עָלָיו חֹפֵף עָלָיו כָּל־הַיּוֹם וּבֵין כְּתֵפָיו שָׁכֵן:

ישראל – וּלְיוֹסֵף אָמַר מְבֹרֶכֶת יהוה אַרְצוֹ מִמֶּגֶד שָׁמַיִם מִטָּל וּמִתְּהוֹם רֹבֶצֶת תָּחַת: וּמִמֶּגֶד תְּבוּאֹת שָׁמֶשׁ וּמִמֶּגֶד גֶּרֶשׁ יְרָחִים: וּמֵרֹאשׁ הַרְרֵי־קֶדֶם וּמִמֶּגֶד גִּבְעוֹת עוֹלָם: וּמִמֶּגֶד אֶרֶץ וּמְלֹאָהּ וּרְצוֹן שֹׁכְנִי סְנֶה תָּבוֹאתָה לְרֹאשׁ יוֹסֵף וּלְקָדְקֹד נְזִיר אֶחָיו: בְּכוֹר שׁוֹרוֹ הָדָר לוֹ וְקַרְנֵי רְאֵם קַרְנָיו בָּהֶם עַמִּים יְנַגַּח יַחְדָּו אַפְסֵי־אָרֶץ וְהֵם רִבְבוֹת אֶפְרַיִם וְהֵם אַלְפֵי מְנַשֶּׁה:

Some congregations stop here; others continue.

רביעי – וְלִזְבוּלֻן אָמַר שְׂמַח זְבוּלֻן בְּצֵאתֶךָ וְיִשָּׂשכָר בְּאֹהָלֶיךָ: עַמִּים הַר־יִקְרָאוּ שָׁם יִזְבְּחוּ זִבְחֵי־צֶדֶק כִּי שֶׁפַע יַמִּים יִינָקוּ וּשְׂפֻנֵי טְמוּנֵי חוֹל: וּלְגָד אָמַר בָּרוּךְ מַרְחִיב גָּד כְּלָבִיא שָׁכֵן וְטָרַף זְרוֹעַ אַף־קָדְקֹד: וַיַּרְא רֵאשִׁית לוֹ כִּי־שָׁם חֶלְקַת מְחֹקֵק סָפוּן וַיֵּתֵא רָאשֵׁי עָם צִדְקַת יהוה עָשָׂה וּמִשְׁפָּטָיו עִם־יִשְׂרָאֵל:

חמישי – וּלְדָן אָמַר דָּן גּוּר אַרְיֵה יְזַנֵּק מִן־הַבָּשָׁן: וּלְנַפְתָּלִי אָמַר נַפְתָּלִי שְׂבַע רָצוֹן וּמָלֵא בִּרְכַּת יהוה יָם וְדָרוֹם יְרָשָׁה: וּלְאָשֵׁר אָמַר בָּרוּךְ מִבָּנִים אָשֵׁר יְהִי רְצוּי אֶחָיו וְטֹבֵל בַּשֶּׁמֶן רַגְלוֹ: בַּרְזֶל וּנְחֹשֶׁת מִנְעָלֶיךָ וּכְיָמֶיךָ דָּבְאֶךָ: אֵין כָּאֵל יְשֻׁרוּן רֹכֵב שָׁמַיִם בְּעֶזְרֶךָ וּבְגַאֲוָתוֹ שְׁחָקִים:

חצי קדיש

After the last *oleh* has completed his closing blessing, the reader recites Half-*Kaddish*.

יִתְגַּדַּל וְיִתְקַדַּשׁ שְׁמֵהּ רַבָּא. (.Cong – אָמֵן.) בְּעָלְמָא דִּי בְרָא כִרְעוּתֵהּ. וְיַמְלִיךְ מַלְכוּתֵהּ, בְּחַיֵּיכוֹן וּבְיוֹמֵיכוֹן וּבְחַיֵּי דְכָל בֵּית יִשְׂרָאֵל, בַּעֲגָלָא וּבִזְמַן קָרִיב. וְאִמְרוּ: אָמֵן.

(.Cong – אָמֵן. יְהֵא שְׁמֵהּ רַבָּא מְבָרַךְ לְעָלַם וּלְעָלְמֵי עָלְמַיָּא.)

יְהֵא שְׁמֵהּ רַבָּא מְבָרַךְ לְעָלַם וּלְעָלְמֵי עָלְמַיָּא.

Levi – *Of Levi he said: Your Tumim and Your Urim befit Your devout one, whom You tested at Massah, and whom You challenged at the waters of Meribah. The one who said of his father and mother, "I have not favored him," he disregarded his brothers and ignored his own children; for they [i.e., the Levites] have observed Your word, and preserved Your covenant. Thus it is they who are worthy to teach Your law to Jacob and Your Torah to Israel; it is they who shall place incense before Your presence, and burnt offerings on Your altar. Bless, O* HASHEM, *his resources, and favor his handiwork. Smash the loins of his foes, and his enemies that they may not rise again.*

Of Benjamin he said: May HASHEM*'s beloved dwell securely by Him; He hovers above him all day long; and rests His Presence among his hills.*

Third – *Of Joseph he said: His land is blessed by* HASHEM *— with the heavenly bounty of dew, and with the deep waters crouching below: with the bounty of the sun's crops, and with the bounty of the moon's yield; with the quick-ripening crops of the ancient mountains, and with the bounty of eternally fertile hills; with the bounty of the land and its fullness, and by the favor of Him Who rested upon the thornbush. May this blessing rest upon Joseph's head, and upon the crown of him who was separated from his brothers. Sovereignty will go to his most distinguished, mighty descendant; and his glory will be like the horns of a re'eim; with both of them together he shall gore nations to the ends of the earth; they are the myriads of Ephraim's victims, and the thousands of Menashe's victims.*

Some congregations stop here; others continue.

Fourth – *Of Zebulun he said: Rejoice, O Zebulun, in your excursions, and Issachar in your tents. The tribes will summon one another to the Temple Mount, there they will bring offerings of righteousness, for they will be nourished by the riches of the sea, and by the treasures concealed in the sand.*

Of Gad he said: Blessed is He Who broadens Gad's boundary; he dwells like a lion tearing off arm and even head. He chose the first portion as his own, for that is where the Lawgiver's plot is hidden. He marched at the head of the nation, carrying out HASHEM*'s justice and His laws with Israel.*

Fifth – *Of Dan he said: Dan is a lion cub, leaping forth from the Bashan.*

Of Naftali he said: Naftali, satiated with favor, and filled with HASHEM*'s blessing; go possess the sea and its south shore.*

Of Asher he said: Asher is most blessed with children, he shall be pleasing to his brothers, and dip his feet in oil.

May your borders be sealed like iron and copper, and like the days of your prime, so may your old age be. There is none like God, O Jeshurun; He rides across heaven to help you, and in His majesty through the upper heights.

HALF KADDISH

After the last *oleh* has completed his closing blessing, the reader recites Half-*Kaddish:*

יִתְגַּדַּל *May His great Name grow exalted and sanctified* (Cong.– *Amen.*) *in the world that He created as He willed. May He give reign to His kingship in your lifetimes and in your days, and in the lifetimes of the entire Family of Israel, swiftly and soon. Now respond: Amen.*

(Cong.– *Amen. May His great Name be blessed forever and ever.*)

May His great Name be blessed forever and ever.

יִתְבָּרַךְ וְיִשְׁתַּבַּח וְיִתְפָּאַר וְיִתְרוֹמַם וְיִתְנַשֵּׂא וְיִתְהַדָּר וְיִתְעַלֶּה וְיִתְהַלָּל שְׁמֵהּ דְּקֻדְשָׁא בְּרִיךְ הוּא (.Cong – בְּרִיךְ הוּא) — לְעֵלָּא מִן כָּל בִּרְכָתָא וְשִׁירָתָא תֻּשְׁבְּחָתָא וְנֶחֱמָתָא, דַּאֲמִירָן בְּעָלְמָא. וְאִמְרוּ: אָמֵן. (.Cong – אָמֵן.)

הגבהה וגלילה

The second Torah is raised in the usual manner. Each person looks at the Torah and recites aloud:

וְזֹאת הַתּוֹרָה אֲשֶׁר שָׂם מֹשֶׁה לִפְנֵי בְּנֵי יִשְׂרָאֵל,[1] עַל פִּי יהוה בְּיַד מֹשֶׁה.[2]

Some add:

עֵץ חַיִּים הִיא לַמַּחֲזִיקִים בָּהּ, וְתֹמְכֶיהָ מְאֻשָּׁר.[3] דְּרָכֶיהָ דַרְכֵי נֹעַם, וְכָל נְתִיבוֹתֶיהָ שָׁלוֹם.[4] אֹרֶךְ יָמִים בִּימִינָהּ, בִּשְׂמֹאלָהּ עֹשֶׁר וְכָבוֹד.[5] יהוה חָפֵץ לְמַעַן צִדְקוֹ, יַגְדִּיל תּוֹרָה וְיַאְדִּיר.[6]

In some congregations, the following *piyutim* are recited after the Torah reading. Some recite them at one or more points during the *Hakafos*.

שִׂישׂוּ וְשִׂמְחוּ[7] בְּשִׂמְחַת תּוֹרָה, וּתְנוּ כָבוֹד לַתּוֹרָה,
כִּי טוֹב סַחְרָהּ מִכָּל סְחוֹרָה,[8] מִפָּז וּמִפְּנִינִים יְקָרָה.[9]
נָגִיל וְנָשִׂישׂ בְּזֹאת הַתּוֹרָה, כִּי הִיא לָנוּ עֹז וְאוֹרָה.

אֲהַלְלָה אֱלֹהַי וְאֶשְׂמְחָה בוֹ, וְאָשִׂימָה תִקְוָתִי בּוֹ,
אֲהוֹדֶנּוּ בְּסוֹד עַם קְרוֹבוֹ, אֱלֹהֵי צוּרִי אֶחֱסֶה בּוֹ.[10]
נָגִיל וְנָשִׂישׂ בְּזֹאת הַתּוֹרָה, כִּי הִיא לָנוּ עֹז וְאוֹרָה.

בְּכָל לֵב אֲרַנֵּן צִדְקוֹתֶיךָ, וַאֲסַפְּרָה תְּהִלָּתֶךָ,
בְּעוֹדִי אַגִּיד נִפְלְאוֹתֶיךָ, עַל חַסְדְּךָ וְעַל אֲמִתֶּךָ.[11]
נָגִיל וְנָשִׂישׂ בְּזֹאת הַתּוֹרָה, כִּי הִיא לָנוּ עֹז וְאוֹרָה.

גּוֹאֵל תָּחִישׁ מְבַשֵּׂר טוֹב,[12] כִּי אַתָּה מִגְדַּל עֹז וְטוֹב,
גְּאוּלִים יוֹדוּךָ בְּלֵב טוֹב, הוֹדוּ לַיהוה כִּי טוֹב.[13]
נָגִיל וְנָשִׂישׂ בְּזֹאת הַתּוֹרָה, כִּי הִיא לָנוּ עֹז וְאוֹרָה.

דָּגוּל גְּאַל נָא הֲמוֹנַי, כִּי אֵין קָדוֹשׁ כַּיהוה.[14]
דְּגוּלִים יוֹדוּךָ יהוה, מִי יְמַלֵּל גְּבוּרוֹת יהוה.[15]
נָגִיל וְנָשִׂישׂ בְּזֹאת הַתּוֹרָה, כִּי הִיא לָנוּ עֹז וְאוֹרָה.

הֲלֹא בְּאַהֲבָתוֹ בָּחַר בָּנוּ, בְּנִי בְכוֹרִי[16] קְרָאָנוּ,
הוֹד וְהָדָר הִנְחִילָנוּ, כִּי לְעוֹלָם חַסְדּוֹ[17] עִמָּנוּ.
נָגִיל וְנָשִׂישׂ בְּזֹאת הַתּוֹרָה, כִּי הִיא לָנוּ עֹז וְאוֹרָה.

אַשְׁרֵיכֶם יִשְׂרָאֵל, אַשְׁרֵיכֶם יִשְׂרָאֵל, אַשְׁרֵיכֶם יִשְׂרָאֵל, אֲשֶׁר בָּחַר בָּכֶם אֵל, וְהִנְחִילְכֶם הַתּוֹרָה מִמִּדְבַּר מַתָּנָה.

Blessed, praised, glorified, exalted, extolled, mighty, upraised, and lauded be the Name of the Holy One, Blessed is He (Cong.— *Blessed is He*) — *beyond any blessing and song, praise and consolation that are uttered in the world. Now respond: Amen.* (Cong.— *Amen.*)

HAGBAHAH AND GELILAH

The second Torah in the usual manner. Each person looks at the Torah and recites aloud:

This is the Torah that Moses placed before the Children of Israel,[1] upon the command of HASHEM, through Moses' hand.[2]

Some add:

עֵץ *It is a tree of life for those who grasp it, and its supporters are praiseworthy.[3] Its ways are ways of pleasantness and all its paths are peace.[4] Lengthy days are at its right; at its left are wealth and honor.[5] HASHEM desired, for the sake of its [Israel's] righteousness, that the Torah be made great and glorious.[6]*

In some congregations, the following *piyutim* are recited after the Torah reading. Some recite them at one or more points during the *Hakafos.*

שִׂישׂוּ *Rejoice and be glad[7] on Simchas Torah, and pay homage to the Torah for it is better than any commerce,[8]*
more precious than finest gold and gems.[9]
Let us exult and rejoice with this Torah, for to us it is strength and light.

א *I shall laud my God and be glad with Him, and place my hope in Him.*
I shall praise Him in the counsel of His intimate people —
God, my Rock — I take refuge in Him.[10]
Let us exult and rejoice with this Torah, for to us it is strength and light.

ב *Wholeheartedly I shall exalt Your righteousness*
and I shall relate Your praise.
While I live I will relate Your wonders, tell of Your kindness and Your truth.[11]
Let us exult and rejoice with this Torah, for to us it is strength and light.

ג *Redeemer, hasten the herald of good tidings,[12]*
for You are a tower of strength and goodness.
The redeemed ones shall thank You in good heart:
'Give thanks to HASHEM, for He is good!'[13]
Let us exult and rejoice with this Torah, for to us it is strength and light.

ד *O Bannered One, redeem now my multitude, for none is as holy as HASHEM.[14]*
The bannered [tribes of Israel] shall thank You,
HASHEM. Who can express the mighty acts of HASHEM?[15]
Let us exult and rejoice with this Torah, for to us it is strength and light.

ה *Has He not chosen us in His love? 'My son! My firstborn!'[16] has He called us.*
Majesty and splendor has he bequeathed us,
for His kindness is forever[17] with us.

אַשְׁרֵיכֶם *You are praiseworthy, Israel. You are praiseworthy, Israel.*
You are praiseworthy, Israel,
for God has chosen you and bequeathed you the Torah — from Sinai a gift.

---

(1) *Deuteronomy* 4:44. (2) *Numbers* 9:23. (3) *Proverbs* 3:18. (4) 3:17. (5) 3:16. (6) *Isaiah* 42:21. (7) Cf. *Psalms* 40:17; 70:5. (8) Cf. *Proverbs* 3:14. (9) Cf. 3:15. (10) Cf. *II Samuel* 22:3; *Psalms* 18:3. (11) Cf. 115:1. (12) Cf. *Isaiah* 52:7. (13) *Psalms* 136:1 et al. (14) *I Samuel* 2:2. (15) *Psalms* 106:2. (16) *Exodus* 4:22. (17) *Psalms* 136:1 et al.

הִתְקַבְּצוּ מַלְאָכִים זֶה אֶל זֶה, זֶה לָקֳבֵל זֶה, וְאָמַר זֶה לָזֶה, מִי הוּא זֶה וְאֵי זֶה הוּא מְאַחֵז פְּנֵי כִסֵּא, פַּרְשֵׁז עָלָיו עֲנָנוֹ, מִי עָלָה לַמָּרוֹם, מִי עָלָה לַמָּרוֹם, מִי עָלָה לַמָּרוֹם, וְהוֹרִיד עֹז מִבְטֶחָה.

מֹשֶׁה עָלָה לַמָּרוֹם, מֹשֶׁה עָלָה לַמָּרוֹם, מֹשֶׁה עָלָה לַמָּרוֹם, נְתַנְאֵל, שְׁמַעְיָה, אֲבִי סוֹכוֹ, אֲבִי זָנוֹחַ, חֶבֶר, יְקוּתִיאֵל, טוֹבִיָּה, יֶרֶד, אֲבִיגְדוֹר, עָלָה לַמָּרוֹם, וְהוֹרִיד עֹז מִבְטֶחָה.

אָגִיל וְאֶשְׂמַח[1] בְּשִׂמְחַת תּוֹרָה, בֹּא יָבֹא צֶמַח בְּשִׂמְחַת תּוֹרָה. תּוֹרָה הִיא עֵץ חַיִּים[2] לְכֻלָּם חַיִּים, כִּי עִמְּךָ מְקוֹר חַיִּים.[3] אַבְרָהָם שָׂמַח בְּשִׂמְחַת תּוֹרָה. יִצְחָק שָׂמַח בְּשִׂמְחַת תּוֹרָה. יַעֲקֹב שָׂמַח בְּשִׂמְחַת תּוֹרָה. מֹשֶׁה וְאַהֲרֹן שָׂמְחוּ בְּשִׂמְחַת תּוֹרָה. אֵלִיָּהוּ שְׁמוּאֵל דָּוִד שְׁלֹמֹה שָׂמְחוּ בְּשִׂמְחַת תּוֹרָה. תּוֹרָה הִיא עֵץ חַיִּים, לְכֻלָּם חַיִּים, כִּי עִמְּךָ מְקוֹר חַיִּים.

The *chazzan* takes the Torah in his right arm and recites:

יְהַלְלוּ אֶת שֵׁם יהוה, כִּי נִשְׂגָּב שְׁמוֹ לְבַדּוֹ –

Congregation responds:

– הוֹדוֹ עַל אֶרֶץ וְשָׁמָיִם. וַיָּרֶם קֶרֶן לְעַמּוֹ, תְּהִלָּה לְכָל חֲסִידָיו, לִבְנֵי יִשְׂרָאֵל עַם קְרֹבוֹ, הַלְלוּיָהּ.[4]

As the Torah is carried to the Ark the congregation recites the following psalm.

תהלים כד

לְדָוִד מִזְמוֹר, לַיהוה הָאָרֶץ וּמְלוֹאָהּ, תֵּבֵל וְיֹשְׁבֵי בָהּ. כִּי הוּא עַל יַמִּים יְסָדָהּ, וְעַל נְהָרוֹת יְכוֹנְנֶהָ. מִי יַעֲלֶה בְהַר יהוה, וּמִי יָקוּם בִּמְקוֹם קָדְשׁוֹ. נְקִי כַפַּיִם וּבַר לֵבָב, אֲשֶׁר לֹא נָשָׂא לַשָּׁוְא נַפְשִׁי וְלֹא נִשְׁבַּע לְמִרְמָה. יִשָּׂא בְרָכָה מֵאֵת יהוה, וּצְדָקָה מֵאֱלֹהֵי יִשְׁעוֹ. זֶה דּוֹר דֹּרְשָׁיו, מְבַקְשֵׁי פָנֶיךָ, יַעֲקֹב, סֶלָה. שְׂאוּ שְׁעָרִים רָאשֵׁיכֶם, וְהִנָּשְׂאוּ פִּתְחֵי עוֹלָם, וְיָבוֹא מֶלֶךְ הַכָּבוֹד. מִי זֶה מֶלֶךְ הַכָּבוֹד, יהוה עִזּוּז וְגִבּוֹר, יהוה גִּבּוֹר מִלְחָמָה. שְׂאוּ שְׁעָרִים רָאשֵׁיכֶם, וּשְׂאוּ פִּתְחֵי עוֹלָם, וְיָבֹא מֶלֶךְ הַכָּבוֹד. מִי הוּא זֶה מֶלֶךְ הַכָּבוֹד, יהוה צְבָאוֹת הוּא מֶלֶךְ הַכָּבוֹד, סֶלָה.

הִתְקַבְּצוּ *The angels gathered to one another, opposite one another, and said to one another, 'Who is the one, which is the one, who is holding onto the face of the throne? Upon whom He has spread His cloud?'*

Who has ascended on high? Who has ascended on high?
Who has ascended on high and taken down the powerful [Torah] from its secure spot [in heaven]?

Moses has ascended on high. Moses has ascended on high.
Nesanel, Shemayah, Avi Socho, Avi Zanoach, Chever, Yekusiel, Toviah, Yered, Avigdor have ascended on high and taken down the powerful [Torah] from its secure spot [in heaven].

אָגִיל *I shall rejoice and be glad*[1] *on Simchas Torah; may Tzemach [Messiah] come on Simchas Torah. The Torah is a tree of life,*[2] *for all of them life, for with You is the source of life.*[3] *Abraham rejoiced on Simchas Torah. Isaac rejoiced on Simchas Torah. Jacob rejoiced on Simchas Torah. Moses and Aaron rejoiced on Simchas Torah. Elijah, Samuel, David and Solomon rejoiced on Simchas Torah. The Torah is a tree of life, for all of them life, for with You is the source of life.*

The *chazzan* takes the Torah in his right arm and recites:

Let them praise the Name of HASHEM,
for His Name alone will have been exalted —

Congregation responds:

— His glory is above earth and heaven. And He will have exalted the pride of His people, causing praise for all His devout ones, for the Children of Israel, His intimate people. Halleluyah![4]

As the Torah is carried to the Ark the congregation recites the following psalm.

Psalm 24

לְדָוִד *Of David a psalm. HASHEM's is the earth and its fullness, the inhabited land and those who dwell in it. For He founded it upon seas, and established it upon rivers. Who may ascend the mountain of HASHEM, and who may stand in the place of His sanctity? One with clean hands and pure heart, who has not sworn in vain by My soul and has not sworn deceitfully. He will receive a blessing from HASHEM and just kindness from the God of his salvation. This is the generation of those who seek Him, those who strive for Your Presence — Jacob, Selah. Raise up your heads, O gates, and be uplifted, you everlasting entrances, so that the King of Glory may enter. Who is this King of Glory? — HASHEM, the mighty and strong, HASHEM, the strong in battle. Raise up your heads, O gates, and raise up, you everlasting entrances, so that the King of Glory may enter. Who then is the King of Glory? HASHEM, Master of Legions, He is the King of Glory. Selah!*

---

(1) Cf. *Psalms* 31:8. (2) Cf. *Proverbs* 3:18. (3) *Psalms* 36:10. (5) 148:13-14.

As the Torah is placed into the Ark, the congregation recites the following verses:

וּבְנֻחֹה יֹאמַר, שׁוּבָה יהוה רִבְבוֹת אַלְפֵי יִשְׂרָאֵל.[1] קוּמָה יהוה לִמְנוּחָתֶךָ, אַתָּה וַאֲרוֹן עֻזֶּךָ. כֹּהֲנֶיךָ יִלְבְּשׁוּ צֶדֶק, וַחֲסִידֶיךָ יְרַנֵּנוּ. בַּעֲבוּר דָּוִד עַבְדֶּךָ, אַל תָּשֵׁב פְּנֵי מְשִׁיחֶךָ.[2] כִּי לֶקַח טוֹב נָתַתִּי לָכֶם, תּוֹרָתִי אַל תַּעֲזֹבוּ.[3] ❖ עֵץ חַיִּים הִיא לַמַּחֲזִיקִים בָּהּ, וְתֹמְכֶיהָ מְאֻשָּׁר.[4] דְּרָכֶיהָ דַרְכֵי נֹעַם, וְכָל נְתִיבוֹתֶיהָ שָׁלוֹם.[5] הֲשִׁיבֵנוּ יהוה אֵלֶיךָ וְנָשׁוּבָה, חַדֵּשׁ יָמֵינוּ כְּקֶדֶם.[6]

קידוש בבית הכנסת

In some congregations, the *chazzan* recites *Kiddush* [although he will repeat *Kiddush* at home]. *Chazzan's Kiddush* consists of the blessings over wine, the holiness of the day, and *Shehecheyanu*. On Saturday night, two *Havdalah* blessings are inserted.

סַבְרִי מָרָנָן וְרַבָּנָן וְרַבּוֹתַי:

בָּרוּךְ אַתָּה יהוה אֱלֹהֵינוּ מֶלֶךְ הָעוֹלָם, בּוֹרֵא פְּרִי הַגָּפֶן.

(Cong. – אָמֵן.)

בָּרוּךְ יהוה אֱלֹהֵינוּ מֶלֶךְ הָעוֹלָם, אֲשֶׁר בָּחַר בָּנוּ מִכָּל עָם, וְרוֹמְמָנוּ מִכָּל לָשׁוֹן, וְקִדְּשָׁנוּ בְּמִצְוֹתָיו. וַתִּתֶּן לָנוּ יהוה אֱלֹהֵינוּ בְּאַהֲבָה מוֹעֲדִים לְשִׂמְחָה חַגִּים וּזְמַנִּים לְשָׂשׂוֹן, אֶת יוֹם הַשְּׁמִינִי חַג הָעֲצֶרֶת הַזֶּה, זְמַן שִׂמְחָתֵנוּ מִקְרָא קֹדֶשׁ, זֵכֶר לִיצִיאַת מִצְרָיִם. כִּי בָנוּ בָחַרְתָּ וְאוֹתָנוּ קִדַּשְׁתָּ מִכָּל הָעַמִּים, וּמוֹעֲדֵי קָדְשֶׁךָ בְּשִׂמְחָה וּבְשָׂשׂוֹן הִנְחַלְתָּנוּ. בָּרוּךְ אַתָּה יהוה, מְקַדֵּשׁ יִשְׂרָאֵל וְהַזְּמַנִּים.

(Cong. – אָמֵן.)

On Saturday night, two candles with flames touching each other are held before the *chazzan*.

בָּרוּךְ אַתָּה יהוה אֱלֹהֵינוּ מֶלֶךְ הָעוֹלָם, בּוֹרֵא מְאוֹרֵי הָאֵשׁ.

(Cong. – אָמֵן.)

The fingers are held up to the flames to see their light reflected on the nails.

בָּרוּךְ אַתָּה יהוה אֱלֹהֵינוּ מֶלֶךְ הָעוֹלָם, הַמַּבְדִּיל בֵּין קֹדֶשׁ לְחוֹל, בֵּין אוֹר לְחֹשֶׁךְ, בֵּין יִשְׂרָאֵל לָעַמִּים, בֵּין יוֹם הַשְּׁבִיעִי לְשֵׁשֶׁת יְמֵי הַמַּעֲשֶׂה. בֵּין קְדֻשַּׁת שַׁבָּת לִקְדֻשַּׁת יוֹם טוֹב הִבְדַּלְתָּ, וְאֶת יוֹם הַשְּׁבִיעִי מִשֵּׁשֶׁת יְמֵי הַמַּעֲשֶׂה קִדַּשְׁתָּ, הִבְדַּלְתָּ וְקִדַּשְׁתָּ אֶת עַמְּךָ יִשְׂרָאֵל בִּקְדֻשָּׁתֶךָ. בָּרוּךְ אַתָּה יהוה, הַמַּבְדִּיל בֵּין קֹדֶשׁ לְקֹדֶשׁ.

(Cong. – אָמֵן.)

בָּרוּךְ אַתָּה יהוה אֱלֹהֵינוּ מֶלֶךְ הָעוֹלָם, שֶׁהֶחֱיָנוּ וְקִיְּמָנוּ וְהִגִּיעָנוּ לַזְּמַן הַזֶּה.

(Cong. – אָמֵן.)

A child who listened to the *Kiddush* and responded אָמֵן is given some of the wine. [If no child is present, the *chazzan* drinks the required amount; see commentary, p. 65.]

As the Torah is placed into the Ark, the congregation recites the following verses:

וּבְנֻחֹה *And when it rested he would say, 'Return, HASHEM, to the myriad thousands of Israel.'*[1] *Arise, HASHEM, to Your resting place, You and the Ark of Your strength. Let Your priests be clothed in righteousness, and Your devout ones will sing joyously. For the sake of David, Your servant, turn not away the face of Your anointed.*[2] *For I have given you a good teaching, do not forsake My Torah.*[3] Chazzan– *It is a tree of life for those who grasp it, and its supporters are praiseworthy.*[4] *Its ways are ways of pleasantness and all its paths are peace.*[5] *Bring us back to You, HASHEM, and we shall return, renew our days as of old.*[6]

KIDDUSH IN THE SYNAGOGUE

In some congregations, the *chazzan* recites *Kiddush* [although he will repeat *Kiddush* at home]. *Chazzan's Kiddush* consists of the blessings over wine, the holiness of the day, and *Shehecheyanu*. On Saturday night, two *Havdalah* blessings are inserted.

By your leave, my masters and teachers:

בָּרוּךְ *Blessed are You, HASHEM, our God, King of the universe, Who creates the fruit of the vine.* (Cong.– *Amen.)*

On Friday night, the words in brackets are included.

בָּרוּךְ *Blessed are You, HASHEM, our God, King of the universe, Who has chosen us from every people, exalted us above every tongue, and sanctified us with His commandments. And You gave us, HASHEM, our God, with love, appointed festivals for gladness, festivals and times of joy, this day of the Shemini Atzeres Festival, the time of our gladness, a holy convocation, a memorial of the Exodus from Egypt. For You have chosen us and You have sanctified us above all the peoples, and Your holy festivals in gladness and in joy have You granted us as a heritage. Blessed are You, HASHEM, Who sanctifies Israel and the seasons.*

(Cong.– *Amen.)*

On Saturday night, two candles with flames touching each other are held before the *chazzan*.

בָּרוּךְ *Blessed are You, HASHEM, our God, King of the universe, Who creates the illumination of the fire.* (Cong. – *Amen.)*

The fingers are held up to the flames to see their light reflected on the nails.

בָּרוּךְ *Blessed are you, HASHEM, our God, King of the universe, Who distinguishes between the sacred and secular, between light and darkness, between Israel and the peoples, between the seventh day and the six days of labor. Between sanctity of the Sabbaths and the sanctity of the holidays You have distinguished, and the seventh day, from among the six days of labor You have sanctified. You have distinguished and You have sanctified Your people Israel with Your holiness. Blessed are You, HASHEM, Who distinguishes between holiness and holiness.* (Cong. – *Amen.)*

בָּרוּךְ *Blessed are You, HASHEM, our God, King of the universe, Who has kept us alive, sustained us, and brought us to this season.*

(Cong.– *Amen.)*

A child who listened to the *Kiddush* and responded *Amen* is given some of the wine. [If no child is present, the *chazzan* drinks the required amount; see commentary p. 65.]

(1) *Numbers* 10:36. (2) *Psalms* 132:8-10. (3) *Proverbs* 4:2. (4) 3:18. (5) 3:17. (6) *Lamentations* 5:21.

The congregation stands while reciting עָלֵינוּ.

עָלֵינוּ לְשַׁבֵּחַ לַאֲדוֹן הַכֹּל, לָתֵת גְּדֻלָּה לְיוֹצֵר בְּרֵאשִׁית, שֶׁלֹּא עָשָׂנוּ כְּגוֹיֵי הָאֲרָצוֹת, וְלֹא שָׂמָנוּ כְּמִשְׁפְּחוֹת הָאֲדָמָה. שֶׁלֹּא שָׂם חֶלְקֵנוּ כָּהֶם, וְגוֹרָלֵנוּ כְּכָל הֲמוֹנָם. (שֶׁהֵם מִשְׁתַּחֲוִים לְהֶבֶל וָרִיק, וּמִתְפַּלְּלִים אֶל אֵל לֹא יוֹשִׁיעַ.[1]) וַאֲנַחְנוּ כּוֹרְעִים וּמִשְׁתַּחֲוִים וּמוֹדִים, לִפְנֵי מֶלֶךְ מַלְכֵי הַמְּלָכִים הַקָּדוֹשׁ בָּרוּךְ הוּא. שֶׁהוּא נוֹטֶה שָׁמַיִם וְיֹסֵד אָרֶץ,[2] וּמוֹשַׁב יְקָרוֹ בַּשָּׁמַיִם מִמַּעַל, וּשְׁכִינַת עֻזּוֹ בְּגָבְהֵי מְרוֹמִים. הוּא אֱלֹהֵינוּ, אֵין עוֹד. אֱמֶת מַלְכֵּנוּ, אֶפֶס זוּלָתוֹ, כַּכָּתוּב בְּתוֹרָתוֹ: וְיָדַעְתָּ הַיּוֹם וַהֲשֵׁבֹתָ אֶל לְבָבֶךָ, כִּי יהוה הוּא הָאֱלֹהִים בַּשָּׁמַיִם מִמַּעַל וְעַל הָאָרֶץ מִתָּחַת, אֵין עוֹד.[3]

Bow while reciting וַאֲנַחְנוּ כּוֹרְעִים וּמִשְׁתַּחֲוִים.

עַל כֵּן נְקַוֶּה לְּךָ יהוה אֱלֹהֵינוּ לִרְאוֹת מְהֵרָה בְּתִפְאֶרֶת עֻזֶּךָ, לְהַעֲבִיר גִּלּוּלִים מִן הָאָרֶץ, וְהָאֱלִילִים כָּרוֹת יִכָּרֵתוּן, לְתַקֵּן עוֹלָם בְּמַלְכוּת שַׁדַּי. וְכָל בְּנֵי בָשָׂר יִקְרְאוּ בִשְׁמֶךָ, לְהַפְנוֹת אֵלֶיךָ כָּל רִשְׁעֵי אָרֶץ. יַכִּירוּ וְיֵדְעוּ כָּל יוֹשְׁבֵי תֵבֵל, כִּי לְךָ תִּכְרַע כָּל בֶּרֶךְ, תִּשָּׁבַע כָּל לָשׁוֹן.[4] לְפָנֶיךָ יהוה אֱלֹהֵינוּ יִכְרְעוּ וְיִפֹּלוּ, וְלִכְבוֹד שִׁמְךָ יְקָר יִתֵּנוּ. וִיקַבְּלוּ כֻלָּם אֶת עוֹל מַלְכוּתֶךָ, וְתִמְלֹךְ עֲלֵיהֶם מְהֵרָה לְעוֹלָם וָעֶד. כִּי הַמַּלְכוּת שֶׁלְּךָ הִיא וּלְעוֹלְמֵי עַד תִּמְלוֹךְ בְּכָבוֹד, כַּכָּתוּב בְּתוֹרָתֶךָ: יהוה יִמְלֹךְ לְעֹלָם וָעֶד.[5] ❖ וְנֶאֱמַר: וְהָיָה יהוה לְמֶלֶךְ עַל כָּל הָאָרֶץ, בַּיּוֹם הַהוּא יִהְיֶה יהוה אֶחָד וּשְׁמוֹ אֶחָד.[6]

Some recite the following after עָלֵינוּ:

אַל תִּירָא מִפַּחַד פִּתְאֹם, וּמִשֹּׁאַת רְשָׁעִים כִּי תָבֹא.[7] עֻצוּ עֵצָה וְתֻפָר, דַּבְּרוּ דָבָר וְלֹא יָקוּם, כִּי עִמָּנוּ אֵל.[8] וְעַד זִקְנָה אֲנִי הוּא, וְעַד שֵׂיבָה אֲנִי אֶסְבֹּל, אֲנִי עָשִׂיתִי וַאֲנִי אֶשָּׂא, וַאֲנִי אֶסְבֹּל וַאֲמַלֵּט.[9]

קדיש יתום

Mourners recite קַדִּישׁ יָתוֹם (see *Laws* §81-83).

יִתְגַּדַּל וְיִתְקַדַּשׁ שְׁמֵהּ רַבָּא. (–Cong. אָמֵן.) בְּעָלְמָא דִּי בְרָא כִרְעוּתֵהּ. וְיַמְלִיךְ מַלְכוּתֵהּ, בְּחַיֵּיכוֹן וּבְיוֹמֵיכוֹן וּבְחַיֵּי דְכָל בֵּית יִשְׂרָאֵל, בַּעֲגָלָא וּבִזְמַן קָרִיב. וְאִמְרוּ: אָמֵן.

(–Cong. אָמֵן. יְהֵא שְׁמֵהּ רַבָּא מְבָרַךְ לְעָלַם וּלְעָלְמֵי עָלְמַיָּא.)

The congregation stands while reciting עָלֵינוּ, *'It is our duty . . .'*

עָלֵינוּ *It is our duty to praise the Master of all, to ascribe greatness to the Molder of primeval creation, for He has not made us like the nations of the lands, and has not emplaced us like the families of the earth; for He has not assigned our portion like theirs nor our lot like all their multitudes. (For they bow to vanity and emptiness and pray to a god which helps not.*[1]*) But we bend our knees, bow, and acknowledge our thanks before the King Who reigns over kings, the Holy One, Blessed is He. He stretches out heaven and establishes earth's foundation,*[2] *the seat of His homage is in the heavens above and His powerful Presence is in the loftiest heights. He is our God and there is none other. True is our King, there is nothing beside Him, as it is written in His Torah: 'You are to know this day and take to your heart that* HASHEM *is the only God — in heaven above and on the earth below — there is none other.'*[3]

Bow while reciting 'But we bend our knees.'

עַל כֵּן *Therefore we put our hope in You,* HASHEM*, our God, that we may soon see Your mighty splendor, to remove detestable idolatry from the earth, and false gods will be utterly cut off, to perfect the universe through the Almighty's sovereignty. Then all humanity will call upon Your Name, to turn all the earth's wicked toward You. All the world's inhabitants will recognize and know that to You every knee should bend, every tongue should swear.*[4] *Before You,* HASHEM*, our God, they will bend every knee and cast themselves down and to the glory of Your Name they will render homage, and they will all accept upon themselves the yoke of Your kingship that You may reign over them soon and eternally. For the kingdom is Yours and You will reign for all eternity in glory as it is written in Your Torah:* HASHEM *shall reign for all eternity.*[5] *And it is said:* HASHEM *will be King over all the world — on that day* HASHEM *will be One and His Name will be One.*[6]

Some recite the following after *Aleinu:*

אַל תִּירָא *Do not fear sudden terror, or the holocaust of the wicked when it comes.*[7] *Plan a conspiracy and it will be annulled; speak your piece and it shall not stand, for God is with us.*[8] *Even till your seniority, I remain unchanged; and even till your ripe old age, I shall endure. I created you and I shall bear you; I shall endure and rescue.*[9]

MOURNER'S KADDISH

Mourners recite the Mourner's *Kaddish* (see *Laws* §81-83).
[A transliteration of this *Kaddish* appears on page 1301.]

יִתְגַּדַּל *May His great Name grow exalted and sanctified* (Cong.— *Amen.*) *in the world that He created as He willed. May He give reign to His kingship in your lifetimes and in your days, and in the lifetimes of the entire Family of Israel, swiftly and soon. Now respond: Amen.*

(Cong.— *Amen. May His great Name be blessed forever and ever.*)

(1) *Isaiah* 45:20. (2) 51:13. (3) *Deuteronomy* 4:39. (4) Cf. *Isaiah* 45:23.
(5) *Exodus* 15:18. (6) *Zechariah* 14:9. (7) *Proverbs* 3:25. (8) *Isaiah* 8:10. (9) 46:4.

יְהֵא שְׁמֵהּ רַבָּא מְבָרַךְ לְעָלַם וּלְעָלְמֵי עָלְמַיָּא.

יִתְבָּרַךְ וְיִשְׁתַּבַּח וְיִתְפָּאַר וְיִתְרוֹמַם וְיִתְנַשֵּׂא וְיִתְהַדָּר וְיִתְעַלֶּה וְיִתְהַלָּל שְׁמֵהּ דְּקֻדְשָׁא בְּרִיךְ הוּא (.Cong – בְּרִיךְ הוּא) – לְעֵלָּא מִן כָּל בִּרְכָתָא וְשִׁירָתָא תֻּשְׁבְּחָתָא וְנֶחֱמָתָא, דַּאֲמִירָן בְּעָלְמָא. וְאִמְרוּ: אָמֵן. (.Cong – אָמֵן.)

יְהֵא שְׁלָמָא רַבָּא מִן שְׁמַיָּא, וְחַיִּים עָלֵינוּ וְעַל כָּל יִשְׂרָאֵל. וְאִמְרוּ: אָמֵן. (.Cong – אָמֵן.)

Take three steps back. Bow left and say . . . עֹשֶׂה; bow right and say . . . הוּא; bow forward and say וְעַל כָּל . . . אָמֵן. Remain standing in place for a few moments, then take three steps forward.

עֹשֶׂה שָׁלוֹם בִּמְרוֹמָיו, הוּא יַעֲשֶׂה שָׁלוֹם עָלֵינוּ, וְעַל כָּל יִשְׂרָאֵל. וְאִמְרוּ: אָמֵן. (.Cong – אָמֵן.)

Many congregations recite either אֲדוֹן עוֹלָם or יִגְדַּל, or both, at this point.

אֲדוֹן עוֹלָם אֲשֶׁר מָלַךְ, בְּטֶרֶם כָּל יְצִיר נִבְרָא.
לְעֵת נַעֲשָׂה בְחֶפְצוֹ כֹּל, אֲזַי מֶלֶךְ שְׁמוֹ נִקְרָא.
וְאַחֲרֵי כִּכְלוֹת הַכֹּל, לְבַדּוֹ יִמְלוֹךְ נוֹרָא.
וְהוּא הָיָה וְהוּא הֹוֶה, וְהוּא יִהְיֶה בְּתִפְאָרָה.
וְהוּא אֶחָד וְאֵין שֵׁנִי, לְהַמְשִׁיל לוֹ לְהַחְבִּירָה.
בְּלִי רֵאשִׁית בְּלִי תַכְלִית, וְלוֹ הָעֹז וְהַמִּשְׂרָה.
וְהוּא אֵלִי וְחַי גֹּאֲלִי, וְצוּר חֶבְלִי בְּעֵת צָרָה.
וְהוּא נִסִּי וּמָנוֹס לִי, מְנָת כּוֹסִי בְּיוֹם אֶקְרָא.
בְּיָדוֹ אַפְקִיד רוּחִי, בְּעֵת אִישַׁן וְאָעִירָה.
וְעִם רוּחִי גְּוִיָּתִי, יהוה לִי וְלֹא אִירָא.

יִגְדַּל אֱלֹהִים חַי וְיִשְׁתַּבַּח, נִמְצָא וְאֵין עֵת אֶל מְצִיאוּתוֹ.
אֶחָד וְאֵין יָחִיד כְּיִחוּדוֹ, נֶעְלָם וְגַם אֵין סוֹף לְאַחְדּוּתוֹ.
אֵין לוֹ דְמוּת הַגּוּף וְאֵינוֹ גוּף, לֹא נַעֲרוֹךְ אֵלָיו קְדֻשָּׁתוֹ.
קַדְמוֹן לְכָל דָּבָר אֲשֶׁר נִבְרָא, רִאשׁוֹן וְאֵין רֵאשִׁית לְרֵאשִׁיתוֹ.
הִנּוֹ אֲדוֹן עוֹלָם לְכָל נוֹצָר, יוֹרֶה גְדֻלָּתוֹ וּמַלְכוּתוֹ.
שֶׁפַע נְבוּאָתוֹ נְתָנוֹ, אֶל אַנְשֵׁי סְגֻלָּתוֹ וְתִפְאַרְתּוֹ.
לֹא קָם בְּיִשְׂרָאֵל כְּמֹשֶׁה עוֹד, נָבִיא וּמַבִּיט אֶת תְּמוּנָתוֹ.
תּוֹרַת אֱמֶת נָתַן לְעַמּוֹ אֵל, עַל יַד נְבִיאוֹ נֶאֱמַן בֵּיתוֹ.
לֹא יַחֲלִיף הָאֵל וְלֹא יָמִיר דָּתוֹ, לְעוֹלָמִים לְזוּלָתוֹ.
צוֹפֶה וְיוֹדֵעַ סְתָרֵינוּ, מַבִּיט לְסוֹף דָּבָר בְּקַדְמָתוֹ.

May His great Name be blessed forever and ever.

Blessed, praised, glorified, exalted, extolled, mighty, upraised, and lauded be the Name of the Holy One, Blessed is He (Cong.— *Blessed is He*) *— beyond any blessing and song, praise and consolation that are uttered in the world. Now respond: Amen.* (Cong.— *Amen.*)

May there be abundant peace from Heaven, and life, upon us and upon all Israel. Now respond: Amen. (Cong.— *Amen.*)

Take three steps back. Bow left and say, *'He Who makes peace . . .'*; bow right and say, *'may He . . .'*; bow forward and say, *'and upon all Israel . . .'* Remain standing in place for a few moments, then take three steps forward.

He Who makes peace in His heights, may He make peace upon us, and upon all Israel. Now respond: Amen. (Cong.— *Amen.*)

Many congregations recite either אֲדוֹן עוֹלָם, *Master of the universe,* or יִגְדַּל, *Exalted be,* or both.

אֲדוֹן עוֹלָם *Master of the universe, Who reigned*
before any form was created,
At the time when His will brought all into being —
then as 'King' was His Name proclaimed.
After all has ceased to be, He, the Awesome One, will reign alone.
It is He Who was, He Who is, and He Who shall remain, in splendor.
He is One — there is no second to compare to Him, to declare as His equal.
Without beginning, without conclusion — His is the power and dominion.
He is my God, my living Redeemer, Rock of my pain in time of distress.
He is my banner, a refuge for me, the portion in my cup on the day I call.
Into His hand I shall entrust my spirit
when I go to sleep — and I shall awaken!
With my spirit shall my body remain.
HASHEM is with me, I shall not fear.

יִגְדַּל *Exalted be the Living God and praised,*
He exists — unbounded by time is His existence.
He is One — and there is no unity like His Oneness.
Inscrutable and infinite is His Oneness.
He has no semblance of a body nor is He corporeal;
nor has His holiness any comparison.
He preceded every being that was created —
the First, and nothing precedes His precedence.
Behold! He is Master of the universe to every creature,
He demonstrates His greatness and His sovereignty.
He granted His flow of prophecy
to His treasured splendrous people.
In Israel none like Moses arose again —
a prophet who perceived His vision clearly.
God gave His people a Torah of truth,
by means of His prophet, the most trusted of His household.
God will never amend nor exchange His law
for any other one, for all eternity.
He scrutinizes and knows our hiddenmost secrets;
He perceives a matter's outcome at its inception.

גּוֹמֵל לְאִישׁ חֶסֶד כְּמִפְעָלוֹ, נוֹתֵן לְרָשָׁע רָע כְּרִשְׁעָתוֹ.
יִשְׁלַח לְקֵץ הַיָּמִין מְשִׁיחֵנוּ, לִפְדּוֹת מְחַכֵּי קֵץ יְשׁוּעָתוֹ.
מֵתִים יְחַיֶּה אֵל בְּרֹב חַסְדּוֹ, בָּרוּךְ עֲדֵי עַד שֵׁם תְּהִלָּתוֹ.

קידוש לליל שמחת תורה

סַבְרִי מָרָנָן וְרַבָּנָן וְרַבּוֹתַי:

בָּרוּךְ אַתָּה יהוה אֱלֹהֵינוּ מֶלֶךְ הָעוֹלָם, בּוֹרֵא פְּרִי הַגָּפֶן.

(—All present respond אָמֵן.)

בָּרוּךְ אַתָּה יהוה אֱלֹהֵינוּ מֶלֶךְ הָעוֹלָם, אֲשֶׁר בָּחַר בָּנוּ מִכָּל עָם, וְרוֹמְמָנוּ מִכָּל לָשׁוֹן, וְקִדְּשָׁנוּ בְּמִצְוֹתָיו. וַתִּתֶּן לָנוּ יהוה אֱלֹהֵינוּ בְּאַהֲבָה מוֹעֲדִים לְשִׂמְחָה חַגִּים וּזְמַנִּים לְשָׂשׂוֹן, אֶת יוֹם הַשְּׁמִינִי חַג הָעֲצֶרֶת הַזֶּה, זְמַן שִׂמְחָתֵנוּ מִקְרָא קֹדֶשׁ, זֵכֶר לִיצִיאַת מִצְרָיִם. כִּי בָנוּ בָחַרְתָּ וְאוֹתָנוּ קִדַּשְׁתָּ מִכָּל הָעַמִּים, וּמוֹעֲדֵי קָדְשֶׁךָ בְּשִׂמְחָה וּבְשָׂשׂוֹן הִנְחַלְתָּנוּ. בָּרוּךְ אַתָּה יהוה, מְקַדֵּשׁ יִשְׂרָאֵל וְהַזְּמַנִּים.

(—All present respond אָמֵן.)

On Saturday night, add the following two *Havdalah*• blessings. Two candles with flames touching each other should be held before the person reciting the *Havdalah*. After the first blessing, hold the fingers up to the flames to see the reflected light.

[It is forbidden to create a new flame — for example, by striking a match — on *Yom Tov*. Therefore, the *Havdalah* candle must be lit from a flame that has been burning from before the Sabbath. It is likewise forbidden to extinguish the flame.]

בָּרוּךְ אַתָּה יהוה אֱלֹהֵינוּ מֶלֶךְ הָעוֹלָם, בּוֹרֵא מְאוֹרֵי הָאֵשׁ.

(—All present respond אָמֵן.)

בָּרוּךְ אַתָּה יהוה אֱלֹהֵינוּ מֶלֶךְ הָעוֹלָם, הַמַּבְדִּיל בֵּין קֹדֶשׁ לְחוֹל, בֵּין אוֹר לְחֹשֶׁךְ, בֵּין יִשְׂרָאֵל לָעַמִּים, בֵּין יוֹם הַשְּׁבִיעִי לְשֵׁשֶׁת יְמֵי הַמַּעֲשֶׂה. בֵּין קְדֻשַּׁת שַׁבָּת לִקְדֻשַּׁת יוֹם טוֹב הִבְדַּלְתָּ, וְאֶת יוֹם הַשְּׁבִיעִי מִשֵּׁשֶׁת יְמֵי הַמַּעֲשֶׂה קִדַּשְׁתָּ, הִבְדַּלְתָּ וְקִדַּשְׁתָּ אֶת עַמְּךָ יִשְׂרָאֵל בִּקְדֻשָּׁתֶךָ. בָּרוּךְ אַתָּה יהוה, הַמַּבְדִּיל בֵּין קֹדֶשׁ לְקֹדֶשׁ.

(—All present respond אָמֵן.)

בָּרוּךְ אַתָּה יהוה אֱלֹהֵינוּ מֶלֶךְ הָעוֹלָם, שֶׁהֶחֱיָנוּ וְקִיְּמָנוּ וְהִגִּיעָנוּ לַזְּמַן הַזֶּה.

(—All present respond אָמֵן.)

Bircas HaMazon appears on page 84.

He recompenses man with kindness according to his deed;
He places evil on the wicked according to his wickedness.
By the End of Days He will send our Messiah,
to redeem those longing for His final salvation.
God will revive the dead in His abundant kindness —
Blessed forever is His praised Name.

KIDDUSH FOR THE NIGHT OF SIMCHAS TORAH

By your leave, my masters, rabbis and teachers:

בָּרוּךְ *Blessed are You,* HASHEM, *our God, King of the universe, Who creates the fruit of the vine.* (All present respond— *Amen.*)

בָּרוּךְ *Blessed are You,* HASHEM, *our God, King of the universe, Who has chosen us from every people, exalted us above every tongue, and sanctified us with His commandments. And You gave us,* HASHEM, *our God, with love, appointed festivals for gladness, festivals and times for joy,* [this day of Sabbath and] *this day of the Shemini Atzeres Festival, the time of our gladness, a holy convocation, a memorial of the Exodus from Egypt. For You have chosen us and You have sanctified us above all the peoples, and Your holy festivals in gladness and in joy have You granted us as a heritage. Blessed are You,* HASHEM, *Who sanctifies* [the Sabbath and] *Israel and the seasons.* (All present respond— *Amen.*)

On Saturday night, add the following two *Havdalah** blessings. Two candles with flames touching each other should be held before the person reciting the *Havdalah*. After the first blessing, hold the fingers up to the flames to see the reflected light.

[It is forbidden to create a new flame — for example, by striking a match — on *Yom Tov*. Therefore, the *Havdalah* candle must be lit from a flame that has been burning from before the Sabbath. It is likewise forbidden to extinguish the flame.]

בָּרוּךְ *Blessed are You,* HASHEM, *our God, King of the universe, Who creates the illumination of the fire.* (All present respond— *Amen.*)

בָּרוּךְ *Blessed are You,* HASHEM, *our God, King of the universe, Who distinguishes between the sacred and secular, between light and darkness, between Israel and the peoples, between the seventh day and the six days of labor. Between sanctity of the Sabbaths and the sanctity of the holidays You have distinguished, and the seventh day, from among the six days of labor You have sanctified. You have distinguished and You have sanctified Your people Israel with Your holiness. Blessed are You,* HASHEM, *Who distinguishes between holiness and holiness.*
(All present respond— *Amen.*)

בָּרוּךְ *Blessed are You,* HASHEM, *our God, King of the universe, Who has kept us alive, sustained us, and brought us to this season.* (All present respond— *Amen.*)

Grace After Meals appears on page 84.

שחרית לשמחת תורה

THE MORNING SERVICE BEGINS WITH PAGES 130-208, THEN CONTINUES HERE.

נִשְׁמַת• מְלַמְּדֵי מוֹרָשָׁה נִקְרָאִים בְּנֵי חֹפֶשׁ,*
נֶצַח יוּנְטָעוּ לְחַיֵּי עוֹלָם וְנֶפֶשׁ,
תּוֹרַת יהוה תְּמִימָה מְשִׁיבַת נָפֶשׁ.[1]

נִשְׁמַת חַכְמֵי חֶמְדָּה בִּגְבוּרָה וְלֹא בַשְּׁתִי,[2]*
תַּמְלִיךְ מוֹרֶה וְשִׂים רְפוּאָתִי,
עֵדוּת יהוה נֶאֱמָנָה מַחְכִּימַת פֶּתִי.[1]

נִשְׁמַת בְּנֵי בִינָה מִתְעַנְּגִים מִטּוּב הַלֵּב,
הִרְגִּישׁוּ רָזֵי דָּרֵי הַלֵּב,
פִּקּוּדֵי יהוה יְשָׁרִים מְשַׂמְּחֵי לֵב.[3]

נִשְׁמַת בְּנֵי נְבוֹנִים בְּשִׁקּוּל וְתַכְרִיעַ מֹאזְנַיִם,
תְּיַשֵּׁר יְוֹפִי חִקּוּר וְתִקּוּן אָזְנַיִם,[4]
מִצְוַת יהוה בָּרָה מְאִירַת עֵינָיִם.[3]

נִשְׁמַת מְבִינֵי מַדָּע תּוֹרָה בְּלִבָּם לְמִסְעָד,
תְּכַבֵּד כּוֹנֵן אֲשׁוּרֵימוֹ לֹא תִמְעַד,[5]
יִרְאַת יהוה טְהוֹרָה עוֹמֶדֶת לָעַד.[6]

נִשְׁמַת יְדִידִים יָדָם זַיֵּן פִּיפִיּוֹת חֲדָיו,[7]
תָּרֹן רוֹמְמוֹת סִלְסוּל עֹז מַחֲמַדָּיו,
מִשְׁפְּטֵי יהוה אֱמֶת צָדְקוּ יַחְדָּו.[6]

נִשְׁמַת וְעוֹדִים בְּאַרְצוֹת שִׁבְיָם,
שְׂרִידֶיךָ פְּזוּרֶיךָ יְרוֹמְמוּךָ בְּעֵת תְּשִׁיבֵם לִצְבִי עֶדְיָם,
בְּאוֹמְרִים אִלּוּ פִינוּ מָלֵא שִׁירָה כַּיָּם.[8]

נִשְׁמַת כָּל חַי תְּבָרֵךְ אֶת שִׁמְךָ יהוה אֱלֹהֵינוּ, וְרוּחַ כָּל בָּשָׂר תְּפָאֵר וּתְרוֹמֵם זִכְרְךָ מַלְכֵּנוּ תָּמִיד. מִן הָעוֹלָם וְעַד הָעוֹלָם אַתָּה אֵל,[9] וּמִבַּלְעָדֶיךָ אֵין לָנוּ מֶלֶךְ[10] גּוֹאֵל וּמוֹשִׁיעַ. פּוֹדֶה וּמַצִּיל וּמְפַרְנֵס וּמְרַחֵם בְּכָל עֵת צָרָה וְצוּקָה, אֵין לָנוּ מֶלֶךְ אֶלָּא אָתָּה. אֱלֹהֵי הָרִאשׁוֹנִים וְהָאַחֲרוֹנִים, אֱלוֹהַּ כָּל בְּרִיּוֹת, אֲדוֹן כָּל תּוֹלָדוֹת, הַמְּהֻלָּל בְּרֹב הַתִּשְׁבָּחוֹת, הַמְנַהֵג עוֹלָמוֹ בְּחֶסֶד

נִשְׁמַת – *The soul.* Calling upon God to encourage and exalt those who study Torah, this *piyut* is based on the verses of Psalm 19:8-10. The acrostic spells the author's name, מְנַחֵם בְּרַבִּי מָכִיר, *Menachem son of R' Machir* (see p. 370).

בְּנֵי חֹפֶשׁ – *Free men.* 'You can have no freer man than the one who engages in the study of Torah' (*Avos* 6:2).

בִּגְבוּרָה וְלֹא בַשְּׁתִי – *In strength but not in weakness.* An alternative rendering [based on the phrase's context in *Ecclesiastes* 10:17] is: *In strength* [of Torah] *but not in drink.*

SHACHARIS FOR SIMCHAS TORAH

THE MORNING SERVICE BEGINS WITH PAGES 130-208, THEN CONTINUES HERE.

מ *The soul* of those who study the heritage [Torah],*
*those who are called free men,**
נ *may they be planted forever for eternal life and contentment —*
[through] the Torah of HASHEM *[which] is perfect, restoring the soul.*[1]
ח *The soul of the scholars of the desirable [Torah],*
in strength but not in weakness,[2]*
מ *cause the teacher [the Torah] to reign,*
and establish my cure [redemption] —
[through] the testimony of HASHEM *[which] is trustworthy,*
making the simple one wise.[1]
ב *The soul of the insightful ones delight with satisfaction of heart,*
ר *may they amass the [Torah's] secrets in the chambers of the heart —*
[through] the orders of HASHEM *[which] are upright,*
gladdening the heart.[3]
ב *The soul of the discerning ones who know how to weigh and tip the scales,*
י *align their beautiful discussions with research and attentive ears*[4] *—*
[through] the command of HASHEM *[which] is clear,*
enlightening the eyes.[3]
מ *The soul of those perceptive in learning,*
who sustain their hearts with Torah,
כ *bring [them] honor, firm their steps that they not falter*[5] *—*
[through] the fear of HASHEM *[which] is pure, enduring forever.*[6]
י *The soul of [God's] beloved whose hands are armed*
with sharp double-edged swords,[7]
may they sing glad song and exalted praise
about the strength of his desire [the Torah] —
[through] the judgments of HASHEM *[which] are true,*
altogether righteous.[6]
The soul of the assembled [in synagogues] in the lands of their captivity,
may Your scattered refugees exalt when You return them to
[Eretz Yisrael], their cherished jewel —
when they sang, 'Were our mouths as full of song as the sea ...'[8]

נִשְׁמַת *The soul of every living being shall bless Your Name,* HASHEM *our God; the spirit of all flesh shall always glorify and exalt Your remembrance, our King. From This World to the World to Come, You are God,*[9] *and other than You we have no king,*[10] *redeemer or savior. Liberator, Rescuer, Sustainer and Merciful One in every time of distress and anguish, we have no king but You! — God of the first and of the last, God of all creatures, Master of all generations, Who is extolled through a multitude of praises, Who guides His world with kindness*

(1) *Psalms* 19:8. (2) *Ecclesiastes* 10:17. (3) *Psalms* 19:9. (4) Cf. *Ecclesiastes* 12:9.
(5) Cf. *Psalms* 40:3 and 37:32. (6) *Psalms* 19:10. (7) Cf. 149:6.
(8) From the *Nishmas* prayer, p. 1110. (9) Cf. *Psalms* 90:2. (10) Cf. *Isaiah* 44:6.

וּבְרִיּוֹתָיו בְּרַחֲמִים. וַיהוה לֹא יָנוּם וְלֹא יִישָׁן.[1] הַמְּעוֹרֵר יְשֵׁנִים, וְהַמֵּקִיץ נִרְדָּמִים, וְהַמֵּשִׂיחַ אִלְּמִים, וְהַמַּתִּיר אֲסוּרִים,[2] וְהַסּוֹמֵךְ נוֹפְלִים, וְהַזּוֹקֵף כְּפוּפִים.[3] לְךָ לְבַדְּךָ אֲנַחְנוּ מוֹדִים. אִלּוּ פִינוּ מָלֵא שִׁירָה כַּיָּם, וּלְשׁוֹנֵנוּ רִנָּה כַּהֲמוֹן גַּלָּיו, וְשִׂפְתוֹתֵינוּ שֶׁבַח כְּמֶרְחֲבֵי רָקִיעַ, וְעֵינֵינוּ מְאִירוֹת כַּשֶּׁמֶשׁ וְכַיָּרֵחַ, וְיָדֵינוּ פְרוּשׂוֹת כְּנִשְׁרֵי שָׁמָיִם, וְרַגְלֵינוּ קַלּוֹת כָּאַיָּלוֹת, אֵין אֲנַחְנוּ מַסְפִּיקִים לְהוֹדוֹת לְךָ, יהוה אֱלֹהֵינוּ וֵאלֹהֵי אֲבוֹתֵינוּ, וּלְבָרֵךְ אֶת שְׁמֶךָ עַל אַחַת מֵאָלֶף אֶלֶף אַלְפֵי אֲלָפִים וְרִבֵּי רְבָבוֹת פְּעָמִים הַטּוֹבוֹת שֶׁעָשִׂיתָ עִם אֲבוֹתֵינוּ וְעִמָּנוּ. מִמִּצְרַיִם גְּאַלְתָּנוּ יהוה אֱלֹהֵינוּ, וּמִבֵּית עֲבָדִים פְּדִיתָנוּ. בְּרָעָב זַנְתָּנוּ, וּבְשָׂבָע כִּלְכַּלְתָּנוּ, מֵחֶרֶב הִצַּלְתָּנוּ, וּמִדֶּבֶר מִלַּטְתָּנוּ, וּמֵחֳלָיִם רָעִים וְנֶאֱמָנִים דִּלִּיתָנוּ. עַד הֵנָּה עֲזָרוּנוּ רַחֲמֶיךָ, וְלֹא עֲזָבוּנוּ חֲסָדֶיךָ. וְאַל תִּטְּשֵׁנוּ יהוה אֱלֹהֵינוּ לָנֶצַח. עַל כֵּן אֵבָרִים שֶׁפִּלַּגְתָּ בָּנוּ, וְרוּחַ וּנְשָׁמָה שֶׁנָּפַחְתָּ בְּאַפֵּינוּ, וְלָשׁוֹן אֲשֶׁר שַׂמְתָּ בְּפִינוּ, הֵן הֵם יוֹדוּ וִיבָרְכוּ וִישַׁבְּחוּ וִיפָאֲרוּ וִירוֹמְמוּ וְיַעֲרִיצוּ וְיַקְדִּישׁוּ וְיַמְלִיכוּ אֶת שִׁמְךָ מַלְכֵּנוּ. כִּי כָל פֶּה לְךָ יוֹדֶה, וְכָל לָשׁוֹן לְךָ תִשָּׁבַע, וְכָל בֶּרֶךְ לְךָ תִכְרַע,[4] וְכָל קוֹמָה לְפָנֶיךָ תִשְׁתַּחֲוֶה, וְכָל לְבָבוֹת יִירָאוּךָ, וְכָל קֶרֶב וּכְלָיוֹת יְזַמְּרוּ לִשְׁמֶךָ, כַּדָּבָר שֶׁכָּתוּב: כָּל עַצְמֹתַי תֹּאמַרְנָה, יהוה מִי כָמוֹךָ, מַצִּיל עָנִי מֵחָזָק מִמֶּנּוּ, וְעָנִי וְאֶבְיוֹן מִגֹּזְלוֹ.[5] מִי יִדְמֶה לָּךְ, וּמִי יִשְׁוֶה לָּךְ, וּמִי יַעֲרָךְ לָךְ.[6] הָאֵל הַגָּדוֹל הַגִּבּוֹר וְהַנּוֹרָא, אֵל עֶלְיוֹן, קֹנֵה שָׁמַיִם וָאָרֶץ. ❖ נְהַלֶּלְךָ וּנְשַׁבֵּחֲךָ וּנְפָאֶרְךָ וּנְבָרֵךְ אֶת שֵׁם קָדְשֶׁךָ, כָּאָמוּר: לְדָוִד, בָּרְכִי נַפְשִׁי אֶת יהוה, וְכָל קְרָבַי אֶת שֵׁם קָדְשׁוֹ.[7]

The *chazzan* of *Shacharis* begins here.

הָאֵל בְּתַעֲצֻמוֹת עֻזֶּךָ, הַגָּדוֹל בִּכְבוֹד שְׁמֶךָ, הַגִּבּוֹר לָנֶצַח וְהַנּוֹרָא בְּנוֹרְאוֹתֶיךָ. הַמֶּלֶךְ הַיּוֹשֵׁב עַל כִּסֵּא רָם וְנִשָּׂא.[8]

שׁוֹכֵן עַד מָרוֹם וְקָדוֹשׁ שְׁמוֹ.[9] וְכָתוּב: רַנְּנוּ צַדִּיקִים בַּיהוה לַיְשָׁרִים נָאוָה תְהִלָּה.[10]

❖ בְּפִי **יְ**שָׁרִים תִּתְהַלָּל.
וּבְדִבְרֵי **צַ**דִּיקִים תִּתְבָּרַךְ.
וּבִלְשׁוֹן **חֲ**סִידִים תִּתְרוֹמָם.
וּבְקֶרֶב **קְ**דוֹשִׁים תִּתְקַדָּשׁ.

and His creatures with mercy. H*ASHEM* *neither slumbers nor sleeps.*[1] *He Who rouses the sleepers and awakens the slumberers, Who makes the mute speak and releases the bound;*[2] *Who supports the fallen and straightens the bent.*[3] *To You alone we give thanks. Were our mouth as full of song as the sea, and our tongue as full of joyous song as its multitude of waves, and our lips as full of praise as the breadth of the heavens, and our eyes as brilliant as the sun and the moon, and our hands as outspread as eagles of the sky and our feet as swift as hinds — we still could not thank You sufficiently,* H*ASHEM* *our God and God of our forefathers, and to bless Your Name for even one of the thousand thousand, thousands of thousands and myriad myriads of favors that You performed for our ancestors and for us. You redeemed us from Egypt,* H*ASHEM* *our God, and liberated us from the house of bondage. In famine You nourished us and in plenty You sustained us. From sword You saved us; from plague You let us escape; and from severe and enduring diseases You spared us. Until now Your mercy has helped us, and Your kindness has not forsaken us. Do not abandon us,* H*ASHEM* *our God, forever. Therefore, the organs that You set within us, and the spirit and soul that You breathed into our nostrils, and the tongue that You placed in our mouth — all of them shall thank and bless, praise and glorify, exalt and revere, sanctify and declare the sovereignty of Your Name, our King. For every mouth shall offer thanks to You; every tongue shall vow allegiance to You; every knee shall bend to You;*[4] *every erect spine shall prostrate itself before You; all hearts shall fear You, and all innermost feelings and thoughts shall sing praises to Your name, as it is written: "All my bones shall say: '*H*ASHEM, who is like You?' You save the poor man from one stronger than he, the poor and destitute from one who would rob him."*[5] *Who is like unto You? Who is equal to You? Who can be compared to You?*[6] *O great, mighty, and awesome God, the supreme God, Creator of heaven and earth.* Chazzan– *We shall laud, praise, and glorify You and bless Your holy Name, as it is said 'Of David: Bless* H*ASHEM, O my soul, and let all my innermost being bless His holy Name!'*[7]

The chazzan of *Shacharis* begins here.

הָאֵל *O God, in the omnipotence of Your strength, great in the glory of Your Name, mighty forever and awesome through Your awesome deeds. O King enthroned upon a high and lofty throne!*[8]

שׁוֹכֵן עַד *He Who abides forever, exalted and holy is His Name.*[9] *And it is written: 'Sing joyfully, O righteous, before* H*ASHEM; for the upright, praise is fitting.'*[10]

Chazzan: *By the mouth of the upright shall You be lauded;*
by the words of the righteous shall You be blessed;
by the tongue of the devout shall You be exalted;
and amid the holy shall You be sanctified.

(1) Cf. *Psalms* 121:4. (2) Cf. 146:7. (3) Cf. 145:14. (4) Cf. *Isaiah* 45:23. (5) *Psalms* 35:10. (6) Cf. 89:7; cf. *Isaiah* 40:25. (7) *Psalms* 103:1. (8) Cf. *Isaiah* 6:1. (9) Cf. 57:15. (10) *Psalms* 33:1.

וּבְמַקְהֲלוֹת רִבְבוֹת עַמְּךָ בֵּית יִשְׂרָאֵל, בְּרִנָּה יִתְפָּאַר שִׁמְךָ מַלְכֵּנוּ בְּכָל דּוֹר וָדוֹר. ❖ שֶׁכֵּן חוֹבַת כָּל הַיְּצוּרִים, לְפָנֶיךָ יהוה אֱלֹהֵינוּ וֵאלֹהֵי אֲבוֹתֵינוּ, לְהוֹדוֹת לְהַלֵּל לְשַׁבֵּחַ לְפָאֵר לְרוֹמֵם לְהַדֵּר לְבָרֵךְ לְעַלֵּה וּלְקַלֵּס, עַל כָּל דִּבְרֵי שִׁירוֹת וְתִשְׁבְּחוֹת דָּוִד בֶּן יִשַׁי עַבְדְּךָ מְשִׁיחֶךָ.

Stand while reciting יִשְׁתַּבַּח . . . The fifteen expressions of praise — שִׁיר וּשְׁבָחָה . . . בְּרָכוֹת וְהוֹדָאוֹת — should be recited without pause, preferably in one breath.

יִשְׁתַּבַּח שִׁמְךָ לָעַד מַלְכֵּנוּ, הָאֵל הַמֶּלֶךְ הַגָּדוֹל וְהַקָּדוֹשׁ, בַּשָּׁמַיִם וּבָאָרֶץ. כִּי לְךָ נָאֶה יהוה אֱלֹהֵינוּ וֵאלֹהֵי אֲבוֹתֵינוּ, שִׁיר וּשְׁבָחָה, הַלֵּל וְזִמְרָה, עֹז וּמֶמְשָׁלָה, נֶצַח גְּדֻלָּה וּגְבוּרָה, תְּהִלָּה וְתִפְאֶרֶת, קְדֻשָּׁה וּמַלְכוּת, בְּרָכוֹת וְהוֹדָאוֹת מֵעַתָּה וְעַד עוֹלָם. ❖ בָּרוּךְ אַתָּה יהוה, אֵל מֶלֶךְ גָּדוֹל בַּתִּשְׁבָּחוֹת, אֵל הַהוֹדָאוֹת, אֲדוֹן הַנִּפְלָאוֹת, הַבּוֹחֵר בְּשִׁירֵי זִמְרָה, מֶלֶךְ אֵל חֵי הָעוֹלָמִים. (.Cong — אָמֵן.)

The *chazzan* recites חֲצִי קַדִּישׁ.

יִתְגַּדַּל וְיִתְקַדַּשׁ שְׁמֵהּ רַבָּא. (.Cong — אָמֵן.) בְּעָלְמָא דִּי בְרָא כִרְעוּתֵהּ. וְיַמְלִיךְ מַלְכוּתֵהּ, בְּחַיֵּיכוֹן וּבְיוֹמֵיכוֹן וּבְחַיֵּי דְכָל בֵּית יִשְׂרָאֵל, בַּעֲגָלָא וּבִזְמַן קָרִיב. וְאִמְרוּ: אָמֵן.

(.Cong — אָמֵן. יְהֵא שְׁמֵהּ רַבָּא מְבָרַךְ לְעָלַם וּלְעָלְמֵי עָלְמַיָּא.)

יְהֵא שְׁמֵהּ רַבָּא מְבָרַךְ לְעָלַם וּלְעָלְמֵי עָלְמַיָּא.

יִתְבָּרַךְ וְיִשְׁתַּבַּח וְיִתְפָּאַר וְיִתְרוֹמַם וְיִתְנַשֵּׂא וְיִתְהַדָּר וְיִתְעַלֶּה וְיִתְהַלָּל שְׁמֵהּ דְּקֻדְשָׁא בְּרִיךְ הוּא (.Cong — בְּרִיךְ הוּא) — לְעֵלָּא מִן כָּל בִּרְכָתָא וְשִׁירָתָא תֻּשְׁבְּחָתָא וְנֶחֱמָתָא, דַּאֲמִירָן בְּעָלְמָא. וְאִמְרוּ: אָמֵן. (.Cong — אָמֵן.)

In some congregations the *chazzan* chants a melody during his recitation of בָּרְכוּ, so that the congregation can then recite יִתְבָּרַךְ.

Chazzan bows at בָּרְכוּ and straightens up at 'ה.

בָּרְכוּ אֶת יהוה הַמְּבֹרָךְ.

Congregation, followed by *chazzan*, responds, bowing at בָּרוּךְ and straightening up at 'ה.

בָּרוּךְ יהוה הַמְּבֹרָךְ לְעוֹלָם וָעֶד.

יִתְבָּרַךְ וְיִשְׁתַּבַּח וְיִתְפָּאַר וְיִתְרוֹמַם וְיִתְנַשֵּׂא שְׁמוֹ שֶׁל מֶלֶךְ מַלְכֵי הַמְּלָכִים, הַקָּדוֹשׁ בָּרוּךְ הוּא. שֶׁהוּא רִאשׁוֹן וְהוּא אַחֲרוֹן, וּמִבַּלְעָדָיו אֵין אֱלֹהִים.[1] סֹלּוּ, לָרֹכֵב בָּעֲרָבוֹת, בְּיָהּ שְׁמוֹ, וְעִלְזוּ לְפָנָיו.[2] וּשְׁמוֹ מְרוֹמָם עַל כָּל בְּרָכָה וּתְהִלָּה.[3] בָּרוּךְ שֵׁם כְּבוֹד מַלְכוּתוֹ לְעוֹלָם וָעֶד. יְהִי שֵׁם יהוה מְבֹרָךְ, מֵעַתָּה וְעַד עוֹלָם.[4]

וּבְמַקְהֲלוֹת *And in the assemblies of the myriads of Your people, the House of Israel, with joyous song shall Your Name be glorified, our King, throughout every generation.* Chazzan– *For such is the duty of all creatures — before You, HASHEM, our God, God of our forefathers, to thank, laud, praise, glorify, exalt, adore, bless, raise high, and sing praises — even beyond all expressions of the songs and praises of David the son of Jesse, Your servant, Your anointed.*

Stand while reciting *'May Your Name be praised . . .'*
The fifteen expressions of praise — *'song and praise. . .blessings and thanksgivings'* — should be recited without pause, preferably in one breath.

יִשְׁתַּבַּח *May Your Name be praised forever — our King, the God, the great and holy King — in heaven and on earth. Because for You is fitting — O HASHEM, our God, and the God of our forefathers — song and praise, lauding and hymns, power and dominion, triumph, greatness and strength, praise and splendor, holiness and sovereignty, blessings and thanksgivings from this time and forever.* Chazzan– *Blessed are You, HASHEM, God, King exalted through praises, God of thanksgivings, Master of wonders, Who chooses musical songs of praise — King, God, Life-giver of the world.*

(Cong.– *Amen.)*

The *chazzan* recites Half-*Kaddish*.

יִתְגַּדַּל *May His great Name grow exalted and sanctified* (Cong.– *Amen.*) *in the world that He created as He willed. May He give reign to His kingship in your lifetimes and in your days, and in the lifetimes of the entire Family of Israel, swiftly and soon. Now respond: Amen.*

(Cong.– *Amen. May His great Name be blessed forever and ever.*)

May His great Name be blessed forever and ever.

Blessed, praised, glorified, exalted, extolled, mighty, upraised, and lauded be the Name of the Holy One, Blessed is He (Cong.– *Blessed is He*) *— beyond any blessing and song, praise and consolation that are uttered in the world. Now respond: Amen.* (Cong.– *Amen.*)

In some congregations the *chazzan* chants a melody during his recitation of *Borchu*, so that the congregation can then recite *'Blessed, praised . . .'*

Chazzan bows at *'Bless'* and straightens up at *'HASHEM.'*

Bless HASHEM, the blessed One.

Congregation, followed by *chazzan*, responds, bowing at *'Blessed'* and straightening up at *'HASHEM.'*

Blessed is HASHEM, the blessed One, for all eternity.

Blessed, praised, glorified, exalted and upraised is the Name of the King Who rules over kings — the Holy One, Blessed is He. For He is the First and He is the Last and aside from Him there is no god.[1] *Extol Him — Who rides the highest heavens — with His Name, YAH, and exult before Him.*[2] *His Name is exalted beyond every blessing and praise.*[3] *Blessed is the Name of His glorious kingdom for all eternity. Blessed be the Name of HASHEM from this time and forever.*[4]

---

(1) Cf. *Isaiah* 44:6. (2) *Psalms* 68:5. (3) Cf. *Nechemiah* 9:5. (4) *Psalms* 113:2.

ברכות קריאת שמע

It is preferable that one sit while reciting the following series of prayers — particularly the *Kedushah* verses, קָדוֹשׁ קָדוֹשׁ קָדוֹשׁ and בָּרוּךְ כְּבוֹד — until *Shemoneh Esrei*.

The following paragraph is recited aloud by the *chazzan,* then repeated by the congregation.

בָּרוּךְ אַתָּה יהוה אֱלֹהֵינוּ מֶלֶךְ הָעוֹלָם, יוֹצֵר אוֹר וּבוֹרֵא חֹשֶׁךְ, עֹשֶׂה שָׁלוֹם וּבוֹרֵא אֶת הַכֹּל.[1]

Congregations that do not recite *yotzros,* continue on page 1120.

Congregations that recite *yotzros,* continue:

אוֹר עוֹלָם בְּאוֹצַר חַיִּים, אוֹרוֹת מֵאֹפֶל אָמַר וַיֶּהִי.

אַשְׁרֵי הָעָם* שֶׁלּוֹ כָּכָה,[2] מֵאֱלֹהָיו וְגוֹאֲלוֹ יִשָּׂא בְרָכָה,
מִתְבָּרֵךְ בַּשָּׁמַיִם וּבָאָרֶץ נֶעֱרָכָה, וְזֹאת הַבְּרָכָה.[3]
בִּפְנוֹת עָנָו לְנוֹחַ שְׁכִיבָה, הִזְהִיר אֲמָרָיו לְאַלְפֵי רְבָבָה,
שְׁמוֹר דָּת בִּזְרוֹעַ כְּתוּבָה, וַיֹּאמַר, יהוה מִסִּינַי בָּא.[4]
גּוֹאֲלָם חָנַן בְּכָל אֻמִּים, וּמְצָאָם כֻּלָּם בַּעֲלֵי מוּמִים,
הִפִּיל חֲבָלִים לוֹ בַּנְּעִימִים,[5] אַף חֹבֵב עַמִּים.[6]
דּוֹדִים מַקְדִּימִים לְנִשְׁמַע נַעֲשֶׂה,[7] הֵשִׁיבוּ זֹאת בַּל תִּמּשֶׁה,[8]
בֹּקֶר וָעֶרֶב לֹא נִגְשָׁה, תּוֹרָה צִוָּה לָנוּ מֹשֶׁה.[9]
הֻכְתַּר אָדוֹן כֶּתֶר לְהִמָּלֵךְ, יְהַב עַם אֵלָיו בְּהִשְׁתַּלֵּךְ,[10]
רַנְּנוּ כָּל גּוֹי וָפֶלֶךְ, וַיְהִי בִישֻׁרוּן מֶלֶךְ.[11]
וּמִיַּד מָחָה כָעָב אֲשָׁמוֹת,[12] כְּנָאֶה לְמֶלֶךְ בְּיוֹם רוֹמֵמוֹת,
שְׂאֵת וְיֶתֶר[13] יְהִי לִתְקוּמוֹת, יְחִי רְאוּבֵן וְאַל יָמֹת.[14]
זֶבֶד טוֹב וְנָעִים כְּנֶאֱמַר, שֶׁבֶת אַחִים יַחַד כְּהִתְאַמַּר,[15]
מִצָּרֵימוֹ הֱיוֹת לָמוֹ לְמִשְׁמָר, וְזֹאת לִיהוּדָה וַיֹּאמַר.[16]

---

(1) Cf. *Isaiah* 45:7. (2) Cf. *Psalms* 144:15. (3) *Deuteronomy* 33:1. (4) 33:2. (5) Cf. *Psalms* 26:6. (6) *Deuteronomy* 33:3. (7) See *Exodus* 24:7 with commentaries. (8) Cf. *Joshua* 1:8; *Isaiah* 59:21. (9) *Deuteronomy* 33:4. (10) Cf. *Psalms* 55:23. (11) *Deuteronomy* 33:5. (12) Cf. *Isaiah* 44:22. (13) See *Genesis* 49:3 with commentaries. (14) *Deuteronomy* 33:6. (15) Cf. *Psalms* 133:1. (16) *Deuteronomy* 33:7.

❧ Interruptions During the Blessings of the Shema

As a general rule, no אָמֵן or other prayer response may be recited between בָּרְכוּ and *Shemoneh Esrei,* but there are exceptions. The main exception is 'between chapters' [בֵּין הַפְּרָקִים] of the *Shema* Blessings — i.e., after יוֹצֵר הַמְּאוֹרוֹת and הַבּוֹחֵר . . . בְּאַהֲבָה, and between the three chapters of *Shema*. At those points, אָמֵן (but not בָּרוּךְ הוּא וּבָרוּךְ שְׁמוֹ) may be responded to any blessing. Some responses, however, are so important that they are permitted at any point in the *Shema* blessings. They are:
(a) In Kaddish, אָמֵן יְהֵא שְׁמֵהּ רַבָּא . . . עָלְמַיָּא and the אָמֵן after דַּאֲמִירָן בְּעָלְמָא; (b) the response to בָּרְכוּ (even of one called to the Torah); and (c) during the *chazzan's* repetition of *Shemoneh Esrei* – 1) in *Kedushah,* the verses קָדוֹשׁ קָדוֹשׁ קָדוֹשׁ . . . כְּבוֹדוֹ and בָּרוּךְ כְּבוֹד ה' מִמְּקוֹמוֹ; 2) the אָמֵן after הָאֵל הַקָּדוֹשׁ; 3) the three words מוֹדִים אֲנַחְנוּ לָךְ.

During the recital of the two verses שְׁמַע and בָּרוּךְ שֵׁם, absolutely no interruptions are permitted.

BLESSINGS OF THE SHEMA

It is preferable that one sit while reciting the following series of prayers — particularly the *Kedushah* verses, *'Holy, holy, holy . . .'* and *'Blessed is the glory . . .'* — until *Shemoneh Esrei.*

The following paragraph is recited aloud by the *chazzan,* then repeated by the congregation.

בָּרוּךְ *Blessed are You,* HASHEM, *our God, King of the universe, Who forms light and creates darkness, makes peace and creates all.*[1]

Congregations that do not recite *yotzros* continue on page 1120.

Congregations that recite *yotzros,* continue:

The primeval light is in the treasury of eternal life;
'Let there be lights from the darkness,' He declared — and so it was!

א *Praiseworthy is the people* for whom this is so,*[2]
that it bears a blessing from its God and [Moses] His redeemer.
מ *It is blessed [by God] in the heavens and [by Moses] on earth*
with the order of 'And this is the blessing ...'[3]

ב *When [Moses] the humble one turned to his restful repose,*
he spoke his admonition to myriad thousands,
ש *'Observe the Law inscribed by [God's] arm;'*
and he said, '[The Torah that] HASHEM *[gave when He] came from Sinai.'*[4]

ג *Their Redeemer turned to all the nations,*
but found them all to be possessed of blemishes.
ה *He made their portions fall to the pleasant ones,*[5]
indeed, the beloved tribal nations.[6]

ד *The beloved who put 'We will do!' before 'We will hear!'*[7]
they responded, 'This [Torah] shall not leave [our mouths].[8]
ב *Morning and evening it shall not be forgotten,*
the Torah with which Moses charged us.'[9]

ה *The Lord was crowned with the sovereign crown,*
when the people [of Israel] cast their burden upon Him.[10]
ר *Each nation and tribe gave forth in glad song,*
'He became King over Jeshurun.'[11]

ו *Immediately, He wiped away sins like a cloud,*[12]
as is fitting for a king on the day of his exaltation.
ש *[May the foremost] rank [of priesthood] and the prerogative [of kingship]*[13] *rise for him again;*
may Reuben live and not die.[14]

ז *A good and pleasant present, as it is said,*
the dwelling of brothers, [Simeon and Judah,] united as one.[15]
מ *Be a guardian for him against his enemies,*
and this to Judah, as He said.[16]

אַשְׁרֵי הָעָם — *Praiseworthy is the people.* The verses of this *piyut* contains an *aleph-beis* acrostic followed by the author's father's name שְׁמוּאֵל יְחִי, *Shmuel, may he live.* The author's own name appears in the initial letters of the third verse of each stanza: משֶׁה בַּר שְׁמוּאֵל בַּר אַבְשָׁלוֹם יִגְדַּל בְּתוֹרָה אָמֵן, *Moshe son of Shmuel son of Avshalom, may he grow in Torah, amen.* This composer probably lived before or in the early years of the twelfth century. Some of his *piyutim* appear in the *machzor* of אפ״ם [Asti, Fossano, Moncalvo] of the Piedmont region of Italy. Not much more is known about him.

The Torah reading for Simchas Torah con-

חֲסִידֶךָ אִישׁ נוֹצֵר מַאֲמָרֶיךָ, נִסִּיתוֹ בְּמַסָּה וַיְּאֻמַּן דְּבָרֶךָ,
וּלְעוֹלָם שָׁרֵת בְּבֵית דְּבִירֶךָ, וּלְלֵוִי אָמַר תֻּמֶּיךָ וְאוּרֶיךָ.[1]
טוֹב בְּשַׁעַר הַמַּחֲנֶה בְּקוּמוֹ, מִי לַיהוה אֵלַי[2] כְּנָאֳמוֹ,
אָסְפוּ חֲסִידָיו כְּאֶחָד לְעִמּוֹ, הָאֹמֵר לְאָבִיו וּלְאִמּוֹ.[3]
יִמָּלֵא פִּימוֹ תְּהִלָּתְךָ לִנְקֹב, שִׁירֶיךָ בְּאַדְמַת נֵכָר[4] מִקֹּב,
לְהַסְלִיל אֹרַח[5] וּלְיַשֵּׁר עָקֹב,[6] יוֹרוּ מִשְׁפָּטֶיךָ לְיַעֲקֹב.[7]
כְּקֶדֶם מִבֵּן בְּכוֹר בְּהִבָּדְלוֹ,[8] קֹדֶשׁ הַקֳּדָשִׁים הֱיוֹת גּוֹרָלוֹ,
בְּכִפְלַיִם כֵּן עוֹד לְאַיָּלוֹ, בָּרֵךְ יהוה חֵילוֹ.[9]
לִשְׁכֹּן בֵּין כִּתְפֵי גְּאוֹנַי, מְקוֹם שִׁירוֹת לְוִיַּי וְכֹהֲנַי,
רֹחַב אֹהָלַי וִירִיעוֹת מִשְׁכָּנַי, לְבִנְיָמִן אָמַר יְדִיד יהוה.[10]
מְבֹרֶכֶת שָׁמַיִם וְתַחַת נִסְמֶכֶת, בִּרְכֹת שָׁדַיִם וָרָחַם[11] מִתְבָּרֶכֶת,
אַרְצוֹ מִכֹּל הֱיוֹת נֶעֱרֶכֶת, וּלְיוֹסֵף אָמַר מְבֹרֶכֶת.[12]
נָא חַסְדּוֹ לֹא יָמֵשׁ, חָשַׂךְ עַצְמוֹ בְּזָרָה מִלְּשַׁמֵּשׁ,[13]
בְּטוּב כָּל גְּבוּלוֹ יִתְגַּמֵּשׁ, וּמִמֶּגֶד תְּבוּאֹת שָׁמֶשׁ.[14]
סָמוּךְ יֵצֶר[15] מֵהֶחָוֵר וְהָאָדֵם,* פִּזּוּ זְרוֹעָיו מִזָּהָב אָדֹם,[16]
שָׁלוֹם יֵצֶר[15] מְרַחֲמוֹ מִקֶּדֶם, וּמֵרֹאשׁ הַרְרֵי קֶדֶם.[17]
עַל קָדְקֹד גֻּלְגֹּלֶת נָאָה, בִּרְכַּת כָּל טוּב תְּבוּאָה,
לְהַשְׁפִּיעַ שֶׁפַע כָּל תְּבוּאָה, וּמִמֶּגֶד אֶרֶץ וּמְלֹאָהּ.[18]
פִּי שְׁנַיִם בְּנַחֲלַת חֶבְלוֹ, תַּחַת מְחַלֵּל יְצוּעַ מְחוֹלְלוֹ,[19]
וְעַד נָחֹל בְּחֵלֶשׁ גּוֹרָלוֹ, בְּכוֹר שׁוֹרוֹ הָדָר לוֹ.[20]
צִידוֹן יַרְכָתוֹ[21] לְהַרְבּוֹת צֶמַח, מִמֵּבִין עִתִּים[22] לִלְחֹם קֶמַח,
מֵאֵת זֶה זֶה יִשְׂמַח, וְלִזְבוּלֻן אָמַר שְׂמַח.[23]

(1) *Deuteronomy* 33:8. (2) *Exodus* 32:26. (3) *Deuteronomy* 33:9. (4) Cf. *Psalms* 137:4. (5) Cf. *Proverbs* 15:19. (6) Cf. *Isaiah* 40:4. (7) *Deuteronomy* 33:10. (8) Cf. *Numbers* 8:14. (9) *Deuteronomy* 33:11. (10) 33:12. (11) Cf. *Genesis* 49:25. (12) *Deuteronomy* 33:13. (13) See *Genesis* 39:7-12. (14) *Deuteronomy* 33:14. (15) Cf. *Isaiah* 26:3. (16) See *Targum Yonasan* to *Genesis* 49:24. (17) *Deuteronomy* 33:15. (18) 33:16. (19) Cf. *Genesis* 49:4; *I Chronicles* 5:1. (20) *Deuteronomy* 33:17. (21) Cf. *Genesis* 49:13. (22) Cf. *I Chronicles* 12:33. (23) *Deuteronomy* 33:18.

tains Moses' final words to the people. In twenty-nine verses, Moses combines blessing, admonition and prophecy for the nation as a whole and for the tribes individually. The present *piyut* is based on these verses in two ways: (a) the themes of the respective stanzas follow those of the Torah verses; and (b) each stanza closes with the opening phrase of its parallel Torah verse [see commentary, beginning page 1158]. Further, the *paytan* relates and unifies Moses' blessing with Jacob's (*Genesis* ch. 49), which he continually alludes to.

מֵהֶחָוֵר וְהָאָדֵם – *From whitening or reddening [in shame].* When a person falls into deep shame or embarrassment, his countenance first reddens, then pales. The Talmud (*Bava Metzia* 58b, see *Tosafos*) speaks of this phenomenon: Anyone

ח *Your devout one [Levi], guardian of Your word,*
You tested him at Massah and he proved faithful to Your word.
ו *May he serve forever in the Holy of Holies of Your Temple,*
for of Levi he said, 'Your perfect one, and Your light.'[1]

ט *When [Moses] the good one stood at the gateway to the camp,*
and cried, 'Whoever is for HASHEM, [come] to me!'[2]
א *His devout ones [the tribe of Levi] gathered to him as one,*
and said, '[We will do our duty] even against father and mother.'[3]

י *May their mouth be filled with articulation of Your praise,*
no longer to recite Your song on foreign soil.[4]
ל *To clear the path,*[5] *to straighten the crooked [road],*[6]
They teach Your laws to Jacob.[7]

כ *As in earlier times when he [Levi's tribe]*
was selected in place of the firstborn,[8]
that holy of holies should be his lot,
ב *May he again be strengthed in double measure,*
when HASHEM blesses his resources.[9]

ל *[The Temple] will dwell between my grand ones [Benjamin and Judah],*
the place of service for Kohanim and Levites,
ר *The expanse of my tent and the curtains of my Tabernacle,*
[in the portion of] Benjamin, of whom he said,
'He is beloved of HASHEM.'[10]

מ *Of the blessings of heaven and the deep he [Joseph] is sustained,*
for the blessings of bosom and womb,[11]
with which he is blessed [by Jacob].
א *His land is better suited than any other,*
for to Joseph he said, 'He is blessed.'[12]

נ *May He please not remove His kindness,*
[from Joseph] who restrained himself from living
with a stranger [Potiphar's wife].[13]
ב *May all [within] his boundaries be abundant,*
with the bounty of the sun's crops.[14]

ס *He [Joseph] suppressed his [Evil] Inclination*[15]
*from whitening or reddening [in shame],**
therefore, his arms were gilded [by Pharaoh] with red gold.[16]
ש *May He Who showed him compassion from the start*
protect his peace,[15]
with the finest crops of ancient mountains.[17]

ע *On the crown of the handsome head,*
may the blessing of all good things come,
ל *To cause a bountiful flow of all crops,*
with the bounty of the land and its fullness.[18]

פ *The heritage of his lot is doubled [to two tribes, Manasseh and Ephraim],*
in place of [Reuben] who desecrated his father's couch.[19]
ו *He was gathered there to inherit the portion of his lot,*
the majesty of the firstborn, ox-like power is due him.[20]

צ *Zidon will be his [Zebulun's] border,*[21] *to increase his crop,*
to supply flour to [Issachar]
who understands the calendrical calculations.[22]
מ *With each one's assets, the other rejoices,*
and so to Zebulun he said, 'Rejoice,'[23]

קִנְיַן חִלָּזוֹן סְפוּן חִבּוּאוֹ, כָּל יוֹעִיל לְמִכְסֶה מַשָּׂאוֹ,[1]
יִזְבְּחוּ זִבְחֵי צֶדֶק וְיִירָאוּ, עַמִּים הַר יִקְרָאוּ.[2]
רֵאשִׁית רָאָה לוֹ וַיֵּאָגֵד, שֶׁשָּׁם חֶלְקַת מְחוֹקֵק יֵאָגֵד,[3]
גְּדוּד יְגוּדֶנּוּ בְּבוֹא גָד,[4] וּלְגָד אָמַר בָּרוּךְ מַרְחִיב גָּד.[5]
שָׁכֵן בְּמִצָד בִּרְאוֹת חֵילוֹ, הַקָּטֹן לְמֵאָה וְלָאֶלֶף גְּדוֹלוֹ,
דָּלָם בְּרֹאשׁ גְּדוּדֵי חֵילוֹ,[6] וַיַּרְא רֵאשִׁית לוֹ.[7]
תַּנִּין עֲלֵי דֶרֶךְ הֱיֵה, שְׁפִיפוֹן עֲלֵי אֹרַח הֱיֵה,[8]
בְּצָרָיו נִלְחַם בְּשֵׁם אֶהְיֶה,[9] וּלְדָן אָמַר דָּן גּוּר אַרְיֵה.[10]
שָׂבֵעַ וְדָשֵׁן בִּפְנִימִי וְחִיצוֹן, יָם וְדָרוֹם יִירַשׁ בְּעֶלְצוֹן,[11]
תִּלְבֹּשֶׁת כָּרִים לְבוּשׁ הַצֹּאן,[12] וּלְנַפְתָּלִי אָמַר נַפְתָּלִי שְׂבַע רָצוֹן.[13]
מְטַבֵּל בַּשֶּׁמֶן רַגְלוֹ בְּאֹשֶׁר, רְצוּי אֶחָיו הָיָה בְּכֹשֶׁר,[14]
וּמַעֲדַנֵּי מֶלֶךְ נוֹתֵן מֵעֹשֶׁר,[15] וּלְאָשֵׁר אָמַר בָּרוּךְ מִבָּנִים אָשֵׁר.[16]
וּכְיָמֶיךָ דָּבְאֶךָ בְּחֹזֶק חֲיָלֶיךָ[17] תִּדְרֹךְ עַל בָּמֳתֵי[18] גּוֹעֲלֶיךָ,
רַגְלְךָ כָּל תִּגֹּף לְהַכְשִׁילֶךָ, בַּרְזֶל וּנְחֹשֶׁת מִנְעָלֶךָ.[19]
אַדִּיר בּוֹרֵא* שְׁחָקֵי שִׁפְרוֹן, רוֹקַע הָאָרֶץ כִּנְסֵי מֵחָרוֹן,
הָעֵינַי כֹּל אֵלֶיךָ יְשַׂבֵּרוּן,[20] אֵין כָּאֵל יְשֻׁרוּן.[21]
לְהַבְדִּיל בֵּין מַיִם לְמַיִם וּלְבוֹדְדֵם, הִתְוִיךְ רָקִיעַ בֵּינָם[22] וַיַּפְרִידֵם,
אֶל מְקוֹמָם הִקְוָם וַיְמַדְּדֵם, מְעֹנָה אֱלֹהֵי קֶדֶם.[23]
יְקַר שְׁנֵי מְאוֹרוֹת חִדֵּד, חַיָּה הִשְׁרִיץ וְצִפּוֹר נִבְדַּד,
מְרֻקָּם בְּצֶלֶם צָר לְהִתְעוֹדֵד, וַיִּשְׁכֹּן יִשְׂרָאֵל בֶּטַח בָּדָד.[24]
יָהּ שָׁבַת מִמִּפְעָל כְּהוֹאֵל, וַיְקַדֵּשׁ שְׁבִיעִי כִּכְתַב יְקוּתִיאֵל,
נִשָּׂא וַיְאַשֵּׁר עַמּוֹ אֵל, אַשְׁרֶיךָ יִשְׂרָאֵל.[25]

(1) See tractate *Megillah* 6a. (2) *Deuteronomy* 33:19. (3) Cf. 33:21. (4) Cf. *Genesis* 49:19; 30:11. (5) *Deuteronomy* 33:20. (6) See *I Samuel* 23:29 and *I Chronicles* 12:8-16. *Midrash Lekach Tov* identifies these two events with each other. (7) *Deuteronomy* 33:21. (8) Cf. *Genesis* 49:17. (9) See *Judges* 16:28. (10) *Deuteronomy* 33:22. (11) Cf. 33:23. (12) Cf. *Psalms* 65:14. (13) *Deuteronomy* 33:23. (14) Cf. 33:24. (15) Cf. *Genesis* 49:20. (16) *Deuteronomy* 33:24. (17) Cf. 33:25. (18) Cf. 33:29. (19) 33:25. (20) Cf. *Psalms* 145:15. (21) *Deuteronomy* 33:26. (22) Cf. *Genesis* 1:6-7. (23) *Deuteronomy* 33:27. (24) 33:28. (25) 33:29.

who whitens the face of another [i.e., embarrasses him] is like one who spills blood . . . For [when one is embarrassed] the red [blood] gathers to flee, and the whiteness comes in its place.

בּוֹרֵא – *Creator.* The *paytan* now describes what was made on each of the Seven Days of Creation respectively. He begins with heaven and earth — day one; the firmament — day two; the seas — day three; the heavenly lights — day four; fish and birds — day five; man — day six; the Sabbath — day seven.

ק *Possessing the chilazon, hidden in its crevices,*
those who steal it will not benefit from it,[1]
י *To bring offerings of righteousness,*
the tribes will summon [one another] to the Mount.[2]

ר *He [Gad] chose the first portion and broadened it,*
for there the Lawgiver's plot is established,[3]
ג *A regiment will be recruited when Gad comes,*[4]
and of Gad he said,
'Blessed is He Who broadens Gad's [boundary].'[5]

ש *When he [David] took refuge in the stronghold [of Ein-Gedi],*
he saw his [Gad's] army,
The least [of Gad's warriors] was equal to a hundred,
the greatest to a thousand.
דל *He drew them to be the chiefs of his army;*[6]
he chose the primary portion as his own.[7]

ת *May he [Dan] be like a serpent on the highway,*
may he be a viper by the road.[8]
ב *He [Dan's descendant Samson] fought his oppressors*
by pronouncing God's Name,[9]
and he [Moses] said of Dan, 'Dan is a lion cub.'[10]

ש *Satiated and wealthy within and without,*
the sea and the south he would possess with joy,[11]
ת *The meadows dress themselves with cloaks of fat sheep,*[12]
for of Naftali he said, 'Naftali [shall be] satiated with favor.'[13]

מ *He dipped his feet in abundant oil,*
powerfully pleasing to his brothers was he.[14]
ו *He provided kingly delicacies from [his] wealth,*[15]
and of Asher he said, 'Asher is the most blessed of children.'[16]

ו *And like the days of your prime, may your possessions be strong,*[17]
may you tread on the high places[18] *of those you despise.*
ר *May your feet not trip and cause you to stumble;*
may your borders be sealed like iron and copper.[19]

א *O Mighty One, Creator* of the clouds of heaven,*
You spread [them over] the earth, but withhold them in wrath,
ה *You to Whom all eyes look with hope,*[20]
there is none like the God of Jeshurun.[21]

ל *To separate the [upper] water from the [lower] water*
and keep them apart,
He interposed the firmament between them[22] *and divided them,*
א *He gathered them to their places [the seas and oceans]*
and measured them,
[The heavens are] the abode of the eternal God.[23]

י *The light of the two luminaries [sun and moon] He clarified;*
ח *He caused [sea] life to swarm, and set the birds [aloft] uniquely;*
מ *To establish [Man] woven in the Creator's image;*
Thus Israel shall dwell secure.[24]

י *God rested from His labors as was His will,*
and He sanctified the seventh, as Yekusiel [Moses] wrote.
נ *God exalted and strengthened His people,*
Fortunate are you, O Israel.[25]

הַמֵּאִיר לָאָרֶץ וְלַדָּרִים עָלֶיהָ בְּרַחֲמִים, וּבְטוּבוֹ מְחַדֵּשׁ בְּכָל יוֹם תָּמִיד מַעֲשֵׂה בְרֵאשִׁית. מָה רַבּוּ מַעֲשֶׂיךָ יהוה, כֻּלָּם בְּחָכְמָה עָשִׂיתָ, מָלְאָה הָאָרֶץ קִנְיָנֶךָ.[1] הַמֶּלֶךְ הַמְּרוֹמָם לְבַדּוֹ מֵאָז, הַמְּשֻׁבָּח וְהַמְּפֹאָר וְהַמִּתְנַשֵּׂא מִימוֹת עוֹלָם. אֱלֹהֵי עוֹלָם, בְּרַחֲמֶיךָ הָרַבִּים רַחֵם עָלֵינוּ, אֲדוֹן עֻזֵּנוּ, צוּר מִשְׂגַּבֵּנוּ, מָגֵן יִשְׁעֵנוּ, מִשְׂגָּב בַּעֲדֵנוּ. אֵל בָּרוּךְ גְּדוֹל דֵּעָה, הֵכִין וּפָעַל זָהֳרֵי חַמָּה, טוֹב יָצַר כָּבוֹד לִשְׁמוֹ, מְאוֹרוֹת נָתַן סְבִיבוֹת עֻזּוֹ, פִּנּוֹת צְבָאָיו קְדוֹשִׁים רוֹמְמֵי שַׁדַּי, תָּמִיד מְסַפְּרִים כְּבוֹד אֵל וּקְדֻשָּׁתוֹ. תִּתְבָּרַךְ יהוה אֱלֹהֵינוּ עַל שֶׁבַח מַעֲשֵׂה יָדֶיךָ, וְעַל מְאוֹרֵי אוֹר שֶׁעָשִׂיתָ, יְפָאֲרוּךָ, סֶּלָה.

תִּתְבָּרַךְ צוּרֵנוּ מַלְכֵּנוּ וְגֹאֲלֵנוּ, בּוֹרֵא קְדוֹשִׁים. יִשְׁתַּבַּח שִׁמְךָ לָעַד מַלְכֵּנוּ, יוֹצֵר מְשָׁרְתִים, וַאֲשֶׁר מְשָׁרְתָיו כֻּלָּם עוֹמְדִים בְּרוּם עוֹלָם, וּמַשְׁמִיעִים בְּיִרְאָה יַחַד בְּקוֹל דִּבְרֵי אֱלֹהִים חַיִּים וּמֶלֶךְ עוֹלָם.[2] כֻּלָּם אֲהוּבִים, כֻּלָּם בְּרוּרִים, כֻּלָּם גִּבּוֹרִים, וְכֻלָּם עֹשִׂים בְּאֵימָה וּבְיִרְאָה רְצוֹן קוֹנָם. ❖ וְכֻלָּם פּוֹתְחִים אֶת פִּיהֶם בִּקְדֻשָּׁה וּבְטָהֳרָה, בְּשִׁירָה וּבְזִמְרָה, וּמְבָרְכִים וּמְשַׁבְּחִים וּמְפָאֲרִים וּמַעֲרִיצִים וּמַקְדִּישִׁים וּמַמְלִיכִים —

אֶת שֵׁם הָאֵל הַמֶּלֶךְ הַגָּדוֹל הַגִּבּוֹר וְהַנּוֹרָא קָדוֹשׁ הוּא.[3] ❖ וְכֻלָּם מְקַבְּלִים עֲלֵיהֶם עֹל מַלְכוּת שָׁמַיִם זֶה מִזֶּה, וְנוֹתְנִים רְשׁוּת זֶה לָזֶה, לְהַקְדִּישׁ לְיוֹצְרָם, בְּנַחַת רוּחַ בְּשָׂפָה בְרוּרָה וּבִנְעִימָה. קְדֻשָּׁה כֻּלָּם כְּאֶחָד עוֹנִים וְאוֹמְרִים בְּיִרְאָה:

Congregation recites aloud:

קָדוֹשׁ קָדוֹשׁ קָדוֹשׁ• יהוה צְבָאוֹת,•
מְלֹא כָל הָאָרֶץ כְּבוֹדוֹ.[4]

❧ קָדוֹשׁ קָדוֹשׁ קָדוֹשׁ — *Holy, holy, holy. Targum Yonasan (Isaiah* 6:3) renders: *Holy* in the most exalted heaven, the abode of His Presence; *holy* on earth, product of His strength; *holy* forever and ever is HASHEM, Master of Legions . . .

כָּבוֹד, *glory,* refers to the glory of God that is present *within* the material world; it is the degree of Godliness that man is capable of perceiving even within creation. קָדוֹשׁ, *holy,* on the other hand, refers to God's essence, which is beyond all comprehension.

צְבָאוֹת — *Master of Legions.* Although it is commonly translated simply as *hosts* or *legions,* the word צְבָאוֹת is a Name of God (see *Shevuos* 35a), which means that He is the *Master* of all

הַמֵּאִיר *He Who illuminates the earth and those who dwell upon it, with compassion; and in His goodness renews daily, perpetually, the work of Creation. How great are Your works,* HASHEM, *You make them all with wisdom, the world is full of Your possessions.*[1] *The King Who was exalted in solitude before Creation, Who is praised, glorified, and upraised since days of old. Eternal God, with Your abundant compassion be compassionate to us — O Master of our power, our rocklike stronghold, O Shield of our salvation, be a stronghold for us. The blessed God, Who is great in knowledge, prepared and worked on the rays of the sun; the Beneficent One fashioned honor for His Name, emplaced luminaries all around His power; the leaders of His legions, holy ones, exalt the Almighty, constantly relate the honor of God and His sanctity. May You be blessed,* HASHEM, *our God, beyond the praises of Your handiwork and beyond the bright luminaries that You have made — may they glorify You — Selah!*

תִּתְבָּרַךְ *May You be blessed, our Rock, our King and our Redeemer, Creator of holy ones; may Your Name be praised forever, our King, O Fashioner of ministering angels; all of Whose ministering angels stand at the summit of the universe and proclaim — with awe, together, loudly — the words of the living God and King of the universe.*[2] *They are all beloved; they are all flawless; they are all mighty; they all do the will of their Maker with dread and reverence.* Chazzan– *And they all open their mouth in holiness and purity, in song and hymn — and bless, praise, glorify, revere, sanctify and declare the kingship of —*

אֶת שֵׁם *The Name of God, the great, mighty, and awesome King; holy is He.*[3] Chazzan– *Then they all accept upon themselves the yoke of heavenly sovereignty from one another, and grant permission to one another to sanctify the One Who formed them, with tranquillity, with clear articulation, and with sweetness. All of them as one proclaim His holiness and say with awe:*

Congregation recites aloud:

'Holy, holy, holy* is HASHEM, Master of Legions,* the whole world is filled with His glory.'[4]

(1) *Psalms* 104:24. (2) Cf. *Jeremiah* 10:10. (3) Cf. *Deuteronomy* 10:17; *Psalms* 99:3. (4) *Isaiah* 6:3.

the heavenly hosts. The word צָבָא is used to refer to an organized, disciplined group. Thus, an army is commonly called צָבָא. In the context of this Divine Name, it refers to the idea that the infinite heavenly bodies are organized according to God's will to do His service.

אֶשְׁנַבֵּי* שְׁחָקִים, נִרְאִים כְּנִבְרְתֵּקִים,
וְכִרְאֵי מוּצָקִים, נוֹעַם שִׁיר מַמְתִּיקִים –
קָדוֹשׁ קָדוֹשׁ קָדוֹשׁ יהוה צְבָאוֹת.[1]
מַרְאֵה הַקֶּשֶׁת, כְּאֵשׁ צְבוּעָה מְאֻשֶּׁשֶׁת,
דְּמוּת מִינִים שְׁלֹשֶׁת,* לְזוֹכֵר הַבְּרִית מְקֻדֶּשֶׁת –
קָדוֹשׁ קָדוֹשׁ קָדוֹשׁ יהוה צְבָאוֹת.
תַּקִּיף מְטַטְרוֹן* שָׂר, הַנֶּהְפַּךְ לְאֵשׁ מִבָּשָׂר,
מְלַמֵּד מוּסָר, לְיַלְדֵי אוֹר נִמְסָר –
קָדוֹשׁ קָדוֹשׁ קָדוֹשׁ יהוה צְבָאוֹת.
יְפֵיפִיָּה שַׂר הַתּוֹרָה, הַחוֹפֵן אֵשׁ שְׁחוֹרָה,*
לִקְשׁוֹר עֲטָרָה, לְאוֹתִיּוֹת הַתּוֹרָה –
קָדוֹשׁ קָדוֹשׁ קָדוֹשׁ יהוה צְבָאוֹת.
יְסוֹד עוֹלָמוֹ, הַנִּקְרָא צַדִּיק שְׁמוֹ,*
בְּהִגָּיוֹן נוֹאֲמוֹ, הוּא הַמַּרְעִישׁ עוֹלָמוֹ –
קָדוֹשׁ קָדוֹשׁ קָדוֹשׁ יהוה צְבָאוֹת.
חַדְרֵי תֵימָן, כְּסִיל וְעָשׁ[2] הַמְּזֻמָּן,
הָאֵל הַנֶּאֱמָן, לְהַקְדִּישׁוֹ מְיַשְּׁבִין טַעֲמָן –
קָדוֹשׁ קָדוֹשׁ קָדוֹשׁ יהוה צְבָאוֹת.
יְפִי קַרְקְסֵי אֵשׁ, הַחֲתוּמִין בְּטַבַּעַת אֵשׁ,
לְאֵשׁ אוֹכְלָה אֵשׁ,[3] בִּשְׁלוֹשׁ קְדֻשּׁוֹת לְהָאֵשׁ –
קָדוֹשׁ קָדוֹשׁ קָדוֹשׁ יהוה צְבָאוֹת.

Congregation, followed by the *chazzan,* recites one of these versions, according to its tradition.

וְהָאוֹפַנִּים וְחַיּוֹת הַקֹּדֶשׁ בְּרַעַשׁ גָּדוֹל מִתְנַשְּׂאִים לְעֻמַּת שְׂרָפִים. לְעֻמָּתָם מְשַׁבְּחִים וְאוֹמְרִים:

וְהַחַיּוֹת יְשׁוֹרֵרוּ, וּכְרוּבִים יְפָאֵרוּ, וּשְׂרָפִים יָרֹנּוּ, וְאֶרְאֶלִּים יְבָרֵכוּ. פְּנֵי כָל חַיָּה וְאוֹפָן וּכְרוּב לְעֻמַּת שְׂרָפִים. לְעֻמָּתָם מְשַׁבְּחִים וְאוֹמְרִים:

Congregation recites aloud:

בָּרוּךְ כְּבוֹד יהוה מִמְּקוֹמוֹ.[4]

אֶשְׁנַבֵּי – *The windows.* The *paytan* peeks through the 'windows' of heaven and describes the angelic recitation of *Kedushah.* Some angels are mentioned by name. The acrostic spells the composer's name: אֲמִתַּי יְחִי, *Amittai, may he live.* He is also the author of אֶרְאֶלִּים, *Erelim,* recited on Shemini Atzeres.

דְּמוּת מִינִים שְׁלֹשֶׁת – *With three different forms.* In relating his *Merkavah* vision, Ezekiel describes the Heavenly Throne in three different analogies: כְּמַרְאֵה אֶבֶן סַפִּיר, *like the appearance of sapphire stone;* כְּמַרְאֵה אֵשׁ, *like the appearance of fire;* and כְּמַרְאֵה הַקֶּשֶׁת, *like the appearance of the rainbow* (*Ezekiel* 1:26-28).

מְטַטְרוֹן – *Metatron.* Chanoch, son of Jared and great-grandfather of Noah, was a righteous man who died comparatively young (see *Genesis,* ch. 5). Many Midrashim discuss the end of his life.

א *The windows* of the clouds, appear as filters,*
and powerful lenses, sweetening the pleasant song —
Holy, holy, holy, is HASHEM, Master of Legions.[1]

מ *The appearance of the rainbow, like strongly colored fire,*
with three different forms, sanctify Him Who remembers the covenant—*
Holy, holy, holy, is HASHEM, Master of Legions.

ת *The mighty prince Metatron,* who had been changed from flesh to fire,*
he teaches the tradition [the Torah],
to the offspring of [Abraham] the one thrown into the fire —
Holy, holy, holy, is HASHEM, Master of Legions.

י *Yefeifiah, prince of the Torah, holds in his fists black fire,**
to attach a crown, to the letters of the Torah —
Holy, holy, holy, is HASHEM, Master of Legions.

י *The foundation of His world, who is called by the name Tzaddik,**
when he utters his words, he thunders through His world —
Holy, holy, holy, is HASHEM, Master of Legions.

ח *The southern chambers of the heavens,*
[the constellations] Ursa Major and Orion[2] *[in their] established [orbits],*
to the faithful God they direct their song of sanctification —
Holy, holy, holy, is HASHEM, Master of Legions.

י *The beautiful fiery hooks [connecting the ocean to the sky on the horizon],*
closed onto a fiery ring, to [God] the Fire that consumes fire,[3]
to powerfully recite three sanctifications —
Holy, holy, holy, is HASHEM, Master of Legions.

Congregation, followed by the *chazzan,* recites one of these versions, according to its tradition.

Then the Ofanim and the holy Chayos, with great noise, raise themselves towards the Seraphim. Facing them they give praise saying:

Then the Chayos sing, the Cherubim glorify, the Seraphim rejoice, and the Erelim bless, in the presence of every Chayah, Ofan, and Cherub towards the Seraphim. Facing them they give praise saying:

Congregation recites aloud:

'Blessed is the glory of HASHEM from His place.'[4]

(1) *Isaiah* 6:3. (2) *Job* 9:9. (3) Cf. *Deuteronomy* 4:24. (4) *Ezekiel* 3:12.

According to *Targum Yonasan (Genesis* 5:24): He ascended to heaven [alive] . . . where he became known as Metatron, the great scholar. According to the Talmud (*Avodah Zarah* 3b), Metatron is the Torah teacher of little children.

אֵשׁ שְׁחוֹרָה — *Black fire.* The spiritual nature of the Torah is described in the simile of fire. White fire takes the place of the parchment, while black fire is used as the ink *(Shir HaShirim* 5:11).

צַדִּיק שְׁמוֹ — *The name Tzaddik.* According to one view in the Talmud (*Chagigah* 12b) the world stands on one 'pillar' whose name is Tzaddik [literally, the righteous one]. This is based on the verse: וְצַדִּיק יְסוֹד עוֹלָם, *the Tzaddik is the foundation of the world (Proverbs* 10:25).

לְאֵל בָּרוּךְ נְעִימוֹת יִתֵּנוּ. לְמֶלֶךְ אֵל חַי וְקַיָּם, זְמִרוֹת יֹאמֵרוּ, וְתִשְׁבָּחוֹת יַשְׁמִיעוּ. כִּי הוּא לְבַדּוֹ פּוֹעֵל גְּבוּרוֹת, עֹשֶׂה חֲדָשׁוֹת, בַּעַל מִלְחָמוֹת, זוֹרֵעַ צְדָקוֹת, מַצְמִיחַ יְשׁוּעוֹת, בּוֹרֵא רְפוּאוֹת, נוֹרָא תְהִלּוֹת, אֲדוֹן הַנִּפְלָאוֹת. הַמְּחַדֵּשׁ בְּטוּבוֹ בְּכָל יוֹם תָּמִיד מַעֲשֵׂה בְרֵאשִׁית. כָּאָמוּר: לְעֹשֵׂה אוֹרִים גְּדֹלִים, כִּי לְעוֹלָם חַסְדּוֹ.[1] ❖ אוֹר חָדָשׁ עַל צִיּוֹן תָּאִיר, וְנִזְכֶּה כֻלָּנוּ מְהֵרָה לְאוֹרוֹ. בָּרוּךְ אַתָּה יהוה, יוֹצֵר הַמְּאוֹרוֹת. (Cong. – אָמֵן.)

אַהֲבָה רַבָּה אֲהַבְתָּנוּ יהוה אֱלֹהֵינוּ, חֶמְלָה גְדוֹלָה וִיתֵרָה חָמַלְתָּ עָלֵינוּ. אָבִינוּ מַלְכֵּנוּ, בַּעֲבוּר אֲבוֹתֵינוּ שֶׁבָּטְחוּ בְךָ, וַתְּלַמְּדֵם חֻקֵּי חַיִּים, כֵּן תְּחָנֵּנוּ וּתְלַמְּדֵנוּ. אָבִינוּ הָאָב הָרַחֲמָן הַמְּרַחֵם, רַחֵם עָלֵינוּ, וְתֵן בְּלִבֵּנוּ לְהָבִין וּלְהַשְׂכִּיל, לִשְׁמֹעַ לִלְמוֹד וּלְלַמֵּד, לִשְׁמֹר וְלַעֲשׂוֹת וּלְקַיֵּם אֶת כָּל דִּבְרֵי תַלְמוּד תּוֹרָתֶךָ בְּאַהֲבָה. וְהָאֵר עֵינֵינוּ בְּתוֹרָתֶךָ, וְדַבֵּק לִבֵּנוּ בְּמִצְוֹתֶיךָ, וְיַחֵד לְבָבֵנוּ לְאַהֲבָה וּלְיִרְאָה אֶת שְׁמֶךָ,[2] וְלֹא נֵבוֹשׁ לְעוֹלָם וָעֶד. כִּי בְשֵׁם קָדְשְׁךָ הַגָּדוֹל וְהַנּוֹרָא בָּטָחְנוּ, נָגִילָה וְנִשְׂמְחָה בִּישׁוּעָתֶךָ.

At this point, gather the four tzitzis between the fourth and fifth fingers of the left hand. Hold tzitzis in this manner throughout the Shema.

וַהֲבִיאֵנוּ לְשָׁלוֹם מֵאַרְבַּע כַּנְפוֹת הָאָרֶץ, וְתוֹלִיכֵנוּ קוֹמְמִיּוּת לְאַרְצֵנוּ. כִּי אֵל פּוֹעֵל יְשׁוּעוֹת אָתָּה, וּבָנוּ בָחַרְתָּ מִכָּל עַם וְלָשׁוֹן. ❖ וְקֵרַבְתָּנוּ לְשִׁמְךָ הַגָּדוֹל סֶלָה בֶּאֱמֶת, לְהוֹדוֹת לְךָ וּלְיַחֶדְךָ בְּאַהֲבָה. בָּרוּךְ אַתָּה יהוה, הַבּוֹחֵר בְּעַמּוֹ יִשְׂרָאֵל בְּאַהֲבָה. (Cong. – אָמֵן.)

שמע

Immediately before its recitation, concentrate on fulfilling the positive commandment of reciting the *Shema* twice daily. It is important to enunciate each word clearly and not to run words together. For this reason, vertical lines have been placed between two words that are prone to be slurred into one and are not separated by a comma or a hyphen. See *Laws* §40-55.

When praying without a *minyan*, begin with the following three-word formula:

אֵל מֶלֶךְ נֶאֱמָן.

Recite the first verse aloud, with the right hand covering the eyes, and concentrate intently upon accepting God's absolute sovereignty.

שְׁמַע | יִשְׂרָאֵל, יהוה | אֱלֹהֵינוּ, יהוה | אֶחָד:[1]

In an undertone – בָּרוּךְ שֵׁם כְּבוֹד מַלְכוּתוֹ לְעוֹלָם וָעֶד.

לְאֵל *To the blessed God they shall offer sweet melodies; to the King, the living and enduring God, they shall sing hymns and proclaim praises. For He alone effects mighty deeds, makes new things, is Master of wars, sows kindnesses, makes salvations flourish, creates cures, is too awesome for praise, is Lord of wonders. In His goodness He renews daily, perpetually, the work of creation. As it is said: '[Give thanks] to Him Who makes the great luminaries, for His kindness endures forever.'*[1] Chazzan— *May You shine a new light on Zion, and may we all speedily merit its light. Blessed are You, HASHEM, Who fashions the luminaries.* (Cong.— *Amen.*)

אַהֲבָה *With an abundant love have You loved us, HASHEM, our God; with exceedingly great pity have You pitied us. Our Father, our King, for the sake of our forefathers who trusted in You and whom You taught the decrees of life, may You be equally gracious to us and teach us. Our Father, the merciful Father, Who acts mercifully, have mercy upon us, instill in our hearts to understand and elucidate, to listen, learn, teach, safeguard, perform, and fulfill all the words of Your Torah's teaching with love. Enlighten our eyes in Your Torah, attach our hearts to Your commandments, and unify our hearts to love and fear Your Name,*[2] *and may we not feel inner shame for all eternity. Because we have trusted in Your great and awesome holy Name, may we exult and rejoice in Your salvation.*

At this point, gather the four *tzitzis* between the fourth and fifth fingers of the left hand. Hold *tzitzis* in this manner throughout the *Shema.*

Bring us in peacefulness from the four corners of the earth and lead us with upright pride to our land. For You effect salvations O God; You have chosen us from among every people and tongue. Chazzan— *And You have brought us close to Your great Name forever in truth, to offer praiseful thanks to You, and proclaim Your Oneness with love. Blessed are You, HASHEM, Who chooses His people Israel with love.* (Cong.— *Amen.*)

THE SHEMA

Immediately before its recitation, concentrate on fulfilling the positive commandment of reciting the *Shema* twice daily. It is important to enunciate each word clearly and not to run words together. See *Laws* §40-55.

When praying without a *minyan,* begin with the following three-word formula:

God, trustworthy King.

Recite the first verse aloud, with the right hand covering the eyes, and concentrate intently upon accepting God's absolute sovereignty.

Hear, O Israel: HASHEM is our God, HASHEM, the One and Only.[3]

In an undertone— *Blessed is the Name of His glorious kingdom for all eternity.*

---

(1) *Psalms* 136:7. (2) Cf. 86:11. (3) *Deuteromony* 6:4.

While reciting the first paragraph (דברים ו:ה-ט), concentrate on accepting the commandment to love God.

וְאָהַבְתָּ אֵת | יהוה | אֱלֹהֶיךָ, בְּכָל־לְבָבְךָ, וּבְכָל־נַפְשְׁךָ, וּבְכָל־מְאֹדֶךָ: וְהָיוּ הַדְּבָרִים הָאֵלֶּה, אֲשֶׁר | אָנֹכִי מְצַוְּךָ הַיּוֹם, עַל־לְבָבֶךָ: וְשִׁנַּנְתָּם לְבָנֶיךָ, וְדִבַּרְתָּ בָּם, בְּשִׁבְתְּךָ בְּבֵיתֶךָ, וּבְלֶכְתְּךָ בַדֶּרֶךְ, וּבְשָׁכְבְּךָ וּבְקוּמֶךָ: וּקְשַׁרְתָּם לְאוֹת | עַל־יָדֶךָ, וְהָיוּ לְטֹטָפֹת בֵּין | עֵינֶיךָ: וּכְתַבְתָּם | עַל־מְזֻזוֹת בֵּיתֶךָ, וּבִשְׁעָרֶיךָ:

While reciting the second paragraph (דברים יא:יג-כא), concentrate on accepting all the commandments and the concept of reward and punishment.

וְהָיָה, אִם־שָׁמֹעַ תִּשְׁמְעוּ אֶל־מִצְוֹתַי, אֲשֶׁר | אָנֹכִי מְצַוֶּה | אֶתְכֶם הַיּוֹם, לְאַהֲבָה אֶת־יהוה | אֱלֹהֵיכֶם וּלְעָבְדוֹ, בְּכָל־לְבַבְכֶם, וּבְכָל־נַפְשְׁכֶם: וְנָתַתִּי מְטַר־אַרְצְכֶם בְּעִתּוֹ, יוֹרֶה וּמַלְקוֹשׁ, וְאָסַפְתָּ דְגָנֶךָ וְתִירֹשְׁךָ וְיִצְהָרֶךָ: וְנָתַתִּי | עֵשֶׂב | בְּשָׂדְךָ לִבְהֶמְתֶּךָ, וְאָכַלְתָּ וְשָׂבָעְתָּ: הִשָּׁמְרוּ לָכֶם, פֶּן־יִפְתֶּה לְבַבְכֶם, וְסַרְתֶּם וַעֲבַדְתֶּם | אֱלֹהִים | אֲחֵרִים, וְהִשְׁתַּחֲוִיתֶם לָהֶם: וְחָרָה | אַף־יהוה בָּכֶם, וְעָצַר | אֶת־הַשָּׁמַיִם, וְלֹא־יִהְיֶה מָטָר, וְהָאֲדָמָה לֹא תִתֵּן אֶת־יְבוּלָהּ, וַאֲבַדְתֶּם | מְהֵרָה מֵעַל הָאָרֶץ הַטֹּבָה | אֲשֶׁר | יהוה נֹתֵן לָכֶם: וְשַׂמְתֶּם | אֶת־דְּבָרַי | אֵלֶּה, עַל־לְבַבְכֶם וְעַל־נַפְשְׁכֶם, וּקְשַׁרְתֶּם | אֹתָם לְאוֹת | עַל־יֶדְכֶם, וְהָיוּ לְטוֹטָפֹת בֵּין | עֵינֵיכֶם: וְלִמַּדְתֶּם | אֹתָם | אֶת־בְּנֵיכֶם, לְדַבֵּר בָּם, בְּשִׁבְתְּךָ בְּבֵיתֶךָ, וּבְלֶכְתְּךָ בַדֶּרֶךְ, וּבְשָׁכְבְּךָ וּבְקוּמֶךָ: וּכְתַבְתָּם | עַל־מְזוּזוֹת בֵּיתֶךָ, וּבִשְׁעָרֶיךָ: לְמַעַן | יִרְבּוּ | יְמֵיכֶם וִימֵי בְנֵיכֶם, עַל הָאֲדָמָה | אֲשֶׁר נִשְׁבַּע | יהוה לַאֲבֹתֵיכֶם לָתֵת לָהֶם, כִּימֵי הַשָּׁמַיִם | עַל־הָאָרֶץ:

Before reciting the third paragraph (במדבר טו:לז-מא), the *tzitzis,* which have been held in the left hand, are taken in the right hand also. The *tzitzis* are kissed at each mention of the word and at the end of the paragraph, and are passed before the eyes at וּרְאִיתֶם אֹתוֹ.

וַיֹּאמֶר | יהוה | אֶל־מֹשֶׁה לֵּאמֹר: דַּבֵּר | אֶל־בְּנֵי | יִשְׂרָאֵל, וְאָמַרְתָּ אֲלֵהֶם, וְעָשׂוּ לָהֶם צִיצִת, עַל־כַּנְפֵי בִגְדֵיהֶם לְדֹרֹתָם, וְנָתְנוּ | עַל־צִיצִת הַכָּנָף, פְּתִיל תְּכֵלֶת: וְהָיָה לָכֶם לְצִיצִת, וּרְאִיתֶם | אֹתוֹ, וּזְכַרְתֶּם | אֶת־כָּל־מִצְוֹת | יהוה, וַעֲשִׂיתֶם | אֹתָם, וְלֹא תָתוּרוּ | אַחֲרֵי לְבַבְכֶם וְאַחֲרֵי | עֵינֵיכֶם, אֲשֶׁר־אַתֶּם זֹנִים | אַחֲרֵיהֶם: לְמַעַן תִּזְכְּרוּ, וַעֲשִׂיתֶם | אֶת־כָּל־מִצְוֹתָי, וִהְיִיתֶם קְדֹשִׁים

While reciting the first paragraph (*Deuteronomy* 6:5-9), concentrate on accepting the commandment to love God.

וְאָהַבְתָּ *You shall love* HASHEM, *your God, with all your heart, with all your soul and with all your resources. Let these matters that I command you today be upon your heart. Teach them thoroughly to your children and speak of them while you sit in your home, while you walk on the way, when you retire and when you arise. Bind them as a sign upon your arm and let them be tefillin between your eyes. And write them on the doorposts of your house and upon your gates.*

While reciting the second paragraph (*Deuteronomy* 11:13-21), concentrate on accepting all the commandments and the concept of reward and punishment.

וְהָיָה *And it will come to pass that if you continually hearken to My commandments that I command you today, to love* HASHEM, *your God, and to serve Him, with all your heart and with all your soul — then I will provide rain for your land in its proper time, the early and late rains, that you may gather in your grain, your wine, and your oil. I will provide grass in your field for your cattle and you will eat and be satisfied. Beware lest your heart be seduced and you turn astray and serve gods of others and bow to them. Then the wrath of* HASHEM *will blaze against you. He will restrain the heaven so there will be no rain and the ground will not yield its produce. And you will swiftly be banished from the goodly land which* HASHEM *gives you. Place these words of Mine upon your heart and upon your soul; bind them for a sign upon your arm and let them be tefillin between your eyes. Teach them to your children, to discuss them, while you sit in your home, while you walk on the way, when you retire and when you arise. And write them on the doorposts of your house and upon your gates. In order to prolong your days and the days of your children upon the ground that* HASHEM *has sworn to your ancestors to give them, like the days of the heaven on the earth.*

Before reciting the third paragraph *(Numbers* 15:37-41) the *tzitzis,* which have been held in the left hand, are taken in the right hand also. The *tzitzis* are kissed at each mention of the word and at the end of the paragraph, and are passed before the eyes at *'that you may see it.'*

וַיֹּאמֶר *And* HASHEM *said to Moses saying: Speak to the Children of Israel and say to them that they are to make themselves tzitzis on the corners of their garments, throughout their generations. And they are to place upon the tzitzis of each corner a thread of techeiles. And it shall constitute tzitzis for you, that you may see it and remember all the commandments of* HASHEM *and perform them; and not explore after your heart and after your eyes after which you stray. So that you may remember and perform all My commandments; and be holy to your*

Concentrate on fulfilling the commandment of remembering the Exodus from Egypt.

לֵאלֹהִֽים: אֲנִי יהוה | אֱלֹהֵיכֶם, אֲשֶׁר הוֹצֵאתִי | אֶתְכֶם | מֵאֶֽרֶץ מִצְרַֽיִם, לִהְיוֹת לָכֶם לֵאלֹהִים, אֲנִי | יהוה | אֱלֹהֵיכֶם: אֱמֶת —

Although the word אֱמֶת belongs to the next paragraph, it is appended to the conclusion of the previous one, as explained in the commentary.

—*Chazzan* repeats **יהוה אֱלֹהֵיכֶם אֱמֶת.**

וְיַצִּיב וְנָכוֹן וְקַיָּם וְיָשָׁר וְנֶאֱמָן וְאָהוּב וְחָבִיב וְנֶחְמָד וְנָעִים וְנוֹרָא וְאַדִּיר וּמְתֻקָּן וּמְקֻבָּל וְטוֹב וְיָפֶה הַדָּבָר הַזֶּה עָלֵינוּ לְעוֹלָם וָעֶד. אֱמֶת אֱלֹהֵי עוֹלָם מַלְכֵּנוּ צוּר יַעֲקֹב, מָגֵן יִשְׁעֵנוּ, לְדֹר וָדֹר הוּא קַיָּם, וּשְׁמוֹ קַיָּם, וְכִסְאוֹ נָכוֹן, וּמַלְכוּתוֹ וֶאֱמוּנָתוֹ לָעַד קַיָּֽמֶת. וּדְבָרָיו חָיִים וְקַיָּמִים, נֶאֱמָנִים וְנֶחֱמָדִים לָעַד (kiss the *tzitzis* and release them) וּלְעוֹלְמֵי עוֹלָמִים. ❖ עַל אֲבוֹתֵינוּ וְעָלֵינוּ, עַל בָּנֵינוּ וְעַל דּוֹרוֹתֵינוּ, וְעַל כָּל דּוֹרוֹת זֶרַע יִשְׂרָאֵל עֲבָדֶיךָ.

עַל הָרִאשׁוֹנִים וְעַל הָאַחֲרוֹנִים, דָּבָר טוֹב וְקַיָּם לְעוֹלָם וָעֶד, אֱמֶת וֶאֱמוּנָה חֹק וְלֹא יַעֲבֹר. אֱמֶת שָׁאַתָּה הוּא יהוה אֱלֹהֵינוּ וֵאלֹהֵי אֲבוֹתֵינוּ, ❖ מַלְכֵּנוּ מֶלֶךְ אֲבוֹתֵינוּ, גֹּאֲלֵנוּ גֹּאֵל אֲבוֹתֵינוּ, יוֹצְרֵנוּ צוּר יְשׁוּעָתֵנוּ, פּוֹדֵנוּ וּמַצִּילֵנוּ מֵעוֹלָם שְׁמֶךָ, אֵין אֱלֹהִים זוּלָתֶךָ.

אָז בְּקֶשֶׁב עָנָו* עֲלֵה אֶל הַר הָעֲבָרִים,[1]
בְּדַעְתּוֹ חִשֵּׁב כַּעֲלִיַּת סִין בְּהִדּוּרִים,
גְּזֵרַת דָּת חֲדָשָׁה וּפִקּוּדִים יְשָׁרִים,
דּוֹד יֶשׁ לוֹ לִתֵּן לְמִשְׁבְּעִים בְּחוּרִים.

הָעֵת כְּקָשַׁב וּמֻת בָּהָר אֲשֶׁר אַתָּה עֹלֶה,[2]
וַי וַי צָוַח בְּפֶה מָלֵא,
זוֹ עֲלִיָּה יְרִידָה הִיא לְהִתְכַּלֶּה,
חַנּוּן אֶעְבְּרָה נָּא וְאֶרְאֶה הָהָר הַטּוֹב[3] וְהַמְּעֻלֶּה.

טָהוֹר עֲנָהוּ רַב לָךְ אַל תּוֹסֶף דַּבֵּר,[4]
יְהוֹשֻׁעַ מְשָׁרְתֶךָ הִגִּיעַ זְמַן הֱיוֹת חָבֵר,
כִּי הַמַּלְכוּת בַּחֲבֶרְתָּהּ כִּמְלֹא נִימָא לֹא תִתְחַבֵּר,
לְהַר נְבוֹ תַּעֲלֶה וְשָׁם תָּמוּת וּבַגַּי תִּקָּבֵר.

Concentrate on fulfilling the commandment of remembering the Exodus from Egypt.

God. I am HASHEM, your God, Who has removed you from the land of Egypt to be a God to you; I am HASHEM your God — it is true —

Although the word אֱמֶת, *'it is true,'* belongs to the next paragraph, it is appended to the conclusion of the previous one, as explained in the commentary.

Chazzan repeats: **HASHEM, your God, is true.**

וְיַצִּיב *And certain, established and enduring, fair and faithful, beloved and cherished, delightful and pleasant, awesome and powerful, correct and accepted, good and beautiful is this affirmation to us forever and ever. True — the God of the universe is our King; the Rock of Jacob is the Shield of our salvation. From generation to generation He endures and His Name endures and His throne is well established; His sovereignty and faithfulness endure forever. His words are living and enduring, faithful and delightful forever* (kiss the *tzitzis* and release them) *and to all eternity;* Chazzan– *for our forefathers and for us, for our children and for our generations, and for all the generations of Your servant Israel's offspring.*

עַל הָרִאשׁוֹנִים *Upon the earlier and upon the later generations, this affirmation is good and enduring forever. True and faithful, it is an unbreachable decree. It is true that You are HASHEM, our God and the God of our forefathers,* Chazzan– *our King and the King of our forefathers, our Redeemer, the Redeemer of our forefathers; our Molder, the Rock of our salvation; our Liberator and our Rescuer — this has ever been Your Name. There is no God but You.*

א *Then, when the humble [Moses] heard,**
'Ascend the mount near the river crossings;'[1]
ב *he thought that it would be as majestic as the ascent on Sinai.*
ג *Newly decreed laws and upright statutes,*
ד *the Beloved [God] would give him, for the [nation] chosen from seventy.*
ה *But when he heard,*
'And you shall die upon the mountain that you ascend;'[2]
ו *he cried, 'Woe! Woe!' with a full mouth,*
ז *'This ascent is a descent, to be destroyed.*
ח *O Gracious One,*
let me please cross over and see the goodly and exalted [Temple] Mount.'[3]
ט *The Pure One replied, 'Enough for you. Do not continue to speak!*[4]
י *Joshua — your attendant — his time to rule has come,*
כ *and one king's reign may not overlap another's even by a hair's breadth.*
ל *Ascend Mount Nebo, and there you shall die and be buried in the valley.'*

(1) *Numbers* 27:12; *Deuteronomy* 32:49. (2) 32:50. (3) Cf. 3:25. (4) 3:26.

⁂ **אָז בְּקֶשֶׁב עָנָו** – *Then when the humble [Moses] heard.* The day's Torah reading tells of Moses' departure from this world (*Deuteronomy* 34:1-12). The *paytan* portrays Moses' last conversation with God before his passing. After following an *aleph-beis* scheme, the composer adds his signature: מֹשֶׁה בַּר שְׁמוּאֵל חֲזַק, *Moshe bar Shmuel, may he grow strong* (see p. 1115).

מֹשֶׁה כְּיָדַע כִּי גְזֵרָה עָלָיו נִגְזְרָה,
נָם לַאֲדוֹן כֹּל הוֹדַע חוֹבָתִי לְיָפָה וּבָרָה,
סְגוּלִים פֶּן יֹאמְרוּ בַּסֵּתֶר עָבַר עֲבֵרָה,
עַל כֵּן לֹא עָנֵהוּ אָיוֹם וְנוֹרָא.

פּוֹדֶה הֱשִׁיבוֹ עַל אֲשֶׁר מְעַלְתֶּם בִּי בְּמֵי מְרִיבָה,[1]
צַעֲקַת שַׁוְעַתְכֶם לָכֵן לְפָנַי לֹא בָא,
קְנִיסָה זוּ עֲלֵיכֶם לָכֵן נִקְנְסָה וְנִקְצָבָה,
רָשׁוּם יֵרָשֵׁם וְיִכָּתֵב בְּדַת נֶפֶשׁ מְשִׁיבָה.

שִׁבְטֵי יְשֻׁרוּן קִבֵּץ וְנִחַת,
תְּמִימַי תִּפְדְּוּנִי מֵרֶדֶת שַׁחַת,
מַר צָרְחוּ כֻּלָּם וְצָוְחוּ כְּאַחַת,
שֶׁאֵין פִּדְיוֹן וְכֹפֶר בִּכְלוּם חֵפֶץ וּדְבַר תּוֹכַחַת.

הִשְׁלִים נַפְשׁוֹ מִיַּד לְמִיתַת נְשִׁיקָה,
בִּרְאוֹתוֹ כִּי אֵין הַצָּלָה בִּתְפִלָּה וּצְעָקָה,
שְׁמָעוּנִי אַחַי וְרֵעַי עִסְקוּ בְּדַת חֲשׁוּקָה,
וְאַל תְּהִי זֹאת לָכֶם לְמִכְשׁוֹל וּלְפוּקָה.[2]

חֲיָלָיו בְּכוּהוּ שְׁלֹשִׁים יָמִים,[3]
זוֹכְרִים צִדְקַת מִשְׁפָּטָיו אֲשֶׁר עִמָּם הִתְמִים,
קָפַץ וְדִלַּג כַּאֲרִי לִפְדוּתָם מִבֵּין עֲנָמִים,
וְהַיָּם בָּקַע לִפְנֵיהֶם וַיַּמְלִיכוּ מַלְכָּם לְעוֹלָמִים.

עֶזְרַת אֲבוֹתֵינוּ אַתָּה הוּא מֵעוֹלָם, מָגֵן וּמוֹשִׁיעַ לִבְנֵיהֶם אַחֲרֵיהֶם בְּכָל דּוֹר וָדוֹר. בְּרוּם עוֹלָם מוֹשָׁבֶךָ, וּמִשְׁפָּטֶיךָ וְצִדְקָתְךָ עַד אַפְסֵי אָרֶץ. אַשְׁרֵי אִישׁ שֶׁיִּשְׁמַע לְמִצְוֹתֶיךָ, וְתוֹרָתְךָ וּדְבָרְךָ יָשִׂים עַל לִבּוֹ. אֱמֶת אַתָּה הוּא אָדוֹן לְעַמֶּךָ וּמֶלֶךְ גִּבּוֹר לָרִיב רִיבָם. אֱמֶת אַתָּה הוּא רִאשׁוֹן וְאַתָּה הוּא אַחֲרוֹן, וּמִבַּלְעָדֶיךָ אֵין לָנוּ מֶלֶךְ[4] גּוֹאֵל וּמוֹשִׁיעַ. מִמִּצְרַיִם גְּאַלְתָּנוּ יהוה אֱלֹהֵינוּ, וּמִבֵּית עֲבָדִים פְּדִיתָנוּ. כָּל בְּכוֹרֵיהֶם הָרָגְתָּ, וּבְכוֹרְךָ גָּאָלְתָּ, וְיַם סוּף בָּקַעְתָּ, וְזֵדִים טִבַּעְתָּ, וִידִידִים הֶעֱבַרְתָּ, וַיְכַסּוּ מַיִם צָרֵיהֶם, אֶחָד מֵהֶם לֹא נוֹתָר.[5] עַל זֹאת שִׁבְּחוּ אֲהוּבִים וְרוֹמְמוּ אֵל, וְנָתְנוּ יְדִידִים זְמִרוֹת שִׁירוֹת וְתִשְׁבָּחוֹת, בְּרָכוֹת וְהוֹדָאוֹת, לְמֶלֶךְ אֵל חַי

מ *When Moses became aware of what was decreed upon him,*
נ *he said to the Master of all,*
"Make my sin known to the beautiful and brilliant [nation].
ס *Lest the treasured ones say, 'He sinned in concealment,*
ע *therefore the Fearsome Awesome One did not answer his prayer!'"*
פ *The Redeemer responded,*
'Because you sinned against Me at the waters of Meribah,[1]
צ *therefore the cries of your prayers cannot come before Me.*
ק *This penalty has been imposed and assessed upon you,*
ר *and so will be inscribed and written in the Torah that restores the soul.'*
ש *'O Tribes of Jeshurun, gather and make an attempt,*
ת *Redeem me, my wholesome ones, from descending to the Pit.'*
מ *They all cried bitterly and screamed out as one,*
ש *that neither redemption nor ransom [will save him],*
nothing, not even persuasive argument.
ה *He immediately readied himself for death by [God's] kiss,*
בר *when he saw that prayer and cry would not avail.*
שמ *'Listen to me, my brothers and friends, engage in the desirable Torah.*
ואל *And may this be unto you neither stumbling block nor snare.'*[2]
ח *His troops [Israel] cried over him for thirty days,*[3]
ז *They remembered the righteousness of his laws*
with which he led them wholesomely.
ק *He had leaped and jumped like a lion*
to redeem them from among the Egyptians,
The sea split before them, and they crowned their King for eternity.

עֶזְרַת *The Helper of our forefathers are You alone, forever, Shield and Savior for their children after them in every generation. At the zenith of the universe is Your dwelling, and Your justice and Your righteousness extend to the ends of the earth. Praiseworthy is the person who obeys Your commandments and takes to his heart Your teaching and Your word. True — You are the Master for Your people and a mighty King to take up their grievance. True — You are the First and You are the Last, and other than You we have no king,*[4] *redeemer, or savior. From Egypt You redeemed us,* HASHEM, *our God, and from the house of slavery You liberated us. All their firstborn You slew, but Your firstborn You redeemed; the Sea of Reeds You split; the wanton sinners You drowned; the dear ones You brought across; and the water covered their foes — not one of them was left.*[5] *For this, the beloved praised and exalted God; the dear ones offered hymns, songs, praises, blessings, and thanksgivings to the King, the living and*

---

(1) Cf. *Deuteronomy* 32:51. (2) Cf. *I Samuel* 25:31.
(3) Cf. *Deuteronomy* 34:8. (4) Cf. *Isaiah* 44:6. (5) *Psalms* 106:11.

וְקַיָּם, רָם וְנִשָּׂא, גָּדוֹל וְנוֹרָא, מַשְׁפִּיל גֵּאִים, וּמַגְבִּיהַּ שְׁפָלִים, מוֹצִיא אֲסִירִים, וּפוֹדֶה עֲנָוִים, וְעוֹזֵר דַּלִּים, וְעוֹנֶה לְעַמּוֹ בְּעֵת שַׁוְּעָם אֵלָיו.

Rise for *Shemoneh Esrei*. Some take three steps backward at this point; others do so before צוּר יִשְׂרָאֵל.

❖ תְּהִלּוֹת לְאֵל עֶלְיוֹן, בָּרוּךְ הוּא וּמְבֹרָךְ. מֹשֶׁה וּבְנֵי יִשְׂרָאֵל לְךָ עָנוּ שִׁירָה בְּשִׂמְחָה רַבָּה וְאָמְרוּ כֻלָּם:

מִי כָמֹכָה בָּאֵלִם יהוה, מִי כָּמֹכָה נֶאְדָּר בַּקֹּדֶשׁ, נוֹרָא תְהִלֹּת עֹשֵׂה פֶלֶא.[1] ❖ שִׁירָה חֲדָשָׁה שִׁבְּחוּ גְאוּלִים לְשִׁמְךָ עַל שְׂפַת הַיָּם, יַחַד כֻּלָּם הוֹדוּ וְהִמְלִיכוּ וְאָמְרוּ:

יהוה יִמְלֹךְ לְעֹלָם וָעֶד.[2]

It is forbidden to interrupt or pause between גָּאַל יִשְׂרָאֵל and *Shemoneh Esrei*, even for *Kaddish, Kedushah* or *Amen*.

❖ **צוּר יִשְׂרָאֵל,*** קוּמָה בְּעֶזְרַת יִשְׂרָאֵל, וּפְדֵה כִנְאֻמֶךָ יְהוּדָה וְיִשְׂרָאֵל. גֹּאֲלֵנוּ יהוה צְבָאוֹת שְׁמוֹ, קְדוֹשׁ יִשְׂרָאֵל.[3] בָּרוּךְ אַתָּה יהוה, גָּאַל יִשְׂרָאֵל.*

❧ שמונה עשרה – עמידה ❧

Take three steps backward, then three steps forward. Remain standing with feet together while reciting *Shemoneh Esrei*. Recite it with quiet devotion and without interruption, verbal or otherwise. Although it should not be audible to others, one must pray loudly enough to hear himself.

אֲדֹנָי שְׂפָתַי תִּפְתָּח, וּפִי יַגִּיד תְּהִלָּתֶךָ.[4]

אבות

Bend the knees at בָּרוּךְ; bow at אַתָּה; straighten up at ה׳.

בָּרוּךְ אַתָּה יהוה אֱלֹהֵינוּ וֵאלֹהֵי אֲבוֹתֵינוּ, אֱלֹהֵי אַבְרָהָם, אֱלֹהֵי יִצְחָק, וֵאלֹהֵי יַעֲקֹב, הָאֵל הַגָּדוֹל הַגִּבּוֹר וְהַנּוֹרָא, אֵל עֶלְיוֹן, גּוֹמֵל חֲסָדִים טוֹבִים וְקוֹנֵה הַכֹּל, וְזוֹכֵר חַסְדֵי אָבוֹת, וּמֵבִיא גוֹאֵל לִבְנֵי בְנֵיהֶם, לְמַעַן שְׁמוֹ בְּאַהֲבָה. מֶלֶךְ עוֹזֵר וּמוֹשִׁיעַ וּמָגֵן.

Bend the knees at בָּרוּךְ; bow at אַתָּה; straighten up at ה׳.

בָּרוּךְ אַתָּה יהוה, מָגֵן אַבְרָהָם.

גבורות

אַתָּה גִּבּוֹר לְעוֹלָם אֲדֹנָי, מְחַיֵּה מֵתִים אַתָּה, רַב לְהוֹשִׁיעַ.

מַשִּׁיב הָרוּחַ וּמוֹרִיד הַגֶּשֶׁם.

enduring God — exalted and uplifted, great and awesome, Who humbles the haughty and lifts the lowly; withdraws the captive, liberates the humble, and helps the poor; Who responds to His people upon their outcry to Him.

Rise for *Shemoneh Esrei.* Some take three steps backward at this point; others do so before צוּר יִשְׂרָאֵל, *'Rock of Israel.'*

Chazzan– *Praises to the Supreme God, the blessed One Who is blessed. Moses and the Children of Israel exclaimed a song to You with great joy and they all said:*

'Who is like You among the heavenly powers, HASHEM! Who is like You, mighty in holiness, too awesome for praise, doing wonders.'[1]
Chazzan– *With a new song the redeemed ones praised Your Name at the seashore, all of them in unison gave thanks, acknowledged [Your] sovereignty, and said:*

'HASHEM shall reign for all eternity.'[2]

It is forbidden to interrupt or pause between *'Who redeemed Israel'* and *Shemoneh Esrei,* even for *Kaddish, Kedushah* or *Amen.*

צוּר יִשְׂרָאֵל Chazzan– *Rock of Israel,* arise to the aid of Israel and liberate, as You pledged, Judah and Israel. Our Redeemer — HASHEM, Master of Legions, is His Name — the Holy One of Israel.*[3] *Blessed are You, HASHEM, Who redeemed Israel.**

❧ SHEMONEH ESREI – AMIDAH ❧

Take three steps backward, then three steps forward. Remain standing with feet together while reciting *Shemoneh Esrei.* Recite it with quiet devotion and without interruption, verbal or otherwise. Although it should not be audible to others, one must pray loudly enough to hear himself.

My Lord, open my lips, that my mouth may declare Your praise.[4]

PATRIARCHS

Bend the knees at *'Blessed'*; bow at *'You'*; straighten up at *'HASHEM.'*

בָּרוּךְ *Blessed are You, HASHEM, our God and the God of our forefathers, God of Abraham, God of Isaac, and God of Jacob; the great, mighty, and awesome God, the supreme God, Who bestows beneficial kindnesses and creates everything, Who recalls the kindnesses of the Patriarchs and brings a Redeemer to their children's children, for His Name's sake, with love. O King, Helper, Savior, and Shield.*

Bend the knees at *'Blessed'*; bow at *'You'*; straighten up at 'HASHEM.'

Blessed are You, HASHEM, Shield of Abraham.

GOD'S MIGHT

אַתָּה *You are eternally mighty, my Lord, the Resuscitator of the dead are You; abundantly able to save.*

He makes the wind blow and He makes the rain descend.

---

(1) *Exodus* 15:11. (2) 15:18. (3) *Isaiah* 47:4. (4) *Psalms* 51:17.

מְכַלְכֵּל חַיִּים בְּחֶסֶד, מְחַיֵּה מֵתִים בְּרַחֲמִים רַבִּים, סוֹמֵךְ נוֹפְלִים, וְרוֹפֵא חוֹלִים, וּמַתִּיר אֲסוּרִים, וּמְקַיֵּם אֱמוּנָתוֹ לִישֵׁנֵי עָפָר. מִי כָמְוֹךָ בַּעַל גְּבוּרוֹת, וּמִי דּוֹמֶה לָּךְ, מֶלֶךְ מֵמִית וּמְחַיֶּה וּמַצְמִיחַ יְשׁוּעָה. וְנֶאֱמָן אַתָּה לְהַחֲיוֹת מֵתִים. בָּרוּךְ אַתָּה יהוה, מְחַיֵּה הַמֵּתִים.

During the *chazzan's* repetition, *Kedushah* (below) is recited at this point.

קדושת השם

INDIVIDUALS RECITE:

אַתָּה קָדוֹשׁ וְשִׁמְךָ קָדוֹשׁ, וּקְדוֹשִׁים בְּכָל יוֹם יְהַלְלוּךָ סֶּלָה. בָּרוּךְ אַתָּה יהוה, הָאֵל הַקָּדוֹשׁ.

CHAZZAN RECITES DURING HIS REPETITION:

לְדוֹר וָדוֹר נַגִּיד גָּדְלֶךָ וּלְנֵצַח נְצָחִים קְדֻשָּׁתְךָ נַקְדִּישׁ, וְשִׁבְחֲךָ אֱלֹהֵינוּ מִפִּינוּ לֹא יָמוּשׁ לְעוֹלָם וָעֶד, כִּי אֵל מֶלֶךְ גָּדוֹל וְקָדוֹשׁ אָתָּה. בָּרוּךְ אַתָּה יהוה, הָאֵל הַקָּדוֹשׁ.

קדושת היום

אַתָּה בְחַרְתָּנוּ מִכָּל הָעַמִּים, אָהַבְתָּ אוֹתָנוּ, וְרָצִיתָ בָּנוּ, וְרוֹמַמְתָּנוּ מִכָּל הַלְּשׁוֹנוֹת, וְקִדַּשְׁתָּנוּ בְּמִצְוֹתֶיךָ, וְקֵרַבְתָּנוּ מַלְכֵּנוּ לַעֲבוֹדָתֶךָ, וְשִׁמְךָ הַגָּדוֹל וְהַקָּדוֹשׁ עָלֵינוּ קָרָאתָ.

קדושה

When reciting *Kedushah,* one must stand with his feet together and avoid any interruptions. One should rise on his toes when saying the words קָדוֹשׁ, קָדוֹשׁ, קָדוֹשׁ; בָּרוּךְ; and יִמְלֹךְ (of בָּרוּךְ כְּבוֹד).

Cong. then *Chazzan* – **נְקַדֵּשׁ** אֶת שִׁמְךָ בָּעוֹלָם, כְּשֵׁם שֶׁמַּקְדִּישִׁים אוֹתוֹ בִּשְׁמֵי מָרוֹם, כַּכָּתוּב עַל יַד נְבִיאֶךָ, וְקָרָא זֶה אֶל זֶה וְאָמַר:

All – קָדוֹשׁ קָדוֹשׁ קָדוֹשׁ יהוה צְבָאוֹת, מְלֹא כָל הָאָרֶץ כְּבוֹדוֹ.[1]

❖ אָז בְּקוֹל רַעַשׁ גָּדוֹל אַדִּיר וְחָזָק מַשְׁמִיעִים קוֹל, מִתְנַשְּׂאִים לְעֻמַּת שְׂרָפִים, לְעֻמָּתָם בָּרוּךְ יֹאמֵרוּ:

All – בָּרוּךְ כְּבוֹד יהוה, מִמְּקוֹמוֹ.[2] ❖ מִמְּקוֹמְךָ מַלְכֵּנוּ תוֹפִיעַ, וְתִמְלֹךְ עָלֵינוּ, כִּי מְחַכִּים אֲנַחְנוּ לָךְ. מָתַי תִּמְלֹךְ בְּצִיּוֹן, בְּקָרוֹב בְּיָמֵינוּ, לְעוֹלָם וָעֶד תִּשְׁכּוֹן. תִּתְגַּדַּל וְתִתְקַדַּשׁ בְּתוֹךְ יְרוּשָׁלַיִם עִירְךָ, לְדוֹר וָדוֹר וּלְנֵצַח נְצָחִים. וְעֵינֵינוּ תִרְאֶינָה מַלְכוּתֶךָ, כַּדָּבָר הָאָמוּר בְּשִׁירֵי עֻזֶּךָ, עַל יְדֵי דָוִד מְשִׁיחַ צִדְקֶךָ:

All – יִמְלֹךְ יהוה לְעוֹלָם, אֱלֹהַיִךְ צִיּוֹן לְדֹר וָדֹר, הַלְלוּיָהּ.[3]

Chazzan continues . . . לְדוֹר וָדוֹר (above).

He sustains the living with kindness, resuscitates the dead with abundant mercy, supports the fallen, heals the sick, releases the confined, and maintains His faith to those asleep in the dust. Who is like You, O Master of mighty deeds, and who is comparable to You, O King Who causes death and restores life and makes salvation sprout! And You are faithful to resuscitate the dead. Blessed are You, HASHEM, Who resuscitates the dead.

During the *chazzan's* repetition, *Kedushah* (below) is recited at this point.

HOLINESS OF GOD'S NAME

INDIVIDUALS RECITE:

אַתָּה *You are holy and Your Name is holy, and holy ones praise You every day, forever. Blessed are You, HASHEM, the holy God.*

CHAZZAN RECITES DURING HIS REPETITION:

לְדוֹר *From generation to generation we shall relate Your greatness and for infinite eternities we shall proclaim Your holiness. Your praise, our God, shall not leave our mouth forever and ever, for You, O God, are a great and holy King. Blessed are You, HASHEM, the holy God.*

SANCTIFICATION OF THE DAY

אַתָּה בְחַרְתָּנוּ *You have chosen us from all the peoples; You loved us and found favor in us; You exalted us above all the tongues and You sanctified us with Your commandments. You drew us close, our King, to Your service and proclaimed Your great and Holy Name upon us.*

KEDUSHAH

When reciting *Kedushah*, one must stand with his feet together and avoid any interruptions. One should rise on his toes when saying the words *Holy, holy, holy; Blessed is;* and *HASHEM shall reign.*

Cong. then Chazzan – **נְקַדֵּשׁ** *We shall sanctify Your Name in this world, just as they sanctify it in heaven above, as it is written by Your prophet, "And one [angel] will call another and say:*

All – *'Holy, holy, holy is HASHEM, Master of Legions, the whole world is filled with His glory.'"*[1] ❖ *Then, with a sound of great noise, mighty and powerful, they make heard a voice, raising themselves toward the seraphim; those facing them say 'Blessed ...':*

All – *'Blessed is the glory of HASHEM from His place.'*[2] ❖ *From Your place, our King, You will appear and reign over us, for we await You. When will You reign in Zion? Soon, in our days — forever and ever — may You dwell there. May You be exalted and sanctified within Jerusalem, Your city, from generation to generation and for all eternity. May our eyes see Your kingdom, as it is expressed in the songs of Your might, written by David, Your righteous anointed:*

All – *'HASHEM shall reign forever — your God, O Zion — from generation to generation, Halleluyah!'*[3]

Chazzan continues לְדוֹר וָדוֹר, *From generation ...* (above).

---

(1) *Isaiah* 6:3. (2) *Ezekiel* 3:12. (3) *Psalms* 146:10.

וַתִּתֶּן לָנוּ יהוה אֱלֹהֵינוּ בְּאַהֲבָה מוֹעֲדִים לְשִׂמְחָה חַגִּים וּזְמַנִּים לְשָׂשׂוֹן, אֶת יוֹם הַשְּׁמִינִי חַג הָעֲצֶרֶת הַזֶּה, זְמַן שִׂמְחָתֵנוּ מִקְרָא קֹדֶשׁ, זֵכֶר לִיצִיאַת מִצְרָיִם.

During the *chazzan's* repetition, congregation responds אָמֵן as indicated.

אֱלֹהֵינוּ וֵאלֹהֵי אֲבוֹתֵינוּ, יַעֲלֶה, וְיָבֹא, וְיַגִּיעַ, וְיֵרָאֶה, וְיֵרָצֶה, וְיִשָּׁמַע, וְיִפָּקֵד, וְיִזָּכֵר זִכְרוֹנֵנוּ וּפִקְדוֹנֵנוּ, וְזִכְרוֹן אֲבוֹתֵינוּ, וְזִכְרוֹן מָשִׁיחַ בֶּן דָּוִד עַבְדֶּךָ, וְזִכְרוֹן יְרוּשָׁלַיִם עִיר קָדְשֶׁךָ, וְזִכְרוֹן כָּל עַמְּךָ בֵּית יִשְׂרָאֵל לְפָנֶיךָ, לִפְלֵיטָה לְטוֹבָה לְחֵן וּלְחֶסֶד וּלְרַחֲמִים, לְחַיִּים וּלְשָׁלוֹם בְּיוֹם הַשְּׁמִינִי חַג הָעֲצֶרֶת הַזֶּה. זָכְרֵנוּ יהוה אֱלֹהֵינוּ בּוֹ לְטוֹבָה (Cong.–אָמֵן), וּפָקְדֵנוּ בוֹ לִבְרָכָה (Cong.–אָמֵן), וְהוֹשִׁיעֵנוּ בוֹ לְחַיִּים (Cong.–אָמֵן). וּבִדְבַר יְשׁוּעָה וְרַחֲמִים, חוּס וְחָנֵּנוּ וְרַחֵם עָלֵינוּ וְהוֹשִׁיעֵנוּ, כִּי אֵלֶיךָ עֵינֵינוּ, כִּי אֵל מֶלֶךְ חַנּוּן וְרַחוּם אָתָּה.[1]

וְהַשִּׂיאֵנוּ יהוה אֱלֹהֵינוּ אֶת בִּרְכַּת מוֹעֲדֶיךָ לְחַיִּים וּלְשָׁלוֹם, לְשִׂמְחָה וּלְשָׂשׂוֹן, כַּאֲשֶׁר רָצִיתָ וְאָמַרְתָּ לְבָרְכֵנוּ. קַדְּשֵׁנוּ בְּמִצְוֹתֶיךָ וְתֵן חֶלְקֵנוּ בְּתוֹרָתֶךָ, שַׂבְּעֵנוּ מִטּוּבֶךָ וְשַׂמְּחֵנוּ בִּישׁוּעָתֶךָ, וְטַהֵר לִבֵּנוּ לְעָבְדְּךָ בֶּאֱמֶת, וְהַנְחִילֵנוּ יהוה אֱלֹהֵינוּ בְּשִׂמְחָה וּבְשָׂשׂוֹן מוֹעֲדֵי קָדְשֶׁךָ, וְיִשְׂמְחוּ בְךָ יִשְׂרָאֵל מְקַדְּשֵׁי שְׁמֶךָ. בָּרוּךְ אַתָּה יהוה, מְקַדֵּשׁ יִשְׂרָאֵל וְהַזְּמַנִּים.

עבודה

רְצֵה יהוה אֱלֹהֵינוּ בְּעַמְּךָ יִשְׂרָאֵל וּבִתְפִלָּתָם, וְהָשֵׁב אֶת הָעֲבוֹדָה לִדְבִיר בֵּיתֶךָ. וְאִשֵּׁי יִשְׂרָאֵל וּתְפִלָּתָם בְּאַהֲבָה תְקַבֵּל בְּרָצוֹן, וּתְהִי לְרָצוֹן תָּמִיד עֲבוֹדַת יִשְׂרָאֵל עַמֶּךָ.

וְתֶחֱזֶינָה עֵינֵינוּ בְּשׁוּבְךָ לְצִיּוֹן בְּרַחֲמִים. בָּרוּךְ אַתָּה יהוה, הַמַּחֲזִיר שְׁכִינָתוֹ לְצִיּוֹן.

וַתִּתֶּן לָנוּ *And You gave us, HASHEM, our God, with love, appointed festivals for gladness, Festivals and times for joy, this day of the Shemini Atzeres Festival, the time of our gladness, a holy convocation, a memorial of the Exodus from Egypt.*

During the *chazzan's* repetition, congregation responds *Amen* as indicated.

אֱלֹהֵינוּ *Our God and God of our forefathers, may there rise, come, reach, be noted, be favored, be heard, be considered, and be remembered — the remembrance and consideration of ourselves; the remembrance of our forefathers; the remembrance of Messiah, son of David, Your servant; the remembrance of Jerusalem, the City of Your Holiness; the remembrance of Your entire people the Family of Israel — before You for deliverance, for goodness, for grace, for kindness, and for compassion, for life, and for peace on this day of the Shemini Atzeres Festival. Remember us on it, HASHEM, our God, for goodness (*Cong.*–Amen); consider us on it for blessing (*Cong.*–Amen); and help us on it for life (*Cong.*–Amen). In the matter of salvation and compassion, pity, be gracious and compassionate with us and help us, for our eyes are turned to You, because You are God, the gracious and compassionate King.*[1]

וְהַשִּׂיאֵנוּ *Bestow upon us, O HASHEM, our God, the blessing of Your appointed Festivals for life and for peace, for gladness and for joy, as You desired and promised to bless us. Sanctify us with Your commandments and grant us our share in Your Torah; satisfy us from Your goodness and gladden us with Your salvation, and purify our heart to serve You sincerely. And grant us a heritage, O HASHEM, our God — with gladness and with joy — the appointed festivals of Your holiness, and may Israel, the sanctifiers of Your Name, rejoice in You. Blessed are You, HASHEM, Who sanctifies Israel and the festive seasons.*

TEMPLE SERVICE

רְצֵה *Be favorable, HASHEM, our God, toward Your people Israel and their prayer and restore the service to the Holy of Holies of Your Temple. The fire-offerings of Israel and their prayer accept with love and favor, and may the service of Your people Israel always be favorable to You.*

וְתֶחֱזֶינָה *May our eyes behold Your return to Zion in compassion. Blessed are You, HASHEM, Who restores His Presence to Zion.*

(1) Cf. *Nechemiah* 9:31.

הודאה

Bow at מוֹדִים; straighten up at ה'. In his repetition the *chazzan* should recite the entire מוֹדִים aloud, while the congregation recites מוֹדִים דְּרַבָּנָן softly.

מוֹדִים אֲנַחְנוּ לָךְ, שָׁאַתָּה הוּא יהוה אֱלֹהֵינוּ וֵאלֹהֵי אֲבוֹתֵינוּ לְעוֹלָם וָעֶד. צוּר חַיֵּינוּ, מָגֵן יִשְׁעֵנוּ אַתָּה הוּא לְדוֹר וָדוֹר. נוֹדֶה לְּךָ וּנְסַפֵּר תְּהִלָּתֶךָ[1] עַל חַיֵּינוּ הַמְּסוּרִים בְּיָדֶךָ, וְעַל נִשְׁמוֹתֵינוּ הַפְּקוּדוֹת לָךְ, וְעַל נִסֶּיךָ שֶׁבְּכָל יוֹם עִמָּנוּ, וְעַל נִפְלְאוֹתֶיךָ וְטוֹבוֹתֶיךָ שֶׁבְּכָל עֵת, עֶרֶב וָבֹקֶר וְצָהֳרָיִם. הַטּוֹב כִּי לֹא כָלוּ רַחֲמֶיךָ, וְהַמְּרַחֵם כִּי לֹא תַמּוּ חֲסָדֶיךָ,[2] מֵעוֹלָם קִוִּינוּ לָךְ.

מודים דרבנן

מוֹדִים אֲנַחְנוּ לָךְ, שָׁאַתָּה הוּא יהוה אֱלֹהֵינוּ וֵאלֹהֵי אֲבוֹתֵינוּ, אֱלֹהֵי כָל בָּשָׂר, יוֹצְרֵנוּ, יוֹצֵר בְּרֵאשִׁית. בְּרָכוֹת וְהוֹדָאוֹת לְשִׁמְךָ הַגָּדוֹל וְהַקָּדוֹשׁ, עַל שֶׁהֶחֱיִיתָנוּ וְקִיַּמְתָּנוּ. כֵּן תְּחַיֵּנוּ וּתְקַיְּמֵנוּ, וְתֶאֱסוֹף גָּלֻיּוֹתֵינוּ לְחַצְרוֹת קָדְשֶׁךָ, לִשְׁמוֹר חֻקֶּיךָ וְלַעֲשׂוֹת רְצוֹנֶךָ, וּלְעָבְדְּךָ בְּלֵבָב שָׁלֵם, עַל שֶׁאֲנַחְנוּ מוֹדִים לָךְ. בָּרוּךְ אֵל הַהוֹדָאוֹת.

וְעַל כֻּלָּם יִתְבָּרַךְ וְיִתְרוֹמַם שִׁמְךָ מַלְכֵּנוּ תָּמִיד לְעוֹלָם וָעֶד.

Bend the knees at בָּרוּךְ; bow at אַתָּה; straighten up at ה'.

וְכֹל הַחַיִּים יוֹדוּךָ סֶּלָה, וִיהַלְלוּ אֶת שִׁמְךָ בֶּאֱמֶת, הָאֵל יְשׁוּעָתֵנוּ וְעֶזְרָתֵנוּ סֶלָה. בָּרוּךְ אַתָּה יהוה, הַטּוֹב שִׁמְךָ וּלְךָ נָאֶה לְהוֹדוֹת.

ON SIMCHAS TORAH ברכת כהנים IS RECITED AT SHACHARIS

When the *chazzan* recites וְכֹל הַחַיִּים, the *Kohanim* recite יְהִי רָצוֹן.

יְהִי רָצוֹן מִלְּפָנֶיךָ, יהוה אֱלֹהֵינוּ וֵאלֹהֵי אֲבוֹתֵינוּ, שֶׁתְּהֵא הַבְּרָכָה הַזֹּאת שֶׁצִּוִּיתָנוּ לְבָרֵךְ אֶת עַמְּךָ יִשְׂרָאֵל בְּרָכָה שְׁלֵמָה, וְלֹא יִהְיֶה בָּהּ שׁוּם מִכְשׁוֹל וְעָוֹן מֵעַתָּה וְעַד עוֹלָם.

The *chazzan* recites the following in an undertone but says the word *'Kohanim'* aloud as a formal summons to the *Kohanim* to bless the people. In some communities the congregation, but not the *Kohanim*, responds, *'Your holy people — as it is said,'* aloud.
If no *Kohanim are present, the chazzan* recites the following paragraph aloud, omits the *blessing,* and proceeds with יְבָרֶכְךָ as he usually does during *Shacharis.*

אֱלֹהֵינוּ וֵאלֹהֵי אֲבוֹתֵינוּ, בָּרְכֵנוּ בַבְּרָכָה הַמְּשֻׁלֶּשֶׁת בַּתּוֹרָה הַכְּתוּבָה עַל יְדֵי מֹשֶׁה עַבְדֶּךָ, הָאֲמוּרָה מִפִּי אַהֲרֹן וּבָנָיו,

כֹּהֲנִים

עַם קְדוֹשֶׁךָ — כָּאָמוּר:

THANKSGIVING [MODIM]

Bow at *'We gratefully thank You';* straighten up at *'HASHEM.'* In his repetition the *chazzan* should recite the entire *Modim* aloud, while the congregation recites *Modim of the Rabbis* softly.

מוֹדִים *We gratefully thank You, for it is You Who are HASHEM, our God and the God of our forefathers for all eternity; Rock of our lives, Shield of our salvation are You from generation to generation. We shall thank You and relate Your praise*[1] *— for our lives, which are committed to Your power and for our souls that are entrusted to You; for Your miracles that are with us every day; and for Your wonders and favors in every season — evening, morning, and afternoon. The Beneficent One, for Your compassions were never exhausted, and the Compassionate One, for Your kindnesses never ended*[2] *— always have we put our hope in You.*

MODIM OF THE RABBIS

מוֹדִים *We gratefully thank You, for it is You Who are HASHEM, our God and the God of our forefathers, the God of all flesh, our Molder, the Molder of the universe. Blessings and thanks are due Your great and holy Name for You have given us life and sustained us. So may You continue to give us life and sustain us and gather our exiles to the Courtyards of Your Sanctuary, to observe Your decrees, to do Your will and to serve You wholeheartedly. [We thank You] for inspiring us to thank You. Blessed is the God of thanksgivings.*

For all these, may Your Name be blessed and exalted, our King, continually forever and ever.

Bend the knees at *'Blessed';* bow at *'You';* straighten up at *'HASHEM.'*

Everything alive will gratefully acknowledge You, Selah! and praise Your Name sincerely, O God of our salvation and help, Selah! Blessed are You, HASHEM, Your Name is 'The Beneficent One' and to You it is fitting to give thanks.

ON SIMCHAS TORAH BIRCAS KOHANIM IS RECITED AT SHACHARIS

When *chazzan* recites וְכֹל הַחַיִּים, *Everything alive, Kohanim* recite יְהִי רָצוֹן, *May it be Your will.*

יְהִי רָצוֹן *May it be Your will, HASHEM, our God and the God of our fathers, that this blessing which You have commanded us to bestow upon Your nation Israel be a full blessing, that there be in it neither stumbling block nor sin from now and forever.*

The *chazzan* recites the following in an undertone but says the word *'Kohanim'* aloud as a formal summons to the *Kohanim* to bless the people. In some communities the congregation, but not the *Kohanim,* responds, *'Your holy people — as it is said,'* aloud.

If no *Kohanim are present, the chazzan* recites the following paragraph aloud, omits the *blessing,* and proceeds with יְבָרֶכְךָ as he usually does during *Shacharis.*

אֱלֹהֵינוּ *Our God and the God of our forefathers, bless us with the three-verse blessing in the Torah that was written by the hand of Moses, Your servant, that was said by Aaron and his sons, the*

Kohanim,

Your holy people — as it is said:

(1) Cf. *Psalms* 79:13. (2) Cf. *Lamentations* 3:22.

The *Kohanim* recite the following blessing aloud, in unison, and the congregation, but not the *chazzan*, responds אָמֵן.

בָּרוּךְ אַתָּה יהוה, אֱלֹהֵינוּ מֶלֶךְ הָעוֹלָם, אֲשֶׁר קִדְּשָׁנוּ בִּקְדֻשָּׁתוֹ שֶׁל אַהֲרֹן, וְצִוָּנוּ לְבָרֵךְ אֶת עַמּוֹ יִשְׂרָאֵל בְּאַהֲבָה.

יְבָרֶכְךָ יהוה, וְיִשְׁמְרֶךָ. (Cong. – אָמֵן.)

יָאֵר יהוה פָּנָיו אֵלֶיךָ וִיחֻנֶּךָּ. (Cong. – אָמֵן.)

יִשָּׂא יהוה פָּנָיו אֵלֶיךָ וְיָשֵׂם לְךָ שָׁלוֹם.[1] (Cong. – אָמֵן.)

The *chazzan* immediately begins שִׂים שָׁלוֹם; the *Kohanim* turn back to the Ark, lower their hands and recite their concluding prayer רִבּוֹנוֹ שֶׁל עוֹלָם; and the congregation recites אַדִּיר בַּמָּרוֹם. All conclude their respective prayers simultaneously with the *chazzan's* conclusion of שִׂים שָׁלוֹם.

Kohanim:

רִבּוֹנוֹ שֶׁל עוֹלָם, עָשִׂינוּ מַה שֶּׁגָּזַרְתָּ עָלֵינוּ, אַף אַתָּה עֲשֵׂה עִמָּנוּ כְּמָה שֶׁהִבְטַחְתָּנוּ: הַשְׁקִיפָה מִמְּעוֹן קָדְשְׁךָ, מִן הַשָּׁמַיִם, וּבָרֵךְ אֶת עַמְּךָ אֶת יִשְׂרָאֵל, וְאֵת הָאֲדָמָה אֲשֶׁר נָתַתָּה לָנוּ – כַּאֲשֶׁר נִשְׁבַּעְתָּ לַאֲבוֹתֵינוּ – אֶרֶץ זָבַת חָלָב וּדְבָשׁ.

Congregation:

אַדִּיר בַּמָּרוֹם, שׁוֹכֵן בִּגְבוּרָה, אַתָּה שָׁלוֹם וְשִׁמְךָ שָׁלוֹם. יְהִי רָצוֹן שֶׁתָּשִׂים עָלֵינוּ וְעַל כָּל עַמְּךָ בֵּית יִשְׂרָאֵל חַיִּים וּבְרָכָה לְמִשְׁמֶרֶת שָׁלוֹם.

שלום

שִׂים שָׁלוֹם, טוֹבָה וּבְרָכָה, חֵן, וָחֶסֶד וְרַחֲמִים עָלֵינוּ וְעַל כָּל יִשְׂרָאֵל עַמֶּךָ. בָּרְכֵנוּ אָבִינוּ, כֻּלָּנוּ כְּאֶחָד בְּאוֹר פָּנֶיךָ, כִּי בְאוֹר פָּנֶיךָ נָתַתָּ לָּנוּ, יהוה אֱלֹהֵינוּ, תּוֹרַת חַיִּים וְאַהֲבַת חֶסֶד, וּצְדָקָה, וּבְרָכָה, וְרַחֲמִים, וְחַיִּים, וְשָׁלוֹם. וְטוֹב בְּעֵינֶיךָ לְבָרֵךְ אֶת עַמְּךָ יִשְׂרָאֵל, בְּכָל עֵת וּבְכָל שָׁעָה בִּשְׁלוֹמֶךָ. בָּרוּךְ אַתָּה יהוה, הַמְּבָרֵךְ אֶת עַמּוֹ יִשְׂרָאֵל בַּשָּׁלוֹם.

יִהְיוּ לְרָצוֹן אִמְרֵי פִי וְהֶגְיוֹן לִבִּי לְפָנֶיךָ, יהוה צוּרִי וְגֹאֲלִי.[2]

Chazzan's repetition of *Shemoneh Esrei* ends here. Individuals continue below.

אֱלֹהַי, נְצוֹר לְשׁוֹנִי מֵרָע, וּשְׂפָתַי מִדַּבֵּר מִרְמָה,[3] וְלִמְקַלְלַי נַפְשִׁי תִדּוֹם, וְנַפְשִׁי כֶּעָפָר לַכֹּל תִּהְיֶה. פְּתַח לִבִּי בְּתוֹרָתֶךָ, וּבְמִצְוֹתֶיךָ תִּרְדּוֹף נַפְשִׁי. וְכֹל הַחוֹשְׁבִים עָלַי רָעָה, מְהֵרָה הָפֵר עֲצָתָם וְקַלְקֵל מַחֲשַׁבְתָּם. עֲשֵׂה לְמַעַן שְׁמֶךָ, עֲשֵׂה לְמַעַן יְמִינֶךָ, עֲשֵׂה לְמַעַן קְדֻשָּׁתֶךָ, עֲשֵׂה לְמַעַן תּוֹרָתֶךָ. לְמַעַן יֵחָלְצוּן יְדִידֶיךָ, הוֹשִׁיעָה יְמִינְךָ וַעֲנֵנִי.[4]

Some recite verses pertaining to their names. See page 1301.

יִהְיוּ לְרָצוֹן אִמְרֵי פִי וְהֶגְיוֹן לִבִּי לְפָנֶיךָ, יהוה צוּרִי וְגֹאֲלִי.[2] עֹשֶׂה שָׁלוֹם בִּמְרוֹמָיו, הוּא יַעֲשֶׂה שָׁלוֹם עָלֵינוּ, וְעַל כָּל יִשְׂרָאֵל. וְאִמְרוּ: אָמֵן.

Bow and take three steps back. Bow left and say ... עֹשֶׂה, bow right and say ... הוּא יַעֲשֶׂה; bow forward and say וְעַל כָּל ... אָמֵן.

The *Kohanim* recite the following blessing aloud, in unison, and the congregation, but not the *chazzan,* responds *Amen.*

בָּרוּךְ *Blessed are You* HASHEM, *our God, King of the universe, Who has sanctified us with the holiness of Aaron, and has commanded us to bless His people Israel with love.* (Cong.– *Amen.)*

May HASHEM *bless you and safeguard you.* (Cong.– *Amen.)*

May HASHEM *illuminate His countenance for you and be gracious to you.* (Cong.– *Amen.)*

May HASHEM *turn His countenance to you and establish peace for you.*[1] (Cong.– *Amen.)*

The *chazzan* immediately begins שִׂים שָׁלוֹם, *Establish peace;* the *Kohanim* turn back to the Ark, lower their hands and recite their concluding prayer רִבּוֹנוֹ שֶׁל עוֹלָם, *Master of the World;* and the congregation recites אַדִּיר, *Mighty One.* All should conclude their respective prayers simultaneously with the *chazzan's* conclusion of שִׂים שָׁלוֹם.

Kohanim:

רִבּוֹנוֹ שֶׁל עוֹלָם *Master of the world, we have done what You have decreed upon us, now may You also do as You have promised us: Look down from Your sacred dwelling, from the heavens, and bless Your people, Israel, and the earth which You have given us — just as You have sworn to our fathers — a land that flows with milk and honey.*

Congregation:

אַדִּיר *Mighty One on high, He Who dwells in power! You are Peace and Your Name is Peace! May it be acceptable that You grant us and all of Your people, the house of Israel, life and blessing for a safeguard of peace.*

PEACE

שִׂים שָׁלוֹם *Establish peace, goodness, blessing, graciousness, kindness, and compassion upon us and upon all of Your people Israel. Bless us, our Father, all of us as one, with the light of Your countenance, for with the light of Your countenance You gave us,* HASHEM, *our God, the Torah of life and a love of kindness, righteousness, blessing, compassion, life, and peace. And may it be good in Your eyes to bless Your people Israel, in every season and in every hour with Your Peace. Blessed are You,* HASHEM, *Who blesses His people Israel with peace.*

May the expressions of my mouth and the thoughts of my heart find favor before You, HASHEM, *my Rock and my Redeemer.*[2]

Chazzan's repetition of *Shemoneh Esrei* ends here. Individuals continue below.

אֱלֹהַי *My God, guard my tongue from evil and my lips from speaking deceitfully.*[3] *To those who curse me, let my soul be silent; and let my soul be like dust to everyone. Open my heart to Your Torah, then my soul will pursue Your commandments. As for all those who design evil against me, speedily nullify their counsel and disrupt their design. Act for Your Name's sake; act for Your right hand's sake; act for Your sanctity's sake; act for Your Torah's sake. That Your beloved ones may be given rest; let Your right hand save, and respond to me.*[4] *May the expressions of my mouth and the thoughts of my heart find favor before You,* HASHEM, *my Rock and my Redeemer.*[2] *He Who makes peace in His heights, may He make peace upon us, and upon all Israel. Now respond: Amen.*

Some recite verses pertaining to their names at this point. See page 1301.

Bow and take three steps back. Bow left and say, *'He Who makes peace . . .';* bow right and say, *'may He make peace . . .';* bow forward and say, *'and upon . . . Amen.'*

(1) *Numbers* 6:24-26. (2) *Psalms* 19:15. (3) Cf. 34:14. (4) 60:7; 108:7. (5) *Malachi* 3:4.

יְהִי רָצוֹן מִלְּפָנֶיךָ יהוה אֱלֹהֵינוּ וֵאלֹהֵי אֲבוֹתֵינוּ, שֶׁיִּבָּנֶה בֵּית הַמִּקְדָּשׁ בִּמְהֵרָה בְיָמֵינוּ, וְתֵן חֶלְקֵנוּ בְּתוֹרָתֶךָ. וְשָׁם נַעֲבָדְךָ בְּיִרְאָה, כִּימֵי עוֹלָם וּכְשָׁנִים קַדְמוֹנִיּוֹת. וְעָרְבָה לַיהוה מִנְחַת יְהוּדָה וִירוּשָׁלָיִם, כִּימֵי עוֹלָם וּכְשָׁנִים קַדְמוֹנִיּוֹת.[1]

THE INDIVIDUAL'S RECITATION OF שְׁמוֹנֶה עֶשְׂרֵה ENDS HERE.

The individual remains standing in place until the *chazzan* reaches *Kedushah* — or at least until the *chazzan* begins his repetition — then he takes three steps forward. The *chazzan* himself, or one praying alone, should remain in place for a few moments before taking three steps forward.

הלל

The *chazzan* recites the blessing. The congregation, after responding אָמֵן, repeats it, and continues with the first psalm.

בָּרוּךְ אַתָּה יהוה אֱלֹהֵינוּ מֶלֶךְ הָעוֹלָם, אֲשֶׁר קִדְּשָׁנוּ בְּמִצְוֹתָיו, וְצִוָּנוּ לִקְרוֹא אֶת הַהַלֵּל. (Cong. — אָמֵן.)

תהלים קיג

הַלְלוּיָהּ הַלְלוּ עַבְדֵי יהוה, הַלְלוּ אֶת שֵׁם יהוה. יְהִי שֵׁם יהוה מְבֹרָךְ, מֵעַתָּה וְעַד עוֹלָם. מִמִּזְרַח שֶׁמֶשׁ עַד מְבוֹאוֹ, מְהֻלָּל שֵׁם יהוה. רָם עַל כָּל גּוֹיִם יהוה, עַל הַשָּׁמַיִם כְּבוֹדוֹ. מִי כַּיהוה אֱלֹהֵינוּ, הַמַּגְבִּיהִי לָשָׁבֶת. הַמַּשְׁפִּילִי לִרְאוֹת, בַּשָּׁמַיִם וּבָאָרֶץ. ❖ מְקִימִי מֵעָפָר דָּל, מֵאַשְׁפֹּת יָרִים אֶבְיוֹן. לְהוֹשִׁיבִי עִם נְדִיבִים, עִם נְדִיבֵי עַמּוֹ. מוֹשִׁיבִי עֲקֶרֶת הַבַּיִת, אֵם הַבָּנִים שְׂמֵחָה, הַלְלוּיָהּ.

תהלים קיד

בְּצֵאת יִשְׂרָאֵל מִמִּצְרָיִם, בֵּית יַעֲקֹב מֵעַם לֹעֵז. הָיְתָה יְהוּדָה לְקָדְשׁוֹ, יִשְׂרָאֵל מַמְשְׁלוֹתָיו. הַיָּם רָאָה וַיָּנֹס, הַיַּרְדֵּן יִסֹּב לְאָחוֹר. הֶהָרִים רָקְדוּ כְאֵילִים, גְּבָעוֹת כִּבְנֵי צֹאן. ❖ מַה לְּךָ הַיָּם כִּי תָנוּס, הַיַּרְדֵּן תִּסֹּב לְאָחוֹר. הֶהָרִים תִּרְקְדוּ כְאֵילִים, גְּבָעוֹת כִּבְנֵי צֹאן. מִלִּפְנֵי אָדוֹן חוּלִי אָרֶץ, מִלִּפְנֵי אֱלוֹהַּ יַעֲקֹב. הַהֹפְכִי הַצּוּר אֲגַם מָיִם, חַלָּמִישׁ לְמַעְיְנוֹ מָיִם.

תהלים קטו:א-יא

לֹא לָנוּ יהוה לֹא לָנוּ, כִּי לְשִׁמְךָ תֵּן כָּבוֹד, עַל חַסְדְּךָ עַל אֲמִתֶּךָ. לָמָּה יֹאמְרוּ הַגּוֹיִם, אַיֵּה נָא אֱלֹהֵיהֶם. וֵאלֹהֵינוּ בַשָּׁמָיִם, כֹּל אֲשֶׁר חָפֵץ עָשָׂה. עֲצַבֵּיהֶם כֶּסֶף וְזָהָב, מַעֲשֵׂה יְדֵי אָדָם. פֶּה לָהֶם וְלֹא יְדַבֵּרוּ, עֵינַיִם לָהֶם וְלֹא יִרְאוּ. אָזְנַיִם לָהֶם וְלֹא יִשְׁמָעוּ, אַף לָהֶם וְלֹא יְרִיחוּן. יְדֵיהֶם וְלֹא יְמִישׁוּן, רַגְלֵיהֶם וְלֹא יְהַלֵּכוּ, לֹא יֶהְגּוּ בִּגְרוֹנָם. כְּמוֹהֶם יִהְיוּ עֹשֵׂיהֶם, כֹּל אֲשֶׁר בֹּטֵחַ בָּהֶם. ❖ יִשְׂרָאֵל בְּטַח בַּיהוה, עֶזְרָם וּמָגִנָּם הוּא. בֵּית אַהֲרֹן בִּטְחוּ בַיהוה, עֶזְרָם וּמָגִנָּם הוּא. יִרְאֵי יהוה בִּטְחוּ בַיהוה, עֶזְרָם וּמָגִנָּם הוּא.

יְהִי רָצוֹן *May it be Your will,* HASHEM, *our God and the God of our forefathers, that the Holy Temple be rebuilt, speedily in our days. Grant us our share in Your Torah, and may we serve You there with reverence, as in days of old and in former years. Then the offering of Judah and Jerusalem will be pleasing to* HASHEM, *as in days of old and in former years.*[1]

THE INDIVIDUAL'S RECITATION OF *SHEMONEH ESREI* ENDS HERE.

The individual remains standing in place until the *chazzan* reaches *Kedushah* — or at least until the *chazzan* begins his repetition — then he takes three steps forward. The *chazzan* himself, or one praying alone, should remain in place for a few moments before taking three steps forward.

HALLEL

The *chazzan* recites the blessing. The congregation, after responding *Amen,* repeats it, and continues with the first psalm.

בָּרוּךְ *Blessed are You,* HASHEM, *our God, King of the universe, Who has sanctified us with His commandments and has commanded us to read the Hallel.* (Cong.– *Amen.)*

Psalm 113

הַלְלוּיָהּ *Halleluyah! Give praise, you servants of* HASHEM; *praise the Name of* HASHEM! *Blessed be the Name of* HASHEM, *from this time and forever. From the rising of the sun to its setting,* HASHEM's *Name is praised. High above all nations is* HASHEM, *above the heavens is His glory. Who is like* HASHEM, *our God, Who is enthroned on high — yet deigns to look upon the heaven and the earth?* Chazzan– *He raises the needy from the dust, from the trash heaps He lifts the destitute. To seat them with nobles, with the nobles of His people. He transforms the barren wife into a glad mother of children. Halleluyah!*

Psalm 114

בְּצֵאת *When Israel went out of Egypt, Jacob's household from a people of alien tongue — Judah became His sanctuary, Israel His dominions. The sea saw and fled: the Jordan turned backward. The mountains skipped like rams, the hills like young lambs.* Chazzan– *What ails you, O sea, that you flee? O Jordan, that you turn backward? O mountains, that you skip like rams? O hills, like young lambs? Before the Lord's Presence — did I, the earth, tremble — before the presence of the God of Jacob, Who turns the rock into a pond of water, the flint into a flowing fountain.*

Psalms 115:1-11

לֹא לָנוּ *Not for our sake,* HASHEM, *not for our sake, but for Your Name's sake give glory, for Your kindness and for Your truth! Why should the nations say, 'Where is their God now?' Our God is in the heavens; whatever He pleases, He does! Their idols are silver and gold, the handiwork of man. They have a mouth, but cannot speak; they have eyes, but cannot see. They have ears, but cannot hear; they have a nose, but cannot smell. Their hands — they cannot feel; their feet — they cannot walk; they cannot utter a sound from their throat. Those who make them should become like them, whoever trusts in them!* Chazzan– *O Israel, trust in* HASHEM; *— their help and their shield is He! House of Aaron, trust in* HASHEM; *their help and their shield is He! You who fear* HASHEM, *trust in* HASHEM; *their help and their shield is He!*

---

(1) *Malachi* 3:4.

תהלים קטו:יב־יח

יהוה זְכָרָנוּ יְבָרֵךְ, יְבָרֵךְ אֶת בֵּית יִשְׂרָאֵל, יְבָרֵךְ אֶת בֵּית אַהֲרֹן. יְבָרֵךְ יִרְאֵי יהוה, הַקְּטַנִּים עִם הַגְּדֹלִים. יֹסֵף יהוה עֲלֵיכֶם, עֲלֵיכֶם וְעַל בְּנֵיכֶם. בְּרוּכִים אַתֶּם לַיהוה, עֹשֵׂה שָׁמַיִם וָאָרֶץ. ❖ הַשָּׁמַיִם שָׁמַיִם לַיהוה, וְהָאָרֶץ נָתַן לִבְנֵי אָדָם. לֹא הַמֵּתִים יְהַלְלוּ יָהּ, וְלֹא כָּל יֹרְדֵי דוּמָה. וַאֲנַחְנוּ נְבָרֵךְ יָהּ, מֵעַתָּה וְעַד עוֹלָם, הַלְלוּיָהּ.

תהלים קטז:א־יא

אָהַבְתִּי כִּי יִשְׁמַע יהוה, אֶת קוֹלִי תַּחֲנוּנָי. כִּי הִטָּה אָזְנוֹ לִי, וּבְיָמַי אֶקְרָא. אֲפָפוּנִי חֶבְלֵי מָוֶת, וּמְצָרֵי שְׁאוֹל מְצָאוּנִי, צָרָה וְיָגוֹן אֶמְצָא. וּבְשֵׁם יהוה אֶקְרָא, אָנָּה יהוה מַלְּטָה נַפְשִׁי. חַנּוּן יהוה וְצַדִּיק, וֵאלֹהֵינוּ מְרַחֵם. שֹׁמֵר פְּתָאִים יהוה, דַּלּוֹתִי וְלִי יְהוֹשִׁיעַ. שׁוּבִי נַפְשִׁי לִמְנוּחָיְכִי, כִּי יהוה גָּמַל עָלָיְכִי. כִּי חִלַּצְתָּ נַפְשִׁי מִמָּוֶת, אֶת עֵינִי מִן דִּמְעָה, אֶת רַגְלִי מִדֶּחִי. ❖ אֶתְהַלֵּךְ לִפְנֵי יהוה, בְּאַרְצוֹת הַחַיִּים. הֶאֱמַנְתִּי כִּי אֲדַבֵּר, אֲנִי עָנִיתִי מְאֹד. אֲנִי אָמַרְתִּי בְחָפְזִי, כָּל הָאָדָם כֹּזֵב.

תהלים קטז:יב־יט

מָה אָשִׁיב לַיהוה, כָּל תַּגְמוּלוֹהִי עָלָי. כּוֹס יְשׁוּעוֹת אֶשָּׂא, וּבְשֵׁם יהוה אֶקְרָא. נְדָרַי לַיהוה אֲשַׁלֵּם, נֶגְדָה נָּא לְכָל עַמּוֹ. יָקָר בְּעֵינֵי יהוה, הַמָּוְתָה לַחֲסִידָיו. אָנָּה יהוה כִּי אֲנִי עַבְדֶּךָ, אֲנִי עַבְדְּךָ, בֶּן אֲמָתֶךָ, פִּתַּחְתָּ לְמוֹסֵרָי. ❖ לְךָ אֶזְבַּח זֶבַח תּוֹדָה, וּבְשֵׁם יהוה אֶקְרָא. נְדָרַי לַיהוה אֲשַׁלֵּם, נֶגְדָה נָּא לְכָל עַמּוֹ. בְּחַצְרוֹת בֵּית יהוה, בְּתוֹכֵכִי יְרוּשָׁלָיִם הַלְלוּיָהּ.

Congregation, then *chazzan:*

תהלים קיז

הַלְלוּ אֶת יהוה, כָּל גּוֹיִם, שַׁבְּחוּהוּ כָּל הָאֻמִּים. כִּי גָבַר עָלֵינוּ חַסְדּוֹ, וֶאֱמֶת יהוה לְעוֹלָם, הַלְלוּיָהּ.

תהלים קיח

Chazzan – **הוֹדוּ** לַיהוה כִּי טוֹב, כִּי לְעוֹלָם חַסְדּוֹ.

Cong. – הוֹדוּ לַיהוה כִּי טוֹב, כִּי לְעוֹלָם חַסְדּוֹ.

יֹאמַר נָא יִשְׂרָאֵל, כִּי לְעוֹלָם חַסְדּוֹ.

Chazzan – יֹאמַר נָא יִשְׂרָאֵל, כִּי לְעוֹלָם חַסְדּוֹ.

Cong. – הוֹדוּ לַיהוה כִּי טוֹב, כִּי לְעוֹלָם חַסְדּוֹ.

יֹאמְרוּ נָא בֵית אַהֲרֹן, כִּי לְעוֹלָם חַסְדּוֹ.

Psalm 115:12-18

יהוה *HASHEM Who has remembered us will bless — He will bless the House of Israel; He will bless the House of Aaron; He will bless those who fear HASHEM, the small as well as the great. May HASHEM increase upon you, upon you and upon your children! You are blessed of HASHEM, maker of heaven and earth.* Chazzan– *As for the heavens — the heavens are HASHEM's, but the earth He has given to mankind. Neither the dead can praise God, nor any who descend into silence; but we will bless God from this time and forever. Halleluyah!*

Psalm 116:1-11

אָהַבְתִּי *I love Him, for HASHEM hears my voice, my supplications. As He has inclined His ear to me, so in my days shall I call. The pains of death encircled me; the confines of the grave have found me; trouble and sorrow I would find. Then I would invoke the Name of HASHEM: 'Please, HASHEM, save my soul.' Gracious is HASHEM and righteous, our God is merciful. HASHEM protects the simple; I was brought low, but He saved me. Return, my soul, to your rest; for HASHEM has been kind to you. For You have delivered my soul from death, my eyes from tears, my feet from stumbling.* Chazzan– *I shall walk before HASHEM in the lands of the living. I have kept faith although I say: 'I suffer exceedingly.' I said in my haste: 'All mankind is deceitful.'*

Psalm 116:12-19

מָה אָשִׁיב *How can I repay HASHEM for all His kindness to me? I will raise the cup of salvations and the Name of HASHEM I will invoke. My vows to HASHEM I will pay, in the presence, now, of His entire people. Difficult in the eyes of HASHEM is the death of His devout ones. Please, HASHEM — for I am Your servant, I am Your servant, son of Your handmaid — You have released my bonds.* Chazzan– *To You I will sacrifice thanksgiving offerings, and the name of HASHEM I will invoke. My vows to HASHEM I will pay, in the presence, now, of His entire people. In the courtyards of the House of HASHEM, in your midst, O Jerusalem, Halleluyah!*

Congregation, then *chazzan:*
Psalm 117

הַלְלוּ *Praise HASHEM, all nations; praise Him, all the states! For His kindness has overwhelmed us, and the truth of HASHEM is eternal, Halleluyah!*

Psalm 118

Chazzan – **הוֹדוּ** *Give thanks to HASHEM for He is good;* *His kindness endures forever!*

Cong. – *Give thanks to HASHEM, for He is good;* *His kindness endures forever!*

Let Israel say now: *His kindness endures forever!*

Chazzan – *Let Israel say now:* *His kindness endures forever!*

Cong. – *Give thanks to HASHEM, for He is good;* *His kindness endures forever!*

Let the House of Aaron say now: *His kindness endures forever!*

Chazzan – יֹאמְרוּ נָא בֵית אַהֲרֹן, כִּי לְעוֹלָם חַסְדּוֹ.
Cong. – הוֹדוּ לַיהוה כִּי טוֹב, כִּי לְעוֹלָם חַסְדּוֹ.
יֹאמְרוּ נָא יִרְאֵי יהוה, כִּי לְעוֹלָם חַסְדּוֹ.
Chazzan – יֹאמְרוּ נָא יִרְאֵי יהוה, כִּי לְעוֹלָם חַסְדּוֹ.
Cong. – הוֹדוּ לַיהוה כִּי טוֹב, כִּי לְעוֹלָם חַסְדּוֹ.

מִן הַמֵּצַר קָרָאתִי יָּהּ, עָנָנִי בַמֶּרְחָב יָהּ. יהוה לִי לֹא אִירָא, מַה יַּעֲשֶׂה לִי אָדָם. יהוה לִי בְּעֹזְרָי, וַאֲנִי אֶרְאֶה בְשֹׂנְאָי. טוֹב לַחֲסוֹת בַּיהוה, מִבְּטֹחַ בָּאָדָם. טוֹב לַחֲסוֹת בַּיהוה, מִבְּטֹחַ בִּנְדִיבִים. כָּל גּוֹיִם סְבָבוּנִי, בְּשֵׁם יהוה כִּי אֲמִילַם. סַבּוּנִי גַם סְבָבוּנִי, בְּשֵׁם יהוה כִּי אֲמִילַם. סַבּוּנִי כִדְבֹרִים דֹּעֲכוּ כְּאֵשׁ קוֹצִים, בְּשֵׁם יהוה כִּי אֲמִילַם. דָּחֹה דְחִיתַנִי לִנְפֹּל, וַיהוה עֲזָרָנִי. עָזִּי וְזִמְרָת יָהּ, וַיְהִי לִי לִישׁוּעָה. קוֹל רִנָּה וִישׁוּעָה, בְּאָהֳלֵי צַדִּיקִים, יְמִין יהוה עֹשָׂה חָיִל. יְמִין יהוה רוֹמֵמָה, יְמִין יהוה עֹשָׂה חָיִל. לֹא אָמוּת כִּי אֶחְיֶה, וַאֲסַפֵּר מַעֲשֵׂי יָהּ. יַסֹּר יִסְּרַנִּי יָּהּ, וְלַמָּוֶת לֹא נְתָנָנִי. ❖ פִּתְחוּ לִי שַׁעֲרֵי צֶדֶק, אָבֹא בָם אוֹדֶה יָהּ. זֶה הַשַּׁעַר לַיהוה, צַדִּיקִים יָבֹאוּ בוֹ. אוֹדְךָ כִּי עֲנִיתָנִי, וַתְּהִי לִי לִישׁוּעָה. אוֹדְךָ כִּי עֲנִיתָנִי, וַתְּהִי לִי לִישׁוּעָה. אֶבֶן מָאֲסוּ הַבּוֹנִים, הָיְתָה לְרֹאשׁ פִּנָּה. אֶבֶן מָאֲסוּ הַבּוֹנִים, הָיְתָה לְרֹאשׁ פִּנָּה. מֵאֵת יהוה הָיְתָה זֹּאת, הִיא נִפְלָאת בְּעֵינֵינוּ. מֵאֵת יהוה הָיְתָה זֹּאת, הִיא נִפְלָאת בְּעֵינֵינוּ. זֶה הַיּוֹם עָשָׂה יהוה, נָגִילָה וְנִשְׂמְחָה בוֹ. זֶה הַיּוֹם עָשָׂה יהוה, נָגִילָה וְנִשְׂמְחָה בוֹ.

The next four lines are recited responsively — *chazzan,* then congregation.

אָנָּא יהוה הוֹשִׁיעָה נָּא.
אָנָּא יהוה הוֹשִׁיעָה נָּא.
אָנָּא יהוה הַצְלִיחָה נָא.
אָנָּא יהוה הַצְלִיחָה נָא.

בָּרוּךְ הַבָּא בְּשֵׁם יהוה, בֵּרַכְנוּכֶם מִבֵּית יהוה. בָּרוּךְ הַבָּא בְּשֵׁם יהוה, בֵּרַכְנוּכֶם מִבֵּית יהוה. אֵל יהוה וַיָּאֶר לָנוּ, אִסְרוּ חַג בַּעֲבֹתִים, עַד קַרְנוֹת הַמִּזְבֵּחַ. אֵל יהוה וַיָּאֶר לָנוּ, אִסְרוּ חַג בַּעֲבֹתִים, עַד קַרְנוֹת הַמִּזְבֵּחַ. אֵלִי אַתָּה וְאוֹדֶךָּ, אֱלֹהַי אֲרוֹמְמֶךָּ. אֵלִי אַתָּה וְאוֹדֶךָּ, אֱלֹהַי אֲרוֹמְמֶךָּ. הוֹדוּ לַיהוה כִּי טוֹב, כִּי לְעוֹלָם חַסְדּוֹ. הוֹדוּ לַיהוה כִּי טוֹב, כִּי לְעוֹלָם חַסְדּוֹ

Chazzan – *Let the House of Aaron say now: His kindness endures forever!*
Cong. – *Give thanks to HASHEM, for He is good;*
His kindness endures forever!
Let those who fear HASHEM say now:
His kindness endures forever!
Chazzan – *Let those who fear HASHEM say now:*
His kindness endures forever!
Cong. – *Give thanks to HASHEM, for He is good;*
His kindness endures forever!

מִן הַמֵּצַר *From the straits did I call upon God; God answered me with expansiveness. HASHEM is with me, I have no fear; how can man affect me? HASHEM is with me through my helpers; therefore I can face my foes. It is better to take refuge in HASHEM than to rely on man. It is better to take refuge in HASHEM than to rely on nobles. All the nations surround me; in the Name of HASHEM I cut them down! They encircle me, they also surround me; in the Name of HASHEM, I cut them down! They encircle me like bees, but they are extinguished as a fire does thorns; in the Name of HASHEM I cut them down! You pushed me hard that I might fall, but HASHEM assisted me. God is my might and my praise, and He was a salvation for me. The sound of rejoicing and salvation is in the tents of the righteous: 'HASHEM's right hand does valiantly. HASHEM's right hand is raised triumphantly; HASHEM's right hand does valiantly!' I shall not die! But I shall live and relate the deeds of God. God has chastened me exceedingly, but He did not let me die.* Chazzan– *Open for me the gates of righteousness, I will enter them and thank God. This is the gate of HASHEM; the righteous shall enter through it. I thank You for You have answered me and become my salvation. I thank You for You have answered me and become my salvation. The stone the builders despised has become the cornerstone. The stone the builders despised has become the cornerstone. This emanated from HASHEM; it is wondrous in our eyes. This emanated from HASHEM; it is wondrous in our eyes. This is the day HASHEM has made; let us rejoice and be glad on it. This is the day HASHEM has made; let us rejoice and be glad on it.*

The next four lines are recited responsively — *chazzan,* then congregation.

אָנָּא *Please, HASHEM, save now!*
Please, HASHEM, save now!
Please, HASHEM, bring success now!
Please, HASHEM, bring success now!

בָּרוּךְ *Blessed is he who comes in the Name of HASHEM; we bless you from the House of HASHEM. Blessed is he who comes in the Name of HASHEM; we bless you from the House of HASHEM. HASHEM is God, He illuminated for us; bind the festival offering with cords until the corners of the Altar. HASHEM is God, He illuminated for us; bind the festival offering with cords until the corners of the Altar. You are my God, and I will thank You; my God, I will exalt You. You are my God, and I will thank You; my God, I will exalt You. Give thanks to HASHEM, for He is good; His kindness endures forever. Give thanks to HASHEM, for He is good; His kindness endures forever.*

יְהַלְלְוּךָ יהוה אֱלֹהֵינוּ כָּל מַעֲשֶׂיךָ, וַחֲסִידֶיךָ צַדִּיקִים עוֹשֵׂי רְצוֹנֶךָ, וְכָל עַמְּךָ בֵּית יִשְׂרָאֵל בְּרִנָּה יוֹדוּ וִיבָרְכוּ וִישַׁבְּחוּ וִיפָאֲרוּ וִירוֹמְמוּ וְיַעֲרִיצוּ וְיַקְדִּישׁוּ וְיַמְלִיכוּ אֶת שִׁמְךָ מַלְכֵּנוּ, ❖ כִּי לְךָ טוֹב לְהוֹדוֹת וּלְשִׁמְךָ נָאֶה לְזַמֵּר, כִּי מֵעוֹלָם וְעַד עוֹלָם אַתָּה אֵל. בָּרוּךְ אַתָּה יהוה, מֶלֶךְ מְהֻלָּל בַּתִּשְׁבָּחוֹת. (Cong. – אָמֵן.)

קדיש שלם

The *chazzan* recites קַדִּישׁ שָׁלֵם:

יִתְגַּדַּל וְיִתְקַדַּשׁ שְׁמֵהּ רַבָּא. (Cong. – אָמֵן.) בְּעָלְמָא דִּי בְרָא כִרְעוּתֵהּ. וְיַמְלִיךְ מַלְכוּתֵהּ, בְּחַיֵּיכוֹן וּבְיוֹמֵיכוֹן וּבְחַיֵּי דְכָל בֵּית יִשְׂרָאֵל, בַּעֲגָלָא וּבִזְמַן קָרִיב. וְאִמְרוּ: אָמֵן.

(Cong. – אָמֵן. יְהֵא שְׁמֵהּ רַבָּא מְבָרַךְ לְעָלַם וּלְעָלְמֵי עָלְמַיָּא.)

יְהֵא שְׁמֵהּ רַבָּא מְבָרַךְ לְעָלַם וּלְעָלְמֵי עָלְמַיָּא.

יִתְבָּרַךְ וְיִשְׁתַּבַּח וְיִתְפָּאַר וְיִתְרוֹמַם וְיִתְנַשֵּׂא וְיִתְהַדָּר וְיִתְעַלֶּה וְיִתְהַלָּל שְׁמֵהּ דְּקֻדְשָׁא בְּרִיךְ הוּא (Cong. – בְּרִיךְ הוּא) — לְעֵלָּא מִן כָּל בִּרְכָתָא וְשִׁירָתָא תֻּשְׁבְּחָתָא וְנֶחֱמָתָא, דַּאֲמִירָן בְּעָלְמָא. וְאִמְרוּ: אָמֵן. (Cong. – אָמֵן.)

(Cong. – קַבֵּל בְּרַחֲמִים וּבְרָצוֹן אֶת תְּפִלָּתֵנוּ.)

תִּתְקַבֵּל צְלוֹתְהוֹן וּבָעוּתְהוֹן דְּכָל בֵּית יִשְׂרָאֵל קֳדָם אֲבוּהוֹן דִּי בִשְׁמַיָּא. וְאִמְרוּ: אָמֵן. (Cong. – אָמֵן.)

(Cong. – יְהִי שֵׁם יהוה מְבֹרָךְ, מֵעַתָּה וְעַד עוֹלָם.[1])

יְהֵא שְׁלָמָא רַבָּא מִן שְׁמַיָּא, וְחַיִּים עָלֵינוּ וְעַל כָּל יִשְׂרָאֵל. וְאִמְרוּ: אָמֵן. (Cong. – אָמֵן.)

(Cong. – עֶזְרִי מֵעִם יהוה, עֹשֵׂה שָׁמַיִם וָאָרֶץ.[2])

Take three steps back. Bow left and say . . . עֹשֶׂה; bow right and say . . . הוּא; bow forward and say וְעַל כָּל . . . אָמֵן. Remain standing in place for a few moments, then take three steps forward.

עֹשֶׂה שָׁלוֹם בִּמְרוֹמָיו, הוּא יַעֲשֶׂה שָׁלוֹם עָלֵינוּ, וְעַל כָּל יִשְׂרָאֵל. וְאִמְרוּ: אָמֵן. (Cong. – אָמֵן.)

הקפות לשמחת תורה

Before the Ark is opened for the *Hakafos,* the following selection of verses is recited responsively:

אַתָּה הָרְאֵתָ לָדַעַת, כִּי יהוה הוּא הָאֱלֹהִים, אֵין עוֹד מִלְּבַדּוֹ.[3]
לְעֹשֵׂה נִפְלָאוֹת גְּדֹלוֹת לְבַדּוֹ, כִּי לְעוֹלָם חַסְדּוֹ.[4]
אֵין כָּמוֹךָ בָאֱלֹהִים, אֲדֹנָי, וְאֵין כְּמַעֲשֶׂיךָ.[5]
יְהִי כְבוֹד יהוה לְעוֹלָם, יִשְׂמַח יהוה בְּמַעֲשָׂיו.[6]
יְהִי שֵׁם יהוה מְבֹרָךְ, מֵעַתָּה וְעַד עוֹלָם.[7]
יְהִי יהוה אֱלֹהֵינוּ עִמָּנוּ, כַּאֲשֶׁר הָיָה עִם אֲבֹתֵינוּ, אַל יַעַזְבֵנוּ וְאַל יִטְּשֵׁנוּ.[8]

יְהַלְלוּךָ *All Your works shall praise You,* HASHEM *our God. And Your devout ones, the righteous, who do Your will, and Your entire people, the House of Israel, with glad song will thank, bless, praise, glorify, exalt, extol, sanctify, and proclaim the sovereignty of Your Name, our King.* Chazzan– *For to You it is fitting to give thanks, and unto Your Name it is proper to sing praises, for from This World to the World to Come You are God. Blessed are You,* HASHEM, *the King Who is lauded with praises.* (Cong.– *Amen.)*

FULL KADDISH

The *chazzan* recites the Full *Kaddish:*

יִתְגַּדַּל *May His great Name grow exalted and sanctified* (Cong.– *Amen.*) *in the world that He created as He willed. May He give reign to His kingship in your lifetimes and in your days, and in the lifetimes of the entire Family of Israel, swiftly and soon. Now respond: Amen.*

(Cong.– *Amen. May His great Name be blessed forever and ever.)*

May His great Name be blessed forever and ever.

Blessed, praised, glorified, exalted, extolled, mighty, upraised, and lauded be the Name of the Holy One, Blessed is He (Cong.– *Blessed is He*) *— beyond any blessing and song, praise and consolation that are uttered in the world. Now respond: Amen.* (Cong.– *Amen.*)

(Cong.– *Accept our prayers with mercy and favor.*)

May the prayers and supplications of the entire Family of Israel be accepted before their Father Who is in Heaven. Now respond: Amen. (Cong.– *Amen.*)

(Cong.– *Blessed be the Name of* HASHEM, *from this time and forever.*[1])

May there be abundant peace from Heaven, and life, upon us and upon all Israel. Now respond: Amen. (Cong.– *Amen.*)

(Cong.– *My help is from* HASHEM, *Maker of heaven and earth.*[2])

Take three steps back. Bow left and say, *'He Who makes peace . . .';* bow right and say, *'may He . . .';* bow forward and say, *'and upon all Israel . . .'* Remain standing in place for a few moments, then take three steps forward.

He Who makes peace in His heights, may He make peace upon us, and upon all Israel. Now respond: Amen. (Cong.– *Amen.*)

THE HAKAFAH-CIRCUITS OF SIMCHAS TORAH

Before the Ark is opened for the *Hakafos,* the following selection of verses is recited responsively:

אַתָּה הָרְאֵתָ *You have been shown to know, that* HASHEM,
He is the God, there is none beside Him.[3]
To Him Who alone performs great wonders,
for His kindness endures forever.[4]
There is none like You among the gods, my Lord,
and there is nothing like Your works.[5]
May the glory of HASHEM *endure forever,*
let HASHEM *rejoice in His works.*[6]
Blessed be the Name of HASHEM, *from this time and forever.*[7]
May HASHEM, *our God, be with us, as He was with our forefathers,*
may He not forsake us nor cast us off.[8]

---

(1) *Psalms* 113:2. (2) 121:2. (3) *Deuteronomy* 4:35.
(4) *Psalms* 136:4. (5) 86:8. (6) 104:31. (7) 113:2. (8) *I Kings* 8:57.

וְאִמְרוּ, הוֹשִׁיעֵנוּ, אֱלֹהֵי יִשְׁעֵנוּ, וְקַבְּצֵנוּ וְהַצִּילֵנוּ מִן הַגּוֹיִם,
לְהֹדוֹת לְשֵׁם קָדְשֶׁךָ, לְהִשְׁתַּבֵּחַ בִּתְהִלָּתֶךָ.[1]
יהוה מֶלֶךְ,[2] יהוה מָלָךְ,[3] יהוה יִמְלֹךְ לְעוֹלָם וָעֶד.[4]
יהוה עֹז לְעַמּוֹ יִתֵּן, יהוה יְבָרֵךְ אֶת עַמּוֹ בַשָּׁלוֹם.[5]
וְיִהְיוּ נָא אֲמָרֵינוּ לְרָצוֹן, לִפְנֵי אֲדוֹן כֹּל.[6]

The Ark is opened and the responsive recitation continues:

וַיְהִי בִּנְסֹעַ הָאָרֹן, וַיֹּאמֶר מֹשֶׁה, קוּמָה יהוה, וְיָפֻצוּ אֹיְבֶיךָ,
וְיָנֻסוּ מְשַׂנְאֶיךָ מִפָּנֶיךָ.[7]
קוּמָה יהוה לִמְנוּחָתֶךָ, אַתָּה וַאֲרוֹן עֻזֶּךָ.
כֹּהֲנֶיךָ יִלְבְּשׁוּ צֶדֶק, וַחֲסִידֶיךָ יְרַנֵּנוּ.
בַּעֲבוּר דָּוִד עַבְדֶּךָ, אַל תָּשֵׁב פְּנֵי מְשִׁיחֶךָ.[8]
וְאָמַר בַּיּוֹם הַהוּא, הִנֵּה אֱלֹהֵינוּ זֶה, קִוִּינוּ לוֹ וְיוֹשִׁיעֵנוּ,
זֶה יהוה קִוִּינוּ לוֹ, נָגִילָה וְנִשְׂמְחָה בִּישׁוּעָתוֹ.[9]
מַלְכוּתְךָ מַלְכוּת כָּל עֹלָמִים, וּמֶמְשַׁלְתְּךָ בְּכָל דּוֹר וָדֹר.[10]
כִּי מִצִּיּוֹן תֵּצֵא תוֹרָה, וּדְבַר יהוה מִירוּשָׁלָיִם.[11]

All, in unison:

אַב הָרַחֲמִים, הֵיטִיבָה בִרְצוֹנְךָ אֶת צִיּוֹן, תִּבְנֶה חוֹמוֹת יְרוּשָׁלָיִם.[12]
כִּי בְךָ לְבַד בָּטָחְנוּ, מֶלֶךְ אֵל רָם וְנִשָּׂא, אֲדוֹן עוֹלָמִים.

All the Torah Scrolls are removed from the Ark and members of the congregation are given the honor of carrying them during the procession. In some congregations, a lit candle, symbolizing the light of Torah, is placed in the Ark while it is empty.

Many congregations repeat the enhanced version of the *hakafah* prayers of the evening beginning on page 1068.

As the Torah Scrolls are carried around the *bimah,* each of the following verses is recited by the *chazzan* or *hakafah* leader and is then repeated by the congregation:

First *hakafah* — אָנָּא יהוה, הוֹשִׁיעָה נָּא
אָנָּא יהוה, הַצְלִיחָה נָא.
אָנָּא יהוה, עֲנֵנוּ בְיוֹם קָרְאֵנוּ.
אֱלֹהֵי הָרוּחוֹת, הוֹשִׁיעָה נָּא.
בּוֹחֵן לְבָבוֹת, הַצְלִיחָה נָא.
גּוֹאֵל חָזָק, עֲנֵנוּ בְיוֹם קָרְאֵנוּ.

Second *hakafah* — דּוֹבֵר צְדָקוֹת, הוֹשִׁיעָה נָּא.
הָדוּר בִּלְבוּשׁוֹ, הַצְלִיחָה נָא.
וָתִיק וְחָסִיד, עֲנֵנוּ בְיוֹם קָרְאֵנוּ.

Third *hakafah* — זַךְ וְיָשָׁר, הוֹשִׁיעָה נָּא.
חוֹמֵל דַּלִּים, הַצְלִיחָה נָא.
טוֹב וּמֵטִיב, עֲנֵנוּ בְיוֹם קָרְאֵנוּ.

Say: 'Save us, O God of our salvation,
gather us and rescue us from the nations,
to thank Your Holy Name and to glory in Your praise.'[1]
HASHEM reigns,[2] *HASHEM has reigned,*[3]
HASHEM shall reign for all eternity.[4]
HASHEM will give might to His people,
HASHEM will bless His people with peace.[5]
May our words find favor, we pray, before the Lord of everything.[6]

The Ark is opened and the responsive recitation continues:

When the Ark would travel, Moses would say,
'Arise, HASHEM, and let Your foes be scattered;
let those who hate You flee from You.'[7]
Arise, HASHEM, to Your resting place,
You and the Ark of Your strength.
Let Your priests be clothed in righteousness,
and Your devout ones will sing joyously.
For the sake of David, Your servant,
turn not away the face of Your anointed.[8] *He shall say on that day, 'Behold! — this is our God,*
we hoped to Him and He saved us; this is HASHEM to whom we hoped,
let us exult and be glad in His salvation.'[9]
Your kingdom is a kingdom spanning all eternities,
and Your dominion is throughout every generation.[10]
For from Zion the Torah will come forth,
and the word of HASHEM from Jerusalem.[11]

All, in unison:

אַב הָרַחֲמִים *Father of compassion, do good to Zion according to Your will; rebuild the walls of Jerusalem.*[12] *For we trust in You alone, O King, God, exalted and uplifted, Master of worlds.*

All the Torah Scrolls are removed from the Ark and members of the congregation are given the honor of carrying them during the procession. In some congregations, a lit candle, symbolizing the light of Torah, is placed in the Ark while it is empty.

Many congregations repeat the enhanced version of the *hakafah* prayers of the evening beginning on page 1068.

As the Torah Scrolls are carried around the *bimah,* each of the following verses is recited by the *chazzan* or *hakafah* leader and is then repeated by the congregation:

First *hakafah* — *Please, HASHEM, save now!*
Please, HASHEM, bring success now!
Please, HASHEM, answer us on the day we call.

God of the spirits, save now!
Tester of hearts, bring success now!
O Powerful Redeemer, answer us on the day we call!

Second *hakafah* — *Speaker of righteousness, save now!*
Majestic One in His garb, bring success now!
Faithful and Devout One, answer us on the day we call!

Third *hakafah* — *Pure and Just One, save now!*
He Who pities the poor, bring success now!
Good and Beneficent One, answer us on the day we call!

---

(1) *I Chronicles* 16:35. (2) *Psalms* 10:16. (3) 93:1 et al. (4) *Exodus* 15:18. (5) *Psalms* 29:11. (6) Cf. 19:15. (7) *Numbers* 10:35. (8) *Psalms* 132:8-10. (9) *Isaiah* 25:9. (10) *Psalms* 145:13. (11) *Isaiah* 2:3; *Micah* 4:2. (12) *Psalms* 51:20.

Fourth *hakafah* – יוֹדֵעַ מַחֲשָׁבוֹת, הוֹשִׁיעָה נָּא.
כַּבִּיר וְנָאוֹר, הַצְלִיחָה נָא.
לוֹבֵשׁ צְדָקוֹת, עֲנֵנוּ בְיוֹם קָרְאֵנוּ.

Fifth *hakafah* – מֶלֶךְ עוֹלָמִים, הוֹשִׁיעָה נָּא.
נָאוֹר וְאַדִּיר, הַצְלִיחָה נָא.
סוֹמֵךְ נוֹפְלִים, עֲנֵנוּ בְיוֹם קָרְאֵנוּ.

Sixth *hakafah* – עוֹזֵר דַּלִּים, הוֹשִׁיעָה נָּא.
פּוֹדֶה וּמַצִּיל, הַצְלִיחָה נָא.
צוּר עוֹלָמִים, עֲנֵנוּ בְיוֹם קָרְאֵנוּ.

Seventh *hakafah* – קָדוֹשׁ וְנוֹרָא, הוֹשִׁיעָה נָּא.
רַחוּם וְחַנּוּן, הַצְלִיחָה נָא.
שׁוֹמֵר הַבְּרִית, עֲנֵנוּ בְיוֹם קָרְאֵנוּ.
תּוֹמֵךְ תְּמִימִים, הוֹשִׁיעָה נָּא.
תַּקִּיף לָעַד, הַצְלִיחָה נָא.
תָּמִים בְּמַעֲשָׂיו, עֲנֵנוּ בְיוֹם קָרְאֵנוּ.

After the *Hakafos* all but three Torah Scrolls are removed from the Ark; one for the main Torah reading, the second for *Chasan Bereishis,* and the third for *Maftir*. The first is presented to the *chazzan,* who accepts it in his right arm. Facing the congregation the *chazzan* raises the Torah and, followed by congregation, recites:

שְׁמַע יִשְׂרָאֵל יהוה אֱלֹהֵינוּ יהוה אֶחָד.[1]

Still facing the congregation, the *chazzan* raises the Torah and, followed by congregation, recites:

אֶחָד (הוּא) אֱלֹהֵינוּ גָּדוֹל אֲדוֹנֵינוּ, קָדוֹשׁ שְׁמוֹ.

The *chazzan* turns to the Ark, bows while raising the Torah, and recites:

גַּדְּלוּ לַיהוה אִתִּי וּנְרוֹמְמָה שְׁמוֹ יַחְדָּו.[2]

The *chazzan* turns to his right and carries the Torah to the *bimah,* as the congregation responds:

לְךָ יהוה הַגְּדֻלָּה וְהַגְּבוּרָה וְהַתִּפְאֶרֶת וְהַנֵּצַח וְהַהוֹד כִּי כֹל בַּשָּׁמַיִם וּבָאָרֶץ, לְךָ יהוה הַמַּמְלָכָה וְהַמִּתְנַשֵּׂא לְכֹל לְרֹאשׁ.[3] רוֹמְמוּ יהוה אֱלֹהֵינוּ, וְהִשְׁתַּחֲווּ לַהֲדֹם רַגְלָיו, קָדוֹשׁ הוּא. רוֹמְמוּ יהוה אֱלֹהֵינוּ, וְהִשְׁתַּחֲווּ לְהַר קָדְשׁוֹ, כִּי קָדוֹשׁ יהוה אֱלֹהֵינוּ.[4]

As the *chazzan* carries the Torah to the *bimah* the congregation recites:

עַל הַכֹּל, יִתְגַּדַּל וְיִתְקַדַּשׁ וְיִשְׁתַּבַּח וְיִתְפָּאַר וְיִתְרוֹמַם וְיִתְנַשֵּׂא שְׁמוֹ שֶׁל מֶלֶךְ מַלְכֵי הַמְּלָכִים הַקָּדוֹשׁ בָּרוּךְ הוּא, בָּעוֹלָמוֹת שֶׁבָּרָא, הָעוֹלָם הַזֶּה וְהָעוֹלָם הַבָּא, כִּרְצוֹנוֹ, וְכִרְצוֹן יְרֵאָיו, וְכִרְצוֹן כָּל בֵּית יִשְׂרָאֵל. צוּר הָעוֹלָמִים, אֲדוֹן כָּל הַבְּרִיּוֹת, אֱלוֹהַּ כָּל הַנְּפָשׁוֹת, הַיּוֹשֵׁב בְּמֶרְחֲבֵי מָרוֹם, הַשּׁוֹכֵן בִּשְׁמֵי שְׁמֵי קֶדֶם. קְדֻשָּׁתוֹ עַל הַחַיּוֹת, וּקְדֻשָּׁתוֹ עַל כִּסֵּא הַכָּבוֹד.

Fourth *hakafah* – *Knower of thoughts, save now!*
Powerful and Illustrious One, bring success now!
He who garbs Himself in righteousness,
answer us on the day we call!

Fifth *hakafah* – *Eternal King, save now!*
Illustrious and Mighty One, bring success now!
Supporter of the fallen, answer us on the day we call!

Sixth *hakafah* – *Helper of the destitute, save now!*
Redeemer and rescuer, bring success now!
Eternal Rock, answer us on the day we call!

Seventh *hakafah* – *Holy and awesome One, save now!*
Merciful and gracious One, bring success now!
Keeper of the covenant, answer us on the day we call!

Supporter of the wholesome, save now!
Eternally strong One, bring success now!
Perfect in His deeds, answer us on the day we call!

After the *Hakafos* all but three Torah Scrolls are returned to the Ark; one for the main Torah reading, the second for *Chasan Bereishis,* and the third for *Maftir.* The first is presented to the *chazzan,* who accepts it in his right arm. Facing the congregation the *chazzan* raises the Torah and, followed by congregation, recites:

Hear, O Israel: HASHEM is our God, HASHEM, the One and Only.[1]

Still facing the congregation, the *chazzan* raises the Torah and, followed by congregation, recites:

One is our God, great is our Master, Holy is His Name.

The *chazzan* turns to the Ark, bows while raising the Torah, and recites:

Declare the greatness of HASHEM with me, and let us exalt His Name together.[2]

The *chazzan* turns to his right and carries the Torah to the *bimah,* as the congregation responds:

לְךָ *Yours, HASHEM, is the greatness, the strength, the splendor, the triumph, and the glory; even everything in heaven and earth; Yours, HASHEM, is the kingdom, and the sovereignty over every leader.*[3] *Exalt HASHEM, our God, and bow at His footstool; He is Holy! Exalt HASHEM, our God, and bow to His holy mountain; for holy is HASHEM, our God.*[4]

As the *chazzan* carries the Torah to the *bimah* the congregation recites:

עַל הַכֹּל *For all this, let the Name of the King of kings, the Holy One, Blessed is He, grow exalted, sanctified, praised, glorified, exalted, and extolled in the worlds that He has created — This World and the World to Come — according to His will, the will of those who fear Him, and the will of the entire House of Israel. Rock of the eternities, Master of all creatures, God of all souls, He Who sits in the expanses on high, Who rests in the loftiest primeval heavens. His holiness is upon the Chayos; His holiness is upon the Throne of Glory.*

(1) *Deuteronomy* 6:4. (2) *Psalms* 34:4. (3) *I Chronicles* 29:11. (4) *Psalms* 99:5,9.

וּבְכֵן יִתְקַדַּשׁ שִׁמְךָ בָּנוּ יהוה אֱלֹהֵינוּ לְעֵינֵי כָּל חָי. וְנֹאמַר לְפָנָיו שִׁיר חָדָשׁ, כַּכָּתוּב: שִׁירוּ לֵאלֹהִים זַמְּרוּ שְׁמוֹ, סֹלּוּ לָרֹכֵב בָּעֲרָבוֹת בְּיָהּ שְׁמוֹ, וְעִלְזוּ לְפָנָיו.[1] וְנִרְאֵהוּ עַיִן בְּעַיִן בְּשׁוּבוֹ אֶל נָוֵהוּ, כַּכָּתוּב: כִּי עַיִן בְּעַיִן יִרְאוּ בְּשׁוּב יהוה צִיּוֹן.[2] וְנֶאֱמַר: וְנִגְלָה כְּבוֹד יהוה, וְרָאוּ כָל בָּשָׂר יַחְדָּו כִּי פִּי יהוה דִּבֵּר.[3]

אַב הָרַחֲמִים הוּא יְרַחֵם עַם עֲמוּסִים, וְיִזְכֹּר בְּרִית אֵיתָנִים, וְיַצִּיל נַפְשׁוֹתֵינוּ מִן הַשָּׁעוֹת הָרָעוֹת, וְיִגְעַר בְּיֵצֶר הָרָע מִן הַנְּשׂוּאִים, וְיָחֹן אוֹתָנוּ לִפְלֵיטַת עוֹלָמִים, וִימַלֵּא מִשְׁאֲלוֹתֵינוּ בְּמִדָּה טוֹבָה יְשׁוּעָה וְרַחֲמִים.

The Torah is placed on the *bimah* and prepared for reading.
The *gabbai* uses the following formula to call a *Kohen* to the Torah:

וְיַעֲזוֹר וְיָגֵן וְיוֹשִׁיעַ לְכֹל הַחוֹסִים בּוֹ, וְנֹאמַר, אָמֵן. הַכֹּל הָבוּ גֹדֶל לֵאלֹהֵינוּ וּתְנוּ כָבוֹד לַתּוֹרָה, כֹּהֵן° קְרָב, יַעֲמֹד (name) בֶּן (father's name) הַכֹּהֵן.

°If no *Kohen* is present, the *gabbai* says:
"אֵין כָּאן כֹּהֵן, יַעֲמֹד (insert name) יִשְׂרָאֵל (לֵוִי) בִּמְקוֹם כֹּהֵן."

בָּרוּךְ שֶׁנָּתַן תּוֹרָה לְעַמּוֹ יִשְׂרָאֵל בִּקְדֻשָּׁתוֹ. (תּוֹרַת יהוה תְּמִימָה מְשִׁיבַת נָפֶשׁ, עֵדוּת יהוה נֶאֱמָנָה מַחְכִּימַת פֶּתִי. פִּקּוּדֵי יהוה יְשָׁרִים מְשַׂמְּחֵי לֵב, מִצְוַת יהוה בָּרָה מְאִירַת עֵינָיִם.[4] יהוה עֹז לְעַמּוֹ יִתֵּן, יהוה יְבָרֵךְ אֶת עַמּוֹ בַשָּׁלוֹם.[5] הָאֵל תָּמִים דַּרְכּוֹ, אִמְרַת יהוה צְרוּפָה, מָגֵן הוּא לְכֹל הַחוֹסִים בּוֹ.[6])

Congregation then *gabbai:*

וְאַתֶּם הַדְּבֵקִים בַּיהוה אֱלֹהֵיכֶם, חַיִּים כֻּלְּכֶם הַיּוֹם.[7]

קריאת התורה

The reader shows the *oleh* (person called to the Torah) the place in the Torah. The *oleh* touches the Torah with a corner of his *tallis,* or the belt or mantle of the Torah, and kisses it. He then begins the blessing, bowing at בָּרְכוּ, and straightening up at 'ה.

בָּרְכוּ אֶת יהוה הַמְּבֹרָךְ.

Congregation, followed by *oleh,* responds, bowing at בָּרוּךְ, and straightening up at 'ה.

בָּרוּךְ יהוה הַמְּבֹרָךְ לְעוֹלָם וָעֶד.

Oleh continues:

בָּרוּךְ אַתָּה יהוה אֱלֹהֵינוּ מֶלֶךְ הָעוֹלָם, אֲשֶׁר בָּחַר בָּנוּ מִכָּל הָעַמִּים, וְנָתַן לָנוּ אֶת תּוֹרָתוֹ. בָּרוּךְ אַתָּה יהוה, נוֹתֵן הַתּוֹרָה. (Cong. – אָמֵן.)

After his Torah portion has been read, the *oleh* recites:

בָּרוּךְ אַתָּה יהוה אֱלֹהֵינוּ מֶלֶךְ הָעוֹלָם, אֲשֶׁר נָתַן לָנוּ תּוֹרַת אֱמֶת, וְחַיֵּי עוֹלָם נָטַע בְּתוֹכֵנוּ. בָּרוּךְ אַתָּה יהוה, נוֹתֵן הַתּוֹרָה. (Cong. – אָמֵן.)

Similarly, may Your Name be sanctified within us, HASHEM, our God, in the sight of all the living. May we chant before Him a new song as it is written: 'Sing to God, make music for His Name, extol the One Who rides in the highest heavens with His Name YAH, and exult before Him.'[1] May we see Him with a perceptive view upon His return to His Abode, as is written: 'For they shall see with a perceptive view as HASHEM returns to Zion.'[2] And it is said: 'The glory of HASHEM shall be revealed and all flesh together shall see that the mouth of HASHEM has spoken.'[3]

אַב הָרַחֲמִים *May the Father of compassion have mercy on the nation that is borne by Him, and may He remember the covenant of the spiritually mighty. May He rescue our souls from the bad times, and upbraid the evil inclination to leave those borne by Him, graciously make us an eternal remnant, and fulfill our requests in good measure, for salvation and mercy.*

The Torah is placed on the *bimah* and prepared for reading.
The *gabbai* uses the following formula to call a *Kohen* to the Torah:

וְיַעֲזוֹר *May He help, shield, and save all who take refuge in Him — Now let us respond: Amen. All of you ascribe greatness to our God and give honor to the Torah. Kohen,° approach. Arise* (name) *son of* (father's name) *the Kohen.*

°If no *Kohen* is present, the *gabbai* says: *'There is no Kohen present, stand* (name) *son of* (father's name) *an Israelite (Levite) in place of the Kohen.'*

Blessed is He Who gave the Torah to His people Israel in His holiness. (The Torah of HASHEM is perfect, restoring the soul; the testimony of HASHEM is trustworthy, making the simple one wise. The orders of HASHEM are upright, gladdening the heart; the command of HASHEM is clear, enlightening the eyes.[4] HASHEM will give might to His nation; HASHEM will bless His nation with peace.[5] The God Whose way is perfect, the promise of HASHEM is flawless, He is a shield for all who take refuge in Him.[6])

Congregation then *gabbai:*

You who cling to HASHEM, your God, you are all alive today.[7]

READING OF THE TORAH

The reader shows the *oleh* (person called to the Torah) the place in the Torah. The *oleh* touches the Torah with a corner of his *tallis,* or the belt or mantle of the Torah, and kisses it. He then begins the blessing, bowing at *'Bless,'* and straightening up at 'HASHEM.'

Bless HASHEM, the blessed One.

Congregation, followed by *oleh,* responds, bowing at 'Blessed,' and straightening up at 'HASHEM.'

Blessed is HASHEM, the blessed One, for all eternity.

Oleh continues:

בָּרוּךְ *Blessed are You, HASHEM, our God, King of the universe, Who selected us from all the peoples and gave us His Torah. Blessed are You, HASHEM, Giver of the Torah.* (Cong.— *Amen.)*

After his Torah portion has been read, the *oleh* recites:

בָּרוּךְ *Blessed are You, HASHEM, our God, King of the universe, Who gave us the Torah of truth and implanted eternal life within us. Blessed are You, HASHEM, Giver of the Torah.* (Cong.— *Amen.)*

---

(1) *Psalms* 68:5. (2) *Isaiah* 52:8. (3) 40:5. (4) *Psalms* 19:8-9. (5) 29:11. (6) 18.31. (7) *Deut.* 4:4.

Because of the large number of *aliyos* distributed on Simchas Torah, many congregations use the following concise *Mi Shebeirach* for each *oleh:*

מִי שֶׁבֵּרַךְ אֶת הָאָבוֹת
הוּא יְבָרֵךְ אֶת הַבָּנִים. וְנֹאמַר: אָמֵן

PRAYER FOR THE OLEH / מי שברך לעולה לתורה

After each *oleh* completes his concluding blessing, the *gabbai* calls the next *oleh* to the Torah, then blesses the one who has just concluded.

מִי שֶׁבֵּרַךְ אֲבוֹתֵינוּ אַבְרָהָם יִצְחָק וְיַעֲקֹב, הוּא יְבָרֵךְ אֶת (name) בֶּן (father's name) בַּעֲבוּר שֶׁעָלָה לִכְבוֹד הַמָּקוֹם, לִכְבוֹד הַתּוֹרָה, לִכְבוֹד הָרֶגֶל. בִּשְׂכַר זֶה, הַקָּדוֹשׁ בָּרוּךְ הוּא יִשְׁמְרֵהוּ וְיַצִּילֵהוּ מִכָּל צָרָה וְצוּקָה, וּמִכָּל נֶגַע וּמַחֲלָה, וְיִשְׁלַח בְּרָכָה וְהַצְלָחָה בְּכָל מַעֲשֵׂה יָדָיו, וְיִזְכֶּה לַעֲלוֹת לְרֶגֶל, עִם כָּל יִשְׂרָאֵל אֶחָיו. וְנֹאמַר: אָמֵן. (Cong.— אָמֵן.)

PRAYER FOR OTHERS / מי שברך לאחרים

It is customary that the following prayer be recited for the family members of the *oleh* and for anyone else that he may wish to include:

מִי שֶׁבֵּרַךְ אֲבוֹתֵינוּ אַבְרָהָם יִצְחָק וְיַעֲקֹב, הוּא יְבָרֵךְ אֶת (names of the recipients) בַּעֲבוּר שֶׁ(name of *oleh*) יִתֵּן לִצְדָקָה בַּעֲבוּרָם. בִּשְׂכַר זֶה, הַקָּדוֹשׁ בָּרוּךְ הוּא יִשְׁמְרֵם וְיַצִּילֵם מִכָּל צָרָה וְצוּקָה, וּמִכָּל נֶגַע וּמַחֲלָה, וְיִשְׁלַח בְּרָכָה וְהַצְלָחָה בְּכָל מַעֲשֵׂה יְדֵיהֶם, וְיִזְכּוּ לַעֲלוֹת לְרֶגֶל, עִם כָּל יִשְׂרָאֵל אֲחֵיהֶם. וְנֹאמַר: אָמֵן. (Cong.— אָמֵן.)

PRAYER FOR A SICK PERSON / מי שברך לחולה

מִי שֶׁבֵּרַךְ אֲבוֹתֵינוּ אַבְרָהָם יִצְחָק וְיַעֲקֹב, מֹשֶׁה אַהֲרֹן דָּוִד וּשְׁלֹמֹה,

for a man

הוּא יְבָרֵךְ וִירַפֵּא אֶת הַחוֹלֶה (patient's name) בֶּן (mother's name) בַּעֲבוּר שֶׁ(supplicant's name) יִתֵּן לִצְדָקָה בַּעֲבוּרוֹ.°° בִּשְׂכַר זֶה, הַקָּדוֹשׁ בָּרוּךְ הוּא יִמָּלֵא רַחֲמִים עָלָיו, לְהַחֲלִימוֹ וּלְרַפְּאתוֹ וּלְהַחֲזִיקוֹ וּלְהַחֲיוֹתוֹ, וְיִשְׁלַח לוֹ מְהֵרָה רְפוּאָה שְׁלֵמָה מִן הַשָּׁמַיִם, לִרְמַ״ח אֵבָרָיו, וּשְׁסָ״ה גִּידָיו, בְּתוֹךְ

for a woman

הוּא יְבָרֵךְ וִירַפֵּא אֶת הַחוֹלָה (patient's name) בַּת (mother's name) בַּעֲבוּר שֶׁ(supplicant's name) יִתֵּן לִצְדָקָה בַּעֲבוּרָהּ.°° בִּשְׂכַר זֶה, הַקָּדוֹשׁ בָּרוּךְ הוּא יִמָּלֵא רַחֲמִים עָלֶיהָ, לְהַחֲלִימָהּ וּלְרַפְּאתָהּ וּלְהַחֲזִיקָהּ וּלְהַחֲיוֹתָהּ, וְיִשְׁלַח לָהּ מְהֵרָה רְפוּאָה שְׁלֵמָה מִן הַשָּׁמַיִם, לְכָל אֵבָרֶיהָ, וּלְכָל גִּידֶיהָ, בְּתוֹךְ

שְׁאָר חוֹלֵי יִשְׂרָאֵל, רְפוּאַת הַנֶּפֶשׁ, וּרְפוּאַת הַגּוּף, יוֹם טוֹב הוּא מִלִּזְעֹק, וּרְפוּאָה קְרוֹבָה לָבֹא, הַשְׁתָּא, בַּעֲגָלָא וּבִזְמַן קָרִיב. וְנֹאמַר: אָמֵן.

(Cong.— אָמֵן.)

°°Many congregations substitute:

בַּעֲבוּר שֶׁכָּל הַקָּהָל מִתְפַּלְּלִים בַּעֲבוּרוֹ (בַּעֲבוּרָהּ)

Because of the large number of *aliyos* distributed on Simchas Torah, many congregations use the following concise *Mi Shebeirach* for each *oleh:*

He who blessed the forefathers — may He bless the children. Now let us respond: Amen.

PRAYER FOR THE OLEH

After each *oleh* completes his concluding blessing, the *gabbai* calls the next *oleh* to the Torah, then blesses the one who has just concluded.

מִי שֶׁבֵּרַךְ *He Who blessed our forefathers Abraham, Isaac, and Jacob — may He bless (* Hebrew name*) son of (* father's Hebrew name*) because he has come up to the Torah in honor of the Omnipresent, in honor of the Torah, in honor of the pilgrimage festival. As reward for this, may the Holy One, Blessed is He, protect him and rescue him from every trouble and distress, from every plague and illness; may He send blessing and success in his every endeavor, and may he be privileged to ascend to Jerusalem for the pilgrimage, together with all Israel, his brethren. Now let us respond: Amen.* (Cong.— *Amen.)*

PRAYER FOR OTHERS

It is customary that the following prayer be recited for the family members of the *oleh* and for anyone else that he may wish to include:

מִי שֶׁבֵּרַךְ *He Who blessed our forefathers Abraham, Isaac, and Jacob — may He bless (* names of recipients*) for (* name of *oleh) will contribute to charity on their behalf. As reward for this, may the Holy One, Blessed is He, protect them and rescue them from every trouble and distress, from every plague and illness; may He send blessing and success in their every endeavor and may they be privileged to ascend to Jerusalem for the pilgrimage, together with all Israel, their brethren. Now let us respond: Amen.* (Cong.— *Amen.)*

PRAYER FOR A SICK PERSON

מִי שֶׁבֵּרַךְ *He Who blessed our forefathers Abraham, Isaac and Jacob, Moses and Aaron, David and Solomon — may He bless and heal the sick person (* patient's Hebrew name*) son/daughter of (* patient's mother's Hebrew name*) because (* name of supplicant*) will contribute to charity on his/her behalf.*°° *In reward for this, may the Holy One, Blessed is He, be filled with*

for a man

compassion for him to restore his health, to heal him, to strengthen him, and to revivify him. And may He send him speedily a complete recovery from heaven for his two hundred forty-eight organs and three hundred sixty-five blood vessels,

for a woman

compassion for her to restore her health, to heal her, to strengthen her, and to revivify her. And may He send her speedily a complete recovery from heaven for all her organs and all her blood vessels,

among the other sick people of Israel, a recovery of the body and a recovery of the spirit though the Festival prohibits us from crying out, may a recovery come speedily, swiftly and soon. Now let us respond: Amen.

(Cong.—*Amen.)*

°°Many congregations substitute:
because the entire congregation prays for him (her)

❧ קריאת התורה לשמחת תורה ❧

As part of the Simchas Torah celebration, the *sidra* is read over and over so that every male in the congregation can be called for an *aliyah.* In most congregations even young boys who are not yet *bar mitzvah* are honored with an *aliyah,* to imbue them with love for the Torah. See *Laws* §231-232.

דברים לג:א-כו

כהן – וְזֹאת הַבְּרָכָה אֲשֶׁר בֵּרַךְ מֹשֶׁה אִישׁ הָאֱלֹהִים* אֶת־בְּנֵי
יִשְׂרָאֵל* לִפְנֵי מוֹתוֹ:* וַיֹּאמַר יהוה מִסִּינַי בָּא* וְזָרַח מִשֵּׂעִיר
לָמוֹ* הוֹפִיעַ מֵהַר פָּארָן וְאָתָה מֵרִבְבֹת קֹדֶשׁ* מִימִינוֹ* אֵשׁ דָּת*
לָמוֹ: אַף חֹבֵב עַמִּים* כָּל־קְדֹשָׁיו* בְּיָדֶךָ וְהֵם תֻּכּוּ לְרַגְלֶךָ*
יִשָּׂא מִדַּבְּרֹתֶיךָ: תּוֹרָה צִוָּה־לָנוּ מֹשֶׁה מוֹרָשָׁה* קְהִלַּת יַעֲקֹב:*
וַיְהִי בִישֻׁרוּן* מֶלֶךְ בְּהִתְאַסֵּף רָאשֵׁי עָם* יַחַד שִׁבְטֵי יִשְׂרָאֵל:
יְחִי רְאוּבֵן* וְאַל־יָמֹת וִיהִי מְתָיו מִסְפָּר: וְזֹאת לִיהוּדָה

⇐§ The Blessing of Moses.

The Midrash teaches that Moses continued the tradition of Jacob in blessing the tribes before his death. These final words of Moses are a combination of blessing and prophecy, in which he blesses them according to their national responsibilities and individual greatness. As discussed above in the introduction to the *Hakafos,* p. 1066. *Simchas Torah* is the day when we complete the Torah-reading cycle, in a mood of joy, reverence, and aspiration. To share in this celebration, every eligible member of the congregation is called to the Torah during this reading.

אִישׁ הָאֱלֹהִים — *The man of God.* This title [which is applied to Moses also in *Joshua* 14:6 and *Psalms* 90:1] indicates that in uttering these blessings Moses was inspired by God (*Ibn Ezra*), and as such, his blessings would be fulfilled (*Ramban*).

בְּנֵי יִשְׂרָאֵל — *The Children of Israel.* Whereas the blessing applied collectively to the entire nation — *the Children of Israel* — Moses directed his blessings to each of the tribes individually, since the welfare of each tribe was dependent upon the others, and collectively the welfare of the nation depended upon all of them (*Pesikta*).

לִפְנֵי מוֹתוֹ — *Before his death,* i.e., very near his death, for he said, "If not now, when?" (*Rashi*).

Introduction

Moses praises God and recalls the merit that makes Israel worthy of His blessing. As the passage notes, God revealed Himself majestically to the people at Mt. Sinai to give them the Torah. But before this, as the Midrashic tradition records, God had offered the Torah to the Edomites, descendants of Esau, inhabitants of Seir, who did not want to inhibit their desires with the restrictions of the Torah, and so declined it. He then offered it to the Ishmaelites, inhabitants of Paran, who also refused it. God, accompanied by some of His myriads of holy angels, then came and presented His fiery Torah to the Israelites who submitted themselves to His sovereignty and accepted His Torah.

Thus Israel, as the only nation worthy of receiving the Torah — and indeed the only nation that accepted it as an eternal heritage — is supremely worthy of receiving Moses' blessing.

In these introductory remarks Moses incorporates three outstanding merits of Israel which make them worthy of the blessings: a) God dwells among them; b) they accepted His Torah; c) they acknowledged His sovereignty (*Ramban*).

ה׳ מִסִּינַי בָּא — *HASHEM approached from Sinai.* To reveal Himself to the Israelites who had gathered there to receive the Torah [see *Exodus* 19:20] (*Rashi*). He caused His Divine Glory to dwell among them and never departed from them again (*Ramban*).

וְזָרַח מִשֵּׂעִיר לָמוֹ — *Having shone forth to them* [the Israelites] *from Seir* — dwelling place of Esau.

The verb זָרַח, *shone forth,* which is the verb that describes sunrise, is used here because Seir is to the east of Sinai, the direction of the rising sun (*Chizkuni*).

מֵרִבְבֹת קֹדֶשׁ — *With some of the holy myriads.* Following *Rashi:* In a display of Divine humility, only *part of,* and not *all,* the myriads of holy angels accompanied God.

מימינו — *From His right hand,* i.e., from the choicest celestial source (*Zohar*). The Torah was communicated directly by God — not by any of the myriads of accompanying angels (*Ramban*).

אֵשׁ דָּת — *Fiery Torah,* which had been written from ancient times in black fire on white fire

TORAH READING FOR SIMCHAS TORAH

As part of the Simchas Torah celebration, the *sidra* is read over and over so that every male in the congregation can be called for an *aliyah*. In most congregations even young boys who are not yet *bar mitzvah* are honored with an *aliyah*, to imbue them with love for the Torah. See *Laws* §231-232.

Deuteronomy 33:1-26

Kohen – *This is the blessing that Moses, the man of God,* bestowed upon the Children of Israel* before his death.**

He said: HASHEM approached from Sinai — having shone forth to them from Seir,* having appeared from Mount Paran, and then approached with some of the holy myriads* — from His right hand* He presented the fiery Torah* to them. Indeed, You greatly loved the tribes,* all His righteous ones* were in Your hands; for they planted themselves at Your feet,* accepting the burden of Your utterances: "The Torah which Moses charged us is the heritage* of the Congregation of Jacob.* He became King over Jeshurun* when the leaders of the nation gathered* — the tribes of Israel in unity."*

May Reuben live and not die, and may his population be counted among the others.*

(*Rashi*). It was presented to them in the midst of fire and lightning (*Ramban*).

עַמִּים — *The tribes,* literally *the peoples,* refers in this context to the various tribes — each one a people unto itself — constituting the people of Israel (*Rashi*).

קְדֹשָׁיו — *His righteous ones,* i.e., the souls of the righteous which are stored up with God in the bond of life. Alternatively: Even in times of adversity the righteous and pious Jews cleave to God (*Rashi*). In a broader sense, the reference is to the righteous and pious ones, over whom God bestows His special providence, protection, and guardianship, leading them on the proper path (*Sifri*).

וְהֵם תֻּכּוּ לְרַגְלֶךָ — *For they planted themselves at Your feet.* This is why the Israelites are worthy of God's special attention — because they planted themselves squarely at God's "feet" — at the foot of Mount Sinai — to receive the Torah (*Rashi*).

תּוֹרָה . . . מוֹרָשָׁה — *The Torah . . . is the heritage.* 'We have accepted it and will not abandon it' (*Rashi*). The Torah is an inalienable possession of Israel, transmitted from generation to generation (*Ramban*).

They 'accepted Your decrees and laws with gladness' (*Rashi*). Upon doing so, they proclaimed the above declaration. Apparently, this passage was habitually recited by the Israelites in the desert, and it is the text they teach their children at an early age (*Daas Soferim*).

Harav Mordechai Gifter explains the difference between 'inheritance' and 'heritage.' An inheritance belongs to the heirs to use and dispose of as they please. A heritage, however, is the property of generations before and after; it is incumbent upon the heirs to preserve it intact.

קְהִלַּת יַעֲקֹב — *The Congregation of Jacob.*

The Torah is the heritage not merely of those born of Jewish parents, but it is shared by every soul that joins the Jewish nation and accepts the Torah (cf. *Ramban*).

יְשֻׁרוּן — *Jeshurun,* i.e., Israel. This title of honor is from the root ישר, *straight, righteous;* it designates Israel in its ideal state as God's *upright nation.*

בְּהִתְאַסֵּף רָאשֵׁי עָם — *When the leaders of the nation gathered.* God can be said to be Israel's king in the fullest sense only when the people are united to do His Will (*Rashi*). The acceptance of God's sovereignty was with the consent of the *entire* Jewish nation, without dissent. Even when they voiced complaints, they were never directed at God, but at Moses and Aaron (*Daas Soferim*).

Reuben

The first to be blessed is Reuben, the firstborn, who was to be the first to receive a portion of the Land (*Ramban*).

יְחִי רְאוּבֵן — *May Reuben live.* May the tribe flourish and not suffer for their ancestor's sin with Bilhah [*Gen.* 35:22] (*Rashi; Ramban*).

Jacob's blessing [*Gen.* 49:3] criticizes Reuben for his impetuosity, which caused him to be stripped of his leadership role. Moses now prays that this impetuosity not bring the tribe to extinction. Moses had a prognostication that the Tribe of Reuben would be one of those destined to be cast off to other lands [*see Deut.* 29:27; *Levit.* 26:38] (*Daas Soferim*).

וַיֹּאמַר֙ שְׁמַ֤ע יהוה֙ ק֣וֹל יְהוּדָ֔ה וְאֶל־עַמּ֖וֹ תְּבִיאֶ֑נּוּ יָדָיו֙ רָ֣ב ל֔וֹ וְעֵ֥זֶר מִצָּרָ֖יו תִּהְיֶֽה׃

לוי – וּלְלֵוִ֣י אָמַ֔ר תֻּמֶּ֥יךָ וְאוּרֶ֖יךָ* לְאִ֣ישׁ חֲסִידֶ֑ךָ אֲשֶׁ֤ר נִסִּיתוֹ֙ בְּמַסָּ֔ה* תְּרִיבֵ֖הוּ עַל־מֵ֥י מְרִיבָֽה׃* הָאֹמֵ֞ר לְאָבִ֤יו וּלְאִמּוֹ֙* לֹ֣א רְאִיתִ֔יו וְאֶת־אֶחָיו֙ לֹ֣א הִכִּ֔יר וְאֶת־בָּנָ֖ו לֹ֣א יָדָ֑ע כִּ֤י שָֽׁמְרוּ֙* אִמְרָתֶ֔ךָ וּבְרִֽיתְךָ֖ יִנְצֹֽרוּ׃ יוֹר֤וּ מִשְׁפָּטֶ֙יךָ֙ לְיַֽעֲקֹ֔ב וְתוֹרָתְךָ֖ לְיִשְׂרָאֵ֑ל יָשִׂ֤ימוּ קְטוֹרָה֙ בְּאַפֶּ֔ךָ וְכָלִ֖יל עַל־מִזְבְּחֶֽךָ׃ בָּרֵ֤ךְ יהוה֙ חֵיל֔וֹ וּפֹ֥עַל יָדָ֖יו* תִּרְצֶ֑ה מְחַ֨ץ מָתְנַ֧יִם קָמָ֛יו וּמְשַׂנְאָ֖יו מִן־יְקוּמֽוּן׃* לְבִנְיָמִ֣ן אָמַ֔ר יְדִ֣יד יהוה יִשְׁכֹּ֥ן לָבֶ֖טַח עָלָ֑יו חֹפֵ֤ף עָלָיו֙ כָּל־הַיּ֔וֹם* וּבֵ֥ין כְּתֵפָ֖יו שָׁכֵֽן׃*

ישראל – וּלְיוֹסֵ֣ף אָמַ֔ר מְבֹרֶ֥כֶת יהוה אַרְצ֑וֹ* מִמֶּ֤גֶד שָׁמַ֙יִם֙ מִטָּ֔ל וּמִתְּה֖וֹם* רֹבֶ֥צֶת תָּֽחַת׃ וּמִמֶּ֖גֶד תְּבוּאֹ֣ת שָׁ֑מֶשׁ וּמִמֶּ֖גֶד גֶּ֥רֶשׁ יְרָחִֽים׃*

Judah

The tribe of Judah — from which the Davidic royal line would descend — was to play a central role in the life of the nation. Accordingly, this princely tribe would lead the nation into the battles for *Eretz Yisrael* [see *Judges* 1:2]. Moses' prayer — like that of Jacob in *Gen.* 49:8 — is that his armies should be victorious, and that his reliance should be only on God Who would respond to his prayers (*Ramban*).

Chronologically, Simeon and Levi, who were older, should have preceded Judah. *Rashi* cites the Talmudic explanation [*Sotah* 7b] that Judah was mentioned immediately after Reuben because Judah, by his personal example of publicly confessing his sin, inspired Reuben to do likewise.

Omission of Simeon

The commentators note that Simeon is omitted. Some explain that this is because Simeon had been castigated in Jacob's blessing [see *Genesis* 49:5] and was conspicuously responsible for the sin of Baal Peor [*Numbers* 25:3].

Ramban maintains that the omission is due to Moses' desire to limit the number of tribes in his blessing to twelve, following the precedent of Jacob who, in mentioning his twelve sons, counted Joseph as one tribe. Moses, however, reckoned Joseph as two — Ephraim and Menashe — basing himself on various precedents [see *Numbers* 7:48,54; 2:18,20; 34:23]. Had Moses mentioned Simeon, the number would have been raised to thirteen. He chose Simeon as the tribe to be omitted because they were few and were to be scattered throughout Southern *Eretz Yisrael* [see *Genesis* 49:7], not having a portion of their own. They were therefore not blessed individually, but would automatically share in the blessing of the nation as a whole. Specifically, since Simeon's cities were within Judah's territory [*Joshua* 19:2], they were included in Judah.

Levi

Moses now turns to God and prays that the privilege of bearing the Urim and Tumim remain with the tribe of Levi, which demonstrated its loyalty to the Divine cause in the desert.

תֻּמֶּיךָ וְאוּרֶיךָ — *Your* [these words are addressed to God (*Rashi*)] *Tumim and Your Urim*. An allusion to the breastplate of the High Priest [see *Exodus* 28:30] — which God bestowed upon His devout ones, the descendants of the tribe of Levi.

בְּמַסָּה — *At Massah*. The reference is to the incident in *Exodus* 17:1 where the people were rebellious. *Rashi* suggests that we may infer from Moses' praise of the Levites in our passage that they did not complain along with the others — and so, withstood the test.

מֵי מְרִיבָה — *At the waters of Meribah*. See *Numbers* 20:13. The punishment Moses and Aaron received far outweighed the apparent insignificance of their offense. They were provoked, and suffered because of the offense of the people (*Ramban*).

הָאֹמֵר לְאָבִיו וּלְאִמּוֹ — *The one who said of his father and mother*. The passage describes the selfless manner with which the tribe of Levi performed its responsibilities when the performance of religious duties was involved: Without regard to family ties, they slew idolaters who worshiped the Golden Calf. See *Exodus* 32:27.

Rashi observes that since the whole tribe of Levi was innocent in that episode, the terms *father, mother*, etc. must be understood in the extended sense as referring to non-Levite rela-

And this to Judah, and he said: Hear, O HASHEM. Judah's prayer, and return him safely to his people; may his hands gain him triumph and may You remain a helper against his enemies.

Levi – *Of Levi he said: Your Tumim and Your Urim* befit Your devout one, whom You tested at Massah,* and whom You challenged at the waters of Meribah.* The one who said of his father and mother,* "I have not favored him," he disregarded his brothers and ignored his own children; for they [i.e., the Levites] have observed* Your word, and preserved Your covenant. Thus it is they who are worthy to teach Your law to Jacob and Your Torah to Israel; it is they who shall place incense before Your presence, and burnt offerings on Your altar. Bless, O HASHEM, his resources, and favor his handiwork.* Smash the loins of his foes, and his enemies that they may not rise again.**

Of Benjamin he said: May HASHEM's beloved dwell securely by Him; He hovers above him all day long; and rests His Presence among his hills.**

Third – *Of Joseph he said: His land is blessed by HASHEM* — with the heavenly bounty of dew, and with the deep waters* crouching below: with the bounty of the sun's crops, and with the bounty of the moon's*

---

tives, such as the maternal grandfather, maternal half-brother, or the son of a daughter married to a non-Levite.

כִּי שָׁמְרוּ — *For they have observed*... Their only motive was loyalty to God, with no personal designs.

וּפֹעַל יָדָיו — *His handiwork.* May the Levites' service in the Sanctuary be found acceptable to God (*Sforno*).

מִן יְקוּמוּן — *That they may not rise again.* May anyone who may oppose the priesthood — like Korach — be utterly defeated (*Sforno*).

Benjamin

Benjamin was Jacob's favorite child, and Moses perceives this as manifested by God in a special love for that tribe and His protection of it.

The blessing refers to the fact that the Temple was located in the territory of Benjamin. It therefore follows the blessing of Levi, whose blessing referred to the Temple service performed by that tribe (*Rashi*).

חֹפֵף עָלָיו כָּל הַיּוֹם — *He hovers above him all day long,* i.e., forever. From the day Jerusalem — which was in Benjamin's territory — was chosen as the site of the Temple, the Divine Presence has never rested anywhere else (*Rashi*).

וּבֵין כְּתֵפָיו שָׁכֵן — *And rests His Presence among his hills* [lit., *and between his shoulders He dwells*]. The Talmud (*Zevachim* 54b; *Yoma* 31a] explains this as a reference to the fact that the Temple was built not on the very highest point of the Land, but slightly lower, just as the shoulder is lower than the head (*Rashi*).

Joseph

This blessing incorporates those of Ephraim and Menashe. In many ways it parallels Jacob's blessing of the tribe [*Genesis* 49:25]

Daas Soferim makes the interesting point that since Moses felt the need to bestow such specific blessings on Joseph's territory, it would seem that Joseph's portion was in need of special Divine grace for it to avoid catastrophe. Indeed Joseph's glorious roots contained dangerous elements, from which would sprout forth the evil kings of the Northern Kingdom, the Ten Tribes, who caused the destruction of the Land.

מְבֹרֶכֶת ה׳ אַרְצוֹ — *His land is blessed by HASHEM.* In fact, no other tribal territory was as abundantly good as Joseph's (*Rashi*).

וּמִתְּהוֹם — *And with the deep waters,* i.e., the subterranean primeval water deep below the earth, from which the fountains spring up. See *Genesis* 1:2.

גֶּרֶשׁ יְרָחִים — *The moon's yield,* i.e., produce which matures at night such as cucumber and melon. Alternately, the phrase refers to the produce which the earth yields month by month (*Rashi*).

וּמֵרֹאשׁ הַרְרֵי־קֶדֶם* וּמִמֶּגֶד גִּבְעוֹת עוֹלָם: וּמִמֶּגֶד אֶרֶץ וּמְלֹאָהּ
וּרְצוֹן שֹׁכְנִי סְנֶה* תָּבוֹאתָה לְרֹאשׁ יוֹסֵף וּלְקָדְקֹד נְזִיר אֶחָיו: בְּכוֹר
שׁוֹרוֹ הָדָר לוֹ* וְקַרְנֵי רְאֵם* קַרְנָיו בָּהֶם עַמִּים יְנַגַּח יַחְדָּו
אַפְסֵי־אָרֶץ וְהֵם רִבְבוֹת* אֶפְרַיִם וְהֵם אַלְפֵי מְנַשֶּׁה:

רביעי – וְלִזְבוּלֻן אָמַר שְׂמַח זְבוּלֻן בְּצֵאתֶךָ* וְיִשָּׂשכָר בְּאֹהָלֶיךָ:* עַמִּים
הַר־יִקְרָאוּ* שָׁם יִזְבְּחוּ זִבְחֵי־צֶדֶק כִּי שֶׁפַע יַמִּים יִינָקוּ* וּשְׂפֻנֵי
טְמוּנֵי חוֹל:* וּלְגָד אָמַר בָּרוּךְ מַרְחִיב גָּד כְּלָבִיא שָׁכֵן* וְטָרַף זְרוֹעַ
אַף־קָדְקֹד: וַיַּרְא רֵאשִׁית* לוֹ כִּי־שָׁם חֶלְקַת מְחֹקֵק סָפוּן* וַיֵּתֵא
רָאשֵׁי עָם* צִדְקַת יהוה עָשָׂה וּמִשְׁפָּטָיו עִם־יִשְׂרָאֵל:

חמישי – וּלְדָן אָמַר דָּן גּוּר אַרְיֵה* יְזַנֵּק מִן־הַבָּשָׁן:* וּלְנַפְתָּלִי אָמַר

הַרְרֵי קֶדֶם — *Ancient mountains.* This is the literal translation. *Rashi* perceives it in the sense of: *the hills of priority;* Joseph's territory is blessed in that its hills are the earliest [קדם] to bring their fruits to maturity.

סְנֶה — *Thornbush,* i.e., the burning bush where God first revealed Himself to Moses [*Exodus* 3:4-5] (*Rashi*). The meaning of the expression is: May Joseph's land be blessed by the grace of God Who revealed Himself on Mt. Sinai, place of the bush (*Ramban*).

בְּכוֹר שׁוֹרוֹ הָדָר לוֹ — *Sovereignty will go to his most distinguished, mighty descendant* [literally, *the majesty of his ox-like one — honor is due him*]. The translation follows *Rashi* who notes that the term בְּכוֹר denotes *greatness* and *sovereignty* [comp. *Exodus* 4:22]; the metaphor of ox, largest animal of the cattle family, alludes to *power.* See Jacob's blessing of Simeon and Levi in *Genesis* 49:6 where the expression *at their whim they maimed an ox* is explained by *Rashi* to refer to their attempt to disable Joseph, who is likened to an ox.

In our context, the text refers to Joshua, the mighty ox-like descendant of Joseph [see *II Samuel* 19:21], who will be the sovereign leader of the Israelites, and whose prowess would subdue many kings (*Rashi*).

רְאֵם — *Re'eim.* The horns of which are noted for beauty (*Rashi*). [See *Numbers* 23:22.]

וְהֵם רִבְבוֹת — *They are the myriads ...* The nations mentioned above who would be gored are the myriads slain by Joshua, a descendant of Ephraim; the thousands are the Midianites slain by Gideon, a desendant of Menashe [*Judges* 8:10] (*Rashi*).

According to *Ramban,* הֵם, *they,* refers to the two *horns* — figuratively representing the two branches of Joseph — the right horn being Ephraim, and the left, Menashe. Both of these tribes will become numerous and will number in the many thousands.

Zebulun and Issachar

The unique partnership of Issachar and Zebulun is emphasized by the Rabbis. Zebulun successfully engaged in maritime commerce and supported Issachar who devoted his time to Torah study as cultivator of the spiritual treasure of the people [see *I Chronicles* 12:32]. Thus, although Issachar was older, his Torah study was made possible by Zebulun, and Zebulun was therefore accorded the honor of being blessed first (*Tanchuma; Rashi*). See *Genesis* 49:13.

בְּצֵאתֶךָ — *In your excursions,* i.e., when you go out by the sea to engage in commerce (*Rashi*).

בְּאֹהָלֶיךָ — *In your tents,* studying Torah. The descendants of Zebulun had a special understanding of the complex procedures for establishing the Jewish calendar, and the science of intercalation (adding a thirteenth month periodically during leap years). They produced two hundred heads of Sanhedrins and their halachic rulings were accepted as authoritative (*Midrash,* based on *I Chronicles* 12:32; *Rashi*).

הַר יִקְרָאוּ — *Summon ... to the Temple Mount* in Jerusalem during the three Pilgrimage Festivals to offer thanksgiving to God (*Sifrei; Rashi*).

As members of the Sanhedrin — which regulates the calendar and hence, the festivals — the scholars of Issachar will "summon" the tribes to the Temple Mount for the Pilgrimage Festivals.

As an alternate interpretation, *Rashi* suggests: In order to trade with Zebulun, merchants from around the world will come to his land and be

yield; with the quick-ripening crops of the ancient mountains,* and with the bounty of eternally fertile hills; with the bounty of the land and its fullness, and by the favor of Him Who rested upon the thornbush.* May this blessing rest upon Joseph's head, and upon the crown of him who was separated from his brothers. Sovereignty will go to his most distinguished, mighty descendant;* and his glory will be like the horns of a re'eim;* with both of them together he shall gore nations to the ends of the earth; they are the myriads* of Ephraim's victims, and the thousands of Menashe's victims.*

Fourth – *Of Zebulun he said: Rejoice, O Zebulun, in your excursions,* and Issachar in your tents.* The tribes will summon one another to the Temple Mount,* there they will bring offerings of righteousness, for they will be nourished* by the riches of the sea, and by the treasures concealed in the sand.**

Of Gad he said: Blessed is He Who broadens Gad's boundary; he dwells like a lion tearing off arm and even head.* He chose the first portion* as his own, for that is where the Lawgiver's plot is hidden.* He marched at the head of the nation, carrying out* HASHEM'*s justice and His laws with Israel.*

Fifth – *Of Dan he said: Dan is a lion cub,* leaping forth from the Bashan.**

---

induced to go to Jerusalem and witness how HASHEM is served. They will be impressed and will offer sacrifices as proselytes.

יִינָקוּ – *They will be nourished. 'They'* refers to Issachar and Zebulun. The sea will yield them abundant wealth *(Rashi).*

טְמוּנֵי חוֹל – *Concealed in the sand* — such as the dye from the *chilazon* fish [used to color the blue thread in the *tzitzis*], and glass *(Sforno).*

Gad

Gad's territory was on the eastern side of the Jordan — the land of Sichon and Og. It extended significantly eastward, and was larger than the territory of any of the western tribes. HASHEM — enlarger of Gad's territory — is the subject of the phrase בָּרוּךְ מַרְחִיב גָּד, *Blessed is He Who broadens Gad's boundary.*

כְּלָבִיא שָׁכֵן – *He dwells like a lion.* The tribe of Gad lived on the border and, like a fierce lion, it defended its own territory and that of the neighboring tribes (*Rashi*).

אַף קָדְקֹד – *Even head.* Those whom the warriors of the tribe of Gad would slay could easily be recognized: They could cut off their victim's head and arm in one blow *(Rashi).*

וַיַּרְא רֵאשִׁית – *He chose* [lit., *perceived*] *the first portion.* Gad had requested for himself the territory of Sichon and Og, which was the first part of *Eretz Yisrael* to be conquered *(Rashi).*

חֶלְקַת מְחֹקֵק סָפוּן – *The Lawgiver's* [i.e., Moses] *plot is hidden.* Gad chose that area because they knew that Moses would be interred there in a grave hidden from all [see Deut. 34:6] *(Rashi).* Moses was thus hinting that his sepulchre had already been divinely prepared since the time of Creation, as stated in *Pirkei Avos* 5:6 *(Daas Soferim).*

וַיֵּתֵא רָאשֵׁי עָם – *He marched at the head of the nation.* During the conquest of *Eretz Yisrael,* the mighty tribe of Gad marched among the first. See *Joshua* 1:14 *(Rashi).* According to *Rashi's* alternate interpretation, the subject of this phrase is the Lawgiver, Moses. Thus the verse explains why the people of Gad wanted Moses' grave to be in their territory.

Dan

The tribe of Dan was located along the Mediterranean coast. It was the first tribe marauding invaders from the sea would encounter.

גּוּר אַרְיֵה – *A lion cub.* Since Dan, like Gad, lived close to the border, he too is described as a lion *(Rashi).* According to some, the simile refers to the nimbleness and adventurous spirit for which the tribe of Dan was noted. One of the most illustrious Danites in Scripture was Samson.

יְזַנֵּק מִן הַבָּשָׁן – *Leaping forth from the Bashan.* This is the literal translation. *Rashi* follows *Onkelos'* translation: *Dan's land drinks of the*

נַפְתָּלִי֙ שְׂבַ֣ע רָצ֔וֹן* וּמָלֵ֖א בִּרְכַּ֣ת יהוָ֑ה יָ֥ם וְדָר֖וֹם* יְרָֽשָׁה׃ וּלְאָשֵׁ֣ר אָמַ֔ר בָּר֥וּךְ מִבָּנִ֖ים אָשֵׁ֑ר יְהִ֤י רְצוּי֙ אֶחָ֔יו* וְטֹבֵ֥ל בַּשֶּׁ֖מֶן רַגְלֽוֹ׃ בַּרְזֶ֥ל וּנְחֹ֖שֶׁת* מִנְעָלֶ֑ךָ וּכְיָמֶ֖יךָ דָּבְאֶֽךָ׃ אֵ֥ין כָּאֵ֖ל יְשֻׁר֑וּן* רֹכֵ֤ב שָׁמַ֙יִם֙ בְּעֶזְרֶ֔ךָ וּבְגַאֲוָת֖וֹ שְׁחָקִֽים׃

⁂ כָּל הַנְּעָרִים ⁂

The last *aliyah* of the previous reading is designated for the children too young to have individual *aliyos*. They all crowd around the adult called for the *aliyah*, and he recites the blessing loudly, slowly, and clearly so that they can recite with him. It is customary to spread a *tallis* over all their heads as a canopy. After the *aliyah* (before or after the blessing, depending on the congregation's custom), all the adults recite the following passage (*Genesis* 48:16), as a blessing for the children. See *Laws* §233-235.

הַמַּלְאָךְ* הַגֹּאֵל אֹתִי מִכָּל רָע יְבָרֵךְ אֶת הַנְּעָרִים, וְיִקָּרֵא בָהֶם שְׁמִי,* וְשֵׁם אֲבֹתַי אַבְרָהָם וְיִצְחָק, וְיִדְגּוּ לָרֹב* בְּקֶרֶב הָאָרֶץ.[1]

Some congregations continue:

יְבָרֶכְךָ יהוה, וְיִשְׁמְרֶךָ. יָאֵר יהוה פָּנָיו אֵלֶיךָ וִיחֻנֶּךָּ. יִשָּׂא יהוה פָּנָיו אֵלֶיךָ וְיָשֵׂם לְךָ שָׁלוֹם.[2]

---

rivers that flow from Bashan. The Jordan [יַרְדֵּן=יֹרֵד דָּן / *Jordan=flows from Dan*] has its source in Bashan.

Bashan lay to the north of the Jordan river in what is today southern Syria. It was a very fertile region, and possessed forests and pastures. [See *Isaiah* 2:13; *Ezekiel* 27:6.]

Naftali

שְׂבַע רָצוֹן – *Satiated with favor.* His territory was most fertile and contained everything its inhabitants could desire *(Rashi)*.

וְדָרוֹם – *And its south shore.* Naftali's territory was in the northwest and included Lake Kinneret. According to the Talmud *[Bava Kamma 81b]*, he received on its south a rope's length of fishing coast for spreading out his nets *(Rashi)*.

Asher

Moses follows the blessing of Jacob [*Genesis* 49:20] and focuses his blessing on the fertility and richness of Asher's territory — and the fruitfulness of his progeny. At that time Asher was the largest tribe [see *Numbers* 26:47], and Moses blessed them that they should remain so and not be diminished because of sin (*Daas Soferim*).

רְצוּי אֶחָיו – *Pleasing to his brothers,* i.e., his fellow tribes. And this was so, for Asher favored his brothers' tribes with oil. [*Dipping his feet in oil* is a metapor for great abundance.] Another interpretation is that he was pleasing because his daughters were beautiful and were much sought in marriage by his fellow tribes *(Rashi)*.

⁂ Epilogue: Moses' Blessing to All of Israel

According to *Rashi,* Moses now addresses the following blessing to all the tribes comprising the nation as a whole. According to *Ibn Ezra (Ramban, Sforno* and *Daas Zekeinim)*, this verse is a continuation of Asher's blessing and the nation's blessing begins with verse 26.

בַּרְזֶל וּנְחֹשֶׁת – *Iron and copper.* In *Rashi*'s view, this verse depicts the security in which the nation would live because of the courage and prowess of its defenders at the borders. In the

Of Naftali he said: Naftali, satiated with favor, and filled with* HASHEM's *blessing; go possess the sea and its south shore.**

Of Asher he said: Asher is most blessed with children, he shall be pleasing to his brothers, and dip his feet in oil.*

May your borders be sealed like iron and copper, and like the days of your prime, so may your old age be. There is none like God, O Jeshurun;* He rides across heaven to help you, and in His majesty through the upper heights.*

ALL THE YOUNG BOYS

The last *aliyah* of the previous reading is designated for the children too young to have individual *aliyos*. They all crowd around the adult called for the *aliyah*, and he recites the blessings loudly, slowly, and clearly so that they can recite with him. It is customary to spread a *tallis* over all their heads as a canopy. After the *aliyah* (before or after the blessing, depending on the congregation's custom), all the adults recite the following passage (*Genesis* 48:16), as a blessing for the children. See *Laws* §233-235.

הַמַּלְאָךְ *May the angel* who redeems me from all evil bless the lads, and may my name be declared upon them* — and the names of my forefathers Abraham and Isaac — and may they proliferate abundantly like fish* within the land.*[1]

Some congregations continue:

יְבָרֶכְךָ *May* HASHEM *bless you and safeguard you. May* HASHEM *illuminate His countenance for you and be gracious to you. May* HASHEM *turn His countenance to you and establish peace for you.*[2]

(1) *Genesis* 48:16. (2) *Numbers* 6:24-26.

---

limited context of Asher, whose territory was situated at the extreme north of *Eretz Yisrael* [*Joshua* 19:24-31], Moses' blessing was that this strategically important area will be divinely protected as if it were sealed by bars of iron and copper; and the tribe will maintain its youthful vigor (*Ramban*).

יְשֻׁרוּן – *Jeshurun.* A reference to the Israelites.

Moses refers to them by the term [from *yashar, upright*] in this context to imply that when they conduct themselves in an upright manner God "rides across heaven to help them" but not when they act sinfully (*Sifre*).

As *R' Hirsch* explains: Nothing can compare to the manner in which God will manifest Himself if the Jewish people remain true to their calling of *Jeshurun;* if they remain *straight* and *upright*, pursuing their life in undeviating loyalty to their duty.

הַמַּלְאָךְ — *May the angel.* The following passages are a collection of Scriptural verses discussing God's 'mercy.' This first verse, *May the angel who redeems,* etc. was Jacob's blessing to his grandsons Ephraim and Menashe (*Genesis* 48:16). The prayer is directed not to the angel, who has no power except as an agent of God, but to God Who dispatched the angel.

וְיִקָּרֵא בָהֶם שְׁמִי – *And may my name be declared upon them.* May they constantly strive to such heights that they will be worthy to have their names coupled with those of the Patriarchs (*R' Avraham ben HaRambam*).

וְיִדְגּוּ לָרֹב – *And may they proliferate abundantly like fish. R' Hirsch* explains that just as fish enjoy contentment hidden from the gaze of human beings, so Jews who live in the sphere assigned them by God will have a degree of serenity and happiness far beyond the comprehension of those around them.

רְשׁוּת לַחֲתַן הַתּוֹרָה

The person designated for the concluding portion of the Torah on Simchas Torah is known as *Chassan Torah,* the groom of the Torah. This is a great honor and is usually reserved for a distinguished Torah Scholar. In honor of the Torah and its 'groom,' he is called up with the following chanted, poetic formula, which praises the Giver of the Torah, the Torah, and its groom. It is customary for people to crowd around the *bimah* with a *tallis* over their heads as a canopy.

מֵרְשׁוּת הָאֵל הַגָּדוֹל הַגִּבּוֹר וְהַנּוֹרָא, וּמֵרְשׁוּת מִפָּז וּמִפְּנִינִים יְקָרָה, וּמֵרְשׁוּת סַנְהֶדְרִין הַקְּדוֹשָׁה וְהַבְּרוּרָה, וּמֵרְשׁוּת רָאשֵׁי יְשִׁיבוֹת וְאַלּוּפֵי תוֹרָה, וּמֵרְשׁוּת זְקֵנִים וּנְעָרִים יוֹשְׁבֵי שׁוּרָה,

אֶפְתַּח פִּי בְּשִׁירָה וּבְזִמְרָה, לְהוֹדוֹת וּלְהַלֵּל לְדָר בִּנְהוֹרָא, שֶׁהֶחֱיָנוּ וְקִיְּמָנוּ בְּיִרְאָתוֹ הַטְּהוֹרָה, וְהִגִּיעָנוּ לִשְׂמֹחַ בְּשִׂמְחַת הַתּוֹרָה,

הַמְשַׂמַּחַת לֵב וְעֵינַיִם מְאִירָה, הַנּוֹתֶנֶת חַיִּים וְעֹשֶׁר וְכָבוֹד וְתִפְאָרָה. הַמְאַשֶּׁרֶת הוֹלְכֶיהָ בְּדֶרֶךְ הַטּוֹבָה וְהַיְשָׁרָה, הַמַּאֲרֶכֶת יָמִים וּמוֹסֶפֶת גְּבוּרָה לְאוֹהֲבֶיהָ וּלְשׁוֹמְרֶיהָ בְּצִוּוּי וְאַזְהָרָה, לְעוֹסְקֶיהָ וּלְנוֹצְרֶיהָ בְּאַהֲבָה וּבְמוֹרָא.

וּבְכֵן יְהִי רָצוֹן מִלִּפְנֵי הַגְּבוּרָה, לָתֵת חַיִּים וָחֶסֶד וָנֵזֶר וַעֲטָרָה, לְרַבִּי (name of honoree) בֶּן (honoree's father's name) שֶׁנִּבְחַר לְהַשְׁלִים הַתּוֹרָה,

לְאַמְּצוֹ לְבָרְכוֹ וּלְגַדְּלוֹ בְּתַלְמוּד תּוֹרָה,
לְדָרְשׁוֹ לְחַיִּים לְהַדְּרוֹ לְוַעֲדוֹ בַּחֲבוּרָה,
לְזַכּוֹתוֹ לְחַיּוֹתוֹ לְטַכְּסוֹ בְּטֶכֶס אוֹרָה,
לְיַשְּׁרוֹ לְכַלְּלוֹ לְלַמְּדוֹ לֶקַח וּסְבָרָא,
לְמַלְּטוֹ לְנַשְּׂאוֹ לְסַעֲדוֹ בְּסַעַד בְּרוּרָה,
לְעַדְּנוֹ לְפַרְנְסוֹ לְצַדְּקוֹ בְּעַם נִבְרָא,
לְקָרְבוֹ לְרַחֲמוֹ וּלְשָׁמְרוֹ מִכָּל צוּקָה וְצָרָה,
לְתָקְפוֹ לְסָמְכוֹ לְתָמְכוֹ בְּרוּחַ נִשְׁבָּרָה.

עֲמוֹד, עֲמוֹד, עֲמוֹד רַבִּי (name of honoree) בֶּן (honoree's father's name) חֲתַן הַתּוֹרָה, וְתֵן כָּבוֹד לָאֵל גָּדוֹל וְנוֹרָא, וּבִשְׂכַר זֶה תִּזְכֶּה מֵאֵל נוֹרָא, לִרְאוֹת בָּנִים וּבְנֵי בָנִים עוֹסְקִים בַּתּוֹרָה, וּמְקַיְּמֵי מִצְוֹת בְּתוֹךְ עַם יָפָה וּבָרָה.

וְתִזְכֶּה לִשְׂמֹחַ בְּשִׂמְחַת בֵּית הַבְּחִירָה, וּפָנֶיךָ לְהָאִיר בִּצְדָקָה בְּאַסְפַּקְלַרְיָא הַמְּאִירָה, כִּנְבוּאַת יְשַׁעְיָהוּ מָלֵא רוּחַ עֵצָה וּגְבוּרָה.

שִׂמְחוּ אֶת יְרוּשָׁלַיִם וְגִילוּ בָהּ מְהֵרָה, שִׂישׂוּ אִתָּהּ מָשׂוֹשׂ, כָּל הַמִּתְאַבְּלִים עָלֶיהָ, בְּאֵבְלָה וְצָרָה.

עֲמוֹד, עֲמוֹד, עֲמוֹד רַבִּי (name of honoree) בֶּן (honoree's father's name) חֲתַן הַתּוֹרָה, מֵרְשׁוּת כָּל הַקָּהָל הַקָּדוֹשׁ הַזֶּה, וְהַשְׁלֵם הַתּוֹרָה.

יַעֲמוֹד (name of honoree) בֶּן (honoree's father's name) חֲתַן הַתּוֹרָה.

INVESTITURE OF THE CHASSAN TORAH

The person designated for the concluding portion of the Torah on Simchas Torah is known as *Chassan Torah,* the groom of the Torah. This is a great honor and is usually reserved for a distinguished Torah Scholar. In honor of the Torah and its 'groom,' he is called up with the following chanted, poetic formula, which praises the Giver of the Torah, the Torah, and its groom. It is customary for people to crowd around the *bimah* with a *tallis* over their heads as a canopy.

מֵרְשׁוּת *With permission of the great, mighty, and awesome God; with permission of [the Torah] that is more precious than the finest gold and gems; with permission of the holy and refined Sanhedrin [of old]; with permission of heads of academies and the nobles of the Torah, with permission of the elders and youths who sit in the ranks —*

I shall open my mouth with song and hymn to thank and praise Him Who dwells amid light, Who has kept us alive and sustained us through His pure reverence and has brought us to rejoice with the gladness of the Torah —

That gladdens the heart and enlightens the eyes; that provides life, prosperity, honor, and glory; that brings good fortune to those who walk its good and just paths; that lengthens days and increases strength of those who love her and observe her commandments and injunctions, for those who occupy themselves with her study and preserve her with love and reverence.

וּבְכֵן *Therefore, may it be the will of the Omnipotent that he bestow life, kindness, diadem and crown upon (* name of honoree*) son of (* honoree's father's name*) who has been chosen to complete the Torah —*

to strengthen, bless, and make him great in the study of the Torah;
to seek him out for life, to glorify him, and to establish him in society;
to grant him merit and life, and to assign him in the council of [the Torah's] light;
to grant him virtue and distinction, to teach him knowledge and logic;
to let him escape danger, to raise him, to succor him with refined support;
to delight him, to support him, to make him righteous among the people for whom the world was created;
to draw him near, to show him mercy, and to protect him against every distress and trouble;
to strengthen, assist, and support him when he is brokenspirited.

עֲמוֹד *Arise, arise, arise (* name of honoree*) son of (* honoree's father's name*) the groom of the Torah, and render honor to the great and awesome God, and in reward for this, may You be deemed worthy by the awesome God to see children and grandchildren occupied with the Torah, and performing commandments among the beautiful and refined people.*

May you be worthy to rejoice in the gladness of the Chosen Temple; may your countenance give illumination with the righteousness as through a clear lens, as Isaiah prophesied [regarding the Messiah who will be] filled with a spirit of counsel and strength.

Be glad with Jerusalem and exult with her speedily, rejoice in her joy, all who grieved for her with grief and distress.

Arise, arise, arise (name of honoree*) son of (* honoree's father's name*) the groom of the Torah, with the permission of this entire holy congregation, and conclude the Torah.*

יַעֲמוֹד *Arise (* name of honoree*) son of (* honoree's father's name*) the groom of the Torah.*

קריאת התורה לחתן התורה

דברים לג:כז־לד:יב

מְעֹנָה אֱלֹהֵי קֶדֶם וּמִתַּחַת זְרֹעֹת עוֹלָם* וַיְגָרֶשׁ מִפָּנֶיךָ אוֹיֵב וַיֹּאמֶר
הַשְׁמֵד: וַיִּשְׁכֹּן יִשְׂרָאֵל בֶּטַח בָּדָד* עֵין יַעֲקֹב* אֶל־אֶרֶץ דָּגָן וְתִירוֹשׁ
אַף־שָׁמָיו יַעַרְפוּ־טָל: אַשְׁרֶיךָ* יִשְׂרָאֵל מִי כָמוֹךָ עַם נוֹשַׁע בַּיהוה
מָגֵן עֶזְרֶךָ וַאֲשֶׁר־חֶרֶב גַּאֲוָתֶךָ וְיִכָּחֲשׁוּ אֹיְבֶיךָ לָךְ וְאַתָּה עַל־
בָּמוֹתֵימוֹ תִדְרֹךְ:* וַיַּעַל מֹשֶׁה מֵעַרְבֹת מוֹאָב אֶל־הַר נְבוֹ רֹאשׁ
הַפִּסְגָּה אֲשֶׁר עַל־פְּנֵי יְרֵחוֹ וַיַּרְאֵהוּ יהוה אֶת־כָּל־הָאָרֶץ* אֶת־
הַגִּלְעָד עַד־דָּן:* וְאֵת כָּל־נַפְתָּלִי וְאֶת־אֶרֶץ אֶפְרַיִם וּמְנַשֶּׁה וְאֵת
כָּל־אֶרֶץ יְהוּדָה עַד הַיָּם הָאַחֲרוֹן:* וְאֶת־הַנֶּגֶב וְאֶת־הַכִּכָּר בִּקְעַת
יְרֵחוֹ עִיר הַתְּמָרִים עַד־צֹעַר: וַיֹּאמֶר יהוה אֵלָיו זֹאת הָאָרֶץ אֲשֶׁר
נִשְׁבַּעְתִּי לְאַבְרָהָם לְיִצְחָק וּלְיַעֲקֹב לֵאמֹר לְזַרְעֲךָ אֶתְּנֶנָּה
הֶרְאִיתִיךָ בְעֵינֶיךָ* וְשָׁמָּה לֹא תַעֲבֹר: וַיָּמָת שָׁם מֹשֶׁה* עֶבֶד־
יהוה* בְּאֶרֶץ מוֹאָב עַל־פִּי יהוה:* וַיִּקְבֹּר אֹתוֹ* בַגַּי בְּאֶרֶץ מוֹאָב

Aliyah of Chassan Torah

This verse begins the reading of *Chassan Torah*, the final *aliyah* of the annual Torah-reading cycle.

זְרֹעֹת עוֹלָם – *The world's mighty ones* [lit., *the arms of the world*]. This follows *Rashi* who explains that the term refers to the world's mighty leaders who, by virtue of being *below*, must tremble at the insignificance of their power in the Presence of God Who dwells Above in the Heavens.

Others render this phrase: *everlasting arms;* arms of inexhaustible strength — a reference to HASHEM who is God Alone, and is their Sustaining Strength on the earth below.

בָּדָד – *Solitary*. Since, as promised in the previous verse, the enemy would be driven out, there would be no need for Jews to band together and live in large groups for fear of invasion. Rather, everyone would dwell individually "each under his vine and under his fig tree" *(Rashi)*.

עֵין יַעֲקֹב – *In the likeness of Jacob's blessing* [lit., *the fountain of Jacob*]. The previously mentioned solitary security will be in conformity with the assurances Jacob had given them [*Genesis* 48:20]: *And God shall be with you and bring you back to the Land of your fathers (Rashi;* cf. *Sifre)*. Jacob is the source of the fountain through which the Land will prosper *(Hirsch)*.

אַשְׁרֶיךָ – *Fortunate*. Israel is unique ... God bestowed upon Israel that eminence among the nations which all the other nations achieve by the sword *(Hirsch)*.

עַל בָּמוֹתֵימוֹ תִדְרֹךְ – *You will trample their haughty ones* [lit., *you will tread upon their high places*], i.e., you will triumph over them as it says: [*Joshua* 10:24] *Put your feet on the necks of these kings (Rashi)*. This figure of speech [see also *Deut.* 32:13] denotes the triumphant and undisputed possession of the Land — even its high mountains and haughty leaders.

Moses' final words

Moses has taken leave of his people with a remarkable mixture of love and praise. In previous portions, he has threatened Israel with a frightening array of punishment if they fall short of God's calling. Indeed, history, more than any commentary, testifies to the gravity of the suffering he prophesied. But in his final words, he displays his true feelings regarding Israel: *Fortunate are you ... Who is like you! ... you will trample their haughty ones.* Even the threats of punishment were uttered only to prevent them from happening, and when that had to be imposed, it was because Israel's lofty status does not permit it to indulge in the excesses that are regarded as "acceptable" by other nations. Moses' last words are of blessing and reassurance — for ultimately Israel will fulfill its promise and be showered with Divine rewards that will eclipse by far the horrors it has endured.

TORAH READING / CHASSAN TORAH

Deuteronomy 33:27-34:12

The heavens are the abode of God immemorial, and below are the world's mighty ones; He drove away the enemy before you, urging you, "Destroy!" Thus Israel shall dwell secure, solitary,* in the likeness of Jacob's blessing, in a land of grain and wine. Even his heavens shall drip with dew.*

Fortunate are you, O Israel: Who is like you! O nation delivered by* HASHEM, *the Shield of your help, Who is the Sword of your grandeur. Your foes will try to deceive you, but you will trample their haughty ones.**

Moses ascended from the plains of Moab, to Mount Nebo, to the summit of the cliff, that faces Jericho, and HASHEM *showed him the entire land: the Gilead as far as Dan;* all of Naftali, and the land of Ephraim and Menashe; the entire land of Judah as far as the Mediterranean;* the Negev; and the Plain — the valley of Jericho, city of date palms — as far as Zoar.*

And HASHEM *said to him, "This is the land of which I have sworn to Abraham, Isaac, and Jacob, saying, 'I will give it to your offspring.' I have let you see it with your own eyes,* but you shall not cross there."*

So Moses, servant of HASHEM,* *died there,* in the land of Moab, by the mouth of* HASHEM.* *He buried him* in the depression, in the land of Moab,*

Death of Moses

Having blessed and prayed for the people, Moses, the faithful servant, ascends the mountain as he had been commanded to do in *Deut.* 32:49.

אֶת כָּל הָאָרֶץ – *The entire land.* It was more than a mere physical glance. God prophetically showed Moses the entire *Eretz Yisrael* in its prosperity, and also the oppressors who would oppress it in the future *(Rashi).*

עַד דָּן – *As far as Dan.* He showed him the children of Dan practicing idolatry [see *Judges* 18:30], and He also showed him Dan's descendant Samson, who would deliver them *(Sifre).*

Targum Yonasan writes: *He showed him all the strong ones of the Land,* i.e., its future leaders throughout history.

עַד הַיָּם הָאַחֲרוֹן – *As far as the Mediterranean* [lit., *the farthest* or *last sea*]. In an alternate explanation *Rashi* cites the *Midrash*: Read this phrase as though it did not state הַיָּם הָאַחֲרוֹן, *the last sea,* but הַיּוֹם הָאַחֲרוֹן, *the last day.* God showed Moses all that would happen to Israel in the future until the last day when the dead will again live.

הֶרְאִיתִיךָ בְעֵינֶיךָ – *I have let you see it with your own eyes* — in order that you may go and say to Abraham, Isaac, and Jacob: HASHEM has fulfilled the promise He has made to you. *But,* it is a decree from Me that *you shall not cross there.* Were this not so I would have kept you alive to see them fully settled in the Land, and you would *then* go and tell the Patriarchs *(Rashi).*

וַיָּמָת שָׁם מֹשֶׁה – *So Moses . . . died there.* There are two opinions among the Sages: Moses wrote up to this point, and Joshua wrote these verses; or the Holy One, Blessed is He, dictated this, and Moses wrote it in tears.

According to tradition, Moses' death occurred on the seventh of Adar, 2490 from Creation.

עֶבֶד ה׳ – Servant of *HASHEM.* Even in dying, Moses was still *HASHEM's servant* — obeying His command willingly *(Ibn Ezra).*

עַל פִּי ה׳ – *By the mouth of HASHEM.* He died by the Divine Kiss *(Rashi).*

וַיִּקְבֹּר אֹתוֹ – *He buried him.* God, in His glory, buried him. According to another opinion in the Talmud, Moses buried himself, the term אתו being reflexive as in *Numbers* 6:13; *Leviticus* 22:16.

מ֥וּל בֵּ֣ית פְּע֑וֹר* וְלֹא־יָדַ֥ע* אִישׁ֙ אֶת־קְבֻ֣רָת֔וֹ עַ֖ד הַיּ֥וֹם הַזֶּֽה׃
וּמֹשֶׁ֗ה בֶּן־מֵאָ֧ה וְעֶשְׂרִ֛ים שָׁנָ֖ה בְּמֹת֑וֹ לֹא־כָהֲתָ֥ה עֵינ֖וֹ וְלֹא־נָ֥ס
לֵחֹֽה׃* וַ֠יִּבְכּוּ בְּנֵ֨י יִשְׂרָאֵ֧ל אֶת־מֹשֶׁ֛ה בְּעַרְבֹ֥ת מוֹאָ֖ב שְׁלֹשִׁ֣ים י֑וֹם
וַיִּתְּמ֔וּ יְמֵ֥י בְכִ֖י אֵ֥בֶל מֹשֶֽׁה׃* וִיהוֹשֻׁ֣עַ בִּן־נ֗וּן מָלֵא֙ ר֣וּחַ חׇכְמָ֔ה
כִּֽי־סָמַ֥ךְ מֹשֶׁ֛ה אֶת־יָדָ֖יו* עָלָ֑יו וַיִּשְׁמְע֨וּ אֵלָ֤יו בְּנֵֽי־יִשְׂרָאֵל֙ וַֽיַּעֲשׂ֔וּ
כַּאֲשֶׁ֛ר צִוָּ֥ה יהוה אֶת־מֹשֶֽׁה׃ וְלֹֽא־קָ֨ם נָבִ֥יא ע֛וֹד בְּיִשְׂרָאֵ֖ל כְּמֹשֶׁ֑ה
אֲשֶׁר֙ יְדָע֣וֹ יהוה פָּנִ֖ים אֶל־פָּנִֽים׃* לְכׇל־הָ֨אֹתֹ֜ת וְהַמּֽוֹפְתִ֗ים אֲשֶׁ֤ר
שְׁלָחוֹ֙ יהוה לַעֲשׂ֖וֹת בְּאֶ֣רֶץ מִצְרָ֑יִם לְפַרְעֹ֥ה וּלְכׇל־עֲבָדָ֖יו וּלְכׇל־
אַרְצֽוֹ׃ (The congregation rises at this point.) וּלְכֹל֙ הַיָּ֣ד הַחֲזָקָ֔ה* וּלְכֹ֖ל הַמּוֹרָ֣א
הַגָּד֑וֹל אֲשֶׁר֙ עָשָׂ֣ה מֹשֶׁ֔ה לְעֵינֵ֖י כׇּל־יִשְׂרָאֵֽל׃*

Congregation then reader:

חֲזַק* חֲזַק וְנִתְחַזֵּק!

הגבהה וגלילה

The first Torah is raised for all to see. To give special honor to the Torah, it is customary to change the usual manner of *hagbahah*, see *Laws* §236.

Each person looks at the Torah and recites aloud:

וְזֹאת הַתּוֹרָה אֲשֶׁר שָׂם מֹשֶׁה לִפְנֵי בְּנֵי יִשְׂרָאֵל,[1] עַל פִּי יהוה בְּיַד מֹשֶׁה.[2]

Some add:

עֵץ חַיִּים הִיא לַמַּחֲזִיקִים בָּהּ, וְתֹמְכֶיהָ מְאֻשָּׁר.[3] דְּרָכֶיהָ דַרְכֵי נֹעַם, וְכָל נְתִיבוֹתֶיהָ שָׁלוֹם.[4] אֹרֶךְ יָמִים בִּימִינָהּ, בִּשְׂמֹאלָהּ עֹשֶׁר וְכָבוֹד.[5] יהוה חָפֵץ לְמַעַן צִדְקוֹ, יַגְדִּיל תּוֹרָה וְיַאְדִּיר.[6]

מוּל בֵּית פְּעוֹר — *Opposite Beth Peor.* According to Rabbinic tradition, Moses' grave was in readiness for him there since the six days of Creation to atone for the incident concerning Peor [see *Numbers* Ch. 15]. It was one of the ten things created 'between the twilights' on the eve of the first Sabbath [see *Avos* 5:6].

וְלֹא יָדַע — *And no one knows.* Even Moses himself did not previously know it, and after his death it remained concealed, so that his tomb might not become a shrine of pilgrimage for those who deify national heroes. It has been noted that this is the seal of his humble self-effacement [see *Sotah* 13a].

וְלֹא נָס לֵחֹה — *And his vigor had not diminished.* Despite old age, he remained fresh. *Rashi* renders: the life-fluids that were in him did not depart; decomposition had no power over him.

וַיִּתְּמוּ יְמֵי בְכִי אֵבֶל מֹשֶׁה — *Then the days of tearful mourning for Moses came to an end.* Although Moses left no equal and his level of prophecy has never been approached, the days of mourning had to end and, as the next verse says, Joshua carried on the legacy.

סָמַךְ . . . יָדָיו — *Had laid his hands.* A symbolic action showing the transference of his authority to Joshua, thus endowing him with a portion of his spirit. See *Numbers* 27:18.

פָּנִים אֶל פָּנִים — *Face to face.* Moses was able to

opposite Beth Peor, and no one knows* his burial place to this very day. Moses was a hundred and twenty years old when he died; his eyes had not dimmed, and his vigor had not diminished.* And the Children of Israel bewailed Moses in the plains of Moab for thirty days; then the days of tearful mourning for Moses came to an end.**

Joshua son of Nun was filled with the spirit of wisdom, because Moses had laid his hands on him. The Children of Israel therefore obeyed him, doing as HASHEM had commanded Moses.*

Never again has there arisen in Israel a prophet like Moses, whom HASHEM had known face to face, as evidenced by all the signs and miracles that HASHEM assigned him to perform in the land of Egypt, against Pharaoh and all his courtiers and all his land.* (The congregation rises at this point.) *And by all the mighty acts* and awesome power that Moses performed before the eyes of all Israel.**

Congregation then reader:

CHAZAK,* CHAZAK, VENIS'CHAZEIK!

Be strong! Be strong! And let us strengthen one another!

HAGBAHAH AND GELILAH

The first Torah is raised for all to see. To give special honor to the Torah, it is customary to change the usual manner of *hagbahah,* see *Laws* §236.

Each person looks at the Torah and recites aloud:

This is the Torah that Moses placed before the Children of Israel,[1] upon the command of HASHEM, through Moses' hand.[2]

Some add:

עֵץ *It is a tree of life for those who grasp it, and its supporters are praiseworthy.[3] Its ways are ways of pleasantness and all its paths are peace.[4] Lengthy days are at its right; at its left are wealth and honor.[5] HASHEM desired, for the sake of its [Israel's] righteousness, that the Torah be made great and glorious.[6]*

(1) *Deuteronomy* 4:44. (2) *Numbers* 9:23. (3) *Proverbs* 3:18. (4) 3:17. (5) 3:16. (6) *Isaiah* 42:21.

speak with God at any time he wished *(Rashi).*

Thus Moses was unique in that he had achieved the highest spiritual level possible. That there will never again arise in Israel a prophet like Moses is one of the basic tenets of our faith.

הַיָּד הַחֲזָקָה – *Mighty acts* [lit., *strong hand*]. This refers to Moses having received in his hands the Tablets of the Ten Commandments, which, according to the Midrash, were of extraordinary weight *(Rashi).* According to *Ramban* this refers to the division of the waters of the Red Sea.

לְעֵינֵי כָּל יִשְׂרָאֵל – *Before the eyes of all Israel.* Moses took it upon himself to shatter the Tablets before their eyes [see *Deut.* 19:17] *(Rashi).*

Moses' prophetic prowess and signs were not limited; his great acts were fully visible to the entire nation. The Divine Presence was revealed through him at the Red Sea, Mount Sinai, and the Tent of Meeting.

⇐§ חֲזַק! – *Chazak!* Following custom, at the completion of the public reading of any of the Five Books of the Torah, the congregation exclaims חֲזַק חֲזַק וְנִתְחַזֵּק, *Be strong, be strong* [i.e., to fulfill the Torah teaching just read] *and let us strengthen one another.*

רְשׁוּת לַחֲתַן בְּרֵאשִׁית

The person designated to begin the Torah reading of *Bereishis* on Simchas Torah is called *Chassan Bereishis,* the groom of *Bereishis.* Like 'the groom of the Torah,' this *aliyah* is a high honor that is generally reserved for a distinguished person. People crowd around with a *tallis* over their heads as a canopy, and the 'groom' is called up with the following chanted, poetic formula:

מֵרְשׁוּת מְרוֹמָם עַל כָּל בְּרָכָה וְשִׁירָה, נוֹרָא עַל כָּל תְּהִלָּה וְזִמְרָה, חֲכַם לֵבָב וְאַמִּיץ כֹּחַ וּגְבוּרָה, וּמוֹשֵׁל עוֹלָם אֲדוֹן כָּל יְצִירָה,

וּמֵרְשׁוּת כְּבוּדָּה בַּת מֶלֶךְ פְּנִימָה עֲצוּרָה, רֵאשִׁית קִנְיָנוֹ אַלְפַּיִם אֲצוּרָה, בָּרָה תְּמִימָה מְשִׁיבַת נֶפֶשׁ וּמַחֲזִירָה,

יְשֻׁרוּן נִתְּנָה מוֹרָשָׁה, לְעָבְדָהּ וּלְשָׁמְרָהּ, מְלַמְּדֶיהָ גְּאוֹנֵי יַעֲקֹב לְפָתְחָהּ וּלְסָגְרָהּ,

כְּלִיל הוֹד נְשִׂיא מַרְבֵּה הַמִּשְׂרָה, יוֹשְׁבֵי עַל מִדִּין מְשִׁיבֵי מִלְחָמָה שַׁעְרָה, רָאשֵׁי יְשִׁיבוֹת רָאשֵׁי גוֹלָה פְּזוּרָה,

וּמֵרְשׁוּת חֲבוּרַת צֶדֶק עֵדָה הַמְּאֻשָּׁרָה, זְקֵנִים וּנְעָרִים בְּכָל שׁוּרָה וְשׁוּרָה, קְבוּצִים פֹּה הַיּוֹם לְשִׂמְחַת הַתּוֹרָה, וְנֶעֱצָרִים לְסַיֵּם וּלְהָחֵל בְּגִיל וּבְמוֹרָא.

אוֹתָהּ מְחַבְּבִים כְּיוֹם נְתִינָתָהּ בַּהֲדָרָהּ, מְסַלְסְלִים בָּהּ כַּחֲדָשָׁה וְלֹא כִּיְשָׁנָה שֶׁעָבְרָה. צְמֵאִים לָמֹץ וּלְהִתְעַנֵּג מִזִּיו יְקָרָהּ, מְשַׂמַּחַת לֵב וְעֶצֶב מְסִירָה. תַּנְחוּמֶיהָ יְשַׁעַשְׁעוּ נַפְשָׁם בָּהּ לְהִתְפָּאֲרָה, וְהוֹגִים בְּמִקְרָא וְהַגָּדָה בְּמִשְׁנָה וּגְמָרָא.

רָצִים וּמְבִיאִים טַפָּם לְבֵית הָעֲתִירָה, וְעוֹשִׂים גַּם מַעֲשִׂים בְּאַזְהָרָה, לָכֵן גָּדוֹל שְׂכָרָם מֵאֵת הַגְּבוּרָה. עַל רֹאשָׁם שִׂמְחַת עוֹלָם קְשׁוּרָה, תְּאֵבִים לִרְאוֹת בְּבִנְיַן בֵּית הַבְּחִירָה.

וּבְכֵן נִסְכַּמְתִּי דַּעַת כֻּלָּם לְבָרְרָה, בָּחוּר הֲרִימוֹתִי מֵעָם תּוֹךְ הַחֲבוּרָה, מְצָאתִיו לֵב נָבוֹן לְהַסְבִּירָה, צֶדֶק וָחֶסֶד רוֹדֵף בְּאֹרַח יְשָׁרָה, וּנְשָׂאוֹ לִבּוֹ וְנָדְבָה רוּחוֹ לְהִתְעוֹרְרָה תְּחִלָּה וְרִאשׁוֹן הֱיוֹת לְהַתְחִיל הַתּוֹרָה. וְעַתָּה, קוּם רַבִּי (name of honoree) בֶּן (honoree's father's name) עֲמֹד לְהִתְאַזְּרָה, בֹּא וְהִתְיַצֵּב וַעֲמֹד לִימִינִי וּקְרָא מַעֲשֵׂה בְּרֵאשִׁית לִכְבוֹד צוּר בָּרָא.

עַל זֹאת מַתְכִּיפִין הַתְחָלָה לְהַשְׁלָמָה בִּתְדִירָה, עַד שֶׁלֹּא יְרַגֵּל בְּעַם זוּ לְשַׁקְּרָה.

יַעַן נַעֲשֵׂיתָ רִאשׁוֹן לְמִצְוָה גְמוּרָה, מָה רַב טוּבְךָ וּמַשְׂכֻּרְתְּךָ יְתֵרָה. טוֹב עַיִן תְּבֹרַךְ בְּנִדְבָתְךָ מִלְּעַצְרָה, וּמִבִּרְכוֹת בּוֹרַאֲךָ תְּבֹרַךְ יָדְךָ מִלְּקַצְּרָה, בַּעֲבוּר שֶׁכָּל הַמְּכַבֵּד תּוֹרָה בִּצְפִירָה, יְהִי גוּפוֹ מְכֻבָּד בְּכֹחַ לְהִתְאַשְּׁרָה.

מַהֵר, עֲמֹד, עֲמֹד, עֲמֹד רַבִּי (name of honoree) בֶּן (honoree's father's name) חֲתַן בְּרֵאשִׁית בָּרָא, מֵרְשׁוּת הַקָּהָל הַקָּדוֹשׁ הַזֶּה, לְבָרֵךְ אֵל גָּדוֹל וְנוֹרָא, אָמֵן יַעֲנוּ אַחֲרֶיךָ הַכֹּל מְהֵרָה.

יַעֲמוֹד רַבִּי (name of honoree) בֶּן (honoree's father's name) חֲתַן בְּרֵאשִׁית בָּרָא.

INVESTITURE OF THE CHASSAN BEREISHIS

The person designated to begin the Torah reading of *Bereishis* on Simchas Torah is called *Chassan Bereishis,* the groom of *Bereishis.* Like 'the groom of the Torah,' this *aliyah* is a high honor that is generally reserved for a distinguished person. People crowd around with a *tallis* over their heads as a canopy, and the 'groom' is called up with the following chanted, poetic formula:

מֵרְשׁוּת *With permission of Him Who is exalted above every blessing and song, awesome above every praise and hymn, the wise-hearted, vigorously strong, mighty One; Ruler of the world, Master of all Creation;*

and with permission of the princess [the Torah] whose glory is confined within [the study hall]; His prime possession that was treasured for two thousand generations [before Creation]; it is pure and perfect, refreshing the soul and restoring it;

[and with permission] of Jeshurun [Israel] to whom it was given as a heritage to perform and to observe; to be started and completed by its students, the great scholars of Jacob;

[and with permission] of the totally glorious Nassi, who enjoys abundant dominion; of those who sit in judgment and bring the battles [for knowledge] to the gates [of the study hall]; the heads of academies, the leaders of the dispersed exile;

and with permission of the righteous company, the praiseworthy congregation; the elders and youths of every single rank, who are gathered here for the gladness of the Torah; and remain to complete it and to begin it with joy and reverence.

They adore it as on the day it was given majestically; they preen themselves with it as with a fresh treasure and not an old thing whose time has passed. They thirst to extract and to enjoy its precious radiance, which gladdens the heart and removes sadness. Their soul enjoys its consolations to glory themselves, and they discuss the Scripture and Aggadah, the Mishnah and Gemara.

They run to bring their children to the house of prayer, and they do good deeds at their parents' bidding; therefore their reward from the Omnipotent One is great. Eternal joy is bound upon their head, for they long to see the rebuilding of the Chosen Temple.

וּבְכֵן *So now I assent to the unanimous decision to select a chosen one, exalted by the people from among the company, I have found him to have an understanding heart to comprehend [the Torah]; he pursues righteousness and kindness in a just manner, and his heart has inspired him to begin, to be the first to start the Torah. So now stand (*name of honoree*) son of (*honoree's father's name*), arise and gird yourself, come and stand erect, and arise to my right and read the story of Creation in honor of Him Who formed and created.*

For this we always hurry to begin the Torah anew as soon as it is completed so that Satan cannot maliciously accuse the Jewish people [of indifference].

Since you are made the first for this perfect mitzvah — how abundant is your goodness and how fulsome your reward! O generous one, may you be blessed without your gift being restrained, and with your Creator's blessings may your hand be blessed that it need never skimp — for whoever honors the Torah beautifully, may his body be honored powerfully to become strong.

*Quickly — Arise, arise, arise (*name of honoree*) son of (*honoree's father's name*) the groom of Bereishis bara — with permission of this holy congregation — to bless the great and awesome God. Let all swiftly respond Amen after you!*

יַעֲמוֹד *Arise (*name of honoree*) son of (*honoree's father's name*) the groom of Bereishis bara.*

❧ קריאת התורה / חתן בראשית ☙

It is customary for the reader to pause before each phrase printed in bold type.
The verses are chanted in unison by the congregation, then repeated by the reader.

בראשית א:א־ב:ג

בְּרֵאשִׁית* בָּרָא* אֱלֹהִים אֵת הַשָּׁמַיִם וְאֵת הָאָרֶץ:* וְהָאָרֶץ הָיְתָה
תֹהוּ וָבֹהוּ* וְחֹשֶׁךְ* עַל־פְּנֵי תְהוֹם וְרוּחַ אֱלֹהִים מְרַחֶפֶת עַל־פְּנֵי
הַמָּיִם: וַיֹּאמֶר אֱלֹהִים יְהִי אוֹר* וַיְהִי־אוֹר: וַיַּרְא אֱלֹהִים אֶת־הָאוֹר
כִּי־טוֹב* וַיַּבְדֵּל אֱלֹהִים בֵּין הָאוֹר וּבֵין הַחֹשֶׁךְ: וַיִּקְרָא אֱלֹהִים | לָאוֹר
יוֹם* וְלַחֹשֶׁךְ קָרָא לָיְלָה **וַיְהִי־עֶרֶב וַיְהִי־בֹקֶר* יוֹם אֶחָד:** וַיֹּאמֶר
אֱלֹהִים יְהִי רָקִיעַ* בְּתוֹךְ הַמָּיִם וִיהִי מַבְדִּיל בֵּין מַיִם לָמָיִם: וַיַּעַשׂ
אֱלֹהִים אֶת־הָרָקִיעַ* וַיַּבְדֵּל בֵּין הַמַּיִם אֲשֶׁר מִתַּחַת לָרָקִיעַ וּבֵין
הַמַּיִם אֲשֶׁר מֵעַל לָרָקִיעַ וַיְהִי־כֵן:* וַיִּקְרָא אֱלֹהִים לָרָקִיעַ שָׁמָיִם
וַיְהִי־עֶרֶב וַיְהִי־בֹקֶר יוֹם שֵׁנִי: וַיֹּאמֶר אֱלֹהִים יִקָּווּ הַמַּיִם מִתַּחַת

☙ Aliyah for Chassan Bereishis

Rav Yitzchak said: Since the Torah is the book of laws, it should have begun with *'This month shall be to you the first of the months'* (*Exodus* 12:2), for that was the first commandment given to all Israel. Why, then, did it begin with the narrative of Creation?

This was done to establish the sovereignty of God over the earth. כֹּחַ מַעֲשָׂיו הִגִּיד לְעַמּוֹ לָתֵת לָהֶם נַחֲלַת גּוֹיִם, *He declared to His people the power of His works in order to give them the heritage of the nations* (*Psalms* 111:6). If the nations accuse Israel of banditry for seizing the lands of the seven nations of Canaan, Israel will tell them: 'The entire universe belongs to God. He created it and He granted it to whomever was deemed fit in His eyes. It was His desire to give it to them and it was then His desire to take it from them and cede it to us.' (Based on *Rashi's* introductory comment.)

בְּרֵאשִׁית — *In the beginning of. Rashi* and others reject the familiar translation — *In the beginning, God created heaven and earth* — on two grounds: (a) The Hebrew word for *in the beginning* is בָּרִאשׁוֹנָה; the word בְּרֵאשִׁית means in the beginning *of something*; (b) The term *in the beginning* implies that we are being told the chronological order in which the components of the universe were created, meaning that heaven and earth were the first things to be created. This, however, cannot be true, because the next verse indicates that the waters pre-existed the earth.

Therefore, *Rashi* explains the verse as we have given it in the translation, i.e., *in the beginning of the creation of heaven and earth — when the earth was astonishingly empty ... — God created light.*

Homiletically, *Rashi* cites the Midrashic interpretation that the world was created for the sake of the things that are called רֵאשִׁית [= בְּרֵאשִׁית בִּשְׁבִיל רֵאשִׁית]. These things are the Torah (*Proverbs* 8:22) and Israel (*Jeremiah* 2:3). Thus, the Torah begins with the declaration that the universe was created for the sake of the Torah and the Jewish people.

בָּרָא — *Creating*. This verb [which Scripture uses exclusively with reference to Divine activity] implies that something is produced out of nothing — יֵשׁ מֵאַיִן [*creatio ex nihilo*].

אֵת הַשָּׁמַיִם וְאֵת הָאָרֶץ — *The heavens and the earth*. The words *heavens and earth* are to be understood as all-embracing terms, including the entire universe as we now know it.

תהו וָבֹהוּ — *Astonishingly empty* [or: *'desolate and void'*]. The desolation was absolute: There was neither tree, nor grass, man nor beast, bird nor fish nor insect; neither darkness nor light, wind [spirit] nor water — an utter vacuum (*B'chor Shor*).

וְחֹשֶׁךְ — *Darkness*. i.e., the utter darkness which enveloped all. The Talmud (*Chagigah* 12a) comments that *'darkness'* is one of the things created on the first day. Therefore, the commentators infer, *darkness* is not merely the absence of light, but a specific creation, as stated in *Isaiah* 45:7 where God describes Himself as יוֹצֵר אוֹר וּבוֹרֵא חֹשֶׁךְ, *He who forms the light and creates darkness.*

Light: From this point onward, we are given a detailed chronology of Creation (*Rashi*).

יְהִי אוֹר — *Let there be light*. God addresses the heavens — and all their potentials. He willed that from their substance there should come forth the brilliance called אוֹר, *light* (*Ramban*).

וַיַּרְא אֱלֹהִים אֶת הָאוֹר כִּי טוֹב — *God saw that the*

⁂ TORAH READING / CHASSAN BEREISHIS ⁂

It is customary for the reader to pause before each phrase printed in bold type. The verses are chanted in unison by the congregation, then repeated by the reader.

Genesis 1:1-2:3

In the beginning of God's creating* the heavens and the earth* — when the earth was astonishingly empty,* with darkness* upon the surface of the deep, and the Divine Presence hovered upon the surface of the waters — God said, 'Let there be light,' and there was light. God saw that the light was good,* and God separated between the light and the darkness. God called to the light: 'Day,'* and to the darkness He called: 'Night.'* **And there was evening and there was morning,* one day.**

God said, 'Let there be a firmament in the midst of the waters, and let it separate between water and water.' So God made the firmament,* and separated between the waters which were beneath the firmament and the waters which were above the firmament. And it was so.* God called to the firmament: 'Heaven.'* **And there was evening and there was morning, a second day.**

God said, 'Let the waters beneath the heaven be gathered into one

---

light was good. God saw that the wicked were unworthy of utilizing His light, and therefore He set it aside for the righteous in the hereafter (*Chagigah* 12a). But in the literal sense, *Rashi* explains the verse thus: He saw that it was good, but it was not proper that light and darkness should function simultaneously in a confused mixture. Consequently he assigned the light to daytime and darkness to nighttime.

וַיִּקְרָא אֱלֹהִים לָאוֹר יוֹם — *God called to the light: Day*. God summoned the light and appointed it for duty by day, and He summoned the darkness and appointed it for duty by night (*Pesachim* 2a), i.e., *calling* does not refer here to giving a name but rather to *summoning*, as a king summons his subject (*Rashi*, ad loc.).

At that time when the original light functioned, the periods of light and darkness were not determined by rotating spheres but by the Will of God, Who separated the time of light from the time of darkness (*Sforno*).

וַיְהִי עֶרֶב וַיְהִי בֹקֶר — *And there was evening and there was morning.* As indicated by this phrase, the day begins with the preceding evening (see *Mishnah Chullin* 5:5). Thus the Sabbaths and festivals begin in the evening — *from evening unto evening* (*Lev.* 23:32).

The intent of the verse, which can be understood to mean that morning and evening are present simultaneously, is: 'When it is evening in one part of the globe it is morning elsewhere . . .' (*Ha'amek Davar* citing *Baal HaMaor, Rosh Hashanah* 20b).

The second day: Creation of the firmament.

יְהִי רָקִיעַ — *Let there be a firmament* (or: *'expanse'*) — i.e., let the expanse solidify. Although the heavens were created on the first day, they were still in a state of flux, solidifying on the second day at God's command, יְהִי רָקִיעַ, *'Let there be a firmament'* (*Rashi; Midrash*).

וַיַּעַשׂ אֱלֹהִים אֶת הָרָקִיעַ — *So God made the firmament.* i.e., God 'completed' the expansion. He allowed the heavens to expand to a certain point and there He stopped further expansion (*R' E. Munk*).

וַיְהִי כֵן — *And it was so.* And so it became (*R' S. R. Hirsch*), i.e., this state of expanse became firmly established. There was to be no further development of the רָקִיעַ [firmament] which had formed between the waters (*Munk*).

Rashi notes that the Torah does not conclude this verse with the phrase כִּי טוֹב, *that it was good*, as it does on the other days of Creation, because the Torah does not describe an element of Creation as 'good' unless it is complete. Since the waters were not completed until the following day [when they were gathered and became seas], they could not yet be described as 'good'. However, on the third day, the expression *'that it was good'* is said twice — once for the completion of the second day's creation, and once for the new creation of the third day [plant life].

The third day: God decrees boundaries for the water, making way for the development of land and vegetation.

Until then the earth was a plain, entirely submerged under water. Scarcely had God's words, *'Let the waters be gathered'*, been uttered, when mountains and hills appeared all over and the waters collected in the deep-lying valleys. But the water threatened to overflow the earth until God forced it back into the sea, encircling

הַשָּׁמַיִם אֶל־מָקוֹם אֶחָד וְתֵרָאֶה הַיַּבָּשָׁה* וַיְהִי־כֵן: וַיִּקְרָא אֱלֹהִים ׀ לַיַּבָּשָׁה אֶרֶץ* וּלְמִקְוֵה הַמַּיִם קָרָא יַמִּים* וַיַּרְא אֱלֹהִים כִּי־טוֹב: וַיֹּאמֶר אֱלֹהִים תַּדְשֵׁא הָאָרֶץ דֶּשֶׁא* עֵשֶׂב מַזְרִיעַ זֶרַע עֵץ פְּרִי עֹשֶׂה פְּרִי לְמִינוֹ אֲשֶׁר זַרְעוֹ־בוֹ עַל־הָאָרֶץ וַיְהִי־כֵן: וַתּוֹצֵא הָאָרֶץ* דֶּשֶׁא עֵשֶׂב מַזְרִיעַ זֶרַע לְמִינֵהוּ וְעֵץ עֹשֶׂה־פְּרִי אֲשֶׁר זַרְעוֹ־בוֹ לְמִינֵהוּ וַיַּרְא אֱלֹהִים כִּי־טוֹב: **וַיְהִי־עֶרֶב וַיְהִי־בֹקֶר יוֹם שְׁלִישִׁי:** וַיֹּאמֶר אֱלֹהִים יְהִי מְאֹרֹת* בִּרְקִיעַ הַשָּׁמַיִם לְהַבְדִּיל בֵּין הַיּוֹם וּבֵין הַלָּיְלָה וְהָיוּ לְאֹתֹת וּלְמוֹעֲדִים* וּלְיָמִים וְשָׁנִים: וְהָיוּ לִמְאוֹרֹת בִּרְקִיעַ הַשָּׁמַיִם לְהָאִיר עַל־הָאָרֶץ וַיְהִי־כֵן: וַיַּעַשׂ אֱלֹהִים אֶת־שְׁנֵי הַמְּאֹרֹת הַגְּדֹלִים* אֶת־הַמָּאוֹר הַגָּדֹל לְמֶמְשֶׁלֶת הַיּוֹם וְאֶת־הַמָּאוֹר הַקָּטֹן לְמֶמְשֶׁלֶת הַלַּיְלָה וְאֵת הַכּוֹכָבִים: וַיִּתֵּן אֹתָם אֱלֹהִים* בִּרְקִיעַ הַשָּׁמָיִם* לְהָאִיר עַל־הָאָרֶץ: וְלִמְשֹׁל בַּיּוֹם וּבַלַּיְלָה וּֽלֲהַבְדִּיל בֵּין הָאוֹר וּבֵין הַחֹשֶׁךְ וַיַּרְא אֱלֹהִים כִּי־טוֹב:* **וַיְהִי־עֶרֶב וַיְהִי־בֹקֶר יוֹם רְבִיעִי:** וַיֹּאמֶר אֱלֹהִים יִשְׁרְצוּ הַמַּיִם שֶׁרֶץ נֶפֶשׁ חַיָּה וְעוֹף יְעוֹפֵף עַל־הָאָרֶץ עַל־פְּנֵי רְקִיעַ הַשָּׁמָיִם: וַיִּבְרָא אֱלֹהִים אֶת־הַתַּנִּינִם הַגְּדֹלִים וְאֵת כָּל־נֶפֶשׁ הַחַיָּה ׀ הָרֹמֶשֶׂת אֲשֶׁר שָׁרְצוּ הַמַּיִם לְמִינֵהֶם וְאֵת כָּל־עוֹף כָּנָף לְמִינֵהוּ וַיַּרְא אֱלֹהִים כִּי־טוֹב: וַיְבָרֶךְ אֹתָם אֱלֹהִים* לֵאמֹר פְּרוּ וּרְבוּ* וּמִלְאוּ אֶת־הַמַּיִם בַּיַּמִּים וְהָעוֹף יִרֶב

---

the sea with sand. Whenever the sea is tempted to transgress its bounds, it beholds the sand and recoils (*Pirkei d'Rabbi Eliezer; Zohar*).

וְתֵרָאֶה הַיַּבָּשָׁה – *That the dry land may appear* [or: *and let the dry land appear*]. This refers to the earth, which was created on the first day but had been neither visible nor dry until the waters were commanded to assemble (*Lekach Tov; Rashbam*).

וַיִּקְרָא אֱלֹהִים לַיַּבָּשָׁה אֶרֶץ – *God called to the dry land: Earth,* i.e., the terrestrial surface that was to be the scene of man's activity.

God named the earth and seas when they assumed their final forms, for initially both the waters and the dry land were referred to collectively as תְּהוֹם, *the deep* (*Ramban*).

וּלְמִקְוֵה הַמַּיִם קָרָא יַמִּים – *And to the gathering of waters He called: Seas.,* i.e., He said, 'Become seas!' Do not remain a single gathering of waters but diversify throughout the dry land and form separate seas. The seas divided the earth into separate continents and countries, thus making possible the development of nations (*R' S. R. Hirsch*).

תַּדְשֵׁא הָאָרֶץ דֶּשֶׁא – *Let the earth sprout vegetation,* i.e., let it be filled and covered with a garment of grasses (*Rashi*).

The earth was granted the power to sprout forth new vegetation forever, but man must first sow — only then will the ground yield up its produce. The exception to this rule was the first vegetation, which sprouted at God's command (*Aderes Eliyahu*).

וַתּוֹצֵא הָאָרֶץ – *And the earth brought forth.* The herbs emerged, but did not yet sprout forth fully as the *Talmud* notes:

Rav Assi perceived an apparent inconsistency between this verse, which says *'and the earth brought forth vegetation'*, and the verse describing the sixth day, which states that *'no shrub of the field was yet in the earth.'* This teaches that the herbs commenced to grow [on the third day], but stopped just as they were about to break through the soil, until Adam came and prayed for them. Then rain fell and they grew. This teaches you that God longs for the prayers of the righteous (*Chullin* 60b).

The fourth day: The luminaries.

R' Hirsch observes that the creations of the first three days are paralleled by those of the next three days: The light of the first day was provided with bearers [מְאֹרֹת] on the fourth day; the water and atmosphere of the second day

area, that the dry land may appear.' And it was so. God called to the dry land: 'Earth,'* and to the gathering of waters He called: 'Seas.'* And God saw that it was good. God said, 'Let the earth sprout vegetation:* herbage yielding seed, fruit trees yielding fruit each after its kind, containing its own seed on the earth.' And it was so. And the earth brought forth* vegetation: herbage yielding seed after its kind and trees yielding fruit, each containing its seed after its kind. And God saw that it was good.* **And there was evening and there was morning, a third day.**

God said, 'Let there be luminaries in the firmament of the heaven to separate between the day and the night; and they shall serve as signs, and for festivals,* and for days and years; and they shall serve as luminaries in the firmament of the heaven to shine upon the earth.' And it was so. And God made the two great luminaries,* the greater luminary to dominate the day and the lesser luminary to dominate the night; and the stars. And God set them* in the firmament of the heaven* to give light upon the earth, to dominate by day and by night, and to separate between the light and between the darkness. And God saw that it was good.** **And there was evening and there was morning, a fourth day.**

God said, 'Let the waters teem with creeping living creatures, and fowl that fly about over the earth across the expanse of the heavens.' And God created the great sea-giants and every living being that creeps, with which the waters teemed after their kinds; and all winged fowl of every kind. And God saw that it was good. God blessed them, saying, 'Be fruitful and multiply,* and fill the waters in the seas; but*

---

were filled with bird and fish life on the fifth day; and the dry land of the third day was provided with inhabitants on the sixth.

יְהִי מְאוֹרֹת — *Let there be luminaries.* They had already been created on the first day but were not suspended in the firmament until the fourth day (*Chagigah* 12a).

וּלְמוֹעֲדִים — *And for festivals.* i.e., as a guide to determining the festivals, which Israel would regulate according to the lunar calendar.

וַיַּעַשׂ אֱלֹהִים אֶת שְׁנֵי הַמְּאֹרֹת הַגְּדֹלִים — *And God made the two great luminaries.* They were originally created of equal size, but the moon was made smaller because it complained and said, 'It is impossible for two kings to make use of the same crown' [it thus demanded more power than the sun, and was punished by being made smaller] (*Chullin* 60b; *Rashi*); see *Overview* to ArtScroll *Bereishis.*

וַיִּתֵּן אֹתָם אֱלֹהִים — *And God set them,* i.e., He put them into fixed orbits (*R' E. Munk*).

בִּרְקִיעַ הַשָּׁמָיִם — *In the firmament of the heaven.* These concepts are beyond man's grasp. 'It is an exceedingly difficult matter and no mortal can fathom it' (*Midrash*).

וַיַּרְא אֱלֹהִים כִּי טוֹב — *And God saw that it was good,* i.e., that it could not be more perfect. Had the sun been larger or closer to the earth, its heat would have scorched the earth; or had its orbit been lower, parts of the earth would have become frozen. Similarly — every constellation is in its proper place (*Abarbanel*).

The fifth day: Marine life and birds.

וַיְבָרֶךְ אֹתָם אֱלֹהִים — *(And) God blessed them. Rashi* notes that fish and fowl needed a special blessing because so many are caught and eaten. The land animals did not receive a blessing so as not to include the serpent, which was destined to be cursed.

פְּרוּ וּרְבוּ — *Be fruitful and multiply.* Had the verse not added וּרְבוּ, *and multiply,* each creature would produce only one offspring — 'multiply' implies multiple birth: One should bring forth many (*Rashi*).

This cannot be a command, because the power of reproduction belongs only to God. Rather it is a Divine blessing and endowment: 'You will be fruitful and multiply.'

וְהָעוֹף יִרֶב בָּאָרֶץ — *But the fowl shall increase on the earth.* Although the fowl were originally created from the water, they would be fruitful

בָּאָרֶץ:* וַיְהִי־עֶרֶב וַיְהִי־בֹקֶר יוֹם חֲמִישִׁי: וַיֹּאמֶר אֱלֹהִים תּוֹצֵא
הָאָרֶץ* נֶפֶשׁ חַיָּה לְמִינָהּ* בְּהֵמָה וָרֶמֶשׂ וְחַיְתוֹ־אֶרֶץ לְמִינָהּ וַיְהִי־
כֵן: וַיַּעַשׂ אֱלֹהִים* אֶת־חַיַּת הָאָרֶץ לְמִינָהּ וְאֶת־הַבְּהֵמָה לְמִינָהּ
וְאֵת כָּל־רֶמֶשׂ הָאֲדָמָה לְמִינֵהוּ וַיַּרְא אֱלֹהִים כִּי־טוֹב:* וַיֹּאמֶר
אֱלֹהִים* נַעֲשֶׂה* אָדָם* בְּצַלְמֵנוּ* כִּדְמוּתֵנוּ* וְיִרְדּוּ בִדְגַת הַיָּם וּבְעוֹף
הַשָּׁמַיִם וּבַבְּהֵמָה וּבְכָל־הָאָרֶץ וּבְכָל־הָרֶמֶשׂ הָרֹמֵשׂ עַל־הָאָרֶץ:
וַיִּבְרָא אֱלֹהִים ׀ אֶת־הָאָדָם בְּצַלְמוֹ בְּצֶלֶם אֱלֹהִים בָּרָא אֹתוֹ זָכָר
וּנְקֵבָה בָּרָא אֹתָם:* וַיְבָרֶךְ אֹתָם אֱלֹהִים וַיֹּאמֶר לָהֶם אֱלֹהִים פְּרוּ
וּרְבוּ וּמִלְאוּ אֶת־הָאָרֶץ וְכִבְשֻׁהָ* וּרְדוּ בִּדְגַת הַיָּם וּבְעוֹף הַשָּׁמַיִם
וּבְכָל־חַיָּה הָרֹמֶשֶׂת עַל־הָאָרֶץ: וַיֹּאמֶר אֱלֹהִים הִנֵּה נָתַתִּי לָכֶם
אֶת־כָּל־עֵשֶׂב ׀ זֹרֵעַ זֶרַע אֲשֶׁר עַל־פְּנֵי כָל־הָאָרֶץ וְאֶת־כָּל־הָעֵץ
אֲשֶׁר־בּוֹ פְרִי־עֵץ זֹרֵעַ זָרַע לָכֶם יִהְיֶה לְאָכְלָה: וּלְכָל־חַיַּת הָאָרֶץ
וּלְכָל־עוֹף הַשָּׁמַיִם וּלְכֹל ׀ רוֹמֵשׂ עַל־הָאָרֶץ אֲשֶׁר־בּוֹ נֶפֶשׁ חַיָּה
אֶת־כָּל־יֶרֶק עֵשֶׂב לְאָכְלָה וַיְהִי־כֵן:* וַיַּרְא אֱלֹהִים אֶת־כָּל־

---

and multiply *on the earth*, for all fowl — even those that live upon the water — lay their eggs on land (*Ramban*).

The sixth day: Animals and man.

תּוֹצֵא הָאָרֶץ – *Let the earth bring forth.* תּוֹצֵא, *bring forth*, implies a concealed presence coming into existence (*Ahavas Yonasan*); for as explained earlier, the potential for everything was created on the first day; it was necessary only to *bring them forth* (*Rashi*).

נֶפֶשׁ חַיָּה לְמִינָהּ – *Living creatures* [lit., *a living soul*] *according to their kind*, i.e., 'Free-living, breathing beings yielding their own species . . . The term could also include any living thing not specifically mentioned, as, for example, germs' (*R' E. Munk*).

וַיַּעַשׂ אֱלֹהִים – *God made;* i.e, He shaped them as they would have wished to be in their full volition and full-grown stature (*Chullin* 60b; *Rashi*).

He endowed each species with whatever senses and faculties it required (*Sforno*).

וַיַּרְא אֱלֹהִים כִּי טוֹב – *And God saw that it was good.* Even though some creatures would prove to be injurious, the overall usefulness of animals was obvious (*Radak*).

Man: Having completed all forms of creation, God said: *'Let us make man.'* Like a person who builds a palace and, having furnished and decorated it, ushers in its owner so it is ready for his immediate dwelling (*R' Saadiah Gaon*) [Cf. *Sanhedrin* 38a].

וַיֹּאמֶר אֱלֹהִים – *And God said.* In recognition of man's superiority, there was a special אֲמִירָה, *utterance*, dedicated to his creation (*Ramban*).

נַעֲשֶׂה אָדָם – *Let us make man.* This preamble indicates that man was created only after great deliberation and wisdom. God did not attribute man's creation to the earth, by decreeing, *'Let the earth bring forth*,' as He did with other creatures. Instead, He attributes it to the deepest involvement of Divine Providence and wisdom (*Abarbanel*).

B'chor Shor notes that the verb נַעֲשֶׂה, *make*, here implies (and throughout this chapter) 'bringing to a state of final completion.' The intent is: 'Let us bring to perfection the as-yet-uncreated man, whose image and form awesomely equip him to rule and govern . . .'

נַעֲשֶׂה – *Let us make.* [The commentators note the use of the plural.]

Targum Yonasan paraphrases: And God said to the ministering angels who had been created on the second day of the creation, 'Let us make man!'

These are the angels who minister before Him continually, such as Michael, Gabriel, et al. They are referred to by the Sages as פַּמַלְיָא שֶׁל מַעְלָה, *the heavenly household*. It was with them, the Sages tell us, that God 'consulted' before creating man (*Ahavas Yonasan*).

Ramban explains that the plural denotes God

*the fowl shall increase on the earth.'** **And there was evening and there was morning, a fifth day.**

God said, 'Let the earth bring forth living creatures according to their kind:* cattle, and creeping things, and beasts of the land according to their kind.' And it was so. God made* the beast of the land after its own kind, and the cattle after its own kind, and every creeping being of the ground after their kind. And God saw that it was good.**

And God said, 'Let us make* man* in Our image,* after Our likeness.* They shall rule over the fish of the sea, the birds of the sky, and over the cattle, the whole earth, and every creeping thing that creeps upon the earth.' So God created man in His image, in the image of God He created him; male and female He created them.**

God blessed them and God said to them, 'Be fruitful and multiply, fill the earth and subdue it; and rule over the fish of the sea, the bird of the sky, and every living thing that moves on earth.'*

God said, 'Behold, I have given to you all herbage yielding seed that is upon the entire earth, and every tree that has seed-yielding fruit; it shall be yours for food. And to every beast of the earth, to every bird of the sky, and to everything that moves on earth, within which there is a living soul, every green herb is for food.' And it was so. And God saw all*

---

and the earth: Concerning the 'living soul' [of animals] God commanded, *'Let the earth bring forth.'* But in the case of man He said, *'Let us make'* — i.e., Me and the earth, the earth to produce the body ... as it did the cattle and beasts, and the higher spirit that would come from the 'mouth' of God.

אָדָם – *Man [Adam].* A general term for mankind as a whole. As evidenced in *Genesis* 5:2, the term applies to both the male and female: 'He called *their* name Adam' (*B'chor Shor; Chizkuni*).

The term is related to *adamah* [ground], from which man was created: When God created man from the upper and lower elements He called him Adam, as if to say, although his spirit is from the heavens, he is nevertheless *adam,* for his body was formed from the *adamah* (*Radak*).

Man's mission on earth is not related to any particular zone or climate ... the whole world being meant to be אֲדָמָה, 'Adam's earth' (*R' S. R. Hirsch*).

בְּצַלְמֵנוּ – *In Our image,* i.e., in the mold that God prepared for man, it being impossible to say that God has an image or 'mold' (*Sifsei Chachomim*).

כִּדְמוּתֵנוּ – *After Our likeness,* i.e., with the power of understanding and intellect (*Rashi*).

זָכָר וּנְקֵבָה בָּרָא אֹתָם – *Male and female He created them. Rashi* notes an apparent contradiction between this verse and *Genesis* 2:21, which says that only Adam was created by God and that Eve was created later from his side.

Rashi comments that the Torah informs us here that both were created on the sixth day, while the *details* of their creation are expanded upon in 2:21. According to the *Midrash,* man was created originally with two פָּנִים, *faces* — i.e., male and female halves — and afterwards God divided them [see *Eruvin* 18a and comm. to 5:2].

The word פָּנִים, *faces,* also means outlook, perspective. The original man contained a duality which was later separated into male and female, each with its own personality and outlook (*Harav Gifter*).

וְכִבְשֻׁהָ – *And subdue it.* Man should bring the creatures of the earth under his control (*Radak*).

Originally, man and beast shared the same diet — all were to eat herbs. Man was not permitted to use animals for food until after the flood [cf. 9:3 and *Sanhedrin* 59b] (*Rashi; Ibn Ezra*).

Ramban explains that meat was prohibited because moving creatures have a certain spiritual superiority — somewhat akin to rational creatures. It was only after they sinned [*Gen.* 6:12] and God decreed that they perish in the Flood that He saved some of them to preserve the species and He permitted Noah's offspring to slaughter and eat them.

וַיְהִי כֵן – *And it was so,* i.e., that all creatures became endowed with the desire for the food which was meant for them (*Radak*).

וַיַּרְא אֱלֹהִים אֶת כָּל אֲשֶׁר עָשָׂה – *And God saw all*

אֲשֶׁר עָשָׂה וְהִנֵּה־טוֹב מְאֹד וַיְהִי־עֶרֶב וַיְהִי־בֹקֶר יוֹם הַשִּׁשִּׁי: וַיְכֻלּוּ הַשָּׁמַיִם וְהָאָרֶץ וְכָל־צְבָאָם: וַיְכַל אֱלֹהִים בַּיּוֹם הַשְּׁבִיעִי מְלַאכְתּוֹ אֲשֶׁר עָשָׂה וַיִּשְׁבֹּת בַּיּוֹם הַשְּׁבִיעִי מִכָּל־מְלַאכְתּוֹ אֲשֶׁר עָשָׂה: וַיְבָרֶךְ אֱלֹהִים אֶת־יוֹם הַשְּׁבִיעִי וַיְקַדֵּשׁ אֹתוֹ כִּי בוֹ שָׁבַת מִכָּל־מְלַאכְתּוֹ אֲשֶׁר־בָּרָא אֱלֹהִים לַעֲשׂוֹת:

חצי קדיש

After the *Chassan Bereishis* has completed his closing blessing, the third Torah Scroll is placed on the *bimah* alongside the second, and the reader recites Half-*Kaddish*.

יִתְגַּדַּל וְיִתְקַדַּשׁ שְׁמֵהּ רַבָּא. (.Cong – אָמֵן.) בְּעָלְמָא דִּי בְרָא כִרְעוּתֵהּ. וְיַמְלִיךְ מַלְכוּתֵהּ, בְּחַיֵּיכוֹן וּבְיוֹמֵיכוֹן וּבְחַיֵּי דְכָל בֵּית יִשְׂרָאֵל, בַּעֲגָלָא וּבִזְמַן קָרִיב. וְאִמְרוּ: אָמֵן.

(.Cong – אָמֵן. יְהֵא שְׁמֵהּ רַבָּא מְבָרַךְ לְעָלַם וּלְעָלְמֵי עָלְמַיָּא.)

יְהֵא שְׁמֵהּ רַבָּא מְבָרַךְ לְעָלַם וּלְעָלְמֵי עָלְמַיָּא.

יִתְבָּרַךְ וְיִשְׁתַּבַּח וְיִתְפָּאַר וְיִתְרוֹמַם וְיִתְנַשֵּׂא וְיִתְהַדָּר וְיִתְעַלֶּה וְיִתְהַלָּל שְׁמֵהּ דְּקֻדְשָׁא בְּרִיךְ הוּא (.Cong – בְּרִיךְ הוּא) – לְעֵלָּא מִן כָּל בִּרְכָתָא וְשִׁירָתָא תֻּשְׁבְּחָתָא וְנֶחֱמָתָא, דַּאֲמִירָן בְּעָלְמָא. וְאִמְרוּ: אָמֵן. (.Cong – אָמֵן.)

הגבהה וגלילה

The second Torah is raised in the usual manner. Each person looks at the Torah and recites aloud:

וְזֹאת הַתּוֹרָה אֲשֶׁר שָׂם מֹשֶׁה לִפְנֵי בְּנֵי יִשְׂרָאֵל,[1] עַל פִּי יהוה בְּיַד מֹשֶׁה.[2]

---

that He had made [even the evil inclination]. Because, as the Sages teach, were it not for the evil inclination, man would neither marry nor have children, with the result that the world would remain barren (*Chizkuni*).

וְהִנֵּה טוֹב מְאֹד – *And behold it was very good*. I.e., everything in creation was suited to its purpose and continually able to act accordingly (*Moreh Nevuchim* 13).

This verse includes the creation of those destructive forces which, when viewed in context with the rest of creation, are necessary and integral (*Ha'amek Davar*).

As *Harav Gifter* notes, the Sages teach that in Time to Come, people will make the same blessing for evil as for good, because they will come to realize that every manifestation of God's will is genuinely good.

וַיְהִי עֶרֶב וַיְהִי בֹקֶר יוֹם הַשִּׁשִּׁי – *And there was evening and there was morning, the sixth day*. The commentators note the unusual use of the definite article ה, *the*, before the word שִׁשִּׁי, *sixth*:

It designates 'the day that is distinguished from the other days of Creation as the day on which His work was completed' (*Chizkuni*).

It is also kabbalistically pointed out in this context that this group of words יוֹם הַשִּׁשִּׁי וַיְכֻלּוּ הַשָּׁמַיִם form an acrostic of the Four-letter Divine Name.

[And so, with the expression of *'very good'*, the six days of creation — preparatory to the seventh day, Sabbath — come to a close.]

The seventh day: Sabbath.

This paragraph attests to the Divine nature of creation and its completion on the Sabbath. Therefore it was appended to the Friday evening service and also recited to introduce the Sabbath *Kiddush* [santification], because Sabbath, too, bears testimony to the fact that the Creator rested after completing the universe in six days (see *Shabbos* 119b and *Orach Chaim* 268.)

וַיְכֻלּוּ הַשָּׁמַיִם וְהָאָרֶץ – *Thus the heaven and the earth were finished*. Now, with the end of the sixth day, the heavens and earth stand before us in their final intended state in complete, harmonious perfection.

that He had made, and behold it was very good.** **And there was evening and there was morning, the sixth day.**

Thus the heaven and the earth were finished,* and all their array.* By the seventh day God completed* His work which He had done,* and He abstained on the seventh day from all His work which He had done.* God blessed the seventh day and hallowed it,* because on it He abstained from all His work which God created to perfect.*

HALF KADDISH

After the *Chassan Bereishis* has completed his closing blessing, the third Torah Scroll is placed on the *bimah* alongside the second, and the reader recites Half-*Kaddish:*

יִתְגַּדַּל *May His great Name grow exalted and sanctified* (Cong.– *Amen.*) *in the world that He created as He willed. May He give reign to His kingship in your lifetimes and in your days, and in the lifetimes of the entire Family of Israel, swiftly and soon. Now respond: Amen.*

(Cong.– *Amen. May His great Name be blessed forever and ever.*)

May His great Name be blessed forever and ever.

Blessed, praised, glorified, exalted, extolled, mighty, upraised, and lauded be the Name of the Holy One, Blessed is He (Cong.– *Blessed is He*) — *beyond any blessing and song, praise and consolation that are uttered in the world. Now respond: Amen.* (Cong.– *Amen.*)

HAGBAHAH AND GELILAH

The second Torah is raised in the usual manner. Each person looks at the Torah and recites aloud:

This is the Torah that Moses placed before the Children of Israel,[1] upon the command of HASHEM, through Moses' hand.[2]

(1) *Deuteronomy* 4:44. (2) *Numbers* 9:23.

וְכָל צְבָאָם – *And all their array.* The *'host' of the earth* refers to the beasts, creeping things, fish, all growing things, and man; *the 'host' of the heavens* refers to the luminaries and the stars. The phrase also alludes to the formation of the angels as part of creation (*Ramban*).

וַיְכַל אֱלֹהִים בַּיּוֹם הַשְּׁבִיעִי – [And] *by the seventh day God completed.* He continued to create until the moment the seventh day began, and ceased from all work thereon — as part of His master plan, for He intended the Sabbath to be a day of rest (*Gur Aryeh*).

מְלַאכְתּוֹ אֲשֶׁר עָשָׂה – *His work which He had done,* i.e., throughout the six days; everything was now in a state of completion (*R' Myuchas*).

Thus, God concluded His purposeful work (מְלַאכְתּוֹ) so that no further creative action would follow, other than the maintenance of the completed universe in its existing working condition (*R' E. Munk*).

וַיְבָרֶךְ אֱלֹהִים אֶת יוֹם הַשְּׁבִיעִי וַיְקַדֵּשׁ אֹתוֹ – [*And*] *God blessed the seventh day and hallowed it. Blessing* refers to abundant goodness, for on Sabbath there is both a renewal of physical strength, and a greater intellectual capacity. *He hallowed it* by doing no work on it as He did on the other days (*Ibn Ezra*).

According to *R' Saadiah Gaon* the blessing and sanctification refer prophetically to those who observe the sanctity of the Sabbath, for they will be blessed and sanctified.

The *blessing* was that people would not experience need because of not working on Shabbos, *'it is the blessing of HASHEM that makes rich'* [*Proverbs* 10:22] . . .

אֲשֶׁר בָּרָא אֱלֹהִים לַעֲשׂוֹת – *Which God created to perfect.* The verb עשה always means putting an object into its ultimate condition (*Ramban* to 1:7).

God created all living creatures with the capacity to reproduce according to their species (*Radak*).

Thus, with the concluding phrase אֲשֶׁר בָּרָא, reminiscent of the introductory phrase בְּרֵאשִׁית בָּרָא, the narrative of the seven days closes (*Minchah Belulah*).

Some add:

עֵץ חַיִּים הִיא לַמַּחֲזִיקִים בָּהּ, וְתֹמְכֶיהָ מְאֻשָּׁר.[1] דְּרָכֶיהָ דַרְכֵי נֹעַם, וְכָל נְתִיבוֹתֶיהָ שָׁלוֹם.[2] אֹרֶךְ יָמִים בִּימִינָהּ, בִּשְׂמֹאלָהּ עֹשֶׁר וְכָבוֹד.[3] יהוה חָפֵץ לְמַעַן צִדְקוֹ, יַגְדִּיל תּוֹרָה וְיַאְדִּיר.[4]

מפטיר

As the second Torah is wound, tied, and covered, the *oleh* for *Maftir* is called to the third Torah.

במדבר כט:לה-ל:א

בַּיּוֹם הַשְּׁמִינִי עֲצֶרֶת* תִּהְיֶה לָכֶם כָּל־מְלֶאכֶת עֲבֹדָה לֹא תַעֲשׂוּ: וְהִקְרַבְתֶּם עֹלָה אִשֵּׁה רֵיחַ נִיחֹחַ לַיהוָה פַּר אֶחָד אַיִל אֶחָד* כְּבָשִׂים בְּנֵי־שָׁנָה שִׁבְעָה תְּמִימִם: מִנְחָתָם וְנִסְכֵּיהֶם לַפָּר לָאַיִל וְלַכְּבָשִׂים בְּמִסְפָּרָם כַּמִּשְׁפָּט: וּשְׂעִיר חַטָּאת אֶחָד מִלְּבַד עֹלַת הַתָּמִיד וּמִנְחָתָהּ וְנִסְכָּהּ: אֵלֶּה תַּעֲשׂוּ לַיהוָה בְּמוֹעֲדֵיכֶם* לְבַד מִנִּדְרֵיכֶם וְנִדְבֹתֵיכֶם לְעֹלֹתֵיכֶם וּלְמִנְחֹתֵיכֶם וּלְנִסְכֵּיכֶם וּלְשַׁלְמֵיכֶם: וַיֹּאמֶר מֹשֶׁה אֶל־בְּנֵי יִשְׂרָאֵל כְּכֹל אֲשֶׁר־צִוָּה יהוָה אֶת־מֹשֶׁה:

הגבהה וגלילה

The *maftir* completes his closing blessing.
The third Torah is raised in the usual manner. Each person looks at the Torah and recites aloud:

וְזֹאת הַתּוֹרָה אֲשֶׁר שָׂם מֹשֶׁה לִפְנֵי בְּנֵי יִשְׂרָאֵל,[5] עַל פִּי יהוה בְּיַד מֹשֶׁה.[6]

Some add:

עֵץ חַיִּים הִיא לַמַּחֲזִיקִים בָּהּ, וְתֹמְכֶיהָ מְאֻשָּׁר.[1] דְּרָכֶיהָ דַרְכֵי נֹעַם, וְכָל נְתִיבוֹתֶיהָ שָׁלוֹם.[2] אֹרֶךְ יָמִים בִּימִינָהּ, בִּשְׂמֹאלָהּ עֹשֶׁר וְכָבוֹד.[3] יהוה חָפֵץ לְמַעַן צִדְקוֹ, יַגְדִּיל תּוֹרָה וְיַאְדִּיר.[4]

After the Torah Scroll has been wound, tied and covered, the *maftir* recites the *Haftarah* blessings.

ברכה קודם ההפטרה

בָּרוּךְ אַתָּה יהוה אֱלֹהֵינוּ מֶלֶךְ הָעוֹלָם, אֲשֶׁר בָּחַר בִּנְבִיאִים טוֹבִים, וְרָצָה בְדִבְרֵיהֶם הַנֶּאֱמָרִים בֶּאֱמֶת, בָּרוּךְ אַתָּה יהוה, הַבּוֹחֵר בַּתּוֹרָה וּבְמֹשֶׁה עַבְדּוֹ, וּבְיִשְׂרָאֵל עַמּוֹ, וּבִנְבִיאֵי הָאֱמֶת וָצֶדֶק: (Cong. – אָמֵן.)

◆§ Maftir

בַּיּוֹם הַשְּׁמִינִי עֲצֶרֶת – *The eighth day ... an assembly. Rashi* comments that the word עֲצֶרֶת derives from עצר, to *restrain*, and offers three interpretations based on this translation: (1) restrain yourselves from work; (2) restrain yourselves from leaving Jerusalem, because one must remain at least overnight after a festival; and (3) after a festival during which *Mussaf* offerings were brought daily to invoke God's protection for the seventy nations, God asks us to remain for one day that is devoted solely to the unique relationship of God and Israel.

פַּר אֶחָד אַיִל אֶחָד – *One bull, one ram.* Unlike

Some add:

עֵץ *It is a tree of life for those who grasp it, and its supporters are praiseworthy.*[1] *Its ways are ways of pleasantness and all its paths are peace.*[2] *Lengthy days are at its right; at its left are wealth and honor.*[3] *HASHEM desired, for the sake of its [Israel's] righteousness, that the Torah be made great and glorious.*[4]

MAFTIR

As the second Torah is wound, tied, and covered, the *oleh* for *Maftir* is called to the third Torah.

Numbers 29:35-30:1

The eighth day shall be an assembly for you; you may not do any laborious work. You are to offer an elevation-offering, a fire-offering, a satisfying aroma to HASHEM; one bull, one ram,* seven lambs within their first years; they are all to be unblemished. Their meal-offerings and libations for the bull, the ram, and the lambs are to be in their proper numbers as required. And one he-goat for a sin-offering; aside from the continual elevation-offering, and its meal-offering and its libation. These are what you should offer to HASHEM on your appointed festivals;* aside from your vows and your free-will offerings for your elevation-offerings, your meal-offerings, your libations, and your peace-offerings.*

Moses spoke to the Children of Israel; according to everything that HASHEM commanded Moses.

HAGBAHAH AND GELILAH

The *maftir* completes his closing blessing.
The third Torah is raised in the usual manner. Each person looks at the Torah and recites aloud:

This is the Torah that Moses placed before the Children of Israel,[5] **upon the command of HASHEM, through Moses' hand.**[6]

Some add:

עֵץ *It is a tree of life for those who grasp it, and its supporters are praiseworthy.*[1] *Its ways are ways of pleasantness and all its paths are peace.*[2] *Lengthy days are at its right; at its left are wealth and honor.*[3] *HASHEM desired, for the sake of its [Israel's] righteousness, that the Torah be made great and glorious.*[4]

After the Torah Scroll has been wound, tied and covered, the *maftir* recites the *Haftarah* blessings.

BLESSING BEFORE THE HAFTARAH

בָּרוּךְ *Blessed are You, HASHEM, our God, King of the universe, Who has chosen good prophets and was pleased with their words that were uttered with truth. Blessed are You, HASHEM, Who chooses the Torah; Moses, His servant; Israel, His nation; and the prophets of truth and righteousness.*

(Cong.— *Amen.*)

(1) *Proverbs* 3:18. (2) 3:17. (3) 3:16. (4) *Isaiah* 42:21. (5) *Deuteronomy* 4:44. (6) *Numbers* 9:23.

Succos when the *Mussaf* offerings symbolize the seventy national groups, on Shemini Atzeres, the *Mussaf* symbolizes God's one, Chosen nation.

בְּמוֹעֲדֵיכֶם — *On your appointed festivals.* This verse sums up the list of *Mussaf* offerings for all respective festival days. The above list is required of the nation; individuals may make private *vows* and bring *free-willed offerings* as they see fit.

הפטרה לשמחת תורה

יהושע א:א-יח

וַיְהִי אַחֲרֵי מוֹת מֹשֶׁה* עֶבֶד יְהוָה וַיֹּאמֶר יְהוָה אֶל־יְהוֹשֻׁעַ בִּן־נוּן מְשָׁרֵת מֹשֶׁה* לֵאמֹר: מֹשֶׁה עַבְדִּי מֵת וְעַתָּה קוּם עֲבֹר אֶת־הַיַּרְדֵּן הַזֶּה אַתָּה וְכָל־הָעָם הַזֶּה אֶל־הָאָרֶץ אֲשֶׁר אָנֹכִי נֹתֵן לָהֶם לִבְנֵי יִשְׂרָאֵל: כָּל־מָקוֹם אֲשֶׁר תִּדְרֹךְ כַּף־רַגְלְכֶם* בּוֹ לָכֶם נְתַתִּיו כַּאֲשֶׁר דִּבַּרְתִּי אֶל־מֹשֶׁה: מֵהַמִּדְבָּר וְהַלְּבָנוֹן הַזֶּה וְעַד־הַנָּהָר הַגָּדוֹל נְהַר־פְּרָת כֹּל אֶרֶץ הַחִתִּים וְעַד־הַיָּם הַגָּדוֹל מְבוֹא הַשָּׁמֶשׁ יִהְיֶה גְּבוּלְכֶם: לֹא־יִתְיַצֵּב אִישׁ* לְפָנֶיךָ כֹּל יְמֵי חַיֶּיךָ כַּאֲשֶׁר הָיִיתִי עִם־מֹשֶׁה אֶהְיֶה עִמָּךְ לֹא אַרְפְּךָ וְלֹא אֶעֶזְבֶךָּ: חֲזַק וֶאֱמָץ כִּי אַתָּה תַּנְחִיל אֶת־הָעָם הַזֶּה אֶת־הָאָרֶץ אֲשֶׁר־נִשְׁבַּעְתִּי לַאֲבוֹתָם לָתֵת לָהֶם: רַק חֲזַק וֶאֱמַץ מְאֹד לִשְׁמֹר לַעֲשׂוֹת כְּכָל־הַתּוֹרָה אֲשֶׁר צִוְּךָ מֹשֶׁה עַבְדִּי אַל־תָּסוּר מִמֶּנּוּ יָמִין וּשְׂמֹאול לְמַעַן תַּשְׂכִּיל* בְּכֹל אֲשֶׁר תֵּלֵךְ: לֹא־יָמוּשׁ* סֵפֶר הַתּוֹרָה הַזֶּה מִפִּיךָ וְהָגִיתָ בּוֹ יוֹמָם וָלַיְלָה* לְמַעַן תִּשְׁמֹר לַעֲשׂוֹת כְּכָל־הַכָּתוּב בּוֹ כִּי־אָז תַּצְלִיחַ אֶת־דְּרָכֶךָ וְאָז תַּשְׂכִּיל: הֲלוֹא צִוִּיתִיךָ חֲזַק וֶאֱמָץ אַל־תַּעֲרֹץ וְאַל־תֵּחָת כִּי עִמְּךָ יְהוָה אֱלֹהֶיךָ בְּכֹל אֲשֶׁר תֵּלֵךְ: וַיְצַו יְהוֹשֻׁעַ אֶת־שֹׁטְרֵי הָעָם לֵאמֹר: עִבְרוּ | בְּקֶרֶב הַמַּחֲנֶה וְצַוּוּ אֶת־הָעָם לֵאמֹר הָכִינוּ לָכֶם צֵדָה כִּי בְּעוֹד | שְׁלֹשֶׁת יָמִים אַתֶּם עֹבְרִים אֶת־הַיַּרְדֵּן הַזֶּה לָבוֹא לָרֶשֶׁת אֶת־הָאָרֶץ אֲשֶׁר יְהוָה אֱלֹהֵיכֶם נֹתֵן לָכֶם לְרִשְׁתָּהּ: וְלָראוּבֵנִי* וְלַגָּדִי וְלַחֲצִי שֵׁבֶט הַמְנַשֶּׁה אָמַר יְהוֹשֻׁעַ לֵאמֹר: זָכוֹר אֶת־הַדָּבָר אֲשֶׁר צִוָּה אֶתְכֶם מֹשֶׁה עֶבֶד־יְהוָה לֵאמֹר יְהוָה אֱלֹהֵיכֶם מֵנִיחַ לָכֶם וְנָתַן לָכֶם אֶת־הָאָרֶץ הַזֹּאת: נְשֵׁיכֶם טַפְּכֶם וּמִקְנֵיכֶם יֵשְׁבוּ בָּאָרֶץ אֲשֶׁר נָתַן לָכֶם מֹשֶׁה בְּעֵבֶר הַיַּרְדֵּן וְאַתֶּם תַּעַבְרוּ חֲמֻשִׁים לִפְנֵי אֲחֵיכֶם כֹּל גִּבּוֹרֵי הַחַיִל וַעֲזַרְתֶּם אוֹתָם: עַד אֲשֶׁר־

Haftarah for Simchas Torah

Having finished the year's Torah reading on Simchas Torah, we continue on to the first chapter of the prophets. A further reason for the choice of this *Haftarah* is that the death of Moses and the succession of his disciple Joshua are closely related.

אַחֲרֵי מוֹת מֹשֶׁה — *After the death of Moses.* Moses died on 7 Adar. The command to Joshua to cross the Jordan came on 7 Nissan, the end of the thirty-day mourning period.

מְשָׁרֵת מֹשֶׁה — *Moses' attendant.* Joshua earned his greatness because of the loyal personal service he rendered Moses. The Talmud (*Berachos* 7b) teaches that one gains more from serving a scholar and learning from his personal behavior than from study alone.

אֲשֶׁר תִּדְרֹךְ כַּף רַגְלְכֶם — *Upon which the sole of your foot will march.* Since the boundaries of *Eretz Yisrael* are given later in the verse, this phrase can only mean that even land outside of those boundaries, if conquered, can become part of *Eretz Yisrael.*

לֹא יִתְיַצֵּב אִישׁ — *No man will challenge you.* Since

HAFTARAH FOR SIMCHAS TORAH

Joshua 1:1-18

And it was after the death of Moses, servant of* HASHEM, *that* HASHEM *said to Joshua son of Nun, Moses' attendant,* saying, 'Moses My servant has died. Now, arise! Cross this Jordan, you and all this people, to the Land which I give to them, to the Children of Israel.*[3] *Every place upon which the sole of your foot will march* I have given to you, as I have spoken to Moses. From the desert and this Lebanon to the great river, the Euphrates River, all the land of the Hittites to the Mediterranean Sea westward will be your boundary. No man will challenge you* all the days of your life. As I was with Moses so will I be with you; I will not let you part from Me nor will I abandon you. Strengthen yourself and persevere because you will cause this people to inherit the Land which I have sworn to their fathers to give to them. O that you will strengthen yourself and persevere very much in order to observe, to do, according to all of the Torah that Moses My servant has commanded you. Do not deviate from it to the right or to the left, that you may succeed* wherever you may go. This Book of the Torah is not to leave* your mouth. You should contemplate it day and night* in order to observe, to do, all that is written in it. For then you will make your ways successful, and then you will become understanding. In truth I commanded you, "Strengthen yourself and persevere." Do not fear and do not lose resolve, because* HASHEM, *your God, is with you wherever you may go.'*

And Joshua commanded the marshals of the people, saying, 'Circulate within the camp and command the people, saying, "Prepare yourselves provisions because in another three days you will cross this Jordan to come to inherit the Land which HASHEM, *your God, is giving you as an inheritance." '*

And to the tribes of Reuben and Gad and part of the tribe of Menashe, Joshua had said, 'Remember that matter which Moses, servant of* HASHEM, *commanded you, saying, "*HASHEM *your God gives you rest, and He will give you this Land." Your wives, your children and your cattle will reside in the Land which Moses had given to you across the Jordan. Then you will cross over, armed, before your brothers — all the mighty warriors — and you will help them, until*

---

no one could take Moses' place, God reassured Joshua by guaranteeing that his position would never be disputed. The prophecy goes on to exhort him several times to be strong and exercise his leadership firmly and confidently.

לְמַעַן תַּשְׂכִּיל — *That you may succeed.* God cautioned Joshua that only through uncompromising adherence to the Torah could he succeed in all his undertakings.

לֹא יָמוּשׁ — *Is not to leave.* According to R' Yishmael this is a prohibition against the neglect of Torah study. R' Shmuel bar Nachman holds that it was a blessing that Joshua would not forget his learning (*Menachos* 99b).

יוֹמָם וָלַיְלָה — *Day and night.* Someone who studies Torah whenever he can is considered to have studied day and night, even though he is forced to work for a living and interrupt his studies for other necessities.

וְלָראוּבֵנִי — *And to the tribes of Reuben ...* In *Numbers* ch. 32, these two and a half tribes asked to receive their portions of *Eretz Yisrael* on

יָנִ֨יחַ יהוָ֜ה ׀ לַאֲחֵיכֶם֮ כָּכֶם֒ וְיָרְשׁ֣וּ גַם־הֵ֔מָּה אֶת־הָאָ֕רֶץ אֲשֶׁר־יהוָ֥ה
אֱלֹהֵיכֶ֖ם נֹתֵ֣ן לָהֶ֑ם וְשַׁבְתֶּ֞ם לְאֶ֤רֶץ יְרֻשַּׁתְכֶם֙ וִירִשְׁתֶּ֣ם אוֹתָ֔הּ אֲשֶׁ֣ר
׀ נָתַ֣ן לָכֶ֗ם מֹשֶׁה֙ עֶ֣בֶד יהוָ֔ה בְּעֵ֥בֶר הַיַּרְדֵּ֖ן מִזְרַ֥ח הַשָּֽׁמֶשׁ׃ וַֽיַּעֲנ֔וּ
אֶת־יְהוֹשֻׁ֖עַ* לֵאמֹ֑ר כֹּ֤ל אֲשֶׁר־צִוִּיתָ֙נוּ֙ נַעֲשֶׂ֔ה וְאֶל־כָּל־אֲשֶׁ֥ר
תִּשְׁלָחֵ֖נוּ נֵלֵֽךְ׃ כְּכֹ֤ל אֲשֶׁר־שָׁמַ֙עְנוּ֙ אֶל־מֹשֶׁ֔ה כֵּ֖ן נִשְׁמַ֣ע אֵלֶ֑יךָ רַ֗ק
יִֽהְיֶ֞ה יהוָ֤ה אֱלֹהֶ֙יךָ֙ עִמָּ֔ךְ כַּאֲשֶׁ֥ר הָיָ֖ה עִם־מֹשֶֽׁה׃ כָּל־אִ֞ישׁ אֲשֶׁר־
יַמְרֶ֣ה אֶת־פִּ֗יךָ וְלֹֽא־יִשְׁמַ֧ע אֶת־דְּבָרֶ֛יךָ לְכֹ֥ל אֲשֶׁר־תְּצַוֶּ֖נּוּ יוּמָ֑ת*
רַ֖ק חֲזַ֥ק וֶאֱמָֽץ׃

ברכות לאחר ההפטרה

After the *Haftarah* is read, the *oleh* recites the following blessings.

בָּרוּךְ אַתָּה יהוה אֱלֹהֵינוּ מֶלֶךְ הָעוֹלָם, צוּר כָּל הָעוֹלָמִים, צַדִּיק בְּכָל הַדּוֹרוֹת, הָאֵל הַנֶּאֱמָן הָאוֹמֵר וְעֹשֶׂה, הַמְּדַבֵּר וּמְקַיֵּם, שֶׁכָּל דְּבָרָיו אֱמֶת וָצֶדֶק. נֶאֱמָן אַתָּה הוּא יהוה אֱלֹהֵינוּ, וְנֶאֱמָנִים דְּבָרֶיךָ, וְדָבָר אֶחָד מִדְּבָרֶיךָ אָחוֹר לֹא יָשׁוּב רֵיקָם, כִּי אֵל מֶלֶךְ נֶאֱמָן (וְרַחֲמָן) אָתָּה. בָּרוּךְ אַתָּה יהוה, הָאֵל הַנֶּאֱמָן בְּכָל דְּבָרָיו.

(Cong. – אָמֵן.)

רַחֵם עַל צִיּוֹן כִּי הִיא בֵּית חַיֵּינוּ, וְלַעֲלוּבַת נֶפֶשׁ תּוֹשִׁיעַ בִּמְהֵרָה בְיָמֵינוּ. בָּרוּךְ אַתָּה יהוה, מְשַׂמֵּחַ צִיּוֹן בְּבָנֶיהָ.

(Cong. – אָמֵן.)

שַׂמְּחֵנוּ יהוה אֱלֹהֵינוּ בְּאֵלִיָּהוּ הַנָּבִיא עַבְדֶּךָ, וּבְמַלְכוּת בֵּית דָּוִד מְשִׁיחֶךָ, בִּמְהֵרָה יָבֹא וְיָגֵל לִבֵּנוּ, עַל כִּסְאוֹ לֹא יֵשֵׁב זָר וְלֹא יִנְחֲלוּ עוֹד אֲחֵרִים אֶת כְּבוֹדוֹ, כִּי בְשֵׁם קָדְשְׁךָ נִשְׁבַּעְתָּ לוֹ, שֶׁלֹּא יִכְבֶּה נֵרוֹ לְעוֹלָם וָעֶד. בָּרוּךְ אַתָּה יהוה, מָגֵן דָּוִד.

(Cong. – אָמֵן.)

עַל הַתּוֹרָה, וְעַל הָעֲבוֹדָה, וְעַל הַנְּבִיאִים, וְעַל יוֹם הַשְּׁמִינִי חַג הָעֲצֶרֶת הַזֶּה שֶׁנָּתַתָּ לָּנוּ יהוה אֱלֹהֵינוּ, לְשָׂשׂוֹן וּלְשִׂמְחָה, לְכָבוֹד וּלְתִפְאָרֶת. עַל הַכֹּל יהוה אֱלֹהֵינוּ, אֲנַחְנוּ מוֹדִים לָךְ, וּמְבָרְכִים אוֹתָךְ, יִתְבָּרַךְ שִׁמְךָ בְּפִי כָּל חַי תָּמִיד לְעוֹלָם וָעֶד. בָּרוּךְ אַתָּה יהוה, מְקַדֵּשׁ יִשְׂרָאֵל וְהַזְּמַנִּים.

(Cong. – אָמֵן.)

Some congregations recite אֲשֶׁר בְּגֹלַל אָבוֹת (p. 1190) and שִׂישׂוּ (p. 1192) at this point.

HASHEM gives your brothers rest as He has given you, and they also take possession of the Land which HASHEM, your God, gives them. Then you may return to the Land of your inheritance and inherit it — that which Moses, servant of HASHEM, gave you across the Jordan on its eastern side.'

And they answered Joshua saying, 'All that you have commanded us we will do, and wherever you send us we will go. As fully as we listened to Moses so shall we listen to you. O that HASHEM, your God, be with you as he had been with Moses! Any man who will rebel against your utterance or will not listen to your words, in whatever you may command him — will be put to death.* O may you strengthen yourself and persevere!'*

BLESSINGS AFTER THE HAFTARAH

After the *Haftarah* is read, the *oleh* recites the following blessings.

בָּרוּךְ *Blessed are You, HASHEM, King of the universe, Rock of all eternities, Righteous in all generations, the trustworthy God, Who says and does, Who speaks and fulfills, all of Whose words are true and righteous. Trustworthy are You, HASHEM, our God, and trustworthy are Your words, not one of Your words is turned back to its origin unfulfilled, for You are God, trustworthy (and compassionate) King. Blessed are You, HASHEM, the God Who is trustworthy in all His words.* (Cong.— *Amen.*)

רַחֵם *Have mercy on Zion for it is the source of our life; to the one who is deeply humiliated bring salvation speedily, in our days. Blessed are You, HASHEM, Who gladdens Zion through her children.* (Cong.— *Amen.*)

שַׂמְּחֵנוּ *Gladden us, HASHEM, our God, with Elijah the prophet, Your servant, and with the kingdom of the House of David, Your anointed, may he come speedily and cause our heart to exult. On his throne let no stranger sit nor let others continue to inherit his honor, for by Your holy Name You swore to him that his heir will not be extinguished forever and ever. Blessed are You, HASHEM, Shield of David.* (Cong.— *Amen.*)

עַל הַתּוֹרָה *For the Torah reading, for the prayer service, for the reading from the Prophets and for this day of the Shemini Atzeres Festival that You, HASHEM, our God, have given us for gladness and joy, for glory and splendor — for all this, HASHEM, our God, we gratefully thank You and bless You. May Your Name be blessed by the mouth of all the living, always, for all eternity. Blessed are You, HASHEM, Who sanctifies Israel and the festival seasons.* (Cong.— *Amen.*)

Some congregations recite אֲשֶׁר בִּגְלַל אָבוֹת (p. 1190) and שִׂישׂוּ (p. 1192) at this point.

---

the eastern bank of the Jordan. In return, they promised to send their fighting men to lead the war against the Canaanites nations in *Eretz Yisrael* proper. Now Joshua reminds them of their pledge.

וַיַּעֲנוּ אֶת יְהוֹשֻׁעַ – *And they answered Joshua.* The reply of the two and a half tribes has great significance. It showed that the nation accepted Joshua's leadership and wanted him to exercise it without compromise.

יוּמָת – *Will be put to death.* In so saying, the tribes gave Joshua the status of a king, for whoever rebels against the king is liable to death by the sword (*Sanhedrin* 49a).

אַשְׁרֵי יוֹשְׁבֵי בֵיתֶךָ, עוֹד יְהַלְלְוּךָ סֶּלָה.[1] אַשְׁרֵי הָעָם שֶׁכָּכָה לּוֹ, אַשְׁרֵי הָעָם שֶׁיהוה אֱלֹהָיו.[2]

תהלים קמה

תְּהִלָּה לְדָוִד,

אֲרוֹמִמְךָ אֱלוֹהַי הַמֶּלֶךְ, וַאֲבָרְכָה שִׁמְךָ לְעוֹלָם וָעֶד.
בְּכָל יוֹם אֲבָרְכֶךָּ, וַאֲהַלְלָה שִׁמְךָ לְעוֹלָם וָעֶד.
גָּדוֹל יהוה וּמְהֻלָּל מְאֹד, וְלִגְדֻלָּתוֹ אֵין חֵקֶר.
דּוֹר לְדוֹר יְשַׁבַּח מַעֲשֶׂיךָ, וּגְבוּרֹתֶיךָ יַגִּידוּ.
הֲדַר כְּבוֹד הוֹדֶךָ, וְדִבְרֵי נִפְלְאֹתֶיךָ אָשִׂיחָה.
וֶעֱזוּז נוֹרְאוֹתֶיךָ יֹאמֵרוּ, וּגְדוּלָּתְךָ אֲסַפְּרֶנָּה.
זֵכֶר רַב טוּבְךָ יַבִּיעוּ, וְצִדְקָתְךָ יְרַנֵּנוּ.
חַנּוּן וְרַחוּם יהוה, אֶרֶךְ אַפַּיִם וּגְדָל חָסֶד.
טוֹב יהוה לַכֹּל, וְרַחֲמָיו עַל כָּל מַעֲשָׂיו.
יוֹדְוּךָ יהוה כָּל מַעֲשֶׂיךָ, וַחֲסִידֶיךָ יְבָרְכוּכָה.
כְּבוֹד מַלְכוּתְךָ יֹאמֵרוּ, וּגְבוּרָתְךָ יְדַבֵּרוּ.
לְהוֹדִיעַ לִבְנֵי הָאָדָם גְּבוּרֹתָיו, וּכְבוֹד הֲדַר מַלְכוּתוֹ.
מַלְכוּתְךָ מַלְכוּת כָּל עֹלָמִים, וּמֶמְשַׁלְתְּךָ בְּכָל דּוֹר וָדֹר.
סוֹמֵךְ יהוה לְכָל הַנֹּפְלִים, וְזוֹקֵף לְכָל הַכְּפוּפִים.
עֵינֵי כֹל אֵלֶיךָ יְשַׂבֵּרוּ, וְאַתָּה נוֹתֵן לָהֶם אֶת אָכְלָם בְּעִתּוֹ.
פּוֹתֵחַ אֶת יָדֶךָ,
וּמַשְׂבִּיעַ לְכָל חַי רָצוֹן.

While reciting the verse פּוֹתֵחַ, concentrate intently on its meaning.

צַדִּיק יהוה בְּכָל דְּרָכָיו, וְחָסִיד בְּכָל מַעֲשָׂיו.
קָרוֹב יהוה לְכָל קֹרְאָיו, לְכֹל אֲשֶׁר יִקְרָאֻהוּ בֶאֱמֶת.
רְצוֹן יְרֵאָיו יַעֲשֶׂה, וְאֶת שַׁוְעָתָם יִשְׁמַע וְיוֹשִׁיעֵם.
שׁוֹמֵר יהוה אֶת כָּל אֹהֲבָיו, וְאֵת כָּל הָרְשָׁעִים יַשְׁמִיד.
❖ תְּהִלַּת יהוה יְדַבֶּר פִּי,
וִיבָרֵךְ כָּל בָּשָׂר שֵׁם קָדְשׁוֹ לְעוֹלָם וָעֶד.
וַאֲנַחְנוּ נְבָרֵךְ יָהּ, מֵעַתָּה וְעַד עוֹלָם, הַלְלוּיָהּ.[3]

---

(1) *Psalms* 84:5. (2) 144:15. (3) 115:18.

אַשְׁרֵי *Praiseworthy are those who dwell in Your house, may they always praise You, Selah![1] Praiseworthy is the people for whom this is so, praiseworthy is the people whose God is* HASHEM.[2]

Psalm 145

A psalm of praise by David:

א *I will exalt You, my God the King,*
and I will bless Your Name forever and ever.
ב *Every day I will bless You,*
and I will laud Your Name forever and ever.
ג HASHEM *is great and exceedingly lauded,*
and His greatness is beyond investigation.
ד *Each generation will praise Your deeds to the next*
and of Your mighty deeds they will tell;
ה *The splendrous glory of Your power*
and Your wondrous deeds I shall discuss.
ו *And of Your awesome power they will speak,*
and Your greatness I shall relate.
ז *A recollection of Your abundant goodness they will utter*
and of Your righteousness they will sing exultantly.
ח *Gracious and merciful is* HASHEM,
slow to anger, and great in [bestowing] kindness.
ט HASHEM *is good to all; His mercies are on all His works.*
י *All Your works shall thank You,* HASHEM,
and Your devout ones will bless You.
כ *Of the glory of Your kingdom they will speak,*
and of Your power they will tell;
ל *To inform human beings of His mighty deeds,*
and the glorious splendor of His kingdom.
מ *Your kingdom is a kingdom spanning all eternities,*
and Your dominion is throughout every generation.
ס HASHEM *supports all the fallen ones and straightens all the bent.*
ע *The eyes of all look to You with hope*
and You give them their food in its proper time;
פ *You open Your hand,* Concentrate intently while reciting the verse, *'You open...'*
and satisfy the desire of every living thing.
צ *Righteous is* HASHEM *in all His ways*
and magnanimous in all His deeds.
ק HASHEM *is close to all who call upon Him —*
to all who call upon Him sincerely.
ר *The will of those who fear Him He will do;*
and their cry He will hear, and save them.
ש HASHEM *protects all who love Him;*
but all the wicked He will destroy.
ת Chazzan— *May my mouth declare the praise of* HASHEM
and may all flesh bless His Holy Name forever and ever.
We will bless God from this time and forever, Halleluyah![3]

Some congregations recite the following *piyutim* before the Torah Scrolls are returned to the Ark:

אֲשֶׁר בִּגְלַל אָבוֹת* בָּנִים גִּדֵּל, וּבַעֲבוּרָם תּוֹרָה נָתַן יהוה.
בְּגַלְגַּלֵּי רוּחַ יהוה נִגְלָה, בְּמַלְאֲכֵי צְבָאוֹת אַלְפֵי שִׁנְאָן.[1]
גִּבּוֹר עַל גֵּאִים אֱלוֹהַּ אַדִּיר, קָרָא לְמשֶׁה לְקַבֵּל לוּחוֹת.
דִּבְרֵי אֵל חַי שָׁמְעָה הָאָרֶץ וְעַמּוּדֶיהָ יִתְפַּלָּצוּן.[2]
הִטָּה שָׁמַיִם וַיֵּרַד, וַיִּרְכַּב עַל כְּרוּב וַיֵּדֶא עַל כַּנְפֵי רוּחַ.[3]
וַיֵּצְאוּ דְבָרִים מִתּוֹךְ הָאֵשׁ וַיִּתְחַקְּקוּ עַל לוּחוֹת הָאֶבֶן.
זְמִרוֹת אָמְרוּ כָּל בְּנֵי אֱלֹהִים, שׁוֹפָר תָּקְעוּ בִּשְׁמֵי מָרוֹם.
חֲרָדָה לָבְשׁוּ כָּל בְּנֵי שֵׂעִיר, כִּי מִשֵּׂעִיר יהוה זָרַח.[4]
טָפְחוּ כֻלָּם בְּנֵי יִשְׁמָעֵאל, כִּי מִפָּארָן יהוה הוֹפִיעַ.[4]
יְמִין יהוה טְפָחַיִם בַּלּוּחוֹת,* וִימִין משֶׁה טְפָחַיִם בַּלּוּחוֹת.
כִּי אֹרֶךְ הַלּוּחוֹת שִׁשָּׁה טְפָחִים, וּטְפָחַיִם מְפֹרָשׁ בֵּין יָד לְיָד.
לֵךְ משֶׁה וּשְׂמַח בִּגְדֻלָּתֶךָ, כִּי אֵין כָּמוֹךָ בְּכָל הַנְּבִיאִים.[5]
מִי עָלָה שָׁמַיִם לְתוֹךְ הֶעָנָן,[6] וּמִי רָאָה תְּמוּנַת אֱלֹהֵינוּ.[7]
משֶׁה עָלָה לְתוֹךְ הֶעָנָן, גַּם הוּא רָאָה תְּמוּנַת אֱלֹהֵינוּ.
נְשִׂיא נְשִׂיאִים הָיָה משֶׁה רַבֵּנוּ, אָב לַחֲכָמִים וְרֹאשׁ לַנְּבִיאִים.
סָגַר הַיָּם בִּתְפִלָּתוֹ, וְעַל יַד שְׁלוּחוֹ חֲרוֹן אַף הֵשִׁיב.[8]
עָנָה יהוה וְאָמַר לְעַמּוֹ, אָנֹכִי יהוה אֱלֹהֶיךָ אֲשֶׁר הוֹצֵאתִיךָ מֵאֶרֶץ
מִצְרַיִם, וּפְדִיתִיךָ מִבֵּית עֲבָדִים.[9]
פָּתְחוּ כֻלָּם פִּיהֶם וְאָמְרוּ, יהוה יִמְלֹךְ לְעוֹלָם וָעֶד.[10]
צָעַק משֶׁה צְעָקָה גְדוֹלָה וּמָרָה, בְּשָׁעָה שֶׁאָמַר לוֹ הַקָּדוֹשׁ בָּרוּךְ הוּא,
עֲלֵה וּמֻת בָּהָר.[11]
קָרַע בְּגָדָיו וְהֵרִים קוֹלוֹ, יְהוֹשֻׁעַ בִּן נוּן, שְׁמַר נָא צֹאנִי.
רָאָה משֶׁה מֵרֹאשׁ הַפִּסְגָּה, נַחֲלַת שְׁבָטִים[12] עוֹמְדִים לְפָנָיו.
שָׁם מֵת משֶׁה עֶבֶד יהוה,[13] מוּל בֵּית פְּעוֹר[14] אֲסָפוֹ אֱלֹהֵינוּ.
תְּפִלַּת משֶׁה קָרַע רָקִיעַ, וְעָנָה צוּר לְעַמּוֹ בְּעֵת צָרוֹתָם.
תְּפִלָּתוֹ לְעוֹלָם לֹא שָׁבָה רֵיקָם, כִּי רוֹעֶה נֶאֱמָן הָיָה משֶׁה לְיִשְׂרָאֵל.
משֶׁה מֵת מִי לֹא יָמוּת. עַל פִּי יהוה מֵת משֶׁה רַבֵּנוּ.[15]

(1) Cf. *Psalms* 68:13 (see Tractate *Shabbos* 88b); 68:18. (2) *Job* 9:6. (3) Cf. *Psalms* 18:10-11; *II Samuel* 22:10-11. (4) Cf. *Deuteronomy* 33:2. (5) Cf. 34:10. (6) Cf. *Exodus* 24:15,18. (7) Cf. *Numbers* 12:8. (8) Cf. *Psalms* 106:23. (9) Cf. *Exodus* 20:2; *Deuteronomy* 5:6. (10) *Exodus* 15:18. (11) *Deuteronomy* 32:49-50. (12) Cf. 34:1-2. (13) Cf. 34:5. (14) 34:6. (15) 34:5.

אֲשֶׁר בִּגְלַל אָבוֹת — *For the sake of the forefathers.* This *piyut* is of extremely early origin (possibly from Talmudic times) and of anonymous authorship. In some ancient communities it was recited as an enhancement to the final blessing recited by the Chassan Torah after the morning Torah reading on Simchas Torah. It draws on a variety of midrashic depictions of the Giving of the Torah at Sinai. It highlights the participation of different classes of angels (*Galgalim, Cherubim, Bnei Elohim*) at that event, and Moses' role as the intermediary. The *piyut* concludes with a eulogy on Moses.

יְמִין ה׳ טְפָחַיִם בַּלּוּחוֹת — *HASHEM's right hand [grasped] two handbreadths of the Tablets.* The Midrash (*Shemos Rabbah* 28:1 et al.) states that the Tablets upon which the Ten Commandments were engraved were six handbreadths long. God held (so to speak) two handbreadths at one side, Moses held the opposite two handbreadths, so that the remaining two handbreadths separated their hands.

Some congregations recite the following *piyutim* before the Torah Scrolls are returned to the Ark:

א *For the sake of the forefathers,* He raised the children,*
and because of them, HASHEM gave the Torah.

ב *HASHEM was revealed among the spiritual Galgalim,*
among angelic legions, thousands of alacritous ones.[1]

ג *Stronger than the haughty, the mighty God,*
called unto Moses, to accept the Tablets.

ד *The earth heard the words of the Living God,*
and its pillars trembled.[2]

ה *He bent down heavens and descended, He rode on a Cherub,*
He soared on the wings of the wind.[3]

ו *Words went forth from the middle of the fire,*
and were engraved upon the stone Tablets.

ז *All the Benai Elohim [i.e., angels] recited zemiros,*
they sounded the shofar from the highest heaven.

ח *Trembling cloaked all the children of Seir [Esau],*
for HASHEM had shown forth from Seir.[4]

ט *All the children of Ishmael clapped hands [in fright],*
for HASHEM had appeared from [Mount] Paran.[4]

י *HASHEM's right hand [grasped] two handbreadths of the Tablets,**
Moses' right hand [grasped] two handbreadths of the Tablets.

כ *For the Tablets' length was six handbreadths,*
two handbreadths separated [God's] hand from [Moses'] hand.

ל *Go, O Moses, and rejoice in your greatness,*
for there is none like you among the prophets.[5]

מ *Who ascended the heaven into the cloud;*[6]
and who perceived the image of our God?[7]

מ *Moses ascended into the cloud,*
and also perceived the image of our God.

נ *Prince of princes was our teacher Moses,*
father to the wise men, head of the prophets.

ס *He [God] sealed the Sea [of Reeds] with his [Moses'] prayer,*
and through His emissary [Moses] He turned aside [His] fiery wrath.[8]

ע *HASHEM proclaimed and said to His people,*
'I am HASHEM, your God, who delivered you from the land of Egypt;
and I redeemed you from the house of slavery.'[9]

פ *They all opened their mouths and said,*
'HASHEM shall reign for all eternity!'[10]

צ *Moses let out a great and bitter cry,*
when the Holy One, Blessed is He, told him,
'Ascend ... and die upon the mountain.'[11]

ק *He rent his garments and called aloud,*
'Joshua son of Nun, guard my flock!'

ר *Moses saw from the summit of the cliff,*
the heritage of the tribes[12] *standing before him.*

ש *There Moses, servant of HASHEM died,*[13]
opposite Beth Peor[14] *our God gathered him in.*

ת *Moses' prayer rent the heavens,*
[in its merit] the Rock answers His people in time of their distress.
His prayer would never return empty-handed,
for Moses was a faithful shepherd unto Israel.
If Moses died, who shall not die?
Our teacher Moses died by the mouth of HASHEM.[15]

שִׂישׂוּ וְשִׂמְחוּ*[1] בְּשִׂמְחַת תּוֹרָה, וּתְנוּ כָבוֹד לַתּוֹרָה,
כִּי טוֹב סַחְרָהּ מִכָּל סְחוֹרָה,[2] מִפָּז וּמִפְּנִינִים יְקָרָה.[3]
נָגִיל וְנָשִׂישׂ בְּזֹאת הַתּוֹרָה, כִּי הִיא לָנוּ עֹז וְאוֹרָה.
אֲהַלְלָה אֱלֹהַי וְאֶשְׂמְחָה בוֹ, וְאָשִׂימָה תִקְוָתִי בּוֹ,
אֲהוֹדֶנּוּ בְּסוֹד עַם קְרוֹבוֹ, אֱלֹהֵי צוּרִי אֶחֱסֶה בּוֹ.[4]
נָגִיל וְנָשִׂישׂ בְּזֹאת הַתּוֹרָה, כִּי הִיא לָנוּ עֹז וְאוֹרָה.
בְּכָל לֵב אֲרַנֵּן צִדְקוֹתֶיךָ, וַאֲסַפְּרָה תְּהִלָּתֶךָ,
בְּעוֹדִי אַגִּיד נִפְלְאוֹתֶיךָ, עַל חַסְדְּךָ וְעַל אֲמִתֶּךָ.[5]
נָגִיל וְנָשִׂישׂ בְּזֹאת הַתּוֹרָה, כִּי הִיא לָנוּ עֹז וְאוֹרָה.
גּוֹאֵל תָּחִישׁ מְבַשֵּׂר טוֹב,[6] כִּי אַתָּה מִגְדַּל עֹז וְטוֹב,
גְּאוּלִים יוֹדוּךָ בְּלֵב טוֹב, הוֹדוּ לַיהוה כִּי טוֹב.[7]
נָגִיל וְנָשִׂישׂ בְּזֹאת הַתּוֹרָה, כִּי הִיא לָנוּ עֹז וְאוֹרָה.
דָּגוּל גְּאַל נָא הֲמוֹנָי, כִּי אֵין קָדוֹשׁ כַּיהוה.[8]
דְּגוּלִים יוֹדוּךָ יהוה, מִי יְמַלֵּל גְּבוּרוֹת יהוה.[9]
נָגִיל וְנָשִׂישׂ בְּזֹאת הַתּוֹרָה, כִּי הִיא לָנוּ עֹז וְאוֹרָה.
הֲלֹא בְּאַהֲבָתוֹ בָּחַר בָּנוּ, בְּנִי בְכוֹרִי[10] קְרָאָנוּ,
הוֹד וְהָדָר הִנְחִילָנוּ, כִּי לְעוֹלָם חַסְדּוֹ[11] עִמָּנוּ.
נָגִיל וְנָשִׂישׂ בְּזֹאת הַתּוֹרָה, כִּי הִיא לָנוּ עֹז וְאוֹרָה.

אַשְׁרֵיכֶם יִשְׂרָאֵל, אַשְׁרֵיכֶם יִשְׂרָאֵל, אַשְׁרֵיכֶם יִשְׂרָאֵל, אֲשֶׁר בָּחַר בָּכֶם אֵל, וְהִנְחִילְכֶם הַתּוֹרָה מִמִּדְבַּר מַתָּנָה.

הִתְקַבְּצוּ מַלְאָכִים* זֶה אֶל זֶה, זֶה לְקַבֵּל זֶה, וְאָמַר זֶה לָזֶה, מִי הוּא זֶה וְאֵי זֶה הוּא מֵאַחֵז פְּנֵי כִסֵּא, פַּרְשֵׁז עָלָיו עֲנָנוֹ,

---

Nezer HaKodesh explains that this Midrash alludes to three planes on which the Torah may be studied: (a) תּוֹרַת ה׳, *the Torah of HASHEM*, i.e., the highest level of Torah knowledge, a level to which no man is privy; God, so to speak, holds on to this segment of the Torah and does not release it; (b) תּוֹרַת הָאָדָם, *the Torah of man*, i.e., the revealed Torah which may be understood superficially without much effort; this section is given over to all men, represented here by Moses; and (c) that portion of the Torah which is not readily comprehended, but may be attained through diligent effort and dedication. This part lies between the other two; God neither 'gave' it to Moses nor prevented him from attaining it.

⌘ **שִׂישׂוּ וְשִׂמְחוּ** – *Rejoice and be glad.* This *piyut* and those that follow it were obviously written especially for Simchas Torah. Each is of unknown authorship and is apparently a fragment of a longer piece. For example, שִׂישׂוּ וְשִׂמְחוּ follows the *aleph-beis* until ה and then stops abruptly; אַשְׁרֵיכֶם, *You are praiseworthy*, is the refrain of an eleven-stanza *piyut* that appears in some *machzorim*.

⌘ **הִתְקַבְּצוּ מַלְאָכִים** – *The angels gathered.* This *piyut* is based on the Talmudic narration of Moses' confrontation with the angels:

When Moses ascended on high, the Ministering Angels said to the Holy One, Blessed is He, 'Master of the Universe, what has one born of woman to do among us?'

He told them, 'He has come to receive the Torah.'

They said before Him, 'The hidden treasure that You have kept concealed for nine hundred

שִׂישׂוּ *Rejoice and be glad*[1]* *on Simchas Torah, and pay homage to the Torah for it is better than any commerce,*[2]
more precious than finest gold and gems.[3]
Let us exult and rejoice with this Torah, for to us it is strength and light.
א *I shall laud my God and be glad with Him, and place my hope in Him.*
I shall praise Him in the counsel of His intimate people —
God, my Rock — I take refuge in Him.[4]
Let us exult and rejoice with this Torah, for to us it is strength and light.
ב *Wholeheartedly I shall exalt Your righteousness*
and I shall relate Your praise.
While I live I will relate Your wonders, tell of Your kindness and Your truth.[5]
Let us exult and rejoice with this Torah, for to us it is strength and light.
ג *Redeemer, hasten the herald of good tidings,*[6]
for You are a tower of strength and goodness.
The redeemed ones shall thank You in good heart:
'Give thanks to HASHEM, for He is good!'[7]
Let us exult and rejoice with this Torah, for to us it is strength and light.
ד *O Bannered One, redeem now my multitude, for none is as holy as HASHEM.*[8]
The bannered [tribes of Israel] shall thank You,
HASHEM. Who can express the mighty acts of HASHEM?[9]
Let us exult and rejoice with this Torah, for to us it is strength and light.
ה *Has He not chosen us in His love? 'My son! My firstborn!'*[10] *has He called us.*
Majesty and splendor has he bequeathed us,
for His kindness is forever[11] *with us.*

אַשְׁרֵיכֶם *You are praiseworthy, Israel. You are praiseworthy, Israel. You are praiseworthy, Israel,*
for God has chosen you and bequeathed you the Torah — from Sinai a gift.

הִתְקַבְּצוּ *The angels gathered** *to one another, opposite one another, and said to one another, 'Who is the one, which is the one, who is holding onto the face of the throne? Upon whom He has spread His cloud?'*

(1) Cf. *Psalms* 40:17; 70:5. (2) Cf. *Proverbs* 3:14. (3) Cf. 3:15. (4) Cf. *II Samuel* 22:3; *Psalms* 18:3. (5) Cf. 115:1. (6) Cf. *Isaiah* 52:7. (7) *Psalms* 136:1 et al. (8) *I Samuel* 2:2. (9) *Psalms* 106:2. (10) *Exodus* 4:22. (11) *Psalms* 136:1 et al.

seventy-four generations before the world was created, You wish to give to flesh and blood?'

The Talmud relates that God told Moses to respond but he was afraid to do so, until God promised to protect him by having him *hold on to the face of the Throne and spreading His cloud over him* (*Job* 26:9). Thereupon, Moses declared that the Torah could only be intended for man. Does the Torah not speak of God who took you out of Egyptian slavery — were the angels ever enslaved? Do the angels require rest on the Sabbath? Do the angels have parents whom they should honor? Do they feel jealousy that impels them to kill, or lust that impels them to be immoral?

Hearing this, the angels admitted Moses was right and befriended him. *What is the frail human that You should remember him; and the son of man that You should be mindful of him? HASHEM, our Lord, how mighty is Your Name throughout the earth, for it were fit that You place Your majesty upon the heavens!* (*Psalms* 8:5,2).

The Holy One, Blessed is He, said to Moses, 'Give them an answer!'

He [Moses] said, 'Master of the Universe, I am afraid they may consume me with the heat of their mouths!'

He [God] told him, 'Hold on to My Throne of Glory and answer them.' As it is said (*Job* 26:9), *He has him hold on to the face of the Throne, and spreads His cloud upon him.*

מִי עָלָה לַמָּרוֹם, מִי עָלָה לַמָּרוֹם, מִי עָלָה לַמָּרוֹם, וְהוֹרִיד עֹז מִבְטֶחָה. מֹשֶׁה עָלָה לַמָּרוֹם, מֹשֶׁה עָלָה לַמָּרוֹם, מֹשֶׁה עָלָה לַמָּרוֹם, נְתַנְאֵל,* שְׁמַעְיָה, אֲבִי סוֹכוֹ, אֲבִי זָנוֹחַ, חֶבֶר, יְקוּתִיאֵל, טוֹבִיָּה, יֶרֶד, אֲבִיגְדוֹר, עָלָה לַמָּרוֹם, וְהוֹרִיד עֹז מִבְטֶחָה.

אָגִיל וְאֶשְׂמַח[1] בְּשִׂמְחַת תּוֹרָה, בֹּא יָבֹא צֶמַח בְּשִׂמְחַת תּוֹרָה. תּוֹרָה הִיא עֵץ חַיִּים[2] לְכֻלָּם חַיִּים, כִּי עִמְּךָ מְקוֹר חַיִּים.[3] אַבְרָהָם שָׂמַח* בְּשִׂמְחַת תּוֹרָה. יִצְחָק שָׂמַח בְּשִׂמְחַת תּוֹרָה. יַעֲקֹב שָׂמַח בְּשִׂמְחַת תּוֹרָה. מֹשֶׁה וְאַהֲרֹן שָׂמְחוּ בְּשִׂמְחַת תּוֹרָה. אֵלִיָּהוּ שְׁמוּאֵל דָּוִד שְׁלֹמֹה שָׂמְחוּ בְּשִׂמְחַת תּוֹרָה. תּוֹרָה הִיא עֵץ חַיִּים, לְכֻלָּם חַיִּים, כִּי עִמְּךָ מְקוֹר חַיִּים.

The *chazzan* takes the Torah in his right arm and recites:

יְהַלְלוּ אֶת שֵׁם יהוה, כִּי נִשְׂגָּב שְׁמוֹ לְבַדּוֹ –

Congregation responds:

– הוֹדוֹ עַל אֶרֶץ וְשָׁמָיִם. וַיָּרֶם קֶרֶן לְעַמּוֹ, תְּהִלָּה לְכָל חֲסִידָיו, לִבְנֵי יִשְׂרָאֵל עַם קְרֹבוֹ, הַלְלוּיָהּ.[4]

As the Torah is carried to the Ark the congregation recites the following psalm.

תהלים כד

לְדָוִד מִזְמוֹר, לַיהוה הָאָרֶץ וּמְלוֹאָהּ, תֵּבֵל וְיֹשְׁבֵי בָהּ. כִּי הוּא עַל יַמִּים יְסָדָהּ, וְעַל נְהָרוֹת יְכוֹנְנֶהָ. מִי יַעֲלֶה בְהַר יהוה, וּמִי יָקוּם בִּמְקוֹם קָדְשׁוֹ. נְקִי כַפַּיִם וּבַר לֵבָב, אֲשֶׁר לֹא נָשָׂא לַשָּׁוְא נַפְשִׁי וְלֹא נִשְׁבַּע לְמִרְמָה. יִשָּׂא בְרָכָה מֵאֵת יהוה, וּצְדָקָה מֵאֱלֹהֵי יִשְׁעוֹ. זֶה דּוֹר דֹּרְשָׁיו, מְבַקְשֵׁי פָנֶיךָ, יַעֲקֹב, סֶלָה. שְׂאוּ שְׁעָרִים רָאשֵׁיכֶם, וְהִנָּשְׂאוּ פִּתְחֵי עוֹלָם, וְיָבוֹא מֶלֶךְ הַכָּבוֹד. מִי זֶה מֶלֶךְ הַכָּבוֹד, יהוה עִזּוּז וְגִבּוֹר, יהוה גִּבּוֹר מִלְחָמָה. שְׂאוּ שְׁעָרִים רָאשֵׁיכֶם, וּשְׂאוּ פִּתְחֵי עוֹלָם, וְיָבֹא מֶלֶךְ הַכָּבוֹד. מִי הוּא זֶה מֶלֶךְ הַכָּבוֹד, יהוה צְבָאוֹת הוּא מֶלֶךְ הַכָּבוֹד, סֶלָה.

The Talmud concludes with Moses' debate with the angels and his victory over them (*Shabbos* 88b).

נְתַנְאֵל ... – *Nesanel* ... Based upon the Talmudic (*Megillah* 13a) and the Midrashic (*Vayikra Rabbah*) interpretations of *II Chronicles* 4:18 and 24:6, Moses was known by a total of ten names. In some congregations, the verse relating Moses' ascent is recited ten times, each

Who has ascended on high? Who has ascended on high?
Who has ascended on high and taken down the powerful [Torah] from its secure spot [in heaven]?

Moses has ascended on high. Moses has ascended on high.
Nesanel, Shemayah, Avi Socho, Avi Zanoach, Chever, Yekusiel, Toviah, Yered, Avigdor have ascended on high and taken down the powerful [Torah] from its secure spot [in heaven].*

אָגִיל *I shall rejoice and be glad[1] on Simchas Torah; may Tzemach [Messiah] come on Simchas Torah. The Torah is a tree of life,[2] for all of them life, for with You is the source of life.[3] Abraham rejoiced* on Simchas Torah. Isaac rejoiced on Simchas Torah. Jacob rejoiced on Simchas Torah. Moses and Aaron rejoiced on Simchas Torah. Elijah, Samuel, David and Solomon rejoiced on Simchas Torah. The Torah is a tree of life, for all of them life, for with You is the source of life.*

The *chazzan* takes the Torah in his right arm and recites:

Let them praise the Name of HASHEM, for His Name alone will have been exalted —

Congregation responds:

— His glory is above earth and heaven. And He will have exalted the pride of His people, causing praise for all His devout ones, for the Children of Israel, His intimate people. Halleluyah![4]

As the Torah is carried to the Ark the congregation recites the following psalm.

Psalm 24

לְדָוִד *Of David a psalm. HASHEM's is the earth and its fullness, the inhabited land and those who dwell in it. For He founded it upon seas, and established it upon rivers. Who may ascend the mountain of HASHEM, and who may stand in the place of His sanctity? One with clean hands and pure heart, who has not sworn in vain by My soul and has not sworn deceitfully. He will receive a blessing from HASHEM and just kindness from the God of his salvation. This is the generation of those who seek Him, those who strive for Your Presence — Jacob, Selah. Raise up your heads, O gates, and be uplifted, you everlasting entrances, so that the King of Glory may enter. Who is this King of Glory? — HASHEM, the mighty and strong, HASHEM, the strong in battle. Raise up your heads, O gates, and raise up, you everlasting entrances, so that the King of Glory may enter. Who then is the King of Glory? HASHEM, Master of Legions, He is the King of Glory. Selah!*

---

(1) Cf. *Psalms* 31:8. (2) Cf. *Proverbs* 3:18. (3) *Psalms* 36:10. (5) 148:13-14.

---

time using a different name. In most congregations, however, the *piyut* is abridged, the nine added names being mentioned all together.

אַבְרָהָם שָׂמַח – *Abraham rejoiced.* This is based on the generally accepted principle that the Patriarchs observed the Scripturally ordained *mitzvos*, the Rabbinical decrees, and even the customs that would later arise among their offspring. [See, e.g., the last *mishnah* in *Kiddushin.*]

As the Torah is placed into the Ark, the congregation recites the following verses:

וּבְנֻחֹה יֹאמַר, שׁוּבָה יהוה רִבְבוֹת אַלְפֵי יִשְׂרָאֵל.[1] קוּמָה יהוה לִמְנוּחָתֶךָ, אַתָּה וַאֲרוֹן עֻזֶּךָ. כֹּהֲנֶיךָ יִלְבְּשׁוּ צֶדֶק, וַחֲסִידֶיךָ יְרַנֵּנוּ. בַּעֲבוּר דָּוִד עַבְדֶּךָ, אַל תָּשֵׁב פְּנֵי מְשִׁיחֶךָ.[2] כִּי לֶקַח טוֹב נָתַתִּי לָכֶם, תּוֹרָתִי אַל תַּעֲזֹבוּ.[3] ❖ עֵץ חַיִּים הִיא לַמַּחֲזִיקִים בָּהּ, וְתֹמְכֶיהָ מְאֻשָּׁר.[4] דְּרָכֶיהָ דַרְכֵי נֹעַם, וְכָל נְתִיבוֹתֶיהָ שָׁלוֹם.[5] הֲשִׁיבֵנוּ יהוה אֵלֶיךָ וְנָשׁוּבָה, חַדֵּשׁ יָמֵינוּ כְּקֶדֶם.[6]

The *chazzan* recites חֲצִי קַדִּישׁ.

יִתְגַּדַּל וְיִתְקַדַּשׁ שְׁמֵהּ רַבָּא. (.Cong – אָמֵן.) בְּעָלְמָא דִּי בְרָא כִרְעוּתֵהּ. וְיַמְלִיךְ מַלְכוּתֵהּ, בְּחַיֵּיכוֹן וּבְיוֹמֵיכוֹן וּבְחַיֵּי דְכָל בֵּית יִשְׂרָאֵל, בַּעֲגָלָא וּבִזְמַן קָרִיב. וְאִמְרוּ: אָמֵן.

(.Cong – אָמֵן. יְהֵא שְׁמֵהּ רַבָּא מְבָרַךְ לְעָלַם וּלְעָלְמֵי עָלְמַיָּא.)

יְהֵא שְׁמֵהּ רַבָּא מְבָרַךְ לְעָלַם וּלְעָלְמֵי עָלְמַיָּא.

יִתְבָּרַךְ וְיִשְׁתַּבַּח וְיִתְפָּאַר וְיִתְרוֹמַם וְיִתְנַשֵּׂא וְיִתְהַדָּר וְיִתְעַלֶּה וְיִתְהַלָּל שְׁמֵהּ דְּקֻדְשָׁא בְּרִיךְ הוּא (.Cong – בְּרִיךְ הוּא) – לְעֵלָּא מִן כָּל בִּרְכָתָא וְשִׁירָתָא תֻּשְׁבְּחָתָא וְנֶחֱמָתָא, דַּאֲמִירָן בְּעָלְמָא. וְאִמְרוּ: אָמֵן. (.Cong – אָמֵן.)

מוסף לשמחת תורה

Take three steps backward, then three steps forward. Remain standing with the feet together while reciting *Shemoneh Esrei*. Recite it with quiet devotion and without interruption, verbal or otherwise. Although its recitation should not be audible to others, one must pray loudly enough to hear himself.

כִּי שֵׁם יהוה אֶקְרָא, הָבוּ גֹדֶל לֵאלֹהֵינוּ.[7]

אֲדֹנָי שְׂפָתַי תִּפְתָּח, וּפִי יַגִּיד תְּהִלָּתֶךָ.[8]

אבות

Bend the knees at בָּרוּךְ; bow at אַתָּה; straighten up at ה׳.

בָּרוּךְ אַתָּה יהוה אֱלֹהֵינוּ וֵאלֹהֵי אֲבוֹתֵינוּ, אֱלֹהֵי אַבְרָהָם, אֱלֹהֵי יִצְחָק, וֵאלֹהֵי יַעֲקֹב, הָאֵל הַגָּדוֹל הַגִּבּוֹר וְהַנּוֹרָא, אֵל עֶלְיוֹן, גּוֹמֵל חֲסָדִים טוֹבִים וְקוֹנֵה הַכֹּל, וְזוֹכֵר חַסְדֵי אָבוֹת, וּמֵבִיא גוֹאֵל לִבְנֵי בְנֵיהֶם, לְמַעַן שְׁמוֹ בְּאַהֲבָה. מֶלֶךְ עוֹזֵר וּמוֹשִׁיעַ וּמָגֵן.

Bend the knees at בָּרוּךְ; bow at אַתָּה; straighten up at ה׳.

בָּרוּךְ אַתָּה יהוה, מָגֵן אַבְרָהָם.

גבורות

אַתָּה גִּבּוֹר לְעוֹלָם אֲדֹנָי, מְחַיֵּה מֵתִים אַתָּה, רַב לְהוֹשִׁיעַ.

מַשִּׁיב הָרוּחַ וּמוֹרִיד הַגֶּשֶׁם.

מְכַלְכֵּל חַיִּים בְּחֶסֶד, מְחַיֵּה מֵתִים בְּרַחֲמִים רַבִּים, סוֹמֵךְ נוֹפְלִים, וְרוֹפֵא חוֹלִים, וּמַתִּיר אֲסוּרִים, וּמְקַיֵּם אֱמוּנָתוֹ לִישֵׁנֵי עָפָר.

As the Torah is placed into the Ark, the congregation recites the following verses:

וּבְנֻחֹה *And when it rested he would say, 'Return, HASHEM, to the myriad thousands of Israel.'*[1] *Arise, HASHEM, to Your resting place, You and the Ark of Your strength. Let Your priests be clothed in righteousness, and Your devout ones will sing joyously. For the sake of David, Your servant, turn not away the face of Your anointed.*[2] *For I have given you a good teaching, do not forsake My Torah.*[3] Chazzan– *It is a tree of life for those who grasp it, and its supporters are praiseworthy.*[4] *Its ways are ways of pleasantness and all its paths are peace.*[5] *Bring us back to You, HASHEM, and we shall return, renew our days as of old.*[6]

The *chazzan* recites Half-*Kaddish:*

יִתְגַּדַּל *May His great Name grow exalted and sanctified* (Cong.– *Amen.*) *in the world that He created as He willed. May He give reign to His kingship in your lifetimes and in your days, and in the lifetimes of the entire Family of Israel, swiftly and soon. Now respond: Amen.*

(Cong.– *Amen. May His great Name be blessed forever and ever.*)

May His great Name be blessed forever and ever.

Blessed, praised, glorified, exalted, extolled, mighty, upraised, and lauded be the Name of the Holy One, Blessed is He (Cong.– *Blessed is He*) — *beyond any blessing and song, praise and consolation that are uttered in the world. Now respond: Amen.* (Cong.– *Amen.*)

MUSSAF FOR SIMCHAS TORAH

Take three steps backward, then three steps forward. Remain standing with the feet together while reciting *Shemoneh Esrei.* Recite it with quiet devotion and without interruption, verbal or otherwise. Although its recitation should not be audible to others, one must pray loudly enough to hear himself.

When I call out the Name of HASHEM, ascribe greatness to our God.[7]

My Lord, open my lips, that my mouth may declare Your praise.[8]

PATRIARCHS

Bend the knees at *'Blessed'*; bow at *'You'*; straighten up at *'HASHEM.'*

בָּרוּךְ *Blessed are You, HASHEM, our God and the God of our forefathers, God of Abraham, God of Isaac, and God of Jacob; the great, mighty, and awesome God, the supreme God, Who bestows beneficial kindnesses and creates everything, Who recalls the kindnesses of the Patriarchs and brings a Redeemer to their children's children, for His Name's sake, with love. O King, Helper, Savior, and Shield.*

Bend the knees at *'Blessed'*; bow at *'You'*; straighten up at *'HASHEM.'*

Blessed are You, HASHEM, Shield of Abraham.

GOD'S MIGHT

אַתָּה *You are eternally mighty, my Lord, the Resuscitator of the dead are You; abundantly able to save.*

He makes the wind blow and He makes the rain descend.

He sustains the living with kindness, resuscitates the dead with abundant mercy, supports the fallen, heals the sick, releases the confined, and maintains His faith to those asleep in the dust. Who is like

(1) *Numbers* 10:36. (2) *Psalms* 132:8-10. (3) *Proverbs* 4:2. (4) 3:18.
(5) 3:17. (6) *Lamentations* 5:21. (7) *Deuteronomy* 32:3. (8) *Psalms* 51:17.

מִי כָמְוֹךָ בַּעַל גְּבוּרוֹת, וּמִי דְּוֹמֶה לָּךְ, מֶלֶךְ מֵמִית וּמְחַיֶּה וּמַצְמִיחַ יְשׁוּעָה. וְנֶאֱמָן אַתָּה לְהַחֲיוֹת מֵתִים. בָּרוּךְ אַתָּה יהוה, מְחַיֵּה הַמֵּתִים.

During the *chazzan's* repetition, *Kedushah* (below) is recited at this point.

קדושת השם

INDIVIDUALS RECITE:

אַתָּה קָדוֹשׁ וְשִׁמְךָ קָדוֹשׁ, וּקְדוֹשִׁים בְּכָל יוֹם יְהַלְּלְוּךָ סֶּלָה. בָּרוּךְ אַתָּה יהוה, הָאֵל הַקָּדוֹשׁ.

CHAZZAN RECITES DURING HIS REPETITION:

לְדוֹר וָדוֹר נַגִּיד גָּדְלֶךָ וּלְנֵצַח נְצָחִים קְדֻשָּׁתְךָ נַקְדִּישׁ, וְשִׁבְחֲךָ אֱלֹהֵינוּ מִפִּינוּ לֹא יָמוּשׁ לְעוֹלָם וָעֶד, כִּי אֵל מֶלֶךְ גָּדוֹל וְקָדוֹשׁ אָתָּה. בָּרוּךְ אַתָּה יהוה, הָאֵל הַקָּדוֹשׁ.

קדושת היום

אַתָּה בְחַרְתָּנוּ מִכָּל הָעַמִּים, אָהַבְתָּ אוֹתָנוּ, וְרָצִיתָ בָּנוּ, וְרוֹמַמְתָּנוּ מִכָּל הַלְּשׁוֹנוֹת, וְקִדַּשְׁתָּנוּ בְּמִצְוֹתֶיךָ, וְקֵרַבְתָּנוּ מַלְכֵּנוּ לַעֲבוֹדָתֶךָ, וְשִׁמְךָ הַגָּדוֹל וְהַקָּדוֹשׁ עָלֵינוּ קָרָאתָ.

קדושה

When reciting *Kedushah,* one must stand with his feet together and avoid any interruptions. One should rise on his toes when saying the words קָדוֹשׁ, קָדוֹשׁ, קָדוֹשׁ; בָּרוּךְ (of בָּרוּךְ כְּבוֹד); and יִמְלֹךְ.

Cong. then *chazzan*:

נַעֲרִיצְךָ וְנַקְדִּישְׁךָ כְּסוֹד שִׂיחַ שַׂרְפֵי קֹדֶשׁ, הַמַּקְדִּישִׁים שִׁמְךָ בַּקֹּדֶשׁ, כַּכָּתוּב עַל יַד נְבִיאֶךָ, וְקָרָא זֶה אֶל זֶה וְאָמַר:

All – קָדוֹשׁ קָדוֹשׁ קָדוֹשׁ יהוה צְבָאוֹת, מְלֹא כָל הָאָרֶץ כְּבוֹדוֹ.[1] ❖ כְּבוֹדוֹ מָלֵא עוֹלָם, מְשָׁרְתָיו שׁוֹאֲלִים זֶה לָזֶה, אַיֵּה מְקוֹם כְּבוֹדוֹ, לְעֻמָּתָם בָּרוּךְ יֹאמֵרוּ:

All – בָּרוּךְ כְּבוֹד יהוה, מִמְּקוֹמוֹ.[2] ❖ מִמְּקוֹמוֹ הוּא יִפֶן בְּרַחֲמִים, וְיָחוֹן עַם הַמְיַחֲדִים שְׁמוֹ, עֶרֶב וָבֹקֶר בְּכָל יוֹם תָּמִיד, פַּעֲמַיִם בְּאַהֲבָה שְׁמַע אוֹמְרִים.

All – שְׁמַע יִשְׂרָאֵל, יהוה אֱלֹהֵינוּ, יהוה אֶחָד.[3] ❖ הוּא אֱלֹהֵינוּ. הוּא אָבִינוּ, הוּא מַלְכֵּנוּ, הוּא מוֹשִׁיעֵנוּ, וְהוּא יַשְׁמִיעֵנוּ בְּרַחֲמָיו שֵׁנִית, לְעֵינֵי כָּל חָי, לִהְיוֹת לָכֶם לֵאלֹהִים, אֲנִי יהוה אֱלֹהֵיכֶם.[4]

All – אַדִּיר אַדִּירֵנוּ, יהוה אֲדֹנֵינוּ, מָה אַדִּיר שִׁמְךָ בְּכָל הָאָרֶץ.[5] וְהָיָה יהוה לְמֶלֶךְ עַל כָּל הָאָרֶץ, בַּיּוֹם הַהוּא יִהְיֶה יהוה אֶחָד וּשְׁמוֹ אֶחָד.[6]

Chazzan – וּבְדִבְרֵי קָדְשְׁךָ כָּתוּב לֵאמֹר:

All – יִמְלֹךְ יהוה לְעוֹלָם, אֱלֹהַיִךְ צִיּוֹן, לְדֹר וָדֹר, הַלְּלוּיָהּ.[7]

You, O Master of mighty deeds, and who is comparable to You, O King Who causes death and restores life and makes salvation sprout! And You are faithful to resuscitate the dead. Blessed are You, HASHEM, Who resuscitates the dead.

During the *chazzan's* repetition, *Kedushah* (below) is recited at this point.

HOLINESS OF GOD'S NAME

INDIVIDUALS RECITE:

אַתָּה *You are holy and Your Name is holy, and holy ones praise You every day, forever. Blessed are You, HASHEM, the holy God.*

CHAZZAN RECITES DURING HIS REPETITION:

לְדוֹר *From generation to generation we shall relate Your greatness and for infinite eternities we shall proclaim Your holiness. Your praise, our God, shall not leave our mouth forever and ever, for You, O God, are a great and holy King. Blessed are You, HASHEM, the holy God.*

SANCTIFICATION OF THE DAY

אַתָּה בְחַרְתָּנוּ *You have chosen us from all the peoples; You loved us and found favor in us; You exalted us above all the tongues and You sanctified us with Your commandments. You drew us close, our King, to Your service and proclaimed Your great and Holy Name upon us.*

KEDUSHAH

When reciting *Kedushah*, one must stand with his feet together and avoid any interruptions. One should rise on his toes when saying the words *Holy, holy, holy; Blessed is; HASHEM shall reign.*

Cong. then *chazzan:*

נַעֲרִיצְךָ *We will revere You and sanctify You according to the counsel of the holy Seraphim, who sanctify Your Name in the Sanctuary, as it is written by Your prophet: "And one [angel] will call another and say:*

All – *'Holy, holy, holy is HASHEM, Master of Legions, the whole world is filled with His glory.' "*[1] ❖*His glory fills the world. His ministering angels ask one another, 'Where is the place of His glory?' Those facing them say 'Blessed':*

All – *'Blessed is the glory of HASHEM from His place.'*[2] ❖*From His place may He turn with compassion and be gracious to the people who declare the Oneness of His Name; evening and morning, every day constantly, twice, with love, they proclaim 'Shema.'*

All – *'Hear O Israel: HASHEM is our God, HASHEM the One and Only.'*[3] ❖*He is our God; He is our Father; He is our King; He is our Savior; and He will let us hear, in His compassion, for a second time in the presence of all the living,' . . . to be a God to you, I am HASHEM, your God.'*[4]

All – *Mighty is our Mighty One, HASHEM, our Master — how mighty is Your name throughout the earth!*[5] *HASHEM will be King over all the world — on that day HASHEM will be One and His Name will be One.*[6]

Chazzan – *And in Your holy Writings the following is written:*

All – *'HASHEM shall reign forever — your God, O Zion — from generation to generation, Halleluyah!'*[7]

---

(1) *Isaiah* 6:3. (2) *Ezekiel* 3:12. (3) *Deuteronomy* 6:4.
(4) *Numbers* 15:41. (5) *Psalms* 8:2. (6) *Zechariah* 14:9. (7) *Psalms* 146:10.

וַתִּתֶּן לָנוּ יהוה אֱלֹהֵינוּ בְּאַהֲבָה מוֹעֲדִים לְשִׂמְחָה חַגִּים וּזְמַנִּים לְשָׂשׂוֹן, אֶת יוֹם הַשְּׁמִינִי חַג הָעֲצֶרֶת הַזֶּה, זְמַן שִׂמְחָתֵנוּ מִקְרָא קֹדֶשׁ, זֵכֶר לִיצִיאַת מִצְרָיִם.

וּמִפְּנֵי חֲטָאֵינוּ גָּלִינוּ מֵאַרְצֵנוּ, וְנִתְרַחַקְנוּ מֵעַל אַדְמָתֵנוּ. וְאֵין אֲנַחְנוּ יְכוֹלִים לַעֲלוֹת וְלֵרָאוֹת וּלְהִשְׁתַּחֲוֹת לְפָנֶיךָ, וְלַעֲשׂוֹת חוֹבוֹתֵינוּ בְּבֵית בְּחִירָתֶךָ, בַּבַּיִת הַגָּדוֹל וְהַקָּדוֹשׁ שֶׁנִּקְרָא שִׁמְךָ עָלָיו, מִפְּנֵי הַיָּד שֶׁנִּשְׁתַּלְּחָה בְּמִקְדָּשֶׁךָ. יְהִי רָצוֹן מִלְּפָנֶיךָ יהוה אֱלֹהֵינוּ וֵאלֹהֵי אֲבוֹתֵינוּ, מֶלֶךְ רַחֲמָן, שֶׁתָּשׁוּב וּתְרַחֵם עָלֵינוּ וְעַל מִקְדָּשְׁךָ בְּרַחֲמֶיךָ הָרַבִּים, וְתִבְנֵהוּ מְהֵרָה וּתְגַדֵּל כְּבוֹדוֹ. אָבִינוּ מַלְכֵּנוּ, גַּלֵּה כְּבוֹד מַלְכוּתְךָ עָלֵינוּ מְהֵרָה, וְהוֹפַע וְהִנָּשֵׂא עָלֵינוּ לְעֵינֵי כָּל חָי. וְקָרֵב פְּזוּרֵינוּ מִבֵּין הַגּוֹיִם, וּנְפוּצוֹתֵינוּ כַּנֵּס מִיַּרְכְּתֵי אָרֶץ. וַהֲבִיאֵנוּ לְצִיּוֹן עִירְךָ בְּרִנָּה, וְלִירוּשָׁלַיִם בֵּית מִקְדָּשְׁךָ בְּשִׂמְחַת עוֹלָם. וְשָׁם נַעֲשֶׂה לְפָנֶיךָ אֶת קָרְבְּנוֹת חוֹבוֹתֵינוּ, תְּמִידִים כְּסִדְרָם, וּמוּסָפִים כְּהִלְכָתָם. וְאֶת מוּסַף יוֹם הַשְּׁמִינִי חַג הָעֲצֶרֶת הַזֶּה נַעֲשֶׂה וְנַקְרִיב לְפָנֶיךָ בְּאַהֲבָה כְּמִצְוַת רְצוֹנֶךָ, כְּמוֹ שֶׁכָּתַבְתָּ עָלֵינוּ בְּתוֹרָתֶךָ, עַל יְדֵי מֹשֶׁה עַבְדֶּךָ, מִפִּי כְבוֹדֶךָ כָּאָמוּר:

בַּיּוֹם הַשְּׁמִינִי, עֲצֶרֶת תִּהְיֶה לָכֶם, כָּל מְלֶאכֶת עֲבֹדָה לֹא תַעֲשׂוּ. וְהִקְרַבְתֶּם עֹלָה אִשֵּׁה רֵיחַ נִיחֹחַ לַיהוה, פַּר אֶחָד, אַיִל אֶחָד, כְּבָשִׂים בְּנֵי שָׁנָה שִׁבְעָה, תְּמִימִם.[1] וּמִנְחָתָם וְנִסְכֵּיהֶם כִּמְדֻבָּר, שְׁלֹשָׁה עֶשְׂרֹנִים לַפָּר, וּשְׁנֵי עֶשְׂרֹנִים לָאָיִל, וְעִשָּׂרוֹן לַכֶּבֶשׂ, וְיַיִן כְּנִסְכּוֹ. וְשָׂעִיר לְכַפֵּר, וּשְׁנֵי תְמִידִים כְּהִלְכָתָם.

אֱלֹהֵינוּ וֵאלֹהֵי אֲבוֹתֵינוּ, מֶלֶךְ רַחֲמָן רַחֵם עָלֵינוּ, טוֹב וּמֵטִיב הִדָּרֶשׁ לָנוּ, שׁוּבָה אֵלֵינוּ בַּהֲמוֹן רַחֲמֶיךָ, בִּגְלַל אָבוֹת שֶׁעָשׂוּ רְצוֹנֶךָ. בְּנֵה בֵיתְךָ כְּבַתְּחִלָּה, וְכוֹנֵן מִקְדָּשְׁךָ עַל מְכוֹנוֹ, וְהַרְאֵנוּ בְּבִנְיָנוֹ, וְשַׂמְּחֵנוּ בְּתִקּוּנוֹ. וְהָשֵׁב כֹּהֲנִים לַעֲבוֹדָתָם, וּלְוִיִּם לְשִׁירָם וּלְזִמְרָם, וְהָשֵׁב יִשְׂרָאֵל לִנְוֵיהֶם. וְשָׁם נַעֲלֶה וְנֵרָאֶה וְנִשְׁתַּחֲוֶה לְפָנֶיךָ, בְּשָׁלשׁ פַּעֲמֵי רְגָלֵינוּ, כַּכָּתוּב בְּתוֹרָתֶךָ: שָׁלוֹשׁ פְּעָמִים בַּשָּׁנָה, יֵרָאֶה כָל זְכוּרְךָ אֶת פְּנֵי יהוה אֱלֹהֶיךָ, בַּמָּקוֹם אֲשֶׁר יִבְחָר, בְּחַג הַמַּצּוֹת, וּבְחַג הַשָּׁבֻעוֹת, וּבְחַג הַסֻּכּוֹת,

(1) *Numbers* 29:35-36.

וַתִּתֶּן לָנוּ *And You gave us,* HASHEM, *our God, with love, appointed festivals for gladness, Festivals and times for joy, this day of the Shemini Atzeres Festival, the time of our gladness, a holy convocation, a memorial of the Exodus from Egypt.*

וּמִפְּנֵי חֲטָאֵינוּ *But because of our sins we have been exiled from our land and sent far from our soil. We cannot ascend to appear and to prostrate ourselves before You, and to perform our obligations in the House of Your choice, in the great and holy House upon which Your Name was proclaimed, because of the hand that was dispatched against Your Sanctuary. May it be Your will,* HASHEM, *our God and the God of our forefathers, O merciful King, that You once more be compassionate upon us and upon Your Sanctuary in Your abundant mercy, and rebuild it soon and magnify its glory. Our Father, our King, reveal the glory of Your Kingship upon us, speedily; appear and be uplifted over us before the eyes of all the living. Draw our scattered ones near from among the nations, and bring in our dispersions from the ends of the earth. Bring us to Zion, Your City, in glad song, and to Jerusalem, home of Your Sanctuary, in eternal joy. There we will perform before You our obligatory offerings, the continual offerings according to their order and the additional offerings according to their law. And the additional offering of this day of the Shemini Atzeres Festival, we will perform and bring near to You with love, according to the commandment of Your will, as You have written for us in Your Torah, through Moses, Your servant, from Your glorious expression, as it is said:*

בַּיּוֹם הַשְּׁמִינִי *On the eighth day, there shall be an Assembly for you, you may not do any laborious work. You are to bring an elevation-offering, a fire-offering, a satisfying aroma to* HASHEM, *one bull, one ram, seven [male] first-year lambs, unblemished.*[1] *And their meal-offerings and their wine-libations as mentioned: three tenth-ephah for each bull; two tenth-ephah for each ram; one tenth-ephah for each lamb; and wine for its libation. A he-goat for atonement, and two continual offerings according to their law.*

אֱלֹהֵינוּ *Our God and the God of our forefathers, O merciful King, have mercy on us; O good and beneficent One, let Yourself be sought out by us; return to us in Your yearning mercy for the sake of the forefathers who did Your will. Rebuild Your House as it was at first, and establish Your Sanctuary on its prepared site; show us its rebuilding and gladden us in its perfection. Restore the Kohanim to their service and the Levites to their song and music; and restore Israel to their dwellings. And there we will ascend and appear and prostrate ourselves before You, during our three pilgrimage seasons, as it is written in Your Torah: Three times a year all your males are to appear before* HASHEM, *your God, in the place He shall choose, on the Festival of Matzos, on the Festival of Shavuos, and on the Festival of Succos, and*

וְלֹא יֵרָאֶה אֶת פְּנֵי יהוה רֵיקָם. אִישׁ כְּמַתְּנַת יָדוֹ, כְּבִרְכַּת יהוה אֱלֹהֶיךָ, אֲשֶׁר נָתַן לָךְ.[1]

וְהַשִּׂיאֵנוּ יהוה אֱלֹהֵינוּ אֶת בִּרְכַּת מוֹעֲדֶיךָ לְחַיִּים וּלְשָׁלוֹם, לְשִׂמְחָה וּלְשָׂשׂוֹן, כַּאֲשֶׁר רָצִיתָ וְאָמַרְתָּ לְבָרְכֵנוּ. קַדְּשֵׁנוּ בְּמִצְוֹתֶיךָ וְתֵן חֶלְקֵנוּ בְּתוֹרָתֶךָ, שַׂבְּעֵנוּ מִטּוּבֶךָ וְשַׂמְּחֵנוּ בִּישׁוּעָתֶךָ, וְטַהֵר לִבֵּנוּ לְעָבְדְּךָ בֶּאֱמֶת, וְהַנְחִילֵנוּ יהוה אֱלֹהֵינוּ בְּשִׂמְחָה וּבְשָׂשׂוֹן מוֹעֲדֵי קָדְשֶׁךָ, וְיִשְׂמְחוּ בְךָ יִשְׂרָאֵל מְקַדְּשֵׁי שְׁמֶךָ. בָּרוּךְ אַתָּה יהוה, מְקַדֵּשׁ יִשְׂרָאֵל וְהַזְּמַנִּים.

עבודה

רְצֵה יהוה אֱלֹהֵינוּ בְּעַמְּךָ יִשְׂרָאֵל וּבִתְפִלָּתָם, וְהָשֵׁב אֶת הָעֲבוֹדָה לִדְבִיר בֵּיתֶךָ. וְאִשֵּׁי יִשְׂרָאֵל וּתְפִלָּתָם בְּאַהֲבָה תְקַבֵּל בְּרָצוֹן, וּתְהִי לְרָצוֹן תָּמִיד עֲבוֹדַת יִשְׂרָאֵל עַמֶּךָ.

IN SOME CONGREGATIONS THE FULL בִּרְכַּת כֹּהֲנִים (PP. 990-1000) IS RECITED AT THIS POINT.

וְתֶחֱזֶינָה עֵינֵינוּ בְּשׁוּבְךָ לְצִיּוֹן בְּרַחֲמִים. בָּרוּךְ אַתָּה יהוה, הַמַּחֲזִיר שְׁכִינָתוֹ לְצִיּוֹן.

הודאה

Bow at מוֹדִים; straighten up at 'ה. In his repetition the *chazzan* should recite the entire מוֹדִים aloud, while the congregation recites מוֹדִים דְּרַבָּנָן softly.

מוֹדִים אֲנַחְנוּ לָךְ, שָׁאַתָּה הוּא יהוה אֱלֹהֵינוּ וֵאלֹהֵי אֲבוֹתֵינוּ לְעוֹלָם וָעֶד. צוּר חַיֵּינוּ, מָגֵן יִשְׁעֵנוּ אַתָּה הוּא לְדוֹר וָדוֹר. נוֹדֶה לְּךָ וּנְסַפֵּר תְּהִלָּתֶךָ[2] עַל חַיֵּינוּ הַמְּסוּרִים בְּיָדֶךָ, וְעַל נִשְׁמוֹתֵינוּ הַפְּקוּדוֹת לָךְ, וְעַל נִסֶּיךָ שֶׁבְּכָל יוֹם עִמָּנוּ, וְעַל נִפְלְאוֹתֶיךָ וְטוֹבוֹתֶיךָ שֶׁבְּכָל עֵת, עֶרֶב וָבֹקֶר וְצָהֳרָיִם. הַטּוֹב כִּי לֹא כָלוּ רַחֲמֶיךָ, וְהַמְּרַחֵם כִּי לֹא תַמּוּ חֲסָדֶיךָ,[3] מֵעוֹלָם קִוִּינוּ לָךְ.

מודים דרבנן

מוֹדִים אֲנַחְנוּ לָךְ, שָׁאַתָּה הוּא יהוה אֱלֹהֵינוּ וֵאלֹהֵי אֲבוֹתֵינוּ, אֱלֹהֵי כָל בָּשָׂר, יוֹצְרֵנוּ, יוֹצֵר בְּרֵאשִׁית. בְּרָכוֹת וְהוֹדָאוֹת לְשִׁמְךָ הַגָּדוֹל וְהַקָּדוֹשׁ, עַל שֶׁהֶחֱיִיתָנוּ וְקִיַּמְתָּנוּ. כֵּן תְּחַיֵּנוּ וּתְקַיְּמֵנוּ, וְתֶאֱסוֹף גָּלֻיּוֹתֵינוּ לְחַצְרוֹת קָדְשֶׁךָ, לִשְׁמוֹר חֻקֶּיךָ וְלַעֲשׂוֹת רְצוֹנֶךָ, וּלְעָבְדְּךָ בְּלֵבָב שָׁלֵם, עַל שֶׁאֲנַחְנוּ מוֹדִים לָךְ. בָּרוּךְ אֵל הַהוֹדָאוֹת.

they shall not appear before HASHEM empty-handed. Every man according to the gift of his hand, according to the blessing of HASHEM, your God, that He gave you.[1]

וְהַשִּׂיאֵנוּ *Bestow upon us, O HASHEM, our God, the blessing of Your appointed Festivals for life and for peace, for gladness and for joy, as You desired and promised to bless us. Sanctify us with Your commandments and grant us our share in Your Torah; satisfy us from Your goodness and gladden us with Your salvation, and purify our heart to serve You sincerely. And grant us a heritage, O HASHEM our God — with gladness and with joy — the appointed festivals of Your holiness, and may Israel, the sanctifiers of Your Name, rejoice in You. Blessed are You, HASHEM, Who sanctifies Israel and the festive seasons.*

TEMPLE SERVICE

רְצֵה *Be favorable, HASHEM, our God, toward Your people Israel and their prayer and restore the service to the Holy of Holies of Your Temple. The fire-offerings of Israel and their prayer accept with love and favor, and may the service of Your people Israel always be favorable to You.*

IN SOME CONGREGATIONS THE FULL PRIESTLY BLESSING (PP. 990-1000) IS RECITED AT THIS POINT.

וְתֶחֱזֶינָה *May our eyes behold Your return to Zion in compassion. Blessed are You, HASHEM, Who restores His Presence to Zion.*

THANKSGIVING [MODIM]

Bow at *'We gratefully thank You'*; straighten up at *'HASHEM.'* In his repetition the *chazzan* should recite the entire *Modim* aloud, while the congregation recites *Modim of the Rabbis* softly.

מוֹדִים *We gratefully thank You, for it is You Who are HASHEM, our God and the God of our forefathers for all eternity; Rock of our lives, Shield of our salvation are You from generation to generation. We shall thank You and relate Your praise*[2] *— for our lives, which are committed to Your power and for our souls that are entrusted to You; for Your miracles that are with us every day; and for Your wonders and favors in every season — evening, morning, and afternoon. The Beneficent One, for Your compassions were never exhausted, and the Compassionate One, for Your kindnesses never ended*[3] *— always have we put our hope in You.*

MODIM OF THE RABBIS

מוֹדִים *We gratefully thank You, for it is You Who are HASHEM, our God and the God of our forefathers, the God of all flesh, our Molder, the Molder of the universe. Blessings and thanks are due Your great and holy Name for You have given us life and sustained us. So may You continue to give us life and sustain us and gather our exiles to the Courtyards of Your Sanctuary, to observe Your decrees, to do Your will and to serve You wholeheartedly. [We thank You] for inspiring us to thank You. Blessed is the God of thanksgivings.*

(1) *Deuteronomy* 16:16-17. (2) Cf. *Psalms* 79:13. (3) Cf. *Lamentations* 3:22.

וְעַל כֻּלָּם יִתְבָּרַךְ וְיִתְרוֹמַם שִׁמְךָ מַלְכֵּנוּ תָּמִיד לְעוֹלָם וָעֶד.

Bend the knees at בָּרוּךְ; bow at אַתָּה; straighten up at ה׳.

וְכֹל הַחַיִּים יוֹדְוּךָ סֶּלָה, וִיהַלְלוּ אֶת שִׁמְךָ בֶּאֱמֶת, הָאֵל יְשׁוּעָתֵנוּ וְעֶזְרָתֵנוּ סֶלָה. בָּרוּךְ אַתָּה יהוה, הַטּוֹב שִׁמְךָ וּלְךָ נָאֶה לְהוֹדוֹת.

ברכת כהנים

The *chazzan* recites the following during his repetition.
He faces right at וְיִשְׁמְרֶךָ; faces left at אֵלֶיךָ וִיחֻנֶּךָּ; faces the Ark for the rest of the blessings.

אֱלֹהֵינוּ, וֵאלֹהֵי אֲבוֹתֵינוּ, בָּרְכֵנוּ בַבְּרָכָה הַמְּשֻׁלֶּשֶׁת בַּתּוֹרָה הַכְּתוּבָה עַל יְדֵי מֹשֶׁה עַבְדֶּךָ, הָאֲמוּרָה מִפִּי אַהֲרֹן וּבָנָיו, כֹּהֲנִים עַם קְדוֹשֶׁךָ, כָּאָמוּר:

יְבָרֶכְךָ יהוה, וְיִשְׁמְרֶךָ. (Cong. – כֵּן יְהִי רָצוֹן.)

יָאֵר יהוה פָּנָיו אֵלֶיךָ וִיחֻנֶּךָּ. (Cong. – כֵּן יְהִי רָצוֹן.)

יִשָּׂא יהוה פָּנָיו אֵלֶיךָ וְיָשֵׂם לְךָ שָׁלוֹם.[1] (Cong. – כֵּן יְהִי רָצוֹן.)

שלום

שִׂים שָׁלוֹם, טוֹבָה, וּבְרָכָה, חֵן, וָחֶסֶד וְרַחֲמִים עָלֵינוּ וְעַל כָּל יִשְׂרָאֵל עַמֶּךָ. בָּרְכֵנוּ אָבִינוּ, כֻּלָּנוּ כְּאֶחָד בְּאוֹר פָּנֶיךָ, כִּי בְאוֹר פָּנֶיךָ נָתַתָּ לָּנוּ, יהוה אֱלֹהֵינוּ, תּוֹרַת חַיִּים וְאַהֲבַת חֶסֶד, וּצְדָקָה, וּבְרָכָה, וְרַחֲמִים, וְחַיִּים, וְשָׁלוֹם. וְטוֹב בְּעֵינֶיךָ לְבָרֵךְ אֶת עַמְּךָ יִשְׂרָאֵל, בְּכָל עֵת וּבְכָל שָׁעָה בִּשְׁלוֹמֶךָ. בָּרוּךְ אַתָּה יהוה, הַמְּבָרֵךְ אֶת עַמּוֹ יִשְׂרָאֵל בַּשָּׁלוֹם.

יִהְיוּ לְרָצוֹן אִמְרֵי פִי וְהֶגְיוֹן לִבִּי לְפָנֶיךָ, יהוה צוּרִי וְגֹאֲלִי.[2]

The *chazzan's* repetition of *Shemoneh Esrei* ends here. The individual continues below:

אֱלֹהַי, נְצוֹר לְשׁוֹנִי מֵרָע, וּשְׂפָתַי מִדַּבֵּר מִרְמָה,[3] וְלִמְקַלְלַי נַפְשִׁי תִדּוֹם, וְנַפְשִׁי כֶּעָפָר לַכֹּל תִּהְיֶה. פְּתַח לִבִּי בְּתוֹרָתֶךָ, וּבְמִצְוֹתֶיךָ תִּרְדּוֹף נַפְשִׁי. וְכֹל הַחוֹשְׁבִים עָלַי רָעָה, מְהֵרָה הָפֵר עֲצָתָם וְקַלְקֵל מַחֲשַׁבְתָּם. עֲשֵׂה לְמַעַן שְׁמֶךָ, עֲשֵׂה לְמַעַן יְמִינֶךָ, עֲשֵׂה לְמַעַן קְדֻשָּׁתֶךָ, עֲשֵׂה לְמַעַן תּוֹרָתֶךָ. לְמַעַן יֵחָלְצוּן יְדִידֶיךָ, הוֹשִׁיעָה יְמִינְךָ וַעֲנֵנִי.[4]

Some recite verses pertaining to their names here. See page 1301.

For all these, may Your Name be blessed and exalted, our King, continually forever and ever.

Bend the knees at *'Blessed'*; bow at *'You'*; straighten up at *'HASHEM.'*

Everything alive will gratefully acknowledge You, Selah! and praise Your Name sincerely, O God of our salvation and help, Selah! Blessed are You, HASHEM, Your Name is 'The Beneficent One' and to You it is fitting to give thanks.

THE PRIESTLY BLESSING

The *chazzan* recites the following during his repetition.

אֱלֹהֵינוּ *Our God and the God of our forefathers, bless us with the three-verse blessing in the Torah that was written by the hand of Moses, Your servant, that was said by Aaron and his sons, the Kohanim, Your holy people, as it is said:*

May HASHEM bless you and safeguard you. (Cong.— *So may it be.*)

May HASHEM illuminate His countenance for you and be gracious to you. (Cong.— *So may it be.*)

May HASHEM turn His countenance to you and establish peace for you.[1] (Cong.— *So may it be.*)

PEACE

שִׂים שָׁלוֹם *Establish peace, goodness, blessing, graciousness, kindness, and compassion upon us and upon all of Your people Israel. Bless us, our Father, all of us as one, with the light of Your countenance, for with the light of Your countenance You gave us, HASHEM, our God, the Torah of life and a love of kindness, righteousness, blessing, compassion, life, and peace. And may it be good in Your eyes to bless Your people Israel at every time and every hour with Your peace. Blessed are You, HASHEM, Who blesses His people Israel with peace.*

May the expressions of my mouth and the thoughts of my heart find favor before You, HASHEM, my Rock and my Redeemer.[2]

The *chazzan's* repetition of *Shemoneh Esrei* ends here. Individuals continue:

אֱלֹהַי *My God, guard my tongue from evil and my lips from speaking deceitfully.*[3] *To those who curse me, let my soul be silent; and let my soul be like dust to everyone. Open my heart to Your Torah, then my soul will pursue Your commandments. As for all those who design evil against me, speedily nullify their counsel and disrupt their design. Act for Your Name's sake; act for Your right hand's sake; act for Your sanctity's sake; act for Your Torah's sake. That Your beloved ones may be given rest; let Your right hand save, and respond to me.*[4]

Some recite verses pertaining to their names at this point. See page 1301.

---

(1) *Numbers* 6:24-26. (2) *Psalms* 19:15. (3) Cf. 34:14. (4) 60:7; 108:7.

יִהְיוּ לְרָצוֹן אִמְרֵי פִי וְהֶגְיוֹן לִבִּי לְפָנֶיךָ, יהוה צוּרִי וְגֹאֲלִי.[1]

Bow and take three steps back. Bow left and say . . . עֹשֶׂה, bow right and say . . . הוּא יַעֲשֶׂה; bow forward and say וְעַל כָּל . . . אָמֵן.

עֹשֶׂה שָׁלוֹם בִּמְרוֹמָיו, הוּא יַעֲשֶׂה שָׁלוֹם עָלֵינוּ, וְעַל כָּל יִשְׂרָאֵל. וְאִמְרוּ: אָמֵן.

יְהִי רָצוֹן מִלְּפָנֶיךָ יהוה אֱלֹהֵינוּ וֵאלֹהֵי אֲבוֹתֵינוּ, שֶׁיִּבָּנֶה בֵּית הַמִּקְדָּשׁ בִּמְהֵרָה בְיָמֵינוּ, וְתֵן חֶלְקֵנוּ בְּתוֹרָתֶךָ. וְשָׁם נַעֲבָדְךָ בְּיִרְאָה, כִּימֵי עוֹלָם וּכְשָׁנִים קַדְמוֹנִיּוֹת. וְעָרְבָה לַיהוה מִנְחַת יְהוּדָה וִירוּשָׁלָיִם, כִּימֵי עוֹלָם וּכְשָׁנִים קַדְמוֹנִיּוֹת.[2]

THE INDIVIDUAL'S RECITATION OF *SHEMONEH ESREI* ENDS HERE.

The individual remains standing in place until the *chazzan* reaches *Kedushah* — or at least until the *chazzan* begins his repetition — then he takes three steps forward. The *chazzan* himself, or one praying alone, should remain in place for a few moments before taking three steps forward.

קדיש שלם

The *chazzan* recites קַדִּישׁ שָׁלֵם.

יִתְגַּדַּל וְיִתְקַדַּשׁ שְׁמֵהּ רַבָּא. (Cong. – אָמֵן.) בְּעָלְמָא דִּי בְרָא כִרְעוּתֵהּ. וְיַמְלִיךְ מַלְכוּתֵהּ, בְּחַיֵּיכוֹן וּבְיוֹמֵיכוֹן וּבְחַיֵּי דְכָל בֵּית יִשְׂרָאֵל, בַּעֲגָלָא וּבִזְמַן קָרִיב. וְאִמְרוּ: אָמֵן.

(Cong. – אָמֵן. יְהֵא שְׁמֵהּ רַבָּא מְבָרַךְ לְעָלַם וּלְעָלְמֵי עָלְמַיָּא.)

יְהֵא שְׁמֵהּ רַבָּא מְבָרַךְ לְעָלַם וּלְעָלְמֵי עָלְמַיָּא.

יִתְבָּרַךְ וְיִשְׁתַּבַּח וְיִתְפָּאַר וְיִתְרוֹמַם וְיִתְנַשֵּׂא וְיִתְהַדָּר וְיִתְעַלֶּה וְיִתְהַלָּל שְׁמֵהּ דְּקֻדְשָׁא בְּרִיךְ הוּא (Cong. – בְּרִיךְ הוּא) — לְעֵלָּא מִן כָּל בִּרְכָתָא וְשִׁירָתָא תֻּשְׁבְּחָתָא וְנֶחֱמָתָא, דַּאֲמִירָן בְּעָלְמָא. וְאִמְרוּ: אָמֵן. (Cong. – אָמֵן.)

(Cong. – קַבֵּל בְּרַחֲמִים וּבְרָצוֹן אֶת תְּפִלָּתֵנוּ.)

תִּתְקַבֵּל צְלוֹתְהוֹן וּבָעוּתְהוֹן דְּכָל בֵּית יִשְׂרָאֵל קֳדָם אֲבוּהוֹן דִּי בִשְׁמַיָּא. וְאִמְרוּ: אָמֵן. (Cong. – אָמֵן.)

(Cong. – יְהִי שֵׁם יהוה מְבֹרָךְ, מֵעַתָּה וְעַד עוֹלָם.[3])

יְהֵא שְׁלָמָא רַבָּא מִן שְׁמַיָּא, וְחַיִּים עָלֵינוּ וְעַל כָּל יִשְׂרָאֵל. וְאִמְרוּ: אָמֵן. (Cong. – אָמֵן.)

(Cong. – עֶזְרִי מֵעִם יהוה, עֹשֵׂה שָׁמַיִם וָאָרֶץ.[4])

Take three steps back. Bow left and say . . . עֹשֶׂה; bow right and say . . . הוּא; bow forward and say וְעַל כָּל . . . אָמֵן. Remain standing in place for a few moments, then take three steps forward.

עֹשֶׂה שָׁלוֹם בִּמְרוֹמָיו, הוּא יַעֲשֶׂה שָׁלוֹם עָלֵינוּ, וְעַל כָּל יִשְׂרָאֵל. וְאִמְרוּ: אָמֵן. (Cong. – אָמֵן.)

May the expressions of my mouth and the thoughts of my heart find favor before You, HASHEM, my Rock and my Redeemer.[1] *He Who makes peace in His heights, may He make peace upon us, and upon all Israel. Now respond: Amen.*

Bow and take three steps back. Bow left and say, *'He Who makes peace . . .'*; bow right and say, *'may He make peace . . .'*; bow forward and say, *'and upon . . . Amen.'*

יְהִי רָצוֹן *May it be Your will, HASHEM, our God and the God of our forefathers, that the Holy Temple be rebuilt, speedily in our days. Grant us our share in Your Torah, and may we serve You there with reverence, as in days of old and in former years. Then the offering of Judah and Jerusalem will be pleasing to HASHEM, as in days of old and in former years.*[2]

THE INDIVIDUAL'S RECITATION OF *SHEMONEH ESREI* ENDS HERE.

The individual remains standing in place until the *chazzan* reaches *Kedushah* — or at least until the *chazzan* begins his repetition — then he takes three steps forward. The *chazzan* himself, or one praying alone, should remain in place for a few moments before taking three steps forward.

FULL KADDISH

The *chazzan* recites the Full *Kaddish*.

יִתְגַּדַּל *May His great Name grow exalted and sanctified* (Cong.– *Amen.*) *in the world that He created as He willed. May He give reign to His kingship in your lifetimes and in your days, and in the lifetimes of the entire Family of Israel, swiftly and soon. Now respond: Amen.*

(Cong.– *Amen. May His great Name be blessed forever and ever.*)

May His great Name be blessed forever and ever.

Blessed, praised, glorified, exalted, extolled, mighty, upraised, and lauded be the Name of the Holy One, Blessed is He (Cong.– *Blessed is He*) — *beyond any blessing and song, praise and consolation that are uttered in the world. Now respond: Amen.* (Cong.– *Amen.*)

(Cong.– *Accept our prayers with mercy and favor.*)

May the prayers and supplications of the entire Family of Israel be accepted before their Father Who is in Heaven. Now respond: Amen. (Cong.– *Amen.*)

(Cong.– *Blessed be the Name of HASHEM, from this time and forever.*[3])

May there be abundant peace from Heaven, and life, upon us and upon all Israel. Now respond: Amen. (Cong.– *Amen.*)

(Cong.– *My help is from HASHEM, Maker of heaven and earth.*[4])

Take three steps back. Bow left and say, *'He Who makes peace . . .'*; bow right and say, *'may He . . .'*; bow forward and say, *'and upon all Israel . . .'* Remain standing in place for a few moments, then take three steps forward.

He Who makes peace in His heights, may He make peace upon us, and upon all Israel. Now respond: Amen. (Cong.– *Amen.*)

---

(1) *Psalms* 19:15. (2) *Malachi* 3:4. (3) *Psalms* 113:2. (4) 121:2.

קַוֵּה אֶל יהוה, חֲזַק וְיַאֲמֵץ לִבֶּךָ, וְקַוֵּה אֶל יהוה.[1] אֵין קָדוֹשׁ כַּיהוה, כִּי אֵין בִּלְתֶּךָ, וְאֵין צוּר כֵּאלֹהֵינוּ.[2] כִּי מִי אֱלוֹהַּ מִבַּלְעֲדֵי יהוה, וּמִי צוּר זוּלָתִי אֱלֹהֵינוּ.[3]

אֵין כֵּאלֹהֵינוּ, אֵין כַּאדוֹנֵינוּ, אֵין כְּמַלְכֵּנוּ, אֵין כְּמוֹשִׁיעֵנוּ. מִי כֵאלֹהֵינוּ, מִי כַאדוֹנֵינוּ, מִי כְמַלְכֵּנוּ, מִי כְמוֹשִׁיעֵנוּ. נוֹדֶה לֵאלֹהֵינוּ, נוֹדֶה לַאדוֹנֵינוּ, נוֹדֶה לְמַלְכֵּנוּ, נוֹדֶה לְמוֹשִׁיעֵנוּ. בָּרוּךְ אֱלֹהֵינוּ, בָּרוּךְ אֲדוֹנֵינוּ, בָּרוּךְ מַלְכֵּנוּ, בָּרוּךְ מוֹשִׁיעֵנוּ. אַתָּה הוּא אֱלֹהֵינוּ, אַתָּה הוּא אֲדוֹנֵינוּ, אַתָּה הוּא מַלְכֵּנוּ, אַתָּה הוּא מוֹשִׁיעֵנוּ. אַתָּה הוּא שֶׁהִקְטִירוּ אֲבוֹתֵינוּ לְפָנֶיךָ אֶת קְטֹרֶת הַסַּמִּים.

כריתות ו.

פִּטּוּם הַקְּטֹרֶת: (א) הַצֳּרִי, (ב) וְהַצִּפֹּרֶן, (ג) הַחֶלְבְּנָה, (ד) וְהַלְּבוֹנָה, מִשְׁקַל שִׁבְעִים שִׁבְעִים מָנֶה; (ה) מוֹר, (ו) וּקְצִיעָה, (ז) שִׁבֹּלֶת נֵרְדְּ, (ח) וְכַרְכֹּם, מִשְׁקַל שִׁשָּׁה עָשָׂר שִׁשָּׁה עָשָׂר מָנֶה; (ט) הַקֹּשְׁטְ שְׁנֵים עָשָׂר, (י) וְקִלּוּפָה שְׁלֹשָׁה, (יא) וְקִנָּמוֹן תִּשְׁעָה. בֹּרִית כַּרְשִׁינָה תִּשְׁעָה קַבִּין, יֵין קַפְרִיסִין סְאִין תְּלָתָא וְקַבִּין תְּלָתָא; וְאִם אֵין לוֹ יֵין קַפְרִיסִין, מֵבִיא חֲמַר חִוַּרְיָן עַתִּיק; מֶלַח סְדוֹמִית רֹבַע הַקָּב; מַעֲלֶה עָשָׁן כָּל שֶׁהוּא. רַבִּי נָתָן הַבַּבְלִי אוֹמֵר: אַף כִּפַּת הַיַּרְדֵּן כָּל שֶׁהוּא. וְאִם נָתַן בָּהּ דְּבַשׁ פְּסָלָהּ. וְאִם חִסַּר אַחַת מִכָּל סַמָּנֶיהָ, חַיָּב מִיתָה.

רַבָּן שִׁמְעוֹן בֶּן גַּמְלִיאֵל אוֹמֵר: הַצֳּרִי אֵינוֹ אֶלָּא שְׂרָף הַנּוֹטֵף מֵעֲצֵי הַקְּטָף. בֹּרִית כַּרְשִׁינָה שֶׁשָּׁפִין בָּהּ אֶת הַצִּפֹּרֶן כְּדֵי שֶׁתְּהֵא נָאָה; יֵין קַפְרִיסִין שֶׁשּׁוֹרִין בּוֹ אֶת הַצִּפֹּרֶן כְּדֵי שֶׁתְּהֵא עַזָּה; וַהֲלֹא מֵי רַגְלַיִם יָפִין לָהּ, אֶלָּא שֶׁאֵין מַכְנִיסִין מֵי רַגְלַיִם בָּעֲזָרָה מִפְּנֵי הַכָּבוֹד.

משנה, תמיד ז:ד

הַשִּׁיר שֶׁהַלְוִיִּם הָיוּ אוֹמְרִים בְּבֵית הַמִּקְדָּשׁ. בַּיּוֹם הָרִאשׁוֹן הָיוּ אוֹמְרִים: לַיהוה הָאָרֶץ וּמְלוֹאָהּ, תֵּבֵל וְיֹשְׁבֵי בָהּ.[4] בַּשֵּׁנִי הָיוּ אוֹמְרִים: גָּדוֹל יהוה וּמְהֻלָּל מְאֹד, בְּעִיר אֱלֹהֵינוּ הַר קָדְשׁוֹ.[5] בַּשְּׁלִישִׁי הָיוּ אוֹמְרִים: אֱלֹהִים נִצָּב בַּעֲדַת אֵל, בְּקֶרֶב אֱלֹהִים יִשְׁפֹּט.[6] בָּרְבִיעִי הָיוּ אוֹמְרִים: אֵל נְקָמוֹת יהוה, אֵל נְקָמוֹת הוֹפִיעַ.[7] בַּחֲמִישִׁי הָיוּ אוֹמְרִים: הַרְנִינוּ לֵאלֹהִים עוּזֵּנוּ, הָרִיעוּ לֵאלֹהֵי יַעֲקֹב.[8] בַּשִּׁשִּׁי הָיוּ אוֹמְרִים: יהוה מָלָךְ גֵּאוּת לָבֵשׁ, לָבֵשׁ יהוה עֹז

קַוֵּה *Hope to* HASHEM, *strengthen yourself and He will give you courage; and hope to* HASHEM.[1] *There is none holy as* HASHEM, *for there is none beside You, and there is no Rock like our God.*[2] *For who is a god beside* HASHEM, *and who is a Rock except for our God.*[3]

אֵין *There is none like our God; there is none like our Master;*
there is none like our King; there is none like our Savior.
Who is like our God? Who is like our Master?
Who is like our King? Who is like our Savior?
Let us thank our God; let us thank our Master;
let us thank our King; let us thank our Savior.
Blessed is our God; blessed is our Master;
blessed is our King; blessed is our Savior.
It is You Who is our God; it is You Who is our Master;
it is You Who is our King; it is You Who is our Savior.
It is You before Whom our forefathers burned the spice-incense.

Talmud, *Kereisos* 6a

פִּטּוּם הַקְּטֹרֶת *The incense mixture was formulated of [eleven spices]:* (1) *stacte,* (2) *onycha,* (3) *galbanum,* (4) *frankincense — each weighing seventy maneh;* (5) *myrrh,* (6) *cassia,* (7) *spikenard,* (8) *saffron — each weighing sixteen maneh;* (9) *costus — twelve [maneh];* (10) *aromatic bark — three; and* (11) *cinnamon — nine. [Additionally] Carshina lye — nine kab; Cyprus wine, three se'ah and three kab — if he has no Cyprus wine, he brings old white wine; Sodom salt, a quarter kab; and a minute amount of smoke-raising herb. Rabbi Nassan the Babylonian says: Also a minute amount of Jordan amber. If he placed fruit-honey into it, he invalidated it. And if he left out any of its spices, he is liable to the death penalty.*

רַבָּן שִׁמְעוֹן *Rabban Shimon ben Gamliel says: The stacte is simply the sap that drips from balsam trees. Carshina lye is used to bleach the onycha to make it pleasing. Cyprus wine is used to soak the onycha to make it pungent. Even though urine is suitable for that, nevertheless they do not bring urine into the Temple out of respect.*

Mishnah, *Tamid* 7:4

הַשִּׁיר *The daily song that the Levites would recite in the Temple was as follows: On the first day [of the week] they would say: '*HASHEM*'s is the earth and its fullness, the inhabited land and those who dwell in it.'*[4] *On the second day they would say: 'Great is* HASHEM *and much praised, in the city of our God, Mount of His Holiness.'*[5] *On the third day they would say: 'God stands in the Divine assembly, in the midst of judges shall He judge.'*[6] *On the fourth day they would say: 'O God of vengeance,* HASHEM, *O God of vengeance, appear.'*[7] *On the fifth day they would say: 'Sing joyously to the God of our might, call out to the God of Jacob.'*[8] *On the sixth day they would say: '*HASHEM *will have reigned, He will have donned grandeur; He will have donned might and*

(1) *Psalms* 27:14. (2) *I Samuel* 2:2. (3) *Psalms* 18:32. (4) 24:1. (5) 48:2. (6) 82:1. (7) 94:1. (8) 81:2.

הִתְאַזָּר, אַף תִּכּוֹן תֵּבֵל בַּל תִּמּוֹט.[1] בַּשַּׁבָּת הָיוּ אוֹמְרִים: מִזְמוֹר שִׁיר לְיוֹם הַשַּׁבָּת.[2] מִזְמוֹר שִׁיר לֶעָתִיד לָבֹא, לְיוֹם שֶׁכֻּלּוֹ שַׁבָּת וּמְנוּחָה לְחַיֵּי הָעוֹלָמִים.

מגילה כח:

תָּנָא דְבֵי אֵלִיָּהוּ: כָּל הַשּׁוֹנֶה הֲלָכוֹת בְּכָל יוֹם, מֻבְטָח לוֹ שֶׁהוּא בֶּן עוֹלָם הַבָּא, שֶׁנֶּאֱמַר: הֲלִיכוֹת עוֹלָם לוֹ,[3] אַל תִּקְרֵי הֲלִיכוֹת, אֶלָּא הֲלָכוֹת.

ברכות סד.

אָמַר רַבִּי אֶלְעָזָר אָמַר רַבִּי חֲנִינָא: תַּלְמִידֵי חֲכָמִים מַרְבִּים שָׁלוֹם בָּעוֹלָם, שֶׁנֶּאֱמַר: וְכָל בָּנַיִךְ לִמּוּדֵי יהוה, וְרַב שְׁלוֹם בָּנָיִךְ,[4] אַל תִּקְרֵי בָּנָיִךְ אֶלָּא בּוֹנָיִךְ. ❖ שָׁלוֹם רָב לְאֹהֲבֵי תוֹרָתֶךָ, וְאֵין לָמוֹ מִכְשׁוֹל.[5] יְהִי שָׁלוֹם בְּחֵילֵךְ, שַׁלְוָה בְּאַרְמְנוֹתָיִךְ. לְמַעַן אַחַי וְרֵעָי, אֲדַבְּרָה נָּא שָׁלוֹם בָּךְ. לְמַעַן בֵּית יהוה אֱלֹהֵינוּ, אֲבַקְשָׁה טוֹב לָךְ.[6] יהוה עֹז לְעַמּוֹ יִתֵּן, יהוה יְבָרֵךְ אֶת עַמּוֹ בַשָּׁלוֹם.[7]

קדיש דרבנן

In the presence of a *minyan,* mourners recite קַדִּישׁ דְּרַבָּנָן (see *Laws* §84-85).

יִתְגַּדַּל וְיִתְקַדַּשׁ שְׁמֵהּ רַבָּא. (.Cong – אָמֵן.) בְּעָלְמָא דִּי בְרָא כִרְעוּתֵהּ. וְיַמְלִיךְ מַלְכוּתֵהּ, בְּחַיֵּיכוֹן וּבְיוֹמֵיכוֹן וּבְחַיֵּי דְכָל בֵּית יִשְׂרָאֵל, בַּעֲגָלָא וּבִזְמַן קָרִיב. וְאִמְרוּ: אָמֵן.

(.Cong – אָמֵן. יְהֵא שְׁמֵהּ רַבָּא מְבָרַךְ לְעָלַם וּלְעָלְמֵי עָלְמַיָּא.)

יְהֵא שְׁמֵהּ רַבָּא מְבָרַךְ לְעָלַם וּלְעָלְמֵי עָלְמַיָּא.

יִתְבָּרַךְ וְיִשְׁתַּבַּח וְיִתְפָּאַר וְיִתְרוֹמַם וְיִתְנַשֵּׂא וְיִתְהַדָּר וְיִתְעַלֶּה וְיִתְהַלָּל שְׁמֵהּ דְּקֻדְשָׁא בְּרִיךְ הוּא (.Cong – בְּרִיךְ הוּא) – לְעֵלָּא מִן כָּל בִּרְכָתָא וְשִׁירָתָא תֻּשְׁבְּחָתָא וְנֶחֱמָתָא, דַּאֲמִירָן בְּעָלְמָא. וְאִמְרוּ: אָמֵן. (.Cong – אָמֵן.)

עַל יִשְׂרָאֵל וְעַל רַבָּנָן, וְעַל תַּלְמִידֵיהוֹן וְעַל כָּל תַּלְמִידֵי תַלְמִידֵיהוֹן, וְעַל כָּל מָאן דְּעָסְקִין בְּאוֹרַיְתָא, דִּי בְאַתְרָא הָדֵין וְדִי בְכָל אֲתַר וַאֲתַר. יְהֵא לְהוֹן וּלְכוֹן שְׁלָמָא רַבָּא, חִנָּא וְחִסְדָּא וְרַחֲמִין, וְחַיִּין אֲרִיכִין, וּמְזוֹנֵי רְוִיחֵי, וּפֻרְקָנָא, מִן קֳדָם אֲבוּהוֹן דִּי בִשְׁמַיָּא (וְאַרְעָא). וְאִמְרוּ: אָמֵן. (.Cong – אָמֵן.)

יְהֵא שְׁלָמָא רַבָּא מִן שְׁמַיָּא, וְחַיִּים (טוֹבִים) עָלֵינוּ וְעַל כָּל יִשְׂרָאֵל. וְאִמְרוּ: אָמֵן. (.Cong – אָמֵן.)

Take three steps back. Bow left and say . . . עֹשֶׂה; bow right and say . . . הוּא; bow forward and say וְעַל כָּל . . . אָמֵן. Remain standing in place for a few moments, then take three steps forward.

עֹשֶׂה שָׁלוֹם בִּמְרוֹמָיו, הוּא בְּרַחֲמָיו יַעֲשֶׂה שָׁלוֹם עָלֵינוּ, וְעַל כָּל יִשְׂרָאֵל. וְאִמְרוּ: אָמֵן. (.Cong – אָמֵן.)

girded Himself; He even made the world firm so that it should not falter.'[1] *On the Sabbath they would say: 'A psalm, a song for the Sabbath day.'*[2] *A psalm, a song for the time to come, to the day that will be entirely Sabbath and contentment for the eternal life.*

Talmud, *Megillah* 28b

תָּנָא *The Academy of Elijah taught: He who studies Torah laws every day has the assurance that he will be in the World to Come, as it is said, 'The ways of the world are His'*[3] *— do not read* [הֲלִיכוֹת] *'ways,' but* [הֲלָכוֹת] *'laws.'*

Talmud, *Berachos* 64a

אָמַר *Rabbi Elazar said on behalf of Rabbi Chanina: Torah scholars increase peace in the world, as it is said: 'And all your children will be students of* HASHEM, *and your children will have peace'*[4] *— do not read* [בָּנָיִךְ] *'your children,' but* [בּוֹנָיִךְ] *'your builders.'* Chazzan– *There is abundant peace for the lovers of Your Torah, and there is no stumbling block for them.*[5] *May there be peace within your wall, serenity within your palaces. For the sake of my brethren and comrades I shall speak of peace in your midst. For the sake of the House of* HASHEM, *our God, I will request your good.*[6] HASHEM *will give might to His people,* HASHEM *will bless His people with peace.*[7]

THE RABBIS' KADDISH

In the presence of a *minyan,* mourners recite the Rabbis' *Kaddish* (see *Laws* §84-85). [A transliteration of this *Kaddish* appears on p. 1304.]

יִתְגַּדַּל *May His great Name grow exalted and sanctified* (Cong.– *Amen.*) *in the world that He created as He willed. May He give reign to His kingship in your lifetimes and in your days, and in the lifetimes of the entire Family of Israel, swiftly and soon. Now respond: Amen.*

(Cong.– *Amen. May His great Name be blessed forever and ever.*)
May His great Name be blessed forever and ever.

Blessed, praised, glorified, exalted, extolled, mighty, upraised, and lauded be the Name of the Holy One, Blessed is He (Cong.– *Blessed is He*) *— beyond any blessing and song, praise and consolation that are uttered in the world. Now respond: Amen.* (Cong.– *Amen.*)

Upon Israel, upon the teachers, their disciples and all of their disciples and upon all those who engage in the study of Torah, who are here or anywhere else; may they and you have abundant peace, grace, kindness, and mercy, long life, ample nourishment, and salvation, from before their Father Who is in Heaven (and on earth). Now respond: Amen. (Cong. – *Amen.*)

May there be abundant peace from Heaven, and (good) life, upon us and upon all Israel. Now respond: Amen. (Cong.– *Amen.*)

Take three steps back. Bow left and say, *'He Who makes peace . . .';* bow right and say, *'may He . . .';* bow forward and say, *'and upon all Israel . . .'* Remain standing in place for a few moments, then take three steps forward.

He Who makes peace in His heights, may He, in His compassion, make peace upon us, and upon all Israel. Now respond: Amen. (Cong.– *Amen.*)

---

(1) *Psalms* 93:1. (2) 92:1. (3) *Habakkuk* 3:6. (4) *Isaiah* 54:13. (5) *Psalms* 119:165. (6) 122:7-9. (7) 29:11.

Stand while reciting עָלֵינוּ.

עָלֵינוּ לְשַׁבֵּחַ לַאֲדוֹן הַכֹּל, לָתֵת גְּדֻלָּה לְיוֹצֵר בְּרֵאשִׁית, שֶׁלֹּא עָשָׂנוּ כְּגוֹיֵי הָאֲרָצוֹת, וְלֹא שָׂמָנוּ כְּמִשְׁפְּחוֹת הָאֲדָמָה. שֶׁלֹּא שָׂם חֶלְקֵנוּ כָּהֶם, וְגוֹרָלֵנוּ כְּכָל הֲמוֹנָם. (שֶׁהֵם מִשְׁתַּחֲוִים לְהֶבֶל וָרִיק, וּמִתְפַּלְּלִים אֶל אֵל לֹא יוֹשִׁיעַ.[1]) וַאֲנַחְנוּ כּוֹרְעִים וּמִשְׁתַּחֲוִים וּמוֹדִים, לִפְנֵי מֶלֶךְ מַלְכֵי הַמְּלָכִים הַקָּדוֹשׁ בָּרוּךְ הוּא. שֶׁהוּא נוֹטֶה שָׁמַיִם וְיֹסֵד אָרֶץ,[2] וּמוֹשַׁב יְקָרוֹ בַּשָּׁמַיִם מִמַּעַל, וּשְׁכִינַת עֻזּוֹ בְּגָבְהֵי מְרוֹמִים. הוּא אֱלֹהֵינוּ, אֵין עוֹד. אֱמֶת מַלְכֵּנוּ, אֶפֶס זוּלָתוֹ, כַּכָּתוּב בְּתוֹרָתוֹ: וְיָדַעְתָּ הַיּוֹם וַהֲשֵׁבֹתָ אֶל לְבָבֶךָ, כִּי יהוה הוּא הָאֱלֹהִים בַּשָּׁמַיִם מִמַּעַל וְעַל הָאָרֶץ מִתָּחַת, אֵין עוֹד.[3]

Bow while reciting וַאֲנַחְנוּ כּוֹרְעִים וּמִשְׁתַּחֲוִים.

עַל כֵּן נְקַוֶּה לְּךָ יהוה אֱלֹהֵינוּ לִרְאוֹת מְהֵרָה בְּתִפְאֶרֶת עֻזֶּךָ, לְהַעֲבִיר גִּלּוּלִים מִן הָאָרֶץ, וְהָאֱלִילִים כָּרוֹת יִכָּרֵתוּן, לְתַקֵּן עוֹלָם בְּמַלְכוּת שַׁדַּי. וְכָל בְּנֵי בָשָׂר יִקְרְאוּ בִשְׁמֶךָ, לְהַפְנוֹת אֵלֶיךָ כָּל רִשְׁעֵי אָרֶץ. יַכִּירוּ וְיֵדְעוּ כָּל יוֹשְׁבֵי תֵבֵל, כִּי לְךָ תִּכְרַע כָּל בֶּרֶךְ, תִּשָּׁבַע כָּל לָשׁוֹן.[4] לְפָנֶיךָ יהוה אֱלֹהֵינוּ יִכְרְעוּ וְיִפֹּלוּ, וְלִכְבוֹד שִׁמְךָ יְקָר יִתֵּנוּ. וִיקַבְּלוּ כֻלָּם אֶת עוֹל מַלְכוּתֶךָ, וְתִמְלֹךְ עֲלֵיהֶם מְהֵרָה לְעוֹלָם וָעֶד. כִּי הַמַּלְכוּת שֶׁלְּךָ הִיא וּלְעוֹלְמֵי עַד תִּמְלוֹךְ בְּכָבוֹד, כַּכָּתוּב בְּתוֹרָתֶךָ: יהוה יִמְלֹךְ לְעֹלָם וָעֶד.[5] ❖ וְנֶאֱמַר: וְהָיָה יהוה לְמֶלֶךְ עַל כָּל הָאָרֶץ, בַּיּוֹם הַהוּא יִהְיֶה יהוה אֶחָד וּשְׁמוֹ אֶחָד.[6]

Some congregations recite the following after עָלֵינוּ.

אַל תִּירָא מִפַּחַד פִּתְאֹם, וּמִשֹּׁאַת רְשָׁעִים כִּי תָבֹא.[7] עֻצוּ עֵצָה וְתֻפָר, דַּבְּרוּ דָבָר וְלֹא יָקוּם, כִּי עִמָּנוּ אֵל.[8] וְעַד זִקְנָה אֲנִי הוּא, וְעַד שֵׂיבָה אֲנִי אֶסְבֹּל, אֲנִי עָשִׂיתִי וַאֲנִי אֶשָּׂא, וַאֲנִי אֶסְבֹּל וַאֲמַלֵּט.[9]

קדיש יתום

In the presence of a *minyan,* mourners recite קַדִּישׁ יָתוֹם, the Mourner's *Kaddish* (see *Laws* §81-83):

יִתְגַּדַּל וְיִתְקַדַּשׁ שְׁמֵהּ רַבָּא. (.Cong – אָמֵן.) בְּעָלְמָא דִּי בְרָא כִרְעוּתֵהּ. וְיַמְלִיךְ מַלְכוּתֵהּ, בְּחַיֵּיכוֹן וּבְיוֹמֵיכוֹן וּבְחַיֵּי דְכָל בֵּית יִשְׂרָאֵל, בַּעֲגָלָא וּבִזְמַן קָרִיב. וְאִמְרוּ: אָמֵן.

(.Cong – אָמֵן. יְהֵא שְׁמֵהּ רַבָּא מְבָרַךְ לְעָלַם וּלְעָלְמֵי עָלְמַיָּא.)

Stand while reciting עָלֵינוּ, *'It is our duty . . .'*

עָלֵינוּ *It is our duty to praise the Master of all, to ascribe greatness to the Molder of primeval creation, for He has not made us like the nations of the lands, and has not emplaced us like the families of the earth; for He has not assigned our portion like theirs nor our lot like all their multitudes. (For they bow to vanity and emptiness and pray to a god which helps not.*[1]*) But we bend our knees, bow, and acknowledge our thanks before the King Who reigns over kings, the Holy One, Blessed is He. He stretches out heaven and establishes earth's foundation,*[2] *the seat of His homage is in the heavens above and His powerful Presence is in the loftiest heights. He is our God and there is none other. True is our King, there is nothing beside Him, as it is written in His Torah: 'You are to know this day and take to your heart that* HASHEM *is the only God — in heaven above and on the earth below — there is none other.'*[3]

Bow while reciting *'But we bend our knees.'*

עַל כֵּן *Therefore we put our hope in You,* HASHEM, *our God, that we may soon see Your mighty splendor, to remove detestable idolatry from the earth, and false gods will be utterly cut off, to perfect the universe through the Almighty's sovereignty. Then all humanity will call upon Your Name, to turn all the earth's wicked toward You. All the world's inhabitants will recognize and know that to You every knee should bend, every tongue should swear.*[4] *Before You,* HASHEM, *our God, they will bend every knee and cast themselves down and to the glory of Your Name they will render homage, and they will all accept upon themselves the yoke of Your kingship that You may reign over them soon and eternally. For the kingdom is Yours and You will reign for all eternity in glory as it is written in Your Torah:* HASHEM *shall reign for all eternity.*[5] Chazzan– *And it is said:* HASHEM *will be King over all the world — on that day* HASHEM *will be One and His Name will be One.*[6]

Some congregations recite the following after *Aleinu*.

אַל תִּירָא *Do not fear sudden terror, or the holocaust of the wicked when it comes.*[7] *Plan a conspiracy and it will be annulled; speak your piece and it shall not stand, for God is with us.*[8] *Even till your seniority, I remain unchanged; and even till your ripe old age, I shall endure. I created you and I shall bear you; I shall endure and rescue.*[9]

MOURNER'S KADDISH

In the presence of a *minyan*, mourners recite קַדִּישׁ יָתוֹם, the Mourner's *Kaddish* (see *Laws* §81-83). [A transliteration of this *Kaddish* appears on p. 1305.]

יִתְגַּדַּל *May His great Name grow exalted and sanctified* (Cong.– *Amen.*) *in the world that He created as He willed. May He give reign to His kingship in your lifetimes and in your days, and in the lifetimes of the entire Family of Israel, swiftly and soon. Now respond: Amen.*

(Cong.– *Amen. May His great Name be blessed forever and ever.*)

---

(1) *Isaiah* 45:20. (2) 51:13. (3) *Deuteronomy* 4:39. (4) Cf. *Isaiah* 45:23. (5) *Exodus* 15:18. (6) *Zechariah* 14:9. (7) *Proverbs* 3:25. (8) *Isaiah* 8:10. (9) 46:4.

יְהֵא שְׁמֵהּ רַבָּא מְבָרַךְ לְעָלַם וּלְעָלְמֵי עָלְמַיָּא.

יִתְבָּרַךְ וְיִשְׁתַּבַּח וְיִתְפָּאַר וְיִתְרוֹמַם וְיִתְנַשֵּׂא וְיִתְהַדָּר וְיִתְעַלֶּה וְיִתְהַלָּל שְׁמֵהּ דְּקֻדְשָׁא בְּרִיךְ הוּא (.Cong – בְּרִיךְ הוּא) — לְעֵלָּא מִן כָּל בִּרְכָתָא וְשִׁירָתָא תֻּשְׁבְּחָתָא וְנֶחֱמָתָא, דַּאֲמִירָן בְּעָלְמָא. וְאִמְרוּ: אָמֵן. (.Cong – אָמֵן.)

יְהֵא שְׁלָמָא רַבָּא מִן שְׁמַיָּא, וְחַיִּים עָלֵינוּ וְעַל כָּל יִשְׂרָאֵל. וְאִמְרוּ: אָמֵן. (.Cong – אָמֵן.)

Take three steps back. Bow left and say . . . עֹשֶׂה; bow right and say . . . הוּא; bow forward and say וְעַל כָּל . . . אָמֵן. Remain standing in place for a few moments, then take three steps forward.

עֹשֶׂה שָׁלוֹם בִּמְרוֹמָיו, הוּא יַעֲשֶׂה שָׁלוֹם עָלֵינוּ, וְעַל כָּל יִשְׂרָאֵל. וְאִמְרוּ: אָמֵן. (.Cong – אָמֵן.)

שיר הכבוד

The Ark is opened and שִׁיר הַכָּבוֹד, *The Song of Glory,* is recited responsively — the *chazzan* reciting the first verse, the congregation reciting the second and so on.

אַנְעִים זְמִירוֹת וְשִׁירִים אֶאֱרוֹג, כִּי אֵלֶיךָ נַפְשִׁי תַעֲרוֹג.
נַפְשִׁי חָמְדָה בְּצֵל יָדֶךָ, לָדַעַת כָּל רָז סוֹדֶךָ.
❖ מִדֵּי דַבְּרִי בִּכְבוֹדֶךָ, הוֹמֶה לִבִּי אֶל דּוֹדֶיךָ.
עַל כֵּן אֲדַבֵּר בְּךָ נִכְבָּדוֹת, וְשִׁמְךָ אֲכַבֵּד בְּשִׁירֵי יְדִידוֹת.
❖ אֲסַפְּרָה כְבוֹדְךָ וְלֹא רְאִיתִיךָ, אֲדַמְּךָ אֲכַנְּךָ וְלֹא יְדַעְתִּיךָ.
בְּיַד נְבִיאֶיךָ בְּסוֹד עֲבָדֶיךָ, דִּמִּיתָ הֲדַר כְּבוֹד הוֹדֶךָ.
❖ גְּדֻלָּתְךָ וּגְבוּרָתֶךָ, כִּנּוּ לְתֹקֶף פְּעֻלָּתֶךָ.
דִּמּוּ אוֹתְךָ וְלֹא כְּפִי יֶשְׁךָ, וַיְשַׁוּוּךָ לְפִי מַעֲשֶׂיךָ.
❖ הִמְשִׁילוּךָ בְּרֹב חֶזְיוֹנוֹת, הִנְּךָ אֶחָד בְּכָל דִּמְיוֹנוֹת.
וַיֶּחֱזוּ בְךָ זִקְנָה וּבַחֲרוּת, וּשְׂעַר רֹאשְׁךָ בְּשֵׂיבָה וְשַׁחֲרוּת.
❖ זִקְנָה בְּיוֹם דִּין וּבַחֲרוּת בְּיוֹם קְרָב, כְּאִישׁ מִלְחָמוֹת יָדָיו לוֹ רָב.
חָבַשׁ כּוֹבַע יְשׁוּעָה בְּרֹאשׁוֹ, הוֹשִׁיעָה לּוֹ יְמִינוֹ וּזְרוֹעַ קָדְשׁוֹ.
❖ טַלְלֵי אוֹרוֹת רֹאשׁוֹ נִמְלָא, קְוֻצּוֹתָיו רְסִיסֵי לָיְלָה.
יִתְפָּאֵר בִּי כִּי חָפֵץ בִּי. וְהוּא יִהְיֶה לִּי לַעֲטֶרֶת צְבִי.
❖ כֶּתֶם טָהוֹר פָּז דְּמוּת רֹאשׁוֹ, וְחַק עַל מֵצַח כְּבוֹד שֵׁם קָדְשׁוֹ.
לְחֵן וּלְכָבוֹד צְבִי תִפְאָרָה, אֻמָּתוֹ לוֹ עִטְּרָה עֲטָרָה.
❖ מַחְלְפוֹת רֹאשׁוֹ כְּבִימֵי בְחֻרוֹת, קְוֻצּוֹתָיו תַּלְתַּלִּים שְׁחוֹרוֹת.
נְוֵה הַצֶּדֶק צְבִי תִפְאַרְתּוֹ, יַעֲלֶה נָּא עַל רֹאשׁ שִׂמְחָתוֹ.

May His great Name be blessed forever and ever.

Blessed, praised, glorified, exalted, extolled, mighty, upraised, and lauded be the Name of the Holy One, Blessed is He (Cong.— *Blessed is He*) — *beyond any blessing and song, praise and consolation that are uttered in the world. Now respond: Amen.* (Cong.— *Amen.*)

May there be abundant peace from Heaven, and life, upon us and upon all Israel. Now respond: Amen. (Cong.— *Amen.*)

Take three steps back. Bow left and say, *'He Who makes peace . . .'*; bow right and say, *'may He . . .'*; bow forward and say, *'and upon all Israel . . .'* Remain standing in place for a few moments, then take three steps forward.

He Who makes peace in His heights, may He make peace upon us, and upon all Israel. Now respond: Amen. (Cong.— *Amen.*)

SONG OF GLORY

The Ark is opened and the *Song of Glory* is recited responsively — the *chazzan* reciting the first verse, the congregation reciting the second and so on.

אַנְעִים זְמִירוֹת *I shall compose pleasant psalms and weave hymns,*
because for You shall my soul pine.
My soul desired the shelter of Your hand,
to know every mystery of Your secret.
∴ *As I speak of Your glory, my heart yearns for Your love.*
Therefore I shall speak of Your glories,
and Your Name I shall honor with loving songs.
∴ *I shall relate Your glory, though I see You not;*
I shall allegorize You, I shall describe You, though I know You not.
Through the hand of Your prophets, through the counsel of Your servants;
You allegorized the splendrous glory of Your power.
∴ *Your greatness and Your strength,*
they described the might of Your works.
They allegorized You, but not according to Your reality,
and they portrayed You according to Your deeds.
∴ *They symbolized You in many varied visions;*
yet You are a Unity containing all the allegories.
They envisioned in You agedness and virility,
and the hair of Your head as hoary and jet black.
∴ *Aged on judgment day and virile on the day of battle,*
like a man of war whose powers are many.
The hat of salvation He put on His head;
salvation for Him, His right hand and His sacred arm.
∴ *With illuminating dew drops His head is filled,*
His locks are the rains of the night.
He shall glory in me for He desires me,
and He shall be for me a crown of pride.
∴ *A form of the very finest gold upon his head,*
and carved on his forehead is His glorious, sacred Name.
For grace and for glory the pride of His splendor;
His nation crowns Him with its prayers.
∴ *The tresses of His head are like His youthful days;*
His locks are jet-black ringlets.
The Abode of righteousness is the pride of His splendor;
may He elevate it to His foremost joy.

❖ סְגֻלָּתוֹ תְּהִי בְיָדוֹ עֲטֶרֶת, וּצְנִיף מְלוּכָה צְבִי תִפְאֶרֶת.
עֲמוּסִים נְשָׂאָם עֲטֶרֶת עִנְּדָם, מֵאֲשֶׁר יָקְרוּ בְעֵינָיו כִּבְּדָם.
❖ פְּאֵרוֹ עָלַי וּפְאֵרִי עָלָיו, וְקָרוֹב אֵלַי בְּקָרְאִי אֵלָיו.
צַח וְאָדוֹם לִלְבוּשׁוֹ אָדוֹם, פּוּרָה בְּדָרְכוֹ בְּבוֹאוֹ מֵאֱדוֹם.
❖ קֶשֶׁר תְּפִלִּין הֶרְאָה לֶעָנָו, תְּמוּנַת יהוה לְנֶגֶד עֵינָיו.
רוֹצֶה בְעַמּוֹ עֲנָוִים יְפָאֵר, יוֹשֵׁב תְּהִלּוֹת בָּם לְהִתְפָּאֵר.
❖ רֹאשׁ דְּבָרְךָ אֱמֶת קוֹרֵא מֵרֹאשׁ, דּוֹר וָדוֹר עַם דּוֹרֶשְׁךָ דְּרוֹשׁ.
שִׁית הֲמוֹן שִׁירַי נָא עָלֶיךָ, וְרִנָּתִי תִּקְרַב אֵלֶיךָ.
❖ תְּהִלָּתִי תְּהִי לְרֹאשְׁךָ עֲטֶרֶת, וּתְפִלָּתִי תִּכּוֹן קְטֹרֶת.
תִּיקַר שִׁירַת רָשׁ בְּעֵינֶיךָ, כַּשִּׁיר יוּשַׁר עַל קָרְבָּנֶיךָ.
❖ בִּרְכָתִי תַעֲלֶה לְרֹאשׁ מַשְׁבִּיר, מְחוֹלֵל וּמוֹלִיד צַדִּיק כַּבִּיר.
וּבְבִרְכָתִי תְנַעְנַע לִי רֹאשׁ, וְאוֹתָהּ קַח לְךָ כִּבְשָׂמִים רֹאשׁ.
יֶעֱרַב נָא שִׂיחִי עָלֶיךָ, כִּי נַפְשִׁי תַעֲרוֹג אֵלֶיךָ.

לְךָ יהוה הַגְּדֻלָּה וְהַגְּבוּרָה וְהַתִּפְאֶרֶת וְהַנֵּצַח וְהַהוֹד, כִּי כֹל בַּשָּׁמַיִם וּבָאָרֶץ; לְךָ יהוה הַמַּמְלָכָה וְהַמִּתְנַשֵּׂא לְכֹל לְרֹאשׁ.[1] מִי יְמַלֵּל גְּבוּרוֹת יהוה, יַשְׁמִיעַ כָּל תְּהִלָּתוֹ.[2]

קדיש יתום

In the presence of a *minyan,* mourners recite קַדִּישׁ יָתוֹם, the Mourner's *Kaddish* (see *Laws* §81-83):

יִתְגַּדַּל וְיִתְקַדַּשׁ שְׁמֵהּ רַבָּא. (.Cong – אָמֵן.) בְּעָלְמָא דִּי בְרָא כִרְעוּתֵהּ. וְיַמְלִיךְ מַלְכוּתֵהּ, בְּחַיֵּיכוֹן וּבְיוֹמֵיכוֹן וּבְחַיֵּי דְכָל בֵּית יִשְׂרָאֵל, בַּעֲגָלָא וּבִזְמַן קָרִיב. וְאִמְרוּ: אָמֵן.

(.Cong – אָמֵן. יְהֵא שְׁמֵהּ רַבָּא מְבָרַךְ לְעָלַם וּלְעָלְמֵי עָלְמַיָּא.)

יְהֵא שְׁמֵהּ רַבָּא מְבָרַךְ לְעָלַם וּלְעָלְמֵי עָלְמַיָּא.

יִתְבָּרַךְ וְיִשְׁתַּבַּח וְיִתְפָּאַר וְיִתְרוֹמַם וְיִתְנַשֵּׂא וְיִתְהַדָּר וְיִתְעַלֶּה וְיִתְהַלָּל שְׁמֵהּ דְּקֻדְשָׁא בְּרִיךְ הוּא (.Cong – בְּרִיךְ הוּא) — לְעֵלָּא מִן כָּל בִּרְכָתָא וְשִׁירָתָא תֻּשְׁבְּחָתָא וְנֶחֱמָתָא, דַּאֲמִירָן בְּעָלְמָא. וְאִמְרוּ: אָמֵן. (.Cong – אָמֵן.)

יְהֵא שְׁלָמָא רַבָּא מִן שְׁמַיָּא, וְחַיִּים עָלֵינוּ וְעַל כָּל יִשְׂרָאֵל. וְאִמְרוּ: אָמֵן. (.Cong – אָמֵן.)

Take three steps back. Bow left and say . . . עֹשֶׂה; bow right and say . . . הוּא; bow forward and say וְעַל כָּל . . . אָמֵן. Remain standing in place for a few moments, then take three steps forward.

עֹשֶׂה שָׁלוֹם בִּמְרוֹמָיו, הוּא יַעֲשֶׂה שָׁלוֹם עָלֵינוּ, וְעַל כָּל יִשְׂרָאֵל. וְאִמְרוּ: אָמֵן. (.Cong – אָמֵן.)

∴ *May His treasured nation be in His hand like a crown,*
and like a royal tiara the pride of His splendor.
From infancy He bore them and affixed them as a crown,
because they are precious in His eyes He honored them.
∴ *His tefillin-splendor is upon me and my tefillin-splendor is upon Him,*
and He is near to me when I call to Him.
He is white and crimson; His garment will be bloody red,
when He tramples as in a press on His coming from Edom.
∴ *He showed the tefillin-knot to the humble [Moses],*
the likeness of HASHEM *before his eyes.*
He desires His people, He will glorify the humble;
enthroned upon praises, He glories with them.
∴ *The very beginning of Your word is truth — one reads it from the*
Torah's start; the people that seeks You expounds each generation's fate.
Place the multitude of my songs before You, please;
and my glad song bring near to You.
∴ *May my praise be a crown for Your head,*
and may my prayer be accepted like incense.
May the poor man's song be dear in Your eyes,
like the song that is sung over Your offerings.
∴ *May my blessing rise up upon the head of the Sustainer —*
Creator, Giver of life, mighty Righteous One.
And to my blessing, nod Your head to me,
and take it to Yourself like the finest incense.
∴ *May my prayer be sweet to You, for my soul shall pine for You.*

לְךָ *Yours,* HASHEM, *is the greatness, the strength, the splendor, the triumph, and the glory; even everything in heaven and earth; Yours,* HASHEM, *is the kingdom, and the sovereignty over every leader.*[1] *Who can express the mighty acts of* HASHEM*? Who can declare all His praise?*[2]

MOURNER'S KADDISH

In the presence of a *minyan,* mourners recite the Mourner's *Kaddish* (see *Laws* §81-83).

יִתְגַּדַּל *May His great Name grow exalted and sanctified* (Cong.– *Amen.*) *in the world that He created as He willed. May He give reign to His kingship in your lifetimes and in your days, and in the lifetimes of the entire Family of Israel, swiftly and soon. Now respond: Amen.*

(Cong.– *Amen. May His great Name be blessed forever and ever.*)
May His great Name be blessed forever and ever.

Blessed, praised, glorified, exalted, extolled, mighty, upraised, and lauded be the Name of the Holy One, Blessed is He (Cong.– *Blessed is He*) *— beyond any blessing and song, praise and consolation that are uttered in the world. Now respond: Amen.* (Cong.– *Amen.*)

May there be abundant peace from Heaven, and life, upon us and upon all Israel. Now respond: Amen. (Cong.– *Amen.*)

Take three steps back. Bow left and say, *'He Who makes peace . . .';* bow right and say, *'may He . . .';* bow forward and say, *'and upon all Israel . . .'* Remain standing in place for a few moments, then take three steps forward.

He Who makes peace in His heights, may He make peace upon us, and upon all Israel. Now respond: Amen. (Cong.– *Amen.*)

---

(1) *I Chronicles* 29:11. (2) *Psalms* 106:2.

שיר של יום

A different psalm is assigned as the שִׁיר שֶׁל יוֹם, *Song of the Day,* for each day of the week.

SUNDAY

הַיּוֹם יוֹם רִאשׁוֹן בַּשַּׁבָּת, שֶׁבּוֹ הָיוּ הַלְוִיִּם אוֹמְרִים בְּבֵית הַמִּקְדָּשׁ:

תהלים כד

לְדָוִד מִזְמוֹר, לַיהוה הָאָרֶץ וּמְלוֹאָהּ, תֵּבֵל וְיֹשְׁבֵי בָהּ. כִּי הוּא עַל יַמִּים יְסָדָהּ, וְעַל נְהָרוֹת יְכוֹנְנֶהָ. מִי יַעֲלֶה בְהַר יהוה, וּמִי יָקוּם בִּמְקוֹם קָדְשׁוֹ. נְקִי כַפַּיִם וּבַר לֵבָב, אֲשֶׁר לֹא נָשָׂא לַשָּׁוְא נַפְשִׁי, וְלֹא נִשְׁבַּע לְמִרְמָה. יִשָּׂא בְרָכָה מֵאֵת יהוה, וּצְדָקָה מֵאֱלֹהֵי יִשְׁעוֹ. זֶה דּוֹר דֹּרְשָׁיו, מְבַקְשֵׁי פָנֶיךָ יַעֲקֹב סֶלָה. שְׂאוּ שְׁעָרִים רָאשֵׁיכֶם, וְהִנָּשְׂאוּ פִּתְחֵי עוֹלָם, וְיָבוֹא מֶלֶךְ הַכָּבוֹד. מִי זֶה מֶלֶךְ הַכָּבוֹד, יהוה עִזּוּז וְגִבּוֹר, יהוה גִּבּוֹר מִלְחָמָה. ❖ שְׂאוּ שְׁעָרִים רָאשֵׁיכֶם, וּשְׂאוּ פִּתְחֵי עוֹלָם, וְיָבֹא מֶלֶךְ הַכָּבוֹד. מִי הוּא זֶה מֶלֶךְ הַכָּבוֹד, יהוה צְבָאוֹת, הוּא מֶלֶךְ הַכָּבוֹד סֶלָה.

The service continues with קַדִּישׁ יָתוֹם, *the Mourner's Kaddish* (page 1220).

TUESDAY

הַיּוֹם יוֹם שְׁלִישִׁי בַּשַּׁבָּת, שֶׁבּוֹ הָיוּ הַלְוִיִּם אוֹמְרִים בְּבֵית הַמִּקְדָּשׁ:

תהלים פב

מִזְמוֹר לְאָסָף, אֱלֹהִים נִצָּב בַּעֲדַת אֵל, בְּקֶרֶב אֱלֹהִים יִשְׁפֹּט. עַד מָתַי תִּשְׁפְּטוּ עָוֶל, וּפְנֵי רְשָׁעִים תִּשְׂאוּ סֶלָה. שִׁפְטוּ דָל וְיָתוֹם, עָנִי וָרָשׁ הַצְדִּיקוּ. פַּלְּטוּ דַל וְאֶבְיוֹן, מִיַּד רְשָׁעִים הַצִּילוּ. לֹא יָדְעוּ וְלֹא יָבִינוּ, בַּחֲשֵׁכָה יִתְהַלָּכוּ, יִמּוֹטוּ כָּל מוֹסְדֵי אָרֶץ. אֲנִי אָמַרְתִּי אֱלֹהִים אַתֶּם, וּבְנֵי עֶלְיוֹן כֻּלְּכֶם. אָכֵן כְּאָדָם תְּמוּתוּן, וּכְאַחַד הַשָּׂרִים תִּפֹּלוּ. ❖ קוּמָה אֱלֹהִים שָׁפְטָה הָאָרֶץ, כִּי אַתָּה תִנְחַל בְּכָל הַגּוֹיִם.

The service continues with קַדִּישׁ יָתוֹם, *the Mourner's Kaddish* (page 1220).

WEDNESDAY

הַיּוֹם יוֹם רְבִיעִי בַּשַּׁבָּת, שֶׁבּוֹ הָיוּ הַלְוִיִּם אוֹמְרִים בְּבֵית הַמִּקְדָּשׁ:

תהלים צד:א-צה:ג

אֵל נְקָמוֹת יהוה, אֵל נְקָמוֹת הוֹפִיעַ. הִנָּשֵׂא שֹׁפֵט הָאָרֶץ, הָשֵׁב גְּמוּל עַל גֵּאִים. עַד מָתַי רְשָׁעִים, יהוה, עַד מָתַי רְשָׁעִים יַעֲלֹזוּ. יַבִּיעוּ יְדַבְּרוּ עָתָק, יִתְאַמְּרוּ כָּל פֹּעֲלֵי אָוֶן. עַמְּךָ יהוה יְדַכְּאוּ, וְנַחֲלָתְךָ יְעַנּוּ. אַלְמָנָה וְגֵר יַהֲרֹגוּ, וִיתוֹמִים יְרַצֵּחוּ. וַיֹּאמְרוּ לֹא יִרְאֶה יָּהּ, וְלֹא יָבִין אֱלֹהֵי יַעֲקֹב. בִּינוּ בֹּעֲרִים בָּעָם, וּכְסִילִים מָתַי תַּשְׂכִּילוּ. הֲנֹטַע אֹזֶן הֲלֹא יִשְׁמָע, אִם יֹצֵר עַיִן הֲלֹא יַבִּיט. הֲיֹסֵר גּוֹיִם הֲלֹא יוֹכִיחַ, הַמְלַמֵּד אָדָם

SONG OF THE DAY

A different psalm is assigned as the Song of the Day for each day of the week.

SUNDAY

Today is the first day of the Sabbath,
on which the Levites would recite in the Holy Temple:

Psalm 24

לְדָוִד *Of David a psalm. HASHEM's is the earth and its fullness, the inhabited land and those who dwell in it. For He founded it upon seas, and established it upon rivers. Who may ascend the mountain of HASHEM, and who may stand in the place of His sanctity? One with clean hands and pure heart, who has not sworn in vain by My soul and has not sworn deceitfully. He will receive a blessing from HASHEM and just kindness from the God of his salvation. This is the generation of those who seek Him, those who strive for Your Presence — Jacob, Selah. Raise up your heads, O gates, and be uplifted, you everlasting entrances, so that the King of Glory may enter. Who is this King of Glory? — HASHEM, the mighty and strong, HASHEM, the strong in battle.* Chazzan— *Raise up your heads, O gates, and raise up, you everlasting entrances, so that the King of Glory may enter. Who then is the King of Glory? HASHEM, Master of Legions, He is the King of Glory. Selah!*

The service continues with קַדִּישׁ יָתוֹם, *the Mourner's Kaddish* (p. 1220).

TUESDAY

Today is the third day of the Sabbath,
on which the Levites would recite in the Holy Temple:

Psalm 82

מִזְמוֹר *A psalm of Assaf: God stands in the Divine assembly, in the midst of judges shall He judge. Until when will you judge lawlessly and favor the presence of the wicked, Selah? Judge the needy and the orphan, vindicate the poor and impoverished. Rescue the needy and destitute, from the hand of the wicked deliver them. They do not know nor do they understand, in darkness they walk; all foundations of the earth collapse. I said, 'You are angelic, sons of the Most High are you all.' But like men you shall die, and like one of the princes you shall fall.* Chazzan— *Arise, O God, judge the earth, for You allot the heritage among all the nations.*

The service continues with קַדִּישׁ יָתוֹם, *the Mourner's Kaddish* (p. 1220).

WEDNESDAY

Today is the fourth day of the Sabbath,
on which the Levites would recite in the Holy Temple:

Psalm 94:1-95:3

אֵל נְקָמוֹת *O God of vengeance, HASHEM; O God of vengeance, appear! Arise, O Judge of the earth, render recompense to the haughty. How long shall the wicked — O HASHEM — how long shall the wicked exult? They speak freely, they utter malicious falsehood, they glorify themselves, all workers of iniquity. Your nation, HASHEM, they crush, and they afflict Your heritage. The widow and the stranger they slay, and the orphans they murder. And they say, 'God will not see, nor will the God of Jacob understand.' Understand, you boors among the people; and you fools, when will you gain wisdom? He Who implants the ear, shall He not hear? He Who fashions the eye, shall He not see? He Who chastises nations, shall He not rebuke? — He Who teaches man*

דָּעַת. יהוה יֹדֵעַ מַחְשְׁבוֹת אָדָם, כִּי הֵמָּה הָבֶל. אַשְׁרֵי הַגֶּבֶר אֲשֶׁר תְּיַסְּרֶנּוּ יָּהּ, וּמִתּוֹרָתְךָ תְלַמְּדֶנּוּ. לְהַשְׁקִיט לוֹ מִימֵי רָע, עַד יִכָּרֶה לָרָשָׁע שָׁחַת. כִּי לֹא יִטֹּשׁ יהוה עַמּוֹ, וְנַחֲלָתוֹ לֹא יַעֲזֹב. כִּי עַד צֶדֶק יָשׁוּב מִשְׁפָּט, וְאַחֲרָיו כָּל יִשְׁרֵי לֵב. מִי יָקוּם לִי עִם מְרֵעִים, מִי יִתְיַצֵּב לִי עִם פֹּעֲלֵי אָוֶן. לוּלֵי יהוה עֶזְרָתָה לִּי, כִּמְעַט שָׁכְנָה דוּמָה נַפְשִׁי. אִם אָמַרְתִּי מָטָה רַגְלִי, חַסְדְּךָ יהוה יִסְעָדֵנִי. בְּרֹב שַׂרְעַפַּי בְּקִרְבִּי, תַּנְחוּמֶיךָ יְשַׁעַשְׁעוּ נַפְשִׁי. הַיְחָבְרְךָ כִּסֵּא הַוּוֹת, יֹצֵר עָמָל עֲלֵי חֹק. יָגוֹדּוּ עַל נֶפֶשׁ צַדִּיק, וְדָם נָקִי יַרְשִׁיעוּ. וַיְהִי יהוה לִי לְמִשְׂגָּב, וֵאלֹהַי לְצוּר מַחְסִי. וַיָּשֶׁב עֲלֵיהֶם אֶת אוֹנָם, וּבְרָעָתָם יַצְמִיתֵם, יַצְמִיתֵם יהוה אֱלֹהֵינוּ.

❖ לְכוּ נְרַנְּנָה לַיהוה, נָרִיעָה לְצוּר יִשְׁעֵנוּ. נְקַדְּמָה פָנָיו בְּתוֹדָה, בִּזְמִרוֹת נָרִיעַ לוֹ. כִּי אֵל גָּדוֹל יהוה, וּמֶלֶךְ גָּדוֹל עַל כָּל אֱלֹהִים.

The service continues with קַדִּישׁ יָתוֹם, *the Mourner's Kaddish* (below).

FRIDAY

הַיּוֹם יוֹם שִׁשִּׁי בַּשַּׁבָּת, שֶׁבּוֹ הָיוּ הַלְוִיִּם אוֹמְרִים בְּבֵית הַמִּקְדָּשׁ:

תהלים צג

יהוה מָלָךְ, גֵּאוּת לָבֵשׁ, לָבֵשׁ יהוה עֹז הִתְאַזָּר, אַף תִּכּוֹן תֵּבֵל בַּל תִּמּוֹט. נָכוֹן כִּסְאֲךָ מֵאָז, מֵעוֹלָם אָתָּה. נָשְׂאוּ נְהָרוֹת יהוה, נָשְׂאוּ נְהָרוֹת קוֹלָם, יִשְׂאוּ נְהָרוֹת דָּכְיָם. מִקֹּלוֹת מַיִם רַבִּים, אַדִּירִים מִשְׁבְּרֵי יָם, אַדִּיר בַּמָּרוֹם יהוה. ❖ עֵדֹתֶיךָ נֶאֶמְנוּ מְאֹד לְבֵיתְךָ נַאֲוָה קֹּדֶשׁ, יהוה לְאֹרֶךְ יָמִים.

קדיש יתום

In the presence of a *minyan,* mourners recite קַדִּישׁ יָתוֹם, the Mourner's *Kaddish* (see *Laws* §81-83):

יִתְגַּדַּל וְיִתְקַדַּשׁ שְׁמֵהּ רַבָּא. (.Cong – אָמֵן.) בְּעָלְמָא דִּי בְרָא כִרְעוּתֵהּ. וְיַמְלִיךְ מַלְכוּתֵהּ, בְּחַיֵּיכוֹן וּבְיוֹמֵיכוֹן וּבְחַיֵּי דְכָל בֵּית יִשְׂרָאֵל, בַּעֲגָלָא וּבִזְמַן קָרִיב. וְאִמְרוּ: אָמֵן.

(.Cong – אָמֵן. יְהֵא שְׁמֵהּ רַבָּא מְבָרַךְ לְעָלַם וּלְעָלְמֵי עָלְמַיָּא.)

יְהֵא שְׁמֵהּ רַבָּא מְבָרַךְ לְעָלַם וּלְעָלְמֵי עָלְמַיָּא.

יִתְבָּרַךְ וְיִשְׁתַּבַּח וְיִתְפָּאַר וְיִתְרוֹמַם וְיִתְנַשֵּׂא וְיִתְהַדָּר וְיִתְעַלֶּה וְיִתְהַלָּל שְׁמֵהּ דְּקֻדְשָׁא בְּרִיךְ הוּא (.Cong – בְּרִיךְ הוּא) – לְעֵלָּא מִן כָּל בִּרְכָתָא וְשִׁירָתָא תֻּשְׁבְּחָתָא וְנֶחֱמָתָא, דַּאֲמִירָן בְּעָלְמָא. וְאִמְרוּ: אָמֵן. (.Cong – אָמֵן.)

יְהֵא שְׁלָמָא רַבָּא מִן שְׁמַיָּא, וְחַיִּים עָלֵינוּ וְעַל כָּל יִשְׂרָאֵל. וְאִמְרוּ: אָמֵן. (.Cong – אָמֵן.)

Take three steps back. Bow left and say . . . עֹשֶׂה; bow right and say . . . הוּא; bow forward and say וְעַל כָּל . . . אָמֵן. Remain standing in place for a few moments, then take three steps forward.

עֹשֶׂה שָׁלוֹם בִּמְרוֹמָיו, הוּא יַעֲשֶׂה שָׁלוֹם עָלֵינוּ, וְעַל כָּל יִשְׂרָאֵל. וְאִמְרוּ: אָמֵן. (.Cong – אָמֵן.)

knowledge. HASHEM knows the thoughts of man, that they are futile. Praiseworthy is the man whom God disciplines, and whom You teach from Your Torah. To give him rest from the days of evil, until a pit is dug for the wicked. For HASHEM will not cast off His people, nor will He forsake His heritage. For justice shall revert to righteousness, and following it will be all of upright heart. Who will rise up for me against evildoers? Who will stand up for me against the workers of iniquity? Had HASHEM not been a help to me, my soul would soon have dwelt in silence. If I said, 'My foot falters,' Your kindness, HASHEM, supported me. When my forebodings were abundant within me, Your comforts cheered my soul. Can the throne of destruction be associated with You? — those who fashion evil into a way of life. They join together against the soul of the righteous, and the blood of the innocent they condemn. Then HASHEM became a stronghold for me, and my God, the Rock of my refuge. He turned upon them their own violence, and with their own evil He will cut them off, HASHEM, our God, will cut them off.

Chazzan– *Come — let us sing to HASHEM, let us call out to the Rock of our salvation. Let us greet Him with thanksgiving, with praiseful songs let us call out to Him. For a great God is HASHEM, and a great King above all heavenly powers.*

The service continues with קַדִּישׁ יָתוֹם, *the Mourner's Kaddish* (below).

FRIDAY

Today is the sixth day of the Sabbath,
on which the Levites would recite in the Holy Temple:

Psalm 93

יהוה מָלָךְ *HASHEM will have reigned, He will have donned grandeur; He will have donned might and girded Himself; He even made the world firm so that it should not falter. Your throne was established from of old, eternal are You. Like rivers they raised, O HASHEM, like rivers they raised their voice; like rivers they shall raise their destructiveness. More than the roars of many waters, mightier than the waves of the sea — You are mighty on high, HASHEM.* Chazzan– *Your testimonies are exceedingly trustworthy about Your House, the Sacred Dwelling — O HASHEM, may it be for long days.*

MOURNER'S KADDISH

In the presence of a *minyan,* mourners recite קַדִּישׁ יָתוֹם, the Mourner's *Kaddish* (see *Laws* §81-83):

יִתְגַּדַּל *May His great Name grow exalted and sanctified* (Cong.– *Amen.*) *in the world that He created as He willed. May He give reign to His kingship in your lifetimes and in your days, and in the lifetimes of the entire Family of Israel, swiftly and soon. Now respond: Amen.*

(Cong.– *Amen. May His great Name be blessed forever and ever.*)
May His great Name be blessed forever and ever.

Blessed, praised, glorified, exalted, extolled, mighty, upraised, and lauded be the Name of the Holy One, Blessed is He (Cong.– *Blessed is He*) — *beyond any blessing and song, praise and consolation that are uttered in the world. Now respond: Amen.* (Cong.– *Amen*).

May there be abundant peace from Heaven, and life, upon us and upon all Israel. Now respond: Amen. (Cong.– *Amen.*)

Take three steps back. Bow left and say, *'He Who makes peace . . .';* bow right and say, *'may He . . .';* bow forward and say, *'and upon all Israel . . .'* Remain standing in place for a few moments, then take three steps forward.

He Who makes peace in His heights, may He make peace upon us, and upon all Israel. Now respond: Amen. (Cong.– *Amen.*)

קידושא רבא

(אֵלֶּה מוֹעֲדֵי יהוה מִקְרָאֵי קֹדֶשׁ אֲשֶׁר תִּקְרְאוּ אֹתָם בְּמוֹעֲדָם.[1]
וַיְדַבֵּר מֹשֶׁה אֶת מֹעֲדֵי יהוה, אֶל בְּנֵי יִשְׂרָאֵל.[2]

סַבְרִי מָרָנָן וְרַבָּנָן וְרַבּוֹתַי:

בָּרוּךְ אַתָּה יהוה אֱלֹהֵינוּ מֶלֶךְ הָעוֹלָם, בּוֹרֵא פְּרִי הַגָּפֶן.

(All present – אָמֵן.)

על המחיה appears on page 92; בִּרְכַּת הַמָּזוֹן, on page 84.

מנחה לשמחת תורה

אַשְׁרֵי יוֹשְׁבֵי בֵיתֶךָ, עוֹד יְהַלְלוּךָ סֶּלָה.[3] אַשְׁרֵי הָעָם שֶׁכָּכָה לּוֹ, אַשְׁרֵי הָעָם שֶׁיהוה אֱלֹהָיו.[4]

תהלים קמה

תְּהִלָּה לְדָוִד,
אֲרוֹמִמְךָ אֱלוֹהַי הַמֶּלֶךְ, וַאֲבָרְכָה שִׁמְךָ לְעוֹלָם וָעֶד.
בְּכָל יוֹם אֲבָרְכֶךָּ, וַאֲהַלְלָה שִׁמְךָ לְעוֹלָם וָעֶד.
גָּדוֹל יהוה וּמְהֻלָּל מְאֹד, וְלִגְדֻלָּתוֹ אֵין חֵקֶר.
דּוֹר לְדוֹר יְשַׁבַּח מַעֲשֶׂיךָ, וּגְבוּרֹתֶיךָ יַגִּידוּ.
הֲדַר כְּבוֹד הוֹדֶךָ, וְדִבְרֵי נִפְלְאֹתֶיךָ אָשִׂיחָה.
וֶעֱזוּז נוֹרְאוֹתֶיךָ יֹאמֵרוּ, וּגְדוּלָּתְךָ אֲסַפְּרֶנָּה.
זֵכֶר רַב טוּבְךָ יַבִּיעוּ, וְצִדְקָתְךָ יְרַנֵּנוּ.
חַנּוּן וְרַחוּם יהוה, אֶרֶךְ אַפַּיִם וּגְדָל חָסֶד.
טוֹב יהוה לַכֹּל, וְרַחֲמָיו עַל כָּל מַעֲשָׂיו.
יוֹדוּךָ יהוה כָּל מַעֲשֶׂיךָ, וַחֲסִידֶיךָ יְבָרְכוּכָה.
כְּבוֹד מַלְכוּתְךָ יֹאמֵרוּ, וּגְבוּרָתְךָ יְדַבֵּרוּ.
לְהוֹדִיעַ לִבְנֵי הָאָדָם גְּבוּרֹתָיו, וּכְבוֹד הֲדַר מַלְכוּתוֹ.
מַלְכוּתְךָ מַלְכוּת כָּל עֹלָמִים, וּמֶמְשַׁלְתְּךָ בְּכָל דּוֹר וָדֹר.
סוֹמֵךְ יהוה לְכָל הַנֹּפְלִים, וְזוֹקֵף לְכָל הַכְּפוּפִים.
עֵינֵי כֹל אֵלֶיךָ יְשַׂבֵּרוּ, וְאַתָּה נוֹתֵן לָהֶם אֶת אָכְלָם בְּעִתּוֹ.
פּוֹתֵחַ אֶת יָדֶךָ,
וּמַשְׂבִּיעַ לְכָל חַי רָצוֹן.

While reciting the verse פּוֹתֵחַ, concentrate intently on its meaning.

KIDDUSHA RABBA

(These are the appointed festivals of HASHEM, holy convocations, which you are to proclaim in their appointed times.[1])

And Moses declared HASHEM's appointed festivals to the Children of Israel.[2]

By your leave, my masters and teachers:

בָּרוּךְ *Blessed are You, HASHEM, our God, King of the universe, Who creates the fruit of the vine.* (All present – *Amen.*)

The blessing after cake and wine appears on page 92; Grace after Meals, on page 84.

MINCHAH FOR SIMCHAS TORAH

אַשְׁרֵי *Praiseworthy are those who dwell in Your house; may they always praise You, Selah![3] Praiseworthy is the people for whom this is so, praiseworthy is the people whose God is HASHEM.[4]*

Psalm 145 *A psalm of praise by David:*

א *I will exalt You, my God the King,*
and I will bless Your Name forever and ever.
ב *Every day I will bless You,*
and I will laud Your Name forever and ever.
ג *HASHEM is great and exceedingly lauded,*
and His greatness is beyond investigation.
ד *Each generation will praise Your deeds to the next*
and of Your mighty deeds they will tell.
ה *The splendrous glory of Your power*
and Your wondrous deeds I shall discuss.
ו *And of Your awesome power they will speak,*
and Your greatness I shall relate.
ז *A recollection of Your abundant goodness they will utter*
and of Your righteousness they will sing exultantly.
ח *Gracious and merciful is HASHEM,*
slow to anger, and great in [bestowing] kindness.
ט *HASHEM is good to all; His mercies are on all His works.*
י *All Your works shall thank You, HASHEM,*
and Your devout ones will bless You.
כ *Of the glory of Your kingdom they will speak,*
and of Your power they will tell;
ל *To inform human beings of His mighty deeds,*
and the glorious splendor of His kingdom.
מ *Your kingdom is a kingdom spanning all eternities,*
and Your dominion is throughout every generation.
ס *HASHEM supports all the fallen ones and straightens all the bent.*
ע *The eyes of all look to You with hope*
and You give them their food in its proper time;
פ *You open Your hand,*
and satisfy the desire of every living thing.

While reciting the verse, *'You open . . .,'* concentrate intently on its meaning.

(1) *Leviticus* 23:4. (2) 23:44. (3) *Psalms* 84:5. (4) 144:15.

צַדִּיק יהוה בְּכָל דְּרָכָיו, וְחָסִיד בְּכָל מַעֲשָׂיו.
קָרוֹב יהוה לְכָל קֹרְאָיו, לְכֹל אֲשֶׁר יִקְרָאֻהוּ בֶאֱמֶת.
רְצוֹן יְרֵאָיו יַעֲשֶׂה, וְאֶת שַׁוְעָתָם יִשְׁמַע וְיוֹשִׁיעֵם.
שׁוֹמֵר יהוה אֶת כָּל אֹהֲבָיו, וְאֵת כָּל הָרְשָׁעִים יַשְׁמִיד.
❖ תְּהִלַּת יהוה יְדַבֶּר פִּי, וִיבָרֵךְ כָּל בָּשָׂר שֵׁם קָדְשׁוֹ לְעוֹלָם וָעֶד.
וַאֲנַחְנוּ נְבָרֵךְ יָהּ, מֵעַתָּה וְעַד עוֹלָם, הַלְלוּיָהּ.[1]

The primary part of וּבָא לְצִיּוֹן is the *Kedushah* recited by the angels. These verses are presented in bold type and it is preferable that the congregation recite them aloud and in unison. However, the interpretive translation in Aramaic (which follows the verses in bold type) should be recited softly.

וּבָא לְצִיּוֹן גּוֹאֵל, וּלְשָׁבֵי פֶשַׁע בְּיַעֲקֹב, נְאֻם יהוה. וַאֲנִי, זֹאת בְּרִיתִי אוֹתָם, אָמַר יהוה, רוּחִי אֲשֶׁר עָלֶיךָ, וּדְבָרַי אֲשֶׁר שַׂמְתִּי בְּפִיךָ, לֹא יָמוּשׁוּ מִפִּיךָ וּמִפִּי זַרְעֲךָ וּמִפִּי זֶרַע זַרְעֲךָ, אָמַר יהוה, מֵעַתָּה וְעַד עוֹלָם:[2] ❖ וְאַתָּה קָדוֹשׁ יוֹשֵׁב תְּהִלּוֹת יִשְׂרָאֵל.[3] וְקָרָא זֶה אֶל זֶה וְאָמַר:

קָדוֹשׁ, קָדוֹשׁ, קָדוֹשׁ יהוה צְבָאוֹת, מְלֹא כָל הָאָרֶץ כְּבוֹדוֹ.[4]

וּמְקַבְּלִין דֵּין מִן דֵּין וְאָמְרִין:
קַדִּישׁ בִּשְׁמֵי מְרוֹמָא עִלָּאָה בֵּית שְׁכִינְתֵּהּ,
קַדִּישׁ עַל אַרְעָא עוֹבַד גְּבוּרְתֵּהּ,
קַדִּישׁ לְעָלַם וּלְעָלְמֵי עָלְמַיָּא, יהוה צְבָאוֹת,
מַלְיָא כָל אַרְעָא זִיו יְקָרֵהּ.[5]

❖ וַתִּשָּׂאֵנִי רוּחַ, וָאֶשְׁמַע אַחֲרַי קוֹל רַעַשׁ גָּדוֹל:

בָּרוּךְ כְּבוֹד יהוה מִמְּקוֹמוֹ.[6]

וּנְטָלַתְנִי רוּחָא, וְשִׁמְעֵת בַּתְרַי קָל זִיעַ סַגִּיא
דִּמְשַׁבְּחִין וְאָמְרִין:
בְּרִיךְ יְקָרָא דַיהוה מֵאֲתַר בֵּית שְׁכִינְתֵּהּ.[7]

יהוה יִמְלֹךְ לְעֹלָם וָעֶד.[8]

יהוה מַלְכוּתֵהּ קָאֵם לְעָלַם וּלְעָלְמֵי עָלְמַיָּא.[9]

יהוה אֱלֹהֵי אַבְרָהָם יִצְחָק וְיִשְׂרָאֵל אֲבֹתֵינוּ, שָׁמְרָה זֹּאת לְעוֹלָם, לְיֵצֶר מַחְשְׁבוֹת לְבַב עַמֶּךָ, וְהָכֵן לְבָבָם אֵלֶיךָ.[10] וְהוּא רַחוּם,

---

✥ וּבָא לְצִיּוֹן / Uva Letzion

The most important part of the וּבָא לְצִיּוֹן prayer is the recitation of the angels' praises of God.

The Talmud (*Sotah* 49a) declares that since the destruction of the Temple, even the physical beauty and pleasures of the world began deteriorating. If so, by what merit does the world endure? Rava teaches: The *Kedushah* in the

צ *Righteous is HASHEM in all His ways and magnanimous in all His deeds.*

ק *HASHEM is close to all who call upon Him — to all who call upon Him sincerely.*

ר *The will of those who fear Him He will do; and their cry He will hear, and save them.*

ש *HASHEM protects all who love Him; but all the wicked He will destroy.*

ת Chazzan– *May my mouth declare the praise of HASHEM and may all flesh bless His Holy Name forever and ever.*

We will bless God from this time and forever, Halleluyah![1]

The primary part of וּבָא לְצִיּוֹן, *'A redeemer shall come . . .',* is the *Kedushah* recited by the angels. These verses are presented in bold type and it is preferable that the congregation recite them aloud and in unison. However, the interpretive translation in Aramaic (which follows the verses in bold type) should be recited softly.

וּבָא לְצִיּוֹן *'A redeemer shall come to Zion and to those of Jacob who repent from willful sin,' the words of HASHEM. 'And as for Me, this is My covenant with them,' said HASHEM, 'My spirit that is upon you and My words that I have placed in your mouth shall not be withdrawn from your mouth, nor from the mouth of your offspring, nor from the mouth of your offspring's offspring,' said HASHEM, 'from this moment and forever.'*[2] Chazzan– *You are the Holy One, enthroned upon the praises of Israel.*[3] *And one [angel] will call another and say:*

'Holy, holy, holy is HASHEM, Master of Legions, the whole world is filled with His glory.'[4]

And they receive permission from one another and say:
'Holy in the most exalted heaven, the abode of His Presence;
holy on earth, product of His strength;
holy forever and ever is HASHEM, Master of Legions —
the entire world is filled with the radiance of His glory.'[5]

Chazzan– *And a wind lifted me; and I heard behind me the sound of a great noise:*

'Blessed is the glory of HASHEM from His place.'[6]

And a wind lifted me and I heard behind me the sound of the powerful movement of those who praised saying:
'Blessed is the honor of HASHEM
from the place of the abode of His Presence.'[7]

HASHEM shall reign for all eternity.[8]

HASHEM — His kingdom is established forever and ever.[9]

HASHEM, God of Abraham, Isaac, and Israel, our forefathers, may You preserve this forever as the realization of the thoughts in Your people's heart, and may You direct their heart to You.[10] *He, the Merciful One,*

---

(1) *Psalms* 115:18. (2) *Isaiah* 59:20-21. (3) *Psalms* 22:4. (4) *Isaiah* 6:3. (5) *Targum Yonasan.* (6) *Ezekiel* 3:12. (7) *Targum Yonasan.* (8) *Exodus* 15:18. (9) *Targum Onkelos.* (10) *I Chronicles* 29:18.

יְכַפֵּר עָוֹן וְלֹא יַשְׁחִית, וְהִרְבָּה לְהָשִׁיב אַפּוֹ, וְלֹא יָעִיר כָּל חֲמָתוֹ.[1] כִּי אַתָּה אֲדֹנָי טוֹב וְסַלָּח, וְרַב חֶסֶד לְכָל קֹרְאֶיךָ.[2] צִדְקָתְךָ צֶדֶק לְעוֹלָם, וְתוֹרָתְךָ אֱמֶת.[3] תִּתֵּן אֱמֶת לְיַעֲקֹב, חֶסֶד לְאַבְרָהָם, אֲשֶׁר נִשְׁבַּעְתָּ לַאֲבֹתֵינוּ מִימֵי קֶדֶם.[4] בָּרוּךְ אֲדֹנָי יוֹם יוֹם יַעֲמָס לָנוּ, הָאֵל יְשׁוּעָתֵנוּ סֶלָה.[5] יהוה צְבָאוֹת עִמָּנוּ, מִשְׂגָּב לָנוּ אֱלֹהֵי יַעֲקֹב סֶלָה.[6] יהוה צְבָאוֹת, אַשְׁרֵי אָדָם בֹּטֵחַ בָּךְ.[7] יהוה הוֹשִׁיעָה, הַמֶּלֶךְ יַעֲנֵנוּ בְיוֹם קָרְאֵנוּ.[8]

בָּרוּךְ הוּא אֱלֹהֵינוּ שֶׁבְּרָאָנוּ לִכְבוֹדוֹ, וְהִבְדִּילָנוּ מִן הַתּוֹעִים, וְנָתַן לָנוּ תּוֹרַת אֱמֶת, וְחַיֵּי עוֹלָם נָטַע בְּתוֹכֵנוּ. הוּא יִפְתַּח לִבֵּנוּ בְּתוֹרָתוֹ, וְיָשֵׂם בְּלִבֵּנוּ אַהֲבָתוֹ וְיִרְאָתוֹ וְלַעֲשׂוֹת רְצוֹנוֹ וּלְעָבְדוֹ בְּלֵבָב שָׁלֵם, לְמַעַן לֹא נִיגַע לָרִיק, וְלֹא נֵלֵד לַבֶּהָלָה.[9]

יְהִי רָצוֹן מִלְּפָנֶיךָ יהוה אֱלֹהֵינוּ וֵאלֹהֵי אֲבוֹתֵינוּ, שֶׁנִּשְׁמֹר חֻקֶּיךָ בָּעוֹלָם הַזֶּה, וְנִזְכֶּה וְנִחְיֶה וְנִרְאֶה וְנִירַשׁ טוֹבָה וּבְרָכָה לִשְׁנֵי יְמוֹת הַמָּשִׁיחַ וּלְחַיֵּי הָעוֹלָם הַבָּא. לְמַעַן יְזַמֶּרְךָ כָבוֹד וְלֹא יִדֹּם, יהוה אֱלֹהַי לְעוֹלָם אוֹדֶךָּ.[10] בָּרוּךְ הַגֶּבֶר אֲשֶׁר יִבְטַח בַּיהוה, וְהָיָה יהוה מִבְטַחוֹ.[11] בִּטְחוּ בַיהוה עֲדֵי עַד, כִּי בְּיָהּ יהוה צוּר עוֹלָמִים.[12] ❖ וְיִבְטְחוּ בְךָ יוֹדְעֵי שְׁמֶךָ, כִּי לֹא עָזַבְתָּ דֹרְשֶׁיךָ, יהוה.[13] יהוה חָפֵץ לְמַעַן צִדְקוֹ, יַגְדִּיל תּוֹרָה וְיַאְדִּיר.[14]

חצי קדיש

Chazzan recites חֲצִי קַדִּישׁ.

יִתְגַּדַּל וְיִתְקַדַּשׁ שְׁמֵהּ רַבָּא. (Cong. – אָמֵן.) בְּעָלְמָא דִּי בְרָא כִרְעוּתֵהּ. וְיַמְלִיךְ מַלְכוּתֵהּ, בְּחַיֵּיכוֹן וּבְיוֹמֵיכוֹן וּבְחַיֵּי דְכָל בֵּית יִשְׂרָאֵל, בַּעֲגָלָא וּבִזְמַן קָרִיב. וְאִמְרוּ: אָמֵן.

(Cong. – אָמֵן. יְהֵא שְׁמֵהּ רַבָּא מְבָרַךְ לְעָלַם וּלְעָלְמֵי עָלְמַיָּא.)

יְהֵא שְׁמֵהּ רַבָּא מְבָרַךְ לְעָלַם וּלְעָלְמֵי עָלְמַיָּא.

יִתְבָּרַךְ וְיִשְׁתַּבַּח וְיִתְפָּאַר וְיִתְרוֹמַם וְיִתְנַשֵּׂא וְיִתְהַדָּר וְיִתְעַלֶּה וְיִתְהַלָּל שְׁמֵהּ דְּקֻדְשָׁא בְּרִיךְ הוּא (Cong. – בְּרִיךְ הוּא) — לְעֵלָּא מִן כָּל בִּרְכָתָא וְשִׁירָתָא תֻּשְׁבְּחָתָא וְנֶחֱמָתָא, דַּאֲמִירָן בְּעָלְמָא. וְאִמְרוּ: אָמֵן.

(Cong. – אָמֵן.)

---

prayer *Uva Letzion,* and the recitation of *Kaddish* following the public study of Torah. *Rashi* explains that after the Destruction, the primary focus of holiness in the universe is Torah study. In *Uva Letzion,* the Sages combined the Scriptural verses containing the angels' praise of God with the interpretive translation of *Yonasan ben Uziel.* Thus, this prayer itself constitutes Torah study and its recitation involves the entire congregation in Torah study. This emphasis on Torah study is further stressed by the latter part of *Uva Letzion* which lauds the study and observance of the Torah. The *Kaddish* recited after public Torah study is a further affirmation of the Torah's central role in Jewish existence.

is forgiving of iniquity and does not destroy; frequently He withdraws His anger, not arousing His entire rage.[1] *For You, my Lord, are good and forgiving, and abundantly kind to all who call upon You.*[2] *Your righteousness remains righteous forever, and Your Torah is truth.*[3] *Grant truth to Jacob, kindness to Abraham, as You swore to our forefathers from ancient times.*[4] *Blessed is my Lord for every single day, He burdens us with blessings, the God of our salvation, Selah.*[5] *HASHEM, Master of Legions, is with us, a stronghold for us is the God of Jacob, Selah.*[6] *HASHEM, Master of Legions, praiseworthy is the man who trusts in You.*[7] *HASHEM, save! May the King answer us on the day we call.*[8]

Blessed is He, our God, Who created us for His glory, separated us from those who stray, gave us the Torah of truth and implanted eternal life within us. May He open our heart through His Torah and imbue our heart with love and awe of Him and that we may do His will and serve Him wholeheartedly, so that we do not struggle in vain nor produce for futility.[9]

May it be Your will, HASHEM, our God and the God of our forefathers, that we observe Your decrees in This World, and merit that we live and see and inherit goodness and blessing in the years of Messianic times and for the life of the World to Come. So that my soul might sing to You and not be stilled, HASHEM, my God, forever will I thank You.[10] *Blessed is the man who trusts in HASHEM, then HASHEM will be his security.*[11] *Trust in HASHEM forever, for in God, HASHEM, is the strength of the worlds.*[12] Chazzan– *Those knowing Your Name will trust in You, and You forsake not those Who seek You, HASHEM.*[13] *HASHEM desired, for the sake of its [Israel's] righteousness, that the Torah be made great and glorious.*[14]

HALF-KADDISH

Chazzan recites Half-*Kaddish.*

יִתְגַּדַּל *May His great Name grow exalted and sanctified* (Cong.– *Amen.*) *in the world that He created as He willed. May He give reign to His kingship in your lifetimes and in your days, and in the lifetimes of the entire Family of Israel, swiftly and soon. Now respond: Amen.*

(Cong.– *Amen. May His great Name be blessed forever and ever.*)

May His great Name be blessed forever and ever.

Blessed, praised, glorified, exalted, extolled, mighty, upraised, and lauded be the Name of the Holy One, Blessed is He (Cong.– *Blessed is He*) — *beyond any blessing and song, praise and consolation that are uttered in the world. Now respond: Amen.* (Cong.– *Amen.*)

---

(1) *Psalms* 78:38. (2) 86:5. (3) 119:142. (4) *Micah* 7:20. (5) *Psalms* 68:20. (6) 46:8. (7) 84:13. (8) 20:10. (9) Cf. *Isaiah* 65:23. (10) *Psalms* 30:13. (11) *Jeremiah* 17:7. (12) *Isaiah* 26:4. (13) *Psalms* 9:11. (14) *Isaiah* 42:21.

שמונה עשרה – עמידה

Take three steps backward, then three steps forward. Remain standing with the feet together while reciting *Shemoneh Esrei*. Recite it with quiet devotion and without interruption, verbal or otherwise. Although its recitation should not be audible to others, one must pray loudly enough to hear himself.

כִּי שֵׁם יהוה אֶקְרָא, הָבוּ גֹדֶל לֵאלֹהֵינוּ.[1]

אֲדֹנָי שְׂפָתַי תִּפְתָּח, וּפִי יַגִּיד תְּהִלָּתֶךָ.[2]

אבות

Bend the knees at בָּרוּךְ; bow at אַתָּה; straighten up at ה'.

בָּרוּךְ אַתָּה יהוה אֱלֹהֵינוּ וֵאלֹהֵי אֲבוֹתֵינוּ, אֱלֹהֵי אַבְרָהָם, אֱלֹהֵי יִצְחָק, וֵאלֹהֵי יַעֲקֹב, הָאֵל הַגָּדוֹל הַגִּבּוֹר וְהַנּוֹרָא, אֵל עֶלְיוֹן, גּוֹמֵל חֲסָדִים טוֹבִים וְקוֹנֵה הַכֹּל, וְזוֹכֵר חַסְדֵי אָבוֹת, וּמֵבִיא גוֹאֵל לִבְנֵי בְנֵיהֶם, לְמַעַן שְׁמוֹ בְּאַהֲבָה. מֶלֶךְ עוֹזֵר וּמוֹשִׁיעַ וּמָגֵן.

Bend the knees at בָּרוּךְ; bow at אַתָּה; straighten up at ה'.

בָּרוּךְ אַתָּה יהוה, מָגֵן אַבְרָהָם.

גבורות

אַתָּה גִּבּוֹר לְעוֹלָם אֲדֹנָי, מְחַיֵּה מֵתִים אַתָּה, רַב לְהוֹשִׁיעַ.

מַשִּׁיב הָרְוּחַ וּמוֹרִיד הַגֶּשֶׁם.

מְכַלְכֵּל חַיִּים בְּחֶסֶד, מְחַיֵּה מֵתִים בְּרַחֲמִים רַבִּים, סוֹמֵךְ נוֹפְלִים, וְרוֹפֵא חוֹלִים, וּמַתִּיר אֲסוּרִים, וּמְקַיֵּם אֱמוּנָתוֹ לִישֵׁנֵי עָפָר. מִי כָמְוֹךָ בַּעַל גְּבוּרוֹת, וּמִי דּוֹמֶה לָּךְ, מֶלֶךְ מֵמִית וּמְחַיֶּה וּמַצְמִיחַ יְשׁוּעָה. וְנֶאֱמָן אַתָּה לְהַחֲיוֹת מֵתִים. בָּרוּךְ אַתָּה יהוה, מְחַיֵּה הַמֵּתִים.

During the *chazzan's* repetition, *Kedushah* (below) is recited at this point.

קדושה

When reciting *Kedushah,* one must stand with his feet together and avoid any interruptions. One should rise on his toes when saying the words קָדוֹשׁ, קָדוֹשׁ, קָדוֹשׁ; בָּרוּךְ (of בָּרוּךְ כְּבוֹד); and יִמְלֹךְ.

Cong. then *Chazzan* – **נְקַדֵּשׁ** אֶת שִׁמְךָ בָּעוֹלָם, כְּשֵׁם שֶׁמַּקְדִּישִׁים אוֹתוֹ בִּשְׁמֵי מָרוֹם, כַּכָּתוּב עַל יַד נְבִיאֶךָ, וְקָרָא זֶה אֶל זֶה וְאָמַר:

All – קָדוֹשׁ קָדוֹשׁ קָדוֹשׁ יהוה צְבָאוֹת, מְלֹא כָל הָאָרֶץ כְּבוֹדוֹ.[3]

Chazzan – לְעֻמָּתָם בָּרוּךְ יֹאמֵרוּ:

All – בָּרוּךְ כְּבוֹד יהוה, מִמְּקוֹמוֹ.[4]

Chazzan – וּבְדִבְרֵי קָדְשְׁךָ כָּתוּב לֵאמֹר:

All – יִמְלֹךְ יהוה לְעוֹלָם, אֱלֹהַיִךְ צִיּוֹן לְדֹר וָדֹר, הַלְלוּיָהּ.[5]

Chazzan only concludes – לְדוֹר וָדוֹר נַגִּיד גָּדְלֶךָ וּלְנֵצַח נְצָחִים קְדֻשָּׁתְךָ נַקְדִּישׁ, וְשִׁבְחֲךָ אֱלֹהֵינוּ מִפִּינוּ לֹא יָמוּשׁ לְעוֹלָם וָעֶד, כִּי אֵל מֶלֶךְ גָּדוֹל וְקָדוֹשׁ אָתָּה. בָּרוּךְ אַתָּה יהוה, הָאֵל הַקָּדוֹשׁ.

Chazzan continues . . . אַתָּה בְחַרְתָּנוּ (page 1230).

SHEMONEH ESREI — AMIDAH

Take three steps backward, then three steps forward. Remain standing with the feet together while reciting *Shemoneh Esrei.* Recite it with quiet devotion and without interruption, verbal or otherwise. Although its recitation should not be audible to others, one must pray loudly enough to hear himself.

When I call out the Name of HASHEM, ascribe greatness to our God.[1]
My Lord, open my lips, that my mouth may declare Your praise.[2]

PATRIARCHS

Bend the knees at *'Blessed'*; bow at *'You'*; straighten up at *'HASHEM.'*

בָּרוּךְ *Blessed are You, HASHEM, our God and the God of our forefathers, God of Abraham, God of Isaac, and God of Jacob; the great, mighty, and awesome God, the supreme God, Who bestows beneficial kindnesses and creates everything, Who recalls the kindnesses of the Patriarchs and brings a Redeemer to their children's children, for His Name's sake, with love.*

Bend the knees at *'Blessed'*; bow at *'You'*; straighten up at 'HASHEM.'

O King, Helper, Savior, and Shield. Blessed are You, HASHEM, Shield of Abraham.

GOD'S MIGHT

אַתָּה *You are eternally mighty, my Lord, the Resuscitator of the dead are You; abundantly able to save.*

He makes the wind blow and He makes the rain descend.

He sustains the living with kindness, resuscitates the dead with abundant mercy, supports the fallen, heals the sick, releases the confined, and maintains His faith to those asleep in the dust. Who is like You, O Master of mighty deeds, and who is comparable to You, O King Who causes death and restores life and makes salvation sprout! And You are faithful to resuscitate the dead. Blessed are You, HASHEM, Who resuscitates the dead.

During the *chazzan's* repetition, *Kedushah* (below) is recited at this point.

KEDUSHAH

When reciting *Kedushah*, one must stand with his feet together and avoid any interruptions. One should rise on his toes when saying the words *Holy, holy, holy; Blessed is;* and *HASHEM shall reign.*

Cong. then Chazzan — **נְקַדֵּשׁ** *We shall sanctify Your Name in this world, just as they sanctify it in heaven above, as it is written by Your prophet, "And one [angel] will call another and say:*

All — *'Holy, holy, holy is HASHEM, Master of Legions, the whole world is filled with His glory.' "*[3]

Chazzan — *Those facing them say 'Blessed':*

All — *'Blessed is the glory of HASHEM from His place.'*[4]

Chazzan — *And in Your holy Writings the following is written:*

All — *'HASHEM shall reign forever — your God, O Zion — from generation to generation, Halleluyah!'*[5]

Chazzan only concludes — *From generation to generation we shall relate Your greatness and for infinite eternities we shall proclaim Your holiness. Your praise, our God, shall not leave our mouth forever and ever, for You, O God, are a great and holy King. Blessed are You HASHEM, the holy God.*

Chazzan continues אַתָּה בְחַרְתָּנוּ, *You have chosen us . . .* (page 1230).

---

(1) *Deuteronomy* 32:3. (2) *Psalms* 51:17. (3) *Isaiah* 6:3. (4) *Ezekiel* 3:12. (5) *Psalms* 146:10.

קדושת השם

אַתָּה קָדוֹשׁ וְשִׁמְךָ קָדוֹשׁ, וּקְדוֹשִׁים בְּכָל יוֹם יְהַלְּלוּךָ סֶּלָה. בָּרוּךְ אַתָּה יהוה, הָאֵל הַקָּדוֹשׁ.

קדושת היום

אַתָּה בְחַרְתָּנוּ מִכָּל הָעַמִּים, אָהַבְתָּ אוֹתָנוּ, וְרָצִיתָ בָּנוּ, וְרוֹמַמְתָּנוּ מִכָּל הַלְּשׁוֹנוֹת, וְקִדַּשְׁתָּנוּ בְּמִצְוֹתֶיךָ, וְקֵרַבְתָּנוּ מַלְכֵּנוּ לַעֲבוֹדָתֶךָ, וְשִׁמְךָ הַגָּדוֹל וְהַקָּדוֹשׁ עָלֵינוּ קָרָאתָ.

וַתִּתֶּן לָנוּ יהוה אֱלֹהֵינוּ בְּאַהֲבָה מוֹעֲדִים לְשִׂמְחָה חַגִּים וּזְמַנִּים לְשָׂשׂוֹן, אֶת יוֹם הַשְּׁמִינִי חַג הָעֲצֶרֶת הַזֶּה, זְמַן שִׂמְחָתֵנוּ מִקְרָא קֹדֶשׁ, זֵכֶר לִיצִיאַת מִצְרָיִם.

During the *chazzan's* repetition, congregation responds אָמֵן as indicated.

אֱלֹהֵינוּ וֵאלֹהֵי אֲבוֹתֵינוּ, יַעֲלֶה, וְיָבֹא, וְיַגִּיעַ, וְיֵרָאֶה, וְיֵרָצֶה, וְיִשָּׁמַע, וְיִפָּקֵד, וְיִזָּכֵר זִכְרוֹנֵנוּ וּפִקְדוֹנֵנוּ, וְזִכְרוֹן אֲבוֹתֵינוּ, וְזִכְרוֹן מָשִׁיחַ בֶּן דָּוִד עַבְדֶּךָ, וְזִכְרוֹן יְרוּשָׁלַיִם עִיר קָדְשֶׁךָ, וְזִכְרוֹן כָּל עַמְּךָ בֵּית יִשְׂרָאֵל לְפָנֶיךָ, לִפְלֵיטָה לְטוֹבָה לְחֵן וּלְחֶסֶד וּלְרַחֲמִים, לְחַיִּים וּלְשָׁלוֹם בְּיוֹם הַשְּׁמִינִי חַג הָעֲצֶרֶת הַזֶּה. זָכְרֵנוּ יהוה אֱלֹהֵינוּ בּוֹ לְטוֹבָה (.Cong – אָמֵן), וּפָקְדֵנוּ בוֹ לִבְרָכָה (.Cong – אָמֵן), וְהוֹשִׁיעֵנוּ בוֹ לְחַיִּים (.Cong – אָמֵן). וּבִדְבַר יְשׁוּעָה וְרַחֲמִים, חוּס וְחָנֵּנוּ וְרַחֵם עָלֵינוּ וְהוֹשִׁיעֵנוּ, כִּי אֵלֶיךָ עֵינֵינוּ, כִּי אֵל מֶלֶךְ חַנּוּן וְרַחוּם אָתָּה.[1]

וְהַשִּׂיאֵנוּ יהוה אֱלֹהֵינוּ אֶת בִּרְכַּת מוֹעֲדֶיךָ לְחַיִּים וּלְשָׁלוֹם, לְשִׂמְחָה וּלְשָׂשׂוֹן, כַּאֲשֶׁר רָצִיתָ וְאָמַרְתָּ לְבָרְכֵנוּ. קַדְּשֵׁנוּ בְּמִצְוֹתֶיךָ וְתֵן חֶלְקֵנוּ בְּתוֹרָתֶךָ, שַׂבְּעֵנוּ מִטּוּבֶךָ וְשַׂמְּחֵנוּ בִּישׁוּעָתֶךָ, וְטַהֵר לִבֵּנוּ לְעָבְדְּךָ בֶּאֱמֶת, וְהַנְחִילֵנוּ יהוה אֱלֹהֵינוּ בְּשִׂמְחָה וּבְשָׂשׂוֹן מוֹעֲדֵי קָדְשֶׁךָ, וְיִשְׂמְחוּ בְךָ יִשְׂרָאֵל מְקַדְּשֵׁי שְׁמֶךָ. בָּרוּךְ אַתָּה יהוה, מְקַדֵּשׁ יִשְׂרָאֵל וְהַזְּמַנִּים.

HOLINESS OF GOD'S NAME

אַתָּה *You are holy and Your Name is holy, and holy ones praise You every day, forever. Blessed are You, HASHEM, the holy God.*

SANCTIFICATION OF THE DAY

אַתָּה בְחַרְתָּנוּ *You have chosen us from all the peoples; You loved us and found favor in us; You exalted us above all the tongues and You sanctified us with Your commandments. You drew us close, our King, to Your service and proclaimed Your great and Holy Name upon us.*

וַתִּתֶּן לָנוּ *And You gave us, HASHEM, our God, with love, appointed festivals for gladness, Festivals and times for joy, this day of the Shemini Atzeres Festival, the time of our gladness, a holy convocation, a memorial of the Exodus from Egypt.*

During the *chazzan's* repetition, congregation responds *Amen* as indicated.

אֱלֹהֵינוּ *Our God and God of our forefathers, may there rise, come, reach, be noted, be favored, be heard, be considered, and be remembered — the remembrance and consideration of ourselves; the remembrance of our forefathers; the remembrance of Messiah, son of David, Your servant; the remembrance of Jerusalem, the City of Your Holiness; the remembrance of Your entire people the Family of Israel — before You for deliverance, for goodness, for grace, for kindness, and for compassion, for life, and for peace on this day of the Shemini Atzeres Festival. Remember us on it, HASHEM, our God, for goodness (*Cong.–*Amen); consider us on it for blessing (*Cong.–*Amen); and help us on it for life (*Cong.–*Amen). In the matter of salvation and compassion, pity, be gracious and compassionate with us and help us, for our eyes are turned to You, because You are God, the gracious and compassionate King.*[1]

וְהַשִּׂיאֵנוּ *Bestow upon us, O HASHEM, our God, the blessing of Your appointed Festivals for life and for peace, for gladness and for joy, as You desired and promised to bless us. Sanctify us withYour commandments and grant us our share in Your Torah; satisfy us from Your goodness and gladden us with Your salvation, and purify our heart to serve You sincerely. And grant us a heritage, O HASHEM our God — with gladness and with joy — the appointed festivals of Your holiness, and may Israel, the sanctifiers of Your Name, rejoice in You. Blessed are You, HASHEM, Who sanctifies Israel and the festive seasons.*

(1) Cf. *Nechemiah* 9:31.

עבודה

רְצֵה יהוה אֱלֹהֵינוּ בְּעַמְּךָ יִשְׂרָאֵל וּבִתְפִלָּתָם, וְהָשֵׁב אֶת הָעֲבוֹדָה לִדְבִיר בֵּיתֶךָ. וְאִשֵּׁי יִשְׂרָאֵל וּתְפִלָּתָם בְּאַהֲבָה תְקַבֵּל בְּרָצוֹן, וּתְהִי לְרָצוֹן תָּמִיד עֲבוֹדַת יִשְׂרָאֵל עַמֶּךָ.

וְתֶחֱזֶינָה עֵינֵינוּ בְּשׁוּבְךָ לְצִיּוֹן בְּרַחֲמִים. בָּרוּךְ אַתָּה יהוה, הַמַּחֲזִיר שְׁכִינָתוֹ לְצִיּוֹן.

הודאה

Bow at מוֹדִים; straighten up at 'ה. In his repetition the *chazzan* should recite the entire מוֹדִים aloud, while the congregation recites מוֹדִים דְּרַבָּנָן softly.

מוֹדִים אֲנַחְנוּ לָךְ, שָׁאַתָּה הוּא יהוה אֱלֹהֵינוּ וֵאלֹהֵי אֲבוֹתֵינוּ לְעוֹלָם וָעֶד. צוּר חַיֵּינוּ, מָגֵן יִשְׁעֵנוּ אַתָּה הוּא לְדוֹר וָדוֹר. נוֹדֶה לְּךָ וּנְסַפֵּר תְּהִלָּתֶךָ[1] עַל חַיֵּינוּ הַמְּסוּרִים בְּיָדֶךָ, וְעַל נִשְׁמוֹתֵינוּ הַפְּקוּדוֹת לָךְ, וְעַל נִסֶּיךָ שֶׁבְּכָל יוֹם עִמָּנוּ, וְעַל נִפְלְאוֹתֶיךָ וְטוֹבוֹתֶיךָ שֶׁבְּכָל עֵת, עֶרֶב וָבֹקֶר וְצָהֳרָיִם. הַטּוֹב כִּי לֹא כָלוּ רַחֲמֶיךָ, וְהַמְּרַחֵם כִּי לֹא תַמּוּ חֲסָדֶיךָ,[2] מֵעוֹלָם קִוִּינוּ לָךְ.

מודים דרבנן

מוֹדִים אֲנַחְנוּ לָךְ, שָׁאַתָּה הוּא יהוה אֱלֹהֵינוּ וֵאלֹהֵי אֲבוֹתֵינוּ, אֱלֹהֵי כָל בָּשָׂר, יוֹצְרֵנוּ, יוֹצֵר בְּרֵאשִׁית. בְּרָכוֹת וְהוֹדָאוֹת לְשִׁמְךָ הַגָּדוֹל וְהַקָּדוֹשׁ, עַל שֶׁהֶחֱיִיתָנוּ וְקִיַּמְתָּנוּ. כֵּן תְּחַיֵּנוּ וּתְקַיְּמֵנוּ, וְתֶאֱסוֹף גָּלֻיּוֹתֵינוּ לְחַצְרוֹת קָדְשֶׁךָ, לִשְׁמוֹר חֻקֶּיךָ וְלַעֲשׂוֹת רְצוֹנֶךָ, וּלְעָבְדְּךָ בְּלֵבָב שָׁלֵם, עַל שֶׁאֲנַחְנוּ מוֹדִים לָךְ. בָּרוּךְ אֵל הַהוֹדָאוֹת.

וְעַל כֻּלָּם יִתְבָּרַךְ וְיִתְרוֹמַם שִׁמְךָ מַלְכֵּנוּ תָּמִיד לְעוֹלָם וָעֶד.

Bend the knees at בָּרוּךְ; bow at אַתָּה; straighten up at 'ה.

וְכֹל הַחַיִּים יוֹדְוּךָ סֶּלָה, וִיהַלְלוּ אֶת שִׁמְךָ בֶּאֱמֶת, הָאֵל יְשׁוּעָתֵנוּ וְעֶזְרָתֵנוּ סֶלָה. בָּרוּךְ אַתָּה יהוה, הַטּוֹב שִׁמְךָ וּלְךָ נָאֶה לְהוֹדוֹת.

TEMPLE SERVICE

רְצֵה *Be favorable, HASHEM, our God, toward Your people Israel and their prayer and restore the service to the Holy of Holies of Your Temple. The fire-offerings of Israel and their prayer accept with love and favor, and may the service of Your people Israel always be favorable to You.*

וְתֶחֱזֶינָה *May our eyes behold Your return to Zion in compassion. Blessed are You, HASHEM, Who restores His Presence to Zion.*

THANKSGIVING [MODIM]

Bow at *'We gratefully thank You'*; straighten up at *'HASHEM.'* In his repetition the *chazzan* should recite the entire *Modim* aloud, while the congregation recites *Modim of the Rabbis* softly.

מוֹדִים *We gratefully thank You, for it is You Who are HASHEM, our God and the God of our forefathers for all eternity; Rock of our lives, Shield of our salvation are You from generation to generation. We shall thank You and relate Your praise*[1] *— for our lives, which are committed to Your power and for our souls that are entrusted to You; for Your miracles that are with us every day; and for Your wonders and favors in every season — evening, morning, and afternoon. The Beneficent One, for Your compassions were never exhausted, and the Compassionate One, for Your kindnesses never ended*[2] *— always have we put our hope in You.*

MODIM OF THE RABBIS

מוֹדִים *We gratefully thank You, for it is You Who are HASHEM, our God and the God of our forefathers, the God of all flesh, our Molder, the Molder of the universe. Blessings and thanks are due Your great and holy Name for You have given us life and sustained us. So may You continue to give us life and sustain us and gather our exiles to the Courtyards of Your Sanctuary, to observe Your decrees, to do Your will and to serve You wholeheartedly. [We thank You] for inspiring us to thank You. Blessed is the God of thanksgivings.*

For all these, may Your Name be blessed and exalted, our King, continually forever and ever.

Bend the knees at *'Blessed'*; bow at *'You'*; straighten up at *'HASHEM.'*

Everything alive will gratefully acknowledge You, Selah! and praise Your Name sincerely, O God of our salvation and help, Selah! Blessed are You, HASHEM, Your Name is 'The Beneficent One' and to You it is fitting to give thanks.

(1) Cf. *Psalms* 79:13. (2) Cf. *Lamentations* 3:22.

שלום

שָׁלוֹם רָב עַל יִשְׂרָאֵל עַמְּךָ תָּשִׂים לְעוֹלָם, כִּי אַתָּה הוּא מֶלֶךְ אָדוֹן לְכָל הַשָּׁלוֹם. וְטוֹב בְּעֵינֶיךָ לְבָרֵךְ אֶת עַמְּךָ יִשְׂרָאֵל, בְּכָל עֵת וּבְכָל שָׁעָה בִּשְׁלוֹמֶךָ. בָּרוּךְ אַתָּה יהוה, הַמְּבָרֵךְ אֶת עַמּוֹ יִשְׂרָאֵל בַּשָּׁלוֹם.

יִהְיוּ לְרָצוֹן אִמְרֵי פִי וְהֶגְיוֹן לִבִּי לְפָנֶיךָ, יהוה צוּרִי וְגֹאֲלִי.[1]

Chazzan's repetition of *Shemoneh Esrei* ends here. Individuals continue below.

אֱלֹהַי, נְצוֹר לְשׁוֹנִי מֵרָע, וּשְׂפָתַי מִדַּבֵּר מִרְמָה,[2] וְלִמְקַלְלַי נַפְשִׁי תִדּוֹם, וְנַפְשִׁי כֶּעָפָר לַכֹּל תִּהְיֶה. פְּתַח לִבִּי בְּתוֹרָתֶךָ, וּבְמִצְוֹתֶיךָ תִּרְדּוֹף נַפְשִׁי. וְכֹל הַחוֹשְׁבִים עָלַי רָעָה, מְהֵרָה הָפֵר עֲצָתָם וְקַלְקֵל מַחֲשַׁבְתָּם. עֲשֵׂה לְמַעַן שְׁמֶךָ, עֲשֵׂה לְמַעַן יְמִינֶךָ, עֲשֵׂה לְמַעַן קְדֻשָּׁתֶךָ, עֲשֵׂה לְמַעַן תּוֹרָתֶךָ. לְמַעַן יֵחָלְצוּן יְדִידֶיךָ, הוֹשִׁיעָה יְמִינְךָ וַעֲנֵנִי.[3]

Some recite verses pertaining to their names. See page 1301.

יִהְיוּ לְרָצוֹן אִמְרֵי פִי וְהֶגְיוֹן לִבִּי לְפָנֶיךָ, יהוה צוּרִי וְגֹאֲלִי.[1]

Bow and take three steps back. Bow left and say . . . עֹשֶׂה, bow right and say . . . הוּא יַעֲשֶׂה; bow forward and say וְעַל כָּל . . . אָמֵן.

עֹשֶׂה שָׁלוֹם בִּמְרוֹמָיו, הוּא יַעֲשֶׂה שָׁלוֹם עָלֵינוּ, וְעַל כָּל יִשְׂרָאֵל. וְאִמְרוּ: אָמֵן.

יְהִי רָצוֹן מִלְּפָנֶיךָ יהוה אֱלֹהֵינוּ וֵאלֹהֵי אֲבוֹתֵינוּ, שֶׁיִּבָּנֶה בֵּית הַמִּקְדָּשׁ בִּמְהֵרָה בְיָמֵינוּ, וְתֵן חֶלְקֵנוּ בְּתוֹרָתֶךָ. וְשָׁם נַעֲבָדְךָ בְּיִרְאָה, כִּימֵי עוֹלָם וּכְשָׁנִים קַדְמוֹנִיּוֹת. וְעָרְבָה לַיהוה מִנְחַת יְהוּדָה וִירוּשָׁלָיִם, כִּימֵי עוֹלָם וּכְשָׁנִים קַדְמוֹנִיּוֹת.[4]

THE INDIVIDUAL'S RECITATION OF שְׁמוֹנֶה עֶשְׂרֵה ENDS HERE.

The individual remains standing in place until the *chazzan* reaches *Kedushah* — or at least until the *chazzan* begins his repetition — then he takes three steps forward. The *chazzan* himself, or one praying alone, should remain in place for a few moments before taking three steps forward.

קדיש שלם

The *chazzan* recites קַדִּישׁ שָׁלֵם.

יִתְגַּדַּל וְיִתְקַדַּשׁ שְׁמֵהּ רַבָּא. (.Cong – אָמֵן.) בְּעָלְמָא דִּי בְרָא כִרְעוּתֵהּ. וְיַמְלִיךְ מַלְכוּתֵהּ, בְּחַיֵּיכוֹן וּבְיוֹמֵיכוֹן וּבְחַיֵּי דְכָל בֵּית יִשְׂרָאֵל, בַּעֲגָלָא וּבִזְמַן קָרִיב. וְאִמְרוּ: אָמֵן.

(.Cong – אָמֵן. יְהֵא שְׁמֵהּ רַבָּא מְבָרַךְ לְעָלַם וּלְעָלְמֵי עָלְמַיָּא.)

יְהֵא שְׁמֵהּ רַבָּא מְבָרַךְ לְעָלַם וּלְעָלְמֵי עָלְמַיָּא.

יִתְבָּרַךְ וְיִשְׁתַּבַּח וְיִתְפָּאַר וְיִתְרוֹמַם וְיִתְנַשֵּׂא וְיִתְהַדָּר וְיִתְעַלֶּה וְיִתְהַלָּל שְׁמֵהּ דְּקֻדְשָׁא בְּרִיךְ הוּא (.Cong – בְּרִיךְ הוּא) — לְעֵלָּא מִן כָּל בִּרְכָתָא וְשִׁירָתָא תֻּשְׁבְּחָתָא וְנֶחֱמָתָא, דַּאֲמִירָן בְּעָלְמָא. וְאִמְרוּ: אָמֵן.

(.Cong – אָמֵן.)

PEACE

שָׁלוֹם *Establish abundant peace upon Your people Israel forever, for You are King, Master of all peace. May it be good in Your eyes to bless Your people Israel at every time and every hour with Your peace. Blessed are You,* HASHEM, *Who blesses His people Israel with peace.*

May the expressions of my mouth and the thoughts of my heart find favor before You, HASHEM, *my Rock and my Redeemer.*[1]

Chazzan's repetition of *Shemoneh Esrei* ends here. Individuals continue below.

אֱלֹהַי *My God, guard my tongue from evil and my lips from speaking deceitfully.*[2] *To those who curse me, let my soul be silent; and let my soul be like dust to everyone. Open my heart to Your Torah, then my soul will pursue Your commandments. As for all those who design evil against me, speedily nullify their counsel and disrupt their design. Act for Your Name's sake; act for Your right hand's sake; act for Your sanctity's sake; act for Your Torah's sake. That Your beloved ones may be given rest; let Your right hand save, and respond to me.*[3]

Some recite verses pertaining to their names at this point. See page 1301.

May the expressions of my mouth and the thoughts of my heart find favor before You, HASHEM, *my Rock and my Redeemer.*[1] *He Who makes peace in His heights, may He make peace upon us, and upon all Israel. Now respond: Amen.*

Bow and take three steps back. Bow left and say, *'He Who makes peace . . .'*; bow right and say, *'may He make peace . . .'*; bow forward and say, *'and upon . . . Amen.'*

יְהִי רָצוֹן *May it be Your will,* HASHEM, *our God and the God of our forefathers, that the Holy Temple be rebuilt, speedily in our days. Grant us our share in Your Torah, and may we serve You there with reverence, as in days of old and in former years. Then the offering of Judah and Jerusalem will be pleasing to* HASHEM, *as in days of old and in former years.*[4]

THE INDIVIDUAL'S RECITATION OF *SHEMONEH ESREI* ENDS HERE.

The individual remains standing in place until the *chazzan* reaches *Kedushah* — or at least until the *chazzan* begins his repetition — then he takes three steps forward. The *chazzan* himself, or one praying alone, should remain in place for a few moments before taking three steps forward.

FULL KADDISH

The *chazzan* recites the Full *Kaddish*.

יִתְגַּדַּל *May His great Name grow exalted and sanctified* (Cong.— *Amen.*) *in the world that He created as He willed. May He give reign to His kingship in your lifetimes and in your days, and in the lifetimes of the entire Family of Israel, swiftly and soon. Now respond: Amen.*

(Cong.— *Amen. May His great Name be blessed forever and ever.*)

May His great Name be blessed forever and ever.

Blessed, praised, glorified, exalted, extolled, mighty, upraised, and lauded be the Name of the Holy One, Blessed is He (Cong.— *Blessed is He*) — *beyond any blessing and song, praise and consolation that are uttered in the world. Now respond: Amen.* (Cong.— *Amen.*)

---

(1) *Psalms* 19:15. (2) Cf. 34:14. (3) 60:7;108:7. (4) *Malachi* 3:4.

(Cong.– קַבֵּל בְּרַחֲמִים וּבְרָצוֹן אֶת תְּפִלָּתֵנוּ.)

תִּתְקַבֵּל צְלוֹתְהוֹן וּבָעוּתְהוֹן דְּכָל בֵּית יִשְׂרָאֵל קֳדָם אֲבוּהוֹן דִּי בִשְׁמַיָּא. וְאִמְרוּ: אָמֵן. (Cong.– אָמֵן.)

(Cong.– יְהִי שֵׁם יהוה מְבֹרָךְ, מֵעַתָּה וְעַד עוֹלָם.[1])

יְהֵא שְׁלָמָא רַבָּא מִן שְׁמַיָּא, וְחַיִּים עָלֵינוּ וְעַל כָּל יִשְׂרָאֵל. וְאִמְרוּ: אָמֵן. (Cong.– אָמֵן.)

(Cong.– עֶזְרִי מֵעִם יהוה, עֹשֵׂה שָׁמַיִם וָאָרֶץ.[2])

Take three steps back. Bow left and say . . . עֹשֶׂה; bow right and say . . . הוּא; bow forward and say וְעַל כָּל . . . אָמֵן. Remain standing in place for a few moments, then take three steps forward.

עֹשֶׂה שָׁלוֹם בִּמְרוֹמָיו, הוּא יַעֲשֶׂה שָׁלוֹם עָלֵינוּ, וְעַל כָּל יִשְׂרָאֵל. וְאִמְרוּ: אָמֵן. (Cong.– אָמֵן.)

Stand while reciting עָלֵינוּ.

עָלֵינוּ לְשַׁבֵּחַ לַאֲדוֹן הַכֹּל, לָתֵת גְּדֻלָּה לְיוֹצֵר בְּרֵאשִׁית, שֶׁלֹּא עָשָׂנוּ כְּגוֹיֵי הָאֲרָצוֹת, וְלֹא שָׂמָנוּ כְּמִשְׁפְּחוֹת הָאֲדָמָה. שֶׁלֹּא שָׂם חֶלְקֵנוּ כָּהֶם, וְגוֹרָלֵנוּ כְּכָל הֲמוֹנָם. (שֶׁהֵם מִשְׁתַּחֲוִים לְהֶבֶל וָרִיק, וּמִתְפַּלְּלִים אֶל אֵל לֹא יוֹשִׁיעַ.[3]) וַאֲנַחְנוּ כּוֹרְעִים וּמִשְׁתַּחֲוִים וּמוֹדִים, לִפְנֵי מֶלֶךְ מַלְכֵי הַמְּלָכִים הַקָּדוֹשׁ בָּרוּךְ הוּא. שֶׁהוּא נוֹטֶה שָׁמַיִם וְיֹסֵד אָרֶץ,[4] וּמוֹשַׁב יְקָרוֹ בַּשָּׁמַיִם מִמַּעַל, וּשְׁכִינַת עֻזּוֹ בְּגָבְהֵי מְרוֹמִים. הוּא אֱלֹהֵינוּ, אֵין עוֹד. אֱמֶת מַלְכֵּנוּ, אֶפֶס זוּלָתוֹ, כַּכָּתוּב בְּתוֹרָתוֹ: וְיָדַעְתָּ הַיּוֹם וַהֲשֵׁבֹתָ אֶל לְבָבֶךָ, כִּי יהוה הוּא הָאֱלֹהִים בַּשָּׁמַיִם מִמַּעַל וְעַל הָאָרֶץ מִתָּחַת, אֵין עוֹד.[5]

Bow while reciting וַאֲנַחְנוּ כּוֹרְעִים וּמִשְׁתַּחֲוִים.

עַל כֵּן נְקַוֶּה לְּךָ יהוה אֱלֹהֵינוּ לִרְאוֹת מְהֵרָה בְּתִפְאֶרֶת עֻזֶּךָ, לְהַעֲבִיר גִּלּוּלִים מִן הָאָרֶץ, וְהָאֱלִילִים כָּרוֹת יִכָּרֵתוּן, לְתַקֵּן עוֹלָם בְּמַלְכוּת שַׁדַּי. וְכָל בְּנֵי בָשָׂר יִקְרְאוּ בִשְׁמֶךָ, לְהַפְנוֹת אֵלֶיךָ כָּל רִשְׁעֵי אָרֶץ. יַכִּירוּ וְיֵדְעוּ כָּל יוֹשְׁבֵי תֵבֵל, כִּי לְךָ תִּכְרַע כָּל בֶּרֶךְ, תִּשָּׁבַע כָּל לָשׁוֹן.[6] לְפָנֶיךָ יהוה אֱלֹהֵינוּ יִכְרְעוּ וְיִפֹּלוּ, וְלִכְבוֹד שִׁמְךָ יְקָר יִתֵּנוּ. וִיקַבְּלוּ כֻלָּם אֶת עוֹל מַלְכוּתֶךָ, וְתִמְלֹךְ עֲלֵיהֶם מְהֵרָה לְעוֹלָם וָעֶד. כִּי הַמַּלְכוּת שֶׁלְּךָ הִיא וּלְעוֹלְמֵי עַד תִּמְלוֹךְ בְּכָבוֹד, כַּכָּתוּב בְּתוֹרָתֶךָ: יהוה יִמְלֹךְ לְעֹלָם וָעֶד.[7] ❖ וְנֶאֱמַר: וְהָיָה יהוה לְמֶלֶךְ עַל כָּל הָאָרֶץ, בַּיּוֹם הַהוּא יִהְיֶה יהוה אֶחָד וּשְׁמוֹ אֶחָד.[8]

(Cong.— *Accept our prayers with mercy and favor.*)

May the prayers and supplications of the entire Family of Israel be accepted before their Father Who is in Heaven. Now respond: Amen. (Cong.— *Amen.*)

(Cong.— *Blessed be the Name of* HASHEM, *from this time and forever.*[1])

May there be abundant peace from Heaven, and life, upon us and upon all Israel. Now respond: Amen. (Cong.— *Amen.*)

(Cong.— *My help is from* HASHEM, *Maker of heaven and earth.*[2])

Take three steps back. Bow left and say, *'He Who makes peace . . .'*; bow right and say, *'may He . . .'*; bow forward and say, *'and upon all Israel . . .'* Remain standing in place for a few moments, then take three steps forward.

He Who makes peace in His heights, may He make peace upon us, and upon all Israel. Now respond: Amen. (Cong.— *Amen.*)

Stand while reciting עָלֵינוּ, *'It is our duty . . .'*

עָלֵינוּ *It is our duty to praise the Master of all, to ascribe greatness to the Molder of primeval creation, for He has not made us like the nations of the lands, and has not emplaced us like the families of the earth; for He has not assigned our portion like theirs nor our lot like all their multitudes. (For they bow to vanity and emptiness and pray to a god which helps not.*[3]*) But we bend our knees, bow, and acknowledge our thanks before the King Who reigns over kings, the Holy One, Blessed is He. He stretches out heaven and establishes earth's foundation,*[4] *the seat of His homage is in the heavens above and His powerful Presence is in the loftiest heights. He is our God and there is none other. True is our King, there is nothing beside Him, as it is written in His Torah: 'You are to know this day and take to your heart that* HASHEM *is the only God — in heaven above and on the earth below — there is none other.'*[5]

Bow while reciting *'But we bend our knees.'*

עַל כֵּן *Therefore we put our hope in You,* HASHEM, *our God, that we may soon see Your mighty splendor, to remove detestable idolatry from the earth, and false gods will be utterly cut off, to perfect the universe through the Almighty's sovereignty. Then all humanity will call upon Your Name, to turn all the earth's wicked toward You. All the world's inhabitants will recognize and know that to You every knee should bend, every tongue should swear.*[6] *Before You,* HASHEM, *our God, they will bend every knee and cast themselves down and to the glory of Your Name they will render homage, and they will all accept upon themselves the yoke of Your kingship that You may reign over them soon and eternally. For the kingdom is Yours and You will reign for all eternity in glory as it is written in Your Torah:* HASHEM *shall reign for all eternity.*[7] Chazzan— *And it is said:* HASHEM *will be King over all the world — on that day* HASHEM *will be One and His Name will be One.*[8]

---

(1) *Psalms* 113:2. (2) 121:2. (3) *Isaiah* 45:20. (4) 51:13. (5) *Deuteronomy* 4:39.
(6) Cf. *Isaiah* 45:23. (7) *Exodus* 15:18. (8) *Zechariah* 14:9.

Some congregations recite the following after עָלֵינוּ:

אַל תִּירָא מִפַּחַד פִּתְאֹם, וּמִשֹּׁאַת רְשָׁעִים כִּי תָבֹא.[1] עֻצוּ עֵצָה וְתֻפָר, דַּבְּרוּ דָבָר וְלֹא יָקוּם, כִּי עִמָּנוּ אֵל.[2] וְעַד זִקְנָה אֲנִי הוּא, וְעַד שֵׂיבָה אֲנִי אֶסְבֹּל, אֲנִי עָשִׂיתִי וַאֲנִי אֶשָּׂא, וַאֲנִי אֶסְבֹּל וַאֲמַלֵּט.[3]

קדיש יתום

In the presence of a *minyan,* mourners recite קַדִּישׁ יָתוֹם, the Mourner's *Kaddish* (see *Laws* §81-83).

יִתְגַּדַּל וְיִתְקַדַּשׁ שְׁמֵהּ רַבָּא. (Cong. – אָמֵן.) בְּעָלְמָא דִּי בְרָא כִרְעוּתֵהּ. וְיַמְלִיךְ מַלְכוּתֵהּ, בְּחַיֵּיכוֹן וּבְיוֹמֵיכוֹן וּבְחַיֵּי דְכָל בֵּית יִשְׂרָאֵל, בַּעֲגָלָא וּבִזְמַן קָרִיב. וְאִמְרוּ: אָמֵן.

(Cong. – אָמֵן. יְהֵא שְׁמֵהּ רַבָּא מְבָרַךְ לְעָלַם וּלְעָלְמֵי עָלְמַיָּא.)

יְהֵא שְׁמֵהּ רַבָּא מְבָרַךְ לְעָלַם וּלְעָלְמֵי עָלְמַיָּא.

יִתְבָּרַךְ וְיִשְׁתַּבַּח וְיִתְפָּאַר וְיִתְרוֹמַם וְיִתְנַשֵּׂא וְיִתְהַדָּר וְיִתְעַלֶּה וְיִתְהַלָּל שְׁמֵהּ דְּקֻדְשָׁא בְּרִיךְ הוּא (Cong. – בְּרִיךְ הוּא) — לְעֵלָּא מִן כָּל בִּרְכָתָא וְשִׁירָתָא תֻּשְׁבְּחָתָא וְנֶחֱמָתָא, דַּאֲמִירָן בְּעָלְמָא. וְאִמְרוּ: אָמֵן. (Cong. – אָמֵן.)

יְהֵא שְׁלָמָא רַבָּא מִן שְׁמַיָּא, וְחַיִּים עָלֵינוּ וְעַל כָּל יִשְׂרָאֵל. וְאִמְרוּ: אָמֵן. (Cong. – אָמֵן.)

Take three steps back. Bow left and say . . . עֹשֶׂה; bow right and say . . . הוּא; bow forward and say וְעַל כָּל . . . אָמֵן. Remain standing in place for a few moments, then take three steps forward.

עֹשֶׂה שָׁלוֹם בִּמְרוֹמָיו, הוּא יַעֲשֶׂה שָׁלוֹם עָלֵינוּ, וְעַל כָּל יִשְׂרָאֵל. וְאִמְרוּ: אָמֵן. (Cong. – אָמֵן.)

מעריב למוצאי יום טוב

When Simchas Torah falls on Sunday, Tuesday or Wednesday, the following Maariv is recited at its conclusion. When Simchas Torah falls on Friday, the regular Friday evening service follows. The service appears on pages 426-450, but the following adjustments should be made:
(a) Insert the phrase מַשִּׁיב הָרוּחַ וּמוֹרִיד הַגָּשֶׁם before the words מְכַלְכֵּל חַיִּים (p. 436).
(b) Omit יַעֲלֶה וְיָבֹא (fourth paragraph, p. 438).

Congregation, then *chazzan:*

וְהוּא רַחוּם יְכַפֵּר עָוֹן וְלֹא יַשְׁחִית, וְהִרְבָּה לְהָשִׁיב אַפּוֹ, וְלֹא יָעִיר כָּל חֲמָתוֹ.[4] יהוה הוֹשִׁיעָה, הַמֶּלֶךְ יַעֲנֵנוּ בְיוֹם קָרְאֵנוּ.[5]

In some congregations the *chazzan* chants a melody during his recitation of בָּרְכוּ so that the congregation can then recite יִתְבָּרַךְ.

Chazzan bows at בָּרְכוּ and straightens up at ה׳.

בָּרְכוּ אֶת יהוה הַמְּבֹרָךְ.

Congregation, followed by *chazzan,* responds, bowing at בָּרוּךְ and straightening up at ה׳.

בָּרוּךְ יהוה הַמְּבֹרָךְ לְעוֹלָם וָעֶד.

יִתְבָּרַךְ וְיִשְׁתַּבַּח וְיִתְפָּאַר וְיִתְרוֹמַם וְיִתְנַשֵּׂא שְׁמוֹ שֶׁל מֶלֶךְ מַלְכֵי הַמְּלָכִים, הַקָּדוֹשׁ בָּרוּךְ הוּא. שֶׁהוּא רִאשׁוֹן וְהוּא אַחֲרוֹן, וּמִבַּלְעָדָיו אֵין אֱלֹהִים.[6] סֹלּוּ, לָרֹכֵב בָּעֲרָבוֹת, בְּיָהּ שְׁמוֹ, וְעִלְזוּ לְפָנָיו.[7] וּשְׁמוֹ מְרוֹמָם עַל כָּל בְּרָכָה וּתְהִלָּה.[8] בָּרוּךְ שֵׁם כְּבוֹד מַלְכוּתוֹ לְעוֹלָם וָעֶד. יְהִי שֵׁם יהוה מְבֹרָךְ, מֵעַתָּה וְעַד עוֹלָם.[9]

Some congregations recite the following after *Aleinu:*

אַל תִּירָא *Do not fear sudden terror, or the holocaust of the wicked when it comes.*[1] *Plan a conspiracy and it will be annulled; speak your piece and it shall not stand, for God is with us.*[2] *Even till your seniority, I remain unchanged; and even till your ripe old age, I shall endure. I created you and I shall bear you; I shall endure and rescue.*[3]

MOURNER'S KADDISH

In the presence of a *minyan,* mourners recite קַדִּישׁ יָתוֹם, the Mourner's *Kaddish* (see *Laws* 81-83). [A transliteration of this *Kaddish* appears on page 1305.]

יִתְגַּדַּל *May His great Name grow exalted and sanctified* (Cong.– *Amen.*) *in the world that He created as He willed. May He give reign to His kingship in your lifetimes and in your days, and in the lifetimes of the entire Family of Israel, swiftly and soon. Now respond: Amen.*

(Cong.– *Amen. May His great Name be blessed forever and ever.)*

May His great Name be blessed forever and ever.

Blessed, praised, glorified, exalted, extolled, mighty, upraised, and lauded be the Name of the Holy One, Blessed is He (Cong.– *Blessed is He*) *— beyond any blessing and song, praise and consolation that are uttered in the world. Now respond: Amen.* (Cong.– *Amen.*)

May there be abundant peace from Heaven, and life, upon us and upon all Israel. Now respond: Amen. (Cong.– *Amen.*)

Take three steps back. Bow left and say, *'He Who makes peace . . .';* bow right and say, *'may He . . .';* bow forward and say, *'and upon all Israel . . .'* Remain standing in place for a few moments, then take three steps forward.

He Who makes peace in His heights, may He make peace upon us, and upon all Israel. Now respond: Amen. (Cong.– *Amen.*)

MAARIV FOR THE CONCLUSION OF YOM TOV

When Simchas Torah falls on Sunday, Tuesday or Wednesday, the following Maariv is recited at its conclusion. When Simchas Torah falls on Friday, the regular Friday evening service follows. The service appears on pages 426-450, but the following adjustments should be made:

(a) Insert the phrase, *'He makes the wind blow and He makes the rain descend,'* before the words, *'He sustains the living . . .'* (p. 436).

(b) Omit יַעֲלֶה וְיָבֹא (fourth paragraph, p. 438).

Congregation, then *chazzan:*

וְהוּא *He, the Merciful One, is forgiving of iniquity and does not destroy. Frequently He withdraws His anger, not arousing His entire rage.*[4] *HASHEM, save! May the King answer us on the day we call.*[5]

In some congregations the *chazzan* chants a melody during his recitation of *Borchu* so that the congregation can then recite *'Blessed, praised . . .'*

Chazzan bows at *'Bless,'* and straightens up at *'HASHEM.'*

Bless HASHEM, the blessed One.

Congregation, followed by *chazzan,* responds, bowing at *'Blessed'* and straightening up at *'HASHEM.'*

Blessed is HASHEM, the blessed One, for all eternity.

Blessed, praised, glorified, exalted and upraised is the Name of the King Who rules over kings — the Holy One, Blessed is He. For He is the First and He is the Last and aside from Him there is no god.[6] *Extol Him — Who rides the highest heavens — with His Name, YAH, and exult before Him.*[7] *His Name is exalted beyond every blessing and praise.*[8] *Blessed is the Name of His glorious kingdom for all eternity. Blessed be the Name of HASHEM from this time and forever.*[9]

(1) *Proverbs* 3:25. (2) *Isaiah* 8:10. (3) 46:4. (4) *Psalms* 78:38. (5) 20:10.
(6) Cf. *Isaiah* 44:6. (7) *Psalms* 68:5. (8) Cf. *Nechemiah* 9:5. (9) *Psalms* 113:2.

ברכות קריאת שמע

בָּרוּךְ אַתָּה יהוה אֱלֹהֵינוּ מֶלֶךְ הָעוֹלָם, אֲשֶׁר בִּדְבָרוֹ מַעֲרִיב עֲרָבִים, בְּחָכְמָה פּוֹתֵחַ שְׁעָרִים, וּבִתְבוּנָה מְשַׁנֶּה עִתִּים, וּמַחֲלִיף אֶת הַזְּמַנִּים, וּמְסַדֵּר אֶת הַכּוֹכָבִים בְּמִשְׁמְרוֹתֵיהֶם בָּרָקִיעַ כִּרְצוֹנוֹ. בּוֹרֵא יוֹם וָלָיְלָה, גּוֹלֵל אוֹר מִפְּנֵי חֹשֶׁךְ וְחֹשֶׁךְ מִפְּנֵי אוֹר. וּמַעֲבִיר יוֹם וּמֵבִיא לָיְלָה, וּמַבְדִּיל בֵּין יוֹם וּבֵין לָיְלָה, יהוה צְבָאוֹת שְׁמוֹ. ❖ אֵל חַי וְקַיָּם, תָּמִיד יִמְלוֹךְ עָלֵינוּ, לְעוֹלָם וָעֶד. בָּרוּךְ אַתָּה יהוה, הַמַּעֲרִיב עֲרָבִים. (Cong. – אָמֵן.)

אַהֲבַת עוֹלָם בֵּית יִשְׂרָאֵל עַמְּךָ אָהָבְתָּ. תּוֹרָה וּמִצְוֹת, חֻקִּים וּמִשְׁפָּטִים, אוֹתָנוּ לִמַּדְתָּ. עַל כֵּן יהוה אֱלֹהֵינוּ, בְּשָׁכְבֵנוּ וּבְקוּמֵנוּ נָשִׂיחַ בְּחֻקֶּיךָ, וְנִשְׂמַח בְּדִבְרֵי תוֹרָתֶךָ, וּבְמִצְוֹתֶיךָ לְעוֹלָם וָעֶד. ❖ כִּי הֵם חַיֵּינוּ, וְאֹרֶךְ יָמֵינוּ, וּבָהֶם נֶהְגֶּה יוֹמָם וָלָיְלָה. וְאַהֲבָתְךָ, אַל תָּסִיר מִמֶּנּוּ לְעוֹלָמִים. בָּרוּךְ אַתָּה יהוה, אוֹהֵב עַמּוֹ יִשְׂרָאֵל. (Cong. – אָמֵן.)

שמע

Immediately before its recitation, concentrate on fulfilling the positive commandment of reciting the *Shema* twice daily. It is important to enunciate each word clearly and not to run words together. For this reason, vertical lines have been placed between two words that are prone to be slurred into one and are not separated by a comma or a hyphen. See *Laws* §40-54.

When praying without a *minyan,* begin with the following three-word formula:

אֵל מֶלֶךְ נֶאֱמָן.

Recite the first verse aloud, with the right hand covering the eyes, and concentrate intently upon accepting God's absolute sovereignty.

שְׁמַע | יִשְׂרָאֵל, יהוה | אֱלֹהֵינוּ, יהוה | אֶחָד:

In an undertone – בָּרוּךְ שֵׁם כְּבוֹד מַלְכוּתוֹ לְעוֹלָם וָעֶד.

While reciting the first paragraph (דברים ו:ה-ט), concentrate on accepting the commandment to love God.

וְאָהַבְתָּ אֵת | יהוה | אֱלֹהֶיךָ, בְּכָל־לְבָבְךָ, וּבְכָל־נַפְשְׁךָ, וּבְכָל־מְאֹדֶךָ: וְהָיוּ הַדְּבָרִים הָאֵלֶּה, אֲשֶׁר | אָנֹכִי מְצַוְּךָ הַיּוֹם, עַל־לְבָבֶךָ: וְשִׁנַּנְתָּם לְבָנֶיךָ, וְדִבַּרְתָּ בָּם, בְּשִׁבְתְּךָ בְּבֵיתֶךָ, וּבְלֶכְתְּךָ בַדֶּרֶךְ, וּבְשָׁכְבְּךָ וּבְקוּמֶךָ: וּקְשַׁרְתָּם לְאוֹת | עַל־יָדֶךָ, וְהָיוּ לְטֹטָפֹת בֵּין | עֵינֶיךָ: וּכְתַבְתָּם | עַל־מְזֻזוֹת בֵּיתֶךָ, וּבִשְׁעָרֶיךָ:

BLESSINGS OF THE SHEMA

בָּרוּךְ *Blessed are You,* H*ASHEM*, *our God, King of the universe, Who by His word brings on evenings, with wisdom opens gates, with understanding alters periods, changes the seasons, and orders the stars in their heavenly constellations as He wills. He creates day and night, removing light before darkness and darkness before light. He causes day to pass and brings night, and separates between day and night —* H*ASHEM*, *Master of Legions, is His Name.* Chazzan– *May the living and enduring God continuously reign over us, for all eternity. Blessed are You,* H*ASHEM*, *Who brings on evenings.* (Cong.– *Amen.*)

אַהֲבַת *With an eternal love have You loved the House of Israel, Your nation. Torah and commandments, decrees and ordinances have You taught us. Therefore* H*ASHEM*, *our God, upon our retiring and arising, we will discuss Your decrees and we will rejoice with the words of Your Torah and with Your commandments for all eternity.* Chazzan– *For they are our life and the length of our days and about them we will meditate day and night. May You not remove Your love from us forever. Blessed are You,* H*ASHEM*, *Who loves His nation Israel.* (Cong.– *Amen.*)

THE SHEMA

Immediately before its recitation, concentrate on fulfilling the positive commandment of reciting the *Shema* twice daily. It is important to enunciate each word clearly and not to run words together. See *Laws* §40-54.

When praying without a *minyan,* begin with the following three-word formula:

God, trustworthy King.

Recite the first verse aloud, with the right hand covering the eyes, and concentrate intently upon accepting God's absolute sovereignty.

Hear, O Israel: HASHEM is our God, HASHEM, the One and Only.[1]

In an undertone– *Blessed is the Name of His glorious kingdom for all eternity.*

While reciting the first paragraph (*Deuteronomy* 6:5-9), concentrate on accepting the commandment to love God.

וְאָהַבְתָּ *You shall love* H*ASHEM*, *your God, with all your heart, with all your soul and with all your resources. Let these matters that I command you today be upon your heart. Teach them thoroughly to your children and speak of them while you sit in your home, while you walk on the way, when you retire and when you arise. Bind them as a sign upon your arm and let them be tefillin between your eyes. And write them on the doorposts of your house and upon your gates.*

(1) *Deuteronomy* 6:4.

While reciting the second paragraph (דברים יא:יג-כא), concentrate on accepting all the commandments and the concept of reward and punishment.

וְהָיָה, אִם־שָׁמֹעַ תִּשְׁמְעוּ אֶל־מִצְוֹתַי, אֲשֶׁר | אָנֹכִי מְצַוֶּה | אֶתְכֶם הַיּוֹם, לְאַהֲבָה אֶת־יהוה | אֱלֹהֵיכֶם וּלְעָבְדוֹ, בְּכָל־לְבַבְכֶם, וּבְכָל־נַפְשְׁכֶם: וְנָתַתִּי מְטַר־אַרְצְכֶם בְּעִתּוֹ, יוֹרֶה וּמַלְקוֹשׁ, וְאָסַפְתָּ דְגָנֶךָ וְתִירֹשְׁךָ וְיִצְהָרֶךָ: וְנָתַתִּי | עֵשֶׂב | בְּשָׂדְךָ לִבְהֶמְתֶּךָ, וְאָכַלְתָּ וְשָׂבָעְתָּ: הִשָּׁמְרוּ לָכֶם, פֶּן־יִפְתֶּה לְבַבְכֶם, וְסַרְתֶּם וַעֲבַדְתֶּם | אֱלֹהִים | אֲחֵרִים, וְהִשְׁתַּחֲוִיתֶם לָהֶם: וְחָרָה | אַף־יהוה בָּכֶם, וְעָצַר | אֶת־הַשָּׁמַיִם, וְלֹא־יִהְיֶה מָטָר, וְהָאֲדָמָה לֹא תִתֵּן אֶת־יְבוּלָהּ, וַאֲבַדְתֶּם | מְהֵרָה | מֵעַל הָאָרֶץ הַטֹּבָה | אֲשֶׁר | יהוה נֹתֵן לָכֶם: וְשַׂמְתֶּם | אֶת־דְּבָרַי | אֵלֶּה, עַל־לְבַבְכֶם וְעַל־נַפְשְׁכֶם, וּקְשַׁרְתֶּם | אֹתָם לְאוֹת | עַל־יֶדְכֶם, וְהָיוּ לְטוֹטָפֹת בֵּין | עֵינֵיכֶם: וְלִמַּדְתֶּם | אֹתָם | אֶת־בְּנֵיכֶם, לְדַבֵּר בָּם, בְּשִׁבְתְּךָ בְּבֵיתֶךָ, וּבְלֶכְתְּךָ בַדֶּרֶךְ, וּבְשָׁכְבְּךָ וּבְקוּמֶךָ: וּכְתַבְתָּם | עַל־מְזוּזוֹת בֵּיתֶךָ, וּבִשְׁעָרֶיךָ: לְמַעַן | יִרְבּוּ | יְמֵיכֶם וִימֵי בְנֵיכֶם, עַל הָאֲדָמָה | אֲשֶׁר נִשְׁבַּע | יהוה לַאֲבֹתֵיכֶם לָתֵת לָהֶם, כִּימֵי הַשָּׁמַיִם | עַל־הָאָרֶץ:

במדבר טו:לז-מא

וַיֹּאמֶר | יהוה | אֶל־מֹשֶׁה לֵּאמֹר: דַּבֵּר | אֶל־בְּנֵי | יִשְׂרָאֵל, וְאָמַרְתָּ אֲלֵהֶם, וְעָשׂוּ לָהֶם צִיצִת, עַל־כַּנְפֵי בִגְדֵיהֶם לְדֹרֹתָם, וְנָתְנוּ | עַל־צִיצִת הַכָּנָף, פְּתִיל תְּכֵלֶת: וְהָיָה לָכֶם לְצִיצִת, וּרְאִיתֶם | אֹתוֹ, וּזְכַרְתֶּם | אֶת־כָּל־מִצְוֹת | יהוה, וַעֲשִׂיתֶם | אֹתָם, וְלֹא תָתֻרוּ | אַחֲרֵי לְבַבְכֶם וְאַחֲרֵי | עֵינֵיכֶם, אֲשֶׁר־אַתֶּם זֹנִים | אַחֲרֵיהֶם: לְמַעַן תִּזְכְּרוּ, וַעֲשִׂיתֶם | אֶת־כָּל־מִצְוֹתָי, וִהְיִיתֶם קְדֹשִׁים לֵאלֹהֵיכֶם: אֲנִי יהוה | אֱלֹהֵיכֶם, אֲשֶׁר הוֹצֵאתִי | אֶתְכֶם | מֵאֶרֶץ מִצְרַיִם, לִהְיוֹת לָכֶם לֵאלֹהִים, אֲנִי | יהוה | אֱלֹהֵיכֶם: אֱמֶת —

Concentrate on fulfilling the commandment of remembering the Exodus from Egypt.

Although the word אֱמֶת belongs to the next paragraph, it is appended to the conclusion of the previous one, as explained in the commentary.

– *Chazzan* repeats **יהוה אֱלֹהֵיכֶם אֱמֶת.**

וֶאֱמוּנָה כָּל זֹאת, וְקַיָּם עָלֵינוּ, כִּי הוּא יהוה אֱלֹהֵינוּ וְאֵין זוּלָתוֹ, וַאֲנַחְנוּ יִשְׂרָאֵל עַמּוֹ. הַפּוֹדֵנוּ מִיַּד מְלָכִים, מַלְכֵּנוּ הַגּוֹאֲלֵנוּ מִכַּף כָּל הֶעָרִיצִים. הָאֵל הַנִּפְרָע לָנוּ מִצָּרֵינוּ,

While reciting the second paragraph (*Deuteronomy* 11:13-21), concentrate on accepting all the commandments and the concept of reward and punishment.

וְהָיָה *And it will come to pass that if you continually hearken to My commandments that I command you today, to love* H*ASHEM*, *your God, and to serve Him, with all your heart and with all your soul — then I will provide rain for your land in its proper time, the early and late rains, that you may gather in your grain, your wine, and your oil. I will provide grass in your field for your cattle and you will eat and be satisfied. Beware lest your heart be seduced and you turn astray and serve gods of others and bow to them. Then the wrath of* H*ASHEM will blaze against you. He will restrain the heaven so there will be no rain and the ground will not yield its produce. And you will swiftly be banished from the goodly land which* H*ASHEM gives you. Place these words of Mine upon your heart and upon your soul; bind them for a sign upon your arm and let them be tefillin between your eyes. Teach them to your children, to discuss them, while you sit in your home, while you walk on the way, when you retire and when you arise. And write them on the doorposts of your house and upon your gates. In order to prolong your days and the days of your children upon the ground that* H*ASHEM has sworn to your ancestors to give them, like the days of the heaven on the earth.*

Numbers 15:37-41

וַיֹּאמֶר *And* H*ASHEM said to Moses saying: Speak to the Children of Israel and say to them that they are to make themselves tzitzis on the corners of their garments, throughout their generations. And they are to place upon the tzitzis of each corner a thread of techeiles. And it shall constitute tzitzis for you, that you may see it and remember all the commandments of* H*ASHEM and perform them; and not explore after your heart and after your eyes after which you stray. So that you may remember and perform all My commandments; and be holy to your God. I am* H*ASHEM, your God, Who has removed you from the land of Egypt to be a God to you; I am* H*ASHEM your God — it is true —*

Concentrate on fulfilling the commandment of remembering the Exodus from Egypt.

Although the word אֱמֶת, *'it is true,'* belongs to the next paragraph, it is appended to the conclusion of the previous one, as explained in the commentary.

Chazzan repeats: **HASHEM, your God, is true.**

וֶאֱמוּנָה *And faithful is all this, and it is firmly established for us that He is* H*ASHEM our God, and there is none but Him, and we are Israel, His nation. He redeems us from the power of kings, our King Who delivers us from the hand of all the cruel tyrants. He is the God Who exacts vengeance for us from our foes and Who*

וְהַמְשַׁלֵּם גְּמוּל לְכָל אֹיְבֵי נַפְשֵׁנוּ. הָעֹשֶׂה גְדֹלוֹת עַד אֵין חֵקֶר, וְנִפְלָאוֹת עַד אֵין מִסְפָּר.[1] הַשָּׂם נַפְשֵׁנוּ בַּחַיִּים, וְלֹא נָתַן לַמּוֹט רַגְלֵנוּ.[2] הַמַּדְרִיכֵנוּ עַל בָּמוֹת אוֹיְבֵינוּ, וַיָּרֶם קַרְנֵנוּ עַל כָּל שׂנְאֵינוּ. הָעֹשֶׂה לָּנוּ נִסִּים וּנְקָמָה בְּפַרְעֹה, אוֹתוֹת וּמוֹפְתִים בְּאַדְמַת בְּנֵי חָם. הַמַּכֶּה בְעֶבְרָתוֹ כָּל בְּכוֹרֵי מִצְרָיִם, וַיּוֹצֵא אֶת עַמּוֹ יִשְׂרָאֵל מִתּוֹכָם לְחֵרוּת עוֹלָם. הַמַּעֲבִיר בָּנָיו בֵּין גִּזְרֵי יַם סוּף, אֶת רוֹדְפֵיהֶם וְאֶת שׂוֹנְאֵיהֶם בִּתְהוֹמוֹת טִבַּע. וְרָאוּ בָנָיו גְּבוּרָתוֹ, שִׁבְּחוּ וְהוֹדוּ לִשְׁמוֹ. ❖ וּמַלְכוּתוֹ בְּרָצוֹן קִבְּלוּ עֲלֵיהֶם. מֹשֶׁה וּבְנֵי יִשְׂרָאֵל לְךָ עָנוּ שִׁירָה, בְּשִׂמְחָה רַבָּה, וְאָמְרוּ כֻלָּם:

מִי כָמֹכָה בָּאֵלִם יהוה, מִי כָּמֹכָה נֶאְדָּר בַּקֹּדֶשׁ, נוֹרָא תְהִלֹּת, עֹשֵׂה פֶלֶא.[3] ❖ מַלְכוּתְךָ רָאוּ בָנֶיךָ בּוֹקֵעַ יָם לִפְנֵי מֹשֶׁה, זֶה אֵלִי[4] עָנוּ וְאָמְרוּ:

יהוה יִמְלֹךְ לְעֹלָם וָעֶד.[5] ❖ וְנֶאֱמַר: כִּי פָדָה יהוה אֶת יַעֲקֹב, וּגְאָלוֹ מִיַּד חָזָק מִמֶּנּוּ.[6] בָּרוּךְ אַתָּה יהוה, גָּאַל יִשְׂרָאֵל.

(–Cong. אָמֵן.)

הַשְׁכִּיבֵנוּ יהוה אֱלֹהֵינוּ לְשָׁלוֹם, וְהַעֲמִידֵנוּ מַלְכֵּנוּ לְחַיִּים, וּפְרוֹשׂ עָלֵינוּ סֻכַּת שְׁלוֹמֶךָ, וְתַקְּנֵנוּ בְּעֵצָה טוֹבָה מִלְּפָנֶיךָ, וְהוֹשִׁיעֵנוּ לְמַעַן שְׁמֶךָ. וְהָגֵן בַּעֲדֵנוּ, וְהָסֵר מֵעָלֵינוּ אוֹיֵב, דֶּבֶר, וְחֶרֶב, וְרָעָב, וְיָגוֹן, וְהָסֵר שָׂטָן מִלְּפָנֵינוּ וּמֵאַחֲרֵינוּ, וּבְצֵל כְּנָפֶיךָ תַּסְתִּירֵנוּ,[7] כִּי אֵל שׁוֹמְרֵנוּ וּמַצִּילֵנוּ אָתָּה, כִּי אֵל מֶלֶךְ חַנּוּן וְרַחוּם אָתָּה.[8] ❖ וּשְׁמוֹר צֵאתֵנוּ וּבוֹאֵנוּ, לְחַיִּים וּלְשָׁלוֹם מֵעַתָּה וְעַד עוֹלָם.[9] בָּרוּךְ אַתָּה יהוה, שׁוֹמֵר עַמּוֹ יִשְׂרָאֵל לָעַד.

(–Cong. אָמֵן.)

Some congregations omit the following prayers and continue with Half-*Kaddish* (p. 1246).

בָּרוּךְ יהוה לְעוֹלָם, אָמֵן וְאָמֵן.[10] בָּרוּךְ יהוה מִצִּיּוֹן, שֹׁכֵן יְרוּשָׁלָיִם, הַלְלוּיָהּ.[11] בָּרוּךְ יהוה אֱלֹהִים אֱלֹהֵי יִשְׂרָאֵל, עֹשֵׂה נִפְלָאוֹת לְבַדּוֹ. וּבָרוּךְ שֵׁם כְּבוֹדוֹ לְעוֹלָם, וְיִמָּלֵא כְבוֹדוֹ אֶת כָּל הָאָרֶץ, אָמֵן וְאָמֵן.[12] יְהִי כְבוֹד יהוה לְעוֹלָם, יִשְׂמַח יהוה בְּמַעֲשָׂיו.[13] יְהִי שֵׁם יהוה מְבֹרָךְ, מֵעַתָּה וְעַד עוֹלָם.[14] כִּי לֹא יִטֹּשׁ

brings just retribution upon all enemies of our soul; Who performs great deeds that are beyond comprehension, and wonders beyond number.[1] *Who set our soul in life and did not allow our foot to falter.*[2] *Who led us upon the heights of our enemies and raised our pride above all who hate us; Who wrought for us miracles and vengeance upon Pharaoh; signs and wonders on the land of the offspring of Ham; Who struck with His anger all the firstborn of Egypt and removed His nation Israel from their midst to eternal freedom; Who brought His children through the split parts of the Sea of Reeds while those who pursued them and hated them He caused to sink into the depths. When His children perceived His power, they lauded and gave grateful praise to His Name.* Chazzan– *And His Kingship they accepted upon themselves willingly. Moses and the Children of Israel raised their voices to You in song with abundant gladness — and said unanimously:*

מִי כָמֹכָה *Who is like You among the heavenly powers, HASHEM! Who is like You, mighty in holiness, too awesome for praise, doing wonders!*[3] Chazzan– *Your children beheld Your majesty, as You split the sea before Moses: 'This is my God!'*[4] *they exclaimed, then they said:*

יהוה *'HASHEM shall reign for all eternity!'*[5] Chazzan– *And it is further said: 'For HASHEM has redeemed Jacob and delivered him from a power mightier than he.'*[6] *Blessed are You, HASHEM, Who redeemed Israel.* (Cong.– *Amen.*)

הַשְׁכִּיבֵנוּ *Lay us down to sleep, HASHEM our God, in peace, raise us erect, our King, to life; and spread over us the shelter of Your peace. Set us aright with good counsel from before Your Presence, and save us for Your Name's sake. Shield us, remove from us foe, plague, sword, famine, and woe; and remove spiritual impediment from before us and behind us, and in the shadow of Your wings shelter us*[7] *— for God Who protects and rescues us are You; for God, the Gracious and Compassionate King, are You.*[8] Chazzan– *Safeguard our going and coming, for life and for peace from now to eternity.*[9] *Blessed are You, HASHEM, Who protects His people Israel forever.* (Cong.– *Amen.*)

Some congregations omit the following prayers and continue with Half-*Kaddish* (p. 1246).

בָּרוּךְ *Blessed is HASHEM forever, Amen and Amen.*[10] *Blessed is HASHEM from Zion, Who dwells in Jerusalem, Halleluyah!*[11] *Blessed is HASHEM, God, the God of Israel, Who alone does wondrous things. Blessed is His glorious Name forever, and may all the earth be filled with His glory, Amen and Amen.*[12] *May the glory of HASHEM endure forever, let HASHEM rejoice in His works.*[13] *Blessed be the Name of HASHEM from this time and forever.*[14] *For HASHEM will not cast off His*

(1) *Job* 9:10. (2) *Psalms* 66:9. (3) *Exodus* 15:11. (4) 15:2. (5) 15:18. (6) *Jeremiah* 31:10. (7) Cf.*Psalms* 17:8. (8) Cf. *Nechemiah* 9:31. (9) Cf. *Psalms* 121:8. (10) *Psalms* 89:53. (11) 135:21. (12) 72:18-19. (13) 104:31. (14) 113:2.

יהוה אֶת עַמּוֹ בַּעֲבוּר שְׁמוֹ הַגָּדוֹל, כִּי הוֹאִיל יהוה לַעֲשׂוֹת אֶתְכֶם לוֹ לְעָם.[1] וַיַּרְא כָּל הָעָם וַיִּפְּלוּ עַל פְּנֵיהֶם, וַיֹּאמְרוּ, יהוה הוּא הָאֱלֹהִים, יהוה הוּא הָאֱלֹהִים.[2] וְהָיָה יהוה לְמֶלֶךְ עַל כָּל הָאָרֶץ, בַּיּוֹם הַהוּא יִהְיֶה יהוה אֶחָד וּשְׁמוֹ אֶחָד.[3] יְהִי חַסְדְּךָ יהוה עָלֵינוּ, כַּאֲשֶׁר יִחַלְנוּ לָךְ.[4] הוֹשִׁיעֵנוּ יהוה אֱלֹהֵינוּ, וְקַבְּצֵנוּ מִן הַגּוֹיִם, לְהוֹדוֹת לְשֵׁם קָדְשֶׁךָ, לְהִשְׁתַּבֵּחַ בִּתְהִלָּתֶךָ.[5] כָּל גּוֹיִם אֲשֶׁר עָשִׂיתָ יָבוֹאוּ וְיִשְׁתַּחֲווּ לְפָנֶיךָ אֲדֹנָי, וִיכַבְּדוּ לִשְׁמֶךָ. כִּי גָדוֹל אַתָּה וְעֹשֵׂה נִפְלָאוֹת, אַתָּה אֱלֹהִים לְבַדֶּךָ.[6] וַאֲנַחְנוּ עַמְּךָ וְצֹאן מַרְעִיתֶךָ, נוֹדֶה לְּךָ לְעוֹלָם, לְדוֹר וָדֹר נְסַפֵּר תְּהִלָּתֶךָ.[7] בָּרוּךְ יהוה בַּיּוֹם. בָּרוּךְ יהוה בַּלָּיְלָה. בָּרוּךְ יהוה בְּשָׁכְבֵנוּ. בָּרוּךְ יהוה בְּקוּמֵנוּ. כִּי בְיָדְךָ נַפְשׁוֹת הַחַיִּים וְהַמֵּתִים. אֲשֶׁר בְּיָדוֹ נֶפֶשׁ כָּל חָי, וְרוּחַ כָּל בְּשַׂר אִישׁ.[8] בְּיָדְךָ אַפְקִיד רוּחִי, פָּדִיתָה אוֹתִי, יהוה אֵל אֱמֶת.[9] אֱלֹהֵינוּ שֶׁבַּשָּׁמַיִם יַחֵד שִׁמְךָ, וְקַיֵּם מַלְכוּתְךָ תָּמִיד, וּמְלוֹךְ עָלֵינוּ לְעוֹלָם וָעֶד.

יִרְאוּ עֵינֵינוּ וְיִשְׂמַח לִבֵּנוּ וְתָגֵל נַפְשֵׁנוּ בִּישׁוּעָתְךָ בֶּאֱמֶת, בֶּאֱמֹר לְצִיּוֹן מָלַךְ אֱלֹהָיִךְ.[10] יהוה מֶלֶךְ,[11] יהוה מָלָךְ,[12] יהוה יִמְלֹךְ לְעֹלָם וָעֶד.[13] ❖ כִּי הַמַּלְכוּת שֶׁלְּךָ הִיא, וּלְעוֹלְמֵי עַד תִּמְלוֹךְ בְּכָבוֹד, כִּי אֵין לָנוּ מֶלֶךְ אֶלָּא אָתָּה. בָּרוּךְ אַתָּה יהוה, הַמֶּלֶךְ בִּכְבוֹדוֹ תָּמִיד יִמְלוֹךְ עָלֵינוּ לְעוֹלָם וָעֶד, וְעַל כָּל מַעֲשָׂיו. (Cong. – אָמֵן.)

The *chazzan* recites חֲצִי קַדִּישׁ.

יִתְגַּדַּל וְיִתְקַדַּשׁ שְׁמֵהּ רַבָּא. (Cong. – אָמֵן.) בְּעָלְמָא דִּי בְרָא כִרְעוּתֵהּ, וְיַמְלִיךְ מַלְכוּתֵהּ, בְּחַיֵּיכוֹן וּבְיוֹמֵיכוֹן וּבְחַיֵּי דְכָל בֵּית יִשְׂרָאֵל, בַּעֲגָלָא וּבִזְמַן קָרִיב. וְאִמְרוּ: אָמֵן.

(Cong. – אָמֵן. יְהֵא שְׁמֵהּ רַבָּא מְבָרַךְ לְעָלַם וּלְעָלְמֵי עָלְמַיָּא.)

יְהֵא שְׁמֵהּ רַבָּא מְבָרַךְ לְעָלַם וּלְעָלְמֵי עָלְמַיָּא.

יִתְבָּרַךְ וְיִשְׁתַּבַּח וְיִתְפָּאַר וְיִתְרוֹמַם וְיִתְנַשֵּׂא וְיִתְהַדָּר וְיִתְעַלֶּה וְיִתְהַלָּל שְׁמֵהּ דְּקֻדְשָׁא בְּרִיךְ הוּא (Cong. – בְּרִיךְ הוּא) — לְעֵלָּא מִן כָּל בִּרְכָתָא וְשִׁירָתָא תֻּשְׁבְּחָתָא וְנֶחֱמָתָא, דַּאֲמִירָן בְּעָלְמָא. וְאִמְרוּ: אָמֵן. (Cong. – אָמֵן.)

nation for the sake of His Great Name, for HASHEM has vowed to make you His own people.[1] Then the entire nation saw and fell on their faces and said, 'HASHEM — only He is God! HASHEM — only He is God!'[2] Then HASHEM will be King over all the world, on that day HASHEM will be One and His Name will be One.[3] May Your kindness, HASHEM, be upon us, just as we awaited You.[4] Save us, HASHEM, our God, gather us from the nations, to thank Your Holy Name and to glory in Your praise![5] All the nations that You made will come and bow before You, My Lord, and shall glorify Your Name. For You are great and work wonders; You alone, O God.[6] Then we, Your nation and the sheep of Your pasture, shall thank You forever; for generation after generation we will relate Your praise.[7] Blessed is HASHEM by day; Blessed is HASHEM by night; Blessed is HASHEM when we retire; Blessed is HASHEM when we arise. For in Your hand are the souls of the living and the dead. He in Whose hand is the soul of all the living and the spirit of every human being.[8] In Your hand I shall entrust my spirit, You redeemed me, HASHEM, God of truth.[9] Our God, Who is in heaven, bring unity to Your Name; establish Your kingdom forever and reign over us for all eternity.

יִרְאוּ *May our eyes see, our heart rejoice and our soul exult in Your salvation in truth, when Zion is told, 'Your God has reigned!'[10] HASHEM reigns,[11] HASHEM has reigned,[12] HASHEM will reign for all eternity.[13]* Chazzan– *For the kingdom is Yours and for all eternity You will reign in glory, for we have no King but You. Blessed are You, HASHEM, the King in His glory — He shall constantly reign over us forever and ever, and over all His creatures.* (Cong.– *Amen.)*

The chazzan recites Half-*Kaddish.*

יִתְגַּדַּל *May His great Name grow exalted and sanctified* (Cong.– *Amen.) in the world that He created as He willed. May He give reign to His kingship in your lifetimes and in your days, and in the lifetimes of the entire Family of Israel, swiftly and soon. Now respond: Amen.*

(Cong.– *Amen. May His great Name be blessed forever and ever.)*

May His great Name be blessed forever and ever.

Blessed, praised, glorified, exalted, extolled, mighty, upraised, and lauded be the Name of the Holy One, Blessed is He (Cong.– *Blessed is He) — beyond any blessing and song, praise and consolation that are uttered in the world. Now respond: Amen.* (Cong.– *Amen.)*

---

(1) *I Samuel* 12:22. (2) *I Kings* 18:39. (3) *Zechariah* 14:9.
(4) *Psalms* 33:22. (5) 106:47. (6) 86:9-10. (7) 79:13. (8) *Job* 12:10. (9) *Psalms* 31:6.
(10) Cf. *Isaiah* 52:7. (11) *Psalms* 10:16. (12) 93:1 et al. (13) *Exodus* 15:18.

❧ שמונה עשרה – עמידה ❧

Take three steps backward, then three steps forward. Remain standing with the feet together while reciting *Shemoneh Esrei.* Recite it with quiet devotion and without interruption, verbal or otherwise. Although its recitation should not be audible to others, one must pray loudly enough to hear himself.

אֲדֹנָי שְׂפָתַי תִּפְתָּח, וּפִי יַגִּיד תְּהִלָּתֶךָ.[1]

אבות

Bend the knees at בָּרוּךְ; bow at אַתָּה; straighten up at ה׳.

בָּרוּךְ אַתָּה יהוה אֱלֹהֵינוּ וֵאלֹהֵי אֲבוֹתֵינוּ, אֱלֹהֵי אַבְרָהָם, אֱלֹהֵי יִצְחָק, וֵאלֹהֵי יַעֲקֹב, הָאֵל הַגָּדוֹל הַגִּבּוֹר וְהַנּוֹרָא, אֵל עֶלְיוֹן, גּוֹמֵל חֲסָדִים טוֹבִים וְקוֹנֵה הַכֹּל, וְזוֹכֵר חַסְדֵי אָבוֹת, וּמֵבִיא גוֹאֵל לִבְנֵי בְנֵיהֶם, לְמַעַן שְׁמוֹ בְּאַהֲבָה. מֶלֶךְ עוֹזֵר וּמוֹשִׁיעַ וּמָגֵן.

Bend the knees at בָּרוּךְ; bow at אַתָּה; straighten up at ה׳.

בָּרוּךְ אַתָּה יהוה, מָגֵן אַבְרָהָם.

גבורות

אַתָּה גִּבּוֹר לְעוֹלָם אֲדֹנָי, מְחַיֵּה מֵתִים אַתָּה, רַב לְהוֹשִׁיעַ.

מַשִּׁיב הָרְוּחַ וּמוֹרִיד הַגֶּשֶׁם.

מְכַלְכֵּל חַיִּים בְּחֶסֶד, מְחַיֵּה מֵתִים בְּרַחֲמִים רַבִּים, סוֹמֵךְ נוֹפְלִים, וְרוֹפֵא חוֹלִים, וּמַתִּיר אֲסוּרִים, וּמְקַיֵּם אֱמוּנָתוֹ לִישֵׁנֵי עָפָר. מִי כָמְוֹךָ בַּעַל גְּבוּרוֹת, וּמִי דּוֹמֶה לָּךְ, מֶלֶךְ מֵמִית וּמְחַיֶּה וּמַצְמִיחַ יְשׁוּעָה. וְנֶאֱמָן אַתָּה לְהַחֲיוֹת מֵתִים. בָּרוּךְ אַתָּה יהוה, מְחַיֵּה הַמֵּתִים.

קדושת השם

אַתָּה קָדוֹשׁ וְשִׁמְךָ קָדוֹשׁ, וּקְדוֹשִׁים בְּכָל יוֹם יְהַלְּלְוּךָ סֶּלָה. בָּרוּךְ אַתָּה יהוה, הָאֵל הַקָּדוֹשׁ.

בינה

אַתָּה חוֹנֵן לְאָדָם דַּעַת, וּמְלַמֵּד לֶאֱנוֹשׁ בִּינָה. אַתָּה חוֹנַנְתָּנוּ לְמַדַּע תּוֹרָתֶךָ, וַתְּלַמְּדֵנוּ לַעֲשׂוֹת חֻקֵּי רְצוֹנֶךָ וַתַּבְדֵּל יהוה אֱלֹהֵינוּ בֵּין קֹדֶשׁ לְחוֹל בֵּין אוֹר לְחְשֶׁךְ, בֵּין יִשְׂרָאֵל לָעַמִּים בֵּין יוֹם הַשְּׁבִיעִי לְשֵׁשֶׁת יְמֵי הַמַּעֲשֶׂה. אָבִינוּ מַלְכֵּנוּ הָחֵל עָלֵינוּ הַיָּמִים הַבָּאִים לִקְרָאתֵנוּ לְשָׁלוֹם חֲשׂוּכִים מִכָּל חֵטְא וּמְנֻקִּים מִכָּל עָוֹן וּמְדֻבָּקִים בְּיִרְאָתֶךָ. וְחָנֵּנוּ מֵאִתְּךָ דֵּעָה בִּינָה וְהַשְׂכֵּל. בָּרוּךְ אַתָּה יהוה, חוֹנֵן הַדָּעַת.

❧ SHEMONEH ESREI – AMIDAH ☙

Take three steps backward, then three steps forward. Remain standing with the feet together while reciting *Shemoneh Esrei*. Recite it with quiet devotion and without interruption, verbal or otherwise. Although its recitation should not be audible to others, one must pray loudly enough to hear himself.

My Lord, open my lips, that my mouth may declare Your praise.[1]

PATRIARCHS

Bend the knees at *'Blessed'*; bow at *'You'*; straighten up at *'HASHEM.'*

בָּרוּךְ *Blessed are You, HASHEM, our God and the God of our forefathers, God of Abraham, God of Isaac, and God of Jacob; the great, mighty, and awesome God, the supreme God, Who bestows beneficial kindnesses and creates everything, Who recalls the kindnesses of the Patriarchs and brings a Redeemer to their children's children, for His Name's sake, with love. O King, Helper, Savior, and Shield.*

Bend the knees at *'Blessed'*; bow at *'You'*; straighten up at 'HASHEM.'

Blessed are You, HASHEM, Shield of Abraham.

GOD'S MIGHT

אַתָּה *You are eternally mighty, my Lord, the Resuscitator of the dead are You; abundantly able to save.*

He makes the wind blow and He makes the rain descend.

He sustains the living with kindness, resuscitates the dead with abundant mercy, supports the fallen, heals the sick, releases the confined, and maintains His faith to those asleep in the dust. Who is like You, O Master of mighty deeds, and who is comparable to You, O King Who causes death and restores life and makes salvation sprout! And You are faithful to resuscitate the dead. Blessed are You, HASHEM, Who resuscitates the dead.

HOLINESS OF GOD'S NAME

אַתָּה *You are holy and Your Name is holy, and holy ones praise You every day, forever. Blessed are You, HASHEM, the holy God.*

INSIGHT

אַתָּה *You graciously endow man with wisdom and teach insight to a frail mortal. You have graced us with intelligence to study Your Torah and You have taught us to perform the decrees You have willed. HASHEM, our God, You have distinguished between the sacred and the secular, between light and darkness, between Israel and the peoples, between the seventh day and the six days of labor. Our Father, our King, begin for us the days approaching us for peace, free from all sin, cleansed from all iniquity and attached to fear of You. And endow us graciously from Yourself with wisdom, insight, and discernment. Blessed are You, HASHEM, gracious Giver of wisdom.*

---

(1) *Psalms* 51:17.

תשובה

הֲשִׁיבֵנוּ אָבִינוּ לְתוֹרָתֶךָ, וְקָרְבֵנוּ מַלְכֵּנוּ לַעֲבוֹדָתֶךָ, וְהַחֲזִירֵנוּ בִּתְשׁוּבָה שְׁלֵמָה לְפָנֶיךָ. בָּרוּךְ אַתָּה יהוה, הָרוֹצֶה בִּתְשׁוּבָה.

סליחה

Strike the left side of the chest with the right fist while reciting the words חָטָאנוּ and פָשָׁעְנוּ.

סְלַח לָנוּ אָבִינוּ כִּי חָטָאנוּ, מְחַל לָנוּ מַלְכֵּנוּ כִּי פָשָׁעְנוּ, כִּי מוֹחֵל וְסוֹלֵחַ אָתָּה. בָּרוּךְ אַתָּה יהוה, חַנּוּן הַמַּרְבֶּה לִסְלֹחַ.

גאולה

רְאֵה בְעָנְיֵנוּ, וְרִיבָה רִיבֵנוּ, וּגְאָלֵנוּ[1] מְהֵרָה לְמַעַן שְׁמֶךָ, כִּי גּוֹאֵל חָזָק אָתָּה. בָּרוּךְ אַתָּה יהוה, גּוֹאֵל יִשְׂרָאֵל.

רפואה

רְפָאֵנוּ יהוה וְנֵרָפֵא, הוֹשִׁיעֵנוּ וְנִוָּשֵׁעָה, כִּי תְהִלָּתֵנוּ אָתָּה,[2] וְהַעֲלֵה רְפוּאָה שְׁלֵמָה לְכָל מַכּוֹתֵינוּ, °°כִּי אֵל מֶלֶךְ רוֹפֵא נֶאֱמָן וְרַחֲמָן אָתָּה. בָּרוּךְ אַתָּה יהוה, רוֹפֵא חוֹלֵי עַמּוֹ יִשְׂרָאֵל.

ברכת השנים

בָּרֵךְ עָלֵינוּ יהוה אֱלֹהֵינוּ אֶת הַשָּׁנָה הַזֹּאת וְאֶת כָּל מִינֵי תְבוּאָתָהּ לְטוֹבָה, וְתֵן בְּרָכָה עַל פְּנֵי הָאֲדָמָה, וְשַׂבְּעֵנוּ מִטּוּבֶךָ, וּבָרֵךְ שְׁנָתֵנוּ כַּשָּׁנִים הַטּוֹבוֹת. בָּרוּךְ אַתָּה יהוה, מְבָרֵךְ הַשָּׁנִים.

קיבוץ גליות

תְּקַע בְּשׁוֹפָר גָּדוֹל לְחֵרוּתֵנוּ, וְשָׂא נֵס לְקַבֵּץ גָּלֻיּוֹתֵינוּ, וְקַבְּצֵנוּ יַחַד מֵאַרְבַּע כַּנְפוֹת הָאָרֶץ.[3] בָּרוּךְ אַתָּה יהוה, מְקַבֵּץ נִדְחֵי עַמּוֹ יִשְׂרָאֵל.

דין

הָשִׁיבָה שׁוֹפְטֵינוּ כְּבָרִאשׁוֹנָה, וְיוֹעֲצֵינוּ כְּבַתְּחִלָּה,[4] וְהָסֵר מִמֶּנּוּ יָגוֹן וַאֲנָחָה, וּמְלוֹךְ עָלֵינוּ אַתָּה יהוה לְבַדְּךָ בְּחֶסֶד וּבְרַחֲמִים, וְצַדְּקֵנוּ בַּמִּשְׁפָּט. בָּרוּךְ אַתָּה יהוה, מֶלֶךְ אוֹהֵב צְדָקָה וּמִשְׁפָּט.

°°At this point one may interject a prayer for one who is ill:

יְהִי רָצוֹן מִלְּפָנֶיךָ יהוה אֱלֹהַי וֵאלֹהֵי אֲבוֹתַי, שֶׁתִּשְׁלַח מְהֵרָה רְפוּאָה שְׁלֵמָה מִן הַשָּׁמַיִם, רְפוּאַת הַנֶּפֶשׁ וּרְפוּאַת הַגּוּף

לַחוֹלֶה (patient's name) בֶּן (mother's name) בְּתוֹךְ שְׁאָר חוֹלֵי יִשְׂרָאֵל. —for a male

לַחוֹלָה (patient's name) בַּת (mother's name) בְּתוֹךְ שְׁאָר חוֹלֵי יִשְׂרָאֵל. —for a female

כִּי אֵל . . . —continue

REPENTANCE

הֲשִׁיבֵנוּ *Bring us back, our Father, to Your Torah, and bring us near, our King, to Your service, and influence us to return in perfect repentance before You. Blessed are You, HASHEM, Who desires repentance.*

FORGIVENESS

Strike the left side of the chest with the right fist while reciting the words *'erred'* and *'sinned.'*

סְלַח *Forgive us, our Father, for we have erred; pardon us, our King, for we have willfully sinned; for You pardon and forgive. Blessed are You, HASHEM, the gracious One Who pardons abundantly.*

REDEMPTION

רְאֵה *Behold our affliction, take up our grievance, and redeem us*[1] *speedily for Your Name's sake, for You are a powerful Redeemer. Blessed are You, HASHEM, Redeemer of Israel.*

HEALTH AND HEALING

רְפָאֵנוּ *Heal us, HASHEM — then we will be healed; save us — then we will be saved, for You are our praise.*[2] *Bring complete recovery for all our ailments,* °°*for You are God, King, the faithful and compassionate Healer. Blessed are You, HASHEM, Who heals the sick of His people Israel.*

YEAR OF PROSPERITY

בָּרֵךְ *Bless on our behalf — O HASHEM, our God — this year and all its kinds of crops for the best, and give a blessing on the face of the earth, and satisfy us from Your bounty, and bless our year like the best years. Blessed are You, HASHEM, Who blesses the years.*

INGATHERING OF EXILES

תְּקַע *Sound the great shofar for our freedom, raise the banner to gather our exiles and gather us together from the four corners of the earth.*[3] *Blessed are You, HASHEM, Who gathers in the dispersed of His people Israel.*

RESTORATION OF JUSTICE

הָשִׁיבָה *Restore our judges as in earliest times and our counselors as at first;*[4] *remove from us sorrow and groan; and reign over us — You, HASHEM, alone — with kindness and compassion, and justify us through judgment. Blessed are You, HASHEM, the King Who loves righteousness and judgment.*

°°At this point one may interject a prayer for one who is ill:

May it be Your will, HASHEM, my God, and the God of my forefathers, that You quickly send a complete recovery from heaven, spiritual healing and physical healing to the patient (name) *son/daughter of* (mother's name) *among the other patients of Israel.*

Continue: *For You are God ...*

---

(1) Cf. *Psalms* 119:153-154. (2) Cf. *Jeremiah* 17:14. (3) Cf. *Isaiah* 11:12. (4) Cf. 1:26.

ברכת המינים

וְלַמַּלְשִׁינִים אַל תְּהִי תִקְוָה, וְכָל הָרִשְׁעָה כְּרֶגַע תֹּאבֵד, וְכָל אֹיְבֶיךָ מְהֵרָה יִכָּרֵתוּ, וְהַזֵּדִים מְהֵרָה תְעַקֵּר וּתְשַׁבֵּר וּתְמַגֵּר וְתַכְנִיעַ בִּמְהֵרָה בְיָמֵינוּ. בָּרוּךְ אַתָּה יהוה, שׁוֹבֵר אֹיְבִים וּמַכְנִיעַ זֵדִים.

צדיקים

עַל הַצַּדִּיקִים וְעַל הַחֲסִידִים, וְעַל זִקְנֵי עַמְּךָ בֵּית יִשְׂרָאֵל, וְעַל פְּלֵיטַת סוֹפְרֵיהֶם, וְעַל גֵּרֵי הַצֶּדֶק וְעָלֵינוּ, יֶהֱמוּ רַחֲמֶיךָ יהוה אֱלֹהֵינוּ, וְתֵן שָׂכָר טוֹב לְכָל הַבּוֹטְחִים בְּשִׁמְךָ בֶּאֱמֶת, וְשִׂים חֶלְקֵנוּ עִמָּהֶם לְעוֹלָם, וְלֹא נֵבוֹשׁ כִּי בְךָ בָּטָחְנוּ. בָּרוּךְ אַתָּה יהוה, מִשְׁעָן וּמִבְטָח לַצַּדִּיקִים.

בנין ירושלים

וְלִירוּשָׁלַיִם עִירְךָ בְּרַחֲמִים תָּשׁוּב, וְתִשְׁכּוֹן בְּתוֹכָהּ כַּאֲשֶׁר דִּבַּרְתָּ, וּבְנֵה אוֹתָהּ בְּקָרוֹב בְּיָמֵינוּ בִּנְיַן עוֹלָם, וְכִסֵּא דָוִד מְהֵרָה לְתוֹכָהּ תָּכִין. בָּרוּךְ אַתָּה יהוה, בּוֹנֵה יְרוּשָׁלָיִם.

מלכות בית דוד

אֶת צֶמַח דָּוִד עַבְדְּךָ מְהֵרָה תַצְמִיחַ, וְקַרְנוֹ תָּרוּם בִּישׁוּעָתֶךָ, כִּי לִישׁוּעָתְךָ קִוִּינוּ כָּל הַיּוֹם. בָּרוּךְ אַתָּה יהוה, מַצְמִיחַ קֶרֶן יְשׁוּעָה.

קבלת תפלה

שְׁמַע קוֹלֵנוּ יהוה אֱלֹהֵינוּ, חוּס וְרַחֵם עָלֵינוּ, וְקַבֵּל בְּרַחֲמִים וּבְרָצוֹן אֶת תְּפִלָּתֵנוּ, כִּי אֵל שׁוֹמֵעַ תְּפִלּוֹת וְתַחֲנוּנִים אָתָּה. וּמִלְּפָנֶיךָ מַלְכֵּנוּ רֵיקָם אַל תְּשִׁיבֵנוּ,°°

°°During the silent *Shemoneh Esrei* one may insert either or both of these personal prayers.

For forgiveness:

אָנָּא יהוה, חָטָאתִי עָוִיתִי וּפָשַׁעְתִּי לְפָנֶיךָ, מִיּוֹם הֱיוֹתִי עַל הָאֲדָמָה עַד הַיּוֹם הַזֶּה (וּבִפְרַט בַּחֵטְא ....). אָנָּא יהוה, עֲשֵׂה לְמַעַן שִׁמְךָ הַגָּדוֹל, וּתְכַפֶּר לִי עַל עֲוֹנַי וַחֲטָאַי וּפְשָׁעַי שֶׁחָטָאתִי וְשֶׁעָוִיתִי וְשֶׁפָּשַׁעְתִּי לְפָנֶיךָ, מִנְּעוּרַי עַד הַיּוֹם הַזֶּה. וּתְמַלֵּא כָּל הַשֵּׁמוֹת שֶׁפָּגַמְתִּי בְּשִׁמְךָ הַגָּדוֹל.

For livelihood:

אַתָּה הוּא יהוה הָאֱלֹהִים, הַזָּן וּמְפַרְנֵס וּמְכַלְכֵּל מִקַּרְנֵי רְאֵמִים עַד בֵּיצֵי כִנִּים. הַטְרִיפֵנִי לֶחֶם חֻקִּי, וְהַמְצֵא לִי וּלְכָל בְּנֵי בֵיתִי מְזוֹנוֹתַי קוֹדֶם שֶׁאֶצְטָרֵךְ לָהֶם, בְּנַחַת וְלֹא בְצַעַר, בְּהֶתֵּר וְלֹא בְאִסּוּר, בְּכָבוֹד וְלֹא בְבִזָּיוֹן, לְחַיִּים וּלְשָׁלוֹם, מִשֶּׁפַע בְּרָכָה וְהַצְלָחָה, וּמִשֶּׁפַע בְּרֵכָה עֶלְיוֹנָה, כְּדֵי שֶׁאוּכַל לַעֲשׂוֹת רְצוֹנֶךָ וְלַעֲסוֹק בְּתוֹרָתֶךָ וּלְקַיֵּם מִצְוֹתֶיךָ. וְאַל תַּצְרִיכֵנִי לִידֵי מַתְּנַת בָּשָׂר וָדָם. וִיקֻיַּם בִּי מִקְרָא שֶׁכָּתוּב: פּוֹתֵחַ אֶת יָדֶךָ, וּמַשְׂבִּיעַ לְכָל חַי רָצוֹן.[1] וְכָתוּב: הַשְׁלֵךְ עַל יהוה יְהָבְךָ וְהוּא יְכַלְכְּלֶךָ.[2]

Continue — כִּי אַתָּה . . .

AGAINST HERETICS

וְלַמַּלְשִׁינִים *And for slanderers let there be no hope; and may all wickedness perish in an instant; and may all Your enemies be cut down speedily. May You speedily uproot, smash, cast down, and humble the wanton sinners — speedily in our days. Blessed are You, HASHEM, Who breaks enemies and humbles wanton sinners.*

THE RIGHTEOUS

עַל הַצַּדִּיקִים *On the righteous, on the devout, on the elders of Your people the Family of Israel, on the remnant of their scholars, on the righteous converts and on ourselves — may Your compassion be aroused, HASHEM, our God, and give goodly reward to all who sincerely believe in Your Name. Put our lot with them forever, and we will not feel ashamed, for we trust in You. Blessed are You, HASHEM, Mainstay and Assurance of the righteous.*

REBUILDING JERUSALEM

וְלִירוּשָׁלַיִם *And to Jerusalem, Your city, may You return in compassion, and may You rest within it, as You have spoken. May You rebuild it soon in our days as an eternal structure, and may You speedily establish the throne of David within it. Blessed are You, HASHEM, the Builder of Jerusalem.*

DAVIDIC REIGN

אֶת צֶמַח *The offspring of Your servant David may You speedily cause to flourish, and enhance his pride through Your salvation, for we hope for Your salvation all day long. Blessed are You, HASHEM, Who causes the pride of salvation to flourish.*

ACCEPTANCE OF PRAYER

שְׁמַע *Hear our voice, HASHEM our God, pity and be compassionate to us, and accept — with compassion and favor — our prayer, for God Who hears prayers and supplications are You. From before Yourself, our King, turn us not away empty-handed,*°°

°°During the silent *Shemoneh Esrei* one may insert either or both of these personal prayers.

For forgiveness:

אָנָּא *Please, O HASHEM, I have erred, been iniquitous, and willfully sinned before You, from the day I have existed on earth until this very day (and especially with the sin of . . .). Please, HASHEM, act for the sake of Your Great Name and grant me atonement for my iniquities, my errors, and my willful sins through which I have erred, been iniquitous, and willfully sinned before You, from my youth until this day. And make whole all the Names that I have blemished in Your Great Name.*

For livelihood:

אַתָּה *It is You, HASHEM the God, Who nourishes, sustains, and supports, from the horns of re'eimim to the eggs of lice. Provide me with my allotment of bread; and bring forth for me and all members of my household, my food, before I have need for it; in contentment but not in pain, in a permissible but not a forbidden manner, in honor but not in disgrace, for life and for peace; from the flow of blessing and success and from the flow of the Heavenly spring, so that I be enabled to do Your will and engage in Your Torah and fulfill Your commandments. Make me not needful of people's largesse; and may there be fulfilled in me the verse that states, 'You open Your hand and satisfy the desire of every living thing'*[1] *and that states, 'Cast Your burden upon HASHEM and He will support you.'*[2]

Continue: *For You hear the prayer . . .*

(1) *Psalms* 145:16. (3) 55:23.

כִּי אַתָּה שׁוֹמֵעַ תְּפִלַּת עַמְּךָ יִשְׂרָאֵל בְּרַחֲמִים. בָּרוּךְ אַתָּה יהוה, שׁוֹמֵעַ תְּפִלָּה.

עבודה

רְצֵה יהוה אֱלֹהֵינוּ בְּעַמְּךָ יִשְׂרָאֵל וּבִתְפִלָּתָם, וְהָשֵׁב אֶת הָעֲבוֹדָה לִדְבִיר בֵּיתֶךָ. וְאִשֵּׁי יִשְׂרָאֵל וּתְפִלָּתָם בְּאַהֲבָה תְקַבֵּל בְּרָצוֹן, וּתְהִי לְרָצוֹן תָּמִיד עֲבוֹדַת יִשְׂרָאֵל עַמֶּךָ.

וְתֶחֱזֶינָה עֵינֵינוּ בְּשׁוּבְךָ לְצִיּוֹן בְּרַחֲמִים. בָּרוּךְ אַתָּה יהוה, הַמַּחֲזִיר שְׁכִינָתוֹ לְצִיּוֹן.

הודאה

Bow at מוֹדִים; straighten up at ה'.

מוֹדִים אֲנַחְנוּ לָךְ שָׁאַתָּה הוּא יהוה אֱלֹהֵינוּ וֵאלֹהֵי אֲבוֹתֵינוּ לְעוֹלָם וָעֶד. צוּר חַיֵּינוּ, מָגֵן יִשְׁעֵנוּ אַתָּה הוּא לְדוֹר וָדוֹר. נוֹדֶה לְּךָ וּנְסַפֵּר תְּהִלָּתֶךָ[1] עַל חַיֵּינוּ הַמְּסוּרִים בְּיָדֶךָ, וְעַל נִשְׁמוֹתֵינוּ הַפְּקוּדוֹת לָךְ, וְעַל נִסֶּיךָ שֶׁבְּכָל יוֹם עִמָּנוּ, וְעַל נִפְלְאוֹתֶיךָ וְטוֹבוֹתֶיךָ שֶׁבְּכָל עֵת, עֶרֶב וָבֹקֶר וְצָהֳרָיִם. הַטּוֹב כִּי לֹא כָלוּ רַחֲמֶיךָ, וְהַמְּרַחֵם כִּי לֹא תַמּוּ חֲסָדֶיךָ,[2] מֵעוֹלָם קִוִּינוּ לָךְ:

וְעַל כֻּלָּם יִתְבָּרַךְ וְיִתְרוֹמַם שִׁמְךָ מַלְכֵּנוּ תָּמִיד לְעוֹלָם וָעֶד.

Bend the knees at בָּרוּךְ; bow at אַתָּה; straighten up at ה'.

וְכֹל הַחַיִּים יוֹדְוּךָ סֶּלָה, וִיהַלְלוּ אֶת שִׁמְךָ בֶּאֱמֶת, הָאֵל יְשׁוּעָתֵנוּ וְעֶזְרָתֵנוּ סֶלָה. בָּרוּךְ אַתָּה יהוה, הַטּוֹב שִׁמְךָ וּלְךָ נָאֶה לְהוֹדוֹת.

שלום

שָׁלוֹם רָב עַל יִשְׂרָאֵל עַמְּךָ תָּשִׂים לְעוֹלָם, כִּי אַתָּה הוּא מֶלֶךְ אָדוֹן לְכָל הַשָּׁלוֹם. וְטוֹב בְּעֵינֶיךָ לְבָרֵךְ אֶת עַמְּךָ יִשְׂרָאֵל, בְּכָל עֵת וּבְכָל שָׁעָה בִּשְׁלוֹמֶךָ. בָּרוּךְ אַתָּה יהוה, הַמְּבָרֵךְ אֶת עַמּוֹ יִשְׂרָאֵל בַּשָּׁלוֹם.

יִהְיוּ לְרָצוֹן אִמְרֵי פִי וְהֶגְיוֹן לִבִּי לְפָנֶיךָ, יהוה צוּרִי וְגֹאֲלִי.[3]

for You hear the prayer of Your people Israel with compassion. Blessed are You, HASHEM, Who hears prayer.

TEMPLE SERVICE

רְצֵה *Be favorable, HASHEM, our God, toward Your people Israel and their prayer and restore the service to the Holy of Holies of Your Temple. The fire-offerings of Israel and their prayer accept with love and favor, and may the service of Your people Israel always be favorable to You.*

וְתֶחֱזֶינָה *May our eyes behold Your return to Zion in compassion. Blessed are You, HASHEM, Who restores His Presence unto Zion.*

THANKSGIVING [MODIM]

Bow at *'We gratefully thank You'*; straighten up at *'HASHEM.'*

מוֹדִים *We gratefully thank You, for it is You Who are HASHEM, our God and the God of our forefathers for all eternity; Rock of our lives, Shield of our salvation are You from generation to generation. We shall thank You and relate Your praise*[1] *— for our lives, which are committed to Your power and for our souls that are entrusted to You; for Your miracles that are with us every day; and for Your wonders and favors in every season — evening, morning, and afternoon. The Beneficent One, for Your compassions were never exhausted, and the Compassionate One, for Your kindnesses never ended*[2] *— always have we put our hope in You.*

For all these, may Your Name be blessed and exalted, our King, continually forever and ever.

Bend the knees at *'Blessed'*; bow at *'You'*; straighten up at *'HASHEM.'*

Everything alive will gratefully acknowledge You, Selah! and praise Your Name sincerely, O God of our salvation and help, Selah! Blessed are You, HASHEM, Your Name is 'The Beneficent One' and to You it is fitting to give thanks.

PEACE

שָׁלוֹם *Establish abundant peace upon Your people Israel forever, for You are King, Master of all peace. May it be good in Your eyes to bless Your people Israel at every time and every hour with Your peace. Blessed are You, HASHEM, Who blesses His people Israel with peace.*

May the expressions of my mouth and the thoughts of my heart
find favor before You, HASHEM, my Rock and my Redeemer.[3]

---

(1) Cf. *Psalms* 79:13. (2) Cf. *Lamentations* 3:22. (3) *Psalms* 19:15.

אֱלֹהַי, נְצוֹר לְשׁוֹנִי מֵרָע, וּשְׂפָתַי מִדַּבֵּר מִרְמָה,[1] וְלִמְקַלְלַי נַפְשִׁי תִדּוֹם, וְנַפְשִׁי כֶּעָפָר לַכֹּל תִּהְיֶה. פְּתַח לִבִּי בְּתוֹרָתֶךָ, וּבְמִצְוֹתֶיךָ תִּרְדּוֹף נַפְשִׁי. וְכֹל הַחוֹשְׁבִים עָלַי רָעָה, מְהֵרָה הָפֵר עֲצָתָם וְקַלְקֵל מַחֲשַׁבְתָּם. עֲשֵׂה לְמַעַן שְׁמֶךָ, עֲשֵׂה לְמַעַן יְמִינֶךָ, עֲשֵׂה לְמַעַן קְדֻשָּׁתֶךָ, עֲשֵׂה לְמַעַן תּוֹרָתֶךָ. לְמַעַן יֵחָלְצוּן יְדִידֶיךָ, הוֹשִׁיעָה יְמִינְךָ וַעֲנֵנִי.[2] Some recite verses pertaining to their names here. See page 1301.

יִהְיוּ לְרָצוֹן אִמְרֵי פִי וְהֶגְיוֹן לִבִּי לְפָנֶיךָ, יהוה צוּרִי וְגֹאֲלִי.[3]

Bow and take three steps back. Bow left and say . . . עֹשֶׂה, bow right and say . . . הוּא יַעֲשֶׂה; bow forward and say וְעַל כָּל . . . אָמֵן.

עֹשֶׂה שָׁלוֹם בִּמְרוֹמָיו, הוּא יַעֲשֶׂה שָׁלוֹם עָלֵינוּ, וְעַל כָּל יִשְׂרָאֵל. וְאִמְרוּ: אָמֵן.

יְהִי רָצוֹן מִלְּפָנֶיךָ יהוה אֱלֹהֵינוּ וֵאלֹהֵי אֲבוֹתֵינוּ, שֶׁיִּבָּנֶה בֵּית הַמִּקְדָּשׁ בִּמְהֵרָה בְיָמֵינוּ, וְתֵן חֶלְקֵנוּ בְּתוֹרָתֶךָ. וְשָׁם נַעֲבָדְךָ בְּיִרְאָה, כִּימֵי עוֹלָם וּכְשָׁנִים קַדְמוֹנִיּוֹת. וְעָרְבָה לַיהוה מִנְחַת יְהוּדָה וִירוּשָׁלָיִם, כִּימֵי עוֹלָם וּכְשָׁנִים קַדְמוֹנִיּוֹת.[4]

SHEMONEH ESREI ENDS HERE.

Remain standing in place for at least a few moments before taking three steps forward.

קדיש שלם

The *chazzan* recites קַדִּישׁ שָׁלֵם.

יִתְגַּדַּל וְיִתְקַדַּשׁ שְׁמֵהּ רַבָּא. (.Cong – אָמֵן.) בְּעָלְמָא דִּי בְרָא כִרְעוּתֵהּ. וְיַמְלִיךְ מַלְכוּתֵהּ, בְּחַיֵּיכוֹן וּבְיוֹמֵיכוֹן וּבְחַיֵּי דְכָל בֵּית יִשְׂרָאֵל, בַּעֲגָלָא וּבִזְמַן קָרִיב. וְאִמְרוּ: אָמֵן.

(.Cong – אָמֵן. יְהֵא שְׁמֵהּ רַבָּא מְבָרַךְ לְעָלַם וּלְעָלְמֵי עָלְמַיָּא.)

יְהֵא שְׁמֵהּ רַבָּא מְבָרַךְ לְעָלַם וּלְעָלְמֵי עָלְמַיָּא.

יִתְבָּרַךְ וְיִשְׁתַּבַּח וְיִתְפָּאַר וְיִתְרוֹמַם וְיִתְנַשֵּׂא וְיִתְהַדָּר וְיִתְעַלֶּה וְיִתְהַלָּל שְׁמֵהּ דְּקֻדְשָׁא בְּרִיךְ הוּא (.Cong – בְּרִיךְ הוּא) — לְעֵלָּא מִן כָּל בִּרְכָתָא וְשִׁירָתָא תֻּשְׁבְּחָתָא וְנֶחֱמָתָא, דַּאֲמִירָן בְּעָלְמָא. וְאִמְרוּ: אָמֵן. (.Cong – אָמֵן.)

(.Cong – קַבֵּל בְּרַחֲמִים וּבְרָצוֹן אֶת תְּפִלָּתֵנוּ.)

תִּתְקַבֵּל צְלוֹתְהוֹן וּבָעוּתְהוֹן דְּכָל בֵּית יִשְׂרָאֵל קֳדָם אֲבוּהוֹן דִּי בִשְׁמַיָּא. וְאִמְרוּ: אָמֵן. (.Cong – אָמֵן.)

(.Cong – יְהִי שֵׁם יהוה מְבֹרָךְ, מֵעַתָּה וְעַד עוֹלָם.[5])

יְהֵא שְׁלָמָא רַבָּא מִן שְׁמַיָּא, וְחַיִּים עָלֵינוּ וְעַל כָּל יִשְׂרָאֵל. וְאִמְרוּ: אָמֵן. (.Cong – אָמֵן.)

אֱלֹהַי *My God, guard my tongue from evil and my lips from speaking deceitfully.*[1] *To those who curse me, let my soul be silent; and let my soul be like dust to everyone. Open my heart to Your Torah, then my soul will pursue Your commandments. As for all those who design evil against me, speedily nullify their counsel and disrupt their design. Act for Your Name's sake; act for Your right hand's sake; act for Your sanctity's sake; act for Your Torah's sake. That Your beloved ones may be given rest; let Your right hand save, and respond to me.*[2]

Some recite verses pertaining to their names at this point. See page 1301.

May the expressions of my mouth and the thoughts of my heart find favor before You, HASHEM, my Rock and my Redeemer.[3] *He Who makes peace in His heights, may He make peace upon us, and upon all Israel. Now respond: Amen.*

Bow and take three steps back. Bow left and say, *'He Who makes peace . . .'*; bow right and say, *'may He make peace . . .'*; bow forward and say, *'and upon . . . Amen.'*

יְהִי רָצוֹן *May it be Your will, HASHEM, our God and the God of our forefathers, that the Holy Temple be rebuilt, speedily in our days. Grant us our share in Your Torah, and may we serve You there with reverence, as in days of old and in former years. Then the offering of Judah and Jerusalem will be pleasing to HASHEM, as in days of old and in former years.*[4]

SHEMONEH ESREI ENDS HERE.

Remain standing in place for a few moments before taking three steps forward.

FULL KADDISH

The *chazzan* recites the Full *Kaddish*.

יִתְגַּדַּל *May His great Name grow exalted and sanctified* (Cong.– *Amen.*) *in the world that He created as He willed. May He give reign to His kingship in your lifetimes and in your days, and in the lifetimes of the entire Family of Israel, swiftly and soon. Now respond: Amen.*

(Cong.– *Amen. May His great Name be blessed forever and ever.)*

May His great Name be blessed forever and ever.

Blessed, praised, glorified, exalted, extolled, mighty, upraised, and lauded be the Name of the Holy One, Blessed is He (Cong.– *Blessed is He*) — *beyond any blessing and song, praise and consolation that are uttered in the world. Now respond: Amen.* (Cong.– *Amen.*)

(Cong.– *Accept our prayers with mercy and favor.*)

May the prayers and supplications of the entire Family of Israel be accepted before their Father Who is in Heaven. Now respond: Amen. (Cong.– *Amen.*)

(Cong.– *Blessed be the Name of HASHEM, from this time and forever.*[5])

May there be abundant peace from Heaven, and life, upon us and upon all Israel. Now respond: Amen. (Cong.– *Amen.*)

---

(1) Cf. *Psalms* 34:14. (2) 60:7;108:7. (3) 19:15. (4) *Malachi* 3:4. (5) *Psalms* 113:2.

(.Cong – עֶזְרִי מֵעִם יהוה, עֹשֵׂה שָׁמַיִם וָאָרֶץ.[1])

Take three steps back. Bow left and say . . . עֹשֶׂה; bow right and say . . . הוּא; bow forward and say וְעַל כָּל . . . אָמֵן. Remain standing in place for a few moments, then take three steps forward.

עֹשֶׂה שָׁלוֹם בִּמְרוֹמָיו, הוּא יַעֲשֶׂה שָׁלוֹם עָלֵינוּ, וְעַל כָּל יִשְׂרָאֵל. וְאִמְרוּ: אָמֵן. (.Cong – אָמֵן.)

הבדלה בבית הכנסת

סַבְרִי מָרָנָן וְרַבָּנָן וְרַבּוֹתַי:

בָּרוּךְ אַתָּה יהוה אֱלֹהֵינוּ מֶלֶךְ הָעוֹלָם, בּוֹרֵא פְּרִי הַגָּפֶן.

(.Cong – אָמֵן.)

בָּרוּךְ אַתָּה יהוה אֱלֹהֵינוּ מֶלֶךְ הָעוֹלָם, הַמַּבְדִּיל בֵּין קֹדֶשׁ לְחוֹל, בֵּין אוֹר לְחֹשֶׁךְ, בֵּין יִשְׂרָאֵל לָעַמִּים, בֵּין יוֹם הַשְּׁבִיעִי לְשֵׁשֶׁת יְמֵי הַמַּעֲשֶׂה. בָּרוּךְ אַתָּה יהוה, הַמַּבְדִּיל בֵּין קֹדֶשׁ לְחוֹל. (.Cong – אָמֵן.)

The *chazzan,* or someone else present for *Havdalah,* should drink most of the cup.

The congregation stands while reciting עָלֵינוּ.

עָלֵינוּ לְשַׁבֵּחַ לַאֲדוֹן הַכֹּל, לָתֵת גְּדֻלָּה לְיוֹצֵר בְּרֵאשִׁית, שֶׁלֹּא עָשָׂנוּ כְּגוֹיֵי הָאֲרָצוֹת, וְלֹא שָׂמָנוּ כְּמִשְׁפְּחוֹת הָאֲדָמָה. שֶׁלֹּא שָׂם חֶלְקֵנוּ כָּהֶם, וְגוֹרָלֵנוּ כְּכָל הֲמוֹנָם. (שֶׁהֵם מִשְׁתַּחֲוִים לְהֶבֶל וָרִיק, וּמִתְפַּלְּלִים אֶל אֵל לֹא יוֹשִׁיעַ.[2]) וַאֲנַחְנוּ כּוֹרְעִים וּמִשְׁתַּחֲוִים וּמוֹדִים, לִפְנֵי מֶלֶךְ מַלְכֵי הַמְּלָכִים הַקָּדוֹשׁ בָּרוּךְ הוּא. שֶׁהוּא נוֹטֶה שָׁמַיִם וְיֹסֵד אָרֶץ,[3] וּמוֹשַׁב יְקָרוֹ בַּשָּׁמַיִם מִמַּעַל, וּשְׁכִינַת עֻזּוֹ בְּגָבְהֵי מְרוֹמִים. הוּא אֱלֹהֵינוּ, אֵין עוֹד. אֱמֶת מַלְכֵּנוּ, אֶפֶס זוּלָתוֹ, כַּכָּתוּב בְּתוֹרָתוֹ: וְיָדַעְתָּ הַיּוֹם וַהֲשֵׁבֹתָ אֶל לְבָבֶךָ, כִּי יהוה הוּא הָאֱלֹהִים בַּשָּׁמַיִם מִמַּעַל וְעַל הָאָרֶץ מִתָּחַת, אֵין עוֹד.[4]

Bow while reciting וַאֲנַחְנוּ כּוֹרְעִים וּמִשְׁתַּחֲוִים.

עַל כֵּן נְקַוֶּה לְּךָ יהוה אֱלֹהֵינוּ לִרְאוֹת מְהֵרָה בְּתִפְאֶרֶת עֻזֶּךָ, לְהַעֲבִיר גִּלּוּלִים מִן הָאָרֶץ, וְהָאֱלִילִים כָּרוֹת יִכָּרֵתוּן, לְתַקֵּן עוֹלָם בְּמַלְכוּת שַׁדַּי. וְכָל בְּנֵי בָשָׂר יִקְרְאוּ בִשְׁמֶךָ, לְהַפְנוֹת אֵלֶיךָ כָּל רִשְׁעֵי אָרֶץ. יַכִּירוּ וְיֵדְעוּ כָּל יוֹשְׁבֵי תֵבֵל, כִּי לְךָ תִּכְרַע כָּל בֶּרֶךְ, תִּשָּׁבַע כָּל לָשׁוֹן.[5] לְפָנֶיךָ יהוה אֱלֹהֵינוּ יִכְרְעוּ וְיִפֹּלוּ, וְלִכְבוֹד שִׁמְךָ יְקָר יִתֵּנוּ. וִיקַבְּלוּ כֻלָּם אֶת עוֹל מַלְכוּתֶךָ, וְתִמְלֹךְ

(Cong.– *My help is from* HASHEM, *Maker of heaven and earth.*[1])

Take three steps back. Bow left and say, *'He Who makes peace ...';* bow right and say, *'may He ...';* bow forward and say, *'and upon all Israel ...'* Remain standing in place for a few moments, then take three steps forward.

He Who makes peace in His heights, may He make peace upon us, and upon all Israel. Now respond: Amen. (Cong.– *Amen.*)

HAVDALAH IN THE SYNAGOGUE

By your leave, my masters and teachers:

בָּרוּךְ *Blessed are You,* HASHEM, *our God, King of the universe, Who creates the fruit of the vine.* (Cong. – *Amen.*)

בָּרוּךְ *Blessed are You,* HASHEM *our God, King of the universe, Who separates between holy and secular, between light and darkness, between Israel and the nations, between the seventh day and the six days of labor. Blessed are You,* HASHEM, *Who separates between holy and secular.* (Cong. – *Amen.*)

The *chazzan,* or someone else present for *Havdalah,* should drink most of the cup.

Stand while reciting עָלֵינוּ, *'It is our duty ...'*

עָלֵינוּ *It is our duty to praise the Master of all, to ascribe greatness to the Molder of primeval creation, for He has not made us like the nations of the lands, and has not emplaced us like the families of the earth; for He has not assigned our portion like theirs nor our lot like all their multitudes. (For they bow to vanity and emptiness and pray to a god which helps not.*[2]*) But we bend our knees, bow, and acknowledge our thanks before the King Who reigns over kings, the Holy One, Blessed is He. He stretches out heaven and establishes earth's foundation,*[3] *the seat of His homage is in the heavens above and His powerful Presence is in the loftiest heights. He is our God and there is none other. True is our King, there is nothing beside Him, as it is written in His Torah: 'You are to know this day and take to your heart that* HASHEM *is the only God — in heaven above and on the earth below — there is none other.'*[4]

Bow while reciting *'But we bend our knees.'*

עַל כֵּן *Therefore we put our hope in You,* HASHEM, *our God, that we may soon see Your mighty splendor, to remove detestable idolatry from the earth, and false gods will be utterly cut off, to perfect the universe through the Almighty's sovereignty. Then all humanity will call upon Your Name, to turn all the earth's wicked toward You. All the world's inhabitants will recognize and know that to You every knee should bend, every tongue should swear.*[5] *Before You,* HASHEM, *our God, they will bend every knee and cast themselves down and to the glory of Your Name they will render homage, and they will all accept upon themselves the yoke of Your kingship that You may reign*

(1) *Psalms* 121:2. (2) *Isaiah* 45:20. (3) 51:13. (4) *Deuteronomy* 4:39. (5) Cf. *Isaiah* 45:23.

עֲלֵיהֶם מְהֵרָה לְעוֹלָם וָעֶד. כִּי הַמַּלְכוּת שֶׁלְּךָ הִיא וּלְעוֹלְמֵי עַד תִּמְלוֹךְ בְּכָבוֹד, כַּכָּתוּב בְּתוֹרָתֶךָ: יהוה יִמְלֹךְ לְעֹלָם וָעֶד.[1] ❖ וְנֶאֱמַר: וְהָיָה יהוה לְמֶלֶךְ עַל כָּל הָאָרֶץ, בַּיּוֹם הַהוּא יִהְיֶה יהוה אֶחָד וּשְׁמוֹ אֶחָד.[2]

Some recite the following after עָלֵינוּ.

אַל תִּירָא מִפַּחַד פִּתְאֹם, וּמִשֹּׁאַת רְשָׁעִים כִּי תָבֹא.[4] עֻצוּ עֵצָה וְתֻפָר, דַּבְּרוּ דָבָר וְלֹא יָקוּם, כִּי עִמָּנוּ אֵל.[5] וְעַד זִקְנָה אֲנִי הוּא, וְעַד שֵׂיבָה אֲנִי אֶסְבֹּל, אֲנִי עָשִׂיתִי וַאֲנִי אֶשָּׂא, וַאֲנִי אֶסְבֹּל וַאֲמַלֵּט.[6]

קדיש יתום

Mourners recite קַדִּישׁ יָתוֹם.

יִתְגַּדַּל וְיִתְקַדַּשׁ שְׁמֵהּ רַבָּא. (.Cong – אָמֵן.) בְּעָלְמָא דִּי בְרָא כִרְעוּתֵהּ. וְיַמְלִיךְ מַלְכוּתֵהּ, בְּחַיֵּיכוֹן וּבְיוֹמֵיכוֹן וּבְחַיֵּי דְכָל בֵּית יִשְׂרָאֵל, בַּעֲגָלָא וּבִזְמַן קָרִיב. וְאִמְרוּ: אָמֵן.

(.Cong – אָמֵן. יְהֵא שְׁמֵהּ רַבָּא מְבָרַךְ לְעָלַם וּלְעָלְמֵי עָלְמַיָּא.)

יְהֵא שְׁמֵהּ רַבָּא מְבָרַךְ לְעָלַם וּלְעָלְמֵי עָלְמַיָּא.

יִתְבָּרַךְ וְיִשְׁתַּבַּח וְיִתְפָּאַר וְיִתְרוֹמַם וְיִתְנַשֵּׂא וְיִתְהַדָּר וְיִתְעַלֶּה וְיִתְהַלָּל שְׁמֵהּ דְּקֻדְשָׁא בְּרִיךְ הוּא (.Cong – בְּרִיךְ הוּא) – לְעֵלָּא מִן כָּל בִּרְכָתָא וְשִׁירָתָא תֻּשְׁבְּחָתָא וְנֶחֱמָתָא, דַּאֲמִירָן בְּעָלְמָא. וְאִמְרוּ: אָמֵן. (.Cong – אָמֵן.)

יְהֵא שְׁלָמָא רַבָּא מִן שְׁמַיָּא, וְחַיִּים עָלֵינוּ וְעַל כָּל יִשְׂרָאֵל. וְאִמְרוּ: אָמֵן. (.Cong – אָמֵן.)

Take three steps back. Bow left and say . . . עֹשֶׂה; bow right and say . . . הוּא; bow forward and say וְעַל כָּל . . . אָמֵן. Remain standing in place for a few moments, then take three steps forward.

עֹשֶׂה שָׁלוֹם בִּמְרוֹמָיו, הוּא יַעֲשֶׂה שָׁלוֹם עָלֵינוּ, וְעַל כָּל יִשְׂרָאֵל. וְאִמְרוּ: אָמֵן. (.Cong – אָמֵן.)

הבדלה

סַבְרִי מָרָנָן וְרַבָּנָן וְרַבּוֹתַי:

בָּרוּךְ אַתָּה יהוה אֱלֹהֵינוּ מֶלֶךְ הָעוֹלָם, בּוֹרֵא פְּרִי הַגָּפֶן.

(all present respond – אָמֵן.)

בָּרוּךְ אַתָּה יהוה אֱלֹהֵינוּ מֶלֶךְ הָעוֹלָם, הַמַּבְדִּיל בֵּין קֹדֶשׁ לְחוֹל, בֵּין אוֹר לְחֹשֶׁךְ, בֵּין יִשְׂרָאֵל לָעַמִּים, בֵּין יוֹם הַשְּׁבִיעִי לְשֵׁשֶׁת יְמֵי הַמַּעֲשֶׂה. בָּרוּךְ אַתָּה יהוה, הַמַּבְדִּיל בֵּין קֹדֶשׁ לְחוֹל. (all present respond – אָמֵן.)

The one who recited *Havdalah,* or someone else present for *Havdalah,* should drink most of the wine from the cup.

over them soon and eternally. For the kingdom is Yours and You will reign for all eternity in glory as it is written in Your Torah: HASHEM shall reign for all eternity.[1] Chazzan– *And it is said: HASHEM will be King over all the world — on that day HASHEM will be One and His Name will be One.*[2]

Some recite the following after *Aleinu.*

אַל תִּירָא *Do not fear sudden terror, or the holocaust of the wicked when it comes.*[3] *Plan a conspiracy and it will be annulled; speak your piece and it shall not stand, for God is with us.*[4] *Even till your seniority, I remain unchanged; and even till your ripe old age, I shall endure. I created you and I shall bear you; I shall endure and rescue.*[5]

MOURNER'S KADDISH

In the presence of a *minyan,* mourners recite קַדִּישׁ יָתוֹם, the Mourner's *Kaddish* (see *Laws* 81-83).

יִתְגַּדַּל *May His great Name grow exalted and sanctified* (Cong.– *Amen.*) *in the world that He created as He willed. May He give reign to His kingship in your lifetimes and in your days, and in the lifetimes of the entire Family of Israel, swiftly and soon. Now respond: Amen.*

(Cong.– *Amen. May His great Name be blessed forever and ever.*)

May His great Name be blessed forever and ever.

Blessed, praised, glorified, exalted, extolled, mighty, upraised, and lauded be the Name of the Holy One, Blessed is He (Cong.– *Blessed is He*) — *beyond any blessing and song, praise and consolation that are uttered in the world. Now respond: Amen.* (Cong.– *Amen*).

May there be abundant peace from Heaven, and life, upon us and upon all Israel. Now respond: Amen. (Cong.– *Amen.*)

Take three steps back. Bow left and say, *'He Who makes peace . . .';*
bow right and say, *'may He . . .';* bow forward and say, *'and upon all Israel . . .'*
Remain standing in place for a few moments, then take three steps forward.

He Who makes peace in His heights, may He make peace upon us, and upon all Israel. Now respond: Amen. (Cong.– *Amen.*)

HAVDALAH

By your leave, my masters and teachers:

בָּרוּךְ *Blessed are You, HASHEM, our God, King of the universe, Who creates the fruit of the vine.* (All present respond– *Amen.*)

בָּרוּךְ *Blessed are You, HASHEM our God, King of the universe, Who separates between holy and secular, between light and darkness, between Israel and the nations, between the seventh day and the six days of labor. Blessed are You, HASHEM, Who separates between holy and secular.* (All present respond– *Amen.*)

The one who recited *Havdalah,* or someone else present for *Havdalah,* should drink most of the wine from the cup.

---

(1) *Exodus* 15:18. (2) *Zechariah* 14:9. (3) *Proverbs* 3:25. (4) *Isaiah* 8:10. (5) 46:4.

❧ Appendices

- פיוטים נוספים
  Additional Piyutim
- הלכות
  Selected Laws
- פסוקים לשמות אנשים
  Verses for People's Names
- קדיש באותיות אנגלית
  Kaddish Transliterated

❧ ADDITIONAL PIYUTIM / פיוטים נוספים ❧

Some congregations recite this *piyut* before the *Kedushah* of *Shacharis* (p. 260) on the first day.

אֶקְחָה בְּרִאשׁוֹן, לְאַחֲרוֹן וְרִאשׁוֹן; פְּרִי עֵץ הָדָר, לְבַקְּדֶשׁ נֶאְדָּר; כַּפּוֹת תָּמָר, לְצַדִּיק כַּתָּמָר; עַנְפֵי הֲדַסִּים, לְצָג בֵּין הַהֲדַסִּים; טַרְפֵּי עֲרָבוֹת, לָרוֹכֵב בָּעֲרָבוֹת; בָּמוֹ לְהַלֵּל, בְּזֶמֶר וְהַלֵּל, בְּיוֹם וְלֹא בְלֵיל, לְאֵין לְפָנָיו לֵיל.

בְּלוּלָב אֶחָד, וְאֶתְרוֹג אֶחָד, לַיהוה אֶחָד, וּשְׁמוֹ אֶחָד. בַּעֲרָבוֹת שְׁתַּיִם, כְּאִמָּהוֹת שְׁתַּיִם, וּכִמְעוֹפְפוֹת שְׁתַּיִם. בְּעָבוֹת שְׁלֹשָׁה, כְּאָבוֹת שְׁלֹשָׁה, כְּמַקְדִּישֵׁי שְׁלֹשָׁה. בַּאֲגֻדּוֹת אַרְבַּע, כִּגְבָעוֹת אַרְבַּע, כְּחַיּוֹת אַרְבַּע, וּכְנָפַיִם אַרְבַּע. בִּשְׂמָחוֹת שֶׁבַע, כִּימֵי שֶׁבַע. בַּחֲגִיגַת שְׁמוֹנָה, כְּמִילַת שְׁמוֹנָה.

בְּהָדָר לְהַזְכִּיר הַדּוּר זְקֵנָה, בְּכַפּוֹת לְהַזְכִּיר לְמֵחִים נִקְנָה, בְּעָבוֹת לְהַזְכִּיר תָּם חַיֵּי עַד קָנָה, בַּעֲרָבָה לְהַזְכִּיר אָח לְעֶבֶד הַקְּנָה.

בְּהָדָר לַחְשֹׁב בְּלוּיַת עֶדְנָה, בְּכַפּוֹת לַחְשֹׁב מְשׁוּלֶּת שׁוֹשַׁנָּה, בְּעָבוֹת לַחְשֹׁב יְחוּמַת דִּינָה, בַּעֲרָבָה לַחְשֹׁב בְּאָחוֹת מְקַנְּאָה.

בְּהָדָר לְהַמְשִׁיל מַפְלִיא עֲגָלָה, בְּכַפּוֹת לְהַמְשִׁיל אַגַּן סְגֻלָּה, בְּעָבוֹת לְהַמְשִׁיל שׁוּרַת דְּגוּלָה, בַּעֲרָבָה לְהַמְשִׁיל מְחוֹקְקֵי מְגִלָּה.

בְּהָדָר לְכַפֵּר סַרְעַפֵּי לֵב, בְּכַפּוֹת לְכַפֵּר שֶׁזָּרָה מוּל לֵב, בְּעָבוֹת לְכַפֵּר סִקּוּר עַיִן וָלֵב, בַּעֲרָבָה לְכַפֵּר נִבּוּל פֶּה עִם לֵב.

בְּהָדָר לְכַנּוֹת שְׁלֵמִים תְּמִימִים, בְּכַפּוֹת לְכַנּוֹת בַּעֲלֵי מַעֲשִׂים נְעִימִים, בְּעָבוֹת לְכַנּוֹת יְשָׁרִים בְּמִצְוֹת חֲתוּמִים, בַּעֲרָבָה לְכַנּוֹת בְּשִׁמְצָה כְּתוּמִים.

וּכְמוֹ בְּעֵץ הָדָר רֵיחַ וָטַעַם, כֵּן בְּעַם זוּ בַּעֲלֵי מִצְוֹת וְדֵעַ נֹעַם; וּכְמוֹ בְּכַף תְּמָר טַעַם וְלֹא רֵיחַ, כֵּן בְּעַם זוּ בַּעֲלֵי מִצְוֹת בְּלֹא דָת וָרֵיחַ; וּכְמוֹ בְּעָבוֹת רֵיחַ וְטַעַם מַר, כֵּן בֵּינֵימוֹ הוֹגֵי דָת וְחִכָּם מַר; וּכְמוֹ עֲרָבָה בְּלֹא טַעַם וָרֵיחַ, כֵּן בֵּינֵימוֹ עִקְּשִׁים אֲטוּמִים מִלְּהָרִיחַ; וּכְמוֹ עֵץ פְּרִי עֲלֵי סָרָק מְחַפִּים, כֵּן יְשָׁרִים עֲלֵי רְשָׁעִים מְחוּפָּפִים; וּכְמוֹ הֵם אֲגוּדִים אֵלֶּה בָּאֵלֶּה, כֵּן תְּלוּיִים אֵלֶּה בָּאֵלֶּה, לִמְשׁוֹךְ אֵלֶּה אֶת אֵלֶּה, וּלְכַפֵּר אֵלֶּה עַל אֵלֶּה, לַעֲשׂוֹת אֵלֶּה כָּאֵלֶּה, לְהַנְעִים זְמִירוֹת אֵלֶּה, לְמִי בָרָא אֵלֶּה.

לְמַלֵּל לְהַלֵּל, לְכַלֵּל לְחוֹלֵל, לְיַשֵּׁר לְאַשֵּׁר, לְהַכְשֵׁר לְהִתְשֵׁר, לְבָרֵר לְשׁוֹרֵר, לְאַדֵּר לְהַדֵּר, לְגַבֵּר לְדַבֵּר, לְהַאֲמֵר לְזַמֵּר, לְחַנֵּן לְרַנֵּן, לְשַׁנֵּן לְהַרְנֵן, לְקַלֵּס לְעַלֵּס, לְנַצֵּחַ לְפַצֵּחַ, לְהַעֲרִיץ וּלְהַעֲלִיץ, לְהַרְגִּישׁ לְהַקְדִּישׁ.

כְּשִׁיר עִירִין, כְּשִׁירַת קַדִּישִׁין, כְּזֶמֶר חַשְׁמַלָּה, כְּזִמְרַת הַמְּלָה, כִּפְאֵר אֵלִים, כְּתִפְאֶרֶת אֶרְאֶלִים, כַּהֲדַר זִקִּים, כְּהַדְרַת בְּרָקִים, כְּנֹעַם גְּלִילִים, כִּנְעִימַת גַּלְגַּלִּים, כְּנִגּוּן רוֹבִים, כִּנְגִינַת כְּרוּבִים, כְּרֶנֶן אוֹפַנִּים, כְּרִנְּנַת מְרֻבְּעֵי פָנִים, כְּחִדּוּשׁ בְּרָקִים, כְּמִתְחַדְּשִׁים לַבְּקָרִים; כְּקִדּוּשׁ עָפִים, כִּקְדֻשַּׁת עוֹפְפִים, כְּרֶגֶשׁ מְעוֹפְפִים, כְּרִגְשַׁת מְתוֹפְפִים, כְּשִׁנּוּן צְפוּפִים, כְּהֶגֶה מְצַפְצְפִים, כְּרַעַשׁ סַפִּים, כְּמַעֲמַד שְׂרָפִים; כְּמַחֲנוֹת קְדוֹשִׁים, לַקָּדוֹשׁ מַקְדִּישִׁים, וּקְדֻשָּׁה מְשַׁלְּשִׁים.

Some Congregations recite this *piyut* before the *Kedushah* of *Shacharis* (p. 278) on the second day.

כִּי אֶקַּח מוֹעֵד, לָבֹא לְקֵץ וּלְמוֹעֵד, כְּמֵאָז לְדַבֵּר מֵאֹהֶל מוֹעֵד, לֵישֵׁב בְּהַר הַמּוֹעֵד, בְּיַרְכְּתֵי צָפוֹן בְּקִרְיַת מוֹעֵד, קְדוֹשִׁים בְּתוֹכָהּ לָוַעַד, לְמוֹעֵד מוֹעֲדִים וַחֲצִי מוֹעֵד, לְהִתְהַלֵּךְ בְּתוֹכָם וּלְהִוָּעֵד, לְהוֹשִׁיבָם בְּאָהֳלֵיהֶם כִּימֵי מוֹעֵד, וְעָנְתָה הַשִּׁירָה הַזֹּאת לְפָנָיו לְעֵד, וְסֻכָּה תִּהְיֶה לְצֵל יוֹמָם לְעֵד, כְּמֵלִיץ מַגִּיד יֹשֶׁר טוּב תָּעֵד, עַל כָּל שֶׁקִּיֵּם מִצְוַת סֻכָּה לְהָעֵד, וְכָל שׁוֹמְרֶיהָ יָבֹא וְיָעֵד, וְאָנֹכִי הַיּוֹדֵעַ וָעֵד.

כִּי עַמִּי קִיְּמוּ מִצוֹתֶיהָ, בְּמִדּוֹתֶיהָ וּבְקִצְבוֹתֶיהָ, בְּאַמּוֹתֶיהָ וּבִמְחִיצוֹתֶיהָ, בִּדְפַנּוֹתֶיהָ וּבְמַצְּבוֹתֶיהָ, בִּסְכוּכֶיהָ וּבְצִלּוֹתֶיהָ, בְּבִיאוֹתֶיהָ וּבִיצִיאוֹתֶיהָ, בִּגְדֵרוֹתֶיהָ וּבִפְרָצוֹתֶיהָ, בַּחֲגִיגוֹתֶיהָ וּבַעֲלִיצוֹתֶיהָ, וְזָר לֹא יִהְיֶה בְּמוֹצָאוֹתֶיהָ, וְנֵכָר לֹא יַעֲבֹר בְּתוֹצְאוֹתֶיהָ, וְעָרֵל לֹא יְשַׁתֵּף בִּמְחִיצוֹתֶיהָ, וְגוֹי לֹא יִרְמֹס חַצְרוֹתֶיהָ, וּלְאֹם לֹא יֵעָרֵב בְּחוּצוֹתֶיהָ, כִּי אִם עֲמוּסֵי נוֹצְרֵי מִצְוֹתֶיהָ, וְגַם לֹא יוּפְרוּ מוֹעֲצוֹתֶיהָ, בְּלֵב שָׁלֵם יָשׁוּבוּ לִקְצָוֹתֶיהָ, וּבְנֶפֶשׁ טוֹבָה יָבֹאוּ חַצְרוֹתֶיהָ, עַתָּה יָבֹאוּ עַמִּי לִקְצָוֹתֶיהָ, כְּמוֹ הֵם לְבַדָּם דִּגְלוּ מִשְׁבְּצוֹתֶיהָ, כֵּן בָּדָד יִשְׁכְּנוּ בִּרְבִיצוֹתֶיהָ, לָתֵת לָמוֹ שְׂכַר מְרוּצוֹתֶיהָ, לְקֵץ סֻכַּת אֵל לִרְצוֹתֶיהָ, לְעֵת חִלּוּק אַרְצוֹתֶיהָ, בְּאֹרֶךְ מִפְּאַת קָדִים לִקְצָוֹתֶיהָ, וְעַד יָם אוֹקְיָנוֹס לִמְצוֹתֶיהָ, בְּרֹחַב שִׁבְעִים וַחֲמִשָּׁה מִיל חֲרִיצוֹתֶיהָ, כְּשׁוּרוֹת הַכֶּרֶם לְחַבְּרָם לְתוֹצְאוֹתֶיהָ, גְּבוּל כָּל שֵׁבֶט וְשֵׁבֶט כַּךְ יַעֲלוּ בִּנְפִיצוֹתֶיהָ.

וְאָז בַּת קוֹל תֵּצֵא בָּאָרֶץ הַזֹּאת, עַל הַר גָּבֹהַּ לְבַשֵּׂר בְּשׂוֹרָה זֹאת, כָּל שֶׁקִּיֵּם מִצְוָה זֹאת, יָבוֹא בְּנֹעַם צוּרוֹ לַחֲזוֹת, לִשְׁקֹד דְּלָתוֹת וְלִשְׁמֹר מְזוּזוֹת, לְהַבִּיט וְלָשׁוּר נֵס עַל זֹאת, יְשׁוּעוֹת עֲלִיזוֹת, עַל כָּל כָּבוֹד חֻפּוֹת מְזוּזוֹת, חֻפּוֹת בְּחֻפּוֹת בְּחֶלְיוֹת אֲחוּזוֹת, עַד כִּסֵּא כָבוֹד מְאֻחָזוֹת, לְיוֹשֵׁב עַל כִּסֵּא בְּיָפְיוֹ לַחֲזוֹת, בְּמַחֲזוֹת הַמְצֻחְצָחוֹת בְּתֵשַׁע מַחֲזוֹת, וְכָל אֲשֶׁר תָּדִיר לַעֲשׂוֹת זֹאת, יִזְכֶּה לְהֵאָמֶר לוֹ כָּזֹאת, אַשְׁרֵי אֱנוֹשׁ יַעֲשֶׂה זֹּאת, יֵחָשֵׁב לוֹ כְּשָׁמַר כָּל הַתּוֹרָה הַזֹּאת, וּמִי שָׁמַע כָּזֹאת, וּמֵאֵת יהוה הָיְתָה זֹּאת, וָאֲחַשְּׁבָה לָדַעַת זֹאת, וְהִיא נִפְלָאת בְּעֵינַי זֹאת, עַד אָבוֹא לְיוֹשְׁבֵי פְּרָזוֹת, וְאֶשְׁאֲלָה לְזִקְנֵי מִי זֹאת, מָה אֶתְנַן עַם שׁוֹמְרֵי מִצְוַת סֻכָּה זֹאת, וְהֵם יְשִׁיבוּנִי תְּשׁוּבוֹת עַזּוֹת, וְיַרְאוּנִי מַצְפּוּנוֹת גְּנוּזוֹת, רַב טוּב הַצָּפוּן בְּבֵית גְּנָזוֹת, לְבַעֲלֵי סֻכָּה יִהוּ נִבְזָזוֹת.

וּמֵחַיִל אֶל חַיִל יִצְעֲדוּ, וּמִסֻּכָּה לְסֻכָּה יִוָּעֲדוּ, וּמֵאֹהֶל אֶל אֹהֶל יוּעָדוּ, בְּסֻכָּה אֲשֶׁר יִצָּמֵדוּ, בְּסֻכַּת שָׁלֵם יִצְמָדוּ, בְּסֻכַּת עֲמָקִים יִמְדָּדוּ, בְּסֻכַּת צִלְצֵל יְעֻדָּדוּ, בְּסֻכַּת סְבִיבָיו יְחֻדָּדוּ, בְּסֻכַּת מַלְכָּם יִתְוַעֲדוּ, בְּסֻכַּת צְפוּנוֹ יְאֻחָדוּ, בְּסֻכַּת נְאוֹת דֶּשֶׁא יְבֻדָּדוּ, בְּסֻכַּת מֵי מְנוּחוֹת יְכֻבָּדוּ, בְּסֻכַּת עֵץ חַיִּים יִתְיַסָּדוּ, בְּסֻכַּת שֶׁתַּחְתָּיו יִסְעָדוּ, בְּסֻכַּת צְלָלוֹתָיו בְּחִיל יְסַלֵּדוּ, בְּמַעֲלוֹתָיו אֵל יְיַחֲדוּ, בְּמַעַרְכוֹתָיו זֵר יְאַפֵּדוּ, בִּרְחוֹבוֹתָיו יִתְרַפֵּדוּ, וְשִׁעוּר תְּפִיסוֹתָיו יְמֻדָּדוּ.

חֲמֵשׁ מֵאוֹת שָׁנָה הֲלִיכוֹתָיו עֲלוֹת, עוֹבֵי עָקְרוֹ בְּזֶה קַו לְהַעֲלוֹת, אֲבָל מִנְיַן עֲנָפָיו אֵין בְּמִדָּה לְהַעֲלוֹת, וְעַל יוּבַל שָׁרָשָׁיו פְּעוּלוֹת, וְכָל מֵי בְרֵאשִׁית מִמֶּנּוּ נִפְעָלוֹת, וּפְלָגִים נִפְלָגִים לְכָל תְּעָלוֹת, וְשֶׁבַע כִּתֵּי קֹדֶשׁ הַמְּעֻלּוֹת, תַּחַת סֻכַּת נוֹפוֹ מִתְעַלְּזוֹת, וּמִתַּחְתֵּיהֶם שְׁלֹשִׁים מַעֲלוֹת, מִסְתּוֹפְפִים בְּצִלָּם בְּשִׁיר הַמַּעֲלוֹת, וְעַל גַּבָּם שִׁשִּׁים מַעֲלוֹת, זוֹ לְמַעְלָה מִזּוֹ עוֹלוֹת, וְעַד כִּסֵּא הַכָּבוֹד טָסוֹת וְעוֹלוֹת, בְּשִׂיחַ נְעִימוֹת שִׁיר הַמַּעֲלוֹת.

וְכָל אֶחָד וְאֶחָד לְפִי כְבוֹדוֹ, בְּכָבוֹד וְהָדָר יִתֵּן הוֹדוֹ, בְּזִיו שְׁכִינָה יְיַחֲדוֹ, בְּמַרְאֵה פָּנִים יְכַבְּדוֹ, בַּעֲשָׂרָה לְבוּשִׁים לְאַפְּדוֹ, בְּרִקְמָה וְעָתִיק לְרַפְּדוֹ, כְּמַרְאֵה הַקֶּשֶׁת לְחַסְדּוֹ, כְּמַרְאֵה הַנֹּגַהּ לְנֶגְדּוֹ, כְּצֵאת הַשֶּׁמֶשׁ בְּעוֹדוֹ, אֲשֶׁר בּוֹ צִדְקוֹ יְעִידוֹ, וּלְפִי הָרָשׁוּם בִּכְתַב יָדוֹ, וּלְפִי מַעֲשָׂיו וּמַעְבָּדוֹ, יְשַׁלֵּם לָמוֹ פָּעֳלָם כְּמַעְבָּדוֹ.

יֵשׁ מִמֵּאָה אַמָּה קוֹמָתָם, כְּתַבְנִית הֵיכָל רִקְמָתָם, יֵשׁ מִמָּאתַיִם וּשְׁלֹשׁ מֵאוֹת תְּקוּמָתָם, כֵּן וְעַד תְּשַׁע מֵאוֹת הֲקָמָתָם, וּלְפִי שִׁעוּר תְּקוּמָתָם, כֵּן תְּהִי בָאָרֶץ מַהֲלַכְתָּם, יֵשׁ מֵהֶם מְלֹא הָעוֹלָם מַהֲלַכְתָּם, וּמִסּוֹף הָעוֹלָם וְעַד סוֹפוֹ הֲלִיכָתָם, יֵשׁ מִשִּׁשָּׁה עָשָׂר עוֹלָמוֹת מַלְכוּתָם, וְיֵשׁ מִשְּׁלֹשׁ מֵאוֹת וַעֲשָׂרָה מֶמְשַׁלְתָּם, וְיֵשׁ מִשְּׁלֹשׁ מֵאוֹת וּשְׁלֹשִׁים וּשְׁלֹשָׁה שְׁלִיחוּתָם, וְשָׁלוֹם גָּדוֹל יֵשׁ בֵּינוֹתָם, וְשִׂנְאָה אֵין בְּמַחֲנוֹתָם, וְתַחֲרוּת אֵין בִּמְחִיצָתָם, וְאֵיבָה אֵין בַּהֲלִיכָתָם, וּפַלְגּוּת אֵין בְּחֻפָּתָם, וְקִנְאָה אֵין בְּמִשְׁכְּנוֹתָם, וְשִׂנְאָה אֵין בִּרְפִידָתָם, וּתְנוּמָה אֵין בִּרְבִיצָתָם, וְאָסוֹן אֵין בִּמְגוּרָתָם, וְדִמְעָה אֵין בְּעַפְעַפּוֹתָם, וְצָרָה אֵין בְּמַחְשְׁבוֹתָם, וְצוּקָה אֵין בְּטוּחוֹתָם, וְיֵצֶר רָע אֵין בְּלִבּוֹתָם, וְרֹעַ עַיִן אֵין בְּדִירָתָם, וּמִיתָה אֵין בִּמְדוּרָתָם, וּמַחֲלָה אֵין בִּגְוִיָּתָם, שָׂשִׂים כָּל אֶחָד וְאֶחָד בְּנַחֲלָתָם, שְׂמֵחִים בְּמִפְעֲלוֹתָם, גָּלִים בִּירֻשָּׁתָם, רוֹנְנִים בְּפוּר חֶלְקָתָם, עוֹלְצִים בְּאָרְחוֹתָם, חָדִים אֶת אֵל בְּחֶדְוָתָם.

וְהוּא יִתְהַלֵּךְ בְּתוֹכָם, עִמּוֹ לְסֻכּוֹ לְמָשְׁכָם, בַּעֲבוֹתוֹת אַהֲבָה לְהַמְשִׁיכָם, בְּאֶבְרָתוֹ לְסוֹכְכָם, תַּחַת כְּנָפָיו לְסַכְּכָם, בְּסֵתֶר אָהֳלוֹ לְמָסְכָם, בֵּינוֹ לְבֵין מְשָׁרְתָיו לְתַוְּכָם.

וְיָנִיחַ רוֹכֵב עֲרָבוֹת, וְיִחַן בְּתוֹךְ מַעֲלוֹת עֲרָבוֹת, בְּצֶדֶק קִיחַת שְׁתֵּי עֲרָבוֹת, וְאָתָה מֵרִבְבוֹת קֹדֶשׁ אַלְפֵי רְבָבוֹת, לַעֲמֹד בֵּין הֲדַסֵּי עָבוֹת, בְּצֶדֶק שְׁלֹשֶׁת אָבוֹת. וְיָרוּם כִּסֵּא מְיֻחָד, וְיֵשֵׁב עִם זִקְנֵי גּוֹי אֶחָד, אוֹגְדֵי לוּלָב אֶחָד, וּמַעֲמִיתִים בָּם אֶתְרוֹג אֶחָד. וְיֶאֱתָיו בְּנֵי אָבוֹת שְׁלֹשָׁה, הַיְחוּסִים אִם מְשֻׁלָּשָׁה, יוֹתֵר מִקּוֹרְאֵי קָדוֹשׁ שְׁלֹשָׁה. וְיֶעֱרַב לוֹ שִׂיחַ אֱמוּנִים, הַמְהַלְּלִים בְּאַרְבַּעַת מִינִים, מֵאַרְבַּע חַיּוֹת מְרֻבְּעֵי פָנִים. וְיַחְפֹּץ בִּמְחוֹלְלֵי חֲמֵשֶׁת וְשֵׁשֶׁת, הַהוֹגִים חֲמֵשֶׁת וְעוֹרְכִים שֵׁשֶׁת, מֵהִלּוּלֵי חַתּוּלֵי כַּנְפֵי שֵׁשֶׁת.

וִיעוֹרֵר אַהֲבַת אֵיתָנִים, וְכִהוּן פְּאֵר חִתּוּנִים, הֱיוֹת לְמַעְלָה מֵהֶם נְתוּנִים, וּמְחִיצָתָם תְּהֵא מִבִּפְנִים, וּמִשְׁתַּעְשְׁעִים בִּיקָרָה מִפְּנִינִים, בְּצֵל שַׁדַּי לִפְנֵי וְלִפְנִים, וְאוֹתָם יִשְׁאֲלוּ שַׁאֲנַנִּים, בְּסֻכַּת נְוֵה שַׁאֲנַנִּים, מַה פָּעַל נוֹצֵר

אֱמוּנִים, וּמָה הוֹרָה בִּמְעוֹנִים, וּמַה גִּלָּה סוֹד לְנֶאֱמָנִים, וּמֶה חָשַׂף מִמַּצְפּוּנִים, וְהֵם יְבָאֲרוּ לָמוֹ חֵךְ צְפוּנִים, קוֹל רִנָּה וִישׁוּעָה אֲשֶׁר בָּם מוֹנִים, כִּי הֵם הָיוּ רִאשׁוֹנִים, חֶרֶב פִּיפִיּוֹת שְׁנוּנִים, הַלֵּל בְּמִשְׁנֶה שׁוֹנִים, חֲדָשִׁים וְגַם יְשָׁנִים, שִׁירוֹת וְתִשְׁבָּחוֹת מְשַׁנְּנִים, וְאַחֲרֵימוֹ זִיעַ חַיּוֹת נוֹתְנִים, בְּקוֹל רַעַשׁ מְנַגְּנִים, קָדוֹשׁ וּבָרוּךְ עוֹנִים, וְשַׂרְפֵי מַעַל עִם כְּנַף רְנָנִים, עוֹמְדִים מִמַּעַל וְרוֹנְנִים, מִמַּעַל לַכִּסֵּא הֲגוּנִים, לְיוֹשֵׁב עַל כִּסֵּא רוֹנְנִים, לְנַעֲרָץ בְּסוֹד קְדוֹשִׁים מְרַנְּנִים, פֶּה אֶחָד עוֹנִים, וְזֶה אֶת זֶה מְכַוְּנִים, וְזֶה אֶל זֶה מְצַיְּנִים, וְזֶה מִזֶּה מִתְבּוֹנְנִים, וְזֶה אֶל זֶה קָרוֹא נְכוֹנִים, וְשִׁלּוּשׁ קְדֻשָּׁה לְקָדוֹשׁ נוֹתְנִים.

תפלת גשם

Some congregations recite the following *piyutim* during the prayer for rain (p. 980).

אָפִיק מַעַן מְעֻטָּר, בְּיוֹם הַמְּעֻטָּר,
אֶעֱרֹךְ שׁוּעַ וְלֹא אֶפְטָר, בְּנִיב הַמְּפֻטָּר.
בְּקֵץ הַמֻּנְטָר שְׁאוֹנֵי הָנְטָר,
בְּמוּסָפֵי לַעְטָר, תְּפִלַּת מָטָר.
גִּילַת פְּעָמַיִם, שׂוֹשׂ יוֹם מִיּוֹמַיִם,
גַּל לִי מִשָּׁמַיִם, בְּשָׁאֲלִי בוֹ מָיִם.
דַּלְתֵי שָׁמַיִם, אֲשֶׁר מוּל שַׁעַר הַמַּיִם,
דּוֹדִי יִפְתַּח מִשָּׁמַיִם, בְּשָׁפְכִי לוֹ לֵב כַּמָּיִם.
הֲגִיגֵי בַּל יַדְמִים, בֶּצַע אֲשֵׁמִים,
הֻלְבְּנוּ בְכִפּוּר אֲשָׁמִים, וְשׂוֹטֵן מַה יַּשְׁמִים.
וְאִמְרֵי רְשׁוּמִים, בְּעֶרְכָּם נִרְשָׁמִים,
וְדִיתִי עִם שָׁמִים, לְהַזְכִּיר גְּבוּרוֹת גְּשָׁמִים.
זַעַק מִמֵּצַר, אֶקְרָא בְּעֵת צָר,
זֶה יַרְחִיב לִי בַּצָּר, שׁוּעַ אֲשֶׁר לֹא בְצָר.
חֹזֶק יָדְךָ לֹא תִקְצָר, מִפְּתוֹחַ אוֹצָר,
חֵטְא אִם עָצָר, יָפֶן בְּעַם נֶעֱצָר.
טְעָמִים אֲחַבֵּר, חֲיָלִים לְגַבֵּר,
טִפֵּי נִתּוּרִים אֲדַבֵּר, וְלֹא כְמִתְגַּבֵּר.
יוֹרוּנִי מָה אֲדַבֵּר, פְּנֵי תֵבָה כְּעוֹבֵר,
יַרְשׁוּנִי בַּעֲדָם לְהַסְבֵּר, כִּי עֵת לַחֲשׁוֹת וְעֵת לְדַבֵּר.
כְּרוֹעַ בֶּרֶךְ לְהַבְרִיךְ, בָּמוֹת לְהַדְרִיךְ,
כִּוּוּן חִין לְהַעֲרִיךְ, בְּעַד עַם מַעֲרִיךְ.
לַחֲבוֹשׁ וּלְהַאֲרִיךְ, חַרְבוֹן חֹרֶב מַפְרִיךְ,
לְדַבֵּר גְּבוּרוֹת אַאֲרִיךְ, כִּי עֵת לְקַצֵּר, וְעֵת לְהַאֲרִיךְ.

מִמַּטַּע דָּרְבוֹנוֹת, אָבִינָה תְּבוּנוֹת,
מֵעַם בִּינוֹת, אֲדַבֵּר נְכוֹנוֹת.
נְאָקוֹת מְכֻוָּנוֹת, לְהַמְטִיר גַּיְא וְלִבְנוֹת,
נְשָׁמוֹת לְבוֹנְנוֹת, בְּרַבּוֹת בָּנוֹת.
שְׂעִירִים לְהַרְבִּיב, חֲזִיזִים לְהַעֲבִיב,
שִׂיחִים לְהַאֲבִיב, עַד זְמַן אָבִיב.
עֲדָנִים לְהַנְבִּיב, מִקְּדִיחַת שְׁבִיב,
עָבִים לְהַלְבִּיב, לְרַווֹת עַם חָבִיב.
פָּנִים לִי יִשָּׂא, בְּצִיגָתִי פְּנֵי כְנִיסָה,
פֹּעַל בְּעֶשֶׂר נִסָּה, יִזְכֹּר לִי לְחוּסָה.
צוּר רָם וְנִשָּׂא, אֵלָיו עַיִן אֶשָּׂא,
צְבָאָיו לוֹ אֲגַיְּסָה, וְלֹא בְרוּחַ גַּסָּה.
קוֹלִי יֶעֱרַב וְרִנָּתִי לְפָנָיו תִּקְרַב,
קַמְתִּי כְּבַקְּרָב, חָגוּר כְּלֵי קְרָב.
רְשׁוּת צָעִיר וָרָב, אֶטֹּל טֶרֶם אֶקְרָב,
רַחַשׁ אֲבַשֵּׂר וְיֶעֱרַב, צֶדֶק בְּקָהָל רָב.
שָׁלִיחַ לְמִסְתּוֹפְפִים, צִיר לַאֲסוּפִים,
שִׁבְעַת יְמֵי חַג אוֹסְפִים, וְנִסּוּךְ הַמַּיִם חוֹסְפִים.
שְׁמִינִי מוֹסִיפִים, וּבוֹ נֶאֱסָפִים,
שַׁוְעַת מַיִם מְחַסְּפִים, בְּחִין מוּסָפִים.
תְּפוּצֶינָה עֵינוֹת מַיִם, בִּרְחוֹבוֹת פַּלְגֵי מַיִם,
תְּמַשֵּׁכְנָה בְּטוּחוֹת לְפֶה מַיִם, לְהִתְגַּבֵּר כְּנַחֲלֵי מָיִם.
✣תִּזְכֹּר לִי אֲתוּי נַהֲרַיִם, מִשּׁוּב אֲחוֹרַיִם,
תַּעֲנֵנִי עֲדֵי אֶפְרַיִם, בְּשָׁפְכִי שִׂיחוֹת צָהֳרָיִם.

אַקַשְּׁטָה כֶּסֶל וָקֶרֶב לְהַבִּיעַ בְּעַד מַיִם,
אֶזּוֹם לְפִי מְעַט גַּעַת בְּלַחֲלוּחַ מְלֶאכֶת מַיִם,
אֲחַסְּפָה מֵעֵין מַעַשׂ מִפְעַל מַיִם,
אֶת פְּנֵי מֵבִין לְהַשְׁמִיעַ גְּבוּרוֹת מָיִם.
בְּגָבְהֵי שָׁמַיִם אָצַר אֲסָמֵי מַיִם,
בְּתַחְתִּיּוֹת אֶרֶץ הֶחְבִּיא תְּהוֹמוֹת מַיִם,
בָּם הֵחֵל וְכָל חוּג אֶרֶץ וְשָׁמַיִם,
בָּם הִרְקִיעַ הֲדוֹם וְקָרָא שָׁמָיִם.
גַּם בְּטֶרֶם יֻצְּרוּ פְּתוּכֵי אֵשׁ וּמַיִם,
גָּמַר וְכָלַל כֹּל בְּמִשְׁוֹלַת מַיִם,
גָּרָה אֶצְלוֹ אָמוֹן לְשַׁעְשְׁעוֹ יוֹמַיִם.
גְּנָזָהּ פֹּעַל אִתּוֹ עוֹלָמוֹת שְׁנַיִם.

דָּרַךְ וְהִשְׁתָּה שָׁתוּת בְּמַשְׁתִּיַּת מַיִם,
דַּעַת כִּי כֹל הוּשְׁתָה, מִשְׁתִיַּת מַיִם,
דִּבֵּר וְהֶעֱרִיךְ תָּפְתֶּה מַשְׁלִיגַת אֵשׁ וּמַיִם,
דָּרַשׁ וְנָטַע שָׁתוּל עַל פַּלְגֵי מָיִם.
הִצְפִּין לַיְשָׁרִים אֱמוּנַת יוֹמַיִם,
הֶעֱבִיר תְּשַׁע מֵאוֹת וְשִׁבְעִים וְאַרְבָּעָה דוֹרוֹת כְּבְשֶׁטֶף מַיִם,
הֵכִין שִׁבְעָה בְרִיאוֹת, עַד לֹא אֶרֶץ וְשָׁמַיִם,
הִשְׁרָה בָם שְׁכִינָה קֶדֶם דָּר שָׁמַיִם.
וְנָכוֹן מֵאָז צָר כֵּס וַיְּחֶסוּ שָׁמַיִם,
וּבְסָסוֹ עַל רוּחַ מְרַחֶפֶת עַל פְּנֵי הַמַּיִם,
וּכְצָר מַעֲשֵׂה בְרֵאשִׁית וּמָדַד בְּשָׁעֳלוֹ מַיִם,
וִיעָדוֹ בֵּין חַשְׁרַת מַיִם לְחֶשְׁכַת מָיִם.
זִמֵּן לוֹ לַעֲמֹס גַּבּוֹת מְלֵאוֹת עֵינַיִם,
זִיו מִסְפַּר רֹבַע פָּנִים חֲמִשִּׁים וָשֵׁשׁ וּמָאתַיִם,
זוֹעוֹת מִמַּשָּׂא וְרוֹעֲשׁוֹת מִקּוֹלוֹת מַיִם,
זְבוּדִים אִתָּם כְּרוּב וְאוֹפָן וְגַלְגַּל מָיִם.
חֵיל שַׂרְפֵי מַעַל גְּוִיָּתָם כְּתַרְשִׁישׁ מַיִם,
חֲקוּקִים וְנִשְׁעָרִים בְּאֹרֶךְ עִמְקֵי מַיִם.
חֶצְיָם בְּרִיַּת אֵשׁ וְחֶצְיָם יְצִירַת מַיִם.
חוֹצְצִים תֵּת מְחִיצָה בֵּין אֵשׁ וּבֵין מָיִם.
טָסִים וּמְעוֹפְפִים בְּכַנְפֵי אֵשׁ וּמַיִם,
טוֹבְלִים בְּנָהָר נָגִיד כְּנַחֲלֵי מַיִם
טִכֵּס אוֹצְרוֹת שֶׁלֶג וָאֵשׁ וּבָרָד וּמַיִם,
טְמוּנִים לְסַעֲרַת חֵמָה לְצַלְמוֹנַת מָיִם.
יָזַם וְאָצַר לְחַיִּים פֶּלֶג מָלֵא מַיִם,
יָעַץ לְפַלֵּג מֶנּוּ לִפְלַגּוֹת מַיִם,
יָהּ כְּבַט בְּכָל פֹּעַל כִּי אֵין חִיּוּת בְּלִי מַיִם,
יִשֵּׁר תֵּת מַתְּנַת חִנָּם לְעוֹלָם מַיִם.
כָּפָץ תֵּת מֵאָז יִשּׁוּב דָּת לְמַיִם,
כֹּל לְהַשְׁקוֹת גֶּשֶׁי מִתַּחְתִּיּוֹת מַיִם,
כִּשֵּׁר בְּבַעֲלֵי זְרוֹעַ כִּי יֶחְמְסוּ מַיִם,
כּוֹנֵן וְשָׁב לְשׁוֹקְקָהּ מֵאוֹצַר שָׁמַיִם.
לְמַעַל לָרָקִיעַ עָשׂ כִּבְרֵכַת מַיִם,
לִנְטוֹת עָלֶיהָ כִּפָּה מַזַּעַת מֵחַמַּת מַיִם,
לְהַטִּיף מִמֶּנָּה מִגְרַע נִטְפֵי מַיִם,
לַהֲלֹךְ מַהֲלַךְ כַּמָּה בְּלִי עֵרוּב מָיִם.
מַרְאֵה הַקֶּשֶׁת כַּעֲשָׁשִׁית בְּמַיִם,

מֶנּוּ כֹּל יָבִינוּ כֹּחַ מוֹרִד מָיִם,
מַרְאָה כָּל מַרְאֶה וּמַרְאָהָ כְּמַרְאִית מַיִם,
מוֹדַעַת לְגֵיא אוֹת בְּרִית בְּלִי טוֹבַעַת מָיִם.
נוֹצֵץ בָּרָק בְּבֶהָל לְהַבְרִיק כְּמֶהַת מַיִם,
נוֹהֵם בְּרַעַשׁ וְקוֹל גַּלְגַּל רַעַם מַרְעִים עַל הַמַּיִם,
נְשִׂיאִים וְרוּחַ מַקְדִּימִים לְמַיִם,
נִרְאִים כְּעוֹלִים מִמַּיִם וְשָׁבִים אֶל הַמָּיִם.
שָׂם מִשְׁקָל לָרוּחַ בּוֹ לְפַלֵּס מַיִם,
סִיֵּם לְפִי כָל אֶרֶץ מַה לְּהַגְרִיל מַיִם,
סִפֵּק וּמָד בְּמִדָּה תִּכֵּן מִדַּת מַיִם,
סִדֵּר לְשֵׁבֶט לָאָרֶץ לְחֶסֶד לְהַמְצִיא מָיִם.
עָב וַחֲזִיז וְנָשִׂיא וְאֵד וַעֲנַן מַיִם,
עָרַךְ בָּם שְׂאֵת מַשָּׂא מֵעִמּוּס מַיִם,
עָפִים וְדָאִים עַל פְּנֵי רָקִיעַ הַשָּׁמַיִם,
עוֹמְדִים צְרוּרִים עַד יֻרְשׁוּ לְהָרִיק מָיִם.
פַּחַד שְׂעִירִים מִשְׁתַּעֲרִים בְּהַרְעִיפָם מַיִם,
פּוֹתְחִים פִּיהֶם כְּנוֹס כַּנֵּד שְׁתִיַּת מַיִם,
פּוֹרְחִים לְהַמְתִּיק בְּשַׁחַק תַּמְלוּחִית מַיִם,
פּוֹנִים שׁוּב לָלֶכֶת אֶל מְקוֹם הַמָּיִם.
צִבְאוֹת רְבִיבִים הַמַּרְבִּיבִים מַיִם,
צוֹמְחִים כַּעֲרָבִים עַל יִבְלֵי מַיִם,
צִיָּה מְמוֹגְגִים בְּנַחַת זִילַת מַיִם,
צִחְיוֹן חַרְבוֹן קַיִץ לְהַשְׂבִּיעַ שׂוֹבַע מָיִם.
קַו מַבְדִּיל אֲשֶׁר הִבְדִּיל לַמַּיִם,
קִצְבָּם תָּלוּי בְּאֹמֶר לְהַפְרוֹת מְטַר מַיִם,
קוֹל צִנּוֹרוֹת כִּי יַזְחִילוּ מֵהֶם מַיִם,
קוֹלוֹת יִתְּנוּ תְהוֹמוֹת שְׁעוֹת לְצִמָּאוֹן מָיִם.
רוֹעֲשִׁים וּמַרְעִישִׁים קוֹל מִקּוֹלוֹת מַיִם.
רוֹגְשִׁים וְנוֹשְׂאִים קוֹל לְאַדִּיר קוֹלוֹ עַל הַמַּיִם,
רֶנֶן מַרְעִימִים לְמַרְעִים עַל רֹב מַיִם,
רִדְתָּם כֹּל יָשִׁירוּ שִׁיר לְמוֹרִד מָיִם.
שֶׁבַח כִּנּוּי שֵׁם כִּנָּה בְּשֵׁם מַיִם,
שִׁתֵּף בְּשֵׁם אַדִּיר אַדִּירִים לְמַיִם,
שָׁת מַעֲטֵה לְבוּשׁוֹ כְּמַחֲזֵה שְׁלִיגַת מַיִם,
שׁוּהָ קוֹל הוֹדוֹ כְּקוֹל רִבּוּי מָיִם.
תִּכֵּן וְכָל וּמָד וְגָזַר וְדָלָה מַיִם,
תֵּת לְכָל גֵּיא וָגֵיא מַעְיָן לִשְׁתּוֹת מַיִם.

✣**תִּ**רְגַּל מֵעֵדֶן נָהָר יוּבַל מַיִם,
תִּוְּכוּ לְהִפָּרֵד לְרִבּוּעַ רָאשֵׁי מָיִם.

תִּכֵּנָם לָאֶרֶץ וְחוּצוֹת לַחֲצוֹת מַיִם,
אִמֵּן לְכָל אֶחָד וְאֶחָד מַה יִּתְּנוּ מָיִם.
שָׁקַל לְרֹאשׁ עַפְרוֹת תֵּבֵל לְבַד פַּלְגֵי מַיִם,
לְמְטַר הַשָּׁמַיִם תִּשְׁתֶּה מָּיִם.
רְצוֹת לָהּ שָׁלוֹם בִּירִידַת מַיִם,
עָמֹק וְתָלוּל גָּלוּי וְחָבוּי כְּאַחַת שָׁתוֹת מָיִם.
קֶרַח וּכְפוֹר וְשֶׁלֶג וְנֶזֶל מַיִם,
זִמְּנוּ לָהּ לְשׁוֹקְקָהּ בְּכָל מִינֵי מָיִם:
צוֹפֶה בָּהּ עַיִן לְהַתְמִידָהּ בְּמַיִם,
רֵאשִׁית וְעַד אַחֲרִית דְּרוּשָׁה רַוּוֹת מָיִם.
פֶּשַׁע אִם הָעֶצֶם וְנִגְזַר עֲדֵי עֲצִירַת מַיִם,
בְּתַחַן וָפֶלֶל יְפַתּוּ מִגְּרַע נִטְפֵי מָיִם.
עַיִן יִשְׂאוּ לָרוֹכֵב בְּעֶזְרָם שָׁמַיִם,
יְשֵׁנִים הֱיוֹת בְּמַצָּע וְהוּא מַסְפִּיק לָמוֹ מָיִם.
שִׂיחַ מֵהַיּוֹם נֶעֱצָרִים לְהַזְכִּיר בְּשִׂיחָם מַיִם,
רוֹגְשִׁים בְּסוֹף שִׁבְעָה לְצַיֵּן בְּמוּסַף מָיִם.
נִסּוּךְ מְנַסְּכִים שְׁלֹשֶׁת לוֹג מַיִם,
בָּם לַעֲרֹךְ כְּסֵדֶר שְׁלֹשֶׁת רְבִיעִיּוֹת מַיִם.
מִמַּעַל לְהַרְבִּיעַ זַכְרוּת רֶבַע מַיִם,
יַעַל בְּכֶפֶל מִתַּחַת פְּרִיַּת נַקְבוּת מָיִם.
לְיִפְתַּח אֶרֶץ וְיִפְרוּ יֶשַׁע מְטַר מַיִם,
קוֹרְאִים זֶה לָזֶה עַד יַשִּׁיקוּ מַיִם לְמַיִם.
(**כִּי**) כַּאֲשֶׁר יֵרֵד הַגֶּשֶׁם וְהַשֶּׁלֶג מִן הַשָּׁמַיִם,
לְצִמָּאוֹן יְשָׁעוּהוּ עֲיָנוֹת וּתְהוֹמוֹת מָיִם.
יַחַד דְּגַת וְקַשְׂקֶשֶׂת הַגְּדֵלִים בַּהֲמוֹן מַיִם,
יִתְאַוּוּ לִרְדִתּוֹ גְּמוֹת מֶנּוּ מְעַט מַיִם.
טְרוּחֵי שְׁחִין וּכְאֵב וְחוֹלֵי מֵעַיִם,
רוֹגְעִים וּמִתְרַוְּחִים בְּאִוּוּי קֶרַת מָיִם.
חַיֵּי כָּל נֶשִׁי מָסַרְתָּ בְּמַזָּלוֹת שָׁמַיִם,
מְמֻנִּים עַל כָּל אֶרֶץ אֵיךְ לְפַרְנְסָהּ מָיִם.
זָבַת חָלָב וּדְבַשׁ אֶרֶץ נַחֲלֵי מַיִם,
קִדַּשְׁתָּ אוֹתָהּ לְשִׁמְךָ לְמוּגָהּ מָיִם.
וְאַתָּה בְּיָדְךָ תַּתָּה מַפְתֵּחַ מְטַר מַיִם,
רְשׁוּת אֵין לְהִנָּתֵן בִּלְעָדֶיךָ לִפְתֹּחַ אוֹצְרוֹת מָיִם.

הָקֵם דְּבָרְךָ הַטּוֹב תֵּת בְּשֶׁפַע מַיִם,
יַחַד לְנֶדֶב לְרָצוֹן לְטֹהַר לְהָנִיף מָיִם.
דֵּי אַרְבָּעִים סְאָה מִשָּׁעֵר מִקְוֵה מַיִם,
תְּמִימֶיךָ אֵיךְ בּוֹ יִטָּהֲרוּ אִם אֵין בּוֹ שִׁעוּר מָיִם.
גְּשָׁמִים שִׁבְעָה מִשִּׁבְעָה רְקִיעֵי מַיִם,
שֶׁבַע אֲרָצוֹת שֶׁבַע וְשִׁבְעַת עַמּוּדֵי מָיִם.
בְּצוּר חוֹגְגִים שִׁבְעָה וְנֶעֱצָרִים עֲדֵי מַיִם,
פְּלוּלָם קְשֹׁב בְּשָׁפְכָם לְךָ לֵב כַּמַּיִם.
❖**אָ**דוֹן הַשְׁקִיפָה מִמְּעוֹן קָדְשְׁךָ מִן הַשָּׁמַיִם,
רֵעֶיךָ לְנַהֵל בְּרֶבֶץ כְּעַל מַבּוּעֵי מָיִם.

יִפְתַּח אֶרֶץ לְיֶשַׁע, לִשְׁבֹּר מַטֵּה רֶשַׁע, מַיִם אִם כִּזְּבוּ בְּפֶשַׁע, זְכֹר נָם יֻקַּח נָא מְעַט מַיִם וְתִישַׁע. **כִּי** אֲרֻבּוֹת שְׁמֵי עֶרֶץ, עַד אָבִיב יִפָּתְחוּ בְּלִי פֶרֶץ, מַיִם אֵד לְהַעֲלוֹת בְּמֶרֶץ, טֶרֶם יִהְיֶה בָּאָרֶץ.

מזל ניסן

טלה

יהוה בְּיָדוֹ מַפְתֵּחַ, זוּלָתוֹ בְּלִי יִפָּתֵחַ, מַיִם בְּצוּל יַרְתִּיחַ, חֲגוֹר בְּנֵי עָקוּד לְפַתֵּחַ. **כַּאֲשֶׁר** בְּחַן וְשָׁפַךְ לֵב כַּמַּיִם, יְחִיוּ טְלָאָיו מִיּוֹמַיִם, מַיִם בְּאֵר חָפַר פַּעֲמַיִם, לְקוֹל תִּתּוֹ הֲמוֹן מַיִם בַּשָּׁמָיִם.

לְךָ גְּשָׁמִים וְשֶׁוַע מַרְהִיטִים, לְהָקֵר חֹרֶב לְהָטִים, מַיִם גָּבַר בְּמִרְהָטִים, בְּחִין פִּצֵּל בָּרְהָטִים. **יֵרֵד** גֶּשֶׁם לְנִדְשָׁאִים, לְעֵדֶן זִיו עַיִן לְךָ נוֹשְׂאִים, מַיִם גְּנוּזִים וּנְשָׂאִים, לַשְּׂאוּתָם מַעֲלֶה נְשִׂיאִים.

מזל אייר

שור

אֶת דְּרוּשָׁה מֵרֹאשׁ, תָּמִיד אוֹתָהּ דְּרוֹשׁ, מַיִם דָּגָן וְתִירוֹשׁ, יִרְווּ בְּשִׂיחַ בְּכוֹר רֹאשׁ. **הַגֶּשֶׁם** דְּשָׁאִים יְרוֹעֲנָן, וְשׁוֹר וּמְרִיא בּוֹ יְחֻנָּן, מַיִם דְּלֵה לָעָב מְעֻנָּן, בְּאוֹת קֶשֶׁת עֲנִינַת עָנָן.

אוֹצָרוֹ הַמָּלֵא, מוֹזַעַת כִּפַּת דּוֹק מִתְמַלֵּא, מַיִם הַמְּצִיַּת מֵי מָלֵא, לְגֵיא מְעַקְּרֵי שׁוֹר תְּמַלֵּא. **וְהַשֶּׁלֶג** הִקְפִּיא לְנִלְקֶשֶׁת, לְרַשּׁוּ בַּשְּׁלִישִׁי מִתְבַּקֶּשֶׁת, מַיִם הַזֵּל לְמִתְנַקֶּשֶׁת, בְּהוֹד נֹגַהּ מַרְאֵה הַקֶּשֶׁת.

מזל סיון

תאומים

הַטּוֹב וְהַנָּעִים, שְׁעֵה זֶמֶר נָעִים, מַיִם וְקוֹל מְזַעְזְעִים, בְּמֵי מְרִיבָה לֹא תְזוּעִים. **מָן** וְדוּי תְּאוֹמִים וְרֵיעִים, תִּתְרַצֶּה בְּשִׂיחַ הַנָּעִים, מַיִם וָעַד לְזוֹרְעִים, בְּקוֹל גַּלְגַּל הַמַּרְעִים.

אֶת זְמַן חָבוּי גְּפֶר, הֻגְבְּלוּ גְבוּלוֹת בַּסֵּפֶר, מַיִם זוּלַת שֶׁפֶר, לְמַדֵּד אַדְמַת גּוֹר עֹפֶר. **הַשָּׁמַיִם** זַעַק לְקַבֵּל, חֹם בְּתַמּוּז מִלְּחַבֵּל, מַיִם זִרְמוּ לְתַבֵּל בְּשֵׁשֶׁת מִינֵי תֵבֵל.

מזל תמוז

סרטן

הַשָּׁמַיִם חַשְׁרַת כְּבָרָה, חָשׁוּר לְרוּחַ נִשְׁבָּרָה, מַיִם חֲזִיז בִּגְבוּרָה, לִמְבִינֵי עִתֵּי בָּרָה. **וְשָׁמָּה** חֶלְקָם בַּחַיִּים, כְּסַרְטָן גָּדֵל בְּמַיִם חַיִּים, מַיִם חֲשׂוּפִים וּבְקַו חֲצוּיִם, הוֹצֵא מִבֵּית מַיִם חַיִּים.

לָתֵת טַעַם וָנֶפֶשׁ, לְהוֹצִיא אֲסִירִים לְחֹפֶשׁ, מַיִם טְבִיעַת רֶפֶשׁ, לְבַל יַבְעִיתוּ מְחָרֵף נֶפֶשׁ. **לֹא** טַרְחוּת כְּמַבּוּלוֹת, וְלֹא בְּחֹרֶב אָב מַחְבִּילוֹת, מַיִם טְמוּנִים בְּתַחְבּוּלוֹת, חָשׂוּף מַצִּיב כָּל גְּבוּלוֹת.

מזל אב

אריה

מָטָר יוֹרֶה לִירוֹת, שָׂדוֹת וִיעָרוֹת, מַיִם יִמָּלְאוּ יְאוֹרוֹת, לִמְגוֹדְדֵי גְדוּד שְׁיָּרוֹת. **יָשׁוּב** יִפְרֶה הַר וְגִבְעָה, יִרְבַּץ כְּאַרְיֵה עֲלֵי תְבוּעָה, מַיִם יְשַׁלְּשׁוּ רְבִיעָה, לְהִפָּרֵד לְרָאשִׁים אַרְבָּעָה.

אַרְצָךְ כִּוּוּן הֲדוֹם רֶגֶל, וְלֹא נִשְׁקֵית כְּגַן בְּרֶגֶל, מַיִם כִּזְנוּק אֵגֶל יְזַנְּקוּ בָּשָׁן בְּמָנוֹחַ עֵגֶל. **כִּי** כֹל בַּשֶּׁקִי יָשִׁישׁ, בְּאָסְפָם בַּר בֶּאֱלוּל בְּטִלּוּל רְסִיס, מַיִם כְּרָמִים לְהַעֲסִיס, בְּנִטְפֵי חָלָב וְעָסִיס.

מזל אלול

בתולה

בְּעִתּוֹ לְהַרְעִים רַעַם, בְּנַחַת וְלֹא בְזַעַם, מַיִם לָתֵת טַעַם, בְּאַדְמַת מַשְׁפִּיר אִמְרֵי נֹעַם. **אִם** לְשֵׁבֶט אִם לְאֶרֶץ נִשְׁלָחִים, לְהַעֲלִיץ בְּתוּלָה בְּאִבֵּי שְׁלָחִים מַיִם לִפְלָגִים נִשְׁלָחִים, לְשַׂמֵּחַ עִיר אֱלֹהִים.

וּלְבָרֵךְ מִמֶּגֶד יְרָחִים, בְּעִדּוּן תְּנוּב פְּרָחִים, מַיִם מֵעָבִים מַטְרִיחִים, וּמַעֲדַנֵּי מֶלֶךְ מַאֲרִיחִים. **הִרְוָה** מְזוֹנִים וְנָטַר, בְּיֶרַח אֵיתָנִים לְהַתִּיר קֶטַר, מַיִם מֵעַתָּה בַּל יֶאְטַר, לְהַרְעִיף שְׂעִירֵי מָטָר.

מזל תשרי

מאזנים

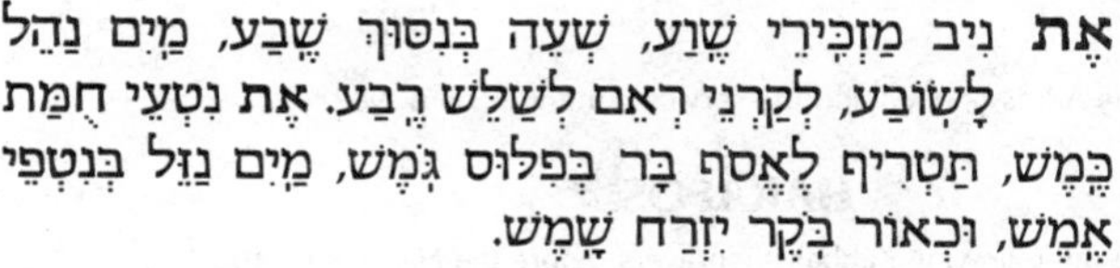

אֵת נִיב מַזְכִּירֵי שֶׁוַע, שְׁעֵה בְּנִסּוּךְ שֶׁבַע, מַיִם נַהֵל לָשׂוֹבַע, לְקַרְנֵי רְאֵם לְשַׁלֵּשׁ רֶבַע. **אֵת** נִטְעֵי חֶמֶת כֶּמֶשׁ, תַּטְרִיף לֶאֱסֹף בָּר בְּפִלּוּס גֹּמֶשׁ, מַיִם נַזֵּל בְּנִטְפֵי אֶמֶשׁ, וּכְאוֹר בֹּקֶר יִזְרַח שָׁמֶשׁ.

כָּל שִׂיחִים בּוֹ יְאֻשָּׁרוּ, יִתְרוֹעֲעוּ אַף יָשִׁירוּ, מַיִם שְׂעִירִים יַחְשֹׁרוּ, וְאַדְמַת רוֹדֵם יַעֲשִׁירוּ. **הָאָרֶץ** סוֹקְרִים כְּבְרַק אֵשׁ, פֶּן כְּמַבּוּל בּוּל תִּתְבַּיֵּשׁ, מַיִם סַפֵּק מְלֻבֵּישׁ, נוֹאֲמִים אָב לַמָּטָר הֲיֵשׁ.

מזל חשון

עקרב

מַעֲשֵׂה עִקּוּשׁ כָּל בְּרִיָּה, לֹא יַעְצְרוּ מִגִּיא פוֹרִיָּה, מַיִם עֲמֻקִּים יַעַטְפוּ פִרְיָה, בְּזֵכֶר עֲנִיַּת מוֹרִיָּה. **וְהוֹלִידָהּ** עָב חִתּוּל בָּשְׁתָהּ, כְּבִמְקוֹם עַקְרָב בְּלִי לְשִׁיתָהּ, מַיִם עֶרֶף רֵאשִׁיתָהּ, הַמְטֵר לְעוֹבְרִים שָׁמָּה לְרִשְׁתָּהּ.

יָדְךָ פְּתַח בִּזְרוֹעַ חָשׂוּף, לִפְתֹּחַ אוֹצָר אָסוּף, מַיִם פָּקַד לְצִיָּה כָּסוּף, בְּזֵכֶר עֲנִיַּת יַם סוּף. **וְהִצְמִיחָהּ** פֵּרוֹת בְּמֵי שֶׁלֶג, בִּימֵי חֲנֻכָּה לְהָצִין מֶלֶג, מַיִם פְּנוֹת אַרְצָה בְּלִי פֶלֶג, מִדּוּק לְהוֹרִיד גֶּשֶׁם וָשֶׁלֶג.

מזל כסלו

קשת

וְהַלְוִיָּת צְבָאֶיךָ רְסִיסֵי אֶגֶל, בְּנַחַת נַהֵל מַעְגָּל, מַיִם צוּק בְּקוֹל גַּלְגַּל, בְּזֵכֶר עֲנִיַּת גִּלְגָּל. **וְנָתַן** צֹאנְךָ לְךָ בְּמֶרֶץ, קֶשֶׁת לְהֵרָאוֹת לְחַיֵּל אֶרֶץ, מַיִם צְרוּרִים לְמִטְרוֹת עֶרֶץ, תַּתִּיר לֵאמֹר לַשֶּׁלֶג הֱוֵא אָרֶץ.

גּוֹיִם קָצְפוּ מִמֵּי הַקְּצָפָה, כְּנִפְתְּחוּ אֲרֻבּוֹת לְהָצִיפָה, מַיִם קָרִים בְּלִי חֲצִיפָה, בְּזֵכֶר עֲנִיַּת מִצְפָּה. **זֶרַע** קֹדֶשׁ מַטָּעָתוֹ, מְכֻפֶּלֶת לְהָכִין מַרְעִיתוֹ, מַיִם קַלִּים מִלְּהַבְעִיתוֹ, צַו לָתֵת מְטַר אַרְצְךָ בְּעִתּוֹ.

מזל טבת

גדי

רַבִּים רְנָנוֹת בְּיִשְׁבִי, הִרְבֵּיתִי לְךָ לְהַקְשִׁיבִי, מַיִם רַוֵּה לְהַשְׁאִיבִי, בְּזֵכֶר עֲנִיַּת תִּשְׁבִּי. **לַזּוֹרֵעַ** רְאֵה שִׂיחַ נִדְכּוּ, כִּגְדִי רוֹבֵץ לְהַשְׁדִּיכוּ, מַיִם רַבָּה כְּגַהַר דַּכּוּ, כְּקָדְרוּ עַד כֹּה וְעַד כֹּה.

מזל שבט

דלי

וְאַתָּה שְׁעֵה נִיב שְׂפָתַי, הַמַּזְכִּירִים מֵאֵימָתַי, מַיִם שׁוֹקֵק עֲמוּתַי, בְּזֵכֶר עֲנִיַּת בֶּן אֲמִתַּי. **וְלֶחֶם** שָׁמֵן וְדָשֵׁן לְרַשֵּׁם, בִּדְלִי שֵׁבֶט יִצְחַצַח כְּלֶשֶׁם, מַיִם שֶׁפַע לִנְפוּחֵי נֶשֶׁם, וְיִמָּלְאוּ הֶעָבִים גֶּשֶׁם.

מזל אדר

דגים

לֹא תִלְוֶה מִלִּפְתֹּחַ כָּל סָגוּר, לַעֲנוֹת מְצַפְצְפִים כְּעָגוּר, מַיִם תָּרִיק לְכָל מָגוּר, בְּזֵכֶר עֲנִיַּת גּוּר וְאָגוּר. **לָאוֹכֵל** תְּלוֹת לְךָ עֵינַיִם, לְאַדְּרוֹ וּלְהַדְגּוֹ מִמֶּגֶד שָׁמַיִם. ❖ מַיִם תֵּן לְהַחֲיוֹת כִּמְיוּמַיִם אֶרֶץ נַחֲלֵי מָיִם.

The Ark is opened and the service continues on p. 982.

HAKAFOS

Some recite the following Kabbalistic prayers before the *Hakafos* (p. 1068) as the Torah Scrolls are removed from the Ark:

לְשֵׁם יִחוּד קֻדְשָׁא בְּרִיךְ הוּא וּשְׁכִינְתֵּהּ, בִּדְחִילוּ וּרְחִימוּ לְיַחֵד שֵׁם י״ה בְּו״ה בְּיִחוּדָא שְׁלִים, בְּשֵׁם כָּל יִשְׂרָאֵל. הִנֵּה אֲנַחְנוּ בָּאִים לְקַיֵּם מִצְוַת מִנְהַג יִשְׂרָאֵל קְדוֹשִׁים לְהַקִּיף שֶׁבַע הַקָּפוֹת לַתֵּבָה שֶׁבָּהּ הַסֵּפֶר תּוֹרָה, וּלְהַרְבּוֹת בְּשִׂמְחַת הַתּוֹרָה, לְתַקֵּן אֶת שָׁרְשָׁהּ בְּמָקוֹם עֶלְיוֹן. וִיהִי רָצוֹן מִלְּפָנֶיךָ יהוה אֱלֹהֵינוּ וֵאלֹהֵי אֲבוֹתֵינוּ, שֶׁבְּכֹחַ הַקָּפוֹת אֵלּוּ תַּפִּיל חוֹמַת בַּרְזֶל הַמַּפְסֶקֶת בֵּינֵינוּ וּבֵינֶךָ, וְנִהְיֶה מֻקָּפִים מִתּוֹרָה וּמִצְוֹת מִבַּיִת וּמִבַּחוּץ, וְנִדְבַּק בְּךָ וּבְתוֹרָתְךָ תָּמִיד, אֲנַחְנוּ וְזַרְעֵנוּ וְזֶרַע זַרְעֵנוּ. וִיהִי נֹעַם אֲדֹנָי אֱלֹהֵינוּ עָלֵינוּ, וּמַעֲשֵׂה יָדֵינוּ כּוֹנְנָה עָלֵינוּ, וּמַעֲשֵׂה יָדֵינוּ כּוֹנְנֵהוּ.

After the first *hakafah* (p. 1070):

יְהִי רָצוֹן מִלְּפָנֶיךָ יהוה אֱלֹהֵינוּ וֵאלֹהֵי אֲבוֹתֵינוּ אָב הָרַחֲמִים, שֶׁבִּזְכוּת הַקָּפָה רִאשׁוֹנָה שֶׁהִקַּפְנוּ לַתֵּבָה בְּשִׂמְחַת תּוֹרָתֶךָ הָרוֹמֶזֶת **לַחֶסֶד**, יְהִי חַסְדְּךָ יהוה עָלֵינוּ, וּתְזַכֵּנוּ לְעָבְדְּךָ בְּיִרְאָה וְאַהֲבָה, וְתִהְיֶה אַהֲבָתְךָ תְּקוּעָה בְּלִבֵּנוּ תָּמִיד כָּל יְמֵי חַיֵּינוּ, וְתִהְיֶה יִרְאָתְךָ עַל פָּנֵינוּ לְבִלְתִּי נֶחֱטָא, וּבְכָל מִדָּה וּמִדָּה שֶׁתְּמַדֵּד לָנוּ נוֹדֶה לְךָ בִּמְאֹד מְאֹד. וּתְזַכֵּנוּ לְהַשְׂכִּיל לְהֵטִיב וְלִגְמוֹל **חֶסֶד** בְּכָל כֹּחֵנוּ, בְּגוּפֵנוּ וּמָמוֹנֵנוּ בְּלֵבָב שָׁלֵם. וְיִהְיוּ כָּל מַעֲשֵׂינוּ לִשְׁמֶךָ וּלְזִכְרְךָ תַּאֲוַת נָפֶשׁ, וּתְזַכֵּנוּ לְהִתְרַחֵק מֵהַקִּנְאָה וְאַכְזָרִיּוּת וְכַעַס, וְלִקְנוֹת מִדַּת **הַחֶסֶד** בְּקִנְיָן גָּמוּר, וּלְמַעַן תּוֹרָתְךָ הַקְּדוֹשָׁה הַנִּתֶּנֶת בְּיָמִין. וּלְמַעַן אַבְרָהָם אֹהַבְךָ אִישׁ **הַחֶסֶד**, תְּמַלֵּא מִשְׁאֲלוֹת לִבֵּנוּ לְטוֹבָה. יִוָּדַע לְעֵינֵי הַכֹּל טוּבְךָ **וְחַסְדְּךָ** עִמָּנוּ.

חַסְדֵי יהוה עוֹלָם אָשִׁירָה, לְדֹר וָדֹר אוֹדִיעַ אֱמוּנָתְךָ בְּפִי.
סִתְרִי וּמָגִנִּי אָתָּה, לִדְבָרְךָ יִחָלְתִּי.
דְּרָכֶיךָ יהוה הוֹדִיעֵנִי, אֹרְחוֹתֶיךָ לַמְּדֵנִי.
יִהְיוּ לְרָצוֹן אִמְרֵי פִי וְהֶגְיוֹן לִבִּי לְפָנֶיךָ, יהוה צוּרִי וְגֹאֲלִי.

After the second *hakafah* (p. 1074):

יְהִי רָצוֹן מִלְּפָנֶיךָ יהוה אֱלֹהֵינוּ וֵאלֹהֵי אֲבוֹתֵינוּ, שֶׁבִּזְכוּת הַקָּפָה הַזֹּאת הַשֵּׁנִית הָרוֹמֶזֶת **לַגְּבוּרָה**, תְּזַכֵּנוּ לְהִתְגַּבֵּר עַל יִצְרֵנוּ, וְתֵן בָּנוּ כֹּחַ לִכְבּוֹשׁ תַּאֲוֹתֵינוּ הַגּוּפָנִיּוֹת, וּלְמַעַן יִצְחָק עֲקֵדְךָ נֶאְזָר **בִּגְבוּרָה**. עוֹרְרָה אֶת גְּבוּרָתֶךָ, וּלְכָה לִישׁוּעָתָה לָנוּ. וּכְמוֹ שֶׁכָּבַשׁ אַבְרָהָם אָבִינוּ אֶת רַחֲמָיו לַעֲשׂוֹת רְצוֹנְךָ בְּלֵבָב שָׁלֵם, כֵּן יִכְבְּשׁוּ רַחֲמֶיךָ אֶת כַּעַסְךָ, וְיִגֹּלּוּ רַחֲמֶיךָ עַל מִדּוֹתֶיךָ, וְתִתְנַהֵג עִמָּנוּ יהוה אֱלֹהֵינוּ בְּמִדַּת הַחֶסֶד, וְתִכָּנֵס לָנוּ לִפְנִים מִשּׁוּרַת הַדִּין, וּבְטוּבְךָ הַגָּדוֹל יָשׁוּב חֲרוֹן אַפְּךָ מֵעַמְּךָ וּמֵעִירְךָ וּמֵאַרְצְךָ וּמִנַּחֲלָתֶךָ. וּתְבַטֵּל מֵעָלֵינוּ כָּל גְּזֵרוֹת קָשׁוֹת וְרָעוֹת, וְתִגְזוֹר עָלֵינוּ גְּזֵרוֹת טוֹבוֹת כְּרֹב רַחֲמֶיךָ.

גַּם מִזֵּדִים חֲשֹׂךְ עַבְדֶּךָ, אַל יִמְשְׁלוּ בִי אָז אֵיתָם.
בְּאֶבְרָתוֹ יָסֶךְ לָךְ וְתַחַת כְּנָפָיו תֶּחְסֶה, צִנָּה וְסֹחֵרָה אֲמִתּוֹ.
וַאֲנַחְנוּ עַמְּךָ וְצֹאן מַרְעִיתֶךָ, נוֹדֶה לְּךָ לְעוֹלָם לְדוֹר וָדוֹר נְסַפֵּר תְּהִלָּתֶךָ.
רֹעֵה יִשְׂרָאֵל הַאֲזִינָה, נֹהֵג כַּצֹּאן יוֹסֵף, יֹשֵׁב הַכְּרֻבִים הוֹפִיעָה.
הוֹרֵנִי יהוה דַּרְכֶּךָ אֲהַלֵּךְ בַּאֲמִתֶּךָ, יַחֵד לְבָבִי לְיִרְאָה שְׁמֶךָ.
יִהְיוּ לְרָצוֹן אִמְרֵי פִי וְהֶגְיוֹן לִבִּי לְפָנֶיךָ, יהוה צוּרִי וְגֹאֲלִי.

After the third *hakafah* (p. 1076):

יְהִי רָצוֹן מִלְּפָנֶיךָ יהוה אֱלֹהֵינוּ וֵאלֹהֵי אֲבוֹתֵינוּ, שֶׁבִּזְכוּת הַקָּפָה שְׁלִישִׁית הָרוֹמֶזֶת **לְתִפְאֶרֶת**, תְּזַכֵּנוּ לִהְיוֹת מֵעֲבָדֶיךָ הַנֶּאֱמַר עֲלֵיהֶם, יִשְׂרָאֵל אֲשֶׁר בְּךָ אֶתְפָּאָר. וּתְזַכֵּנוּ לַעֲסֹק בְּתוֹרָתְךָ הַקְּדוֹשָׁה תּוֹרַת אֱמֶת, וְתִהְיֶה כָּל מְגַמָּתֵנוּ לְבַקֵּשׁ הָאֱמֶת, וּתְחָנֵּנוּ לְמַעַן דַּעַת אֲמִתּוּת דִּינֵי הַתּוֹרָה, וּתְזַכֵּנוּ לְהִתְרַחֵק מֵהַשֶּׁקֶר וְהַכָּזָב, וְכָל פְּנוֹת

שֶׁנִּפְנֶה יִהְיוּ עַל דְּבַר אֱמֶת, וּבִזְכוּת תּוֹרַת אֱמֶת וּזְכוּת יַעֲקֹב אָבִינוּ עָלָיו הַשָּׁלוֹם הֶחָתוּם **בְּתִפְאֶרֶת** מִדַּת אֱמֶת, וּכְתִיב תִּתֵּן אֱמֶת לְיַעֲקֹב, תַּעֲנֵנוּ וְתַעֲשֶׂה בַּקָּשָׁתֵנוּ, וְנִקְרֵאת יְרוּשָׁלַיִם עִיר הָאֱמֶת. עַל כֵּן נְקַוֶּה לְּךָ יהוה אֱלֹהֵינוּ לִרְאוֹת מְהֵרָה **בְּתִפְאֶרֶת** עֻזֶּךָ.

תִּקְרַב רִנָּתִי לְפָנֶיךָ יהוה, כִּדְבָרְךָ הֲבִינֵנִי.
פְּעָמַי הָכֵן בְּאִמְרָתֶךָ, וְאַל תַּשְׁלֶט בִּי כָל אָוֶן.
אַשְׁרֵי אָדָם עוֹז לוֹ בָךְ, מְסִלּוֹת בִּלְבָבָם.
רַחֲמֶיךָ רַבִּים, יהוה, כְּמִשְׁפָּטֶיךָ חַיֵּנִי.
תְּהִלַּת יהוה יְדַבֶּר פִּי, וִיבָרֵךְ כָּל בָּשָׂר שֵׁם קָדְשׁוֹ לְעוֹלָם וָעֶד.
יִהְיוּ לְרָצוֹן אִמְרֵי פִי וְהֶגְיוֹן לִבִּי לְפָנֶיךָ, יהוה צוּרִי וְגֹאֲלִי.

After the fourth *hakafah* (p. 1080):

יְהִי רָצוֹן מִלְּפָנֶיךָ יהוה אֱלֹהֵינוּ וֵאלֹהֵי אֲבוֹתֵינוּ, אֵל מָלֵא רַחֲמִים, שֶׁתַּעֲשֶׂה לְמַעַן זְכוּת הַקָּפָה רְבִיעִית הָרוֹמֶזֶת לְמִדַּת **נֶצַח**, בְּרַחֲמֶיךָ הָרַבִּים אַל יַעַזְבֵנוּ **נֶצַח** סֶלָה וָעֶד, וְנִשְׂמְחָה וְנִרְאֶה נְעִימוֹת בִּימִינְךָ **נֶצַח**. וּתְזַכֵּנוּ לְכָל הַהַבְטָחוֹת וְנֶחָמוֹת שֶׁהִבְטַחְתָּנוּ עַל יְדֵי נְבִיאֶיךָ הַקְּדוֹשִׁים, וְגַם **נֵצַח** יִשְׂרָאֵל לֹא יְשַׁקֵּר וְלֹא יִנָּחֵם, וּתְחַזְּקֵנוּ וּתְאַמְּצֵנוּ **לָנֶצַח**, וּתְ**נַצֵּחַ** אוֹיְבֵינוּ וְתִסְתֹּם וְתַחְסֹם פִּי כָל הַמְקַטְרְגִים עָלֵינוּ, וּלְמַעַן זְכוּת מֹשֶׁה רַעְיָא מְהֵימְנָא הֶחָתוּם בְּמִדַּת **הַנֶּצַח**, תָּאִיר עֵינֵינוּ בְּתוֹרָתֶךָ, וְאַחֲרֵי מִצְוֹתֶיךָ תִּרְדֹּף נַפְשֵׁנוּ, וְתִגְאָלֵנוּ גְאֻלַּת עוֹלָם מִגָּלוּת הַחֵל הַזֶּה, בִּזְכוּת מֹשֶׁה רַעְיָא מְהֵימְנָא, וְתִבְנֶה בֵּית הַמִּקְדָּשׁ בִּמְהֵרָה בְיָמֵינוּ, וְקוֹל בֶּן לֵוִי תִּסֹּב עַל שִׁירָה וּנְבָלָה עִמּוֹ, כִּנּוֹר נָעִים עִם נֶבֶל. **לְנַצֵּחַ** עַל מְלֶאכֶת בֵּית יהוה.

נוֹדָע בִּיהוּדָה אֱלֹהִים, בְּיִשְׂרָאֵל גָּדוֹל שְׁמוֹ.
צֶדֶק לְפָנָיו יְהַלֵּךְ, וְיָשֵׂם לְדֶרֶךְ פְּעָמָיו.
חָנֵּנִי יהוה, כִּי אֵלֶיךָ אֶקְרָא כָּל הַיּוֹם.
יִהְיוּ לְרָצוֹן אִמְרֵי פִי וְהֶגְיוֹן לִבִּי לְפָנֶיךָ, יהוה צוּרִי וְגֹאֲלִי.

After the fifth *hakafah* (p. 1082):

יְהִי רָצוֹן מִלְּפָנֶיךָ יהוה אֱלֹהֵינוּ וֵאלֹהֵי אֲבוֹתֵינוּ, שֶׁתַּעֲשֶׂה לְמַעַן רַחֲמֶיךָ וּלְמַעַן הַקָּפָה חֲמִישִׁית הָרוֹמֶזֶת לְמִדַּת **הַהוֹד**, וּתְזַכֵּנוּ לְכַבֵּד הַתּוֹרָה וְלוֹמְדֶיהָ, וּלְהַחֲזִיק וּלְאַמֵּץ בִּרְכַּיִם כּוֹשְׁלוֹת, הַנֵּי בִּרְכֵּי דְרַבָּנָן דְּשַׁלְהֵי, וּתְזַכֵּנוּ שֶׁלֹּא נֵלֵךְ בַּעֲצַת רְשָׁעִים, וְלֹא נִהְיֶה מֵהוֹלְכֵי רָכִיל, וּלְמַעַן זְכוּת אַהֲרֹן קְדוֹשׁ יהוה הֶחָתוּם בְּמִדַּת **הוֹד** לְטוֹבָה, וּתְזַכֵּנוּ לִרְדֹּף שָׁלוֹם וּלְבַקֵּשׁ שָׁלוֹם וְלָשִׂים שָׁלוֹם, וּלְהַרְבּוֹת שָׁלוֹם בָּעוֹלָם, וּלְמֶעְבַּד עוּבְדָא דְאַהֲרֹן, וְתָשִׂים שָׁלוֹם בֵּינֵינוּ וּתְבָרְכֵנוּ לְחַיִּים טוֹבִים וּלְשָׁלוֹם, וּבָא לְצִיּוֹן גּוֹאֵל. גָּדוֹל כְּבוֹדוֹ בִּישׁוּעָתֶךָ, **הוֹד** וְהָדָר תְּשַׁוֶּה עָלָיו בִּמְהֵרָה בְיָמֵינוּ.

הַשָּׂם נַפְשֵׁנוּ בַּחַיִּים, וְלֹא נָתַן לַמּוֹט רַגְלֵנוּ.
וַיְהִי יהוה לִי לְמִשְׂגָּב, וֵאלֹהַי לְצוּר מַחְסִי.
דֶּרֶךְ מִצְוֹתֶיךָ אָרוּץ, כִּי תַרְחִיב לִבִּי.
יִהְיוּ לְרָצוֹן אִמְרֵי פִי וְהֶגְיוֹן לִבִּי לְפָנֶיךָ, יהוה צוּרִי וְגֹאֲלִי.

After the sixth *hakafah* (p. 1084):

יְהִי רָצוֹן מִלְּפָנֶיךָ יהוה אֱלֹהֵינוּ וֵאלֹהֵי אֲבוֹתֵינוּ, שֶׁתַּעֲשֶׂה לְמַעַן רַחֲמֶיךָ וּלְמַעַן זְכוּת הַקָּפָה הַשִּׁשִּׁית הָרוֹמֶזֶת **לַיְסוֹד**, וְתַצִּילֵנוּ מִכָּל חֵטְא וְעָוֹן וְהִרְהוּר רָע. וְאַתָּה בְּטוּבְךָ הַגָּדוֹל תְּלַקֵּט אֲשֶׁר פִּזַּרְנוּ, וּתְיַחֵד אֲשֶׁר הִפְרַדְנוּ, וּתְתַקֵּן אֲשֶׁר עִוַּתְנוּ, וְתוֹצִיא לָאוֹר כָּל הַנִּיצוֹצוֹת שֶׁל קְדֻשָּׁה אֲשֶׁר נִטְמְעוּ בֵּין הַקְּלִפּוֹת, חַיִל בָּלַע וַיְקִיאֶנּוּ, מִבִּטְנוֹ יוֹרִישֶׁנּוּ אֵל. וּתְזַכֵּנוּ לִשְׁמֹר עַצְמֵנוּ וּדְרָכֵינוּ מִכָּל חֵטְא, וְלֹא יִמָּצֵא בָנוּ וְלֹא בְזַרְעֵנוּ שׁוּם פְּגָם, וְיִהְיֶה כָּל זַרְעֵנוּ זֶרַע קֹדֶשׁ, וּבִזְכוּת יוֹסֵף צַדִּיקֶךָ הֶחָתוּם בְּמִדַּת **הַיְסוֹד** תְּרַחֵם עָלֵינוּ אֵל שַׁדַּי, **יַסֵּד** יְסוֹד צִיּוֹן תְּרוֹמֵמְנָה קַרְנוֹת צַדִּיק. וּבִזְכוּת יוֹסֵף יֹסִיף יהוה שֵׁנִית יָדוֹ וְיִגְאָלֵנוּ גְּאֻלַּת עוֹלָם בִּמְהֵרָה בְיָמֵינוּ.

יִשָּׂא בְרָכָה מֵאֵת יהוה, וּצְדָקָה מֵאֱלֹהֵי יִשְׁעוֹ.
סוּר מֵרָע וַעֲשֵׂה טוֹב, בַּקֵּשׁ שָׁלוֹם וְרָדְפֵהוּ.
וְהָיָה כְּעֵץ שָׁתוּל עַל פַּלְגֵי מָיִם, אֲשֶׁר פִּרְיוֹ יִתֵּן בְּעִתּוֹ וְעָלֵהוּ לֹא יִבּוֹל, וְכֹל אֲשֶׁר יַעֲשֶׂה יַצְלִיחַ.
דְּרָכַי סִפַּרְתִּי וַתַּעֲנֵנִי, לַמְּדֵנִי חֻקֶּיךָ.
יִהְיוּ לְרָצוֹן אִמְרֵי פִי וְהֶגְיוֹן לִבִּי לְפָנֶיךָ, יהוה צוּרִי וְגֹאֲלִי.

After the seventh *hakafah* (p. 1088):

יְהִי רָצוֹן מִלְּפָנֶיךָ יהוה אֱלֹהֵינוּ וֵאלֹהֵי אֲבוֹתֵינוּ, אֵל מָלֵא רַחֲמִים, שֶׁתַּעֲשֶׂה לְמַעַן רַחֲמֶיךָ, וּבִזְכוּת הַקָּפָה שְׁבִיעִית הָרוֹמֶזֶת **לַמַּלְכוּת**, וְתִגָּלֶה וְתֵרָאֶה **מַלְכוּתְךָ** עָלֵינוּ מְהֵרָה, וּמְלֹךְ עַל כָּל הָעוֹלָם כֻּלּוֹ בִּכְבוֹדֶךָ, וְהָיְתָה לַיהוה הַמְּלוּכָה, וְהָיָה יהוה לְמֶלֶךְ עַל כָּל הָאָרֶץ, בַּיּוֹם הַהוּא יִהְיֶה יהוה אֶחָד וּשְׁמוֹ אֶחָד. וַעֲשֵׂה לְמַעַן דָּוִד הַמֶּלֶךְ עָלָיו הַשָּׁלוֹם הֶחָתוּם בְּמִדַּת **מַלְכוּת**, וְתַשְׁרֶה שְׁכִינָתְךָ עָלֵינוּ. יְהִי יהוה אֱלֹהֵינוּ עִמָּנוּ כַּאֲשֶׁר הָיָה עִם אֲבוֹתֵינוּ אַל יַעַזְבֵנוּ וְאַל יִטְּשֵׁנוּ.

מְהֻלָּל אֶקְרָא יהוה, וּמִן אֹיְבַי אִוָּשֵׁעַ.
לְעוֹלָם יהוה, דְּבָרְךָ נִצָּב בַּשָּׁמָיִם.
כִּי חַסְדְּךָ גָּדוֹל עָלָי, וְהִצַּלְתָּ נַפְשִׁי מִשְּׁאוֹל תַּחְתִּיָּה.
וַאֲנִי כְּזַיִת רַעֲנָן בְּבֵית אֱלֹהִים, בָּטַחְתִּי בְחֶסֶד אֱלֹהִים עוֹלָם וָעֶד.
תַּאֲוַת עֲנָוִים שָׁמַעְתָּ יהוה, תָּכִין לִבָּם תַּקְשִׁיב אָזְנֶךָ.
יִהְיוּ לְרָצוֹן אִמְרֵי פִי וְהֶגְיוֹן לִבִּי לְפָנֶיךָ, יהוה צוּרִי וְגֹאֲלִי.

After all the *hakafos* have been completed, some recite the following:

רִבּוֹנוֹ שֶׁל עוֹלָם, הִנֵּה אֲנַחְנוּ בָּאִים בְּיִרְאָה וְאַהֲבָה וְשִׂמְחָה רַבָּה, לְהוֹדוֹת לְךָ עַל אֲשֶׁר קִדַּשְׁתָּנוּ בְּמִצְוֹתֶיךָ, וּבָחַרְתָּ בָּנוּ מִכָּל הָעַמִּים, אָהַבְתָּ אוֹתָנוּ וְרָצִיתָ בָּנוּ, וַתִּתֶּן לָנוּ אֶת תּוֹרָתְךָ הַקְּדוֹשָׁה, תּוֹרָה שֶׁבִּכְתָב וְתוֹרָה שֶׁבְּעַל פֶּה, וְקֵרַבְתָּנוּ לַעֲבוֹדָתֶךָ. מָה אָנוּ,

מַה חַיֵּינוּ, אֲשֶׁר עָשִׂיתָ עִמָּנוּ חֲסָדִים גְּדוֹלִים רַבִּים וַעֲצוּמִים כָּאֵלֶּה. וְעַתָּה יהוה אֱלֹהֵינוּ, מוֹדִים אֲנַחְנוּ לָךְ וּמְהַלְלִים לְשֵׁם תִּפְאַרְתֶּךָ. אָמְנָם גָּדוֹל צַעֲרֵנוּ בְּהַעֲלוֹתֵנוּ עַל לְבָבֵנוּ כֹּל אֲשֶׁר נִתְרַשַּׁלְנוּ מִלַּעֲסוֹק בְּתוֹרָתְךָ הַקְּדוֹשָׁה וְכֹל אֲשֶׁר פָּגַמְנוּ בְּלִמּוּדֵנוּ, הֵן מִצַּד לִמּוּד לְהִתְגַּדֵּל, הֵן מִצַּד שֶׁלֹּא לָמַדְנוּ בִּקְדֻשָּׁה וְיִרְאָה כַּדָּת מַה לַּעֲשׂוֹת, וְהֵן שֶׁלֹּא טָרַחְנוּ לְהָבִין דָּבָר עַל בֻּרְיוֹ מִצּוּי הַדִּין וְעֹמֶק הַהֲלָכָה, וְהֵן אֲשֶׁר קָטַפְנוּ מַלּוּחַ עֲלֵי שִׂיחַ, וְהֵן אֲשֶׁר לֹא תָמַכְנוּ וְחִזַּקְנוּ בִּרְכֵּי דְּרַבָּנָן דְּשַׁלְהֵי, וְלֹא אִמַּצְנוּ בִּרְכַּיִם כּוֹשְׁלוֹת, וְכָזֹאת וְכָזֹאת פָּגַמְנוּ בְּכ״ב אוֹתִיּוֹת תּוֹרָתֶךָ, וְטָעִינוּ בְּלִמּוּד וּבְהוֹרָאָה, וְלֹא נָהַגְנוּ בְּטַכְסִיס תַּלְמִיד חָכָם, וְעוֹד אַחֶרֶת לַאֲשֶׁר נָפְלוּ נִיצוֹצֵי תּוֹרָתֵנוּ וּמִצְוֹתֵינוּ לְבוֹרוֹת נִשְׁבָּרִים וַיִּשְׁבְּ מִמֶּנּוּ שֶׁבִי.

עַל הַכֹּל בֹּשְׁנוּ וְנִכְלַמְנוּ וּבְמִסְתָּרִים תִּבְכֶּה נַפְשֵׁנוּ, יִרְאָה וָרַעַד יָבֹא בָנוּ וַתְּכַסֵּנוּ פַּלָּצוּת. וְהֵן עַתָּה בְּבֹשֶׁת פָּנִים אָנוּ שָׁבִים וּמִתְחָרְטִים וְאָנוּ רוֹצִים לַעֲשׂוֹת רְצוֹנְךָ כִּרְצוֹנֵנוּ, וִיהִי רָצוֹן מִלְּפָנֶיךָ יהוה אֱלֹהֵינוּ וֵאלֹהֵי אֲבוֹתֵינוּ, אֵל רַחוּם וְחַנּוּן הַטּוֹב וְהַמֵּטִיב שֶׁתְּקַבֵּל כַּוָּנָתֵנוּ, כִּי אַתָּה בּוֹחֵן לְבּוֹת וְיָדַעְתָּ שֶׁרְצוֹנֵנוּ לַעֲשׂוֹת רְצוֹנֶךָ וְלַעֲסוֹק בְּתוֹרָתְךָ הַקְּדוֹשָׁה כַּדָּת מַה לַּעֲשׂוֹת, וְאַתָּה הִבְטַחְתָּנוּ עַל יְדֵי עֲבָדֶיךָ חַכְמֵי יִשְׂרָאֵל, הַבָּא לִטַּהֵר מְסַיְּעִין אוֹתוֹ. וּבְכֵן יֶהֱמוּ נָא רַחֲמֶיךָ, וּרְאֵה כִּי אָזְלַת יָד וְאֶפֶס עָצוּר וְעָזוּב, וַאֲוִיר אֶרֶץ הָעַמִּים וּבִטּוּל הַטָּהֳרָה וְתֹקֶף גָּלוּת גּוּף וָנֶפֶשׁ הֵן הֵנָּה הָיוּ בְּעוֹכְרֵינוּ, כִּי גָּבַר אוֹיֵב יִצְרֵנוּ הָרָע וְעָשָׂה אֲשֶׁר זָמַם לְהַדִּיחֵנוּ מִתּוֹרָתְךָ וּמֵעֲבוֹדָתֶךָ.

וּבְכֵן אֵין לָנוּ גּוֹאֵל וּמוֹשִׁיעַ בִּלְתֶּךָ. הַנְּשָׁמָה לָךְ וְהַגּוּף פָּעֳלָךְ, חוּסָה עַל עֲמָלָךְ. וּבְכֹחַ שֶׁבַע הַקָּפוֹת שֶׁהִקַּפְנוּ לַתֵּבָה שֶׁבָּהּ סֵפֶר הַתּוֹרָה וְשָׂמַחְנוּ לִכְבוֹד תּוֹרָתֶךָ, תִּתְמַלֵּא רַחֲמִים עָלֵינוּ. הֲשִׁיבֵנוּ אָבִינוּ לְתוֹרָתֶךָ וְקָרְבֵנוּ מַלְכֵּנוּ לַעֲבוֹדָתֶךָ, וְיִתְמַתְּקוּ הַדִּינִים וְיִכְבְּשׁוּ רַחֲמֶיךָ אֶת כַּעַסְךָ, וְיִגֹּלּוּ רַחֲמֶיךָ עַל מִדּוֹתֶיךָ, וְתוֹצִיא לָאוֹר כָּל נִיצוֹצֵי תּוֹרָתֵנוּ וּמִצְוֹתֵינוּ, וְיָשׁוּב הַכֹּל לְאֵיתָנוֹ הָרִאשׁוֹן, וְלֹא יִדַּח מִמֶּנּוּ נִדָּח, וּתְזַכֵּנוּ לַעֲסוֹק בַּתּוֹרָה לִשְׁמָהּ, לִלְמוֹד וּלְלַמֵּד, לִשְׁמוֹר וְלַעֲשׂוֹת, לְהוֹצִיא לָאוֹר כָּל חֶלְקֵי פַּרְדֵּ״ס תּוֹרָתֵנוּ הַשַּׁיָּכִים לְנַפְשֵׁנוּ רוּחֵנוּ וְנִשְׁמָתֵנוּ. וּתְחָנֵּנוּ מֵאִתְּךָ חָכְמָה בִּינָה וָדַעַת, לְחַדֵּשׁ חִדּוּשִׁים רַבִּים אֲמִתִּיִּים בְּפַרְדֵּ״ס תּוֹרָתְךָ הַקְּדוֹשָׁה, וְקוּשְׁיוֹת וַהֲוָיוֹת וְיִשּׁוּבִים אֲמִתִּיִּים וְחִדּוּשֵׁי דִינִים לַאֲמִתָּהּ שֶׁל תּוֹרָה. וּבְרֹב רַחֲמֶיךָ תְּזַכֵּנוּ לְזֶרַע קָדוֹשׁ, בָּנִים חֲכָמִים וַחֲסִידִים, זֶרַע אֲנָשִׁים, וּבָרִיא מַזָּלַיְהוּ, וְלֹא יִמָּצֵא בָנוּ וְלֹא בְזַרְעֵנוּ שׁוּם פְּגַם וְשׁוּם פְּסוּל. וְאַתָּה בְּרַחֲמֶיךָ, תִּתֵּן בָּנוּ כֹּחַ וּבְרִיאוּת, וִיכֹלֶת מַסְפִּיק, וְחֹזֶק וְאֹמֶץ בְּאֵבָרֵינוּ וְגִידֵינוּ וְגוּפֵינוּ לַעֲמוֹד עַל הַמִּשְׁמָר, וְלֹא יֶאֱרַע לָנוּ שׁוּם מֵחוּשׁ וְשׁוּם כְּאֵב, וְנִהְיֶה שְׂמֵחִים וְטוֹבִים וּבְרִיאִים לַעֲבוֹדָתֶךָ, וְתַצִּילֵנוּ מִכָּל רָע. אֱלֹהֵינוּ וֵאלֹהֵי אֲבוֹתֵינוּ, מְלוֹךְ עַל כָּל הָעוֹלָם כֻּלּוֹ בִּכְבוֹדֶךָ, וְהִנָּשֵׂא עַל כָּל הָאָרֶץ בִּיקָרֶךָ, וְהוֹפַע בַּהֲדַר גְּאוֹן עֻזֶּךָ עַל כָּל יוֹשְׁבֵי תֵבֵל אַרְצֶךָ, וְיֵדַע כָּל פָּעוּל כִּי אַתָּה פְעַלְתּוֹ, וְיָבִין כָּל יָצוּר כִּי אַתָּה יְצַרְתּוֹ, וְיֹאמַר כֹּל אֲשֶׁר נְשָׁמָה בְאַפּוֹ, יהוה אֱלֹהֵי

יִשְׂרָאֵל מֶלֶךְ, וּמַלְכוּתוֹ בַּכֹּל מָשָׁלָה. קַדְּשֵׁנוּ בְּמִצְוֹתֶיךָ, וְתֵן חֶלְקֵנוּ בְּתוֹרָתֶךָ, שַׂבְּעֵנוּ מִטּוּבֶךָ, וְשַׂמַּח נַפְשֵׁנוּ בִּישׁוּעָתֶךָ, וְטַהֵר לִבֵּנוּ לְעָבְדְּךָ בֶּאֱמֶת, וְאַל תַּדִּיחֵנוּ מִפְּנֵי שׁוּם נִבְרָא שֶׁבָּעוֹלָם. וְתַאֲרִיךְ יָמֵינוּ בַּטּוֹב וּשְׁנוֹתֵינוּ בַּנְּעִימִים. וּמַלֵּא שְׁנוֹתֵינוּ (שְׁמוֹנִים שָׁנָה) אֹרֶךְ יָמִים וּשְׁנוֹת חַיִּים תּוֹסִיף לָנוּ לַעֲבוֹדָתֶךָ, וּבְצֵל כְּנָפֶיךָ תַּסְתִּירֵנוּ, וְתַצִּילֵנוּ לָנוּ וּלְכָל בְּנֵי בֵיתֵנוּ מִכָּל גְּזֵרוֹת קָשׁוֹת וְרָעוֹת, וּתְחַדֵּשׁ עָלֵינוּ שָׁנָה טוֹבָה, וְנִהְיֶה שְׁקֵטִים וְשַׁאֲנַנִּים דְּשֵׁנִים וְרַעֲנַנִּים לַעֲבוֹדָתֶךָ וּלְיִרְאָתֶךָ. כִּי עִמְּךָ מְקוֹר חַיִּים בְּאוֹרְךָ נִרְאֶה אוֹר.

יְהִי חַסְדְּךָ יהוה עָלֵינוּ כַּאֲשֶׁר יִחַלְנוּ לָךְ.
הַרְאֵנוּ יְיָ חַסְדֶּךָ וְיֶשְׁעֲךָ תִּתֶּן לָנוּ.
וַאֲנִי בְּחַסְדְּךָ בָטַחְתִּי, יָגֵל לִבִּי בִּישׁוּעָתֶךָ, אָשִׁירָה לַיהוה כִּי גָמַל עָלָי.
הִנֵּה אֵל יְשׁוּעָתִי, אֶבְטַח וְלֹא אֶפְחָד, כִּי עָזִּי וְזִמְרָת יָהּ יהוה,
וַיְהִי לִי לִישׁוּעָה.

On *Simchas Torah*, some congregations recite the following *piyut* either between the *Haftarah* blessing and the first verse of the *Haftarah* or between the first two verses of the *Haftarah* (p. 1184). Written by the famous commentator of Scripture and *paytan* Rabbi Avraham ibn Ezra (11th-12th century Spain), the *piyut* is a eulogy on Moses. The acrostic formed by the stanzas reads אַבְרָהָם.

אַשְׁרֶיךָ הַר הָעֲבָרִים, עַל הֶהָרִים הַגְּבוֹהִים,
יַעַן בָּךְ מִבְחַר קְבָרִים, הַקֶּבֶר אִישׁ הָאֱלֹהִים.

בִּלְבָבִי לַבָּה וְכַף אַף, עַל מוֹת צִיר נֶאֱמָן, אֲשֶׁר לֹא
קָם עוֹד כָּמוֹהוּ, וּמַלְאָךְ נִרְאָה מִתּוֹךְ הַסְּנֶה לוֹ,
בּוֹעֵר בָּאֵשׁ הַסְּנֶה, אַךְ לֹא אֻכַּל עַצְמוֹ וְחֵילוֹ.
וַיּוֹאֶל עֵינָיו לְהָרִים, וַיִּקְרָא אֵלָיו אֱלֹהִים,
הִסְתִּיר פָּנָיו הַיְּקָרִים, מֵהַבִּיט אֶל הָאֱלֹהִים. אַשְׁרֶיךָ...

רַב מוֹפְתָיו אַף בֶּאֱמוּנָה, אֵל חַי עִצְּמוֹ בְּעָצְמָה,
הוּא הִנְחִיל דָּת נֶאֱמָנָה, דָּת מְלֵאָה דַּעַת וְחָכְמָה,
כַּבֵּד מוֹרֶיךָ וְאַל נָא תִשְׁאַל, אֵיךְ הָיָה וְכַמָּה.
הַנִּפְלָאִים הַזְּכוּרִים, לָמָּה יִקְצֹף הָאֱלֹהִים,
הַדּוֹבְרִים עָלָיו שְׁקָרִים, לֹא הֶאֱמִינוּ בֵּאלֹהִים. אַשְׁרֶיךָ...

הוּא הוֹרִיד לוּחוֹת שְׁתַּיִם, וּבְעֵת תַּעְיִתִי בְּמַעְלִי,
אַרְבָּעִים יוֹם פַּעֲמַיִם, לֹא אָכַל לֶחֶם בְּשֶׁלִי,
אֵיךְ אֹכַל לֶחֶם וּמַיִם אֶשְׁתֶּה, כִּי נֶאְסַף פְּלִילִי.
שֶׁפֵּרַשׁ לִי סוֹד אֲמָרִים, שֶׁאָמַר לוֹ הָאֱלֹהִים,
וּבְמוֹתוֹ בֵּרַךְ יְשָׁרִים, וַיְבָרֵךְ אוֹתָם אֱלֹהִים. אַשְׁרֶיךָ...

מַה נִּכְבָּד מִפְקָד וּמִדְרָשׁ, דָּת הָיְתָה אָמוֹן בְּשַׁחַק,
הוֹרִישָׁהּ עָנָו וְיָרַשׁ, דּוֹר מִדּוֹר קָרוֹב לְמֶרְחָק,
וִיסוֹד הַשֵּׁם הַמְּפֹרָשׁ, עַל סֵפֶר וְאֵלֶּה שְׁמוֹת חָק.
וַיִּקְרָא סוֹד הַסְּפָרִים, וַיְדַבֵּר אִתּוֹ אֱלֹהִים,
דִּבֵּר אֵלֶּה הַדְּבָרִים וּבְרֵאשִׁית בָּרָא אֱלֹהִים. אַשְׁרֶיךָ...

☙ Selected Laws and Customs

compiled by Rabbi Hersh Goldwurm

Although most of the applicable laws are cited in the main text of the *Machzor,* in some cases they are too involved or lengthy to be given fully where they apply. A selection of such laws is compiled here. This digest cannot cover all eventualities and should be regarded merely as a guide; in case of doubt, one should consult a competent halachic authority. When a particular *halachah* is in dispute, we generally follow the ruling of *Mishnah Berurah.* On occasion, however (usually when *Mishnah Berurah* does not give a definitive ruling or when a significant number of congregations do not follow *Mishnah Berurah's* ruling), we cite more than one opinion. As a general rule, each congregation is bound by its tradition and the ruling of its authorities.

These laws and customs have been culled, in the main, from the most widely accepted authorities: the *Shulchan Aruch Orach Chaim* [here abbreviated *O.C.*]; and *Mishnah Berurah* [*M.B.*]; and R' Ephraim Zalman Margulies' classic work, *Matteh Ephraim,* on the laws and customs of the period from Rosh Chodesh Elul through Succos. We have also included many of the general laws of prayer that apply to the Yom Tov.

We have added a detailed section on the laws of the *succah* and the Four Species, to enable the reader to familiarize himself with the complex laws of the *mitzvos* central to the Yom Tov. These digests, too, are not a substitute for the source texts. They are meant only as a learning and familiarizing tool. For halachic questions, one should consult the *Shulchan Aruch* and its commentaries and/or a halachic authority.

☙ The Days before Succos

1. One should begin to build the *succah,* if possible, on *Motza'ei Yom Kippur* (the evening following Yom Kippur), in order to go from one *mitzvah* to the next (*Rama O.C.* 624:5), and complete its construction on the next day (*M.B.* 624:19; *Rama* 625:1).

2. One should begin *Shacharis* early on the morning after Yom Kippur (*Magen Avraham* 624:7), so as not give Satan the pretext to denounce Israel by saying that the people shirk their duties as soon as Yom Kippur is over (*Shelah* cited in *Machatzis HaShekel*).

3. The days between Yom Kippur and Succos are festive, because they are the anniversary of the fourteen-day dedication of the Holy Temple by King Solomon (see *I Kings* 8:2, 65; *II Chronicles* 5:3, *Moed Kattan* 9a), which began on the eighth day of Tishrei. We commemorate this by assigning quasi-festival status to these days. *Tachanun* is omitted, as is the prayer אַב הָרַחֲמִים, *Father of Compassion,* before Mussaf. Also, one may not fast on a *yahrzeit* (*Matteh Ephraim* 624:2; cf. *Rama* in *O.C.* 284:7).

4. On the *Minchah* of the Sabbath afternoon before Succos, צִדְקָתְךָ, *Your Righteousness,* is not said (*Rama O.C.* 624:5 *Magen Avraham*); nor are *Pirkei Avos* or בָּרְכִי נַפְשִׁי, *Bless HASHEM, O my soul* (*M.B.* 624:18).

5. Some communities do not say לַמְנַצֵּחַ, *For the Conductor,* (between *Ashrei* and *U'va L'Zion*) *on Erev Succos.* However, all agree that אֵל אֶרֶךְ אַפַּיִם, *O God slow to anger,* (before the reading of the Torah) is said (*M.B.* 624:18).

☙ The Eve of Yom Tov

6. The eve of Succos is a propitious time for distributing charity (*Matteh Ephraim* 625:21, *Sha'arei Teshuvah* to *O.C.* 625). One should invite those unable to have their own Yom Tov meal (*Matteh Ephraim* 625:21) *Rambam* (*Hil. Yom Tov* 6:18) rules: "When one eats and drinks [on Yom Tov] he is obligated to feed the proselyte, orphan, widow, as well as other unfortunate poor people. However if one locks the gates of his courtyard and eats and drinks . . . but does not feed and give drink to the poor and embittered, this is not a rejoicing of *mitzvah,* rather it is a rejoicing of his own stomach . . . Such a rejoicing is a disgrace to them . . ."

7. On the afternoon preceding the first day of Succos, one may not eat a meal after about three o'clock (standard time) so that he will be able to eat at night in the *succah* with a good appetite (authorities cited by *M.B.* 639:27).

[More precisely, the day (from morning until night) is divided into twelve equal parts called שָׁעוֹת זְמַנִּיּוֹת, or proportional hours. The prohibition against eating begins with the onset of the tenth hour. *Rama* rules that this prohibition begins from noon. *Matteh Ephraim* (625:7) rules that it is preferable to follow *Rama,* but if one did not eat before noon he may do so until mid-afternoon, the tenth hour.]

8. A 'meal' is defined as anything such as bread or cake, that is made from the five types of grain (wheat, rye, barley, oats, and spelt). Snacks of fruit, vegetables, meat, etc. are permitted in small amounts, but one should not 'fill his stomach' with them (*O.C.* 639:3 with *M.B.*; *O.C.* 471:1 with *M.B.* §3).

9. If one did not cut his hair before Rosh Hashanah, and his hair is long, he is obligated to have a haircut in honor of *Yom Tov.* Although one may cut hair all day, it is preferable to do so before noon (*Matteh Ephraim* 625:11).

Similarly one should cut his finger nails and toe nails on the eve of *Yom Tov,* if necessary (*Matteh Ephraim* 625:13). However, it is preferable that the fingernails and toenails not be cut on the same day (*M.B.* 260 §6).

10. It is a *mitzvah* to bathe in warm water on *Erev Yom Tov,* and one should also immerse himself in a *mikveh* in honor of the *Yom Tov* (*Matteh Ephraim* 625:14).

11. Even if everyone will eat in the *succah,* one should cover the tables in the house, as one does for the Sabbath (*Matteh Ephraim* 625:31).

12. The *Yom Tov* candles should be lit in the *succah* (*Matteh Ephraim* 625:33). [One may bring the candles into the house because of lack of space, but some of the candles should be left in the *succah*. If more than one woman lit candles in the *succah,* each should leave at least one of her candles there (see *M.B.* 263:48).]

GENERAL LAWS OF PRAYER

◆§ The Obligation

13. Prayer is a major ingredient of every Jew's daily religious life. The Sages teach us that in the post-Temple era, prayer was substituted for the Temple service, and according to some authorities it is a Scriptural obligation to pray every single day (see *Rambam, Hil. Tefillah*).

14. Before praying, one should set aside a few minutes to collect his thoughts and to prepare himself mentally to stand before his Maker. Also, one should not rush away immediately after ending his prayer so as not to give the impression that he regards prayer as a burdensome task (*O.C.* 93:1).

15. Before beginning to pray, one should meditate upon God's infinite greatness and man's insignificance, and thereby remove from his heart any thoughts of physical pleasure (*O.C.* 98:1). By pondering God's works, man recognizes His infinite wisdom and comes to love and laud Him. This makes man cognizant of his own puny intelligence and flawed nature and puts him in a proper frame of mind to plead for God's mercy (*Rambam, Yesodei HaTorah* 2:2).

16. The prayers should be said with a feeling of awe and humility, and surely not in an atmosphere of levity, frivolity, or mundane concerns, nor should one pray while angry. Rather one should pray with the feeling of happiness brought on by the knowledge of God's historic kindness to Israel and His mercy to all creatures (*O.C.* 93:2).

◆§ Concentration on the Prayers

17. During *Shemoneh Esrei* one should imagine that he is in the Holy Temple and concentrate his feelings and thoughts toward Heaven, clearing his mind of all extraneous matters (*O.C.* 95:2). His eyes should be directed downward, either closed or reading from the *machzor* (*O.C.* 95:2, *M.B.* 5). One should not look up during *Shemoneh Esrei,* but when he feels his concentration failing he should raise his eyes heavenward to renew his inspiration (*M.B.* 90:8).

18. One should know the meaning of his prayers. If one had an audience with a human ruler he would take the utmost care in his choice of words and be aware of their meaning. Surely, therefore, when one stands before the King of Kings Who knows his innermost thoughts, he must be careful how he speaks (*O.C.* 98:1). Especially in regard to the benedictions of *Shemoneh Esrei,* one should at least meditate on the meaning of the concluding sentence of each benediction, which summarizes its theme (e.g., בָּרוּךְ ... הָאֵל הַקָּדוֹשׁ, *Blessed ... the holy God; M.B.* 101 §1). The first benediction of the *Shemoneh Esrei* is treated with special stringency in this regard. According to the *halachah* as stated in the Talmud, this benediction must be repeated if it was said without concentration on its meaning (*O.C.* 101:1). However, *Rama (loc. cit.)* rules that it is best *not* to repeat the benediction because it is likely that one will not concentrate properly even during the repetition. *Chayei Adam* (cited in *M.B.* 101:4) advises that if one realized his inattentiveness before saying the word HASHEM in the concluding formula of the first blessing (בָּרוּךְ . . . מָגֵן אַבְרָהָם), he should start over from אֱלֹהֵי אַבְרָהָם. Thus it is of utmost importance that one learn the meaning of the prayers in order to develop his power of concentration (*M.B.* 101:2).

19. The prayers of *Yom Tov* differ from the regular weekday prayers. This is especially true in communities where *piyutim* are said. Thus it is desirable that one learn the meaning of the prayers before *Yom Tov* so that he will understand what he is reciting. One should also leaf through the *machzor* to familiarize himself with the relatively unfamiliar sequence of the prayers, so that he not have to interrupt the flow of the prayer to find the place. This is especially important in congregations that skip some of the *piyutim*. Likewise one should teach his children where to find the prayers so that they will not distract him during the services (*Matteh Ephraim* 625:26).

◆§ Women's Obligation to Pray

20. Women are obligated to pray, and according to *Rambam* and *Shulchan Aruch* (*O.C.* 106:1) this obligation has Scriptural status. However, there are various opinions regarding the extent of their obligation.

According to the views preferred by *M.B.* (106:4), women are required to recite the *Shemoneh Esrei* of *Shacharis* and *Minchah;* they must recall the Exodus by reciting אֱמֶת וְיַצִּיב, *true and certain* (the prayer after the *Shacharis* recitation of *Shema,* p. 238), and אֱמֶת וֶאֱמוּנָה, *true and faithful* (the parallel prayer after the *Maariv* recitation of *Shema,* p. 42), because it recalls the Exodus (*M.B.* 70:2); and it is urged that they recite at least the first verse of *Shema* because it constitutes קַבָּלַת עוֹל מַלְכוּת שָׁמַיִם, *acceptance of God's sovereignty* (*O.C.* 70:1).

Some authorities rule that women should also recite all the morning benedictions (p. 136-140). According to one view, *Pesukei D'zimrah* is introductory to *Shemoneh Esrei* and, consequently, is obligatory upon women too (*M.B.* 70:2).

Women should recite בִּרְכַּת הַתּוֹרָה, *blessings of the Torah* [p. 136] (O.C. 47:14, see *Be'ur Halachah*).

According to *Magen Avraham* (*O.C.* 106:2), women are required by the Torah to pray once a day and they may formulate the prayer as they wish. In many countries, this ruling became the basis for the custom that women recite a brief prayer early in the morning and do not recite any of the formal prayers from the Siddur.

◆§ Miscellaneous Laws

21. One should not eat nor drink in the morning before praying (*O.C.* 89:3). However, it is permitted to drink water, tea, or coffee (*M.B.* 89:22) with milk (*Daas Torah* 89:5).

22. One may not pray in the presence of immodestly clad women, or facing a window through which they can be observed (see *O.C.* 75 for details).

23. It is forbidden to pray while one feels the need to discharge his bodily functions (*O.C.* 92:1-3).

24. One must wash his hands before praying, but no benediction is required (*O.C.* 92:4).

PRAYER WITH THE CONGREGATION

◆§ Prayer with a Minyan of Ten

25. One should do his utmost to pray in the synagogue together with the congregation (*O.C.* 90:9), for the Almighty does not reject the prayer of the many. Contrary to the popular misconception that it is sufficient to respond to בָּרְכוּ and קְדוּשָׁה, the main objective of prayer with a *minyan* is to recite *Shemoneh Esrei* with the *minyan*. Therefore one must arrive at the synagogue early enough to keep up with the congregation (*M.B.* §28).

◆§ Instructions for Latecomers

26. If one arrived at the synagogue too late to recite the entire order of the prayer and still recite the *Shemoneh Esrei* together with the congregation, he may omit certain parts of the service and recite them after the end of *Shacharis*. If time is extremely short, it suffices to recite the benedictions עַל נְטִילַת יָדַיִם; אֲשֶׁר יָצַר; אֱלֹהַי נְשָׁמָה; the benedictions over the Torah; בָּרוּךְ שֶׁאָמַר; אַשְׁרֵי; נִשְׁמַת; and from יִשְׁתַּבַּח through *Shemoneh Esrei*. If time permits, the following sections (listed in descending order of importance) should be recited:
(1) הַלְלוּיָהּ הַלְלוּ אֵל בְּקָדְשׁוֹ;
(2) הַלְלוּיָהּ הַלְלוּ אֶת ה׳ מִן הַשָּׁמַיִם;
(3) the other three הַלְלוּיָהּ psalms;
(4) from וַיְבָרֶךְ דָּוִיד until לְשֵׁם תִּפְאַרְתֶּךָ;
(5) הודו until וְהוּא רַחוּם;
(6) the rest of *Pesukei D'zimrah* (*O.C.* 52:1, *M.B.* 4, *Ba'er Heitev* §3).

27. All of the psalms that are recited daily take precedence over those that are added on the Sabbath and Festival (with the exception of נִשְׁמַת, as noted above). Among the Sabbath additions themselves, some selections have priority over the others. They are: לַמְנַצֵּחַ, לְדָוִד בְּשַׁנּוֹתוֹ, and תְּפִלָּה לְמשֶׁה (*M.B.* 52:5).

28. The above is only an emergency solution. One should not rely on this to arrive late for the *Pesukei D'zimrah*, because the proper order of the prayers is of utmost importance. Indeed, some authorities contend that recitation of the prayers in their proper order takes priority over the obligation to recite *Shemoneh Esrei* together with the congregation (*M.B.* 52:1).

RESPONSES DURING THE PRAYER

◆§ During Pesukei D'zimrah

29. Other than the exceptions noted below, it is prohibited to interrupt from the beginning of בָּרוּךְ שֶׁאָמַר until the conclusion of the *Shemoneh Esrei* (*O.C.* 51:4). Wherever one may not talk, it is forbidden to do so even in Hebrew (*M.B.* 51:7).

30. With the exception of *Shemoneh Esrei*, parts of *Shacharis* may be interrupted for certain responses to the *chazzan* or for certain blessings, but the rules vary widely, depending on the section of *Shacharis* and the response. In this regard, the most lenient part of *Shacharis* is *Pesukei D'zimrah*, i.e., the unit that includes the verses between בָּרוּךְ שֶׁאָמַר and יִשְׁתַּבַּח. There, one may respond with *Amen* to any benediction, but may not say בָּרוּךְ הוּא וּבָרוּךְ שְׁמוֹ. It is permitted to respond to *Kedushah* and מודים (in the repetiton of *Shemoneh Esrei*), בָּרְכוּ, and *Kaddish*. If the congregation is reciting the *Shema*, one should recite the first verse (*Shema Yisrael ...*) together with them. If one discharged his bodily functions, he may recite the benediction אֲשֶׁר יָצַר (*M.B.* 51:8).

31. If one did not yet recite the *Shema* and

calculates that the congregation will reach it after the deadline (see §55 below) or if he had forgotten to say the daily *berachos* on the Torah, he should say them in the *Pesukei D'zimrah* (*M.B.* 51:10).

◆§ During the Pesukei D'zimrah Blessings

32. The second level of stringency regarding interruptions includes the two benedictions of *Pesukei D'zimrah* — בָּרוּךְ שֶׁאָמַר and יִשְׁתַּבַּח.

בָּרוּךְ שֶׁאָמַר is composed of three parts:
(a) From בָּרוּךְ שֶׁאָמַר until the first בָּרוּךְ אַתָּה ה׳ is but a preamble; all responses are permitted.
(b) From the first בָּרוּךְ אַתָּה ה׳ until the final one, all the interruptions permitted in §30 for the rest of *Pesukei D'zimrah* are also permitted here. However, the following interruptions are *not* permitted at this point: אֲשֶׁר יָצַר and the *Amen* after the benedictions בָּרוּךְ שֶׁאָמַר and יִשְׁתַּבַּח.
(c) The last, brief blessing, בָּרוּךְ ... בְּתִשְׁבָּחוֹת, during which no interruption at all is permitted (*M.B.* 51:2).

יִשְׁתַּבַּח is composed of two parts:
(a) From the beginning of יִשְׁתַּבַּח to בָּרוּךְ אַתָּה ה׳, which has the same rules as (b) above.
(b) From בָּרוּךְ אַתָּה ה׳ to the end, which has the same rules as (c) above (*M.B.* 51:2, 65:11, 54:11).

◆§ Between the Shema Blessings of Shacharis and Maariv

33. The third level of stringency concerns the 'intervals' between the various sections of the *Shema* and the benedictions bracketing it. The intervals are as follows: After בָּרוּךְ ... יוֹצֵר הַמְּאוֹרוֹת; after בָּרוּךְ ... בְּאַהֲבָה; and after the first and second sections of the *Shema*. [The end of the *Shema* is immediately followed by the first word of the following paragraph (אֱמֶת) so that there is no 'interval' there. Similarly, it is forbidden to interrupt between the benediction גָּאַל יִשְׂרָאֵל and *Shemoneh Esrei* (O.C. 66:5,9).]

Corresponding 'intervals' exist in *Maariv* following each blessing and after the first and second sections of the *Shema* (*M.B.* 66:27; *Be'ur Halachah* there).

34. During the 'intervals' one may respond with *Amen* to all benedictions (*M.B.* 66:23). Regarding קַדִּישׁ, קְדוּשָּׁה, בָּרְכוּ, and other interruptions, the 'intervals' are treated in the same way as are interruptions in the fourth level (see below §35). During the interval between בְּאַהֲבָה and שְׁמַע, however, only the *Amen* after בְּאַהֲבָה is permitted (*Derech HaChaim*; see *M.B.* 59:25).

◆§ During the Shema and its Blessings in Shacharis and Maariv

35. The fourth level concerns the *Shema* itself and the benedictions bracketing it. The benedictions may be separated into two parts for this purpose: (1) During the concluding, brief blessing, and during the verses of שְׁמַע ... אֶחָד and בָּרוּךְ שֵׁם, no interruption whatever is permitted (*O.C.* 66:1; *M.B.* §11, 12). (2) During the rest of the fourth level, one may respond with *Amen* only to the two blessings הָאֵל הַקָּדוֹשׁ and שׁוֹמֵעַ תְּפִלָּה in *Shemoneh Esrei.* It is permitted to respond to בָּרְכוּ of both the *chazzan* and one who is called up to the Torah. In *Kaddish* one may respond with ... אָמֵן יְהֵא שְׁמֵהּ רַבָּא and with the *Amen* to דַּאֲמִירָן בְּעָלְמָא. In *Kedushah* one may say only the verses beginning קָדוֹשׁ and בָּרוּךְ. To *Modim*, one may respond only with the three words מוֹדִים אֲנַחְנוּ לָךְ (*O.C* 66:3; (*M.B.* §17,18).

A person who is reciting the *Shema* or its benedictions should not be called up to the Torah, even if he is the only *Kohen* or Levite present; in such a case it is preferable that he leave the room. However, if he *was* called up to the Torah, he may recite the benedictions, but should not read along with the reader. If possible he should attempt to get to an 'interval' in his prayers before doing so (*M.B.* 66:26).

If one had to discharge his bodily functions he should merely wash his hands and defer the recitation of אֲשֶׁר יָצַר until after *Shemoneh Esrei* (*M.B.* 66:23).

36. If one has not yet responded to בָּרְכוּ, קְדוּשָּׁה or מוֹדִים and is nearly up to *Shemoneh Esrei*, he should stop before שִׁירָה חֲדָשָׁה in order to make the responses. If he has already said שִׁירָה חֲדָשָׁה, but has not yet concluded the benediction, he may respond, but after the response he should start again from שִׁירָה חֲדָשָׁה (*M.B.* 66:52).

37. Regarding גָּאַל יִשְׂרָאֵל of *Shacharis, Rama*, followed by most Ashkenazi congregations, rules that it is permitted to answer *Amen*, while others, particularly Chassidic congregations, follow R' Yosef Caro's ruling against *Amen* at this point. To avoid the controversy, many individuals recite the blessing in unison with the *chazzan* (*O.C.* 66:7, *M.B.* §35).

38. The fifth level concerns the *Shemoneh Esrei* prayer. Here any interruption is forbidden. Even motioning to someone is prohibited (O.C. 104:1; *M.B.* §1). If the *chazzan* is up to קַדִּישׁ, קְדוּשָּׁה, or בָּרְכוּ, one should stop and listen silently to the *chazzan's* recitation; his own silent concentration is considered as if he had responded (*O.C.* 104:7; *M.B.* §26-28).

39. From the time one has concluded the last benediction of *Shemoneh Esrei* with בַּשָּׁלוֹם until the end of the standard prayers (i.e., יִהְיוּ לְרָצוֹן at the end of אֱלֹהַי נְצוֹר), one is restricted to the responses listed in level four. However, whenever possible, one should hurry to say the verse יִהְיוּ לְרָצוֹן ... וְגוֹאֲלִי before making any kind of response. It is preferable to take the usual three steps backward before making the responses (*O.C.* 122:1; *M.B.* §2-4).

LAWS OF RECITING THE SHEMA

40. It is a Scriptural precept to recite the *Shema* twice daily, once in the morning and again in the evening. When one recites the *Shema* he must have in mind that he is fulfilling a Scriptural precept; otherwise it must be repeated (*O.C.* 60:4). However, if the circumstances make it obvious that the intention was present — e.g., he recited it during the prayer with the benedictions preceding and following it — he need not repeat the *Shema* even if he did not make a mental declaration of purpose (*M.B.* 60:10).

41. The third section of *Shema*, whose recitation is Rabbinical in origin according to almost all authorities, contains a verse whose recitation fulfills the Scriptural obligation to commemorate the Exodus from Egypt twice daily (see *Berachos* 12b; *Rambam, Hil. Kerias Shema* 1:3). The above rule concerning a mental declaration of intent applies here, too.

42. One should concentrate on the meaning of all the words, and read them with awe and trepidation (*O.C.* 61:1). He should read the *Shema* as if it were a new proclamation containing teachings never yet revealed (*O.C.* 61:2). The first verse of *Shema* is the essential profession of our faith. Therefore the utmost concentration on its meaning is necessary. If one said it without such concentration, he has not fulfilled his obligation and must repeat it (*O.C.* 60:5, 63:4), but he should repeat the verse quietly, for one may not (publicly) say the first verse of *Shema* repeatedly (ibid.).

43. While reciting the first verse, it is customary to cover the eyes with the right hand to avoid distraction and to enhance concentration (*O.C.* 61:5).

44. Although *Shema* may be recited quietly, one should recite it loudly enough to hear himself. However, one has discharged his obligation even if he does not hear himself, as long as he has enunciated the words (*O.C.* 62:3).

45. The last word of the first verse, אֶחָד, must be pronounced with special emphasis, while one meditates on God's exclusive sovereignty over the seven heavens and earth, and the four directions — east, south, west, and north (*O.C.* 61:6).

46. Some consider it preferable to recite the entire *Shema* aloud (except for the passage בָּרוּךְ שֵׁם) while others say it quietly; our custom follows the latter usage. However, the first verse should be said aloud in order to arouse one's full concentration (*O.C.* 61:4,26). It is customary for the *chazzan* to lead the congregation in the recitation of the first verse so that they all proclaim the Kingdom of Heaven together (*Kol Bo* cited in *Darkei Moshe* to *O.C.* 61; *Levush*).

47. Every word must be enunciated clearly and uttered with the correct grammatical pronunciation (*O.C.* 62:1, 61:23, 16-19). It is especially important to enunciate each word clearly and to avoid run-on words by pausing briefly between words ending and beginning with the same consonant, such as וַאֲבַדְתֶּם מְהֵרָה, בְּכָל לְבַבְכֶם, and to pause between a word that ends with a consonant and the next one that begins with a silent letter [i.e., א or ע], such as אֲשֶׁר אָנֹכִי ,הַיּוֹם עַל ,וּרְאִיתֶם אֹתוֹ (*O.C.* 61:20, 21).

48. Although it is not the universal custom to chant the *Shema* with the cantillation melody used during the synagogue Torah reading, it is laudable to do so, unless one finds that such chanting interferes with his concentration. In any event, the proper punctuation must be followed so that words are grouped into the proper phrases in accordance with the syntax of each word-group and verse (*O.C.* 61:24, *M.B.* §37,38).

49. While reciting the first two portions of the *Shema*, one may not communicate with someone else by winking or motioning with his lips or fingers (*O.C.* 63:6, *M.B.* §18).

50. It is incumbent that each paragraph of the *Shema* be read word for word as it appears in the Torah. If one erred and skipped a word, he must return to the place of his error and continue the section from there (*O.C.* 64:1-2).

51. The *Shema* should be said in one uninterrupted recitation, but, if one interrupted, whether by talking or waiting silently, he does not have to repeat the *Shema*. However, if the interruption was involuntary in nature, [e.g., one had to relieve himself], and the interruption was long enough for him to have recited all three paragraphs of the *Shema* at his own normal speed, he must repeat the entire *Shema* (*Rama* *O.C.* 65:1). Multiple interruptions interspersed in the recitation of *Shema* are not added together to constitute one long, invalidating interruption (*M.B.* 65:4).

52. If one is present in the synagogue when the congregation recites the *Shema*, he must recite at least the first verse and the verse בָּרוּךְ שֵׁם together with them. If he is in the midst of a prayer that he may not interrupt (see above §29-39), he should at least give the appearance of saying *Shema* by praying loudly in the tune the congregation uses for the *Shema* (*O.C.* 65:2,3; *M.B.* §10).

53. During morning services, one should gather together the four *tzitzis* when he says the words וַהֲבִיאֵנוּ לְשָׁלוֹם מֵאַרְבַּע כַּנְפוֹת הָאָרֶץ, *Bring us in peacefulness from the four corners of the earth*, in the paragraph preceding the *Shema*. From then on and throughout the *Shema*, he should hold the *tzitzis* — according to some customs, between the fourth and little fingers of the left hand — against the heart (*Ba'er Heitev*, *O.C.* 59:3; *Derech HaChaim*).

54. When reciting the third portion of the *Shema,* וַיֹּאמֶר ה׳, during the morning services, one should grasp the *tzitzis* with the right hand also, and look at them, until after he has said the words נֶאֱמָנִים וְנֶחֱמָדִים לָעַד in the אֱמֶת וְיַצִּיב prayer following *Shema.* At that point one should kiss the *tzitzis* and release them from his hand (ibid.). [According to the prevalent custom, one also kisses the *tzitzis* every time he says the word צִיצִית, at אֱמֶת, at the end of *Shema,* and at לָעַד קַיֶּמֶת.]

◆§ Kerias Shema on Yom Tov

55. It is absolutely required that the *Shema* be recited within the requisite time — the first quarter of the day. There are various opinions among the *poskim* as to how to calculate the first quarter of a day, and these are noted in many Jewish calendars. Since many congregations begin *Shacharis* late on *Yom Tov,* one should be careful to check the deadline for *Krias Shema* and, if necessary, recite all three passages of the *Shema* before the communal prayers.

◆§ Shemoneh Esrei

56. On Chol HaMoed the prayer יַעֲלֶה וְיָבֹא is inserted in the benediction רְצֵה, *Be favorable,* of *Shemoneh Esrei.* If it is forgotten the *Shemoneh Esrei* must be repeated. [The omission of יַעֲלֶה וְיָבֹא on *Yom Tov* is a rare occurrence, since it is an integral part of the *Yom Tov Shemoneh Esrei.* On Chol HaMoed, however, it is merely an insertion in the standard weekday prayer.]

Thus, if one realized his error before uttering the word HASHEM in the formula concluding the benediction, he returns to יַעֲלֶה וְיָבֹא. If he has already concluded with הַמַּחֲזִיר שְׁכִינָתוֹ לְצִיּוֹן but not yet begun the benediction מוֹדִים he should recite יַעֲלֶה וְיָבֹא there (till מֶלֶךְ חַנּוּן וְרַחוּם אָתָּה) and continue with מוֹדִים. If he had already begun to say מוֹדִים he must return to the beginning of the benediction רְצֵה. If he had concluded *Shemoneh Esrei,* he must repeat it in its entirety (*O.C.* 422:1; 490:2).

One is considered to have 'concluded' in this context when one has recited the verse יִהְיוּ לְרָצוֹן at the conclusion of the prayer אֱלֹהַי (before עֹשֶׂה שָׁלוֹם; see M.B. 422:9).

If one is in doubt whether he has said יַעֲלֶה וְיָבֹא he must assume he has not said it. However, if he knows that while praying he was aware that he had to recite יַעֲלֶה וְיָבֹא, but is in doubt some time after concluding the prayer, he may assume that he fulfilled his intention and recited יַעֲלֶה וְיָבֹא (*M.B.* 422:10).

◆§ The Chazzan's Repetition of the Shemoneh Esrei

57. The *chazzan's* repetition of *Shemoneh Esrei* is a congregational, rather than an individual, worship. By definition a 'congregation' consists of a *minyan* (quorum of at least ten males over *bar mitzvah,* including the *chazzan*), present and listening to the recitation. If the congregants do not pay attention it is almost as if the *chazzan* were taking God's Name in vain. Every person should imagine that there are only ten congregants present and that he is one of the nine whose attentive listening is vital to the recitation (*O.C.* 124:4).

If one of the ten is in the middle of the silent *Amidah,* he may still be counted as part of the *minyan.* However, it is preferable that not more than one such person be included (*M.B.* 55:32-34).

58. One should respond with *Amen* to every benediction he hears, and should teach his young children to do so (*O.C.* 124:6,7).

59. When one says *Amen,* it is important to enunciate all of the vowels and consonants distinctly. One should not respond until the *chazzan* has concluded the benediction, and then the response should be immediate (*O.C.* 124:8). *Mishnah Berurah* (§17) cautions even against Torah study or recitation of psalms and other prayers during the *chazzan's* recitation of the *Shemoneh Esrei.*

60. It is absolutely forbidden to talk during the repetition of *Shemoneh Esrei* even if one makes sure to respond with *Amen* at the conclusion of each benediction (*O.C.* 124:7).

THE READING OF THE TORAH

61. On Succos, as on every Festival, five people are called to the Torah. If Succos falls on the Sabbath, the same Torah portion is divided into seven *aliyos* to allow for the mandatory number of seven people who must be called to the Torah on the Sabbath. It is customary not to add to the prescribed amount of *aliyos* on festivals. However, when it falls on the Sabbath it is permitted to add *aliyos* although it is rarely done (*O.C.* 282:1, *M.B.* §6).

62. The first *aliyah* belongs to a *Kohen* and the second to a *Levi* (if any are present). If no *Kohen* is present, there is no obligation to call a *Levi* in his place, but if no *Levi* is present the same *Kohen* who has been called for his own *aliyah* is called again to replace the *Levi.* He recites both blessings again. According to the prevalent custom, a *Kohen* or *Levi* may not be called up for any other regular *aliyah* except *Maftir.* They may also be called for *Acharon,* the last *aliyah* of the weekly Sabbath portion (*sidra*), after the prescribed number of seven *aliyos* has been completed (*O.C.* 135:10, *M.B.* §35).

63. Time-honored custom has established that certain occasions entitle one to an *aliyah.* These are listed in *Levush* and *Magen Avraham* to *Orach Chaim* 282, and in *Be'ur Halachah* to *O.C.* 136. [They are summarized in the *Laws* section of the ArtScroll *Siddur* §99-101.]

◆§ Close Relatives in Successive Aliyos

64. Two brothers, or a father and a son, should not be called up to the Torah in succession. Some authorities feel that this stringency should be followed even in regard to a grandfather and his grandson (*O.C.* 141:6; *M.B.* there). However, when *Maftir* is read from a second Torah scroll as on Succos, even a father and son may be called up in succession (*Ba'er Heitev* 141:6).

◆§ Procedure of the Aliyah

65. Before the person called to the Torah for an *aliyah* recites the benediction, he must open the Torah and find the passage that will be read for him (*O.C.* 139:4). In order to dispel any notion that he is reading the benedictions from the Torah, one should avert his face while reciting them; it is preferable to turn to the left side (*Rama* there). Some authorities maintain that it is better to face the Torah while saying the benedictions but to close his eyes (*M.B.* §19). Others say that it is better to close the Torah during the recitation of the benedictions (*Be'ur Halachah* there). All three modes are practiced today in various congregations.

66. In many congregations it is customary to touch the Torah with the *tallis* (or the Torah's mantle or girdle) at the beginning of the passage to be read, and to kiss the edge which touched the Torah (*Sha'arei Ephraim* 4:3). One should be careful not to rub on the Torah script forcefully for this can cause words to become erased and thus invalidate the Torah scroll.

67. It is extremely important that the benedictions be said loud enough for the congregation to hear (*O.C.* 139:6). If the congregation did not hear the recitation of בָּרְכוּ they may not respond with בָּרוּךְ . . . וָעֶד (*Be'ur Halachah* to *O.C.* 57:1). However, if the congregation (or at least a *minyan*) heard בָּרְכוּ, then even someone who has not heard בָּרְכוּ may respond along with the congregation (*M.B.* 57:2).

68. While reciting the benedictions, one should hold the poles (*atzei chaim*) upon which the Torah is rolled. During the reading the reader holds one pole and the person called to the Torah holds the other one (*O.C.* 139:11; *M.B.* §35). *Arizal* says one should hold the *atzei chaim* with both hands during the benedictions and with the right hand only during the reading (cited in *Magen Avraham* 139:13).

69. Upon completion of the reading it is customary for the person who has been called up to touch the Torah with his *tallis* (or the Torah's mantle or girdle) and to kiss the edge that has touched the Torah (see *M.B.* 139:35).

70. After the Torah passage has been read, he closes the Torah scroll and then recites the benediction (*Rama O.C.* 139:5). If the Torah reading will not be resumed immediately, (e.g., a מִי שֶׁבֵּרַךְ is said), then a covering should be spread out over the Torah (*M.B.* 139:21).

71. In Talmudic times the person called for an *aliyah* would also read aloud from the Torah. This practice was still followed in Greek and Turkish communities up to the sixteenth century (see *Beis Yosef* to *Tur O.C.* 141), and the tradition persists to this day in Yemenite communities. However, since ancient times the Ashkenazic custom has been for a designated reader (*baal korei*) to read the Torah aloud to the congregation (see *Rosh* cited in *Tur* loc. cit). Nevertheless, the person who recites the benedictions should read quietly along with the reader (*O.C.* 141:2).

72. The reader and the one called up to the Torah must stand while reading the Torah in public. It is forbidden even to lean upon something (*O.C.* 141:1).

73. When going up to the *bimah* to recite the benedictions one should pick the shortest route possible, and when returning to his seat, he should take a longer route. If two routes are equidistant, one should go to the *bimah* via the route which is to his right and descend via the opposite route (*O.C.* 141:7).

74. After one has finished reciting the concluding benediction he should not return to his place at least until the next person called up to the Torah has come to the *bimah* (*O.C.* 141:7). However, it is customary to wait until the next person has finished his passage of the Torah (*M.B.* §26).

75. It is forbidden to talk or even to discuss Torah topics while the Torah is being read (*O.C.* 146:2).

76. It is forbidden to leave the synagogue while the Torah is being read (*O.C.* 146:1), even if one has already heard the reading of the passage elsewhere (*M.B.* §1). However, if necessary, one may leave during the pause between one portion and the next (*O.C.* 146:1), provided that a *minyan* remains in the synagogue (*M.B.* §2).

KADDISH

77. The conclusion of a section of prayer is usually signified by the recitation of the *Kaddish*. Many of these *Kaddish* recitations are the privilege of mourners (within the eleven months following the death or burial of a parent, or in some instances, of other close relatives), or of those observing *yahrzeit*, i.e., the anniversary of the death of a parent (and in some congregations, of a grandparent who has no living sons; see *Matteh Ephraim, Dinei Kaddish* 3:14). However, many recitations of *Kaddish* are exclusively the prerogative of the *chazzan*.

78. Basically there are four types of *Kaddish:*

(a) חֲצִי קַדִּישׁ, Half-*Kaddish,* which ends with דַּאֲמִירָן בְּעָלְמָא וְאִמְרוּ אָמֵן;

(b) קַדִּישׁ יָתוֹם, the Mourner's *Kaddish,* which consists of Half *Kaddish,* with the addition of יְהֵא שְׁלָמָא and עוֹשֶׂה שָׁלוֹם;

(c) קַדִּישׁ שָׁלֵם, the Full *Kaddish,* the same as the Mourner's *Kaddish* with the addition of תִּתְקַבֵּל before יְהֵא שְׁלָמָא; and

(d) קַדִּישׁ דְּרַבָּנָן, the Rabbis' *Kaddish,* the same as the Mourner's *Kaddish* with the addition of עַל יִשְׂרָאֵל.

79. The function of the Half-*Kaddish* is to link different segments of the prayer, e.g., it is recited between *Pesukei D'zimrah* and the *Shema* benedictions, between *Shemoneh Esrei* (or *Tachanun)* and the prayers that conclude the service *(Pri Megadim* in *Mishbetzos Zahav, Orach Chaim* 55:1). Thus it is recited by the *chazzan.*

Nevertheless, in some congregations it is customary for a mourner to recite the *Kaddish* following the reading of the Torah if he has been called to the Torah for the concluding segment *(Sha'arei Ephraim* 10:9). The rationale for this custom is that the person called to the Torah is also a *chazzan* of sorts, since he too must read from the Torah, albeit quietly. In some congregations, a mourner recites this *Kaddish* even if he was not called to the Torah.

80. The Full *Kaddish* is recited only after the communal recitation of *Shemoneh Esrei* (or *Selichos).* It includes the *chazzan's* prayer that the just-concluded service be accepted by God. Consequently it must be recited by the *chazzan.*

81. The Mourner's *Kaddish* is recited after the recital of Scriptural verses that supplement the main body of prayer. The recital of *Kaddish* after this portion of the service is not obligatory, and is not recited if no mourners are present. Since *Kaddish* in these parts of the service is recited exclusively by mourners, it has become customary that one whose parents are living should not recite it, since this would be a mark of disrespect to his parents (see *Rama* O.C. 132:2; *Pis'chei Teshuvah, Yoreh Deah* 376:4).

If no mourners are present, the Mourner's *Kaddish* is not recited, with one exception. After *Aleinu,* which also contains Scriptural verses, *Kaddish* should be recited even if no mourner is present. In such a case, it should be recited by the *chazzan* or one of the congregants, preferably one whose parents are no longer alive, or one whose parents have not explicitly expressed their opposition to his recitation of *Kaddish (O.C.* 132:2 with *M.B.* §11).

82. Ideally, each Mourner's *Kaddish* should be recited by only one person. Where more than one mourner is present, the *poskim* developed a system of rules establishing an order of priorities for those who must recite *Kaddish* (see *M.B.* in *Be'ur Halachah* to *O.C.* 132, et al.). However, since adherence to these rules can often cause discord in the congregation, it has become widely accepted for all the mourners to recite the *Kaddish* simultaneously (see *Aruch HaShulchan* O.C. 132:8; *Siddur R' Yaakov Emden; Teshuvos Chasam Sofer,* O. C. 159).

83. In many congregations it is customary that someone observing a *yahrzeit* is given the exclusive privilege of reciting a *Kaddish,* usually the one after *Aleinu.* In that case, an additional psalm (usually *Psalm* 24) is recited at the conclusion of the services so that all the mourners can recite *Kaddish* after it.

84. The Rabbis' *Kaddish (Kaddish D'Rabbanan)* is recited after segments of the Oral Torah (e.g., Talmud) have been studied or recited by a quorum of ten adult males *(Rambam, Seder Tefilos Kol HaShanah).* The Talmud *(Sotah* 49a) refers to the great significance of יְהֵא שְׁמֵיהּ רַבָּא (a reference to *Kaddish)* that is said after *Aggadah,* indicating that this *Kaddish* has a special relevance to the Midrashic portion of the Torah. Therefore, it is customary to append a brief *Aggadic* selection to Torah study and then to recite the Rabbis' *Kaddish (M.B.* 54:9).

85. Although *Kaddish D'Rabbanan* is not reserved for mourners and may be recited even by one whose parents are alive *(Pis'chei Teshuvah, Yoreh Deah* 376:4), it is generally recited by mourners. However, when one celebrates the completion of a tractate of the Talmud, or when the rabbi delivers a *derashah* (homiletical discourse), it is customary for the celebrant or the rabbi to recite the *Kaddish* himself.

☙ The Sabbath

86. If *Yom Tov* falls on the Sabbath several additions are made to the liturgy of the *Shemoneh Esrei* and *Kiddush.* Some of them are essential and, if omitted, the *Amidah* must be repeated, while others are not. In the passage beginning וַתִּתֶּן לָנוּ, *and You gave us,* the word בְּאַהֲבָה *with love,* is added after the mention of the Sabbath and *Yom Tov.* This addition is not essential, and the prayer need not be repeated if it has been omitted *(Matteh Ephraim* 582:16). Also, if one erred and added בְּאַהֲבָה on a weekday he need not repeat the phrase. The same applies if יִשְׂמְחוּ is omitted from *Mussaf* or וַיְכֻלּוּ from *Kiddush.*

87. A different group of additions, essential in nature, consists of the inclusion of the Sabbath wherever the *Yom Tov* is mentioned (except in יַעֲלֶה וְיָבֹא where our custom omits the mention of the Sabbath). Thus we say וַתִּתֶּן לָנוּ ... **אֶת יוֹם הַשַּׁבָּת הַזֶּה** וְאֶת יוֹם חַג הַסֻּכּוֹת הַזֶּה זְמַן שִׂמְחָתֵנוּ and בָּרוּךְ אַתָּה ה׳ ... מְקַדֵּשׁ **הַשַּׁבָּת** וְיִשְׂרָאֵל וְהַזְּמַנִּים. If *both* of these additions were omitted — so that the Sabbath was not mentioned at all — then that blessing (beginning with אַתָּה בְחַרְתָּנוּ) must be repeated. Thus if one has not yet finished the *Shemoneh Esrei* [or *Kiddush],* he returns to the beginning of that blessing, and continues from there. If he has already concluded it he must start again from the beginning of *Shemoneh Esrei* [or *Kiddush]*. The 'conclusion of *Shemoneh Esrei*' in this regard is defined as the recitation of the verse יִהְיוּ לְרָצוֹן . . . וְגוֹאֲלִי just before . . . עוֹשֶׂה שָׁלוֹם

88. There are cases, however, regarding both *Shemoneh Esrei* and *Kiddush*, where it is not clear whether or not the blessing must be repeated. If one mentioned the Sabbath at the beginning of the blessing [i.e., in וַתִּתֶּן לָנוּ], but failed to do so in the concluding formula [i.e., . . . בָּרוּךְ אַתָּה ה'], it is questionable whether the blessing has to be repeated (see *M.B.* 487:7, *Be'ur Halachah* there). *Mishnah Berurah* does not give a clear ruling on these questions (although he implies his preference for some of the views). In the absence of a ruling from a competent halachic authority, one should not repeat *Shemoneh Esrei* in this case, since the general rule is that סָפֵק בְּרָכוֹת לְהָקֵל, *when there is doubt whether a blessing should be repeated, we rule leniently*, in order to avoid the possibility of reciting a blessing that is not required.

89. Conversely, if one mentioned the *Yom Tov* in וַתִּתֶּן לָנוּ but concluded the blessing with a mention only of the Sabbath, there is controversy over whether the blessing must be repeated. According to *Magen Avraham* (*O.C.* 487:2), in this case one should not repeat the blessing. However, many authorities differ (*Pri Chadash, Be'ur Halachah*, et. al.; see *Hagahas R' Akiva Eiger)*.

If the omission occurred in the concluding formula, one can correct it by immediately saying only the words הַשַּׁבָּת וְיִשְׂרָאֵל וְהַזְּמַנִּים. This correction is valid only if it was begun before enough time to say the words שָׁלוֹם עָלֶיךָ רַבִּי has elapsed from when the erroneously phrased formula was concluded.

90. If, however, the blessing has not yet been completed, there are cases where the error can be corrected and the above halachic problem avoided. If one omitted the Sabbath in וַתִּתֶּן לָנוּ, he simply goes back to וַתִּתֶּן לָנוּ and continues from there. If he has said the three words בָּרוּךְ אַתָּה ה' of the concluding formula, he should add the words לַמְּדֵנִי חֻקֶּיךָ. [By doing so he has recited the verse בָּרוּךְ אַתָּה ה' לַמְּדֵנִי חֻקֶּיךָ, *Blessed are you* HASHEM, *teach me Your statutes (Psalms* 119:12); thus no wrong or needless blessing has been recited.] Then he can go back to וַתִּתֶּן לָנוּ and correct his omission. However, if he has recited more than three words of the blessing [i.e., . . . בָּרוּךְ אַתָּה ה' מְקַדֵּשׁ], he must finish the blessing.

☙ The End of Sabbath

91. When the second day of *Yom Tov* follows the Sabbath, it is necessary to recite a prayer differentiating between the greater sanctity of the Sabbath and the lesser sanctity of the Festival. In the *Amidah*, this prayer — וַתּוֹדִיעֵנוּ — is recited in the fourth benediction. The rules outlined for אַתָּה חוֹנַנְתָּנוּ (see below §93) apply here as well *(Be'ur Halachah* to *O.C.* 294:1). If the Sabbath has already ended and one wishes to do work permitted on the Festival, but he has not said וַתּוֹדִיעֵנוּ, he must say the following formula: בָּרוּךְ הַמַּבְדִּיל בֵּין קֹדֶשׁ לְקֹדֶשׁ, *Blessed is He Who separates between holy and holy (M.B.* 299:36).

92. One should not begin to eat a meal in the three-hour period preceding the Sabbath *(O.C.* 249:2). If the second day of Yom Tov occurred on Friday and one began the festival meal within the three-hour period, he should have a smaller meal than usual, so that he will have an appetite to eat the Sabbath meal in the evening *(Matteh Ephraim* 601:5).

SABBATH, HAVDALAH, THE SECOND NIGHT

☙ The End of Yom Tov

93. In the first weekday *Maariv* prayer following the first two day Festival, a special prayer אַתָּה חוֹנַנְתָּנוּ, *You have favored us*, is inserted in the fourth benediction of *Shemoneh Esrei*. The function of this prayer is to declare the distinction between the higher holiness of the Festivals and the more mundane nature of Chol HaMoed [Intermediate Days]. If one forgets to insert this prayer he may not repeat the benediction, nor should he insert this prayer in the benediction שְׁמַע קוֹלֵנוּ. Rather he should rely on the *Havdalah* which will be recited over wine after *Maariv* (*O.C.* 294:1; *M.B.* §6).

Even after the *Yom Tov* has ended, it is prohibited to do any forbidden work before reciting אַתָּה חוֹנַנְתָּנוּ or *Havdalah*. Therefore, if one has not yet recited either, one should be very careful not to do any work even after dark. Since women generally do not recite *Maariv*, they should be careful not do any work before hearing *Havdalah*. However, by saying the words: בָּרוּךְ הַמַּבְדִּיל בֵּין קוֹדֶשׁ לְחוֹל, *Blessed is He Who separates between holy and secular*, one becomes permitted to do work (*O.C.* 299:10; see *Sha'ar HaTziyun* §51).

☙ Preparing for the Second Day

94. It is forbidden to cook on the first day of *Yom Tov* for the second day, or to make any kind of preparations on one day for the other *(O.C.* 503:1 with *M.B.).* Even in the twilight period between the two days [בֵּין הַשְּׁמָשׁוֹת] it is forbidden to make any preparations for the night; one must wait until it is definitely night *(Pri Megadim* cited in *Be'ur Halachah* to 503:1).

[See page 2 for laws regarding preparations for the Sabbath when *Yom Tov* falls on Friday.]

95. It is customary not to begin *Maariv* until it is definitely night because most families assume that they are permitted to prepare the evening meal upon commencement of the service (*Matteh Ephraim* 599:2).

96. One may light candles at the end of the afternoon of the first day (except on the Sabbath) if their light is needed at the time they are lit, even though their main use will be at night (*Matteh Ephraim* 598:8). However, the Festival candles, which are lit with the recitation of a blessing, should be lit only after it is definitely night (preface of *Prishah* to *Yoreh Deah;* see *Eleph LaMatteh* 625:51 and *K'tzei HaMatteh* there). [The candles may only be lit from an existing fire, such as a gas pilot light; in no case may a match or cigarette lighter be struck on the Festival.]

97. Likewise it should be noted that Chol HaMoed too has restrictions on the types of labor which may be performed. However, as already noted these laws are not within the purview of this digest.

SHEMINI ATZERES

מַשִּׁיב הָרוּחַ וּמוֹרִיד הַגֶּשֶׁם

98. Beginning with the recitation of *Mussaf* on Shemini Atzeres, the passage מַשִּׁיב הָרוּחַ וּמוֹרִיד הַגֶּשֶׁם, *He makes the wind blow and He makes the rain descend*, is inserted into the second benediction of the *Shemoneh Esrei* (before מְכַלְכֵּל חַיִּים). This formula is said until the *Mussaf* prayer of the first day of Pesach (see further). This is not an actual prayer for rain, but merely a הַזְכָּרָה, *a mention*, of God's raingiving power. The actual prayer for rain (in בָּרֵךְ עָלֵינוּ, *Bless on our behalf*, of the weekday prayer) is begun at a later date (*O.C.* 114:1).

99. Just before the silent *Mussaf* prayer is begun, the *shamash* should announce מַשִּׁיב הָרוּחַ וּמוֹרִיד הַגֶּשֶׁם. If this announcement is not made, the phrase should *not* be recited in the silent *Shemoneh Esrei*. The *chazzan*, however, recites the prayer in his public repetition even in the absence of an announcement (*Rama O.C.* 114:2; *M.B.* §4). Because the proclamation is absolutely essential one must be extremely careful not to recite the *mussaf* prayer before the communal proclamation has been made (*O.C.* 114:2).

100. Although מוֹרִיד הַגֶּשֶׁם is not said before the public announcement, some poskim rule that if one *did* recite מוֹרִיד הַגֶּשֶׁם before the proclamation, he need not repeat the *Shemoneh Esrei*. Moreover even if he did so during the *Maariv* or *Shacharis* prayers of Shemini Atzeres, he need not repeat the *Shemoneh Esrei* (see *Ba'er Heitev* 114:1, *Derech Chaim, Be'ur Halachah* to *O.C* 114:2 s.v. אסור).

101. The essential part of the proclamation is the phrase מוֹרִיד הַגֶּשֶׁם. Thus if the *shamash* said only מַשִּׁיב הָרוּחַ, the proclamation is not valid, and the congregation should not include the insertion in the silent prayer (*M.B.* 114:6). If, however, one of the congregants said מוֹרִיד הַגֶּשֶׁם out loud during his silent prayers, the other congregants may also say it (*M.B.* 114:4). Nevertheless the validity of a proclamation not made by an officer of the congregation is questionable. Therefore, if someone failed to recite מוֹרִיד הַגֶּשֶׁם, after such a proclamation, he need not repeat *Mussaf* (ibid.)

102. If one entered the synagogue and found that the congregation had already begun the silent *Mussaf*, he should recite מוֹרִיד הַגֶּשֶׁם on the assumption that the proclamation had been made in the customary manner (*O.C.* 114:2).

103. If one forgot to recite מַשִּׁיב הָרוּחַ וּמוֹרִיד הַגֶּשֶׁם he must start again from the beginning of the *Shemoneh Esrei* (*O.C.* 114:5), even if the omission occurred in the *Mussaf* prayer of Shemini Atzeres (*M.B.* §25). [But see below.]

104. If one recited מוֹרִיד הַטָּל, as is customary during the summer in the *Nusach Sefard* ritual and in most congregations in Israel, he need not repeat *Shemoneh Esrei*, even if he forgot מוֹרִיד הַגֶּשֶׁם. This is because he has praised God for giving dew, which is one aspect of His role as sustainer of the world's moisture. However the phrase מַשִּׁיב הָרוּחַ alone — without mention of rain or dew — cannot serve as a substitute for מוֹרִיד הַגֶּשֶׁם (*O.C.* 114:5, *M.B.* §26,27).

105. If one is not sure whether he recited מוֹרִיד הַגֶּשֶׁם, the rule is as follows: It is assumed that someone recited whatever he has been accustomed to, until a different recitation becomes habitual. The Sages set down the presumption that until someone has recited a new addition for thirty days, it has not yet become habitual with him. Consequently, until thirty days after Shemini Atzeres it is assumed that he either said nothing or מוֹרִיד הַטָּל (*O.C.* 114:8).

106. One is not required to repeat *Shemoneh Esrei* unless he has begun the word אַתָּה of the next benediction, אַתָּה קָדוֹשׁ. If he realizes his omission after having concluded מְחַיֵּה הַמֵּתִים (or said the word HASHEM in the concluding formula), but has not yet begun אַתָּה קָדוֹשׁ (or *Kedushah* of the *chazzan's Shemoneh Esrei*), he says the words מַשִּׁיב הָרוּחַ וּמוֹרִיד הַגֶּשֶׁם and continues with אַתָּה קָדוֹשׁ. If he has not begun the concluding formula of the benediction (בָּרוּךְ . . . מְחַיֵּה הַמֵּתִים) or has at least not yet said the word HASHEM in that formula, he should recite מַשִּׁיב הָרוּחַ וּמוֹרִיד הַגֶּשֶׁם and then conclude the benediction (*O.C.* 114:6 with *Be'ur Halachah*). [However if he realized his error after saying the word וְנֶאֱמָן, he should say מַשִּׁיב הָרוּחַ וּמוֹרִיד הַגֶּשֶׁם, and start over from וְנֶאֱמָן (see *M.B.* 114:29).]

THE SUCCAH

Many of the laws discussed below deal with the measurements of the *succah* and the Four Species, and are expressed in terms of טְפָחִים, *fists.* Contemporary *poskim* (halachic authorities) do not agree on the translation of the Mishnaic measurements into present-day terminology. For the convenience of the reader, we present three of the most prevalent views for the equivalent of the fist. *Chazon Ish,* as presented by R' Yisrael Yaakov Kanievsky (the Steipler) in *Shiurin shel Torah,* maintains that the fist measures 3.8 inches. However, in cases of Scriptural law (דְאוֹרַיְתָא) one must follow the more stringent view, as the case may be (see *Shiurin shel Torah,* p. 67). R' Moshe Feinstein *(Igros Moshe)* reckons the fist at 3.75 inches, and in the opinion of R' Avraham Chaim No'eh *(Shiurei Torah)* it measures 3.2 inches.

107. The laws regarding the minimum number of the walls — in the event one will not have four full walls — are complicated, so it is advisable to make four sturdy walls (*Rama* in O.C. 630:5).

108. The walls may be of any material (*O.C.* 630:1) but must be sturdy enough to withstand an ordinary wind (*O.C.* 630:10). If one uses cloth for the walls, it must be tied down securely so that it does not flap in the wind; otherwise the *succah* does not qualify for the *mitzvah.* If possible, however, one should not use a cloth *succah* at all, because of the apprehension that one of the flaps may become detached (and not be noticed) thus disqualifying the *succah* (*O.C.* 630:10). In the case of canvas *succos* manufactured especially for this purpose nowadays, this apprehension is probably non-existent. [This writer has not found the problem discussed in contemporary halachic literature. In view of the widespread custom to use canvas *succos,* we must assume that the *rabbanim* distinguish between a specially manufactured canvas *succah,* which is designed for sturdiness, and one erected on a make-shift basis.]

109. The minimum height of the walls must be ten *tefachim* (fists), totalling approximately forty inches.

110. The area enclosed by the walls must be at least 7 *tefachim* (fists; approx. 23-28 inches) wide and 7 *tefachim* long (O.C. 634:1). If the *succah* is narrower than this minimum it is not qualified for the *mitzvah* even if the total area is equal to or greater than 7x7 *tefachim;* for example, if the dimensions are 5x10 *tefachim* (*Acharonim* cited in M.B. 630:1). If a cove adjoins the *succah,* one may not eat in it unless the cove has the minimum dimensions on its own (*M.B.* 634:1).

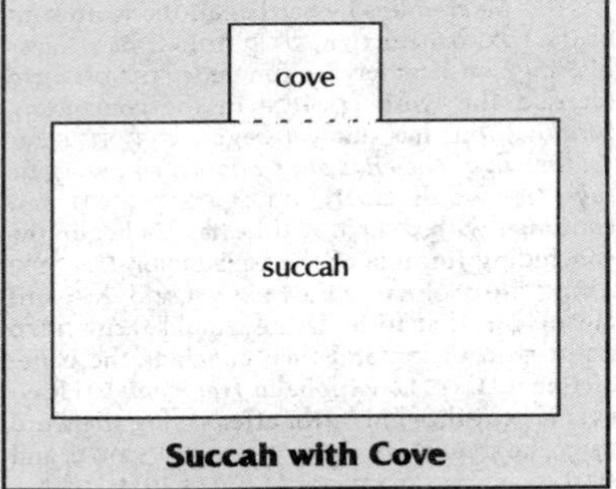

Succah with Cove

111. The material of the *succah* walls may be borrowed, but not stolen. Therefore, one may not use a *succah* against the owner's wishes. When the owner is not present, one may enter and use his *succah* on the assumption that he is willing to lend his property for the performance of a *mitzvah.* When the owner is present one may not use the *succah* without his explicit permission, since the owner may regard this as an intrusion on his privacy. Moreover if one entered a *succah* under such circumstances he may not recite the blessing for the *succah.* Even if the owner is not present when one enters the *succah* but may soon arrive, one may not use the *succah* without prior permission from the owner or his wife (O.C. 637:3 with *M.B.*).

112. One may not erect his *succah* on someone else's property without permission. Thus one may not erect a *succah* on public property (e.g., streets, parks) unless he is granted explicit permission by the appropriate authorities (*Rama* in O.C 637:3). If one has done so without obtaining such permission, *post facto* (בְּדִיעֲבַד), he is considered to have discharged his duty and may even recite the *berachah* (*Acharonim* in M.B. 637:10 and *Be'ur Halachah* there).

◆§ The S'chach

113. The covering of the *succah,* or as it is more commonly known, the *s'chach,* must be composed of materials which: a) grew from the earth; b) have been detached from the earth; and c) are not susceptible to *tumah* [contamination] (O.C. 629:1-2). Thus metals and leather, growing trees, and foodstuffs, are excluded respectively for the above three reasons. Cloth and thread (or the prepared raw material they are made of) are also excluded, as are discarded parts of materials or furniture, for they are now, or had been, susceptible to *tumah* (O.C. 629:1-2,4).

114. Mats made of reeds are not qualified for *s'chach* if they are manufactured to be used as cots (or for some other use). If the intent of the manufacture is unknown, a competent *rav* should be consulted. However, if this type of mat is generally manufactured to be used as a cot, it is not qualified even if the individual manufacturer made it expressly for use as *s'chach* (*O.C.* 629:6 with *M.B.* sec. 17).

115. Bundles of reeds containing more than twenty-five pieces do not qualify while they are still bundled. However, one may place the entire bundle upon the *succah* and open it afterward, in which case the individual reeds qualify (*O.C.* 629:15,17).

116. One should not use *s'chach* materials that emit an unpleasant odor or whose leaves drop off continually (*O.C.* 629:14).

117. Boards or beams measuring more than four fists in width (approx. 12-16 inches) may not be used even if they are stood on edge, because such wide boards are similar to the roof of a house. Some authorities maintain that since nowadays even boards less than four fists wide are used as roofing materials, these boards should not be used for *s'chach* (*O.C.* 629:18 with *M.B.* 49). Some maintain that even narrow slats should not be used because they can be placed so tightly together as to be rainproof (*M.B.* 49; see below §120).

118. Ideally (לְכַתְּחִילָּה), one should not support the *s'chach* upon something susceptible to *tumah*. Thus one should not place the *s'chach* on metal poles. However, it is permissible to support the *s'chach* on the walls of the *succah* although they are made of materials not fit for *s'chach* (e.g., a stone or metal wall; *O.C.* 629:7 with *M.B.* 22). However, some prohibit even this (see *Ran* cited in *Magen Avraham* 629:9). Therefore some people place a wooden slat upon the walls and support the *s'chach* upon the slat (see *R' Tzvi Pesach Frank, Mikra'e Kodesh* p. 92).

119. The *s'chach* must be spread over the *succah* so that it covers most of the open space and the "shade is greater than the sun" (*O.C.* 631:1).

120. The *s'chach* should be porous enough to enable one to see the stars at night (*O.C.* 631:3), but it is sufficient if the stars can be sighted from even one spot in the *succah* (*M.B.* 631 §3). Moreover, in general one may assume that stars can be sighted even when the *s'chach* is thick, for it is virtually impossible for *s'chach* not to have some openings (*M.B.* §5).

◂§ Disqualified S'chach in the Succah

121. *S'chach* not qualified for use in a *succah* may be used in small amounts without disqualifying the *succah* as a whole. If this *s'chach* does not cover an area three fists wide (or long; approximately 9-12 inches) one may even eat or sleep directly underneath it (see *M.B.* 632:3).

122. If invalid *s'chach* measuring four *tefachim* (approximately 12-16 inches), or an empty air space measuring three *tefachim* wide (9-12 inches) runs across the full length (or width) of the *succah*, it is possible that the entire *succah* (even those parts covered with *kosher s'chach)* may be disqualified. A competent authority should be consulted. The details of this law are too complicated to be discussed here (see *O.C.* 632:1).

123. If the invalid *s'chach* is placed immediately adjacent to the walls of the *succah* it does not disqualify the *succah* as long as its width does not equal four cubits (approx. 72 in.). Thus one may open a skylight in the roof of his home, cover the open area with *s'chach* and have a kosher *succah*, provided that not more than one side of the skylight is four cubits removed from the walls. In such cases, the unfit *s'chach* or the ceiling adjacent to the skylight is considered as if it were part of an overhanging wall [דוֹפֶן עֲקוּמָה, *a bent wall*]. However one may not eat under the area not covered by *s'chach* (and that area is not included in the computation determining whether the *succah* contains the minimum necessary area as outlined in §110). This distinction does not apply to air spaces; even a three fist air space may (under certain conditions) disqualify the *succah*, whether it occurs in the middle of the *succah* or along the walls (*O.C.* 632:1-2).

124. Even if *succah* decorations are made from materials not qualified to be *s'chach*, they do not disqualify the *succah*, provided they are hung within four *tefachim* (appr. 12-16 inches) of the *s'chach*. One may even eat beneath them (*O.C.* 627:4). If they are hung four fists or more below the *s'chach*, they are judged as invalid *s'chach*. Therefore *Rama* rules that one should not hang any decorations four *tefachim* below the *s'chach* (ibid.). Lighting fixtures are treated as decorations. However, if suspending them within four *tefachim* of the *s'chach* will create a fire hazard, they may and should be suspended more than four *tefachim* below the *s'chach* (see *M.B.* 627:15).

125. If any opening in the *s'chach* is long enough to admit the head and most of the body of a person lengthwise (see *Aruch HaShulchan* 632:5) one may not eat beneath that space, although the *succah* as a whole is kosher. The same is true if even a small air space runs uninterruptedly across the entire *succah* (*O.C.* 632:2). [Therefore when the *succah* is covered with bamboo poles or slats placed parallel to each other, one should place some poles at right angles to the rest of the *s'chach*, so as to break up the long spaces usually created by this type of *s'chach*.]

126. A *succah* may not be erected under a tree or the overhang of a house (*O.C.* 626:1). If a branch covers part of a *succah* a competent authority should be consulted, since the subject is complex.

◂§ Removable Roofs

127. One may construct a portable roof for the *succah* to enable him to cover the *succah* when it rains. Indeed some urge that such a device be constructed (*Matteh Ephraim* 625:29).

128. Many authorities maintain that *s'chach* placed upon the *succah* while the portable roof is in place is disqualifed. Their opinion should be followed (*M.B.* 626:18). Therefore, if this had been done, the *s'chach* should be picked up and placed on the *succah* again, piece by piece, after the roof has been removed. [It is not necessary to remove all the *s'chach* before replacing it.]

◆§ Miscellaneous Laws of S'chach

129. One should first erect the walls and then place the *s'chach* upon them (*Rama O.C.* 635:1). If the procedure was reversed, the *s'chach* is disqualified according to some and each piece must be removed and placed on the *succah* again after the walls have been completed (*M.B.* 635:10).

130. A *succah* may be left to stand from year to year with its *s'chach*. However one must cover at least a small part of the *succah* with *s'chach* within thirty days before the festival to demonstrate that this hut has been thatched over to serve as a *succah* (*O.C.* 636:1 with *M.B.* 7). One may comply with this requirement by covering an area running the entire length or width of the *succah* (ibid.). However a *succah* erected expressly for this year's festival may be covered with *s'chach* any time of the year, and the thirty-day limitation does not apply (ibid.).

◆§ Living in the Succah

131. The essence of the *mitzvah* of *succah* is to establish one's residence in the *succah* for the duration of the festival. The Torah commands us to *'dwell' in succos for seven days* (*Lev.* 23:42), meaning that any activity normally done in one's home should be done in the *succah*. Thus, one should eat, drink, sleep, and pass one's time (מְטַיֵּל) in the *succah* (*O.C.* 639:1). If he wishes to converse with his friend he should do so in the *succah*. However, in deference to the great sanctity of the *succah* one should refrain as much as possible from idle talk while in it and devote his time to Torah and matters of sanctity (*M.B.* 639:2).

132. One should treat the *succah* with the greatest respect and endeavor to adorn it as much as possible. One's finest table utensils should be used in the *succah*. Pots and pans should never be brought into the *succah* and dirty plates should be removed immediately after eating, but drinking utensils may be left there (*O.C.* 639:1; *M.B.* §4-6).

◆§ Eating in the Succah

133. Although in general one should establish the *succah* as his dwelling for the duration of the festival, the obligation of the *mitzvah* is the most stringent and is spelled out in the greatest detail in regard to eating and sleeping — the most characteristic components of 'dwelling.'

134. What is considered a snack? As formulated in *Shulchan Aruch* (*O.C.* 639:2), even large quantities of beverages are in the category of a snack. However, since some authorities are more stringent in this regard and rule that one should not drink beverages in a formal setting (e.g., in a group) or in great quantity (דֶּרֶךְ קֶבַע) outside of the *succah*, it is preferable to follow this view, if possible. However the *succah*-blessing should not be recited when drinking beverages (*M.B.* 639:13). Moreover, some hold that in regard to wine, the law is even more stringent and the even a *revi'is* (3-6 fl. oz.) may not be drunk outside the *succah* (*Be'ur Halachah O.C.* 639:2).

The same difference of opinion applies to fruits, vegetables, meat, and fish. *Shulchan Aruch* (ibid.) rules that they may be eaten outside the *succah* in any quantity. Some authorities, however, rule that a *meal* of meat, fish, or cheese should not be eaten outside the *succah* (*M.B.* 639:15). Some are stringent even regarding a meal of fruit, but *Mishnah Berurah* (*Sha'ar HaTziyun* 38) leans to the lenient view in the case of fruits (or vegetables).

As stated above in regard to beverages, no *succah*-blessing should be recited for these foods.

135. Bread and cake up to the volume of an egg may be eaten outside the *succah*; but an amount greater than this must be eaten in the *succah*. In regard to the recitation of a blessing, it must definitely be recited even over the above quantity of bread. In regard to cake the halachah is not clear.

If enough cake is eaten to constitute a meal there is no question that it requires a *succah* and the *succah* blessing should be recited. Thus if one has coffee and cake for breakfast, he must eat in the *succah* and recite the blessing over it (*M.B.* 639:16). If the cake is slightly more than the volume of an egg, there are conflicting views (although bread would surely require a *succah* in this instance), and one should eat it in the *succah* but not recite the *berachah*. However, there is a widespread custom to recite a *berachah* even in this instance. Therefore one should spend some time in the *succah* after eating so that the *berachah* will apply not only to the eating but also to the time in the *succah* (see 131, 140) which is surely a *mitzvah*. However when one makes *Kiddush* after *Mussaf* on the Sabbath or *Yom Tov*, and eats cake, this is definitely considered a meal, and a *berachah* must be recited (*M.B.* 639:16).

Cooked foods (like cereals) made of the 'five grains' (wheat, barley, rye, oats and spelt) may be consumed outside of the *succah* unless they are considered a 'meal.' For the purpose of this halachah a 'meal' means either when a group is assembled to eat together, or if the grain food is eaten in an amount (greatly exceeding the volume of an egg) sufficient for a full meal (*O.C.* 639:2). This is the lenient view stated in *Shulchan Aruch*. However, the later authorities contend that if foods made from these grains exceed the volume of an egg, they should be considered in the category of bread and must be eaten in the *succah*. However, no *succah* blessing should be recited unless the standard stated in *Shulchan Aruch* is met (M.B. 639:15).

136. The above articulates only the parameters for the *obligation* to eat in the *succah*. However, one who is stringent with himself and abstains from drinking even water outside the *succah* is to be commended (O.C. 639:2).

◆§ Sleeping in the Succah

137. With regard to sleep, the law is more stringent. It is forbidden even to nap outside of the *succah* (*O.C.* 639:2). However, nowadays most people do not sleep in the *succah* and their behaviour is condoned by *Rama* (ibid.) based on the premise that it is too cold to sleep comfortably in the outdoors in the northern latitudes, and because of other contributing factors. Nevertheless many of those who are punctilious in the performance of the *mitzvos* observe even this facet of dwelling in the *succah* (ibid.).

◆§ Exemptions from the Mitzvah

138. One to whom any facet of 'dwelling' in the *succah* causes physical distress is exempt from performing that activity in the *succah*. Therefore if a significant amount of rain penetrates the *succah* one may leave and eat his entire meal in the house. The amount of rain that exempts one from his *succah* obligation is an amount sufficient to spoil a food that is very susceptible to water spoilage (O.C. 639:5). Similarly, if one is ill, even slightly, he is exempted from the performance of this *mitzvah* and may eat (and sleep) outside the *succah* (O.C. 640:3). Other examples of this exemption are one who is distressed by the wind, flies, foul smells, or is afraid of being robbed (O.C. 640:4). However, one must not erect his *succah* in a place where he can anticipate hindrances to his performance of the *mitzvah* (ibid.).

Someone who must travel on the Intermediate Days and will not have access to a *succah* should ask a competent *rav* as to how to conduct himself.

◆§ The Blessing

139. Just as one is required to recite a benediction before the performance of most *mitzvos*, so must he say the blessing לֵישֵׁב בַּסֻּכָּה, *to dwell in the succah*, before fulfilling this particular *mitzvah*. However, one recites it only if he will perform a function requiring him to be present in the *succah*. Thus, if one enters the *succah* to eat, he recites the blessing only if the food is of sufficient quantity and quality to obligate him to consume it in the *succah* (see §134-135; see also *M.B.* end of 639:16).

140. If one enters the *succah* to spend time there, the blessing is required (see *M.B.* 639:46), but the custom is to defer the recitation of the blessing until the beginning of the meal (O.C. 639:8). It is better, though, to eat something requiring the *berachah* (see §134-135) immediately upon entering the *succah* (M.B. 639:46).

141. If one leaves the *succah* temporarily in the middle of a meal with the intent to return immediately, the blessing need not be recited when the meal is resumed (*M.B.* 639:47).

142. If one remained in the *succah* from one meal to the next, the blessing need not be recited before the second meal. According to most opinions, one need not recite the blessing even if he left temporarily (as above) between meals, but this opinion is not held by all. However if one left the *succah* to attend the synagogue or to attend to business or other matters, all agree that a new blessing must be recited upon his return (ibid.).

143. If one leaves his *succah* during his meal to visit his friend's *succah*, he need not recite the blessing again; the blessing he recited in his own *succah* suffices (*M.B.* 639:48).

144. If one had begun to eat and only later realized that he had forgotten to remove the covering from the *succah*, he must recite the blessing again before resuming the meal. If this happened on the first two nights of the festival he is obligated to eat another *kezayis* of bread after the covering was removed (see §148). He should not, however, recite the *Kiddush* and the *shehecheyanu* blessing again (*M.B.* 639:48).

145. On the Intermediate Days of the festival the blessing is recited after the *hamotzi* and before one eats the bread. On the first (two) night(s) of the festival, or on the Sabbath, when *Kiddush* is said, the blessing follows *Kiddush* and is said before drinking the wine (O.C. 643:3; see §152). On the Sabbath and *Yom Tov* mornings, some recite the blessing immediately after *Kiddush*, whereas others defer it until after *hamotzi* (*M.B.* 643:9).

146. Women are exempt from the *mitzvah* of *succah* (O.C. 640:1), but they may perform it if they wish and recite the blessing (*M.B.* 640:1).

147. A male child who does not need the constant supervision of his mother is obligated in this *mitzvah* under Rabbinic law (מִדְּרַבָּנָן), so as to train him in the performance of *mitzvos* (O.C. 640:2).

◆§ The First Night of the Festival

148. The first night (and in the Diaspora the first two nights) differs from the rest of the festival in regard to the *mitzvah* of *succah*. On this night one is obligated to eat bread of at least the volume of an olive (*kezayis*) in the *succah*. One cannot discharge this *mitzvah* with cake (see *Sha'arei Teshuvah to O.C.* 639:3 *Mishnah Berurah* there §21; and at length in *Mikra'e Kodesh* pp. 133-5). This obligatory *kezayis* should be consumed within a time span not exceeding כְּדֵי אֲכִילַת פְּרָס (*M.B.* 639:22; see *Shiurei Torah* 3:15 about the length of the duration of אֲכִילַת פְּרָס; according to divergent opinions, this time span ranges from four to nine minutes). An olive's volume of bread is the smallest amount upon which one may recite the blessing for the *mitzvah* of *succah*, even on the first night. Various estimates are given for the volume of an olive (*kezayis)*, but *Shulchan Aruch* (*O.C.* 486) rules that it equals half an egg. Since the *mitzvah* of eating this volume on the first night is of Scriptural origin (דְאוֹרַיְיתָא), this ruling should be followed (see *M.B.* 486:1). Moreover some hold that the average egg nowadays equals only approximately *half* the volume of the eggs referred to by the Sages, so that it is necessary to eat the equivalent of an average egg (see *Tzlach* toward end of *Pesachim*, *Sha'arei Teshuvah* and *M.B.* to *O.C.* 486; *Chazon Ish O.C.* ch. 17; *Shiurin shel Torah)*. However according to many *poskim* one does not fulfill the *mitzvah* (nor can one recite the blessing) unless he eats slightly more than the volume of an egg. All agree that it is preferable to eat this amount in order to ensure that one has fulfilled the *mitzvah* (*M.B.* 639:22). During other meals of Succos all agree that one must eat a quantity slightly greater than the volume of an egg (see *O.C.* 639:2; see above §135).

149. Since there is an obligation to eat in the *succah* on the first night of the *Yom Tov*, one should not begin the meal, or even recite *Kiddush* before it is halachically night (*Rama O.C.* 639:3 with *Magen Avraham)*. If one ate during the twilight period [בֵּין הַשְּׁמָשׁוֹת], he should eat at least an olive's volume of bread again after nightfall, but not repeat the blessing (*M.B.* 25). In the Diaspora, one should follow this practice on the second night as well.

150. The first night differs also in regard to the stringency of the obligation. On the rest of the festival one need not eat in the *succah* when heavy rain penetrates the *s'chach* or one feels some other form of distress through eating in the *succah* in any way (see above §138), but on the first night this does not pertain. One must eat (the minimum amount) in the *succah* even when it is raining (*Rama* in *O.C.* 639:5). However, many authorities dispute this ruling. Therefore no blessing should be recited in such an instance. Moreover one should wait for an hour or two for the rain to stop, so that he can perform the *mitzvah* properly according to all opinions. If it is not possible to wait so long (e.g., there are guests, little children, etc.) or the rain has not stopped even after this wait, one should make *Kiddush* and eat the minimum amount required to be eaten in the *succah* (but without reciting the *succah* blessing) and then he may finish the meal indoors. If the rain stops later he should again go into the *succah*, recite the blessing and eat the minimum requirement. This should be done even when one has already recited the *Bircas HaMazon* after the meal, in which case he must wash his hands again with the appropriate blessing (M.B. 639:35-36 with *Sha'ar HaTziyun* §67).

151. In the Diaspora the above applies to the second night as well, with one difference: If it rains on the second night, one may recite the *Kiddush* in the house and eat the meal without waiting for the rain to stop, and then go to the *succah* and eat the minimum there. If possible, however, one should wait a reasonable time for the rain to stop, even on the second night (*M.B.* 639:36).

152. In the *Kiddush* of the first night the blessing over the *mitzvah* of *succah* follows the blessing of *Kiddush. Shehecheyanu* is recited last. On the second night some reverse this sequence, placing *shehecheyanu* immediately after *Kiddush.* Others maintain the same order as on the first day (*O.C.* 643:1 and 661 with *M.B.* and *Sha'ar HaTziyun*).

153. One should make sure to eat the minimum requirement before midnight (*Rama* 639:3). However if he had been detained until midnight, he may still recite the blessing on the *succah* just as he does at any time during the rest of the festival (*M.B.* 439:26).

154. When one eats the first *kezayis* on the first night, he should concentrate on the reason given by the Torah for this *mitzvah: So that your generations shall know that I settled the Children of Israel in succos when I took them out of Egypt* (*Lev.* 23:43). This is in addition to the mental intent common to all *mitzvos* that the act is being done because it has been bidden by God. On Succos one should meditate on the status of the *succah* as a commemoration of the Exodus from Egypt, and that God surrounded Israel at that time with Heavenly Clouds (עֲנָנֵי הַכָּבוֹד) to protect them from the elements (*M.B.* 625:1).

THE FOUR SPECIES

155. The Torah (*Lev.* 23:40) commands us to *take on the first day of the Succos festival, the Four Species.* As identified by the oral tradition handed down to the Sages, they are an *esrog* (citron), a *lulav* (branch of a date palm), three myrtle twigs *(hadassim)*, and two willow twigs *(aravos)*. The specifications for each of these species will be described later at length. Here only the general laws applying to the Four Species as a unit will be discussed.

156. The essence of the *mitzvah* is *taking* these species in one's hands, as indicated by the phraseology used by the Torah in the above cited verse (*And you shall take for yourselves . . .)*. The well-known rite of 'waving' the Four Species to the points of the compass and to 'heave' them up and down, although a Rabbinical *mitzvah*, is not essential to the fulfillment of the Scriptural obligation.

157. The Scriptural *mitzvah* of taking the Four Species was not the same in all places. A seven day observance of 'taking' is mandated for the Temple, whereas outside it only on the first day of Succos were the species taken. However after the destruction of the Temple, the Sages decreed that, in commemoration of the Temple observance, the species be taken everywhere for seven days (*O.C.* 658:1 with *M.B.*).

158. A very important provision of the *mitzvah* on the first (or the first two days; see *M.B.* 658:23 and *O.C.* 649:5) day of the festival is that the species must belong to the person performing the *mitzvah*. However, one may ask a friend to give him the Four Species as a gift, on the condition that he will return then (*O.C.* 658:3-4). Nevertheless, if someone gives the species to a friend on the condition that they will be his only for the duration of the *mitzvah*, after which they will automatically revert to their original owner, it is considered a loan, since the acquisition is terminated after a certain time has elapsed (*O.C.* 658:3). One should not give the species to a minor on such a condition because, as a minor, he is not legally empowered to transfer ownership back to the original owner; thus the species will remain in the minor's possession. Nor will the child be deprived of his ownership for not having fulfilled the conditions, because such conditions are not legally binding on a minor (*O.C.* 658:6).

159. On the Intermediate Days, when the *mitzvah* is performed only in commemoration of the Temple, one may borrow the species from his colleague without acquiring ownership (ibid. and *O.C.* 649:5).

160. As with every *mitzvah*, a blessing (עַל נְטִילַת לוּלָב) is recited before 'taking' the species. The procedure common to all *mitzvos* is that one holds the object used for the *mitzvah* in his hand and recites the blessing prior to the performance. For example, one holds the Four Species before reciting the blessing. This presents a difficulty in regard to the Four Species, for once one has 'taken' them in his hand, the *mitzvah* has been fulfilled and it is too late to recite the blessing.

The most widely practiced solution to this problem is based on the rule that the species must be held in the direction in which they grew. Accordingly, if the *esrog* is held facing down (with the *pitam* toward the ground) the *mitzvah* is not fulfilled although one has 'taken' the species in hand (*O.C.* 651:5). Only after the *berachah* has been recited is the *esrog* inverted so that the *pitam* (see diagram further) faces up. Another method is to hold only the *lulav* (which has the myrtles and willows attached to it). After the blessing the *esrog* is picked up (ibid.).

161. Since the Four Species is a *mitzvah* dependent on time, women are exempt from it, but they have taken this *mitzvah* upon themselves as an obligation. Thus they may recite the blessing (*O.C.* 17:2; cf. *O.C.* 589:6).

162. On the first day that one performs the *mitzvah*, an additional *shehecheyanu* blessing is recited immediately following the blessing over the *mitzvah*, and before the performance of the *mitzvah* (*O.C.* 651:5).

163. Three of the species — the *lulav*, myrtle twigs and willows — should be tied together (*O.C.* 651:1). It is customary to tie them with *lulav* fronds. The *lulav* is held with its 'backbone' facing the person. The three myrtle twigs should be on the right and the two willows on the left as one faces the *lulav* (*M.B.* 651:12; *Shelah* cited in *Magen Avraham* 651:8; *M.B.* 650:8). Some people arrange the willows and myrtle twigs in different ways and some even add to the number of myrtle twigs in accordance with the kabbalistic teachings of *Arizal* and his disciples. The above is the custom most widely practiced.

164. The myrtles should be placed so that their tops are higher than the willows, but both should be attached to the lower end of the *lulav*, so that when one grasps the *lulav* he holds the myrtles and willows as well (*Rama O.C.* 651:1). Moreover, at least a *tefach* (fist; approx. 3-4 inches) of the *lulav's* 'backbone' should be visible above the tips of the myrtle and willow twigs (*O.C.* 650:2).

165. The *lulav* should be tied in three places with palm fronds. Some consider the attachment of the myrtles and willows to the *lulav* as one of the places and tie the *lulav* in only two more places, while others maintain that the three ties are in addition to the attachment. At least one *tefach* (fist; approx. 3-4 in.) from the top of the backbone should be left untied so that its leaves rustle when the *lulav* is shaken (*M.B.* 651:14).

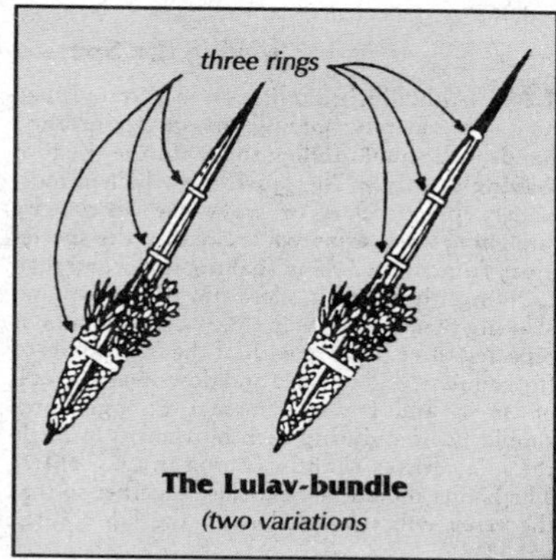

The Lulav-bundle
(two variations

166. The *esrog* should be held in the left hand and the *lulav* in the right (*O.C.* 651:2). If one reversed this order he should 'take' the species again (without reciting the blessing), because according to some the reversal invalidates the performance (*M.B.* 651:19).

167. A lefthanded person should hold the *lulav* in his left hand and the *esrog* in his right, but someone who is ambidextrous should hold the *lulav* in his right (*Rama* 651:3). There are differences of opinion how the *hadassim* and *aravos* should be arranged on the *lulav* of a lefthanded person (see *Reishis Bikurim)*.

168. There are two views as to how the Four Species should be picked up when one is ready to perform the *mitzvah*. According to a widely held view one first takes the *lulav* in the right hand, and takes the *esrog* (upside down) in his left (*Dagul Mer'vavah* and *Sha'arei Teshuvah* to O.C. 651:3). Others reverse the procedure: First the *esrog* is picked up (upside down) in the left hand, and only then is the *lulav* taken. When putting away the species this procedure is reversed; the *lulav* is put away first and then the *esrog (Magen Avraham* 651:8; see *Dagul Mervavah* and *Sha'arei Teshuvah* for divergent views).

169. If the *esrog* and *lulav* were held in one hand during the performance of the *mitzvah* the 'taking' is invalid according to some authorities and the *mitzvah* should be performed again (without a blessing; *M.B.* 651:15).

170. Nothing should cover the hand or be in it while one performs the *mitzvah,* so that there will be no barrier (חֲצִיצָה) between the hand and the species (see O.C. 651:7). The custom is to remove even the straps of the *tefillin* (for those who wear *tefillin* on the Intermediate Days) and rings from one's fingers, to avoid even this partial interposition (*Rama O.C.* 651:7). Some authorities are stringent in this matter and rule that if this is not done the species should be taken again, without recital of the *berachah* (*M.B.* 651:36).

◆§ Waving the Species

171. Although the *mitzvah* is accomplished by merely holding the species in one's hands, one should follow this with the ritual of waving (נַעֲנוּעִים). The procedure which is most widely practiced is to wave the species by stretching one's arms while holding the species away from his body and shaking them, and then bringing them back close to the chest and shaking them again (*M.B.* 651:37). This motion is repeated three times to each of the four points of the compass, and upward and downward (a total of 36 to and fro movements). Enough force should be used during each movement to rustle the *lulav* leaves slightly (*Rama* in *O.C.* 651:9). The hands should be held close together so that the *esrog* will remain close to the *lulav* (O.C. 651:11).

172. There are varying customs regarding the sequence of these movements. The following is the mode practiced in Ashkenazic communities. One begins by waving the species to the east (the direction directly ahead of him), then he turns clockwise toward the other three directions, and finally move the species up and down. Thus the sequence is east, south, west, north, up and down (see *Shulchan Aruch* O.C. 651:10). However, *Arizal* (see *Ba'er Heitev* and *Sha'arei Teshuvah* 651:20) teaches that the sequence should be south, north, east, upward, downward, and west. Communities following the Chassidic custom of prayer (commonly known as *Nusach Sfard)* and many Sephardic Jews follow *Arizal's* practice.

The species are pointed horizontally in the direction toward which they are being waved (*Rama* in O.C. 651:9). However, it is preferable that the tips of the species not be lower than the stems, even during the downward motion (ibid. *M.B.* §45). According to *Arizal* the species should be kept upright throughout the waving, with only the arms extended in the appropriate directions (cited by *Kaf HaChaim* 651:47,99 and *Siddur Baal HaTanya)*.

Some remain facing eastward and merely point the species to the indicated directions in accordance with *Maharil's* custom (*M.B.* 651:37), while others conduct themselves as indicated by *Arizal* and turn in the direction of the waving (*Kaf HaChaim* 651:96).

173. The species should also be held during the recital of *Hallel* and *Hoshanos* (see O.C. 660:2). During certain verses of *Hallel,* the species should be waved again in the manner described above. The custom recorded by *Rama (O.C.* 651:8) is to wave during each of the four times the verse הודו is repeated, each of the the two times the verse אָנָּא ה׳ הוֹשִׁיעָה נָּא is said, and finally, the two times the verse הודו is repeated (again) toward the end of the *Hallel* (a total of eight times). This custom is practiced in the communities using the *Ashkenazic* rite of prayer.

174. The most widely accepted custom is to recite the word הודו during or after the first movement (i.e., the complete set of three back-and-forth motions toward the east or south) then to recite the word לַה׳; the word כִּי is recited during or after the next movement; and so on for the remaining four words of this verse. For the verse אָנָּא, which contains only four words, the procedure is as follows: The words אָנָּא ה׳ are said in conjunction with the first two movements: הוֹשִׁיעָה in conjunction with the next two movements; and נָּא in conjunction with the last two movements (*M.B.* 651:37).

175. The *mitzvah* of taking the species may be fulfilled only during daytime, i.e., after sunrise (*O.C.* 652:1). Therefore one should be careful when praying with an early *minyan* to delay the 'taking' of the species as much as possible. However if one performed this *mitzvah* before sunrise but after dawn (i.e., seventy-two minutes before sunrise), he has, *post facto* (בְּדִיעֲבַד), discharged his obligation (*M.B.* 652:3).

176. One who must leave his home early may 'take' the 'species' before sunrise, providing it is after dawn (O.C. 652:1).

177. According to the view expressed in *Shulchan Aruch* (*O.C.* 644:1), one should perform the *mitzvah* of taking the species after the *Shacharis* prayer — immediately before *Hallel*. However, many conduct themselves in accordance with *Arizal* who teaches that it is highly desirable to perform the *mitzvah* in the *succah*. Since it is not practical to go home to one's *succah* between *Shacharis* and *Hallel*, they perform the *mitzvah* before *Shacharis* (*M.B.* 652:4, *Shelah*). In many communities it is customary to have a *succah* near the synagogue, to enable people to perform the *mitzvah* in the *succah* at its most desirable time — before *Hallel*.

178. It is prohibited to eat before performance of the *mitzvah* (*O.C.* 652:2), but one may have a snack if this is absolutely necessary. If the species are not available in the morning, however, one should not defer his meal until past noon, for it is forbidden to fast on the Festival or the Intermediate Days (*M.B.* 652:7). Many people desist even from drinking before the performance of the *mitzvah* (see *Da'as Torah* to *O.C.* 652:2; *Arba'as Haminim HaShalem* p. 25-6).

GENERAL RULES OF THE FOUR SPECIES

◆§ General Disqualifications

Although the *halachos* vary for each of the Four Species, there are nevertheless general rules that apply across the board, and that are the basis for most of the other laws. A description of these general *halachos* will permit a better understanding of the laws which flow from them.

a) לָכֶם – *Possession.* The command to *take* the Four Species is expressed as (*Lev.* 23:40) *You shall take* לָכֶם*, for yourselves . . .* The expression *for yourselves* means that one must own the Four Species before he can use them to perform the *mitzvah* (see *Sifra* there, *Gem. Succah* 41b). Thus, one cannot discharge his obligation with a set of borrowed species (see §158).

b) גָּזוּל – *Stolen.* If any of the species had been stolen they are disqualified (see *Succah* 29b). This disqualification is not unique to the Four Species; rather it derives from the general rule that disqualifies מִצְוָה הַבָּאָה בַּעֲבֵירָה, *the performance of any mitzvah through a transgression.* This invalidation applies even in some instances where the species have become the property of the thief by the time he performs the *mitzvah* (see *M.B.* 649:32).

c) הָדָר – *Beauty.* Esthetic beauty is a precondition for the validity of all of the Four Species. One example of this is the disqualification of a withered *lulav* (see Succah 29b). The *mitzvah* of the Four Species differs in this respect from other *mitzvos* where — although it is *commendable* to beautify objects used for *mitzvos* — it is not *essential* to the point where an object is disqualified if it is not beautiful.

d) שָׁלֵם – *Completeness.* The species must be whole, as they were in their natural state. A common example is the disqualification of an *esrog* whose rind with some of the underlying flesh has been peeled off.

e) שִׁיעוּר – *Minimum dimensions.* Each of the species must have certain minimum dimensions. Thus the *lulav* may not measure less than four fists in its length, et. al.

◆§ General Disqualification on the Intermediate Days

The mitzvah of taking the Four Species on the Intermediate Days is Rabbinic; (see §157) accordingly the Sages did not apply some of the Scriptural disqualifications that are in effect on the first day. According to the view accepted by *Rama*, all the above disqualifications apply also after the first day, (and in the Diaspora after the first two days) except a. (Possession) and d. (Completeness). Thus one may perform the mitzvah with borrowed species, and one may use an esrog which is not whole (*O.C.* 649:6).

All the other disqualifications, and also species that do not have the required physical characteristics are invalid throughout Succos. Examples of this are *hadassim* whose leaves do not grow from the stem in threefold clusters (מְשֻׁלָּשׁ), and *aravos* whose leaves have substantial serrations (*O.C.* 649:6 with *M.B.* 46).

◆§ The Lulav

179. The leaves of the *lulav* should point upward in the general direction of its 'backbone' and be bunched closely together; if they sag and are only slightly separated, the *lulav* is kosher. Ideally (לְכַתְּחִילָּה), however, such a *lulav* should not be used. But if the leaves sag downward so much that they do not point at all in the general direction of the *lulav's* backbone, it is invalid (*O.C.* 645:1,2).

180. *Lulav* leaves usually grow 'doubled over' lengthwise. If most of the leaves grew singly or were split lengthwise (along most of the length of the leaf; *M.B.* 645:11) the *lulav* is invalid (O.C. 645:3). *Ritva* ponders whether a *lulav* whose leaves *grew* singly is invalid for the

The Lulav

entire duration of the festival or if it may be used on the Intermediate Days (*M.B.* 645:13; see General Rules of the Four Species).

181. The middle-leaf, extending uppermost from the *lulav's* backbone, enjoys a special status. If this leaf is split until the point where it meets the backbone, the *lulav* is invalid even if the rest of the leaves are intact (*Rama* in O.C. 645:3). If there are two middle leaves, both have this status and if either one is split the *lulav* is invalid (*M.B.* 645:15). *Vilna Gaon* invalidates the *lulav* even if only most of the middle leaf is split. Similarly, if the middle leaf grew singly (i.e., it was not doubled over as in §180) the *lulav* is invalid (*Rama O.C.* 645:3).

Furthermore, *Rama* (there) cautions that ideally one should look for a *lulav* that is not split at all. Thus if one has a choice of two *lulavim*, one split slightly and the other not at all, he should prefer the latter *lulav*. However, if someone's own *lulav* is not split for most of its length, he need not go so far as to use someone else's unsplit *lulav* (*M.B.* 645:17-8). Moreover, in *Turei Zahav's* view, as long as the split does not measure a fist (טֶפַח), one need not even attempt to look for another *lulav*, but *Chaye Adam* maintains that ideally one should seek a *lulav* whose middle leaf is entirely intact (*M.B.* 645:19).

182. If the middle leaf was so split that the two parts are separated by a space and they seem like two separate leaves, the *lulav* is invalid even if the length of the split is not enough to invalidate it *per se* (*O.C.* and *Rama* 645:7). One should be very careful in regard to this (*M.B.* 645:32). The same is true if the middle leaf is intact but most of the other leaves are split in the manner described above (*Be'ur Halachah* to *O.C.* 645:7).

183. The disqualifications arising out of a split middle leaf are in effect only on the first day of the festival (in the Diaspora, the first two days). On the Intermediate Days they do not apply (*M.B.* 645:17).

184. A *lulav* is invalid if it has dried out to the point where its leaves have lost their green color and are now whitish (*O.C.* 645:5).

185. If most of the points of the leaves growing out of the tip of the *lulav's* backbone were broken or snipped off (i.e., the tips of the middle double leaf and those of the two double leaves to either side of it) the *lulav* is invalid (O.C. 645:6; see *Be'ur Halachah* there). *Rama* (loc. cit.) rules that even if only the middle leaf was mutilated in this manner one should not use this *lulav*. This invalidation is in effect for the entire festival (see *M.B.* 645:27). *Rama* adds that in the latter case if one has no other *lulav* he may use it and even recite the blessing over it (ibid.). However, this ruling is complicated by a controversy among the *Acharonim* if even a slight (מַשֶׁהוּ) mutilation along the length of these leaves invalidates the *lulav*, or if it is disqualified only if most of the leaf is missing (*M.B.* 645:26). Based on this, *Mishnah Berurah* (§30) rules that Rama's lenient ruling be relied upon only in the case of a slight mutilation. However, if most of the middle leaf is missing one should not recite the blessing. Similarly if the mutilation occurred on most of the upper leaves (the first case) the blessing should not be recited (*M.B.* 645:30).

186. The *lulav* may not be crooked. If it is curved like a sickle to the sides or forward (i.e., when the *lulav* is held with its backbone toward the person, it curves away from him) it is invalid. However if it curves backward (i.e., toward the person) it is valid, for this is a normal curvature (*O.C.* 645:8).

187. If the backbone [שִׁדְרָה] of the *lulav* is straight for most of its length and is bent (hooklike) at its top, it is invalid (*O.C.* 645:9) even if it is bent backward (*M.B.* 645:38). However, if only the tops of the leaves were bent, the *lulav* is kosher (*O.C.* 645:9); indeed many prefer such a *lulav* because its leaves will be unlikely to split (see *Tur* 645 citing *Rosh; Sha'arei Teshuvah* to *O.C.* 645:9; *M.B.* §40). But if the leaves were doubled over it is invalid (*M.B.* 645:40).

188. All invalidations listed above are in effect for the whole duration of the festival except that concerning split leaves (see §180-183), which applies only on the first (two) day(s) of the festival (*Magen Avraham* 645:6).

189. The minimum length for the *lulav's* backbone is four fists (*Rama* in *O.C.* 650:1). According to *Chazon Ish* this equals approx. 16 inches (40 centimeters) while according to *Shiurei Torah* approx. 13 inches (32 centimeters) suffices. If the *lulav's* backbone is slightly shorter than four fists it is kosher *post facto* if it meets the minimum dimensions accepted by the most lenient view in *Shulchan Aruch O.C.* 650:1 (see there), but a *lulav* shorter than that is invalid for the entire duration of the festival (*M.B.* 650:8). The backbone of the *lulav* should jut out one fist above the myrtle and willow twigs (*O.C.* 650:2).

◆§ The Myrtle Twigs (Hadassim)

190. The myrtle twigs must have three leaves growing out of each level of the twig. This is called a threefold myrtle (הֲדַס מְשֻׁלָּשׁ). If only two leaves grow at each level it is invalid (*O.C.* 646:3).; see *Be'ur Halachah* there).

191. Ideally the leaves along the entire required length (3 fists) of the myrtle twigs should be threefold. Nevertheless if only most of this length (slightly more than $1\frac{1}{2}$ fists) was threefold, it is kosher (*O.C.* 646:5) even if the threefold leaves are not situated at the upper segment of the twig (*Rama* there). If the threefold leaves are not found in one continuous stretch there is a question whether it is kosher (*Be'ur Halachah* to 646:5). [Thus, according to *Chazon Ish* the total minimum length of the myrtle is slightly less than 12 inches (30 cm.) and 'most of its length' is 6 inches. According to the dimensions given in *Shiurei Torah* the total length of the myrtle is slightly less than 10 inches (25 cm.) and 'most of its length' would be 5 inches.]

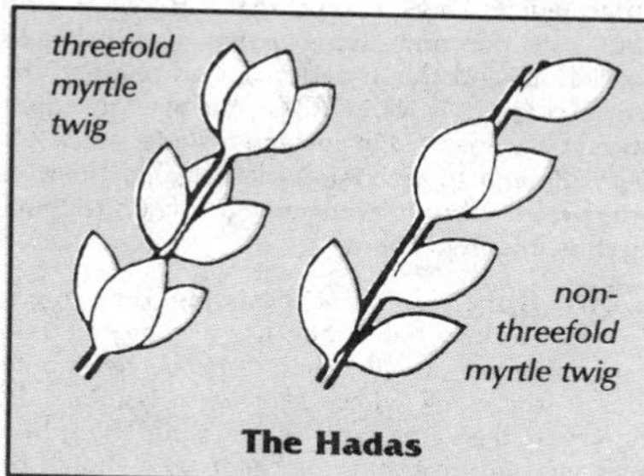

The Hadas

192. If most of the leaves (within the top 3 fists) fell off it is invalid. But if only a minority fell off it is valid (*O.C.* 646:2,4) providing that there are two remaining leaves in each threefold set (*M.B.* 646:17,18). In the latter case, however, the myrtle twigs should be used only in cases of emergency (ibid.). One should be very careful when inserting the twigs into the palm frond receptable which is used to attach them to the *lulav* not to invalidate the twigs by tearing off the leaves (see *Magen Avraham* 647:1).

193. If all of the leaves in a twig have dried up it is invalid, but if they are merely wilted it may be used. The definition of 'dry' is that the leaf has lost its green color and has become whitish (*O.C.* 646:6-7).

194. However, if the threefold set of leaves at the top of the twig are still fresh, it is kosher although all the others are dry (*O.C.* 646:8 with *M.B.* §21). If the top leaves are not fresh but wilted and the rest are dry there it is questionable whether the twig is kosher (*O.C.* 646:9); therefore one should be stringent on the first day of the festival, but one may use it on the second [even in the Diaspora] (*M.B.* 646:27). But if all of the other leaves (or at least most of them) were fresh, then the wilted leaves at the top do not disqualify the twig (see *O.C.* 646:6).

195. If the top set of leaves dried up, the twig is invalid according to *Bach* even if the rest of the leaves are fresh. This is disputed by many authorities and one may rely on their view (see *M.B.* 646:34 and *Be'ur Halachah)*. However, if one removes the dry top leaves, the twig is valid even according to *Bach* (ibid., see below §19).

196. If the top of the twig was broken off there is a question as to its validity (*O.C.* 646:10). Therefore one should not use it if he can get another twig *(Rama)*.

197. The above is true only in reference to the stem of the twig itself. If only the top leaves are ripped [or even if they fell off entirely] it is valid (ibid.).

198. The small branches sometimes growing out of the stems of the twig should be removed before *Yom Tov (M.B.* 646:33; *Sha'ar HaTziun* §36).

199. All the disqualifications of the myrtle twigs apply for the entire duration of the festival (*Be'ur Halachah* to 646:1). Where no kosher twig is available, a competent *rav* should be consulted (see *M.B.* 649:53).

200. Three myrtle twigs, each three *tefachim* (fists) long, are required for the performance of the *mitzvah* (*O.C.* 651:1). However if only one kosher twig is available one may discharge his obligation with it *(Rama)* and recite the blessing (*M.B.* 651:6).

◆§ The Willow Twigs (Aravos)

201. Many species are similar to the twigs mandated by the Torah. The prime means of identifying the proper twigs are the leaves. They should be elongated with smooth edges and the stems should be red. However green-stemmed willows are also kosher since they tend to turn red if exposed to the sun. Only those with whitish stems are invalid (*M.B.* 647:2). The sub-species whose leaves are slightly serrated, but otherwise resemble the species described above, is also kosher (*O.C.* 647:1), although some people prefer to use twigs whose leaves have no readily discernible serration. One should be careful when buying willow twigs, for many times the people selling them are not knowledgeable (*M.B.* 647:6).

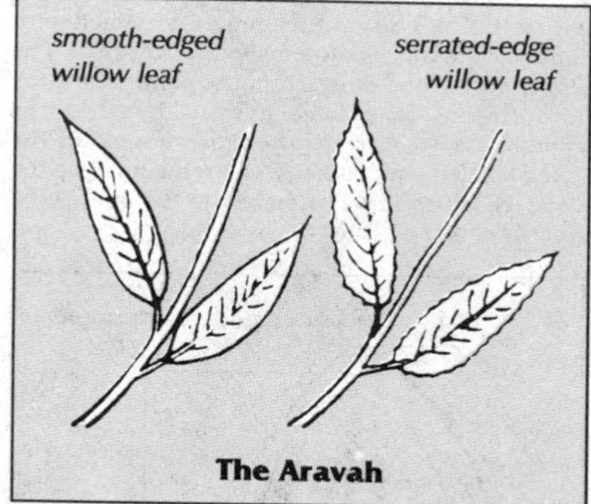

The Aravah

202. If most of the leaves on a twig fell off or dried up it is invalid (*O.C.* 647:2 with *M.B.)*. Dryness is defined as a total loss of the green color (*Sha'ar HaTziyun* 647:6). If the leaves are merely wilted the twig is kosher (*O.C.* 647:2). However, there is a difference of opinion among the *Acharonim* whether twigs that had lost less than the majority of their leaves should be used initially (לְכַתְּחִילָה). *Mishnah Berurah* (647:11) advises conformance with the stringent ruling since willow twigs are easy to attain. One should be very careful in regard to tearing off the leaves, because this often happens when the *lulav* is handled or when the twigs are inserted into the palm frond receptable attaching them to the *lulav (M.B.* 647:8).

203. If the twig's tip was broken off it is invalid (*O.C.* 647:2 with *M.B.* §12). However, if only the tip of the topmost leaf is missing [or the entire leaf was torn off] it is kosher (*M.B.* 647:10).

204. If most of the leaves of a twig are split or partly detached from the stem one should not use it (*M.B.* 647:9).

205. All disqualifications of the willow twigs are in effect for the entire duration of the festival (see *M.B.* 647:10; but cf. *M.B.* 649:48). If kosher willows are not available, a competent *rav* should be consulted.

206. Two willow twigs, each measuring three *tefachim* (fists), are required for the fulfillment of the *mitzvah* (651:1).

◆§ The Esrog

207. The laws concerning the validity of the *esrog* are complicated and numerous, and an exhaustive digest would be beyond the scope of this book. We will limit ourselves to a discussion of the most common problems. Any condition out of the ordinary should be shown to a competent *rav*.

208. Even a rudimentary understanding of the laws of the *esrog* is predicated upon an acquaintance with the *esrog's* parts and the terms used to refer to them. The *esrog* is topped by a woodlike protuberance which is called the *pitam* (פִּיטָם). This protuberance is crowned with a flowerlike top — the *shoshanta* (שׁוֹשַׁנְתָּא). The upper part of the *esrog*, from the point where the *esrog* begins to become narrow, is called the *chotam* (חוֹטָם), *nose*. At the broad bottom of the *esrog* is the stem, actually the remainder of the twig by which it was attached to the tree — the *ukatz* (עוּקָץ).

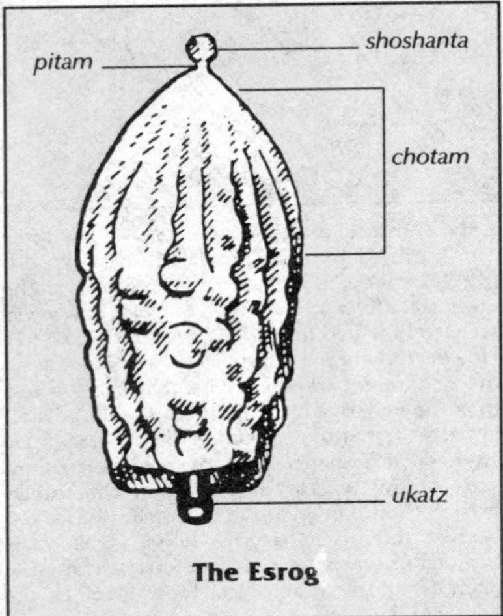

The Esrog

209. The *esrog* must be whole. If even the minutest part is missing it is invalid for the first (two) day(s). It is however valid for the Intermediate Days. If only the thin yellow rind (but not the underlying flesh) was partially peeled off, and the underlying rind retained the *esrog* color it is valid (*O.C.* 648:6). An expert should be consulted in such an instance since it is very difficult to ascertain whether only the rind was peeled off or if even some of the underlying flesh is missing.

210. If the *shoshanta* is missing, the *esrog* is kosher, but if one has a choice of two *esrogim* equal in all other respects, he should choose the *esrog* whose *shoshanta* is intact. If, however, the *esrog* with the missing *shoshanta* was superior (in beauty or *kashrus)* it should be first choice (*Rama O.C.* 648:7 with *M.B.* 31). The above refers to an instance where only the *shoshanta* was missing and the *pitam* under it is fully intact. But if part of the *pitam* is missing, although the *esrog* is kosher, another *esrog* would be preferred, regardless of the former's superiority in other respects (ibid.). According to one view, one should not recite the blessing over such an *esrog* on the first (two) day(s) of the festival, but he may do so on the Intermediate Days *(Bikkurei Yaakov* 648:23; cf. *Daas Torah).*

211. If the entire *pitam*, including the part that was embedded in the tip of the *esrog*, is missing, thus leaving a cavity, it is invalid. It is valid, however, if only the part of the *pitam* jutting out above the tip of the *esrog* was broken off *(Rama O.C.* 648:7). Some authorities rule that the *esrog* remains kosher only if part of the *pitam* remains above the tip of the *esrog;* but if it is broken off flush with the top of the *esrog*, it is invalid (*M.B.* 30). If this happened, a competent *rav* should be consulted.

212. A missing *pitam* disqualifies the *esrog* only if it was broken off. If the *esrog* grew without a *pitam*, as do many strains of this fruit, it is kosher (*Rama* 648:7) and should not be judged as inferior because of this (*M.B.* 648:32).

213. Although the disqualification caused by missing portions (חָסֵר) of an *esrog* does not apply on the Intermediate Days (see §209 and General Rules of the Four Species), some authorities feel that a (totally) missing *pitam* carries with it the additional disqualification of lacking beauty (הָדָר) and is therefore invalid even on the Intermediate Days. Thus one should endeavor to perform the *mitzvah* with an *esrog* which retains its *pitam*, at least partially, even on the Intermediate Days.

If none is available one can fulfill his obligation with an *esrog* lacking the *pitam* (even where a cavity was caused by the break). It is however questionable whether a *berachah* may be recited in such a case (*M.B.* 649:36).

214. If the entire *ukatz* (stem) was missing, leaving a small cavity at the bottom of the *esrog*, it is invalid on the first (two) day(s)

(O.C. 648:8) but kosher on the Intermediate Days. But if enough of the *ukatz* remained so that there is no cavity, it is kosher even on the first day (*Rama* O.C. 648:8 with *M.B.*).

215. A hairline puncture in the *esrog* may be a disqualification and an authority should be consulted, for the laws governing punctures are complex (see O.C. 648:2-3). However where a hole was made by the thorns on the tree while the *esrog* was growing and a scab covers the hole it is valid (*Rama* O.C. 648:2 with *M.B.*).

216. A blister-like growth called *chazazis* (חֲזָזִית), caused by rot and the like (see *Be'ur Halachah* to O.C. 648:13), may invalidate an *esrog* if it is noticeably higher than the rest of the *esrog* so that it can be felt (O.C. 648:13), and is of a different color than the rest of the *esrog* (see *Pri Megadim* in *Eshel Avraham* 648:19; *Sha'ar HaTziyun* 648:56). *Pri Megadim* seems to hold that a *chazazis* disqualifies only if it is of a color which, in itself, would disqualify the *esrog* (see §217). *R' Meir Arik* (*Minchas Pittim* O.C. 648:13) disputes this and maintains that a *chazazis* disqualifies whenever its color differs from the general coloring of that particular *esrog*.

217. Certain discolorations of the *esrog's* rind may disqualify it under the conditions outlined below. Black and white are disqualifying colors (O.C. 648:16); red discoloration may disqualify the *esrog*, depending on the intensity of the color (see *Be'ur Halachah* to O.C. 648:16). An authority should be consulted.

218. Discolorations and *chazazis* disqualify an *esrog* in any of the following ways:

(a) If it occurs on the *chotam* (the upper part of the *esrog* which slopes toward the tip) it disqualfies even if it covers only a most minute area (O.C. 648:12). However it must be easily visible to the naked eye. A discoloration that can be seen only upon close inspection is, from a halachic viewpoint, considered non-existent (*M.B.* 648:46).

(b) It occupies most of the surface area of the *esrog*.

(c) Two or more discolorations or *chazazis* cover even less than half of the surface of the *esrog*. In this instance the *esrog* is disqualified only if the major part of the *esrog's* circumference is covered by the discolorations or blisters plus the space between them. If they are all on one side of the *esrog* it is kosher (O.C. 648:10 with *M.B.*). However if there were more than three spots it is doubtful if it is kosher even in such an instance (*Be'ur Halachah* there s.v. שכולם). There is controversy concerning discolorations dispersed in more than one spot: According to one view, in this case, too, disqualification will apply only where the discoloration was of the specific colors listed in §217. Others, however, hold that any spotted *esrog* (מְנוּמָּר) is disqualified even if the discoloration is of other colors (*M.B.* 648:55).

219. The disqualifications arising out of discolorations and *chazazis* apply even on the Intermediate Days (*Rama* 649:5).

220. Some discolorations, specifically black dots, are very common and many are disqualifications. In cases of doubt a *rav* should be consulted. However if these spots are merely specks of dirt adhering to the surface of the *esrog* they do not constitute a disqualification.

221. The minimum size for an *esrog* is the volume of an egg (כְּבֵיצָה). According to many *poskim* (*Noda BiYehudah, Chazon Ish*; cf. *Teshuvos Chasam Sofer Orach Chaim* 181) the volume should be that of two medium eggs. An *esrog* weighing approximately 3.53 oz. is definitely the equivalent of two eggs. [This above figure has been arrived at using the following figures. *Shiurin shel Torah* (p. 4 and 65) fixes the weight of the water displaced by a *kebeitzah* at 100 grams or 3.53 oz. av. Since an *esrog* weighs less than its equivalent volume of water, an *esrog* weighing less than this may also be kosher. Another way of approximating is to bear in mind that adding approximately 1/5 to the circumference of an egg will double its volume (*Shiurin shel Torah*, p. 66).]

222. Some authorities (*Teshuvos Beis Yitzchok, Yoreh Deah* §135) maintain that it is not sufficient that the total volume of the *esrog* be equal to that of an egg, but hold that the *esrog* must also have an egg's overall dimensions. Thus an *esrog* which is narrower than an egg but makes up for the volume in its length is invalid. However many *poskim* (*Teshuvos, Maharsham* 2:129; *Chazon Ish* cited in *Shiurin shel Torah* p. 66) dispute this (see *R' E. Weissfish, Arbaas HaMinim HaShalem* p. 263-4).

223. Most *Poskim* invalidate an *esrog* grown on an *esrog* twig that was grafted onto another tree species or vice versa. They rule that even if such an *esrog* is the only one available it should be taken without reciting the blessing (*M.B.* 648:65, *Da'as Torah* there, *Sha'arei Teshuvah* 649:7, *Arbaas HaMinim HaShalem*).

◆§ Disqualified Species

224. If some of a person's Four Species are invalid, and no kosher set is available in the entire town, he should 'take' what he has without a blessing. Even if some of the species are missing entirely, one should take whatever species he has, but without a blessing (O.C. 649:6). However, under no circumstances should one substitute another species, e.g., willows similar to the prescribed one, or stolen species for the missing one (*M.B.* 649:53). Regarding the very complex question of what is defined as stolen in this regard see O.C. 649:1 with *M.B.*

225. If the disqualification was because of dryness, a blessing may be recited if no valid specimens of this species are available in the entire town (*M.B.* 649:58).

226. The second day of *Yom Tov* in the Diaspora is, generally speaking, accorded the same stringency as is the first day, and the disqualifications in effect on the first day are in effect on the second. Nevertheless, if one does not have a completely kosher set of the Four Species, he may 'take' species that are disqualified only on the first day but acceptable during the Intermediate Days. In such an instance, however, one should not recite the blessing (*O.C.* 649:6). On the first day this may be done only if there is no valid specimen to be obtained in the entire town, whereas on the second day it is sufficient that a valid specimen is available only with great exertion (*M.B.* 649:50). The above holds true only for disqualifications not in effect on the Intermediate Days, e.g., if it is difficult to obtain an *esrog* that will be one's own, he may borrow an *esrog* and 'take' it without a blessing.

☙ Simchas Torah

227. Because Simchas Torah marks the completion of the yearly reading of the Torah, many customs have been introduced to honor the Torah on this day. We will limit ourselves to pointing out some of the customs regarding the reading of the Torah on this day.

228. In most Ashkenazic congregations (based on the Eastern European rite) the Torah is also read on the night of Simchas Torah. In olden days there were many customs as to what was read, but in our days, one custom is virtually universal: The first five sections in וְזֹאת הַבְּרָכָה (*Deuteronomy* 33:1-26) is read and five people (and in some congregations three people) are called up to the Torah (see *O.C.* 669; *Sha'arei Ephraim* 8:57; cf *M.B.* §15). At the completion of the reading, Half *Kaddish* is recited followed by *Aleinu* (*M.B.* §15).

229. After *Shacharis* the Torah is read as usual. The portion for the day is the last *sidra* of the Torah — וְזֹאת הַבְּרָכָה – instead of a Festival reading. To this we add a passage from the beginning of *Bereisis* to demonstrate that we continuously begin the Torah anew (see *Tur O.C.* 669). This is followed by the Half *Kaddish*, *Maftir* and *Haftarah* as usual.

230. The passage in וְזֹאת הַבְּרָכָה until מְעוֹנָה is read for five people, corresponding to the five *aliyos* which are obligatory on every *Yom Tov*. The reading from מְעוֹנָה and further and the beginning of *Bereishis* are additional. The person called to read the former passage is the one who completes the year's Torah reading, and he is honored with the title חָתָן תּוֹרָה, *the Groom of the Torah*. The person called to begin the reading of *Bereishis* is honored as the חָתָן בְּרֵאשִׁית, *groom of Bereishis*. Both *aliyos* are considered great honors, and in most congregations they are given to people distinguished for their Torah scholarship and other attributes (*M.B.* 669:1). It is customary for the 'grooms' to serve a feast (*Kiddush*) to the congregants (*O.C.* 669).

231. As part of the Simchas Torah celebration, the *sidra* וְזֹאת הַבְּרָכָה is read over and over so that every male in the congregation can be called for an *aliyah* (*O.C.* 669; *M.B.* §12). In most congregations even young boys who are not yet *bar-mitzvah* are honored with an *aliyah*, to imbue them with love for the Torah (see *Shaarei Ephraim* 8:57).

232. Great care should be exercised to ensure that, throughout these repeated readings, there will always be ten adult males who listen attentively to the Torah reading and the blessings (*M.B.* 669:12).

233. Even very young children who cannot themselves recite the blessings are given the honor of an *aliyah* (see *Sha'arei Ephraim* 8:57 with *Pis'chei She'arim*). This is accomplished in the following manner: An adult is designated to be called for an *aliyah* עִם כָּל הַנְּעָרִים, *with all the young boys*. He is called for the last *aliyah* before the *Chassan Torah*, and his *aliyah* is aptly named *Kol HaNe'arim* (כָּל הַנְּעָרִים), lit. *all the young boys*, and is considered a great honor. The designated person recites the blessings slowly and clearly so that all the children who are able to, recite along with him. The others simply answer *Amen* (see ibid.).

234. It is also customary to recite the verse הַמַּלְאָךְ הַגּוֹאֵל אֹתִי, *May the angel who redeems me* (*Genesis* 48:16), with the children. In some communities it is customary to recite the verse immediately after the Torah reading, before the blessing is recited (*M.B.* 669:14); other communities recite it after the *berachah*.

235. One of the virtually universal customs is for the congregants to crowd around the *bimah* during the *aliyos* of *Chassan Torah*, *Chassan Bereishis*, and *Kol HaNearim*. Over their heads, they hold a canopy of *taleisim*. This writer has not found the source and reason for this custom. Perhaps it commemorates the giving of the Torah, regarding which the Sages say (*Shabbos 88a*) that Mount Sinai was perched above the heads of the Jewish people.

236. In many congregations it is customary to change the usual manner of *hagbahah* [הַגְבָּהָה] *raising the Torah*, after the *Chassan Torah's aliyah*. The reason for the change is to give special honor to the Torah on this day. While the Torah is still resting on the *bimah*, the person given this honor grasps the right *etz chaim* [lit. *tree of life*, the pole upon which the scroll is rolled] with his left hand, and the left *etz chaim* with his right hand. He lifts the Torah cross-handed, and then straightens out his hands, thereby turning the written side of the scroll toward the congregation. Care should be taken, however, that the individual be strong or that the Torah not be heavy, in order to avoid the danger that the Torah may be dropped — God forbid (*Sha'arei Ephraim* 8:62).

VERSES FOR PEOPLE'S NAMES / פסוקים לשמות אנשים

Kitzur Sh'lah teaches that it is a source of merit to recite a Scriptural verse symbolizing one's name before יִהְיוּ לְרָצוֹן at the end of *Shemoneh Esrei.* The verse should either contain the person's name, or else begin and end with the first and last letters of the name.

Following is a selection of first and last letters of names, with appropriate verses:

א...א אָנָּא יהוה הוֹשִׁיעָה נָּא, אָנָּא יהוה הַצְלִיחָה נָּא.[1]

א...ה אַשְׁרֵי מַשְׂכִּיל אֶל דָּל, בְּיוֹם רָעָה יְמַלְּטֵהוּ יהוה.[2]

א...ו אַשְׁרֵי שֶׁאֵל יַעֲקֹב בְּעֶזְרוֹ, שִׂבְרוֹ עַל יהוה אֱלֹהָיו.[3]

א...י אֲמָרַי הַאֲזִינָה יהוה בִּינָה הֲגִיגִי.[4]

א...ך אָמַרְתְּ לַיהוה אֲדֹנָי אָתָּה, טוֹבָתִי בַּל עָלֶיךָ.[5]

א...ל אֶרֶץ רָעָשָׁה אַף שָׁמַיִם נָטְפוּ מִפְּנֵי אֱלֹהִים זֶה סִינַי, מִפְּנֵי אֱלֹהִים אֱלֹהֵי יִשְׂרָאֵל.[6]

א...ם אַתָּה הוּא יהוה הָאֱלֹהִים, אֲשֶׁר בָּחַרְתָּ בְּאַבְרָם, וְהוֹצֵאתוֹ מֵאוּר כַּשְׂדִּים, וְשַׂמְתָּ שְׁמוֹ אַבְרָהָם.[7]

א...ן אֵלֶיךָ יהוה אֶקְרָא, וְאֶל אֲדֹנָי אֶתְחַנָּן.[8]

א...ע אָמַר בְּלִבּוֹ בַּל אֶמּוֹט, לְדֹר וָדֹר אֲשֶׁר לֹא בְרָע.[9]

א...ר אֵלֶּה בָרֶכֶב וְאֵלֶּה בַסּוּסִים, וַאֲנַחְנוּ בְּשֵׁם יהוה אֱלֹהֵינוּ נַזְכִּיר.[10]

ב...א בְּרִיתִי הָיְתָה אִתּוֹ הַחַיִּים וְהַשָּׁלוֹם, וָאֶתְּנֵם לוֹ מוֹרָא וַיִּירָאֵנִי, וּמִפְּנֵי שְׁמִי נִחַת הוּא.[11]

ב...ה בַּעֲבוּר יִשְׁמְרוּ חֻקָּיו, וְתוֹרֹתָיו יִנְצֹרוּ, הַלְלוּיָהּ.[12]

ב...ז בְּיוֹם קָרָאתִי וַתַּעֲנֵנִי, תַּרְהִבֵנִי בְנַפְשִׁי עֹז.[13]

ב...ך בָּרוּךְ אַתָּה יהוה, לַמְּדֵנִי חֻקֶּיךָ.[14]

ב...ל בְּמַקְהֵלוֹת בָּרְכוּ אֱלֹהִים, אֲדֹנָי מִמְּקוֹר יִשְׂרָאֵל.[15]

ב...ן בָּרוּךְ יהוה אֱלֹהֵי יִשְׂרָאֵל מֵהָעוֹלָם וְעַד הָעוֹלָם, אָמֵן וְאָמֵן.[16]

ב...ע בְּחֶסֶד וֶאֱמֶת יְכֻפַּר עָוֹן, וּבְיִרְאַת יהוה סוּר מֵרָע.[17]

ג...ה גּוֹל עַל יהוה דַּרְכֶּךָ, וּבְטַח עָלָיו וְהוּא יַעֲשֶׂה.[18]

ג...ל גַּם אֲנִי אוֹדְךָ בִכְלִי נֶבֶל, אֲמִתְּךָ אֱלֹהָי אֲזַמְּרָה לְךָ בְכִנּוֹר, קְדוֹשׁ יִשְׂרָאֵל.[19]

ג...ן גַּם בְּנֵי אָדָם גַּם בְּנֵי אִישׁ, יַחַד עָשִׁיר וְאֶבְיוֹן.[20]

ד...ב דִּרְשׁוּ יהוה בְּהִמָּצְאוֹ, קְרָאֻהוּ בִּהְיוֹתוֹ קָרוֹב.[21]

ד...ד דִּרְשׁוּ יהוה וְעֻזּוֹ, בַּקְּשׁוּ פָנָיו תָּמִיד.[22]

ד...ה דְּאָגָה בְלֶב אִישׁ יַשְׁחֶנָּה, וְדָבָר טוֹב יְשַׂמְּחֶנָּה.[23]

ד...ל דָּן יָדִין עַמּוֹ, כְּאַחַד שִׁבְטֵי יִשְׂרָאֵל.[24]

ה...א הַצּוּר תָּמִים פָּעֳלוֹ, כִּי כָל דְּרָכָיו מִשְׁפָּט, אֵל אֱמוּנָה וְאֵין עָוֶל, צַדִּיק וְיָשָׁר הוּא.[25]

ה...ה הַסְתֵּר פָּנֶיךָ מֵחֲטָאָי, וְכָל עֲוֹנֹתַי מְחֵה.[26]

ה...ל הַקְשִׁיבָה לְקוֹל שַׁוְעִי מַלְכִּי וֵאלֹהָי, כִּי אֵלֶיךָ אֶתְפַּלָּל.[27]

ז...ב זֵכֶר צַדִּיק לִבְרָכָה, וְשֵׁם רְשָׁעִים יִרְקָב.[28]

ז...ה זֹאת מְנוּחָתִי עֲדֵי עַד, פֹּה אֵשֵׁב כִּי אִוִּתִיהָ.[29]

ז...ח זָכַרְתִּי יָמִים מִקֶּדֶם, הָגִיתִי בְכָל פָּעֳלֶךָ, בְּמַעֲשֵׂה יָדֶיךָ אֲשׂוֹחֵחַ.[30]

ז...ן זְבוּלֻן לְחוֹף יַמִּים יִשְׁכֹּן, וְהוּא לְחוֹף אֳנִיֹּת וְיַרְכָתוֹ עַל צִידֹן.[31]

---

(1) *Psalms* 118:25. (2) 41:2. (3) 146:5. (4) 5:2. (5) 16:2. (6) 68:9. (7) *Nehemiah* 9:7. (8) *Psalms* 30:9. (9) 10:6. (10) 20:8. (11) *Malachi* 2:5. (12) *Psalms* 105:45. (13) 138:3. (14) 119:12. (15) 68:27. (16) 41:14. (17) *Proverbs* 16:6. (18) *Psalms* 37:5. (19) 71:22. (20) 49:3. (21) *Isaiah* 55:6. (22) *Psalms* 105:4. (23) *Proverbs* 12:25. (24) *Genesis* 49:16. (25) *Deuteronomy* 32:4. (26) *Psalms* 51:11. (27) 5:3. (28) *Proverbs* 10:7. (29) *Psalms* 132:14. (30) 143:5. (31) *Genesis* 49:13.

ח...ה חָגְרָה בְעוֹז מָתְנֶיהָ, וַתְּאַמֵּץ זְרוֹעֹתֶיהָ.[1]
ח...ך חֲצוֹת לַיְלָה אָקוּם לְהוֹדוֹת לָךְ, עַל מִשְׁפְּטֵי צִדְקֶךָ.[2]
ח...ם חֹנֶה מַלְאַךְ יהוה סָבִיב לִירֵאָיו, וַיְחַלְּצֵם.[3]
ט...א טוֹב יַנְחִיל בְּנֵי בָנִים, וְצָפוּן לַצַּדִּיק חֵיל חוֹטֵא.[4]
ט...ה טָמְנוּ גֵאִים פַּח לִי, וַחֲבָלִים פָּרְשׂוּ רֶשֶׁת לְיַד מַעְגָּל, מֹקְשִׁים שָׁתוּ לִי סֶלָה.[5]
י...א יִשְׂרָאֵל בְּטַח בַּיהוה, עֶזְרָם וּמָגִנָּם הוּא.[6]
י...ב יַעַנְךָ יהוה בְּיוֹם צָרָה, יְשַׂגֶּבְךָ שֵׁם אֱלֹהֵי יַעֲקֹב.[7]
י...ד יָסַד אֶרֶץ עַל מְכוֹנֶיהָ, בַּל תִּמּוֹט עוֹלָם וָעֶד.[8]
י...ה יהוה הַצִּילָה נַפְשִׁי מִשְּׂפַת שֶׁקֶר, מִלָּשׁוֹן רְמִיָּה.[9]
י...י יהוה לִי בְּעֹזְרָי, וַאֲנִי אֶרְאֶה בְשֹׂנְאָי.[10]
י...ל יְמִין יהוה רוֹמֵמָה, יְמִין יהוה עֹשָׂה חָיִל.[11]
י...ם יַעְלְזוּ חֲסִידִים בְּכָבוֹד, יְרַנְּנוּ עַל מִשְׁכְּבוֹתָם.[12]
י...ן יָשֵׂם נְהָרוֹת לְמִדְבָּר, וּמֹצָאֵי מַיִם לְצִמָּאוֹן.[13]
י...ע יָחֹס עַל דַּל וְאֶבְיוֹן, וְנַפְשׁוֹת אֶבְיוֹנִים יוֹשִׁיעַ.[14]
י...ף יהוה יִגְמֹר בַּעֲדִי, יהוה חַסְדְּךָ לְעוֹלָם, מַעֲשֵׂי יָדֶיךָ אַל תֶּרֶף.[15]
י...ץ יְבָרְכֵנוּ אֱלֹהִים וְיִירְאוּ אוֹתוֹ כָּל אַפְסֵי אָרֶץ.[16]
י...ק יוֹצִיאֵם מֵחֹשֶׁךְ וְצַלְמָוֶת, וּמוֹסְרוֹתֵיהֶם יְנַתֵּק.[17]
י...ר יהוה שִׁמְךָ לְעוֹלָם, יהוה זִכְרְךָ לְדֹר וָדֹר.[18]
י...ת יהוה שֹׁמֵר אֶת גֵּרִים, יָתוֹם וְאַלְמָנָה יְעוֹדֵד, וְדֶרֶךְ רְשָׁעִים יְעַוֵּת.[19]
כ...ב כִּי לֹא יִטֹּשׁ יהוה עַמּוֹ, וְנַחֲלָתוֹ לֹא יַעֲזֹב.[20]
כ...ל כִּי מֶלֶךְ כָּל הָאָרֶץ אֱלֹהִים, זַמְּרוּ מַשְׂכִּיל.[21]
ל...א לֹא תִהְיֶה מְשַׁכֵּלָה וַעֲקָרָה בְּאַרְצֶךָ, אֶת מִסְפַּר יָמֶיךָ אֲמַלֵּא.[22]
ל...ה לְדָוִד בָּרוּךְ יהוה צוּרִי הַמְלַמֵּד יָדַי לַקְרָב, אֶצְבְּעוֹתַי לַמִּלְחָמָה.[23]
ל...י לוּלֵי תוֹרָתְךָ שַׁעֲשֻׁעָי, אָז אָבַדְתִּי בְעָנְיִי.[24]
ל...ת לַמְנַצֵּחַ עַל שֹׁשַׁנִּים לִבְנֵי קֹרַח, מַשְׂכִּיל שִׁיר יְדִידֹת.[25]
מ...א מִי כָמֹכָה בָּאֵלִם יהוה מִי כָּמֹכָה נֶאְדָּר בַּקֹּדֶשׁ, נוֹרָא תְהִלֹּת עֹשֵׂה פֶלֶא.[26]
מ...ה מַחֲשָׁבוֹת בְּעֵצָה תִכּוֹן, וּבְתַחְבֻּלוֹת עֲשֵׂה מִלְחָמָה.[27]
מ...ו מַה דּוֹדֵךְ מִדּוֹד הַיָּפָה בַּנָּשִׁים, מַה דּוֹדֵךְ מִדּוֹד שֶׁכָּכָה הִשְׁבַּעְתָּנוּ.[28]
מ...י מָה אָהַבְתִּי תוֹרָתֶךָ, כָּל הַיּוֹם הִיא שִׂיחָתִי.[29]
מ...ל מַה טֹּבוּ אֹהָלֶיךָ יַעֲקֹב, מִשְׁכְּנֹתֶיךָ יִשְׂרָאֵל.[30]
מ...ם מְאוֹר עֵינַיִם יְשַׂמַּח לֵב, שְׁמוּעָה טוֹבָה תְּדַשֶּׁן עָצֶם.[31]
מ...ר מִי זֶה הָאִישׁ יְרֵא יהוה, יוֹרֶנּוּ בְּדֶרֶךְ יִבְחָר.[32]
נ...א נַפְשֵׁנוּ חִכְּתָה לַיהוה עֶזְרֵנוּ וּמָגִנֵּנוּ הוּא.[33]
נ...ה נָחַלְתִּי עֵדְוֹתֶיךָ לְעוֹלָם, כִּי שְׂשׂוֹן לִבִּי הֵמָּה.[34]
נ...י נִדְבוֹת פִּי רְצֵה נָא יהוה, וּמִשְׁפָּטֶיךָ לַמְּדֵנִי.[35]
נ...ל נֶחְשַׁבְתִּי עִם יוֹרְדֵי בוֹר, הָיִיתִי כְּגֶבֶר אֵין אֱיָל.[36]
נ...ם נַחֲמוּ נַחֲמוּ עַמִּי, יֹאמַר אֱלֹהֵיכֶם.[37]

---

(1) *Proverbs* 31:17. (2) *Psalms* 119:62. (3) 34:8. (4) *Proverbs* 13:22. (5) *Psalms* 140:6. (6) 115:9. (7) 20:2. (8) 104:5. (9) 120:2. (10) 118:7. (11) 118:16. (12) 149:5. (13) 107:33. (14) 72:13. (15) 138:8. (16) 67:8. (17) 107:14. (18) 135:13. (19) 146:9. (20) 94:14. (21) 47:8. (22) *Exodus* 23:26. (23) *Psalms* 144:1. (24) 119:92. (25) 45:1. (26) *Exodus* 15:11. (27) *Proverbs* 20:18. (28) *Song of Songs* 5:9. (29) *Psalms* 119:97. (30) *Numbers* 24:5. (31) *Proverbs* 15:30. (32) *Psalms* 25:12. (33) 33:20. (34) 119:111. (35) 119:108. (36) 88:5. (37) *Isaiah* 40:1.

נ...ן נֵר יהוה נִשְׁמַת אָדָם, חֹפֵשׂ כָּל חַדְרֵי בָטֶן.[1]

ס...ה סֹבּוּ צִיּוֹן וְהַקִּיפוּהָ סִפְרוּ מִגְדָּלֶיהָ.[2]

ס...י סֵעֲפִים שָׂנֵאתִי, וְתוֹרָתְךָ אָהָבְתִּי.[3]

ע...א עַתָּה אָקוּם, יֹאמַר יהוה, עַתָּה אֵרוֹמָם, עַתָּה אֶנָּשֵׂא.[4]

ע...ב עַד אֶמְצָא מָקוֹם לַיהוה, מִשְׁכָּנוֹת לַאֲבִיר יַעֲקֹב.[5]

ע...ה עָזִּי וְזִמְרָת יָהּ, וַיְהִי לִי לִישׁוּעָה.[6]

ע...ל עַל דַּעְתְּךָ כִּי לֹא אֶרְשָׁע, וְאֵין מִיָּדְךָ מַצִּיל.[7]

ע...ם עֲרֹב עַבְדְּךָ לְטוֹב, אַל יַעַשְׁקֻנִי זֵדִים.[8]

ע...ר עֹשֶׂה גְדֹלוֹת וְאֵין חֵקֶר, נִפְלָאוֹת עַד אֵין מִסְפָּר.[9]

פ...ה פִּתְחוּ לִי שַׁעֲרֵי צֶדֶק, אָבֹא בָם אוֹדֶה יָהּ.[10]

פ...ל פֶּן יִטְרֹף כְּאַרְיֵה נַפְשִׁי, פֹּרֵק וְאֵין מַצִּיל.[11]

פ...ס פֶּלֶס וּמֹאזְנֵי מִשְׁפָּט לַיהוה, מַעֲשֵׂהוּ כָּל אַבְנֵי כִיס.[12]

פ...ץ פִּנִּיתָ לְפָנֶיהָ וַתַּשְׁרֵשׁ שָׁרָשֶׁיהָ וַתְּמַלֵּא אָרֶץ.[13]

צ...ה צִיּוֹן בְּמִשְׁפָּט תִּפָּדֶה, וְשָׁבֶיהָ בִּצְדָקָה.[14]

צ...ח צִיּוֹן יִשְׁאָלוּ דֶּרֶךְ הֵנָּה פְנֵיהֶם, בֹּאוּ וְנִלְווּ אֶל יהוה, בְּרִית עוֹלָם לֹא תִשָּׁכֵחַ.[15]

צ...י צַר וּמָצוֹק מְצָאוּנִי, מִצְוֹתֶיךָ שַׁעֲשֻׁעָי.[16]

ק...ל קַמְתִּי אֲנִי לִפְתֹּחַ לְדוֹדִי, וְיָדַי נָטְפוּ מוֹר וְאֶצְבְּעֹתַי מוֹר עֹבֵר עַל כַּפּוֹת הַמַּנְעוּל.[17]

ק...ן קוֹלִי אֶל יהוה אֶזְעָק, קוֹלִי אֶל יהוה אֶתְחַנָּן.[18]

ק...ת קָרוֹב אַתָּה יהוה, וְכָל מִצְוֹתֶיךָ אֱמֶת.[19]

ר...ה רִגְזוּ וְאַל תֶּחֱטָאוּ, אִמְרוּ בִלְבַבְכֶם עַל מִשְׁכַּבְכֶם, וְדֹמּוּ סֶלָה.[20]

ר...ל רְאוּ עַתָּה כִּי אֲנִי אֲנִי הוּא, וְאֵין אֱלֹהִים עִמָּדִי, אֲנִי אָמִית וַאֲחַיֶּה, מָחַצְתִּי וַאֲנִי אֶרְפָּא, וְאֵין מִיָּדִי מַצִּיל.[21]

ר...ן רְאֵה זֶה מָצָאתִי, אָמְרָה קֹהֶלֶת, אַחַת לְאַחַת לִמְצֹא חֶשְׁבּוֹן.[22]

ש...א שַׂמֵּחַ נֶפֶשׁ עַבְדֶּךָ, כִּי אֵלֶיךָ אֲדֹנָי נַפְשִׁי אֶשָּׂא.[23]

ש...ה שְׂאוּ יְדֵכֶם קֹדֶשׁ, וּבָרְכוּ אֶת יהוה.[24]

ש...ח שָׁמַע יהוה תְּחִנָּתִי, יהוה תְּפִלָּתִי יִקָּח.[25]

ש...י שָׂנֵאתִי הַשֹּׁמְרִים הַבְלֵי שָׁוְא, וַאֲנִי אֶל יהוה בָּטָחְתִּי.[26]

ש...ל שָׁלוֹם רָב לְאֹהֲבֵי תוֹרָתֶךָ וְאֵין לָמוֹ מִכְשׁוֹל.[27]

ש...ם שְׁמָר תָּם וּרְאֵה יָשָׁר, כִּי אַחֲרִית לְאִישׁ שָׁלוֹם.[28]

ש...ן שִׁיתוּ לִבְּכֶם לְחֵילָה פַּסְּגוּ אַרְמְנוֹתֶיהָ, לְמַעַן תְּסַפְּרוּ לְדוֹר אַחֲרוֹן.[29]

ש...ר שְׂפַת אֱמֶת תִּכּוֹן לָעַד, וְעַד אַרְגִּיעָה לְשׁוֹן שָׁקֶר.[30]

ש...ת שִׁיר הַמַּעֲלוֹת, הִנֵּה בָּרְכוּ אֶת יהוה כָּל עַבְדֵי יהוה, הָעֹמְדִים בְּבֵית יהוה בַּלֵּילוֹת.[31]

ת...ה תַּעֲרֹךְ לְפָנַי שֻׁלְחָן נֶגֶד צֹרְרָי, דִּשַּׁנְתָּ בַשֶּׁמֶן רֹאשִׁי, כּוֹסִי רְוָיָה.[32]

ת...י תּוֹצִיאֵנִי מֵרֶשֶׁת זוּ, טָמְנוּ לִי, כִּי אַתָּה מָעוּזִּי.[33]

ת...ם תְּנוּ עֹז לֵאלֹהִים עַל יִשְׂרָאֵל גַּאֲוָתוֹ, וְעֻזּוֹ בַּשְּׁחָקִים.[34]

---

(1) *Proverbs* 20:27. (2) *Psalms* 48:13. (3) 119:113. (4) *Isaiah* 33:10. (5) *Psalms* 132:5. (6) 118:14. (7) *Job* 10:7. (8) *Psalms* 119:122. (9) *Job* 5:9. (10) *Psalms* 118:19. (11) 7:3. (12) *Proverbs* 16:11. (13) *Psalms* 80:10. (14) *Isaiah* 1:27. (15) *Jeremiah* 50:5. (16) *Psalms* 119:143. (17) *Song of Songs* 5:5. (18) *Psalms* 142:2. (19) 119:151. (20) 5:4. (21) *Deuteronomy* 32:39. (22) *Ecclesiastes* 7:27. (23) *Psalms* 86:4. (24) 134:2. (25) 6:10. (26) 31:7. (27) 119:165. (28) 37:37. (29) 48:14. (30) *Proverbs* 12:19. (31) *Psalms* 134:1. (32) 23:5. (33) 31:5. (34) 68:35.

THE RABBIS' KADDISH / KADDISH D'RABBANAN

TRANSLITERATED WITH ASHKENAZIC PRONUNCIATION

Yisgadal v'yiskadash sh'mei rabbaw (Cong. — *Amein*).
B'allmaw dee v'raw chir'usei v'yamlich malchusei,
b'chayeichon, uv'yomeichon, uv'chayei d'chol beis yisroel,
ba'agawlaw u'vizman kawriv, v'imru: Amein.
(Cong. – *Amein. Y'hei sh'mei rabbaw m'vawrach l'allam u'l'allmei allmayaw.*)
Y'hei sh'mei rabbaw m'vawrach, l'allam u'l'allmei allmayaw.

Yis'bawrach, v'yishtabach, v'yispaw'ar, v'yisromam, v'yis'nasei,
v'yis'hadar, v'yis'aleh, v'yis'halawl
sh'mei d'kudshaw b'rich hu (Cong. – *b'rich hu*).
L'aylaw min kol
bir'chawsaw v'shirawsaw,
tush'b'chawsaw v'nechemawsaw,
da'ami'rawn b'allmaw, v'imru: Amein (Cong. – *Amein*).

Al yisroel v'al rabaw'nawn v'al talmidei'hon,
v'al kol talmidei salmidei'hon,
v'al kol mawn d'awskin b'oray'saw,
dee v'as'raw haw'dain, v'dee b'chol asar va'asar.
Y'hei l'hon u'l'chon shlaw'maw rabbaw,
chee'naw v'chisdaw v'rachamin,
v'chayin arichin, u'm'zonei r'vichei,
u'furkawnaw min kaw'dawm a'vu'hone dee vi'sh'ma'yaw
v'imru: Amein (Cong. – *Amein*).
Y'hei shlawmaw rabbaw min sh'mayaw,
v'chayim awleinu v'al kol yisroel, v'imru: Amein (Cong. – *Amein*).

Take three steps back, bow left and say, *'Oseh . . .'*; bow right and say, *'hu b'rachamawv ya'aseh . . .'*; bow forward and say, *'v'al kol yisroel v'imru: Amein.'*

Oseh shawlom bim'ro'mawv,
hu b'rachamawv ya'aseh shawlom awleinu,
v'al kol yisroel v'imru: Amein (Cong. – *Amein*).

Remain standing in place for a few moments, then take three steps forward.

⁂ THE MOURNER'S KADDISH ⁂

TRANSLITERATED WITH ASHKENAZIC PRONUNCIATION

Yisgadal v'yiskadash sh'mei rabbaw (Cong. — *Amein*).
B'allmaw dee v'raw chir'usei v'yamlich malchusei,
b'chayeichon, uv'yomeichon, uv'chayei d'chol beis yisroel,
ba'agawlaw u'vizman kawriv, v'imru: Amein.
(Cong. — *Amein. Y'hei sh'mei rabbaw m'vawrach l'allam u'l'allmei allmayaw.*)
Y'hei sh'mei rabbaw m'vawrach, l'allam u'l'allmei allmayaw.

Yis'bawrach, v'yishtabach, v'yispaw'ar,
v'yisromam, v'yis'nasei,
v'yis'hadar, v'yis'aleh, v'yis'halawl
sh'mei d'kudshaw b'rich hu (Cong. — *b'rich hu*).
L'aylaw min kol
bir'chawsaw v'shirawsaw,
tush'b'chawsaw v'nechemawsaw,
da'ami'rawn b'allmaw, v'imru: Amein (Cong. – *Amein*).
Y'hei shlawmaw rabbaw min sh'mayaw,
v'chayim awleinu v'al kol yisroel, v'imru: Amein (Cong. – *Amein*).

Take three steps back, bow left and say, *'Oseh . . .'*; bow right and say, *'hu ya'aseh . . .'*; bow forward and say, *'v'al kol yisroel v'imru: Amein.'*

Oseh shawlom bim'ro'mawv,
hu ya'aseh shawlom awleinu,
v'al kol yisroel v'imru: Amein (Cong. – *Amein*).

Remain standing in place for a few moments, then take three steps forward.

Mesorah Publications, Ltd.
1969 Coney Island Avenue
Brooklyn, New York 11223
(718) 339-1700